Air-Britain

Civil Aircraft Registers of the United Kingdom, Republic of Ireland and the Isle of Man 2008

Published by:

Air-Britain (Historians) Limited

Sales Department:

41 Penshurst Road, Leigh, Tonbridge, Kent TN11 8HL
e-mail: sales@air-britain.co.uk

Membership Enquiries:

1 Rose Cottages, 179 Penn Road,
Hazlemere, Bucks HP15 7NE
e-mail: membership@air-britain.co.uk

Web-site:

http://www.air-britain.com

ISBN 978-0-85130-392-5

Printed by Bell & Bain Ltd,
Thornliebank, Glasgow G46 7UQ

COVER PHOTOGRAPHS:

Front: Extra EA.300/L G-IIEX displaying its abilities at Biggin Hill on 2.6.07. (Roger Birchall)

Rear: Folland Gnat T.1 G-TIMM at North Weald on 16.6.07 is one of many ex-RAF aircraft with dispensation to wear military marks, in this case the incorrect serial XS111. (Roger Birchall)

Illustrating the new Isle of Man civil register, Cessna 560 Citation XLS M-BWFC (for Bolton Wanderers Football Club) arriving at Nottingham/East Midlands Airport on 29.9.07. (Steve Blood)

Our Irish contribution is Tecnam P2002 Sierra EI-DRO at home at Kilkenny airfield 29.6.07. (Bill Teasdale)

CIVIL AIRCRAFT REGISTERS OF THE UNITED KINGDOM, REPUBLIC OF IRELAND AND THE ISLE OF MAN 2008

44th Year of Publication – Collated and Edited by Barrie Womersley

© Air-Britain (Historians) Ltd 2008

ISBN 978-0-85130-392-5   ISSN 0264-5270

INTRODUCTION AND EDITORIAL

Welcome to the 44th Air-Britain United Kingdom and Ireland Civil Aircraft and Glider Register. This is my tenth and final edition as Editor but I hope to be involved in the compilation of future editions.

My main rôle has been to maintain the basic details of the UK Register listed in SECTION 1. Generally, this is as provided by the Civil Aviation Authority (CAA) from their G-INFO database. This is now achieved with the unfailing support of Alan Johnson, Bernard Martin and Graham Slack. The Irish data in SECTION 2 is updated by myself. The other important members of the team are Paul Hewins who maintains responsibility for updating details of Overseas civil registered aircraft located in the UK & Ireland (SECTION 5) and Richard Cawsey who oversees the British Gliding Association registration details (SECTION 6) . Duirng my time I introducedI SECTION 4 which focuses on the thriving UK preservation scene and specifically concentrates on the historical aspects of those aircraft which have been listed on the UK & Irish civil aircraft registers over many years and are still extant worldwide. Most of these are de-registered but they can still be located albeit, sometimes, with different identities. The main proviso is that it is possible to view them in Museums around the world and in easily accessible private collections. Finally, SECTION 7 consists of a series of Indices designed to help the reader track down speciific aircraft.

A fair percentage of the UK Register is devoted to amateur kit-built aircraft, microlights or hot air balloons. This is the area where the CAA devolves some regulatory tasks to other bodies although overall responsibility for safety regulation remains with them. This devolved segment is a broad one and covers four large groups involved in recrreational aviation. These are the British Balloon and Airship Club (BBAC) which governs balloon and airship activity, the Light Aircraft Association (LAA), formerly the Popular Flying Association, which regulates amateur-built aircraft and the British Microlight Aircraft Association (BMAA) which regulates microlight activity, The fourth body, which is outside this ambit of this book, is the British Parachute Association (BPA) which controls parachuting. As the majority of balloons and airships are produced commercially we are more conceerned with the role of the BMAA and LAA. The BMAA is responsible for regulating those microlights which meet certain criteria. They must either have a wing that is flexible, and can move relative to the main body of the aircraft, or a fixed wing that is rigidly attached to the aircraft's body. The total number of microlight aircraft under BMAA regulations on the current register is over 400. They all operate on a Permit to Fly rather than a CofA. The LAA is responsible for the supervision of aircraft that are amateur-built by individuals, as opposed to commercial manufacturers. They, also, operate on a Permit to Fly rather than a Certificate of Airworthiness (CofA). The total number of amateur-built aircraft under LAA regulations on the current register is about 2,500. The LAA also regulates a significant number of microlight aircraft, and a few vintage and classic aircraft, mainly types which do not qualify for an International Civil Aviation Organisation (ICAO) compliant CofA because of the demise of the manufacturer or other design authority.

Many amateur-built aircraft and microlights are now assembled by owners from kits of components supplied by commercial manufacturers to aid construction. To keep within the regulations it is important to avoid identifyng an aircraft as a factory built specimen as this would exclude it from the BMAA and LAA Permit system and require it to hold an ICAO compliant CofA. Thereby, both the BMAA and LAA have introduced their own dedicated plans numbering system designed to identify, specifically, those aircraft falling under their devolved regulatory powers. It is this BMAA and LAA reference which is used when a builder-owner seeks to register his aircraft with the CAA and it is this reference which is shown on the CAA's G-INFO database. Unfortunately for the aviation historian, this methodology has the effect of obscuring the real commercial construction (kit) number of the aircraft. Our thanks are due to those devoted members, notably Bernard Martin and Barry Taylor, who for a number of years have set out to establish and record the missing details by either developing commercial contacts or by physical examination of such aircraft. Elsewhere, some kit data has also been unearthed from web-sites, notably those of Europa and Jabiru. A look at SECTION 1 shows that there are still many new aircraft where little prime identity data is recorded other than BMAA and LAA project details. So, it is important to hunt out and record this information before it disappears!

I am grateful to all the following contributors this year. My thanks go to Jeff Bell, Pete Bish, Jim Brazier, Tony Broadhurst, Peter Budden, Nigel Burch, Phil Butler, Ian Burnett, Mike Cain, Ian Callier, Richard Cawsey, Ian Collins,,Ken Dalton, Terry Dann, Phil Dunnington, Nigel Dupuy, Ken Ede, Alan Faupel, Nick Foden, Bryan Foster, Colin Frost, Peter Gerhardt, Roy Goodwill, Dave Haines, Kenneth Hearn, Paul Hewins, Nigel Hitchman, Kenneth James, Alan Johnson, Nigel and Phil Kemp, Bob Kent, Andy Mac, Bernard Martin, Ken Parfitt, Dave Partington, Tony Pither, Nigel Ponsford, Brian Print, Geoff Pott, Dave Reid, Bob Sauvary, Rod Simpson, Graham Slack, Andy Smith, Terry Smith, Tony Smith, Martyn Steggalls, Mike Stroud, Pyul Sweatman, Barry V Taylor, D Theobald, John Tietjen, Barry Towey, Richard A Ward and Pete Webber, and to all those members who supply regular updates either direct or via ABIX and, or the A-B Sightings web-site. Once again I am indebted to Dave Partington for his work in completing the book. A final very special thanks goes to Angela for a last year (she hopes!) of patience.

On 11th January 2008 the UK Register of Civil Aircraft exceeded 20,000 currently registered aircraft for the first time. The rapid growth in numbers on the UK Register, which has seen an increase of 2,000 aircraft since 2006, is primarily due to the addition of gliders as part of the transition to EASA requirements. As at that date there were 1,210 gliders on the UK Register. This is likely to be approaching 2,000 by now. Elsewhere you can find the CAA's summary of UK registered aircraft from 1st January 1984 to 1st January 2008. Other statistical data is available on their web-site. By the end of February 2008 over 52,000 aircraft had received registrations since 1919 of which almost 34,500 fall within the G-A, G-B and G-C series. All official UK aircraft registration and ownership information shown is published by the CAA and this includes the issue and status of each Certificate of Airworthiness. The CAA registration and British Gliding Association data is correct to the end of February 2008. The Irish Aviation Authority data is correct to the end of January 2008.

BARRIE WOMERSLEY
19 The Pastures, Westwood,
Bradford-on-Avon, Wiltshire BA15 2BH

email: barrie.womersley@air-britain.co.uk   March 2008

A BRIEF HISTORICAL LOOK AT THE UK's CIVIL AIRCRAFT REGULATIONS

BACKGROUND

The Air Board was formed in May 1916 and established the Civil Aerial Transport Committee (CATC) a year later. The CATC's primary brief was to report on the measures necessary to develop aviation for civil and commercial purposes. Meantime the Air Force Bill received the Royal Assent in November 1917 leading to the creation of the Air Council and the Air Ministry. Although the Armistice was negotiated in November 1918 official restrictions on civil flying were not lifted as, technically, a state of war continued until the signing of the Peace Treaty in July 1919.

During the ensuing years, and largely instigated by de Havillands, there was considerable pressure on the Air Ministry to relax control of private aviation. In July 1933 the Secretary of State, Marquess of Londonderry appointed an independent committee under Lord Gorrell, chairman of the Royal Aeronautical Society. The Committee was charged *"To examine the requirements of the present air navigation regulations, with particular reference to those governing private flying in such matters as certificates of airworthiness; to consider whether, and in what respects, the present system of control by the Air Ministry should be modified by way of devolution or otherwise; to make recommendations in regard to these and any cognate questions which might remitted to them by the Secretary of State"*. Initial investigations seemed to be directed towards opposing proposals for the UK to relinquish control to an international authority as discussed at a League of Nation's Disarmament Conference held at Geneva earlier that year. The UK Government had no desire to follow such thinking: although the country was in depression private flying continued to progress. In fact the early 1930s saw an expansion of private flying with an increase in licensed civil aerodromes including several new municipal airfields and, in addition, there was a steady growth in international and internal air services. But there was little increase in privately owned aeroplanes: in 1933 there were just 1055 aircraft on the Register of Aircraft of which only 400 were so defined.

The report of the Gorrell Committee on *"Control of Private Flying"* was issued in July 1934. The Committee was not unanimous in its findings: one member wanted control to remain with the Air Ministry whilst two others recommended immediate divorce in every aspect of civil aviation. Broadly the Committee agreed that airworthiness regulations and the system of checking design and construction should be handed to an independent body to be named "The Air Registration Board". The Air Ministry duly agreed that the new body would control the system of approved firms, airworthiness requirements, modification procedure, renewal of Certificates of Airworthiness, inspection certificates and supervision of competency of ground engineers. It was also agreed in principle that foreign C of As should have validity on a reciprocal basis. Although required for club aircraft the Air Council was prepared to make them optional for private flying and aerial work. Third party insurance became mandatory. Interestingly, gliders came under these general provisions.

In 1936 the Air Navigation Bill became law and provided for the formation of an Air Registration Board (ARB) based on the Gorrell Report proposal that the Certification of Airworthiness of civil aircraft should devolve upon a "statutory autonomous board" formed from the the the British Corporation Register and Lloyds Register. The constituent groups were drawn from the Society of British Aircraft Constructors (SBAC), the two Insurance registers, commercial operators, and the Royal Aeronautical Society. The board was registered as a company on 26th February 1937. By 1939 the ARB's responsibilites had grown. The Register of Aircraft now contained 1,725 machines and some 75% were airworthy whilst several prototypes were flying under "B" Conditions procedures, see Section 7 Part 3.

Despite the title the ARB had little to do with the issue of Certificates of Registration for civil aircraft. This was left to the Ministry of Civil Aviation which was created in 1944. In the mid 1950s this department merged with the Ministry of Transport to become the Ministry of Transport and Civil Aviation (MTCA). Responsibility passed through a series of departments before the CAA was born. In 1967 the Government set up a committee under the chairmanship of Sir Ronald Edwards to inquire into Britain's civil air transport. The committee's findings were published in 1969 and included a recommendation to establish a civil aviation authority. The Civil Aviation Act of 1971 created the new authority, as a public corporation, and it assumed full responsibilities on 1 April 1972. Thus, the Air Registration Board was embodied into the new CAA. Originally the CAA was established as an independent specialist aviation regulator and provider of air traffic services but following the separation of National Air Traffic Services from the CAA in 2001, the CAA now functions solely in the former role with all civil aviation regulatory functions (economic regulation, airspace policy, safety regulation and consumer protection) integrated within a single specialist body. It should be noted that the UK Government requires that the CAA's costs are met entirely from the charges on those whom it regulates. Unlike many other countries there is no direct Government funding of the CAA's work.

REGISTRATION OF AIRCRAFT

There were no international regulations controlling the registration of civil aircraft within the United Kingdom at the end of the First World War. Consequently the Air Ministry's Civil Air Department specified a system of temporary registration marks in May 1919 but this practice prevailed only until July of that year. Two temporary registers were established for (i) military aircraft sold for civil purposes and already bearing Service serials - existing aircraft would be allocated their serials as registration marks with the Service ring markings obliterated and (ii) new aircraft and those built from spares - they were allocated marks in a special Service sequence commencing at K100. Subsequently, a number of these aircraft were re-allocated registrations in the first permanent register which replaced the two temporary registers. This was inaugurated on 31st July 1919 and ran until 29th July 1928 when the registration G-EBZZ had been issued - see Section 1 Part 1. Meantime, the civil use of Airships and Balloons came under the supplementary air traffic regulations of the Air Navigation Act 1911-1919. and a separate lighter-than-air register series, G-FAAA to G-FAAZ, was established until the end of 1928.

With the growth of international civil aviation the Director-General of Civil Aviation decided to terminate the first series and he authorised a new sequence of registration marks commencing at G-AAAA including airships and balloons. This second permanent register was introduced retrospectively from 30th July 1928 and, in effect, continues today - see Section 1 Part 2. Registrations were usually allocated in alphabetical sequence until the late 1970s although there have been numerous sporadic exceptions to this rule throughout this time. The G-AAAA to G-AZZZ series was allocated by July 1972 and a new series G-BAAA onwards was used in the same month: this series became exhausted in June 2001. Notwithstanding this, and commencing in 1974, many registrations were issued ahead of the natural alphabetical sequence and came from all of the forthcoming G-Bxxx to G-Zxxx series, examples being Accountant G-ATEL (August 1957), Concorde G-BSST (May 1968) and Harrier G-VSTO (June 1971). The advance G-Bxxx registrations were eventually subsumed within the proper sequence and we have moved on to the G-Cxxx series which has been in regular use since June 2001.

Small parts of an original G-Cxxx series were allocated to Canadian civilian aircraft from 20th April 1920 until 31st December 1928 commencing with G-CAAA. Registration G-CAWI was the last to be issued although G-CAXP had been formally allocated earlier in May 1928 being ex G-EBXP. On 1st January 1929 Canada adopted the nationality marks CF, followed by a hyphen, and three registration marks running from AAA to ZZZ. Those aircraft registered previously with G-CAxxx markings continued to display them until they were retired from service. At least two aircraft were still known to carry the old series markings in 2005, namely Fairchild FC-2W2, G-CART and DH.60X Moth G-CAUA. In addition, two separate series of quasi-military markings were created for aircraft operated on Canadian Government Air Operations by the Royal Canadian Air Force (RCAF). Series G-CYAA to G-CYHD was used from 18th June 1920 to 11th June 1926 and G-CYUR to G-CYZZ, but not sequentially, from 15th March 1927 to 18th July 1931. The batch from G-CYHE to G-CYUQ were not allotted as the RCAF were using a numerical series for registration marks on aircraft in their use by this time and marks were being displayed in an abbreviated form, that is the last two letters only. Aircraft still wearing these marks were absorbed into the existent RCAF numerical series by 1939. Consequently, the Civil Aviation Authority has not allocated any further registrations from the G-CAxx range although nine advance registrations were issued between December 1977 and March 1999 and remain extant. These were not allocated previously although two were reserved in 1928.

In addition, two special registrations series have been used as shown below:

i)   During 1979 and 1980 specific alpha-numeric registrations G-N81AC and G-N94AA to G-N94AE which were used for British Airways' Concordes,

ii) From 1981 until 1998 registration batches G-MBAA to G-MBZZ, G-MGAA to G-MGZZ, G-MJAA to G-MJZZ, G-MMAA to G-MNZZ, G-MTAA to G-MTZZ and G-MYAA to G-MZZZ which were allocated originally for microlight aircraft use. Subsequently, other aircraft can now be found within these batches.

A third series was established in January 1982 when registration blocks G-FYAA to G-FYZZ were confined to Minimum Lift Balloons. G-FYAA was allocated on 4th January 1982 and G-FYNC, the latest, was allocated on 4th August 1986. This series is still in existence.

The CAA web-site explains the Availability and Reservation of UK Registration Marks and is recommended reading.

USER GUIDE

There are a number of purposes to this annual volume. The primary one is to list all aircraft on the current civil aircraft registers, giving full details of types and previous identities, registered ownership and/or operator, probable home base and certification of airworthiness status. This information reproduces, expands upon and amplifies the official country registers. However, we go well beyond that; included are all other known, but no longer currently registered, UK and Irish aircraft noted in a reasonably identifiable condition and which are displayed or on/for rebuild. Some of these are held for instructional, fire or spares use. The majority of these are in located in the UK and Ireland but a few are resident abroad. In addition we detail the extensive numbers of foreign registered aircraft now located in both the UK and Ireland, some of which may aspire to G-, M- or EI- registrations in due course. Finally, we include a comprehensive listing of all gliders in use throughout the area in order to present an all-inclusive guide of the civil aviation scene.

Secondly, on a more technical level, we cater for the aviation specialist and historian who wishes to know more about a particular aircraft by providing detailed information such as the reasons for that aircraft's non-airworthy state where known and if applicable. Also, it has been our policy for many years to record engine details in the text, for example the modification of an airframe to receive a non standard engine has to be approved by the CAA and is then recorded in their Register. When the first microlights appeared in 1981 there was little standardisation and, consequently, we recorded all engine information. Now the majority are produced commercially, either in whole or kit form, engine fitment is standard to type in many cases. Accordingly, a default fit is shown in the Index at Section 7 Part 10 whilst variations remain identified in Section 1. A similar situation exists for LAA and BMAA approved, and other miscellaneous imported, home-build types.

A guide to the main text is as follows:

Registration   Current UK registrations are set out in alphabetic order in Section 1, Parts 1 and 2. Aircraft no longer currently registered shown in Part 3. Those aircraft allocated and cancelled in the period since the last register are shown in Part 4. A few aircraft, either real or static reproductions are identified in fictitious UK civil marks for display purposes and are identified in Section 7. Those marks which have been re-issued or re-allotted, particularly either if the first holder or allottee did not use the marks or they were not allocated at the time, are shown with a suffix, for example (2) after the registration.

Type   We adopt the official type description as set down by the manufacturer or designer. Where there is doubt, reference is made to the relevant editions of "Jane's All the World Aircraft", "Airlife's World Aircraft", "The General Aviation Handbook" and the "World Directory of Leisure Aviation". Indication is given if the manufacturer is a successor company or a licence builder - although not always if it is merely a sub-contractor. Under this column, we show engine types in parenthesis if the engine is non-standard for all LAA and BMAA approved and other home-build types and for those vintage and classic aircraft where engines do vary. Standard fit engines for most LAA and BMAA approved types are shown in the respective Indices in Section 7. In addition, and especially for the aforementioned types, we show the manufacturer. Final explanatory notes comment on the airframe's identity and the true position where it is at variance with official records. Numbers quoted in brackets for certain BMAA homebuilt types and their engines refer to detailed variants listed in their Homebuild Aircraft Data Sheets. These can be accessed at www.bmaa.org/techinfo.asp from which the HADS option can be selected and for each type listed the numbered variants can be displayed in full.

Construction Number   Also often referred to as the "Manufacturer's Serial Number (MSN)" the construction number (c/n) is quoted in all official registers. The c/n should be a constant traceable reference throughout an airframe's life by means of a unique identification plate or stamp contained somewhere on the airframe. Homebuilt and kit build examples may have a home-builder's personal reference number as well. Some aircraft have more than one build number, for example LAA and BMAA approved types. Both Associations use dedicated project number (pr.no.) series for their approved designs and these are often accepted as "construction numbers" in the absence of a more specific reference. The CAA records these as their prime identifier. However, most LAA and BMAA examples will have Manufacturers' Plans or Kit numbers and we quote these as our prime reference where known. In these cases the LAA and BMAA pr.nos. are shown with the individual builder details. In the case of self-assembly often main components carry adhesive labels with individual kit numbers when packed by manufacturers but during build these are often discarded and, without any visible identity on a particular airframe, traceability is lost, unfortunately.

The Irish equivalent of the LAA is the Society of Amateur Aircraft Constructors (SAAC), and various aircraft use a SAAC allocation as their construction number.

Production of early weightshift microlights were identfied with two separate construction numbers covering the Trike unit and the Sailwing respectively. As a rule the CAA only records the latter number although we record both numbers where known. Nonetheless, manufacturers Hornet, Mainair and Medway issue a composite construction number comprising of both units and this is generally adopted by the CAA. For example, Mainair Rapier G-BYBV is officially registered as c/n 1183-1198-7-W986 but only the first nine digits form the trike c/n.

Previous Identities   These are set out in reverse order with the most recent identity first. Some of these may have been issued several times and are noted with a suffix as stated above. Registrations shown in parenthesis have been allotted but were never officially used to the best of our knowledge. The nationality of foreign military serials is indicated only where it may not be apparent. Manufacturers' test marks, also known as "B Conditions" identities, are given where known.

Registration Date   This is the date of the original registration for those particular marks even where subsequently removed and restored.

Owner (*Operator*)   This is the registered owner for current aircraft as recorded in CAA records. Where the operator is known to be different this is shown in parenthesis. Included under this column are details of the latest reported status, for example if the C of A is not current or the aircraft is known to be under repair plus details of any names and, in particular, any military colour schemes and marks worn. Some aircraft are shown as temporary un-registered ("Temp unregd"); this is where the CAA has not received an application from a new owner following a sale. Usually the CAA gives a period of discretion and if no response is received the Certificate is cancelled and the aircraft is not permitted to fly. Such action usually stimulates the new owner to produce the relevant documentation.

(Unconfirmed) Base   The information in this column is not guaranteed: there is no official information. Reports by members and other readers who visit airfields and strips are perused to compile this column. Aircraft change base frequently. Balloons are generally shown as being based at their owners' registered address unless we have further information. Bases for active flexwing aircraft can present a problem as trikes are often stored at owners' homes after flying whilst corresponding sailwings are pegged out at base airfields. When the location is uncertain the owner's hometown is shown in parenthesis.

Readers are reminded that the identification of a base, particularly if it is a private strip, is not an invitation to visit and in a number of cases visiting is actively discouraged because of previous abuses. We recognise the need for privacy in this area and consequently not all information held is published. Readers are also directed to the AB-IX Bases database which has current details of airfields and listings of occupants. This is updated frequently.

CERTIFICATES OF AIRWORTHINESS (CofA) STATUS

The formation of the European Aviation Safety Agency (EASA) and the implementation of the associated European legislation has changed the responsibilities and procedures for the regulation of continuing airworthiness. Consistent with these developments, substantial changes have been made to CAA mandatory airworthiness information.

As a direct result of the European legislation, and with effect from 28th September 2004, UK-registered aircraft are now divided into two groups:
- *"EASA aircraft"*; that is, aircraft subject to regulation by EASA; and
- *"Non-EASA aircraft"*; that is, aircraft that remain subject to regulation by the CAA.

The specific aircraft are detailed in CAP747. Therefore, a new "EASA Standard Certificate of Airworthiness" has been introduced for those UK-registered aircraft now defined as *"EASA aircraft"*. CAA definitions for Private, Aerial Work and Transport categories remain for *"Non-EASA aircraft"*. These changes are in transition but it is already affecting the way we show CofA information. Two specific points to note are (i) all type certificated balloons are now deemed EASA aircraft and (ii) all gliders with a structural mass of 80kg or more (single seater) or 100 kg or more (two seater) are now being issued with a CofA.

CofA Expiry Date: Information is taken from information published by the CAA. The date indicates the currency of the aircraft's certificate and details of the coding suffix letters applied are set out below. In Section 1 the codings shown after the date of expiry indicate the CofA Certification category. The absence of a code letter means an aircraft holds a Private category CofA of either one or three year's duration. Where a CofA has expired or lapsed and an aircraft has been reported since that date further details are shown.

Codes used are as follows:-

   E: EASA Standard CofA - replacing **T** below

   S: Standard - national leglislation.

   T: Transport - issued to any Passenger aircraft operated for hire or reward, usually for either one or three years duration.

   T (C): Transport (Cargo) - issued to any aircraft operated for carrying cargo for hire or reward only, usually for either one or three years duration. Very few aircraft remain in this category.

   P: Permit to Fly - originally introduced in December 1935, but then lapsed during the Second World War, this system was re-activated in 1950. It covers homebuilder, vintage and microlight aircraft. The major criterion set out by the LAA is that the aircraft must be amateur built by it's owner in the UK. A homebuilder must spend at least 500 hours in completing the project for it to qualify under the Permit scheme as homebuilt. Permits are issued by the CAA on the recommendation of the LAA. It is the "prime document" and legalises flight of a Permit aircraft. The Permit is issued for the life of the aircraft but is only valid when certain conditions are fulfilled. The most fundamental of these is the Certificate of Validity (CofV) which is issued by the LAA following a satisfactory report concerning the annual inspection and test flying of the aircraft.

   A: Aerial Work - this category normally indicates aerial advertising, mainly by hot air balloons, and a few banner towing aircraft.

   X: Non-expiring Exemptions were issued originally to early microlights and hot air balloons. As at early 2007 only a few remained. However, a number of aircraft have now been declared to the BMAA as withdrawing from (or not requiring) the permit to fly scheme and they are now operating under the "Sub-115" exemption granted by the CAA whereby the aircraft effectively becomes "self-certified" by the pilot (type as listed by BMAA)

UK REGISTERED AIRCRAFT AS AT 1ST JANUARY EACH YEAR

Aircraft Class	MTOW kg	1985	1986	1987	1988	1989	1990	1991	1992	1993	1994	1995	1996	1997	1998	1999	2000	2001	2002	2003	2004	2005	2006	2007	2008	change since 2007
AIRSHIP (GAS-FILLED)	1 - 750 kg	2	2	3	2	3	5	5	5	5	4	4	4	3	3	3	3	0	0	0	0	0	0	0	0	0
AIRSHIP (GAS-FILLED)	751 - 5700 kg	3	3	3	3	4	5	7	7	7	6	6	3	3	3	3	3	3	4	5	5	5	5	3	3	0
AIRSHIP (GAS-FILLED)	5701 - 15000 kg	6	6	6	7	6	3	4	2	2	1	1	1	0	0	0	0	0	0	0	0	0	0	0	0	0
AIRSHIP (HOT AIR)	1 - 750 kg	17	21	20	23	29	31	28	28	29	27	27	26	21	19	16	18	14	10	11	10	10	9	8	8	0
AIRSHIP (HOT AIR)	751 - 5700 kg	4	4	2	4	4	4	6	9	9	9	9	10	13	15	18	18	16	18	15	15	14	13	13	13	0
BALLOON (GAS-FILLED)	1 - 750 kg	4	4	4	4	4	4	5	4	4	3	3	5	8	8	8	9	8	7	9	9	9	7	6	6	0
BALLOON (GAS-FILLED)	751 - 5700 kg	0	0	0	0	0	0	0	0	0	0	0	0	0	0	0	0	0	0	0	0	0	0	2	2	0
BALLOON (GAS/HOT AIR)	Not known	1	0	0	0	0	0	2	2	2	2	3	3	2	2	2	2	2	2	2	2	2	2	1	1	0
BALLOON (GAS/HOT AIR)	1 - 750 kg	0	0	0	0	1	0	2	1	0	0	0	1	1	2	2	2	3	2	2	1	1	0	1	2	1
BALLOON (GAS/HOT AIR)	751 - 5700 kg	0	0	0	0	2	2	2	1	2	2	3	2	2	2	2	2	2	2	2	3	3	2	2	2	0
BALLOON (HOT AIR)	Not known	99	114	118	134	147	159	167	162	168	156	158	157	154	148	134	138	142	116	114	107	108	105	102	102	0
BALLOON (HOT AIR)	1 - 750 kg	315	354	402	443	502	584	636	662	659	635	660	674	684	673	663	680	699	624	612	626	636	641	652	657	5
BALLOON (HOT AIR)	751 - 5700 kg	109	133	175	237	310	396	490	606	660	705	756	801	869	881	871	912	965	936	955	961	1000	1043	1056	1090	34
BALLOON (MINIMUM LIFT)	Not known	506	500	504	497	246	245	243	245	245	163	172	171	168	169	150	150	150	118	99	99	99	99	100	100	0
FIXED-WING AMPHIBIAN	1 - 750 kg	4	3	4	3	4	5	5	5	5	5	6	6	7	7	8	8	6	9	6	8	7	7	7	8	1
FIXED-WING AMPHIBIAN	751 - 5700 kg	2	3	3	3	6	5	6	7	9	9	9	8	9	8	10	10	6	9	8	8	9	10	11	12	1
FIXED-WING AMPHIBIAN	5701 - 15000 kg	0	0	0	0	0	0	0	0	0	0	0	0	0	1	0	1	1	1	0	1	1	1	1	1	0
FIXED-WING LANDPLANE	1 - 750 kg	1766	1845	1855	1879	1969	2143	2295	2289	2385	2507	2593	2657	2712	2758	2827	2813	2824	2832	2859	2914	2994	3022	3077	3153	76
FIXED-WING LANDPLANE	751 - 5700 kg	4019	4219	4291	4459	4807	5003	5176	5228	5187	5130	5075	5043	5111	5190	5292	5347	5429	5442	5461	5556	5647	5711	5822	5887	65
FIXED-WING LANDPLANE	5701 - 15000 kg	175	185	191	204	221	255	255	282	298	279	285	285	279	257	247	247	262	276	267	264	254	254	253	258	5
FIXED-WING LANDPLANE	15001 - 50000 kg	200	196	200	218	243	251	273	274	261	263	261	241	246	251	280	289	288	296	307	264	271	256	272	257	-15
FIXED-WING LANDPLANE	>50000 kg	229	233	231	254	284	324	336	358	380	388	396	401	406	439	499	541	592	624	645	644	662	679	712	760	48
FIXED-WING SEAPLANE	1 - 750 kg	0	0	0	0	0	0	0	1	0	0	0	0	0	0	0	0	0	0	0	0	0	0	0	0	0
FIXED-WING SEAPLANE	751 - 5700 kg	0	0	1	1	1	1	1	1	2	3	3	2	2	2	2	2	2	2	2	3	3	3	2	2	0
FIXED-WING SEAPLANE	15001 - 50000 kg	0	0	0	0	0	0	0	0	0	0	0	0	0	0	0	0	0	0	0	0	0	0	0	0	0
FIXED-WING SELF-LAUNCHING MOTOR GLIDER	1 - 750 kg	111	121	126	131	143	145	157	162	184	186	193	193	196	199	201	202	203	203	199	204	203	204	204	206	2
FIXED-WING SELF-LAUNCHING MOTOR GLIDER	751 - 5700 kg	25	35	52	52	50	51	52	52	54	48	46	46	49	56	62	66	70	70	71	70	73	76	76	80	4
GLIDER	1 - 750 kg	13	14	13	7	7	6	6	9	9	8	8	8	8	7	7	7	0	7	0	0	0	2	147	1094	947
GLIDER	751 - 5700 kg	0	0	0	0	0	0	0	0	0	0	0	0	0	0	0	0	0	0	0	0	0	1	2	13	11
GYROPLANE	1 - 750 kg	115	120	129	132	160	200	226	209	217	227	243	254	258	258	263	242	233	242	244	247	250	248	259	277	18
GYROPLANE	751 - 5700 kg	1	1	1	2	1	2	2	1	1	2	3	3	3	3	2	2	7	10	11	12	12	1	1	1	0
HANG GLIDER	1 - 750 kg	17	27	43	66	124	188	231	245	254	244	235	228	231	242	262	270	275	267	273	277	291	13	13	13	0
HELICOPTER	1 - 750 kg	17	27	43	66	124	188	231	245	254	244	235	228	231	242	262	270	275	267	273	277	291	293	288	289	1
HELICOPTER	751 - 5700 kg	413	448	448	446	491	573	595	574	541	507	515	532	552	591	642	673	715	755	794	814	882	952	1026	1120	94
HELICOPTER	5701 - 15000 kg	93	92	92	85	85	81	86	83	81	81	78	78	76	73	76	67	67	68	67	68	68	69	72	81	9
HELICOPTER	15001 - 50000 kg	4	4	1	3	0	0	0	0	0	0	0	0	0	0	0	0	0	0	0	0	0	0	0	0	0
MICROLIGHT	1 - 750 kg	1580	1901	2300	2629	3012	3298	3050	3194	3347	3337	3266	3207	3231	3314	3450	3548	3478	3531	3618	3828	4070	4118	4254	4392	138
TOTAL		9836	10594	11225	11934	12872	13958	14350	14710	15017	14941	15015	15059	15303	15594	16013	16293	16473	16474	16663	17013	17588	17894	18445	19890	1445

Aircraft Class	Weight group	1985	1986	1987	1988	1989	1990	1991	1992	1993	1994	1995	1996	1997	1998	1999	2000	2001	2002	2003	2004	2005	2006	2007	2008	change since 2007
AIRSHIP	All weights	32	35	34	38	46	53	50	51	54	47	47	44	40	40	40	42	33	28	31	30	29	27	24	24	0
BALLOON	All weights	529	608	702	821	966	1146	1302	1437	1499	1505	1586	1650	1730	1727	1693	1757	1829	1694	1700	1713	1763	1806	1822	1862	40
BALLOON (MINIMUM LIFT)	All weights	506	500	504	497	246	245	243	245	245	163	172	171	168	169	150	150	150	118	99	99	99	99	100	100	0
FIXED WING	All weights	6397	6688	6777	7024	7538	7970	8350	8448	8531	8585	8623	8645	8761	8915	9165	9263	9412	9487	9555	9650	9848	9943	10157	10338	181
FIXED WING SLMG	All weights	136	156	178	183	193	196	209	214	238	234	239	239	245	255	263	268	273	270	270	274	276	280	280	286	6
GLIDER	All weights	13	14	7	7	7	6	6	9	9	8	8	8	7	7	7	7	10	9	0	2	2	45	149	1107	958
GYROPLANE	All weights	116	121	130	134	161	202	228	210	218	229	246	257	261	261	265	244	233	242	244	247	251	249	260	278	18
HANG GLIDER	All weights	0	0	0	0	0	0	0	0	0	0	0	0	0	0	0	0	0	0	0	0	0	13	13	13	0
HELICOPTER	All weights	527	571	587	601	703	842	912	902	876	832	828	838	859	906	980	1013	1057	1090	1134	1159	1238	1314	1386	1490	104
MICROLIGHT	All weights	1580	1901	2300	2629	3012	3298	3050	3194	3347	3337	3266	3207	3231	3314	3450	3548	3478	3531	3618	3828	4070	4118	4254	4392	138
TOTAL	All weights	9836	10594	11225	11934	12872	13958	14350	14710	15017	14941	15015	15059	15303	15594	16013	16293	16473	16474	16663	17013	17588	17894	18445	19890	1445

Data produced on 02/01/2008 by the CAA Aircraft Registration Section, 45-59 Kingsway, London WC2B 6TE. Tel 020 7453 6666, E-mail aircraft.reg@caa.co.uk

GLOSSARY of TERMS and ABBREVIATIONS

AA	Automobile Association
AAC	Army Air Corps
AAIB	Air Accidents Investigation Branch
AB	Aktiebolaget (1)
ABAC	Assocation of British Aero Clubs and Centres
AC	Awaiting Certification
AERONCA	Aeronautical Corporation of America
AESL	Aero Engine Services Ltd
AIA	Atelier Industriel de l'Aéronautique d'Alger
AIRCO	Aircraft Manufacturing Co
ALAT	Aviation Légère de l'Armée de Terre
AMD-BA	Avions Marcel Dassault-Breguet and Aviation
ANEC	Air Navigation and Engineering Co
ANG	Air National Guard
ApS	Anpartsselskab (2)
APSS	Aviation Preservation Society of Scotland
ASS	Air Signallers School
AVIA	Azionara Vercellese Ind.Areo
A/c	Aircraft
Aka	also known as
Assn	Association
BA	British Aircraft Manufacturing Co Ltd
BAC	British Aircraft Company
BAC	British Aircraft Corporation
BAT	British Aerial Transport Co Ltd
BoBMF	Battle of Britain Memorial Flight
BMAA	British Microlight Aircraft Association
BV	Besloten Vennootschap (3)
CAARP	Coopérative des Ateliers Aéronautiques de la Région Parisienne
CAB	Constructions Aéronautiques de Béarn
CAB	Constructions Aéronautiques de Bourgogne
CAF	Canadian Air Force
CASA	Construcciones Aeronáuticas SA
CC	County Council
CCF	Canadian Car and Foundry
CDG	Charles de Gaule
CEA	Centre Est Aviation
Cobelavia	Compagnie Belge d'Aviation
CSS	Centralne Studium Samolotów
CZAL	Ceskoslovenske Zavody Automobilove a Letecke
Corp	Corporation
c	circa
C of A	Certificate of Airworthiness
C of R	Certificate of Registration
c/s	Colour scheme
DBF	Destroyed by fire
DEFRA	Department for Environment, Food and Rural Affairs
DEFTS	Defence Elementary Flying Training School
DF	Defence Force
DOSAAF	Dobrovol'noe Obshchestvo Sodeistviya Armii, Aviasii i Flotu
EASA	European Aviation Safety Agency
EKW	Eidgenössiche Konstruktions Werkstätte

EMBRAER	Empresa Brasileira de Aeronautica SA
EoN	Elliotts of Newbury Ltd
ERCO	Engineering and Research Corporation
ETPS	Empire Test Pilots' School
FAA	Fleet Air Arm
FAAM	Facility for Airborne Atmospheric Measurements
FLPH	Foot Launched Propelled Hang-glider
FTS	Flying Training School
f/f	First flight
fsm	Full Scale Model
GAF	Government Aircraft Factory
GC	Gliding Club
GmbH	Gesellschaft mit beschränkter Haftung (4)
IAA	Irish Aviation Authority
IAC	Integrated Avation Consortium
IAC	Irish Air Corps
IAR	Industria Aeronautica Romania
IAV	Intreprinderea de Avioane
ICA	Intreprinderea de Constructii Aeronautice-Brasov
ICAO	International Civil Aviation Organisation
IDF/AF	Israel Defence Force/Air Force
III	Iniziative Industriali Italiane
IMCO	Intermountain Manufacturing Co
IMES	Irish Marine Emergency Services
IPTN	Industri Pesawat Terbang Nusantara
IWM	Imperial War Museum
Intl	International
JAA	Joint Aviation Authority
JAR	Joint Aviation Regulations
KG	Kommanditgesellschaft (5)
KK	Kabushiki Kaisha (6)
LAA	Light Aircraft Association
LAK	Litovskaya Aviatsyonnaya Konstruktsiya
LET	Letecky Narodny Podnik
LLC	Limited Liability Corporation (7)
LLP	Limited Liability Partnership (8)
LVG	Luft-Verkehrs Gesellschaft
Lda	Limitada (9)
Lsg	Leasing
Ltd	Limited (10)
MBA	Micro Biplane Aviation
MBB	Messerschmitt-Bölkow-Blohm
MPA	Man Powered Aircraft
NV	Naamloze Vennootschap (11)
NK	Not known
Ntu	Not taken up
n/w	nose-wheel
OGMA	Oficinas Gerais de Material Aeronautico
Op	Operated by

PAP	Propulsion Auxiliare Parapente		t/a	Trading as
PFA	Popular Flying Association		tr	Trustee of
PIK	Polytecknikkojen Ilmailukerho		t/w	tail-wheel
PLC	Public Limited Company (12)		**U**AS	University Air Squadron
pr.no.	Project Number		ULM	Ultra-Léger Motorisé
PRC	Peoples' Republic of China		USAAC	United States Army Air Corps
PS	Plane Set			
PT	Pesawat Terbang (13)		**V**TC	Vazduhoplovno Tehnicki Centar
PWFU	Permanently Withdrawn from Use		VW	Volkswagen
PZL	Panstwowe Zaklady Lotnicze (State Aviation Works)			
			WACO	Weaver Aircraft Corp
			WFU	Withdrawn from Use
Qv	Which see		WSK	Wytwornia Sprzetu Komunikacy Jnego Okecie
R	Reservation			
RAF	Royal Aircraft Factory		**Z**RiPS	Zaklad Remontów i Produkcji Sprzetu Lotniczego
RAF	Royal Air Force			
RAFC	RAF College			
RAFGSA	RAF Gliding and Soaring Association			
RCAF	Royal Canadian Air Force			
Rep	Reproduction			

Company Constitution Notes

(1)	Sweden	Joint Stock
(2)	Denmark	Limited Liability
(3)	Netherlands	Private
(4)	Germany	Private Limited
(5)	Germany	Limited Partnership
(6)	Japan	
(7)	USA	Limited Partnership
(8)	UK	Limited Partnership
(9)	Portugal	Private Limited
(10)	UK	Private Limited
(11)	Belgian and Netherlands	
(12)	UK	Public Limited
(13)	Indonesia	
(14)	France and Romania	Public Limited
(15)	Spain	Public Limited
(16)	Poland	
(17)	France	Joint Stock
(18)	Italy	Limited Liability
(19)	Italy	Joint Stock

RFC — Royal Flying Corps
RJAF — Royal Jordanian Air Force
RN — Royal Navy
RNAS — Royal Naval Air Service
RSAF — Royal Saudi Air Force
RTS — Reduced to spares

SA — Société Anonyme (14)
SA — Sociedad Anónima (15)
SA — Spoika Akeyjna (16)
SAAC — Society of Amateur Aircraft Constructors
SA(AF) — South Arabian Federation (South Yemen)
SAI — Skandinavsk Aero Industri
SAN — Société Aéronautique Normande
SAR — Search and Rescue
SAS — Société par Actions Simplifiées (17)
SE — Scouting Experimental
SEAE — School of Electrical and Aeronautical Engineering
SIPA — Société Industrielle pour l'Aéronautique
SMA — Société de Motorisations Aeronautiques

SMD — Southern Microlight Developments
SNCAC — Société Nationale de Constructions Aéronautiques du Centre
SNCAN — Société Nationale de Constructions Aéronautiques du Nord
SOCATA — Société de Construction d'Avions de Tourisme et d'Affaires
SoS — Secretary of State
SpA — Società per Azioni (18)
SPP — Strojirny Prvni Petilesky
SRCM — Société de Recherches et de Constructions Mécaniques
Srl — Società a Responsabilità Limata (19)
Srs. — Series
SS — Special Shape (Balloon)
SZD — Szybowcowy Zaklad Dowswiadczalny
s/n — Serial Number

TAD — Technical Aid and Demonstrator
TBA — To be advised
TEAM — Tennessee Engineering and Manufacturing
TWU — Tactical Weapons Unit

SECTION 1 - UNITED KINGDOM

PART 1 – FIRST PERMANENT REGISTER (1919 to 1928)

Registration	Type	Construction No	Previous Identity	Reg.date	Registered Owner (*Operator*)	(Unconfirmed) Base	CofA Expy

G-EAAA - G-EAZZ

Registration	Type	Construction No	Previous Identity	Reg.date	Registered Owner (*Operator*)	(Unconfirmed) Base	CofA Expy
G-EASD	Avro 504L *(Clerget 130hp)*	E 5	S-AHAA S-AAP, G-EASD, (RAF)	26. 3.20	G M New *(Under restoration for Avro Heritage Centre 3.04)*	Woodford	

G-EBAA - G-EBZZ

Registration	Type	Construction No	Previous Identity	Reg.date	Registered Owner (*Operator*)	(Unconfirmed) Base	CofA Expy
G-EBHX	de Havilland DH.53 Humming Bird *(ABC Scorpion II)*	98	No.8* *("Lympne 1923 trials)*	22. 9.23	Richard Shuttleworth Trustees *"L'Oiseau-Mouche" (Noted 10.06)*	Old Warden	21. 8.04P
G-EBIA	Royal Aircraft Factory SE.5a *(Built Wolseley Motors Ltd) (Wolseley Viper 200hp)*	654/2404	F904 "D7000", G-EBIA, F904	26. 9.23	Richard Shuttleworth Trustees *(As "F904" in RFC 56 Sqdn c/s: noted 10.06)*	Old Warden	5. 5.06P
G-EBIR	de Havilland DH.51 *(AirDisco Renault 120bhp)*	102	VP-KAA G-KAA, G-EBIR	22. 1.24	Richard Shuttleworth Trustees *"Miss Kenya"*	Old Warden	12.10.07P
G-EBJO	Air Navigation and Engineering ANEC II *(ABC Scorpion II)*	1	No.7* *(*Lympne 1924 trials)*	17. 7.24	Richard Shuttleworth Trustees	Old Warden	111. 6.08P
G-EBKY	Sopwith Pup *(Built Sopwith Aviation Co Ltd as "Dove") (Le Rhône 80hp)*	w/o 3004/14	"N5180" "N5184", G-EBKY	27. 3.25	Richard Shuttleworth Trustees *"Happy"* *(As "9917" in RFC c/s to represent Beardmore built Pup)*	Old Warden	12.07.08P
G-EBLV	de Havilland DH.60 Moth *(ADC Cirrus III)*	188		22. 6.25	BAE Systems (Operations) Ltd *(On loan to Richard Shuttleworth Trustees)*	Old Warden	21. 8.08P
G-EBNV	English Electric S.1 Wren *(ABC 398cc)*	4	(BAPC.11) G-EBNV	9. 4.26	Richard Shuttleworth Trustees *(Composite - principally c/n 3 rebuilt 1955/56: noted 10.06 as "No.4")*	Old Warden	23. 6.87P
G-EBQP	de Havilland DH.53 Humming Bird *(Bristol Cherub III)*	114	J7326	?. 4.27	M C Russell tr G-EBQP Syndicate	Salisbury Hall, London Colney	
					(Fuselage on rebuild 5.04: will use wings ex Martin Monoplane G-AEYY and carry "J7326")		
G-EBWD	de Havilland DH.60X Moth *(ADC Hermes 2)*	552		2. 3.28	Richard Shuttleworth Trustees	Old Warden	10. 4.08P

PART 2 – SECOND PERMANENT REGISTER (1928 onwards)

G-AAAA - G-AAZZ

Registration	Type	Construction No	Previous Identity	Reg.date	Registered Owner (*Operator*)	(Unconfirmed) Base	CofA Expy
G-AADR (2)	American Moth Corporation DH.60GM Moth *(DH Gipsy I)*	138	NC939M	2. 6.86	E V Moffatt	Woodlow Farm, Bosbury	20.11.07P
G-AAEG	de Havilland DH.60G Moth	1027	D-EUPI D-1599, G-AAEG	4. 2.29	I B Grace *(New owner 1.02)*	(Ada, Michigan, US)	
G-AAHI	de Havilland DH.60G Moth *(DH Gipsy I) (Original fuselage used in 1953 rebuild of G-AAWO)*	1082		25. 5.29	N J W Reid	Lee-on-Solent	9. 4.08P
G-AAHY	de Havilland DH.60M Moth *(DH Gipsy I)*	1362	HB-AFI G-AAHY	10. 5.29	D J Elliott *(Brooklands Flying Club titles)*	Thruxton	15. 8.08P
G-AAIN	Parnall Elf II *(ADC Hermes 2)*	2 & J 6		11. 6.29	Richard Shuttleworth Trustees *(Noted 10.06)*	Old Warden	16. 7.05P
G-AAJT	de Havilland DH.60G Moth	1084	NC947M G-AAJT	4. 7.29	M R Paul *(New owner 6.05)*	Lee-on-Solent	
G-AALY	de Havilland DH.60G Moth *(DH Gipsy I) (Composite: rebuilt from components*	1175	F-AJKM G-AALY	9. 9.29	K M Fresson	Lee-on-Solent	15. 5.05T
G-AAMY (2)	American Moth Corporation DH.60GMW Moth *(Wright Gipsy L320)*	86	N585M NC585M	2. 5.80	Totalsure Ltd	Seppe-Hoeven, Netherlands	11. 8.04P
G-AANG (2)	Bleriot Type XI *(1910 original) (Anzani 25hp)*	14	BAPC.3	29.11.81	Richard Shuttleworth Trustees *(No external marks)*	Old Warden	22. 9.07P
G-AANH (2)	Deperdussin Monoplane *(Anzani Y 35hp) (Possibly c/n 143)*	43	BAPC.4	29.10.81	Richard Shuttleworth Trustees *(No external marks)*	Old Warden	4. 4.08P
G-AANI (2)	Blackburn Single Seat Monoplane *(Gnome 50hp no.683)*	"9"	BAPC.5 No.9* *(*Lympne 1923 trials)*	29.10.81	Richard Shuttleworth Trustees *(No external marks)*	Old Warden	22. 6.08P
G-AANL (2)	de Havilland DH.60M Moth *(DH Gipsy II) (Composite rebuild)*	1446	OY-DEH RDAF S-357, S-107	26. 6.87	A L Berry *(National Flying Services titles)*	Glenrothes	22.11.08P
G-AANM (2)	Bristol F 2b Fighter composite *(Built British and Coloniial Aero Co 1917) (RR Falcon)*	"67626"	BAPC.166	16. 7.87	Aero Vintage Ltd *(To Canada Aviation Museum 12.06 as "D7889")*	Ottawa, Ontario, Canada	25. 6.07P
G-AANO (2)	American Moth Corporation DH.60GMW Moth *(Composite rebuild 11.91)*	165	N590N NC590N	3. 3.88	A W and M E Jenkins *(New owner 3.03)*	(Comberton, Cambridge)	
G-AANV (2)	de Havilland DH.60M Moth *(Built Morane Saulnier) (DH Gipsy I)*	13	HB-OBU CH-349, F-AJNY	8. 3.84	R A Seeley	Hill Farm, Durley	22. 6.08P
G-AAOK (2)	Curtiss-Wright Travel Air 12Q Travelair *(Warner Scarab 125hp)*	12Q-2026	N370N NC370N, NC352M	18.11.81	Shipping and Airlines Ltd	Biggin Hill	11. 7.08P
G-AAOR (2)	de Havilland DH.60G Moth *(DH Gipsy I) (C/n uncertain: probably a composite)*	1075	EC-AAO	15. 4.85	B R Cox and N J Stagg *(Noted 6.06)*	Frogland Cross	17.11.05P
G-AAPZ	Desoutter I *(ADC Hermes 2)*	D 25		?. ?.31	Richard Shuttleworth Trustees	Old Warden	24. 4.07P
G-AAUP	Klemm L 25-1a *(Salmson AD9)*	145		19. 2.30	J I Cooper t/a Newbury Aeroplane Co *(On rebuild 10.01)* *"Clementine"*	Denford Manor, Hungerford	21.11.84P
G-AAWO	de Havilland DH.60G Moth *(DH Gipsy I) (1953 rebuild substituted original fuselage of G-AAHI)*	1235		2. 5.30	N J W Reid	Lee-on-Solent	1. 4.08P
G-AAYT	de Havilland DH.60G Moth	1233	DR606 G-AAYT	?. 5.30	P Groves *(Noted 9.04)*	Lee-on-Solent	
G-AAYX	Southern Martlet *(AS Genet Major 1A)*	202		14. 5.30	Richard Shuttleworth Trustees	Old Warden	14. 6.07P

G-AAZG	de Havilland DH.60G Moth	1253	EC-AAE	23. 5.30	C C J M Lovell and J A Pothecary	Chilbolton	
			EC-MMA, M-CMMA, MW-133, G-AAZG *(On rebuild 9.04)*				
G-AAZP	de Havilland DH.80A Puss Moth	2047	HL537	4. 6.30	R P Williams	Folly Farm, Hungerford	17. 6.09S
	(DH Gipsy Major)		G-AAZP, SU-AAC, G-AAZP *"British Heritage"*				

G-ABAA - G-ABZZ

G-ABAG	de Havilland DH.60G Moth	1259		23. 6.30	A and P A Wood	Audley End	6. 5.08P
	(DH Gipsy I)						
G-ABDA	de Havilland DH.60G Moth	1284	N60GD	7.30	R A Palmer	White Waltham	24. 5.08P
			N1284A, G-ABDA, 2595M, DG583, G-ABDA				
G-ABDX	de Havilland DH.60G Moth	1294	HB-UAS	22. 8.30	M D Souch	Hill Farm, Durley	13.10.05P
	(DH Gipsy I)		G-ABDX				
G-ABEV (2)	de Havilland DH.60G Moth	1823	N4203E	10. 3.77	S L G Darch	East Chinnock, Yeovil	29.11.75P
	(DH Gipsy I)		G-ABEV (2), HB-OKI, CH-217				
G-ABLS	de Havilland DH.80A Puss Moth	2164		7. 5.31	R A Seeley	Turweston	28. 5.08P
	(DH Gipsy Major)						
G-ABNT	Civilian CAC.1 Coupe	O 2.3		10. 9.31	Shipping and Airlines Ltd	Biggin Hill	25. 5.07P
	(AS Genet Major 1A) *(C/n also quoted as O 3)*						
G-ABNX	Robinson Redwing 2	9		2. 7.31	R J Burgess tr Redwing Syndicate	Redhill	12. 5.03P
					(Noted 4.06)		
G-ABOX (2)	Sopwith Pup	-	N5195	2. 9.84	C M D and A P St Cyrien	AAC Middle Wallop	22. 4.93P
	(80hp Le Rhône)				*(On loan to Museum of Army Flying as "N5195")*		
G-ABSD	de Havilland DH.60G Moth	1883	A7-96	21.11.31	M E Vaisey tr Chiltern Flying Club		
			VH-UTN, G-ABSD		*(On rebuild)*	(Hemel Hempstead)	
G-ABUS	Comper CLA.7 Swift	S 32/4		27. 2.32	R C F Bailey	(France)	19. 6.79P
	(Pobjoy Niagara 3)				*(Believed extant 2007)*		
G-ABVE	Arrow Active 2	2		19. 3.32	R A Fleming	Breighton	3. 5.08P
	(DH Gipsy III)						
G-ABWP	Spartan Arrow 1	78		?. 4.32	R E Blain	Redhill	3. 1.06P
	(Cirrus Hermes 2)						
G-ABXL	Granger Archaeopteryx	3A		3. 6.32	J R Granger	Radcliffe-on-Trent	22. 9.82P
	(Cherub III)				*(New owner 4.02)*		
G-ABYA	de Havilland DH.60G Moth	1906		?. 7.32	D A Hay and J F Moore	Biggin Hill	30 3.08
	(DH Gipsy I)						
G-ABZB (2)	de Havilland Moth Major	5011	SE-AEL	11. 9.80	G M Turner and N Child	(Siddington, Cirencester)	8. 7.08P
	(DH Gipsy Major 1C)		OY-DAK				

G-ACAA - G-ACZZ

G-ACCB	de Havilland DH.83 Fox Moth	4042		24. 1.33	E A Gautrey	(Nuneaton)	20. 7.57
					(Crashed off Southport 25. 9.56 and on rebuild 10.95)		
G-ACDA	de Havilland DH.82A Tiger Moth	3175	BB724	6. 2.33	B D Hughes	Rotary Farm, Hatch	26. 6.82
			G-ACDA		*(Crashed and burned out near Cirencester 27. 6.79: on rebuild 2007)*		
G-ACDC	de Havilland DH.82A Tiger Moth	3177	BB726	6. 2.33	The Tiger Club (1990) Ltd	Sywell	20. 6.08T
	(Composite airframe)		G-ACDC				
G-ACDI	de Havilland DH.82A Tiger Moth	3182	BB742	6. 2.33	J A Pothecary	Old Sarum	
	(Composite rebuild)		G-ACDI		*(Noted on rebuild 1.08)*		
G-ACEJ	de Havilland DH.83 Fox Moth	4069		21. 4.33	J I Cooper	Boscombe Down	16. 8.10S
					(Scottish Motor Traction titles)		
G-ACET	de Havilland DH.84 Dragon	6021	2779M	21. 4.33	M D Souch	Hill Farm, Durley	
			AW171, G-ACET		*(On rebuild 5.06 composite based on original wings)*		
G-ACGZ	de Havilland Moth Major	5038	VT-AFW	30. 5.33	N H Lemon	(Cookham, Maidenhead)	
			G-ACGZ		*(On rebuild 2000)*		
G-ACLL	de Havilland DH.85 Leopard Moth	7028	AW165	16. 1.34	D C M and V M Stiles	Jurby, Isle of Man	6.12.95P
			G-ACLL		*(New owners 1.03)*		
G-ACMA	de Havilland DH.85 Leopard Moth	7042	BD148	14. 3.34	S J Filhol	(Castlefreke, County Cork)	3. 2.94P
			G-ACMA		*(Noted 2005)*		
G-ACMD (2)	de Havilland DH.82A Tiger Moth	3195	N182DH	20. 1.88	M J Bonnick	Rectory Farm, Abbotsley	18. 7.08S
			EC-AGB, Sp AF 33-5 *(Provenance doubtful: EC-AGB had interim Spanish AF serial 30-104)*				
G-ACMN	de Havilland DH.85 Leopard Moth	7050	X9381	?. 4.34	M R and K E Slack	Duxford	25. 7.09S
			G-ACMN				
G-ACNS	de Havilland Moth Major	5068	ZS-???	?. 3.34	R I and D Souch	Hill Farm, Durley	19. 9.08S
			G-ACNS				
G-ACOJ (2)	de Havilland DH.85 Leopard Moth	7035	F-AMXP	5. 6.87	A J Norman tr Norman Aeroplane Trust	Rendcomb	24. 10.10S
	(Composite with wings from HB-OXO)						
G-ACSP	de Havilland DH.88 Comet	1994	CS-AAJ	21. 8.34	T M, M L, D A and P M Jones	Derby	
			G-ACSP, E-1		*(Under restoration 2005)*		
G-ACSS	de Havilland DH.88 Comet	1996	K5084	4. 9.34	Richard Shuttleworth Trustees	Old Warden	2. 6.94P
	(DH Gipsy Queen 2)		G-ACSS		*"Grosvenor House/" "34" (Noted 10.06)*		
	(In addition, four other replicas exist as "G-ACSS" - (1) at Mount Waverley, Victoria, Australia, (2) BAPC.216, (3) BAPC.257						
	- details in SECTION 5, Part 2,.and (4) N88XD [T7] built Repeat Aircraft, Riverside CA, US in 1993 for T J Wathen)						
G-ACTF	Comper CLA.7 Swift	S 32/9	VT-ADO	24. 5.34	Richard Shuttleworth Trustees	Old Warden	24. 4.07P
	(Pobjoy Niagara 2)						
G-ACUS (2)	de Havilland DH.85 Leopard Moth	7082	HB-OXA	17.11.77	R A and V A Gammons	RAF Henlow	18.12.08S
	(Composite including parts ex HB-OXO c/n 7045)		(G-ACUS)				
G-ACXB (2)	de Havilland Moth Major	5098	EC-ABY	24. 1.89	D F Hodgkinson	(Gravesend)	
			EC-BAX, Sp AF 30-53, EC-YAY *(On rebuild 2000)*				
G-ACXE	British Klemm L 25c1 Swallow	21		29.10.34	J G Wakeford	Bexhill-on-Sea	7. 4.40
	(On rebuild using components to re-draw plans and produce a substantially "new-build" airframe: progress continuing 2006 at Newbury)						
G-ACZE	de Havilland DH.89A Dragon Rapide	6264	G-AJGS	20.11.34	Wessex Aviation and Transport Ltd	(Haverfordwest)	2. 7.10S
			G-ACZE, Z7266, G-ACZE				

G-ADAA - G-ADZZ

Reg	Type	C/n	Prev ID	Date	Owner	Location	Date
G-ADEV (2)	Avro 504K	R3/LE/61400	G-ACNB	18. 4.84	Richard Shuttleworth Trustees	Old Warden	24. 4.08P
	(110 hp Le Rhône)		"E3404"		(As "H5199" in RAF c/s)		
	(P/i not confirmed but, if correct, full p/i is 3118M, BK892, G-ADEV, H5199)						
G-ADGP	Miles M.2L Hawk Speed Six	160	G-ADGP	20. 5.35	R A Mills "8"	Lasham	4. 6.08P
G-ADGT	de Havilland DH.82A Tiger Moth	3338	BB697	23. 5.35	Aviation Ventures Ltd	Sywell	4. 5.09S
			G-ADGT		(Also carries "BB697")		
G-ADGV	de Havilland DH.82A Tiger Moth	3340	(D-E...)	23. 5.35	K J and P J Whitehead		
			G-ADGV, (G-BACW), BB694, G-ADGV		Whitchurch Hill, Reading		1.10.09S
G-ADHD (2)	de Havilland Moth Major	5105	EC-...	17. 2.88	M E Vaisey	RAF Henlow	
	(Rebuild of ex Spanish components ex US)		Spanish AF 34-5, EC-W32		(Noted 7.02)		
G-ADIA	de Havilland DH.82A Tiger Moth	3368	BB747	13. 8.35	S J Beaty	Wold Lodge, Finedon	5. 5.08
			G-ADIA				
G-ADJJ	de Havilland DH.82A Tiger Moth	3386	BB819	29. 8.35	J M Preston	Watchford Farm, Yarcombe	20.12.08S
			G-ADJJ				
G-ADKC	de Havilland DH.87B Hornet Moth	8064	X9445	27. 3.36	A J Davy	White Waltham	30. 3.08
			G-ADKC				
G-ADKK	de Havilland DH.87B Hornet Moth	8033	W5749	9.11.35	R M and D R Lee	Oaksey Park	18. 4.10
			G-ADKK				
G-ADKL	de Havilland DH.87B Hornet Moth	8035	F-BCJO	?.11.35	P R and M J F Gould		
			G-ADKL, W5750, G-ADKL		Coulommiers, Seine-et-Marne, France		8. 7.08
G-ADKM	de Havilland DH.87B Hornet Moth	8037	W5751	12.11.35	L V Mayhead	Hill Farm, Durley	6. 7.01
			G-ADKM		(Fuselage noted 8.06)		
G-ADLY	de Havilland DH.87B Hornet Moth	8020	W9388	5.10.35	Totalsure Ltd	Perth	1. 1.11
			G-ADLY		"Leicestershire Foxhound II"		
G-ADMT	de Havilland DH.87B Hornet Moth	8093		8. 5.36	S and H Roberts "Curlew"	Oaksey Park	30. 7.10
G-ADND	de Havilland DH.87B Hornet Moth	8097	W9385	4. 8.36	D M and S M Weston	Hullavington	22. 3.08P
			G-ADND		(As "W9385:YG-L" and "3" in RAF 502 Sqdn c/s)		
G-ADNE	de Havilland DH.87B Hornet Moth	8089	X9325	10. 3.36	R Felix tr G-ADNE Group	Oaksey Park	16. 5.09
			G-ADNE		"Ariadne"		
G-ADNL	Miles M.5 Sparrowhawk	239		12. 8.35	A P Pearson	(Ramsbottom, Bury)	13. 5.58S
	(Reconstructed c1953 as M 77 Sparrowjet)				(On rebuild in Bristol area 4.04)		
G-ADNZ (2)	de Havilland DH.82A Tiger Moth	85614	6948M	10.10.74	D C Wall	Tibenham	12. 8.09S
			DE673		(As "DE673" in RAF c/s)		
G-ADPC	de Havilland DH.82A Tiger Moth	3393	BB852	24. 9.35	D J Marshall	Charity Farm, Baxterley	2. 8.06
			G-ADPC				
G-ADPJ	BAC Drone 2	7		21. 8.35	N H Ponsford	(Selby)	17. 5.55
	(Douglas Sprite)				(Crashed Leicester 3. 4.55: on rebuild 12.99 using parts from G-AEJR c/n 22)		
G-ADPS	BA L.25c Swallow II	410		4. 9.35	J F Hopkins	Watchford Farm, Yarcombe	23. 4.08P
	(Pobjoy Cataract 2)						
G-ADRA (2)	Pietenpol AirCamper	PFA 1514		10. 4.78	A J Mason	Bicester	19. 4.08P
	(Built A J Mason) (Continental A65)				"Edna May"		
G-ADRH (2)	de Havilland DH.87B Hornet Moth	8038	G-ADRH	6. 8.82	R G Grocott	Mandeville, Gore, New Zealand	
	(Originally regd with c/n IMC/8164, amended 20.5.85)		F-AQBY, HB-OBE		(On rebuild 2000 - reserved as ZK-ANR)		
G-ADRR (2)	Aeronca C.3	A.734	N17423	6. 9.88	S J Rudkin	(Oakham)	
			NC17423		(On rebuild 2007: wings noted at Skycraft, Spalding 11.01)		
G-ADUR	de Havilland DH.87B Hornet Moth	8085	N9026Y	10. 3.36	W A Gerdes	Swanborough Farm, Lewes	1. 8.08
			G-ADUR				
G-ADWJ	de Havilland DH.82A Tiger Moth	3450	BB803	9.12.35	C Adams	(Madley)	
			G-ADWJ		(Under restoration 3.97)		
G-ADWT	Miles M.2W Hawk Trainer	215	CF-NXT	18.11.35	R Earl and B Morris	Landmead Farm, Garford	10. 6.08P
			G-ADWT, NF750, G-ADWT				
G-ADXT	de Havilland DH.82A Tiger Moth	3436		9.12.35	J R Hanauer	Goodwood	15. 6.09S
	(Mainly rebuild of components)						
G-ADYS	Aeronca C.3	A.600		?. 1.36	J I Cooper	Frogland Cross	6. 5.04P
	(Aeronca E113C)				(London Air Park Flying Club titles)		

G-AEAA - G-AEZZ

Reg	Type	C/n	Prev ID	Date	Owner	Location	Date
G-AEBB	Mignet HM.14 Pou-Du-Ciel	KWO.1		24. 1.36	Richard Shuttleworth Trustees	Old Warden	31. 5.39
	(Built K W Owen)				(Noted 8.06)		
G-AEBJ	Blackburn B 2	6300/8		4. 2.36	BAE Systems (Operations) Ltd	Old Warden	30. 6.05
	(DH Gipsy Major)				(On loan to Richard Shuttleworth Trustees)		
G-AEDB	BAC Drone 2	13	BGA 2731	18. 3.36	P L Kirk and R E Nerou	Hucknall	26. 5.87P
	(Bristol Cherub III)		G-AEDB (Composite with wings of G-AEJH and tail of G-AEEN) (Noted 6.07)				
G-AEDU (2)	de Havilland DH.90A Dragonfly	7526	N190DH	4. 6.79	A J Norman tr Norman Aeroplane Trust	Rendcomb	11. 8.08
			G-AEDU, ZS-CTR, CR-AAB				
G-AEEG	Miles M.3A Falcon Major	216	SE-AFN	14. 3.36	P R Holloway	Old Warden	12. 7.10S
			Fv913, SE-AFN, G-AEEG, U-20				
G-AEFT	Aeronca C.3	A.610		17. 4.36	N C Chittenden	(Herodsfoot, Liskeard)	8. 5.04P
	(JAP J 99) (Rebuilt 1976 with major parts of G-AETG (qv))						
G-AELO	de Havilland DH.87B Hornet Moth	8105	AW118	30. 7.36	M J Miller	Audley End	16. 8.10S
			G-AELO				
G-AEML	de Havilland DH.89 Dragon Rapide	6337	X9450	1. 9.36	Fundacion Infante de Orleans	Cuatro Vientos, Spain	4. 7.08
			G-AEML				
G-AENP (2)	Hawker Afghan Hind	41H/81902	(BAPC.78)	29.10.81	Richard Shuttleworth Trustees	Old Warden	5. 6.08P
	(Kestrel V)		R Afghan AF		(As "K5414:XV"in RAF 15 Sqdn c/s)		
G-AEOA	de Havilland DH.80A Puss Moth	2184	ES921	1.10.36	A and P A Wood	(Audley End)	27. 6.95P
	(DH Gipsy Major)		G-AEOA, YU-PAX, UN-PAX				
G-AEOF (2)	Rearwin 8500 Sportster	462	N15863	1.12.81	Shipping and Airlines Ltd	Biggin Hill	5.10.01P
	(85hp Le Blond 5DF)		NC15863				

G-AEPH	Bristol F 2b Fighter	7575	D8096	13.11.36	Richard Shuttleworth Trustees	Old Warden	24. 4.08P
	(RR Falcon 3) *(Original c/n 3746 and rebuilt C 1931)*		G-AEPH, D8096		*(As "D8096:D" in RAF c/s)*		
G-AERV	Miles M.11A Whitney Straight	307	EM999	30.12.36	R A Seeley	Hill Farm, Durley	9. 4.66
			G-AERV		*(On rebuild 9.07)*		
G-AESB (2)	Aeronca C.3	A.638	N15742	5. 8.88	R J M Turnbull	Rydinghurst Farm, Cranleigh	
			NC15742		*(On rebuild 6.06)*		
G-AESE	de Havilland DH.87B Hornet Moth	8108	W5775	13. 1.37	J G Green	Grange Farm, Frogland Cross	10. 8.09S
			G-AESE		"Sheena"		
G-AESZ	Chilton DW.1	DW.1/1		?. 1.37	R E Nerou	(Old Warden)	16. 8.08P
	(Carden Ford 32 hp)						
G-AETG	Aeronca 100	AB.110		?. 2.37	J J Teague tr J Teague and Partners (Barton Ashes)		
	(Crashed on take-off Booker 7. 4.69 : cancelled 29. 2.72 as destroyed: major parts to G-AEFT in 1976 - on rebuild with parts from G-AEWV 1996) (New owner 1.07)						
G-AEUJ	Miles M.11A Whitney Straight	313		19. 2.37	R E Mitchell *(Stored 11.06)*	Sleap	4. 6.70
G-AEVS	Aeronca 100	AB.114		3.37	R A Fleming	Breighton	11. 4.07P
	(JAP J 99) *(Composite including parts of original G-AEXD)*				"Jeeves" *(Noted 12.07)*		
G-AEXD	Aeronca 100	AB.124		1. 4.37	M A and R W Mills	Sywell	20. 4.70P
	(JAP J 99) *(Mainly comprises parts of G-AESP after rebuild in 1958)*				*(On rebuild 10.07)*		
G-AEXF	Percival Type E Mew Gull	E 22	ZS-AHM	18. 5.37	R A Fleming	Breighton	17. 6.08P
	(Rebuilt as pr.no.PFA 013-10020)						
G-AEXT	Dart Kitten II	123		?. 4.37	A J Hartfield	Marsh Hill Farm, Aylesbury	2. 7.07P
	(JAP J 99)						
G-AEXZ	Piper J-2 Cub	997		5. 2.38	J R and M Dowson	(Leicester)	2.11.78S
	(Built Taylor Aircraft Co Inc) (Continental A75)				*(On rebuild: by 3.00 wings only and remainder with owner at home)*		
G-AEZJ	Percival Type K Vega Gull	K 65	SE-ALA	2. 7.37	D P H Hulme	Biggin Hill	5. 8.10S
			D-IXWD, PH-ATH, G-AEZJ				

G-AFAA - G-AFZZ

G-AFAX	BA Eagle 2	138	VH-ACN	26.10.37	Fundacion Infante de Orleans Cuatro Vientos, Spain		15. 5.08
	(DH Gipsy Major)		G-AFAX				
G-AFCL	BA L 25c Swallow II	462		3.11.37	C P Bloxham	Shotteswell	16. 8.04P
	(Pobjoy Niagara 3)				*(New owner 5.07)*		
G-AFDO (2)	Piper J-3C-65 Cub	2593	N21697	7. 6.88	R Wald	Hill Farm, Durley	27. 7.99P
	(Frame No.2633)		NC21697		"Butter Cub" *(On rebuild 12.02)*		
G-AFEL (2)	Monocoupe 90A	A 782	N19432	7. 6.82	M Rieser	Little Staughton	22.12.05P
	(Lambert R266)		NC194323		*(On rebuild 2007)*		
G-AFFD	Percival Type Q Six	Q.21	(G-AIEY)	12. 2.38	B D Greenwood	Fenland	31. 8.56
			X9407, G-AFFD		*(On rebuild 2007)*		
G-AFFH	Piper J-2 Cub	1166	EC-ALA	26. 3.38	M J Honeychurch	(Charlton, Pewsey)	29. 8.53
	(Built Taylor Aircraft Co Inc) (Continental A40)		G-AFFH		*(On restoration at owner's home 10.01)*		
G-AFGC	BA L 25c Swallow II	467	BK893	4. 4.38	G E Arden	Thorns Cross Farm, Chudleigh	20. 3.51
	(Pobjoy Niagara 3)		G-AFGC		*(Stored 1.98)*		
G-AFGE	BA L 25c Swallow II	470	BK894	4. 4.38	C W N and A A M Huke	Manor Farm, Dinton	27. 7.98P
	(Pobjoy Niagara 2)		G-AFGE		*(Noted 4.98)*		
G-AFGH	Chilton DW.1	DW.1/2		20. 3.38	M L and G L Joseph	Denford Manor, Hungerford	7. 7.83P
	(Lycoming O-145-A2) *(To be re-engined with Carden-Ford)*				*(On rebuild 2006)*		
G-AFGI	Chilton DW.1	DW.1/3		30. 3.38	J E and K A A McDonald	White Waltham	15. 8.07P
	(Walter Mikron 2)						
G-AFGM (2)	Piper J-4A Cub Coupé	4-943	N26895	30.12.81	P H Wilkinson	Wigtown	9.10.06P
			NC26895				
G-AFGZ	de Havilland DH.82A Tiger Moth	3700	G-AMHI	9. 5.38	M R Paul	Lee-on-Solent	16. 5.09S
			BB759, G-AFGZ				
G-AFHA (2)	Moss MA.1	MA.1/2		27. 2.67	C V Butler	(Allesley, Coventry)	
					(Small components only stored)		
G-AFIN	Chrislea LC.1 Airguard	LC.1	BAPC.203	7. 7.38	N H Wright	Queach Farm, Bury St Edmunds	
					(Stored 2.06)		
G-AFIR	Luton LA-4 Minor	JSS.2		7. 7.38	A J Mason	(Aylesbury)	30. 7.71
	(Built J S Squires) (JAP J-99)				*(Damaged near Cobham 14. 3.71 and on rebuild 5.05)*		
G-AFJA	Taylor-Watkinson Dingbat	DB.100		2. 8.38	A T Christian	Walkeridge Farm, Overton	23. 6.75S
	(Built Taylor Watkinson Aircraft Co) (Carden-Ford 32hp)				*(Damaged Headcorn 19. 5.75 and partially rebuilt: new owner 11.06)*		
G-AFJB	Foster-Wikner GM.1 Wicko	5	DR613	15. 8.38	J Dible	Hill Farm, Durley	16. 7.08P
	(DH Gipsy Major 1)		G-AFJB				
G-AFJU	Miles M.17 Monarch	789	X9306	25. 8.38	P W Bishop	Oaksey Park	18. 5.64
	(Built Phillips and Powis Aircraft Ltd)		G-AFJU		*(Noted for rebuild 11.07)*		
G-AFJV (2)	Moss MA.2	MA.2/2		27. 2.67	C V Butler	(Allesley, Coventry)	
					(Small components only stored)		
G-AFNG	de Havilland DH.94 Moth Minor	94014	AW112	2. 5.39	D Saunders tr The Gullwing Trust		
	(Cabin)		G-AFNG		*(Stored 10.05)*	(Galway, Counth Galway)	21.10.98P
G-AFNI	de Havilland DH.94 Moth Minor	94035	W7972	11. 5.39	J Jennings	Fenland	26. 5.67
			G-AFNI		*(On rebuild 2002)*		
G-AFOB	de Havilland DH.94 Moth Minor	94018	X5117	16. 5.39	K Cantwell	(Royston)	11. 5.93P
			G-AFOB		*(New owner 2.02)*		
G-AFOJ	de Havilland DH.94 Moth Minor	9407	E-1	21. 7.39	R M Long "Bugs 2" Salisbury Hall, London Colney		27. 8.69P
	(Cabin)		E-0236, G-AFOJ		*(On loan to de Havilland Heritage Museum) (Noted 5.04)*		
G-AFPN	de Havilland DH.94 Moth Minor	94044	X9297	23. 5.39	J W and A R Davy	Redhill	2. 6.08
	(Now regd with c/n 94016)		G-AFPN				
G-AFRZ	Miles M.17 Monarch	793	G-AIDE	24. 3.39	R E Mitchell	Sleap	29. 6.70
			W6463, G-AFRZ		*(Noted 10.06)*		
G-AFSC	Tipsy Trainer 1	11		15. 7.39	D M Forshaw	Panshanger	31. 5.07P
	(Walter Mikron 2)						
G-AFSV	Chilton DW.1A	DW.1A/1		5. 4.39	R E Nerou	(Coventry)	12. 7.72
	(Train 4T 40 hp)				*(On restoration 2006)*		

Reg	Type	C/n	Prev id	Date	Owner	Base	Status
G-AFTA	Hawker Tomtit (Mongoose 3C)	30380	K1786 G-AFTA, K1786	26. 4.39	Richard Shuttleworth Trustees (As "K1786" in RAF c/s)	Old Warden	31. 7.07P
G-AFUP (2)	Luscombe 8A Silvaire (Continental A65)	1246	N25370 NC25370	7. 6.88	R Dispain	(Fordingbridge)	12. 3.97P
G-AFVE (2)	de Havilland DH.82A Tiger Moth (Built Morris Motors Ltd)	83720	T7230	1. 2.78	J Mainka (As "T-7230" in RAF c/s)	(Warsaw, Poland)	30. 4.10T
G-AFWH (2)	Piper J-4A Cub Coupé (Continental A65)	4-1341	N33093 NC33093	14. 1.82	C W Stearn and R D W Norton (Stored 4.04)	(Ely)	2. 7.01P
G-AFWI	de Havilland DH.82A Tiger Moth	82187	BB814 G-AFWI	19. 7.39	E Newbigin Brown Shutters Farm, Norton St Philips, Somerset		28. 2.10
G-AFWT	Tipsy Trainer 1 (Walter Mikron 2)	13		1. 8.39	N Parkhouse	Old Warden	20. 5.08P
G-AFYD (2)	Luscombe 8F Silvaire (Continental C90)	1044	N25120 NC25120	29. 7.75	J D Iliffe	Chilbolton	4.11.10
G-AFYO (2)	Stinson HW-75 Voyager	7039	F-BGQP NC22586 (Probably ex French.Military with identity "22586")	25. 4.77	M Lodge	Westfield Farm, Hailsham	21. 5.07P
G-AFZA (2)	Piper J-4A Cub Coupé (Continental A65)	4-873	N26198 NC26198	27. 6.84	R A Benson (Wings noted at Trenchard Farm, Eggesford 9.05)	(Exeter)	2.12.02P
G-AFZK (2)	Luscombe 8A Silvaire (Continental A65)	1042	N25118 NC25118	24.10.88	M G Byrnes	Haverfordwest	29. 5.08P
G-AFZL (2)	Porterfield CP-50 (Continental A50)	581	N25401 NC25401	18. 3.82	P G Lucus and S H Sharpe	White Waltham	17. 7.08P
G-AFZN (2)	Luscombe 8A Silvaire (Continental A65)	1186	N25279 NC25279	5.10.81	R J Griffin and J L Truscott	Ranston Farm, Iwerne Courtney	25. 7.08P

G-AGAA - G-AGZZ

Reg	Type	C/n	Prev id	Date	Owner	Base	Status
G-AGAT (2)	Piper J-3F-50 Cub (Franklin 4AC-150 Series 50)	4062	N26126 NC26126	17. 7.87	A S Bathgate	Castleton Farm, Gorebridge	29. 7.08P
G-AGEG (2)	de Havilland DH.82A Tiger Moth	82710	N9146 D-EDIL, R Neth AF A-32, PH-UFK, A-32, R4769	16. 8.82	A J Norman tr Norman Aeroplane Trust	Rendcomb	15. 5.10S
G-AGFT (2)	Avia FL.3 (CNA D4S)	176	I-TOLB MM....	21. 8.84	K Joynson and K Cracknell (As "8110" in Croatian Air Force c/s)	Breighton	31. 1.08P
G-AGHY (2)	de Havilland DH.82A Tiger Moth	82292	N9181	17. 2.88	P Groves	Lee-on-Solent	29. 4.10
G-AGIV (2)	Piper J-3C-65 Cub (L-4J-PI) (Frame No.12506)	12676	OO-AFI OO-GBA, 44-80380	13. 8.82	T Welsh tr J3 Cub Group	Compton Abbas	6. 3.08P
G-AGJG	de Havilland DH.89A Dragon Rapide	6517	X7344	25.10.43	M J and D J T Miller	Duxford	9.10.10S
G-AGLK	Taylorcraft J Auster 5D	1137	RT475	25. 8.44	C R Harris	Rochester	10. 6.10S
G-AGMI (2)	Luscombe 8E Silvaire Deluxe (Continental C85)	1569	N28827 NC28827	15.11.88	P J Laycock and D J R Pike tr Oscar Flying Group	Twineham, West Sussex	16. 4.08P
G-AGNJ (2)	de Havilland DH.82A Tiger Moth (Built de Havilland Aircraft Proprietary Ltd Australia)	660	VP-YOJ ZS-BGF, SAAF 2366	21. 2.89	A J, B P and P J Borsberry (Kidmore End, Reading) (On rebuild 6.95:)		
G-AGOH	Auster V J/1 Autocrat	1442		19. 4.45	Leicestershire County Council Museums (On loan to Newark Air Museum)	Winthorpe	24. 8.95
G-AGPK (2)	de Havilland DH.82A Tiger Moth (Fitted with wings, tailplane, fin and rudder ex G-ANLH 2002)	86566	N657DH F-BGDN, French AF, PG657	27.10.88	Aviation Ventures Ltd (Operated Delta Aviation)	Sywell	23. 4.08E
G-AGSH	de Havilland DH.89A Dragon Rapide 6 (Built Brush Coachworks Ltd)	6884	EI-AJO G-AGSH, NR808	25. 7.45	Techair London Ltd (BEA titles) "Jemma Meeson"	Bournemouth	20. 9.07
G-AGTM	de Havilland DH.89A Dragon Rapide 6 (Built Brush Coachworks Ltd)	6746	JY-ACL D-ABP, G-AGTM, NF875	19. 9.45	Aviation Heritage Ltd	Coventry	31. 5.10S
G-AGTO	Auster V J/1 Autocrat	1822		2.10.45	M J Barnett and D J T Miller	Duxford	9. 3.09S
G-AGTT	Auster V J/1 Autocrat	1826		2.10.45	R Farrer (Stored 12.97)	(Bromham, Bedford)	11. 2.93
G-AGVG	Auster V J/1 Autocrat (Lycoming O-360-A2A) (Modified tail surfaces)	1858		7.12.45	P J Benest "Pamela IV"	Hamstead Marshall	13. 7.09S
G-AGVN	Auster V J/1 Autocrat	1873	EI-CKC G-AGVN	18. 1.46	R Taggart	(Clonard, Enfield, County Meath)	24. 8.09S
G-AGVV (2)	Piper J-3C-65 Cub (L-4H-PI)	11163	F-BCZK French AF, 43-29872	19. 2.81	M Molina-Ruano	(Malaga, Spain)	2. 9.04P
G-AGXN	Auster J/1N Alpha	1963		22. 1.46	J J Teagle tr Gentleman's Aerial Touring Carriage Group	Barton Ashes	19. 6.08
G-AGXU	Auster J/1N Alpha	1969		24. 1.46	B H Austen	Oaksey Park	13. 8.06
G-AGXV	Auster V J/1 Autocrat	1970		1. 2.46	B S Dowsett and I M Oliver "Pamela IV"	Little Gransden	2.11.09S
G-AGYD	Auster J/1N Alpha	1985		4. 2.46	P R Hodson (Damaged near Felthorpe 25.11.90: on rebuild 4.94)	Little Gransden	24.11.90
G-AGYH	Auster J/1N Alpha (Built Taylor Aeroplanes)	1989		4. 2.46	I M Staves (New owner 1.05)	(Northallerton)	10.10.72
G-AGYK	Auster V J/1 Autocrat	2002		4. 2.46	M C Hayes tr Autocraft Syndicate	Bidford	17. 8.07
G-AGYT	Auster J/1N Alpha	1862		18. 1.46	P J Barrett (On overhaul 6.94)	(Lightwater)	27. 2.91
G-AGYU	de Havilland DH.82A Tiger Moth (Built Morris Motors Ltd)	85265	DE208	10. 1.46	P L Jones (As "DE-208" in RAF c/s)	Tuam, Galway, County Galway	14. 9.10S
G-AGYY (2)	Ryan ST3KR (PT-21-RY) (Kinner R56)	1167	N56792	15. 6.83	H de Vries (As "27" in USAAC c/s)	(Haskerdijken, Netherlands)	3. 7.08P
G-AGZZ (2)	de Havilland DH.82A Tiger Moth (Built de Havilland Aircraft Proprietary Ltd Australia)	T256 & 926	N3862 VH-BTU, VH-RNM, VH-BMY, A17-503	14. 5.82	M C Jordan	Eaglescott	9. 9.10

G-AHAA - G-AHZZ

Reg	Type	C/n	Prev id	Date	Owner	Base	Status
G-AHAG	de Havilland DH.89A Dragon Rapide (Built Brush Coachworks Ltd)	6926	RL944	31. 1.46	S G Jones (New owner 8.05)	Membury	15. 7.73
G-AHAL	Auster J/1N Alpha (Built Taylor Aeroplanes)	1870		31. 1.46	J W Frecklington and R Merwood t/a Wickenby Aviation	Wickenby	4. 5.10S
G-AHAM	Auster V J/1 Autocrat	1885		21. 1.46	C P L Jenkins	Rush Green	11. 5.08S

G-AHAN (2)	de Havilland DH.82A Tiger Moth	86553	N90406	31. 5.85	Tiger Associates Ltd	Bicester	26. 7.10S
	(Built Morris Motors Ltd)		F-BGDG, French AF, PG644				
G-AHAP	Auster V J/1 Autocrat	1887		8. 2.46	W D Hill	Fenland	20. 2.91P
	(Rover V-8)				(Noted 7.07)		
G-AHAU	Auster V J/1-160 Autocrat	1850	(HB-EOL)	11. 2.46	A C Webber tr Andreas Auster Group		
	(Lycoming O-320-A) (Built-up fin/fuselage fillet)					Andreas, Isle of Man	21. 4.09S
G-AHBL	de Havilland DH.87B Hornet Moth	8135	P6786	6. 2.46	H D Labouchere	Blue Tile Farm, Langham	10. 8.09S
			CF-BFN				
G-AHBM	de Havilland DH.87B Hornet Moth	8126	P6785	6. 2.46	E P and P A Gliddon Northfield Farm, Mavis Enderby		21. 6.02
			CF-BFJ, (CF-BFO), CF-BFJ		(Noted 7.06)		
G-AHCL	Auster J/1N Alpha	1977	G-OJVC	13. 5.46	Electronic Precision Ltd	RAF Mona	22.10.10S
	(Originally regd as J/1 Autocrat) (Lycoming 0-320-A2B)		G-AHCL				
G-AHCN	Auster J/1N Alpha	1980	OY-AVM	25. 3.46	C L Towell and E Martinsen	Bakersfield	8. 9.08S
	(Originally regd as J/1 Autocrat)		G-AHCN, OY-AVM, G-AHCN				
G-AHCR	Gould-Taylorcraft Plus D Special	211	LB352	15. 4.46	D R Shepherd and D E H Balmford	Dunkeswell	7. 9.07P
	(Continental C90)						
G-AHEC (2)	Luscombe 8A Silvaire	3428	N72001	28.10.88	P G Baxter	Hill Farm, Nayland	14. 7.05P
	(Continental A65)		NC72001		(Noted 2.06)		
G-AHGD	de Havilland DH.89A Dragon Rapide	6862	NR786	1. 4.46	S G Jones	Membury	20. 9.92
	(Built Brush Coachworks Ltd)				(New owner 1.06)		
G-AHGW	Taylorcraft Plus D	222	LB375	2. 9.46	C V Butler	Shenington	3. 5.96P
					(Operated Military Auster Flight as "LB375")		
G-AHGZ	Taylorcraft Plus D	214	LB367	24. 4.46	M Pocock	Henstridge	13.10.05
					(As "LB367" in RAF c/s) (Operated S White)		
G-AHHH	Auster J/1N Alpha	2011	F-BAVR	11. 5.46	H A Jones	Duxford	18. 6.08P
			G-AHHH				
G-AHHT	Auster J/1N Alpha	2022		11. 5.46	A C Barber and N J Hudson tr Southdowns Auster Group		
						Durleighmarsh Farm, Rogate	1.12.07
G-AHIP (2)	Piper J-3C-65 Cub (L-4H-PI)	12122	OO-GEJ (2)	3. 7.85	A R M Mangham	Rayne Hall Farm, Braintree	11.12 03P
	(Frame No.11950)		OO-ALY, 44-79826		(Noted 1.07)		
	(Officially regd with c/n 12008: see G-AJAD)						
G-AHIZ	de Havilland DH.82A Tiger Moth	86533	PG624	23. 4.46	CFG Flying Ltd	Cambridge	4. 6.09S
	(Built Morris Motors Ltd) (Regd with fuselage no.4610)						
G-AHKX	Avro 19 Series 2	1333		18. 5.46	BAE Systems (Operations) Ltd	Old Warden	21. 8.08P
					(On loan to Richard Shuttleworth Trustees)		
G-AHLK	Taylorcraft E Auster III	700	NJ889	1. 5.46	J H Powell-Tuck	(St Briavels, Lydney)	21. 9.97
					(New owner 2.08)		
G-AHLT	de Havilland DH.82A Tiger Moth	82247	N9128	2. 5.46	M P Waring	(Hrenley-on-Thames)	13 8.09S
G-AHNR (2)	Taylorcraft BC-12D	7204	N43545	15.11.88	J C Holland	Chilton Foliat, Hungerford	2. 6.08P
	(Continental A65)		NC43545				
G-AHOO (2)	de Havilland DH.82A Tiger Moth	86150	6940M	6. 6.85	J T and A D Milsom	Little Farm, Hamstead Marshall	14. 8.09S
	(Built Morris Motors Ltd) (Regd with c/n 86149)		EM967				
G-AHPZ	de Havilland DH.82A Tiger Moth	83794	EI-AFJ	22. 5.46	N J Wareing	Lee-on-Solent	21.11.10S
			G-AHPZ, T7280				
G-AHSA	Avro 621 Tutor	-	K3215	21. 6.46	Richard Shuttleworth Trustees	Old Warden	30. 8.08P
	(Lynx IVM)		G-AHSA, K3215		(As "K3241" in RAF Central Flying School 1930s c/s)		
G-AHSD	Taylorcraft Plus D	182	LB323	1. 7.46	A L Hall-Carpenter	Shipdham	10. 9.62
					(Restored and noted 8.06)		
G-AHSO	Auster J/1N Alpha	2123		8. 8.46	W P Miller	Northfield Farm, Mavis Enderby	6. 4.95T
					(On rebuild 9.05)		
G-AHSP	Auster V J/1 Autocrat	2134	F-BGRO	8. 8.46	R M Weeks	Earls Colne	1.10.10S
			G-AHSP				
G-AHSS	Auster J/1N Alpha	2136		8. 8.46	A M Roche "Sunday Sierra"	Great Massingham	23. 7.09S
G-AHTE	Percival Proctor V	Ae58		26. 6.46	D K Tregilgas	New Farm House, Great Oakley	10. 8.61
					(On rebuild 1.06)		
G-AHUF (2)	de Havilland DH.82A Tiger Moth	86221	A2123	26. 2.85	Dream Ventures Ltd	Full Sutton	12. 7.09S
	(Built Morris Motors Ltd)		NL750		(As "T-7997" in RAF c/s)		
G-AHUG	Taylorcraft Plus D	153	LB282	5. 6.46	D Nieman	(Thame)	12. 7.70
G-AHUN (2)	Globe GC-1B Swift	3536/766	EC-AJK	24. 7.86	R J Hamlet	North Weald	4. 8.95P
			OO-KAY, NC77764		(On rebuild 6.07)		
G-AHUV	de Havilland DH.82A Tiger Moth	3894	N6593	24. 6.46	A D Gordon	Blair Athol	27. 7.09S
G-AHVU	de Havilland DH.82A Tiger Moth	84728	T6313	14. 8.46	J B Steel	Blue Tile Farm, Langham	29.12.08E
					(As "T6313" in RAF c/s)		
					(Made heavy landing Goodwood 8.7.06 with substantial damage)		
G-AHVV	de Havilland DH.82A Tiger Moth	86123	EM929	24. 6.46	Ace Flight Training LLP	Dunkeswell	5. 3.10T
	(Built Morris Motors Ltd)						
G-AHWJ	Taylorcraft Plus D	165	LB294	20. 6.46	M Pocock (New owner 1.03)	Kemble	30. 6.71
G-AHXE	Taylorcraft Plus D	171	LB312	9. 7.46	J M C Pothecary	AAC Netheravon	16. 7.08P
					(As "LB312" in RAF c/s)		

G-AIAA - G-AIZZ

G-AIBH	Auster J/1N Alpha	2113		19. 8.46	M J Bonnick	Standalone Farm, Meppershall	5. 9 10S
G-AIBM	Auster V J/1 Autocrat	2148		2. 9.46	R Greatrex	Colthrop Manor, Thatcham	21.11.10
G-AIBR	Auster V J/1 Autocrat	2151		2. 9.46	P R Hodson	Felthorpe	26.10.09S
G-AIBW	Auster J/1N Alpha	2158		2. 9.46	W B Bateson	Blackpool	12. 7.09S
G-AIBX	Auster V J/1 Autocrat	2159		2. 9.46	B H Beeston tr The Wasp Flying Group	Little Gransden	5.12.08S
G-AIBY	Auster V J/1 Autocrat	2160		2. 9.46	D Morris (Stored 6.97)	Sherburn-in-Elmet	13. 4.81
G-AICX (2)	Luscombe 8A Silvaire	2568	N71141	27. 1.88	R V Smith	Henstridge	10. 8.07P
	(Continental A65)		NC71141		"Easy Grace"		
G-AIDL	de Havilland DH.89A Dragon Rapide 6	6968	TX310	23. 8.46	Air Atlantique Ltd	Coventry	4. 7.08T
	(Built Brush Coachworks Ltd)				(As "TX310" in RAF c/s)		

Reg	Type	c/n	Prev id	Date	Owner	Location	Date
G-AIDS	de Havilland DH.82A Tiger Moth	84546	T6055	22. 8.46	K D Pogmore and T Dann Benson's Farm, Laindon		11. 8.09S
					"The Sorcerer"		
G-AIEK	Miles M.38 Messenger 2A	6339	U-9	27. 8.46	J Buckingham	New Farm, Felton	26. 7.10
					(As "RG333" in RAF 2 TAF Comm Sqdn c/s)		
G-AIFZ	Auster J/1N Alpha	2182		2.11.46	M D Anstey	Rushett Farm, Chessington	20. 8.01
					(Noted 2004)		
G-AIGD	Auster V J/1 Autocrat	2186		2.11.46	R B Webber *(Noted 8.07)* Trenchard Farm, Eggesford		3. 5.07P
G-AIGF	Auster J/1N Alpha	2188		5.11.46	A R C Mathie	Carlisle	17.11.08S
G-AIGT	Auster J/1N Alpha	2176		12.10.46	R R Harris *(New owner 4.02)*	(Crowfield)	22.10.76
G-AIIH	Piper J-3C-65 Cub (L-4H-PI)	11945	44-79649	14. 9.46	M S Pettit	Oxford	19.12.06P
G-AIJM	Auster V J/4 Archer	2069	EI-BEU	13.11.46	N Huxtable *"Priscilla"*	Cheddington	28. 3.97
			G-AIJM		*(Damaged near Tring 5. 1.97: stored pending overhaul and /repairs)*		
G-AIJT	Auster V J/4 Series 100 Archer	2075		13.11.46	J L Thorogood tr The Aberdeen Auster Flying Group		
	(Continental O-200-A)					Pittrichie Farm, Whiterashes	10.11.08S
G-AIKE	Taylorcraft J Auster 5	1097	NJ728	15.11.46	C J Baker	Carr Farm, Thorney, Newark	3. 2.66
	(Built Taylorcraft Aeroplanes Ltd) (Frame No.TAY 2450)				*(Crashed Luton 1. 9.65: dismantled 1.05)*		
G-AIPR	Auster V J/4 Archer	2084		9. 1.47	R W and M A Mills tr The MPM Flying Group		
						Popham	27. 9.07P
G-AIPV	Auster V J/1 Autocrat	2203		9. 1.47	W P Miller	Northfield Farm, Mavis Enderby	7. 2.05
					"Buttercup"		
G-AIRC	Auster V J/1 Autocrat	2215		13. 1.47	Z J Rockey	Trenchard Farm, Eggesford	2. 8.07
G-AIRK	de Havilland DH.82A Tiger Moth	82336	N9241	22.10.46	J S and P R Johnson		
					(Bradfield St Clare, Bury St Edmunds)		1. 8.07
G-AISA	Tipsy Trainer 1	17		24. 4.47	S Slater	Bicester	19. 4.08P
G-AISC	Tipsy Trainer 1	19		24. 4.47	D R Shepherd tr Wagtail Flying Group	(Prestwick)	23. 5.79P
					(Stored 5.02)		
G-AISD	Miles M.65 Gemini 1A	6285	OO-RLD	26.11.46	William Tompkins Ltd	Spanhoe	8. 3.10S
			VP-KDH, OO-RLD, G-AISD				
G-AISS (2)	Piper J-3C-65 Cub (L-4H-PI)	12077	D-ECAV	3. 9.85	K W Wood and F Watson	Insch	25. 6.97P
	(Frame No.11904)		SL-AAA, 44-79781		*(Fuselage noted 9.07 hanging from hangar roof unmarked).*		
G-AIST	Vickers Supermarine 300 Spitfire IA WASP/20/2		AR213	25.10.46	Sheringham Aviation UK Ltd	Wycombe Air Park	26. 3.02P
	(Built Westland Aircraft Ltd) (Also Heston Aircraft Company c/n HA1 6S/5 139)				*(First post restoration flight 12.11.07 as G-AIST)*		
G-AISX	Piper J-3C-85 Cub (L-4H-PI)	11663	43-303722	8.10.46	A M Turney tr Cubfly	Wycombe Air Park	21. 5.07P
	(Frame No.11489) (Rebuilt with ex Spanish airframe)						
G-AIUA	Miles M.14A Hawk Trainer 3	2035	T9768	11.11.46	D S Hunt	Redhill	13. 7.67P
	(Wings fitted 1960s from G-ANWO: crashed Roborough 26.9.65 and original centre section used to rebuild G-AKPF: fuselage stored) (New owner 1.06)						
G-AIXJ	de Havilland DH.82A Tiger Moth	85434	DE426	28.11.46	D Green	(Pulborough)	13. 8.09S
	(Built Morris Motors Ltd) (Probably rebuilt with composite airframe by Newbury Aeroplane Co mpany c 1991)						
G-AIXN	Automobilove Zavody Mraz M 1C Sokol	112	OK-BHA	22. 4.47	A J Wood	Breighton	12. 4.08P
G-AIYG (2)	SNCAN Stampe SV-4B	21	OO-CKZ	31. 8.89	M Lageirse and E Henny	Antwerp, Belgium	30. 3.08
			F-BCKZ, French AF				
G-AIYR	de Havilland DH.89A Dragon Rapide	6676	HG691	11.12.46	Spectrum Leisure Ltd	Duxford	1. 5..08T
	(Built Brush Coachworks Ltd)				*(As "HG691" in RAF c/s) (Operated Classic Wings)*		
G-AIYS	de Havilland DH.85 Leopard Moth	7089	YI-ABI	16.12.46	R A and V A Gammons	RAF Henlow	3. 6.10S
			SU-ABM				
G-AIZU	Auster V J/1 Autocrat	2228		31. 1.47	C J and J G B Morley	Popham	2. 8.09
G-AIZY	Auster V J/1 Autocrat	2233		31. 1.47	B J Richards		
					(City of Bristol College, Ashley Down, Bristol)		20. 9.78
					(Damaged Portskewett, Caldicot 8.89: on rebuild 6.91)		

G-AJAA - G-AJZZ

Reg	Type	c/n	Prev id	Date	Owner	Location	Date
G-AJAD (2)	Piper J-3C-65 Cub (L-4H-PI)	12008	OO-GEJ (1)	26. 6.84	C R Shipley	(Bristol)	28. 8.07P
	(Frame No.11835) (Regd with c/n 11700)		44-79712		*(Airframe has original fuselage of OO-GEJ discarded in a rebuild in 1970s)*		
	OO-GEJ rebuilt with Frame No.11950 (c/n 12122) ex OO-ALY/44-79826 and now G-AHIP: OO-ALY rebuilt from c/n 11700 ex OO-TON (ex 43-30409)						
G-AJAE	Auster J/1N Alpha	2237		4. 2.47	J Cooke tr Lichfield Auster Group		
						Streathay Farm, Lichfield	7. 9.09S
G-AJAJ	Auster J/1N Alpha	2243		4. 2.47	R B Lawrence	Watchford Farm, Yarcombe	1. 4.07
G-AJAM	Auster V J/2 Arrow	2371		8. 2.47	D A Porter	Griffins Farm, Temple Bruer	20. 6.07P
G-AJAP (2)	Luscombe 8A Silvaire	2305	N45778	26. 1.89	M Flint	Fenland	28. 5.08P
	(Continental A65)		NC45778				
G-AJAS	Auster J/1N Alpha	2319		14. 3.47	C J Baker	Carr Farm, Thorney, Newark	11. 4.90
					(Noted complete 1.05)		
G-AJCP (2)	Druine D 31 Turbulent	PFA 512		9. 2.59	B R Pearson tr Turbulent Group	Eaglescott	4. 9.78S
	(Built Rollason Aircraft and Engines) (Ardem 4C02)				*(Stored 10.95)*		
G-AJEE	Auster V J/1 Autocrat	2309		14. 3.47	P Bate and A C Whitehead	Barton	3. 4.10S
G-AJEH	Auster J/1N Alpha	2312		14. 3.47	J Powell-Tuck	(Mamhilad, Pontypool)	28. 5.90
G-AJEI	Auster J/1N Alpha	2313		14. 3.47	J Siddall	North Moor, Scunthorpe	13. 6.08T
	(Originally regd as Auster J/1 Autocrat) (Composite rebuild 1976 with fuselage of F-BFUT c/n 3357)						
G-AJEM	Auster V J/1 Autocrat	2317	F-BFPB	14. 3.47	C D Wilkinson	Rosemarket	17. 5.10
			G-AJEM				
G-AJES (2)	Piper J-3C-65 Cub (L-4H-PI)	11776	OO-ACB	21. 9.84	G W Jarvis	Mill Farm, Shifnal	14. 9.07P
	(Frame No.11602)		43-30485		*(As "330485:C-44" in USAAC c/s)*		
G-AJGJ	Taylorcraft J Auster 5	1147	RT486	31. 1.47	D Gotts and E J Downing tr Auster RT486 Flying Group		
					(As "RT486:PF-A" in RAF c/s)	Lee-on-Solent	4. 6.10S
G-AJHS	de Havilland DH.82A Tiger Moth	82121	N6866	12. 2.47	J M Voeten and H van Der Paauw		
					(Operated Vliegend Museum)	Seppe, Netherlands	22. 7.09S
G-AJIH	Auster V J/1 Autocrat	2318		2. 4.47	D G Curran	Newtownards	2. 6.07
G-AJIS	Auster J/1N Alpha	2336		30. 4.47	J D Smith and J M Hodgson tr Husthwaite Auster Group		
						Baxby Manor, Husthwaite	3. 7.09S
G-AJIT	Auster V J/1 Kingsland	2337		30. 4.47	S J Rick tr G-AJIT Group	Netherthorpe	17. 6.07P
	(Continental O-200-A)				*(New owner 12.07)*		
G-AJIU	Auster V J/1 Autocrat	2338		30. 4.47	M D Greenhalgh	Netherthorpe	20. 6.03

G-AJIW	Auster J/1N Alpha	2340		30. 4.47	Truman Aviation Ltd	Tollerton	22. 8.04
G-AJJS (2)	Cessna 120	13047	8R-GBO	7. 1.87	R W Marchant, I D Ranger and S C Parsons tr Robhurst Flying Group		
	(Continental O-200-A)		VP-GBO VP-TBO, N1106M, YV-T-CTA, NC2786N			Little Robhurst Farm, Woodchurch	9. 5.08P
	(Rebuilt 1994 with new airframe?)						
G-AJJT (2)	Cessna 120	12881	N2621N	27. 1.88	J S Robson	Franklyn's Field, Chewton Mendip	15.10.07P
	(Continental C85)		NC2621N				
G-AJJU (2)	Luscombe 8E Silvaire Deluxe	2295	N45768	10. 1.89	S C Weston and R J Hopcraft	Enstone	16. 8.08P
	(Continental C85)		NC45768		*"Juliet Uniform"*		
G-AJKB (2)	Luscombe 8E Silvaire Deluxe	3058	N71631	4. 1.89	L Jump and T Carter	(Liverpool)	1. 7.05P
	(Continental C85)		NC71631		*(New owners 8.07)*		
G-AJOE	Miles M.38 Messenger 2A	6367		28. 4.47	P W Bishop	(France)	18.12.07
					(On rebuild 2007 after forced landing in Holland in 2006? which tore off starboard wing)		
G-AJON (2)	Aeronca 7AC Champion	7AC-2633	OO-TWH	3. 1.86	J M Gale	Dunkeswel	10. 6.08P
G-AJPI	Fairchild 24R-46A Argus III	851	HB614	26. 4.47	R Sijben	(Heel, Netherlands)	27. 6.10S
	(UC-61A-FA)		43-14887		*(As "314887" in USAAF c/s)*		
G-AJRB	Auster V J/1 Autocrat	2350		12. 5.47	P D Hamilton-Box	Trenchard Farm, Eggesford	8. 3.04T
					(Noted 8.07)		
G-AJRE	Auster V J/1 Autocrat	2603		12. 5.47	P Slater t/a Air Tech Spares Wellesbourne Mountford		17. 5.10S
G-AJRS	Miles M.14A Hawk Trainer 3	1750	P6382	30. 4.47	Richard Shuttleworth Trustees	Old Warden	11. 4.08P
	(Composite a/c which flew as "G-AJDR" 1.54/3.71)		G-AJDR, G-AJRS, P6382		*(As "P6382:C" in RAF 16 EFTS c/s)*		
G-AJTW	de Havilland DH.82A Tiger Moth	82203	N6965	21. 5.47	J A Barker (As "N6965:FL-J")	Tibenham	9. 9.00
					(Crashed landing Raydon near Ipswich 7. 6.99 and extensively damaged: wreck noted 7.02)		
G-AJUE	Auster V J/1 Autocrat	2616		5. 6.47	P H B Cole	Craysmarsh Farm, Melksham	22. 6.06
G-AJUL	Auster J/1N Alpha	2624		18. 6.47	M J Crees	Halstead, Essex	11. 9.81
					(On rebuild 12.90)		
G-AJVE	de Havilland DH.82A Tiger Moth	85814	DE943	28. 5.47	R A Gammons	RAF Henlow	10. 6.09S
	(Composite rebuild 1981 including substantial parts of G-APGL c/n 86460 ex NM140)						
G-AJWB	Miles M.38 Messenger 2A	6699		17. 6.47	P W Bishop	(Woodley, Reading)	8. 5.08
G-AJXC	Taylorcraft J Auster 5	1409	TJ343	11. 6.47	R D Helliar-Symons, K A and S E W Williams		
					(New owners 1.08) Bourne Park, Hurstbourne Tarrant		2. 8.82
G-AJXV	Taylorcraft G Auster 4	1065	F-BEEJ	8. 9.47	B A Farries	Carr Farm, Thorney, Newark	13. 7.09S
			G-AJXV, NJ695		*(As "NJ695" in RAF c/s) "Little Lulu"*		
G-AJXY	Taylorcraft G Auster 4	792	MT243	4. 5.48	D A Hall	(Melton Mowbray)	10.11.70
					(On rebuild 1993: new owner 7.00)		
G-AJYB	Auster J/1N Alpha	847	MS974	3. 2.49	P J Shotbolt		
					Ingthorpe Farm, Ingtthorpe, Great Casterton, Stamford		25. 7.08

G-AKAA - G-AKZZ

G-AKAT	Miles M.14A Hawk Trainer 3	2005	F-AZOR	2. 7.47	R A Fleming	Breighton	9. 9.08P
			G-AKAT, T9738		*(As "T9738" in RAF c/s)*		
G-AKAZ (2)	Piper J-3C-65 Cub (L-4A-PI)	AN.1 & 8499	F-BFYL	19. 4.82	Frazerblades Ltd	Duxford	12. 4.08P
	(Frame No.8616)		French AF, 42-36375		*(As "G-57" in 83rd FS/78th FG USAAC c/s)*		
G-AKDN	de Havilland DHC-1A Chipmunk 10	11		14. 8.47	P S Derry	Saskatoon, Canada	31. 5.07
G-AKDW	de Havilland DH.89A Dragon Rapide	6897	F-BCDB	25. 8.47	de Havilland Aircraft Museum Trust Ltd		
	(Built Brush Coachworks Ltd)		G-AKDW, YI-ABD, NR833		*"City of Winchester"* Salisbury Hall, London Colney		8. 5.59
					(On long term restoration 5.04)		
G-AKEN	Miles M.65 Gemini 1A	6486	VH-GBB	8. 9.47	C W P Turner (Snitterfield, Stratford-upon-Avon)		7.10.54
			VH=BTP (1)		*(New owner 1.08)*		
G-AKEX	Percival P.34 Proctor III	H 549	SE-BTR	26. 8.47	M Biddulph	(Bildeston, Ipswich)	
	(Built F Hills and Sons Ltd)		LZ791		*(Shipped to UK 12.07 for eventual restoration)*		
G-AKHP	Miles M.65 Gemini 1A	6519		3.10.47	M Hales	Little Staughton	11. 6.09S
G-AKHU	Miles M.65 Gemini 1A	6522	VH-BOB (2)	18.10.47	C W P Turner (Snitterfield, Stratford-upon-Avon)		28. 2.49
			VH-WEK, VH-WEJ, (VH-DFP) VH-BMV *(New owner 1.08)*				
G-AKIB (2)	Piper J-3C-90 Cub (L-4H-PI)	12311	OO-RAY	18. 4.84	M C Bennett	Higherlands Farm, Branscombe	19. 8.06P
	(Frame No.12139)		44-80015		*(As "480015:M-44" in USAAC c/s)*		
					(Caught by gust of wind and overturned beside runway.Perranporth 2. 7.06 with substantial damage: on rebuild 2007)		
G-AKIF	de Havilland DH.89A Dragon Rapide	6838	LN-BEZ	24. 9.47	Airborne Taxi Services Ltd		
			G-AKIF, NR750			Duxford and Wycombe Air Park	5. 7.10S
G-AKIN	Miles M.38 Messenger 2A	6728		19. 9.47	D L Sentance tr Sywell Messenger Group	Sywell	11. 7.09S
G-AKIU	Percival Proctor V	Ae129		20. 2.48	Air Atlantique Ltd	Seaton Ross	24. 1.65
					(Under restoration by Hornet Aviation 2.04)		
G-AKKB	Miles M.65 Gemini 1A	6537		28.10.47	J Buckingham *(Air Total c/s)*	New Farm, Felton	19. 5.08
G-AKKH	Miles M.65 Gemini 1A	6479	OO-CDO	23. 7.48	J S Allison	Bicester	5.10.09S
G-AKPF	Miles M.14A Hawk Trainer 3	2228	V1075	27. 1.48	P R Holloway (As "N3788" in RAF c/s)	Old Warden	10. 4.08P
	(Rebuilt 1955 as composite with centre-section from G-AIUA, fuselage from G-ANLT, wings from G-AHYL: rebuilt 1970/80 with about 10%						
	of fuselage from G-AKPF: tail unit also from G-ANLT)						
G-AKRA (2)	Piper J-3C-65 Cub (L-4H-PI)	11255	I-FIVI	15. 6.84	W R Savin	(Cambridge)	
	(Frame No.11080)		43-29964		*(On rebuild 5.05)*		
G-AKRP	de Havilland DH.89A Dragon Rapide 4	6940	CN-TTO	26. 1.48	B R Pearson tr Eaglescott Dominie Group Eaglescott		6. 1.08S
			(F-DAFS), G-AKRP, RL958		*"Northamptonshire Rose"*		
G-AKSY	Taylorcraft J Auster 5	1567	F-BGOO	10. 2.48	A Brier	Breighton	17. 5.10S
			G-AKSY, TJ534		*(As "TJ534" in AAC c/s)*		
G-AKSZ	Taylorcraft J Auster 5C	1503	F-BGPQ	10. 2.48	P W Yates and R G Darbyshire (Adlington, Chorley)		9. 5.02
	(DH Gipsy Major 1) *(Large fin and rudder)*		G-AKSZ, TJ457				
G-AKTH (2)	Piper J-3C-65 Cub (L-4J-PI)	13211	OO-AGL	14. 7.86	G J Harry, The Viscount Goschen		
	(Frame No.13041) (Regd with incorrect c/n 13047)		PH-UCR, 45-4471			Bradleys Lawn, Heathfield	14. 5.08P
G-AKTI (2)	Luscombe 8A Silvaire	4101	N1374K	27. 5.87	J D May	(London W6)	4. 4.08P
	(Continental A65)		NC1374K				
G-AKTK (2)	Aeronca 11AC Chief	11AC-1017	N9379E	13. 3.89	R W Marshall tr Aeronca Tango Kilo Group		
	(Continental A65)		NC9379E			Waits Farm, Belchamp Walter	11. 9.03P
G-AKTN (2)	Luscombe 8A Silvaire	3540	N77813	22. 7.88	P C Hignett and PG Ward	(Harwich)	1. 6.04P
	(Continental A65)		NC77813		*(New owners 9.07)*		

G-AKTO (2)	Aeronca 7BCM Champion	7AC-940	N8515X	19. 5.88	D C Murray	Lee-on-Solent	15. 5.08P
	(Continental A75) *(Modified ex 7AC standard 1950)* N82311, NC82311						
G-AKTP (2)	Piper PA-17 Vagabond	17-82	N4683H	24. 6.88	P J B Lewis tr Golf Tango Papa Group	Swansea	5. 8.03P
	(Continental C85)		NC4683H				
G-AKTR (2)	Aeronca 7AC Champion	7AC-3017	N58312	19. 6.89	C Fielder	Oaksey Park	17. 6.07P
			NC58312		*"Eddie"*		
G-AKTS (2)	Cessna 120	11875	N77434	26. 5.88	M Isterling	Insch	24.10.08P
			NC77434				
G-AKTT (2)	Luscombe 8A Silvaire	3279	N71852	21. 7.88	S J Charters (Eddsfield, Octon Lodge Farm, Thwing)		23. 6.92P
	(Continental A65)		NC71852		*(Crashed 6. 7.91: stored 1.96)*		
G-AKUE (2)	de Havilland DH.82A Tiger Moth	P 68	ZS-FZL	12. 2.86	D F Hodgkinson	Maypole Farm, Chislet	6.11.10S
	(Built OGMA)		CR-AGM, Portuguese AF FAP ????				
G-AKUF (2)	Luscombe 8F Silvaire	4794	N2067K	1. 8.88	M O Loxton	Parsonage Farm, Eastchurch	7. 8.03P
	(Continental C90)		NC2067K		*(New owner 3.07)*		
G-AKUH (2)	Luscombe 8E Silvaire Deluxe	4644	N1917K	24.10.88	E J Lloyd	Cardington	27. 7.08P
	(Continental O-200-A)		NC1917K		*"Lucy Too"*		
G-AKUI (2)	Luscombe 8E Silvaire Deluxe	2464	N45937	24.10.88	D A Sims	Yeatsall Farm, Abbots Bromley	30. 3.08P
	(Continental O-200-A)		NC45937 *(Involved in mid-air collision with Pacific Aerospace 570XL ZK-KAY (107),*				
	crashed in field Rectory Farm, near Admaston, Staffordshire 16.12.07.and substantially damaged)						
G-AKUJ (2)	Luscombe 8E Silvaire Deluxe	5282	N2555K	4. 8.88	R C Green	Coventry	31. 7.07P
	(Continental C85)		NC2555K				
G-AKUK (2)	Luscombe 8A Silvaire	5793	N1166B	28.10.88	O R Watts	Roughay Farm, Bishops Waltham	15. 9.08P
	(Continental A65)		NC1166B				
G-AKUL (2)	Luscombe 8A Silvaire	4189	N1462K	9. 2.89	E A Taylor	Southend	21. 5.90P
	(Continental A65)		NC1462K		*(Stored 2.08)*		
G-AKUM (2)	Luscombe 8F Silvaire	6452	N2025B	17. 2.88	D A Young	North Weald	27. 9.07P
	(Continental C90)						
G-AKUN (2)	Piper J-3C-85 Cub	6914	N38304	13. 1.89	W R Savin	Coldharbour Farm, Willingham	31. 5.08P
			NC38304				
G-AKUO (2)	Aeronca 11AC Chief	11AC-1376	N9730E	16. 1.89	L W Richardson		
			NC9730E		Ventfield Farm, Horton-cum-Studley,Oxford		19. 9.07P
G-AKUP (2)	Luscombe 8E Silvaire Deluxe	5501	N2774K	9. 5.89	D A Young	North Weald	
	(Lycoming O-320)		NC2774K		*(Dismantled awaiting rebuild 6.07)*		
G-AKUR (2)	Cessna 140	13819	N1647V	26. 1.89	J Greenaway and C A Davis *(Noted 10.07 on slow rebuild)*		
			NC1647V			Phoenix Farm, Lower Upham	21. 9.95
G-AKUW	Chrislea CH.3 Series 2 Super Ace	105		8. 3.48	J and S Rickett	North Coates	12. 3.08P
G-AKVF	Chrislea CH.3 Series 2 Super Ace	114	AP-ADT	8. 3.48	B Metters	Little Rissington	15. 4.08P
			G-AKVF				
G-AKVM (2)	Cessna 120	13431	N3173N	10. 1.89	N and S Wise	Croft Farm, Croft-on-Tees	7. 6.08P
			NC3173N				
G-AKVN (2)	Aeronca 11AC Chief	11AC-469	N3742B	13. 1.89	P A Jackson	Priory Farm, Tibenham	29 2.08P
			N86047, NC86047		*(Carries "3742B" on fin)*		
G-AKVO (2)	Taylorcraft BC-12D	9845	N44045	10. 1.89	A Weir	(Cranwell Village, Sleaford)	4 7.07P
	(Continental A65)		NC44045				
G-AKVP (2)	Luscombe 8A Silvaire	5549	N2822K	21. 7.48	J M Edis	Charity Farm, Baxterley	25. 4.07P
	(Continental A65)		NC2822K				
G-AKVR	Chrislea CH.3 Series 4 Skyjeep	125	VH-OLD	8. 3.48	R B Webber	Trenchard Farm, Eggesford	7. 9.07P
			VH-RCD, VH-BRP, G-AKVR				
G-AKVZ	Miles M.38 Messenger 4B	6352	RH427	25. 6.48	Shipping and Airlines Ltd	Biggin Hill	11. 3.10S
G-AKWS	Auster 5A-160	1237	RT610	1. 4.48	A J Collins t/a Interesting Aircraft Company	Bidford	19. 9.09S
	(Lycoming O-320)				*(As "RT610" in AAC c/s)*		
G-AKXP	Taylorcraft J Auster 5	1017	NJ633	13. 4.48	A D Pearce	Eastbach Farm, Coleford	19.12.70
					(Crashed St Mary's, Isles of Scilly 9. 4.70: noted as "NJ633" 8.07)		
G-AKXS	de Havilland DH.82A Tiger Moth	83512	T7105	13. 4.48	J and G J Eagles	Oaksey Park	21. 3.03T
					(Spun into ground White Waltham 21. 7.02 and badly damaged)		

G-ALAA - G-ALZZ

G-ALBD	de Havilland DH.82A Tiger Moth	84130	T7748	27. 5.48	C H Schoonbeek	Midden Zeeland, Netherlands	31.10.81
			(Damaged Leopoldsburg, Belgium 24. 5.81: noted 10.05 with Gyrocopter Aviation being rebuilt for static display)				
G-ALBJ	Taylorcraft J Auster 5	1831	TW501	3. 6.48	P N Elkington	Bloxholm, Sleaford	23. 8.07
G-ALBK	Taylorcraft J Auster 5	1273	RT644	3. 6.48	K Wheatcroft	(Wigston)	29. 6.09S
G-ALEH (2)	Piper PA-17 Vagabond	17-87	N4689H	17. 8.81	A D Pearce	White Waltham	28. 3.08P
	(Continental A65)		NC4689H				
G-ALFA	Taylorcraft J Auster 5	1236	RT607	20.10.48	G M Rundle	(Overton, Basingstoke)	6.12.10
	(P/i uncertain as c/n 1236 considered sold as HB-EOC 4.48: reported as c/n 826 (MS958) but doubtful)						
G-ALGA (2)	Piper PA-15 Vagabond	15-348	N4575H	3.12.86	G A Brady	Enstone	22. 5.07P
	(Lycoming O-145)		NC4575H				
			(Struck ground during approach Marshland 22. 7.06 with substantial damage: stored engineless 7.07)				
G-ALGT	Vickers Supermarine 379 Spitfire F XIVc		RM689	9. 2.49	Rolls-Royce PLC	Filton	31 .7.92P
		6S/432263	"RM619", G-ALGT, RM689 *(Destroyed in crash Woodford 27. 6.92: on restoration Sandown, IoW 8.04)*				
G-ALIJ (2)	Piper PA-17 Vagabond	17-166	N4866H	13. 2.87	A S Cowan tr Popham Flying Group G-ALIJ		
	(Continental A65					Popham	21. 5.08P
G-ALIW	de Havilland DH.82A Tiger Moth	82901	N27WB	17. 8.81	F R Curry	Sywell	16. 9.09S
			ZK-ATI, NZ899, R5006		*(Operated Delta Aviation)*		
G-ALJF	Percival Proctor III	K 427	Z7252	3. 3.49	J F Moore	Biggin Hill	12. 9.10S
G-ALJL	de Havilland DH.82A Tiger Moth	84726	T6311	7. 3.49	D and R I Souch	Hill Farm, Durley	28. 9.50
	(Built Morris Motors Ltd)				*(On long term rebuild from components 8.00)*		
G-ALJR	Abbott-Baynes Scud III	2	BGA 283-ACF	16. 3.49	L P Woodage	Dunstable	4. 3.06
			G-ALJR, BGA 283-ACF				
G-ALLF	Slingsby T 30A Kirby Prefect	548	BGA 599	29. 3.49	J F Hopkins and K M Fresson	RNAS Yeovilton	
			PH-1, BGA 599, G-ALLF, BGA 599 *"ARK"*				

G-ALNA	de Havilland DH.82A Tiger Moth	85061	T6774	11. 4.49	R J Doughton	(Nomansland, Tiverton)	6. 6.10S
	(Brooklands Aviation titles)						
G-ALND	de Havilland DH.82A Tiger Moth	82308	N9191	12. 4.49	J Powell-Tuck	(Mamhilad, Pontypool)	11. 4.82
	(Crashed Panshanger 8. 3.81 and on rebuild 3.96)						
G-ALOD (2)	Cessna 140	14691	N2440V	14.10.83	J R Stainer	Whitehall Farm, Benington	11. 1.08E
G-ALRI	de Havilland DH.82A Tiger Moth	83350	ZK-BAB	2. 5.51	T W Smallwood	(Woodstock)	22. 6.07
	(Built Morris Motors Ltd)		G-ALRI, T5672		(As "T5672" in RAF c/s) (New owner 11.07)		
G-ALTO (2)	Cessna 140	14253	N2040V	19. 1.82	T M, P M and M L Jones	Derby	29. 6.08E
	(Continental C85)						
G-ALUC	de Havilland DH.82A Tiger Moth	83094	R5219	28. 6.49	D R and M Wood	Fowle Hall Farm, Paddock Wood	31. 5.08
G-ALWB	de Havilland DHC-1 Chipmunk 22A	C1/0100	OE-ABC	28.12.49	D J Neville and P A Dear Neville	Little Gransden	17. 3.08
			G-ALWB				
G-ALWS	de Havilland DH.82A Tiger Moth	82415	N9328	24. 1.50	A P Beynon	Trehelig, Welshpool	
	(Officially regd with c/n 82413)				(On rebuild 8.00)		
G-ALWW	de Havilland DH.82A Tiger Moth	86366	NL923	24. 1.50	D E Findon tr Stratford-upon-Avon Tiger Moth Group		
	(Built Morris Motors Ltd)					Bidford	11. 3.09
G-ALXZ	Taylorcraft J Auster 5-150	1082	D-EGOF	1. 2.50	D J Langrick tr G-ALXZ Syndicate	Sywell	14. 9.09S
	(Lycoming O-320) (Frame No.TAY24070)		PH-NER, G-ALXZ, NJ689				
G-ALYG	Taylorcraft J Auster 5D	835	MS968	14. 3.50	A L Young	Henstridge	19. 1.70
	(Officially regd with incorrect identity MT968:)				(Frame stored 8.02: for rebuild as Auster 5)		

G-AMAA - G-AMZZ

G-AMAW	Luton LA-4 Minor	JRC.01		29. 4.50	The Real Aeroplane Company Ltd	Breighton	6. 8.88P
	(Built J R Coates) (Aka as Swalesong SA.I with c/n SA.I) (Bristol Cherub 3)				(Noted dismantled 12.07)		
G-AMBB	de Havilland DH.82A Tiger Moth	85070	T6801	1. 5.50	J Eagles	Oaksey Park	
	(Composite rebuild - parts to "G-MAZY" ? - details in SECTION 6, Part 4)				(On rebuild 6.95)		
G-AMCK	de Havilland DH.82A Tiger Moth	84641	N65N	15. 6.50	Aviation Ventures Ltd	Sywell	7. 5.10S
			C-GBBF, SLN-05, D-EGXY, HB-UAC, G-AMCK, T6193 (Operates as Delta Aviation)				
G-AMCM	de Havilland DH.82A Tiger Moth	85295	DE249	14.12.50	A K and J.I Cooper	Denford Manor, Hungerford	28. 5.56
	(Regd with c/n "89259")		(Crashed near Somerton 25. 9.55: rear fuselage frame on restoration 10.01 but not original G-AMCM!)				
G-AMEN (2)	Piper PA-18 Super Cub 95 (L-18C-PI)	18-1998	(G-BJTR)	29.12.81	A Lovejoy and W Cook tr The G-AMEN Flying Group		
	(Frame No.18-1963) (Italian rebuild c/n OMA.71-08)		MM52-2398 "EI.71", I-EIAM, MM52-2398, 52-2398 (New owner 4.07)			Popham	26. 7.03P
G-AMHF	de Havilland DH.82A Tiger Moth	83026	R5144	6. 2.51	Wavendon Social Housing Ltd	Sywell	14. 9.03
	(Rebuilt with components from G-BABA c/n 86584 ex F-BGDT/PG687)				(On rebuild 10.07)		
G-AMIU	de Havilland DH.82A Tiger Moth	83228	T5495	9. 4.51	M D Souch	Hill Farm, Durley	9. 9.71
			(Crashed Booker 15.10.69: frame reported on restoration Denford Manor 10.01: now departed for completion)				
G-AMIV	de Havilland DH.82A Tiger Moth	83105	R5246	9. 4.51	K F Crumplin (Noted 8.07)	(Croscombe, Wells)	12.11.65
G-AMKU	Auster V J/1B Aiglet	2721	ST-ABD	10. 7.51	P G Lipman	Romney Street Farm, Sevenoaks	11. 7.09S
			SN-ABD, G-AMKU				
G-AMMS	Auster J/5K Aiglet Trainer	2745		11.10.51	R B Webber	Trenchard Farm, Eggesford	30. 5.08
G-AMNN	de Havilland DH.82A Tiger Moth	86457	NM137	24.12.51	I J Perry	Shoreham	23. 3.09S
	(Composite rebuild with unidentified airframe: original G-AMNN posssibly absorbed into G-BPAJ qv)						
G-AMPG (2)	Piper PA-12 Super Cruiser	12-985	N2647M	25. 3.85	A G and S M Measey	Leicester	22.10.08P
	(Hoerner wing-tips)		NC2647				
G-AMPI (2)	SNCAN Stampe SV-4C	213	N6RA	13. 2.84	T W Harris	Wycombe Air Park	20.11.10
			F-BCFX				
G-AMPY	Douglas C-47B-15-DK Dakota 3	15124 & 26569	(EI-BKJ)	8. 3.52	Air Atlantique Ltd (As "KK116" in RAF c/s)	Coventry	4. 7.08E
			G-AMPY, N15751, G-AMPY, TF-FIO, G-AMPY, JY-ABE, G-AMPY, KK116, 43-49308				
G-AMRA	Douglas C-47B-15-DK Dakota 6	15290 & 26735	XE280	8. 3.52	RVL Aviation Ltd	Coventry	13. 7.08T
			G-AMRA, KK151, 43-49474		(Atlantic c/s with Air Atlantique titles)		
G-AMRF	Auster J/5F Aiglet Trainer	2716	VT-DHA	20. 3.52	D A Hill	Fenland	31. 3.07
			G-AMRF				
G-AMRK	Gloster Gladiator I	?	L8032	16. 5.52	Richard Shuttleworth Trustees	Old Warden	17. 4.08P
	(Bristol Mercury XXX)		"K8032", G-AMRK, L8032		(As "K7985 "in 73 Sqdn RAF c/s)		
G-AMSG	SIPA 903	77	OO-VBL	25.11.81	S W Markham	Valentine Farm, Odiham	13. 7.08P
			F-BGHB				
G-AMTA	Auster J/5F Aiglet Trainer	2780		24. 5.52	J D Manson	Tollerton	24.10.09S
G-AMTF	de Havilland DH.82A Tiger Moth	84207		11. 6.52	H A D Monro	Headcorn	11.12.07
			G-AMTF, ZK-AVE, G-AMTF, T7842 (As "T-7842" in RAF c/s)				
G-AMTK	de Havilland DH.82A Tiger Moth	3982	N6709	18. 6.52	S W McKay and M E Vaisey	(Berkhamsted)	27. 5.66
					(Stored 12.99)		
G-AMTM	Auster V J/1 Autocrat	3101	G-AJUJ	3. 7.52	R J Stobo	Oaklands Farm, Stonesfield, Witney	5. 7.06P
	(Auster rebuild - originally c/n 2622)		(Struck telegraph pole laid across end of runway landing Oaklands 22. 4.06 and substantially damaged)				
G-AMTV	de Havilland DH.82A Tiger Moth	3858	OO-SOE	5. 8.52	Aviation Ventures Ltd	Sywell	4. 3.07
			G-AMTV, N6545		(Operated Delta Aviation) (Noted 10.07)		
G-AMUF	de Havilland DHC-1 Chipmunk 21	C1/0832		2. 9.52	Redhill Tailwheel Flying Club Ltd	Dunsfold	8. 2.08
G-AMUI	Auster J/5F Aiglet Trainer	2790		29. 8.52	R B Webber (Noted 2.06) Trenchard Farm, Eggesford		15. 2.66T
G-AMVD	Taylorcraft J Auster 5	1565	F-BGTF	6.10.52	M Hammond	Airfield Farm, Hardwick	7. 6.10S
			G-AMVD, TJ565		(As "TJ565" in RAF camouflage & D-Day stripes c/s: 652 Sqdn crest)		
G-AMVP	Tipsy Junior	J 111	OO-ULA	23.10.52	A R Wershat	Sandown, Isle of Wight	1. 2.08P
	(Walter Mikron 2)						
G-AMVS	de Havilland DH.82A Tiger Moth	82784	OO-SOJ	12.11.52	J Powell-Tuck	(Mamhilad, Pontypool)	21.12.53
			G-AMVS, R4852		(On rebuild 8.92)		
G-AMYD	Auster J/5L Aiglet Trainer	2773		13. 2.53	S Vince	(Bradfield, North Walsham)	3. 9.04
					(New owner 10.05)		
G-AMZI	Auster J/5F Aiglet Trainer	3104		4. 5.53	J F Moore	Rexden, Rye	16. 2.07
G-AMZT	Auster J/5F Aiglet Trainer	3107		28. 5.53	D Hyde, J W Saull, and J C Hutchinson		
						Wycombe Air Park	18. 4.10S
G-AMZU	Auster J/5F Aiglet Trainer	3108		28. 5.53	J A Longworth, A R M and C B A Eagle tr Flying Flicks		
						White Waltham	5.10.08S

G-ANAA - G-ANZZ

G-ANAF Douglas C-47B-35-DK Dakota 3 16688 & 33436 N170GP 17. 6.53 Air Atlantique Ltd Coventry 9. 4.10S
G-ANAF, KP220, 44-77104 (THALES titles - special radar fit under nose)

G-ANCS de Havilland DH.82A Tiger Moth 82824 R4907 12. 9.53 C E Edwards and E A Higgins Rush Green 23. 7.09

G-ANCX de Havilland DH.82A Tiger Moth 83719 T7229 15. 9.53 D R Wood Fowle Hall Farm, Paddock Wood 28. 7.02
(Built Morris Motors Ltd)

G-ANDE de Havilland DH.82A Tiger Moth 85957 G-YVFS 21. 6.06 Aviation Ventures Ltd Sywell 29. 3.10S
(Built Morris Motors Ltd) G-ANDE, EM726 (Operated Delta Aviation)

G-ANDM de Havilland DH.82A Tiger Moth 3946 EI-AGP 23. 9.53 N J Stagg (Frogland Cross) 14. 8.06
G-ANDM, EI-AGP, G-ANDM, (G-ANDI), N6642

G-ANDP de Havilland DH.82A Tiger Moth 82868 D-EBEC 22. 9.53 A H Diver Newtownards 10. 5.08
N9920F, G-ANDP, R4960

G-ANEH de Havilland DH.82A Tiger Moth 82067 N6797 29. 9.53 G J Wells (As "N-6797" in RAF c/s) (Wycombe Air Park) 18. 7.10

G-ANEL de Havilland DH.82A Tiger Moth 82333 N9238 1.10.53 Totalsure Ltd Blue Tile Farm, Langham 14.11.08S

G-ANEM de Havilland DH.82A Tiger Moth 82943 EI-AGN 1.10.53 P J Benest Hamstead Marshall 19. 7.08
G-ANEM, R5042

G-ANEN de Havilland DH.82A Tiger Moth 85418 OO-ACG 2.10.53 A J D Douglas-Hamilton Goodwood 9. 5.08
G-ANEN, DE410 (Tipped onto nose on take off Goodwood 13. 7.05 and substantially damaged)

G-ANEW de Havilland DH.82A Tiger Moth 86458 NM138 6.10.53 K F Crumplin Henstridge 18. 6.62T
(Built Morris Motors Ltd) (Noted 4.07)

G-ANEZ de Havilland DH.82A Tiger Moth 84218 T7849 20.10.53 C D J Bland Sandown, Isle of Wight 9. 7.08

G-ANFC de Havilland DH.82A Tiger Moth 85385 DE363 13.10.53 J E Pierce Ley Farm, Chirk 9.10.03T
(Built Morris Motors Ltd) (Noted 5.05)

G-ANFI de Havilland DH.82A Tiger Moth 85577 DE623 16.10.53 G P Graham (As "DE623" in RAF c/s) Shobdon 4. 7.09
(Built Morris Motors Ltd) (Note Tiger Moth D-EDON is displayed at Auto und Technik Museum, Sinsheim, Germany also as "DE623")

G-ANFL de Havilland DH.82A Tiger Moth 84617 T6169 22.10.53 Felthorpe Tiger Group Ltd Felthorpe 5. 7.10S
(Built Morris Motors Ltd)

G-ANFM de Havilland DH.82A Tiger Moth 83604 T5888 22.10.53 A J Coker and N H Lemon tr Reading Flying Group
(Built Morris Motors Ltd) White Waltham 8. 3.08

G-ANFP de Havilland DH.82A Tiger Moth 82530 N9503 28.10.53 G D Horn (Frame only 1.00) (Fordingbridge) 1. 7.63

G-ANFV de Havilland DH.82A Tiger Moth 85904 DF155 1.12.53 R A L Falconer Shempston Farm, Lossiemouth 2.10.09S
(Built Morris Motors Ltd) (As "DF155" in RAF c/s)

G-ANGK (2) Cessna 140A 15396 N9675A 10. 3.89 I J F MacDonald tr Shempston Cessna Group
Shempston Farm, Lossiemouth 12. 8.07

G-ANHK de Havilland DH.82A Tiger Moth 82442 F-BHIM 4.12.53 J D Iliffe Hampstead Norrey's 14. 7.10
G-ANHK, N9372

G-ANHR Taylorcraft J Auster 5 759 MT192 5.12.53 H L Swallow (Stored 6.04) Hibaldstow 20. 7.86

G-ANHS Taylorcraft G Auster 4 737 MT197 5.12.53 M Stewart and C Tyers tr Mike Tango Group Spanhoe 18. 8.08E
(As "MT197" in RAF c/s)

G-ANHU Taylorcraft G Auster 4 799 EC-AXR 5.12.53 D J Baker Carr Farm, Thorney, Newark 22.10.66
G-ANHU, MT255 (Noted dismantled, camouflaged 1.05)

G-ANHX Taylorcraft J Auster 5D 2064 TW519 5.12.53 D J Baker Carr Farm, Thorney, Newark 2.11.73
(Crashed 28. 3.70: noted dismantled 1.05)

G-ANIE Taylorcraft J Auster 5 1809 TW467 5.12.53 R T Ingram New Farm House, Great Oakley 27.11.08S
(As "TW467" in AAC c/s)

G-ANIJ Taylorcraft J Auster 5D 1680 TJ672 5.12.53 M Pocock Eggesford 5. 5.71
(On rebuild 2007 as "TJ672: DT-S")

G-ANJA de Havilland DH.82A Tiger Moth 82459 N9389 7.12.53 The Tiger Club 1990 Ltd Headcorn 17. 1.09S
(As "N9389" in RAF c/s)

G-ANJD de Havilland DH.82A Tiger Moth 84652 T6226 8.12.53 I Laws Audley End 8. 7.09S
(Built Morris Motors Ltd)

G-ANKK de Havilland DH.82A Tiger Moth 83590 T5854 24.12.53 P A Cambridge tr Halfpenny Green Tiger Group
(As "T-5854" in RAF c/s) Charity Farm, Baxterley 12. 1.08

G-ANKT de Havilland DH.82A Tiger Moth 85087 T6818 24.12.53 Richard Shuttleworth Trustees Old Warden 21. 8.08P
(As "K-2585" in RAF CFS c/s)

G-ANKZ de Havilland DH.82A Tiger Moth 3803 (N) 30.12.53 D W Graham Bossington 24. 7.09S
F-BHIO, G-ANKZ, N6466 (As "N-6466" in RAF c/s)

G-ANLD de Havilland DH.82A Tiger Moth 85990 OO-DPA 30.12.53 K Peters White Waltham 17.12.08S
G-ANLD, EM773

G-ANLS de Havilland DH.82A Tiger Moth 85862 DF113 7. 1.54 P A Gliddon Great Fryup, Egton, Whitby 29. 6.03
(Built Morris Motors Ltd)

G-ANMO de Havilland DH.82A Tiger Moth 3255 F-BHIU 22. 1.54 Aviation Ventures Ltd Sywell 26. 8.09S
G-ANMO, K4259 (As "K-4259:71" in RAF c/s) (Operated Delta Aviation)

G-ANMY de Havilland DH.82A Tiger Moth 85466 OO-SOL 22. 1.54 F P Le Coyte tr Lotmead Flying Group
(Built Morris Motors Ltd) "OO-SOC", G-ANMY, DE470 (As "DE470:16" in RAF c/s) Landmead Farm, Garford 28. 9.07

G-ANNB de Havilland DH.82A Tiger Moth 84233 N6037 22. 1.54 G C Bates (Hemingford Grey) 12. 6.58
D-EGYN, G-ANNB, T6037 (New owner 7.06)

G-ANNE (2) de Havilland DH.82A Tiger Moth "83814" 15. 4.94 C R Hardiman Shobdon 30. 5.58
(Composite airframe) (On rebuild 9.02)

G-ANNG de Havilland DH.82A Tiger Moth 85504 DE524 22. 1.54 P F Walter Wycombe Air Park 8.12.07
(Built Morris Motors Ltd)

G-ANNI de Havilland DH.82A Tiger Moth 85162 T6953 22. 1.54 C E, O C and M E Ponsford Shoreham 13. 9.09S
(As "T-6953" in RAF c/s)

G-ANNK de Havilland DH.82A Tiger Moth 83804 F-BFDO 22. 1.54 D R Wilcox Sywell 25. 9.87
(Built Morris Motors Ltd) G-ANNK, T7290 (New owner 5.02) (Wings only noted Spanhoe 4.03)

G-ANOH de Havilland DH.82A Tiger Moth 86040 EM838 22. 2.54 N Parkhouse Redhill 25. 1.09
(Built Morris Motors Ltd)

G-ANOM de Havilland DH.82A Tiger Moth 82086 N6837 2. 3.54 T G I Dark (Chedworth, Cheltenham) 3. 5.62T
(Crashed Fairoaks 17.12.61: on rebuild 6.00: new owner 11.06)

G-ANON de Havilland DH.82A Tiger Moth 84270 T7909 4. 3.54 R C Hields t/a Hields Aviation Sherburn-in-Elmet 12. 7.09S
(Built Morris Motors Ltd) (As "T7909" in RAF c/s)

G-ANOO	de Havilland DH.82A Tiger Moth	85409	DE401	11. 3.54	R K Packman	Little Staughton	17. 4.10
	(Built Morris Motors Ltd)						
G-ANPE	de Havilland DH.82A Tiger Moth	83738	G-IESH	27. 3.54	I E S Hudleston	Duxford	9. 8.09S
	(Built Morris Motors Ltd)		G-ANPE, F-BHAT, G-ANPE, T7397				
G-ANRF	de Havilland DH.82A Tiger Moth	83748	T5850	24. 5.54	C D Cyster	Glenrothes	28. 8.10S
	(Built Morris Motors Ltd)						
G-ANRM	de Havilland DH.82A Tiger Moth	85861	DF112	8. 6.54	Spectrum Leisure Ltd	Duxford	31. 7.10S
	(Built Morris Motors Ltd)				*(As "DF112" in RAF c/s) (Operated Classic Wings)*		
G-ANRN	de Havilland DH.82A Tiger Moth	83133	T5368	24. 5.54	J J V Elwes	Old Sarum	19. 5.07
G-ANRP	Taylorcraft J Auster 5	1789	TW439	21. 5.54	P R and J S Johnson *(As "TW439" in RAF c/s)*		
						(Bradfield St Clare, Bury St Edmunds)	4. 5.08S
G-ANSM	de Havilland DH.82A Tiger Moth	82909	R5014	3. 6.54	Modi Aviation Ltd	Sibson	28. 8.09T
	(Built Morris Motors Ltd)						
G-ANTE	de Havilland DH.82A Tiger Moth	84891	T6562	20. 9.54	Aviation Adventures Ltd	Sywell	16. 7.05T
	(Built Morris Motors Ltd)				*(On rebuild 10.07)*		
G-ANWB	de Havilland DHC-1 Chipmunk 21	C1/0987	G-5-17	15. 2.55	G Briggs *(Noted 10.07)*	Blackpool	17.12.04T
G-ANWO	Miles M.14A Hawk Trainer 3	718	L8262	31.12.58	A G Dunkerley	(Bristol)	18. 4.63
	(DBR Kirton-in-Lindsey 21. 4.62 and cancelled as damaged: restored 24. 6.87 but unlikely little residue: wings to G-AIUA in 1960s and fuselage remnants slight of substance: for possible incorporation into rebuild of G-ADNL (qv))						
G-ANXC	Auster J/5R Alpine	3135	5Y-UBD	4.12.54	R B Webber tr Alpine Group		
			VP-UBD, G-ANXC, (AP-AHG), G-ANXC			Trenchard Farm, Eggesford	14. 9.06
G-ANXR	Percival P.31C Proctor IV	H 803	RM221	14.12.54	L H Oakins	Le Touquet, France	24. 5.10S
	(Built F Hills and Sons Ltd)				*(As "RM221" in RAF c/s)*		
G-ANZT	Thruxton Jackaroo	84176	T7798	4. 3.55	D J Neville and P J Dear	Wycombe Air Park	14. 8.08
G-ANZU	de Havilland DH.82A Tiger Moth	3583	L6938	9. 3.55	M I Lodge *(New owner 4.05)*	Walton Wood	17. 3.91
G-ANZZ	de Havilland DH.82A Tiger Moth	85834	DE974	14. 3.55	J I B Bennett and P P Amershi	(Hatfield)	28. 2.69T
	(Built Morris Motors Ltd)						

G-AOAA - G-AOZZ

G-AOAA	de Havilland DH.82A Tiger Moth	85908	DF159	14. 3.55	R C P Brookhouse	Thruxton	8.12.91T
	(Built Morris Motors Ltd)				*(Damaged Redhill 4. 6.89: under restoration 2002)*		
G-AOBG	Somers-Kendall SK-1	1		30. 3.55	P W Bishop *(Stored 2007)*	(Woodley, Reading)	26. 6.58
G-AOBH	de Havilland DH.82A Tiger Moth	84350	T7997	31. 3.55	P Nutley	Higherlands Farm, Branscombe	2.12.09
	(Built Morris Motors Ltd) (Officially regd with c/n 83818 ex T7439)				*(As "NL750" in RAF c/s)*		
G-AOBO	de Havilland DH.82A Tiger Moth	3810	N6473	23. 4.55	J S and S V Shaw	Perranporth	15. 8.08S
					(As "N-6473" in RAF c/s)		
G-AOBU	Hunting Percival P 84 Jet Provost T 1	P84/6	XM129	2. 5.55	T J Manna t/a Kennet Aviation	North Weald	13. 3.07P
			G-AOBU, G-42-1		*(As "XD693:Z-Q" in RAF 2 FTS c/s) (Noted 6.07)*		
G-AOBX	de Havilland DH.82A Tiger Moth	83653	T7187	26. 4.55	S Bohill-Smith tr David Ross Flying Group		
	(Built Morris Motors Ltd)					White Waltham	27. 6.09
G-AOCR (2)	Taylorcraft J Auster 5D	1060	EI-AJS	25. 5.56	K E Ballington	Yeatsall Farm, Abbots Bromley	1. 3.09S
			G-AOCR, NJ673		*(As "NJ673" in RAF c/s)*		
G-AOCU (2)	Taylorcraft J Auster 5	986	MT349	8. 6.56	S J Ball	Leicester	4. 4.10
G-AODR	de Havilland DH.82A Tiger Moth	86251	G-ISIS	4. 8.55	T Groves tr G-AODR Group	Lee-on-Solent	29. 3.62
	(Built Morris Motors Ltd)		G-AODR, NL779		*(New owner 9.05)*		
G-AODT	de Havilland DH.82A Tiger Moth	83109	R5250	4. 8.55	R A Harrowven	Tibenham	15. 4.10S
G-AOEH	Aeronca 7AC Champion	7AC-2144	N79854	8. 9.55	A Gregori	Nethershields Farm, Chapelton	20. 6.07P
	(Continental A65)		OO-TWF				
G-AOEI	de Havilland DH.82A Tiger Moth	82196	N6946	14. 9.55	CFG Flying Ltd	Cambridge	27. 6.08T
	(Regd with fuselage no.MCO/DH3409 which should correspond to ex DE298 [85332]: a/c is probably composite airframe)						
G-AOES	de Havilland DH.82A Tiger Moth	84547	T6056	6.10.55	K A and A J Broomfield	Charity Farm, Baxterley	15. 6.02
	(Built Morris Motors Ltd 1941)				*(Dismantled 10.05)*		
G-AOET	de Havilland DH.82A Tiger Moth	85650	DE720	7.10.55	Techair London Ltd	Bossington	22. 4.10
	(Built Morris Motors Ltd)						
G-AOEX	Thruxton Jackaroo	86483	NM175	10.10.55	A T Christian	Walkeridge Farm, Overton	3. 2.68T
					(Rebuild nearing completion 4.05)		
G-AOFE	de Havilland DHC-1 Chipmunk 22A	C1/0150	WB702	13. 9.56	W J Quinn *(As "WB702" in RAF c/s)*	Dunsfold	21.12.07
G-AOFJ (2)	Auster Alpha 5	3401		3.10.56	R J Bentley	Carnmore, Galway, County Galway	9.12.10S
G-AOFS	Auster J/5L Aiglet Trainer	3143	EI-ALN	28.10.55	P N A Whitehead	Leicester	29. 5.10S
			G-AOFS				
G-AOGI	de Havilland DH.82A Tiger Moth	85922	(N　　)	14.12.55	W J Taylor	(Friskney, Boston)	23. 8.91
	(Built Morris Motors Ltd)		OO-SOA, G-AOGI, DF186		*(Stored 10.92)*		
G-AOGR	de Havilland DH.82A Tiger Moth	84566	XL714	20. 1.56	R J S G Clark	(Cranwell Village, Sleaford)	9.11.08S
	(Built Morris Motors Ltd)		G-AOGR, T6099		*(As "XL714": in RAF c/s)*		
G-AOGV	Auster J/5R Alpine	3302		2. 2.56	R E Heading	Walnut Tree Farm, Thorney, Whittlesey	17. 7.72
					(Stored 12.97)		
G-AOHY	de Havilland DH.82A Tiger Moth	3850	N6537	23. 2.56	R H and S J Cooper	(Stow, Lincoln)	20. 8.60
					(On rebuild 9.00: new owners 7.04)		
G-AOHZ	Auster J/5P Autocar	3252		28. 2.56	A D Hodgkinson *(Stored 10.07)* Farley Farm, Romsey		25. 9.03
G-AOIL	de Havilland DH.82A Tiger Moth	83673	XL716	20. 8.56	C D Davidson	Compton Abbas	17. 9.08S
	(Built Morris Motors Ltd)		G-AOIL, T7363		*(As "XL-716" in RN c/s)*		
G-AOIM	de Havilland DH.82A Tiger Moth	83536	T7109	27. 8.56	C R Hardiman	Shobdon	21. 3.08
	(Built Morris Motors Ltd)						
G-AOIR	Thruxton Jackaroo	82882	R4972	13. 1.56	K A and A J Broomfield	Charity Farm, Baxterley	6. 9.08S
G-AOIS	de Havilland DH.82A Tiger Moth	83034	R5172	13. 1.56	J K Ellwood	Breighton	16. 8.08S
					(As "R5172:FIJE" in RAF c/s)		
G-AOIY	Auster J/5V Series 160 Autocar	3199		1. 3.56	R A Benson	Trenchard Farm, Eggesford	14. 5.10
	(Lycoming O-320)						
G-AOJH	de Havilland DH.83C Fox Moth	FM.42	AP-ABO	29. 3.56	Connect Properties Ltd	Rendcomb	1. 3.09S
	(Built de Havilland Canada)						
G-AOJJ	de Havilland DH.82A Tiger Moth	85877	DF128	5. 4.56	E and K M Lay	White Waltham	27. 3.09
	(Built Morris Motors Ltd)				*(As "DF128:RCO-U" in RAF c/s)*		

G-AOJK	de Havilland DH.82A Tiger Moth	82813	R4896	5. 4.56	R J Willies	Sywell	18. 8.08
G-AOJR	de Havilland DHC-1 Chipmunk 22	C1/0205	SE-BBS	9. 4.56	G J G-H Caubergs and N Marien	Spa, Belgium	28. 7.08
			OY-DFB, D-EGIM, G-AOJR, D-EGIM, G-AOJR, WB756				
G-AOKL	Percival P 40 Prentice 1	PAC-208	VS610	13. 4.56	Richard Shuttleworth Trustees	Old Warden	20. 9.96
					(Under restoration 8.06)		
G-AOLK	Percival P 40 Prentice 1	PAC-225	VS618	25. 4.56	A Hilton	Southend	17. 9.10S
G-AOLU	Percival P 40 Prentice 1	B3/1A/PAC/283	EI-ASP	25. 4.56	N J Butler	(Montrose)	8. 5.76
	(Regd with c/n 5830/3)		G-AOLU, VS356		*(As "VS356" in RAF c/s) (Noted 4.02)*		
G-AORB (2)	Cessna 170B	20767	OO-SIZ	13. 2.84	A R Thompson tr Hawley Farm Group	Englefield	9. 4.08
			N2615D				
G-AORG	de Havilland DH.114 Heron	214101	XR441	1. 5.56	Duchess of Brittany (Jersey) Ltd	Coventry	26. 6.07S
	(Built as Sea Heron C 1)		G-AORG, G-5-16		*"Duchess of Brittany" (Jersey Airlines titles) (On overhaul 1.08)*		
G-AORW	de Havilland DHC-1 Chipmunk 22A	C1/0130	WB682	28. 5.56	Skylark Aviation Ltd	Prestwick	29. 1.09S
G-AOSF	de Havilland DHC-1 Chipmunk 22	C1/0023	D-EIIZ	25. 6.56	T S Olsen	(Trier, Germany)	6. 4.06
			G-AOSF, HB-TUA, G-AOSF, WB571 *(As "WB571:34" in RAF c/s)*				
G-AOSK	de Havilland DHC-1 Chipmunk 22A	C1/0178	WB726	26. 6.56	L J Irvine	RAF Halton	30. 3.09
					(As "WB726:E" in RAF Cambridge UAS c/s)		
G-AOSY	de Havilland DHC-1 Chipmunk 22	C1/0037	WB585	29. 6.56	I A Davies tr WFG Chipmunk Group	Seething	26. 6.08
					(As "WB585:M in RAF red and white c/s)		
G-AOTD	de Havilland DHC-1 Chipmunk 22	C1/0040	WB588	30. 6.56	S Piech	Old Sarum	5.11.09
					(As "WB588:D" in RAF Oxford UAS c/s)		
G-AOTF	de Havilland DHC-1 Chipmunk 23	C1/0015	WB563	2. 7.56	T M Holloway tr RAF Gliding and Soaring Association		
	(Lycoming O-360)				*(Operated Clevelands Gliding Club)*	AAC Dishforth	28.10.07
G-AOTK	Druine D 53 Turbi	1		1.11.56	T J Adams	Old Warden	15.10.08P
	(Built TK Flying Group - pr.no.PFA 230) (Walter Mikron 3)						
G-AOTR	de Havilland DHC-1 Chipmunk 22	C1/0045	HB-TUH	12. 7.56	Propshop Ltd	Duxford	12. 6.06
			D-EGOG, G-AOTR, WB604				
G-AOTY	de Havilland DHC-1 Chipmunk 22	C1/0522	WG472	12. 7.56	A A Hodgson tr Bryn Gwyn Bach Chipmunk Group		
					(As "WG472" in RAF c/s)	Bryn Gwyn Bach	5. 4.10S
G-AOUO	de Havilland DHC-1 Chipmunk 22	C1/0179	WB730	10. 8.56	T M Holloway tr RAF Gliding and Soaring Association		
	(Lycoming O-360)				*(Operated Wrekin Gliding Club)*	RAF Cosford	16. 3.08
G-AOUP	de Havilland DHC-1 Chipmunk 22	C1/0180	WB731	10. 8.56	A R Harding	Leicester	3. 8.06
G-AOVW	Taylorcraft J Auster 5	894	MT119	16.11.59	B Marriott	Wilsford, Sleaford	15.11.09
G-AOXN	de Havilland DH.82A Tiger Moth	85958	EM727	31.10.56	S L G Darch	(East Chinnock, Yeovil)	21.12.01
	(Built Morris Motors Ltd)						
G-AOZH	de Havilland DH.82A Tiger Moth	86449	NM129	18. 1.57	M H Blois-Brooke	Sywell	10. 6.08T
	(Built Morris Motors Ltd)				*(As "K2572" in RAF c/s)*		
G-AOZL	Auster J/5Q Alpine	3202		5. 2.57	R M Weeks *(On rebuild 8.06)*	Earls Colne	28. 5.88
G-AOZP	de Havilland DHC-1 Chipmunk 22A	C1/0183	WB734	14. 2.57	S J Davies	Sandtoft	15. 5.08

G-APAA - G-APZZ

G-APAF	Auster Alpha 5	3404	G-CMAL	25. 3.57	J J J Mostyn	Draycott Farm, Chiseldon	14. 8.08
			G-APAF		*(As "TW511" in AAC c/s)*		
G-APAH	Auster Alpha 5	3402		29. 3.57	T J Goodwin	New Farm House, Great Oakley	5. 4.04
					(Noted 1.06)		
G-APAJ	Thruxton Jackaroo	83314	VH-KRK	3. 4.57	J T H and S J Page	Crawley, Barton Ashes	
			G-APAJ, T5616		*(Noted 6.07)*		
G-APAL	de Havilland DH.82A Tiger Moth	82102	N6847	3. 4.57	P J Shotbolt *(As "N6847" in RAF c/s)*		
					Ingthorpe Farm, Ingtthorpe, Great Casterton, Stamford		9. 7.06T
G-APAM	de Havilland DH.82A Tiger Moth	3874	N6580	3. 4.57	R P Williams tr Myth Group Folly Farm, Hungerford		1.10.10S
					"Myth"		
G-APAO	de Havilland DH.82A Tiger Moth	82845	R4922	3. 4.57	H J Maguire *(Operated Classic Wings)*	Duxford	23. 4.09S
G-APAP	de Havilland DH.82A Tiger Moth	83018	R5136	3. 4.57	J C Wright *(As "R-5136" in RAF c/s)*	RAF Henlow	17. 7.09S
G-APBE	Auster Alpha 5	3403		7. 5.57	R B Woods	Hampstead Norrey's	11. 5.08
G-APBI	de Havilland DH.82A Tiger Moth	86097	EM903	16. 5.57	C J Zeal	(Twyford, Reading)	19. 4.82
	(Built Morris Motors Ltd)				*(Damaged Audley End 7. 7.80: on rebuild 12.90: new owner 5.05)*		
G-APBO	Druine D 53 Turbi	PFA 229		3. 6.57	R C Hibberd	Lower Upham Farm, Chiseldon	12. 7.08P
	(Built F Roche) (Continental C75)						
G-APBW	Auster Alpha 5A	3405		23. 5.57	C R W Brown	(Cornillon-Confoux, France)	1. 6.09
G-APCB	Auster J/5Q Alpine	3204		5. 6.57	A A Beswick	Thruxton	11. 7 07
G-APCC	de Havilland DH.82A Tiger Moth	86549	PG640	11. 6.57	L J Rice	Quebec Farm, Knook, Warminster	15.11.09
G-APFA	Druine D 52 Turbi	PFA 232		5. 2.57	F J Keitch	(Smiths Farm, Brixham)	22. 9.92P
	(Built Britten-Norman Ltd) (Continental A65)						
G-APFU	de Havilland DH.82A Tiger Moth	86081	EM879	28. 8.57	Leisure Assets Ltd	Goodwood	11. 4.09S
G-APFV (1)	Piper PA-23-160 Apache	23-1686	G-MOLY	11.12.59	J L Thorogood	Pittrichie Farm, Whiterashes	25. 4.08E
			EI-BAW, G-APFV, EI-ALK, N10F				
G-APGL	de Havilland DH.82A Tiger Moth	86460	NM140	6. 9.57	K A Broomfield (Charity Farm, Baxterley, Atherstone)		
	(Built Morris Motors Ltd) (Substantial parts used in rebuild of G-AJVE)						
G-APIE	Tipsy Belfair	535	(OO-TIE)	22.10.57	D Beale	Witchford	15. 4.08P
	(Walter Mikron 2)						
G-APIH	de Havilland DH.82A Tiger Moth	82981	N111DH	25.10.57	K Stewering	Borken-Gemen, Germany	3. 5.09S
			OY-DGJ, D-EMEX, G-APIH, R5086				
G-APIK	Auster J/1N Alpha	3375		11.11.57	J H Powell-Tuck	Gloucestershire	7. 3.09
G-APIZ	Druine D 31 Turbulent	PFA 478		22.11.57	G M Rundle	RAF Shawbury	6. 2.08P
	(Built Rollason Aircraft and Engines) (Volkswagen 1600)						
G-APJB	Percival P 40 Prentice 1	PAC-086	VR259	28.11.57	Air Atlantique Ltd	Coventry	24. 7.08T
					(As "VR259:M" in RAF 2 ASS c/s)		
G-APJO	de Havilland DH.82A Tiger Moth	86446	NM126	23.12.57	D R and M Wood	Tunbridge Wells	27. 3.59T
	(Built Morris Motors Ltd) (C/n quoted as "17712":)				*(Crashed Ross-on-Wye 5. 8.58: on rebuild and may include components from G-APJR)*		
G-APJZ	Auster J/1N Alpha	3382	5N-ACY	3. 1.58	P G Lipman	Romney Street Farm, Sevenoaks	15. 7.77
			(VR-NDR), G-APJZ		*(Damaged Thornicombe 10.11.75: on rebuild 12.97)*		

Reg	Type	C/n	Prev identity	Date	Owner	Location	Status date
G-APKN	Auster J/1N Alpha	3387		27. 1.58	P R Hodson	Felthorpe	8. 9.05
	(Badly damaged in arson attack Felthorpe 8. 2.03: new owner 9.05)						
G-APLO	de Havilland DHC-1 Chipmunk 22	C1/0144	EI-AHU WB696	1. 5.58	Lindholme Aircraft Ltd	Coventry	2.11.09S
	(As "WD379:K" in RAF Cambridge UAS c/s)						
G-APLU	de Havilland DH.82A Tiger Moth	85094	VR-AAY F-OBKK, G-APLU, T6825	2. 4.58	R A Bishop and M E Vaisey	Rush Green	13. 2.08
	(Built Morris Motors Ltd)						
G-APMH	Auster J/1U Workmaster	3502	F-OBOA G-APMH	15. 4.58	J L Thorogood	Insch	2. 6.10S
G-APMX	de Havilland DH.82A Tiger Moth	85645	DE715	9. 5.58	T A P Hubbard tr Foley Farm Flying Group	Meon	17. 7.10S
	(Built Morris Motors Ltd)						
G-APNS	Garland-Bianchi Linnet	001		17. 6.58	P M Busaidy	Scaynes Hill, Haywards Heath	6.10.78
	(Continental C90)				*(Stored 2004)*		
G-APNT	Currie Wot	P 6399		18. 6.58	B J Dunford	Longwood Farm, Morestead	29. 6.07P
	(Built Hampshire Aero Club - c/n HAC-3) (Continental PC60)				*"Airymouse"*		
G-APNZ	Druine D 31 Turbulent	PFA 482		17. 4.58	J Knight	(Hailsham)	13.12.95P
	(Built Rollason Aircraft and Engines) (Ardem 4C02)				*(Damaged River Rother near Iden 3. 9.95: on rebuild)*		
G-APOI	Saunders-Roe Skeeter Series 8	S2/5081		29. 7.58	B Chamberlain *(Noted 6.06)*	AAC Middle Wallop	2. 8.00
G-APPA	de Havilland DHC-1 Chipmunk 22	C1/0792	N5073E G-APPA, WP917	11. 9.58	D M Squires	(Wellesbourne Mountford)	14. 7.85
					(On slow rebuild 1.03)		
G-APPL	Percival P 40 Prentice 1	PAC-013	VR189	7.10.58	S J Saggers	Biggin Hill	10. 9.10S
G-APPM	de Havilland DHC-1 Chipmunk 22	C1/0159	WB711	14.10.58	S D Wilch *(As "WB711" in RAF c/s)*	Sywell	7. 9.08
G-APPN	de Havilland DH.82A Tiger Moth	83839	T7328	26. 9.03	John Colours SRL	Phoenix Farm, Lower Upham	4.11.07
	(As "T7328" in RAF c/s)						
G-APRR	SPP Super Aero 45 Series 04	04-014	OK-KFQ	5. 1.59	R E Dagless	Holly Hill Farm, Guist, Dereham	21. 7.07
G-APRS	Scottish Aviation Twin Pioneer 3	561	G-BCWF XT610, G-APRS, (PI-C430)	9. 1.59	Aviation Heritage Ltd	Coventry	15. 7.08T
	"Primrose" (Raspberry ripple c/s with ETPS titles)						
G-APRT	Taylor JT.1 Monoplane	PFA 537		15. 1.59	R A Keech	(Woodvale)	26. 5.07P
	(Built J Taylor) (Ardem 4C02)						
G-APSA	Douglas DC-6A	45497	4W-ABQ HZ-ADA, G-APSA, CF-MC	12. 2.59	Air Atlantique Ltd.	Coventry	11. 4.08T
					(KLM 1950s London - Christchurch c/s - "TGA" & "21")		
G-APSR	Auster J/1U Workmaster	3499	OO-HXA G-APSR, VP-JCD, G-APSR, (F-OBHR)	22. 4.59	D and K Aero Services Ltd (Operated P de Liens)	Namur-Temploux, Belgium	22.11.08S
G-APTR	Auster J/1N Alpha	3392		15. 4.59	C J and D J Baker	Carr Farm, Thorney, Newark	11. 4.87
					(Noted complete 1.05)		
G-APTU	Auster Alpha 5	3413		20. 4.59	A J and J M Davis tr G-APTU Flying Group		
					(On rebuild 3.00)	Leicester	8. 6.98
G-APTY	Beech G35 Bonanza	D-4789	EI-AJG	4. 6.59	G E Brennand *(Noted 10.07)*	Blackpool	11. 6.06
G-APTZ	Druine D 31 Turbulent	PFA 508		18. 3.59	Tiger Club (1990) Ltd	Headcorn	18. 6.07P
	(Built Rollason Aircraft and Engines) (Volkswagen 1600)						
G-APUE	Orlican L-40 Meta-Sokol	150708	OK-NMB	2. 6.59	S E and M J Aherne	Top Farm, Croydon, Royston	20. 5.09
G-APUR	Piper PA-22-160 Tri-Pacer	22-6711		3. 7.59	S T A Hutchinson	Gransha, Rathfriland	11.11.10S
G-APUW	Auster J/5V Series 160 Autocar	3273		23. 6.59	E A J Hibbard *(Noted 2.06)*	Hill Farm, Nayland	18.12.03
G-APUY	Druine D 31 Turbulent	PFA 509		24. 6.59	C Jones	Barton	10. 6.86P
	(Built K F W Turner) (Volkswagen 1300)				*(On slow rebuild 7.06)*		
G-APVF	Putzer Elster B	006	D-EEQX 97+04, D-EJUH	29.12.83	A and E A Wiseman	Breighton	5. 7.08P
	(Continental O-200-A)				*(As "97+04" in Luftwaffe c/s)*		
G-APVG	Auster J/5L Aiglet Trainer	3306	(ZK-BQW)	10. 7.59	R Farrer	Cranfield	20. 3.00
G-APVL	Saunders-Roe P531-2	S2/5311	XP166 G-APVL	23. 7.59	C J Marsden	RNAS Yeovilton	
					(New owner 6.07)		
G-APVN	Druine D 31 Turbulent	PFA 511		24. 7.59	R Sherwin	Swanborough Farm, Lewes	24. 6.94P
	(Built J P Knight) (Volkswagen 1600)				*(Stored 6.04)*		
G-APVS	Cessna 170B	26156	N2512C	7. 8.59	N Simpson *"Stormin' Norman"*	East Kirkby	23. 6.08E
G-APVU	Orlican L-40 Meta-Sokol	150706	OK-NMI	21. 8.59	S A and M J Aherne	(Smallford, St Albans)	27. 6.79
					(Damaged Manchester 12. 9.78: on rebuild 1993)		
G-APVZ	Druine D 31 Turbulent	PFA 545		23. 7.59	The Tiger Club 1990 Ltd	Headcorn	3.12.08P
	(Built Rollason Aircraft and Engines) (Ardem 4C02)						
G-APWL	EoN AP.10 460 Standard Series 1A	EoN/S/001	BGA 1172 -BRK G-APWL, RAFGSA.268, G-APWL *(Noted 2000)*	2. 9.59	D G Andrew	Eaglescott	26. 4.00
G-APWP	Druine D 31 Turbulent	PFA 497		14. 9.59	C F Rogers	(Wheathampstead, St Albans)	27. 6.67
	(Built C F Rogers)						
G-APXJ	Piper PA-24-250 Comanche	24-291	VR-NDA N10F	11.12.59	T Wildsmith	Gamston	15. 10.07E
G-APXR	Piper PA-22-160 Tri-Pacer	22-7172	N10F	29. 1.60	A Troughton	Belfast International	5.12.07E
G-APXT	Piper PA-22-150 Tri-Pacer	22-3854	N4545A	16. 2.60	A E Cuttler	Oaksey Park	22. 5.08E
	(Rebuilt to PA-20 Pacer configuration)						
G-APXU	Piper PA-22 Tri-Pacer	22-474	N1723A	10. 2.60	The Scottish Aero Club Ltd	Perth	20. 2.85
					"The Cloth Bomber" (Noted 8.07)		
G-APXY	Cessna 150	17711	N7911E	15. 1.60	Well Clinics Ltd	Exeter	1. 4.08E
G-APYB	Tipsy Nipper T 66 Series 3	T66/39		28. 1.60	B O Smith	Yearby	12. 6.96P
	(Built Avions Fairey SA) (Volkswagen 1834)				*(On rebuild 12.08)*		
G-APYG	de Havilland DHC-1 Chipmunk 22	C1/0060	WB619	11.11.60	P A and J M Doyle	Little Gransden	27. 8.10
G-APYI	Piper PA-22-135 Tri-Pacer	22-2218	N8031C	8. 2.60	R E Dagless	Holly Hill Farm, Guist, Dereham	9. 5.08E
	(Modified to PA-20 Pacer configuration)						
G-APYN	Piper PA-22-160 Tri-Pacer	22-6797	N2804Z	24. 2.60	J Vipond and M Lamb tr Fishburn Tripacer Group	Morgansfield, Fishburn	24. 7.10S
G-APYT	Champion 7FC Tri-Traveler	387		9. 5.60	B J Anning	Watchford Farm, Yarcombe	29. 6.06P
G-APZJ	Piper PA-18-150 Super Cub	18-7233	N10F	29. 1.60	R Jones t/a Southern Sailplanes	Membury	27. 5.08
	(Rebuilt 1986 after accident 12. 6.83 using fuselage frame believed ex G-ATRH {18-7830})						
G-APZL	Piper PA-22-160 Tri-Pacer	22-7054	EI-ALF N10F	27. 1.60	B Robins	(Catcott, Bridgwater)	14. 5.99
G-APZX	Piper PA-22-150 Tri-Pacer	22-5181	N7420D	28. 4.60	V A Holliday	Tatenhill	19. 4.08E
	(Modified to PA-20 Pacer configuration)						

G-ARAA - G-ARZZ

Reg	Type	C/n	Prev id	Date	Owner/Operator	Location	Date
G-ARAI	Piper PA-22-160 Tri-Pacer	22-7421	N10F	17. 5.60	P McCabe	Newtownards	31. 3.08E
	(Fitted witn wings from G-ARSX in 2005/6)						
G-ARAM	Piper PA-18-150 Super Cub	18-7312	N10F	17. 5.60	Skymax (Aviation) Ltd	Sywell	22. 6.02T
					(Noted on rebuild 9.06)		
G-ARAN	Piper PA-18-150 Super Cub	18-7307	N10F	28. 4.60	A P Docherty	Redhill	8. 6.10S
G-ARAO	Piper PA-18 Super Cub 95	18-7327	N10F	17. 5.60	R G Manton	Manor Farm, Haddenham	6. 7.08E
G-ARAS	Champion 7FC Tri-Traveler	7FC-396		12. 9.60	G J Taylor tr Alpha Sierra Flying Group		
					(Noted 8.07)	Yeatsall Farm, Abbots Bromley	22. 6.01P
G-ARAT	Cessna 180C	50827	N9327T	18. 5.60	S D Pryke and J Graham		
						(Great Witchingham, Norwich)	22. 6.08E
G-ARAW	Cessna 182C Skylane	52843	N8943T	18. 5.60	R P Beck, G and R L McLean t/a Ximango UK		
						Rufforth	27. 3.08E
G-ARAX	Piper PA-22-150 Caribbean	22-3830	N4523A	22. 4.60	J W Iliffe	Derby	3. 5.08E
G-ARAZ	de Havilland DH.82A Tiger Moth	82867	R4959	25. 3.60	D A Porter	Griffins Farm, Temple Bruer	4. 6.10S
G-ARBE	de Havilland DH.104 Dove 8	04517		6. 5.60	M Whale and M W A Lunn	Little Rissington	3.10.02
					(Noted 1.08)		
G-ARBG	Tipsy Nipper T 66 Series 2	ABAC.1		11. 5.60	D Shrimpton	(Oakhill, Bath)	17. 8.84P
	(Originally built Avions Fairey SA as c/n T66.57) (Volkswagen 1834 Acro)				*(On rebuild 2006)*		
G-ARBO	Piper PA-24-250 Comanche	24-2117	N10F	15. 6.60	Tatenhill Aviation Ltd	Tatenhill	27. 5.84
					(New owner 7.06)		
G-ARBS	Piper PA-22-160 Tri-Pacer	22-6858	N2868Z	24. 8.60	S D Rowell	Valley Farm, Winwick	7. 3.08E
	(Modified to PA-20 Pacer configuration)				"Greta"		
G-ARBV	Piper PA-22-160 Tri-Pacer	22-5836	N8633D	29. 6.60	L M Williams	Mendlesham	3. 7.06
	(Rebuilt 1983/84 using fuselage of G-ARDP ex N7004B [22-4254])						
G-ARBZ	Druine D 31 Turbulent	PFA 553		6. 5.60	G Richards	Headcorn	15.10.99P
	(Built Rollason Aircraft and Engines) (Ardem 4C02)				*(New owner 2.03)*		
G-ARCF	Piper PA-22-150 Caribbean	22-4563	N5902D	28. 6.60	M J Speakman	North Coates	24. 5.08E
G-ARCS	Auster D 6 Series 180	3703		4. 7.60	E A Matty	Shobdon	3. 9.03
G-ARCV	Cessna 175A Skylark	17556757	N8057T	7.11.60	R Francis and C Campbell	Church Farm, Askern	3. 9.05
	(Continental O-300D)				*(Noted damaged 9.07)*		
G-ARCW	Piper PA-23 Apache	23-796	N2187P	7. 7.60	F W Ellis	Cranfield	24. 8.07T
	(Modified to PA-23-160 standard)						
G-ARDB	Piper PA-24-250 Comanche	24-2166	PH-RON	15. 8.60	P Crook	Rochester	9. 7.08E
			G-ARDB, N7019P				
G-ARDD	Scintex CP.301-C1 Emeraude	549		4. 7.60	N C Grayson	Boscombe Down	15. 8.08P
	(Rebuilt EMK Aeroplanes Ltd- c/n EMK.004)						
G-ARDJ	Auster D 6 Series 180	3704		15. 7.60	R E Neal t/a RN Aviation (Leicester Airport) Leicester		7. 7.88T
					(Damaged near Leicester 30. 5.86: noted 10.07)		
G-ARDO	Jodel D 112J	146	F-PBTE	22. 8.60	W R Prescott	Ballymageough, Kilkeel	30. 5.07P
	(Built Etablissement Couesnon)		F-BBTE, F-WBTE		*(Composite with fuselage of G-AYEO ex F-BIGG [684] c 1974)*		
G-ARDS	Piper PA-22-160 Tri-Pacer	22-7154	N3214Z	4. 9.60	N P McGowan	Newtownards	26. 3.08E
G-ARDT	Piper PA-22-160 Tri-Pacer	22-6210	N9158D	15. 9.60	B W Haston	Cheyene Farm, Stonehaven	29. 6.08E
G-ARDV	Piper PA-22-160 Tri-Pacer	22-7487	EI-APA	28. 7.60	P Heffron	Dreemore Road, Dungannon	18. 4.08E
			G-ARDV, N10F				
G-ARDY	Tipsy Nipper T 66 Series 2	T66/55		10. 8.60	J K Davies	Green Farm, Chester	12.12.00P
	(Built Avions Fairey SA) (Martlet Volkswagen)				*(New owner 7.07)*		
G-AREH	de Havilland DH.82A Tiger Moth	85287	(G-APYV)	4. 7.60	C D Cyster and A J Hastings	Glenrothes	19. 4.66T
	(Built Morris Motors Ltd)		6746M, DE241		*(New owner 2.02)*		
G-AREI	Taylorcraft E Auster III	518	9M-ALB	14.12.60	R B Webber	Trenchard Farm, Eggesford	18. 4.10
			VR-RBM, VR-SCJ, MT438		*(As "MT438" in SEAC c/s) "Akyab"*		
G-AREL	Piper PA-22-150 Caribbean	22-7284	N3344Z	14. 9.60	R Gibson tr The Caribbean Flying Club White Waltham		12. 5.08E
G-AREO	Piper PA-18-150 Super Cub	18-7407	N10F	24. 8.60	The Vale of the White Horse Gliding Club		
						Sandhill Farm, Shrivenham	17. 9.07
G-ARET	Piper PA-22-160 Tri-Pacer	22-7590	N10F	2. 9.60	I S Runnalls	Enstone	20. 5.83T
					(Frame noted hangared 3.07)		
G-AREV	Piper PA-22-160 Tri-Pacer	22-6540	N9628D	25.10.60	D J Ash "Smart Cat"	Barton	29. 1.08
G-AREX	Aeronca 15AC Sedan	15AC-61	CF-FNM	12. 9.60	R J M Turnbull	Rydinghurst Farm, Cranleigh	12.10.10S
G-ARFB	Piper PA-22-150 Caribbean	22-7518	N3625Z	8. 9.60	S Young tr The Tripacer Group	Derby	11. 5.08E
G-ARFD	Piper PA-22-160 Tri-Pacer	22-7565	N3667Z	8. 9.60	J R Dunnett	Priory Farm, Tibenham	7. 6.08E
G-ARFI	Cessna 150A	15059100	N41836	1. 2.61	A R Abrey	Gloucestershire	18.10.07
			G-ARFI, N7000X				
G-ARFO	Cessna 150A	15059174	N7074X	23. 3.61	A P Amor	Phoenix Farm, Lower Upham	18. 9.08E
G-ARFT	SAN Jodel DR.1050 Ambassadeur	170		27.10.60	R Shaw	(Sowerby Bridge)	13.10.84
					(Damaged Prestwick 15.. 6.84)		
G-ARFV	Tipsy Nipper T 66 Series 2	T66/44		5.10.60	T J Butler	Watchford Farm, Yarcombe	12. 9.08P
	(Built Avions Fairey SA) (Volkswagen 1834)						
G-ARGG	de Havilland DHC-1 Chipmunk 22	C1/0247	WD305	19.10.60	D Curtis	Prestwick	27. 2.10S
G-ARGO	Piper PA-22-108 Colt	22-8034		18. 1.61	D R Smith	Halfpenny Green	18. 7.08E
G-ARGV	Piper PA-18-150 Super Cub	18-7559	N10F	20.12.60	Wolds Gliding Club Ltd	Pocklington	14. 4.08E
	(Lycoming O-360-A4)						
G-ARGY	Piper PA-22-160 Tri-Pacer	22-7620	G-JEST	20.12.60	D H and R T Tanner	Wellesbourne Mountford	9. 4.08E
	(Modified to PA-20 configuration)		G-ARGY, N10F				
G-ARGZ	Druine D 31 Turbulent	PFA 562		7.11.60	The Tiger Club (1990) Ltd	Headcorn	10.12.07P
	(Built Rollason Aircraft and Engines) (Volkswagen 1600)						
G-ARHB	Forney F-1A Aircoupe	5733		17. 4.61	K J Peacock and S F Turner	Earls Colne	14. 3.09S
G-ARHC	Forney F-1A Aircoupe	5734		26. 5.61	A P Gardner	Little Gransden	13.12.10S
G-ARHI	Piper PA-24 Comanche	24-2260	N7299P	20.12.60	D D Smith	Hardwick	8. 8.08E
			N10F				
G-ARHM	Auster 6A	2515	VF557	5. 1.61	R C P Brookhouse *(Noted 3.05)*	Wycombe Air Park	9.12.01
G-ARHN	Piper PA-22-150 Caribbean	22-7514	N3622Z	10. 1.61	I S Hodge and S Haughton	East Winch	5. 3.07
	(Rebuilt with parts of G-ATXB which was damaged beyond repair 26.8.74)				*(Noted 5.07)*		

Reg	Type	c/n	Prev id	Date	Owner	Location	Date
G-ARHP	Piper PA-22-160 Tri-Pacer	22-7549	N3652Z	10. 1.61	A S Cowan tr Popham Flying Group G-ARHP	Popham	22. 5.10
G-ARHR	Piper PA-22-150 Caribbean	22-7576	N3707Z	10. 1.61	A R Wyatt	Cottered, Hertford	2. 2.08E
G-ARHW	de Havilland DH.104 Dove 8	04512		10. 1.61	Aviation Heritage Ltd	Coventry	19. 5.06T
G-ARHZ	Druine D 62A Condor	PFA 247		13.12.60	E Shouler	Beeches Farm, South Scarle	6.11.07P
	(Built Rollason Aircraft and Engines with c/n RAE 602)						
G-ARID	Cessna 172B Skyhawk	48209	N7709X	2. 2.61	L M Edwards	Sleap	3. 8.08E
G-ARIF	Ord-Hume O-H 7 Minor Coupe	PAL 1401		22. 8.60	N H Ponsford	Wigan	
	(Built A W J G Ord-Hume - c/n O-H 7) (Modified Luton LA-4C Minor)				*(Stored incomplete 3.96)*		
G-ARIH	Auster 6A	2463	TW591	23. 1.61	M C Jordan	(Dolton, Winkleigh)	27. 4.10S
					(As "TW591" in RAF 664 (AOP) Sqdn c/s)		
G-ARIK	Piper PA-22-150 Caribbean	22-7570	N3701Z	26. 1.61	A Taylor	Manor Farm, Binham	5. 6.06
G-ARIL	Piper PA-22-150 Caribbean	22-7574	N3705Z	26. 1.61	AJW Construction Ltd.	(Hordle, Lymington)	23.10.10E
G-ARIM	Druine D 31 Turbulent	PFA 510		27. 2.61	J G McTaggart	Archerfield Estate, Direlton	
	(Built A Schima)				*(New owner 2.08)*		
G-ARJB	de Havilland DH.104 Dove 8	04518		29. 9.60	M Whale and M W A Lunn	Little Rissington	10.12.73T
					"Exporter" (JCB titles: noted 1.08)		
G-ARJE	Piper PA-22-108 Colt	22-8184		29. 3.61	C I Fray *(New owner 10.00)*	(Disley)	29. 4.73
G-ARJF	Piper PA-22-108 Colt	22-8199		23. 3.61	Tandycel Co Ltd	Glebe Farm, Stockton	16. 3.07
G-ARJH	Piper PA-22-108 Colt	22-8249		29. 3.61	F Vogels	Le Plessis-Bellville, Picardy, France	8.10.06
G-ARJS	Piper PA-23-160 Apache G	23-1977	N10F	3. 3.61	Bencray Ltd	Blackpool	26. 4.08E
					(Operated Blackpool and Fylde Aero Club)		
G-ARJT	Piper PA-23-160 Apache G	23-1981	N10F	3. 3.61	J A Cole	Netherthorpe	18. 8.07T
G-ARJU	Piper PA-23-160 Apache G	23-1984	N10F	3. 3.61	G R Manley	Biggin Hill	29. 8.08E
G-ARJV	Piper PA-23-160 Apache G	23-1985	N10F	3. 3.61	M Corbett	Dunsfold	22. 6.08E
G-ARKG	Auster J/5G Cirrus Autocar	3061	AP-AHJ VP-KKN	22. 2.61	S J Cooper	Wickenby	19. 6.10S
G-ARKJ	Beech N35 Bonanza	D-6736		5. 5.61	P D and J L Jenkins	Goodwood	20. 1.08E
G-ARKK	Piper PA-22-108 Colt	22-8290		12. 4.61	R D Welfare	Rochester	20. 1.08E
G-ARKM	Piper PA-22-108 Colt	22-8313		12. 4.61	D Dytch and J Moffat	Perth	25. 4.08E
G-ARKN	Piper PA-22-108 Colt	22-8327		9. 5.61	R Redfern	Derby	29. 1.11S
G-ARKP	Piper PA-22-108 Colt	22-8364		19. 5.61	J P A Freeman and Shenley Farms (Aviation) Ltd	Headcorn	12.12.07E
G-ARKS	Piper PA-22-108 Colt	22-8422		7. 6.61	R A Nesbitt-Dufort	Bradleys Lawn, Heathfield	28.11.11S
	(Lycoming O-320)						
G-ARLB	Piper PA-24-250 Comanche	24-2352	G-BUTL G-ARLB, N10F	21. 3.61	D Heater	Blackbushe	12. 9.08E
G-ARLG	Auster D 4/108	3606		4. 4.61	R D Helliar-Symons tr Auster D4 Group		
	(Lycoming O-235)				Bourne Park, Hurstbourne Tarrant	12. 6.08P
G-ARLK	Piper PA-24-250 Comanche	24-2433	EI-ALW G-ARLK, N10F	25. 5.61	R P Jackson	(Harpenden)	16. 5.08E
G-ARLP (2)	Beagle A 61 Terrier 1	3724 (1)	VX123	11. 4.61	D R Whitby tr Gemini Flying Group	(Fakenham)	31.10.91
	(C/n officially quoted as 2573 (VF631) which became G-ARLM (2) then G-ASDK)				*(Damaged Truleigh Farm, Edburton 4. 8.91: on rebuild 2000)*		
G-ARLR	Beagle A 61 Terrier 2	3721 & B 601	VW996	11. 4.61	M Palfreman *(Noted 2.08)*	Bagby	9. 9.01
G-ARLX	SAN Jodel D 140B Mousquetaire II	66		12. 4.61	J S and S V Shaw	Perranporth	12. 9.10
G-ARLZ	Druine D 31A Turbulent	RAE 578		7. 4.61	J A Thomas	(Hamstreet, Ashford)	10. 9.07P
	(Built Rollason Aircraft and Engines) (Ardem 4C02)						
G-ARMA	Piper PA-23-160 Apache G	23-1967	N4448P	8. 5.61	C J Hopewell *(Stored 10.01)*	Sibson	22. 7.77
G-ARMC	de Havilland DHC-1 Chipmunk 22A	C1/0151	WB703	26. 4.61	J T H Henderson tr John Henderson Childrens Trust		
					(As "WB703" in RAF c/s)	Wycombe Air Park	26. 4.10S
G-ARMD	de Havilland DHC-1 Chipmunk 22A	C1/0237	WD297	26. 4.61	D M Squires *(Stored 2.04)*	(Redditch)	5. 6.76
G-ARMF	de Havilland DHC-1 Chipmunk 22A	C1/0394	WG322	26. 4.61	D M Squires	(Redditch)	12.10.98
					(As "WZ868:H" in RAF c/s) (Damaged 1996: wings stored Husbands Bosworth 10.07)		
G-ARMG	de Havilland DHC-1 Chipmunk 22A	C1/0575	WK558	26. 4.61	J Archer tr MG Group	Bidford	21. 3.10S
G-ARML	Cessna 175B Skylark	17556995	N8295T	12. 7.61	G A Copeland	Popham	1. 9.07T
G-ARMN	Cessna 175B Skylark	17556994	N8294T	18. 8.61	B R Nash	Lower Wasing Farm, Brimpton	18. 7.08
G-ARMO	Cessna 172B Skyhawk	48560	N8060X	12. 6.61	I M Latiff	Little Staughton	23.12.05
G-ARMR	Cessna 172B Skyhawk	48566	N8066X	12. 6.61	Sunsaver Ltd	Barton	25. 9.08E
G-ARMZ	Druine D 31 Turbulent	PFA 565		2. 5.61	The Tiger Club 1990 Ltd Headcorn	Headcorn	16. 8.08P
	(Built Rollason Aircraft and Engines) (Volkswagen 1500)						
G-ARNB	Auster J/5G Cirrus Autocar	3169	AP-AHL VP-KNL	18. 5.61	R F Tolhurst	Lenham, Maidstone	19. 2.77
					(Possibly on rebuild 1995)		
G-ARND	Piper PA-22-108 Colt	22-8484		6. 6.61	C D Hardwick	Perranporth	15.11.10S
G-ARNE	Piper PA-22-108 Colt	22-8502		15. 6.61	T D L Bowden	Knettishall	11. 7.10S
	(Lycoming O-320)						
G-ARNG	Piper PA-22-108 Colt	22-8547		26. 6.61	F B Rothera	Stoneacre Farm, Farthing Corner	27.1.11S
	(Lycoming O-320)				*"Awful Red"*		
G-ARNJ	Piper PA-22-108 Colt	22-8587		3. 8.61	R A Keech	Liverpool	29. 1.11E
G-ARNK	Piper PA-22-108 Colt	22-8622		5. 9.61	I P Burnett	Landmead Farm, Garford	6. 2.11S
	(Tail-wheel conversion)						
G-ARNL	Piper PA-22-108 Colt	22-8625		3. 8.61	Miss J A Dodsworth	White Waltham	24. 5.08
G-ARNN	Globe GC-1B Swift	1272	VP-YMJ VP-RDA, ZS-BMX, NC3279K	11. 5.61	K E Sword *(Crashed Hucknall 1. 9.73)*	(Leicester)	11. 7.74
G-ARNO	Beagle A 61 Terrier 1	3722	VX113	8. 5.61	R Webber	Trenchard Farm, Eggesford	26. 2.09S
	(Official p/i shown as VX115)				*(As "VX113:36" in AAC c/s)*		
G-ARNP	Beagle A 109 Airedale	B 503		10. 5.61	S T and M Isbister	Spanhoe	27. 4.09S
	(Originally regd with c/n A109-P1)						
G-ARNY	SAN Jodel D 117	595	F-BHXQ	13. 6.61	P Jenkins	Inverness	12. 4.08P
G-ARNZ	Druine D 31 Turbulent	PFA 579		28. 6.61	The Tiger Club (1990) Ltd	Headcorn	12. 3.08P
	(Built Rollason Aircraft and Engines) (Volkswagen 1600)						
G-AROA	Cessna 172B Skyhawk	48628	N8128X	19. 9.61	D E Partridge tr The D and P Group		
						Rayne Hall Farm, Braintree	18. 9.08E
G-AROC	Cessna 175BX Skylark	17556997	G-OTOW G-AROC, N8297T	2.10.61	A J Symms	High Ham, Yeovil	23. 5.08
	(Modified to 172 configuration)						

Reg	Type	c/n	Prev id	Date	Owner / Notes	Location	Date
G-ARON	Piper PA-22-108 Colt	22-8822		23.11.61	R Gibson tr The G-ARON Flying Group		
					(New owners 11.04)	White Waltham	5. 7.01
G-AROO	Forney F-1A Aircoupe	5750	N25B	3.11.61	W J McMeekan	Newtownards	13. 4.08
G-AROW	SAN Jodel D 140B Mousquetaire II	71		13. 9.61	A R Crome New Farm House, Great Oakley		7. 6.08E
G-AROY	Boeing Stearman A75N1 (PT-17) Kaydet	75-4775	N56418	6. 6.61	I T Whitaker-Bethel and J Mann	Spanhoe	19. 7.07
	(Pratt and Whitney R985)		42-16612		*(New owners 10.07)*		
G-ARRD	SAN Jodel DR.1051 Ambassadeur	274		20. 7.61	D J Taylor and J P Brady	RAF Benson	24.10.07P
G-ARRE	SAN Jodel DR.1050 Ambassadeur	275		20. 7.61	W C Mansfield	Little Gransden	16. 7.08
G-ARRI	Cessna 175B Skylark	17557001	N8301T	5.10.61	M V Eckley tr G-ARRI Partnership	Pembrey	24. 6.08E
G-ARRL	Auster J/1N Alpha	2115	VP-KFK	13. 6.61	A C Ladd Romney Street Farm, Sevenoaks		24. 7.08
			VP-KPF, VP-KFK, VP-UAK				
G-ARRO	Beagle A 109 Airedale	B 507	EI-AYL (2)	16. 6.61	M and S W Isbister	Spanhoe	17. 1.74
	(Originally regd with c/n A 109-P5)		G-ARRO, (EI-AVP), G-ARRO		*(Stored for spares as "EI-AYL" 10.07)*		
G-ARRS	Menavia Piel CP.301A Emeraude	226	F-BIMA	29. 6.61	J F Sully	Sturgate	24. 7.08P
G-ARRT	Wallis WA-116/Mc	2		28. 6.61	K H Wallis Reymerston Hall, Norfolk		24. 5.83P
	(McCulloch 4318A) *(Originally regd as a Wallis Gyroplane then became WA-116/Mc)* *(Noted 8.01)*						
G-ARRU	Druine D 31 Turbulent	PFA 502		28. 6.61	D G Huck	Rugby	27. 2.97P
	(Built J O'Connor) (Volkswagen 1600)				*(New owner 8.03)*		
G-ARRX	Auster 6A	2281	VF512	4. 7.61	J E D Mackie	Popham	22. 6.09
					(As "VF512:PF-M" in RAF 43 OTU c/s) "Peggy Too"		
G-ARRY	SAN Jodel D 140B Mousquetaire II	72		13. 9.61	Fictionview Ltd	Bodmin	25. 1.08E
G-ARRZ	Druine D 31 Turbulent	PFA 580		21. 8.61	T W Harris	Wycombe Air Park	21.12.90P
	(Built Rollason Aircraft and Engines) (Ardem 4C02)		*(Damaged Horley, Surrey 21. 7.90: rear fuselage Priory Farm, Tibenham 6.04: new owner 5.05)*				
G-ARSG	Avro Triplane Type IV replica	TRI-1	(BAPC.1)	29.10.81	Richard Shuttleworth Trustees	Old Warden	8. 9.08P
	(Built Hampshire Aero Club) (ADC Cirrus III) *(Built for "Those Magnificent Men in Their Flying Machines" film)* *(As "12")*						
G-ARSL	Beagle A 61 Terrier 2	2539	VF581	13. 7.61	D J Colclough Trenchard Farm, Eggesford		1. 5.10S
					(As "VF581" in AAC c/s)		
G-ARSU	Piper PA-22-108 Colt	22-8835	EI-AMI	23.11.61	D Hawkins tr Sierra Uniform Flying Group		
			G-ARSU		(Rotherfield Greys, Henley-on-Thames)		26. 9.08E
G-ARTH	Piper PA-12 Super Cruiser	12-3278	EI-ADO	22. 9.61	R I Souch and B J Dunford	Bournemouth	21. 4.95P
					(On rebuild 3.07)		
G-ARTL	de Havilland DH.82A Tiger Moth		"T7281"	22. 9.61	F G Clacherty Longwood Farm, Morestead		9. 6.09S
	(P/i is doubtful - if correct the c/n is 83795)				*(As "T7281" in RAF c/s)*		
G-ARTZ (2)	McCandless M 4 Gyroplane	M4/1		24.10.61	W R Partridge	St Merryn	13.10.69P
	(Volkswagen 1500)				*(Noted 5.03)*		
G-ARUG	Auster J/5G Cirrus Autocar	3272		2. 1.62	D P H Hulme	Biggin Hill	18. 4.03
G-ARUH	SAN Jodel DR.1050 Ambassadeur	284		5.12.61	P R Bentley Roughay Farm, Bishops Waltham		4. 7.88
					(New owner 12.07)		
G-ARUI	Beagle A 61 Terrier 1	2529	VF571	9. 3.62	T W J Dann	Southend	31. 3.08
G-ARUL	LeVier Cosmic Wind	103	N22C	28.11.61	P G Kynsey *"Ballerina"*	Duxford	4. 7.08P
	(Built Tony LeVier Associates Inc: rebuilt 1973 as pr.no.PFA 1511 but original fuselage, wings and data plate held elsewhere) (Continental O-200-A)						
G-ARUV	Piel CP.301 Emeraude Series 1	PFA 700		2. 2.62	P O'Fee	RAF Keevil	25. 4.08P
	(Built M N Harrison) (Continental C90)				*"Emma"*		
G-ARUY	Auster J/1N Alpha	3394		2. 2.62	D Burnham *(Being restored 1.08)*	Andrewsfield	27.11.05
G-ARUZ	Cessna 175C Skylark	17557080	N8380T	23. 2.62	M Lowe and L E Brown tr Cardiff Skylark Group		
					(Noted 10.07)	Bodmin	18. 5.06
G-ARVO	Piper PA-18 Super Cub 95	18-7252	D-ENFI	18. 1.83	D S Brown and R M Kimbrell tr Victor Oscar Group		
			N3376Z		(Rushton, Kettering)	16.12.10E
G-ARVT	Piper PA-28-160 Cherokee	28-379		21. 3.62	Red Rose Aviation Ltd	Liverpool	15. 3.08E
G-ARVU	Piper PA-28-160 Cherokee	28-410	PH-ONY	30. 3.62	Barton Mudwing Ltd	Barton	10. 7.08E
			G-ARVU				
G-ARVV	Piper PA-28-160 Cherokee	28-451		11. 7.62	G E Hopkins	Shobdon	25. 1.08E
G-ARVZ	Druine D 62B Condor	RAE 606		6.12.61	A A M Huke Manor Farm, Dinton		6. 5.08P
	(Built Rollason Aircraft and Engines)						
G-ARWB	de Havilland DHC-1 Chipmunk 22A	C1/0621	WK611	2. 1.62	P G Alston tr Thruxton Chipmunk Flying Group		
					(As "WK611" in RAF c/s)	Thruxton	21.11.08S
G-ARWO	Cessna 172C Skyhawk	49187	N1487Y	10. 4.62	D Bentley (Nenagh, County Tipperary)		2. 7.08
G-ARWR	Cessna 172C Skyhawk	49172	N1472Y	13. 4.62	M McCann tr Devanha Flying Group	Insch	22.12.07E
G-ARWS	Cessna 175C Skylark	17557102	N8502X	12. 4.62	M D Fage	Derby	28.10.07E
G-ARXB	Beagle A 109 Airedale	B 509	EI-BBK	5. 2.62	M Isbister	Spanhoe	9. 9.76
	(Originally regd with c/n A 109-2)		G-ARXB, EI-ATE, G-ARXB		*(Stored for spares as "EI-BBK" 10.07)*		
G-ARXD	Beagle A 109 Airedale	B 511		19. 4.62	D Howden	Lumphanan	13. 6.86
	(Originally regd with c/n A 109-4)				*(Under restoration 6.00)*		
G-ARXG	Piper PA-24-250 Comanche	24-3154	N10F	21. 2.62	R F Corstin t/a Fairoaks Comanche	Dunsfold	8. 9.08E
G-ARXH	Bell 47	G 40	N120B	13. 2.62	A B Searle	Cranfield	6. 7.90
			NC120B		*(Noted 8.06)*		
G-ARXP	Phoenix Luton LA-4A Minor	PAL 1119		23. 2.62	E Evans Benson's Farm, Laindon		17.10.95P
	(Built W C Hymas - pr.no.PFA 816) (Walter Mikron 3)				*(Stored 1.08)*		
G-ARXT	SAN Jodel DR.1050 Ambassadeur	355		14. 3.62	M F Coy tr CJM Flying Group Wellesbourne Mountford		25.11.10S
G-ARXU	Auster 6A	2295	VF526	5. 3.62	E C Tait and M Pocock AAC Netheravon		4.10.08S
					(As "VF526:T" in AAC c/s)		
G-ARXW	Morane Saulnier MS.885 Super Rallye	100		30. 3.62	M J Kirk *(Noted 5.05)*	Haverfordwest	4. 5.04
G-ARYH	Piper PA-22-160 Tri-Pacer	22-7039	N3102Z	9. 3.62	C Watt	Crosland Moor	28. 6.08E
G-ARYI	Cessna 172C	49260	N1560Y	13. 7.62	J Rhodes *(Noted 2.06)*	Blackbushe	10. 8.03T
G-ARYK	Cessna 172C	49288	N1588Y	13. 7.62	A Winnicott	Lydd	26. 4.08E
G-ARYR	Piper PA-28-160 Cherokee B	28-770		12. 7.62	R P Synge and C S Wilkinson tr GARYR Flying Group		
						Turweston	22. 3.08E
G-ARYS	Cessna 172C Skyhawk	49291	N1591Y	13. 7.62	G Cockerton tr Lucon Chasnais Flying Amis Coventry		7.12.07E
					(New owner 2.08)		
G-ARYV	Piper PA-24-250 Comanche	24-2516	N7337P	17. 4.62	D C Hanss	Elstree	2.11.07E
G-ARYZ	Beagle A 109 Airedale	B 512		9. 4.62	C W Tomkins *(Noted 10.07)*	Spanhoe	26. 2.01
G-ARZB	Wallis WA-116 Series 1 Agile	B 203	XR943	18. 4.62	K H Wallis Reymerston Hall, Norfolk		29. 6.93P
	(Built Beagle-Miles Aircraft Ltd) (McCulloch 4318A) G-ARZB				*"Little Nellie"*		
	(Flown as "XR943" for evaluation 1962 and remained on UK Register: used in 1966 for James Bond film "You Only Live Twice") *(Noted 8.01)*						

G-ARZN	Beech N35 Bonanza	D-6795	N215DM	23. 5.62	S R Cleary	Kirknewton	20.12.07E
G-ARZS	Beagle A 109 Airedale	B 515	EI-BAL	11. 5.62	M and S W Isbister	Spanhoe	23. 5.75
			G-ARZS		*(Fuselage noted 10.07)*		
G-ARZW	Phoenix Currie Wot	1		25. 5.62	B R Pearson	Eaglescott	7. 1.89P
	(Built J H B Urmston) (Walter Mikron 3)				*(Damaged near Headcorn 12. 2.88: on rebuild 10.99 as Pfalz D VII scale replica)*		

G-ASAA - G-ASZZ

G-ASAA	Phoenix Luton LA-4A Minor	O-H/4		19. 4.62	M J Aubrey	Kington, Hereford	7. 6.01P
	(Built P D Lea and Partners) (JAP J 99)				*(Notod 2002)*		
G-ASAI	Beagle A 109 Airedale	B 516		26. 6.62	K R Howden *(On rebuild 6.00)*	(Lumphanan)	20. 5.773
G-ASAJ	Beagle A 61 Terrier 2	B 605	WE569	26. 6.62	T A Collins	(Little Faringdon, Lechlade)	29.11..09E
	(Initially allocated c/n 3732)				*(As "WE569" (Auster T 7) in AAC c/s)*		
G-ASAL (2)	Scottish Aviation Bulldog Series 100/101		(G-BBHF)	5. 9.73	Pioneer Flying Company Ltd	Prestwick	9.11.07P
		BH120/239	G-31-17				
G-ASAT	Morane Saulnier MS.880B Rallye Club	178		21. 6.62	M Cutovic	Oaksey Park	2. 8.08E
G-ASAU	Morane Saulnier MS.880B Rallye Club	179		21. 6.62	M S Lonsdale	Full Sutton	9. 7.08E
G-ASAX	Beagle A 61 Terrier 2	B 609	TW533	12. 6.62	A D Hodgkinson	(Luton)	1. 9.96
	(Converted from Auster 6 c/n 1911)				*(New owner 1.07)*		
G-ASAZ	Hiller UH-12E-4	2070	N5372V	18. 6.62	R C Hields t/a Hields Aviation	Hawarden	17. 1.08E
					(As "XS165:37" in RAF c/s)		
G-ASBA	Phoenix Currie Wot	AE.1		16. 8.62	J C Lister	Valley Farm, Winwick	9. 5.08P
	(Built A Etherbridge - pr.no.PFA 3005) (Continental C90)						
G-ASBH	Beagle A 109 Airedale	B 519		26. 6.62	D T Smollett	Bratton Clovelly, Okehampton	19. 2.99
G-ASBY	Beagle A 109 Airedale	B 523		23. 7.62	F A Forster *(New owner 4.02)*	Lydd	22. 3.80
G-ASCC	Beagle E 3 Mk.11	B 701	(G-25-12)	23. 7.62	T A Collins	(Little Faringdon, Lechlade)	11. 8.07P
			XP254		*(As "XP254" in 'AAC c/s)*		
				(Struck tree during go-around Filkins near Lechlade 29. 7.07 and fell into field incurring substantial damage)			
G-ASCM	Isaacs Fury II	1		1. 8.62	E C and P King	Eastbach Farm, Coleford	24.10.02P
	(Built J O Isaacs - pr.no.PFA 2002/1B - builder's membership no.) (Lycoming O-290) (As "K2050" in pre-war RAF c/s)						
G-ASCZ	Menavia Piel CP.301A Emeraude	233	F-BIMG	1.10.62	P Johnson *(In pseudo military marks)*	Goodwood	1. 7.08P
G-ASDK	Beagle A 61 Terrier 2	B 702	G-ARLM (2)	26.10.62	J Swallow	Hibaldstow	26.10.09S
	(Converted from Auster AOP.6 c/n 2573)		G-ARLP(1), VF631				
G-ASDY	Beagle-Wallis WA-116/F	B 205	XR944	9.11.62	K H Wallis	Reymerston Hall, Norfolk	28.10.97P
	(Franklin 2A-120-B)		(G-ARZC (1))		*(Noted 8.01)*		
	(Regd with c/n B 204 as Beagle-Wallis WA.116 Srs 1 and powered by McCulloch 4318A: fitted with 990cc Hillman Imp engine 1965						
	and re-styled WA.119: re-engined 1971 with 60hp 2-cylinder Franklin 2A-120-A and re-designated)						
G-ASEA	Phoenix Luton LA-4A Minor	PAL 1154		14.11.62	D Underwood	(Totternhoe, Dunstable)	16. 8.89P
	(Built G P Smith and M Fawkes - pr.no.PFA 1154) (JAP J 99)				*(New owner 11.05)*		
G-ASEB	Phoenix Luton LA-4A Minor	PAL 1149		26.11.62	S R P Harper	Siege Cross Farm, Thatcham	13. 1.09P
	(Built J A Anning) (Lycoming O-145)						
G-ASEO	Piper PA-24-250 Comanche	24-3367	(G-ASDX)	23. 1.63	M Scott t/a Pixies Day Nursery	Bournemouth	19. 6.08
			N10F				
G-ASEP	Piper PA-23-235 Aztec	27-541		28. 1.63	Air Warren Ltd	Denham	21. 7.08E
					"Miss Max Power" (Maxim titles)		
G-ASEU	Druine D 62A Condor	RAE 607		12. 2.63	W M Grant	Inverness	13. 5.08P
	(Built Rollason Aircraft and Engines) (Continental C90-8F)						
G-ASFA	Cessna 172D Skyhawk	17250182	N2582U	21. 2.63	D Halfpenny	Maypole Farm,Chislet	18. 6.04
G-ASFD	SPP Morava L-200A	170808	OK-PHH	26. 2.63	M Emery *(New owner 12.02)*	(Redhill)	12. 7.84T
G-ASFK	Auster J/5G Cirrus Autocar	3276		7. 3.63	T D G Lancaster	Landmead Farm, Garford	6. 7.09
G-ASFL	Piper PA-28-180 Cherokee B	28-1170		7. 3.63	M R O Thompson and S M R Hickman	Lee-on-Solent	6. 3.08
G-ASFR	Bölkow BÖ.208C Junior	522	D-EGMO	12. 3.63	S T Dauncey *(Stored 2.08)*	Yearby	29. 3.90P
G-ASFX	Druine D 31 Turbulent	PFA 513		18. 3.63	E F Clapham and W B S Dobie	Oldbury-on-Severn	12.12.07P
	(Built E F Clapham) (Volkswagen 1600)						
G-ASHH	Piper PA-23-250 Aztec	27-63	N455SL	25. 3.63	C Fordham and L Barr	(Leicester)	29. 8.03
			N4557P		*(Reportedly destroyed by fire on ground c 2005 and removed)*		
G-ASHS	SNCAN Stampe SV-4C(G)	265	F-BCFN	23. 4.63	D G Girling	(Liverpool)	6. 2.08T
	(Original fuselage for rebuild of G-AWEF 1980: rebuilt 1984 with fuselage of G-AZIR c/n 452 ex F-BCXR)						
G-ASHT	Druine D 31 Turbulent	PFA 1610		23. 4.63	C W N Huke	Manor Farm, Dinton	2.10.08P
	(Built Rollason Aircraft and Engines) (Volkswagen 1600)						
G-ASHU	Piper PA-15 Vagabond	15-46	N4164H	1. 5.63	T J Ventham tr The Calybe Flying Group		
			NC4164H		*"Calybe"*	Farley Farm, Romsey	21.10.08P
	(Rotax 912-UL)						
G-ASHX	Piper PA-28-180 Cherokee B	28-1266	N7382W	3. 5.63	Powertheme Ltd	Barton	11. 5.08E
G-ASIB	Cessna F172D Skyhawk	F172-0006	F-WLIR	9. 5.63	A Jones tr G-ASIB Flying Group	Hawarden	5. 6.08E
	(Built Reims Aviation SA) (Wichita c/n 17250091)						
G-ASII	Piper PA-28-180 Cherokee B	28-1264		21. 5.63	T R Hart and R W S Matthews	Exeter	25. 5.08E
G-ASIJ	Piper PA-28-180 Cherokee B	28-1333	N7445W	21. 5.63	S A King tr G-ASIJ Group	Andrewsfield	6. 6.08E
G-ASIL	Piper PA-28-180 Cherokee B	28-1350	N7461W	21. 5.63	C D Powell	Leicester	8. 8.08E
G-ASIS	Wassmer Jodel D 112	1166	EI-CKX	24. 2.81	W R Prescott	Ballymageough, Kilkeel	20. 8.08P
			G-ASIS, F-BKNR				
G-ASIT	Cessna 180	32567	N7670A	24. 5.63	R A Seeley	Turweston	7. 6.08E
G-ASIY	Piper PA-25-235 Pawnee	25-2446		30. 5.63	T M Holloway tr RAF Gliding and Soaring Association		
	(250hp Lycoming O-540-A1D5)				*(Operated Chilterns Glidng Centre)*	RAF Halton	20. 2.08E
G-ASJL	Beech H35 Bonanza	D-5132	N5582D	14. 6.63	A J Orchard and R L Dargue	Biggin Hill	24. 7.08E
G-ASJV	Vickers Supermarine 361 Spitfire LF.IXb		OO-ARA	3. 7.63	Merlin Aviation Ltd	Duxford	27. 6.08P
		CBAF.IX.552	Belgian AF SM-41, Fokker B-13, R Neth AF H-68, H-105, MH434				
				(Operated The Old Flying Machine Company as "MH434:ZD-B" in RAF 316 Sqdn c/s)			
G-ASJY	Sud-Aviation Gardan GY-80-160 Horizon	13		9. 7.63	L W Quigley tr No. 6 Group *(Noted 2.08)*	Bagby	14.11.07E
G-ASKL	SAN Jodel D 150 Mascaret	27		18. 7.63	J M Graty	Nuthampstead	9. 9.07P
G-ASKP	de Havilland DH.82A Tiger Moth	3889	N6588	22. 7.63	The Tiger Club (1990) Ltd	Headcorn	14. 3.09S
G-ASKT	Piper PA-28-180 Cherokee B	28-1410	N7497W	24. 7.63	T J Herbert	Biggin Hill	14. 6.08
G-ASLH	Cessna 182F Skylane	18254905	N3505U	19. 8.63	A L Brown and A L Butcher	Bourn	17.10.07E
G-ASLV	Piper PA-28-235 Cherokee Pathfinder	28-10048		11. 9.63	I L Harding tr Sackville Flying Group		
						Sackville Lodge, Riseley	10. 2.08E

G-ASLX	Menavia Piel CP.301A Emeraude	292	F-BISV	12. 9.63	J J Reilly	(Thurles, County Tipperary)	1. 3.08P
G-ASMA	Piper PA-30 Twin Comanche	30-143	N10F	17. 9.63	K Cooper	Farley Farm, Romsey	5. 1.03
	(Modified to PA-39 C/R status)				(Stored 10.07)		
G-ASME	Bensen B 8M	12		24. 9.63	R M Harris	North Coates	19. 8.08P
	(Rotax 582)						
G-ASMF	Beech D95A TravelAir	TD-565		26. 9.63	M J A Hornblower	White Waltham	11. 8.08T
G-ASMJ	Cessna F172E	F172-0029		25.10.63	Aeroscene Ltd	Sherburn-in-Elmet	3. 8.08E
	(Built Reims Aviation SA) (Wichita c/n 17250584)						
G-ASML	Phoenix Luton LA-4A Minor	PAL 1148		28.10.63	R W Vince	(Stansted, Sevenoaks)	16. 7.08P
	(Built R M Kirby - pr.no.PFA 802) (Volkswagen 1600)						
G-ASMM	Druine D 31 Turbulent	PFA 1611		31.10.63	W J Browning	Redhill	11. 7.08P
	(Built Rollason Aircraft and Engines) (Ardem 4C02)				"Mouche Miel"		
G-ASMS	Cessna 150A	15059204	N7104X	18.11.63	M Smith (New owner 12.07)	(Brighouse)	4. 4.07
G-ASMT	Fairtravel Linnet 2	004		20.11.63	P Harrison	Swanborough Farm, Lewes	17. 7.08P
G-ASMV	Scintex CP.1310-C3 Super Emeraude	919		22.11.63	P F D Waltham	(Thurlton, Norwich)	7.11.94
					(New owner 7.07)		
G-ASMW	Cessna 150D	15060247	N4247U	26.11.63	C Brown	Netherthorpe	27. 9.08E
G-ASMY	Piper PA-23-160 Apache H	23-2032	N4309Y	3.12.63	R D Forster (Noted 10.07)	Ellough, Beccles	25.11.95T
G-ASMZ	Beagle A 61 Terrier 2	B 629	G-35-11	4.12.63	B Andrews	Trenchard Farm, Eggesford	11. 5.09
	(Conversion of Auster AOP.10 c/n 2285)		VF516		(As "VF516" in RAF c/s)		
G-ASNC	Beagle D 5/180 Husky	3678		9.12.63	Peterborough and Spalding Gliding Club Ltd		
						Crowland	4. 4.10S
G-ASNI	Scintex CP.1310-C3 Super Emeraude	925		20.12.63	D Chapman	Wickenby	5. 9.08E
G-ASNK	Cessna 205	205-0400	N8400Z	27.12.63	Justgold Ltd	Blackpool	29. 6.06T
					(Operated Blackpool Air Centre) (Noted 10.07)		
G-ASNW	Cessna F172E	F172-0031		13. 1.64	B M Tremain tr G-ASNW Group		
	(Built Reims Aviation SA) (Wichita c/n 17250613)					Draycott Farm, Chiseldon	14.10.07E
G-ASOC	Auster 6A Tugmaster	2544	VF603	21. 1.64	M J Kirk (New owner 4.03)	Haverfordwest	18. 5.02
G-ASOH	Beech 95-B55A Baron	TC-656		31. 1.64	G S Goodsir tr GMD Group	Biggin Hill	21. 9.07
G-ASOI	Beagle A 61 Terrier 2	B 627	G-35-11	31. 1.64	G D B Delmege	Kemble	19. 6.98
			WJ404		(Stored dismantled 7.05)		
G-ASOK	Cessna F172E	F172-0057		31. 1.64	D W Disney	Derby	27. 9.08E
	(Built Reims Aviation SA)						
G-ASOM	Beagle A 61 Terrier 2	B 622	G-JETS	3. 2.64	D Humphries	Spanhoe	5. 7.09S
			G-ASOM, G-35-11, VF505				
G-ASOX	Cessna 205A	205-0556	N4856U	3. 2.64	S M C Harvey	Hinton-in-the-Hedges	1. 8.92
					(New owner 1.06)		
G-ASPF	Wassmer Jodel D 120 Paris-Nice	02	F-BFNP	26. 2.64	T J Bates	Dairy House Farm, Worleston	19. 6.08P
G-ASPP	Bristol Boxkite replica	BOX.1 & BM.7279	(BAPC.2)	29.10.81	Richard Shuttleworth Trustees	Old Warden	26. 7.08P
	(Built F G Miles Ltd) (Continental O-200-B) (Built for "Those Magnificent Men in Their Flying Machines" film) (As No."12A")						
G-ASPS	Piper J-3C-65 Cub Special	22809	N3571N	2. 3.64	A J Chalkley	Rhoshirwaun, Pwllheli	27. 5.08P
	(Frame No.21971)		NC3571N				
G-ASPV (2)	de Havilland DH.82A Tiger Moth	84167	T7794	5. 3.64	Z J Rockey	Higherlands Farm, Branscombe	31. 8.97
	(Built Morris Motors Ltd) (P/i obscure - original G-ASPV sold Norway 7.75 and rebuilt as LN-MAX) (On rebuild 2007)						
G-ASRB	Druine D 62B Condor	RAE 608		11. 3.64	R J Bentley Pallas West, Toomyvvara, County Tipperary		4. 6.08P
	(Built Rollason Aircraft and Engines)						
G-ASRC	Druine D 62C Condor	RAE 609		11. 3.64	C R Isbell	(Felstead, Dunmow)	22.11.08P
	(Built Rollason Aircraft and Engines) (Continental O-240-A)						
G-ASRK	Beagle A 109 Airedale	B 538		26. 3.64	Bio Pathica Ltd	Lydd	27. 6.10S
G-ASRO	Piper PA-30 Twin Comanche	30-395	N10F	31. 3.64	D W Blake tr Five Star Flying Group		
						(Bourne End, Walsall)	18. 9.08E
G-ASRT	SAN Jodel D 150 Mascaret	45		6. 4.64	P Turton(Stored 6.94)	(Holmes Chapel, Crewe)	3. 6.94P
G-ASRW	Piper PA-28-180 Cherokee B	28-1606	N11C	21. 4.64	G N Smith	(Thorpe Abbots, Diss)	7. 6.08E
G-ASSF	Cessna 182G Skylane	18255593	N2493R	5. 5.64	M E Falkingham	(Rudston, Driffield)	10. 4.08E
G-ASSP	Piper PA-30 Twin Comanche	30-458	N10F	7. 5.64	P H Tavener	(Rochester)	22.12.07E
G-ASSS	Cessna 172E	17251467	N5567T	7. 5.64	P R March and P Turner	Filton	26. 5.08E
G-ASST	Cessna 150D	15060630	N5930T	7. 5.64	F R H Parker Pear Tree Farm, Marsh Gibbon, Bicester		10. 9.08E
G-ASSV	Kensinger KF	2	N23S	11. 5.64	C I Jefferson	Priory Farm, Tibenham	30. 7.69P
	(Built N Kensinger - pr.no.PFA 168-13923) (Continental C85)				(Noted 8.05)		
G-ASSW	Piper PA-28-140 Cherokee	28-20055	N11C	11. 5.64	D K Roberts	Biggin Hill	5. 9.08E
G-ASSY	Druine D 31 Turbulent	PFA 586		12. 5.64	V E Booth	(Prestbury, Cheltenham)	20. 4.84P
	(Built F J Parker) (Volkswagen 1500)				(New owner 8.06)		
G-ASTA	Druine D 31 Turbulent	152	F-PJGH	12. 5.64	P A Cooke	(Chippenham)	13.11.97P
	(Built M Barboni) (Ardem 4C02)				(Fuselage noted 11.06 on lorry at Lechlade)		
G-ASTG	Nord 1002 Pingouin II	183	F-BGKI	21. 5.64	L M Walton	Duxford	26.10.73S
			French AF 183		(On rebuild and unmarked 4.03)		
G-ASTI	Auster 6A Tugmaster	3745	WJ359	27. 5.64	J D Samson-Snell	Headcorn	9. 1.10S
G-ASUB	Mooney M 20E Super 21	397	N7158U	24. 6.64	S C Coulbeck	North Coates	17. 9.08E
G-ASUD	Piper PA-28-180 Cherokee B	28-1654	N7673W	29. 6.64	P J Wilkinson and A J Rogers tr G-ASUD Flying Group		
						Andrewsfield	29. 1.08E
G-ASUE	Cessna 150D	15060718	N6018T	30. 6.64	D Huckle (Stored 6.94)	West Thurrock	1. 8.90
G-ASUI	Beagle A 61 Terrier 2	B 641	VF628	6. 7.64	R J Bentley		
	(Conversion of Auster AOP.10 c/n 2570)				Pallas West, Toomyvara, County Tipperary		11. 1.10
G-ASUP	Cessna F172E	F172-0071		22. 7.64	P T and L.E Trivett t/a Gasup Air	Cardiff	24. 5.08
	(Built Reims Aviation SA)						
G-ASUR	Dornier Do.28A-1	3051	D-IBOM	28. 7.64	P R Dyson	Thruxton	14. 3.08E
G-ASUS	Jurca MJ.2E Tempête	PFA 2001		28. 7.64	R Targonski	Coventry	20. 8.04P
	(Built D G Jones) (Continental O-200-A)				"67" (Noted late 2007)		
G-ASVG	Rousseau Piel CP.301B Emeraude	109	F-BILV	7. 8.64	K R H Wingate	Halwell	31. 5.08P
					"Emma II" (Also carries "F-BILV")		
G-ASVM	Cessna F172E	F172-0077		11. 8.64	R Seckington	Popham	6.12.07E
	(Built Reims Aviation SA)						
G-ASVN	Cessna 206 Super Skywagon	206-0275	N5275U	12. 8.64	Skydive Brid Ltd	East Leys Farm, Grindale	18. 5.08E
G-ASVP	Piper PA-25-235 Pawnee	25-2978	N10F	17. 8.64	Aquila Gliding Club Ltd	Hinton-in-the-Hedges	27. 3.08E

G-ASVZ	Piper PA-28-140 Cherokee	28-20357	N11C	24. 8.64	J S Garvey	Sleap	9.11.07E
G-ASWL	Cessna F172F	F172-0087		10. 9.64	Ensiform Aviation Ltd	Elstree	5. 7.08E
	(Built Reims Aviation SA)						
G-ASWN	Bensen B 8M	14		15. 9.64	D R Shepherd	(Prestwick)	
	(Built D R Shepherd)				(Components stored 2003)		
G-ASWW	Piper PA-30 Twin Comanche	30-556	N7531Y N10F	1.10.64	N C Scanlan tr G-WW Group	RAF Waddington	6.11.07
G-ASWX	Piper PA-28-180 Cherokee C	28-1932	N11C	1.10.64	A F Dadds	Biggin Hill	16. 4.08E
G-ASXD	Brantly B 2B	435		7.10.64	Lousada PLC		
						Crawley Park, Husborne Crawley, Bedford	2. 7.05
G-ASXI	Tipsy Nipper T 66 Series 3	T66/56	VH-CGH OO-KOC, (VH-CGC)	13.10.64	P G Blenkinsopp	Old Sarum	14. 8.07P
	(Built Avions Fairey SA) (Jabiru 2200A)						
G-ASXJ	Phoenix Luton LA-4A Minor	PFA 801		14.10.64	A D Parsons	Brock Farm, Billericay	1. 6.07P
	(Built P D Lea and E A Linguard) (Lycoming O-145)				(Noted 2.08)		
G-ASXR	Cessna 210	57532	5Y-KPW VP-KPW, N6532X	16.10.64	A Schofield	Barton	3. 1.93
					(Noted dismantled 11.04)		
G-ASXS	SAN Jodel DR.1050 Ambassadeur	133	F-BJNG	19.10.64	R A Hunter	Finmere	17.12.06
G-ASXU	Wassmer Jodel D 120A Paris-Nice	196	F-BKAG	19.10.64	M Ferid tr G-ASXU Group		
						Stoneacre Farm, Farthing Corner Corner	2. 5.08P
G-ASXY	SAN Jodel D 117A	914	F-BIVA	27.10.64	P A, R A Davies and D G Claxton	Cardiff	23. 3.08P
G-ASXZ	Cessna 182G Skylane	18255738	N3238S	28.10.64	Last Refuge Ltd Gedney Marsh Farm, Gedney, Wells		20.12.07E
G-ASYG	Beagle A 61 Terrier 2	B 637	VX927	3.11.64	T K Rumble tr Terrane Auster Group RAF Scampton		7 6.09S
	(Rebuilt to T 7 standard)				(As "VX927" in AAC c/s)		
G-ASYJ	Beech D95A TravelAir	TD-595	N8675Q	6.11.64	Crosby Aviation (Jersey) Ltd (Noted 1.08)	Jersey	31.10.07E
G-ASYP	Cessna 150E	15060794	N6094T	23.11.64	A C Melmore tr Henlow Flying Group	RAF Henlow	25.10.07E
G-ASZB	Cessna 150E	15061113	N3013J	16.12.64	R J Scott	(Binfield, Bracknell)	19. 4.07
G-ASZD	Bölkow BÖ.208A-2 Junior	563	D-ENKI	16.12.64	M J Ayres	Full Sutton	23. 6.03P
G-ASZE	Beagle A 61 Terrier 2	B 636	VF552	17.12.64	D R Ockleton	RNAS Yeovilton	7. 7.09S
	(Conversion of Auster 6 c/n 2510)						
G-ASZR	Fairtravel Linnet 2	005		5. 1.65	R Hodgson	(Guildford)	28. 6.08P
G-ASZS	Sud-Aviation Gardan GY-80-160 Horizon	70		6. 1.65	L R Burton tr ZS Group	Wellesbourne Mountford	21.12.07
G-ASZU	Cessna 150E	15061152	N3052J	13. 1.65	L J Baker and S L Bassett	Cranfield	29. 8.08E
G-ASZV	Tipsy Nipper T 66 Series 2	T66/45	5N-ADE 5N-ADY, VR-NDD	14. 1.65	D H Greenwood	Barton	23. 5.90P
	(Built Avions Fairey SA) (Volkswagen 1835)				(New owner 5.06)		
G-ASZX	Beagle A 61 Terrier 1	3742	(SE-ELO) WJ368	18. 1.65	R B Webber	Trenchard Farm, Eggesford	18. 7.10S

G-ATAA - G-ATZZ

G-ATAF	Cessna F172F	F172-0135		25. 1.65	Summit Media Ltd	(Norwich)	15. 8.08E
	(Built Reims Aviation SA)						
G-ATAG	CEA Jodel DR.1050 Ambassadeur	226	F-BKGG	25. 1.65	T M Dawes-Gamble Wishanger Farm, Frensham		4.10.02
					(Noted 8.06)		
G-ATAS	Piper PA-28-180 Cherokee C	28-2137	N11C	4. 2.65	R Osborn tr Atlas Group	Andrewsfield	24. 8.08E
G-ATAU	Druine D 62B Condor	RAE 610		10. 2.65	W J Forrest		
	(Built Rollason Aircraft and Engines)				Ventfield Farm, Horton-cum-Studley,Oxford		29.12.08P
G-ATAV	Druine D 62C Condor	RAE 611		10. 2.65	V A Holliday	Streethay Farm, Lichfield	11. 9.08P
	(Built Rollason Aircraft and Engines) (Continental O-240-A)						
G-ATBG	Nord 1002 Pingouin II	121	F-BGVX F-OTAN-5, French.Military	24. 2.65	T W Harris	Wycombe Air Park	13. 9.08P
					(As "NJ+C11" in Luftwaffe c/s)		
G-ATBH	SPP Aero 145	20-015		24. 2.65	P D Aviram	Redhill	26.10.81
					(On rebuild 1.06)		
G-ATBI	Beech A23 Musketeer II	M-696		26. 2.65	A C Dent tr Three Musketeers Flying Group	Oxford	13. 2.08
G-ATBJ	Sikorsky S-61N	61-269	N10043?	12. 3.65	Veritair Ltd t/a British International	Plymouth	2. 6.07E
G-ATBL	de Havilland DH.60G Moth	1917	HB-OBA CH-353	2. 3.65	J M Greenland Blackacre Farm, Holt, Trowbridge		23. 7.08P
	(DH Gipsy I)						
G-ATBP	Fournier RF3	59		11. 3.65	D McNicholl	Inverness	22. 8.09S
G-ATBS	Druine D 31 Turbulent	PFA 1620		16. 3.65	J A Lear	Pittrichie Farm, Whiterashes	29.11.08P
	(Built C R Shilling) (Volkswagen 1500)				"Fly Baby Fly"		
G-ATBU	Beagle A 61 Terrier 2	B 635	VF611	17. 3.65	T Jarvis	(Charlton, Banbury)	19 6.08
	(Conversion of Auster 6 c/n 2552)						
G-ATBW	Tipsy Nipper T 66 Series 2	T66/52	OO-MAG	19. 3.65	S Bloomfield and C Firth tr Stapleford Nipper Group		
	(Built Cobelavia SA) (Volkswagen 1834 Acro)					Stapleford	26 3.08P
G-ATBX	Piper PA-20-135 Pacer	20-904	VP-KRX VR-TCH, VP-KKE	19. 3.65	G D and P M Thomson		
					Standalone Farm, Meppershall		29. 6.08E
G-ATCC	Beagle A 109 Airedale	B 542		25. 3.65	J R Bowden	Headcorn	24. 3.08
G-ATCD	Beagle D 5/180 Husky	3683		25. 3.65	D J O'Gorman	Enstone	4. 4.09S
G-ATCE	Cessna U206 Super Skywagon	U2060380	N2180F	25. 3.65	Performance Aviation Ltd t/a British Skysports Parachute Centre		
					(Fuselage noted 8.07) East Leys Farm, Grindale		2. 8.08E
G-ATCJ	Phoenix Luton LA-4A Minor	PAL1163		5. 4.65	T D Boyle	Errol	16 7.08P
	(Built R M Sharphouse - pr.no.PFA 812) (Volkswagen 1600)						
G-ATCL	Victa Airtourer 100	93		5. 4.65	A D Goodall (Noted 8.06)	Oaksey Park	25. 7.05
G-ATCX	Cessna 182H Skylane	18255848	N3448S	26. 4.65	Softnotes Ltd	Cranfield	22.12.07E
					(Note fuselage of cancelled G-OLSC is also marked as "G-ATCX")		
G-ATDA	Piper PA-28-160 Cherokee	28-206	EI-AME (G-ARUV)	27. 4.65	Portway Aviation Ltd	Shobdon	19. 1.08E
G-ATDB	SNCAN 1101 Noralpha	186	F-OTAN-6 French.Military	27. 4.65	J W Hardie	Prestwick	22.11.78S
					(Partially dismantled 10.07)		
G-ATDN	Beagle A 61 Terrier 2	B 638	TW641	7. 5.65	S J Saggers	Biggin Hill	5. 8.10S
	(Conversion of Auster 6 c/n 2499)				(As "TW641" in AAC c/s)		
G-ATDO	Bölkow BÖ.208C Junior	576	D-EGZU	10. 5.65	P Thompson	Crosland Moor	24. 1.08P
G-ATEF	Cessna 150E	15061378	N3978U	25. 5.65	A J White and B M Scott t/a Swans Aviation Blackbushe		15.11.07E
G-ATEM	Piper PA-28-180 Cherokee C	28-2329	N11C	26. 5.65	G D Wyles	Bovingdon	31. 5.08E

Reg	Type	C/n	Prev id	Date	Owner	Base	Expiry
G-ATEV	CEA Jodel DR.1050 Ambassadeur	18	F-BJHL	31. 5.65	J C Carter and J L Altrip *(On rebuild 9.00:)*	(Cambridge)	13. 8.71
G-ATEW	Piper PA-30 Twin Comanche	30-719	N7640Y	3. 6.65	Air Northumbria (Woolsington) Ltd	Newcastle	10.11.07E
G-ATEX	Victa Airtourer 100	110	(VH-MTU)	3. 6.65	D R Henson tr Halton Victa Group *"Matilda"*	RAF Halton	29. 9.06
G-ATEZ	Piper PA-28-140 Cherokee	28-21044	N11C	8. 6.65	EFI Aviation Ltd	Norwich	5. 6.08E
G-ATFD	CEA Jodel DR.1050 Ambassadeur	311	F-BKIM	14. 6.65	K D Hills tr G-ATFD Group	Lee-on-Solent	31. 8.08E
G-ATFF	Piper PA-23-250 Aztec C	27-2898	N5769Y	16. 6.65	T J Wassell *(Noted 10.07 engineless) "53"*	Halfpenny Green	15. 5.05
G-ATFM	Sikorsky S-61N Mk.II	61-270	CF-OKY N10052 *(US p/i not confirmed) (Noted 11.07)*	21. 6.65	British International Ltd	Aberdeen	1.10.06T
G-ATFR	Piper PA-25 Pawnee	25-135	OY-ADJ N10F	28. 6.65	Borders (Milfield) Gliding Club Ltd	Milfield	18. 7.08E
G-ATFW	Phoenix Luton LA-4A Minor *(Built G W Shield)*	PFA 811		2. 7.65	P A Rose	Walney Island	2.12.97P
G-ATFY	Cessna F172G *(Built Reims Aviation SA)*	F172-0199		8. 7.65	J M Vinall	Kemble	8. 3.08E
G-ATGE	SAN Jodel DR.1050 Ambassadeur	114	F-BJJF	9. 7.65	H A McKnight	Ballymageough, Kilkeel	8. 3.08E
G-ATGY	Sud-Aviation Gardan GY-80-160 Horizon	121		20. 7.65	D Cowen	Henstridge	10. 6.08E
G-ATGZ	Griffiths GH-4 Gyroplane *(Built G Griffiths)*	G 1		20. 7.65	R W J Cripps *(Stored 7.91)*	(Shardlow, Derby)	
G-ATHD	de Havilland DHC-1 Chipmunk 22	C1/0837	WP971 G-ATHD, WP971	26. 7.65	O L Cubitt and N Keveren tr Spartan Flying Group *(As "WP971" in RAF c/s)*	Denham	30. 6.09
G-ATHK	Aeronca 7AC Champion *(Continental A75)*	7AC-971	N82339 NC82339	2. 8.65	D A G Fraser tr The Chase Flying Group	Compton Abbas	31. 5.08P
G-ATHM	Wallis WA-116/F *(Originally McCulloch - 60hp Franklin fitted 1974)*	402 & 211	4R-ACK G-ATHM	3. 8.65	Wallis Autogyros Ltd *(Noted 8.01)*	Reymerston Hall, Norfolk	23. 5.93P
G-ATHR	Piper PA-28-180 Cherokee C	28-2343	EI-AOT N11C	11. 8.65	Thomsonfly Ltd	Cranfield	8. 8.08E
G-ATHT	Victa Airtourer 115	120		16. 8.65	D A Beese tr Cotswold Flying Group	Badminton	5.10.09S
G-ATHU	Beagle A 61 Terrier 1	AUS/127/FM	7435M WE539	16. 8.65	J A L Irwin	Park Farm, Eaton Bray	15. 9.08
G-ATHV	Cessna 150F	15062019	N8719S	16. 8.65	S Greenwood tr Cessna Hotel Victor Group	Sherburn-in-Elmet	2. 3.08E
G-ATHZ	Cessna 150F	15061586	(EI-AOP) N6286R	20. 8.65	R D Forster *(Noted 10.07)*	Ellough, Beccles	27. 3.98T
G-ATIC	CEA Jodel DR.1050 Ambassadeur	6	F-BJCJ	23. 8.65	T A Major	Porthtowan	17. 9.08
G-ATIN	SAN Jodel D 117	437	F-BHNV	8. 9.65	A Ayre *(New owner 7.04)*	(St Andrews)	18. 4.96P
G-ATIR	AIA Stampe SV-4C	1047	F-BNMC G-ATIR, F-BMKQ, Aéronavale, F-BCDM, Aéronavale	9. 9.65	Austin Trueman Ltd	Little Gransden	19. 5.08
G-ATIS	Piper PA-28-160 Cherokee C	28-2713	N11C	9. 9.65	M J Barton	Lee-on-Solent	19. 3.08E
G-ATIZ	SAN Jodel D 117	636	F-BIBR	15. 9.65	R A Smith	Tower Farm, Wollaston	31. 5.08P
G-ATJA	SAN Jodel DR.1050 Ambassadeur	378	F-BKHL	15. 9.65	D A Head and G W Cunningham tr Bicester Flying Group	Bicester	9. 5.08E
G-ATJC	Victa Airtourer 100	125		16. 9.65	Aviation West Ltd	Kirknewton	22. 2.10S
G-ATJG	Piper PA-28-140 Cherokee	28-21299		20. 9.65	C A McGee and L K G Manning	Biggin Hilll	12. 1.08T
G-ATJL	Piper PA-24-260 Comanche	24-4203	N8752P N10F	23. 9.65	C G Sims tr Juliet Lima Flying Group	Enstone	17. 7.08E
G-ATJM	Fokker Dr.1 Triplane replica *(Built Bitz Flugzeugbau GmbH) (Siemens SH-14A-165)*	002	N78001 EI-APY, G-ATJM	23. 9.65	R J Lamplough *(As "152/17"in German Army Air Service c/s)*	Manor Farm, East Garston	3..7.07P
G-ATJN	Jodel D 119 *(Built Etablissement Dormois)*	863	F-PINZ	23. 9.65	R C Smith	(Partridge Green, Horsham)	27. 6.08P
G-ATJT	Sud-Aviation Gardan GY-80-160 Horizon	108		4.10.65	N Huxtable	Cheddington	8. 6.08
G-ATJV	Piper PA-32-260 Cherokee Six	32-103	TF-GOS G-ATJV, N11C	7.10.65	Wingglider Ltd	Hibaldstow	23. 8.08E
G-ATKF	Cessna 150F	15062386	N3586L	20.10.65	P Asbridge	Sleap	27.4.06T
G-ATKH	Phoenix Luton LA-4A Minor *(Built E B W Woodhall) (Lycoming O-145)*	PFA 809		25.10.65	H E Jenner	Brenchley, Kent	27. 8.06P
G-ATKI	Piper J-3C-65 Cub *(Continental A75)*	17545	N70536 NC70536	25.10.65	B Ryan	Lower Wasing Farm, Brimpton	27. 4.08P
G-ATKT	Cessna F172G *(Built Reims Aviation SA)*	F172-0206		9.11.65	J R Waterman tr KT Group	Shipdham	21. 6.08E
G-ATKX	SAN Jodel D 140C Mousquetaire III	163		19.11.65	I V Sharman tr Kilo Xray Syndicate	Redhill	17. 7.08S
G-ATLA	Cessna 182J Skylane	18256923	N2823F	24.11.65	J W and J T Whicher	Full Sutton	8. 2.08E
G-ATLB	SAN Jodel DR.1050M Excellence	78	F-BIVG	29.11.65	D J Gibson tr Le Syndicate du Petit Oiseau	New Farm House, Great Oakley	15.11.10E
G-ATLM	Cessna F172G *(Built Reims Aviation SA)*	F172-0252		6.12.65	Airfotos Ltd	Newcastle	30 3.06T
G-ATLP	Bensen B 8M *(Built C D Julian) (McCulloch Motors 4318F)*	17		9.12.65	R F G Moyle *(Noted 3.07)*	St Merryn	19. 5.97P
G-ATLT	Cessna U206A Super Skywagon	U2060523	N4823F	13.12.65	Skydive UK Ltd	Dunkeswell	8. 4.08E
G-ATLV	Wassmer Jodel D 120 Paris-Nice	224	F-BKNQ	15.12.65	L S Thorne	(Grendon, Atherstone)	8. 7.07P
G-ATMC	Cessna F150F *(Built Reims Aviation SA) (Wichita c/n 15062806)*	F150-0020		28.12.65	G H Farrah and D Cunnane	Abbeyshrule, County Longford	4. 9.08E
G-ATMH	Beagle D 5/180 Husky	3684		3. 1.66	Dorset Gliding Club Ltd	Eyres Field	16. 7.09S
G-ATMJ	Hawker Siddeley HS.748 Series 2A/225	1593	VP-LAJ G-ATMJ, 6Y-JFJ, G-ATMJ	4. 1.66	PTB (Emerald) Proprietary Ltd *(Stored externally 2.08)*	Blackpool	7. 9.06T
G-ATML	Cessna F150F *(Built Reims Aviation SA) (Wichita c/n 15062722)*	F150-0014		6. 1.66	G I Smith	Eddsfield, Octon Lodge Farm, Thwing	10.11.07E
G-ATMM	Cessna F150F *(Built Reims Aviation SA) (Wichita c/n 15062775)*	F150-0016	(N) G-ATMM	6. 1.66	R Marshall	(Sheffield City)	24. 6.08E
G-ATMT	Piper PA-30 Twin Comanche	30-439	XW938 G-ATMT, N7385Y	10. 1.66	Montagu-Smith and Company Ltd	Turweston	8. 8.08E

G-ATMY	Cessna 150F	15062642	SE-ETD	13. 1.66	AV8 (UK) Ltd	Derby	20.10.08
			N8542G				
G-ATNB	Piper PA-28-180 Cherokee C	28-3057	N11C	20. 1.66	K N Macdonald t/a Ken Macdonald and Co	Stornoway	31. 7.08E
G-ATNE	Cessna F150F	F150-0042		20. 1.66	A D Revill	Tatenhill	26. 3.08E
	(Built Reims Aviation SA) (Wichita c/n 15063252)						
G-ATNL	Cessna F150F	F150-0066		25. 1.66	D F Ranger	Popham	28. 9.07E
	(Built Reims Aviation SA) (Wichita c/n 15063652)						
G-ATNV	Piper PA-24-260 Comanche	24-4350	N8896P	28. 1.66	A Heydn and K Powell	King's Farm, Thurrock	6. 1.08E
G-ATOA	Piper PA-23-160 Apache G	23-1954	N4437P	31. 1.66	Oscar Alpha Ltd *(Noted 9.05)*	Stapleford	13. 6.03
G-ATOD	Cessna F150F	F150-0003		1. 2.66	D Lugg	RNAS Culdrose	10.10.07E
	(Built Reims Aviation SA) (Wichita c/n 15062342)						
G-ATOH	Druine D 62B Condor	RAE 612		3. 2.66	J Cooke tr Three Spires Flying Group		
	(Built Rollason Aircraft and Engines)					Streethay Farm, Lichfield	4.10.07P
G-ATOI	Piper PA-28-140 Cherokee	28-21556	N11C	3. 2.66	R Ronaldson	RAF Brize Norton	7. 6.08E
G-ATOJ	Piper PA-28-140 Cherokee	28-21584	N11C	3. 2.66	A Flight Aviation Ltd	Prestwick	5.11.07E
					(Operated Prestwick Flying Club)		
G-ATOK	Piper PA-28-140 Cherokee	28-21612	N11C	3. 2.66	G T S Done and P R Harrison tr ILC Flying Group		
						White Waltham	22. 3.08E
G-ATOL	Piper PA-28-140 Cherokee	28-21626	N11C	3. 2.66	L J and G Nation tr G-ATOL Flying Group		
						(Pontypridd)	23. 1.98
G-ATOM	Piper PA-28-140 Cherokee	28-21640	N11C	3. 2.66	A Flight Aviation Ltd	Prestwick	28. 8.08E
					(Operated Prestwick Flying Club)		
G-ATON	Piper PA-28-140 Cherokee	28-21654	N11C	3. 2.66	R G Walters tr Stirling Flying Syndicate	Shobdon	14.11.07E
G-ATOO	Piper PA-28-140 Cherokee	28-21668	N11C	3. 2.66	A K Komosa	Biggin Hill	23.11.07E
G-ATOP	Piper PA-28-140 Cherokee	28-21682	N11C	3. 2.66	P R Coombs tr The Aero 80 Flying Group	Popham	12. 6.08E
G-ATOR	Piper PA-28-140 Cherokee	28-21696	N11C	3. 2.66	D Palmer tr Aligator Group	Shobdon	22. 6.08E
G-ATOT	Piper PA-28-180 Cherokee C	28-3061	N11C	3. 2.66	Totair Ltd *"Totty"*	Shipdham	17. 8.08E
G-ATOU	Mooney M 20E Super 21	961	N5946Q	3. 2.66	A D Morgan tr Mooney M 20 Flying Group		
						Sherburn-in-Elmet	7. 8.08E
G-ATOZ	Bensen B 8M	18		7. 2.66	N C White	Sorbie Farm, Kingsmuir	9.12.05P
	(Built J D M Wilson) (Rotax 503 (Substantially rebuilt in 1986, original airframe stored Wimborne: noted 12.07 unmarked)						
G-ATPN	Piper PA-28-140 Cherokee	28-21899	N11C	18. 2.66	R W Harris, M F Hatt, P E Preston and A Jahanfar		
					(Operated Southend Flying Club)	Southend	7. 4.08E
G-ATPT	Cessna 182J Skylane	18257056	N2956F	22. 2.66	C Beer tr Papa Tango Group	Elstree	16. 8.08E
G-ATPV	Gardan GY-20 Minicab	JB-01	F-PJKA	22. 2.66	J K Davies	(Newtownards)	25. 8.08P
	(Continental C90) (Rebuild of GY-20 F-PHUC c/n A 155 by J Barritault-Bauge as JB.01 Minicab)						
G-ATRG	Piper PA-18-150 Super Cub	18-7764	5B-CAB	1. 3.66	Lasham Gliding Society Ltd	Lasham	6. 6.10S
	(Lycoming O-360-A4)		N4985Z				
G-ATRI	Bölkow BÖ.208C Junior	602	D-ECGY	3. 3.66	S S A Withams tr Kingsmuir Group		
						Sorbie Farm., Kingsmuir	26. 9.08E
G-ATRK	Cessna F150F	F150-0049	(G-ATNC)	4. 3.66	G G and J G Armstrong t/a Armstrong Aviation		
	(Built Reims Aviation SA) (Wichita c/n 15063381)					Wigtown	7. 8.06T
G-ATRM	Cessna F150F	F150-0053	(G-ATNJ)	4. 3.66	J Redfearn	Durham Tees Valley	14. 7.07T
	(Built Reims Aviation SA) (Wichita c/n 15063454)						
G-ATRO	Piper PA-28-140 Cherokee	28-21871	N11C	4. 3.66	G M Malpass	Exeter	24. 8.08E
G-ATRR	Piper PA-28-140 Cherokee	28-21892	N11C	4. 3.66	Keen Leasing (IOM) Ltd	Ronaldsway	11. 7.08E
					(Operated Manx Flyers Aero Club)		
G-ATRW	Piper PA-32-260 Cherokee Six	32-360	N11C	8. 3.66	J Pringle t/a Pringle Brandon Architects and Moxley Architects		
						Biggin Hill	20.10.07E
G-ATRX	Piper PA-32-260 Cherokee Six	32-390	N11C	8. 3.66	A M., A C M and M.R Harrhy	Bembridge	12. 5.08E
G-ATSI	Bölkow BÖ.208C Junior	605	D-EFNU	14. 3.66	N C Ravine *(Noted 10.07)*	Sywell	16. 4.06
G-ATSL	Cessna F172G	F172-0260		16. 3.66	G F Robinson tr Alpha Aviation	Enniskillen	14. 9.08E
	(Built Reims Aviation SA)						
G-ATSR	Beech M35 Bonanza	D-6236	EI-ALL	29. 3.66	C B Linton	Gloucestershire	19. 7.08E
G-ATSX	Bölkow BÖ.208C Junior	608	D-EJUC	7. 4.66	Little Bear Ltd *(Noted 12.05)*	Exeter	1. 7.02
G-ATSY	Wassmer WA.41 Super Baladou IV	117		12. 4.66	R L and K P McLean t/a McLean Aviation		
					(Spares use for G-ATZS 5.01)	Rufforth	23.11.91
G-ATSZ	Piper PA-30 Twin Comanche B	30-1002	EI-BPS	13. 4.66	Sierra Zulu Aviation Ltd	Little Staughton	19. 7.08E
				G-ATSZ, (AN-...), G-ATSZ, (EI-BBS), G-ATSZ, N7912Y				
G-ATTB	Wallis WA-116/F	214		19. 4.66	D A Wallis	Reymerston Hall, Norfolk	27. 5.06P
	(Built Beagle-Wallis Ltd) (Franklin 2A) (Originally regd as Wallis WA.116 Srs 1 (McCulloch) being rebuild of WA-116 G-ARZC () ex XR944 c/n 205)						
	(As "XR944" in RAF c/s) (Made heavy landing Swanton Morley 18. 5.06 with substantial damage)						
G-ATTI	Piper PA-28-140 Cherokee	28-21951	N11C	24. 4.66	T Marsh tr G-ATTI Flying Group	Bristol	28.10 07T
G-ATTK	Piper PA-28-140 Cherokee	28-21959	N11C	25. 4.66	D J E Fairburn tr G-ATTK Flying Group	Southend	3. 6.08E
G-ATTM	CEA Jodel DR.250/160 Capitaine	65		26. 4.66	R W Tomkinson	Seletar, Singapore	2. 3.08E
G-ATTR	Bölkow BÖ.208C Junior	612	D-EHEH	28. 4.66	S Luck	Audley End	24.10.07E
G-ATTV	Piper PA-28-140 Cherokee	28-21991	N11C	2. 5.66	N E Leech tr G-ATTV Group	Andrewsfield	7. 3.08E
G-ATTX	Piper PA-28-180 Cherokee C	28-3390	PH-VDP	2. 5.66	IPAC Aviation Ltd	Earls Colne	14. 2.08E
			(G-ATTX), N11C				
G-ATUB	Piper PA-28-140 Cherokee	28-21971	N11C	2. 5.66	R H Partington and M J Porter	Wombleton	3. 4.08E
G-ATUD	Piper PA-28-140 Cherokee	28-21979	N11C	2. 5.66	J J Ferguson	Belle Vue Farm, Yarnscombe	25. 9.08E
G-ATUF	Cessna F150F	F150-0040		4. 5.66	D P Williams	Hill Farm, Nayland	16. 5.08E
	(Built Reims Aviation SA) (Wichita c/n 15063229)					*"Honeysuckle"*	
G-ATUG	Druine D 62B Condor	RAE 614		4. 5.66	C Gill	AAC Netheravon	31. 8.07P
	(Built Rollason Aircraft and Engines) (Continental C90-14F)						
G-ATUH	Tipsy Nipper T 66 Series 1	T66/6	OO-NIF	4. 5.66	M D Barnard and C Voelger	Glebe Farm, Southam	1. 5.08P
	(Built Avions Fairey SA) (Volkswagen 1600)						
G-ATUI	Bölkow BÖ.208C Junior	611	D-EHEF	4. 5.66	M J Grundy	Stapleford	26.11.05
G-ATUL	Piper PA-28-180 Cherokee C	28-3033	N9007J	6. 5.66	Barry Fielding Aviation Ltd	Ronaldsway	21. 6.08E
G-ATVF	de Havilland DHC-1 Chipmunk 22	C1/0265	WD327	25. 5.66	T M Holloway tr RAF Gliding and Soaring Association		
	(Lycoming AEIO-360)					RAF Halton	8. 7.10S
G-ATVK	Piper PA-28-140 Cherokee	28-22006	N11C	27. 5.66	Broadland Flyers Ltd	Norwich	21. 3.08E
G-ATVO	Piper PA-28-140 Cherokee	28-22020	N11C	27. 5.66	G R Bright	Little Gransden	29. 3.08E
G-ATVS	Piper PA-28-180 Cherokee C	28-3041	N9014J	1. 6.66	T A Buckley	Sandown, Isle of Wight	13.12.07E

G-ATVW	Druine D 62B Condor		RAE 615		7. 6.66	G G Roberts	Rayne Hall Farm, Braintree	19. 6.08P
	(Built Rollason Aircraft and Engines)							
G-ATVX	Bölkow BÖ.208C Junior		615	D-EHER	9. 6.66	A M Witt	(Bradwell Common, Milton Keynes)	2. 4.08P
G-ATWA	SAN Jodel DR.1050 Ambassadeur		296	F-BKHA	10. 6.66	C R Elliott tr One Twenty Group	Tollerton	15. 1.11S
G-ATWB	SAN Jodel D 117		423	F-BHNH	10. 6.66	D P Ash tr Andrewsfield Whisky Bravo Group		
							Andrewsfield	23. 4.08P
G-ATWJ	Cessna F172F		F172-0095	EI-ANS	21. 6.66	Shenley Farm (Aviation) and J P A Freeman		
	(Built Reims Aviation SA)						Headcorn	25. 7.08E
G-ATXA	Piper PA-22-150 Tri-Pacer		22-3730	N4403A	8. 7.66	S Hildrop	Top Farm, Croydon, Royston	17. 5.08S
	(Modified to PA-20 Super Pacer configuration)							
G-ATXD	Piper PA-30 Twin Comanche B		30-1166	N8053Y	12. 7.66	P A Brook	Shoreham	21. 8.08E
G-ATXM	Piper PA-28-180 Cherokee C		28-2759	N8809J	19. 7.66	M J Stack tr G-ATXM Flying Group	Stapleford	12.10.02
						(Noted 9.05)		
G-ATXN	Mitchell-Procter Kittiwake I		1		19. 7.66	R G Day	Biggin Hill	22. 5.07P
	(Built R Procter - pr.no.PFA 1306) (Lycoming O-290)							
G-ATXO	SIPA 903		41	F-BGAP	19. 7.66	C H Morris	Deanland	30. 6.08P
G-ATXZ	Bölkow BÖ.208C Junior		624	D-ELNE	28. 7.66	M R Kaye tr G-ATXZ Group	Tatenhill	12. 7.08P
G-ATYM	Cessna F150G		F150-0074		15. 8.66	A J Cooke	(Sempringham Fen, Sleaford)	12. 2.08E
	(Built Reims Aviation SA)							
G-ATYS	Piper PA-28-180 Cherokee C		28-3296	N9226J	19. 8.66	E Baker tr G-ATYS Flying Group	Lydd	24. 5.08E
G-ATZK	Piper PA-28-180 Cherokee C		28-3128	N9090J	21. 9.66	I A Eddy tr G-ZK Group	Oaksey Park	14. 5.08T
				(D-EFUN), N9090J				
G-ATZM	Piper J-3C-90 Cub Special		20868	N2092M	26. 9.66	N D Marshall	RAF Halton	1. 2.08P
	(Frame No.21310)			NC2092M				
G-ATZS	Wassmer WA 41 Super Baladou IV		128		30. 9.66	C J Cauwood tr G-ATZS Flying Group	Spanhoe	28.11.07E
G-ATZY	Cessna F150G		F150-0135		14.10.66	Aircraft Engineers Ltd	Prestwick	14. 3.08E
	(Built Reims Aviation SA)							

G-AVAA - G-AVZZ

G-AVAR	Cessna F150G		F150-0122		27.10.66	J A Rees	Haverfordwest	24.10.08E
	(Built Reims Aviation SA)							
G-AVAW	Druine D 62C Condor		RAE 617		10.11.66	S Banyard tr Condor Aircraft Group	Tibenham	21. 7.08P
	(Built Rollason Aircraft and Engines) (Continental O-240-A)							
G-AVAX	Piper PA-28-180 Cherokee C		28-3798	N11C	11.11.66	J J Parkes	Halfpenny Green	30. 5.08E
G-AVBG	Piper PA-28-180 Cherokee C		28-3801	N11C	11.11.66	M C Plomer-Roberts	Wellesbourne Mountford	19. 4.08E
G-AVBH	Piper PA-28-180 Cherokee C		28-3802	N11C	11.11.66	T R Smith (Agricultural Machinery) Ltd		
							New Lane Farm, North Elmham	18. 5.08E
G-AVBS	Piper PA-28-180 Cherokee C		28-3938	N11C	14.11.66	A G Arthur	Perranporth	5. 7.08E
G-AVBT	Piper PA-28-180 Cherokee C		28-3945	N11C	14.11.66	J F Mitchell	Shoreham	1. 7.08E
G-AVCM	Piper PA-24-260 Comanche B		24-4520	N9054P	5.12.66	R F Smith	Stapleford	18. 7.08E
G-AVCN	Britten-Norman BN-2A-8 Islander		3	N290VL	6.12.66	Airstream International Group Ltd	Bembridge	5.11.76T
	(Originally regd as BN-2)			F-OGHG, G-AVCN		*(For restoration by Britten-Norman Aircraft Preservation Society)*		
G-AVCV	Cessna 182J Skylane		18257492	N3492F	15.12.66	University of Manchester, School of Earth, Atmospheric and		
						Environmental Sciences	Liverpool	29. 4.08E
G-AVDA	Cessna 182K Skylane		18257959	N2759Q	16.12.66	F W Ellis	Water Leisure Park, Skegness	16. 7.08E
G-AVDG	Wallis WA-116 Series 1 Agile		215		28.12.66	K H Wallis	Reymerston Hall, Norfolk	23. 5.92P
	(Variously powered by McCulloch: Fuji 440, Norton twin-rotor Wankel and now Rotax 532) (Stored 8.01)							
G-AVDT	Aeronca 7AC Champion		7AC-6932	N3594E	5. 1.67	D Cheney and G Moore	(Gransha, Rathfriland)	8.11.07P
				NC3594E				
G-AVDV	Piper PA-22-150 Tri-Pacer		22-3752	N4423A	5. 1.67	S C Brooks	Wellcross Grange, Slinfold	23.10.03
	(Modifed to PA-20 Super Pacer configuration)							
G-AVDY	Phoenix Luton LA-4A Minor		PAL 1183		10. 1.67	R Targonski	(Coventry)	9. 8.00P
	(Built M E Pendlebury - pr.no.PFA 808) (Lycoming O-145)					*(Damaged landing Stapleford 18.12.99: on rebuild 2006)*		
G-AVEB	Morane Saulnier MS.230Et2		1076	N230EB	13. 1.67	T McG Leaver	Church Farm, North Moreton	17. 1.08P
	(Built Societé Levasseur)			G-AVEB, F-BGJT, French AF		*(As "No.157-01" in French AF c/s)*		
G-AVEC	Cessna F172H		F172-0405		13. 1.67	S M Furner	Earls Colne	11. 5.08E
	(Built Reims Aviation SA)							
G-AVEF	SAN Jodel D 150 Mascaret		16	F-BLDK	19. 1.67	Prop-Air Corporation Ltd	Headcorn	5.11.10E
G-AVEH	SIAI-Marchetti S 205-20R		346		20. 1.67	K Fear tr EH Aviation	Shipdham	26. 9.08E
G-AVEM	Cessna F150G		F150-0198		23. 1.67	T D and J A Warren	Redhill	6. 5.08E
	(Built Reims Aviation SA)							
G-AVEN	Cessna F150G		F150-0202		23. 1.67	R A Lambert	Bourn	8.12.07E
	(Built Reims Aviation SA)							
G-AVEO	Cessna F150G		F150-0204	G-DENA	23. 1.67	M Howells	Barton	22. 8.08E
	(Built Reims Aviation SA)			G-AVEO, EI-BOI, G-AVEO				
G-AVER	Cessna F150G		F150-0206		23. 1.67	Upperstack Ltd t/a LAC Flying School	Barton	10. 1.08E
	(Built Reims Aviation SA)					*(Operated Lancashire Aero Club)*		
G-AVEU	Wassmer WA.41 Super Baladou IV		136		27. 1.67	H and S Roberts	Oaksey Park	10.11.07E
G-AVEX	Druine D 62B Condor		RAE 616		31. 1.67	C A Macleod	Hinton-in-the-Hedges	8. 7.08P
	(Built Rollason Aircraft and Engines)							
G-AVEY	Phoenix Currie Super Wot		SE.100		31. 1.67	C K Farley	Halfpenny Green	3. 7.07P
	(Built K Sedgwick - pr.no.PFA 3006) (Pobjoy "R")					*(Noted 10.07) (Also as "2-B-7" in pseudo-WW2 early US Navy c/s)*		
G-AVFR	Piper PA-28-140 Cherokee		28-22747	N11C	1. 2.67	R R Orr	Newtownards	21. 8.08E
G-AVFU	Piper PA-32-300 Cherokee Six		32-40182	N11C	1. 2.67	Tri-Star Farms Ltd	Andreas, Isle of Man	11. 4.08E
G-AVFX	Piper PA-28-140 Cherokee		28-22757	N11C	1. 2.67	J Watson	Strathaven	18.11.07E
G-AVFZ	Piper PA-28-140 Cherokee		28-22767	N11C	1. 2.67	C M Toyne tr G-AVFZ Flying Group	Yeovil	14.10.07E
G-AVGA	Piper PA-24-260 Comanche B		24-4489	N9027P	31. 1.67	G McD.Moir	Derby	7. 9.08E
G-AVGC	Piper PA-28-140 Cherokee		28-22777	N11C	31. 1.67	D Matthews	Bournemouth	12. 6.08
G-AVGD	Piper PA-28-140 Cherokee		28-22782	N11C	31. 1.67	T Akeroyd tr Falconer Flying Group	Cranfield	10. 2.08E
	(Force landed in field nr NE of Deanland 16. 9.07 due to engine failure on approach: both wings torn off)							
G-AVGE	Piper PA-28-140 Cherokee		28-22787	N11C	31. 1.67	J D C Lea	(Tenerife, Spain)	25. 4.08
G-AVGI	Piper PA-28-140 Cherokee		28-22822	N11C	31. 1.67	R D A Gilchrist tr GI Group	Barton	16.12.07E

G-AVGK	Piper PA-28-180 Cherokee C	28-3639	N9516J	2. 2.67	M A Bush	Andrewsfield	7. 9.08E
G-AVGU	Cessna F150G	F150-0199		8. 2.67	Coulson Flying Services Ltd	Cranfield	13. 3.08E
	(Built Reims Aviation SA)						
G-AVGY	Cessna 182K Skylane	18258112	N3112Q	17. 2.67	R M C Sears	Stoke Ferry	21. 9.08E
G-AVGZ	CEA Jodel DR.1050 Sicile	341	F-BKPR	14. 2.67	D C Webb *(Stored 2.08)*	Bagby	13. 7.97
G-AVHH	Cessna F172H	F172-0337		20. 2.67	Business Brokers Ltd t/a HMC Funding	Bristol	12.10.07E
	(Built Reims Aviation SA)						
G-AVHL	SAN Jodel DR.105A Ambassadeur	90	F-BIVY	23. 2.67	I A Davies tr Seething Jodel Group	Seething	24. 8.08E
G-AVHM	Cessna F150G	F150-0181		24. 2.67	W D Hill	Fenland	18. 8.08E
	(Built Reims Aviation SA) (Rebuilt 1997 with wings from G-ATRL qv)						
G-AVHT	Beagle E 3	Not known	WZ711	1. 3.67	J Pyett	Spanhoe	26. 9.10S
	(Built Auster Aircraft Ltd as Auster AOP.9M) (Lycoming O-360)						
G-AVHY	Fournier RF4D	4009		10. 3.67	I K G Mitchell	Dunkeswell	16.10.07P
G-AVIA	Cessna F150G	F150-0184		10. 3.67	S Lynn t/a American Airplane Breakers	Sibson	5. 5.08E
	(Built Reims Aviation SA)						
G-AVIB	Cessna F150G	F150-0180		10. 3.67	Far North Aviation	Wick	14.11.07E
	(Built Reims Aviation SA)						
G-AVIC	Cessna F172H	F172-0320	N17011	10. 3.67	Leeside Flying Ltd	Cork, County Cork	18. 7.08E
	(Built Reims Aviation SA)						
G-AVID	Cessna 182K	18257734	N2534Q	10. 3.67	Jaguar Aviation Ltd	Eroll	18. 4.06
	(Operated Fife Parachute Centre) (Noted dismantled 9.07)						
G-AVII	Agusta-Bell 206B-2 JetRanger II	8011		10. 3.67	Bristow Helicopters Ltd *"Brighton Belle"*	Norwich	26. 3.08E
G-AVIL	Alon A-2	A 5	N5471E	14. 3.67	D J Hulks	Fridd Farm, Bethersden, Kent	4.11.07E
	(As "VX147" in RAF c/s)						
G-AVIN	SOCATA MS.880B Rallye Club	884		14. 3.67	R Bunce	Compton Abbas	6. 8.08E
G-AVIP	Brantly B 2B	471		14. 3.67	M Richardson t/a Ilkeston Contractors	Ilkeston	3. 4.08E
G-AVIS	Cessna F172H	F172-0413		14. 3.67	J P A Freeman	Headcorn	22. 2.08E
	(Built Reims Aviation SA)						
G-AVIT	Cessna F150G	F150-0217		14. 3.67	P Cottrell	Wellesbourne Mountford	20.12.07E
	(Built Reims Aviation SA)						
G-AVIZ	Scheibe SF25A Motorfalke	4552	(D-KOFY)	21. 3.67	T J Wiltshire tr Splisby Soaring Trust		
	(Hirth F10A)					(Great Steeping, Spilsby)	19. 9.91
G-AVJF	Cessna F172H	F172-0393		31. 3.67	J A and G M Rees c/o Haverfordwest Air Charter		
	(Built Reims Aviation SA)					Haverfordwest	1. 4.08E
G-AVJJ	Piper PA-30 Twin Comanche B	30-1420	N8285Y	7. 4.67	A H Manser	Gloucestershire	8. 9.07T
G-AVJK	SAN Jodel DR.1050M Excellence	453	F-BLJH	7. 4.67	D A Sutton tr Juliet Kilo Syndicate		
	(Originally built as DR.1051)					Sackville Lodge, Riseley	14.11.07
G-AVJO	Fokker E III replica	PPS/REP/6		12. 4.67	Bianchi Aviation Film Services Ltd	Compton Abbas	5. 4.04P
	(Built Personal Plane Services Ltd - c/n PPS/FOK/6) (Continental C85)						
	(In Flying Aces Movie Aeroplane Collection 1.06 as "E III 422/15" in German Army Air Service c/s)						
G-AVJV	Wallis WA-117 Series 1	K/402/X		12. 4.67	K H Wallis	Reymerston Hall, Norfolk	21. 4.89P
	(RR Continental O-200-B) (Used major parts of G-ATCV c/n 301)					*(Stored 8.01)*	
G-AVJW	Wallis WA-118/M Meteorite	K/502/X		12. 4.67	K H Wallis	Reymerston Hall, Norfolk	21. 4.83P
	(Meteor Alfa 1) (Originally regd as Wallis WA.118 Srs 2: used major components of G-ATPW c/n 401) (Stored 8.01)						
G-AVKB	Brochet MB.50 Pipistrelle	02	F-PFAL	17. 4.67	(M G Rummey)	(Binderton, West Sussex)	30.10.96P
	(Walter Mikron 3)					*(On long term rebuild 4.06)*	
G-AVKD	Fournier RF4D	4024		19. 4.67	R E Cross tr Lasham RF4 Group	Lasham	17. 7.08P
G-AVKG	Cessna F172H	F172-0345		21. 4.67	P R Brown-John	Oxford	2. 5.08E
	(Built Reims Aviation SA) (Rebuilt with fuselage of G-AVDC c/n F172-0382 in 1986)						
G-AVKI	Nipper T 66 RA.45 Series 3	S 102		24. 4.67	J M Greenway	(Lapley, Stafford)	7. 8.91P
	(Ardem Mk.10)						
	(Originally built using Avions Fairey SA c/n T66/31 then rebuilt Slingsby Sailplanes Ltd as c/n 1587 for Nipper Aircraft Ltd) (New owner 9.06)						
G-AVKK	Nipper T 66 RA.45 Series 3	S 104	EI-BJH	24. 4.67	C Watson	Newtownards	6. 4.08P
	(Ardem 4C02)		G-AVKK				
	(Originally built using Avions Fairey SA c/n T66/74 then re-built Slingsby Sailplanes Ltd as c/n 1588 for Nipper Aircraft Ltd)						
G-AVKN	Cessna 401	401-0082	(N3282Q)	26. 4.67	Law Leasing Ltd	Rochester	2. 8.08E
G-AVKP	Beagle A 109 Airedale	B 540	SE-EGA	26. 4.67	D R Williams *(Stored 11.07)*	Peplow	26. 9.03
G-AVKR	Bölkow BÖ.208C Junior	648	D-EGRA	28. 4.67	E J F McEntee	Kirdford	30. 4.08E
G-AVLB	Piper PA-28-140 Cherokee	28-23158	N11C	8. 5.67	M Wilson	Sywell	30. 8.08E
G-AVLC	Piper PA-28-140 Cherokee	28-23178	N11C	8. 5.67	C M Tyers	Spanhoe	13. 3.08E
G-AVLE	Piper PA-28-140 Cherokee	28-23223	N11C	8. 5.67	G E Wright t/a Video Security Services		
						South Lodge Farm, Widmerpool	23.12.07E
G-AVLF	Piper PA-28-140 Cherokee	28-23268	N11C	8. 5.67	D Kimpton tr Woodbine Group	(Greenford)	29. 3.08E
G-AVLG	Piper PA-28-140 Cherokee	28-23358	N11C	8. 5.67	C H R Hewitt	Poplar Hall Farm, Elmsett	12. 9.08E
G-AVLI	Piper PA-28-140 Cherokee	28-23388	N11C	8. 5.67	D P Ward and I Richmond tr Lima India Aviation Group		
						Southend	31. 3.08E
G-AVLJ	Piper PA-28-140 Cherokee	28-23393	9H-AAZ	8. 5.67	Cherokee Aviation Holdings Jersey Ltd	Jersey	5. 8.08E
			G-AVLJ, N11C				
G-AVLM	Beagle B 121 Pup Series 2	B121-003		8. 5.67	T M and D A Jones	Derby	29. 4.69S
					(On slow restoration 1.03)		
G-AVLN	Beagle B 121 Pup Series 2	B121-004		8. 5.67	A P Marks tr Dogs Flying Group	Sywell	17. 5.08E
G-AVLO	Bölkow BÖ.208C Junior	650	D-EGUC	8. 5.67	P J Swain	Sandford Hall, Knockin	8. 6.07P
G-AVLT	Piper PA-28-140 Cherokee	28-23328	G-KELC	9. 5.67	Transcourt Ltd and Turweston Flying School Ltd		
			G-AVLT, N11C			Turweston	14. 4.08E
G-AVLY	Wassmer Jodel D 120A Paris-Nice	331		11. 5.67	M E Wills and N V de Candole		
						Stancombe Farm, Litton Cheney	4. 5.08P
G-AVMA	Sud-Aviation Gardan GY-80-180 Horizon	196		12. 5.67	Z R Hildick	Shenstone Hall Farm, Shenstone	10. 9.08E
G-AVMB	Druine D 62B Condor	RAE 621		12. 5.67	L J Dray	Watchford Farm, Yarcombe	25. 4.08P
	(Built Rollason Aircraft and Engines) (Continental C90-14F)					*"Spirit of Silver City"*	
G-AVMD	Cessna 150G	15065504	N2404J	16. 5.67	T A White t/a Bagby Aviation	Bagby	3. 2.08E
G-AVMF	Cessna F150G	F150-0203		17. 5.67	J F Marsh	Newton Farm, Sudbury	14. 9.08E
	(Built Reims Aviation SA)						
G-AVNC	Cessna F150G	F150-0200		18. 5.67	J Turner	Popham	24. 5.04
	(Built Reims Aviation SA)					*(Noted 9.06)*	

Reg	Type	c/n	Prev id	Date	Owner	Location	Status
G-AVNN	Piper PA-28-180 Cherokee C	28-4049	N11C	26. 5.67	J Acres tr G-AVNN Flying Group	Eaglescott	7. 4.08
G-AVNO	Piper PA-28-180 Cherokee C	28-4105	N11C	26. 5.67	A F Cornell tr November Oscar Flying Group		
					(Noted 1.08)	Southend	11.10.07E
G-AVNS	Piper PA-28-180 Cherokee C	28-4129	N11C	26. 5.67	W Bagnall	North Weald	27. 7.08E
G-AVNU	Piper PA-28-180 Cherokee C	28-4153	N11C	26. 5.67	O Durrani	Lydd	24. 4.08E
G-AVNW	Piper PA-28-180 Cherokee C	28-4210	N11C	26. 5.67	Len Smith's (Aviation) Ltd	Fairoaks	16. 5.08T
G-AVNZ	Fournier RF4D	4030		26. 5.67	C D Pidler	Watchford Farm, Yarcombe	21. 9.08E
G-AVOA	SAN Jodel DR.1050 Ambassadeur	195	F-BJYY	31. 5.67	D A Willies	Anwick	2.10.06
G-AVOC	CEA Jodel DR.221 Dauphin	67		2. 6.67	J P Coulter and J Chidley tr Alpha One Flying Group		
						Nuthampstead	25. 5.08E
G-AVOH	Druine D 62B Condor	RAE 622		6. 6.67	Transcourt Ltd	Hinton-in-the-Hedges	16. 5.08T
	(Built Rollason Aircraft and Engines)						
G-AVOM	CEA Jodel DR.221 Dauphin	65		6. 6.67	C J S Drewett tr Avon Flying Group	Bickmarsh	29. 7.08E
G-AVOO	Piper PA-18-150 Super Cub	18-8511	N10F	7. 6.67	Dublin Gliding Club Ltd Gowran Grange, County Kildare		14. 5.08E
	(Lycoming O-360-A4)						
G-AVOZ	Piper PA-28-180 Cherokee C	28-3711	N9574J	13. 6.67	P Hoskins and R Flavell tr Oscar Zulu Flying Group		
						Wycombe Air Park	5. 6.08
G-AVPD	Jodel D 9 Bébé	MAC.1		15. 6.67	S W McKay	(Berkhamsted)	6. 6.75S
	(Built S W McKay using Jodel c/n 521 as-pr.no.PFA 927) (Volkswagen 1500)				(Stored 12.99)		
G-AVPI	Cessna F172H	F172-0409		20. 6.67	D R Larder t/a Air-Tech Water Leisure Park, Skegness		30. 5.03
	(Built Reims Aviation SA)				(On rebuild using fuselage and parts ex EI-AOK 4.04 - new owner 4.05)		
G-AVPJ	de Havilland DH.82A Tiger Moth	86326	NL879	20. 6.67	C C Silk Bericote Farm, Blackdown, Leamington Spa		5. 9.10S
	(Built Morris Motors Ltd)						
G-AVPM	SAN Jodel D 117	593	F-BHXO	20. 6.67	L B Clark and J C Haynes	Breighton	17. 9.08P
G-AVPO	Hindustan HAL-26 Pushpak	PK-127	9M-AOZ	31. 3.83	M B Johns	(Leamington Spa)	27.11.08P
	(Continental C90)		VT-DWL				
G-AVPV	Piper PA-28-180 Cherokee C	28-2705	9J-RBP	27. 6.67	K A Passmore	Rayne Hall Farm, Braintree	8. 3.03
			N11C		(Derelict 1.08)		
G-AVPY	Piper PA-25-235 Pawnee C	25-4330	N4636Y	7. 7.67	Southdown Gliding Club Ltd	Parham Park	5. 9.08E
			N10F				
G-AVRK	Piper PA-28-180 Cherokee C	28-4041	N11C	11. 7.67	N D Wyndow tr Sir W G Armstrong-Whitworth Flying Group		
						Coventry	5. 4.08E
G-AVRP	Piper PA-28-140 Cherokee	28-23153	N11C	14. 7.67	M Rhodes	Sittles Farm, Lichfield	6. 8.08E
G-AVRS	Sud-Aviation Gardan GY-80-180 Horizon	224		14. 7.67	N M Robbins	Sleap	19. 7.08E
G-AVRU	Piper PA-28-180 Cherokee C	28-4025	N11C	17. 7.67	D M Barnett t/a Lanpro	Elstree	23.11.07E
G-AVRW	Gardan GY-20 Minicab	OH-1549		18. 7.67	D J Smith tr Kestrel Flying Group	Hucknall	2. 9.07P
	(Built R Hart - pr.no.PFA 1800 to JB.01 Minicab standard) (Continental C90)						
G-AVRY	Piper PA-28-180 Cherokee C	28-4089	N11C	24. 7.67	Brigfast Ltd	Popham	2. 5.08E
G-AVRZ	Piper PA-28-180 Cherokee C	28-4137	N11C	24. 7.67	Mantavia Group Ltd	Guernsey	22.11.07E
G-AVSA	Piper PA-28-180 Cherokee C	28-4184	N11C	24. 7.67	P A Wells	Ronaldsway	5. 6.08E
G-AVSB	Piper PA-28-180 Cherokee C	28-4191	N11C	24. 7.67	D L Macdonald	Denham	18. 5.08E
G-AVSC	Piper PA-28-180 Cherokee C	28-4193	N11C	24. 7.67	P M Tucker tr G-AVSC Syndicate	Dunkeswell	10. 8.08E
G-AVSD	Piper PA-28-180 Cherokee C	28-4195	N11C	24. 7.67	C B D Owen	Haverfordwest	22.11.07E
G-AVSE	Piper PA-28-180 Cherokee C	28-4196	N11C	24. 7.67	F Glendon (Noted 5.06) Kilrush, County Kildare		30. 4.00T
G-AVSF	Piper PA-28-180 Cherokee C	28-4197	N11C	24. 7.67	S E Pick and D A Rham tr Monday Club	Blackbushe	28. 4.08
G-AVSI	Piper PA-28-140 Cherokee	28-23148	N11C	24. 7.67	C M Royle tr G-AVSI Flying Group	White Waltham	12. 4.08
G-AVSP	Piper PA-28-180 Cherokee C	28-3952	N11C	8. 8.67	Airways Flight Training (Exeter) Ltd RNAS Yeovilton		30. 1.08E
			(PJ-ACT)				
G-AVSR	Beagle D 5/180 Husky	3689		8. 8.67	G R Greenfield and S D J Holwill	Dukeswell	3. 5.09A
G-AVSZ	Agusta-Bell 206B-2 JetRanger II	8032	VH-BEQ	8. 8.67	R P Harper	(Egmere, Walsingham)	16. 6.99T
			PK-HBZ, VR-BCR, PK-HBD, VR-BCR, G-AVSZ (New owner 8.06)				
G-AVTC	Nipper T 66 RA.45 Series 3	S 106		8. 8.67	R M Laver	Shoreham	30 9.08P
	(Built Slingsby Aircraft Co Ltd as c/n 1583 for Nipper Aircraft Ltd) (Ardem Mk.10)						
G-AVTP	Cessna F172H	F172-0458		17. 8.67	K Bartholomew and M J Green tr Tango Papa Group		
	(Built Reims Aviation SA)					White Waltham	13. 9.08E
G-AVTV	SOCATA MS.893A Rallye Commodore 180	10725		24. 8.67	P Storey	Husbands Bosworth	6. 8.06
G-AVUG	Cessna F150H	F150-0234		11. 9.67	N J Gensler and V J Larkin tr Skyways Flying Group		
	(Built Reims Aviation SA)				(Nuthall, Nottingham and Sheffield)		21. 6.08E
G-AVUH	Cessna F150H	F150-0244		11. 9.67	A G Mclaren	Great Ponton	26. 8.07
	(Built Reims Aviation SA)						
G-AVUO	Phoenix Luton LA-4A Minor	PAL 1313		21. 9.67	M E Vaisey	(Hemel Hempstead)	
	(Built C P Butterfield)				(Initially not completed: parts used in construction of G-AXKH - possible long-term build project)		
G-AVUS	Piper PA-28-140 Cherokee	28-24065	(G-AVUT)	25. 9.67	D J Hunter	Shipdham	18. 4.08E
			N11C				
G-AVUT	Piper PA-28-140 Cherokee	28-24085	(G-AVUU)	25. 9.67	Bencray Ltd	Blackpool	21. 8.08E
			N11C		(Operated Blackpool and Fylde Aero Club)		
G-AVUU	Piper PA-28-140 Cherokee	28-24100	(G-AVUS)	25. 9.67	R W Harris, A Jahanfar, P E Preston and M F Hatt		
			N11C		(Operated Southend Flying Club)	Southend	11. 5.08E
G-AVUZ	Piper PA-32-300 Cherokee Six	32-40302	N11C	29. 9.67	Ceesix Ltd	Jersey	1. 4.08E
G-AVVC	Cessna F172H	F172-0443		29. 9.67	C W Wilson tr Babs Flying Group		
	(Built Reims Aviation SA)					Durham Tees Valley	17. 6.08E
G-AVVJ	SOCATA MS.893A Rallye Commodore 180	10752		6.10.67	M Powell	Felthorpe	13.11.07E
G-AVVL	Cessna F150H	F150-0257		6.10.67	A L Hather	Gamston	5.11.08E
	(Built Reims Aviation SA) (Wilksch WAM-120)						
G-AVWA	Piper PA-28-140 Cherokee	28-23660	N11C	19.10.67	SFG Ltd	Shipdham	27. 2.08E
G-AVWD	Piper PA-28-140 Cherokee	28-23700	N11C	19.10.67	C Bentley and B Marlowe t/a Evelyn Air		
						Leeds-Bradford	23. 3.08E
G-AVWG	Piper PA-28-140 Cherokee	28-23760		19.10.67	Bencray Ltd	Blackpool	11. 8.91T
	(Badly damaged in forced landing Tal-y-Fan, Conwy, Gwynedd 11.12.88: major components used to rebuild G-BBEF 1998 - wings only 4.06)						
G-AVWI	Piper PA-28-140 Cherokee	28-23800	N11C	19.10.67	L M Middleton	Cranfield	21. 2.08E
G-AVWJ	Piper PA-28-140 Cherokee	28-23940	N11C	19.10.67	A C M Harrhy	Bembridge, Isle of Wight	27. 7.08E
G-AVWL	Piper PA-28-140 Cherokee	28-24000	N11C	19.10.67	S H and C L Maynard	Durham Tees Valley	4.10 07
G-AVWM	Piper PA-28-140 Cherokee	28-24005		19.10.67	A Jahanfar, P E Preston, M F Hatt and R W Harris		
					(Operated Southend Flying Club)	Southend	6. 8.08E

G-AVWN	Piper PA-28R-180 Cherokee Arrow	28R-30170	N11C	19.10.67	Vawn Air Ltd	Jersey	10. 4.08E
G-AVWO	Piper PA-28R-180 Cherokee Arrow	28R-30205	N11C	19.10.67	I P Scobell	Biggin Hill	9. 2.07
G-AVWR	Piper PA-28R-180 Cherokee Arrow	28R-30242	N11C	19.10.67	R W Scarr tr G-AVWR Flying Group	Dunkeswell	14. 6.08E
G-AVWT	Piper PA-28R-180 Cherokee Arrow	28R-30362	N11C	19.10.67	F Brecha	(St Mawes, Truro)	21. 5.08E
G-AVWU	Piper PA-28R-180 Cherokee Arrow	28R-30380	N11C	19.10.67	A M Alam	Elstree	9. 8.08E
G-AVWV	Piper PA-28R-180 Cherokee Arrow	28R-30404	N11C	19.10.67	R V Thornton and R Barron tr Strathtay Flying Group		
						Perth	23. 6.08E
G-AVWY	Fournier RF4D	4031		26.10.67	P Turner	(Weston-super-Mare)	10.10.08P
G-AVXA	Piper PA-25-235 Pawnee C	25-4244	N4576Y	26.10.67	South Wales Gliding Club Ltd	Usk	21. 5.08E
	(Re-built using new frame - c/n unknown)						
G-AVXD	Nipper T 66 RA.45 Series 3	S 109		26.10.67	J A Brompton	Dundee	19.12.03P
	(Built Slingsby Aircraft Co Ltd as c/n 1606 for Nipper Aircraft Ltd) (Volkswagen 1834 Acro) *(Noted 6.07)*						
G-AVXF	Piper PA-28R-180 Cherokee Arrow	28R-30044	N11C	26.10.67	A D C McNeile tr GAVXF Group	North Weald	5. 7.08E
G-AVXW	Druine D 62B Condor	RAE 625		3.11.67	J M Alexander	Streethay Farm, Lichfield	16. 5.08P
	(Built Rollason Aircraft and Engines)						
G-AVXY	Auster AOP.9	xxxx	XK417	7.11.67	G J Siddall	South Lodge Farm, Widmerpool	9. 7.00P
	(Officially regd with Frame no.AUS/120 - believed to be AUS.10/92)				*(New owner 8.04)*		
G-AVYK	Beagle A 61 Terrier 3	B 642	WJ357	20.11.67	R Burgun	Derby	28. 8.93
G-AVYL	Piper PA-28-180 Cherokee D	28-4622	N11C	24.11.67	A C Hogben tr G-AVYL Flying Group	Full Sutton	1. 6.08E
G-AVYM	Piper PA-28-180 Cherokee D	8-4638	N11C	24.11.67	Carlisle Aviation (1985) Ltd	Carlisle	11. 7.08E
G-AVYR	Piper PA-28-140 Cherokee	28-24226	N11C	24.11.67	R M Weeks	Earls Colne	18. 6.08E
G-AVYS	Piper PA-28R-180 Cherokee Arrow	28R-30456	N11C	24.11.67	Musicbank Ltd	Ludham	5. 3.08E
G-AVYT	Piper PA-28R-180 Cherokee Arrow	28R-30472	N11C	24.11.67	G N Smith	(Rotherham)	28. 3.08E
G-AVYV	Wassmer Jodel D 120A Paris-Nice	252	F-BMAM	27.11.67	A J Sephton	Old Warden	24. 8.08P
G-AVZI	Bölkow BÖ.208C Junior	673	D-EGZF	19.12.67	C F Rogers *(Stored 10.00)*	(Wheathampstead)	24. 7.76
G-AVZN	Beagle B 121 Pup Series 1	B121-006		19.12.67	B L Elvy tr Shipdham Aviators Flying Group		
						Shipdham	27. 1.08
G-AVZP	Beagle B 121 Pup Series 1	B121-008		19.12.67	T A White *(Noted 2.08)*	Bagby	21. 9.07
G-AVZR	Piper PA-28-180 Cherokee C	28-4114	N4779L	19.12.67	Lincoln Aero Club Ltd	Sturgate	28. 6.08E
G-AVZU	Cessna F150H	F150-0283		29.12.67	R D Forster	Ellough, Beccles	23.12.07E
	(Built Reims Aviation SA)				*(Rain Air, Beccles titles on tail)*		
G-AVZV	Cessna F172H	F172-0511		29.12.67	E L King and D S Lightbown	Crosland Moor	5. 6.08E
	(Built Reims Aviation SA)						
G-AVZW	EAA Biplane Model P	PFA 1314		29.12.67	R G Maidment and G R Edmondson		
	(Built R G Maidment) (Lycoming O-290)					Lower Wasing Farm, Brimpton	4. 7.08P
G-AVZX	SOCATA MS.880B Rallye Club	1165		29.12.67	J Nugent	Kilrush, County Kildare	19.11.06

G-AWAA - G-AWZZ

G-AWAC	Sud-Aviation Gardan GY-80-180 Horizon	234		29.12.67	P B Hodgson *"Le Fantome"*	Enstone	11. 6.04
					(Force landed wheels-up Semley, Wiltshire 22. 7.03: on rebuild 3.07)		
G-AWAJ	Beech D55 Baron	TE-536		1. 1.68	Aflex Hose Ltd	Blackpool	29. 9.07E
G-AWAT	Druine D 62B Condor	RAE 627		8. 1.68	M D Burns	Cumbernauld	16. 4.08P
	(Built Rollason Aircraft and Engines)						
G-AWAX	Cessna 150D	15060153	OY-TRJ	5. 1.68	P L Lovegrove	Bournemouth	1.12.07E
	(Tail-wheel conversion)		N4153U				
G-AWAZ	Piper PA-28R-180 Cherokee Arrow	28R-30512	N11C	8. 1.68	P J Manders tr G-AWAZ Flying Group		
						Poplar Hall Farm, Elmsett	3. 8.08E
G-AWBA	Piper PA-28R-180 Cherokee Arrow	28R-30528	N11C	8. 1.68	A Taplin and G A Dunster tr March Flying Group		
						Stapleford	20. 2.08E
G-AWBB	Piper PA-28R-180 Cherokee Arrow	28R-30552	N11C	8. 1.68	P J Young	Ringstead, Hunstanton	18. 5.08E
G-AWBC	Piper PA-28R-180 Cherokee Arrow	28R-30572	N11C	8. 1.68	Anglo Aviation (UK) Ltd	Bournemouth	28.12.07
G-AWBE	Piper PA-28-140 Cherokee	28-24266	N11C	8. 1.68	B E Boyle	Shenington	24.11.05
G-AWBG	Piper PA-28-140 Cherokee	28-24286	N11C	8. 1.68	B Patrick	Oxford	17. 5.08E
G-AWBH	Piper PA-28-140 Cherokee	28-24306	N11C	8. 1.68	Proofgolden Ltd t/a Mainstreet Aviation	Newcastle	30.12.04T
					(Stored for spares 3.06)		
G-AWBJ	Fournier RF4D	4055		12. 1.68	N J Arthur	Bicester	25. 4.08P
G-AWBM	Druine D 31A Turbulent	PFA 1647		17. 1.68	A D Pratt	(Welwyn Garden City)	20. 7.95P
	(Built J R D Bygrave) (Volkswagen 1700)				*(New owner 8.04)*		
G-AWBN	Piper PA-30 Twin Comanche B	30-1472	N8517Y	18. 1.68	Stourfield Investments Ltd *(Noted 1.08)*	Jersey	18.12.07
G-AWBS	Piper PA-28-140 Cherokee	28-24331	N11C	22. 1.68	T M Brown	Little Snoring	7. 7.08E
G-AWBU	Morane Saulnier Type N Rep	PPS/REP/7		22. 1.68	Bianchi Aviation Film Services Ltd	Compton Abbas	28. 4.04P
	(Built D E Bianchi) (Continental C90-8F)				*(In Flying Aces Movie Aeroplane Collection 1.06 as "MS824" in French AF c/s)*		
G-AWBX	Cessna F150H	F150-0286		22. 1.68	G G L James	Sleap	5. 9.08E
	(Built Reims Aviation SA)						
G-AWCN	Reims FR172E Rocket	FR17200020		25. 1.68	B and C Stobart-Hook	Sandown, Isle of Wight	12. 8.08S
G-AWCP	Cessna F150H	F150-0354		29. 1.68	C E Mason	Shobdon	14. 2.08E
	(Built Reims Aviation SA) (Tail-wheel conversion)						
G-AWDA	Nipper T 66 RA.45 Series 3	S 117		7. 2.68	J A Cheesbrough	Ottringham	27. 5.08P
	(Built Slingsby Aircraft Co Ltd as c/n 1624 for Nipper Aircraft Ltd) (Volkswagen Acro 1834)						
G-AWDO	Druine D 31 Turbulent	PFA 1649		21. 2.68	R N Crosland	Deanland	18. 5.08P
	(Built R Watling-Greenwood) (Volkswagen 1600)						
G-AWDP	Piper PA-28-180 Cherokee D	28-4870	N11C	21. 2.68	B H and P M Illston	Norwich	29. 6.08E
					(Operated Norwich School of Flying)		
G-AWDR	Reims FR172E Rocket	FR17200004		21. 2.68	B A Wallace	Nuthampstead	9. 4.08E
G-AWDU	Brantly B 2B	481		23. 2.68	B M Freeman	(Stourport-on-Severn)	17. 3.08
G-AWDW	Campbell-Bensen CB.8MS	DS.1330		26. 2.68	M R Langton	(Taplow)	7.10.71P
	(Built D J C Summerfield) (McCulloch.Motors 4318C)				*(Stored 12.00)*		
G-AWEF	SNCAN Stampe SV-4C(G)	549	F-BDCT	29. 3.68	R A F Buchanan	Headcorn	29. 1.11S
G-AWEI	Druine D 62B Condor	RAE 628		6. 3.68	A M Noble	Roughay Farm, Bishops Waltham	10.11.98T
	(Built Rollason Aircraft and Engines)				*(On long term rebuild 2.06)*		
G-AWEK	Fournier RF4D	4071		6. 3.68	M P J Hill	(Macclesfield)	23 .8.74
					(New owner 1.08)		

G-AWEL	Fournier RF4D	4077		7. 3.68	A B Clymo	Halfpenny Green	11. 9.08P
G-AWEM	Fournier RF4D	4078		7. 3.68	B J Griffin	Wickenby	20. 6.08P
G-AWEP	Gardan GY-20 Minicab	PFA 1801		12. 3.68	D A Porter	Griffins Farm, Temple Bruer	17. 8.04P
	(Built F S Jackson 1969 to JB.01 Minicab standard) (Continental C90)				*(New owner 2.08)*		
G-AWES	Cessna 150H	15068626	N22933	20. 3.68	D W Vincent	Redhill	21. 9.08E
G-AWEV	Piper PA-28-140 Cherokee	28-24460	N11C	21. 3.68	Norflight Ltd	Ludham	10. 8.08E
G-AWEX	Piper PA-28-140 Cherokee	28-24472	N11C	21. 3.68	N D Wyndow tr Sir W G Armstrong-Whitworth Flying Group	Coventry	29. 5.08E
G-AWEZ	Piper PA-28R-180 Cherokee Arrow	28R-30592	N11C	21. 3.68	T R Leighton, R G E Simpson and D A C Clissett	Stapleford	15. 1.08
G-AWFB	Piper PA-28R-180 Cherokee Arrow	28R-30689	N11C	21. 3.68	J C Luke	Filton	7. 8.08E
G-AWFC	Piper PA-28R-180 Cherokee Arrow	28R-30670	N11C	21. 3.68	B J Hines	Wycombe Air Park	30. 9.07E
G-AWFD	Piper PA-28R-180 Cherokee Arrow	28R-30669	N11C	21. 3.68	D J Hill	Moorlands Farm, Farway Common	14. 8.08E
G-AWFF	Cessna F150H	F150-0280		25. 3.68	R J Colver	(Coddington, Ledbury)	31.10.07E
	(Built Reims Aviation SA)						
G-AWFJ	Piper PA-28R-180 Cherokee Arrow	28R-30688	N11C	26. 3.68	Parplon Ltd	Liverpool	23. 3.08E
G-AWFN	Druine D 62B Condor	RAE 629		27. 3.68	P B Lowry	Deanland	3. 7.08P
	(Built Rollason Aircraft and Engines)						
G-AWFO	Druine D 62B Condor	RAE 630		27. 3.68	R E and T A Major	Porthtowan, Truro	7.11.08P
	(Built Rollason Aircraft and Engines)						
G-AWFP	Druine D 62B Condor	RAE 631		27. 3.68	D J Taylor tr Blackbushe Flying Club	White Waltham	1. 7.08P
	(Built Rollason Aircraft and Engines)						
G-AWFT	Jodel D 9 Bébé	PFA 932		29. 3.68	W H Cole	Spilstead Farm, Sedlescombe	22. 7.69P
	(Built W H Cole) (Volkswagen 1200)				*(Noted 3.07)*		
G-AWFW	SAN Jodel D 117	599	PH-VRE	2. 4.68	C J Rodwell	Hawksbridge Farm, Oxenhope	30. 8.08P
			F-BHXU				
G-AWFZ	Beech 19A Musketeer Sport	MB-323	N2811B	3. 4.68	Bob Crowe Aircraft Sales Ltd	Cranfield	20.12.07T
G-AWGD	Cessna F172H	F172-0503		5. 4.68	R P Vincent	Shoreham	18. 7.08E
	(Built Reims Aviation SA)						
G-AWGK	Cessna F150H	F150-0347		8. 4.68	G E Allen	(Saxilby, Lincoln)	1. 5.08E
	(Built Reims Aviation SA)						
G-AWGN	Fournier RF4D	4084		9. 4.68	R J Grimstead	(Tillington, Petworth)	9. 6.07P
					(New owner 1.08)		
G-AWGZ	Taylor JT.1 Monoplane	M 1		17. 4.68	R L Sambell	Stoke Golding	29.10.08P
	(Built J Morris - pr.no.PFA 1406) (Ardem 4C02)						
G-AWHX	Rollason Beta B 2	RAE 04	(G-ATEE)	17. 4.68	S G Jones *"Vertigo" (On rebuild 5.05)*	Membury	14. 6.87P
G-AWHY	Falconar F-11-3	PFA 1322	G-BDPB	17. 4.68	D Holroyd tr Why Fly Group	Goodwood	10. 4.08P
	(Built A E Pritchard and A E Riley-Gale) (Continental C90) (G-AWHY)						
G-AWIF	Brookland Mosquito	LC-1 & 3		17. 4.68	C A Reeves	Henstridge	7. 1.82P
	(Built Brooklands Aero Ltd)				*(Noted 10.03)*		
G-AWII	Vickers Supermarine 349 Spitfire LF.Vc		AR501	25. 4.68	Richard Shuttleworth Trustees	Old Warden	20. 5.06P
	(Built Westland Aircraft Ltd)	WASP/20/223			*(As "AR501:NN-A" in RAF 310 Sqdn c/s) (Noted 8.06)*		
G-AWIP	Phoenix Luton LA-4A Minor	PAL 1308		30. 4.68	J Houghton	(North Ferriby)	8. 5.89P
	(Built T Reagan - pr.no.PFA 830) (Continental A65)				*(Damaged near Holme-on-Spalding Moor 20.7.88: stored 2000)*		
G-AWIR	Bushby-Long Midget Mustang	PFA 1315		30. 4.68	K E Sword	Leicester	6. 3.90P
	(Built A F Jarman and Co Ltd) (Continental O-200-A)				*(On overhaul 1991)*		
G-AWIT	Piper PA-28-140 Cherokee D	28-4987	N11C	30. 4.68	G-AWIT Ltd	Andreas, Isle of Man	12. 4.08E
G-AWIV	Storey TSR.3	PFA 1325		30. 4.68	P K Jenkins	(Redditch)	18. 6.08P
	(Built J M Storey) (Continental PC60) (Offcially regd as c/n "1325")						
G-AWIW	SNCAN Stampe SV-4B	532	F-BDCC	2. 5.68	R E Mitchell *(Noted 10.06)*	Sleap	6. 5.73
G-AWJE	Nipper T 66 RA.45 Series 3	S 121		8. 5.68	K G G Howe	Barton	30. 1.08P
	(Built Slingsby Aircraft Co Ltd as c/n 1628 for Nipper Aircraft Ltd) (Volkswagen 1834)						
G-AWJX	Moravan Zlin Z-526 Trener Master	1049		22. 5.68	P A Colman	Luxter's Farm, Hambleden	29. 5.85A
					(New owner 11.02)		
G-AWJY	Moravan Zlin Z-526 Trener Master	1050		22. 5.68	M Gainza	Freiburg, Germany	26. 4.03
					(Noted dismantled 9.07)		
G-AWKD	Piper PA-17 Vagabond	17-192	F-BFMZ	27. 5.68	A T and M R Dowie	Scotland Farm, Hook	5.10.07P
	(Continental A65)		N4892H				
G-AWKO	Beagle B 121 Pup Series 1	B121-019		11. 6.68	N Davidson and L George	Duxford	19.12.07
G-AWKT	SOCATA MS.880B Rallye Club	1235		17. 6.68	A Ringland and P Keating	Enniskillen	22. 5.08E
G-AWLA	Cessna F150H	F150-0269	N13175	27. 6.68	T A White t/a Bagby Aviation	Bagby	13. 8.08E
	(Built Reims Aviation SA)						
G-AWLF	Cessna F172H	F172-0536		27. 6.68	H Sharp and A Mackey tr Gannet Aviation		
	(Built Reims Aviation SA)					Mullaghmore, Coleraine	5. 1.07
G-AWLG	SIPA 903	82	F-BGHG	27. 6.68	S W Markham	Valentine Farm, Odiham	22. 8.79P
					(Stored 1997)		
G-AWLI	Piper PA-22-150 Caribbean	22-5083	N7256D	1. 7.68	J S Lewery *"Little Peach"*	Shoreham	21. 6.08P
G-AWLO	Boeing Stearman E75 (PT-13D) Kaydet	75-5563	5Y-KRR	9. 7.68	N D Pickard	Panshanger	9. 6.08
	(Pratt and Whitney R985)		VP-KRR, 42-17400		*(Operated Sky High Advertising Ltd)*		
G-AWLP	Mooney M 20F Executive	680200		9. 7.68	I C Lomax *(Noted 1.05)*	Gamston	7. 7.00
G-AWLR	Nipper T 66 RA.45 Series 3	S 125		9. 7.68	T D Reid	Newtownards	16. 5.05P
	(Built Slingsby Aircraft Co Ltd as c/n 1662 for Nipper Aircraft Ltd) (Ardem 4C02)						
G-AWLS	Nipper T 66 RA.45 Series 3	S 126		9. 7.68	G A Dunster and B Gallagher	(Loughton, Essex)	25. 3.88P
	(Built Slingsby Aircraft Co Ltd as c/n 1663 for Nipper Aircraft Ltd) (Ardem Mk.10)				*(Damaged Stapleford 14. 1.88)*		
G-AWLX	Auster 5 J/2 Arrow	2378	F-BGJQ	10. 7.68	W J Taylor	(Friskney, Boston)	23. 4.70P
			OO-ABZ		*(New owner 9.06)*		
G-AWLZ	Fournier RF4D	4099		12. 7.68	J H Taylor tr Nympsfield RF4 Group	Nympsfield	12. 6.08P
G-AWMD	Jodel D 11	PFA 904		19. 7.68	D L King and J R Cooper	(Swansea)	27. 6.08P
	(Built F H French) (Continental C90)						
G-AWMF	Piper PA-18-150 Super Cub	18-8674	N4356Z	23. 7.68	Booker Gliding Club Ltd	Wycombe Air Park	31. 1.08
	(Lycoming O-360-A4)						
G-AWMI	AESL Airtourer T2 (115)	505		24. 7.68	M Furse	Cardiff	8. 5.08
	(Built Glos Air Ltd)						

G-AWMN	Phoenix Luton LA-4A Minor	PFA 827		30. 7.68	S Penfold	(Halstead)	15. 8.07P
	(Built R Wilks) (Volkswagen 1800)				(New owner 11.07)		
G-AWMP	Cessna F172H	F172-0488		31. 7.68	R J D Blois	Yoxford, Saxmundham	23.12.07E
	(Built Reims Aviation SA)						
G-AWMR	Druine D 31 Turbulent	43		1. 8.68	M J Freeman	Shobdon	20. 7.07P
	(Built S J Hargreaves- pr.no.PFA 1661) (Volkswagen 1390)				"Demelza"		
G-AWMT	Cessna F150H	F150-0360		1. 8.68	Strategic Syngernies Ltd	Insch	16 11.07E
	(Built Reims Aviation SA)						
G-AWNT	Britten-Norman BN-2A Islander	32		2. 8.68	Precision Terrain Surveys Ltd		
						(Crockham Hill, Edenbridge)	18. 9.08E
G-AWOA	SOCATA MS.880B Rallye Club	1258		2. 8.68	A F Walters	Elstree	22. 8.08E
G-AWOE	Aero Commander 680E	680E-753-41	N3844C	5. 8.68	J M Houlder t/a Elstree Flying Club	Elstree	12. 6.08E
G-AWOF	Piper PA-15 Vagabond	15-227	F-BETF	6. 8.68	C M Hicks	Barton	7. 8.08P
	(Continental C90) (Officially registered as "PA-17")						
G-AWOH	Piper PA-17 Vagabond	17-191	F-BFMY	6. 8.68	A Lovejoy and K Downes	(Basingstoke)	24. 7.03P
	(Continental C90)		N4891H		(New owners 2.05)		
G-AWOT	Cessna F150H	F150-0389		14. 8.68	M J Willoughby	Cranfield	5. 2.08E
	(Built Reims Aviation SA)						
G-AWOU	Cessna 170B	25829	VQ-ZJA	16. 8.68	S Billington	Ashcroft Farm, Winsford	12. 7.08E
			ZS-CKY, CR-ADU, N3185A				
G-AWPH	Percival P 56 Provost T 1	PAC/F/003	WV420	6. 9.68	J A D Bradshaw	Three Mile Cross, Reading	29. 8.08P
G-AWPJ	Cessna F150H	F150-0376		9. 9.68	W J Greenfield	Humberside	8. 5.08E
	(Built Reims Aviation SA)				(Operated Humberside Flying Club)		
G-AWPN	Shield Xyla	2		13. 9.68	P N Stacey	Sandown, Isle of Wight	3. 5.07P
	(Built G W Shield - pr.no.PFA 1320) (Continental A65)						
G-AWPS	Piper PA-28-140 Cherokee	28-20196	5N-AEK	16. 9.68	A R Matthews	Sittles Farm, Alrewas	17. 3.08E
G-AWPU	Cessna F150J	F150-0411		18. 9.68	Upperstack Ltd t/a LAC Flying School	Barton	15. 3.08E
	(Built Reims Aviation SA)				(Operated Lancashire Aero Club)		
G-AWPW	Piper PA-12 Super Cruiser	12-3947	N78572	23. 9.68	AK Leasing (Jersey) Ltd	Jersey	26. 4.08E
			NC78572				
G-AWPY	Bensen B 8M	CA-314		20. 9.68	J Jordan	(Melrose Farm, Melbourne)	
	(Built Campbell Aircraft Ltd)						
G-AWPZ	Andreasson BA-4B	1	SE-XBS	24. 9.68	J M Vening	Duxford	5.11.03P
	(Built B Andreasson) (Continental O-200A)				(On rebuild since early 2007)		
	(Malmö Flygindustri (MFI) c/n plate on rear fuselage (port) shows c/n as 01)						
G-AWRK	Cessna F150J	F150-0410		8.10.68	Systemroute Ltd	Shoreham	23. 7.08E
	(Built Reims Aviation SA)				(Operated Southern Strut Flying Group)		
G-AWRY	Hunting Percival P 56 Provost T 1	PAC/F/339	XF836	29.10.81	A J House	Lower Wasing Farm, Brimpton	22. 8.88P
			8043M		(As "XF836" in RAF c/s) (New owner 3.05)		
G-AWSH	Moravan Zlin Z-526 Trener Master	1052	OK-XRH	23.11.68	Avia Special Ltd	White Waltham	23.12.04T
			G-AWSH				
G-AWSL	Piper PA-28-180 Cherokee D	28-4907	N11C	30.10.68	Fascia Services Ltd	King's Farm, Thurrock	14.12.06
G-AWSM	Piper PA-28-235 Cherokee Pathfinder	28-11125	N11C	30.10.68	N A Wright t/a Aviation Projects	Shoreham	13. 5.07T
G-AWSN	Druine D 62B Condor	RAE 632		31.10.68	M K A Blyth	Little Gransden	16. 4.08P
	(Built Rollason Aircraft and Engines)						
G-AWSP	Druine D 62B Condor	RAE 634		31.10.68	R Q and A S Bond	Enstone	23. 1.95
	(Built Rollason Aircraft and Engines)				(Noted 3.07)		
G-AWSS	Druine D 62B Condor	RAE 636		31.10.68	N J and D Butler	(Laurencekirk)	19.10.94P
	(Built Rollason Aircraft and Engines)				(Stored at owner's home? 3.98)		
G-AWST	Druine D 62B Condor	RAE 637		31.10.68	T P Lowe	Fenland	31. 5.07P
	(Built Rollason Aircraft and Engines)						
G-AWSW	Beagle D 5/180 Husky	3690	XW635	4.11.68	C Tyers t/a Windmill Aviation	Spanhoe	4. 9.08S
			G-AWSW		(As "XW635" in RAF c/s)		
G-AWTJ	Cessna F150J	F150-0419		8.11.68	P L Jameson	Elstree	8.12.04T
	(Built Reims Aviation SA)						
G-AWTL	Piper PA-28-180 Cherokee D	28-5068	N11C	12.11.68	G Lloyd and M Day	King's Farm, Thurrock	28. 7.08E
G-AWTS	Beech 19A Musketeer Sport	MB-412	OO-BGN	14.11.68	A Newall	Cumbernauld	13.10.07E
			G-AWTS, N2763B				
G-AWTV	Beech 19A Musketeer Sport	MB-424	N2770B	14.11.68	J Whittaker	Trehelig, Welshpool	26.10.07E
G-AWTX	Cessna F150J	F150-0404		18.11.68	R D Forster	Ellough, Beccles	16.12.07E
	(Built Reims Aviation SA)						
G-AWUB	Gardan GY-201 Minicab	A 205	F-PERX	22.11.68	R A Hand	Black Spring Farm, Castle Bytham	5. 4.08P
	(Built Aéronautique Havraise) (Continental A65)						
G-AWUE	SAN Jodel DR.1050 Ambassadeur	299	F-BKHE	22.11.68	K W and F M Wood (On rebuild 4.07)	Insch	17.10.87
G-AWUG	Cessna F150H	F150-0299		25.11.68	Aircraft Engineers Ltd	Prestwick	21. 5.08E
	(Built Reims Aviation SA)						
G-AWUJ	Cessna F150H	F150-0332		25.11.68	S R Hughes	Netherthorpe	19. 4.08E
	(Built Reims Aviation SA)						
G-AWUL	Cessna F150H	F150-0346		25.11.68	A J Baron	Ventfield Farm, Oxfordshire	5. 3.08E
	(Built Reims Aviation SA)						
G-AWUN	Cessna F150H	F150-0377		25.11.68	S G Brown tr G-AWUN Group		
	(Built Reims Aviation SA)					Eddsfield, Octon Lodge Farm, Thwing	12. 5.08E
G-AWUO	Cessna F150H	F150-0380		25.11.68	R Grigg tr Uniform Oscar Flying Group	(Thatcham)	22. 7.07
	(Built Reims Aviation SA)						
G-AWUT	Cessna F150J	F150-0405		25.11.68	B F Spafford	(Scunthorpe)	15.11.07E
	(Built Reims Aviation SA)						
G-AWUU	Cessna F150J	F150-0408	EI-BRA	25.11.68	W J Hockenhull tr G-AWUU Flying Group		
	(Built Reims Aviation SA)		G-AWUU			RAF Waddington	4. 8.08E
G-AWUX	Cessna F172H	F172-0577		25.11.68	B J Portch tr G-AWUX Group	St Just	24. 5.08E
	(Built Reims Aviation SA)						
G-AWUZ	Cessna F172H	F172-0587		25.11.68	I R Judge tr Five Per Cent Flying Group	Shoreham	19. 6.08E
	(Built Reims Aviation SA)						
G-AWVA	Cessna F172H	F172-0597		25.11.68	Barton Air Ltd	Barton	12.10.07E
	(Built Reims Aviation SA)						

Reg	Type	C/n	Prev id	Date	Owner	Location	Date2
G-AWVB	SAN Jodel D 117	604	F-BIBA	26.11.68	H Davies	Haverfordwest	31. 5.08P
G-AWVC	Beagle B 121 Pup Series 1	B121-026	(OE-CUP)	27.11.68	J J West	Sturgate	23. 8.08S
G-AWVE	CEA Jodel DR.1050/M1 Sicile Record	612	F-BMPQ	27.11.68	E A Taylor *(Stored 2.08)*	Southend	18. 5.00
G-AWVF	Hunting Percival P 56 Provost T 1	PAC/F/375	XF877	28.11.68	A J House	Lower Wasing Farm, Brimpton	2. 8.08P
					(As "XF877:JX" in RAF c/s)		
G-AWVG	AESL Airtourer T2 (115)	513	OO-WIC G-AWVG	29.11.68	C J Scholfield	Top Farm, Croydon, Royston	25. 9.10S
	(Built Glos Air Ltd)						
G-AWVN	Aeronca 7AC Champion	7AC-6005	N2426E NC2426E	4.12.68	P K Brown tr Champ Flying Group	Rush Green	25. 4.08P
G-AWVZ	Jodel D 112	898	F-PKVL	12.12.68	D C Stokes	Dunkeswell	1. 8.08P
	(Built J Coupe)						
G-AWWE	Beagle B 121 Pup Series 2	B121-032	G-35-032	12.12.68	A Bleetman	Coventry	6. 8.10E
G-AWWI	SAN Jodel D 117	728	F-BIDU	13.12.68	W J Evans	Rhigos	13. 6.04P
G-AWWM	Gardan GY-201 Minicab	A 195	F-BFOQ	1. 1.69	P J Brayshaw		
	(Built M Heron) (Continental A65)					(Haddock Stone Farm, Markington, Harrogate)	10.12.92P
G-AWWN	SAN Jodel DR.1050 Sicile	398	F-BLJA	8. 1.69	R A J Hurst	Nuthampstead	9.10.10S
G-AWWP	Aerosport Woody Pusher Mk.3	WA/163		7. 1.69	M S and R D Bird	Pepperbox, Salisbury	
	(Built Woods Aeroplanes - pr.no.PFA 1323)				*(Stored 6.93)*		
G-AWWU	Reims FR172F Rocket	FR17200111		15. 1.69	Westward Airways (Lands End) Ltd	St Just	16. 4.08E
G-AWXR	Piper PA-28-180 Cherokee D	28-5171	N11C	24. 1.69	Aero Club de Portugal	(Lisbon, Portugal)	12. 7.08E
G-AWXS	Piper PA-28-180 Cherokee D	28-5283	N11C	24. 1.69	C R and S A Hardiman,	Shobdon	6. 1.08E
G-AWXZ	SNCAN Stampe SV-4C	360	F-BHMZ French.Army, F-BCOI	30. 1.69	Bianchi Aviation Film Services Ltd	Wycombe Air Park	18. 5.08S
G-AWYB	Reims FR172F Rocket	FR17200075		30. 1.69	J R Sharpe	(Southend)	22. 9.07
G-AWYI	Royal Aircraft Factory BE.2c replica	001	N1914B G-AWYI	5. 2.69	M C Boddington and S Slater	Sywell	
	(Built C Boddington)				*(On rebuild 10.07)*		
G-AWYJ	Beagle B 121 Pup Series 2	B121-038	G-35-038	10. 2.69	H C Taylor	Popham	28. 8.08
G-AWYL	CEA Jodel DR.253B Régent	143		11. 2.69	K Gillam	Radley Farm, Hungerford	30. 5.08E
G-AWYO	Beagle B 121 Pup Series 1	B121-041	G-35-041	11. 2.69	B R C Wild	Popham	21.12.08S
G-AWYX	SOCATA MS.880B Rallye Club	1311		11. 2.69	M J Edwards *(Noted 8.03)*	St Just	27. 6.86

G-AXAA - G-AXZZ

Reg	Type	C/n	Prev id	Date	Owner	Location	Date2
G-AXAB	Piper PA-28-140 Cherokee	28-20238	EI-AOA N6206W	17. 2.69	Bencray Ltd	Blackpool	19. 8.08E
					(Operated Blackpool and Fylde Aero Club)		
G-AXAN	de Havilland DH.82A Tiger Moth	85951	F-BDMM French AF, EM720	21. 2.69	Leading Edge Marketing Ltd	Old Warden	27. 8.09E
					(As "EM720" in RAF c/s)		
G-AXAS	Wallis WA-116-T/Mc	217		25. 2.69	K H Wallis	Reymerston Hall, Norfolk	22. 5.07P
	(72hp McCulloch 4318A) (Originally registered as Wallis WA-116-T two-seater tandem version: used major components from G-AVDH c/n 216)						
G-AXAT	SAN Jodel D 117A	836	F-BITJ	26. 2.69	P S Wilkinson	Garton, Insch	29. 4.08P
G-AXBF	Beagle D 5/180 Husky	3691	OE-DEW	17.10.84	J H Powell-Tuck	(St Briavels, Lydney)	20. 9.10S
G-AXBG	Bensen B 8M	RC.1		12. 3.69	R Curtis	(Great Barton, Bury St Edmunds)	
	(Built R Curtis)						
G-AXBH	Cessna F172H	F172-0571		12. 3.69	D F Ranger	Popham	20. 3.08E
	(Built Reims Aviation SA)						
G-AXBJ	Cessna F172H	F172-0573		12. 3.69	S E Goodman tr BJ Flying Group	Leicester	29. 3.08E
	(Built Reims Aviation SA)						
G-AXBW	de Havilland DH.82A Tiger Moth	83595	6854M T5879	12. 3.69	G-AXBW Ltd	Frensham, Wilshanger	24. 4.10S
					(As "T-5879:RUC-W" in RAF c/s)		
G-AXBZ	de Havilland DH.82A Tiger Moth	86552	F-BGDF French AF, PG643	14. 3.69	W J de Jong Cleyndert	(Dereham)	28.11.08E
	(Built Morris Motors Ltd)						
G-AXCA	Piper PA-28R-200 Cherokee Arrow II	28R-35053	N11C	18. 3.69	W H Nelson	Southend	16. 4.08E
G-AXCG	SAN Jodel D 117	510	PH-VRA F-BHXI	19. 3.69	C A White tr The Charlie Golf Group	Andrewsfield	25. 4.07P
G-AXCM	SOCATA MS.880B Rallye Club	1322		25. 3.69	D C Maniford	Bidford	23. 1.08E
G-AXCX	Beagle B 121 Pup Series 2	B121-046	G-35-046	31. 3.69	L A Pink	Glebe Farm, Stockton	10. 7.94
					(On restoration 9.06)		
G-AXCY	SAN Jodel D 117A	499	F-BHXB	31. 3.69	S Marom	Whitehall Farm, Benington	29. 5.08P
					"La Dame en Rouge"		
G-AXCZ	SNCAN Stampe SV-4C	186	ZS-VFW G-AXCZ, F-BCFG	31. 3.69	J Price	Trenchard Farm, Eggesford	10. 7.83
					(Fuselage noted 2.06)		
G-AXDC	Piper PA-23-250 Aztec D	27-4169	N6829Y	8. 4.69	N J Lilley *(Noted 3.07)*	Bodmin	24. 8.98
G-AXDI	Cessna F172H	F172-0574		14. 4.69	M F and J R Leusby t/a Jeanair		
	(Built Reims Aviation SA)					Maypole Farm, Chislet	14. 3.08E
G-AXDK	CEA Jodel DR.315 Petit Prince	378		16. 4.69	M R Weatherhead and J C Lowe tr Delta Kilo Flying Group		
						Sywell	20.12.07
G-AXDV	Beagle B 121 Pup Series 1	B121-049		18. 4.69	T A White	Bagby	13. 7.08S
G-AXDW	Beagle B 121 Pup Series 1	B121-053		18. 4.69	I Beaty, P J Abbott and A M Chester	Cranfield	27. 3.08
					tr Cranfield Delta Whiskey Group		
G-AXED	Piper PA-25-235 Pawnee B	25-3586	OH-PIM OH-CPY, N7540Z	24. 4.69	Wolds Gliding Club Ltd	Pocklington	18. 5.08E
G-AXEO	Scheibe SF25B Falke	4645	D-KEBC	1. 5.69	The Borders (Milfield) Gliding Club Ltd	Milfield	28. 6.07
	(Stark-Stamo MS1500)						
G-AXEV	Beagle B 121 Pup Series 2	B121-070		6. 5.69	G Benson and D S Russell	Gloucestershire	6. 8.09
G-AXFN	Jodel D 119 *(Built M Ganu)*	980	F-PHBU	19. 5.69	D M Jackson	Netherthorpe	20.12.07P
G-AXGE	SOCATA MS.880B Rallye Club	1353		23. 5.69	R P Loxton	(Bridport)	8. 2.08E
G-AXGG	Cessna F150J	F150-0440		28. 5.69	A J Simpson and I Coughlan	Kilrush, County Kildare	8.11.07E
	(Built Reims Aviation SA)						
G-AXGP	Piper J-3C-90 Cub (L-4J-PI)	12544	F-BGPS F-BDTM, 44-80248	2. 6.69	L J Brinkley	Standalone Farm, Meppershall	31. 5.08P
	(Frame No.12374) (Reported as c/n 9542 ex 43-28251)						
G-AXGR	Phoenix Luton LA-4A Minor	PAL 1125		2. 6.69	B A Schlussler	(Hanthorpe, Bourne)	23. 9.06P
	(Built R Spall) (JAP J 99)						

G-AXGS	Druine D 62B Condor	RAE 638		3. 6.69	P J Huxley tr SAS Flying Group	Compton Abbas	15. 8.08P
	(Built Rollason Aircraft and Engines)						
G-AXGV	Druine D 62B Condor	RAE 641		3. 6.69	S B Robson	Watchford Farm, Yarcombe	6.11.08P
	(Built Rollason Aircraft and Engines)						
G-AXGZ	Druine D 62B Condor	RAE 643		3. 6.69	A J Cooper	Rochester	6. 7.08P
	(Built Rollason Aircraft and Engines)						
G-AXHA	Cessna 337A Super Skymaster	3370484	(EI-ATH)	5. 6.69	I M Latiff	Little Staughton	30. 8.02
			N5384S		(Noted 9.05)		
G-AXHC	SNCAN Stampe SV-4C	293	F-BCFU	6. 6.69	D L Webley	Wickenby	9. 7.09S
G-AXHO	Beagle B 121 Pup Series 2	B121-077		9. 6.69	L H Grundy	King's Farm, Thurrock	31. 7.08S
G-AXHP	Piper J-3C-65 Cub (L-4J-PI)	12932	F-BETT	9. 6.69	Witham (Specialist) Vehicles Ltd	Spanhoe	12. 9.08P
	(Frame No.12762)		NC74121, 44-80636		(As "480636:A-58" in USAAC c/s)		
	(Regd with c/n "AF36506" which is USAAC contract no)						
G-AXHR	Piper J-3C-65 Cub (L-4H-PI)	10892	F-BETI	9. 6.69	K B Raven and E Cundy tr G-AXHR Cub Group		
			43-29601		(As "329601:D-44" in USAAC c/s) Hill Farm, Nayland		20. 8.08P
G-AXHS	SOCATA MS.880B Rallye Club	1357		9. 6.69	W B and A Swales (Noted 2.08)	Bagby	14. 7.06
G-AXHT	SOCATA MS.880B Rallye Club	1358		9. 6.69	P M Murray (Noted 2.08)	Bagby	19. 4.07
G-AXHV	SAN Jodel D 117A	695	F-BIDF	9. 6.69	J S Ponsford tr Derwent Flying Group	Hucknall	10. 9.08P
G-AXIA	Beagle B 121 Pup Series 1	B121-078		17. 6.69	C K Parsons	Kemble	28.10.07T
G-AXIE	Beagle B 121 Pup Series 2	B121-087		17. 6.69	J P Thomas	(Chesham)	15. 8.08S
G-AXIF	Beagle B 121 Pup Series 2	B121-088	(SE-FGV)	17. 6.69	J R Faulkner	Derby	13.10.08S
G-AXIG	Scottish Aviation Bulldog Series 100/104			24. 6.69	A A Douglas-Hamilton	Cumbernauld	22. 8.08S
		BH120/002					
G-AXIO	Piper PA-28-140 Cherokee B	28-25764	N11C	26. 6.69	T Akeroyd	Cranfield	20. 3.08E
G-AXIR	Piper PA-28-140 Cherokee B	28-25795	N11C	26. 6.69	R W Howard	Lasham	24. 7.08E
G-AXIW	Scheibe SF25B Falke	4657	(D-KABJ)	3. 7.69	M Pedley	Nympsfield	8. 3.08E
	(Stark-Stamo MS1500)						
G-AXIX	AESL Airtourer T4 (150)	A 527		3. 7.69	J C Wood	Shobdon	13 .6.10
	(Built Glos Air Ltd)						
G-AXJB	Omega 84 Balloon (Hot Air)	04		9. 7.69	Semajan Ltd tr Southern Balloon Group	Romsey	20. 8.73S
	(Initially flown as G-AXDT)				"Jester"		
G-AXJH	Beagle B 121 Pup Series 2	B121-089		11. 7.69	D Collings tr The Henry Flying Group	Popham	2. 5.10S
G-AXJI	Beagle B 121 Pup Series 2	B121-090		11. 7.69	J J Sanders	Derby	3. 6.08
G-AXJJ	Beagle B 121 Pup Series 2	B121-091		11. 7.69	M L, T M, D A and P M Jones	Derby	13.12.09S
G-AXJO	Beagle B 121 Pup Series 2	B121-094		11. 7.69	J A D Bradshaw "Joey" Three Mile Cross, Reading		20. 8.09S
G-AXJR	Scheibe SF25B Falke	4652	D-KICD	4. 7.69	R I Hey tr The Falke Syndicate	Nympsfield	14. 8.08E
	(Stark-Stamo MS1500)						
G-AXJV	Piper PA-28-140 Cherokee B	28-25572	N11C	14. 7.69	British Disabled Flying Association	Lasham	7. 6.08E
G-AXJX	Piper PA-28-140 Cherokee B	28-25990	N11C	14. 7.69	C W Hall	Popham	4.11.07E
G-AXKH	Phoenix Luton LA-4A Minor	PAL 1316		21. 7.69	M E Vaisey tr Chiltern Flying Club		
	(Built M E Vaisey - pr.no.PFA 823) (Volkswagen 1600)					(Hemel Hempstead)	18. 4.84P
G-AXKJ	Jodel D 9 Bébé	SAS.002		22. 7.69	L B Roberts	Halwell	16. 8.07P
	(Built Southdown Aero Services Ltd - pr.no.PFA 941: also originally PFA 928B) (Volkswagen 1600)						
G-AXKO	Westland-Bell 47G-4A	WA/720	G-17-5	22. 7.69	M Gallagher	(Ballinamore, County Leitrim)	23. 4.10S
G-AXKX	Westland-Bell 47G-4A	WA/728	G-17-13	22. 7.69	South Yorkshire Aviation Ltd	Gamston	4.12.10S
G-AXKY	Westland-Bell 47G-4A	WA/729	G-17-14	22. 7.69	C P Golborne	(Whittlesey, Peterborough)	15. 5.06
G-AXLG	Cessna 310K	310K0204	N3804X	25. 7.69	C Koscso	(King's Lynn)	26.10 07E
G-AXLI	Nipper T 66 RA.45 Series 3	S 131		25. 7.69	D and M Shrimpton		
	(Built Slingsby Aircraft Co Ltd as c/n 1701 for Nipper Aircraft Ltd) (Ardem Mk.10)					Franklyn's Field, Chewton Mendip	2. 7.08P
G-AXLS	SAN Jodel DR.105A Ambassadeur	86	F-BIVR	31. 7.69	J J Boon tr Axle Flying Club	Popham	9. 4.08E
G-AXLZ	Piper PA-18 Super Cub 95	18-2052	PH-NLB	31. 7.69	R J Quantrell	(Low Farm, South Walsham)	23. 4.00
	(L-18C-PI) (Frame No.18-2065)		R Neth.AF R-45, 8A-45, 52-2452 (Damaged Low Farm 14. 8.97)				
G-AXMA	Piper PA-24 Comanche	24-3467	N8214P	5. 8.69	J A and S M Fletcher	Humberside	26. 5.08
G-AXMN	Auster J/5B Autocar	2962	F-BGPN	14. 8.69	C D Wilkinson	Trenchard Farm, Eggesford	15. 4.04
G-AXMT	Bücker Bü.133C Jungmeister	46	N133SJ	19. 8.69	R A Fleming	Breighton	3. 5.08P
	(Built AG Fur Dornier-Flugzeuge)		G-AXMT, HB-MIY, Swiss AF U-99 (As "U-99" in Swiss AF c/s)				
G-AXMW	Beagle B 121 Pup Series 1	B121-101		19. 8.69	DJP Engineering (Knebworth) Ltd	Cambridge	22. 7.07
G-AXMX	Beagle B 121 Pup Series 2	B121-103		19. 8.69	S A Jones	(Cannes, France)	8.10.09S
			G-AXMX, G-35-103				
G-AXNJ	Wassmer Jodel D 120 Paris-Nice	52	F-BHYO	29. 8.69	D I Vernon tr Clive Flying Group	Sleap	15.10.08P
G-AXNN	Beagle B 121 Pup Series 2	B121-104		3. 9.69	Gabrielle Aviation Ltd "Gabrielle"	Shoreham	17. 9.08S
G-AXNP	Beagle B 121 Pup Series 2	B121-106		3. 9.69	J W Ellis and R J Hemmings	Hawarden	24. 6.08
G-AXNR	Beagle B 121 Pup Series 2	B121-108		3. 9.69	M Brown tr November Romeo Group		
						Raby's Farm, Great Stukeley	25. 3.08
G-AXNS	Beagle B 121 Pup Series 2	B121-110		3. 9.69	D Beckwith and D Long tr Derwent Aero Group	Gamston	6. 6.08S
G-AXNW	SNCAN Stampe SV-4C	381	F-BFZX	11. 9.69	Carolyn S Grace Blooms Farm, Sible Hedingham		12. 6.09S
			French AF				
G-AXNX	Cessna 182M	18259322	N70606	16. 9.69	H A Harper	Biggin Hill	5.10.07E
G-AXNZ	Pitts S-1C	EB.1		16. 9.69	C D Baglin	(Gamlingay, Sandy)	30. 8.91P
	(Built W Berry and B Etheridge - pr.no.PFA 1383: official c/n shown as EBX2)				(New owner 3.05)		
G-AXOH	SOCATA MS.894A Rallye Minerva 220	11062	D-EAGU	17. 9.69	T A D Crook	White Waltham	25. 9.06
G-AXOJ	Beagle B 121 Pup Series 2	B121-109	G-35-109	24. 9.69	T J Martin tr Pup Flying Group	Rochester	9. 7.08S
G-AXOS	SOCATA MS.894A Rallye Minerva 220	11079		3.10.69	A L Hall-Carpenter	Shipdham	15. 2.08E
G-AXOT	SOCATA MS.893A Rallye Commodore 180	11433		3.10.69	P Evans	Dalscote, Northampton	26. 3.08E
G-AXOZ	Beagle B 121 Pup Series 1	B121-115	N70290	7.10.69	R J Ogborn	Hawarden	3. 6.10
			G-AXOZ, G-35-115				
G-AXPA	Beagle B 121 Pup Series 1	B121-116	D-EATL	7.10.69	A J C Hawks and D Griffiths tr Papa-Alpha Group		
			G-AXPA, G-35-116				Derby	21.11.08S
G-AXPB	Beagle B 121 Pup Series 1	B121-117	G-35-117	7.10.69	M J K Seary and R T Austin tr Beagle Flying Group		
						Leicester	22. 2.08
G-AXPC	Beagle B 121 Pup Series 1	B121-119	PH-VRS	7.10.69	T A White	Bagby	21.11.08E
			G-AXPC				
G-AXPF	Reims Cessna F150K	F15000543		14.10.69	D R Marks (Stored 7.07)	Enstone	22. 4.02
G-AXPG	Mignet HM.293	PFA 1333		14.10.69	W H Cole	Spilstead Farm, Sedlescombe	20. 1.77P
	(Built W H Cole) (Volkswagen 1300)				(Noted 3.07)		

G-AXPM	Beagle B 121 Pup Series 1	B121-122	G-35-122	20.10.69	S C Stanton		Panshanger	1.12.08S
G-AXPN	Beagle B 121 Pup Series 2	B121-123	G-35-123	20.10.69	A Richardson		Derby	26. 5.08
G-AXPZ	Campbell Cricket	CA-320		3.11.69	W R Partridge		St Merryn	20. 5.08P
	(Rotax 582)							
G-AXRC	Campbell Cricket	CA-323		3.11.69	L R Morris	(Newry, County Armagh)	18. 5.78S
	(Volkswagen 1600)			*(Damaged Wittering 22.10.77: stored Tattershall Thorpe 7.91) (New owner 12.02)*				
G-AXRP	SNCAN Stampe SV-4C	554	G-BLOL	7.11.69	C C Manning		Rotary Farm, Hatch	20.11.06
			G-AXRP, F-BDCZ		*(See entry for G-BLOL)*			
G-AXRR	Auster AOP.9	B5/10/178	XR241	7.11.69	R B Webber	Trenchard Farm, Eggesford	11. 5.07P
	(Frame no.AUS/178)		G-AXRR, XR241		*(As "XR241" in AAC c/s)*			
G-AXRT	Reims Cessna FA150K Aerobat	FA1500018		12.11.69	C C Walley		Elstree	25. 1.06T
	(Tail-wheel conversion)							
G-AXSC	Beagle B 121 Pup Series 1	B121-138	G-35-138	13.11.69	R J MacCarthy		Derby	28. 4.07
G-AXSD	Beagle B 121 Pup Series 1	B121-139	G-35-139	13.11.69	AURS Aviation Ltd		Prestwick	10. 5.08T
G-AXSF	Nash Petrel	P 003		17.11.69	Nash Aircraft Ltd		Lasham	?. 4.94P
	(Built Nash Aircraft Ltd - pr.no.PFA 1516) (Lycoming O-360)				*(Stored 10.95)*			
G-AXSG	Piper PA-28-180 Cherokee E	28-5605	N11C	17.11.69	The Tago Island Company Ltd	(London SW1Y)	2.11 07E
G-AXSI	Reims Cessna F172H	F17200687	G-SNIP	19.11.69	R Collins		Humberside	8..9.07
			G-AXSI					
G-AXSM	CEA Jodel DR.1051 Sicile	512	F-BLRH	20.11.69	T R G Barnby and M S Regendanz	Headcorn	14. 6.08E
G-AXSW	Reims Cessna FA150K Aerobat	FA1500003		25.11.69	R Mitchell	(Chalfont St Giles)	2. 4.08E
G-AXSZ	Piper PA-28-140 Cherokee B	28-26188	N11C	26.11.69	B J Collins tr The White Wings Flying Group			
							White Waltham	24. 4.08T
G-AXTA	Piper PA-28-140 Cherokee B	28-26301	N11C	26.11.69	P J Farrell tr G-AXTA Aircraft Group	Shoreham	25. 5.08E
G-AXTC	Piper PA-28-140 Cherokee B	28-26265	N11C	26.11.69	W J Knott tr G-AXTC Group	North Coates	16. 2.08E
G-AXTJ	Piper PA-28-140 Cherokee B	28-26241	N11C	26.11.69	K Patel		Elstree	26. 2.07T
G-AXTL	Piper PA-28-140 Cherokee B	28-26247	N11C	26.11.69	S F Pickering tr Pegasus Aviation Midlands	Tatenhill	1.12.07E
G-AXTO	Piper PA-24-260 Comanche C	24-4900	N9449P	28.11.69	J L Richardson		RAF Wittering	4. 8.08E
			N9705N		*"Betsy Baby"*			
G-AXTP	Piper PA-28-180 Cherokee C	28-3791	OH-PID	1.12.69	M Whyte	Carnmore, Galway, County Galway	6. 2.08E
G-AXUA	Beagle B 121 Pup Series 1	B121-150	G-35-150	4.12.69	P Wood		Audley End	5. 6.08
G-AXUB	Britten-Norman BN-2A Islander	121	5N-AIJ	4.12.69	Headcorn Parachute Club Ltd		Headcorn	18. 5.08E
			G-AXUB, N859JA, G-51-47					
G-AXUC	Piper PA-12 Super Cruiser	12-621	5Y-KFR	5.12.69	J J Bunton	Clipgate Farm, Denton	18. 7.08E
			VP-KFR, ZS-BIN					
G-AXUF	Reims Cessna FA150K Aerobat	FA1500043		9.12.69	W B Bateson *(Noted 10.07)*		Blackpool	6. 5.07T
G-AXUJ	Auster V J/1 Autocrat	1957	G-OSTA	11.12.69	P Gill	Yeatsall Farm, Abbots Bromley	6. 5.07
			G-AXUJ, PH-OTO		*(Noted 8.07)*			
G-AXUK	SAN Jodel DR.1050 Ambassadeur	292	F-BJYU	11.12.69	G J Keegan tr Downland Flying Group (2KI)		
							Deanland	21. 5.08E
G-AXVB	Reims Cessna F172H	F17200703		22.12.69	R and J Turner	Charlton Park, Malmesbury	5. 7.08
G-AXVK	Campbell Cricket	CA-327		1. 1.70	B Jones	Melrose Farm, Melbourne	16. 4.07P
	(Volkswagen 1600)							
G-AXVM	Campbell Cricket	CA-329		1. 1.70	D M Organ		Gloucestershire	18.12.07P
	(Volkswagen 1834)							
G-AXVN	McCandless M 4	M4/6		5. 1.70	W R Partridge		St Merryn	
	(Volkswagen 1700)				*(Stored 5.03)*			
G-AXWA	Auster AOP.9	B5/10/133	XN437	13. 1.70	C M Edwards *(On rebuild 6.07)*	North Weald	
G-AXWT	Jodel D 11	PFA 911		26. 1.70	R C Owen	(Danehill, Haywards Heath)	2. 6.00P
	(Built C King and R C Owen) (Continental C90)							
G-AXWV	CEA Jodel DR.253 Régent	104	F-OCKL	2. 2.70	R Friedlander and D C Ray	Grateley, Andover	11. 5.08E
G-AXWZ	Piper PA-28R-200 Cherokee Arrow II		N11C	3. 2.70	P Walkley		Lydd	15.11.07E
		28R-35605						
G-AXXC	Rousseau Piel CP.301B Emeraude	117	F-BJAT	4. 2.70	R S C Andrews tr Emy Group		
						Green Farm, Wellesbourne	9. 1.08P
G-AXXV	de Havilland DH.82A Tiger Moth	85852	F-BGJI	24. 2.70	C N Wookey		Membury	1. 7.07
	(Built Morris Motors Ltd)		French AF, DE992		*(As "DE992" in RAF c/s)*			
			(Caught by gust of wind landing Membury 19. 6.07, swung to right and tipped on to nose incurring damage)					
G-AXXW	SAN Jodel D 117	632	F-BIBN	26. 2.70	D F Chamberlain and M A Hughes	Haverfordwest	5. 9.07P
G-AXYK	Taylor JT.1 Monoplane	PFA 1409		2. 3.70	P F Gandy		(Heathfield)	30. 4.08P
	(Built G Oakins) (Volkswagen 1600)							
G-AXYU	Jodel D 9 Bébé	547	EI-BVE	5. 3.70	P Turton and H C Peake-Jones		
	(Volkswagen 1600)		G-AXYU		(Ashcroft Farm, Winsford)	13. 9.01P
G-AXZD	Piper PA-28-180 Cherokee E	28-5609	N11C	12. 3.70	G M Whitmore	High Cross, Ware	9. 1.08E
G-AXZF	Piper PA-28-180 Cherokee E	28-5688	N11C	12. 3.70	Haimoss Ltd		Old Sarum	6. 8.08E
					(Operated Old Sarum Flying Club)			
G-AXZH	Glasflügel H201B Standard Libelle	82	BGA 2247-DNL,	12. 3.70	M C Gregorie	Gransden Lodge	6. 6.08
			RAFGSA 742, RAFGSA 16, G-AXZH					
G-AXZK	Britten-Norman BN-2A-26 Islander	153	V2-LAD	12. 3.70	B-N Group Ltd		Bembridge	16. 4.06
			VP-LAD, G-AXZK, G-51-153					
G-AXZM	Nipper T 66 RA.45 Series 3A	S 133		16. 3.70	G R Harlow		Newcastle	24. 8.89P
	(Re-built S J Booth and A Young - pr.no.PFA 1378) (Volkswagen 1600)				*(Damaged near Eshott 21. 8.89)*			
	(Originally built as c/n 1709 Slingsby Aircraft Co Ltd for Nipper Aircraft Ltd)							
G-AXZO	Cessna 180	31137	N3639C	17. 3.70	J C King tr Bourne Park Flyers		
						Bourne Park, Hurstbourne Tarrant	2.11.07E
G-AXZP	Piper PA-E23-250 Aztec D	27-4464	N13819	17. 3.70	D M Harbottle		Fairoaks	28.11.07E
G-AXZT	SAN Jodel D 117A	607	F-BIBD	17. 3.70	P Guest		(Leeds)	22.11.08P
G-AXZU	Cessna 182N Skylane	18260104	N92233	19. 3.70	W Gollan		Errol	2. 8.08E

G-AYAA - G-AYZZ

G-AYAB	Piper PA-28-180 Cherokee E	28-5804	N11C	24. 3.70	J R Green		Turweston	21. 8.08E
G-AYAC	Piper PA-28R-200 Cherokee Arrow III		N11C	24. 3.70	R I Willcox tr Fersfield Flying Group	Knettishall	13. 3.08E
		28R-35606						

G-AYAN	Slingsby Cadet III Motor Glider	003	BGA 1224 RAFGSA.223	6. 4.70	D C Pattison "Thermal Hopper"	Brunton	23. 7.07P
	(Re-built P J Martin and D R Wilkinson - pr.no.PFA 1385 from Slingsby T 31B [Frame no.SSK/FF776]) (Volkswagen 1600)						
G-AYAR	Piper PA-28-180 Cherokee E	28-5797	N11C	8. 4.70	A Jahanfar	Southend	9. 3 08E
					(Operated Seawing Flying Club)		
G-AYAT	Piper PA-28-180 Cherokee E	28-5801	N11C	8. 4.70	A Goodchild tr G-AYAT Flying Group	Seething	26. 3.08E
G-AYAW	Piper PA-28-180 Cherokee E	28-5805	N11C	14. 4.70	N S Nixon and R S Scott tr GAYAW Group	Denham	7. 7.08E
G-AYBD	Reims Cessna F150K	F15000583		7. 4.70	Apollo Aviation Advisory Ltd	Shoreham	13.10.07E
					(Operated Ace Aviation)		
G-AYBG	Scheibe SF25B Falke	4696	(D-KECJ)	13. 4.70	H H T Wolf	(Eyres Field)	4. 4.97
	(Volswagen Danum 1600/1)						
G-AYBO	Piper PA-23-250 Aztec D	27-4510	N13874	15. 4.70	A G Gutknecht	(Langenwang, Austria)	7. 5.06
G-AYBP	Jodel D 112	1131	F-PMEK	16. 4.70	G J Langston	Bidford	20.12.08P
	(Built Aero Club du Rousillon)						
G-AYBR	Wassmer Jodel D 112	1259	F-BMIG	16. 4.70	I S Parker	Damyn's Hall, Upminster	14. 6.08P
G-AYCC	Campbell Cricket	CA-336		20. 4.70	D J M Charity	Hinton-in-the-Hedges	16. 5.07P
	(Rotax 582)						
G-AYCE	Scintex CP.301-C1 Emeraude	530	F-BJFH	20. 4.70	S D Glover	Charterhall	24.10.08P
G-AYCF	Reims Cessna FA150K Aerobat	FA1500055		22. 4.70	E J Atkins	Popham	27. 6.08
G-AYCG	SNCAN Stampe SV-4C	59	F-BOHF F-BBAE, French AF	24. 4.70	N Bignall	White Waltham	4. 7.10
G-AYCJ	Cessna TP206D Turbo Super Skylane	P206-0552	N8752Z	27. 4.70	White Knuckle Airways Ltd	Leeds-Bradford	10. 7.08E
	(Regd with c/n T206-0552)						
G-AYCK	AIA Stampe SV-4C(G)	1139	G-BUNT G-AYCK, F-BANE, Aeronavale	28. 4.70	The Real Flying Company Ltd	Shoreham	18.10.07T
	(Officially regd as built SNCAN)						
G-AYCN	Piper J-3C-65 Cub	"13365"	F-BCPO	28. 4.70	W R and B M Young *(Stored 4.91)*		
	(Frame No.not known: c/n quoted became PH-UCM in 11.46 and p/i is doubtful)					Furze Hill Farm, Rosemarket, Milford Haven	27. 1.89P
G-AYCO	CEA Jodel DR.360 Chevalier	362	F-BRFI	29. 4.70	P L Buckley tr Charlie Oscar Club Hill Farm, Nayland		12. 3.08E
G-AYCP	SAN Jodel D 112	67	F-BGKO	30. 4.70	E C Murgatroyd tr Charlie Papa Group	Cranfield	28. 6.07P
G-AYCT	Reims Cessna F172H	F17200724		1. 5.70	P A and J Rose	Full Sutton	9.12.07E
G-AYDI	de Havilland DH.82A Tiger Moth	85910	F-BDOE French AF, DF174	7. 5.70	R B and E W Woods and J D M Barr	Hampstead Norrey's	15. 6.09S
G-AYDR	SNCAN Stampe SV-4C	307	F-BCLG	13. 5.70	A J McLuskie (Quebec Farm, Knook, Warminster)		27. 3.75
					(Damaged 16. 6.73 and on rebuild 8.93)		
G-AYDV	Coates Swalesong SA.II Series 1	PFA 1353		18. 5.70	D F Coates	Breighton	8. 8.07P
	(Built J R Coates)				*(Noted 12.07)*		
G-AYDX	Beagle A 61 Terrier 2	B 647	VX121	20. 5.70	R A Kirby	Spanhoe	28. 8.09S
G-AYDY	Phoenix Luton LA-4A Minor	PAL 1302		21. 5.70	J Dible	(Sandyford, Dublin)	15. 8.97P
	(Built L J E Goldfinch - pr.no.PFA 817) (Volkswagen 1600)				*(New owner 10.05)*		
G-AYDZ	CEA Jodel DR.200	01	F-BLKV F-WLKV	21. 5.70	D Nickson tr Zero One Group	Enstone	29. 3.08
	(Lycoming O-235)						
G-AYEB	Wassmer Jodel D 112	586	F-BIQR	26. 5.70	P Goring	Sturgate	31. 3.07P
G-AYEC	Menavia Piel CP.301A Emeraude	249	F-BIMV	26. 5.70	J J Shepherd tr Red Wing Flying Group "Antoinette"	Netherthorpe	26. 7.07P
G-AYEE	Piper PA-28-180 Cherokee E	28-5813	N11C	28. 5.70	Demero Ltd	Hinton-in-the-Hedges	5. 7.08E
G-AYEF	Piper PA-28-180 Cherokee E	28-5815	N11C	28. 5.70	P A Coleman and K Lloyd tr G-AYEF Group	Barton	10. 2.08E
G-AYEG	Falconar F-9	PFA 1321		29. 5.70	A L Smith	Sackville Lodge, Riseley	5. 9.07P
	(Built G R Gladstone) (Volkswagen 1600)						
G-AYEH	SAN Jodel DR.1050 Ambassadeur	455	F-BLJB	8. 6.70	J W Scott tr John Scott Jodel Group "Jemima"	Bidford	17. 6.08
G-AYEJ	SAN Jodel DR.1050 Ambassadeur	253	F-BJYG	1. 6.70	J M Newbold	Enstone	3. 5.08
G-AYEN	Piper J-3C-65 Cub (L-4H-PI)	12184	F-BGQD	4. 6.70	P J Warde and C F Morris	Old Warden	18.12.07P
	(Frame No.12012)			(F-BGQA), French AF, 44-79888			
	(Official identity is c/n 9696/43-835 but fuselages probably exchanged with F-BGQA on conversion in 1952/53)						
G-AYEV	SAN Jodel DR.1050 Ambassadeur	179	F-BERH F-OBTH, F-OBRH	10. 6.70	L G Evans tr Echo Victor Group	Redhill	17. 4.08E
G-AYEW	CEA Jodel DR.1050 Sicile	443	F-BLMJ	11. 6.70	J M Gale and J R Hope	Dunkeswell	18. 8.08E
G-AYFC	Druine D 62B Condor	RAE 644		19. 6.70	A R Chadwick	Breighton	11.12.08P
	(Built Rollason Aircraft and Engines)						
G-AYFD	Druine D 62B Condor	RAE 645		19. 6.70	B G Manning	Little Down Farm, Milson	24. 7.08P
	(Built Rollason Aircraft and Engines)				*(Hourds Travel titles) '94'*		
G-AYFF	Druine D 62B Condor	RAE 647		19. 6.70	A W Maycock and I Macleod	Lower Upham Farm, Chiseldon	19. 8.08P
	(Built Rollason Aircraft and Engines)						
G-AYFG	Druine D 62C Condor	RAE 648		19. 6.70	C Jobling and A J Mackay	RAF Waddington	31. 3 08P
	(Built Rollason Aircraft and Engines) (Continental O-240-A)						
G-AYFP	SAN Jodel D 140 Mousquetaire	18	F-BMSI F-OBLH, F-WNDO	24. 6.70	J J L Girardot	(Montmorency, France)	29. 1.11P
G-AYFV	Andreasson BA-4B	002		26. 6.70	A R C Mathie	(Burgate, Diss)	16.10.08P
	(Built Crosby Aviation Ltd - pr.no.PFA 1359) (Lycoming IO-320)						
G-AYGA	SAN Jodel D 117	436	F-BHNU	30. 6.70	J W Bowes) Hawksbridge Farm, Oxenhope		13. 4.07P
					(Noted 7.07)		
G-AYGC	Reims Cessna F150K	F15000556		2. 7.70	M J Kelly tr Alpha Aviation Group	Barton	6. 7.08E
G-AYGD	CEA Jodel DR.1050 Sicile	515	F-BLRE	3. 7.70	J F M Bartlett and J P Liber	Oaksey Park	25. 1.08
G-AYGE	SNCAN Stampe SV-4C	242	F-BCGM	6. 7.70	I, L J and S Proudfoot	Duxford	4. 6.03
G-AYGG	Wassmer Jodel D 120 Paris-Nice	184	F-BJPH	10. 7.70	J M Dean	Stoneacre Farm, Farthing Corner	24. 3.08P
G-AYGX	Reims FR172G Rocket	FR17200208		15. 7.70	D Waterhouse tr Reims Rocket Group	Barton	14.11.07E
G-AYHA	American AA-1A Trainer	AA1-0396	N6196L	21. 7.70	S J Carr	RAF Leuchars	23. 3.08E
G-AYHX	SAN Jodel D 117A	903	F-BIVE	23. 7.70	L J E Goldfinch tr Jodel Flying Group	Old Sarum	9. 4.08P
G-AYIA	Hughes 369HS	99-0120S		29. 7.70	G D E Bilton	Sywell	16. 7.88
	(Hughes 500) (Badly damaged in heavy landing S of France 1. 6.88. to March Helicopters - stored for spares use 8.97)						
G-AYIG	Piper PA-28-140 Cherokee C	28-26878	N11C	31. 7.70	R W Hinton	(Woolpit, Bury St Edmunds)	6.12.07E
G-AYII	Piper PA-28R-200 Cherokee Arrow II	28R-35736	N11C	4. 8.70	P W J Gove tr Double India Group	Exeter	23. 4.08E
G-AYIJ	SNCAN Stampe SV-4B	376	F-BCOM	4. 8.70	D Savage	(Staplehurst, Tonbridge)	23. 6.09S

Reg	Type	c/n	Prev id	Date	Owner/Operator	Base	Date
G-AYIM	Hawker Siddeley HS.748 Series 2A/270	1687	G-11-687 CS-TAG/G-AYIM, G-11-5	11. 8.70	PTB (Emerald) Proprietary Ltd *(Stored externally 2.08)*	Blackpool	21.12.07E
G-AYJA	SAN Jodel DR.1050 Ambassadeur	150	F-BJJJ	8. 9.70	G Connell	Weston, Leixlip, County Kildare	11. 7.08
G-AYJB	SNCAN Stampe SV-4C(G)	560	F-BDDF	8. 9.70	F J M and J P Esson *"Odette"* Bere Farm, Warnford		24. 9.10
G-AYJD	Fournier RF3	11	F-BLXA	8. 9.70	I O Bull tr Juliet Delta Group	Ringmer	1. 9.08P
G-AYJP	Piper PA-28-140 Cherokee C	28-26403	N11C	15. 9.70	RAF Brize Norton Flying Club Ltd	RAF Brize Norton	21. 6.08T
G-AYJR	Piper PA-28-140 Cherokee C	28-26694	N11C	15. 9.70	Transcourt Ltd and Turweston Flying School Ltd	Turweston	25. 2.08T
G-AYJW	Reims FR172G Rocket	FR17200225		17. 9.70	N D Wyndow tr Sir W G Armstrong-Whitworth Flying Group	Coventry	19 .4.08E
G-AYJY	Isaacs Fury II *(Built A V Francis) (RR Continental C90)*	PFA 1373		23. 9.70	M S Pettit tr The G-AYJY Group	Bidford	22. 2.08P
G-AYKD	SAN Jodel DR.1050 Ambassadeur	351	F-BKHR	30. 9.70	M D L Weston *"Isis"*	Popham	23. 7.08
G-AYKJ	SAN Jodel D 117A	730	F-BIDX	6.10.70	R J Hughes	(Hepworth, Diss)	20 6.08P
G-AYKK	SAN Jodel D 117	378	F-BHGM	6.10.70	J M Whitham (Delves Farm, Delves, Huddersfield) *(New owner 3.04)*		22. 5.85S
G-AYKS	Leopoldoff L 7 Colibri *(Continental A65)*	125	F-PCZX F-APZQ	8.10.70	W B Cooper	Walkeridge Farm, Overton	11.11.08P
G-AYKT	SAN Jodel D 117	507	F-BGYY F-OAYY	9.10.70	D I Walker	Popham	22. 2.08P
G-AYKW	Piper PA-28-140 Cherokee C	28-26931	N11C	12.10.70	S P Rooney and D Griffiths	Southend	11. 5.08E
G-AYKZ	SAI Kramme KZ-VIII *(DH Gipsy Major 7)*	202	HB-EPB OY-ACB	13.10.70	R E Mitchell *(Stored 11.06)*	Sleap	17. 7.81P
G-AYLA	AESL Airtourer T2 (115) *(Built Glos Air Ltd)*	524		12.10.70	D S P Disney	Bristol	28. 6.09
G-AYLC	CEA Jodel DR.1051 Sicile	536	F-BLZG	12.10.70	E W B Trollope	Wing Farm, Longbridge Deverill	15. 4.08P
G-AYLF	CEA Jodel DR.1051 Sicile	547	F-BLZQ	14.10.70	R Twigg and L Daglish tr Sicile Flying Group	Rectory Farm, Abbotsley	8. 8.08E
G-AYLL	CEA Jodel DR.1050 Ambassadeur	11	F-BJHK	27.10.70	C Joly	Lee-on-Solent	9. 2.10S
G-AYLP	American AA-1 Yankee	AA1-0445	EI-AVV G-AYLP	21.10.70	D Nairn *(Noted 5.05)*	Haverfordwest	10. 2.02
G-AYLV	Wassmer Jodel D 120 Paris-Nice	300	F-BNCG	27.10.70	M R Henham *(Noted 11.06)*	Stancombe Farm, Askerswell	13. 9.83P
G-AYLZ	SPP Super Aero 45 Series 04	06-014	9M-AOF F-BILP	2.11.70	M J Cobb *(Damaged Andrewsfield 2. 1.76: stored 7.05)*	(Charlwood)	11. 6.76
G-AYME	Fournier RF5	5089		6.11.70	R D Goodger and C J Norman	Fowle Hall Farm, Laddingford	3. 9.08P
G-AYMK	Piper PA-28-140 Cherokee C	28-26772	N11C (PT-DPU)	17.11.70	T J Parish tr Piper Flying Group	Newcastle	18.11.07E
G-AYMO	Piper PA-23-250 Aztec C	27-2995	5Y-ACX N5845Y, (N5844Y)	18.11.70	J A D Richardson	Wellesbourne Mountford	1. 8.08E
G-AYMP	Phoenix Currie Wot Special *(Built E H Gould)*	PFA 3014		8.11.70	R C Hibberd *(New owner 11.06)*	(Chiseldon, Swindon)	4.10.94P
G-AYMR	Lederlin 380L Ladybug *(Built J S Brayshaw - pr.no.PFA 1513) (Continental C90)*	EAA/55189		19.11.70	P Brayshaw *(Last reported under construction 1992)*	(Harrogate)	
G-AYMU	Wassmer Jodel D 112	1015	F-BJPB	23.11.70	M R Baker *(Damaged Hailsham, East Sussex 7.1.92: on rebuild 2004)*	(Eastbourne)	5. 6.92P
G-AYMV	Western 20 Balloon (Hot Air)	002		23.11.70	R G Turnball *"Tinkerbelle" (Active 10.05)*	Clyro, Hereford	
G-AYNA	Phoenix Currie Wot *(Built R W Hart) (Continental A65)*	PFA 3016		25.11.70	J James	Enstone	6. 8.08P
G-AYND	Cessna 310Q	310Q0110	N7610Q	2.12.70	Source Group Ltd	Bournemouth	12. 4.08
G-AYNF	Piper PA-28-140 Cherokee C	28-26778	N11C (PT-DPV)	3.12.70	BW Aviation Ltd	Wellesbourne Mountford	9. 8.08E
G-AYNJ	Piper PA-28-140 Cherokee C	28-26810	N11C	3.12.70	P C Bird tr Cherry Tree Group	Haverfordwest	12.12.07E
G-AYNN	Cessna 185B Skywagon	185-0518	8R-GCC VP-GCC, N2518Z	11.12.70	Bencray Ltd *(Operated Blackpool and Fylde Aero Club)*	Blackpool	31 5.08T
G-AYOW	Cessna 182N Skylane	18260481	N8941G	6. 1.71	D W and S E Suttill	Full Sutton	25. 6.08E
G-AYOY	Sikorsky S-61N	61-476		7. 1.71	British International Ltd	Plymouth	21. 4.08E
G-AYOZ	Reims Cessna FA150L Aerobat	FA1500085		7. 1.71	P D Stell	Fenland	15. 3.08E
G-AYPE	MBB BÖ.209 Monsun 160RV	123	D-EFJA	11. 1.71	Papa Echo Ltd *"Buswells Spirit"*	Biggin Hill	10.11.06
G-AYPG	Reims Cessna F177RG Cardinal RG *(Wichita c/n 17700102)*	F177RG0007		11. 1.71	D P McDermott	Haverfordwest	17. 3.08E
G-AYPH	Reims Cessna F177RG Cardinal RG *(Wichita c/n 17700146)*	F177RG0018		11. 1.71	M R and K E Slack	Cambridge	27. 5.07
G-AYPJ	Piper PA-28-180 Cherokee E	28-5821	N11C	12. 1.71	R B Petrie *(Noted 3.07)*	Caernarfon	1.10.04T
G-AYPM	Piper PA-18 Super Cub 95 *(L-18C-PI) (Frame No.18-1282)*	18-1373	French Army 18-1373 13. 1.71 51-15373		R Horner Trenchard Farm, Eggesford *(As "115373-A-373" in US Army c/s)*		27. 7.08P
G-AYPO	Piper PA-18 Super Cub 95 *(L-18C-PI) (RR Continental O-200-A)*	18-1615	French Army 18-1615 13. 1.71 51-15615		A W Knowles	Plymouth	25. 7.08E
	(Rebuilt 1984 using OO-TSJ c/n 18-1398 (Frame No.18-1325) and ex LN-TSJ, OO-HMH, 51-15398)						
G-AYPS	Piper PA-18 Super Cub 95 *(L-18C-PI)*	18-2092	French Army 18-2092 13. 1.71 52-2492		B C Hockley, R J Hamlett, D G and L G Callow	North Weald	20. 4.08P
G-AYPT	Piper PA-18 Super Cub 95 *(L-18C-PI) (RR Continental O-200-A) (Frame No.18-1508)*	18-1533	(D-EALX) 13. 1.71 French Army 18-1533, 51-15533		R G Brooks and T F Lyddon	Dunkeswell	28. 6.08E
G-AYPU	Piper PA-28R-200 Cherokee Arrow II	28R-7135005	N11C	13. 1.71	Monalto Investments Ltd	Jersey	20. 4.08E
G-AYPV	Piper PA-28-140 Cherokee D	28-7125039	N11C	13. 1.71	Ashley Gardner Flying Club Ltd	Ronaldsway	6. 9.08E
G-AYPZ	Campbell Cricket *(Volkswagen 1600)*	CA-343		13. 1.71	A Melody	Henstridge	21. 4.04P
G-AYRF	Reims Cessna F150L	F15000665		14. 1.71	D T A Rees	Haverfordwest	25.11.00T
	(Crashed Upper Welson Farm, Haverfordwest 13. 3.99)						
G-AYRG	Reims Cessna F172K	F17200761		14. 1.71	I G Harrison	Derby	8.12.07E

G-AYRH	GEMS MS.892A Rallye Commodore 150	10558	F-BNBX	14. 1.71	S O'Ceallaigh and J Barry	Haverfordwest	13. 1.03
					(Noted 11.05)		
G-AYRI	Piper PA-28R-200 Cherokee Arrow II		N11C	15. 1.71	A E Thompson and J C Houdret	White Waltham	6.11.07E
		28R-7135004					
G-AYRM	Piper PA-28-140 Cherokee D	28-7125049	N11C	19. 1.71	M J Saggers	Biggin Hill	15.10.07E
G-AYRO	Reims Cessna FA150L Aerobat	FA15000102		21. 1.71	S M C Harvey tr Fat Boys Flying Club		
						Hinton-in-the-Hedges	3. 8.07T
G-AYRS	Wassmer Jodel D 120A Paris-Nice	255	F-BMAV	22. 1.71	L R H D'Eath	Knettishall	8. 5.08P
G-AYRT	Reims Cessna F172K	F17200777		22. 1.71	P E Crees	Rhosgoch	15. 4.08E
G-AYRU	Britten-Norman BN-2A-6 Islander	181	G-51-181	22. 1.71	Skydive Aircraft Ltd	AAC Netheravon	16. 6.08E
			OH-BNA, G-51-181				
G-AYSB	Piper PA-30 Twin Comanche C	30-1916	N8760Y	1. 2.71	M J Abbott	(Cereste, France)	18.11.07E
G-AYSD	Slingsby T 61A Falke	1726		4. 2.71	P W Hextall (Stored 1.95)	Tatenhill	29. 4.94
G-AYSH	Taylor JT.1 Monoplane	PFA 1413		10. 2.71	C J Lodge	Retreat Farm, Little Baddow	21. 5.08P
	(Built C J Lodge)						
G-AYSX	Reims Cessna F177RG Cardinal RG			17. 2.71	A P R Dean	Liverpool	16. 5.08E
	(Wichita c/n 17700175)	F177RG0024					
G-AYSY	Reims Cessna F177RG Cardinal RG			17. 2.71	S A Tuer	Waterstones Farm, Newby Wiske	17.12.07E
	(Wichita c/n 17700180)	F177RG0026			(Noted 2.08)		
G-AYTR	Menavia Piel CP.301A Emeraude	229	F-BIMD	3. 3.71	G Herbert tr Croft Farm Flying Group		
						Croft Farm, Defford	9. 9.06P
G-AYTT	Phoenix PM-3 Duet	PFA 841		4. 3.71	R B Webber and J K Houlgrave		
	(Built A J Knowles) (Officially regd as "Luton Minor III Duet") (Continental C90)					Trenchard Farm, Eggesford	11. 9.08P
G-AYTV	Jurca MJ.2D Tempête	PFA 2002		10. 3.71	C W Kirk tr Shoestring Flying Group		
	(Built A Baggallay) (Continental C90)					Swanborough Farm, Lewes	4. 9.07P
G-AYUA	Auster AOP.9	B5/10/119	7855M	12. 3.71	P T Bolton	(Widmerpool. Keyworth, Nottingham)	
			XK416				
G-AYUB	CEA Jodel DR.253B Régent	185		15. 3.71	D S Brown and V H R Gray tr Rothwell Group		
						Rothwell Lodge Farm, Kettering	19.10.07E
G-AYUH	Piper PA-28-180 Cherokee F	28-7105042	N11C	17. 3.71	Broadland Flying Group Ltd	Old Buckenham	11. 4.08E
G-AYUJ	Evans VP-1 Series 2	PFA 1538		17. 3.71	T N Howard	Barton Ashes	6. 8.08P
	(Built J A Wills) (Volkswagen 1776)				"Unforgettable Juliet"		
G-AYUM	Slingsby T 61A Falke	1730		19. 3.71	N A Stone and M H Simms	Shipdham	10. 6.02
					(Unmarked and on rebuild 8.06)		
G-AYUN	Slingsby T 61A Falke	1731		19. 3.71	R J Watts tr G-AYUN Group	Rattlesden	15. 6.08E
G-AYUP	Slingsby T 61A Falke	1735	XW983	19. 3.71	P R Williams	Bicester	15. 7.96
			G-AYUP		(Stored 2.97)		
G-AYUR	Slingsby T 61A Falke	1736		19. 3.71	R Hannigan and R Lingard tr Falke G-AYUR Flying Group		
						Strubby	14. 4.08
G-AYUS	Taylor JT.1 Monoplane	PFA 1412		19. 3.71	S P Collins	Hill Farm, Nayland	5. 8.05P
	(Built D G J Barker)				(Noted 2.06)		
G-AYUT	SAN Jodel DR.1050 Ambassadeur	479	F-BLJZ	22. 3.71	M L Robinson "Roland"	Kirkbride	20. 7.08
G-AYUV	Reims Cessna F172H	F17200752		26. 3.71	Justgold Ltd (Noted 10.07)	Blackpool	15. 3.07E
G-AYVO	Wallis WA-120 Series 1	K/602/X		6. 4.71	K H Wallis	Reymerston Hall, Norfolk	31.12.75P
	(130hp RR Continental O-240-B)				(Stored 8.01)		
G-AYVP	Aerosport Woody Pusher	181		6. 4.71	J R Wraight	(Chatham)	
	(Built J R Wraight - pr.no.PFA 1344)				(Stored incomplete)		
G-AYWD	Cessna 182N Skylane	18260468	N8928G	15. 4.71	S I Zorb tr Wild Dreams Group	Leicester	22.12.07E
G-AYWE	Piper PA-28-140 Cherokee C	28-26826	N5910U	16. 4.71	Intelcomm (UK) Ltd	Andrewsfield	30. 5.05
	(Had accident Denham 2004/5?: dismantled and to local scrap yard 11.05: wings noted 1.06 - remains on CAA UK Register 2.08)						
G-AYWH	SAN Jodel D 117A	844	F-BIVO	16. 4.71	D Kynaston	Cold Harbour Farm, Willingham	16. 7.08P
G-AYWM	AESL Airtourer T5 (Super 150)	A 534		16. 4.71	J E Gittins tr Star Flying Group	Gloucestershire	8. 7.09
G-AYWT	AIA Stampe SV-4C(G)	1111	F-BLEY	21. 4.71	R A Palmer	(Weybridge)	20. 3.06T
			F-BAGL				
G-AYXP	SAN Jodel D 117A	693	F-BIDD	27. 4.71	G N Davies	Shobdon	25. 9.08P
G-AYXS	SIAI-Marchetti S 205-18R	4-165	OY-DNG	28. 4.71	P J Bloore and J M Biles		
						Wellesbourne Mountford	26. 6.08E
G-AYXU	Champion 7KCAB Citabria	232-70	N7587F	28. 4.71	A G Hatton	(Cwm Head, Church Stretton)	16. 4.08E
G-AYYL	Slingsby T 61A Falke	1738		10. 5.71	C Wood	(Aston Clinton, Aylesbury)	2. 6.83
					(Suffered gale damage Manston 15.12.82: on rebuild 7.90)		
G-AYYO	CEA Jodel DR.1050/M1 Sicile Record	622	EI-BAI	11. 5.71	D J M White tr Bustard Jodel Group		
			G-AYYO, F-BMPZ			Boscombe Down	3. 7.08
G-AYYT	CEA Jodel DR.1050/M1 Sicile Record	587	F-BMGU	13. 5.71	W R Prescott tr Yankee Tango Group		
					(Dismantled 7.07)	Ballymageough, Kilkeel	7. 9.06P
G-AYYU	Beech C23 Musketeer Custom	M-1353		14. 5.71	D M Powell tr G-AYYU Group	Sturgate	6. 6.08E
G-AYYX	SOCATA MS.880B Rallye Club	1812		18. 5.71	J G MacDonald	Morgansfield, Fishburn	13. 7.08E
G-AYZE	Piper PA-39 Twin Comanche C/R	39-92	N8934Y	20. 5.71	J E Balmer	Gloucestershire	18. 9.08
G-AYZH	Taylor JT.2 Titch	PFA 060-1316		21. 5.71	T D Gardner	Halfpenny Green	30. 5.08P
	(Built T D Gardner) (Original regd to K Munro as pr.no. PFA 1316)						
G-AYZI	SNCAN Stampe SV-4C	15	(EI- . . .)	24. 5.71	D M and P A Fenton	(Sheffield City)	13.11.06
			G-AYZI, F-BBAA, French AF				
G-AYZK	CEA Jodel DR.1050/M1 Sicile Record	590	F-BMGY	24. 5.71	D G Hesketh	Streethay Farm, Lichfield	8.10.06
G-AYZS	Druine D 62B Condor	RAE 650		4. 6.71	M N Thrush	Manor Farm, Inglesham	5.12.05P
	(Built Rollason Aircraft and Engines)						
G-AYZU	Slingsby T 61A Falke	1740		4. 6.71	A J Harpley	Waterstones Farm, Newby Wiske	10. 6.07
					(Dismantled 2.08)		
G-AYZW	Slingsby T 61A Falke	1743		4. 6.71	I D Walton t/a G-ZW Group	Long Mynd	13. 9.08E

G-AZAA - G-AZZZ

G-AZAB	Piper PA-30 Twin Comanche B	30-1475	5H-MNM	8. 6.71	Bickertons Aerodromes Ltd	Denham	22. 9.07T
			5Y-AGB				
G-AZAJ	Piper PA-28R-200 Cherokee Arrow II		N11C	18. 6.71	J C McHugh and P Woulfe	Stapleford	13. 7.08E
		28R-7135116					

Reg	Type	C/n	Prev id	Date	Owner/operator	Location	Fate
G-AZAW	Sud-Aviation Gardan GY-80-160 Horizon	104	F-BMUL	24. 6.71	J W Foley tr G-AZAW Group	Inverness	1.11.07E
G-AZBB	MBB BÖ.209 Monsun 160FV	137	D-EFJO	1. 7.71	G N Richardson t/a GN Richardson Motors	Oaksey Park	3. 5.08
G-AZBE	AESL Airtourer T5 (Super 150)	A 535		5. 7.71	R G Vincent tr BE Flying Group	Gloucestershire	8. 3.09
G-AZBI	SAN Jodel D 150 Mascaret	43	F-BMFB	12. 7.71	F M Ward	AAC Dishforth	4. 3.08P
G-AZBL	Jodel D 9 Bébé	PFA 938		12. 7.71	J Hill	(Dudley)	15.10.85P
	(Built D S Morgans) (Volkswagen 1500)				(On rebuild 1993 ?)		
G-AZBN	Noorduyn AT-16-ND Harvard IIB	14A-1431	PH-HON	13. 7.71	Swaygate Ltd	Goodwood	23. 5.08P
			R Neth.AF B-97, FT391, 43-13132 (As "FT391" in RAF c/s)				
G-AZBU	Auster AOP.9	xxxx	7862M	15. 7.71	K Brooks tr Auster Nine Group	Tollerton	19. 5.08P
	(Officially regd with Frame no.AUS/183)		XR246		(As "XR246" in RAE c/s)		
G-AZCB	SNCAN Stampe SV-4C	140	F-BBCR	21. 7.71	M L Martin	Shoreham	11. 9.10S
G-AZCE	Pitts S-1C	373.H		26. 7.71	R J Oulton	(Tutshill, Chepstow)	18. 6.76S
	(Built R J Oulton - pr.no.PFA 1527) (Lycoming O-235)				(Crashed Eastbach Farm, Coleford 2. 9.75)		
G-AZCK	Beagle B 121 Pup Series 2	B121-153		30. 7.71	D R Newell	Newtownards	29. 8.08
G-AZCL	Beagle B 121 Pup Series 2	B121-154		30. 7.71	J J Watts and D Fletcher	Bournemouth	8. 7.08T
					(Operated Bournemouth Flying Club)		
G-AZCN	Beagle B 121 Pup Series 2	B121-156	HB-NAY	30. 7.71	D M Callaghan, E J and T M Spencer	Derby	5. 7.08S
			G-AZCN				
G-AZCP	Beagle B 121 Pup Series 1	B121-158	(D-EKWA)	30. 7.71	T J Watson	Elstree	17. 7.08E
			G-AZCP				
G-AZCT	Beagle B 121 Pup Series 1	B121-161		30. 7.71	J Coleman	Sywell	4. 8.08T
G-AZCU	Beagle B 121 Pup Series 1	B121-162		30. 7.71	A A Harris	Shobdon	13. 9.08S
G-AZCV	Beagle B 121 Pup Series 2	B121-163	HB-NAR	30. 7.71	N R W Long	Henstridge	15. 9.08S
			G-AZCV			(Great Circle Design titles)		
G-AZCZ	Beagle B 121 Pup Series 2	B121-167		30. 7.71	L and J M Northover	Cardiff	21. 8.08T
G-AZDA	Beagle B 121 Pup Series 1	B121-168		30. 7.71	B D Deubelbeiss	Elstree	23. 7.09
G-AZDD	MBB BÖ.209 Monsun 150FF	143	D-EBJC	3. 8.71	J D Hall and D Lawrence tr Double Delta Flying Group	Rochester	20. 3.07
G-AZDE	Piper PA-28R-200 Cherokee Arrow II	28R-7135141	N11C	3. 8.71	A M Alam	Cranfield	20. 4.08E
G-AZDG	Beagle B 121 Pup Series 2	B121-145	(G-BLYM)	17. 6.85	J R Heaps	Elstree	2. 8.08S
			HB-NAM, (VH-EPT), G-35-145 (DHL titles)				
G-AZDJ	Piper PA-32-300 Cherokee Six D	32-7140068	OY-AJK	23. 8.71	Delta Juliet Ltd	Cardiff	16. 4.08E
			G-AZDJ, N5273S				
G-AZDX	Piper PA-28-180 Cherokee F	28-7105186	N11C	25. 8.71	M Cowan	Hundon	3. 4.08
G-AZDY	de Havilland DH.82A Tiger Moth	86559	F-BGDJ	25. 8.71	J B Mills	(Sawbridgeworth)	18. 8.97
	(Built Morris Motors Ltd)		French AF, PG650		(New owner 11.04)		
G-AZEE	Morane Saulnier MS.880B Rallye Club	74	F-BKKA	1. 9.71	J Shelton	Water Leisure Park, Skegness	27. 9.98
	(Composite including fuselage of G-AZNJ c/n 5375 in 1980)				(Noted 4.04)		
G-AZEF	Wassmer Jodel D 120 Paris-Nice	321	F-BNZS	1. 9.71	P R Sears	(Tamworth)	29. 5.08P
G-AZEG	Piper PA-28-140 Cherokee D	28-7125530	N11C	1. 9.71	The Ashley Gardner Flying Club Ltd	Ronaldsway	3. 7.08E
G-AZET	Scottish Aviation Bulldog Series 100/101	BH100/122	SE-LNN	9. 9.71	P S Shuttleworth	East Winch	31. 1.72S
			Swedish Army Fv61019, G-AZET (Noted 5.07)				
G-AZEV	Beagle B 121 Pup Series 2	B121-131	VH-EPM	15. 9.71	C J Partridge	Popham	23. 8.08
			G-35-131				
G-AZEW	Beagle B 121 Pup Series 2	B121-132	VH-EPN	15. 9.71	D and M Bonsall t/a Dukeries Aviation	Netherthorpe	24. 3.09S
			G-35-132				
G-AZEY	Beagle B 121 Pup Series 2	B121-136	HB-NAK	15. 9.71	M E Reynolds	(Iping, Midhurst)	8. 7.08
			G-AZEY, VH-EPP, G-35-136				
G-AZFA	Beagle B 121 Pup Series 2	B121-143	VH-EPR	15. 9.71	J Smith	Sandown, Isle of Wight	18. 6.09
			G-35-143				
G-AZFC	Piper PA-28-140 Cherokee D	28-7125486	N11C	16. 9.71	P Hennessy tr WLS Flying Group	White Waltham	22.11.07E
G-AZFF	Wassmer Jodel D 112	1175	F-BLFI	17. 9.71	J Bolger	(Bennetts Bridge, County Kilkenny)	26. 1.08P
G-AZFI	Piper PA-28R-200 Cherokee Arrow II	28R-7135160	N11C	21. 9.71	GAZFI Ltd	Sherburn-in-Elmet	6. 4.08E
G-AZFM	Piper PA-28R-200 Cherokee Arrow II	28R-7135218	N11C	24. 9.71	P J Jenness	Compton Abbas	21. 9 07
					(Noted 1.08)		
G-AZFR	Cessna 401B	401B0121	N7981Q	30. 9.71	R E Wragg	(St Andrew, Guernsey)	17. 1.08E
G-AZGA	Wassmer Jodel D 120 Paris-Nice	144	F-BIXV	30. 9.71	A F Vizoso	RAF Halton	11. 4.08P
G-AZGC	SNCAN Stampe SV-4C	120	F-BCGE	4.10.71	V Lindsay	Folly Farm, Hungerford	22. 2.91
	(Damaged taxying Folly Farm, Hungerford 28. 5.90: cancelled 19. 9.00 by CAA: fuselage stored 7.06)						
G-AZGE	SNCAN Stampe SV-4C	576	F-BDDV	6.10.71	M R L Astor (Stored 3.97)	(East Hatley, Tadlow)	15. 8.94
G-AZGF	Beagle B 121 Pup Series 2	B121-076	PH-KUF	6.10.71	K Singh	Barton	2. 5.98
			G-35-076			(Noted 10.07)		
G-AZGL	SOCATA MS.894A Rallye Minerva 220	119291		7.10.71	The Cambridge Aero Club Ltd	Cambridge	20.12.07T
G-AZGY	Rousseau Piel CP.301B Emeraude	122	F-BRAA	12.10.71	R H Braithwaite	Barton	5. 7.08P
G-AZGZ	de Havilland DH.82A Tiger Moth	86489	F-BGCF	13.10.71	R J King	Rush Green	19. 9.08S
	(Built Morris Motors Ltd)		French AF, NM181		(As "NM181" in RAF c/s)		
G-AZHB	Robin HR.100-200B Royal	118		14.10.71	P Fenwick	Headcorn	4. 7.08E
G-AZHC	Wassmer Jodel D 112	585	F-BIQQ	18.10.71	T N Appleyard tr Aerodel Flying Group	Netherthorpe	24. 8.06P
G-AZHD	Slingsby T 61A Falke	1753		18.10.71	R J Shallcrass	Challock	4. 9.08E
G-AZHH	K & S SA 102.5 Cavalier	PFA 1393		20.10.71	D W Buckle	Morton Carr Farm, Nunthorpe	20. 1.00P
	(Built D Buckle) (Lycoming O-290)						
G-AZHI	AESL Airtourer T5 (Super 150)	A 540		20.10.71	Flying Grasshoppers Ltd	Rochester	23. 4.09S
G-AZHK	Robin HR.100-200B Royal	113	G-ILEG	22.10.71	G I Applin	Fairoaks	6. 6.08E
			G-AZHK				
G-AZHR	Piccard Ax6 Balloon (Hot Air)	617	N17US	27.10.71	C Fisher tr Halcyon Balloon Group	Aston, Sheffield	
					"Happiness"		
G-AZHT	AESL Airtourer 115	525		29.10.71	Aviation West Ltd	(Glasgow)	29. 1.89T
	(Continental O-240)				(New owner 3.03)		
G-AZHU	Phoenix Luton LA-4A Minor	PFA 839		1.11.71	W Cawrey	Netherthorpe	7. 5.07P
	(Built A E Morris) (Volkswagen 1834)						
G-AZIB	SOCATA ST-10 Diplomate	141		4.11.71	W B Bateson (Noted 10.07)	Blackpool	17. 2.07

Reg	Type	C/n	Prev id	Date	Owner/Operator	Location	Status
G-AZID	Reims Cessna FA150L Aerobat	FA1500083	N9447	8.11.71	Aerobat Ltd	Halfpenny Green	1. 5.08E
G-AZII	SAN Jodel D 117	A 848	F-BNDO F-OBFO	12.11.71	P J Brayshaw	Haddock Stone Farm, Markington	11. 4.01P
G-AZIJ	Robin DR.360 Chevalier	634		15.11.71	F M Carter	Fenland	9. 7.08E
G-AZIK	Piper PA-34-200 Seneca	34-7250018	N2392T	15.11.71	Silvergate Leisure Ltd	Earls Colne	2. 6.08E
G-AZIL	Slingsby T 61A Falke	1756		16.11.71	D W Savage	Arbroath	8. 3.08E
G-AZIP	Cameron O-65 Balloon (Hot Air)	29		24.11.71	P G Dunnington tr Dante Balloon Group	Hungerford	5. 5.81A
	"Dante" (Non-airworthy - inflated 9.05)						
G-AZJC	Fournier RF5	5108		30.11.71	W S V Stoney	(Arezzo, Italy)	1. 5.02P
G-AZJE	Gardan GY-20 Minicab	JBE.1		1.12.71	J B Evans	Ventnor, Isle of Wight	7. 7.82P
	(Built J B Evans - pr.no.PFA 1806 to JB.01 Minicab standard) (Continental C90)				*(Stored 1.98)*		
G-AZJN	Robin DR.300-140 Major	642		6.12.71	J F Wright	Cherry Tree Farm, Monewden	7. 8.08E
G-AZJV	Reims Cessna F172L	F17200810		8.12.71	M W Smith tr GAZJV Flying Group	Exeter	23. 3.08
G-AZJY	Reims Cessna FRA150L Aerobat	FRA1500126		8.12.71	P J McCartney	Barton	7. 7.07
G-AZKC	SOCATA MS.880B Rallye Club	1914		8.12.71	L J Martin	Sandown, Isle of Wight	25. 2.08E
G-AZKE	SOCATA MS.880B Rallye Club	1950	(LX-SDT)	8.12.71	J D Headlam tr Kayee Flyers	Southend	11. 4.08E
G-AZKK	Cameron O-56 Balloon (Hot Air)	32		13.12.71	P J Green and C Bosley tr Gemini Balloon Group		
					"Gemini" (Inflated 4.06)	Oakley, Basingstoke	23.12.82A
G-AZKO	Reims Cessna F337F Super Skymaster	F33700041		20.12.71	G James	Sleap	30. 8.08E
	(Wichita c/n 33701380)				*"Bird Dog"*		
G-AZKP	SAN Jodel D 117	419	F-BHND	20.12.71	A M and J L Moar	Wick	31. 5.08P
G-AZKR	Piper PA-24 Comanche	24-2192	N7044P	23.12.71	J van der Kwast	Rochester	19. 6.08E
G-AZKS	American AA-1A Trainer	0334	N6134L	23.12.71	M D Henson	Coventry	2.. 1.08E
G-AZKW	Reims Cessna F172L	F17200836		23.12.71	J C C Wright	Hinton-in-the-Hedges	5. 6.08E
G-AZKZ	Reims Cessna F172L	F17200814		23.12.71	R D Forster	Ellough, Beccles	9. 9.07T
G-AZLE	Boeing Stearman E75 (N2S-5) Kaydet	75-8543	CF-XRD N5619N, Bu43449	29.12.71	A E Poulsom	Manor Farm, Tongham	31. 5.10
	(Continental W670)				*(As "1102:102" in US Navy c/s)*		
G-AZLF	Wassmer Jodel D 120 Paris-Nice	230	F-BLFL	30.12.71	M S C Ball	Garston Farm, Marshfield	21. 3.08P
G-AZLH	Reims Cessna F150L	F15000757		31.12.71	L Papatheocharis and I Buck	Cranfield	30.11.03T
					(Noted 1.07)		
G-AZLN	Piper PA-28-180 Cherokee F	28-7105210	N11C	3. 1.72	Liteflite Ltd	Oxford	5. 3.08E
G-AZLV	Cessna 172K	17257908	4X-ALM N79138	10. 1.72	M N Baker tr G-AZLV Flying Group	RAF Waddington	27. 5.08E
G-AZLY	Reims Cessna F150L	F15000771		10. 1.72	S Roberts	Spanhoe	26. 1.08E
G-AZMC	Slingsby T 61A Falke	1757		12. 1.72	B Molloy tr G-AZMC Group	Challock	7. 8.08E
G-AZMD	Slingsby T 61C Falke	1758		12. 1.72	R A Rice	Wellesbourne Mountford	21. 6.08E
G-AZMJ	American AA-5 Traveler	0019		27. 1.72	W R Partridge	St Merryn	31. 5.08E
G-AZMZ	SOCATA MS.893A Rallye Commodore 180	11927		8. 2.72	D R Wilcox	Lyveden	31. 8.08E
G-AZNK	SNCAN Stampe SV-4A	290	F-BKXF F-BCGZ	15. 2.72	R A G Lucas tr November Kilo Group	Redhill	2. 9.10S
					"Globird"		
G-AZNL	Piper PA-28R-200 Cherokee Arrow II	28R-7235006	N11C	16. 2.72	B P Liversidge	Poplar Hall Farm, Elmsett	11. 4.08E
G-AZNO	Cessna 182P Skylane	18261005	N7365Q	18. 2.72	A I Bird	Guernsey	4. 4.08E
G-AZNT	Cameron O-84 Balloon (Hot Air)	34		21. 2.72	N Tasker *"Oberon"*	Bristol	5. 6.85
G-AZOA	MBB BÖ.209 Monsun 150FF	183	D-EAAY	21. 2.72	M W Hurst	Seighford	15. 7.07
G-AZOB	MBB BÖ.209 Monsun 150FF	184	D-EAAZ	21. 2.72	G N Richardson	Shelsley Beauchamp, Worcester	9. 7.84
					(Crashed Droitwich 21. 8.83: stored 8.92)		
G-AZOE	AESL Airtourer T2 (115)	528		21. 2.72	B J Edmondson and J K Smithson tr G-AZOE 607 Group		
						Shotton Colliery, Peterlee	1.11.09S
G-AZOF	AESL Airtourer T5 (Super 150)	A 549		21. 2.72	C Goldsmith and R C Thursby	(Barry)	3. 5.08
G-AZOG	Piper PA-28R-200 Cherokee Arrow II	28R-7235009	N11C	21. 2.72	Atromin Ltd t/a Southend Flying Club	Southend	18. 8.07
					(Noted 1.08)		
G-AZOL	Piper PA-34-200 Seneca	34-7250075	N4348T	28. 2.72	Stapleford Flying Club Ltd	Stapleford	3. 9.08E
G-AZOO	Western O-65 Balloon (Hot Air)	015		1. 3.72	Semajan Ltd *(Inflated 4.06)*	Newbury	6. 6.77S
					"Carousel" (On loan to British Balloon Museum and Library)		
G-AZOT	Piper PA-34-200 Seneca	34-7250073	N4340T	3. 3.72	M Soojeri	Prestwick	13. 9.08E
G-AZOU	SAN Jodel DR.1050 Sicile	354	F-BJYX	7. 3.72	D Elliott and D Holl tr Horsham Flying Group		
						Wellcross Grange, Slinfold	30. 6.08
G-AZOZ	Reims Cessna FRA150L Aerobat	FRA1500136		7. 3.72	Seawing Flying Club Ltd	Southend	23. 8.08E
					"The Wizard of Oz"		
G-AZPA	Piper PA-25-235 Pawnee C	25-5223	N8797L N9749N	7. 3.72	Black Mountains Gliding Club Ltd	Talgarth	17. 2.07
G-AZPC	Slingsby T 61C Falke	1767		7. 3.72	The Surrey Hills Gliding Club Ltd	Kenley	31. 7.07
G-AZPF	Fournier RF5	5001	D-KOLT	10. 3.72	R Pye	(Barton, Preston)	23. 8.07P
G-AZPV	Phoenix Luton LA-4A Minor	PFA 833		14. 3.72	J R Faulkner	(Derby)	18. 9.97P
	(Built J Scott) (Lycoming O-145)				*(Noted 3.07)*		
G-AZPX	Western O-31 Balloon (Hot Air)	011		20. 3.72	B L King tr Eugena Rex Balloon Group	Coulsdon	
					"Eugena Rex" (Inflated 4.06)		
G-AZRA	MBB BÖ.209 Monsun 150FF	192	D-EAIH	21. 3.72	Alpha Flying Ltd	Wycombe Air Park	6. 4.08
G-AZRD	Cessna 401B	401B0218	N7999Q	22. 3.72	G Hatton tr Romeo Delta Group	Blackpool	6. 4.06T
					(Noted 10.07)		
G-AZRH	Piper PA-28-140 Cherokee D	28-7125585	N11C	23. 3.72	H B Carter tr Trust Flying Group	Jersey	19.10.07E
					(Noted 1.08)		
G-AZRI	Payne Free Balloon (Hot Air) (56,500 cu.ft)GFP.1			21. 3.72	C A Butter and J J T Cooke t/a Aardvark Balloon Company		
	(Built G F Payne)				*"Shoestring"*	Newbury and Southall	
G-AZRK	Fournier RF5	5112		23. 3.72	J F Rogers and A B Clymo	Shenington	17. 6.08E
G-AZRL	Piper PA-18 Super Cub 95	18-1331	OO-SBR	23. 3.72	M G Fountain	Leicester	22.12.07
	(L-18C-PI) *(Frame No.18-1213)*		OO-HML, French Army 18-1331, 51-15331				
G-AZRM	Fournier RF5	5111		24. 3.72	R Speer and M Millar tr Romeo Mike Group		
	(Volkswagen 1834)					Ringmer	7. 5.07P
G-AZRN	Cameron O-84 Balloon (Hot Air)	28		28. 3.72	C J Desmet	Brussels, Belgium	4. 7.81A
G-AZRP	AESL Airtourer T2 (115)	529		28. 3.72	B F Strawford	Shobdon	28. 1.11
G-AZRS	Piper PA-22-150 Caribbean	22-5141	XT-AAH	28. 3.72	R H Hulls	Oaksey Park	30. 7.08E
			F-OCGZ, French Army 22-5141, "FMKAC", N10F *"Sandpiper"*				

G-AZRZ	Cessna U206F Stationair	U20601803	N9603G	4. 4.72	Hinton Skydiving Centre Ltd	Perranporth	19. 6.08
G-AZSA	Stampe et Renard Stampe SV-4B	1203	Belgian AF V-61	5. 4.72	M R Dolman	(Cliddesden, Basingstoke)	2.12.10S
	(Officially regd with c/n 64)						
G-AZSC	Noorduyn AT-16-ND Harvard IIB	14A-1363	PH-SKK	7. 4.72	Goodwood Road Racing Company Ltd	Goodwood	5. 9.08S
			R Neth AF B-19, FT323, 43-13064 *(As "43:SC" in USAAF c/s)*				
G-AZSF	Piper PA-28R-200 Cherokee Arrow II		N11C	10. 4.72	Plane Talking Ltd	Elstree	5. 9.08E
		28R-7235048					
G-AZSW	Beagle B 121 Pup Series 1	B121-140	PH-VRT	24. 4.72	T A White	Bagby	15. 6.09
			G-35-140		*(Hulk only 2.08)*		
G-AZTA	MBB BÖ.209 Monsun 150FF	190	D-EAIF	25. 4.72	A J Court	Franklyn's Field, Chewton Mendip	27.10.07E
G-AZTF	Reims Cessna F177RG Cardinal RG			28. 4.72	R Burgun	Derby	15. 8.08E
		F177RG0054					
G-AZTK	Cessna F172F	F17200116	PH-CON	27. 4.72	S O'Ceallaigh	Haverfordwest	20.10.00
	(Built Reims Aviation SA)		OO-SIR		*(Noted 6.05 unmarked)*		
G-AZTS	Reims Cessna F172L	F17200866		28. 4.72	R Murray and A Bagley-Murray	Humberside	1. 5.08E
G-AZTV	Stolp SA.500 Starlet	SSM.2		19. 5.72	G G Rowland	Old Sarum	19.11.92
	(Built S S Miles - pr.no.PFA 1584) (Continental C90)				*(Damaged Manor Farm, Grateley, Hampshire 4.7.92: on rebuild 1.08)*		
G-AZTW	Reims Cessna F177RG Cardinal RG			28. 4.72	I M Richmond	Panshanger	11.12.08E
		F177RG0043					
G-AZUM	Reims Cessna F172L	F17200863		11. 5.72	M S Hills tr Fowlmere Flyers	Fowlmere	20. 2.08E
G-AZUP	Cameron O-65 Balloon (Hot Air)	36		11. 5.72	R S Bailey and A B Simpson *"Eight of Hearts"* Aylesbury		23.10.77S
G-AZUT	SOCATA MS.893A Rallye Commodore 180	10963	VH-TCH	12. 5.72	J Palethorpe tr Rallye Flying Group		
						Blakedown, Kidderminster	13. 3.08E
G-AZUY	Cessna 310L	310L0012	SE-FEC	15. 5.72	W B Bateson	Blackpool	5.11.05T
			LN-LMH, N2212F		*(Noted 11.07)*		
G-AZUZ	Reims Cessna FRA150L Aerobat	FRA1500146		16. 5.72	D J Parker	Netherthorpe	18.12.08E
G-AZVA	MBB BÖ.209 Monsun 150FF	177	(D-EAAQ)	16. 5.72	C Elder	New Farm, Felton	8.11.07
G-AZVB	MBB BÖ.209 Monsun 150FF	178	(D-EAAS)	16. 5.72	E and P M L Cliffe	Tibenham	18. 7.08E
G-AZVF	SOCATA MS.894A Rallye Minerva 220	11999	(F-OCSR)	16. 5.72	J R Hepburn tr Minerva Flying Group		
						Upfield Farm, Usk	6. 4.08E
G-AZVG	American AA-5 Traveler	AA5-0075		16. 5.72	K M Whelan tr G-AZVG Group	Cranfield	8.11.07E
G-AZVH	SOCATA MS.894A Rallye Minerva 220	12017		16. 5.72	P L Jubb	Suton, Norwich	12. 7.08E
G-AZVI	SOCATA MS.892A Rallye Commodore 150	12039		6. 5.72	G C Jarvis	Henstridge	3. 6.08
G-AZVJ	Piper PA-34-200 Seneca	34-7250125	N4529T	16. 5.72	Andrews Professional Colour Laboratories Ltd		
					(Noted 8.05 less engines)	Headcorn	21. 8.03A
G-AZVL	Jodel D 119	794	F-BILB	19. 5.72	S P Collins	Hill Farm, Nayland	31. 8.07P
	(Built Etablissement Valladeau)				*(Noted 9.07)*		
G-AZVP	Reims Cessna F177RG Cardinal RG			22. 5.72	C R Brown	Oxford	28.10.07E
		F177RG0057					
G-AZWB	Piper PA-28-140 Cherokee E	28-7225244	N11C	5. 6.72	J A Tyndall tr G-AZWB Flying Group	Oaksey Park	19. 2.08E
G-AZWD	Piper PA-28-140 Cherokee E	28-7225298	N11C	6. 6.72	Whisky Delta Ltd	(Bethersden, Ashford)	6. 5.08E
G-AZWF	SAN Jodel DR.1050 Ambassadeur	130	F-BJJT	7. 6.72	J A D Reedie tr Cawdor Flying Group	Perth	17. 2.08
	(Composite including fuselage of DR.1050M F-BLJX c/n 492)						
G-AZWS	Piper PA-28R-180 Cherokee Arrow	28R-30749	N4993J	8. 6.72	G S Blair tr Arrow 88 Flying Group	Eshott	7. 8.08E
G-AZWT	Westland Lysander IIIA	Y1536	RCAF 1582	9. 6.72	Richard Shuttleworth Trustees	Old Warden	24. 4.08P
			V9552		*(As "V9367:MA-B" in RAF 161 Sqdn c/s)*		
G-AZWY	Piper PA-24-260 Comanche C	24-4806	N9310P	16. 6.72	Keymer, Son and Company Ltd	Biggin Hill	15. 6.08E
G-AZXB	Cameron O-65 Balloon (Hot Air)	48		20. 6.72	R J Mitchener and P F Smart t/a Balloon Collection		
					"London Pride II"	Andover	6. 5.81A
G-AZXD	Reims Cessna F172L	F17200878		20. 6.72	R J R Williams and D Palmer	Shobdon	28. 1.08E
G-AZYA	Sud-Aviation Gardan GY-80-160 Horizon	57	F-BLPT	7. 7.72	R G Whyte	Turweston	4. 6.08E
G-AZYD	GEMS MS.893A Rallye Commodore 180	10645	F-BNSE	30. 6.72	Staffordshire Gliding Club Ltd	Seighford	12. 9.08E
G-AZYF	Piper PA-28-180 Cherokee D	28-5227	N7813M	23. 6.72	R N Bourne tr AZYF Group	Leicester	10. 5.08E
			G-AZYF, 5Y-AJK, N7813N				
	(Landed heavily on the Isles of Scilly 3. 7.06 and nosewheel detached with substantial damage)						
G-AZYS	Scintex CP.301-C1 Emeraude	568	F-BJAY	7. 7.72	C G Ferguson and D Drew	Jericho Farm, Lambley	10. 5.08P
G-AZYU	Piper PA-23-250 Aztec E	27-4601	N13983	13. 7.72	L J Martin	Bembridge, Isle of Wight	12.12.07E
G-AZYY	Slingsby T 61A Falke	1770		12. 7.72	J A Towers	Yearby	21. 8.08P
G-AZYZ	Wassmer WA.51A Pacific	30	F-OCSE	14. 7.72	C R Buxton	(Gourvillette, France)	8. 7.10
G-AZZH	Practavia Pilot Sprite 115	PFA 1532		13. 7.72	A Moore	(Hutton, Brentwood)	
	(Built K G Stewart)				*(New owner 9.04)*		
G-AZZO	Piper PA-28-140 Cherokee	28-22887	N4471J	18. 7.72	R J Hind *(Noted 9.05)*	Stapleford	6. 8.03
G-AZZR	Reims Cessna F150L	F15000690	LN-LJX	24. 7.72	E B Atalay	Kimbolton	15. 8.08E
G-AZZV	Reims Cessna F172L	F15000883		18. 7.72	Zentelligence Ltd	Rochester	7. 7.08E
G-AZZZ	de Havilland DH.82A Tiger Moth	86311	F-BGJE	27. 7.72	S W McKay	RAF Henlow	30. 1.11
	(Built Morris Motors Ltd)		French AF, NL864				

G-BAAA - G-BAZZ

G-BAAD	Evans VP-1	PFA 1540		27. 7.72	K Wigglesworth tr Breighton VP-1 Group	Breighton	20.12.07P
	(Built R W Husband) (Volkswagen 1600)						
G-BAAF	Manning-Flanders MF.1 replica	PPS/REP/8		27. 7.72	Bianchi Aviation Film Services Ltd	Compton Abbas	6. 8.96P
	(Built Personal Plane Services Ltd) (Continental C75)				*(In Flying Aces Movie Aeroplane Collection 1.06: no external marks)*		
G-BAAI	SOCATA MS.893A Rallye Commodore 180	10705	F-BOVG	31. 7.72	R D Taylor *(Noted 8.06)*	Thruxton	11. 9.00
G-BAAT	Cessna 182P Skylane	18260835	N399JF	10. 8.72	T E Earl	Blackbushe	16. 6.08E
			G-BAAT, N9295G				
G-BAAW	Jodel D 119	366	F-BHMY	11. 8.72	P J Newson tr Alpha Whiskey Flying Group		
	(Built Etablissement Valladeau) (Continental 0-200-A)					Cherry Tree Farm, Monewden	20. 7.07P
G-BABC	Reims Cessna F150L	F15000831		15. 8.72	B B Singh	(Hitchin)	30. 8.08E
G-BABD	Reims Cessna FRA150L Aerobat	FRA1500153		3. 8.72	K F Mason and D Featherby t/a Anglia Flight Norwich		5. 7.08E
G-BABE	Taylor JT.2 Titch	PEB/01		3. 8.72	M Bonsall	Netherthorpe	3. 2.05P
	(Built P E Barker - pr.no.PFA 1394) (Continental 0-200-A)				*(Overturned Elmton 15. 5.04 with serious damage to fuselage, starboard wing and engine)*		
G-BABG	Piper PA-28-180 Cherokee C	28-2031	PH-APU	15. 8.72	C E Dodge tr Mendip Flying Group	Bristol	16.12.07E
			N7978W				

Reg	Type	C/n	Prev Id	Date	Owner	Base	Expiry
G-BABK	Piper PA-34-200 Seneca	34-7250219	PH-DMN, G-BABK, N5203T	18. 8.72	D F J Flashman *(Noted 6.05)*	Biggin Hill	9. 1.05
G-BACB	Piper PA-34-200 Seneca	34-7250251	N5354T	25. 8.72	A R Braybrooke t/a Milbrooke Motors *(Noted 1.08)*	Southend	16.10.07E
G-BACE	Sportavia-Pützer Fournier RF5	5102	(PT-DVZ) D-KCID	25. 8.72	N P Harrison tr G-BACE Fournier Group	Dunkeswell	2.12.07E
G-BACJ	Wassmer Jodel D 120 Paris-Nice	315	F-BNZC	1. 9.72	J M Allan tr Wearside Flying Association	Eshott	25. 4.08P
G-BACL	SAN Jodel D 150 Mascaret	31	F-BSTY CN-TYY	4. 9.72	D F Micklethwait	Yearby	23. 2.08E
G-BACN	Reims Cessna FRA150L Aerobat	FRA1500161		4. 9.72	F Bundy	Bodmin	7. 3.08E
G-BACO	Reims Cessna FRA150L Aerobat	FRA1500163		4. 9.72	A J Hobbs	Bridge Farm, Acle, Norwich	18. 3.08E
G-BACP	Reims Cessna F150L Aerobat *(Built originally as FRA150L)*	FRA1500164		4. 9.72	M Markwick	Shoreham	23. 5.08E
G-BADC	Rollason Beta B 2A	PFA 002-10140		7. 9.72	D H Greenwood	Barton	31. 1.85P

(Built H M Mackenzie) (Originally regd to J J Feely as c/ns JJF.1 and PFA 1384 - then adopted c/n of Beta G-BETA when cancelled 3. 2.87 by CAA as "not completed": probably incorporated into final build: noted 1.07)

Reg	Type	C/n	Prev Id	Date	Owner	Base	Expiry
G-BADH	Slingsby T 61A Falke	1774		6. 9.72	A P Askwith	Rhosgoch	9. 2.08E
G-BADJ	Piper PA-E23-250 Aztec E	27-4841	N14279	11. 9.72	C Papadakis	Cranfield	2. 8.08E
G-BADM	Druine D 62B Condor	RAE 653		8. 9.72	D J Wilson	Compton Abbas	16. 7.07P

(Built K Worksworth and M Harris - pr.no.PFA 049-11442 using uncompleted Rollason build frame)

Reg	Type	C/n	Prev Id	Date	Owner	Base	Expiry
G-BADV	Brochet MB.50 Pipistrelle *(Built A Bouriquat)*	78	F-PBRJ	13. 9.72	W B Cooper *(New owner 1.05)*	Walkeridge Farm, Overton	9. 5.79P
G-BADW	Pitts S-2A *(Built Aerotek Inc)*	2035		21. 9.72	R E Mitchell *(Noted 10.06)*	Sleap	16. 9.95T
G-BAEB	Robin DR.400-160 Knight	733		19. 9.72	R Hatton	Andreas, Isle of Man	18. 4.08E
G-BAEE	CEA Jodel DR.1050/M1 Sicile Record	579	F-BMGN	29. 9.72	R Little	Jackrell's Farm, Southwater	14. 6.10
G-BAEM	Robin DR.400-120 Petit Prince	728		25. 9.72	M A Webb	Denham	2. 6.08E
G-BAEN	Robin DR.400-180 Régent	736		25. 9.72	European Soaring Club Ltd	Membury	23. 9.08E
G-BAEO	Reims Cessna F172M	F17200911		14. 9.72	L W Scattergood	Sandtoft	10 1.08E

(Re-built with original fuselage and remains of G-YTWO)

Reg	Type	C/n	Prev Id	Date	Owner	Base	Expiry
G-BAEP	Reims Cessna F150L Aerobat *(Built originally as FRA150L)*	FRA1500170		14. 9.72	A M Lynn t/a Busy Bee *(Operated RAF Marham Flying Club)*	RAF Marham	12. 5.08E
G-BAER	LeVier Cosmic Wind *(Built R S Voice - pr.no.PFA 1571) (Continental O-200-A)*	106		14. 9.72	A G Truman *(New owner 12,07)*	Lasham	18. 9.06P
G-BAET	Piper J-3C-65 Cub (L-4H) *(Frame No.11430)*	11605	OO-AJI 43-30314	26. 9.72	C J Rees	Valley Farm, Winwick	10.11.05P
G-BAEU	Reims Cessna F150L	F15000873		26. 9.72	L W Scattergood	Sandtoft	1. 7.07T
G-BAEV	Reims Cessna FRA150L Aerobat	FRA1500173		27. 9.72	B Doyle	(Kilmaley, Ennis, County Clare)	15. 4.08E
G-BAEY	Reims Cessna F172M	F17200915		28. 9.72	Skytrax Aviation Ltd	Derby	6. 4.08E
G-BAEZ	Reims Cessna FRA150L Aerobat	FRA1500169		28. 9.72	Donair Flying Club Ltd	East Midlands	26 8.07E
G-BAFA	American AA-5 Traveler	AA5-0201	N6136A	6.10.72	C F Mackley *(Noted 8.04)*	Sleap	31. 8.01
G-BAFG	de Havilland DH.82A Tiger Moth *(Built Morris Motors Ltd)*	85995	F-BGEL French.AF, EM778	13.10.72	Meinl Capital Markets Ltd	Boones Farm, Braintree	10.10.10S
G-BAFL	Cessna 182P Skylane	18261469	N21180	15. 8.72	M Langhammer	Old Sarum	20. 3.08E
G-BAFP	Robin DR.400-160 Knight	735		19.10.72	M H Hoffmann and M W Bodger	Yeatsall Farm, Abbots Bromley	5. 4.07
G-BAFT	Piper PA-18-150 Super Cub	18-5340	(D-E...) French Army 18-5340, N10F	3. 8.72	C A M Neidt	(Roosendaal, Netherlands)	2. 5.09S
G-BAFU	Piper PA-28-140 Cherokee	28-20759	PH-NLS	11.10.72	D A Carter	Standalone Farm, Meppershall	20. 6.08E
G-BAFV	Piper PA-18 Super Cub 95 *(L-18C-PI) (Frame No.18-2055)*	18-2045	PH-WJK R Neth AF R-40, 8A-40, 52-2445	24.10.72	T F and S J Thorpe	Coldharbour Farm, Willingham	22.11.10S
G-BAFW	Piper PA-28-140 Cherokee	28-21050	PH-NLT	24.10.72	A J Peters	Derby	29 4.08E
G-BAFX	Robin DR.400-140 Earl	739		30.10.72	R Foster	(Marston, Oxford)	8. 5.08E
G-BAGB	SIAI-Marchetti SF.260	1-07	LN-BIV	20.10.72	British Midland Airways Ltd	East Midlands	4. 7.08E
G-BAGC	Robin DR.400-140 Earl	737		13.10.72	S J York	(Arkendale, Knaresborough)	7.10.07E
G-BAGF	Jodel D 92 Bébé *(Built Aero Club Basse-Moselle)*	59	F-PHFC	13.11.72	E Evans	(Fobbing, Stanford-le-Hope)	

(Fuselage stored Fobbing: wings stored Benson's Farm, Laindon 1.08)

Reg	Type	C/n	Prev Id	Date	Owner	Base	Expiry
G-BAGG (2)	Piper PA-32-300 Cherokee Six	32-7340186	N9562N	7.12.73	Channel Islands Aero Club (Jersey)Ltd	Jersey	19. 2.08E
G-BAGN	Reims Cessna F177RG Cardinal RG	F177RG0068		24.10.72	R W J Andrews	Halfpenny Green	15. 3.08E
G-BAGR	Robin DR.400-140 Petit Prince	753		30.10.72	J D Last	Caernarfon	7. 6.08E
G-BAGS	Robin DR.400-100 2+2	760		30.10.72	M Whale and M W A Lunn *(On rebuild 2.08)*	Little Rissington	16. 1.03T
G-BAGT	Helio H 295 Super Courier	1288	CR-LJG	31.10.72	D C Hanss	Elstree	11.11.07E
G-BAGV	Cessna U206F Stationair	U20601867	N9667G	31.10.72	K Brady tr The Scottish Parachute Club	Strathallan	14. 5.04

(Badly damaged 5. 5.02: fuselage used for parachute training 1.05)

Reg	Type	C/n	Prev Id	Date	Owner	Base	Expiry
G-BAGX	Piper PA-28-140 Cherokee	28-23633	N3574K	30.10.72	J R Clayton tr The Golf X-Ray Group	Conington	14.12.07E
G-BAGY	Cameron O-84 Balloon (Hot Air)	54		17.10.72	P G Dunnington tr Dante Balloon Group "Beatrice" *(Stored 5.07)*	Hungerford	16. 6.81A
G-BAHD	Cessna 182P Skylane	18261501	N21228	25.10.72	J W Hardy tr Lambley Flying Group	Jericho Farm, Lambley	2. 8.08E
G-BAHE	Piper PA-28-140 Cherokee C	28-26494	N5696U	30.10.72	A O Jones and M W Kilvert *(Noted heading north from Rhayader on trailer 5.06)*	Trehelig, Welshpool	8. 6.95
G-BAHF	Piper PA-28-140 Fliteliner	28-7125215	N431FL	30.10.72	BJ Services (Midlands) Ltd	Coventry	25. 7.08E
G-BAHH	Wallis WA-121/Mc *(Wallis modified McCulloch)*	K/701/X		7.11.72	K H Wallis *(Noted 8.01)*	Reymerston Hall, Norfolk	27. 5.98T
G-BAHI	Cessna F150H *(Built Reims Aviation SA)*	F150-0330	PH-EHA	6.11.72	M Player t/a MJP Aviation and Sales	Little Staughton	14.12.07E
G-BAHJ	Piper PA-24-250 Comanche	24-1863	PH-RED N6735P	6.11.72	K Cooper	Halfpenny Green	19.12.07E
G-BAHL	Robin DR.400-160 Knight	704	F-OCSR	8.11.72	J B McVeighty	Breighton	8.11.07E
G-BAHO	Beech C23 Sundowner	M-1456		7.11.72	S C Carty	(Great Cheverell, Devizes)	18. 6.08E
G-BAHP	Volmer VJ.22 Sportsman *(Built J P Crawford) (Continental C90)*	PFA 1313		9.11.72	G K Holloway tr Seaplane Group *(Noted 4.07 on restoration)*	Aboyne	18.10.93P
G-BAHS	Piper PA-28R-200 Cherokee Arrow II	28R-7335017	N15147	9.11.72	A R N Morris	Shobdon	31. 8.08E

G-BAHX	Cessna 182P Skylane	18261588	N21363	16.11.72	A P Stone tr Dupost Group *(Noted 10.07)*	Blackpool	14. 8.06
G-BAIG	Piper PA-34-200 Seneca	34-7250243	OY-BSU	21.11.72	Mid-Anglia Flying Centre Ltd t/a Mid-Anglia School of Flying		
			G-BAIG, N5257T			Cambridge	31 1.08E
G-BAIH	Piper PA-28R-200 Cherokee Arrow II		N11C	21.11.72	M G West	King's Farm, Thurrock	13. 3.08E
		28R-7335011					
G-BAII	Reims Cessna FRA150L Aerobat	FRA1500178		22.11.72	Cornwall Flying Club Ltd	Plymouth	14. 6.03T
	(Force landed Hendra Farm, Bodmin 9.9.01 and severely damaged) (Wreck noted 4.02)						
G-BAIK	Reims Cessna F150L	F15000903		22.11.72	J W Frecklington and R Merewood t/a Wickenby Aviation		
						Wickenby	9. 4.08E
G-BAIP	Reims Cessna F150L	F15000898		13.11.72	G and S A Jones	(Linley Hill, Leven)	28. 9.97T
					(Damaged Linley Hill 30. 5.95)		
G-BAIS	Reims Cessna F177RG Cardinal RG			13.11.72	R M Graham and E P Howard tr Cardinal Syndicate		
		F177RG0069				Seething	21. 2.08E
G-BAIW	Reims Cessna F172M	F17200928		14.11.72	W J Greenfield	Humberside	13. 1.07T
G-BAIX	Reims Cessna F172M	F17200931		14.11.72	I S Mcleod and J L Yourell	(Bedford and Luton)	6. 4.06
					(New owners 7.07)		
G-BAIZ	Slingsby T 61A Falke	1776		27.11.72	R G Sangster and J J Doswell tr Falke Syndicate		
						Hinton-in-the-Hedges	25.10.07E
G-BAJA	Reims Cessna F177RG Cardinal RG			29.11.72	D W Ward	Biggin Hill	19. 6.08E
		F177RG0078					
G-BAJB	Reims Cessna F177RG Cardinal RG			29.11.72	J D Loveridge	Guernsey	19. 9.08E
		F177RG0080					
G-BAJC	Evans VP-1 Series 2	PFA 1548		30.11.72	S J Greer	Shenington	10. 6.04P
	(Built J R Clements) (Volkswagen 1834)						
G-BAJE	Cessna 177 Cardinal	17700812	N29322	30.11.72	D M Dawson tr Juliet Echo Group	Blackpool	15. 5.08E
G-BAJN	American AA-5 Traveler	AA5-0259		29.11.72	J M Cuddy	Blackpool	5. 5.08E
G-BAJO	American AA-5 Traveler	AA5-0260		29.11.72	Montgomery Aviation Ltd	Blackpool	10.10.07E
G-BAJR	Piper PA-28-180 Cherokee Challenger		N11C	1.12.72	Belfast Flying Club Ltd	Belfast International	21. 5.08E
		28-7305008					
G-BAJY	Robin DR.400-180 Régent	758		4.12.72	L J Murray	Bournemouth	28. 8.07T
G-BAJZ	Robin DR.400-2+2	759		4.12.72	Weald Air Services Ltd	Headcorn	19. 9.08E
G-BAKD	Piper PA-34-200 Seneca	34-7350013	N1378T	28.11.72	Andrews Professional Colour Laboratories Ltd	Lydd	30.12.07E
					(Operated Foto Flite)		
G-BAKH	Piper PA-28-140 Cherokee F	28-7325014	N11C	12.12.72	Keen Leasing (IOM) Ltd	Belfast International	21.11.07E
					(Operated Ulster Flying Club)		
G-BAKJ	Piper PA-30 Twin Comanche B	30-1232	TJ-AAI	13.12.72	G D Colover, R Jones and N O'Connor	Biggin Hill	19. 2.08E
			TJ-ADH, N8122Y				
G-BAKM	Robin DR.400-140 Earl	755		15.12.72	D V Pieri	Carlisle	17. 4.08E
G-BAKN	SNCAN Stampe SV-4C	348	F-BCOY	15.12.72	M Holloway	Watchford Farm, Yarcombe	25. 9.08S
G-BAKR	SAN Jodel D 117	814	F-BIOV	27.12.72	R W Brown	Stoneacre Farm, Farthing Corner	18. 9.08P
G-BAKV	Piper PA-18-150 Super Cub	18-8993	N9744N	22.12.72	W J Murray	Thruxton	17. 8.07T
G-BAKW	Beagle B 121 Pup Series 2	B121-175		15.12.72	M A Stock tr Cunning Stunts Flying Group	Redhill	21. 8.09S
G-BAKY	Slingsby T 61C Falke	1777		20.12.72	T J Wiltshire *(Noted 2.08)*	Saltby	7. 8.98
G-BALD	Cameron O-84 Balloon (Hot Air)	58		2. 1.73	C A Gould *"Puffin"*	Ipswich	7. 6.06S
G-BALF	Robin DR.400-140 Earl	772		5. 1.73	G and Dawn A Wasey	Oaksey Park	5. 7.08
G-BALG	Robin DR.400-180 Régent	771		5. 1.73	R Jones t/a Southern Sailplanes	Membury	24. 5.08
G-BALH	Robin DR.400-140B Earl	766		5. 1.73	C Johnson tr G-BALH Flying Group	Fenland	29. 3.08E
G-BALI	Robin DR.400 2+2	764		5. 1.73	A Brinkley	Standalone Farm, Meppershall	3. 9.88
					(On rebuild 3.96)		
G-BALJ	Robin DR.400-180 Régent	767		5. 1.73	D A Batt and D de Lacey-Rowe		
						Standalone Farm, Meppershall	13. 6.08E
G-BALN	Cessna T310Q	310Q0684	N7980Q	8. 1.73	O'Brien Properties Ltd	Shoreham	24. 5.08E
G-BALY	Practavia Pilot Sprite 150	"OS-10009"		10. 1.73	A L Young t/a Aly Aviation	(Henstridge)	
	(Built A L Young - pr.no.PFA 005-10009)				*(Believed not commenced)*		
G-BALZ	Bell 212	30542	EC-IPD	10. 1.73	Bristow Helicopters Ltd	Mauritania	26. 7.08E
			G-BALZ, EC-GCR, EC-931, G-BALZ, 9Y-TIL, G-BALZ, VR-BIB, N99040, G-BALZ, EI-AWK, G-BALZ, VR-BEK, N2961W					
G-BAMB	Slingsby T 61C Falke	1778		9. 1.73	N J Clemens tr Flying Group G-BAMB	Eaglescott	21. 1.07
G-BAMC	Reims Cessna F150L	F15000892		12. 1.73	K Evans	Welshpool	8. 8.08E
G-BAMJ	Cessna 182P	18261650	N21469	10. 1.73	A E Kedros	Oxford	26. 4.08E
G-BAMM	Piper PA-28-235 Cherokee Pathfinder	28-10642	SE-EOA	16. 1.73	D Clare and P Holhurst tr Group 235	Headcorn	4. 4.08
G-BAMR	Piper PA-16 Clipper	16-392	F-BFMS	12. 1.73	H Royce	Bradleys Lawn, Heathfield	29. 9.07E
	(Lycoming O-290)		CU-P339				
G-BAMS	Robin DR.400-160 Knight	774		15. 1.73	G-BAMS Ltd	Biggin Hill	8. 4.08E
G-BAMT	Robin DR.400-160 Knight	775		15. 1.73	S G Jones	(Membury)	15. 5.79
	(Crashed Cudham 8.1.78: cancelled 24.4.78 as WFU: wreck stored 1.92) (New owner 1.05)						
G-BAMU	Robin DR.400-160 Knight	778		15. 1.73	N P Tyne tr Alternative Flying Group	Sywell	22. 4.08E
G-BAMV	Robin DR.400-180 Régent	777		15. 1.73	K Jones and E A Anderson	Wycombe Air Park	8. 5.08E
G-BAMY	Piper PA-28R-200 Cherokee Arrow II		N11C	9. 1.73	S R Pool	Lydd	7. 6.08E
		28R-7335015					
G-BANA	CEA Jodel DR.221 Dauphin	73	F-BOZR	22. 1.73	G T Pryor	Tibenham	27. 9.08E
G-BANB	Robin DR.400-180 Régent	776		22. 1.73	D R L Jones	Oaksey Park	28. 4.08T
G-BANC	Gardan GY-201 Minicab	A 203	F-PCZV	22. 1.73	C R Shipley	Frogland Cross	31. 5.02P
	(Built M Ducreuzet) (Continental C90)		F-BCZV		*(New owner 9.03)*		
G-BANF	Phoenix Luton LA-4A Minor	PFA 838		22. 1.73	W J McCollum	Coagh, County Londonderry	5. 6.92P
	(Built D W Bosworth) (Continental A65)				*(Damaged Mullaghmore, Coleraine 27.6.92: noted 11.01)*		
G-BANU	Wassmer Jodel D 120 Paris-Nice	247	F-BLNZ	31. 1.73	W M and C H Kilner Shacklewell Farm, Empingham		26. 7.07P
G-BANV	Phoenix Currie Wot	PFA 3010		25. 1.73	K Knight	(Malvern)	26. 6.84P
	(Built C Turner) (Lycoming O-290)				*(Damaged near Leek, Staffs 15. 9.83)*		
G-BANW	CAARP CP.1330 Super Emeraude	941	PH-VRF	30. 1.73	P S Milner	Popham	12. 7.07P
	(Lycoming 0-235-C1)						
G-BANX	Reims Cessna F172M	F17200941		31. 1.73	Oakfleet 2000 Ltd	Biggin Hill	24. 6.08E
G-BAOB	Reims Cessna F172M	F17200949		2. 2.73	R H Taylor and S O Smith	Andrewsfield	12. 5.07T
G-BAOH	SOCATA MS.880B Rallye Club	2250		6. 2.73	A P Swain *(Noted in bare metal 6.05)*	Haverfordwest	28. 7.01
G-BAOJ	SOCATA MS.880B Rallye Club	2252		6. 2.73	R E Jones	Caernarfon	24. 5.08E

G-BAOP	Reims Cessna FRA150L Aerobat	FRA1500190		5. 2.73	R D Forster (Fuselage noted 10.07) Ellough, Beccles		11. 4.02
G-BAOS	Reims Cessna F172M	F17200946		6. 2.73	Wingtask 1995 Ltd	Seething	19. 7.08E
	(Overturned after landing on soft ground in crop field at Seething 30. 5.06 with substantial damage)						
G-BAOU	Grumman AA-5 Traveler	AA5-0298		8. 2.73	R C Mark	Shobdon	27. 2.08E
G-BAPB	de Havilland DHC-1 Chipmunk 22A	C1/0001	WB549	26. 2.73	G V Bunyan	(Bidford)	31. 5.98
G-BAPI	Reims Cessna FRA150L Aerobat	FRA1500195		8. 2.73	Marketing Management Services Ltd	Glasgow	24. 6.08E
G-BAPJ	Reims Cessna FRA150L Aerobat	FRA1500196		8. 2.73	M D Page	Manston	10. 6.08E
G-BAPL	Piper PA-23-250 Aztec E	27-7304966	N14377	12. 2.73	Donington Aviation Ltd	East Midlands	7.10.07E
G-BAPP	Evans VP-1 Coupe	PFA 1580		13. 2.73	A Sharp	Sleap	27. 5.98P
	(Built M J Drybanski and M Crow) (Volkswagen 1834)				(Noted 8.07)		
G-BAPR	Jodel D 11	295		14. 2.73	J P Liber and J F M Bartlett	Oaksey Park	17. 4.06P
	(Built Crantech Flying Group - pr.no.PFA 914) (Continental PC60)						
G-BAPV	Robin DR.400-160 Knight	742	F-OCSR	19. 2.73	J D and M Millne	(Bedlington)	22. 8.03
G-BAPW	Piper PA-28R-180 Cherokee Arrow	28R-30697	5Y-AIR	21. 2.73	A G Bourne and M W Freeman Hinton-in-the-Hedges		22. 1.08E
			N4951J				
G-BAPX	Robin DR.400-160 Knight	789		21. 2.73	D Whitton tr G-BAPX Group	Sywell	1. 6.08E
G-BAPY	Robin HR.100-210 Safari II	153		21. 2.73	D M J Williams tr G-BAPY Group	Fairoaks	4. 8.08E
G-BARC	Reims FR172J Rocket	FR17200356	(D-EEDK)	5. 3.73	C H Porter tr Severn Valley Aviation Group		
						Croft Farm, Defford	24. 4.08E
G-BARF	Wassmer Jodel D 112	1019	F-BJPF	5. 3.73	J J Penney	Rhigos	14.10.08P
G-BARG	Cessna E310Q	310Q0712	N8237Q	2. 3.73	IT Factor Ltd	Oxford	31. 3.06T
G-BARH	Beech C23 Sundowner	M-1473		2. 3.73	G Moorby and J Hinchcliffe	Sherburn-in-Elmet	18. 3.08E
G-BARN	Taylor JT.2 Titch	PFA 060-11136		5. 3.73	R G W Newton	Hailsham	11. 7.08P
	(Built R G W Newton) (Continental C90)						
G-BARP	Bell 206B-2 JetRanger II	967	N18092	5. 3.73	Western Power Distribution (South West) PLC Bristol		17. 5.08T
G-BARS	de Havilland DHC-1 Chipmunk 22	C1/0557	WK520	26. 2.73	J Beattie	RNAS Yeovilton	11. 8.08
					(As "1377" in Portuguese AF c/s)		
G-BARV	Cessna 310Q	310Q-0774		7. 3.73	Old England Watches Ltd	Elstree	18. 8.08E
G-BARZ	Scheibe SF28A Tandem Falke	5724	(D-KAUK)	8. 3.73	K Kiely	AAC Dishforth	21. 9.08E
G-BASH	Grumman AA-5 Traveler	AA5-0319	EI-AWV	12. 3.73	G Jenkins tr BASH Flying Group	Popham	18.10.07E
			G-BASH, N5419L				
G-BASJ	Piper PA-28-180 Cherokee Challenger		N11C	13. 3.73	Bristol Aero Club	Filton	20. 2.08E
		28-7305136					
G-BASM	Piper PA-34-200 Seneca	34-7350120	N16272	13. 3.73	M Gipps	Denham	24. 2.08E
G-BASN	Beech C23 Sundowner	M-1476		13. 3.73	O M O'Neill	(Leigh Woods, Bristol)	15.12.07E
G-BASO	Lake LA-4-180 Amphibian	358	N2025L	16. 3.73	C J A Macaulay	City of Derry	19. 6.06
	(Built Consolidated Aeronautics Inc)				(Stored 9.07)		
G-BASP	Beagle B 121 Pup Series 1	B121-149	SE-FOC	14. 3.73	B J Coutts	Sibson	15. 9.08S
			G-35-149				
G-BATC	MBB BÖ.105DB	S 45	D-HDAW	9. 3.73	Bond Air Services	Stromness	22. 6.08E
	(Originally registered as BÖ.105D: rebuilt using new MBB pod 1989 c/n unknown) (Operated North Wales Air Ambulance)						
G-BATJ	Jodel D 119	287	F-PIIQ	21. 3.73	M G Davis	Maypole Farm, Chislet	11. 7.08P
	(Built Ecole Technique Aéronautique de Ville) (Continental C90)						
G-BATN	Piper PA-23-250 Aztec E	27-7304987	N14391	26. 3.73	Marshall of Cambridge Aerospace Ltd	Cambridge	26. 2.08E
G-BATR	Piper PA-34-200 Seneca	34-7250290	9H-ABH	23. 3.73	A S Bamrah t/a Falcon Flying Services	Biggin Hill	24. 4.05
			G-BATR, LN-BDT		(Overran landing Woodchurch 4.8.02: struck hedge and badly damaged)		
G-BATV	Piper PA-28-180 Cherokee F	28-7105022	N5168S	26. 3.73	J N Rudsdale tr The Scoreby Flying Group		
						Full Sutton	10. 1.08E
G-BATW	Piper PA-28-140 Cherokee Fliteliner	28-7225587	N742FL	26. 3.73	C D Sainsbury	Swansea	2. 2.08E
G-BAUC	Piper PA-25-235 Pawnee C	25-5243	N8761L	26. 3.73	Southdown Gliding Club Ltd	Parham Park	25. 4.08E
G-BAUH	Dormois Jodel D 112	870	F-BILO	29. 3.73	G A and D Shepherd tr G-BAUH Flying Group		
						Seething	5. 2.08P
G-BAVB	Reims Cessna F172M	F17200965		10. 4.73	T S Sheridan-McGinnitty	Halfpenny Green	16. 5.08E
G-BAVH	de Havilland DHC-1 Chipmunk 22	C1/0841	WP975	10. 4.73	D C Murray tr Portsmouth Naval Gliding Club		
	(Lycoming O-360)					Lee-on-Solent	27. 3.09S
G-BAVL	Piper PA-23-250 Aztec E	27-4671	N14063	10. 4.73	S P and A V Chilcott	Durham Tees Valley	30. 7.08E
G-BAVO	Boeing Stearman A75N1 Kaydet	?	4X-AIH	13. 4.73	M Shaw	Old Buckenham	11. 7.10S
	(Continental W670) (Registered with c/n "3250-1405" which is part number: original identity unknown) (As "26" in US Army c/s)						
G-BAVR	Grumman AA-5 Traveler	AA5-0348		12. 4.73	G E Murray	Swansea	13.12.07E
G-BAWG	Piper PA-28R-200 Cherokee Arrow II		N11C	18. 4.73	Solent Air Ltd	Goodwood	19. 3.08E
		28R-7335133					
G-BAWK	Piper PA-28-140 Cherokee Cruiser	28-7325243		24. 4.73	J Stanley	(South Shields)	2.11.07T
G-BAWR	Robin HR.100-210 Safari II	156		27. 4.73	T Taylor (Noted 3.05)	Oxford	8. 6.00
G-BAXE	Hughes 269A-1	113-0313	N8931F	2. 5.73	Reeve Newfields Ltd	Sywell	21.12.93S
	(Hughes 300)				(Frame only noted 11.01)		
G-BAXS	Bell 47G-5	7908	5B-CFB	11. 5.73	R M Kemp t/a RK Helicopters	Fairoaks	5. 6.08S
			G-BAXS, N4098G				
G-BAXU	Reims Cessna F150L	F15000959		14. 5.73	M W Sheppardson	Sibson	5. 7.08E
G-BAXV	Reims Cessna F150L	F15000966		14. 5.73	G and S A Jones	Linley Hill, Leven	21. 6.08E
G-BAXY	Reims Cessna F172M	F17200905	N10636	15. 5.73	Eaglesoar Ltd	Humberside	2.11.07E
G-BAXZ	Piper PA-28-140 Cherokee C	28-26760	PH-NLX	15. 5.73	C Kearsley and D England tr G-BAXZ (87) Syndicate		
			N11C			Turweston	18. 4.08E
G-BAYO	Cessna 150L	15074435	N19471	18. 5.73	J A, G M, D T A and J A Rees		
					t/a Messrs Rees of Poyston West	Haverfordwest	27. 6.07T
G-BAYP	Cessna 150L	15074017	N18651	18. 5.73	D I Thomas tr Yankee Papa Flying Group	Popham	2. 6.08E
G-BAYR	Robin HR.100-210 Safari II	164		18. 5.73	P D Harries	Pembrey	14. 6.08
G-BAZC	Robin DR.400-160 Knight	824		29. 5.73	R Jones t/a Southern Sailplanes	Membury	24. 6.88
					(Damaged Crosland Moor 21.5.88: stored 10.01)		
G-BAZM	Jodel D 11	PAL 1416		31. 5.73	A F Simpson	Watchford Farm, Yarcombe	9. 8.07P
	(Built Bingley Flying Group - pr.no.PFA 915 and identified as "D 113") (Continental O-200-A) "L'oiseau jaune"						
G-BAZS	Reims Cessna F150L	F15000954		1. 6.73	L W Scattergood	Sandtoft	16.12.07E
G-BAZT	Reims Cessna F172M	F17200996		1. 6.73	Exeter Flying Club Ltd	Exeter	16. 7.08E

G-BBAA - G-BBZZ

Reg	Type	C/n	Prev ID	Date	Owner/Operator	Location	Date2
G-BBAW	Robin HR.100-210 Safari II	167		12. 6.73	F A Purvis (Noted 2.08)	Bagby	27.10.07E
G-BBAX	Robin DR.400-140 Earl	835		12. 6.73	G J Bissex and P H Garbutt	Nortom Malreward	3. 5.08
G-BBAY	Robin DR.400-140 Earl	841		12. 6.73	J C Stubbs	Sibson	25. 5.08E
G-BBBB	Taylor JT.1 Monoplane	SAM/01		4. 6.73	P J Burgess	(Navenby, Lincoln)	
	(Built S A MacConnacher - pr.no.PFA 1422)				(New owner 7.05)		
G-BBBC	Reims Cessna F150L	F15000864	N10635	14. 6.73	W J Greenfield	Humberside	24. 1.08E
G-BBBI	Grumman AA-5 Traveler	AA5-0392		15. 6.73	W Haddow tr Go Baby Aviation Group	Prestwick	2. 4.08E
G-BBBN	Piper PA-28-180 Cherokee Challenger		N11C	20. 6.73	Estuary Aviation Ltd	Southend	9. 1.08E
		28-7305365					
G-BBBO	SIPA 903	67	F-BGBQ	16. 1.74	G E Morris	Bolt Head, Salcombe	1. 7.08P
G-BBBW	Clutton FRED Series II	DLW.1		26. 6.73	M Palfreman	Waterstones Farm, Newby Wiske	19. 6.08P
	(Built D Webster - pr.no.PFA 1551)						
G-BBBY	Piper PA-28-140 Cherokee Cruiser	28-7325533	N9501N	28. 6.73	W R and R Davies	RAF Mona	25. 6.08E
G-BBCA	Bell 206B-2 JetRanger II	1101	N18091	29. 6.73	Heliflight (UK) Ltd	Gloucestershire	24.10.08E
G-BBCB	Western O-65 Balloon (Hot Air)	018		29. 6.73	G M Bulmer "Cee Bee"	Credenhill, Hereford	19. 5.76S
G-BBCC	Piper PA-23-250 Aztec D	27-4317	N6953Y	29. 6.73	G J Conley	(Villeneuve St Denis, France)	11. 4.08E
G-BBCH	Robin DR.400 2+2	850		4. 7.73	S M Braithwaite and C R Thomas	Bicester	31. 5.08E
					tr Oilburners (2006) Flying Association		
G-BBCI	Cessna 150H	15069282	N50409	4. 7.73	A L and Farideh Alam	Cranfield	9. 8.08E
G-BBCK	Cameron O-77 Balloon (Hot Air)	76		4. 7.73	W R Teasdale	Maidenhead	15. 6.89S
					"Mary Gloster" (Inflated 4.02)		
G-BBCN	Robin HR.100-210	168		11. 7.73	J C King	Bourne Park, Hurstbourne Tarrant	22. 9.06
G-BBCS	Robin DR.400-140B Earl	851		12. 7.73	B N Stevens	Breighton	31. 5.08E
G-BBCY	Phoenix Luton LA-4A Minor	PFA 825		17. 7.73	J Angiolini and T D Boyle	Errol	15. 4.08P
	(Built C H Difford) (Volkswagen 1600)						
G-BBCZ	Grumman AA-5 Traveler	AA5-0382		18. 7.73	No.1 Investments Ltd	Compton Abbas	11.10.07E
G-BBDC	Piper PA-28-140 Cherokee Cruiser	28-7325437	N11C	18. 7.73	B Scragg and C M O'Connell tr G-BBDC Group		
						Earls Colne	6. 6.08E
G-BBDE	Piper PA-28R-200 Cherokee Arrow II		(EI-...)	18. 7.73	R L Coleman, A Holt and A Crozier	Panshanger	18.10.07E
		28R-7335250	G-BBDE, N11C				
G-BBDH	Reims Cessna F172M	F17200990		19. 7.73	J D Woodward	Franklyn's Field, Chewton Mendip	7. 8.08E
G-BBDJ	Thunder Ax6-56 Balloon (Hot Air)	006		20. 7.73	A D Kent tr Balloon Preservation Flying Group		
					"Jack Tar"	Petworth	5. 8.82A
G-BBDL	Grumman AA-5 Traveler	AA5-0406		18. 7.73	P F Robertshaw tr Delta Lima Flying Group		
						Durham Tees Valley	16.11.07E
G-BBDM	Grumman AA-5 Traveler	AA5-0407		18. 7.73	J Rees tr Jackeroo Aviation Group	Thruxton	1.11.07E
G-BBDO	Piper PA-23-250 Aztec E	27-7305120	N40361	24. 7.73	J W Anstee tr G-BBDO Flying Group	(Filton)	30. 6.08T
G-BBDP	Robin DR.400-160 Major	853		25. 7.73	Robin Lance Aviation Associates Ltd	Rochester	9.11.07E
G-BBDS	Piper PA-31 Turbo Navajo B	31-7300956	N97RJ	26. 7.73	Fly (CI) Ltd	Southend	17. 4.08E
			G-SKKB, G-BBDS, N7565L		(Operated Trans Euro Air)		
G-BBDT	Cessna 150H	15068839	N23272	26. 7.73	J G N Wilson tr Delta Tango Group	Full Sutton	11. 7.08E
G-BBDV	SIPA 903	7/21	F-BEYY	26. 7.73	W McAndrew	Cardington	20. 6.07P
	(Continental C90) (Originally ex F-BEYJ c/n 7 but rebuilt in 1978 from F-BEYY c/n 21)						
G-BBEA	Phoenix Luton LA-4A Minor	PFA 843		30. 7.73	M Howland tr Echo Alpha Syndicate	Wickenby	14 12.06P
	(Built G J Hewitt) (Volkswagen 1600)				(New owner 1.08)		
G-BBEB	Piper PA-28R-200 Cherokee Arrow II		N9514N	31. 7.73	R D W Rippingale tr Anvils Flying Group		
		28R-7335292				Anvil Farm, Hungerford	18. 4.08
G-BBEC	Piper PA-28-180 Cherokee Challenger		N11C	30. 7.73	A L Gardner	Ronaldsway	30. 5.08E
		28-7305478					
G-BBED	SOCATA MS.894A Rallye Minerva 220	12097		30. 7.73	C A Shelley t/a Vista Products		
					(Noted 7.05) The Mill Industrial State, Alcester		13. 9.87T
G-BBEF	Piper PA-28-140 Cherokee Cruiser	28-7325527	N9500N	31. 7.73	CC Helicopters Ltd	Blackpool	7. 9.08E
	(Rebuilt using major components from damaged G-AVWG by 4.99)						
G-BBEN	Bellanca 7GCBC Citabria	496-73	(D-EAUT)	7. 8.73	C A G Schofield	Harpsden, Henley-on-Thames	10. 5.02
			N36416				
G-BBEX	Cessna 185A Skywagon	185-0491	EI-CMC	7. 8.73	F Byrne and V McCarthy tr Falcon Parachute Centre		
			G-BBEX, 4X-ALD, N99992, N1691Z			Hackettstown, County Carlow	27. 2.08E
G-BBFD	Piper PA-28R-200 Cherokee Arrow II		N9517N	8. 8.73	C H Rose and A R Annable	White Waltham	3. 7.08T
		28R-7335342					
G-BBFL	Gardan GY-201 Minicab	21	F-BHCQ	17. 8.73	R Smith	Griffins Farm, Temple Bruer	1. 1.08P
	(Built SRCM) (Continental A65)						
G-BBFV	Piper PA-32-260 Cherokee Six	32-778	5Y-ADF	13. 8.73	D T Wright tr G-BBFV Syndicate	Wickenby	20. 7.08E
G-BBGC	SOCATA MS.893E Rallye 180GT	12215	F-BUCV	16. 8.73	P M Nolan	Kilkenny, County Kilkenny	2. 9.08E
G-BBGI	Fuji FA.200-160 Aero Subaru	FA200-228		21. 8.73	Tandycel Co Ltd	Dunkeswell	12. 3.08E
G-BBGL	Oldfield Baby Lakes	7223-B412-B		22. 8.73	F J Ball	Jubilee Farm, Wisbech St Mary	21. 3.02P
	(Built D S Morgan - pr.no.PFA 1593) (Continental C90)						
G-BBGR	Cameron O-65 Balloon (Hot Air)	85		20. 8.73	M L and L P Willoughby	Woodcote, Reading	26. 5.81A
					"Jabberwock"		
G-BBGZ	Cambridge Balloon (Hot Air)A 42 Balloon (Hot Air)	CBalloon (Hot Air)A 42		31. 8.73	J L Hinton, G Laslett and R A Laslett		
					"Phlogiston" (Inflated 4.02)	Bishopston, Bristol	
G-BBHF	Piper PA-23-250 Aztec E	27-7305166	N40453	5. 9.73	G J Williams	Sherburn-in-Elmet	4. 7.08E
G-BBHI	Cessna 177RG Cardinal RG	177RG0225	5Y-ANX	7. 9.73	T G W Bunce	Newtownards	14.12.07E
			N1825Q				
G-BBHJ	Piper J-3C-85 Cub	16378	OO-GEC	7. 9.73	P Dyer tr Wellcross Flying Group		
	(Frame No.16037)					Wellcross Grange, Slinfold	4. 6.07P
G-BBHK	Noorduyn AT-16-ND Harvard IIB	14-787	PH-PPS	7. 9.73	Sheringham Aviation UK Ltd	Wycombe Air Park	5. 7.08P
			(PH-HTC), R Neth AF B-158, FH153, 42-12540 (As "FH153: 58" in RCAF c/s)				
G-BBHL	Sikorsky S-61N Mk.II	61-712	N4032S	7. 9.73	Bristow Helicopters Ltd	Stornoway	4.12.07E
					"Glamis" (Operated Marine and Coastguard Agency)		
G-BBHY	Piper PA-28-180 Cherokee Challenger		EI-BBS	7. 9.73	Air Operations Ltd	Guernsey	5. 7.08E
		28-7305474	G-BBHY, N9508N				

Reg	Type	C/n	Prev ID	Date	Owner/Operator	Location	Expiry
G-BBIF	Piper PA-23-250 Aztec E	27-7305234	N9736N	10. 9.73	D M Davies "Flying Miss Daisie"	Tatenhill	14.11.07E
G-BBIH	Enstrom F-28A-UK	026	N4875	12. 9.73	Stephenson Marine Co Ltd (Noted 9.06)	Goodwood	28. 6.02T
G-BBII	Fiat G 46-3B	44	I-AEHU MM52801	13. 9.73	G-BBII Ltd	Wycombe Air Park	19. 6.08P
					(As "44mm52801:"97" [black]-"4" [red] in Italian AF c/s)		
G-BBIL	Piper PA-28-140 Cherokee	28-22567	SE-FAR N4219J	13. 9.73	John West Consulting Ltd	Biggin Hill	18. 7.08E
G-BBIO	Robin HR.100-210 Safari II	178		14. 9.73	R P Caley	Eddsfield, Octon Lodge Farm, Thwing	27. 9.07E
G-BBIX	Piper PA-28-140 Cherokee E	28-7225442	LN-AEN	17. 9.73	F A Griffiths and R A Lee tr Sterling Aviation	White Waltham	21. 2.08E
G-BBJI	Isaacs Spitfire	2		18. 9.73	R F Cresswell	Gamston	26. 6.07P
	(Built J O Isaacs - pr.no.PFA 027-10055) (Continental O-200-A)						
	(Collided with hangar during prop. swing Gamston mid 2006 and substantially damaged: wings only noted Shipdham 3.07)						
G-BBJU	Robin DR.400-140 Earl	874		19. 9.73	J C Lister tr Victor Sierra Aero Club	Valley Farm, Winwick	13. 6.08E
G-BBJV	Reims Cessna F177RG Cardinal RG	F177RG0098		20. 9.73	3GRCOMM Ltd	Shobdon	2. 4.08E
G-BBJX	Reims Cessna F150L	F15001017		20. 9.73	L W Scattergood	Sherburn-in-Elmet	2.11.07E
G-BBJY	Reims Cessna F172M Skyhawk II	F17201075		20. 9.73	Cardinal Sin Ltd t/a Staverton Flying School	Gloucestershire	28. 6.08E
G-BBJZ	Reims Cessna F172M Skyhawk II	F17201035		20. 9.73	J K and J A Green	Gamston	29. 2.08E
G-BBKA	Reims Cessna F150L	F15001029		20. 9.73	W M Wilson	North Moor, Scunthorpe	29. 2.08E
G-BBKB	Reims Cessna F150L	F15001030		20. 9.73	Justgold Ltd	Blackpool	10. 1.03T
	(Operated Blackpool Air Centre) (Noted 10.07)						
G-BBKE	Reims Cessna F150L	F15001026		20. 9.73	Xpedite (UK) Ltd	Cranfield	25. 8.07T
G-BBKG	Reims FR172J Rocket	FR17200465		20. 9.73	R Wright	Coventry	3. 4.08E
G-BBKI	Reims Cessna F172M Skyhawk II	F17201069		20. 9.73	C W and S A Burman (Dismantled 1.07)	East Winch	8. 2.08E
G-BBKL	Menavia Piel CP.301A Emeraude	237	F-BIMK	21. 9.73	R K Griggs tr Piel G-BBKL	Perth	13. 6.03P
	(Substantially damaged in heavy landing Perth 3. 5.03: dismantled 8.07)						
G-BBKX	Piper PA-28-180 Cherokee Challenger	28-7305581	N9550N	26. 9.73	RAE Aero Club Ltd	Farnborough	25.11.07E
G-BBKY	Reims Cessna F150L	F15000991		26. 9.73	Telesonic Ltd	Barton	22. 2.08E
G-BBKZ	Cessna 172M Skyhawk	17261495	N20694	27. 9.73	R S Thomson tr KZ Flying Group	Exeter	13. 5.08T
G-BBLH	Piper J-3C-65 Cub (L-4B-PI)	10006	F-BFQY French.Military, 43-1145	24. 9.73	Shipping and Airlines Ltd	Biggin Hill	22. 5.08E
	(Frame No.9838) (Regd with c/n 10549)				(As "31145:G-26" in 183rd Field Battalion US Army c/s)		
G-BBLM	SOCATA Rallye 100S	2392		3.10.73	J R Rodgers	Halfpenny Green	8. 5.08E
G-BBLS	Grumman AA-5 Traveler	AA5-0440	EI-AYM G-BBLS	8.10.73	A Grant	Perth	6. 6.08
G-BBLU	Piper PA-34-200 Seneca	34-7350271	N55984	8.10.73	R H R Rue	Turweston	21. 5.08T
G-BBMB	Robin DR.400-180 Régent	848	5Y-ASB	27. 9.73	I James tr Régent Flying Group	King's Farm, Thurrock	24. 4.08E
G-BBMH	EAA Biplane Sport Model P1	PFA 1348		11.10.73	M V Batin tr G-BBMH Flying Group	(Turville, Henley-on-Thames)	5.10.05P
	(Built K Dawson) (Continental C90-14F)						
G-BBMJ	Piper PA-23-250 Aztec E	27-7305150	N40387	12.10.73	Nationwide Caravan Rental Services Ltd	Hawarden	19.12.07E
G-BBMN	de Havilland DHC-1 Chipmunk 22	C1/0300	WD359	12.10.73	R Steiner "3"	North Weald	18.11.07
G-BBMO	de Havilland DHC-1 Chipmunk 22	C1/0550	WK514	12.10.73	D M Squires	Wellesbourne Mountford	10. 6.10E
	(As "WK514" in RAF c/s)						
G-BBMR	de Havilland DHC-1 Chipmunk 22	C1/0213	WB763	12.10.73	P J Wood (Noted 11.05)	Tollerton	
G-BBMT	de Havilland DHC-1 Chipmunk 22	C1/0712	WP831	12.10.73	J Evans and D Withers tr MT Group	Graveley Hall Farm, Graveley	27. 6.10S
G-BBMV	de Havilland DHC-1 Chipmunk 22	C1/0432	WG348	12.10.73	S G Howell and S P Tilling	Biggin Hill	28. 4.09
	(As "WG348" in RAF c/s)						
G-BBMW	de Havilland DHC-1 Chipmunk 22	C1/0641	WK628	12.10.73	G Fielder and A Wilson	Goodwood	15.12.04
	(As "WK628" in RAF c/s) (New owners 5.06)						
G-BBMX	de Havilland DHC-1 Chipmunk 22	C1/0800	WP924	12.10.73	M I Koch	Sonderberg, Denmark	24. 8.08S
G-BBMZ	de Havilland DHC-1 Chipmunk 22	C1/0563	WK548	12.10.73	D P Copse tr G-BBMZ Chipmunk Symdicate	Wycombe Air Park	28. 2..10
G-BBNA	de Havilland DHC-1 Chipmunk 22	C1/0491	WG417	12.10.73	Coventry Gliding Club Ltd	Husbands Bosworth	20. 7.09
	(Lycoming O-360)						
G-BBND	de Havilland DHC-1 Chipmunk 22	C1/0225	WD286	12.10.73	W Norton and D Fradley tr Bernoulli Syndicate	Little Gransden	18. 5.07S
				(As "WD286" in RAF silver with yellow bands c/s)			
G-BBNG	Bell 206B-2 JetRanger II	134	VH-BHX G-BBNG, VR-BEY, G-BBNG, PK-HBO, N6268N	16.10.73	MB Air Ltd (Operated Eagle Helicopters)	Winchester Farm, Ouston	13. 6.08E
G-BBNH	Piper PA-34-200 Seneca	34-7350339	N56492	16.10.73	A L Howell, A P Barrow and M G D Baverstock	Bournemouth	22. 4.08E
G-BBNI	Piper PA-34-200 Seneca	34-7350312	N56286	16.10.73	Noisy Moose Ltd	Cranfield	22. 9.07T
G-BBNJ	Reims Cessna F150L	F15001038		16.10.73	Sherburn Aero Club Ltd	Sherburn-in-Elmet	21.11.07E
G-BBNT	Piper PA-31-350 Navajo Chieftain	31-7305107	EI-CNM N1201H, G-BBNT, N74958	22.10.73	M P Goss (Operated British North West Airlines)	Belfast City	19. 1.08E
G-BBNZ	Reims Cessna F172M Skyhawk II	F17201054		23.10.73	R E Nunn	Clipgate Farm, Denton	31. 7.08E
G-BBOA	Reims Cessna F172M Skyhawk II	F17201066		23.10.73	J D and A M Black	Lodge Farm, St Osyth	24. 7.08E
G-BBOC	Cameron O-77 Balloon (Hot Air)	86		24.10.73	J A B Gray "Bacchus"	Daglingworth, Cirencester	6. 1.90A
G-BBOD	Thunder O 5 Balloon (Hot Air)	013		24.10.73	B R and M.Boyle "Little Titch"	Budbrooke, Warwick	
G-BBOE	Robin HR.200-100 Club	26		24.10.73	R J Powell	(Wickham, Hampshire)	7. 7.02
	(Badly damaged striking hedge and concrete post landing Wells Cross Farm, Horsham 24.6.01: dismantled)						
G-BBOH	Craft-Pitts S-1S	AJEP-P-S1-S-1		25.10.73	Techair London Ltd	Rotary Farm, Hatch	8. 9.97P
	(Built Pitts Aviation Enterprises Inc - pr.no.PFA 1570)				(Noted 5.07)		
G-BBOL	Piper PA-18-150 Super Cub	18-7561	D-EMFE N3821Z	26.10.73	N Artt	Aston Down	18. 7.10
G-BBOO	Thunder Ax6-56 Balloon (Hot Air)	012		4.10.73	K Meehan "Tiger Jack"	Much Wenlock	31. 5.03A
G-BBOR	Bell 206B-2 JetRanger II	1197	(SE-) G-BBOR	30.10.73	M J Easey	Town Farm, Hoxne, Eye	29. 7.08E
G-BBOX	Thunder Ax7-77 Balloon (Hot Air)	011		24.10.73	The British Balloon Museum and Library Ltd "Rocinante" (Inflated 4.06)	Newbury	23.12.82A
G-BBPN	Enstrom F-28A-UK	166		30.10.73	D W C Holmes Ormonde Fields, Codnor, Derbyshire		31. 5.08E
	(Crashed into trees near Ormonde Fields Golf Course, Codnor, Derbyshire 12. 6.07 and substantially damaged)						

Reg	Type	C/n	Prev id	Date	Owner/Operator	Location	Status
G-BBPO	Enstrom F-28A	176		30.10.73	Henfield Lodge Aviation Ltd	Shoreham	13.12.07E
G-BBPP	Piper PA-28-180 Cherokee Archer	28-7405007	G-WACP	5. 4.89	Big Red Kite Ltd	RAF Benson	30. 7.07E
			G-BBPP, N9559N				
G-BBPS	SAN Jodel D 117	597	F-BHXS	30.10.73	A Appleby	Westfield Farm, Hailsham ·	29. 4.08P
G-BBPX	Piper PA-34-200 Seneca	34-7250262	N1202T	7.11.73	M Corbett tr The G-BBPX Flying Group	Dunsfold	5. 3.08
G-BBPY	Piper PA-28-180 Cherokee Challenger	28-7305590	N9554N	8.11.73	Sunsaver Ltd	Barton	21. 8.08E
G-BBRA	Piper PA-23-250 Aztec E	27-7305197	N40479	12.11.73	R C Lough	Stapleford	23. 7.08E
G-BBRB	de Havilland DH.82A Tiger Moth	85934	OO-EVB	21.11.73	R Barham	(West Wickham)	
			Belgian AF T-8, ETA-8, DF198 *(Damaged Biggin Hill 16. 1.87)*				
G-BBRC	Fuji FA.200-180 Aero Subaru	FA200-235		8.11.73	G-BBRC Ltd	Blackbushe	25. 6.08E
G-BBRI	Bell 47G-5A	25158	N18092	8.11.73	Alan Mann Helicopters Ltd	(Fairoaks)	28. 7.02T
	(Composite following several major rebuilds)						
G-BBRN	Mitchell-Procter Kittiwake I	02	XW784	20.11.73	H M Price	RNAS Yeovilton	8. 9.05P
	(Built Air Engineering, HMS Daedalus - pr.no.PFA 1352) (Continental O-200-A)				*(As "XW784:VL" in RN c/s) (Noted 3.06)*		
G-BBRV	de Havilland DHC-1 Chipmunk 22	C1/0284	WD347	13.11.73	C W Tomkins	Spanhoe	7. 8.09S
			(As "WD347" in RAF grey and orange dayglo stripes)				
G-BBRX	SIAI-Marchetti S 205-18F	342	LN-VYH OO-HAQ	13.11.73	C T Findon and J B Owens	Errol	21.12.07E
G-BBRZ	Grumman AA-5 Traveler	AA5-0471	(EI-AYV) G-BBRZ	15.11.73	B McIntyre	(Movenis)	30. 4.99
					(New owner 1.07)		
G-BBSA	Grumman AA-5 Traveler	AA5-0472		15.11.73	Usworth 84 Flying Associates Ltd	Durham Tees Valley	16. 4.08E
G-BBSB	Beech C23 Sundowner 180	M-1516		15.11.73	L J Welsh	Perth	2. 8.08E
G-BBSM	Piper PA-32-300 Cherokee Six	32-7440005	N9577N	14.11.73	G C Collings	Hardwick	28. 8.08E
G-BBSS	de Havilland DHC-1 Chipmunk 22	C1/0520	WG470	21.11.73	Coventry Gliding Club Ltd	Husbands Bosworth	21. 5.10S
	(Lycoming O-360)						
G-BBSW	Pietenpol AirCamper	PFA 1506		21.11.73	J K S Wills	(London SE3)	
	(Built J K S Wills)						
G-BBTB	Reims Cessna FRA150L Aerobat	FRA1500224		26.11.73	Global Engineering and Maintenance Ltd	Bournemouth	31. 7.08E
G-BBTG	Reims Cessna F172M Skyhawk II	F17201097		26.11.73	L W Huson tr Triple X Flying Group	Biggin Hill	15. 5.08E
G-BBTH	Reims Cessna F172M Skyhawk II	F17201089		26.11.73	Tayside Aviation Ltd	Glenrothes	20. 9.08E
G-BBTJ	Piper PA-23-250 Aztec E	27-7305131	N40369	27.11.73	Cooper Aerial Surveys Ltd	Wickenby	16. 4.08E
G-BBTS	Beech V35B Bonanza	D-9551	N3051W	29.11.73	S Wenham t/a Eastern Air	Cannes-Mandelieu, Monaco	5. 6.03
G-BBTY	Beech C23 Sundowner 180	M-1525		29.11.73	A W Roderick and W Price tr TY Group	Cardiff	6. 8.08E
G-BBUE	Grumman AA-5 Traveler	0479		6.12.73	O Balland and T Shotton	Tatenhill	13. 1.08E
G-BBUF	Grumman AA-5 Traveler	0480		6.12.73	G S McNaughton	Prestwick	22.12.07E
G-BBUG	Piper PA-16 Clipper	16-29	F-BFMC	6.12.73	J Dolan	Enniskillen	28. 8.08E
G-BBUT	Western O-65 Balloon (Hot Air)	020		11.12.73	R G Turnbull *"Christabelle II"*	Clyro, Hereford	5. 6.06A
G-BBUU	Piper J-3C-75 Cub (L-4A-PI)	10529	F-BBSQ	14. 1.74	C Stokes	Hulcote Farm, Milton Keynes	11. 5.08P
	(Frame No.10354)		F-OAEZ, French AF, 43-29238				
G-BBVA	Sikorsky S-61N Mk.II	61-718		12. 2.74	Bristow Helicopters Ltd	Lee-on-Solent	24. 2.08E
					"Vega" (Operated Marine and Coastguard Agency)		
G-BBVO	Isaacs Fury II	PFA 011-10091		20.12.73	R W Hinton	(Woolpit, Biry St Edmunds)	16. 6.07P
	(Built D Silsbury) (Lycoming O-320)				*(As "S1579:571" {Hawker Nimrod} of RN FAA 408 Flight, HMS Glorious)*		
G-BBWZ	Grumman AA-1B Trainer	AA1B-0334		4. 1.74	A C Jacobs	Muchiamel, Alicante, Spain	7. 6.08E
G-BBXB	Reims Cessna FRA150L Aerobat	FRA1500236		16. 1.74	C and M Laycock	Full Sutton	8.11.07E
G-BBXH	Reims FR172F Rocket	FR17200113	SE-FKG	21. 1.74	D Ridley	(High Flatts Farm, Chester-le-Street)	8.11.03
G-BBXK	Piper PA-34-200 Seneca	34-7450056	N54366	21. 1.74	J A Rees	Haverfordwest	7. 4.08E
					(Operated Haverfordwest Flight Centre)		
G-BBXL	Cessna 310Q II	310Q1076	EI-CLX G-BBXL, (N1223G)	21. 1.74	D H Madden and J Phelan tr MD Aviation Group	(Craigavon and Lisburn)	19. 9.08E
G-BBXS	Piper J-3C-65 Cub (L-4H-PI)	12214	N9865F G-ALMA, 44-79918	25. 1.74	M J Butler	Spanhoe	14. 9.00P
	(Continental C90) (Frame No.12042)				*(Officially regd as c/n "9865") (Noted 11.01)*		
G-BBXW	Piper PA-28-151 Cherokee Warrior	28-7415050	PH-CPL G-BBXW, N9599N	21. 1.74	Bristol Aero Club	Filton	4.11.07E
G-BBXY	Bellanca 7GCBC Citabria	614-74	N57639	1. 2.74	R R L Windus	Truleigh Manor Farm, Edburton	12. 3.08E
G-BBXZ	Evans VP-1	PFA 1562		31. 1.74	R W Burrows	Swanton Morley	8. 3.96P
	(Built G D Price) (Volkswagen 1600)				*(Noted wingless 4.02)*		
G-BBYB	Piper PA-18 Super Cub 95	18-1627	PH-TMA	4. 2.74	The Tiger Club (1990) Ltd	Headcorn	26. 7.07T
	(L-18C-PI) (Frame No.18-1628)		(D-ENCH), French Army 18-1627, 51-15627				
					(Nosed over on take-off Headcorn 17. 3.07: damage to wings and tail)		
G-BBYH	Cessna 182P	18262814	N52744	6. 2.74	Ramco (UK) Ltd	Poplar Farm, Croft, Skegness	18. 5.08E
G-BBYP	Piper PA-28-140 Cherokee F	28-7425158	N9620N	19. 2.74	E Williams	(Abergele)	6. 7.07E
G-BBYS	Cessna 182P Skylane	18261520	5Y-ATE N21256	14. 2.74	I M Jones	Gamston	9. 6.08E
G-BBZF	Piper PA-28-140 Cherokee F	28-7425195	N9501N	19. 2.74	J McGuinness and R Stamp t/a East Coast Aviation	Waterford, County Waterford	10. 9.08E
G-BBZH	Piper PA-28R-200 Cherokee Arrow II	28R-7435102	N9608N	22. 2.74	ZH Flying Ltd	Exeter	13. 6.08E
G-BBZN	Fuji FA.200-180 Aero Subaru	FA200-230		26. 2.74	D Kynaston, J S V Westwood and P D Wedd	Cambridge	27.11.07E
G-BBZV	Piper PA-28R-200 Cherokee Arrow II	28R-7435105	N9609N	11. 3.74	P B Mellor	Standalone Farm, Meppershall	19.10.07E

G-BCAA - G-BCZZ

Reg	Type	C/n	Prev id	Date	Owner/Operator	Location	Status
G-BCAH	de Havilland DHC-1 Chipmunk 22	C1/0372	WG316	6. 5.74	A W Eldridge *(As "WG316" in RAF c/s)*	Leicester	25. 6.08T
G-BCAZ	Piper PA-12 Super Cruiser	12-2312	5Y-KGK VP-KGK, ZS-BYJ, ZS-BPH	12. 3.74	A D Williams	Rhos-y-Gilwen Farm, Rhos Hill	21. 2.08E
G-BCBG	Piper PA-23-250 Aztec E	27-7305224	VP-BBN VR-BBN, (VR-BDM), G-BCBG, N40494	13. 3.74	M J L Batt	Redhill	24.11.07E

G-BCBH	Fairchild 24R-46A Argus III	975	(VH-AAQ)	13. 3.74	Dreamticket Promotions Ltd	Spanhoe	28. 6.09S
	(UC-61K-FA)		G-BCBH, ZS-AXH, HB737, 43-15011				
G-BCBJ	Piper PA-25-235 Pawnee C	25-2380/R		18. 3.74	Deeside Gliding Club (Aberdeenshire) Ltd	Aboyne	2. 9.08E
	(Rebuild of G-ASLA {25-2380})						
G-BCBL	Fairchild 24R-46A Argus III	989	OO-EKE	19. 3.74	F J Cox	(Woolsery, Bideford)	31. 3.96
	(UC-61K-FA)		D-EKEQ, HB-AEC, HB751, 43-15025				
G-BCBR	Wittman W.8 Tailwind	TW3-380		20. 3.74	D P Jones	Top Farm, Croydon, Royston	30. 7.07P
	(Built AJEP Developments)						
G-BCBX	Reims Cessna F150L	F15001001	F-BUEO	25. 3.74	Merseyflight Ltd	Liverpool	15. 4.08E
G-BCBZ	Cessna 337C Super Skymaster	3370942	SE-FKB	28. 3.74	J Haden	Jersey	30. 5.08E
	(Robertson STOL conversion)		N2642S				
G-BCCC	Reims Cessna F150L	F15001041		8. 4.74	A Mitchell tr Treble Charlie Flying Group	Cranfield	25. 4.08E
G-BCCD	Reims Cessna F172M Skyhawk II	F17201144		8. 4.74	R M Austin t/a Austin Aviation	Rochester	30. 6.07T
G-BCCE	Piper PA-23-250 Aztec E	27-7405282	N40544	3. 4.74	Golf Charlie Echo Ltd	Shoreham	7.11.08T
					(Operated The Flying Hut)		
G-BCCF	Piper PA-28-180 Cherokee Archer	28-7405069	N9632N	3. 4.74	Top Cat Aviation Ltd	Sleap	15. 7.08E
					(Operated Manchester School of Flying)		
	(Left wing struck post while taxiing Sleap 4. 4.07 and substantially damaged: noted 8.07)						
G-BCCG	Thunder Ax7-65 Balloon (Hot Air)	020		4. 4.74	N H Ponsford t/a Rango Balloon and Kite Company		
					"Zephyr" (Active 1999)	Leeds	7.11.83A
G-BCCJ	Grumman AA-5 Traveler	AA5-0546		8. 4.74	T Needham	Exeter	26. 4.08
G-BCCK	Grumman AA-5 Traveler	AA5-0547		8. 4.74	Prospect Air Ltd	Manchester	19. 9.08E
					(Operated Manchester School of Flying)		
G-BCCR	Piel CP.301A Emeraude	PFA 712		8. 4.74	J H and C J Waterman		
	(Built Korist Flying Group) (Continental O-200-A)					Armshold Farm, Kingston, Cambridge	23. 2.08P
G-BCCX	de Havilland DHC-1 Chipmunk 22	C1/0531	WG481	17. 4.74	T M Holloway tr RAF Gliding and Soaring Association		
	(Lycoming O-360)				(Operated Clevelands Gliding Club)	AAC Dishforth	11. 5.09S
G-BCCY	Robin HR.200-100 Club	37		18. 4.74	Charlie Yankee Ltd	Filton	24. 4.08E
G-BCDJ	Piper PA-28-140 Cherokee	28-24276	PH-NLV	29. 4.74	R J Whyham	Blackpool	24. 6.08E
			N1841J		(Operated Air Navigation and Trading) (Noted 10.07)		
G-BCDK (2)	Partenavia P68B	32	A6-ALN	4. 7.75	Compass Air SRL	(Trino, Italy)	11. 9.08E
			G-BCDK				
G-BCDL	Cameron O-42 Balloon (Hot Air)	115		24. 4.74	D P and B O Turner Leigh upon Mendip, Radstock		13. 7.83A
					"Chums"		
G-BCDY	Reims Cessna FRA150L Aerobat	FRA1500237		7. 5.74	R L Nunn and T R Edwards	King's Farm, Thurrock	20. 8.08E
G-BCEA	Sikorsky S-61N Mk.II	61-721		7. 6.74	British International Ltd	Plymouth	13. 7.08E
G-BCEB	Sikorsky S-61NM Mk.II	61-454	N4023S	2.10.74	Veritair Ltd "The Isles of Scilly"	Penzance Heliport	16.12.07E
G-BCEE	Grumman AA-5 Traveler	AA5-0571		7. 5.74	P J Marchant	Standalone Farm, Meppershall	17.12.07E
G-BCEF	Grumman AA-5 Traveler	AA5-0572		7. 5.74	D G Price tr G-BCEF Group	Enstone	9. 6.08E
G-BCEN	Fairey Britten-Norman BN-2A-26 Islander	403	4X-AYG	6. 5.74	Reconnaissance Ventures Ltd	Manston	7.11.07E
			SX-BFB, 4X-AYG, N90JA, G-BCEN (Operated Marine and Coastguard Agency)				
G-BCEP	Grumman AA-5 Traveler	AA5-0576		7. 5.74	S Bradshaw	Biggin Hill	6. 9.08E
G-BCER	Gardan GY-201 Minicab	8	F-BGJP	8. 5.74	D Beaumont	West Freugh	21. 5.08P
	(Built Con. Aéronautique de Bearn) (Continental A65)						
G-BCEU	Cameron O-42 Balloon (Hot Air)	111		9. 5.74	P Glydon (New owner 8.07)	Knowle, Bristol	31. 5.85A
G-BCEX	Piper PA-23-250 Aztec E	27-7305024	N40225	13. 5.74	DJ Aviation Ltd	(Bulkington, Devizes)	14. 5.08E
G-BCEY	de Havilland DHC-1 Chipmunk 22	C1/0515	WG465	14. 5.74	T C B Dehn and C A Robey tr Gopher Flying Group		
					(As "WG465" in RAF c/s)	White Waltham	2.10.08S
G-BCEZ	Cameron O-84 Balloon (Hot Air)	107		13. 5.74	P F Smart and R J Mitchener t/a Balloon Collection		
					"Stars and Bars"	Romsey and Andover	20. 7.82A
G-BCFF	Fuji FA.200-160 Aero Subaru	FA200-237		21. 5.74	S A Cole	Exeter	23. 4.08E
G-BCFN	Cameron O-65 Balloon (Hot Air)	109		23. 5.74	W G Johnston and H M Savage	Edinburgh	15. 5.77S
					"Fireball" (Noted 6.00)		
G-BCFO	Piper PA-18-150 Super Cub	18-5335	(D-EIOZ)	29. 5.74	D C Murray tr Portsmouth Naval Gliding Club		
			French Army 18-5335, N10F			Lee-on-Solent	13. 5.07
G-BCFR	Reims Cessna FRA150L Aerobat	FRA1500244		30. 5.74	M Garrard tr Foxtrot Romeo Group,	Earls Colne	15. 1.08T
G-BCFW	SAAB 91D Safir	91-437	PH-RLZ	29. 5.74	D R Williams (Stored 11.07)	Peplow	24. 7.06
G-BCFY	Phoenix Luton LA-4A Minor	PAL 1301		29. 5.74	G Capes	(Welton, Brough)	17. 1 92P
	(Built G F M Garner - pr.no.PFA 824) (Ardem Mk.6)				(Stored 8.92: new owner 10.00)		
G-BCGB	Bensen B 8	PCL-14		3. 6.74	J W Birkett	Henstridge	19. 8.08P
	(Built P C Lovegrove) (Rotax 503)						
G-BCGC	de Havilland DHC-1 Chipmunk 22	C1/0776	WP903	13. 3.74	J C Wright tr Henlow Chipmunk Group	RAF Henlow	2. 8.10S
					(As "WP903" in Queen's Flight c/s)		
G-BCGH	SNCAN NC.854S	122	F-BAFG	10. 6.74	T J N H Palmer tr Nord Flying Group Hill Farm, Nayland		28. 5.08P
G-BCGI	Piper PA-28-140 Cherokee Cruiser	28-7425283	N9573N	10. 6.74	G Hurst	(Dukinfield)	12. 6.08E
G-BCGJ	Piper PA-28-140 Cherokee Cruiser	28-7425286	N9574N	10. 6.74	Demero Ltd and Transcourt Ltd Hinton-in-the-Hedges		12.10.07E
G-BCGM	Wassmer Jodel D 120 Paris-Nice	50	F-BHQM	15. 7.74	T J Roberts	Rochester	18. 5.07P
			F-BHYM				
G-BCGN	Piper PA-28-140 Cherokee F	28-7425323	N9595N	10. 6.74	Golf November Ltd	Oxford	13. 9.08E
G-BCGS	Piper PA-28R-200 Cherokee Arrow II	28R-7235133	N4893T	13. 6.74	S Rayne tr Arrow Aviation Group	Little Gransden	14. 6.08E
G-BCGW	Jodel D 11	CC.001		14. 6.74	G H and M D Chittenden	(London NW7)	30. 1.85P
	(Built G H and M D Chittenden - pr.no.PFA 912 & EAA/61554) (Lycoming O-290)						
G-BCHK	Reims Cessna F172H	F17200716	9H-AAD	19. 6.74	D Darby (Noted 7.04)	Haverfordwest	23.11.03T
G-BCHL	de Havilland DHC-1 Chipmunk 22A	C1/0680	WP788	20. 6.74	Shropshire Soaring Ltd	Sleap	2. 2.10S
					(As "WP788" in RAF c/s)		
G-BCHM	Westland SA.341G Gazelle 1	1168	G-17-20	14. 6.74	MW Helicopters Ltd	Stapleford	23. 8.99
					(New owner 5.02)		
G-BCHP	Scintex CP.1310-C3 Super Emeraude	902	G-JOSI	24. 6.74	G and AG Hughes	Earls Colne	2. 7.08P
			G-BCHP, F-BJVQ				
G-BCHT	Schleicher ASK 16	16021	BGA 1996	25. 6.74	D E Cadisch tr Dunstable K16 Group	Dunstable	31. 5.07
			D-KAMY				
G-BCHV	de Havilland DHC-1 Chipmunk 22	C1/0703	WP807	27. 6.74	K I Sutherland	(Stevington, Bedford)	20. 6.98
G-BCID	Piper PA-34-200 Seneca	34-7250303	N1381T	3. 7.74	Shenley Farms (Aviation) Ltd	Headcorn	22. 3.08E

G-BCIH	de Havilland DHC-1 Chipmunk 22	C1/0304	WD363	3. 7.74	J M Hosey (As "WD363" in RAF c/s)	Audley End	12. 6.09S
G-BCIJ	Grumman AA-5 Traveler	AA5-0603	N6143A	3. 7.74	D G Page t/a Arrow Association	Elstree	11. 7.08E
G-BCIN	Thunder Ax7-77 Balloon (Hot Air)	030		5. 7.74	R A ,P M G and N T M Vale Hurcott, Kidderminster		5. 5.84A
					(Tethered 9.05)		
G-BCIR	Piper PA-28-151 Cherokee Warrior	28-7415401	N9587N	9. 7.74	R W Harris	Southend	28.11.07E
					(Operated Willowair Flying Club) (Noted 1.08)		
G-BCJM	Piper PA-28-140 Cherokee F	28-7425321	N9592N	17. 7.74	APB Leasing Ltd	(Edgerley, Oswestry)	18. 2.08E
G-BCJN	Piper PA-28-140 Cherokee Cruiser	28-7425350	N9618N	17. 7.74	Top Cat Aviation Ltd	Manchester	8. 9.08E
					(Operated Manchester School of Flying)		
G-BCJO	Piper PA-28R-200 Cherokee Arrow II		N9640N	17. 7.74	R Ross	Inverness	19. 9.07
		28R-7435272					
G-BCJP	Piper PA-28-140 Cherokee	28-24187	N1766J	15. 8.74	D J and D Pitman tr Omletair Flying Group		
						Bournemouth	17. 5.08
G-BCKN	de Havilland DHC-1 Chipmunk 22	C1/0707	WP811	5. 8.74	T M Holloway tr RAF Gliding and Soaring Association		
	(Lycoming O-360)				(Operated Cranwell Gliding Club)	RAF Cranwell	20. 2.10S
G-BCKS	Fuji FA.200-180AO Aero Subaru	FA200-250		2. 8.74	S Hyland	Dunkeswell	14. 6.08E
G-BCKT	Fuji FA.200-180 Aero Subaru	FA200-251		2. 8.74	P Chilcott tr Kilo Tango Group	Shoreham	29. 6.08E
G-BCKU	Reims Cessna FRA150L Aerobat	FRA1500256		1. 8.74	Stapleford Flying Club Ltd	Stapleford	9.11.07E
G-BCKV	Reims Cessna FRA150L Aerobat	FRA1500251		1. 8.74	S N Bower and P W Brown t/a Huck Air		
						(Sheffield City)	19. 2.08E
G-BCLD	Sikorsky S-61N Mk.II	61-739	9M-BED	4. 2.75	Bristow Helicopters Ltd	Aberdeen	7. 8.08E
			G-BCLD				
G-BCLI	Grumman AA-5 Traveler	AA5-0643		12. 8.74	W D Smith	Lee-on-Solent	14. 8.07T
G-BCLL	Piper PA-28-180 Cherokee C	28-2400	SE-EON	13. 8.74	J Nash tr G-BCLL Group	Popham	14.11.07E
G-BCLS	Cessna 170B	20946	N8094A	23. 8.74	N Simpson	(Chapel Hill, Lincoln)	6. 6.08E
G-BCLT	SOCATA MS.894A Rallye Minerva 220	12003	EI-BBW	1. 8.74	K M Bowen	Upfield Farm, Whitson	17. 7.05
			G-BCLT, F-BTRL				
G-BCLU	SAN Jodel D 117	506	F-BHXG	28. 8.74	J B Dovey	Crowfield	3. 4.08P
G-BCLW	Grumman AA-1B Trainer	AA1B-0463		29. 8.74	J R Faulkner (Noted10.07)	Spanhoe	22. 8.05T
G-BCMD	Piper PA-18 Super Cub 95	18-2055	OO-SPF	4. 9.74	P Stephenson	(Clacton)	2. 6.08E
	(L-18C-PI) (Frame No.18-2071)		R Neth AF R-70, 52-2455				
G-BCMJ	K & S SA.102.5 Cavalier	MJ.1		9. 9.74	N F Andrews	(Oakham)	8. 8.85P
	(Built M Johnson - pr.no.PFA 001-1546) (Tailwheel u/c)						
G-BCMT	Isaacs Fury II	PFA 1522		9. 9.74	R W Burrows	Priory Farm, Tibenham	
	(Built M H Turner) (Continental O-200-A)				(New owner 2.02)		
G-BCNC	Gardan GY-201 Minicab	A 202	F-BICF	9. 9.74	J R Wraight	(Chatham)	
	(Built Nouvelle Soc Cometal)						
G-BCNP	Cameron O-77 Balloon (Hot Air)	117		16. 9.74	P Spellward "Blue Fret"	Bristol	28. 7.00A
G-BCNX	Piper J-3C-65 Cub (L-4H-PI)	11168	F-BEGM	17. 9.74	K J Lord tr The Grasshopper Flying Group		
	(Frame No.10993)		French AF, 43-29877			Cherry Tree Farm, Monewden	18. 2.08P
G-BCNZ	Fuji FA.200-160 Aero Subaru	FA200-257		16. 9.74	W Dougan	Prestwick	23. 2.08P
G-BCOB	Piper J-3C-65 Cub (L-4H-PI)	10696	F-BCPV	19. 9.74	J W Marjoram Low Farm, South Walsham		23. 2.08P
	(Frame No.10521)		43-29405		(As "329405:A-23" in USAAC c/s)		
G-BCOI	de Havilland DHC-1 Chipmunk 22	C1/0759	WP870	24. 9.74	M J Diggins Rayne Hall Farm, Braintree		25. 8.07
					(As "WP870:12" in RAF grey c/s)		
G-BCOJ	Cameron O-56 Balloon (Hot Air)	124		25. 9.74	T J Knott and M J Webber tr Phoenix Balloon Group		
					"Red Squirrel"	Rickmansworth	12. 7.87A
G-BCOL	Reims Cessna F172M Skyhawk II	F17201233		25. 9.74	M Power tr November Charlie Flying Group Gamston		10. 7.08E
G-BCOM	Piper J-3C-90 Cub (L-4A-PI)	10478	F-BDTP	27. 9.74	S L McKinnon tr Dougal Flying Group "Dougal"		
	(Frame No.10303)		F-BFQP, OO-ADI, 43-29187		(On rebuild 8.03) Butlers Gyhll, Southwater		8. 7.02P
	(Officially regd as c/n 12040 which is correct identity of G-BGPD; fuselages probably exchanged in France)						
G-BCOO	de Havilland DHC-1 Chipmunk 22	C1/0209	WB760	10.10.74	T G Fielding and M S Morton	Hawarden	1. 6.08
G-BCOR	SOCATA Rallye 100ST	2544	F-OCZK	7. 1.75	P R W Goslin and I M Speight	Henstridge	26. 7.08E
G-BCOU	de Havilland DHC-1 Chipmunk 22	C1/0559	WK522	10.10.74	P J Loweth	Duxford	30. 3.95
					"Thunderbird 5" (As "WK522" in RAF c/s) (Noted 1.07)		
G-BCOY	de Havilland DHC-1 Chipmunk 22	C1/0212	WB762	10.10.74	Coventry Gliding Club Ltd Husbands Bosworth		24. 1.09S
	(Lycoming O-360)						
G-BCPD	Gardan GY-201 Minicab	18	F-BGKN	24.10.74	P R Cozens	Hinton-in-the-Hedges	2. 8.08P
	(Built Con. Aéronautique de Bearn) (Continental A65)						
G-BCPG	Piper PA-28R-200 Cherokee Arrow II		N4985S	16.10.74	A G Antoniades tr Roses Flying Group	Barton	18. 9.08E
		28R-35705					
G-BCPH	Piper J-3C-65 Cub (L-4H-PI)	11225	F-BCZA	13.12.74	M J Janaway Siege Cross Farm, Thatcham		1. 5.08P
	(Frame No.11050)		French AF, 43-29934		(As "329934:B-72" in 25th AOP French Armoured Divn of US 3rd Army c/s)		
G-BCPJ	Piper J-3C-65 Cub (L-4J-PI)	13206	F-BDTJ	5.11.74	S Hollingsworth tr Piper Cub Group	Popham	17. 4.08P
	(Frame No.13036)		45-4466				
G-BCPK	Reims Cessna F172M Skyhawk II	F17201194	(D-ELOB)	21.10.74	D C C Handley (Noted 4.07)	Little Staughton	12. 1.01T
G-BCPN	Grumman AA-5 Traveler	AA5-0665	N6155A	21.10.74	J R Walker tr G-BCPN Group	Gamston	11. 3.08E
G-BCPU	de Havilland DHC-1 Chipmunk 22	C1/0839	WP973	24.10.74	P Waller	Wycombe Air Park	3.10.08S
G-BCRB	Reims Cessna F172M Skyhawk II	F17201209		29.10.74	Wingtask 1995 Ltd	Seething	9. 5.08E
G-BCRI	Cameron O-65 Balloon (Hot Air)	135		5.11.74	V J Thorne "Joseph"	Nailsea, Bristol	26. 8.81A
G-BCRK	K & S SA 102.5 Cavalier	PFA 001-10049		5.11.74	P G R Brown Trenchard Farm, Eggesford		14. 7.00P
	(Built R Y Kendal) (Lycoming O-235)				(In external store 11.06)		
G-BCRL	Piper PA-28-151 Cherokee Warrior	28-7415689	N9564N	5.11.74	BCRL Ltd (Operated Soloflight)	Humberside	7. 8.08E
G-BCRP	Piper PA-E23-250 Aztec E	27-7305082	N40269	7.11.74	Aeros Air Charter Ltd	Gloucestershire	24. 8.08E
G-BCRR	Grumman AA-5B Tiger	AA5B-0006		7.11.74	P A Rutherford tr Tiger Group	Popham	16. 1.08
G-BCRT	Reims Cessna F150M	F15001164		18.11.74	Almat Flying Club Ltd	Coventry	11. 6.08E
G-BCRX	de Havilland DHC-1 Chipmunk 22	C1/0232	WD292	22.11.74	M I Robinson and P J Tuplin	White Waltham	4. 9.09S
					(As "WD292" in RAF c/s)		
G-BCSA	de Havilland DHC-1 Chipmunk 22	C1/0691	WP799	25.11.74	T M Holloway tr RAF Gliding and Soaring Association		
	(Lycoming O-360)				(Operated Fulmar Gliding Club)	Easterton	6. 4.09S
G-BCSL	de Havilland DHC-1 Chipmunk 22	C1/0524	WG474	26.11.74	Chipmunk Flyers Ltd	Liverpool	26. 3.08T
G-BCST	SOCATA MS.893A Rallye Commodore 180	10748	F-BPQD	18.11.74	D R Wilcox	Spanhoe	5.10.07E
G-BCSX	Thunder Ax7-77 Balloon (Hot Air)	031		2.12.74	C Wolstenholme	Macclesfield	5. 7.86A
					"Woophski" (Tethered 9.05)		

Reg	Type	c/n	Prev id	Date	Owner/Operator	Base / Status
G-BCTF	Piper PA-28-151 Cherokee Warrior	28-7515033	N9585N	11.12.74	E Reed t/a St George Flight Training	
	(Rebuilt 1989/90 using major components from G-BFXZ)					Durham Tees Valley 27.11.07E
G-BCTI	Schleicher ASK 16	16029	D-KIWA	23.12.74	J G Batch tr Tango India Syndicate	
						Hinton-in-the-Hedges 17. 9.08E
G-BCTK	Reims FR172J Rocket	FR17200546		23.12.74	C F Dukes	(Starcross, Exeter) 11. 4.08
G-BCTT	Evans VP-1	PFA 1543		24.12.74	E R G Ludlow	(Harleston, Norfolk) 25. 3.05P
	(Built B J Boughton) (Volkswagen 1600)				*(Crashed Priory Farm, Tibenham: wreck stored 7.05)*	
G-BCUB	Piper J-3C-65 Cub (L-4J-PI)	13370	F-BFBU	13.12.74	A L Brown	Bourn 13. 6.01P
	(Lippert Reed conversion)		45-4630		*(Noted 10.05)*	
	(Officially regd with c/n 13186 which is G-BDOL (qv): airframes switched during conversion in UK)					
G-BCUF	Reims Cessna F172M Skyhawk II	F17201279		3. 1.75	R N Howell t/a Howell Plant Hire and Construction	
						Water Leisure Park, Skegness 22. 8.08E
G-BCUH	Reims Cessna F150M	F15001195		7. 1.75	M G Montgomerie tr G-BCUH Group	Elstree 25. 3.08E
G-BCUJ	Reims Cessna F150M	F15001176		9. 1.75	J Oleksyn and G Astle	Kemble 24. 4.08E
G-BCUO	Scottish Aviation Bulldog Series 120/122	BH120/371	Ghana AF G-107 G-BCUO	9. 1.75	Cranfield University	Cranfield 10. 5.10S
G-BCUS	Scottish Aviation Bulldog Series 120/122	BH120/373	Ghana AF G-109 G-BCUS	9. 1.75	C D Hill	North Weald 22. 6.08
G-BCUV	Scottish Aviation Bulldog Series 120/122	BH120/376	Ghana AF G-112 G-BCUV	9. 1.75	Dolphin Property (Management) Ltd	Old Sarum 15. 6.09T
	(As "XX704" in RAF c/s)					
G-BCUY	Reims Cessna FRA150M Aerobat	FRA1500269		14. 1.75	J C Carpenter	Clipgate Farm, Denton 27. 3.08E
G-BCVB	Piper PA-17 Vagabond	17-190	F-BFMT N4890H	22. 1.75	A T Nowak	Popham 16. 7.08P
	(Continental A65)					
G-BCVC	SOCATA Rallye 100ST	2548	F-OCZO	16. 1.75	W Haddow	Prestwick 17. 3.08E
G-BCVF	Practavia Pilot Sprite 115	GBC.1		27. 1.75	D G Hammersley	Tatenhill 18. 9.06P
	(Built G B Castle - pr.no.PFA 1362) (Continental C125)					
G-BCVG	Reims Cessna FRA150L Aerobat	FRA1500245	(I-AFAD)	16. 1.75	I G Cooper tr G-BCVG Flying Group	Compton Abbas 18. 1.08
G-BCVH	Reims Cessna FRA150L Aerobat	FRA1500258		16. 1.75	M A James	Perth 7.12.07E
G-BCVJ	Reims Cessna F172M Skyhawk II	F17201305		16. 1.75	Rothland Ltd	RAF Woodvale 20. 3.08E
G-BCVY	Piper PA-34-200T Seneca II	34-7570022	N32447	28. 1.75	Oxford Aviation Training Ltd	Oxford 9. 8.08E
G-BCWB	Cessna 182P Skylane II	18263566	N5848J	29. 1.75	M F Oliver and A J Mew	White Waltham 17. 2.08E
G-BCWH	Practavia Pilot Sprite 115	PFA 1366		3. 2.75	R Tasker	Blackpool 12. 6.08P
	(Built K B Parkinson and R Tasker) (Continental O-240-A)					
G-BCWK	Fournier RF3	24	F-BMDD	7. 2.75	T J Hartwell *(New owner 2.05)*	Thurleigh 13. 8.02P
G-BCXB	SOCATA Rallye 100ST	2546	F-OCZM	7. 2.75	T Gillespie tr The Rallye Group	Bagby 28. 5.08E
G-BCXE	Robin DR.400 2+2	1015		19. 2.75	Weald Air Services Ltd	Headcorn 27. 7.08E
G-BCXJ	Piper J-3C-65 Cub (L-4J-PI)	13048	F-BFFH OO-SWA, 44-80752	21. 2.75	W Readman	Old Sarum 15. 8.08P
	(Frame No.12878)				*(As "480752:E-39" in USAAC c/s)*	
G-BCXN	de Havilland DHC-1 Chipmunk 22	C1/0692	WP800	7. 3.75	G M Turner	RAF Halton 29. 5.09S
	(As "WP800:2" in RAF Southampton UAS c/s)					
G-BCYH	Slingsby Cadet III Motor Glider	2	BGA 1158 RAFGSA.264, XA297	10. 3.75	R O Johnson tr G-BCYH Group	5 10.07P
						Stoneacre Farm, Farthing Corner
	(Re-built D C Pattison - pr.no.PFA 1568)					
	(Formerly Slingsby T 31B c/n 839 now officially regd as Cadet III Motor Glider) (Volkswagen 1600)					
G-BCYM	de Havilland DHC-1 Chipmunk 22	C1/0598	WK577	13. 3.75	C H Nicholls tr G-BCYM Group	Little Rissington 29.11.09S
	(As "WK577" in RAF c/s)					
G-BCYR	Reims Cessna F172M Skyhawk II	F17201288		20. 3.75	Highland Flying School Ltd	Inverness 27. 1.08E
G-BCZM	Reims Cessna F172M Skyhawk II	F17201350		3. 4.75	Cornwall Flying Club Ltd	Bodmin 12. 2.08T
G-BCZO	Cameron O-77 Balloon (Hot Air)	158		27. 3.75	W O T Holmes *"Leo" (Inflated 6.02)*	Shrewsbury 11.10.86A

G-BDAA - G-BDZZ

Reg	Type	c/n	Prev id	Date	Owner/Operator	Base / Status
G-BDAD	Taylor JT.1 Monoplane	PFA 1453		2. 4.75	J N Hanson	Tarn Farm, Cockerham 7. 5.08P
	(Built J F Bakewell) (Volkswagen 1700)					
G-BDAG	Taylor JT.1 Monoplane	PFA 1430		1. 4.75	N R Osborne	Longside, Peterhead 5. 2.08P
	(Built R S Basinger)					
G-BDAI	Reims Cessna FRA150M Aerobat	FRA1500266		21. 4.75	D F Ranger	Popham 25. 7.08T
G-BDAK	Rockwell Commander 112A	252	N1252J	10. 4.75	M C Wilson	Top Farm, Croydon, Royston 29. 4.08E
G-BDAO	SIPA S91	2	F-BEPT	10. 4.75	S B Churchill	Eastbach Farm, Coleford 10. 5.08P
	(Continental C85)					
G-BDAP	Wittman W.8 Tailwind	0387		9. 4.75	J Whiting	Bagby 28. 2.06P
	(Built J and A Whiting - pr.no.PFA 3507)					
G-BDAR	Evans VP-1 Series 2	PFA 062-10461		10. 4.75	R B Valler	(Waterlooville) 20. 7.84P
	(Built S C Foggin and M J Dunmore - pr.no.PFA 1537) (Volkswagen 1600)					
G-BDAY	Thunder Ax5-42A Balloon (Hot Air)	042		8. 4.75	T M Donnelly *"Meconium"*	Sprotbrough, Doncaster 16. 1.93A
G-BDBD	Wittman W.8 Tailwind	133	N1198S	25. 4.75	W S Siebert and B Ohrman tr Tailwind Group	
	(Built Hamilton Tool Company)					Wellesbourne Mountford 22. 2.08P
G-BDBF	Clutton FRED Series II	PFA 1528		15. 4.75	G E and R E Collins	Derby 18. 3.98P
	(Built W T Morrell) (Volkswagen 1600)				*(New owners 10.04)*	
G-BDBH	Bellanca 7GCBC Citabria	758-74	OE-AOL	15. 4.75	C J Gray	Finmere 26. 9.10S
G-BDBI	Cameron O-77 Balloon (Hot Air)	162		15. 4.75	C Jones *"Funny Money"*	Sonning Common, Reading 11. 7.87A
G-BDBJ	Cessna 182P Skylane II	18263646	N4644K	18. 4.75	H C Wilson	Great Ashfield, Suffolk 11. 4.08E
G-BDBU	Reims Cessna F150M	F15001174		30. 4.75	Cumbernauld Flying School Ltd	Enniskillen 26. 8.08E
G-BDBV	Aero Jodel D 11A	V 3	D-EGIB	23. 4.75	S Pavey tr Seething Jodel Group	Seething 17.12.07E
	(Buillt Schwabach W Wolfrum) (Continental C90)					
G-BDCD	Piper J-3C-65 Cub (L-4J-PI)	12429	OO-AVS 44-80133	28. 4.75	S Willard tr Cubby Cub Group	Shoreham 15. 8.08P
	(Continental C90) (Frame No.12257)				*(As "480133:B-44" in US Army c/s)*	
G-BDCI	Menavia Piel CP.301C Emeraude	503	F-BIRC	25. 4.75	D L Sentance	Rothwell Lodge Farm, Kettering 9. 2.08P
G-BDCL	Grumman AA-5 Traveler	AA5-0773	EI-CCI	5. 5.75	J Crowe	Coventry 29.11.93T
			G-BDCL, EI-BGV, G-BDCL, N1373R *(Fuselage stored 5.00)*			
G-BDCO	Beagle B 121 Pup Series 1	B121-171		6. 5.75	R J Page and M H Simms *(New owner 4.01)*	
					(Bolney, Haywards Heath and Shipdham, Thetford)	28. 7.97
G-BDDD	de Havilland DHC-1 Chipmunk 22	C1/0326	WD387	16. 5.75	RAE Aero Club Ltd	Farnborough 27. 6.10T
G-BDDF	Wassmer Jodel D 120 Paris-Nice	97	F-BIKZ	20. 5.75	J V Thompson *(New owner 4.04)*	(Leeds) 10.11.03P

G-BDDG	Dormois Jodel D 112	855	F-BILM	20. 5.75	D G Palme *(Noted 6.05)*	Sturgate	28. 7.04P
G-BDDS	Piper PA-25-260 Pawnee C	25-4757	CS-AIU N10F	22. 5.75	T J Price tr Vale of Neath Gliding Club	Rhigos	21. 7.08E
G-BDDZ	Menavia Piel CP.301A Emeraude	253	F-BIMZ	30. 5.75	E C Mort	(Winwick, Warrington)	20. 6.84P
					(Damaged Cranwell North 3.6.84: on rebuild 1.01)		
G-BDEC	SOCATA Rallye 100ST	2552	F-OCZS	28. 5.75	J Fingleton	Kilkenny, County Kilkenny	19.12.07E
G-BDEH	Wassmer Jodel D 120A Paris-Nice	239	F-BLNE	2. 6.75	A J Warman tr EH Group	Oaksey Park	27. 8.08P
G-BDEI	Jodel D 9 Bébé	585		2. 6.75	R Q.T Newns tr The Noddy Group	White Waltham	20.10.08P
	(Built L T Dix - pr.no.PFA 936) (Volkswagen 1600)				*"Noddy"*		
G-BDEU	de Havilland DHC-1 Chipmunk 22	C1/0704	WP808	17. 6.75	Skylark Aviation Ltd	Prestwick	17.12.09
					(As "WP808" in RAF c/s)		
G-BDEX	Reims Cessna FRA150M Aerobat	FRA1500279		12. 6.75	R A Powell	Belle Vue Farm, Yarnscombe	30. 7.06T
G-BDEY	Piper J-3C-65 Cub (L-4J-PI)	12538	OO-AAT OO-GAC, 44-80242	17. 6.75	W J and J.Morecraft tr Ducksworth Flying Club	Highfield Farm, Empingham	17. 5.08P
	(Frame No.12366)						
G-BDEZ	Piper J-3C-65 Cub (L-4J-PI)	12383	OO-SOC OO-EPI, 44-80087	17. 6.75	R J M Turnbull	Rydinghurst Farm, Cranleigh	7. 8.08P
	(Frame No.12211)						
G-BDFB	Phoenix Currie Wot	PFA 3008		20. 6.75	J Jennings	Little Gransden	12.10.07P
	(Built D F Faulkner-Bryant and J Jennings) (Walter Mikron III)						
G-BDFH	Auster AOP.9	B5/10/176	XR240	24. 6.75	R B Webber	Trenchard Farm, Eggesford	17. 6.08P
	(Officially regd with Frame No.AUS/177)				*(As "XR240" in AAC c/s)*		
G-BDFJ	Reims Cessna F150M	F15001182		25. 6.75	C J Hopewell	Sibson	13. 7.02T
G-BDFR	Fuji FA.200-160 Aero Subaru	FA200-262		7. 7.75	M S Bird *(Noted 9.06)*	Glebe Farm, Stockton	1.11.04
G-BDFW	Rockwell Commander 112A	308	N1308J	18. 6.75	M E and E G Reynolds	Standalone Farm, Meppershall	22.11.07E
G-BDFX	Taylorcraft J Auster 5	2060	F-BGXG TW517	9. 7.75	J Eagles	Oaksey Park	3. 6.94T
					(Damaged Oaksey Park 10.10.93: on rebuild 4.02)		
G-BDFY	Grumman AA-5 Traveler	AA5-0806		10. 7.75	G Robertson tr The Grumman Group	Edinburgh	17. 6.06E
					(Operated Edinburgh Flying Club)		
G-BDFZ	Reims Cessna F150M	F15001184	(D-EIWB) (F-BXIH)	14. 7.75	L W Scattergood	Full Sutton	27. 6.08E
G-BDGB	Gardan GY-20 Minicab	PFA 1819		23. 6.75	D G Burden	Armshold Farm, Kingston, Cambridge	12. 6.01P
	(Built D G Burden to JB.01 Minicab standard) (Continental PC-60)						
G-BDGH	Thunder Ax7-77 Balloon (Hot Air)	049		16. 7.75	R J Mitchener and P F Smart t/a Balloon Collection "London Pride III"	Andover	30. 8.83A
G-BDGM	Piper PA-28-151 Cherokee Warrior	28-7415165	N41307	30. 7.75	J H Mitchell	Bagby	8. 9.07T
G-BDHK	Piper J-3C-65 Cub (L-4A-PI)	8969	F-PHFZ 42-38400	24. 7.75	S Pritchard tr Knight Flying Group		
					(As "329417" in USAAC c/s) Eastbach Farm, Coleford		18.10.08P
	(Official c/n quoted as "261" with p/i 42-36414 but this corresponds to c/n 8538/N75366)						
G-BDIE	Rockwell Commander 112A	342	N1342J	14. 8.75	R J Adams	RAF Brize Norton	5. 9.07T
G-BDIG	Cessna 182P Skylane II	18263938	N9877E	26. 8.75	P B Barrett and A R Bruce tr Air Group 6	Gamston	5. 9.08E
	(Reims-assembled with c/n F18200020)						
G-BDIH	SAN Jodel D 117	812	F-BIOT	22. 8.75	N D H Stokes	Trenchard Farm, Eggesford	13. 7.07P
					(Noted 8.07)		
G-BDIJ	Sikorsky S-61N Mk.II	61-751	9M-AYF G-BDIJ	3.10.75	Bristow Helicopters Ltd	Lee-on-Solent	31. 5.08E
	(SAR conversion)				*"Crathes" (Operated Marine and Coastguard Agency)*		
G-BDJD	Jodel D 112	PFA 910		3. 9.75	J E Preston	Linley Hill, Leven	29. 5.08P
	(Built J V Derrick) (Continental A65)				*"Marianne"*		
G-BDJG	Phoenix Luton LA-4A Minor	PFA 828		3. 9.75	S K Rose tr Very Slow Flying Club	(Bournemouth)	1. 7.04P
	(Built D J Gaskin) (Volkswagen 1835)				*(Address change 12.07)*		
G-BDJP	Piper J-3C-65 Cub Special	22992	OO-SKZ PH-NCV, NC3908K	11.12.75	S T Gilbert	Enstone	18. 5.03T
	(Continental C90) *(Frame No.21017)*						
G-BDJR	SNCAC NC.858	2	F-BFIY	30. 9.75	R F M Marson *(On rebuild 9.00)*	(Fleet)	23. 5.92T
G-BDJV	Britten-Norman BN-2A-21 Islander	476	Belgian Army B-03 G-BDJV	29. 9.75	Cormack (Aircraft Services) Ltd	Cumbernauld	
					(Noted 9.06)		
G-BDKC	Cessna A185F Skywagon	185-02569	N1854R	30. 9.75	Bridge of Tilt Company Ltd	Blair Atholl	23. 4.08E
G-BDKD	Enstrom F-28A	319		30. 9.75	P J Price	(Warrington)	8.11.07E
G-BDKH	Menavia Piel CP.301A Emeraude	241	F-BIMN	15.10.75	C Lobban tr G-BDKH Group	Perth	10. 8.08P
G-BDKJ	K & S SA.102.5 Cavalier	72207		14.10.75	D A Garner	(Swansea)	5. 6.95P
	(Built H B Yardley - pr.no.PFA 1589) (Continental O-240-A)				*(Damaged Gloucestershire 14. 9.97)*		
G-BDKM	SIPA 903	98	F-BGHX	17.11.75	S W Markham	Valentine Farm, Odiham	17. 7.08P
G-BDKW	Rockwell Commander 112A	106	N1277J ZS-MIB, N1106J	3.11.75	J T Klaschka	Poplar Hall Farm, Elmsett	26.10.07E
G-BDLO	Grumman AA-5A Cheetah	AA5A-0026	N6154A	3.11.75	S and J Dolan	Elstree	4. 8.07T
G-BDLT	Rockwell Commander 112A	363	N1363J	4.11.75	D L Churchward	Exeter	12. 6.08E
G-BDLY	K & S SA 102.5 Cavalier	PFA 001-10011		14.11.75	P R Stevens	Thruxton	2. 6.04P
	(Built B S Reeve) (Lycoming O-290)						
G-BDMS	Piper J-3C-65 Cub (L-4J-PI)	13049	F-BEGZ 44-80753	4.11.75	A T H Martin	Old Sarum	2. 8.08P
					(As "FR886" in RAF c/s)		
G-BDMW	SAN Jodel DR.100A Ambassadeur	79	F-BIVM	2.12.75	P R H Moore tr G-Mike Whisky Group	(Tarporley)	7. 8.08E
G-BDNC	Taylor JT.1 Monoplane	PFA 1454		8.12.75	D W Mathie	(Diss)	2. 8.08P
	(Built N J Cole) (Walter Mikron III)						
G-BDNG	Taylor JT.1 Monoplane	PFA 1405		12.12.75	W Long	Shobdon	14. 7.06P
	(Built D J Phillips) (Volkswagen 1834)						
G-BDNO	Taylor JT.1 Monoplane	PFA 1431		15.12.75	S D Glover	Perranporth	4. 9.04P
	(Built A J Gray)				*(Noted 10.07)*		
G-BDNT	Jodel D 92 Bébé	397	F-PINL	2. 1.76	R J Stobo	Oaklands Farm, Stonesfield, Witney	8. 6.08P
	(Volkswagen 1600)						
G-BDNU	Reims Cessna F172M Skyhawk II	F17201405		2. 1.76	J and K G McVicar	Elstree	21. 8.08E
G-BDNW	Grumman AA-1B Trainer	AA1B-0588		8. 1.76	P Mitchell	Deenethorpe	14. 5.08E
G-BDNX	Grumman AA-1B Trainer	AA1B-0590		8. 1.76	D M and P A Fenton	(Seaton Ross, York)	23. 8.08E
G-BDOC	Sikorsky S-61N Mk.II	61-765		20. 3.76	Bristow Helicopters Ltd	Den Helder, Netherlands	2. 7.08E
	(SAR conversion)				*"Tolquhoun"*		
G-BDOD	Reims Cessna F150M	F15001266		20. 1.76	P R Green tr OD Group	RAF Benson	2. 7.08E
G-BDOE	Reims FR172J Rocket	FR17200559		20. 1.76	D Sansome	Little Chase Farm, Kenilworth	24. 4.08E

G-BDOG	Scottish Aviation Bulldog Series 200 BH200/381			18.12.75	D C Bonsall	Netherthorpe	3. 9.07P
					(Phoenix Flying Group titles)		
G-BDOL	Piper J-3C-65 Cub (L-4J-PI)	13186	F-BCPC	18.12.75	L R Balthazor	Lee-on-Solent	10. 9.07P
	(Frame No.13016)		45-4446				
	(Officially regd as c/n 13370: holds c/n & USAAC plates which relate to correct 13370 - G-BCUB (qv) as airframes switched during UK conversion)						
G-BDON	Thunder Ax7-77A Balloon (Hot Air)	063		17.12.75	M J Smith *"Fred"*	Westow, York	24. 6.94A
G-BDOT	Fairey Britten-Norman BN-2A Mk.III-2 Trislander		ZK-SFF	21. 1.76	Lyddair Ltd	Lydd	2. 3.08T
		1025	N900TA, N903GD, N3850K, VH-BPB, G-BDOT				
G-BDOW	Reims Cessna FRA150M Aerobat FRA1500296			26. 1.76	Joystick Aviation Ltd	Cranfield	3. 4.08E
G-BDPA	Piper PA-28-151 Cherokee Warrior 28-7615033		N9630N	26. 1.76	Aircraft Engineers Ltd	Prestwick	19.11.07E
G-BDPJ	Piper PA-25-235 Pawnee B	25-3665	(PH-VBF)	2. 2.76	T M Holloway tr RAF Gliding and Soaring Association		
	(Lycoming O-540A1B5)		G-BDPJ, SE-EPZ			RAF Halton	22.11.07E
G-BDPK	Cameron O-56 Balloon (Hot Air)	191		4. 2.76	K J and G R Ibbotson	Abbeydale, Gloucester	29.12.88A
					(New owners 2.05)		
G-BDPN	Britten-Norman BN-2A-21 Islander	498	Belgian Army B-04	5. 2.76	Fly BN Ltd	Bembridge	
			G-BDPN		*(New owner 8.06)*		
G-BDRD	Reims Cessna FRA150M Aerobat FRA1500289			9. 2.76	Aircraft Engineers Ltd	Prestwick	19.10.07E
G-BDRG	Taylor JT.2 Titch	PFA 060-10295		19.12.78	D R Gray	*(Wilmslow)*	
	(Built D R Gray)						
G-BDRJ	de Havilland DHC-1 Chipmunk 22	C1/0742	WP857	19. 2.76	D MacDonald and D Friel tr WP857 Aircraft Trust		
					(As "WP857:24" in RAF c/s)	Prestwick	8.12.08E
G-BDRK	Cameron O-65 Balloon (Hot Air)	205		12. 2.76	R J Mitchener and P F Smart *"Smirk"* (Tethered 9.05)		
						Andover and Oakley, Basingstoke	20. 6.86A
G-BDSB	Piper PA-28-181 Cherokee Archer II		N8221C	23. 2.76	Testfair Ltd	Fairoaks	2. 5.08
		28-7690107					
G-BDSE	Cameron O-77 Balloon (Hot Air)	210		27. 2.76	British Airways PLC	Worplesdon	31. 3.90A
					"Concorde" (Tethered 9.05)		
G-BDSF	Cameron O-56 Balloon (Hot Air)	209		1. 3.76	J H Greensides *"Itzuma"*	Burton Pidsea, Hull	24. 5.93A
G-BDSH	Piper PA-28-140 Cherokee Cruiser 28-7625063		N9638N	1. 3.76	D Jones tr The Wright Brothers Flying Group		
						Tollerton	30. 8.08E
G-BDSK	Cameron O-65 Balloon (Hot Air)	166		3. 3.76	Semajan Ltd tr Southern Balloon Group	France	15. 9.08A
					"Carousel II"		
G-BDSL	Reims Cessna F150M	F15001306		5. 3.76	M Howells	Willey Park Farm, Caterham	24. 6.04E
	(Lost power on take-off Netherthorpe 16. 2.04 and substantially damaged: to Nalson Aviation Ltd for spares recovery and noted 3.06)						
G-BDSM	Slingsby T.31 Motor Cadet III	2464/3B		5. 3.76	F C J Wevers	*(Amersfoort, Netherlands)*	22. 5.02P
	(Re-built D W Savage - pr.no.PFA 042-10507)				*(New owner 4.04)*		
G-BDTB	Evans VP-1 Series 2	PFA 7009		15. 3.76	P F Moffatt	Breighton	29.10.04P
	(Built T E Boyes) (Volkswagen 1834)				*(Noted 12.07)*		
G-BDTL	Evans VP-1	PFA 7012		17. 3.76	A K Lang	*(Ilton, Ilminster)*	5. 9.85P
	(Built A K Lang) (Volkswagen 1600)				*(Addrses change 3.07)*		
G-BDTN	Fairey Britten-Norman BN-2A Mk.III-2 Trislander		S7-AAN	16. 3.76	Aurigny Air Services Ltd	Guernsey	10. 6.98T
		1026	VQ-SAN, G-BDTN		*(Stored 3.03)*		
G-BDTO	Fairey Britten-Norman BN-2A Mk.III-2 Trislander		G-RBSI	16. 3.76	Aurigny Air Services Ltd	Guernsey	31. 3.08E
		1027	G-OTSB, G-BDTO, 8P-ASC, G-BDTO, (C-GYOX), G-BDTO *(Aurigny.com titles)*				
G-BDTU	Van Den Bemden Omega III Gas Balloon (20,000 cu.ft)			16. 3.76	R G Turnbull	Clyro, Hereford	4. 8.99A
	(Also Abingdon Free Balloon c/n AFB.4) VDB-35				*"Omega III"*		
G-BDTV	Mooney M 20F Executive	22-1307	N6934V	16. 3.76	S Redfearn	Gamston	6. 8.08E
G-BDTX	Reims Cessna F150M	F15001275		19. 3.76	F W Ellis	Water Leisure Park, Skegness	14. 8.08E
G-BDUI	Cameron V-56 Balloon (Hot Air)	218		19. 3.76	D C Johnson *"True Brit"*	Farnham	6. 7.91A
G-BDUL	Evans VP-1	PFA 1557		25. 3.76	J C Lindsay	*(Inworth, Colchester)*	17. 3.07P
	(Built C Goodman) (Volkswagen 1834)				*(New owner 11.07)*		
G-BDUM	Reims Cessna F150M	F15001301	F-BXZB	29. 3.76	S G Bishop tr G-BDUM Group	Earls Colne	2. 5.08E
G-BDUN	Piper PA-34-200T Seneca II	34-7570163	(EI-BLR)	29. 3.76	R Paris	Oxford	26. 2.08E
			G-BDUN, SE-GIA				
G-BDUO	Reims Cessna F150M Commuter	F15001304		29. 3.76	D W Locke	*(Teddington)*	16. 5.07T
G-BDUY	Robin DR.400-140B Major	1120		5. 4.76	J G Anderson	Pittrichie Farm, Whiterashes	13. 4.08E
G-BDUZ	Cameron V-56 Balloon (Hot Air)	213		30. 3.76	P J Bish t/a Zebedee Balloon Service		
					"Hot Lips"	Newtown, Hungerford	19. 2.00A
G-BDVA	Piper PA-17 Vagabond	17-206	CN-TVY	23. 4.76	I M Callier	*(Berry Grove Farm, Liss)*	13. 8.03P
	(Continental C90)		F-BFFE				
G-BDVB	Piper PA-15 Vagabond	15-229	F-BHHE	23. 4.76	B P Gardner	Whittles Farm, Mapledurham	5. 6.08P
	(Continental C90) (Regd as "PA-17")		SL-AAY, F-BETG				
G-BDVC	Piper PA-17 Vagabond	17-140	F-BFBL	29. 9.76	A R Caveen	Sandford Hall, Knockin	21. 8.08P
	(Continental C90)						
G-BDWA	SOCATA Rallye 150ST	2695		20. 4.76	J T Wilson *(Noted 8.07)*	Derrytrasna Glen, Bannfoot	7. 6.01
G-BDWE	Flaglor Sky Scooter	DWE-01		12. 4.76	P King	Eastbach Farm, Coleford	27. 6.05P
	(Built D W Evernden - pr.no.PFA 1332 & KF-S-66) (Volkswagen 1600)						
G-BDWH	SOCATA Rallye 150ST	2697		20. 4.76	M A Jones Upper Harford Farm, Bourton-on-the-Water		28.10.07E
G-BDWJ	Replica Plans SE.5a	PFA 020-10034	"C1904"	27. 4.76	D W Linney	*(Langport)*	15. 8.08P
	(Built M L Beach) (Continental C90)		"F8010"		*(As "F8010/Z" in RFC c/s)*		
G-BDWM	Bonsall DB-1 Mustang	PFA 073-10200		3. 5.76	D C Bonsall	Netherthorpe	15. 6.98T
	(Built D C Bonsall) (Lycoming IO-360)				*(As "FB226:MT-A" in RAF c/s: on rebuild 5.04)*		
G-BDWO	Howes Ax6 Balloon (Hot Air)	RBH.2		5. 5.76	R Band C Howes	Keysoe	
	(Built R B and C Howes)				*"Griffin" (Complete 11.88)*		
G-BDWP	Piper PA-32R-300 Cherokee Lance 32R-7680176		N8784E	7. 5.76	W M Brown	Coventry	7. 3.08E
G-BDWX	Wassmer Jodel D 120A Paris-Nice	311	F-BNHT	13. 5.76	R P Rochester	Wombleton	22. 2.08P
G-BDWY	Piper PA-28-140 Cherokee E	28-7225378	PH-NSC	14. 5.76	A Boorman and D Bishop	Oxford	19. 7.08E
			N11C				
G-BDWZ	Slingsby T.59J Kestrel 22	1867	BGA.2470-DXU	17. 5.76	T J Wilkinson	Sackville Lodge, Riseley	29. 4.08
	(Converted from T.59H 1979)						
G-BDXJ	Boeing 747-246B	21831	N1792B	2.5.80	Aces High Ltd	Dunsfold	18.11.07E
G-BDXX	SNCAN NC.858S	110	F-BEZO	17. 5.76	K M Davis	North Weald	3. 7.96P
					(On rebuild 5.04) (New owner 7.04)		
G-BDYD	Rockwell Commander 114	14014	N1914J	21. 5.76	J R Pybus	Sherburn-in-Elmet	21.11.07E

G-BDYH	Cameron V-56 Balloon (Hot Air)	233		24. 5.76	B J Godding "Novocastrian"	Didcot	25.11.90A
G-BDZA	Scheibe SF25E Super Falke (Limbach SL-1700)	4320	(D-KECW)	1. 6.76	G Pybus tr Hereward Flying Group	Crowland	13. 4.08
G-BDZC	Reims Cessna F150M	F15001316		1. 6.76	A M Lynn	Sibson	21. 7.08E
G-BDZD	Reims Cessna F172M Skyhawk II	F17201478		1. 6.76	Skydive Aircraft Ltd	AAC Netheravon	7. 8.08T
G-BDZG	Slingsby T.59H Kestrel 22	1868	BGA 2481-DYG G-BDZG	3. 6.76	R E Gretton	Crowland	19. 4.08
G-BDZI	Britten-Norman BN-2A-21 Islander	531	Belgian Army B-08 G-BDZI	9. 6.76	Fly BN Ltd *(New owner 8.06)*	Bembridge	

G-BEAA - G-BEZZ

G-BEAB	CEA Jodel DR.1051 Sicile	228	F-BKGH	18. 8.76	R C Hibberd	(Chiseldon, Swindon)	13. 7.07
G-BEAC	Piper PA-28-140 Cherokee	28-21963	4X-AND	4. 6.76	R Murray and A Bagley-Murray	Humberside	10. 7.08E
G-BEAG	Piper PA-34-200T Seneca II	34-7670204	N9395K	18. 6.76	Oxford Aviation Training Ltd	Oxford	21. 9.08E
G-BEAH	Auster V J/2 Arrow (Continental C85)	2366	F-BFUV F-BFVV, OO-ABS	28. 6.76	J G Parish tr Bedwell Hey Flying Group "Llewellyn" Bedwell Hey Farm, Little Thetford, Ely		26. 4.08P
G-BEBE	Grumman AA-5A Cheetah	AA5A-0154		28. 6.76	Bills Aviation Ltd	Biggin Hill	31. 5.08E
G-BEBG	PZL-Bielsko SZD-45A Ogar	B-655		29. 6.76	D W Coultrip tr The Ogar Syndicate	Hinton-in-the-Hedges	21. 6.08E
G-BEBN	Cessna 177B Cardinal	17701631	4X-CEW N34031	1. 7.76	R Turrell and P Mason	King's Farm, Thurrock	9. 4.08E
G-BEBR	Gardan GY-201 Minicab (Built A S Jones) (Originally officially regd with c/n PFA 1670)	PFA 1824		5. 7.76	K G G Howe	Barton	6.11.08P
G-BEBS	Andreasson BA-4B (Built D M Fenton [t/a Hornet Aviation] - pr.no.PFA 038-10157) (Continental O-200-A)	HA/01		7. 7.76	N J W Reid	Lee-on-Solent	19. 5.08P
G-BEBU	Rockwell Commander 112A	272	N1272J	8. 7.76	Aeros Engineering Ltd *(Noted 1.06)*	Gloucestershire	19. 6.04T
G-BEBZ	Piper PA-28-151 Cherokee Warrior	28-7615328	N6193J	14. 7.76	Airways Flight Training (Exeter) Ltd	RNAS Yeovilton	27. 4.08E
G-BECA	SOCATA Rallye 100ST	2751		14. 7.76	A C Stamp	Redhill	24.10.07
G-BECB	SOCATA Rallye 100ST	2783		14. 7.76	D H Tonkin	Bugle, St Austell	4. 8.08E
G-BECF	Scheibe SF25A Motorfalke (Hirth F23A)	4555	OO-WIZ (D-KARA)	14. 7.76	North County Ltd *(Fuselage noted 5.05)*	Barton	1. 3.94P
G-BECK	Cameron V-56 Balloon (Hot Air)	136		27. 7.76	A M and N H Ponsford	Leeds	9. 5.06A
G-BECN	Piper J-3C-65 Cub (L-4J-PI)	12776	HB-OCI (1), 44-80480	27. 7.76	G Denney *(As "480480:E-44" in USAAC c/s) "Miss Monica"*	Audley End	16.10.08S
G-BECS	Thunder Ax6-56A Balloon (Hot Air)	074		4. 8.76	A Sieger	Munster, Germany	5. 6.08A
G-BECT	CASA 1-131E Jungmann	"3974"	Spanish AF E3B-338	3. 8.76	G M S Scott tr Alpha 57 Group *(As "A-57" in Swiss AF c/s)*	(London SW18)	19. 2.07P
G-BECW	CASA 1-131E Jungmann (Incorporating parts of G-BECY ex E3B-459)	2037	Spanish AF E3B-423	3. 8.76	C M Rampton *(As "A-10" in Swiss AF c/s)*	(Lyminge, Folkestone)	4.11.06P
G-BECZ	Mudry CAP.10B	68	F-BXHK	26. 7.76	Avia Special Ltd	Little Gransden	2. 6.07T
G-BEDD	SAN Jodel D 117A	915	F-BITY	3. 8.76	M D Howlett tr Dubious Group	Shrove Furlong Farm, Ilmer	7. 6.08P
G-BEDF	Boeing B-17G-105-VE Fortress	8693	N17TE F-BGSR, 44-85784	5. 8.76	B-17 Preservation Ltd *(As "124485:DF-A" in USAAC c/s) "Sally B" (port)/"Memphis Belle" (starboard)*	Duxford	22. 5.08P
G-BEDG	Rockwell Commander 112A	482	N1219J	5. 8.76	Hotels International Ltd	Blackbushe	3. 4.08E
G-BEDJ	Piper J-3C-65 Cub (L-4J-PI) (Frame No.12720)	12890	F-BDTC 44-80594	5. 8.76	R Earl *(Stored frame 2.07)*	White Waltham	8.10.96P
G-BEDP	Fairey Britten-Norman BN-2A Mk.III-2 Trislander	1039	ZK-SFG N902TA, N1FY, N401JA, G-BEDP	17. 8.76	Airx Ltd t/a Blue Islands	Alderney	28. 5.08E
G-BEDW	Britten-Norman BN-2A-21 Islander	541	Belgian Army B-10 G-BEDW	25. 8.76	Fly BN Ltd *(New owner 8.06)*	Bembridge	
G-BEEG	Fairey Britten-Norman BN-2A-26 Islander	550	(C-GYUH) G-BEEG	25. 8.76	M D Carruthers and S F Morris t/a North West Parachute Centre	Cark-in-Cartmel	5. 4.05T
G-BEEH	Cameron V-56 Balloon (Hot Air)	250		24. 8.76	Sade Balloons Ltd "Tywi"	Coulsdon	29.11.07A
G-BEER	Isaacs Fury II (Built M J Clark) (Lycoming O-235)	PFA 1588		31. 8.76	R S C Andrews *(As "K2075" in RAF c/s)*	Bidford	14. 6.07P
G-BEEU	Piper PA-28-140 Cherokee F	28-7325247	PH-NSE N11C	9. 9.76	H and E Merkado	Panshanger	6. 3.08E
G-BEFA	Piper PA-28-151 Cherokee Warrior	28-7615416	N6978J	8. 9.76	M A Verran t/a Verran Freight	RAF Benson	2. 5.08E
G-BEFF	Piper PA-28-140 Cherokee F	28-7325228	PH-NSF N11C	27. 9.76	H and E Merkado	Panshanger	22. 5.08E
G-BEGG	Scheibe SF25E Super Falke (Limbach SL1700)	4326	(D-KDFB)	15.10.76	H Altmann tr G-BEGG Motorfalke	Turweston	6. 6.08E
G-BEHH	Piper PA-32R-300 Cherokee Lance	32R-7680323	N6172J	29.10.76	K Swallow	Sherburn-in-Elmet	5. 9.08E
G-BEHU	Piper PA-34-200T Seneca II	34-7670265	N6175J	3.11.76	Pirin Aeronautical Ltd	Stapleford	6. 4.08E
G-BEHV	Reims Cessna F172N Skyhawk II	F17201541		3.11.76	Edinburgh Air Centre Ltd	Edinburgh	3.10.07E
G-BEIA	Reims Cessna FRA150M Aerobat	FRA1500317		8.11.76	C J Hopewell *(New owner 9.05)*	Sibson	27.10.03T
G-BEIF	Cameron O-65 Balloon (Hot Air)	259		17.11.76	C Vening *"Solitaire" (Operated Balloon Preservation Group)*	Petworth	22. 4.07A
G-BEIG	Reims Cessna F150M	F15001361		18.11.76	R D Forster and M S B Thorp	Ellough, Beccles	1. 8.08E
G-BEII	Piper PA-25-235 Pawnee D	25-7656059	N54918	16.11.76	Burn Gliding Club Ltd	Burn	7. 4.08E
G-BEIL	SOCATA Rallye 150T	2653	F-BXDL	1.12.76	J I Oakes and R A Harris tr The Rallye Flying Group	Hill Farm, Nayland	23. 7.08E
G-BEIP	Piper PA-28-181 Cherokee Archer II	28-7790158	N6628F	22.11.76	S Pope	Barton	13. 9.08E
G-BEIS	Evans VP-1 (Built D J Park) (Volkswagen 1600)	PFA 7029		25.11.76	P J Hunt *(Stored 2.99)*	Thruxton	16. 7.90P
G-BEJD	Avro 748 Series 1/105	1543	LV-HHE LV-PUF	17.12.76	PTB (Emerald) Proprietary Ltd *"Sisyphus" (Stored internally 2.08)*	Blackpool	29. 3.06E
G-BEJK	Cameron S-31 Balloon (Hot Air)	256		1.12.76	A M and N H Ponsford t/a Rango Balloon and Kite Company *"L'Essence" (Amended owners 8.07)*	Leeds	16. 2.92A
G-BEJV	Piper PA-34-200T Seneca II	34-7770062	N7657F	31.12.76	Oxford Aviation Training Ltd	Oxford	19. 9.08E

Reg	Type	C/n	Prev id	Date	Owner / Location	Date
G-BEKL	Bede BD-4E-150　　151 & BD4E/2		(G-AYKB)	11. 1.77	F E Tofield　　　　　　(Farnborough)	14.10.80P
	(Built Brookmoor Bede Aircraft) (Lycoming O-320)				*(New owner 4.02)*	
G-BEKM	Evans VP-1　　PFA 7025			12. 1.77	G J McDill　　Westmoor Far, Thirsk	23. 3.95P
	(Built G J McDill) (Volkswagen 1834)				*(Stored 7.98: new owner 1.03)*	
G-BEKN	Reims Cessna FRA150M Aerobat　FRA1500318			12. 1.77	A L Brown *(Derelict 10.05 - for rebuild)*　Bourn	8.10.89T
G-BEKO	Reims Cessna F182Q Skylane II　F18200037			12. 1.77	G J and F J Leese　Sherburn-in-Elmet	21. 4.08E
G-BELT	Cessna F150J　　F150-0409X			26. 1.77	A Kumar　　Blackpool	10. 9.08E
	(Built Reims Aviation SA) (Mainly rebuild of G-AWUV and parts of G-ATND)					
G-BEMB	Reims Cessna F172M Skyhawk II　F17201487			27. 1.77	Stocklaunch Ltd　　Goodwood	23. 4.08E
G-BEMM	Slingsby Cadet III Motor Glider　1247		BGA 942	27. 1.77	E and P McEvoy　Kilrush, County Kildare	10.10.06P
	(Re-built M N Martin from Slingsby T 31B)		RAFGSA 289, BGA 942		(Volkswagen 1600)	
G-BEMU	Thunder Ax5-42 Balloon (Hot Air)　097			9. 2.77	M A Hall *"Chrysophylax"*　Stoneleigh	16. 1.99A
G-BEMW	Piper PA-28-181 Cherokee Archer II		N9566N	9. 2.77	Touch and Go Ltd　White Waltham	30.11.07E
		28-7790243				
G-BEMY	Reims Cessna FRA150M Aerobat　FRA1500315			9. 2.77	J R Power　Kilrush, County Kildare	13.12.07E
G-BEND	Cameron V-56 Balloon (Hot Air)　260			14. 2.77	P J Bish tr Dante Balloon Group *"Le Billet"*	1. 1.94A
					(Tethered 9.05)　Newtown, Hungerford	
G-BENJ	Rockwell Commander 112B　522		N1391J	7. 3.77	D J Gibney tr BENJ Flying Group	21. 8.08E
					Top Farm, Croydon, Royston	
G-BENK	Reims Cessna F172M Skyhawk II　F17201509			2. 3.77	Bulldog Aviation Ltd　Earls Colne	14. 6.08E
G-BENN	Cameron V-56 Balloon (Hot Air)　278			4. 3.77	S J Hollingsworth and M K Bellamy	15. 3.87A
					"English Rose" (Inflated 4.06)　Bleasby, Nottingham	
G-BEOD	Cessna 180　32092		OO-SPZ	14. 3.77	I Addy　　Spanhoe	6. 9.91
			D-EDAH, SL-AAT, N3294D		*(Noted stored 10.07)*	
G-BEOE	Reims Cessna FRA150M Aerobat　FRA1500322			21. 3.77	W J Henderson t/a Air Images　Kilbride	21. 8.08E
G-BEOH	Piper PA-28R-201T Turbo Arrow III		N1905H	11. 3.77	K G Harper tr Gloucestershire Flying Club	
		28R-7703038			Gloucestershire	23. 6.08E
G-BEOI	Piper PA-18-150 Super Cub　18-7709028		N54976	11. 3.77	Southdown Gliding Club Ltd　Parham Park	23. 2.08E
	(Lycoming O-360-A4)					
G-BEOK	Reims Cessna F150M　F15001366			14. 3.77	J Woodthorpe tr Oscar Kilo Flying Group　Gamston	11. 5.08E
G-BEOL	Short SC.7 Skyvan 3 Variant 100　SH1954		ZS-OIO	16. 3.77	Invicta Aviation Ltd　Hibaldstow	23. 4.08E
			JA8803 (2), G-BEOL, G-14-122			
G-BEOY	Reims Cessna FRA150L Aerobat　FRA1500150		F-BTFS	30. 3.77	J H Ponsford　(Chichester)	28. 7.08E
G-BEPC	SNCAN Stampe SV-4C　64		F-BFUM	17.10.77	Papa Charlie's Flying Circus Ltd　Little Rissington	7.11.09S
			F-BFZM, French.Military			
G-BEPF	SNCAN Stampe SV-4C　424		F-BCVD	30. 3.77	C C Rollings and F J Hodson　Gloucestershire	
					(New owners 10.06)	
G-BEPV	Fokker S 11.1 Instructor　6274		PH-ANK	13. 4.77	S W M Isbister and C Tyers　North Weald	13. 2.08P
			Dutch Navy 174, Dutch AF E-31		*(As "174:K:" in Royal Netherlands Navy c/s)*	
G-BEPY	Rockwell Commander 112B　524		N1399J	20. 4.77	V Parsons tr PAM Aero Group　Cranfield	1. 7.07
G-BERA	SOCATA Rallye 150ST　2821		F-ODEX	13. 4.77	E L L Burbidge　(London SW6)	3.12.07E
G-BERC	SOCATA Rallye 150ST　2858			13. 4.77	R S Jones tr The Severn Valley Aero Group	
					Welshpool	20. 4.08E
G-BERD	Thunder Ax6-56A Balloon (Hot Air)　106			25. 4.77	P M Gaines *"Goldfinger"*　Stockton-on-Tees	14. 5.04A
G-BERI	Rockwell Commander 114　14234		N4909W	6. 5.77	K B Harper　Blackbushe	12. 5.08
G-BERN	Saffery S 330 BALLOON (MINIMUM LIFT)　4			19. 4.77	B Martin　Somersham, Huntingdon	
					"Beeze I" (Extant 5.07)	
G-BERT	Cameron V-56 Balloon (Hot Air)　273			19. 4.77	Semajan Ltd tr Southern Balloon Group *"Bert"*　(France)	15. 9.08A
G-BERY	Grumman AA-1B Trainer　0193		N9693L	27.10.77	R H J Levi *"79"*　Stapleford	2. 8.08E
G-BETD	Robin HR.200-100 Club　20		PH-SRL	28. 4.77	C L Wilsher　Sywell	24. 1.08
G-BETE	Rollason Beta B 2A　PFA 002-10169			26. 4.77	T M Jones　Derby	
	(Built T Jones) (Incorporates parts from PFA 1304)				*(Under construction 4.04)*	
G-BETG	Cessna 180K Skywagon　180-52873		N64146	17. 5.77	J A Hart　Dunkeswell	13. 3.08E
G-BETI	Pitts S-1D　7-0314		G-PIII	28. 4.77	D R Puleston tr On A Roll Aerobatics Group	
	(Built B Bray - pr.no.PFA 009-10156) (Lycoming O-320) G-BETI				Leicester	1. 3.08P
G-BETL	Piper PA-25-235 Pawnee D　25-7656016		N54874	27. 5.77	Cambridge Gliding Club Ltd　Gransden Lodge	22.10.07
G-BETM	Piper PA-25-235 Pawnee D　25-7656066		N54927	5. 5.77	Yorkshire Gliding Club (Proprietary) Ltd　Sutton Bank	1. 5.08
G-BETW	Rand Robinson KR-2　PFA 129-10251			26. 4.77	S C Solley　Clipgate Farm, Denton	
	(Original c/n allocated as KR-2/TAW.1 (T A Wiffen) but PFA pr.no issued to VP-1 [62-10251]: re-allocated to S C Solley)					
G-BEUA	Piper PA-18-150 Super Cub　18-8212		D-ECSY	21. 6.77	London Gliding Club Proprietary Ltd　Dunstable	27. 2.08E
	(Lycoming O-360-A4)		N4146Z		*(Landing gear collapsed Dunstable 8.4.06 due to fatigue failure with substantial damage)*	
G-BEUD	Robin HR.100-285 Tiara　534		F-BXRC	8. 6.77	E A and L M C Payton　Cranfield	11. 8.08E
G-BEUI	Piper J-3C-65 Cub (L-4H-PI)　12174		F-BFEC	19. 5.77	M C Jordan　Eaglescott	5. 3.08P
	(Frame No.12002)		F-OAJF, French AF, 44-79878		*(Regd as ex 43-29245 which is actually G-KIRK)*	
G-BEUM	Taylor JT.1 Monoplane　PFA 1438			8. 6.77	J M Burgess　Aboyne	28. 7.04P
	(Built Speedwell Sailplanes) (Volkswagen 1700)				*(Noted under restoration 4.07)*	
G-BEUP	Robin DR.400-180 Régent　1228			19. 5.77	Legal Week Ltd t/a Samuels Aviation　Biggin Hill	24. 7.08E
G-BEUU	Piper PA-18 Super Cub 95　18-1551		F-BOUU	27. 6.77	F Sharples　Sandown, Isle of Wight	18. 5.08P
	(L-18C-PI) *(Frame No.should be 18-1523)*		French Army 18-1551, 51-15551			
G-BEUX	Reims Cessna F172N Skyhawk II　F17201596			30. 5.77	Multiflight Ltd　Hawarden	15. 3.08E
G-BEUY	Cameron N-31 Balloon (Hot Air)　283			31. 5.77	M L and L P Willoughby　Woodcote, Reading	17.10.90A
					(Typhoo Tea titles) (Inflated 4.02)	
G-BEVB	SOCATA Rallye 150ST　2860			2. 6.77	M Smullen　(Lullymore, Rathangan, County Kildare)	23. 6.08E
G-BEVC	SOCATA Rallye 150ST　2861			2. 6.77	I R Chaplin　Andrewsfield	10. 8.08E
G-BEVG	Piper PA-34-200T Seneca II　34-7570060		VQ-SAM	31. 5.77	Direct Aviation Management Ltd　Humberside	26. 3.08E
			N32854			
G-BEVO	Fournier RF5　5107		5N-AIX	27. 6.77	M Hill　(Stratford-upon-Avon)	24. 8.08E
			D-KAAZ			
G-BEVS	Taylor JT.1 Monoplane　PFA 1429			8. 6.77	D Hunter　Chavenage, Tetbury	17. 4.08P
	(Built D Hunter) (Volkswagen 1835)					
G-BEVT	Fairey Britten-Norman BN-2A Mk.III-2 Trislander			10. 6.77	Aurigny Air Services Ltd　Guernsey	15.11.07E
		1057			*(Aberdeen Asset Management titles)*	
G-BEVW	SOCATA Rallye 150ST　2928			2. 6.77	A L Hall-Carpenter　Old Buckenham	8. 2.08E

Reg	Type	c/n	Prev id	Date	Owner/Operator	Location	Date
G-BEWN	de Havilland DH.82A Tiger Moth	952	VH-WAL RAAF A17-529	16. 6.77	H D Labouchere	Blue Tile Farm, Langham	22. 7.09S

(Built de Havilland Aircraft Pty Ltd Australia - rebuild as official c/n T305)

Reg	Type	c/n	Prev id	Date	Owner/Operator	Location	Date
G-BEWO	Moravan Zlin Z-326 Trener Master	915	CS-ALU	23.11.77	P A Colman	Luxter's Farm, Hambledon	2. 7.03
G-BEWR	Reims Cessna F172N Skyhawk II	F17201613		13. 6.77	Cheshire Air Training Services Ltd	Liverpool	25. 5.08E
G-BEWX	Piper PA-28R-201 Cherokee Arrow III	28R-7737070	N5723V	23. 6.77	A Vickers	North Weald	23. 5.08E
G-BEWY	Bell 206B-2 JetRanger II	348	G-CULL EI-BXQ, G-BEWY, 9Y-TDF	27. 6.77	Polo Aviation Ltd	Bristol	13. 5.08E
G-BEXN	Grumman AA-1C Lynx	AA1C-0045	N6147A	7. 9.77	H Sykes and M Holliday "0045"	North Weald	27. 4.08E
G-BEXO	Piper PA-23 Apache	23-213	OO-APH N1176P	4. 7.77	Aviation Advisory Services Ltd	Stapleford	10.10.07E
G-BEXW	Piper PA-28-181 Cherokee Archer II	28-7790521	N38122	11. 7.77	J O'Keefe	Waterford, County Waterford	10. 9.08E
G-BEXX	Cameron V-56 Balloon (Hot Air)	274		29. 6.77	K A Schlussler "Rupert of Rutland"	Bourne, Lincoln	2. 7.86A
G-BEXZ	Cameron N-56 Balloon (Hot Air)	294		7. 7.77	D C Eager and G C Clark "Valor"	Bracknell and Worcester	6. 3.08A
G-BEYA	Enstrom 280C Shark	1104		15. 8.77	Hovercam Ltd	Staddon Heights, Plymouth	11. 7.08E
G-BEYL	Piper PA-28-180 Cherokee Archer	28-7405098	PH-SDW N9518N	6. 9.77	D W Gerrard tr Yankee Lima Group Compton Abbas		2. 4.08
G-BEYT	Piper PA-28-140 Cherokee	28-20330	D-EBWO N6280W	19. 7.77	R M Dene	Oxford	14. 5.08E
G-BEYV	Cessna T210M Turbo Centurion II	21061583	N732KX	19. 7.77	Castleridge Ltd	Bagby	7. 6.08E
G-BEYW	Taylor JT.1 Monoplane	RJS.100		22. 7.77	R A Abrahams "Red Hot"	Barton	5. 6.08P

(Built R A Abrahams - pr.no.PFA 055-10279) (Volkswagen 1834)

Reg	Type	c/n	Prev id	Date	Owner/Operator	Location	Date
G-BEYZ	CEA Jodel DR.1050/M1 Sicile Record	588	F-BMGV	22. 7.77	M L Balding	Biggin Hill	5.10.07E
G-BEZC	Grumman AA-5 Traveler	AA5-0493	F-BUYN (N7193L)	29. 7.77	C M O'Connell	Southend	11. 8.08E
G-BEZE	Rutan VariEze	PFA 074-10207		26. 7.77	S K Cockburn	(Stanford-Le-Hope)	2. 6.04P

(Built J Berry) (Continental O-200-A)
(Force-landed 5ms from Rayleigh 17.12.03 and badly damaged)

Reg	Type	c/n	Prev id	Date	Owner/Operator	Location	Date
G-BEZF	Grumman AA-5 Traveler	AA5-0538	F-BVJP	29. 7.77	M D Moaby tr BEZF Group	Conington	21.12.07E
G-BEZG	Grumman AA-5 Traveler	AA5-0561	F-BVRJ	29. 7.77	M D R Harling	Shobdon	31. 5.08E
G-BEZH	Grumman AA-5 Traveler	AA5-0566	F-BVRK N9566L	29. 7.77	L and S M Sims	Fenland	22. 5.08E
G-BEZI	Grumman AA-5 Traveler	AA5-0567	F-BVRL N9567L	29. 7.77	H Matthews tr The BEZI Flying Group	Cranfield	27. 9.08E
G-BEZK (2)	Cessna F172H	F172-0462	D-EBUD D-ENHC, SLN-07, N20462	17. 8.77	S Jones	Ellough, Beccles	30. 7.08E

(Built Reims Aviation SA)

Reg	Type	c/n	Prev id	Date	Owner/Operator	Location	Date
G-BEZL	Piper PA-31 Navajo C	31-7712054	SE-GPA	1. 8.77	A Jahanfar	Southend	20. 7.08E
G-BEZO	Reims Cessna F172M Skyhawk II	F17201392		24. 8.77	Cardinal Sin Ltd t/a Staverton Flying School Gloucestershire		1. 4.08E
G-BEZP	Piper PA-32-300 Cherokee Six	32-7740087	N38572	19. 8.77	T P McCormack and J K Zealley	White Waltham	19. 5.08
G-BEZR	Reims Cessna F172M Skyhawk II	F17201395		24. 8.77	Kirmington Aviation Ltd	Thruxton	8. 5.08E
G-BEZV	Reims Cessna F172M Skyhawk II	F17201474	(I-CCAY)	24. 8.77	A T Wilson tr Insch Flying Group	Insch	28. 4.08E
G-BEZY	Rutan VariEze	1167		26. 7.77	I J Pountney	(Malvern)	18. 5.96P

(Built R J Jones - pr.no.PFA 074-10225) (Continental PC60)

Reg	Type	c/n	Prev id	Date	Owner/Operator	Location	Date
G-BEZZ	Jodel D 112	397	F-BHMC	12. 8.77	K R Nestor tr G-BEZZ Group	Barton	19.11.87P

(Built Passot Aviation)

G-BFAA - G-BFZZ

Reg	Type	c/n	Prev id	Date	Owner/Operator	Location	Date
G-BFAA	Sud-Aviation Gardan GY-80-160 Horizon	78	F-BLVY	20.10.77	G R Williams	(Biddulph, Stoke-on-Trent)	18.11.90

(New owner 8.04)

Reg	Type	c/n	Prev id	Date	Owner/Operator	Location	Date
G-BFAF	Aeronca 7BCM Champion (L-16A-AE)	7BCM-11	N797US N2552B, 47-797	15. 8.77	D C W Harper	Finmere	30. 8.01P

(As "7797" in US Army c/s) (Noted 8.06)

Reg	Type	c/n	Prev id	Date	Owner/Operator	Location	Date
G-BFAH	Phoenix Currie Wot	PFA 058-11376		22. 8.77	R W Clarke	(Cheadle)	

(Built N Hamilton-Wright) (Initially allocated as c/n PFA 3017: on build as Replica SE.5a project probably confused with PFA 101-11376, a Sopwith Pup replica)

Reg	Type	c/n	Prev id	Date	Owner/Operator	Location	Date
G-BFAI	Rockwell Commander 114	14304	N4984W	17. 8.77	A J Procter tr BFAI Flying Group Sherburn-in-Elmet		20.12.07E
G-BFAK	GEMS MS.892A Rallye Commodore 150	10595	F-BNNJ	9. 8.77	J M Hedges "54"	Lower Upham Farm, Chiseldon	31. 5.08E
G-BFAP	SIAI-Marchetti S 205-20R	4-213	I-ALEN	1. 9.77	A O'Broin	Raby's Farm, Great Stukeley	7.11.07E
G-BFAS	Evans VP-1 Series 2	PFA 7033		15. 8.77	A I Sutherland	Fearn	17. 7.08P

(Built A I Sutherland) (Volkswagen 1834)

Reg	Type	c/n	Prev id	Date	Owner/Operator	Location	Date
G-BFAW	de Havilland DHC-1 Chipmunk 22	C1/0733	8342M WP848	31. 8.77	R V Bowles	Husbands Bosworth	6. 6.08S
G-BFAX	de Havilland DHC-1 Chipmunk 22	C1/0496	8394M WG422	31. 8.77	N Rushton Trenchard Farm, Eggesford		23. 6.05

(As "WG422:16" in RAF c/s) (Noted 2.06)

Reg	Type	c/n	Prev id	Date	Owner/Operator	Location	Date
G-BFBA	SAN Jodel DR.100A Ambassadeur	88	F-BIVU	12. 9.77	W H Sherlock Drayton Manor, Drayton St Leonard		24.10.07E
G-BFBB	Piper PA-23-250 Aztec E	27-7405294	SE-GBI	1. 9.77	D Byrne	Elstree	5. 6.08E
G-BFBC	Taylor JT.1 Monoplane	PFA 055-10280		5. 9.77	G Heins	(Rochdale)	

(Built A Brooks)
(Under construction 2.93: new owner 1.02)

Reg	Type	c/n	Prev id	Date	Owner/Operator	Location	Date
G-BFBE	Robin HR.200-100 Club	12	PH-SRK	9. 9.77	A C Pearson	Rochester	15. 3.08E
G-BFBM	Saffery S 330	7		1. 9.77	B Martin	Somersham, Huntingdon	

"Beeze II" (Extant 5.07)

Reg	Type	c/n	Prev id	Date	Owner/Operator	Location	Date
G-BFBR	Piper PA-28-161 Cherokee Warrior II	28-7716277	N38845	15. 9.77	Moore Flying Ltd	Fairoaks	8. 5.08T
G-BFBU	Partenavia P68B	24	SE-FTM	25. 1.78	Geminair Services Ltd	Thruxton	24. 4.08E
G-BFBY	Piper J-3C-65 Cub (L-4H-PI)	10998	F-BDTG 43-29707	29. 9.77	M Shaw	Old Buckenham	30. 8.07P
G-BFCT	Cessna TU206F Turbo Stationair II	U20603202	(LN-TVF) N8341Q	15. 9.77	D I Schellingerhout Mount Airey Farm, South Cave		21. 5.08E
G-BFDC	de Havilland DHC-1 Chipmunk 22	C1/0525	7989M WG475	15.11.77	N F O'Neill	Newtownards	29.10.09S
G-BFDF	SOCATA Rallye 235E	12834	F-GAKT	6.10.77	M A Wratten	Bourne Park, Hurstbourne Tarrant	2. 5.08E

G-BFDI	Piper PA-28-181 Cherokee Archer II	28-7790382	N2205Q	5.10.77	Truman Aviation Ltd	Tollerton	10.10.07E
G-BFDK	Piper PA-28-161 Cherokee Warrior II	28-7816010	N40061	23. 9.77	S T Gilbert	Kemble	14. 6.08E
G-BFDL	Piper J-3C-65 Cub (L-4J-PI) 13277 (Continental O-200-A) *(Frame No.13107)*		HB-OIF 45-4537	30.11.77	B A Nicholson and P J Lochhead Shempston Farm, Lossiemouth *(As "454537:J-04" in US Army c/s)*		20. 5.08P
G-BFDO	Piper PA-28R-201T Turbo Arrow III	28R-7703212	N38396	3.10.77	J Blackburn and J Driver	Elstree	21.12.07E
G-BFDZ	Taylor JT.1 Monoplane PFA 055-10185 *(Built D C Barber)*			5.10.77	R A Collins Garston Farm, Marshfield *(Struck ground heavily on approach Garston Farm, Marshfield 23. 6.07 and substantially damaged)*		14. 9.07P
G-BFEB	SAN Jodel D 150 Mascaret 34		F-BMJR OO-LDY, F-BLDX	14.10.77	A W Russell tr Jodel Syndicate	Portmoak	17. 6.07P
G-BFEF	Agusta-Bell 47G-3B1 1541		XT132	11.10.77	I F Vaughan	Guernsey	8. 7.08E
G-BFEH	SAN Jodel D 117A 828		F-BITG	5.10.77	J A Crabb	Dunkeswell	18.11.05P
G-BFEK	Reims Cessna F152 II F15201442			11.10.77	Cardinal Sin Ltd t/a Staverton Flying School Gloucestershire		20. 2.08E
G-BFER	Bell 212 30835		N18099	7.11.77	FB Leasing Ltd	Kazakhstan	27.11.07E
G-BFEV	Piper PA-25-235 Pawnee D 25-7756060		N82547	20.10.77	Trent Valley Aerotowing Club Ltd	Kirton-in-Lindsey	18. 3.08A
G-BFFC	Reims Cessna F152 II F15201451			27.10.77	Multiflight Ltd	Leeds-Bradford	9.12.07E
G-BFFE	Reims Cessna F152 II F15201454			27.10.77	A J Hastings	Prestwick	4. 7.08E
G-BFFJ	Sikorsky S-61N Mk.II 61-777		N6231	17. 1.78	Veritair Ltd *"Tresco"*	Sumburgh	22. 3.08E
G-BFFP	Piper PA-18-150 Super Cub 18-8187 (Lycoming O-360-A4) *(Frame No.18-8402)*		PH-OTC N10F	9.11.77	East Sussex Gliding Club Ltd	Ringmer	14. 6.08S
G-BFFT	Cameron V-56 Balloon (Hot Air) 360			7.11.77	R I McKean Kerr and D C Boxall Bristol tr The Red Section Balloon Group *"Red Leader"*		16. 2.03A
G-BFFW	Reims Cessna F152 II F15201447			14.11.77	Aircraft Engineers Ltd	Prestwick	3. 7.08E
G-BFGD	Reims Cessna F172N Skyhawk II F17201545		F-WZDT	14.11.77	J T Armstrong	Fairoaks	18.11.07E
G-BFGG	Reims Cessna FRA150M Aerobat FRA1500321		F-WZDS	14.11.77	J M Machin	Netherthorpe	16. 4.08E
G-BFGH	Reims Cessna F337G Super Skymaster F33700081 *(Wichita c/n 33701754)*			14.11.77	T Perkins	Bagby	12. 1.08
G-BFGK	SAN Jodel D 117 644		F-BIBT	27. 6.78	B F J Hope Stoneacre Farm, Farthing Corner		26 6.07P
G-BFGL	Reims Cessna FA152 Aerobat FA1520339			14.11.77	Multiflight Ltd	Leeds-Bradford	12. 7.08E
G-BFGO	Fuji FA.200-160 Aero Subaru FA200-219		PH-KDB	25.11.77	R J Everett (Sproughton, Ipswich) *(Damaged taxying Rush Green 18. 8.93)*		23. 8.92
G-BFGS	SOCATA MS.893E Rallye 180GT 12571		F-BXYK	31. 8.76	Chiltern Flyers Ltd Eaton Bray		8.11.07E
			French AF 12571 FSCAZ, "41-AZ" *(Noted Turweston 1.08)*				
G-BFGX	Reims Cessna FRA150M Aerobat FRA1500328		F-BUDX	28.11.77	Aircraft Engineers Ltd *(Noted 10.07)* Prestwick		22. 9.07T
G-BFGZ	Reims Cessna FRA150M Aerobat FRA1500329			28.11.77	C M Barnes Garden Piece, Basingstoke		4. 4.08T
G-BFHH	de Havilland DH.82A Tiger Moth 85933 *(Built Morris Motors Ltd)*		F-BDOH French AF, DF197	25.11.77	P Harrison and M J Gambrell Swanborough Farm, Lewes		26. 5.07
G-BFHI	Piper J-3C-65 Cub (L-4J-PI) 12532		F-BFBT 44-80236	25.11.77	N Glass and A J Richardson Derrytrasna Glen, Bannfoot *(Noted 8.07)*		28. 5.04P
G-BFHP	Champion 7GCAA Citabria 114		HB-UAX	8.12.77	M P Edwards tr Citabriation Group	Barton	10.10.10S
G-BFHR	CEA Jodel DR.220 2+2 30		F-BOCX	1.12.77	J E Sweetman (Kingston, Sturminster Newton)		29. 6.08
G-BFHU	Reims Cessna F152 II F15201461			7.12.77	D J Cooke and Company Ltd Liverpool *(Operated Cheshire Air Training Services Ltd)*		30.11.07E
G-BFHV	Reims Cessna F152 II F15201470			21.12.77	A S Bamrah t/a Falcon Flying Services (Rochester)		29.12.07E
G-BFIB	Piper PA-31 Turbo Navajo 31-684		LN-NPE OY-DVH, LN-RTJ	21.12.77	Richard Hannon Ltd	Thruxton	15. 4.08E
G-BFID	Taylor JT.2 Titch PFA 060-10311 *(Built W F Adams)* (Continental O-200-A)			13.12.77	R W Kilham (Langtoft, Peterborough) *(Damaged Breighton 31. 5.99) (New owner 5.04)*		23. 8.99P
G-BFIE	Reims Cessna FRA150M Aerobat FRA1500331			12. 1.78	J P A Freeman	Headcorn	28. 1.08E
G-BFIG	Reims Cessna FR172K Hawk XP FR17200615			12. 1.78	Tenair Ltd	Barton	6. 3.08E
G-BFIJ	Grumman AA-5A Cheetah AA5A-0486		N6160A	1. 3.78	T H and M G Weetman	Prestwick	2. 5.08E
G-BFIN	Grumman AA-5A Cheetah AA5A-0520		N6145A	22. 3.78	Aircraft Engineers Ltd	Prestwick	23. 5.08E
G-BFIT	Thunder Ax6-56Z Balloon (Hot Air) 136			20.12.77	J A G Tyson *"Folly"*	Torphins, Banchory	3. 5.91
G-BFIU	Reims Cessna FR172K Hawk XP FR17200591		N96098	12. 1.78	B M Jobling tr The G-BFIU Flying Group Hinton-in-the-Hedges		20. 9.08E
G-BFIV	Reims Cessna F177RG Cardinal RG F177RG0161		N96106	12. 1.78	C Fisher	Blackbushe	25. 5.08E
G-BFIX	Thunder Ax7-77A Balloon (Hot Air) 133			9.12.77	R Owen *"Animal Magic"*	Standish, Wigan	23. 1.79
G-BFIY	Reims Cessna F150M F15001381		OE-CMT	11. 1.78	R J Scott	Blackbushe	25. 9.08E
G-BFJJ	Evans VP-1 PFA 062-10273 *(Built P R Pykett)* (Volkswagen 1800)			30.12.77	M A Watts Farley Farm, Romsey *(New owner 10.07)*		23. 6.96P
G-BFJR	Reims Cessna F337G Super Skymaster F33700082 *(Wichita c/n 33701761)*		N46297 (N53658)	4. 1.78	Columbus Systems Ltd (Laxey, Isle of Man)		18. 5.08E
G-BFJZ	Robin DR.400-140B Major 1290			20. 1.78	Weald Air Services Ltd	Headcorn	26. 8.07E
G-BFKB	Reims Cessna F172N Skyhawk II F17201601		PH-AXO	16. 1.78	R L Clarke and D Tench tr Shropshire Flying Group Sleap		22. 3.08E
G-BFKF	Reims Cessna FA152 Aerobat FA1520337			26. 1.78	Aerolease Ltd	Conington	13. 5.08E
G-BFKH	Reims Cessna F152 II F15201464			26. 1.78	TG Aviation Ltd Manston *(Operated Thanet Flying Club)*		26. 3.08E
G-BFKL	Cameron N-56 Balloon (Hot Air) 369			23. 1.78	Merrythought Ltd	Telford	17. 7.92A
G-BFLH	Piper PA-34-200T Seneca II 34-7870065		N2126M	16. 2.78	Air Medical Ltd	Oxford	8. 6.06T
G-BFLI	Piper PA-28R-201T Turbo Arrow III 28R-7803134		N2582M	16. 2.78	J K Chudzicki *"Spirit of Rita May"*	Elstree	16. 6.08E
G-BFLU	Reims Cessna F152 II F15201433			15. 2.78	Atlantic Flight Training Ltd Coventry *(Atlantic old style c/s but no titles)*		21. 6.08E
G-BFLX	Grumman AA-5A Cheetah AA5A-0524		N6147A	14. 3.78	A M Verdon	Blackbushe	27. 7.08E
G-BFLZ	Beech 95-A55 Baron TC-220		PH-ILE HB-GOV	16. 3.78	K A Graham t/a Caterite Food Service	Carlisle	23. 8.08E
G-BFMF	Cassutt Racer IIIM PFA 034-10147 *(Built P H Lewis)* (Continental C90)			17. 2.78	M C R Sims (Chichester) *(New owner 5.06)*		24. 5.91P

Reg	Type	C/n	Prev ID	Date	Owner/Operator	Location	Status
G-BFMG	Piper PA-28-161 Cherokee Warrior II	28-7716160	N3506Q	11. 5.78	Stardial Ltd	Fairoaks	18.10.07E
G-BFMH	Cessna 177B Cardinal	17702034	N34836	18. 4.78	Aerofoil Aviation Ltd	Leeds-Bradford	10. 7.08E
G-BFMK	Reims Cessna FA152 Aerobat	FA1520344		6. 3.78	The Leicestershire Aero Club Ltd	Leicester	4. 4.08E
G-BFMR	Piper PA-20 Pacer 125	20-130	N7025K	20. 2.78	J Knight	Headcorn	6. 3.06
G-BFMX	Reims Cessna F172N Skyhawk II	F17201732		24. 8.78	A2Z Wholesale Fashion Jewellery Ltd	Halfpenny Green	15. 5.08E
G-BFMZ	Payne Ax7-62 Balloon (Hot Air) (Built G F Payne)	GFP.2		1. 3.78	E G Woolnough (Inflated 4.06)	Halesworth, Suffolk	
G-BFNG	Wassmer Jodel D 112	1321	F-BNHI	6. 3.78	M Cooke and P H Jeffcote	Leicester	21. 5.08P
G-BFNI	Piper PA-28-161 Cherokee Warrior II	28-7816215	N9505N	8. 3.78	P R J Welch t/a Lion Services	Hawarden	26. 7.08E
G-BFNK	Piper PA-28-161 Cherokee Warrior II	28-7816282	N9527N	8. 3.78	Oxford Aviation Training Ltd	Oxford	12. 1.08T
G-BFNM	Globe GC-1B Swift	2205	N78205 NC78205	15. 6.78	M J Butler	Spanhoe	25.10.08P
G-BFOE	Reims Cessna F152 II	F15201475		23. 3.78	Redhill Air Services Ltd	Redhill	19. 1.08E
G-BFOF	Reims Cessna F152 II	F15201448		9. 3.78	Cardinal Sin Ltd t/a Staverton Flying School	Derby	21. 6.08E
G-BFOG	Cessna 150M	15076223	N66706	13. 3.78	C L Day	Haverfordwest	12. 5.08E
G-BFOJ	American AA-1 Yankee	AA1-0395	OH-AYB (LN-KAJ), (N6195L)	4. 4.78	N W Thomas	Bournemouth	17.11.07E
G-BFOP	Wassmer Jodel D 120 Paris-Nice	32	F-BHTX	23. 3.78	R J Wesley and G D Western "Jean"	Sampsons Hall, Kersey	12. 6.04P
G-BFOS	Thunder Ax6-56A Balloon (Hot Air)	147		20. 3.78	N T Petty "Milton Keynes"	Sudbury	25.11.93A
G-BFOU	Taylor JT.1 Monoplane (Built I N M Cameron)	PFA 055-10333		17. 3.78	G Bee	(Stockton-on-Tees)	
G-BFOV	Reims Cessna F172N Skyhawk II	F17201675		18. 5.78	D J Walker	Shoreham	18.10.07E
G-BFPA	Scheibe SF25B Falke (Volkswagen Danum 1600/1)	46179	D-KAGM	29. 3.78	R Gibson and R Hamilton (Noted 7.06)	Portmoak	13. 9.98
G-BFPH	Reims Cessna F172K	F17200802	PH-VHN	23. 3.78	T Marriott tr Linc-Air Flying Group	Derby	14. 8.08E
G-BFPM	Reims Cessna F172M Skyhawk II	F17201384	PH-MIO	13. 4.78	M P Wimsey and J M Cope	Strubby	22. 4.08E
G-BFPO	Rockwell Commander 112B	530	N1412J	10. 5.78	J G Hale Ltd	Shoreham	15. 1.08E
G-BFPP	Bell 47J-2 Ranger	2851	F-BJAN TR-LKD, F-OCBU	23. 5.78	M R Masters (Phoenix Farm, Lower Upham)		11.11.99
G-BFPR	Piper PA-25-235 Pawnee D	25-7856007	SE-KGY I-TOZU, G-BFPR, N82591	4. 4.78	The Windrushers Gliding Club Ltd	Bicester	5. 3.08
G-BFPS	Piper PA-25-235 Pawnee D	25-7856013	N82598	4. 4.78	Kent Gliding Club Ltd	Challock	19. 8.08E
G-BFPZ	Reims Cessna F177RG Cardinal RG	F177RG0079	N56PZ G-BFPZ, PH-AUK, D-EGBM, (OO-DVE), G-BFPZ	3. 4.78	D M Glinternick	Swansea	16. 5.08E
G-BFRD	Bowers Fly Baby 1A (Built F R Donaldson and R A Phillips)	PFA 016-10300		27. 1.78	R A Phillips (Under construction 6.00)	(Elgin)	
G-BFRI	Sikorsky S-61N Mk.II	61-809		26. 5.78	Veritair Ltd t/a British International (Noted 11.06)	Plymouth	14. 6.04T
G-BFRR	Reims Cessna FRA150M Aerobat	FRA1500326	LN-ALO	19. 4.78	S Cosgrove tr Romeo Romeo Flying Group	Tatenhill	21. 9.08E
G-BFRS	Reims Cessna F172N Skyhawk II	F17201555	LN-ALP	19. 4.78	Aerocomm Ltd	King's Farm, Thurrock	6. 6.08E
G-BFRV	Reims Cessna FA152 Aerobat	FA1520345		17. 4.78	Solo Services Ltd	Shoreham	3.10.07E
G-BFRY	Piper PA-25-260 Pawnee D	25-7405789	SE-GIB	23. 5.78	Yorkshire Gliding Club (Proprietary) Ltd	Sutton Bank	30. 6.08E
G-BFSA	Reims Cessna F182Q Skylane II	F18200074	F-WZDG	17. 4.78	Ensiform Aviation Ltd	Cranfield	27.11.07E
G-BFSC	Piper PA-25-235 Pawnee D	25-7656068	N82302	2. 6.78	Essex Gliding Club Ltd	North Weald	11. 1.08E
G-BFSD	Piper PA-25-235 Pawnee D	25-7656084	N82338	2. 6.78	Deeside Gliding Club (Aberdeenshire) Ltd	Aboyne	18. 4.08E
G-BFSR	Cessna F150J (Built Reims Aviation SA)	F150-0504	OH-CBN	7. 7.78	W Ali	Cranfield	17. 7.08E
G-BFSS	Reims FR172G Rocket	FR17200167	OH-CDY	7. 7.78	Albedale Farms Ltd	Grateley, Andover	29. 5.08
G-BFSY	Piper PA-28-181 Cherokee Archer II	28-7890200	N9503N	19. 4.78	A S Domone t/a Downland Aviation	Goodwood	2. 2.08E
G-BFTC	Piper PA-28R-201T Turbo Arrow III	28R-7803197	N3868M	19. 4.78	D Petty tr Top Cat Flying Group (New owner 2.08)	Sherburn-in-Elmet	19.10.07E
G-BFTF	Grumman AA-5B Tiger	AA5B-0879		7. 9.78	F C Burrow Ltd	Sherburn-in-Elmet	17. 7.08E
G-BFTG	Grumman AA-5B Tiger	AA5B-0777		15. 5.78	D Hepburn and G R Montgomery	Perth	16.11.07E
G-BFTH	Reims Cessna F172N Skyhawk II	F17201671		3. 5.78	T W Oakley	Bagby	15. 9.08E
G-BFTT	Cessna 421C Golden Eagle	421C-0462	N6789C	3. 5.78	M A Ward	Goodwood	11. 7.08E
G-BFTX	Reims Cessna F172N Skyhawk II	F17201715		2. 5.78	F P Hall tr Tri Society	Clipgate Farm, Denton	6. 5.06
	(Abandoned take-off Clipgate Farm, Denton 15.7.04 resulting in extensive damage: cancelled 30.12.04 as destroyed: noted wrecked 4.6.05 but restored 7.6.05).						
G-BFUB	Piper PA-32RT-300 Lance II	32R-7885052	N9509C	18. 5.78	Jolida Holdings Ltd	Jersey	18. 5.08E
G-BFUD	Scheibe SF25E Super Falke (Limbach SL1700)	4313	D-KLDC	19. 5.78	P A Lewis tr The Lakes Libelle Syndicate	Walney Island	30. 5.08
G-BFUZ	Cameron V-77 Balloon (Hot Air)	398		24. 5.78	A W Macdonald tr Servowarm Balloon Syndicate	Leigh-on-Sea	11. 4.08A
G-BFVG	Piper PA-28-181 Cherokee Archer II	28-7890408	N31746 N9558N	1. 6.78	P Anderson	Blackpool	22. 6.08E
G-BFVH	AirCo DH.2 fsm (Built Westward Airways (Lands End) Ltd) (125 hp Kinner B54)	WA/4		1. 6.78	M J Kirk (Noted in poor condition as "5964" 9.03) (Note BAPC.112 also marked as "5964")	(RAF Lyneham)	20. 7.01P
G-BFVS	Grumman AA-5B Tiger	0784	N28736	11. 8.78	S W Biroth and T Chapman	Denham	1. 3.08E
G-BFVU	Cessna 150L Commuter	15074684	N75189	10. 8.78	Aviation South West Ltd	Exeter	2. 8.08E
G-BFWB	Piper PA-28-161 Cherokee Warrior II	28-7816584	N31752	22. 6.78	Mid-Anglia Flight Centre Ltd t/a Mid-Anglia School of Flying	Cambridge	24. 7.08E
G-BFWD	Phoenix Currie Wot (Built F E Nuthall) (Walter Mikron 3)	PFA 3009		22. 6.78	D Silsbury and B Proctor (On restoration 12.05 as "C3009/B" in RFC c/s)	Dunkeswell	6.10.96P
G-BFWE	Piper PA-23-250 Aztec E	27-4583	9M-AQT 9V-BDI, N13968	13. 7.78	Air Navigation and Trading Company Ltd (Noted 9.07)	Sleap	15. 2.03T
G-BFXF	Andreasson BA-4B (Built A Brown - pr.no.PFA 038-10351) (Lycoming O-290-G)	AAB-001		10. 7.78	P N Birch	Ludham	30. 8.07P
G-BFXG	Druine D 31 Turbulent (Built S Griffin)	PFA 1663		10. 7.78	E J I Musty and M J Whatley (Partially complete 6.07)	(White Waltham)	
G-BFXK	Piper PA-28-140 Cherokee F	28-7325387	PH-NSK	1. 8.78	D M Wheeler	Rochester	11. 6.08E

G-BFXR	Wassmer Jodel D 112	247	F-BFTM	27. 7.78	M R Coreth	Henstridge	17. 7.08P
G-BFXS	Rockwell Commander 114	14271	N4949W	3. 8.78	Romeo Whiskey Ltd	Old Buckenham	22. 8.08E
G-BFXW	Gulfstream AA-5B Tiger	AA5B-0940		21. 2.79	Campsol Ltd	Leeds-Bradford	12. 7.08E
G-BFXX	Gulfstream AA-5B Tiger	AA5B-0917		3.10.78	W R Gibson	North Weald	23. 1.08E
G-BFYA	MBB BÖ.105DB	S 321	D-HJET	31.10.78	Sterling Helicopters Ltd	Norwich	25. 5.08E
					(Operated Norfolk Police)		
G-BFYC	Piper PA-32RT-300 Lance II	32R-7885200	N36645	31. 7.78	A A Barnes t/a Cyril Silver and Partners	Biggin Hill	12. 1.08E
G-BFYI	Westland-Bell 47G-3B1	WA/326	XT167	24. 1.79	K P Mayes (New owner 10.06)	Hawarden	13. 7.06
G-BFYK	Cameron V-77 Balloon (Hot Air)	433	EI-BAY	16. 8.78	L E Jones	Worcester	31.12.99A
			G-BFYK				
G-BFYL	Evans VP-2	PFA 063-10146		15. 8.78	W C Brown	(Camberley)	17.12.98P
	(Built A G Wilford) (Volkswagen 1834)						
G-BFYM	Piper PA-28-161 Cherokee Warrior II		N812E	14. 8.78	Sheffield City Flying School Ltd	(Sheffield City)	9. 5.08E
		28-7816586	N480X, G-BFYM, N31813				
G-BFZA	Fournier RF3	5	F-BLEL	14. 9.78	T J Hartwell	(Sackville Lodge, Riseley)	
G-BFZB	Piper J-3C-65 Cub (L-4J-PI)	13019	D-ECEL	21. 9.78	M S Pettit	Bidford	26. 1.08P
	(Continental C85) (Frame No.12849)		HB-OSP, 44-80723		(As "480723:E5" and "J" in USAF c/s)		
G-BFZD	Reims Cessna FR182 Skylane RG II	FR18200010		9.10.78	R B Lewis t/a R B Lewis and Company	Sleap	1. 2.08E
G-BFZH	Piper PA-28R-200 Cherokee Arrow II		OY-BDB	25.10.78	A Mason t/a Mason Aviation	Prestwick	25. 9.08E
		28R-35307					
G-BFZM	Rockwell Commander 112TC-A	13191	N4661W	9.10.78	J A Hart and R J Lamplough	Filton	28. 9.07
G-BFZN	Reims Cessna FA152 Aerobat	FA1520348		20.10.78	A S Bamrah t/a Falcon Flying Services	Biggin Hill	29.11.81T
					(Crashed Narborough, Leicestershire 4.10.80: on rebuild 2.95)		
G-BFZO	Gulfstream AA-5A Cheetah	AA5A-0697		1.11.78	J W Cross and A E Kempson	Elstree	16. 8.08E
G-BFZT	Reims Cessna FA152 Aerobat	FA1520356		4. 7.79	Herefordshire Aero Club Ltd	Shobdon	13. 3.08E
G-BFZU	Reims Cessna FA152 Aerobat	FA1520355		29. 6.79	BJ Aviation Ltd	Welshpool	4. 4.08E
G-BFZV	Reims Cessna F172M	F17201093	SE-FZR	2.11.78	The Royal Artillery Aero Club Ltd t/a The Army Flying Association		
						AAC Middle Wallop	16. 3.08T

G-BGAA - G-BGZZ

G-BGAA	Cessna 152 II	15281894	N67529	18. 7.78	PJC (Leasing) Ltd	Stapleford	24. 6.08E
G-BGAB	Reims Cessna F152 II	F15201531		13.10.78	TG Aviation Ltd	Manston	7. 4.03T
					(Operated Thanet Flying Club)		
G-BGAE	Reims Cessna F152 II	F15201540		8.11.78	Aerolease Ltd	Conington	1. 6.08T
G-BGAF	Reims Cessna FA152 Aerobat	FA1520349		13.10.78	P E Preston tr G-BGAF Group	Southend	15. 5.08E
					(Operated Southend Flying Club)		
G-BGAG	Reims Cessna F172N Skyhawk II	F17201754	"G-KING"	13.10.78	R Clarke	Tatenhill	25. 5.07T
G-BGAJ	Reims Cessna F182Q Skylane II	F18200096		13.10.78	Ground Airport Services Ltd	Guernsey	4. 5.08E
G-BGAX	Piper PA-28-140 Cherokee F	28-7325409	PH-NSH	20.10.78	B L Newbold tr G-BGAX Group	Breighton	13. 2.08E
G-BGAZ	Cameron V-77 Balloon (Hot Air)	439		20.10.78	C.J Madigan and D H McGibbon	Bristol	
	(Rebuilt envelope)				(Cameron Balloons titles) (Noted 8.03)		
G-BGBA	Robin R2100A Club	133	F-OCBJ	2. 5.78	Cotswold Aviation Services Ltd	Gloucestershire	11. 9.08E
G-BGBE	SAN Jodel DR.1050 Ambassadeur	260	F-BJYT	29.11.78	J A and B.Mawby Graveley Hall Farm, Graveley		20. 4.08E
G-BGBG	Piper PA-28-181 Archer II	28-7990012	N39730	2.11.78	Harlow Printing Ltd	Carlisle	10. 7.08E
G-BGBI	Reims Cessna F150L	F15000688	PH-LUA	28.11.78	C P Tapp	Bourn	5.12.07E
G-BGBK	Piper PA-38-112 Tomahawk	38-78A0433	N9738N	2.11.78	Truman Aviation Ltd	Tollerton	25. 7.08E
G-BGBN	Piper PA-38-112 Tomahawk	38-78A0511	N9657N	29.11.78	Bonus Aviation Ltd	Cranfield	27. 9.08E
G-BGBR	Reims Cessna F172N Skyhawk II	F17201772		8.11.78	S Papi (Operated Willowair Flying Club)	Southend	2. 5.08E
G-BGBW	Piper PA-38-112 Tomahawk	38-78A0670	N9710N	8.11.78	Truman Aviation Ltd	Tollerton	18. 7.08E
G-BGBZ	Rockwell Commander 114	14423	N5878N	9.10.78	G W Dimmer (On overhaul 1.08)	Old Sarum	9. 8.04
G-BGCM	Gulfstream AA-5A Cheetah	AA5A-0835		23. 3.79	G and S A Jones	Linley Hill, Leven	21. 9.07T
G-BGCO	Piper PA-44-180 Seminole	44-7995128	N2103D	20.12.78	BAE Systems (Operations) Ltd	Warton	19.12.07E
G-BGCY	Taylor JT.1 Monoplane	PFA 055-10370		23.11.78	A T Lane	Fenland	19. 7.08P
	(Built M T Taylor)						
G-BGEH	Monnett Sonerai II	209		1.12.78	D and Vivienne T Hubbard	(Basingstoke)	16. 8.96P
	(Built R E Finlay- p/no PFA 015-10254) (Volkswagen 2234)						
G-BGEI	Oldfield Baby Lakes	PFA 015-10370		1.12.78	M T Taylor	Griffins Farm, Temple Bruer	1. 5.08P
	(Built D H Greenwood) (Fuselage of PFA 1576 incorporated during construction) (Continental A65)						
G-BGEW	SNCAN NC.854S	63	F-BFSJ	13.12.78	S A Francis Bourne Park, Hurstbourne Tarrant		10. 4.08P
	(Continental A65)						
G-BGFC	Evans VP-2	V2-1278		15.12.78	S W C Hollins	(Shavington, Crewe)	29. 9.93P
	(Built J A Jones - pr.no.PFA 063-10441) (Volkswagen 1834)						
G-BGFF	Clutton FRED Series II	PFA 029-10261		18.12.78	I Pearson and P C Appleton	Bodmin	28. 6.05P
	(Built G R G Smith) (Volkswagen 1834)				(New owner 12.07)		
G-BGFG	Gulfstream AA-5A Cheetah	AA5A-0687	N6158A	25. 1.79	R C Willis-Fleming tr Cheetah Flying Group	Exeter	30. 5.08E
G-BGFI	Gulfstream AA-5A Cheetah	AA5A-0733	N6142A	5. 3.79	I J Hay and A Nayyar tr GFI Group	Biggin Hill	22. 2.08E
G-BGFJ	Jodel D 9 Bébé	PFA 1324		11.12.78	O G Jones	RAF Mona	28.10.08P
	(Built C M Fitton) (Volkswagen 1600)						
G-BGFT	Piper PA-34-200T Seneca II	34-7870218	N9714C	17. 1.79	Oxford Aviation Training Ltd	Oxford	14. 9.08E
G-BGFX	Reims Cessna F152 II	F15201555		28.12.78	A J Gomes (New owner 2.08)	Biggin Hill	23. 6.91T
G-BGGA	Bellanca 7GCBC Citabria 150S	1104-79		5. 2.79	L A King (Noted 9.07)	Perth	2. 3.07
G-BGGB	Bellanca 7GCBC Citabria 150S	1105-79		7. 2.79	R S Kiddy tr Citabria Syndicate	Rattlesden	17. 3.08E
G-BGGC	Bellanca 7GCBC Citabria 150S	1106-79		5. 2.79	R P Ashfield and J M Stone tr G-BGGC Flying Group		
						Stancombe Farm, Askerswell	19.10.07E
G-BGGD	Bellanca 8GCBC Scout	284-78		5. 2.79	The Bristol Gliding Club Proprietary Ltd	Nympsfield	1.12.07E
G-BGGE	Piper PA-38-112 Tomahawk	38-79A0161	N9673N	10. 1.79	Truman Aviation Ltd	Tollerton	25. 6.08E
G-BGGI	Piper PA-38-112 Tomahawk	38-79A0165	N9675N	10. 1.79	Truman Aviation Ltd	Tollerton	11. 3.08E
G-BGGL	Piper PA-38-112 Tomahawk	38-79A0169	N9696N	10. 1.79	Grunwick Processing Laboratories Ltd	Cranfield	4. 7.08E
					(Operated Bonus Aviation)		
G-BGGM	Piper PA-38-112 Tomahawk	38-79A0170	N9698N	10. 1.79	Grunwick Processing Laboratories Ltd	Cranfield	30.11.07E
					(Operated Bonus Aviation)		
G-BGGN	Piper PA-38-112 Tomahawk	38-79A0171	N9706N	10. 1.79	Bell Aviation Ltd	Cranfield	5. 9.08E

Reg	Type	C/n	Prev id	Date	Owner/Operator	Base	Expiry
G-BGGO	Reims Cessna F152 II	F15201569		8. 3.79	East Midlands Flying School Ltd	East Midlands	31. 7.08E
G-BGGP	Reims Cessna F152 II	F15201580		8. 3.79	East Midlands Flying School Ltd	East Midlands	23.11.07E
G-BGGU	Wallis WA-116 RR	702		28.12.78	K H Wallis	Reymerston Hall, Norfolk	
	(Subaru EA61)				*(Noted 8.01)*		
G-BGGV	Wallis WA-120 Series 2	703		28.12.78	K H Wallis	Reymerston Hall, Norfolk	
					(Not completed)		
G-BGGW	Wallis WA-122 RR	704		28.12.78	K H Wallis	Reymerston Hall, Norfolk	30. 5.08P
	(RR Continental O-240-A)						
G-BGHI	Reims Cessna F152 II	F15201560		15. 1.79	V R McCready	Shoreham	4. 6.08E
G-BGHJ	Reims Cessna F172N Skyhawk II	F17201777	EI-BVF	15. 1.79	Airplane Ltd	Humberside	18. 8.08E
			G-BGHJ				
G-BGHM	Robin R1180T Aiglon	227		19. 2.79	H Price	Blackpool	13..5.08E
G-BGHP	Beech 76 Duchess	ME-190	N60132	16. 1.79	Magenta Ltd	Exeter	6. 8.08E
					(Operated Airways Flight Training)		
G-BGHS	Cameron N-31 Balloon (Hot Air)	501		15. 1.79	W R Teasdale *"Baby Champion"*	Newbury	17. 1.00A
					(On loan to British Balloon Museum and Library) (Inflated 4.06)		
G-BGHT	Falconar F-12	PFA 022-10040		17. 1.79	C R Coates	(Sneaton Thorpe, Whitby)	
	(Built T K Baillie) (Lycoming O-290)						
G-BGHU	North American T-6G-NF Texan	182-729	FAP1707	22. 1.79	C E Bellhouse	Headcorn	30. 5.08P
			French AF 115042, 51-15042 *"Carly" (As "115042:T/A-042" in USAF c/s)*				
G-BGHV	Cameron V-77 Balloon (Hot Air)	483		12. 1.79	E Davies t/a Adeilad Claddings		
					"Adclad"	Penlan Farm, Llanwrda	28. 9.03A
G-BGHY	Taylor JT.1 Monoplane	PFA 1455		12. 1.79	G W Hancox	Priory Farm, Tibenham	2. 9.08P
	(Built J Prowse)						
G-BGHZ	Clutton FRED Series II	PFA 029-10445		12. 1.79	A J Perry	(Bognor Regis)	
	(Built A G Edwards)				*(New owner 11.06)*		
G-BGIB	Cessna 152 II	15282161	N68169	3. 7.79	Redhill Air Services Ltd	Redhill	2. 1.08E
G-BGIG	Piper PA-38-112 Tomahawk	38-78A0773	N2607A	23. 1.79	Air Claire Ltd	Glasgow	12. 4.08E
					(Operated Glasgow Flying Club)		
G-BGIO	Montgomerie-Bensen B 8MR	GJ.1		11. 1.79	R M Savage tr Great Orton Group	Kirkbride	13. 2.08P
	(Built C G Johns and R M Savage - pr.no.PFA G/01-1259) (Rotax 503)						
G-BGIU	Cessna F172H	F172-0620	PH-VIT	26. 2.79	A G Arthur	Perranporth	24. 5.08E
	(Built Reims Aviation SA)						
G-BGIX	Helio H 295 Super Courier	1467	(G-BGAO)	17.10.79	C M Lee	Fanners Farm, Great Waltham	9. 3.08E
			N68861				
G-BGIY	Reims Cessna F172N Skyhawk II	F17201824		31. 1.79	Air Claire Ltd	Glasgow	13.11.07E
					(Operated Glasgow Flying Club)		
G-BGJU	Cameron V-65 Balloon (Hot Air)	499		5. 2.79	J A Folkes *"Spoils"*	Loughborough	4. 4.93A
G-BGKC	SOCATA Rallye 110ST	3262		25. 4.79	J H Cranmer *(Dumped 4.07)*	Bidford	8. 9.99
G-BGKO	Gardan GY-20 Minicab	PFA 1827		14. 2.79	M N King.	Higherlands Farm, Branscombe	
	(Built R B Webber)				*(On long term rebuild 8.06)*		
G-BGKS	Piper PA-28-161 Warrior II	28-7916221	N9562N	12. 2.79	Mid America (UK) Ltd	Inverness	4. 6.08E
G-BGKT	Auster AOP.9	B5/10/137	XN441	28.12.78	G T Gimblett tr Kilo Tango Group *(Noted 8.07)*		11. 5.07P
	(Officially regd with Frame no.AUS/137)				*(As "XN441" in AAC c/s)* Trenchard Farm, Eggesford		
G-BGKU	Piper PA-28R-201 Arrow III	28R-7837237	N31585	8. 3.79	Aerolease Ltd	Conington	6. 3.08E
G-BGKV	Piper PA-28R-201 Cherokee Arrow III		N44985	21. 5.79	R Haverson and A K Lake	Little Snoring	12. 5.08E
		28R-7737156					
G-BGKY	Piper PA-38-112 Tomahawk	38-78A0737	N9732N	2. 3.79	APB Leasing Ltd	(Edgerley, Oswestry)	26. 9.08E
G-BGKZ	Auster J/5F Aiglet Trainer	2776	F-BGKZ	15.12.78	R B Webber *(Noted 2.06)* Trenchard Farm, Eggesford		25. 2.95
G-BGLA	Piper PA-38-112 Tomahawk	38-78A0741	N9699N	9. 3.79	B H and P M Illston t/a Norwich School of Flying		
						Norwich	15 1.08E
G-BGLF	Evans VP-1 Series 2	PFA 062-10388		28. 2.79	B A Schlussler	Black Spring Farm, Castle Bytham	2. 5.08P
	(Built R A Abrahams) (Volkswagen 1834)						
G-BGLG	Cessna 152 II	15282092	N67909	11. 4.79	L W Scattergood	(Sheffield City)	24. 7.08E
G-BGLK	Monnett Sonerai IIL	PFA 015-10304		24. 2.78	J Bradley	City of Derry	1. 6.05P
	(Built G L Kemp) (Volkswagen 1783)				*(Noted 7.07)*		
G-BGLN	Reims Cessna FA152 Aerobat	FA1520354		8. 3.79	Bflying Ltd	Bournemouth	18. 9.06T
				(Forced landed Ingleby Cross, Northallerton 27. 7.04 and substantially damaged: wreck stored 1.07)			
G-BGLO	Reims Cessna F172N Skyhawk II	F17201900		8. 3.79	J R Isabel	Southend	29. 1.08E
G-BGLS	Oldfield Baby Lakes	PFA 010-10237		11.12.78	J F Dowe	Parham	18. 6.88P
	(Built D S Morgan) (Lycoming O-235)				*(Stored dismantled 1.08)*		
G-BGLZ	Stits SA-3A Playboy	71-100	N9996	19. 6.79	P C Sheard	Strubby	15. 5.07P
	(Built D J Stadler) (Continental C90)						
G-BGME	SIPA 903	96	G-BCML	1. 1.81	M Emery	Redhill	17. 6.94P
			"G-BCHU", F-BGHU		*(New owner 8.07)*		
G-BGMJ	Gardan GY-201 Minicab	12	F-BGMJ	19. 6.78	A W Wakefield tr G-BGMJ Group	Sibson	22.11.08P
	(Built Con. Aéronautique de Bearn) (Continental A65)						
G-BGMO	Hawker Siddeley HS.748 Series 2A/347	1767	ZK-MCB	9. 3.79	PTB (Emerald) Proprietary Ltd	Blackool	22. 4.08E
			G-BGMO, 9Y-TGI, V2-LDB, 9Y-TGI, (G-BGMO) *(Stored externally 2.08)*				
G-BGMP	Cessna F172G	F172-0240	PH-BNV	26. 3.79	R W Collings	(Southam, Coventry)	10. 9.08P
	(Built Reims Aviation SA)						
G-BGMR	Gardan GY-20 Minicab	PFA 056-10153		12. 3.79	R A M Smith tr Mike Romeo Flying Group		
	(Built A B Holloway to JB.01 Minicab standard) (Continental C90)				*(Noted 6.06)*	White Waltham	29. 9.04P
G-BGMS	Taylor JT.2 Titch	MS.1		20.10.78	M A J Spice	(Middlewich, Cheshire)	
	(Built M A J Spice - pr.no.PFA 060-10400)						
G-BGMT	SOCATA Rallye 235E	13126		14. 9.78	C G Wheeler	Morgansfield, Fishburn	15.1.08E
G-BGMV	Scheibe SF25B Falke	4648	D-KEBG	15. 5.79	C A Bloom and A P Twort	(Kittyhawk Farm, Deanland)	16.11.01
	(Stark-Stamo MS1500)				*(Stored 2004)*		
G-BGND	Reims Cessna F172N Skyhawk II	F17201576	PH-AYI	3. 3.78	A J M Freeman	Andrewsfield	31.10.07E
			(F-GAQA)				
G-BGNT	Reims Cessna F152 II	F15201644		23.10.79	Aerolease Ltd	Conington	2. 4.08E
G-BGNV	Gulfstream GA-7 Cougar	GA7-0078	N790GA	20. 4.79	G J Bissex	Nortom Malreward	3. 5.08T
G-BGOD	Colt 77A Balloon (Hot Air)	040		4. 4.79	C and M D Steuer *"Harvey Wallbanger"*	London NW1	18. 6.97A
G-BGOG	Piper PA-28-161 Warrior II	28-7916350	N9639N	8. 6.79	W D Moore	Cranfield	30. 4.08E

Reg	Type	c/n	Prev id	Date	Owner/Operator	Base	Expiry
G-BGOI	Cameron O-56 Balloon (Hot Air)	526		4. 4.79	M J Streat "Skymaster"	Bristol	21. 5.08A
G-BGOJ	Reims Cessna F150L	F15000931	G-MABI	19. 4.79	D J Hockings	(Hailsham)	21. 7.97
			G-BGOJ, PH-KDA				
G-BGOL	Piper PA-28R-201T Turbo Arrow III	28R-7803335	N36705	11. 4.79	R G Jackson	Bournemouth	19. 2.08E
G-BGON	Gulfstream GA-7 Cougar	GA7-0095	N9527Z	24. 4.79	J P E Walsh t/a Walsh Aviation	Cranfield	30. 8.08E
					(Operated Cabair)		
G-BGOR	North American AT-6D-NT Harvard III 88-14863		FAP1508	28. 3.79	P Meyrick	Rednal	18. 9.07P
	(Reported as c/n 88-14880)		SAAF 7504, EX935, 41-33908 *(As "14863" in USAAF c/s)*				
G-BGPA	Cessna 182Q Skylane II	18266538	C-GYBW	11. 7.79	Hydestile Business Systems Ltd	Dunsfold	26. 4.08E
			(N94935)				
G-BGPB	CCF Harvard 4 (T-6J-CCF Texan)	CCF4-538	FAP1747	4. 4.79	1959 Ltd	Duxford	11. 4.09P
			WGAF BF+050, WGAF AA+050, 53-4619 *(As "1747" in Portuguese AF c/s)*				
G-BGPD	Piper J-3C-65 Cub (L-4H-PI)	12040	F-BFQP	18. 4.79	P R Whiteman	Marsh Hill Farm, Aylesbury	20. 6.07P
	(Frame No.11867)		F-BDTP, 44-79744 *(As "479744:49-M" in 92nd Armoured FA Btn, US 9th Army c/s)*				
	(Officially regd as c/n 10478 which is ex 43-29187/OO-ADI/F-BFQP: G-BGPD is ex 44-79744/F-BDTP: presumably fuselages exchanged in France - see G-BCOM)						
G-BGPH	Gulfstream AA-5B Tiger	AA5B-1248	(G-BGRU)	14. 8.79	Shipping and Airlines Ltd	Biggin Hill	13. 1.08E
G-BGPI	Plumb BGP-1 Biplane	PFA 083-10359		26. 6.78	B G Plumb	Hinton-in-the-Hedges	2. 4.08P
	(Built B G Plumb) (Continental O-200A)						
G-BGPJ	Piper PA-28-161 Warrior II	28-7916288	N9602N	24. 4.79	West Lancs Warrior Co Ltd	RAF Woodvale	23. 4.08E
G-BGPL	Piper PA-28-161 Warrior II	28-7916289	N9603N	20. 4.79	Montash Properties Ltd	Manston	9. 9.08E
G-BGPM	Evans VP-2	PFA 063-10335		17. 4.79	E Stinton tr Cheap as Chips Group	(Cheltenham)	29. 4.86P
	(Built T Painter)				*(New owners 2.07)*		
G-BGPN	Piper PA-18-150 Super Cub	18-7909044	N9750N	12. 4.79	D McHugh and A R Darke	Wycombe Air Park	29.11.07E
G-BGPU	Piper PA-28-140 Cherokee F	28-7325282	PH-GNT	25. 4.79	Air Navigation and Trading Company Ltd	Blackpool	3. 9.06T
					(Noted 10.07)		
G-BGRC	Piper PA-28-140 Cherokee B	28-26208	SE-FHF	12. 6.79	Tecair Aviation Ltd and G F Haigh	Shipdham	26.10.97T
			N5501U		*(Stored and dismantled 8.05)*		
G-BGRE	Beech 200 Super King Air	BB-568		8. 5.79	Martin-Baker (Engineering) Ltd	Chalgrove	23.10.07E
G-BGRG	Beech 76 Duchess	ME-233		8. 5.79	S J Skilton t/a Aviation Rentals	Bournemouth	7. 4.08E
					(Operated Professional Air Training)		
G-BGRH	Robin DR.400 2+2	1411		21. 5.79	C R Beard Grassthorpe Grange, Sutton-on-Trent		5. 4.08E
G-BGRI	CEA Jodel DR.1050 Sicile	540	F-BLZJ	27. 4.79	B J L P and W J A L de Saar	Shipdham	8.11.07E
G-BGRM	Piper PA-38-112 Tomahawk	38-79A1067	N9673N	1. 8.79	Iris W Goodger t/a Classair	Biggin Hill	22. 6.08E
G-BGRO	Reims Cessna F172M Skyhawk II	F17201129	PH-KAB	4. 5.79	A N Pirie t/a Cammo Aviation	Kirknewton	14. 1.08E
G-BGRR	Piper PA-38-112 Tomahawk	38-78A0336	OO-FLT	8. 5.79	Pure Air Aviation Ltd	(Mersham, Ashford)	27. 3.08E
			N9685N				
G-BGRS	Thunder Ax7-77Z Balloon (Hot Air)	203		21. 5.79	P M Gaines	Stockton-on-Tees	26. 4.03A
G-BGRT	Steen Skybolt	RCT.001		12. 9.78	O Meier	St Johann In Tirol, Austria	7. 1.08P
	(Built R C Teverson - pr.no.PFA 064-10171)						
G-BGRX	Piper PA-38-112 Tomahawk	38-79A0609	N9662N	11. 5.79	Bonus Aviation Ltd	Cranfield	16.11.07E
G-BGSA	SOCATA MS.892E Rallye 150GT	12838	F-GAKC	29. 5.79	D H Tonkin	Bodmin	10. 3.08E
G-BGSH	Piper PA-38-112 Tomahawk	38-79A0562	N9719N	11. 5.79	S Padidar-Nazar	Carlisle	31.10.07E
G-BGSJ	Piper J-3C-65 Cub (L-4A-PI)	8781	F-BGXJ	21. 5.79	A J Higgins	Dunkeswell	5 12.07P
	(Frame No.8917)		French AF, 42-36657 *(As "236657:D-72" in USAAC c/s)*				
G-BGSV	Reims Cessna F172N Skyhawk II	F17201830		1. 8.79	Southwell Air Services Ltd	Linley Hill, Leven	18. 3.08E
G-BGSW	Beech F33 Bonanza	CD-1253	OH-BDD	30. 5.79	C Wood	Wellesbourne Mountford	11. 9.08E
G-BGSY	Gulfstream GA-7 Cougar	GA7-0096		4. 6.79	N D Anderson	Old Sarum	9. 2.08E
G-BGTC	Auster AOP.9	xxxx	XP282	12.10.79	T K Rumble tr Terranne Auster Group	(Scampton)	9. 6.97P
	(Officially regd with Frame no.AUS/168)				*(New owner 6.06)*		
G-BGTF	Piper PA-44-180 Seminole	44-7995287	N2131Y	20. 6.79	Shemburn Ltd	Weston, Lucan, Dublin	19. 6.08E
G-BGTG	Piper PA-23-250 Aztec F	27-7954061	N2454M	23. 5.79	ASG Leasing Ltd	Guernsey	21.10.06T
G-BGTI	Piper J-3C-65 Cub (L-4J-PI)	12940	F-BFFL	17. 5.79	A P Broad	Brandy Wharf, Waddingham	23. 9.08P
	(Rotax 582) (Frame No.12770)		44-80644				
G-BGTJ	Piper PA-28-180 Cherokee Archer	28-7405083	OY-BIO	3. 7.79	Serendipity Aviation Ltd	Gloucestershire	20.12.07E
			SE-GAH				
G-BGTT	Cessna 310R II	310R1641	N1AN	13. 7.79	Capital Trading (Aviation) Ltd	(Filton)	14. 6.08E
			(N2635D)				
G-BGTX	SAN Jodel D 117	698	F-BIDI	22. 6.79	C Adams and H F Young tr Madley Flying Group (Cisavia)	Shobdon	20. 8.08P
G-BGUB (2)	Piper PA-32-300 Six	32-7940252	N2387U	29.11.79	A J Diplock	Biggin Hill	28. 5.08E
G-BGVB	CEA Jodel DR.315 Petit Prince	308	F-BPOP	20. 7.79	P J Leggo	Leicester	18. 5.08E
G-BGVE	Scintex CP.1310-C3 Super Emeraude	931	F-BMJE	8. 6.79	H T Morris	Stapleford	14. 7.06P
G-BGVH	Beech 76 Duchess	ME-260		8. 6.79	W J and J.C M Golden t/a Valco Marketing	Bowerchalke, Salisbury	6. 9.08E
G-BGVK	Piper PA-28-161 Cherokee Warrior II	28-7816400	PH-WPT	13. 6.79	Aviation South West Ltd	Exeter	29. 5.08E
			G-BGVK, N6244C				
G-BGVN	Piper PA-28RT-201 Arrow IV	28R-7918168	N2846U	22. 6.79	John Wailing Ltd	Fairoaks	15.11.07E
G-BGVS	Reims Cessna F172M	F17200992	PH-HVS	3. 5.79	J W Tulloch tr Kirkwall Flying Club	Kirkwall	22.12.07E
			(PH-LUK)				
G-BGVV	Gulfstream AA-5A Cheetah	AA5A-0750		27. 6.79	W A Davidson	Prestwick	26. 5.08E
G-BGVY	Gulfstream AA-5B Tiger	AA5B-1080	(G-BGVU)	21. 8.79	R J C Neal-Smith	Compton Abbas	1.12.06
			(F-GBOO)		*(Noted 2.08)*		
G-BGVZ	Piper PA-28-181 Archer II	28-7990528	N2886A	12. 7.79	W Walsh and S R Mitchell	RAF Woodvale	9. 7.08E
G-BGWC	Robin DR.400-180 Régent	1420		26. 6.79	M A Newman	(Quarley, Andover)	29. 8.08E
G-BGWH	Piper PA-18-150 Super Cub	18-7605	ST-ABR,	18. 6.79	Spectrum Leisure Ltd	Clacton	27. 5.07T
			G-ARSR, N10F				
	(Veered to right landing Great Oakley 6. 9.05 and ground looped, damaging the rear fuselage)						
G-BGWJ	Sikorsky S-61N Mk.II	61-819		20. 8.79	Bristow Helicopters Ltd "Monadh Mor"	Aberdeen	4. 6.08E
G-BGWK	Sikorsky S-61N Mk.II	61-820	N1346C	10. 9.79	Bristow Helicopters Ltd	Egypt	28.11.07E
			G-BGWK		"Dun Robin"		
G-BGWM	Piper PA-28-181 Archer II	28-7990458	N2817Y	29. 6.79	Thames Valley Flying Club Ltd	Wycombe Air Park	10. 5.08E
G-BGWN	Piper PA-38-112 Tomahawk	38-79A0918	N9693N	2. 7.79	R T Callow Aslackby Decoy Farm, Aslackby, Bourne		17. 7.08E
G-BGWO	Jodel D 112	227	F-BHGQ	22. 6.79	R C Williams tr G-BGWO Group	Breighton	25. 4.07P
	(Built Etablissement Valladeau)				*(Noted 12.07)*		

G-BGWR	Cessna U206A Super Skywagon	U2060653	G-DISC	6. 7.79	Airkix Aircraft Ltd	Sibson	26. 1.08E
			G-BGWR, PH-OTD, N4953F				
G-BGWV	Aeronca 7AC Champion	7AC-4082	OO-GRI	23. 8.79	J A Webb tr RFC Flying Group	(Alton)	10.10.86P
			OO-TWR		*(Damaged Popham 8. 6.86)*		
G-BGXA	Piper J-3C-65 Cub (L-4H-PI)	10762	F-BGXA	1. 3.78	E C and P King tr G-XA Group *(As "329471:F-44" in USAAC c/s)*		
	(Frame No.10587 - regd with c/n 11170)		French AF, 43-29471			Eastbach Farm, Coleford	24. 4.07P
G-BGXB	Piper PA-38-112 Tomahawk	38-79A1007	N9728N	2. 7.79	Signtest Ltd	Alton	16. 8.04T
					(Noted Air Salvage International 8.07)		
G-BGXC	SOCATA TB-10 Tobago	35		19.10.79	D H Courtley	Alderney	19. 8.08E
G-BGXD	SOCATA TB-10 Tobago	39		19.10.79	D F P Finan	Durham Tees Valley	6. 8.08E
G-BGXO	Piper PA-38-112 Tomahawk	38-79A0982	N9703N	5. 7.79	Goodwood Road Racing Company Ltd	Goodwood	12. 2.08E
					(Operated Goodwood Flying Club)		
G-BGXR	Robin HR.200-100 Club	53	F-BVYH	1.10.79	J R Cross	Derby	29. 3.08E
G-BGXS	Piper PA-28-236 Dakota	28-7911198	N2836Z	12. 7.79	M Holland tr G-BGXS Group	Gamston	18. 4.08E
G-BGXT	SOCATA TB-10 Tobago	40		3.10.79	J L Alexander	(Cilgwyn, Newport)	31.10.07E
G-BGYH	Piper PA-28-161 Warrior II	28-7916313	N209LG	17. 7.79	Paper Space Ltd	Full Sutton	1. 5.08E
			N580X, G-BGYH, N9619N				
G-BGYN	Piper PA-18-150 Super Cub	18-7709137	N62747	19. 7.79	B J Dunford	Long Wood, Morestead	21.11.10E
G-BGZF	Piper PA-38-112 Tomahawk	38-79A1015	N9700N	26. 7.79	Fly Me Ltd	Hawarden	2.12.07E

G-BHAA - G-BHZZ

G-BHAA	Cessna 152 II	15281330	N49809	12. 2.79	Herefordshire Aero Club Ltd	Shobdon	10. 5.08T
G-BHAD	Cessna A152 Aerobat	A1520807	N7390L	12. 2.79	Shropshire Aero Club Ltd	Sleap	11. 4.08E
G-BHAI	Reims Cessna F152 II	F15201625	(D-EJAY)	14. 8.79	S Fyfe t/a Scottish Aircraft Sales	Strathallan	18. 2.08E
G-BHAJ	Robin DR.400-160 Major 80	1430		22. 8.79	Rowantask Ltd	Rochester	25. 3.06E
G-BHAR	Westland-Bell 47G-3B1	WA/353	XT194	7. 8.79	T J Wright	(Mullingar, County Westmeath)	8. 7.07
					(New owner 1.08)		
G-BHAV	Reims Cessna F152 II	F15201633		15. 8.79	T M and M L Jones *(Operated Derby Aero Club)*	Derby	17. 3.08E
G-BHAW	Reims Cessna F172N Skyhawk II	F17201858		15. 8.79	A Wright	(Cawood, Selby)	28. 6.08E
G-BHAX	Enstrom F-28C-2-UK	486-2	N5689N	22.10.79	J L Ferguson	Barton	12.10.07E
G-BHAY	Piper PA-28RT-201 Arrow IV	28R-7918213	N2910N	17. 8.79	Alpha Yankee Ltd	Newcastle	9. 6.08E
G-BHBA	Campbell Cricket	SMI-1		15. 8.79	S N McGovern	Henstridge	10 . 5.08P
	(Built S M Irwin) Rotax 503)						
G-BHBE	Westland-Bell 47G-3B1	WA/422	XT510	29.10.79	T R Smith (Agricultural Machinery) Ltd		
	(Soloy conversion)				*(Stored 6.05)* New Lane Farm, North Elmham		21.12.01
G-BHBF	Sikorsky S-76A II Plus	760022	N4247S	9.11.79	Bristow Helicopters Ltd *"Spirit of Paris"*	Aberdeen	2. 1.08E
G-BHBG	Piper PA-32R-300 Lance	32R-7780515	N408RC	18. 9.79	D E Gee	Blackbushe	29. 9.07E
			N9590N				
G-BHBI	Mooney M 20J Mooney 201	24-0842	N4764H	24. 9.79	D Caron	(Dompierre sur Ner, France)	10. 5.08
G-BHBT	Marquart MA.5 Charger	PFA 068-10190		3. 9.79	R G and C J Maidment	Goodwood	31.10.08P
	(Built R G Maidment) (Lycoming O-320)						
G-BHBZ	Partenavia P68B	191		10. 9.79	Geminair Services Ltd	Thruxton	20. 7.08E
G-BHCC	Cessna 172M Skyhawk II	17266711	(G-BGLY)	26.10.79	D Wood-Jenkins	Gloucestershire	7. 8.08E
			N80713				
G-BHCE	SAN Jodel D 117A	381	F-BHME	1.10.79	D G Jones	Pool Quay, Breidden	16. 2.08P
	(Originally built as D 112A and converted during rebuild between 1985 and 2004)						
G-BHCM	Cessna F172H	F172-0468	SE-FBD	25. 9.79	J Dominic	North Weald	9. 4.08E
	(Built Reims Aviation SA)						
G-BHCP	Reims Cessna F152 II	F15201640		31.10.79	Eastern Air Executive Ltd	Sturgate	4. 5.08E
G-BHCZ	Piper PA-38-112 Tomahawk	38-78A0321	N214MD	26. 9.79	J E Abbott	(Storrington, Pulborough)	19.10.07E
G-BHDD	Vickers 668 Varsity T 1	?	WL626	18.10.79	G Vale	East Midlands	
					(Noted Aeropark museum as "WL626:P" 3.06)		
G-BHDE	SOCATA TB-10 Tobago	58		2. 1.80	Alpha-Alpha Ltd	Liverpool	7. 3.09E
G-BHDM	Reims Cessna F152 II	F15201684		15.10.79	Big Red Kite Ltd	RAF Benson	19. 4.08E
G-BHDP	Reims Cessna F182Q Skylane II	F18200131		15.10.79	Zone Travel Ltd	Wycombe Air Park	4. 7.08
G-BHDR	Reims Cessna F152 II	F15201680		15.10.79	Heron-Air Ltd	(Glasgow)	29. 7.07T
	(Rebuilt 2003/4 using parts from G-BPGM)				*(Incurred accident 1. 8.06: removed from Cumbernauld 2.07)*		
G-BHDS	Reims Cessna F152 II	F15201682		15.10.79	Tayside Aviation Ltd	Glenrothes	14. 7.08E
G-BHDV	Cameron V-77 Balloon (Hot Air)	585		1. 2.80	P Glydon *"Dorm Ouse"*	Barnt Green, Birmingham	23. 3.08A
G-BHDW	Reims Cessna F152 II	F15201652		15.10.79	Aircraft Engineers Ltd	Prestwick	3. 7.08E
G-BHDX	Reims Cessna F172N Skyhawk II	F17201889		5.10.79	GDX Ltd	Cranfield	26. 7.08E
G-BHDZ	Reims Cessna F172N Skyhawk II	F17201911		3.12.79	Abbey Security Services Ltd		
						Great Ashfield, Bury St Edmunds	31. 5.08E
G-BHEC	Reims Cessna F152 II	F15201676		3.12.79	Stapleford Flying Club Ltd	Stapleford	22. 7.08E
G-BHED	Reims Cessna FA152 Aerobat	FA1520359		3.12.79	TG Aviation Ltd	Manston	26. 6.08E
					(Operated Thanet Flying Club)		
G-BHEG	SAN Jodel D 150 Mascaret	46	PH-ULS	3. 7.80	D M Griffiths	RAF Mona	25. 6.07P
			OO-SET				
G-BHEK	Scintex CP.1315-C3 Super Emeraude	923	F-BJMU	11.10.79	D B Winstanley	Barton	4.12.08P
G-BHEL	SAN Jodel D 117	735	F-BIOA	8.10.79	N Wright and C M Kettlewell Priory Farm, Tibenham		22.10.08P
G-BHEM	Bensen B 8MV	EK.14		8.10.79	G C Kerr	Kirkbride	5.10.00P
	(Built E Kenny - pr.no.PFA G/01-1016) (Rotax 503)				*(Noted 8.07)*		
G-BHEN	Reims Cessna FA152 Aerobat	FA1520363		3. 1.80	The Leicestershire Aero Club Ltd	Leicester	5. 1.08E
G-BHEU	Thunder Ax7-65 Series 1 Balloon (Hot Air)	238		16.10.79	D G Such *"Polomoche"*	Barkway, Royston	4. 4.07A
G-BHEV	Piper PA-28R-200 Cherokee Arrow II		PH-BOY	23.10.79	P Hardy tr 7-Up Group	Gamston	16. 4.08E
		28R-7435159	N41244				
G-BHEX	Colt 56A Balloon (Hot Air)	056		15.10.79	A S Dear, R B Green and W S Templeton Fordingbridge		5. 8.08A
					tr Hale Hot Air Balloon Group *"Superwasp"*		
G-BHEZ	SAN Jodel D 150 Mascaret	22	F-BLDO	31. 1.80	A Shorter tr Air Yorkshire Group	Sherburn-in-Elmet	27.11.08P
G-BHFC	Reims Cessna F152 II	F15201436		7. 4.78	Premier Flight Training Ltd	Old Buckenham	1. 8.08E
G-BHFE	Piper PA-44-180 Seminole	44-7995324	Abu Dhabi AF 0052 2.10.79		Grunwick Processing Laboratories Ltd	Cranfield	9. 2.08E
			G-BHFE, N2383U		*(Operated Bonus Aviation)*		

Reg	Type	c/n	Prev ID	Date	Owner	Location	Expiry
G-BHFF	Dormois Jodel D 112	322	F-BEKJ	19.10.79	G H Gilmour-White	(Thorverton, Exeter)	28. 3.02P
	(Force landed in field 4 nm W of Marlborough 1.9.01: damage to port u/c, port wing and engine: wing donated to G-BIVB 2003) (New owner 3.03)						
G-BHFG	SNCAN Stampe SV-4C	45	F-BJDN	31.10.79	C C Rollings and T F J Hodson t/a Tiger Airways		
			Aeronavale, Fr.AF			Gloucestershire	17. 4.08T
G-BHFH	Piper PA-34-200T Seneca II	34-7970482	N8075Q	23.10.79	Oxford Aviation Training Ltd	Oxford	19. 4.08E
G-BHFI	Reims Cessna F152 II	F15201685		22.10.79	R Bilson and D Turner tr BAe Warton Flying Club		
						Blackpool	22. 5.08E
G-BHFJ	Piper PA-28RT-201T Turbo Arrow IV		N8072R	22.10.79	A D R Northeast and S A Cook	White Waltham	26.10.07E
		28R-7931298					
G-BHFK	Piper PA-28-151 Cherokee Warrior	28-7615088	N8325C	12.12.79	Ilkeston Car Sales Ltd	Jericho Farm, Lambley	23. 3.08E
G-BHGC	Piper PA-18-150 Super Cub	18-8793	PH-NKH	3. 4.79	Vectis Gliding Club Ltd	Bembridge	29. 2.08E
			N4447Z				
G-BHGF	Cameron V-56 Balloon (Hot Air)	574		5.11.79	P Spellward *"Biggles"*	Bristol	29. 8.00A
G-BHGJ	Wassmer Jodel D 120 Paris-Nice	336	F-BOYB	15. 1.80	Q.M B Oswell	RAF Halton	12. 4.08P
G-BHGO	Piper PA-32-260 Cherokee Six	32-7800007	PH-BGP	16.11.79	L C Myall	(Maidenhead)	19. 1.08E
			N9656C		*(New owner 2.08)*		
G-BHGY	Piper PA-28R-200 Cherokee Arrow II		PH-NSL	23.11.79	Truman Aviation Ltd	Tollerton	8. 8.08E
		28R-7435086	N57365				
G-BHHB	Cameron V-77 Balloon (Hot Air)	170		26.11.79	R M Powell *"Pax"*	Stockbridge	1. 6.08A
G-BHHE	CEA Jodel DR.1051/M1 Sicile Record	628	F-BMZC	26. 4.80	P Bridges and P C Matthews		
						Fowle Hall Farm, Laddingford	13. 4.08
G-BHHG	Reims Cessna F152 II	F15201725		4. 3.80	TG Aviation Ltd	Manston	18. 7.08E
					(Operated Thanet Flying Club)		
G-BHHH	Thunder Ax7-65 Bolt Balloon (Hot Air)	245		5.12.79	C A Hendley (Essex) Ltd	Oakwood Hill, Loughton	27. 9.87A
					"Christmas" (Inflated 4.06)		
G-BHHK	Cameron N-77 Balloon (Hot Air)	547		5.12.79	I S Bridge	Newbury	7.12.87A
					"Shadowfax II" (On loan to British Balloon Museum and Library)		
G-BHHN	Cameron V-77 Balloon (Hot Air)	549		29.11.79	P Gooch tr The Itchen Valley Balloon Group		
					"Valley Crusader"	Alresford	5. 4.08A
G-BHHX	Jodel D 112	223	F-BFAJ	19. 2.80	M J Wells tr G-BHHX Group		
	(Built Etablissement Valladeau)					Watchford Farm, Yarcombe	15. 8.08P
G-BHIB	Reims Cessna F182Q Skylane II	F18200134		18.12.79	S N Chater and B Payne	Sherburn-in-Elmet	30. 4.08E
G-BHIG	Colt 31A Air Chair Balloon (Hot Air)	060	SE-...	12.12.79	P A Lindstrand	Upplands Vasby, Sweden	3. 3.00A
			G-BHIG		*(Operated S Ericsson)*		
G-BHII	Cameron V-77 Balloon (Hot Air)	548		10.12.79	R V Brown *"Tosca"*	Maidenhead	2. 9.96A
G-BHIJ	Eiriavion PIK-20E	20241		9. 1.80	P M Yeoman	(Scalford, Melton Mowbray)	15.11.07E
G-BHIK	Adam RA.14 Loisir	11-bis	F-PHLK	6. 2.80	L Lewis	(Redcar)	20. 8.85P
	(Continental A65)				*(Damaged near Lancaster 17.4.85: stored 1.02)*		
G-BHIN	Reims Cessna F152 II	F15201715		28. 1.80	Sussex Flying Club Ltd	Shoreham	18.11.07E
G-BHIS	Thunder Ax7-65 Bolt Balloon (Hot Air)	254		26.11.79	J R Wilson tr The Hedgehoppers Balloon Group		
					"Yo-Yo"	Didcot	21. 3.96A
G-BHIT	SOCATA TB-9 Tampico	63		7.12.79	C J P Webster	Biggin Hill	31. 1.01T
					(Reported at Mahon, Menorca 6.03 apparently abandoned)		
G-BHIY	Cessna F150K	F15000627	F-BRXR	18.12.79	G J Ball	Old Sarum	18. 4.08E
G-BHJF	SOCATA TB-10 Tobago	83		2. 1.80	D J Saunders tr Flying Fox Group	Fairoaks	17.12.07
G-BHJI	Mooney M 20J Mooney 201	24-0925	N3753H	11. 2.80	Hearing Centre Aarhus	Exeter	6. 3.08E
G-BHJK	Maule M-5-235C Lunar Rocket	7296C	N56359	25. 2.80	P J Kelsey	Glenrothes	23. 6.08E
G-BHJN	Fournier RF4D	4021	F-BORH	3. 1.80	R F Wondrak tr RF4 Flying Group	Enstone	23. 3.08P
G-BHJO	Piper PA-28-161 Cherokee Warrior II		OO-FLD	4. 1.80	A Sangster, I Young and T R Whittome	Inverness	16. 5.08E
		28-7816213	N9507N, N6034H		tr Brackla Flying Group		
G-BHJS	Partenavia P68B	172	I-KLUB	28.12.79	J J Watts and D Fletcher	Bournemouth	15. 7.08E
G-BHJU	Robin DR.400 2+2	1288	D-ECDK	9. 1.80	J Barlow and P Crow tr Ageless Aeronauts	Lydd	29. 5.08E
G-BHKH	Cameron O-65 Balloon (Hot Air)	592		7. 1.80	P Donkin *"Daisy"*	Caerwent, Caldicot	6. 2.08A
G-BHKJ	Cessna 421C Golden Eagle	421C0848	(N26596)	25. 1.80	Totaljet Ltd	Hawarden	6.10.07E
	(Robertson STOL conversion)						
G-BHLE	Robin DR.400-180 Régent	1466		25. 1.80	B D Greenwood	Ronaldsway	17. 4.08E
G-BHLH	Robin DR.400-180 Régent	1320	F-GBIG	11. 2.80	A Hegner tr G-BHLH Group	Wycombe Air Park	22. 4.08E
G-BHLJ	Saffery-Rigg S 200 Skyliner Balloon (Minimum Lift)			23. 1.80	I A Rigg	Pendlebury, Swinton	
	(Built C Saffery)	IAR/01			*"Skyliner"*		
G-BHLT	de Havilland DH.82A Tiger Moth	84997	ZS-DGA	9. 6.80	Skymax (Aviation) Ltd	Damyn's Hall, Upminster	26. 2.90
	(Built Morris Motors Ltd)		SAAF 2272, T6697		*(New owner 4.06)*		
G-BHLU	Fournier RF3	79	F-BMTN	14. 4.80	G Sabatino	(Uxbridge)	19. 4.08P
G-BHLW	Cessna 120	10210	N73300	24. 3.80	L W Scattergood	Sherburn-in-Elmet	24. 9.08P
	(Continental C85)		NC73005		*"Sky Ranger"*		
G-BHLX	Grumman AA-5B Tiger	AA5B-0573	OY-GAR	1. 2.80	M D McPherson	Cranfield	22. 7.08E
G-BHMA	SIPA 903	61	OO-FAE	13. 3.80	H J Taggart	Ballymoney, County Antrim	2. 7.08P
			F-BGBK				
G-BHMG	Reims Cessna FA152 Aerobat	FA1520368		10. 6.80	R D Smith	Popham	7. 7.08E
G-BHMI	Reims Cessna F172N Skyhawk II	F17202036	G-WADE	6. 8.80	GMI Aviation Ltd	(Ormskirk)	9. 3.08E
			G-BHMI				
G-BHMJ	Avenger T 200-2112 Balloon (Minimum Lift) 002			29. 1.80	R Light	Stockport	
	(Built R Light)				*"Lord Anthony I"*		
G-BHMK	Avenger T 200-2112 Balloon (Minimum Lift) 003			29. 1.80	P Kinder	Stockport	
	(Built P Kinder)				*"Lord Anthony II"*		
G-BHMR	Stinson 108-3 Voyager	108-4352	F-BABO	12. 2.80	G Cormack	Cumbernauld	23.11.90
	(Built Consolidated Vultee Aircraft)		F-DABO, NC6352M		*(New owner 12.07)*		
G-BHMT	Evans VP-1	PFA 062-10473		18. 2.80	P E J Sturgeon	Queach Farm, Bury St Edmunds	8. 7.05P
	(Built P E J Sturgeon) (Volkswagen 1834)						
G-BHNC	Cameron O-65 Balloon (Hot Air)	588		7. 2.80	D Bareford and C Charley *"Hot N'Cold"*		
					Cookley, Kidderminster and Wymeswold, Loughborough		5. 3.94A
G-BHND	Cameron N-65 Balloon (Hot Air)	582		7. 2.80	S M Wellband	Little Keyford, Frome	24. 6.89A
G-BHNK	Wassmer Jodel D 120A Paris-Nice	243	F-BLNK	26. 3.80	D A Bates tr G-BHNK Flying Group		
						St Mary's, Isles of Scilly	19. 4.08P
G-BHNL	Wassmer Jodel D 112	1206	F-BLNL	30. 1.80	M D Mold tr HNL Group	Watchford Farm, Yarcombe	21.10.08P

Reg	Type	c/n	Prev id	Date	Owner	Location	Date
G-BHNO	Piper PA-28-181 Archer II	28-8090211	N81413	7. 2.80	B J Richardson	RAF Cosford	21. 8.08E
G-BHNP	Eiriavion PIK-20E	20253		29. 2.80	D A Sutton *"NP"*	Sackville Lodge, Riseley	26. 5.08E
G-BHNV	Westland-Bell 47G-3B1	WA/700	F-GHNM	11. 3.80	Leyline Helicopters Ltd	Trenholme Farm, Billingham	28. 5.89T
			G-BHNV, XW180		*(Noted 10.02)*		
G-BHNX	SAN Jodel D 117	493	F-BHNX	7. 9.78	A J Chalkley *(On rebuild 4.91)*	(Pwllheli)	12. 1.87P
G-BHOA	Robin DR.400-160 Major 80	1478		27. 1.80	Goudhurst Service Station Ltd	Goudhurst	11. 9.08E
G-BHOG	Sikorsky S-61N Mk.II	61-825	PT-YEK	25. 3.80	Veritair Ltd t/a British International	Plymouth	
			G-BHOG, (LN-ONK), G-BHOG		*(Noted 11.06)*		
G-BHOJ	Colt 12A Cloudhopper Balloon (Hot Air)	080		27. 2.80	J A Folkes	Bulcote, Nottingham	
	(Originally registered as Colt 14A)				*(Inflated 4.06)*		
G-BHOL	CEA Jodel DR.1050 Ambassadeur	35	F-BJQL	6. 2.80	S P Tilling	Old Hay, Paddock Wood	15.12.07
G-BHOM	Piper PA-18 Super Cub 95	18-1391	OO-PIU	7. 3.80	P Myers tr Oscar Mike Flying Group		
	(L-18C-PI) *(Frame No.18-1272)*		OO-HMT, French Army 51-15391			Whitehall Farm, Benington	2. 5.08P
G-BHOO	Yorkshire Air Balloon A66 Balloon (Hot Air)	001		26. 2.80	D Livesey and J M Purves	Brampton and York	
	(Built D Livesey and J M Purves)				*"Scraps"*		
G-BHOR	Piper PA-28-161 Warrior II	28-8016331	N82162	12. 6.80	A J Harewood tr Oscar Romeo Flying Group		
						Biggin Hill	15. 8.08E
G-BHOT	Cameron V-65 Balloon (Hot Air)	777		15. 9.81	J A Baker tr The Dante Balloon Group	Hungerford	8. 8.99A
					"Le Billet Doux"		
G-BHOZ	SOCATA TB-9 Tampico	84		11. 3.80	G-BHOZ Management Ltd	Kemble	29. 4.08E
G-BHPK	Piper J-3C-65 Cub (L-4A-PI)	8979	F-BEPK	26. 2.80	L B Smith tr L4 Group	Priory Farm, Tibenham	3. 4.08P
	(Frame No.9098: official c/n 12161/44-79865 [F-BFYU]}		French Military, 42-38410		*(As "238410:A-44" in USAAF c/s)*		
G-BHPL	CASA 1-131E Jungmann	1058	Spanish AF E3B-350	17. 7.80	A Burroughes	Compton Abbas	18. 7.08E
					(As "E3B-350:05 97" in Spanish AF c/s)		
G-BHPS	Wassmer Jodel D 120A Paris-Nice	148	F-BIXI	11. 6.80	T J Price	Rhigos	16. 7.08P
G-BHPY	Cessna 152 II	15282983	N46009	26. 3.80	TGD Leasing Ltd	Wellesbourne Mountford	4.10.07T
G-BHPZ	Cessna 172N Skyhawk II	17272017	N6411E	26. 3.80	O'Brien Properties Ltd	Shoreham	22. 4.08E
G-BHRB	Reims Cessna F152 II	F15201707		20. 3.80	Upperstack Ltd t/a LAC Flying School	Barton	6. 3.08E
					(Operated Lancashire Aero Club)		
G-BHRC	Piper PA-28-161 Warrior II	28-7916430	N9527N	3. 4.80	The Sherwood Flying Club Ltd	Tollerton	9. 3.08E
G-BHRH	Reims Cessna FA150K Aerobat	FA1500056	PH-ECB	24. 3.80	Merlin Flying Club Ltd	Hucknall	25. 6.08E
			D-ECBL, (D-EKKW)				
G-BHRN	Reims Cessna F152 II	F15201728	F-GCHV	8. 4.80	Flight Academy Scotland Ltd	Cumbernauld	5. 9.08E
G-BHRO	Rockwell Commander 112A	364	N1364J	20. 3.80	R A Blackwell	North Weald	20. 9.08E
G-BHRP	Piper PA-44-180 Seminole	44-8095021	N81602	1. 4.80	Shemburn Ltd	Weston, Lucan, County Dublin	20. 5.07T
					(New owner 12.07)		
G-BHRR	Menavia Piel CP.301A Emeraude	270	F-BISK	28. 3.80	T W Offen *(Noted 8.07)*	Maypole Farm, Chislet	28. 5.87P
G-BHRW	CEA Jodel DR.221 Dauphin	93	F-BPCP	10. 7.80	D H Williams and I Bell tr Dauphin Flying Group		
						Gloucestershire	9. 5.08
G-BHRY	Colt 56A Balloon (Hot Air)	030		2. 4.80	A S Davidson *"Turkish Delight"*	Burton-on-Trent	29. 4.95A
G-BHSB	Cessna 172N Skyhawk II	17272977	(N1225F)	25. 6.80	SB Aviation Ltd	Leeds-Bradford	5. 2.08E
G-BHSD	Scheibe SF25E Super Falke	4357	D-KDGG	21. 7.80	L Barber tr Upwood Motorglider Group	Upwood	25. 7.08
	(Limbach SL1700						
G-BHSE	Rockwell Commander 114	14161	N4831W	15. 5.80	604 Squadron Flying Group Ltd	Wycombe Air Park	16. 5.08E
			AN-BRL, (N4831W)				
G-BHSN	Cameron N-56 Balloon (Hot Air)	595		10. 4.80	I Bentley	Bath	9. 7.05A
G-BHSP	Thunder Ax7-77Z Balloon (Hot Air)	272		15. 4.80	G A Fisher tr Out-of-the Blue	Guildford	23. 2.94A
	(Originally built as D-TRIER c/n 221)				*"Chicago" (Inflated 4.06)*		
G-BHSS	Pitts S-1S	C 1461M	N1704	19. 9.80	C W Burkett	Little Gransden	19. 2.08P
	(Built C H McClendon) (Lycoming O-320)						
G-BHSY	CEA Jodel DR.1050 Sicile	546	F-BLZO	6. 5.80	T R Allebone	Easton Maudit	23. 2.08
G-BHTA	Piper PA-28-236 Dakota	28-8011102	N8197H	22. 4.80	Dakota Ltd *(Noted 1.08)*	Jersey	26. 9.07
G-BHTC	CEA Jodel DR.1051/M1 Sicile Record	581	F-BMGR	1. 5.80	A H Macaskill and G Clark	Oaksey Park	27. 1.08
G-BHTG	Thunder Ax6-56 Bolt Balloon (Hot Air)	273		18. 4.80	F R and S.H MacDonald	Newgate, Dorking	18.12.91A
					"Halcyon"		
G-BHUE	SAN Jodel DR.1050 Ambassadeur	185	F-BERM	21. 4.80	M J Harris	(Lower Broadheath, Worcester)	19.10.92
			F-OBRM				
G-BHUG	Cessna 172N Skyhawk II	17272985	N1283F	24. 6.80	F G Baulch t/a FGT Aircraft Hire	Dunkeswell	29. 3.08E
G-BHUI	Cessna 152 II	15283144	N46932	27. 5.80	Galair International Ltd	Wellesbourne Mountford	9. 3.08E
G-BHUJ	Cessna 172N Skyhawk II	17271932	N5752E	27. 5.80	K B Dupuy tr Uniform Juliet Group	Southend	6. 6.08E
G-BHUM	de Havilland DH.82A Tiger Moth	85453	VT-DGA	9. 6.80	S G Towers	Beckwithshaw, Harrogate	10. 7.09S
			VT-DDN, RIAF, SAAF 4622, DE457				
G-BHUR	Thunder Ax3 Mini Sky Chariot Balloon (Hot Air)			9. 5.80	B F G Ribbans	Newbury	6. 6.06A
		277			*"Ben Hur" (On loan to British Balloon Museum and Library)*		
G-BHUU	Piper PA-25-235 Pawnee D	25-8056035	N2440Q	28. 5.80	Booker Gliding Club Ltd	Wycombe Air Park	5. 4.07
	(Modified to PA-25-260 standard)						
G-BHVB	Piper PA-28-161 Warrior II	28-8016260	N9638N	16. 5.80	P J Clarke	Halfpenny Green	9. 9.07E
G-BHVC	Cessna 172RG Cutlass II	172RG0550	N9048K	30. 5.80	K O'Connor	Weston, Leixlip, County Kildare	7. 5.08E
			G-BHVC, N372SA, G-BHVC, N5515V				
G-BHVF	SAN Jodel D 150A Mascaret	11	F-BLDF	28.10.80	J D Walton	Swanborough Farm, Lewes	5.12.08P
G-BHVP	Cessna 182Q Skylane II	18267071	N97374	15.12.80	R J W Wood	Gregory Farm, Mirfield	7.10.07E
G-BHVR	Cessna 172N Skyhawk II	17270196	N738SG	27. 5.80	C Vincent tr Victor Romeo Group	Elstree	9. 7.08E
G-BHVV	Piper J-3C-65 Cub (L-4A-PI)	8953	F-BGXF	27. 6.80	C A Ward and C A Cash	Perranporth	2. 4.08P
	(Frame No.9048)		French Military, 42-38384		*(As "31430" in USAAF c/s)*		
	(Regd with c/n 10291/43-1430 ex F-BEGF: frames probably exchanged in 1953 rebuild)						
G-BHWA	Reims Cessna F152 II	F15201775		28. 3.80	Lincoln Enterprises Ltd	Wickenby	12. 7.08E
G-BHWB	Reims Cessna F152 II	F15201776	(G-BHWA)	14. 4.80	Lincoln Enterprises Ltd	Wickenby	22.11.07E
G-BHWH	Weedhopper JC-24A	0074		23. 4.80	G A Clephane	Basingstoke	X
	(Fuji-Robin EC-34-PM) *(Modified to JC-24C)*				*(As "Bu.126603" in US Navy c/s) "Dream Machine"*		
G-BHWK	SOCATA MS.880B Rallye Club	870	F-BONK	27. 8.80	W O Wright and D-J Spencer		
						Shotton Colliery, Peterlee	16.12.07
G-BHWY	Piper PA-28R-200 Cherokee Arrow II		N56904	17. 6.80	I C Rogers and R B Cheek tr Kilo Foxtrot Flying Group		
		28R-7435059				Sandown, Isle of Wight	26. 5.08E
G-BHWZ	Piper PA-28-181 Cherokee Archer II		N3379M	8. 4.80	M A Abbott	Fairoaks	16. 8.07T
		28-7890299					

G-BHXA	Scottish Aviation Bulldog Series 120/1210		Botswana DF OD1	9. 6.80	Air Plan Flight Equipment Ltd	Derby	10. 8.09S
		BH120/407	G-BHXA		*(Deltair Aviation titles)*		
G-BHXD	Wassmer Jodel D 120 Paris-Nice	258	F-BMIA	3. 7.80	D A Garner	Rhigos	29. 9.07P
G-BHXK	Piper PA-28-140 Cherokee	28-21106	VR-HGB	14. 7.80	J Moreland tr GXK Flying Group	Thruxton	3. 5.08
			9V-BAJ, (9M-AOM)				
G-BHXS	Wassmer Jodel D 120 Paris-Nice	133	F-BIXS	27. 8.80	R I Walker tr Plymouth Jodel Group	Plymouth	19. 7.08P
G-BHXY	Piper J-3C-65 Cub (L-4H-PI)	11905	D-EAXY	1. 7.80	F W Rogers	Callington, Plymouth	7. 5.07P
	(Frame No.11733)		F-BFQX, 44-79609		*(As "44-79609:S-44 in USAAF c/s)*		
G-BHYA	Cessna R182 Skylane RG II	R18200532	N1717R	10. 7.80	B Davies	Aberporth	27. 3.08E
G-BHYC	Cessna 172RG Cutlass II	172RG0404	(N4868V)	24. 6.80	IB Aeroplanes Ltd	City of Derry	12.12.07
G-BHYD	Cessna R172K Hawk XP	R1722734	N736RS	11.12.80	Sylmar Aviation and Services Ltd		
						Lower Wasing Farm, Brimpton	3. 5.08E
G-BHYG	Piper PA-34-200T Seneca II	34-8070235	N8225X	30. 6.80	Oxford Aviation Training Ltd	Oxford	27.10.07E
G-BHYI	SNCAN Stampe SV-4A	18	F-BAAF	11. 7.80	D Hicklin	(Brightlingsea, Colchester)	25. 7.07
			French AF				
G-BHYP	Reims Cessna F172M Skyhawk II	F17201108	OY-BFR	30. 6.80	Avior Ltd	Oxford	16. 6.08E
G-BHYR	Reims Cessna F172M	F17200922	OY-DZH	30. 6.80	R G Forster tr G-BHYR Group	Stapleford	10. 7.08E
			SE-FZH, (OH-CFQ)				
G-BHYV	Evans VP-1	LC.2		2. 7.80	L Chiappi	White Waltham	
	(Built L Chiappi - pr.no.PFA 1569) (Volkswagen 1600)				*(Noted 6.07 dumped outside less engine - far side black hangar*		
G-BHYX	Cessna 152 II	15281832	N67434	4. 7.80	Stapleford Flying Club Ltd	Stapleford	10. 4.08E
G-BHZE	Piper PA-28-181 Cherokee Archer II		OO-FLR	4.11.80	Zegruppe Ltd	White Waltham	24. 1.08T
		28-7890291	(OO-HCM), N3053M				
G-BHZH	Reims Cessna F152 II	F15201786		25. 7.80	Plymouth Flying School Ltd	Plymouth	27. 9.08E
G-BHZK	Grumman AA-5B Tiger	AA5B-0743	N28670	8. 9.80	R G Seth-Smith tr Zulu Kilo Group	Elstree	29. 5.08E
G-BHZO	Gulfstream AA-5A Cheetah	AA5A-0692	N26750	21. 7.80	Global Engineering and Maintenance Ltd		
					(New oener 7.07)	Bournemouth	23.12.04T
G-BHZR	Scottish Aviation Bulldog Series 120/1210		Botswana DF OD4	23. 7.80	White Knuckle Air Ltd	Pembrey	9. 7.09S
		BH120/410	G-BHZR		*"Winston"*		
G-BHZS	Scottish Aviation Bulldog Series 120/1210		Botswana DF OD5	23. 7.80	Air Plan Flight Equipment Ltd	Derby	20. 2.06T
		BH120/411	G-BHZS				
G-BHZT	Scottish Aviation Bulldog Series 120/1210		Botswana DF OD6	23. 7.80	D M Curties	Kemble	20. 3.08T
		BH120/412	G-BHZT				
G-BHZU	Piper J-3C-65 Cub (L-4B-PI)	9775	F-BETO	17. 7.80	J K Tomkinson	Brook Farm, Boylestone	16. 7.07P
	(Continental O-200-A)		(F-BFKH), 43-914				
	(Regd with Frame No.9606 fitted to F-BETO in 1961 rebuild replacing c/n 13164 ex 45-4424)						
G-BHZV	Wassmer Jodel D 120A Paris-Nice	278	F-BMON	23. 7.80	K J Scott	Rochester	19. 6.07P
G-BHZX	Thunder Ax7-69A Balloon (Hot Air)	288		25. 7.80	R J and H.M Beattie	Wendover, Aylesbury	10. 6.94A
					"After Eight"		

G-BIAA - G-BIZZ

G-BIAC	SOCATA Rallye 235E Gabier	13323		17. 7.80	D R Watson and A J Haigh	Maypole Farm, Chislet	12. 7.08E
G-BIAH	Wassmer Jodel D 112	1218	F-BMAH	20. 8.80	P S Grellier	Barton Ashes	22. 7.08P
G-BIAI	Wallingford WMB.2 Windtracker Balloon (Minimum Lift)			1. 7.80	I Chadwick tr Unicorn Group *"Amanda I"*		
		008				Partridge Green, Horsham	
G-BIAP	Piper PA-16 Clipper	16-732	F-BBGM	25. 6.80	P J Bish	Draycott Farm, Chiseldon	12. 4.08E
	(Frame No.16-733)		F-OAGS				
G-BIAR	Rigg Skyliner II Balloon (Minimum Lift)	AKC-59		9. 7.80	I A Rigg	Pendlebury, Swinton	
	(Built I A Rigg - c/n IAR/02)						
G-BIAX	Taylor JT.2 Titch	GFR-1		30. 7.80	D M Bland	(Malvern)	11. 5.04P
	(Built J T Everest and G F Rowley - pr.no.PFA 3228) (Continental O-200)				*(New owner 7.07)*		
G-BIAY	Grumman AA-5 Traveler	AA5-0423	OY-GAD	26. 8.80	P Moderate tr Group AY	Headcorn	30. 7.08E
			N7123L				
G-BIBA	SOCATA TB-9 Tampico	149		17. 7.80	TB Aviation Ltd	Denham	1. 5.08E
G-BIBB	Mooney M 20C Mark 21	2803	OH-MOD	22. 7.80	Lefay Engineering Ltd	Popham	23. 6.08E
G-BIBG	Sikorsky S-76A II Plus	760083	5N-BCE	18. 8.80	Bristow Helicopters Ltd	Aberdeen	18. 8.08E
			G-BIBG		*"Loch Seaforth"*		
G-BIBJ	Enstrom 280C-UK-2 Shark	1187		13. 8.80	C J Swift	Little Snoring	18. 2.08E
G-BIBN	Reims Cessna FA150K Aerobat	FA1500078	F-BSHN	29.10.80	B V Mayo	Maypole Farm, Chislet	20. 1.08E
G-BIBO	Cameron V-65 Balloon (Hot Air)	667		7. 8.80	D M Hoddinott	Bristol	13. 8.08A
G-BIBS	Cameron P-20 Balloon (Hot Air)	671		14. 8.80	Cameron Balloons Ltd *(Stored 2006)*	Bristol	
G-BIBT	Gulfstream AA-5B Tiger	AA5B-1047	N4518V	8. 9.80	Horizon Aviation Ltd *(Noted 11.07)*	Swansea	3.10.07E
G-BIBW	Reims Cessna F172N Skyhawk II	F17201756		13.10.78	Drawflight Ltd	Lydd	19. 4.08E
G-BIBX	Wallingford WMB.2 Windtracker Balloon (Minimum Lift)			18. 8.80	I A Rigg	Pendlebury, Swinton	
		9			*"Bumble"*		
G-BICD	Taylorcraft J Auster 5	735	F-BFXH	20. 8.80	T R Parsons	Beeches Farm, South Scarle	25. 4.08P
			MT166		*(Carries "MT166")*		
G-BICE	North American AT-6C-1-NT Harvard IIA	88-9755	FAP1545	3. 9.80	C M L Edwards	New Farm House, Great Oakley	12. 7.07P
			SAAF 7084, EX302, 41-33275		*(As "41-33275:CE" in USAAF c/s)*		
G-BICG	Reims Cessna F152 II	F15201796		3. 9.80	A S Bamrah t/a Falcon Flying Services	Biggin Hill	12. 4.08E
G-BICJ	Monnett Sonerai II	726		22. 8.80	P Daukas	Connington	24. 1.06P
	(Built J R Heaton - pr.no.PFA 015-10531) (Volkswagen 1834)						
G-BICM	Colt 56A Balloon (Hot Air)	095		1. 9.80	W S Templeton and R B Green	Fordingbridge	5. 8.08A
					tr The Avon Advertiser Balloon Club *"Ladybird"*		
G-BICP	Robin DR.360 Chevalier	610	F-BSPH	2.10.80	J B McVeighty *(On rebuild 2008)*	(Huntingdon, York)	28. 7.08E
G-BICR	Wassmer Jodel D 120A Paris-Nice	135	F-BIXR	5. 9.80	G L Perry tr Beehive Flying Group	White Waltham	21.12.08P
G-BICS	Robin R2100A Club	128	F-GBAC	4.12.80	I Young	Sandown, Isle of Wight	18. 7.08
G-BICU	Cameron V-56 Balloon (Hot Air)	680		9. 9.80	G A Chadwick t/a Black Pearl Balloons		
						Partridge Green, Horsham	31. 1.08A
G-BICW	Piper PA-28-161 Warrior II	28-7916309	N2091U	8.10.80	S Morley tr Charlie Whisky Flying Group	Blackbushe	23. 2.08E
G-BICX	Maule M-5-235C Lunar Rocket	7287C	(G-MAUL (1))	2. 2.81	A T Jeans and J F Clarkson		
			N56352			Compton Chamberlayne, Salisbury	22. 5.08E

G-BIDD	Evans VP-1	PFA 062-10974			27.10.78	J Hodgkinson	(Hill Farm, Nayland)	2.12.00P
	(Built J Wedgebury and regd initially as c/n PFA 062-10167 but combined project) (Volkswagen 1600) (Reported 7.05)							
G-BIDF	Reims Cessna F172P Skyhawk II	F17202045	(PH-JPO)	18. 9.80		C J Chaplin and N J C Howard	Redhill	19. 7.08E
G-BIDG	SAN Jodel D 150A Mascaret	08	F-BLDG	11. 9.80		D R Gray	Barton	17. 9.08P
G-BIDH	Cessna 152 II	15280546	G-DONA	12. 9.80		Hull Aero Club Ltd	Linley Hill, Leven	4. 8.08E
			G-BIDH, N25234					
G-BIDI	Piper PA-28R-201 Arrow III	28R-7837135	N3759M	11.11.80		A Lidster and T A N Brierley *(New owners 1.08)*		9. 5.05
							(East Cowton, Northallerton and York)	
G-BIDJ	Piper PA-18A-150 Super Cub	18-6007	PH-MAY	22. 9.80		Flight Solutions Ltd	Panshanger	19. 7.08E
	(Frame No.18-6089)		N7798D					
G-BIDK	Piper PA-18-150 Super Cub	"18-6591"	PH-MAI	22. 9.80		J and M.A McCullough	Newtownards	12. 6.08E
	(L-21A-PI)		R Neth AF R-211, 51-15679, N7194K					
	(Composite of PH-MAI originally Frame No.18-6714 [c/n 18-6591] ex LN-TVB/N9285D rebuilt 1976 with Frame No.18-503 [c/n 18-565] ex R Neth AF R-211)							
G-BIDO	Piel CP.301A Emeraude	327	F-POIO	25. 3.81		A R Plumb	Hill Farm, Nayland	2. 8.08P
G-BIDX	Dormois Jodel D 112	876	F-BIQY	19. 9.80		P Turton and H C Peake-Jones	Ash Farm, Winsford	5. 9.05P
						(Noted 11.07)		
G-BIEF	Cameron V-77 Balloon (Hot Air)	679		25. 9.80		D S Bush	Hertingfordbury, Hereford	6. 3.94A
						"Daedalus" (Inflated 4.06)		
G-BIEJ	Sikorsky S-76A II Plus	760097		21.10.80		Bristow Helicopters Ltd *"Glen Lossie"*	Norwich	21. 2.08E
G-BIEN	Wassmer Jodel D 120A Paris-Nice	218	F-BKNK	3. 6.81		C Newton	(Tilhouse, France)	19. 5.06P
G-BIEO	Wassmer Jodel D 112	1296	F-BMOK	19. 3.82		S C Solley tr Clipgate Flyers Clipgate Farm, Denton		15. 8.08P
G-BIES	Maule M-5-235C Lunar Rocket	7334C	N56394	24. 7.81		W Procter t/a William Procter Farms		
							Stowe Farm, Tillingham	23. 5.08E
G-BIET	Cameron O-77 Balloon (Hot Air)	674		30. 9.80		G M Westley *"Archimedes"*	London SW15	11. 1.02A
G-BIEY	Piper PA-28-151 Cherokee Warrior	28-7715213	PH-KDH	10.11.80		A S Bamrah	Biggin Hill	15. 2.07T
			OO-HCB, N9540N					
G-BIFA	Cessna 310R II	310R1606	N36868	29. 1.81		J S Lee	Wycombe Air Park	18.12.07
G-BIFB	Piper PA-28-150 Cherokee C	28-1968	4X-AEC	6.10.80		P Coombs	Sturgate	17. 4.08E
G-BIFO	Evans VP-1	PFA 062-10411		29. 9.80		R Broadhead Eddsfield, Octon Lodge Farm, Thwing		26. 4.08P
	(Built P Raggett) (Volkswagen 1834)							
G-BIFY	Reims Cessna F150L	F15000829	PH-CEZ	9.10.80		Bonus Aviation Ltd	Cranfield	25.10.07E
G-BIGJ	Reims Cessna F172M	F17200936	PH-SKT	2.12.80		Cirrus Aviation Ltd	Clacton	9. 6.08E
G-BIGK	Taylorcraft BC-12D	8302	N96002	29.10.80		N P St J Ramsay	Sywell	6. 6.08P
	(Continental A65)		NC96002			*(Also carries "NC96002")*		
G-BIGL	Cameron O-65 Balloon (Hot Air)	690		22.10.80		P L and S V Mossman	Llanishen, Chepstow	24. 3.08A
						"Biggles"		
G-BIGP	Bensen B 8M	PFA G/01-1005		14.10.80		R H S Cooper	(Shrewsbury)	20.10.97P
	(Built R H S Cooper) (McCulloch Motors O-100-1)							
G-BIGR	Avenger T 200-2112 Balloon (Minimum Lift) 004			6.10.80		R Light	Stockport	
	(Built R Light)							
G-BIGZ	Scheibe SF25B Falke	46142	D-KCAI	22.12.80		C N Jones tr Big-Z Owners Group	RAF Henlow	19.10.07E
	(Stark-Stamo MS1500)							
G-BIHD	Robin DR.400-160 Major 80	1510		29.10.80		G I J Thomson and R A Hawkins	Little Snoring	13. 3.08E
G-BIHF	Replica Plans SE.5a	079275		27.10.80		S H O'Connell	White Waltham	13.11.08P
	(Built K J Garrett - pr.no.PFA 020-10548) (Continental O-200-A)					*(As "F-943" in RFC 92 Sqdn c/s) "Lady Di"*		
G-BIHI	Cessna 172M Skyhawk II	17266854	(G-BIHA)	18.11.80		L R Haunch t/a Fenland Flying School	Fenland	30.10.07E
			N1125U					
G-BIHO	de Havilland DHC-6-310 Twin Otter	738	A6-ADB	9. 1.81		Isles of Scilly Skybus Ltd	St Just	18. 4.08E
			G-BIHO					
G-BIHP (2)	Van Den Bemden 1000m3 Gas Balloon VDB-38	OO-VBA		19.12.80		J J Harris	London SW6	3. 5.01
	(C/n quoted as "18" by Belgian owner: believed rebuilt with 600m3 canopy c/n VDB-47) "Belgica"							
G-BIHT	Piper PA-17 Vagabond	17-41	N138N	9. 1.81		B Carter	Old Sarum	9. 7.08P
	(Continental A65)		N8N, N4626H, NC4626H					
G-BIHU	Saffery S 200 Balloon (Minimum Lift)	25		5.11.80		B L King	Coulsdon	
	(Built Cupro Sapphire Ltd)							
G-BIHX	Bensen B 8MR	PFA G/01-1003		12.11.80		P P Willmott	North Coates	30. 7.08P
	(Built P P Willmott) (Rotax 503)							
G-BIIA	Fournier RF3	51	F-BMTA	14.11.80		J D Webb and J D Bally	Rhosgoch	26. 4.08P
G-BIIB	Reims Cessna F172M Skyhawk II	F17201110	PH-GRE	18.11.80		Civil Service Flying Club (Biggin Hill) Ltd	Rochester	24. 4.08E
G-BIID	Piper PA-18 Super Cub 95	18-1606	OO-LPA	5. 1.81		D A Lacey	Cumbernauld	17. 7.08P
	(L-18C-PI) *(Frame No.18-1558)*		OO-HMK, French Army 18-1606, 51-15606					
G-BIIE	Reims Cessna F172P Skyhawk II	F17202051		31.12.80		Sterling Helicopters Ltd	Norwich	12. 3.08E
G-BIIK	SOCATA MS.883 Rallye 115	1552	F-BSAP	28.11.80		N J Garbett	Fenland	1. 9.08E
G-BIIL	Thunder Ax6-56 Bolt Balloon (Hot Air)	306		12.11.80		R Powell	Craswall, Hereford	14. 3.06A
G-BIIT	Piper PA-28-161 Warrior II	28-8116052	N82744	1.12.80		Highland Flying School Ltd	Inverness	1. 4.08E
G-BIIV	Piper PA-28-181 Archer II	28-7990028	N20875	19.12.80		J Thuret	(Montpellier, France)	21. 8.08E
G-BIIZ	Great Lakes 2T-1A	57	N603K	1. 4.81		Circa 42 Ltd	(Great Horkesley, Colchester)	4. 2.99P
	(Warner Super Scarab 165D-5)		NC603K			*(Damaged Upper Harford, Gloucestershire 8. 8.98)*		
G-BIJB	Piper PA-18-150 Super Cub	18-8009001	N23923	18. 8.80		James Aero Ltd	Stapleford	9. 8.08E
			N2573H					
G-BIJD	Bölkow BÖ.208C Junior	636	PH-KAE	9.12.80		P Singh tr Sikh Syndicate	Leicester	20. 1.08E
			(PH-DYM), OO-SIS, (D-EGFA)					
G-BIJE	Piper J-3C-65 Cub (L-4A-PI)	8367	F-BIGN	5. 5.81		R L Hayward and A G Scott	(Cardiff and Usk)	
	(Frame No.8504)		French Military, 42-15248			*(On rebuild 4.91)*		
G-BIJS	Phoenix Luton LA-4A Minor	PAL 1348		18. 5.78		I J Smith	(Brook Farm, Boylestone)	14.11.95P
	(Built I J Smith - pr.no.PFA 835) (Volkswagen 1600)							
G-BIJU	Menavia Piel CP.301A Emeraude	221	G-BHTX	10. 6.80		J R Large tr Eastern Taildraggers Flying Club		
			F-BIJU				Stapleford	18. 7.07P
G-BIJV	Reims Cessna F152 II	F15201813		22.12.80		A S Bamrah t/a Falcon Flying Services	Lydd	21. 3.08E
G-BIJW	Reims Cessna F152 II	F15201820		22.12.80		A S Bamrah t/a Falcon Flying Services	Rochester	26. 2.08E
G-BIKC	Boeing 757-236	22174		31. 1.83		DHL Air Ltd	Brussels, Belgium	9. 2.08E
G-BIKE	Piper PA-28R-200 Cherokee Arrow II		OY-DVT	18. 4.80		R V Webb	Elstree	25.11.07E
		28R-7335173	N55047					
G-BIKF (2)	Boeing 757-236	22177	(G-BIKG)	28. 4.83		DHL Air Ltd	Brussels, Belgium	14. 9.08E

G-BIKG (2)	Boeing 757-236	22178	(G-BIKH)	26. 8.83	DHL Air Ltd	Brussels, Belgium	26. 8.08E
G-BIKI (2)	Boeing 757-236	22180	OO-DLO	30.11.83	DHL Air Ltd	Brussels, Belgium	23. 6.08E
			G-BIKI (2)				
G-BIKJ (2)	Boeing 757-236	22181	(G-BIKK)	9. 1.84	DHL Air Ltd	Brussels, Belgium	11. 1.07T
G-BIKK (2)	Boeing 757-236	22182	(G-BIKL)	1. 2.84	DHL Air Ltd	Brussels, Belgium	1. 2.07T
G-BIKM (2)	Boeing 757-236	22184	N8293V	21. 3.84	DHL Air Ltd	Brussels, Belgium	22. 3.07T
			(G-BIKN)				
G-BIKN (2)	Boeing 757-236	22186	(G-BIKP)	23. 1.85	DHL Air Ltd	Brussels, Belgium	22. 9.08E
G-BIKO (2)	Boeing 757-236	22187	(G-BIKR)	14. 2.85	DHL Air Ltd	Brussels, Belgium	18. 2.08E
G-BIKP (2)	Boeing 757-236	22188	(G-BIKS)	11. 3.85	DHL Air Ltd	Brussels, Belgium	14. 3.08E
G-BIKS (2)	Boeing 757-236	22190	(G-BIKU)	31. 5.85	DHL Air Ltd	Brussels, Belgium	2. 6.08E
G-BIKU (2)	Boeing 757-236	23399		7.11.85	DHL Air Ltd	Brussels, Belgium	7.11.07E
G-BIKV	Boeing 757-236	23400		9.12.85	DHL Air Ltd	Brussels, Belgium	11.12.07E
G-BIKZ	Boeing 757-236	23532		15. 5.86	DHL Air Ltd	Brussels, Belgium	30. 9.07T
G-BILB	Wallingford WMB.2 Windtracker Balloon (Minimum Lift)			22. 1.81	B L King	Coulsdon	
		14					
G-BILE	Morris Scruggs BL-2B Balloon (Minimum Lift)			13. 3.81	P D Ridout	Botley	
		81231					
G-BILG	Morris Scruggs BL-2B Balloon (Minimum Lift)			13. 3.81	P D Ridout	Botley	
		81232					
G-BILI	Piper J-3C-65 Cub (L-4J-PI)	13207	F-BDTB	14. 1.81	S C Wilson and J A Goodridge tr G-BILI Flying Group		
	(Frame No.13044)		45-4467		(As "454467:J-44" in US Army c/s)	White Waltham	27. 7.08P
G-BILJ	Reims Cessna FA152 Aerobat	FA1520376		31.12.80	D G Baverstock	Wycombe Air Park	25. 8.08E
G-BILL	Piper PA-25-235 Pawnee D	25-7856028	N9174T	3. 1.79	A E and W J Taylor t/a Pawnee Aviation	East Winch	27. 7.08A
	(260hp Lycoming O-540-G2A5)						
G-BILR	Cessna 152 II	15284822	N4822P	19. 3.81	Shropshire Aero Club Ltd	Sleap	8. 5.08E
G-BILS	Cessna 152 II	15284857	N4954P	3. 6.81	Mona Aviation Ltd t/a Mona Flying Club	RAF Mona	5. 8.07T
G-BILU	Cessna 172RG Cutlass II	172RG0564	N5540V	29. 1.81	Full Sutton Flying Centre Ltd	Full Sutton	27. 7.08E
G-BILZ	Taylor JT.1 Monoplane	PFA 055-10244		15.12.80	A Petherbridge	(Sibsey)	29. 2.91P
	(Built G Beaumont and regd officially as c/n PFA 055-10124)				(Damaged Ingoldmells 10. 6.90: stored 8.00)		
G-BIMK	Baron Tiger T 200 Series 1 Balloon (Minimum Lift)			22.12.80	M K Baron	Woodley, Stockport	
	(Built M K Baron)	7/MKB-01					
G-BIMM	Piper PA-18-150 Super Cub	18-3868	PH-VHO	8. 1.81	Spectrum Leisure Ltd	Clacton	15.11.10S
	(L-21B-PI)(Frame No.18-3881)		R Neth AF R-178, 54-2468				
G-BIMN	Steen Skybolt	PFA 064-10329		31.12.80	R J Thomas	(Ashford)	3. 4.08P
	(Built C R Williamson)						
G-BIMO	SNCAN Stampe SV-4C	394	F-BADG	5. 3.81	E L P A Dupont	Goodwood	3. 5.10S
			French AF		(As "394" in French AF c/s)		
G-BIMT	Cessna FA152 Aerobat	FA1520361	N8062L	9. 1.81	Cardinal Sin Ltd t/a Staverton Flying School		
	(Built Reims Aviation SA)					Gloucestershire	26. 5.08E
G-BIMU	Sikorsky S-61N Mk.II	61-752	N8511Z	9. 1.81	Bristow Helicopters Ltd	Stornoway	23.10.07E
	(SAR conversion)		VH-CRU, N4042S		"Stac Pollaidh" (Operated Marine and Coastguard Agency)		
G-BIMX	Rutan VariEze	PFA 074-10544		6. 1.81	D G Crew	Biggin Hill	9. 9.08P
	(Built A S Knowles) (Continental O-200-A)						
G-BIMZ	Beech 76 Duchess	ME-169	N6021K	20. 3.81	R P Smith	Gloucestershire	5. 7.08T
G-BINL	Morris Scruggs BL-2B Balloon (Minimum Lift)			5. 2.81	P D Ridout	Eastleigh	
		81216					
G-BINM	Morris Scruggs BL-2B Balloon (Minimum Lift)			5. 2.81	P D Ridout	Eastleigh	
		81217					
G-BINR	Unicorn UE-1A Balloon (Minimum Lift)	81004		20. 1.81	I Chadwick tr Unicorn Group "Lady Diana"		
					(Extant 5.07)	Partridge Green, Horsham	
G-BINS	Unicorn UE-2A Balloon (Minimum Lift)	80002		22.12.80	I Chadwick tr Unicorn Group "Caroline"		
					(Extant 5.07)	Partridge Green, Horsham	
G-BINT	Unicorn UE-1A Balloon (Minimum Lift)	80001		22.12.80	D E Bint	Downham Market	
G-BINX	Morris Scruggs BL-2B Balloon (Minimum Lift)			5. 2.81	P D Ridout	Eastleigh	
		81219					
G-BINY	Morton Oriental Air-Bag Balloon (Minimum Lift)			22. 1.81	J L Morton	Wokingham	
	(Built J L Morton)	OAB-001					
G-BIOA	Hughes 369D	120-0880D	OO-HFS	9. 2.81	AH Helicopter Services Ltd	Newton Abbot	25. 7.08E
	(Hughes 500)		LX-HLE, OO-HFS, G-BIOA				
G-BIOB	Reims Cessna F172P Skyhawk II	F17202042		23. 1.81	Flight Images LLP	Fairoaks	15. 5.08E
G-BIOC	Reims Cessna F150L	F15000848	F-BUEC	3. 2.81	M Taylor	(Hollym, Withernsea)	19. 9.08E
G-BIOI	SAN Jodel DR.1050M Excellence	477	F-BLJQ	21. 1.81	A A Alderdice	(Kilkeel, Newry)	21. 4.08P
G-BIOJ	Rockwell Commander 112TC-A	13192	N4662W	22. 1.82	A T Dalby (Noted 9.05)	Sibson	13.12.02
G-BIOK	Reims Cessna F152 II	F15201810		2. 2.81	A D H MacDonald	Glenrothes	27. 4.08E
G-BIOU	SAN Jodel D 117A	813	F-BIOU	9. 8.78	M R Routh and T de Salis tr Jemalk Group		
					(Noted 7.07)	Ballymageough, Kilkeel	23. 5.04P
G-BIOW	Slingsby T 67A	1988		26. 2.81	A B Slinger tr Slingsby T.67A Group	Sherburn-in-Elmet	27. 9.08E
G-BIPA	Grumman AA-5B Tiger	AA5B-0200	OY-GAM	24. 3.81	Tri-Star Developments Ltd	Andreas, Isle of Man	4. 8.08E
G-BIPH	Morris Scruggs BL-2B Balloon (Minimum Lift)			10. 2.81	C M Dewsnap	(Owlsmoor, Sandhurst)	
		81224					
G-BIPI	Everett Gyroplane	001		30. 4.81	C A Reeves	Apperley, Gloucestershire	19. 6.01P
	(Volkswagen 1834)				(Noted 5.03)		
G-BIPN	Fournier RF3	35	F-BMDN	26. 2.81	J C R Rogers and I F Fairhead tr G-BIPN Group		
						RAF Cranwell	16. 8.08P
G-BIPO	Mudry CAP.20 LS 200	03	F-GAUB	5. 3.81	A McClean tr The CAP 20 Group	White Waltham	8. 5.05S
G-BIPT	Wassmer Jodel D 112	1254	F-BMIB	11. 3.81	C R Davies	Allensmore, Hereford	23. 7.08P
G-BIPV	Gulfstream AA-5B Tiger	AA5B-0981	N28266	10. 3.81	Echo Echo Ltd	Bournemouth	14. 6.08T
G-BIPW	Avenger T 200-2112 Balloon (Minimum Lift)	10		24. 2.81	B L King	Coulsdon	
	(Built R Light)						
G-BIPY	Montgomerie-Bensen B 8MR	AJW.01		25. 2.81	P A Clare	North Connel, Oban	14. 3.08P
	(Built A J Wood - pr.no.PFA G/01-1007) (Rotax 532)						
G-BIRD	Pitts S-1D	PFA 1596		3.11.77	P Metcalfe	(Stockton-on-Tees)	4. 9.07P
	(Built R N York - c/n 707-H)						

Reg	Type	C/n	Prev id	Date	Owner/Operator	Base	
G-BIRE	Colt Bottle 56 SS Balloon (Hot Air) *(Satzenbrau Bottle)*	323		4. 3.81	J Edwards	Northampton	24. 5.08A
G-BIRH	Piper PA-18-150 Super Cub (L-21B-PI) 18-3853 (Lycoming O-360-A4) *(Frame No.18-3857)*		PH-LET R Neth AF R-163, 54-2453	19. 3.81	Aquila Gliding Club Ltd *(As 54-2453:R-163" in R Neth AF c/s)*	Bidford	3. 5.09S
G-BIRI	CASA 1-131E Jungmann	1074	Spanish AF E3B-113	14. 4.81	D Watt	Sibson	25. 4.08P
G-BIRL	Avenger T 200-2112 Balloon (Minimum Lift) 008 *(Built R Light)*			10. 3.81	R Light	Stockport	
G-BIRP	Ridout Arena Mk.17 Skyship Balloon (Minimum Lift)	01		13. 3.81	A S Ridout	Eastleigh	
G-BIRT	Robin R1180TD Aiglon	276		25. 3.81	W D'A Hall	White Waltham	21.12.07E
G-BISG	Clutton FRED Series III	RAC 01-224		13. 3.81	T Littlefair	Lymington	29.10.86P
	(Built R A Coombe - pr.no.PFA 029-10675) (Volkswagen 1600)				*"Fuzz Bee" (New owner 10.00)*		
G-BISH	Cameron V-65 Balloon (Hot Air)	707		16. 3.81	P J Bish *"Tsaritsa"*	Newtown, Hungerford	18. 9.07A
G-BISL	Morris Scruggs BL-2B Balloon (Minimum Lift)	81233		13. 3.81	P D Ridout	Eastleigh	
G-BISM	Morris Scruggs BL-2B Balloon (Minimum Lift)	81234		13. 3.81	P D Ridout	Eastleigh	
G-BISS	Morris Scruggs BL-2C Balloon (Minimum Lift)	81235		13. 3.81	P D Ridout	Eastleigh	
G-BIST	Morris Scruggs BL-2C Balloon (Minimum Lift)	81236		13. 3.81	P D Ridout	Eastleigh	
G-BISX	Colt 56A Balloon (Hot Air)	324		18. 3.81	C D Steel *(Active 7.05)*	St Boswells	18. 8.99A
G-BISZ	Sikorsky S-76A II Plus	760156		19. 3.81	Bristow Helicopters Ltd	Redhill	23.10.07E
G-BITA	Piper PA-18-150 Super Cub	18-8109037	N82585	24. 3.81	D J Gilmour	Dunsfold	26.10.07E
G-BITE	SOCATA TB-10 Tobago	193		7. 5.81	M A Smith	Eshott	23. 3.08E
G-BITF	Reims Cessna F152 II	F15201822		27. 3.81	J Parker tr G-BITF Owners	Glenrothes	30. 8.08E
G-BITH	Reims Cessna F152 II	F15201825	G-TFSA G-BITH	27. 3.81	J R Hyde	Derby	31. 8.08E
G-BITK	Clutton FRED Series II	PFA 029-10369		23. 3.81	D J Wood	(Eythorne, Dover)	
	(Built B J Miles) (Volkswagen 1500)						
G-BITM	Reims Cessna F172P Skyhawk II	F17202046		13. 4.81	Dreamtrade Ltd	Barton	6.11.07E
G-BITO	Wassmer Jodel D 112D	1200	F-BIUO	20. 3.81	A Dunbar *(Noted 7.04)*	Barton	5. 9.02P
G-BITS	Drayton B-56 Balloon (Hot Air)	MJB-01/81		16. 3.81	M J Betts	Drayton, Norwich	
					"Hedger" (Operated Eastern Region, British Balloon and Airship Club)		
G-BITY	Bell FD.31T Flying Dodo Balloon (Minimum Lift)	2604		25. 3.81	A J Bell	Luton	
G-BIUM	Reims Cessna F152 II	F15201807		3. 4.81	Sheffield Aero Club Ltd	Netherthorpe	21 11.07E
G-BIUP	SNCAN NC.854S	54	(G-AMPE) G-BIUP, F-BFSC	4. 6.81	J Greenaway and T D Cooper tr BIUP Flying Group	Popham	10. 7.07P
G-BIUV	Hawker Siddeley HS.748 Series 2A/275LFD	1701	5W-FAN G-AYYH, G-11-8	11. 5.81	PTB (Emerald) Proprietary Ltd *"City of Liverpool" (Stored externally 2.08)*	Blackpool	16. 6.08E
G-BIUW	Piper PA-28-161 Warrior II	28-8116128	N9506N	14. 4.81	D R Staley	Gamston	27. 6.08E
G-BIUY	Piper PA-28-181 Archer II	28-8190133	N8318X	3. 4.81	J S Develin and Z Islam	Shoreham	9. 3.08E
G-BIVA	Robin R2112	137	F-GBAZ	6. 5.81	I G McDonald tr Seahawk Flying Group	RNAS Culdrose	17.11.07E
G-BIVB	Wassmer Jodel D 112	1009	(G-BIVC) F-BJII	18. 9.81	N M Harwood Roughay Farm, Bishops Waltham		20.11.08P
	(Continental A65)						
G-BIVC	Wassmer Jodel D 112	1219	F-BMAI	1. 6.81	M J Barnby	Frogland Cross	13. 7.00P
	(Continental A65)						
G-BIVF	Scintex CP.301-C3 Emeraude	594	F-BJVN	4.11.81	R J Moore *"Emma"*	Sywell	11.12.08P
G-BIVK	Bensen B 8MV	PFA G/01-1008		10. 4.81	M J Atyeo	(Bognor Regis)	19.11.03P
	(Built J G Toy) (Registered as B 8M) (Volkswagen 1834)				*"Skyrider"*		
G-BIVV	Gulfstream AA-5A Cheetah	AA5A-0857	N26979	26. 5.81	R Afia t/a Robert Afia Consulting Engineer	North Weald	18. 7.05T
					(Hulk dumped 1.06 - fire services trainer as "G-PRAT")		
G-BIWA	Ridout Stevendon Skyreacher Balloon (Minimum Lift)	102		8. 6.81	S D Barnes (	Eastleigh	
G-BIWB	Morris Scruggs RS.5000 Balloon (Minimum Lift)	81541		8. 6.81	P D Ridout	Eastleigh	
G-BIWC	Morris Scruggs RS.5000 Balloon (Minimum Lift)	81546		26. 6.81	P D Ridout *"Waterloo"*	Eastleigh	
G-BIWF	Ridout Warren Windcatcher Balloon (Minimum Lift)	WW.013		3. 7.81	P D Ridout	Eastleigh	
G-BIWG	Ridout Zelenski Mk.2 Balloon (Minimum Lift) *(Officially regd with c/n 2401)*	Z 401		3. 7.81	P D Ridout	Eastleigh	
G-BIWJ	Unicorn UE-1A Balloon (Minimum Lift)	81014		14. 7.81	B L King	Coulsdon	
G-BIWK	Cameron V-65 Balloon (Hot Air)	719		22. 4.81	I R Williams and R G Bickerdike *"Double Fantasy"* Bedford and Huntingdon		19. 2.08A
G-BIWN	Wassmer Jodel D 112	1314	F-BNCN	5. 6.81	C R Coates Eddsfield, Octon Lodge Farm, Thwing		8.10.07P
G-BIWR	Mooney M 20F Executive	22-1339	N6972V	1. 6.81	A C Brink	Bourn	3. 3.08E
G-BIWU	Cameron V-65 Balloon (Hot Air)	717		15. 5.81	J Tyrrell and W Rousell Wollaston, Wellingborough *(New owners 6.07)*		12.11.05A
G-BIWW	American AA-5 Traveler	AA5-0263	OY-AYV	2. 6.81	S J Perkins and D Dobson	Little Staughton	27. 4.08E
G-BIXA	SOCATA TB-9 Tampico	205		7. 5.81	W Maxwell	Perth	17.11.07E
G-BIXB	SOCATA TB-9 Tampico	208		7. 5.81	B G Adams	Shobdon	3. 4.08E
G-BIXH	Reims Cessna F152 II	F15201840		30. 4.81	Northern Aviation Ltd	Durham Tees Valley	13. 4.08E
G-BIXL	North American P-51D-20-NA Mustang	122-38675	Israel DFAF2343 Swedish AF Fv.26116, 44-72216	3. 7.81	R J Lamplough Manor Farm, East Garston *"Miss Helen"*		12. 6.08P
					(As "472216:HO-M" in 487th Fighter Sqdn/352nd Fighter Group USAF c/s)		
G-BIXN	Boeing Stearman A75N1 (PT-17-BW) Kaydet *(Continental W670)*	75-2248	N51132 41-8689	15. 6.81	V S E Norman	(Rendcomb)	3. 8.96
G-BIXV	Bell 212	30870	N16931	27. 5.81	Bristow Helicopters Ltd	Kazakhstan	22. 7.08E
G-BIXW	Colt 56B Balloon (Hot Air)	348		18. 5.81	N A P Bates *"Spam"*	Tunbridge Wells	17. 8.97A
G-BIXX	Pearson Series 2 Balloon (Minimum Lift) 00327			8. 5.81	D Pearson	Solihull	

G-BIXZ	Grob G109	6019	D-KGRO	14. 5.81	D L Nind and I Allum Wycombe Air Park and Enstone	15. 6.07
G-BIYI	Cameron V-65 Balloon (Hot Air)	722		21. 5.81	P F Smart tr The Sarnia Balloon Group	
					"Penny" Oakley, Basingstoke	19. 6.08A
G-BIYJ	Piper PA-18 Super Cub 95	18-1000	MM51-15303	5. 6.81	S Russell Pilmuir Farm, Lundin Links	30. 1.08P
	(L-18C-PI)		I-EIST, MM51-15303, 51-15303			
G-BIYK	Isaacs Fury II	PFA 011-10418		20. 5.81	S M Roberts (Guernsey)	4. 7.07P
	(Built R S Martins) (Continental C90)					
G-BIYP	Piper PA-20 Pacer 125	20-802	CN-TYP	25. 5.83	A W Hoy and S W M Johnson tr G-BIYP Flying Group	
			F-DACJ, OO-ADP		Berry Grove Farm, Liss	3. 6.08E
G-BIYR	Piper PA-18-150 Super Cub	18-3841	(G-BIYB)	26. 5.81	B H and M J Fairclough tr The Delta Foxtrot Flying Group	
	(L-21B-PI) (Frame No. 18-3843)		PH-GER, R Neth AF R-151, 5G-96, 54-2441		Watchford Farm, Yarcombe	30. 8.10S
			(As "R-151" in R Neth AF c/s)			
G-BIYT	Colt 17A Cloudhopper Balloon (Hot Air)	344		13. 7.81	J-M Francois Salles-Courbatiers, France	18. 1.05A
G-BIYU	Fokker S 11.1 Instructor	6206	(PH-HOM)	13. 5.81	C Briggs Bagby	14.10.04P
			R Neth AF E-15		(As "E-15" in R Neth AF c/s: noted 2.08)	
G-BIYW	Wassmer Jodel D 112	1209	F-BLNR	26. 5.81	K Balaam tr Pollard/Balaam/Bye Flying Group	
					Poplar Hall Farm, Elmsett	6.11.08P
G-BIYX	Piper PA-28-140 Cherokee Cruiser	28-7625064	OY-BLD	19. 6.81	W B Bateson Blackpool	22. 3.08E
G-BIYY	Piper PA-18 Super Cub 95	18-1979	MM52-2379	2. 6.81	A E and W J Taylor Fenland	6. 3.08T
	(L-18C-PI) (Frame No.18-1914)		I-EIGA, MM52-2379, 52-2379			
G-BIZE	SOCATA TB-9 Tampico	209	9H-ABJ	15. 6.81	C Fordham Bourn	3. 7.08E
			G-BIZE			
G-BIZF	Reims Cessna F172P Skyhawk II	F17202070		16. 6.81	R S Bentley Bourn	23. 8.08E
G-BIZG	Reims Cessna F152 II	F15201873		16. 6.81	M A Judge tr Aero Group 78 Netherthorpe	2. 8.08E
G-BIZI	Robin DR.400 2+2	1543		29. 5.81	BIZI Club Ltd (Colden Common, Winchester)	10. 5.08T
G-BIZK	Nord 3202B1	78	N2255E	22.11.85	A I Milne Little Snoring	29. 1.08P
			French Army		(As "78" in all-yellow French AF c/s)	
G-BIZM	Nord 3202B	91	N2256K	22.11.85	Global Aviation Ltd Humberside	31. 8.07P
			French Army			
G-BIZO	Piper PA-28R-200 Cherokee Arrow II		OY-DLH	16. 6.81	P J Mason and J F Leather tr Lemas Air (Bristo)	4. 4.08E
		28R-7535339	N1578X			
G-BIZR	SOCATA TB-9 Tampico	210	G-BSEC	15. 6.81	E S Murphy and G Ward tr Fenland Flying Group	
			G-BIZR		Fenland	23. 8.08E
G-BIZU	Thunder Ax6-56Z Balloon (Hot Air)	358		15. 6.81	M J Loades "Greenall Whitley" Southampton	6. 7.03A
G-BIZV	Piper PA-18 Super Cub 95 (L-18C-PI)	18-2001	EI-74	12. 6.81	R W Skelton Mullahead, Tandragee	5. 7.07P
			I-EIDE, MM52-2401, 52-2401		(As "18-2001" in US Army c/s)	
G-BIZW	Champion 7GCBC Citabria	0157	D-EGPD	16. 7.81	J C Read t/a G Read and Sons North Reston	30. 8.04
G-BIZY	Wassmer Jodel D 112	1120	F-BKJL	13. 7.81	W Tunley t/a Wayland Tunley and Associates	
					Hinton-in-the-Hedges	25. 5.08P

G-BJAA - G-BJZZ

G-BJAD	Clutton FRED Series II	CA.1		11. 6.81	Newark (Nottinghamshire and Linclonshire) Air Museuem Ltd	
	(Built C Allison - pr.no..PFA 29-10586)				Newark	
G-BJAE	Starck AS.80 Holiday	04	F-PGGA	17. 6.81	D J and S.A E Phillips (Leamington Spa)	8. 8.92P
	(Built J R Lavadoux) (Continental A65)		F-WGGA		(Damaged Woburn 17. 8.91)	
G-BJAF	Piper J-3C-65 Cub (L-4A-PI)	8437	D-EJAF	23. 6.81	P J Cottle Craysmarsh Farm, Melksham	18. 2.08P
	(Frame No.8540)		HB-OAD, 42-15318			
G-BJAG	Piper PA-28-181 Archer II	28-7990353	PH-LDB	23. 6.81	C R Chubb Manston	18. 9.08E
			(PH-BEG), (OO-FLM), N2244W			
G-BJAJ	Gulfstream AA-5B Tiger	AA5B-1177	N4532V	2. 7.81	A J Byrne tr Draycott Tiger Club	
					Draycott Farm, Chisledon	17.9.08T
G-BJAL	CASA 1-131E Jungmann	1028	Spanish AF E3B-114	11. 9.78	I C Underwood and S B J Chandler tr G-BJAL Group	
	(Spanish AF serial no. conflicts with G-BUCC)				Breighton	1. 8.08P
G-BJAO	Montgomerie-Bensen B 8MR	GLS-01		28. 8.81	A P Lay Henstridge	2. 4.01P
	(Built A Gault - pr.no.PFA G/01-1001: officially regd as c/n GL5-01) (Rotax 582)					
G-BJAP	de Havilland DH.82A Tiger Moth	0482		15. 6.81	K Knight Shobdon	9. 9.08P
	(Built J A Pothecary - pr.no.PFA 157-12897) (Composite rebuild)				(As "K2587" in pre-war RAF 32 Sqdn/CFS c/s)	
G-BJAS	Rango NA-9 Balloon (Minimum Lift)	TL-19		22. 6.81	A Lindsay Twickenham	
G-BJAV	Sud-Aviation Gardan GY-80-160 Horizon	28	OO-AJP	8. 9.81	L Stanton Seething	9.11.07E
			F-BLVB			
G-BJAW	Cameron V-65 Balloon (Hot Air)	745		19. 6.81	G A McCarthy "Breezin" Shepton Mallet	16. 4.86A
G-BJAY	Piper J-3C-65 Cub (L-4H-PI)	12086	F-BFBN	1.11.78	D W Finlay (Lamourache Nord, Aquitaine, France)	12. 6.06P
	(Frame No.11914)		OO-EAC, 44-79790			
G-BJBK	Piper PA-18 Super Cub 95	18-1431	F-BOME	21. 8.81	M S Bird Pepperbox, Salisbury	9. 7.08P
	(L-18C-PI) (Continental O-200-A) (Frame No.18-1370)		French Army 51-15431			
G-BJBM	Monnett Sonerai I	MEA-117		2. 7.81	N J Cowley Popham	9. 1.97P
	(Built Lyster Aviation Ltd - pr.no.PFA 015-10022) (Volkswagen 2074)				"The Answer" (Noted 8.06)	
G-BJBO	CEA Jodel DR.250/160 Capitaine	40	F-BNJG	24. 8.81	J A Hobby tr Wiltshire Flying Group Oaksey Park	21. 2.08E
G-BJBW	Piper PA-28-161 Warrior II	28-8116280	N2913Z	22. 7.81	T G Phillips and C Greenland tr 152 Group Popham	22. 1.08
G-BJBX	Piper PA-28-161 Warrior II	28-8116269	N8414H	17. 7.81	Haimoss Ltd Old Sarum	23. 5.08E
					(Operated Old Sarum Flying Club)	
G-BJCA	Piper PA-28-161 Warrior II	28-7916473	N2846D	30. 7.81	Plane Sailing (South West) Ltd Plymouth	17. 2.08E
G-BJCF	Scintex CP.1310-C3 Super Emeraude	936	F-BMJH	19.11.81	K M Hodson and C G H Gurney Little Snoring	9. 8.08P
G-BJCI	Piper PA-18-150 Super Cub	18-6658	N9388D	10. 9.81	The Borders (Milfield) Gliding Club Ltd Milfield	15. 5.08E
	(Lycoming O-360-A4)					
G-BJCW	Piper PA-32R-301 Saratoga II SP	32R-8113094	N2866U	6. 8.81	Golf Charlie Whisky Ltd Fairoaks	11. 5.08E
G-BJDE	Reims Cessna F172M	F17200984	OO-MSS	25. 8.81	J K P Amor Sandown, Isle of Wight	26. 6.08E
			D-EGBR			
G-BJDF	SOCATA MS.880B Rallye 100T	3000	F-GAKP	21. 9.81	A J Wilkinson tr G-BJDF Group	
					Coldharbour Farm, Willingham	20. 3.08E
G-BJDK	Ridout European E 157 Balloon (Minimum Lift)	S 2		17. 8.81	E Osborn t/a Aeroprint Tours Eastleigh	
G-BJDO	Gulfstream AA-5A Cheetah	AA5A-0823	N26936	3. 8.81	J J Woodhouse t/a Flying Services	
					Sandown, Isle of Wight	6. 8.08E

Reg	Type	C/n	Prev id	Date	Owner/Operator	Location	
G-BJDW	Reims Cessna F172M Skyhawk II	F17201417	PH-JBE	10. 8.81	J Rae	Earls Colne	26. 1.08E
G-BJEE	Pilatus Britten-Norman BN-2T Turbine Islander		C9-TAH	28. 7.81	Cormack (Aircraft Services) Ltd	Cumbernauld	
	(Originally regd as a BN-2B)	2120	G-BJEE		(New owner 8.04)		
G-BJEF	Pilatus Britten-Norman BN-2T Turbine Islander		C9-TAK	28. 7.81	Cormack (Aircraft Services) Ltd	Cumbernauld	
	(Originally regd as a BN-2B)	2121	G-BJEF		(New owner 8.04)		
G-BJEI	Piper PA-18 Super Cub 95	18-1988	EI-66	27. 7.81	H J Cox	Wendover Farm, Sheepwash	22. 8.07P
	(L-18C-PI) (Frame No.18-1938)		I-EILO, MM52-2388, 52-2388				
G-BJEJ	Pilatus Britten-Norman BN-2T Turbine Islander		C9-TAJ	28. 7.81	Cormack (Aircraft Services) Ltd	Cumbernauld	
	(Originally regd as a BN-2B)	2124	G-BJEJ		(New owner 8.04)		
G-BJEL	SNCAN NC.854S	113	F-BEZT	7. 8.81	C A James "Jessie"	Doynton	13. 6.08P
G-BJEV	Aeronca 11AC Chief	11AC-270	N85897	12. 8.81	R F Willcox	Eastbach Farm, Coleford	18. 3.08P
			NC85897		(As "897:E" in US Navy c/s)		
G-BJEX	Bölkow BÖ.208C Junior	690	F-BRHY	27. 8.81	G D H Crawford	(Henley-on-Thames)	28. 1.88
			D-EEAM				
G-BJFC	Ridout European E 8 Balloon (Minimum Lift) S 1			17. 8.81	P D Ridout (Extant 5.07)	Eastleigh	
G-BJFE	Piper PA-18 Super Cub 95	18-2022	EI-91	17. 8.81	P H Wilmot-Allistone	Watchford Farm, Yarcombe	22. 8.07P
	(L-18C-PI)		I-EISU, MM52-2422, 52-2422 (Noted 10.07)				
G-BJFL	Sikorsky S-76A II Plus	760056	N106BH	28. 8.81	Bristow Helicopters Ltd	(Khazakstan)	17. 9.08E
			N1546T, (G-BHRK)		"Glen Moray"		
G-BJFM	Wassmer Jodel D 120 Paris-Nice	227	F-BLFM	8.10.81	J V George and P A Smith	Popham	20. 7.07P
G-BJGK	Cameron V-77 Balloon (Hot Air)	696		3. 9.81	M E Orchard	Bristol	29. 8.08A
G-BJGM	Unicorn UE-1A Balloon (Minimum Lift)	81015		21. 8.81	D Eaves and P D Ridout	Southampton and Eastleigh	
					"Capricorn" (Extant 5.07)		
G-BJGX	Sikorsky S-76A II Plus	760026	N103BH	4. 9.81	Bristow Helicopters Ltd	Norwich	8.10.07E
			N4251S		"Glen Elgin"		
G-BJGY	Reims Cessna F172P Skyhawk II	F17202128		13.10.81	K and S Martin	Gunton Hall, Somerton	18. 4.08E
G-BJHB	Mooney M 20J Mooney 201	24-1190	N1145G	23.12.81	Zitair Flying Club Ltd	Wycombe Air Park	23. 5.08E
G-BJHK	EAA Acrosport	PFA 072-10470		20. 3.80	M R Holden	Stoneacre Farm, Farthing Corner	31. 8.04P
	(Built J H Kimber) (Lycoming IO-360)						
G-BJIA	Allport Hot Air Free Balloon (Minimum Lift)	1		2. 9.81	D J Allport	Bourne	
G-BJIC	Eaves Dodo 1A Balloon (Minimum Lift)	DD.3		4. 9.81	P D Ridout (Extant 5.07)	Eastleigh	
G-BJID	Chown Osprey Lizzieliner Mk-1B Balloon (Minimum Lift)	28		4. 9.81	P D Ridout	Eastleigh	
G-BJIG	Slingsby T 67A	1992		16. 9.81	A D Hodgkinson (New owner 8.05)	(Luton)	15. 4.04
G-BJIV	Piper PA-18-150 Super Cub	18-8262	N5972Z	17. 9.81	Yorkshire Gliding Club (Proprietary) Ltd	Sutton Bank	5. 4.08E
	(Lycoming O-360-A4)						
G-BJKF	SOCATA TB-9 Tampico	240		30. 9.81	C J Archer tr G-BJKF Group (Petts Wood, Orpington)		26. 4.08
G-BJKW	Wills Aera 2	A3JKW		1. 3.78	J K S Wills	(London SE3)	
	(Built J K S Wills)						
G-BJKY	Reims Cessna F152 II	F15201886		22. 9.81	Manx Aero Marine Management Ltd	Blackpool	29. 2.08E
					(Operated Westair Flying Services)		
G-BJLB	SNCAN NC.854S	58	(OO-MVM)	5.11.81	M J Barmby	(Llanishen, Cardiff)	30. 6.83P
			F-BFSG		(Crashed near Newport, Gwent 29. 7.84: stored 8.90)		
G-BJLC	Monnett Sonerai IIL	942L		18. 9.81	P D Yeo	AAC Netheravon	11. 5.98P
	(Built J P Whitham - pr.no.PFA 015-10634) (Volkswagen 1835)				(Noted 1.08)		
G-BJLF	Unicorn UE-1C Balloon (Minimum Lift)	81018		21. 9.81	I Chadwick tr Unicorn Group		
					(Extant 5.07)	Partridge Green, Horsham	
G-BJLG	Unicorn UE-1B Balloon (Minimum Lift)	81017		21. 9.81	I Chadwick tr Unicorn Group		
						Partridge Green, Horsham	
G-BJLX	Cremer Cracker Balloon (Minimum Lift)	711		24. 9.81	P W May	Wilmslow	
G-BJLY	Cremer Cracker Balloon (Minimum Lift)	709		24. 9.81	P Cannon (Extant 5.07)	Luton	
G-BJML	Cessna 120	10766	N76349	5.10.81	R A Smith	Great Yeldham Hall, Halstead	28. 6.08P
	(Continental C90)		NC76349				
G-BJMO	Taylor JT.1 Monoplane	PFA 055-10612		30. 9.81	R C Mark	(Orelton, Ludlow)	
	(Built R C Mark)						
G-BJMR	Cessna 310R II	310R1624	N2631Z	16. 7.79	J M Robinson	Rufforth	24. 4.08E
G-BJMW	Thunder Ax8-105 Series 2 Balloon (Hot Air)	369		14.10.81	G M Westley	London SW15	11. 1.02A
G-BJMX	Ridout Jarre JR-3 Balloon (Minimum Lift)	81601		6.10.81	P D Ridout	Eastleigh	
G-BJMZ	Ridout European EA-8A Balloon (Minimum Lift)	S 5		6.10.81	P D Ridout	Eastleigh	
					(Extant 5.07)		
G-BJNA	Ridout Arena Mk.117P Balloon (Minimum Lift)	202		6.10.81	P D Ridout	Eastleigh	
					(Extant 5.07)		
G-BJND	Chown Osprey Mk.1E Balloon (Minimum Lift)	AKC.53		7.10.81	A Billington and D Whitmore	Liverpool	
G-BJNF	Reims Cessna F152 II	F15201882		21.10.81	D M and B Cloke	Dunkeswell	16. 2.08E
G-BJNG	Slingsby T 67AM	1993		16.10.81	D F Hodgkinson (Noted dismantled 7.05) Dunkeswell		23. 7.01T
G-BJNH	Chown Osprey Mk.1E Balloon (Minimum Lift)	AKC.57		8.10.81	D A Kirk	Manchester	
G-BJNN	Piper PA-38-112 Tomahawk	38-80A0064	N9684N	15.10.81	S Padidar-Nazar	Carlisle	10. 8.08E
G-BJNY	Aeronca 11CC Super Chief	11CC-264	CN-TYZ	28.10.81	P I and Doris.M Morgans (Stored 4.91)		
			F-OAEE		Furze Hill Farm, Rosemarket, Milford Haven		9. 8.90P
G-BJNZ	Piper PA-23-250 Aztec F	27-7954099	G-FANZ	5.10.81	Bonus Aviation Ltd	Cranfield	27. 7.08E
			N6905A, C-GTJG				
G-BJOB	SAN Jodel D 140C Mousquetaire III	118	F-BMBD	2.11.81	T W M Beck and M J Smith		
						Southwater Farm, Horsham	20. 6.08E
G-BJOE	Wassmer Jodel D 120A Paris-Nice	177	F-BJIU	12.11.81	J F Govan tr Forth Flying Group	East Fortune	31. 7.08P
G-BJOP	Pilatus Britten-Norman BN-2B-26 Islander	2132		29.10.81	Loganair Ltd	Kirkwall	5. 9.08E
G-BJOT	SAN Jodel D 117	688	F-BJCO	12.11.81	R H Ryle tr R H Ryle and Partners		
			CN-TVH, F-DABU		High Flatts Farm, Chester-le-Street		19.12.08P
G-BJOV	Reims Cessna F150K	F15000558	PH-VSD	4. 2.82	J A Boyd tr Mid Kent Flying Group		
						Baker Street Farm, Maidstone	15. 8.08E
G-BJPI	Bede BD-5G	1		30.10.81	M D McQueen	(Beckenham)	
	(Built M D McQueen - pr.no.PFA 014-10218) (Hirth 230R)						
G-BJPL	Chown Osprey Mk.4A Balloon (Minimum Lift)	AKC-39		13.10.81	M Vincent	St Helier, Jersey	

G-BJRA	Chown Osprey Mk.4B Balloon (Minimum Lift)			23.10.81	E Osborn t/a Aeroprint Tours	Eastleigh
			AKC.87			
G-BJRG	Chown Osprey Mk.4B Balloon (Minimum Lift)			26.10.81	A de Gruchy	St Brelade, Jersey
			AKC.95			
G-BJRH	Rango NA-36 Ax3 Balloon (Minimum Lift)			4.11.81	N H Ponsford t/a Rango Balloon and Kite Company	
			NHP-23			Leeds
G-BJRP	Cremer Cracker Balloon (Minimum Lift)			29.10.81	M D Williams	Houghton Regis, Dunstable
			15.712 PAC		*(Extant 5.07)*	
G-BJRR	Cremer Cracker Balloon (Minimum Lift)			29.10.81	M D Williams	Houghton Regis, Dunstable
			15.715 PAC		*(Extant 5.07)*	
G-BJRV	Cremer Cracker Balloon (Minimum Lift)			29.10.81	M D Williams	Houghton Regis, Dunstable
			15.713 PAC		*(Extant 5.07)*	
G-BJSS	Allport Hot Air Free Balloon (Minimum Lift)	2		9.11.81	D J Allport	Bourne
G-BJST	CCF Harvard 4 (T-6J-CCF Texan)	CCF4-...	MM53-795	21.12.81	P J Tuplin *(and estate of P W Portelli)*	Thruxton	29. 7.08P
			SC-66		*(As "KF729" in RAF c/s)*	
G-BJSV	Piper PA-28-161 Warrior II	28-8016229	PH-VZL	25.11.81	Airways Flight Training (Exeter) Ltd	Exeter	19.10.07E
			(OO-HLM), N35787			
G-BJSW	Thunder Ax7-65Z Balloon (Hot Air)	378		16.11.81	J Edwards	Northampton	8. 7.08A
G-BJSZ	Piper J-3C-65 Cub (L-4H-PI)	12047	D-EHID	20.11.81	H Gilbert	Enstone	22. 6.07P
	(Regd with c/n 11874)		(D-ECAX), (D-EKAB), PH-NBP, 44-79751			
G-BJTB	Cessna A150M Aerobat	A1500627	(G-BIVN)	28.10.82	Cirrus Aviation Ltd	Clacton	27.11.07E
			N9818J			
G-BJTF	Kirk Skyrider Mk.1 Balloon (Minimum Lift)			18.11.81	D A Kirk	Manchester
			KSR-01			
G-BJTN	Solent Osprey Mk.4B Balloon (Minimum Lift)			23.11.81	M Vincent	St Helier, Jersey
			ASC-112			
G-BJTO	Piper J-3C-65 Cub (L-4H-PI)	11527	F-BEGK	1.12.81	R Horner	Eggesford	16. 7.08P
	(Frame No.11352)		OO-AAL, 43-30236			
G-BJTP	Piper PA-18 Super Cub 95	18-999	EI-51	26.11.81	J T Parkins	Croft Farm, Defford	30.10.08P
	(L-18C-PI)		I-EICO, MM51-15302, 51-15302 *(As "115302:TP" in VMO-6 Sqdn, US Marines c/s) "Sittin' Duck"*			
G-BJTY	Solent Osprey Mk.4B Balloon (Minimum Lift)			23.11.81	A E de Gruchy)	St Brelade, Jersey
			ASC-115			
G-BJUB	Wild BVS Special 01 Balloon (Minimum Lift)			25.11.81	P G Wild	Linley Hill, Leven
			VS/PW01			
G-BJUC	Robinson R22	0228		13. 1.82	B C Seedle t/a Brian Seddle Helicopters	Blackpool	14.11.07E
G-BJUD	Robin DR.400-180R Remorqueur	870	PH-SRM	27.11.81	Lasham Gliding Society Ltd	Lasham	5. 1.08
	(Rebuilt using new fuselage: original scrapped Membury 11.88)					
G-BJUE	Solent Osprey Mk.4B Balloon (Minimum Lift)			23.11.81	M Vincent	St Helier, Jersey
			ASC-114			
G-BJUR	Piper PA-38-112 Tomahawk	38-79A0915	N9722N	5. 2.82	Truman Aviation Ltd	Tollerton	23.11.07E
					(Operated Nottingham School of Flying)	
G-BJUS	Piper PA-38-112 Tomahawk	38-80A0065	N9690N	10.12.81	Panshanger School of Flying Ltd	High Cross, Ware	2. 1.08E
G-BJUU	Solent Osprey Mk.4B Balloon (Minimum Lift)			23.11.81	M Vincent	St Helier, Jersey
			ASC-113			
G-BJUV	Cameron V-20 Balloon (Hot Air)	792		9.12.81	P Spellward *"Busy Bee"*	Bristol
G-BJVC	Evans VP-2	PFA 063-10599		17. 2.82	S J Greer and S E Clarke	Shenington	19. 6.91P
	(Built R G Fenn) (Volkswagen 1911)				*(New owners 8.06)*	
G-BJVH	Reims Cessna F182Q Skylane II	F18200106	D-EJMO	21.12.81	R J D Cuming	Salcombe	26. 9.08
			PH-AXU (2)			
G-BJVJ	Reims Cessna F152 II	F15201906		6. 1.82	Wilkins and Wilkins (Special Auctions) Ltd t/a Henlow Flying Club		
						RAF Henlow	5. 8.08E
G-BJVK	Grob G109	6074		11. 3.82	B A Kimberley	(Hook Norton, Banbury)	22. 5.92
G-BJVS	Scintex CP.1310-C3 Super Emeraude	903	F-BJVS	5. 1.79	J M Hoblyn tr G-BJVS Group		
						Watchford Farm, Yarcombe	9.11.08P
G-BJVT	Reims Cessna F152 II	F15201904		12. 1.82	Northern Aviation Ltd	Durham Tees Valley	30. 1.08E
G-BJVU	Thunder Ax6-56 Bolt Balloon (Hot Air)	397		31.12.81	G V Beckwith	Xanten, Germany	26. 4.91A
					"Cooper"	
G-BJVV	Robin R1180TD Aiglon II	79		5.11.81	P Hawkins	Cardiff	18. 6.08E
G-BJWH	Reims Cessna F152 II	F15201919		7. 5.82	J D Baines	Elstree	27. 9.08E
G-BJWI	Reims Cessna F172P Skyhawk II	F17202172		14. 5.82	Bflying Ltd	Bournemouth	28. 8.07T
					(Operated Bournemouth Flying Club)	
G-BJWJ	Cameron V-65 Balloon (Hot Air)	802		25. 1.82	R G Turnbull and S G Farse	Glasbury, Hereford	15. 4.06A
					"Gawain"	
G-BJWO	Fairey Britten-Norman BN-2A-26 Islander	334	4X-AYR	16. 2.82	Metachem Diagnostics Ltd	Turweston	3. 5.08A
			SX-BBX, 4X-AYR, G-BAXC			
G-BJWT	Wittman W.10 Tailwind	PFA 031-10688		5. 1.82	J F Bakewell tr Tailwind Group	Hucknall	8. 2.08P
	(Built J F Bakewell) (Lycoming O-290-G)					
G-BJWV	Colt 17A Cloudhopper Balloon (Hot Air)	391		22. 1.82	D T Meyes	Leamington Spa	26. 3.97A
					(Bryant Homes titles)	
G-BJWW	Reims Cessna F172P Skyhawk II	F17202148	(D-EFTV)	1. 2.82	Manx Aero Marine Management Ltd	Blackpool	13.11.07E
					(Operated Westair Flying Services)	
G-BJWX	Piper PA-18 Super Cub 95	18-1985	EI-64	23. 2.82	R A G Lucas tr G-BJWX Syndicate	Sleap	26. 4.08P
	(L-18C-PI) (Continental O-200-A)		I-EIME, MM52-2385, 52-2385			
G-BJWZ	Piper PA-18 Super Cub 95	18-1361	OO-HMO	18. 1.82	R C Dean tr G-BJWZ Syndicate	Redhill	24. 5.08P
	(L-18C-PI) *(Frame No.18-1262)*		French Army 18-1361, 51-15361			
G-BJXA	Slingsby T 67A	1994		8. 2.82	Aircraft Grouping Ltd	Blackpool	20. 1.07T
					(New owner 1.08)	
G-BJXB	Slingsby T 67A	1995		8. 2.82	XRay Bravo Ltd	Barton	21.10.07E
G-BJXK	Fournier RF5	5054	D-KINB	3. 2.82	S J Jenkins tr RF5 Syndicate	Usk	9. 7.08E
G-BJXP	Colt 56B Balloon (Hot Air)	393		29. 3.82	H J Anderson *"Bart"*	Oswestry	9. 9.00A
G-BJXR	Auster AOP.9	xxxx	XR267	2. 2.82	I Churm and J Hanson		
	(Officially regd with {Frame no.AUS/} 184)				(Mickleover, Derby and Duffield, Belper)	
G-BJXX	Piper PA-23-250 Aztec E	27-4692	F-BTCM	7. 4.82	V Bojovic	Padinska Skela, Serbia	23. 6.01
			N14094		*(Noted 3.04)*	

G-BJXZ	Cessna 172N Skyhawk II	17273039	PH-CAA	24. 3.82	T M Jones	Derby	19.10.07E
			N1949F		*(Operated Derby Aero Club)*		
G-BJYD	Reims Cessna F152 II	F15201915		25. 3.82	N J James	Welshpool	26. 2.08E
G-BJYF	Colt 56A Balloon (Hot Air)	401		1. 3.82	Helena Dos Santos SA	Corroios, Portugal	28.10.06A
					"Fanta" (New owner 3.07)		
G-BJYK	Wassmer Jodel D 120A Paris-Nice	185	(G-BJWK)	11. 5.82	M R Baker	(Eastbourne)	20. 8.08P
			F-BJPK				
G-BJYN	Piper PA-38-112 Tomahawk	38-79A1076	G-BJTE	12. 3.82	Panshanger School of Flying Ltd	High Cross, Ware	6. 3.00T
			N24310, N9671N				
G-BJZA	Cameron N-65 Balloon (Hot Air)	820		4. 3.82	N D Hepworth *(New owner 7.05)*	Stockport	3. 6.97A
G-BJZB	Evans VP-2	PFA 063-10633		10. 3.82	I P Manley and J Pearce	Marsh Farm, Sidlesham	15. 1.03P
	(Built A Graham) (Volkswagen 1834) *(Scrapped 2002/3 - fuselage noted 4.03: wings and engine to be fitted to a new VP-2 on site and believed to be G-CCEI)*						
G-BJZF	de Havilland DH.82A Tiger Moth	NAS-100		8. 3.82	M I Lodge	Lavenham	24. 4.07P
	(Built Norfolk Aerial Spraying Ltd from spares and officially redesignated "NAS Tiger Moth")						
G-BJZN	Slingsby T 67A	1997		31. 3.82	P B Rice	Breighton	9. 9.08E
G-BJZR	Colt 42A Balloon (Hot Air)	402		18. 3.82	A F Selby tr Selfish Balloon Group	Loughborough	21. 9.08A
					"Selfish"		

G-BKAA - G-BKZZ

G-BKAE	Wassmer Jodel D 120 Paris-Nice	200	F-BKCE	5. 5.82	S J Harris	Sleap	2. 4.08P
G-BKAF	Clutton FRED Series II	PFA 029-10337		23. 3.82	J M Robinson	(Achill Island, County Mayo)	30. 5.97P
	(Built L G Millen) (Volkswagen 1835)						
G-BKAM	Slingsby T 67M-160 Firefly	1999		26. 4.82	R C P Brookhouse	Maypole Farm, Chislet	30. 5.08E
G-BKAO	Wassmer Jodel D 112	249	F-BFTO	22. 3.82	R Broadhead	Eddsfield, Octon Lodge Farm, Thwing	29. 5.08P
G-BKAS	Piper PA-38-112 Tomahawk	38-79A1075	N24291	16. 4.82	E Reed t/a St George Flight Training		
			N9670N			Durham Tees Valley	11. 8.08E
G-BKAY	Rockwell Commander 114	14411	SE-GSN	28. 9.81	D L Bunning	Dunkeswell	5. 6.08E
G-BKAZ	Cessna 152 II	15282832	N89705	27. 4.82	L W Scattergood	Sandtoft	5. 6.08E
G-BKBB	Hawker Fury replica	WA/6	OO-HFU	2. 4.82	Brandish Holdings Ltd	Wevelgem, Belgium	3. 6.04P
	(Built Westward Airways (Lands End) Ltd) (RR Kestrel 5)		OO-XFU, G-BKBB		*(As "K1930" in RAF 43 Sqdn c/s)* *(Noted 11.05)*		
G-BKBD	Thunder Ax3 Maxi Sky Chariot Balloon (Hot Air)			5. 4.82	M J Casson	Lyth, Kendal	
		418					
G-BKBF	SOCATA MS.894A Rallye Minerva 220	11622	F-BSKZ	8. 9.82	K A Hale and L C Clark	Draycott Farm, Chiseldon	13. 9.08E
G-BKBN	SOCATA TB-10 Tobago	287		4. 6.82	F L Hunter	(Sheffield City)	25. 8.07
G-BKBO	Colt 17A Cloudhopper Balloon (Hot Air)	342		1. 9.82	J Armstrong, M A Ashworth and H Davey	Newquay	19. 2.04A
					"Captain Courageous"		
G-BKBP	Bellanca 7GCBC Citabria	465-73	N8693	1. 6.82	M G and J R Jefferies t/a H G Jefferies and Son		
						Little Gransden	1.12.06T
G-BKBS	Bensen B 8MV	PFA G/01-1027		14. 4.82	L Harrison	(Southend-on-Sea)	30. 7.08P
	(Built G Dawe) (Rotax 532)						
G-BKBV	SOCATA TB-10 Tobago	288	F-BNGO	4. 6.82	A P Orchard *"Cocoa"*	(Cottesmore, Oakham)	17. 2.08E
G-BKBW	SOCATA TB-10 Tobago	289		4. 6.82	P J Bramhall and D F Woodhouse tr Merlin Aviation		
						Bristol	26. 5.08E
G-BKCC	Piper PA-28-180 Cherokee Archer	28-7405099	OY-BGY	13. 5.82	DR Flying Club Ltd	Gloucestershire	15.10.08E
G-BKCE	Reims Cessna F172P Skyhawk II	F17202135	N9687R	26. 4.82	The Leicestershire Aero Club Ltd	Leicester	18. 6.08E
G-BKCI	Brügger MB.2 Colibri	PFA 043-10692		22. 4.82	M R Walters	Leicester	
	(Built E R Newall) (Volkswagen 1600)				*(Noted 11.06)*		
G-BKCN	Phoenix Currie Wot	PFA 3018		27. 4.82	N A A Pogmore	Benson's Farm, Laindon	22.11.08P
	(Built S E O Tomlinson) (Continental A65)						
G-BKCR	SOCATA TB-9 Tampico	297		6. 5.82	P A Little *(Noted 11.05)*	Haverfordwest	3. 8.98T
G-BKCV	EAA Acrosport II	430		5. 5.82	M J Clark	Dunsfold	11.12.07P
	(Built M J Clark) - pr.no.PFA 072A-10776) (Lycoming 0-360)						
G-BKCW	Wassmer Jodel D 120A Paris-Nice	285	(G-BKCP)	1. 6.82	I C Waddell tr Dundee Flying Group	Perth	12.12.08P
			F-BMYF				
G-BKCX	Mudry CAP.10B	149		28. 7.82	G P Gorvett	Rhosgoch	28. 9.08E
G-BKCZ	Wassmer Jodel D 120A Paris-Nice	207	F-BKCZ	23. 4.82	I K Ratcliffe	(Eastbourne)	27. 3.08P
G-BKDC	Monnett Sonerai IIL	876		2. 7.82	K J Towell	(Guildford)	18. 6.90P
	(Built J Boobyer) - pr.no.PFA 15-10597) (Volkswagen 1834)				*(Damaged Breighton 7. 8.90)*		
G-BKDH	Robin DR.400-120 Dauphin 80	1582	PH-CAB	25. 5.82	Dauphin Flying Group Ltd	Draycott Farm, Chiseldon	25.11.07E
G-BKDI	Robin DR.400-120 Dauphin 80	1583	PH-CAD	25. 5.82	Mistral Aviation Ltd	Perth	19. 7.08E
G-BKDJ	Robin DR.400-120 Dauphin 80	1584	PH-CAC	25. 5.82	I C Colwell and S Pritchard		
						Eastbach Farm, Monmouth	26. 5.07
G-BKDK	Thunder Ax7-77Z Balloon (Hot Air)	428		21. 6.82	A J Byrne *"Cider Riser"*	Thatcham	17. 9.95A
G-BKDP	Clutton FRED Series III	PFA 029-10650		24. 5.82	M Whittaker	(Wolverhampton)	
	(Built M Whittaker)						
G-BKDR	Pitts S-1S	PFA 009-10654		14. 6.82	J H Milne and T H Bishop	(Norwich)	21. 5.08P
	(Built Maypole Engineering Ltd)						
G-BKDS	Colt 14A Cloudhopper Balloon (Hot Air)	340	SE-ZBZ	1. 6.82	D M and K R Sandford	Knutsford and Nortwich	
			G-BKDS		*(Noted tethered 10.06)*		
G-BKDX	SAN Jodel DR.1050 Ambassadeur	55	F-BITX	1. 6.82	G J Slater	Ventfield Farm, Oxfordshire	6. 7.08E
G-BKEK	Piper PA-32-300 Cherokee Six	32-7540091	OY-TOP	30. 6.82	Favourites Racing Ltd	Wellesbourne Mountford	19. 7.08E
G-BKEP	Reims Cessna F172M Skyhawk II	F17201095	OY-BFJ	8. 7.82	R M Dalley	Perth	15. 3.08E
	(Thielert TAE 125-01)						
G-BKER	Replica Plans SE.5a	PFA 020-10641		15. 6.82	N K Geddes	South Barnbeth Farm, Bridge of Weir	28. 5.08P
	(Built N K Geddes) (Continental O-200A)				*(As "F5447:N" in RAF c/s)*		
G-BKET	Piper PA-18 Super Cub 95	18-1990	EI-67	17. 6.82	H M MacKenzie	Inverness	27. 5.08P
	(L-18C-PI)		I-EIBI, MM52-2390, 52-2390				
G-BKEU	Taylor JT.1 Monoplane	PFA 055-10553		18. 6.82	A J Moore	(Turweston, Brackley)	20. 7.95P
	(Built R J Whybrow and J M Springham)				*(New owner 1.05)*		
G-BKEV	Reims Cessna F172M Skyhawk II	F17201443	PH-WLH	8. 7.82	G Henn tr Derby Arrows	Derby	18. 4.08E
			OO-CNE				
G-BKEW	Bell 206B-3 JetRanger III	3010	D-HDAD	8. 7.82	N R Foster t/a Foster Associates	Biggin Hill	14. 8.08E

Reg	Type	c/n	Prev id	Date	Owner/Operator	Location	Date
G-BKEY	Clutton FRED Series III	PFA 029-10208		27. 5.82	G S Taylor	(Rock, Kidderminster)	
	(Built G S Taylor) (Volkswagen 1600)						
G-BKFA	Monnett Sonerai IIL	PFA 015-10524		21. 6.82	S J N Robbie Roughay Farm, Bishops Waltham		
	(Built R F Bridge)				(On long term rebuild 2.06)		
G-BKFC	Reims Cessna F152 II	F15201443	OO-AWB	1. 9.82	C Walton Ltd t/a Sulby Aerial Surveys Bruntingthorpe		19. 1.08E
G-BKFI	Evans VP-1 Series 2	PFA 062-10491		24. 6.82	P L Naylor	Morgansfield, Fishburn	7. 5.08P
	(Built R F A Lavergne) (Volkswagen 1834)						
G-BKFK	Isaacs Fury II	PFA 011-10038		25. 6.82	G C Jones	Waits Farm, Belchamp Walter	27. 8.02P
	(Built G C Jones) (Lycoming O-290-D)				"Cia Cia San" (Persian AF c/s)		
G-BKFL	Aerosport Scamp	PFA 117-10814		17. 8.82	J Sherwood	(Royston, Barnsley)	
	(Built I D Daniels)						
G-BKFM	QAC Quickie 1	PFA 094-10570		28. 6.82	G E Meakin	(Ruddington)	29. 6.98P
	(Built R I Davidson and P Cheney) (Rotax 503)				(Damaged on take off Cranfield 4.7.98: new owner 7.01)		
G-BKFR	Scintex CP.301-C Emeraude	519	F-BUUR F-BJFF	30. 6.82	D G Burgess tr Devonshire Flying Group	Trenchard Farm, Eggesford	18. 7.08P
G-BKFW	Percival P 56 Provost T 1	PAC/F/303	XF597	21. 9.82	Sylmar Aviation and Services Ltd		27. 7.07P
					(As "XF597:AH" in RAF College c/s) Lower Wasing Farm, Brimpton		
G-BKFZ	Piper PA-28R-200 Cherokee Arrow II	28R-7635127	OY-BLE	17. 8.82	R S Watt tr Shacklewell Flying Group	Shacklewell Farm, Empingham	3. 1.08E
G-BKGA	SOCATA MS.892E Rallye 150GT	13287	F-GBXJ	15. 7.82	C J Spradbery	Coventry	20. 3.08E
G-BKGB	Wassmer Jodel D 120 Paris-Nice	267	F-BMOB	21. 6.82	B A Ridgway	Rhigos	20. 3.08P
G-BKGC	Maule M-6-235C Super Rocket	7413C	N56465	23. 7.82	The Vale of the White Horse Gliding Centre Ltd	Sandhill Farm, Shrivenham	25. 9.08E
G-BKGL	Beech D18S (3TM)	CA-164	CF-QPD RCAF 5193, 1564	14. 7.82	A T J Darrah	Duxford	30. 3.08
		(Beech c/n A-764)			(As "1164" in {1942} USAAC c/s)		
G-BKGM	Beech 3NM (D18S)	CA-203	N5063N	14. 7.82	Skyblue Aviation Ltd	Exeter	17. 9.09S
		(Beech c/n A-853)	G-BKGM, CF-SUQ, RCAF 2324		(As "HB275" in RAF SEAC c/s)		
G-BKGR	Cameron O-65 Balloon (Hot Air)	864		6. 8.82	K Kidner and L E More	Newton Abbot	8. 5.93P
G-BKGT	SOCATA Rallye 110ST Galopin	3361		23. 7.82	A G Morgan tr Long Marston Flying Group	Wellesbourne Mountford	12. 2.08E
G-BKGW	Reims Cessna F152 II	F15201878	N9071N	11. 8.82	The Leicestershire Aero Club Ltd	Leicester	15. 5.08E
G-BKHD	Oldfield Baby Lakes	8133-F-802B		5. 8.82	P J Tanulak	(Myddle, Shrewsbury)	11. 4.96P
	(Built P J Tanulak - pr.no.PFA 010-107182) (Continental O-200-A)				(Damaged Shrewsbury 22.10.95)		
G-BKHG	Piper J-3C-65 Cub (L-4H-PI)	12062	F-BCPT NC79807, 44-79766	13. 9.82	H C Cox	Frogland Cross	12. 7.07P
					(As "479766:63-D" in HQ 9th Army, USAAC c/s) "Puddle Jumper"		
G-BKHJ	Cessna 182P Skylane II	18264129	PH-CAT D-EATV, N6223F	25. 8.82	Augur Films Ltd	Shipdham	9. 1.08E
	(Reims c/n F18200040)						
G-BKHW	Stoddard-Hamilton Glasair RG	357		27.8.82	P J Mansfield	(Newark)	18. 9.08P
	(Built N Clayton - pr.no.PFA 149-11312) (Lycoming O-320)						
G-BKHY	Taylor JT.1 Monoplane	PFA 1416		8. 9.82	B C J O'Neill	Benson's Farm, Laindon	29.10.08P
	(Built J Hall)						
G-BKIB	SOCATA TB-9 Tampico	323		25. 8.82	G A Vickers	Hawarden	15. 2.08E
G-BKIF	Fournier RF6-100	3	F-GADR	8.10.82	C C Rollings and F J Hodgson t/a Tiger Airways	Gloucestershire	17. 2.07
G-BKII	Reims Cessna F172M Skyhawk II	F17201370	PH-PLO (D-EGIA)	8.10.82	Sealand Ap Ltd	Goodwood	6. 3.08E
G-BKIJ	Reims Cessna F172M	F17200920	PH-TGZ	15.10.82	Cirrus Aviation Ltd	Clacton	8. 8.08E
G-BKIR	SAN Jodel D 117	737	F-BIOC	30. 9.82	D M Hardaker	(Gomersal, Cleckheaton)	28. 8.92P
					(On rebuild 3.96)		
G-BKIS	SOCATA TB-10 Tobago	329		22. 9.82	R J Burrows and S M Cuthill, tr Wessex Flyers	Thruxton	7. 7.08E
G-BKIT	SOCATA TB-9 Tampico	330		22. 9.82	Cavendish Aviation UK Ltd	Earls Colne	30. 6.08E
G-BKIU	Colt 17A Cloudhopper Balloon (Hot Air)	420		29. 9.82	S R J Pooley (New owner 1.08)	Elstree	
G-BKIX	Cameron V-31 Air Chair Balloon (Hot Air)	863	(G-BKGJ)	23. 9.82	(P Gooch) (Extant 2007)	Alresford	12. 4.03
G-BKJB	Piper PA-18-135 Super Cub	18-574	PH-GAI	1. 8.83	Haimoss Ltd	Old Sarum	6.11.08E
	(L-21A-PI) (Frame No.18-522)		R Neth AF R-204, 51-15657, N1003A		(Operated Old Sarum Flying Club)		
G-BKJF	SOCATA MS.880B Rallye 100T	2300	F-BULF	16.12.82	Journeyman Aviation Ltd (Noted 10.07)	Sywell	26. 7.07
G-BKJS	Wassmer Jodel D 120A Paris-Nice	191	F-BJPS	4.10.82	B F Baldock and T J Nicholson Clipgate Farm, Denton		10. 9.07P
G-BKJW	Piper PA-23-250 Aztec E	27-4716	N14153	3.11.78	Alan Williams Entertainments Ltd	Southend	26. 5.05
					(Noted 1.08)		
G-BKKN	Cessna 182R Skylane II	18267801	N6218N	30.11.82	R A Marven t/a Marvagraphic (Sandridge, St Albans)		23. 5.08E
G-BKKO	Cessna 182R Skylane II	18267852	N4907H	30.11.82	E L King and D S Lightbown	Crosland Moor	11. 5.08E
G-BKKZ	Pitts S-1S	PFA 009-10525	(G-BIVW)	10.11.82	G M Huffen	Sherburn-in-Elmet	7. 8.08P
	(Built J A Coutts)						
G-BKLO	Reims Cessna F172M Skyhawk II	F17201380	PH-BET D-EFMS	22. 3.83	Stapleford Flying Club Ltd	Stapleford	11. 6.08E
G-BKMA	Mooney M 20J Mooney 201	24-1316	N1170N	13.12.82	C A White t/a Foxtrot Whisky Aviation	Cambridge	9. 6.08E
G-BKMB	Mooney M 20J Mooney 201	24-1307	N1168P	15.12.82	W A Cook, B Pearson and P Turnbull Sherburn-in-Elmet		30. 1.08E
G-BKMG	Handley Page 0/400 replica	TPG-1		8.12.82	M G King tr The Paralyser Group	(Wroxham, Norwich)	
	(Built The Paralyser Group)						
G-BKMI	Vickers Supermarine 359 Spitfire HF.VIIIc	6S/583793	A58-671 MV154	23.12.82	R J Lamplough	Filton	27. 6.08P
					(As "MT928:ZX-M" in RAF 145 Sqdn c/s)		
G-BKMT	Piper PA-32R-301 Saratoga II SP	32R-8213013	N8005Z	4. 2.83	P Squires	Blackpool	20. 4.08E
G-BKMX	Short SD.3-60 Variant 100	SH3608	G-14-3608	13.12.82	BAC Leasing Ltd "City of Bristol"	Inverness	31. 7.08E
G-BKNI	Sud-Aviation Gardan GY-80-160D Horizon	249	F-BRJN	28. 1.83	A Hartigan tr Blue Horizon Flying Group	Bourn	13. 5.02
					"Blue Lady" (Stored 10.05)		
G-BKNO	Monnett Sonerai IIL	792		11. 3.83	S Hardy	(Northchurch, Hemel Hempstead)	15. 6.99P
	(Built S Tattersfield and K Bailey - pr.no.PFA 015-10528) (Volkswagen 1834)				(New owner 8.05)		
G-BKNP	Cameron V-77 Balloon (Hot Air)	874		22.12.82	K Jakobsson	Goteborg, Sweden	25. 2.06A
G-BKNZ	Menavia Piel CP.301A Emeraude	296	F-BISZ	21. 1.83	A D Heath	Sleap	13. 9.08P
G-BKOA	SOCATA MS.893E Rallye 180GT	12432	F-BOFB F-ODAT, F-BVAT	2. 3.83	M Jarrett	(Yaxley, Peterborough)	31.10.05
					(New owner 4.07)		
G-BKOB	Moravan Zlin Z-326 Trener Master	757	F-BKOB	28. 9.81	A L Rae	Luxter's Farm, Hambleden	30. 5.08
G-BKOT	Wassmer WA.81 Piranha	813	F-GAIP	17. 2.87	B N Rolfe (Noted 10.05)	Bourn	

G-BKOU	Hunting Percival P 84 Jet Provost T 3	PAC/W/13901	XN637	17. 2.83	M P Grimshaw tr G-BKOU Group	North Weald	31. 8.08P
					"Where Eagles Share"		
G-BKPA	Hoffmann H 36 Dimona	3522		16. 6.83	D E Puttock	Perranporth	25. 8.08E
G-BKPB	Aerosport Scamp	PFA 117-10736		23. 2.83	B R Thompson	Hucknall	8. 8.07P
	(Built R Scroby) (Volkswagen 1834)						
G-BKPC	Cessna A185F AGcarryall	185-03809	N4599E	10. 7.80	The Black Knights Parachute Centre Ltd		
						Bank End Farm, Cockerham	10.11.07E
G-BKPD	Viking Dragonfly	302		11. 3.83	E P Browne and G J Sargent	(Cambridge)	20. 1.00P
	(Built P E J Sturgeon - pr.no.PFA 139-10897) (Revmaster 2100D)				*(Damaged Cambridge 17. 7.99)*		
G-BKPE	CEA Jodel DR.250/160 Capitaine	35	F-BNJD	18. 3.83	J S and J D Lewer	Dunkeswell	16.12.04
G-BKPN	Cameron N-77 Balloon (Hot Air)	923		9. 3.83	R H Sanderson	Nuneaton	21. 5.87A
					"Do It All" (Donated to Balloon Preservation Group 1.03)		
G-BKPS	Grumman AA-5B Tiger	AA5B-0007	OO-SAS	7. 3.83	A E T Clarke	Manston	26.11.07E
			OO-HAO, (OO-WAY), N1507R				
G-BKPX	Wassmer Jodel D 120A Paris-Nice	240	F-BLNG	19. 1.84	D M Garrett and C A Jones	Defford	9. 7.08P
G-BKPZ	Pitts S-1T	PFA 009-10852		4. 3.83	P R Rutterford	Redhill	10. 7.08P
	(Built G C Masterton)						
G-BKRA	North American T-6G-NH Texan	188-90	MM53-664	19. 8.83	First Air Ltd	Shoreham	21. 3.10S
			RM-9, 51-15227		*(As "115227 in US Navy c/s)*		
G-BKRF	Piper PA-18 Super Cub 95	18-1525	F-BOUI	7.11.83	K M Bishop	Croft Farm, Defford	20. 5.08P
	(L-18C-PI) (Frame No.18-1502)		French Army, 51-15525				
G-BKRH	Brügger MB.2 Colibri	142		15. 3.83	M R Benwell	Bodmin	9. 8.08P
	(Built M R Benwell - pr no.PFA 043-10150) (Volkswagen 1835)						
G-BKRK	SNCAN Stampe SV-4C	57	Aeronavale	30. 3.83	J R Bisset tr Strathgadie Stampe Group	(Aboyne)	28. 6.98
G-BKRN	Beech D18S	A-675	CF-DTN	14. 4.83	A A Marshall and P L Turland	Bruntingthorpe	26. 6.83P
	(Offcial c/n is CA-75 and suggests Canadian rebuild)		RCAF A675, RCAF 1500		*(Under restoration 3.02)*		
G-BKRS	Cameron V-56 Balloon (Hot Air)	908		23. 3.83	D N and L J Close	Chute Forest, Andover	17. 7.97A
					"Bonkers" (Noted 8.06)		
G-BKRZ	Dragon 77 Balloon (Hot Air)	001		11. 4.83	J R Barber *"Rupert"*	Newbury	5. 3.94A
					(On loan to British Balloon Museum and Library)		
G-BKSD	Colt 56A Balloon (Hot Air)	361		11. 4.83	M J Casson *"Entwhistle Green"*	Kendal	2. 6.96A
G-BKSE	QAC Quickie 1	PFA 094-10748		6. 4.83	M D Burns	(Kirkintilloch, Glasgow)	8. 5.89P
	(Built Taylor, M D Burns and Ibbott and officially regd with c/n PFA 094-10784) (Onan B48M) (Stored 6.00)						
G-BKSP	Schleicher ASK 14	14028	D-KOMO	25. 5.83	J H Bryson	Bellarena	11. 9.08E
G-BKST	Rutan VariEze	12718-001		20. 4.83	R Towle	(Barrasford, Hexham)	
	(Built R Towle)						
G-BKSX	SNCAN Stampe SV-4C	61	F-BBAF	16. 5.83	C A Bailey and J A Carr	(Eggesford)	15. 6.89
			French AF		*(Stored 11.02)*		
G-BKTA	Piper PA-18 Super Cub 95	18-3223	OO-HBA	10. 5.83	M J Dyson	Roddige	10. 8.05P
	(L-18C-PI) (Frame No.18-3246)		Belg AF OL-L49, L-149, 53-4823				
G-BKTH	Hawker Sea Hurricane IB	CCF/41H/4013	Z7015	24. 5.83	Richard Shuttleworth Trustees	Old Warden	10. 5.08P
	(Built Canadian Car and Foundry Co)				*(As "Z7015:7-L" in RN 880 Sqdn c/s)*		
G-BKTM	PZL-Bielsko SZD-45A Ogar	B-656		31. 5.83	J T Pajdak	Challock	2. 9.08E
G-BKTR	Cameron V-77 Balloon (Hot Air)	951		6. 6.83	C M Morley and C Williamson		
					Upchurch, Sittingbourne and Goudhurst, Cranbrook		25. 9.08A
G-BKTV	Reims Cessna F152 II	F15201450	OY-BJB	8. 8.83	ACS Aviation Ltd	Cumbernauld	31. 8.08E
G-BKTZ	Slingsby T 67M Firefly	2004	G-SFTV	26. 8.83	P R Elvidge Eddsfield, Octon Lodge Farm, Thwing		15.12.07E
					(Fuselage marked as "G-BKTZ" noted Blackpool 10.07)		
G-BKUE	SOCATA TB-9 Tampico	369	F-BNGX	31. 5.83	R N Swinney tr Fife TB9ers	Glenrothes	28. 3.08E
G-BKUR	Menavia Piel CP.301A Emeraude	280	(G-BKBX)	19.10.83	R Wells	Morgansfield, Fishburn	25. 6.08P
			F-BMLX, F-OBLY				
G-BKUU	Thunder Ax7-77 Series 1 Balloon (Hot Air)	522		3. 8.83	M A Mould *"Tanglefoot"*	Winchester	12. 4.03A
G-BKVA	SOCATA Rallye 180T Galerien	3274	SE-GFS	30. 6.83	Buckminster Gliding Club Ltd	Saltby	20. 8.08E
			F-GBXA				
G-BKVB	SOCATA Rallye 110ST Galopin	3258	OO-PIP	22. 6.83	A and K Bishop	Haverfordwest	11.12.05
G-BKVC	SOCATA TB-9 Tampico	372	F-BNGQ	4. 7.83	D M Hook	Bicester	21. 4.08E
G-BKVF	Clutton FRED Series III	PFA 029-10791		29. 7.83	G E and R E Collins	Derby	
	(Built N E Johnson)				*(New owners 10.04)*		
G-BKVG	Scheibe SF25E Super Falke	4362	(D-KNAE)	25. 8.83	G-BKVG Ltd	North Hill	4. 6.08
	(Limbach SL1700)						
G-BKVK	Auster AOP.9	xxxx	WZ662	8. 8.83	J K Houlgrave Trenchard Farm, Eggesford		5. 7.08P
	(Officially regd with Frame no.AUS/10/2)				*(As "WZ662" in AAC c/s)*		
G-BKVL	Robin DR.400-160 Major	1625		26. 7.83	Tatenhill Aviation Ltd t/a Tatenhill Aviation	Tatenhill	2. 4.08E
G-BKVM	Piper PA-18-150 Super Cub	18-849	PH-KAZ	26. 8.83	D G Caffrey	Strubby	26.10.08
	(L-21A-PI) (Frame No.18-824)		R Neth AF R-214, 51-15684		*(As "115684:VM" in US Army c/s) "Spirit of Goxhill"*		
G-BKVO	Pietenpol AirCamper	PFA 047-10799		8. 8.83	M C Hayes	(Woonton, Hereford)	26. 9.07P
	(Built M J Honeychurch) (Continental A65)						
G-BKVP	Pitts S-1D	002		19. 8.83	S W Doyle	Popham	26. 7.07P
	(Built P J Leggo - pr.no.PFA 009-10800)						
G-BKVS	Campbell Cricket	PFA G/01-1047		11. 8.83	K Hughes	(Amlwch, Gwynedd)	10. 8.05P
	(Built V Scott) (Volkswagen 1834)						
G-BKVT	Piper PA-23-250 Aztec F	27-7754002	G-HARV	6. 2.84	BKS Surveys Ltd	Belfast International	3. 4.08E
			N62760				
G-BKVW	Airtour AH-56 Balloon (Hot Air)	AH.003		27. 6.84	L D and H Vaughan *"Lunardi"*	Wilstone, Tring	
G-BKVX	Airtour AH-56C Balloon (Hot Air)	AH.002		27. 6.84	P Aldridge	Halesworth, Suffolk	
					"Featherspin" or "Liebling"		
G-BKVY	Airtour B-31 Balloon (Hot Air)	AH.001		9. 8.83	M Davies *"Day Dream"*	Callington, Plymouth	15. 8.01A
G-BKWD	Taylor JT.2 Titch	PFA 060-10232		17. 8.83	J F Sully	Sturgate	23. 6.07P
	(Built E H Booker and originally regd as c/n PFA 060-10143 - presumed absorbed into this project on build) (Continental PC60)						
G-BKWR	Cameron V-65 Balloon (Hot Air)	970		26. 8.83	Window on the World Ltd	London SW4	18. 1.07A
G-BKWW	Cameron O-77 Balloon (Hot Air)	984		13. 9.83	A M Marten *"Kouros"*	Woking	18. 1.89A
G-BKWY	Reims Cessna F152	F15201940		22. 9.83	Northern Aviation Ltd	Durham Tees Valley	30. 1.08T
G-BKXA	Robin R2100	114	F-GAOS	24.11.83	M Wilson *(New owner 8.01)*	Little Gransden	22.10.99
G-BKXD	Aérospatiale SA.365N Dauphin 2	6088	F-WMHD	7. 9.83	CHC Scotia Ltd	Blackpool	8.12.07E

G-BKXF	Piper PA-28R-200 Cherokee Arrow II		OY-DZN	10.11.83	P L Brunton	Welshpool	12. 7.08E
		28R-7335351	N56092				
G-BKXM	Colt 17A Cloudhopper Balloon (Hot Air)	531		3.10.83	R G Turnbull	Glasbury, Hereford	15. 4.06A
G-BKXN	ICA IS-28M2A	48		24.10.83	S P Moles tr Skyways Aviation Group	Headcorn	2. 8.08E
G-BKXO	Rutan LongEz	PFA 074A-10580		24.10.83	M G Parsons	RAF Kinloss	11. 4.08P
	(Built P Wareham) (Continental O-200-A)						
G-BKXP	Auster AOP.6	2830	A-14	12.10.83	B J Ellis	Thruxton	
	(Frame No.TAY841BJ)		Belg AF, VT987		*(On rebuild 7.91: new owner 12.01)*		
G-BKXR	Druine D 31A Turbulent	303	OY-AMW	1.11.83	M B Hill	Draycott Farm, Chiseldon	27.11.05P
	(Built H Husted) (Volkswagen 1700)						
G-BKZB	Cameron V-77 Balloon (Hot Air)	995		11.11.83	K B Chapple Montastruc, Hautes-Pyrenees, France		6. 7.01A
G-BKZE	Aérospatiale AS.332L Super Puma	2102	F-WKQE	30. 9.83	CHC Scotia Ltd	Aberdeen	25. 9.08E
G-BKZF	Cameron V-56 Balloon (Hot Air)	246	F-BXUK	14.11.83	C F Sanger-Davies	Eldersfield, Gloucester	18. 3.97A
					(New owner 11.04)		
G-BKZG	Aérospatiale AS.332L Super Puma	2106	HB-ZBT	30. 9.83	CHC Scotia Ltd	Aberdeen	25. 8.08E
			G-BKZG				
G-BKZI	Bell 206A JetRanger	118	(5B-CGC or 'CGD) 7.12.83		Bucklefields Business Developments Ltd		
			G-BKZI, N6238N			(Ogbourne St George, Marlborough)	19. 9.08E
G-BKZM	Isaacs Fury	PFA 011-10742		27. 9.83	D A Weldon	Kilrush, County Kildare	1.10.90P
	(Built R J Smith and J Evans)				*(New owner 6.07)*		
G-BKZT	Clutton FRED Series II	PFA 029-10715		20.10.83	U Chakravorty	Clipgate Farm, Denton	2. 7.02P
	(Built A E Morris) (Volkswagen 1834)				*(Noted 6.05)*		
G-BKZV	Bede BD-4	380	ZS-UAB	31. 8.84	G I J Thomson	Little Snoring	28.10.05P
	(Built A L Bergamasgo) (Lycoming O-320)						

G-BLAA - G-BLZZ

G-BLAC	Reims Cessna FA152 Aerobat	FA1520370		25. 3.80	D C C Handley	Little Staughton	30. 5.08E
G-BLAF	Stolp SA.900 V-Star	PFA 106-10651		13. 9.83	P R Skeels	Yew Tree Farm, Lymm Dam	15. 4.08P
	(Built J E Molloy) (Continental O-200-A)						
G-BLAG	Pitts S-1D	PFA 009-10195		1.12.83	I S Grosz	Stornoway	21.12.07P
	(Built B Bray)						
G-BLAH	Thunder Ax7-77 Series 1 Balloon (Hot Air)	526		3.10.83	T M Donnelly	Sprotbrough, Doncaster	19. 8.01A
					"Blah" (Active Albuquerque , New Mexico 10.03)		
G-BLAI	Monnett Sonerai IIL	PFA 015-10583		6.12.83	T Simpson	(Kirkcaldy)	12. 1.99P
	(Built T Simpson and officially regd with c/n PFA 15-10584)				*(Noted 12.01)*		
G-BLAM	CEA Jodel DR.360 Chevalier	345	F-BRCM	6. 2.84	D J Durell	Rochester	18. 8.08E
G-BLAT	SAN Jodel D 150 Mascaret	56	F-BNID	30. 1.84	N T Coote and I R Willis tr G-BLAT Flying Group		
						Glenrothes	28.11.07P
G-BLAX	Reims Cessna FA152 Aerobat	FA1520385		11.10.83	N C and M L Scanlan	RAF Waddington	28. 5.08E
G-BLCC	Thunder Ax7-77Z Balloon (Hot Air)	532		7.12.83	W J Treacy and P Murphy	(Trim, County Meath)	27. 9.06A
G-BLCG	SOCATA TB-10 Tobago	61	G-BHES	17. 3.80	R Deery and D Tunks tr Charlie Golf Flying Group		
						Shoreham	10. 8.08
G-BLCH	Colt 65D Balloon (Hot Air)	392	G-BJHT (1)	14.11.83	Balloon Flights Club Ltd	Kings Norton, Leicester	
					"Geronimo" (New owner 9.05)		
G-BLCI	EAA Acrosport P	P-10A	N6AS	29. 2.84	M R Holden	(Stoneacre Farm, Farthing Corner)	16. 6.97P
					"Bluebottle" (Damaged Farthing Corner 1996)		
G-BLCM	SOCATA TB-9 Tampico	194	OO-TCT	2.12.83	K J Steele and D J Hewitt		
			(OO-TBC)			(Kynnersley, Telford and Himley, Dudley)	5. 7.08E
G-BLCT	CEA Jodel DR.220 2+2	23	F-BOCQ	22.12.83	D I Scott	Swanborough Farm, Lewes	7. 8.08E
G-BLCU	Scheibe SF25B Falke	4699	D-KECC	30.12.83	J D Johnson tr Charlie Uniform Syndicate	Rufforth	23.11.07E
	(Stark-Stamo MS1500)						
G-BLCV	Hoffmann H 36 Dimona	36113	EI-CJO	21. 3.84	R and M Weaver	Usk	20. 7.08E
			G-BLCV				
G-BLCW	Evans VP-1	PFA 062-10835		19.12.83	M Flint	Fenland	25. 4.06P
	(Built K D Pearce) (Volkswagen 1600)				*"Le Plank"*		
G-BLCY	Thunder Ax7-65Z Balloon (Hot Air)	487		13. 1.84	C M George	Newton Ferrers, Plymouth	26. 2.99A
					"Warsteiner" (Active Germany 2005)		
G-BLDB	Taylor JT.1 Monoplane	PFA 055-10506		28.12.83	C J Bush	New Farm House, Great Oakley	12. 5.08P
	(Built C J Bush)						
G-BLDD	Wag-Aero CUBy AcroTrainer	PFA 108-10653		29.12.83	A F Stafford	Combrook	4.10.06P
	(Built C A Lacock) (Lycoming O-320)						
G-BLDG	Piper PA-25-235 Pawnee C	25-4501	SE-FLB	9. 1.84	York Gliding Centre Ltd	Rufforth	23. 6.08E
	(Modified to PA-25-260 standard)		LN-VYM				
G-BLDK	Robinson R22	0139	C-GSGU	17. 1.84	Flight Academy (Gyrocopters) Ltd	Blackpool	23. 8.08E
G-BLDN	Rand Robinson KR-2	PFA 129-10913		12. 1.84	P R Diffey	Top Farm, Croydon, Royston	18. 9.07P
	(Built R Y Kendal) (Volkswagen 1834)						
G-BLDV	Pilatus Britten-Norman BN-2B-26 Islander	2179	D-INEY	13. 1.84	Loganair Ltd	Glasgow	19. 7.08E
			G-BLDV		*(Highland Park titles)*		
G-BLEB	Colt 69A Balloon (Hot Air)	537		20. 1.84	I R M Jacobs	Padworth Common, Reading	30. 3.85A
G-BLEP	Cameron V-65 Balloon (Hot Air)	102		27. 2.84	D Chapman tr The Ground Hogs	Maidstone	10. 9.96A
					"Manor Marquees"		
G-BLES	Stolp SA.750 Acroduster Too	197		8.12.83	C J Kingswood	RAF Church Fenton	26. 5.07P
	(Built W G Hosie - pr.no.PFA 089-10428) (Lycoming O-360)						
G-BLET	Thunder Ax7-77 Series 1 Balloon (Hot Air)	539		16. 2.84	Servatruc Ltd *"Servatruc"*	Nottingham	15. 8.97E
G-BLEZ	Aérospatiale SA.365N Dauphin 2	6131		24. 1.84	CHC Scotia Ltd	Blackpool	27. 8.08E
G-BLFI	Piper PA-28-181 Archer II	28-8490034	N4333Z	22. 2.84	Bonus Aviation Ltd	Cranfield	31. 7.08E
G-BLFW	Grumman AA-5 Traveler	AA5-0786	OO-GLW	22. 2.84	D C A Milne tr Grumman Club		
						Draycott Farm, Chiseldon	11.10.07E
G-BLFY	Cameron V-77 Balloon (Hot Air)	1030		16. 3.84	A N F Pertwee *"Groupie"*	Frinton-on-Sea	5. 4.92A
G-BLFZ	Piper PA-31 Navajo C	31-7912106	PH-RWS	21. 3.84	London Executive Aviation Ltd	Stapleford	17. 9.07E
			(PH-ASV), N3538W				
G-BLGH	Robin DR.300-180R Remorqueur	570	D-EAFL	10. 4.84	Booker Gliding Club Ltd	Wycombe Air Park	24. 5.08E

G-BLGS	SOCATA Rallye 180T	3206		7. 7.78	A Waters t/a London Light Aircraft	Dunstable	21. 5.99
					(Gutted fuselage noted 6.00)		
G-BLGV	Bell 206B-2 JetRanger II	982	5B-JSB	2. 5.84	Heliflight (UK) Ltd	Gloucestershire	22. 5.08E
			C-FDYL, CF-DYL				
G-BLHH	CEA Jodel DR.315 Petit Prince	324	F-BPRH	3. 7.84	S J Luck	Bodmin	24. 7.08E
G-BLHI	Colt 17A Cloudhopper Balloon (Hot Air)	506		8. 9.86	J A Folkes *"Hopping Mad"*	Loughborough	24.11.01A
G-BLHJ	Reims Cessna F172P Skyhawk II	F17202182		26. 3.84	Flight Academy Scotland Ltd	Perth	2. 2.08E
G-BLHK	Colt 105A Balloon (Hot Air)	576		19. 6.84	A S Dear, R B Green and W S Templeton	Fordingbridge	12. 7.97A
					tr Hale Hot Air Balloon Group *"Gloworm"*		
G-BLHM (2)	Piper PA-18 Super Cub 95	18-3120	LX-AIM	23. 7.84	A G Edwards	(Llandegla)	8. 8.08P
	(L-18C-PI) *(Frame No.18-3088)*		D-EOAB, Belgian AF OL-L46, L-46, 53-4720				
G-BLHN	Robin HR.100-285 Tiara	539	F-GABF	20. 2.78	E A and L M C Payton	Spanhoe	18.12.06
					(Fuselage on trailer, wings stacked 10.07)		
G-BLHR	Gulfstream GA-7 Cougar	GA7-0109	OO-RTI	12. 4.84	Affair Aircraft Leasing LLP	Leeds-Bradford	1. 3.08E
			(OO-HRC), N751G				
G-BLHS	Bellanca 7ECA Citabria 115	1342-80	OO-RTQ	12. 4.84	N J F Campbell and D J Lockett tr Hotel Sierra Group		
						Inverness	5. 5.08E
G-BLHW	Varga 2150A Kachina	VAC161-80		17. 7.84	J R Surbey tr Wilburton Flying Group		
					Mitchells Farm, Wilburton and Blockmoor Farm, Barway, Ely		21. 9.08E
G-BLID	de Havilland DH.112 Venom FB.50 (FB.1)	815	Swiss AF J-1605	13. 7.84	P G Vallance Ltd	Charlwood, Surrey	
	(Built F + W)				*(In Gatwick Aviation Museum: as "J-1605" in Swiss AF c/s)*		
G-BLIH	Piper PA-18-135 Super Cub	18-3828	(PH-KNG)	12.11.84	I R F Hammond	(Titchfield, Fareham)	
	(L-21B-PI)*(Frame No.18-3827)*		R Neth AF R-138, (PH-KNG), (PH-GRC), R-138, 54-2428				
G-BLIK	Wallis WA-116/F/S	K-218X		30. 4.84	K H Wallis	Reymerston Hall, Norfolk	31 5.07P
	(Franklin 2A-120)						
G-BLIT	Thorp T-18CW	PFA 076-10550		24. 4.84	A P Tyrwhitt-Drake	Ellough, Beccles	15. 8.08P
	(Built A J Waller) (Lycoming O-320)						
G-BLIW	Percival P 56 Provost T 51	PAC/F/125	IAC.177	12. 6.85	A D Mand K B Edie	Shoreham	16. 5.05P
					(As "177" in IAC c/s) (Noted 11.05)		
G-BLIX	Saro Skeeter AOP.12	S2/5094	PH-HOF	3. 5.84	K M Scholes	Wilden	2. 6.06
			(PH-SRE), XL809		*(As "XL809" in AAC c/s)*		
G-BLIY	SOCATA MS.892A Rallye Commodore 150	11639	F-BSCX	9. 5.84	A J Brasher	Landmead Farm, Garford	26. 9.08
G-BLJD	Glaser-Dirks DG-400	4-85		15. 6.84	M I Gee	Lasham	21. 6.08E
G-BLJH	Cameron N-77 Balloon (Hot Air)	1047		14. 5.84	D , Glenis and DJ Phillips t/a Phillair		
					"Daydream"	Dosthill, Tamworth	27. 6.89A
G-BLJM	Beech 95-B55 Baron	TC-1997	SE-GRT	3. 3.78	A Nitsche	(Bensheim, Germany)	25. 9.08E
G-BLJO	Reims Cessna F152 II	F15201627	OY-BNB	21. 6.84	J S Develin and Z Islam	Redhill	28.10.07E
					(Operated Redhill Flying Club)		
G-BLKM	CEA Jodel DR.1051 Sicile	519	F-BLRO	26. 6.84	F H Lissimore tr Kilo Mike Group	Biggin Hill	27. 6.08E
G-BLKY	Beech 58 Baron	TH-1440		22. 8.84	R A Perrot	Guernsey	30. 7.08E
G-BLKZ	Pilatus P 2-05	600-45	Swiss AF U-125	30. 7.84	R W Hinton	Duxford	19. 2.08P
	(Official c/n is "45")		Swiss AF A-125		*(As "A-125" in Swiss AF c/s)*		
G-BLLA	Bensen B 8M	PFA G/01-1055		27. 6.84	K T Donaghey	Henstridge	21. 5.07P
	(Built K T Donaghey) (Volkswagen 1834)						
G-BLLB	Bensen B 8MR	PFA G/01A-1059		4. 9.84	D H Moss	Henstridge	14. 6.01P
	(Built D H Moss) (Rotax 532)				*(Noted 12.02)*		
G-BLLD	Cameron O-77 Balloon (Hot Air)	1060		16. 7.84	G Birchall	Ormskirk	24. 8.07A
G-BLLH	CEA Jodel DR.220A/B 2+2	131	F-BROM	17. 7.84	M D Hughes	Pauncefoot, Romsey	22. 8.08E
G-BLLN	Piper PA-18 Super Cub 95 (L-18C-PI)	18-3447	D-ECLN	27. 6.84	P L Pilch and C G Fisher	Rochester	13. 1.11S
	(Continental O-200A) *(Frame No.18-3380)*		96+23, PY+901, QZ+011, AC+508, AS+507, 54-747				
G-BLLO	Piper PA-18 Super Cub 95 (L-18C-PI)	18-3099	D-EAUB	11. 7.84	D G Margetts	Sleap	2. 8.08P
	(Frame No 18-3058)		Belgian AF OL-L25, L-25, 53-4699				
G-BLLP	Slingsby T 67B Firefly	2008		19. 7.84	Air Navigation and Trading Company Ltd	Blackpool	4.12.00T
					(On rebuild 11.06)		
G-BLLR	Slingsby T 67C Firefly	2011		19. 7.84	R L Brinklow	Exeter	17. 3.08E
	(Lycoming O-320) *(Regd as "T 67B (mod)")*						
G-BLLS	Slingsby T 67B Firefly	2013		19. 7.84	Freedom Aviation Ltd	RAF Lyneham	12. 7.08E
G-BLLW	Colt 56B Balloon (Hot Air)	578		11. 9.84	G Fordyce, R Wickens and S A Sawyer	Olney	7. 5.08A
					"Angel Clare"		
G-BLLZ	Rutan LongEz	PFA 074A-10830		16. 7.84	R S Stoddart-Stones	(Woldingham, Caterham)	22. 6.94P
	(Built G E Relf, D G Machin and E F Braddon) (Lycoming O-235)						
G-BLMA	Moravan Zlin Z-526 Trener Master	922	F-BORS	23. 7.84	G P Northcott	Redhill	26. 5.06
G-BLME	Robinson R22HP	0032	N90261	16. 4.85	Heli Air Ltd	Denham	17. 1.08E
G-BLMG	Grob G109B	6322		27. 9.84	R W Littledale tr Mike Golf Syndicate	Enstone	16.11.07E
G-BLMI	Piper PA-18 Super Cub 95	18-2066	D-ENWI	5. 6.84	I Mackinnon tr G-BLMI Flying Group	White Waltham	12. 7.08P
	(L-18C-PI) *(Frame No.18-2086)*		R Neth AF R-55, 52-2466		*(As "52-2466:R-55" in R Neth AF c/s)*		
G-BLMN	Rutan LongEz	PFA 074A-10643		3. 7.84	S E Bowers tr G-BLMN Flying Group	Thruxton	8. 3.07P
	(Built Farrington and Farrington and officially regd as c/n PFA 074A-10648) (Lycoming O-235)						
G-BLMP	Piper PA-17 Vagabond	17-193	F-BFMR	15. 5.84	D and M Shrimpton	Watchford Farm, Yarcombe	29. 6.08P
	(Continental C90)		N4893H				
G-BLMR	Piper PA-18-150 Super Cub (L-18C-PI)	18-2057	PH-NLD	29. 5.84	Limadelta Aviation Ltd	Shoreham	8. 9.08E
	(Lycoming O-320) *(Frame No.18-2070)*		R Neth AF R-72, 52-2457				
G-BLMT	Piper PA-18-135 Super Cub	18-2706	D-ELGH	12. 9.84	I S Runnalls	Enstone	14.11.10E
	(Frame No.18-2724)		N8558C				
G-BLMW	Nipper T 66 Series 3	PFA 025-11020		31. 8.84	S L Millar	Crowland	5.12.07P
	(Built S L Millar) (Ardem 10)						
G-BLMZ	Colt 105A Balloon (Hot Air)	404		24. 9.84	Mandy D Dickinson *"Zulu"*	Bristol	28. 3.97A
G-BLNH	Pilatus Britten-Norman BN-2B-26 Islander	2187	D-IOLA	30. 8.07	B-N Group Ltd	Bembridge	
			G-BLNH				
G-BLNJ	Pilatus Britten-Norman BN-2B-26 Islander	2189		3. 9.84	Panhispanica Digital SL	(Madrid, Spain)	3.12.07E
G-BLNO	Clutton FRED Series III	PFA 029-10559		17.10.84	L W Smith	(Sale, Cheshire)	
	(Built L W Smith)						
G-BLOL	SNCAN Stampe SV-4A	SS-SV-R1		12. 2.85	T Moore t/a Skysport Engineering		
	(Officialy regd for rebuild of G-AXRP but restored as such)				*(New owner 1.06)*	Rotary Farm, Hatch	

G-BLOR	Piper PA-30 Twin Comanche	30-59	HB-LAE	19. 7.85	R L C Appleton	Wendover Farm, Sheepwash	21. 5.08E
			N7097Y, N10F				
G-BLOS	Cessna 185A Skywagon	185-0359	LN-BDS	17. 9.84	D C Minshaw	Sywell	20. 6.08E
			N4159Y				
G-BLOT	Colt 56B Balloon (Hot Air)	424		11. 9.84	H J Anderson *"Pathfinder"*	Oswestry	17. 7.96A
G-BLOV	Thunder Ax5-42 Series 1 Balloon (Hot Air)	590		11. 9.84	A G R Calder *"Puff The Magic Dragon"*	(California, US)	29.11.02A
G-BLPA	Piper J-3C-65 Cub (L-4H-PI)	11327	OO-AJL	27. 9.84	A C Frost	Rectory Farm, Abbotsley	26. 8.08P
	(Frame No.11152)		OO-JOE, 43-30036				
G-BLPB	Turner TSW Hot Two Wot	PFA 046-10606		19.10.84	I R Hannah	Shoreham	25. 7.08P
	(J R Woolford and K M Thomas) (Lycoming O-320-A)						
G-BLPE	Piper PA-18 Super Cub 95 (L-18C-PI)	18-3084	D-ECBE	28. 9.84	A A Haig-Thomas	Thorpe-le-Soken	11. 7.08P
	(Continental O-200-A) (Also quoted as 18-3083)		Belgian Army L-10, 53-4684				
G-BLPF	Reims FR172G Rocket	FR17200187	N4594Q	29. 1.85	P Kohl	Southend	2. 5.06T
			D-EEFL		*(Noted 1.08)*		
G-BLPG	Auster J/1N Alpha	3395	G-AZIH	21. 5.82	P J Gill t/a Annic Marketing	Carlisle	29. 6.08
					(As "16693:693" in RCAF c/s)		
G-BLPH	Cessna FRA.150L Aerobat	FRA1500239	EI-BHH	19. 9.84	N P Lake	Farley Farm, Romsey	25. 2.08
	(Built Reims Aviation SA)		PH-ASH				
G-BLPI	Slingsby T 67B Firefly	2016		24. 9.84	The Pathfinder Flying Club Ltd	RAF Wyton	6. 3.08E
G-BLPM	Aérospatiale AS.332L Super Puma	2122	LN-ONB	5.10.84	Bristow Helicopters Ltd	Aberdeen	27. 7.08E
			G-BLPM, C-GQCB, G-BLPM				
G-BLPP	Cameron V-77 Balloon (Hot Air)	432		19. 9.78	R J Gooch	Alresford	23. 3.08A
G-BLRA	British Aerospace BAe 146 Series 100	E1017	N117TR	3.10.84	BAE Systems (Operations) Ltd	Warton	15.10.07E
			N462AP, CP-2249, N462AP, G-BLRA, G-5-02				
G-BLRC	Piper PA-18-135 Super Cub (L-21B-PI)	18-3602	OO-DKC	27.11.84	S Hornung tr Supercub Group	Seething	11. 3.10S
	(Frame No.18-3790)		PH-DKC, R NethAF R-112, 54-2402				
	(Original fuselage (Frame No: 18-3790) reported removed and used in 1984 rebuild of OO-POU (c/n 18-7860 ex-D-EHRY). If so then OO-DKC has no connection with the original aircraft or the fuselage frame was not used in the rebuild of OO-POU)						
G-BLRF	Slingsby T 67C Firefly	2014		30.11.84	R C Nicholls	Wellesbourne Mountford	21. 6.08T
G-BLRG	Slingsby T 67B Firefly	2020		30.11.84	R L Brinklow	(Buckingham)	17. 7.00T
					(Believed fuselage dumped pre 2007)		
G-BLRL	Scintex CP.301-C1 Emeraude	552	(G-BLNP)	5.11.84	J A Macleod and I M Macleod	Stornoway	16. 7.08P
			F-BJFT				
G-BLRM	Glaser-Dirks DG-400	4-107		5. 2.85	J A and W S Y Stephen	Aboyne	23. 4.08E
G-BLST	Cessna 421C Golden Eagle	421C0623	N88638	29.11.78	Cecil Aviation Ltd	Cambridge	10. 2.08E
G-BLTA	Colt 77A Coil Balloon (Hot Air)	525		8. 6.84	K A Schlussler *"James Sadler"*	Bourne, Lincoln	7. 8.91A
G-BLTC	Druine D 31A Turbulent	PFA 048-10964		18.12.84	S J Butler	(Henlow)	15. 5.08P
	(Built G P Smith and A W Burton) (Volkswagen 1600)						
G-BLTF	Robinson R22 Alpha	0428	N8526A	10. 1.85	Brian Seedle Helicopters Ltd	Blackpool	5. 4.04T
					(Noted 10.07)		
G-BLTK	Rockwell Commander 112TC-A	13106	SE-GSD	11.12.84	T A Stoate and I M Mackay tr Commander TC Group	Blackbushe	6. 6.08
G-BLTM	Robin HR.200-100 Club Club	96	F-GAEC	21.11.84	J S Swale tr Barton Robin Group	Barton	15. 1.07
G-BLTN	Thunder Ax7-65 Balloon (Hot Air)	621		4. 1.85	A H Symonds	Little Leighs, Chelmsford	13. 4.08A
G-BLTR	Scheibe SF25B Falke	4823	D-KHEC	23. 1.85	V Mallon	(Kleve-Wisseler Dünen, Germany)	1. 4.94
	(Built Sportavia-Pützer) (Stark-Stamo MS1500)						
G-BLTS	Rutan LongEz	PFA 074A-10741		14. 1.85	R W Cutler	(Thorverton, Exeter)	
	(Built R W Cutler)						
G-BLTW	Slingsby T 67B Firefly	2026		16. 1.85	R L Brinklow	Hinton-in-the-Hedges	15. 9.06T
G-BLTY	Westland WG.30 Series 160	019	VT-EKG	14. 1.85	D Brem-Wilson	(Joydens Farm, Westerham)	
			G-17-9, G-BLTY, G-17-19		*(Amended owner 8.04)*		
G-BLUI	Thunder Ax7-65 Balloon (Hot Air)	553		22. 2.85	S Jones *"Rhubarb and Custard"*	Thornton-Cleveleys	31. 7.00A
G-BLUM	Aérospatiale SA.365N Dauphin 2	6101		21. 1.85	CHC Scotia Ltd	Blackpool	14. 4.08E
G-BLUN	Aérospatiale SA.365N Dauphin 2	6114	PH-SSS	21. 1.85	CHC Scotia Ltd	Blackpool	5. 3.08E
			G-BLUN		*(Crashed into Morecambe Bay 27.12.06 and substantially damaged)*		
G-BLUV	Grob G109B	6336		1. 2.85	S K D'Urso and J Bailey tr The 109 Flying Group	North Weald	6.12.07E
G-BLUX	Slingsby T 67M-200 Firefly	2027	G-7-145	31. 1.85	R L Brinklow t/a Richard Brinklow Aviation	Rochester	27. 4.07T
			G-BLUX, G-7-113				
G-BLUZ	de Havilland DH.82B Queen Bee	1435 & SAL.150	LF858	9. 4.85	C I Knowles and J Flynn tr The Bee Keepers Group		
					(As "LF858" in RAF c/s)	RAF Henlow	7.11.07P
G-BLVA	Airtour AH-31 Balloon (Hot Air)	AH.004		12. 2.86	A van Wyk *(Noted active 11.02)* Caxton, Cambridge		
G-BLVB	Airtour AH-56 Balloon (Hot Air)	AH.005		12. 2.86	J J Daly	Halfway House, County Waterford	
					(New owner 6.07)		
G-BLVI	Slingsby T 67M Firefly II	2017	(PH-KIF)	1. 2.85	Brooke Park Ltd	(Darlington)	20. 3.08E
			G-BLVI				
G-BLVK	Mudry CAP.10B	141	JY-GSR	11. 3.85	E K Coventry	Childerditch	17. 5.08E
G-BLVL	Piper PA-28-161 Warrior II	28-8416109	N43677	11. 2.85	TG Aviation Ltd	Manston	16. 5.08E
G-BLVS	Cessna 150M Commuter	15076869	EI-BLS	19. 2.85	R Collier	Fenland	14.12.07E
			N45356				
G-BLVW	Cessna F172H	F172-0422	D-ENQU	16. 5.85	R and D Holloway (Theydon Mount Nursery) Ltd		
	(Built Reims Aviation SA)				(Stapleford Tawney, Romford)		10. 7.00
G-BLWD	Piper PA-34-200T Seneca II	34-8070334	ZS-KKV	14. 3.85	Bencray Ltd	Blackpool	7. 5.05T
			ZS-XAT, N8253E		*(Noted 10.07)*		
G-BLWF	Robin HR.100-210 Safari II	183	F-BUSR	8. 3.85	Starguide Ltd *(Noted 2.08)*	North Weald	18.10.07E
G-BLWH	Fournier RF6-100	7	F-GADF	3. 4.85	I R March	Wycombe Air Park	5. 9.03
					(Noted stored dismantled 4.04)		
G-BLWP	Piper PA-38-112 Tomahawk	38-78A0367	OY-BTW	7. 6.85	J E Rowley	Hawarden	23.10.07T
G-BLWT	Evans VP-1 Series 2	PFA 062-10639		27. 3.85	N Clark	(New Milton)	30. 9.08P
	(Built G B O'Neill) (Volkswagen 1834)						
G-BLWV	Reims Cessna F152 II	F15201843	EI-BIN	25. 2.85	J S Develin and Z Islam	Redhill	27. 6.08E
					(Operated Redhill Flying Club)		
G-BLWY	Robin R2160	176	F-GCUV	15. 4.85	K D Boardman	Perth	6.12.07E
			SE-GXE				

G-BLXA	SOCATA TB-20 Trinidad	284	SE-IMO F-ODOH	11. 4.85	Trinidad Flyers Ltd	Blackbushe	27. 9.08E
G-BLXG	Colt 21A Cloudhopper Balloon (Hot Air)	605		2. 5.85	A Walker *"Britannia Park"*	Richmond, Surrey	6. 5.98A
G-BLXH	Fournier RF3	39	F-BMDQ	25. 3.85	J E Dallison	(Thatcham)	24.10.08P
G-BLXI (2)	Scintex CP.1310-C3 Super Emeraude	937	F-BMJI	1. 4.85	R Howard	Grove Moor Farm, Grassthorpe	11. 4.08P
G-BLXO	SAN Jodel D 150 Mascaret	10	F-BLDB	9. 5.85	P R Powell *(Noted 11.06)*	Shobdon	6.11.08P
G-BLXP	Piper PA-28R-200 Cherokee Arrow II 28R-7235200		N5226T	29. 7.85	M B Hamlett	Le Plessis-Belleville, France	5. 8.08E
G-BLXR	Aérospatiale AS.332L Super Puma	2154		14. 5.85	Bristow Helicopters Ltd *"Cromarty"*	Aberdeen	1. 7.08E
G-BLYD	SOCATA TB-20 Trinidad	518		1. 5.85	Yankee Delta Corporation Ltd	Biggin Hilll	23. 3.08E
G-BLYE	SOCATA TB-10 Tobago	521		1. 5.85	Silverstar Aviation Ltd	Blackpool	6. 6.07T
G-BLYK	Piper PA-34-220T Seneca III	34-8433083	N4371J	30. 5.85	Fly (CI) Ltd *(Operated Trans Euro Air)*	Southend	6. 1.08E
G-BLYP	Robin R3000/120	109		15. 5.85	Weald Air Services Ltd *(Noted dismantled 8.05)*	Headcorn	5. 5.01T
G-BLYT	Airtour AH-77 Balloon (Hot Air)	AH.008		7. 7.87	I J Taylor and R C Kincaid *"Signal 2"*	Bristol	9. 8.03A
G-BLZA	Scheibe SF25B Falke (Sauer S1800S)	4684	D-KBAJ	22. 5.85	G W L Howarth tr Zulu Alpha Syndicate	RAF Halton	4.12.07E
G-BLZE	Reims Cessna F152 II	F15201579	G-CSSC PH-AYF (2)	3. 5.85	Redhill Aviation Ltd *(Operated Redhill Flying Club)*	Redhill	25. 6.08E
G-BLZF	Thunder Ax7-77 Balloon (Hot Air)	660		3. 6.85	H M Savage *"Hector"*	Edinburgh	10. 9.03A
G-BLZH	Reims Cessna F152 II	F15201965		21. 6.85	P D'Costa	(London N11)	13. 6.08E
G-BLZN	Bell 206B-2 JetRanger II	314	ZS-HMV C-GWDH, N1408W	12. 7.85	E Miles	Biggin Hill	26.10.07E
G-BLZP	Reims Cessna F152 II	F15201959		10. 7.85	East Midlands Flying School Ltd	East Midlands	18. 1.08E
G-BLZS	Cameron O-77 Balloon (Hot Air)	479		22. 5.85	C D Steel	St Boswells, Melrose	26.11.04A

G-BMAA - G-BMZZ

G-BMAD	Cameron V-77 Balloon (Hot Air)	1166		10. 6.85	M A Stelling *"Nautilus" (Inflated 4.06)*	Barton-le-Clay, Bedford	29. 9.99A
G-BMAL	Sikorsky S-76A II Plus	760120	F-WZSA G-BMAL	27.11.80	CHC Scotia Ltd	Humberside	9. 5.08E
G-BMAO	Taylor JT.1 Monoplane *(Built V A Wordsworth)*	PFA 1411		29. 7.85	S J Alston	Hinton-in-the-Hedges	19.11.07P
G-BMAX	Clutton FRED Series II	PFA 029-10322		20.12.78	D A Arkley	(Little Green, Chelmsford)	24. 8.99P
	(Built P Cawkwell and D A Arkley) (Volkswagen 1834)						
G-BMAY	Piper PA-18-135 Super Cub *(L-21B-PI) (Frame No.18-3961)*	18-3925	OO-LWB "EI-229", I-EIJZ, MM54-2525, 54-2525	3. 7.85	R W Davies	Little Robhurst Farm, Woodchurch	10. 1.08T
G-BMBB	Reims Cessna F150L	F15001136	OO-LWM PH-GAA	2. 8.85	G.P.Robinson	Netherthorpe	21. 1.08E
G-BMBJ	Schempp-Hirth Janus CM	20/209	(G-BLZL)	9. 9.85	M Critchlow tr BJ Flying Group *"BJ"*	RAF Keevil	30. 6.08E
G-BMBS	Colt 105A Balloon (Hot Air)	704		18. 7.85	H G Davies	Cheltenham	27. 8.91A
G-BMBW	Bensen B 8MR	MV-001		27. 8.85	M E Vahdat-Hagh	(Uxbridge)	30. 6.93P
	(Built M E Vahdat-Hagh - pr.no.PFA G/01-1064) (Rotax 503)						
G-BMBZ	Scheibe SF25E Super Falke (Limbach SL1700)	4322	D-KEFQ	17. 7.85	K E Ballington	Yeatsall Farm, Abbots Bromley	26. 9.08E
G-BMCC	Thunder Ax7-77 Balloon (Hot Air)	705		12. 7.85	A K and C.M Russell *"Charlie Charlie"*	Wheaton Aston, Stafford	23. 2.99A
G-BMCD	Cameron V-65 Balloon (Hot Air)	1234		26. 6.85	R Lillyman	Irchester, Wellingborough	21. 4.07A
G-BMCG	Grob G109B	6362	(EAF673)	25. 7.85	Lagerholm Finnimport Ltd	Wycombe Air Park	15. 6.08E
G-BMCI	Reims Cessna F172H	F17200683	OO-WID	19. 8.85	A B Davis *(Operated Edinburgh Flying Club)*	Edinburgh	1. 2.08E
G-BMCN	Reims Cessna F152 II	F15201471	D-ELDM	7. 8.85	M C R Wills	Doncaster-Sheffield	9. 3.07T
	(Noted with Marshall Aerospace Engineering College 11.07 as Instructional airframe)						
G-BMCS	Piper PA-22-135 Tri-Pacer	22-1969	5Y-KMH VP-KMH, ZS-DJI	6. 9.85	T A Hodges *(New owner 2.08)*	(Brynteg)	15. 7.01
G-BMCV	Reims Cessna F152 II	F15201963		2.10.85	The Leicestershire Aero Club Ltd	Leicester	7. 6.08E
G-BMCW	Aérospatiale AS.332L Super Puma	2161	F-WYMG G-BMCW	4.10.85	Bristow Helicopters Ltd *"Monifieth"*	(China)	7.11.07E
G-BMCX	Aérospatiale AS.332L Super Puma	2164		7.10.85	Bristow Helicopters Ltd *"Lossiemouth"*	(Kenya)	14.11.07T
G-BMDB	Replica Plans SE.5a *(Built D Biggs) (Continental O-200-A)*	PFA 020-10931		12. 8.85	D Biggs *(As "F235:B" in RFC c/s)*	Lee-on-Solent	21. 5.08P
G-BMDC	Piper PA-32-301 Saratoga	32-8006075	OO-PAC OO-HKK, N8242A	13. 8.85	TGD Leasing Ltd	Wellesbourne Mountford	12.11.07E
G-BMDE	Pietenpol AirCamper *(Built D Silsbury) (Continental O-200-A)*	PFA 047-10989		12. 8.85	P B Childs	New Farm, Felton	18. 8.03P
G-BMDJ	Price Ax7-77S Balloon (Hot Air) *(Built T P Price - c/n TPB.1) (Regd as Price TPB.1)*	003		1. 8.85	R A Benham *"Wings of Phoenix" (New owner 10.01)*	Burton-on-Trent	
G-BMDK	Piper PA-34-220T Seneca III	34-8133155	ZS-LOS N84209, N9553N	16. 9.85	Air Medical Fleet Ltd	Oxford	22.12.07E
G-BMDP	Partenavia P64B Oscar 200	08	HB-EPQ	20. 8.85	S T G Lloyd	Cardiff	21. 7.08S
G-BMDS	Wassmer Jodel D 120 Paris-Nice	281	F-BMOS	12. 8.85	R T Mosforth	Netherthorpe	6. 4.08P
G-BMEA	Piper PA-18 Super Cub 95 *(L-18C-PI)*	18-3204	(D-ECZF) Belg AF OL-L07, L-130, 53-4804	27. 8.85	M J Butler	Spanhoe	3.12.08P
	(Frame No. reported as 18-3206 [c/n 18-3194 ex OL-L20/L-120/53-4794]: c/n 18-3204 has Frame No.18-3216)						
G-BMEE	Cameron O-105 Balloon (Hot Air)	1189		4. 9.85	A G R Calder	Los Angeles, CA, US	8.10.89A
G-BMEH	Jodel D 150 Special Super Mascaret	PFA 151-11047		15. 8.85	R J and C J Lewis	Garston Farm, Marshfield	21. 5.08P
	(Built E J Horsfall as rebuild of incomplete SAN Jodel D 150 Mascaret c/n 62) (Lycoming O-235) "Noir Coupar"						
G-BMET	Taylor JT.1 Monoplane *(Built M Blythe)*	PFA 1465		4. 9.85	M K A Blyth	Little Gransden	2. 5.08P
G-BMEU	Isaacs Fury II *(Built G R G Smith) (Salmson 90hp)*	PFA 011-10179		11. 9.85	I G Harrison *(90% complete 6.99: new owner 11.02)*	Derby	
G-BMEX	Cessna A150K Aerobat	A1500169	N8469M	18. 9.85	R Barry	Shoreham	2. 6.08E

Reg	Type	C/n	Prev ID	Date	Owner/Operator	Base	Date
G-BMFD	Piper PA-23-250 Aztec F	27-7954080	N6834A, N9741N	6. 9.79	Air Partner Private Jets Ltd	Cambridge	14. 4.08E
G-BMFG	Dornier Do.27A-1	27-1003-342	FAP 3460 AC+955	23. 9.85	R F Warner (Whittington, King's Lynn) *(On rebuild 2.99)*		
G-BMFI	PZL-Bielsko SZD-45A Ogar	B-657		23. 9.85	S L Morrey	Andreas, Isle of Man	30. 5.08E
G-BMFP	Piper PA-28-161 Warrior II	28-7916243	N3032L	1.11.85	T J Froggatt and C A Lennard tr Bravo Mike Fox Papa Group	Blackbushe	8. 8.08E
G-BMFU	Cameron N-90 Balloon (Hot Air)	628		1.10.85	J J Rudoni	Great Haywood, Stafford	19. 5.03T
G-BMFY	Grob G109B	6401		8.10.85	P J Shearer	Kirkwall	20. 8.08E
G-BMFZ	Reims Cessna F152 II	F15201953		3.12.85	Cornwall Flying Club Ltd	Bodmin	12. 3.08E
G-BMGB	Piper PA-28R-200 Cherokee Arrow II	28R-7335099	N15864	8.11.85	A L Ings t/a Malmesbury Specialist Cars	Kemble	21. 4.08E
G-BMGG	Cessna 152 II	15279592	OO-ADB PH-ADB, D-EHUG, F-GBLM, N757AT	10.10.85	A S Bamrah t/a Falcon Flying Services	Biggin Hill	24.10.06T
G-BMGR	Grob G109B	6396		27.11.85	M Clarke tr BMGR Group	Lasham	18. 4.08E
G-BMHA	Rutan LongEz	PFA 074A-10973		18.10.85	S F Elvins	(Staple Hill, Bristol)	
	(Built S F Elvins)						
G-BMHC	Cessna U206F Stationair II	U20603427	N10TB G-BMHC, N8571Q	17.11.76	Performance Aviation Ltd t/a British Skysports Parachute Centre *(Fusealge noted 8.07)*	East Leys Farm, Grindale	19. 2.07T
G-BMHJ	Thunder Ax7-65 Series 1 Balloon (Hot Air)	743		2. 1.86	M G Robinson *"Kittylog"*	Great Milton, Oxford	19. 5.92A
G-BMHL	Wittman W.8 Tailwind	PFA 031-10503		28.11.85	O M Nash	Barton Ashes	25. 5.08P
	(Built T G Hoult)						
G-BMHS	Reims Cessna F172M	F17200964	PH-WAB	7. 4.86	R A Hall tr Tango Xray Flying Group	Rayne Hall Farm, Braintree	21. 7.08E
G-BMHT	Piper PA-28RT-201T Turbo Arrow IV	28R-8231010	ZS-LCJ N8462Y	18.11.85	G Lungley and P A Lamming tr G-BMHT Flying Group	Sherburn-in-Elmet	17. 7.08E
G-BMID	Wassmer Jodel D 120 Paris-Nice	259	F-BMID	18. 8.81	P E S Latham tr G-BMID Flying Group	RAF Shawbury	13. 4.08P
G-BMIG	Cessna 172N Skyhawk II	17272376	ZS-KGI (N48630)	13. 5.86	R B Singleton-McGuire tr BMIG Group	Elstree	21. 7.07T
G-BMIM	Rutan LongEz	8102/160	OY-CMT OY-8102	12.12.85	R M Smith	Biggin Hill	13. 2.08P
	(Built K A I Christensen) (Lycoming O-235)						
G-BMIO	Stoddard-Hamilton Glasair RG	PFA 149-11016		25.11.85	P Bint and L McMahon	Kemble	8 7.08P
	(Buillt A H Carrington) (Lycoming O-360)						
G-BMIP	Wassmer Jodel D 112	1264	F-BMIP	7.12.78	F J E Brownsill	(Fairford)	14. 3.08P
G-BMIS	Monnett Sonerai II	755	VR-HIS	26. 2.87	S R Edwards	Kemble	24. 9.08P
	(Built B A Bower - pr.no.PFA 015A-10813) (Revmaster R2100DQ)						
G-BMIV	Piper PA-28R-201T Turbo Arrow III	28R-7703154	ZS-JZW N5816V	7. 1.86	Firmbeam Ltd	Wycombe Air Park	12. 7.08
G-BMIW	Piper PA-28-181 Archer II	28-8190093	ZS-KTJ N8301J	6.12.85	Oldbus Ltd	Shoreham	28. 4.08E
G-BMIX	SOCATA TB-20 Trinidad	579	EI-BSV G-BMIX	5.12.85	Air Touring Ltd *(Noted as "EI-BSV" 6.07)*	Biggin Hill	
G-BMIY	Oldfield Baby Lakes	PFA 010-10194	G-NOME	3.12.85	J B Scott	(Thornton-Cleveleys)	27. 8.87P
	(Built J B Scott, Parkinson and Brown) (Continental O-200-A)						
G-BMJA	Piper PA-32R-301 Saratoga II SP	32R-8113019	ZS-KTH N8309E	23.12.85	H Merkado	Panshanger	18.10.07E
G-BMJC	Cessna 152 II	15284989	N623AP	3. 2.86	Northern Aviation Ltd	Durham Tees Valley	22. 8.08E
G-BMJD	Cessna 152 II	15279755	N757HP	21.11.85	Donair Flying Club Ltd	East Midlands	19 8.08E
G-BMJL	Rockwell Commander 114	14006	A2-JRI ZS-JRI, N1906J	8. 1.86	D J and S M Hawkins	(Woking)	20. 8.08E
G-BMJM	Evans VP-1	PFA 062-10763		21.11.85	S E Clarke *(Noted 2.07)*	Shenington	1. 9.05P
	(Built J A Mawby) (Volkswagen 1834)						
G-BMJN	Cameron O-65 Balloon (Hot Air)	1212		6.12.85	P M Traviss *"F'red"*	Yarm	11. 5.08A
G-BMJO	Piper PA-34-220T Seneca III	34-8533036	N6919K N9565N	5.12.85	Deep Cleavage Ltd	Exeter	5. 3.08E
G-BMJR	Cessna T337H Super Skymaster	33701895	G-NOVA N1259S	10. 7.84	Eastcote Services Ltd	Sturgate	27.10.07E
G-BMJX	Wallis WA-116/X Series 1	K/219/X		31.12.85	K H Wallis *(Stored 8.01)*	Reymerston Hall, Norfolk	1. 4.89P
	(Limbach L-2000)						
G-BMJY	SPP Yakovlev Yak C-18A	?	(France) Egypt AF 627	21. 1.86	R J Lamplough *(As "07" (yellow) in Russian AF c/s)*	Manor Farm, East Garston	27.11.01P
G-BMJZ	Cameron N-90 Balloon (Hot Air)	1219		16.12.85	P Spellward tr Bristol University Hot Air Ballooning Society *"Uvistat" (Inflated 7.06)*	Bristol	31. 3.94A
G-BMKB	Piper PA-18-135 Super Cub	18-3817	OO-DKB PH-DKB, (PH-GRP), R Neth AF R-127, 54-2417	11.12.85	Cubair Flight Training Ltd	Redhill	3. 7.06T
	(L-21B-PI) (Frame No.18-3818)						
G-BMKC	Piper J-3C-65 Cub (L-4H-PI)	11145	F-BFBA 43-29854	2. 1.86	E P Parkin *(As "329854:R-44" in USAAC 533rd BS/381st Bomb Group c/s) "Little Rockette Jnr"*	Derby	22.10.08P
	(Continental C90)(Frame No.10970)						
G-BMKD	Beech C90A King Air	LJ-1069	N223CG N67516	30.12.85	A E Bristow	Fairoaks	13. 4.08E
G-BMKF	CEA Jodel DR.221 Dauphin	96		3. 2.86	S T and Lynda.J Gilbert	Enstone	22. 3.08
G-BMKG	Piper PA-38-112 Tomahawk II	38-82A0050	ZS-LGC N91544	3. 2.86	Glasgow Aviation Ltd	Perth	15.12.07E
G-BMKI	Colt 21A Cloudhopper Balloon (Hot Air)	753		30.12.85	A C Booth	Bristol	31.12.04A
G-BMKJ	Cameron V-77 Balloon (Hot Air)	1235		2. 1.86	R C Thursby	Barry	7. 4.08A
G-BMKK	Piper PA-28R-200 Cherokee Arrow II	28R-7535265	ZS-JNY N9537N	16. 1.86	P M Murray *(Noted 2.08)*	Bagby	5. 4.07T
G-BMKP	Cameron V-77 Balloon (Hot Air)	724	(G-BMFX)	10. 1.86	R Bayly *"And Baby Makes 10" (Noted 8.02)*	Clutton, Bristol	7. 8.93A
G-BMKR	Piper PA-28-161 Warrior II	28-7916220	G-BGKR N9561N	14. 6.84	D R Shrosbee tr Field Flying Group	Goodwood	5. 6.08E
G-BMKY	Cameron O-65 Balloon (Hot Air)	1246		4. 3.86	A R Rich *"Orion"*	Hyde	24. 4.08A
G-BMLB	Wassmer Jodel D 120A Paris-Nice	295	F-BNCI	20. 1.86	C A Croucher	Headcorn	19. 6.08P

Reg	Type	C/n	Prev ID	Date	Owner/Operator	Base	Date
G-BMLJ	Cameron N-77 Balloon (Hot Air)	1263		7. 3.86	C J Dunkley t/a Wendover Trailers *"Mr Funshine"*	Aylesbury	28. 3.08A
G-BMLK	Grob G109B	6424		24. 2.86	J J Mawson tr Brams Syndicate	Rufforth	11. 6.08E
G-BMLL	Grob G109B	6420		13. 3.86	C Rupasinha tr G-BMLL Flying Group	Denham	25. 8.08E
G-BMLM	Beech 95-58 Baron	TH-405	N111LM	2. 7.79	Atlantic Bridge Aviation Ltd	Lydd	22. 5.08E
			G-BMLM, F-GEPV, 3D-ADF, ZS-LOZ, G-BMLM, G-BBJF				
G-BMLS	Piper PA-28R-201 Cherokee Arrow III 28R-7737167		N47496	11. 2.86	R M Shorter	Wycombe Air Park	24. 4.08E
G-BMLT	Pietenpol AirCamper PFA 047-10949 *(Built R A and F Hawke)* (Continental C90)			28. 1.86	W E R Jenkins	Waits Farm, Belchamp Walter	20. 6.08P
G-BMLW	Cameron O-77 Balloon (Hot Air)	813		6. 2.86	M L and L P Willoughby *"Stelrad"*	Woodcote, Reading	7. 8.95A
G-BMLX	Reims Cessna F150L	F15000700	PH-VOV	21. 3.86	J P A Freeman	Headcorn	27. 1.08E
G-BMMF	Clutton FRED Series II PFA 029-10296 *(Built J M Jones)* (Volkswagen 1834)			20. 2.86	R C Thomas *(New owner 9.05)*	(Llantwit Major)	18. 7.03P
G-BMMI	Pazmany PL-4A PFA 017-10149 *(Built M L Martin)* (Continental PC 60)			6. 2.86	P I Morgans *(Noted 11.05)*	Haverfordwest	18. 7.03P
G-BMMK	Cessna 182P Skylane II 18264117 *(Reims-assembled c/n F18200038)*		OO-AVU N6129F	24. 3.86	G G Weston	Denham	7.10.07E
G-BMMM	Cessna 152 II	15284793	N4652P	10. 9.86	A S Bamrah t/a Falcon Flying Services	Fairoaks	22.11.07E
G-BMMP	Grob G109B	6432		27. 6.86	E W Reynolds tr G-GBMMP Syndicate	Tatenhill	24. 5.08E
G-BMMV	ICA IS-28M2A	57		10. 3.86	C D King	Trenchard Farm, Eggesford	10.12.07E
G-BMMW	Thunder Ax7-77 Balloon (Hot Air)	782		10. 3.86	P A George *"Ethos"*	Princes Risborough	3. 6.96A
G-BMMY	Thunder Ax7-77 Balloon (Hot Air)	716		11. 3.86	S M Wade and S E Hadley *"Winco"*	Salisbury	7. 4.08A
G-BMNL	Piper PA-28R-200 Cherokee Arrow II 28R-7535040		N32280 (N18MW), N32280	17. 9.86	Elston Ltd tr Arrow Flying Group	Elstree	30. 5.08E
G-BMNV	SNCAN Stampe SV-4C	108	F-BBNI	14. 3.86	Wessex Aviation and Transport Ltd *(Noted 5.05)*	Haverfordwest	29. 8.03P
G-BMOE	Piper PA-28R-200 Cherokee Arrow II 28R-7635226		PH-PCB OO-HAS, N9221K	20. 5.86	Piper Leasing Ltd	Exeter	16.11.07E
G-BMOF	Cessna U206G Stationair 6	U20603658	N7427N	17. 4.86	D M Penny tr Wild Geese Skydiving Centre	(Movenis, Coleraine)	23. 3.08E
G-BMOG	Thunder Ax7-77 Balloon (Hot Air)	793		2. 4.86	R M Boswell	Bawburgh, Norwich	28. 8.95A
G-BMOH	Cameron N-77 Balloon (Hot Air)	1270		2. 4.86	P J Marshall and M A Clarke *"Ellen Gee"*	Rye and Wokingham	24.11.03A
G-BMOI	Partenavia P68B	103	I-EEVA	4. 4.86	Simmette Ltd	Exeter	4. 7.08
G-BMOK	ARV Aviation ARV-1 Super 2	011		14. 4.86	R E Griffiths	Stoke, Isle of Grain	31. 8.07E
G-BMOM	ICA IS-28M2A	50		30. 6.86	M E Todd	Sandtoft	12. 1.08
	(Rebuilt 2001 with forward fuselage of G-BKAB)						
G-BMOT	Bensen B 8M PFA G/01-1066 *(Built R S W Jones)* (Volkswagen 1834)			17. 4.86	A J Thomas *(New owner 9.07)*	(Sutton Coldfield)	13. 8.01P
G-BMOV	Cameron O-105 Balloon (Hot Air)	1307		11. 4.86	C Gillott *"Up and Down"*	Stroud	1. 7.99A
G-BMPC	Piper PA-28-181 Cherokee Archer II 28-7790436		LN-NAT	23. 4.86	C J and R J Barnes	East Midlands	15. 3.08E
G-BMPD	Cameron V-65 Balloon (Hot Air)	1200		4. 6.86	D Triggs	Alresford	6. 4.07A
G-BMPL	Optica OA.7 Optica	016		14. 4.86	J K Edgley *(New owner 1.08)*	Thruxton	2. 8.97T
G-BMPP	Cameron N-77 Balloon (Hot Air)	1303		15. 4.86	P F Smart tr The Sarnia Balloon Group *"Tuppence" (Inflated 4.06)*	Oakley, Basingstoke	14. 5.93A
G-BMPR	Piper PA-28R-201 Arrow III 28R-7837175		ZS-LMF N417GH	22. 4.86	T J Brammer and D T Colley	(London SE5)	6. 6.08E
G-BMPS	Strojnik S-2A 045 *(Built T J Gardiner)*			18. 4.86	G J Green	(Darley Bridge, Matlock)	
G-BMPY	de Havilland DH.82A Tiger Moth	"82619"	ZS-CNR SAAF??	25. 4.86	N M Eisenstein	Sandford Hall, Knockin	3. 5.08
G-BMRA	Boeing 757-236	23710		2. 3.87	DHL Air Ltd	Brussels, Belgium	2. 8.08E
G-BMRB	Boeing 757-236	23975		25. 9.87	DHL Air Ltd	Brussels, Belgium	29. 9.08E
G-BMRC	Boeing 757-236	24072	(N....)	2.12.87	DHL Air Ltd	Brussels, Belgium	26. 1.07T
G-BMRD	Boeing 757-236	24073	(N....) G-BMRD	2.12.87	DHL Air Ltd	East Midlands	3. 3.08E
G-BMRE	Boeing 757-236	24074	(N)	2.12.87	DHL Air Ltd	East Midlands	28. 4.08E
G-BMRF	Boeing 757-236	24101		13. 5.88	DHL Air Ltd	Brussels, Belgium	17. 5.08E
G-BMRH	Boeing 757-236	24266		21. 2.89	DHL Air Ltd	Brussels, Belgium	29. 2.08E
G-BMRJ	Boeing 757-236	24268		6. 3.89	DHL Air Ltd	Brussels, Belgium	13. 3.08E
G-BMSA	Stinson HW-75 Voyager	7040	G-BCUM F-BGQO, NC21189	26. 3.86	M A Thomas tr The Stinson Group *"Iron Eagle" (On major overhaul 1.07)*	Barton	9. 9.05P
G-BMSB	Vickers Supermarine 509 Spitfire Tr.9 CBAF.7722		G-ASOZ IAC158, G-15-171, MJ627	3. 5.78	M S Bayliss *(As "MJ627:9G-P" in RAF 441 Sqdn c/s)*	RAF Coningsby	25. 4.08P
G-BMSC	Evans VP-2 V2-482MSC *(Built Youth Opportunity Project -pr.no.PFA 063-10785)* (Volkswagen 1834)			25. 8.82	L G Hunt *(Noted 4.06)*	Sittles Farm, Alrewas	29. 4.05P
G-BMSD	Piper PA-28-181 Cherokee Archer II 28-7690070		EC-CVH N9646N	2. 7.86	H Merkado	Panshanger	21. 9.08E
G-BMSE	Valentin Taifun 17E	1082	D-KHVA(17)	20. 5.86	A Wiseman	Breighton	4. 6.08E
G-BMSF	Piper PA-38-112 Tomahawk	38-78A0524	N4277E	9. 2.79	B Catlow	Haverfordwest	13. 6.08E
G-BMSG	SAAB 32A Lansen	32028	Swedish AF Fv32028	22. 7.86	J E Wilkie *(Open store in bare-metal finish.1.06)*	Cranfield	
G-BMSL	Clutton FRED Series III PFA 029-11142 *(Built A C Coombe)*			19. 5.86	M J Veary	Long Marston	31. 8.06P
G-BMSU	Cessna 152 II	15279421	N714TN	29. 8.86	S Waite tr LBA Flying Group	(Sheffield City)	4. 7.08E
G-BMTA	Cessna 152 II	15282864	N89776	27. 8.86	ACS Aviation Ltd	Perth	2. 6.08E
G-BMTB	Cessna 152 II	15280672	N25457	19. 8.86	Sky Leisure Aviation (Charters) Ltd	Blackbushe	14. 9.08E
G-BMTC	Aérospatiale AS.355F1 Ecureuil 2	5302	G-EPOL G-SASU, G-BSSM, G-BMTC, G-BKUK	9.12.83	Sterling Helicopters Ltd	Norwich	12.11.10E
G-BMTJ	Cessna 152 II	15285010	N6389P	19. 6.86	The Pilot Centre Ltd	Denham	17. 6.08E
G-BMTN	Cameron O-77 Balloon (Hot Air)	1305		4. 6.86	Industrial Services (Material Handling) Ltd t/a Flete Rental *"Fletie"*	Westbury-on-Trym, Bristol	1. 6.97A

Reg	Type	C/n	Prev id	Date	Owner/Operator	Location	Date
G-BMTO	Piper PA-38-112 Tomahawk II	38-81A0051	N25679	28.11.86	A S Bamrah t/a Falcon Flying Services	Biggin Hill	11. 8.08E
G-BMTR	Piper PA-28-161 Warrior II	28-8116119	N83179	19. 6.86	Aeros Leasing Ltd	Gloucestershire	4. 4.08E
G-BMTU	Pitts S-1E	PFA 009-10801		4. 6.86	C Lambropoulos	(Kippax, Leeds)	25.11.08P
	(Built O R Howe)						
G-BMTX	Cameron V-77 Balloon (Hot Air)	733		19. 6.86	J A Langley	Stroud	7. 9.08A
	(Buses for Bristol titles) "Boondoggle"						
G-BMUD	Cessna 182P Skylane	18261786	OY-DVS N78847	6.11.81	Mescal E Taylor	RAF Waddington	31. 3.08E
G-BMUG	Rutan LongEz	PFA 074A-10987		17. 6.86	A G Sayers	RAF Kinloss	12. 1.06P
	(Built P Richardson) (Lycoming O-235)				(Noted 3.06)		
G-BMUO	Cessna A152 Aerobat	A1520788	4X-ALJ N7328L	4. 6.86	Sky Leisure Aviation (Charters) Ltd	Shoreham	14. 9.07T
G-BMUT	Piper PA-34-200T Seneca II	34-7570320	EC-CUH N3935X	23. 1.87	G-DAD Air Ltd	Cranfield	14.11.07E
G-BMUU	Thunder Ax7-77 Balloon (Hot Air)	827		1. 8.86	A R Hill	Rolvenden, Cranbrook	29.10.98A
					"Fiesta" (Noted 2005)		
G-BMUZ	Piper PA-28-161 Warrior II	28-8016329	EC-DMA N9559N	24. 7.86	Northumbria Flying School Ltd	Newcastle	5. 4.08E
G-BMVA	Scheibe SF25B Falke	46223	RAFGGA.512 D-KAEN	28. 7.86	M L Jackson	Rochester	5. 6.08
	(Limbach SL1700						
G-BMVB	Reims Cessna F152 II	F15201974		10. 9.86	M P Barnard	Cranfield	24. 4.08E
G-BMVG	QAC Quickie Q.1	PFA 094-10749		11. 6.86	P M Wright	Waldringfield, Woodbridge	1. 1.02P
	(Built P M Wright) (Rotax 503)				(Noted 2.06)		
G-BMVL	Piper PA-38-112 Tomahawk	38-79A0033	N2391B	5. 9.86	John Reynolds Racing Ltd	Tollerton	20.12.07E
G-BMVM	Piper PA-38-112 Tomahawk	38-79A0025	N2359B	5. 9.86	R Davitt and C J Wheeler tr Brimpton Flying Group		
						Lower Wasing Farm, Brimpton	4. 6.08T
G-BMVS	Cameron Benihana 70 SS Balloon (Hot Air)	1252		27.10.86	Benihana (UK) Ltd	London W1	9. 2.07A
	(Aka Chef''s Hat)						
G-BMVT	Thunder Ax7-77A Balloon (Hot Air)	102	SE-ZYY	15. 7.86	M L and L P Willoughby	Woolcote, Reading	
					"Trygg Hansa"		
G-BMVU	Monnett Moni	PFA 142-10948		14. 8.86	D Prentice	(Sheffield)	20. 9.99P
	(Built S R Lee) (KEF-107)				(New owner 6.07)		
G-BMVW	Cameron O-65 Balloon (Hot Air)	1331		27. 6.86	S P Richards "Olau Ferries"	Cranbrook	15. 8.91A
G-BMWA	Hughes 269C	14-0271	N8998F	1. 7.86	D G Lewendon	(Chantrigne, Mayenne, France)	19.12.07E
	(Hughes 300)						
G-BMWF	ARV Aviation ARV-1 Super 2	013		1. 7.86	G E Collard	(Frensham, Farnham)	2. 4.90T
					(New owner 11.06)		
G-BMWM	ARV Aviation ARV-1 Super 2	020		30. 3.87	G B Thomas	Wishanger Farm, Frensham	14. 8.06P
G-BMWR	Rockwell Commander 112A	365	N1365J	23. 9.86	M and J Edwards	Blackbushe	30. 1.08E
G-BMWU	Cameron N-42 Balloon (Hot Air)	1346		22.12.88	I Chadwick tr Balloon Preservation Group		
					(Helix Motor Oil titles)	Partridge Green, Horsham	8. 3.08E
G-BMWV	Putzer Elster B	024	D-EEKB 97+14, D-EBGI	5. 8.86	E A J Hibbard tr Magpie Group	Hill Farm, Nayland	27.10,06P
G-BMXA	Cessna 152 II	15280125	N757ZC	14. 7.86	ACS Aviation Ltd	Durham Tees Valley	28. 9.07E
					(New owner 1.08)		
G-BMXB	Cessna 152 II	15280996	N48840	14. 7.86	C I J Young	Leicester	13.12.07E
G-BMXC	Cessna 152 II	15280416	N24858	14. 7.86	MK Aero Support Ltd	Andrewsfield	2. 6.08E
G-BMXD	Fokker F 27 Friendship 500	10417	TF-FLR	6.10.86	BAC Group Ltd	Edinburgh	12.12.05E
				HL5210, (HL5206), PH-FOR	"Scottish Trader" (Dismantled - to Airport Fire Service 12.07)		
G-BMXJ	Reims Cessna F150L	F15000853	F-BUBA	18. 7.86	R Harman tr Arrow Aircraft Group	Tatenhill	20. 6.03
G-BMXM	Colt 180A Balloon (Hot Air)	838	(C-) G-BMXM	28. 7.86	D A Michaud	Edmonton, Alberta, Canada	20.12.04A
					(Noted 2005)		
G-BMXX	Cessna 152 II	15284953	N5469P	10. 9.86	Evensport Ltd (Noted 10.07)	Halfpenny Green	1. 9.02T
G-BMYC	SOCATA TB-10 Tobago	696		1. 9.86	E A Grady	Old Buckenham	9. 5.08E
G-BMYD	Beech A36 Bonanza	E-2350		28.11.86	Seabeam Partners Ltd	Wellesbourne Mountford	21. 3.08E
G-BMYF	Bensen B 8M	PE-01		18. 8.86	G Callaghan	Rich Hill, County Armagh	
	(Built P Entwistle)						
G-BMYG	Cessna FA152 Aerobat	FA1520365	OO-JCA	23.10.86	Greer Aviation Ltd	Prestwick	14. 6.08E
	(Built Reims Aviation SA)		(OO-JCC), PH-AXG				
G-BMYI	Grumman AA-5 Traveler	AA5-0568	EI-BJF	1. 9.86	W C and S C Westran	Shoreham	16. 2.07T
			F-BVRM, N9568L				
G-BMYJ	Cameron V-65 Balloon (Hot Air)	726		8. 9.86	S P Harrowing "Skylark II"	Port Talbot	23. 3.08A
G-BMYN	Colt 77A Balloon (Hot Air)	873		2. 9.86	J E Wetters and M H Read	Timperley, Altrincham	24. 3.07A
G-BMYS	Thunder Ax7-77Z Balloon (Hot Air)	887		3.11.86	J E Weidema	Baambrugge, Netherlands	1. 6.01A
					(Operated Pinkel Balloons)		
G-BMYU	Wassmer Jodel D 120 Paris-Nice	289	F-BMYU	23. 6.78	A J L Gordon (New owner 7.07)	(Bicester)	4.11.05P
G-BMZB	Cameron N-77 Balloon (Hot Air)	1370		30.10.86	D C Eager "Dreamland"	Bracknell	30. 4.95A
G-BMZN	Everett Gyroplane Series 1	008		13.11.86	K Ashford	(Walsall)	2.12.02P
	(Volkswagen 1835)						
G-BMZP	Everett Gyroplane Series 1	010		14.11.86	D H Kirton	(Wendover, Aylesbury)	10. 4.02P
	(Volkswagen 1835)				(Noted Henstridge 8.07)		
G-BMZS	Everett Gyroplane Series 1	012		13.11.86	L W Cload	St Merryn	6.11.06P
	(Volkswagen 1835)						
G-BMZW	Bensen B 8MR	PFA G/01-1021		16.10.86	P D Widdicombe	Huntingdon, York	25. 8.99P
	(Built P D Widdicombe) (Rotax 532)						
G-BMZX	Wolf W-11 Boredom Fighter	PFA 146-11042		31.10.86	J Nugent	Kilrush, County Kildare	10.12.04P
	(Built J Penney) (Continental A65)				(As "6-1042:7" in USAAC c/s)		

G-BNAA - G-BNZZ

Reg	Type	C/n	Prev id	Date	Owner/Operator	Location	Date
G-BNAG	Colt 105A Balloon (Hot Air)	906		31.10.86	R W Batchelor	Thame	19.12.89A
G-BNAI	Wolf W-11 Boredom Fighter	PFA 146-11083		31.10.86	C M Bunn	Haverfordwest	12. 4.08P
	(Built PJ Gronow to represent Spad replica) (Continental A65)				(As "5:146-11083" in USAAC c/s)		

G-BNAJ	Cessna 152 II	15282527	C-GZWF	3.11.86	Galair Ltd	Biggin Hill	11. 3.08E
			(N69173)		*(Operated Surrey and Kent Flying Club)*		
G-BNAN	Cameron V-65 Balloon (Hot Air)	1333		28.10.86	A M and N H Ponsford t/a Rango Balloon and Kite Company		
					"Actually" (Amended owners 8.07)	Leeds	7. 7.01A
G-BNAU	Cameron V-65 Balloon (Hot Air)	1395		13.11.86	T J Ellenrieder tr 4-Flight Group	Bristol	4.11.05E
G-BNAW	Cameron V-65 Balloon (Hot Air)	1366		24.10.86	A and P A Walker	Richmond, Surrey	24. 8.08A
					(HMS Recruitment titles) "Hippo-Thermia"		
G-BNBL	Thunder Ax7-77 Balloon (Hot Air)	910		7. 1.87	F W Ewer Lighthorne Heath, Leamington Spa		4.10.06A
G-BNBW	Thunder Ax7-77 Balloon (Hot Air)	914		11.12.86	I S and S W Watthews *"Mutley"*	Grange-over-Sands	9. 9.99A
G-BNBY	Beech 95-B55A Baron	TC-1347	G-AXXR	14. 2.83	J Butler	(Lisle Sur Tarn, France)	19. 7.08E
G-BNCB	Cameron V-77 Balloon (Hot Air)	1401		2.12.86	C W Brown	Melton Mowbray	25. 5.08A
G-BNCC	Thunder Ax7-77 Balloon (Hot Air)	924		11.12.86	C J Burnhope *"Charlie"*	(US)	9.10.99A
G-BNCJ	Cameron V-77 Balloon (Hot Air)	815		16.12.86	D Johnson *(New owner 12.06)*	Bromley	17.10.05A
G-BNCO	Piper PA-38-112 Tomahawk	38-79A0472	N2482F	8. 1.87	D K Walker	Gamston	20. 4.08E
G-BNCR	Piper PA-28-161 Warrior II	28-8016111	G-PDMT	10.12.86	Airways Aero Associations Ltd Wycombe Air Park		19. 5.08E
			ZS-LGW, N8103D		*(Operated British Airways Flying Club) (British Airways titles)*		
G-BNCS	Cessna 180	30022	OO-SPA	7. 1.87	C Elwell Transport (Repairs) Ltd	Tatenhill	17. 2.95
			D-ENUX, N2822A				
G-BNCU	Thunder Ax7-77 Balloon (Hot Air)	928		7. 1.87	W De Bock	Peterborough	14. 7.00A
G-BNDE	Piper PA-38-112 Tomahawk	38-79A0363	EI-BUR	13. 1.87	M Magrabi	Bournemouth	25. 4.08E
			G-BNDE, N2541D				
G-BNDG	Wallis WA-201/R Series 1	K/220/X		22. 1.87	K H Wallis	Reymerston Hall, Norfolk	3. 3.88P
	(Rotax 64hp x 2)				*(Stored 8.01)*		
G-BNDN	Cameron V-77 Balloon (Hot Air)	1443		8. 1.87	A Hornshaw	Ugborough, Ivybridge	21. 1.08A
G-BNDO	Cessna 152 II	15284574	N5387M	11. 2.87	Simair Ltd	Andrewsfield	6.10.07E
		(Crashed Wick Farm, Layer Marney, Colchester 11. 7.06 and badly damaged: wreck noted 9.07)					
G-BNDP	Brügger MB.2 Colibri	PFA 043-10956		8. 1.87	A C Barber	(Newmarket	30. 8.08P
	(Built M Black) (Volkswagen 1834)						
G-BNDR	SOCATA TB-10 Tobago	740		12. 2.87	Delta Fire Ltd	Norwich	15. 3.08E
G-BNDT	Brügger MB.2 Colibri	PFA 043-10981		8. 1.87	H Haigh tr Colibri Flying Group	Bagby	14. 7.08P
	(Built A Szep) (Volkswagen 1834)						
G-BNDV	Cameron N-77 Balloon (Hot Air)	1427		25. 2.87	R E Jones	Lytham St Annes	9. 5.93A
					(English Lake Hotels titles)		
G-BNDW	de Havilland DH.82A Tiger Moth	3942	N6638	10.12.86	N D Welch *(Noted 5.03)*	(Stafford)	
G-BNEE	Piper PA-28R-201 Arrow III	28R-7837084	N630DJ	28. 1.87	J W Reid tr Britannic Management Aviation		
			N9518N			Turweston	22.11.07
G-BNEK	Piper PA-38-112 Tomahawk II	38-82A0081	N9096A	28. 1.87	APB Leasing Ltd	Trehelig, Welshpool	17. 5.00T
G-BNEL	Piper PA-28-161 Warrior II	28-7916314	N2246U	27. 4.87	S C Westran	Shoreham	30.10.07E
G-BNEN	Piper PA-34-200T Seneca II	34-8070262	N8232V	18. 2.87	Jet Options Ltd	Coventry	25.10.07E
G-BNEO	Cameron V-77 Balloon (Hot Air)	1408		9. 2.87	J G O'Connell *"Rowtate"*	Braintree	2.11.00
G-BNEV	Viking Dragonfly	PFA 139-10935		28.11.86	N W Eyre	(Kirkbymoorside, York)	
	(Built N W Eyre) (Volkswagen 1834)						
G-BNFG	Cameron O-77 Balloon (Hot Air)	1416		5. 3.87	Capital Balloon Club Ltd *"Dolores"*	London NW1	13. 1.94A
G-BNFI	Cessna 150J	15069417	N50588	8. 1.87	A Waters	Enstone	5. 11.07E
G-BNFM	Colt 21A Cloudhopper Balloon (Hot Air)	668		5. 3.87	M E Dworski	Vermenton, France	24. 7.01A
G-BNFN	Cameron N-105 Balloon (Hot Air)	1442		13. 3.87	P Glydon	Barnt Green, Birmingham	17. 6.97T
G-BNFO	Cameron V-77 Balloon (Hot Air)	816		5. 3.87	T J Ellenrieder tr 4-Flight Group	Bristol	24. 3.08A
G-BNFP	Cameron O-84 Balloon (Hot Air)	1474		29. 4.87	M Clarke	Egham	25.11.07A
G-BNFR	Cessna 152 II	15282035	N67817	8. 4.87	A Jahanfar	Southend	29. 4.08E
					(Operated Seawing Flying Club)		
G-BNFS	Cessna 152 II	15283899	N5545B	10. 4.87	P J Clarke	Tatenhill	14. 7.08E
G-BNFV	Robin DR.400-120 Dauphin 80	1767		4. 3.87	J P A Freeman	Headcorn	11. 1.08E
G-BNGE	Auster AOP.6	1925	7704M	18. 3.87	M Pocock	AAC Netheravon	3. 7.08P
			TW536		*(As "TW536:T-SV" in RAF 657 AOP Sqdn c/s) (Operated Military Auster Flight)*		
G-BNGJ	Cameron V-77 Balloon (Hot Air)	1487		18. 3.87	Lathams Ltd *"Latham Timber"*	High Wycombe	15. 8.08A
G-BNGN	Cameron N-77 Balloon (Hot Air)	817		3. 4.87	N Dykes	Tostock, Bury St Edmunds	16. 4.08A
					"Falcon" (New owner 7.06)		
G-BNGO	Thunder Ax7-77 Balloon (Hot Air)	971		26. 3.87	J S Finlan tr The G-BNGO Group		
					"Thunderbird" (Philips titles) Hamilton, New Zealand		16. 4.06A
G-BNGT	Piper PA-28-181 Archer II	28-8590036	N149AV	29. 4.87	Edinburgh Flying Club Ltd	Edinburgh	18. 5.08E
			N9559N				
G-BNGV	ARV Aviation ARV-1 Super 2	021		4. 6.87	N A Onions *(Noted 8.07)*	(North End, Dunmow)	28. 4.06
G-BNGW	ARV Aviation ARV-1 Super 2	022		4. 6.87	Southern Gas Turbines Ltd	(Bognor Regis)	8. 7.90T
					(Stored 6.94)		
G-BNGY	ARV Aviation ARV-1 Super 2	019	(G-BMWL)	9. 6.87	S C Smith	Shobdon	25. 3.08P
G-BNHB	ARV Aviation ARV-1 Super 2	026		13. 7.87	C J Challener	Barton	23.11.06E
G-BNHG	Piper PA-38-112 Tomahawk II	38-82A0030	N91435	23. 3.87	D A Whitmore	Stornaway	31. 5.06T
					(Operated Highland Flying School: noted 2007)		
G-BNHI	Cameron V-77 Balloon (Hot Air)	1249		26. 3.87	C M Duggan *(Address change 5.07)*	Barlby, Selby	8. 9.05A
G-BNHJ	Cessna 152 II	15281249	N49418	4. 6.87	The Pilot Centre Ltd	Denham	19.12.07E
G-BNHK	Cessna 152 II	15285355	N80161	30. 3.87	N Houghton tr Wayfarers Flying Group		
						(South Normanton, Alfreton)	1. 8.08E
G-BNHT	Fournier RF3	80	(D-KITX)	13. 4.87	D G Hey tr G-BNHT Group	Little Gransden	27. 2.08P
			G-BNHT, F-BMT				
G-BNID	Cessna 152 II	15284931	N5378P	24. 4.87	MK Aero Support Ltd	Andrewsfield	5. 7.08E
G-BNII	Cameron N-90 Balloon (Hot Air)	1497		15. 4.87	S M Ratcliffe tr Topless Balloon Group		
						Lower Bourne, Farnham	13. 3.05
G-BNIK	Robin HR.200-120 Club	43	LX-AIK	15. 4.87	P A Guest tr G-BNIK Group	Leicester	23. 5.08E
			LX-PAA				
G-BNIM	Piper PA-38-112 Tomahawk	38-78A0148	N9631T	18. 6.87	Air Claire Ltd	Glasgow	30. 3.08E
G-BNIN	Cameron V-77 Balloon (Hot Air)	1079	G-RRSG (1)	15. 4.87	MJL Hilditch t/a Cloud Nine Balloon Group		
			(G-BLRO)		*"Cloud Nine"*	Southwick, Brighton	10. 6.02A
G-BNIO	Luscombe 8A Silvaire	2120	N45593	15. 4.87	R C Dyer	(Felixstowe)	17. 9.08P
	(Continental A75)		NC45593				

G-BNIP	Luscombe 8A Silvaire (Continental A65)	3547	N77820 NC77820	15. 4.87	M J Diggins	White Waltham	19.12.07P
G-BNIU	Cameron O-77 Balloon (Hot Air)	1499		28. 4.87	MC VH SA	Brussels, Belgium	22. 9.08A
G-BNIV	Cessna 152 II	15284866	N4972P	24. 4.87	Aerohire Ltd (Fuselage dumped 8.05)	Wellesbourne Mountford	17. 8.03T
G-BNIW	Boeing Stearman A75N1 (PT-17) Kaydet (Pratt and Whitney R985)	75-1526	N49291 41-7967	22. 4.87	R C Goold	East Winch	17. 7.10S
G-BNJB	Cessna 152 II	15284865	N4970P	27. 4.87	Aerolease Ltd	Conington	20. 7.08E
G-BNJC	Cessna 152 II	15283588	N4705B	27. 4.87	Stapleford Flying Club Ltd	Stapleford	26. 8.08E
G-BNJD	Cessna 152 II	15282044	N67833	27. 4.87	M Howells	Barton	6. 5.06T
G-BNJG	Cameron O-77 Balloon (Hot Air)	1502		9. 5.89	A M Figiel	High Wycombe	4. 4.97
G-BNJH	Cessna 152 II	15285401	C-GORA (N93101)	21. 7.87	ACS Aviation Ltd	Perth	23. 6.08E
G-BNJL	Bensen B 8MR (Built C G Ponsford) (Rotax 532)	PFA G/01-1020		30. 4.87	S Ram (New owner 2.04)	(Lowestoft)	29. 3.03P
G-BNJO	QAC Quickie Q.2 (Revmaster 2100D)	2217	N17LM	6.10.87	J D McKay	(Exeter Street, North Tawton)	14. 5.93P
G-BNJR	Piper PA-28RT-201T Turbo Arrow IV	28R-8031104	N8212U	8. 5.87	D Crocker	Blackbushe	27. 9.08E
G-BNJT	Piper PA-28-161 Warrior II	28-8116184	N8360T	11. 6.87	M Jones tr Hawarden Flying Group	Hawarden	15. 1.08E
G-BNJZ	Cassutt Racer IIIM (Built Miller Aerial Spraying)	PFA 034-11228		14. 5.87	J Cull	Popham	17. 5.08P
G-BNKC	Cessna 152 II	15281036	N48894	26. 5.87	Herefordshire Aero Club Ltd	Shobdon	14.12.07E
G-BNKD	Cessna 172N Skyhawk II	17272329	N4681D	19. 5.87	Barnes Olson Aero Leasing Ltd (Operated Bristol Flying Centre)	Bristol	2. 4.08E
G-BNKE	Cessna 172N Skyhawk II	17273886	N6534J	20. 5.87	T Jackson tr Kilo Echo Flying Group	Barton	3. 6.08E
G-BNKH	Piper PA-38-112 Tomahawk II	38-81A0078	N25874	14. 5.87	Goodwood Road Racing Company Ltd (Operated Goodwood Flying Club)	Goodwood	10. 8.08E
G-BNKI	Cessna 152 II	15281765	N67337	19. 5.87	RAF Halton Aeroplane Club Ltd	RAF Halton	7. 7.08E
G-BNKP	Cessna 152 II	15281286	N49460	18. 5.87	Spectrum Leisure Ltd	Clacton	3. 4.08E
G-BNKR	Cessna 152 II	15281284	N49458	18. 5.87	Keen Leasing (IoM) Ltd (Operated Ulster Flying Club)	Newtownards	12. 2.08E
G-BNKS	Cessna 152 II	15283186	N47202	18. 5.87	Shropshire Aero Club Ltd	Sleap	18. 5.08T
G-BNKT	Cameron O-77 Balloon (Hot Air)	1356		13. 2.87	British Airways PLC "Katie II"	Harmondsworth, West Drayton	4. 9.08A
G-BNKV	Cessna 152 II	15283079	N46604	18. 5.87	S C Westran	Shoreham	13.11.07E
G-BNLA	Boeing 747-436	23908	N60665	30. 6.89	British Airways PLC	London Heathrow	29. 6.08E
G-BNLB	Boeing 747-436	23909		31. 7.89	British Airways PLC	London Heathrow	13. 3.08E
G-BNLC	Boeing 747-436	23910		21. 7.89	British Airways PLC	London Gatwick	26. 7.08E
G-BNLD	Boeing 747-436	23911	N6018N	5. 9.89	British Airways PLC	London Heathrow	5. 9.08E
G-BNLE	Boeing 747-436	24047		14.11.89	British Airways PLC	London Heathrow	16.11.07E
G-BNLF	Boeing 747-436	24048		23. 2.90	British Airways PLC	London Heathrow	11.10.07E
G-BNLG	Boeing 747-436	24049		23. 2.90	British Airways PLC	London Heathrow	1.10.07E
G-BNLH	Boeing 747-436	24050	VH-NLH G-BNLH	28. 3.90	British Airways PLC	London Heathrow	5. 5.08E
G-BNLI	Boeing 747-436	24051		19. 4.90	British Airways PLC	London Heathrow	20. 4.08E
G-BNLJ	Boeing 747-436	24052	N60668	23. 5.90	British Airways PLC	London Heathrow	24. 5.08E
G-BNLK	Boeing 747-436	24053	N6009F	25. 5.90	British Airways PLC	London Heathrow	28. 5.08E
G-BNLL	Boeing 747-436	24054		13. 6.90	British Airways PLC	London Heathrow	13. 6.08E
G-BNLM	Boeing 747-436	24055	N6009F	28. 6.90	British Airways PLC	London Gatwick	27. 6.08E
G-BNLN	Boeing 747-436	24056		26. 7.90	British Airways PLC	London Heathrow	26. 7.08E
G-BNLO	Boeing 747-436	24057		25.10.90	British Airways PLC	London Heathrow	24.10.08E
G-BNLP	Boeing 747-436	24058		17.12.90	British Airways PLC	London Gatwick	10. 9.08E
G-BNLR	Boeing 747-436	24447	N6005C	15. 1.91	British Airways PLC	London Heathrow	16. 1.08E
G-BNLS	Boeing 747-436	24629		13. 3.91	British Airways PLC	London Heathrow	12. 3.08E
G-BNLT	Boeing 747-436	24630		19. 3.91	British Airways PLC	London Gatwick	14.11.07E
G-BNLU	Boeing 747-436	25406		28. 1.92	British Airways PLC	London Heathrow	27. 1.08E
G-BNLV	Boeing 747-436	25427		20. 2.92	British Airways PLC	London Gatwick	19. 2.08E
G-BNLW	Boeing 747-436	25432		4. 3.92	British Airways PLC	London Heathrow	4. 3.08E
G-BNLX (2)	Boeing 747-436	25435		1. 4.92	British Airways PLC	London Heathrow	2. 4.08E
G-BNLY (3)	Boeing 747-436	27090	N60659	10. 2.93	British Airways PLC	London Heathrow	9. 2.08E
G-BNLZ (3)	Boeing 747-436	27091		4. 3.93	British Airways PLC	London Heathrow	3. 3.08E
G-BNMA	Cameron O-77 Balloon (Hot Air)	830		15.12.87	A Wilkes and N Woodham "Finian" Temple Cloud, Bristol and Fawley, Southampton		4. 4.03A
G-BNMB	Piper PA-28-151 Cherokee Warrior	28-7615369	N6826J	6.10.87	Thomsonfly Ltd (Operated Britannia Flying Club)	Liverpool	27. 1.08E
G-BNMC	Cessna 152 II	15282564	N69218	29. 5.87	M L Jones (Operated Derby Aero Club)	Derby	10. 8.03T
G-BNMD	Cessna 152 II	15283786	N5170B	28. 5.87	T M Jones (Stored 9.02)	Derby	28. 7.01T
G-BNME	Cessna 152 II	15284888	N5159P	25. 9.87	A R Jury	(Oakham)	19.12.07E
G-BNMF	Cessna 152T	15285563	N93858	21. 7.87	Central Aircraft Leasing Ltd (Operated Midland Flight Centre) (Noted 10.07)	Halfpenny Green	8. 7.07T
G-BNMG	Cameron O-77 Balloon (Hot Air)	1500		27. 5.87	J H Turner	Bridgnorth	4. 4.03A
G-BNMH	Pietenpol AirCamper (Built N M Hitchman)	NH-1-001		2. 6.87	N M Hitchman	(Burbage, Leicester)	
G-BNML	Rand Robinson KR-2 (Built R J Smyth) (Volkswagen 1834)	PFA 129-11240		23. 6.87	P J Brookman (New owner 8.07)	(Shepshed, Loughborough)	17. 8.00P
G-BNMO	Cessna R182 Skylane RG II	R18200956	N738RK	3. 7.87	Kenrye Developments Ltd	Enniskillen	10. 7.06
G-BNMX	Thunder Ax7-77 Balloon (Hot Air)	1003		15. 6.87	S A D Beard	Cheltenham	20. 6.06A
G-BNNA	Stolp SA.300 Starduster Too (Built T C Maxwell) (Lycoming O-360)	1462	N8SD	29. 6.87	M A Neeves tr Banana Group	Leicester	11. 4.08P
G-BNNE	Cameron N-77 Balloon (Hot Air)	1413		15. 6.87	J A Hibberd (New owner 6.06)	Rotterdam, Netherlands	
G-BNNO	Piper PA-28-161 Cherokee Warrior II	28-8116099	N8307X	15. 6.87	I A Anderson	Little Snoring	5. 8.08E

Reg	Type	C/n	Prev id	Date	Owner/Operator	Location	Code
G-BNNR	Cessna 152 II	15285146	N40SX	15. 6.87	J H Sandham t/a J H Sandham Aviation	Carlisle	28.10.07E
			N40SU, N6121Q				
G-BNNS	Piper PA-28-161 Warrior II	28-8116061	N8283C	26. 6.87	S J French	Turweston	29. 5.08E
G-BNNT	Piper PA-28-151 Cherokee Warrior	28-7615056	N7624C	12. 6.87	S T Gilbert and D J Kirkwood	RAF Lyneham	12. 7.08T
G-BNNU	Piper PA-38-112 Tomahawk II	38-81A0037	N25650	12. 6.87	Edinburgh Flying Club Ltd	Edinburgh	13.12.07E
G-BNNX	Piper PA-28R-201T Turbo Arrow III		N9005F	14. 7.87	Bristol Flying Centre Ltd	Bristol	12. 1.08E
		28R-7703009					
G-BNNY	Piper PA-28-161 Warrior II	28-8016084	N8092M	1. 9.87	A S Bamrah t/a Falcon Flying Services	Biggin Hill	14.12.07E
G-BNNZ	Piper PA-28-161 Warrior II	28-8016177	N8135Y	24. 7.87	R West	(Shorne, Gravesend)	3.11.07E
G-BNOB	Wittman W.8 Tailwind	258/DH1		13. 7.87	M Robson-Robinson	(Abbots Bromley)	14. 5.02P
	(Built D G Hammersley - pr.no.PFA 3502) (Continental.PC60)				"Imogen"		
G-BNOE	Piper PA-28-161 Warrior II	2816013	N9121X	26. 6.87	Sherburn Aero Club Ltd	Sherburn-in-Elmet	27. 2.08E
			N9568N				
G-BNOF	Piper PA-28-161 Warrior II	2816014	N9122B	26. 6.87	Tayside Aviation Ltd	Dundee	29. 3.08E
G-BNOH	Piper PA-28-161 Warrior II	2816016	N9122L	26. 6.87	Sherburn Aero Club Ltd	Sherburn-in-Elmet	29. 1.08E
G-BNOJ	Piper PA-28-161 Warrior II	2816018	N9122R	26. 6.87	R D Turner and W M Brown tr BAE (Warton) Flying Club		
						Blackpool	9. 8.08E
G-BNOM	Piper PA-28-161 Warrior II	2816024		26. 6.87	Air Navigation and Trading Company Ltd	Blackpool	20.10.07E
G-BNON	Piper PA-28-161 Warrior II	2816025		26. 6.87	Tayside Aviation Ltd	Dundee	13. 3.08E
G-BNOP	Piper PA-28-161 Warrior II	2816027		26. 6.87	R D Turner and F J Smith tr BAE (Warton) Flying Club		
						Blackpool	13. 8.08E
G-BNOZ	Cessna 152 II	15281625	EI-CCP	22. 6.87	E J Haythornthwaite tr OZ Flying Group	Blackpool	21. 3.08E
			G-BNOZ, N65570				
G-BNPE	Cameron N-77 Balloon (Hot Air)	1519	(G-BNPX)	25. 8.87	Zebedee Balloon Service Ltd	Newtown, Hungerford	27. 6.08A
G-BNPF	Slingsby Cadet III Motor Glider	826	XA284	3.11.87	S Luck, P Norman and D R Winder	Audley End	10. 8.00P
	(Re-built S Luck and Partners - pr.no.PFA 042-11122 from Slingsby T 31M: with wings from XE791 which became OO-ZDQ) (Stark Stamo MS.1400A) "Noddy"						
G-BNPH	Percival P 66 Pembroke C 1	P66/41	WV740	30. 6.87	A and G A Gainsford Dixon	Bournemouth	19. 5.08P
	(Officially regd with c/n "PAC66/027")				(As "WV740" in RAF 60 Sqdn c/s)		
G-BNPM	Piper PA-38-112 Tomahawk	38-79A0374	N2561D	28. 7.87	D and L K Britten t/a Papa Mike Aviation	Cranfield	19. 5.08T
G-BNPO	Piper PA-28-181 Cherokee Archer II		N47720	28. 7.87	Bonus Aviation Ltd	Cranfield	19. 6.08E
		28-7890123					
G-BNPV	Bowers Fly Baby 1A	PFA 016-11120		2. 7.87	J G Day and R Gauld-Galliers		
	(Built J G Day)				Rushett Farm, Chessington	21.11.05P	
	(As "C L .1801/18" in German Army Air Service c/s to represent Junkers CL1)						
G-BNPY	Cessna 152 II	15280249	N24388	30. 6.87	Traffic Management Services Ltd	Gamston	29. 2.08E
G-BNRA	SOCATA TB-10 Tobago	772		15. 7.87	S N Kingan tr Double D Airgroup	Tollerton	27. 2.08E
					"Triple One"		
G-BNRG	Piper PA-28-161 Warrior II	28-8116217	N83810	7. 7.87	RAF Brize Norton Flying Club Ltd	RAF Brize Norton	23. 5.08T
G-BNRK	Cessna 152 II	15284659	N6297M	29. 7.87	Redhill Aviation Ltd	Redhill	9. 3.08E
G-BNRL	Cessna 152 II	15284250	N5084L	13. 7.87	Modi Aviation Ltd	Earls Colne	15. 6.08E
G-BNRP	Piper PA-28-181 Cherokee Archer II		N984BT	25.11.87	Bonus Aviation Ltd	Cranfield	19. 6.08E
		28-7790528					
G-BNRR	Cessna 172P Skyhawk II	17274013	N5213K	13. 7.87	P H Archard t/a PHA Aviation	Elstree	22. 5.08E
G-BNRX	Piper PA-34-200T Seneca II	34-7970336	N2898A	25.11.87	Truman Aviation Ltd	Tollerton	3. 8.08E
G-BNRY	Cessna 182Q Skylane II	18265629	N735RR	20. 7.87	K F and S J Farey	Wycombe Air Park	6. 6.08E
G-BNSG	Piper PA-28R-201 Arrow III	28R-7837205	N9516C	30. 7.87	Stronghold Trust Ltd	Top Farm, Croydon, Royston	7. 1.08E
G-BNSI	Cessna 152 II	15284853	N4945P	6. 8.87	Sky Leisure Aviation (Charters) Ltd	Shoreham	15. 2.08E
G-BNSL	Piper PA-38-112 Tomahawk II	38-81A0086	N25956	21. 7.87	APB Leasing Ltd	Manchester	1. 7.08E
G-BNSM	Cessna 152 II	15285342	N68948	23. 7.87	Cornwall Flying Club Ltd	Bodmin	26. 7.08E
G-BNSN	Cessna 152 II	15285776	N94738	21. 7.87	The Pilot Centre Ltd	Denham	19. 3.08E
G-BNSO	Slingsby T 67M Firefly II	2021		20. 8.87	R M Rennoldson	Full Sutton	3. 4.08E
G-BNSP	Slingsby T 67M Firefly II	2044		20. 8.87	M S Roadhouse tr Slingsby Group	Netherthorpe	4. 6.08E
G-BNSR	Slingsby T 67M Firefly II	2047		20. 8.87	E Whitehead tr Slingsby SR Group		
					(Newchapel, Lingfield)	26. 6.08E	
G-BNST	Cessna 172N Skyhawk II	17273661	N4670J	21. 9.87	J Revill t/a CSG Bodyshop	Netherthorpe	23. 4.08E
G-BNSU	Cessna 152 II	15281245	N49410	2.12.87	A L Brown t/a Channel Aviation	Bourn	13.10.07E
					(Operated Rural Flying Corps)		
G-BNSV	Cessna 152 II	15284531	N5322M	4.12.87	A L Brown t/a Channel Aviation	Bourn	12. 7.97T
					(Fuselage noted 10.05)		
G-BNSY	Piper PA-28-161 Warrior II	28-8016017	N4512M	18. 8.87	Light Aircraft Leasing Ltd	(Sheffield City)	26. 4.08E
G-BNSZ	Piper PA-28-161 Warrior II	28-8116315	N8433B	20. 8.87	Haimoss Ltd	Old Sarum	19.12.09T
G-BNTC	Piper PA-28RT-201T Turbo Arrow IV		N83428	4.11.87	Central Aircraft Leasing Ltd	Halfpenny Green	7. 7.08E
		28R-8131081					
					(Operated Halfpenny Green Flight Centre)		
G-BNTD	Piper PA-28-161 Cherokee Warrior II		N38490	5. 8.87	A M and F.Alam	Elstree	14.11.07E
		28-7716235	N9539N				
G-BNTP	Cessna 172N Skyhawk II	17272030	N6531E	4. 9.87	Westnet Ltd	Liverpool	15. 3.08E
G-BNTT	Beech 76 Duchess	ME-228	N54SB	8.10.87	Plane Talking Ltd (Operated Cabair)	Bournemouth	18. 6.08E
G-BNTW	Cameron V-77 Balloon (Hot Air)	1574		13. 8.87	P Goss "Cecilia"	Alton	6.11.99A
G-BNTZ	Cameron N-77 Balloon (Hot Air)	1518		27. 8.87	P M Watkins t/a Balloon Team	Chippenham	26. 8.02A
G-BNUC	Cameron O-77 Balloon (Hot Air)	1575		18. 8.87	T J Bucknall "Bridges Van Hire II"	Hawarden	
G-BNUL	Cessna 152 II	15284486	N4852M	2.10.87	Big Red Kite Ltd	RAF Benson	4. 5.08E
					(RAF Benson Flying Club titles)		
G-BNUN	Beech 58PA Baron	TJ-256	N6732Y	19. 8.87	British Midland Airways Ltd	East Midlands	8. 5.08E
G-BNUO	Beech 76 Duchess	ME-250	N6635Y	29. 9.87	G A F Tilley	Bournemouth	31. 5.08E
G-BNUS	Cessna 152 II	15282166	N68179	26. 8.87	Stapleford Flying Club Ltd	Stapleford	10. 7.08E
G-BNUT	Cessna 152 II	15279458	N714VC	26. 8.87	Stapleford Flying Club Ltd	Stapleford	5. 6.08E
G-BNUV	Piper PA-23-250 Aztec F	27-7854038	N97BB	2.10.87	L J Martin	Sandown, Isle of Wight	19.10.07E
			N63894				
G-BNUX	Hoffmann H 36 Dimona	36236		26. 8.87	G Hill tr Buckminster Dimona Syndicate	Saltby	21. 9.08E
G-BNUY	Piper PA-38-112 Tomahawk II	38-81A0093	N26006	10. 9.87	D C Storey (Noted 10.07)	Bodmin	17. 8.03T
G-BNVB	Grumman AA-5A Cheetah	AA5A-0758	N26843	28. 8.87	V R Coultan tr Grumman Group	Turweston	9. 4.08E
	(Regd as such but plate indicates Gulfstream American production)						
G-BNVD	Piper PA-38-112 Tomahawk	38-79A0055	N2421B	16.11.87	D Sharp	Bagby	14. 4.08E
G-BNVE	Piper PA-28-181 Archer II	28-8490046	N4338D	28. 8.87	Solent Flight Ltd	Lee-on-Solent	13.12.07E
	(Left wing tip struck gate at Lee-on-Solent 12.7.06 with substantial damage)						

Reg	Type	C/n	Prev id	Date	Owner/Operator	Location	Date
G-BNVT	Piper PA-28R-201T Turbo Arrow III	28R-7703157	N5863V	26. 1.88	T Yeung tr Victor Tango Group	Prestwick	4. 3.08E
G-BNWA	Boeing 767-336	24333	N6009F	19. 4.90	British Airways PLC	London Heathrow	24. 4.08E
G-BNWB	Boeing 767-336	24334	N6046P	2. 2.90	British Airways PLC	London Heathrow	12. 2.08E
G-BNWC	Boeing 767-336	24335		2. 2.90	British Airways PLC	London Heathrow	21. 2.08E
G-BNWD	Boeing 767-336	24336	N6018N	2. 2.90	British Airways PLC	London Heathrow	31. 8.08E
G-BNWH	Boeing 767-336	24340	N6005C	31.10.90	British Airways PLC	London Heathrow	30.10.08E
G-BNWI	Boeing 767-336	24341		18.12.90	British Airways PLC	London Heathrow	17.12.08E
G-BNWM	Boeing 767-336	25204		24. 6.91	British Airways PLC	London Heathrow	24. 6.08E
G-BNWN	Boeing 767-336	25444		30.10.91	British Airways PLC	London Heathrow	29.10.07E
G-BNWO	Boeing 767-336	25442		2. 3.92	British Airways PLC	London Heathrow	1. 3.08E
G-BNWR	Boeing 767-336	25732		20. 3.92	British Airways PLC	London Heathrow	19. 3.08E
G-BNWS	Boeing 767-336	25826	N6018N	19. 2.93	British Airways PLC	London Heathrow	18. 2.08E
G-BNWT	Boeing 767-336	25828		8. 2.93	British Airways PLC	London Heathrow	29.11.07E
G-BNWU	Boeing 767-336	25829		16. 3.93	British Airways PLC	London Heathrow	15. 3.08E
G-BNWV	Boeing 767-336	27140		29. 4.93	British Airways PLC	London Heathrow	28. 4.08E
G-BNWW	Boeing 767-336	25831		3. 2.94	British Airways PLC	London Heathrow	18. 3.08E
G-BNWX	Boeing 767-336	25832		1. 3.94	British Airways PLC	London Heathrow	28. 2.08E
G-BNWY	Boeing 767-336	25834	N5005C	22. 4.96	British Airways PLC	Birmingham	21. 4.08E
G-BNWZ	Boeing 767-336	25733		25. 2.97	British Airways PLC	London Heathrow	24. 2.08E
G-BNXD	Cessna 172N Skyhawk II	17272692	N6285D	25. 9.87	M and N Jahanfar	Southend	2. 7.08E
					(Operated The Flight Centre)		
G-BNXE	Piper PA-28-161 Warrior II	28-8116034	N8262D	24. 9.87	M S Brown	Leicester	26. 1.08
G-BNXK	Nott-Cameron NCA ULD/3 Balloon (Hot Air)		(G-BLJN)	23. 9.87	J R P Nott Twain-Harte, California, US and Bristol		
	(Built Airship Industries (UK) Ltd)	7 & 1110		*(Hot air envelope stored Twain-Harte 7.03 - helium inner envelope stored Bristol 1995)*			
G-BNXL	Glaser-Dirks DG-400	4-216		2.10.87	C I Cowley tr G-BNXL Syndicate Husbands Bosworth		2. 5.08E
G-BNXM	Piper PA-18 Super Cub 95 (L-21B-PI)	18-4019	MM54-2619	23.11.87	R Thorp tr G-BNXM Group		
	(Continental O-200-A) (Italian Frame rebuild No.0006)	EI-276, I-EIVC, MM54-2619, 54-2619				Gipsy Wood Farm, Warthill	16. 4.08P
G-BNXR	Cameron O-84 Balloon (Hot Air)	1515		23. 9.87	J A B Gray	Daglingworth, Cirencester	9.12.04T
					"Bacchus II" (Noted 8.06)		
G-BNXT	Piper PA-28-161 Cherokee Warrior II	28-7716168	N4047Q	23. 9.87	A S Bamrah t/a Falcon Flying Services	Biggin Hill	30.11.07E
					(Operated Euroflyers)		
G-BNXU	Piper PA-28-161 Warrior II	28-7916129	N2082C	23. 9.87	R E Woolsey tr Friendly Warrior Group Newtownards		31. 5.08E
G-BNXV	Piper PA-38-112 Tomahawk	38-79A0826	N2399N	10.12.87	W B Bateson *(Noted 10.07)*	Blackpool	5.10.01T
G-BNXX	SOCATA TB-20 Trinidad	664	N20GZ	15. 9.87	D M Carr	Wellesbourne Mountford	4. 7.08E
G-BNXZ	Thunder Ax7-77 Balloon (Hot Air)	1105		13.10.87	W S Templeton, R B Green and A S Dear	Fordingbridge	5. 8.084A
					tr Hale Hot Air Balloon Group *"Dragonfly"*		
G-BNYB	Piper PA-28-201T Turbo Dakota	28-7921040	N2856A N9533N	27. 1.88	Rosetta Sourcing Ltd	(London W1)	8. 3.08E
G-BNYD	Bell 206B-2 JetRanger II	1911	N3254P C-GTWM, N49712	1.10.87	Fast Helicopters Ltd	Hawarden	12.11.07E
G-BNYK	Piper PA-38-112 Tomahawk II	38-82A0059	N2376V	23.10.87	APB Leasing Ltd	(Sheffield City)	24. 5.08E
G-BNYL	Cessna 152 II	15280671	N25454	6.10.87	V J Freeman	Headcorn	24.11.06T
G-BNYM	Cessna 172N Skyhawk II	17273854	N6089J	13.11.87	D J Skinner tr Kestrel Syndicate	AAC Netheravon	17. 4.08
G-BNYN	Cessna 152 II	15285433	N93185	2.10.87	Redhill Aviation Ltd	Redhill	17. 2.03T
					(Damaged overnight 14/15.4.03)		
G-BNYO	Beech 76 Duchess	ME-78	N2010P	28.10.87	Multiflight Ltd	Leeds-Bradford	26. 4.08E
G-BNYP	Piper PA-28-181 Archer II	28-8490027	N4330K	19.10.87	R D Cooper	Turweston	13. 3.08E
					(Operated Sandra's Flying Group)		
G-BNYX	Denney Kitfox Model 1	PFA 172-11285		28.10.87	W J Husband	Blackbrook Farm, Sheffield	20. 2.08P
	(Built R W Husband) (Rotax 532)						
G-BNYZ	SNCAN Stampe SV-4E	200	F-BFZR Aeronavale	10.12.87	M J Parr	Wycombe Air Park	13. 3.10S
	(Also reported as ex N180SV(?) with c/n "200-53" but may be ex Belgian V-53 c/n 1195)						
G-BNZB	Piper PA-28-161 Warrior II	28-7916521	N2900U	18.11.87	Falcon Flying Services Ltd	Biggin Hill	31. 1.08E
G-BNZC	de Havilland DHC-1 Chipmunk 22	C1/0778	G-ROYS 7438M, WP905	11.11.87	Richard Shuttleworth Trustees	Old Warden	12. 4.10
					(As "RCAF 671" in RCAF c/s)		
G-BNZK	Thunder Ax7-77 Balloon (Hot Air)	1104		10.11.87	T D Marsden *"Shropshire Lass"*	Limber, Grimsby	28. 5.97A
G-BNZL	RotorWay Scorpion 133	2839		2.11.87	J R Wraight (Stoneacre Farm, Farthing Corner)		
	(Built J Evans)				*(Complete and stored 5.95)*		
G-BNZM	Cessna T210N Turbo Centurion II	21063640	N4828C	9.11.87	A J M Freeman	North Weald	9. 4.08E
G-BNZN	Cameron N-56 Balloon (Hot Air)	1471	SE-ZFA G-BNZN	9.11.87	Balloon Sports HB	Partille, Sweden	17. 2.08A
G-BNZO	RotorWay Executive	RW152/3535		9.11.87	J S David	Street Farm, Takeley	7. 9.07P
	(Built M J Wiltshire) (RotorWay RW162)				*(Noted 2.08)*		
G-BNZR	Clutton FRED Series II	PFA 029-10727		10.11.87	R M Waugh	(Belfast)	25. 5.99P
	(Built R M Waugh)						
G-BNZV	Piper PA-25-235 Pawnee D	25-7405649	C-GSKU N9548P	22. 2.88	Aeroklub Alpski Letalski Center Lesce		
						Lesce-Bled, Slovenia	6. 6.08E
G-BNZZ	Piper PA-28-161 Warrior II	28-8216184	N8253Z	17.11.87	Providence Aviation Ltd	Wellesbourne Mountford	8. 3.08E

G-BOAA - G-BOZZ

Reg	Type	C/n	Prev id	Date	Owner/Operator	Location	Date
G-BOAH	Piper PA-28-161 Warrior II	28-8416030	N43401 N9554N	21. 1.88	Aircraft Engineers Ltd	Prestwick	18.12.07E
G-BOAI	Cessna 152 II	15279830	C-GSJH N757LS	8. 1.88	Aviation Spirit Ltd	Shobdon	12. 1.08E
G-BOAL	Cameron V-65 Balloon (Hot Air)	1600		5.11.87	A M and N H Ponsford	Leeds	7. 2.02A
					"Nameless" (Amended owners 8.07)		
G-BOAO	Thunder Ax7-77 Balloon (Hot Air)	1162		2.12.87	D V Fowler	Cranbrook	17.10.02A
G-BOAS	Air Command 503 Commander	0388		3.12.87	R Robinson	(Leighton Buzzard)	
	(Built R Robinson - pr.no.PFA G/04-1094)						
G-BOAU	Cameron V-77 Balloon (Hot Air)	1606		10.12.87	G T Barstow	Llandrindod Wells	9.12.96A
					"Flying Colours/Duster I"		

G-BOBA	Piper PA-28R-201 Arrow III	28R-7837232	N31249	4. 1.88	GT Ventures Ltd	Coventry	9. 7.08E
G-BOBH	Airtour AH-77B Balloon (Hot Air)	009		2.12.87	J and K Francis	Dibden Purlieu, Southampton	29. 6.02A
					"Gloworm" (Noted 8.06)		
G-BOBR	Cameron N-77 Balloon (Hot Air)	1623		10.12.87	Trigger Concepts Ltd	Swallowfield, Reading	24. 4.06A
G-BOBT	Stolp SA.300 Starduster Too	CJ-01	N690CM	15.12.87	S C Lever tr G-BOBT Group	White Waltham	19. 9.07P
	(Built C J Anderson) (Lycoming O-360)						
G-BOBV	Cessna F150M	F15001415	EI-BCV	14.12.87	Sheffield Aero Club Ltd	Netherthorpe	12. 5.08E
	(Built Reims Aviation SA)						
G-BOBY	Monnett Sonerai II	PFA 015-10223		26.10.78	R G Hallam	(Netherthorpe)	8.11.82P
	(Built R G Hallam) (Volkswagen 2233)				*Damaged near Barton 31.10.82: stored 9.96)*		
G-BOCG	Piper PA-34-200T Seneca II	34-7870359	N36759	30.12.87	Oxford Aviation Training Ltd	Oxford	22. 1.08E
G-BOCI	Cessna 140A	15497	N5366C	17.11.87	J B Bonnell	Thruxton	12. 1.08
	(Continental C90)				*"Whitey"*		
G-BOCK	Sopwith Triplane replica	NAW-1		26. 1.88	Richard Shuttleworth Trustees	Old Warden	31. 7.08P
	(Built Northern Aeroplane Workshops) (Sopwith c/n 153) (130hp Clerget Rotary 9B)				*(As "N6290" in RNAS 8 Sqdn c/s) "DIXIE II"*		
G-BOCL	Slingsby T 67C Firefly	2035		5. 1.88	Richard Brinklow Aviation Ltd	Shoreham	26. 2.07T
					(Operated The Flying Hut)		
G-BOCM	Slingsby T 67C Firefly	2036		5. 1.88	Richard Brinklow Aviation Ltd	RAF Benson	18. 1.08T
G-BOCN	Robinson R22 Beta	0726	N... G-BOCN	8. 1.88	Aga Property Development Ltd (Brideswell, Athlone, County Westmeath)		2. 4.08E
G-BODB	Piper PA-28-161 Warrior II	2816042	N9606N	23. 2.88	Sherburn Aero Club Ltd	Sherburn-in-Elmet	13.11.07E
G-BODC	Piper PA-28-161 Warrior II	2816041	N9605N	23. 2.88	Sherburn Aero Club Ltd	Sherburn-in-Elmet	12. 7.08E
G-BODD	Piper PA-28-161 Warrior II	2816040	N9604N	23. 2.88	L W Scattergood	Sandtoft	19.10.07E
G-BODE	Piper PA-28-161 Warrior II	2816039	N9603N	23. 2.88	Sherburn Aero Club Ltd	Sherburn-in-Elmet	1. 8.08E
G-BODI	Stoddard-Hamilton Glasair III SH-3R		(HB-...)	14. 4.89	R R Arias	(Soto del Real, Madrid, Spain)	19. 5.07P
	(Built Jackson Barr Ltd) EMK .030 & 3088		G-BODI		*(Lycoming O-360)*		
G-BODM	Piper PA-28-180 Cherokee Challenger	28-7305519	N56016	2. 2.88	R Emery	Clutton Hill Farm, Clutton	8.11.07E
G-BODO	Cessna 152 II	15282404	N68923	29. 1.88	M and D C Brooks	Bidford	29. 5.08E
G-BODP	Piper PA-38-112 Tomahawk II	38-81A0010	N25616	5. 1.88	Bethan Petrie	Hawarden	23. 2.08e
G-BODR	Piper PA-28-161 Warrior II	28-8116318	N8436B	5. 1.88	Airways Aero Associations Ltd	Wycombe Air Park	23. 1.08E
					(Operated British Airways Flying Club with British Airways titles)		
G-BODS	Piper PA-38-112 Tomahawk	38-79A0410	N2379F	3. 2.88	Coulson Flying Services Ltd	Cranfield	25. 8.08E
G-BODT	Jodel D 18	173		14. 1.88	L D McPhillips tr Jodel G-BODT Syndicate	Portmoak	29. 5.08P
	(Built R A Jarvis - pr.no.PFA 169-11290) (Rotax 912-UL)						
G-BODU	Scheibe SF25C-2000 Falke	44434	D-KIAA	19. 1.88	Hertfordshire County Scout Council		
	(Limbach L2000)					Gransden Lodge	11. 5.08E
G-BODX	Beech 76 Duchess	ME-309	N67094	26. 2.88	S J Skilton t/a Aviation Rentals	Bournemouth	3. 9.08E
					(Operated Professional Air Training)		
G-BODY	Cessna 310R II	310R1503	N4897A	17.12.87	Reconnaissance Ventures Ltd	Coventry	23. 2.08E
					(Atlantic Flight Training on tip tanks)		
G-BODZ	Robinson R22 Beta	0729		8. 1.88	Langley Aviation Ltd	Gamston	26. 4.08E
G-BOEE	Piper PA-28-181 Cherokee Archer II	28-7690359	N6168J	20. 1.88	T B Parmenter	Lodge Farm, St Osyth	13. 6.08E
G-BOEG	Short SD.3-60 Variant 100	SH3733	CS-TLS N133PC, G-14-3733	27. 1.88	BAC Group Ltd *(Noted 2.08)*	Southend	22.11.06
G-BOEH	Robin DR.340 Major	434	F-BRVN	4. 1.88	G Bowles tr Piper Flyers Group	Bradleys Lawn, Heathfield	24. 5.08E
G-BOEK	Cameron V-77 Balloon (Hot Air)	1658		25. 1.88	R I M Kerr, R S McLean and P McCheyne *"Secret Leader"*	Bristol	29. 4.08A
G-BOEM	Pitts S-2A *(Built Aerotek Inc)*	2255	N31525	17. 2.88	M Murphy *(Noted 10.07)*	Spanhoe	21. 7.01P
G-BOEN	Cessna 172M Skyhawk	17261325	N20482	12. 2.88	C Barlow	Standalone Farm, Meppershall	16. 4.08E
G-BOER	Piper PA-28-161 Warrior II	28-8116094	N83030	21. 1.88	M and W Fraser-Urquhart	Blackpool	18. 4.08
G-BOET	Piper PA-28RT-201 Arrow IV	28R-8018020	G-IBEC G-BOET, N8116V	28. 1.88	B C Chambers *(Noted 1.08)*	Jersey	28. 9.07E
G-BOEW	Robinson R22 Beta	0750		27. 1.88	Plane Talking Ltd	Cranfield	13. 4.06T
G-BOFC	Beech 76 Duchess	ME-217	N6628M	28. 1.88	Magenta Ltd) *(Operated Airways Flight Training)*	Exeter	8. 4.08E
G-BOFD	Cessna U206G Stationair 6	U20604181	N756LS	27. 1.88	D M Penny	(Coleraine)	16. 8.08E
G-BOFE	Piper PA-34-200T Seneca II	34-7870381	N39493	22. 2.88	Alstons Upholstery Ltd	Earls Colne	3. 9.08E
G-BOFF	Cameron N-77 Balloon (Hot Air)	1666		26. 1.88	R C Corcoran *(Systems 80 titles)*	Bristol	23. 7.03A
G-BOFL	Cessna 152 II	15284101	N5457H	28. 1.88	Gem Rewinds Ltd	Coventry	9. 8.08E
G-BOFM	Cessna 152 II	15284730	N6445M	28. 1.88	Gem Rewinds Ltd	Halfpenny Green	29. 8.08E
G-BOFW	Cessna A150M Aerobat	A1500612	N9803J	15. 2.88	D F Donovan	Elstree	23.11.08E
G-BOFX	Cessna A150M Aerobat	A1500678	N9869J	15. 2.88	M R Woodgate	Newtownards	9. 4.08E
G-BOFY	Piper PA-28-140 Cherokee Cruiser	28-7425374	N43521	3. 2.88	Light Aircraft Leasing Ltd	(Sheffield City)	6. 5.08E
G-BOFZ	Piper PA-28-161 Cherokee Warrior II	28-7816255	N2189M	10. 2.88	R W Harris *(Operated The Flight Centre)*	Southend	3. 8.08E
G-BOGC	Cessna 152 II	15284500	N5346M	8. 2.88	Cloud 9 Aviation (Leasing) Ltd	Full Sutton	3. 2.08E
G-BOGI	Robin DR.400-180 Régent	1821		15. 2.88	A L M Shepherd	Rochester	30. 5.08E
G-BOGK	ARV Aviation ARV-1	K 006		10. 2.88	M K Field	Sleap	23. 7.08P
	(Built Monewden Flying Group - pr.no.PFA 152-11138)						
G-BOGM	Piper PA-28RT-201T Turbo Arrow IV	28R-8031077	N8173C	10. 2.88	R J Pearce t/a RJP Aviation *(Operated RJP Flying School)*	Halfpenny Green	3. 4.08E
G-BOGO	Piper PA-32R-301T Turbio Saratoga II SP	32R-8029064	N8165W	6. 4.88	A S Doman	Biggin Hill	28. 7.08E
G-BOGP	Cameron V-77 Balloon (Hot Air)	896		30. 3.88	T Gunn tr Wealden Balloon Group *"Dire Straits"*	Crowborough	10. 7.00A
G-BOGV	Air Command 532 Elite	0399		10. 3.88	G M Hobman	Heworth, York	10. 1.91P
	(Built Deandell Products Ltd - pr.no.PFA G/04-1102)						
G-BOGY	Cameron V-77 Balloon (Hot Air)	1650		15. 2.88	P Spellward and A Reimann	Bristol and Merrenberg, Germany	4. 8.08E
G-BOHA	Piper PA-28-161 Cherokee Warrior II	28-7816352	N3526M	16. 3.88	S J Gardiner	Shoreham	12. 6.08E

G-BOHD	Colt 77A Balloon (Hot Air)	1214		4. 3.88	D B Court "Bluebird"	Ormskirk	5. 8.02A
G-BOHF	Thunder Ax8-84 Balloon (Hot Air)	1197		8. 4.88	J A Harris	Stalbridge, Sturminster Newton	1. 9.05A
G-BOHH	Cessna 172N Skyhawk II	17273906	N131FR	19. 2.88	N King tr G-BOHH Group	Swansea	23. 5.08E
			N7333J				
G-BOHI	Cessna 152 II	15281241	N49406	29. 2.88	Cirrus Aviation Ltd	Clacton	5. 6.08E
G-BOHJ	Cessna 152 II	15280558	N25259	29. 2.88	A G Knight t/a Airlaunch	Tibenham	22. 3.08E
G-BOHL	Cameron A-120 Balloon (Hot Air)	1701		11. 3.88	T J Bucknall "Son of City of Bath"	Colwyn Bay	12.10.02
G-BOHM	Piper PA-28-180 Cherokee Challenger		N55000	18. 2.88	B F Keogh and R A Scott		
		28-7305287				Lockmead Farm, South Marston	8. 5.08E
G-BOHO	Piper PA-28-161 Warrior II	28-8016196	N747RH	25. 2.88	H M Sherriff and D G Buchanan tr Egressus Flying Group		
			N9560N			Duxford	1. 1.08E
G-BOHR	Piper PA-28-151 Cherokee Warrior	28-7515245	C-GNFE	29. 2.88	R M E Garforth	Southend	20. 4.08E
G-BOHS	Piper PA-38-112 Tomahawk	38-79A0988	N2418P	26. 2.88	A S Bamrah t/a Falcon Flying Services	Earls Colne	15. 4.07T
G-BOHT	Piper PA-38-112 Tomahawk	38-79A1079	N25304	14. 4.88	E Reed t/a St George Flight Training		
			C-GAYW, N24052			Durham Tees Valley	15.10.07E
G-BOHU	Piper PA-38-112 Tomahawk	38-80A0031	N25093	26. 2.88	D A Whitmore	Pembrey	18. 5.08E
G-BOHV	Wittman W 8.Tailwind	621		3. 3.88	R A Povall	Yearby	10. 9.08P
	(Built R A Povall - pr.no.PFA 031-11151)						
G-BOHW	Van's RV-4	PFA 181-11309		16. 6.88	P J Robins	Deenethorpe	22. 8.08P
	(Built R W H Cole) (Lycoming O-320)						
G-BOIA	Cessna 180K Skywagon II	18053121	N2895K	3. 3.88	R E.,P E R.,J E R and R J W Styles	Rush Green	26. 7.08E
					tr Old Warden Flying and Parachute Group		
G-BOIB	Wittman W.10 Tailwind	PFA 031-10551		3. 3.88	R F Bradshaw	Valley Farm, Winwick	17. 4.08P
	(Built P H Lewis) (Continental O-300-D)						
G-BOIC	Piper PA-28R-201T Turbo Arrow III		N2336M	7. 4.88	M J Pearson	North Weald	17. 6.08E
		28R-7803123					
G-BOID	Bellanca 7ECA Citabria	1092-75	N8676V	3. 3.88	D Mallinson	Birds Edge, Penistone	11. 6.08E
G-BOIG	Piper PA-28-161 Warrior II	28-8516027	N4390B	1. 3.88	D Vallance-Pell	Gamston	2. 8.08E
			N9519N				
G-BOIJ	Thunder Ax7-77 Series 1 Balloon (Hot Air)	964		11. 3.88	K Dodman	Stowmarket	6. 7.07A
G-BOIK	Air Command 503 Commander	0420		8. 3.88	F G Shepherd	Alston, Cumbria	22. 1.90P
	(Built G R Horner - pr.no.PFA G/04-1090)						
G-BOIL	Cessna 172N Skyhawk II	17271301	N23FL	2. 3.88	Upperstack Ltd	Barton	1. 8.08E
			N23ER, (N2494E)				
G-BOIO	Cessna 152 II	15280260	N24445	7. 3.88	J H Sandham t/a J H Sandham Aviation	Perth	30. 5.08E
G-BOIR	Cessna 152 II	15283272	N48041	7. 3.88	Shropshire Aero Club Ltd	Sleap	13. 6.08E
G-BOIT	SOCATA TB-10 Tobago	810		10. 3.88	M J Ryan t/a G-BOIT Flying Group	RNAS Yeovilton	19.12.07E
					(FLY NAVY titles)		
G-BOIV	Cessna 150M Commuter	15078620	N704HH	30. 3.88	M J Page tr India Victor Group	Seething	4.12.07E
G-BOIX	Cessna 172N Skyhawk II	17271206	C-GMMX	9. 3.88	JR Flying Ltd	Bournemouth	29. 2.08E
			N2253E				
G-BOIY	Cessna 172N Skyhawk II	17267738	N73901	9. 3.88	L W Scattergood	Sandtoft	6. 9.08E
G-BOIZ	Piper PA-34-200T Seneca II	34-8070014	N81081	25. 2.88	R W Tebby t/a S F Tebby and Son	Bristol	2.10.07E
					(Operated Bristol Flying Centre)		
G-BOJB	Cameron V-77 Balloon (Hot Air)	1615		11. 3.88	I M and S D Warner (New owners 8.06)	(Luton)	5. 4.08A
G-BOJI	Piper PA-28RT-201 Arrow IV	28R-7918221	N2919X	31. 3.88	K B Frost and M J Berry tr Arrow Two Group		
						Blackbushe	14. 5.08E
G-BOJK	Piper PA-34-220T Seneca III	3433020	G-BRUF	11. 3.88	Redhill Aviation Ltd	Blackbushe	24. 8.08E
			N9113D		(Operated Redhill Flying Club)		
G-BOJM	Piper PA-28-181 Archer II	28-8090244	N8155L	21. 3.88	R P Emms	Gamston	12. 5.08E
G-BOJR	Cessna 172P Skyhawk II	17275574	N64539	22. 4.88	Exeter Flying Club Ltd	Exeter	14. 6.08E
G-BOJS	Cessna 172P Skyhawk II	17274582	N52699	29. 3.88	B A Paul	Denham	23.1.07E
G-BOJU	Cameron N-77 Balloon (Hot Air)	1718		21. 3.88	M A Scholes "GB Transport"	London SE25	7. 9.97A
G-BOJW	Piper PA-28-161 Cherokee Warrior II		N1668H	28. 3.88	Brewhamfield Farm Ltd	Enstone	26. 2.08E
		28-7716038					
G-BOJZ	Piper PA-28-161 Warrior II	28-7916223	N2113J	28. 3.88	A S Bamrah t/a Falcon Flying Services	Biggin Hill	1. 4.08E
G-BOKA	Piper PA-28-201T Turbo Dakota	28-7921076	N2860S	15. 3.88	CBG Aviation Ltd	Fairoaks	14. 5.08
G-BOKB	Piper PA-28-161 Warrior II	28-8216077	N8013Y	29. 3.88	Apollo Aviation Advisory Ltd	Shoreham	20. 8.08E
G-BOKF	Air Command 532 Elite	0404		28. 3.88	J K Padden	(Leeds)	22. 9.99P
	(Built N J Brunskill - pr.no.PFA G/04-1101)						
G-BOKH	Whittaker MW7	PFA 171-11281	(G-MTWT)	21. 3.88	G J Chater	Landmead Farm, Garford	23. 5.07P
	(Built M Whittaker and officially regd as PFA 171-11231)						
G-BOKW	Bölkow BÖ.208C Junior	689	G-BITT	6. 1.88	S Yelland	Bagby	11 11.08P
			F-BRHX, (D-EEAL)				
G-BOKX	Piper PA-28-161 Cherokee Warrior II		N39709	28. 3.88	Shenley Farms (Aviation) Ltd	Headcorn	21. 9.03T
		28-7816680					
G-BOKY	Cessna 152 II	15285298	N67409	6. 4.88	D F F and J E Poore	Bournemouth	1. 7.08E
G-BOLB	Taylorcraft BC-12-65	3165	N36211	17. 5.88	J C Lovell	Eastbach Farm, Coleford	6. 2.08P
	(Continental A65)		NC36211				
G-BOLC	Fournier RF6-100	1	F-BVKS	28. 3.88	J D Cohen	Dunkeswell	5. 8.08E
G-BOLD	Piper PA-38-112 Tomahawk	38-78A0180	N9740T	8. 7.88	B R Pearson tr BOLD Group	Eaglescott	7. 3.08E
G-BOLE	Piper PA-38-112 Tomahawk	38-78A0475	N2506E	13. 7.88	J and G Stevenson tr Double S Group	Tollerton	28. 5.08E
G-BOLF	Piper PA-38-112 Tomahawk	38-79A0375	N583P	13. 7.88	P W Carlton	Durham Tees Valley	5. 5.08E
			YV-583P, YV-133E, YV-1696P, N9666N				
G-BOLG	Bellanca 7KCAB Citabria	517-75	N8706V	25.11.88	B R Pearson t/a Aerotug	Eaglescott	21. 5.08E
G-BOLI	Cessna 172P Skyhawk II	17275484	N63794	30. 3.88	W White tr BOLI Flying Club	Denham	8. 8.08E
G-BOLL	Lake LA-4-200 Skimmer	295	(F-GRMX)	4. 5.88	M C Holmes	Mullaghmore, Coleraine	3. 5.08
			G-BOLL, EI-ANR, N1133L				
G-BOLN	Colt 21A Cloudhopper Balloon (Hot Air)	1226		4. 5.88	G Everatt	Maidstone	26. 9 08A
G-BOLO	Bell 206B-2 JetRanger II	1522	N59409	2.11.87	Hargreaves Leasing Ltd (Rustington, Littlehampton)		15. 3.08E
					(Operated Blades Helicopters)		
G-BOLP	Colt 21A Cloudhopper Balloon (Hot Air)	1227		4. 5.88	J E Rose	Abingdon	1. 5.02A
G-BOLR	Colt 21A Cloudhopper Balloon (Hot Air)	1228		3. 5.88	C J Sanger-Davies	Hawarden, Deeside	15. 4.08A

Reg	Type	C/n	Prev id	Date	Owner/Operator	Base	
G-BOLS	Clutton FRED Series II	PFA 029-10676		6. 4.88	I F Vaughan	(St Martin, Guernsey)	
	(Built R J Goodburn)				"The Ruptured Uck"		
G-BOLT	Rockwell Commander 114	14428	N5883N	16.10.78	I R Harnett	Elstree	9. 7.08E
G-BOLU	Robin R3000/120	106	F-GFAO	14. 4.88	M A Hogbin	Biggin Hill	18. 7.08E
			SE-IMS				
G-BOLV	Cessna 152 II	15280492	N24983	8. 4.88	Synergy Aircraft Leasing Ltd	Fairoaks	28. 3.08E
G-BOLW	Cessna 152 II	15280589	N25316	9. 6.88	A Jahanfar (	Southend	30. 8.08E
					Operated Seawing Flying Club)		
G-BOLY	Cessna 172N Skyhawk II	17269004	N734PJ	31. 3.88	Simair Ltd	Biggin Hill	20. 6.08E
G-BOLZ	Rand Robinson KR-2	PFA 129-10866		6. 4.88	B Normington	Coventry	18. 9.08P
	(Built B Normington) (Volkswagen 1834)						
G-BOMB	Cassutt Racer IIIM	PFA 034-10386		18.12.78	R S Grace	Audley End	23. 5.08P
	(Built D Ford)				"Blind Panic" and "3"		
G-BOMN	Cessna 150F	15063089	N6489F	25. 4.89	P A Chamberlaine tr Auburn Flying Group		
						Movenis, Coleraine	16.10.07E
G-BOMO	Piper PA-38-112 Tomahawk II	38-81A0161	N91324	8. 4.88	APB Leasing Ltd	Swansea	28. 6.08E
G-BOMP	Piper PA-28-181 Cherokee Archer II	28-7790249	N8482F	8. 4.88	Dawne Carter	Little Gransden	12. 2.08T
G-BOMS	Cessna 172N Skyhawk II	17269448	N737JG	11. 4.88	Almat Flying Club Ltd and Penchant Ltd	Coventry	25.10.07E
G-BOMU	Piper PA-28-181 Cherokee Archer II	28-7790318	N1631H	8. 4.88	J Sawyer	Blackbushe	22. 8.08E
G-BOMY	Piper PA-28-161 Warrior II	28-8216049	N8457S	28. 6.88	D A Cobham tr BOMY Group	Headcorn	16. 2.08E
G-BOMZ	Piper PA-38-112 Tomahawk	38-78A0635	N2315A	30. 6.88	I C Barlow and I Cummins tr BOMZ Aviation		
						Wycombe Air Park	19. 3.08T
G-BONC	Piper PA-28RT-201 Arrow IV	28R-7918007	C-GXYX	13. 5.88	Finglow Ltd	Fowlmere	15. 8.08E
			N3069K				
G-BONG	Enstrom F-28A-UK	154	N9604	22. 4.88	J D Beeson	Barton	9. 8.08E
G-BONP	CFM Streak Shadow	108		4. 5.88	R Lawes	(Hayling Island)	17. 5 08P
	(Built CFM Metal-Fax as c/n SS-01P and pr.no.PFA 161A-11344) (Rotax 582)						
G-BONR	Cessna 172N Skyhawk II	17268164	C-GYGK	18. 4.88	D I Claik	Biggin Hill	5. 7.08E
			(N733BH)				
G-BONS	Cessna 172N Skyhawk II	17268345	C-GIUF	18. 4.88	M G Montgomerie tr G-BONS Group	Elstree	17. 9.08E
G-BONT	Slingsby T 67M Firefly II	2054		3. 5.88	Babcock Support Services Ltd t/a Babcock Defence Services		
						AAC Middle Wallop	23.11.07E
G-BONU	Slingsby T 67B Firefly	2037		3. 5.88	R L Brinklow (Noted 5.06)	Hinton-in-the-Hedges	29. 6.00T
G-BONW	Cessna 152 II	15280401	OY-CPL	15. 4.88	Lincoln Aero Club Ltd	Sturgate	22. 8.08E
			N24825				
G-BONY	Denney Kitfox Model 1	166		11. 5.88	M J Blanchard	Old Sarum	3.10.08P
	(Built J S Penny - pr.no.PFA 172-11351) (Rotax 532) (Inscribed as "Mk.2")						
G-BONZ	Beech V35B Bonanza	D-10282	N6661D	6. 4.88	P M Coulten	Boughton, Norfolk	16. 2.07
G-BOOB	Cameron N-65 Balloon (Hot Air)	515		12.11.79	P J Hooper	Southville, Bristol	24. 8.08A
G-BOOC	Piper PA-18-150 Super Cub	18-8279	SE-EPC	29. 4.88	S A C Whitcombe	Meon, Petersfield	1. 1.09E
G-BOOD	Slingsby T.31	PFA 042-11264		4. 5.88	K A Hale	Lotmead Farm, Wanborough	10. 1.08P
	(Built P J Titherington with wings ex XE810 c/n 923) (Fuji-Robin EC-44-2PM)						
G-BOOE	Gulfstream GA-7 Cougar	GA7-0093	N718G	7. 6.88	N Gardner	Bournemouth	6. 8.08E
G-BOOF	Piper PA-28-181 Cherokee Archer II	28-7890084	N47510	16. 6.88	H Merkado	Panshanger	13.11.07E
G-BOOG	Piper PA-28RT-201T Turbo Arrow IV	28R-8331036	N4303K	6. 5.88	Simair Ltd	Earls Colne	2. 6.08E
G-BOOH	Jodel D 112	481	F-BHVK	16. 5.88	R M MacCormac	Tibenham	9. 8.08P
	(Built Etablissement Valladeau)						
G-BOOI	Cessna 152 II	15280751	N25590	22. 8.88	Stapleford Flying Club Ltd	Stapleford	19. 5.08E
G-BOOJ	Air Command 532 Elite II	PB206		4. 5.88	Roger Savage (Penrith) Ltd	Kirkbride	6.12.91P
	(Built H P Barlow - pr.no.PFA G/04-1098)				(New owner 1.07)		
G-BOOL	Cessna 172N Skyhawk II	17272486	C-GJSY	27. 4.88	Surrey and Kent Flying Club Ltd	Biggin Hill	21.12.07T
			N5271D				
G-BOOW	Aerosport Scamp	PFA 117-10709		10. 5.88	D A Weldon	Kilrush, County Kildare	7. 9.08P
	(Built C Tyers) (Volkswagen 1834)						
G-BOOX	Rutan LongEz	PFA 074A-10844		3. 5.88	I R Wilde	Deenethorpe	23. 5.08P
	(Built I R Thomas and I R Wilde) (Lycoming O-235)						
G-BOOZ	Cameron N-77 Balloon (Hot Air)	904	(G-BKSJ)	21. 6.83	J E F Kettlety	Littleton Drew, Chippenham	8. 4.08E
	(New home built envelope c 6.98)				"Bluebell"		
G-BOPA	Piper PA-28-181 Archer II	28-8490024	N43299	28. 4.88	Flyco Ltd	Denham	5. 9.08E
G-BOPB	Boeing 767-204ER	24239	TF-ATP	1.11.88	XL Airways UK Ltd	London Gatwick	20. 4.08E
			G-BOPB, N6009F				
G-BOPC	Piper PA-28-161 Warrior II	28-8216006	N2124X	6. 5.88	Aeros Leasing Ltd	Gloucestershire	3. 8.08E
G-BOPD	Bede BD-4	632	N632DH	25. 5.88	S T Dauncey	Yearby	17. 6.08P
	(Built D E Hewes) (Lycoming O-320						
G-BOPH	Cessna TR182 Turbo Skylane RG II	R18201031	N756BJ	11. 5.88	R D Masters	Standalone Farm, Meppershall	7. 3.08E
G-BOPO	FLS Aerospace OA.7 Optica Series 301	021	EC-FVM	17. 5.88	J K Edgley	Thruxton	27. 5.96T
			EC-435, G-BOPO		(New owner 1.08)		
G-BOPR	FLS Aerospace OA.7 Optica Series 301	023		17. 5.88	Aeroelvira Ltd (New owner 1.08)	Thruxton	
G-BOPT	Grob G115	8046		10. 5.88	Upperstack Ltd t/a LAC Flying School	Barton	25.12.07E
					(Operated Lancashire Aero Club)		
G-BOPU	Grob G115	8059		10. 5.88	Upperstack Ltd t/a LAC Flying School	Barton	5. 2.08E
					(Operated Lancashire Aero Club)		
G-BOPX	Cessna A152 Aerobat	A1520932	N761BK	11. 5.88	A J Gomes (Noted dismantled 10.07)	Rochester	24. 1.98T
G-BORB	Cameron V-77 Balloon (Hot Air)	1348		24. 8.88	M H Wolff	Liskeard	9. 7.02A
G-BORD	Thunder Ax7-77 Balloon (Hot Air)	1164		26. 5.88	D D Owen "Marvin"	Wotton-under-Edge	11.12.99A
G-BORE	Colt 77A Balloon (Hot Air)	642		24. 5.88	J D Medcalf and C Wilson	Enfield	24. 8.02A
					tr Little Secret Hot Air Balloon Group "My Little Secret"		
G-BORG	Campbell Cricket	PFA G/03-1085		8. 6.88	R L Gilmore	(Cressage, Shrewsbury)	25. 4.05P
	(Built N G Bailey) (Rotax 503)				(New owner 6.07)		
G-BORH	Piper PA-34-200T Seneca II	34-8070352	N8261V	7. 6.88	The Construction Workers Guild Ltd	Elstree	25. 3.08E

Registration	Type	c/n	Prev id	Date	Owner/Operator	Location	Date
G-BORJ	Cessna 152 II	15282649	N89148	27. 5.88	Silverstar Aviation Ltd	Blackpool	10. 1.08E
G-BORK	Piper PA-28-161 Warrior II	28-8116095	G-IIIC		T W Eagles tr Warrior Group	Turweston	21.12.07E
			G-BORK, N83036		*(Orange Communications titles)*		
G-BORL	Piper PA-28-161 Cherokee Warrior II	28-7816256	N2190M	28. 9.88	Westair Flying School Ltd	Blackpool	11. 2.08E
G-BORN	Cameron N-77 Balloon (Hot Air)	1777		13. 5.88	I Chadwick *"Ian"*	Partridge Green, Bolney	3.10.08A
G-BORR	Thunder AX8-90 Balloon (Hot Air)	1256		13. 6.88	W J Harris	Schwarzhofen, Germany	10. 9.05A
G-BORS	Piper PA-28-181 Archer II	28-8090156	N8127C	31. 5.88	Silverstar Aviation Ltd *(New owner 5.07)*	Blackpool	29. 6.06T
G-BORT	Colt 77A Balloon (Hot Air)	1255		7. 6.88	J Triquet	St Gemmes-Le-Robert, France	10. 9.01A
G-BORW	Cessna 172P Skyhawk II	17274301	N51357	23. 8.88	Briter Aviation Ltd	Coventry	3.10.07E
G-BORY	Cessna 150L	15072292	N6792G	27. 5.88	C J Twelves t/a Alexander Aviation	Fenland	21. 7.08E
G-BOSB	Thunder Ax7-77 Balloon (Hot Air)	1199		7. 6.88	M Gallagher	Consett	5. 4.08A
	(Regd as c/n 581 but built as above)						
G-BOSD	Piper PA-34-200T Seneca II	34-7570085	N33086	7. 6.88	Bristol Flying Centre Ltd	Bristol	16. 8.08E
G-BOSE	Piper PA-28-181 Archer II	28-8590007	N143AV	17. 5.88	J Lemon and R Pawsey tr G-BOSE Group	White Waltham	4. 6.08E
G-BOSJ	Nord 3400	124	N9048P	26. 5.88	A I Milne	Etthornes Farm, Swaffham	1.11.94P
			French Army "MOO"		*(As "124" in French AF c/s) (Damaged Fenland 12.6.94: stored 9.02)*		
G-BOSM	CEA Jodel DR.253B Régent	168	F-BSBH	24. 5.88	A G Stevens	Full Sutton	20. 1.08E
G-BOSN	Aérospatiale AS.355F1 Ecureuil 2	5266	N2109L	22. 8.88	L L F Smith t/a Helicopter Services	Wycombe Air Park	10. 3.08E
			5N-AYL, G-BOSN, 5N-AYL				
G-BOSO	Cessna A152 Aerobat	A1520975	N761PD	25. 5.88	J S Develin and Z Islam	Redhill	16. 9.07T
G-BOSR	Piper PA-28-140 Cherokee	28-22092	N7464R	26. 5.88	C R Guggenheim tr Sierra-Romeo Group	Bournemouth	6.11.07T
G-BOTD	Cameron O-105 Balloon (Hot Air)	1611		6. 6.88	P J Beglan	Marminiac, France	21. 5.08A
G-BOTF	Piper PA-28-151 Cherokee Warrior	28-7515436	C-GGIF	8. 6.88	P E Preston tr G-BOTF Group	Southend	15.10.07E
					(Operated Southend Flying Club) (Noted 1.08)		
G-BOTG	Cessna 152 II	15283035	N46343	9. 6.88	Donington Aviation Ltd	East Midlands	12.11.07E
G-BOTH	Cessna 182Q Skylane II	18267558	N202PS	9. 6.88	A Beviss tr G-BOTH Group	Liverpool	13. 6.08E
			N114SP, N5172N				
G-BOTI	Piper PA-28-151 Warrior	28-7515251	C-GNFF	9. 6.88	A J Bamrah t/a Falcon Flying Services	Biggin Hill	31. 8.08E
	(Converted to PA-28-161 model)						
G-BOTK	Cameron O-105 Balloon (Hot Air)	1765		9. 6.88	N Woodham	Fawley, Southampton	23. 4.07T
G-BOTN	Piper PA-28-161 Warrior II	28-7916261	N2173N	9. 6.88	Apollo Aviation Advisory Ltd	Shoreham	8. 2.07T
G-BOTO	Bellanca 7ECA Citabria	939-73	N57398	9. 6.88	A K Hulme tr G-BOTO Group	Rayne Hall Farm, Braintree	21.12.07E
G-BOTP	Cessna 150J	15070736	N61017	2. 8.88	R F Finnis and C P Williams	Thruxton	2. 6.08
G-BOTU	Piper J-3C-65 Cub	19045	N98803	8. 7.88	T L Giles	Browns Farm, Hitcham	15. 4.08P
	(Continental A75)		NC98803				
G-BOTV	Piper PA-32RT-300 Lance II	32R-7885153	N36039	7. 6.88	Robin Lance Aviation Associates Ltd	Rochester	20. 1.08E
G-BOTW	Cameron V-77 Balloon (Hot Air)	1761		14. 6.88	M R Jeynes *(Inflated 4.06)*	Inkberrow, Worcester	17. 6.03A
G-BOUE	Cessna 172N Skyhawk II	17273235	N6535F	8. 8.88	P Gray and G N R Bradley	Gamston	4. 4.08E
G-BOUF	Cessna 172N Skyhawk II	17271900	N5605E	24. 6.88	B P and M I Sneap	Ripley, Derby	11. 9.08E
G-BOUJ	Cessna 150M Commuter	15076373	N3058V	25. 8.88	R D Billins tr UJ Flying Group	Cranfield	25. 1.08E
G-BOUK	Piper PA-34-200T Seneca II	34-7570124	N33476	31. 8.88	C J and R J Barnes	East Midlands	10.10.05T
G-BOUL	Piper PA-34-200T Seneca II	34-7670157	N8936C	28. 6.88	Oxford Aviation Training Ltd	Oxford	18. 4.08E
G-BOUM	Piper PA-34-200T Seneca II	34-7670136	N8401C	3. 8.88	Oxford Aviation Training Ltd	Oxford	2..4.08E
G-BOUN	Rand Robinson KR-2	PFA 129-10945		9. 6.88	P J Brookman	Knapthorpe Lodge, Caunton	30.11.07P
	(Propeller blade detached after touch-and-go Horse Leys Farm, Burton-on-the-Wolds 28. 3.07: forced landed, overturned and substantially damaged)						
G-BOUP	Piper PA-28-161 Warrior II	2816059	N9139X	12. 7.88	Aeros Holdings Ltd	Gloucestershire	10. 2.08E
G-BOUT	Colomban MC-12 Cri-Cri	12-0135	N120JN	14. 6.88	C K Farley	(Wolverhampton)	
	(Built J A Nelson)						
G-BOUV	Montgomerie-Bensen B 8MR	PFA G/01-1092		23. 6.88	L R Phillips	(Shafton, Barnsley)	13. 6.03P
	(Built P Wilkinson) (Rotax 532)				*(New owner 10.06)*		
G-BOUZ	Cessna 150G	15065606	N2606J	15. 6.88	Atlantic Bridge Aviation Ltd	Lydd	19. 1.08E
G-BOVB	Piper PA-15 Vagabond	15-180	N4396H	23. 6.88	J R Kimberley	(Lawford, Manningtree)	18. 5.05P
	(Lycoming O-145)		NC4396H				
					(Failed to gain height on take-off Whitefields Farm, South Molton, Devon 16.10.04 and suffered major damage)		
G-BOVK	Piper PA-28-161 Warrior II	28-8516061	N69168	7. 9.88	Multiflight Ltd	Leeds-Bradford	23. 5.08E
G-BOVT	Cessna 150M Commuter	15078032	N8962U	1.12.88	C J Hopewell	Fenland	13. 4.07T
G-BOVU	Stoddard-Hamilton Glasair III	3090		16. 9.88	B R Chaplin	Deenethorpe	19. 6.08P
	(Builllt A H Carrington) (Lycoming IO-540)						
G-BOVV	Cameron V-77 Balloon (Hot Air)	1724		26. 9.88	P Glydon *"Debs Delight"*	Knowle, Bristol	1. 6.08A
G-BOVW	Colt 69A Balloon (Hot Air)	1286		13. 7.88	V Hyland *"*	Turnditch, Derby	6. 4.94A
					"Enderby-Hyland Painting"		
G-BOVX	Hughes 269C	38-0673	N58170	12. 7.88	P E Tornberg	Hannington, Rushden	27. 1.08E
	(Hughes 300)						
G-BOWB	Cameron V-77 Balloon (Hot Air)	1767		13. 7.88	R A Benham	Chellaston, Derby	14. 4.08A
G-BOWE	Piper PA-34-200T Seneca II	34-7870405	N39668	14. 7.88	Oxford Aviation Services Ltd	Oxford	15 2.08E
G-BOWL	Cameron V-77 Balloon (Hot Air)	1780		26. 7.88	P G and G R Hall *"Matrix"*	Mranwood, Chard	12. 5.00A
G-BOWM	Cameron V-56 Balloon (Hot Air)	1781		26. 7.88	C G Caldecott and Georgina.Pitt	Woore, Crewe	30. 7.00A
G-BOWN	Piper PA-12 Super Cruiser	12-1912	N3661N	26. 7.88	T L Giles	Brown Farm, Hitcham, Ipswich	1.11.10S
	(Lycoming O-235)		NC3661N				
G-BOWO	Cessna R182 Skylane RG II	R18200146	(G-BOTR)	20. 7.88	D A H Morris	Halfpenny Green	29.12.07E
			N2301C				
G-BOWP	Wassmer Jodel D 120A Paris-Nice	319	F-BNZM	26. 7.88	J M Pearson	Crosland Moor	19. 3.08P
	(Continental O-200-A)						
G-BOWU	Cameron O-84 Balloon (Hot Air)	1779		1. 8.88	C F Pooley and D C Ball tr St Elmos Fire Syndicate *"Elmo"*	Barnwood, Gloucester	7. 8.01A
G-BOWV	Cameron V-65 Balloon (Hot Air)	1800		24. 8.88	R A Harris *"Sigmund"*	Axminster	12 3.08A
G-BOWY	Piper PA-28RT-201T Turbo Arrow IV	28R-8131114	N404EL	8. 8.88	J S Develin and Z Islam	Blackbushe	4.10.07E
			N83648				
G-BOWZ	Bensen B 80V	PFA G/01-1060		27. 7.88	M D Cole	Morgansfield, Fishburn	29.10.08P
	(Built W M Day) (Rotax 532)						

G-BOXA	Piper PA-28-161 Warrior II	2816075	N9149Q	1.11.88	Channel Islands Aero Club (Jersey) Ltd	Jersey	8. 7.08E
G-BOXC	Piper PA-28-161 Warrior II	2816063	N9142D	12. 8.88	Channel Islands Aero Club (Jersey) Ltd	Jersey	21. 5.08E
G-BOXG	Cameron O-77 Balloon (Hot Air)	1792		26. 8.88	R A Wicks	Norwich	12. 6.08A
G-BOXJ	Piper J-3C-90 Cub (L-4H-PI)	12193	OO-ADJ	1. 8.88	A Bendkowski	Rochester	4. 8.07P
	(Continental C90) *(Regd as L-4H)* (Frame No.12021)		44-79897		*(As "479897:JD" in USAF c/s)*		
G-BOXR	Grumman American GA-7 Cougar	GA7-0059	N772GA	19.10.88	Plane Talking Ltd	Cranfield	11. 9.08E
	(C/n plate shows manufacturer as Gulfstream American)				*(Operated Cabair)*		
G-BOXT	Hughes 269C	104-0367	SE-HMR	1. 8.88	Jetscape Leisure Ltd	Gloucestershire	23. 3.08E
	(Hughes 300)		PH-JOH, D-HBOL				
G-BOXU	Grumman AA-5B Tiger	AA5B-0026	N1526R	28. 7.88	M Hamer tr Marcher Aviation Group	Welshpool	19. 5.08E
G-BOXV	Pitts S-1S	7-0433	N27822	8. 8.88	C Waddington	Shobdon	6.11.08P
	(Built J R Castrillo)						
G-BOXW	Cassutt Racer IIIM	PFA 034-11317		11. 8.88	D I Johnson	(Leigh-on-Sea)	
	(Built D I Johnson)						
G-BOYB	Cessna A152 Aerobat	A1520928	N761AW	29. 7.88	Modi Aviation Ltd	Sibson	27. 9.08E
G-BOYC	Robinson R22 Beta	0837		22. 8.88	M D Thorpe t/a Yorkshire Helicopters	Coney Park, Leeds	9. 6.08E
G-BOYF	Sikorsky S-76B	760343		15. 9.88	Darley Stud Management Company Ltd	Cambridge	24.11.07E
					(Operated Air Hanson)		
G-BOYH	Piper PA-28-151 Cherokee Warrior	28-7715290	N8795F	8. 8.88	D Wood-Jenkins, Skytime Flight Training Ltd and D A Keen		
	(Converted to PA-28-161 model)					Gloucestershire	20. 3.08E
G-BOYI	Piper PA-28-161 Cherokee Warrior II		N9032K	8. 8.88	A P Ware and S Hoy tr G-BOYI Group	Sleap	3. 6.08E
		28-7816183					
G-BOYL	Cessna 152 II	15284379	N6232L	11. 8.88	Redhill Air Services Ltd *(New owner 2.08)*	Redhill	26. 2.01T
G-BOYM	Cameron O-84 Balloon (Hot Air)	1796		25. 8.88	M P Ryan *"Frontline"*	Newbury	
G-BOYO	Cameron V-20 Balloon (Hot Air)	1843		27. 9.88	J M Willard	Burgess Hill	
G-BOYP	Cessna 172N Skyhawk II	17270349	N738YU	22. 8.88	I D and Delia Brierley	North Weald	19. 5.08E
G-BOYR	Reims Cessna F337G Super Skymaster	F33700070	RA-04147	9. 9.88	Tri-Star Farms Ltd	Andreas, Isle of Man	30. 4.08E
	(Wichita c/n 33701589)		G-BOYR, PH-RPE				
G-BOYS	Cameron N-77 Balloon (Hot Air)	1759		16. 6.88	Julie King	Chippenham	8. 3.05T
G-BOYU	Cessna A150L Aerobat	A1500497	N8121L	31. 8.88	Upperstack Ltd	Barton	14.11.07E
G-BOYV	Piper PA-28R-201T Turbo Arrow III		N1143H	1. 9.88	Arrow Air Ltd	Wellesbourne Mountford	1. 8.08E
		28R-7703014					
G-BOYX	Robinson R22 Beta	0862	N90813	25. 8.88	R Towle	(Barrasford, Hexham)	28. 9.91T
					(Damaged Teesside 18. 7.90)		
G-BOZI	Piper PA-28-161 Warrior II	28-8116120	(G-BOSZ)	14. 7.88	Aerolease Ltd	Conington	20.12.07E
			N8318A				
G-BOZN	Cameron N-77 Balloon (Hot Air)	1807		1. 9.88	Calarel Developments Ltd	Chipping Campden	10. 5.06A
					"Calarel Developments"		
G-BOZO	Gulfstream AA-5B Tiger	AA5B-1282	N4536Q	12. 8.88	Caslon Ltd	Biggin Hill	29. 1.08E
G-BOZR	Cessna 152 II	15284614	N6083M	7. 9.88	Gem Rewinds Ltd	Coventry	1. 4.07T
G-BOZS	Pitts S-1C	221-H	N10EZ	31. 8.88	T A S Rayner	Perth	1. 8.08P
	(Built W A Orr) (Lycoming O-320-A2B)						
G-BOZU	Aero Dynamics Sparrow Hawk Mk II	PFA 184-11371		12.12.88	R V Phillimore	(Bexhill-on-Sea)	
	(Built R V Phillimore)						
G-BOZV	Robin DR.340 Major	416	F-BRTS	9. 8.88	C J Turner and S D Kent	Garston Farm, Marshfield	21.12.07E
G-BOZW	Bensen B 8MR	PFA G/01-1096		1. 9.88	M E Wills	Lytchett Matravers	8. 6.07P
	(Built M E Wills) (Rotax 532)						
G-BOZY	Cameron RTW-120 Balloon (Hot Air)	1770		1. 9.88	Magical Adventures Ltd		
						West Bloomfield, Michigan, US	21. 4.97A
G-BOZZ	Gulfstream AA-5B Tiger	AA5B-1155	N4530N	22. 8.88	A W Matthews tr Solent Tiger Group	Lee-on-Solent	1. 3.08E

G-BPAA - G-BPZZ

G-BPAA	Acro Advanced	AA-001		26. 8.88	B O and F A Smith	Yearby	7. 8.08P
	(Built B O Smith - pr.no.PFA 200-11528) (Volkswagen Acro 2100)						
G-BPAB	Cessna 150M Commuter	15077244	N63335	21. 9.88	M J Diggins	Rayne Hall Farm, Braintree	18. 9.09E
G-BPAF	Piper PA-28-161 Cherokee Warrior II		N3199Q	6. 9.88	RAF Brize Norton Flying Club Ltd	RAF Brize Norton	16. 7.08E
		28-7716142					
G-BPAJ	de Havilland DH.82A Tiger Moth	83472	G-AOIX	5.11.80	P A Jackson	Raby's Farm, Great Stukeley	11. 7.09S
	(Built Morris Motors Ltd)		T7087		*(May be composite rebuild from original G-AMNN qv)*		
G-BPAL	de Havilland DHC-1 Chipmunk 22	C1/0437	G-BCYE	29.10.86	K F and Phyllis .Tomsett	(Carvoeiro, Portigal)	12. 9.09
			WG350		*(As "WG350" in RAF c/s)*		
G-BPAS	SOCATA TB-20 Trinidad	283	A2-ADR	9.11.88	Syndicate Clerical Services Ltd	Exeter	5. 7.08T
			F-GDBO				
G-BPAW	Cessna 150M Commuter	15077923	N8348U	5. 9.88	P D Sims tr G-BPAW Group		
						Lower Wasing Farm, Brimpton	17.10.07E
G-BPAX	Cessna 150M Commuter	15077401	N63571	5. 9.88	M K Casely and C J Horlock tr The Dirty Dozen		
						Shoreham	23. 9.08E
G-BPAY	Piper PA-28-181 Archer II	28-8090191	N3568X	12. 9.98	D A C Smith	(Gosberton, Spalding)	13. 5.07T
G-BPBB	Evans VP-2	PFA 063-11261		2. 9.88	A Bleese	Hill Farm, Nayland	9. 6.97P
	(Built J S Penny)				*(Noted 5.03: new owner 5.05)*		
G-BPBJ	Cessna 152 II	15283639	N4793B	9. 9.88	W Shaw and P G Haines		
						Whaley Farm, New York, Lincoln	4. 5.08E
G-BPBK	Cessna 152 II	15283417	N49095	9. 9.88	Atlantic Flight Training Ltd	Coventry	21. 8.08E
G-BPBM	Piper PA-28-161 Warrior II	28-7916272	N3050N	12. 9.88	Redhill Air Services Ltd	Redhill	1.12.07T
G-BPBO	Piper PA-28RT-201T Turbo Arrow IV		N8431H	28. 9.88	Tile Holdings Ltd	Sandtoft	18. 7.08E
		28R-8131195					
G-BPBP	Brügger MB.2 Colibri Mk.II	PFA 043-10246		6. 2.78	D A Preston	(Ulverston)	16. 9.08P
	(Built B Perkins) (Volkswagen 1600)						
G-BPBV	Cameron V-77 Balloon (Hot Air)	1821		21. 9.88	S J Farrant	Hydestile, Godalmimg	10. 6.05A
					"Sugar Plumb" (Noted 8.06)		
G-BPBW	Cameron O-105 Balloon (Hot Air)	1841		14.10.88	R J Mansfield	Bowness-on-Windermere	23. 2.08A
					"October Gold"		

Reg	Type	C/n	Prev id	Date	Owner/Operator	Location	Date
G-BPBY	Cameron V-77 Balloon (Hot Air)	1818	(G-BPCS)	9.12.88	C Kunert	Johannesburg, South Africa	30. 4.08A
G-BPCA	Pilatus Britten-Norman BN-2B-26 Islander	2198	G-BLNX	28. 1.88	Loganair Ltd (*Highland Park titles*)	Kirkwall	16. 2.08E
G-BPCF	Piper J-3C-65 Cub	4532	N140DC	12. 5.89	J S Evans	Wycombe Air Park	1. 9.08P
	(Continental O-200-A)		N28033, NC28033		(*Lippert Reed clipped-wing conversion - s/n SA811SW*)		
G-BPCG	Colt AS-80 Mk.II Airship (Hot Air)	1300		14.10.88	N Charbonnier	Aosta, Italy	10.10.96A
					"*Greensport*" and "*Napapijri*"		
G-BPCI	Cessna R172K Hawk XP	R1722360	N9976V	3. 1.89	W B Bateson	Blackpool	11. 4.08E
G-BPCK	Piper PA-28-161 Warrior II	28-8016279	N8529N	26. 9.88	Compton Abbas Airfield Ltd	Compton Abbas	12. 9.08E
			C-GMEI, N9519N				
G-BPCL	Scottish Aviation Bulldog Series 120/128		HKG-6	20. 9.88	Isohigh Ltd t/a 121 Group	North Weald	6. 9.10S
		BH120/393	G-31-19		(*As "HKG-6" in Royal Hong Kong AAF c/s*)		
G-BPCM	RotorWay Executive	E 3293	N979WP	21. 9.88	D Rigby	(Barnsley)	25.11.91P
	(*Built W Petrie*) (RotorWay RW152)				(*New owner 3.06*)		
G-BPCR	Mooney M 20K Mooney 231	25-0532	N98433	23. 9.88	T and R Harris "*Over The Moony*"	Biggin Hill	7. 9.08E
G-BPCV	Montgomerie-Bensen B 8MR	PFA G/01-1088		11.10.88	M A Hayward	(Liskeard)	25. 7.91P
	(*Built J Fisher*) (Rotax 532)				(*New owner 2.03*)		
G-BPCX	Piper PA-28-236 Dakota	28-8211004	N8441S	25.10.88	Blue Yonder Aviation Ltd	Earls Colne	17. 9.08E
G-BPDG	Cameron V-77 Balloon (Hot Air)	1839		21.10.88	F R Battersby "*Pretty Damn Good*"	Worsley, Manchester	5.11.08A
G-BPDJ	Chris Tena Mini Coupe	275	N13877	4.10.88	J J Morrissey	(Teddington)	
	(Volkswagen 1835)				(*Wings only noted Durham Tees Valley 4.05*)		
G-BPDM	CASA 1-131E Jungmann	2058	Spanish AF E3B-369	24.10.88	J D Haslam	(Northallerton)	22. 6.96P
					(*As "E3B-369:781-32" in Spanish AF c/s*)		
G-BPDT	Piper PA-28-161 Warrior II	28-8416004	N4317Z	22.12.88	Channel Islands Aero Club (Jersey) Ltd	Jersey	18.12.07T
					(*Noted 1.08*)		
G-BPDV	Pitts S-1S	27P	N330VE	15. 9.88	J Vize	Leicester	29.10.07P
	(*Built C H Pitts*)						
G-BPEC	Boeing 757-236	24882		6.11.90	British Airways PLC	London Heathrow	12.11.07E
G-BPED	Boeing 757-236	25059		30. 4.91	British Airways PLC	London Heathrow	29. 4.08E
G-BPEE	Boeing 757-236	25060		3. 5.91	British Airways PLC	London Heathrow	2. 5.08E
G-BPEI	Boeing 757-236	25806	(G-BMRK)	9. 3.94	British Airways PLC	London Heathrow	8.12.07E
					"*Chatham Historic Dockyard*"		
G-BPEJ	Boeing 757-236	25807	(G-BMRL)	22. 4.94	British Airways PLC	London Heathrow	24. 4.08E
					(*Operated Open Skies 6.08*)		
G-BPEK	Boeing 757-236	25808	(G-BMRM)	17. 3.95	British Airways PLC	London Heathrow	16. 3.08E
					(*Operated Open Skies 6.08*)		
G-BPEM	Cessna 150K	15071707	N6207G	24.10.88	C G Rice	Henstridge	24. 2.08E
G-BPEO	Cessna 152 II	15283775	C-GQVO	10.10.88	JHP Aviation Ltd	Coventry	17. 7.08E
			(N5147B)				
G-BPES	Piper PA-38-112 Tomahawk II	38-81A0064	N25728	2.11.88	The Sherwood Flying Club Ltd	Tollerton	27. 1.07T
G-BPEZ	Colt 77A Balloon (Hot Air)	1324		14.10.88	J W Adkins	Market Harborough	8. 7.08A
G-BPFB	Colt 77A Balloon (Hot Air)	1334		26.10.88	S Ingram	Oldham	5. 7.04A
G-BPFC	Mooney M 20C Mark 21	20-1243	N3606H	21.10.88	D P Wring	Dunkeswell	6.11.07E
G-BPFD	Jodel D 112	312	F-PHJT	3.11.88	C P Whitwell	Fenland	26. 4.08P
	(*Built Aero Club de L`Orne*)						
G-BPFF	Cameron DP-70 Airship (Hot Air)	1831		24.10.88	John Aimo Balloons SAS	Mondovi, Italy	22. 5.08A
G-BPFH	Piper PA-28-161 Warrior II	28-8116201	N83723	3.11.88	M H Kleiser (*Operated Edinburgh Flying Club*)	Edinburgh	5. 2.08E
G-BPFI	Piper PA-28-181 Archer II	28-8090113	N8103G	5. 1.89	F Teagle	Bodmin	18. 7.08
G-BPFL	Davis DA-2A	051	N72RJ	27.10.88	B W Griffiths	Coventry	11. 1.09P
	(*Built A Tribling*) (Continental O-200-A)						
G-BPFM	Aeronca 7AC Champion	7AC-4751	N1193E	13.10.88	D Boyce	Bodmin	7. 8.08P
			NC1193E				
G-BPFN	Short SD.3-60 Variant 100	SH3747	N747HH	2.11.88	Aurigny Air Services Ltd	Guernsey	8. 9.07E
			N747SA, G-BPFN, G-14-3747		(*Aurigny.com titles*) (*Stored 2.07*)		
G-BPFZ	Cessna 152 II	15285741	N94594	27.10.88	Devon and Somerset Flight Training Ltd	Dunkeswell	13. 2.08E
G-BPGC	Speich Air Command Gyroplane	0440		11.10.88	A G W Davis	(West Bridgford, Nottingham)	15.12.06P
	(*Built G A Speich - pr.no.PFA G/04-1108 as modified Air Command 532 Elite*)				(*Noted Henstridge 8.07*)		
G-BPGD	Cameron V-65 Balloon (Hot Air)	2000		9. 9.88	Gone With The Wind Ltd	Schwieberdingen, Germany	6. 7.08A
	(*Rebuilt with new envelope c/n 4969 c 8.01*)				"*Silver Lining*"		
G-BPGE	Cessna U206C Super Skywagon	U2061013	N29017	7.11.88	K Brady tr The Scottish Parachute Club	Strathallan	18.11.07E
G-BPGF	Thunder Ax7-77 Balloon (Hot Air)	1355		22.11.88	M Schiavo "*Dovetail*"	Manchester	25. 8.95A
G-BPGH	EAA Acrosport II	422	N12JE	14.11.88	G M Bradley	Redhill	22.10.08P
	(*Built J Ellenbaas*) (Continental IO-346)						
G-BPGK	Aeronca 7AC Champion	7AC-7187	N4409E	7. 2.89	D A Crompton and G C Holmes		
	(Continental A65)					Yeatsall Farm, Abbots Bromley	15. 5.08P
G-BPGT	Colt AS-80 Mk.II Airship (Hot Air)	1248	(I -. . . .)	14.11.88	P Porati	Milano, Italy	20. 7.00A
			G-BPGT				
G-BPGU	Piper PA-28-181 Archer II	28-8490025	N4330B	26.10.88	G Underwood	Tollerton	8. 3.08E
G-BPGV	Robinson R22 Beta	0887		3.11.88	G Gazza	(Monte Carlo, Monaco)	24. 5.06T
G-BPGZ	Cessna 150G	15064912	N3612J	14.11.88	J B Scott	Blackpool	20. 5.08E
G-BPHD	Cameron N-42 Balloon (Hot Air)	1863		21. 2.89	P J Marshall and M A Clarke "*Ellen Gee II*"	Ruislip	9. 6.02A
G-BPHG	Robin DR.400-180 Régent	1887		29.11.88	A B Brock	(Great Billing, Northampton)	25. 6.08E
G-BPHH	Cameron V-77 Balloon (Hot Air)	1840		2.12.88	C D Aindow "*Office Angels*"	Tonbridge	16. 6.06A
G-BPHI	Piper PA-38-112 Tomahawk	38-79A0002	N2535T	22.11.88	J S Develin and Z Islam	Blackbushe	22. 7.07T
G-BPHJ	Cameron V-77 Balloon (Hot Air)	1881		23.11.88	C W Brown "*Twiggy*"	Nottingham	14. 4.06A
G-BPHK	Whittaker MW7	PFA 171-11389		24.11.88	J S Shufflebottom	(Chepstow)	23. 6.04P
	(*Built J G Beesley*)						
G-BPHL	Piper PA-28-161 Warrior II	28-7916315	N555PY	2.12.88	J D Swales	Bagby	19. 7.04T
			N2247U		(*Noted 3.05*)		
G-BPHO	Taylorcraft BC-12D	8497	N96197	10. 1.89	B J Swanton	Ballymageough, Kilkeel	31. 5.07P
			NC96197		"*Spirit of Missouri*" (*Noted 7.07*)		
G-BPHP	Taylorcraft BC-12-65	2799	N33948	12.12.88	J S Jackson	(Nottingham)	2.11.99P
	(Continental A65)		NC33948		(*New owner 8.04*)		
G-BPHR	de Havilland DH.82A Tiger Moth	45	N48DH	3. 1.89	N Parry tr A17-48 Group (*As "A17-48" in RAustralianAF c/s*)		
	(*Built de Havilland Aircraft Proprietary Ltd Australia*)		VH-BLX, A17-48			Lotmead Farm, Wanborough	15. 5.09

Reg	Type	C/n	Prev ID	Date	Owner/Operator	Base	Date
G-BPHT	Cessna 152 II	15282401	N961LP	5.12.88	I A Anderson	(Little Snoring)	22. 6.08E
G-BPHU	Thunder Ax7-77 Balloon (Hot Air)	1365		19.12.88	R P Waite	St Helens	11. 4.08A
G-BPHW	Cessna 140 (Continental C85)	11035	N76595 NC76595	13. 1.89	L J A Bell	White Waltham	18. 6.08E
G-BPHX	Cessna 140 (Continental C85)	12488	N2252N NC2252N	2.12.88	M McChesney	(Enniskillen)	23. 5.93
G-BPHZ	Morane Saulnier MS.505 Criquet	53/7	F-BJQC French Military	17. 4.89	Aero Vintage Ltd *(As "DM+BK in I/JG54 Luftwaffe c/s)*	Audley End	18. 4.08P
G-BPIF	Bensen-Parsons Two-Place Gyroplane *(Built W Parsons)* (Rotax 532)	UK-01		19.12.88	B J L P and W J A Lde Saar *(Noted 8.06)*	Shipdham	28. 3.96P
G-BPII	Denney Kitfox Model 1 *(Built R Derbyshire - pr.no.PFA 172-11496)* (IAME KFM 112)	213		15.12.88	P Etherington tr G-BPII Group	Sandtoft	17. 9.08P
G-BPIJ	Brantly B 2B	465	N2293U	23. 3.89	I Davies tr Seething Brantly Group	Seething	3. 4.08E
G-BPIK	Piper PA-38-112 Tomahawk II	38-82A0028	N3947M ZP-EAP, N91423	2.12.88	Fly Me Ltd	Carlisle	22. 5.08E
G-BPIL	Cessna 310B	35620	N620GS OO-SEF, N5420A	16.11.89	A L Brown *"Fast Lady" (On slow rebuild 10.05)*	Bourn	28. 4.00T
G-BPIN	Glaser-Dirks DG-400	4-242		14.12.88	C E Griffiths and J N Stevenson	Lasham	11. 4.08E
G-BPIP	Slingsby T.31 Motor Cadet III *(Re-built J H Beard)* (Volkswagen 1600)	PFA 042-10771		14.11.88	V K Meers Pendeford, Wolverhampton *(New owner 12.07)*		27. 9.96P
G-BPIR	Scheibe SF25E Super Falke (Limbach SL1700)	4332	N25SF (D-KDFX)	15.12.88	A P Askwith	Rhosgoch	17. 4.08E
G-BPIT	Robinson R22 Beta	0907	N80011	22.12.88	NA Air Ltd	Blacklaw Farm, Aberbothrie	8. 8.08E
G-BPIU	Piper PA-28-161 Warrior II	28-7916303	N3028T	28.12.88	T S Rafter tr Golf India Uniform Group	Fairoaks	14. 4.07
G-BPIV	Bristol 149 Blenheim IV *(Built Fairchild Aircraft Ltd as Bollingbroke IVT)*	?	"Z5722" 152.89 RCAF 10201		Blenheim (Duxford) Ltd Duxford *(As "R3821:UX-N"in RAF c/s) "Spirit of Britain First" (On rebuild 6.05)*		19. 6.04P
G-BPIZ	Gulfstream AA-5B Tiger	AA5B-1154	N4530L	14. 2.89	N R F McNally	Shoreham	21. 8.08E
G-BPJB	Schweizer 269C *(Schweizer 300)*	S 1331	N75065	7.11.88	Elborne Holdings Ltd	Cascais, Portugal	14.11.07
G-BPJD	SOCATA Rallye 110ST	3253	OY-CAV	22.12.88	L P Claydon	(Gedding, Bury St Edmunds)	26. 9.08E
G-BPJE	Cameron A-105 Balloon (Hot Air)	1864		8.11.88	A Parsons tr Loughborough Students Hot Air Balloon Club	Loughborough	13. 4.08A
G-BPJG	Piper PA-18-150 Super Cub	18-8350	SE-EZG N4172Z	4. 1.89	M W Stein	Oaksey Park	12. 9.10
G-BPJH	Piper PA-18 Super Cub 95 (L-18C-PI)	18-1980	EI-59 24. 5.83 I-EICA, MM52-2380, 52-2380		P J Heron	Blackhill, Draperstown	22. 4.08P
G-BPJK	Colt 77A Balloon (Hot Air)	1362		22.12.88	Saran UK Ltd	Cheltenham	10.10.04A
G-BPJO	Piper PA-28-161 Cadet	2841014	N9153Z	15.12.88	S J Skilton t/a Aviation Rentals	Bournemouth	22.12.07E
G-BPJP	Piper PA-28-161 Cadet *(Thielert TAE 125)*	2841015	N9154K	22.12.88	S J Skilton t/a Aviation Rentals *(Operated Solent Flight)*	Bournemouth	28. 6.08E
G-BPJR	Piper PA-28-161 Cadet	2841024	N9154X	17. 1.89	Plane Talking Ltd	Denham	22.11.07E
G-BPJS	Piper PA-28-161 Cadet	2841025	EC-IBG 12. 1.89 G-BPJS, N9154Z		Abraxas Aviation Ltd	Denham	18.12.07T
G-BPJU	Piper PA-28-161 Cadet	2841032	N9156Z	11. 1.89	S J Skilton t/a Aviation Rentals *(Operated Bookajet Operations Ltd)*	Lee-on-Solent	15. 4.08E
G-BPJV	Taylorcraft F-21	F-1005	N2004L	12. 1.89	P Glennon tr TC Flying Group *(Crashed in field near Corn Dean Lane, Winchcombe 28.11.05 and substantially damaged)*	Enstone	9. 9.05P
G-BPJW	Cessna A150K Aerobat	A1500127	C-FAJX CF-AJX, N8427M	4. 1.89	Heald Ltd	Bagby	2. 8.07T
G-BPKF	Grob G115	8075		3. 1.89	W R Field tr Dorset Aviation Group *(Operated Bournemouth Flying Club)*	Bournemouth	27. 1.07
G-BPKK	Denney Kitfox Model 1 *(Built R W Holmes - pr.no.PFA 172-11411) (Originally laid down as Model 2)* (Rotax 532)	264		19.12.88	D Moffat	Lochview House, Limerigg	11.10.02P
G-BPKM	Piper PA-28-161 Warrior II	28-7916341	PH-CKO 6. 1.89 N2140X, N9630N		R Cass	Durham Tees Valley	17. 7.08E
G-BPKO	Cessna 140	8936	N89891 12. 1.89 NC89891		M G Rummey *(Dismantled 4.06)*	(Binderton, West Sussex)	18. 5.06
G-BPKR	Piper PA-28-151 Cherokee Warrior	28-7515446	N4341X	13. 3.89	Aeros Leasing Ltd	Gloucestershire	20. 5.08E
G-BPLH	CEA Jodel DR.1051 Sicile *(Potez 4E20A)*	401	F-BLAE	27. 2.89	C K Farley	Halfpenny Green	29. 1.08E
G-BPLM	AIA Stampe SV-4C *(Officially regd as built SNCAN)*	1004	F-BHET 8. 2.89 French Army, F-BDKC		C J Jesson	Headcorn	30. 1.09S
G-BPLV	Cameron V-77 Balloon (Hot Air) *(Rebuilt1998)*	1822		23. 1.89	MC VH SA *(Noted 8.06)*	Brussels, Belgium	22. 9.08A
G-BPLY	Pitts S-2B *(Built Christen Industries Inc)* (Lycoming AEIO-540)	5149		25. 1.89	P A Greenhalgh	Spilstead Farm, Sedlescombe	7. 8.08S
G-BPLZ	Hughes 369HS *(Hughes 500)*	91-0342S	N126CM	15. 2.89	M A and R J Fawcett	(Leeds)	27. 9.07E
G-BPMB	Maule M-5-235C Lunar Rocket	7284C	N5635T	13. 8.79	R G Marshall	Crosland Moor	25. 4.08E
G-BPME	Cessna 152 II	15285585	N94021	24. 1.89	A Jahanfar *(Operated Southend School of Flying) (Damaged Southend, 28. 4.07: noted 1.08)*	Southend	24. 8.07T
G-BPMF	Piper PA-28-151 Cherokee Warrior	28-7515050	C-GOXL	2. 2.89	A Hill and P A Lewis tr Mike Foxtrot Group (Harrogate and Barrow-in-Furness)		5. 5.08E
G-BPML	Cessna 172M Skyhawk II	17267102	N1435U	17.11.89	N A Bilton	Priory Farm, Tibenham	26. 9.08E
G-BPMR	Piper PA-28-161 Warrior II	28-8416119	N4373S N9620N	25. 1.89	Aeros Holdings Ltd	Gloucestershire	17. 5.07T
G-BPMU	Nord 3202B	70	(G-BIZJ) 26. 1.89 N22546, French Army		A I Milne *"AIX" (Stored owner's workshop 2007)*	(Swanton Morley, Dereham)	19.10.90P
G-BPMW	QAC Quickie Q.2 *(Built R Davidson-Outbridge) (Revmaster R2100DQ)*	PFA 094A-10790	G-OICI G-OGKN	13. 3.89	P M Wright *(Damaged near Basingstoke 16. 2.91: on repair 9.00)*	(Waldringfield, Woodbridge)	17. 8.91P
G-BPMX	ARV Aviation ARV-1 Super 2 *(Built B Houghton - pr.no.PFA 152-11128)*	K 005		30. 1.89	R A Collins *(New owner 11.07)*	(Chippenham)	22. 9.06P
G-BPNA	Cessna 150L	15073042	N1742Q	10. 2.89	M P Whitley and G W Todd tr Wolds Flyers Syndicate Eddsfield, Octon Lodge Farm, Thwing		1. 6.08E

Reg	Type	C/n	Prev ID	Date	Owner/Operator	Location	Date
G-BPNI	Robinson R22 Beta	0948		6. 2.89	Heliflight (UK) Ltd	Gloucestershire	12. 4.08E
G-BPNJ	Hawker Siddeley HS.748 Series 2A/263	1680	ZS-ODJ	3. 2.89	PTB (Emerald) Proprietary.Ltd	Blackpool	
			F-GHKA, G-BPNJ, 9J-ABW, G-11-4 *(On fire dump as "ZS-ODJ" 6.06)*				
G-BPNN	Montgomerie-Bensen B 8MR	MV-003		3. 2.89	M E Vahdat-Hagh	(Uxbridge)	
	(Built M E Vahdat-Hagh)						
G-BPNO	Moravan Zlin Z-526 Trener Master	930	F-BPNO	18. 2.86	J A S Baldry and S T Logan	RAF Cranwell	21. 6.08E
G-BPNT	British Aerospace BAe 146 Series 300	E3126		4. 1.89	Flightline Ltd	Rotterdam, Netherlands	31. 5.08E
					(Operated VLM Airlines in VLM c/s) "Spirit of Rotterdam".		
G-BPNU	Thunder Ax7-77 Balloon (Hot Air)	1011		9. 2.89	M J Barnes *"Firefly"*	Ivybridge	16. 8.02T
G-BPOB	Sopwith Camel F 1 replica	TM-10	N8997	14. 3.89	Bianchi Aviation Film Services Ltd	Compton Abbas	24. 7.05P
	(Built Tallmantz Aviation Inc) (Warner Scarab 165)				*(In Flying Aces Movie Aeroplane Collection 1.06 as "B2458:R" in RFC c/s))*		
G-BPOM	Piper PA-28-161 Warrior II	28-8416118	N4373Q	15. 2.89	C Dale tr POM Flying Group	Humberside	25. 4.08E
			N9619N		*(Operated Soloflight)*		
G-BPON	Piper PA-34-200T Seneca II	34-7570040	N675ES	13. 2.89	Aeros Leasing Ltd	Gloucestershire	11. 7.07T
			N32644				
G-BPOO	Montgomerie-Bensen B 8MR	MV-002		3. 2.89	M E Vahdat-Hagh	(Uxbridge)	
	(Built M E Vahdat-Hagh - pr.no.PFA G/01A-1109)				*(Believed not constructed)*		
G-BPOS	Cessna 150M	15075905	N66187	21. 2.89	Brooke Park Ltd	Durham Tees Valley	13. 2.08E
G-BPOT	Piper PA-28-181 Cherokee Archer II	28-7790267	N8807F	7. 2.89	Icarus Flyers Ltd	Rochester	6. 1.08E
G-BPOU	Luscombe 8A Silvaire	4159	N1432K	14. 2.89	J L Grayer	(Danehill, Haywards Heath)	4.11.02P
	(Continental A65)		NC1432K		*(New owner 1.06)*		
G-BPPA	Cameron O-65 Balloon (Hot Air)	1930		15. 2.89	Rix Petroleum Ltd *"Rix Petroleum"*	Hull	29. 1.08E
G-BPPE	Piper PA-38-112 Tomahawk	38-79A0189	N2445C	15. 2.89	First Air Ltd	Haverfordwest	24. 4.08E
					(Noted 11.04 for major surgery with G-BNPL to provide a single flyer)		
G-BPPF	Piper PA-38-112 Tomahawk	38-79A0578	N2329K	15. 2.89	D J Bellamy tr Bristol Strut Flying Group	Bristol	13. 1.08E
G-BPPK	Piper PA-28-151 Cherokee Warrior	28-7615054	N7592C	10. 3.89	Idfit Ltd	Headcorn	30. 6.08E
G-BPPO	Luscombe 8A Silvaire	2541	N3519M	15. 2.89	M G Rummey	(Binderton, West Sussex)	23. 7.08P
	(Continental A65)		N71114, NC71114				
G-BPPP	Cameron V-77 Balloon (Hot Air)	1700		29. 2.88	P F Smart tr The Sarnia Balloon Group		
					"Thruppence" (Inflated 4.06)	Oakley, Basingstoke	28. 6.97A
G-BPPS	Mudry CAP.21	09	F-GDTD	3. 5.85	L van Vuuren	Durham Tees Valley	27. 9.07E
G-BPPU	Air Command 532 Elite	0438		22. 2.89	J Hough	Alresford	18.10.91P
	(Built J Hough - pr.no.PFA G/04-1120)						
G-BPPY	Hughes 269B	20-0448	N9554F	10. 3.89	M D Lenney	(Patrington, Hull)	11. 5.08E
	(Hughes 300)						
G-BPPZ	Taylorcraft BC-12D	7988	N28286	22. 3.89	I R Henderson	Mosside Farm, Carluke	31. 5.08P
	(Continental C85)		NC28286				
G-BPRA	Aeronca 11AC Chief	11AC-1344	N9702E	22. 3.89	P L Clements	Beeches Farm, South Scarle	9. 5.08P
			NC9702E				
G-BPRC	Cameron Elephant 77 SS Balloon (Hot Air)	1871		21. 2.89	A Schneider *"Elefant Benjamin"*	Borken, Germany	27. 3.08A
G-BPRD	Pitts S-1C	ZZ.1	N10ZZ	21. 2.89	P Rhodes and R Trickey tr Parrot Aerobatic Group		
	(Built P C Serkland)					Pittrichie Farm, Whiterashes	17. 7.06P
G-BPRI	Aérospatiale AS.355F1 Ecureuil 2	5181	G-TVPA	22. 2.89	MW Helicopters Ltd	Stapleford	5. 11.07E
			G-BPRI, N364E				
G-BPRJ	Aérospatiale AS.355F1 Ecureuil 2	5201	N368E	22. 2.89	PLM Dollar Group Ltd	Cumbernauld	14.12.07E
G-BPRL	Aérospatiale AS.355F1 Ecureuil 2	5154	N362E	22. 2.89	MW Helicopters Ltd	Stapleford	4.10.07T
G-BPRM	Reims Cessna F172L	F17200825	G-AZKG	20. 4.88	BJ Aviation Ltd	Welshpool	24. 1.08E
G-BPRN	Piper PA-28-161 Warrior II	28-8116109	N83112	6. 3.89	Air Navigation and Trading Company Ltd	Blackpool	2. 6.08E
G-BPRR	Rand Robinson KR-2	PFA 129-11105		1. 3.89	P E Taylor	(Ferndown)	
	(Built M W Albery)				*(New owner 1.03)*		
G-BPRX	Aeronca 11AC Chief	11AC-94	N86288	3. 3.89	M G Rummey	Preston Farm, Binderton	23. 8.99P
	(Continental A75)		NC86288		*(New owner 5.06)*		
G-BPRY	Piper PA-28-161 Warrior II	28-8416120	N4373Y	2. 3.89	R C White t/a White Wings Aviation	East Midlands	30. 6.08E
			N9621N		*"17"*		
G-BPSH	Cameron V-77 Balloon (Hot Air)	1837		21. 2.89	P G Hossack *"Coconut Ice"*	Pewsey	5. 4.97T
G-BPSJ	Thunder Ax6-56 Balloon (Hot Air)	1479		13. 3.89	V Hyland	(Turnditch, Derby)	5. 6.04A
G-BPSK	Montgomerie-Bensen B 8M	PFA G/01-1100		15. 3.89	P T Ambrozik	(Great Orton)	25.11.99P
	(Built P Harrison) (Rotax 532)						
G-BPSL	Cessna 177 Cardinal	17701138	N659SR	3. 3.89	K S Herbert	Elstree	5.12.07E
G-BPSO	Cameron N-90 Balloon (Hot Air)	1959		10. 3.89	J Oberprieler	Mauern, Germany	21. 9.08A
G-BPSR	Cameron V-77 Balloon (Hot Air)	1962		10. 3.89	K J A Maxwell	Haywards Heath	11. 5.05T
					"Norma Jean" (Noted 5.07)		
G-BPSS	Cameron A-120 Balloon (Hot Air)	1947		27. 2.89	Anglian Countryside Balloons Ltd	Burnham-on-Crouch	17. 3.06T
G-BPTA	Stinson 108-2 Voyager	108-3429	N429C	22. 3.89	M L Ryan	Garston Farm, Marshfield	29.10.10
	(Built Consolidated Vultee Aircraft)		NC429C				
G-BPTD	Cameron V-77 Balloon (Hot Air)	2001		14. 3.89	J Lippett *"Visions 2001"*	South Petherton, Somerset	31. 5.04A
G-BPTE	Piper PA-28-181 Cherokee Archer II	28-7690178	N8553E	9. 3.89	J S Develin and Z Islam	Redhill	25. 8.07T
G-BPTG	Rockwell Commander 112TC	13067	N4577W	31. 3.89	B Ogunyemi	Kirknewton	15. 8.08E
G-BPTI	SOCATA TB-20 Trinidad	414	N41BM	21. 4.89	N Davis	Blackbushe	3. 7.08
G-BPTL	Cessna 172N Skyhawk II	17268652	N733YJ	22. 3.89	Tindon Engineering Ltd	Little Snoring	5. 6.08E
G-BPTS	CASA 1-131E Jungmann	?	Spanish AF E3B-153	23. 5.89	Aerobatic Displays Ltd	Duxford	16. 3.07P
			"781-75"		*(As "E3B-153:781-75" in Spanish AF c/s) (Operated The Old Flying Machine Company)*		
G-BPTU	Cessna 152 II	15282955	N45946	22. 3.89	A M Alam *(On rebuild 6.07)*	North Weald	21.10.06T
G-BPTV	Bensen B 8	PFA G/01-1058		30. 3.89	C Munro	(Trawden, Colne)	
	(Built L Chiappi)						
G-BPTX	Cameron O-120 Balloon (Hot Air)	1972		29. 3.89	S J Colin t/a Skybus Ballooning	Cranbrook	2. 6.05T
G-BPTZ	Robinson R22 Beta	0958		22. 3.89	Aero Maintenance Ltd	Gamston	17. 1.08E
G-BPUA	EAA Biplane Sport	xxxx	EI-BBF	30. 3.89	J F Heath and R Hatton	Kirkbride	21. 5.07P
	(Built B B Feeley - pr.no.SAAC-02) (Lycoming O-235)						
G-BPUB	Cameron V-31 Air Chair Balloon (Hot Air)	1114		15. 3.89	M T Evans *(Noted 1.04)*	Peasedown St John, Bath	3. 6.94A
G-BPUE	Air Command 532 Elite	0441		29. 3.89	J K Padden	(Longhirst, Morpeth)	11. 9.91P
	(Built R A Fazerkerley - pr.no.PFA G/04-1136)				*(New owner 2.05)*		

Reg	Type	C/n	Prev Id	Date	Owner/Operator	Location	Date
G-BPUF	Thunder Ax6-56Z Balloon (Hot Air)	270	(G-BHRL)	30. 4.80	R C and M A Trimble *"Buf Puf"*	Henley-on-Thames	10. 2.90A
G-BPUG	Air Command 532 Elite	0401		29. 3.89	T A Holmes	(Melrose Farm, Melbourne)	18. 4.91P
	(Built C Slater - pr.no.PFA G/04-1157)				*(Possibly moved to Spain by 2000)*		
G-BPUJ	Cameron N-90 Balloon (Hot Air)	1977		17. 4.89	D Grimshaw	Preston	29.12.02T
G-BPUL	Piper PA-18A-150 Super Cub	18-2517	OO-LUL	12. 4.89	C D Duthy-James	Chauvigny, France	14. 7.08E
	(L-18C-PI) (Frame no. may be in 18-25xx series)		PH-NEV				
G-BPUM	Cessna R182 Skylane RG II	R18200915	N738DZ	2. 5.89	R C Chapman	Marley Hall, Ledbury	30. 4.08
G-BPUP	Whittaker MW7	PFA 171-11473		2. 8.89	J H Beard	(Buckfastleigh, Devon)	
	(Built J H Beard)						
G-BPUR	Piper J-3L-65 Cub	4708	N30228	14. 6.89	H A D Monro	(Westfield, Hastings)	
	(Frame No.4764)		NC30228		*(Noted 10.07: as "VM286" in RAF c/s)*		
G-BPUU	Cessna 140	13722	N4251N	31. 3.89	D R Speight	Full Sutton	16. 1.08E
			NC4251N				
G-BPUW	Colt 90A Balloon (Hot Air)	1436		12. 4.89	Gefa-Flug GmbH	Aachen, Germany	9. 7.08A
G-BPVA	Cessna 172F Skyhawk	17252286	N8386U	13. 4.89	J Pilkington and P Makin tr South Lancashire Flyers Group		
						Barton	17. 8.08E
G-BPVC	Cameron V-77 Balloon (Hot Air)	1302		7. 4.89	B D Pettitt	Barningham, Bury St Edmunds	16. 8.05A
					(Active 5.07)		
G-BPVE	Bleriot Type XI 1909 replica	1	N1197	20. 6.89	Bianchi Aviation Film Services Ltd	Compton Abbas	29. 6.01P
	(Built R D Henry, Texas, 1967)				*(As "01") (Noted in Flying Aces Movie Aeroplane Collection 9.05)*		
G-BPVH	Piper Cub J-3 Prospector	178C	CF-DRY	7. 4.89	D E Cooper-Maguire	Washington, West Sussex	18. 8.05P
	(Continental C85)				*(Incurred damage 17. 7.05)*		
G-BPVI	Piper PA-32R-301 Saratoga II SP	3213021	N91685	24. 4.89	M T Coppen	Goodwood	23. 8.08E
G-BPVK	Varga 2150A Kachina	VAC-85-77	N4626V	4. 5.89	H W Hall	Southend	12.12.07P
G-BPVM	Cameron V-77 Balloon (Hot Air)	1970		4. 4.89	J Dyer	Farnborough	22..4.05A
G-BPVN	Piper PA-32R-301T Turbo Saratoga		N8178W	14. 4.89	R Weston	Elstree	15. 9.07T
		32R-8029073					
G-BPVO	Cassutt Racer IIIM	DG.1	N19DD	13. 4.89	R S Grace	Audley End	23. 6.07P
	(Built D Giorgi)				*"VooDoo" and "2" (Noted 10.07)*		
G-BPVW	CASA 1-131E Jungmann	2133	Spanish AF E3B-559	17. 5.89	C and J-W Labeij	Goodwood	19. 7.07P
G-BPVY	Cessna 172D Skyhawk	17250568	N2968U	20. 4.89	S J Davies and D Toft	Sandtoft	4. 7.08E
G-BPVZ	Luscombe 8E Silvaire Deluxe	5565	N2838K	9. 5.89	W E Gillham and P Ryman		
	(Continental C85)		NC2838K			Croft Farm, Croft-on-Tees	3. 6.08P
G-BPWB	Sikorsky S-61N Mk.II	61-822	EI-BHO	4. 5.89	Bristow Helicopters Ltd	Portland	10. 7.08E
			G-BPWB, EI-BHO		*"Portland Castle" (Operated Marine and Coastguard Agency)*		
G-BPWC	Cameron V-77 Balloon (Hot Air)	1986		12. 4.89	H B Roberts *"Hot Flush"*	Failand, Bristol	10. 8.08T
G-BPWD	Cessna 120	10026	N72839	14. 4.89	L L Bee tr Peregrine Flying Group	Hucknall	13. 9.08P
	(Continental O-240-E)		NC72839				
G-BPWE	Piper PA-28-161 Warrior II	28-8116143	N8330P	2. 5.89	RPR Associates Ltd	Swansea	22. 6.08E
G-BPWG	Cessna 150M	15076707	(G-BPTK)	10. 4.89	G Addison tr G-B Pilots Wilsford Group		
			N45029			Nanbeck Farm, Wilsford, Grantham	20. 9.08E
G-BPWI	Bell 206B-3 JetRanger III	3087	9M-BSR	14. 4.89	M J Coates t/a Warren Aviation	Goodwood	12. 9.07T
			VH-HXZ, ZK-HXX, XC-PFH				
G-BPWK	Sportavia-Pützer RF5B Sperber	51036	N56JM	17. 4.89	S L Reed tr G-BPWK Flying Group	Usk	3. 12.07P
			(D-KEAR)				
G-BPWL	Piper PA-25-235 Pawnee	25-2304	N6690Z	14. 4.89	Tecair Aviation Ltd	Seething	17. 5.08E
			G-BPWL, N6690Z				
G-BPWM	Cessna 150L	15072820	N1520Q	17. 4.89	B R Whitehead	AAC Netheravon	1.12.07E
G-BPWN	Cessna 150L	15074325	N19308	17. 4.89	A J and N J Bissex	New Farm, Felton	1.12.07E
G-BPWP	Rutan LongEz	PFA 074A-11132		17. 4.89	D A Field	Biggin Hill	29. 6.08P
	(Built J F O'Hara and A J Voyle) (Continental O-240)						
G-BPWR	Cessna R172K Hawk XP	R1722953	N758AZ	21. 4.89	J A, D T A, J and G M Rees t/a Messrs Rees		
						Haverfordwest	14.11.07E
G-BPWS	Cessna 172P Skyhawk II	17274306	N51387	21. 4.89	Chartstone Ltd	Redhill	4. 5.08E
G-BPXA	Piper PA-28-181 Archer II	28-8390064	N4305T	12. 5.89	D Howdle and D L Heighington tr Cherokee Flying Group		
						Netherthorpe	4. 6.08E
G-BPXB	Glaser-Dirks DG-400	4-248		2. 5.89	V A S de Brederode	(Queluz, Portugal)	25. 7.08E
G-BPXE	Enstrom 280C Shark	1089	N379KH	21. 4.89	A Healy		
			C-GMLH, N660H		Hampden Manor, Little Hampden, Great Missenden		5. 5.08E
G-BPXF	Cameron V-65 Balloon (Hot Air)	2003		21. 4.89	D Pascall *(Noted 2003)*	Croydon	
G-BPXG	Colt 42A Balloon (Hot Air)	1445		25. 4.89	Zebedee Balloon Service Ltd	Newtown, Hungerford	18. 9.08A
G-BPXH	Colt 17A Cloudhopper Balloon (Hot Air)	667	OO-BWG	21. 4.89	Sport Promotion SRL (Active 5.07)	Belbo, Italy	8. 9.00A
G-BPXJ	Piper PA-28RT-201T Turbo Arrow IV		N8061U	21. 4.89	J France and M Holubecki	Bagby	5.10.07E
		28R-8231023			*(Noted 2.08)*		
G-BPXX	Piper PA-34-200T Seneca II	34-7970069	N923SM	21. 4.89	Yorkshire Aviation Ltd	Sherburn-in-Elmet	18. 9.08E
			N9556N				
G-BPXY	Aeronca 11AC Chief	11AC-S-50	N3842E	10. 4.89	P L Turner	Morgansfield, Fishburn	29.10.08P
G-BPYJ	Wittman W.8 Tailwind	PFA 031-11028		12. 5.89	Y Tutt and J P Mills	(Stockport)	17. 8.08P
	(Built J Dixon) (Continental PC60)						
G-BPYL	Hughes 369D	100-0796D	N65AM	10. 5.89	Morcorp (BVI) Ltd	Halfpenny Green	5. 9.07T
	(Hughes 500)		G-BPYL, HB-XKT				
G-BPYN	Piper J-3C-65 Cub (L-4H-PI)	11422	F-BFYN	14. 3.79	D W Stubbs tr The Aquila Group	White Waltham	5. 9.08P
			HB-OFN, 43-30131				
G-BPYO	Piper PA-28-181 Archer II	2890114	SE-KIH	22. 5.89	Sherburn Aero Club Ltd	Sherburn-in-Elmet	12. 9.08E
G-BPYR	Piper PA-31 Navajo C	31-7812032	G-ECMA	15. 5.89	Synergy Aircraft Leasing Ltd	Fairoaks	11. 5.08E
			N27493				
G-BPYS	Cameron O-77 Balloon (Hot Air)	2008		9. 5.89	D J Goldsmith *"Aqualisa II"*	Edenbridge	11. 9.08A
G-BPYT	Cameron V-77 Balloon (Hot Air)	1984		9. 5.89	M H Redman	Stalbridge, Sturminster Newton	
					(New owner 5.05)		
G-BPYV	Cameron V-77 Balloon (Hot Air)	1992		17. 5.89	R J Shortall	Peasedown St John, Bath	31. 3.08A
					(Spa Vehicle Electrics titles)		
G-BPYZ	Thunder Ax7-77 Balloon (Hot Air)	1521		11. 5.89	J E Bayly	Clutton, Bristol	7. 7.96A
					"Axis" Stolen Crewkerne, Somerset 23.10.97)		

G-BPZA	Luscombe 8A Silvaire	4326	N1599K	18. 4.89	M J Wright	St Junien, Haute-Vienne, France	2.10.08P
	(Continental A65)		NC1599K				
G-BPZB	Cessna 120	8898	N89853	25. 5.89	J F Corkin tr Cessna 120 Group	White Waltham	14. 9.08P
	(Continental C90)		NC89853				
G-BPZC	Luscombe 8A Silvaire	4322	N1595K	6. 6.89	C C and Jeninfer M Lovel		
	(Continental A65)		NC1595K			(South Wonston, Winchester)	5. 7.90P
	(Damaged by gales Cranfield 25.1.90: used for spares 10.96)						
G-BPZD	SNCAN NC.858S	97	F-BEZD	26. 1.79	G Richards tr Zula Delta Syndicate	Headcorn	26. 6.07P
	(Continental C90) *(Built as NC.854S with Continental C65)*						
	(Right hand main landing gear collapsed due to heavy landing London City 1.7.06 with substantial damage)						
G-BPZE	Luscombe 8E Silvaire Deluxe	3904	N1177K	6. 6.89	A V Harmer	(Hardwick)	2. 5.08P
	(Continental C85)		NC1177K		*(Failed to get airborne Hardwick 8. 7.07, struck crops and overturned)*		
G-BPZK	Cameron O-120 Balloon (Hot Air)	1982		7. 4.89	D L Smith *"Hot Stuff"*	Newbury	12. 5.97T
G-BPZM	Piper PA-28RT-201 Arrow IV	28R-7918238	G-ROYW	12. 5.89	Magenta Ltd	Exeter	28.10.08E
			G-CRTI, SE-ICY				
G-BPZP	Robin DR.400-180R Remorqueur	1471	D-EFZP	4. 5.89	S G Jones	Membury	23. 5.07
G-BPZS	Colt 105A Balloon (Hot Air)	1312		25. 5.89	L E Giles	Westbury-on-Trym, Bristol	13. 4.08A
					(Carousel Carpets titles)		
G-BPZU	Scheibe SF25C-2000 Falke	44471	D-KIAV	21. 7.89	Southdown Gliding Club Ltd	Parham Park	12. 8.08E
	(Limbach L2000)						
G-BPZY	Pitts S-1C	RN-1	N1159	15. 5.89	J S Mitchell	White Waltham	10. 4.08P
	(Built R N Newbauer) (Lycoming O-320)						
G-BPZZ	Thunder Ax8-105 Balloon (Hot Air)	1441		25. 5.89	Capricorn Balloons Ltd	Loughborough	5. 8.08A

G-BRAA - G-BRZZ

G-BRAA (2)	Pitts S-1C	101-GM	N14T	12. 5.89	G Hunter	(Direlton, North Berwick)	26. 4.91P
	(Built G R Miller)				*(New owner 1.08)*		
G-BRAF	Vickers Supermarine 394 Spitfire FR.XVIIIe		Indian AF HS877	29.12.78	Patina Ltd	Duxford	23. 9.93P
		6S/663052	SM969		*(Stored 10.07 unmarked)*		
	(More recent research confirms Indian AF serial as HS977 although photos exist showing HS877 applied).						
G-BRAK	Cessna 172N Skyhawk II	17273795	C-GBPN	23. 6.88	The Burnett Group Ltd	Kemble	11. 3.07T
			(N5438J)		*(Noted 4.07)*		
G-BRAR	Aeronca 7AC Champion	7AC-6564	N2978E	14. 6.89	R B Armitage	Maypole Farm, Chislet	18.10.06P
			NC2978E				
G-BRAX	Payne Knight Twister KT-85B	203	N9792	4. 5.89	R Earl	Landmead Farm, Garford	29. 9.93P
	(Built M Anderson and C Sunderland) (Continental O-200-A)				*(Fuselage noted 4.05)*		
G-BRBA	Piper PA-28-161 Warrior II	28-7916109	N2090B	25. 5.89	B Willis	Full Sutton	9.12.07E
G-BRBB	Piper PA-28-161 Warrior II	28-8116030	N8260W	28. 6.89	M A and A J Bell	Gloucestershire	3.11.07E
G-BRBC	North American T-6G-NH Texan	182-156	Italian AF MM54-099	4. 9.92	A P Murphy	Audley End	
			51-14470		*(Under construction 2008)*		
G-BRBD	Piper PA-28-151 Cherokee Warrior	28-7415315	N41702	28. 6.89	Compton Abbas Airfield Ltd	Compton Abbas	10. 4.08E
					"Shaftesbury Belle"		
G-BRBE	Piper PA-28-161 Warrior II	28-7916437	N2815D	13. 6.89	Solo Services Ltd	Shoreham	20. 1.08E
					(Operated Sussex Flying Club)		
G-BRBG	Piper PA-28-180 Cherokee Archer	28-7505248	N3927X	12. 6.89	M D N Fisher and B J Millington	Fenland	6. 9.08E
					tr Piper PA-28-180 Cherokee Archer G-BRBG Group		
G-BRBH	Cessna 150H	15069283	N50410	13. 6.89	J Maffia	Panshanger	8. 8.08E
G-BRBI	Cessna 172N Skyhawk II	17269613	N737RJ	7. 7.89	N A J Robinson tr Skyhawk Flying Group	Popham	12. 9.08E
G-BRBJ	Cessna 172M Skyhawk II	17267492	N73476	26. 5.89	W J Howe *(New owner 6.07)*	Carlisle	12. 1.02
G-BRBK	Robin DR.400-180 Régent	1915		31. 5.89	R Kemp	Thruxton	25.11.07E
G-BRBL	Robin DR.400-180 Régent	1920		5. 7.89	C A Marren	Trenchard Lines, Upavon	6. 3.08
G-BRBM	Robin DR.400-180 Régent	1921		5. 7.89	R W Davies	Little Robhurst Farm, Woodchurch	5. 7.08E
G-BRBN	Pitts S-1S	G 3	N81BG	14. 7.89	D R Evans	Gloucestershire	5. 7.08P
	(Built W L Garner)						
G-BRBO	Cameron V-77 Balloon (Hot Air)	1877		30. 5.89	M B Murby *"Patches"*	Cheltenham	20. 4.08A
G-BRBP	Cessna 152 II	15284915	N5324P	14. 6.89	Cardinal Sin Ltd t/a Staverton Flying School		
						Gloucestershire	24. 7.08E
G-BRBS	Bensen B 8M	PFA G/01-1039		30. 5.89	K T MacFarlane	(Kilmacolm)	
	(Built J Simpson) (Rotax 503)				*(Under construction 6.00)*		
G-BRBT	Trotter Ax3-20 Balloon (Hot Air)	RMT-001		13. 6.89	R M Trotter	Chew Magna, Bristol	
	(Built R M Trotter)						
G-BRBV	Piper J-4A Cub Coupé	4-1080	N27860	13. 6.89	P Clarke *(New owner 9.07)*	(Drefach, Llanybydder)	6. 9.05P
G-BRBW	Piper PA-28-140 Cherokee Cruiser	28-7425153	N40737	3. 7.89	Air Navigation and Trading Company Ltd	Blackpool	1.11.04
					(Noted 10.07)		
G-BRBX	Piper PA-28-181 Cherokee Archer II		N8674E	20. 7.89	C M Oldham and R Perks tr Trent 199 Flying Group		
		28-7690185				Tatenhill	27. 4.08E
G-BRBY	Robinson R22 Beta	1027		15. 6.89	Helijaf Ltd	Glenrothes	13. 8.08E
G-BRCA	Jodel D 112	1203	F-BLIU	11. 7.89	R C Jordan	Marsh Hill Farm, Aylesbury	14. 9.07P
	(Built Etablissement Valladeau)						
G-BRCE	Pitts S-1C	1001	N4611G	22. 6.89	R D Rogers	Hulcote Farm, Salford, Bedford	25.11.97P
	(Built Davis and Blake) (Lycoming O-290)				*(Operated Skylark Aerobatic Company)*		
G-BRCF	Montgomerie-Bensen B 8MR	PFA G/01A-1131		12. 6.89	J S Walton	(Nannerch, Mold)	30.10.91P
	(Built B E Trinder) (Rotax 532)						
G-BRCJ	Cameron H-20 Balloon (Hot Air)	2028	(OO-BXV)	13. 6.89	P A Sweatman	Birmingham	1. 1.08A
			G-BRCJ				
G-BRCM	Cessna 172L Skyhawk	17259960	N3860Q	19. 6.89	S G E Plessis and D C C Handley	Little Staughton	17. 9.08E
G-BRCO	Cameron H-20 Balloon (Hot Air)	2030		19. 6.89	P Lawman *(New owner 9.07)*	Northampton	10. 1.03A
G-BRCT	Denney Kitfox Model 2	396		23. 6.89	M L Roberts	Bodmin	11. 4.08P
	(Built M L Roberts - pr.no.PFA 172-11521)						
G-BRCV	Aeronca 7AC Champion	7AC-282	N81661	19. 9.89	M J Whitwell	Kemble	24.10.08P
	(Continental A65)		NC81661				
G-BRCW	Aeronca 11BC Chief	11AC-386	N85964	16.10.89	R B McComish	Bow, Totnes	26.11.08P
	(Continental C85)		NC85964		*(Officially regd with incorrect c/n 11AC-366)*		

G-BRDB	Zenair CH.701 STOL	7-1300		11. 7.89	D L Bowtell and N C Pettengell	Benington	24.10.08P
	(Built D L Bowtell - pr.no.PFA 187-11412)						
G-BRDD	Mudry CAP.10B	224		3. 8.88	R D Dickson	Gamston	17. 5.07
G-BRDE	Thunder Ax7-77 Balloon (Hot Air)	1538		22. 6.89	D J Keys	Bailieborough, County Cavan	9. 6.08A
G-BRDF	Piper PA-28-161 Cherokee Warrior II	N1139Q		26. 6.89	White Waltham Airfield Ltd	White Waltham	16. 8.08E
		28-7716085			*(Operated West London Aero Services)*		
G-BRDG	Piper PA-28-161 Cherokee Warrior II	N44934		26. 6.89	A S Bamrah t/a Falcon Flying Services	Biggin Hill	18. 5.08E
		28-7816047					
G-BRDJ	Luscombe 8A Silvaire	3411	N71984	28. 6.89	P G Stewart	Popham	6. 3.08P
	(Continental A65)		NC71984				
	(Officially regd as Luscombe 8F with Contintental C90)						
G-BRDM	Piper PA-28-161 Cherokee Warrior II	N8464F		26. 6.89	White Waltham Airfield Ltd	White Waltham	18. 1.08E
		28-7716004			*(Operated West London Aero Services)*		
G-BRDN	SOCATA MS.880B Rallye Club	1212	OY-DTV	14. 7.89	A J Gomes	Sandown, Isle of Wight	27. 4.02
	(Noted dismantled 6.06)						
G-BRDO	Cessna 177B Cardinal	17702166	N35030	13. 7.89	C R Granton and I S Jane tr Cardinal Aviation		
						Durham Tees Valley	30. 1.08E
G-BRDT	Cameron DP-70 Airship (Hot Air)	2029		3. 7.89	Tim Balloon Promotion Airships Ltd	Nailsea, Bristol	7. 6.07A
	(Konig SD 570)						
G-BRDW	Piper PA-24 Comanche	24-1733	N6612P	12. 3.90	I P Gibson	Sion, Switzerland	1.10.07E
G-BREB	Piper J-3C-65 Cub	7705	N41094	3. 7.89	J R Wraight	Pent Farm, Postling	3.12.07P
			NC41094				
G-BREE	Whittaker MW7	PFA 171-11497		22. 6.89	D A Couchman	Lower Upham Farm, Chiseldon	4. 7.05P
	(Built M J Hayman) (Rotax 503)						
G-BREH	Cameron V-65 Balloon (Hot Air)	2049		7. 7.89	S E and V D Hurst *"Promise"*	Mansfield	13. 5.04A
G-BREP	Piper PA-28RT-201 Arrow IV	28R-7918119	EC-HZN	19. 6.90	B W Gomez	Halfpenny Green	10. 3.08E
			G-BREP, N2230Z				
G-BRER	Aeronca 7AC Champion	7AC-6758	N3157E	12. 7.89	I Sinnett tr Rabbit Flight	Bodmin	9. 6.06P
	(Continental A65)		NC3157E		*(Noted 10.07)*		
G-BREU	Montgomerie-Bensen B 8MR PFA G/01A-1137			20. 7.89	J S Firth	Sherburn-in-Elmet	16. 5.08P
	(Built M Hayward) (Rotax 582)						
G-BREX	Cameron O-84 Balloon (Hot Air)	2019		14. 7.89	P Hegarty	Magherafelt, Belfast	8. 8.08A
G-BREY	Taylorcraft BC-12D	7299	N43640	14. 7.89	R J Pitts tr BREY Group	Leicester	18. 5.08P
			NC43640				
G-BRFB	Rutan LongEz	PFA 074A-10646		14. 7.89	A R Oliver	Duxford	20. 4.08P
	(Built R A Gardiner) (Lycoming O-290)						
G-BRFC	Percival P 57 Sea Prince T 1	P57/71	N7SY	10. 9.80	A and G A Gainsford Dixon	Bournemouth	
			G-BRFC, WP321		*(On display Aviation Museum: on overhaul 2008)*		
G-BRFE	Cameron V-77 Balloon (Hot Air)	1835		20. 7.89	D L C Nelmes tr Ezmerelda Balloon Syndicate		
					"Ezmerelda"	Abbots Leigh, Bristol	21. 4.06A
G-BRFI	Aeronca 7DC Champion	7AC-4609	N1058E	1. 8.89	A C Lines	Leicester	19. 2.91P
	(Continental C85)		NC1058E		*(Damaged 1990: on rebuild 4.96)*		
G-BRFJ	Aeronca 11AC Chief	11AC-796	N9163E	28. 7.89	J M Mooney	Lochview House, Limerigg	11. 9.02P
	(Continental A65)		NC9163E		*(Stored 2.03)*		
G-BRFL	Piper PA-38-112 Tomahawk	38-79A0431	N2416F	17. 8.89	D P Chowen	(Seaford)	6. 6.08E
G-BRFM	Piper PA-28-161 Warrior II	28-7916279	N2234P	17.10.89	GT Ventures Ltd	Coventry	25. 1.08E
G-BRFO	Cameron V-77 Balloon (Hot Air)	2025		6. 7.89	N J Bland tr Hedgehoppers Balloon Group	Oxford	31. 7.00A
					"Lurcher"		
G-BRFW	Montgomerie-Bensen B 8 Two-Seat PFA G/01-1073			20. 7.89	A J Barker	Sorbie Farm, Kingsmuir	7. 9.06P
	(Built J M Montgomerie) (Rotax 582)						
G-BRFX	Pazmany PL-4A	PFA 017-10079		14. 7.89	D E Hills	(Ipswich)	
	(Built D E Hills) (Volkswagen 1700)						
G-BRGD	Cameron O-84 Balloon (Hot Air)	2043		20. 7.89	R G Russell *(New owner 7.07)*	Henllys, Cwmbran	
G-BRGF	Luscombe 8E Silvaire Deluxe	5475	N23FP	20. 7.89	N Surman tr Luscombe Flying Group		
	(Continental C85)		N944BL, N2748K, NC2748K			Hinton-in-the-Hedges	1. 8.08P
G-BRGG	Luscombe 8A Silvaire	3795	N1068K	20. 7.89	M A Lamprell	Popham	6.10.05P
	(Continental A65)		NC1068K				
G-BRGI	Piper PA-28-180 Cherokee E	28-5827	N77VG	24. 7.89	R A Buckfield	Rochester	20. 6.06E
			NIIVG		*(New owner 10.06)*		
G-BRGO	Air Command 532 Elite	0615		7. 8.89	A McCredie	Sorbie Farm, Kingsmuir	13. 2.91P
	(Built D A Wood - pr.no.PFA G/04-1149)				*(Frame noted 5.05)*		
G-BRGT	Piper PA-32-260 Cherokee Six	32-658	N3744W	7.11.89	D A Hitchcock		
					(St Germain de Longue Chaume, France)		19.10.07E
G-BRGW	Gardan GY-20 Minicab	PFA 1823		13.11.78	R G White	Bossington	17. 7.08P
	(Built R G White to JB.01 Minicab standard) (Continental O-200-A)						
G-BRHA	Piper PA-32RT-300 Lance II	32R-7985076	N2093P	27. 7.89	D J Chatterton and P MacKinnon tr Lance G-BRHA Group		
						Earls Colne	8.12.07E
G-BRHG	Colt 90A Balloon (Hot Air)	1568		11. 9.89	Bath University Students Union	Bath	17. 8.04A
					(Badgerline titles)		
G-BRHL	Montgomerie-Bensen B 8MR PFA G/01A-1123			7. 8.89	T M Jones and B Moore	Kirkbride	26. 8.03P
	(Built N D Marshall) (Rotax 503)				*(Noted 8.07)*		
G-BRHO	Piper PA-34-200 Seneca	34-7350037	N15222	20. 9.89	A S Bamrah t/a Falcon Flying Services	Biggin Hill	20.10.07E
G-BRHP	Aeronca O-58B Grasshopper	058B-8533	N58JR	2. 8.89	C J Willis	Dunkeswell	22. 2.01P
	(Continental A65)		N46536, 43-1923		*(As "3-1923" in US Army c/s)*		
	(If US Army serial is correct, type should be L-3C-AE)						
G-BRHR	Piper PA-38-112 Tomahawk	38-79A0969	N2377P	21. 8.89	Bell Investments Ltd (Stony Stratford, Milton Keynes)		9.11.07E
G-BRHW	de Havilland DH.82A Tiger Moth	85612	7Q-YMY	26. 7.89	P J and A J Borsberry (Sonning Common, Reading)		
	(Built Morris Motors Ltd)		VP-YMY, ZS-DLB, SAAF 4606, DE671				
G-BRHX	Luscombe 8E Silvaire Deluxe	5114	N176M	8. 8.89	J Lakin	Eaglescott	5. 8.08P
	(Continental C90)		N2387K, NC2387K				
G-BRHY	Luscombe 8E Silvaire Deluxe	5138	N2411K	8. 8.89	A R W Taylor	Sleap	29. 4.08P
	(Continental C85)		NC2411K				
G-BRIA	Cessna 310L	310L0010	N2210F	4. 8.89	B J Tucker	Kemble	29. 6.08E
G-BRIE	Cameron N-77 Balloon (Hot Air)	2076		8. 8.89	S F Redman	Stalbridge, Sturminster Newton	12. 7.06A

Reg	Type	C/n	Prev id	Date	Owner/operator	Location	Expiry
G-BRIH	Taylorcraft BC-12D *(Continental A75)*	7421	N43762 NC43762	24. 8.89	A D Duke tr IH Flying Group	Leicester	17. 4.08P
G-BRII	Zenair CH.600 Zodiac *(Built A C Bowdrey)*	PFA 162-11392		18. 8.89	A C Bowdrey *(Under build 2000)*	(Hemel Hempstead)	
G-BRIJ	Taylorcraft F-19	F-119	N3863T	23. 8.89	M W Olliver *(New owner 3.03)*	Farley Farm, Romsey	12. 6.01P
G-BRIK	Nipper T 66S Series 3 *(Built C W R Piper as rebuild of G-AVKH) (Volkswagen 1834)*	PFA 025-10174		26. 4.77	P R Bentley	Roughay Farm, Bishops Waltham	17. 5.08P
G-BRIL	Piper J-5A Cub Cruiser *(Continental A75)*	5-572	N35183 NC35183	2. 8.89	P L Jobes and D J Bone	Spite Hall Farm, Pinchinthorpe	19.12.08P
G-BRIO	Turner Super T-40A *(Built D McIntyre and officially regd incorrectly as c/n PFA 104-10736)) (Continental O-200-A)*	PFA 104-10636		7. 8.89	S Bidwell	(Brighton)	8. 9.06P
G-BRIR	Cameron V-56 Balloon (Hot Air) *(Skyviews Windows titles) "Spirit of Century"*	2056		17. 8.89	H G Davies and C Dowd	Cheltenham	6. 9.97A
G-BRIS	Steen Skybolt *(Built M.K.Callen)*	01	N870MC	30. 8.89	M R Jones *(New owner 12.07)*	(Windsor)	4. 3.04P
G-BRIV	SOCATA TB-9 Tampico Club	939		24. 8.89	S J Taft	Sturgate	6. 3.08E
G-BRIY	Taylorcraft DF-65 *(Continental A65) (Built as TG-6 glider)*	6183	N59687 NC59687, 42-58678	1. 2.90	S R Potts *(As "42-58678:IY" in L-2A USAAC c/s: noted on rebuild 8.07)*	Stanton, Morpeth	10. 7.98P
G-BRJA	Luscombe 8A Silvaire *(Continental A65)*	3744	N1017K NC1017K	12. 9.89	A D Keen	Halwell	4.12.07P
G-BRJB	Zenair CH.601HD Zodiac *(Built D Collinson - pr.no.PFA 162-11573)*	6-1283		2. 8.89	C A Hasell	Audley End	19. 3.08P
G-BRJC	Cessna 120 *(Continental C85)*	12077	N1833N NC1833N	21. 8.89	A L Hall-Carpenter *(New owner 1.05)*	Shipdham	21. 3.04P
G-BRJK	Luscombe 8A Silvaire *(Continental A65)*	4205	N1478K NC1478K	21. 8.89	C J L Peat and M Richardson	Chilbolton	19.12.08P
G-BRJL	Piper PA-15 Vagabond *(Continental C85)*	15-157	N4370H NC4370H	21. 8.89	A R Williams	Garston Farm, Marshfield	20. 9.07P
G-BRJN	Pitts S-1C *(Built M G Acker) (Lycoming O-320)*	1-MA	N6A	23. 8.89	W Chapel	Sherburn-in-Elmet	20. 5.04P
G-BRJR	Piper PA-38-112 Tomahawk	38-79A0144	N2598B	31. 8.89	M McGovern *(Noted 1.07)*	Hawarden	27. 5.05T
G-BRJT	Cessna 150H	15068426	N44SS	31. 8.89	M R Winter tr Romeo Tango Group	Welshpool	26. 9.07T
G-BRJV	Piper PA-28-161 Cadet	2841167	N9185G	24. 8.89	Northumbria Flying School Ltd	Carlisle	20. 3.08E
G-BRJW	Bellanca 7GCBC Citabria 150S *(Crashed Old Buckenham 27.10.07: damaged fuselage noted 12.07 on trailer westbound on A47 at Thorney, Peterborough)*	1200-80	OO-LPG	7. 4.82	P G Smith	(Old Buckenham)	10.12.07E
G-BRJX	Rand Robinson KR-2 *(Built C Willcocks)*	PFA 129-11386		22. 8.89	J R Bell *(New owner 11.03)*	(Parcllyn, Cardigan)	15. 4.97P
G-BRJY	Rand Robinson KR-2 *(Built J M Scott) (Revmaster 2100D)*	PFA 129-11308		22. 8.89	R E Taylor *(Under restoration 6.00)*	(Bonar Bridge)	23. 5.96P
G-BRKC	Auster V J/1 Autocrat	2749	F-BFYT	31. 8.89	J W Conlon	High Easter	5. 3.08P
G-BRKH	Piper PA-28-236 Dakota	28-7911003	N21444	30. 8.89	A P H Hay and C C Bennett	Popham	22. 2.08E
G-BRKR	Cessna 182R Skylane II	18268468	N9896E	2. 6.89	A R D Brooker	Springfield Farm, Ettington	28. 4.08E
G-BRKW	Cameron V-77 Balloon (Hot Air)	2093		1. 9.89	T J Parker	Burnham-on-Crouch	7. 3.07
G-BRKY	Viking Dragonfly Mk II *(Built G D Price) (Volkswagen 2180)*	PFA 139-11117		7. 9.89	G D Price *(Stored less engine 6.04)*	Deanland	8. 6.94P
G-BRLB	Air Command 532 Elite *(Built H R Bethune)*	0622		4. 9.89	F G Shepherd	(Great Orton)	
G-BRLF	Campbell Cricket replica *(Built D Wood) (Rotax 503)*	PFA G/03-1077		6. 9.89	J L G McLane	(Gilling East, York)	7. 9.08P
G-BRLG	Piper PA-28RT-201T Turbo Arrow IV	28R-8431027	N4379P N9600N	12. 9.89	P Lodge and J G McVey	Liverpool	4. 2.08E
G-BRLI	Piper J-5A Cub Cruiser *(Lycoming O-290)*	5-822	N35951 NC35951	23. 8.89	Little Bear Ltd	Exeter	28. 7.06P
G-BRLL	Cameron A-105 Balloon (Hot Air)	2032		7. 9.89	Aerosaurus Balloons Ltd *(Extant 5.07)*	Whimple, Exeter	4. 4.06T
G-BRLO	Piper PA-38-112 Tomahawk	38-78A0621	N2397K N9680N	26.10.89	E Reed t/a St George Flight Training	Durham Tees Valley	15. 3.08E
G-BRLP	Piper PA-38-112 Tomahawk	38-78A0011	N9301T	4.10.89	P D Brooks	Inverness	10. 4.08E
G-BRLR	Cessna 150G	15064822	N4772X	4.10.89	D Carr and M R Muter	Bagby	2. 8.08E
G-BRLS	Thunder Ax7-77 Balloon (Hot Air)	1603		29. 9.89	E C Meek	Oswestry	27. 9.08A
G-BRLT	Colt 77A Balloon (Hot Air)	1588		12. 9.89	D Bareford *"Pro-Sport"*	Kidderminster	13. 6.05A
G-BRLV	CCF Harvard 4 (T-6J-CCF Texan)	CCF4-194	N90448 RCAF 20403	14. 9.89	Extravation Ltd *"Texan Belle"* *(As "93542:LTA-542" in USAF 6148th TCS c/s) (Noted 6.07)*	North Weald	10. 9.08P
G-BRME	Piper PA-28-181 Cherokee Archer II	28-7790105	OY-BTA	14. 9.89	Keen Leasing Ltd	Belfast International	17. 7.08E
G-BRMI	Cameron V-65 Balloon (Hot Air)	2104		14. 9.89	M Davies *"Sapphire"*	Callington, Plymouth	25. 8.01A
G-BRMT	Cameron V-31 Air Chair Balloon (Hot Air)	2038		31. 8.89	B M Reed *(New owner 6.06)*	Paizay le Sec, France	
G-BRMU	Cameron V-77 Balloon (Hot Air)	2109		19. 9.89	K J and G R Ibbotson *"Hyperion"*	Gloucester	15. 4.08A
G-BRMV	Cameron O-77 Balloon (Hot Air)	2103		25. 9.89	P D Griffiths *"Viscount"*	Southampton	10. 7.03A
G-BRMW	Whittaker MW7 *(Built M Grunwell)*	PFA 171-11395		25. 9.89	G S Parsons	(Coventry)	21. 4.03P
G-BRNC	Cessna 150M Commuter	15078833	N704SG	29. 9.89	Penny Hydraulics Ltd	(Sheffield City)	30. 6.08E
G-BRND	Cessna 152 II	15283776	N5148B	7.11.89	T M and M L Jones *(Operated Derby Aero Club)*	Derby	27. 7.08E
G-BRNE	Cessna 152 II	15284248	N5082L	4.10.89	Redhill Air Services Ltd *(Airbase titles on tail)*	Rochester	20. 3.08E
G-BRNK	Cessna 152 II	15280479	N24969	22. 9.89	Sheffield Aero Club Ltd	Netherthorpe	17. 4.08E
G-BRNN	Cessna 152 II	15284735	N6452M	22. 9.89	Sheffield Aero Club Ltd	Netherthorpe	6. 2.08E
G-BRNT	Robin DR.400-180 Régent	1935		3.10.89	C E., O C and M E Ponsford *(Operated Cega Aviation)*	Shoreham	23. 3.08
G-BRNU	Robin DR.400-180 Régent	1937		31.10.89	November Uniform Travel Syndicate Ltd	White Waltham	23. 6.08E
G-BRNV	Piper PA-28-181 Cherokee Archer II	28-7790402	N2537Q	7.12.89	B S Hobbs	Goodwood	10. 3.08E

Reg	Type	c/n	Prev ident	Date	Owner/Operator	Location	Expiry
G-BRNW	Cameron V-77 Balloon (Hot Air)	2138		2.10.89	G Smith and N Robertson "Mr Blue Sky"	Alveston, Bristol and Walton-on-Thames	4. 8.06A
G-BRNX	Piper PA-22-150 Caribbean	22-2945	N2610P	3.10.89	S N Askey	Draycott Farm, Chiseldon	19.12.07E
G-BRNZ	Piper PA-32-300 Cherokee Six B	32-40594	N4229R	7. 2.90	W Anderson tr Longfellow Flying Group	Headcorn	20. 6.08E
	(Substantially damaged in gales Fenland 1.07: wreck noted 4.07)						
G-BROE	Cameron N-65 Balloon (Hot Air)	2098		5.10.89	A I Attwood	(Inverness)	3. 4.08A
G-BROG	Cameron V-65 Balloon (Hot Air)	2121		6. 9.89	R Kunert "The Dodger"	Finchampstead, Wokingham	18. 9.08A
G-BROI	CFM Streak Shadow	K 115-SA		16.11.89	A Collinson	Brook Farm, Pilling	13. 6.08P
	(Built G W Rowbotham - pr.no.PFA 161-11586) (Rotax 532)						
G-BROJ	Colt 31A Balloon (Hot Air)	1468		6.10.89	N J Langley	Clapton in Gordano, Bristol	10. 5.06A
	(Fly Virgin, Pocara Sweat and Nature Mate titles)						
G-BROO	Luscombe 8E Silvaire Deluxe	6154	N75297	28. 9.89	P R Bush	(Milford Haven)	1. 5.08P
	(Continental O-200-A)		N1527B, NC1527B				
G-BROR	Piper J-3C-65 Cub (L-4H-PI)	10885	F-BHMQ	7.12.89	J H Bailey and A P J Wiseman tr White Hart Flying Group		
			43-29594			Sturgate	29. 8.08P
G-BROX	Robinson R22 Beta	1127	N8061V	13.10.89	J G Burgess	(Waldron, Heathfield)	29. 8.08E
G-BROY	Cameron O-90 Balloon (Hot Air)	2173		6. 9.89	T G S Dixon *(Dixon Furnace Division tiles)*	Bromsgrove	4. 8.07A
G-BROZ	Piper PA-18-150 Super Cub	18-6754	HB-ORC	20. 9.89	P G Kynsey	Rushett Farm, Chessington	9. 2.11E
			N9572D				
G-BRPE	Cessna 120	13326	N3068N	11.10.89	W B Bateson	Blackpool	7. 7.05P
	(Continental C85)		NC3068N		*(Noted 10.07)*		
G-BRPF	Cessna 120	9902	N72723	11.10.89	A L Hall-Carpenter	Shipdham	15. 5.05P
	(Continental C85)		NC72723				
G-BRPG	Cessna 120	9882	N72703	11.10.89	I C Lomax	(Thirtlebury, Hull)	29. 8.94P
	(Continental C85)		NC72703				
G-BRPH	Cessna 120	12137	N1893N	11.10.89	J A Cook	Pent Farm, Postling	22. 6.06P
	(Continental C85)		NC1893N				
G-BRPJ	Cameron N-90 Balloon (Hot Air)	2071		11. 9.89	P Johnson t/a Cloud Nine Balloon Company		
					"Presto"	Ebchetser, Consett	10. 3.99T
G-BRPK	Piper PA-28-140 Cherokee Cruiser	28-7325070	N15449	17.11.89	G R Bright tr G-BRPK Group	Little Gransden	14. 6.08E
G-BRPL	Piper PA-28-140 Cherokee Cruiser	28-7325160	N15771	13.10.89	Silverstar Aviation Ltd *(New owner 2.08)*	Blackpool	6.11.05T
G-BRPM	Nipper T 66 Series 3B	PFA 025-11038		4. 3.85	T C Horner	(Barrhead)	
	(Built R Morris)				*(Under construction 6.00)*		
G-BRPP	Gyroflight Brookland Hornet	DC-1		16.10.89	B J L P and W J A L de Saar	(Great Yarmouth)	23. 8.93P
	(Volkswagen 1776)				*(For rebuild 2000)*		
G-BRPR	Aeronca O-58B Grasshopper	058B-8823	N49880	17.10.89	C S Tolchard	Earls Colne	30. 5.08P
	(Continental A65)		43-1952		*(As "31952" in US Army c/s)*		
	(If US Army serial is correct, type should be L-3C-AE)						
G-BRPS	Cessna 177B Cardinal	17702101	N34935	23.10.89	R C Tebbett	Shobdon	16. 6.08E
G-BRPT	Rans S-10 Sakota	0589.052		18.10.89	A R Hawes	Mendlesham	14.12.06P
	(Built J G Beesley - pr.no.PFA 194-11554)						
G-BRPU	Beech 76 Duchess	ME-140	N6007Z	17.10.89	Plane Talking Ltd *(Operated Cabair)*	Bournemouth	19.10.07E
G-BRPV	Cessna 152 II	15285228	N6311Q	6.11.89	Eastern Air Executive Ltd	Sturgate	23. 3.08E
G-BRPX	Taylorcraft BC-12D	6462	N39208	12.12.89	R A C Lees tr The BRPX Group	Leicester	25. 9.08P
	(Continental A65)		NC39208				
G-BRPY	Piper PA-15 Vagabond	15-141	N4356H	23.10.89	J and V Hobday	Barton	26. 4.08P
	(Continental C85)		NC4356H				
G-BRPZ	Luscombe 8A Silvaire	911	N22089	13.12.89	G L Brown	Shacklewell Farm, Empingham	25.10.08P
	(Continental A65)		NC22089				
G-BRRB	Luscombe 8E Silvaire Deluxe	2611	N71184	23.10.89	J Nicholls	(Bishops Waltham)	14. 5.00P
	(Continental C85)		NC71184		*(New owner 5.04)*		
G-BRRD	Scheibe SF25B Falke	4811	D-KBAT	30.10.89	P J Gill tr G-BRRD Group	Seighford	18. 6.08E
	(Built Sportavia-Pützer) (Stark-Stamo MS1500)						
G-BRRF	Cameron O-77 Balloon (Hot Air)	2101		24.10.89	K P and G J Storey	Sawbridgeworth	20. 7.08A
G-BRRG	Glaser-Dirks DG-500M	5E7-M5		7.11.89	P J Fincham tr G-BRRG Syndicate	(Milton Keynes)	8. 4.08E
G-BRRJ	Piper PA-28RT-201T Turbo Arrow IV		N4353T	27.11.89	M Stower	Elstree	8. 8.08E
		28R-8431021					
G-BRRK	Cessna 182Q Skylane II	18266160	N759PW	30.10.89	Werewolf Aviation Ltd	Elstree	30. 5.08E
G-BRRL	Piper PA-18 Super Cub 95 (L-18C-PI)	18-1615	G-AYPO (1)	17. 9.90	A J White tr Acebell G-BRRL Syndicate	(Redhill)	
	(Regd using paperwork of wrecked D-EMKE [18-2050])		French Army 18-1615, 51-15615				
G-BRRR	Cameron V-77 Balloon (Hot Air)	2070		13.10.89	K P and G J Storey "Breezy"	Sawbridgeworth	20. 7.08A
G-BRRU	Colt 90A Balloon (Hot Air)	1591		1.11.89	Reach For The Sky Ltd	Guildford	31. 7.08E
G-BRRY	Robinson R22 Beta	1193		14.11.89	Fast Helicopters Ltd	Shoreham	9. 1.08E
G-BRSA (2)	Cameron N-56 Balloon (Hot Air)	2113		8.11.89	C Wilkinson	Newcastle	5. 4.08A
G-BRSD (2)	Cameron V-77 Balloon (Hot Air)	2174		8.11.89	M E Granger	Little Bytham, Grantham	9. 4.08A
G-BRSE (2)	Piper PA-28-161 Warrior II	28-8016276	N8163R	5.12.89	Falcon Flying Services Ltd	Biggin Hill	12. 7.08E
G-BRSF (2)	Vickers Supermarine 361 Spitfire HF.IXc	56322	SAAF 5632	2.11.89	M B Phillips	(Newton St Cyres, Exeter)	
			RR232		*(As "RR232" in RAF c/s) (Noted 2007)*		
	(Composite including tail and parts ex Mk.VIII, JF629 from Western Australia and wings ex Mk.XIV, R Thai AF U14-6/93, RAF RM873)						
G-BRSJ (2)	Piper PA-38-112 Tomahawk II	38-81A0044	N25664	29.12.89	APB Leasing Ltd	(Sheffield City)	7. 4.08E
G-BRSK	Boeing Stearman B75N1 (N2S-3) Kaydet	75-1180	N5565N	15.11.89	M Burpitt	Priory Farm, Tibenham	20. 1.97
	(Continental W670)		Bu.3403		*(Noted on rebuild 2.08)*		
G-BRSN	Rand Robinson KR-2	PFA 129-11178		10.11.89	K W Darby	(Teignmouth)	
	(Built K W Darby) (Volkswagen 1834)						
G-BRSO	CFM Streak Shadow	K 133-SA		16.11.89	B C Norris	Trenchard Farm, Eggesford	14.11.03P
	(Built P H Slade - pr.no.PFA 161A-11601) (Rotax 618)				*(Noted 8.07)*		
G-BRSP	MODAC (Air Command) 503	0626		13.11.89	G M Hobman	Melrose Farm, Melbourne	19. 4.07P
	(Built D R G Griffith - pr.no.PFA G04-1158)				*(Noted 9.07)*		
G-BRSW	Luscombe 8A Silvaire	3249	N71822	15.11.89	P H Needham tr Bloody Mary Aviation	Fenland	3. 5.08P
	(Continental A75)		NC71822		"Bloody Mary"		
G-BRSX	Piper PA-15 Vagabond	15-117	N4334H	27.10.89	M R Holden	(Hagworthingham, Spilsby)	3. 8.06P
	(Continental A65)		NC4334H				
G-BRSY	Hatz CB-1	6	N2257J	15.11.89	W Senior	Breighton	21. 1.08P
	(Built M Ondrus) (Lycoming O-290-D)						

Reg	Type	c/n	Prev id	Date	Owner	Location	Date
G-BRTD	Cessna 152 II	15280023	N757UW	11. 1.90	R G Prince, T G Phillips and C Greenland tr 152 Group		
						Popham	21. 6.08E
G-BRTJ	Cessna 150F	15061749	N8149S	22.11.89	Avon Aviation Ltd	Bristol	19. 7.08E
G-BRTK	Boeing Stearman E75 (PT-13D) Kaydet 75-5949		N16716	29.11.89	Eastern Stearman Ltd	Rendcomb	24. 4.93
	(Continental W670)		42-17786, Bu.38728		*(Parts donated to N52485 by 12.01)*		
G-BRTL	Hughes 369E	0356E	(F-GHLF)	5. 1.90	Crewhall Ltd	Sywell	3. 4.08E
	(Hughes 500)						
G-BRTP	Cessna 152 II	15281275	N49448	28.11.89	R Lee	(Hull)	1. 9.08E
G-BRTT	Schweizer 269C	S 1411		29.11.89	Technical Exponents Ltd	Bennett's Field, Denham	18. 9.08E
	(Schweizer 300)						
G-BRTV	Cameron O-77 Balloon (Hot Air)	2182		1.12.89	R J Clements	Lower Weston, Bath	16.12.07A
G-BRTW	Glaser-Dirks DG-400	4-259		22.12.89	I J Carruthers	(Great Orton)	13. 6.08E
G-BRTX	Piper PA-28-151 Cherokee Warrior 28-7615085		N8307C	27.12.89	J Phelan and D G Scott tr Spectrum Flying Group		
						Belfast International	16. 5.08E
G-BRUB	Piper PA-28-161 Warrior II	28-8116177	N8351Y	27.12.89	Flytrek Ltd	Compton Abbas	9. 2.08E
G-BRUD	Piper PA-28-181 Archer II	28-8390010	N8300S	9. 2.90	Wilkins and Wilkins (Special Auctions) Ltd t/a Henlow Flying Club		
						RAF Henlow	18. 3.08E
G-BRUG	Luscombe 8E Silvaire Deluxe	4462	N1735K	15.12.89	N W Barratt and K Reeve		
	(Continental C85)		NC1735K			Ranston Farm, Iwerne Courtney	21. 3.08P
G-BRUH	Colt 105A Balloon (Hot Air)	1650		15.12.89	D C Chipping	Grantham	29. 7.93T
G-BRUI	Piper PA-44-180 Seminole	44-7995150	N2230E	15.12.89	F Pilkington	Hawarden	25..7.08E
			G-BRUI, N2230E				
G-BRUJ	Boeing Stearman A75N1 (PT-17) Kaydet 75-4299		N55557	6. 4.90	R M Hughes	Liverpool	25. 7.10S
	(Continental R670)		42-16136		*(As "16136:205" in USN c/s)*		
G-BRUM	Cessna A152 Aerobat	A1520870	N4693A	12. 3.86	Central Aircraft Leasing Ltd	Kemble	15. 8.08E
G-BRUN	Cessna 120	9294	G-BRDH	29. 8.89	O C Brun	Great Massingham	23. 4.08P
	(Continental C85)		N72127, NC72127				
G-BRUO	Taylor JT.1 Monoplane	PFA 055-10859		15.12.89	R Hatton	Kirkbride	17. 1.08P
	(Built P C Cardno)						
G-BRUV	Cameron V-77 Balloon (Hot Air)	2100		16. 8.89	T W and R F Benbrook *"biG-BRUVver"*	Romford	5. 4.08A
G-BRUX	Piper PA-44-180 Seminole	44-7995151	N2245E	8. 3.79	C J Thomas	Tatenhill	13.12.06
G-BRVB	Stolp SA.300 Starduster Too	409	N33MH	21.12.89	M N Petchey tr G-VB Group	Andrewsfield	21. 6.08P
	(Built M Hoover) (Lycoming O-360)						
G-BRVE	Beech D17S Traveller Mk.1 (UC-43-BH)	6701	N1193V	12. 3.90	Patina Ltd	Duxford	5. 6.08
			NC1193V, Bu.32874, FT475, 44-67724, (Bu.23689) *(Operated The Fighter Collection)*				
G-BRVF	Colt 77A Balloon (Hot Air)	1651		19.12.89	J Adkins	Market Harborough	5. 5.08A
G-BRVG	North American SNJ-7C Texan	88-17676	N830X		D J Gilmour	Dunsfold	4. 9.10S
			N4134A, Bu.90678, (42-85895) *(As "90678:27" in USN VS-932 Sqdn c/s)*				
G-BRVI	Robinson R22 Beta	1240		27.12.89	M D Thorpe t/a Yorkshire Helicopters		
						Coney Park, Leeds	7.11.07E
G-BRVJ	Slingsby Cadet III Motor Glider	701	BGA 3360	24. 1.90	B Outhwaite	Yearby	11.10.08P
			WT906				
	(Re-built D F Micklethwaite and J R Paskins - pr.no.PFA 042-11382 and modified ex T 31B) (Volkswagen 1600)						
G-BRVL	Pitts S-1C	559H	N2NW	10. 1.90	M F Pocock	RAF Leeming	9. 4.08P
	(Built N Williams) (Lycoming IO-320)						
G-BRVN	Thunder Ax7-77 Balloon (Hot Air)	1614		28.12.89	D L Beckwith	Kislingbury, Northampton	9. 8.08A
G-BRVO	Aérospatiale AS.350B Ecureuil	2315		3. 1.90	Rotorhire LLP	(Allington, Maidstone)	20.12.07E
G-BRVR	Barnett Rotorcraft J4B-2	216-2		20. 2.90	M Richardson t/a Ilkeston Contractors	Ilkeston	
G-BRVS	Barnett Rotorcraft J4B-2	210-2		20. 2.90	M Richardson t/a Ilkeston Contractors	Ilkeston	
	(Built M Richardson)						
G-BRVT	Pitts S-2B	5189		6. 4.90	R Woollard	Biggin Hill	4. 5.06E
	(Built Christen Industries Inc) (Lycoming AEIO-540)				*"The Tart" (New owner 8.06)*		
G-BRVU	Colt 77A Balloon (Hot Air)	1652		4. 1.90	J K Woods *"Concorde Watches"*	Chatham	25. 6.02A
G-BRVY	Thunder Ax8-90 Balloon (Hot Air)	1676		9. 1.90	G E and J V Morris *"Golden Gem"*	Cheltenham	6. 5.04A
G-BRVZ	SAN Jodel D 117	433	F-BHNR	22.12.89	L Holland	(Nottingham)	29. 5.08P
G-BRWA	Aeronca 7AC Champion	7AC-351	N81730	20. 3.90	D D Smith and J R Edwards	Scotland Farm, Hook	10. 4.08P
			NC81730				
G-BRWD	Robinson R22 Beta	1231	N8064U	15. 1.90	ACS Aviation Ltd	Durham Tees Valley	5. 6.08E
G-BRWO	Piper PA-28-140 Cherokee Cruiser 28-7325548		N55985	11. 1.90	B and Claire Taylor	Humberside	26. 8.08E
G-BRWP	CFM Streak Shadow	K 122		17. 1.90	R Biffin	Kirknewton	24. 7.07P
	(Built D F Gaughan - pr.no.PFA 161A-11596) (Rotax 532)						
G-BRWR	Aeronca 11AC Chief	11AC-1319	N9676E	17. 1.90	A W Crutcher	Cardiff	2. 7.08P
	(Continental A65)						
G-BRWT	Scheibe SF25C-2000 Falke	44480	D-KIAY	11. 1.90	Booker Gliding Club Ltd	Wycombe Air Park	24. 4.08E
	(Limbach L2000)						
G-BRWU	Phoenix Luton LA-4A Minor	PAL 1141		18. 1.90	R B Webber	Trenchard Farm, Eggesford	9. 9.08P
	(Built R B Webber and P K Pike - pr.no.PFA 1141) (JAP J 99)						
G-BRWV	Brügger MB.2 Colibri	PFA 043-11027		18. 1.90	M P Wakem	Barton	15.10.08P
	(Built S J McCollom) (Volkswagen 1834)						
G-BRWX	Cessna 172P Skyhawk II	17274729	N53363	17. 1.90	Light Aircraft Leasing Ltd	(Sheffield City)	26. 4.08E
	(Thielert TAE 125-01)						
G-BRWZ	Cameron Macaw 90 SS Balloon (Hot Air)	2206		29. 1.90	Forbes Global Inc	Balleroy, Calvados, France	17. 4.08E
					"Capitalist Tool"		
G-BRXA	Cameron O-120 Balloon (Hot Air)	2217		19. 1.90	R J Mansfield	Bowness-on-Windermere	23. 2.08T
G-BRXB	Thunder Ax7-77 Balloon (Hot Air)	1631		18. 1.90	H Peel	Petworth	22. 7.02A
					(Donated to Balloon Preservation Group 2004)		
G-BRXD	Piper PA-28-181 Archer II	28-8290126	D-EHWN	19. 2.90	D D Stone	Wellesbourne Mountford	15. 4.08E
			N9690N, N8203E				
G-BRXE	Taylorcraft BC-12D	9459	N95059	25. 1.90	B T Morgan and W J Durrad		
	(Continental A65)		NC95059		*"Flying Fishes"*	Eastbach Farm, Coleford	13. 3.08P
G-BRXF	Aeronca 11AC Chief	11AC-1033	N9396E	25. 1.90	C G Nice tr Aeronca Flying Group	Andrewsfield	6. 4.08P
	(Continental A65)		NC9396E				
G-BRXG	Aeronca 7AC Champion	7AC-3910	N85178	1. 3.90	J D Webb tr X-Ray Golf Flying Group		
	(Continental A65)		NC85178			Hill Farm, Nayland	15. 9.08P

G-BRXH	Cessna 120	10462	N76068	25. 1.90	A C Garside tr BRXH Group	Headcorn	9. 4.08P
	(Continental C85)		NC76068				
G-BRXL	Aeronca 11AC Chief	11AC-1629	N3254E	31. 1.90	P L Green	(Haverhill)	9. 7.08P
	(Continental A65)		NC3254E		(As "42-78044" in US Army AC L-3F c/s)		
G-BRXN	Montgomerie-Bensen B 8MR	PFA G/01-1160		31. 1.90	C M Frerk	Spanhoe	14. 9.07P
	(Built J C Aitken) (Rotax 532)						
G-BRXP	SNCAN Stampe SV-4C	678	N33528	2. 2.90	T Brown	Maypole Farm, Chislet	5. 9.10S
			F-BGGU, French AF 678, (F-BDNX) "SFASA SAINT-YAN"				
G-BRXS	Howard Special T-Minus	REC-1	N2278C	14. 2.90	A Shuttleworth	Barton	12. 4.08P
	(Built C Howard) (Lycoming O-290) (Modified Taylorcraft BC)						
G-BRXV	Robinson R22 Beta	1246		7. 2.90	Heliflight (UK) Ltd	Gloucestershire	30.11.07E
G-BRXW	Piper PA-24-260 Comanche	24-4069	N8621P	16. 2.90	P A Jenkins tr Oak Group	Farley Farm, Romsey	11. 2.06
					(On rebuild 10.07)		
G-BRXY	Pietenpol AirCamper	PFA 047-11416		7. 2.90	P S Ganczakowski	Great Eversden	3.12.08P
	(Built A E Morris) (Continental C90)						
G-BRZA	Cameron O-77 Balloon (Hot Air)	2231		7. 2.90	L and R J Mold "Breezy"	High Wycombe	5. 4.05A
	(Originally regd with c/n 2237 - see G-BSCA)				(Phil Dunson and Wycombe Insurance titles)		
G-BRZD	HAPI Cygnet SF-2A	PFA 182-11443		8. 2.90	C I Coghill	(Farnham)	7.10.04P
	(Built L G Millen) (Volkswagen 2078)						
G-BRZE	Thunder Ax7-77 Balloon (Hot Air)	1633		8. 2.90	G V Beckwith and F Schoeder		
					"Jenlain" Zanten and Mulheim Ruhr, Germany		31. 8.97A
G-BRZG	Enstrom F-28A	169	N9053	8. 2.90	J E Preston	Linley Hill, Leven	3. 9.08E
G-BRZI	Cameron N-180 Balloon (Hot Air)	2215		8. 2.90	C E Wood t/a Eastern Balloon Rides	Witham	24. 2.00T
G-BRZK	Stinson 108-2 Voyager	108-2846	N9846K	17. 4.90	P C G Wyld tr Voyager G-BRZK Syndicate		
	(Built Consolidated Vultee Aircraft)		NC9846K			Wycombe Air Park	1. 1.10
G-BRZL	Pitts S-1D	01	N899RN	26. 2.90	T R G Barnby	Headcorn	2. 8.96P
	(Built R C Nelson)				(Noted on rebuild 5.00: new owner 8.03)		
G-BRZS	Cessna 172P Skyhawk II	17275004	N54585	2.10.90	M H Seville and P F Hughes tr YP Flying Group		
						Blackpool	5. 3.08E
G-BRZT	Cameron V-77 Balloon (Hot Air)	2241		21. 2.90	B Drawbridge "Hoopla"	Cranbrook	19. 2.01A
G-BRZV	Colt Flying Apple SS Balloon (Hot Air)	1662		26. 2.90	Obst Vom Bodensee Marketing Gbr		
					Tettnang-Siggenweiler, Germany		14. 9.97A
G-BRZW	Rans S-10 Sakota	0789.058		21. 2.90	D L Davies	Emlyn's Field, Rhuallt	6. 8.98P
	(Built D L Davies - pr.no.PFA 194-11932)				(Noted 8.07)		
G-BRZX	Pitts S-1S	711-H	N272H	22. 2.90	J S Dawson	Sherburn-in-Elmet	30. 4.08P
	(Built M M Lotero) (Lycoming O-320)						
G-BRZZ	CFM Streak Shadow	K 135		22. 2.90	J A Weston	Sumburgh	13. 5.08P
	(Built P R Oakes - pr.no.PFA 161A-11628) (Rotax 532)						

G-BSAA - G-BSZZ

G-BSAI	Stoddard-Hamilton Glasair III	3102		31. 1.90	K J and P.J Whitehead	Wycombe Air Park	21. 8.08P
	(Builllt K J Whitehead) (Lycoming IO-540)						
G-BSAJ	CASA 1-131E Jungmann	2209	Spanish AF E3B-209	23. 1.90	P G Kynsey	Headcorn	15. 7.08P
G-BSAK	Colt 21A Sky Chariot Balloon (Hot Air)	1696		26. 2.90	G A Chadwick t/a Black Pearl Balloons		
					(New owners 10.06) Partridge Green, Horsham		16. 7.08A
G-BSAS	Cameron V-65 Balloon (Hot Air)	2191		27. 2.90	J R Barber	King's Lynn	4. 7.07A
G-BSAV	Thunder Ax7-77 Balloon (Hot Air)	1555		26. 2.90	I G Lloyd "Burnt Savings"	Derby	22. 6.03A
G-BSAW	Piper PA-28-161 Warrior II	28-8216152	N8203C	27. 2.90	Haimoss Ltd	Old Sarum	10. 8.08E
			YV-2265P, N8203C				
G-BSAZ	Denney Kitfox Model 2	602	(G-BRVW)	5. 3.90	A J Lloyd, D M Garrett and J T Lane		
	(Built P E Hinkley - pr.no.PFA 172-11664)				(Ullingswick, Hereford, Bromyard and Brierley Hill)		26. 6.97P
G-BSBA	Piper PA-28-161 Warrior II	28-8016041	N2574U	1. 3.90	Falcon Flying Services Ltd	Fairoaks	27. 5.08E
G-BSBG	CCF Harvard 4 (T-6J-CCF Texan)	CCF4-483	Moz.PLAF 1753	5. 3.90	A P St John	Tatenhill	27. 9.08P
			FAP 1753,WGAF BF+053, WGAF AA+053, 52-8562 (As "20310:310" in RCAF c/s)				
G-BSBI	Cameron O-77 Balloon (Hot Air)	2245		6. 3.90	D M Billing "Calibre"	Uckfield	4. 8.07A
G-BSBR	Cameron V-77 Balloon (Hot Air)	2247		26. 2.90	R P Wade "Honey"	Wigan	13. 4.08A
G-BSBT	Piper J-3C-65 Cub	17712	N70694	9. 3.90	A Ward	Sherburn-in-Elmet	17. 5.07P
			NC70694				
G-BSBV	Rans S-10 Sakota	1089.064		9. 3.90	J D C Henslow	(Ingrams Green, Midhurst)	16.12.07P
	(Built J Whiting - pr.no.PFA 194-11769)						
G-BSBW	Bell 206B-3 JetRanger III	3664	N43EA	12. 3.90	D T Sharpe	Shoreham	17. 8.08E
			N6498V, 9Y-THC				
G-BSBX	Montgomerie-Bensen B 8MR	PFA G/01A-1135		12. 3.90	W Toulmin and R J Roan	(Peterborough)	26. 5.93P
	(Built B Ibbott) (Rotax 503)				(New owner 3.03)		
G-BSBZ	Cessna 150M	15077093	N63086	29. 3.90	D T Given t/a DTG Aviation	Newtownards	28. 8.08E
G-BSCA	Cameron N-90 Balloon (Hot Air)	2237	(9M-)	12. 3.90	J Steiner	Kuala Lumpur, Malaysia	21. 5.05A
	(Originally regd with c/n 2239 - also see G-BRZA)		G-BSCA				
G-BSCC	Colt 105A Balloon (Hot Air)	1006		15. 3.90	Capricorn Balloons Ltd	Loughborough	5. 8.08T
G-BSCE	Robinson R22 Beta	1245		15. 3.90	H.Sugden (Operated Soloflight)	Humberside	17. 3.08E
G-BSCF	Thunder Ax7-77 Balloon (Hot Air)	1537		14. 3.90	V P Gardiner "Charlie Farley"	Stoke-on-Trent	22.11.02A
G-BSCG	Denney Kitfox Model 2	PFA 172-11602		23. 4.90	A Levitt	(Hebden Bridge)	17. 9.08P
	(Built A C and T G Pinkstone)						
G-BSCH	Denney Kitfox Model 2	510		16. 3.90	J D Cheeseman	(Poole)	30.10.08P
	(Built Baldoon Leisure Flying Co Ltd - pr.no.PFA 172-11621)						
G-BSCI	Colt 77A Balloon (Hot Air)	1683		16. 3.90	J L and S Wrigglesworth "Brody"	Ilminster	15. 8.08A
G-BSCK	Cameron H-24 Balloon (Hot Air)	2263		16. 3.90	J D Shapland "Monacle"	Wadebridge	11. 6.95A
G-BSCN	SOCATA TB-20 Trinidad	1070	D-EGTC	27. 3.90	B W Dye	Biggin Hill	1. 6.02
			G-BSCN		(Noted 6.05)		
G-BSCO	Thunder Ax7-77 Balloon (Hot Air)	1635		6. 3.90	F J Whalley "Bluebell"	Cleish	8. 9.02A
G-BSCP	Cessna 152 II	15283289	N48135	20. 3.90	Moray Flying Club (1990) Ltd	RAF Kinloss	15.10.07E
G-BSCS	Piper PA-28-181 Cherokee Archer II		N47392	3. 4.90	Wingtask 1995 Ltd	Seething	16. 5.08E
		28-7890064					

G-BSCV	Piper PA-28-161 Cherokee Warrior II		C-GQXW	22. 3.90	R J L Beynon tr Southwood Flying Group	Earls Colne	6. 1.06
		28-7816135			*(Noted 2007)*		
G-BSCW	Taylorcraft BC-65	1798	N24461	22. 3.90	S Leach	Plymouth	11. 6.08P
			NC24461		*(Carries "C24461" on fin)*		
G-BSCX	Thunder Ax8-105 Balloon (Hot Air)	1748		21. 3.90	Balloon Flights Club Ltd *"Balloon Flights"*	Leicester	14. 7.99T
G-BSCY	Piper PA-28-151 Cherokee Warrior	28-7515046	C-GOBE	22. 3.90	Take Flight Aviation Ltd	Wellesbourne Mountford	20. 7.08E
	(Converted to PA-28-161 model)						
G-BSCZ	Cessna 152 II	15282199	N68226	22. 3.90	The Royal Air Force Halton Aeroplane Club Ltd		
						RAF Halton	7. 9.08E
G-BSDA	Taylorcraft BC-12D	7316	N43657	15.11.90	D G Edwards	Ellens Green, West Sussex	16. 8.08P
			NC43657		*(Noted 7.03 minus engine)*		
G-BSDD	Denney Kitfox Model 2	639		28. 3.90	D C Crawley	*(Calverton, Nottingham)*	10. 5.08P
	(Built M Richardson and J Cook - pr.no.PFA 172-11797)						
G-BSDH	Robin DR.400-180 Régent	1980		18. 4.90	R L Brucciani	Leicester	10. 5.08E
G-BSDI	Corben Junior Ace Model E	3961	N91706	28. 3.90	J R Ravenhill	Chavenage, Tetbury	12. 1.07P
	(Built Oliver and Clark)						
G-BSDJ	Piper J-4E Cub Coupé	4-1456	N35975	13. 2.91	W J Siertsema	Bicester	10. 5.08P
	(Continental C85)		NC35975				
G-BSDK	Piper J-5A Cub Cruiser	5-175	N30337	28. 3.90	J E Mead	Oaksey Park	6. 9.07P
	(Continental A75)		NC30337				
G-BSDL	SOCATA TB-10 Tobago	156		7.10.80	P Middleton and G Corbin tr Delta Lima Group		
						Sherburn-in-Elmet	13. 7.08E
G-BSDN	Piper PA-34-200T Seneca II	34-7970335	N2893A	2. 4.90	Aircraft Asset Management Ltd	Cardiff	15. 6.08E
G-BSDO	Cessna 152 II	15281657	N65894	23. 5.90	L W Scattergood	*(Sheffield City)*	27. 7.08E
G-BSDP	Cessna 152 II	15280268	N24468	11. 6.90	B A Paul	Denham	3. 4.08E
G-BSDS	Boeing Stearman E75 (PT-13A) Kaydet	75-118	N57852	6. 4.90	A Basso	Biel-Kappelen, Switzerland	16. 5.08E
	(Continental W670)		38-470		*(As "118" in US Army c/s)*		
G-BSDV	Colt 31A Balloon (Hot Air)	1722		30. 3.90	S J Roake	Frimley, Camberley	16. 8.08A
G-BSDW	Cessna 182P Skylane II	18264688	N9125M	9. 4.90	Parker Diving Ltd	St Just	27. 6.08E
G-BSDX	Cameron V-77 Balloon (Hot Air)	541	(G-BGWA)	30. 3.90	G P and S J Allen	Abingdon	
	(Officially regd with c/n 2050)		G-SNOW (1)		*(Active 2005)*		
G-BSDZ	Enstrom 280FX	2051	OO-MHV	3. 4.90	Avalon Group Ltd	Botany Bay, Chorley	25. 7.05
			(OO-JMH), G-ODSC, G-BSDZ		*(Noted 2007)*		
G-BSED	Piper PA-22-160 Tri-Pacer	22-6377	N9404D	7. 6.90	Tayflite Ltd	Perth	5. 9.03
	(Hoerner wing-tips: tail-wheel conversion)				*(Had accident Stonehaven 21. 6.02 - dismantled 2.07)*		
G-BSEE	Rans S-9	PFA 196-11635		2. 3.90	R P Hothersall	St Michaels	26.11.01P
	(Built P M Semler) (Rotax 532)				*(New owner 1.05)*		
G-BSEF	Piper PA-28-180 Cherokee C	28-1846	N7831W	18. 4.90	I D Wakeling	Franklyn's Field, Chewton Mendip	2.11.06
G-BSEG	Ken Brock KB-2	PFA G/06-1106		3. 4.90	S J M Ledingham	Carlisle	2. 7.02P
	(Built H Bancroft-Wilson)						
G-BSEJ	Cessna 150M Commuter	15076261	N66767	4. 5.90	D J Dimmer and B Robins	High Ham, Langport	22. 8.08E
G-BSEK	Robinson R22	0027	N45AD	10. 4.90	S J Strange	Blackpool	12. 5.08E
			N90193				
G-BSEL	Slingsby T 61G Super Falke	1986		31. 3.80	D G Holley	RAF Keevil	29. 8.08E
G-BSEP	Cessna 172	46555	N6455E	12. 4.90	R J Watts tr EP Aviation	Redhill	15. 3.08E
G-BSER	Piper PA-28-160 Cherokee B	28-790	N5665W	19. 4.90	Yorkair Ltd	Breighton	16.10.08E
G-BSEU	Piper PA-28-181 Cherokee Archer II		N47639	1. 5.90	Euro Aviation 91 Ltd	Blackbushe	25. 5.08E
		28-7890108					
G-BSEV	Cameron O-77 Balloon (Hot Air)	2271		20. 4.90	P B Kenington	Devauden, Chepstow	23. 3.08A
					(Donor Card titles)		
G-BSEY	Beech A36 Bonanza	E-1873	N1809F	17. 5.90	P Malam-Wilson	Coventry	6.10.07E
G-BSFA	Aero Designs Pulsar	176		18. 4.90	P F Lorriman	Rochester	8. 6.06P
	(Built S A Gill - pr.no.PFA 202-11754) (Tri-cycle u/c)						
G-BSFB	CASA 1-131E Jungmann Series 2000	2053	Spanish AF E3B-449	27. 4.90	M L J Goff	Old Buckenham	3. 9.07P
					(As "S5+B06" in Luftwaffe c/s)		
G-BSFD	Piper J-3C-65 Cub	16037	N88419	25. 5.90	B R Emerson	Moat Farm, Milden	9. 7.08P
			NC88419		*(As "16037" in US Army c/s)*		
G-BSFE	Piper PA-38-112 Tomahawk II	38-82A0033	N91452	26. 4.90	D J Campbell	Perth	10. 6.07T
G-BSFF	Robin DR.400-180R Remorqueur	1295	D-ELMM	20. 4.90	Lasham Gliding Society Ltd	Lasham	4. 7.08E
G-BSFP	Cessna 152T	15285548	N93764	9. 5.90	The Pilot Centre Ltd	Denham	18. 8.08E
G-BSFR	Cessna 152 II	15282268	N68341	9. 5.90	Galair Ltd	Biggin Hill	8. 7.08E
G-BSFV	Woods Woody Pusher	201	N16WP	30. 4.90	M G Parsons	RAF Kinloss	17. 7.08P
	(Built P E Hall) (Continental C85)						
G-BSFW	Piper PA-15 Vagabond	15-273	N4484H	26. 4.90	J R Kimberley	Bounds Farm, Ardleigh	21.12.05P
	(Continental A65)		NC4484H		*(Noted 11.06)*		
G-BSFX	Denney Kitfox Model 2	506		23. 4.90	H Hedley-Lewis	Croft Farm, Defford	19. 7.08P
	(Built D A McFadyean - pr.no.PFA 172-11723)						
G-BSFY	Denney Kitfox Model 2	PFA 172-11632		16. 3.90	C I Bates	Long Marston	8. 6.04P
	(Built J R Howard - PFA pr.no. duplicates Kitfox G-MWCH)						
G-BSGB	Gaertner Ax4 Skyranger Balloon (Hot Air)			30. 3.90	B Gaertner	Biddenden, Ashford	
	(Built B Gaertner)	SR.0001					
G-BSGD	Piper PA-28-180 Cherokee E	28-5691	N3463R	4. 5.90	R J Cleverley	Draycott Farm, Chiseldon	6. 6.08E
G-BSGF	Robinson R22 Beta	1383		1. 5.90	L B Clark	Breighton	28. 6.08T
G-BSGG	Denney Kitfox Model 2	PFA 172-11666		1. 5.90	C G Richardson	Fulbeck, Lincoln	16. 6.07P
	(Built C G Richardson) (Jabiru 2200A)						
G-BSGH	Airtour AH-56B Balloon (Hot Air)	014		1. 5.90	A R Hardwick	Shefford	
					"Battle of Britain" (Active 8.04)		
G-BSGJ	Monnett Sonerai II	300	N34WH	1. 5.90	G A Brady	Enstone	6. 9.91P
	(Built W Hossink) (Volkswagen 1835)				*(Noted 5.06)*		
G-BSGK	Piper PA-34-200T Seneca II	34-7870331	N36450	22. 5.90	Aeros Holdings Ltd	Gloucestershire	20. 3.08T
G-BSGL	Piper PA-28-161 Warrior II	28-8116041	N82690	10. 5.90	Keywest Air Charter Ltd	Liverpool	26.10.07E
					"Liverbird V" (Operated Cheshire Air Training Services Ltd)		
G-BSGP	Cameron N-65 Balloon (Hot Air)	2293		1. 5.90	T D Gibbs	Billingshurst	16. 5.07A

Reg	Type	C/N	Prev ID	Date	Owner	Location	Date2
G-BSGS	Rans S-10 Sakota	1289.076		9. 5.90	M R Parr	Kirkbride	18. 9.07P
	(Built R Handley - pr.no.PFA 194-11724)						
G-BSGT	Cessna 210N Turbo Centurion II	21063361	LX-ATL	21. 5.90	E A T Brenninkmeyer	Biggin Hill	14. 1.08E
	(Reims-assembled c/n F2100020)		D-EOGB, N5308A				
G-BSHA	Piper PA-34-200T Seneca II	34-7670216	N9707K	2. 5.90	Justgold Ltd	Blackpool	29. 3.08E
G-BSHC	Colt 69A Balloon (Hot Air)	1668		8. 5.90	Magical Adventures Ltd	West Bloomfield, Michigan, US	12.10.98A
G-BSHD	Colt 69A Balloon (Hot Air)	1736		8. 5.90	F W Ewer)	Lighthorne Heath, Leamington Spa	22. 5.08A
G-BSHH	Luscombe 8E Silvaire Deluxe	3981	N1254K	11. 5.90	S L Lewis	Lower Upham Farm, Chiseldon	6. 2.08P
	(Continental C85)		NC1254K				
G-BSHI	Luscombe 8F Silvaire	1821	N39060	11. 5.90	P R Bush	(Mastlebridge, Milford Haven)	14. 8.01P
	(Continental C90)		NC39060		(New owner 5.07)		
G-BSHK	Denney Kitfox Model 2	449		11. 5.90	D Doyle and C Aherne	Kilrush, County Kildare	29. 8.08P
	(Built A C Cree - pr.no.PFA 172-11752) (Rotax 532)						
G-BSHO	Cameron V-77 Balloon (Hot Air)	2313		16. 5.90	C Stewart and D J Duckworth		
					London E7 and Bellingdon, Chesham		21. 9.07A
G-BSHP	Piper PA-28-161 Warrior II	28-8616002	N190X	31. 5.90	S J Skilton t/a Aviation Rentals	(Cranfield)	28.11.07E
			G-BSHP, N9107Y		(Noted 6.07 on trailer - M25 clockwise between Junctions 16 and 17)		
G-BSHS	Colt 105A Balloon (Hot Air)	1674	(D-OCAT)	16. 5.90	I Novosad	Planegg, Germany	9. 9.01A
			G-BSHS				
G-BSHT	Cameron V-77 Balloon (Hot Air)	2321		30. 5.90	E C Moore "Buckshot Too"	Great Missenden	19.11.03T
G-BSHV	Piper PA-18-135 Super Cub	18-3123	OO-GDG	5. 7.90	G T Fisher	Northside, Thorney	20. 5.04
	(L-18C-PI)		Belgian Army L-49, 53-4723				
G-BSHY	EAA Acrosport	PFA 072-10928		17. 4.90	R J Hodder	Eastfield Farm, Manby	20.12.05P
	(Built T Butterworth and R J Hodder) (Lycoming O-290)				(Landed long Keal Coates, Lincoln 2.5.05 and substantially damaged)		
G-BSIC	Cameron V-77 Balloon (Hot Air)	2322		17. 5.90	T R Tillson (New owner 10.07)	Ilkeston	14. 8.05A
G-BSIF	Denney Kitfox Model 2	563		5. 7.90	R J Humphries	Walkeridge Farm, Overton	29. 8.08P
	(Built R M Kimbell and M H Wylde - pr.no.PFA 172-11889)						
G-BSIG	Colt 21A Cloudhopper Balloon (Hot Air)	1322		18. 5.90	S J Humphreys	Great Missenden	27. 4.07A
G-BSIH	Rutan LongEz	1200-1		31. 5.90	W S Allen	(Cheltenham)	
	(Built W S Allen - pr.no.PFA 074A-11492)						
G-BSII	Piper PA-34-200T Seneca II	34-8070336	N8253N	16. 5.90	T Belso	Fowlmere	11. 5.08E
G-BSIJ	Cameron V-77 Balloon (Hot Air)	2164		23. 5.90	G B Davies	Thorney, Peterborough	16. 7.08A
G-BSIK	Denney Kitfox Model 1	51		5. 6.90	M Bromage	(Stonehouse)	26. 6.06P
	(Built R L Cunliffe) (Rotax 503)						
G-BSIM	Piper PA-28-181 Archer II	28-8690017	N9092Y	22. 5.90	Central Aircraft Leasing Ltd	Halfpenny Green	7. 9.08E
G-BSIO	Cameron Furness House 56 SS Balloon (Hot Air)	2310		25. 5.90	R E Jones "Pinkie"	Lytham St Annes	17. 3.06A
G-BSIU	Colt 90A Balloon (Hot Air)	1774		25. 5.90	S Travaglia	Firenze, Italy	12. 7.04A
G-BSIY	Schleicher ASK 14	14005	5Y-AID	4. 6.90	P W Andrews	Husbands Bosworth	8. 9.07
			D-KOIC				
G-BSIZ	Piper PA-28-181 Archer II	28-7990377	N2162Y	25. 5.90	M J Cunnliffe	Liverpool	21. 6.08E
G-BSJB	Bensen B 8	PFA G/01-1080		5. 6.90	J W Limbrick	(Bewdley)	
	(Built J W Limbrick)						
G-BSJU	Cessna 150M	15076430	N3230V	14. 6.90	A C Williamson	Crowfield	17. 4.08E
					(Operated Crowfield Flying Club)		
G-BSJX	Piper PA-28-161 Warrior II	28-8216084	N8036N	30. 5.90	MK Aero Supprt Ltd	Andrewsfield	23. 7.08E
G-BSJZ	Cessna 150J	15070485	N60661	7. 5.91	M H Campbell	Kemble	10. 7.08E
G-BSKA	Cessna 150M	15076137	N66588	31. 7.90	R J Cushing	Ellough, Beccles	13. 3.08E
G-BSKD	Cameron V-77 Balloon (Hot Air)	2336		4. 6.90	M J Gunston "Skulduggery"	Blackwater, Camberley	4. 8.06A
G-BSKE	Cameron O-84 Balloon (Hot Air)	1604	ZS-HYD	4. 6.90	S F Redman	Stalbridge, Sturminster Newton	19. 8.03A
			G-BSKE				
G-BSKG	Maule MX-7-180 Super Rocket	11072C		7. 6.90	J R Surbey	Blockmoor Farm, Soham, Ely	10. 2.06
					(On rebuild East Winch 7.07 following accident at Top Farm 20.11.05)		
G-BSKI	Thunder Ax8-90 Balloon (Hot Air)	1623		18. 5.90	K P Barnes and L A Pibworth	(Bristol)	11.10.07A
G-BSKL	Piper PA-38-112 Tomahawk	38-78A0509	N4252E	11. 6.90	A S Bamrah t/a Falcon Flying Services	Biggin Hill	22.11.07E
G-BSKU	Cameron O-84 Balloon (Hot Air)	2330		8. 6.90	Alfred Bagnall and Sons (West) Ltd "Bagnalls II"	Bristol	7. 6.02A
G-BSKW	Piper PA-28-181 Archer II	2890138	N91940	1. 6.90	Shropshire Aero Club Ltd	Sleap	9. 4.08E
G-BSLA	Robin DR.400-180 Régent	1997		22. 6.90	A B McCoig tr Robin Lima Alpha Group	Rochester	19. 3.08E
G-BSLH	CASA 1-131E Jungmann Series 2000	2222	Spanish AF E3B-622	27. 7.90	P Warden	Biel-Kappelen, Switzerland	12. 8.08P
	(Officially quoted c/n and p/i incorect: built new Bücker Prado SL, Albacete, Spain)						
G-BSLI	Cameron V-77 Balloon (Hot Air)	2115		15. 6.90	R C Corcoran	Thornbury, Bristol	11. 8.08T
G-BSLK	Piper PA-28-161 Warrior II	28-7916018	N20849	15. 6.90	R A Rose	Wellesbourne Mountford	23. 6.08E
G-BSLM	Piper PA-28-160 Cherokee	28-308	N5262W	22. 6.90	R Fulton	Popham	25. 4.08
G-BSLT	Piper PA-28-161 Warrior II	28-8016303	N81817	19. 6.90	L W Scattergood	Sherburn-in-Elmet	30. 1.08E
G-BSLU	Piper PA-28-140 Cherokee	28-24733	OY-PJL	19. 6.90	W E Lewis	Shobdon	6. 2.08E
			OH-PJL, SE-FFA				
G-BSLV	Enstrom 280FX	2054	D-HHAS	26. 6.90	EVI (UK) Ltd	Hawarden	2. 2.08E
			G-BSLV				
G-BSLW	Champion 7ECA Citabria	431-66	N9696S	16. 7.90	D W Mann tr Shoreham Citabria Group	Shoreham	6. 9.03
	(Officially regd as "Bellanca 7ECA Citabria")						
G-BSLX	WAR Focke-Wulf FW190 replica	24	N698WW	19. 6.90	D Featherby tr FW190 Gruppe	Norwich	2. 8.02P
	(Built W Wilson)				(As "1+4" in Luftwaffe c/s)		
G-BSMD	SNCAN 1101 Noralpha	139	F-GDPQ	26. 6.90	J W Hardie	Prestwick	1. 5.08P
			F-YEEE, F-YCZK, CAN-11, French.Military (As "+14" in Luftwaffe c/s)				
G-BSME	Bölkow BÖ.208C Junior	596	D-ECGA	25. 6.90	D J Hampson	Popham	14.12.07E
G-BSMG	Montgomerie-Bensen B 8M	PFA G/01-1170		22. 6.90	A C Timperley	(Dull, Aberfeldy)	16. 7.97P
	(Built A C Timperley) (Rotax 532)						
G-BSMK	Cameron O-84 Balloon (Hot Air)	2328		26. 6.90	D F Maine and D M Newton tr G-BSMK Shareholders	Redditch	27. 8.08A
G-BSML	Schweizer 269C	S 1462	PH-HUH	10.10.90	K P Foster and B I Winsor t/a Moorgoods Helicopters	Liskeard Heliport	9. 5.08E
	(Schweizer 300)		N134DM				
G-BSMM	Colt 31A Sky Chariot Balloon (Hot Air)	1779		27. 6.90	D V Fowler	Cranbrook	11. 7.04A
G-BSMN	CFM Streak Shadow	K 137-SA		26. 6.90	P J Porter	Henstridge	29. 8.08P
	(Built K Daniels - pr.no.PFA 161A-11656) (Rotax 582)						

G-BSMS	Cameron V-77 Balloon (Hot Air)	2356		26. 6.90	R Ashford	Petworth	30. 6.07A
G-BSMT	Rans S-10 Sakota	1289.077		29. 6.90	S J Kidd	Redhill	8. 6.05P
	(Built N Woodworth - pr.no.PFA 194-11793)						
G-BSMU	Rans S-6-116N Coyote II	1089.090	G-MWJE	27. 6.90	A Wright	Church Farm, Askern	30. 6.07P
	(Built W D Walker - pr.no.PFA 204-11732)				(Noted 9.07)		
G-BSMV	Piper PA-17 Vagabond	17-94	N4696H	29. 6.90	A Cheriton	Wellesbourne Mountford	8. 8.07P
	(Continental C85)		NC4696H		"Sophie" (Carries 'N4696H' on tail)		
G-BSMX	Bensen B 8MR	PFA G/01-1171		3. 7.90	J S E R McGregor	(Birmingham)	
	(Built J S E R McGregor)						
G-BSND	Air Command 532 Elite	PFA G/04-1180		16. 7.90	T A Holmes	(Leeds)	
	(Built B J Castle)				(New owner 7.06)		
G-BSNE	Luscombe 8E Silvaire Deluxe	5757	N1130B	2.11.90	N Reynolds and C Watts	Dunsfold	16. 8.07P
	(Continental C85)		NC1130B				
G-BSNF	Piper J-3C-65 Cub	3070	N23317	17. 8.90	D A Hammant	Bere Farm, Warnford	17. 9.07P
	(Continental O-200-A) (Frame No.3116)		NC23317		(Lippert Reed conversion)		
G-BSNG	Cessna 172N Skyhawk II	17270192	N738SB	19. 7.90	A J and P C MacDonald	Edinburgh	14.12.07E
G-BSNJ	Cameron N-90 Balloon (Hot Air)	2335		6. 7.90	D P H Smith	Ilkley	8. 6.04A
G-BSNL	Bensen B 8MR	PFA G/01-1181		16. 7.90	A C Breane	(Ballybofey, County Donegal)	20. 7.97P
	(Built T R Grief) (Rotax 532)						
G-BSNP	Piper PA-28R-201T Turbo Arrow III		N38537	18. 7.90	D F K Singleton	(Teck, Germany)	29. 9.07E
		28R-7703236					
G-BSNT	Luscombe 8A Silvaire	1679	N37018	16. 7.90	P K Jordan tr Luscombe Quartet		
	(Continental A65) (Built as Model 8C)		NC37018			Stoneacre Farm, Farthing Corner	1. 4.08P
G-BSNU	Colt 105A Balloon (Hot Air)	1811		23. 7.90	M P Rich tr Gone Ballooning	Warmley, Bristol	9. 4.07A
					(Sun Rise titles)		
G-BSNX	Piper PA-28-181 Archer II	28-7990311	N3028S	19. 7.90	Central Aircraft Leasing Ltd	Halfpenny Green	25. 8.08E
					(Operated Halfpenny Green Flight Centre?)		
G-BSNY	Bensen B 8M	PFA G/01-1176		16. 7.90	H McCartney	(Stockport)	6. 9.01P
	(Built A S Deakin) (Arrow GT500R)						
G-BSNZ	Cameron O-105 Balloon (Hot Air)	2364		16. 7.90	J Francis "Firefly"	Dibden Purlieu, Southampton	9. 7.08A
G-BSOE	Luscombe 8A Silvaire	4331	N1604K	22. 8.90	S B Marsden	Sturgate	
	(C/n would indicate Model 8E)		NC1604K		(Stored dismantled as "N1604K" 8.05)		
G-BSOF	Colt 25A Sky Chariot Mk.II Balloon (Hot Air)	1820		27. 7.90	L P Hooper	St George, Bristol	20.10.04A
G-BSOG	Cessna 172M Skyhawk II	17263636	N1508V	16. 7.90	S Eustace	Crowfield	25. 1.08E
G-BSOJ	Thunder Ax7-77 Balloon (Hot Air)	1818	JA-...	31. 7.90	R J S Jones	Stourbridge	15. 3.04A
			G-BSOJ				
G-BSOK	Piper PA-28-161 Cherokee Warrior II		N9749K	19. 7.90	Aeros Leasing Ltd	Gloucestershire	5. 2.08E
		28-7816191					
G-BSOM	Glaser-Dirks DG-400	4-126	LN-GMC	12. 7.90	M J Watson tr G-BSOM Group	Sutton Bank	29. 5.08E
			D-KGDG		"403"		
G-BSON	Green S-25 Balloon (Hot Air)	001		7. 6.90	J J Green	Newbury	
	(Built J J Green)						
G-BSOO	Cessna 172F	17252431	N8531U	19. 7.90	P W Lawrence tr Double Oscar Flying Group	Seething	8.11.07E
G-BSOR	CFM Streak Shadow	K 131-SA		23.10.89	A Parr	(Lewes, Sussex)	11. 6.08P
	(Built J P Sorensen - pr.no.PFA 161A-11602) (Rotax 532)						
G-BSOT	Piper PA-38-112 Tomahawk II	38-81A0053	N25682	23. 7.90	APB Leasing Ltd	Sleap	26. 9.08E
G-BSOU	Piper PA-38-112 Tomahawk II	38-81A0130	N23373	23. 7.90	D J Campbell	Perth	22. 2.08E
G-BSOX	Luscombe 8AE Silvaire	2318	N45791	7. 8.90	R S Lanary	Sixpenny Handley, Dorset	15. 6.08P
	(Continental O-200-A)		NC45791		"Bobby Sox"		
G-BSOZ	Piper PA-28-161 Warrior II	28-7916080	N30220	14. 8.90	Grampian Airways Ltd	Aberdeen	28.12.07E
G-BSPA	QAC Quickie Q.2	2227	N227T	16. 8.90	G V Mckirdy and B K Glover	Enstone	25. 5.06P
	(Built C C and MA Wilde) (Revmaster R2100DQ)						
G-BSPB	Thunder Ax8-84 Balloon (Hot Air)	1803		24. 7.90	A N F Pertwee	Great Holland, Frinton-on-Sea	22. 9.00T
					(New owner 8.04)		
G-BSPE	Reims Cessna F172P Skyhawk II	F17202073		31.12.80	T W Williamson	Hinkle Grange Farm, Barton	30. 6.08E
G-BSPG	Piper PA-34-200T Seneca II	34-8070168	N8176S	8. 8.90	Andrews Professional Colour Laboratories Ltd	Lydd	12. 7.08E
G-BSPI	Piper PA-28-161 Warrior II	28-8116025	N8258V	26. 7.90	TGD Leasing Ltd	Wellesbourne Mountford	30. 4.08E
G-BSPJ	Campell Cricket replica	PFA G/01-1061		3. 8.90	D Ross	(Londonderry)	8. 1.04P
	(Built P Barlow ,A Scott and C Jones)						
G-BSPK	Cessna 195A	7691	N1079D	14. 8.90	A G and D.L Bompas	Biggin Hill	4. 5.08E
	(Jacobs R-755-9)						
G-BSPL	CFM Streak Shadow	K 140-SA		26. 7.90	G L Turner	Pittrichie Farm, Whiterashes	18. 6.08P
	(Built CFM Metal-Fax) (Rotax 582)						
G-BSPM	Piper PA-28-161 Warrior II	28-8116046	N82679	27. 7.90	S J Skilton t/a Aviation Rentals	White Waltham	12. 1.07T
	(Thielert TAE 125)				(Operated West London Aero Services)		
G-BSPN	Piper PA-28R-201T Turbo Arrow III		N5965V	31. 7.90	V E H Taylor	Haverfordwest	23. 2.08E
		28R-7703171					
G-BSPT	Pilatus Britten-Norman BN-2B-20 Islander	2240	TF-VEG	3. 8.90	Hebridean Air Services Ltd	Cumbernauld	29. 3.08E
	(Originally regd as BN-2B-26)		N52WA, OY-PHY, JA5316, G-BSPT				
G-BSPW	Avid Speed Wing	PFA 189-11840		17. 7.90	M J Sewell	(Haydock, St Helens)	4. 9.04P
	(Built P D Wheatland)						
G-BSRD	Cameron N-105 Balloon (Hot Air)	1568	D-ORSD	3. 8.90	A Ockelmann t/a Ballon Reisen	Buchholz, Germany	4. 9.04A
			G-BSRD				
G-BSRH	Pitts S-1C	LS-2	N4111	7. 8.90	C D Swift	(Bexhill-on-Sea)	9. 5.07P
	(Built L Smith)				(Carries "N4111" on rudder)		
G-BSRI	Neico Lancair 235	PFA 191-11467		9. 8.90	G Lewis	Liverpool	7. 8.08P
	(Built G Lewis) (Lycoming O-235) (Tri-cycle u/c)						
G-BSRK	ARV Aviation ARV-1 Super 2	K 007	ZK-FSQ	8. 8.90	D M Blair	RAF Mona	19. 6.08P
G-BSRL	Campbell Cricket Mk.4 replica	PFA G/03-1325		8. 8.90	I Rosewall	Henstridge	3. 8.05P
	(Built I Rosewall from Everett Gyroplane Series 2 c/n 0022)				(Noted 4.07)		
G-BSRP	RotorWay Executive	3824		15. 8.90	R J Baker	Hawarden	1. 5.08P
	(Built J P Dennison) (RotorWay RW 152)						
G-BSRR	Cessna 182Q Skylane II	18266915	N96961	25. 7.90	C M Moore	Thornborough Grounds, Buckingham	1. 4.08E

Reg	Type	C/n	Prev id	Date	Owner/Operator	Location	CofA
G-BSRT	Denney Kitfox Model 2	742		9. 8.90	A Rooker	(Histon, Cambridge)	20.12.07P
	(Built L R James - pr.no.PFA 172-11873)						
G-BSRX	CFM Streak Shadow	K 148-SA		15. 8.90	W Southcott	Old Sarum	24.11.08P
	(Built C Penman - pr.no.PFA 206-11870) (Rotax 618)						
G-BSSA	Luscombe 8E Silvaire Deluxe	4176	N1449K NC1449K	15. 8.90	K R Old tr Luscombe Flying Group	White Waltham	24.10.08P
	(Continental C85)						
G-BSSB	Cessna 150L Commuter	15074147	N19076	15. 8.90	D T A Rees	Haverfordwest	30. 6.06T
					(Operated Haverfordwest Air Charter Services)		
G-BSSC	Piper PA-28-161 Warrior II	28-8216176	N81993 N9529N, N8234B	15. 8.90	G-BSSC Ltd	Norwich	13. 3.08E
G-BSSE	Piper PA-28-140 Cherokee Cruiser	28-7525192	N33440	22.10.90	D Hoyle	Blackpool	14.11.07E
G-BSSF	Denney Kitfox Model 2	738		15. 8.90	A M Smith	(Broughton, Brigg)	9.10.08P
	(Built D M Orrock - pr.no.PFA 172-11796)						
G-BSSI	Rans S-6-116N Coyote II	0190.112	(G-MWJA)	17. 8.90	J Currell	(Bangor, County Down)	16.11.99P
	(Built D A Farnwroth - pr.no.PFA 204-11782)				(Believed stored)		
G-BSSK	QAC Quickie Q.200	PFA 094A-11354		5. 9.90	D G Greatrex	(Crookham, Thatcham)	23. 9.99P
	(Built D G Greatrex) (Continental O-200-A)				(Address change 9.07)		
G-BSSP	Robin DR.400-180R Remorqueur	2015		24. 9.90	Soaring (Oxford) Ltd	RAF Syerston	8. 1.08E
					(Operated Air Cadets Gliding School)		
G-BSSV	CFM Streak Shadow	K 129-SA		21. 8.90	R W Payne (Eddsfield, Octon Lodge Farm, Thwing)		5. 5.98P
	(Built A M Green - pr.no.PFA 206-11532) (Rotax 532)						
G-BSSW	Piper PA-28-161 Cherokee Warrior II	N47850 28-7816143		29. 8.90	D J Skidmore and E F Rowland	Filton	5. 9.08E
G-BSTC	Aeronca 11AC Chief	11AC-1660	N3289E NC3289E	15.10.90	J Armstrong and D Lamb	(Crook)	26. 6.93P
	(Continental A65)				(Damaged Henstridge 18.4.93: on rebuild 12.95: new owners 1.02)		
G-BSTE	Aérospatiale AS.355F2 Ecureuil 2	5453		29. 8.90	Oscar Mayer Ltd	Redhill	6.12.07E
G-BSTH	Piper PA-25-235 Pawnee C	25-5009	N8599L	25. 9.90	Scottish Gliding Union Ltd	Portmoak	1. 5.08E
G-BSTI	Piper J-3C-65 Cub	19144	N6007H NC6007H	31. 8.90	J A Scott	Chesnut Farm, Tipps End, Welney	13. 7.08P
	(Continental C85) (Frame No.19073)						
G-BSTK	Thunder Ax8-90 Balloon (Hot Air)	1838		17. 9.90	M Williams	Wadhurst, East Sussex	28. 1.08A
G-BSTL	Rand Robinson KR-2	PFA 129-11863		6. 9.90	C S Hales and N Brauns	Shenington	30. 6.05P
	(Built C S Hales and believed to incorporate G-BYLP (qv))				(Noted 3.06)		
G-BSTM	Cessna 172L Skyhawk	17260143	N4243Q	25. 9.90	A C G Brown tr G-BSTM Group	Duxford	18. 3.08E
G-BSTO	Cessna 152 II	15282133	N68005	4. 9.90	Plymouth Flying School Ltd	Plymouth	16. 1.08E
G-BSTP	Cessna 152 II	15282925	N89953	4. 9.90	Cobham Leasing Ltd	Bournemouth	18. 3.08E
G-BSTR	Grumman AA-5 Traveler	AA5-0688	OO-ALR OO-HAN, (OO-WAZ)	8.10.90	B D Jones	Wellesbourne Mountford	1. 3.08E
G-BSTT	Rans S-6 Coyote II	0190.115		5. 9.90	D G Palmer	Mintlaw, Peterhead	2.12.02P
	(Built M W Holmes - pr.no.PFA 204-11880) (Rotax 582)						
G-BSTV	Piper PA-32-300 Cherokee Six	32-40378	N4069R	13. 9.90	B C Hudson (In open store 10.06)	Popham	
G-BSTX	Luscombe 8A Silvaire	3301	EI-CDZ G-BSTX, N71874, NC71874	10. 9.90	G R Nicholson	Derryogue	31. 5.07P
	(Continental A65)				(Noted 7.07)		
G-BSTY	Thunder Ax8-90 Balloon (Hot Air)	394		12. 9.90	High On Adventure Balloons Ltd	Storrington, Pulborough	23. 4.08A
G-BSTZ	Piper PA-28-140 Cherokee Cruiser	28-7725153	N1674H	10.10.90	Air Navigation and Trading Company Ltd	Blackpool	15. 7.08E
G-BSUA	Rans S-6 Coyote II	0190.109		29.10.90	A J Todd	Abbey Warren Farm, Bucknall	1. 2.08P
	(Built P S Dopson - pr.no.PFA 204-11910) (Rotax 582)						
G-BSUB	Colt 77A Balloon (Hot Air)	1801		30.10.90	M P Hill and J M Foster	Flax Bourton, Bristol	3. 5.08A
					"Bristol Blue"		
G-BSUD	Luscombe 8A Silvaire	1745	N37084 NC37084	14. 9.90	I G Harrison	Derby	16. 9.08P
	(Continental A65)						
G-BSUE	Cessna U206G Stationair 6	U20604334	N756TB	6. 9.90	I C Austin, G S Chapman and J Dyer Little Gransden		6. 6.08E
G-BSUF	Piper PA-32RT-300 Lance II	32R-7885240	N32PL ZP-PJQ, N9641N	17. 9.90	S A Fell and J Gibbs	Guernsey	6. 2.08E
G-BSUK	Colt 77A Balloon (Hot Air)	1374		21. 9.90	A J Moore	Northwood, Harrow	22. 7.08A
G-BSUO	Scheibe SF25C-2000 Falke	44501	D-KIOK	6.12.90	J G Smith and J L Riley tr Portmoak Falke Syndicate	Portmoak	9. 7.08E
	(Limbach L2000)						
G-BSUV	Cameron O-77 Balloon (Hot Air)	2407		26. 9.90	J F Trehern	Edinburgh	4. 5.08A
G-BSUW	Piper PA-34-200T Seneca II	34-7870081	N2360M	26. 9.90	NPD Direct Ltd	Fenland	9. 2.08E
G-BSUX	Carlson Sparrow II	PFA 209-11794		5.10.90	J Stephenson	Wombleton	17. 6.06P
	(Built J Stephnson) (Rotax 532)						
G-BSUZ	Denney Kitfox Model 3	745		10. 9.90	P C Avery	Fenland	22. 8.05P
	(Built E T Wicks - pr.no.PFA 172-11875) (Converted from Model 2)						
G-BSVB	Piper PA-28-181 Archer II	2890098	N9155S	10. 9.90	K A Boost	Stapleford	2. 2.08E
G-BSVE	Binder CP.301S Smaragd	113	HB-SED	27. 9.90	R E Perry tr Smaragd Flying Group	Smalls Farm, Charterhouse	18. 4.08P
G-BSVG	Piper PA-28-161 Warrior II	28-8516013	C-GZAV	2.10.90	Airways Aero Associations Ltd Wycombe Air Park		22.12.07E
					(Operated British Airways Flying Club) (British Airways titles)		
G-BSVH	Piper J-3C-65 Cub	15360	N87702 NC87702	2.10.90	C R and K A Maher	RAF Woodvale	18. 7.08P
	(Continental A75) (Frame No.15003)						
G-BSVI	Piper PA-16 Clipper	16-186	N5379H	7.11.90	J Watkins and S Northway tr Clipper Aviation	Wadswick Manor Farm , Corsham	19.12.10P
G-BSVK	Denney Kitfox Model 2	PFA 172-11731		2.10.90	R Jelbert	(Easebourne, Midhurst)	5. 4.94P
	(Built K P Wordsworth)				(New owner 9.07)		
G-BSVM	Piper PA-28-161 Warrior II	28-8116173	N8351N	7.11.90	EFG Flying Services Ltd	Southend	31. 1.08E
					(Operated Willowair Flying Club)		
G-BSVN	Thorp T-18	107	N4881	17. 9.90	D Prentice	(Sheffield)	8. 7.05P
	(Built M R Miller) (Lycoming O-290)				(New owner 5.06)		
G-BSVP	Piper PA-23-250 Aztec F	27-7754115	N959JB G-BSVP, N63787	9. 2.78	S G Spier	Elstree	1. 5.08E
G-BSVR	Schweizer 269C	S 1236	OO-JWW D-HLEB	14.11.90	M K E Askham	(Low Catton, York)	25. 7.08E
	(Schweizer 300)						
G-BSVS	Robin DR.400-100 Cadet	2017		22.10.90	D M Chalmers	Upper Harford Farm, Bourton-on-the-Water	23. 3.08E

G-BSWB	Rans S-10 Sakota	0489.046		8.10.90	F A Hewitt	Garston Farm, Marshfield	17.10.07P
	(Built F A Hewitt - pr.no.PFA 194-11560)						
G-BSWC	Boeing Stearman E75 (PT-13D) Kaydet	75-5560	N17112	16.11.90	Richard Thwaites Aviation Ltd	Gloucestershire	22. 6.08E
	(Lycoming R-680)		N5021V, 42-17397		(As "112" in US Army c/s)		
G-BSWF	Piper PA-16 Clipper	16-475	N5865H	12.10.90	P E Bates tr Durham Clipper Group		
	(Lycoming O-320)					High Flatts Farm, Chester le Street	14. 4.08E
G-BSWG	Piper PA-17 Vagabond	15-99	N4316H	8.10.90	P E J Sturgeon	Queach Farm, Bury St Edmunds	31.10.08P
	(Continental A65-8)		NC4316H				
G-BSWH	Cessna 152 II	15281365	N49861	15.10.90	Airspeed Aviation Ltd	Derby	14. 3.02T
G-BSWL	Slingsby T 61F Venture T 2	1974	EI-CCQ	15.10.90	Bidford Gliding Ltd	Bidford	10. 7.08E
			G-BSWL, ZA655				
G-BSWM	Slingsby T 61F Venture T 2	1965	ZA629	12.10.90	P S Holmes tr Venture Gliding Group	Bellamena	5. 6.08E
G-BSWR	Pilatus Britten-Norman BN-2T Islander	2245		22.10.90	Police Service of Northern Ireland		
						Belfast International	2. 3.10S
G-BSWV	Cameron N-77 Balloon (Hot Air)	2369		22.10.90	S Charlish "Leicester Mercury"	Leicester	10. 8.08A
G-BSWX	Cameron V-90 Balloon (Hot Air)	2401		22.10.90	B J Burrows "Beeswax"	Bristol	24. 7.08A
G-BSWY	Cameron N-77 Balloon (Hot Air)	2428		12.10.90	A S Davidson tr Nottingham Hot Air Balloon Club		
						Woodville, Swadlincote	5. 7.05A
G-BSWZ	Cameron A-180 Balloon (Hot Air)	2419	C-FGWZ	22.10.90	G C Ludlow	Hythe	19. 7.99T
			G-BSWZ		"Keep Britain Farming" (Operated Balloon Preservation Group)		
G-BSXA	Piper PA-28-161 Warrior II	28-8416121	N4373Z	11.12.90	A S Bamrah t/a Falcon Flying Services	Biggin Hill	3. 8.08E
			N9622N				
G-BSXB	Piper PA-28-161 Warrior II	28-8416125	N4374D	4.12.90	Aeros Leasing Ltd	Gloucestershire	10. 5.08E
			N9626N				
G-BSXC	Piper PA-28-161 Warrior II	28-8416126	N4374F	4.12.90	L T Halpin	Cameley, Somerset	5.10.07E
			N9627N				
G-BSXD	Soko P-2 Kraguj	030	Yugoslav AF 30146	22.10.90	N C Stone	Stanton, Morpeth	16. 4.08P
					(As "146" in Yugoslav Air Force c/s)		
G-BSXI	Mooney M 20E Super 21	700056	N6766V	31.10.90	A N Pain	Southend	1. 6.08E
G-BSXM	Cameron V-77 Balloon (Hot Air)	2446		5.11.90	C A Oxby "Oxby"	Doncaster	31. 8.05A
G-BSXS	Piper PA-28-181 Archer II	28-7990151	N3055C	26.11.90	J K Milner	(Baunton, Cirencester)	10. 8.08E
G-BSXT	Piper J-5A Cub Cruiser	5-498	N33409	8.11.90	L Jobes	Spite Hall Farm, Pinchinthorpe	26. 7.03P
	(Continental C85)		NC33409		(New owner 2.06)		
G-BSXX	Whittaker MW7	PFA 171-11469		16.10.90	H J Stanley	(Abingdon)	
	(Built H J Stanley)						
G-BSYA	Jodel D 18	PFA 169-11316		7.11.90	K Wright	Andreas, Isle of Man	1.10.07P
	(Built S Harrison) (Volkswagen 1834)						
G-BSYB	Cameron N-120 Balloon (Hot Air)	2406		7.11.90	M Buono (Cameron Balloon titles)	Mondovi, Italy	24. 7.03A
G-BSYC	Piper PA-32R-300 Lance	32R-7780159	N7745T	2. 4.91	B W Gomez	Halfpenny Green	11. 8.06
			N1435H		(New owner 11.07)		
G-BSYD	Cameron A-180 Balloon (Hot Air)	2426		18.10.90	R H Etherington	Montisi, Siena, Italy	16. 6.08E
G-BSYF	Luscombe 8A Silvaire	3455	N72028	12.11.90	Atlantic Connexions Ltd t/a Atlantic Aviation		
	(Continetnal C85)		NC72028			Old Warden	7. 1.08P
G-BSYG	Piper PA-12 Super Cruiser	12-2106	N3228M	12.11.90	E R Newall tr Fat Cub Group	Breighton	9. 8.07P
	(Lycoming O-235)		NC3228M		(Noted 12.07)		
G-BSYH	Luscombe 8A Silvaire	2842	N71415	13.11.90	N R Osborne	Insch	30. 4.08P
	(Continental A65)		NC71415				
G-BSYI	Aérospatiale AS.355F1 Ecureuil 2	5197	M-MJI	14.11.90	Sky Charter UK Ltd	Manston	28.11.07E
G-BSYO	Piper J-3C-65 Cub (L-4B-PI)	12809	(G-BSMJ)	19. 2.91	C R Reynolds and J D Fuller	Pent Farm, Postling	17. 5.08P
	(Continental O-200-A) (Frame No.12639)		(G-BRHE), EC-AIY, HB-ODO, HB-OUA, 44-80513				
	(Officially regd as c/n 10244 which is HB-OVG ex 43-1383/F-BFYF)						
G-BSYU	Robin DR.400-180 Régent	2027		26.11.90	P D Smoothy	Hinton-in-the-Hedges	20. 4.08
G-BSYV	Cessna 150M	15078371	N9423U	16.11.90	L R Haunch t/a Fenland Flying School	Fenland	14. 4.08E
G-BSYW	Cessna 150M	15078446	N9498U	16.11.90	Cada Vliegtuilgen BV	(The Hague, Netherlands)	26. 4.08E
G-BSYY	Piper PA-28-161 Warrior II	2816009	N440X	26.11.90	S J Skilton t/a Aviation Rentals	Compton Abbas	17. 1.08T
	(Thielert TAE 125)		G-BSYY, N9100X		(Operated Solent Flight)		
G-BSYZ	Piper PA-28-161 Warrior II	28-8516051	N6908H	22.11.90	S W Cowie tr Yankee Zulu Group	Glasgow	29.10.07E
					(Operated Glasgow Flying Club)		
G-BSZB	Stolp SA.300 Starduster Too	545	N5495M	3.12.90	D T Gethin	Haverfordwest	17. 5.08P
	(Built J W Matthews) (Lycoming O-360)						
G-BSZC	Beech C-45H-BH Expeditor	AF-258	N9541Z	14.12.90	Weston Ltd	Weston, Leixlip, County Kildare	4. 6.06
	(Built as AT-7 42-2490 [4166]: re-manufactured 4.52) 51-11701				(As "51-11701A:AF258/" in USAF c/s) "Southern Comfort"		
G-BSZD	Robin DR.400-180 Régent	2029		21.11.90	M Rowland	Draycott Farm, Chiseldon	24. 4.08
G-BSZF	CEA Jodel DR.250/160 Capitaine	32	F-BNJB	29.11.90	J B Randle	Biggin Hill	11. 7.08E
G-BSZG	Stolp SA.100 Starduster	101	N70P	27.11.90	D F Chapman	Headcorn	4. 7.00P
	(Built L Stolp and G Adams) (Lycoming O-320)				(Noted 6.05)		
G-BSZH	Thunder Ax7-77 Balloon (Hot Air)	1848		27.11.90	P K Morris	Cleethorpes	30. 6.07
G-BSZI	Cessna 152 II	15285856	N95139	17.12.90	Eglinton Flying Club Ltd	City of Derry	11. 4.08E
G-BSZJ	Piper PA-28-181 Archer II	28-8190216	N8373Z	6.12.90	R D Fuller and M L A Pudney "21"		
					West Newlands Farm, St Lawrence, Bradwell-on-Sea		3. 5.08E
G-BSZM	Montgomerie-Bensen B 8MR	PFA G/01-1193		30.11.90	A McCredie	Kirkbride	13. 8.07P
	(Built J H H Turner) (Rotax 582)						
G-BSZO	Cessna 152 II	15280221	N24334	30.11.90	M and N Jahanafar	Southend	18. 1.08E
					(Operated The Flight Centre)		
G-BSZT	Piper PA-28-161 Warrior II	28-8116027	N8260D	31.12.90	Golf Charlie Echo Ltd	Shoreham	26. 4.08E
					(Operated The Flying Hut)		
G-BSZU	Cessna 150F Commuter	15063481	N6881F	3.12.90	C Partington	Ronaldsway	18.12.07E
G-BSZV	Cessna 150F	15062304	N3504L	3.12.90	C A Davis	Sandown, Isle of Wight	15.11.07E
G-BSZW	Cessna 152 II	15281072	N48958	3.12.90	Haimoss Ltd	Old Sarum	9.12.06T
					(Operated Old Sarum Flying Club)		

G-BTAA - G-BTZZ

G-BTAG	Cameron O-77 Balloon (Hot Air)	2454		12.11.90	R A Shapland "Tag-Along"	Petworth	13. 1.02A

Reg	Type	C/n	Prev ID	Date	Owner	Location	Date
G-BTAK	EAA Acrosport II	1468	N440X	27.12.90	S E Ford	Mitchells Farm, Wilburton	22. 4.08P
	(Built A P Savage) (Lycoming O-320)						
G-BTAL	Reims Cessna F152 II	F15201444		7. 4.78	TG Aviation Ltd	Manston	16. 3.08E
					(Operated Thanet Flying Club)		
G-BTAM	Piper PA-28-181 Archer II	2890093	RA-01765	10. 1.91	Tri-Star Farms Ltd	Glenforsa, Isle of Mull	7.12.07T
			G-BTAM, N9153D		(Noted engineless after propeller strike 7.06)		
G-BTAN	Thunder Ax7-65Z Balloon (Hot Air)	517		4. 5.83	A S Newnham	Southampton	23. 8.06A
G-BTAS	Piper PA-38-112 Tomahawk	38-79A0545	F-GTAS	21. 2.91	Ravenair Aircraft Ltd	Ronaldsway	17. 2.07T
			G-BTAS, N2492G				
G-BTAT	Denney Kitfox Model 2	689		6.11.90	M Lawton	Otherton, Cannock	11. 6.08P
	(Built D G Marwick - pr.no.PFA 172-11832)						
G-BTAU	Thunder Ax7-77 Balloon (Hot Air)	1429		13.12.90	S and G Gebauer	Lippstadt, Germany	13. 6.08A
G-BTAW	Piper PA-28-161 Warrior II	28-8616031	N9259T	14.12.90	A J Wiggins	Gloucestershire	16. 5.06T
					(Operated Gloucester and Cheltenham Flying School)		
G-BTAZ	Evans VP-2	PFA 063-11474		13.12.90	G S Poulter	Norwich	
	(Built G S Poulter)				(Noted complete 10.05)		
G-BTBA	Robinson R22 Beta	1717		18. 3.91	Heliflight (UK) Ltd	Gloucestershire	30. 4.08E
G-BTBB	Thunder Ax8-105 Series 2 Balloon (Hot Air)	1871		23.11.90	G J Boulden	Ash, Aldershot	14.10.07T
G-BTBC	Piper PA-28-161 Warrior II	28-7916414	N28755	19.12.90	Synergy Aircraft Leasing Ltd	Fairoaks	9. 5.08E
G-BTBF	Fisher Super Koala	SK.067	(G-MWOZ)	24.12.90	E A Taylor	(Southend-on-Sea)	
	(Built E A Taylor - pr.no.PFA 158-11954)				(Construction suspended 2.08)		
G-BTBG	Denney Kitfox Model 2	PFA 172-11845		18.12.90	R Noble	Shobdon	31. 5.06P
	(Built J Catley)				(Noted 8.06)		
G-BTBH	Ryan ST3KR (PT-22-RY)	2063	N854	18. 2.91	P R Holloway	Old Warden	10. 5.08P
	(Kinner R56)		N50993, 41-20854		(As "854" in US Army Air Corp c/s)		
G-BTBL	Montgomerie-Bensen B 8MR	PFA G/01A-1183		21.12.90	N H Collins t/a AES Radionic Surveillance Systems		
	(Built J M Montgomerie) (Rotax 532)				(Noted 4.04)	Melrose Farm, Melbourne	2. 9.01P
G-BTBP	Cameron N-90 Balloon (Hot Air)	2464		21.12.90	M Catalani	Pistoia, Italy	15. 2.08A
G-BTBU	Piper PA-18-150 Super Cub	18-7509010	N9665P	3. 1.91	A J White tr G-BTBU Syndicate	Redhill	31. 1.08e
G-BTBW	Cessna 120	14220	N2009V	24. 1.91	M J Willies	Sywell	19. 8.10S
	(Continental C90)		NC2009V		"40"		
G-BTBX	Piper J-3C-65 Cub	6334	N35367	29. 1.91	J B Hargrave and D T C Collins tr Henlow Taildraggers		
			NC35367			RAF Henlow	6.12.09
G-BTBY	Piper PA-17 Vagabond	17-195	N4894H	4. 1.91	G W Miller	Jenkin's Farm, Navestock	21. 4.08P
	(Continental C85)						
G-BTCA	Piper PA-32R-300 Lance	32R-7780381	N5941V	10. 1.91	R Page tr Lance Group	Sleap	11. 6.08E
G-BTCB	Air Command 582 Sport	0634		9. 1.91	G Scurrah	(Duddon Bridge, Millom)	
	(Built G Scurrah - pr.no.PFA G/04-1198)						
G-BTCC	Grumman F6F-5K Hellcat	A-11286	(N10CN)	31.12.90	Patina Ltd	Duxford	6. 7.08P
			N100T, FN80142, Bu.80141		(As "40467:19" in VF-6 Sqdn:US Navy c/s)		
	(Composite with centre section ex Bu.08831 [A-218] ex F6F-3)				(Operated The Fighter Collection)		
G-BTCD	North American P-51D-25-NA Mustang	122-39608	N51JJ	11. 1.91	Pelham Ltd	Duxford	19. 5.08P
			N6340T, RCAF 9568, 44-73149		(As "413704:B7-H" in 374th FG:USAAF c/s)		
					(Operated The Old Flying Machine Company)		
G-BTCE	Cessna 152 II	15281376	N49876	10. 1.91	S T Gilbert	Enstone	22. 6.07T
	(Tail-wheel conversion)						
G-BTCH	Luscombe 8E Silvaire Deluxe	6403	N1976B	11. 2.91	J Grewcock and R C Carroll tr G-BTCH Flying Group		
	(Continental C85)		NC1976B			Popham	26. 9.07P
G-BTCI	Piper PA-17 Vagabond	17-136	N4839H	11. 1.91	T R Whittome	Inverness	9. 8.05P
	(Continental A65)		NC4839H				
G-BTCJ	Luscombe 8AE Silvaire	1869	N41908	16. 1.91	J M Lovell	Chilbolton	9. 6.08P
	(Continental O-200A)		NC41908				
G-BTCM	Cameron N-90 Balloon (Hot Air)	1306	(G-BMPW)	8. 5.86	G Everett	Maidstone	16. 4.06A
G-BTCR	Rans S-10 Sakota	0290.091		11. 1.91	B J Hewitt	Newtownards	6. 2.08P
	(Built S H Barr - pr.no.PFA 194-11877)				(Noted 4.06)		
G-BTCS	Colt 90A Balloon (Hot Air)	1895		11. 1.91	L A Watts	Pangbourne	14. 6.08A
G-BTCZ	Cameron Chateau-84 SS Balloon (Hot Air)	2246		18. 1.91	Forbes Global Inc	London SW11	22.12.06
	(Forbes Chateau de Balleroy shape)				"Chateau II"		
G-BTDA	Slingsby T 61F Venture T 2	1870	XZ550	17. 4.91	T M Holloway tr RAF Gliding and Soaring Association		
					(Operated Anglia Gliding Club)	AAC Wattisham	23. 5.08E
G-BTDC	Denney Kitfox Model 2	405		11. 1.91	D M Smith	Halwell	26. 6.07P
	(Built D Collinson and O Smith - pr.no.PFA 172-11483)						
G-BTDD	CFM Streak Shadow	K 127-SA		14. 1.91	S H Merrony	(Egham)	12.10.06P
	(Built S J Evans - pr.no.PFA 161A-11622) (Rotax 582)						
G-BTDE	Cessna C-165 Airmaster	551	N21911	18. 1.91	R H Screen	Liverpool	24. 4.10
			NC21911				
G-BTDF	Luscombe 8A Silvaire	2205	N45678	17. 4.91	D M Watts	(Eastleigh)	19 .8.93P
			NC45678		(New owner 6.07)		
G-BTDI	Robinson R-22 Beta	1670	PH-HTA	29. 1.91	ACS Aviation Ltd	Glenrothes	29. 3.08E
			G-BTDI				
G-BTDN	Denney Kitfox Model 2	688		22. 1.91	S D Arnold tr Foxy Flyers Group		
	(Built A B Butler - pr.no.PFA 172-11826)					Wellesbourne Mountford	29. 6.05P
G-BTDR	Aero Designs Pulsar	PFA 202-11962		24. 1.91	R A Blackwell	North Weald	4. 1.08P
	(Built R M Hughes and T Packe)						
G-BTDS	Colt 77A Balloon (Hot Air)	1897		29. 1.91	CP Witter Ltd "Witters II"	Chester	31. 5.08A
G-BTDT	CASA 1-131E Jungmann Series 2000	2131	Spanish AF E3B-505	5. 2.91	T A Reed	Headcorn	24. 5.08P
G-BTDV	Piper PA-28-161 Cherokee Warrior II	28-7816355	N3548M	25. 2.91	Central Aircraft Leasing Ltd	Halfpenny Green	21. 6.07T
					(Noted 10.07)		
G-BTDW	Cessna 152 II	15279864	N757NC	25. 2.91	Border Air Training Ltd	Carlisle	23.11.07E
G-BTDZ	CASA 1-131E Jungmann Series 2000	2104	Spanish AF E3B-524	5. 2.91	M and R J Pickin	Headcorn	29.11.08P
					('Fliegerschule Luxeuil' - silver with Nazi tail flash)		
G-BTEA	Cameron N-105 Balloon (Hot Air)	284		31. 5.77	M W A Shemilt "Big Red"	Henley-on-Thames	8. 5.99A

Regn	Type	C/n	Prev id	Date	Owner/Operator	Location	Status
G-BTEE	Cameron O-120 Balloon (Hot Air)	2499		24. 1.91	W H and J P Morgan	Swansea	17. 5.02T
	"Y Ddraig Goch" and "The Red Dragon"						
G-BTEF	Pitts S-1	515H	N88PR	19. 2.91	C Davidson	Blackpool	28.10.97P
	(Built D R Brewer)				(Noted 10.07)		
G-BTEL	CFM Streak Shadow	K 125-SA		31. 1.91	J E Eatwell	Boscombe Down	19.11.08P
	(Built J E Eatwell - pr.no.PFA 206-11667) (Rotax 618)						
G-BTES	Cessna 150H	15068371	N22575	29. 4.91	R A Forward	Biggin Hill	14.10.07E
G-BTET	Piper J-3C-65 Cub	18296	N98141 NC98141	5. 2.91	K Handley	Higher Barn Farm, Houghton	29.11.07P
					(New owner 12.06)		
G-BTEU	Aérospatiale AS.365N2 Dauphin 2	6392		11. 2.91	CHC Scotia Ltd	Humberside	1. 4.08E
G-BTEW	Cessna 120	10238	CF-ELE	29. 4.91	S D Pryke and L M Hamblyn	Old Buckenham	29. 6.10S
	(Continental C90)						
G-BTEX	Piper PA-28-140 Cherokee	28-23773	CF-XXL N3907K	24. 4.91	E Latimer	Little Snoring	11. 2.08E
G-BTFC	Reims Cessna F152 II	F15201668		23. 5.79	Aircraft Engineers Ltd	Prestwick	6. 8.08E
G-BTFE	Parsons Gyroplane Model 1	38		13. 2.91	J R Goldspink	Haverfordwest	27.10.01P
	(Built I Brewster) (Rotax 582) (Tandem Trainer)						
G-BTFF	Cessna T310R II	310R0718	N1363G	25. 2.91	M C Daniels	Lee-on-Solent	15. 8.08E
G-BTFG	Boeing Stearman A75N1 (N2S-4) Kaydet	75-3441	N4467N Bu.30010	20. 2.91	TG Aviation Ltd	Manston	2. 7.08T
	(Continental W670)				(As "441" in USN c/s)		
G-BTFJ	Piper PA-15 Vagabond	15-159	N4373H NC4373H	13. 2.91	C W Thirtle	Old Sarum	31.10.07P
	(Continental C 90)						
G-BTFK	Taylorcraft BC-12D	10540	N599SB N5240M	13. 2.91	A O'Rourke	Pallas West, Toomyvara, County Tipperary	10. 6.08P
	(Continental A65)						
G-BTFL	Aeronca 11AC Chief	11AC-1727	N3403E NC3403E	18. 2.91	J G Vaughan tr BTFL Group	Eastbach Farm, Coleford	1.12.08P
G-BTFM	Cameron O-105 Balloon (Hot Air)	2623		12. 8.91	P Forster and J Trehern	Edinburgh	22.12.07A
					tr Edinburgh University Hot Air Balloon Club		
G-BTFO	Piper PA-28-161 Cherokee Warrior II	28-7816580	N31728	12. 3.91	Flyfar Ltd	RAF Woodvale	22. 5.08E
G-BTFS	Cessna A150M Aerobat	A1500719	N20331	20. 2.91	M A Segar	Pitrichie Farm, Whiterashes	1. 8.08E
G-BTFT	Beech 58 Baron	TH-979	N2036W	14. 3.91	Fastwing Air Charter Ltd (Noted 11.07)	Thruxton	8. 4.07T
G-BTFU	Cameron N-90 Balloon (Hot Air)	2391		28. 2.91	J J Rudoni and A C K Rawson	Stafford	26. 3.05A
					t/a Wickers World Hot Air Balloon Co mpany "Maltesers II"		
G-BTFV	Whittaker MW7	PFA 171-11722		8. 2.91	S J Luck	Tower Farm, Wollaston	12.12.05P
	(Built S J Luck)						
G-BTFW	Montgomerie-Bensen B 8MR	PFA G/01A-1141		20. 2.91	C G Ponsford	Willingale	14. 6.06P
	(Built A Mansfield) (Rotax 532)						
G-BTFX	Bell 206B-2 JetRanger II	1648	N400MH N90219	20. 2.91	J W Moss	(Parbold, Wigan)	12. 6.07E
G-BTGD	Rand Robinson KR-2	PFA 129-11150		22. 2.91	M D Gorlov	Top Farm, Croydon, Royston	2. 8.08P
	(Built D W Mullin) (Volkswagen 1915)						
G-BTGG	Rans S-10 Sakota	0790.113		20. 2.91	C A James	Doynton	22. 6.96P
	(Built A R Cameron - pr.no.PFA 194-11944)				(New owner 12.03)		
G-BTGH	Cessna 152 II	15281048	N48919	2. 4.91	P J Clarke	Halfpenny Green	25. 4.07T
G-BTGI	Rearwin 175 Skyranger	1517	N32308 NC32308	26. 2.91	J M Fforde	Lane Farm, Clyro, Hereford	6.11.07P
	(Continental A75)						
G-BTGJ	Smith DSA-1 Miniplane	NM.II	N1471	25. 3.91	G J Knowles	Goodwood	18. 9.07P
	(Built S J Malovic) (Continental C90)						
G-BTGL	Avid Speed Wing	PFA 189-11885		27. 2.91	I Kazi	Stoneacre Farm, Farthing Corner	4. 9.03P
	(Built A J Maxwell)				(Noted 1.07)		
G-BTGM	Aeronca 7AC Champion	7AC-3665	N84943 NC84943	11. 3.91	G P Gregg	Shacklewell Farm, Empingham	18. 7.08P
	(Continental A65)						
G-BTGO	Piper PA-28-140 Cherokee D	28-7125613	N1998T	20. 2.91	Demero Ltd and Transcourt Ltd	Oxford	16. 8.08E
G-BTGP	Cessna 150M Commuter	15078921	N704WA	28. 2.91	Billins Air Services Ltd	Bournemouth	30. 5.08E
G-BTGR	Cessna 152 II	15284447	N6581L	28. 2.91	A J Gomes	Shoreham	25. 7.00T
					(Crashed Mile Oak, Portslade, Sussex 7.10.99:)		
G-BTGS (2)	Stolp SA.300 Starduster Too	EAA/50553	G-AYMA	30. 9.87	G N Elliott tr G N Elliott and Partners	Shoreham	25. 7.06P
	(Build initiated T G Solomon - pr.no.PFA 035-10076: completed P G Leggo) (Lycoming O-320)						
G-BTGT	CFM Streak Shadow	K 164-SA	(G-MWPY)	1. 3.91	G J Sargent	Bourn	29.11.07P
	(Built M Allison - pr.no.PFA 206-11964) (Rotax 582)						
G-BTGV	Piper PA-34-200T Seneca II	34-7970077	N3004H	26. 3.91	Oxford Aviation Training Ltd	Oxford	16. 8.08E
G-BTGW	Cessna 152 II	15279812	N757KY	5. 3.91	Stapleford Flying Club Ltd	Stapleford	13. 8.08E
G-BTGX	Cessna 152 II	15284950	N5462P	5. 3.91	Stapleford Flying Club Ltd	Stapleford	24. 8.08E
G-BTGY	Piper PA-28-161 Warrior II	28-8216199	N209FT N9574N	5. 3.91	Stapleford Flying Club Ltd	Stapleford	23. 6.08E
G-BTGZ	Piper PA-28-181 Cherokee Archer II	28-7890160	N47956	8. 4.91	Allzones Ltd	Biggin Hill	5.12.07E
G-BTHE	Cessna 150L	15075340	N11348	7. 3.91	J H Loose and F P White tr Humberside Police Flying Club	Mount Airey Farm, South Cave	3. 9.08E
G-BTHF	Cameron V-90 Balloon (Hot Air)	2543		7. 3.91	N J and S J Langley	Bristol	12. 4.08A
G-BTHH	CEA Jodel DR.100A Ambassadeur	5	F-BJCH	28. 2.91	H R Leefe	Bourg-en-Bresse, France	20.12.10E
G-BTHI	Robinson R22 Beta	1732		26. 3.91	Summerline Aviation Ltd	Coventry	25. 4.08E
G-BTHJ	Evans VP-2	PFA 063-10901		14. 3.91	C J Moseley	Bournemouth	
	(Built C J Moseley)				(Under construction 8.92)		
G-BTHK	Thunder Ax7-77 Balloon (Hot Air)	1906		11. 3.91	M S Trend	Maidstone	25. 6.06A
G-BTHM	Thunder Ax8-105 Balloon (Hot Air)	1925		11. 3.91	J K Woods	Chatham	25. 9.08A
G-BTHN	Murphy Renegade 912	384		12. 3.91	D Baker	(Enfield, County Meath)	8. 8.06P
	(Built Meridian Ultralights Ltd - pr.no.PFA 188-12005)				(New owner 9.07)		
G-BTHP	Thorp T 211	101		13. 6.91	M J Newton	Barton	21. 4.08E
G-BTHU	Avid Flyer	PFA 189-11427		14. 3.91	R C Bowley	(Earls Croome, Worcester)	
	(Built M Morris)				(Damaged Field Head Farm, Denholme, Bradford 7. 6.92: on rebuild 5.95)		
G-BTHV	MBB BÖ.105DBS-4	S 855	D-HMBV G-BTHV, D-HFHM	20. 3.91	Bond Air Services Ltd	Welshpool	22. 5.08E
					(Operated County Air Ambulance)		

G-BTHW	Beech F33C Bonanza	CJ-130	PH-BNA	18. 3.91	Robin Lance Aviation Associates Ltd	Rochester	25. 9.06
			N23787				
G-BTHX	Colt 105A Balloon (Hot Air)	1939		18. 3.91	PSH Skypower Ltd	Pewsey	16. 4.08A
G-BTHY	Bell 206B-3 JetRanger III	2290	N6606M	20. 3.91	Suffolk Helicopters Ltd	Southend	19. 5.08E
			VH-BIQ, ZK-HBQ, DQ-FEN, ZK-HLU				
G-BTHZ	Cameron V-56 Balloon (Hot Air)	486	OO-BBC	20. 3.91	(C N Marshall)	Not known	
	(UK regn believed not taken up and remains as "OO-BBC" 2008)						
G-BTID	Piper PA-28-161 Warrior II	28-8116036	N82647	25. 6.91	Aviation South West Ltd	Exeter	6. 4.08E
G-BTIE	SOCATA TB-10 Tobago	187		30. 3.81	Aviation Spirit Ltd	Shobdon	19. 9.08E
G-BTIF	Denney Kitfox Model 3	684		27. 2.91	D A Murchie	(Blackwaterfoot, Arran)	10. 8.01P
	(Built C R Thompson and J Scott - pr.no.PFA 172-11862) (Converted from Model 2)						
G-BTII	Gulfstream AA-5B Tiger	AA5B-1256	N4560S	5. 6.91	S A Niechial and P W Gillott tr BTII Group	Biggin Hill	13. 5.08E
G-BTIJ	Luscombe 8E Silvaire Deluxe	5194	N2467K	3. 4.91	S J Hornsby	Ranston Farm, Iwerne Courtney	9. 1.08P
	(Continental C85)		NC2467K				
G-BTIK	Cessna 152 II	15282993	N46068	26. 3.91	P Ashley	Prestwick	15. 6.08E
G-BTIL	Piper PA-38-112 Tomahawk	38-80A0004	N24730	26. 3.91	B J Pearson	Eaglescott	
					(Noted as "N24730" dismantled 7.05)		
G-BTIM	Piper PA-28-161 Cadet	2841159	N9185D	24. 8.89	S J Skilton t/a Aviation Rentals	Bournemouth	28.11.07E
			(SE-KIO)				
G-BTIO	SNCAN Stampe SV-4C	303	N73NS	28. 3.91	M D and C F Garratt	RNAS Yeovilton	9.10.08S
			F-BCLC				
G-BTIR	Denney Kitfox Model 2 PFA 172-11952			26. 3.91	R B Wilson	(Levens, Kendal)	30.10.08P
	(Built J N C Shields and D J Millar) (Hewland AE75)						
G-BTIU	SOCATA MS.892A Rallye Commodore 150	10914	F-BPQS	7. 5.91	Cole Aviation Ltd Willey Park Farm, Caterham		16. 6.05
					(Noted Nalson Aviation 3.06)		
G-BTIV	Piper PA-28-161 Warrior II	28-8116044	N82697	10. 5.91	B R Pearson tr Warrior Group	Eaglescott	24. 7.06T
					(Noted 8.07)		
G-BTIZ	Cameron A-105 Balloon (Hot Air)	2546		11. 3.91	W A Board t/a Glen Board Promotions		
						Java, Alicante, Spain	10. 7.08A
G-BTJA	Luscombe 8E Silvaire Deluxe	5037	N2310K	4. 4.91	M W Rudkin	Blackpool	26. 2.08P
	(Continental O-200A)		NC2310K				
G-BTJB	Luscombe 8E Silvaire Deluxe	6194	N1567B	4. 4.91	M Loxton	Parsonage Farm, Eastchurch	2. 5.06P
	(Continental C85)		NC1567B				
G-BTJC	Luscombe 8F Silvaire	6589	N2162B	4. 4.91	A M Noble	Chilbolton	18.10.99P
	(Lycoming O-290D2)				*(Damged Glebe Farm, Stockton, Warminster 31. 7.99: noted 7.04)*		
G-BTJD	Thunder Ax8-90 Series 2 Balloon (Hot Air)	1865		28. 3.91	R E Vinten "Beez Neez"	Wellingborough	25. 5.08A
G-BTJH	Cameron O-77 Balloon (Hot Air)	2559		3. 4.91	H Stringer "Oriel"	Scarborough	31. 5.05T
G-BTJK	Piper PA-38-112 Tomahawk	38-79A0838	N2427N	3. 4.91	Ravenair Aircraft Ltd	Liverpool	26.10.07E
G-BTJL	Piper PA-38-112 Tomahawk	38-79A0863	N2477N	3. 4.91	J S Develin and Z Islam	Shoreham	1. 2.08E
G-BTJN	Montgomerie-Bensen B 8MR PFA G/01-1194			3. 4.91	A Hamilton	Strathaven	9.12.00P
	(Built A Hamilton) (Rotax 532)						
G-BTJO	Thunder Ax9-140 Balloon (Hot Air)	1948		3. 4.91	G P Lane	USA	28. 4.92A
					(Pacific Flyer titles) (Stored 5.07)		
G-BTJS	Montgomerie-Bensen B 8MR PFA G/01-1083			8. 4.91	T A Holmes	(Leeds)	13. 3.08P
	(Built J M P Annand) (Rotax 532)						
G-BTJU	Cameron V-90 Balloon (Hot Air)	2554		8. 4.91	Flambe Balloons Ltd	Shipham, Winscombe	29. 6.07A
G-BTJX	Rans S-10 Sakota	0790.114		9. 4.91	P C Avery	Lower Mountplesant, Chatteris	15. 9.04P
	(Built M Goacher - pr.no.PFA 194-12014) (Rotax 582)				*(New owner 9.07)*		
G-BTKA	Piper J-5A Cub Cruiser	5-954	N38403	11. 4.91	J M Lister	Valley Farm, Winwick	9. 5.08P
			NC38403				
G-BTKB	Murphy Renegade 912	376		11. 4.91	P and J Calvert	Rufforth	27. 9.08P
	(Built G S Blundell - pr.no.PFA 188-11876)						
G-BTKD	Denney Kitfox Model 4	853		15. 4.91	R A Hills	Dunkeswell	30. 9.08P
	(Built J F White - pr.no.PFA 172-11941) (Denny kit no.indicates Model 3 and conflicts with N653CP)						
G-BTKG	Avid Flyer PFA 189-12037			16. 4.91	J Dennedy tr Avid Group	(Blanchardstown, Dublin)	4.10.06P
	(Built P R Snowden)						
G-BTKL	MBB BÖ.105DB-4	S 422	D-HDMU	2. 5.91	Veritair Ltd	(Halfpenny Green)	2. 3.08E
			Swedish Army, D-HDMU		*(Operated Central Counties Police Air Operations Unit)*		
G-BTKN	Cameron O-120 Balloon (Hot Air)	2579	OO-BQQ	24. 4.91	R H Etherington	Siena, Italy	16. 4.03A
G-BTKP	CFM Streak Shadow	K 174		24. 4.91	C D Creasey and C A Sargent *(New owners 11.07)*		
	(Built K S Woodward - pr.no.PFA 206-12036) (Rotax 582)					Wickambrook, Newmarket	20. 8.02P
G-BTKT	Piper PA-28-161 Warrior II	28-8216218	N429FT	9. 5.91	Biggin Hill Flying Club Ltd	Shoreham	16. 4.08E
			N9606N				
G-BTKV	Piper PA-22-160 Tri-Pacer	22-7157	N3216Z	25. 4.91	R A Moore	Gransha, Rathfriland	23. 9.10S
G-BTKW	Cameron O-105 Balloon (Hot Air)	2566		25. 4.91	P Spellward tr Bristol University Hot Air Ballooning Society		
					(Inflated 5.06)	Bristol	9. 3.01A
G-BTKX	Piper PA-28-181 Cherokee Archer II		N47866	14. 5.91	R M Pannell	Eaglescott	30. 5.08E
		28-7890146					
G-BTKZ	Cameron V-77 Balloon (Hot Air)	2573		26. 4.91	S P Richards "Lancaster Jaguar"	Tonbridge	7. 6.97T
G-BTLB	Wassmer WA.52 Europa	42	F-BTLB	17. 4.89	A S Cowan tr Popham Flying Group G-BTLB		
						Popham	12.11.08E
G-BTLG	Piper PA-28R-200 Cherokee Arrow II		N5045S	29. 4.91	P J Moore	Lee-on-Solent	15. 3.08E
		28R-35811					
G-BTLM	Piper PA-22-160	22-6162	N9025D	16. 5.91	A C and M D N Fisher	Leicester	6. 7.08E
	(Tail-wheel conversion)						
G-BTLP	Grumman AA-1C Lynx	AA1C-0109	N9732U	13. 5.91	Partlease Ltd	Stapleford	2. 2.08E
					"28" *(Operated Stapleford Flying Club)*		
G-BTMA	Cessna 172N Skyhawk II	17273711	N5136J	2. 5.91	East of England Flying Group Ltd	North Weald	9.11.07T
G-BTMK	Cessna R172K Hawk XP	R1722787	N736TZ	10. 6.91	K E Halford	Garston Farm, Marshfield	25. 3.08E
G-BTMN	Thunder Ax9-120 Series 2 Balloon (Hot Air)			17. 5.91	M E White	Dublin	8. 3 99T
		2003			*(Inflated 4.02)*		
G-BTMO	Colt 69A Balloon (Hot Air)	2004		20. 5.91	Cameron Balloons Ltd t/a Thunder and Colt	Bristol	
G-BTMP	Everett Campbell Cricket	024		20. 5.91	P W McLaughlin	Henstridge	30. 5.08P
	(Built D G Hill - pr.no.PFA G/03-1226) (Rotax 532)						

Reg	Type	C/n	Prev ID	Date	Owner	Location	CofA
G-BTMR	Cessna 172M Skyhawk II	17264985	N64047	20. 5.91	Linley Aviation Ltd	Linley Hill, Leven	20. 7.08E
C-BTMS	Avid Speed Wing	908	(CS-)	24. 4.91	J Makonnen	(Plumpton Green, Lewes)	9. 4.08P
	(Built D L Docking and M J Kay - pr.no.PFA 189-12023)	G-BTMS					
G-BTMT	Denney Kitfox Model 1	66		10. 5.91	L G Horne	(Ashford, Kent)	5.11.04P
	(Built J Lindzalone) (Rotax 532)						
G-BTMV	Everett Gyroplane Series 2	025		21. 5.91	L Armes	(Pitsea, Basildon)	
G-BTMW	Zenair CH.701 STOL	PFA 187-11808		21. 5.91	L Lewis	Yearby	9. 4.96P
	(Built L Lewis) (Rotax 582)				(Stored 2.08)		
G-BTMY	Cameron Train 80 SS Balloon (Hot Air)	2561	(SE-...) G-BTMY	22. 5.91	Balloon Sports HB	Partille, Sweden	9. 2.97A
G-BTNA	Robinson R22 Beta	1800	N40820	23. 5.91	Helicopter Training and Hire Ltd	Newtownards	6. 6.08E
G-BTNC	Aérospatiale AS.365N2 Dauphin 2	6409		21. 6.91	CHC Scotia Ltd	Humberside	9.10.07T
G-BTND	Piper PA-38-112 Tomahawk	38-78A0155	N9671T	23. 5.91	Ravenair Aircraft Ltd	Biggin Hill	1. 8.08E
G-BTNE	Piper PA-28-161 Warrior II	28-8116212	N8379H	22. 7.91	Fly Welle Ltd	Wellesbourne Mountford	18. 7.08E
G-BTNH	Piper PA-28-161 Warrior II	28-8216202	G-DENH G-BTNH, N253FT, N9577N	28. 5.91	A S Bamrah t/a Falcon Flying Services	Biggin Hill	8.10.07E
					(Noted 12.07)		
G-BTNO	Aeronca 7AC Champion	7AC-3132	N84441 NC84441	31. 5.91	B J and G B Robe	(Hexham and Riding Mill)	13. 8.08P
G-BTNR	Denney Kitfox Model 3	921		31. 5.91	J Beirne tr High Notions Flying Group		
	(Built J W G Ellis - pr.no.PFA 172-12035)					Klrush, County Kildare	14. 9.08P
G-BTNT	Piper PA-28-151 Cherokee Warrior	28-7615401	N6929J	31. 5.91	Britannia Airways Ltd	Cranfield	24.11.07E
					(Operated Britannia Airways Flying Club)		
G-BTNV	Piper PA-28-161 Cherokee Warrior II	28-7816590	N31878	20. 6.91	G M Bauer and A M Davies	Wickenby	18. 8.08T
G-BTNW	Rans S-6-ESA Coyote II	0391.174		3. 6.91	R H Hughes	Emlyn's Field, Rhuallt	8. 8.06P
	(Built A Barbone - pr.no.PFA 204-12077) (Rotax 582)				(Noted 8.07)		
G-BTOC	Robinson R22 Beta	1801	N23004	10. 6.91	Summerline Aviation Ltd	Damyn's Hall, Upminster	20. 9.08E
G-BTOG	de Havilland DH.82A Tiger Moth	86500	F-BGCJ	5. 9.91	S W Barratt tr TOG Group	(Silsoe, Bedford)	
	(Built Morris Motors Ltd)		French AF, NM192		(New owner 3.07)		
G-BTOL	Denney Kitfox Model 3	919		26. 6.91	P J Gibbs	(Woodlands Barton Farm, Roche)	28. 7.07P
	(Built C R Phillips - pr.no.PFA 172-12052)						
G-BTON	Piper PA-28-140 Cherokee Cruiser	28-7425343	N43193	15. 7.91	P Quinn tr Group G-BTON		
						Cherry Tree Farm, Monewden	20. 7.07T
G-BTOO	Pitts S-1C	5215-24A	N37H	12. 6.91	G H Matthews	(Fareham)	
	(Built E Lawrence)				(On overhaul 5.92)		
G-BTOP	Cameron V-77 Balloon (Hot Air)	2484		14. 6.91	J J Winter	Michaelston-y-Fedw, Cardiff	
					"Big Top" (Active 4.05)		
G-BTOS	Cessna 140	8353	N89325 NC89325	7. 6.91	J L Kaiser	Nancy-Essey, France	1. 7.99
	(Continental C85)						
G-BTOT	Piper PA-15 Vagabond	15-60	N4176H NC4176H	22. 5.91	S J Raw tr Vagabond Flying Group		
	(Continental O-200)					Morgansfield, Fishburn	11. 5.08P
G-BTOU	Cameron O-120 Balloon (Hot Air)	2606		2. 7.91	J J Daly	Halfway House, County Waterford	29. 9.08A
G-BTOW	SOCATA Rallye 180T Galerien	3360	F-BNGZ	9.11.82	Cambridge Gliding Club Ltd	Gransden Lodge	1. 4.08E
G-BTOZ	Thunder Ax9-120 Series 2 Balloon (Hot Air)	2008		28. 6.91	H G Davies	(Cheltenham)	1. 4.08T
G-BTPA	British Aerospace ATP	2007	EC-HGC G-BTPA, EC-GYE, G-BTPA, (N377AE)	19. 8.88	Capital Bank Leasing 12 Ltd	Bucharest, Romania	18.11.98T
					(Noted 2.06)		
G-BTPE	British Aerospace ATP	2012	EC-HGE G-BTPE, EC-GZH, G-BTPE, (N382AE)	1. 9.88	Capital Bank Leasing 3 Ltd	Coventry	12. 3.99T
					(Noted 10.07 operated Atlantic Airlines		
G-BTPF	British Aerospace ATP	2013	EC-HCY G-BTPF, G-11-013, G-BTPF, (N383AE)	2. 9.88	Capital Bank Leasing 5 Ltd	Coventry	17. 4.99T
					(Noted 11.07 operated Atlantic Airways)		
G-BTPG	British Aerospace ATP	2014	EC-HEH G-BTPG, (N384AE)	2. 9.88	Capital Bank Leasing 5 Ltd	Bucharest, Romania	22. 5.99T
					(Noted 7.05)		
G-BTPH	British Aerospace ATP	2015	(G-JEMF) EC-HFM, G-BTPH, (N385AE)	2. 9.88	Capital Bank Leasing 6 Ltd	Coventry	23. 7.08E
					Operated Atlantic Airlines)		
G-BTPJ	British Aerospace ATP	2016	EC-HFR G-BTPJ, (N386AE)	2. 9.88	Capital Bank Leasing 7 Ltd	Bucharest, Romania	9. 7.99T
					(Noted 10.05)		
G-BTPL	British Aerospace ATP	2042	EC-HES G-BTPL, (PH-MJK), EC-GLH, G-BTPL, G-11-042 "Brandon"	3.10.91	Trident Aviation Leasing Services (Jersey) Ltd	Coventry	1. 6.08E
	(Operated Atlantic Airlines: stored 8.07 less engines in Magic Bird livery - PH-MGB reserved since 9.06)						
G-BTPN	British Aerospace ATP	2044	EC-GSI EC-GNJ, G-BTPN, G-11-044	19.11.91	Trident Aviation Leasing Services (Jersey) Ltd	Lidköping, Sweden	19.12.98T
				(Noted 6.07)				
G-BTPT	Cameron N-77 Balloon (Hot Air)	2575		10. 6.91	H J Andrews "Hi Society"	Selborne, Alton	6. 7.07A
G-BTPV	Colt 90A Balloon (Hot Air)	1956		14. 6.91	R S Kent tr Balloon Preservation Flying Group		
					(Mondial titles)	Petworth	15. 4.08A
G-BTRB	Colt Mickey Mouse SS Balloon (Hot Air)	1959		4. 7.91	Stratos Ballooning Gmbh and Co KG		
					"Calibre"	Ennigerloh, Germany	18. 3.05A
G-BTRC	Avid Speed Wing	913		2. 7.91	Grangecote Ltd	Goodwood	11. 8.07P
	(Built A A Craig - pr.no.PFA 189-12076) (BMW R100)						
G-BTRF	Aero Designs Pulsar	PFA 202-12051		4. 7.91	C Smith	Spilstead Farm, Sedlescombe	19.10.08P
	(Built C Smith) (Tri-cycle u/c)						
G-BTRG	Aeronca 65C Super Chief	C4149	N22466 NC22466	4. 7.91	A Welburn	Mount Airey Farm, South Cave	14. 9.06P
	(Continental A65)						
G-BTRI	Aeronca 11CC Super Chief	11CC-246	N4540E NC4540E	4. 7.91	P A Wensak	Bounds Farm, Ardleigh	16. 7.06P
	(Continental C85)				(Noted 11.06)		
G-BTRK	Piper PA-28-161 Warrior II	28-8216206	N297FT N9594N	8. 7.91	Stapleford Flying Club Ltd	Stapleford	26.10.07T
G-BTRL	Cameron N-105 Balloon (Hot Air)	2622		5. 7.91	J Lippett "Harrods"	South Petherton, Somerset	24. 8.02A
G-BTRN	Thunder Ax9-120 Series 2 Balloon (Hot Air)	1983		11. 7.91	A R Hardwick	Shefford	10. 9.07A
G-BTRO	Thunder Ax8-90 Balloon (Hot Air)	1872		11. 7.91	Capital Balloon Club Ltd	Hounslow	29. 7.07A
G-BTRP	Hughes 369E	0475E	N1607D	11. 7.91	P C Shann and P C Shann Management and Research Ltd		
	(Hughes 500)					Fulford, York	25. 3.05
G-BTRR	Thunder Ax7-77 Balloon (Hot Air)	1905		12. 7.91	P J Wentworth	Stanford in the Vale, Faringdon	9. 6.06A

G-BTRS	Piper PA-28-161 Warrior II	28-8116004	N8248V	12. 7.91	K D Taylor and T Bailey tr Airwise Flying Group Barton	9. 3.08E
G-BTRT	Piper PA-28R-200 Cherokee Arrow II		N1189X	24. 7.91	C D Barden and D G Smith tr Romeo Tango Group	
		28R-7535270			Barton	18. 3.08E
G-BTRU	Robin DR.400-180 Régent	2089		12. 7.91	R H Mackay Perth	24. 7.08E
G-BTRW	Slingsby T 61F Venture T 2	1968	ZA632	5. 7.91	G B Monslow tr The Falke Syndicate Long Marston	3.12.07E
G-BTRY	Piper PA-28-161 Warrior II	28-8116190	N8363L	18. 7.91	Oxford Aviation Training Ltd Oxford	4. 4.08E
G-BTRZ	Jodel D 18	148		16. 7.91	A P Aspinall Little Gransden	31. 5.07P
	(Built R Collin - pr.no.PFA 169-11271) (Volkswagen 1834)					
G-BTSB	Corben Baby Ace D	JC-1	N3599	16. 7.91	S E Leach Perth	11. 7.08P
	(Built J Cole) (Continental A65)				(Camouflage scheme with RFC roundels)	
G-BTSJ	Piper PA-28-161 Cherokee Warrior II		N9417C	23. 7.91	Plymouth School of Flying Ltd Plymouth	29. 1.08E
		28-7816473				
G-BTSM	Cessna 180A	32678	P2-DEQ	9. 7.91	C Couston tr Sierra Mike Group	
			VH-DEQ, VH-DEC, N7781A		Landmead Farm, Garford	17. 4.08E
G-BTSN	Cessna 150G	15065106	N3806J	30. 8.91	M L F Langrick (Marloes, Haverfordwest)	23. 5.08E
G-BTSP	Piper J-3C-65 Cub	7647	N41013	30. 8.91	J A Walshe and A Corcoran	
			NC41013		Strandhill, Sligo, County Sligo	17. 5.08P
G-BTSR	Aeronca 11AC Chief	11AC-785	N9152E	30. 8.91	S M McBride New Farm House, Great Oakley	19.11.07P
	(Continental A65)		NC9152E			
G-BTSV	Denney Kitfox Model 3	PFA 172-11920		24. 7.91	R J Folwell Wishanger Farm, Frensham	6. 7.07P
	(Built D J Sharland)					
G-BTSW	Colt AS-105 GD Airship (Hot Air)	1999		24. 7.91	Gefa-Flug GmbH Aachen, Germany	10. 3.08A
					(Adler Modemarkt titles)	
G-BTSX	Thunder Ax7-77 Balloon (Hot Air)	2027		24. 7.91	C Moris-Gallimore Sao Bras de Alportel, Portugal	18. 9.94
G-BTSZ	Cessna 177A Cardinal	17701198	N30332	30. 7.91	W J Peachment Popham	17. 5.08E
G-BTTB	Cameron V-90 Balloon (Hot Air)	2624		22. 7.91	D C Mitchell tr Royal Engineers Balloon Club	
					"Sapper IV" Codford, Warminster	21. 6.08A
G-BTTD	Montgomerie-Bensen B 8MR	PFA G/01-1204		31. 7.91	A J P Herculson Little Snoring	28. 4.05P
	(Built K J Parker) (Rotax 582)				(Noted 5.06)	
G-BTTE	Cessna 150L	15075558	N11602	31. 7.91	C A Wilson and W B Murray Hill Farm, Nayland	29.11.07E
					"The Sky's the Limit"	
G-BTTL	Cameron V-90 Balloon (Hot Air)	2649		12. 8.91	A J Baird "Hyde Farm Dairy" Cheltenham	4. 5.08A
G-BTTO	British Aerospace ATP	2033	EC-HNA	16. 8.91	Trident Aviation Leasing Services (Jersey) Ltd Coventry	7.12.07E
			EC-GJU, G-BTTO, G-OEDE, G-BTTO, TC-THV, G-BTTO, S2-ACZ, G-11-033 (Operated Atlantic Airlines)			
G-BTTR	Pitts S-2A	2208	N38MP	16. 8.91	Yellowbird Adventures Ltd Popham	27. 6.08E
	(Built Aerotek Inc)					
G-BTTS	Colt 77A Balloon (Hot Air)	1861		16. 8.91	J A Lomas tr Rutland Balloon Club Melton Mowbray	4. 5.08A
G-BTTW	Thunder Ax7-77 Balloon (Hot Air)	2016		27. 8.91	J Kenny Athlone, County Roscommon	29.11.07A
G-BTTY	Denney Kitfox Model 2	PFA 172-11823		29. 7.91	K J Fleming (Liverpool)	
	(Built K J Fleming)					
G-BTTZ	Slingsby T 61F Venture T 2	1961	ZA625	30. 7.91	M W Olliver Halesland	3. 9.03
G-BTUA	Slingsby T 61F Venture T 2	1985	ZA666	20. 8.91	C Edmunds tr Shenington Gliding Club Shenington	24. 6.07
G-BTUB	LET Yakovlev C-11	172623	(France)	29. 8.91	M G and J R Jefferies Little Gransden	4. 1.08P
	(Identity of 039 quoted)		Egyptian AF 543		(Soviet AF c/s without serial)	
G-BTUG	SOCATA Rallye 180T	3208		10. 7.78	Herefordshire Gliding Club Ltd Shobdon	8. 2.08E
G-BTUH	Cameron N-65 Balloon (Hot Air)	1452		28. 8.91	J S Russon Cheadle Hulme, Cheadle	15. 4.08E
G-BTUJ	Thunder Ax9-120 Balloon (Hot Air)	2022		30. 8.91	ECM Construction Ltd Great Missenden	20. 5.02T
G-BTUK	Pitts S-2A	2260	N5300J	2. 9.91	S H Elkington Wickenby	24.10.07E
	(Built Aerotek Inc)					
G-BTUL	Pitts S-2A	2200	N900RS	2. 9.91	J M Adams RAF Syerston	15. 5.08E
	(Built Aerotek Inc)					
G-BTUM	Piper J-3C-65 Cub	19516	N6335H	6. 9.91	I M Mackay tr G-BTUM Syndicate White Waltham	6. 8.08P
	(Continental C85) (Frame No.19586)		NC6335H		"Jingle-Belle"	
G-BTUR	Piper PA-18 Super Cub 95 (L-18C-PI)	18-3205	OO-LVM	11. 9.91	N T Oakman Andrewsfield	11. 4.08E
	(Continental C90) (Frame No.18-3218)		Belgian AF OL-L08, L-131, 53-4805			
G-BTUS	Whittaker MW7	PFA 171-11999		5. 9.91	C T Bailey Croft Farm, Defford	27. 6.05P
	(Built J F Bakewell) (Rotax 503)					
G-BTUU	Cameron O-120 Balloon (Hot Air)	2669		16. 9.91	P Dubois-Dauphin Montfrim, France	8. 4.03T
G-BTUV	Aeronca 65TAC Defender	C 1661TA	N36816	12. 9.91	M B Hamlett Le Plessis-Belleville, France	27. 7.08P
			NC36816		(As "C1661:T/A" in USAF c/s)	
G-BTUW	Piper PA-28-151 Cherokee Warrior	28-7415066	N54458	12. 9.91	T S Kemp Enstone	22. 9.07T
G-BTUZ	American General AG-5B Tiger	10075	N11939	3.10.91	R V Grocott Sleap	26. 2.08E
G-BTVA	Thunder Ax7-77 Balloon (Hot Air)	2009		16. 9.91	Claire M Waters Holbeach, Spalding	10. 4.08A
G-BTVB	Everett Gyroplane Series 3	026		24. 9.91	J P Whitter (Leigh)	5. 5.06P
	(Rotax 532)					
G-BTVC	Denney Kitfox Model 2	PFA 172-11784		23. 9.91	M J Downes Pool Quay, Breidden	7. 8.08P
	(Built R Swinden)					
G-BTVE	Hawker Demon I	?	2292M	18. 9.91	Demon Displays Ltd Rotary Farm, Hatch	
	(Built Boulton Paul Aircraft Ltd) (Kestrel V)		K8203		(As "K8203" in RAF 64 Sqdn c/s) (On final rebuild 4.05)	
G-BTVV	Reims Cessna F337G Super Skymaster	F33700058	PH-RPD	25. 9.91	C Keane Weston, Leixlip, County Kildare	12. 1.03T
	(Wichita c/n 33701476)		N1876M		(Noted 5.06)	
G-BTVW	Cessna 152 II	15279631	N757CK	23. 9.91	TGD Leasing Ltd Wellesbourne Mountford	24. 1.08E
G-BTVX	Cessna 152 II	15283375	N48786	23. 9.91	Traffic Management Services Ltd Gamston	2. 4.07T
					(New owner 1.08)	
G-BTWB	Denney Kitfox Model 3	920	(G-BTTM)	21. 8.91	J E Tootell Strathaven	19. 6.08P
	(Built J E Toothill - pr.no.PFA 172-12278)					
G-BTWC	Slingsby T 61F Venture T 2	1975	ZA656	23. 9.91	T M Holloway tr RAF Gliding and Soaring Association	
					Trenchard Lines, Upavon	30. 5.08
					(Operated Wyvern (Army) Gliding Club)	
G-BTWD	Slingsby T 61F Venture T 2	1976	ZA657	23. 9.91	York Gliding Centre Ltd t/a York Gliding Centre	
					Rufforth	10. 4.08E
G-BTWE	Slingsby T 61F Venture T 2	1980	ZA661	23. 9.91	J L Clegg tr Aston Down G-BTWE Syndicate	
					Aston Down	24. 6.08E
G-BTWF	de Havilland DHC-1 Chipmunk 22	C1/0564	WK549	30. 9.91	J A and V G Simms (As "WK549"in RAF c/s) (York)	31. 5.10S

G-BTWI   EAA Acrosport   230   N10JW   2.10.91   S Alexander and W M Coffee   Bidford   3. 6.05P
(Built J N Wharton) (Lycoming O-290)

G-BTWJ   Cameron V-77 Balloon (Hot Air)   2670   3.10.91   C Gingell and M Holden-Wadsworth   Nailsea, Bristol   2. 8.08A

G-BTWL   Wag-Aero CUBy Sport Trainer   PFA 108-10893   3.10.91   I M Ashpole   Preston Court, Ledbury   15.10.07P
(Built Penair) (Lycoming O-235)

G-BTWM   Cameron V-77 Balloon (Hot Air)   2163   4.10.91   R C Franklin *"Aerolus"*   Chesham   13. 9.04A

G-BTWV   Cameron O-90 Balloon (Hot Air)   2675   10.10.91   C F Sanger-Davies   Eldersfield, Gloucester   2. 2.08A

G-BTWX   SOCATA TB-9 Tampico Club   1401   14.10.91   Archer Two Ltd   Lydd   12. 2.08E

G-BTWY   Aero Designs Pulsar   PFA 202-12040   15.10.91   R Bishop   Headcorn   12.11.08P
(Built J J Pridal and A K Pirie) (Tail-wheel u/c)

G-BTWZ   Rans S-10 Sakota   0990.117   15.10.91   P C Avery   Lower Mountpleasant Farm, Chatteris   1.10.07P
(Built D G Hey - pr.no.PFA 194-12117) (Rotax 912 - officially regd with Rotax 582)

G-BTXD (2)   Rans S-6-ESA Coyote II   0591.191   22.10.91   A I Sutherland   Fearn   25. 7.08P
(Built M Isterling - pr.no.PFA 204-12104) (Rotax 582) (Tail-wheel u/c)

G-BTXF   Cameron V-90 Balloon (Hot Air)   2692   2.10.91   G Thompson   Ambleside   3. 3.03

G-BTXG   British Aerospace Jetstream Series 3102   719   23.10.91   Highland Airways Ltd   Inverness   9. 7.08E
G-BTXG, OK-REJ, G-BTXG, OY-EEC, G-BTXG, N418MX, G-31-719

G-BTXH   Colt AS-56 Airship (Hot Air)   2078   23.10.91   L Kiefer   March-Flugstetten, Germany   26. 3.93A

G-BTXI   Noorduyn AT-16-ND Harvard IIB   14-429   Swedish Fv16105   25.10.91   Patina Ltd   Duxford   12. 4.08P
RCAF FE695, FE695, 42-892 *(As "FE695:94" in RAF c/s) (Operated The Fighter Collection)*

G-BTXK   Thunder Ax7-65 Balloon (Hot Air)   1910   ZS-HYP   28.10.91   A F Selby   Woodhouse Eaves , Loughborough   5. 4.08
G-BTXK

G-BTXM   Colt 21A Cloudhopper Balloon (Hot Air)   2082   29.10.91   H J Andrews   Selborne, Alton   22 .8.97A

G-BTXS   Cameron O-120 Balloon (Hot Air)   2141   16.10.91   Semajan Ltd tr Southern Balloon Group   (France)   16. 9.08A

G-BTXT   Maule MXT-7-180 Super Rocket   14027C   7.10.91   E A Gibson tr G-BTXT Group   Morgansfield, Fishburn   10. 6.08E

G-BTXW   Cameron V-77 Balloon (Hot Air)   2717   31.10.91   P C Waterhouse   Wadhurst, East Sussex   19. 9.07A
"Scott's Whisky"

G-BTXX   Bellanca 8KCAB Decathlon   595-80   OY-CYC   1.10.91   Tatenhill Aviation Ltd   Tatenhill   20. 5.08E
SE-IEP, N5063G

G-BTXZ   Zenair CH.250   PFA 113-12170   24.10.91   I Parris and P W J Hull   Hinton-in-the-Hedges   13. 2.08P
(Built B F Arnall) (Lycoming O-290)

G-BTYC   Cessna 150L   15075767   N66002   4.11.91   Polestar Aviation Ltd   Jersey   5. 3.08E

G-BTYE   Cameron A-180 Balloon (Hot Air)   2704   5.11.91   K J A Maxwell and D S Messmer   Uckfield   26. 3.00T
"Rolling Rock" (Active 5.07)

G-BTYF   Thunder Ax10-180 Series 2 Balloon (Hot Air)   2086   7.11.91   I Bentley   Bath   6.10.08T
(Operated Innovation Balloons)

G-BTYH   Pottier P 80S   PFA 160-11121   11.11.91   G E Livings   RAF Halton   7. 1.08P
(Built R Pickett) (Volkswagen 1834)

G-BTYI   Piper PA-28-181 Archer II   28-8190078   N8287T   15.11.91   G B Jeffery   (Wisbech)   29. 2.08E

G-BTYT   Cessna 152 II   15280455   N24931   25.11.91   Cristal Air Ltd   Shoreham   21. 9.08E

G-BTYW   Cessna 120   11725   N77283   27.11.91   A R Dix and R Nisbet
(Continental C85)   NC77283   Shacklewell Farm, Empingham   27.11.10S

G-BTYY   Curtiss Robertson C-2 Robin   475   N348K   8.10.91   R R L Windus   Truleigh Manor Farm, Edburton   1. 9.97P
(Continental W-670)   NC348K   *(Noted 7.04)*

G-BTYZ   Colt 210A Balloon (Hot Air)   2083   17.10.91   T M Donnelly *(Active 5.07)*   Sprotbrough, Doncaster   19.10.03T

G-BTZA   Beech F33A Bonanza   CE-957   PH-BNT   22.11.91   H Mendelssohn tr G-BTZA Group   Kirknewton   26. 6.08E

G-BTZB   Yakovlev Yak-50   801810   DOSAAF 77   27.11.91   D H Boardman   Lee-on-Solent   29. 9.08P
(As "10" in DOSAAF c/s)

G-BTZD   Yakovlev Yak-1 Series 1   8188   1342   10.12.91   Historic Aircraft Collection Ltd   (Westfield, Hastings)
(C/n stamped on engine bearers)   (Soviet AF)
(Salvaged from lake in N Russia mid 1991 after forced landing c.1942: for completion by 2009)

G-BTZE   LET Yakovlev C-11   171312   (France)   11. 2.92   M V Rijkse   (London W8)
(C/n noted on plate as 172503)   Egypt AF, OK-JIK   *(New owner 7.07)*

G-BTZG   British Aerospace ATP   2046   PK-MTV   11.12.91   Trident Aviation Leasing Services (Jersey) Ltd   Woodford
(PK-MAA), G-BTZG   *(Stored as "PK-MTV" 3.06)*

G-BTZH   British Aerospace ATP   2047   PK-MTW   11.12.91   Trident Aviation Leasing Services (Jersey) Ltd   Woodford
(PK-MAC), G-BTZH   *(Stored 3.06)*

G-BTZK   British Aerospace ATP   2050   PK-MTZ   11.12.91   Trident Aviation Leasing Services (Jersey) Ltd   Woodford
G-BTZK, (PK-MAF), G-BTZK   *(Stored 3.06)*

G-BTZL   Oldfield Baby Lakes   8506-M-28B   N2288B   12.12.91   M R Winter   Sleap   1. 7.08P
(Built H R Swack) (Continental C85)

G-BTZO   SOCATA TB-20 Trinidad   1409   18.12.91   A P Howells   Cardiff   1. 5.08E

G-BTZP   SOCATA TB-9 Tampico Club   1421   18.12.91   M W Orr   Oxford   18. 6.08E

G-BTZS   Colt 77B Balloon (Hot Air)   2088   18.12.91   P T R Ollivere *"Petal"*   Sutton   27. 5.04A

G-BTZU   Cameron Concept 60 Balloon (Hot Air)   2734   20.12.91   S A Simington   Eccles, Norwich   1. 5.04A

G-BTZV   Cameron V-77 Balloon (Hot Air)   2410   20.12.91   D J and H M Brown *"Vulcan"*   Redditch   27. 6.08A

G-BTZX   Piper J-3C-65 Cub   18871   N98648   27. 2.92   D A Woodhams and J T Coulthard tr ZX Cub Group
NC98648   Bidford   28. 6.08P

G-BTZY   Colt 56A Balloon (Hot Air)   2084   17.10.91   S J Wardle   Kettering   21. 9.05A

G-BTZZ   CFM Streak Shadow   K 169-SA   23.12.91   D R Stennett   Mendlesham   6.11.07P
(Built D R Stennett - pr.no.PFA 206-12155) (Rotax 582)

G-BUAA - G-BUZZ

G-BUAA   Corben Baby Ace D   561   N516DH   19.11.91   C J Bragg   Hill Farm, Nayland   20.11.08P
(Built D E Hale) (Continental A65)   *(New owner 9.06)*

G-BUAB   Aeronca 11AC Chief   11AC-1759   N3458E   17. 1.92   J Reed   Craysmarsh Farm, Melksham   9. 8.08P
(Continental A65)   NC3458E

G-BUAC   Slingsby T.31 Motor Cadet III   PFA 042-12059   (??)   17. 1.92   D A Wilson and C R Partington   Milfield   4.10.94P
(Re-built D C Pattison) (Volkswagen 1200) (P/i unknown, possibly home-built)   *(Noted 1.04)*

G-BUAF   Cameron N-77 Balloon (Hot Air)   2746   2. 1.92   Zebedee Balloon Service Ltd   Szekszárd, Hungary   7. 7.08
(Rebuilt from 5N-ATT)

G-BUAG   Jodel D 18   PFA 169-11651   3. 1.92   A L Silcox   Bodmin   1. 7.03P
(Built A L Silcox) (Volkswagen 1834)

G-BUAI	Everett Gyroplane Series 3	030		6. 1.92	D Bateson	(Haslemere)	9. 4.04P
	(Rotax 532)						
G-BUAJ	Cameron N-90 Balloon (Hot Air)	2735		7. 1.92	Skyview Ballooning Ltd t/a Kent Ballooning		
						Stanford, Ashford	12.10.07E
G-BUAM	Cameron V-77 Balloon (Hot Air)	2470		10. 1.92	N Florence *"J and E Page Flowers"*	London SW11	3. 5.06A
G-BUAO	Luscombe 8A Silvaire	4089	N1362K	15. 1.92	K E Ballington	Yeatsall Farm, Abbots Bromley	11. 8.04P
	(Continental A65)		NC1362K		*(New owner 11.04)*		
G-BUAT	Thunder Ax9-120 Balloon (Hot Air)	2093		24. 1.92	J Fenton *"Calor"*	Preston	17. 3.00T
G-BUAV	Cameron O-105 Balloon (Hot Air)	2767		27. 1.92	C D Monk	Wells	28. 7.07E
G-BUAX	Rans S-10 Sakota	0390.095		28. 1.92	A W McKee	(London W12)	10. 8.07P
	(Built J W Topham - pr.no.PFA 194-11848) (Rotax 582)						
G-BUBN	Pilatus Britten-Norman BN-2B-26 Islander	2270		14. 2.92	Isles of Scilly Skybus Ltd	St Just	18. 2.06T
G-BUBS	Lindstrand LBL 77B Balloon (Hot Air)	144 (2)		10.10.94	Beaulah J Bower *"Bubbles Balloon"*	Perugia, Italy	27. 4.08A
G-BUBT	Stoddard-Hamilton Glasair IIS RG	2026		6. 2.92	DOC Tiles Ltd	(Watford)	3. 6.08P
	(Buillt M D Evans - pr.no.PFA 149-11633) (Lycoming IO-320)						
G-BUBU	Piper PA-34-220T Seneca III	34-8233060	N8043B	9. 7.87	Brinor (Holdings) Ltd	Poplar Hall Farm, Elmsett	13. 8.08E
G-BUBW	Robinson R22 Beta	2048		7. 2.92	Staske Construction Ltd	(Bletchley)	9. 9.07T
G-BUBY	Thunder Ax8-105 Series 2 Balloon (Hot Air)			3. 2.92	T M Donnelly	Sprotbrough, Doncaster	10. 6.03T
		2115			*"Jorvik Viking Centre"*		
G-BUCA	Cessna A150K Aerobat	A1500220	N5920J	14. 6.89	D Featherby tr BUCA Group	Norwich	4. 5.08E
G-BUCB	Cameron H-34 Balloon (Hot Air)	2777		11. 2.92	A S Jones	Halfpenny Green	30. 6.07A
G-BUCC	CASA 1-131E Jungmann	1109	G-BUEM	11. 9.78	P L Gaze	Goodwood	5. 5.07P
	(Spanish AF serial conflicts with G-BJAL)				G-BUCC, Spanish AF E3B-114 *(As "BU+CC: w/no.1109" in Luftwaffe c/s)*		
G-BUCG	Schleicher ASW 20L TOP	20396	BGA 3140	19. 2.92	W B Andrews	Davidstow Moor	3. 8.08E
	(Konig SD430)		I-FEEL		*"344"*		
G-BUCH	Stinson V-77 (AT-19) Reliant	77-381	N9570H	21. 2.92	Gullwing Trading Ltd	White Waltham	8. 8.09
			FB531 *(RN)*				
G-BUCK	CASA 1-131E Jungmann Series 1000	1113	Spanish AF E3B-322	11. 9.78	J G Brander tr Jungmann Flying Group		
					(As "BU+CK" in Luftwaffe c/s)	White Waltham	27. 4.07P
G-BUCM	Hawker Sea Fury FB.11	-	VX653	26. 2.92	Patina Ltd	Duxford	
					(Operated The Fighter Collection) (On rebuild 11.07)		
G-BUCO	Pietenpol AirCamper	PFA 047-11829		10. 2.92	A James	Siege Cross Farm, Thatcham	10. 9.08P
	(Built A James) (Continental C90)						
G-BUCS	Cessna 150F	15062368	N3568L	25. 8.89	London Ashford Airport Ltd *(New owners 2.08)*	Lydd	1. 4.04T
G-BUCT	Cessna 150L	15075326	N11320	14. 6.89	Aircraft Engineers Ltd	Prestwick	31.10.07E
G-BUDA	Slingsby T 61F Venture T 2	1963	ZA627	18. 2.92	T M Holloway tr RAF Gliding and Soaring Association		
						RAF Cranwell	18. 8.07
G-BUDB	Slingsby T 61F Venture T 2	1964	ZA628	18. 2.92	T M Holloway tr RAF Gliding and Soaring Association		
					(Operated Fenland Gliding Club)	RAF Marham	5. 9.07
G-BUDC	Slingsby T 61F Venture T 2	1971	ZA652	18. 2.92	I P Litchfield tr T 61 Group	Enstone	3. 7.08E
					(As "ZA652" in RAF c/s)		
G-BUDE	Piper PA-22-135 Tri-Pacer	22-980	N1144C	9. 4.92	P Robinson		
	(Tail-wheel conversion)					Upper Harford Farm, Bourton-on-the-Water	20.11.07E
G-BUDF	Rand Robinson KR-2	PFA 129-11155		26. 2.92	M Stott	(Bedford)	3.12.03P
	(Built J B McNab) (HAPI Magnum 75)						
G-BUDI	Aero Designs Pulsar	PFA 202-12185		25. 2.92	R W L Oliver	Popham	7. 8.07P
	(Built R W L Oliver)				*(Nose undercarriage collapsed landing Popham 13.10.06 with substantial damage)*		
G-BUDK	Thunder Ax7-77 Balloon (Hot Air)	2076		2. 3.92	W Evans	Wrexham	15. 4.08A
G-BUDL	Taylorcraft E Auster III	458	PH-POL	5. 3.92	M Pocock	AAC Middle Wallop	
	(Regd with Frame No.TAY 5810)		8A-2, R Neth AF R-17, NX534 *(On rebuild 9.05)*				
G-BUDN	Cameron Shoe 90 SS Balloon (Hot Air)	2761		6. 3.92	Magical Adventures Ltd	West Bloomfield, Mi, US	1. 8.00A
	(Converse Allstar Trainers shape)				*"Converse Allstar Boot"*		
G-BUDO	PZL-110 Koliber 150	03900045	(D-EIVT)	12. 3.92	A S Vine	Haverfordwest	27. 7.06
G-BUDR	Denney Kitfox Model 3	1066		16. 3.92	N J P Mayled	Dunkeswell	26.11.08P
	(Built D Silsbury - pr.no.PFA 172-12107)						
G-BUDS	Rand Robinson KR-2	PFA 129-10937		31.12.85	D W Munday	Kemble	
	(Built D W Munday)				*(Noted 10.05)*		
G-BUDT	Slingsby T 61F Venture T 2	1883	XZ563	30. 3.92	R V Andrews tr G-BUDT Group		
						Belle Vue Farm, Yarnscombe	4. 8.07P
G-BUDU	Cameron V-77 Balloon (Hot Air)	2447		16. 3.92	T M G Amery	Llandeilo	18. 9.03A
G-BUDW	Brügger MB.2 Colibri	PFA 043-10644	G-GODS	19. 3.92	S P Barrett	(Irby-in-the-Marsh, Skegness)	17. 7.08P
	(Built J M Hoblyn) (Volkswagen 1600)						
G-BUEC	Van's RV-6	21015		17. 3.92	A H Harper	High Ham, Langport	29. 3.08P
	(Built D W Richardson and R D Harper - pr.no.PFA 181C-11884) (Lycoming O-360)						
G-BUED	Slingsby T 61F Venture T 2	1979	ZA660	12. 3.92	F B Rutterford tr 617 VGS Flying Group		
						Waldershare Park	5. 7.07
G-BUEF	Cessna 152 II	15280862	N25928	17. 3.92	A L Brown t/a Channel Aviation	Bourn	7. 9.08E
G-BUEG	Cessna 152 II	15280347	N24736	17. 3.92	Aviation South West Ltd	Exeter	2.10.08E
G-BUEI	Thunder Ax8-105 Balloon (Hot Air)	2172		23. 3.92	K P Barnes and L A Pibworth	Bristol	13. 4.08T
G-BUEK	Slingsby T 61F Venture T 2	1879	XZ559	30. 3.92	G E Draycott and B L Owen tr G-BUEK Group		
						Shipdham	12.12.07
G-BUEN	Magni M-14 Scout	VPM14-UK101		19. 3.92	J L G McLane	(Gilling East, York)	14. 8.08P
	(Arrow GT1000R)						
G-BUEP	Maule MXT-7-180 Super Rocket	14023C		24. 3.92	N J B Bennett	Henstridge	13. 6.08E
G-BUEV	Cameron O-77 Balloon (Hot Air)	2810	EI-CFW	31. 3.92	K C Tanner	Thame	30. 4.06A
			G-BUEV				
G-BUEW	Rans S-6 Coyote II	0190-111	G-MWYF	1. 4.92	J D Clabon	Shobdon	15. 8.08P
	(Built D J O'Gorman - pr.no.PFA 204-12021)		(EI-CEL) *(Rotax 582) (Tri-cycle u/c)*				
G-BUEX	Schweizer 269C	S 1412	G-HFLR	14. 4.92	M R S Trumble	(Bantham, Kingsbridge)	20.11.07E
	(Schweizer 300)						
G-BUFA	Cameron R-77 Gas/Balloon (Hot Air)	2712		19. 3.92	Noble Adventures Ltd *(Stored 1996)*	(Netherlands)	10. 6.93A
G-BUFC	Cameron R-77 Gas/Balloon (Hot Air)	2823		19. 3.92	Noble Adventures Ltd *(Stored 1996)*	(Netherlands)	23. 6.93A
G-BUFE	Cameron R-77 Gas/Balloon (Hot Air)	2825		19. 3.92	Noble Adventures Ltd *(Stored 1996)*	(Netherlands)	21. 6.93A
G-BUFG	Slingsby T 61F Venture T 2	1977	ZA658	3. 4.92	Transcourt Ltd	Hinton-in-the-Hedges	16. 8.07

Reg	Type	C/n	Prev id	Date	Owner/Operator	Location	Date2
G-BUFH	Piper PA-28-161 Warrior II	28-8416076	N43520	15. 4.92	R J Gibson	Sleap	2. 7.08E
G-BUFJ	Cameron V-90 Balloon (Hot Air)	2809		7. 4.92	S P Richards	Tonbridge	7. 7.06T
G-BUFN	Slingsby T 61F Venture T 2	1967	ZA631	8. 4.92	S C Foggin tr BUFN Group		
						Sandhill Farm, Shrivenham	16.11.07
G-BUFR	Slingsby T 61F Venture T 2	1880	XZ560	9. 4.92	East Sussex Gliding Club Ltd	Ringmer	16. 12.07
	(Rollason RS Mk.2)						
G-BUFT	Cameron O-120 Balloon (Hot Air)	2814		9. 4.92	D Bron	St Barthelemy, France	2. 3.08A
G-BUFV	Avid Speed Wing Mk.4	PFA 189-12192		15. 4.92	M and B Gribbin	(Antrim, County Antrim)	16. 9.05P
	(Built S C Ord) (BMW R100)				(Lost power on take-off Toomebridge and ditched in Lough Neagh 10. 6.05)		
G-BUFW	Aérospatiale AS.355F1 Ecureuil 2	5112	5N-BAK	21. 4.92	RCR Aviation Ltd	Thruxton	31. 5.92A
			G-BUFW, N57904				
G-BUFY	Piper PA-28-161 Warrior II	28-8016211	N130CT	14. 4.92	Bickertons Aerodromes Ltd	Denham	1. 7.08E
			N8TS, N3571K		(Operated The Pilots Centre)		
G-BUGB	Stolp SA.750 Acroduster Too	PFA 089-11942		22. 4.92	R M Chaplin	Rochester	15. 3.08P
	(Built D Burnham) (Lycoming O-360)						
G-BUGD	Cameron V-77 Balloon (Hot Air)	2195		23. 4.92	P Haslett	Arcy sur Cure, France	11. 9.04A
G-BUGE	Bellanca 7GCAA Citabria	339-77	N4165Y	23. 4.92	V Vaughan and N O'Brien	Glountha, Kilkenny	14.10.10S
G-BUGG	Cessna 150F	15062479	N8379G	24. 3.92	C P J Taylor and D M Forshaw	Panshanger	28. 9.07E
G-BUGJ	Robin DR.400-180 Régent	2137		28. 4.92	W E R Jenkins	Little Gransden	3.11.07E
G-BUGL	Slingsby T 61F Venture T 2	1966	ZA630	29. 4.92	S Bradford and M Bean tr VMG Group	Tibenham	20. 1.08
					(Also carries "ZA630" on tail)		
G-BUGM	CFM Streak Shadow	K 176-SA		29. 4.92	S J Welch and W D Berry tr The Shadow Group		
	(Built W J de Gier - pr.no.PFA 206-12069) (Rotax 582)					Sywell	24.10.08P
G-BUGO	Colt 56B Balloon (Hot Air)	2143		18. 5.92	Escuela de Aerostacion Mica	Valencia, Spain	19. 7.00A
G-BUGP	Cameron V-77 Balloon (Hot Air)	2278	OO-BEE	10. 3.92	R Churcher	Canterbury	17. 6.08A
G-BUGS	Cameron V-77 Balloon (Hot Air)	2482		14. 4.92	S J Dymond "Bugs Bunny"	Tidworth	14. 9.01T
G-BUGT	Slingsby T 61F Venture T 2	1871	XZ551	22. 4.92	R W Hornsey tr Bambi Aircraft Group	Rufforth	3. 8.08
G-BUGV	Slingsby T 61F Venture T 2	1884	XZ564	28. 4.92	Oxfordshire Sportflying Ltd	Enstone	28. 6.08E
G-BUGW	Slingsby T 61F Venture T 2	1962	ZA626	22. 4.92	Transcourt Ltd	Hinton-in-the-Hedges	13.10.07
G-BUGY	Cameron V-90 Balloon (Hot Air)	2800		9. 4.92	I J Culley tr Dante Balloon Group	Hungerford	4.10.08A
					"Florence""		
G-BUGZ	Slingsby T 61F Venture T 2	1981	ZA662	22. 4.92	R W Spiller tr Dishforth Flying Group	AAC Dishforth	13. 6.08
G-BUHA	Slingsby T 61F Venture T 2	1970	ZA634	29. 4.92	Buckminster Gliding Club Ltd	Saltby	16.11.07E
					(As "ZA634:C" in RAF c/s) (Noted 2.08)		
G-BUHM	Cameron V-77 Balloon (Hot Air)	2481		7. 5.92	J Skinner "Blue Horizon"	Chart Sutton, Maidstone	9. 6.08A
G-BUHO	Cessna 140	14402	N2173V	1. 5.92	W B Bateson	Blackpool	19.11.04T
	(Continental C90)				(Noted 10.07)		
G-BUHR	Slingsby T 61F Venture T 2	1874	XZ554	8. 5.92	W G Miller tr Connel Motor Glider Group		
						North Connel, Oban	16.10.07E
G-BUHS	Stoddard-Hamilton Glasair SH TD-1	149	C-GYMB	8. 5.92	T F Horrocks	Wick	21. 1.08P
	(Built F L Binder) (Lycoming O-360)						
G-BUHU	Cameron N-105 Balloon (Hot Air)	2785		13. 5.92	Unipart Group Ltd tr Unipart Balloon Club		
						Cowley, Oxford	21.11.96A
G-BUHZ	Cessna 120	14950	N3676V	1. 5.92	M R Houseman tr C140 Group	RAF Henlow	15. 5.08P
G-BUIE	Cameron N-90 Balloon (Hot Air)	2863		22. 5.92	B Conway	Wheatley, Oxford	24. 1.01A
G-BUIF	Piper PA-28-161 Warrior II	28-7916406	N28375	29. 5.92	Northumbria Flying School Ltd	Newcastle	4. 7.08E
G-BUIG	Campbell Cricket	PFA G/03-1173		27. 5.92	J A English	Kirkbride	27. 4.05P
	(Built T A Holmes) (Rotax 532)				(Noted 8.07)		
G-BUIH	Slingsby T 61F Venture T 2	1876	XZ556	29. 5.92	L E Ingram tr Falcon Gliding Group		
						Wellesbourne Mountford	5. 7.08E
G-BUIJ	Piper PA-28-161 Warrior II	28-8116210	N83784	3. 6.92	Tradecliff Ltd	Popham	25. 8.08E
G-BUIK	Piper PA-28-161 Warrior II	28-7916469	N2845P	2. 6.92	A S Bamrah t/a Falcon Flying Services	Biggin Hill	25.10.07E
G-BUIL	CFM Streak Shadow	K 182-SA		8. 5.92	J A McKie	Stoke, Isle of Grain	31.10.07P
	(Built P N Bevan and L M Poor - pr.no.PFA 206-12121) (Rotax 582)						
G-BUIN	Thunder Ax7-77 Balloon (Hot Air)	1882		5. 6.92	P C Johnson	Gloucester	23. 5.08A
G-BUIP	Denney Kitfox Model 2	710		8. 6.92	Avcomm Developments Ltd	Enstone	7. 8.08P
	(Built G D Lean - pr.no.PFA 172-11874)						
G-BUIR	Avid Speed Wing Mk.4	PFA 189-12213		9. 6.92	E Stinton	Gloucestershire	9. 7.07P
	(Buillt K N Pollard)						
G-BUIU	Cameron V-90 Balloon (Hot Air)	2641		11. 6.92	H Micketeit	Bielefeld, Germany	18. 4.03A
G-BUIZ	Cameron N-90 Balloon (Hot Air)	2850		12. 6.92	R S Kent tr Balloon Preservation Flying Group		
	(Telecoms Shape)				"Hutchinson"	Petworth	6. 6.08A
G-BUJA	Slingsby T 61F Venture T 2	1972	ZA653	22. 5.92	T M Holloway tr RAF Gliding and Soaring Association		
					(Operated Wrekin Gliding Club)	RAF Cosford	28. 3.08E
G-BUJB	Slingsby T 61F Venture T 2	1978	ZA659	21. 5.92	O F Vaughan and D A Fall tr Falke Syndicate		
						Shobdon	11. 7.08
G-BUJE	Cessna 177B Cardinal	17701920	N34646	10. 6.92	J Flux tr FG93 Group	Old Sarum	6. 4.08E
G-BUJH	Colt 77B Balloon (Hot Air)	2207		23. 6.92	R P Cross and R Stanley	Luton and Harpenden	12. 4.08A
G-BUJI	Slingsby T 61F Venture T 2	1882	XZ562	22. 5.92	Solent Venture Syndicate Ltd	Lee-on-Solent	15. 4.07
G-BUJJ	Avid Speed Wing	213	N614JD	20.10.92	R A Dawson	(Totnes)	13. 9.06P
	(Built M Cox)						
G-BUJK	Montgomerie-Bensen B 8MR	PFA G/01-1211		25. 6.92	P C W Raine	Walkeridge Farm, Overton	7. 8.08P
	(Built J M Montgomerie) (Rotax 582)						
G-BUJL	Aero Designs Pulsar	PFA 202-11892		16. 6.92	J J Lynch	(Dunstable)	
	(Built J J Lynch)						
G-BUJM	Cessna 120	11784	N77343	19. 6.92	D H Mackay tr Cessna 120 Flying Group		
	(Continental C85)		NC77343			RNAS Yeovilton	14. 3.08E
G-BUJN	Cessna 172N Skyhawk II	17272713	N6315D	19. 6.92	M Djukic and J Benfell	(Newcastle, Staffordshire)	8..3.08E
G-BUJO	Piper PA-28-161 Cherokee Warrior II		N1014Q	19. 6.92	A S Bamrah t/a Falcon Flying Services	Lydd	22. 6.08E
		28-7716077					
G-BUJP	Piper PA-28-161 Warrior II	28-7916047	N21624	19. 6.92	J M C Manson (Operated Ace Aviation)	Shoreham	1.11.07E
G-BUJR	Cameron A-180 Balloon (Hot Air)	2821		22. 6.92	Dragon Balloon Company Ltd Castleton, Hope Valley		16.10.00T
G-BUJV	Avid Speed Wing Mk.4	PFA 189-12250		3. 7.92	C Thomas	Shenstone	28. 7.94P
	(Built D N Anderson)				(Damaged 13. 8.93 Caernarfon - remnants dumped 8.06)		

G-BUJW	Thunder Ax8-90 Series 2 Balloon (Hot Air) 2208			6. 7.92	G J Grimes	Farnham	19. 9.07A
G-BUJX	Slingsby T 61F Venture T 2	1873	XZ553	7. 7.92	K E Ballington *(Noted 2.08)*	Saltby	4.10.07E
G-BUJZ	RotorWay Executive 90	5119/6973		9. 7.92	M P Swoboda	Street Farm, Takeley	7. 9.07P
	(Built T W Aisthorpe and R J D Crick) (RotorWay RI 162)				*(Landed in field near Willingdale 27. 6.07 and substantially damaged: noted 2.08)*		
	(Originally regd as c/n 5119: rebuilt 2004/5 after accident 6.03 with new official c/n 5119/6973 although c/n plate states "5218/6973")						
G-BUKB	Rans S-10 Sakota	0790.112		13. 7.92	M K Blatch	RAF Brize Norton	18. 4.07P
	(Built M K Blatch - pr.no.PFA 194-12078) (Rotax 582)						
G-BUKF	Denney Kitfox Model 4	PFA 172A-12247		2. 6.92	A G V McClintock tr Kilo Foxtrot Group		
	(Built M R Crosland)					East Fortune	16. 7.08P
G-BUKH	Druine D 31 Turbulent	PFA 048-11419		14. 8.92	R B Armitage	Maypole Farm,Chislet	16.10.08P
	(Built J S Smith) (Volkswagen 1600)						
G-BUKI	Thunder Ax7-77 Balloon (Hot Air)	2239		8. 7.92	Airxcite Ltd t/a Virgin Balloon Flights	Wembley	31. 5.08A
G-BUKJ	British Aerospace ATP	2052	(PH-MGC)	5. 8.92	Trident Aviation Leasing Services (Jersey) Ltd *(Noted 9.07)*		
	G-BUKJ, EC-HCO, G-BUKJ, (PH-MJL), EC-GLD, G-OEDF, G-BUKJ, TC-THZ, G-BUKJ				Bucharest, Romania		15. 4.08E
G-BUKK	Bücker Bü.133D Jungmeister	27	N44DD	15.11.89	E J F McEntee	Kirdford	18.10.07P
	(Built Dornier-Werke AG)		HB-MKG, Swiss AF U-80		*(As "U-80" in Swiss AF c/s)*		
G-BUKN	Piper PA-15 Vagabond	15-215	N4427H	15. 7.92	M A Goddard	(Southampton)	
			NC4427H		*(New owner 1.05)*		
G-BUKO	Cessna 120	13089	N2828N	15. 7.92	S Warrener	Fenland	31. 7.98P
			NC2828N		*(On rebuild 2007 using components ex G-GAWA)*		
G-BUKP	Denney Kitfox Model 2	PFA 172-12301		22. 7.92	K N Cobb	Weston Zoyland	19.10.07P
	(Built T D Reid)						
G-BUKR	SOCATA MS.880B Rallye 100T	2923	LN-BIY	27. 7.92	G R Russell tr G-BUKR Flying Group		
						Middle Pymore Farm , Bridport	23. 2.08E
G-BUKS	Colt 77B Balloon (Hot Air)	2241		6. 7.92	R and M Bairstow	Middlewich, Cheshire	22. 6.08A
G-BUKT	Luscombe 8E Silvaire Deluxe	2197	N45670	30. 7.92	R J F Swain	Sleap	27. 3.08P
	(Continental C85)		NC45670				
G-BUKU	Luscombe 8E Silvaire Deluxe	4720	N1993K	30. 7.92	D J Warren tr Silvaire Flying Group	Rochester	17. 6.08P
	(Continental C85)		NC1993K				
G-BUKX	Piper PA-28-161 Cherokee Warrior II		N231PA	5. 8.92	LNP Ltd	Dunkeswell	13.12.07E
		28-7816674			*(Noted 2.08)*		
G-BUKY	CCF Harvard 4 (T-6J-CCF Texan)	CCF4-464	N455V	13. 7.92	R A Fleming	Breighton	17.12.08P
			G-BUKY, FAP 1766 , WGAF	BF-063 , WGAF AA-063, 52-8543			
					(As "52-8543-'66" in US Navy c/s)		
G-BUKZ	Evans VP-2	PFA 063-10761		5. 8.92	P R Farnell	Wombleton	
	(Built P R Farnell)				*(Noted 7.02)*		
G-BULB	Thunder Ax7-77 Balloon (Hot Air)	1968		3. 7.92	G B Davies	Thorney, Peterborough	2. 3.08E
G-BULC	Avid Flyer Mk.4	PFA 189-12202		6. 7.92	C Nice	Popham	17.10.07P
	(Built C Nice)						
G-BULD	Cameron N-105 Balloon (Hot Air)	2136		6. 8.92	R J Collins	Hurtmore, Godalming	14.11.05T
G-BULF	Colt 77A Balloon (Hot Air)	2043		10. 8.92	P Goss and T C Davies *"Nursery"*	Christchurch	4. 6.08A
G-BULG	Van's RV-4	JRV4-1	C-FELJ	28. 7.92	V D Long tr BULG Group		
	(Built L Johnson) (Lycoming O-320)					(Firgrove, Wreningham, Norfolk)	16. 7.08P
G-BULH	Cessna 172N Skyhawk II	17269869	N738CJ	2. 7.92	Aircraft Grouping Ltd	Blackpool	16. 1.06T
G-BULJ	CFM Streak Shadow	K 191-SA		10. 8.92	C C Brown	Wellesbourne Mountford	24.10.08P
	(Built C C Brown - pr.no.PFA 206-12199) (Rotax 582)						
G-BULK	Thunder Ax9-120 Series 2 Balloon (Hot Air)			3. 7.92	S J Colin t/a Skybus Ballooning	Cranbrook	11.10.04T
		2237					
G-BULL	Scottish Aviation Bulldog Series 120/128		HKG-5	20. 9.88	N V Sills	Old Sarum	17.10.10S
		BH120/392	G-31-18		*(Also carries "HKG-5" in Royal Hong Kong AAF c/s)*		
G-BULN	Colt 210A Balloon (Hot Air)	2265		13. 8.92	H G Davies	Woodmancote, Cheltenham	16. 7.08T
G-BULO	Luscombe 8F Silvaire	4216	N1489K	13. 8.92	A F S Caldecourt	Popham	12. 7.08P
	(Continental O-200A)		NC1489K				
G-BULR	Piper PA-28-140 Cherokee B	28-25230	HB-OHP	8. 7.92	G R Bright	Little Gransden	4. 7.08E
			N7320F				
G-BULT	Everett Gyroplane Series 1	PFA G/03A-1213		20. 8.92	A T Pocklington	(Bishops Stortford)	26. 5.05P
	(Built A T Pocklington)						
G-BULY	Avid Flyer	PFA 189-12309		12. 8.92	J Angiolini	Cumbernauld	23. 7.06P
	(Built M O Breen)				*(New owner 7.07)*		
G-BULZ	Denney Kitfox Model 2	PFA 172-11546		31. 7.92	T G F Trenchard		
	(Built D J Dumulo)					Newton Peverill Farm, Sturminster Marshall	22.11.05P
G-BUMP	Piper PA-28-181 Cherokee Archer II		PH-MVA	17. 1.79	A J Keen	(Colby, Isle of Man)	13. 9.08E
		28-7790437	OO-HCH, N3105Q				
G-BUNB	Slingsby T 61F Venture T 2	1969	ZA633	25. 8.92	T M Holloway tr RAF Gliding and Soaring Association		
						Lee-on-Solent	23. 7.08E
G-BUNC	PZL-104 Wilga 35A	129444	SP-TWP	2. 9.92	R F Goodman	Husbands Bosworth	6. 7.08
G-BUND	Piper PA-28RT-201T Turbo Arrow IV		N8219V	18. 7.88	L J Martin	Sandown, Isle of Wight	20. 8.04
		28R-8031107			*(New owner 12.06)*		
G-BUNG	Cameron N-77 Balloon (Hot Air)	2905		2. 9.92	A Kaye tr The Bungle Balloon Group		
					(Aspen titles) "Bungle"	Wellingborough	13. 4.07A
G-BUNH	Piper PA-28RT-201T Turbo Arrow IV		N8255H	26. 8.92	J H Sandham t/a JH Sandham Aviation	Carlisle	8. 3.08E
		28R-8031166					
G-BUNJ	K & S SA 102.5 Cavalier	PFA 001-10058		10. 9.92	J A Smith	Great Massingham	
	(Built J S Smith)				*(On build 9.97)*		
G-BUNM	Denney Kitfox Model 3	PFA 172-12111		15. 9.92	P N Akass	(Ireland)	5. 5.04P
	(Built P J Carter) (Floatplane)						
G-BUNO	Neico Lancair 320	PFA 191-12332		11. 9.92	J Softley	(Newbury)	
	(Built J Softley)				*(On build 2000)*		
G-BUNV	Thunder Ax7-77 Balloon (Hot Air)	1967		23. 9.92	R Stone and R M Garnett *(New owners 12.06)*		
						(Romsey and Bursledon, Southampton)	18. 7.07A
G-BUNZ	Thunder Ax10-180 Series 2 Balloon (Hot Air)			7. 9.92	M A Scholes	Haywards Heath	27. 2.06T
		2271			*(WFU and dismembered 2006)*		
G-BUOA	Whittaker MW6-S Fatboy Flyer Series A			25. 9.92	H N Graham	(Lisbellaw, Enniskillen)	30.10.06P
	(Built D A Izod) (Rotax 582)	PFA 164-11959					

G-BUOB	CFM Streak Shadow	K 186-SA		29. 9.92	W J White	Insch	21.10.08P
	(Built A M Simmons - pr.no.PFA 206-12156) (Rotax 582)						
G-BUOD	Replica Plans SE.5a	PFA 020-10474		5.10.92	M D Waldron	Croft Farm, Defford	29. 8.08P
	(Built M D Waldron) (Continental C90)				(As "B595:W" in RFC 56 Sqdn c/s)		
G-BUOE	Cameron V-90 Balloon (Hot Air)	2938		6.10.92	B and Joy.Smallwood	Marshfield, Chippenham	1. 4.08A
	(New envelope 7.05 - c/n not known)				"Flying Colours 2"		
G-BUOF	Druine D 62B Condor	PFA 049-11236		6.10.92	R P Loxton	Wyke Farm, Sherbourne	11.12.08P
	(Built K Jones)						
G-BUOI	Piper PA-20-135 Pacer	20-571	OY-ALS	18. 9.92	T A P Hubbard tr Foley Farm Flying Group	Meon	15. 5.08E
	(Lycoming O-320) (Hoerner wing-tips)		D-EHEN, N7750K				
G-BUOK	Rans S-6-116 Coyote II	0692.314		9.10.92	M Morris	Fieldhead Farm, Denholme, Bradford	25. 5.08P
	(Built M Morris - pr.no.PFA 204A-12317) (Rotax 912-UL)						
G-BUOL	Denney Kitfox Model 3	PFA 172-12142		12.10.92	E C King	Eastbach Farm, Coleford	12. 8.04P
	(Built J G D Barbour)						
G-BUON	Avid Aerobat	PFA 189-12160		13.10.92	S R Winder	(Bolton)	6.11.01P
	(Built I A J Lappin)						
G-BUOR	CASA 1-131E Jungmann Series 2000	2134	N89542	21.10.92	M I M Schermer Voest	Den Helder, Netherlands	15. 6.04P
			EC-336, Spanish AF E3B-508				
G-BUOS	Vickers Supermarine 394 Spitfire FR.XVIIIe	6S/672224	Indian AF HS687 SM845	19.10.92	Historic Flying Ltd	Duxford	21. 8.08P
					(As "SM845:GZ-J" in RAF c/s) (Operated Aircraft Restoration Company)		
G-BUOW	Aero Designs Pulsar XP	PFA 202-12206		22.10.92	T J Hartwell	Sackville Lodge, Riseley	8. 6.95P
	(Built P F Gaughan)				(New owner 7.01)		
G-BUOX	Cameron V-77 Balloon (Hot Air)	2925		23.10.92	I G H Woodmansey "High Flyer"	Thame	21. 8.08A
G-BUOZ	Thunder Ax10-180 Balloon (Hot Air)	1962	(SX-)	29.10.92	Zebedee Balloon Service Ltd	Cranbrook	3.11.08T
			G-BUOZ		(Operated Skybus Ballooning)		
G-BUPA	Rutan LongEz	750	N72SD	22. 9.92	N G Henry	(Gloucester)	27. 4.06P
	(Built D Moore) (Lycoming O-235)						
G-BUPB	Stolp SA.300 Starduster Too	RH.100	N8035E	3.11.92	J R Edwards tr Starduster PB Group	Popham	16. 4.08P
	(Built R Harte) (Lycoming IO-360)						
G-BUPC	Rollason Beta B 2	PFA 002-12369		29.10.92	C A Rolph	Liverpool	3. 6.03P
	(Built C A Rolph) (Continental C90)				(Veered off runway Clutton Hill Farm, Clutton and overturned 12. 9.02)		
G-BUPF	Bensen B 8MR	PFA G/01-1209		5.11.92	P W Hewitt-Dean	(Wootton Bassett)	1. 8.02P
	(Built G M Hobman) (Rotax 532)						
G-BUPG	Cessna 180K Skywagon	18052490	N52086	15.10.92	T P A Norman	Blue Tile Farm, Langham	6.11.07E
G-BUPH	Colt 25A Balloon (Hot Air)	2023		10.11.92	BAB-Ballonwerbung GmbH	Hanover, Germany	11. 2.05A
G-BUPI	Cameron V-77 Balloon (Hot Air)	1778	G-BOUC	28. 7.88	H W R Stewart	Burslecombe, Tiverton	6. 9.08A
					(New owner 8.07)		
G-BUPJ	Fournier RF4D	4119	N7752	10.11.92	M R Shelton	Tatenhill	
G-BUPM	Magni M-16 Tandem Trainer	VPM16-UK-102		16.10.92	Roger Savage (Penrith) Ltd	Kirkbride	18. 7.08P
	(Rotax 914)						
G-BUPP	Cameron V-42 Balloon (Hot Air)	2789		21. 7.92	L J Schoeman	Basildon	13. 5.04A
G-BUPR	Jodel D 18	PFA 169-11289		23.11.92	R W Burrows	Priory Farm, Tibenham	15. 5.08P
	(Built R W Burrows) (Limbach L2000)						
G-BUPU	Thunder Ax7-77 Balloon (Hot Air)	2305		25.11.92	R C Barkworth and D G Maguire "Puzzle"	Pulborough	26. 3.01A
G-BUPV	Great Lakes 2T-1A	126	N865K	26.11.92	R J Fray	Sibson	17. 5.08P
	(Gladden Kinner R55)		NC865K				
G-BUPW	Denney Kitfox Model 3	PFA 172-12281		22.10.92	G M Park tr Forfoxake Flyers	Newtownards	1. 8.08P
	(Built D Sweet) (Rotax 912)						
G-BURD	Reims Cessna F172N Skyhawk II	F17201677	PH-AXI	26. 4.78	Tayside Aviation Ltd	Glenrothes	12.12.07E
G-BURE	Jodel D 9 Bébé	PFA 944		30.11.92	L J Kingsford	Headcorn	
	(Built P B Shilling and C R Kingsford)				(Noted 6.05)		
G-BURG	Colt 77A Balloon (Hot Air)	2042		12. 1.93	S T Humphreys "Lily"	Great Missenden	13. 7.08A
G-BURH	Cessna 150E	15061225	EI-AOO	2.12.92	C A Davis	Sandown, Isle of Wight	4.11.06
			G-BURH, EI-AOO, N2125J				
G-BURJ	Hawker Siddeley HS.748 Series 2A/256	1667	9N-ACP	14.12.92	Clewer Aviation Ltd	Blackpool	
G-BURI	Enstrom F-28C	433	N51743	11.12.92	R L Heath tr India Helicopters Group	Goodwood	5. 6.08E
G-BURL	Colt 105A Balloon (Hot Air)	2297		18.11.92	J E Rose "Isis"	Abingdon	9. 6.06T
G-BURN	Cameron O-120 Balloon (Hot Air)	2793		18. 2.92	Innovation Ballooning Ltd "Innovations"	Bath	17. 9.05T
G-BURP	RotorWay Executive 90	5116		8.10.92	N K Newman	(Buckingham)	13. 9.96P
	(Built A GA Edwards) (RotorWay RI 162)				(Stored 7.99)		
G-BURS	Sikorsky S-76A II Plus	760040	(HP-)	4. 5.89	Premiair Aviation Services Ltd	Denham	25.10.07E
			G-BURS, G-OHTL				
G-BURT	Piper PA-28-161 Cherokee Warrior II	28-7716105	N2459Q	10. 6.81	B A Paul	Denham	3. 5.08E
G-BURX	Cameron N-105 Balloon (Hot Air)	2959	G-NPNP	8. 1.93	R S Kent tr Balloon Preservation Flying Group		
			G-BURX		"National Power III"	Petworth	11. 7.08A
G-BURZ	Hawker Nimrod II	41H-59890	K3661	22.12.91	Historic Aircraft Collection Ltd	Duxford	
					(As "K3661:562" in RAF 802 Sqdn c/s) (First post-rebuilt flight 16.11.06)		
G-BUSG	Airbus A320-211	0039	F-WWDM	30. 5.89	British Airways PLC	London Heathrow	30. 5.08E
					(To be retired 2.08)		
G-BUSH	Airbus A320-211	0042	F-WWDT	19. 6.89	British Airways PLC	London Heathrow	18. 6.08E
					(To be retired 5.08)		
G-BUSI	Airbus A320-211	0103	F-WWDB	23. 3.90	British Airways PLC	London Heathrow	21. 3.08E
					(To be retired 4.08)		
G-BUSJ	Airbus A320-211	0109	F-WWIC	6. 8.90	British Airways PLC	London Heathrow	5. 8.08E
					(To be retired 9.08)		
G-BUSK	Airbus A320-211	0120	F-WWIN	12.10.90	British Airways PLC	London Heathrow	11.10.08E
					(To be retired 10.08)		
G-BUSN	RotorWay Executive 90	5141		6. 1.93	J A McGinley(Noted 2.08)	Street Farm, Takeley	7. 1.09P
G-BUSR	Aero Designs Pulsar	PFA 202-12356		15.12.92	S S Bateman and R A Watts	Cheddington	21. 6.07P
	(Built S S Bateman and R A Watts) (Tail-wheel u/c)						
G-BUSS	Cameron Bus 90 SS Balloon (Hot Air)	1685		11. 3.88	Magical Adventures Ltd (National Express tiles)		
						West Bloomfield, Michigan, US	31. 1.96A
G-BUSV	Colt 105A Balloon (Hot Air)	2324		12. 1.93	M N J Kirby	Northwich	24. 5.08

Reg	Type	C/n	Prev id	Date	Owner/Operator	Base	Expiry
G-BUSW	Rockwell Commander 114	14079	N4749W	18. 1.93	J M J Palmer	Biggin Hill	12. 9.08E
G-BUTB	CFM Streak Shadow	K 190		20. 1.93	H O Maclean and S MacKechnie		
	(Built F A H Ashmead - pr.no.PFA 206-12243) (Hirth 2706 R05)					North Connel, Oban	17. 7.07P
G-BUTD	Van's RV-6	PFA 181-12152		21. 1.93	N W Beadle	Airfield Farm, Hardwick	26.11.08P
	(Built N Reddish) (Lycoming O-320)						
G-BUTE	Anderson EA-1 Kingfisher Amphibian		G-BRCK	15. 8.91	T Crawford	Cumbernauld	15.10.99P
	(Built T Crawford) (Lycoming O-235) PFA 132-10798				(Damaged by storms 1.07)		
G-BUTF	Aeronca 11AC Chief	11AC-1578	N3231E	21. 1.93	D Horne tr Fox Flying Group	High Easter	28. 5.08P
			NC3231E				
G-BUTG	Zenair CH.601HD Zodiac	PFA 162-12225		22. 1.93	I J McNally	Bourn	7. 6.06P
	(Built J M Scott) (Continental C90-14F)		(Substantially damaged after hitting obstruction on landing Upper Wellingham Farm, Ringmer 14.8.05)				
G-BUTH	CEA Jodel DR.220 2+2	6	F-BNVK	10. 2.93	P J Gristwood tr Phoenix Flying Group	Dunkeswell	28. 6.08E
G-BUTJ	Cameron O-77 Balloon (Hot Air)	2991		25. 1.93	D Hoddinott	Nottingham	12. 2.08A
G-BUTK	Murphy Rebel	PFA 232-12091		25. 1.93	G S Claybourn	Walton Wood	27. 6.08P
	(Built D Webb) (Rotax 912-UL)						
G-BUTM	Rans S-6-116 Coyote II	0792.323		22. 1.93	N D White tr G-BUTM Group		
	(Built M Rudd - pr.no.PFA 204A-12414) (Rotax 912-UL) (Tailwheel u/c)					Buttermilk Hall Farm, Blisworth	2. 7.07P
G-BUTT	Reims Cessna FA150K Aerobat	FA1500029	G-AXSJ	18. 8.86	Global Engineering and Maintenance Ltd		
					(New owner 1.08)	Bournemouth	24.10.99T
G-BUTX	Bücker Bü.133C Jungmeister	1010?	Spanish AF E1-4 3. 2.93		J G Brander tr Bücker Flying Group	White Waltham	9. 2.07P
	(Warner Super Scarab) (Possibly a CASA 1.133L?)		Spanish AF ES.1-4, 35-4		(New owners 10.07)		
G-BUTY	Brügger MB.2 Colibri	PFA 043-12387		30.11.92	R M Lawday	(Milford, Derby)	
	(Built R M Lawday)						
G-BUTZ	Piper PA-28-180 Cherokee C	28-3107	G-DARL	23. 4.93	M H Canning	Leicester	9. 8.08E
			4R-ARL, 4R-ONE, SE-EYD				
G-BUUA	Slingsby T 67M Firefly II	2111		17. 3.93	Babcock Support Services Ltd t/a Babcock Defence Services		
						AAC Middle Wallop	22. 7.08E
G-BUUB	Slingsby T 67M Firefly II	2112		17. 3.93	Babcock Support Services Ltd t/a Babcock Defence Services		
						AAC Middle Wallop	25. 7.08E
G-BUUC	Slingsby T 67M Firefly II	2113		17. 3.93	Babcock Support Services Ltd t/a Babcock Defence Services		
						AAC Middle Wallop	5.10.07E
G-BUUE	Slingsby T 67M Firefly II	2115		17. 3.93	J R Bratty	Tollerton	4.10.07E
G-BUUF	Slingsby T 67M Firefly II	2116		17. 3.93	C C Rollings and F J Hodson t/a Tiger Airways		
						Gloucestershire	3.12.07E
G-BUUI	Slingsby T 67M Firefly II	2119		17. 3.93	Bustard Flying Club Ltd	Boscombe Down	22. 1.08E
G-BUUJ	Slingsby T 67M Firefly II	2120		17. 3.93	A C Lees	Bagby	20. 8.08E
G-BUUK	Slingsby T 67M Firefly II	2121		17. 3.93	Babcock Support Services Ltd t/a Babcock Defence Services		
						AAC Middle Wallop	29. 2.08E
G-BUUL	Slingsby T 67M Firefly II	2122		17. 3.93	C Hunter	Compton Abbas	19. 9.08E
G-BUUM	Piper PA-28RT-201 Arrow IV	28R-7918090	N2145X	14. 1.93	J Phelan and D G Scott tr Bluebird Flying Group		
						Belfast International	3. 4.08E
G-BUUO	Cameron N-90 Balloon (Hot Air)	2994		9. 2.93	M P Rich tr Gone Ballooning Group	Bristol	19. 6.03A
G-BUUP	British Aerospace ATP	2008	G-MANU	18. 2.93	Trident Aviation Leasing Services (Jersey) Ltd		
			G-BUUP, CS-TGA, G-11-8, (N378AE) (Noted 1.08)				Coventry	24. 3.03T
G-BUUR	British Aerospace ATP	2024	EC-GUX	18. 2.93	Trident Aviation Leasing Services (Jersey) Ltd		
			G-OEDJ, G-BUUR, CS-TGC, G-11-024				Coventry	29. 9.07T
					(Operated Atlantic Airlines)		
G-BUUT	Interavia 70TA Balloon (Hot Air)	04509-92		21. 1.93	Aero Vintage Ltd	(Northiam, Rye)	
G-BUUX	Piper PA-28-180 Cherokee D	28-5128	OY-BCW	17. 2.93	M A Judge tr Aero Group 78	Netherthorpe	22.12.07E
G-BUVA	Piper PA-22-135 Tri-Pacer	22-1301	N8626C	12. 2.93	K W Thomas tr Oaksey VA Group	Oaksey Park	21. 8.08E
G-BUVC	British Aerospace Jetstream Series 3202	970	F-GMVP	10. 3.93	Airx Ltd t/a Blue Islands	Jersey	5. 3.08E
			F-GLPY, G-BUVC, F-GLPY, (F-OHFS), G-BUVC, G-31-970					
G-BUVD	British Aerospace Jetstream Series 3202	977	F-GMVK	10. 3.93	Air Kilroe Ltd t/a Eastern Airways	Humberside	26. 4.08E
			G-BUVD, (F-OHFR), (F-OHFW), G-31-977 (Stored 2007)					
G-BUVE	Colt 77B Balloon (Hot Air)	2376		8. 3.93	G D Philpot "Trident"	Hemel Hempstead	4. 4.07A
G-BUVL	Fisher Super Koala	PFA 228-11399		3. 3.93	A D Malcolm Park Farm, Throwley, Faversham		30. 9.04P
	(Built A D Malcolm) (Jabiru 2200A)				"Spirit of Throwley"		
G-BUVM	CEA Jodel DR.250/160 Capitaine	54	OO-NJR	11. 3.93	M Lodge tr G-BUVM Group	Crosland Moor	18. 9.08E
			F-BNJR				
G-BUVN	CASA 1-131E Jungmann Series 2000	2092	Spanish AF EC-333 12. 3.93		W van Egmond	Hoogeveen, Netherlands	1. 7.08P
			Spanish AF E3B-487		(As "BI:005" in R Neth AF c/s)		
G-BUVO	Reims Cessna F182P Skylane II	F18200022	G-WTFA	10. 3.93	P N Stapleton tr Romeo Mike Flying Group		
			PH-VDH, D-EJCL				Plymouth	20. 6.08E
G-BUVR	Christen A-1 Husky	1162		12. 3.93	A E Poulsom	Manor Farm, Tongham	3. 7.08E
G-BUVS	Colt 77A Balloon (Hot Air)	2381		12. 3.93	Justine Pelling (New owner 4.07)	Cranleigh	11. 5.04A
G-BUVT	Colt 77A Balloon (Hot Air)	2382		12. 3.93	N A Carr	Leicester	13. 4.08A
G-BUVW	Cameron N-90 Balloon (Hot Air)	3020		19. 3.93	P Spellward (New owner 5.06)	Bristol	7. 2.01A
G-BUVX	CFM Streak Shadow SA	K 214-SA		22. 3.93	T J Shaw	North Coates	3. 4.08P
	(Built G K R Linney -pr.no.PFA 206-12410) (Rotax 582)						
G-BUVZ	Thunder Ax10-180 Series 2 Balloon (Hot Air)			24. 3.93	A van Wyk	Caxton	4. 9.04T
		2380					
G-BUWE	Replica Plans SE.5a	PFA 020-11816		25. 3.93	Airpark Flight Centre Ltd	Coventry	21. 8.08P
	(Built D Biggs) (Continental C90)				(As "C9533:M" in RFC c/s)		
G-BUWF	Cameron N-105 Balloon (Hot Air)	3036		26. 3.93	R E Jones "British Aerospace II"	Lytham St Annes	23. 2.08T
G-BUWH	Parsons Two-Place Gyroplane	PFA G/08-1215		1. 4.93	R V Brunskill	Melrose Farm, Melbourne	22. 8.95P
	(Built R V Brunskill) (Rotax 532)						
G-BUWI	Lindstrand LBL 77A Balloon (Hot Air)	023		5. 4.93	Capital Balloon Club Ltd "Throw Up"	London NW1	16. 8.08A
G-BUWJ	Pitts S-1C (Built J T Griffins)	2002	N110R	25. 3.93	R V Barber	Audley End	29. 5.08P
G-BUWK	Rans S-6-116N Coyote II	1292.410		7. 4.93	R Warriner	Maypole Farm, Chislet	3. 6.08P
	(Built R Warriner - pr.no.PFA 204A-12448) (Rotax 912)						
G-BUWL	Piper J-4A Cub Coupé	4-1047	N27828	8. 4.93	M L Ryan	Garston Farm, Marshfield	
			NC27828				
G-BUWM	British Aerospace ATP	2009	CS-TGB	19. 4.93	BAE Systems (Operations) Ltd	Woodford	
			G-BUWM, CS-TGB, G-11-9 (Stored 3.06)					

G-BUWR	CFM Streak Shadow	K 177-SA		26. 4.93	T Harvey	Grove Farm, Raveningham	24. 4.07P
	(Built T Harvey - pr.no.PFA 206-12068) (Rotax 582)						
G-BUWS	Denney Kitfox Model 2	PFA 172-11831		26. 4.93	J E Brewis	(Castletown, Isle of Man)	
	(Built J E Brewis)						
G-BUWT	Rand Robinson KR-2	PFA 129-10952		5. 4.93	C M Coombe	(Ruislip)	
	(Built C M Coombe)						
G-BUWU	Cameron V-77 Balloon (Hot Air)	3053		27. 4.93	T R Dews	Hill Deverill, Warminster	25. 6.08A
G-BUXC	CFM Streak Shadow	K 188		20. 4.93	J P Mimnagh	Guy Lane Farm, Waverton	20.12.07P
	(Built T Hosier - pr.no.PFA 206-12177) (Rotax 582)						
G-BUXD	Maule MXT-7-160 Super Rocket	17001C	N9231R	4. 5.93	S Baigent	East Winch	19.10.07E
	(Tri-cycle u/c)						
G-BUXI	Steen Skybolt	PFA 064-10755		16. 3.93	D Tucker	Kemble	16. 8.08P
	(Built M Frankland)						
G-BUXJ	Slingsby T 61F Venture T 2	1878	XZ558	6. 5.93	D Mihailovic tr Venture Motor Glider Club	Dunsfold	26. 6.08
G-BUXK	Pietenpol AirCamper	PFA 047-11901		12. 5.93	B M D Nelson	Finmere	31. 8.07P
	(Built G R G Smith) (Continental C90))						
G-BUXL	Taylor JT.1 Monoplane	PFA 055-11819		12. 5.93	P J Hebdon	(Milton, Banbury)	12. 5.07P
	(Built M W Elliott)						
G-BUXN	Beech C23 Sundowner 180	M-1752	N9256S	13. 5.93	D G Tudor tr Private Pilots Syndicate	Bournemouth	21.12.07
G-BUXO	Pober P-9 Pixie	PFA 105-10647		17. 5.93	J Mangiapane tr P-9 Flying Group	(Matlock)	
	(Built T Moore)				(Nearing completion 2000)		
G-BUXR	Cameron A-250 Balloon (Hot Air)	3056		13. 5.93	D S King t/a Celebration Balloon Flights		
					(Active 5.07)	Keyworth, Nottingham	18. 6.03T
G-BUXS	MBB BÖ.105DBS-4	S 913	G-PASA	19. 5.93	Bond Air Services "Irn Bru"	Aberdeen	25. 5.08E
	(Originally c/n S 41: rebuilt 1993)		G-BGWP, F-ODMZ, G-BGWP, HB-XFD, N153BB, D-HDAS (Operated Northern Lighthouse)				
G-BUXV	Piper PA-22-160 Tri-Pacer	22-6685	N9769D	20. 5.93	J Mathews tr Romeo Delta Juliet Group		
	(Super Pacer Tail-wheel conversion)			(Noted 5.06 damaged and stored) Weston, Leixlip, County Kildare				18.10.03
G-BUXW	Thunder Ax8-90 Series 2 Balloon (Hot Air)	2405		25. 5.93	A S Davidson tr Nottingham Hot Air Balloon Club		
					"Silver Lady"	Woodville, Swadlincote	18. 7.08A
G-BUXX	Piper PA-17 Vagabond	17-28	N4611H	31. 3.93	R H Hunt	Old Sarum	12. 7.08P
	(Continental A75)		NC4611H				
G-BUXY	Piper PA-25-235 Pawnee	25-2705	C-GZCR	18. 3.93	Bath, Wilts and North Dorset Gliding Club Ltd		
			N6959Z			Kingston Deverill	1.12.07E
G-BUYB	Aero Designs Pulsar	PFA 202-12193		28. 5.93	A P Fenn	Shobdon	14. 5.07P
	(Built A P Fenn) (Tail-wheel u/c)						
G-BUYC	Cameron Concept 80 Balloon (Hot Air)	3095		28. 5.93	R P Cross (Windrush titles)	Luton	20. 9.07A
G-BUYD	Thunder Ax8-90 Balloon (Hot Air)	2422		28. 5.93	S and S McGuigan	Draperstown, Magherafelt	7. 6.08A
G-BUYF	American Aircraft Falcon XP	600179	N512AA	13. 5.93	M J Hadland	Tarn Farm, Cockerham	21. 5.04P
	(Built R W Harris) (Rotax 503)				(New owner 11.04)		
G-BUYJ	Lindstrand LBL 105A Balloon (Hot Air)	039		1. 6.93	D K Fish and G Fordyce	Manchester and Olney	7. 3.08A
G-BUYK	Denney Kitfox Model 4	PFA 172A-12214		1. 6.93	M S Shelton	Hill Farm, Nayland	25. 4.08P
	(Built R D L Mayes) (Rotax 912-UL)						
G-BUYL	Rotary Air Force RAF 2000	H2-92-361	C-FPFN	2. 6.93	Newtonair Gyroplanes Ltd		
	(Built D A Lafleur: rebuilt by Newtonair using parts from G-TXSE)					Watchford Farm, Yarcombe	6. 9.06P
G-BUYO	Colt 77A Balloon (Hot Air)	2398		4. 6.93	S F Burden	Noordwijk, Netherlands	25. 6.07A
G-BUYS	Robin DR.400-180 Régent	2197		21. 6.93	P R Currer tr G-BUYS Flying Group	Nuthampstead	7. 4.08E
G-BUYU	Bowers Fly Baby 1A	PFA 016-12222		7. 6.93	R Metcalfe	Rushett Farm, Chessington	3. 4.07P
	(Built J A Nugent) (Continental A65)			(As "C L 1.1803/18" in German Army Air Service c/s to represent Junkers CL1)				
G-BUYY	Piper PA-28-180 Cherokee B	28-1028	C-FXDP	18. 3.93	A J Hedges and C E Yates tr G-BUYY Group		
			CF-XDP, N7214W			Bristol	9.10.07E
G-BUZA	Denney Kitfox Model 3	1178		10. 6.93	A O'Brien	Abbeyshrule, County Longford	4. 4.08P
	(Built R Hill - pr.no.PFA 172-12547)						
G-BUZB	Aero Designs Pulsar XP	PFA 202-12312		14. 6.93	S M Lancashire	(Timperley, Altrincham)	19. 8.08P
	(Built M J Whatley) (Tail-wheel u/c)						
G-BUZC	Everett Gyroplane Series 3A	034		14. 7.93	M P Lhermette	(Sproughton, Ipswich)	
					(Damaged 7.94: stored 12.95)		
G-BUZD	Aérospatiale AS.332L Super Puma	2069	C-GSLJ	11. 2.93	CHC Scotia Ltd	Aberdeen	14.12.07E
			N189EH, C-GSLJ, HC-BNB, C-GSLJ, PT-HRN, C-GSLJ				
G-BUZE	Avid Speed Wing	PFA 189-12047		16. 6.93	P B Harrison	(Wirral)	7. 9.06P
	(Built N L E Nupee)				(New owner 12.07)		
G-BUZG	Zenair CH.601HD Zodiac	PFA 162-12457		17. 6.93	P G Morris	Cheyne Farm, Stonehaven	10. 6.08P
	(Built N C White) (Continental O-200-A)						
G-BUZH	Star-Lite SL-1	119	N4HC	17. 6.93	C A McDowall	(Blackfield, Southampton)	8. 9.00P
	(Built H M Cottle) (Rotax 447)		(Damaged Farley Farm, Romsey 10. 8.00: in container 9.00 - fuselage only)				
G-BUZJ	Lindstrand LBL 105A Balloon (Hot Air)	038		17. 6.93	A M Holly	Breadstone, Berkeley	16. 4.08T
G-BUZK	Cameron V-77 Balloon (Hot Air)	2962		17. 6.93	J T Wilkinson	Blackland, Calne	15. 6.08A
G-BUZM	Avid Speed Wing Mk.3	PFA 189-12179		30. 4.93	R McLuckie and O G Jones	RAF Mona	14. 5.07P
	(Built R McLuckie and O G Jones) (Jabiru 2200) (Officially regd with Rotax 582)						
G-BUZN	Cessna 172H	17256056	N2856L	24. 6.93	H D Jones	Barton	18.12.07
G-BUZO	Pietenpol AirCamper	PFA 047-12408		28. 6.93	D A Jones	(Maidenhead)	
	(Built D A Jones) (Salmson AD9)						
G-BUZR	Lindstrand LBL 77A Balloon (Hot Air)	044		29. 6.93	Lindstrand Technologies Ltd	Oswestry	3.11.07A
G-BUZS	Colt Flying Pig SS Balloon (Hot Air)	2415		2. 7.93	Banco Bilbao Vizcaya	Bilbao, Spain	20. 5.96A
G-BUZT	Kolb Twinstar Mk.3	K0009-0193		1. 7.93	J A G Robb	Caim, County Wexford	3. 7.07P
	(Built A C Goadby - pr.no.PFA 205-12367)						
G-BUZV	Ken Brock KB-2	PFA G/06-1152		1. 7.93	K Hughes	(Amlwch, Gwynedd)	
	(Built K Hughes)						
G-BUZZ	Agusta-Bell 206B-2 JetRanger II	8178	F-GAMS	13. 4.78	Rivermead Aviation Ltd	Gloucestershire	23. 2.08E
			HB-XGI, OE-DXF		(Operated Rise Helicopters)		

G-BVAA - G-BVZZ

G-BVAB	Zenair CH.601HDS Zodiac	PFA 162-12475		26. 5.93	B N Rides	Garston Farm, Marshfield	27. 6.08P
	(Built A R Bender)						

Reg	Type	C/n	Prev id	Regd	Owner	Location	
G-BVAC	Zenair CH.601HD Zodiac	PFA 162-12504		1. 6.93	J A Tyndall and S Wisedale	Oaksey Park	6. 9.08P
	(Built A G Cozens)						
G-BVAF	Piper J-3C-65 Cub	4645	OO-UBU	14. 6.93	N M Hitchman	Garston Farm, Marshfield	19. 6.08P
	(Continental C85)		N28199, NC28199				
G-BVAH	Denney Kitfox Model 3	PFA 172-12031		22.10.91	S Allinson	Shobdon	7. 8.08P
	(Built V A Hutchinson) (Rotax 912)						
G-BVAI	PZL-110 Koliber 150	03900040	OY-CYJ	7. 7.93	P R Powell	Shobdon	12.11.07E
G-BVAM	Evans VP-1	PFA 062-12132		7. 7.93	R F Selby	(East Preston, Littlehampton)	
	(Built R F Selby)						
G-BVAO	Colt 25A Balloon (Hot Air)	2024		9. 7.93	M E Dworski	Vermenton, France	5. 5.06A
G-BVAW	Staaken Z-1 Flitzer	PFA 223-12058		12. 7.93	L R Williams t/a Flitzer Sportflugverein	Rhigos	22. 6.07P
	(Built L R Williams and D J Evans) (Volkswagen 1834)				*(As "D692")*		
G-BVAX	Colt 77A Balloon (Hot Air)	1213		30. 3.88	P H Porter *"Vax"*	Tenbury Wells	5. 8.95A
G-BVAY	Rutan VariEze	RS.8673/345	N5MS	3. 9.93	D A Young	(Sunderland)	11.11.02P
	(Built R N Saunders)						
G-BVAZ	Montgomerie-Bensen B 8MR	PFA G/01-1190		12. 7.93	N Steele	Newtownards	22. 7.04P
	(Built R Patrick) (Rotax 582)				*(Suffered engine failure on take off Newtownards 30. 8.03, rolled over to right damaging rotors)*		
G-BVBR	Avid Speed Wing	PFA 189-12085		3. 8.93	P D Thomas	(Whitchurch)	25.11.08P
	(Built H R Rowley)						
G-BVBS	Cameron N-77 Balloon (Hot Air)	3128		4. 8.93	S M Gabb t/a Heart of England Balloons		
						Haselor, Alcester	27. 3.08A
G-BVBU	Cameron V-77 Balloon (Hot Air)	3076	(OO-BYS)	5. 8.93	J Manclark *(Operated Alba Ballooning)*	Haddington	15. 3.04A
G-BVBV	Avid Speed Wing	PFA 189-12187		4. 8.93	L W M Summers	Popham	19. 5.07P
	(Built D A Jarvis)						
G-BVCA	Cameron N-105 Balloon (Hot Air)	3129		11. 8.93	Unipart Group Ltd tr Unipart Balloon Club	Cowley	25. 6.00A
G-BVCC	Monnett Sonerai IILT	PFA 015-10547		12. 8.93	J Eggleston	(Ainderby Steeple, Northallerton)	
	(Built J Eggleston)						
G-BVCG	Van's RV-6	PFA 181-11783		17. 8.93	P C J Stone and K Dennison	(Lytham St Annes)	6.11.08P
	(Built G J Newby and E M Farquharson) (Lycoming O-320)						
G-BVCL	Rans S-6-116 Coyote II	0493.486		25. 8.93	J Powell	Roughay Farm, Bishops Waltham	8. 8.08P
	(Built W E Willetts - pr.no.PFA 204A-12551) (Rotax 912-UL) (Tri-cycle u/c)						
G-BVCM	Cessna 525 CitationJet	525-0022	N1329N	2. 5.94	Kenmore Aviation Ltd and BLP 2003-19 Ltd	Edinburgh	22. 5.08E
					(both) as Trustees of the Aircraft Trust		
G-BVCN	Colt 56A Balloon (Hot Air)	2445		25. 8.93	J A W Dyer	Farnborough	7. 4.08E
G-BVCO	Clutton FRED Series II	PFA 029-10947		25. 8.93	I W Bremner	(Dornoch, Sutherland)	21. 6.06P
	(Built I W Bremner)						
G-BVCP	Piper CP.1 Metisse	PFA 253-12512		24. 6.93	B M Diggins	RAF Mona	2. 5.08P
	(Built C W R Piper) (Revmaster 2200)						
G-BVCS	Aeronca 7AC Champion	7AC-1346	N69BD	1. 9.93	A C Lines	Leicester	30. 5.07P
	(Continental A65)		N82702, NC82702		*(Noted 10.07)*		
G-BVCT	Denney Kitfox Model 4-1200	1761		27. 8.93	A F Reid	Comber, County Down	7. 9.07P
	(Built A F Reid - pr.no.PFA 172A-12456) (Rotax 912-UL)						
G-BVCX	Sikorsky S-76A	760183	OY-HIW	21. 9.93	CHC Scotia Ltd	North Denes Heliport	21. 4.08E
			G-BVCX, N951L, N5450M				
G-BVCY	Cameron H-24 Balloon (Hot Air)	3136		3. 9.93	A C K Rawson and J J Rudoni	Stafford	18.12.07A
					t/a Wickers World Hot Air Balloon Company *(Bryant Homes titles)*		
G-BVDB	Thunder Ax7-77 Balloon (Hot Air)	2364	G-ORDY	6. 9.93	M J Smith and J Towler	York	17.10.99A
G-BVDC	Van's RV-3	PFA 099-12218		12. 7.93	R J Hodder	Eastfield Farm, Manby	2.10.07P
	(Built D Calibritto) (Lycoming O-235)						
G-BVDD	Colt 69A Balloon (Hot Air)	2170		6. 9.93	R M Cambidge	Oswestry	27. 8.02P
					"Delta Dawn Fantasia" (New owner 4.03)		
G-BVDH	Piper PA-28RT-201 Arrow IV	28R-7918030	N2176L	13. 9.93	Oxford Aviation Services Ltd	Oxford	28. 5.08E
G-BVDI	Van's RV-4	2058	N55GJ	13. 9.93	J Glen-Davis Gorman	Redhill	10. 4.08P
	(Built G P Larson) (Lycoming O-320)						
G-BVDJ	Campbell Cricket replica	PFA G/03-1189		13. 9.93	S Jennings	St Merryn	17. 1.08P
	(Built C D Julian and S Jennings) (Rotax 582)						
G-BVDM	Cameron Concept 60 Balloon (Hot Air)	3141		15. 9.93	M P Young	Dover	31. 5.01A
G-BVDO	Lindstrand LBL 105A Balloon (Hot Air)	055		16. 9.93	A E Still	Edgcott, Aylesbury	17. 7.08T
G-BVDP	Sequoia F 8L Falco	PFA 100-10879		17. 9.93	N M Turner	Slinfold	8. 6.08P
	(Built T G Painter)						
G-BVDR	Cameron O-77 Balloon (Hot Air)	2452		21. 9.93	N J Logue	Pembroke Dock	5. 7.07T
G-BVDS	Lindstrand LBL 69A Balloon (Hot Air)	102		23. 9.93	Lindstrand Hot Air Balloons Ltd	Oswestry	26. 6.01A
G-BVDT	CFM Streak Shadow SA-I	K 223		23. 9.93	H J Bennet	North Connel, Oban	24.10.08P
	(Built H J Bennet - pr.no.PFA 206-12462) (Rotax 582)						
G-BVDW	Thunder Ax8-90 Balloon (Hot Air)	2507		30. 9.93	S C Vora *"Cosmic"*	Oadby	14. 8.07
G-BVDX	Cameron V-90 Balloon (Hot Air)	3159	OO-BMY	30. 9.93	R K Scott	North Perrott, Crewkerne	25. 9.05A
			G-BVDX		*"Merlin" (Address change 3.07)*		
G-BVDY	Cameron Concept 60 Balloon (Hot Air)	3167		30. 9.93	P Baker	Abbeyview, Trim, County Meath	30. 6.07A
G-BVDZ	Taylorcraft BC-12D	9043	N96743	21. 1.94	P N W England	(Hove)	
			NC96743				
G-BVEA	Nostalgair N 3 Pup	01-GB	G-MWEA	7. 6.93	N Lynch	Red Moor Farm, Dufield	30. 8.08P
	(Built B D Godden - pr.no.PFA 212-11837) and officially regd as "Mosler Motors N-3 Pup") (Mosler MM-CB35)						
G-BVEH	Wassmer Jodel D 112	1294	F-BMOH	29.10.93	M L Copland	Breighton	22 .8.08P
G-BVEK	Cameron Concept 80 Balloon (Hot Air)	3133		5.10.93	A D Malcolm	Devizes	1. 4.08A
G-BVEL	Evans VP-1 Series 2	PFA 062-11983		6.10.93	M J and S J Quinn	(Scholes, Holmfirth)	
	(Built M J Quinn)				*(New owners 5.06)*		
G-BVEN	Cameron Concept 80 Balloon (Hot Air)	3164		6.10.93	R M Powell	Broughton, Stockbridge	30. 5.08A
					(New owner 7.07)		
G-BVEP	Luscombe 8A Silvaire	1468	N28707	8.10.93	B H Austen	Oaksey Park	21.10.09S
	(Continental A-65)		NC28707				
G-BVER	de Havilland DHC-2 Beaver 1	1648	G-BTDM	13. 8.91	Seaflite Ltd	Cumbernauld	23. 4.95T
			XV268		*(As "XV268" in AAC c/s) (Fuselage stored 1.05)*		
G-BVES	Cessna 340A II	340A0077	N1378G	8. 9.93	K P Gibbin and I M Worthington	East Midlands	9. 5.08E
G-BVEU	Cameron O-105 Balloon (Hot Air)	3145		12.10.93	G J Bell	Petersfield	26. 7.07E

Reg	Type	C/n	Prev id	Date	Owner / Operator	Location	Last noted
G-BVEV	Piper PA-34-200 Seneca	34-7250316	N1428T	8.10.93	R W Harris, D Quick, A Jahanfar and Atromin Ltd		
			HB-LLN, D-GHSG, N1428I		*(Operated Southend Flying Club)*	Southend	9. 8.08E
G-BVEW	Lindstrand LBL 150A Balloon (Hot Air)	057		14.10.93	A van Wyk	Cambridge	15. 8.02T
G-BVEY	Denney Kitfox Model 4-1200	PFA 172A-12527		14.10.93	J H H Turner	(Houston)	7. 7.07P
	(Built J S Penny)						
G-BVEZ	Hunting Percival P 84 Jet Provost T 3A	PAC/W/9287	XM479	13.10.93	N T McCarthy tr Newcastle Jet Provost Group		
					(As "XM479:54" in RAF c/s)	Newcastle	5. 9.08P
G-BVFA	Rans S-10 Sakota	1090.116		7. 9.93	D S Wilkinson	Kemble	27. 3.03P
	(Built D Allam and D Parkinson - pr.no.PFA 194-12298) (Rotax 582)				*(Noted 1.05)*		
G-BVFB	Cameron N-31 Balloon (Hot Air)	3175		20.10.93	P Lawman	Northampton	13.10.07A
G-BVFF	Cameron V-77 Balloon (Hot Air)	3161		26.10.93	R J Kerr and G P Allen	Abingdon	7. 7.06A
G-BVFM	Rans S-6-116 Coyote II	0793.522		2.11.93	F D C de Beer	Wishanger Farm, Frensham	21. 6.87P
	(Built P G Walton - pr.no.PFA 204A-12579) (Rotax 912-UL) *(Tri-cycle u/c)*						
G-BVFO	Avid Speed Wing	PFA 189-12053		9. 9.93	M S Moat	(Scunthorpe)	20. 4.07P
	(Built P Chisman)						
G-BVFP	Cameron V-90 Balloon (Hot Air)	3179		2.11.93	D E and J M Hartland	Hognaston, Ashbourne	12. 4.08A
G-BVFR	CFM Streak Shadow	K 237-SA		3.11.93	R W Chatterton	Griffins Farm, Temple Bruer	16.11.05P
	(Built M G B Stebbing - pr.no.PFA 206-12567) (Rotax 582)						
G-BVFS	Slingsby T.31M Cadet III	PFA 042-11387	ex RAF?	3.11.93	S R Williams	Southend	
	(Re-built M Gagffney and R Jones to Motor Tutor standard)				*(Stored dismantled 1.08)*		
G-BVFT	Maule M-5-235C Lunar Rocket	7183C	N6180M	5.11.93	S R Clark tr Newnham Joint Flying Syndicate		
						Newnham, Baldock	6. 6.08E
G-BVFU	Cameron Sphere 105 SS Balloon (Hot Air) 3137			18.11.93	Stichting Phoenix	Amsterdam, Netherlands	23. 7.08A
					(Greenpeace titles)		
G-BVFZ	Maule M-5-180C Lunar Rocket	8082C	N5664D	21. 2.94	P J Brand	High Cross, Ware	20. 4.08E
G-BVGA	Bell 206B-3 JetRanger III	2922	N54AJ	11.11.93	J L Leonard t/a Findon Air Services	Southend	30. 1.08E
			VH-SBC				
G-BVGB	Thunder Ax8-105 Series 2 Balloon (Hot Air)			11.11.93	M E Dunstan-Sewell	Bristol	5. 7.05A
		2408					
G-BVGE	Westland WS-55 Whirlwind HAR.10	WA/100	8732M	18.11.93	J F Kelly Cloghan, Mullingar, County Westmeath		17 6.08P
			XJ729		*(As "XJ729" in RAF Rescue c/s)*		
G-BVGF	Europa Aviation Europa	034		18.11.93	A Graham and G G Beal	Morgansfield, Fishburn	23.10.08P
	(Built A Graham - pr.no.PFA 247-12565) (Tri-gear u/c)						
G-BVGG	Lindstrand LBL 69A Balloon (Hot Air)	011		30.11.93	L P Hooper	St George, Bristol	21. 5.08A
G-BVGH	Hawker Hunter T 7	HABL 004328	XL573	26.11.93	Global Aviation Services Ltd	Exeter	19.11.08P
	(Centre fuselage no.is HABL 003360)		*(As "XL573" in RAF c/s)*				
G-BVGI	Pereira Osprey 2	PFA 070-10536		29.11.93	A A Knight	North Connel, Oban	25.11.03P
	(Built B Weare) (Lycoming O-320)						
G-BVGJ	Cameron Concept 80 Balloon (Hot Air)	3099		7.12.93	J M J and V F Roberts *(Pizza Express titles)*	Epping	5. 4.08A
G-BVGK	Lindstrand LBL Newspaper SS Balloon (Hot Air)	SE-ZHC		3.12.93	H Holmqvist	Lund, Sweden	23. 5.97A
		059	G-BVGK				
G-BVGO	Denney Kitfox Model 4-1200	PFA 172A-12362		15.11.93	G Edwards	Walkeridge Farm, Overton	9. 7.08P
	(Built R K Dunford)						
G-BVGP	Bücker Bü.133C Jungmeister	42	F-AZMN	3.12.93	M V Rijkse *(As "U-95" Swiss AF c/s)* Wycombe Air Park		1. 1.08P
	(Built Dornier-Werke AG)		F-BVGP, F-AZFQ, N15696, HB-MIE, D-EIII, MB-MIE, Swiss AF U-95				
G-BVGS	Robinson R22 Beta	2389	N2363S	9.12.93	R C Hayward and J H Garrioch t/a Polar Helicopters		
						Manston	6. 8.08E
G-BVGT	Crofton Auster V J/1A Special	PFA 000-220		19.11.93	K D and C S Rhodes	Henstridge	20. 6.08P
	(Built L A Groves from unknown J/1 Autocrat frame used as engine test rig) (Blackburn Cirrus 2)						
G-BVGW	Luscombe 8A Silvaire	4823	N2096K	18.11.93	J Smith	(Eccleshall, Stafford)	14. 7.08P
	(Continental A65)		NC2096K				
G-BVGY	Luscombe 8E Silvaire Deluxe	4754	N2027K	18.11.93	M C Burlock	Lower Wasing Farm, Brimpton	17. 6.08P
	(Continental C85)		NC2027K				
G-BVGZ	Fokker Dr.1 Triplane replica	VHB-10		20.12.93	R A Fleming	Breighton	22. 7.08P
	(Built V H Bellamy - pr.no.PFA 238-12654) (Lycoming AIO-360)				*(As "450/17" in German Army Air Service c/s)*		
G-BVHC	Grob G115D-2 Heron	82005	D-EARG	14.12.93	Tayside Aviation Ltd	Dundee	6. 6.08E
G-BVHD	Grob G115D-2 Heron	82006	D-EARJ	14.12.93	Tayside Aviation Ltd	Glenrothes	8. 6.08E
G-BVHE	Grob G115D-2 Heron	82008	D-EASR	14.12.93	Tayside Aviation Ltd	Glenrothes	25. 1.08E
			G-BVHE, D-EARQ				
G-BVHF	Grob G115D-2 Heron	82011	D-EARV	14.12.93	Tayside Aviation Ltd	Dundee	18. 5.08E
G-BVHG	Grob G115D-2 Heron	82012	D-EARX	14.12.93	Tayside Aviation Ltd	Dundee	11. 5.08E
G-BVHI	Rans S-10 Sakota	0990.119		20.12.93	J D Amos	Hawarden	9. 6.07P
	(Built P D Rowley - pr.no.PFA 194-12608) (Rotax 582)						
G-BVHK	Cameron V-77 Balloon (Hot Air)	3209		23.12.93	A R Rich *"Intel Inside"*	Hyde	24. 4.08A
G-BVHL	Nicollier HN.700 Ménestrel II	PFA 217-12614		24.12.93	W Goldsmith	(Boldon Colliery)	
	(Built I H R Walker and C Herbert)						
G-BVHM	Piper PA-38-112 Tomahawk	38-79A0313	G-DCAN	14.11.91	A J Gomes	Shoreham	12. 9.08E
			N2490D		*(Operated Sky Leisure Aviation)*		
G-BVHO	Cameron V-90 Balloon (Hot Air)	3158		29.12.93	N W B Bews	Tenbury Wells	18. 7.03
G-BVHR	Cameron V-90 Balloon (Hot Air)	3174		5. 1.94	G P Walton	Bagshot	6. 2.08T
G-BVHS	Murphy Rebel	050		5. 1.94	S T Raby	Grange Farm, Woodwalton	16. 8.08P
	(Built J Brown, B Godden and M Hanley - pr.no.PFA 232-12180)						
G-BVHT	Avid Speed Wing Mk.4	PFA 189-12226		28.10.93	H B S Stephens *(New owner 5.06)*		
	(Built R S Holt)					Lausanne-La Blecherette, Switzerland	4. 6.07P
G-BVHV	Cameron N-105 Balloon (Hot Air)	3215		6. 1.94	Wye Valley Aviation Ltd *(Rover titles)* Ross-on-Wye		25. 9.07T
G-BVIA	Rand Robinson KR-2	PFA 129-11004		14. 1.94	K Atkinson	(Ulverston)	2. 3.08P
	(Built K Atkinson)						
G-BVIE	Piper PA-18 Super Cub 95 (L-18C-PI)	18-1549	G-CLIK	26. 1.94	J C Best tr C'est La Vie Group	Andrewsfield	9. 4.08P
	(Continental O-200-A) (Frame No.18-1521)		(G-BLMB), D-EDRB, French Army 18-1549, 51-15549 *"C'est La Vie"*				
G-BVIF	Montgomerie-Bensen B 8MR	PFA G/01A-1228		26. 1.94	R Mand D Mann	(Brodick, Arran)	21. 8.95P
	(Built R M Mann) (Rotax 582)				*(Last noted 4.00)*		
G-BVIK	Maule MXT-7-180 Super Rocket	14056C		31. 1.94	D S Simpson tr Graveley Flying Group		
						Graveley Hall Farm, Graveley	9.10.07E
G-BVIL	Maule MXT-7-180 Super Rocket	14059C		31. 1.94	K and S C Knight	Shobdon	8. 3.08E

G-BVIN	Rans S-6-ESA Coyote II	1292.406		25.10.93	P C Davis	Sackville Lodge, Riseley	27. 9.06P
	(Built K J Vincent - pr.no.PFA 204-12533) (Tail-wheel u/c)						
G-BVIR	Lindstrand LBL 69A Balloon (Hot Air)	079		2. 2.94	Aerial Promotions Ltd (*Vauxhall titles*)	Cannock	25. 5.01A
G-BVIS	Brügger MB.2 Colibri	PFA 043-10666		2. 2.94	B H Shaw	Spanhoe	15. 1.08P
	(Built B H Shaw) (Volkswagen 1600)						
G-BVIT	Campbell Cricket replica	PFA G/03-1229		4. 2.94	D R Owen	Kirkbride	24. 7.97P
	(Built A N Nesbit) (Rotax 582)				*(Noted 8.07)*		
G-BVIV	Avid Speed Wing	PFA 189-12034		25.10.93	R C Holmes	(Lleweni Parc)	17. 5.08P
	(Built V and J Hobday - rebuilt R C Holmes)						
G-BVIW	Piper PA-18-150 Super Cub	18-8277	SE-EPD	4. 2.94	I H Logan	Popham	29. 6.08E
G-BVIX	Lindstrand LBL 180A Balloon (Hot Air)	082		8. 2.94	European Balloon Display Co Ltd	Great Missenden	31. 3.01T
					"*Drifter*"		
G-BVIZ	Europa Aviation Europa	052		24. 1.94	T J Punter and P G Jeffers tr The Europa Group		
	(Built T J Punter and P G Jeffers - pr.no.PFA 247-12601) (Tri-gear u/c)					Wycombe Air Park	25. 4.08P
G-BVJE	Aérospatiale AS.350B1 Ecureuil	1991	SE-HRS	3. 2.94	PLM Dollar Group Ltd	Inverness	24. 2.08E
G-BVJF	Montgomerie-Bensen B 8MR	PFA G/01-1082		18. 2.94	D M F Harvey	(Yate, Bristol)	
	(Built D M F Harvey)						
G-BVJG	Cyclone AX3K/582	C 3123187	G-69-14	15. 2.94	T D Reid	Newtownards	23. 4.07P
	(Built T D Reid - pr.no.PFA 245-12663)		(G-MYOP)				
G-BVJK	Glaser-Dirks DG-800A	8-24-A21		30. 3.94	J S Forster	Ringmer	2. 4.08E
G-BVJN	Europa Aviation Europa	066		2. 3.94	P Gibson tr JN Europa Group	Cumbernauld	30. 6.08P
	(Built N Adam - pr.no.PFA 247-12666) (Tri-gear u/c)						
G-BVJT	Reims Cessna F406 Caravan II	F406-0073		2. 2.94	M Evans and A Jay t/a Nor Leasing	Farnborough	29. 3.08E
G-BVJU	Evans VP-1	PFA 062-10691		10. 3.94	B A Schlussler	(Hanthorpe, Bourne)	
	(Built R Waring and B A Schlussler)						
G-BVJX	Marquart MA.5 Charger	PFA 068-11239		12. 1.94	A E Cox	Yearby	8. 7.05P
	(Built M L Martin) (Lycoming O-360)				*(Noted 2.08)*		
G-BVJZ	Piper PA-28-161 Cherokee Warrior II		N2088M	22. 3.94	J Brown	(Chesterfield)	9.10.07E
		28-7816248					
G-BVKB	Boeing 737-59D	27268	SE-DNM	24. 3.94	British Midland Airways Ltd	East Midlands	11. 4.08E
					"*Foxy Baby*" (Operated bmiBaby)		
G-BVKD	Boeing 737-59D	26421	SE-DNK	25.11.94	British Midland Airways Ltd	East Midlands	15.12.07E
					(Operated bmiBaby)		
G-BVKF	Europa Aviation Europa	050		11. 3.94	T R Sinclair	Lamb Holm Farm, Orkney	18. 5.08P
	(Built T R Sinclair - pr.no.PFA 247-12638) (Tri-gear u/c)						
G-BVKH	Thunder Ax8-90 Balloon (Hot Air)	2574		15. 3.94	L Ashill "*Pisces*"	Combe Down, Bath	4. 4.07
G-BVKK	Slingsby T 61F Venture T 2	1984	ZA665	22. 2.94	Buckminster Gliding Club Ltd	Saltby	30. 5.08
G-BVKL	Cameron A-180 Balloon (Hot Air)	3255		17. 3.94	Dragon Balloon Company Ltd Castleton, Hope Valley		1. 4.01T
G-BVKM	Rutan VariEze	1933	N7137G	5. 4.94	J P G Lindquist	Neuchatel, Switzerland	25.10.06P
	(Built K H Duncan) (Continental O-200-A)						
G-BVKU	Slingsby T 61F Venture T 2	1877	XZ557	22. 3.94	N R Bowers tr G-BVKU Syndicate	Kingston Deverill	6.12.07
G-BVKZ	Thunder Ax9-120 Balloon (Hot Air)	2547		23. 3.94	D J Head	Newbury	25. 7.00T
G-BVLD	Campbell Cricket	PFA G/01A-1163		29. 3.94	C Berry	Bruntingthorpe	15.10.08P
	(Built C Berry) (Arrow GT500)						
G-BVLE	McCandless M 4	PFA G/10-1232		29. 3.94	H Walls (Stonewalls , Victoria Bridge, Strabane)		
	(Built H Walls)				*(Stored 2006)*		
G-BVLF	CFM Starstreak Shadow SS-D	K 250-SSD		4. 3.94	R W Chatterton	Griffins Farm, Temple Bruer	11. 6.08P
	(Built B R Johnson- pr.no.PFA 206-12662)						
G-BVLG	Aérospatiale AS.355F1 Ecureuil 2	5011	N57745	31. 3.94	PLM Dollar Group Ltd	Cumbernauld	6. 4.08E
G-BVLL	Lindstrand LBL 210A Balloon (Hot Air)	101		9. 3.94	Airborne Balloon Flights Ltd		
						Paddock Wood, Tonbridge	6. 2.08T
G-BVLN	Aero Designs Pulsar XP	PFA 202-12530		6. 4.94	D A Campbell	(Cheadle, Stoke-on-Trent)	
	(Built D A Campbell)						
G-BVLP	Piper PA-38-112 Tomahawk II	38-82A0002	N91355	8. 4.94	M Housley	Derby	26. 5.08E
G-BVLR	Van's RV-4	PFA 181-12306		13. 4.94	S D Arnold and S J Moody tr RV4 Group		
	(Built M Weaver and S D Arnold) (Lycoming 0320-E2A)				*(Under construction 7.99)* (Leamington Spa and Coventry)		
G-BVLT	Bellanca 7GCBC Citabria 150S	1103-79	SE-GHV	6. 4.94	M A N Newall	Breighton	2.12.10S
G-BVLU	Druine D 31 Turbulent	PFA 1604		18. 4.94	C D Bancroft	Litlte Down Farm,Milson	17.11.08P
	(Built C D Bancroft) (Jabiru 2200A)						
G-BVLV	Europa Aviation Europa	039		10. 3.94	J T Naylor tr Euro 39 Group	Bidford	18. 9.08P
	(Built J T Naylor - pr.no.PFA 247-12585) (Monowheel u/c)						
G-BVLW	Avid Hauler Mk.4	PFA 189-12577		24. 3.94	J P Chappell (Newbiggin-on-Lune, Kirkby Stephen)		20.10.07P
	(Built D M Johnstone) (Hirth F30)						
G-BVLX	Slingsby T 61F Venture T 2	1973	ZA654	19. 4.94	T M Holloway tr RAF Gliding and Soaring Association		
					(Operated Fulmar Gliding Club)	Easterton	2. 5.08E
G-BVLZ	Lindstrand LBL 120A Balloon (Hot Air)	063		4. 3.94	Balloon Flights Club Ltd Kings Norton, Leicester		6.10.03T
G-BVMA	Beech 200 Super King Air	BB-797	G-VPLC	22. 7.93	Dragonfly Aviation Services LLP	Cardiff	26.10.07E
			N84B				
G-BVMC	Robinson R44 Astro	0060		15. 4.94	Tiger Helicopters Ltd	(Not known)	23. 7.06T
G-BVMF	Cameron V-77 Balloon (Hot Air)	3195		22. 4.94	P A Meecham	Milton-under-Wychwood	28. 1.08A
G-BVMH	Wag-Aero CUBy Sport Trainer PFA 108-12647			28. 4.94	J Mathews	(Trim, County Meath)	13. 6.08P
	(Built D M Jagger) (Continental C90-8)				*(As "624:D-39" in US Army c/s)*		
G-BVMI	Piper PA-18-150 Super Cub	18-4649	D-EIAC	6. 4.94	S Sampson	Morgansfield, Fishburn	3. 4.08E
	(Frame No.18-4613)		(PH-WDP), D-EIAC, D-EKAF, N10F				
	(Officially regd with c/n 18-8482 ex OH-PIN/N4262Z but rebuilt from D-EIAC [18-4649] after crash 15. 8.95)						
G-BVMJ	Cameron Eagle 95 SS Balloon (Hot Air)	3262		28. 4.94	R D Sargeant	Wollerau, Switzerland	23. 8.05A
G-BVML	Lindstrand LBL 210A Balloon (Hot Air)	094		29. 4.94	Ballooning Adventures Ltd	Hexham	25. 3.03T
G-BVMM	Robin HR.200-100 Club	41	F-BVMM	18. 8.80	J J Burch tr Gloster Aero Group	Gloucestershire	19.10.07E
G-BVMN	Ken Brock KB-2	PFA G/06-1218		29. 4.94	S A Scally	Kirkbride	7. 5.08P
	(Built S McCullagh)						
G-BVMR	Cameron V-90 Balloon (Hot Air)	3269		28. 3.94	I R Comley	Churchdown, Gloucester	8. 6.08A
					"*Midnight Rainbow*"		
G-BVMU	Aerostar Yakovlev Yak-52	9411809	YR-013	11. 5.94	Ascendances SPRL	Sint-Truiden, Belgium	14. 3.08P
					(As "09" in DOSAAF c/s)		

G-BVNG	de Havilland Moth Major		?	EC-AFK	17. 5.94	P and T.Groves	Lee-on-the-Solent	
				EE1-81, 30-81		*(On rebuild 4.03)*		
G-BVNI	Taylor JT.2 Titch	PFA 060-11107			20. 5.94	T V Adamson	Rufforth	
	(Built T V Adamson)					*(Noted 8.06)*		
G-BVNR	Cameron N-105 Balloon (Hot Air)		3288		24. 5.94	Liquigas SpA	Milan, Italy	22. 5.08A
	(New envelope c/n 4994@ 2001)							
G-BVNS	Piper PA-28-181 Cherokee Archer II			N6163J	13. 4.94	Scottish Airways Flyers (Prestwick) Ltd	Prestwick	9.10.07E
			28-7690358					
G-BVNU	FLS Aerospace Sprint Club		004		25. 5.94	M D R Elmes	(Bradfield, Manningtree)	27.10.07E
G-BVNY	Rans S-7 Courier		0290.072		24. 5.94	D M Byers-Jones	(Medstead, Alton)	19. 6.07P
	(Built J Whiting - pr.no.PFA 218-11951) (Rotax 532)							
G-BVOB	Fokker F 27 Friendship 500		10366	PH-FMN	5. 7.94	BAC Group Ltd	Southend	6.10.06T
				PT-LZM, F-BPNA, PH-FMN		*"Euro Trader" (In open store 2.08 less engines)*		
G-BVOC	Cameron V-90 Balloon (Hot Air)		3291		8. 6.94	H W R Stewart	Exton, Oakham	6. 9.08A
G-BVOH	Campbell Cricket replica	PFA G/03-1220			14. 6.94	G A Kitson	RAF Mona	14. 8.08P
	(Built B F Pearson) (Rotax 532)							
G-BVOI	Rans S-6-116 Coyote II		0893.524		14. 6.94	W G Goodall	(Adlingfleet, Goole)	23. 6.07P
	(Built A P Bacon - pr.no.PFA 204A-12712) (Rotax 582) (Tail-wheel u/c)							
G-BVOK	Aerostar Yakovlev Yak-52		9111505	RA-9111505	14. 6.94	Trans Holdings Ltd	Shoreham	3. 9.08P
				DOSAAF55		*(As "55" in DOSAAF c/s)*		
G-BVON	Lindstrand LBL 105A Balloon (Hot Air)		001	N532LB	16. 6.94	D J Farrar	Tadcaster	5. 3.06
				G-BVON				
G-BVOP	Cameron N-90 Balloon (Hot Air)		3317		21. 6.94	October Gold Ballooning Ltd t/a Mr.Lazenbys		
							Windermere	10. 2.07T
G-BVOR	CFM Streak Shadow	K 238-SA			31. 3.94	J M Chandler	Oakley	22.11.08P
	(Built J Lord -pr.no.PFA 206-12695) (Rotax 582)							
G-BVOS	Europa Aviation Europa		003		11. 4.94	D A Young tr Durham Europa Group		
	(Built D Collinson and D A Young- pr.no.PFA 247-12562) (Mid-West AE100R) (Monowheel u/c)						Shotton Colliery, Peterlee	13. 3.08P
						(Bounced landing Sandtoft 23. 3.06 and substantially damaged)		
G-BVOU	Hawker Siddeley HS.748 Series 2A/270		1721	CS-TAH	21. 6.94	PTB (Emerald) Proprietary Ltd	Blackpool	30. 7.07T
				G-11-6		*(Stored externally 2.08)*		
G-BVOV	Hawker Siddeley HS.748 Series 2A/372		1777	CS-TAO	21. 6.94	PTB (Emerald) Proprietary Ltd	Blackpool	11. 5.07T
				G-11-4		*(Stored externally 2.08)*		
G-BVOW	Europa Aviation Europa		084		27. 6.94	H P Brooks	(Haywards Heath)	30.10.07P
	(Built M W Cater - pr.no.PFA 247-12679) (Monowheel u/c)							
G-BVOX	Taylorcraft F-22		2208	N221UK	20. 5.94	R K Jordan	Leicester	30. 8.08E
G-BVOY	RotorWay Executive 90		5238		17. 6.94	Southern Helicopters Ltd	Street Farm, Takeley	
	(Built N J Bethell) (RotorWay RI 162)					*(Stored 2.08)*		
G-BVOZ	Colt 56A Balloon (Hot Air)		2595		21. 6.94	Balloon School (International) Ltd t/a British School of Ballooning		
							Colhook Common, Petworth	23. 4.08A
G-BVPA	Thunder Ax8-105 Series 2 Balloon (Hot Air)				24. 6.94	J Fenton t/a Firefly Balloon Promotions	Preston	2. 3.08T
			2600					
G-BVPD	CASA 1-131E Jungmann		2086	F-AZNG	12. 7.94	D Bruton	Abbeyshrule, County Longford	13. 3.07P
				Spanish AF E3B-482				
G-BVPK	Cameron O-90 Balloon (Hot Air)		3313		1. 7.94	D V Fowler	Cranbrook	10. 6.07T
G-BVPL	Zenair CH.601HD Zodiac	PFA 162-12693			4. 7.94	D A Trueman	Perth	10.11.08P
	(Built D Harker) (Continental O-200-A)							
G-BVPM	Evans VP-2		V2-1016		6.11.78	P Marigold	(Locking, Weston-super-Mare)	31. 5.94P
	(Built P Marigold - pr.no.PFA 7205) (Continental A65-8)					*(Stored 7.95)*		
G-BVPN	Piper J-3C-65 Cub		6917	G-TAFY	6. 7.94	K I Munro	Plymouth	11. 9.08P
				N31073, N38207, N38307, NC38307				
	(Officially regd with c/n 5298 but has Frame No.7002 which was N38207: probably used in rebuild of N31073 in early 1970s)							
G-BVPP	Folland Gnat T 1		FL.536	8620M	22. 4.94	Red Gnat Ltd	North Weald	14. 1.05P
				XP534		*(As "XR993" in RAF Red Arrows c/s 6.07)*		
G-BVPR	Robinson R22 Beta		1612	G-KNIT	17. 6.94	Helicentre Blackpool Ltd	Blackpool	4. 2.08E
G-BVPS	Jodel D 11		1403		6. 7.94	P J Sharp	Rush Green	25.10.08P
	(Built P J Sharp - pr.no.PFA 917) (Continental A65)							
G-BVPV	Lindstrand LBL 77B Balloon (Hot Air)		119		13. 7.94	A R Greensides	Burton Pidsea, Hull	20. 9.08A
						"Reverend Leonard"		
G-BVPW	Rans S-6-116 Coyote II		0294.587		12. 7.94	T B Woolley	(Narborough, Leicester)	17. 3.05P
	(Built J G Beesley - pr.no.PFA 204A-12737) (Rotax 582) (Tri-cycle u/c)							
G-BVPX	Bensen B 8 Tyro Gyro Mk.II		PCL125		13. 7.94	A W Harvey	Henstridge	19. 9.08P
	(Built P C Lovegrove - pr.no.PFA G/11-1237)							
G-BVPY	CFM Streak Shadow	K 204			14. 6.94	R J Mitchell	(Scalloway, Shetland)	24. 5.08P
	(Built R J Mitchell - pr.no.PFA 206-12375) (Rotax 582)					*(Operates from Tingwall)*		
G-BVRA	Europa Aviation Europa		008		25. 7.94	N E Stokes Haughton Farm, Haughton, Ellesmere		17.12.07P
	(Built E J J Pels - pr.no.PFA 247-12635) (Monowheel u/c)					*"Hummingbird"*		
G-BVRH	Taylorcraft BL-65		1657	N23929	15. 7.94	M J Kirk	Haverfordwest	23. 9.06
				G-BVRH, N24322, NC24322		*(New owner 10.06)*		
G-BVRK	Rans S-6-ESA Coyote II		1193.566	G-MYPK	14. 7.94	J Secular	(Beckenham)	
	(Built J Secular)							
G-BVRL	Lindstrand LBL 21A Balloon (Hot Air)		130		3. 8.94	A M Holly t/a Exclusive Ballooning	Berkeley	17. 1.05A
G-BVRR	Lindstrand LBL 77A Balloon (Hot Air)		133		9. 8.94	M Icam	Carquefou, France	11. 7.04A
G-BVRU	Lindstrand LBL 105A Balloon (Hot Air)		131		15. 8.94	R P Nash	Beighton, Norwich	16. 6.07A
G-BVRV	Van's RV-4		793	N144TH	23. 6.94	A Troughton	Armagh Field, Woodview	9. 5.07P
	(Built C Thomas Hahn) (Lycoming AEIO-320)							
G-BVRZ	Piper PA-18 Super Cub 95		18-3442	SE-ITP	22.11.94	R W Davison	Rhedyn Coch Farm, Rhuallt	13. 9.10S
	(Regd with Frame No.18-3381)				LN-LJG, D-EDCM, 96+19, QW+901, QZ+001, AC+507, AS+506, 54-752			
G-BVSB	TEAM Mini-MAX 91A	PFA 186-12241			1. 7.94	D G Palmer	Fetterangus	20.12.07P
	(Built C Nice) (Rotax 503)							
G-BVSD	Sud-Aviation SE.3130 Alouette II		1897	Swiss AF V-54	8. 9.94	M J Cuttell	Gloucestershire	28. 4.08E
						(As "V-54" in Swiss AF c/s)		
G-BVSF	Aero Designs Pulsar	PFA 202-12071			1. 7.94	S N and R J Freestone	Deanland	21.10.08P
	(Built S N and R J Freestone) (Tri-cycle u/c)							

G-BVSM	Rotary Air Force RAF 2000	EW-42		24. 8.94	S Ram	(Lowestoft)	24. 1.97P

G-BVSM Rotary Air Force RAF 2000　　　　EW-42　　　24. 8.94　S Ram　(Lowestoft)　24. 1.97P
(Built K Quigley and T M Truesdale) (Subaru EA82)　　(Noted eastbound on A303 at Amesbury 30.8.05)
G-BVSN Avid Speed Wing　　　PFA 189-12088　24. 8.94　R C Bowley　(Kerswell Green, Worcester)　26.10.06P
(Built D J Park)　　　　　　　　　　　(New owner 1.07)
G-BVSO Cameron A-120 Balloon (Hot Air)　3339　25. 8.94　A Kaye t/a Khaos Ballooning　Wellingborough　16. 6.08T
　　　　　　　　　　　　　　　　　　　(Cameron Balloons titles)
G-BVSP Hunting Percival P 84 Jet Provost T 3A PAC/W/6327 XM370　31. 8.94　H G Hodges and Son Ltd (Noted 1.07)　Hawarden　10. 6.04P
G-BVSS Jodel D 150 Mascaret　　118　22. 8.94　A P Burns　RAF Woodvale　19. 5.08P
(Built A P Burns - pr.no.PFA 151-11878 (Continental O-200-A)
G-BVST Jodel D 150 Mascaret　　130　11. 8.94　A Shipp　Full Sutton　9. 1.08P
(Built A Shipp - pr.no.PFA 235-12198) (Continental O-200-A)
G-BVSX TEAM Mini-MAX 91A　　PFA 186-12463　9. 9.94　J A Clark　Orchard Farm, Sittingbourne　18. 7.03P
(Built G N Smith) (Mosler MM CB-35)
G-BVSZ Pitts S-1E　　PFA 009-11235　9. 9.94　H J Morton　(L'Huisserie, France)　24.10.08P
(Built K Garrett and R P Millinship)
G-BVTA Tri-R KIS　　PFA 239-12450　26. 8.94　P J Webb　Dunkeswell　2. 8.08P
(Built P J Webb) (Continental O-240-E)
G-BVTC British Aircraft Corporation BAC 145 Jet Provost T 5A XW333　7. 9.94　Global Aviation Ltd　Humberside　22. 7.08P
　　　　EEP/JP/997　　　　　　　　(As "XW333" in RAF c/s)
G-BVTD CFM Streak Shadow　K 159-SA　14. 9.94　M Walton　Old Sarum　29. 8.07P
(Built M Walton - pr.no.PFA 206-11972) (Rotax 582)
G-BVTL Colt 31A Air Chair Balloon (Hot Air)　2572　5. 7.94　A Lindsay　Twickenham　15. 5.97
G-BVTM Reims Cessna F152 II　F15201827 G-WACS　31. 8.94　RAF Halton Aeroplane Club Ltd　RAF Halton　19. 9.08T
　　　　　　　　　D-EFGZ
G-BVTN Cameron N-90 Balloon (Hot Air)　3361　16. 9.94　P Zulehner　Peterskirchen, Austria　17. 7.08A
G-BVTV RotorWay Executive 90　5243/6599　16. 9.94　D W J Lee　(Northiam, Rye)　7. 9.08P
(Built J J Bull) (RotorWay RI 162)
G-BVTW Aero Designs Pulsar　PFA 202-12172　14. 9.94　R J Panther　(Stoke Golding, Nuneaton)　13.11.08P
(Built J D Webb)
G-BVTX de Havilland DHC-1 Chipmunk 22A　C1/0705 WP809　2. 8.94　P W Skinner tr TX Flying Group　Husbands Bosworth　20. 2.08E
　　　　　　　　　　　　　　　　　(As "WP809:78" in RN c/s)
G-BVUA Cameron O-105 Balloon (Hot Air)　3369　27. 9.94　D C Eager　Bracknell　28. 5.00A
G-BVUC Colt 56A Balloon (Hot Air)　2608 G-639　30. 9.94　J F Till　Welburn, York　3. 4.08A
("B" Conditions markings carried 9.94 as shown)　　(Corks and Cans Norton titles)
G-BVUG Betts TB.1　　PFA 265-12770　3.10.94　H F Fekete　(Melsomvik, Norway)　23. 5.07P
(Built T A Betts from modified AIA Stampe SV.4C c/n 1045 ex G-BEUS) (Tigre G IV-A2 120hp) (New owner 1.08)
G-BVUH Thunder Ax7-65B Balloon (Hot Air)　243 JA-A0075　3.10.94　K B Chapple　Montastruc, Hautes-Pyrenees, France　26. 4.08E
G-BVUI Lindstrand LBL 25A Cloudhopper Balloon (Hot Air)　5.10.94　J W Hole　Mondovi, Italy.　3. 8.08A
　　　　148
G-BVUJ Ken Brock KB-2　　PFA G/06-1244　10.10.94　R J Hutchinson　Kemble　17. 5.99P
(Built R J Hutchinson) (Rotax 503)
G-BVUK Cameron V-77 Balloon (Hot Air)　3372　11.10.94　H G Griffiths and W A Steel　Reading　30. 8.08A
G-BVUM Rans S-6-116 Coyote II　0893.528　11.10.94　M A Abbott　Glenrothes　16. 4.08P
(Built J L Donaldson - pr.no.PFA 204A-12685) (Rotax 582)
G-BVUN Van's RV-4　　3363UK　11.10.94　D J Harvey　(Bedale)　10. 5.08P
(Built I G Glenn - pr.no.PFA 181-12488) (Lycoming O-360)
G-BVUT Evans VP-1 Series 2　PFA 062-12092　24.10.94　M J Barnett　Shobdon　29. 9.99P
(Built P J Weston) (Volkswagen 1600)　　(Damaged on take off Pepperbox, Wiltshire 13. 3.99: on restoration 8.06)
G-BVUU Cameron C-80 Balloon (Hot Air)　3383　11.10.94　T M C McCoy　Peasedown St John, Bath　15. 6.05T
　　　　　　　　　　　　　　　　　"Ascent" (Stored 2007
G-BVUV Europa Aviation Europa　141　23. 9.94　R J Mills　Gamston　8. 8.08P
(Built R J Mills - pr.no.PFA 247-12762) (Monowheel u/c)
G-BVUZ Cessna 120　　11334 Z-YGH　20. 9.94　M J Medland　Leicester
　　　　　VP-YGH, VP-NAM, VP-YGH　(New owner 2.08)
G-BVVA IAV-Bacau Yakovlev Yak-52　8776109 LY-ANN　24.10.94　S T G Lloyd　Swansea　21. 3.08P
　　　　　DOSAAF 52
G-BVVB Carlson Sparrow II　PFA 209-11809　26. 9.94　L M McCullen　(North Ballachulish, Onich)　1. 8.06P
(Built L M McCullen) (Rotax 532)　　(Noted 5.07)
G-BVVE Wassmer Jodel D 112　1070 F-BKAJ　28.10.94　G D Gunby　Crowfield　11. 7.08P
G-BVVG Nanchang CJ-6A　2751219 (F-....)　10.10.94　R Davy tr Nanchang CJ6A Group　White Waltham　12.12.07P
(Yak 18)　　　　G-BVVG, Chinese PLAAF　(As "68" in Chinese AF c/s)
G-BVVH Europa Aviation Europa　014　31.10.94　T G Hoult　Octon Grange Farm, Foxholes　23. 8.07P
(Built T G Hoult and M P Whitley - pr.no.PFA 247-12505) (Monowheel u/c)
G-BVVI Hawker Audax I　? 2015M　3.11.94　Aero Vintage Ltd　(Northiam, Rye)
(Built Avro Aircraft Ltd)　K5600　　(On rebuild 8.95)
G-BVVK de Havilland DHC-6-310 Twin Otter　666 LN-BEZ　21.12.94　Loganair Ltd　Glasgow　12. 1.07E
G-BVVL EAA Acrosport II　PFA 072A-10887　11.11.94　G A Breen　Portimão, Faro, Portugal　6. 9.07P
(Built D Park, A J Maxwell and P Price) (Lycoming O-360)
G-BVVM Zenair CH.601HD Zodiac　PFA 162-12539　3.10.94　D Macdonald　Popham　6. 2.08P
(Built J G Small)
G-BVVN Brügger MB.2 Colibri　PFA 043-10979　12.10.94　T C Darters　Valley Farm, Winwick　19. 5.08P
(Built N F Andrews) (Volkswagen 1834)
G-BVVP Europa Aviation Europa　088　20. 9.94　I Mansfeld　Kemble　24. 4.08P
(Built J S Melville - pr.no.PFA 247-12697) (Monowheel u/c)
G-BVVR Stits SA-3A Playboy　P-736 N4620S　14.11.94　R A Chapman　Breighton　23.11.08P
(Built S Goins) (Continental A65)
G-BVVS Van's RV-4　　PFA 181-12324　15.11.94　E C and N S C English　North Weald　22. 5.08P
(Built E C English) (Lycoming O-320)
G-BVVU Lindstrand LBL Four SS Balloon (Hot Air)　155 HB-QAP　18.11.94　Magical Adventures Ltd
　　　　　　　G-BVVU　　West Bloomfield, Michigan, US　6.12.01P
G-BVVW IAV-Bacau Yakovlev Yak-52　844605 RA-01361　16.11.94　M Blackman　Cherry Tree Farm, Monewden　19.10.08P
(Official c/n suspect as plate shows 833519)　DOSAAF 15, DOSAAF 95
G-BVVZ Corby CJ-1 Starlet　PFA 134-12293　9.11.94　P V Flack　Lasham　27. 1.04P
(Built A E Morris) (Volkswagen 1834)

G-BVWB	Thunder Ax8-90 Series 2 Balloon (Hot Air)	3000		2.12.94	M A Stelling, K C and K Tanner		
					"Starship" Barton-Le-Clay, Thame and Sutton		18. 6.08
G-BVWC	English Electric Canberra B 2	71399	WK163	2.12.94	Classic Aviation Projects Ltd	Coventry	29. 6.08P
	(Built Avro Aircraft Ltd) (Regd as B 6 but c/n relates to nose section originally fitted to XH568) (As "WK163" in RAF 617 Sqdn c/s)						
G-BVWI	Cameron Light Bulb 65 SS Balloon (Hot Air)			8.12.94	A D Kent tr Balloon Preservation Flying Group		
		3405			"Phillips Energy Saver" (New owner 6.04)	Petworth	2. 6.97A
G-BVWM	Europa Aviation Europa	070		14.12.94	A Aubeelack tr Europa Syndicate	White Waltham	13. 3.07P
	(Built A Aubeelack and C J Hadley - pr.no.PFA 247-12620) (Monowheel u/c)						
G-BVWW	Lindstrand LBL 90A Balloon (Hot Air)	169		28.12.94	Drawflight Ltd "Double Whiskey"	Hastings	29. 3.07A
G-BVWY	Porterfield CP-65	720	N27223	23.11.94	R L Earl and B Morris Landmead Farm, Garford		28. 3.08P
	(Continental A65)		NC27223				
G-BVWZ	Piper PA-32-301 Saratoga	3206055	I-TASP	3. 1.95	M A Kesteven tr The Saratoga (WZ) Group (Ryton)		4. 4.08E
			N9184N				
G-BVXA	Cameron N-105 Balloon (Hot Air)	3441		4. 1.95	R E Jones (Ribby Hall titles) Lytham St Annes		19. 3.05T
G-BVXB	Cameron V-77 Balloon (Hot Air)	3442		4. 1.95	J A Lawton "Pat McLean"	Godalming	7.11.07A
G-BVXD	Cameron O-84 Balloon (Hot Air)	3432		5. 1.95	J R Wilson tr Hedge Hoppers Balloon Group	Oxford	18. 7.08A
G-BVXE	Steen Skybolt	PFA 064-11123	G-LISA	5. 1.95	J Buglass	Sleap	30. 6.08P
	(Built T C Humphreys and T J Reeve)				"Billie"		
G-BVXF	Cameron O-120 Balloon (Hot Air)	3400		21. 9.94	Off The Ground Balloon Co Ltd Lyth, Kendal		6. 2.08T
G-BVXJ	Bücker Bü.133 Jungmeister	?	Spanish AF E1-9	11. 1.95	A C Mercer	Breighton	22. 5.06P
	(Built CASA) (Official c/n is "E1-9")		Spanish AF ES1-9, 35-9		*(Also carries "ES-9" on tail in Spanish Air Force c/s) (Noted 12.07)*		
G-BVXK	Aerostar Yakovlev Yak-52	9111306	RA-44508 (1)	12. 1.95	E G Gavazzi	White Waltham	12. 5.08P
			DOSAAF 26		*(As "26" in DOSAAF c/s)*		
G-BVXM	Aérospatiale AS.350B Ecureuil	2013	I-AUDI	10. 1.95	The Berkeley Leisure Group Ltd	Sparkford	5. 3.08E
			I-CIOC				
G-BVXR	de Havilland DH.104 Devon C 2	04436	XA880	13. 1.95	M Whale and M W A Lunn Little Rissington		
					(Stored as "XA880" in RAE c/s 1.08)		
G-BVXS	Taylorcraft BC-12D	9284	N96984	27. 1.95	M Hickin and R I Biddles tr XRay Sierra Group		
	(Continental A65)		NC96984			Leicester	4. 7.08P
G-BVYF	Piper PA-31-350 Navajo Chieftain	31-7952102	G-SAVE	8. 2.95	J A, G M, D T A and J A Rees		
			N3518T		t/a Messrs Rees of Poynston West	Haverfordwest	23. 1.08E
G-BVYG	Robin DR.300-180R Remorqueur	611	F-BSQB	9. 1.95	Ulster Gliding Club Ltd	Bellarena	11. 4.08E
			F-BSPI				
G-BVYK	TEAM Mini-MAX 91A	PFA 186-12598		13. 2.95	A G Ward Longacre Farm, Sandy		14.10.07P
	(Built S B Churchill) (DAF) (Officially regd with Rotax 447)						
G-BVYM	Robin DR.300-180R Remorqueur	656	F-BTBL	9.12.94	London Gliding Club Proprietary Ltd Dunstable		19. 7.08E
G-BVYO	Robin R2160	288		11. 1.95	D J S McClean	City of Derry	30. 4.08E
G-BVYP	Piper PA-25-235 Pawnee B	25-3481	N7475D	13. 2.95	Bidford Gliding Ltd	Bidford	23. 5.08E
			OY-CLT, N7475Z				
G-BVYU	Cameron A-140 Balloon (Hot Air)	3544		17. 2.95	Balloon Flights Club Ltd	Leicester	20.11.07T
G-BVYX	Avid Speed Wing Mk.4	PFA 189-12370		16. 2.95	M E Lloyd (Totton, Southampton)		5. 4.06P
	(Built G J Keen)						
G-BVYY	Pietenpol AirCamper	PFA 047-12559		20. 2.95	T F Harrison tr Pietenpol G-BVYY Group		
	(Built J R Orchard)				(New owners 9.04) (Perton, Wolverhampton)		
G-BVYZ	Stemme S 10-V	14-011	D-KGDD	6. 3.95	A D Gubbay	Bicester	4. 5.08E
G-BVZD	Tri-R KIS	PFA 239-12416		21. 2.95	G A Haines	Carlisle	24. 7.08P
	(Built R T Clegg) (Canadian Air Motive CAM.100) (Tri-cycle u/c)						
G-BVZE	Boeing 737-59D	26422	SE-DNL	7. 3.95	British Midland Airways Ltd East Midlands		22. 3.08E
					"Little Costa Baby" (Operated bmiBaby)		
G-BVZG	Boeing 737-5Q8	25160	SE-DNF	12. 4.95	British Midland Airways Ltd East Midlands		1. 5.08E
					(Operated bmiBaby)		
G-BVZI	Boeing 737-5Q8	25167	SE-DNH	15. 5.95	British Midland Airways Ltd East Midlands		11. 6.08E
					(Operated bmiBaby)		
G-BVZJ	Rand Robinson KR-2	PFA 129-11049		21. 2.95	P D'Arcy Button	AAC Netheravon	25. 2.08P
	(Built J P McConnell-Wood) (Revmaster) (Damaged 15. 7.98 and rebuilt with KR2 fuselage pr.no.PFA 129-11174 c 2004-5)						
G-BVZN	Cameron C-80 Balloon (Hot Air)	3546		28. 2.95	S J Clarke	Watford	16. 2.07A
G-BVZO	Rans S-6-116 Coyote II	0494.606		1. 3.95	P J Brion	Barton Ashes	5. 3.08P
	(Built P Atkinson pr.no.PFA 204A-12710) (Rotax 582) (Tri-cycle u/c)						
G-BVZR	Zenair CH.601HD Zodiac	PFA 162-12417		2. 3.95	R A Perkins	Bicester	10. 9.08P
	(Built J D White) (Tri-cycle u/c)						
G-BVZT	Lindstrand LBL 90A Balloon (Hot Air)	183		9. 3.95	J W Adkins and J Edwards		
					Market Harborough and Northampton		27. 6.08A
G-BVZV	Rans S-6-116N Coyote II	1294.708		16. 2.95	A R White	Popham	13. 6.05P
	(Built J Fothergill - pr.no.PFA 204A-12832: kit no.reported also as 0195.719 and possibly repaired with kit no.0493.471) (Rotax 582)						
G-BVZX	Cameron H-34 Balloon (Hot Air)	3564		15. 3.95	J B Turnau tr Chianti Balloon Club Siena, Italy		16. 6.08A
G-BVZZ	de Havilland DHC-1 Chipmunk 22	C1/0687	WP795	5. 1.95	D C Murray tr Portsmouth Naval Gliding Club (Noted 5.05)		
					(As "WP795:901" in RN c/s) Husbands Bosworth		14. 6.04

G-BWAA - G-BWZZ

G-BWAA	Cameron N-133 Balloon (Hot Air)	3471		9. 3.95	C and J M Bailey t/a Bailey Balloons	Bristol	14.11.04T
					(Brunel Ford titles)		
G-BWAB	Jodel D 140 Mousquetaire	PFA 251-12469		25. 1.95	W A Braim	(Driffield)	25.11.08P
	(Built W A Braim) (Lycoming O-360)						
G-BWAC	Waco YKS-7	4693	N50RA	19. 8.92	D N Peters	Little Gransden	18. 7.08
	(Jacobs R-755)		N2896D, NC50				
G-BWAD	Rotary Air Force RAF 2000	147		27. 2.95	Newtonair (Gyroplanes) Ltd	Henstridge	22.11.08P
	(Built J R Legge - pr.no.PFA G/13-1254) (Subaru EA82)				(Operated A Melody)		
G-BWAF	Hawker Hunter F 6A	S4/U/3393	8831M	24. 2.95	RV Aviation Ltd	Bournemouth	
	(Built Armstrong-Whitworth Aircraft)		XG160		*(As "XG160:U" in CFS Black Arrows c/s: displayed Aviation Museum 12.07)*		
G-BWAG	Cameron O-120 Balloon (Hot Air)	3478		3. 2.95	P M Skinner "Joker" Chart Sutton, Maidstone		9. 6.08A
G-BWAH	Montgomerie-Bensen B 8MR	PFA G/01-1208		16. 3.95	J B Allan (Corringham, Stanford-le-Hope)		13. 6.07P
	(Built S J O Tinn) (Rotax 582)				"The Flyng Sealander" and "The Flying Scotsman" (Noted Henstridge 8.07)		

G-BWAI	CFM Streak Shadow SA	K 235-SA		21. 3.95	C M James	Kemble	15. 7.04P

(Built J M Heath - pr.no.PFA 206-12556 but originally allocated as pr.no.BMAA/HB/052 C 1990) (Rotax 582) (Noted 1.05)

G-BWAJ	Cameron V-77 Balloon (Hot Air)	3579		22. 3.95	K Graham *(New owner 2.08)*	Spennymoor	8. 7.07A
G-BWAN	Cameron N-77 Balloon (Hot Air)	3499		24. 3.95	I Chadwick tr Balloon Preservation Flying Group		
					(BPG tiltes)	Partridge Green, Horsham	3.10.08A
G-BWAO	Cameron C-80 Balloon (Hot Air)	3436		24. 3.95	S Mitchell and M D Freeston	(Hertford)	5. 4.08E
G-BWAP	Clutton FRED Series III	PFA 029-10959		24. 3.95	G A Shepherd	(Mutford, Beccles)	

(Built R J Smyth)

G-BWAR	Denney Kitfox Model 3	PFA 172-12432		16. 3.95	I Wightman	(Berwick-upon-Tweed)	10. 9.08P

(Built C E Brookes)

G-BWAT	Pietenpol AirCamper	PFA 047-11594		15. 3.95	P W Aitchison	Enstone	10. 2.06P

(Built D R Waters) (Continental C90)   *(Stored 7.07)*

G-BWAU	Cameron V-90 Balloon (Hot Air)	3569		27. 3.95	A M and K M Hall	London N10	3. 5.08A
G-BWAV	Schweizer 269C	S 1204	SE-JAY	28. 2.95	B Maggs t/a Helihire	Shere, Guildford	31. 8.07T
	(Schweizer 300)		LN-OTS, OY-HDW, N41S		*(Noted 10.07)*		
G-BWAW	Lindstrand LBL 77A Balloon (Hot Air)	207		28. 3.95	D Bareford *(Seton Healthcare titles)*	Kidderminster	29. 5.06A
G-BWBA	Cameron V-65 Balloon (Hot Air)	3456		27. 2.95	P G Dunnington tr Dante Balloon Group		
					(British Airways titles)	Newtown, Hungerford	2. 2.08A
G-BWBB	Lindstrand LBL 14A Balloon (Hot Air) *(Gas filled)*			3. 4.95	Oxford Promotions (UK) Ltd	(Kentucky, US)	
		222			*(Operated F Prell)*		
G-BWBE	Colt Flying Ice Cream Cone SS Balloon (Hot Air)			3. 4.95	Stratos Ballooning Gmbh and Co KG		
		3560				Ennigerloh, Germany	5. 5.05A
G-BWBF	Colt Flying Ice Cream Cone SS Balloon (Hot Air)			3. 4.95	Stratos Ballooning Gmbh and Co KG		
		3561				Ennigerloh, Germany	17. 4.03A
G-BWBI	Taylorcraft F-22A	2207	N22UK	3. 4.95	R T G Preston	Little Rissington	5. 8.08E
G-BWBJ	Colt 21A Balloon (Hot Air)	3532		6. 4.95	U Schneider	Giessen, Germany	28. 3.08A
G-BWBO	Lindstrand LBL 77A Balloon (Hot Air)	157		10. 4.95	T J Orchard, N J Glover and S R Godfrey	Aylesbury	29. 8.08A
G-BWBT	Lindstrand LBL 90A Balloon (Hot Air)	184		3. 4.95	British Telecommunications PLC *(BT titles)*	Newbury	9. 4.05A
G-BWBY	Schleicher ASH 26E	26076		30. 8.95	J S Wand	Bidford	24.11.07E
G-BWBZ	ARV Aviation ARV-1 Super 2	PFA 152-12802		10. 3.95	J A Straw	Langar	23. 4.07P

(Built J N C Shields and officially regd as "ARV K1 Super 2") (Mid-West AE.100R) (Noted 6.07)

G-BWCA	CFM Streak Shadow	K 160		19. 4.95	I C Pearson	(Horsham)	11. 7.07P

(Built R Thompson - pr.no.PFA 206-11985) (Rotax 582)

G-BWCC	Van Den Bemden 460m3 (Gas) Free Balloon "022"	PH-BOX		5. 4.95	R W Batchelor tr Piccard Balloon Group	Thame	
	(C/n may be a corruption of Netherlands owner 622)				*"Prof A Piccard"*		

(Netherlands records indicate some parts came from OO-BGX which itself became G-BBFS)

G-BWCG	Lindstrand LBL 42A Balloon (Hot Air)	223		25. 4.95	Oxford Promotions (UK) Ltd	(Kentucky, US)	10. 1.97A
					(Operated F Prell)		
G-BWCK	Everett Gyroplane Series 3	036		26. 4.95	B F Pearson	(Eakring, Newark)	28. 3.08P
	(Rotax 582)						
G-BWCO	Dornier Do.28D-2 Skyservant	4337	EI-CJU	19. 6.95	Wingglider Ltd	Hibaldstow	19. 5.99A
			(N5TK), 5N-AOH, D-ILIF		*(Stored 7.04)*		
G-BWCS	British Aircraft Corporation BAC 145 Jet Provost T 5A	XW293		28. 4.95	J H Ashcroft	Bournemouth	15. 3.02P
		EEP/JP/957			*(As "XW293:Z" in RAF c/s) (Test flown 23. 8.07 after overhaul)*		
G-BWCT	Tipsy Nipper T 66 Series 1	T66/11	"OO-NIC"	27. 4.95	J S Hemmings and C R Steer		
	(Built Avions Fairey SA)		PH-MEC, D-EMEC, OO-NIC			(Heathfield and Bexhill-on-Sea)	
G-BWCV	Europa Aviation Europa	041		4. 5.95	G V McKirdy	Enstone	13. 7.07P
	(Built M P Chetwynd-Talbot - pr.no.PFA 247-12591) (NSI EA-81/100) (Monowheel u/c) (Struck hedge landing Portbury 16.7.06 and substantially damaged)						
G-BWCY	Murphy Rebel	058R		15. 5.95	S Burrow	(Wentbridge, Pontefract)	11. 7.08P
	(Built A Jones, R Hallam and A Koneczek - pr.no.PFA 232-12135)						
G-BWDA	Aérospatiale-Alenia ATR 72-202	444	F-WQNG	29. 6.95	Aurigny Air Services Ltd	Guernsey	28. 8.08E
			G-BWDA, (9M-AMB), G-AWDA, F-WWEQ				
G-BWDB	Aérospatiale-Alenia ATR 72-202	449	F-WQNI	14. 6.95	Aurigny Air Services Ltd	Guernsey	16. 9.08E
			G-BWDB, (9M-AMA) G-AWDB, F-WWEE				
G-BWDF	PZL-104 Wilga 35A	21950955		17. 5.95	Sky Banners Ltd	Dunsfold	3. 6.07A
					(Substantially damaged Dunsfold 6.8.06)		
G-BWDH	Cameron N-105 Balloon (Hot Air)	3549		22. 5.95	Bridges Van Hire Ltd	Awsworth, Nottingham	2.10.08T
G-BWDM	Lindstrand LBL 120A Balloon (Hot Air)	263	(F-GYDM)	26. 5.95	A N F Pertwee	Frinton-on-Sea	14. 2.02T
			(F-GUMP), G-BWDM		*(New owner 10.05)*		
G-BWDP	Europa Aviation Europa	062		7. 6.95	S Attubato	Bodmin	23. 8.07P
	(Built I Valentine - pr.no.PFA 247-12637) (Monowheel u/c)						
G-BWDR	Hunting Percival P 84 Jet Provost T 3A	PAC/W/6603	XM376	6. 6.95	Global Aviation Ltd *(New owner 12.05)*	Humberside	24.10.02P
G-BWDS	Hunting Percival P 84 Jet Provost T 3A "PAC/W/932"		XM424	6. 6.95	A W Brown tr XM424 Group	(Manchester)	4.10.06P
	(Correct c/n PAC/W/9231?)		(N77506?), XM424		*(As "XM424" in RAF c/s) (New owner 1.08)*		
G-BWDT	Piper PA-34-220T Seneca III	34-8233045	PH-TWI	21. 9.88	H R Chambers	Blackbushe	19.11.06T
			G-BKHS, N8472H				
G-BWDU	Cameron V-90 Balloon (Hot Air)	3143		19. 6.95	D M Roberts	Llandeilo	1. 2.08A
G-BWDV	Schweizer 269C	S 1712	N86G	16. 6.95	Flightframe Ltd	(Pontardawe, Swansea)	5. 9.08E
	(Schweizer 300)						
G-BWDX	Europa Aviation Europa	056		13. 6.95	J Robson	(Church Crookham, Fleet)	6. 8.07P
	(Built J B Crane - pr.no.PFA 247-12603) (Monowheel u/c)						
G-BWDZ	Sky 31-24 Balloon (Hot Air)	002		13. 6.95	Westcountry Ballooning Ltd	Queen Camel, Yeovil	25. 4.08T
G-BWEA	Lindstrand LBL 120A Balloon (Hot Air)	252		14. 6.95	S R Seager *(Parrott and Coales titles)*	Aylesbury	8. 7.00T
G-BWEB	British Aircraft Corporation BAC 145 Jet Provost T 5A	XW422		19. 6.95	S Patrick	Hawarden	27. 7.08P
		EEP/JP/1044			*(As "XW422" in RAF c/s)*		
G-BWEE	Cameron V-42 Balloon (Hot Air)	3480		8. 3.95	A J Davey	Aschaffenburg, Germany	14.10.08A
G-BWEF	SNCAN Stampe SV-4C(G)	208	G-BOVL	13. 5.93	D A Smith tr Acebell BWEF Syndicate	Redhill	4. 6.10S
			N20SV, F-BHES, F-BBLC				
G-BWEG	Europa Aviation Europa	053		4. 4.95	R J Marsh	Exeter	5. 6.08P
	(Built B A Selmes and R J Marsh - pr.no.PFA 247-12600) (Conventional u/c)						
G-BWEM	Vickers Supermarine 358 Seafire L III	?	IAC.157	28. 6.95	C J Warrilow and S W Atkins	(Exeter)	
	(Build Westland Aircraft Ltd)		RX168		*(On rebuild 10.01)*		
G-BWEN	Macair Merlin GT	050194		20. 6.95	D A Hill (Terrington St Clement, King's Lynn)		7.12.95P
	(Built B W Davies - pr.no.PFA 208A-12859) (Subaru EA81)				*(New owner 5.04)*		

G-BWEU	Reims Cessna F152 II	F15201894	EI-BNC	15. 6.95	Affair Aircraft Leasing LLP	Leeds-Bradford	23. 9.07T
			N9097Y				
G-BWEV	Cessna 152 II	15283182	EI-BVU	28. 6.95	MK Aero Support Ltd	Andrewsfield	9.11.07E
			N47184		*(Force landed in field Sandon, Chelmsford 2. 5.07 and damaged: noted 10.07)*		
G-BWEW	Cameron N-105 Balloon (Hot Air)	3637		30. 6.95	Unipart Group Ltd tr Unipart Balloon Club	Cowley	3. 3.06A
					(Unipart titles)		
G-BWEY	Bensen B 8	PFA G/01-1197		3. 7.95	F G Shepherd	(Leadgate, Alston)	
	(Built F G Shepherd)						
G-BWEZ	Piper J-3C-85 Cub	6021	N29050	3. 7.95	J G McTaggart	Archerfield Estate, Dirleton	9. 5.08P
			NC29050		*(As "436021" in USAAF c/s)*		
G-BWFG	Robin HR.200-120	293		20. 7.95	RVL Aviation Ltd	Coventry	15. 3.08E
G-BWFH	Europa Aviation Europa	201		14. 7.95	B L Wratten	Deanland	10. 8.07P
	(B L Wratten and R W Baylie - pr.no.PFA 247-12842) (Monowheel u/c)						
G-BWFI	HOAC DV.20 Katana	20128		17. 7.95	Air Aqua Ltd	Scotland Farm, Hook	22. 8.08E
G-BWFJ	Evans VP-1	PFA 062-10349		1. 9.78	P A West	(Middle Spillmans, Stroud)	27. 1.93P
	(Built W E Jones) (Volkswagen 1600)				*(Stored 5.94)*		
G-BWFK	Lindstrand LBL 77A Balloon (Hot Air)	289		17. 7.95	R S Kent tr Balloon Preservation Flying Group		
					"Mr Orange"	Petworth	7. 8.06A
G-BWFM	Yakovlev Yak-50	781208	NX5224R	19. 7.95	J Hurrell tr Fox Mike Group	Blackpool	6.10.06P
			DDR-WQX, DM-WQX		*(Noted 10.07)*		
G-BWFN	HAPI Cygnet SF-2A	PFA 182-11335		19. 7.95	K Shelton and G J Green tr G-BWFN Group Hucknall		
	(Built T Crawford)				*Noted hangared 6.07 and still not flown)*		
G-BWFO	Colomban MC-15 Cri-Cri	PFA 133-11253		19. 7.95	K D and C S Rhodest		
	(Built O G Jones) (JPX PUL-212)				*(Noted 1.08)*	Bourne Park, Hurstbourne Tarrant	
G-BWFP	IAV-Bacau Yakovlev Yak-52	855503	RA-44501 (1)	20. 7.95	M C Lee	Spanhoe	11.10.08P
	(Official c/n suspect as plate shows 855606 - composite?)		DOSAAF 43, DOSAAF 61 *(blue)*				
G-BWFR	Hawker Hunter F 58	41H-697398	Swiss AF J-4031	24. 7.95	Classic Aviation Ltd	RAF Scampton	3. 8.99P
					(New owner 7.06 - stored as "J-4031")		
G-BWFT	Hawker Hunter T 8M	41H-695332	XL602	24. 7.95	Global Aviation Services Ltd	Exeter	23. 7.99P
					(As "XL602": on rebuild 1.07)		
G-BWFV	HOAC DV.20 Katana	20132		26. 7.95	J P E Walsh t/a Walsh Aviation	Cranfield	10.10.07E
G-BWFX	Europa Aviation Europa	038		26. 7.95	A D Stewart	Rayne Hall Farm, Braintree	11. 3.08P
	(Built A D Stewart - pr.no.PFA 247-12586) (Monowheel u/c)						
G-BWFZ	Murphy Rebel	PFA 232-12536	G-SAVS	19. 7.95	S Beresford	Gamston	10. 7.08P
	(Built I E Spencer)						
G-BWGA	Lindstrand LBL 105A Balloon (Hot Air)	295		2. 8.95	R Thompson	Berry Grove Farm, Liss	29. 7.08A
G-BWGF	British Aircraft Corporation BAC 145 Jet Provost T 5A		XW325	10. 8.95	Viper Jet Provost Group Ltd	Hawarden	30. 9.08P
		EEP/JP/989			*(As "XW325:E" in RAF c/s)*		
G-BWGG	Max Holste MH.1521C1 Broussard	20	F-GGKG	10. 7.95	M J Burnett Jnr and R B Maalouf	Kemble	16. 9.06
			F-WGKG, French Military		*(As "20:315-SQ" in French Army c/s)*		
G-BWGJ	Chilton DW.1A	PFA 225-12615		11. 8.95	T J Harrison	Phoenix Farm Lower Upham	
	(Built T J Harrison) (Lycoming O-145-A2)				*(Complete 5.00)*		
G-BWGK	Hawker Hunter GA.11	HABL-003032	XE689	15. 8.95	B R Pearson tr GA11 Group	Kemble	11. 7.01P
	(Centre fuselage no.is 41HR HABL 003032)				*(Stored as "XE689:864-VL" 8.06)*		
G-BWGL	Hawker Hunter T 8C	HABL-003086	XF357	15. 8.95	Stichting Hawker Hunter Foundation		
	(Officially regd with c/n 41H-695946)				Leeuwarden, Netherlands		12. 3.08P
					(As "N-321" in R Netherlands AF c/s)'		
G-BWGM	Hawker Hunter T 8C	HABL-003008	XE665	15. 8.95	B J Pearson tr The Admirals Barge	Kemble	24. 6.98P
	(Officially regd with c/n 41H-695940)				*(Noted 3.07 as "XE665:876:VL")*		
G-BWGN	Hawker Hunter T 8C	41H-670689	WT722	15. 8.95	B J Pearson tr T8C Group	(Exeter)	3. 9.97P
					(In open store as "WT722:878:VL" 12.05)		
G-BWGO	Slingsby T 67M-200 Firefly	2048	SE-LBC	15. 8.95	R Gray	Fairoaks	10. 7.08E
G-BWGP	Cameron C-80 Balloon (Hot Air)	3631		17. 8.95	Zebedee Balloon Service Ltd	Newtown, Hungerford	9. 4.07A
G-BWGS	British Aircraft Corporation BAC 145 Jet Provost T 5A		XW310	18. 8.95	G-BWGS Ltd	North Weald	2. 9.08P
		EEP/JP/974			*"Where Eagles Share"*		
G-BWGT	Hunting Percival P 84 Jet Provost T 4	PAC/W/21624	8991M	21. 8.95	G M Snow	(Wigan)	20 7.06P
	(Reported as c/n PAC/W/19992)		XR679		*(New owner 2.08)*		
G-BWGX	Cameron N-42 Balloon (Hot Air)	3633		21. 8.95	Newbury Building Society	Newbury	25.10.05A
					(Newbury Building Society titles)		
G-BWGY	HOAC DV.20 Katana	20134		22. 8.95	Stars Fly Ltd	Elstree	18.11.07E
G-BWHC	Cameron N-77 Balloon (Hot Air)	3647		25. 8.95	R B Craik	Naseby, Northampton	23. 6.04A
					(Travelsphere Holidays titles) (Inflated 4.06)		
G-BWHD	Lindstrand LBL 31A Balloon (Hot Air)	292		29. 8.95	Directorate Army Aviation	Middle Wallop	20. 3.08A
G-BWHF	Piper PA-31-325 Navajo C/R	31-7612076	F-GECA	7. 9.95	Awyr Cymru Cyf	Welshpool	1.11.07E
			D-IBIS, N59862				
G-BWHG	Cameron N-65 Balloon (Hot Air)	3619		7. 9.95	M Stefanini and F B Alaoui	Firenze, Italy	31. 3.07A
G-BWHI	de Havilland DHC-1 Chipmunk 22	C1/0637	WK624	8. 9.95	N E M Clare	Blackpool	2. 3.08T
	(Hulk of WK624/M may have been used in rebuild of G-AOSY c1998/99)				*(As "WK624:M" in RAF c/s)*		
G-BWHK	Rans S-6-116 Coyote II	0695.834		15. 9.95	D A Buttress	Charity Farm, Baxterley	12. 5.07P
	(Built N D White - pr.no.PFA 204A-12908) (Tri-cycle u/c)						
G-BWHP	CASA 1-131E Jungmann	2109	Spanish AF E3B-513	18. 8.95	J F Hopkins	Watchford Farm, Yarcombe	19. 6.08P
					(As "S4+A07" in Luftwaffe c/s)		
G-BWHR	Tipsy Nipper T 66 Series 1	PFA 025-12843	(OO-KAM)	19. 9.95	L R Marnef	(Koningshooikt, Belgium)	
	(Built L R Marnef)		OO-69 *(Composite homebuild of original Fairey build c/ns 29 and 71)*				
G-BWHS	Rotary Air Force RAF 2000	PFA G/13-1253		25. 9.95	A W Findlay and B J Payne	(Aberdeen)	28. 9.07P
	(Built V G Freke) (Subaru EA82)				*(New owners 12.07)*		
G-BWHU	Westland Scout AH.1	F9517	XR595	27. 9.95	N J F Boston	North Weald	11. 6.08P
					(As "XR595:M" in AAC c/s)		
G-BWHY	Robinson R22	0098	N90366	24. 3.87	P Boal	Newtownards	30. 8.08E
G-BWIA	Rans S-10 Sakota	xxxx.xxx		15. 9.95	L H and M van Cleeff	Lydd	24. 7.07P
	(Built P A Beck - pr.no.PFA 194-12044) (Rotax 582)				*(Engine failed during touch and go Kingsnorth, Kent 7. 4.07 and substantially damaged)*		
G-BWIB	Scottish Aviation Bulldog Series 120/122		Ghana AF G-103	10.10.95	B I Robertson	(Pontiac, Michigan, US)	16. 6.08T
		BH120/227			*(As "XX514" in RAF c/s)*		

G-BWID	Druine D 31 Turbulent	201	F-PHFR	16.10.95	A M Turney	Cheddington	21. 7.05P
	(Built R Druine and H Gindre) (Volkswagen 1200)						
G-BWII	Cessna 150G	15065308		22. 9.95	J D G Hicks	Sturgate	25. 2.08E
			(G-BSKB), N4008J				
G-BWIJ	Europa Aviation Europa	006		19.10.95	R Lloyd	(Upper Dormington, Hereford)	
	(Built R Lloyd - pr.no.PFA 247-12513)			*(Landed with u/c fully retracted position Kemble 23. 5.07 and substantially damaged)*			
G-BWIK	de Havilland DH.82A Tiger Moth	86417	7015M	20.10.95	B J Ellis	Little Gransden	
			NL985		*(On rebuild as "NL985")*		
G-BWIL	Rans S-10 Sakota	1089.065	G-WIEN	4.10.95	S H Leahy	Lower Mountpleasant Farm, Chatteris	12. 4.07P
	(Built J C Longmore - pr.no.PFA 194-11770) (Rotax 582)				*(New owner 8.07)*		
G-BWIP	Cameron N-90 Balloon (Hot Air)	3668		20.10.95	S H Fell *(New owner 9.02)*	Carlisle	27.10.96A
G-BWIR	Dornier 328-100	3023	D-CDXF	18.10.95	Suckling Airways (Cambridge) Ltd t/a Scot Airways		
			N328DA, D-CDHH			London City	19.10.07E
G-BWIV	Europa Aviation Europa	210		27.10.95	T G Ledbury	(Holyport, Maidenhead)	9. 9.99P
	(Built J R Lockwood-Goose - pr.no.PFA 247-12871) (Rotax 912) (Monowheel u/c)						
G-BWIW	Sky 180-24 Balloon (Hot Air)	008		1.11.95	T M Donnelly	Sprotborough, Doncaster	24. 4.08T
G-BWIX	Sky 120-24 Balloon (Hot Air)	009		31.10.95	J M Percival	Bourton-on-the-Wolds, Loughborough	20.12.07
					"Mayfly III" (Inflated 4.06)		
G-BWIZ	QAC Quickie Tri-Q 200	PFA 094-12330		21. 8.95	M C Davies	Turweston	23. 6.98P
	(Built B Cain) (Continental O-200)				*(Noted dismantled 1.08)*		
G-BWJG	Mooney M 20J Model 201	24-3319	N1083P	7.11.95	S Nahum	Elstree	28. 4.08E
G-BWJH	Europa Aviation Europa	007		10.11.95	T P Cripps	Haverfordwest	3. 7.07P
	(Built D, J and A R D Hood - pr.no.PFA 247-12643) (Tri-gear u/c)						
G-BWJI	Cameron V-90 Balloon (Hot Air)	3727		13.11.95	Calarel Developments Ltd	Chipping Camden	4. 5.08A
G-BWJM	Bristol 20 M 1C replica	NAW-2		23.11.95	Richard Shuttleworth Trustees	Old Warden	13. 5.08P
	(Built Northern Aeroplane Workshops)				*(As "C4918" in RFC 72 Sqdn c/s)*		
G-BWJN	Montgomerie-Bensen B 8MR	PFA G/01-1262		16.11.95	G C Kerr	Kirkbride	13. 7.07P
	(Built M G Mee) (Rotax 582)						
G-BWJR	Sky 120-24 Balloon (Hot Air)	007		22.11.95	W J Brogan *"Filzmooser"*	Steiermark, Austria	21.12.96
G-BWJW	Westland Scout AH.1	F9705	XV130	29.11.95	S Dadak and G Sobell	Thruxton	25. 1.06P
					(As "XV130:R" in RAF 666 Sqdn c/s)		
G-BWJY	de Havilland DHC-1 Chipmunk 22	C1/0519	WG469	5.12.95	K J Thompson	Strandhill, Sligo, County Sligo	7. 8.09S
					(As "WG469:72" in RAF c/s)		
G-BWKD	Cameron O-120 Balloon (Hot Air)	3773		8.12.95	L J and M Schoeman	Basildon	7. 3.03T
G-BWKE	Cameron AS-105GD Airship (Hot Air)	3685		8.12.95	W Arnold	Kassel, Germany	10. 1.08A
G-BWKF	Cameron N-105 Balloon (Hot Air)	3736		8.12.95	R M M Botti	Grosseto, Italy	30. 3.08A
G-BWKG	Europa Aviation Europa	004		28.11.95	E H Keppert	Bad Voslau, Austria	19. 8.08P
	(Built T C Jackson - pr.no.PFA 247-12451) (Monowheel u/c)						
G-BWKJ	Rans S-7 Courier	xxxx.xxx		14.12.95	B Tierney tr Three Point Aviation		
	(Built J P Kovacs - pr.no.PFA 218-12918) (Verner SVS1400) (Officially recorded as Rotax 582)					Kilrush, County Kildare	4.11.04P
G-BWKK	Auster AOP.9	B5/10/165	XP279	30. 7.79	C A Davis and D R White	(Winchester)	1. 8.96P
	(Officially regd with Frame no.AUS/166)				*(As "XP279" in AAC c/s)*		
G-BWKR	Sky 90-24 Balloon (Hot Air)	014		18.12.95	B Drawbridge	Cranbrook	16. 3.03T
G-BWKT	Laser Lazer Z200	PFA 123-11421		19.12.95	P D Begley	Deenethorpe	29. 3.08P
	(Built P D Begley) (Lycoming IO-360)						
G-BWKU	Cameron A-250 Balloon (Hot Air)	3730		21.12.95	Balloon School (International) Ltd t/a British School of Ballooning		
						Colhook Common, Petworth	2. 5.08T
G-BWKV	Cameron V-77 Balloon (Hot Air)	3780		27.12.95	Poppies (UK) Ltd	Wootton Fitzpaine	27. 6.07A
G-BWKW	Thunder Ax8-90 Balloon (Hot Air)	3770		28.12.95	Venice Simplon-Orient Express Ltd	Bristol	1. 9.08A
					"Road to Mandalay"		
G-BWKX	Cameron A-250 Balloon (Hot Air)	3731		2. 1.96	Balloon School (International) Ltd t/a Hot Airlines		
					(Hot Airlines titles) Colhook Common, Petworth		4. 7.06T
G-BWKZ	Lindstrand LBL 77A Balloon (Hot Air)	340		21.12.95	J H Dobson	Reading	4. 2.07T
G-BWLA	Lindstrand LBL 69A Balloon (Hot Air)	339		3. 1.96	I Chadwick tr Balloon Preservation Flying Group		
						Partridge Green, Horsham	21 6.07A
G-BWLD	Cameron O-120 Balloon (Hot Air)	3774	(I-. . . .)	16. 1.96	D., P Pedri and C Nicolodi		
						Villa Lagarina, Rovereto, Italy	20. 1.08A
G-BWLF	Cessna 404 Titan	404-0414	G-BNXS	26.10.94	Blom Aerofilms Ltd	Cranfield	3.12.07E
			HKG-4, (N8799K)				
G-BWLJ	Taylorcraft DCO-65	O-4331	C-GUSA	16. 1.96	C Evans	New Farm House, Great Oakley	4.10.07P
			?, 42-35870		*(As "42-35870:129" in USNavy c/s) "Grasshopper"*		
G-BWLL	Murphy Rebel	PFA 232-12499		22. 1.96	F W Parker	Richmond, North.Yorkshire	28. 7.08P
	(Built F W Parker)						
G-BWLN	Cameron O-84 Balloon (Hot Air)	3737		24. 1.96	Reggiana Riduttori SRL San Polo d'Enza, Reggio, Italy		25. 9.05A
G-BWLP	HOAC DV.20 Katana	20141	OE-UDV	6. 2.96	Flight Academy Scotland Ltd	Cumbernauld	9. 9.07T
G-BWLR	Max Holste MH.1521C1 Broussard	185	F-GGKJ	25. 1.96	Chicory Crops Ltd	Gloucestershire	20. 9.09S
			F-WGKJ, French AF		*(As "185:44-CA" in French AF c/s)*		
G-BWLS	HOAC DV.20 Katana	20142	OE-UHK	6. 2.96	M Reed t/a Shadow Aviation	Blackbushe	29. 8.08E
G-BWLY	RotorWay Executive	5142		11. 1.93	P W and I P Bewley	Ley Farm, Chirk	1. 5.08P
	(Built P W and I P Bewley) (RotorWay RI 162)						
G-BWLZ	Wombat Gyrocopter	PFA G/09-1255		28.12.95	M R Harrisson	(Breccqhou, Guernsey)	
	(Built J M Shippen)				*(Stored 3.98)*		
G-BWMA	Colt 105A Balloon (Hot Air)	1853		31.10.90	L Lacroix St Paul en Chablais, Haute-Savoie, France		24. 4.06A
G-BWMB	Wassmer Jodel D 119	77-1492	F-BGMA	17. 2.78	C Hughes	Finmere	22. 5.08P
	(Orig F-BGMA [77] became F-PHQH and rebuilt as Larrieu JL.2: presumed a rebuild using some components of c/n 77 and new build c/n 1492)						
G-BWMC	Cessna 182P Skylane II	18263117	N5462J	30. 1.96	P F N Burrow and E N Skinner tr Eggesford Eagles Flying Group		
			G-BWMC, OO-RGM, (OO-RAN), F-BVOU, N7333N		Trenchard Farm, Eggesford		11. 7.08
G-BWMF	Gloster Meteor T 7	G5/356460	7917M	15.12.95	M Jones tr Meteor Flight	Yatesbury	
			WA591		*(Noted 1.04)*		
G-BWMH	Lindstrand LBL 77B Balloon (Hot Air)	152		7. 2.96	J W Hole	Much Wenlock	10. 6.03A
G-BWMI	Piper PA-28RT-201T Turbo Arrow IV		F-GCTG	31. 1.96	O Cowley	Fairoaks	31. 1.08E
		28R-8031131	N82482, N9571N				
G-BWMJ	Nieuport Scout 17/23 replica	PFA 121-12351		8. 2.96	R Gauld-Galliers and L J Day	Popham	27. 7.08P
	(Built R Gauld-Galliers and L J Day) (Warner Scarab 165)				*(As "N1977:8" in French AF c/s)*		

Reg	Type	C/n	Prev ID	Date	Owner/Operator	Location	
G-BWMK	de Havilland DH.82A Tiger Moth	84483	T8191	9. 2.96	APB Leasing Ltd	Trehelig, Welshpool	
	(Built Morris Motors Ltd)				*(New owner 2.02)*		
G-BWML	Cameron A-275 Balloon (Hot Air)	3725		12. 2.96	A J Street *(Exeter Balloons titles)*	Exeter	17. 8.01T
G-BWMN	Rans S-7 Courier	0193.104		14. 2.96	G J Knee	Turweston	10. 4.08P
	(Built T M Turnbull - pr.no.PFA 218-12446) (Rotax 912-UL)						
G-BWMO	Oldfield Baby Lakes	JAL.3	G-CIII	14. 2.96	D Maddocks	Sleap	12. 3.08P
	(Built J A List) (Continental C85)		N11JL				
G-BWMS	de Havilland DH.82A Tiger Moth	82712	OO-EVJ	14. 2.96	Foundation Early Birds	(Nederhorst, Netherlands)	
			T-29, R4771				
G-BWMU	Cameron Monster Truck 105 SS Balloon (Hot Air)			20. 2.96	Magical Adventures Ltd		
		3607			*"Skycrusher"*	West Bloomfield, Michigan, US	2. 8.01A
G-BWMV	Colt AS-105 Mk.II Airship (Hot Air)	3775		22. 2.96	D Stuber	Schwabenheim, Germany	1. 7.08E
G-BWMX	de Havilland DHC-1 Chipmunk 22	C1/0481	WG407	19. 2.96	K S Kelso tr 407th Flying Group *(As "WG407:67" in RAF c/s)*		
						Fen End Farm, Smithy Fen, Cottenham	5. 5.08
G-BWMY	Cameron Bradford and Bingley 90 SS Balloon (Hot Air)			23. 2.96	Magical Adventures Ltd		
		3808				West Bloomfield, Michigan, US	20. 4.00A
G-BWNB	Cessna 152 II	15280051	N757WA	23. 8.96	Galair International Ltd	Wellesbourne Mountford	13.11.05T
G-BWNC	Cessna 152 II	15284415	N6487L	23. 8.96	Galair International Ltd	Wellesbourne Mountford	23. 7.08E
G-BWND	Cessna 152 II	15285905	N95493	23. 8.96	Galair International Ltd and G Davies		
						Wellesbourne Mountford	23. 7.08E
G-BWNI	Piper PA-24 Comanche	24-136	N5123P	15. 2.96	W A Stewart	North Connel, Oban	5.10.07E
G-BWNJ	Hughes 269C	86-0528	N42LW	29. 2.96	L R Fenwick	Long Fosse House, Beelsby, Grimsby	12. 6.08E
	(Hughes 300)		N27RD, N7458F				
G-BWNK	de Havilland DHC-1 Chipmunk 22	C1/0317	WD390	4. 3.96	S Smith tr WD390 Group	(Wragby, Market Rasen)	1. 8.09S
					(As "WD390:68" in RAF c/s)		
G-BWNM	Piper PA-28R-180 Cherokee Arrow	28R-30435	N934BD	5. 3.96	M and Rosa C Ramnial	Gloucestershire	17.10.07E
G-BWNO	Cameron O-90 Balloon (Hot Air)	3716		5. 3.96	T Knight	Ightfield, Whitchurch	31. 8.07A
					(Action Research titles)		
G-BWNP	Cameron Club-90 SS Balloon (Hot Air)	1717	EI-BVQ	6. 3.96	C J Davies and P Spellward	Castleton, Hope Valley	4. 7.04
	(Club Orange Soft Drink Can shape)						
G-BWNS	Cameron O-90 Balloon (Hot Air)	3842		6. 3.96	Smithair Ltd	Billingshurst	22. 9.08T
					(Self Assessment Tax titles) "Hector"		
G-BWNT	de Havilland DHC-1 Chipmunk 22	C1/0772	WP901	7. 3.96	P G D Bell and R A Stafford	East Midlands	28. 5.09S
					(As "WP901:B" in RAF c/s)		
G-BWNU	Piper PA-38-112 Tomahawk	38-78A0334	N9294T	8. 3.96	Kemble Aero Club Ltd	Kemble	14.12.07E
G-BWNY	Aeromot AMT-200 Super Ximango	200055		11. 6.96	Powell-Brett Associates Ltd	(Leamington Spa)	27. 6.08T
G-BWNZ	Agusta A109C	7654		3. 4.96	Anglo Beef Processors Ltd	(Ardlee, County Louth)	14. 4.08E
G-BWOA	Sky 105-24 Balloon (Hot Air)	027		13. 3.96	Akhter Group PLC	(Harlow)	11. 7.02A
G-BWOB	Luscombe 8F Silvaire	6179	N1552B	14. 3.96	P J Tanulak and H T Law	Sleap	
			NC1552B		*(Noted 8.07)*		
G-BWOD	IAV-Bacau Yakovlev Yak-52	833810	LY-ALY	14. 3.96	Insurefast Ltd	Whitland	12. 7.08P
			DOSAAF 139		*(As "139" in DOSAAF c/s)*		
G-BWOF	British Aircraft Corporation BAC 145 Jet Provost T 5		XW291	18. 3.96	Techair London Ltd	Bournemouth	18. 2.08P
		EEP/JP/955					
G-BWOH	Piper PA-28-161 Cadet	2841061	EC-IBH	18. 3.96	Abraxas Aviation Ltd	Elstree	11.12.07E
			G-BWOH, D-ENXG, N9142S				
G-BWOI	Piper PA-28-161 Cadet	2841307	N270X	18. 3.96	S J Skilton t/a Aviation Rentals	Lee-on-Solent	12. 8.07T
			G-BWOI, D-EJTM, N9264N, N9208P				
G-BWOJ	Piper PA-28-161 Cadet	2841331	N630X	18. 3.96	S J Skilton t/a Aviation Rentals	Halfpenny Green	26. 8.08E
	(Thielert TAE 125-01)		G-BWOJ, D-ESTM, N92242, (N123ND), N92242 *(Centurion built by Thielert titles)*				
G-BWON	Europa Aviation Europa	112		29. 1.96	R L Hitchcock tr Ripley Technical Flyers		
	(Built G T Birks - pr.no.PFA 247-12720) (Conventional u/c)					(Blackbrook, Belper)	19. 9.07P
G-BWOR	Piper PA-18-135 Super Cub (L-18C)	18-2547	OO-WIS	21. 3.96	C D Baird	Roughay Farm, Bishops Waltham	24. 8.08E
			OO-HMF, French Army, 52-6229				
G-BWOT	Hunting Percival P 84 Jet Provost T 3A	PAC/W/10138	XN459	25. 3.96	Red Pelicans Ltd	Hawarden	27. 3.08P
	(C/n reported as PAC/W/949267)				*(As "XN459" in RAF Red Pelicans c/s)*		
G-BWOU	Hawker Hunter F 58A	HABL.003067	Swiss AF J-4105	26. 3.96	Classic Aviation Ltd	RAF Scampton	20. 1.99P
			G-9-315, A2565, XF303		*(New owner 3.05)*		
	(May be a composite: regd with c/n 41H-003067 ex XF306/7776M/G-9-402: this became J-4133)						
G-BWOV	Enstrom F-28A	222	N690BR	26. 3.96	P A Goss	Draycott Farm, Chiseldon	4. 6.08E
			G-BWOV, F-BVRG				
G-BWOW	Cameron N-105 Balloon (Hot Air)	3805		31. 1.96	S J Colin t/a Skybus Ballooning	Cranbrook	30. 5.06T
					"Skybus"		
G-BWOX	de Havilland DHC-1 Chipmunk 22	C1/0728	WP844	27. 3.96	J St Clair-Quentin *(As "WP844" in RAF c/s)* Spanhoe		10. 7.00
G-BWOY	Sky 31-24 Balloon (Hot Air)	029		28. 3.96	C Wolstenholme	Bristol	4. 7.06A
G-BWOZ	CFM Streak Shadow SA	K 154-SA		1. 4.96	J A Lord	Stapleford	31. 1.08P
	(Built H Witt - pr.no.PFA 206-12988) (Rotax 582)						
G-BWPC	Cameron V-77 Balloon (Hot Air)	3867		1. 4.96	H Vaughan *(Cancer Research UK titles)*	Tring	26.10.07A
G-BWPE	Murphy Renegade 912	PFA 188-12791		2. 4.96	J Hatswell	Clipgate Farm, Denton	23. 5.08P
	(Built G Wilson)				*(Also wears "83-EB" under starboard wing)*		
G-BWPF	Sky 120-24 Balloon (Hot Air)	028		3. 4.96	Zebedee Balloon Service Ltd	Newtown, Hungerford	4. 5.08T
					"Whisper"		
G-BWPH	Piper PA-28-181 Cherokee Archer II		N1408H	4. 4.96	H and E Merkado	Panshanger	4. 5.08E
		28-7790311					
G-BWPJ	Steen Skybolt	PFA 064-12854		9. 4.96	D Houghton	Croft Farm, Defford	23. 1.08P
	(Built W R Penaluna) (Continental IO-346)						
G-BWPP	Sky 105-24 Balloon (Hot Air)	031		9. 4.96	P F Smart tr The Sarnia Balloon Group		
					(nice day titles)	Oakley, Basingstoke	19. 6.08A
G-BWPS	CFM Streak Shadow SA	K 275-SA		9. 2.96	P J Mogg	Stour Row, Sturminster Newton	8. 6.07P
	(Built P G A Sumner - pr.no.PFA 206-12954) (Rotax 618)						
G-BWPT	Cameron N-90 Balloon (Hot Air)	3838		5. 3.96	G Everet	Sandway, Maidstone	26. 9.07A
G-BWPZ	Cameron N-105 Balloon (Hot Air)	3889		19. 4.96	D M Moffat	Bristol	2.10.04A
G-BWRA	Sopwith LC-1T Triplane replica	PFA 021-10035	G-PENY	19. 4.96	S M Truscott and J M Hoblyn	RNAS Yeovilton	28. 4.08P
	(Built J S Penny) (Warner Scarab 165)				*(As "N500" in RAF c/s)*		

Reg	Type	C/n	Prev id	Date	Owner/Operator	Base	Expiry
G-BWRC	Avid Hauler Mk.4	PFA 189-12979		22. 2.96	M J E Walsh	Stancombe Farm, Askerswell	10. 7.07P
	(Built B Williams) (Hirth F30)						
G-BWRM	Colt 105A Balloon (Hot Air)	3734		23. 4.96	N Charbonnier (Espace Mont Blanc titles) Aosta, Italy		21. 1.07A
G-BWRO	Europa Aviation Europa	196		22. 4.96	J G Murphy tr G-BWRO Group		
	(Built E C Clark - pr.no.PFA 247-12849) (Monowheel u/c)					Morgansfield, Fishburn	8. 3.08P
G-BWRR	Cessna 182Q Skylane II	18266660	N95861	29. 3.94	D Ridley	Bagby	25. 7.08E
G-BWRS	SNCAN Stampe SV-4C	437	(N . . .)	24. 4.96	G P J M Valvekens	(Diest, Belgium)	
			F-BCVQ		(Stored 2006)		
G-BWRT	Cameron Concept 60 Balloon (Hot Air)	3078	EI-BYP	22.10.96	W R Teasdale (Tethered 9.05)	Maidenhead	
G-BWRY	Cameron N-105 Balloon (Hot Air)	3817		24. 4.96	G Aimo "Ferodo"	Mondovi, Italy	6. 5.06A
G-BWRZ	Lindstrand LBL 105A Balloon (Hot Air)	383		26. 4.96	D J Palmer	Bury St Edmunds	16. 6.04A
G-BWSB	Lindstrand LBL 105A Balloon (Hot Air)	384		26. 4.96	R Calvert-Fisher	Abingdon	18. 7.08A
G-BWSC	Piper PA-38-112 Tomahawk	38-81A0125	N23203	29. 4.96	J Hornby	(Riby, Grimsby)	5. 9.08E
G-BWSD	Campbell Cricket	PFA G/03-1216		3. 5.96	R F G Moyle	(Penryn)	
	(Built R F G Moyle)						
G-BWSG	British Aircraft Corporation BAC 145 Jet Provost T 5	XW324		13. 5.96	J Bell	(Nottingham)	23.10.07P
		EEP/JP/988			(As "XW324:K" in RAF 6FTS c/s)		
G-BWSH	Hunting Percival P 84 Jet Provost T 3A	PAC/W/10159	XN498	13. 5.96	Global Aviation Ltd (Noted 12.05)	Humberside	8. 7.03P
G-BWSI	K & S SA.102.5 Cavalier	PFA 001-10624		18. 4.84	B W Shaw	Waterstones Farm, Newby Wiske	19. 4.08P
	(Built B W Shaw) (Lycoming O-235)						
G-BWSJ	Denney Kitfox Model 3	PFA 172-12204		15. 5.96	J M Miller	Sutton Meadows	6. 6.07P
	(Built J M Miller)						
G-BWSL	Sky 77-24 Balloon (Hot Air)	004		16. 5.96	D Baggley	Stoke-on-Trent	29. 5.06A
G-BWSN	Denney Kitfox Model 3	PFA 172-12141		16. 5.96	M J Laundy	(London W5)	19. 3.08P
	(Built W J Forrest)						
G-BWSO	Cameron Apple 90 Balloon (Hot Air)	3915		17. 5.96	Flying Pictures Ltd	Chilbolton, Stockbridge	11. 6.02A
					"Sainsbury's Apple"		
G-BWSP	Cameron Carrots 80 Balloon (Hot Air)	3914		17. 5.96	Flying Pictures Ltd	Chilbolton, Stockbridge	5. 7.02A
					"Sainsbury's Carrots"		
G-BWST	Sky 200-24 Balloon (Hot Air)	036		20. 5.96	S A Townley t/a Sky High Leisure	Wrexham	28. 4.06T
G-BWSU	Cameron N-105 Balloon (Hot Air)	3848		20. 5.96	A M Marten "Wonder Bra"	Guildford	2. 9.03A
G-BWSV	IAV-Bacau Yakovlev Yak-52	877601	DOSAAF 43	20. 5.96	M W Fitch	North Weald	13. 3.08P
G-BWSZ	Montgomerie-Bensen B 8MR	PFA G/01-1268		14. 5.96	D Cawkwell	Goole	6. 1.98P
	(Built D Cawkwell) (Rotax 582)						
G-BWTB	Lindstrand LBL 105A Balloon (Hot Air)	374		29. 5.96	Servatruc Ltd	Nottingham	22. 5.08A
G-BWTC	Moravan Zlin Z-242L	0697		2. 8.96	A G Bell	Sturgate	2. 2.08E
G-BWTD	Moravan Zlin Z-242L	0698		2. 8.96	Oxford Aviation Training Ltd	Oxford	7.11.07E
G-BWTE	Cameron O-140 Balloon (Hot Air)	3885		30. 5.96	R J and A J Mansfield	Bowness-on-Windermere	23. 2.07T
G-BWTG	de Havilland DHC-1 Chipmunk 22	C1/0119	WB671	4. 6.96	P M M de Graaf tr Chipmunk 4 Ever Foundation		
					(As "WB671:910" in RN c/s)	Teuge, Netherlands	24. 9.06
G-BWTH	Robinson R22 Beta	1767	HB-XYD	5. 6.96	L Smith t/a Helicopter Services	Wycombe Air Park	13. 7.08E
			N4052R				
G-BWTJ	Cameron V-77 Balloon (Hot Air)	3917		7. 6.96	A J Montgomery	Yeovil	12. 6.07A
G-BWTK	Rotary Air Force RAF 2000 GTX-SE	PFA G/13-1264		7. 6.96	M Love	Blackbushe	4. 6.08P
	(Built M P Lehermette)						
G-BWTN	Lindstrand LBL 90A Balloon (Hot Air)	357		12. 6.96	Clarks Drainage Ltd	Oakham	28. 7.05A
					(Clark's Drainage and Polypipe titles)		
G-BWTO	de Havilland DHC-1 Chipmunk 22	C1/0852	WP984	5. 6.96	Skycraft Services Ltd	Little Gransden	22. 6.08
					(As "WP984:H" in RAF c/s)		
G-BWTR	Slingsby T 61F Venture T 2	1881	XZ561	12. 6.96	P R Williams	(Stow on the Wold)	
G-BWTW	Mooney M 20C Mark 21	20-1188	EI-CHI	5. 6.96	T J Berry	Little Rissington	17. 7.08E
			N6955V				
G-BWUA	Campbell Cricket replica	PFA G/03-1248		17. 6.96	N J Orchard	(Portishead, Bristol)	31.10.07P
	(Built R T Lancaster)						
G-BWUB	Piper PA-18S-135 Super Cub	18-3986	N786CS	13. 6.96	Caledonian Seaplanes Ltd	St Fillans, Loch Earn	12. 5.08T
	(L-21C) (Floatplane) (Regd with c/n 18-3786)		G-BWUB, SX-AHB, EI-263, I-EIUO, MM54-2586, 54-2586				
G-BWUE	Hispano HA.1112-MIL Buchon	223	N9938	14. 6.96	Spitfire Ltd	Duxford	21. 6.08P
	(Reported as c/n 172: C4K-155 was c/n 223)		G-AWHK, C4K-102		(As "1" (Red) in Luftwaffe c/s)		
G-BWUH	Piper PA-28-181 Archer III	2843048	N9272E	30. 8.96	B K Ambrose tr G-BWUH Flying Group	Duxford	26.10.07E
			(G-BWUH)				
G-BWUJ	RotorWay Executive 162F	6153		2. 7.96	Southern Helicopters Ltd	Street Farm, Takeley	7. 8.08P
	(Built Southern Helicopters Ltd) (RotorWay RI 162F)						
G-BWUK	Sky 160-24 Balloon (Hot Air)	043		2. 7.96	Cameron Flights Southern Ltd		
						Woodborough, Pewsey	22. 2.08T
G-BWUL	Noorduyn AT-16 Harvard IIB	14A-1415	N16NA	4. 7.96	P Fama and F Scichilone	(Rome, Italy)	25. 5.06P
			G-BWUL, FT375, 43-13116		(As "FT375" in RAF c/s) (New owners 9.07)		
G-BWUN	de Havilland DHC-1 Chipmunk 22	C1/0253	WD310	5. 7.96	T Henderson (As "WD310:B" in RAF c/s)	Deanland	6. 6.09
G-BWUP	Europa Aviation Europa	104		3. 7.96	G W Grant	(Nairn)	22. 6.07P
	(Built T J Harrison - pr.no.PFA 247-12703) (NSI EA-81/100) (Conventional u/c)				(Stored 9.07)		
G-BWUS	Sky 65-24 Balloon (Hot Air)	040		16. 7.96	N A P Bates	Tunbridge Wells	24. 5.08A
G-BWUT	de Havilland DHC-1 Chipmunk 22	C1/0918	WZ879	4. 6.96	Aero Vintage Ltd	Duxford	15. 6.09S
					As "WZ879:X" in RAF red and white c/s)		
G-BWUU	Cameron N-90 Balloon (Hot Air)	3954		17. 7.96	Bailey Balloons Ltd	Pill, Bristol	11. 7.07A
G-BWUV	de Havilland DHC-1 Chipmunk 22A	C1/0655	WK640	18. 7.96	P Ray (As "WK640:C" in RAF c/s)	Bagby	24. 2.11S
G-BWUZ	Campbell Cricket replica	PFA G/03-1267		24. 6.96	K A Touhey	Henstridge	22.10.08P
	(Built M A Concannon) (Rotax 582)						
G-BWVB	Pietenpol AirCamper	PFA 047-11777		24. 7.96	M W Olliver	Farley Farm, Romsey	11. 7.07P
	(Built M J Whatley) (Continental O-200-A)				(New owner 9.07)		
G-BWVC	Jodel D 18	PFA 169-11331		29. 7.96	R W J Cripps	(Spondon, Derby)	
	(Built R W J Cripps)						
G-BWVF	Pietenpol AirCamper	PFA 047-11936		5. 8.96	N Clark	(New Milton)	
	(Built R M Sharphouse)				(New owner 10.07)		
G-BWVH	Robinson R44 Astro	0072	SX-HDE	10. 9.96	Heli Air Ltd	Wellesbourne Mountford	17. 1.08E
			(D-HBBT)				

G-BWVI	Stern St 80 Balade	PFA 166-11190			7. 8.96	I M Godfrey-Davies	Bourne Park, Hurstbourne Tarrant	11. 8.06P
	(Built P E Parker) (Volkswagen 1834)							
G-BWVN	Whittaker MW7	PFA 171-11839			19. 8.96	L C Coyne	(Bishop's Stortford)	
	(Built J W May)					*(New owner 4.06)*		
G-BWVP	Sky 16-24 Balloon (Hot Air)	044			21. 8.96	JK (England) Ltd	London W1	7. 5.06
G-BWVR	IAV-Bacau Yakovlev Yak-52	878202	LY-AKQ		27. 8.96	I Parkinson	Eshott	7.12.06P
			DOSAAF 134			*"52"*		
G-BWVS	Europa Aviation Europa	085			28. 8.96	D R Bishop	Kemble	1. 7.08P
	(Built D R Bishop - pr.no.PFA 247-12686) (Monowheel u/c)							
G-BWVT	de Havilland DHA.82A Tiger Moth	1039	N1350		27. 8.96	R Jewitt	(Tunbridge Wells)	20. 6.08
	(Built de Havilland Aircraft Proprietary Ltd Australia)		VH-SNZ, A17-604, VH-AIN, A17-604					
G-BWVU	Cameron O-90 Balloon (Hot Air)	3204			28. 8.96	J Atkinson	Dorchester	3. 9.08A
G-BWVV	Jodel D 18	PFA 169-12699			29. 8.96	D S Howarth	Hawksbridge Farm, Oxenhope	20. 8.08P
	(Built P Cooper) (Volkswagen 1834)							
G-BWVY	de Havilland DHC-1 Chipmunk 22	C1/0766	WP896		3. 9.96	(P W Portelli) *(As "WP896" in RAF c/s)*	Niot known	6. 1.11E
G-BWVZ	de Havilland DHC-1 Chipmunk 22	C1/0614	WK590		16. 7.96	D Campion	Grimbergen, Belgium	18.10.07S
						(As "WK590:69" in RAF c/s)		
G-BWWA	Ultravia Pelican Club GS	PFA 165-12242			6. 9.96	J S Aplin	Tirley, Gloucestershire	22. 5.08P
	(Built E F Clapham) (Rotax 912-UL)							
G-BWWB	Europa Aviation Europa	080			9. 9.96	S M O'Reilly	Redhill	21. 1.08P
	(Built M G Dolphin- pr.no.PFA 247-12670) (Monowheel u/c)							
G-BWWC	de Havilland DH.104 Dove 7	04498	XM223		14. 6.96	Air Atlantique Ltd	(Coventry)	
	(Wings from G-APSO fitted early 2000)					*(As "XM223" in RAF c/s) (Stored 6.02)*		
G-BWWE	Lindstrand LBL 90A Balloon (Hot Air)	410			11. 9.96	B J Newman	Rushden, Northampton	1. 5.08T
G-BWWF	Cessna 185A Skywagon	185-0240	N4893K		13. 9.96	S M Craig Harvey	Hackettstown, County Carlow	7. 6.08E
			G-BWWF, 9J-MCK, 5Y-BBG, ET-ACI, N4040Y					
			(Sold 3.07 to F.Byrne and V.McCarthy tr Naas Falcons Parachute Centre: noted 9.07)					
G-BWWG	SOCATA Rallye 235E Gabier	13121	EI-BIF		23.10.96	J J Frew	City of Derry	28. 7.06
			HB-EYT, N344RA					
G-BWWI	Aérospatiale AS.332L Super Puma	2040	OY-HMF		11. 9.96	Bristow Helicopters Ltd	Aberdeen	8.11.07E
			(G-TIGT)			*"Johnshaven"*		
G-BWWK	Hawker Nimrod I	41H-43617	S1581		13. 9.96	Patina Ltd	Duxford	25. 6.08P
	(RR Kestrel)					*(As "S1581:573" in RN 802 Sqdn c/s)*		
G-BWWL	Colt Flying Egg SS Balloon (Hot Air)	1813	JA-A0513		19. 9.96	Magical Adventures Ltd		
							West Bloomfield, Michigan, US	2. 8.01A
G-BWWN	Isaacs Fury II	PFA 011-10957			23. 9.96	F J Ball	Jubilee Farm, Wisbech St Mary	13. 6.08P
	(Built D H Pattison) (Lycoming O-235-H2C)					*(As "K8303:D" in RAF c/s)*		
G-BWWP	Rans S-6-116 Coyote II	1293.570			2.10.96	P Lewis	Park Farm, Eaton Bray	13. 9.08P
	(Built S A Beddus - pr.no.PFA 204A-12648) (Rotax 582) (Tailwheel u/c)							
G-BWWT	Dornier 328-100	3022	D-CDXO		12.11.96	Suckling Airways (Cambridge) Ltd t/a Scot Airways		
			VT-VIG, D-CDHG				London City	12.11.06E
G-BWWU	Piper PA-22-150 Caribbean	22-5002	N7139D		9.10.96	K M Bowen	Upfield Farm, Whitson	17. 5.08
	(Hoerner wing-tips: tail-wheel conversion)							
G-BWWW	British Aerospace Jetstream Series 3102	614	G-31-614		8. 7.83	BAE Systems (Operations) Ltd	Cranfield	4.12.07E
G-BWWX	Yakovlev Yak-50	853003	LY-AOI		11.10.96	D P McCoy	Weston, Leixlip, County Kildare	9. 3.08P
			DOSAAF					
G-BWWY	Lindstrand LBL 105A Balloon (Hot Air)	411			14.10.96	M J Smith *(Corks and Cans Norton titles)*	Westow, York	3. 4.08T
G-BWWZ	Denney Kitfox Model 3	PFA 172-13054			15.10.96	A I Eskander	Yew Tree Farm, Lymm Dam	1. 2.08P
	(Built K M Allan) (Rotax 912)							
G-BWXA	Slingsby T 67M-260 Firefly	2236			19. 3.96	Babcock Support Services Ltd t/a Babcock Defence Services		
							RAF Barkston Heath	9. 8.08E
G-BWXB	Slingsby T 67M-260 Firefly	2237			19. 3.96	Babcock Support Services Ltd t/a Babcock Defence Services		
							RAF Barkston Heath	19.10.07E
G-BWXC	Slingsby T 67M-260 Firefly	2238			19. 3.96	Babcock Support Services Ltd t/a Babcock Defence Services		
						(Operated DEFTS)	RAF Barkston Heath	19. 9.08E
G-BWXD	Slingsby T 67M-260 Firefly	2239			19. 3.96	Babcock Support Services Ltd t/a Babcock Defence Services		
						(Operated DEFTS)	RAF Barkston Heath	22.11.07E
G-BWXE	Slingsby T 67M-260 Firefly	2240			19. 3.96	Babcock Support Services Ltd t/a Babcock Defence Services		
							RAF Barkston Heath	8. 7.08E
G-BWXF	Slingsby T 67M-260 Firefly	2241			19. 3.96	Babcock Support Services Ltd t/a Babcock Defence Services		
						(Operated DEFTS)	RAF Barkston Heath	14.11.07E
G-BWXG	Slingsby T 67M-260 Firefly	2242			19. 3.96	Babcock Support Services Ltd t/a Babcock Defence Services		
						(Operated DEFTS)	RAF Barkston Heath	27. 6.08E
G-BWXH	Slingsby T 67M-260 Firefly	2243			19. 3.96	Babcock Support Services Ltd t/a Babcock Defence Services		
							AAC Middle Wallop	20.10.07E
G-BWXI	Slingsby T 67M-260 Firefly	2244			19. 3.96	Babcock Support Services Ltd t/a Babcock Defence Services		
						(Operated DEFTS)	RAF Barkston Heath	28.11.07E
G-BWXJ	Slingsby T 67M-260 Firefly	2245			19. 3.96	Babcock Support Services Ltd t/a Babcock Defence Services		
						(Operated DEFTS)	RAF Barkston Heath	18.12.07E
G-BWXK	Slingsby T 67M-260 Firefly	2246			19. 3.96	Babcock Support Services Ltd t/a Babcock Defence Services		
							RAF Barkston Heath	22.11.07E
G-BWXL	Slingsby T 67M-260 Firefly	2247			19. 3.96	Babcock Support Services Ltd t/a Babcock Defence Services		
							RAF Barkston Heath	26. 1.08E
G-BWXM	Slingsby T 67M-260 Firefly	2248			19. 3.96	Babcock Support Services Ltd t/a Babcock Defence Services		
							RAF Barkston Heath	1. 5.08E
G-BWXN	Slingsby T 67M-260 Firefly	2249			19. 3.96	Babcock Support Services Ltd t/a Babcock Defence Services		
							RAF Barkston Heath	26. 2.08E
G-BWXO	Slingsby T 67M-260 Firefly	2250			19. 3.96	Babcock Support Services Ltd t/a Babcock Defence Services		
						(Operated DEFTS)	RAF Barkston Heath	19. 2.08E
G-BWXP	Slingsby T 67M-260 Firefly	2251			19. 3.96	D S McGregor	Rayne Hall Farm, Braintree	14. 3.08E
G-BWXR	Slingsby T 67M-260 Firefly	2252			19. 3.96	Babcock Support Services Ltd t/a Babcock Defence Services		
						(Operated DEFTS)	RAF Barkston Heath	15.11.07E
G-BWXS	Slingsby T 67M-260 Firefly	2253			19. 3.96	Babcock Support Services Ltd t/a Babcock Defence Services		
						(Operated DEFTS) "6"	RAF Barkston Heath	10. 4.08E

G-BWXT	Slingsby T 67M-260 Firefly	2254		19. 3.96	Babcock Support Services Ltd t/a Babcock Defence Services		
					(Operated DEFTS)	RAF Barkston Heath	5. 3.08E
G-BWXU	Slingsby T 67M-260 Firefly	2255		19. 3.96	Babcock Support Services Ltd t/a Babcock Defence Services		
						RAF Barkston Heath	30. 3.08E
G-BWXV	Slingsby T 67M-260 Firefly	2256		19. 3.96	Babcock Support Services Ltd t/a Babcock Defence Services		
						RAF Barkston Heath	20. 4.08E
G-BWXW	Slingsby T 67M-260 Firefly	2257		19. 3.96	Babcock Support Services Ltd t/a Babcock Defence Services		
						RAF Barkston Heath	24. 3.06T
G-BWXX	Slingsby T 67M-260 Firefly	2258		19. 3.96	Babcock Support Services Ltd t/a Babcock Defence Services		
						RAF Barkston Heath	18. 5.08E
G-BWXY	Slingsby T 67M-260 Firefly	2259		19. 3.96	Babcock Support Services Ltd t/a Babcock Defence Services		
					(Operated DEFTS)	RAF Barkston Heath	6. 4.08E
G-BWXZ	Slingsby T 67M-260 Firefly	2260		19. 3.96	Babcock Support Services Ltd t/a Babcock Defence Services		
						RAF Barkston Heath	20. 6.08E
G-BWYB	Piper PA-28-160 Cherokee	28-263	N6374A	16. 9.96	I M Latiff	Little Staughton	21. 7.08E
			G-BWYB, 6Y-JLO, 6Y-JCH, VP-JCH				
G-BWYD	Europa Aviation Europa	072		28. 8.96	F H Mycroft	Kirknewton	3. 4.08P
	(Built H J Bendiksen - pr.no.PFA 247-12621) (Monowheel u/c)						
G-BWYE	Cessna 310R II	310R1654	F-GBPE	6. 9.96	ACS Contracts Ltd	Perth	20. 3.08E
			(N26369)				
G-BWYG	Cessna 310R II	310R1580	F-GBMY	28.10.96	R F Jones t/a Kissair Aviation	Biggin Hill	28. 8.08E
			(N1820E)				
G-BWYI	Denney Kitfox Model 3	PFA 172-12143		30.10.96	M J Blanchard	Old Sarum	25. 4.07P
	(Built J Adamson) (Rotax 912)				*(New owner 7.07)*		
G-BWYK	Yakovlev Yak-50	812004	RA-01386	9. 8.96	R A L Hubbard tr Foley Farm Flying Group	Meon	22. 1.09P
			DOSAAF 51				
G-BWYM	HOAC DV.20 Katana	20067	D-EWAU	27. 1.97	Plane Talking Ltd	Blackbushe	18. 6.08E
G-BWYN	Cameron O-77 Balloon (Hot Air)	1162	G-ODER	13.11.96	W H Morgan *"Hobo"*	Swansea	29. 4.01A
G-BWYO	Sequoia F 8L Falco	PFA 100-10920		7.11.96	M C R Sims	Goodwood	26. 9.08P
	(Built S Harper) (Lycoming O-320-E2A)						
G-BWYP	Sky 56-24 Balloon (Hot Air)	053		8.11.96	S A Townley t/a Sky High Leisure	Wrexham	9.11.01A
G-BWYR	Rans S-6-116 Coyote II	1294-700		8.11.96	E A Pearson	Weston Zoyland	18.10.07P
	(Built S Palmer - pr.no.PFA 204A-13058) (Rotax 912-UL) (Tailwheel u/c)						
G-BWYS	Cameron O-120 Balloon (Hot Air)	3997		30. 9.96	J M Stables t/a Aire Valley Balloons		
						Arkendale, Knaresborough	20. 5.08T
G-BWYU	Sky 120-24 Balloon (Hot Air)	052		13.11.96	D G Such and M Tomlin	Barkway, Royston	10. 7.08A
G-BWZA	Europa Aviation Europa	063		1.11.96	T G Cowlishaw	Full Sutton	31.10.08P
	(Built M C Costin - pr.no.PFA 247-12626) (Monowheel u/c)						
G-BWZG	Robin R2160	311	F-WZZZ	6.11.96	Sherburn Aero Club Ltd	Sherburn-in-Elmet	2.10.07E
G-BWZJ	Cameron A-250 Balloon (Hot Air)	4021		2.12.96	Balloon School (International) Ltd t/a Balloon Club of Great Britain		
						Colhook Common, Petworth	23. 4.08T
G-BWZK	Cameron A-210 Balloon (Hot Air)	4020		2.12.96	Balloon School (International) Ltd t/a Balloon Club of Great Britain		
						Colhook Common, Petworth	10. 8.06T
G-BWZU	Lindstrand LBL 90B Balloon (Hot Air)	418		12.12.96	K D Pierce	Cranbrook	10. 6.07
G-BWZX	Aérospatiale AS.332L Super Puma	2120	F-WQDX	12.12.96	Bristow Helicopters Ltd *"Muchalls"*	Aberdeen	5. 5.08T
			G-BWZX, F-WQDX, 5V-MCD, 5V-TAH, LN-OLE				
G-BWZY	Hughes 269A	95-0378	G-FSDT	4.12.96	Reeve Newfields Ltd	Sywell	5. 1.08E
	(Hughes 300)		N269CH, N1336D, 64-18066				

G-BXAA - G-BXZZ

G-BXAB	Piper PA-28-161 Warrior II	28-8416054	G-BTGK	7.10.96	TG Aviation Ltd	Manston	10. 5.08E
			N4344C				
G-BXAC	Rotary Air Force RAF 2000 GTX-SE PFA G/13-1279			21.11.96	J A Robinson	Eaglescott	13. 6.08P
	(Built D C Fairbrass)						
G-BXAD	Thunder Ax11-225 Series 2 Balloon (Hot Air) 4052			18.12.96	M E White	Trim, County Meath	24. 7.04T
					(Address change 9.07)		
G-BXAF	Pitts S-1D	PFA 009-12258		6.12.96	N J Watson	Sandown, Isle of Wight	23. 5.08P
	(Built F Sharples)						
G-BXAH	Piel CP.301A Emeraude	AB.422	D-EBAH	29.10.96	A P Goodwin	Compton Abbas	12. 6.07P
	(Built Fliegerclub Eichstatt EV) (Continental C90)				*(Noted 8.07)*		
G-BXAJ	Lindstrand LBL 14A Balloon (Gas-Filled)	425		23.12.96	Oscair Project AB	Täby, Sweden	
G-BXAK	IAV-Bacau Yakovlev Yak-52	811508	LY-ASC	23.12.96	J Calverley	Tatenhill	14. 8.08P
			DOSAAF				
G-BXAL	Cameron Bertie Bassett 90 SS Balloon (Hot Air)	4034		13. 1.97	Trebor Bassett Ltd	Petworth	27. 1.02A
					"Bertie Bassett" (Operated Balloon Preservation Group)		
G-BXAM	Cameron N-90 Balloon (Hot Air)	4035		13. 1.97	Trebor Bassett Ltd	Shoreham	22. 4.04A
					"Bertie Junior" (Bassett's titles)		
G-BXAN	Scheibe SF25C Falke	44299	D-KDGQ	13. 1.97	J P Harrison tr C Falke Syndicate	Winthorpe	25.10.07E
	(Limbach SL1700)						
G-BXAO	Avtech Jabiru SK	0099		14. 1.97	P J Thompson	(Llanddaniel, Gaerwen)	23. 4.99P
	(Built I M Donnelly - pr.no.PFA 274-13066)				*(Damaged Ledicot near Shobdon 3. 5.98)*		
G-BXAR	British Aerospace Avro 146-RJ100	E3298	G-6-298	27. 3.97	BA Cityflyer Ltd	London City	29. 3.08E
G-BXAS	British Aerospace Avro 146-RJ100	E3301	G-6-301	23. 4.97	BA Cityflyer Ltd	Manchester	29. 4.08E
G-BXAU	Pitts S-1	GHG.9	N9GG	22. 1.97	L Westnage		
	(Built G Goodrich) (Lycoming O-320)				(Shipton-under-Wychwood, Chipping Norton)		3. 1.08P
G-BXAV	Aerostar Yakovlev Yak-52	9111608	RA-01325	24. 1.97	RA 293 Group Ltd	Tatenhill	3. 7.08P
			DOSAAF 73				
G-BXAY	Bell 206B-3 JetRanger III	3946	N85EA	24. 1.97	Viewdart Ltd	Cranfield	11. 9.08E
			N521RC, N3210D				
G-BXBA	Cameron A-210 Balloon (Hot Air)	4072		10. 1.97	Reach For The Sky Ltd	Guildford	31. 7.08T
G-BXBC	Anderson EA-1 Kingfisher Amphibian PFA 132-11302			28. 1.97	S Bichan	Lamb Holm Farm, Orkney	
	(Built S Bichan)				*(Noted 12.05)*		

Reg	Type	c/n	Prev id	Date	Owner	Location	Status
G-BXBG	Cameron A-275 Balloon (Hot Air)	4023		28. 1.97	M L Gabb	Haselor, Alcester	20. 3.04T
G-BXBK	Mudry CAP.10B	17	N170RC French AF "307-SO"	30. 1.97	S Skipworth	White Waltham	12. 4.08
G-BXBL	Lindstrand LBL 240A Balloon (Hot Air)	317		31. 1.97	J Fenton t/a Firefly Balloon Promotions	(Preston)	17. 7.07T
G-BXBM	Cameron O-105 Balloon (Hot Air)	3990		31. 1.97	P Spellward tr Bristol University Hot Air Ballooning Society	Bristol	10. 2.07A
G-BXBP	Denney Kitfox Model 2 (Built G S Adams)	PFA 172-12149		3. 2.97	G S Adams	Enniskillen	18.11.06P
G-BXBR	Cameron A-120 Balloon (Hot Air)	1983	SE-ZDY	4. 2.97	M G Barlow (Active 5.07))	Carelton, Skipton	
G-BXBU	Mudry CAP.10B	103	N173RC French AF	11. 2.97	J F Cosgrave and H R Pearson	Luxter's Farm, Hambledon	31. 7.08E
G-BXBY	Cameron A-105 Balloon (Hot Air)	4077		13. 2.97	S P Watkins (Roman Baths titles) (Operated D Littlewood)	Bristol	31. 3.08A
G-BXBZ	PZL-104 Wilga 80	CF21930941	EC-GDA ZK-PZQ	13. 2.97	J H Sandham t/a J H Sandham Aviation	Carlisle	2. 7.08E
G-BXCA	Hapi Cygnet SF-2A (Built G E Collard) (Rotax 912-UL)	PFA 182-12921		22. 1.97	J N Harley "Fighting Cygnets"	Popham	5. 9.07P
G-BXCC	Piper PA-28-201T Turbo Dakota	28-7921068	D-EKBM N2855A	19. 2.97	Greer Aviation Ltd	(Prestwick)	22.10 07E
G-BXCD	TEAM Mini-MAX 91A (Built R Davies) (Rotax 503)	PFA 186-12393		18. 2.97	R Davies	RAF Halton	7. 8.07P
G-BXCG	Jodel DR.250 (Built J M Scott - pr.no.PFA 299-13146)	060	D-EHGG	22. 5.97	J C Carter tr CG Group	Cambridge	22. 8.08P
G-BXCH	Europa Aviation Europa (Built D M Stevens - pr.no.PFA 247-12980) (Monowheel u/c)	186		19. 2.97	R E T Hatton	Enstone	18. 6.07P
G-BXCJ	Campbell Cricket replica (Built R A Friend) (Rotax 532)	PFA G/03-1177		24. 2.97	A G Peel (New owner 9.07)	(Waterlooville)	11. 7.05P
G-BXCL	Montgomerie-Bensen B 8MR (Built A V Francis) (Rotax 582)	PFA G/01-1287		26. 2.97	M L L Temple (Noted 8.05)	Kirkbride	14.12.04P
G-BXCM	Lindstrand LBL 150A Balloon (Hot Air)	443		26. 2.97	Aerosaurus Balloons Ltd	Whimple, Exeter	4. 7.07E
G-BXCN	Sky 105-24 Balloon (Hot Air)	047	(PH-RTH)	27. 2.97	A S Davidson tr Nottingham Hot Air Balloon Club "Rainbow"	Woodville, Swadlincote	18. 7.08
G-BXCO	Colt 120A Balloon (Hot Air)	4086		3. 3.97	T G Church (Super Golf Invicta titles)	Clayton le Dale, Blackburn	20.10.08T
G-BXCP	de Havilland DHC-1 Chipmunk 22	C1/0744	WP859	27. 2.97	Propshop Ltd (As "WP859:E" in RAF c/s)	Duxford	12. 4.08
G-BXCT	de Havilland DHC-1 Chipmunk 22	C1/0145	WB697	3. 3.97	J W Frecklington and R Merewood t/a Wickenby Aviation (As "WB697:95" in RAF c/s)	Wickenby	2. 5.09S
G-BXCU	Rans S-6-116 Coyote II (Built M R McNeil - pr.no.PFA 204A-13105) (Rotax 912-UL) (Tri-cycle u/c)	1096.1044		6. 3.97	R S Gent	Leicester	11. 5.08P
G-BXCV	de Havilland DHC-1 Chipmunk 22	C1/0807	WP929	3. 3.97	Ocean Flight Holdings Ltd (As "WP929" in RAF c/s)	Duxford	18. 2.10S
G-BXCW	Denney Kitfox Model 3 (Built M J Blanchard)	PFA 172-12619		6. 3.97	M J Blanchard	Old Sarum	7.11.06P
G-BXDA	de Havilland DHC-1 Chipmunk 22	C1/0747	WP860	7. 3.97	S R Cleary and D Mowat (As "WP860:6" in RAF c/s)	Kirknewton	17. 8.09S
G-BXDB	Cessna U206F Stationair	U20602233	G-BMNZ F-BVJT, N1519U	18.12.96	D A Howard	Colonsay, Isle of Colonsay	2. 9.08E
G-BXDE	Rotary Air Force RAF 2000 GTX-SE (Built A McCredie)	PFA G/13-1280		14. 1.97	D Beevers (New owner 7.07)	Melrose Farm, Melbourne	23. 1.02P
G-BXDF	Beech 95-B55 Baron	TC-2011	SE-IXG OY-ASB	7. 3.97	Chesh-Air Ltd	Liverpool	6. 2.08E
G-BXDG	de Havilland DHC-1 Chipmunk 22	C1/0644	WK630	7. 3.97	Felthorpe Flying Group Ltd (As "WK630" in RAF c/s)	Felthorpe	4. 11.10S
G-BXDH	de Havilland DHC-1 Chipmunk 22	C1/0270	WD331	10. 3.97	D F Ranger (As "WD331" in RAF c/s)	Popham	26. 5.08
G-BXDI	de Havilland DHC-1 Chipmunk 22	C1/0312	WD373	10. 3.97	Propshop Ltd (As "WD373:12" in RAF red and white c/s)	Duxford	22.10.09S
G-BXDL	Hunting Percival P 84 Jet Provost T 3A	PAC/W/9286	(8983M) XM478	18. 3.97	Noras SRL (As "XM478" in RAF c/s and test flown 23. 8.07after overhaul)	Bournemouth)	12. 9.08P
G-BXDM	de Havilland DHC-1 Chipmunk 22	C1/0723	WP840	28. 2.97	Ace Leasing Ltd (As "WP840:9" in RAF c/s)	Conington	12. 4.09S
G-BXDN	de Havilland DHC-1 Chipmunk 22	C1/0618	WK609	18. 3.97	W D Lowe and L A Edwards (As "WK609:93" in RAF c/s)	Wycombe Air Park	15. 2.10
G-BXDO	Rutan Cozy (Built C R Blackburn) (Lycoming O-235) (Force landed near Junction 12 on M5 10. 7.04 and substantially damaged: on rebuiltd 2008 from remnants of LongEz G-BLZH)	PFA 159-12032		21. 3.97	D G Foreman	(Swanley)	4. 7.05P
G-BXDP	de Havilland DHC-1 Chipmunk 22	C1/0659	WK642	27. 2.97	T A McBennet and J Kelly (As "WK642" in RAF c/s)	Kilrush, County Kildare	7.10.06
G-BXDR	Lindstrand LBL 77A Balloon (Hot Air)	441		25. 3.97	British Telecommunications PLC "Bright Future"	Thatcham	7. 4.08A
G-BXDT	Robin HR.200-120B	315		25. 3.97	Multiflight Ltd	Leeds-Bradford	8. 6.08E
G-BXDU	Aero Designs Pulsar (Built M P Board) (Tri-cycle u/c)	PFA 202-11991		25. 3.97	M P Board	Damyn's Hall, Upminster	18. 6.08P
G-BXDV	Sky 105-24 Balloon (Hot Air)	049		26. 3.97	A Parsons tr Loughborough Students Union Hot Air Balloon Club	Loughborough	13. 4.08
G-BXDY	Europa Aviation Europa (Built D G Watts - pr.no.PFA 247-12914: sequence no.conflicts with G-MYZP) (Monowheel u/c) "The Rocketeer"	229		27. 3.97	D G and S.Watts	Fowle Hall Farm, Laddingford	15. 5.08P
G-BXDZ	Lindstrand LBL 105A Balloon (Hot Air)	437		4. 4.97	D J and A D Sutcliffe	Harrogate	21. 9.08A
G-BXEA	Rotary Air Force RAF 2000 GTX-SE (Built R Firth)	PFA G/13-1270		2. 4.97	R Firth	Netherthorpe	23. 5.06P
G-BXEC	de Havilland DHC-1 Chipmunk 22	C1/0647	WK633	3. 4.97	D S Hunt (As "WK633:B" in RAF c/s)	Redhill	28. 6.07
G-BXEJ	Magni M-16 Tandem Trainer (Arrow GT 1000)	D-9302	D-MIFF	8. 4.97	N H Collins t/a AES Radionic Surveillance Systems	Cork Farm, Streethay	21. 5.08P

G-BXEN	Cameron N-105 Balloon (Hot Air)	4090		11. 4.97	G Aimo	Mondovi, Piedmont, Italy	23. 5.07A
	(New envelope c/n 10288, 3.03)				"Liquigas"		
G-BXES	Hunting Percival P 66 Pembroke C 1	P66/101	N4234C	14. 4.97	Air Atlantique Ltd	Coventry	9. 5.07P
	(Regd with c/n PAC/W/3032)		9042M, XL954		(As "XL954" in RAF 60 Sqdn c/s)		
G-BXET	Piper PA-38-112 Tomahawk	38-80A0028	N25089	14. 4.97	Highland Flying School Ltd	Inverness	5. 5.06E
G-BXEX	Piper PA-28-181 Cherokee Archer II		N3562Q	16. 4.97	R Mayle	Shoreham	23. 8.08E
		28-7790463					
G-BXEY	Colt AS-105 GD Airship (Hot Air)	3936		15. 4.97	D Mayer "Luftwerbung"	Felsberg, Germany	8. 2.08E
G-BXEZ	Cessna 182P Skylane II	18264344	OH-CHJ	16. 4.97	Forhawk Ltd	Perranporth	16. 2.08T
	(Reims assembled c/n F18200054)		N1479M				
G-BXFB	Pitts S-1	9543	N77ZZ	16. 4.97	O P Sparrow tr Foxtrot Bravo Flying Group (Lingfield)		28. 3.08P
	(Built B J Dziuba)						
G-BXFC	Jodel D 18	PFA 169-11322		17. 4.97	B S Godbold	Little Gransden	26. 7.07P
	(Builtt B S Godbold) (Revmaster 2100D)						
G-BXFD	Enstrom 280C Shark	1084	N88MD	18. 4.97	Buckland Newton Hire Ltd		
			N632H			Buckland Newton, Dorchester	15. 2.08T
G-BXFE	Mudry CAP.10B	135	N175RC	18. 4.97	Avion Aerobatic Ltd	White Waltham	4. 4.08E
			French AF				
G-BXFG	Europa Aviation Europa	018		21. 4.97	A Rawicz-Szczerbo	Eaglescott	24. 5.07P
	(Built A Rawicz-Szczerbo - pr.no.PFA 247-12500) (Monowheel u/c)						
G-BXFI	Hawker Hunter T 7	41H-670815	WV372	24. 4.97	Fox-One Ltd	Kemble	15. 3.08P
					(As "WV372:R" in RAF 2 Sqdn c/s)		
G-BXFK	CFM Streak Shadow	K 206		24. 4.97	W J Bernasinski (Crawley Down, Crawley)		18.11.03P
	(Built D Adcock - pr.no.PFA 206-12329) (Rotax 582)				(New owner 8.07)		
G-BXFN	Cameron Colt 77A Balloon (Hot Air)	4145		25. 4.97	Charter Ballooning Ltd	Liphook	3. 4.08A
G-BXFY	Cameron Bierkrug 90 SS Balloon (Hot Air)	4133	D-OIBP	29. 4.97	D G Such and M Tomlin	Barkway, Royston	13.10.08A
			G-BXFY				
G-BXGA	Eurocopter AS.350B2 Ecureuil	2493	OO-RCH	30. 4.97	PLM Dollar Group Ltd	(Cumbernauld)	27. 8.08E
			OO-XCH, F-WZFX				
		(Main rotor blades struck boulder and damaged Corrie of Clova, north-west Forfar, Scotland 20. 1.06)					
G-BXGC	Cameron N-105 Balloon (Hot Air)	4137		6. 5.97	Cliveden House Ltd	Bath	16. 3.05T
					(Royal Crescent Hotel titles) (Stored 2007)		
G-BXGD	Sky 90-24 Balloon (Hot Air)	067		6. 5.97	Servo and Electronic Sales Ltd		
					(Operated Cameron Flights Southern)	Woodborough, Pewsey	22. 2.07T
G-BXGG	Europa Aviation Europa	178		29. 4.97	C J H and P A J Richardson		
	(Built B W Faulkner - pr.no.PFA 247-12803) (Monowheel u/c)					Bremridge Farm, Shillingford	10. 4.08P
G-BXGH	Diamond DA.20-A1 Katana	10151		20. 5.97	Cumbernauld Flying School Ltd	Enniskillen	24. 6.08E
					(Operated Enniskillen Flying Club)		
G-BXGL	de Havilland DHC-1 Chipmunk 22	C1/0924	WZ884	12. 5.97	Airways Aero Associations Ltd	Wycombe Air Park	30. 1.10S
					(Operated British Airways Flying Club)		
G-BXGM	de Havilland DHC-1 Chipmunk 22	C1/0806	WP928	9. 5.97	D Parkinson tr Chipmunk G-BXGM Group	Shoreham	17.11.09S
					(As "WP928:D" in AAC c/s)		
G-BXGO	de Havilland DHC-1 Chipmunk 22	C1/0097	WB654	13. 5.97	I C Barlow and T J Orchard tr Trees Group		
					(As "WB654:U" in AAC c/s)	Wycombe Air Park	26.10.09
G-BXGP	de Havilland DHC-1 Chipmunk 22	C1/0927	WZ882	12. 5.97	T K Pullen tr Eaglescott Chipmunk Group		
					(As "WZ882:K" in AAC c/s)	Eaglescott	20. 8.07T
G-BXGS	Rotary Air Force RAF 2000	PFA G/13-1290		14. 5.97	C R Gordon	(Cupar)	4.12.08P
	(Built N C White)						
G-BXGT	III Sky Arrow 650 T	PFA 298-13085		7. 5.97	D., B D C Barnard and J S C Goodale	Popham	15. 8.08P
	(Built Sky Arrow (Kits) UK Ltd)						
G-BXGV	Cessna 172R Skyhawk	17280240	N9300F	7. 1.98	P Cooke tr Skyhawk Group	White Waltham	18. 2.08T
G-BXGW	Robin HR.200-120B	317		16. 5.97	Multiflight Ltd	Leeds-Bradford	19.10.07E
					(Operated Multiflight Flying Club)		
G-BXGX	de Havilland DHC-1 Chipmunk 22	C1/0609	WK586	19. 5.97	Interflight (Air Charter) Ltd)	Duxford	6. 8.10S
					(As "WK586:V" in AAC c/s)		
G-BXGY	Cameron V-65 Balloon (Hot Air)	4125		18. 4.97	R J Plume tr Dante Balloon Group	Mondovi, Italy	2. 8.08A
G-BXGZ	Stemme S 10-V	14-023	D-KSTE	18. 8.97	D Tucker and K Lloyd	Aston Down	20. 3.08E
			EC-GGD, D-KGDF		"S10"		
G-BXHA	de Havilland DHC-1 Chipmunk 22	C1/0801	WP925	20. 5.97	F A de Munck and C S Huijers	Seppe, Netherlands	14. 9.06
					(As "WP925:C" in AAC c/s)		
G-BXHD	Beech 76 Duchess	ME-284	OY-ARM	22. 5.97	Plane Talking Ltd	Bournemouth	16. 8.08E
			N223JC		(Operated Cabair)		
G-BXHE	Lindstrand LBL 105A Balloon (Hot Air)	459		23. 5.97	L H Ellis	Burcott, Leighton Buzzard	4. 9.08T
G-BXHF	de Havilland DHC-1 Chipmunk 22	C1/0808	WP930	28. 5.97	R A Wallis tr Hotel Fox Sydicate	Redhill	13. 5.10
					(As "WP930:J" in AAC c/s)		
G-BXHH	Grumman AA-5A Cheetah	AA5A-0105	N9705U	3. 6.97	M G Greenslade t/a Oaklands Flying	Biggin Hill	12. 6.08E
G-BXHJ	Hapi Cygnet SF-2A	PFA 182-12159		29. 5.97	I J Smith	Brook Farm, Boylestone	
	(Built I J Smith) (Volkswagen 1835)						
G-BXHL	Sky 77-24 Balloon (Hot Air)	055		29. 5.97	R K Gyselynck "Harlequin"	Port Erin, Isle of Man	14. 6.07
G-BXHN	Lindstrand LBL Pop Can SS Balloon (Hot Air)			30. 5.97	R S Kent t/a Ornithological Desires Balloon Group		
		465				Petworth	29. 5.06A
G-BXHO	Lindstrand Telewest Sphere SS Balloon (Hot Air)			30. 5.97	Magical Adventures Ltd		
		474				West Bloomfield, Michigan, US	25. 2.03A
G-BXHR	Stemme S 10-V	14-030	D-KSTE	23. 7.97	J H Rutherford	(Norbury, Bishops Castle)	10.12.07E
G-BXHT	Bushby-Long Midget Mustang	PFA 168-13077		3. 6.97	P P Chapman	Headcorn	18. 3.08P
	(Built P P Chapman)						
G-BXHU	Campbell Cricket Mk.6	PFA G/16-1293		3. 6.97	P J Began	Henstridge	18. 8.06P
	(Built P C Lovegrove) (Rotax 503)						
G-BXHY	Europa Aviation Europa	022		6. 6.97	A L Thorne and B Lewis tr Jupiter Flying Group		
	(Built A L Thorne - pr.no.PFA 247-12514) (Monowheel u/c)					White Waltham	26. 2.08P
G-BXIA	de Havilland DHC-1 Chipmunk 22	C1/0056	WB615	9. 6.97	W Askew and C Duckett t/a Dales Aviation		
					(As "WB615:E" in AAC c/s)	Blackpool	12. 6.09S
G-BXIC	Cameron A-275 Balloon (Hot Air)	4162		9. 6.97	Aerosaurus Balloons Ltd	Whimple, Exeter	12. 3.08T

Regn	Type	C/n	Previous Identity	Date	Owner or Operator	Base	Expiry
G-BXID	IAV-Bacau Yakovlev Yak-52	888802	LY-ALG DOSAAF 74	10. 6.97	E S Ewen	Oaksey Park	1. 4.08P
G-BXIE	Cameron Colt 77B Balloon (Hot Air)	4181		11. 6.97	L C Sanders *(New owner 3.07)*	Marden, Hereford	24. 4.08A
G-BXIF	Piper PA-28-181 Cherokee Archer II	28-7690404	PH-SWM OO-HAY, N6827J	12. 6.97	Piper Flight Ltd	Swansea	10. 7.08E
G-BXIG	Zenair CH.701 STOL (Built A J Perry)	PFA 187-12065		16. 6.97	A J Perry	Marsh Farm, Bracklesham	19.11.07P
G-BXIH	Sky 200-24 Balloon (Hot Air)	076		16. 6.97	Skyview Ballooning Ltd t/a Kent Ballooning	Ashford	19.10.07T
G-BXII	Europa Aviation Europa (Built D A McFadyean - pr.no.PFA 247-12812) (Tailwheel u/c)	175		30. 4.97	D A McFadyean	Long Marston	26. 8.08P
G-BXIJ	Europa Aviation Europa (Built D G and E A Bligh - pr.no.PFA 247-12698) (Monowheel u/c)	076		16. 6.97	R James	Shobdon	27. 4.08P
G-BXIM	de Havilland DHC-1 Chipmunk 22 (As "WK512:A" in AAC c/s)	C1/0548	WK512	13. 5.97	P R Joshua and A B Ascroft	RAF Brize Norton	5. 7.09
G-BXIO	SAN Jodel DR.1050M Excellence	493	F-BNIO	16. 5.97	R S Palmer	Sandown, Isle of Wight	29. 8.08E
G-BXIT	Zebedee V-31 Balloon (Hot Air) (Built Zebedee Balloon Service)	Z1/3999		8. 5.97	P J Bish (Active 10.06)	Newtown, Hungerford	
G-BXIW	Sky 105-24 Balloon (Hot Air)	073		24. 6.97	Idea Balloon SAS	Tavarnelle Val Di Pesa, Firenze, Italy	27. 4.08
G-BXIX	Magni M-16 Tandem Trainer (Built D Beevers) (Arrow GT1000R)	PFA G/12-1292		13. 6.97	D Beevers	Melrose Farm, Melbourne	20. 8.08P
G-BXIY	Blake Bluetit (Built W H C Blake) (Gnat 32hp) (Pre-war composite from Spartans G-AAGN, G-AAJB and Avro 504K) (Noted 2.06)	01	BAPC.37	26. 6.97	J Bryant	Old Warden	
G-BXIZ	Lindstrand LBL 31A Balloon (Hot Air)	476		3. 7.97	I Chadwick tr Balloon Preservation Flying Group	Partridge Greem, Horsham	15. 4.08A
G-BXJA	Cessna 402B	402B0356	N5753M XA-RFK, N5753M	17. 7.97	CK Fasteners Ltd	Perth	17.10.07T
G-BXJB	IAV-Bacau Yakovlev Yak-52	877403	LY-ABR DOSAAF 15	30. 6.97	A M Playford, D J Young and N Willson "15"	Poplar Hall Farm, Elmsett	22. 1.09P
G-BXJC	Cameron A-210 Balloon (Hot Air)	419		12. 7.97	Balloon School (International) Ltd t/a British School of Ballooning	Colhook Common, Petworth	23. 4.08T
G-BXJD	Piper PA-28-180 Cherokee C	28-4215	OY-BBZ	27. 6.97	M A Powell	Shobdon	5. 3.08E
G-BXJG	Lindstrand LBL 105B Balloon (Hot Air)	478		11. 7.97	C E Wood	Witham	12. 6.08T
G-BXJH	Cameron N-42 Balloon (Hot Air)	4194		15. 7.97	B Conway	Wheatley, Oxford	22. 9.01A
G-BXJJ	Piper PA-28-161 Cadet	2841200	EC-IGN G-BXJJ, G-GFCC, N9189N	26. 6.97	S J Skilton t/a Aviation Rentals	Bournemouth	8.12.07E
G-BXJM	Cessna 152 II	15282380	OO-HOQ F-GHOQ, N68797	15. 7.97	ACS Aviation Ltd	Cumbernauld	16. 9.08E
G-BXJO	Cameron O-90 Balloon (Hot Air)	4190		16. 7.97	Dragon Balloon Company Ltd	Castleton, Hope Valley	3. 4.08T
G-BXJP	Cameron C-80 Balloon (Hot Air)	4171		17. 7.97	AR Cobaleno Pasta Fresca SRL (Arco Baleno titles)	Basta Umbria, Perugia, Italy	1. 4.06A
G-BXJS	Schempp-Hirth Janus CM	35/265	OH-819	7. 7.97	R A Hall tr Janus Syndicate	Enstone	3. 4.08E
G-BXJT	Sky 90-24 Balloon (Hot Air)	072		18. 7.97	J G O'Connell	(Braintree)	18.11.07A
G-BXJV	Diamond DA.20-A1 Katana	10152	C-GKAH	23. 7.97	Enniskillen Flying School Ltd	Cumbernauld	3. 8.08E
G-BXJW	Diamond DA.20-A1 Katana	10211	(OE- VPX) N811CH, C-FDVA	23. 7.97	Enniskillen Flying School Ltd	Enniskillen	20. 8.08E
G-BXJY	Van's RV-6 (Built D J Sharland) (Lycoming O-320-D3G)	PFA 181-12447		23. 7.97	D J Sharland	Popham	10. 5.08P
G-BXJZ	Cameron C-60 Balloon (Hot Air)	4168		23. 7.97	R S Mohr	Ditteridge, Box, Chippenham	23. 7.08A
G-BXKF	Hawker Hunter T 7 (Regd with c/n 41H-003315)	HABL-003314	8676M XL577	28. 7.97	R F Harvey (As "XL577/V" in colours of RAF 92 Sqdn "Blue Diamonds" aerobatic team)	Kemble	9.10.08P
G-BXKH	Cameron Colt Sparkasse Box 90SS Balloon (Hot Air)	4161		4. 8.97	Westfälisch-Lippischer Sparkassen und Giroverband "Spardueschen"	Münster, Germany	7. 8.08A
G-BXKL	Bell 206B-3 JetRanger III	3006	N5735Y	8.10.97	Swattons Aviation Ltd	Thruxton	18.11.07T
G-BXKM	Rotary Air Force RAF 2000 GTX-SE (Built J R Huggins)	PFA G/13-1291		5. 8.97	J R Huggins	Lamberhurst Farm, Faversham	21.10.04P
G-BXKO	Sky 65-24 Balloon (Hot Air)	083		11. 8.97	J-M Reck	Evette-Salbert, France	20. 1.08
G-BXKU	Colt AS-120 Mk.II Airship (Hot Air)	4165		15. 8.97	D C Chipping	Grantham	19. 4.01A
G-BXKW	Slingsby T 67M-200 Firefly (As "HKG-13" in Royal Hong Kong AAF c/s)	2061	VR-HZS HKG-13, G-7-129	15. 8.97	N A Whatling	Spanhoe	17. 6.08E
G-BXKX	Taylorcraft J Auster 5	803	D-EMXA HB-EOK, MS938	19. 8.97	J A Clark	Orchard Farm, Sittingbourne	5. 6.08
G-BXLC	Sky 120-24 Balloon (Hot Air)	085		20. 8.97	Dragon Balloon Company Ltd	Mexico City, Mexico	23. 3.08A
G-BXLF	Lindstrand LBL 90A Balloon (Hot Air)	487		3. 9.97	J Tyrrell and W Rousell (Variohm Components titles)	Wollaston, Wellingborough	6. 7.08A
G-BXLG	Cameron C-80 Balloon (Hot Air)	4250		5. 3.98	S M Anthony	Northam, Bideford	27. 5.07A
G-BXLK	Europa Aviation Europa (Built R G Fairall - pr.no.PFA 247-12613) (Monowheel u/c)	074		11. 9.97	R G Fairall	Redhill	25. 6.07P
G-BXLN	Fournier RF4D	4022	F-BORK	15. 9.97	P W Cooper	(Eaton, Congleton)	7. 5.08E
G-BXLO	Hunting Percival P 84 Jet Provost T 4 (As "XR673" in RAF c/s)	PAC/W/19986	9032M XR673	14. 8.97	S J Davies and S Eagle	(Rotherham and Doncaster)	19. 9.08P
G-BXLP	Sky 90-24 Balloon (Hot Air)	084		18. 9.97	G B Lescott "Heart of Gold"	Oxford	23. 8.08A
G-BXLR	PZL-110 Koliber 160A	04980077	SP-WGF (2) (SP-WGF (1)), (N150CD)	10. 6.98	I Foster tr Sligo Koliber Group	Strandhill, Sligo, County Sligo	21. 2.08S
G-BXLS	PZL-110 Koliber 160A	04980078	SP-WGG (2) SP-PEB (2), (SP-WGG (1) (N150CP)	23. 6.98	D C Bayes	Gamston	20. 9.08E
G-BXLT	SOCATA TB-200 Tobago XL	1457	F-GRBB EC-FNX, EC-234, F-GLFP	28. 4.97	R M Shears	Fairoaks	18. 6.07E
G-BXLW	Enstrom F-28F	734	N279SA G-BXLW, Thai Government/KASET 1712	11. 9.97	I Martin	Barton	14.10.07E
G-BXLY	Piper PA-28-151 Cherokee Warrior	28-7715220	G-WATZ N7641F	19. 9.97	Multiflight Ltd	Leeds-Bradford	13. 5.08E
G-BXMF	Cassutt Racer IIIM (Built J F Bakewell)	PFA 034-13003		19. 9.97	P R Fabish	Coldharbour Farm, Willingham	1. 1.08P
G-BXMG	Rotary Air Force RAF 2000 (Built G Hansen)	H2-92-3-59	PH-TEN	18. 8.97	J S Wright (New owner 2.04)	(Huddersfield)	17.12.03P

Reg	Type	C/n	Prev id	Date	Owner/Operator	Location	Expiry
G-BXML	Mooney M 20A	1594	OY-AIZ	26. 9.97	G Kay	Crosland Moor	28. 7.08E
G-BXMM	Cameron A-180 Balloon (Hot Air)	4252		28.10.97	B Conway	Wheatley, Oxford	3.11.00A
G-BXMV	Scheibe SF25C Falke	44223	D-KDFV	7. 8.97	K E Ballington	Yeatsall Farm, Abbots Bromley	24. 7.08E
	(Limbach SL1700)						
G-BXMX	Phoenix Currie Wot	PFA 058-13055		23. 9.97	M J Hayman	Watchford Farm, Yarcombe	10. 6.08P
	(Built M J Hayman)						
G-BXMY	Hughes 269C	74-0328	N9599F	20.10.97	Oxford Aviation Services Ltd	Oxford	15. 5.08E
	(Hughes 300)						
G-BXMZ	Diamond DA.20-A1 Katana	10236	C-GDMB	4.12.97	Flight Academy Scotland Ltd	Perth	12. 2.08E
G-BXNA	Avid Flyer	118	N5531J	10.10.97	A P Daines	(Great Yeldham, Halstead)	14.10.08P
	(Built L Pickett) (Rotax 503)						
G-BXNC	Europa Aviation Europa	122		13.10.97	J K Cantwell	(Ashton-under-Lyne)	
	(Built J K Cantwell - pr.no.PFA 247-12970)						
G-BXNN	de Havilland DHC-1 Chipmunk 22	C1/0849	WP983	4. 8.97	J N Robinson	Trenchard Farm, Eggesford	24. 4.08
	(As "WP983:B" in AAC c/s)						
G-BXNS	Bell 206B-3 JetRanger III	2385	N16822	3.11.97	Sterling Helicopters Ltd	Norwich	19.12.06T
G-BXNT	Bell 206B-3 JetRanger III	2398	N94CA N123AL	11.11.97	Sterling Helicopters Ltd	Hawarden	7.11.07E
G-BXNV	Colt AS-105 GD Airship (Hot Air)	4231		19. 2.98	The Sleeping Society	Edegem, Belgium	24. 7.04A
G-BXNX	Lindstrand LBL 210A Balloon (Hot Air)	318		3.11.97	Balloon School (International) Ltd		
						Colhook Common, Petworth	24. 3.05T
G-BXOA	Robinson R22 Beta	1614	N41132 JA7832	10.11.97	MG Group Ltd	Sywell	8. 3.08E
G-BXOC	Evans VP-2	PFA 063-10305		29. 9.97	H J and E M Cox	(Bideford)	29. 4.08P
	(Built H J Cox)						
G-BXOF	Diamond DA.20-A1 Katana	10256	C-FDVP	4.12.97	Cumbernauld Flying School Ltd	Cumbernauld	30. 1.08E
G-BXOI	Cessna 172R Skyhawk	17280145	N9990F	17.11.97	E J Watts	Bodmin	4. 2.08E
G-BXOJ	Piper PA-28-161 Warrior III	2842010	N9265G	15.12.97	Craigard Property Trading Ltd	(Southampton)	5. 3.08E
G-BXOM	Isaacs Spitfire	PFA 027-12768		25.11.97	J H Betton	(Betws, Ammanford)	
	(Built J H Betton)						
G-BXON	Auster AOP.9	xxxx	WZ729	1.12.97	C J and D J Baker	Carr Farm, Thorney, Newark	
	(Officially regd with Frame no.AUS/10/60)				(On rebuild 1.05)		
G-BXOR	Robin HR.200-120B	321		1.12.97	Multiflight Ltd	Leeds-Bradford	22. 4.08E
G-BXOS	Cameron A-200 Balloon (Hot Air)	4286		19. 2.98	Airborne Balloon Management Ltd		
						Paddock Wood, Tonbridge	22. 5.04T
G-BXOT	Cameron C-70 Balloon (Hot Air)	4200		21.10.97	R J Plume tr Dante Balloon Group	Hungerford	19. 6.08A
G-BXOU	CEA Jodel DR.360 Chevalier	312	F-BPOU	6.10.97	J A Lofthouse	Blackpool	20. 5.08E
G-BXOW	Cameron Colt 105A Balloon (Hot Air)	4228		9. 1.98	M E White	Dublin	13. 7.08A
G-BXOX	Grumman American AA-5A Cheetah	AA5A-0694	F-GBDS	27. 2.98	R L Carter and P J Large	Turweston	16. 4.08E
G-BXOY	QAC Quickie Q.235	PFA 094-12183		17.11.97	C C Clapham	Enstone	3. 9.04P
	(Built C C Clapham) (Lycoming O-235)				(Noted 5.06)		
G-BXOZ	Piper PA-28-181 Cherokee Archer II	28-7790173	N6927F	14.10.97	Oz Air Ltd	Panshanger	9. 5.08T
G-BXPC	Diamond DA.20-A1 Katana	10258	C-GKAN	4.12.97	Cubair Flight Training Ltd	Redhill	18. 5.08E
G-BXPD	Diamond DA.20-A1 Katana	10259	C-GDMU	4.12.97	Cubair Flight Training Ltd	Redhill	13. 5.08E
G-BXPI	Van's RV-4	PFA 181-12426		2. 1.98	Cavendish Aviation Ltd	Gamston	23. 6.08P
	(Built E M Marsh) (Lycoming O-360-A1A)						
G-BXPK	Cameron A-250 Balloon (Hot Air)	4226		2. 2.98	Alba Ballooning Ltd	Edinburgh EH9	27. 3.08T
G-BXPL	Piper PA-28-140 Cherokee	28-24560	N7224J	10.12.97	C R Guggenheim	Bournemouth	22. 5.08T
G-BXPM	Beech 58 Baron	TH-1677	N207ZM	10.10.97	Foyle Flyers Ltd	City of Derry	17. 5.08E
G-BXPP	Sky 90-24 Balloon (Hot Air)	092		17.12.97	S J Farrant	Hydestile, Godalming	14. 3.08A
G-BXPR	Cameron Can 110 SS Balloon (Hot Air)	4218		2. 2.98	P O Wagner	Blankenhagen, Germany	10. 4.08A
G-BXPT	Ultramagic H-77 Balloon (Hot Air)	77/140		22.12.97	G D O Bartram	Ordino, Andorra	6. 4.05A
G-BXRA	Mudry CAP.10B	03	French AF 03	12.12.97	J W Scott	Bidford	22. 9.07
					(P/i F-TFVR also quoted but this may be c/n 3) (New owner 2.08)		
G-BXRB	Mudry CAP.10B	100	FrAF 100	12.12.97	T T Duhig	Spilstead Farm, Sedlescombe	29. 7.08E
G-BXRC	Mudry CAP.10B	134	FrAF 134	12.12.97	I F Scott tr Group Alpha	Fenland	31. 3.08E
G-BXRD	Enstrom 280FX	2012	PH-JVM N213M	22.12.97	K Payne and M A Stephenson		
						(Maxey, Peterborough)	25. 3.08E
G-BXRF	Scintex CP.1310-C3 Super Emeraude	935	OO-NSF F-BMJG	9. 1.98	D T Gethin	Swansea	30. 6.06
G-BXRG	Piper PA-28-181 Archer II	28-7990036	PH-LEC N21173	29. 1.98	Alderney Flying Training Ltd	Alderney	1. 3.08E
G-BXRH	Cessna 185A Skywagon	185-0413	HB-CRX N1613Z	10.12.97	R E M Holmes	Ronaldsway	7. 6.08E
	(Hoerner wing-tips)						
G-BXRM	Cameron A-210 Balloon (Hot Air)	4237		23. 4.98	Dragon Balloon Company Ltd	Castleton, Hope Valley	3.11.07T
G-BXRO	Cessna U206G Stationair II	U20604217	OH-ULK N756NE	9. 2.98	Maggie.Penny	(Movenis, Coleraine)	17. 4.08E
G-BXRP	Schweizer 269C	S 1334	OH-HSP N7506U	27. 1.98	Exmouth Developments Ltd	Dunkeswell	20. 3.08E
	(Schweizer 300)						
G-BXRR	Westland Scout AH.1	F9740	XW612	28. 1.98	BN Helicopters Ltd	Bembridge	13.10.06P
G-BXRS	Westland Scout AH.1	F9741	XW613	28. 1.98	B-N Group Ltd	Bembridge	15. 5.08P
G-BXRT	Robin DR.400-180 Régent	2382		23. 2.98	R A Ford	White Waltham	21. 6.08E
G-BXRV	Van's RV-4	PFA 181-12482		12. 1.98	B J Oke tr Cleeve Flying Group	Gloucestershire	9. 6.08P
	(Built B J Oke) (Lycoming O-320)						
G-BXRY	Bell 206B-2 JetRanger II	208	N4054G	19. 3.98	Corbett Holdings Ltd	Hawarden	23. 9.08E
G-BXRZ	Rans S-6-116 Coyote II	0897.1146		3. 2.98	J R Pearce	Chilbolton	13. 2.08P
	(Built C M White - pr.no.PFA 204A-13195) (Rotax 912-UL) (Tailwheel u/c)						
G-BXSC	Cameron C-80 Balloon (Hot Air)	4251		12.12.97	N A Apsey	Hazlemere, High Wycombe	10. 4.08A
G-BXSD	Cessna 172R Skyhawk	17280310	N431ES	12. 3.98	R Paston	Wellesbourne Mountford	6. 3.08E
G-BXSE	Cessna 172R Skyhawk	17280352	N9321F	19. 5.98	MK Aero Support Ltd	Andrewsfield	15. 7.08E
G-BXSG	Robinson R22 Beta II	2789		3. 2.98	Rivermead Aviation Ltd	Goodwood	18. 4.07T
G-BXSH	DG Flugzeugbau DG-800B	8-121B50		5. 2.98	R O'Conor	Sutton Bank	16.11.07E
G-BXSI	Avtech Jabiru SK	0139		5. 2.98	Leath Ltd	Wellcross Grange, Slinfold	11. 7.08P
	(Built V R Leggott pr.no.PFA 274-13204)						

Reg	Type	C/n	Prev id	Date	Owner/Operator	Location	
G-BXSJ	Cameron C-80 Balloon (Hot Air)	4330		24. 3.98	Balloon School (International) Ltd t/a British School of Ballooning Colhook Common, Petworth		26. 7.05T
G-BXSP	Grob G109B	6335	D-KNEA	25. 3.98	J R Dransfield tr Deeside Grob Group	Aboyne	13.10.07
G-BXSR	Reims Cessna F172N Skyhawk II	F17202003	PH-SPY D-EITH	6. 2.98	N C K G Copeman	(Fulbourn, Cambridge)	21. 4.08E
G-BXST	Piper PA-25-235 Pawnee C *(Frame No.25-4971)*	25-4952	PH-BAT N8532L	9. 2.98	The Northumbria Gliding Club Ltd	Currock Hill	19. 7.08E
G-BXSU	TEAM Mini-MAX 91A *(Built A R Carr)* (Rotax 503)	PFA 186-12357	G-MYGL	20. 2.98	M R Overall	Wethersfield, Braintree	30. 7.08P
G-BXSV	SNCAN Stampe SV-4C *(Noted 2.06 for rebuild)*	556	N21PM F-BDDB	10.10.02	B A Bower	(Crawley)	
G-BXSX	Cameron V-77 Balloon (Hot Air)	4329		6. 4.98	D R Medcalf *"All Tech"*	Bromsgrove	18. 5.08A
G-BXSY	Robinson R22 Beta II	2778		27. 1.98	N M G Pearson	Bristol	5. 2.07T
G-BXTB	Cessna 152 II	15282516	OH-CMS N69151	25. 2.98	N Clark	Newcastle	8. 5.08E
G-BXTD	Europa Aviation Europa *(Built P R Anderson - pr.no.PFA 247-12772)* (Monowheel u/c)	155		26. 2.98	P R Anderson	Hucknall	31. 5.08P
G-BXTE	Cameron A-275 Balloon (Hot Air)	4028		30. 3.98	Global Ballooning Ltd	Uckfield	16. 5.07T
G-BXTF	Cameron N-105 Balloon (Hot Air)	4304		2. 4.98	Flying Pictures Ltd *"Sainsbury's Strawberry"*	Chilbolton, Stockbridge	30. 6.06A
G-BXTG	Cameron N-42 Balloon (Hot Air)	4305		2. 4.98	P M Watkins and S M M Carden	Chippenham	13. 9.07A
G-BXTH	Westland SA.341D Gazelle HT.3	WA1120	XW866	13. 3.98	Armstrong Aviation Ltd *"E"*	Kirkbride	5. 7.08P
G-BXTI	Pitts S-1S *(Built N J Pesch)*	NP-1	ZS-VZX N96MM	9. 3.98	A B Theherne-Pollock tr BXTI Group	White Waltham	25. 7.08P
G-BXTJ	Cameron N-77 Balloon (Hot Air)	4332		6. 4.98	J M Albury *(Chubb titles)*	Cirencester	1. 9.08A
G-BXTN	Aérospatiale-Alenia ATR 72-202	483	F-WQNR G-BXTN, F-WWEV	24.10.97	Aurigny Air Services Ltd	Guernsey	19. 2.08E
G-BXTO	Hindustan HAL-26 Pushpak *(Continental C90-8F)*	PK-128	9V-BAI VT-DWM	12. 2.98	P Q.Benn	Draycott Farm, Chiseldon	22. 5.08P
G-BXTS	Diamond DA.20-A1 Katana	10308	N638DA C-GKAC	10. 3.98	I M Armitage	Bristol	26. 8.07T
G-BXTT	Grumman AA-5B Tiger	AA5B-0749	F-GBDH	27. 2.98	M N Stevens	(Oakley, Basingstoke)	16. 4.08E
G-BXTV	Cope Bug	BUG.2		12. 3.98	B R Cope	(Bewdley)	
G-BXTW	Piper PA-28-181 Archer III	2843137	N41279 (G-BXTW), N41279	26. 5.98	J N Davison t/a Davison Plant Hire	Compton Abbas	28. 6.08
G-BXTY	Piper PA-28-161 Cadet	2841179	PH-LED	11. 3.98	Bflying Ltd) *(Operated Bournemouth Flying Club)*	Bournemouth	27. 6.08E
G-BXTZ	Piper PA-28-161 Cadet	2841181	PH-LEE	11. 3.98	Bflying Ltd *(Operated Bournemouth Flying Club)*	Bournemouth	16. 4.08E
G-BXUA	Campbell Cricket Mk.5 *(Built P C Lovegrrove)* (Rotax 582)	PFA G/03-1272		12. 3.98	R N Bodley	Henstridge	9. 1.08P
G-BXUC	Robinson R22 Beta	0908	OY-HFB	17. 3.98	Rivermead Aviation Ltd	Goodwood	29. 4.08T
G-BXUE	Sky 240-24 Balloon (Hot Air)	098		30. 4.98	G M Houston t/a Scotair Balloons	Lesmahagow	11. 4.08T
G-BXUF	Agusta-Bell 206B-2 JetRanger II	8633	EC-DUS	12. 5.98	SJ Contracting Services Ltd	Beckley, Oxford	13. 8.08T
G-BXUG	Lindstrand Baby Bel SS Balloon (Hot Air)	512		14. 5.98	Karl-Heinz Gruenauer	Schwaebisch Hall, Germany	5. 6.08E
G-BXUH	Lindstrand LBL 31A Balloon (Hot Air)	513		2. 6.98	A D Kent tr Balloon Preservation Flying Group	Petworth	26.10.07A
G-BXUI	DG Flugzeugbau DG-800B	8-105B39	BGA 4382 D-KKLC	12. 5.98	J Le Coyte	Sandhill Farm, Shrivenham	22. 3.08
G-BXUM	Europa Aviation Europa *(Built D Bosomworth - pr.no.PFA 247-12611)* (Monowheel u/c)	067		19. 3.98	D Bosomworth *(Transported from home for flying)*	Popham	8. 5.07P
G-BXUO	Lindstrand LBL 105A Balloon (Hot Air)	520		27. 3.98	Lindstrand Technologies Ltd *(New owner 6.07)*	Oswestry	18.12.05A
G-BXUS	Sky 65-24 Balloon (Hot Air)	111		6. 4.98	PSH Skypower Ltd	Woodborough, Pewsey	16. 5.08A
G-BXUU	Cameron V-65 Balloon (Hot Air)	4362		23. 4.98	M D Freeston and S Mitchell	Hertford	5. 4.08A
G-BXUW	Cameron Colt 90A Balloon (Hot Air)	4317		23. 4.98	Zycomm Electronics Ltd	Ripley	25. 5.08A
G-BXUX	Brandli BX-2 Cherry *(Built M F Fountain)* (Continental C90-12F)	PFA 179-12571		4. 4.98	M F Fountain	Clipgate Farm,Denton	26.11.08P
G-BXUY	Cessna 310Q	310Q0231	N137SA D-IHMT, N7731Q	16. 4.98	Massair Ltd	Liverpool	28.11.07E
G-BXVA	SOCATA TB-200 Tobago XL	1325	F-GJXL F-WJXL	15. 4.98	H R Palser	Cardiff	24. 7.08E
G-BXVB	Cessna 152 II	15282584	N69250	15. 4.98	PJC (Leasing) Ltd	Stapleford	25. 9.08E
G-BXVD	CFM Streak Shadow SA *(Built CFM Aircraft Ltd - pr.no..PFA 206-13304)* (Rotax 912)	K 301-SA		1. 4.98	R C Osler	Over Farm, Gloucester	9. 2.08P
G-BXVG	Sky 77-24 Balloon (Hot Air)	99		28. 5.98	M Wolf	Wallingford	22. 7.08
G-BXVJ	Cameron O-120 Balloon (Hot Air)	2201	PH-VVJ G-IMAX	12. 3.98	Aerosaurus Balloons Ltd	Whimple, Exeter	4. 4.06T
G-BXVK	Robin HR.200-120B	326		1. 7.98	Modi Aviation Ltd	Sibson	23. 6.08E
G-BXVL	Sky 180-24 Balloon (Hot Air)	113		16. 6.98	A W Talbott *(New owner 5.06)*	Birmingham	24. 7.05T
G-BXVM	Van's RV-6A *(Built J G Small)* (Lycoming O-320)	PFA 181-13103		26. 2.98	J C Lomax	Andreas, Isle of Man	22. 5.08P
G-BXVO	Van's RV-6A *(Built P J Hynes)* (Lycoming O-320-D1A)	PFA 181-12575		28. 4.98	M E and P J Hynes	Sleap	24. 8.08P
G-BXVP	Sky 31-24 Balloon (Hot Air)	056		28. 4.98	T Dudman *(Sky Balloon titles)*	Cleeve, Bristol	13. 4.08A
G-BXVR	Sky 90-24 Balloon (Hot Air)	061		20. 7.98	P Hegarty	Magherafelt, County Londonderry	8. 6.08
G-BXVS	Brügger MB.2 Colibri *(Built G T Snoddon)* (Volkswagen 1834)	PFA 043-11948		5. 5.98	G T Snoddon	Newtownards	19. 5.03P
G-BXVT	Cameron O-77 Balloon (Hot Air)	1444	PH-MKB	30. 7.98	R P Wade	Shevington, Wigan	
G-BXVU	Piper PA-28-161 Cherokee Warrior II	28-7816063	N47372	5. 5.98	Jet Connections Ltd	Lydd	24. 8.08E
G-BXVV	Cameron V-90 Balloon (Hot Air)	4369		5. 5.98	Floating Sensations Ltd	Thatcham	28. 4.08A
G-BXVW	Colt Piggy Bank SS Balloon (Hot Air)	4366		2. 7.98	G Binder	Sonnennbuhl, Germany	2. 8.03A
G-BXVX	Rutan Cozy Classic *(Built G E Murray)* (Lycoming O-320)	PFA 159-12680		6. 5.98	G E Murray	Swansea	21.10.03P

Reg	Type	C/n	Prev id	Date	Owner/Operator	Base	Status
G-BXVY	Cessna 152	15279808	N757KU	11. 5.98	Stapleford Flying Club Ltd	Stapleford	18.11.07E
G-BXVZ	WSK-PZL Mielec TS-11 Iskra	3H-1625	SP-DOF	27. 3.98	J Ziubrzynski (Noted 7.05)	Manston	
G-BXWA	Beech 76 Duchess	ME-232	OY-CYM	8. 4.98	Aviation South West Ltd	Exeter	18. 7.08E
			(SE-IUY), D-GBTD				
G-BXWB	Robin HR.100-200B Royal	08	HB-EMT	29. 4.98	W A Brunwin	Oaksey Park	14.10.07E
G-BXWC	Cessna 152	15283640	N4794B	11. 5.98	PJC (Leasing) Ltd	Stapleford	12. 7.07T
G-BXWG	Sky 120-24 Balloon (Hot Air)	114		28. 5.98	M E White	Trim, County Meath	30. 6.07T
G-BXWH	Denney Kitfox Model 4-1200 Speedster			4. 3.98	B J Finch	Long Marston	11. 6.08P
	(Built B J Finch)	PFA 172A-12343			"Bumble 2"		
G-BXWK	Rans S-6-ESA Coyote II	0298.1020		19. 5.98	M A Newbould	Baxby Manor, Husthwaite	26. 4.08P
	(Built J Whiting - pr.no.PFA 204-13317) (Rotax 582) (Tri-cycle u/c)						
G-BXWL	Sky 90-24 Balloon (Hot Air)	117		20. 7.98	D J Baggley	Stoke-on-Trent	8 .6.07A
G-BXWO	Piper PA-28-181 Archer II	28-8190311	D-ENHA (2)	22. 5.98	J S Develin and Z Islam	Redhill	5. 6.08E
			N8431C				
G-BXWP	Piper PA-32-300 Cherokee Six	32-7340088	N8143D	26. 5.98	J M Hill and I Jones tr Alliance Aviation	Barton	8. 2.08E
			G-BXWP, OE-DRR, N16452				
G-BXWR	CFM Streak Shadow SA	K 289-SA	G-MZMI	22. 5.98	M A Hayward	Bodmin	19.11.08P
	(Built M Hayward - pr.no.PFA 206-13205) (Rotax 912)						
G-BXWT	Van's RV-6	PFA 181-12639		19. 7.96	R C Owen	Danehill	25. 9.07P
	(Built R C Owen) (Lycoming O-360						
G-BXWU	FLS Aerospace Sprint 160	003	G-70-503	5. 6.98	Eurojet Aircraft Leasing 3 Ltd	(Bexhill-on-Sea)	
					(New owner 12.06)		
G-BXWV	FLS Aerospace Sprint 160	005	G-70-505	5. 6.98	Eurojet Aircraft Leasing 3 Ltd	(Bexhill-on-Sea)	
					(New owner 12.06)		
G-BXWX	Sky 25-16 Balloon (Hot Air)	082		29. 5.98	C O'Neill and G Davis	Crosserlough, County Cavan	
					(New owners 12.07)		
G-BXXG	Cameron N-105 Balloon (Hot Air)	3662		19. 6.98	Allen Owen Ltd	Wotton-under-Edge	2. 4.02A
G-BXXH	Hatz CB-1	PFA 143-12445		9. 6.98	R F Shingler	Forest Farm, Welshpool	18. 6.08P
	(Built R F Shingler)						
G-BXXI	Grob G109B	6400	F-CAQR	9. 6.98	M N Martin	Saltby	23.10.07
			F-WAQR		(Noted 2.08)		
G-BXXJ	Colt Flying Yacht SS Balloon (Hot Air)	1797	JA-A0515	10. 6.98	Magical Adventures Ltd		
						West Bloomfield, Michigan, US	7. 9.01A
G-BXXK	Reims Cessna F172N Skyhawk II	F17201806	D-EOPP	15. 6.98	I R Chaplin	North Weald	6. 9.08E
G-BXXL	Cameron N-105 Balloon (Hot Air)	4408		16. 7.98	Flying Pictures Ltd	Chilbolton, Stockbridge	11. 9.05A
					(Blue Peter titles)		
G-BXXN	Robinson R22 Beta	0720	N720HH	16. 6.98	L L Smith t/a Helicopter Services	Wycombe Air Park	26. 7.08T
G-BXXO	Lindstrand LBL 90B Balloon (Hot Air)	534		6. 7.98	K Temple	Tivetshall St Margaret, Norwich	7. 8.07A
G-BXXP	Sky 77-24 Balloon (Hot Air)	124		20. 7.98	C J James	Wincanton	31. 7.08A
G-BXXR	Lovegrove AV-8 Gyroplane	PFA G/15-1263		29. 6.98	P C Lovegrove	(Didcot)	
	(Built P C Lovegrove and officially regd. as "Lovegrove BGL Four Runner" with c/n PFA G/15-1273)						
G-BXXS	Sky 105-24 Balloon (Hot Air)	116		30. 7.98	L D and H Vaughan "Skylark"	Tring	4. 7.08A
G-BXXT	Beech 76 Duchess	ME-212	(N212BE)	17. 7.98	Pridenote Ltd	Sturgate	29. 9.07E
			F-GBOZ				
G-BXXU	Colt 31A Balloon (Hot Air)	4427		21. 8.98	Sade Balloons Ltd	Coulsdon	23. 3.08
G-BXXW	Enstrom F-28F	771	G-SCOX	2. 7.98	Fast Helicopters Ltd	Shoreham	8.12.07E
			N330SA, G-BXXW, JA7823				
G-BXYD	Eurocopter EC.120B Colibri	1006		7. 7.98	Aero Maintenance Ltd	Walton Wood	13.12.07E
G-BXYE	Scintex CP.301-C1 Emeraude	559	F-BTEO	8. 7.98	D T Gethin	Swansea	
			F-PTEO, F-WTEO, F-BJFV				
G-BXYF	Colt AS-105 GD Airship (Hot Air)	4433		7. 8.98	LN Flying Ltd	(Germany)	14.11.05E
G-BXYG	Cessna 310D	39089	HB-LSF	14. 8.98	Equitus SARL	Merville-Calonne, France	27. 2.08E
			F-GEJT, 3A-MCA, F-BBOT, F-OBOT, (N6789T)				
G-BXYH	Cameron N-105 Balloon (Hot Air)	4441		7. 8.98	N J Langley	Clapton in Gordano, Bristol	10. 5.06A
G-BXYI	Cameron H-34 Balloon (Hot Air)	4442		7. 8.98	S P Harrowing	Margam, Port Talbot	23. 6.07A
G-BXYJ	SAN Jodel DR.1050 Ambassadeur	143	F-BJNA	28. 7.98	C Brooke tr G-BXYJ Group	Netherthorpe	16. 1.08S
G-BXYK	Robinson R22 Beta	1579	N4037B	27. 7.98	D N Whittlestone	(Oxenhope)	8. 1.08E
G-BXYM	Piper PA-28-235 Cherokee Pathfinder	28-10858	SE-FAM	18. 8.98	Redfly Aviation Ltd	Shoreham	22.12.07E
G-BXYO	Piper PA-28RT-201 Arrow IV	28R-8018046	PH-SDD	18. 8.98	Airways Flight Training (Exeter) Ltd	Exeter	30.12.07E
			N8164M				
G-BXYP	Piper PA-28RT-201 Arrow IV	28R-8018050	PH-SBO	18. 8.98	G I Cooper	(Raydon, Ipswich)	7.12.07E
			N8168H				
G-BXYR	Piper PA-28RT-201 Arrow IV	28R-8018101	PH-SDA	3. 8.98	A Dayani	Exeter	29. 3.08E
			N8251B				
G-BXYT	Piper PA-28RT-201 Arrow IV	28R-7918198	PH-SBN	3. 8.98	Aviation Asset Management Ltd	Kemble	9. 9.07T
			(PH-SBM), OO-HLA, N2878W				
G-BXYX	Van's RV-6	22293	N2399C	31. 7.98	A G Palmer	Wellesbourne Mountford	30. 3.08P
	(Built A G Palmer) (Lycoming O-320-E2D)						
G-BXZA	Piper PA-38-112 Tomahawk	38-79A0864	N2480N	6. 8.98	P D Brooks	Inverness	29.10.07E
G-BXZB	Nanchang CJ-6A	2632019	Chinese AF	18. 9.98	Wingglider Ltd (As "2632019")	Hibaldstow	31. 5.02P
G-BXZF	Lindstrand LBL 90A Balloon (Hot Air)	575		8. 1.99	R G Carrell	Havant	21. 3.08A
G-BXZI	Lindstrand LBL 90A Balloon (Hot Air)	543		14. 8.98	J A Viner	Caterham	25. 6.08A
G-BXZK	MD Helicopters MD.900 Explorer	900-00057	N9238T	27. 8.98	Dorset Police Air Support Unit	Winfrith	17. 2.08E
			G-76-057				
G-BXZM	Cessna 182S Skylane	18280310	N2683L	8.10.98	AB Integro Aviation Ltd	White Waltham	18.11.07E
G-BXZO	Pietenpol AirCamper	PFA 047-12818		10. 7.98	P J Cooke	Westfield Farm, Hailsham	14. 7.07P
	(Built P J Cooke) (Continental A65)						
G-BXZT	Morane Saulnier MS.880B Rallye Club	1733	OO-EDG	2. 9.98	C O'Connor tr Naas Flying Group		
			D-EBDG, F-BSVL			(Naas, County Kildare)	1. 3.08E
G-BXZU	Micro Aviation B 22S Bantam	98-015	ZK-JJL	21. 9.98	M E Whapham and R W Hollamby		
						Corn Wood Farm, Adversane	11. 7.08P
G-BXZY	CFM Shadow Series DD	296-DD		21. 9.98	P A James t/a Cloudbase Aviation G-BXZY	Redhill	16.12.07P

G-BYAA - G-BYZZ

G-BYAA	Boeing 767-204ER	25058	PH-AHM	23. 4.91	Thomsonfly Ltd		Luton	13.11.07E
			G-BYAA, N60659		"Sir Matt Busby CBE"			
G-BYAB	Boeing 767-204ER	25139	(PH-AHN)	11. 6.91	Thomsonfly Ltd		Luton	26. 3.08E
			G-BYAB		"Brian Johnston CBE MC"			
G-BYAD	Boeing 757-204ER	26963		6. 5.92	Thomsonfly Ltd		Luton	22. 2.08E
G-BYAE	Boeing 757-204ER	26964		12. 5.92	Thomsonfly Ltd		Luton	26. 4.08E
G-BYAF	Boeing 757-204ER	26266		13. 1.93	Thomsonfly Ltd		Exeter	19. 1.08E
G-BYAH	Boeing 757-204	26966		5. 2.93	Thomsonfly Ltd		Luton	10. 2.08E
G-BYAI	Boeing 757-204	26967		1. 3.93	Thomsonfly Ltd		Luton	4. 3.08E
G-BYAJ	Boeing 757-204ER	25623		4. 3.93	Thomsonfly Ltd		Luton	23. 1.08E
G-BYAK	Boeing 757-204	26267		6. 4.93	Thomsonfly Ltd		Luton	13. 4.08E
G-BYAL	Boeing 757-204	25626		13. 5.93	Thomsonfly Ltd		Luton	18. 5.08E
G-BYAO	Boeing 757-204	27235		3. 2.94	Thomsonfly Ltd "Eric Morecambe OBE"		Luton	2. 2.08E
G-BYAP	Boeing 757-204	27236		15. 2.94	Thomsonfly Ltd "John Lennon"		Luton	14. 2.08E
G-BYAR	Boeing 757-204	27237	PH-AHT	1. 3.94	Thomsonfly Ltd		Luton	11. 6.08E
			G-BYAR					
G-BYAS	Boeing 757-204	27238		9. 3.94	Thomsonfly Ltd "Gordon Hill"		Luton	31. 1.08E
G-BYAT	Boeing 757-204	27208		21. 3.94	Thomsonfly Ltd		Luton	24. 3.08E
G-BYAU	Boeing 757-204	27220		18. 5.94	Thomsonfly Ltd		Luton	17. 5.08E
G-BYAV	Taylor JT.1 Monoplane	PFA 055-11010		27. 8.98	J S Marten-Hale		RAF Henlow	1. 5.08P
	(Built C J Pidler)							
G-BYAW	Boeing 757-204	27234		3. 4.95	Thomsonfly Ltd "Phil Stanley"		Luton	2. 4.08E
G-BYAX	Boeing 757-204	28834		24. 2.99	Thomsonfly Ltd		Luton	28. 2.08E
G-BYAY	Boeing 757-204	28836	N1786B	13. 4.99	Thomsonfly Ltd		Luton	12. 4.08E
G-BYAZ	CFM Streak Shadow SA	K 244		1. 9.98	A G Wright		Old Sarum	15. 8.08P
	(Built A G Wright - pr.no.PFA 206-12656) (Rotax 582)							
G-BYBA	Agusta-Bell 206B-3 JetRanger III	8596	G-BHXV	31. 3.98	D L and S M Dennett		Shobdon	9.10.07E
			G-OWJM, G-BHXV					
G-BYBC	Agusta-Bell 206B-2 JetRanger II	8567	G-BTWW	31. 3.98	Sky Charter UK Ltd		Hawarden	21.11.07E
			EI-BJV, G-BTWW					
G-BYBD	Cessna F172H	F172-0487	G-OBHX	6. 7.98	D G Bell and J Cartmell		Derby	29. 6.08T
	(Built Reims Aviation SA)		G-AWMU					
G-BYBE	Wassmer Jodel D 120A Paris-Nice	269	OO-FDP	24. 7.98	P G Wiggett and O Downes		Shipdham	14. 6.08E
G-BYBF	Robin R2160i	329 (2)		1.10.98	D J R Lloyd-Evans		Bournemouth	25 5.08E
	(Airframe replaced after collision with Kitfox G-LEED 9.02 but c/n retained)							
G-BYBH	Piper PA-34-200T Seneca II	34-8070078	N119SA	9. 6.00	Goldspear (UK) Ltd	(Holyport, Maidenhead)		7. 6.07
			(G-BYBH), N4023K, N3567B					
G-BYBI	Bell 206B-3 JetRanger III	3668	ZS-RGP	19.10.98	Winkburn Air Ltd		Elstree	3. 4.08E
			N5757M					
G-BYBJ	Medway Hybred 44XLR-C	MR156/135-C		22. 1.99	M Gardner		Rochester	25. 4.01P
	(Rotax 503)							
G-BYBK	Murphy Rebel	260R	N95LD	19. 8.98	M J Whiteman-Haywood			
	(Built L A Dyer)					Pound Green, Buttonoak, Bewdley		13. 4.06P
G-BYBL	Sud-Aviation Gardan GY-80-160D Horizon	127	F-BMUY	25. 9.98	R H W Beath		Exeter	11. 7.08E
G-BYBM	Avtech Jabiru SK	0201		18. 9.98	P J Hatton	(Bridestowe, Okehampton)		30.10.08P
	(Built M Rudd - pr.no.PFA 274-13377)							
G-BYBN	Cameron N-77 Balloon (Hot Air)	3082	N6004M	30. 9.98	M G and Renee.D Howard	Timperley, Altrincham		7. 4.08A
G-BYBO	Medway EclipseR	155/134		14. 9.98	D R Purslow	Pound Green, Buttonoak, Bewdley		16.12.07P
	(Jabiru 2200A)							
G-BYBP	Cessna A185F	185-03804	OO-DCD	15.10.98	G M S Scott	Bradley's Lawn, Heathfield		28. 2 08E
			F-GDCD, F-ODIA, N4593E					
G-BYBR	Rans S-6-116 Coyote II	0996.1042		10. 7.98	S and A F Williams		Exeter	5.11.07P
	(Built J B Robinson - pr.no.PFA 204A-13081) (Rotax 912-UL) (Tri-cycle u/c)							
G-BYBS	Sky 80-16 Balloon (Hot Air)	136		27.10.98	J E Rose (New owner 10.07)		Abingdon	10. 8.04
G-BYBU	Murphy Renegade Spirit UK	PFA 188-13229		12.10.98	L C Cook		Sywell	14. 9.08P
	(Built K R Anderson)							
G-BYBV	Mainair Rapier	1183-1198-7-W986		20.10.98	M W Robson		York	1.11.02P
G-BYBW	TEAM Mini-MAX 88	PFA 186-12120		19.10.98	D W Pearce		Redlands, Swindon	10. 4.08P
	(Built J E Johnson)							
G-BYBX	Slingsby T 67M-260 Firefly	2261		21.10.98	Slingsby Aviation Ltd	(Kirkbymoorside, York)		
G-BYBY	Thorp T-18C Tiger	492	N77KK	17. 7.98	P G Mair	(Lundin Links, Leven)		24. 7.08P
	(Built K K Knowles)							
G-BYBZ	Avtech Jabiru SK	0162		7. 9.98	N P D Smith		Little Gransden	18. 3.08P
	(Built A W Harris - pr.no.PFA 274-13290)							
G-BYCA	Piper PA-28-140 Cherokee D	28-7125223	PH-VRZ	24. 9.98	A Reay		Caernarfon	21. 3.08E
			N11C					
G-BYCB	Sky 21-16 Balloon (Hot Air)	142		28.10.98	S J Colin (Active 5.07)	Headcorn, Ashford		
G-BYCD	Cessna 140	13744	N4273N	28. 9.98	G P James	(Oak Farm, Cowbit)		12. 5.08E
	(Continental O-200-A)		NC4273N					
G-BYCE	Robinson R44 Astro	0520		12.10.98	C A Rosenberg	(Groesfaen, Pontyclun)		30.10.07T
G-BYCF	Robinson R22 Beta II	2866		12.10.98	R F McLachlan	(Rodsley, Ashbourne)		29. 2.08E
G-BYCJ	CFM Shadow Series DD	K 294-DD		14.10.98	P I Hodgson	(Ilford)		19. 7.08P
	(Built J W E Pearson - pr.no.PFA 161-13258)							
G-BYCL	Raj Hamsa X'Air Jabiru(1)	331		15.10.98	D O'Keefe, K Rutter and A J Clarke	London Colney		31. 7.08P
	(Built G A J Salter - pr.no.BMAA/HB/088)							
G-BYCM	Rans S-6-ES Coyote II	0298.1204		15. 9.98	E W McMullan	(Dunnyvadden, County Antrim)		7.11.00P
	(Built E W McMullan - pr.no.PFA 204-13315)							
G-BYCN	Rans S-6-ES Coyote II	0298.1205		15. 9.98	T J Croskery		City of Derry	7. 8.08P
	(Built J K and R L Dunseath - pr.no.PFA 204-13314) (Rotax 582)							
G-BYCP	Beech B200 Super King Air	BB-966	F-GDCS	15.10.98	London Executive Aviation Ltd		Stapleford	11. 2.08E
G-BYCS	CEA Jodel DR.1051 Sicile	201	F-BJUJ	28.10.98	M C Bennett		Perranporth	11. 5.08

Reg	Type	C/n	Prev id	Date	Owner	Location	Code
G-BYCT	Aero L-29A Delfin	395142	ES-YLH Estonian AF, Soviet AF	29.10.98	Propeller BVBA (Noted 6.06)	North Weald	2. 6.04P
G-BYCV	Murphy Maverick	PFA 259-12925		24. 9.98	M Martin	(Leverington, Wisbech)	19. 8.08P
	(Built P C Vallance) (Rotax 503)						
G-BYCW	Mainair Blade	1185-1198-7-W988		5.11.98	P C Watson	St Michaels	14. 6.08P
G-BYCX	Westland Wasp HAS.1	F9754 & WA-B-Z3	ZK-HOX South African Navy 92	9.11.98	BN Helicopters Ltd (As "92" in South African Navy c/s) (Noted 1.08)	Thruxton	12. 7.06P
G-BYCY	III Sky Arrow 650 T	PFA 298-13332		10.11.98	K A Daniels	Upfield Farm,Whitson	7. 8.08P
	(Built A S Spriglings)						
G-BYCZ	Avtech Jabiru SK	xxxx		16.10.98	R Scroby (Noted 10.07)	Leicester	12. 9.07P
	(Built C Hewer - pr.no.PFA 274-13388)						
G-BYDB	Grob G115B	8025	VH-JVL D-EFCG	26. 3.99	J B Baker	Tatenhill	28. 4.08E
G-BYDE	Vickers Supermarine 361 Spitfire IX		Soviet AF PT879	11.11.98	P A Teichman (Noted 1.06)	North Weald	
		CBAF IX.2922					
G-BYDF	Sikorsky S-76A	760364	JA6615	9. 1.98	Brecqhou Development Ltd	Guernsey	12. 7.08E
G-BYDG	Beech C24R Sierra	MC-627	OY-AZL	9.11.98	Professional Flight Simulation Ltd	Bournemouth	14. 6.08E
G-BYDJ	Colt 120A Balloon (Hot Air)	3527		17.11.98	D K Hempleman-Adams	Corsham	8. 8.08A
G-BYDK	SNCAN Stampe SV-4C	55	F-BCXY French AF	20.11.98	Bianchi Aviation Film Services Ltd (Wycombe Air Park) (Stored in rafters in hangar 6.06)		
	(Official p/i quoted as F-BCXV which is c/n 298)						
G-BYDL	Hawker Hurricane IIB	Not known	Soviet AF Z5207	17.11.98	P J Lawton (New owner 9.07)	Thruxton	
G-BYDT	Cameron N-90 Balloon (Hot Air)	4499		28. 1.99	N J Langley (Tesco titles)	Clapton in Gordano, Bristol	10. 5.06A
G-BYDU	Cameron Cart SS Balloon (Hot Air)	4500		28. 1.99	N J Langley (Tesco titles)	Clapton in Gordano, Bristol	3. 4.04A
G-BYDV	Van's RV-6	PFA 181-13264		3.12.98	R G Andrews	King's Farm, Thurrock	8. 6.08P
	(Built G L Carpenter) (Lycoming O-320)						
G-BYDY	Beech 58 Baron	TH-1852	C-GBWF	10.11.98	Pilot Services Flying Group Ltd	Fairoaks	13. 1.08E
G-BYDZ	Cyclone Airsports Pegasus Quantum 15-912	7493		22.12.98	P Newson	Sutton Meadows	30. 4.08P
G-BYEA	Cessna 172P Skyhawk	17275464	PH-ILL N63661	7.10.98	Falcon Flying Services Ltd	Biggin Hill	20. 9.08E
G-BYEC	DG Flugzeugbau DG-800B	8-102B36	D-KSDG	13.11.98	P R Redshaw "23"	Walney Island	6. 3.08E
G-BYEE	Mooney M 20K Mooney 231	25-0282	N231JZ	20. 7.88	R J Baker and W Woods tr Double Echo Flying Group	Coventry	11. 5.07
G-BYEH	CEA Jodel DR.250/160 Capitaine	15	OO-SOL F-BMZL	6.10.98	Nicholson Decommissioning Ltd	Derryogue	17. 4.08E
G-BYEJ	Scheibe SF28A Tandem Falke	5713	OE-9070 (D-KDAM)	18.12.98	D Shrimpton	RAF Keevil	13.11.07E
G-BYEK	Stoddard-Hamilton GlaStar	PFA 295-13087	ZK-NEW G-BYEK	14. 9.98	G M New (Noted Tauranga, New Zealand 2.06)	Bagby	29.10.07P
	(Built G M New) (Continental IO-240) (Tailwheel u/c)						
G-BYEL	Van's RV-6	PFA 181-12568		7. 1.99	D Millar	Bidford	7. 8.08P
	(Built D T Smith) (Lycoming O-320)						
G-BYEM	Cessna R182 Skylane RG II	R18200822	N494 D-ELVI, N737FT	8. 1.99	Wycombe Air Centre Ltd	Wycombe Air Park	30. 1.08E
G-BYEO	Zenair CH.601HDS Zodiac	PFA 162-13345		11. 1.99	B S Carpenter	Strubby	20. 7.08P
	(Built B S Carpenter and M W Elliott) (Tail-wheel u/c)						
G-BYER	Cameron C-80 Balloon (Hot Air)	4513		19.11.98	J M Langley	Ebley, Stroud	7. 9.08A
G-BYES	Cessna 172P Skyhawk	17274514	PH-ILN N172TP, N52424	7.10.98	Redhill Air Services Ltd	Redhill	25.11.07E
G-BYET	Cessna 172P Skyhawk	17275122	PH-ILP N55158	7.10.98	Redhill Air Services Ltd (Noted 2.08)	Rochester	4.11.07E
G-BYEW	Cyclone Airsports Pegasus Quantum 15-912	7499		15. 1.99	D Martin "Attitude not Altitude"	Strathaven	30. 6.08P
G-BYEX	Sky 120-24 Balloon (Hot Air)	135		21. 1.99	Ballongflyg Upp and Ner AB	Stockholm, Sweden	5. 3.08A
G-BYEY	Lindstrand LBL 21 Silver Dream Balloon (Hot Air)	577		15. 1.99	Oscair Project Ltd	Täby, Sweden	
G-BYEZ	Dyn'Aéro MCR-01 Club	47		25.11.98	J P Davies	Leicester	14. 9.08P
	(Built J P Davies - pr.no.PFA 301-13185)						
G-BYFA	Reims Cessna F152 II	F15201968	G-WACA	19.11.98	A J Gomes	Rochester	16. 3.08E
G-BYFC	Avtech Jabiru SK	0209		5. 2.99	I P Fisher	Cherry Tree Farm, Monewden	10. 5.08P
	(Built A C N Freeman - pr.no.PFA 274-13344)						
G-BYFD	Grob G115A	8100	EI-CCN G-BSGE	15. 1.99	M Kane tr Kane Group	Kilrush, County Kildare	25. 8.08E
G-BYFE	Cyclone Airsports Pegasus Quantum 15-912	7496		21. 6.99	J L Pollard tr G-BYFE Syndicate	Knapthorpe Lodge, Caunton	17. 3.08P
G-BYFF	Cyclone Airsports Pegasus Quantum 15-912	7500		1. 2.99	D Young tr Kemble Flying Club	Kemble	2. 4.08P
G-BYFG	Europa Aviation Europa XS	396		22. 1.99	R Hawkes tr BDR Flying Group	Tatenhill	2.12.07P
	(Built P R Brodie - pr.no.PFA 247-13407) (Jabiru 3300) (Tri-gear u/c)						
G-BYFI	CFM Starstreak Shadow SA-II	xxx		11. 2.99	J A Cook	(Aldringham, Leiston)	3. 9.08P
	(Built D G Cook - pr.no.PFA 206-13300)						
G-BYFJ	Cameron N-105 Balloon (Hot Air)	4545		4. 3.99	R J Mercer	Belfast	8. 6.08E
G-BYFL	Diamond HK 36 TTS Super Dimona	36.623		5. 2.99	C N J Squibb tr Seahawk Gliding Club	RNAS Culdrose	26. 7.08E
G-BYFM	Jodel DR.1050-M1 Sicile Record	PFA 304-13237		26. 2.99	A J Roxburgh	Barton	5. 6.08P
	(Built P M Standen and A J Roxburgh) (Continental O-200-A)						
G-BYFR	Piper PA-32R-301 Saratoga II HP	3246133	N4135P G-BYFR, N9515N	13. 4.99	Buckleton Ltd	Fairoaks	12. 7.08T
G-BYFT	Pietenpol AirCamper	PFA 047-13057		22.12.98	G Everett	(Sandway, Maidstone)	7.11.08P
	(Built M W Elliott) (Subaru EA81)						
G-BYFU	Lindstrand LBL 105B Balloon (Hot Air)	594		9. 3.99	Balloons Lindstrand France	Curcay-sur-Dive, France	25. 4.06A
G-BYFV	TEAM Mini-MAX 91	PFA 186-13431		5. 2.99	W E Gillham	Croft Farm, Croft-on-Tees	16. 7.08P
	(Built W E Gillham)						
G-BYFX	Colt 77A Balloon (Hot Air)	4547		4. 3.99	Wye Valley Aviation Ltd (New owner 9.07)	Bridstowe, Ross-on-Wye	5. 5.05A
G-BYFY	Mudry CAP.10B	263	F-GKKD	9. 3.99	R N Crosland	Deanland	1. 8.08E
G-BYGA	Boeing 747-436	28855		15.12.98	British Airways PLC	London Heathrow	13.12.07E

G-BYGB	Boeing 747-436	28856		17. 1.99	British Airways PLC	London Heathrow	3. 7.08E
G-BYGC	Boeing 747-436	25823		19. 1.99	British Airways PLC	London Heathrow	23.10.07E
G-BYGD	Boeing 747-436	28857		26. 1.99	British Airways PLC	London Heathrow	23.10.07E
G-BYGE	Boeing 747-436	28858		5. 2.99	British Airways PLC	London Heathrow	4. 2.08E
G-BYGF	Boeing 747-436	25824		17. 2.99	British Airways PLC	London Heathrow	16. 2.08E
G-BYGG	Boeing 747-436	28859		29. 4.99	British Airways PLC	London Heathrow	28. 4.08E
G-BYHC	Cameron Z-90 Balloon (Hot Air)	4555		16. 3.99	S M Sherwin *(Darlows titles)*	Morton, Bourne	25. 2.07
G-BYHE	Robinson R22 Beta	2023	N82128 LV-VAB	14. 1.99	Helicopter Services Ltd	Wycombe Air Park	3. 3.08E
G-BYHG	Dornier 328-100	3098	D-CDAE	7. 4.99	Suckling Aviation (Cambridge) Ltd t/a Scot Airways *(Blue Islands c/s)*	Guernsey	6. 4.08E
G-BYHH	Piper PA-28-161 Warrior III	2842050	N4126Z G-BYHH, N9527N	15. 6.99	Stapleford Flying Club Ltd	Stapleford	19. 6.08E
G-BYHI	Piper PA-28-161 Warrior II	28-8116084	SE-IDP	4. 1.99	Haimoss Ltd *(Operated Old Sarum Flying Club)*	Old Sarum	27. 3.08T
G-BYHJ	Piper PA-28R-201 Arrow	2844020	N41675 G-BYHJ, N41675	25. 2.00	Bflying Ltd *(Operated Bournemouth Flying Club)*	Bournemouth	4. 5.08E
G-BYHK	Piper PA-28-181 Archer II	2843240	N4128V (G-BYHK), N9519N	20. 5.99	T-Air Services Ltd	Ronaldsway	25. 4.08E
G-BYHL	de Havilland DHC-1 Chipmunk 22	C1/0361	WG308	15. 3.99	M R and I D Higgins *(As "WG308:8" in RAF c/s)*	RAF Cranwell	15.11.09
G-BYHM	British Aerospace BAe 125 Series 800B *(Build Corporate Jets Ltd)*	258233	VP-BTM VR-BTM, (VR-BQH), F-WQCD, D-CAVW, G-5-770	12. 2.99	Club 328 Ltd	Biggin Hill	5. 5.08E
G-BYHN	Mainair Blade 912	1191-0399-7-W994		9. 4.99	R Stone	(Stoke-on-Trent)	24.11.06P
G-BYHO	Mainair Blade 912	1197-0599-7-W1000		16. 3.99	K Bailey	St Michaels	30. 3.08P
G-BYHP	CEA Jodel DR.253B Régent	161	OO-CSK	29. 3.99	C P Course, M Walker and J C Harmon t/a The G-BYHP Group	Sywell	15. 9.08E
G-BYHR	Cyclone Airsports Pegasus Quantum 15-912	7518		6. 4.99	I D Chantler	Longacre Farm, Sandy	1.11.08P
G-BYHS	Mainair Blade 912	1187-0299-7-W990		11. 3.99	T J Widdison	Little Snoring	26. 4.08P
G-BYHT	Robin DR.400-180R Remorqueur	811	HB-EUU	9. 4.99	R C Wilson tr Deeside Robin Group	Aboyne	1. 9.08E
G-BYHU	Cameron N-105 Balloon (Hot Air)	4567		30. 4.99	ABC Flights Ltd	Clapton in Gordano, Bristol	2. 5.08A
G-BYHV	Raj Hamsa X'Air 582(6) *(Built J Bowditch - pr.no.BMAA/HB/090)*	381		25. 3.99	P M Yeoman and J S Mason	Knapthorpe Lodge, Caunton	27. 6.08P
G-BYHX	Cameron A-250 Balloon (Hot Air)	4565		16. 4.99	Balloon School (International) Ltd *(New owner 5.06)*	Colhook Common, Petworth	9. 9.05T
G-BYHY	Cameron V-77 Balloon (Hot Air)	4493		22. 3.99	P Spellward *"Biggles"*	Bristol	16. 4.08A
G-BYIA	Avtech Jabiru SK *(Built M F Cottam - pr.no.PFA 274-13436)*	0237		10. 2.99	B J Spence tr Teesside Aviators Group	Durham Tees Valley	13. 2.08P
G-BYIB	Rans S-6-ESA Coyote II *(Built G A Clayton - pr.no.PFA 204-13387)* (Rotax 582) *(Tail-wheel u/c)*	0498 1222		26. 3.99	W Anderson	Polmont	26. 9.09P
G-BYIC	Cessna TU206G Turbo Stationair	U20605476	OY-NUA N113RS, N3RS, N6398U	27. 4.99	D M Penny t/a Wild Geese Parachute Club	Shotton Colliery, Peterlee	29. 7.08E
G-BYID	Rans S-6-ES Coyote II *(Built D J Brotherhood - pr.no.PFA 204-13348)* (Rotax 582) *(Tri-cycle u/c)*	0498.1218		11. 5.99	J A E Bowen	Davidstow Moor	16. 1.08P
G-BYIE	Robinson R22 Beta II	2933		22. 4.99	G Givens t/a Givens Aviation	(Ewenny, Bridgend)	6. 6.08E
G-BYII	TEAM Mini-MAX 91 *(Built J S R Moodie)*	PFA 186-11820		22. 1.99	J Edwards	Barton	20. 3.08P
G-BYIJ	CASA 1-131E Jungmann	2110	Spanish AF E3B-514	16. 7.90	P R Teager and R N Crosland	Deanland	12. 6.08P
G-BYIK	Europa Aviation Europa *(Built P M Davis - pr.no.PFA 247-12771)* (Monowheel u/c)	154		2. 2.99	P M Davis	Oxford	7.10.07P
G-BYIL	Cameron N-105 Balloon (Hot Air)	4591		29. 4.99	Oakfield Farm Products Ltd *(Oakfield Farm Products Ltd titles)*	Broadway	3. 5.08A
G-BYIM	Avtech Jabiru UL *(Built W J Dale and R F Hinton - pr.no.PFA 274A-13397)*	xxxx		22.12.98	A and J McVey	Ince Blundell	27. 3.08P
G-BYIN	Rotary Air Force RAF 2000 GTX-SE *(Built J R Legge)*	PFA G/13-1305		19. 1.99	J R Legge	(Rossendale)	30. 9.07P
G-BYIO	Colt 105A Balloon (Hot Air)	4601		30. 4.99	N Charbonnier *(Lindt titles)*	Aosta, Italy	17. 1.08A
G-BYIP	Pitts S-2A *(Built Aerotek Inc)*	2244	N109WA TC-ECN	23. 2.99	D P Heather-Hayes	Perth	1..8.08S
G-BYIR	Pitts S-1S *(Built Aerotek Inc)*	1-0063	N103WA TC-ECP	23. 2.99	Hampshire Aeroplane Company Ltd	Perranporth	26. 9.08
G-BYIS	Cyclone Airsports Pegasus Quantum 15-912	7508		25. 2.99	L M Tidman	North Coates	4. 5.08P
G-BYIT	Robin DR.500-200i Président *(Officially regd as DR.400-500)*	0010		27. 1.99	D Quirke	Rochester	23. 5.08E
G-BYIU	Cameron V-90 Balloon (Hot Air)	4552		6. 4.99	H Micketeit	Bielefeld, Germany	6. 3.08A
G-BYIV	Cameron PM-80 Balloon (Hot Air) *(Coca Cola bottle)*	4595		14. 5.99	A Schneider	Borken, Germany	27. 3.08A
G-BYIX	Cameron PM-80 Balloon (Hot Air) *(Coca Cola bottle)*	4597		14. 5.99	A Schneider	Borken, Germany	27. 4.06A
G-BYIY	Lindstrand LBL 56B Balloon (Hot Air)	601		26. 3.99	J H Dobson	Streatley, Reading	1. 6.08A
G-BYIZ	Cyclone Airsports Pegasus Quantum 15-912	7504		8. 2.99	J D Gray	Eshott	28. 5.08P
G-BYJA	Rotary Air Force RAF 2000 GTX-SE *(Built B Errington-Weddle)*	PFA G/13-1297		6. 4.99	B Errington-Weddle *(New owner 7.07)*	Henstridge	18. 7.02P
G-BYJB	Mainair Blade 912	1192-0499-7-W995		6. 4.99	M Atkinson	Tarn Farm, Cockerham	26. 4.08P
G-BYJC	Cameron N-90 Balloon (Hot Air)	4562		30. 4.99	A G Merry *(Bentleys of Knaresborough titles)*	Alresford	11. 4.08A
G-BYJD	Avtech Jabiru UL *(Built G Wallis and M W Knights - pr.no.PFA 274-13376 although type prefix should be "274A")*	0172		16. 4.99	M W Knights	Blue Tile Farm, Hindolveston	21. 5.08P
G-BYJE	TEAM Mini-MAX 91 *(Built A W Austin and M F Cottam)*	PFA 186-12327		6. 4.99	P K Jenkins	(Redditch)	17. 7.08P
G-BYJF	Thorp T 211 *(Built Venture Light Aircraft Resources)*	107	N2545C	20. 5.99	AD Aviation Ltd	Liverpool	22. 5.08E
G-BYJG	Lindstrand LBL 77A Balloon (Hot Air)	600		16. 4.99	Lindstrand Hot Air Balloons Ltd	Oswestry	22.12.07A
G-BYJH	Grob G109B	6512	D-KFRI	19. 5.99	A J Buchanan	Parham Park	26. 6.08E

Reg	Type	C/n	Prev id	Date	Owner/Operator	Base	Expiry
G-BYJI	Europa Aviation Europa	F0004	G-ODTI	19. 4.99	P S Jones	Halfpenny Green	20. 6.08P
	(Built Europa Aviation Ltd - pr.no.PFA 247-13010 (Monowheel u/c)						
G-BYJJ	Cameron C-80 Balloon (Hot Air)	4436	SX-MAX	20. 4.99	Proxim Franchising SRL Agrate Brianza, Milan, Italy		30. 3.08A
					(RF/Max titles)		
G-BYJK	Cyclone Airsports Pegasus Quantum 15-912	7524		7. 5.99	B S Smy	East Fortune	2. 6.08P
G-BYJL	Aero Designs Pulsar 3	PFA 202-13311		20. 4.99	F A H Ashmead	(Barton-on-Sea, New Milton))	4. 7.08P
	(Built F A H Ashmead) (Tricycle u/c)						
G-BYJM	Cyclone AX2000	7523		25. 5.99	A M Smith tr Caunton Ax2000 Syndicate		
						Knapthorpe Lodge, Caunton	30. 5.08P
G-BYJN	Lindstrand LBL 105A Balloon (Hot Air)	605		30. 4.99	B Meeson	Pwllheli	29. 4.00A
G-BYJO	Rans S-6-ES Coyote II	0498.1217		4. 3.99	G Ferguson	Blue Tile Farm, Hindolveston	18. 9.08P
	(Built G Ferguson - pr.no.PFA 204-13338) (Rotax 582) (Tail-wheel u/c)						
G-BYJP	Pitts S-1S	1-0064	N105WA	16. 3.99	T Riddle tr Eaglescott Pitts Group	Eaglescott	18. 4.08
	(Built Aerotek Inc)		TC-ECR, Turkish AF?				
G-BYJR	Lindstrand LBL 77B Balloon (Hot Air)	608		30. 4.99	C D Duthy-James	Poitiers, France	5. 4.08A
G-BYJS	SOCATA TB-20 Trinidad	1875	F-OIGE	15. 1.99	A P Bedford tr Juliet Sierra Group	Oxford	30. 5.08E
G-BYJT	Zenair CH.601HDS Zodiac	PFA 162-13130		4. 5.99	J D T Tannock	Tollerton	9. 4.08P
	(Built J D T Tannock) (Tri-cycle u/c)						
G-BYJU	Raj Hamsa X'Air 582(1)	429		6. 5.99	G P Morling	Andreas, Isle of Man	22. 8.08P
	(Built C W Payne - pr.no.BMAA/HB/098)						
G-BYJW	Cameron Sphere 105 SS Balloon (Hot Air)	4585		15. 6.99	Forbes Global Inc	Far Hills, New Jersey, US	5. 8.07A
G-BYJX	Cameron C-70 Balloon (Hot Air)	4580		30. 4.99	B Perona	Torino, Italy	21. 5.08A
G-BYJZ	Lindstrand LBL 105A Balloon (Hot Air)	609		27. 5.99	M A..Webb	Chard	26. 7.02A
G-BYKA	Lindstrand LBL 69A Balloon (Hot Air)	612		7. 5.99	B Meeson *(Vauxhall titles)*	Rhiw, Pwllheli	21. 6.07A
G-BYKB	Rockwell Commander 114	14121	SE-GSM	18. 5.99	A Walton	Little Staughton	18. 7.08P
			N4801W				
G-BYKC	Mainair Blade 912	1196-0599-7-W999		7. 5.99	G J Wharmby	Ince Blundell	6. 9.08P
G-BYKD	Mainair Blade 912	1198-0599-7-W1001		7. 5.99	D C Boyle	(Chorley)	11. 4.08P
G-BYKF	Enstrom F-28F	725	JA7684	19. 5.99	G T Williams and S C Severeyns		
						(Newcastle Emlyn and Llandysul))	28. 8.08E
G-BYKG	Pietenpol AirCamper	PFA 047-12827		17. 3.99	K B Hodge	(Mynydd Isa, Mold)	
	(Built K B Hodge)				*(Last known nearing completion 2000!)*		
G-BYKI	Cameron N-105 Balloon (Hot Air)	4635		4. 6.99	J A Leahy	Navan, County Meath	26. 3.08A
G-BYKJ	Westland Scout AH.1	F9696	XV121	6. 8.99	B H Austen t/a Austen Associates	Edinburgh	21.12.08P
G-BYKK	Robinson R44 Astro	0572		4. 3.99	M N Cowley t/a Dragonfly Aviation		
						Red House Farm, Preston Capes	5. 4.08E
G-BYKL	Piper PA-28-181 Archer II	28-8090162	HB-PFB	15. 7.99	Transport Command Ltd	Shoreham	25.10.07E
			N8129Y				
G-BYKP	Piper PA-28RT-201T Turbo Arrow IV	28R-7931029	HB-PDB	22. 6.99	D L Grimes and D W Knox	Bristol	9.10.07E
			N3010G				
G-BYKS	Leopoldoff L 6 Colibri	129	N10LC	19. 4.99	I M Callier	(Hungerford)	
	(Continental C90)		F-BGIT, F-WGIT		*(Stored 2007)*		
G-BYKT	Cyclone Airsports Pegasus Quantum 15-912	7529		28. 5.99	D A Bannister and N J Howarth		
						Sackville Farm, Riseley	7. 6.08P
G-BYKU	BFC Challenger II	PFA 177A-13252		25. 5.99	K W Seedhouse	Otherton, Cannock	7. 8.08P
	(Built K W Seedhouse)						
G-BYKW	Lindstrand LBL 77B Balloon (Hot Air)	620		22. 6.99	K Allemand	Plassal, France	16. 4.08A
G-BYKZ	Sky 140-24 Balloon (Hot Air)	147		25. 2.99	D J Head	Newbury	6. 8.05T
G-BYLB	de Havilland DH.82A Tiger Moth	83286	T5595	24. 5.99	P A Layzell *(Noted 8.07)*	Old Buckenham	
G-BYLC	Cyclone Airsports Pegasus Quantum 15-912	7528		25. 6.99	A Cordes	Deenethorpe	22. 8.08P
G-BYLD	Pietenpol AirCamper	PFA 047-13392		27. 4.99	S Bryan	(Chipping Warden, Banbury)	
	(Built S Bryan)						
G-BYLF	Zenair CH.601HDS Zodiac	PFA 162-13179		3. 6.99	G Waters	Swansea	21.10.08P
	(Built M and J S Thomas and G Waters) (Tricycle u/c)						
G-BYLH	Robin HR.200-120B	335		9. 7.99	Multiflight Ltd	Leeds-Bradford	6.10.07E
G-BYLI	Nova Vertex 22	14319		9. 4.99	M Hay *(New owner 1.03)*	(Dundee)	
G-BYLJ	Letov LK-2M Sluka	PFA 263-13464		9. 6.99	W J McCarroll	Mullaghmore, Coleraine	
	(Built N E Stokes) (Rotax 447)				*(New owner 6.06)*		
G-BYLL	Sequoia F 8L Falco	PFA 100-10843		6.12.85	N J Langrick	Breighton	6. 3.08P
	(Built N J Langrick) (Lycoming O-320-A3C)						
G-BYLO	Tipsy Nipper T 66 Series 1	T66/04	OO-NIA	27. 4.99	M J A Trudgill	RAF Henlow	24. 6.04P
	(Built Avions Fairey SA) (Volkswagen 1600)						
G-BYLP	Rand Robinson KR-2	PFA 129-11431		19. 4.99	C S Hales	(Walsall)	
	(Built C S Hales)				*(See G-BSTL)*		
G-BYLS	Bede BD-4	PFA 037-11288		13.12.90	G H Bayliss	Welshpool	28. 1.08P
	(Built G H Bayliss) (Lycoming O-320-E2F)						
G-BYLT	Raj Hamsa X'Air 582(1)	411		8. 6.99	T W Phipps	Craysmarsh Farm, Melksham	23. 9.05P
	(Built R J Turner - pr.no.BMAA/HB/095)				*(New owner 7.07)*		
G-BYLV	Thunder Ax8-105 Series 2 Balloon (Hot Air)			6. 7.99	KB Voli S.A.S Di Bartolomeo Chiozzio and Cia		
		4061				Cappella Cantone, Italy	1. 8.08A
G-BYLW	Lindstrand LBL 77A Balloon (Hot Air)	615		11. 6.99	Associazione Gran Premio Italiano	Perugia, Italy	10. 6.00A
G-BYLX	Lindstrand LBL 105A Balloon (Hot Air)	614		11. 6.99	Italiana Aeronavi	Cervignano, Italy	9. 5.04A
G-BYLY	Cameron V-77 Balloon (Hot Air)	3375	G-ULIA (2)	16. 7.97	R Bayly *(See G-ULIA)*	Clutton, Bristol	3. 2.08A
G-BYLZ	Rutan Cozy Mk.4	PFA 159-12464		21. 5.99	E R Allen	Dunsfold	18.11.08P
	(Built E R Allen)						
G-BYMB	Diamond DA.20-C1 Katana	C0051	C-GDMB	9. 7.99	S C Brown t/a Enstone Flying Club	Enstone	7. 3.08E
G-BYMC	Piper PA-38-112 Tomahawk II	38-82A0034	N91457	18. 6.99	Central Aircraft Leasing Ltd	Halfpenny Green	2. 7.06T
					(Noted 10.07)		
G-BYMD	Piper PA-38-112 Tomahawk II	38-82A0009	N91342	18. 6.99	J E Rowley and M A Petrie	Hawarden	23. 8.08E
G-BYME	Sud-Aviation Gardan GY-80-180 Horizon	207	F-BPAA	24. 5.99	Air Venturas Ltd *(Noted 2.08)*	Bagby	17. 1.08E
G-BYMF	Cyclone Airsports Pegasus Quantum 15-912	7540		9. 7.99	G R Stockdale	Rufforth	26. 1.08P
G-BYMG	Cameron A-210 Balloon (Hot Air)	4631		17. 9.99	P Johnson t/a Cloud Nine Balloon Company		
						Ebchester, Consett	12. 3.08T
G-BYMH	Cessna 152	15284980	N6127P	15. 7.99	PJC (Leasing) Ltd	Stapleford	21. 7.08E

G-BYMI	Cyclone Airsports Pegasus Quantum 15	7533		9. 7.99	N C Grayson	Knapthorpe Lodge, Caunton	18. 7.08P
	(Rotax 503)						
G-BYMJ	Cessna 152	15285564	N93865	16. 7.99	Stapleford Flying Club Ltd	Stapleford	26.11.07E
G-BYMK	Dornier 328-100	3062	LN-ASK	9. 6.99	Suckling Aviation (Cambridge) Ltd t/a Scot Airways		
			D-CDXE			London City	8. 6.08E
G-BYML	Dornier 328-100	3069	D-CDUL	27. 7.99	Suckling Aviation (Cambridge) Ltd t/a Scot Airways		
			LN-ASL, D-CDXT (2)		(CityJet titles)	London City	14. 8.08E
G-BYMN	Rans S-6-ESA Coyote II	0199.1292		16. 6.99	R L Barker	Chase Farm, Little Bursted	19. 2.08P
	(Built H Smith - pr.no.PFA 204-13477) (Rotax 582) (Tri-cycle u/c)						
G-BYMO	Campbell Cricket	PFA G/03-1266		16. 7.99	P G Rawson	(Huddersfield)	23. 5.06P
	(Built D G Hill) (Rotax 532)						
G-BYMP	Campbell Cricket Mk.1	PFA G/03-1265		16. 6.99	J J Fitzgerald	(Newtownards)	
	(Built J J Fitzgerald)						
G-BYMR	Raj Hamsa X'Air R100(3)	434		18. 6.99	W Drury Slieve Croob, Slievenamoney, Castlewellen		26.12.06P
	(Built W M McMinn - pr.no.BMAA/HB/094)				(Noted 7.07)		
G-BYMT	Cyclone Airsports Pegasus Quantum 15-912	7549		16. 7.99	C M Mackinnon	Strathaven	30. 7.08P
G-BYMU	Rans S-6-ESN Coyote II	0498.1219		25. 6.99	I R Russell and S Palmer	Swinford, Rugby	21. 6.08P
	(Built I R Russell - pr.no.PFA 204-13424) (Verner VM133)						
G-BYMV	Rans S-6-ESN Coyote II	0998.1265		25. 6.99	J A Kentzer	(Sheffield)	25. 7.08P
	(Built G A Squires - pr.no.PFA 204-13444) (Rotax 582) (Tri-cycle u/c)						
G-BYMW	Boland 52-12 Balloon (Hot Air)	001		25. 6.99	C Jones	Sonning Common, Reading	
	(Built C Jones)				(Noted active 1.08)		
G-BYMX	Cameron A-105 Balloon (Hot Air)	4629		16. 7.99	H Reis	Aachen, Germany	21. 2.07A
				(ZENTIS titles and "Einfach traumhaft gut" lettering =Simply Fantastically Good)			
G-BYMY	Cameron N-90 Balloon (Hot Air)	4653		19. 7.99	A Cakss (New owner 11.06)	Segny, France	4. 8.08A
G-BYNA	Cessna F172H	F172-0626	OO-VDW	15. 1.99	D M White	Blackbushe	15. 4.08E
	(Built Reims Aviation SA)		PH-VDW, (G-AWTH), F-WLIT				
G-BYND	Cyclone Airsports Pegasus Quantum 15	7546		16. 7.99	D G Baker	(East Meon. Petersfield)	3.11.08P
	(Rotax 582)						
G-BYNE	Pilatus PC-6/B2-H4 Turbo Porter	631	HB-FLW	10. 8.99	D M Penny	Le Luc, Cennes, France	3.10.07E
			C-FRAV, N631SA, N62148, HS-..., N62148, XW-PFC, XW-PDK, HB-FCR				
G-BYNF	North American NA-64 Yale I	64-2171	N55904	10. 1.00	R S van Dijk	Duxford	4. 3.08P
			RCAF 3349		(As "3349" in RCAF c/s)		
G-BYNH	RotorWay Executive 162F	6323		5. 7.99	R C Mackenzie	(Clavering, Saffron Walden)	
	(Built R Mackenzie) (RotorWay RI 162F)						
G-BYNI	RotorWay Executive 90	5216		16. 7.99	M Bunn	(Wacton, Norwich)	17.10.08P
	(Built M Bunn) (RotorWay RI 162)						
G-BYNJ	Cameron N-77 Balloon (Hot Air)	4661		26. 7.99	G Aimo (Primagaz titles)	Mondovi, Italy	28. 5.05A
G-BYNK	Robin HR.200-160	338		28. 7.99	R J Stainer and D A Healey tr Penguin Flight Group		
						Bodmin	28. 9.08E
G-BYNM	Mainair Blade 912	1204-0799-7-W1007		20. 7.99	J P Hanlon and A C McAllister	Ince Blundell	4. 8.07P
G-BYNN	Cameron V-90 Balloon (Hot Air)	4643		16. 7.99	J L Hilditch t/a Cloud Nine Balloon Group		
					"Cloud Nine"	Southwick, Brighton	4 .6.08
G-BYNP	Rans S-6-ES Coyote II	1098.1269		22. 7.99	R J Lines	Sandtoft	16. 8.08P
	(Built R J Lines - pr.no.PFA 204-13414) (Rotax 582)						
G-BYNR	Avtech Jabiru UL	0129	EI-MAT	23. 7.99	M P Maughan	Rufforth	14. 7.07P
	(Built A Parker - pr.no.SAAC 66 and also UL series no.UL0001)				(Noted 10.07)		
G-BYNS	Avtech Jabiru SK	0159		23. 7.99	D K Lawry	Tibenham	10. 8.05P
	(Built D K Lawry - pr.no.PFA 274-13235)				(Noted 11.07)		
G-BYNT	Raj Hamsa X'Air V2(1)	457		20. 7.99	A Evans	Longside, Peterhead	14. 7.08P
	(Built G R Wallis - pr.no.BMAA/HB/107)						
G-BYNU	Thunder AX7-77 Balloon (Hot Air)	3520		29. 7.99	P M Gaines "Soup Dragon"	Sedgefield, Stockton-on-Tees	4. 8.06A
G-BYNV	Sky 105-24 Balloon (Hot Air)	165		11. 8.99	Par Rovelli Construzioni SRL	Mazzini, Italy	31. 3.07
G-BYNW	Cameron H-34 Balloon (Hot Air)	4666		27. 7.99	I M Ashpole (Energis titles)	Bridstow, Ross-on-Wye	13. 9.08A
G-BYNX	Cameron RX-105 Balloon (Hot Air)	4656		26. 7.99	Cameron Balloons Ltd	Bristol	1.11.00A
G-BYNY	Beech 76 Duchess	ME-247	N247ME	4. 8.99	Magenta Ltd	Exeter	30.10.07E
			OE-FES, N6635H		(Operated European Flight Training)		
G-BYOB	Slingsby T 67M-260 Firefly	2263		8. 6.99	Stapleford Flying Club Ltd	Stapleford	6.10.07E
G-BYOD	Slingsby T 67C Firefly	2265		13. 6.00	TDR Aviation Ltd	Newtownards	27. 1.08E
G-BYOG	Cyclone Airsports Pegasus Quantum 15-912	7555		15. 9.99	M D Hinge	Old Sarum	14. 4.08P
G-BYOH	Raj Hamsa X'Air 582(2)	443		23. 7.99	P H J Kent	Belle Vue Farm, Yarnscombe	3. 5.08P
	(Built G A J Salter - pr.no.BMAA/HB/101)						
G-BYOI	Sky 80-16 Balloon (Hot Air)	163		5. 8.99	I S and S W Watthews	Cark-in-Cartmel	7. 6.08
G-BYOJ	Raj Hamsa X'Air 582(1)	458		23. 7.99	H M Owen	Haverfordwest	11. 8.08P
	(Built R R Hadley - pr.no.BMAA/HB/108)				(Noted 6.05)		
G-BYOK	Cameron V-90 Balloon (Hot Air)	3726		9. 8.99	D S Wilson	Norwich	26. 3.08A
G-BYOM	Sikorsky S-76C	760464	G-IJCB	25. 8.99	Starspeed Ltd	Blackbushe	30. 3.08E
G-BYON	Mainair Blade	1199-0599-7-W1002		4. 8.99	P G Mallon	Redlands, Swindon	17. 6.08P
	(Rotax 503)						
G-BYOO	CFM Streak Shadow SA	K 270		6. 8.99	G R Eastwood	Full Sutton	18. 6.08P
	(Built C I Chegwen - pr.no.PFA 206-12806) (Rotax 912-UL)						
G-BYOR	Raj Hamsa X'Air 582(2)	478		11. 8.99	R V Horlock	Grayshott, (Hindhead)	23. 7.07P
	(Built A R Walker - pr.no.BMAA/HB/117)				(New owner 1.08)		
G-BYOS	Mainair Blade 912	1209-0899-7-W1012		6. 8.99	R M Wigman	Mapperley, Nottingham	4. 9.08P
G-BYOT	Rans S-6-ES Coyote II	0498.1221		29. 7.99	H F Blakeman	Arclid Green, Sandbach	7. 5.08P
	(Built H F Blakeman - pr.no.PFA 204-13363) (Tri-cycle u/c)				(Noted 3.07)		
G-BYOU	Rans S-6-ES Coyote II	1298.1288		1. 6.99	P G Bright and P L Parker	(South Cave, Brough)	22.10.08P
	(Built Light Flight Ltd and R Germany - pr.no.PFA 204-13460) (Rotax 582) (Tri-cycle u/c)						
G-BYOW	Mainair Blade	1207-0899-7-W1010		9. 8.99	M Forsyth	East Fortune	23. 3.08P
	(Rotax 582)						
G-BYOX	Cameron Z-90 Balloon (Hot Air)	4672		31. 8.99	D G Such (Virgin Atlantic titles)	Barkway, Royston	12. 8.08A
G-BYOZ	Mainair Rapier	1208-0899-7-W1011		12. 8.99	D P Harvey	Arclid Green, Sandbach	2. 8.08P
G-BYPA	Aérospatiale AS.355F2 Ecureuil 2	5348	G-NWPI	20. 8.99	P and J Carter	Redhill	28. 3.08E
			F-GMAO	(Crashed in woods Wansford near Peterborough 2. 5.07 and substantially damaged)			

G-BYPB	Cyclone Airsports Pegasus Quantum 15-912	7566		3. 9.99	S Graham	Redlands, Swindon	23. 9.06P
G-BYPD	Cameron A-105 Balloon (Hot Air)	4680		6. 1.00	Headland Hotel Company Ltd	Newquay	19. 2.07A
					(Headland Hotel titles)		
G-BYPE	Sud-Aviation Gardan GY-80-160 Horizon	180	F-BNYD	10. 8.99	H I Smith and P R Hendry-Smith	Little Snoring	17. 5.08E
G-BYPF	Thruster T 600N Sprint	9089-T600N-034		17. 8.99	R J Oakley tr Canary Syndicate	Shobdon	26. 1.08P
	(Rotax 582UL)						
G-BYPG	Thruster T 600N Sprint	9089-T600N-035		17. 8.99	R Bowden tr G-BYPG Syndicate	Dunkeswell	20. 7.08P
	(Rotax 582UL)						
G-BYPH	Thruster T 600N	9089-T600N-036		17. 8.99	D M Canham	Leicester	30. 4.08P
	(Rotax 582UL) (Officially regd with incorrect c/n as 9099-T600N-036)						
G-BYPJ	Cyclone Airsports Pegasus Quantum 15-912	7565		17. 9.99	M E Oakman	(Watton-at-Stone, Hertford)	10.12.07P
G-BYPL	Cyclone Airsports Pegasus Quantum 15-912	7558		9. 9.99	I T Carlse	(Fowlmere)	26. 9.08P
G-BYPM	Europa Aviation Europa XS	404		16.12.98	P Mileham	Dunkeswell	30. 7.08P
	(Built P Mileham - pr.no.PFA 247-13418) (Tri-gear u/c)						
G-BYPN	SOCATA MS.880B Rallye Club	2043	F-BTPN	23. 7.99	R and T C Edwards, S A and D Bell	Sturgate	26. 7.08E
G-BYPO	Raj Hamsa X'Air 582(1)	439		25. 8.99	D W Willis tr X'Air Group	Brook Farm, Pilling	1.10.07P
	(Built N G Woodhall and A S Leach - pr.no.BMAA/HB/111)						
G-BYPP	Medway Rebel SS	168/146		25.10.99	J L Gowens	(Leeds, Maidstone)	17. 3.01P
	(2 Stroke International 690L70)						
G-BYPR	Zenair CH.601HD Zodiac	PFA 162-12816		25. 8.99	S C Ord	(Chester)	7. 8.08P
	(Built D Clark) (Lycoming O-235-C2C)						
G-BYPT	Rans S-6-ESN Coyote II	0499.1316		27. 8.99	M A Sims	(Swindon)	7.12.07P
	(Built G R Pritchard - pr.no.PFA 204-13508) (Jabiru 2200A) (Tri-cycle u/c)						
G-BYPU	Piper PA-32R-301 Saratoga II HP	3246150	N4160K	2.12.99	AM Blatch Electrical Contractors Ltd	East Winch	17. 1.08E
			G-BYPU, N9518N				
G-BYPW	Raj Hamsa X'Air 582(3)	441		1. 9.99	M A Petrie and J E Rowley	Tarn Farm, Cockerham	22.12.07P
	(Built P A Mercer - pr.no.BMAA/HB/113)						
G-BYPY	Ryan ST3KR	1001	F-AZEV	5.10.99	T Curtis-Taylor	Old Warden	27. 8.08P
			N18926		*(As "001" in US Army c/s)*		
G-BYPZ	Rans S-6-S-116 Super Six	0299.1304		14. 7.99	R A Blackbourn	Perth	26. 3.08P
	(Built P G Hayward - pr.no.PFA 204A-13448) (Rotax 912-UL) (Tri-cycle u/c)						
G-BYRC	Westland Wessex HC.Mk.2	WA539	XT671	23. 9.99	D Brem-Wilson	Joydens Farm, Westerham	
					(Change of Type notified 10.06)		
G-BYRG	Rans S-6-ES Coyote II	1298.1289		9. 9.99	S J Macmillan	Easter Poldar Farm, Thornhill	20. 9.08P
	(Built J Whiting - pr.no.PFA 204-13518) (Rotax 582) (Tri-cycle u/c)						
G-BYRH	Medway Hybred 44XLR	MR165/143		25.10.99	G R Puffett	Landmead Farm, Garford	5. 9.05P
	(Rotax 503)				*(Noted 2.06)*		
G-BYRJ	Cyclone Airsports Pegasus Quantum 15-912	7548		24. 9.99	A L Brown	Long Marston	28. 6.08P
G-BYRK	Cameron V-42 Balloon (Hot Air)	4662		14. 7.99	R Kunert *(Inflated 4.06)*	Finchamstead, Wokingham	17. 7.08A
G-BYRO	Mainair Blade	1210-0899-7-W1013		20. 8.99	P W F Coleman	Corn Wood Farm, Adversane	2 6.07P
	(Rotax 582)x						
G-BYRP	Mainair Blade 912	1075-1295-7-W877		15. 9.99	J T and A C Swannick	Ince Blundell	17. 4.07P
	(C/n amended to 1075-0999-7-W877 by Mainair)						
G-BYRR	Mainair Blade 912	1211-0999-7-W1015		17. 8.99	G R Sharples	(Harrow)	18. 6.04P
	(C/n amended to 1222-0999-7-W1015 by Mainair)						
G-BYRS	Rans S-6-ES Coyote II	0998.1266		17. 9.99	A E Turner	Longacre Farm, Sandy	11.10.08P
	(Built R Beniston - pr.no.PFA 204-13425) (Rotax 582) (Tri-cycle u/c)						
G-BYRU	Cyclone Airsports Pegasus Quantum 15-912	7574		24. 9.99	V R March tr The Sarum QTM912 Group	Old Sarum	28. 9.08P
G-BYRV	Raj Hamsa X'Air 582(2)	387		10. 9.99	A D Russell (Coolboy, Letterkenny, County Donegal)		22. 7.08P
	(Built A Hipkin - pr.no.BMAA/HB/106)						
G-BYRX	Westland Scout AH.1	F9640	XT634	5.10.99	Historic Helicopters Ltd	Thruxton	2.11.08P
					(As "XT634" in AAC c/s)		
G-BYRY	Slingsby T 67M-200 Firefly	2042	B-HZQ	28. 9.99	T R Pearson	Oxford	4. 5.08E
			VR-HZQ, HKG-11		*(As "HKG-11" in Royal Hong Kong AAF c/s)*		
G-BYRZ	Lindstrand LBL 77M Balloon (Hot Air)	643		28. 9.99	Challenge Transatlantique	Metz, France	5.12.00A
	(Reported to be rebuild of G-BXDX)				*"Conseil Régional de Lorraine"*		
G-BYSA	Europa Aviation Europa XS	360		23. 8.99	B Allsop	Bentley Farm, Coal Aston	31. 5.08P
	(Built B Allsop - pr.no.PFA 247-13199) (Monowheel u/c)				*"Sadie"*		
G-BYSE	Agusta-Bell 206B-2 JetRanger II	8553	G-BFND	3.11.81	Alspath Properties Ltd	Coventry	19. 9.08P
G-BYSF	Avtech Jabiru UL	0195		5.10.99	M W Sayers	Sittles Farm, Alrewas	13.11.08P
	(Built M M Smith - pr.no.PFA 274A-13356)						
G-BYSG	Robin HR.200-120B	339		22.11.99	Modi Aviation Ltd	Earls Colne	22.12.07E
G-BYSI	PZL-110 Koliber 160A	04990081	SP-WGI	21. 1.00	J and Dawn.F Evans	Gamston	29. 3.08S
G-BYSJ	de Havilland DHC-1 Chipmunk 22	C1/0021	SE-BON	12.10.99	C H Green	(Tresham, Wotton-under-Edge)	2. 1.10S
			WB569		*(As "WB569:R" in RAF c/s)*		
G-BYSK	Cameron A-275 Balloon (Hot Air)	4699		23. 2.00	Balloon School (International) Ltd *(British School of Ballooning titles)*	Colhook Common, Petworth	23. 4.08T
G-BYSM	Cameron A-210 Balloon (Hot Air)	4698		12. 4.00	Balloon School (International) Ltd	Bath	23. 4.08T
					"Bath Heritage" (Operated Heritage Balloons)		
G-BYSN	Rans S-6-ES Coyote II	1098.1270		19.10.99	A L and A R Roberts	RAF St Athan	3.12.07P
	(Built A L Roberts - pr.no.PFA 204-13459) (Rotax 582) (Tri-cycle u/c)						
G-BYSP	Piper PA-28-181 Archer II	28-8590047	D-EAUL	12.10.99	Take Flight Aviation Ltd	Wellesbourne Mountford	27.11.07E
			N6909D				
G-BYSR	Cyclone Airsports Pegasus Quantum 15-912	7560		7. 3.00	A C Stuart	Seattle, Washington, US	10. 5.05P
G-BYSS	Medway EclipseR	167/145		25.10.99	D W Allen	Popham	20.11.08P
G-BYSV	Cameron N-120 Balloon (Hot Air)	4704		15.10.99	S Simmington	Eccles, Norwich	2. 2.08A
G-BYSW	Enstrom 280FX Shark	2026	I-LUST	19. 9.00	D A Marks	(Milbrook, Bedford)	30. 1.08E
			N88CV				
G-BYSX	Cyclone Airsports Pegasus Quantum 15-912	7586		23.11.99	D W Ormond	Deenethorpe	28. 1.08P
G-BYSY	Raj Hamsa X'Air 582(2)	448		21.10.99	J M Davidson		
	(Built J M Davidson - pr.no.BMAA/HB/109)				(Oxleaze Grange, Hawling, Cheltenham)		9. 7.06P
G-BYTA	Kolb Twinstar Mk.3	PFA 205-13240		2. 9.99	L R Morris	Ballymageough, Kilkeel	14. 2.08P
	(Built R E Gray)				*(Suffered engine failure on flight 10 or 11.07 and substantially damaged)*		
G-BYTB	SOCATA TB-20 Trinidad	2002	F-OILE	18. 5.00	Mogato Ltd	Goodwood	6. 9.08P

G-BYTC	Cyclone Airsports Pegasus Quantum Q.2 Sport	15-912		25.10.99	R J Marriott	Headon Farm, Retford	22.11.06P
		7571					
G-BYTE	Robinson R22 Beta	1250		18. 4.90	Patriot Aviation Ltd	Cranfield	17. 6.02T
G-BYTG	Glaser-Dirks DG-400	4-211	D-KBBP	18.11.99	P R Williams and B Sebestik	Fuentemilanos, Spain	18. 4.08E
G-BYTH	Airbus A320-231	0429	C-GTDM	21. 1.00	Thomas Cook Airlines Ltd t/a MyTravel Airways		
	G-BYTH, C-GTDM, G-BYTH, C-GTDM, G-BYTH, D-ASSR, (D-AUKT), G-BYTH, EI-TLE, D-AORX, N429RX, F-WWIZ					East Midlands	27. 4.08E
G-BYTI	Piper PA-24-250 Comanche	24-3489	D-ELOP	9.11.99	M Carruthers and G Auchterlonie	Gamston	5. 5.07
			N8297P, N10F				
G-BYTJ	Cameron Concept 80 Balloon (Hot Air)	4703		19.11.99	M White (*Rapido titles*)	Cirencester	14. 7.08A
G-BYTK	Avtech Jabiru SPL-450	0265		8.11.99	P J Reilly	Old Sarum	9. 7.08P
	(Built K A Fagan and S R Pike - pr.no.PFA 274A-13465)						
G-BYTL	Mainair Blade 912	1224-0999-7-W1017		19.10.99	P B Spencer	(Barton, Preston)	17.10.08P
G-BYTM	Dyn'Aéro MCR-01 Club	83		1.10.99	I Lang	Shobdon	1. 5.08P
	(Built I Lang - pr.no.PFA 301-13440)						
G-BYTN	de Havilland DH.82A Tiger Moth	3993	7014M	18.11.99	J W Freckington and R Merewood	Wickenby	2. 9.10S
			N6720		(As "N6720:VX" in RAF c/s)		
G-BYTR	Raj Hamsa X'Air 582(1)	460		5.10.99	D R Western and J F Northey	Weston Zoyland	26. 9.08P
	(Built A P Roberts and R Dunn - pr.no.BMAA/HB/105)						
G-BYTS	Montgomerie-Bensen B 8MR	MGM-2		22. 9.99	M G Mee	Kirkbride	18. 7.08P
	(Built M G Mee) (Rotax 912)						
G-BYTU	Mainair Blade 912	1225-1099-7-W1018		26.11.99	J E Morgan	Caernarfon	16. 5.08P
G-BYTV	Avtech Jabiru UL-450	0264		3.11.99	M G Speers	Andreas, Isle of Man	7.10.08P
	(Built E Bentley - pr.no.PFA 274A-13454)						
G-BYTW	Cameron O-90 Balloon (Hot Air)	4747		11. 4.00	Sade Balloons Ltd	London EC2	21. 9.08A
G-BYTX	Whittaker MW6-S Fatboy Flyer	PFA 164-12819		2.12.99	J K Ewing	Mapperton Farm, Newton Peverill	15. 8.06P
	(Built J K Ewing) (Rotax 532)						
G-BYTZ	Raj Hamsa X'Air 582(6)	472		26.10.99	R Armstrong	(Dungannon)	29. 6.08P
	(Built A B Wilson and K C Millar - pr.no.BMAA/HB/120)						
G-BYUA	Grob G115E Tutor	82086E	D-EUKB	22. 7.99	VT Aerospace Ltd	RAF Wyton	5. 8.08E
					(Operated Cambridge UAS [5 AEF] and University of London AS)		
G-BYUB	Grob G115E Tutor	82087E		22. 7.99	VT Aerospace Ltd	RAF Cranwell	5. 8.08E
					(Operated East Midlands UAS [7 AEF])		
G-BYUC	Grob G115E Tutor	82088E		22. 7.99	VT Aerospace Ltd	RAF Cranwell	5. 8.08E
					(Operated East Midlands UAS [7 AEF])		
G-BYUD	Grob G115E Tutor	82089E		22. 7.99	VT Aerospace Ltd	Glasgow	5. 8.08E
					(Operated Universities of Glasgow and Strathclyde AS [4 AEF])		
G-BYUE	Grob G115E Tutor	82090E		12. 8.99	VT Aerospace Ltd	RAF Cranwell	30. 8.08E
					(Operated East Midlands UAS [7 AEF])		
G-BYUF	Grob G115E Tutor	82091E		12. 8.99	VT Aerospace Ltd	RAF Cosford	30. 8.08E
					(Operated University of Birmingham AS [8 AEF])		
G-BYUG	Grob G115E Tutor	82092E		22. 9.99	VT Aerospace Ltd	RAF Leuchars	27. 9.08E
					(Operated East of Scotland UAS [12 AEF])		
G-BYUH	Grob G115E Tutor	82093E		22. 9.99	VT Aerospace Ltd	Boscombe Down	27. 9.08E
					(Operated Southampton UAS [2 AEF])		
G-BYUI	Grob G115E Tutor	82094E		24. 9.99	VT Aerospace Ltd	RAF Woodvale	27. 9.08E
					(Operated Liverpool UAS and Manchester and Salford Universities AS [10 AEF])		
G-BYUJ	Grob G115E Tutor	82095E		24. 9.99	VT Aerospace Ltd	RAF Church Fenton	27. 9.08E
					(Operated Yorkshire Universities AS [9 AEF])		
G-BYUK	Grob G115E Tutor	82096E		18.10.99	VT Aerospace Ltd	RAF Cosford	28.10.07E
					(Operated University of Birmingham AS [8 AEF])		
G-BYUL	Grob G115E Tutor	82097E		18.10.99	VT Aerospace Ltd	RAF Wyton	28.10.07E
					(Operated Cambridge UAS [5 AEF] and University of London AS)		
G-BYUM	Grob G115E Tutor	82098E		18.10.99	VT Aerospace Ltd	RAF Leuchars	28.10.07E
					(Operated East of Scotland UAS [12AEF])		
G-BYUN	Grob G115E Tutor	82099E		18.10.99	VT Aerospace Ltd	RAF St Athan	28.10.07E
					(Operated University of Wales AS [1 AEF])		
G-BYUO	Grob G115E Tutor	82100E		19.11.99	VT Aerospace Ltd	RAF Wyton	28.11.07E
					(Operated Cambridge UAS [5 AEF] and University of London AS)		
G-BYUP	Grob G115E Tutor	82101E		19.11.99	VT Aerospace Ltd	RAF Cranwell	28.11.07E
					(Operated CFS Tutor Sqdn)		
G-BYUR	Grob G115E Tutor	82102E		19.11.99	VT Aerospace Ltd	RAF Leuchars	28.11.07E
					(Operated East of Scotland UAS [12 AEF])		
G-BYUS	Grob G115E Tutor	82103E		19.11.99	VT Aerospace Ltd	RAF Wyton	28.11.07E
					(Operated Cambridge UAS [5 AEF] and University of London AS)		
G-BYUT	Grob G115E Tutor	82104E		7.12.99	VT Aerospace Ltd	RAF St Athan	14.12.07E
					(Operated University of Wales AS [1 AEF])		
G-BYUU	Grob G115E Tutor	82105E		7.12.99	VT Aerospace Ltd	RAF Leuchars	14.12.07E
					(Operated East of Scotland UAS [12 AEF])		
G-BYUV	Grob G115E Tutor	82106E		7.12.99	VT Aerospace Ltd	RAF Benson	14.12.07E
					(Operated Oxford University AS [6 AEF])		
G-BYUW	Grob G115E Tutor	82107E		7.12.99	VT Aerospace Ltd	RAF Leuchars	16.12.07E
					(Operated East of Scotland UAS [12 AEF])		
G-BYUX	Grob G115E Tutor	82108E		18. 1.00	VT Aerospace Ltd	RAF Leuchars	31. 1.08E
					(Operated East of Scotland UAS [12 AEF])f		
G-BYUY	Grob G115E Tutor	82109E		18. 1.00	VT Aerospace Ltd	RAF Leuchars	31. 1.08E
					(Operated East of Scotland UAS [12 AEF])		
G-BYUZ	Grob G115E Tutor	82110E		18. 1.00	VT Aerospace Ltd	RAF Woodvale	31. 1.08E
					(Operated Liverpool UAS and Manchester and Salford Universities AS [10 AEF])		
G-BYVA	Grob G115E Tutor	82111E		18. 1.00	VT Aerospace Ltd	RAF Cranwell	31. 1.08E
					(Operated East Midlands UAS [7 AEF])		
G-BYVB	Grob G115E Tutor	82112E		17. 2.00	VT Aerospace Ltd	RAF Benson	29. 2.08E
					(Operated Oxford University AS [6 AEF])		
G-BYVC	Grob G115E Tutor	82113E		17. 2.00	VT Aerospace Ltd	Colerne	2. 3.08E
					(Operated Bristol UAS [3 AEF])		

G-BYVD	Grob G115E Tutor	82114E	17. 2.00	VT Aerospace Ltd	RAF Wyton	2. 4.08E
				(Operated Cambridge UAS [5 AEF] and University of London AS)		
G-BYVE	Grob G115E Tutor	82115E	17. 2.00	VT Aerospace Ltd	Boscombe Down	2. 4.08E
				(Operated Southampton UAS [2 AEF])		
G-BYVF	Grob G115E Tutor	82116E	22. 2.00	VT Aerospace Ltd	RNAS Yeovilton	29. 2.08E
				(Operated 727 Sqdn)		
G-BYVG	Grob G115E Tutor	82117E	22. 3.00	VT Aerospace Ltd	RAF Church Fenton	2. 4.08E
				(Operated Yorkshire Universities AS [9 AEF])		
G-BYVH	Grob G115E Tutor	82118E	22. 3.00	VT Aerospace Ltd	RAF Leuchars	4. 4.08E
				(Operated East of Scotland UAS [12 AEF])		
G-BYVI	Grob G115E Tutor	82119E	22. 3.00	VT Aerospace Ltd	RAF Church Fenton	4. 4.08E
				(Operated Yorkshire Universities AS [9 AEF])		
G-BYVJ	Grob G115E Tutor	82120E	14. 4.00	VT Aerospace Ltd	RAF Church Fenton	25. 4.08E
				(Operated Yorkshire Universities AS [9 AEF])		
G-BYVK	Grob G115E Tutor	82121E	14. 4.00	VT Aerospace Ltd	RNAS Yeovilton	25. 4.08E
				(Operated 727 Sqdn)		
G-BYVL	Grob G115E Tutor	82122E	14. 4.00	VT Aerospace Ltd	RAF Benson	26. 4.08E
				(Operated Oxford University AS [6 AEF])		
G-BYVM	Grob G115E Tutor	82123E	14. 4.00	VT Aerospace Ltd	Glasgow	26. 4.08E
				(Operated Universities of Glasgow and Strathclyde AS [4 AEF])		
G-BYVN	Grob G115E Tutor	82124E	18. 5.00	VT Aerospace Ltd	RNAS Yeovilton	31. 5.08E
				(Operated 727 Sqdn)		
G-BYVO	Grob G115E Tutor	82125E	18. 5.00	VT Aerospace Ltd	RAF Cranwell	31. 5.08E
				(Operated CFS Tutor Sqdn)		
G-BYVP	Grob G115E Tutor	82126E	18. 5.00	VT Aerospace Ltd	RAF Benson	31. 5.08E
				(Operated Oxford University AS [6 AEF])		
G-BYVR	Grob G115E Tutor	82127E	18. 5.00	VT Aerospace Ltd	RAF Cranwell	31. 5.08E
				(Operated CFS Tutor Sqdn)		
G-BYVS	Grob G115E Tutor	82128E	20. 6.00	VT Aerospace Ltd	RAF Cranwell	29. 6.08E
				(Operated CFS Tutor Sqdn)		
G-BYVT	Grob G115E Tutor	82129E	20. 6.00	VT Aerospace Ltd	RAF Wyton	29. 6.08E
				(Operated Cambridge UAS [5 AEF] and University of London AS)		
G-BYVU	Grob G115E Tutor	82130E	20. 6.00	VT Aerospace Ltd	RAF Benson	29. 6.08E
				(Operated Oxford University AS [6 AEF])		
G-BYVV	Grob G115E Tutor	82131E	20. 6.00	VT Aerospace Ltd	RAF Leeming	29. 6.08E
				(Operated Northumbrian Universities AS [11 AEF])		
G-BYVW	Grob G115E Tutor	82132E	21. 7.00	VT Aerospace Ltd	RAF St Athan	6. 8.08E
				(Operated University of Wales AS [1 AEF])		
G-BYVX	Grob G115E Tutor	82133E	21. 7.00	VT Aerospace Ltd	RAF Church Fenton	6. 8.08E
				(Operated Yorkshire Universities AS [9 AEF])		
G-BYVY	Grob G115E Tutor	82134E	21. 7.00	VT Aerospace Ltd	RAF Cosford	6. 8.08E
				(Operated University of Birmingham AS [8 AEF])		
G-BYVZ	Grob G115E Tutor	82135E	21. 7.00	VT Aerospace Ltd	RAF Church Fenton	6. 8.08E
				(Operated Yorkshire Universities AS [9 AEF])		
G-BYWA	Grob G115E Tutor	82136E	21. 8.00	VT Aerospace Ltd	RAF Leeming	30. 8.08E
				(Operated Northumbrian Universities AS [11 AEF])		
G-BYWB	Grob G115E Tutor	82137E	21. 8.00	VT Aerospace Ltd	RAF Cranwell	30. 8.08E
				(Operated CFS Tutor Sqdn)		
G-BYWC	Grob G115E Tutor	82138E	18. 9.00	VT Aerospace Ltd	Colerne	27. 9.08E
				(Operated Bristol UAS [3 AEF])		
G-BYWD	Grob G115E Tutor	82139E	18. 9.00	VT Aerospace Ltd	RAF Woodvale	27. 9.08E
				(Operated Liverpool UAS and Manchester and Salford Universities AS [10 AEF])		
G-BYWE	Grob G115E Tutor	82140E	18. 9.00	VT Aerospace Ltd	Colerne	27. 9.08E
				(Operated Bristol UAS [3 AEF])		
G-BYWF	Grob G115E Tutor	82141E	18. 9.00	VT Aerospace Ltd	RAF Cranwell	27. 9.08E
				(Operated East Midlands UAS [7 AEF])		
G-BYWG	Grob G115E Tutor	82142E	13.10.00	VT Aerospace Ltd	RAF Cranwell	29.10.08E
				(Operated CFS Tutor Sqdn)		
G-BYWH	Grob G115E Tutor	82143E	13.10.00	VT Aerospace Ltd	RAF Leeming	29.10.08E
				(Operated Northumbrian Universities AS [11 AEF])		
G-BYWI	Grob G115E Tutor	82144E	13.10.00	VT Aerospace Ltd	Colerne	29.10.08E
				(Operated Bristol UAS [3 AEF])		
G-BYWJ	Grob G115E Tutor	82145E	13.10.00	VT Aerospace Ltd	RAF Woodvale	29.10.08E
				(Operated Liverpool UAS and Manchester and Salford Universities AS [10 AEF])		
G-BYWK	Grob G115E Tutor	82146E	17.11.00	VT Aerospace Ltd	Boscombe Down	28.11.08E
				(Operated Southampton UAS [2 AEF])		
G-BYWL	Grob G115E Tutor	82147E	17.11.00	VT Aerospace Ltd	RAF Cranwell	28.11.08E
				(Operated CFS Tutor Sqdn)		
G-BYWM	Grob G115E Tutor	82148E	17.11.00	VT Aerospace Ltd	RNAS Yeovilton	28.11.08E
				(Operated 727 Sqdn)		
G-BYWN	Grob G115E Tutor	82149E	17.11.00	VT Aerospace Ltd	RAF Woodvale	28.11.08E
				(Operated Liverpool UAS and Manchester and Salford Universities AS [10 AEF])		
G-BYWO	Grob G115E Tutor	82150E	7.12.00	VT Aerospace Ltd	RAF Church Fenton	14. 1.08E
				(Operated Yorkshire Universities AS [9 AEF])		
G-BYWP	Grob G115E Tutor	82151E	7.12.00	VT Aerospace Ltd	RAF Church Fenton	14. 1.08E
				(Operated Yorkshire Universities AS [9 AEF])		
G-BYWR	Grob G115E Tutor	82152E	18. 5.00	VT Aerospace Ltd	RAF Wyton	5. 2.08E
				(Operated Cambridge UAS [5 AEF] and University of London AS)		
G-BYWS	Grob G115E Tutor	82153E	7.12.00	VT Aerospace Ltd	RAF Church Fenton	16. 1.08E
				(Operated Yorkshire Universities AS [9 AEF])		
G-BYWT	Grob G115E Tutor	82154E	12.12.00	VT Aerospace Ltd	RAF Leeming	16. 1.08E
				(Operated Northumbrian Universities AS [11 AEF])		
G-BYWU	Grob G115E Tutor	82155E	19. 1.01	VT Aerospace Ltd	RAF Cranwell	28. 1.08E
				(Operated CFS Tutor Sqdn)		

G-BYWV	Grob G115E Tutor	82156E		19. 1.01	VT Aerospace Ltd	RAF Church Fenton	28. 1.08E
					(Operated Yorkshire Universities AS [9 AEF])		
G-BYWW	Grob G115E Tutor	82157E		19. 1.01	VT Aerospace Ltd	Boscombe Down	28. 1.08E
					(Operated Southampton UAS [2 AEF])		
G-BYWX	Grob G115E Tutor	82158E		14. 2.01	VT Aerospace Ltd	RAF Church Fenton	25. 2.08E
					(Operated Yorkshire Universities AS [9 AEF])		
G-BYWY	Grob G115E Tutor	82159E		14. 2.01	VT Aerospace Ltd	RAF Cranwell	25. 2.08E
					(Operated East Midlands UAS [7 AEF])		
G-BYWZ	Grob G115E Tutor	82160E		14. 2.01	VT Aerospace Ltd	RAF Cranwell	4. 3.08E
					(Operated East Midlands UAS [7 AEF])		
G-BYXA	Grob G115E Tutor	82161E		14. 2.01	VT Aerospace Ltd	RAF Woodvale	4. 3.08E
					(Operated Liverpool UAS and Manchester and Salford Universities AS [10 AEF])		
G-BYXB	Grob G115E Tutor	82162E		19. 3.01	VT Aerospace Ltd	Boscombe Down	1. 4.08E
					(Operated Southampton UAS [2 AEF])		
G-BYXC	Grob G115E Tutor	82163E		19. 3.01	VT Aerospace Ltd	RAF Benson	1. 4.08E
					(Operated Oxford University AS [6 AEF])		
G-BYXD	Grob G115E Tutor	82164E		19. 3.01	VT Aerospace Ltd	Boscombe Down	1. 4.08E
					(Operated Southampton UAS [2 AEF])		
G-BYXE	Grob G115E Tutor	82165E		19. 3.01	VT Aerospace Ltd)	RAF Church Fenton	1. 4.08E
					(Operated Yorkshire Universities AS [9 AEF])		
G-BYXF	Grob G115E Tutor	82166E		12. 4.01	VT Aerospace Ltd	RAF Cosford	25. 4.08E
					(Operated University of Birmingham AS [8 AEF])		
G-BYXG	Grob G115E Tutor	82167E		12. 4.01	VT Aerospace Ltd)	RAF Cosford	25. 4.08E
					(Operated University of Birmingham AS [8 AEF])		
G-BYXH	Grob G115E Tutor	82168E		12. 4.01	VT Aerospace Ltd	RAF Wyton	29. 4.08E
					(Operated Cambridge UAS [5 AEF] and University of London AS)		
G-BYXI	Grob G115E Tutor	82169E		12. 4.01	VT Aerospace Ltd	RAF Woodvale	29. 4.08E
					(Operated Liverpool UAS and Manchester and Salford Universities AS [10 AEF])		
G-BYXJ	Grob G115E Tutor	82170E		16. 5.01	VT Aerospace Ltd	Boscombe Down	28. 5.08E
					(Operated Southampton UAS [2 AEF])		
G-BYXK	Grob G115E Tutor	82171E		16. 5.01	VT Aerospace Ltd	RNAS Yeovilton	28. 5.08E
					(Operated 727 Sqdn)		
G-BYXL	Grob G115E Tutor	82172E		16. 5.01	VT Aerospace Ltd	RAF Cosford	28. 5.08E
					(Operated University of Birmingham AS [8 AEF])		
G-BYXM	Grob G115E Tutor	82173E		16. 5.01	VT Aerospace Ltd	RAF Cranwell	28. 5.08E
					(Operated CFS Tutor Sqdn)		
G-BYXN	Grob G115E Tutor	82174E		8. 6.01	VT Aerospace Ltd	RAF Cranwell	11. 6.08E
					(Operated East Midlands UAS [7 AEF]) "XN"		
G-BYXO	Grob G115E Tutor	82175E		8. 6.01	VT Aerospace Ltd	RAF Cosford	11. 6.08E
					(Operated University of Birmingham AS [8 AEF])		
G-BYXP	Grob G115E Tutor	82176E		8. 6.01	VT Aerospace Ltd	RAF Wyton	11. 6.08E
					(Operated Cambridge UAS [5 AEF] and University of London AS)		
G-BYXR	Grob G115E Tutor	82177E		8. 6.01	VT Aerospace Ltd	RAF Benson	11. 6.08E
					(Operated Oxford University AS [6 AEF])		
G-BYXS	Grob G115E Tutor	82178E		18. 7.01	VT Aerospace Ltd	RNAS Yeovilton	29. 7.08E
					(Operated 727 Sqdn)		
G-BYXT	Grob G115E Tutor	82179E		18. 7.01	VT Aerospace Ltd	Boscombe Down	1.11.07E
					(Operated Southampton UAS [2 AEF])		
G-BYXV	Medway EclipseR	162/140		25.10.99	K A Christie	Easter Balgillo Farm, Finavon	10. 5.04P
		(C/n not confirmed)					
G-BYXW	Medway EclipseR	166/147		25.10.99	G A Hazell	Redlands, Swindon	25. 5.08P
		(Officially registered as c/n 166/144)					
G-BYXX	Grob G115E Tutor	82180E		18. 7.01	VT Aerospace Ltd	RAF Woodvale	1.11.07E
					(Operated Liverpool UAS and Manchester and Salford Universities AS [10 AEF])		
G-BYXY	Grob G115E Tutor	82181E		18. 7.01	VT Aerospace Ltd	RAF Leeming	30. 9.07E
					(Operated Northumbrian Universities AS [11 AEF])		
G-BYXZ	Grob G115E Tutor	82182E		15. 8.01	VT Aerospace Ltd	RAF Cranwell	17. 9.08E
					(Operated CFS Tutor Sqdn)		
G-BYYA	Grob G115E Tutor	82183E		15. 8.01	VT Aerospace Ltd	RAF Leeming	23. 9.08E
					(Operated Northumbrian Universities AS [11 AEF])		
G-BYYB	Grob G115E Tutor	82184E		15. 8.01	VT Aerospace Ltd	RAF Cosford	17. 9.08E
					(Operated University of Birmingham AS [8 AEF])		
G-BYYC	Hapi Cygnet SF-2A	PFA 182-12311		25.11.99	G H Smith	Shenstone Hall Farm, Shenstone	18. 6.08P
		(Built C D Hughes and G H Smith) (Volkswagen 2180)					
G-BYYD	Cameron A-250 Balloon (Hot Air)	4712		31. 3.00	C and J.M Bailey	Bristol	1. 5.08T
G-BYYE	Lindstrand LBL 77A Balloon (Hot Air)	151		25.11.99	D J Cook	Norwich	8. 6.07A
G-BYYG	Slingsby T 67C Firefly	2101	PH-SGI	30.11.99	The Pathfinder Flying Club Ltd	RAF Wyton	6. 4.08E
G-BYYJ	Lindstrand LBL 25A Cloudhopper Balloon (Hot Air)			10.12.99	A M Barton	Coulsdon	14. 8.07A
		651					
G-BYYL	Avtech Jabiru UL-450	xxxx		10.12.99	K C Lye	Edington Hill, Keevil	16. 7.08P
		(Built C Jackson - pr.no.PFA 274A-13480)					
G-BYYM	Raj Hamsa X'Air 582(1)	476		21.10.99	S M S Smith	(Malborough, Kingsbridge)	6.10.08P
		(Built J J Cozens - pr.no.BMAA/HB/119)					
G-BYYN	Cyclone Airsports Pegasus Quantum 15-912	7601		6. 1.00	S E Robinson	Tarn Farm Cockerham	14. 6.08P
G-BYYO	Piper PA-28R-201 Arrow	2837061	(N182ND)	11. 2.00	Stapleford Flying Club Ltd	Stapleford	26. 4.08E
			N9249C, G-BYYO, N9249C				
G-BYYP	Cyclone Airsports Pegasus Quantum 15	7603		11. 2.00	D A Linsey-Bloom	(Long Ashton, Bristol)	21. 4.08P
		(Rotax 582)					
G-BYYR	Raj Hamsa X'Air 582(4)	453		23.12.99	T D Bawden	Weston Zoyland	11. 5.04P
		(Built T D Bawden - pr.no.BMAA/HB/115)					
G-BYYT	Avtech Jabiru UL-450	0259		18.11.99	A J Young and A C Gale	Marley Hall, Ledbury	25. 5.07P
		(Built T D Saveker - pr.no.PFA 274A-13452)					
G-BYYX	TEAM Mini-MAX 91	PFA 186-13410		6. 1.00	J Batchelor	Gerpins Farm, Upminster	7. 6.07P
		(Built P L Turner)					

G-BYYY	Cyclone Airsports Pegasus Quantum 15-912 7564			8.12.99	Clearprop Microlight School Ltd	Redlands, Swindon	24. 1.08P
G-BYYZ	Staaken Z-21A Flitzer	PFA 223-13324		12.11.99	T White	Headcorn	26. 3.08P
	(Built A E Morris) (Volkswagen 1834)						
G-BYZA	Aérospatiale AS.355F2 Ecureuil 2	5518	JA6784	20.12.99	MMAir Ltd	Redhill	17. 4.08E
			F-OHNK				
G-BYZB	Mainair Blade	1229-1299-7-W1022		14. 1.00	A M Thornley	(Acthorp Top, Louth)	29. 9.08P
G-BYZD	Tri-R KIS Cruiser	PFA 302-13156		22.11.99	M G Thatcher	Sleap	18. 6.08P
	(Built R T Clegg) (Lycoming IO-360) (Tri-cycle u/c)						
G-BYZF	Raj Hamsa X'Air 582(1)	461		7. 1.00	R P Davies	(Eccleston, Chorley)	
	(Built S W Grainger - pr.no.BMAA/HB/110)				(Crashed during test-flying Brook Farm, Pilling: stored dismantled 6.07)		
G-BYZG	Cameron A-275 Balloon (Hot Air)	4706		23. 2.00	Cameron Flights Southern Ltd		
					(New owner 1.08)	Woodborough, Pewsey	1. 3.07T
G-BYZJ	Boeing 737-3Q8	24962	G-COLE	11. 1.00	British Midland Airways Ltd	East Midlands	20.11.07E
			PP-VOX		"Pudsey Baby" (Operated bmiBaby)		
G-BYZL	Cameron GP-65 Balloon (Hot Air)	4494		6. 4.00	P Thibo	Junglinster, Luxembourg	28.10.08A
G-BYZO	Rans S-6-ES Coyote II	1298.1287		14. 1.00	B E J Badger and J E Storer	Long Marston	6. 8.08P
	(Built S C Jackson - pr.no.PFA 204-13560) (Rotax 582) (Tri-cycle u/c)						
G-BYZP	Robinson R22 Beta II	3018		9.12.99	Propwash Investments Ltd	Swansea	18. 1.08E
G-BYZR	III Sky Arrow 650 TC	C001	D-ENGF	24. 1.00	J O Harkness and R Moncrieff tr G-BYZR Flying Group		
	(Built Iniziative Industriali Italian)		I-TREI			Gamston	14. 8.08P
G-BYZS	Avtech Jabiru UL-450	xxxx		25. 1.00	N Fielding	Ince Blundell	17. 7.08P
	(Built N Fielding - pr.no.PFA 274A-13489)						
G-BYZT	Nova Vertex 26	13345		21. 1.00	M Hay (New owner 1.03)	(Dundee)	
G-BYZU	Cyclone Airsports Pegasus Quantum 15-	7613		15. 2.00	N I Clifton	East Fortune	25. 4.08P
	(Rotax 582)						
G-BYZV	Sky 90-24 Balloon (Hot Air)	174		15. 8.00	P Farmer	Wadhurst	19. 1.01
G-BYZW	Raj Hamsa X'Air 582(1)	499		19. 1.00	J Magill	(Braystones, Beckermet)	5. 7.08P
	(Built P A Gilford - pr.no.BMAA/HB/129)						
G-BYZX	Cameron R-90 Balloon (Hot Air)	4751		31. 3.00	D K Hempleman-Adams	Corsham	22. 3.05A
	(Rebuilt with envelope c/n 10369)				"Britannic Challenge"		
G-BYZY	Pietenpol AirCamper	PFA 047-12190		2.12.99	D N Hanchet	Siege Cross Farm, Thatcham	31.10.07P
	(Built D N Hanchet)						
G-BYZZ	Robinson R22 Beta II	3000		1.12.99	Astra Helicopters Ltd	Kemble	8.11.08T

G-BZAA - G-BZZZ

G-BZAA	Mainair Blade 912	1142-0198-7-W945		22.11.99	G P Spittles	(Brackley)	4. 4.08P
	(Rotax 462) (Trike c/n amended to 1142-1299-7 by Mainair Sports Ltd)						
G-BZAB	Mainair Rapier	1228-1299-7-W1021		23.12.99	R H Stockton	(Christleton, Chester)	11. 4.08P
G-BZAD	Cessna 152	15279563	N303MA	22. 3.00	Cristal Air Ltd	Deanland	18.11.07E
			N714ZN				
G-BZAE	Cessna 152	15281300	N49480	22. 3.00	APB Leasing Ltd	Sleap	6 12.07E
G-BZAF	Raj Hamsa X'Air 582(1)	503		18. 1.00	Y A Evans	Rufforth	18.11.07P
	(Built P Hassett - pr.no.BMAA/HB/130)						
G-BZAG	Lindstrand LBL 105A Balloon (Hot Air)	542		29..2.00	A M Figiel	High Wycombe	7. 9.76A
G-BZAH	Cessna 208B Grand Caravan	208B0811	N5196U	28. 2.00	R Durie tr Army Parachute Association		
						AAC Netheravon	13. 4.08E
G-BZAI	Cyclone Airsports Pegasus Quantum 15	7614		9. 2.00	LW Harris	(Freiston, Boston)	3. 5.08P
	(Rotax 503)						
G-BZAK	Raj Hamsa X'Air 582(9)	477		20. 1.00	R J Ripley	Field Farm, Oakley	25. 5.08P
	(Built B W Austen - pr.no.BMAA/HB/114)						
G-BZAL	Mainair Blade 912	1205-0799-7-W1008		27. 1.00	J Potts	Tarn Farm, Cockerham	27. 7.07P
G-BZAM	Europa Aviation Europa	265		6.12.99	D Corbett	Shobdon	1. 6.08P
	(Built D U Corbett - pr.no.PFA 247-12969) (Monowheel u/c)						
G-BZAO	Rans S-12XL Airaile	PFA 307-13394		1. 2.00	M L Robinson	Kirkbride	11. 7.08P
	(Built M L Robinson) (Rotax 582)						
G-BZAP	Avtech Jabiru UL-450	0280		13.12.99	D R Griffiths and I J Grindley		
	(Built S Derwin - pr.no.PFA 274A-13479)					Top Farm, Croydon, Royston	30. 6.08P
G-BZAR	Denney Kitfox Model 4-1200 Speedster	G-LEZJ		17. 2.00	C E Brookes Little Battleflats Farm, Ellistown, Coalville		19. 6.08P
	(Built L A James) (Rotax 912-UL)	PFA 172B-12529			"Ol' Red"		
G-BZAS	Isaacs Fury II	PFA 011-10837		10. 2.00	H A Brunt and H Frick	Bournemouth	4. 7.04P
	(Built H A Brunt and H Frick) (Canadian Air Motive CAM100)				(On display Aviation Museum 1.07 as "K5673" in RAF c/s) "Spirit of Dunsfold"		
G-BZAT	British Aerospace Avro 146-RJ100	E3320	G-6-320	18.11.97	BA Cityflyer Ltd	Birmingham	8. 1.08E
G-BZAU	British Aerospace Avro 146-RJ100	E3328		25. 4.98	BA Cityflyer Ltd	Birmingham	11. 6.08E
G-BZAV	British Aerospace Avro 146-RJ100	E3331		19. 5.98	BA Cityflyer Ltd	Birmingham	23. 7.08E
G-BZAW	British Aerospace Avro 146-RJ100	E3354		11. 6.99	BA Cityflyer Ltd	Manchester	15. 7.08E
G-BZAX	British Aerospace Avro 146-RJ100	E3356	G-6-356	9. 7.99	BA Cityflyer Ltd	Manchester	16. 8.08E
G-BZAY	British Aerospace Avro 146-RJ100	E3368		15. 2.00	BA Cityflyer Ltd	Manchester	27. 3.08E
G-BZAZ	British Aerospace Avro 146-RJ100	E3369		15. 2.00	BA Cityflyer Ltd	Manchester	13. 4.08E
G-BZBC	Rans S-6-ES Coyote II	0499.1314		2. 2.00	A J Baldwin	Derby	29. 8.08P
	(Built A J Baldwin - pr.no.PFA 204-13525) (Rotax 582) (Tri-cycle u/c)						
G-BZBE	Cameron A-210 Balloon (Hot Air)	4708		9. 5.00	Dragon Balloon Company Ltd Castleton, Hope Valley		16. 6.07T
G-BZBF	Cessna 172M	17262258	N126SA	20.12.99	L W Scattergood	(Cawood, Selby)	20. 9.08E
	(Lycoming O-360)		G-BZBF, 9H-ACV, N12785				
G-BZBH	Thunder Ax7-65 Bolt Balloon (Hot Air)	173		28.11.78	P J Hebdon and Charlotte A Fraser	Milton, Banbury	19. 3.08A
					"Serendipity II"		
G-BZBI	Cameron V-77 Balloon (Hot Air)	4740		4. 4.00	C and A I Gibson "Flying Colours"	Stockport	8. 6.08A
G-BZBJ	Lindstrand LBL 77A Balloon (Hot Air)	646		29. 2.00	P T R Ollivere	Eastbourne	9. 7.08A
G-BZBL	Lindstrand LBL 120A Balloon (Hot Air)	676		23. 2.00	East Coast Balloons Ltd	York	1. 4.08A
G-BZBO	Stoddard-Hamilton Glasair III	3032		21. 2.00	M B Hamlett	(Lagny le Sec, France)	
	(Built M B Hamlett)						
G-BZBP	Raj Hamsa X'Air 582(5)	470		29. 2.00	D P Sudworth	Maypole Farm, Chislet	27. 8.08P
	(Built D F Hughes - pr.no.BMAA/HB/131)						

G-BZBR	Cyclone Airsports Pegasus Quantum 15	7631		26. 5.00	A Asslanian	Hunsdon	15. 8.08P
	(Rotax 503)						
G-BZBS	Piper PA-28-161 Warrior III	2842080	N4180H	10. 5.00	S J Skilton t/a Aviation Rentals	White Waltham	21. 5.08E
			G-BZBS, N9529N				
G-BZBT	Cameron Hopper H-34 Balloon (Hot Air)	4730		18. 5.00	British Telecommunications PLC	Thatcham	9. 4.05A
G-BZBU	Robinson R22	0131	OH-HLB	23. 5.00	I C Macdonald	Blackpool	26. 4.07T
			SE-HOH		(Noted 10,07)		
G-BZBW	RotorWay Executive 162F	6415		23. 2.00	Southern Helicopters Ltd	Street Farm, Takeley	28.11.08P
	(Built M Gardiner) (RotorWay RI 162F)						
G-BZBX	Rans S-6-ES Coyote II	0499.1317		26. 1.00	P E De-Ville and M W Shepherd	Otherton, Cannock	6. 7.07P
	(Built R Johnstone - pr.no.PFA 204-13501) (Rotax 582) (Tri-cycle u/c)						
G-BZBZ	Jodel D 9 Bébé	519	OO-48	29. 2.00	S Marom	Whitehall Farm, Benington	28. 7.06P
	(Built Etienne de Schrevel, Gent 1970-77) (Volkswagen 1600)						
G-BZDA	Piper PA-28-161 Warrior III	2842087	N41814	29. 6.00	S J Skilton t/a Aviation Rentals	White Waltham	5. 7.08T
			G-BZDA, N41814				
G-BZDB	Thruster T 600T Sprint 450 Jab	0030-T600T-041		7. 3.00	R M Raikes	Clench Common	7. 7.08P
G-BZDC	Mainair Blade	1232-0100-7-W1025		13. 3.00	E J Wells and P J Smith	Over Farm, Gloucester	17. 4.08P
	(Rotax 462)						
G-BZDD	Mainair Blade 912	1238-0200-7-W1031		21. 1.00	A S Facey tr Barton Blade Group	Barton	13. 4.08P
G-BZDE	Lindstrand LBL 210A Balloon (Hot Air)	665		6. 3.00	Toucan Travel Ltd (Toucan Travel titles) Basingstoke		20. 9.07T
G-BZDF	CFM Streak Shadow SA	K 241	(EI-)	7. 3.00	W M Moylan Glencorrig, Shinrone Birr, County Offaly		11. 7.08P
	(Built J W Beckett - pr.no.PFA 206-12609) (Rotax 582) G-BZDF						
G-BZDH	Piper PA-28R-200 Cherokee Arrow II		5B-CJU	8. 3.00	G-BZDH Ltd	Manston	10. 7.09E
		28R-7235028	G-BZDH, HB-OHH, N4390T				
G-BZDI	Aero L-39C Albatros	031822	ES-ZLB	7. 6.00	C C Butt	Hawarden	25.1.08P
			Soviet AF				
G-BZDJ	Cameron Z-105 Balloon (Hot Air)	4832		27. 6.00	BWS Security Systems Ltd	Corston, Bath	2. 5.08A
					(BWS Security Systems titles)		
G-BZDK	Raj Hamsa X'Air 582(2)	447		8. 2.00	B Park	(Lanner Moor, Redruth)	20. 1.06P
	(Built B Park and R Barnes - pr.no.BMAA/HB/124)				(Operates from Truro and noted 10.06)		
G-BZDL	Cyclone Airsports Pegasus Quantum 15-912 7629			18. 4.00	D M Merritt-Colman	(Benicolet, Spain)	8. 7.07P
G-BZDM	Stoddard-Hamilton GlaStar	PFA 295-13283		13. 3.00	F G Miskelly	Newtownards	26. 7.08P
	(Built F G Miskelly)						
G-BZDN	Cameron N-105 Balloon (Hot Air)	2840	D-OABB	26. 4.00	I R Warrington and P A Foot	Stamford	2. 3.08T
			D-Saxonia (2)		(Wir Geben Gas and E W S titles)		
G-BZDP	Scottish Aviation Bulldog Series 120/121		XX551	31. 3.00	D J Rae	Colerne	8. 7.10S
		BH120/244			(As "XX551:E" in RAF c/s)		
G-BZDR	Tri-R KIS	9403		8. 3.00	J A and J M Jackson	Sleap	28. 6.08P
	(Built B S Neilson) (Continental IO-240)						
G-BZDS	Cyclone Airsports Pegasus Quantum 15-912 7633			17. 4.00	K C Yeates	(Bitteswell, Luterworth)	11. 2.09P
G-BZDU	de Havilland DHC-1 Chipmunk 22	C1/0714	WP833	31. 3.00	M R Clark (As "WP833" in RAF c/s)	Newcastle	6. 7.09S
G-BZDV	Westland SA.341C Gazelle HT.2	1150	3D-HXL	31. 3.00	A Murphy tr European Plant and Machinery Sales		8. 5.08P
			G-BZDV, XW884			(Hayling Island)	
G-BZDX	Cameron Colt Sugarbox 90 SS Balloon (Hot Air)			17. 5.00	Stratos Ballooning GmbH and Co KG		6. 5.04A
		4814				Ennigerloh, Germany	
G-BZDY	Cameron Colt Sugarbox 90 SS Balloon (Hot Air)			22. 5.00	Stratos Ballooning GmbH and Co KG		7. 4.04A
		4815				Ennigerloh, Germany	
G-BZDZ	Avtech Jabiru SP-430	0232	ZU-BVB	14. 5.01	R M Whiteside	Shoreham	14. 3.07P
	(Built R M Whiteside)				(Carries name "Jooney Bird" in script at top of fin)		
G-BZEA	Cessna A152	A1520824	N7606L	13. 3.00	Sky Leisure Aviation (Charters) Ltd	Blackbushe	19. 7.08E
G-BZEB	Cessna 152	15282772	N89532	31. 1.00	Sky Leisure Aviation (Charters) Ltd	Redhill	24. 9.03T
					(Noted 9.07)		
G-BZEC	Cessna 152	15284475	N4655M	21. 1.00	Sky Leisure Aviation (Charters) Ltd	Shoreham	14. 8.08E
G-BZED	Cyclone Airsports Pegasus Quantum 15-912 7600			17. 3.00	D Crozier	Shotton Colliery, Peterlee	9. 6.08P
G-BZEE	Agusta-Bell 206B-2 JetRanger II	8554	G-OJCB	22 .2.00	Yateley Helicopters Ltd	Blackbushe	17.11.06T
G-BZEG	Mainair Blade	1239-0200-7-W1032		3. 3.00	R P Cookson	Ince Blundell	8. 5.08P
	(Rotax 912-UL)						
G-BZEH	Piper PA-28-235 Cherokee Pathfinder 28-10838		9M-ARW	31. 3.00	G-BZEH Aviation Ltd	(Banstead)	22. 5.08E
			RP-C704, PI-C704, N9182W				
G-BZEJ	Raj Hamsa X'Air 582(7)	500		31. 3.00	P J Perry tr X'Air Flying Group	Otherton, Cannock	27.10.08P
	(Built H Hall - pr.no.BMAA/HB/134)						
G-BZEK	Cameron C-70 Balloon (Hot Air)	4860		30. 5.00	Ballooning 50 Degrees Nord Fouhren, Luxembourg		27. 3.08A
G-BZEL	Mainair Blade	1245-0300-7-W1038		27. 3.00	M W Bush	Belle Vue Farm, Yarnscombe	17. 4.08P
	(Rotax 582)						
G-BZEN	Avtech Jabiru UL	0161		4. 4.00	B W Stockil	Bagby	4. 1.07P
	(Built B W Stockil - pr.no.PFA 274-13272)				(Noted 2.08)		
G-BZEP	Scottish Aviation Bulldog Series 120/121		XX561	4. 4.00	A J Amato	Biggin Hill	25. 5.05T
		BH120/257			(As "XX561:7" in RAF c/s)		
G-BZER	Raj Hamsa X'Air R100(1)	526		22. 3.00	N P Lloyd and H Lloyd-Hughes		
	(Built N P Lloyd and H Lloyd-Hughes - pr.no.BMAA/HB/133)					Emlyn's Field, Rhuallt	27.12.07P
G-BZES	RotorWay Executive 90	6191	G-LUFF	25. 4.00	Southern Helicopters Ltd	(Street Farm, Takeley)	
	(Built D C Luffingham)				(Noted 2.03)		
G-BZET	Robin HR.200-120B	345	F-GTZG	9. 5.00	Modi Aviation Ltd	Earls Colne	22. 5.08E
G-BZEU	Raj Hamsa X'Air 582(8)	518		20. 4.00	K J Brereton	Otherton, Cannock	2. 2.08P
	(Built J C Harris - pr.no.BMAA/HB/140)						
G-BZEV	Vahdat-Hagh Semicopter 1	002		10.10.00	M E Vahdat-Hagh	(Uxbridge)	
	(Built M E Vahdat-Hagh)						
G-BZEW	Rans S-6-ES Coyote II	0998 1268		5. 4.00	M J Wooldridge	(Siege Cross Farm, Thatcham)	24. 6.08P
	(Built D Kingslake - pr.no.PFA 204-13450) (Rotax 582) (Tri-cycle u/c) (Rebuilt and redated after accident ? as kit no.0998.1268.0199)						
G-BZEX	Raj Hamsa X'Air R100(2)	530		5. 4.00	R Johnston	Newtownards	23. 3.08P
	(Built J M McCullough and R T Henry - pr.no.BMAA/HB/135)						
G-BZEY	Cameron N-90 Balloon (Hot Air)	4829		15. 5.00	Northants Auto Parts and Service Ltd Northampton		9. 8.08A
G-BZEZ	CFM Streak Shadow SA	K 332		1 .2.00	G J Pearce	Jackrells Farm, Southwater	10. 5.08P
	(Built M F Cottam - pr.no.PFA 206-13503) (Rotax 582)						

G-BZFB	Robin R2112A Alpha	175	EI-BIU	7. 4.00	T F Wells	Sackville Lodge, Riseley	12. 7.08E
G-BZFC	Cyclone Airsports Pegasus Quantum 15	7640		14. 4.00	G Addison	East Fortune	6 9.08P
G-BZFD	Cameron N-90 Balloon (Hot Air)	2725	OO-BFD	24. 5.00	David Hathaway Holdings Ltd	Yate, Bristol	23. 3.08E
					(David Hathaway Transport titles)		
G-BZFF	Raj Hamsa X'Air 582(2)	521		6. 4.00	L H S Stephens	Davidstow Moor	24. 8.08P
	(Built G Chatwick, A L H Seed and G Statham - pr.no.BMAA/HB/137)						
G-BZFH	Cyclone Airsports Pegasus Quantum 15-912	7660		15. 5.00	J S Hamilton t/a Kent Scout Microlights	(Edenbridge)	6. 7.08P
G-BZFI	Avtech Jabiru UL-450	0271		27. 3.00	A W J Findlay tr Group Family	(Wolvey)	10. 7.08P
	(Built A W J and A I Findlay - pr.no.PFA 274-13497)						
G-BZFK	TEAM Mini-MAX 88	PFA 186-12060		17. 4.00	I Macleod	Lower Upham Farm, Chiseldon	9. 9.08P
	(Built C Vandenberghe)						
G-BZFN	Scottish Aviation Bulldog Series 120/121		XX667	18. 4.00	Risk Logical Ltd	Ronaldsway	25. 1.08E
		BH120/325			*(As "XX667:16" in RAF c/s)*		
G-BZFO	Mainair Blade (Rotax 503)	1235-0100-7-W1028		29. 3.00	G S McCombie	Insch	5.12.08P
G-BZFP	de Havilland DHC-6-310 Twin Otter	696	C-GGNF	11. 8.00	Loganair Ltd	Glasgow	13. 8.06E
			N712PV, N696WJ, F-ODUH, TR-LZN, C-GKIQ				
G-BZFR	Extra EA.300/L	203		26. 6.00	T C Beadle	North Weald	14. 6.08E
	(Official c/n outside normal EA300L c/n batch: possibly ex D-EDGE [03?])						
G-BZFS	Mainair Blade 912	1243-0300-7-W1036		23. 3.00	A Sorah and D G Barnes	(Glossop and Hyde)	4. 5.08P
G-BZFT	Murphy Rebel	PFA 232-13224		7. 4.00	N A Evans	Higherlands Farm, Branscombe	12. 6.08P
	(Built N A Evans) (Lycoming O-320)						
G-BZFU	Lindstrand LBL HS-110 Airship (Hot Air)	671		25. 4.00	Lindstrand Hot Air Balloons Ltd	Oswestry	11. 1.03A
					(New owners 11.05)		
G-BZFV	Zenair CH.601UL Zodiac	PFA 162A-13547		14. 4.00	M E Caton	Sibson	22. 4.08P
	(Built I M Donnelly)						
G-BZGA	de Havilland DHC-1 Chipmunk 22	C1/0608	WK585	31. 3.00	The Real Flying Company Ltd	Shoreham	30. 4.10S
					(As "WK585" in RAF c/s)		
G-BZGB	de Havilland DHC-1 Chipmunk 22	C1/0905	WZ872	31. 3.00	Silverstar Aviation Ltd	Blackpool	18. 8.06
					(As "WZ872:E" in RAF c/s) (Noted 10.07)		
G-BZGD	Piper PA-18-150 Super Cub	18-8109049	N90943	15. 5.00	M G and S J White t/a Proline Aviation		
						Edmondsham, Wimborne	31. 8.08T
G-BZGF	Rans S-6-ES Coyote II	0199 1297		25. 4.00	C A Purvis	London Colney	30. 8.07P
	(Built D F Castle - pr.no.PFA 204-13594) (Rotax 582) (Original kit no.was 0899.1334 but changed - possibly after accident 22. 7.01)						
G-BZGG	Sud-Aviation SE.313B Alouette II	1430	G-POSE	22. 2.00	J T Meall	(Liverpool)	21. 2.08E
			G-BZGG, EI-CTH, F-GKML, French Army				
G-BZGH	Reims Cessna F172N Skyhawk II	F17201789	EI-BGH	1.12.98	D Behan tr Golf Hotel Group		
						Weston, Leixlip, County Kildare	2.11.07E
G-BZGI	Ultramagic M-145 Balloon (Hot Air)	145/12		9. 6.00	European Balloon Company Ltd	Great Missenden	7. 8.08T
G-BZGJ	Thunder Ax10-180 Series 2 Balloon (Hot Air)		LN-CBT	8. 5.00	M Wady t/a Merlin Balloons	Hamstreet	3. 5.08T
		3956					
G-BZGK	North American OV-10B Bronco	338-17	Luftwaffe 9932	9. 6.00	Invicta Aviation Ltd	Duxford	11.11.08P
			D-9561, Bu 158308		*(Operated Aircraft Restoration Company as "99+32")*		
G-BZGL	North American OV-10B Bronco	338-11	Luftwaffe 9926	9. 6.00	Invicta Aviation Ltd	Duxford	
			D-9555, Bu 158302		*(Operated Aircraft Restoration Company: noted 11.06)*		
G-BZGM	Mainair Blade 912	1247-0400-7-W1040		14. 4.00	D Young	North Coates	25. 7.07P
G-BZGN	Raj Hamsa X'Air 582(2)	445		3. 5.00	C S Warr and P A Pilkington	North Coates	20. 8.06P
	(Built B G M Chapman - pr.no.BMAA/HB/128)						
G-BZGO	Robinson R44 Astro	0757		14. 4.00	P Durkin	(Blackpool)	17. 5.08E
G-BZGR	Rans S-6-ES Coyote II	0999.1338		3. 5.00	J M Benton	Hadzor Farm, Worcester	23. 7.07P
	(Built J M Benton and G R Pritchard - pr.no.PFA 204-13595) (Jabiru 2200A) (Tri-cycle u/c) (Carries "J M Benton" in script on nose)						
G-BZGS	Mainair Blade 912	1242-0300-7-W1035		10. 5.00	R J Coppin	Broadmeadow Farm, Hereford	28. 4.08P
G-BZGT	Avtech Jabiru UL-450	0291		4. 5.00	J White	(Burnham-on-Sea)	16. 7.08P
	(Built P H Ronfel - pr.no.PFA 274A-13539)						
G-BZGU	Raj Hamsa X'Air 582(4)	512		4. 5.00	W Bracken	Limetree, Portarlington, County Laois	8.10.05P
	(Built C Kiernan - pr.no.BMAA/HB/138)					*(Noted 4.06)*		
G-BZGV	Lindstrand LBL 77A Balloon (Hot Air)	695		9. 5.00	J H Dryden *"Skylark"*	Okehampton	9. 4.08A
G-BZGW	Mainair Blade	1246-0400-7-W1039		5. 5.00	C S M Hallam	Barton	15 8.08P
G-BZGX	Raj Hamsa X'Air 582(6)	400		2. 6.00	A Crowe	Newtownards	9 6.08P
	(Built A Crowe - pr.no.BMAA/HB/099)						
G-BZGY	Dyn'Aéro CR100C	21	F-TGCI	7. 6.00	D Hayes	Spilstead Farm, Sedlescombe	2. 5.08P
G-BZGZ	Cyclone Airsports Pegasus Quantum 15-912	7674		7. 6.00	D W Beech	Ince Blundell	16. 1.08P
G-BZHA	Boeing 767-336	29230	N60668	22. 5.98	British Airways PLC	London Heathrow	21. 5.08E
G-BZHB	Boeing 767-336	29231		30. 5.98	British Airways PLC	London Heathrow	29. 5.08E
G-BZHC	Boeing 767-336	29232		29. 6.98	British Airways PLC	London Heathrow	28. 6.08E
G-BZHE	Cessna 152	15281303	D-EAOC	20. 4.00	Simair Ltd	Andrewsfield	24. 7.08E
			N49484				
G-BZHF	Cessna 152	15283986	D-EMJA	20. 4.00	Modi Aviation Ltd	Earls Colne	24. 7.08E
			N4858H				
G-BZHG	Tecnam P92-EM Echo	PFA 318-13606		24. 5.00	R W F Boarder	Field Farm, Oakley	25. 2.08P
	(Built M Rudd)						
G-BZHI	Enstrom F-28A-UK	281	G-BPOZ	14.12.99	Tindon Engineering Ltd	Little Snoring	5. 6.08
			N246Q				
G-BZHJ	Raj Hamsa X'Air 582(7)	482		10. 5.00	P J Smith	Otherton, Cannock	1. 6.08P
	(Built A P Harvey and B Baker - pr.no.BMAA/HB/126)						
G-BZHK	Piper PA-28-181 Archer III	2843347	N41647	14. 7.00	J Middlemass	Duxford	15. 8.08E
			N9519N				
G-BZHL	North American AT-16 Harvard IIB	14A-1158	FT118	6. 6.00	R H Cooper and S Swallow	Hemswell	
	(Built Noorduyn Aviation, Canada)		43-12859		*(Stored 1.02)*		
	(Officially quoted USAF p/i is "43-12959")						
G-BZHN	Cyclone Airsports Pegasus Quantum 15-912	7677		20. 6.00	P L Cummings t/a Eaglescott Microlights	Eaglescott	17. 6.08P
G-BZHO	Cyclone Airsports Pegasus Quantum 15-	7658		19. 5.00	R L Williams	Roddige	23. 7.08P
	(Rotax 582)						
G-BZHP	Quad City Challenger II	CH2-0995-CW-1398		11. 5.00	G Cousins	Rochester	16. 7.07P
	(Built F Payne - pr.no.PFA 177-13153) (Rotax 582)						

G-BZHR	Avtech Jabiru UL-450	0267		16. 5.00	G W Rowbotham	(Loughborough)	29. 8.07P
	(Built G W Rowbotham - pr.no.PFA 274A-13493)						
G-BZHS	Europa Aviation Europa	207		16. 5.00	P Waugh	(Caudeval, France)	25. 8.07P
	(Built P Waugh - pr.no.PFA 247-12865) (Monowheel u/c)						
G-BZHT	Piper PA-18A-150 Super Cub	18-5886	ZK-BTF	25. 5.00	The Furness Gliding Club Proprietary Ltd t/a Lakes Gliding Club		
						Walney Island	9. 1.08E
G-BZHU	Wag-Aero CUBy Sport Trainer	AACA/351	ZK-MPH	25. 5.00	S D Clark tr Teddy Boys Flying Group		
	(Built D C Hoffman)					Gloucestershire	26.11.07P
G-BZHV	Piper PA-28-181 Archer III	2843382	N41848	17.10.00	M J Hill	(Southsea)	1.10.07T
			G-BZHV, N41848				
G-BZHX	Thunder Ax11-250 Series 2 Balloon (Hot Air)			21. 6.00	T H Wilson	Shieldaig, Strathcarron	13. 9.08T
		4880			"Slim Your Bin"		
G-BZIA	Raj Hamsa X'Air 700(1)	475		1. 6.00	J L Pritchett	(Gloucester)	14. 4.08P
	(Built A U I Hudson - pr.no.BMAA/HB/116)						
G-BZIC	Lindstrand LBL Sun SS Balloon (Hot Air)	702		8. 6.00	Ballongaventyr I Skane AB	Lund, Sweden	25. 2.07A
G-BZID	Montgomerie-Bensen B 8MR	PFA G/01-1315		31. 5.00	S C Gillies	(Buckie)	
	(Built A Gault from cannibalised Air Command Elite G-BOGW)				(New owner 10.02)		
G-BZIG	Thruster T 600N Sprint	0400-T600N-042		25. 4.00	Ultra Air Ltd	Leicester	8. 5.08P
	(Rotax 582 UL)						
G-BZIH	Lindstrand LBL 31A Balloon (Hot Air)	700		7. 6.00	R S Kent t/a Skyart Balloons "Budweiser"	Lancing	10.10.07A
G-BZII	Extra EA.300/L	119		13. 9.00	R J Verrall	Luxter's Farm, Hambledon	20. 9.08E
G-BZIJ	Robin DR.500-200i Président	0023		9. 3.00	Rob Airways Ltd	Guernsey	13. 4.08E
	(Officially regd as DR.400-500)						
G-BZIK	Cameron A-250 Balloon (Hot Air)	4890		27. 6.00	Breckland Balloons Ltd	Dereham	31. 3.08T
G-BZIL	Cameron Colt 120A Balloon (Hot Air)	4876		7. 7.00	S R Seager t/a Champagne Flights	Aylesbury	3. 4.08T
					(Parrott and Coles Solicitors titles)		
G-BZIM	Cyclone Airsports Pegasus Quantum 15-912 7678			20. 6.00	A Cuthbertson	Swansea	20. 5.08P
G-BZIO	Piper PA-28-161 Warrior III	2842085	EC-IBJ	29.06.00	S J Skilton t/a Aviation Rentals	White Waltham	11.12.06T
			G-BZIO, N41796, (VH-PWF), N41796				
G-BZIP	Montgomerie-Bensen B 8MR	PFA G/01A-1319		11. 5.00	S J Boxall	Church Farm, Askern	12. 6.07P
	(Built S J Boxall) (Rotax 582)						
G-BZIS	Raj Hamsa X'Air 582(2)	520		12. 6.00	M D Bell	Ince Blundell	29. 1.08P
	(Built J Way and R Bonnett - pr.no.BMAA/HB/142)						
G-BZIT	Beech 95-B55 Baron	TC-564	HB-GBS	12. 6.00	Propellorhead Aviation Ltd	Turweston	17.10.07E
			I-ALGE, HB-GBS, N6845Q		(Noted 1.08)		
G-BZIV	Avtech Jabiru SPL-450	0341		20. 6.00	V R Leggott	Coldharbour Farm, Willingham	7. 9.08P
	(Built V R Leggott - pr.no.PFA 274A-13587)						
G-BZIW	Cyclone Airsports Pegasus Quantum 15-912 7681			17. 7.00	J M Hodgson	Baxby Manor, Husthwaite	7. 9.08P
G-BZIX	Cameron N-90 Balloon (Hot Air)	4867		3. 8.00	M Stefanini and P Marmugi	Florence, Italy	22. 5.07A
G-BZIY	Raj Hamsa X'Air 582(5)	488		19. 6.00	A L A Gill	Kirkbride	28. 2.07P
	(Built I K Hogg - pr.no.BMAA/HB/141)						
G-BZIZ	Ultramagic H-31 Balloon (Hot Air)	31/02		12. 6.00	G D O Bartram	Andorra la Vella, Spain	28. 2.07A
G-BZJA	Cameron Fire 90 SS Balloon (Hot Air)	4757		5. 5.00	Chubb Fire Ltd	Sunbury-on-Thames	31. 8.08A
	(Chubb Fire Extinguisher shape)				(Chubb titles)		
G-BZJB	Aerostar Yakovlev Yak-52	811601	ZU-YAK	18. 9.00	Matristar Ltd	Elstree	4. 4.08P
			ZS-YAK, RA-01356, DOSAAF				
G-BZJC	Thruster T 600N Sprint	0070-T600N-044		21. 6.00	M H Moulai	Sandtoft	12. 6.08P
G-BZJD	Thruster T 600T 450 Jab	0070-T600T-045		21. 6.00	P G Valentine	(Rochechouart, France)	28. 5.05P
G-BZJF	Cyclone Airsports Pegasus Quantum 15-	7696		21. 7.00	R S McMaster	Sackville Lodge, Riseley	20. 7.08P
	(Rotax 582)				(Crashed Knotting, Bedfordshire 26. 8.07 and substantially damaged)		
G-BZJH	Cameron Z-90 Balloon (Hot Air)	4920		10. 7.00	Cameron Balloons Ltd "Greeco"	(Italy)	2.11.04A
G-BZJI	Nova X-Large 37	18946		28. 6.00	M Hay (New owner 1.03)	(Dundee)	
G-BZJJ	Robinson R22 Beta II	3081		12. 6.00	M J Burgess	(Caernarfon)	29. 6.08E
G-BZJL	Mainair Blade 912S	1252-0600-7-W1046		4. 7.00	D N Powell	(Bootle)	20. 2.04P
G-BZJM	Magni M-16 Tandem Trainer	PFA G/12-1301		19. 6.00	J Musil	Mount Airey Farm, South Cave	26. 9.07P
	(Built J Musil)						
G-BZJN	Mainair Blade 912	1254-0600-7-W1048		13. 7.00	L Campbell and M A Haughey	Newtownards	10. 8.08P
G-BZJO	Cyclone Airsports Pegasus Quantum 15	7699		6. 9.00	J D Doran Shinglis, Ballymore County Westmeath		29. 9.05P
	(Rotax 503)						
G-BZJP	Zenair CH.701UL STOL	PFA 187-13579		30. 6.00	J A Ware	Haverfordwest	17.12.07P
	(Built D Jerwood) (Verner SVS1400)						
G-BZJU	Cameron A-200 Balloon (Hot Air)	4810		30. 6.00	Leeds Castle Enterprises Ltd		
					(Leeds Castle titles)	Leeds Castle, Maidstone	23. 5.05T
G-BZJV	CASA 1-131E Jungmann Series 1000	1075	Spanish AF E3B-367	31. 7.00	J A Sykes	Stretton	20.12.07P
G-BZJW	Cessna 150F	15062054	OO-WIH	27. 6.01	P Ligertwood	Ventfield Farm, Oxfordshire	1. 4.08E
			OO-SIH, N8754S				
G-BZJX	Ultramagic N-250 Balloon (Hot Air)	250/12		4. 7.00	Hot Air Balloons Ltd	Henley-on-Thames	8. 6.08T
					(e-homes titles)		
G-BZJZ	Cyclone Airsports Pegasus Quantum 15	7697		2. 8.00	S Baker	Long Marston	28. 8.07P
	(Rotax 503)						
G-BZKC	Raj Hamsa X'Air 582(2)	502		12. 7.00	B J V Gardiner	(Wanborough, Guildford)	31. 7.08P
	(Built P J Cheyney and M C Reed - pr.no.BMAA/HB/144)						
G-BZKD	Stolp SA.300 Starduster Too	1	N70DM	3. 7.00	P and C Edmunds	Enstone	26. 7.07P
	(Built R D Merritt) (Lycoming IO-360)						
G-BZKE	Lindstrand LBL 77B Balloon (Hot Air)	708		17. 7.00	D B Green	Llantysilio, Llangollen	1.11.08A
G-BZKF	Rans S-6-ES Coyote II	0499.1315		17. 7.00	J T Spencer	Eshott	2.11.07P
	(Built A W Hodder - pr.no.PFA 204-13610) (Rotax 582) (Tri-cycle u/c)						
G-BZKG	Extreme/Silex	E761 01A		17. 7.00	R M Hardy	(Radwell, Baldock)	
G-BZKH	Flylight Doodle Bug-Target	DB023		17. 7.00	B Tempest	(Halifax)	
G-BZKI	Flylight Doodle Bug-Target	DB063		17. 7.00	S Bond	(Golcar, Huddersfield)	
G-BZKJ	Flylight Doodle Bug-Target	DB067		17. 7.00	Flylight Airsports Ltd	Sywell	
G-BZKK	Cameron V-56 Balloon (Hot Air)	396		2. 8.78	P J Green and C Bosley tr Gemini Balloon Group		
					"Gemini II"	Oakley, Basingstoke	13. 8.96A
G-BZKL	Piper PA-28R-201 Cherokee Arrow III		D-EFFZ	20. 7.00	S Empson	Wycombe Air Park	17. 8.08E
		28R-7737152	N40000				

Reg	Type	C/n	Prev id	Date	Owner	Location	Date
G-BZKN	Campbell Cricket Mk.4	PFA G/03-1304		20. 7.00	C G Ponsford	Willingale	
	(Built C G Hooghkirk)				(Noted 8.07)		
G-BZKO	Rans S-6-ES Coyote II	0199.1293		20. 7.00	S G Beeson	(Stoke-on-Trent)	3. 1.07P
	(Built J A R Hartley - pr.no.PFA 204-13564) (Rotax 912-UL) (Tri-cycle u/c)						
G-BZKR	Cameron Colt Sugarbox 90 SS Balloon (Hot Air)			4. 8.00	Stratos Ballooning GmbH and Co KG		
		4922				Enningerloh, Germany	6. 6.08A
G-BZKU	Cameron Z-105 Balloon (Hot Air)	4931		21. 7.00	N A Fishlock	Welland, Malvern	4. 5.08P
G-BZKV	Cameron Sky 90-24 Balloon (Hot Air)	4857		5. 9.00	Omega Selection Services Ltd	Stonehouse	9. 6.08A
					(Omega titles)		
G-BZKW	Ultramagic M-77 Balloon (Hot Air)	77/179		25. 7.00	T G Church	Clayton le Dale, Blackburn	6. 2.08T
					(Pendle titles)		
G-BZKX	Cameron V-90 Balloon (Hot Air)	4505		19. 7.00	Cameron Balloons Ltd	Dalien, PRC	26. 7.01A
G-BZLC	PZL-110 Koliber 160A	04980084	SP-WGL	13. 9.00	G F Smith	Cranfield	26. 5.08S
G-BZLE	Rans S-6-ES Coyote II	0499.1311		12. 7.00	J C Rose	Manor Farm, Haddenham	13. 4.08P
	(Built W S Long - pr.no.PFA 204-13608) (Jabiru 2200A) (Tri-cycle u/c)						
G-BZLF	CFM Shadow Series CD	K 236		31. 7.00	D W Stacey	(St Albans)	
	(Built D W Stacey - pr.no.BMAA/HB/053)				(Possibly not built)		
G-BZLG	Robin HR.200-120B	353		7. 7.00	M C Turner	(Campbeltown)	24.11.07E
G-BZLH	Piper PA-28-161 Warrior II	28-8316075	N43069	23. 8.00	S J Skilton t/a Aviation Rentals	Lasham	21. 9.08E
	(Thielert TAE 125)				(Operated British Disabled Flying Association)		
G-BZLI	SOCATA TB-21 Trinidad TC	500	F-GENI	29. 9.00	K B Hallam	Fairoaks	14. 1.08E
G-BZLK	Slingsby Cadet III Motor Glider	683	BGA 2976	2. 8.00	I P Manley	Swanborough Farm, Lewes	15. 8.08P
	(Re-built I P Manley - pr.no.PFA 042-13629 ex Slingsby T 31B WT873) (Volkswagen 1834)						
G-BZLL	Cyclone Airsports Pegasus Quantum 15-912 7693			9. 8.00	J L Merriman tr Caunton Graphites Syndicate		
						Knapthorpe Lodge, Caunton	22.11.08P
G-BZLP	Robinson R44 Raven	0814		17. 7.00	R C Hayward and J H Garrioch t/a Polar Helicopters		
						Manston	11. 9.08P
G-BZLS	Cameron Sky 77-24 Balloon (Hot Air)	4858		17. 8.00	D W Young	Stenhousemuir	15. 3.04A
G-BZLT	Raj Hamsa X'Air 582(1)	486		10. 8.00	G S Millar	Moygashel, County Tyrone	7. 8.08P
	(Built G S Millar - pr.no.BMAA/HB/125)						
G-BZLU	Lindstrand LBL 90A Balloon (Hot Air)	719		9. 8.00	A E Lusty "Tetris 1"	(Morton, Bourne)	2. 3.07A
G-BZLV	Avtech Jabiru UL-450	xxxx		15. 8.00	G Dalton	Bodmin	6. 8.08P
	(Built G Dalton - pr.no.PFA 274A-13537)						
G-BZLX	Cyclone Airsports Pegasus Quantum 15-912 7714			30. 8.00	D McCabe	Eshott	19. 5.08P
G-BZLY	Grob G109B	6242	D-KLMG	24. 8.00	A Baker	(Brough)	1.12.07E
			G-BZLY, OE-9230				
G-BZLZ	Cyclone Airsports Pegasus Quantum 15-912 7721			13. 9.00	A S Martin	Eaglescott	29. 4.08P
G-BZMB	Piper PA-28R-201 Arrow III	28R-7837144	HB-PBY	20. 4.00	S J White tr Thurrock Arrow Group		7. 4.08E
			N3963M			King's Farm, Thurrock	
G-BZMC	Avtech Jabiru UL-450	xxxx		18. 8.00	D G Harkness	Newtownards	29. 8.08P
	(Built J R Banks - pr.no.PFA 274A-13593)						
G-BZMD	Scottish Aviation Bulldog Series 120/121	XX554		18. 8.00	D Ridley tr Mad Dog Flying Group	Shoreham	17. 4.08
		BH120/247			(As "XX554:09" in RAF c/s)		
G-BZME	Scottish Aviation Bulldog Series 120/121	XX698		18. 8.00	S J Whitworth (As "XX698:9" in RAF c/s)	Breighton	2.12.10S
		BH120/347					
G-BZMF	Rutan LongEz	PFA 074-10698		30. 8.00	R A Gardiner	Cumbernauld	13. 6.08P
	(Built A McCaughlin)						
G-BZMG	Robinson R44 Raven	0815		16. 8.00	Total Digital Solutions Ltd	(Bolton)	14. 9.08E
G-BZMH	Scottish Aviation Bulldog Series 120/121	XX692		21. 8.00	M E J Hingley and Co Ltd	Wellesbourne Mountford	29. 1.11S
		BH120/341			(As "XX692:A" in RAF c/s)		
G-BZMI	Cyclone Airsports Pegasus Quantum 15-912 7716			22. 9.00	P L Jarvis	(Ruislip)	17.12.08P
G-BZMJ	Rans S-6-ES Coyote II	0899.1337ES		31. 8.00	E Foster and J H Peet	St Michaels	12. 7.08P
	(Built J Seddon, F J Lloyd and T I Bull - pr.no.PFA 204-13631) (Jabiru 2200A) (Tri-cycle u/c) (New owners 5.07)						
G-BZML	Scottish Aviation Bulldog Series 120/121	XX693		1. 9.00	I D Anderson	Poplar Hall Farm, Elmsett	4. 1.08
		BH120/342			(As "XX693:07" in RAF c/s)		
G-BZMM	Robin DR.400-180R Remorqueur	918	OE-KIR	17. 7.00	N A C Norman	Feshiebridge	21. 9.08E
			D-EAWR				
G-BZMO	Robinson R22 Beta	1219	N24282	31. 7.00	Heli Charter Ltd	Manston	4. 9.08E
			JA7814, N8056H				
G-BZMR	Raj Hamsa X'Air 582(2)	480		11. 9.00	M Grime	Brook Farm, Pilling	4. 6.08P
	(Built M Grime - pr.no.BMAA/HB/149)						
G-BZMS	Mainair Blade	1256-0700-7-W1050		2. 8.00	T R Villa	Priory Farm, Tibenham	3.11.07P
	(Rotax 582)						
G-BZMT	Piper PA-28-161 Warrior III	2842107	N4147D	29.11.00	S J Skilton t/a Aviation Rentals	White Waltham	28.11.07T
			G-BZMT, N9519N, N4147D				
G-BZMV	Cameron Concept 80 Balloon (Hot Air)	4930		26. 9.00	KB Voli S.A.S Di Bartolomeo Chiozzio and Cia		
						Cappela Cantone, Italy	1. 8.08A
G-BZMW	Cyclone Airsports Pegasus Quantum 15-912 7720			26. 9.00	G C Kemp	Stoke, Isle of Grain	31. 5.08P
G-BZMY	SPP Yakovlev Yak C-11	171314	F-AZSF	4.10.00	Classic Displays Ltd	North Weald	15. 8.06P
			Egyptian AF		(As "1" in Soviet AF c/s) (New owner 2.08)		
G-BZMZ	CFM Streak Shadow	K 265-CD		13. 9.00	J F F Fouche	Old Sarum	11.12.08P
	(Built J F F Fouche - original pr.no.BMAA/HB/051 but completed as pr.no,PFA 206-13848) (Rotax 582)						
G-BZNB	Cyclone Airsports Pegasus Quantum 15 7739			10.11.00	T J Drew	Weston Zoyland	22.11.06P
	(Rotax 503)				(Noted 5.07)		
G-BZNC	Cyclone Airsports Pegasus Quantum 15-912 7736			25.10.00	D E Wall	Long Marston	11. 8.08P
G-BZND	Sopwith Pup replica	PFA 101-11815		27. 9.00	M A Goddard	Watchford Farm, Yarcombe	29. 7.08P
	(Built B F Goddard)				(As "N5199" in RNAS c/s)		
G-BZNE	Beech B300 Super King Air	FL-286	N4486V	17.10.00	Skyhopper LLP	Gloucestershire	16.11.07E
	(Aka "King Air 350")						
G-BZNF	Cameron Colt 120A Balloon (Hot Air)	4866		13.11.00	N Charbonnier	Aosta, Italy	17. 1.08A
					(Grand St Bernard - Le Tunnel titles)		
G-BZNG	Raj Hamsa X'Air Jabiru(2)	571		4.10.00	J Walsh	Newtownards	10. 8.06P
	(Built G L Craig - pr.no.BMAA/HB/147)						
G-BZNH	Rans S-6-ES Coyote II	0899.1333		18.10.00	L J Field	(Peacehaven)	21. 8.08P
	(Built V Whiting - pr.no.PFA 204-13660) (Rotax 582) (Tri-cycle u/c)						

Reg	Type	C/n	Prev id	Date	Owner / Operator	Location	CofA
G-BZNI	Bell 206B-2 JetRanger II	2142	G-ODIG	4.10.00	Dorset Country Homes Ltd		
			G-NEEP, N777FW, N3CR			(Thornicombe, Blandford Forum)	9. 1.08E
G-BZNJ	Rans S-6-ES Coyote II	0700.1382		23.10.00	R A McKee	(Newry)	25. 4.08P
	(Built S P Read - pr.no.PFA 204-13640) (Rotax 582)		*(Tailwheel u/c)*				
G-BZNK	Morane Saulnier MS.315E D2	354	F-BCNY	2.11.00	R H Cooper and S Swallow	(Wickenby)	
			French AF		*(Dismantled, in advanced stage of restoration 1.05).*		
G-BZNM	Cyclone Airsports Pegasus Quantum 15	7754		20.11.00	M Tomlinson	(Burton-on-Trent)	21. 4.08P
	(Rotax 582)						
G-BZNN	Beech 76 Duchess	ME-343	N6133P	25.10.00	S J Skilton t/a Aviation Rentals	Bournemouth	14.12.07T
			F-GHSU, N6722L		*(Operated Bournemouth Flying Club)*		
G-BZNO	Ercoupe 415C	2118	N99495	9.11.00	D K Tregilgas	New Farm House, Great Oakley	
G-BZNP	Thruster T 600N 450	0100-T600N-047		27.10.00	J D Gibbons	Derryogue	1. 2.08P
	(Rotax 582)						
G-BZNS	Mainair Blade	1263-1000-7-W1057		23.11.00	A G Laycock	Arclid Green, Sandbach	1. 4.08P
	(Rotax 582)						
G-BZNT	Aero L-29 Delfin	893019	ES-YLG	3.11.00	E Harper	Caernarfon	10.11.04P
			Estonian AF, Soviet AF		*(Noted 8.07)*		
G-BZNU	Cameron A-300 Balloon (Hot Air)	4960		29.11.00	Balloon School (International) Ltd		
	(New envelope reported fitted as c/n 4960 (2))					Colhook Common, Petworth	23. 4.08T
G-BZNV	Lindstrand LBL 31A Balloon (Hot Air)	741		12.12.00	G R Down	Gillingham	9. 6.08A
G-BZNW	Isaacs Fury II	PFA 011-13402		10.11.00	J E D Rogerson	Morgansfield, Fishburn	19. 6.08P
	(Built J E D Rogerson)				*(As "K2048" in RAF c/s)*		
G-BZNX	SOCATA MS.880B Rallye Club	2113	F-BTVX	17.11.00	P C Avery	Lower Mountpleasant Farm, Chatteris	30. 1.08E
G-BZNY	Europa Aviation Europa XS	401		14.11.00	W J Harrison	Cambridge	1. 1.08P
	(Built A K Middlemas - pr.no.PFA 247-13355) (Tri-gear u/c)						
G-BZNZ	Lindstrand LBL Cake SS Balloon (Hot Air)	747		21.12.00	Oxford Promotions (UK) Ltd	(Kentucky, US)	3. 4.03A
					(Operated F Prell)		
G-BZOB	Slepcev Storch	PFA 316-13592		21.11.00	B J Chester-Master	Shobdon	18. 8.07P
	(Built J E Ashby)				*(As "6G+ED" in Luftwaffe c/s)*		
G-BZOD	Cyclone Airsports Pegasus Quantum 15-912	7763		18.12.00	S M Wilson	Perth	2. 9.08P
G-BZOE	Cyclone Airsports Pegasus Quantum 15	7723		14. 9.00	B N Thresher	Dunkeswell	27. 4.08P
	(Rotax 582)						
G-BZOF	Montgomerie-Bensen B 8MR	MGM3 & SJML1		7.11.00	S J M Ledingham	Carlisle	24. 8.08P
	(Built M G Mee and S J M Ledingham) (Rotax 912-UL)						
G-BZOG	Dornier 328-100	3088	D-CDXN (5)	19.12.00	Suckling Airways (Cambridge) Ltd t/a Scot Airways		
			F-GNPR			London City	18.11.07E
G-BZOI	Nicollier HN.700 Ménestrel II	122		27.10.00	S J McCollum	Newtownards	22. 5.08P
	(Built S J McCollum - pr.no.PFA 217-12604) (Volkswagen 2180)						
G-BZOL	Robin R3000/140	124	F-GEKZ	20.12.00	S D Baker	Exeter	31. 8.07T
G-BZOM	RotorWay Executive 162F	6243	N767SG	27. 3.01	R L Cole	(Haverfordwest)	6. 6.08P
	(Built G and S Waugh)						
G-BZON	Scottish Aviation Bulldog Series 120/121		XX528	19.12.00	D J Critchley	Earls Colne	18. 4.10S
		BH120/214			*(As "XX528:D" in RAF c/s)*		
G-BZOO	Cyclone Airsports Pegasus Quantum 15-912	7702		15. 8.00	T A Dobbins	Otherton, Cannock	3. 9.08P
G-BZOP	Robinson R44	0958		11. 1.01	J D Caudwell	(Eccleshall, Stafford)	1. 2.08E
G-BZOR	TEAM Mini-MAX 91	PFA 186-13312		9. 8.00	A Watt	Insch	13. 5.07P
	(Built A Watt)						
G-BZOU	Cyclone Airsports Pegasus Quantum 15-912	7768		22. 3.01	M J Canty	(Raheen, Limerick, County Limerick	12. 4.08P
G-BZOV	Cyclone Airsports Pegasus Quantum 15-912	7769		22. 3.01	D Turner	(Bicester)	29. 5.03P
G-BZOW	Whittaker MW7	PFA 171-13118		15.12.00	G W Peacock	(Kirk Sandall, Doncaster)	
	(Built G W Peacock)						
G-BZOX	Cameron Colt 90B Balloon (Hot Air)	10000		8. 2.01	D J Head	Newbury	21. 3.07A
G-BZOY	Beech 76 Duchess	ME-144	EC-ICJ	3.1.01	S J Skilton t/a Aviation Rentals	Bournemouth	9. 6.08T
			G-BZOY, F-GFFH, 5T-AOH, F-ODJQ, F-GBLO	*(Operated CTC Aviation)*			
G-BZOZ	Van's RV-6	PFA 181A-12455		14. 9.00	M and S Sheppard	Cambridge	17. 1.08P
	(Built V Edmundson)						
G-BZPA	Mainair Blade 912S	1264-1100-7-W1058		13.12.00	J McGoldrick		
						Slieve Croob, Slievenamoney, Castlewellen	3. 5.08P
G-BZPB	Hawker Hunter GA.11	41H-670758	WV256	15. 1.01	B R Pearson	Kemble	17. 7.03P
					(Noted as "WB188" Hunter prototype in duck-egg green c/s 5.07)		
G-BZPC	Hawker Hunter GA.11	HABL-003061	XF300	15. 1.01	B R Pearson	Kemble	
					(Noted as "WB188" Hunter prototype in all-red c/s 5.07)		
G-BZPD	Cameron V-65 Balloon (Hot Air)	4700		10.11.00	P Spellward "Buzbee"	Heidelburg, Germany	28. 5.08A
G-BZPE	Lindstrand LBL 310A Balloon (Hot Air)	746		16. 2.01	Aerosaurus Balloons Ltd	Whimple, Exeter	12. 3.08T
G-BZPF	Scheibe SF24B Motorspatz I	4028	D-KROA	19. 1.01	J S Gorrett	(Skenfrith, Abergavenny)	24. 8.08E
			PH-971, OE-9005, (D-KECO)				
G-BZPG	Beech C24R Sierra	MC-556	N23840	27. 3.01	Plane Talking Ltd	Elstree	18. 6.08T
G-BZPH	Van's RV-4	PFA 181-12867		6. 9.00	A G Truman tr G-BZPH RV-4 Group	Lasham	7. 2.08P
	(Built A G Truman) (Lycoming O-360)						
G-BZPI	SOCATA TB-20 Trinidad	1814	SX-ATT	20.12.00	K M Brennan	Leicester	24. 5.08E
G-BZPJ	Beech 76 Duchess	ME-227	N6630Z	2. 3.01	S J Skilton t/a Aviation Rentals	Bournemouth	23. 3.08T
					(Operated Bournemouth Flying Club)		
G-BZPK	Cameron C-80 Balloon (Hot Air)	4183		23. 2.01	Horizon Ballooning Ltd	Alton	6.12.07T
G-BZPL	Robinson R44 Clipper	0948		10. 1.01	M K Shaw	San Bonet, Majorca, Spain	17. 2.07T
G-BZPM	Cessna 172S Skyhawk SP	172S8561	N72760	11. 1.01	Pooler-LMT Ltd	Lower Grounds Farm, Sherlowe	28. 3.08E
G-BZPN	Mainair Blade 912S	1268-0101-7-W1062		25. 1.01	G R Barker *(New owner 6.07)*	(Epping)	14. 9.08P
G-BZPP	Westland Wasp HAS.1	F9675	XT793	15. 1.01	C J Marsden	RNAS Yeovilton	21. 8.08P
					(As "XT793:456" in RN c/s)		
G-BZPR	Ultramagic N-210 Balloon (Hot Air)	210/14		16. 1.01	European Balloon Display Company Ltd		
					(MIX 96 titles)	Great Missenden	24. 5.07T
G-BZPS	Scottish Aviation Bulldog Series 120/121		XX658	8. 1.01	D M Squires	(Wellesbourne Mountford)	
		BH120/316			*(As "XX658:03" in RAF c/s 1.03)*		
G-BZPT	Ultramagic N-210 Balloon (Hot Air)	210/15		16. 1.01	European Balloon Display Company Ltd		
					(Bucks Free Press titles)	Great Missenden	19. 4.08T

Reg	Type	C/n	Prev id	Date	Owner/Operator	Location	Date2
G-BZPV	Lindstrand LBL 90B Balloon (Hot Air)	727		17. 1.01	D P Hopkins	Pidley, Huntingdon	22. 8.08A
					(Lakeside Lodge Golf Centre titles)		
G-BZPW	Cameron V-77 Balloon (Hot Air)	6245	N4463V	2. 2.01	J Vonka	New Malden	12. 8.08A
G-BZPX	Ultramagic S-105 Balloon (Hot Air)	105/78		12. 2.01	G M Houston t/a Scotair Balloons	Lesmahagow	11. 4.08T
G-BZPY	Ultramagic H-31 Balloon (Hot Air)	31/03		12. 2.01	G M Houston t/a Scotair Balloons	Lesmahagow	11. 4.08A
G-BZPZ	Mainair Blade	1265-1200-7-W1059		23. 1.01	K Lynn	Sywell	14. 6.08P
	(Rotax 582)						
G-BZRA	Rans S-6-ES Coyote II	0600-1376		16. 1.01	K J Warburton	Derby	9. 3.08P
	(Built A W Fish - pr.no.PFA 204-13683) (Rotax 912-UL)						
G-BZRB	Mainair Blade	1270-0201-7-W1064		7. 3.01	J-B Weber	Mill Farm, Shifnal	3.11.08P
	(Rotax 582)						
G-BZRG	Hunt Avon 582(3)/Hunt Wing	0009090		16. 1.01	W G Reynolds	(Overstrand, Cromer)	12. 6.08P
	(Built W G Reynolds - pr.no.BMAA/HB/154)						
G-BZRJ	Cyclone Airsports Pegasus Quantum 15-912	7783		5. 2.01	P J Fletcher tr G-BZRJ Group	Longacre Farm, Sandy	14. 4.08P
G-BZRO	Piper PA-30 Twin Comanche C	30-1923	SE-IYL	2. 3.01	Comanche Hire Ltd	Gloucestershire	51. 9.08E
			D-GATI, I-KATI, N8767Y				
G-BZRP	Cyclone Airsports Pegasus Quantum 15-912	7758		24. 1.01	S Hutchinson	(Hollybush, Ayr)	27. 2.08P
G-BZRR	Cyclone Airsports Pegasus Quantum 15-912	7727		4.10.00	S E Garner	(Stone)	29.10.08P
G-BZRS	Eurocopter EC.135 T2	0166		22. 3.01	Bond Air Services Ltd	Aberdeen	8. 4.08E
G-BZRT	Beech 76 Duchess	ME-89	EC-HYO	21. 3.01	S J Skilton t/a Aviation Rentals	Bournemouth	11.11.07E
			G-BZRT, F-GHBL, N2074G				
G-BZRU	Cameron V-90 Balloon (Hot Air)	10053		1. 5.01	R Trombetti tr Aerostatica Monte	Villanteto, Italy	22. 9.08A
G-BZRV	Van's RV-6	PFA 181A-13573		12.10.00	N M Hitchman	Leicester	11. 8.08P
	(Built E Hicks, P Hicks and N M Hitchman) (Lycoming O-320)						
G-BZRW	Mainair Blade 912S	1266-0101-7-W1060		6. 2.01	S E Kearney	Newtownards	1. 2.08P
G-BZRX	Ultramagic M-105 Balloon (Hot Air)	105/80		3. 5.01	P A Foot and I R Warrington	Stamford	2. 3.07A
G-BZRY	Rans S-6-ES Coyote II	0600-1375		1. 2.01	A G Smith	Longacre Farm, Sandy	5.10.08P
	(Built S Forman - pr.no.PFA 204-13666) (Rotax 582)						
G-BZRZ	Thunder Ax11-250 Series 2 Balloon (Hot Air)	10013		11.10.01	A C K Rawson and J J Rudoni	Stafford	3.10.08T
G-BZSA	Cyclone Airsports Pegasus Quantum 15	7784		25. 1.01	M Skrinar	(Feltham)	21. 7.08P
	(Rotax 503)						
G-BZSB	Pitts S-1S	PFA 009-13697		2. 2.01	A D Ingold	(Harlow)	
	(Built A D Ingold)				(On build 2004)		
G-BZSC	Sopwith Camel F 1 replica	NAW-3		15. 1.01	Richard Shuttleworth Trustees	Old Warden	
	(Built Northern Aeroplane Workshops)				(Under consruction 3.02)		
G-BZSE	Hawker Hunter T 8C	41H-670788	9096M	6. 2.01	Towerdrive 2000 Ltd	Exeter	19.11.08P
	(Officially.regd as T 8B (c/n 41H-670792) see G-FFOX)		WV322		(As "WV322:Y" in RAF c/s)		
G-BZSG	Cyclone Airsports Pegasus Quantum 15-912	7766		22. 2.01	S Andrews (Noted 1.07)	Newtownards	18. 4.08P
G-BZSH	Ultramagic H-77 Balloon (Hot Air)	77/191		12. 4.01	P M G Vale	Hurcote, Kidderminster	10. 8.08A
G-BZSI	Cyclone Airsports Pegasus Quantum 15	7787		12. 3.01	M O O'Brien	Rufforth	4. 5.08P
	(Rotax 582)						
G-BZSL	Sky 25-16 Balloon (Hot Air)	138		31. 1.01	A E Austin	Naseby	29.10.07A
G-BZSM	Cyclone Airsports Pegasus Quantum 15	7788		23. 2.01	J Walker and A J Johnson	Deenethorpe	11.10.08P
	(Rotax 503)						
G-BZSO	Ultramagic M-77C Balloon (Hot Air)	77/190		22. 3.02	C C Duppa-Miller	Warwick	18. 7.08A
G-BZSP	Stemme S 10-V	10-14	HB-2217	10. 5.01	A Flewelling and L Bleaken	Aston Down	8. 8.07
			D-KDNE		"626"		
	(Officially regd as S-10 but converted to S-10-V when HB-2217: in theory c/n should now be 14-014M)						
G-BZSS	Cyclone Airsports Pegasus Quantum 15-912	7770		6. 2.01	T R Marsh		
					Brown Shutters Farm, Norton St Philips, Somerset		9. 6.08P
G-BZST	Avtech Jabiru UL-450	0400		13. 2.01	G Hammond	Headcorn	4. 9.08P
	(Built G Hammond - pr.no.PFA 274A-13616)						
G-BZSU	Cameron A-315 Balloon (Hot Air)	10009		13. 6.01	Ballooning Network Ltd	Bristol	20. 8.07T
					(Bath Building Society titles)		
G-BZSV	Aherne Barracuda (Built M J Aherne)	631		20. 2.01	M J Aherne	(St Albans)	
G-BZSX	Cyclone Airsports Pegasus Quantum 15-912	7789		23. 2.01	G L Hall		9. 6.08P
G-BZSY	SAN Stampe SV-4A	677	N12426	12. 3.01	G P J M Valvekens	Diest, Belgium	
			F-BGGT, French AF, (F-BDNV)			(Stored 2006)	
G-BZSZ	Avtech Jabiru UL-450	0220		16. 2.01	M P Gurr and D R Burridge	Clipgate Farm, Denton	22. 8.07P
	(Built R Riley and F Overall - pr.no.PFA 274A-13432)						
G-BZTA	Robinson R44 Raven	0968		20. 2.01	Jarretts Motors Ltd	Redhill	27. 3 08E
G-BZTC	TEAM Mini-MAX 91	PFA 186-13336		23. 1.01	G G Clayton	Woodlands Barton Farm, Roche	24. 1.07P
	(Built G G Clayton)						
G-BZTD	Thruster T 600T 450 Jab	0021-T600T-049		22. 2.01	B O and B C McCartan	Newry Road, Banbridge	18. 7.08P
G-BZTF	IAV-Bacau Yakovlev Yak-52	866703	LY-AKE	28. 2.01	A C Pledger tr KY Flying Group	Duxford	15.10.08P
			DOSAAF				
G-BZTG	Piper PA-34-220T Seneca V	3449126	EC-HGK	4. 4.01	Mainstreet Aviation Ltd	Newcastle	1. 6.08E
			N4141N				
G-BZTH	Europa Aviation Europa	010		21.12.00	T J Houlihan	Croft Farm, Defford	14. 2.08P
	(Built T J Houlihan - pr.no.PFA 247-12494) (Monowheel u/c)						
G-BZTI	Europa Aviation Europa XS	124		30. 3.01	W Hoolachan	Perranporth	21. 5.08P
	(Built W Hoolachan - pr.no.PFA 247-13172) (Rotax 914-UL) (Tri-gear u/c)						
G-BZTJ	Bücker Bü.133C Jungmeister	41	Spanish AF ES1-41	7. 3.01	R A Seeley	Turweston	4.12.07P
	(Officially recorded as built CASA but c/n dubious and believed to be built Bücker)				(As "17+TF" in Luftwaffe c/s) (Noted 1.08)		
G-BZTK	Cameron V-90 Balloon (Hot Air)	10083		6. 3.01	E Appollodorus	London W12	25. 5.08A
G-BZTL	Cameron Colt Flying Ice Cream Cone SS Balloon (Hot Air)	10008		16. 5.01	Stratos Ballooning GmbH and Co KG	Ennigerloh, Germany	5. 6.08A
G-BZTM	Mainair Blade	1273-0201-7-W1068		16. 3.01	B A Richards	Watnall	16. 8.08P
G-BZTN	Europa Aviation Europa XS	504		16. 3.01	M K McGreavey and S A Smith	Perth	6. 8.08P
	(Built W Pringle and J Dewberry - pr.no.PFA 247-13715) (Tri-gear u/c)						
G-BZTR	Mainair Blade	1276-0301-7-W1071		8. 3.01	A Raithby and N McCusker	Rufforth	9. 4.08P
G-BZTS	Cameron Bertie Bassett 90 SS Balloon (Hot Air)	10050		3. 5.01	Trebor Bassett Ltd	Shoreham	16. 7.08A

G-BZTT	Cameron A-275 Balloon (Hot Air)	4953		28. 8.01	Cameron Flights Southern Ltd		
						Woodborough, Pewsey	22. 2.08T
G-BZTV	Mainair Blade 912S	1278-0301-7-W1073		2. 4.01	R D McManus	(Bignall End, Stoke-on-Trent)	30. 5.08P
G-BZTW	Hunt Avon 582(1)/Huntwing	9906092		17. 1.01	T S Walker	(Sandbach)	12. 5.08P
	(Built T S Walker- pr.no.BMAA/HB/136)						
G-BZTX	Mainair Blade 912	1267-0101-7-W1061		9. 2.01	K A Ingham *(Noted 8.05)*	Shipdham	20. 7.05P
G-BZTY	Avtech Jabiru UL-450	0288		1. 3.01	R P Lewis	White House Farm, Southery	2. 8.08P
	(Built R P Lewis - pr.no.PFA 274A-13533)						
G-BZUB	Mainair Blade	1274-0201-7-W1069		27. 3.01	J Campbell and T Scott		
						(Immingham and Hemswell, Gainsborough)	15. 5.08P
G-BZUC	Cyclone Airsports Pegasus Quantum 15-912	7796		10. 4.01	G A Breen	Portimão, Faro, Portugal	10. 4 08P
G-BZUD	Lindstrand LBL 105A Balloon (Hot Air)	780		27. 3.01	A Nimmo *(HSBC titiles)*	Dubai, UAE	13. 9.08A
G-BZUE	Cyclone Airsports Pegasus Quantum 15	7800		23. 4.01	M P and R A Wells	Croft Farm, Defford	28. 5.08P
	(Rotax 503)						
G-BZUF	Mainair Rapier	1277-0301-7-W1072		27. 3.01	C A Denver	St Michaels	24. 3.08P
G-BZUG	TLAC RL7A XP Sherwood Ranger	xxxx		23. 3.01	J G Boxall	Pittrichie Farm, Whiterashes	23. 9.08P
	(Built S P Sharp- pr.no.PFA 237-13040) (Rotax 618)				*(In pseudo RAF c/s as false serial "SR-XP020")*		
G-BZUH	Rans S-6-ES Coyote II	0600.1371		26. 3.01	J D Sinclair-Day	Eshott	13. 7.07P
	(Built G M Prowling - pr.no.PFA 204-13716) (Tri-cycle u/c) (Jabiru 2200A)				*(Noted 9.07)*		
G-BZUI	Cyclone Airsports Pegasus Quantum 15-912	7798		8. 5.01	A P Slade	Field Farm, Oakley	18. 1.07P
G-BZUK	Lindstrand LBL 31A Balloon (Hot Air)	776		7. 3.01	G R J Luckett	Fort Collins, Colorado, US	4.10.08A
G-BZUL	Avtech Jabiru UL-450	xxxx		28. 3.01	A M Hemmings	North Moor, Scunthorpe	22. 8.08P
	(Built P Hawkins - pr.no.PFA 274A-13678)						
G-BZUN	Mainair Blade 912	1279-0301-7-W1074		18. 4.01	A D Jones *(New owner 11.05)*	Ince Blundell	2. 6.05P
G-BZUO	Cameron A-340HL Balloon (Hot Air)	4952		18. 5.01	Anglian Countryside Balloons Ltd	Burnham-on-Crouch	11. 3.08T
G-BZUP	Raj Hamsa X'Air 582(5)	624		24. 4.01	I A J Lappin	Newtownards	21. 8.08P
	(Built I A J Lappin - pr.no.BMAA/HB/164)						
G-BZUU	Cameron O-90 Balloon (Hot Air)	10058		14. 6.01	D C Ball and C F Pooley		
					"Elmo II"	London SE1 and Barnwood, Gloucester	8. 8.08A
G-BZUV	Cameron H-24 Balloon (Hot Air)	2665	LX-JLW	27. 4.01	J N Race *"The Gerkin"*	Lewes	9. 5.05A
G-BZUX	Cyclone Airsports Pegasus Quantum 15-	7819		22. 5.01	K M MacRae, J D and C A Capewell	East Fortune	23. 6.08P
	(Rotax 582)						
G-BZUY	Van's RV-6	PFA 181A-13471		23. 5.01	D A Healey	Bodmin	6. 7.07P
	(Built D M Gale and K F Crumplin) (Lycoming O-320)				*(Noted 10..07)*		
G-BZUZ	Hunt Avon-Blade R100(1)	BMAA/HB/162		9. 2.01	C Hershaw	Doynton	15. 3.07P
	(Built J A Hunt) (Uses Mainair Sailwing c/n W1067)						
G-BZVA	Zenair CH.701UL STOL	PFA 187-13635		21. 3.01	M W Taylor	Insch	18. 4.08P
	(Built M W Taylor)						
G-BZVB	Reims FR172H Rocket	FR17200327	G-BLMX	29. 8.00	K G Worcester	Wing Farm, Longbridge Deverill	18. 1.08E
			PH-RPC				
G-BZVC	Mickleburgh L107 Sparrow	PFA 256-12549		21. 3.01	D R Mickleburgh	(Sutton St James, Spalding)	27. 2.08P
	(Built D R Mickleburgh)						
G-BZVD	Cameron Colt Forklift 105 SS Balloon (Hot Air)			15. 6.01	Stratos Ballooning GmbH and Co KG		
		10084			*"JungHeinrich"*	Ennigerloh, Germany	19. 4.07A
G-BZVE	Cameron N-133 Balloon (Hot Air)	10092		20. 6.01	I M Ashpole	Bridstow, Ross-on-Wye	10. 6.08A
					"American Chopper"		
G-BZVH	Raj Hamsa X'Air 582(1)	561		20. 4.01	M Smullen	(Lullymore, Rathangan, County KIldare)	13.10.07P
	(Built B and D Bergin - pr.no.BMAA/HB/160)						
G-BZVI	Nova Vertex 24	13379		24. 5.01	M Hay *(New owner 1.03)*	(Dundee)	
G-BZVJ	Cyclone Airsports Pegasus Quantum 15	7821		12. 6.01	O P Gall	(Lerwick, Shetland)	1. 7.08P
	(Rotax 582)						
G-BZVK	Raj Hamsa X'Air 582(11)	592		22. 2.01	A P and J M Cadd	Field Farm, Oakley	7. 1.08P
	(Built K P Taylor - pr.no.BMAA/HB/152)						
G-BZVM	Rans S-6-ES Coyote II	1000.1394ES		1. 3.01	N N Ducker	Tatenhill	20. 7.08P
	(Built N N Ducker - pr.no.PFA 204-13705) (Rotax 912-UL)						
G-BZVN	Van's RV-6	PFA 181-13188		25. 4.01	J A Booth	(Sheffield City)	27. 6.05P
	(Built J A Booth) (Lycoming O-360)						
G-BZVO	Cessna TR182 Turbo Skylane RG II		D-EPOL	3. 4.01	Swiftair Ltd	Elstree	21.10.07E
		R18200990	N739CX				
G-BZVR	Raj Hamsa X'Air 582(8)	566		13. 3.01	P Travis tr Hummingbird Club	Davidstow Moor	2. 3.08P
	(Built R P Sims, E Bowen and P Travis - pr.no.BMAA/HB/146)						
G-BZVT	III Sky Arrow 650 T	PFA 298-13333		23. 3.01	D J Goldsmith	Headcorn	22. 8.08P
	(Built R N W Wright)						
G-BZVU	Cameron Z-105 Balloon (Hot Air)	10078		9. 8.01	The Mall Balloon Team Ltd	Bristol	2. 4.07A
					(The Mall and Cribbs Causeway titles)		
G-BZVV	Cyclone Airsports Pegasus Quantum 15-912	7793		12. 3.01	C Cox	Jackrell's Farm, Southwater	2. 6.08P
G-BZVW	Ilyushin Il-2 Stormovik	1870710	Soviet AF 1870710	16. 5.01	S Swallow and R H Cooper	Wickenby	
					(Noted 10.06)		
G-BZVX	Ilyushin Il-2 Stormovik	1878576	Soviet AF 1878576	16. 5.01	S Swallow and R H Cooper	Wickenby	
					(Noted 10.06)		
G-BZWB	Mainair Blade 912	1284-0507-7-W1079		26. 4.01	L Parker	Newtownards	24. 8.08P
G-BZWC	Raj Hamsa X'Air Falcon 912(1)	587		9. 5.01	C McAfee	Nether Glastry, Dunblane	21. 8.06P
	(Built G A J Salter - pr.no.BMAA/HB/157)						
G-BZWG	Piper PA-28-140 Cherokee Cruiser 28-7625188		N9656K	17. 5.01	H and E Merkado	Panshanger	12. 7.08E
G-BZWH	Cessna 152	15281339	N49819	17. 5.01	J and H Aviation Services Ltd	North Weald	5. 7.08E
G-BZWI	Medway EclipseR	170/148		3. 5.01	R A Keene	Over Farm, Gloucester	28. 3.05P
G-BZWJ	CFM Streak Shadow SA	K 338		8. 5.01	T A Morgan	Popham	17. 8.08P
	(Built T A Morgan - pr.no.PFA 206-13553) (Rotax 582)				*"Harmony Angel"*		
G-BZWK	Avtech Jabiru SK	xxxx		8. 5.01	G M R Abrey	East Winch	16. 8.08P
	(Built R Thompson - pr.no.PFA 274-13292)						
G-BZWM	Cyclone Airsports Pegasus XL-Q	7792		18. 5.01	D T Evans	Broadmeadow Farm, Hereford	24. 6.04P
	(Built using Trike SW-TE-0136 from G-MVKM)				*(Noted 11.07)*		
G-BZWN	Van's RV-8	PFA 303-13692		14. 5.01	A J Symms and R D Harper	High Ham, Langport	17. 4.08P
	(Built A J Symms and R D Harper) (Lycoming IO-360)						

G-BZWS	Cyclone Airsports Pegasus Quantum 15-912	7813		26. 4.01	G B Smith tr G-BZWS Syndicate		
						Knapthorpe Lodge, Caunton	9. 5.08P
G-BZWT	Tecnam P92-EA Echo	PFA 318-13681		17. 5.01	R F Cooper	Field Farm, Oakley	7. 2.08P
	(Built R F Cooper) (Marked as "P92S")						
G-BZWU	Cyclone Airsports Pegasus Quantum 15-912	7831		19. 7.01	J Needham	Roddige	23. 6.08P
G-BZWV	Steen Skybolt	PFA 064-10751		30. 5.01	P D and K Begley	Sywell	6. 4.08P
	(Built P D Begley)						
G-BZWX	Whittaker MW5-D Sorcerer	PFA 163-13599		1. 6.01	B J Syson	Landmead Farm, Garford	24. 7.08P
	(Built P G Depper)						
G-BZWY	CFM Streak Shadow SA	xxxx		31. 5.01	B Cartwright	The Polo Field, Lurgan	17.10.05P
	(Built B Cartwright - pr.no.PFA 206-13601)						
G-BZWZ	Van's RV-6	PFA 181A-13419		26. 4.01	J Shanley	Croft Farm, Croft-on-Tees	9. 4.08P
	(Built J Shanley) (Lycoming O-320)						
G-BZXA	Raj Hamsa X'Air V2(2)	560		31. 5.01	D W Mullin	Ash Farm, Winsford	3. 9.08P
	(Built D W Mullin - pr.no.BMAA/HB/148)						
G-BZXB	Van's RV-6	PFA 181A-13625		4. 6.01	B J King-Smith and D J Akerman	Goodwood	6. 3.08P
	(Built B J King-Smith and D J Akerman) (Lycoming O-360)						
G-BZXC	Scottish Aviation Bulldog Series 120/121	XX612		8. 6.01	A R Oliver	Duxford	15. 1.09S
		BH120/260			(As "XX612:A03" in RAF c/s)		
G-BZXD	RotorWay Executive 162F	6494		5. 6.01	P G King	Street Farm, Takeley	27. 4.06P
	(Built P G King) (RotorWay RI 162F)				(Noted 2.08)		
G-BZXE	de Havilland DHC-1 Chipmunk 22	C1/0722	WP839	5. 6.01	K Moore	(Thornton-Cleveleys)	
G-BZXF	Cameron A-210 Balloon (Hot Air)	4999		5. 2.02	Off The Ground Balloon Co mpanyLtd	Lyth, Kendal	6. 2.08T
G-BZXG	Dyn'Aéro MCR-01 ULC	156		26.10.01	J L Ker	Longframlington	19. 2.08P
	(Built J M Scott and G J Sargent - pr.no.PFA 301B-13815)						
G-BZXI	Nova Philou 26	11207		16. 5.01	M Hay (New owner 1.03)	(Dundee)	
G-BZXJ	Schweizer 269C-1	0128		20. 6.01	Helicentre Liverpool Ltd	Liverpool	15. 8.08E
	(Schweizer 300)						
G-BZXK	Robin HR.200-120B	286	F-GNNV	12. 6.01	Helicopter One Ltd	Bournemouth	15. 7.07T
G-BZXL	Whittaker MW5-D Sorcerer	PFA 163-13738		7. 6.01	R Hatton	Kirkbride	2. 7.04P
	(Built K Wright and C Gale) (Rotax 503)						
G-BZXM	Mainair Blade 912	1283-0501-7-W1078		20. 4.01	M E Fowler	Steeple Claydon, Buckingham	1. 8 08P
G-BZXN	Avtech Jabiru UL-450	xxxx		7. 6.01	D A Hall and V G J Davies	Lee-on-Solent	9. 4.08P
	(Built A R Silvester - pr.no.PFA 274A-13747)						
G-BZXO	Cameron Z-105 Balloon (Hot Air)	10125		27. 6.01	D K Jones and K D Thomas	(Alton and Epsom)	13.10.08A
G-BZXP	Air Création 582(1)/Kiss 400	FL001		14. 6.01	A Fairbrother	Sywell	20. 4.08P
	(Built P M Dewhurst - pr.no.BMAA/HB/169 for Flylight kit comprising Trike s/n T00100 and Wing s/n A00056-0054)						
G-BZXR	Cameron N-90 Balloon (Hot Air)	10124		3. 9.01	H J Andrews	Selborne, Alton	6. 7.07A
G-BZXS	Scottish Aviation Bulldog Series 120/121	XX631		21. 6.01	K J Thompson	Strandhill, Sligo, County Sligo	7. 5.10S
		BH120/296			(As "XX631:W" in RAF c/s: noted 9.06)		
G-BZXT	Mainair Blade 912	1286-0501-7-W1081		25. 5.01	S R Vinsun tr Barton 912 Flyers	Barton	4. 5.08P
G-BZXV	Cyclone Airsports Pegasus Quantum 15-912	7828		28. 6.01	P I Oliver	Rufforth	9. 6.08P
G-BZXW	Magni M-16 Tandem Trainer	PFA G/12-1249	G-NANA	30. 4.01	S J Tyler	(Cumwhinton, Carlisle)	31. 8.00P
	(Built J W P Lewis) (Rotax 912S)						
G-BZXX	Cyclone Airsports Pegasus Quantum 15-912	7812		20. 4.01	C S Povey tr G-BZXX Group	Tarn Farm, Cockerham	24. 4 08P
G-BZXY	Robinson R44 Raven	1027		12. 6.01	Helicopter Services Ltd	Wycombe Air Park	8. 7.07T
G-BZXZ	Scottish Aviation Bulldog Series 120/121	XX629		1. 6.01	J A D Richardson	Wellesbourne Mountford	5.12.10S
		BH120/294			(As "XX629:V" in RAF c/s)		
G-BZYA	Rans S-6-ES Coyote II	0499.1313		12. 6.01	M R Osbourn	Long Marston	10.10.07P
	(Built D J Clack - pr.no.PFA 204-13529) (Rotax 582) (Tri-cycle u/c)						
G-BZYD	Westland SA.341G Gazelle AH.1	1648	XZ329	14. 6.01	Aerocars Ltd	Filton	15. 6.08P
	(C/n 1652 quoted also)				(As "XZ329" in AAC c/s)		
G-BZYE	Robinson R22 Beta II	3231		15. 6.01	Plane Talking Ltd	Redhill	11. 7.08E
G-BZYG	DG Flugzeugbau DG-500MB	(5E220B15)		25. 9.01	R C Bromwich "94"	Aboyne	28.11.07E
G-BZYI	Nova Phocus 123	9748		8. 6.01	M Hay (New owner 1.03)	(Dundee)	
G-BZYK	Avtech Jabiru UL-450	0140		21. 6.01	P A James tr Cloudbase Aviation G-BZYK	Redhill	12.11.08P
	(Built A S Forbes - pr.no.PFA 274A-13227)						
G-BZYL	Rans S-6-ES Coyote II	1000.1395ES		22. 6.01	C B Heslop	Lower Wasing Farm, Brimpton	29. 5.07P
	(Build J D Harris - pr.no.PFA 204-13718) (Jabiru 2200A) (Tri-cycle u/c)						
G-BZYM	Raj Hamsa X'Air 133(1)	649		21. 6.01	D R Sutton	Brook Farm, Pilling	14. 7.08P
	(Built G Fleck - pr.no.BMAA/HB/172) (Verner VM133)						
G-BZYN	Cyclone Airsports Pegasus Quantum 15-912	7835		15. 8.01	J Cannon	Graveley Hall Farm, Graveley	26.10.08P
G-BZYO	Colt 210A Balloon (Hot Air)	3523	D-OSPM	19. 7.01	P M Forster (Operated Alba Ballooning)	Edinburgh	17. 3.04T
	(Understood stripped for spares with envelope to Art College for non aviation use 2006)						
G-BZYR	Cameron N-31 Balloon (Hot Air)	10137		6. 8.01	C J Sanger-Davies	Hawarden	15. 4.08A
G-BZYS	Micro Aviation B 22S Bantam	94-001	ZK-JDO	12. 7.01	D L Howell (Noted 10.05)	Stoke, Isle of Grain	12. 9.02P
G-BZYT	Interavia 80TA Balloon (Hot Air)	04309-92		6. 7.01	J King (New owner 10.03)	Leighton Buzzard	
G-BZYU	Whittaker MW6 Merlin	PFA 164-13647		2. 7.01	K J Cole	Over Farm, Gloucester	8. 7.04P
	(Built K J Cole) (Rotax 582)						
G-BZYV	Noble Hardman Snowbird Mk.V 582(1)			5. 7.01	S Jones	(Llangeitho, Tregaron)	
	(Built S Jones)	BMAA/HB/175					
G-BZYW	Cameron N-90 Balloon (Hot Air)	10134		6. 8.01	C and J M Bailey t/a Bailey Balloons	Pill, Bristol	29. 5.07T
					(Bass titles)		
G-BZYX	Raj Hamsa X'Air 700(1A)	653		15. 6.01	A M Sutton	Otherton, Cannock	25. 8.08P
	(Built A G Marsh - pr.no.BMAA/HB/173)						
G-BZYY	Cameron N-90 Balloon (Hot Air)	10130		30. 8.01	Mason Zimbler Ltd (Oracle titles)	Bristol	7. 7.08A
G-BZZD	Reims Cessna F172M Skyhawk II	F172O1436	G-BDPF	14. 4.98	R H M Richardson-Bunbury	Bodmin	3. 8.08E

G-CAAA - G-CAZZ

G-CAHA	Piper PA-34-200T Seneca II	34-7770010	N23PL	7. 7.98	Aeros Holdings Ltd	Gloucestershire	13. 1.08E
			SE-GPY, (D-IIIC), SE-GPY				
G-CAIN	CFM Shadow Series CD	062	G-MTKU	26. 1.99	G D Haimes	(Newton Bank Farm, Daresbury)	19. 2.08P

G-CALL	Piper PA-23-250 Aztec F	27-7754061	N62826	21.12.77	J D Moon		Belfast International	22. 6.08E
G-CAMB	Aérospatiale AS.355F2 Ecureuil 2	5416	N813LP	17.12.96	Tiger Helicopters Ltd		Shobdon	31. 5.08E
G-CAMM	Hawker Cygnet replica	PFA 077-10245	(G-ERDB)	30. 5.91	R W Cashmore		Old Warden	25. 7.08P

(Built D M Cashmore) (Mosler MM-CB35)   *(On loan to Richard Shuttleworth Trustees) ("6":and carries "G-CAMM" on wings only)*

G-CAMP	Cameron N-105 Balloon (Hot Air)	4546		24. 3.99	R D Parry		Hong Kong, PRC	18. 8.07A

(Operated Hong Kong Balloon and Airship Club)

G-CAMR	BFC Challenger II	xxxxx	26. 3.99	P R A Walker		(Kingston, Ringwood)	

(Built P R A Walker - pr.no.PFA 177-12569 - should be 177A type prefix)

G-CAPI	Mudry CAP.10B	76	G-BEXR	16. 3.99	C Wills tr PI Group	Orchard House, Littleport	27.11.06T
G-CAPX	Akrotech Europe CAP.10B	280		21. 9.98	H J Pessall	Leicester	6. 5.08E

G-CBAA - G-CBZZ

G-CBAB	Scottish Aviation Bulldog Series 120/121		XX543	14. 6.01	Propshop Ltd		Duxford	19. 7.08
		BH120/235			*(As "XX543:F" in RAF c/s)*			
G-CBAD	Mainair Blade 912	1287-0601-7-W1082		8. 6.01	S D Morris		(LLay, Wrexham)	7. 7.08P
G-CBAE	British Aerospace BAe 146 Series 200	E2057	SE-DRB	30. 4.02	BAE Systems (Operations) Ltd		Exeter	
			N698AA, N146AC, G-5-057		*(In open storage as "SE-DRB" Malmo Aviation c/s 1.07)*			
G-CBAF	Neico Lancair 320	PFA 191-13567		11. 6.01	L N and M van Cleef		Lydd	17. 7.05P
	(Built R W Fairless) (Lycoming IO-320)		*(Nose undercarriage collapsed landing Lydd 11.6.05: propeller struck ground shock loading engine)*					
G-CBAH	Raj Hamsa X'Air 133(1)	640		4. 7.01	D N B Hearn Little Heathfield Farm, Atherfield, Ventnor			27. 4.07P
	(Built D N B Hearn - pr.no.BMAA/HB/174)				*(Change of Type 5.06)*			
G-CBAI	Flight Design CT2K	01-02-04-07	G-69-52	4. 7.01	K Maxwell tr Newtownards Microlight Group			
	(Assembled Pegasus Aviation - no Pegasus c/n issued)						Newtownards	21. 7.08P
G-CBAK	Robinson R44 Clipper	1089		2. 8.01	CEL Electrical Logistics Ltd		(Tadcaster)	14. 8.08E
G-CBAL	Piper PA-28-161 Warrior II	28-8116087	LN-MAD	25. 3.94	Thomsonfly Ltd		Rochester	13. 4.08E
			N83007					
G-CBAN	Scottish Aviation Bulldog Series 120/121		XX668	26. 7.01	C Hilliker		Colerne	21. 5.10S
		BH120/326			*(As "XX668:I" in RAF c/s)*			
G-CBAP	Zenair CH.601UL Zodiac	PFA 162A-13656		12. 7.01	A G Marsh		Kirknewton	13. 3.08P
	(Built L J Lowry)							
G-CBAR	Stoddard-Hamilton GlaStar	PFA 295-13133		18. 5.01	C M Barnes		Garden Piece, Basingstoke	10. 5.08P
	(Built C M Barnes) (Tri-cycle u/c)							
G-CBAS	Rans S-6-ES Coyote II	1100.1399ES		4. 7.01	S Stockill		(Buckingham)	11. 4.08P
	(Built S R Green - pr.no.PFA 204-13688) (Rotax 912-UL) (Tailwheel u/c)							
G-CBAT	Cameron Z-90 Balloon (Hot Air)	10099		1. 6.01	British Telecommunications PLC		Thatcham	7. 4.08A
G-CBAU	Rand Robinson KR-2	PFA 129-12789		11. 7.01	B Normington		(Leamington Spa)	
	(Built B Normington)							
G-CBAV	Raj Hamsa X'Air V2(2)	399		7. 9.01	D W Stamp and G J Lampitt		Otherton, Cannock	15. 9.08P
	(Built D W Stamp and G J Lampitt - pr.no.BMAA/HB/127)							
G-CBAW	Cameron A-300 Balloon (Hot Air)	10148		16. 4.02	D K Hempleman-Adams		Corsham	
G-CBAX	Tecnam P92-EM Echo	PFA 318-13698		26. 6.01	R P Reeves		Dunkeswell	1.12.08P
	(Built R P Reeves)							
G-CBAY	Cyclone Airsports Pegasus Quantum 15-912 7829			4. 6.01	P R Jones		Felthorpe	18. 6.03P
					(Damaged Felthorpe in arson attack 18.2.03)			
G-CBAZ	Rans S-6-ES Coyote II	0998.1267		12. 7.01	J G J McDill		(Westmoor Farm,, Thirsk)	5. 1.06P
	(Built G V Willder - pr.no.PFA 204-13596) (Rotax 582)				*(New owner 3.06)*			
G-CBBA	Robin DR.400-180 Régent	2505		27. 7.01	Whitby Seafoods Ltd		Durham Tees Valley	15. 8.08E
G-CBBB	Cyclone Airsports Pegasus Quantum 15-912 7827			22. 6.01	D Workman		(Brierley Hill)	21. 6.08P
G-CBBC	Scottish Aviation Bulldog Series 120/121		XX515	8. 6.01	Bulldog Flyers Ltd		Blackbushe	4. 1.08T
		BH120/201			*(As "XX515:4" in RAF c/s)*			
G-CBBF	Beech 76 Duchess	ME-352	OY-BED	23. 7.01	Bflying Ltd		Bournemouth	6.11.07E
			EI-BHS		*(Operated Bournemouth Flying Club)*			
G-CBBG	Mainair Blade	1291-0601-7-W1086		23. 7.01	S L Cogger		Willingale	19. 4.08P
G-CBBH	Raj Hamsa X'Air V2(2)	435		19. 7.01	S P Macdonald			
	(Built W G Colyer - pr.no.BMAA/HB/143)						Lower Mountpleasant Farm, Chatteris	13. 8.07P
G-CBBK	Robinson R22 Beta	3233	EI-CWP	26. 7.01	R J Everett		(Sproughton, Ipswich)	14. 8.08E
			G-CBBK					
G-CBBL	Scottish Aviation Bulldog Series 120/121		XX550	8. 8.01	A Cunningham		(Swords, County Dublin)	2. 3.08
		BH120/243						
G-CBBM	ICP MXP-740 Savannah Jabiru(1) 01-03-51-062			10. 8.01	C E Passmore		East Barling, Essex	10. 7.08P
	(Built P J Wilson and S Whittaker - pr.no.BMAA/HB/176)							
G-CBBN	Cyclone Airsports Pegasus Quantum 15-912 7844			9. 8.01	N I Garland tr G-CBBN Group		Dunkeswell	31. 8.08P
G-CBBO	Whittaker MW5-D Sorcerer	PFA 163-13443		23. 7.01	P J Gripton		Baxby Manor, Husthwaite	14. 5.08P
	(Built P J Gripton)							
G-CBBP	Cyclone Airsports Pegasus Quantum 15-912 7843			31. 7.01	C Thompson		(Wombourne, Wolverhampton)	30. 7.08P
G-CBBR	Scottish Aviation Bulldog Series 120/121		XX625	8. 8.01	G V Crowe and D L Thompson		Norwich	
		BH120/290			*(Noted 5.06 as "XX625:01")*			
G-CBBS	Scottish Aviation Bulldog Series 120/121		XX694	8. 8.01	Newcastle Aerobatic Academy Ltd		Newcastle	6. 7.09S
		BH120/343			*(As "XX694:E" in RAF c/s)*			
G-CBBT	Scottish Aviation Bulldog Series 120/121		XX695	8. 8.01	Newcastle Bulldog Group Ltd		Durham Tees Valley	7. 3.10T
		BH120/344			*(As "XX695:3" in RAF c/s)*			
G-CBBU	Scottish Aviation Bulldog Series 120/121		XX711	6. 8.01	Newcastle Bulldog Group Ltd		Derby	
		BH120/360			*(Noted 6.06)*			
G-CBBW	Scottish Aviation Bulldog Series 120/121		XX619	1. 8.01	S E Robottom-Scott		Coventry	27. 8.03T
		BH120/277			*(As "XX619:T" in RAF c/s)*			
G-CBBX	Lindstrand LBL 69A Balloon (Hot Air)	805		2. 8.01	J L F Garcia		Guadalajara, Spain	5. 8.02A
G-CBCB	Scottish Aviation Bulldog Series 120/121		XX537	25. 9.01	The General Aviation Trading Company Ltd			
		BH120/223			*(As "XX537:C" in RAF c/s)*		North Weald	22. 3.08T
G-CBCD	Cyclone Airsports Pegasus Quantum 15 7845			6. 8.01	I A Lumley		(Penrith)	5. 6.08P
	(Rotax 582)							
G-CBCF	Cyclone Airsports Pegasus Quantum 15-912 7846			23. 8.01	S Speake tr G-CBCF Group		(Newton Bank, Daresbury)	17.12.07P
G-CBCH	Zenair CH.701UL STOL	PFA 187-13568		8. 8.01	L G Millen		(Sittingbourne)	
	(Built L G Millen)							

G-CBCI	Raj Hamsa X'Air 582(11)	659		9. 8.01	C P Lincoln	Stoke, Isle of Grain 10. 4.08P
	(Built P A Gilford - pr.no.BMAA/HB/180)					
G-CBCJ	Rotary Air Force RAF 2000 GTX-SE	PFA G/13-1331		13. 8.01	B Errington-Weddle	Henstridge 9.10.07P
	(Built J P Comerford)					
G-CBCK	Nipper T 66 Series 3	T66/30	G-TEDZ	14. 8.01	N M Bloom Abbots Hill Farm, Hemel Hempstead 14.12.06P
	(Originally built Avions Fairey SA: rebuilt C Edwards C 1998 as G-TEDZ - pr.no.PFA 25-11051: later rebuilt N Bloom c 2001 and re-regd) (Jabiru 2200A)					
G-CBCL	Stoddard-Hamilton GlaStar	PFA 295-13089		5. 9.97	M I Weaver	Coventry 21. 5.08P
	(Built C J Norman) (Tri-cycle u/c)					
G-CBCM	Raj Hamsa X'Air 700(1A)	656		23. 7.01	G Firth	(Barnsley) 21. 8.06P
	(Built A Hipkin - pr.no.BMAA/HB/177)					
G-CBCN	Schweizer 269C-1	0129	EI-CWS	17. 9.01	Helicentre Liverpool Ltd	Liverpool 29. 9.08E
	(Schweizer 300)		G-CBCN			
G-CBCP	Van's RV-6A *(Built AM Smith)*	PFA 181A-13643		6. 8.01	A M Smith tr G-CBCP Group	Crowfield 27. 5.08P
G-CBCR	Scottish Aviation Bulldog Series 120/121	XX702		5. 9.01	D Wells	Derby 22. 6.08S
		BH120/351			*(As "XX702" in RAF c/s)*	
G-CBCV	Scottish Aviation Bulldog Series 120/121	XX699		30. 8.01	C A Patter	North Coates 24. 8.08S
		BH120/348			*(As "XX699:F" in RAF c/s)*	
G-CBCX	Cyclone Airsports Pegasus Quantum 15	7848		10. 9.01	T J Heaton	(Sleaford) 9. 9.08P
	(Rotax 582)					
G-CBCY	Beech C24R Sierra	MC-491	N881RS	26. 9.01	Plane Talking Ltd	Bournemouth 8. 3.08E
			PH-HLA		*(Operated Cabair)*	
G-CBCZ	CFM Streak Shadow SLA	K 340-SLA		13. 9.01	J O'Malley Kane Great Yeldham Hall, Halstead 30. 1.08P
	(Built J A Hambleton - pr.no.PFA 206-13586) (Rotax 582)				"Alana Rose"	
G-CBDC	Thruster T 600N 450 Jab Sprint	0071-T600N-054		12. 7.01	E Maguire	Enniskillen 14. 7.08P
G-CBDD	Mainair Blade	1293-0701-7-W1088		1. 8.01	M Turner	(Nantwich) 31. 8.08P
G-CBDG	Zenair CH.601HD Zodiac	PFA 162-13375		3. 9.01	R E Lasnier	Sleap 15. 6.08P
	(Built R E Lasnier)					
G-CBDH	Flight Design CT2K	01-07-02-17		4.10.01	K Tuck	(Horningtoft, Dereham) 31. 3.07P
	(Assembled Pegasus Aviation with c/n 7849)					
G-CBDI	Denney Kitfox Model 2	PFA 172-11888		4. 9.01	J G D Barbour	Sherriff Hall Estate, Balgone 12. 6.08P
	(Built J G D Barbour)					
G-CBDJ	Flight Design CT2K	01-07-01-17		11.10.01	P J Walker	Griffins Farm, Temple Bruer 25.10.08P
	(Assembled Pegasus Aviation with c/n 7850)					
G-CBDK	Scottish Aviation Bulldog Series 120/121	XX611		26. 9.01	J N Randle	Coventry 9. 4.08S
		BH120/259			*(As "XX611:7" in RAF c/s)*	
G-CBDL	Mainair Blade	1292-0701-7-W1087		1. 8.01	D Lightwood	(Macclesfield) 14.11.03P
G-CBDM	Tecnam P92-EM Echo	PFA 318-13756		11. 7.01	J J Cozens	Dunkeswell 19. 6.08P
	(Built J J Cozens and C J Willy)					
G-CBDN	Mainair Blade	1297-0801-7-W1092		20. 9.01	T Peckham	(Graveney, Faversham) 16.11.08P
G-CBDO	Raj Hamsa X'Air 582(1)	583		12.11.01	A Campbell	Newtonwards 22.10.07P
	(Built R T Henry - pr.no.BMAA/HB/170)					
G-CBDP	Mainair Blade 912	1295-0801-7-W1090		17. 8.01	D S Parker	Carlisle 16. 8.08P
G-CBDS	Scottish Aviation Bulldog Series 120/121	XX707		27. 7.01	J R Parry	Caernarfon 20.12.07T
		BH120/356			*(As "XX707:4" in RAF c/s)*	
G-CBDT	Zenair CH.601HD Zodiac	PFA 162-12474		17. 9.01	D G Watt	Cark-in-Cartmell 8. 7.08P
	(Built D G Watt)					
G-CBDU	Quad City Challenger II	PFA 177-13000		14. 9.01	Hiscox Cases Ltd	Otherton, Cannock
	(Built B A Hiscox)				*(Noted 8.05)*	
G-CBDV	Raj Hamsa X'Air 582(6)	616		6. 8.01	T S Davis	Davidstow Moor 7. 7.08P
	(Built R J Brown and D J Prothero - pr.no.BMAA/HB/161)					
G-CBDW	Raj Hamsa X'Air Jabiru(1)	575		18. 9.01	P C Bishop	Dunkeswel 5.10.07P
	(Built P R Reynolds - pr.no.BMAA/HB/150)					
G-CBDX	Cyclone Airsports Pegasus Quantum 15	7857		11.10.01	P Sinkler	Shobdon 5. 1.08P
	(Rotax 582)					
G-CBDY	Raj Hamsa X'Air V2(2)	588		26. 9.01	P M Stoney	Willingale 29. 5.08P
	(Built D Mahajan - pr.no.BMAA/HB/155)					
G-CBDZ	Cyclone Airsports Pegasus Quantum 15-912	7852		11. 9.01	J J Brutnell	Sutton Meadows 6.10.08P
G-CBEB	Air Création 582(1)/Kiss 400	FL003/135		3.10.01	M Harris	Redlands, Swindon 27. 5.08P
	(Built P J R Bradshaw.and A R R Williams - pr.no.BMAA/HB/184 for Flylight kit)					
G-CBEC	Cameron Z-105 Balloon (Hot Air)	10105		16.10.01	A L Ballarino	Piedimonte Matese, Italy 3. 8.08A
G-CBED	Cameron Z-90 Balloon (Hot Air)	10121		15.10.01	John Aimo Balloons SAS	Mondovi, Italy 3.11.07A
					(Citta di Mondovi titles)	
G-CBEE	Piper PA-28R-200 Cherokee Arrow II	N4479X		5.10.01	IHC Ltd	Biggin Hill 12. 1.08E
		28R-7635055				
G-CBEF	Scottish Aviation Bulldog Series 120/121	XX621		3.10.01	J A Ingram	Leicester 15. 2.08
		BH120/286			*(As "XX621:H" in RAF c/s)*	
G-CBEG	Robinson R44 Raven	1124		28. 9.01	MGB Trading Ltd	Headcorn 22.12.07E
G-CBEH	Scottish Aviation Bulldog Series 120/121	XX521		28. 9.01	J E Lewis	Enstone 9. 9.08E
		BH120/207			*(As "XX521:H" in RAF c/s)*	
G-CBEI	Piper PA-22-108 Colt	22-9136	SE-CZR	5. 6.02	D Sharp	Breighton 9. 1.11S
G-CBEJ	Colt 120A Balloon (Hot Air)	10181		11.10.01	J A Gray	Daglingworth, Cirencester 6. 3.07T
G-CBEK	Scottish Aviation Bulldog Series 120/121	XX700		26. 9.01	S Landregan	Blackbushe 23.11.07T
		BH120/349			*(As "XX700:17" in RAF c/s)*	
G-CBEL	Hawker Iraqi Fury FB.11	37579	N36SF	6. 8.01	J A D Bradshaw	Bournemouth 30.10.08P
			Iraqi AF 315		*(Also carries "361 NAVY")*	
G-CBEM	Mainair Blade	1294-0801-7-W1089		17. 8.01	M Earp	Calton Moor Farm, Ashbourne 14.11.08P
G-CBEN	Cyclone Airsports Pegasus Quantum 15-912	7855		8.10.01	S Clarke	Swinford, Rugby 12. 3.08P
G-CBES	Europa Aviation Europa	061		27. 9.01	M R Hexley	(Penmaenmawr) 7. 5.07P
	(Built M R Hexley - pr.no.PFA 247-12691) (Monowheel u/c)					
G-CBET	Mainair Blade 912S	1296-0801-7-W1091		6. 9.01	D F Kenny	Finmere 26. 1.08P
G-CBEU	Cyclone Airsports Pegasus Quantum 15-912	7869		16.10.01	C Lee	Longacre Farm, Sandy 15.10.07P
G-CBEV	Cyclone Airsports Pegasus Quantum 15-912	7854		16.10.01	P J Barton tr G-CBEV Group	Longacre Farm, Sandy 10.12.07P
G-CBEW	Flight Design CT2K	01-08-02-23		19.10.01	A J Webb tr Shy Talk Group	Oxford 23.12.07P
	(Assembled Pegasus Aviation with c/n 7868)					

Reg	Type	c/n	Prev id	Date	Owner/Operator	Location	Expiry
G-CBEX	Flight Design CT2K	01-08-01-23		29.10.01	A G Quinn	Knapthorpe Lodge, Caunton	13. 4.08P
	(Assembled Pegasus Aviation with c/n 7867)						
G-CBEY	Cameron C-80 Balloon (Hot Air)	10190		31.10.01	D V Fowler	Cranbrook	5.10.07A
G-CBEZ	Robin DR.400-180 Régent	2511		26. 2.02	K V Field	Turweston	8. 4.08E
G-CBFA	Diamond DA.40 Star	40063		25.10.01	Lyrastar Ltd	Redhill	30. 3.08E
G-CBFE	Raj Hamsa X'Air 582(1)	636		19.10.01	M L Powell	Brook Farm, Pilling	14. 7.08P
	(Built S Whittle - pr.no.BMAA/HB/186)						
G-CBFF	Cameron O-120 Balloon (Hot Air)	10167		20.11.01	T M C McCoy	Peasedown St John, Bath	30. 5.08T
	(Operated Ascent Balloons) (Ascent titles)						
G-CBFH	Thunder AX8-105 Series 2 Balloon (Hot Air)			13.11.01	D V Fowler and A N F Pertwee		
		10188			Sandhurst, Cranbrook and Great Holland, Frinton-on-Sea		10.11.06A
G-CBFJ	Robinson R44 Raven	1131		7.11.01	Safedem Ltd	(Doune)	8.11.07E
G-CBFK	Murphy Rebel	PFA 232-13340		13. 9.01	P J Gibbs	Truro	13.10.03P
	(Built D Webb)				*(New owner 8.04)*		
G-CBFM	SOCATA TB-21 Trinidad GT	710	PH-BLM	2. 1.02	Execflight Ltd	Southend	21. 3.08E
			D-EFAK (4)				
G-CBFN	Robin HR.100-200B Royal	112	F-BTBP	1. 3.02	T H A Alington tr Foxtrot November Group		
					(Noted 1.08)	Bourne Park, Hurstbourne Tarrant	11. 6.05T
G-CBFO	Cessna 172S Skyhawk SP	172S8929	N3520A	22.10.01	Transcourt Ltd	Oxford	29.10.07E
G-CBFP	Scottish Aviation Bulldog Series 120/121	XX636		29.10.01	D J Scott *(As "XX636:Y" in RAF c/s)*	Cranfield	3. 3.08T
		BH120/306					
G-CBFU	Scottish Aviation Bulldog Series 120/121	XX628		12.11.01	J R and S J Huggins	Chalksole Green Farm, Alkham	30. 5.08
		BH120/293			*(As "XX628:9" in RAF c/s)*		
G-CBFV	Comco Ikarus C42 FB UK	PFA 322-13774		5.11.01	A W Leadley		
	(Built P A D Chubb)					(Lismonaghan, Letterkenny, County Donegal)	28. 4.08P
G-CBFW	Montgomerie-Bensen B 8MR	PFA G/01-1312		6.11.01	I Mclean	Kirkbride	21.12.07P
	(Built B F Pearson)						
G-CBFX	Rans S-6-ESN Coyote II	1000.1392		8.11.01	J R Lowman	Lower Mountpleasant Farm, Chatteris	16. 8.08P
	(Built J Whiting - pr.no.PFA 204-13820) (Rotax 582) (Tri-cycle u/c)						
G-CBFY	Cameron Z-250 Balloon (Hot Air)	10023		9.11.01	M L Gabb	Haselor, Alcester	9. 3.07A
G-CBFZ	Avtech Jabiru SPL-450	0353		8.11.01	A H King	(Orpington)	26. 5.07P
	(Built A H King - pr.no.PFA 274A-13617) (Originally designated with addtional UL series c/n "UL0103")						
G-CBGA	PZL-110 Koliber 160A	04010086	SP-WGM	14.11.01	STG Fabrications Ltd	Old Sarum	14. 2.08E
G-CBGB	Zenair CH.601UL Zodiac	PFA 162A-13819		12.11.01	J F Woodham	Hollow Hill Farm, Granborough	27. 4.08P
	(Built R Germany) (Tri-cycle u/c)						
G-CBGC	SOCATA TB-10 Tobago	1584	VH-YHB	21. 9.01	Tobago Aviation Ltd *(Noted 2.06)*	Blackbushe	6.12.05E
G-CBGD	Zenair CH.701UL STOL	PFA 187-13785		13.11.01	I S Walsh	Dunkeswell	24. 7.07P
	(Built I S Walsh)						
G-CBGE	Tecnam P92-EM Echo	PFA 318-13680		9.11.01	I D Rutherford	(Calvert, Buckingham)	19. 8.07P
	(Built T C Robson)						
G-CBGG	Cyclone Airsports Pegasus Quantum 15	7874		27.11.01	T E Davies	Headon Farm, Retford	25. 3.08P
	(Rotax 503)						
G-CBGH	Teverson Bisport	PFA 267-12784		7.11.01	R C Teverson	Waits Farm, Belchamp Walter	14. 3.08P
	(Built R C Teverson)						
G-CBGI	CFM Streak Shadow SLA	K 336		30.10.01	M W W Clotworthy	Wadswick Manor Farm, Corsham	20. 6.08P
	(Built M W W Clotworthy - pr.no.PFA 206-13559)						
G-CBGJ	Aeroprakt A22 Foxbat	PFA 317-13803		14.11.01	M McCall	(Moira, Craigavon)	29. 8.08P
	(Built W R Davis-Smith)				*(Marked "002" possibly indicating second UK Foxbat built)*		
G-CBGL	Max Holste MH.1521M Broussard	19	F-BMJO	3.12.01	A I Milne tr Broussard Flying Group	Horsford	
			F-BNEN, French AF		*(Stored awaiting rebuild 4.06)*		
G-CBGO	Murphy Maverick 430	PFA 259-13470		24.10.01	C R Ellis and E A Wrathall	(Chapel-en-le-Frith)	15.10.08P
	(Built C R Ellis) (Jabiru 2200A)						
G-CBGP	Comco Ikarus C42 FB UK	PFA 322-13741		22.11.01	G F Welby	Bakersfield	20. 5.08P
	(Built A R Lloyd)						
G-CBGR	Avtech Jabiru UL-450	xxxx		21.11.01	R G Kirkland	RAF Henlow	10..4.08P
	(Built K R Emery - pr.no.PFA 274A-13682)						
G-CBGS	Cyclone AX2000 HKS	7866		8. 3.02	S M Newton	Enstone	3. 7.07P
G-CBGU	Thruster T 600N 450	0121-T600N-055		21.11.01	B R Cardosi	Wick	2.12.07P
G-CBGV	Thruster T 600N 450 Sprint	0121-T600N-056		21.11.01	J R Nutter	(Shanklin)	1. 4.08P
G-CBGW	Thruster T 600N 450 Sprint	0121-T600N-058		21.11.01	M C Arnold and A R Pluck	Damyn's Hall, Upminster	18. 4.08P
G-CBGX	Scottish Aviation Bulldog Series 120/121	XX622		26.11.01	Henfield Lodge Aviation Ltd	Shoreham	6.12.08T
		BH120/287			*(As "XX622:B" in RAF c/s)*		
G-CBGZ	Westland SA.341C Gazelle HT.2	1923	ZB646	30.10.01	D Weatherhead Ltd	Cambridge	19. 9.08P
G-CBHA	SOCATA TB-10 Tobago	1583	VH-YHA	6.11.01	Oscar Romeo Aviation Ltd	Redhill	8. 6.08E
G-CBHB	Raj Hamsa X'Air 582(5)	611		22.11.01	R A J Graham	Kirkbride	27. 2.08P
	(Built G Fleck - pr.no.BMAA/HB/189)						
G-CBHC	Rotary Air Force RAF 2000 GTX-SE	PFA G/13-1326		22.11.01	A J Thomas	(Sutton Coldfield)	30. 9.08P
	(Built A J Thomas)						
G-CBHD	Cameron Z-160 Balloon (Hot Air)	10225		1. 3.02	Ballooning 50 Degrees Nord	Fouhren, Luxembourg	28. 3.08A
					(Nichobetzen Founzen titles.)		
G-CBHG	Mainair Blade 912S	1298-1001-7-W1093		12.12.01	B S Hope	(Marsh Gibbon, Bicester)	9. 7.08P
G-CBHI	Europa Aviation Europa XS	373		31.10.01	B Price tr Hotel India Group	(Southampton)	14.12.04P
	(Built B Price - pr.no.PFA 247-13245) (Monowheel u/c)						
G-CBHJ	Mainair Blade 912	1305-1201-7-W1100		28. 1.02	B C Jones	(Altrincham)	29. 4.08P
G-CBHK	Cyclone Airsports Pegasus Quantum 15	7871		6.12.01	B Dossett	Plaistows Farm, St Albans	5. 4.08P
	(HKS 700E)						
G-CBHL	Eurocopter AS.350B2 Ecureuil	2673	C-GKHS	28. 1.02	C S Mcrae	(Lanark)	1. 5.08E
			JA6123		*(Crashed Jerviswood House, Lanark 15. 9.07 and substantially damaged*		
G-CBHM	Mainair Blade 912	1301-1100-7-W1096		3.12.01	W T Milburn	Barton	24. 5.08P
G-CBHN	Cyclone Airsports Pegasus Quantum 15-912	7872		6.12.01	G G Cook	Clench Common	28. 1.08P
G-CBHO	Gloster Gladiator II	?	N5719 (?)	11.12.01	Retro Track and Air (UK) Ltd	(Dursley)	
G-CBHP	Corby CJ-1 Starlet	PFA 134-12498		12.12.01	D H Barker	Turweston	29. 8.08P
	(Built J D Muldowney and D H Barker)						
G-CBHR	Laser Lazer Z200	Q056	VH-IAC	31.12.01	J R Hallam tr G-CBHR Flying Group	White Waltham	6. 4.08P
	(Built H Selvey)						

G-CBHT	Dassault Falcon 900EX	48	G-GPWH F-WWFP	3. 1.02	TAG Aviation (UK) Ltd	Farnborough	23.11.07E
G-CBHU	TLAC RL5B XP Sherwood Ranger *(Built M J Gooch - pr.no. PFA 237-12477) (Jabiru 2200A)*	xxxx		12.12.01	A J Glading tr G-CBHU Group	(Leafield, Witney)	2.10.07P
G-CBHV	Raj Hamsa X'Air 582(5) *(Built J D Buchanan - pr.no.BMAA/HB/139)*	525		12.12.01	G E MacCuish	North Connel, Oban	18.12.08P
G-CBHW	Cameron Z-105 Balloon (Hot Air)	10217		16. 1.02	Bristol Chamber of Commerce, Industry and Shipping *(Crea8ive and Business West titles) "Bridg-it"* Bristol		3. 5.08A
G-CBHX	Cameron V-77 Balloon (Hot Air)	3950		19.12.01	N A Apsey *"Irene"*	Hazlemere, High Wycombe	5. 4.08A
G-CBHY	Cyclone Airsports Pegasus Quantum 15-912	7859		7. 1.02	A Hope	Miiddle Stoke, Isle of Grain	6. 3.08P
G-CBHZ	Rotary Air Force RAF 2000 GTX-SE PFA G/13-1321 *(Built M P Donnelly)*			2. 1.02	M P Donnelly	(Thurso)	
G-CBIB	Flight Design CT2K *(Assembled Pegasus Aviation with c/n 7878)*	01-08-06-23		21. 1.02	J A Moss	Grove Farm, Needham	14. 3.07P
G-CBIC	Raj Hamsa X'Air V2(2) *(Built J T Blackburn and D R Sutton - pr.no.BMAA/HB/156)*	608		2. 1.02	J T Blackburn and D R Sutton	Brook Farm, Pilling	17. 4.07P
G-CBID	Scottish Aviation Bulldog Series 120/121 BH120/242	XX549		14.12.01	D A Steven tr Red Dog Group *(As "XX549:6" in RAF c/s)*	White Waltham	25. 1.10S
G-CBIE	Flight Design CT2K *(Assembled Pegasus Aviation with c/n 7879)*	01-09-01-23		10. 1.02	S R McKiernan	Ince Blundell	24. 4.08P
G-CBIF	Avtech Jabiru SPL-450 *(Built J A Iszard - pr.no.PFA 274A-13789)*	xxxx		3. 1.02	S N J Huxtable	Weston Zoyland	12. 7.08P
G-CBIH	Cameron Z-31 Balloon (Hot Air)	10243		4. 1.02	Gone With The Wind Ltd	Bristol	13.10.08A
G-CBII	Raj Hamsa X'Air 582(2) *(Built A Worthington - pr.no.BMAA/HB/185)*	676		7. 1.02	G H Speakman	Tarn Farm, Cockerham	13. 7.08E
G-CBIJ	Comco Ikarus C42 FB UK *(Built A Jones - pr.no.PFA 322-13720) (Kit no. not confirmed)*	0102-6319		3. 1.02	J A Smith	(Royal Oak, Filey)	16. 6.08P
G-CBIK	RotorWay Executive 162F *(Built J Hodson) RotorWay RI 162F)*	6112		9. 1.02	J Hodson	Street Farm, Takeley *(Noted 2.08)*	
G-CBIL	Cessna 182K Skylane	18257804	(G-BFZZ) D-ENGO, N2604Q	9.10.78	E Bannister and J R C Spooner	East Midlands	27. 6.08E
G-CBIM	Lindstrand LBL 90A Balloon (Hot Air)	817		28. 1.02	R K Parsons	South Petherton, Somerset	27. 4.06A
G-CBIN	TEAM Mini-MAX 91 PFA 186-13111 *(Built D E Steade) (Rotax 503) (Enclosed cockpit)*			7. 1.02	K J Walton	RAF Halton	7. 8.07P
G-CBIO	Thruster T 600N 450 Jab	0022-T600N-062		7. 1.02	J Kenyon tr Sandown Microlights 	Sandown, Isle of Wight	8. 8.08P
G-CBIP	Thruster T 600N 450	0022-T600N-060		7. 1.02	K D Mitchell tr G-CBIP Group	Deanland	15. 6.08P
G-CBIR	Thruster T 600N 450	0022-T600N-061		7. 1.02	E G White	Landmead Farm, Garford	7. 7.08P
G-CBIS	Raj Hamsa X'Air 582(2) *(Built P T W T Derges - pr.no.BMAA/HB/199)*	708		15. 1.02	P T W T Derges	Long Marston	17. 4.08P
G-CBIT	Rotary Air Force RAF 2000 GTX-SE PFA G/13-1340 *(Built M P Lehermette)*			27.11.01	Terrafirma Services Ltd 	Lamberhurst Farm, Faversham	
G-CBIU	Cameron Flame 95 SS Balloon (Hot Air)	10222		6. 2.02	PSH Skypower Ltd *(British Gas-Think Energy titles)*	Woodborough, Pewsey	16. 5.08A
G-CBIV	Best Off Sky Ranger 912(1) SKRxxxxxxx *(Built P M Dewhurst - pr.no.BMAA/HB/201)*			25. 1.02	K Brown	Bakersfield	4.10.08P
G-CBIW	Lindstrand LBL 310A Balloon (Hot Air)	821		24. 1.02	C E Wood	Witham	12. 3.08T
G-CBIX	Zenair CH.601UL Zodiac PFA 162A-13765 *(Built M F Cottam)*			24.12.01	R A and B M Roberts	Griffins Farm, Temple Bruer	15. 6.07P
G-CBIY	Evektor EV-97 Eurostar PFA 315-13846 *(Built E M Middleton)*			23. 1.02	R Soltysik	Otherton, Cannock	22. 3.08P
G-CBIZ	Cyclone Airsports Pegasus Quantum 15-912	7870		6.12.01	M P Duckett	(Bradford)	5. 4.08P
G-CBJD	Stoddard-Hamilton GlaStar PFA 295-13853 *(Built K F Farey)*			23. 1.02	K F Farey	(Bourne End)	
G-CBJE	Rotary Air Force RAF 2000 GTX-SE PFA G/13-1342 *(Built K F Farey)*			23. 1.02	V G Freke *(Noted Henstridge 8.07)*	(Swallowfield, Reading)	13. 5.08P
G-CBJG	de Havilland DHC-1 Chipmunk 22 *(Built OGMA)*	63	CS-AZT Portuguese AF FAP 1373	8. 2.02	C J Rees *(As "1373" in Portuguese AF c/s)*	Dalkeith Farm, Winwick	29. 4.10S
G-CBJH	Aeroprakt A22 Foxbat PFA 317-13847 *(Built H Smith)*			30. 1.02	H Smith	Morgansfield, Fishburn	17.10.07P
G-CBJJ	Scottish Aviation Bulldog Series 120/121 BH120/211	XX525		3.12.01	G V Crowe and D L Thompson *(As "XX525:8")*	Norwich	4. 4.09S
G-CBJK	Scottish Aviation Bulldog Series 120/121 BH120/362	XX713		3.12.01	G V Crowe and D L Thompson *(As "XX713:2": noted 5.06)*	Norwich	
G-CBJL	Air Création 582(1)/Kiss 400 FL005 *(Built R E Morris - pr.no.BMAA/HB/205 for Flylight kit comprising Trike s/n T01099 and s/n Wing A01158-1164)*			8. 2.02	R E Morris	(Kidwelly, Dyfed)	30. 7.04P
G-CBJM	Avtech Jabiru SP-470 xxxx *(Built A T Moyce - pr.no.PFA 274B-13769)*			11.12.01	G R T Elliott	Newtownards	22. 5.08P
G-CBJN	Rotary Air Force RAF 2000 GTX-SE PFA G/13-1335 *(Built R Hall)*			30. 1.02	R Hall	(Truro)	
G-CBJO	Cyclone Airsports Pegasus Quantum 15-912	7861		10.12.01	P A Martland	Arclid Green, Sandbach	5. 8.07P
G-CBJP	Zenair CH.601UL Zodiac PFA 162A-13590 *(Built R E Peirse) (Tri-cycle u/c)*			31. 1.02	R E Peirse	Armshold Farm, Kingston, Cambridge	31. 8.08P
G-CBJR	Evektor EV-97 Eurostar PFA 315-13845 *(Buillt B J Crockett)*			31. 1.02	R B Skinner	Belle Vue Farm, Yarnscombe	22. 3.08P
G-CBJS	Cameron C-60 Balloon (Hot Air)	10253		17. 4.02	N Ivison	Barton Seagrave, Kettering	3. 3.08A
G-CBJT	Mainair Blade	1302-1101-7-W1097		12.12.01	D Maddison	Headon Farm, Retford	3.10.08P
G-CBJU	Van's RV-7A PFA 323-13868 *(Built T W Waltham)*			1. 2.02	T W Waltham	(Teffont Evias, Salisbury)	
G-CBJV	RotorWay Executive 162F *(Built Southern Helicopters Ltd) (RotorWay RI 162F)*	6589		13. 2.02	R J Green *(Noted 2.08)*	Street Farm, Takeley	2. 11.07P
G-CBJW	Comco Ikarus C42 FB UK PFA 322-13811 *(Built T J Cale)*			13. 2.02	J A Robinson *(New owner 10.07)*	Tarn Farm, Cockerham	14. 5.07P
G-CBJX	Raj Hamsa X'Air Falcon Jabiru(1) *(Built M R Coreth - pr.no.BMAA/HB/181)*	622		13. 2.02	P M and M Stoney	Willingale	3.11.08P

G-CBJY	Avtech Jabiru UL-450	xxxx		14. 2.02	D L H Person	Great Ashfield, Suffolk	18. 8.08P
	(Built D L H Person - pr.no.PFA 274A-13613)						
G-CBJZ	Westland SA.341G Gazelle HT.3	1734	3D-HGW	13. 2.02	K G Theurer	Sion, Switzerland	10. 4.08P
			XZ932				
G-CBKA	Westland SA.341G Gazelle HT.3	1746	XZ937	20. 2.02	J Windmill	(Ilkeston)	12.12.08P
G-CBKB	Bücker Bü.181C Bestmann	121	F-PCRL	28. 1.02	W R and G D Snadden	(Alexandria)	
			F-BCRU				
G-CBKC	Westland SA.341D Gazelle HT.3	1104	XW862	20. 2.02	C R Onslow	(Heyton, Royston)	9. 4.08P
G-CBKD	Westland SA.341C Gazelle HT.2	1130	XW868	20. 2.02	Flying Scout Ltd	Welshpool	25. 4.08P
G-CBKE	Air Création 582(1)/Kiss 400	FL010		18. 2.02	P Blackbourn	(Sheffield)	20. 6.07P
	(Built R J Howell - pr.no.BMAA/HB/206 for Flylight kit comprising Trike s/n T02011 and s/n Wing A02014-2007) (New owner 9.07)						
G-CBKF	Reality Easy Raider J2.2(2)	0003		24. 1.02	R R Armstrong	Headcorn	5. 4.08P
	(Built R J Creasey - pr.no.BMAA/HB/202)						
G-CBKG	Thruster T 600N 450	0022-T600N-059		1. 3.02	A S Mitchell	Shobdon	6. 3.08P
G-CBKI	Cameron Z-90 Balloon (Hot Air)	10236		22. 3.02	Wheatfields Park Ltd	Churchill, Winscombe	19. 3.05A
					(Roundtrees Garden Centres titles)		
G-CBKJ	Cameron Z-90 Balloon (Hot Air)	10251		6. 3.02	Invista (UK) Holdings Ltd	Brockworth, Gloucester	3. 5.08A
G-CBKK	Ultramagic S-130 Balloon (Hot Air)	130/32		19. 3.02	Airborne Adventures Ltd	Rylestone, Skipton	8. 6.06E
					(co.uk titles)		
G-CBKL	Raj Hamsa X'Air 582(12)	682		18. 2.02	S Smith tr Caithness X-Air Group	Wick	2. 3.08P
	(Built J Garcia - pr.no.BMAA/HB/203)						
G-CBKM	Mainair Blade 912	1310-0102-7-W1105		21. 1.02	N Purdy	Headon Farm, Retford	16. 4.08P
G-CBKN	Mainair Blade 912S	1316-0302-7-W1111		11. 3.02	D S Clews	Headon Farm, Retford	19. 4.08P
G-CBKO	Mainair Blade 912S	1311-0102-7-W1106		11. 2.02	P W Jordan	(Bradford)	26. 3.08P
G-CBKR	Piper PA-28-161 Warrior III	2842143	N5334N	15. 3.02	Devon and Somerset Flight Training Ltd	Dunkeswell	30. 3.08E
G-CBKS	Air Création 582(1)/Kiss 400	FL007		28. 1.02	S Kilpin	Manor Farm, Haddenham	6.10.08P
	(Built S Kilpin - pr.no.BMAA/HB/197 for Flylight kit comprising.Trike s/n T01113 and Wing s/n A01193-1203)						
G-CBKU	Comco Ikarus C42 FB UK	0112-6431	(EI-)	4. 3.02	C Blackburn	Carnowen, County Donegal	4. 6.08P
	(Built R G Q Clarke and P Walton - pr.no.PFA 322-13862)						
G-CBKV	Cameron Z-77 Balloon (Hot Air)	4946		15. 3.02	J F Till	Welburn, York	3. 4.08A
G-CBKW	Cyclone Airsports Pegasus Quantum 15-912	7892		25. 3.02	W G Coulter	Perth	18. 6.08P
G-CBKY	Avtech Jabiru SP-470	xxxx		6. 3.02	P R Sistern	City of Derry	14.10.08P
	(Built P R Sistern - pr.no.PFA 274B-13764)						
G-CBLA	Aero Designs Pulsar XP	367	N367JR	15. 2.02	J P Kynaston	Graveley Hall Farm, Graveley	11.10.08P
	(Built J L Reeves)						
G-CBLB	Tecnam P92-EM Echo	PFA 318-13770		12. 3.02	F G Walker	(Lleweni Parc)	2. 8.08P
	(Built M A Lomas)						
G-CBLD	Mainair Blade 912S	1306-1201-7-W1101		21. 3.02	N E King	St Michaels	21. 4.08P
G-CBLE	Robin R2120U Alpha 120T	364		16. 4.02	Cardiff Academy of Aviation Ltd	Cardiff	2. 8.08E
G-CBLF	Raj Hamsa X'Air 582(11)	696		18. 3.02	B J Harper and P J Soukup	Eaglescott	29. 4.08P
	(Built E G Bishop and E N Dunn - pr.no.BMAA/HB/194)						
G-CBLH	Raj Hamsa X'Air 582(11)	673		18. 3.02	P Sykes	Mapperton Farm, Newton Peverill	6. 7.08P
	(Built S Rance - pr.no.BMAA/HB/182)						
G-CBLJ	IAV-Bacau Yakovlev Yak-52	888615	RA-44472	19. 4.02	A R Richards	(White Waltham)	25. 4.07P
			LY-AHF, DOSAAF 57 *(yellow) (Also as "61" (black)) (Noted 1.08)*				
G-CBLK	Hawker Hind	41H-82971	R Afghan AF L7181	20. 3.02	Aero Vintage Ltd *(Noted unmarked 11.06)*	Duxford	
G-CBLL	Cyclone Airsports Pegasus Quantum 15-912	7891		22. 3.02	P R Jones	Felthorpe	16. 6.08P
G-CBLM	Mainair Blade 912	1308-0102-7-W1103		12. 2.02	P A Flaherty	(Thetford)	26. 4.08P
G-CBLN	Cameron Z-31 Balloon (Hot Air)	10285		26. 4.02	L P Hooper	St George, Bristol	21. 5.08A
G-CBLO	Lindstrand LBL 42A Balloon (Hot Air)	854		3. 4.02	N K and R H Calvert	Bradley Stoke, Bristol	20. 4.08A
G-CBLP	Raj Hamsa X'Air Falcon Jabiru(2)	646		26. 3.02	A C Parsons	Dunkeswell	17. 5.06P
	(Built M J Kay and S Litchfield - pr.no.BMAA/HB/213)					*(Noted 8.07)*		
G-CBLS	Fiat CR.42 Falco	920	Swedish AF 2542	20. 7.05	Patina Ltd	Duxford	
					(Operated The Fighter Collection) (Stored 11.06)		
G-CBLT	Mainair Blade 912	1315-0202-7-W1110		25. 4.02	B J Bader	(Taunton)	25. 5.08P
G-CBLU	Cameron C-90 Balloon (Hot Air)	10128		30. 4.02	A G Martin *"Harlequin"*	Bristol	5. 4.08A
G-CBLV	Flight Design CT2K	02-01-04-04		11. 4.02	A K Pickering	(Villefollett, Deux-Sèvres, France)	31. 3.06P
	(Assembled Pegasus Aviation with c/n 7886)						
G-CBLW	Raj Hamsa X'Air Falcon V2(1)	641		13. 3.02	R G Halliwell	Ince Blundell	30.10.08P
	(Built R R Hadley - pr.no.BMAA/HB/209)						
G-CBLX	Air Création 582(1)/Kiss 400	FL008		3. 4.02	J P Doswell	(St Dominick, Saltash)	30.10.08P
	(Built J H Hayday - pr.no.BMAA/HB/208 being Flylight kit comprising Trike s/n T02010 and Wing s/n A02013-2003)						
G-CBLY	Grob G109B	6403	D-KITZ (2)	12. 3.02	D A Smith tr G-CBLY Syndicate		23. 5.08E
			(F-WAQS)			Wing Farm, Longbridge Deverill	
G-CBLZ	Rutan LongEz	1046	F-PYYV	5. 6.02	S K Cockburn	Southend	22.11.08P
	(Built N W Ruston) (Lycoming O-235)						
G-CBMA	Raj Hamsa X'Air 582(10)	739		14. 2.02	A J Baker	Stoke, Isle of Grain	24.11.08P
	(Built K Angel - pr.no.BMAA/HB/204)						
G-CBMB	Cyclone AX2000 HKS	7894		18. 6.02	York Microlight Centre Ltd	Rufforth	24. 6.08P
G-CBMC	Cameron Z-105 Balloon (Hot Air)	10274		30. 4.02	The Balloon Company Ltd t/a First Flight		1. 8.08T
						Langford, Bristol	
					(Edward Ware Homes titles)		
G-CBMD	IAV-Bacau Yakovlev Yak-52	822710	RA-44460	4.11.02	R J Hunter	Headcorn	28.11.07P
			LY-AHE, DOSAAF 100 *(yellow)*				
G-CBME	Cessna F172M	F17201060	TF-FTV	28. 2.02	Skytrax Aviation Ltd	Derby	27. 4.08P
	(Built Reims Aviation SA)		TF-POP, SE-FZP				
G-CBMI	IAV-Bacau Yakovlev Yak-52	855907	LY-AOZ	24. 7.02	D P Holland	Tatenhill	16. 5.08P
			RA-02050, DOSAAF 107 *(blue) (Empire Test Pilots' School c/s)*				
G-CBMK	Cameron Z-120 Balloon (Hot Air)	10293		11. 4.02	G Davies	Thorney, Peterborough	16. 4.08A
G-CBML	de Havilland DHC-6-310 Twin Otter	695	C-FZSP	5. 6.02	Isles of Scilly Skybus Ltd	St Just	4. 6.08E
			HB-LSN, C-FZSP, TR-LZO, C-GJZK				
G-CBMM	Mainair Blade 912	1312-0202-7-W1107		9. 9.02	L E Donaldson	Headon Farm, Retford	14.10.07P
					(Noted 2.08)		
G-CBMO	Piper PA-28-180 Cherokee D	28-4806	ZS-ONK	16. 5.02	C Woodliffe	Bagby	16. 6.08E
			9J-RHN, N6391J				

G-CBMP	Cessna R182 Skylane RG II	R18201325	ZS-MWT N38MH, YV-2034P, N2286S	9. 4.02	Orman (Carrolls Farm) Ltd	Great Massingham	26. 9.08T
G-CBMR	Medway EclipseR	172/150		27. 3.02	D S Blofeld	Stoke, Isle of Grain	30. 6.08P
G-CBMS	Medway EclipseR	173/151		27. 3.02	R R Bagge *(Noted 1.06)*	Field Farm, Oakley	31.10.05P
G-CBMT	Robin DR.400-180 Régent	2538		3. 5.02	A C Williamson	Crowfield	12. 7.08E
G-CBMU	Whittaker MW6-S Fatboy Flyer PFA 164-13339 *(Built F J Brown)*			30. 4.02	F J Brown	Sackville Farm, Riseley	22.11.08P
G-CBMV	Cyclone Airsports Pegasus Quantum 15 7893 *(Rotax 582)*			3. 5.02	B Hamilton	Long Marston	12.10.08P
G-CBMW	Zenair CH.701UL STOL PFA 187-13788 *(Built C Long) (Jabiru 2200A)*			9. 4.02	I Park *(New owner 2.08)*	(Gretna)	17. 4.07P
G-CBMX	Air Création 582(1)/Kiss 400 FL009 *(Built D L Turner - pr.no.BMAA/HB/207 being Flylight kit comprising Trike s/n T02009 and Wing s/n A02012-2004)*			28. 3.02	D L Turner	(Sidcup)	7. 9.08P
G-CBMZ	Evektor EV-97 Eurostar PFA 315-13890 *(Built P Grenet and J C O'Donnell)*			12. 4.02	J C O'Donnell	Church Farm, Shotteswell	29. 7.08P
G-CBNA	Flight Design CT2K 02-01-06-04 *(Assembled Pegasus Aviation with c/n 7887)*			31. 5.02	D M Wood	Hook, Norton	16. 6.08P
G-CBNB	Eurocopter EC.120B Colibri	1040		8. 6.99	Arenberg Consultadoria e Servicos LDA	(Madeira, Portugal)	26. 7.08E
G-CBNC	Mainair Blade 912	1319-0402-7-W1114		17. 4.02	A C Rowlands	Dalscote, Northamptonshire	26. 4.08P
G-CBNF	Rans S-7 Courier *(Built T R Grief - pr.no.PFA 218-13762*	xxxx		12. 4.02	M Rockliff *(New owner 12.03)*	(Leeds)	
G-CBNG	Robin R2112 Alpha	180	PH-ROL F-GCAF	20. 5.02	B Scott and D J Wilson tr Solway Flyers Group	Carlisle	14. 8.08E
G-CBNI	Lindstrand LBL 90A Balloon (Hot Air)	857		16. 4.02	Cancer Research UK *(Cancer Research UK titles)* Bath		30. 3.08A
G-CBNJ	Raj Hamsa X'Air 912(1) *(Built M K Slaughter, J L Francis and M Hunt - pr.no.BMAA/HB/187)*	680		23. 4.02	M G Lynes	(East Woodhay, Newbury)	8. 7.08P
G-CBNL	Dyn'Aéro MCR-01 Club PFA 301A-13805 *(Built D H Wilson)*			12. 4.02	D H Wilson	Coal Aston	20. 9.08P
G-CBNM	North American P-51D-20-NA Mustang 122-31590 *(As ""463864/HL-W" in 78th Fighter Group USAAF c/s)*		SE-BKG 4X-AIM, Israeli DFAF 2338, Swedish AF Fv26158, 44-63864 *"Twilight Tear"*	29. 4.02	Patina Ltd	Duxford *(Operated The Fighter Collection)*	9. 7.08P
G-CBNO	CFM Streak Shadow *(Built D J Goldsmith - pr.no.PFA 206-13809)*	xxxx		8. 3.02	D J Goldsmith	(Crockham Hill, Edenbridge)	9.10.04P
G-CBNT	Cyclone Airsports Pegasus Quantum 15-912 7860			14. 5.02	B H Goldsmith	Clench Common	9. 7.08P
G-CBNU	Vickers Supermarine 361 Spitfire LF.IX CBAF IX 2115		Turkish AF ML411	27. 8.02	M Aldridge *(New owner 4.03)*	(Ashford)	
G-CBNV	Rans S-6-ES Coyote II 1000 1393 ES *(Built C W J Davis - pr.no.PFA 204-13817) (Rotax 582) (Tri-cycle u/c)*			23. 4.02	F H Cook	Chilbolton	14.11.08P
G-CBNW	Cameron N-105 Balloon (Hot Air)	10283		16. 5.02	C and J M Bailey t/a Bailey Balloons *(Bristol and West titles)*	Pill, Bristol	1. 6.08T
G-CBNX	Montgomerie-Bensen B 8MR PFA G/01A-1345 *(Built C Hewer) (Rotax 912-UL)*			26. 4.02	A C S M Hart	Farley Farm, Romsey	25. 4.08P
G-CBNY	Air Création 582(1)/Kiss 400 FL013 *(Built R Redman - pr.no.BMAA/HB/218 being Flylight kit comprising Trike s/n T02035 and Wing A02051-2047)*			30. 4.02	R Redman	(Grantham)	10. 6.08P
G-CBNZ	TEAM Hi-MAX 1700R PFA 272-13624 *(Built J J Penny)*			30. 4.02	A P S John	(Conderton, Tewkesbury)	15.11.08P
G-CBOA	Auster B 8 Agricola Series 1 AIRP/860 *(Built Airepair, New Zealand 1966 from spares using parts of ZK-BMN c/n B 106)*		ZK-BXO ZK-BMN	22. 4.02	C J Baker Carr Farm, Thorney, Newark *(Outer wings removed 1.05)*		
G-CBOC	Raj Hamsa X'Air 582(5) *(Built A J McAleer - pr.no.BMAA/HB/166) (Undercarriage struck trees Crocknagaran, Pomeroy 22. 6.05 and damaged)*	623		1. 5.02	A J McAleer	(Dungannon)	3. 4.06P
G-CBOE	Hawker Hurricane IIB R30040 *(Built Canadian Car and Foundry Co)*		RCAF 5487	24. 5.02	P J Tuplin (and P W Portelli) *(New owners 2.05)*	Thruxton	
G-CBOF	Europa Aviation Europa XS *(Built I W Ligertwood - pr.no.PFA 247-13462)*	431		1. 5.02	I W Ligertwood	Sleap	12. 2.08P
G-CBOG	Mainair Blade 912S	1309-0102-7-W1104		26. 3.02	J S Littler	(Standish)	9. 5 07P
G-CBOK	Rans S-6-ES Coyote II 1201.1426 *(Built C J Arthur - pr.no.PFA 204-13864) (Rotax 912-UL)*			19. 4.02	I Johnson	New Farm House, Great Oakley	30.10.08P
G-CBOM	Mainair Blade 912	1314-0202-7-W1109		30. 4.02	G Suckling	Graveley Hall Farm, Graveley	30. 4.08P
G-CBON	Cameron Bull-110 SS Balloon (Hot Air)	10261		14. 6.02	Stratos Ballooning GmbH and Co KG	Ennigerloh, Germany	26. 5.05A
G-CBOO	Mainair Blade 912S	1317-0302-7-W1112		4. 4.02	N J Holt	Weston Zoyland	15. 8.08P
G-CBOP	Avtech Jabiru UL-450 *(Built D W Batchelor - pr.no.PFA 274A-13611)*	0355		2. 5.02	D W Batchelor	Sandtoft	6. 3.07P
G-CBOR	Reims Cessna F172N Skyhawk II F17201656		PH-BOR PH-AXG (1)	28. 5.87	P Seville	Barton	24. 5.08E
G-CBOS	Rans S-6-ES Coyote II 1201.1428 *(Built R Skene - pr.no.PFA 204-13859) (Jabiru 2200A) (Tri-cycle u/c)*			8. 5.02	W Gillam	(Henstridge)	18. 6.07P
G-CBOT	Robinson R44 Raven	1194		11. 4.02	Helicopter One Ltd	Bournemouth	10. 5.08E
G-CBOU	Bensen-Parsons Two-Place Gyroplane PFA G/8-1311 *(Built R Collin)*			8. 5.02	R Collin and M S Sparkes	Kirkbride	6.11.08P
G-CBOV	Mainair Blade	1327-0502-7-W1122		16. 5.02	H D Lynch	(Knock, Fermoy, County Cork)	25. 6.08P
G-CBOW	Cameron Z-120 Balloon (Hot Air)	10302		7. 8.02	Associated Technologies Ltd Hook Norton Banbury *(Torex titles)*		26. 9.08A
G-CBOY	Cyclone Airsports Pegasus Quantum 15-912 7898			17. 4.02	I W Barlow	Mapperley, Nottingham	16. 4.08P
G-CBOZ	IAV-Bacau Yakovlev Yak-52	811308	LY-AOC DOSAAF 30	15.11.02	T M Knight	Headcorn	10. 5.08P
G-CBPC	Sportavia-Pützer RF5B Sperber	51013	OY-XKC	27. 6.02	J Bennett tr Lee RF5B Group	Lee-on-Solent	30.11.07E
G-CBPD	Comco Ikarus C42 FB UK 0112-6444 *(Built M L Robinson - pr.no.PFA 322-13863)*			14. 5.02	A Haslam tr Waxwing Group	Kirkbride	9. 4.08P
G-CBPE	SOCATA TB-10 Tobago	129	HB-EZR	13. 6.02	A F Welch	(Cambridge)	24. 5.08E
G-CBPG	The Balloon Works Firefly 7 Balloon (Hot Air) FS7-001		N9045C	14. 6.02	I Chadwick tr Balloon Preservation Flying Group	Partridge Green, Horsham	

G-CBPH	Lindstrand LBL 105A Balloon (Hot Air)	850		29. 5.02	Vastano Ivan	Firenze, Italy	18. 8.05A
G-CBPI	Piper PA-28R-201 Arrow	2844073	N53496	23. 5.02	Atsi Aviation Ltd	(Chalfont St Giles)	23. 7.08E
G-CBPL	TEAM Mini-MAX 93	PFA 186-13100		24. 5.02	K M Moores	(Boston)	
	(Built K M Moores)						
G-CBPM	Yakovlev Yak-50	812101	LY-ASG	10. 7.02	P W Ansell	North Weald	15. 7.08P
			DOSAAF 58 ?		"50" (black)		
G-CBPN	Thruster T 600N 450	0052-T600N-065		23. 5.02	J S Webb	Old Sarum	6.10.08P
G-CBPP	Avtech Jabiru UL-450	0359		23. 4.02	D G Bennett	Headon Farm, Retford	1. 8.08P
	(Built J N Pearson - pr.no.PFA 274A-13607)						
G-CBPR	Avtech Jabiru UL-450	xxxx		16. 5.02	F B Hall	Bodmin	12. 4.06P
	(Built P L Riley and F B Hall - pr.no.PFA 274A-13492)						
G-CBPU	Raj Hamsa X'Air R100(3)	442		27. 5.02	G Humphrey tr X'Air Group	Long Marston	23.10.08P
	(Built M S McCrudden and W P Byrne - pr.no.BMAA/HB/123)						
G-CBPV	Zenair CH.601UL Zodiac	PFA 162A-13689		28. 5.02	R D Barnard	Calton Moor Farm, Ashbourne	16. 9.08P
	(Built R D Barnard)						
G-CBPW	Lindstrand LBL 105A Balloon (Hot Air)	863		12. 6.02	Flying Pictures Ltd	Chilbolton, Stockbridge	2. 7.04A
					(Samsung titles)		
G-CBPY	IAV-Bacau Yakovlev Yak-52	800708	RA-44474	8. 1.03	Lyttondale Associates Ltd	Sherburn-in-Elmet	12. 2.08P
			LY-AMP, DOSAAF 52		(Also carries "52" in red and white DOSAAF c/s)		
G-CBPZ	Ultramagic N-300 Balloon (Hot Air)	300/04		25. 6.02	Skyview Ballooning Ltd t/a Kent Ballooning	Ashford	28. 5.08T
G-CBRB	Ultramagic S-105 Balloon (Hot Air)	105/103		19. 6.02	I S Bridge	Shrewsbury	11. 4.08A
G-CBRC	Jodel D 18	PFA 169-11408		31. 5.02	B W Shaw	Waterstones Farm, Newby Wiske	
	(Built B W Shaw)				(Noted 2.08)		
G-CBRD	Jodel D 18	PFA 169-11484		31. 5.02	J D Haslam	Waterstones Farm, Newby Wiske	29. 8.08P
	(Built J D Haslam)						
G-CBRE	Mainair Blade 912	1330-0602-7-W1125		19. 6.02	R G McCron	Broadmeadow Farm. Hereford	13. 6.08P
G-CBRF	Comco Ikarus C42 FB100 VLA	0202-6454		7. 6.02	T W Gale	Trim, County Meath	14.11.08P
	(Built T W Gale - pr.no.PFA 322-13900)						
G-CBRG	Cessna 560XL Citation Excel	560-5266	N5245D	13. 8.02	Queensway Aviation Ltd	Belfast International	14. 8.08T
G-CBRH	IAV-Bacau Yakovlev Yak-52	844815	LY-ALO	6. 9.02	B M Gwynnett	Haverfordwest	29. 2.08P
			DOSAAF 135				
G-CBRJ	Mainair Blade 912	1321-0502-7-W1116		24. 4.02	R W Janion	Humberside	30. 5.08P
	(Rotax 582-2V)						
G-CBRK	Ultramagic M-77 Balloon (Hot Air)	77/212		8. 7.02	R T Revel	Great Missenden	6. 7.08P
					(UltraMAGIC Balloons titles)		
G-CBRL	IAV-Bacau Yakovlev Yak-52	833708	RA-44468	2.12.02	P S Mirams tr Norbert Group	Biggin Hill	18. 1.08P
			LY-AOX, DOSAAF 122?				
G-CBRM	Mainair Blade	1326-0502-7-W1121		19. 6.02	M H Levy	(Northwich)	25.10.08P
G-CBRO	Robinson R44 Raven	1221		17. 6.02	R D Jordan	Cranfield	8. 7.08E
G-CBRP	IAV-Bacau Yakovlev Yak-52	822603	RA-02041	22. 9.04	R J Pinnock	Gloucestershire	18. 1.07P
			LY-AID, DOSAAF 105				
G-CBRR	Evektor EV-97 Eurostar	PFA 315-13919		18. 6.02	S J Galloway tr G-CBRR Group	Redhill	25.10.08P
	(Built C M Theakstone)						
G-CBRT	Murphy Elite	PFA 232-13461		19. 6.02	R W Baylie	(Hailsham)	
	(Built R W Baylie) (Wilksch WAM-120)				(Flying 11.07)		
G-CBRU	IAV-Bacau Yakovlev Yak-52	888911	RA-02042	21. 1.03	G M Smith and J E Pasquale	Rochester	29. 6.08P
			DOSAAF 98 (yellow)		(As "42" (red) in Soviet Air Force c/s)		
G-CBRV	Cameron C-90 Balloon (Hot Air)	10323		31. 7.02	C J Teall	Salford, Chipping Norton	5. 8.08
G-CBRW	Aerostar Yakovlev Yak-52	9111415	RA-44464	4. 2.03	M A Gainza	White Waltham	20. 4.08P
			DOSAAF 50		(As "50" in DOSAAF c/s)		
G-CBRX	Zenair CH.601UL Zodiac	PFA 162A-13833		21. 6.02	J B Marshall	Eddsfield, Octon Lodge Farm, Thwing	9. 5.08P
	(Built J B Marshall)						
G-CBRY	Cyclone Airsports Pegasus Quik	7902		24. 6.02	Cyclone Airsports t/a Pegasus Aviation		
						(Elm Tree Farm, Manton)	
G-CBRZ	Air Création 582(1)/Kiss 400	FL015	(EI-)	21. 6.02	J J Ryan		
			G-CBRZ			Ardenagh Great, Taghmon, County Wexford	16. 6.08P
	(Built B Chantry - pr.no.BMAA/HB/226 being Flylight kit comprising Trike s/n T02052 and s/n Wing A02086-2080)						
G-CBSD	Westland SA.341C Gazelle HT.2	1045	XW854	6. 6.02	Mexsky Ltd (As "XW854" in RN c/s)	Earls Colne	20. 2.08P
G-CBSF	Westland SA.341C Gazelle HT.2	1924	ZB647	6. 6.02	Falcon Aviation Ltd	(Tileshurst, Reading)	
					(As "ZB647:40")		
G-CBSH	Westland SA.341G Gazelle HT.3	1344	XX406	28.10.02	Alltask Ltd (As "XX406:P" in RAF c/s)	Rochester	17. 4.08P
G-CBSI	Westland SA.341G Gazelle HT.3	1736	XZ934	6. 6.02	P S Unwin	Bourne Park, Hurstbourne Tarrant	24. 7.08P
					(As "XZ934:U" in RAF red and white c/s)		
G-CBSK	Westland SA.341G Gazelle HT.3	1914	ZB627	6. 6.02	P J Whitaker and B W Stuart tr Falcon Flying Group		
						Bourne Park, Hurstbourne Tarrant	11.12.08P
					(As "ZB627:A" in RAF c/s)		
G-CBSL	IAV-Bacau Yakovlev Yak-52	822013	RA-44534	13. 1.03	N and A D Barton	Leicester	20. 8.08P
G-CBSM	Mainair Blade 912	1331-0602-7-W1126		10. 5.02	Mainair Sports Ltd	Rochdale	
G-CBSO	Piper PA-28-181 Cherokee Archer II		D-EOFL	18. 7.02	Archer One Ltd	Lydd	12. 8.08E
		28-7690376	N9595N				
G-CBSP	Cyclone Airsports Pegasus Quantum 15-912	7903		9. 7.02	D S Carstairs	Perth	7. 7.08P
G-CBSR	IAV-Bacau Yakovlev Yak-52	877913	LY-AQB	10. 7.02	L Olivier tr Pegasus U2W	Wevelgem, Belgium	20. 8.08P
			Ukraine AF 10 (yellow), DOSAAF 100 (yellow?)				
G-CBSS	IAV-Bacau Yakovlev Yak-52	833707	RA-44475	19. 2.03	E J F Verhellen	Namur, Belgium	28 .3.08P
			LY-AIJ, DOSAAF 121?				
G-CBSU	Avtech Jabiru UL-450	xxxx		15. 7.02	P K Sutton	Coventry	23. 6.05P
	(Built P K Sutton - pr.no.PFA 274A-13812)				(Noted engineless 6.05)		
G-CBSV	Montgomerie-Bensen B 8MR	PFA G/01A-1344		1. 7.02	J A McGill	Damyn's Hall, Upminster	17. 2.08P
	(Built J A McGill) (Rotax912-UL)						
G-CBSX	Air Création Clipper/Kiss	FL014		3. 7.02	G A G Parnell	Sywell	10. 7.07P
	(Built N Hartley - pr.no.BMAA/HB/225 being Flylight kit comprisong Trike s/n T02051 and Wing s/n A02085-2079) (Noted 10.07)						
G-CBSZ	Mainair Blade 912S	1334-0602-7-W1129		6. 8.02	D M Newton	Easter Balgillo Farm, Finavon	1. 3.07P
G-CBTB	III Sky Arrow 650 T	PFA 298-13832		25. 6.02	D A and J A S T Hood	Fenland	12.11.08P
	(Built D A .and J A S T Hood)						

G-CBTD	Cyclone Airsports Pegasus Quantum 15-912	7904		9. 7.02	D Baillie	Glassonby	19. 7.08P
G-CBTE	Mainair Blade 912S	1328-0602-7-W1123		10. 7.02	K J Miles	St Michaels	10. 8.08P
G-CBTG	Comco Ikarus C42 FB UK	PFA 322-13849		25. 6.02	R McLaughlin	(Letterkenny, County Donegal)	10. 4.08P
	(Built J A Way and R Bonnett)						
G-CBTK	Raj Hamsa X'Air 582(5)	589		9. 7.02	A R Cook	Lower Upham Farm, Chiseldon	18.11.08P
	(Built C D Wood - pr.no.BMAA/HB/168)						
G-CBTL	Monnett Moni	PFA 142-11558		8. 7.02	G Dawes	(Dover)	
	(Built G Dawes)						
G-CBTM	Mainair Blade	1322-0502-7-W1117		2. 7.02	D A A Hewitt	Headon Farm, Retford	14. 8.08P
	(Rotax 582)						
G-CBTN	Piper PA-31 Navajo C	31-7812073	OO-VLH	7. 8.02	Durban Aviation Services Ltd	Biggin Hill	19.10.07E
			N27636				
G-CBTO	Rans S-6-ES Coyote II	1201.1427		16. 7.02	C G Deeley	Sittles Farm, Alrewas	8.11.08P
	(Built B J Mould and M Walsh - pr.no.PFA 204-13910) (Rotax 912-UL) (Tri-cycle u/c)						
G-CBTR	Lindstrand LBL 120A Balloon (Hot Air)	733		22. 7.02	R H Etherington	Siena, Italy	13. 8.05A
G-CBTS	Gloster Gamecock replica	GA 97		17. 7.02	Retro Track and Air (UK) Ltd	(Dursley)	
	(Built Retro Track and Air (UK) Ltd)						
G-CBTT	Piper PA-28-181 Cherokee Archer II		G-BFMM	22. 7.02	Citicourt Aviation Ltd	Denham	4.10.07E
		28-7890127	N47735				
G-CBTW	Mainair Blade 912	1329-0602-7-W1124		20. 6.02	D Hyatt	Stoke, Isle of Grain	1. 8.08P
G-CBTX	Denney Kitfox Model 2	PFA 172-11721		19. 7.02	G I Doake	(Craigavon, County Armagh)	
	(Built W M Farrell and G I Doake)						
G-CBTZ	Cyclone Airsports Pegasus Quantum 15-912	7909		29. 7.02	J Waite	(Farnham Common, Slough)	15.10.08P
G-CBUA	Extra EA.230	009	N230KR	5. 9.02	R Howarth	White Waltham	28. 3.08P
			N286PA				
G-CBUC	Raj Hamsa X'Air 582(5)	779		22. 7.02	M N Watson	Sackville Lodge, Riseley	7. 4.08P
	(Built A P Fenn and D R Lewis - pr.no.BMAA/HB/228)						
G-CBUD	Cyclone Airsports Pegasus Quantum 15-912	7906		30. 7.02	G N S Farrant	Drayton Manor. Drayton St Leonard	21. 6.08P
G-CBUE	Ultramagic N-250 Balloon (Hot Air)	250/25		5.12.02	Elinore French Ltd t/a Imagination Balloon Flights		
						Longframlington	29. 2.08T
G-CBUF	Flight Design CT2K	02-04-04-18		26. 7.02	B G Cox	Hunsdon	13.11.06P
	(Assembled Pegasus Aviation with c/n 7901)				*(Engine failure at High Wych 10.6.06 with major damage)*		
G-CBUG	Tecnam P92-EM Echo	PFA 318-13662		20. 6.01	J J Bodnarec	Hawksbridge Farm, Oxenhope	15. 5.08P
	(Built R C Mincik) (Rotax 912-ULS) (Marked as "P92S")						
					(Directional control lost landing Oxenhope 1. 9.07, struck earth bank and substantially damaged)		
G-CBUH	Westland Scout AH.1	F9475	XP849	5. 8.02	C J Marsden	(Thruxton)	21. 8.08P
					(Wears old Raspberry Ripple scheme)		
G-CBUI	Westland Wasp HAS.1	F9590	XT420	5. 8.02	BN Helicopters Ltd	Bembridge	4. 2.08P
					(As "XT420:606" in RN c/s)		
G-CBUJ	Raj Hamsa X'Air 582(10)	651		1. 8.02	J T Laity tr G-CBUJ Flying Group	Kemble	21. 8.07P
	(Built J T Laity - pr.no.BMAA/HB/212)						
G-CBUK	Van's RV-6A	PFA 181A-13614		25. 7.02	P G Greenslade	(Billingshurst)	14.11.08P
	(Built P G Greenslade)						
G-CBUN	Barker Charade	PFA 166-13520		31. 7.02	T Coldwell and D R Wilkinson		
	(Built P E Barker) (Jabiru 2200A)					Sackville Lodge, Riseley	7. 9.08P
G-CBUO	Cameron O-90 Balloon (Hot Air)	3353	CC-PMH	15. 8.02	W J Treacy and P M Smith	Trim, County Meath	6. 7.08A
G-CBUP	Magni M-16 Tandem Trainer	SA-M16-10M	ZU-AIH	28. 8.02	J S Firth	Burn	12. 6.08P
	(Built R W Husband - pr.no.PFA G/12-1346)						
G-CBUR	Zenair CH.601UL Zodiac	PFA 162A-13891		19. 7.02	N A Jack	Insch	18. 9.03P
	(Built R J Kelly)				*(On rebuild 2007)*		
G-CBUS	Cyclone Airsports Pegasus Quantum 15	7916		29. 8.02	J Liddiard	Yatesbury	19.11.08P
	(Rotax 582)						
G-CBUU	Cyclone Airsports Pegasus Quantum 15-912	7917		27. 8.02	I D Town	Longacre Farm, Sandy	27. 8.07P
G-CBUW	Cameron Z-133 Balloon (Hot Air)	10322		29. 8.02	Balloon School (International) Ltd		
						Colhook Common, Petworth	4. 7.08T
G-CBUX	Cyclone AX2000	7918		2.10.02	R Thompson	(Sawbridgeworth)	27. 8.08P
	(Rotax 582)						
G-CBUY	Rans S-6-ES Coyote II	0302.1436		13. 8.02	K R Crawley	Rufforth	20.12.07P
	(Built S C Jackson - pr.no.PFA 204-13954) (Rotax 582) (Tri-cycle u/c)						
G-CBUZ	Cyclone Airsports Pegasus Quantum 15	7907		31. 7.02	D G Seymour	Craysmarsh Farm, Melksham	22. 8.08P
	(Rotax 503)						
G-CBVA	Thruster T 600N 450	0082-T600N-068		14. 8.02	D J Clingan (Noted 2.08)	Derryogue	6.12.05P
G-CBVB	Robin R2120U	365		26. 7.02	Cardiff Academy of Aviation Ltd	Cardiff	8. 6.08T
G-CBVC	Raj Hamsa X'Air 582(5)	792		15. 8.02	M J Male	Dunkeswell	15.12.07P
	(Built M J Male - pr.no.BMAA/HB/230)						
G-CBVD	Cameron C-60 Balloon (Hot Air)	10338		31.10.02	Phoenix Balloons Ltd *"Popeye"*	Bristol	20. 4.08
G-CBVE	Raj Hamsa X'Air Falcon 912(1)	766		19. 8.02	P K Bennett	Stoke, Isle of Grain	15. 3.08P
	(Built D F Hughes - pr.no.BMAA/HB/229)						
G-CBVF	Murphy Maverick	PFA 259-12876		19. 8.02	H A Leek	(Scalford, Melton Mowbray)	
	(Built J Hopkinson)				*(New owner 11.07)*		
G-CBVG	Mainair Blade 912S	1338-0802-7-W1133		27. 8.02	A M Buchanan	Kirkbride	10. 2.08P
G-CBVH	Lindstrand LBL 120A Balloon (Hot Air)	870		2. 9.02	Line Packaging and Display Ltd	Gillingham, Kent	9. 6.08A
G-CBVI	Robinson R44 Raven	1259		21. 8.02	Happy Chopper Ltd	Hawarden	15. 9.08E
G-CBVK	Schroeder Fire Balloons G Balloon (Hot Air)	408	D-OVHS	30. 9.02	S Travaglia t/a Idea Balloon	Fiorentino, Italy	
G-CBVL	Robinson R22 Beta II	3353	N71650	23. 8.02	Beechview Aviation Ltd	Toome	26. 9.08E
G-CBVM	Evektor EV-97 Eurostar	PFA 315-13932		8. 8.02	R J Butler	Guy Lane, Waverton	6.11.08P
	(Built J Cunliffe and A Costello)						
G-CBVN	Mainair Sports Pegasus Quik	7919		27. 8.02	C Kearney	Ince Blundell	20.12.07P
G-CBVO	Raj Hamsa X'Air 582(5)	627		27. 8.02	C J Burley	Sackville Lodge, Riseley	5. 6.08P
	(Built W E Richards - pr.no.BMAA/HB/227)						
G-CBVR	Best Off Sky Ranger 912(2)	SKRxxxx209		6. 9.02	S H Lunney	Ince Blundell	18. 5.08P
	(Built R H J Jenkins - pr.no.BMAA/HB/231)						
G-CBVS	Best Off Sky Ranger 912(2)	SKR0207215		19. 8.02	S C Cornock	(Streethay Farm, Lichfield)	17. 7.08P
	(Built S C Cornock - pr.no.BMAA/HB/234)						

G-CBVT	IAV-Bacau Yakovlev Yak-52	9010305	LY-AGR	19. 9.02	Lancair Espana SL	(Alicante, Spain)	14. 2.08P
	Ukraine AF 02 (yellow), DOSAAF 02 (yellow)						
G-CBVU	Piper PA-28R-200 Cherokee Arrow	28R-7135007	ZS-RER N11C	12. 9.02	E W Guess (Holdings) Ltd	Spanhoe	22.12.07E
G-CBVV	Cameron N-120 Balloon (Hot Air)	10331		13. 9.02	John Aimo Balloons SAS (Warsteiner titles)	Mondovi, Italy	19. 8.05A
G-CBVX	Cessna 182P Skylane	18263419	ZS-IYZ N9653G	16.12.02	P and A de Weerdt	Old Sarum	26. 6.08E
G-CBVY	Comco Ikarus C42 FB UK	0112-6436		4. 9.02	M J Hendra and R Gossage	Brook Farm, Pilling	3. 4.08P
	(Built M J Hendra and R Gossage - pr.no.PFA 322-13835)						
G-CBVZ	Flight Design CT2K	02-05-06-04		19. 9.02	A N D Arthur	Denham	29. 7.08P
	(Assembled Pegasus Aviation Ltd with c/n "9714" - this should be "7914")						
G-CBWA	Flight Design CT2K	02-06-01-04		11.10.02	C A Hasell and D J Collier tr G-CBWA Group		
	(Assembled Pegasus AviationLtd with c/n 7921)				(Noted 2.08) Lower Mountpleasant Farm, Chatteris		4.11.07P
G-CBWB	Piper PA-34-200T Seneca II	34-7770188	N2495Q	31.10.02	Fairoaks Airport Ltd	Fairoaks	17.1 .08E
G-CBWD	Piper PA-28-161 Warrior III	2842160	N5357G	1.10.02	Fleetwash Ltd	Blackbushe	16.10.07E
G-CBWE	Evektor EV-97 Eurostar	PFA 315-13958		16. 9.02	J and C W Hood	Longframlington	28.10.08P
	(Built E Clarke)						
G-CBWG	Evektor EV-97A Eurostar	03-1162		17. 9.02	A B Cameron and B Waterson tr Southside Flyers		
	(Built M Rhodes - pr.no.PFA 315-13918)					Prestwick	14.11.08P
G-CBWI	Thruster T 600N 450	0102-T600N-071		20. 9.02	Tina Lee	Longacre Farm, Sandy	17.10.08P
G-CBWJ	Thruster T 600N 450 Sprint	0092-T600N-069		20. 9.02	D Cioffi tr Voliamo Group	Broad Farm, Eastbourne	18 .1.08P
G-CBWK	Ultramagic H-77 Balloon (Hot Air)	77/218		4.11.02	H C Peel	Worcester	14. 9.08P
G-CBWM	Mainair Blade 912	1339-0802-7-W1134		22. 8.02	G Homan	(Appleton, Warrington)	19. 6.08P
	(Rotax 503) (Built with major components of G-BZUM)						
G-CBWN	Campbell Cricket Mk.6	PFA G/16-1328		24. 9.02	P G Rawson	Crosland Moor	7. 5.08P
	(Built G J Layzell) (Marked as "Layzell AV-18A")						
G-CBWO	RotorWay Executive 162F	6597		24. 9.02	Handyvalue Ltd	Street Farm, Takeley	14. 2.09P
	(Built S P Tetley) (RotorWay RI 162F)						
G-CBWP	Europa Aviation Europa	233		1.10.02	T W Greaves	(Gardon Field, Hull)	15. 4.08P
	(Built T W Greaves - pr.no.PFA 247-12930) (Monowheel u/c)				("Flying Yorkshireman" on fin)		
G-CBWS	Whittaker MW6 Merlin	PFA 164-12863		7.10.02	D W McCormack	(Atherstone)	
	(Built D W McCormack)						
G-CBWU	RotorWay Executive 162F	6416		4.10.02	F A Cavaciuti t/a Usk Valley Trout Farm		
	(Built F A Cavciuti) (RotorWay RI 162F)					Street Farm, Takeley	17.12.08P
G-CBWV	Falconar F-12A Cruiser	PFA 22-13904		7.10.02	A Ackland	(Reading)	
	(Built A Ackland)						
G-CBWW	Best Off Sky Ranger 912(2)	SKRxxxx210		30. 8.02	S H and R L Tosswill	Kirkbride	9.11.08P
	(Built R L and S H Tosswill - pr.no.BMAA/HB/232)						
G-CBWX	Slingsby T 67M-260 Firefly	2282	G-7-194	11.10.02	Slingsby Aviation Ltd	Wombleton	10.12.05T
G-CBWY	Raj Hamsa X'Air 582(6)	775		17.10.02	G C Linley	Eastbach Farm, Coleford	9. 4.08P
	(Built T Collins - pr.no.BMAA/HB/244)						
G-CBWZ	Robinson R22 Beta II	3101	N141DC	23.10.02	Plane Talking Ltd	Blackbushe	15.11.07E
G-CBXA	Raj Hamsa X'Air 582(5)	790		18.10.02	A J Sharratt	Sackville Lodge, Riseley	4. 3.08P
	(Built N Stevenson-Guy - pr.no.BMAA/HB/245)						
G-CBXC	Comco Ikarus C42 FB UK	PFA 322-13955		23.10.02	B J Mould	Halfpenny Green	29. 2.08P
	(Built A R Lloyd)						
G-CBXD	Bell 206L-3 LongRanger III	51328	D-HAUA N21AH, N21830	22.10.02	Whirlybird Charters Ltd-Automotive and General Supply Co Ltd	Stapleford	9. 2.08E
G-CBXE	Reality Easy Raider J2.2(2)	0006		22. 8.02	A Appleby	(Hailsham)	
	(Built A Appleby - pr.no.BMAA/HB/198)						
G-CBXF	Reality Easy Raider J2.2(2)	0001		19.11.02	F Colman	Eshott	12. 7.07P
	(Built F Colman - pr.no.BMAA/HB/196) (Forced landed and overturned in cornfield Seaton Delaval, Newcastle 3. 6.07 with substantial damage)						
G-CBXG	Thruster T 600N 450 Sprint	0112-T600N-073		29.10.02	K Maxwell tr Newtownards Microlight Group		
						Newtownards	6. 8.08P
G-CBXH	Thruster T 600N 450 Sprint	0122-T600N-075		29.10.02	Airbourne Aviation Ltd	Popham	22. 4.08P
G-CBXJ	Cessna 172S Skyhawk SP	172S8125	N2391J	30.10.02	Caernarfon Airworld Ltd	Caernarfon	16. 1.08E
G-CBXK	Robinson R22 Mariner	2302M	N3052P LQ-BLD, N80524	4.11.02	Helicentre Liverpool Ltd	Liverpool	31.10.07E
G-CBXM	Mainair Blade	1335-0802-7-W1130		19. 8.02	B A Coombe	(Billingshurst)	21. 9.08P
G-CBXN	Robinson R22 Beta II	3385		11.11.02	N M Pearson	Bristol	29.11.07E
G-CBXR	Raj Hamsa X'Air Falcon 582(1)	612		11.11.02	A R Rhodes	Kirkbride	2.10.08P
	(Built J F Heath - pr.no..BMAA/HB/224)						
G-CBXS	Best Off Sky Ranger J2.1(1)	SKRxxxx246		13.11.02	C J Erith	Lower Wasing Farm, Brimpton	
	(Built C J Erith - pr.no.BMAA/HB/248)				(Noted 5.07 less wings)		
G-CBXT	Westland SA.341G Gazelle HT.3	1191	XW898	26. 9.02	C D Evans and R Paskey (As "XW898:G" in RN c/s)		
					(Baxterley, Atherstone and Tamworth)		18. 6.08P
G-CBXU	TEAM Mini-MAX 91A	PFA 186-13037		13.11.02	C D Hatcher	Bakersfield	27. 8.08P
	(Built T J Shaw)						
G-CBXV	Mainair Blade	1343-1002-7-W1138		4.10.02	S E Harper	Priory Farm, Tibenham	13. 1.08P
G-CBXW	Europa Aviation Europa XS	494		18.11.02	R G Fairall	Redhill	
	(Built R G Fairall - pr.no.PFA 247-13674) (Monowheel u/c)						
G-CBXZ	Rans S-6-ESN Coyote II	0302.1438		20.11.02	D Tole	Long Marston	12. 4.05P
	(Built D Tole - pr.no.PFA 204-13988) (Rotax 582)				(Noted 4.06)		
G-CBYB	RotorWay Executive 162F	6623		20.11.02	T Clark t/a Clark Contracting	(Amersham)	
	(Built T Clark) (RotorWay RI 162F)						
G-CBYC	Cameron Z-275 Balloon (Hot Air)	10342		20. 3.03	The Balloon Company Ltd t/a First Flight		
					(Park Furnishers titles)	Langford, Bristol	6. 4.08T
G-CBYD	Rans S-6-ESA Coyote II	1201.1429		21.11.02	R Burland	Perth	18. 1.08P
	(Built R Burland - pr.no.PFA 204-13871) (Rotax 912)						
G-CBYE	Cyclone Airsports Pegasus Quik	7933		27. 1.03	C E Morris	Enstone	23. 2.08P
G-CBYF	Mainair Blade	1349-1202-7-W1144		2. 1.03	C P Lemon	(Chorley)	7. 6.08P
G-CBYH	Aeroprakt A22 Foxbat	PFA 317-13902		2.12.02	G C Moore tr G-CBYH Foxbat Group		
	(Built G C Moore and P C de-Ville)					Otherton, Cannock	1. 5.08P
	(Crashed Otherton 5.7.04 and stripped-out remains dumped Chirk 5.05: rebuilt 2005						

G-CBYI	Cyclone Airsports Pegasus Quantum 15	7931		2. 1.03	J M Hardy	Deenethorpe	8. 2.08P
	(Rotax 503)						
G-CBYJ	Steen Skybolt	PFA 064-13354		2.12.02	F G Morris	Newtownards	26. 7.08P
	(Built F G Morris)						
G-CBYM	Mainair Blade	1323-0502-7-W1118		13. 9.02	A Clarke	Rochdale	27. 4.07P
	(Rotax 582)				(Noted 10.07)		
G-CBYN	Europa Aviation Europa XS	518		5.12.02	A B Milne	Lower Wasing Farm, Brimpton	31. 8.08P
	(Built A B Milne - pr.no.PFA 247-13751) (Tri-gear u/c)						
G-CBYO	Cyclone Airsports Pegasus Quik	7928		5.12.02	P F Mayo and C J Roper	East Fortune	2.12.07P
G-CBYP	Whittaker MW6-S LW Fatboy Flyer	PFA 164-13131		6.12.02	R J Grainger	(Sywell)	6.11.06P
	(Built R J Grainger)						
G-CBYS	Lindstrand LBL 21A Balloon (Hot Air)	156		17.12.02	B M Reed	Paizay Le Sec, France	5. 4.08A
G-CBYT	Thruster T 600N 450	0102-T600N-072		10.10.02	B E Smith	Eshott	8.11.08P
G-CBYU	Piper PA-28-161 Warrior III	2842173	N53606	12. 2.03	Stapleford Flying Club Ltd	Stapleford	19. 2.08E
G-CBYV	Cyclone Airsports Pegasus Quantum 15-912	7920		19. 9.02	A R Vincent	Chiltern Park, Wallingford	11.11.08P
G-CBYW	Hatz CB-1	PFA 143-13710		16. 1.03	T A Hinton	Doynton	19. 9.07P
	(Built T A Hinton)						
G-CBYX	Bell 206B-3 JetRanger III	480	HB-ZBX	5. 3.03	Sky Charter UK Ltd	Manston	20. 7.08E
			N203WB, C-GRGP, N2502M				
G-CBYY	Robinson R44 Raven	1250	N71837	11. 9.02	Helicopter Training and Hire Ltd	Newtownards	10.10.07E
G-CBYZ	Tecnam P92-EA Echo-Super	PFA 318A-13984		17.12.02	B Weaver	(Osmington, Weymouth)	12. 8.08P
	(Built M Rudd)						
G-CBZA	Mainair Blade	1344-1002-7-W1139		28.10.02	R K Johnson	(Darnhall, Winsford)	12. 3.08P
G-CBZB	Mainair Blade	1346-1102-7-W1141		6.12.02	A Bennion	Arclid Green, Sandbach	7. 2.08P
G-CBZD	Mainair Blade	1348-1102-7-W1143		12.12.02	G F Jones	Mill Farm, Shifnal	24. 7.08P
G-CBZE	Robinson R44 Clipper	1276		12.12.02	Alps (Scotland) Ltd	(Kilwinning)	4. 2.08E
G-CBZF	Robinson R22 Beta II	3393	N71878	6.12.02	J Drake	(Knebworth)	4. 5.08E
G-CBZG	Rans S-6-ES Coyote II	1201.1430		9. 1.03	S Bayes	Bagby	21. 5.08P
	(Built N McKenzie - pr.no.PFA 204-13894) (Jabiru 2200) (Tri-cycle u/c)						
G-CBZH	Cyclone Airsports Pegasus Quik	7934		30. 1.03	G M Yule and M Bond		
						Broadmeadow Farm, Hereford	3. 9.08P
G-CBZI	RotorWay Executive 162F	6718		3. 1.03	T D Stock	Street Farm, Takeley	
	(Built T Stock) (RotorWay RI 162F)				(Noted 2.08)		
G-CBZJ	Lindstrand LBL 25A Cloudhopper Balloon (Hot Air)			9. 1.03	J L and T J Hilditch t/a Pegasus Ballooning		
		892			(Lindstrand Balloons titles)	Southwick, Brighton	5. 4.08A
G-CBZK	Robin DR.400-180 Régent	2543		12. 2.03	R A Fleming (Noted 12.07)	Breighton	17. 4.07E
G-CBZL	Westland SA.341D Gazelle HT.3	WA2010	ZB629	17. 1.03	Armstrong Aviation Ltd	Kirkbride	25. 8.04P
	(As "ZB629" in RAF c/s) (Struck power cables landing Mouswald near Dumfries 22.11.03 and substantially damaged)						
G-CBZM	Avtech Jabiru SPL-450	xxxx		2. 1.03	M E Ledward	Old Sarum	27.11.08P
	(Built M E Ledward - pr.no.PFA 274A-13827)						
G-CBZN	Rans S-6-ES Coyote II	0600.1374		6. 1.03	A James	Otherton, Cannock	12. 6.07P
	(Built A James - pr.no.PFA 204-13652) (Rotax 582) (Tri-cycle u/c)						
G-CBZP	Hawker Fury 1	41H-67550	SAAF??	2. 4.03	Historic Aircraft Collection Ltd	(Duxford)	
					(On rebuild 2008)		
G-CBZR	Piper PA-28R-201 Arrow	2837029	EC-IJX	13. 1.03	Plane Talking Ltd	Bournemouth	24. 2.08E
			N175ND		(Operated Cabair)		
G-CBZS	Lynden Aurora	PFA 313-13534		13. 1.03	J Lynden	Brook Farm, Pilling	10. 4.08P
	(Built J Lynden)						
G-CBZT	Cyclone Airsports Pegasus Quik	7936		6. 1.03	A P Portsmouth	(Gateshead)	8. 2.08P
G-CBZU	Lindstrand LBL 180A Balloon (Hot Air)	877		13. 1.03	European Balloon Co Ltd	Great Missenden	14. 1.08T
G-CBZV	Ultramagic S-130 Balloon (Hot Air)	130/36		5. 3.03	P Goldschmidt	San Casciano, Italy	4. 4.08T
G-CBZW	Zenair CH.701UL STOL	PFA 187-13731		13. 1.03	T M Stiles	(Heathfield)	14.11.08P
	(Built T M Stiles)						
G-CBZX	Dyn'Aéro MCR-01 ULC	221		15. 1.03	A C N Freeman and M P Wilson	Bournemouth	7. 4.08P
	(Built S L Morris - pr.no.PFA 301B-13957)						
G-CBZY	Flylight Doodle Bug-Target	DB022		22.11.02	A I Calderhead-Lea	(Basildon)	
G-CBZZ	Cameron Z-275 Balloon (Hot Air)	10346		12. 2.03	A C K Rawson and J J Rudoni	Stafford	29. 3.08T
					t/a Wickers World Hot Air Balloon Company		

G-CCAA - G-CCZZ

G-CCAB	Mainair Blade	1345-1002-7-W1140		28. 1.03	A J Morris	Sutton Meadows	3. 3.08P
G-CCAC	Evektor EV-97A Eurostar	PFA 315-13979		26.11.02	J S Holden	Wadswick Manor Farm, Corsham	16. 3.08P
	(Built P J Ladd and J S Holden)				"Slightly Dangerous"		
G-CCAD	Cyclone Airsports Pegasus Quik	7924		3.12.02	E G Cartwright	Mapperley, Nottingham	28. 3.08P
G-CCAE	Avtech Jabiru UL-450	xxxx		17. 1.03	M P and R A Wells	Croft Farm, Defford	23. 7.08P
	(Built C E Daniels - pr.no.PFA 274A-13938)						
G-CCAF	Best Off Sky Ranger 912(1)	SKRxxxx212		28.11.02	D W and M.L Squire	(Hewas Water, St Austell)	
	(Built D W Squire - pr.no.BMAA/HB/235)						
G-CCAG	Mainair Blade 912	1350-1202-7-W1145		22.11.02	W Cope	(Warslow, Buxton)	26. 1.07P
G-CCAH	Magni M-16C Tandem Trainer	16-06-3494		19. 6.06	Magni Gyro Ltd	(Waddington, Clitheroe)	
	(Rotax 914)				(Noted NEC Birmingham 11.07)		
G-CCAK	Zenair CH.601HD Zodiac	PFA 162-13469		11.12.02	A Kinmond	(Blairgowrie)	
	(Built A Kinmond)						
G-CCAL	Tecnam P92-EM Echo	PFA 318-13842		6.12.02	S Clegg	Maypole Farm, Chislet	14. 6.07P
	(Built D Cassidy)				(New owner 9.07)		
G-CCAM	Mainair Blade	1347-1102-7-W1142		6.12.02	M D Peacock	Cottage Farm, Norton Juxta	1. 8.08P
G-CCAN	Cessna 182P Skylane	18264069	SE-LON	16. 1.03	D J Hunter	Priory Farm, Tibenham	12. 5.08E
			OH-COZ, C-GWXC, (N6052F)				
G-CCAP	Robinson R22 Beta II	3413		11. 2.03	S G Simpson t/a HJS Helicopters		
						Lower Baads, Peterculter	22. 3.08E
G-CCAR	Cameron N-77 Balloon (Hot Air)	464		5.12.78	D P Turner	Leigh-on-Mendip	2. 6.05A
	(Rebuilt with envelope c/n 670 8.80: with c/n 2108 in 1989 and with c/n 2658 in 1992) (Mitsubishi Cars titles)						

G-CCAS	Cyclone Airsports Pegasus Quik	7935		11. 2.03	C M Addison	Knapthorpe Lodge, Caunton	17. 3.07P
G-CCAT	Gulfstream AA-5A Cheetah	AA5A-0893	G-OAJH	16. 1.92	A Ohringer	Blackbushe	31.10.07E
			G-KILT, G-BJFA, N27169				
G-CCAU	Eurocopter EC.135 T1	0040	G-79-01	30. 6.98	West Mercia Constabulary	Halfpenny Green	21. 7.10S
					(Operated Central Counties Police)		
G-CCAV	Piper PA-28-181 Archer II	28-8090353	D-EXRT	31. 3.03	S Turner tr Alpha Victor Group	Southend	3. 5.08E
			N8233A				
G-CCAW	Mainair Blade 912	1351-0103-7-W1146		5. 2.03	R H Stockton	(Christleton, Chester)	21. 5.08P
G-CCAY	Cameron Z-42 Balloon (Hot Air)	10373		27. 2.03	P Stern	Deggendorf, Germany	6. 9.07A
G-CCAZ	Cyclone Airsports Pegasus Quik	7927		3.12.02	J P Floyd	Sywell	26. 4.08P
G-CCBA	Best Off Sky Ranger R100(1)	SKR0211277		23. 1.03	R M Bremner tr Fourstrokes Group	Barton Ashes	23.10.08P
	(Built R M Bremner - pr.no.BMAA/HB/256)						
G-CCBB	Cameron N-90 Balloon (Hot Air)	10085	G-TEEZ (2)	11. 2.03	L E and S C A Craze	Berkhamsted	6. 6.08A
	(Note: G-TEEZ (1) stolen and cut up)				"Fresh Air"		
G-CCBC	Thruster T 600N 450	0013-T600N-077		23. 1.03	E J Girling and J A E Bowen	Davidstow Moor	18. 4.08P
G-CCBF	Maule M-5-235C Lunar Rocket	7276C	G-NHVH	29.11.02	R Windley	Northfield Farm, Mavis Enderby	27. 3.05
			N5634N		*(Damaged Leicester 15. 5.03: noted 7.06)*		
G-CCBG	Best Off Sky Ranger 912(2)	SKR0207214		28. 1.03	P R Mailer	Longacre Farm, Sandy	15. 6.05P
	(Built G R Wallis - pr.no.BMAA/HB/240)				*(New owner 1.08)*		
G-CCBH	Piper PA-28-235 Cherokee Pathfinder	28-10648	PH-ABL	29. 1.03	J R Hunt and S M Packer	Thruxton	30. 8.08E
			F-BNFY, N9054W				
G-CCBJ	Best Off Sky Ranger 912(2)	SKRxxxx285		4. 2.03	A T Hayward	Mill Farm, Hughley, Much Wenlock	4. 8.08P
	(Built A T Hayward - pr.no.BMAA/HB/262)						
G-CCBK	Evektor EV-97 Eurostar	03-1198(?)		5. 2.03	B S Waycott	Eastbach Farm, Coleford	3. 4.08P
	(Built J A and G R Pritchard - pr.no.PFA 315-14025)						
G-CCBL	Agusta-Bell 206B-2 JetRanger II	8732	OO-VCI	5. 3.03	Wilson Aviation Ltd	Southend	17. 6.08E
			PH-VCP, OO-VCI, (OO-XCI)				
G-CCBM	Evektor EV-97 Eurostar	PFA 315-14023		5. 2.03	W Graves	Sackville Lodge, Riseley	8. 5.08P
	(Built W Graves)						
G-CCBN	Replica Plans SE.5a	077246	PH-WWI	2. 4.03	V C Lockwood	(Boscombe Down)	14.11.08P
	(Built B Barra)		N8010S		*(As "80105:19" in US Air Service c/s)*		
G-CCBP	Lindstrand LBL 60X Balloon (Hot Air)	908		12. 2.03	D Strasmann	Mulheim ad Ruhr, Germany	6. 6.08A
G-CCBR	Wassmer Jodel D 120 Paris-Nice	59	OO-JAL	18. 2.03	A Dunne and M Munnelly	Kilrush, County Kildare	19. 6.06P
			(OO-CMF), F-BHYP		*(Departed runway landing Kilrush 14.4.06 with substantial damage)*		
G-CCBT	Cameron Z-90 Balloon (Hot Air)	10340		24. 3.03	I J Sharpe	Caterham	25. 6.08A
G-CCBU	Raj Hamsa X'Air 582(9)	756		19. 2.03	J S Rakkar	Stoke, Isle of Grain	22. 6.07P
	(Built M L Newton - pr.no.BMAA/HB/237)						
G-CCBV	Cameron Z-225 Balloon (Hot Air)	10365		10. 4.03	Compagnie Aéronautique du Grand-Duché de Luxembourg		
						Junglister, Luxembourg	28. 3.08A
G-CCBW	TLAC RL5A LW Sherwood Ranger	xxxx		18. 2.03	P H Wiltshire	Barton Ashes	21.11.08P
	(Built P H Wiltshire - pr.no.PFA 237-13002) (Rotax 582)						
G-CCBX	Raj Hamsa X'Air 133(2)	745		28. 5.03	A D'Amico	Longacre Farm, Sandy	10. 4.08P
	(Built A D'Amico - pr.no.BMAA/HB/286)						
G-CCBY	Avtech Jabiru UL-450	xxxx		21. 2.03	D M Goodman	Baxby Manor, Husthwaite	3. 7.07P
	(Built D M Goodman - PFA 274A-13528)				*(Noted 9.07)*		
G-CCBZ	Aero Designs Pulsar	1936	N4075X	17. 2.03	J M Keane	(Brighton)	18. 1.06P
	(Built R N Wasserman) (Tri-cycle u/c)				*(Force-landed in field near Deanland 2.7.05 and substantially damaged)*		
G-CCCA	Vickers Supermarine 509 Spitfire Tr.IX		G-TRIX	18. 2.03	Historic Flying Ltd	Duxford	21. 2.08P
		CBAF.9590	(G-BHGH), IAC 161, G-15-174, PV202 *(As "H-98" in R Netherlands AF c/s)*				
G-CCCB	Thruster T 600N 450 Sprint	0033-T600N-078		24. 2.03	J Williams *(Noted 10.07)*	Leicester	2. 9.06P
G-CCCD	Cyclone Airsports Pegasus Quantum 15	7929		12. 6.03	R N Gamble	Plaistows Farm, St Albans	17. 6.08P
	(Rotax 582)						
G-CCCE	Aeroprakt A22 Foxbat	PFA 317-14002		16. 1.03	C V Ellingworth	Henstridge	9. 2.08P
	(Built C V Ellingworth)						
G-CCCF	Thruster T 600N 450 Sprint	0033-T600N-081		24. 2.03	G A Fowler *(Noted 10.07)*	Leicester	24. 3.07P
G-CCCG	Mainair Sports Pegasus Quik	7946		16. 4.03	C J Haste	Easter Poldar Farm, Thornhill	21. 4.08P
G-CCCI	Medway EclipseR	174/152		11. 2.03	V Grayson	Stoke, Isle of Grain	25. 3.08P
G-CCCJ	Nicollier HN.700 Ménestrel II	PFA 217-13707		26. 2.03	G A Rodmell	(North Bar Without, Beverley)	20.12.06P
	(Built R Y Kendall)						
G-CCCK	Best Off Sky Ranger 912(2)	SKRxxxx289		26. 2.03	P L Braniff	Newtownards	1. 8.08P
	(Built J S Liming - pr.no.BMAA/HB/265)						
G-CCCM	Best Off Sky Ranger 912(2)	SKRxxxx292		3. 3.03	I A Forrest and C K Richardson	(East Fortune)	23. 9.08P
	(Built J R Moore - pr.no.BMAA/HB/263)						
G-CCCN	Robin R3000/160	167	OE-KOM	5. 3.03	R W Denny	Poplar Hall Farm, Elmsett	8. 6.08E
G-CCCO	Evektor EV-97 Eurostar	03-1181		11. 3.03	D R G Whitelaw	North Connel, Oban	29. 4.08P
	(Built Connel Flying Club Eurostar Group - pr.no.PFA 315-14006)						
G-CCCP	IAV-Bacau Yakovlev Yak-52	899404	LY-AKV	30.11.93	A H Soper	Jenkin's Farm, Navestock	13. 9.08P
			DOSAAF16 *(yellow)*				
G-CCCR	Best Off Sky Ranger 912(2)	SKR0301290		19. 3.03	D M Robbins	Goodwood	23. 6.08P
	(Built T C Viner - pr.no.BMAA/HB/266)						
G-CCCT	Comco Ikarus C42 FB UK	0211-6504		19. 3.03	J Kilpatrick	(Convoy, Lifford, County Donegal)	25. 9.08P
	(Built G A Pentelow - pr.no.PFA 322-13975)						
G-CCCU	Thruster T 600N 450	0034-T600N-084		29. 4.03	A F Cashin	Stoke, Isle of Grain	13. 5.08P
	(Official c/n incorrect - date of manufacture [April 2003] indicates correct version should be 0043-T 600N-084)						
G-CCCV	Raj Hamsa X'Air Falcon 133(1)	614		20. 3.03	G J Boyer	Weston Zoyland	15. 9.05P
	(Built G A J Salter - pr.no.BMAA/HB/252)				*(New owner 1.08)*		
G-CCCW	Pereira Osprey 2	PFA 070-13408		10. 4.03	D J Southward	Kirkbride	16. 5.08P
	(Built D J Southward)						
G-CCCY	Best Off Sky Ranger 912(2)	SKR0211278		25. 3.03	A Watson	Siege Cross Farm, Thatcham	16. 9.08P
	(Built D M Cottingham - pr.no.BMAA/HB/260)						
G-CCDB	Mainair Sports Pegasus Quik	7948		8. 4.03	C J van Dyke	Maypole Farm, Chislet	10. 4.08P
G-CCDC	Rans S-6-ES Coyote II	0302.1439		28. 1.03	A S Luketa	Stoke, Isle of Grain	11. 6.07P
	(Built G N Smith - pr.no.PFA 204-13992) (Rotax 582) (Tri-cycle u/c)						
G-CCDD	Mainair Sports Pegasus Quik	7951		31. 3.03	M P Hadden and M H Rollins	Long Marston	4. 6.08P

G-CCDE	Robinson R22 Beta II	3400	N71906	2. 4.03	J K, Mavis, A J, C and Charlotte.A Houldcroft		
					t/a J K.and M Houldcroft and Sons	Hawarden	15. 5.08T
G-CCDF	Mainair Sports Pegasus Quik	7949		23. 4.03	R P McGann	Headon Farm, Retford	29. 4.08P
G-CCDG	Best Off Sky Ranger 912(1)	SKR0302294		1. 4.03	T H Filmer	Newtownards	26. 9.08P
	(Built W P Byrne - pr.no.BMAA/HB/271)						
G-CCDH	Best Off Sky Ranger 912(2)	SKRxxxx211		5. 2.03	P and V C Reynolds	Haddington	8.12.07P
	(Built D M Hepworth - pr.no.BMAA/HB/233)						
G-CCDJ	Raj Hamsa X'Air Falcon 582(2)	692		18. 2.03	J M Spitz	Longacre Farm, Sandy	23. 4.08P
	(Built J M Spitz - pr.no.BMAA/HB/214)						
G-CCDK	Cyclone Airsports Pegasus Quantum 15	7947		19. 3.03	S Brock	Bourn	15. 6.08P
G-CCDL	Raj Hamsa X'Air Falcon 582(2)	819		1. 4.03	G M Brown	Craysmarsh Farm, Melksham	3. 8.08P
	(Built H Burroughs - pr.no.BMAA/HB/274)						
G-CCDM	Mainair Blade	1352-0203-7-W1147		21. 3.03	P R G Morley	Newnham, Baldock	5. 5.08P
G-CCDO	Mainair Sports Pegasus Quik	7944		19. 3.03	R J Erlam	(St Helens)	26. 4.08P
G-CCDP	Raj Hamsa X'Air 582(14)	847		10. 4.03	F J McGuigan	Stoke, Isle of Grain	14. 3.08P
	(Built J A McKie - pr.no.BMAA/HB/276)						
G-CCDR	Raj Hamsa X'Air Falcon Jabiru(3)	787		16. 4.03	P D Sibbons	Duxford	22. 6.08P
	(Built P D Sibbons - pr.no.BMAA/HB/253)						
G-CCDS	Nicollier HN.700 Ménestrel II	PFA 217-13915		13. 3.03	B W Gowland	(Rhoshirwaun, Pwllheli)	
	(Built B W Gowland)						
G-CCDU	Tecnam P92-EM Echo	PFA 318-13721		23. 4.03	M J Barrett	Eaglescott	30. 9.08P
	(Built M J Barrett)						
G-CCDV	Thruster T 600N 450 Sprint	0034-T600N-082		24. 4.03	D J Whysall	(Ripley)	14. 6.08P
	(Official c/n incorrect - manufactured April 2003 and should be 0043-T600N-082)						
G-CCDW	Best Off Sky Ranger 582(1)	SKR0302309		27. 3.03	P Reed tr Debts R Us Family Group		
	(Built P Reed - pr.no.BMAA/HB/268)					Sackville Lodge, Riseley	26. 1.08P
	(Engine failed on take-off Cromer 13. 3.07 and forced landing in field with substantial damage)						
G-CCDX	Evektor EV-97 Eurostar	PFA 315-14013		18. 2.03	J M Swash	Sittles Farm, Alrewas	8.11.07P
	(Built H F Breakwell and R A Morris)						
G-CCDY	Best Off Sky Ranger 912(1)	SKRxxxx310		10. 4.03	N H Copperthwaite	(Baildon, Shipley)	30.11.07P
	(Built A V Dunne and G S Gee-Carter - pr.no.BMAA/HB/275)						
G-CCDZ	Mainair Sports Pegasus Quantum 15	7952		24. 4.03	K D Baldwin	Graveley Hall Farm, Graveley	27. 4.08P
G-CCEA	Mainair Sports Pegasus Quik	7950		8. 4.03	G D Ritchie	East Fortune	25. 4.08P
G-CCEB	Thruster T 600N 450 Sprint	0035-T600N-085		24. 4.03	V Goddard	Craysmarsh Farm, Melksham	15. 6.08P
	(Official c/n incorrect - manufactured May 2003 and should be 0053-T600N-085)						
G-CCED	Zenair CH.601UL Zodiac	PFA 162A-13946		4. 4.03	R P Reynolds	(Walsall)	15.11.08P
	(Built R P Reynolds)						
G-CCEE	Piper PA-15 Vagabond	15-248	G-VAGA	31. 3.03	I M Callier	Berry Grove Farm, Liss	11. 1.08P
	(Continental C-90)		N4458H, NC4458H				
G-CCEF	Europa Aviation Europa	302		24. 4.03	C P Garner	Eaglescott	10. 9.08P
	(Built C P Garner - pr.no.PFA 247-13038) (Monowheel u/c)						
G-CCEG	Rans S-6-ES Coyote II	1000.1391		24. 4.03	W F Whitfield	Eshott	25. 4.08P
	(Built E O Bartle - pr.no.PFA 204-13831) (Rotax 582) (Tri-cycle u/c)						
G-CCEH	Best Off Sky Ranger 912(2)	SKRxxxx291		28. 4.03	A Eastham tr ZC Owners	Tarn Farm, Cockerham	4.11.08P
	(Built A Eastham - pr.no.BMAA/HB/267)						
G-CCEI	Evans VP-2	PFA 063-11377		16. 4.03	I P Manley and J Pearce	Marsh Farm, Sidlesham	
	(Built I P Manley and J Pearce) (Volkswagen 1834) (Incorporates wings and engine from G-BJZB [PFA 063-10633] scrapped 2002/-: new fuselage noted 4.03)						
G-CCEJ	Evektor EV-97 Eurostar	PFA 315-14011		1. 5.03	K R Haskell and N A Quintin	Henstridge	9. 4.08P
	(Built C R Ashley)						
G-CCEK	Air Création 582(1)/Kiss 400	xxxxx		2. 5.03	G S Sage	RAF Henlow	17.12.07P
	(Built G S Sage - pr.no.BMAA/HB/272)						
G-CCEL	Avtech Jabiru UL-450	xxxx		12. 2.03	S K Armstrong	(Dundrum, Newcastle)	2. 5.07P
	(Built R Pyper - pr.no.PFA 247A-13976)						
G-CCEM	Evektor EV-97A Eurostar	03-1148		19. 2.03	R L Wademan tr Oxenhope Flying Group		
	(Built E Atherden - pr.no.PFA 315-13987)					Hawksbridge Farm, Oxenhope	10. 8.08P
G-CCEN	Cameron Z-120 Balloon (Hot Air)	10399		9. 5.03	R Hunt	Ripley	1. 9.08A
G-CCEO	Thunder Ax10-180 Series 2 Balloon (Hot Air)	OE-RZH	10. 6.03	P Heitzeneder	Desselbrunn, Austria	14. 7.04A
		4634			t/a 1 Oberösterreichischer and t/a Ballonfahrerverein		
G-CCEP	Raj Hamsa X'Air Falcon Jabiru(4)	716		6. 5.03	K Angel	Stoke, Isle of Grain	14. 9.06P
	(Built A McIvor - pr.no.BMAA/HB/264)						
G-CCES	Raj Hamsa X'Air 2706(2)	401		8. 5.03	G V McCloskey	Blackhill, Draperstown	
	(Built G V McCloskey - pr.no.BMAA/HB/104)				(Noted 2007)		
G-CCET	Nova Vertex 28	14296		25. 3.03	M Hay (New owner 1.04)	Dundee	
G-CCEU	Rotary Air Force RAF 2000 GTX-SE	001	N97ZP	24. 6.03	N G Dovaston	Morgansfield, Fishburn	30. 9.08P
	(Built J L Rollins)						
G-CCEW	Mainair Sports Pegasus Quik	7966		17. 6.03	N F Mackenzie	Perth	10. 7.08P
G-CCEY	Raj Hamsa X'Air 582(11)	833		12. 5.03	P J F Spedding	(Ashford)	11.11.06P
	(Built P J F Spedding - pr.no.BMAA/HB/258)						
G-CCEZ	Reality Easy Raider J2.2(2)	0010		7. 5.03	M Peters	Broomclose Farm, Longbridge Deverill	
	(Built S A Chambers - pr.no.BMAA/HB/220)				(Noted 9.07)		
G-CCFA	Air Création 582(1)/Kiss 400	xxxxx		16. 5.03	N Hewitt	Sywell	12. 3.08P
	(Built N Hewitt - pr.no.BMAA/HB/282)						
G-CCFB	Mainair Sports Pegasus Quik	7955		16. 6.03	W T Davis	Perth	15. 6.08P
G-CCFC	Robinson R44 Raven II	10151		16. 9.03	M Entwistle	Wycombe Air Park	4.11.07T
G-CCFD	Quad City Challenger II	CH-0597-UK-1617		20. 5.03	W Oswald	Longside, Peterhead	
	(Built W Oswald - pr.no.PFA 177-13180)				(On build 4.07)		
G-CCFE	Tipsy Nipper T 66 Series 2	T66/37	OO-PLG	12. 6.03	D R Smith tr G-CCFE Group		
	(Built Avions Fairey SA)					(Ottery St Mary, Devon)	18.12.07P
G-CCFG	Dyn'Aéro MCR-01 Club	PFA 301A-14047		8. 4.03	A Jones	Headon Farm, Retford	7. 9.08P
	(Built M P Sargent)						
G-CCFI	Piper PA-32-260 Cherokee Six	32-7400002	OO-PCT	30. 6.03	McManus Truck and Trailer Spares Ltd		
			N56630			Trim, County Meath	22. 8.08E
G-CCFJ	Kolb Twinstar Mk.3 Extra	PFA 205-14014		29. 5.03	D Travers	(Ealand, Scunthorpe)	30. 7.08P
	(Built M H Moulai)						

G-CCFK	Europa Aviation Europa	502		29. 5.03	C R Knapton	(Humbleton)	21. 8.08P
	(Built C R Knapton - pr.no.PFA 247-13744)						
G-CCFL	Mainair Sports Pegasus Quik	7960		16. 6.03	J C Higham	Otherton, Cannock	15. 6.08P
G-CCFM	Mainair Blade 912	1354-0603-7-W1149		8. 5.03	M J Devane	(Killarney,County Kerry)	29. 7.08P
G-CCFN	Cameron N-105 Balloon (Hot Air)	10442		5. 8.03	ABC Flights Ltd	Clapton in Gordano, Bristol	12. 4.08A
					(Clairol titles)		
G-CCFO	Pitts S-1S	001	C-FYXO	28. 5.03	R J Anderson	Priory Farm, Tibenham	8.11.08P
	(Built R B Innes)						
G-CCFP	Diamond DA.40D Star	D4.026		3. 9.03	Diamond Aircraft UK Ltd	Halfpenny Green	15.10.07E
G-CCFR	Diamond DA.40D Star	D4.032		3. 9.03	B Wronski	(Oxford)	12.10.07E
G-CCFS	Diamond DA.40D Star	D4.034		3. 9.03	R H Butterfield and A M Dyson t/a Principle Aircraft		
						(Sheffield City)	15. 1.08E
G-CCFT	Mainair Sports Pegasus Quantum 15-912	7961		17. 6.03	D J Gardner	Dunkeswell	8. 8.08P
G-CCFU	Diamond DA.40D Star	D4.035		3. 9.03	Egnatia Aviation Ltd	Kavala, Greece	6. 3.08E
G-CCFV	Lindstrand LBL 77A Balloon (Hot Air)	934		23. 6.03	Alton Aviation Ltd	Oswestry	21. 8.08A
G-CCFW	WAR Focke-Wulf FW190 replica	PFA 081-12729		27. 5.03	D B Conway	Little Rissington	1. 6.08P
	(Builtb D B Conway)				*(As "- + 9" in Luftwaffe c/s)*		
G-CCFX	EAA Acrosport II	PFA 072-11221		23. 6.03	C D Ward	(Leyburn)	
	(Built C D Ward)						
G-CCFY	RotorWay Executive 162F	6719		27. 6.03	Southern Helicopters Ltd	Street Farm, Takeley	
	(Built M Hawley)				*(Noted 2.08)*		
G-CCFZ	Comco Ikarus C42 FB UK	PFA 322-14040		2. 5.03	B W Drake	Over Farm, Gloucester	23.11.07P
	(Built B W Drake)						
G-CCGB	TEAM Mini-MAX 91	PFA 186-13767		4. 6.03	A D Pentland	Baxby Manor, Husthwaite	16. 8.08P
	(Built A D Pentland)						
G-CCGC	Mainair Sports Pegasus Quik	7958		27. 5.03	R W Street	(Edinburgh)	1. 6.08P
G-CCGE	Robinson R22 Beta II	3453		25. 6.03	Heli Aitch Be Ltd	Redhill	9. 7.08E
G-CCGF	Robinson R22 Beta II	3454		25. 6.03	A Tallis	Halfpenny Green	13. 7.08E
	(Tail rotor struck ground during hover taxi Skinstown, County Kilkenny 10. 4.07 incurring substantial damage: noted wrecked 5.07)						
G-CCGG	Avtech Jabiru J400	0xxx		16. 6.03	G E Hall	Dunkeswell	23. 4.08P
	(Built K D Pearce - pr.no.PFA 325-14055)						
G-CCGH	Super Marine Spitfire Mk.26	021		17. 6.03	K D Pearce	Shoreham	16. 4.08P
	(Built K D Pearce - pr.no.PFA 324-14054) (Jabiru 5100)				*(As "AB196" in RAF c/s)*		
G-CCGI	Mainair Sports Pegasus Quik	7967		7. 7.03	M C Kerr	Clench Common	7. 9.08P
G-CCGK	Mainair Blade	1355-0603-7-W1150		18. 7.03	C M Babiy and M Hurn	Graveley Hall Farm, Graveley	19. 7.08P
G-CCGL	SOCATA TB-20 Trinidad	2187	F-OIMN	28. 5.03	Pembroke Motor Services Ltd	Haverfordwest	22. 6.08E
G-CCGM	Air Création 582(2)/Kiss 450	xxxxx		23. 5.03	A I Lea	Benson's Farm, Laindon	23. 6.08P
	(Built G P Masters - pr.no.BMAA/HB/277 being Flylight kit comprising Trike s/n T03026 and Wing s/n A2049-2044)						
G-CCGO	Medway AV8R	176/154		11. 4.03	C J Draper t/a Medway Microlights		
	(Rotax 582 - no. 5589987)					Stoke, Isle of Grain	
G-CCGP	Holman Bristol Type 2000	PFA 270-12858		1. 7.03	R G Holman	Kemble	
	(Built R G Holman)				*(On build 1.04)*		
G-CCGR	Raj Hamsa X'Air 133(1)	865		12. 6.03	C M Wilkes	Barton Ashes	24. 6.08P
	(Built J M Weston - pr.no.BMAA/HB/284)						
G-CCGS	Dornier 328-100	3101	D-CPRX	18. 3.04	Suckling Airways (Cambridge) Ltd t/a Scot Airways		
			D-CDXR			London City	17. 3.08E
G-CCGT	Cameron Z-425 Balloon (Hot Air)	10398		16. 6.03	A A Brown	Guildford	17. 6.08A
G-CCGU	Van's RV-9A	PFA 320-13798		10. 7.03	B J Main, C W Hague and A Strachan	Henstridge	4. 6.08P
	(Built B J Main)						
G-CCGW	Europa Aviation Europa	026		8. 7.03	G C Smith	Bourn	17. 6.05P
	(Built G C Smith - pr.no.PFA 247-12548)						
G-CCGY	Cameron Z-105 Balloon (Hot Air)	10422		8. 7.03	Cameron Balloons Ltd	Bristol	30. 8.07A
					(Cameron Balloons titles)		
G-CCGZ	Cameron Z-250 Balloon (Hot Air)	10438		4. 9.03	Ballooning Adventures Ltd	Hexham	1. 8.08T
G-CCHA	Diamond DA.40D Star	D4.046		14. 7.03	Diamond Hire UK Ltd	(Renishaw, Sheffield)	4. 9.08E
G-CCHB	Diamond DA.40D Star	D4.047		16. 7.03	Diamond Aircraft UK Ltd	Gamston	7. 9.08E
					(Blown over in gales and noted in compound 4.07, reportedly written-off)		
G-CCHC	Diamond DA.40D Star	D4.050		26. 8.03	Diamond Aircraft UK Ltd	Gamston	24. 9.08E
G-CCHD	Diamond DA.40D Star	D4.051		3. 9.03	Diamond Aircraft UK Ltd	Belfast International	21. 9.08E
G-CCHE	Diamond DA.40D Star	D4.054		29. 8.03	Diamond Aircraft UK Ltd	Gamston	21. 9.08E
					(Blown over in gales and noted in compound 4.07, reportedly written-off)		
G-CCHF	Diamond DA.40D Star	D4.055		3. 9.03	Diamond Aircraft UK Ltd	Gamston	24. 9.08E
G-CCHG	Diamond DA.40D Star	D4.058		3. 9.03	Diamond Aircraft UK Ltd	Shoreham	30. 9.07E
G-CCHH	Mainair Sports Pegasus Quik	7963		24. 6.03	C A Green	(Shalford, Guildford)	27. 8.08P
G-CCHI	Mainair Sports Pegasus Quik	7971		29. 7.03	M R Starling	(Swafield, North Walsham)	16. 9.08P
G-CCHJ	Air Création 582(1)/Kiss 400	FL016		28. 4.03	H C Jones	(Wolvey)	3. 9.06P
	(Built H C Jones - pr.no.BMAA/HB/257 being Flylight kit comprising, Trike s/n T02117 and Wing s/n A02184-02179)						
G-CCHK	Diamond DA.40D Star	D4.059		3. 9.03	Diamond Aircraft UK Ltd	Gamston	24. 9.08E
G-CCHL	Piper PA-28-181 Archer III	2843176	OY-JAA	4. 8.03	Archer Three Ltd	Lydd	23. 8.08E
			N9501N				
G-CCHM	Air Création 582(1)/Kiss 450	FL022		15. 7.03	M J Jessup	(Edenbridge)	10. 6.08P
	(Built W G Colyer - pr.no.BMAA/HB/292 being Flylight kit comprising Trike s/n T03057 and Wing s/n A03099-3016)						
G-CCHN	Corby CJ-1 Starlet	PFA 134-12848		15. 7.03	D C Mayle	(Woodcote, Reading)	
	(Built D C Mayle)						
G-CCHO	Mainair Sports Pegasus Quik	7968		9. 7.03	M Allan	(Dalkeith)	8. 7.08P
G-CCHP	Cameron Z-31 Balloon (Hot Air)	10443		20. 8.03	M H Redman	Stalbridge, Sturminster Newton	9. 9.08P
G-CCHR	Reality Easy Raider 503(1)	0008		24. 6.03	R B M Etherington	Halwel	
	(Built R B Hawkins - pr.no.BMAA/HB/223)				*(New owner 9.06)*		
G-CCHS	Raj Hamsa X'Air 582(10)	840		4. 7.03	M Howes tr HS Flying Group		
	(Built I Lonsdale - pr.no.BMAA/HB/291)					Tarn Farm, Cockerham	13. 8.08P
G-CCHT	Cessna 152	15285176	9H-ACW	17. 7.03	J S Devlin and Z Islam	Blackbushe	1.11.07E
			N6159Q				
G-CCHV	Mainair Rapier	1353-0403-7-W1148		15. 9.03	A Butterworth	(Poynton)	10. 2.07P
G-CCHW	Cameron Z-77 Balloon (Hot Air)	10426		26. 6.03	A Murphy	Dunshaughlin, County West Meath	13. 6.08A

G-CCHX	Scheibe SF25C Falke	44694	D-KBCI	25. 9.03	Lasham Gliding Society Ltd	Lasham	3.11.07E
	(Rotax 912S)						
G-CCHY	Bücker Bü.131 Jungmann	21	I-CABI	12.11.03	M V Rijkse	(London WC1)	16. 7.08P
	(Built Dornier-Werke AG)		HB-UTZ, Swiss AF A-12		(As "A-12" in Swiss AF c/s)		
G-CCID	Avtech Jabiru J400	0xxx		25. 7.03	J Bailey	Crowfield	19.11.07P
	(Built J Bailey - pr.no.PFA 325-14059)						
G-CCIE	Colt 315A Balloon (Hot Air)	10176		25. 7.03	T M Donnelly	Sprotbrough, Doncaster	21. 7.07T
G-CCIF	Mainair Blade	1356-0703-7-W1151		28. 7.03	S P Moores	(Biddulph, Stoke-on-Trent)	30..1.08P
G-CCIG	Aero Designs Pulsar	PFA 202-12133		15. 7.03	P Maguire	(Accrington)	
	(Built P Maguire)						
G-CCIH	Mainair Sports Pegasus Quantum 15	7973		31. 7.03	R Bennett	Rochester	12. 8.08P
	(Rotax 582)						
G-CCII	ICP MXP-740 Savannah Jabiru(4) 01-04-51-063			6. 6.03	J R Livett and D Chaloner	Redlands, Swindon	15.10.08P
	(Built M J Kaye - pr.no.BMAA/HB/285)						
G-CCIJ	Piper PA-28R-180 Cherokee Arrow	28R-30873	SE-FDZ	14. 7.03	S A Hughes	Andrewsfield	14. 9.08E
G-CCIK	Best Off Sky Ranger 912(2)	SKR0212279		30. 7.03	M D Kirby	Chase Farm, Little Bursted	24. 2.08P
	(Built L E Cowling and A P Chapman - pr.no.BMAA/HB/278)						
G-CCIO	Best Off Sky Ranger 912(2)	SKR0212284		4. 8.03	B Berry	Crosland Moor	2. 4.07P
	(Built B Berry - pr.no.BMAA/HB/261)						
G-CCIR	Van's RV-8	PFA 303-13732		7. 8.03	G Johnson	Earls Colne	1. 3.08P
	(Built D Marsh)						
G-CCIS	Scheibe SF28A Tandem Falke	5791	OE-9154	15.10.03	P T Ross	St Merryn	9.11.07E
			(D-KDFZ)				
G-CCIT	Zenair CH.701UL STOL	PFA 187-13911		30. 6.03	I M Sinclair	Glenrothes	16.10.08P
	(Built I M Sinclair) (Jabiru 2200A)						
G-CCIU	Cameron N-105 Balloon (Hot Air)	10485		18. 8.03	Bianchi Aviation Film Services Ltd		
						Wycombe Air Park	14. 9.04A
G-CCIV	Mainair Sports Pegasus Quik	7977		13. 8.03	F Omaraie-Hamdanie	Hunsdon	2. 9.08P
G-CCIW	Raj Hamsa X'Air 582(5)	838		11. 8.03	N Watts	(Rugeley)	14. 5.06P
	(Built G Wilkinson - pr.no.BMAA/HB/281)				(New owner 12.07)		
G-CCIY	Best Off Sky Ranger 912(2)	SKR0210244		14. 8.03	L F Tanner	Sywell	14. 4.08P
	(Built L F Tanner -pr.no.BMAA/HB/250)						
G-CCIZ	PZL-110 Koliber 160A	04010087	SP-WGN (2)	21. 8.03	Horizon Aviation Ltd	Swansea	21.11.07E
G-CCJA	Best Off Sky Ranger 912(2)	SKR0307364		6. 8.03	C Day	(Salisbury)	22. 5.08P
	(Built T R Southall - pr.no.BMAA/HB/299)						
G-CCJB	Zenair CH.701 STOL	7-3659		24. 6.03	E G Brown	(Luton)	
	(Built E G Brown - pr.no.PFA 187-13270)						
G-CCJC	British Aerospace BAe 146 Series 200	E2060	EI-DDE	12 .9.03	BAE Systems (Operations) Ltd	Exeter	
	G-CCJC, D-AZUR, N352BA, CP-2260, N352BA, XA-RMO, N402XV, G-5-060 (New owner 1.08)						
G-CCJD	Mainair Sports Pegasus Quantum 15	7974		3. 9.03	P Clark	Yatesbury	5. 8.08P
	(Rotax 582)						
G-CCJF	Cameron C-90 Balloon (Hot Air)	10483		14.10.03	Balloon School (International) Ltd		
						Colhook Common, Petworth	20. 9.08E
G-CCJG	Cameron A-200 Balloon (Hot Air)	10484		12. 2.04	J M Stables t/a Aire Valley Balloons	Knaresborough	23. 3.08T
G-CCJH	Lindstrand LBL 90A Balloon (Hot Air)	906		5. 8.03	J R Hoare	Plymouth	12. 3.08A
G-CCJI	Van's RV-6	PFA 181A-13572		4. 7.03	N A Thomas	Hunsdon	17. 9.08P
	(Built E M Marsh)				"jadeair.co.uk".		
G-CCJJ	Medway SLA 80 Executive	18803		20. 8.03	K J Draper	Stoke, Isle of Grain	7.12.07P
	(Originally regd as Medway Piranah until 10.03)						
G-CCJK	Aerostar Yakovlev Yak-52	9612001	RA-02622	3. 3.04	R K Howell	White Waltham	4. 6.08P
			LY-AFH				
G-CCJL	Super Marine Spitfire Mk.26	PFA 324-14053		22. 8.03	M W Hanley and P M Whitaker	Perranporth	30. 8.08P
	(Built P M Whitaker and M Hanley)				(As "PV303:ON-B" in RAF c/s)"		
G-CCJM	Mainair Sports Pegasus Quik	7970		24. 7.03	P Crosby	Ince Blundell	24. 7.07P
G-CCJN	Rans S-6-ES Coyote II	0899.1336		28. 8.03	M G A Wood	Church Farm, Askern	20. 7.08P
	(Built M G A Wood - pr.no.PFA 204-13575) (Rotax 582) (Tri-cycle u/c)						
G-CCJO	ICP MXP-740 Savannah Jabiru(4) 03-05-01-213			28. 8.03	R and I Fletcher	Sandtoft	25. 8.08P
	(Built R and I Fletcher - pr.no.BMAA/HB/295)						
G-CCJP	British Aerospace BAe 146 Series 200	E2066	I-TERK	17.10.03	BAE Systems (Operations) Ltd (Stored 8.07) Kemble		
	G-CCJP D-ALOA, N356BA, C-FHNX, N356BA, XA-RTI, N405XV, C-FHNX, N405XV, G-5-066, N405XV						
G-CCJT	Best Off Sky Ranger 912(2)	SKRxxxx317		30. 7.03	M S R Burak tr Juliet Tango Group		
	(Built J W Taylor - pr.no.BMAA/HB/300)					Over Farm, Gloucester	13. 8.08P
G-CCJU	ICP MXP-740 Savannah Jabiru(4) 03-05-01-214			3. 9.03	K R Wootton and A Colverson		
	(Built K R Wootton and A Colverson - pr.no.BMAA/HB/294)				(Withernsea and Patrington, Hull)	15.11.08P
G-CCJV	Aeroprakt A22 Foxbat	PFA 317-14082		3. 9.03	J C Forrester tr Foxbat UK015 Syndicate		
	(Built M J Barrett, A Dace, S McRoberts and J C Forrester)					Otherton, Cannock	19. 7.08P
G-CCJW	Best Off Sky Ranger 912(2)	SKRxxxx366		3. 9.03	J R Walter	Hunterson Farm, Stair	8. 6.08P
	(Built J R Walter - pr.no.BMAA/HB/303)						
G-CCJX	Europa Aviation Europa XS	509		9. 9.03	J S Baranski	Wycombe Air Park	12. 6.08P
	(Built J S Baranski - pr.no.PFA 247-13727)						
G-CCJY	Cameron Z-42 Balloon (Hot Air)	10465		12. 9.03	D J Griffin	Bowerhill, Melksham	10.11.07E
					(Cameron Balloons titles)		
G-CCKF	Best Off Sky Ranger 912(2)	SKRxxxx314		4. 9.03	T P M Turnbull	Eshott	10. 6.08P
	(Built S A Owen - pr.no.BMAA/HB/289)						
G-CCKG	Best Off Sky Ranger 912(2)	SKRxxxx375		26. 8.03	J Hannibal	Pound Green, Buttonoak, Bewdley	27. 7.08P
	(Built J Hannibal - pr.no.BMAA/HB/302)						
G-CCKH	Diamond DA.40D Star	D4.039		23.10.03	Flying Time Ltd	Shoreham	28. 1.08E
G-CCKI	Diamond DA.40D Star	D4.038		23.10.03	S C Horwood	(Broxbourne)	14.12.07E
G-CCKJ	Raj Hamsa X'Air 582(5)	855		2.10.03	D Robertson	Ince Blundell	3.10.07P
	(Built S Thompson - pr.no.BMAA/HB/306)						
G-CCKL	Evektor EV-97 Eurostar	PFA 315-14117		15. 9.03	A C and B A Aiken	Plaistows Farm, St Albans	18.11.08P
	(Built J S Liming and A U I Hudson)						
G-CCKM	Mainair Sports Pegasus Quik	7985		22. 9.03	C I Poole	(Southport)	5. 2.08P

G-CCKN	Nicollier HN.700 Ménestrel II	PFA 217-13943		23. 9.03	C R Partington	Stanton, Morpeth	16. 1.08P
	(Built C R Partington)						
G-CCKO	Mainair Sports Pegasus Quik	7982		27. 8.03	M J Mawle, C R Bunce and C D Waldron		
						Redlands, Swindon	31. 8.08P
G-CCKP	Robin DR.400-120 Dauphin 2+2	2044	F-GKQD	15. 9.04	B A Mills t/a Duxford Flying Group	Duxford	
G-CCKR	Pietenpol Aircamper	PFA 047-12295		22. 8.03	T J Wilson	Bodmin	16. 8.08P
	(Built T J Wilson) (Continental O-200-A)						
G-CCKS	Hughes 369E	0303E	N7065C	22.10.03	Eastern Atlantic Helicopters Ltd	Shoreham	25. 4.08E
	(Hughes 500)		N314JP				
G-CCKT	HAPI Cygnet SF-2A	PFA 182-13366		15. 7.03	P W Abraham	Upfield Farm, Whitson	13. 5.08P
	(Built P W Abraham)						
G-CCKU	Canadian Home Rotors Safari	S2113		7.10.03	J C Collingwood	(Cranbrook)	
	(Built J C Collingwood) (Verner VM133)						
G-CCKV	Isaacs Fury II	PFA 011-13695		10.10.03	S T G Ingram	St Just	
	(Built S T G Ingram)				(As "K7271" in RAF c/s: noted 10.07)		
G-CCKW	Piper PA-18-135 Super Cub	18-3535	G-GDAM	16. 9.03	G T Fisher	(Northside, Thorney)	11. 8.91
	(L-21B-PI) (Frame No.18-3648)		PH-PVW, (PH-DKE), R Neth AF R-107, 54-2335 (New owner 11.03: also see G-CUBI)				
G-CCKX	Lindstrand LBL 210A Balloon (Hot Air)	931		23. 1.04	Alba Ballooning Ltd	Edinburgh	19.10.07T
G-CCKY	Lindstrand LBL 240A Balloon (Hot Air)	943		21.11.03	Cameron Flights Southern Ltd		
						Woodborough, Pewsey	18.10.08T
G-CCKZ	Customcraft A25 Balloon (Hot Air)	CC005		10.10.03	A van Wyk (Noted 2004)	Higham, Bury St Edmunds	
G-CCLB	Diamond DA.40D Star	D4.074		19. 1.04	R J Millen and M J Millen t/a The Millen Corporation		
						Rochester	17. 5.08E
G-CCLC	Diamond DA.40D Star	D4.073		22. 1.04	Diamond Aircraft UK Ltd	Gamston	7. 8.08E
	(Marked as DA40TDi)						
G-CCLF	Best Off Sky Ranger 912(2)	SKRxxxx380		16.10.03	J Bannister and N J Sutherland	Perth	22. 9.08P
	(Built G K R Linney - pr.no.BMAA/HB/311)						
G-CCLH	Rans S-6-ES Coyote II	0600.1372		24.10.03	K R Browne	(Sackville Lodge, Riseley)	23. 4.08P
	(Built K R Browne - pr.no.PFA 204-13658) (Tri-cycle u/c)						
G-CCLJ	Piper PA-28-140 Cherokee Cruiser	28-7525049	OY-TOJ	1. 9.03	A M George	(Thornwood, Epping)	2. 8.08E
G-CCLL	Zenair CH.601XL Zodiac	PFA 162B-14081		4. 9.03	L Lewis	Yearby	
	(Built L Lewis)						
G-CCLM	Mainair Sports Pegasus Quik	7986		7.10.03	P M Ryder and D J Shippen	Newton Bank, Daresbury	6.10.08P
G-CCLO	Ultramagic H-77 Balloon (Hot Air)	77/244		19. 2.04	J P Moore	Great Missenden	6 6.08T
G-CCLP	ICP MXP-740 Savannah Jabiru(4)	xx-xx-xx-xxx		31.10.03	S Woolmington	Earls Colne	13. 7.08P
	(Built M J Kaye - pr.no.BMAA/HB/314)						
G-CCLR	Schleicher ASH 26E	26209		26.11.03	M T Burton and S Edwards "26E"	Dunstable	26.11.07E
G-CCLS	Comco Ikarus C42 FB UK	0302-6534		19. 9.03	SLS Computing Services Ltd	Swinford, Rugby	30. 3.08P
	(Built J Spinks and T Greenhill - pr.no.PFA 322-14050) (Kit no.not confirmed)						
G-CCLU	Best Off Sky Ranger 912(2)	SKR0309379		11.11.03	M Hurn	Graveley Hall Farm, Graveley	7. 8.07P
	(Built L Stanton - pr.no.BMAA/HB/316)				"Annie's Dream"		
G-CCLV	Diamond DA.40D Star	D4.052		22.12.03	D J Watson	Blackpool	19. 4.08E
G-CCLW	Diamond DA.40D Star	D4.068		19.12.03	Diamond Aircraft UK Ltd	Gamston	1. 5.08E
G-CCLX	Mainair Sports Pegasus Quik	7996		13.11.03	S D Pain	Rayne Hall Farm, Braintree	13. 3.08P
G-CCMC	Avtech Jabiru UL-450	xxxx		9. 9.03	J Johnston	(Knocklong, County Limerick)	28. 6.08P
	(Built J T McCormack - pr.no.PFA 274A-13775)						
G-CCMD	Mainair Sports Pegasus Quik	7991		23.10.03	J T McCormack	Broomhill Farm, West Calder	4. 1.08P
G-CCME	Mainair Sports Pegasus Quik	7995		7.11.03	A Bloomfield and A Underwood		
						Headon Farm, Retford	22. 4.08P
G-CCMF	Diamond DA.40D Star	D4.075		19.12.03	Diamond Aircraft UK Ltd	Gamston	23. 3.07T
G-CCMH	Miles M.2H Hawk Major	172	EC-ABI	20.10.03	J A Pothecary	(Newton Toney, Salisbury)	
			EC-CAS, EC-DDB, EC-W44				
G-CCMI	Scottish Aviation Bulldog Series 120/121		G-KKKK	20.11.03	H R M Tyrrell	Sleap	15. 3.08E
		BH120/199	XX513		(As "XX513:10" in RAF c/s)		
G-CCMJ	Reality Easy Raider Jab22	0009		13.11.03	G F Clews	(Burton-on-Trent)	
	(Built G F Clews - pr.no..BMAA/HB/254)						
G-CCMK	Raj Hamsa X'Air Falcon Jabiru(3)	827		17.11.03	G Taylor	Armshold Farm, Kingston, Cambridge	6. 7.08P
	(Built M A Beadman - pr.no.BMAA/HB/301)						
G-CCML	Mainair Sports Pegasus Quik	7992		14.10.03	D Seiler (New owner 11.07)	(Ossett)	21.10.08P
G-CCMM	Dyn'Aéro MCR-01 ULC	131		8. 9.03	J D Harris	Garston Farm, Marshfield	7. 6.08P
	(Built J P Davis - pr.no.PFA 301B-13945)						
G-CCMN	Cameron C-90 Balloon (Hot Air)	10519		27. 1.04	A E Austin	Sibbertoft, Market Harborough	7. 4.08A
G-CCMO	Evektor EV-97A Eurostar	PFA 315-14155		11.11.03	E M Woods	Lydney-St Briavels	15. 3.08P
	(Built E M Woods)						
G-CCMP	Evektor EV-97A Eurostar	PFA 315-14127		23.10.03	E K McAlinden	Derryogue	5. 3.08P
	(Built W K Wilkie)						
G-CCMR	Robinson R22 Beta II	3497	N75273	9. 1.04	G F Smith	Cranfield	14. 1.08E
G-CCMS	Mainair Sports Pegasus Quik	7997		1.12.03	A J Roche	Elm Farm, Wickford	21. 4.08P
G-CCMT	Thruster T 600N 450	1031-T600N-092		14.11.03	S P McCaffrey	(Abingdon)	27. 6.08P
G-CCMU	Rotorway Executive 162F	6720		20.11.03	D J Fravigar and J Smith		
	(Built M Irving)					Clough Farm, Croft, Skegness	28. 8.07P
G-CCMW	CFM Shadow Series DD	K 348		2. 9.03	M Wilkinson	Enstone	2.10.07P
	(Built M Wilkinson - pr.no.PFA 161-13869) (Rotax 582)						
G-CCMX	Best Off Sky Ranger 912(2)	SKR0210243		25.11.03	K J Cole	Over Farm, Gloucester	27. 3.08P
	(Built K J Cole - pr.no.BMAA/HB/255)						
G-CCMZ	Best Off Sky Ranger 912(2)	SKR0304316		23.10.03	D D Appleford	Draycott Farm, Chiseldon	13. 6.08P
	(Built D D Appleford - pr.no.BMAA/HB/288)						
G-CCNA	Jodel DR.100A replica	PFA 304-13519		21.11.03	W R Davis-Smith and R Everitt	Ley Farm, Chirk	
	(Built R Everitt) -reported as rebuild of G-ATHX)				(Noted 6.07)		
G-CCNB	Rans S-6-ES Coyote II	1202.1469		2. 9.03	M S Lawrence	Mill Farm, Shifnal	7. 6.05P
	(Built D Bedford - pr.no.PFA 204-14027)				(Stalled and crashed Weston Park, Shifnal 28.3.05 and substantially damaged)		
G-CCNC	Cameron Z-275 Balloon (Hot Air)	10504		16. 4.04	Ladybird Balloons Ltd	Bingham, Nottingham	25. 4.08T
G-CCND	Van's RV-9A	PFA 320-14142		10.12.03	K S Woodard	Airfield Farm, Hardwick	22.10.07P
	(Built K S Woodard)						

G-CCNE	Cyclone Airsports Pegasus Quantum 15	7093	T2-2795	11.12.03	P R Hanman	Over Farm, Gloucester	21. 4.08P
	(Rotax 582(						
G-CCNF	Raj Hamsa X'Air Falcon 133(1)	644		9.12.03	M F Eddington	Henstridge	13.11.08P
	(Built M F Eddington - pr.no.BMAA/HB/211)						
G-CCNG	Flight Design CT2K	03-06-02-27		5. 1.04	David Goode Sculpture Ltd	Enstone	13.12.07P
	(Assembled Mainair Sports Ltd with c/n 8004)						
G-CCNH	Rans S-6-ES Coyote II	0503.1498		11. 9.03	N C Harper tr Coyote Group	Grove Farm, Needham	12.12.08P
	(Built N C Harper - pr.no.PFA 204-14114) (Rotax 912)						
G-CCNJ	Best Off Sky Ranger 912(2)	SKR0310392		17.12.03	J D Buchanan	Coldharbour Farm, Willingham	10.11.08P
	(Built J D Buchanan - pr.no..BMAA/HB/330)						
G-CCNM	Mainair Sports Pegasus Quik	8002		2.12.03	H M N and N M Corr	Newtownards	10.12.08P
G-CCNN	Cameron Z-90 Balloon (Hot Air)	10512		8. 1.04	J H Turner (Gottex titles)	Broad Chalke, Salisbury	11.12.07A
G-CCNP	Flight Design CT2K	03.07.03.34		22. 1.04	M J Hawkins	(Ansty, Dorchester)	20. 4.08P
	(Assembled Mainair Sports Ltd with (official) c/n 8005: now reported by P&M Aviation as c/n 8104 but inspection shows c/n 8124)						
G-CCNR	Best Off Sky Ranger 912(2)	SKR0309381		4.12.03	A J Lewis	(Lydney)	18. 5.08P
	(Built S J Huxtable - pr.no.BMAA/HB/315)						
G-CCNS	Best Off Sky Ranger 912(2)	SKR0401434		24. 2.04	G G Rowley and M Liptrot	Glassonby	25. 5.08P
	(Built G G Rowley and M Liptrot - pr.no.BMAA/HB/356)						
G-CCNT	Comco Ikarus C42 FB80	0311-6585		19.12.03	D J Collier t/a Sunfun Group		
	(Rotax 912-UL)					Lower Mountpleasant Farm, Chatteris	25. 1.08P
G-CCNU	Best Off Sky Ranger J2.2(2)	SKRxxxx319		9. 1.04	P D Priestley	Wickenby	27.11.07P
	(Built D P Toulson and R L Nyman - pr.no.BMAA/HB/297)						
G-CCNV	Cameron Z-210 Balloon (Hot Air)	10505		22. 4.04	J A Cooper	Ugborough, Ivybridge	4. 4.08T
G-CCNW	Mainair Sports Pegasus Quantum 15	8010		28. 1.04	J Childs	Deenethorpe	23. 8.08P
	(Rotax 582)						
G-CCNX	CAB CAP.10B	311		6. 1.04	Arc Input Ltd	New Farm House, Great Oakley	31. 3.08E
	(Marked as "CAP.10C")						
G-CCNY	Robinson R44 Raven	1349		18.11.03	C M Evans and J W Blaylock	(Kirton, Boston)	10. 1.08E
G-CCNZ	Raj Hamsa X'Air 133(1)	888		5.11.03	A A Passmore	Dunkeswell	17.10.08P
	(Built K J Foxall - pr.no.BMAA/HB/308)						
G-CCOB	Aero C 104	247	N2348	21. 1.04	William Tomkins Ltd	Spanhoe	17. 7.08P
	(Bücker Bü.131 Jungmann)		LN-BNG, OK-AXV, Czech AF				
G-CCOC	Mainair Sports Pegasus Quantum 15	7999		16.12.03	MJ Dean	Tarn Farm, Cockerham	9. 2.08P
	(Rotax 582)						
G-CCOF	Rans S-6-ESA Coyote II	1202.1472		8. 1.04	A J Wright and M Govan		
	(Built A J Wright and M Govan - pr.no.PFA 204-14037)					Yeatsall Farm, Abbots Bromley	2. 7.08P
G-CCOG	Mainair Sports Pegasus Quik	8001		16.12.03	A O Sutherland	Latch Farm, Kirknewton	28. 1.08P
G-CCOH	Raj Hamsa X'Air Falcon 133(1)	831		13. 1.04	M O Roach	Otherton, Cannock	4.10.05P
	(Built A R Emerson - pr.no.BMAA/HB/338)						
G-CCOI	Lindstrand LBL 90A Balloon (Hot Air)	945		21. 1.04	D J Groombridge	Portishead, Bristol	2. 5.08A
G-CCOK	Mainair Sports Pegasus Quik	8000		5. 1.04	A G Woodward	Heckington, Sleaford	28. 6.08P
G-CCOM	Westland Lysander IIIA	Y1363	N3093K	10.12.03	Propshop Ltd	Duxford	
			RCAF V9312		(Noted for restoration 11.06)		
G-CCOO	Raj Hamsa X'Air 133(1)	754		12.11.03	A Hipkin	Droppingwell Farm, Bewdley	10. 3.08P
	(Built A Hipkin - pr.no.BMAA/HB/320)						
G-CCOP	Ultramagic M-105 Balloon (Hot Air)	105/113		19. 1.04	G Holtam	Heage, Belper	24. 5.08
G-CCOR	Sequoia F 8L Falco	PFA 100-10588		9.12.03	D J and K S Thomas	Fenland	17. 6.08P
	(Built D J Thomas)						
G-CCOS	Cameron Z-350 Balloon (Hot Air)	10513		8. 3.04	M L Gabb	Haselor, Alcester	19. 3.08T
G-CCOT	Cameron Z-105 Balloon (Hot Air)	10517		14. 1.04	Airborne Adventures Ltd (Invista titles)	Skipton	3. 5.08A
G-CCOU	Mainair Sports Pegasus Quik	8012		21. 1.04	D E J McVicker	Newtownards	4. 4.08P
G-CCOV	Europa Aviation Europa XS	543		19. 1.04	G N Drake	Fowle Hall Farm, Laddingford	14.10.08P
	(Built G N Drake - pr.no.PFA 247-13998)						
G-CCOW	Mainair Sports Pegasus Quik	8008		28. 1.04	G P Couttie	Perth	25. 2.08P
G-CCOX	Piper J-3C-65 Cub	7278	EI-CCH	21. 1.04	R P Marks	Dunkeswell	
			N38801, NC38801		(On build 9.06)		
G-CCOY	North American AT-6D Harvard II	88-14555	Portuguese AF 1513	22. 3.04	Classic Aero Services Ltd	Mendlesham	
			SAAF 7426, EX884, 41-33857	(Parts noted 8.06)			
G-CCOZ	Monnett Sonerai II	0197		31. 5.78	P R Cozens	Spilstead Farm, Sedlescombe	26. 3.04P
	(Built P R Cozens - pr.no.PFA 015-10107) (Volkswagen 1900)				(Noted 10.07)		
G-CCPA	Air Création 582(1)/Kiss 400	FL023		13. 1.04	C P Astridge	Sywell	17. 8.08P
	(Built C P Astridge - pr.no.BMAA/HB/334 being Flylight kit comprising Trike s/n T03102 and Wing s/n A03183-3172)						
G-CCPC (2)	Mainair Sports Pegasus Quik	7994		26.11.03	P M Coppola	East Fortune	14.12.07P
G-CCPD	Campbell Cricket Mk.4	PFA G/03-1333		27. 1.04	N C Smith	(Newport, Isle of Wight)	
	(Built N C Smith)						
G-CCPE	Steen Skybolt	PFA 064-12830		10.12.03	C Moore	Kirkbride	20. 6.08P
	(Built C Moore)						
G-CCPF	Best Off Sky Ranger 912(2)	SKR0311396		26. 1.04	R K and T A Willcox	Chase Farm,Chipping Sodbury	23. 6.08P
	(Built T A Willcox - pr.no.BMAA/HB/340)						
G-CCPG	Mainair Sports Pegasus Quik	8016		13. 5.04	A W Lowrie	Eshott	12. 5.08P
G-CCPH	Evektor EV-97 teamEurostar UK	1814		9. 1.04	A H Woolley	(Hucknall)	30. 3.08P
G-CCPJ	Evektor EV-97 teamEurostar UK	1909		13. 2.04	S R Winter	Willingale	12. 2.08P
G-CCPK	Murphy Rebel	274R	N2283B	20. 1.04	B A Bridgewater and D Webb	Shobdon	27. 4.08P
	(Built M C Sentall)						
G-CCPL	Best Off Sky Ranger 912(2)	SKR0310385		29. 1.04	John Charles Turner tr G-CCPL Group		
	(Built P Openshaw and Partners - pr.no.BMAA/HB/342)					Tarn Farm, Cockerham	15.12.07P
G-CCPM	Mainair Blade 912	1360-1203-7-W1155		12. 1.04	T D Thompson	(Knutsford)	11. 1.08P
G-CCPN	Dyn'Aéro MCR-01 Club	271		28.11.03	P H Nelson	Higherlands Farm, Branscombe	7. 7.08P
	(Built P H Nelson - pr.no.PFA 301A-14133)						
G-CCPO	Cameron N-77 Balloon (Hot Air)	3217	(ZS-HPR)	4. 2.04	M J Woodcock and A C Woodcock		
			G-MITS			East Grinstead and Bristol	15. 6.08A
	(Originally built as c/n 1115 and regd G-MITS (qv), re-built with unknown new envelope C 1994 and then third envelope c/n 3217 and re-registered)						
G-CCPP	Cameron Concept-70 Balloon (Hot Air)	10515		16. 3.04	P F Smart tr The Sarnia Balloon Group		
						Oakley, Basingstoke	19. 6.08A

G-CCPS	Comco Ikarus C42 FB100 VLA	0310-6584		5. 2.04	H Cullens	Charterhall	11. 8.07P
	(Built H Cullens -pr.no.PFA 322-14138)						
G-CCPT	Cameron Z-90 Balloon (Hot Air)	10534		14. 4.04	Charter Ballooning Ltd (Castlepoint titles)	Liphook	3. 4.08A
G-CCPV	Avtech Jabiru J400	0xxx		12. 2.04	J R Lawrence	Charterhall	19.12.08P
	(Built J R Lawrence - pr.no.PFA 325-14058)						
G-CCPW	British Aerospace Jetstream Series 3102	785	SE-LDI	23. 4.04	Highland Airways Ltd	Inverness	18. 9.08E
			C-FHOE, G-31-785		"www.jetstreamexpress.com"		
G-CCPX	Diamond DA.40D Star	D4.092		18. 3.04	R T Dickinson	(Sheffield City)	10. 3.08E
G-CCPY	Hughes 369D	20-0674D	N622WA	22. 3.04	Hughes Helicopter Co Ltd t/a Biggin Hill Helicopters		
	(Hughes 500)		N833RW, N58388		(New owner 2.07)	Biggin Hill	
G-CCPZ	Cameron Z-225 Balloon (Hot Air)	10506		11. 3.04	Cameron Flights Southern Ltd		
						Woodborough, Pewsey	15. 3.08T
G-CCRA	DG Flugzeugbau DG-800B	8-308B208		19. 1.04	R Arkle "RA"	Aboyne	4. 4.08E
G-CCRB	Kolb Twinstar Mk.3	PFA 205-13993		9.12.03	R W Burge	(Ilfracombe)	7. 6.08P
	(Built R W Burge)						
G-CCRC	Cessna TU206G Turbo Stationair 6	U20607001	9A-DLC	24. 2.04	D M Penny	(Movenis, Coleraine)	6. 4.08E
			YU-DLC, N9960R				
G-CCRF	Mainair Sports Pegasus Quantum 15	8009		3. 3.04	R D Ballard	(Bexhill-on-Sea)	21. 4.08P
	(Rotax 582)						
G-CCRG	Ultramagic M-77 Balloon (Hot Air)	77/249		19. 4.04	Aerial Promotions Ltd	Cannock	30. 6.07A
G-CCRH	Cameron Z-315 Balloon (Hot Air)	10489		19. 3.04	Ballooning Network Ltd	Bristol	30. 7.08T
					(Bath Building Society titles)		
G-CCRI	Raj Hamsa X'Air 582(5)	891		26. 2.04	B M Tibenham	Longside, Peterhead	3. 6.08P
	(Built R A Wright - pr.no.BMAA/HB/354)						
G-CCRJ	Europa Aviation Europa	259		27. 2.04	J F Cliff	(Binfield, Bracknell)	
	(Built J F Cliff -pr.no.PFA 247-12966)						
G-CCRK	Luscombe 8A Silvaire	3186	N71759	16. 2.04	J R Kimberley	(Bounds Farm, Ardleigh)	26. 4.08P
	(Continental A65)		NC71759				
G-CCRN	Thruster T 600N 450 Sprint	1031-T600N-096		25. 2.04	R A Wright	(Hundleby, Spilsby)	5. 9.08P
G-CCRP	Thruster T.600N 450 Sprint	0043-T600N-099	G-ULLY	17. 3.04	M R Jones	Wing Farm, Longbridge Deverill	8.10.07
	(Rotax 582)		G-CCRP				
G-CCRR	Best Off Sky Ranger 912(1)	SKR0310393		16. 1.04	M Cheetham	Plaistows Farm, St Albans	9. 6.08P
	(Built J A Hunt - pr.no.BMAA/HB/329)						
G-CCRS	Lindstrand LBL 210A Balloon (Hot Air)	981		4. 3.04	Aerosaurus Balloons Ltd	Whimple, Exeter	12. 3.08T
G-CCRT	Mainair Sports Pegasus Quantum 15	8014		3. 2.04	C R Whitton	East Fortune	1. 6.08P
	(Rotax 582)						
G-CCRV	Best Off Sky Ranger 912(2)	SKRxxxx315		20. 2.04	A C Thomson	Parkhill Farm, Ilkeston	15. 8.08P
	(Built M R Mosley - pr.no.BMAA/HB/283)						
G-CCRW	Mainair Sports Pegasus Quik	8003		16. 3.04	S D Hutchinson	St Michaels	15. 3.07P
G-CCRX	Avtech Jabiru UL-450	xxxx		3. 3.04	M Everest	Cottage Farm, Norton Juxta	23. 5.07P
	(Built M Everest - pr.no.PFA 274A-14032)						
G-CCSA	Cameron Z-350 Balloon (Hot Air)	10490		19. 3.04	Ballooning Network Ltd	Southville, Bristol	30. 7.08T
					(Bristol Balloons titles)		
G-CCSD	Mainair Sports Pegasus Quik	8023		19. 3.04	A G Woodward	Heckington, Sleaford	10. 3.08P
G-CCSF	Mainair Sports Pegasus Quik	8030		1. 4.04	J S Walton	(Mold)	31. 3.08P
G-CCSG	Cameron Z-275 Balloon (Hot Air)	10518		2. 4.04	M L Gabb	Haselor, Alcester	3. 1.08T
G-CCSH	Mainair Sports Pegasus Quik	8020		1. 3.04	D G Adley	Weston Zoyland	14. 3.08P
G-CCSI	Cameron Z-42 Balloon (Hot Air)	10563		30. 3.04	Ikea Ltd	Eastgate, Bristol	20. 4.08A
G-CCSJ	Cameron A-275 Balloon (Hot Air)	10510		7. 5.04	Dragon Balloon Company Ltd	Castleton, Hope Valley	5. 4.08T
G-CCSK	Zenair CH.701SP STOL	PFA 187-14188		11. 3.04	J E W Mayhew	(Netherthorpe)	23. 4.08P
	(Built S J Thomas)		(Heavy landing Netherthorpe 2.8.07: nose under-carriage collapsed:, damage to propeller and engine shock-loaded)				
G-CCSL	Mainair Sports Pegasus Quik	8029		26. 4.04	A J Harper	Croughton	29. 4.08P
G-CCSM	Lindstrand LBL 105A Balloon (Hot Air)	991		18. 3.04	M A Webb (Gulf Air c/s)	Muscat	7. 5.08A
G-CCSN	Cessna U206G Stationair 6	U20604224	F-GECP	26. 3.04	K Brady	Strathallan	14. 5.08E
			D-EKAX, (OY-ASG), N756NM (Operated Strathallan Parachute Club)				
G-CCSO	Raj Hamsa X'Air Falcon VM133(1)	921		15. 3.04	K N Rigley and D Thorpe		
	(Built P Richardson - pr.no.BMAA/HB/364)				(Carlton-le-Moorland, Lincoln and Grantham)		3. 9.08P
G-CCSP	Cameron N-77 Balloon (Hot Air)	2882	SE-ZFV	17. 3.04	Ballongforeningen Oscair I Goteborg		
						Giteborg, Karlstad, Sweden	17. 2.08E
G-CCSR	Evektor EV-97A Eurostar	PFA 315-14174		18. 3.04	A Galante tr Sierra Romeo Group	Netherthorpe	20. 6.08P
	(Built M Lang)						
G-CCSS	Lindstrand LBL 90A Balloon (Hot Air)	973		11. 2.04	British Telecommunications PLC	Thatcham	7. 4.08A
G-CCST	Piper PA-32R-301 Saratoga II HP	3246182	N4180T	14. 2.01	G R Balls	Biggin Hill	30. 3.08T
G-CCSU	IAV-Bacau Yakovlev Yak-52	888712	LY-APO	26. 4.04	S Ullrich	Bad Worishofen, Germany	27 .4.08P
			DOSAAF 69 (yellow)				
G-CCSV	ICP MXP-740 Savannah Jabiru(4) 03-12-51-261			18. 3.04	R D Wood	Rochester	12. 3.08P
	(Built R D Wood - pr.no.BMAA/HB/362)						
G-CCSW	Nott PA Balloon (Hot Air)	9		24. 3.04	J R P Nott	London NW3	
G-CCSX	Best Off Sky Ranger 912(2)	SKR0401425		24. 3.04	T Jackson	The Chase, Wickwar	5.10.08P
	(Built T Jackson - pr.no.BMAA/HB/366)						
G-CCSY	Mainair Sports Pegasus Quik	8022		27. 2.04	C H Henderson	Perth	14. 8.08P
G-CCTA	Zenair CH.601UL Zodiac	PFA 162A-13725		4. 2.04	R E Gray and G T Harris	(Oxted)	17.10.08P
	(Built R E Gray and G T Harris)						
G-CCTC	Mainair Sports Pegasus Quik	8021		23. 2.04	D R Purslow	(Cleobury Mortimer, Kidderminster)	9. 7.08P
G-CCTD	Mainair Sports Pegasus Quik	8040		16. 3.04	R N S Taylor	Headon Farm, Retford	9. 6.08P
G-CCTE	Dyn'Aéro MCR-01 Club	61		22 .3.04	J T M McNie and P G Mackintosh	RAF Kinloss	14. 5.08P
	(Built G J Slater - pr.no.PFA 301-13268)						
G-CCTF	Pitts S-2A	2146	N51ST	26. 3.04	M S Hill	Crosland Moor	18. 8.07P
	(Built Aerotek Inc)						
G-CCTG	Van's RV-3B	PFA 099-10518		9. 3.04	M R Tingle	Ludham	12. 6.08P
	(Built I G Glenn) (PFA pr.no.identical to Van's RV-3 G-BHXN [c/n EAA 105098] builder P Hing which was cancelled 2. 9.91 by CAA)						
G-CCTH	Evektor EV-97 teamEurostar UK	2005		12. 3.04	P R Whitmore and S J Downing		
					(Talbot Green, Pontyclun and Romsley, Halesowen)		14. 3.08P
G-CCTI	Evektor EV-97 teamEurostar UK	2009		6. 4.04	Flylight Airsports Ltd	Sywell	26. 4.08P

G-CCTL	Robinson R44 Raven II	10309		30. 3.04	Aerocorp Ltd	Liverpool	25. 4.08E
G-CCTM	Mainair Blade	1363-0504-7-W1158		5. 4.04	J N Hanson	Tarn Farm, Cockerham	4. 6.08P
G-CCTN	Ultramagic T-180 Balloon (Hot Air)	180/48		5. 7.04	A Derbyshire	Woodseaves, Stafford	16. 4.08T
G-CCTO	Evektor EV-97 Eurostar	PFA 315-14136		17. 3.04	A J Boulton	Sittles Farm, Alrewas	21. 8.08P
	(Built A J Boulton)						
G-CCTP	Evektor EV-97 Eurostar	PFA 315-14185		18. 2.04	P E Rose	Ince Blundell	30. 5.08P
	(Built G M Yule)						
G-CCTR	Best Off Sky Ranger 912(2)	SKR0401410		2. 3.04	A H Trapp	(Kidderminster)	21. 3.08P
	(Built A H Trapp - pr.no.BMAA/HB/350)						
G-CCTS	Cameron Z-120 Balloon (Hot Air)	10570		22. 6.04	F R Hart *(Snap Survey titles)*	Bishop Sutton, Bristol	5. 3.08A
G-CCTT	Cessna 172SP Skyhawk	172S8157	N957SP	12. 2.04	A Reay	Caernarfon	2. 4.08E
G-CCTU	Mainair Sports Pegasus Quik	8024		21. 4.04	B J Syson	Landmead Farm, Garford	2. 5.08P
G-CCTV	Rans S-6-ES Coyote II	0302.1437		19. 6.03	G and S Simons	Jackrells Farm, Southwater	14. 6.06P
	(Built R M Broom - pr.no.PFA 204-14069) (Tri-cycle u/c)				*(New owners 11.07)*		
G-CCTW	Cessna 152	15279882	N757NW	26. 4.04	R J Dempsey	Lower Wasing Farm, Brimpton	8. 8.08E
G-CCTX	Rans S-6-ES Coyote II	1003.1524		19. 2.04	D A Tibbals	Rufforth	9. 6.07P
	(Built L M Leachman - pr.no.PFA 204-14143) (Tri-cycle u/c)				*(Noted 9.07)*		
G-CCTZ	Mainair Sports Pegasus Quik	8031		13. 4.04	S Baker	Long Marston	10. 5.08P
G-CCUA	Mainair Sports Pegasus Quik	8032		27. 4.04	H M Manning	Damyn's Hall, Upminster	28. 4.08P
G-CCUB	Piper J-3C-65 Cub	2362A	N33528	2. 4.81	Cormack (Aircraft Services) Ltd	Rothesay	
			NC33528, NX33528		*(On rebuild 2001)*		
G-CCUD	Best Off Sky Ranger J2.2(1)	SKRxxxx454		13. 4.04	A D Haughey	Newtownards	20.11.08P
	(Built J Johnston - pr.no.BMAA/HB/374)						
G-CCUE	Ultramagic T-180 Balloon (Hot Air)	180/45		10. 5.04	Espiritu Balloon Flights Ltd	Minsterley, Shrewsbury	23 .7.08T
G-CCUF	Best Off Sky Ranger 912(2)	SKRxxxx459		15. 4.04	R E Parker	Hunsdon	15.10.08P
	(Built C D Hogbourne and D J Parrish - pr.no.BMAA/HB/375)						
G-CCUH	Rotary Air Force RAF 2000 GTX-SE	PFA G/13-1356		16. 4.04	J H Haverhals	(Graffham, Petworth)	3. 7.08P
	(Built D R Lazenby)						
G-CCUI	Dyn'Aéro MCR-01	236		1. 4.04	J T Morgan	Sywell	9. 8.08P
	(Built J T Morgan - pr.no.PFA 301-13963)						
G-CCUJ	Cameron C-90 Balloon (Hot Air)	10576		5. 7.04	R D Jones t/a Rudgleigh Inn *(The Rudgleigh Inn titles)*		
						Easton-in-Gordano, Bristol	27. 5.05A
G-CCUK	Agusta A109A II	7263	RP-C109	5. 4.04	Churchgate Aviation LLP	(Battlesbridge, Wickford)	4.10.07E
			I-SEIE, N109AE				
G-CCUL	Europa Aviation Europa XS	336		20. 4.04	I P Dole tr Europa 6	Rayne Hall Farm, Braintree	25. 4.08P
	(Built I Dole - pr.no.PFA 247-13119) (Monowheel u/c)						
G-CCUO	Hughes 369D	40-0711D	N655WA	30. 4.04	M and K Pinfold t/a Claremont Air Services		
	(Hughes 500)		C-GKHI			Halfpenny Green	14. 2.08E
G-CCUP	Westland Wessex HC.Mk.2	WA/127	XR502	12.11.04	D Brem-Wilson and J Buswell		
	(Built Avions Fairey SA)				(Joydens Farm, Westerham and Sevenoaks)		
G-CCUR	Mainair Sports Pegasus Quantum 15-912	8034		30. 4.04	D W Power and D James	(Ammanford and Neath)	22. 5.08P
G-CCUS	Diamond DA.40D Star	D4.082		29. 4.04	R J and M J Millen t/a The Millen Corporation		
						Rochester	29. 8.08E
G-CCUT	Evektor EV-97 Eurostar	PFA 315-14191		9. 3.04	C C Pagett tr Doctor and the Medics		
	(Built C K Jones)					Croft Farm, Defford	17. 8.08P
G-CCUU	Vahdat-Hagh Shiraz	MV-009		15. 3.04	M E Vahdat-Hagh	(Uxbridge)	
	(Built M E Vahdat-Hagh)						
G-CCUV	Piper PA-25-260 Pawnee C	25-5201	VT-EBH	31. 1.05	D B Almey	(Weston Hills, Spalding)	
			N8745L				
G-CCUY	Europa Aviation Europa	xxx		14. 4.04	N Evans	Old Buckenham	27.11.06P
	(Built N Evans pr.no.PFA 247-13189)				*(Noted 9.07)*		
G-CCUZ	Thruster T 600N 450 Sprint	0044-T600N-102		29. 4.04	Fly 365 Ltd	Wickenby	14. 6.08P
G-CCVA	Evektor EV-97 Eurostar	PFA 315-14226		21. 4.04	D A Palmer	Halfpenny Green	29. 8.08P
	(Built T A Jones)						
G-CCVB	Mainair Sports Pegasus Quik	8033		6. 5.04	L Chesworth	(Malpas)	17. 5.08P
G-CCVD	Cameron Z-105 Balloon (Hot Air)	10583		25. 5.04	Associazione Sportiva Sorvolare	Crevalcore, Italy	1. 6.05A
					(Casanova titles)		
G-CCVF	Lindstrand LBL 105A Balloon (Hot Air)	953		6. 5.04	S Villiers and A W Patterson t/a Alan Patterson Design		
						Bangor	7. 8.08A
G-CCVG	Schweizer 269C-1	0164		2. 4.04	Radcliffe Engineering Services Ltd	Liverpool	18. 4.07T
	(Schweizer 300)						
G-CCVH	Curtiss H75A-1	12881	NX80FR	25. 5.04	Patina Ltd	Duxford	5. 6.08P
			G-CCVH, French AF 82		*(Operated The Fighter Collection)*		
G-CCVI	Zenair CH.701SP STOL	PFA 187-14181		5. 5.04	C R Hoveman	Bidford	30. 5.08P
	(Built C R Hoveman)						
G-CCVJ	Raj Hamsa X'Air Falcon 133(1)	916		7. 5.04	F J Rodrigues	Rhedyn Coch Farm, Rhuallt	8. 3.08P
	(Built G A J Salter - pr.no.BMAA/HB/381)						
G-CCVK	Evektor EV-97 teamEurostar UK	2016		19. 5.04	S A Kirk tr Kent Eurostar Group	Rochester	4. 6.08P
G-CCVL	Zenair CH.601XL Zodiac	PFA 162B-14204		22. 4.04	A Y-T Leung and G Constantine	Beccles	5. 4.08P
	(Built A Y-T Leung and G Constantine) (Tri-cycle u/c)						
G-CCVM	Van's RV-7A	PFA 323-14213		12. 3.04	J G Small	(Southport)	28.10.08P
	(Built J G Small)						
G-CCVN	Avtech Jabiru SP-470	xxxx		10. 5.04	J C Collingwood	Wittersham, Tenterden	6. 6.07P
	(Built J C Collingwood - pr.no.PFA 274B-13677)						
G-CCVO	Bell 206B-3 JetRanger III	4326	N471M	22. 6.04	Bell Trailers (Rental) Ltd	(Nelson)	29. 7.08E
			JA6150, N20334, C-GLZU				
G-CCVP	Beech 58 Baron	TH-1948	PH-ZEM	13. 5.04	Richard Nash Cars Ltd	Norwich	27. 6.08E
			N80VS				
G-CCVR	Best Off Sky Ranger 912(2)	SKR0311407		29. 4.04	M J Batchelor	The Chase, Wickwar	14. 9.08P
	(Built M J Batchelor - pr.no.BMAA/HB/353)						
G-CCVS	Van's RV-6A	PFA 181A-13413	G-CCVC	29. 3.04	J Edgeworth	(Darlington)	
	(Built J Edgeworth)						
G-CCVT	Zenair CH.601UL Zodiac	PFA 162A-14160		2. 4.04	P Millar	Kirknewton	19. 6.08P
	(Built D McCormack) (Tri-cycle u/c)						

Reg	Type	C/n	Prev id	Date	Owner	Location	Date
G-CCVU	Robinson R22 Beta II	3600		11. 5.04	Helieagle Ltd	Leicester	5. 6.08P
G-CCVW	Nicollier HN.700 Ménestrel II	PFA 217-11950		13. 5.04	B F Enock	(Leamington Spa)	
	(Built B F Enock)						
G-CCVX	Mainair Tri Flyer 250/Flexiform Striker	AS-001		18. 5.04	J A Shufflebotham	(Macclesfield)	
G-CCVY	Robinson R22 Beta	1666	N101SK	9. 7.04	S Klinge	Prestwick	9. 8.08P
			N4041W, C-GJKD, N4041W				
G-CCVZ	Cameron O-120 Balloon (Hot Air)	10586		27. 7.04	T M C McCoy	Peasedown St John, Bath	11. 6.08T
					(Operated Ascent Balloons)		
G-CCWA	Piper PA-28-181 Archer III	2843328	D-ELEM	16. 6.04	T P Gooley	White Waltham	24. 6.08T
			PH-AEG, N41776				
G-CCWB	Aero L-39ZA Albatros	132036	N404ZA	4. 6.04	Freespirit Charters Ltd	Duxford	
			Romanian AF 136		(Noted 11.06)		
G-CCWC	Best Off Sky Ranger 912(2)	SKRxxxx422		4. 5.04	R M Nutt, E B Maxwell and M J Richardson	Carlisle	21. 9.08P
	(Built C Hewer - pr.no.BMAA/HB/367)				tr Carlisle Sky Rangers		
G-CCWD	Robinson R44 Raven	1296		10. 3.03	Mulroy Car Sales (Letterkenny) Ltd		
						Letterkenny, County Donegal	3. 4.08E
G-CCWE	Lindstrand LBL 330A Balloon (Hot Air)	984		22. 4.04	Adventure Balloons Ltd	Hartley Wintney, Hook	7.10.08A
G-CCWF	Raj Hamsa X'Air 133(1)	675		19. 5.04	F Loughran	(Kildarky, County Meath	6.10.05P
	(Built G A J Salter - pr.no.BMAA/HB/331)				(New owner 10.07)		
G-CCWG	Whittaker MW6 Merlin	PFA 164-11998		8. 4.04	D E Williams	(Llangynwyd, Maesteg)	
	(Built D E Williams)						
G-CCWH	Dyn'Aéro MCR-01 Club	233		20. 4.04	B J Mills and N J Mines		
	(Built M G Rasch - pr.no.PFA 301-13949)					Wadswick Manor Farm, Corsham	8. 5.08P
G-CCWI	Robinson R44 Clipper II	10362		16. 6.04	Saxon Logistics Ltd	Elstree	26. 9.08E
	(Officially regd as "Raven II")						
G-CCWJ	Robinson R44 Clipper II	10363		16. 6.04	Saxon Logistics Ltd	Denham	26. 9.08E
	(Officially regd as "Raven II")						
G-CCWK	Aérospatiale AS.355F2 Ecureuil 2	5439	N8066G	10. 9.04	RCR Aviation Ltd	Thruxton	13. 9.07T
			LN-OES, F-GGRS		(New owners 2.08)		
G-CCWL	Mainair Blade	1364-0504-7-W1159		19. 5.04	T J Burrow	St Michaels	23. 5.08P
G-CCWM	Robin DR.400-180 Régent	2457	F-GTZM	3. 6.04	M R Clark	Newcastle	9. 8.08E
G-CCWN	Mainair Sports Pegasus Quantum 15-912	8045		11. 6.04	T H Ferguson	Sutton Meadows	16. 8.08P
G-CCWO	Mainair Sports Pegasus Quantum 15-912	8042		16. 6.04	R Fitzgerald	(London N10)	16. 6.08P
G-CCWP	Evektor EV-97 teamEurostar UK	2010		9. 6.04	N P de G Lambert	(Farnham)	23. 4.08P
G-CCWR	Mainair Sports Pegasus Quik	8053		1. 6.04	J A Robinson	Tarn Farm, Cockerham	5. 7.08P
G-CCWT	Balony Kubicek BB20GP Balloon (Hot Air)	298	OK-0298	18. 5.04	H C J and S L G Williams	Langford, Bristol	25. 5.08A
					"Little Roo"		
G-CCWU	Best Off Sky Ranger 912(2)	SKR0403461		1. 6.04	S P Clifton tr G-CCWU Syndicate	Long Marston	28. 5.08P
	(Built D M Lane - prr/no.BMAA/HB/386)						
G-CCWV	Mainair Sports Pegasus Quik	8043		1. 6.04	W J Dawson	(Ilton, Ripon)	6. 6.07P
G-CCWW	Mainair Sports Pegasus Quantum 15-912	8035		4. 5.04	Virginia G Concannon tr Double Whisky Syndicate		
						Knapthorpe Lodge, Caunton	3. 5.08P
G-CCWY	Pilatus PC-12/45	568		8. 9.04	Harpin Ltd	Leeds-Bradford	10.10.07E
G-CCWZ	Raj Hamsa X'Air Falcon 133(1)	925		4. 5.04	M A Evans	Weston Zoyland	26. 9.08P
	(Built M A Evans - pr.no.BMAA/HB/380)						
G-CCXA	Boeing Stearman A75N1 Kaydet	75-3616	N75TL	1. 6.04	Skymax (Aviation) Ltd	Damyns Hall, Upminster	6. 9.07P
	(N2S-4 Kaydet)		N5148N, Bu.37869		(As "669" in USAAC c/s)		
G-CCXB	Boeing Stearman B75N1 Kaydet	75-7854	N1363M	26. 7.05	Skymax (Aviation) Ltd	Damyns Hall, Upminster	3.10.08S
	(N2S-3 Kaydet)		Bu.38233		(As "699" in USAAC c/s)		
G-CCXC	Mudry CAP.10B	165	N4247M	26. 5.04	Skymax (Aviation) Ltd	Damyns Hall, Upminster	6. 9.07T
			Mexican AF EPC-162				
G-CCXD	Lindstrand LBL 105B Balloon (Hot Air)	996		14. 6.04	J H Dobson "Rainbow Blue"	Streatley, Reading	1. 6.08T
G-CCXE	Cameron Z-120 Balloon (Hot Air)	10596		3. 6.04	Hans-Juergen Haas-Wittmuess		
						Gmund-St Quirin, Germany	5. 9.08E
G-CCXF	Cameron Z-90 Balloon (Hot Air)	10593		3. 8.04	R G March and T J Maycock	Market Harborough	6. 7.08A
					(Unison titles)		
G-CCXG	Replica Plans SE.5a	PFA 020-11785		11. 6.04	C Morris	Gresford, Wrexham	10. 9.07P
	(Built C Morris)				(As "C5430:V" in RFC c/s)		
G-CCXH	Best Off Sky Ranger J2.2(1)	SKR0403458		4. 6.04	M J O'Connor	(Carshalton)	2. 8.07P
	(Built Sky Ranger UK Ltd - pr.no.BMAA/HB/323)				(New owner 9.07)		
G-CCXI	Thorp T 211	PFA 305-13504		22. 9.03	J Gilroy	(Worth, Crawley)	
	(Built S G R and J Gilroy)						
G-CCXJ	Cessna 340A	340A0912	N25PJ	13. 7.04	Kilo Aviation Ltd	Liverpool	25. 7.08E
			HB-LNM, LN-TEA, N27026				
G-CCXK	Pitts S-1S	AACA/1061	ZK-ECO	14. 6.04	P G Bond	Shipdham	20.11.08P
	(Built E C Roberts)						
G-CCXL	Best Off Sky Ranger 912(2)	SKRxxxx411		18. 6.04	F W McCann	Strathaven	5. 6.08P
	(Built R G Cameron - pr.no.BMAA/HB/335)						
G-CCXM	Best Off Sky Ranger 912(2)	SKR0311394		16. 6.04	C J Finnigan	Enstone	4.11.07P
	(Built C J Finnigan - pr.no.BMAA/HB/337)						
G-CCXN	Best Off Sky Ranger 912(2)	SKRxxxx833		4. 6.04	C I Chegwen	Mill Farm, Hughley, Much Wenlock	25. 8.08P
	(Built C I Chegwen - pr.no.BMAA/HB/323)						
G-CCXO	Corby CJ-1 Starlet	PFA 134-13267		21. 6.04	I W L Aikman	Lower Wasing Farm, Brimpton	16. 9.08P
	(Built I W L Aikman)						
G-CCXP	ICP MXP-740 Savannah Jabiru(4)	03-09-51-231		30. 4.04	B J Harper	Eaglescott	1. 4.08P
	(Built B J Harper - pr.no.BMAA/HB/318)						
G-CCXR	Mainair Blade	1367-0604-7-W1162		5. 7.04	J McErlain	(Tralee, County Kerry)	10. 8.08P
G-CCXS	Montgomerie-Bensen B 8MR	PFA G/01A-1350		26. 5.04	S A Sharp	Kirkbride	
	(Built S A Sharp)				(Noted 8.07)		
G-CCXT	Mainair Sports Pegasus Quik	8046		18. 6.04	C Turner	Priory Farm, Tibenham	23. 6.08P
G-CCXU	Diamond DA.40D Star	D4.037	ZK-SFH	28. 6.04	R J and L Hole	Norwich	16. 8.08E
G-CCXV	Thruster T 600N 450	0045-T600N-103		18. 6.04	W G Dunn	Dowland, Winkleigh	9. 7.08P
G-CCXW	Thruster T 600N 450	0045-T600N-104		15. 7.04	J Walsh	North Weald	14. 7.08P
					(Operated Saxon Microlights)		

G-CCXX	American General AG-5B Tiger	10160	PH-MLG YL-CAH	19. 4.04	N R Dick and D O'Donnell tr Osprey Flying Group (Banchory)	21. 7.08E
G-CCXZ	Mainair Sports Pegasus Quik	8038		24. 5.04	K J Sene	Barton	21. 5.08P
G-CCYA	Avtech Jabiru J430	0xxx		22. 6.04	D J Royce	Ludham	20. 6.08P
	(Built D J Royce - pr.no.PFA 336-14060)					
G-CCYB	Reality Escapade 912(1)	JAESC 0034		24. 6.04	B E and S M Renehan	Lasham	6. 7.08P
	(Built B E Renehan - pr.no.BMAA/HB/391)					
G-CCYC	Robinson R44 Raven II	10388		24. 6.04	Derg Developments Ltd Ballyvally, Killaloe, County Clare	20. 7.08E
G-CCYE	Mainair Sports Pegasus Quik	8050		30. 7.04	J Lane	Clench Common	29. 7.08P
G-CCYF	Aerophile 5500 Tethered Balloon (Gas-filled)	6	F-GPRS	30. 6.04	High Point Balloons Ltd (GWR titles) Alveston, Bristol	27. 5.06T
G-CCYG	Robinson R44 Raven II	10424		9. 7.04	P Durkin t/a Moorland Windows	Blackpool	8. 8.08E
G-CCYH	Embraer EMB-145EP	145070	SE-DZA PT-SAO	23. 9.04	British Midland Regional Ltd	Aberdeen	22. 9.08E
G-CCYI	Cameron O-105 Balloon (Hot Air)	10604		30. 7.04	Media Balloons	Policoro, Italy	15. 8.07A
G-CCYJ	Mainair Sports Pegasus Quik	8054		2. 8.04	R J Griffiths	Perth	17.11.08P
G-CCYL	Mainair Sports Pegasus Quantum 15	8055		26. 7.04	M J L Morris	Swansea	4.11.08P
	(Rotax 582)					
G-CCYM	Best Off Sky Ranger 912(2)	SKR0401412		16. 7.04	K A O'Neill	Plaistows Farm, St Albans	27. 1.08P
	(Built D McDonagh - pr.no.BMAA/HB/390)					
G-CCYN	Cameron C-80 Balloon (Hot Air)	10133		2. 8.04	D R Firkins	Beckford, Tewkesbury	19. 7.07A
G-CCYO	Christen Eagle II	HAYNER 0001	N56RJ	13. 9.04	P C Woolley	Cadwell Park, Louth	20.11.07P
	(Built R Hayner)				(New owner 1.08)	
G-CCYP	Colt 56A Balloon (Hot Air)	302	SE-ZXG	23. 7.04	Magical Adventures Ltd	Oswestry	3. 4.08E
	(Special Shape Beefburger)					
G-CCYR	Comco Ikarus C42 FB80	0408-6612		20. 9.04	Airbourne Aviation Ltd	Popham	20 .9.0P
G-CCYS	Reims Cessna F182Q Skylane	F18200126	OY-BNG	31. 8.04	S Dyson	Netherthorpe	25. 6.08E
G-CCYT	Robinson R44 Raven II	10443		28. 7.04	B E Llewellyn t/a Bell Commercials	Swansea	13. 9.07T
G-CCYU	Ultramagic S-90 Balloon (Hot Air)	90/70		17. 8.04	A R Craze	St Leonards-on-Sea	26. 8.07T
G-CCYX	Bell 412	34001	PK-HMI	2. 8.04	RCR Aviation Ltd	Thruxton	
	(Built Ndustri Pesawat Terbang Nusantara)					
G-CCYY	Piper PA-28-161 Warrior II	2816094	HB-PML	17. 6.04	Flightcontrol Ltd	Fairoaks	15. 8.08E
G-CCYZ	Dornier EKW C-3605	338	N31624 Swiss AF C-558	30. 9.04	William Tomkins Ltd	Wickenby	
	(Built Federal Aircraft Factory)				(Noted 10.06)	
G-CCZA	SOCATA MS.894A Rallye Minerva 220	12094	D-EBWL F-BUVI	14. 7.05	J Greenwood	Morgansfield, Fishburn	5. 6.08P
G-CCZB	Mainair Sports Pegasus Quantum 15	8052		21. 7.04	J Hartley	Deenethorpe	15. 3.08P
	(Rotax 582)					
G-CCZD	Van's RV-7	PFA 323-14087		28. 5.04	D Powell	Shenstone	24.10.08P
	(Built R T Clegg)					
G-CCZG	Robinson R44 Raven II	10474		2. 9.04	JLC Aviation Ltd	(Gormersal, Cleckheaton)	7.10.07E
	(Marked as R44 Clipper II)					
G-CCZH	Robinson R44 Raven	1423		6. 9.04	Newtown Aviation Ltd	(Enfield, County Meath)	17.10.07E
G-CCZI	Cameron A-275 Balloon (Hot Air)	10626		4. 4.05	Balloon School (International) Ltd Colhook Common, Petworth	2. 5.08E
G-CCZJ	Raj Hamsa X'Air Falcon 582(2)	xxx		5. 8.04	P A Linford	(Denby Dale, Huddersfield)	17. 8.08P
	(Built A B Gridley - pr.no.BMAA/HB/401)					
G-CCZK	Zenair CH.601UL Zodiac	PFA 162A-14270		11. 8.04	R J Hopkins	Popham	7. 5.08P
	(Built R J Hopkins)					
G-CCZL	Comco Ikarus C42 FB80	0410-6620		29.11.04	D Stokes	(The Gambia)	28.11.05P
					(New owner 1.06)	
G-CCZM	Best Off Sky Ranger 912S(1)	SKRxxxx455		1. 7.04	D Woodward	(Marple, Stockport)	2. 2.08P
	(Built D M Hepworth - pr.no.BMAA/HB/372)					
G-CCZN	Rans S-6-ES Coyote II	0404 1561 ES		9. 8.04	R D Proctor	(Yarwell, Peterborough)	4.12.07P
	(Built M Taylor - pr.no.PFA 204-14275)					
G-CCZO	Mainair Sports Pegasus Quik	8066		2. 9.04	J V Clewer Harringe Court, Seliindge, Folkestone	7. 9.08P
G-CCZP	Super Marine Spitfire Mk.26	25		10. 6.04	J W E Pearson	Panshanger	19.12.08P
	(Built J W E Pearson and H Luck - pr.no.PFA 324-14062)				(As "JF343:JW-P" in RAF c/s)	
G-CCZR	Medway EclipseR	177/155		15. 7.04	R A Keene	Over Farm, Gloucester	15.10.07P
G-CCZS	Raj Hamsa X'Air Falcon 582(2)	xxxx		16. 8.04	A T Kilpatrick	(Convoy, Lifford, Co Donegal)	9.10.08P
	(Built P J Sheehy - pr.no.BMAA/HB/403)					
G-CCZT	Van's RV-9A	PFA 320-13777		10. 8.04	N A Henderson	Bicester	23. 4.08P
	(Built N A Henderson)					
G-CCZU	Diamond DA.40D Star	D4.125	OE-VPU	24. 8.04	Diamond Finance Services GmbH	Perth	17.10.07E
					(Operated Tayflite)	
G-CCZV	Piper PA-28-151 Cherokee Warrior	28-7715089	OY-CHR SE-GNY	7. 7.04	P D P Deal	Elstree	6. 4.08E
G-CCZW	Mainair Blade	1368-0904-7-W1163		21.10.04	C J Wright	(Endmoor, Kendal)	27.11.08P
G-CCZX	Robin DR.400-180 Régent	2127	F-GLKY	15. 9.04	M Conrad	North Weald	10. 5.08E
G-CCZY	Van's RV-9A	PFA 320-14154		23. 8.04	G Williams tr Mona RV-9 Group	RAF Mona	3. 7.08P
	(Built G Williams and Partners)					
G-CCZZ	Evektor EV-97 Eurostar	PFA 315-14158		28. 5.04	B M Starck and J P Aitken	Bourn	5. 8.07P
	(Built B M Starck and R Bastin)					

G-CDAA - G-CDZZ

G-CDAA	Mainair Sports Pegasus Quantum 15-912	8069		27. 8.04	I A Macadam	Damyn's Hall, Upminster	26. 8.08P
G-CDAB	Stoddard-Hamilton Glasair IIS RG	PFA 149-13231		7. 7.04	W L Hitchins	Landmead Farm, Garford	
	(Built W L Hitchins)				(On build 11.06)	
G-CDAC	Evektor EV-97 teamEurostar UK	2116		30. 9.04	Nene Valley Microlights Ltd Sackville Farm, Riseley	29. 9.08P
G-CDAD	Lindstrand LBL 25A Cloudhopper Balloon (Hot Air)	1003		21. 9.04	G J Madelin	Farnham	6.11.08A
G-CDAE	Van's RV-6A	PFA 181A-13018		5. 8.04	K J Fleming	RAF Woodvale	8. 2.08P
	(Built K J Fleming)					

Reg	Type	C/n	Prev id	Date	Owner/Operator	Location	Expiry
G-CDAF	Bell 412	33105	PK-HMS	2. 8.04	RCR Aviation Ltd	Thruxton	
G-CDAG	Mainair Blade	1325-0502-7-W1120		10. 9.04	D K May	Tarn Farm, Cockerham	26. 4.08P
G-CDAI	Robin DR.400-140B	2574	D-EEAQ	13.12.04	Cole Aviation Ltd	Elstree	13.11.07E
			G-CDAI				
G-CDAK	Zenair CH.601UL Zodiac	PFA 162A-14210		21. 7.04	K Kerr	Sleap	5. 2.08P
	(Built K Kerr) (Tri-cycle u/c)						
G-CDAL	Zenair CH.601UL Zodiac	PFA 162A-14195		7. 6.04	R J Howell	(Cleeve, Bristol)	28. 9.08P
	(Built D Cassidy) (Tri-cycle u/c)						
G-CDAM	Sky 77-24 Balloon (Hot Air)	057	CS-BAO	16. 8.04	M Morris and P A Davies	Park Hall, Oswestry	25. 1.08A
G-CDAO	Mainair Sports Pegasus Quantum 15-912	8061		17. 8.04	J C Duncan	(High Askomil, Campbeltown)	12. 9.07P
G-CDAP	Evektor EV-97 teamEurostar UK	2114		28. 7.04	R W Caress	Fenland	27. 7.08P
G-CDAR	Mainair Sports Pegasus Quik	8060		17. 8.04	A R Pitcher	(Rye)	16. 8.08P
G-CDAT	ICP MXP-740 Savannah Jabiru(4) 03-05-51-211			7. 7.04	R Simpson	Eshott	23. 8.08P
	(Built R Simpson - pr.no.BMAA/HB/327)						
G-CDAW	Robinson R22 Beta	3703		11.10.04	Airtask Group PLC	Stapleford	10.11.07E
G-CDAX	Mainair Sports Pegasus Quik	8068		8. 9.04	I D Nuttall	Over Farm, Gloucester	22. 9.08P
G-CDAY	Best Off Sky Ranger 912(2)	SKR0404473		7. 7.04	D A Perkins tr G-CDAY Group		
	(Built M E Furniss - pr.no.BMAA/HB/394)					Tarn Farm, Cockerham	4.12.08P
G-CDAZ	Evektor EV-97 Eurostar	2004 21.10		13. 8.04	M C J Ludlow Harringe Court, Sellindge, Folkestone		29.10.08P
	(Built M C J Ludlow - pr.no.PFA 315-14268)						
G-CDBA	Best Off Sky Ranger 912(2)	SKR0404484		21.10.04	P J Brennan	Ashcroft Fam, Winsford	2. 6.08P
	(Built P J Brennan - pr.no.BMAA/HB/406)						
G-CDBB	Mainair Sports Pegasus Quik	8062		16. 8.04	J P Witcher and A H Mackinnon Redlands, Swindon		23.10.08P
G-CDBC	Aviation Enterprises Magnum	001	G-61-2	27. 8.04	Aviation Enterprises Ltd	Membury	
					(Noted derelict outside premises 5.05 and less wings and tail by 4.06)		
G-CDBD	Avtech Jabiru J400	0xxx		16. 8.04	S Derwin and E Bentley	Morgansfield, Fishburn	12. 4.08P
	(Built S Derwin and E Bentley - pr.no.PFA 325-14077)						
G-CDBE	Montgomerie-Bensen B 8M	PFA G/01-1360		7. 9.04	P Harwood	Kirkbride	8. 8.07P
	(Built P Harwood)						
G-CDBF	Robinson R22 Beta II	3681		11.10.04	Wiksy Charter Ltd	Hawarden	31.10.07E
G-CDBG	Robinson R22 Beta II	3682		11.10.04	CC Helicopters Ltd	Blackpool	28.10.07E
G-CDBJ	Yakovlev Yak-3	02-03	RA-44553	1.11.07	C E Bellhouse	Headcorn	
	(Official p/i and c/n appear incorrect - thought, as new-build, to be 0470203)				*(Noted 8.07 as "21" (white) in Russian AF c/s)*		
G-CDBK	Rotorway Executive 162F	6834		20. 9.04	Car Builder Solutions Ltd	(Staplehurst, Tonbridge)	13. 8.08P
	(Built N and M Foreman)						
G-CDBM	CAB Robin DR.400-180 Régent	2573		16.11.04	C M Simmonds	St Just	23.11.07E
G-CDBO	Best Off Sky Ranger 912(2)	SKRxxxx424		13. 8.04	A C Turnbull	Perth	2.11.06P
	(Built A M Dalgetty - pr.no.BMAA/HB/370)				*(Noted 2.07)*		
G-CDBR	Stolp SA.300 Starduster Too	PFA 035-13036		15. 9.04	R J Warren	(West Drayton)	
	(Built R J Warren)				*(Fuselage noted 4.06 heading West Drayton to M4)*		
G-CDBS	MBB BÖ.105DBS-4	S 738	D-HDRZ	29. 9.89	Bond Air Services Ltd	Glasgow City Heliport	8.11.07E
			VH-MBK, N970MB, D-HDRZ				
G-CDBU	Comco Ikarus C42 FB100	0411-6632		26. 1.05	S E Meehan and J K Agarwala	Ince Blundell	22. 4.08P
G-CDBV	Best Off Sky Ranger 912S(1)	SKRxxxx499		23. 9.04	K Hall	Harringe Court, Sellindge	6. 4.08P
	(Built K Hall - pr.no.BMAA/HB/409)						
G-CDBX	Europa Aviation Europa XS	568		16. 9.04	R Marston	Shenstone	17. 2.08P
	(Built R Marston - pr.no.PFA 247-13971)						
G-CDBY	Dyn'Aéro MCR-01 ULC	288		23. 8.04	R Clark	(Sherburn-in-Elmet)	18. 1.08P
	(Built R Germany- pr.no.PFA 301B-14269)						
G-CDBZ	Thruster T 600N 450	0047-T600N-106		24. 9.04	J A Lynch	Sandown, Isle of Wight	29. 9.08P
G-CDCB	Robinson R44 Raven II	10532		8.11.04	Microwave Sales and Services Ltd	Enniskillen	9.12.07E
G-CDCC	Evektor EV-97A Eurostar	PFA 315A-14262		11. 8.04	R E and N G Nicholson		
	(Built R E and N G Nicholson)				"The Dream" Higherlands Farm, Branscombe		8. 2.08P
G-CDCD	Van's RV-9A	PFA 320-13925		20. 1.04	M Weaver and S D Arnold tr RV9ers	(Coleshill)	
	(Built M Weaver and S D Arnold)				*(Exhibited incomplete Kemble 7.05)*		
G-CDCE	Mudry CAP.10B	39	F-BNDC	3.11.04	The Tiger Club 1990 Ltd	Headcorn	11. 5.08E
			CN-TBW, F-BUDG				
G-CDCF	Mainair Sports Pegasus Quik	8076		8.11.04	T J Gayton-Polley	(Billingshurst)	17.11.08P
G-CDCG	Comco Ikarus C42 FB UK	0408-6625		16. 8.04	N E Ashton and R H J Jenkins	Ince Blundell	27. 6.08P
	(Built N E Ashton and R H J Jenkins - pr.no.PFA 322-14281)						
G-CDCH	Best Off Sky Ranger 912(2)	SKR0401436		28. 9.04	K Laud	Nottage Farm, Swadlincote	17. 8.08P
	(Built K Laud - pr.no.BMAA/HB/384)						
G-CDCI	Mainair Sports Pegasus Quik	8077		14. 1.05	S G Murray	Fowle Hall Farm, Laddingford	5. 5.08P
G-CDCK	Mainair Sports Pegasus Quik	8078		22.10.04	S G Ward	(Chatham)	9.11.07P
	(Original trike fitted to G-CDEVP 10.07 qv)						
G-CDCM	Comco Ikarus C42 FB UK	0408-6624		26.10.04	S T Allen	Craysmarsh Farm, Melksham	21. 9.07P
	(Built S T Allen as pr.no.PFA 322-14280) (Carries "Icarus C42B" titles)						
G-CDCO	Comco Ikarus C42 FB UK	PFA 322-14315		7.10.04	Churchill Trading Ltd	(London N4)	27.11.08P
	(Built G G Bevis)						
G-CDCP	Avtech Jabiru J400	0xxx		7.10.04	M W T Wilson	Morgansfield, Fishburn	1. 5.08P
	(Built M W T Wilson - pr.no.PFA 325-14094)						
G-CDCR	ICP MXP-740 Savannah Jabiru(4) 04-06-51-291			14. 1.05	T Davidson and G McKinstry		
	(Built T Davidson and G McKinstry - pr.no.BMAA/HB/405)				Slieve Croob, Slievenamoney, Castlewellan		21. 9.08P
G-CDCS	Piper PA-12 Super Cruiser	12-2907	N854CC	29. 9.04	D Todorovic	Spanhoe	14. 5.08P
			CS-ACC				
G-CDCT	Evektor EV-97 teamEurostar UK	2117		15. 9.04	J Lynch	Barton	17.10.08P
G-CDCU	Mainair Blade	1369-1004-7-W1164		19.10.04	W S Clare	(Stratford-upon-Avon)	3. 4.08P
G-CDCV	Robinson R44 Clipper II	10536		28.10.04	Central Chiswick Developments Ltd	Denham	29.11.07E
G-CDCW	Reality Escapade 912(1)	JAESC 0050		4.10.04	P Nicholls	(Ludlow)	13. 3.07P
	(Built P Nicholls - pr.no.BMAA/HB/413)						
G-CDCX	Cessna 750 Citation X	750-0194	N194CX	26. 6.03	P W Harris t/a Pendley Farm	Luton	25. 6.08E
			N5192E				
G-CDCY	Mainair Sports Pegasus Quantum 15	8065		29.10.04	H Kearns	(Sallins, County Kildare)	23.10.07P
	(Rotax 582)						

Reg	Type	C/n	Prev id	Date	Owner	Location	Expiry
G-CDDA	SOCATA TB-20 Trinidad	1860	PH-SXE F-OIGL	22.10.04	Oxford Aviation Training Ltd	Oxford	4. 1.08E
G-CDDB	Standard Cirrus (Built Burkhart Grob Flugzeugbau)	577G	BGA 5102-KHJ F-CEMG	13.10.04	K D Barker (St Nicholas de la Grave, France) "KM"		5. 2.08
G-CDDC	Cameron Z-275 Balloon (Hot Air)	10656		19. 7.05	Airborne Balloon Management Ltd Paddock Wood		4. 9.08E
G-CDDD	Robinson R22 Beta II	3658		24. 8.04	TDR Aviation Ltd (Mullahead, Tandragee)		27. 9.07E
G-CDDE	PZL-110 Koliber 160A	04020088	SP-WGO	26.10.04	Horizon Aviation Ltd	Swansea	21.12.07T
G-CDDF	Mainair Sports Pegasus Quantum 15-912	8079		8.11.04	B C Blackburn (Noted 2.07)	Perth	8.11.05P
G-CDDG	Piper PA-28-161 Warrior II	2816065	HB-PLU	4.10.04	A Oxenham	Hinton-in-the-Hedges	30.11.07E
G-CDDH	Raj Hamsa X'Air Falcon Jabiru(3) (Built B Stanbridge - pr.no.BMAA/HB/419)	944		26.10.04	B and Lorna Stanbridge	Wickenby	18. 9.08P
G-CDDI	Thruster T 600N 450	1040-T600N-109		26.10.04	R Nayak	North Coates	28.11.07P
G-CDDK	Cessna 172M Skyhawk	17265258	TF-SIX N64478	1.12.04	M H and P R Kevern	Enstone	12. 3.08E
G-CDDL	Cameron Z-350 Balloon (Hot Air)	10632		24. 5.05	Balloon School (International) Ltd Colhook Common, Petworth		21. 5.08E
G-CDDM	Lindstrand LBL 90A Balloon (Hot Air)	902	ZS-HAI	14. 1.05	S P Harrowing	Margam, Port Talbot	23. 3.08E
G-CDDN	Lindstrand LBL 90A Balloon (Hot Air)	903	ZS-HAK	14. 1.05	I J Martin and D J Groombridge t/a Flying Enterprises (Fishtank.com titles)	Bristol	23. 7.08E
G-CDDO	Raj Hamsa X'Air 133(2) (Built R N Tarrant - pr.no.BMAA/HB/407)	941		2.11.04	N C Marciano	Ince Blundell	13. 1.08P
G-CDDP	Laser Lazer Z230 (Built F L Thomson)	001	N230RT	16.11.04	A Smith	Bagby	14. 8.08P
G-CDDR	Best Off Sky Ranger 582(1) (Built R J Milward - pr.no.BMAA/HB/418)	SKR0406502		26.10.04	M J Saywell	Kimbolton	9. 6.08P
G-CDDS	Zenair CH.601HD Zodiac (Built S Foreman)	PFA 162-14223		8.10.04	S Foreman	Tibenham	20. 5.08P
G-CDDT	SOCATA TB-20 Trinidad	1858	PH-SXC F-OIGJ	24.11.04	Oxford Aviation Training Ltd (New owner 8.07)	Oxford	12. 4.07E
G-CDDU	Best Off Sky Ranger 912(2) (Built R C Reynolds - pr.no.BMAA/HB/422)	SKR0404506		10.11.04	A Rastall	Darley Moor	16. 4.08P
G-CDDV	Cameron Z-250 Balloon (Hot Air)	10625		22. 3.05	Off The Ground Balloon Co Ltd t/a High Adventure Lyth, Kendal		6. 2.08E
G-CDDW	Aeroprakt A22 Foxbat (Built D A A Wineberg)	PFA 317-14261		8. 9.04	M Raflewski	(Dungannon)	8. 5.08P
G-CDDX	Thruster T 600N 450	0049-T600N-107		11.11.04	P A G Harper	Priory Farm, Tibenham	13. 1.08P
G-CDDY	Van's RV-8 (Built C S Ziekle)	80912	N701CZ	24.11.04	C A Foss tr The AV8ors	Shoreham	22. 5.08P
G-CDEA	SAAB-Scania 2000	2000-009	SE-LOX HB-IZF, (D-ADIC), SE-009	20. 1.05	Air Kilroe Ltd t/a Eastern Airways	Aberdeen	19. 1.08E
G-CDEB	SAAB-Scania 2000	2000-036	SE-036 HZ-IZT, SE-036	30.11.04	Air Kilroe Ltd t/a Eastern Airways	Aberdeen	29.11.07E
G-CDEC	Mainair Sports Pegasus Quik	8081		27. 1.05	S Bradie and A Huyton (Noted 11.06) Broomhill Farm, West Calder		26. 1.06P
G-CDED	Robinson R22 Beta II	3747	N74365	19. 1.05	Flight Solutions Ltd	Panshanger	13. 2.08E
G-CDEF	Piper PA-28-161 Cadet	2841341	D-ESTD N9184X, N621FT, (OH-PFB)	12.11.04	Western Air (Thruxton) Ltd	Thruxton	12.12.07E
G-CDEG	Boeing 737-8BK	33022		21. 3.05	Globespan Airways Ltd t/a Flyglobespan.com Edinburgh		20. 3.08E
G-CDEH	ICP MXP-740 Savannah LS(1) (Built S Whittaker and P J Wilson - pr.no.BMAA/HB/349) (Suzuki LS1000)	03-03-51-200		18.11.04	A J Webb	Oxford	1.11.08P
G-CDEJ	Diamond DA.40D Star	D4.142	OE-VPU	1.12.04	Diamond Aircraft UK Ltd	Cumbernauld	23. 2.08E
G-CDEK	Diamond DA.40D Star	D4.143	OE-VPW	1.12.04	A D and C Realff t/a ADR Aviation	Shoreham	23. 2.08E
G-CDEL	Diamond DA.40D Star	D4.144	OE-VPW	1.12.04	Diamond Aircraft UK Ltd	Gamston	23. 2.08E
G-CDEM	Raj Hamsa X'Air 133(1) (Built R J Froud - pr.no.BMAA/HB/421)	939		17.11.04	R J Froud	(Newport, Isle of Wight)	
G-CDEN	Mainair Sports Pegasus Quantum 15-912	8087		30.11.04	J D J Spragg	Roddige	8.12.07P
G-CDEO	Piper PA-28-180 Cherokee Archer	28-7405011	HB-OQE N9568N	17. 2.05	G G Hammond	Biggin Hill	23. 6.08E
G-CDEP	Evektor EV-97 teamEurostar UK	2128		6.12.04	N Morrison and P S Rose tr Echo Papa Groupr Wycombe Air Park		23. 6.08P
G-CDER	Piper PA-28-161 Warrior II	28-8116222	HB-PHL D-EBKC, N9537N, N8383S	18. 2.05	Cinque Ports Aviation Ltd	Lydd	20. 3.08E
G-CDET	Culver LCA Cadet (Continental O-200-A)	129	N29261 NC29261	10.11.86	J Gregson Durham Tees Valley (Noted 12.07 as "29261" in USAAF c/s)		15. 8.07P
G-CDEU	Lindstrand LBL 90B Balloon (Hot Air)	1015		7. 2.05	N Florence and P J Marshall	Ruislip	24. 5.08E
G-CDEV	Reality Escapade 912(1) (Built M B Devenport - pr.no.BMAA/HB/360)	JAESC 0024		26.10.04	M B Devenport	Popham	20. 9.08P
G-CDEW	Mainair Sports Pegasus Quik	8083		13. 1.05	K M Sullivan	Newtownards	14. 3.08P
G-CDEX	Europa Aviation Europa (Built S Collins - pr.no.PFA 247-12507) (Tri-Gear u/c)	012		21.10.04	J M Carter	Morgansfield, Fishburn	31.10.08P
G-CDFA	Kolb Twinstar Mk.3 Extra (Built M H Moulai - pr.no.PFA 205-14274)	M3X-04-7-00057		25.11.04	S Soar and W A Douthwaite	Tarn Farm, Cockerham	16. 6.08P
G-CDFC	Ultramagic S-160 Balloon (Hot Air)	160/39		30. 3.05	Over The Rainbow Balloon Flights Ltd Forest Town, Mansfield		17. 5.06E
G-CDFD	Scheibe SF25C Falke (Rotax 912S)	44705	D-KEOQ	1.12.04	T M Holloway tr RAF Gliding and Soaring Association (Operated Bannerdown Gliding Club) RAF Keevil		3. 2.08E
G-CDFE	IAV-Bacau Yakovlev Yak-52	855712	LY-APU G-CDFE, N151PA, Kyrgyz AF, DOSAAF 82 (blue)?	29.11.04	D R Farley	Little Gransden	28. 3.08P
G-CDFF	Aérospatiale-Alenia ATR 42-300	331	LN-FAI (5) G-BVEF, (F-GKNF), F-WWLP	30. 3.04	Aurigny Air Services Ltd	(Germany)	1. 4.08E
			(In basic Air Wales c/s with Aurigny Air Services titles at rear and Flightline titles on forward door)				
G-CDFG	Mainair Sports Pegasus Quik	8082		21.12.04	D Gabbott	Ince Blundell	22.12.07P

G-CDFI	Cameron Colt 31A Balloon (Hot Air)	10655		6.12.04	A M Holly t/a Exclusive Ballooning	Berkeley	2. 3.08E
					(Sloggi titles)		
G-CDFJ	Best Off Sky Ranger 912(2)	SKR0404490		6.12.04	A Worthington tr Heskin Flyers Group		
	(Built W C Yates - pr.no.BMAA/HB/424)					Tarn Farm, Cockerham	19. 9.08P
G-CDFK	Avtech Jabiru SPL-450	xxxx		2.12.04	H J Bradley	(Bridgnorth)	7. 8.08P
	(Built H J Bradley - pr.no.PFA 274A-14144)						
G-CDFL	Zenair CH.601UL Zodiac	PFA 162A-14309		30.11.04	F G Green tr Caunton Zodiac Group		
	(Built F G Green, R Welch and V Causey) (Tri-cycle u/c)					Knapthorpe Lodge, Caunton	11. 3.08P
G-CDFM	Raj Hamsa X'Air 582(5)	920		2.12.04	W A Keel-Stocker	Norton, Gloucestershire	3. 4.08P
	(Built J Griffiths - pr.no.BMAA/HB/417)						
G-CDFN	Thunder Ax7-77 Balloon (Hot Air)	3697	I-FMCL (2)	22. 2. 06	E Rullo	Caulonia Marina (RC), Italy	
G-CDFO	Mainair Sports Pegasus Quik	8080		17. 1.05	C J Gordon	Perth	18. 3.07P
G-CDFP	Best Off Sky Ranger 912(2)	SKR0409522		10.12.04	J M Gammidge	Sywell	4. 9.08P
	(Built J M Gammidge - pr.no.BMAA/HB/431)						
G-CDFR	Cyclone Airsports Pegasus Quantum 15	6943	CS-UGX	8. 3.05	C J E Hartshorne, (J Madhvani) and L M Pickles		
	(Rotax 582)					Plaistows Farm, St Albans	17. 3.08P
G-CDFS	Embraer EMB-135ER	145431	EI-ORK	23.12.04	British Midland Airways Ltd	East Midlands	13. 1.07E
			PT-SUC, (CN-RLG), PT-SUC				
G-CDFU	Rans S-6-ES Coyote II	0304.1560		3.11.04	P W Taylor	Priory Farm, Tibenham	31. 5.08P
	(Built P W Taylor - pr.no.PFA 204-14232) (Tri-cycle u/c)						
G-CDFW	Sheffy Gyroplane	PFA G/19-1366		5. 9.05	P C Lovegrove	(Didcot)	
	(Built P C Lovegrove)						
G-CDFY	Beech B200 Super King Air	BB-1715	N607TA	4. 2.05	BAE Systems Marine Ltd	Walney Island	3. 2.08E
G-CDGA	Taylor JT.1 Monoplane	6020/1		28.12.78	R M Larimore	(Spondon, Derby)	
	(Built D G Anderson - pr.no.PFA 055-10382)						
G-CDGB	Rans S-6-116 Coyote II	0696.1006		21.12.04	S Penoyre	(Windlesham)	15.10.08P
	(Built S Penoyre - pr.no.PFA 204A-13047)						
G-CDGC	Mainair Sports Pegasus Quik	8090		26. 1.05	A T K Crozier	Kirknewton	5. 2.08P
G-CDGD	Mainair Sports Pegasus Quik	8086		11.11.04	I D and V A Milne *(Noted 5.07)*	St Michaels	12.12.06P
G-CDGE	AirBorne XT912-B-Streak III-B	XT912-028	T2-2253	22.12.04	M R Leyshon	(Brierley Hill)	30. 5.08P
	(Wing s/n S3B-009)						
G-CDGF	Ultramagic S-105 Balloon (Hot Air)	105/127		9. 3.05	D and Karin Bareford	Cookley, Kidderminster	17. 5.08E
G-CDGG	Dyn'Aéro MCR-01 Club	291		26.10.04	N Rollins	Hawksbridge Farm, Oxenhope	1. 3.08P
	(Built P Simpson and P A B Morgan - pr.no.PFA 301A-14267)						
G-CDGH	Rans S-6-ES Coyote II	1203.1537 ES		22.12.04	K T Vinning tr G-CDGH Group	Long Marston	29. 8.07P
	(Built K T Vinning -pr.no.PFA 204-14209) (Tri-cycle u/c)						
	(Stalled on take-off Broadmeadow 25. .8.07 and substantially damaged in collision with Quiks G-CCJM and G-CDFG)						
G-CDGI	Thruster T 600N 450 Sprint	1041-T600N-108		5. 1.05	R L J Goodridge	Beeches Farm, South Scarle	5. 3.08P
G-CDGJ	American Champion 7ECA Citabria Aurora			14.12.04	K Fast	(Billund, Denmark)	16. 5.08E
		1391-2004					
G-CDGN	Cameron C-90 Balloon (Hot Air)	10641		24. 2.05	M C Gibbons *"Betty"*	Bristol	6. 3.06E
G-CDGO	Mainair Sports Pegasus Quik	8084		11.11.04	Mainair Sports Ltd	(Rochdale)	10. 5.08P
G-CDGP	Zenair CH.601XL Zodiac	PFA 162B-14313		6. 1.05	T J Bax	Henstridge	29. 7.08P
	(Built T J Bax) (Tailwheel u/c)						
G-CDGR	Zenair CH.701UL STOL	PFA 187-14327		6. 1.05	M Morris	Tarn Farm, Cockerham	10. 7.08P
	(Built M Morris)						
G-CDGS	American General AG-5B Tiger	10097	PH-BMA	7. 2.05	K Hennessy tr Premier Flying Group		
			N1195Q			Waterford, County Waterford	6. 3.08E
G-CDGT	Montgomerie-Parsons Two-Place Gyroplane			10. 1.05	A A Craig	Kirkbride	30. 8.08P
	(Built A A Craig)	PFA G/08-1361					
G-CDGU	Vickers Supermarine 300 Spitfire I	6S-75156	X4276	7. 1.05	A J E Smith	(Gateforth, Selby)	
G-CDGW	Piper PA-28-181 Archer II	28-7990402	HB-PDZ	13. 1.05	Stamp Aviation Ltd	(Ballasalla, Isle of Man)	22. 6.08E
			N2156Z				
G-CDGX	Mainair Sports Pegasus Quantum 15-912	8096		28. 1.05	S R Green	(Bishops Itchington, Southam)	5. 4.08P
G-CDGY	Vickers Supermarine 349 Spitfire Vc	WWA3832	ZK-MKV	19. 1.05	Aero Vintage Ltd	(Northiam, Rye)	
	(Built Westland Aircraft Ltd)		A58-149, EF545				
G-CDHA	Best Off Sky Ranger 912S(1)	SKR0407508		18. 1.05	A T Cameron	(Limavady)	12. 8.08P
	(Built K J Gay - pr.no.BMAA/HB/428)						
G-CDHB	British Aircraft Corporation 167 Strikemaster Mk.80A		R Saudi AF 1130	31. 1.05	S J Davies	(South Grove, Rotherham)	30. 5.08P
		EEP/JP/4096	G-27-296				
G-CDHC	Slingsby T 67C Firefly	2081	PH-SGC	20. 1.05	N J Morgan	Tatenhill	19. 4.08E
			(PH-SBC), G-7-138				
G-CDHD	Balony Kubicek BB22 Balloon (Hot Air)	342	OK-0342	22. 2.05	R C Franklin	Aylesbury	3. 4.07E
G-CDHE	Best Off Sky Ranger 912(2)	SKRxxxx500		26. 1.05	E Clayton tr Barton Syndicate	Barton	5. 7.08P
	(Built S Owen - pr.no.BMAA/HB/412)						
G-CDHF	Piper PA-30 Twin Comanche B	30-1111	LX-AML	17. 2.05	Raid International (Guernsey) Ltd		
			F-BJCC, N8005Y			Le Plessis-Bellville, Picardy, France	8. 6.08E
G-CDHG	Mainair Sports Pegasus Quik	8092		21. 2.05	T W Pelan	Balgrummo Steading, Bonnybank	13. 5.08P
G-CDHH	Robinson R44 Raven II	10660		4. 3.05	Forest Fencing Ltd t/a Abwood Homes		
						(Newcastle, County Wicklow)	19. 4.08E
G-CDHK	Lindstrand LBL 330A Balloon (Hot Air)	1022		9. 2.05	Richard Nash Cars Ltd	Norwich	19. 5.08E
G-CDHL	Lindstrand LBL 330A Balloon (Hot Air)	1028		9. 2.05	Richard Nash Cars Ltd	Norwich	19. 5.08E
G-CDHM	Mainair Sports Pegasus Quantum 15	8085		18. 1.05	M K Morgan	Swansea	21. 3.08P
	(Rotax 582))						
G-CDHN	Lindstrand LBL 317A Balloon (Hot Air)	1027		6. 4.05	Aerosaurus Balloons Ltd	Exeter	12. 3.08E
G-CDHO	Raj Hamsa X'Air 133(1)	902		8. 2.05	J D Aitchison	Damyn's Hall, Upminster	22.11.06P
	(Built W E Corps - pr.no.BMAA/HB/408)				*(Noted 9.07)*		
G-CDHP	Lindstrand LBL 150A Balloon (Hot Air)	754	G-OHRH	11. 2.05	Floating Sensations Ltd	Llandeilo	31. 5.08E
G-CDHR	Comco Ikarus C42 FB80	0502-6652		21. 2.05	Airbourne Aviation Ltd	Popham	7. 3.08P
G-CDHS	Cameron N-90 Balloon (Hot Air)	4367	LX-BIS	10. 3.05	C Moulin	Neville le Liene, France	28. 3.08E
G-CDHU	Best Off Sky Ranger 912(2)	SKRxxxx546		22. 2.05	S J Smith	Chase Farm, Chipping Sodbury	6.10.08P
	(Built S J Smith - pr.no.BMAA/HB/444)						
G-CDHX	Aeroprakt A22 Foxbat	PFA 317-14297		28. 2.05	N E Stokes and B N Searle		
	(Built N E Stokes and B N Searle)					Haughton Farm, Haughton, Ellesmere	15.10.08P

Reg	Type	C/n	Prev id	Date	Owner/Operator	Location	Exp
G-CDHY	Cameron Z-90 Balloon (Hot Air)	10675		6. 7.05	D M Roberts	(Ffairfach, Llandeilo)	1. 2.08E
G-CDHZ	Nicollier HN.700 Ménestrel II	PFA 217-14163		1. 3.05	G E Whittaker	(Formby, Liverpool)	
	(Built G E Whittaker)						
G-CDIA	Thruster T 600N 450 Sprint	0051-T600N-111		8. 3.05	A D Tomlins	Andreas, Isle of Man	9 12.08P
G-CDIB	Cameron Z-350 Balloon (Hot Air)	10622		11.5.05	Ballooning Network Ltd	Southville, Bristol	30. 7.06E
G-CDIF	CAB CAP.10B	302	N126SM	21. 6.05	J D Gordon	Shobdon	18. 7.08E
			F-GYKD				
G-CDIG	Evektor EV-97 Eurostar	2004-2208		22. 2.05	M Sanders	Ince Blundell	15. 5.08P
	(Built J Cunliffe and A Costello - pr.no.PFA 315-14353)						
G-CDIH	Cameron Z-275 Balloon (Hot Air)	10613		6. 4.05	Bailey Balloons Ltd (Bailey Balloons titles) Pill, Bristol		16. 8.08E
G-CDIJ	Best Off Sky Ranger 912(2)	SKR0501553		3. 3.05	E B Toulson	Baxby Manor, Husthwaite	
	(Built E B Toulson - pr.no.BMAA/HB/445)				(Noted 9.07)		
G-CDIK	Cameron Z-120 Balloon (Hot Air)	10698		8. 3.05	Cameron Balloons Ltd	Bristol	2. 1.08E
					(Cameron Balloons titles)		
G-CDIL	Mainair Sports Pegasus Quantum 15-912	8093		21.12.04	G W Hillidge	Dunkeswell	5. 2.08P
G-CDIM	Robin DR.400-180 Régent	2584		6. 4.05	L R Marks	Lasham	25. 4.08E
G-CDIO	Cameron Z-90 Balloon (Hot Air)	10695		28. 4.05	P Oggioni	Fossano, Italy	27. 4.08E
G-CDIP	Best Off Sky Ranger 912S(1)	SKR0407507		11. 1.05	M S McCrudden	Newtownards	17. 8.08P
	(Built M S McCrudden - pr.no.BMAA/HB/429)						
G-CDIR	Mainair Sports Pegasus Quantum 15-912	8108		8. 3.05	A S Turner	Dunkeswell	7. 3.08P
G-CDIS	Cessna 150F	15062718	SE-ETR	23. 5.05	S P Fox	RAF Marham	24. 5.08E
			N11B, N8618G		(Operated RAF Marham Flying Club)		
G-CDIT	Cameron Z-105 Balloon (Hot Air)	10702		6. 4.05	Bailey Balloons Ltd (EDF Energy titles) Pill, Bristol		26. 3.07E
G-CDIU	Best Off Sky Ranger 912S(1)	SKR0401405		15. 3.05	C P Dawes and J English Darley Moor, Ashbourne		4. 9.08P
	(Built C P Dawes and R A Budd - pr.no.BMAA/HB/376)						
G-CDIV	Lindstrand LBL 90A Balloon (Hot Air)	1021		18. 3.05	The Packhouse Ltd	Farnham	18. 7.08E
G-CDIX	Comco Ikarus C42 FB100	0504-6669		20. 4.05	Assured Quality Catering Mangement Services Ltd		
						Stoke Golding	24. 4.08E
G-CDIY	Evektor EV-97 Eurostar	2004.21.27		30.12.04	E J and M P Hill	Milton, Cleobury Mortimer	21. 3.08P
	(Built G R Pritchard - pr.no.PFA 315-14345)						
G-CDIZ	Reality Escapade 912(1)	JAESC 0033		7. 1.05	E G Bishop and E N Dunn		
	(Built E G Bishop and E N Dunn - pr.no.BMAA/HB/393)				Dunkery, Wootton Courtenay, Minehead		
G-CDJB	Van's RV-4	1270	N21RP	21. 1.05	G J Slater	Clench Common	16. 5.07P
	(Built T A Rudisill and R G Pettyjohn)				(New owner 8.07)		
G-CDJC	Best Off Sky Ranger 912(2)	SKRxxxx540		16. 3.05	J L A Campbell	Dunkeswell	
	(Built J L A Campbell - pr.no.BMAA/HB/440)				(Noted 7.07)		
G-CDJD	ICP MXP-740 Savannah Jabiru(1)	03-05-51-209		22. 3.05	D W Mullin	Hawarden	
	(Built D W Mullin - pr.no.BMAA/HB/321)						
G-CDJE	Thruster T 600N 450 Sprint	0053-T600N-112		24. 3.05	K R Ford	Wickenby	5. 4.08P
G-CDJF	Flight Design CT2K	03-07-04-35		8. 7.05	P A James	Redhill	7. 7.08P
	(Assembled Mainair Sports Ltd with (official) c/n 8104: now reported by P&M Aviation as c/n 8005)						
G-CDJG	Zenair CH.601UL Zodiac	PFA 162A-14374		9. 3.05	J Garcia	Moscow, Galston	29. 2.08P
	(Built J Garcia)						
G-CDJI	Ultramagic M-120 Balloon (Hot Air)	120/12		17. 5.05	The Ballooning Business Ltd	Walcote, Alcester	26. 3.08E
					(Zirtec titles)		
G-CDJJ	IAV Bacau Yakovlev Yak-52	899912	LY-AQI	26. 5.05	J J Miles	Shoreham	25. 6.08P
			HA-HUY, LY-AFR, 99 (yellow) DOSAAF				
G-CDJK	Comco Ikarus C42 FB80	0504-6666		26. 4.05	Cornish Aviation Ltd	Davidstow Moor	25. 4.08P
G-CDJL	Avtech Jabiru J400	0xxx		4. 2.05	T R Sinclair and T Clyde Lamb Holm Farm, Orkney		16. 6.08P
	(Built T R Sinclair - pr.no.PFA 325-14215)						
G-CDJM	Zenair CH.601XL Zodiac	PFA 162B-14303		30.12.04	T J Adams-Lewis	Haverfordwest	26. 4.08P
	(Built T J Adams-Lewis)						
G-CDJN	Rotary Air Force RAF 2000 GTX-SE			11. 3.05	D J North	(Andover)	15. 8.08P
	(Built D J North)	PFA G/13-1363					
G-CDJO	de Havilland DH.82A Tiger Moth	915	VH-BGH (2)	11. 4.05	D Dal Bon	Ventfield Farm, Oxfordshire	
	(Built de Havilland Aircraft Proprietary Ltd, Australia)		VH-BGA, A17-492		(Noted 8.06)		
G-CDJP	Best Off Sky Ranger 912(2)	SKRxxxxx501		18. 1.05	J S Potts	Hunterston Farm, Stair	3. 9.08P
	(Built J S Potts - pr.no.BMAA/HB/435) (Tailwheel u/c)						
G-CDJR	Evektor EV-97 teamEurostar UK	2318		24. 3.05	P G Gale t/a W J Gale and Son Edington Hill, Keevil		23. 3.07P
G-CDJT	Aérospatiale SA.341G Gazelle 1	1509	N401S	19. 8.05	Simlot Ltd	Oxton, Nottingham	29. 9.07E
G-CDJU	CASA 1-131E Jungmann Series 1000	1078	OO-OLE	25. 8.05	B Roemer	Strandhill, Sligo, County Sligo	19.12.07P
			EC-DKV, Spanish AF E3B-379		(As "OO-DLE" and "E3B-379")		
G-CDJV	Beech A36 Bonanza	E-951	HB-EJP	27. 4.05	Atlantic Bridge Aviation Ltd	Lydd	14. 6.08P
			D-EICH, N4296S				
G-CDJW	Van's RV-7	PFA 323-14045		17. 3.05	J B Shaw	(Bramhope, Leeds)	12. 2.07P
	(Built D J Williams)				(New owner 11.07)		
G-CDJX	Cameron N-56 Balloon (Hot Air)	10715		6. 4.05	Cameron Balloons Ltd	Bristol	29. 9.08E
G-CDJY	Cameron C-80 Balloon (Hot Air)	10677		16. 5.05	British Airways PLC	West Drayton	26. 4.08E
G-CDKA	SAAB-Scania 2000	2000-006	SE-006	10. 3.05	Air Kilroe Ltd t/a Eastern Airways	Norwich	9. 3.08E
			HB-IZC, SE-006		(Aberdeen City And Shire titles and artwork)"		
G-CDKB	SAAB-Scania 2000	2000-032	SE-032	22. 4.05	Air Kilroe Ltd t/a Eastern Airways	Humberside	21. 4.08E
			LY-SBG, HB-IZQ, SE-032				
G-CDKC	Raj Hamsa X'Air 582(3)	531		14. 4.05	F G Walker	(Hawarden)	3 .4.08P
	(Built G Walker - pr.no.BMAA/HB/159)						
G-CDKD	Boeing 737-683	28302	SE-DNT	15. 4.05	Globespan Airways Ltd t/a Flyglobespan.com		
			N1786B			Edinburgh	14. 4.08E
G-CDKE	Rans S-6-ES Coyote II	0603.1506		9. 5.05	J E Holloway	(Saltash)	4.12.08P
	(Built J E Holloway - pr.no.PFA 204-14119)						
G-CDKF	Reality Escapade 912(1)	JAESC 0035		15. 2.05	N Forman	Barton	22. 1.08P
	(Built P J Little - pr.no.BMAA/HB/389)						
G-CDKH	Best Off Sky Ranger 912S(1)	SKRxxxxx545		14. 4.05	R J Gilbert	Kirkbride	17. 8.08P
	(Built W P Byrne - pr.no.BMAA/HB/448)						
G-CDKI	Best Off Sky Ranger 912S(1)	SKR0209242		15. 4.05	J M Hucker	Broadmeadow Farm, Hereford	18.10.08P
	(Built J M Hucker - pr.no.BMAA/HB/434)						

G-CDKJ	Silence Twister	PFA 329-14336		5. 5.05	European Land Solutions Ltd		
	(Built A Stansfield)					Radley Farm, Hungerford	29. 8.08P
G-CDKK	Mainair Sports Pegasus Quik	8097		4. 3.05	P M Knight	(Billericay)	23. 4.08P
G-CDKL	Reality Escapade 912(1)	JAESC 0023		21. 4.05	D Harker	Morgansfield, Fishburn	
	(Built D Harker - pr.no.BMAA/HB/359) (Change of Type 9.07)						
G-CDKM	Mainair Sports Pegasus Quik	8091		28. 1.05	P Lister	Ince Blundell	26. 4.08P
G-CDKN	ICP MXP-740 Savannah Jabiru(4) 04-05-51-293			7. 4.05	N R Benson	Kirkbride	12.10.08P
	(Built F McGuigan - pr.no.BMAA/HB/397)						
G-CDKO	ICP MXP-740 Savannah Jabiru(4) 04-01-51-274			25. 4.05	C Jones and B Hunter	Barton	5. 9.08P
	(Built C Jones and B Hunter - pr.no.BMAA/HB/402)						
G-CDKP	Avtech Jabiru UL-D Calypso	0636		18. 2.05	Rochester Microlights Ltd Damyn's Hall, Upminster		12. 2.08P
G-CDKR	Diamond DA.42 Twin Star	42.029	(D-GAAA)	28. 6.05	R H Butterfield and A M Dyson t/a Principle Aircraft		
						Newcastle	11. 7.08E
G-CDKT	Boeing 737-683	28303	SE-DNU	18. 5.05	Globespan Airways Ltd t/a Flyglobespan.com		
			N1786B			Edinburgh	17. 5.08E
G-CDKU	Robinson R44 Raven	1480		29. 4.05	J M McCullagh t/a Blackberry Aviation		
					Blackberry Farm, Great Smeaton, Northallerton		23. 5.08E
G-CDKX	Best Off Sky Ranger J2.2(1)	SKR0404474		23. 5.05	M S Ashby	(Kingsbridge)	2. 4.08P
	(Built M S Ashby - pr.no.BMAA/HB/395)						
G-CDKY	Robinson R44 Raven	1470		11. 3.05	Bernard Hunter Ltd Gilmerton Helipad, Edinburgh		7. 4.08E
G-CDKZ	Thunder Ax10-160 Series 2 Balloon (Hot Air)			13. 4.05	D J Head	Newbury	24. 3.08E
		10648					
G-CDLA	Mainair Sports Pegasus Quik	8102		4. 4.05	C R Stevens	(Egerton, Ashford)	24. 4.08P
G-CDLB	Cameron Z-120 Balloon (Hot Air)	10672		8. 6.05	Interbrew UK Ltd *(Bass titles)*	Luton	7. 6.06E
G-CDLC	CASA 1-131E Jungmann Series 2000	2095	N46923	10. 6.05	R D and M Loder Lower Upham Farm, Chisledon		8. 8.07P
			Spanish AF E3B-494		*(As "E3B-494:81-47" in Spanish AF c/s)*		
	(C/n 2095 is quoted also for Jungmann D-EEGN ex-Spanish AF E3B-351)						
G-CDLD	Mainair Sports Pegasus Quik	8106		16. 3.05	W Williams	(Todwick, Sheffield)	24. 3.08P
G-CDLE	Reality Escapade 912(1)	JAESC 0005		12. 5.05	R A J Paddock	Eastbach Farm, Coleford	16.12.07P
	(Built R A J Paddock - pr.no.BMAA/HB/317)						
G-CDLG	Best Off Sky Ranger 912(2)	SKRxxxxx457		19. 5.05	D J Saunders	(Ashdon, Saffron Walden)	7. 6.08P
	(Built D J Saunders - pr.no.BMAA/HB/387)						
G-CDLI	Airco DH.9	1414	E8894	31. 5.05	Aero Vintage Ltd	(Northiam, Rye)	
	(Built Aircraft Maufacturing Co Ltd 1918) (Siddeley Puma)				*(On rebuild as "E8894" 2007)*		
G-CDLJ	Mainair Sports Pegasus Quik	8111		9. 5.05	M L Johnston Graveley Hall Farm, Graveley		8. 5.08P
G-CDLK	Best Off Sky Ranger 912S(1)	SKRxxxx570		11. 7.05	L E Cowling and A P Chapman		
	(Built L E Cowling and A P Chapman - pr.no.BMAA/HB/452)					Hawksbridge Farm, Oxenhope	13.12.08P
G-CDLL	Dyn'Aéro MCR-01 ULC	PFA 301B-14348		23. 3.05	D Cassidy	Gildridge Farm, Hailsham	16. 6.08P
	(Built D Cassidy)						
G-CDLP	Aérospatiale AS.355F1 Ecureuil 2	5012	G-GRID	18. 4.05	Valley Helicopter Services Ltd	(Rossendale)	18. 6.08E
			TG-BOS				
G-CDLR	ICP MXP-740 Savannah Jabiru(4) 04-06-51-292			9. 5.05	R Locke	Headon Farm, Retford	
	(Built R Locke - pr.no.BMAA/HB/399)				*(Noted 8.05)*		
G-CDLS	Avtech Jabiru J400	Jxxxx		9. 3.05	G M Geary	Morgansfield, Fishburn	24. 5.08P
	(Built G M Geary - pr.no.PFA 325-14319)						
G-CDLT	Raytheon Hawker 800XP	258710	N37010	27. 5.05	Gama Aviation Ltd	Farnborough	26. 5.08E
G-CDLV	Lindstrand LBL 105A Balloon (Hot Air)	1050		1. 7.05	Smartfusion SV Ltd *(Nokia titles)*	London SW8	12. 4.08E
G-CDLW	Zenair CH.601UL Zodiac	PFA 162-13944		23. 6.05	W A Stephen	Popham	21.12.07P
	(Built W A Stephen)						
G-CDLY	Cirrus SR20	1519	N54212	10. 6.05	Partside Aviation Ltd	(Newport)	14. 6.08E
G-CDLZ	Mainair Sports Pegasus Quantum 15-912	8113		19. 4.05	L C Brown	(Humbie)	18. 4.08P
G-CDMA	Piper PA-28-151 Cherokee Warrior 28-7415650		OY-TFL	3. 5.05	A Cabre	(Hainford, Norwich)	10. 8.08E
			SE-GBV				
G-CDMC	Cameron Z-105 Balloon (Hot Air)	10671		14. 3.05	The Balloon Company Ltd t/a First Flight		
					(A-Gas titles)	Langford, Bristol	4. 4.08E
G-CDMD	Robin DR.500-200i Président	42		14.10.05	P R Liddle	Rochester	10.11.07E
	(Officially regd as DR.400-500)						
G-CDME	Van's RV-7	PFA 323-14151		13. 5.05	M W Elliott	Shenstone	8. 8.08P
	(Built M W Elliott)						
G-CDMF	Van's RV-9A	PFA 320-14157		29. 6.05	S R Neale and T R Donovan	Oaksey Park	11. 4.08P
	(Built J Shanley)						
G-CDMG	Robinson R22 Beta	1874	N2305J	7. 4.05	Heli Aitch Be Ltd	Redhill	1. 8.08E
G-CDMH	Cessna P210N Pressurized Centurion		LX-ACP	25. 7.05	J G Hinley	Wellesbourne Mountford	29.11.07E
		P21000131	N33CP, C-GRAT, N4901P				
G-CDMI	Robinson R44 Raven II	10779		7. 6.05	Faser Court Ltd t/a Casey Enterprises		
					(Gorey, County Wexford)		6. 7.08E
G-CDMJ	Mainair Sports Pegasus Quik	8107		17. 3.05	J Rodgers *(Noted 4.06)*	Barton	19. 3.08P
G-CDMK	Montgomerie-Bensen B 8MR PFA G/01A-1358			8. 7.05	P Rentell	(St Clement, Truro)	
	(Built P Rentell)						
G-CDML	P&M Pegasus Quik	8127		15. 7.05	H T Beattie	Perth	18. 8.08P
G-CDMM	Cessna 172P Skyhawk	17275124	N55161	8. 7.05	Cristal Air Ltd	North Weald	9. 2.08E
G-CDMN	Van's RV-9	PFA 320-14108		8. 6.05	G J Smith	(Manton)	29. 5.08P
	(Built G J Smith)						
G-CDMO	Cameron S Can-100 Balloon (Hot Air)	2178	OE-ZCU	22. 7.05	A Schneider	Borken, Germany	10. 7.08E
			OE-CZU				
G-CDMP	Best Off Sky Ranger 912S(1)	SKRxxxxx600		8. 7.05	J A Charlton	(Ashbourne)	5. 4.08P
	(Built J A Charlton - pr.no.BMAA/HB/457)						
G-CDMS	Comco Ikarus C42 FB80	0506-6689		19. 7.05	Airbourne Aviation Ltd	Popham	18. 7.08P
G-CDMT	Zenair CH.601XL Zodiac	PFA 162B-14359		17. 6.05	L Hogan	Glenrothes	4. 8.08P
	(Built D McCormack) (Tri-cycle u/c)						
G-CDMU	P&M Pegasus Quik	8121		19. 8.05	A M Burrows and T M Bolton	Barton	6. 9.08P
G-CDMV	Best Off Sky Ranger 912S(1)	SKRxxxxx575		28. 7.05	D O'Keeffe and K E Rutter	London Colney	23.11.08P
	(Built D O'Keeffe, K E Rutter and A J Clarke - pr.no.BMAA/HB/455)						

G-CDMX	Piper PA-28-161 Warrior II	28-7916006	PH-SBY N39746	4. 8.05	FlyUK.com Ltd	Wendover Farm, Sheepwash	10. 9.08E
G-CDMY	Piper PA-28-161 Warrior II	28-7916007	PH-SBZ N30768	25. 8.05	J S Develin and Z Islam	Shoreham	29. 9.07E
G-CDMZ	P&M Pegasus Quik	8116		3. 8.05	R Solomons	(Pembury, Tunbridge Wells)	7. 8.08P
G-CDNA	Grob G109B	6324	D-KEOJ	28. 7.05	J W Sage tr Army Gliding Association		
						Trenchard Lines, Upavon	23. 8.08E
G-CDND	Gulfstream American GA-7 Cougar	GA7-0057	(OY-GAV)	19. 7.05	C J Chaplin	Redhill	30. 1.08E
	G-CDND, OY-GAV, (OY-SVO), LN-ALY, OY-GAV, N770GA						
G-CDNE	Best Off Sky Ranger 912S(1)	SKRxxxxx574		28. 7.05	C D London	Plaistows Farm, St Albans	14. 9.08P
	(Built G S Gee-Carter and A Dunne - pr.no.BMAA/HB/454)						
G-CDNF	Aero Designs Pulsar 3	PFA 202-13253		28. 4.05	D Ringer	Perth	7. 5.08P
	(Built D Ringer)						
G-CDNG	Evektor EV-97 teamEurostar UK	2319		18. 5.05	G E Hillyer-Jones	Shobdon	17. 5.08P
G-CDNH	P&M Pegasus Quik	8126		2. 8.05	C D Andrews	Swinford, Rugby	16. 9.08P
G-CDNI	Evektor EV-97 teamEurostar UK	2321		11. 7.05	Fly CB Ltd	Oxford	10. 7.08P
G-CDNJ	Colomban MC-15 Cri-Cri	69	F-PEAH	16. 6.05	N J Johnson	(Exeter)	
	(Built E Ahlrichs)						
G-CDNK	Learjet Model 45	45-280	N40079	17.10.05	Air Partner Private Jets Ltd	London Stansted	16.10.07E
G-CDNM	Evektor EV-97 teamEurostar UK	2407		5. 8.05	H C Lowther	(Penrith)	24. 8.08P
G-CDNO	Westland SA.341B Gazelle AH.1	1385	XX432	23. 9.05	Falcon Aviation Ltd (Noted 5.07)		
						Bourne Park, Hurstbourne Tarrant	
G-CDNP	Evektor EV-97 teamEurostar UK	2320		13. 6.05	B R Pearson tr Eaglescott Eurostar Group	Eaglescott	27. 6.08P
G-CDNR	Comco Ikarus C42 FB100	0507-6696		12. 8.05	R S O'Carroll	Mullahead, Tandragee	11. 8.08P
G-CDNS	Westland SA.341B Gazelle AH.1	1614	XZ321	23. 9.05	Falcon Aviation Ltd		
						Bourne Park, Hurstbourne Tarrant	
G-CDNT	Zenair CH.601XL Zodiac	PFA 162B-14360		17. 6.05	W McCormack	Broomhill Farm, West Calder	14. 8.08P
	(Built W McCormack)						
G-CDNW	Comco Ikarus C42 FB UK	PFA 322-14426		6. 7.05	W Gabbott	Barton	10. 4.08P
	(Built W Gabbott)						
G-CDNY	Avtech Jabiru SP-470	xxxx		4. 8.05	G Lucey	Popham	13. 8.08P
	(Built G Lucey - pr.no.PFA 274B-14020)						
G-CDNZ	Ultramagic M-120 Balloon (Hot Air)	120/08	D-OHFJ	12. 8.05	R H Etherington	Montisi, Siena, Italy	16. 6.08E
G-CDOA	Evektor EV-97 teamEurostar UK	2506		12. 9.05	T K Duffy	Ellough, Beccles	11. 9.08P
G-CDOB	Cameron C-90 Balloon (Hot Air)	10756		10. 8.05	G D and S M Philpot	Hemel Hempstead	27. 6.08E
G-CDOC	P&M Quik GT450	8123		20.10.05	P J Clegg	Tarn Farm, Cockerham	1. 3.08P
G-CDOD	Aviat A-1B Husky	2292	(D-E) G-CDOD, N322PA	30. 8.05	K Anspach	Kempten, Germany	8. 9.08P
G-CDOG	Lindstrand LBL Dog SS Balloon (Hot Air)	938		7. 1.04	ABC Flights Ltd "Churchill"	Clapton-in-Gordano, Bristol	14. 9.08A
G-CDOI	Cameron Z-90 Balloon (Hot Air)	10765		12. 8.05	Cameron Balloons Ltd (Cameron Balloons titles)	Bristol	9. 1.08E
G-CDOJ	Schweizer 269C-1	0218	N86G	1.11.05	Sterling Helicopters Ltd	Norwich	16.11.07E
	(Schweizer 300)						
G-CDOK	Comco Ikarus C42 FB100	0509-6757		4.10.05	B S Keene	Compton Abbas	11.10.08P
G-CDOM	Mainair Sports Pegasus Quik	8118		20. 5.05	J A Dearn tr G-CDOM Flying Group	Barton	4. 8.08P
G-CDON	Piper PA-28-161 Warrior II	28-8216185	N8254D	24. 5.88	A Logan and A Martin tr G-CDON Group		
						East Midlands	1. 6.08E
G-CDOO	P&M Pegasus Quantum 15-912	8130		2. 8.05	O C Harding	Mapperley	10. 9.08P
G-CDOP	P&M Pegasus Quik	8129		16. 8.05	G R Craig and A W Hay	Insch	31. 5.08P
G-CDOR	Mainair Blade	1372-0805-7-W1167		8. 9.05	J D Otter (New owner 4.07)	(Boston)	4.10.06P
G-CDOT	Comco Ikarus C42 FB100	0505-6678		24. 6.05	A C Anderson	Dunkeswell	24. 6.08P
G-CDOV	Best Off Sky Ranger 912(2)	SKRxxxx606		5. 9.05	B Richardson	Eshott	3. 4.08P
	(Built B Richardson - pr.no.BMAA/HB/459)						
G-CDOW	P&M Pegasus Quik	8132		11.10.05	D H Marsh	(Sheffield)	13.10.06P
G-CDOY	Robin DR.400-180R Remorqueur	1206	D-EGRY SE-GRY	25.10.05	Lasham Gliding Society Ltd	Lasham	18.11.07E
G-CDOZ	Evektor EV-97 Eurostar	2005.25.07		2. 9.05	J P McCall	Jenkin's Farm, Navestock	22. 4.08P
	(Built J P McCall - pr.no.PFA 315-14437)						
G-CDPA	Alpi Pioneer 300	17		26. 8.05	N D White and N G Dowding		
	(Built A R Lloyd - pr.no.PFA 330-14415)					(Northampton and Towcester)	11.11.08P
G-CDPB	Best Off Sky Ranger 582(1)	SKRxxxxx423		24.10.05	N S Bishop	Manor Farm, Fencott	7. 7.08P
	(Built N S Bishop - pr.no.BMAA/HB/385)						
G-CDPC	Cameron C-90 Balloon (Hot Air)	10754		14. 3.07	Cameron Balloons Ltd	Bristol	
G-CDPD	Mainair Sports Pegasus Quik	8051		5. 8.04	P C Davis	Weston Zoyland	15. 8.08P
G-CDPE	Best Off Sky Ranger 912(2)	SKRxxxxx382		13. 9.05	P A Mercer	Tarn Farm, Cockerham	17. 5.08P
	(Built P A Mercer - pr.no.BMAA/HB/432)						
G-CDPG	Crofton Auster V J/1A	PFA 000-325		11. 8.05	P and T Groves	(Lee-on-the-Solent)	
	(Built P Groves aka Crofton Aeroplane Service)						
G-CDPH	TLAC RL5A LW Sherwood Ranger ST	xxxx		23. 9.05	K F Crumplin	Henstridge	
	(Built K F Crumplin - pr.no.PFA 237-12920)				(Noted 4.07)		
G-CDPI	Zenair CH.601UL Zodiac	PFA 162A-14406		24. 6.05	M J Kaye	(Swinton, Mexborough)	
	(Built M J Kaye)						
G-CDPJ	Van's RV-8	80661		5. 5.05	P Johnson	Morgansfield, Fishburn	2.11.08P
	(Built P Johnson - pr.no.PFA 303-13295)						
G-CDPL	Evektor EV-97 teamEurostar UK	2207		13. 1.05	C D H Garrison	Sutton Meadows	12. 1.08P
G-CDPM	Jurca MJ.100 Spitfire	PFA 130-12007		22. 9.05	J E D Rogerson	(East Howle, Ferryhill)	
	(Built J E D Rogerson) (80% scale replica Spitfire) (Walter Lom 6-cylinder 250hp inline)						
					(As "X4683 EB-N" to represent 41 Sqdn Spitfire) (Substantially complete 5.07)		
G-CDPN	Ultramagic S-105 Balloon (Hot Air)	105/135		3. 1.06	Horizon Ballooning Ltd	Blacknest, Alton	6.12.07E
G-CDPO	Aerochute Dual	240		4.10.05	G Martin	(Lisburn)	
G-CDPP	Comco Ikarus C42 FB100 VLA	PFA 322-14423		22. 9.05	H M Owen	(Foelgastell, Llanelli)	17. 7.08P
	(Built H M Owen)						

G-CDPR	Piper PA-18 Super Cub 95	18-3202	OY-AVT	17.11.05	J P Hibble	(St Peter Port, Guernsey)	20.12.07P
			D-ELFT, OL-L05 Belgian Army, L-128, 53-4802				
G-CDPS	Raj Hamsa X'Air Falcon 133(1)	919		31. 8.05	P R Smith	(Eccleston, Chorley)	
	(Built P R Smith - pr.no.BMAA/HB/332)				(Noted 11.06)		
G-CDPT	Boeing 767-319ER	29388	ZK-NCN	6. 4.06	Globespan Airways Ltd t/a Flyglobespan.com		
						London Heathrow	6. 4.08E
G-CDPV	Piper PA-34-200T Seneca II	34-8070086	PH-MRM	14.10.05	Partside Aviation Ltd	Shobdon	6.11.07E
			D-GIGF, N99GN, C-FJRN, N35717				
G-CDPW	P&M Pegasus Quantum 15-912	8138		14.10.05	T P R Wright	(Ilkeston)	20.10.08P
G-CDPX	Schleicher ASH 25Mi	25256		5. 1.06	P Pozerskis and M C Costin	Husbands Bosworth	6. 4.08E
	(Officially regd as ASH 25M) (Diamond IAE50R-AA)				"260"		
G-CDPY	Europa Aviation Europa	303		8. 3.00	A Burrill	(Calcot, Reading)	
	(Built A Burrill - pr.no.PFA 247-13029) (Monowheel u/c)						
G-CDPZ	Flight Design CT2K	03-06-03-28		23. 6.05	M E Henwick	Popham	22. 6.08P
	(Assembled Mainair Sports Ltd with (official) c/n 8124 but thought to be c/n 8104)						
G-CDRA	Boeing 737-683	28304	SE-DNX	8.11.05	Globespan Airways Ltd t/a Flyglobespan.com		
			EC-INT, SE-DNX, N1787B		(Stored 2.08)	Edinburgh	7.11.07E
G-CDRB	Boeing 737-683	28305	SE-DOR	1.12.05	Globespan Airways Ltd t/a Flyglobespan.com		
			EC-IND, OY-KKE, N1787B		(Stored 2.08)	Edinburgh	30.11.07E
G-CDRC	Cessna 182Q Skylane	18267085	N97418	2. 9.05	A G Hill t/a R S Hill and Sons	Bournemouth	31. 1.08E
G-CDRD	AirBorne XT912-B-Streak III-B	XT912-096		24.10.05	Fly NI Ltd	Newtownards	17.10.07P
	(Wing s/n SB3-80)						
G-CDRF	Cameron Z-90	10763		20. 1.06	Chalmers Ballong Corps	(Goteborg, Sweden)	19. 2.08E
G-CDRG	P&M Pegasus Quik	8137		19.10.05	R J Gabriel	Yatesbury	20.10.08P
G-CDRH	Thruster T 600N	0056-T600N-114		30. 6.05	A Cope and G L Pritt	Carlisle	29. 6.08P
G-CDRI	Cameron O-105 Balloon (Hot Air)	10794		22.12.05	R J Fuller tr Snapdragon Balloon Group	Godalming	15. 3.08E
G-CDRJ	Air Création Tanarg 912S/iXess 15	FLT003		23.11.05	J H Hayday	Plaistows Farm, St Albans	4. 6.08P
	(Built J H Hayday - pr.no.BMAA/HB/464 being Flylight kit comprising Trike s/n T05071 and Wing s/n A05148-5135)						
G-CDRK	British Aerospace Avro 146-RJ100	E3265	TC-THO	25. 1.06	Trident Jet (Dublin) Ltd	Kemble	
			G-6-265		(Stored 8.07)		
G-CDRM	Van's RV-7A	PFA 323-14203		26. 7.05	R A Morris	St Just	22.10.07P
	(Built R A Morris)		(Nose gear dug in after landing Croft Farm, north of Gloucester 9. 6.07: overturned causing substantial damage)				
G-CDRN	Cameron Z-225 Balloon (Hot Air)	10750		25. 4.06	Balloon School (International) Ltd		
						Colhook Common, Petworth	2. 5.08E
G-CDRO	Comco Ikarus C42 FB80	0507-6750		17. 8.05	Airbourne Aviation Ltd	Popham	16. 8.08P
G-CDRP	Comco Ikarus C42 FB80	0509-6762		26.10.05	D S Parker	Carlisle	26.10.08P
G-CDRR	P&M Pegasus Quantum 15-912	8134		12. 9.05	A W Buchan	Knapthorpe Lodge, Caunton	13. 9.08P
G-CDRS	Rotorway Executive 162F	6956		30. 8.05	R C Swann	(Blofield, Norwich)	
	(Built R C Swann)						
G-CDRT	P&M Pegasus Quik	8131		22.11.05	R Tetlow	(Uppermill, Oldham)	7. 5.08P
G-CDRU	CASA 1-131E Jungmann	2321	EC-DRU	19. 1.90	P Cunniff	White Waltham	10. 5.08P
			Spanish AF E3B-530		"Yen a Bon"		
G-CDRV	Van's RV-9A	PFA 320-14186		29. 6.05	R J Woodford	(Danbury, Chelmsford)	
	(Built R J Woodford)						
G-CDRW	P&M Pegasus Quik	8141		21. 9.05	G Fearon	Oxton, Nottingham	7.10.07P
G-CDRX	Cameron Z-275 Balloon (Hot Air)	10773		25. 4.06	Balloon School (International) Ltd		
						Colhook Common, Petworth	2. 5.08E
G-CDRY	Comco Ikarus C42 FB100 VLA	PFA 322-14448		26. 9.05	R J Mitchell	Tingwall	
	(Built R J Mitchell)						
G-CDRZ	Balony Kubicek BB22 Balloon (Hot Air)	395		6. 3.06	Club Amatori Del Volo In Mongolfiera	Macherio, Italy	14. 3.07E
G-CDSA	P&M Pegasus Quik	8144		9.11.05	D J Cornelius (New owner 5.07)	Lee-on-Solent	24.11.08P
G-CDSB	Alpi Pioneer 200	xxx		4.11.04	T A and Phyllis M Pugh	Shobdon	12. 3.08P
	(Built T W Skinner - pr.no.PFA 334-14443)						
G-CDSC	Scheibe SF25C Falke	44643	D-KIEX	2.12.05	I K G Mitchell tr Devon & Somerset Motorglider Group		
	(Rotax 912-S)					North Hill	8. 2.08E
G-CDSD	Alpi Pioneer 300	xxx		3.11.05	J A Ball and S D Barnard	Leicester	11. 1.08P
	(Built F A Cavaciuti - pr.no.PFA 330-14439)						
G-CDSF	Diamond DA.40D Star	D4.190	OE-VPU	24. 2.06	Flying Time Ltd	Shoreham	9. 4.08E
	(Marked as "DA40TDi")						
G-CDSG	Sud-Aviation SA.316B Alouette III	14	Romanian AF 07	11.11.05	G Snook	(Leeds)	
	(Built ICA-Brasov as type IAR.316B)						
G-CDSH	ICP MXP-740 Savannah Jabiru(5)	05-07-51-413		9.11.05	J P Bell	Eshott	25. 9.08P
	(Built S Whittaker and P J Wilson - pr.no.BMAA/HB/463)						
G-CDSI	Avtech Jabiru J400	0xxx		17.11.05	G H Gilmour-White	(Thorverton, Exeter)	
	(Built G H Gilmour-White - pr.no.PFA 325-14183)						
G-CDSJ	Sud-Aviation SA.316B Alouette III	20	Romanian AF12	17.11.05	S Atherton	(Tadcaster)	
	(Built ICA-Brasov as "IAR.316B")				(Noted 6.07)		
G-CDSK	Reality Escapade Jabiru(3)	UKESC 0004		15.11.05	R H Sear	(Lincoln)	27. 2.08P
	(Built R H Sear - pr.no.BMAA/HB/469)						
G-CDSL	Cessna 182R Skylane	18267970	N9606H	5.12.05	A G Craig	(Easterton, Devizes)	2. 9.08
G-CDSM	P&M Quik GT450	8146		20.10.05	B A Ritchie	Perth	18.12.07P
G-CDSN	Raj Hamsa X'Air Jabiru(3)	1042		16.11.05	G W Cole	(Christchurch, Newport)	
	(Built G W Cole - pr.no.BMAA/HB/472)						
G-CDSO	Thruster T 600N 450	1051-T600N-115		9.12.05	W G Reynolds	(Overstrand, Cromer)	11. 2.08P
G-CDSR	Learjet Model 45	45-286	N50126	30. 1.06	Air Partner Private Jets Ltd	London Stansted	31. 1.08E
G-CDSS	P&M Pegasus Quik	8142		16.11.05	P A Bass	Wilby, Wellingborough	15.12.07P
G-CDST	Ultramagic N-250 Balloon (Hot Air)	250/37		27. 7.05	S A Towney t/a Sky High Leisure	Ellesmere Port	26. 6.08E
G-CDSU	Robinson R22 Beta	3464	EI-MUR	15.12.05	C Poundes	(Crownhill, Milton Keynes)	9. 1.08E
G-CDSV	Aérospatiale AS.332L Super Puma	2058	N171EH	1.12.05	CHC Helicopters International Inc	Aberdeen	
			C-GSLA, PT-HRM, C-GSLA		(Noted 12.05)		
G-CDSW	Comco Ikarus C42 FB80	0511-6772		23.11.05	P J Barton	Longacre Farm, Sandy	2. 2.08P
G-CDSX	English Electric Canberra T Mk.4	71367	WJ874	27. 3.06	Aviation Heritage Ltd	Coventry	
					(As "VN799" to represent the A1 Canberra prototype)		

G-CDSY	Robinson R44 Raven	1534		3. 1.06	E Meegan		
					Bloomfield , Castle Blayney, County Monaghan		23. 2.08E
G-CDSZ	Diamond DA.42 Twin Star	42.084		1. 3.06	Aviation Services Ltd	Ronaldsway	23. 3.08E
G-CDTA	Evektor EV-97 teamEurostar UK	2509		19.10.05	R D Stein	Redlands, Swindon	22.10.08P
G-CDTB	P&M Pegasus Quantum 15-912	8136		6.10.05	D W Corbett	Cottage Farm, Norton Juxta	4.10.08P
G-CDTC	P&M Pegasus Quantum 15-912	8135		12.10.05	C W J Davis	(Swadlincote)	4.10.08P
G-CDTD	Eurocopter AS.350B2 Ecureuil	9072	F-GUAZ	20. 2.06	London Helicopter Centres Ltd	Redhill	20. 2.08E
			F-WQED,F-WW..				
G-CDTE	Tecnam P2002-JF Sierra	029		23. 1.06	Tecnam Gen. Aviation Ltd	Clench Common	16. 2.08E
G-CDTF	Whittaker MW5-D Sorcerer	PFA 163-14469		28.11.05	R J Smyth	(York)	
	(Built R J Smyth)						
G-CDTG	Diamond DA.42 Twin Star	42.083		6. 2.06	Twinstar Ltd	Liverpool	9. 3.08E
G-CDTH	Schempp-Hirth Nimbus 4DM	65		7. 7.06	M A V Gatehouse	North Hill	27. 7.08E
G-CDTI	Messerschmitt Bf109E-1	4034		12.12.05	Rare Aero Ltd	(Jersey)	
	(Built Focke-Wulf at Bremen 1939?)						
G-CDTJ	Reality Escapade Jabiru(1)	UKESC 0003		13.12.05	D Little	(Crawley)	13.12.07P
	(Built D Little - pr.no.BMAA/HB/461)						
G-CDTK	Schweizer 269C-1	0216	N86G	13.12.05	Caseright Ltd	Bournemouth	5. 1.08E
	(Schweizer 300)				(Operated Bournemouth Helicopters)		
G-CDTL	Avtech Jabiru J400	0xxx		13.12.05	M I Sistern	Sleap	9.11.08P
	(Built M I Sistern - pr.no.PFA 325-14386)						
G-CDTM	Vickers Supermarine 384 Seafire F XVII	?	A2054	21.12.05	T J Manna	North Weald	
	(Built Westland Aircraft Ltd)		A646, SX300		(Parts only, stored in boxes (for restoration?) 1.06)		
G-CDTO	P&M Quik GT450	8149		11. 1.06	J R Houston	Perth	30. 1.08P
G-CDTP	Best Off Sky Ranger 912S(1)	SKRxxxxx617		21.12.05	J R S Heaton	Hawksbridge Farm, Oxenhope	27. 7.08P
	(Built J R S Heaton - pr.no.BMAA/HB/475)						
G-CDTR	P&M Quik GT450	8153		20.12.05	D J Collier t/a Sunfun Group		
					Lower Mountpleasant Farm, Chatteris		2. 1.08P
G-CDTT	ICP MXP-740 Savannah Jabiru(4) 04-01-51-273			29. 9.05	M P Middleton	(Rhosgoch)	29.10.07P
	(Built M P Middleton - pr.no.BMAA/HB/383)						
G-CDTU	Evektor EV-97 teamEurostar UK	2522		5.1.06	I Shaw tr G-CDTU Group	(Wilmslow)	22.12.07P
G-CDTV	Tecnam P2002-EA Sierra	PFA 333-14501		19.1.06	M Rudd	Hermitage, Dorchester	13. 6.08P
	(Built M Rudd						
G-CDTX	Reims Cessna F152	F15201662	D-EERU	22.12.05	Z Islam and J S Develin	Blackbushe	8. 6.08E
			N1659C				
G-CDTY	ICP MXP-740 Savannah Jabiru(5) 05-09-51-414			5. 1.06	D McCormack and Senga Bradie		
	(Built J N Anyan - pr.no.BMAA/HB/467)				Broomhill Farm, West Calder		26. 6.08P
G-CDTZ	Aeroprakt A22 Foxbat	PFA 317-14433		21.12.05	P C Piggott and M E Hughes	Husbands Bosworth	31. 5.08P
	(Built P C Piggott and M E Hughes)						
G-CDUE	Robinson R44 Raven	1549		24. 1.06	Scotia Helicopters Ltd	Cumbernauld	7. 2.08E
G-CDUH	P&M Quik GT450	8167		14. 2.06	R W Thornborough	Ince Blundell	29. 2.08P
G-CDUJ	Lindstrand LBL 31A Balloon (Hot Air)	1080		27. 1.06	J M Frazer	Holystone, Morpeth	11. 3.08E
G-CDUK	Comco Ikarus C42 FB80	0511-6770		21.11.05	D M Lane	(Poole)	14.12.07P
G-CDUL	Best Off Sky Ranger 912(2)	SKR0506615		23. 1.06	T W Thiele and C D Hogbourne	Radwell	19. 5.08P
	(Built T W Thiele - pr.no.BMAA/HB/471)						
G-CDUS	Best Off Sky Ranger 912S(1)	SKR0508643		26. 1.06	C S Robinson	Newtownards	11. 9.08P
	(Built W P Byrne - pr.no.BMAA/HB/490)						
G-CDUT	Avtech Jabiru J400	0xxx		2. 2.06	T W and A Pullin	(Barrow-in-Furness)	26. 7.08P
	(Built T W and A Pullin - pr.no.PFA 325-14352)						
G-CDUU	P&M Quik GT450	8165		16. 3.06	A Rose tr Caunton Charlie Delta Group		
					Knapthorpe Lodge, Caunton		8. 5.08P
G-CDUV	ICP MXP-740 Savannah Jabiru(5) 05-09-51-415			5. 1. 06	D M Blackman	Rochester	26. 6.08P
	(Built M Leachman - pr.no.BMAA/HB/465)						
G-CDUW	Aeronca C 3	A 517	(F-AZKE)	20. 2.06	N K Geddes South Barnbeth Farm, Bridge of Weir		
			N64765, NC14631				
G-CDUX	Piper PA-32-300 Cherokee Six	32-7340074	EC-DUX	31. 7.02	D J Mason	Ronaldsway	29.1.08E
			F-BSGY, 5T-TJR, N11C				
G-CDUY	Colt 77A Balloon (Hot Air)	600	D-HIPPO	9. 2.06	G D D Jones tr De Hippo Balloon Group		
			D-WESTFALEN (2)			Tarleton, Preston	
G-CDVA	Best Off Sky Ranger 912(2)	SKR0211247		21.12.05	D C Mole	Mullahead, Tandragee	27. 7.07P
	(Built R J Hoare - pr.no.BMAA/HB/269)				(New owner 10.07)		
G-CDVD	Evektor EV-97 Eurostar	PFA 315-14485		6. 1.06	P Ritchie	Glenrothes	6. 3.08P
	(Built G R Pritchard)						
G-CDVF	Rans S-6-ES Coyote II	xxxx		2. 2.06	G P Jones	Stoke-on-Trent	21. 9.08P
	(Built G P Jones - pr.no.PFA 204-14464)						
G-CDVG	P&M Pegasus Quik	8152		24. 1.06	M Overend	(Long Clawson, Melton Mowbray)	21. 2.08P
G-CDVH	P&M Pegasus Quantum 15	8166		20. 2.06	M J Hyde	Deenethorpe	21. 8.08P
G-CDVI	Comco Ikarus C42 FB80	0602-6794		13. 3.06	Airbourne Aviation Ltd	Popham	1. 5.08P
G-CDVJ	Montgomerie-Bensen B 8MR PFA G/01A-1355			17. 1.06	D J Martin	(Leigh End, Glazebury, Warrington)	
	(Built D J Martin)						
G-CDVK	ICP MXP-740 Savannah Jabiru(5) 05-02-51-372			24. 1.06	M Peters	Wing Farm, Longbridge Deverill	25. 9.08P
	(Built M Peters - pr.no.BMAA/HB/449)						
G-CDVL	Alpi Pioneer 300	xxx		27. 1.06	T C Robson and A N Pascoe	Great Massingham	7. 8.08P
	(Built T C Robson and A N Pascoe - pr.no.PFA 330-14379)				(Noted 5.06)		
G-CDVN	P&M Quik GT450	8176		11. 4.06	R E J Pattenden	Rochester	20. 4.08P
G-CDVO	P&M Pegasus Quik	8147		9.12.05	S D J Harvey	Broadmeadow Farm, Hereford	12.12.06P
G-CDVP	Evektor EV-97 teamEurostar UK	2521		14. 2.06	I Seurre and V Nolan tr Victor Papa Group		
					(Maidenhead and Winnersh, Wokingham)		26. 2.08P
G-CDVR	P&M Quik GT450	8160		27. 1.06	A V Cosser	East Fortune	30. 1.08P
G-CDVS	Europa Aviation Europa XS	364		20. 2.06	J F Lawn	(Holy Cross, Norwich)	21.11.07P
	(Built J F Lawn - pr.no.PFA 247-13217)						
G-CDVT	Van's RV-6	20206	N391DS	7. 2.06	P D Wood	(Leigh, Worcester)	31. 5.08P
	(Built D W Sorrels)						
G-CDVU	Evektor EV-97 teamEurostar UK	2525		13. 3.06	D J Dick	Shobdon	23. 3.08P

G-CDVV	Scottish Aviation Bulldog Series 120/121	BH120/291	9290M XX626	27. 1.06	D M Squires	Wellesbourne Mountford	13. 7.09S
	(As "XX626: 02" and "9290M")						
G-CDVX	Republic TP-47G-10-CU Thunderbolt	21953	N47DG N42354, 42-25068	20. 2.06	Patina Ltd *"Little Demon"*	Duxford	
	(Built Curtiss-Wright Corporationas				*(As "28476:YJ-X").(To Chino, California, US 9.06 for completion)*		
G-CDVZ	P&M Quik GT450	8151		30. 1.06	A K Burden	Colliers Elm, Churcham	2. 5.07P
G-CDWA	Balony Kubicek BB37 Balloon (Hot Air)	424		2. 3.06	Fly In Balloons SRL	Villafalletto, Italy	19. 4.07E
G-CDWB	Best Off Sky Ranger 912(2)	SKRxxxx627		19. 1.06	V J Morris	Forest Farm, Redruth	16. 7.08P
	(Built V J Morris - pr.no.BMAA/HB/477)						
G-CDWD	Cameron Z-105 Balloon (Hot Air)	10827		3. 5.06	P Spellward t/a Bristol University Ballooning Society		
					"Eric".	Bristol	3. 2.08E
G-CDWE	Nord NC.856 Norvigie	01	F-WFKF F-BFKF	10. 3.06	R H and S J Cooper	(Stow, Lincolnshire)	
G-CDWG	Dyn'Aéro MCR-01 Club	PFA 301A-14132		10. 2.06	S E Gribble	Sywell	17. 5.08P
	(Built S E Gribble)						
G-CDWH	Curtiss P-40B	16073	N80FR G-CDWH, 41-13297	27. 1.06	Patina Ltd	Duxford	
	(Built Curtiss-Wright Corporation)				*(Operated.The Fighter Collection) (Noted 6.07)*		
	(Restored c 1990 using parts ex 39-285 and 39-287)						
G-CDWI	Comco Ikarus C42 FB80	0601-6783		9. 1.06	A E Broughton	(Laughton, Gainsborough)	12. 3.08P
G-CDWJ	Flight Design CTSW	05.11.16		9. 3.06	B W T Rood	Sywell	27. 6.08P
	(Assembled P&M Aviation Ltd with c/n 8157)						
G-CDWK	Robinson R22 Raven II	11116		3. 4.06	J O'Connor t/a Speedyparts Direct		
						(Mullingar, County Westmeath)	20. 4.08E
G-CDWL	Raj Hamsa X'Air 582(5)	xxxx		30. 1.06	C Lenaghan	(Crossmaglen, Newry)	14. 9.08P
	(Built C Lenaghan - pr.no.BMAA/HB/484)						
G-CDWM	Best Off Sky Ranger 912S(1)	SKRxxxx616		15.12.05	W H McMinn		
	(Built W H McMinn- pr.no.BMAA/HB/470)					Slieve Croob, Slievenamoney, Castlewellen	4. 6.08P
G-CDWN	Ultramagic N-210 Balloon (Hot Air)	210/33		22. 5.06	S R Seager	Weedon, Aylesbury	25. 5.07E
G-CDWO	P&M Quik GT450	8175		3. 4.06	M D Harris	(Earls Barton, Northampton)	6. 4.08E
G-CDWP	P&M Quik GT450	8173		16. 3.06	S M Hall	Headon Farm, Retford	3. 4.08E
G-CDWR	P&M Quik GT450	8181		10. 4.06	D P Creedy	(Haslington, Crewe)	9. 4.08E
G-CDWS	P&M Quik GT450	8178		26. 4.06	H N Barrott	East Fortune	1. 5.08P
G-CDWT	Flight Design CTSW	05.12.10		9. 3.06	R Scammell	Sywell	2. 7.08P
	(Assembled P&M Aviation Ltd with c/n 8162)						
G-CDWU	Zenair CH.601UL Zodiac	PFA 162A-14332		16. 3.06	A D Worrall	Tarn Farm, Cockerham	31.10.07P
	(Built A D Worrall)						
G-CDWV	Lindstrand LBL House SS Balloon (Hot Air) 1089			13. 3.06	LSB Public Relations Ltd	Abergavenny	10. 8.07E
					(Stroud and Swindon Building Society titles).		
G-CDWW	P&M Quik GT450	8156		6. 1.06	J H Bradbury	Arclid Green, Sandbach	30. 1.08P
G-CDWX	Lindstrand LBL 77A Balloon (Hot Air)	1088		13. 3.06	LSB Public Relations Ltd	Abergavenny	26. 3.08E
					(Stroud and Swindon Building Society titles).		
G-CDWY	Agusta A109S Grand	22011		15. 6.06	Sports World International Ltd	Sywell	14. 6.08E
G-CDWZ	P&M Quik GT450	8154		2. 2.06	B J Holloway	Bicester	5. 2.08P
G-CDXA	Robinson R44 Raven	1584		31. 3.06	R A J Graham t/a J and D Graham		
					(Operated Northumbrian Helicopters)	Newcastle	27. 4.08E
G-CDXB	Robinson R44 Raven	1578		31. 3.06	HJS Helicopters Ltd	Lower Baads, Peterculter	4. 5.08E
G-CDXD	Medway SLA 100 Executive	070306		8. 3.06	K J Draper	Stoke, Isle of Grain	23.11.07P
G-CDXE	Westland Gazelle AH.Mk.1	1524	XZ299	29. 3.06	S Atherton *(On rebuild 2008)*	Thruxton	
G-CDXF	Lindstrand LBL 31A Balloon (Hot Air)	1076		7. 4.06	Roman Trading Ltd	Box, Corsham	23. 7.08E
G-CDXG	P&M Pegasus Quantum 15-912	8180		28. 4.06	E H Gatehouse Pound Green, Buttonoak, Bewdley		19. 5.08P
G-CDXH	British Aerospace Avro 146-RJ100	E3237	TC-THD G-6-237	21. 4.06	Trident Jet Leasing (Ireland) Ltd	Kemble	
					(Stored 8.07)		
G-CDXI	Cessna 182P Skylane	18263554	SE-GXY OY-ANT, N5820J	2. 3.06	B G McBeath	(Erith)	11. 9.08P
G-CDXJ	Avtech Jabiru J400	0xxx		27. 3.06	J C Collingwood	Wittersham, Tenterden	5.12.07P
	(Built J C Collingwood - pr.no.PFA 325-14356)						
G-CDXK	Diamond DA.42 Twin Star	42.136		6. 6.06	A M Healy	Cranfield	5. 7.08E
G-CDXL	Flight Design CTSW	06.05.17		4. 7.06	A K Paterson	(Pointon, Sleaford)	9. 7.08P
	(Assembled P&M Aviation Ltd with c/n 8191)						
G-CDXM	P&M Pegasus Quik	8159		8. 2.06	Mainair Microlight Centre Ltd	Barton	10. 2.08P
	(Believed rebuilt with Trike c/n 8197 in 4.06 taking original build no)						
G-CDXN	P&M Quik GT450	8171		15. 5.06	Microflight Aviation Ltd	Headon Farm, Retford	22. 5.08P
G-CDXO	Zenair CH.601UL Zodiac	PFA 162A-14524		6. 4.06	D P W Smith	(Barrow-in-Furness)	15. 8.08P
	(Built R O Lewthwaite and R E Welche)						
G-CDXP	Evektor EV-97 Eurostar	PFA 315-14530		6. 4.06	B J Crockett	Broadmeadow Farm, Hereford	18 .5.08P
	(Built B J Crockett)						
G-CDXR	Fokker Dr.1 Triplane replica	PFA 238-14043		13. 4.06	J G Gray	Rushett Farm, Chessington	26. 7.08P
	(Built J G Gray)				*(As "403/17" in German Army Air Service c/s)*		
G-CDXS	Evektor EV-97 teamEurostar UK	2005.26.27		22. 2.06	R T P Harris	Manor Farm, Haddenham	3. 4.08P
	(Officially regd with c/n 2627)						
G-CDXT	Van's RV-9	PFA 320-14376		11. 4.06	T M Storey	Newells Farm, Lower Beeding	13. 7.08P
	(Built T M Storey)						
G-CDXU	Chilton DW.1A	PFA 225-12038		19. 4.06	M Gibbs	(London SW11)	
	(Built R W Burrows)				*(New owner 6.07)*		
G-CDXV	Campbell Cricket Mk.6A	PGA G/16-1339		19. 4.06	W G Spencer	(Blandford Forum)	
	(Built W G Spencer) (Marked as "Layzell AV-18A").						
G-CDXW	Cameron Orange 120 SS Balloon (Hot Air) 2947		HB-BXL	22. 5.06	A Biasioli	Padova, Veneto, Italy	
G-CDXX	Robinson R44 Raven II	10624		31. 1.05	Emsway Developments Ltd	(Cannock)	23. 3.08P
G-CDXY	Skystar Kitfox Mk.7	PFA 172D-14112		24. 2.06	D E Steade	Croft Farm, Defford	12. 3.08P
	(Built D E Steade)						
G-CDYA	Gippsland GA-8 Airvan	GA8-05-090	VH-IMI	7. 4.06	P Marsden	South Cerney	4. 5.08E
G-CDYB	Rans S-6-ES Coyote II	xxxxx		28. 3.06	D Sykes and J M Hardstaff	Rufforth	15. 6.08P
	(Built D Sykes - pr.no.PFA 204-14416)						
G-CDYC	Piper PA-28RT-201 Arrow IV	28R-7918164	N2835D	26. 4.06	Arrowflight Ltd	Swansea	22. 7.08E
G-CDYD	Comco Ikarus C42 FB80	0604-6812		9. 6.06	F A Stephens tr C42 Group Baxby Manor, Husthwaite		15. 8.08P

G-CDYF	Rotorsport UK MT-03	RSUK/MT-03/003		21. 8.06	A J P Herculson	Little Snoring	30. 8.07P
G-CDYG	Cameron Z-105 Balloon (Hot Air)	10870		10. 5.06	A Service Di Tartaglini Emanuela		
					(Vodaphone titles).	Recanati, Marche, Italy	21. 5.08E
G-CDYI	British Aerospace Jetstream Series 4102	41019	N305UE	8. 6.06	Air Kilroe Ltd t/a Eastern Airways	Humberside	
	(Built Jetstream Aircraft Ltd)		G-4-019				
G-CDYJ	Best Off Sky Ranger 912(1)	SKRxxxx681		16. 5.06	D S Taylor	(Leeds, Maidstone)	
	(Built D S Taylor - pr.no.BMAA/HB/498)						
G-CDYL	Lindstrand LBL 77A Balloon (Hot Air)	1098		20. 6.06	J H Dobson	Streatley, Reading	1. 6.08E
					(Lambert Smith Hampton titles)		
G-CDYM	Murphy Maverick 430	PFA 259-12981		20. 3.06	M R Cann	Roche, Cornwall	4.12.07P
	(Built G T Leedham)						
G-CDYN	Extra EA.300/L	1222	D-EXTT	9. 5.06	C M Kritzinger	Dusseldorf, Germany	11. 5.08E
G-CDYO	Comco Ikarus C42 FB80	0604-6810		10.10.06	B Goodridge	Dunkeswel	9.10.07P
G-CDYP	Evektor EV-97 teamEurostar UK	2628		1. 6.06	R V Buxton and R Cranborne	(Wymondham)	4..7.08P
G-CDYR	Bell 206L-3 LongRanger III	51237	N341AJ	20. 9.07	M D Thorpe t/a Yorkshire Helicopters		
			5Y-BFL			Coney Park, Leeds	24. 9.08E
G-CDYS	Bell 206B-3 JetRanger III	3881	G-BOTM	15.11.05	Cardy Construction Ltd	Manston	19. 8.08E
			N31940				
G-CDYT	Comco Ikarus C42 FB80	0603-6798		4. 5.06	J W D Blythe	Swansea	3. 5.08P
G-CDYU	Zenair CH.701UL STOL	PFA 187-14489		8. 5.06	A Gannon	Glenrothes	12.12.07P
	(Built M Henderson)						
G-CDYW	Schweizer 269C-1	0247	N86G	20. 6.06	C R and S E Hewgill t/a CSL Industrial		
	(Schweizer 300)					(Sheffield City)	7. 9.08E
G-CDYX	Lindstrand LBL 77B Balloon (Hot Air)	1094		6. 7.06	H M Savage	Edinburgh	7. 9.08E
G-CDYY	Alpi Pioneer 300	xxx		14. 2.06	B Williams	(Llanddewi, Llandrindod Wells)	24.10.08P
	(Built B Williams - pr.no.PFA 330-14323)						
G-CDYZ	Van's RV-7	PFA 323-14276		1. 2.06	G A Martin and W D Garlick	Brock Farm, Billericay	26. 4.08P
	(Built G A Martin and W D Garlick) (Tailwheel u/c)						
G-CDZA	Alpi Pioneer 300	xxx		15. 3.06	J F Dowe	Parham	18. 9.08P
	(Built J Dowe - pr.no.PFA 330-14329)						
G-CDZB	Zenair CH.601UL Zodiac	PFA 162A-14431		10. 5.06	L J Dutch	Tarn Farm, Cockerham	3.11.07P
	(Built L J Dutch)						
G-CDZD	Van's RV-9A	PFA 320-13966	G-DUGS	24. 1.06	R T Clegg	Netherthorpe	1. 5.08P
	(initially built D M Provost and completed R T Clegg) (Wilksch WAM120 diesel)						
G-CDZG	Comco Ikarus C42 FB80	0604-6808		20. 4.06	Mainair Microlight School Ltd	Barton	1. 5.07P
G-CDZH	Boeing 737-804	28227	SE-DZH	19. 5.06	Thomsonfly Ltd	Sheffield-Doncaster	18. 5.08E
			N1786B				
G-CDZI	Boeing 737-804	28229	SE-DZI	24. 5.06	Thomsonfly Ltd	Sheffield-Doncaster	23. 5.08E
G-CDZJ	Tecnam P92-JS	050		15. 6.06	Tecnam General Aviation Ltd	Clench Common	24. 7.08E
G-CDZK	Tecnam P92-JS	052		7. 8.06	Tecnam General Aviation Ltd	Clench Common	21..9.08E
G-CDZL	Boeing 737-804	30465	D-ATUA	28. 4.06	Thomsonfly Ltd	Luton	27. 4.08E
			SE-DZL, PH-AAV, G-BYNC, N1786B, (SE-DZK)				
G-CDZM	Boeing 737-804	30466	D-ATUB	23.11.05	Thomsonfly Ltd	Coventry	22.11.07E
			SE-DZM, PH-ABE, G-BYNB, N1786B				
G-CDZO	Lindstrand LBL 60X Balloon (Hot Air)	1104		7. 7.06	R D Parry	Chalford, Stroud	30. 8.08E
					(Chelsea Financial Services titles)		
G-CDZP	British Aerospace Avro 146-RJ85	E2346	N521XJ	3.08R	(CityJet Ltd)	Cologne, Germany	
			G-6-346		*(Noted 12.06 in Air France c/s) (To become EI-RJI 2008)*		
G-CDZR	Nicollier HN.700 Menestrel II	PFA 217-13773		17. 5.06	T M Williams	(Pembrey, Burry Port)	
	(Built T M Williams)						
G-CDZS	Kolb Twinstar Mk.3 Extra	PFA 205-14278		23. 5.06	P W Heywood	Trewince Manor, Portscatho	
	(Built P W Heywood)						
G-CDZT	Beech B200 Super King Air	BB-1619	N240AJ	3. 7.06	BAE Systems Marine Ltd	Walney Island	2. 7.08E
			N719TA				
G-CDZU	ICP MXP-740 Savannah Jabiru(5)	04-06-51-295		17. 5.06	P J Cheyney	New House Farm, Birds Edge	9. 8.08P
	(Built P J Cheyney - pr.no.BMAA/HB/398)						
G-CDZW	Cameron N-105 Balloon (Hot Air)	2204	SE-ZEK	23. 5.06	P Lesser	Partille, Sweden	18. 2.08E
G-CDZY	Medway SLA 80 Executive	180406		19. 4.06	K J Draper t/a Medway Microlights		
					(Noted 8.06)	Stoke, Isle of Grain	
G-CDZZ	Rotorsport UK MT-03	RSUK/MT-03/002	G-94-1	4. 8.06	S J Boxall	Church Farm, Askern	8. 8.08P

G-CEAA - G-CEZZ

G-CEAE	Boeing 737-229	20912	OO-SDF	25. 1.00	European Skybus Ltd	Bournemouth	28. 2.08E
G-CEAF	Boeing 737-229	20910	G-BYRI	13. 1.00	European Skybus Ltd	Bournemouth	3. 4.08E
			OO-SDD, EC-EEG, OO-SDD		*(Operated Palmair)*		
G-CEAG	Boeing 737-229	21136	OO-SDL	6. 6.00	European Aviation Air Charter Ltd	Bournemouth	14. 6.06T
			(OO-SDM)		*(Stored 10.07)*		
G-CEAH	Boeing 737-229	21135	OO-SDG	1. 8.00	European Aviation Air Charter Ltd	Manchester	14.11.07E
					(Operated Jet 2.com)		
G-CEAK	Comco Ikarus C42 FB80	0606-6826		20. 7.06	M J Rhodes tr Barton Heritage Flying Group	Barton	13. 8.08P
G-CEAM	Evektor EV-97 teamEurostar UK	2729		13. 6.06	Flylight Airsports Ltd	Sywell	15. 6.08P
G-CEAN	Comco Ikarus C42 FB80	0606-6825		20. 6.06	Airbourne Aviation Ltd	Popham	31. 7.08P
G-CEAO	Jurca MJ.5 Sirocco	PFA 2209		23. 5.06	P S Watts	(Cam, Dursley)	
	(Built P S Watts)				*(Noted 3.07)*		
G-CEAR	Alpi Pioneer 300	xxx		25. 5.06	A Parker	Rufforth	26. 2.08P
	(Built A Parker - pr.no.PFA 330-14511)				"SW-1"		
G-CEAT	Zenair CH.601HDS Zodiac	PFA 162-13930		11. 5.06	T B Smith	(Yeovil)	
	(Built T B Smith)						
G-CEAU	Robinson R44 Clipper II	11311		22. 6.06	Mullahead Property Company Ltd		
						(Mullahead, Tandragee)	20. 7.08E
G-CEAV	Ultramagic M-105 Balloon (Hot Air)	105/140		24. 5.06	G Everett	Sandway, Maidstone	19. 6.07E
					(Saga Insurance titles)		

G-CEAW	Schweizer 269C-1	0241	N15120	24. 5.06	Aerocorp Ltd	(Sheffield City)	23. 7.08E
	(Schweizer 300)		N86G				
G-CEAX	UltraMagic S-130 Balloon (Hot Air)	130/49		14. 7.06	Anglian Countryside Balloons Ltd		
						Burnham-on-Crouch	14. 2.07E
G-CEAY	UltraMagic H-42 Balloon (Hot Air)	42/13		24. 7.06	J D A Shields	Hastings	25. 7.07E
G-CEBA	Zenair CH.601XL Zodiac PFA 162B-13426			21. 4.06	I J M Donnelly	Aboyne	16. 4.08P
	(Built I J M Donnelly)						
G-CEBC	ICP MXP-740 Savannah Jabiru(5) xx-xx-xx-xxx			25. 5.06	E W Chapman	North Moor, Scunthorpe	14. 3.08P
	(Built E W Chapman - pr.no.BMAA/HB/503)						
G-CEBD	P&M Quik GT450	8193		22. 5.06	E J Douglas	East Fortune	22. 5.08P
G-CEBE	Schweizer 269C-1	0253	N86G	19. 6.06	Milburn World Travel Services Ltd	Edinburgh	7. 9.08E
	(Schweizer 300)						
G-CEBF	Evektor EV-97A Eurostar PFA 315A-14525			6. 6.06	M Lang	Netherthorpe	2.11.08P
	(Built M Lang)						
G-CEBG	Balony Kubicek BB26 Balloon (Hot Air)	442		26. 6.06	P M Smith	Trim, County Meath	6. 7.08P
					(Beechwood Lodge titles)		
G-CEBH	Air Création Tanarg 912S/iXess 15 FLT.xxx			14. 6.06	D A Chamberlain	Sywell	17. 1.08P
	(Built D A Chamberlain - pr.no.BMAA/HB/481 being Flylight kit comprising Trike s/n T05098 and Wing s/n A05186-5193)						
G-CEBI	Kolb Twinstar Mk 3 Extra PFA 205-14361			6. 6.06	R W Livingstone	(Lisnaskea, Enniskillen)	
	(Built R W Livingstone)						
G-CEBK	Piper PA-31-350 Navajo Chieftain 31-7652056		PH-SAV	31. 8.06	Skydrift Ltd	Norwich	8.10.07E
			N59818				
G-CEBL	Balony Kubicek BB20GP Balloon (Hot Air)	456		23. 8.06	Associazione Sportiva Aerostatica Lombada		
					(X BIANCHI GROUP titles)	Milan, Italy	31. 8.87E
G-CEBM	P&M Quik GT450	8197		23. 5.06	P&M Aviation Ltd	Over Farm, Gloucester	19. 6.07P
G-CEBN	British Aerospace Avro 146-RJ100	E3238	TC-THE	20. 7.06	Trident Jet Leasing (Ireland) Ltd	Southend	
			G-6-238		(In open store 2.08)		
G-CEBO	Ultramagic M-65C Balloon (Hot Air)	65/77	D-OWBZ	26. 6.06	Renee D Howard	Timperley, Altrincham	15. 6.08P
G-CEBP	Evektor EV-97 teamEurostar UK	2825		3. 7.06	T R Southall "Lady Jean"	Shobdon	29. 6.08P
G-CEBT	P&M Quik GT450	8199		22. 6.06	A J Ridell	Henstridge	29. 6.08P
G-CEBV	Europa Aviation Europa XS	573		28. 6.06	S Vestuti	Swansea	29. 3.08P
	(Built S Vestuti - pr.no.PFA 247-14007)						
G-CEBW	North American P-51D-20-NA Mustang 122-38640		44-72181	5. 7.06	Classic (UW) Ltd	(Norwich)	
G-CEBY	Air Création Tanarg 912S(2)/iXess 15 FLT.xxx			30. 6.06	P S Bewley	(Saltford, Bristol)	18.10.08P
	(Built P S Bewley - pr.no.BMAA/HB/504 being Flylight kit comprising Trike s/n xxxx and Wing s/n xxxx)						
G-CEBZ	Zenair CH.601UL Zodiac PFA 162A-13942			12. 5.06	I M Ross and A Watt	Insch	5.12.08P
	(Built I M Ross and A Watt)						
G-CECA	P&M Quik GT450	8185		16. 8.06	A Whetherall	Blair Atholl	21. 8.08P
G-CECB	ELA Aviacion ELA 07S	11050710722		14. 7.06	A D Gordon	Blair Atholl	
G-CECC	Comco Ikarus C42 FB80	0607-6832		14. 6.06	K D Mitchell tr G-CECC Group	Deanland	3. 9.08P
G-CECD	Cameron C-90 Balloon (Hot Air)	10898		7. 8.06	A M Holly t/a Exclusive Holdings		
					(Adez titles)	Breadstone, Berkeley	2. 3.08E
G-CECE	Avtech Jabiru UL-D	656		8. 6.06	ST Aviation Ltd		
						Oaklands Farm, Horsham and Southery	1. 8.08P
G-CECF	Reality Escapade Jabiru(3) UKESC 0007			8. 6.06	T F Francis	Old Sarum	9.10.08P
	(Built T F Francis - pr.no.BMAA/HB/496) (Tailwheel u/c)						
G-CECG	Avtech Jabiru UL-D	661		18. 7.06	R K Watson "Pauline"	Damyn's Hall, Upminster	21. 8.08P
G-CECH	Jodel D 150	174		19. 7.06	J Simpson and D Kennedy	Lee-on-Solent	5.12.08P
	(Built D Kennedy - pr.no.PFA 235-13889)						
G-CECI	Pilatus PC-6/B2-H4 Turbo Porter	936	N2TS	3. 3.06	D M Penny	(Movenis, Coleraine)	22. 3.08E
			N424PS, HB-FMD				
G-CECJ	Aeromot AMT-200S Super Ximango	200168	PR-AMU	14.11.06	C J and S C Partridge	Lasham)	11.12.07P
G-CECK	ICP MXP-740 Savannah Jabiru(5) 06-01-51-453			11. 7.06	K W Eskins	Weston Zoyland	24. 4.08P
	(Built K W Eskins - pr.no.BMAA/HB/495)						
G-CECL	Comco Ikarus C42 FB80	0607-6834		4. 7.06	C Lee	Longacre Farm, Sandy	11.10.08P
G-CECM	P&M Quik GT450	8195		4. 9.06	C S Mackenzie	Perth	4. 9.08P
G-CECO	Hughes 269C	114-0377	D-HAEK	14. 9.06	P A Leverton	(Kirkby-in-Ashfield, Nottingham)	19.10.07E
			JA7574				
G-CECP	Best Off Sky Ranger 912(2) SKR0508639			13. 7.06	F Omaraie-Hamdanie	Hunsdon	20. 5.08P
	(Built D C Davies - pr.no.BMAA/HB/483) (C/n possibly SKR0509639)						
G-CECR	Bilsam Sky Cruiser S-CR-7B-XHP-2006			16.11.06	J C Collingwood	Wittersham, Tenterden	
G-CECS	Lindstrand LBL 105A Balloon (Hot Air)	1121		25. 7.06	Beam Global Distribution (UK) Ltd	Telford	11. 7.08E
					(Harvey's Orange titles)		
G-CECU	Boeing 767-222	21864	N603UA	2. 1 07	UK International Airlines Ltd	East Midlands	15. 3.08E
					(Airline suspended 2008)		
G-CECV	Van's RV-7 PFA 323-14338			30. 5.06	D M Stevens	Haverfordwest	18.10.07P
	(Built D M Stevens)						
G-CECW	Robinson R44 Raven II	11446		9.10.06	VHE Construction Ltd	(Rethmines, Dublin)	2.11.07E
G-CECX	Robinson R44 Raven II	11390		6. 9.06	Dolphin Property (Management) Ltd	Thruxton	28. 9.07E
G-CECY	Evektor EV-97 Eurostar PFA 315-14551			21. 7.06	M R M Welch	Goodwood	4. 9.08P
	(Built M R M Welch)						
G-CECZ	Zenair CH.601XL Zodiac PFA 162B-14458			17. 7.06	G M Johnson	(Ramsey, Huntingdon)	11.12.08P
	(Built G M Johnson) (Tail-wheel u/c)						
G-CEDA	Cameron Z-105 Balloon (Hot Air)	10910		9. 8.06	N Charbonnier (Sanpaulo Leasint titles) Aosta, Italy		17. 1.08E
G-CEDB	Reality Escapade Jabiru(3) UKESC.0002			12. 4.06	P Travis	Davidstow Moor	
	(Built D Bedford - pr.no.BMAA/HB/456)				(New owner 1.08)		
G-CEDC	Comco Ikarus C42 FB100	0607-6831		14. 8.06	P D Ashley	Dunkeswell	31. 8.08P
G-CEDD	Piper PA-28RT-201 Arrow IV	28R-8018100	N82507	16. 6.06	R Hammond	Southend	11. 6.08P
G-CEDE	Flight Design CTSW	06.06.14		16. 8.06	F Williams and J A R Hartley		
	(Assembled P&M Aviation Ltd with c/n 8212)					Combrooke, Stratford-upon-Avon	20. 8.08P
G-CEDF	Cameron N-105 Balloon (Hot Air)	10884		31. 7.06	Bailey Balloons Ltd (EDF Energy titles)	Bristol	16. 8.08E
G-CEDG	Robinson R44 Raven	1639		31. 8.06	Wiksy Charter Ltd	Hawarden	14. 9.08P
G-CEDI	Best Off Sky Ranger 912(2) SKRxxxx700			10..8.06	P B Davey	(Wittersham, Tenterden)	
	(Built P B Davey - pr.no.BMAA/HB/513)						

Reg	Type	c/n	Prev id	Date	Owner/Operator	Location	Date
G-CEDJ	Aero Designs Pulsar XP	207	N383B	21.12.06	R R Walters	Parham	15.11.08P
	(Built W Becker)						
G-CEDK	Cessna 750 Citation X	750-0252	N252CX	20. 3.07	The Duke of Westminster	Hawarden)	19. 3.08E
			N5000R				
G-CEDL	TEAM miniMAX 91	PFA 186-12546		18. 7.06	J W Taylor	Over Farm, Gloucester	2.10.08P
	(Built J W Taylor)						
G-CEDM	Flight Design CTSW	06.06.14		17. 8.06	S A Fair	Sywell	17. 8.07P
	(Assembled P&M Aviation Ltd with c/n 8214)				*(Noted 10.07)*		
G-CEDN	P&M Pegasus Quik	8206		15. 8.06	N J Hargreaves	(Southport)	19. 9.08P
G-CEDO	Raj Hamsa X'Air Falcon 133(1)	xxxxx		3. 8.06	A P Lambert and J Lane		
	(Built A P Lambert and J Lane - pr.no.BMAA/HB/511) (Change of Type 10.06)				*(Noted 3.07)*	Lower Upham Farm, Chisledon	
G-CEDP	ELA Aviacion ELA 07R	04040270712		21. 8.06	Roger Savage (Penrith) Ltd *(Noted 8.07)*	Kirkbride	
G-CEDR	Comco Ikarus C42 FB80	0606-6833		1. 8.06	R S O'Carroll	Mullahead, Tandragee	3. 8.08P
G-CEDT	Air Création Tanarg 912S/iXess 15	FLT.xxx		14. 7.06	R A Taylor	RAF Cranwell	20. 5.08P
	(Built R A Taylor - pr.no.BMAA/HB/510 being Flylight kit comprising Trike s/n T06033 and Wing s/n xxxx)						
G-CEDV	Evektor EV-97 teamEurostar UK	2826		29. 9.06	Airbourne Aviation Ltd	Popham	5.10.08P
G-CEDW	TEAM miniMAX 91	PFA 186-12472		22. 6.06	A T Peatman	(Dursley)	
	(Built A T Peatman)				*(Noted unmarked and unfinished PFA Kemble 8.06)*		
G-CEDX	Evektor EV-97 teamEurostar UK	2827		6. 9.06	M W Houghton	Bakersfield	10. 9.08P
G-CEDZ	Best Off Sky Ranger 912(2)	SKRxxxx685		28. 7.06	I Bell and J E Walendowski	Sandtoft	
	(Built J E Walendowski - pr.no.BMAA/HB/505)				*(New owner 1.07)*		
G-CEEA	ELA Aviacion ELA 07R	04040430712		30. 8.06	S J Tyler	Kirkbride	
G-CEEB	Cameron C-80 Balloon (Hot Air)	10923		18. 8.06	Cameron Balloons Ltd	Bristol	8. 3.08E
G-CEEC	Raj Hamsa X'Air Hawk	1096		23. 8.06	G A J Salter	(Taunton)	26. 7.08P
	(Built G A J Salter - pr.no.PFA 340-14559)						
G-CEED	ICP MXP-740 Savannah Jabiru(5)	06-03-51-470		24. 8.06	A U I Hudson	Bracon Ash	1. 4.08P
	(Built A U I Hudson - pr.no.BMAA/HB/500)						
G-CEEE	Robinson R44 Raven II	10005		26.11.02	Caswell Environmental Services Ltd	(Stevenage)	17.12.07E
G-CEEF	ELA Aviacion ELA 07R	06040440712		8. 9.06	G Millward	(Calow, Chesterfield)	
G-CEEG	Alpi Pioneer 300	26		31. 8.06	D McCormack	Kirknewton	9.11.07P
	(Built D McCormack - pr.no.PFA 330-14556)						
G-CEEI	P&M Quik GT450	8218		16.10.06	R A Hill	Enstone	30.10.08P
G-CEEJ	Rans S-7S Courier	0105-392		31. 8.06	J G J McDill	Felixkirk	
	(Built J G J McDill - pr.no.PFA 218-14557)				*(Noted 5.07)*		
G-CEEK	Cameron Z-105 Balloon (Hot Air)	10909		9.11.06	PSH Skypower Ltd	Woodborough, Pewsey	16.10.08E
G-CEEL	Ultramagic S-90 Balloon (Hot Air)	90/89		12. 9.06	Impresa San Paolo SRL	Reggio Emilia, Italy	28. 9.07E
					(Impresa S Paolo titles)		
G-CEEM	P&M Quik GT450	8216		29. 9.06	T Griffiths	(Whitemill, Carmarthen)	3.10.07P
G-CEEN	Piper PA-28-161 Cadet	2841293	EC-IHA	22. 9.06	Plane Talking Ltd	Denham	10.10.07E
			N9202N				
G-CEEO	Flight Design CTSW	06.08.12		29. 9.06	E McCallum	Longframlington	5.10.08P
	(Assembled P&M Aviation Ltd with c/n 8225)						
G-CEEP	Van's RV-9A	90062	N966AM	7.09.06	J M Ghosh and M P Wiseman		
	(Built R A Jones)					Mount Airey Farm, South Cave	20.12.08P
G-CEER	ELA Aviacion ELA 07R	04040420712		8. 9.06	F G Shepherd	Kirkbride	
G-CEES	Cameron C-90 Balloon (Hot Air)	11916		11.10.06	P C May	Poling, Arundel	24.10.07E
G-CEEU	Piper PA-28-161 Cadet	2841038	N224FT	8. 2.07	Plane Talking Ltd	Elstree	
			EC-IIF, N9158J				
G-CEEV	Piper PA-28-161 Warrior III	2842162	N5352X	11.12.06	Plane Talking Ltd	Cranfield	6. 2.08E
G-CEEW	Comco Ikarus C42 FB100	0609-6847		18. 9.06	Autocom Products Ltd	Long Marston	19.11.07P
G-CEEX	ICP MXP-740 Savannah Jabiru(5)	xx-xx-xx-xxx		21. 8.06	M A Jones	(Bracebridge Heath, Lincoln)	8. 2.08P
	(Built T Brumpton and M Hicks - pr.no.BMAA/HB/508)						
G-CEEY	Piper PA-28-161 Warrior III	2842168	N53583	11.12.06	Plane Talking Ltd	Elstree	19. 4.08E
G-CEEZ	Piper PA-28-161 Warrior III	2842161	N53513	11.12.06	Plane Talking Ltd	Elstree	8. 2.08E
G-CEFA	Comco Ikarus C42 FB UK	0609-6851		7.11.06	J Little	Barton	30. 5.08P
	(Built J Little - pr.no.PFA 322-14570)						
G-CEFB	Ultramagic H-31 Balloon (Hot Air)	31/06		30.10.06	P Dickinson	St Martins, Oswestry	8.11.07E
G-CEFC	Super Marine Spitfire Mk.26	PFA 324-14417		21. 9.06	D R Bishop	Kemble	
	(Built D R Bishop)				*(As "RB412:DW-B" in RAF c/s)*		
G-CEFG	Boeing 767-319ER	26264	ZK-NCH	27.10.06	Globespan Airways Ltd t/a Flyglobespan.com	Glasgow	1.11.07E
G-CEFH	ELA Aviacion ELA 07S	03060950722		2.10.06	M L L Temple	Kirkbride	
G-CEFJ	Sonex Aircraft Sonex	FF05-4-00048		9.10.06	M H Moulai	Sandtoft	11.11.08P
	(Built M H Moulai - pr.no.PFA 337-14518) (Hirth F33)						
G-CEFK	Evektor EV-97 teamEurostar UK	2823		13.11.06	P Morgan	Ince Blundell	12.11.07P
G-CEFM	Cessna 152	15284357	N6102L	19.10.06	Cristal Air Ltd	Deanland	
G-CEFP	Avtech Jabiru J430	0xxx		23.10.06	G Hammond	Headcorn	8. 8.08P
	(Built G Hammond - pr.no.PFA 336-14452)						
G-CEFS	Cameron C-100 Balloon (Hot Air)	11000		2. 1.07	Gone With The Wind Ltd Schwieberdingen, Germany		17. 1.08E
					'Stairway to Heaven"		
G-CEFT	Whittaker MW5-D Sorcerer	PFA 163-14335		20.10.06	W Bruce	(Immingham)	
	(Built W Bruce)						
G-CEFV	Cessna 182T Skylane	18281538	N66167	2.11.06	D H, P M, A H and R H Smith t/a G H Smith and Son		
						Bagby	30.11.07E
G-CEFW	British Aerospace Avro 146-RJ100	E3243	TC-THH	13.11.06	Trident Jet (Dublin) Ltd	Kemble	
			G-6-243		*(Stored as "TC-THH" 8.07)*		
G-CEFX	Diamond DA.42 Twin Star	42.187	OE-VPY	17. 1.07	Spirit Communications (UK) Ltd	Gamston	15. 3.08E
G-CEFY	ICP MXP-740 Savannah Jabiru(4)	04-07-51-316		17.11.06	B Hartley	(Rossendale)	4. 7.08P
	(Built B Hartley - pr.no.BMAA/HB/453)						
G-CEFZ	Evektor EV-97 teamEurostar UK	2824		9.11.06	G Robertson and D Young tr Robo Flying Group		
						Kemble	21.11.08P
G-CEGC	Cameron Z-105 Balloon (Hot Air)	10930		2.11.06	The Balloon Company Ltd t/a First Flight		
					(HUMBERTS titles)	Langford, Bristol	10.10.08E
G-CEGE	Swearingen SA.226TC Metro II	TC-258	OY-NPA	14. 3.07	Blue City Aviation Ltd	Coventry	13. 3.08E
			(SP-MRB), OY-NPA, C-GBDF, 4X-CSA, N5463M				

Reg	Type	C/n	Prev id	Date	Owner/Operator	Location	Date
G-CEGG	Lindstrand LBL 25A Cloudhopper Balloon (Hot Air) 1120			20. 7.06	C G Dobson	Streatley, Reading	17. 9.08E
G-CEGH	Van's RV-9A PFA 320-14468 (Built M E Creasey)			5. 9.06	M E Creasey	Crowfield	18.12.08P
G-CEGI	Van's RV-8 81480 (Built R Faller)		N747RF	10.10.06	W H Greenwood *(Also carries "N747RF")*	Swanborough Farm, Lewes	14. 3.08P
G-CEGJ	P&M Quik GT450 8234			5. 1.07	Flylight Airsports Ltd	Sywell	4. 1.08P
G-CEGK	ICP MXP-740 Savannah VG Jabiru(1) 06-03-51-474 (Built S Whittaker and P J Wilson - pr.no.BMAA/HB/515)			9.11.06	S Whittaker and P J Wilson t/a Sandtoft Ultralights Partnership	Sandtoft	24.10.08P
G-CEGL	Comco Ikarus C42 FB80 0609-6848			21. 9.06	Aerosport Ltd	Halfpenny Green	27.11.07P
G-CEGM	Mainair Blade 582 996-0694-7-W793		I-3844	22. 6.07	N S Bellwood	Baxby Manor, Husthwaite	21. 6.08P
G-CEGO	Evektor EV-97A Eurostar PFA 315A-14552			25. 8.06	N J Keeling, R F McLachlan and J A Charlton	Ashbourne	18.10.08P
G-CEGP	Beech 200 Super King Air BB-726 (N58AJ), G-BXMA, N622JA, N522JA, N222JD		G-BXMA 14. 5.01		Cega Aviation Ltd	Bournemouth	7. 8.08E
G-CEGR	Beech 200 Super King Air BB-351 N351FW, N6666C, N6666K		N68CP 23. 7.97		Henfield Lodge Aviation Ltd *(Operated Cega Aviation)*	Shoreham	18. 8.08E
G-CEGS	Piper PA-28-161 Warrior II 28-7816418 (Thielert TAE 125)		N6391C	20.11.06	S J Skilton t/a Aviation Rentals *(Operated Solent Flight) (Noted 10.06)*	Bournemouth	
G-CEGT	P&M Quik GT450 8208			15. 8.06	J Plenderleith	Inverness	3. 9.08P
G-CEGU	Piper PA-28-151 Cherokee Warrior 28-7715165 (Thielert TAE 125)		N575DM N5990F	20.11.06	S J Skilton t/a Aviation Rentals *(Operated Solent Flight)*	Bournemouth	
G-CEGV	P&M Quik GT450 8203			18. 8.06	D J Collier t/a Sunfun Group	Lower Mountpleasant Farm, Chatteris	31. 8.08P
G-CEGW	P&M Quik GT450 8223			2.11.06	P Barrow	Arclid Green, Sandbach	1.11.07P
G-CEGY	ELA Aviacion ELA 07R 02050570712			21.11.06	A Buchanan *(Noted 8.07)*	Kirkbride	
G-CEGZ	Comco Ikarus C42 FB80 0609-6852			14.12.06	G E Spark tr Ikarus Flying Group	Barton	17. 1.08E
G-CEHC	P&M Quik GT450 8231			4.12.06	G H Sharwood-Smith	(Edinburgh)	13.12.07P
G-CEHD	Best Off Sky Ranger 912(2) SKR0604716 (Built A A Howland - pr.no.BMAA/HB/520)			17.11.06	A A Howland	(Battle)	14. 6.08P
G-CEHE	Medway SLA 100 Executive 171106			11. 2.08	R P Stoner	(London W3)	
G-CEHG	Comco Ikarus C42 FB100 0612-6861			17.11.06	G E Cole	Over Farm, Gloucester	19. 4.08P
G-CEHH	AirBorne XT912-B-Streak III-B XT912-065		5B-HAZ	15.11.06	(J Madhvani) and K Bolton	Plaistows Farm, St Albans	16. 1.08P
G-CEHI	P&M Quik GT450 8229			14.12.06	A Costello	Brook Farm, Pilling	13.12.07P
G-CEHJ	Short S312 Tucano T Mk.1 S 116 & T87 *(Officially regd as T166)*		ZF373	14. 2.07	C C Butt	Hawarden	
G-CEHK	Robinson R44 Raven II 11513			11.12.06	C Gallagher and Rathcoole Construction Ltd	(Ennis, County Clare and Dublin)	19.12.07E
G-CEHL	Evektor EV-97 teamEurostar UK 2928			16. 1.07	B P Connally	Shobdon	17. 1.08P
G-CEHM	Rotorsport UK MT-03 RSUK/MT-03/004		G-94-1	18.10.06	K O Maurer	Stoke, Isle of Grain	20.11.08P
G-CEHN	Rotorsport UK MT-03 RSUK/MT-03/008			8.12.06	P A Harwood	Rufforth	19.12.08P
G-CEHO	ELA Aviacion ELA 07R 06040480712			6. 2.07	C Gilholm	(Selkirk)	
G-CEHR	Auster AOP.9 B5/10/149		XP241	7.12.06	J Cooke and R B Webber *(Noted 8.07)*	Trenchard Farm, Eggesford	
G-CEHS	CAB CAP.10B 304		HS-BCS	8. 3.07	Cole Aviation Ltd *(Noted 11.07 as "HS-BCS")*	Spilstead Farm, Sedlescombe	
G-CEHT	Rand Robinson KR-2 PFA 129-14288 (Built P P Geoghegan)			7.12.06	P P Geoghegan	(Bromley)	
G-CEHU	Cameron Z-105 Balloon (Hot Air) 10973			8.12.06	Cameron Balloons Ltd *(Dubailand titles)*	Bristol	19.12.07E
G-CEHV	Comco Ikarus C42 FB80 0610-6854			14.12.06	Mainair Microlight School Ltd	Barton	13.12.08P
G-CEHW	P&M Quik GT450 8241 *(Sailwing used as demonstrator with G-CERW trike: frequently interchanges with sailwing from G-CERW (standard Quik) on G-CEHW trike)*			8.12.06	P&M Aviation Ltd	Barton	7.12.07P
G-CEHX	Lindstrand LBL 9A Balloon (Hot Air) 1147			19.12.06	P Baker	Abbeyview, Trim, County Meath	5.12.08E
G-CEHZ	AirBorne XT912-B-Streak III-B XT912-144			14.12.06	Fly NI Ltd	Tarsan Lane, Portadown	21. 1.08P
G-CEIA	Rotorsport UK MT-03 RSUK/MT-03/009			12.12.06	M P Chetwynd-Talbot	(Coxwold, York)	19.12.08P
G-CEIB	Yakovlev Yak-18A 1160402		RA-3336K	23. 5.07	G M Bauer	Wickenby	11. 7.08P
G-CEIC	British Aerospace Avro 146-RJ85 E2345		N520XJ G-6-345	28. 6.07	BAE Systems (Funding One) Ltd *(To become EI-RJH 2008)*	Cologne, Germany	
G-CEID	Van's RV-7 PFA 323-14403 (Built A Moyce)			29.11.06	A Moyce	Newtownards	2. 4.08P
G-CEIE	Flight Design CTSW 06.10.01 (Assembled P&M Aviation Ltd with c/n 8243)			14.12.06	D K Ross	Sittles Farm, Alrewas	15.10.08P
G-CEIG	Van's RV-7 PFA 323-14402 (Built W K Wilkie)			5.12.06	W K Wilkie	Newtownards	2. 4.08P
G-CEIH	British Aerospace Avro 146-RJ100 E3232		TC-THA G-6-232	23. 2.07	Trident Jet Leasing (Ireland) Ltd *(Noted 2.08)*	Bacau, Romania	
G-CEII	Medway SLA 80 Executive 010107			27. 7.07	F J Clarehugh	Eshott	11. 7.08P
G-CEIK	Ultramagic M-90 Balloon (Hot Air) 90/92			19. 2.07	Elinore Frence Ltd t/a Imagination Balloon Flights	Longframlington	21. 2.08E
G-CEIL	Reality Escapade 912(2) JAESC xxxx (Built D E Bassett - pr.no.BMAA/HB/506)			5.12.06	D E Bassett	(Marple Bridge, Stockport)	
G-CEIM	Robinson R44 Raven II 11583			29. 1.07	Helieagle Ltd	Coventry	8. 2.08E
G-CEIN	Cameron Z-105 Balloon (Hot Air) 10989			18.12.06	Cameron Balloons Ltd	Bristol	29. 1.08E
G-CEIO	Britten-Norman BN-2T-4S Islander 4015			20.12.06	Britten-Norman Aircraft Ltd	Bembridge	
G-CEIP	Britten-Norman BN-2T-4S Islander 4016			20.12.06	Britten-Norman Aircraft Ltd	Bembridge	
G-CEIR	Britten-Norman BN-2T-4S Islander 4017			20.12.06	Britten-Norman Aircraft Ltd	Bembridge	
G-CEIS	SAN Jodel DR.1050 Ambassadeur 469		F-BLJL	9. 1.07	M Hales	Little Staughton	
G-CEIT	Van's RV-7 PFA 323-13696 (Built S S Gould)			21.12.06	S S Gould	(Bedford)	
G-CEIV	Air Création Tanarg 912S/iXess 15 FLT.xxx (Built G Brown - pr.no.BMAA/HB/516 being Flylight kit comprising Trike s/n T06079 and Wing s/n A06121-6106)			17.10.06	Focus Property Services Ltd	Long Marston	
G-CEIW	Europa Aviation Europa xxxx (Built R Scanlan - pr.no.PFA 247-12707)			6.11.06	R Scanlan	(Woodbury, Exeter)	

Reg	Type	C/n	Prev id	Date	Owner/Operator	Location	Date
G-CEIX	Alpi Pioneer 300	xxx		10. 4.07	R F Bond	(Box, Corsham)	
	(Built R F Bond - pr.no.PFA 330-14656)						
G-CEIY	Ultramagic M-120 Balloon (Hot Air)	120/23		20. 3.07	Societa Cooperativa Sociale Il Paraticchio		
						Barletta, Italy	18 .6.08P
G-CEIZ	Piper PA-28-161 Warrior II	28-8116076	D-EIAL	21. 2.07	Altus Aviation Ltd	Headcorn	1. 3.08E
			N8291D				
G-CEJA	Cameron V-77 Balloon (Hot Air)	2469	G-BTOF	17. 6.91	L and Cindy Gray	Farnborough	5. 5.06A
G-CEJB	PIper PA-46-500TP Malibu Meridian	4697240	OY-PHO	12. 1.07	The van Meeuwen Flying Company Ltd	Fairoaks	24. 1.08E
			N31278, N9512N				
G-CEJC	Cameron N-77 Balloon (Hot Air)	4164	G-VODA (2)	12. 1.07	Zebedee Balloon Service Ltd	Newtown, Hungerford	3. 4.08E
					(Also see G-VODA (1))		
G-CEJD	Piper PA-28-161 Warrior III	2842244	D-EGVY	5. 2.07	Western Air (Thruxton) Ltd	Thruxton	18. 2.08E
			N31044				
G-CEJE	Wittman W.10 Tailwind	PFA 031-14003		15..1.07	R A Povall	Yearby	
	(Built R A Povall)						
G-CEJF	Piper PA-28-161 Cadet	2841224	N230FT	14.11.07	S J Skilton t/a Aviation Rentals	Bournemouth	
					(Marked as G-CEJF and stored 2.07)		
G-CEJG	Ultramagic M-56 Balloon (Hot Air)	56/37		2. 8.07	M J Warne	Tavistock	29. 7.08E
G-CEJI	Lindstrand LBL 105A Balloon (Hot Air)	1144		29. 1.07	Richard Nash Cars Ltd	Norwich	29. 1.08E
G-CEJJ	P&M Quik GT450	8236		2. 1.07	I M Bracegirdle tr Juliet Juilet Group		
						(Knapthorpe Lodge, Caunton)	2. 1.08P
G-CEJK	Lindstrand LBL 260A Balloon (Hot Air)	1141		26. 3.07	T G Church t/a Pendle Balloon Company		
					(Bowker Titles titles)	Clayton-le-Dale, Blackburn	10. 4.08E
G-CEJL	Ultramagic H-31 Balloon (Hot Air)	31/08		4. 6.07	Robert Wiseman Dairies PLC	Skirling, Biggar	6. 6.08E
					(Fresh n'lo milk titles)		
G-CEJM	Boeing 757-28A	26276	TF-FIK	23. 3.07	Globespan Airways Ltd t/a Flyglobespan.com		
					(Stored 11.07 less one engine)	Lasham	23. 3.08E
G-CEJN	Mooney M 20F Executive	670216	N237MM	12. 2.07	I Watson tr Mooney M 20F Club	Bournemouth	25. 4.08E
			F-BOJP, N9639M				
G-CEJO	Boeing 737-8BK	29643		27. 6.07	Globespan Airways Ltd t/a Flyglobespan.com		
						Lasham	27. 6.08E
G-CEJP	Boeing 737-8BK	29646		8. 6.07	Globespan Airways Ltd t/a Flyglobespan.com		
						Glasgow	10. 6.08E
G-CEJR	Cameron Z-90 Balloon (Hot Air)	10967		29. 1.07	Cameron Balloons Ltd	Bristol	
G-CEJT	Cameron Z-31 Balloon (Hot Air)	10972		29. 1.07	Cameron Balloons Ltd	Bristol	
G-CEJU	Bell P-39Q-6-BE Airacobra	26E-397	N793QG	21. 2.07	Patina Ltd "Brooklyn Bum-2nd"	Duxford	1. 7.08E
			(N139DP), 42-19993		(Operated The Fighter Collection as "219993" in USAAF c/s)		
G-CEJV	Piper PA-28-161 Cadet	2841225	N144ND	1. 2.07	S J Skilton t/a Aviation Rentals	Bournemouth	
					(Noted 3.07)		
G-CEJW	Comco Ikarus C42 FB80	0612-6860		4. 1.07	M I Deeley	Otherton, Cannock	8. 1.08P
G-CEJX	P&M Quik GT450	8249		13. 3.07	P Stewart and A J Huntly		
						Easter Poldar Farm, Thornhill	19. 3.08P
G-CEJY	Aerospool WT9 UK Dynamic	DY165/2007		9. 3.07	R G Bennett	Sywell	1. 5.08P
	(Official c/n is "DY165")"						
G-CEJZ	Cameron C-90 Balloon (Hot Air)	10970		20. 4.07	A M Holly	Breadstone, Berkeley	26. 4.08E
G-CEKA	Robinson R44 Raven II	11639		5. 3.07	M Virdee t/a Heligift.com	(Plaistow, Billingshurst)	27. 3.08E
G-CEKB	Taylor JT.1 Monoplane	PFA 055-12113		14. 2.07	C J Bush	New Farm House, Great Oakley	
	(Built C J Bush)						
G-CEKD	Flight Design CTSW	06.11.05		28. 3.07	M K Arora	Long Marston	23. 7.08P
	(Assembled P&M Aviation Ltd with c/n 8255)						
G-CEKE	Robin DR.400-180 Régent	943	HB-EXG	12. 4.07	M F Cuming	Shenington	2. 5.08E
G-CEKF	Robinson R44 Raven II	11650		18. 4.07	Aughakilmore Developments Ltd		
						(Ballinalee, County Longford)	10. 5.08E
G-CEKG	P&M Quik GT450	8261		16. 4.07	I W Trench	East Fortune	15. 4.08P
G-CEKH	Ultramagic M-105 Balloon (Hot Air)	105/149		3. 5.07	A Derbyshire	Woodseaves, Stafford	29. 4.08E
G-CEKI	Cessna 172P Skyhawk	17274356	N51829	19. 4.07	Zentelligence Ltd	Maypole Farm, Chislet	7. 6.08E
G-CEKJ	Evektor EV-97A Eurostar	PFA 315A-14584		20.11.06	C W J Vershoyle-Greene	Kilrush, County Kildare	25. 2.08P
	(Built C W J Vershoyle-Greene)						
G-CEKK	Best Off Sky Ranger Swift 912S(1)	SKR0610744		15. 2.07	J A Hunt	(Clydach, Abergavenny)	29. 4.08P
	(Built J A Hunt - pr.no.BMAA/HB/522)						
G-CEKL	Replica Plans SE.5a	PFA 020-13793		28. 2.07	B P North	RAF Halton	
	(Built B P North)				(Noted 2.08 as "C6468:A" in RFC c/s)		
G-CEKM	Avtech Jabiru UL-450			15. 2.07	D R Morton and R H Bain	Headon Farm, Retford	10. 9.08P
	(Built D R Morton and R H Bain - pr.no.PFA 274A-14436)						
G-CEKO	Robin DR.400-100 Cadet	1932	PH-VSU	30. 3.07	Exavia Ltd	Exeter	1. 4.08E
			OO-KPF, PH-VSU				
G-CEKS	Cameron Z-105 Balloon (Hot Air)	11003		13. 6.07	Phoenix Balloons Ltd	Bristol	18. 6.08E
G-CEKT	Flight Design CTSW	07.02.14		5. 4.07	G Lund tr Charlie Tango Group	Wycombe Air Park	4. 4.08P
	(Assembled P&M Aviation Ltd with c/n 8272)						
G-CEKU	Bushby-Long Midget Mustang	XU-5	C-GFPF	3. 5.07	Longacre Aviation Ltd		
	(Built R W Eaves)					(Middleton Cheyney, Banbury	22. 8.08P
G-CEKV	Europa Aviation Europa	xxx		19. 3. 07	K Atkinson	(Greenodd, Ulverston)	
	(Built K Atkinson - pr.no.PFA 247-12493)						
G-CEKW	Avtech Jabiru J430	0xxx		12. 1.07	J G Culley tr J430 Syndicate		
	(Buit J G Culley and 3 partners - pr.no.PFA 336-14340)				Hall Farm, Lillingstone Lovell, Buckingham		13. 6.08P
G-CEKX	Robinson R44 Raven II	11680		17. 4.07	Heli Air Ltd	Perth	26. 4.08E
G-CELA	Boeing 737-377QC	23663	VH-CZK	15. 8.03	Dart Group PLC	Blackpool	20. 1.08E
					"jet 2 Newcastle" (Operated.Jet2.com)		
G-CELB	Boeing 737-377	23664	VH-CZL	3. 7.03	Dart Group PLC	Leeds-Bradford	10. 5.08E
					(YORKSHIRE titles) (Operated.Jet2.com)		
G-CELC	Boeing 737-33A	23831	N190FH	4. 7.03	Dart Group PLC	Leeds-Bradford	12.10.07E
			VH-CZV, G-OBMA		"jet2 Prague" (Operated.Jet2.com)		
G-CELD	Boeing 737-33A	23832	N191FH	4. 7.03	Dart Group PLC	Leeds-Bradford	1. 2.08E
			VH-CZW, G-OBMB		"jet2 Espana" (Operated.Jet2.com)		

Reg	Type	C/n	Prev id	Date	Owner/Operator	Location	Expiry
G-CELE	Boeing 737-33A	24029	VH-CZX G-MONN	11. 7.03	Dart Group PLC "jet2 Belfast" (Operated.Jet2.com)	Leeds-Bradford	18. 8.08E
G-CELF	Boeing 737-377	24302	S7-ABB VH-CZM, N113AW, VH-CZM	5.10.04	Dart Group PLC "jet2 Valencia" (Operated.Jet2.com)	Leeds-Bradford	7.11.07E
G-CELG	Boeing 737-377	24303	S7-ABD VH-CZN	26.10.04	Dart Group PLC "jet2 London" (Operated.Jet2.com)	Leeds-Bradford	19.12.07E
G-CELH	Boeing 737-330	23525	D-ABXD (PR-GLB), D-ABXD, TF-ABL, D-ABXD "jet2 Faro" (Operated.Jet2.com)	23. 8.04	Dart Group PLC	Manchester	24. 9.08E
G-CELI	Boeing 737-330	23526	D-ABXE (PR-GLC), D-ABXE	21. 9.04	Dart Group PLC (MANCHESTER titles) (Operated.Jet2.com)	Manchester	17.11.07E
G-CELJ	Boeing 737-330	23529	LZ-BOG (PR-GLF), (D-ABXI), LZ-BOG, D-ABXI "jet 2 Italia (Operated.Jet2.com)	23.12.04	Dart Group PLC	Leeds Bradford	12. 2.08E
G-CELK	Boeing 737-330	23530	LZ-BOH (PR-GLJ), (D-ABXK), LZ-BOH, D-ABXK "jet 2 Edinburgh" (Operated.Jet2.com)	11. 2.05	Dart Group PLC	Blackpool	9. 3.08E
G-CELM	Cameron C-80 Balloon (Hot Air)	10931		10. 5.07	L Greaves	Doulting, Shepton Mallet	9. 5.08E
G-CELN	Ultramagic S-105 Balloon (Hot Air)	105/155		15. 6.07	B S Smith	Congleton	17. 6.08E
G-CELO	Boeing 737-33A(QC)	24028	TF-ELO G-CELO, TF-ELO, F-GIXK, G-MONP	17. 2.06	Dart Group PLC	London Stansted	22. 1.09E
G-CELP	Boeing 737-330	23522	TF-ELP D-ABXA, N1786B	27.10.03	Dart Group PLC (Operated.Channel Express)	London Stansted	26.10.07E
G-CELR	Boeing 737-330	23523	TF-ELR D-ABXB	4.11.03	Dart Group PLC (Operated Flyglobespan)	Glasgow	3.11.07E
G-CELS	Boeing 737-377	23660	VH-CZH	17. 5.02	Dart Group PLC "jet2 Leeds Bradford" (Operated.Jet2.com)	Leeds-Bradford	19. 6.08E
G-CELU	Boeing 737-377	23657	VH-CZE	13. 6.02	Dart Group PLC "jet2 Barcelona" (Operated.Jet2.com)	Leeds-Bradford	30. 7.08E
G-CELV	Boeing 737-377	23661	VH-CZI	2.10.02	Dart Group PLC "jet2 Amsterdam" (Operated.Jet2.com)	Leeds-Bradford	10. 2.08E
G-CELW	Boeing 737-377	23659	N659DG G-CELW, VH-CZG	4. 7.02	Dart Group PLC (Operated Jet2)	London Stansted	14.10.07E
G-CELX	Boeing 737-377	26354	VH-CZB N5573B	5. 3.03	Dart Group PLC "jet2 Malaga" (Operated.Jet2.com)	Leeds-Bradford	15. 4.08E
G-CELY	Boeing 737-377	23662	N662DG G-CELY, VH-CZJ	29. 4.03	Dart Group PLC "jet2 Ireland" (Operated.Jet2.com)	Belfast City	22. 4.08E
G-CELZ	Boeing 737-377	23658	VH-CZF	22. 9.03	Dart Group PLC "jet2 Paris" (Operated.Jet2.com)	Blackpool	2. 8.08E
G-CEMA	Alpi Pioneer 200	xxx		5. 3.07	D M Bracken	Shobdon	22. 4.08P
	(Built D M Bracken - pr.no.PFA 334-14569)						
G-CEMB	P&M Quik GT450	8262		13. 4.07	M E Howard tr RAF Microlight Flying Association	RAF Halton	12. 4.08P
G-CEMC	Robinson R44 Raven II	11620		26. 2.07	Aerocorp Ltd	Liverpool	14. 3.08E
G-CEMD	Piper PA-28-161 Warrior II	2842263	D-EVCC N31367	10. 4.07	Caernarfon Airworld Ltd	Caernarfon	18. 4.08E
G-CEME	Evektor EV-97 Eurostar PFA 315-14632			20. 2.07	G R and J A Pritchard	(Hardwicke, Hay-on-Wye)	20. 3.08P
	(Built G R Pritchard)						
G-CEMF	Cameron C-80 Balloon (Hot Air)	10892		22. 6.07	Linear Communications Consultants Ltd	Devauden, Chepstow	29. 7.08E
G-CEMG	Ultramagic M-105 Balloon (Hot Air)	105/153		16. 4.07	Comunicazione In Volo SRL	Carpineti, Italy	6. 6.08E
G-CEMH	Cessna 172S Skyhawk	172S10420	N12067	16. 4.07	Siverstar Aviation Ltd	Blackpool	2. 5.08E
G-CEMI	Europa Aviation Europa XS	xxxx		2. 4.07	B D A Morris	(Cheltenham)	
	(Built B D A Morris - pr.no.PFA 247-13989)						
G-CEMK	Boeing 767-222	21865	N604UA	23. 2.07	UK International Airlines Ltd (Airline suspended and not delivered 2008)	(East Midlands)	
G-CEML	P&M Pegasus Quik	8260		5. 4.07	C J Kew	Longacre Farm, Sandy	13. 4.08P
G-CEMM	P&M Quik GT450	8253		23. 4.07	M A Rhodes	(Congleton)	22. 4.08P
G-CEMN	Ultramagic S-130 Balloon (Hot Air)	130/56		9. 5.07	Associazione Sportiva Sorvoolare	Crevalcore, Italy	
G-CEMO	P&M Quik GT450	8265		8. 5.07	L E Craig	(Welling)	29. 5.08E
G-CEMP	BB Ultralight BB-03 UK Trya 503(1)	xxxxx		14. 3.07	P Robshaw	Rufforth	
	(Built P Robshaw - pr.no.BMAA/HB/527)				(Noted 11.07)		
G-CEMR	Mainair Blade 912	1066-0196-7-W868	I-4651	13. 4.07	D A Valentine	(Hargrave, Wellingborough)	13. 4.08P
G-CEMS	MD Helicopters MD.900 Explorer	900-00089	PK-OCR N70089	30. 3.07	Yorkshire Air Ambulance Ltd	Leeds-Bradford	15. 8.08E
G-CEMT	P&M Quik GT450	8251		22. 2.07	A Dixon	Tarn Farm, Cockerham	21. 2.08P
G-CEMU	Cameron C-80 Balloon (Hot Air)	11029		13. 7.07	J G O'Connell	Pattiswick, Braintree	29. 7.08E
G-CEMV	Lindstrand LBL 105A Balloon (Hot Air)	1164		22. 6.07	R G Turnbull	Glasbury, Hereford	19. 7.08E
G-CEMW	Lindstrand LBL Bananas SS Balloon (Hot Air)	388	G-OCAW	23. 4.07	T G Read t/a Top Banana Balloon Team	Mobberley, Knutsford	25. 5.08A
G-CEMX	P&M Quik	8281		30. 8.07	J H Askew	Wickenby	29. 8.08P
G-CEMY	Alpi Pioneer 300	xxx		24. 4.07	J C A Garland and P F Salter	(Bromham, Chippenham and Edington, Westbury)	21. 8.08P
	(Built J C A Garland, P F and C M Salter - pr.no.PFA 330-14440)						
G-CEMZ	P&M Pegasus Quik	8280		31. 5.07	D Jessop	Abbey Warren Farm, Bucknall	30. 5.08E
G-CENA	Dyn'Aéro MCR-01 ULC Banbi PFA 301B-14640			25. 5.07	R Germany	Knapthorpe Lodge, Caunton	28. 8.08P
	(Built R Germany)						
G-CENB	Evektor EV-97 teamEurostar UK	2913		16. 4.07	G Suckling and S J Joseph	Graveley Hall Farm, Graveley	15. 4.08P
G-CENC	Christen Eagle II PFA 138-14627			20. 4.07	J R Pearce	Compton Abbas	
	(Built J R Pearce)				(Noted 1.08)		
G-CEND	Evektor EV-97 teamEurostar UK	2916		10. 5.07	Flylight Airsports Ltd	Sywell	9. 5.08P
G-CENE	Flight Design CTSW	07.03.20		1. 5.07	G K Kenealey tr KT Flying Group	Barton	30. 4.08P
	(Assembled P&M Aviation Ltd with c/n 8273)						
G-CENF	ELA Aviacion ELA 07S	01071220722		3. 9.07	D G Hill	(Blackpool)	
G-CENG	Best Off Sky Ranger 912(2)	SKRxxxx701		1. 5.07	R A Knight	Chilbolton	
	(Built R A Knight - pr.no.BMAA/HB/518)						

Reg	Type	C/n	Prev id	Date	Owner/Operator	Location	Expiry
G-CENH	Tecnam P2002-EA Sierra	PFA 333-14564		3. 5.07	M W Taylor	Insch	14.11.08P
	(Built M W Taylor and J P Kovacs)						
G-CENI	Super Marine Spitfire Mk.26	PFA 324-14102		24. 4.07	D B Smith	(Netherley, Stonehaven)	
	(Built D B Smith)						
G-CENJ	Medway SLA 95I	240407		2. 5.07	M Ingleton	Cripps Farm, Eastchurch	
G-CENK	Schempp-Hirth Nimbus 4DT	9/40	BGA 4482-JFQ	4. 5.07	P Whitt and D Towson tr 651 Syndicate	Shobdon	9. 7.08
					"JFQ" and "651"		
G-CENL	P&M Quik GT450	8267		26. 5.07	S Baker and P von Sydow	Long Marston	25. 5.08P
G-CENM	Evektor EV-97 Eurostar	PFA 315-14247		20. 3.07	N D Meer	Tamworth	31. 5.08E
	(Built N D Meer)						
G-CENN	Cameron C-60 Balloon (Hot Air)	11013		15. 3.07	Stonebee Ltd	Chedworth, Cheltenham	10. 4.08E
G-CENO	Aerospool WT9 UK Dynamic	DY188/2007		8. 5.07	Yeoman Light Aircraft CompanyLtd		
	(Official c/n is "DY188")					Manor Farm, Drayton St Leonard	17.12.08P
G-CENP	Ace Magic Laser	AA00126	G-93-1	19. 6.07	P & M Aviation Ltd ((Noted 5.07)	Rochdale	
G-CENR	ELA Aviacion ELA 07S	03061030722		2.11.07	M S Gough	(Trottiscliffe, West Malling)	
G-CENS	Best Off Sky Ranger Swift 912S(1)	SKR0701769		9. 5.07	N D and M Stannard	Sywell	
	(Built N D Stannard - pr.no.BMAA/HB/536)				(Noted 10.07)		
G-CENU	ICP MXP-740 Savannah Jabiru(5)	04-11-51-344		15. 5.07	N Farrell	(Tarmonbarry, County Roscommon)	
	(Built N Farrell - pr.no.BMAA/HB/534)						
G-CENV	P&M Quik GT450	8275		4. 6.07	M E Howard tr RAF Microlight Flying Association (NV)		
						RAF Halton	3. 8.08P
G-CENW	Evektor EV-97 Eurostar	PFA 315-14612		14. 3.07	W S Long	Mayfield Farm, Stevenston	1. 7.08P
	(Built W S Long)						
G-CENX	Lindstrand LBL 360A	1160		4. 6.07	Richard Nash Cars Ltd	Norwich	12. 6.08E
G-CENY	Robinson R44 Raven II	11820		31. 7.07	Envision Aviation Ltd	(Ballymoney)	22 .8.08E
G-CENZ	Aeros Discus-Alizé	014.07 and 001		19. 7.07	S A Kirk	(Tenterden)	
	(Discus wing and DTA Alizé trike)						
G-CEOB	Pitts S-1 Special	DIH-1	N8036J	30. 5.07	P A Moslin and I Gallacher	RAF Halton	
	(Built D I Heaps)		C-FQEZ				
G-CEOC	Tecnam P2002-EA Sierra	PFA 333-14604		31. 5.07	M A Lomas	Leicester	14. 1.09P
	(Built M A Lomas)						
G-CEOD	Boeing 767-319ER	30586	ZK-NCO	6. 9.07	Globespan Airways Ltd t/a Flyglobespan.com		
						(Edinburgh)	27. 9.08E
G-CEOE	American Champion 8KCAB Super Decathlon	803-97	N748PH	27. 4.07	R Boucher	Griffins Farm, Temple Bruer	15. 7.08E
G-CEOF	Piper PA-28R-201 Arrow III	2837008	N805ND	4. 6.07	J H Sandham t/a J H Sandham Aviation	Carlisle	
G-CEOG	Piper PA-28R-201 Arrow III	2837025	N173ND	4. 6.07	J H Sandham t/a J H Sandham Aviation	Carlisle	
G-CEOH	Raj Hamsa X'Air Falcon ULP(1)	666		13. 6.07	Miles Blackburn Ltd	(Blackburn)	
	(Built J C Miles - pr.no.BMAA/HB/525) (UL250i)						
G-CEOI	Cameron C-60 Balloon (Hot Air)	10977		27. 6.07	M E White	Abbeyview, Trim, County Meath	21. 6.08E
G-CEOJ	Eurocopter EC.155B	6575	C-FORE	1. 8.07	Starspeed Ltd	Blackbushe	4. 9.08E
G-CEOK	Cessna 150M	15077928	N8375U	12. 6.07	M Howell	Barton	
G-CEOL	Flylight Lightfly-Discus	001		12. 6.07	Flylight Airsports Ltd	Sywell	X
	(Ukraine built Aeros Discus T sailwing on basic trike unit and marketed as "Flylight Dragonfly Discus") (Noted 12.07)						
G-CEOM	Avtech Jabiru UL-450	xxx		12. 6.07	J R Caylow	Headon Farm, Retford	10. 9.08P
	(Built J R Caylow - pr.no.PFA 274A-14455)						
G-CEON	Raj Hamsa X'Air Hawk	xxx		15. 6.07	A Anderson	Carlisle	
	(Built A Anderson - pr.no.PFA 340-14673)				(Noted 10.07)		
G-CEOO	P&M Quik GT450	8257		30. 3.07	S Moran	(Werrington, Stoke-on-Trent)	4. 4.08P
G-CEOP	Aeroprakt A22-L Foxbat	PFA 317A-14671		15. 6.07	P M Ford	(South Weald, Brentwood)	20. 8.08P
	(Built P M Ford)						
G-CEOS	Cameron C-90 Balloon (Hot Air)	11047		4. 9.07	Balloon School (International) Ltd t/a British School of Ballooning		
						Colhook Common, Petworth	31. 8.08E
G-CEOT	Bailey Quattro 175-Dudek reAction Sport			30. 5.07	J Kelly	Longstanton, Cambridge	X
		P 02908					
G-CEOU	Lindstrand LBL 31A Balloon (Hot Air)	1157		15. 6.07	Lindstrand Hot Air Balloons Ltd	Oswestry	12. 7.08E
G-CEOV	Lindstrand LBL 120A Balloon (Hot Air)	1158		18. 7.07	Lindstrand Hot Air Balloons Ltd	Oswestry	29. 7.08E
G-CEOW	Europa Aviation Europa XS	xxx		4. 6.07	R W Wood	(Little Cowarne, Bromyard)	
	(Built R W Wood - pr.no.PFA 247-13877)						
G-CEOX	Rotorsport UK MT-03	RSUK/MT-03/014		27. 6.07	L C Griffiths	(Temple Guiting, Cheltenham)	12. 7.08P
G-CEOY	Schweizer 269C-1	0234	EI-DOJ	2. 7.07	C R and S E Hewgill t/a CBL Industrial	Gamston	28. 6.08E
	(Schweizer 300)						
G-CEOZ	Passion'Ailes Chariot Z-Paramania Action GT26	1006148		21. 6.07	A M Shepherd	(Silverstone, Towcester)	
	(Powered paraglider (PPG) consisting of Paramania Action GT26 sailwing and Passion'Ailes (PAP = Propulsion Auxiliare Parapente) Chariot Z)						
G-CEPA	McDonnell Douglas MD-82	49425	B-2104 N1005T	10. 5.07	PL Aviation Ltd (Noted as "B-2104 "10.07)	Bucharest, Romania	
G-CEPB	McDonnell Douglas MD-82	49428	B-2105 N1005U	17. 5.07	PL Aviation Ltd (Noted as "B-2105" 10.07)	Bucharest, Romania	
G-CEPC	McDonnell Douglas MD-82	49502	B-2108	22. 3.07	PL Aviation Ltd (Noted as "B-2108" 10.07)	Bucharest, Romania	
G-CEPD	McDonnell Douglas MD-82	49505	B-2121	17. 5.07	PL Aviation Ltd (Noted as "B-2121" 10.07)	Bucharest, Romania	
G-CEPE	McDonnell Douglas MD-82	49506	B-2122	10. 5.07	PL Aviation Ltd (Noted as "B-2122" 10.07)	Bucharest, Romania	
G-CEPF	McDonnell Douglas MD-82	49510	B-2126	17. 5.07	PL Aviation Ltd (Noted as "B-2126" 10.07)	Bucharest, Romania	
G-CEPH	McDonnell Douglas MD-82	53162	B-2146	22. 3.07	PL Aviation Ltd (Noted as "B-2146" 10.07)	Bucharest, Romania	
G-CEPI	McDonnell Douglas MD-82	53169	B-2148 N838AU	8. 6.07	PL Aviation Ltd (Noted as "B-2148" 10.07)	Bucharest, Romania	
G-CEPJ	McDonnell Douglas MD-82	53170	B-2149 N839AU	8. 6.07	PL Aviation Ltd (Noted as "B-2149" 10.07)	Bucharest, Romania	
G-CEPK	McDonnell Douglas MD-82	53171	B-2150 N840AU	8. 6.07	PL Aviation Ltd (Noted as "B-2150" 10.07)	Bucharest, Romania	

Reg	Type	c/n	Prev id	Date	Owner/Operator	Location	
G-CEPL	Super Marine Spitfire Mk.26	PFA 324-14507		19. 6.07	S R Marsh	(Grays)	
	(Built S R Marsh)						
G-CEPN	New Kolb Firefly	FF05.4.00048		20 06.07	M H Moulai	Sandtoft	
	(Built M H Moulai)						
G-CEPM	Avtech Jabiru J430	xxxx		1. 5.07	T R Sinclair	Lamb Holm Farm, Orkney	
	(Built T R Sinclair - pr.no.PFA 336-14517)						
G-CEPP	P&M Quik GT450	8266		10. 5.07	W M Studley	Middle Pymore Farm, Bridport	9. 5.08P
G-CEPR	Cameron Z-90 Balloon (Hot Air)	11057		4. 9.07	Sport Promotion SRL	La Morra, Italy	30. 8.08E
G-CEPS	TL Ultralight TL-2000 Sting	PFA 347-14705		2. 7.07	P A Saunders	Otherton, Cannock	
	(Built P A Saunders)						
G-CEPT	SOCATA TB-20 Trinidad	1240	G-BTEK	27. 8.04	P J Caiger	Biggin Hill	13.11.07E
G-CEPU	Cameron Z-77 Balloon (Hot Air)	11030		31. 8.07	Liquigas SpA	Milan, Italy	9. 7.08E
G-CEPV	Cameron Z-77 Balloon (Hot Air)	11031		31. 8.07	Liquigas SpA	Milan, Italy	9. 7.08E
G-CEPW	Alpi Pioneer 300	xxx		27. 6.07	N K Spedding	(Hatton Green)	
	(Built N K Spedding - pr.no.PFA 330-14293)						
G-CEPX	Cessna 152	15285792	N94808	13. 6.07	Cristal Air Ltd	Shoreham	13. 9.08E
G-CEPY	Comco Ikarus C42 FB80	0707-6900		6. 8.07	L Lay	Clench Common	5. 8.08P
G-CEPZ	Dan Rihn DR.107 One Design	0038	N107TH	14. 5.07	P J Pengilly	(Chuch Crookham, Fleet)	
	(Built J J Tomlinson)						
G-CERA	Flight Design CTSW	07.04.05		4. 6.07	Mainair Microlight School Ltd	Barton	6. 6.08P
	(Assembled P&M Aviation Ltd with c/n 8287)						
G-CERB	Best Off Sky Ranger Swift 912S(1)	SKRxxxx772		31. 5.07	J J Littler (Limmer Pomd, Aldingbourne, Chichester)		
	(Built J J Littler - pr.no.BMAA/HB/537)						
G-CERC	Cameron Z-350 Balloon (Hot Air)	11028		20.12.07	Ballooning Network Ltd	Southville, Bristol	
G-CERD	de Havilland DHC-1 Chipmunk 22	7	CS-AZM	25. 7.07	A C Darby	(Aylesbury)	
	(Built OGMA)		Portuguese AF 1317				
G-CERE	Evektor EV-97 teamEurostar UK	2931		4. 7.07	Airbourne Aviation Ltd	Popham	3. 7.08P
G-CERF	Rotorsport UK MT-03	RSUK/MT-03/017		24. 7.07	P J Robinson	Kirkbride	21. 8.08P
G-CERG	Magni M16C Tandem Trainer	892851		10. 8.07	D C Fairbrass	Willingale	
	(Officially regd as c/n 16-07-4344)						
G-CERH	Cameron C-90 Balloon (Hot Air)	10941		17. 7.07	R J Percival and P Linaker	Wellingborough	24. 7.08E
G-CERI	Europa Aviation Europa XS	511		20. 8.03	S J M Shepherd	(Bodelwyddan, Rhyl)	
	(Built S J M Shepherd - pr.no.PFA 247-13970)						
G-CERK	Van's RV-9A	PFA 320-14049		2. 7.07	P E Brown	(Ton Kenfig, Bridgend)	
	(Built P E Brown)						
G-CERL	Ultramagic M-77 Balloon (Hot Air)	77/309		17. 9.07	A M Holly	Breadstone, Berkeley	
G-CERM	Kubicek BB-22Z Balloon (Hot Air)	528		25. 7.07	A M Holly	Breadstone, Berkeley	5. 8.08E
G-CERN	P&M Quik GT450	8299		26. 7.07	N D Leak	Clench Common	30. 7.08P
G-CERO	Agusta A109C	7627	G-OBEK	31. 5.07	Castle Air Charters Ltd	Yeovil	4. 8.08E
			G-CDDJ, RP-C2877, TC-HCM, D-HAAV, JA9999 (Operated Agusta Westland)				
G-CERP	P&M Quik GT450	8285		12. 7.07	A Morrison	East Fortune	11. 7.08P
G-CERR	Ultramagic M-77C Balloon (Hot Air)	77/305		29. 8.07	G M Houston t/a Scotair Balloons	Skirling, Biggar	27. 7.08E
G-CERS	Robinson R44 Raven II	11840		23. 7.07	P J Egan t/a Egan Helicopters	Ellough, Beccles	23. 8.08E
G-CERT	Mooney M 20K Mooney 231	25-1134		5.10.87	J A Nisbet	Fowlmere	13. 6.08E
G-CERV	P&M Quik GT450	8300		31. 7.07	J MacDonald tr East Fortune Flyers	East Fortune	30. 7.08P
G-CERW	P&M Pegasus Quik	8294		3. 5.07	P&M Aviation Ltd (Noted 2.08)	Rochdale	
G-CERX	Raytheon Hawker 850XP	258810	OE-GJA	21. 8.07	Hangar 8 Ltd	Oxford	6. 9.08E
G-CERY	SAAB-Scania 2000	2000-008	D-AOLA, ,	21. 9.07	Air Kilroe Ltd t/a Eastern Airways	Humberside	20. 9.08E
			SE-008, HB-!ZE, (D-ADIB), SE-008				
G-CERZ	SAAB-Scania 2000	2000-042	SE-LSA	24. 8.07	Air Kilroe Ltd t/a Eastern Airways	Humberside	
G-CESA	Jodel DR.1050M-1 Excellence replica			9. 7.07	P D Thomas and T J Bates		
	(Built P D Thomas and T J Bates) PFA 304-13753					Dairy House Farm, Worleston	
G-CESB	Robinson R44 Raven I	1369	OO-FXS	5. 6.07	GCS Helicopters Ltd	Perth	26. 6.08E
G-CESC	Cameron Z-105 Balloon (Hot Air)	11055		30. 7.07	Klober Ltd	Shepshed, Loughborough	31. 7.08E
G-CESD	Best Off Sky Ranger Swift 912S(1)	SKRxxxx770		15. 5.07	S E Dancaster	Newton Bank Farm, Daresbury	19.12.08P
	(Built S E Dancaster - pr.no.BMAA/HB/535)						
G-CESG	P&M Quik GT450	8211	I-8211	19. 7.07	L Greco	Centallo, Italy	
G-CESH	Cameron Z-90 Balloon (Hot Air)	11061		30. 7.07	The Balloon Company Ltd t/a First Flight		
						Langford, Bristol	10. 8.08E
G-CESI	Aeroprakt A22-L Foxbat	PFA 317A-14643		25. 7.07	D J Ashley	(Llandrindod Wells)	12.12.08P
	(Built D J Ashley)						
G-CESJ	Raj Hamsa X'Air Hawk	PFA 340-14677		8. 8.07	B K Harrison and R G Cameron	Strathaven	
	(Built B K Harrison and R G Cameron)					(Noted 8.07)	
G-CESL	Fresh Breeze Muller & Werner Flyke-Silex L-Monster			1. 6.07	T J Gayton-Polley	(Billingshurst)	X
		F1073, 19609 and M0114					
G-CESN	Robinson R-22 Beta	4176	N30667	27. 9.07	Helieagle Ltd	Coventry	
G-CESO	Robinson R44 Raven II	11859		3. 8.07	Heliverne	(La Vilie Aux Dames, France)	20. 9.08P
G-CESP	Rutan Cozy Mk.4	PFA 159A-13860		29. 6.07	T N Craigie	(Kirkcaldy)	
	(Built T N Craigie)						
G-CESR	P&M Quik GT450	8304		20. 8.07	G Kerr	East Fortune	19. 8.08P
G-CESS	Cessna F172G	F172-0181	G-ATGO	23. 7.07	Keenair Ltd	Liverpool	22.11.07E
	(Built Reims Aviation SA)						
G-CEST	Robinson R44 Raven	1424	D-HALZ	19. 7.07	Roofline Scotland Ltd	Lower Baads, Peterculter	19. 8.08E
G-CESU	Robinson R22 Beta	4139	N30804	4. 9.07	Alcock and Brown Aviation Ltd		
						(Ballybrit,County Galway)	
G-CESV	Evektor EV-97 teamEurostar UK	3011		17. 9.07	N Jones	Andrewsfield	16. 9.08P
G-CESW	Flight Design CTSW	07.06.04		20. 6.07	J Cunliffe and A Costello	St Michaels	29. 6.08P
	(Assembled P&M Aviation Ltd with c/n 8296)						
G-CESX	Cameron Z-31 Balloon (Hot Air)	11074		6. 9.07	Knucklehead Ltd	London W1	8. 9.08E
G-CESY	Cameron Z-31 Balloon (Hot Air)	11075		6. 9.07	Knucklehead Ltd	London W1	8. 9.08E
G-CESZ	CZAW Sportcruiser	PFA 338-14652		8. 8.07	J A and J M Iszard	Parham	
	(Built J A Iszard)					(F/f Bentwaters 12.11.07)	
G-CETB	Robin DR.400-180 Régent	1369	D-EFQR	31. 7.07	M W Cater tr QR Flying Club	Husbands Bosworth	5. 9.08E
G-CETD	Piper PA-28-161 Warrior III	2842152	N5351Y	17. 7.07	Plane Talking Ltd	Elstree	

Reg	Type	c/n	Prev id	Date	Owner/Operator	Location	
G-CETE	Piper PA-28-161 Warrior III	2842079	N120FT	17. 7.07	Plane Talking Ltd	Elstree	
G-CETF	Flight Design CTSW	07.06.05		24. 8.07	P and M Aviation Ltd	Whilton	23. 8.08P
	(Assembled P&M Aviation Ltd with c/n 8318)						
G-CETG	Alpha Aviation Alpha R2160i	160Ai-0008		01. 2.08	D J Lawrence	(Stoke by Nayland, Colchester)	
	(Marked as "Alpha 160 Ai")				(Noted 2.08)		
G-CETH	Flight Design CTSW	07.07.17		29. 8.07	R A Morris	Shenstone	28. 8.08P
	(Assembled P&M Aviation Ltd with c/n 8317)						
G-CETI	Van's RV-8	PFA 303-14466		11. 7.07	Cavendish Aviation Ltd	Gamston	
	(Built E M Marsh)						
G-CETJ	Slingsby T 59D Kestrel 19	1863	BGA 1988-DBQ	17. 8.07	S M Sanderson	Sutton Bank	10.10.07
G-CETK	Cameron Z-145 Balloon (Hot Air)	4770	OO-BWN	12. 9.07	R H Etherington	Siena, Italy	
G-CETL	P&M Quik GT450	8307		13. 8.07	J I Greenshields	Dunkeswell	12. 8.08P
G-CETM	P&M Quik GT450	8298		31. 7.07	I Burnside	East Fortune	30. 7.08P
G-CETN	Haseldine Hummelbird	PFA 127-13044		31. 8.07	A A Haseldine	(Craswell, Hereford)	
	(Built A A Haseldine)						
G-CETO	Best Off Sky Ranger Swift 912S(1)	SKRxxxxxx		13. 7.07	P J Shergold	Old Sarum	
	(Built P J Shergold - pr.no.BMAA/HB/541)						
G-CETP	Van's RV-9A	PFA 320-14012		3. 9.07	D Boxall and S Hill	(Bath)	
	(Built D Boxall and S Hill)						
G-CETR	Comco Ikarus C42 FB100	0706-6898		2. 8.07	A E Lacy-Hulbert	Redlands, Swindon	12. 8.08P
G-CETS	Van's RV-7	70529	N557WM	23. 8.07	W H Greenwood	Swanborough Farm, Lewes	15. 1.09P
	(Built M R Wyatt)						
G-CETT	Evektor EV-97 teamEurostar UK	3006		24. 7.07	S R Pike	Wycombe Air Park	17. 7.08P
G-CETU	Best Off Sky Ranger Swift 912S(1)	SKRxxxx803		12. 9.07	M A Sweet	St. Michaels	
	(Built M A Sweet- pr.no.BMAA/HB/551)						
G-CETV	Best Off Sky Ranger Swift 912S(1)	SKRxxxx759		22. 6.07	K J Gay	Newtownards	22. 8.08P
	(Built K J Gay - pr.no.BMAA/HB/532)						
G-CETW	ELA Aviacion ELA 07S	06071650722		1.10.07	C Hewer (Noted 10.07)	Kirkbride	
G-CETX	Alpi Pioneer 300	PFA 330-14573		23. 7.07	M C Ellis	(Medstead, Alton)	
	(Built M C Ellis)						
G-CETY	Rans S-6-ES Coyote II	PFA 204-14654		17. 7.07	J North	(Felmersham, Bedford)	
	(Built J North)						
G-CETZ	Comco Ikarus C42 Cyclone FB100	0706-6899		8.11.07	Airways Airsports Ltd	Darley Moor	7.11.08P
G-CEUA	Britten-Norman BN-2B-20 Islander	2305		27. 7.07	Britten-Norman Aircraft Ltd	Bembridge	
G-CEUB	Britten-Norman BN-2B-20 Islander	2306		27. 7.07	Britten-Norman Aircraft Ltd	Bembridge	
G-CEUC	Britten-Norman BN-2B-20 Islander	2307		27. 7.07	Britten-Norman Aircraft Ltd	Bembridge	
G-CEUD	Britten-Norman BN-2B-20 Islander	2309		27. 7.07	Britten-Norman Aircraft Ltd	Bembridge	
G-CEUE	Britten-Norman BN-2B-20 Islander	2310		27. 7.07	Britten-Norman Aircraft Ltd	Bembridge	
G-CEUF	P&M Quik GT450	8325		12.10.07	G T Snoddon	Newtownards	11.10.08P
G-CEUG	Schleicher ASW 27	27114	BGA 4696-JQM	13. 9.07	R J Smith	Wycombe Air Park	29.11.07
G-CEUH	P&M Quik GT450	8316		25.10.07	North West Turf Ltd	(Ormskirk)	28.10.08P
G-CEUI	Rotorsport UK MT-03	RSUK/MT-03/021		18.10.07	A D Lysser	(Keswick)	25.10.08P
G-CEUJ	Best Off Sky Ranger Swift 912S(1)	SKRxxxx802		14.12.07	J P Batty and J R C Brightman		
	(Built - J P Batty and J R C Brightman - pr.no.BMAA/HB/548)					Sackville Lodge, Riseley	
G-CEUK	Eurocopter AS.365N3 Dauphin 2	6785	F-WWOZ	1.11.07	McAlpine Helicopters Ltd	Oxford	
G-CEUL	Ultramagic M-105 Balloon (Hot Air)	105/157		4. 1.08	R A Vale	Hurcott, Kidderminster	
G-CEUM	Ultramagic M-120 Balloon (Hot Air)	120/30		28.11.07	Bridges Van Hire Ltd	Awsworth, Nottingham	
G-CEUN	Schempp-Hirth Discus CS	075CS	BGA 4694-JQK	8.10.07	J G Arnold tr RAF Gliding and Soaring Association		
			RAFGGA 501		(Operated Chilterns Gliding Centre)	RAF Halton	15. 1.08
G-CEUO	Cessna 550 Citation II	550-0033	LX-GDL	26.11.07	Unique Air International Ltd	Farnborough	
			LX-JET, LX-GDL, F-WPLT, F-GPLT, N46DA, N755CM, N59MJ, TR-LYE, (N3252M)				
G-CEUP	PZL-Swidnik PW-5 Smyk	17.04.010	BGA 4988-KCQ	27. 9.07	P H Young	Chipping	27. 3.08
			OY-XYE				
G-CEUR	Schempp-Hirth Ventus 2cxT	109/303	BGA 5060-KFQ	26. 9.07	P R Hamblin	Lasham	6. 9.08
			D-KKAO				
G-CEUS	Cessna 152	15281906	N67548	17. 1.08	R Germany	(Coltishall, Norwich)	
G-CEUT	Hoffman H 36 Dimona	36270	LY-GDW	5.10.07	P Pozerskis	Husbands Bosworth	
			F-CGAX				
G-CEUU	Robinson R44 Raven II	11949		12.10.07	A Stafford-Jones	(Churt, Farnham)	
G-CEUV	Cameron C-90 Balloon (Hot Air)	11078		18.12.07	A M Holly	Breadstone, Berkeley	
G-CEUW	Zenair CH.601XL Zodiac	PFA 162B-14554		4.10.07	M Taylor	(Hollym, Withernsea)	
	(Built M Taylor)						
G-CEUX	Robinson R44 Raven II	11864		12.10.07	O'Reilly Aviation Ltd	(Wicklow, County Wicklow)	
G-CEUY	American Champion 8KCAB Super Decathlon	1044-2007		18.12.07	Blue Yonder Aviation Ltd	Earls Colne	
					(Noted 2.08)		
G-CEUZ	P&M Quik GT450	8321		25.10.07	M Gallagher	(Kiln Pitt Hill, Consett)	24.10.08P
G-CEVA	Comco Ikarus C42 FB80	0709-6915		25.10.07	Sport Aviation Training Ltd	(Nunnington, York)	28.10.08P
G-CEVB	P&M Quik GT450	8315		3.10.07	J L Guy and N Hartley	Baxby Manor, Husthwaite	2.10.08P
G-CEVC	Van's RV-4	2726	N2063Z	21. 9.07	P A Brook	Shoreham	14. 1.09P
	(Built K W Pabo)						
G-CEVD	Rolladen-Schneider LS3	3024	BGA 2979-EVD	21.12.07	C H Appleyard	Lasham	14. 2.08
			N63LS, D-7914				
G-CEVE	Centrair 101A Pégase	101A0141	BGA 2980-EVE	17. 9.07	J W North and T Newham	Lasham	28. 9.08
G-CEVF	British Aerospace BAe 146 Series 200	E2068	EI-CSK	22.11.07	BAE Sysyems (Operations) Ltd	Exeter	
			N810AS, N880DV, G-5-062, N406XV, (G-BNDR), G-5-062				
G-CEVG	P&M Pegasus Quik	8319		25.10.07	R Higton tr Barton Quik Group	Barton	24.10.08P
G-CEVH	Cameron V-65 Balloon (Hot Air)	2765	OO-BGG	12.10.07	J A Atkinson	Dorchester	
G-CEVI	Robinson R44 Raven II	11993		12.11.07	Redwood Properties Ltd		
						Weston, Leixlip, County Kildare	15. 1.09P
G-CEVJ	Alpi Pioneer 200	PFA 334-14710		16.10.07	B W Bartlett	(North Wootton, Shepton Mallet)	
	(Built B W Bartlett)						
G-CEVK	Schleicher Ka 6CR	6541	BGA 2870-EQQ	11.10.07	C R Reese tr K6 Syndicate	Challock	28. 9.08
			AGA 24, BGA 1353-BYZ				
G-CEVL	Fairchild M-62A-4 Cornell	T43-4361	N9606H	22.11.07	T K Rumble tr UK Cornell Group	Wickenby	
			FJ662, 42-15491		(On rebuild 2008)		

Reg	Type	C/n	Prev ID	Date	Owner/Operator	Location	Date2
G-CEVM	Tecnam P2002-EA Sierra	PFA 333-14709		27. 7.07	R C Mincik	Bournemouth	
	(Built R C Mincik)				(Noted 2.08)		
G-CEVN	Rolladen-Schneider LS7	7029	BGA 3438-FQH D-1316	25.10.07	B C Toon and N Gaunt	Sutton Bank	28. 9.08
G-CEVP	P&M Quik GT450	8329		30.10.07	S G Ward	(Chatham)	29.10.08P
	(Fitted with trike ex G-CDCK qv)						
G-CEVS	Evektor EV-97 team Eurostar UK	3102		16.11.07	R Joy tr Eurostar Group	Leicester	15.11.08P
G-CEVT	Bailey Quattro 175-Dudek Reaction 27	P 03193		3. 8.07	J Kelly	Longstanton, Cambridge	
G-CEVU	ICP MXP-740 Savannah VG Jabiru(1)	07-05-51-600		2.11.07	B L Cook	Sandtoft	
	(Built B L Cook - pr.no.BMAA/HB/552)				(Noted NEC Birmingham 11.07)		
G-CEVV	Rolladen-Schneider LS3	3035	BGA 2251-DNQ	25.10.07	M C Cooper tr LS3 307 Syndicate	Challock	8. 3.08
G-CEVW	P&M Quik GT450	8314		25. 9.07	A M Dalgetty	Perth	20. 9.08P
G-CEVX	Aeriane Swift'Light PAS	111		19.10.07	J S Firth	Sherburn-in-Elmet	
G-CEVY	Rotorsport UK MT-03	RSUK/MT-03/025		20.12.07	P Robinson	Willingale	8. 1.09P
G-CEVZ	Centrair ASW 20FL	20184	BGA 2726-EJQ	1.10.07	J R Rayner and J R Matthews	Parham Park	4. 4.08
G-CEWC	Schleicher ASK 21	21157	BGA 2871-EQR	2.11.07	London Gliding Club Proprietary Ltd "EQR"	Dunstable	28. 9.08
G-CEWD	P&M Quik GT450	8330		15.11.07	J Murphy	Eshott	14.11.08P
G-CEWE	Schempp-Hirth Nimbus 2	4	BGA 1725-CQP	29.10.07	D Caunt	Wycombe Air Park	8. 1.08
G-CEWF	Jacobs V35 Airchair Balloon (Hot Air)	EJ-194	ZS-HYU	28. 1.08	D J Farrar	Tadcaster	
	(Built E J Jacobs)						
G-CEWG	Aerola Alatus-M	AS 01-011		17.12.07	Flylight Airsports Ltd (Noted 12.07)	Sywell	
G-CEWH	Mainair Pegasus Quik	8324		5.11.07	B W Hunter	East Fortune	4.11.08P
G-CEWI	Schleicher ASW 19B	19086	BGA 4410-JCQ PH-562	31.10.07	K Steele and S R Edwards	Hinton-in-the-Hedges	22. 2.08
G-CEWL	Alpi Pioneer 200	PFA 334-14712		29.10.07	M A Hogg	(Finchampstead, Wokingham)	
	(Built M A Hogg)						
G-CEWN	Diamond DA.42 Twin Star	42.32		11. 1 08	Diamond Aircraft UK Ltd	Gamston	
G-CEWO	Schleicher Ka 6CR	1065	BGA 2301-DQS D-5144	10. 8.07	J M Robinson tr DQS Group	North Hill	9. 2.08
G-CEWP	Grob G102 Astir CS	1258	BGA 2155-DJQ	8.11.07	R D Slater	Usk	27. 2.08
G-CEWR	Aeroprakt A22-L Foxbat	PFA 317A-14736		22.11.07	C S Bourne and G P Wiley	Otherton ,Cannock	
	(Built C S Bourne and G P Wiley)						
G-CEWS	Zenair CH.701SP STOL	PFA 187A-14692		13.11.07	I J M Donnelly	Aboyne	
	(Built I J M Donnelly)						
G-CEWT	Flight Design CTSW	07.10.10		21.11.07	I M Sinclair	Glenrothes	20.11.08P
	(Assembled P&M Aviation Ltd with c/n 8333)						
G-CEWV	Robinson R44 Raven II	12008		4.12.07	J Kleinschmidt (New owner 1.08)	(Monaco)	
G-CEWW	Grob G102 Astir CS77	1758	BGA 2442-DWQ	25.10.07	M R Woodiwiss	Sleap	14. 4.08
G-CEWY	Murphy Quicksilver GT500	PFA 348-14707		21.11.07	W Murphy	(Twyford, Reading)	
	(Built W Murphy)						
G-CEWZ	Schempp-Hirth Discus bT	128/490	BGA 4032-HLQ	17. 8.07	J F Goudie	Portmoak	17.11.07
G-CEXL	Comco Ikarus C42 FB80	0711-6927		23.11.07	R S O'Carroll	(Mullahead, Tandragee)	15. 1.09P
G-CEXM	Best Off Sky Ranger Swift 912S(1)	SKRxxxx812		1.11.07	A F Batchelor	Rayne Hall Farm, Braintree	
	(Built A F Batchelor - pr.no.BMAA/HB/556)						
G-CEXN	Cameron A-120 Balloon (Hot Air)	11089		3. 1.08	Dragon Balloon Company Ltd	Castleton, Hope Valley	
G-CEXO	Piper PA-28-161 Warrior III	2842041	N250ND	28.11.07	Plane Talking Ltd (Noted 12.07)	Denham	
G-CEXR	Piper PA-28-161 Warrior III	2842076	N70FT	28.11.07	Plane Talking Ltd (Noted 12.07)	Elstree	
G-CEXX	Rotorsport UK MT-03	RSUK/MT-03/022		12.11.07	D B Roberts	(Kinoulton, Nottingham)	22.11.08P
					(Noted NEC Birmingham 11.07		
G-CEXY	Schleicher ASW 19B	19265	BGA 2862-EQG PH-665	16.10.07	B A Tansley tr ASW 239 Syndicate	Challock	28. 9.08
G-CEXZ	Eurocopter EC.155 B1	6789	F-WQDF	1. 2.08	Eurocopter UK Ltd	Oxford	
G-CEYA	Robinson R44 Clipper II	11892		2.11.07	Fast Helicopters Ltd	Shoreham	
G-CEYB	Robinson R44 Raven II	11910	N3061S	2.11.07	Fast Helicopters Ltd	Shoreham	
G-CEYC	DG Flugzeugbau DG-505 Elan Orion	5E194X38	BGA 4690-JQF S5-7516	27.11.07	Scottish Gliding Union Ltd	Portmoak	28. 2.08
G-CEYD	Cameron N-31 Balloon (Hot Air)	3558	G-LLYD	22. 6.07	G A Chadwick t/a Black Pearl Balloons	Partridge Green	17. 7.08E
G-CEYE	Piper PA-32R-300 Cherokee Lance	32R-7780533	SE-KCD OH-PAS	24.10.02	D L Claydon	Andrewsfield	31. 1.08E
G-CEYJ	Aérospatiale AS.332L Super Puma	2083	LN-OLC	21.12.07	Bristow Helicopters Ltd	Aberdeen	
G-CEYK	Europa Aviation Europa XS	xxx		10.12.07	A B Milne	Lower Wasing Farm, Brimpton	
	(Built A B Milne - pr.no.PFA 247-14476)						
G-CEYM	Van's RV-6	xxxx		12.12.07	H Gordon-Roe	(Cambridge)	
	(Built H Gordon-Roe - pr.no.PFA 181A-14595)						
G-CEYN	Grob G109B	6256	D-KGFY	12.12.07	Lasham Gliding Society Ltd	Lasham	
G-CEYP	North Wing Design Stratus-ATF	7642		21.12.07	S G Murphy	(Luppitt, Honiton)	
G-CEYR	Rotorsport UK MT-03	RSUK/MT-03-032		14. 2.08	N Wright	(Baxterley, Atherstone)	
G-CEYS							
G-CEYT	Fuji FA.200-180AO Aero Subaru	FA200-249	PH-PDZ	7. 2.08	T R Cooper	Dunkeswell	
	(Officially regn as FA200-244 which was JA3707 and w/o 19. 2.75)				(Noted 11.07)		
G-CEYU							
G-CEYV							
G-CEYW							
G-CEYX							
G-CEYY	Evektor EV-97 teamEurostar UK	3123		7. 1.08	N J James	Welshpool	6. 1.09P
G-CEYZ	Sikorsky S-76C	760669	N4514R	10. 1.08	Bristow Helicopters Ltd	Aberdeen	
G-CEZA	Comco Ikarus C42 Cyclone FB80	0711-6923		13.11.07	P Harper and P J Morton	(Fleetwood and New Mills, High Peak)	16.12.08P
G-CEZB	ICP MXP-740 Savannah VG Jabiru(1)	07-05-51-599		14.12.07	J N Anyan	Glentham Grange, Market Rasen	
	(Built J N Anyan - pr.no.BMAA/HB/549)						
G-CEZC							
G-CEZD	Evektor EV-97 teamEurostar UK	3107		22.12.07	G P Jones	(Stoke-on-Trent)	21.12.08P

G-CEZE	Best Off Sky Ranger Swift 912S(1) SKRxxxx811			9.11.07	L Robinson , N McAllister and R N Tarrant		
	(Built N McAllister - pr/no.BMAA/HB/555)					Sackville Lodge, Riseley	
G-CEZF	Evektor EV-97 teamEurostar UK	3205		18. 2.08	D J Dick	Broadmeadow Farm, Hereford	17. 2.09P
G-CEZG							
G-CEZH	Aerochute Dual	321		14. 1.08	A Kay	(Croston, Leyland)	
	(C/n refers to trike unit – wing c/n 1288 and engine s/n 6478655)						
G-CEZI	Piper PA-28-161 Cadet II	2841228	N131ND	4. 1.08	Plane Talking Ltd	Elstree	
G-CEZJ							
G-CEZK	Stolp SA.750 Acroduster Too	PFA 089-13726		24. 1.08	R I M Hague	(Baildon, Shipley)	
	(Built R I M Hague)						
G-CEZL	Piper PA-28-161 Cadet II	2841247	OO-JAG N9192Z	14. 1.08	Plane Talking Ltd	Elstree	
G-CEZM	Cessna 152	152-85179	N6167Q	7. 1.08	Cristal Air Ltd	Shoreham	
G-CEZN	Pacific Airwave Pulse 2-Skycycle			30. 1.08	G W Cameron	(Edinburgh)	
		IR008-10157-11					
G-CEZO	Piper PA-28-161 Cadet II	2841226	N145ND	4. 1.08	Plane Talking Ltd	Elstree	
G-CEZP							
G-CEZR							
G-CEZS	Zenair CH.601HDS Zodiac	PFA 162-14030		1. 2.08	R Wyness	Bicester	
	(Built R Wyness)						
G-CEZT	P&M Quik GT450	8349		22. 2.08	B C Blackburn	Perth	21. 2.09P
G-CEZU	CFM Streak Shadow SA	K337		5. 2.08	M R Foreman	(Priorslees, Telford)	
	(Built M R Foreman - pr no.PFA 206-13597)						
G-CEZV	Zenair CH.601HDS Zodiac	PFA 162-13748		4. 2.08	G Waters	Swansea	
	(Built G Waters)						
G-CEZW	Jodel D.150 Mascaret	PFA 235-13866		5. 2.08	N J Kilford	(New Barn Farm, Whitchurch)	
	(Buiit N J Kilford)						
G-CEZX	P&M Quik GT450	8360		3.08R	(Noted 90% complete 2.08	Rochdale	
G-CEZZ	Flight Design CTSW	07.08.05		20. 9.07	S Emery	Damyn's Hall, Upminster	18. 9.08P
	(Assembled P&M Aviation Ltd with c/n 8326)						

G-CFAA - G-CFZZ

G-CFAA	British Aerospace Avro 146-RJ100	E3373		9. 5.00	BA Cityflyer Ltd	Manchester	15. 6.08E
G-CFAI	Rotorsport UK MT-03	RSUK/MT-03-027		23. 1.08	Airbourne Aviation Ltd	Popham	
G-CFAJ	DG Flugzeugbau DG-300 Elan	3E50	BGA 3103-FAJ	7. 1.08	B A Brown	Milfield	11. 3.08
G-CFAK	Rotorsport UK MT-03	RSUK/MT-03-030		14. 2.08	Capallini LLP	(Derby)	
G-CFAM	Schempp-Hirth Nimbus 3/24.5	79	BGA 3106-FAM	19.10.07	K J Hartley tr Nimbus III Syndicate J15	Bicester	11. 6.08
G-CFAN	Robinson R44 Clipper	0689	N829PM	4. 6.07	A M Payne	(Worsley, Manchester)	
G-CFAO	Rolladen-Schneider LS4	4465	BGA 3109-FAQ	5.11.07	C A Meir	Seighford	9. 3.08
G-CFAP	Interplane ZJ-Viera	VIERAA5-08M		14. 2.08	Flylight Airsports Ltd (Noted 2.08)	Sywell	
G-CFAR	Rotorsport UK MT-03	RSUK/MT-03/026		20.12.07	P M Twose	(Acton Bridge, Northwich)	8. 1.09P
G-CFAS	Reality Escapade Jabiru(3)	xxxxx		7. 1.08	C G N Boyd	(Malahide, County Dublin)	
	(Built C G N Boyd - pr.no.BMAA/HB/473)						
G-CFAT	P&M Pegasus Quik GT450	8355		28. 2.08	T A Jackson	(Donhead St Mary, Shaftesbury)	
					(Noted 2.08)		
G-CFAY	Sky 120-24 Balloon (Hor Air)	74	OE-ZAY	8. 1.08	G B Lescott	Oxford	
G-CFAZ	Flight Design CTSW	07.10.17		3.12.07	M Cusack tr CT Aviation Group	Barton	2.12.08P
	(Assembled P&M Aviation Ltd with c/n 8347)						
G-CFBA	Schleicher ASW 20BL	20665	BGA 3119-FBA	21. 1.08	A.Docherty	Long Mynd	31. 3.08
G-CFBB	Schempp-Hirth Standard Cirrus	327G	BGA 3120-FBB RAFGGA 312	25. 9.07	R Andrewartha and B F R Smyth	Nympsfield	26. 8.08
G-CFBC	Schleicher ASW 15B	15356	BGA 3121-FBC OH-439	10.12.07	C Knock and J J A Myrdal	Sandhill Farm, Shrivenham	26. 8.08
G-CFBD	Cessna 150M	15076736	N45103	21. 1.08	J S Willcocks	(Horley)	
G-CFBF	Lindstrand LBL 203T Balloon (Gas Filled) HF010			13. 2.08	S and D Leisure (Europe) Ltd	Manchester	
G-CFBH	Glaser-Dirks DG-100G Elan	E156G123	BGA 3126-FBH	22.11.07	N Riggott	Lasham	22. 3.08
G-CFBI	Colt 56A Balloon (Hot Air)	570		11. 7.84	G A Fisher tr Out-of-the-Blue	Petworth	24. 7.91A
					"Air O" (Operated Balloon Preservation Group)		
G-CFBK	British Aircraft Corporation 167 Strikemaster Mk.80A	R Saudi AF 1125	12. 2.08	Trans Holdings Ltd	Shoreham	
		EEP/JP/409	G-27-291				
G-CFBL	Best Off Sky Ranger Swift 912S(1) SKRxxxx824			14. 2.08	S R Isaac	Fyfield	
	(Built S R Isaac - pr.no.BMAA/HB/558)						
G-CFBM	P&M Pegasus Quantum 15-912	8352		14. 2.08	F W and N A Milne	(Chedburgh, Bury St Edmunds)	13. 2.09P
G-CFBN	Glasflügel H303 Mosquito B	167	BGA 3131-FBN D-6364	5. 9.07	S R and J Nash	Sandhill Farm, Shrivenham	28. 9.08
G-CFBO	Reality Escapade Jabiru(3)	UK ESC 0011		14. 2.08	J F Thornton	Old Sarum	
	(Built J F Thornton - pr.no.BMAA/HB/538)						
G-CFBS	Best Off Sky Ranger Swift 912S(1) SKRxxxxxxx			21. 2.08	A J Tyler	(Blackboys, Uckfield)	
	(Built A J Tyler - pr.no.BMAA/HB/563)						
G-CFBT	Schempp-Hirth Ventus bT	35/218	BGA 3136-FBT	6.12.07	S H Gibson tr 488 (Gransden) Group		
						Gransden Lodge	18.12.07
G-CFBV	Schleicher ASK 21	21223	BGA 3138-FBV	8. 1.08	London Gliding Club Proprietary Ltd	Dunstable	8. 3.08
G-CFBW	Glaser-Dirks DG-100G Elan	E174G140	BGA 3139-FBW	12.12.07	G N Phillips tr G-CFBW Syndicate	Lasham	9. 2.08
G-CFBY	Best Off Sky Ranger Swift 912S(1) SKRxxxxxxx			26. 2.08	J A Armin	(Morpeth)	
	(Built J A Armin - pr.no BMAA/HB/562)						
G-CFBZ	Schleicher Ka 6CR	6016	BGA 3142-FBZ D-4667, D-KIMN, D-4667	4.12.07	R E Branch Wycombe Air Park	10. 2.08	
G-CFCA	Schempp-Hirth Discus b	336	BGA 4117-HQJ D-1762	7. 2.08	M R Hayden	(Edelsborough, Dunstable)	23. 3.07
G-CFCB	Centrair 101 Pégase	10100178	BGA 3144-FCB F-CGEA	11. 9.07	M Forster and N Stratton	Portmoak	7. 2.08
G-CFCC	Cameron Z-275 Balloon (Hot Air)	11103		27. 2.08	The Balloon Company Ltd t/a First Flight		
						Langford, Bristol	

G-CFCD	Best Off Sky Ranger Swift 912S(1) SKRxxxx801			18.12.07	R J Gilbert	Dunnyvadden	
	(Built R J Gilbert - pr.no,BMAA/HB/554)						
G-CFCE	Raj Hamsa X'Air Hawk		xxx	20. 2.08	P C Bishop	(Chard)	
	(Built P C Bishop -pr.no.PFA 340-14751)						
G-CFCH	Campbell Cricket Mk.4	PFA G/03-1347		28. 2.08	E J Barton	(Bramley, Tadley)	
	(Built E J Barton)						
G-CFCJ	Grob G102 Astir CS	1231	BGA 3151-FCJ	13.11.07	I Ashby and M Levitt	Aston Down	28. 9.08
			D-4205				
G-CFCK	Best Off Sky Ranger Swift 912S(1) SKRxxxxxxx			28. 2.08	C M Sperring	(Weston-super-Mare)	
	(Built C M Sperring - pr.no,BMAA/HB/565)						
G-CFCL	Rotorsport UK MT-03	RSUK/MT-03/043		29. 2.08	A Parker	(Bingley)	
G-CFCN	Schempp-Hirth Standard Cirrus	131	BGA 3155-FCN	22.10.07	S M Robinson	Nympsfield	3. 3.08
			D-0191				
G-CFCP	Rolladen-Schneider LS6-a	6030	BGA 3156-FCP	8. 1.08	R E Robertson	Dunstable	1. 4.08
G-CFCR	Schleicher Ka 6 E	4223	BGA 3158-FCR	7.11.07	R F Whittaker	Lasham	27. 2.08
			OH-375, OH-REC				
G-CFCS	Schempp-Hirth HS.5 Nimbus 2C	233	BGA 3159-FCS	7.11.07	J Luck and P Dolling	Hinton-in-the-Hedges	13.12.07
G-CFDA	Schleicher ASW 15	15050	BGA 3167-FDA	12.10.07	N I Newton tr 7 Delta Group	Wycombe Air Park	13.11.07
			D-0511				
G-CFDE	Schempp-Hirth Ventus bT	53/256	BGA 3171-FDE	6. 9.07	P Clay	Sutton Bank	27. 3.08
G-CFDM	Schempp-Hirth Discus b	87	BGA 3185-FDU	1.10.07	J L and T G M Whiting	Edgehill	28. 3.08
G-CFDR	Schleicher Ka 6CR	6119	BGA 3182-FDR	25. 1.08	Dartmoor Gliding Society Ltd	Brentor	1. 8.08
			D-8456				
G-CFDV	Sikorsky S-76C	760666	N45140	26. 2.08	Bristow Hleicopters Ltd	Aberdeen	
G-CFEE	Evektor EV-97 Eurostar	LAA 315-14778		21. 2.08	G R Pritchard	Hardwicke, Hay-on-Wye	
	(Built G R Pritchard)						
G-CFEF	Grob G102 Astir CS	1164	BGA 3196-FEF	8. 2.08	M Bacic tr Oxford University Gliding Club	Bicester	4. 3.08
			OY-XGC				
G-CFEG	Schempp-Hirth Ventus b/16.6	279	BGA 3197-FEG	23.11.07	K F Moorhouse and R W Partridge	Lasham	27. 3.08
G-CFEH	Centrair 101A Pégase	101A0268	BGA 3198-FEH	13.12.07	Booker Gliding Club Ltd	Wycombe Air Park	21. 3.08
	(Rebuilt with new fuselage c/n 01304: original fuselage rebuilt as BGA 3560)						
G-CFEJ	Schempp-Hirth Discus b	76	BGA 3199-FEJ	17.12.07	L Coles	Wycombe Air Park	4. 2.08
G-CFEN	PZL-Bielsko SZD-50-3 Puchacz	B-1326	BGA3203-FEN	17. 1.08	The Northumbria Gliding Club Ltd	Currock Hill	23. 9.08
G-CFES	Schempp-Hirth Discus b	88	BGA 3207-FES	22.11.07	P W Berridge	Sandhill Farm, Shrivenham	2. 2.08
G-CFEZ	CZAW Sportcruiser	PFA 338-14675		14. 2.08	J F Barbe and J R Large	Stapleford	
	(Built J F Barbe and J R Large)						
G-CFFB	Grob G102 Astir CS	1123	BGA 3216-FFB	8.10.07	J G Arnold tr RAF Gliding and Soaring Association		
			RAFGSA R9, RAFGSA R97, BGA 3216-FFB, D-6977			RAF Halton	28. 9.08
					(Operated Chilterns Gliding Centre)		
G-CFFC	Centrair 101A Pégase	101A0255	BGA 3217-FFC	21.12.07	B Douglas	Rufforth	16. 4.08
G-CFFK	Schempp-Hirth Nimbus 3/24.5	87	BGA 3224-FFK	21.12.07	I Ashdown	Parham Park	28. 9.08
G-CFFS	Centrair 101A Pégase	101A0265	BGA 3231-FFS	9.11.07	W Murray	Gransden Lodge	3. 4.08
G-CFFT	Schempp-Hirth Discus b	110	BGA 3232-FFT	28.11.07	R Maskell	Gransden Lodge	4. 4.08
G-CFFU	Glaser-Dirks DG-100G Elan	E200G166	BGA 3233-FFU	17.10.07	K T Tutthill tr FFU Group	Chipping	31. 3.08
G-CFFV	PZL-Bielsko SZD-51-1 Junior	B-1616	BGA 3234-FFV	12. 2.08	Herefordshire Gliding Club Ltd	Shobdon	5. 4.08
			F-WGJA				
G-CFFX	Schempp-Hirth Discus b	109	BGA 3236-FFX	10.12.07	P J Tiller	Husbands Bosworth	5. 4.08
G-CFFY	PZL-Bielsko SZD-51-1 Junior	W-938	BGA 3237-FFY	17. 1.08	Scottish Gliding Union Ltd	Portmoak	2. 4.08
G-CFGF	Schempp-Hirth Nimbus 3T	25/91	BGA 3244-FGF	5.10.07	R E Cross	Lasham	14. 1.08
G-CFGK	Grob G102 Astir CS	1323	BGA 3248-FGK,	20.12.07	P Allingham	Eyres Field	15. 4.08
			RAFGSA R61, RAFGSA 316				
G-CFGP	Schleicher ASW 19	19121	BGA 3252-FGP	3.12.07	A E Prime tr Foxtrot Golf Alpha Group	Tibenham	20. 3.08
			C-GJXG				
G-CFGR	Schleicher ASK 13	13655AB	BGA 3254-FGR	6. 2.08	T World tr Portsmouth Naval Gliding Centre		
						Lee-on-Solent	10. 8.07
G-CFGW	Centrair 101A Pégase	101A0275	BGA 3259-FGW	2.11.07	L.P.Smith	Kingston Deverill	18. 3.08
G-CFHD	Schleicher ASW 20BL	20694	BGA 3266-FHD	18.12.07	D P Smith tr 196 Syndicate	Bicester	30. 4.08
			RAFGGA				
G-CFHF	PZL-Bielsko SZD-51-1 Junior	W-952	BGA 3268-FHF	1.12.07	Black Mountains Gliding Club	Talgarth	30. 4.08
G-CFHG	Schempp-Hirth Mini Nimbus C	140	BGA 3269-FHG	12.10.07	R W and M P Weaver	Usk	21.12.06
			(BGA 3213-FEY), ZS-GNI				
G-CFHL	Rolladen-Schneider LS4	4633	BGA 3273-FHL	28.11.07	I P Hicks	Dunstable	19. 2.08
G-CFHM	Schleicher ASK 13	13662AB	BGA 3274-FHM	16.11.07	Lasham Gliding Society Ltd	Lasham	13.12.07
G-CFHO	Grob G103 Twin Astir II	3566	BGA 5275-KPI	19. 4.07	The Surrey Hills Gliding Club Ltd	Kenley	27. 4.08
			F-CFHO		"KPI"		
G-CFHR	Schempp-Hirth Discus b	152	BGA 3278-FHR	7. 2.08	J Jervis, M Fursedon and T Turner	Edgehill	8. 2.08
G-CFHT	Grob G102 Astir CS	1234	BGA 3280-FHT	18. 1.08	E K Sharp	Bicester	9. 5.08
			D-4208				
G-CFHV	PZL-Bielsko SZD-48-1 Jantar Standard 2	B-1036	BGA 3282-FHV	17. 9.07	R A Williams tr Jantar FHV Syndicate	Long Mynd	10. 5.08
			D-4516				
G-CFHW	Grob G102 Astir CS	1087	BGA 3283-FHW	7.12.07	P Haliday tr Astir 698 Group	Lasham	18. 2.08
			D-6987				
G-CFJE	Schleicher ASW 20BL	20953	BGA 3291-FJE	25.10.07	A Groves	Lasham	28. 9.08
G-CFJK	Centrair 101A Pégase	101070	BGA 3296-FJK	4.12.07	A W McKee and T J Parker	Hinton-in-the-Hedges	26. 4.08
			N4429W				
G-CFJM	Rolladen-Schneider LS4-a	4665	BGA 3298-FJM	21.12.07	K Woods and S Hill	Dunstable	22. 6.08
			D-1431		"143"		
G-CFJR	DG Flugzeugbau DG-300 Club Elan	3E270C2	BGA 3302-FJR	17. 1.08	H Smith and W.J.Palmer	Lasham	11. 3.08
G-CFJS	DG Flugzeugbau DG-300 Club Elan	3E271C3	BGA 3303-FJS	7.11.07	K L Goldsmith	Rattlesden	9. 4.08
G-CFJW	Schleicher K 7 Rhönadler	980	BGA 3307-FJW	1. 2.08	A J Pettitt tr K7 Group	Rivar Hill	9. 6.08
			OH-241, OH-KKF				
G-CFJX	DG Flugzeugbau DG-300 Elan	3E261	BGA 3308-FJX	10.12.07	Crown Service Gliding Club	Lasham	4. 2.08

Reg	Type	Serial	BGA	Date	Owner	Location	Date
G-CFJZ	Schempp-Hirth SHK-1	14	BGA 3310-FJZ D-9330	13.11.07	B S Irwin and R H Hanna	Bellarena	24. 6.08
G-CFKG	Rolladen-Schneider LS4-a	4673	BGA 3317-FKG	27.11.07	D A Smith	Kingston Deverill	16. 3.08
G-CFKL	Schleicher ASW 20BL	20954	BGA 3321-FKL	19.12.07	J Ley	Wormingford	18.12.07
G-CFKY	Schleicher Ka 6CR	822	BGA 3329-FKU D-0025	12. 2.08	J A Timmis	Camphill	25. 6.08
G-CFLC	DG Flugzeugbau DG-300 Elan	3E310	BGA 3337-FLC	12.11.07	J L Hey	Rufforth	19. 3.08
G-CFLE	Schempp-Hirth Discus b	207	BGA 3339-FLE	15.10.07	Booker Gliding Club Ltd	Wycombe Air Park	28. 9.08
G-CFLH	Schleicher K 8B	22	BGA 3342-FLH OH-361, OH-RTW	25. 1.08	The South Wales Gliding Club Ltdb	Usk	14. 4.08
G-CFLW	Schempp-Hirth Standard Cirrus 75	656	BGA 3355-FLW F-CEMT	4.10.07	J Pack	Lasham	28. 9.08
G-CFLX	DG Flugzeugbau DG-300 Club Elan	3E304C19	BGA 3356-FLX	4.12.07	R Emms tr Felix Flying Group	Upwood	16. 3.08
G-CFME	SOCATA TB-10 Tobago	1795	F-GNHU	15. 4.98	Charles Funke Associates Ltd	Goodwood	12. 7.08E
G-CFMH	Schleicher ASK 13	13673AB	BGA 3366-FMH	31.10.07	Lasham Gliding Society Ltd	Lasham	28. 9.08
G-CFMK	Centrair 101 Pégase Club	10100293	BGA 3368-FMK	11.12.07	D Hatch	Nympsfield	28. 1.08
G-CFML	Schleicher ASW 15B	15294	BGA 3369-FML F-CEGR	13. 9.07	G H Macmillan tr ASW 15B Syndicate	Snitterfield	6. 1.08
G-CFMN	Schempp-Hirth Ventus cT	123/397	BGA 3371-FMN	15. 2.08	R E Matthews tr FMN Glider Syndicate	Lasham	1. 2.08
G-CFMO	Schempp-Hirth Discus b	243	BGA 3373-FMQ	28.11.07	P D Bagnall	Nympsfield	5. 4.08
G-CFMS	Schleicher ASW 15	15061	BGA 3375-FMS N111SP	15. 2.08	A F Brind and W Orson	Rivar Hill	22. 6.08
G-CFMT	Schempp-Hirth Standard Cirrus	249	BGA 3376-FMT N2HM	30. 1.08	S R Westlake	North Hill	20. 6.08
G-CFMU	Schempp-Hirth Standard Cirrus	236	BGA 3377-FMU N3LB	31.10.07	A Harrison and J Gammage	Aston Down	16. 2.08
G-CFMY	Rolladen-Schneider LS7	7004	BGA 3381-FMY D-1256	16. 1.08	N J Howes tr G-CFMY Group	Camphill	17. 4.08
G-CFNA	Schleicher K 8B	8499	BGA 3383-FNA D-5670	4. 9.07	Bowland Forest Gliding Club Ltd	Chipping	28. 9.08
G-CFND	Schleicher Ka 6E	4069	BGA 3386-FND PH-366	20. 9.07	T Barton	Talgarth	12. 2.08
G-CFNG	Schleicher ASW 24	24015	BGA 3389-FNG	17. 9.07	P H Pickett	Snitterfield	28. 9.08
G-CFNH	Schleicher ASW 19	19194	BGA 3390-FNH D-7969	10.12.07	S N and P E S Longland	Gransden Lodge	8. 4.08
G-CFNL	Schempp-Hirth Discus b	253	BGA 3393-FNL	3.12.07	A S Ramsay and P P Musto	Long Mynd	31. 1.08
G-CFNM	Centrair 101B Pegase	101B0289	BGA 3394-FNM F-CGSE	25.10.07	D T Hartley	Husbands Bosworth	28. 9.08
G-CFNN	Schempp-Hirth Ventus cT	130	BGA 3395-FNN	27.11.07	D G Every	Eyres Field	6.12.07
G-CFNR	Schempp-Hirth Discus b	255	BGA 3398-FNR	22.10.07	R A Amor	Nympsfield	13. 4.08
G-CFNS	DG Flugzeugbau DG-300 Club Elan	3E314C23	BGA 3399-FNS	14. 1.08	J M Price, K F Byrne and P.E.Williams	Portmoak	2. 7.08
G-CFNT	Glaser-Dirks DG-600	6-12	BGA 3400-FNT	21. 9.07	M R Johnson tr G-CFNT Group	Sutton Bank	29. 3.08
G-CFNU	Rolladen-Schneider LS4-a	4732	BGA 3401-FNU D-1376	23. 8.07	R J Simpson	Nympsfield	6. 1.08
G-CFOB	Schleicher ASW 15B	15340	BGA 3432-FQB D-2345	1. 2.08	A Maitland	Drumshade	16. 3.08
G-CFOF	Scheibe SF27A Zugvögel V	6025	BGA 3436-FQF D-0009	5. 2.08	S Maddex	Darlton	6. 5.08
G-CFOG	Comco Ikarus C42 FB UK (Built P D Coppin - pr.no.PFA 322-14482)	0511-6773		19. 4.06	P D Coppin	Lee-on-Solent	7. 8.08P
G-CFOK	Grob G103C Twin III Acro	34123	BGA 3440-FOK	16.10.07	York Gliding Centre Ltd	Rufforth	29. 3.08
G-CFON	Wittman W.8 Tailwind (Built C F O'Neill)	PFA 031-11789		7.11.07	C F O'Neill	Newtownards	
G-CFOT	PZL Bielsko SZD-48-3 Jantar Standard 3 (BGA 3409-FPC)	B-1891	BGA 3448-FQT	29. 2.08	T H Greenwood	Rivar Hill	18. 5.08
G-CFOU	Schleicher K 7 Rhönadler	1139	BGA 3449-FQU D-8614, HB-709	20.11.07	Channel Gliding Club Ltd	Waldershare Park	3. 3.08
G-CFOX	Marganski MDM-1 Fox	224	BGA 4566-JKC SP-P632	26. 9.07	M Newman tr Fox Glider Syndicate	Saltby	28. 9.08
G-CFOY	Schempp-Hirth Discus b	274	BGA 3453-FQY	21. 9.07	B W Mills and J W Slater	Dunstable	28. 9.08
G-CFOZ	Rolladen-Schneider LS1-f	391	BGA 3454-FQZ F-CEKH	12. 2.08	A G Wallace tr L51 Group	Bidford	26. 2.08
G-CFPE	Schempp-Hirth Ventus cT	131/408	BGA 3411-FPE	28. 2.08	R Palmer	Bidford	5. 4.08
G-CFPH	Centrair ASW 20F	20132	BGA 3414-FPH F-CFFX	4.12.07	G Burkert	Bidford	11. 3.08
G-CFPL	Schempp-Hirth Ventus c	409	BGA 3417-FPL	23. 8.07	R V Barrett	Nympsfield	28. 9.08
G-CFPM	PZL-Bielsko SZD-51-1 Junior	B-1788	BGA 3418-FPM	29.10.07	Kent Gliding Club Ltd	Challock	28. 9.08
G-CFPN	Schleicher ASW 20	20376	BGA 3419-FPN RAFGGA 545, D-8780	15. 2.08	M Rayner	Lasham	19. 8.08
G-CFPX	Schleicher ASK 13	13325	BGA 3428-FPX F-CDYR	3. 1.08	R B Witter	Lleweni Parc	17. 8.07
G-CFRB	Schempp-Hirth Ventus c	404	BGA 3456-FRB	19. 9.07	C J Ratcliffe	Seighford	14. 3.08
G-CFRK	Schleicher ASW 15 B	15214	BGA 3464-FRK	29.11.07	M Hill	Edgehill	21.10.07
G-CFRL	Grob G102 Astir CS	1373	BGA 3465-FRL D-7402	25. 1.08	The South Wales Gliding Club Ltd	Usk	13. 4.08
G-CFRR	Centrair 101A Pégase	101034	BGA 3470-FRR (BGA3451-FQW), F-CFQA	27.11.07	P A Lewis	Walney Island	4. 6.08
G-CFRS	Scheibe Zugvögel IIIB	1097	BGA 3471-FRS D-2171, HB-749	29. 1.08	S W Vallei and R C Theobald	Rivar Hill	26. 4.08
G-CFRV	Centrair 101A Pégase	101A0325	BGA 3474-FRV	2.11.07	P J Britten	Wycombe Air Park	15. 1.08
G-CFRW	Schleicher ASW 20L	20202	BGA 3475-FRW D-5981	11. 1.08	S R Jarvis	Lasham	4. 3.08
G-CFRX	Centrair 101A Pégase	101A0315	BGA 3476-FRX	10. 1.08	S Woolrich	(Auchtermuchty, Cupar)	13. 2.08

Reg	Type	C/n	Prev id	Date	Owner/Operator	Base	Date2
G-CFRY	Zenair CH.601UL Zodiac (Built C K Fry)	PFA 162A-14302		5. 1.05	C K Fry	(Lytchett Minster, Poole)	
G-CFSA	Piper PA-44-180 Seminole	4496170	N492AF G-CCDA, N53487	27. 9.06	Northern Aviation Ltd	Durham Tees Valley	29.10.07E
G-CFSD	Schleicher ASK 13	13367	BGA 3482-FSD D-0863	29. 1.08	T World tr Portsmouth Naval Gliding Centre	Lee-on-Solent	16. 8.08
G-CFSH	Grob G102 Astir CS Jeans	2090	BGA 3486-FSH D-7532	23. 1.08	Buckminster Gliding Club Ltd	Saltby	7. 7.08
G-CFSR	DG Flugzeugbau DG-300 Elan	3E343	BGA 3494-FSR	18.12.07	A P Montague and J E May	Nympsfield	22. 1.08
G-CFST	Schleicher ASH 25E	25073	BGA 3496-FST (BGA 3530)	30. 8.07	D Tucker and K H Lloyd	Aston Down	18. 3.08
G-CFSZ	Grob G102 Astir CS77	1841	BGA 3502-FSZ D-2908	16.11.07	N Greenwood	Aston Down	17. 3.08
G-CFTB	Schleicher Ka 6CR	019	BGA 3504-FTB D-8900	31.10.07	P J F Blair	Bidford	24. 1.08
G-CFTC	PZL-Bielsko SZD-51-1 Junior	B-1860	BGA 3505-FTC	07.02.08	J G Kosak tr Seahawk Gliding Club	RNAS Culdrose	20. 3.08
G-CFTD	Schleicher ASW 15B	15191	BGA 3506-FTD D-0872	11. 1.08	E Stephenson	Milfield	29. 4.08
G-CFTH	PZL-Bielsko SZD-50-3 Puchacz	B-1881	BGA 3510-FTH	24.10.07	Buckminster Gliding Club Ltd (Noted 2.08)	Saltby	17.12.07
G-CFTJ	Evektor EV-97A Eurostar (Built C B Flood)	PFA 315-14504		13. 2.06	C B Flood	Ince Blundell	9. 8.08P
G-CFTK	Grob G102 Astir CS Jeans	2059	BGA 3512-FTK OE-5152	5.10.07	Ulster Gliding Club Ltd	Bellarena	8. 9.07
G-CFTL	Schleicher ASW 20CL	20751	BGA 3513-FTL	9.10.07	J S and S V Shaw	Perranporth	22. 4.08
G-CFTP	Schleicher ASW 20CL	20733	BGA 3516-FTP D-3640	14. 2.08	D J Pengilley and M S Hawkins	Kingston Deverill	31. 5.08
G-CFTR	Grob G102 Astir CS77	1606	BGA 3518-FTR D-4807	5.12.07	The Furness Gliding Club Proprietary Ltd t/a Lakes Gliding Club	Walney Island	9. 3.08
G-CFTS	DG Flugzeugbau DG-300 Club Elan	3E349C38	BGA 3519-FTS	15. 1.08	A J E Taylor	Parham Park	23. 5.08
G-CFTV	Rolladen-Schneider LS7-WL	7073	BGA 3522-FTV	6.12.07	D Hilton	Wycombe Air Park	6. 3.08
G-CFTW	Schempp-Hirth Discus b	292	BGA 3523-FTW	17. 9.07	P A Startup	North Hill	28. 9.08
	(Rebuilt with new fuselage after accident 21. 6.91; original fuselage rebuilt as BGA 3879)						
G-CFTY	Rolladen-Schneider LS7-WL	7075	BGA 3525-FTY	14. 1.08	A Burgess and J D Thomson	Easterton	4. 4.08
G-CFUH	Schempp-Hirth Ventus c	438	BGA 3533-FUH	6. 9.07	M A Gale and S D Wright tr 192 Syndicate	Eyres Field	28. 9.08
G-CFUJ	DG Flugzeugbau DG-300 Elan	3E353	BGA 3534-FUJ	7.11.07	V A Leitch tr Foxtrot Uniform Juliet Group	Portmoak	4. 3.08
G-CFUL	Schempp-Hirth Discus b	293	BGA 3535-FUL	1.12.07	J Greenwood tr Discus 803 Syndicate	Dunstable	22. 2.08
G-CFUN	Schleicher ASW 20CL	20813	BGA 3537-FUN D-3432	5.11.07	S Economu and W H Parker	Wycombe Air Park	6. 3.08
G-CFUS	PZL-Bielsko SZD-51-1 Junior	B-1912	BGA 3541-FUS	2.11.07	Scottish Gliding Union Ltd	Portmoak	28. 9.08
G-CFUU	DG Flugzeugbau DG-300 Club Elan	3E360C45	BGA 3543-FUU	6. 9.07	D S Penny	Perranporth	28. 9.08
G-CFUV	Rolladen-Schneider LS7-WL	7068	BGA 3544-FUV	9.11.07	E Alston	North Hill	28. 9.08
G-CFUY	PZL-Bielsko SZD-50-3 Puchacz	B-1983	BGA 3546-FUY	19. 2.08	The Bath, Wilts and North Dorset Gliding Club Ltd	Kingston Deverill	6. 5.08
G-CFVC	Schleicher ASK 13	13682AB	BGA 3550-FVC	22.12.07	Mendip Gliding Club Ltd	Halesland	25. 1.08
G-CFVE	Schempp-Hirth Nimbus 2C	202	BGA 3553-FVE	28.11.07	L Mitchell	Chipping	19. 6.08
G-CFVH	Rolladen-Schneider LS7	7067	BGA 3555-FVH (BGA 3527-FUA)	18. 1.08	B.R.Forrest	Wycombe Air Park	11. 4.08
G-CFVM	Centrair 101A Pégase	101A0345	BGA 3559-FVM	10.12.07	S H North	Kingston Deverill	11. 4.08
G-CFVN	Centrair 101A Pégase	101A0268/2	BGA 3560-FVN	6. 2.08	G G Butler	Snitterfield	1. 2.08
G-CFVP	Centrair 101A Pégase	101A0350	BGA 3561-FVP	27. 9.07	J R Parry tr Foxtrot Victor Papa Group	Long Mynd	8. 3.08
G-CFVS	Schempp-Hirth Standard Cirrus	359G	BGA 3564-FVS D-2168	29.10.07	P A Clark	Lasham	24. 1.08
G-CFVU	Schleicher ASK 13	13062	BGA 3566-FVU D-1348	1.11.07	The Vale of the White Horse Gliding Centre Ltd	Sandhill Farm, Shrivenham	28. 9.08
G-CFVV	Centrair 101A Pégase	101A0353	BGA 3567-FVV	29. 2.08	Cambridge Gliding Club Ltd	Gransden Lodge	1. 7.08
G-CFVW	Schempp-Hirth Ventus bT	51-252	BGA 3568-FVW D-KORN	4.12.07	I C Champness and R F Barber	Lasham	28. 9.08
G-CFVZ	Schleicher Ka 6E	4007	BGA 3571-FVZ D-4104	12.12.07	R C Fisher	Kingston Deverill	21. 6.08
G-CFWA	Schleicher Ka 6CR	6227	BGA 3572-FWA D-1062	10. 9.07	A Parker and D Cousins	Usk	5.10.07
G-CFWB	Schleicher ASK 13	13224	BGA 3573-FWB HB-989	21. 1.08	R Birch tr Cotswold Gliding Club	Aston Down	19. 1.08
G-CFWC	Grob G103C Twin III Acro	34154	BGA 3574-FWC	25. 1.08	The South Wales Gliding Club Ltd	Usk	17. 3.08
G-CFWE	PZL-Bielsko SZD-50-3 Puchacz	B-1984	BGA 3576-FWE (BGA 3547-FUZ)	25.10.07	Deeside Gliding Club (Aberdeenshire) Ltd	Aboyne	28. 9.08
G-CFWK	Schempp-Hirth Nimbus 3DT	32	BGA 3581-FWK	7. 1.08	A J Dibdin tr 29 Syndicate	Gransden Lodge	27. 3.08
G-CFWL	Schleicher K 8B	106-58	BGA 3582-FWL D-7151	11. 2.08	M Staniscia	(Kettering)	3. 8.08
G-CFWM	DG Flugzeugbau DG-300 Club Elan	3E373C50	BGA 3583-FWM	26.10.07	S A Gunn-Russell tr FWM Group	Long Mynd	28. 9.08
G-CFWP	Schleicher ASW 19B	19262	BGA 3585-FWP D-5980	3. 1.08	B Spriggs	Dunstable	17. 3.08
G-CFWR	Best Off Sky Ranger 912(2) (Built R W Clarke - pr.no.BMAA/HB/426)	SKRxxxx525		2.12.04	A M Wood and J Mills	(London SW4 and NW1)	19. 3.08P
G-CFWS	Schleicher ASW 20C	20765	BGA 3588-FWS D-6623	10.12.07	R Hawtree tr 662 Syndicate	Ridgewell	3. 4.08
G-CFWT	PZL-Bielsko SZD-50-3 Puchacz	B-1988	BGA 3589-FWT	3.10.07	Coventry Gliding Club Ltd t/a The Gliding Centre "FWT"	Husbands Bosworth	11. 1.08
G-CFWU	Rolladen-Schneider LS7-WL	7080	BGA 3590-FWU	21.12.07	G E Thomas	Husbands Bosworth	29. 3.08
G-CFWW	Schleicher ASH 25E	25093	BGA 3592-FWW	24. 3.06	A T Farmer tr FWW Syndicate	Bicester	28. 2.08
G-CFWY	Centrair 101A Pégase	101071	BGA 3594-FWY F-CFRZ	17. 1.08	R Johnson tr Foxtrot Whiskey Yankee	Lasham	5. 4.08
G-CFWZ	Schleicher ASW 19B	19342	BGA 3595-FWZ D-2603	21. 2.08	C M Worrall tr G-CFWZ Flying Group	Camphill	15.12.07

G-CFXA	Grob G104 Speed Astir IIB	4083	BGA 3596-FXA 16. 8.07 D-2671	C M Hawkes and D C White	Ringmer	29.11.07
G-CFXD	Centrair 101A Pégase	101A0346	BGA 3599-FXD 2.10.07 (BGA 3563-FVR)	Coventry Gliding Club Ltd t/a The Gliding Centre Husbands Bosworth		27.12.07
G-CFXH	Schleicher K 7 Rhönadler	353	BGA 3603-FXH 11. 1.08 D-4040	T J Price tr Vale of Neath Gliding Club	Rhigos	6. 9.08
G-CFXJ	Schleicher ASW 24	24086	BGA 3604-FXJ 21. 8.07	A K Laylee	Lasham	28. 5.08
G-CFXO	PZL-Bielsko SZD-50-3 Puchacz	B-2024	BGA 3658-FXQ 3.10.07 (BGA 3637-FYT)	Coventry Gliding Club Ltd t/a The Gliding Centre "FXQ" Husbands Bosworth		28. 9.08
G-CFXU	Schleicher Ka 6E	4071	BGA 3614-FXU 4. 1.08 OH-343, OH-RSY	T Ward	Lasham	14. 3.08
G-CFXW	Schleicher K 8B	8651	BGA 3616-FXW 25. 1.08 D-7203, D-KOLA, D-7203	The South Wales Gliding Club Ltd	Usk	24. 3.07
G-CFYA	PZL-Bielsko SZD-50-3 Puchacz	B-2022	BGA 3620-FYA 8.11.07	W R Longstaff tr Cairngorm Gliding Club Feshie Bridge		25. 3.08
G-CFYB	Rolladen-Schneider LS7	7102	BGA 3621-FYB 6. 9.07	A T Macdonald and V P Haley	Wormingford	28. 9.08
G-CFYC	Schempp-Hirth Ventus b	83	BGA 3622-FYC 8. 1.08 F-CEDR, F-WEDR	K Fear	Crowland	20. 4.08
G-CFYJ	Schempp-Hirth Standard Cirrus	581G	BGA 3628-FYJ 16.11.07 D-8931	S A Gibson tr FYJ Syndicate	Pocklington	29.12.07
G-CFYK	Rolladen-Schneider LS7-WL	7108	BGA 3629-FYK 19.11.07	R R Ward	Gransden Lodge	26. 1.08
G-CFYL	PZL-Bielsko SZD-50-3 Puchasz	B-1990	BGA 3630-FYL 16.11.07	Deeside Gliding Club (Aberdeenshire) Ltd	Aboyne	28. 9.08
G-CFYM	Schempp-Hirth Discus bT	31	BGA 3631-FYM 5.10.07	B F Laverick-Smith	Challock	28. 9.08
G-CFYN	Schempp-Hirth Discus b	179	BGA 3632-FYN 12.11.07 N75J	N White and P R Foulger	Wormingford	21. 3.08
G-CFYU	Glaser-Dirks DG-100 Elan	E111	BGA 3638-FYU 14. 2.08 OY-XMR, SE-TYO	I M and C Shepherd RAF Weston-on-the-Green		5. 7.08
G-CFYV	Schleicher ASK 21	21468	BGA 3639-FYV 6.11.07	The Bristol Gliding Club Proprietary Ltd	Nympsfield	28. 9.08
G-CFYW	Rolladen-Schneider LS7	7111	BGA 3640-FYW 10.12.07	D S Lodge	Pocklington	19. 1.08
G-CFZA	PZL-Bielsko SZD-51-1 Junior	B-1913	BGA 3644-FZA 13.12.07	Booker Gliding Club Ltd	Wycombe Air Park	29. 1.08
G-CFZB	Glasflügel H201B Standard Libelle	669	BGA 3645-FZB 3. 1.08 OH-388, OH-GLA	J C Meyer	Nympsfield	2. 1.08
G-CFZF	PZL-Bielsko SZD-51-1 Junior	B-1861	BGA 3649-FZF 30.11.07	Devon & Somerset Gliding Club Ltd	North Hill	28. 9.08
G-CFZH	Schempp-Hirth Ventus c	455	BGA 3651-FZH 12.11.07	G D Clack tr FZH Group	Lasham	22. 1.08
G-CFZL	Schleicher ASW 20CL	20764	BGA 3654-FZL 25. 9.07 D-5937	A L and R M Housden	Aboyne	8.11.07
G-CFZN	Schleicher ASK 13	13045	BGA 3656-FZN 1.12.07 D-5759	Black Mountains Gliding Club	Talgarth	16. 5.08
G-CFZO	Schempp-Hirth Numbus-3DT	31	BGA 3610-FXQ 17.11.07	D Tanner	Lasham	28. 9.08
G-CFZP	PZL-Bielsko SZD-51-1 Junior	B-1926	BGA 3657-FZP 28. 1.08	T World tr Portsmouth Naval Gliding Centre Lee-on-Solent		19. 6.08
G-CFZV	Rolladen-Schneider LS7	7116	BGA 3663-FZV 18. 1.08	R N Boddy	Wycombe Air Park	8. 3.08
G-CFZW	DG Flugzeugbau DG-300 Club Elan	3E378C53	BGA 3664-FZW 16. 1.08	D O'Flanagan, G Rogers and G Stilgoe	Parham Park	7. 3.08

G-CGAA - G-CGZZ

G-CGAF	Schleicher ASK 21	21152	BGA 3673-GAF 16. 1.08 ZD652, BGA 2892-ERO	Lasham Gliding Society Ltd	Lasham	15. 3.08
G-CGAG	Schleicher ASK 21	21143	BGA 3674-GAG 24. 9.07 ZD645, BGA 2885-ERF	Stratford on Avon Gliding Club Ltd	Snitterfield	28. 9.08
G-CGAH	Schempp-Hirth Standard Cirrus	572	BGA 3675-GAH 19.12.07 HB-1240	J W Williams	Nympsfield	30. 3.08
G-CGAM	Schleicher ASK 21	21144	BGA 3679-GAM 8. 2.08 ZD646, BGA 2886-ERG	M Bacic tr Oxford University Gliding Club	Bicester	24. 2.08
G-CGAS	Schempp-Hirth Ventus cT	157/509	BGA 3684-GAS 3.10.07	M W Edwards	Kingston Deverill	28. 9.08
G-CGAV	Scheibe SF27A Zugvögel V	6073	BGA 3687-GAV 8. 2.08 D-5287	R A Kempton tr GAV Syndicate	Darlton	1. 9.08
G-CGAW	Beech 200 Super King Air	BB-700	N440WA 24. 5.07 N200PY, N101TS, N101SK	G A Warburton	Guernsey	26. 7.08P
G-CGBB	Schleicher ASK 21	21073	BGA 3693-GBB 25. 2.08 D-3239	I R McTernan tr Edinburgh University Gliding Club Portmoak		17. 3.08
G-CGBD	PZL-Bielsko SZD-50-3 Puchacz	B-2028	BGA 3695-GBD 3. 1.08	The Northumbria Gliding Club Ltd	Currock Hill	17. 6.08
G-CGBF	Schleicher ASK 21	21142	BGA 3697-GBF 4.12.07 ZD644, BGA 2883-ERD	R E Neal tr BBC (London) Club	Lasham	28. 9.08
G-CGBG	Rolladen-Schneider LS6-c	6214	BGA 3698-GBG 6.12.07 D-3482	C M and M A Greaves	Rufforth	7. 2.08
G-CGBJ	Grob G102 Astir CS	1107	BGA 3700-GBJ 6.11.07 D-4167	Aquila Gliding Club Ltd	Hinton-in-the-Hedges	16. 4.08
G-CGBK	Grob G102 Astir CS	1461	BGA 3701-GBK 29.11.07	B J Griffiths	Saltby	28. 9.08
G-CGBL	Rolladen-Schneider LS7-WL	7119	BGA 3702-GBL 14. 1.08	M J Aldridge	Rougham	2. 3.08
G-CGBN	Schleicher ASK 21	21141	BGA 3704-GBN 13.12.07 ZD643, BGA 2883-ERD	Essex & Suffolk Gliding Club Ltd	Wormingford	1. 3.08
G-CGBO	Rolladen-Schneider LS6	6082	BGA 3706-GBQ 6. 2.08 D-3725	G D Sutherland tr C30 Group	Wycombe Air Park	17. 3.08
G-CGBU	Centrair 101A Pegase 90	101A0394	BGA 3710-GBU 1. 2.08	A D Wood, P S Tickner and S I Ross	Parham Park	15. 2.08
G-CGBR	Rolladen-Schneider LS6-c	6196	BGA 3707-GBR 7.12.07	V L Brown	Snitterfield	12. 9.08
G-CGBV	Schleicher ASK 21	21149	BGA 3711-GBV 10.10.07 ZD649, BGA 2889	Wolds Gliding Club Ltd	Pocklington	27. 3.08
G-CGBX	Schleicher ASW 22	22029	BGA 3713-GBX 21.12.07 D-4325	D A Ashby	Sutton Bank	26. 2.08
G-CGBZ	DG Flugzeugbau DG-500 Elan Trainer	5E34T10	BGA 3715-GBZ 23.11.07	Needwood Forest Gliding Club Ltd	Cross Hayes	11. 5.08

G-CGCA	Schleicher ASW 19B	19281	BGA 3716-GCA D-3179	21.12.07	Deeside Gliding Club (Aberdeenshire) Ltd	Aboyne	30. 1.08
G-CGCC	PZL-Bielsko SZD-51-1 Junior	B-1928	BGA 3718-GCC	2.10.07	Coventry Gliding Club Ltd t/a The Gliding Centre	Husbands Bosworth	31. 3.08
G-CGCF	Schleicher ASK 23	23010	BGA 3721-GCF AGA 9	20.11.07	Needwood Forest Gliding Club Ltd	Cross Hayes	18. 2.08
G-CGCL	Grob G .102 Astir CS	1194	BGA 3726-GCL D-7311	17. 8.07	J A Williams	Parham Park	23. 6.07
G-CGCM	Rolladen-Schneider LS6-c	6216	BGA 3727-GCM	12.10.07	G R Glazebrook	Dunstable	28. 9.08
G-CGCP	Schleicher Ka 6CR	6416	BGA 3729-GCP D-6369	23. 1.08	B Clarke and D Clarke	Burn	28. 5.08
G-CGCR	Schleicher ASW 15B	15447	BGA 3731-GCR D-6887	10. 1.08	R C Page	Nympsfield	17. 3.08
G-CGCT	Schempp-Hirth Discus b	360	BGA 3733-GCT	14. 2.08	D A White	Dunstable	17. 2.08
G-CGCU	PZL-Bielsko SZD-50-3 Puchacz	B-2023	BGA 3734-GCU (BGA 3619-FXZ)	23. 1.08	Buckminster Gliding Club Ltd	Saltby	27. 2.08
G-CGDA	Rolladen-Schneider LS3-17	3448	BGA 3739-GDA RAFGGA 546	15.10.07	A R Fish	Saltby	1. 2.08
G-CGDB	Schleicher K 8B	8152	BGA 3740-GDB HB-738	11.12.07	The Welland Gliding Club Ltd	Lyveden	7. 8.08
G-CGDE	Schleicher Ka 6CR	6570SI	BGA 3743-GDE D-5306	29. 8.07	P D Rowlands tr K6 Syndicate	North Hill	7.10.07
G-CGDJ	Piper PA-28-161 Warrior II	28-8116256	G-ETDA N84051	12. 9.06	C G D Jones	Blackbushe	13. 4.08E
G-CGDK	Schleicher K 8B	8240	BGA 3748-GDK D-5381, D-KANU, D-5381	23. 1.08	T J Price tr Vale of Neath Gliding Club	Rhigos	24. 7.08
G-CGDO	Grob G102 Astir CS	1145	BGA 3753-GDQ D-7229	16.11.07	P Lowe and R Bostock	Seighford	28. 9.08
G-CGDS	Schleicher ASW 15B	15205	BGA 3755-GDS D-0902	9. 1.08	B Birk and P A Crouch	Ringmer	17. 2.08
G-CGDT	Schleicher ASW 24	24120	BGA 3756-GDT	19. 2.08	R D Mcvean tr Tango 54 Syndicate	Chipping	4. 4.08
G-CGDU	Schleicher ASW 24	24118	BGA 3757-GDU	21. 9.07	G J Moore	Dunstable	28. 9.08
G-CGDX	Schempp-Hirth Discus CS	023CS	BGA 3760-GDX	3.10.07	Coventry Gliding Club Ltd t/a The Gliding Centre "HB2"	Husbands Bosworth	28. 9.08
G-CGDY	Schleicher ASW 15B	15220	BGA 3761-GDY D-0947	13.12.07	G A Stewart tr Cloud Nine Syndicate	Bidford	20. 2.08
G-CGDZ	Schleicher ASW 24	24116	BGA 3762-GDZ	5.12.07	J M Norman tr 24 Group	Pocklington	1. 4.08
G-CGEL	PZL-Bielsko SZD-50-3 Puchacz	B-20308	BGA 3772-GEL	3. 1.08	The Northumbria Gliding Club Ltd	Currock Hill	7. 5.08
G-CGEP	Schempp-Hirth Standard Cirrus	205G	BGA 3775-GEP D-0917	14.12.07	D J Bundock	Wycombe Air Park	30. 3.08
G-CGGG	Robinson R44 Astro	0626	G-SJDI	24. 8.07	R D Masters	Standalone Farm, Meppershall	31. 7.08E
G-CGHM	Piper PA-28-140 Cruiser	28-7425143	PH-NSM N9614N	25. 4.79	A Reay	Caernarfon	10. 2.07T
G-CGIJ	Agusta AW139	31203		27. 2.08	CHC Scotia Ltd *(Operated Marine and Coastguard Agency)*	Lee-on-Solent	
G-CGMU	Sikorsky S-92A	920034	N8010S	5. 6.07	CHC Scotia Ltd *(Operated HM Coastguard)*	Stornoway	14. 6.08E
G-CGOC	Sikorsky S-92A	920051	N45165	30.11.07	CHC Scotia Ltd	Aberdeen	
G-CGOD	Cameron N-77 Balloon (Hot Air)	2647		5. 9.91	G P Lane "Neptune"	Waltham Abbey	12. 8.05A
G-CGRD	Cirrus SR22	2234	N613SR	16. 2.07	Craigard Property Trading Ltd	Goodwood	22. 2.08E
G-CGRI	Agusta A109S Grand	22003	I-RAID	3. 8.05	C G Roach	Liskeard Heliport	2. 8.08E
G-CGWB	Agusta AW139			4.08R	CHC Scotia Ltd *(Operated Marine and Coastguard Agency)*	Portland	
G-CGWD	Robinson R44 Raven	1695		23. 3.07	J M Henderson	Newtownards	11. 4.08E

G-CHAA - G-CHZZ

G-CHAB	Schleicher Ka 6CR	6596	BGA 3778-HAB D-1596	12.10.07	P Saunders	Usk	18. 1.08
G-CHAD	Aeroprakt A22 Foxbat *(Built D Winsper)*	PFA 317-13909		30. 4.02	R A Neal tr DJB Foxbat	Otherton, Cannock	19. 7.08P
G-CHAF	PZL-Bielsko SZD-50-3 Puchacz	B-2031	BGA 3782-HAF	29.11.07	J G Kosak tr Seahawk Gliding Club	RNAS Culdrose	13. 3.08
G-CHAH	Europa Aviation Europa XS *(Built T Higgins - pr.no.PFA 247-12949)*	252		14. 6.04	T Higgins	Welshpool	18.11.07P
G-CHAI	Bombardier CL-600-2B16 *(CL-601-3R Challenger)*	5152	G-FBFI N601FB, G-FBFI, N388PG, (N933PG), N18RF, N605BA, VP-COJ, VR-COJ, N777XX, C-GLWX	9.10.07	Hangar 8 Ltd	Oxford	20. 1.08E
G-CHAM	Cameron Pot 90 SS Balloon (Hot Air) *(Chambourcy Pot shape)*	2912		29. 9.92	B J Reeves and C Walker t/a High Exposure Balloons "Yogpot"	Brighouse	7. 6.08A
G-CHAN	Robinson R22 Beta	3794		16. 3.05	Artall Air LLP	Panshanger	17. 4.08E
G-CHAO	Rolladen-Schneider LS 6b	6150	BGA 3791-HAQ D-8079	30.11.07	A R J Hughes	Wycombe Air Park	13. 4.08
G-CHAP	Robinson R44 Astro	0326		9. 4.97	Brierley Lifting Tackle Company Ltd	Halfpenny Green	10. 5.08E
G-CHAR	Grob G109B	6435		21. 5.86	T M Holloway tr RAF Gliding and Soaring Association *(Operated RAFGSA Chilterns Centre)*	RAF Halton	7. 5.08E
G-CHAS	Piper PA-28-181 Archer II	28-8090325	N82228	18. 3.91	C H Elliott	Stapleford	20. 6.08E
G-CHAX	Schempp-Hirth Standard Cirrus	2	BGA 3798-HAX ZS-GHZ, ZS-TIM, ZS-GGR, D-0302	21.11.07	C Keating and R Jarvis	Rivar Hill	28. 4.08
G-CHAY	Rolladen-Schneider LS7	7154	BGA 3799-HAY	28. 2.08	N J Leaton	Gransden Lodge	19. 3.08
G-CHBA	Rolladen-Schneider LS7	7156	BGA 3801-HBA D-6041	29.10.07	P O'Donald	Gransden Lodge	28. 9.08
G-CHBB	Schleicher ASW 24	24132	BGA 3802-HBB	3.12.07	London Gliding Club Proprietary Ltd	Dunstable	28. 9.08
G-CHBC	Rolladen-Schneider LS6-c	6209	BGA 3803-HBC D-xxxx	20.10.07	R Crowden	Talgarth	28. 9.08

Reg	Type	c/n	Prev id	Date	Owner/Operator	Base	Date
G-CHBD	Glaser-Dirks DG-200	2-12	BGA 3804-HBD HB-1384	29. 8.07	D A Clempson	Portmoak	28. 9.08
G-CHBE	DG Flugzeugbau DG-300 Elan	3E237	BGA 3805-HBE SE-UFB	12.11.07	G Dixon and M J Weston tr DG 356 Group	Aston Down	28. 9.08
G-CHBG	Schleicher ASW 24	24133	BGA 3807-HBG	14. 2.08	Imperial College of Science, Technology and Medicine	Lasham	25. 3.08
G-CHBH	Grob G103C Twin III Acro	36006	BGA 3808-HBH	14. 2.08	Imperial College of Science, Technology and Medicine	Lasham	3. 3.08
G-CHBT	Grob G102 Astir CS Jeans	2235	BGA 3819-HBT PH-675	20.12.07	M D Evans tr Astir Syndicate	Darlton	23. 3.08
G-CHBV	Schempp-Hirth Nimbus 2B	143	BGA 3821-HBV D-7850	22. 2.08	G J Evison, J Lynas and R Strerup	Sutton Bank	11. 4.08
G-CHCM	Eurocopter EC.225LP Super Puma	2675		21.12.07	CHC Scotia Ltd	Aberdeen	
G-CHBU	Centrair ASW 20F	20527	BGA 3820-HBU F-CFSI	2.11.07	R Williams	Ringmer	28. 4.08
G-CHCD	Sikorsky S-76A II Plus	760101	OY-HEZ	16. 1.98	CHC Scotia Ltd	North Denes Heliport	28.11.07E
	G-CHCD, G-CBJB, N288SP, C-GIMN, YV-326C						
G-CHCF	Eurocopter AS.332L2 Super Puma	2567		30.11.01	CHC Scotia Ltd	Aberdeen	15. 1.08E
G-CHCG	Eurocopter AS.332L2 Super Puma	2592		1. 7.03	CHC Scotia Ltd	Aberdeen	23. 7.08E
G-CHCH	Eurocopter AS.332L2 Super Puma	2601		16.12.03	CHC Scotia Ltd	Aberdeen	26. 1.08E
G-CHCI	Eurocopter AS.332L2 Super Puma	2395	LN-OHD F-WQDN	30. 9.05	CHC Scotia Ltd	Aberdeen	29. 9.07E
G-CHCK	Sikorsky S-92A	920030	N8001N	28. 2.06	CHC Scotia Ltd	Aberdeen	30. 3.08E
G-CHCL	Eurocopter EC.225 LP Super Puma	2674	F-WWOS	14.11.07	CHC Scotia Ltd	Aberdeen	
G-CHCM	Eurocopter EC.225 LP Super Puma	2675	F-WWOV	21.12.07	CHC Scotia Ltd	Aberdeen	
G-CHCP	Agusta AB139	31046	PH-IEH	12. 9.06	CHC Scotia Ltd	Aberdeen	12. 9.08E
G-CHCT	Agusta AB139	31042	PH-TRH	13. 7.06	CHC Scotia Ltd	North Denes	13. 7.08E
G-CHCV	Agusta AW139	41005	N106AW	17. 1.08	CHC Scotia Ltd	Aberdeen	
G-CHDA	Pilatus B4-PC11AF	17	BGA 3851-HDA D-0964	13. 2.08	F P and C M E Bois	Lasham	5. 6.08
G-CHDB	PZL-Bielsko SZD-51-1 Junior	B-1997	BGA 3852-HDB	24. 9.07	Stratford on Avon Gliding Club Ltd	Snitterfield	12. 1.08
G-CHDD	Centrair 101B Pégase 90	101B0425	BGA 3854-HDD	30.10.07	P M Weston tr 591 Glider Syndicate	Gransden Lodge	28. 9.08
G-CHDE	Pilatus B4-PC11AF	223	BGA 3855-HDE VH-XOZ, VH-WQP	25. 1.08	A A Jenkins	Wycombe Air Park	5. 5.08
G-CHDJ	Schleicher ASW 20CL	20828	BGA 3859-HDJ D-8442	6. 2.08	G E G Lambert and L M M Sebreights	Weelde, Belgium	30. 4.08
G-CHDL	Schleicher ASW 20	20082	BGA 3861-HDL D-1617, OH-495	14. 2.08	C R Faulkner tr 137 Syndicate	Currock Hill	21. 5.08
G-CHDN	Schleicher K 8B	2	BGA 3863-HDN D-8017	14. 2.08	Upward Bound Trust	Thame	28. 4.08
G-CHDY	Schleicher K 8B	8277	BGA 3873-HDY D-4094	7. 2.08	V Mallon	Kleve-Wisseler, Germany	13. 4.08
G-CHDP	PZL-Bielsko SZD-50-3 Puchacz	B-2050	BGA 3864-HDP	23. 1.08	D J Marpole tr Heron Gliding Club	RNAS Yeovilton	30. 3.08
G-CHDR	DG Flugzeugbau DG-300 Elan	3E95	BGA 3866-HDR RAFGSA R30	7. 1.08	R Robins	Pocklington	22. 1.08
G-CHDX	Rolladen-Schneider LS7-WL	7161	BGA 3872-HDX	23. 1.08	D Holborn and R T Halliburton	Pocklington	15. 3.08
G-CHDU	PZL-Bielsko SZD-51-1 Junior	B-1996	BGA 3869-HDU	18.10.07	Cambridge Gliding Club Ltd	Gransden Lodge	28. 9.08
G-CHEB	Europa Aviation Europa	263		16. 9.96	P Whittingham	Sittles Farm, Alrewas	9.11.07P
	(Built C H P Bell - pr.no.PFA 247-12967) (NSI EA-81/100)						
G-CHEC	PZL-Bielsko SZD-55-1 Promyk	551191019	BGA 3877-HEC	1.11.07	D Pye	Challock	24. 4.08
G-CHEF	DG Flugzeugbau DG-500 Elan Trainer	5E53T20	BGA 3880-HEF	17. 1.08	Yorkshire Gliding Club (Proprietary) Ltd	Sutton Bank	20. 3.08
G-CHEH	Rolladen-Schneider LS7-WL	7163	BGA 3882-HEH D-6078	17. 9.07	P Candler	Dunstable	30. 1.08
G-CHEJ	Schleicher ASW 15B	15441	BGA 3883-HEJ D-6871	20.11.07	A F F Webb	Wycombe Air Park	11. 1.08
G-CHEK	PZL-Bielsko SZD-51-1 Junior	B-2009	BGA 3884-HEK BGA 3893-HEU, (BGA 3884-HEK)	11.12.07	Cambridge Gliding Club Ltd	Gransden Lodge	16. 3.08
G-CHEL	Colt 77B Balloon (Hot Air)	4823		18. 5.00	Chelsea Financial Services PLC (Chelsea Financial Service titles)	Chalford, Stroud	7. 7.08A
G-CHEM	Piper PA-34-200T Seneca II	34-8170032	N8292Y	26. 8.87	London Executive Aviation Ltd	Stapleford	27. 2.08E
G-CHEN	Schempp-Hirth Discus b	422	BGA 3887-HEN	22.12.07	M D Kerley tr G-CHEN Group	Challock	8. 3.08
G-CHEO	Schleicher ASW 20	20410	BGA 3889-HEQ D-6747	4.12.07	P Morrison tr The Eleven Group	North Hill	27. 2.08
G-CHEP	PZL-Bielsko SZD-50-3 Puchacz	B-2057	BGA 3888- HEP	28. 2.08	Peterborough & Spalding Gliding Club Ltd	Crowland	5. 4.08
G-CHER	Piper PA-38-112 Tomahawk II	38-82A0004	G-BVBL N91339	19.12.00	C L Goodsell (Operated Central Aviation Training School)	Halfpenny Green	15. 5.08E
G-CHES	Pilatus Britten-Norman BN-2A-21 Islander	2011	EI-IPC	19. 4.94	Auxiliar de Actividades Aerea SL	(Barcelona, Spain)	29 .7.08E
	G-CHES, G-PASY, G-BPCB, G-BEXA, G-MALI, (ZB503), G-DIVE, G-BEXA						
G-CHET	Europa Aviation Europa XS	376		12. 2.98	H H R Lagache	Leicester	19. 4.08P
	(Built C R Arkle - pr.no.PFA 247-13277) (Rotax 914-UL) (Tri-gear u/c)						
G-CHEY	Piper PA-31T2 Cheyenne IIXL	31T-8166033	N67PD N42NE, N42ND, N59WA, N9092Y	27. 7.05	Air Medical Fleet Ltd	Oxford	16.10.07P
G-CHEZ	Pilatus Britten-Norman BN-2B-20 Islander	2234	9M-TAM G-BSAG	30. 4.01	The Cheshire Police Authority	Hawarden	11. 8.08T
G-CHFB	Schleicher Ka 6CR	6344SI	BGA 3900-HFB D-5825	12.11.07	P J Galloway	Rhigos	25. 9.07
G-CHFF	Schempp-Hirth Standard Cirrus	539	BGA 3904-HFF D-8916	2.11.07	R S Morrisroe tr Foxtrot 2 Group	Upwood	4. 4.08
G-CHFH	PZL-Bielsko SZD-50-3 Puchacz	B-2059	BGA 3906-HFH	18.12.07	Trent Valley Aerotowing Club Ltd	Kirton-in-Lindsey	6. 3.08
G-CHFV	Schempp-Hirth Ventus b-16.6	204	BGA 3918-HFV D-5235	5.12.07	A Cliffe and B Pearson	Seighford	4. 4.08
G-CHFX	Schempp-Hirth Nimbus 4T	12	BGA 3920-HFX	7.11.07	R Jones	Lasham	26. 3.08

G-CHFY	Schempp-Hirth Ventus cT	168	BGA 3921-HFY	21.12.07	D J Ellis and M Day	Lasham	28. 9.08
			(BGA 3916-HFT), (BGA 3867-HDS)				
G-CHGB	Grob G102 Astir CS	1356	BGA 3924-HGB	13. 2.08	A A M Wahlberg, G Clark and P Hollamby		
			D-7386			Lee-on-Solent	11. 9.08
	(Rebuilt with wings and components from RAFGGA 507)						
G-CHGG	Schempp-Hirth Standard Cirrus	362	BGA 3929-HGG	28. 1.08	N P Holifield	(Bicester)	21. 3.08
			HB-1172				
G-CHGK	Schempp-Hirth Discus bT	96/435	BGA 3932-HGK	29.10.07	C C Redrup tr HGK Syndicate	Lasham	28. 9.08
G-CHGL	Bell 206B-2 JetRanger II	1669	EI-WSN	29. 4.98	Engineaward Ltd	(Westbury)	14.10.08E
			G-CHGL, G-BPNG, G-ORTC, G-BPNG, N20EA, C-GHVB				
G-CHGR	Sportline Aviacija LAK-12 Lietuva	6186	BGA 3938-HGR	21. 9.07	F R and R G Stevens	Husbands Bosworth	28. 9.08
G-CHGS	Schempp-Hirth Discus b	439	BGA 3939-HGS	8.10.07	M J Armes tr G-CHGS Syndicate	Lasham	28. 9.08
G-CHGT	FFA Diamant 16.5	40	BGA 3940-HGT	15. 1.08	E Gibson and R.W.Collins	Burn	30. 4.08
			HB-929				
G-CHGV	DG Flugzeugbau DG-500/22 Elan	5E70S11	BGA 3942-HGV	12.11.07	A J Hulme tr Hotel Golf Victor Syndicate		
						Gransden Lodge	14. 1.08
G-CHGW	Centrair ASW 20F	20102	BGA 3943	23. 8.07	M Dixon	Nympsfield	3.11.07
			F-CFFB				
G-CHGZ	Schempp-Hirth Discus bT	95-434	BGA 3946-HGZ	23. 1.08	S H Baker tr HUA Syndicate	Lasham	6. 3.08
G-CHHE	PZL-Bielsko SZD-51-1 Junior	B-2008	BGA 3951-HHE	21. 9.07	Bowland Forest Gliding Club Ltd	Chipping	28. 9.08
G-CHHH	Rolladen-Schneider LS6-c	6289	BGA 3954-HHH	18.10.07	P H Rackham	Dunstable	28. 9.08
G-CHHK	Schleicher ASW 19B	19384	BGA 3956-HHK	29.11.07	M Walker	Burn	11. 5.07
			ZD661, BGA 2897-ERT				
G-CHHM	Sportline Aviacija LAK-12 Lietuva	6195	BGA 3958-HHM	24.10.07	D Martin	(Bordeaux, France)	17. 1.08
G-CHHO	Schempp-Hirth Discus bT	106/453	BGA 3961-HHO	30.10.07	P J Tratt and M Davis tr 97Z Syndicate	Parham Park	27. 3.08
G-CHHR	PZL-Bielsko SZD-55-1 Promyk	551191020	BGA 3962-HHR	27. 9.07	R T and G Starling	Nympsfield	28. 9.08
G-CHHS	Schleicher ASW 20	20008	BGA 3963-HHS	8. 2.08	D Britt and P J Rocks	Kirton-in-Lindsey	1. 4.08
			SE-TTU				
G-CHHT	Rolladen-Schneider LS6-c	6292	BGA 3964-HHT	13.11.07	G O Humphries	Kingston Deverill	1. 3.08
G-CHHU	Rolladen-Schneider LS6-c	6296	BGA 3965-HHU	17. 8.07	J S Weston	Bellarena	28. 9.08
G-CHHW	Sportline Aviacija LAK-12 Lietuva	6212	BGA 3967-HHW	8.12.07	A J Dibdin	Dunstable	4. 3.08
G-CHIK	Reims Cessna F152 II	F15201628	G-BHAZ	19.10.81	Stapleford Flying Club Ltd	Stapleford	7.12.07T
			(D-EHLE)				
G-CHIP	Piper PA-28-181 Archer II	28-8290095	N81337	22. 2.82	J A Divis	(Angmering, Littlehampton)	14. 6.08E
G-CHIS	Robinson R22 Beta	1740		5. 4.91	Staffordshire Helicopters Ltd	Tatenhill	1. 4.08E
G-CHIX	Robin DR.500-200i Président	0036	F-GXGD	29.11.01	P A and R Stephens	Moor Farm, West Haslerton	10. 1.08E
	(Officially regd as DR.400-500)		F-WQPN				
G-CHJA	VFW-Fokker FK-3	0008	BGA 3971-HJA	14.12.07	M A Johnson	Sackville Lodge, Riseley	17. 3.08
			D-0409				
G-CHJC	Rolladen-Schneider LS6-c	6290	BGA 3973-HJC	25.10.07	F J Davies and I C Woodhouse	Husbands Bosworth	28. 9.08
G-CHJF	Rolladen-Schneider LS6-c	6291	BGA 3976-HJF	17.10.07	J L Bridge	Gransden Lodge	28. 9.08
G-CHJH	Schempp-Hirth Discus bT	65	BGA 3978-HJH	29. 1.08	J C Leonard tr Hotel Juliet Hotel Group	Bembridge	25. 4.08
			N224WT				
G-CHJL	Schempp-Hirth Discus bT	105/451	BGA 3981-HJL	16.10.07	M J Huddart	Saltby	28. 9.08
G-CHJP	Schleicher Ka 6CR	616	BGA 3985-HJQ	4.1.08	D M Cornelius	Dunstable	5. 5.08
			OH-210, OH-RSB				
G-CHJR	Glasflügel H201B Standard Libelle	102	BGA 3986-HJR	14. 2.08	B O Marcham and B Magnani	Tibenham	29. 5.08
			SE-TIO				
G-CHJY	Schempp-Hirth Standard Cirrus	459	BGA 3992-HJY	19. 2.08	J M Hogbin tr The Cirrus Group	Currock Hill	28. 7.08
			HB-1207				
G-CHKA	Schempp-Hirth Discus CS	120CS	BGA 3994-HKA	12.10.07	R W and M P Weaver	Usk	13.12.07
G-CHKB	Grob G102 Astir CS77	1658	BGA 3995-HKB	19. 2.08	R Peach tr G-CHKB Group	RAF Keevil	5. 4.08
			D-7491				
G-CHKC	Schempp-Hirth Standard Cirrus	520G	BGA 3996-HKC	11.12.07	The Welland Gliding Club Ltd	Lyveden	1. 5.08
			D-3268				
G-CHKD	Schempp-Hirth Standard Cirrus	576G	BGA 3997-HKD	12.11.07	A Liran and M Truelove	Rivar Hill	24. 4.08
			F-CEMF				
G-CHKK	Schleicher K 8 B	8886	BGA 4003-HKK	7.12.07	W Rossmann tr HKK Syndicate	Drumshade	3. 4.08
			D-0866				
G-CHKN	Air Création 582(1)/Kiss 400	FL002/134		18. 9.01	D A Edwards	Deenethorpe	13. 3.08P
	(Built I Tomkins - pr.no.BMAA/HB/183 being Flylight kit comprising Trike s/n xxxxx and Wing s/n xxxx)						
G-CHKR	Jastreb Standard Cirrus G/81	276	BGA 4009-HKR	22. 1.08	N White and S Crozier	Crowland	30. 5.08
			OH-663				
G-CHKS	Jastreb Standard Cirrus G/81	361	BGA 4010-HKS	6. 2.08	G G Butler	Snitterfield	1. 4.08
			SE-TZS				
G-CHKV	Scheibe Zugvögel IIIB	1034	BGA 4013-HKV	31. 1.08	Dartmoor Gliding Society	Brenttor	11. 9.08
			D-8294				
G-CHKX	Rolladen-Schneider LS4-b	4933	BGA 4015-HKX	3.10.07	D J Hughes tr HKX Group	Long Mynd	19. 2.08
G-CHKY	Schempp-Hirth Discus b	461	BGA 4016-HKY	30.11.07	C V Hill and O J Anderson	Bellarena	3. 4.08
G-CHLC	Pilatus B4-PC11AF	177	BGA 4020-HLC	25. 2.08	E A Lockhart	Lasham	2. 5.08
			SE-UFX, OH-455				
G-CHLL	Lindstrand LBL 90A Balloon (Hot Air)	941		7. 1.04	P J Hollingsworth	Grappenhall, Warrington	12. 4.08A
					(www.churchill.com titles)		
G-CHLM	Schleicher ASW 19B	19269	BGA 4029-HLM	14. 2.08	R A Colbeck	Dunstable	24. 5.05
			OH-538				
G-CHLN	Schempp-Hirth Discus CS	143CS	BGA 4030-HLN	28. 1.08	T World tr Portsmouth Naval Gliding Centre		
						Lee-on-Solent	6. 4.07
G-CHLP	Schleicher ASK 21	21597	BGA 4031-HLP	9.11.07	Southdown Gliding Club Ltd	Parham Park	25. 3.08
G-CHLS	Schempp-Hirth Discus b	114	BGA 4034-HLS	7. 9.07	R A Lennard	Dunstable	8. 1.08
			RAFGSA R11				
G-CHLV	Schleicher ASW 19B	19325	BGA 4038-HLW	18.12.07	P J Belcher and R I Brickwood	Gransden Lodge	15. 1.08
			D-8799				
G-CHLX	Schleicher ASH 25	25124	BGA 4039-HLX	21.12.07	P Armstrong tr HLX Group	Husbands Bosworth	9. 3.08
			D-3988				

G-CHLY	Schempp-Hirth Discus CS	161CS	BGA 4040-HLY	17. 1.08	T Barton	Talgarth	14. 4.08
G-CHMA	PZL-Bielsko SZD-51-1 Junior	B-2132	BGA 4042-HMA	2.10.07	Coventry Gliding Club Ltd t/a The Gliding Centre		
						Husbands Bosworth	15. 1.08
G-CHMB	DG Flugzeugbau DG-300 Elan	3E105	BGA 4043-HMB	15.11.07	A D and P Langlands	Edgehill	31. 1.08
			D-4676				
G-CHMK	Rolladen-Schneider LS6-18W	6324	BGA 4046-HMK	16.10.07	A S Decloux	Gransden Lodge	11. 3.08
			D-1245				
G-CHMM	Jastreb Glasflügel 304B	322	BGA 4048-HMM	3.12.07	A P Cullen tr Delta 19 Group	Husbands Bosworth	20.12.07
			SE-UGZ, D-1005				
G-CHMO	Schempp-Hirth Discus CS	099CS	BGA 4051-HMO	23.10.07	S Barter	Ringmer	28. 9.08
			D-7160				
G-CHMT	Glasflügel H303 Mosquito B	153	BGA 4054-HMT	29.10.07	R J Pirie and J Taberham	North Hill	28. 9.08
			F-CEDY				
G-CHMU	CARMAM JP-15/36AR Aiglon	22	BGA 4055-HMU	20.11.07	J R Holmes tr HMU Syndicate	Kingston Deverill	9. 3.08
			F-CETT				
G-CHMX	Rolladen-Schneider LS4-a	4230	BGA 4058-HMX	15. 1.08	J M Hall and P Shuttleworth	Long Mynd	16. 4.08
			OO-ZNN, F-CEIO				
G-CHMY	Schempp-Hirth Standard Cirrus	121	BGA 4059-HMY	20. 2.08	D Nisbet tr HMY Syndicate		
			HB-1034			RAF Weston-on-the-Green	2. 5.08
G-CHNA	DG Flugzeugbau DG-500/20 Elan	5E128W3	BGA 4061-HNA	30.11.07	M S Armstrong tr G-CHNA Group	Camphill	28. 9.08
G-CHNC	Schleicher ASW 19B	19297	BGA 4063-HNC	9.11.07	T J Highton	Tibenham	4. 4.08
			OH-515				
G-CHNF	Schempp-Hirth Duo Discus	11	BGA 4066-HNF	15.10.07	Booker Gliding Club Ltd	Wycombe Air Park	28. 9.08
G-CHNH	Schempp-Hirth HS.5 Nimbus 2C	187	BGA 4068-HNH	27.11.07	R J Hart	Tibenham	6. 2.08
			D-2830				
G-CHNK	PZL-Bielsko SZD-51-1 Junior	B-1496	BGA 4070-HNK	15.10.07	Booker Gliding Club Ltd	Wycombe Air Park	28. 9.08
			SP-3299, (SP-3290)		"HNK"		
G-CHNM	Jastreb Standard Cirrus G-81	360	BGA 4072-HNM	30.11.07	N C Harrison tr Harrison Pozerskis Group		
			SE-TZT			Husbands Bosworth	9. 4.08
G-CHNU	Schempp-Hirth Nimbus 4DT	3/5	BGA 4079-HNU-	20. 9.07	D E Findon	Bidford	28. 9.08
			D-KHIA				
G-CHNV	Rolladen-Schneider LS4-b	4960	BGA 4080-HNV	2.11.07	P H Dixon and S K Armstrong	Kirton-in-Lindsey	2. 5.08
G-CHNW	Schempp-Hirth Duo Discus	25	BGA 4081-HNW	23.10.07	W J Head tr G-CHNW Group	Gransden Lodge	21. 3.08
G-CHNZ	Centrair 101A Pégase	101032	BGA 4084-HNZ	26.10.07	R H Partington	Milfield	19. 2.08
			F-CFRY				
G-CHOM	Schempp-Hirth Discus b	44	BGA 4120-HQM	25.10.07	Cambridge Gliding Club Ltd	Gransden Lodge	28. 9.08
G-CHOP	Westland-Bell 47G-3B1	WA/380	XT221	19.12.78	Classic Rotors Ltd	(Thruxton)	20. 3.08E
G-CHOR	Schempp-Hirth Discus b	531	BGA 4123-HQR	25. 2.08	A Twigg and L Brandt	Bicester	31. 3.08
G-CHOV	PZL-Bielsko SZD-51-1 Junior	B-2139	BGA 4127-HQV	5.10.07	Coventry Gliding Club Ltd t/a The Gliding Centre		
					"HQV"	Husbands Bosworth	28. 9.08
G-CHOW	Schempp-Hirth Discus b	538	BGA 4128-HQW	29. 8.07	M H Hardwick	Wycombe Air Park	13.11.07
G-CHOX	Europa Aviation Europa XS	566		2. 4.03	Chocks Away Ltd	(Chertsey)	
	(Built P Field - pr.no.PFA 247-13974)						
G-CHOY	Schempp-Hirth Mini Nimbus C	113	BGA 4130-HQY	18.10.07	A H Sparrow	Rivar Hill	26. 2.08
			D-3364				
G-CHOZ	Rolladen-Schneider LS6-18W	6353	BGA 4131-HQZ	18. 1.08	R E Scott	(Henfield)	21. 1.08
			D-1486				
G-CHPA	Robinson R22 Beta	3442	EI-EHC	18. 4.07	Rivermead Aviation Ltd	(Vaud, Switzerland)	27 .8.08E
			N71850				
G-CHPC	Schleicher ASW 20CL	20787	BGA 4087-HPC	4. 1.08	B L Liddiard and P J Willimiams		
			D-3424		(Eastbourne) and Ninfield, Battle		27. 3.08
G-CHPD	Rolladen-Schneider LS6-c18	6331	BGA 4088-HPD	29.10.07	S A Hughes and J A Kane	Sutton Bank	28. 9.08
			D-1054				
G-CHPE	Schleicher ASK 13	13510	BGA 4089-HPE	23. 1.08	Dumfries and District Gliding Club	Falgunzeon	13. 7.08
			D-3992				
G-CHPH	Schempp-Hirth Discus CS	174CS	BGA 4092-HPH	26.11.07	A D Johnson and J E Kelk	Wormingford	8. 5.08
G-CHPL	Rolladen-Schneider LS4-b	4959	BGA 4095-HPL	9.11.07	Southdown Gliding Club Ltd	Parham Park	30. 1.08
			(BGA 4071-HNL)				
G-CHPO	Schleicher Ka 6 CR	6200	BGA 4099-HPQ	26.11.07	A and M Ewer	Crowland	23. 3.08
			D-1933				
G-CHPR	Robinson R22 Beta	3854		25. 5.05	Neptune Property Developments Ltd	Sywell	27. 6.08E
G-CHPT	Fedorov Me7 Mechta	M006	BGA 4102-HPT	8. 2.08	A E Griffiths	Long Mynd	4. 4.08
G-CHPV	Schleicher ASK 21	21608	BGA 4104-HPV	27.11.07	Scottish Gliding Union Ltd	Portmoak	28. 9.08
G-CHPW	Schleicher ASK 21	21609	BGA 4105-HPW	2.11.07	Scottish Gliding Union Ltd	Portmoak	28. 9.08
G-CHPX	Schempp-Hirth Discus CS	177CS	BGA 4106-HPX	14.11.07	M A Whitehead tr G-CHPX Group	Gransden Lodge	28. 9.08
G-CHPY	de Havilland DHC-1 Chipmunk 22	C1/0093	WB652	7. 3.97	Devonair Executive Business Transport Ltd		
						Little Rissington	6. 7.08T
G-CHRA	Grob G102 Astir CS	1109	BGA 4132-HRA	29. 1.08	T World tr Portsmouth Naval Gliding Centre		
			D-4169			Lee-on-Solent	29. 3.08
G-CHRB	Sportline Aviacija LAK-12 Lietuva	6223	BGA 4133-HRB	15.10.07	J E Nevill	Aboyne	28. 9.08
G-CHRC	DG Flugzeugbau DG-500/22 Elan	5E136W5	BGA 4134-HRC	10.10.07	D Rhys-Jones tr DG500-390 Syndicate	Parham Park	24. 4.08
G-CHRG	PZL-Bielsko SZD-51-1 Junior	B-2013	BGA 4138-HRG	17. 1.08	Scottish Gliding Union Ltd	Portmoak	3. 6.08
			B-2013				
G-CHRN	Schleicher ASK 18	18026	BGA 4143-HRN	3.10.07	Stratford on Avon Gliding Club Ltd	Snitterfield	9. 3.08
			HB-1308				
G-CHRS	Schempp-Hirth Discus CS	100CS	BGA 4147-HRS	25.10.07	M E Hughes	Husbands Bosworth	14. 3.08
			D-5100				
G-CHRW	Schempp-Hirth Duo Discus	43	BGA 4151-HRW	17. 9.07	A J Davis tr 802 Syndicate	Nympsfield	28. 9.08
			(BGA 4160), BGA 4151-HRW				
G-CHRX	Schempp-Hirth Discus a	545	BGA 4152-HRX	21. 1.08	G S Bird & N Worrell	Lasham	15. 2.08
G-CHSA	Rolladen-Schneider LS6-18W	6361	BGA 4155-HSA	11.10.07	D A Benton	Snitterfield	11.10.07
G-CHSC	PZL-Bielsko SZD-50-3 Puchacz	B-2079	BGA 4157-HSC	8.11.07	British Gliding Association Ltd	Husbands Bosworth	5. 4.08
G-CHSD	Schempp-Hirth Discus b	258/1	BGA 4158-HSD	1.11.07	J R Reed tr G-CHSD Group	Dunstable	27. 3.08
			(BGA 4142-HRM)				

G-CHSE	Grob G102 Astir CS77	1635	BGA 4159-HSE 15. 1.08	A Mutch	Portmoak	8. 3.08
			RAFGSA R68, RAFGSA 548			
G-CHSM	Schleicher ASK 13	13145	BGA 4166-HSM- 24. 9.07	Stratford on Avon Gliding Club Ltd	Snitterfield	2. 3.08
			D-0168			
G-CHSN	Schleicher Ka 6CR	6218	BGA 4167-HSN 20.11.07	Needwood Forest Gliding Club Ltd	Cross Hayes	16. 2.08
			OO-ZZF, D-8546			
G-CHSO	Schempp-Hirth Discus b	99	BGA 4169-HSQ 10.12.07	Midland Gliding Club Ltd	Long Mynd	28. 9.08
			D2943			
G-CHSU	Eurocopter EC.135 T1	0079	4. 2.99	Thames Valley Police Authority	RAF Benson	12. 4.08T
				(Operated Chiltern Air Support Unit)		
G-CHSV	Schempp-Hirth Standard Cirrus	195	BGA 4174-HSV 29.11.07	C D Morrow	Rivar Hill	27. 4.06
			D-0785			
G-CHSW	Schempp-Hirth Duo Discus	48	BGA 4175-HSW 19.12.07	M P S Roberts	Gransden Lodge	28. 9.08
G-CHSX	Scheibe SF27A Zugvögel V	6031	BGA 4176-HSX 6.11.07	C Downes and G M Wright	Wormingford	7. 2.08
			SE-TDT			
G-CHTA	Grumman AA-5A Cheetah	AA5A-0631	G-BFRC 3. 3.86	T Hale	Biggin Hill	9. 4.08E
G-CHTB	Schempp-Hirth Janus	7	BGA 4180-HTB 20. 2.08	J B Maddison tr Janus G-CHTB Syndicate		
			D-3114		Kirton-in-Lindsey	1. 5.08
G-CHTD	Grob G102 Astir CS	1012	BGA 4182-HTD 7. 1.08	C R Little and T Hatton tr Tango Delta Group		
			D-6508		Halesland	8. 3.08
G-CHTE	Grob G102 Astir CS77	1716	BGA 4183-HTE 20.11.07	P R Crabb tr HTE Group	Challock	9. 4.08
			RAFGSA R82, RAFGSA 882			
G-CHTF	Sportline Aviacija LAK-12 Lietuva	6180	BGA 4184-HTF 19.12.07	N C Harrison and S Pozerskis Husbands Bosworth		30. 4.08
G-CHTG	RotorWay Executive 90	5118	G-BVAJ 19.11.99	G Cooper Calton Moor Farm, Ashbourne		1. 5.07P
	(Built Rotorbuild Helicopters Ltd) (RotorWay RI 162)					
G-CHTM	Rolladen-Schneider LS8-18	8036	BGA 4190-HTM 5.10.07	M J Chapman	Seighford	28. 9.08
G-CHTN	Schleicher ASW 22	22013	BGA 4191-HTN 17. 8.07	R C Hodge	Dunstable	23.10.07
			ZS-GLN			
G-CHTR	Grob G102 Astir CS	1190	BGA 4194-HTR 25.10.07	I P and D M Wright	Kingston Deverill	11. 3.08
			D-7307			
G-CHTS	Rolladen-Schneider LS8-18	8040	BGA 4195-HTS 23.10.07	A R Head and P Rowden	Gransden Lodge	27. 3.08
G-CHTU	Schempp-Hirth Cirrus	88	BGA 4197-HTU 19. 2.08	G V Higgins tr Open Cirrus Group	Burn	12. 4.08
			D-0478			
G-CHTV	Schleicher ASK 21	21624	BGA 4198-HTV 1. 2.08	Cambridge Gliding Club Ltd	Gransden Lodge	20. 3.08
			D-8355			
G-CHTY	LET L-13 Blanik	026318	BGA 4201-HTY 26.11.07	T Taberham tr North Devon Gliding Club Blanik Syndicate		
			LY-GDT, DOSAAF		Eaglescott	8. 6.08
G-CHUA	Schleicher ASW 19B	19091	BGA 4203-HUA 16. 1.08	G D Vaughan East Hardwick, Pontefract		5. 5.07
			D-3840			
G-CHUD	Schleicher ASK 13	13018	BGA 4206-HUD 12.10.07	London Gliding Club Proprietary Ltd	Dunstable	28. 9.08
			D-9203			
G-CHUF	Schleicher ASK 13	13109	BGA 4208-HUF 11.12.07	The Welland Gliding Club Ltd	Lyveden	25. 3.08
			OO-ZWE			
G-CHUG	Europa Aviation Europa	260	29. 7.96	C M Washington	Sleap	21.12.07P
	(Built C M Washington - pr.no.PFA 247-12960) (Monowheel u/c)					
G-CHUH	Schempp-Hirth Janus	15	BGA 4210-HUH 18. 1.08	R A Gardiner tr Janus D31 Syndicate		
			D-3116		(Uppingham, Oakham)	14. 7.08
G-CHUJ	Centrair ASW 20F	20170	BGA 4211-HUJ 3.10.07	D M Cornish tr HUJ Group	Rattlesden	30. 5.08
			F-CFLY			
G-CHUK	Cameron O-77 Balloon (Hot Air)	2773	6. 3.92	R Ashford	Petworth	11. 7.08A
G-CHUM	Robinson R44 Raven	0839	2. 8.00	Just Plane Trading Ltd Top Farm, Croydon, Royston		7. 9.08E
G-CHUN	Grob G102 Astir CS Jeans	2089	BGA 4215-HUN 3. 1.08	Staffordshire Gliding Club Ltd	Seighford	12. 3.08
			D-7531			
G-CHUO	Fedorov Me7 Mechta	M007	BGA 4217-HUQ 10. 1.08	E A Hull	Dunstable	9. 4.08
G-CHUR	Schempp-Hirth HS.2 Cirrus	12	BGA 4218-HUR 30.11.07	A F Thomas and M Rossiter	Talgarth	23. 4.08
			HB-927			
G-CHUT	Centrair ASW 20F	20187	BGA 4220-HUT 6. 9.07	G Macfadyen	Nympsfield	28. 9.08
			F-CEUQ			
G-CHUV	Rolladen-Schneider LS8-18	8056	BGA 4222-HUV 19.10.07	C P A Jeffery	Gransden Lodge	22. 3.08
			D-3823			
G-CHUU	Schleicher ASK 13	AB13527	BGA 4221-HUU 12.12.07	Upward Bound Trust	Thame	21. 9.08
			D-7506, D-8945			
G-CHUW	Rolladen-Schneider LS8-a	8058	BGA 4223-HUW 12.12.07	S E Bort tr S8 Group	Challock	17. 3.08
G-CHUY	Schempp-Hirth Ventus cT	84/329	BGA 4225-HUY 30. 8.07	M H and M N Challans	Lasham	28. 9.08
			D-KILZ			
G-CHUZ	Schempp-Hirth Discus bT	158/559	BGA 4226-HUZ 30.11.07	P A Gelsthorpe (Blackwater, Camberley)		1. 3.08
G-CHVE	Schempp-Hirth Ventus 2cT	8/19	BGA 4231-HVE 17. 8.07	R B Witter	Lleweni Parc	28. 9.08
			D-KHIA			
G-CHVF	Rolladen-Schneider LS8-18	8059	BGA 4232-HVF 23. 8.07	J Haigh and R B Coote	Parham Park	28. 9.08
			D-1683			
G-CHVK	Grob G102 Astir CS	1161	BGA 4236-HVK 10. 1.08	P G Goulding	Crowland	7. 5.08
			D-4182			
G-CHVL	Rolladen-Schneider LS8-18	8060	BGA 4237-HVL 19.10.07	M W Durham tr Cumulus Gliding Syndicate Bicester		30. 3.08
G-CHVP	Schleicher ASW 20	20374	BGA 4240-HVP 7. 1.08	E J P Smallbone tr 930 Syndicate	Lasham	13. 2.08
			D-1961			
G-CHVT	Schempp-Hirth Ventus 2b	37	BGA 4244-HVT 12.11.07	G Alison tr Victor Tango Group Wycombe Air Park		28. 9.08
G-CHVU	Rolladen-Schneider LS8-a	8066	BGA 4245-HVU 14. 1.08	B T Spreckley	(France)	20. 3.08
				(Operated European Soaring Club)		
G-CHVV	Rolladen-Schneider LS4-b	41009	BGA 4246-HVV 6.11.07	A J Bardgett	Milfield	28. 9.08
G-CHVW	Schleicher ASK 13	13431	BGA 4247-HVW 31. 1.08	Rattlesden Gliding Club Ltd	Rattlesden	17.12.07
			D-2140			
G-CHVX	Centrair ASW 20F	20528	BGA 4248-HVX 1.12.07	J A Castle	Hinton-in-the-Hedges	8. 4.08
			F-CFSJ			

G-CHVZ	Schempp-Hirth Standard Cirrus	567G	BGA 4250-HVZ	27.11.07	P H V Alexander tr ABC Soaring	(Glossop)	6. 4.08
			HB-1269				
G-CHWC	Glasflugel H201B Standard Libelle	310	BGA 4253-HWC	12.12.07	J C R Rogers tr Whiskey Charlie Group		
			HB-1076			RAF Cranwell	24. 8.08
G-CHWW	Grob G103A Twin II Acro	3658-K-27	BGA 4271-HWW	10.12.07	Crown Service Gliding Club	Lasham	27. 3.08
			OE-5285				
G-CHWH	Schempp-Hirth Ventus cT	182/599	BGA 4258-HWH	20. 8.07	H R Browning	Lasham	28. 9.08
			RAFGGA 506				
G-CHWL	Rolladen-Schneider LS8-a	8076	BGA 4261-HWL	18. 1.08	W M Coffee	Snitterfield	9. 2.08
G-CHWS	Rolladen-Schneider LS8-18	8080	BGA 4267-HWS	15.11.07	G A and H B Chalmers	Easterton	15. 2.08
G-CHWX	PZL-Bielsko SZD-59 Acro	B-2170	BGA 4272-HWX	16. 1.08	D W F Gosden	Talgarth	10. 8.08
G-CHXC	Rolladen-Schneider LS8-18	8094	BGA 4278-HXC	17.10.07	S M Smith	Gransden Lodge	28. 9.08
G-CHXD	Schleicher ASW 27	27030	BGA 4279-HXD	3.12.07	J Quartermaine and M Jerman	Wormingford	28. 9.08
G-CHXE	Schleicher ASW 19B	19053	BGA 4280-HXE	6.11.07	M Hargreaves and V Bettle	Wormingford	29. 5.08
			D-6699				
G-CHXH	Schempp-Hirth Discus b	573	BGA 4283-HXH	16.11.07	Deeside Gliding Club (Aberdeenshire) Ltd	Aboyne	28. 9.08
			BGA 4375-JBD, (BGA 4283-HXH)				
G-CHXJ	Schleicher ASK 13	13216	BGA 4284-HXJ	23.10.07	R Birch tr Cotswold Gliding Club	Aston Down	28. 9.08
			D-0417				
G-CHXO	Schleicher ASH 25B	25187	BGA 4290-HXQ	4.12.07	P Morrison tr The Eleven Group	North Hill	13. 3.08
			OH-874				
G-CHXP	Schleicher ASK 13	13023	BGA 4289-HXP	28.11.07	The Vale of the White Horse Gliding Centre Ltd		
			D-3656			Sandhill Farm, Shrivenham	7. 3.08
G-CHXR	Schempp-Hirth Ventus cT	88/333	BGA 4291-HXR	19.10.07	J W a'Court and M Benson	Lasham	28. 9.08
			D-KESH				
G-CHXT	Rolladen-Schneider LS 4a	4325	BGA 4293-HXT	3.12.07	B T Spreckley	Ontur, Spain	5. 4.08
			ZS-GNV		(Operated European Soaring Club)		
G-CHXU	Schleicher ASW 19B	19359	BGA 4294-HXU	1. 2.08	D P Binney	Pocklingtonn	7. 9.08
			SE-TXN				
G-CHXZ	Rolladen-Schneider LS4	4249	BGA 4299-HXZ	1. 2.08	E J Foggin, G N Turner and J D Huband		
			SE-TXF			Sandhill Farm, Shrivenham	8. 2.08
G-CHXV	Schleicher ASK 13	13080	BGA 4295-HXV	17.10.07	Aquila Gliding Club Ltd	Hinton-in-the-Hedges	20. 1.08
			D-5462				
G-CHXW	Rolladen-Schneider LS8-18	8097	BGA 4296-HXW	19.12.07	W Aspland	Wycombe Air Park	23. 3.08
G-CHXY	Grob G102 Astir CS Jeans	1781	BGA 4298-HXY	8. 1.08	G W Powell	Edgehill	25. 3.08
			D-7689				
G-CHYA	Rolladen-Schneider LS6c-18	6349	BGA 4300-HYA	5.11.07	R H Dixon	(Mere, Warminster)	2. 3.08
			D-2162				
G-CHYD	Schleicher ASW 24	24039	BGA 4303-HYD	20.11.07	E B Adlard	Long Mynd	5. 2.08
			OE-5460				
G-CHYE	DG Flugzeugbau DG-500 Elan Orion		BGA 4304-HYE	12. 9.07	The Bristol Gliding Club Proprietary Ltd	Nympsfield	9. 4.08
		5E167X22					
G-CHYF	Rolladen-Schneider LS8-18	8106	BGA 4305-HYF	26.10.07	R E Francis	Nympsfield	28. 9.08
G-CHYL	Robinson R22 Beta	1197		28.11.89	C M Gough-Cooper	(Macclesfield)	28. 4.08E
G-CHYR	Schleicher ASW 27	27013	BGA 4315-HYR	20.11.07	A P Brown and A R Hutchings	Dunstable	21. 2.07
G-CHYT	Schleicher ASK 21	21568	BGA 4317-HYT	29. 1.08	J W Sage tr Army Gliding Association		
			AGA20			Trenchard Lines, Upavon	7. 2.08
G-CHYW	Schleicher K 8B	8163A	BGA 4320-HYW	29. 2.08	Lincolnshire Gliding Club Ltd	Strubby	5. 4.08
			D-5316, D-3202				
G-CHYX	Schleicher K 8B	686	BGA 4321-HYX	8. 2.08	M Bacic tr Oxford University Gliding Club	Bicester	2. 2.08
			D-5742				
G-CHYY	Schempp-Hirth Nimbus 3dT	21	BGA 4322-HYY	6.11.07	A C Broadbridge tr The Nimbus 3 Group	Bidford	28. 9.08
			RAFGSA R26, D-KAFA				
G-CHZA	Schempp-Hirth Nimbus 3/24.5	94	BGA 4324-HZA	16.10.07	P J Kite tr 374 Syndicate	Lasham	13.12.07
			SE-UFO				
G-CHZD	Schleicher ASW 15B	15327	BGA 4327-HZD	4.12.07	C P Ellison and W C Davis	Rivar Hill	13. 4.08
			D-2191				
G-CHZE	Schempp-Hirth Discus CS	121CS	BGA 4328-HZE	27. 7.07	S B Marshall tr HZE Glider Syndicate	Portmoak	28. 9.08
			D-6946				
G-CHZG	Rolladen-Schneider LS8-18	8118	BGA 4330-HZG	15.11.07	M J and T J Webb	RAF Halton	22. 3.08
G-CHZJ	Schempp-Hirth Standard Cirrus	23	BGA 4332-HZJ	27.11.07	P Fletcher and R H D Adams	Edgehill	28. 3.08
			HB-981				
G-CHZM	Rolladen-Schneider LS4-a	4762	BGA 4335-HZM	15.11.07	B Toulson and J M Bevan	Husbands Bosworth	17. 3.08
			D-1394				
G-CHZN	Robinson R22 Beta	0884	G-GHZM	9. 4.99	Cloudbase Ltd	Welshpool	5. 4.08E
			G-FENI				
G-CHZO	Schleicher ASW 27	27018	BGA 4338-HZQ	23. 1.08	A A Gilmore	Husbands Bosworth	6. 4.08
			D-4499				
G-CHZR	Schleicher ASK 21	21079	BGA 4339-HZR	17.12.07	D J Brookman tr K21 HZR Group	Aston Down	29. 3.08
			D-4491				
G-CHZU	Schempp-Hirth Standard Cirrus	366	BGA 4342-HZU	28.11.07	N S Murning	Eyres Field	31. 1.08
			HB-1258, N71KW				
G-CHZY	Rolladen-Schneider LS4	4479	BGA 4346-HZY	7.11.07	N P Wedi	Wycombe Air Park	28. 9.08
			D-3458				
G-CHZZ	Schleicher ASW 20L	20353	BGA 4347-HZZ	6.11.07	C M Davey tr LD Syndicate	RAF Wittering	31. 5.08
			N727AM				

G-CIAA - G-CIZZ

G-CIAO	III Sky Arrow 650 T	PFA 298-13095		23. 7.97	G Arscott	Popham	21. 8.08P
	(Built J Hosier)						
G-CIAS	Pilatus Britten-Norman BN-2B-21 Islander	2162	HC-BNS	1. 5.91	Channel Island Air Search Ltd	Guernsey	11. 3.08E
			G-BKJM				

G-CIBO	Cessna 180K Skywagon	18053177	VH-JNS N19029	23. 7.04	CIBO Ops Ltd	Blue Tile Farm, Langham	22.10.07E
G-CICI	Cameron R-15 Gas/Balloon (Hot Air)	673	(N) G-CICI, (G-BIHP)	11.11.80	Noble Adventures Ltd	Bristol	5. 6.91P
G-CIDA	Robinson R44 Raven II	11611		19. 2.07	Warrenpark Ltd	(Tiverton)	8. 3.08E
G-CIDD	Bellanca 7ECA Citabria	1002-74	N86577	29.11.00	A and P West	Dunkeswell	4.11.10S
G-CIEL	Cessna 560XL Citation Excel	560-5247	N57RL N7RL, N51038	29. 4.05	Enerway Ltd *(Operated London Executive Aviation)*	London Stansted	9. 5.08E
G-CIFR	Piper PA-28-181 Cherokee Archer II	28-7790208	PH-MIT OO-HBB, N7654F	18. 6.97	Shropshire Aero Club Ltd	Sleap	4. 9.08E
G-CIGY	Westland-Bell 47G-3B1	WA/350	G-BGXP XT191	26.10.98	Heli-Highland Ltd	Glastullich Farm, Tain	24. 9.08E
G-CIRI	Cirrus SR20 GTS	1791	N473SR	15. 5.07	C D Palfreyman tr Cirrus Flyers Group	Turweston	16. 5.08E
G-CITJ	Cessna 525 CitationJet	525-0084	D-ITSV (N5092D)	23. 2.07	Centreline Air Charter Ltd	Bristol	1. 3.08E
G-CITR	Cameron Z-105 Balloon (Hot Air)	10278		22. 2.02	Flying Pictures Ltd *(Citroën C3 titles)*	Chilbolton, Stockbridge	19. 5.04A
G-CITY	Piper PA-31-350 Navajo Chieftain	31-7852136	N27741	12. 9.78	Woodgate Aviation (IoM) Ltd	Ronaldsway	21.12.06T
G-CIVA	Boeing 747-436	27092		19. 3.93	British Airways PLC	London Heathrow	18. 3.08E
G-CIVB	Boeing 747-436	25811	(G-BNLY)	15. 2.94	British Airways PLC	London Heathrow	14. 2.08E
G-CIVC	Boeing 747-436	25812	(G-BNLZ)	26. 2.94	British Airways PLC	London Heathrow	25. 2.08E
G-CIVD	Boeing 747-436	27349		14.12.94	British Airways PLC	London Heathrow	3. 8.08E
G-CIVE	Boeing 747-436	27350		20.12.94	British Airways PLC	London Heathrow	22. 8.08E
G-CIVF	Boeing 747-436	25434	(G-BNLY)	29. 3.95	British Airways PLC	London Heathrow	20. 9.08E
G-CIVG	Boeing 747-436	25813	N6009F	20. 4.95	British Airways PLC	London Heathrow	18. 4.08E
G-CIVH	Boeing 747-436	25809		23. 4.96	British Airways PLC	London Heathrow	22. 4.08E
G-CIVI	Boeing 747-436	25814		2. 5.96	British Airways PLC	London Heathrow	1. 5.08E
G-CIVJ	Boeing 747-436	25817		11. 2.97	British Airways PLC	London Heathrow	10. 9.08E
G-CIVK	Boeing 747-436	25818		28. 2.97	British Airways PLC	London Heathrow	30. 8.08E
G-CIVL	Boeing 747-436	27478		28. 3.97	British Airways PLC	London Heathrow	26.11.08E
G-CIVM	Boeing 747-436	28700		5. 6.97	British Airways PLC *(Change For Good titles)*	London Heathrow	4. 6.08E
G-CIVN	Boeing 747-436	28848		29. 9.97	British Airways PLC	London Heathrow	28. 9.08E
G-CIVO	Boeing 747-436	28849	N6046P	5.12.97	British Airways PLC	London Heathrow	4.12.08E
G-CIVP	Boeing 747-436	25850		17. 2.98	British Airways PLC	London Heathrow	16. 2.08E
G-CIVR	Boeing 747-436	25820		2. 3.98	British Airways PLC	London Heathrow	21. 2.08E
G-CIVS	Boeing 747-436	28851		13. 3.98	British Airways PLC	London Heathrow	12. 3.08E
G-CIVT	Boeing 747-436	25821	(G-CIVN)	20. 3.98	British Airways PLC	London Heathrow	9.11.06T
G-CIVU	Boeing 747-436	25810	(G-CIVO)	24. 4.98	British Airways PLC	London Heathrow	23. 4.08E
G-CIVV	Boeing 747-436	25819	N6009F (G-CIVP)	23. 5.98	British Airways PLC	London Heathrow	10. 4.08E
G-CIVW	Boeing 747-436	25822	(G-CIVR)	15. 5.98	British Airways PLC	London Heathrow	14. 5.07T
G-CIVX	Boeing 747-436	28852		3. 9.98	British Airways PLC	London Heathrow	2. 9.07T
G-CIVY	Boeing 747-436	28853		29. 9.98	British Airways PLC	London Heathrow	28. 9.07T
G-CIVZ	Boeing 747-436	28854		31.10.98	British Airways PLC	London Heathrow	30.10.07E
G-CIZZ	Beech 58 Baron	TH-2041	N5000S	16. 1.08	Bonanza Flying Club Ltd *(Noted 2.08)*	Wycombe Air Park	

G-CJAA - G-CJZZ

G-CJAB	Dornier 328-300	3200	OE-HAA D-BDXN, (G-CJAB), D-BDXN, N328BC, D-BDMO, D-BDXN, (V5-NMC), (D-BMAH)	16. 9.05	Corporate Jet Realisations Ltd	Southampton	19. 9.08E
G-CJAD	Cessna 525 CitationJet	525-0453	N525AD N5244F	28. 6.02	A B Davis t/a Davis Aircraft Operations	Edinburgh	27. 6.08E
G-CJAG	Raytheon RB390 Premier 1	RB-122	N3722Z	20.12.05	Corporate Jet Realisations Ltd	Southampton	8. 1.08E
G-CJAH	Raytheon RB390 Premier 1	RB-131	N36731	20.12.05	Corporate Jet Realisations Ltd	Southampton	4. 1.08E
G-CJAI	P&M Quik GT450	8198		19.10.07	J C Kitchen	Hunsdon	8.11.08P
	(Possibly fitted with trike c/n 7979 ex G-CJAY qv)						
G-CJAO	Schempp-Hirth Discus b	190	BGA 4362-JAQ	11. 1.08	A Lyth and J Weddell	Ringmer	18. 3.08
G-CJAS	Glasflügel H201 Standard Libelle	109	BGA 4364-JAS SE-TIS	1.12.07	M J Collett	Wycombe Air Park	21.12.07
G-CJAT	Schleicher K 8B	8150	BGA 4365-JAT D-4390	10.10.07	Wolds Gliding Club Ltd	Pocklington	19. 7.07
G-CJAV	Schleicher ASK 21	21662	BGA 4367-JAV	10.10.07	Wolds Gliding Club Ltd	Pocklington	1. 2.08
G-CJAW	Glaser-Dirks DG-200-17	2-180-1759	BGA 4368-JAW D-5618	19.12.07	J P Kirby and T McKinley	Bembridge	21. 3.08
G-CJAX	Schleicher ASK 21	21665	BGA 4369-JAX	10.10.07	Wolds Gliding Club Ltd	Pocklington	28. 9.08
G-CJAY	P&M Quik	7979		18. 8.03	J C Kitchen	Stoke, Isle of Grain	1.10.07P
	(Originally built by Maiinair as Sports Pegasus Quik: new Sailwing (c/n 8198) fitted 6.06 and re-registered as Quik GT450: subsequently reverted to Quik status c.2007 and believed trike donated to G-CJAI qv)				*(Noted 2.08)*		
G-CJBC	Piper PA-28-180 Cherokee D	28-5470	OY-BDE	28.11.80	J B Cave	Halfpenny Green	15. 9.08E
G-CJBH	Eiriavion PIK-20D	20621	BGA 4379-JBH OH-529	14.11.07	S R Domoney tr 537 Syndicate	Parham Park	29. 1.08
G-CJBK	Schleicher ASW 19B	19204	BGA 4381-JBK D-4099, PH-602	7.11.07	D Caielli and P Sharpe	Dunstable	9. 1.08
G-CJBM	Schleicher ASK 21	21089	BGA 4383-JBM D-6391	10.12.07	Midland Gliding Club Ltd	Long Mynd	5. 6.08
G-CJBR	Schempp-Hirth Discus b	90	BGA 4387-JBR F-CGGD, F-WGGD	8. 2.08	M R C Corrance, M Pointon and R Fitch	Kenley	20. 9.08
G-CJBS	Sportline Aviacija LAK-12 Lietuva	6115	BGA 4388-JBS	8. 2.08	N G Davies tr Bravo Sierra Bigwigs Flying Group	(Seaford)	14. 3.08
G-CJBT	Schleicher ASW 19B	19075	BGA 4389-JBT D4477	14.11.07	C H Braithwaite	Kingston Deverill	29. 7.08

G-CJBW	Schempp-Hirth Discus bT	34/337	BGA 4392-JBW D-KBJR	17.10.07	N Pringle tr G-CJBW Syndicate	Lasham	23. 1.08
G-CJBX	Rolladen-Schneider LS4	4293	BGA 4393-JBX D-9111	21. 3.07	P W Lee and P A Ivens *"JBX" (Noted 11.07)*	Nympsfield	27. 3.07
G-CJBY	Sportline Aviacija LAK-12 Lietuva	6185	BGA 4394-JBY	26. 2.08	N Clarke and P G Steggles	Rattlesden	25. 7.08
G-CJCD	Schleicher ASW 24	24101	BGA 4399-JCD D-6091	24. 9.07	M D Evershed	Gransden Lodge	1. 3.08
G-CJCF	Grob G102 Astir CS77	1705	BGA 4401-JCF PH-1012, D-7634	3. 1.08	The Northumbria Gliding Club Ltd	Currock Hi	2. 6.08
G-CJCG	PZL-Swidnik PW-5 Smyk	17.09.003	BGA 4402-JCG	3. 9.07	J Lavery	Bellarena	20.12.07
G-CJCI	Pilatus P 2-06	600-63	Swiss AF U-143	30. 7.84	J Briscoe and P G Bond tr Pilatus P2 Flying Group *(As "CC+43" in Luftwaffe c/s in Arado Ar.96B guise)* Norwich		27. 6.05P
G-CJCJ	Schempp-Hirth Standard Cirrus	434G	BGA 4404-JCJ SE-TNC	23.10.07	R Johnson and R Carter	Husbands Bosworth	18. 4.08
G-CJCK	Schempp-Hirth Discus bT	92/430	BGA 4405-JCK D-KIDE	29. 8.07	D C Coppin	Lasham	28.10.07
G-CJCM	Schleicher ASW 27	27064	BGA 4407-JCM	8. 1.08	J R Klunder and K E Singer	Camphill	4. 5.08
G-CJCN	Schempp-Hirth Standard Cirrus 75	646	BGA 4408-JCN D-7247	8.12.07	S C J Barker	Pocklington	28. 9.08
G-CJCP	Rolladen-Schneider LS8-18	8146	BGA 4409-JCP	16. 8.07	D P Francis	Bicester	28. 9.08
G-CJCT	Schempp-Hirth Nimbus 4T	21	BGA 4413-JCT D-KKKL	22. 1.08	D S Innes	Lasham	8. 5.08
G-CJCU	Schempp-Hirth Standard Cirrus B	688	BGA 4414-JCU D-6604	21.11.07	R A Davenport	Aston Down	13. 3.08
G-CJCX	Schempp-Hirth Discus bT	93	BGA 4417-JCX D-KJOB	8. 1.08	R Starmer	Bidford	27. 3.08
G-CJDB	Cessna 525 CitationJet	525-0648		8. 8.07	Breed Aircraft Ltd.	Jersey	8. 8.08E
G-CJDC	Schleicher ASW 27	27010	BGA 4422-JDC D-6209	17.10.07	J J Marshall	Dunstable	28. 9.08
G-CJDE	Rolladen-Schneider LS8-18	8151	BGA 4424-JDE	29.10.07	B Kerby and M Davies	Snitterfield	16. 4.08
G-CJDG	Rolladen-Schneider LS6-b	6145	BGA 4426-JDG D-5675	5.10.07	A and R H Moss	Nympsfield	2. 3.08
G-CJDJ	Rolladen-Schneider LS3	3010	BGA 4428-JCJ D-7729	16.10.07	J C Burdett	Walney Island	10. 2.08
G-CJDK	Rolladen-Schneider LS8-18	8153	BGA 4429-JDK	1.10.07	G K and S Drury	Challock	28. 9.08
G-CJDM	Schleicher ASW 15B	15280	BGA 4431-JDM F-CEGL	19. 2.08	W Ellis	Wormingford	20. 4.08
G-CJDP	Glaser-Dirks DG-202/17	2-134/1732	BGA 4433-JDP D-6545	4.12.07	M Downie and R Fielding tr The Owners of JDP	Camphill	28. 9.08
G-CJDR	Schleicher ASW 15	15053	BGA 4435-JDR D-6910	20.11.07	M J Waters *"Rocinante"*	Waldershare Park	2. 4.08
G-CJDS	Schempp-Hirth Standard Cirrus 75	638	BGA 4436-JDS D-4057, OY-XCZ	13. 9.07	S Holland	Rivar Hil	16. 3.08
G-CJDT	Rolladen-Schneider LS8-a	8172	BGA 4437-JDT	28. 2.08	H A Rebbeck	Dunstable	14. 5.08
G-CJDU	LET L-13 Blanik	026303	BGA 4438-JDU D-8919	19.10.07	Herefordshire Gliding Club Ltd *(Noted 12.07)*	Shobdon	14. 7.07
G-CJDV	DG Flugzeugbau DG-300 Elan Acro	3E481A24	BGA 4439-JDV	24.10.07	J Herman and S C Williams	Wycombe Air Park	6.12.07
G-CJDX	Wassmer WA-28F Espadon	101	BGA 4441-JDX F-CDZU	11. 1.08	K J Woods	(Impington, Cambridge)	10. 5.08
G-CJEA	Rolladen-Schneider LS8-18	8159	BGA 4444-JEA D-2411	26.10.07	D J Westwood and R I Davidson	Husbands Bosworth	25. 4.08
G-CJEB	Schleicher ASW 24	24172	BGA 4445-JEB D-9344	16.11.07	M A Taylor and S L Barnes	Rattlesden	28. 2.08
G-CJEC	PZL-Bielsko SZD-50-3 Puchacz	B-2197	BGA 4446-JEC	16.10.07	Cambridge Gliding Club Ltd	Gransden Lodge	28. 9.08
G-CJED	Schempp-Hirth Nimbus 3/24.5	37	BGA 4822-JVT D-3176	26. 2.08	J R Edyvean	Bicester	23. 5.08
G-CJEE	Schleicher ASW 20L	20073	BGA 4448-JEE (BGA 4456-JEQ)	1.11.07	J C Baldock	Nympsfield	28. 9.08
G-CJEH	Glasflügel H303 Mosquito B	172	BGA 4451-JEH	19.12.07	M J Vickery	Lasham	22. 3.08
G-CJEL	Schleicher ASW 24	24044	BGA 4454-JEL PH-866	8. 2.08	D Robson	Milfield	12. 5.08
G-CJEM	Schempp-Hirth Duo Discus	146	BGA 4455-JEM	22.11.07	D W Briggs tr Duo Discus 572 Flying Group	Aston Down	28. 9.08
G-CJEP	Rolladen-Schneider LS4-b	41021	BGA 4457-JEP	22.11.07	C F Carter and N Backes	Long Mynd	16. 4.08
G-CJER	Schempp-Hirth Standard Cirrus 75	654	BGA 4459-JER D-6475, OO-ZBM	20.11.07	S R Brown tr Cirrus Group	Snitterfield	7. 4.08
G-CJEU	Glasflügel H201 Standard Libelle	55	BGA 4462-JEU SE-TIC	21.11.07	D B Johns	Aston Down	30. 3.08
G-CJEV	Schempp-Hirth Standard Cirrus B	650	BGA 4463-JEV OE-5072	25. 9.07	G F King and E Perrin	North Hill	22. 1.08
G-CJEW	Schleicher Ka 6CR	6493	BGA 4464-JEW D-4116	14. 1.08	S Blundell	(Birmingham)	1. 3.08
G-CJEX	Schempp-Hirth Ventus 2a	64	BGA 4465-JEX	3.10.07	D S Watt	Bicester	21. 2.08
G-CJFA	Schempp-Hirth Standard Cirrus	225	BGA 4468-JFA D-0974	14. 1.08	P.M.Sheahan	Lasham	21. 3.08
G-CJFC	Schempp-Hirth Discus CS	054CS	BGA 4470-JFC RAFGSA R55	9. 5.07	T M Holloway tr RAF Gliding and Soaring Association *"JFC" and "R55"* RAF Marham *(Operated Fenland Gliding Club)*		28.10.07
G-CJFE	Schempp-Hirth Janus Ce	(21)/299	BGA 4472-JFE- RAFGSA R16	26. 9.07	J G Arnold tr RAF Gliding and Soaring Association *(Operated Bannerdown Gliding Club)* RAF Keevil		30.10.07
G-CJFF	Schempp-Hirth Duo Discus	131	BGA 4473-JFF RAFGSA R26	17.10.07	J G Arnold tr RAF Gliding and Soaring Association *(Operated Chilterns Gliding Centre)* RAF Halton		28. 9.08
G-CJFH	Schempp-Hirth Duo Discus	118	BGA 4475-JFH RAFGSA R1	27. 2.08	J G Arnold tr RAF Gliding and Soaring Association *(Operated Fulmar Gliding Club)* Easterton		4. 4.08

G-CJFJ	Schleicher ASW 20 CL	20830	BGA 4476-JFJ	29. 1.08	R J Stirk	Burn	1. 4.08
			D-8307, F-CGCS				
G-CJFK	Schleicher ASW 20L	20201	BGA 4477-JFK	19. 4.07	D Holt	Llantisilio	16. 5.08
			D-5979		*"JFK"*		
G-CJFL	Rolladen Schneider LS8-18	8178	BGA 4478-JFL	19.11.07	G Smith and N Hoare	Dunstable	18. 2.08
G-CJFR	Schemmp-Hirth Ventus cT	170/560	BGA 4483-JFR	24.10.07	J G Allen	Bicester	9. 1.08
			RAFGSA R24				
G-CJFT	Schleicher K 8B	8451	BGA 4485-JFT	15.11.07	The Surrey Hills Gliding Club Ltd	Kenley	31. 8.06
			D-1883				
G-CJFU	Schleicher ASW 19 B	19038	BGA 4486-JFU	28. 1.08	M T Stanley	Sutton Bank	9. 3.08
			D-4531				
G-CJFX	Rolladen-Schneider LS8-a	8174	BGA 4489-JFX	16.10.07	P E Baker	Gransden Lodge	28. 9.08
G-CJGD	Schleicher K 8B	8214A-SH	BGA 4495-JGD	30. 1.08	C A McLay and R E Pettifer	Chipping	21. 4.08
	(Officially regd as c/n 8214)		D-....				
G-CJGG	P&M Quik GT450	8305		30. 8.07	J M Pearce	(Sandbank, Dunoon)	17.10.08P
G-CJGJ	Schleicher ASK 21	21039	BGA 4500-JGJ	10.12.07	Midland Gliding Club Ltd	Long Mynd	28. 9.08
			RAFGSA R22				
G-CJGK	Eiriavion PIK-20D	20571	BGA 4501-JGK	22.10.07	R Cassidy and W Stephen	Milfield	20. 4.08
			OO-ZDL, D-6707				
G-CJGL	Schempp-Hirth Discus CS	148CS	BGA 4502-JGL	14. 1.08	J G Arnold t/a RAF Gliding and Soaring Association		
			RAFGSA R27		*(Operated Chilterns Glding Centre)* RAF Halton		28. 9.08
G-CJGM	Schempp-Hirth Discus CS	036CS	BGA 4503-JGM	27. 2.08	J G Arnold t/a RAF Gliding and Soaring Association		
			RAFGSA R53		*(Operated Fulmar Gliding Club)*	Easterton	6. 5.08
G-CJGN	Schempp-Hirth Standard Cirrus	554	BGA 4504-JCN	29. 1.08	P A Shuttleworth	Long Mynd	21. 5.08
			D-8674				
G-CJGR	Schempp-Hirth Discus bT	10/275	BGA 4507-JGR	3. 1.08	D A Sinclair	Lasham	19. 3.08
			D-KGPS, D-5461				
G-CJGS	Rolladen-Schneider LS8-18	8180	BGA 4508-JGS	16.10.07	M D Allan	Shobdon	28. 9.08
G-CJGW	Schleicher ASK 13	13146	BGA 4512-JGW	11. 1.08	Darlton Gliding Club Ltd	Darlton	3. 2.08
			D-0169				
G-CJHD	Schleicher Ka 6E	4307	BGA 4519-JHD	30. 8.07	M A King	Lyveden	25. 3.08
			OY-XGS, D-0272				
G-CJHJ	Glasflügel H201B Standard Libelle	495	BGA 4524-JHJ	18.10.07	M E Hahnefeld tr G-CJHU Group	Parham Park	9. 2.08
			HB-1187				
G-CJHK	Schleicher K 8B	558	BGA 4525-JHK	3.10.07	Stratford on Avon Gliding Club Ltd	Snitterfield	12. 4.08
			(BGA 4319-HYV)				
G-CJHL	Schleicher Ka 6E	4073	BGA 4526-JHL	20. 2.08	J R Gilbert and M R Doran	Wormingford	4. 4.08
			SE-TFB				
G-CJHM	Schempp-Hirth Discus b	373	BGA 4527-JHM	5. 2.08	J H May	Sutton Bank	13. 3.08
			OO-ZGZ				
G-CJHO	Schleicher ASK 18	18021	BGA 4530-JHQ	23. 1.08	J G Arnold tr RAF Gliding and Soaring Association		
			RAFGSA R43, RAFGSA 713, RAFGSA 113			RAF Cosford	5. 3.08
					(Operated Wrekin Gliding Club)		
G-CJHP	Flight Design CTSW	07.08.06		2.11.07	J Prentice	Perth	1.11.08P
	(Assembled P&M Aviation Ltd with c/n 8327)						
G-CJHR	Centrair SNC-34C Alliance	34026	BGA 4531-JHR	25. 2.08	The Borders (Milfield) Gliding Club Ltd	Milfield	21. 6.08
G-CJHY	Rolladen-Schneider LS8-18	8181	BGA 4538-JHY	21. 9.07	L E N Tanner and N Wall	Nympsfield	10. 2.08
			D-9988				
G-CJHZ	Schleicher ASW 20	20313	BGA 4539-JHZ	6. 9.07	T J Stanley	Sutton Bank	28. 9.08
			D-6532				
G-CJJB	Rolladen-Schneider LS4	4542	BGA 4541-JJB	9. 1.08	M Tomlinson	Talgarth	3. 4.08
			D-2397				
G-CJJF	Schleicher ASW 27	27086	BGA 4545-JJF	12.10.07	G F Read *"JJF"*	Wycombe Air Park	28. 9.08
G-CJJH	DG Flugzeugbau DG-800S	8-137S30	BGA 4547-JJH	29. 1.08	W R Brown	Husbands Bosworth	15. 5.08
G-CJJJ	Schempp-Hirth Standard Cirrus	284	BGA 4548-JJJ	21. 9.07	F R and R G Stevens	Husbands Bosworth	28. 9.08
			D-2946		*(Also carries "2946")*		
G-CJJK	Rolladen-Schneider LS 8-18	8199	BGA 4549-JJK	26.11.07	J White	Dunstable	28. 9.08
G-CJJP	Schempp-Hirth Duo Discus	180	BGA 4553-JJP	25. 9.07	N Clements	Long Mynd	28. 9.08
G-CJJR	Schleicher ASK 21	21054	BGA 4555-JJR	8.10.07	J G Arnold tr RAF Gliding and Soaring Association		
			RAFGSA R73, RAFGGA 513		*(Operated Chilterns Gliding Centre)* RAF Halton		9.11.07
G-CJJT	Schleicher ASW 27	27070	BGA 4557-JJT	6. 2.08	T World tr Portsmouth Naval Gliding Centre		
			D-6209			Lee-on-Solent	5. 5.08
G-CJJX	Schleicher ASW 15B	15323	BGA 4561-JJX	31.10.07	M D Brooks	Saltby	26. 3.08
			D-2312				
G-CJJZ	Schempp-Hirth Discus bT	156/556	BGA 4563-JJZ	27. 9.07	S J C Parker	Nympsfield	28. 9.08
			OO-ZQX				
G-CJKA	Schleicher ASK 21	21059	BGA 4564-JKA	18. 1.08	East Sussex Gliding Club Ltd	Ringmer	14. 6.08
			D-8835				
G-CJKD	Rolladen-Schneider LS8-18	8215	BGA 4567-JKD	14.11.07	D Abbey and G Glover	Husbands Bosworth	29. 4.08
G-CJKG	Schleicher ASK 18	18036	BGA 4570-JKG	17.10.07	J G Arnold tr RAF Gliding and Soaring Association		
			RAFGSA R48, RAFGSA 444		*(Operated Chilterns Gliding Centre)* RAF Halton		10.12.07
G-CJKJ	Schleicher ASK 21	21679	BGA 4572-JKJ	17.10.07	J G Arnold tr RAF Gliding and Soaring Association *"R 21"*		
			(RAFGSA R21)		*(Operated Chilterns Gliding Centre)* RAF Halton		7. 1.08
G-CJKL	Rolladen-Schneider LS8-18	8218	BGA 4574-JKL	21.11.07	R J Welford	Gransden Lodge	26. 3.08
G-CJKM	Glaser-Dirks DG-200/17	2-148/1746	BGA 4575-JKM	8. 1.08	E W Russell	Wormingford	28. 9.08
			D-4155				
G-CJKN	Rolladen-Schneider LS8-18	8214	BGA 4576-JKN	2.11.07	D A Booth	Husbands Bosworth	28. 9.08
G-CJKO	Schleicher ASK 21	21098	BGA 4578-JKQ	18. 1.08	J G Arnold t/a RAF Gliding and Soaring Association		
			RAFGSA R20			RAF Wittering	20. 7.07
					(Operated Four Counties Gliding Club)		
G-CJKP	Rolladen-Schneider LS4-b	41000	BGA 4577-JKP	17.10.07	D M Hope	Wycombe Air Park	18. 2.08
			PH-1089				
G-CJKR	Schempp-Hirth Discus b	151	BGA 4579-JKR	21.12.07	T Wright	Husbands Bosworth	4. 3.08

G-CJKS	Schleicher ASW 19B	19362	BGA 4580-JKS 18. 1.08 D-1273	D.M.Brown and P D F Adshead	Dunstable	19. 6.08
G-CJKU	Schleicher ASK 18	18022	BGA 4582-JKU, 19.12.07 RAFGSA R33, RAFGSA 223	J G Arnold tr RAF Gliding and Soaring Association (Operated Clevelands Gliding Club) AAC Dishforth		28. 9.08
G-CJKV	Grob G103A Twin II Acro	34042-K-273	BGA 4583-JKV 11.12.07 RAFGSA R52	The Welland Gliding Club Ltd	Lyveden	13. 6.08
G-CJKW	Grob G102 Astir CS77	1666	BGA 4584-JKW 22.12.07 RAFGSA R60, RAFGSA 560	The Bath, Wilts and North Dorset Gliding Club Ltd	Kingston Deverill	24. 6.08
G-CJKX	Schempp-Hirth Discus b	247	BGA 4585-JKX 10. 7.07 RAFGSA R17	A R Armstrong	RAF Keevil	13. 4.08
G-CJKY	Schempp-Hirth Ventus cT	181/597	BGA 4586-JKY 29.10.07 RAFGSA R24, RAFGGA 557	M P Osborn and G V Matthews	RAF Cosford	13. 1.08
G-CJKZ	Schleicher ASK 21	21123	BGA 4587-JKZ 17.10.07 RAFGSA R25	J G Arnold tr RAF Gliding and Soaring Association “R 25” (Operated Chilterns Gliding Centre) RAF Halton		19. 2.08
G-CJLA	Schempp-Hirth Ventus 2cT	26/94	BGA 4588-JLA 28. 2.08 PH-1129	E C and P M Neighbour	Camphill	19. 9.08
G-CJLC	Schempp-Hirth Discus CS	193CS	BGA 4590-JLC 5. 2.08 RAFGSA R10	J G Arnold tr RAF Gliding and Soaring Association (Operated Four Counties Gliding Club) RAF Wittering		25. 3.08
G-CJLG	PZL-Bielsko SZD-51-1 Junior	B-1933	BGA 4594-JLG 18. 2.08 AGA 5, (BGA 3699-GBH)	J W Sage tr Army Gliding Association	Trenchard Lines, Upavon (Operated Wyvern Gliding Club)	17. 2.08
G-CJLP	Schempp-Hirth Discus CS	034CS	BGA 4601-JLP 1. 2.08 RAFGSA R39	J G Arnold tr RAF Gliding and Soaring Association (Operated Cranwell Gliding Club) RAF Cranwell		7. 2.08
G-CJLH	Rolladen-Schneider LS4	4256	BGA 4595-JLH 1.11.07 AGA 1	C A Sorace tr JLH Syndicate “JLH”	Dunstable	19. 4.08
G-CJLJ	Rolladen-Schneider LS4-B	4997	BGA 4596-JLJ 29. 1.08 AGA 2	J W Sage tr Army Gliding Association	Trenchard Lines, Upavon (Operated Wyvern Gliding Club)	9. 5.08
G-CJLK	Rolladen-Schneider LS7	7112	BGA 4597-JLK 9. 1.08 AGA 3	D N Munro and S G Hamilton	Rougham	5. 5.08
G-CJLL	Robinson R44 Raven II	11588	29. 1.07	AT and P Rentals Ltd	Durham Tees Valley	27. 2.08E
G-CJLN	Rolladen-Schneider LS8-18	8169	BGA 4600-JLN 25.10.07 RAFGSA R4	J G Arnold tr RAF Gliding and Soaring Association (Operated Cranwell Gliding Club) RAF Cranwell		28. 9.08
G-CJLO	Schleicher ASK 13	13608	BGA 4602-JLQ 20. 9.07 RAFGSA R40, RAFGSA R4	Bowland Forest Gliding Club Ltd	Chipping	28. 9.08
G-CJLR	Grob G102 Astir CS	1509	BGA 4603-JLR, 17.12.07 RAFGSA R57, RAFGSA 507	J G Arnold tr RAF Gliding and Soaring Association (Operated Cranwell Gliding Club) RAF Cranwell		28. 9.08
G-CJLS	Schleicher K 8B	8950	BGA 4604-JLS 9. 1.08 RAFGSA R75, RAFGSA 285	J G Arnold tr RAF Gliding and Soaring Association (Operated Crusaders Gliding Club) Kingsfield, Cyprus		1.12.07
G-CJLW	Schempp-Hirth Discus CS	033CS	BGA 4608-JLW 11. 2.08 RAFGSA R87	J G Arnold tr RAF Gliding and Soaring Association (Operated Wrekin Gliding Club) RAF Cosford		17. 3.08
G-CJLY	Schleicher ASW 27	27111	BGA 4610-JLY 26.11.07	L M Astle and P C Piggott	Husbands Bosworth	16. 5.08
G-CJLZ	Grob G103A Twin II Acro	3633-K-15	BGA 4611-JLZ 2.11.07 D-7912	B L Eppy tr 21 Syndicate Flying Group	Lasham	28. 3.08
G-CJMB	Bombardier CL-600-2B19 (CL-600 Regional Jet)	8055	N850RJ 21. 8.07	Corporate Jet Management Ltd	Farnborough	23. 8.08E
G-CJMD	Embraer EMB-135BJ Legacy	14500994	P4-SAO 2.11.07 PT-SKN	Corporate Jet Management Ltd	Farnborough	
G-CJMH	Schempp-Hirth Standard Cirrus	571	BGA 4619-JMH 19. 2.08 HB-1263	J G Walker	Pocklington	28. 4.08
G-CJMK	Schleicher ASK 18	18023	BGA 4621-JMK 9. 1.08 RAFGSA R49, RAFGSA 318	J G Arnold tr RAF Gliding and Soaring Association (Operated Crusaders Gliding Club) Kingsfield, Cyprus		2. 8.07
G-CJMN	Schempp-Hirth Nimbus 2	38	BGA 4624-JMN 26. 9.07 D-1129, HB-1159	R.A.Holroyd	Pocklington	28. 9.08
G-CJMO	Rolladen-Schneider LS8-18	8225	BGA 4625-JMO 12.11.07	D J Langrick	Husbands Bosworth	20. 4.08
G-CJMP	Schleicher ASK 13	13436	BGA 4626-JMP 18. 1.08 D-2984	East Sussex Gliding Club Ltd	Ringmer	11. 3.08
G-CJMT	Rolladen-Schneider LS8-18	8223	BGA 4630-JMT 1.11.07	D P and K M Draper	Lasham	28. 9.08
G-CJMU	Rolladen-Schneider LS8-18	8246	BGA 4631-JMU 15. 1.08	J G Guy	Portmoak	27. 2.08
G-CJMV	Schempp-Hirth Nimbus 2C	179	BGA 4632-JMV 4. 1.08 D-6738	G Tucker	Lee-on-Solent	10. 3.08
G-CJMW	Schleicher ASK 13	13688AB	BGA 4633-JMW 11.10.07 RAFGGA 567	J G Arnold tr RAF Gliding and Soaring Association (Operated Bannerdown Gliding Club) RAF Keevil		11. 4.08
G-CJMY	PZL-Bielsko SZD-51-1 Junior	W-959	BGA 4635-JMY 11. 2.08 OO-ZRH	Highland Gliding Club Ltd	Easterton	27. 8.08
G-CJMZ	Schleicher ASK 13	13099	BGA 4636-JMZ 9. 1.08 RAFGSA R37, RAFGSA 378	J G Arnold tr RAF Gliding and Soaring Association	RAF Keevil	27. 4.08
G-CJNE	Schempp-Hirth Discus 2a	18	BGA 4641-JNE 4.12.07 D-4499	R Priest	Wycombe Air Park	19. 4.08
G-CJNG	Glasflügel H201B Standard Libelle	006	BGA 4643-JNG 1.10.07 SE-TFU	C A Willson	Rivar Hill	17. 8.08
G-CJNJ	Rolladen-Schneider LS8-18	8226	BGA 4645-JNJ 12.11.07	A B Laws	Crowland	15. 3.08
G-CJNN	Schleicher K 8B	8744	BGA 4649-JNN 23. 1.08 D-8583	Buckminster Gliding Club Ltd	Saltby	3. 6.08
G-CJNO	DG Flugzeugbau DG-300 Elan	3E341	BGA 4651-JNQ 15. 1.08 SE-UHO	R Friend	Husbands Bosworth	24. 4.08
G-CJNP	Rolladen-Schneider LS6-b	6109	BGA 4650-JNP 31.10.07 D-5853	P.S.Fink	Lasham	21. 4.08
G-CJNR	Glasflügel H303 Mosquito B	159	BGA 4652-JNR 12.11.07 D-5908	B R Smith and I H Agutter	Wormingford	2. 3.08
G-CJNT	Schleicher ASW 19B	19371	BGA 4654-JNT 20.12.07 D-2233	M D Borrowdale	Lasham	18. 3.08

G-CJNX	LET L-13 Blanik	827408	BGA 4658-JNX OK-2712	27.11.07	Vectis Gliding Club Ltd	Bembridge	28. 9.08
G-CJNZ	Glaser-Dirks DG-100	70	BGA 4660-JNZ (D-7324), HB-1324	13. 2.08	R Jones and T Tordoff	Rufforth	4. 8.08
G-CJOA	Schempp-Hirth Discus b	265	BGA 4685-JQA RAFGGA 547, RAFGGA 500	4.10.07	J G Arnold tr RAF Gliding and Soaring Association *(Operated Bannerdown Gliding Club)* RAF Keevil		28. 9.08
G-CJOC	Schempp-Hirth Discus bT	127/488	BGA 4687-JQC D-KITT	16.11.07	D Cooper tr 287 Syndicate	Wycombe Air Park	2.12.07
G-CJOD	Rolladen-Schneider LS8-18	8224	BGA 4688-JQD	20. 9.07	J G Arnold tr RAF Gliding and Soaring Association *(Operated Bannerdown Gliding Club)* RAF Keevil		28. 9.08
G-CJOG	Grob G103A Twin II Acro	33964-K-197	BGA 4691-JQG RAFGSA R50	19.12.07	R G J Tait tr Acro Syndicate	Easterton	25. 5.08
G-CJOJ	Schleicher K 8B	8795	BGA 4693-JQJ RAFGSA R47, BGA 1564	15. 1.08	P W Burgess	Seighford	27. 5.08
G-CJOO	Schempp-Hirth Duo Discus	227	BGA 4699-JQQ	24. 1.08	K G Reid tr 185 Syndicate	Rivar Hill	10. 3.08
G-CJOR	Schempp-Hirth Ventus 2cT	49/152	BGA 4700-JQR	17. 9.07	A M George and N A MacLean	Lasham	28. 9.08
G-CJOS	Schempp-Hirth Standard Cirrus	251G	BGA 4701-JQS D-1147	20. 2.08	R K Arkley tr G-CJOS Group	Milfield	7. 7.08
G-CJOU	AB Sportine Aviacija LAK-17A	102	BGA 4703-JQU	5.10.07	N G R Moffat	Walney Island	18. 1.08
G-CJOW	Schempp-Hirth Cirrus VTC	47	BGA 4705-JQW D-0186	1. 2.08	G Stilgoe and D G Smith	Parham Park	19. 1.08
G-CJOX	Schleicher ASK 21	21702	BGA 4706-JQX	11. 9.07	Southdown Gliding Club Ltd	Parham Park	28. 9.08
G-CJPA	Schempp-Hirth Duo Discus	201	BGA 4661-JPA	3.10.07	Coventry Gliding Club Ltd t/a The Gliding Centre	Husbands Bosworth	20. 3.08
G-CJPH	Rolladen-Schneider LS8-18	8259	BGA 4668-JPH	31.10.07	J P Ben-David	Lasham	6. 4.08
G-CJPL	Rolladen-Schneider LS8-18	8249	BGA 4671-JPL D-2562	12.10.07	I A Reekie	Dunstable	8. 3.08
G-CJPO	Schleicher ASK 18	18002	BGA 4675-JPQ RAFGSA R32, RAFGSA 213, D-3978	5.10.07	J G Arnold tr RAF Gliding and Soaring Association *(Operated Bannerdown Gliding Club)* RAF Keevil		16. 3.08
G-CJPP	Schempp-Hirth Discus b	206	BGA 4674-JPP AGA 4	23. 8.07	Scottish Gliding Union Ltd	Portmoak	28. 9.08
G-CJPR	Rolladen-Schneider LS 8-18	8245	BGA 4676-JPR	28.11.07	D M Byass and J A McCoshim	Wycombe Air Park	5. 4.08
G-CJPS	Schleicher ASW 27	27108	BGA 4677-JPS	23.11.07	E W and P T Healy	Lasham	22. 1.08
G-CJPT	Schleicher ASW 27	27113	BGA 4678-JPT	20. 2.08	R C Willis-Fleming	North Hill	16. 4.08
G-CJPV	Schleicher ASK 13	13312	BGA 4680-JPV RAFGSA R88, RAFGSA 186	9. 1.08	J G Arnold tr RAF Gliding and Soaring Association *(Operated Crusaders Gliding Club)* Kingsfield, Cyprus		5. 6.08
G-CJPX	Schleicher ASW 15	15160	BGA 4682-JPX D-0823	21. 1.08	P Daly and R Hayden	Upwood	14. 4.08
G-CJPY	Schleicher ASK 13	13653AB	BGA 4683-JPY RAFGSA 509	22.12.07	J G Arnold tr RAF Gliding and Soaring Association *(Operated Cranwell Gliding Club)* RAF Cranwell		5. 1.08
G-CJPZ	Schleicher ASK 18	18027	BGA 4684-JPZ RAFGGA 563	17.12.07	J G Arnold tr RAF Gliding and Soaring Association *(Operated Cranwell Gliding Club)* RAF Cranwell		19. 1.08
G-CJRA	Rolladen-Schneider LS8-18	8263	BGA 4709-JRA	30.10.07	J Williams	Kirton-in-Lindsey	28. 9.08
G-CJRB	Schleicher ASW 19B	19227	BGA 4710-JRB D-2713	5. 2.08	J W Baxter tr S33 Syndicate	Long Mynd	12. 3.07
G-CJRC	DG Flugzeugbau DG-300 Elan	3E20	BGA 4711-JRC HB-1718	18. 1.08	P.J.Sillett	Tibenham	3.11.07
G-CJRE	Schleicher ASW 15	15048	BGA 4713-JRE LN-GGL, OH-391, OH-RWA	5. 9.07	R A Starling	Darlton	28. 9.08
G-CJRF	PZL-Bielsko SZD-50-3 Puchacz	B-1395	BGA 4714-JRF OO-ZTX, D-8213, SP-3285	10.10.07	Wolds Gliding Club Ltd	Pocklington	11. 8.08
G-CJRG	Schempp-Hirth HS.4 Standard Cirrus	146	BGA 4715-JRG D-0297	5.11.07	D P and K M Draper	Lasham	28. 9.08
G-CJRH	Schleicher ASW 27	27118	BGA 4716-JRH	23. 8.07	C Jackson and P C Jarvis	Lasham	28. 9.08
G-CJRJ	PZL-Bielsko SZD-50-3 Puchacz	503199327	BGA 4717-JRJ	11. 2.08	Bidford Gliding Ltd	Bidford	18. 7.08
G-CJRL	Glaser-Dirks DG-101G Elan	E185G151	BGA 4719-JRL D-1246	29.10.07	P Lazenby	Aston Down	20. 2.08
G-CJRR	Schempp-Hirth Discus bT	50/367	BGA 4724-JRR PH-1087, D-KBHM	15.10.07	J P Walker and M W Cater	Husbands Bosworth	17. 5.08
G-CJRT	Schempp-Hirth Standard Cirrus	99	BGA 4726-JRT D-0734	29. 8.07	J A Tipler tr JRT Syndicate	Husbands Bosworth	28. 9.08
G-CJRU	Schleicher ASW 24	24168	BGA 4727-JRU D-7085	2.11.07	S A Kerby	Snitterfield	28. 9.08
G-CJSD	Grob G102 Astir CS	1133	BGA 4736-JSD RAFGSA R77, D-4177	24. 1.08	J G Arnold tr RAF Gliding and Soaring Association *(Operated Fenland Gliding Club)* RAF Marham		16. 2.08
G-CJSE	Schempp-Hirth Discus b	365	BGA 4737-JSE PH-918	14. 2.08	Imperial College of Science, Technology and Medicine	Lasham	9. 3.08
G-CJSG	Schleicher Ka 6E	4248	BGA 4739-JSG D-0090	4.10.07	A J Emck	Lasham	17. 1.07
G-CJSJ	Rolladen-Schneider LS7-WL	7058	BGA 4741-JSJ D-5774	6.11.07	S P Woolcock	Gransden Lodge	24. 2.08
G-CJSK	Grob G102 Astir CS	1521	BGA 4742-JSK D-7455	22.12.07	J D Hanton and P T Pearce	Brentor	28. 9.08
G-CJSL	Schempp-Hirth Ventus cT	121	BGA 4743-JSL D-KIFL	7.11.07	P Jackson and R H Gisby	Bidford	30.12.07
G-CJSS	Schleicher ASW 27	27121	BGA 4749-JSS	4. 2.08	J H Belk	Dunstable	28. 2.08
G-CJST	Rolladen-Schneider LS1-c	86	BGA 4750-JST OO-ZPA, D-0766	7. 1.08	M W Hands	Saltby	5. 4.08
G-CJSU	Rolladen-Schneider LS8-18	8297	BGA 4751-JSU D-0543	22. 1.08	J G Bell	Parham Park	17. 1.08
G-CJSW	Rolladen-Schneider LS4-a	4262	BGA 4753-JSW ZS-GOP	22.11.07	B T Spreckley *(Operated European Soaring Club)*	Ontur, Spain	28. 9.08

G-CJSZ	Schleicher ASK 18	18012	BGA 4756-JSZ D-6878	27. 2.08	C J N Weston	Challock	1. 5.08
G-CJTB	Schleicher ASW 24	24017	BGA 4758-JTB D-3465	2.10.07	M E Knell tr V17 Syndicate	RAF Keevil	28. 9.08
G-CJTH	Schleicher ASW 24	24218	BGA 4764-JTH D-7681	13. 2.08	R J and J E Lodge	Dunstable	9. 4.08
G-CJTJ	Schempp-Hirth Mini-Nimbus B	73	BGA 4765-JTJ D-7620	15. 1.08	A Richards	(Gweek, Helston)	6. 4.08
G-CJTK	DG Flugzeugbau DG-303 Elan Acro 3E487A28		BGA 4766-JTK	22. 1.08	A Jorgensen	Wycombe Air Park	6. 3.08
G-CJTM	Rolladen-Schneider LS8-18	8268	BGA 4768-JTM	7. 1.08	A D Holmes	Nympsfield	26. 2.08
G-CJTN	DG Flugzeugbau DG-300 Elan	3E19	BGA 4769-JTN HB-1717	11. 1.08	I P McKavney	Nympsfield	24. 2.08
G-CJTO	Glasflügel H303A Mosquito	88	BGA 4771-JTQ OO-ZYL	17. 1.08	I.Hamilton tr Tango Oscar Group	Chipping	20. 4.08
G-CJTP	Schleicher ASW 20L	20569	BGA 4770-JTP D-4688	12. 2.08	C A Sheldon	Pocklington	4. 5.08
G-CJTR	Rolladen-Schneider LS7-WL	7104	BGA 4772-JTR D-5309	8.11.07	G W L Howarth tr D53 Syndicate	RAF Halton	14. 1.08
G-CJTY	Rolladen-Schneider LS 8a	8102	BGA 4779-JTY SE-USA	30.11.07	R E Neal tr BBC (London) Club	Wycombe Air Park	28. 9.08
G-CJTU	Schempp-Hirth Duo Discus T	4/234	BGA 4775-JTU	28 .2.08	M J Philpott tr G-CJTU Syndicate	(Ruislip)	30. 3.08
G-CJUD	Denney Kitfox Model 3 (Built C W Judge - pr.no.PFA 172-11939)	847		17. 1.91	A Thomas t/a AV8 Air	Shobdon	13.11.08P
G-CJUE	Rolladen-Schneider LS8-18	8295	BGA 4785-JUE	30. 8.07	G Goudie and S Waterfall	Gransden Lodge	28. 9.08
G-CJUM	Schempp-Hirth Duo Discus T	243	BGA 4792-JUM	10.10.07	B A Bateson tr 2 UP Group	Parham Park	25. 3.08
G-CJUP	Schempp-Hirth Discus-2b	60	BGA 4794-JUP	6. 2.08	N Parkin and O Ward	Aston Down	29. 3.08
G-CJUS	Grob G102 Astir CS	1403	BGA 4797-JUS (BGA 4774), D-4269	18. 1.08	East Sussex Gliding Club Ltd	Ringmer	25. 5.08
G-CJUU	Schempp-Hirth Standard Cirrus	450	BGA 4799-JUU PH-500	1.12.07	H R Fraser	Milfield	14. 5.08
G-CJUV	Schempp-Hirth Discus b	551	BGA 4800-JUV D-8257	22. 1.08	North Downs Gliding Trust Ltd	Lasham	29. 3.08
G-CJUZ	Schleicher ASW 19B	19146	BGA 4804-JUZ D-7932	6. 9.07	D Heaton	Seighford	28. 9.08
G-CJVA	Schempp-Hirth Ventus 2cT	66/203	BGA 4805-JVA	15.10.07	M S Armstrong	Camphill	28. 9.08
G-CJVB	Schempp-Hirth Discus bT	111/462	BGA 4806-JVB D-KUNK	11.10.07	C J Edwards	Nympsfield	28. 9.08
G-CJVC	PZL-Bielsko SZD-51-1 Junior	B-1799	BGA 4807-JVC SP-3434	29.10.07	York Gliding Centre Ltd	Rufforth	28. 9.08
G-CJVE	Eiriavion PIK-20D	20631	BGA 4809-JVE OY-XJC	18.12.07	S R Wilkinson	Kirton-in-Lindsey	1. 5.08
G-CJVJ	AB Sportine Aviacija LAK-17A	108	BGA 4813-JVJ	14. 1.08	J.A.Sutton	Milfield	6. 3.08
G-CJVL	DG Flugzeugbau DG-300 Elan	3E158	BGA 4815-JVL HB-1833	4.12.07	A T Vidion and A Griffiths	Tibenham	11. 1.08
G-CJVM	Schleicher ASW 27B	27138	BGA 4816-JVM	18.12.07	G K Payne	Dunstable	28. 9.08
G-CJVP	Glaser-Dirks DG-200	2-1	BGA 4818-JVP D-8200	9. 1.08	M S Howey and S Leadbeater	Burn	1. 4.08
G-CJVS	Schleicher ASW 28	28003	BGA 4821-JVS D-4008	11. 9.07	S J Kelman	Gransden Lodge	28. 9.08
G-CJVU	Schempp-Hirth Standard Cirrus CS 11-75L	28	BGA 4823-JVU F-CEVT	7. 1.08	H C Yorke tr Cirrus 75 Syndicate	Snitterfield	14. 1.08
G-CJVW	Schleicher ASW 15	15042	BGA 4825-JVW HB-992	10. 9.07	J M Taylor	Dunstable	12.10.07
G-CJVX	Schempp-Hirth Discus CS	087CS	BGA 4826-JVX D-0263	23.11.07	M P Kemp tr G-CJVX Syndicate	(West Malling)	26. 3.08
G-CJVZ	Schleicher ASK 21	21721	BGA 4828-JVZ	6.11.07	Yorkshire Gliding Club (Proprietary) Ltd "Sharpe's Classique"	Sutton Bank	28. 9.08
G-CJWA	Schleicher ASW 28	28005	BGA 4829-JWA	21. 8.07	M J Taylor and P R Porter	Lyveden	28. 9.08
G-CJWB	Schleicher ASK 13	13671AB	BGA 4830-JWB D-1066	18. 1.08	East Sussex Gliding Club Ltd	Ringmer	8. 5.08
G-CJWD	Schleicher ASK 21	21724	BGA 4832-JWD	8. 1.08	London Gliding Club Proprietary Ltd "JWD"	Dunstable	27. 3.08
G-CJWG	Schempp-Hirth Nimbus 3DT	11	BGA 4835-JWG D-KMGD	15.11.07	P G Kynsey tr 880 Group	Lasham	5.11.07
G-CJWJ	Schleicher ASK 13	13599	BGA 4837-JWJ RAFGSA R38, RAFGSA R3	11. 1.08	J G Arnold tr RAF Gliding and Soaring Association (Operated Wrekin Gliding Club)	RAF Cosford	13. 1.08
G-CJWK	Schempp-Hirth Discus bT	453/1	BGA 4838-JWK	14. 2.08	R Thompson tr 722 Syndicate	Nympsfield	14. 2.08

(Officially regd as c/n "122" - correct c/n 122 was BGA 4021 w/o Parham 7. 5.95) (Composite airframe built up from BGA 4687 (127/488) (fuselage) and BGA 3961 (106/453) (left wing) and right wing ex New Zealand. The c/n plate shows 127. (BGA 4838) was originally registered with BGA as c/n 106 but changed to "453/1" when found BGA noted a duplicate c/n 106)

G-CJWM	Grob G103 Twin Astir II	3536	BGA 4840-JWM D-8730	15. 2.08	Norfolk Gliding Club Ltd	Tibenham	17. 4.08
G-CJWR	Grob G102 Astir CS	1271	BGA 4844-JWR D-7366	18.12.07	G J Hunter tr Astir JWR	Portmoak	20. 1.08
G-CJWT	Glaser-Dirks DG-200	2-42	BGA 4846-JWT D-6560	12.11.07	K R Nash	RNAS Yeovilton	28. 9.08
G-CJWV	Glasflügel H201B Standard Libelle	411	BGA 4848-JWV OY-XBG	12.10.07	A Beatty	(Welwyn Garden City)	28. 9.08
G-CJWX	Schempp-Hirth Ventus 2cT	63/198	BGA 4850-JWX	31.10.07	S.G.Olender	Santo Tome del Puerto, Spain	28. 9.08
G-CJWZ	Schleicher ASW 22	22037	BGA 4852-JWZ D-3422	29.11.07	D Prosolek	Saltby	7.12.07
G-CJXA	Schempp-Hirth Nimbus 3dT	9	BGA 4853-JXA D-KKYY, D-4444	2.11.07	B C Morris tr Y44 Syndicate	Lasham	17. 2.08

G-CJXB	Centrair 201B Marianne	201015	BGA 4854-JXB F-CGMN	12. 2.08	C A Sheldon tr Marianne Syndicate	Pocklington	27. 3.08
G-CJXC	Wassmer WA-28 Espadon	102	BGA 4855-JXC F-CDZV	22.12.07	A P Montague	Nympsfield	5. 6.08
G-CJXG	Eiriavion PIK-20D	20660	BGA 4859-JXG PH-670	19.12.07	D Ingledew	Lee-on-Solent	21. 4.08
G-CJXL	Schempp-Hirth Discus CS	278CS	BGA 4863-JXL	1.12.07	J Hall and M J Hasluck	Parham Park	23. 1.08
G-CJXM	Schleicher ASK 13	13542	BGA 4864-JXM RAFGSA R34, F-CERF	7. 2.08	The Windrushers Gliding Club Ltd	Bicester	23. 3.08
G-CJXN	Centrair 201B Marianne	201B035	BGA 4865-JXN F-CBLI	13.12.07	J D Trussell	(Ilkeston)	
G-CJXP	Glaser-Dirks DG-100	18	BGA 4866-JXP PH-520	13. 2.08	R M Wootten	Eyres Field	19. 3.08
G-CJXR	Schempp-Hirth Discus b	540	BGA 4868-JXR D-9152	29. 2.08	Cambridge Gliding Club Ltd	Gransden Lodge	25. 3.08
G-CJXT	Schleicher ASW 24B	24233	BGA 4870-JXT D-6706	11.10.07	P McAuley	Snitterfield	10.12.07
G-CJXW	Schempp-Hirth Duo Discus T	7/250	BGA 4873-JXW D-KOZX	16.11.07	C Bainbridge	Wormingford	7. 6.08
G-CJXX	Pilatus B4-PC11AF	13	BGA 4874-JXX HB-1112	21.12.07	N H Buckenham	Rattlesden	6. 6.08
G-CJXZ	Schleicher ASW 27	27152	BGA 4876-JXZ	27.11.07	P R H Starey	Wycombe Air Park	28. 9.08
G-CJYC	Grob G102 Astir CS	1429	BGA 4880-JYC RAFGSA R19, RAFGGA 742, D-7425	14. 8.07	R A Christie	Easterton	4.11.07
G-CJYD	Schleicher ASW 27	27155	BGA 4881-JYD	1.11.07	J E Gatfield	Wycombe Air Park	17.10.07
G-CJYE	Schleicher ASK 13	13191	BGA 4882-JYE D-0347	23. 1.08	North Wales Gliding Club Ltd	Llantisilio	15. 5.08
G-CJYF	Schempp-Hirth Discus CS	281CS	BGA 4883-JYF	4.12.07	R D Stroud	Wycombe Air Park	17. 3.08
G-CJYN	Schempp-Hirth Discus 2b	94	BGA 4890-JYN	7. 1.08	R Brigliadori	Alzate Brianza, Italy	27. 6.08
G-CJYP	Grob G102 Astir CS	5018C	BGA 4891-JYP D-8743	7. 2.08	Norfolk Gliding Club Ltd	Tibenham	25. 9.08
G-CJYS	Schempp-Hirth Mini-Nimbus C	106	BGA 4894-JYS HB-1437	9. 1.08	A Jenkins	Shobdon	5. 7.08
G-CJYU	Schempp-Hirth Ventus 2cT	70/216	BGA 4896-JYU	8.10.07	J G Arnold tr RAF Gliding and Soaring Association "R11" (Operated Chilterns Gliding Centre)	RAF Halton	3. 4.08
G-CJZB	DG Flugzeugbau DG-500 Elan Orion	5E223X61	BGA 4903-JZB	7. 1.08	J I May tr Bicester JZB Syndicate "Jezabel"	Bicester	28. 9.08
G-CJZE	Schleicher ASK 13	13423	BGA 4906-JZE OY-XPJ, D-2125	20.11.07	Needwood Forest Gliding Club Ltd	Cross Hayes	16. 3.08
G-CJZG	Schempp-Hirth Discus bT	9/272	BGA 4908-JZG D-KISM	7. 9.07	R H C Acreman	Nympsfield	2. 5.08
G-CJZH	Schleicher ASW 20CL	20754	BGA 4909-JZH D-5932	11. 9.07	C P Gibson and C A Hunt	Lasham	28. 9.08
G-CJZK	DG Flugzeugbau DG-500 Elan Orion	5E225X63	BGA 4911-JZK	18.12.07	Devon & Somerset Gliding Club Ltd	North Hill	29. 7.08
G-CJZL	Schempp-Hirth Mini Nimbus B	92	BGA 4912-JZL HB-1453	2.11.07	S J Aldridge	Saltby	16. 5.08
G-CJZM	Schempp-Hirth Ventus 2a	117	BGA 4913-JZM	7. 1.08	M D Wells	Nympsfield	28. 9.08
G-CJZN	Schleicher ASW 28	28038	BGA 4914-JZN	19.10.07	P J Coward	Husbands Bosworth	8.12.07
G-CJZX	Schleicher ASW 27B	27166	BGA 4923-JZX	18.10.07	D M Jones and P R Barley	RAF Halton	28. 9.08
G-CJZZ	Rolladen-Schneider LS7-WL	7128	BGA 4925-JZZ SE-UIU	8.12.07	J H Tucker	Crowland	22. 3.08

G-CKAA - G-CKZZ

G-CKAH	Schempp-Hirth Discus bT	112-464	BGA 4933-KAH D-KNZZ	10.12.07	R M Brown	Bicester	28. 9.08
G-CKAJ	Schempp-Hirth Ventus 2cT	86/...	BGA 4934-KAJ	08.11.07	A N Redington	RNAS Culdrose	23. 4.08
G-CKAL	Schleicher ASW 28	28031	BGA 4936-KAL	30.10.07	P A Ivens and D A Smith	Nympsfield	16. 2.08
G-CKAM	Glasflügel H205 Club Libelle	83	BGA 4937-KAM D-8928	14. 9.07	P A Cronk and R C Tallowin	Lyveden	9.12.07
G-CKAN	PZL-Bielsko SZD-50-3 Puchacz	B-2106	BGA 4938-KAN PH-1104	26.11.07	The Bath, Wilts and North Dorset Gliding Club Ltd	Kingston Deverill	28. 2.08
G-CKAP	Schempp-Hirth Discus CS	290CS	BGA 4939-KAP	5.10.07	A A Stewart tr KAP Syndicate	Portmoak	28. 9.08
G-CKAS	Schempp-Hirth Ventus 2cT	93-271	BGA 4942-KAS (BGA 4995-KCX), (BGA 4942-KAS)	24. 1.08	R E Fletcher tr KAS Club (Finchampstead, Wokingham)		29. 8.08
G-CKAV	Rolladen-Schneider LS4-a	4696	BGA 4945-KAV D-1055	17.11.07	A J Cockerell "GG"	Pormoak	28. 9.08
G-CKAW	DG Flugzeugbau DG-500 Elan Orion	5E228X66	BGA 4946-KAW	30. 8.07	Midland Gliding Club Ltd	Long Mynd	16. 9.09
G-CKAX	DG Flugzeugbau DG-500 Elan Orion	5E229X67	BGA 4947-KAX	29.11.07	York Gliding Centre Ltd	Rufforth	7. 5.08
G-CKAY	Grob G102 Astir CS	1452	BGA 4948-KAY D-7433	18. 1.08	Lincolnshire Gliding Club	Strubby	17. 2.08
G-CKBA	Centrair 101A Pégase 90	101A0435	BGA 4950-KBA HB-3096	27. 2.08	C Weston tr KBA Pégase 101A Syndicate	Challock	18. 4.08
G-CKBD	Grob G102 Astir CS	1217	BGA 4953-KBD D-7290	29.10.07	R A Morriss	(RAF Cranwell)	3. 3.07
G-CKBF	DG Flugzeugbau DG-303 Elan	3E498	BGA 4955-KBF	21. 9.07	A L Garfield	Dunstable	28. 9.08
G-CKBG	Schempp-Hirth Ventus 2cT	83-250	BGA 4956-KBG	14. 2.08	J F d'Arcy tr 71 Syndicate	Lasham	7. 4.08
G-CKBH	Rolladen-Schneider LS6	6072	BGA 4957-KBH D-7798	24.10.07	F C Ballard anf P Walker	Nympsfield	5. 5.08

G-CKBK	Schempp-Hirth Ventus 2cT	79/244	BGA 4959-KBK	9.10.07	D Rhys-Jones	Parham Park	4. 3.08
G-CKBL	Grob G102 Astir CS	1464	BGA 4960-KBL D-7436	15. 2.08	Norfolk Gliding Club Ltd	Tibenham	9. 2.08
G-CKBM	Schleicher ASW 28	28046	BGA 4961-KBM D-0001	2.11.07	M E Newland-Smith and M Poole	Dunstable	28. 9.08
G-CKBN	PZL-Bielsko SZD-55-1 Promyk	551190004	BGA 4962-KBN SE-ULV	1.10.07	N D Pearson	Ringmer	15. 3.08
G-CKBS	Glaser-Dirks DG-600	6-42	BGA 4966-KBS OO-YPH, D-4882	20. 8.07	M S Szymkowicz	Bicester	21. 2.08
G-CKBU	Schleicher ASW 28	28040	BGA 4968-KBU	15.10.07	G C Metcalfe	Lasham	28. 9.08
G-CKBV	Schleicher ASW 28	28045	BGA 4969-KBV	2.11.07	P Whipp	Dunstable	6. 9.08
G-CKCB	Rolladen-Schneider LS4-a	4776	BGA 4975-KCB PH-887, D-1597	26. 9.07	The Bristol Gliding Club Proprietary Ltd	Nympsfield	28. 9.08
G-CKCH	Schempp-Hirth Ventus 2cT	56/186	BGA 4981-KCH PH-1191	12.11.07	J J Pridal and L R Marks	Lasham	24. 4.08
G-CKCK	Enstrom 280FX Shark	2071	OO-PVL	5. 5.95	Rhoburt Ltd	(Styal, Wilmslow)	23. 1.08E
G-CKCN	Schleicher ASW 27	27188	BGA 4986-KCN D-0001	23.10.07	A Walford and W J Head	Gransden Lodge	28. 9.08
G-CKCR	AB Sportine Aviacija LAK-17A	132	BGA 4989-KCR	26. 2.08	L Bertoncini	Alzate Brianza, Italy	29. 6.08
G-CKCT	Schleicher ASK 21	21751	BGA 4991-KCT	31. 8.07	Kent Gliding Club Aircraft Ltd	Challock	28. 9.08
G-CKCV	Schempp-Hirth Duo Discus T	54/339	BGA 4993-KCV D-KOZZ	20. 9.07	A J Buchanan tr WE4 Group	Parham Park	28. 9.08
G-CKCY	Schleicher ASW 20	20068	BGA 4996-KCY PH-597, (OY-XTM), PH-597	12. 2.08	A J Wilson and S R Tromans	Nympsfield	3. 3.08
G-CKCZ	Schleicher ASK 21	21749	BGA 4997-KCZ	25. 1.08	Booker Gliding Club Ltd	Wycombe Air Park	21. 3.08
G-CKDA	Schemm-Hirth Ventus 2B	138	BGA 4998-KDA (BGA 5008-KDL), D-4999	19.10.07	D J Eade	Lasham	25. 2.08
G-CKDB	Schleicher Ka 6CR	6431	BGA 4999-KDB HB-805	17.10.07	Aquila Gliding Club Ltd	Hinton-in-the-Hedges	20. 1.08
G-CKDC	Centrair ASW 20F	20524	BGA 5000-KDC F-CFSF	11. 9.07	A R Blanchard and D J Graham	Rattlesden	5. 5.07
G-CKDF	Schleicher ASK 21	21006	BGA 5003-KDF D-6539	29. 1.08	T World tr Portsmouth Naval Gliding Centre Lee-on-Solent		30. 3.08
G-CKDH	Schleicher K 8B	E4	BGA 5005-KDH D-8428	20.12.07	Midland Gliding Club Ltd	Long Mynd	29. 9.08
G-CKDK	Rolladen-Schneider LS4-a	4352	BGA 5007-KDK	21.12.07	M C Ridger	Long Mynd	13. 4.08
G-CKDN	Schleicher ASW 27	27208	BGA 5010-KDN-	17. 8.07	J S McCullagh	Lasham	28. 9.08
G-CKDO	Schempp-Hirth Ventus 2cT	97/..	BGA 5012-KDQ	27. 9.07	A R Milne	Kingston Deverill	6.12.07
G-CKDS	Schleicher ASW 27	27202	BGA 5014-KDS	31.10.07	A W Gillett and G D Morris	Nympsfield	28. 9.08
G-CKDU	Glaser-Dirks DG-200/17	2-161/1752	BGA 5016-KDU D-6000	8. 1.08	P.G.Noonan	Edgehill	28. 3.08
G-CKDV	Schempp-Hirth Ventus b/16.6	224	BGA 5017-KDV HB-1770	21. 9.07	M A Codd	Talgarth	28. 9.08
G-CKDW	Schleicher ASW 27	27196	BGA 5018-KDW	21.11.07	C Colton	Gransden Lodge	16. 3.08
G-CKDX	Glaser-Dirks DG-200	2-11	BGA 5019-KDX D-7218	26. 2.08	A M Bailey	Aston Down	21. 3.08
G-CKDY	Glaser-Dirks DG-100	78	BGA 5020-KDY D-2591	2.11.07	P T Claiden tr 503 Group	Dunstable	27.11.07
G-CKEA	Schempp-Hirth Cirrus 18	11	BGA 5022-KEA D-8807, HB-911	9.11.07	C M Reed	Rattlesden	5. 1.08
G-CKEB	Schempp-Hirth Standard Cirrus	436G	BGA 5023-KEB F-CEFN	22. 2.08	P J D Smith	Rivar Hill	27. 3.08
G-CKEC	Rolladen-Schneider LS4-a	4469	BGA 5024-KEC D-5170	22.11.07	B T Spreckley (Operated European Soaring Club)	Ontur, Spain	28. 9.08
G-CKED	Schleicher ASW 27B	27203	BGA 5025-KED D-0001	6.11.07	M H Bull	Crowland	28. 9.08
G-CKEE	Grob G102 Astir CS	1135	BGA 5026-KEE D-4179	13.12.07	Essex & Suffolk Gliding Club Ltd	Wormingford	17. 1.08
G-CKEK	Schleicher ASK 21	21767	BGA 5031-KEK	12.11.07	Devon & Somerset Gliding Club Ltd	North Hill	28. 9.08
G-CKEL	Rolladen-Schneider LS8-18	8454	BGA 5032-KEL	8. 2.08	C W Nicolson and P Kaye	Gransden Lodge	16. 4.08
G-CKEM	Robinson R44 Clipper II	11375		24. 8.06	True Course Helicopter Ltd	Gibraltar	5. 9.08E
G-CKER	Schleicher ASW 19B	19224	BGA 5037-KER OY-XJI	6.11.07	B Van Woerden tr G-CKER Syndicate	Feshiebridge	15. 4.08
G-CKES	Schempp-Hirth Cirrus 18	46	BGA 5038-KES D-6955, HB-955	28.11.07	D Judd	RAF Cosford	30. 5.08
G-CKEV	Schempp-Hirth Duo Discus	368	BGA 5041-KEV	25.10.07	J G Arnold tr RAF Gliding and Soaring Association (Operated Cranwell Gliding Club)	RAF Cranwell	28. 9.08
G-CKEX	Schleicher ASW 19B	19115	BGA 5043-KEX I-IUUH, D-7551	6.12.07	E D Johnson	Lyveden	28. 9.08
G-CKEY	Piper PA-28-161 Warrior II	28-7916061	N510PU N22166	4. 1.07	B W Gomez	Halfpenny Green	13. 6.08E
G-CKEZ	DG Flugzeugbau LS8-t	8464	BGA 5045-KEZ D-KSAB	25.10.07	D A Jesty	Brentor	19. 6.08
G-CKFA	Schempp-Hirth Standard Cirrus 75	644	BGA 5046-KFA D-2124, F-CEMQ	8. 2.08	C F Jordan	(Banchory, Aberdeen)	23. 5.08
G-CKFB	Schempp-Hirth Discus 2T	30-179	BGA 5047-KFB D-KOZZ	12.12.07	P L and P A G Holland	Kirton-in-Lindsey	23. 9.08
G-CKFC	Schempp-Hirth Ventus 2cT	105	BGA 5048-KFC D-KOZZ	3.10.07	M R Emmett	Wycombe Air Park	28. 9.08
G-CKFD	Schleicher ASW 27	27211	BGA 5049-KFD	30. 1.08	W T Craig	Dunstable	14. 2.08
G-CKFE	Eiriavion PIK 20D	20520	BGA 5050-KFE D-8103, OE-5103	11. 1.08	M J McSorley	Bellarena	24. 8.07
G-CKFG	Grob G103A Twin II Acro	3771-K-57	BGA 5052-KFG D-1339	6. 2.08	The Surrey Hills Gliding Club Ltd	Kenley	23. 6.08

G-CKFH	Schempp-Hirth HS-7 Mini Nimbus	15	BGA 5053-KFH D-4819	26.11.07	D Nichols	Aston Down	16. 4.07
G-CKFJ	Schleicher ASK 13	13136	BGA 5054-KFJ PH-383	29.11.07	York Gliding Centre Ltd	Rufforth	11. 3.08
G-CKFK	VTC Standard Cirrus	203	BGA 5055-KFK S5-3058, SL-3058, YU-4295	29.10.07	R J Clarke tr G-CKFK Group	North Hill	29. 3.08
G-CKFL	Rolladen-Schneider LS4	4080	BGA 5056-KFL HB-1619	17. 1.08	D R Taylor and D A O'Brien	Tibenham	23. 2.08
G-CKFM	Rolladen-Schneider LS8-18	8475	BGA 5057-KFM D-9502	13. 9.07	A J H Smith	Rougham	13. 7.08
G-CKFN	DG Flugzeugbau DG-1000S	10-29S28	BGA 5058-KFN	5.12.07	Yorkshire Gliding Club (Proprietary) Ltd	Sutton Bank	22.12.07
G-CKFP	Schempp-Hirth Ventus 2cT	110/304	BGA 5059-KFP D-KKAH	9.11.07	C R Sutton	Saltby	25. 1.08
G-CKFT	Schempp-Hirth Duo Discus T	77/383	BGA 5063-KFT D-KIIH	12. 2.08	L R Merritt tr Duo Discus Syndicate	Saltby	4. 4.08
G-CKFV	DG Flugzeugbau LS8-t	8476	BGA 5065-KFV D-KOBP	11. 1.08	G A Rowden and K I Arkley	Sutton Bank	16. 4.08
G-CKFY	Schleicher ASK 21	21776	BGA 5068-KFN	23. 1.06	Cambridge Gliding Club Ltd	Gransden Lodge	28 .9.08
G-CKGA	Schempp-Hirth Ventus 2cxT	115/312	BGA 5070-KGA D-KIBL	24. 4.06	D R Campbell "370"	Wycombe Air Park	28. 9.08
G-CKGB	Schempp-Hirth Ventus 2CT	117	BGA 5071-KGB	3. 1.06	D R Irving "T3"	Portmoak	28. 9.08
G-CKGC	Schempp-Hirth Ventus 2cxT	118/317	BGA 5072-KGC D-KMAF	7.10.05	C P A Jeffery "J6"	Gransden Lodge	28. 9.08
G-CKGD	Schempp-Hirth Ventus 2cT	119/318	BGA 5073-KGD D-KEAD	7.10.05	C Morris ""V9"	Bidford	28. 9.08
G-CKGF	Schempp-Hirth Duo Discus T	84/397	BGA 5075-KGF	17.10.05	J P McNamee tr Duo 233 Group "233"	Gransden Lodge	7.12.07
G-CKGH	Grob G102 Club Astir II	5057C	BGA 5077-KGH OO-ZVS	6. 9.06	I M Gavan	Kenley	22.11.07
G-CKGK	Schleicher ASK 21	21766	BGA 5079-KGK	21.12.05	T M Holloway tr RAF Gliding and Soaring Association "R28" (Operated Clevelands Gliding Club)	AAC Dishforth	28. 9.08
G-CKGL	Schempp-Hirth Ventus 2cT	88/263	BGA 5080-KGL EI-152	13. 2.06	Bidford Airfield Ltd "X4"	Bidford	26. 4.08
G-CKGN	Schleicher ASW 28-18	28505	BGA 5082-KGN D-3063, D-0001	15. 3.06	M Jerman	Sutton Bank	17. 3.07
G-CKGT	Standard Cirrus 75-VTC (Built Jastreb Fabrika Aviona I Jedrilica)	294	BGA 5087-KGT HA-4283	4.10.06	D M Raffello "41"	Enemonzo, Italy	1. 7.08
G-CKGU	Schleicher ASW 19B	19208	BGA 5088-KGU Belgian Air Cadets PL68	21. 4.06	D M Ruttle "690"	Strubby	22. 4.07
G-CKGV	Schleicher ASW 28-18	28512	BGA 5089-KGV D-7062	4.10.05	A H Reynolds	Long Mynd	30. 3.08
G-CKGX	Scheicher ASK 21	21782	BGA 5091-KGX	9. 5.06	Coventry Gliding Club Ltd "KGX"	Husbands Bosworth	4. 5.08
G-CKGY	Scheibe Bergfalke IV	5839	BGA 5092-KGY SE-TLL	17. 1.06	B R Pearson tr North Devon Gliding Club	Eaglescott	23. 6.07
G-CKHA	PZL-Bielsko SZD-51-1 Junior	B-1918	BGA 5094-KHA (SP-3691), D-2843, DDR-2803	1.12.05	Devon & Somerset Gliding Club Ltd	North Hill	28. 9.08
G-CKHB	Rolladen-Schneider LS3	3316	BGA 5095-KHB D-2635	28. 3.06	P A Dunthorne	Nympsfield	13. 4.08
G-CKHC	DG Flugzeugbau DG-500/20 Elan	5E178W11	BGA 5096-KHC D-6401	12.12.05	G M Brightman and J Donovan tr G-CKHC Group 	Lyveden	23. 3.08
G-CKHD	Schleicher ASW 27	27222	BGA 5097-KHD	1.12.05	N D Tillett "T4"	Dunstable	28. 9.08
G-CKHE	AB Sportine Aviacija LAK-17A	122	BGA 5098-KHE OM-0118	17. 1.07	A J Garrity and N J Gough	RAF Wittering	25. 5.08
G-CKHF	Schleicher ASW 20	20229	BGA 5099-KHF D-3162	21. 9.05	C H Brown "XD2"	AAC Dishforth	14. 5.08
G-CKHG	Schleicher ASW 27	27223	BGA 5100-KHG	28.11.05	R A F King "K5"	Bicester	7. 2.08
G-CKHH	Schleicher ASK 13	13171	BGA 5101-KHH LN-GAX	15. 3.06	Lincolnshire Gliding Club Ltd	Strubby	6. 3.08
G-CKHK	Schempp-Hirth Duo Discus T	100/426	BGA 5103-KHK	29. 6.06	I Ashton tr Duo Discus Syndicate	Chipping	23. 6.08
G-CKHM	Centrair 101A Pégase 90	101A0359	BGA 5105-KHM F-CHDE	23.11.05	A Bland tr G-CKHM Group	Lasham	4. 4.08
G-CKHN	PZL-Bielsko SZD-51-1 Junior	B-2142	BGA 5106-KHN OE-5614, SP-3612	17. 3.06	The Nene Valley Gliding Club Ltd	Upwood	10. 6.07
G-CKHP	Rolladen-Schneider LS8-18	8337	BGA 5107-KHP N818FD	28. 3.06	A D May "70"	Dunstable	2. 5.08
G-CKHR	PZL-Bielsko SZD-51-1 Junior	B-1775	BGA 5109-KHR HB-1928	15.11.06	Wolds Gliding Club Ltd	Pocklington	19. 3.08
G-CKHS	Rolladen-Schneider LS7-WL	7043	BGA 5110-KHS PH-862, D-5157	20.12.05	G F Coles and E W Russell "KO"	Wormingford	15. 3.08
G-CKHT	Standard Cirrus (Built Burkhart Grob Flugzeugbau)	259G	BGA 5111-KHT D-1139	31. 8.06	M Holden "424"	Lasham	8. 3.08
G-CKHV	Glaser-Dirks DG-100	77	BGA 5112-KHV HB-1331	8. 2.08	M E Laxaback and M J Brown	Chipping	29. 7.08
G-CKHW	PZL-Bielsko SZD-50-3 Puchacz	503.A 004.001	BGA 5113-KHW	14. 8.07	Derbyshire and Lancashire Gliding Club Ltd	Camphill	16. 8.06
G-CKHX	Schleicher ASW 28-18E	28720	BGA 5114-KHX D-KAMF	10. 2.06	P J O'Connell and M C Foreman "6X"	Lasham	11. 4.08
G-CKJA	Schleicher ASW 28-18	28712	BGA 5117-KJA D-6051	27. 1.06	J Vella-Grech "28E"	(Shrewsbury)	7. 2.08
G-CKJB	Schempp-Hirth Ventus bT	26/191	BGA 5118-KJB D-KBST	9. 3.06	J D Sorrell "LW"	Usk	16. 7.07
G-CKJC	Schempp-Hirth Nimbus 3T	6/57	BGA 5119-KJC D-KUPA, OY-KHX, D-KHXB	16. 1.06	A C Wright "617"	Sutton Bank	9. 2.08

G-CKJD	Schempp-Hirth Standard Cirrus 75-VTC	241	BGA 5120-KJD	30. 3.07	L Rebbeck	Wycombe Air Park	4. 5.08
	(Built Vazduhoplovno Tehnicki Centar)		F-CDOZ		*"KJD"*		
G-CKJE	DG Flugzeugbau LS8-18	8498	BGA 5121-KJE	6. 9.06	M D Wells *"321"*	Bidford	28. 9.08
G-CKJF	Schempp-Hirth Standard Cirrus	414G	BGA 5122-KJF	16. 1.06	J G Wilson tr G-CKJF Group	Bicester	23. 3.08
			OY-XGW, D-9247		*"GW"*		
G-CKJG	Schempp-Hirth Cirrus	153Y	BGA 5123-KJG	11.10.05	S J Wright	Rattlesden	23. 3.08
			EC-CKO		*"901"*		
G-CKJH	DG Flugzeugbau DG-300 Elan	3E506	BGA 5124-KJH	9.12.05	Yorkshire Gliding Club (Proprietary) Ltd	Sutton Bank	28. 9.08
G-CKJJ	DG Flugzeugbau DG-505 Elan Orion	5E249X79	BGA 5125-KJJ	29. 3.06	Ulster Gliding Club Ltd	Bellarena	28. 9.08
			S5-AMS01				
G-CKJK	Schempp-Hirth Janus Ce	283	BGA 5126-KJK	30. 1.06	M P Drayton tr Janus Syndicate	Pocklington	25. 4.08
			D-3666		*"C66"*		
G-CKJL	Schleicher ASK 13	13468	BGA 5127-KJL	18. 9.06	Lincolnshire Gliding Club Ltd	Strubby	22. 9.07
			D-2338				
G-CKJM	Schempp-Hirth Ventus cT	120/394	BGA 5128-KJM	10.11.05	J Ferguson	Portmoak	28. 9.08
	(Officially regd with c/n 120)		D-KAHE, OH-781		*"7A"*		
G-CKJN	Schleicher ASW 20	20052	BGA 5129-KJN	22.12.05	R Logan	Bellarena	17.11.07
			D-7964		*"9E"*		
G-CKJP	Schleicher ASK 21	21783	BGA 5130-KJP	17. 1.06	T M Holloway tr RAF Gliding and Soaring Association		
			D-0001		*"R12"*	RAF Keevil	24.11.07
					(Operated Bannerdown Gliding Club)		
G-CKJS	Schleicher ASW 28-18E	28713	BGA 5132-KJS	9. 3.06	J R Warren and A Hegner	Wycombe Air Park	15. 3.08
			D-KHJW		*"JW"*		
G-CKJV	Schleicher ASW 28-18E	28725	BGA 5145-KJV	25. 1.06	A C Price	Nympsfield	19. 3.08
			D-KFAP, D-KOAB		*"AP"*		
G-CKJZ	Schempp-Hirth Discus bT	75/403	BGA 5149-KJZ	28.11.05	A I Mawer tr G-CKJZ Group	Kirton-in-Lindsey	13. 2.08
			OE-9367		*"E17"*		
G-CKKB	Centrair 101A Pégase	101A0209	BGA 5151-KKB	8. 3.06	D M Rushton	Lyveden	9. 6.08
			SE-TZU				
G-CKKC	DG Flugzeugbau DG-303 Elan Acro	3E509A41	BGA 5152-KKC	8. 5.06	M P Ellis tr Charlie Kilo Kilo Charlie Syndicate	Burn	14. 5.08
G-CKKD	Schleicher ASW 28-18E	28734	BGA 5153-KKD	28. 4.06	A Palmer *"AP1"*	Dunstable	29. 3.08
G-CKKE	Schempp-Hirth Duo Discus T	103/429	BGA 5154-KKE	30. 1.06	T Moyes and M Powell-Brett	Husbands Bosworth	29. 3.08
			D-KOZZ		*"F94"*		
G-CKKF	Schempp-Hirth Ventus 2cT	139/364	BGA 5155-KKF	23. 9.05	A R MacGregor *"306"*	Kingston Deverill	28. 9.08
G-CKKH	Schleicher ASW 27	27231	BGA 5157-KKH	20.10.05	P L Hurd	Wycombe Air Park	28. 9.08
			D-0001		*"AG"*		
G-CKKK	AB Sportine Aviacija LAK-17A	161	BGA 5159-KKK	12. 9.06	C J Nicolas	Ridgewell	13. 4.08
			LY-GGF		*"960"*		
G-CKKM	Schleicher ASW 28-18	28502	BGA 5161-KKM	16.10.06	R F Thirkell	Lasham	17. 3.07
			D-9004, D-0001		*"B3"*		
G-CKKN	Schempp-Hirth Duo Discus	165	BGA 5162-KKN	10. 3.06	M Jordy tr Golf Bravo One	Husbands Bosworth	22. 2.08
			D-8215		*"GB1"*		
G-CKKP	Schleicher ASK 21	21795	BGA 5163-KKP	24. 4.06	Bowland Forest Gliding Club Ltd *"BF1"*	Chipping	23. 6.08
G-CKKR	Schleicher ASK 13	13065	BGA 5164-KKR	5.12.05	Aquila Gliding Club Ltd	Hinton-in-the-Hedges	26. 4.08
			PH-391				
G-CKKV	DG Flugzeugbau DG-1000S	10-57T2	BGA 5167-KKV	10. 2.06	Lasham Gliding Society Ltd *"776"*	Lasham	14. 5.08
G-CKKX	Rolladen-Schneider LS4-a	4827	BGA 5169-KKX	19. 1.06	B W Svenson tr 449 Syndicate	Pocklington	2. 2.08
			PH-928, D-3529		*"449"*		
G-CKKY	Schempp-Hirth Duo Discus T	124/...	BGA 5170-KKY	19. 1.06	P D Duffin tr G-CKKY Group *"440"*	Wormingford	29. 3.08
G-CKLA	Schleicher ASK 13	13363	BGA 5172-KLA	16. 6.06	Booker Gliding Club Ltd	Wycombe Air Park	14. 6.07
			PH-1084, D-0857		*"KLA" (Noted 2.08)*		
G-CKLB	Schleicher ASW 27	27234	BGA 5173-KLB	19.10.05	S J Riddington and C Curtis *"Z27"*	Husbands Bosworth	28. 9.08
G-CKLC	Glasflügel H206 Hornet	39	BGA 5174-KLC	16. 2.06	P R Thomas	Dunstable	9. 6.08
			SE-TPL				
G-CKLD	Schempp-Hirth Discus 2cT	1	BGA 5175-KLD	27.10.05	J P Galloway	Portmoak	28. 9.08
			D-KDCC		*"797"*		
G-CKLF	Schempp-Hirth Janus	59	BGA 5177-KLF	15. 9.06	T J Edmunds	RAF Marham	21. 9.08
			D-2170, I-ANUS		*"08"*		
G-CKLG	Rolladen-Schneider LS 4	4264	BGA 5178	7. 8.06	P M Scheiwiller, P S Graham and J P Heath		
			F-CAEQ, D-5530			Sandhill Farm, Shrivenham	29. 8.08
G-CKLN	Rolladen-Schneider LS4-a	4791	BGA 5183-KLN	12. 6.06	K E Jenkinson	Husbands Bosworth	5. 7.08
			D-2823		*"M11"*		
G-CKLP	Schleicher ASW 28-18E	28737	BGA 5184-KLP	16. 3.06	J T Birch	Gransden Lodge	29. 8.08
			D-KOAB		*"205"*		
G-CKLR	PZL-Bielsko SZD-55-1 Promyk	551193056	G-CKLM-KLR	25. 1.06	D T King and A Gibson tr Zulu Five Gliding Group		
			BGA 5185, F-CHSP, F-WHSP		*"Z55"*	Trenchard Lines, Upavon	22. 4.08
G-CKLS	Rolladen-Schneider LS4	4637	BGA 5186-KLS	29. 6.06	Wolds Gliding Club Ltd	Pocklington	16. 6.08
			D-6786				
G-CKLT	Schempp-Hirth Nimbus 3/24.5	1	BGA 5187-KLT	22. 5.06	G N Thomas	AAC Wattisham	5. 4.08
			D-5052, EC-EBP, D-2111		*"GT"*		
G-CKLV	Schempp-Hirth Discus 2cT	20/27	BGA 5188-KLV	8. 2.06	J Iglehart	Lasham	15. 3.08
			D-KKFC"				
G-CKLW	Schleicher ASK 21	21799	BGA 5189-KLW	9.12.05	Yorkshire Gliding Club (Proprietary) Ltd	Sutton Bank	29. 8.08
G-CKLX	Bölkow Phoebus B1	757	BGA 5190-KLX	17. 4.07	D R Poleck	Camphill	15. 5.08
	(Built Waggon-U Maschinenbau AG)		OE-0851		*"KLX"*		
G-CKLY	DG Flugzeugbau DG-1000T	10-66T6	BGA 5191-KLY	3.10.05	R J Large tr G-CKLY Group	Husbands Bosworth	8. 5.08
			D-KAAD		*"D6"*		
G-CKMA	DG Flugzeugbau LS8-T	8510	BGA 5192-KMA	5.12.05	G Rizk *"GR8"*	Saltby	30.11.06
G-CKMB	AB Sportine Aviacija LAK-19T	018	BGA 5193-KMB	7. 3.07	D J McKenzie	Camphill	14. 3.08
			LY-GJE		*"KMB"*		
G-CKMC	Grob G102 Astir CS77	1625	BGA 5194-KMC	20. 9.05	L J Gregoire	Lasham	8.11.07
			LN-GBA, D-4799				
G-CKMD	Schempp-Hirth Standard Cirrus	31	BGA 5195-KMD	8.11.05	C I Roberts	Snitterfield	13. 3.08
			SE-TIX, D-0528		*"V12"*		

G-CKME	DG Flugzeugbau LS8-T	8504	BGA 5196-KME	22.12.05	D Bradley "DB"	Sutton Bank	16. 2.08
G-CKMF	Centrair 101A Pégase	101038	BGA 5197-KMF F-CFQE	8. 5.06	D L M Jamin	Dunstable	29. 4.08
G-CKMG	Glaser-Dirks DG-100G Elan	E159G126	BGA 5198-KMG HB-1733	27. 9.06	A W Roberts "AD"	Dunstable	4. 4.08
G-CKMI	Schleicher K 8C	81006	BGA 5200-KMI RAFGGA 562"	6. 9.06	V Mallon	Kleve-Wisseler Dünen, Germany	28. 8.08
G-CKMJ	Schleicher Ka 6CR	6109	BGA 5201-KMJ RAFGGA 555. D-8455	15. 8.06	V Mallon	Kleve-Wisseler Dünen, Germany	27. 9.06
G-CKML	Schempp-Hirth Duo Discus T	52/336	BGA 5203-KML PH-1256	12. 4.06	J J Pridal tr KML Group "KA"	Lasham	12. 4.08
G-CKMM	Schleicher ASW 28-18E	28742	BGA 5204-KMM	23. 1.06	R G Munro "RM"	Wycombe Air Park	18.12.07
G-CKMO	Rolladen-Schneider LS7-WL	7007	BGA 5206-KMO PH-861, D-1264	15.12.05	G E M Turpin "L7"	RAF Keevll	5. 4.08
G-CKMP	AB Sportine Aviacija LAK-17A	173	BGA 5207-KMP LY-GMZ	17. 1.06	J L Mciver	Portmoak	29. 8.08
G-CKMR	Letov LF-107 Lunak	54	BGA 5208-KMR OK-0838	6.12.05	W Seitz	Pohlheim, Germany	10. 4.08
G-CKMT	Grob G103C Twin III Acro	34157	BGA 5210-KMT PH-1151, D-0659	3. 1.06	The Borders (Milfield) Gliding Club Ltd	Milfield	14. 1.08
G-CKMV	Rolladen-Schneider LS3-17	3329	BGA 5212-KMV D-6931	8.11.05	F Roles	Husbands Bosworth	29. 8.08
G-CKMW	Schleicher ASK 21	21798	BGA 5213-KMW	9.12.05	T M Holloway tr RAF Gliding and Soaring Association "R18" RAF Cranwell (Operated Cranwell Gliding Club)		29. 8.08
G-CKMY	Schleicher ASW20L	20392	BGA 5215-KMY PH-803, D-8833	17. 1.06	C M Davey tr WR Soaring Group "W81"	RAF Wittering	18. 4.08
G-CKMZ	Schleicher ASW 28-18	28716	BGA 5216-KMZ D-KBJM	6. 1.06	J R Martindale "J5"	Walney Island	7. 2.08
G-CKNB	Schempp-Hirth Standard Cirrus	222	BGA 5218-KNB S5-3056, SL-3056, YU-4209	17. 3.06	A Booker "505"	Lasham	16. 4.08
G-CKNC	Caproni Vizzola Calif A-21S	240	BGA 5219-KNC F-CEUE	8. 2. 06	J J and M E Pritchard "NC"	Lasham	19. 5.08
G-CKND	DG Flugzeugbau DG-1000T	10-76T15	BGA 5220-KND	12. 6.06	S Heaton tr KND Group	Sutton Bank	11. 6.08
G-CKNE	Schempp-Hirth Standard Cirrus 75-VTC (Built Vzaduhoplovno Tehnicki Centar)	199	BGA 5221-KNE S5-3057, SL-3057, YU-4293	27. 7.06	G D E Macdonald	Lasham	
G-CKNF	DG Flugzeugbau DG-1000T	10-81T20	BGA 5222-KNF	12. 7.06	R Johnson tr Six November Fox	Lasham	9. 7.08
G-CKNG	Schleicher ASW 28-18E	28747	BGA 5223-KNG	16. 8.06	M P Brockington	Talgarth	6. 8.07
G-CKNI	Glasflügel H205 Club Libelle	150	BGA 5225-KNI F-CEQG	3.08R	K Sleigh "W9"	Rattlesden	
G-CKNJ	Schempp-Hirth Duo Discus xT	142/...	BGA 5224-KNJ	6. 6.06	P Hurd tr Duo D11 Flying Group "D11"	Dunstable	28. 9.08
G-CKNK	DG Flugzeugbau DG-500 Elan Trainer	5E116T48	BGA 5226-KNK D-5661	27. 3.06	R Birch tr Cotswold Gliding Club	Aston Down	1. 5.08
G-CKNL	Schleicher ASK 21	21811	BGA 5228-KNL	15. 5.06	Buckminster Gliding Club Ltd "KNL"	Saltby	29. 4.08
G-CKNM	Schleicher ASK 18	18037	BGA 5229-KNM PH-908, D-4539	4. 7.06	I L Pattingale "K18"	RAF Odiham	28. 9.08
G-CKNN	Slingsby T 21B Sedbergh (Built Martin Hearn Ltd)	MHL.012	BGA 5230-KNN OY-XSI, SE-SMA, WB985	21. 4.06	R Wassermann	Donxdorf, Germany	26. 4.08
G-CKNO	Schempp-Hirth Ventus 2cxT	179/429	BGA 5231-KNO	6. 7.06	C McEwen	Aston Down	28. 9.08
G-CKNR	Schempp-Hirth Ventus 2cxT	181/...	BGA 5233-KNR	27. 7.06	R J Nicholls	Husbands Bosworth	23. 7.07
G-CKNS	Rolladen-Schneider LS4-a	4398	BGA 5234-KNS SE-UEP, OH-714	5. 6.06	I R Willows	Husbands Bosworth	6. 6.08
G-CKNV	Schleicher ASW 28-18E	28749	BGA 5237-KNV	24. 7.06	D G Brain	Dunstable	28. 9.08
G-CKOD	Schempp-Hirth Discus bT	11/282	BGA 5245-KOD HB-2157, D-KCCE	1.12.06	A L Harris and M W Talbot	Nympsfield	28. 9.08
G-CKOE	Schleicher ASG 29	29024	BGA 5246-KOE D-9729	3.08R	D Strange and R C Bromwich "290"	RAF Keevil	
G-CKOH	DG Flugzeugbau DG-1000T	10-87T25	BGA 5249-KOH	20.11.06	Lasham Gliding Society Ltd "45"	Lasham	22.11.07
G-CKOI	AB Sportine Aviacija LAK-17AT	183	BGA 5250-KOI LY-GQF	6.12.06	C G Corbett	Dunstable	28. 9.08
G-CKOJ	Schempp-Hirth Duo Discus	188	BGA 5251-KOJ OE-5583	21.11.06	M R Dawson	Saintes, France	28. 9.08
G-CKOK	Schempp-Hirth Discus 2cT	50	BGA 5252-KOK	17. 4.07	B D Scougall "KOK"	Portmoak	12. 4.08
G-CKOL	Schempp-Hirth Duo Discus T	164	BGA 5253-KOL	24. 4.07	P M Harmer tr Oscar Lima Syndicate "KOL"	North Hill	22. 4.08
G-CKOM	Schleicher ASW 27-18	29023	BGA 5254-KOM D-9529, D-0001	11. 1.08	M D Wells "LE"	Nympsfield	28. 9.08
G-CKON	Schleicher ASG 29E	29512	BGA 5255-KON D-KBJG	3.08R	J Gorringe (Reserved as G-CKON)	Lasham	
G-CKOO	Schleicher ASG 29E	29519	BGA 5256-KOO D-KAAD	3.08R	A Darlington "7"	Lasham	
G-CKOR	DG Flugzeugbau DG-300 Elan	3E110	BGA 5258-KOR PH-768	20.12.06	C D Prescott and J A Sparrow	Gransden Lodge	15.12.07
G-CKOT	Schleicher ASK 21	21818	BGA 5260-KOT	17. 5.07	Ulster Gliding Club Ltd "KOT"	Bellarena	29. 5.08
G-CKOU	AB Sportine Aviacija LAK-19T	027	BGA 5261-KOU LY-GNP	25. 5.07	D Le Roux, R Walker and A Challoner "KOU" & "1UP" (Operated Southdown Gliding Club)	Parham Park	4. 6.08
G-CKOV	Issoire E-78B Silene	05	BGA 5262-KOV F-CFEB	16. 3.07	I P Stork "KOV"	(Alviazere, Portugal)	26. 4.08
G-CKOW	DG Flugzeugbau DG-500 Elan Orion	5E260X89	BGA 5263-KOW	16. 5.07	Southdown Gliding Club Ltd "KOW"	Parham Park	15. 5.08
G-CKOX	DG Flugzeugbau DG-500 Elan Orion	5E258X87	BGA 5264-KOX	4. 9.07	M Blowers tr Seahawk Gliding Club	RNAS Culdrose	1. 9.08
G-CKOY	Schleicher ASG 29E	29510	BGA 5265-KOY D-KNZG	3.08R	P Wells (Zulu Glasstek Ltd) "Z"	Wycombe Air Park	

G-CKOZ	Schleicher ASG 29E	29513	BGA 5266-KOZ 3.08R	E Johnston	Dunstable	
			D-KEEJ	"G9"		
G-CKPA	AB Sportine Aviacija LAK-19T	020	BGA 5267-KPA 14. 2.07	Baltic Sailplanes Ltd	Husbands Bosworth	28. 9.08
			(BGA 5214), LY-GMV	"KPA" and L19"		
G-CKPB	Schempp-Hirth Discus b	166	BGA 5268 15. 2.07	M F Cuming	Edgehill	7. 5.08
			SE-UFE, LN-GFE	"KPB"		
G-CKPE	Schempp-Hirth Duo Discus	56	BGA 5271-KPE 27. 4.07	M F Cuming	Edgehill	9. 4.08
			HB-3088	"KPE"		
G-CKPG	Schempp-Hirth Discus 2cT	59	BGA 5273-KPG 25. 7.07	G Knight and R Baker	Gransden Lodge	26. 7.08
G-CKPJ	Neukom S-4D Elfe	411AB	BGA 5276-KPJ 26. 3.07	J Szladowski	Camphill	
	(Built Jubi GmbH)		D-4598	"KPJ"		
G-CKPK	Schempp-Hirth Ventus 2cxT	197	BGA 5277-KPK 19. 7.07	I C Lees	Pocklington	17. 7.08
G-CKPL	Schempp-Hirth Standard Cirrus 75	649	BGA 5278-KPL 2. 4.07	L B Roberts	Nympsfield	28. 9.08
			F-CEMS	"KPL"		
G-CKPM	DG Flugzeugbau LS8-st	8517	BGA 5279-KPM 1. 6.07	J Bayford tr 8T Soaring "KPM"	Gransden Lodge	19. 5.08
G-CKPN	PZL-Bielsko SZD-51-1 Junior	B-1927	BGA 5280-KPN 1. 2.08	Rattlesden Gliding Club Ltd	Rattlesden	12. 9.08
			HB-3036			
G-CKPO	Schempp-Hirth Duo Discus xT	171	BGA 5281-KPO 19. 7.07	B F Walker	Nympsfield	15. 7.08
			(D-KDWF)			
G-CKPP	Schleicher ASK 21	21824	BGA 5282-KPP 25. 7.07	Coventry Gliding Club Ltd t/a The Gliding Centre		
				"KPP"	Husbands Bosworth	19. 7.08
G-CKPV	Schempp-Hirth HS.7 Mini-Nimbus B	63	BGA 5287-KPV 20. 6.07	C J Pollard	Rougham	
			PH-607, (PH-606)	"KPV"		
G-CKPX	PZL-Swidnik PW-6U	78.04.03	25. 9.07	J C Gibson tr KPX Syndicate	Chipping	
G-CKPY	Schempp-Hirth Duo Discus xT	174	BGA 5290-KPY 30.11.07	C A Marren tr Duo-Discus Syndicate		
					Trenchard Lines, Upavon	
G-CKPZ	Schleicher ASW 20	20360	BGA 5291-KPZ 5. 9.07	T Davies	RAF Cranwell	7. 9.08
			D-4090			
G-CKRB	Schleicher ASK 13	13292	BGA 5293-KRB 13. 9.07	Derbyshire and Lancashire Gliding Club Ltd	Camphill	12. 9.08
			D-0220			
G-CKRC	Schleicher ASW 28-18 E	28735	BGA 5294-KRC 19.10.07	M Woodcock	(Mickle Trafford, Chester)	26. 9.08
			D-KUPC			
G-CKRF	DG Flugzeugbau DG-300 Elan	3E392	BGA 5297-KRF 5.12.07	G A King	Talgarth	
			PH-923			
G-CKRH	Grob G103 Twin Astir II	3596	BGA 5299-KRH 22.11.07	Staffordshire Gliding Club Ltd	Seighford	
			F-CFYJ, D-3963			
G-CKRM	Schleicher ASW 27	27174	BGA 5304-KRM, 14. 2.08	C Luton	Husbands Bosworth	
			EI-GMA, EI-151			
G-CKRN	Grob G102 Astir CS	1261	BGA 5305-KRN 31. 1.08	P Sallis	(Brixworth, Northampton)	
			D-7356			
G-CKRR	Schleicher ASW 15B	15393	BGA 5308-KRR 26. 2.08	S A Day	(Winsford)	
			D-9288			

G-CLAA - G-CLZZ

G-CLAC	Piper PA-28-161 Warrior II	28-8116241	N8396U 18. 5.87	J M Holley tr G-CLAC Group	Blackbushe	7. 3.08
G-CLAS	Short SD.3-60 Variant 200	SH3635	EI-BEK 28. 7.93	BAC Group Ltd	Edinburgh	7. 8.08E
			G-BLED, G-14-3635			
G-CLAV	Europa Aviation Europa	060	11.10.02	C Laverty	Glenforsa, Isle of Mull	24. 4.08P
	(Built C Laverty - pr.no.PFA 247-12612) (Monowheel u/c)					
G-CLAX	Jurca MJ.5 Sirocco	PFA 2204	G-AWKB 22. 4.99	G D Claxton	(Talbot Green, Pontyclun)	
	(Built G D Claxton)					
G-CLAY	Bell 206B-3 JetRanger III	4409	G-DENN 16. 9.02	Claygate Distribution Ltd	Paynetts Farm, Goudhurst	10. 8.08E
			N75486, C-GFNO			
G-CLEA	Piper PA-28-161 Warrior II	28-7916081	N30296 28. 8.80	R J Harrison and A R Carpenter	Oaksey Park	26. 4.08E
G-CLEE	Rans S-6-ES Coyote II	0600.1373 ES	29. 6.01	R Holt	Mill Farm, Shifnal	30. 9.08P
	(Built R Holt - pr.no.PFA 204-13670) (Jabiru 2200A) (Tri-cycle u/c)					
G-CLEG	Flight Design CTSW	07.02.13	12. 4.07	P J Clegg	Barton	11. 4.08P
	(Assembled P&M Aviation Ltd with c/n 8269)					
G-CLEM	Bölkow BÖ.208A-2 Junior	561	G-ASWE 22. 9.81	J J Donely and K Herbert tr Bölkow Group		
			D-EFHE		Coventry	25. 9.08P
G-CLEO	Zenair CH.601HD Zodiac	PFA 162-13500	9. 8.99	K M Bowen	(Whitson, Newport)	
	(Built K M Bowen)					
G-CLFC	Mainair Blade	1324-0502-7-W1119	11. 6.02	G N Cliffe and G Marshall	(Winsford)	20. 6.08P
G-CLHD	British Aerospace BAe 146 Series 200	E2023	G-DEBF 2. 5.00	Flightline Ltd	Southend	26. 9.08E
			N165US, N347PS	(In open store in IAC c/s 2.08 with some engines out)		
G-CLIC	Cameron A-105 Balloon (Hot Air)	2557	18. 4.91	R S Mohr (Clic Trust titles)	Box, Corsham	25. 9.08A
	(Second envelope fitted as c/n 3395, 4.95: third envelope fitted as c/n 10514, 4.04)					
G-CLIF	Comco Ikarus C42 FB UK	PFA 322-14377	14. 3.05	C Sims	Old Sarum	31. 7.07P
	(Built C Sims)					
G-CLOE	Sky 90-24 Balloon (Hot Air)	019	11. 3.96	J Skinner	Chart Sutton, Maidstone	9. 6.08A
G-CLOP	Piper PA-32R-301T Saratoga TC	3257257	OY-PHW 12.12.06	G F A Craig	(Felsted, Dunmow)	18. 1.08E
			SX-ACV, N5346S			
G-CLOS	Piper PA-34-200T Seneca II	34-7870361	HB-LKE 17. 6.86	P S Kirby	Coventry	3. 2.08
			N36783			
G-CLOW	Beech 200 Super King Air	BB-821	N821RC 2.11.99	Clowes Estates Ltd	East Midlands	9.11.07E
			TC-DBY, N144TM, F-GDCB			
G-CLRK	Sky 77-24 Balloon (Hot Air)	101	3. 3.98	William Clark and Son (Parkgate) Ltd	Dumfries	1. 8.07A
G-CLUB	Reims Cessna FRA150N Aerobat	FRA1500347	OO-AWZ 10. 2.83	D C C Handley	Little Staughton	23. 7.08E
			F-WZAZ, (F-WZDZ)			
G-CLUE	Piper PA-34-200T Seneca II	34-7970502	N8089Z 15. 9.92	J P Spencer Ltd	Fowlmere	25. 4.08E
G-CLUX	Reims Cessna F172N Skyhawk II	F17201996	PH-AYG (3) 1. 5.80	J G Jackman and K M Drewitt	Hawarden	20. 8.08E
G-CLWN	Cameron Clown SS Balloon (Hot Air)	2857	SE-ZGU	Magical Adventures Ltd	Oswestry	21. 2.97A
			G-UBBE	(New owner 8.07)		

G-CMAA - G-CMZZ

Reg	Type	c/n	Prev. id	Date	Owner/Operator	Location	Status
G-CMAF	Embraer EMB-135BJ Legacy	14501011	PT-SVE	18.10.07	TAG Aviation (UK) Ltd	Farnborough	
G-CMBL	Bombardier CL-600-2B19	8067	C-FLKA C-FMMN	23. 1.08	TAG Aviation (UK) Ltd	Farnborough	
	(CL-600 Regional Jet)						
G-CMBS	MD Helicopters MD.900 Explorer	900-00111	N70124 N7011V, (PH-PXG)	24. 4.06	Cambridgeshire Constabulary	RAF Wyton	16. 5.09S
G-CMCC	Robinson R44 Raven II	11837		2. 8.07	C McCann	(Lanark)	29. 8.08E
G-CMED	SOCATA TB-9 Tampico Club	1867	F-GSZK	19. 3.01	S C Brown t/a Enstone Flying Club	Enstone	15. 4.08E
G-CMGC	Piper PA-25-235 Pawnee D	25-7756042	G-BFEX N82525	19.11.91	Midland Gliding Club Ltd	Long Mynd	2. 7.08
G-CMLS	Cirrus SR20	1315	N1298C	24. 4.07	Cumulus Aircraft Rentals Ltd	Bournemouth	18. 6.08E
G-CMOR	Best Off Sky Ranger 912(2)	SKR0412542		25. 2.05	P Moore	Bakersfield	22. 8.07P
	(Built C Moore - pr.no.BMAA/HB/441)						
G-CMOS	Cessna T303 Crusader	T30300222	D-IPMG N121JH, N9858C	15.12.06	C J Moss	Goodwood	8. 2.08E
G-CMSN	Robinson R22 Beta	1669	G-MGEE G-PHEL, G-RUMP, N2405T	29. 6.04	S Meadows	Gamston	22. 4.08E
G-CMXX	Robinson R44 Raven II	10661		9. 3.05	Northern Excavators Ltd	Ballinderry	14. 4.08E

G-CNAA - G-CNZZ

Reg	Type	c/n	Prev. id	Date	Owner/Operator	Location	Status
G-CNAB	Avtech Jabiru UL-450	xxxx		27. 9.00	W A Brighouse		
	(Built W A Brighouse - pr.no.PFA 274-13651 although type prefix should be "274A")					Eddsfield, Octon Lodge Farm, Thwing	17.12.07P
G-CNCN	Rockwell Commander 112TC-A	13151	HB-NCN N4620W	1. 6.05	R A and P A Symmonds	Southend	21. 7.08E

G-COAA - G-COZZ

Reg	Type	c/n	Prev. id	Date	Owner/Operator	Location	Status
G-COAI	Cranfield A 1-400 Eagle	001	G-BCIT	1. 6.98	Cranfield University	Cranfield	
	(Built Cranfield Institute of Technology)				*(Noted 1.07)*		
G-COCO	Reims Cessna F172M Skyhawk II	F17201373	PH-SMO OO-ADI	27.10.80	P C Sheard and R C Larder	Strubby	14. 4.08E
G-CODY	Kolb Twinstar Mk.3 Extra	M3X05·2·00070		8. 2.06	J W Codd	(Broughton, Brigg)	17. 6.08P
	(Built J W Codd - pr.no.PFA 205-14456)						
G-COIN	Bell 206B-2 JetRanger II	897	EI-AWA	11. 3.85	S Pool, J Woodward and P J Niehorster	(Stevenage, Buntingford and Ramsey, Isle of Man)	12. 9.07
G-COLA	Beech F33C Bonanza	CJ-137	G-BUAZ PH-BNH	31. 3.92	J R C Spooner and P M Scarratt	East Midlands	3.11.07
G-COLH	Piper PA-28-140 Cherokee	28-23143	G-AVRT N11C	13.10.00	Full Sutton Flying Centre Ltd	Full Sutton	10. 3.08E
G-COLL	Enstrom 280C-UK-2 Shark	1223		17. 8.81	M G Roberts	Biggin Hill	20 8.08E
G-COLS	Van's RV-7A	PFA 323-14312		6.10.04	C Terry	(Grampound. Truro)	
	(Built C Terry)						
G-COMB	Piper PA-30 Twin Comanche B	30-1362	G-AVBL N8236Y	14. 9.84	M R Booker	(Bridlington)	7. 3.08E
G-COMU	Flight Design CT2K	03-03-01-08		16. 6.03	Comunica Industries International Ltd	Roughay Farm, Bishops Waltham	29. 1.08P
	(Assembled Mainair Sports Ltd with c/n 7965)						
G-CONB	Robin DR.400-180 Régent	2176	G-BUPX	14. 4.93	M D Souster	Redhill	3. 3.08E
G-CONC	Cameron N-90 Balloon (Hot Air)	2139		13.11.89	British Airways PLC "Concorde"	West Drayton	4. 9.08T
G-CONL	SOCATA TB-10 Tobago	173	F-GCOR	22.12.98	J M Huntington	Full Sutton	16. 5.08E
G-CONR	Champion 7GCBC Citabria	280-70	YU-CAB	15. 5.06	N O'Brien	Glountha, Kilkenny	11. 8.08E
G-COOT	Aerocar Taylor Coot A	EE-1A		16. 9.81	P M Napp	Stanton, Morpeth	
	(Built D A Hood)				*(Noted stored 8.07)*		
G-COPS	Piper J-3C-65 Cub (L-4H-PI)	11911	F-BFYC French AF, 44-79615	17. 7.79	R W Sproat	Lenox Plunton Farm, Borgue	9. 5.08P
	(Frame No.11739)						
	(Officially regd with c/n 36-817 which is USAAC contract no)						
G-COPZ	Van's RV-7	71605		8.12.03	R S Horan	(Melrose)	
	(Built R S Horan - pr.no.PFA 323-14150)						
G-CORA	Europa Aviation Europa XS	467	G-ILUM	30. 5.06	A P Gardner	Little Gransden	
	(Built A R Haynes - pr.no.PFA 247-13565) (Tri-gear u/c)						
G-CORB	SOCATA TB-20 Trinidad	1178	F-GKUX	12. 4.99	G D Corbin	Flamstone Park, Bishopstone	10. 5.08E
G-CORD	Nipper T 66 RA.45 Series 3	S 129	G-AVTB	21. 3.88	A V Lamprell *(Noted 10.05)*	Charity Farm, Baxterley	3. 7.08P
	(Built Slingsby Sailplanes Ltd as c/n 1565 (G-AVTB) for Nipper Aircraft Ltd with c/n S 105 then rebuilt as c/n 1676 (G-CORD) with Nipper c/n S 129)						
G-CORN	Bell 206B-3 JetRanger III	3035	G-BHTR N18098	4. 6.99	Looporder Ltd t/a East Midlands Helicopters	Costock	25. 4.08E
G-COSY	Lindstrand LBL 56A Balloon (Hot Air)	017		18. 2.93	D D Owen	Wotton-under-Edge	2. 4.03A
G-COTT	Cameron Flying Cottage 60 SS Balloon (Hot Air)	687	"G-HOUS"	13. 2.81	Dragon Balloon Company Ltd	Castleton, Hope Valley	7. 9.05A
G-COUP	Ercoupe 415C	1903	N99280 NC99280	27. 5.93	S M Gerrard	Goodwood	2. 3.10S
	(Continental C75)				"Jenny Lin"		
G-COVA	Piper PA-28-161 Warrior III	2842217	G-CDCL N3072G	18. 2.05	Coventry (Civil) Aviation Ltd	Coventry	16.11.07E
G-COVB	Piper PA-28-161 Warrior III	2842234	N3094S	13. 6.05	Coventry (Civil) Aviation Ltd	Coventry	21. 6.08E
G-COVE	Avtech Jabiru UL	0214		23. 7.99	A A Rowson	Emlyn's Field, Rhuallt	14. 9.07P
	(Built A A Rowson - pr.no.PFA 274A-13409)						
G-COXS	Aeroprakt A22 Foxbat	PFA 317-14168		9. 3.04	S Cox	(Hinckley)	30. 6.08P
	(Built S Cox)						
G-COXY	Air Création 582(1)/Kiss 400	FL.025		11. 3.04	B G Cox	Hunsdon	30. 6.07P
	(Built B G Cox - pr.no.BMAA/HB/351 being Flylight kit comprising Trike s/n T03107 and s/n Wing A03186-3184)						
G-COZI	Rutan Cozy	PFA 159-12162		19. 7.93	R Machin	Ronaldsway	9. 4.08P
	(Built D G Machin) (Lycoming O-320)						

G-CPAA - G-CPZZ

G-CPCD	CEA Jodel DR.221 Dauphin	81	F-BPCD	11.12.90	D J Taylor	Enstone	12. 7.08
G-CPDA	de Havilland DH.106 Comet 4C	6473	XS235	10. 8.00	C Walton Ltd (As "XS235") (Noted 3.04)	Bruntingthorpe	
G-CPDW	Mudry CAP.10B	195	N502DW	23.04.07	Hilfa Ltd	Sywell	6. 6.08P
G-CPEL	Boeing 757-236	24398	N602DF	24. 8.92	British Airways PLC	London Heathrow	26.10.07E
			EC-EOL, EC-597, G-BRJE, EC-EOL, EC-278, G-BRJE				
G-CPEM	Boeing 757-236	28665		28. 3.97	British Airways PLC	London Heathrow	27. 3.08E
G-CPEN	Boeing 757-236	28666		23. 4.97	British Airways PLC	London Heathrow	22. 4.08E
G-CPEO	Boeing 757-236	28667		11. 7.97	British Airways PLC	London Heathrow	10. 7.08E
G-CPEP	Boeing 757-2Y0	25268	C-GTSU	16. 4.97	First Choice Airways Ltd	Manchester	9. 7.08E
			EI-CLP, N400KL, XA-TAE				
G-CPER	Boeing 757-236	29113		29.12.97	British Airways PLC	London Gatwick	28.12.08E
G-CPES	Boeing 757-236	29114		17. 3.98	British Airways PLC	London Heathrow	16. 3.08E
G-CPET	Boeing 757-236	29115		12. 5.98	British Airways PLC	London Heathrow	11. 5.08E
G-CPFC	Reims Cessna F152 II	F15201430		1.12.77	A S Bamrah ta Falcon Flying Services	Biggin Hill	20. 7.08E
G-CPMK	de Havilland DHC-1 Chipmunk 22	C1/0866	WZ847	28. 6.96	P A Walley (As "WZ847:F" in RAF c/s)	Elstree	12. 1.09S
G-CPMS	SOCATA TB-20 Trinidad	1607	F-GNHA	7. 4.98	Charlotte Park Management Services Ltd	Goodwood	13. 6.08E
G-CPOL	Aérospatiale AS.355F1 Ecureuil 2	5007	N5775T	30.11.95	MW Helicopters Ltd	(Stapleford)	22. 5.08E
			C-GJJB, N5775T				
G-CPPM	North American Harvard II	81-4013	RCAF 3019	2. 3.07	S D Wilch	Bruntingthorpe	
G-CPSF	Cameron N-90 Balloon (Hot Air)	3747	G-OISK	21. 4.99	S A Simington and J D Rigden	Norwich	1. 5.04A
G-CPSH	Eurocopter EC.135 T1	0209	D-HECJ	8. 4.02	Thames Valley Police Authority	Luton	20. 6.08T
G-CPTM	Piper PA-28-151 Cherokee Warrior	28-7715012	G-BTOE	9. 7.91	C and T J Mackay	(Wettenhall, Winsford)	11. 3.08E
			N4264F				
G-CPTS	Agusta-Bell 206B-2 JetRanger II	8556		1. 6.78	A R B Aspinall	Skipton	28. 8.08E
G-CPXC	CAB CAP.10C	301		11.12.01	J M Wicks	Boones Farm, Braintree	31. 7.08E

G-CRAA - G-CRZZ

G-CRAB	Best Off Sky Ranger 912(1)	SKR0210245		1.11.02	R A Weller	Priory Farm, Tibenham	16. 9.08P
	(Built R A Bell - pr.no.BMAA/HB/246)						
G-CRAY	Robinson R22 Beta	0919		12. 1.89	P Durkin t/a Moorland Windows	(Lytham St Annes)	16. 3.08P
G-CRBV	Balony Kubicek BB26 Balloon (Hot Air)	373	OK-0373	22. 7.05	Charter Ballooning Ltd	Liphook	3. 4.08E
					(Reading Business Venue titles)		
G-CRDY	Agusta-Bell 206A JetRanger	8112	G-WHAZ	22.12.03	Cardy Construction Ltd	(Manston)	11.11.07E
			OH-HRE, G-WHAZ, OH-HRE				
G-CRES	Denney Kitfox Model 2	PFA 172-11574		7. 6.90	J McGoldrick	Newtownards	14. 6.07P
	(Built R J Cresswell) (Rotax 912)						
G-CREY	Progressive Aerodyne Searey Amphibian			2. 1.07	A F Reid and P J Gallagher		
	(Built A F Reid and P J Gallagher) PFA 343-14619					(Newtownards and Bangor)	
G-CRIB	Robinson R44 Raven	0980	G-JJWL	28. 3.03	D G Williams t/a Cribarth Helicopters	Builth Wells	11. 4.08T
G-CRIC	Colomban MC-15 Cri-Cri	PFA 133-10915		22. 7.83	R S Stoddart-Stones	(Woldingham, Caterham)	5. 5.99P
	(Built A J Maxwell) (JPX PUL.212)						
G-CRIK	Colomban MC-15 Cri-Cri	PFA 133-13289		10.11.04	A R Robinson	(Prestbury, Macclesfield)	
	(Built A R Robinson)						
G-CRIL	Rockwell Commander 112B	521	N1388J	22. 6.79	J W Reynolds tr Rockwell Aviation Group	Cardiff	14.12.07
G-CRIS	Taylor JT.1 Monoplane	PFA 055-10318		5. 6.79	C R Steer	(Spilstead Farm, Sedlescombe)	
	(Built C J Bragg)				(Bare fuselage noted 5.01)		
G-CROB	Europa Aviation Europa XS	442		25. 4.02	R G Hallam	Sleap	21. 2.08P
	(Built R G Hallam - pr.no.PFA 247-13510) (Jabiru 3300) (Tri-Gear u/c)						
G-CROL	Maule MXT-7-180 Super Rocket	14032C	N9232F	24.11.93	W E Willets (New owner 1.08)	(Bewdley)	4. 3.04
G-CROW	Robinson R44 Raven	0754		19. 4.00	Longmoore Ltd	Shoreham	22. 5.06T
					(Operated FAST Helicopters Ltd)		
G-CROY	Europa Aviation Europa	101		7. 2.97	M T Austin	Kirkwall	26. 4.08P
	(Built A T Croy - pr.no.PFA 247-12896) (Monowheel u/c)						
G-CRPH	Airbus A320-231	0424	F-WQBB	10. 4.95	Thomas Cook Airlines Ltd t/a MyTravel Airways		
			F-WWIV			Manchester	14. 4.08E
G-CRUM	Westland Scout AH.1	F9712	XV137	17. 3.98	D O Sears tr G-CRUM Group		
					(As "XV137" in AAC c/s)	Draycott Farm, Chiseldon	30. 1.09P
G-CRUZ	Cessna T303 Crusader	T30300004	N9336T	7.12.90	Bank Farm Ltd	Bank Farm, Benwick, March	10. 7.08E

G-CSAA - G-CSZZ

G-CSAM	Van's RV-9A	PFA 320-14384		1. 3.07	B G Murray	(Teignmouth)	
	(Built B G Murray)						
G-CSAV	Thruster T 600N 450	0032-T600N-064		14. 3.02	R C Best	Wickenby	12. 8.08P
G-CSBD	Piper PA-28-236 Dakota	28-8211019	G-CSBO	18. 7.05	S B and S-J Dunnett	Upfield Farm, Whitson	15. 8.08E
			N8471Y				
G-CSBM	Reims Cessna F150M	F15201359	PH-AYC	24. 5.78	Transcourt Ltd	Hinton-in-the-Hedges	18. 1.08T
G-CSCS	Reims Cessna F172N Skyhawk II	F17201707	PH-MEM	28.11.86	C Sullivan	Stapleford	10. 6.08E
			(PH-WEB), N9899A				
G-CSDJ	Avtech Jabiru UL	0201		23. 3.99	D W and J Johnston, C D and S Slater		
	(Built D W Johnston and C D Slater - pr.no.PFA 274A-13337)					Redlands, Swindon	22. 5.08P
G-CSFC	Cessna 150L	15075360	(G-BFLX)	21. 3.78	S J Williams tr Foxtrot Charlie Flying Group		
			N11370			RNAS Culdrose	3. 4.08E
G-CSFD	Ultramagic M-90 Balloon (Hot Air)	90/56		12.12.02	L A Watts (Chelmsford titles)	Pangbourne, Reading	2. 6.08A
G-CSGT	Piper PA-28-161 Warrior II	2816069	G-BPHB	31. 1.06	M J Wade	Turweston	1. 4.08E
			N9148G				
G-CSIX	Piper PA-32-300 Cherokee Six	32-7840030	ZS-OMX	15. 6.01	A J Hodge	Hinton-in-the-Hedges	8. 8.08E
			Z-WJM, VP-WJM, HB-PCX, ZS-KBR, N9857K				
G-CSMK	Evektor EV-97 Eurostar	PFA 315-13813		4.12.01	R Frey	Derby	4. 4.08P
	(Built N R Beale)						

G-CSNA	Cessna 421C Golden Eagle	421C0677	(D-IOSS) N26522	11. 6.79	Blue Swan Aviation Ltd	Lee-on-Solent	18. 8.06E
G-CSPR	Van's RV-6A *(Built D L Reed)*	25584	N9004F	16. 5.07	P J Pengilly	(Chuch Crookham, Fleet)	22. 7.08P
G-CSUE	ICP MXP-740 Savannah Jabiru(5) 06-07-51-505 *(Built J R Stratton - pr.no.BMAA/HB/517)*			26.10.06	J R Stratton	Dunkeswell	3. 9.08P
G-CSWH	Piper PA-28R-180 Cherokee Arrow 28R-30541		N4647J G-CSWH, N4647J	5. 4.02	J F Gould	(Yoxall, Burton-on-Trent)	10. 1.08T
G-CSWL	Bell 206L-1 LongRanger	45565	G-VOLK G-GBAY, G-CSWL, G-SIRI, G-CSWL, F-GDAD	6. 5.97	Milford Garage Ltd t/a Milford Aviation	Cranfield	10.10.07E
G-CSZM	Zenair CH.601XL Zodiac PFA 162B-14367 *(Built C Budd)*			9.12.05	C Budd	(Tairgwaith, Ammanford)	

G-CTAA - G-CTZZ

G-CTAA	Schempp-Hirth Janus	16	BGA 5133-KJT N2AA	9.11.05	D Catt tr AA Group "AA"	Bicester	27. 1.08
G-CTAG	Rolladen-Schneider LS8-18	8150	BGA 4450-JEG	11. 9.07	C D R Tagg	Pocklington	15.11.07
G-CTAV	Evektor EV-97 teamEurostar UK	2129		25.11.04	P Simpson	Bourn	3.12.08P
G-CTCD	Diamond DA.42 Twin Star	42.079	OE-VPI	8. 2.06	CTC Aviation Group PLC	Bournemouth	2. 3.08E
G-CTCE	Diamond DA.42 Twin Star	42.043	OE-VPI	25. 8.05	CTC Aviation Group PLC	Bournemouth	21. 9.08E
G-CTCF	Diamond DA.42 Twin Star	42.045	OE-VPY	25. 8.05	CTC Aviation Group PLC	Bournemouth	21. 9.08E
G-CTCG	Diamond DA.42 Twin Star	42.046		25. 8.05	I Annenskiy	(Sheffield City)	10.10.07E
G-CTCH	Diamond DA.42 Twin Star	42.238	(ZK-CTP) OE-VPY	4. 5.07	CTC Aviation Group PLC	Bournemouth	22. 5.08E
G-CTCL	SOCATA TB-10 Tobago	1107	G-BSIV	16. 7.90	Gift Aviation Ltd	Tatenhill	30. 9.08E
G-CTDH	Flight Design CT2K 02-08-01-31 *(Assembled Mainair Sports Ltd with c/n 7939)*			1. 5.03	A D Thelwall	Baxby Manor, Husthwaite	25. 5.08P
G-CTDW	Flight Design CTSW 07.05.05 *(Assembled P&M Aviation Ltd with c/n 8295)*			22. 6.07	D Watson	Tarn Farm, Cockerham	21. 6.08P
G-CTEC	Stoddard-Hamilton GlaStar PFA 295-13260 *(Built A J Clarry)*			9.11.99	B N C Mogg	(Bibberne Farm, Stalbridge)	
G-CTED	Van's RV-7A PFA 323-14631 *(Built E W Lyon)*			24. 5.07	E W Lyon	(Gattonside, Melrose)	
G-CTEL	Cameron N-90 Balloon (Hot Air)	3933		27. 8.96	M R Noyce *(Gabletop titles)*	Hatherden, Andover	11. 4.08A
G-CTFF	Cessna T206H Turbo Stationair	T20608150	N24309	29.10.01	Oxford Aviation Services Ltd	Oxford	4 11.07E
G-CTGR	Cameron N-77 Balloon (Hot Air)	1775	G-CCDI	28. 8.97	T G Read *(Charles Church titles)*	Knutsford	13. 9.03T
G-CTIO	SOCATA TB-20 Trinidad GT	2174	F-OIMH	7.11.02	I R Hunt	Biggin Hill	1.12.07E
G-CTIX	Vickers Supermarine 509 Spitfire Tr.9 Not known *(Major rebuild from parts pre 1994)*		N462JC G-CTIX, IDF/AF 2067, 0607, MM4100, PT462	9. 4.85	A A Hodgson *(As "PT462:SW-A" in RAF c/s)*	Bryn Gwyn Bach	20. 5.08P
G-CTKL	Noorduyn AT-16 Harvard IIB 07-30 *(C/n also quoted as "76-80")*		(G-BKWZ) MM54-137, RCAF3064	22.11.83	M R Simpson *(As "FE788" in RAF c/s)*	Rochester	22. 2.08P
G-CTOY	Denney Kitfox Model 3 *(Built G S Cass and G C Brooke - pr.no.PFA 172-12150)*	1176		14.10.91	B McNeilly	(Newtownards)	10. 5.93P
G-CTRL	Robinson R22 Beta II	3601		13. 5.04	Central Helicopters Ltd	Tollerton	12. 6.08E
G-CTSW	Flight Design CTSW 05.11.15 *(Assembled P&M Aviation Ltd with c/n 8158)*			7.12.05	C J Powell *(New owner 11.07)*	Upfield Farm, Whitson	20. 8.07P
G-CTUG	Piper PA-25-235 Pawnee	25-4448	N4713Y	13. 9.04	The Borders (Milfield) Gliding Club Ltd	Milfield	27.10.07E
G-CTWO	Schempp-Hirth Standard Cirrus	256	BGA 4836-JWH SE-TMZ	11. 7.07	R J Griffin	Edgehill	26. 1.08
G-CTWW	Piper PA-34-200T Seneca II	34-7970191	G-ROYZ G-GALE, N3052X	21. 7.93	Centreline Air Charter Ltd	(Filton)	9. 2.08E
G-CTZO	SOCATA TB-20 Trinidad GT	2166	F-OIME	7.10.02	M R Munn *(Noted 1.08)*	Turweston	13.10.07E

G-CUAA - G-CUZZ

G-CUBB	Piper PA-18-150 Super Cub (L-18C-PI) 18-3111 *(Lycoming O-360-C2) (Frame No.18-3009)*		PH-WAM Belgian AF OL-L37, 53-4711	5.12.78	Bidford Gliding Ltd	Bidford	18. 4.08E
G-CUBE	Best Off Sky Ranger 912(2) SKR0311409 *(Built T R Villa - pr.no.BMAA/HB/336)*			13. 1.04	T R Villa	Priory Farm, Tibenham	6. 7.08P
G-CUBI	Piper PA-18-125 Super Cub 18-3181 (L-18C-PI)		PH-GAV PH-VCV, R Neth AF R-43, Belgian AF L-107, 53-4781	26. 2.79	G T Fisher	(Northside, Thorney)	4.11.94T
	(Official c/n 18-559 related to PH-GAV prior to 1970 rebuild when it incorporated Frame No.18-3170 from PH-VCV: possible link to G-CCKW qv)						
G-CUBJ	Piper PA-18-150 Super Cub 18-2036 (L-18C-PI) (Frame No.18-2035)		PH-MBF PH-NLF, R Neth AF R-43, 8A-43, 52-2436	15.12.82	A L Grisay *(As "18-5395:CDG" in French Army c/s)*	Old Warden	9.11.07E
	(Regd with c/n 18-5395 after 1974 rebuild of PH-NLF: acquired data plate from, and took identity of, PH-MBF - note G-SUPA also carries this c/n)						
G-CUBN	Piper PA-18-150 Super Cub	18-7902	SE-ECN	17.11.05	N J R Minchin *(Noted 1.06)*	East Winch	
G-CUBP	Piper PA-18-150 Super Cub 18-8482 *(Frame No.18-8725)*		N1136Z G-BVMI, OH-PIN, N4262Z	8. 8.96	D W Berger	Trenchard Farm, Eggesford	24. 6.08E
	(Regd with c/n 18-8823 the "official" identity of N1136Z/D-EIAC: rebuilt 1984/85 with Frame No.18-4613 ex D-EKAF: this frame fitted to G-BVMI following accident on 15.8.95: repaired frame of G-BVMI has now become G-CUBP)						
G-CUBS	Piper J-3C-65 Cub "17792" *(Frame No.17792)*		G-BHPT F-BSGQ, LX-AIH, N70688, NC70688	26.10.01	S M Rolfe t/a Sunbeam Aviation	Willington, Bedford	13. 7.05P
	(Official p/i is frame no. - possibly c/n 18105 ex NC71076, N71076)						
G-CUBW	Wag-Aero AcroTrainer PFA 108-13581 *(Built B G, N D Plumb and A G Bourne)*			26.11.02	B G, N D Plumb and A G Bourne	Hinton-in-the-Hedges	29. 2.08P
G-CUBY	Piper J-3C-65 Cub 16317 *(Rebuilt with new fuselage 1996/97)*		G-BTZW N88689, NC88689	2. 3.95	C A Bloom	Shoreham	11. 7.08P
G-CUCU	Colt 180A Balloon (Hot Air)	3869		22. 4.96	S R Seager	Aylesbury	28. 5.06T
G-CUIK	QAC Quickie Q.200 PFA 094A-11204 *(Built C S Rayner)*			15.12.04	C S Rayner *(Noted 3.08)*	Enstone	

G-CULF	Robinson R44 Raven II	11770		8. 6.07	Broadfield Properties Ltd	Southend	28. 6.08E
G-CUPP	Pitts S-2A	2166	N42XX	27. 3.07	Avmarine Ltd	(Rusper, Horsham)	
	(Built Aerotek Inc)		N86PS				
G-CUPS	IAV Bacau Yakovlev Yak-52	9010312	LY-AMD	13. 6.03	L R Haunch t/a Fenland Flying School	Fenland	29. 6.07P
	Ukraine AF 09 (yellow), DOSAAF 09 (yellow)						
G-CURV	Avid Speed Wing	PFA 189-12169		28. 3.00	K S Kelso	Fen End Farm, Smith Fen, Cottenham	
	(Built K S Kelso)				(On build 3.06)		
G-CUTE	Dyn'Aéro MCR-01 Club	132		7. 9.99	E G Shimmin	Shobdon	8. 2.08P
	(Built E G Shimmin - pr.no.PFA 301-13511)						
G-CUTY	Europa Aviation Europa	224		20. 8.96	D J and M Watson		
	(Built D J and M Watson - pr.no.PFA 247-12910) (Tri-gear u/c)				(San Miguel de Salinas, Alicante, Spain)		

G-CVAA - G-CVZZ

G-CVAL	Comco Ikarus C42 FB100	0608-6836		15. 8.06	J I Greenshields tr G-CVAL Group	Dunkeswell	3.10.08P
G-CVBF	Cameron A-210 Balloon (Hot Air)	3588		2. 6.95	Airxcite Ltd t/a Virgin Balloon Flights	Wembley	15. 8.01T
G-CVII	Dan Rihn DR.107 One Design	PFA 264-14478		9. 3.06	R M Davies tr One Design Group	(Melton Mowbray)	
G-CVIP	Bell 206B-3 JetRanger III	3228	SX-HDJ	29. 4.02	Apple International Inc Ltd	Southend	4. 5.08E
			N824C, N824H, N3902L				
G-CVIX	de Havilland DH.110 Sea Vixen D 3	10125	XP924	26. 2.96	Drilling Systems Ltd	Bournemouth	18. 5.07P
	(Regd as FAW.2 with c/n 10132)				(As "XP524:134" in RN c/s)		
G-CVLH	Piper PA-34-200T Seneca II	34-8070332	F-GCPK	5. 9.02	Atlantic Aviation Ltd	St Brieuc, France	12. 9.05T
			N8252D, N8250H				
G-CVMI	Piper PA-18-150 Super Cub	18-5700	SE-CEE	23. 5.05	D Heslop and T P Spurge		
						New Farm House, Great Oakley	24. 5.08E
G-CVPM	Magni M-16 Tandem Trainer	VPM16-UK-110		26. 3.98	P J Troy-Davies	(Fleetwood)	2. 6.08P
	(Arrow GT1000R)						
G-CVST	Jodel D 140 Mousquetaire	PFA 251-13384		21. 5.03	A Shipp	Full Sutton	
	(Built A Shipp)				(Noted 4.05)		

G-CWAA - G-CWZZ

G-CWAG	Sequoia F 8L Falco	PFA 100-10895		11. 5.92	D R Austin	Standalone Farm, Meppershall	19. 8.08P
	(Built C C Wagner) (Lycoming O-320)						
G-CWAL	Raj Hamsa X'Air 133(1)	777		27. 4.04	C Walsh	Woodlands Barton Farm, Roche	31.10.08P
	(Built C Walsh - pr.no.BMAA/HB/339)						
G-CWAY	Comco Ikarus C42 FB100	0707-6907		6. 9.07	M Conway	(Cookstown, Belfast)	18.10.08P
G-CWBM	Phoenix Currie Wot	PFA 3020	G-BTVP	28. 3.94	B V Mayo	Maypole Farm, Chislet	3.10.08P
	(Built B V Mayo) (Continental C85)						
G-CWEB	P&M Quik GT450	8343		20. 2.08	K A and M Forsyth	(Lempitlaw, Kelso)l	19. 2.09P
G-CWFA	Piper PA-38-112 Tomahawk	38-78A0120	G-BTGC	17. 8.99	K R W Scull and J Watkins	Upfield Farm, Whitson	26. 6.08E
			N9507T				
G-CWFB	Piper PA-38-112 Tomahawk	38-78A0623	G-OAAL	13. 1.00	P M Moyle	Bodmin	8. 2.07T
			N4471E		(Noted 10.07)		
G-CWIC	Mainair Sports Pegasus Quik	8067		21. 9.04	A Battersby tr G-CWIC Group	Barton	30.11.07P
G-CWIK	Mainair Sports Pegasus Quik	8018		23. 4.04	C D Jackson	Easter Poldar Farm, Thornhill	15 .5.08P
G-CWLC	Schleicher ASH 25	25105	BGA 3720-GCE	9. 1.08	C.L.Withall	Dunstable	1. 4.08
G-CWMC	P&M Quik GT450	8201		26. 8.06	A R Hughes	Yatesbury	3. 9.07P
G-CWMT	Dyn'Aéro MCR-01	PFA 301-14347		7. 9.05	J Jones	(Pontardawe. Swansea)	22.10.08P
	(Built J Jones)						
G-CWOT	Phoenix Currie Wot	PFA 3019		31. 1.78	D Doyle and Helena Duggan	Kilrush, County Kildare	19. 1.04P
	(Built D A Lord) (Walter Mikron 2)				(Noted 5.06)		
G-CWTD	Aeroprakt A22 Foxbat	PFA 317-14131		21.10.03	J V Harris	Ley Farm, Chirk	11. 4.08P
	(Built J V Harris)						
G-CWVY	Mainair Sports Pegasus Quik	7984		29. 9.03	R K Jenkins	(Rhossili, Swansea)	26. 1.08P

G-CXAA - G-CXZZ

G-CXCX	Cameron N-90 Balloon (Hot Air)	1242		14. 3.86	Cathay Pacific Airways (London) Ltd	Swindon	6. 7.03A
	(Replacement envelope c/n 3332)				"Cathay Pacific IV"		
G-CXDZ	Cassutt Speed Two	PFA 034-13816		27.12.02	J A H Chadwick	Little Staughton	
	(Build R Whinsper, J A H Chadwick and S Thompson)				(Noted 4.07)		
G-CXHK	Cameron N-77 Balloon (Hot Air)	4978		22. 2.01	Cathay Pacific Airways (London) Ltd	London SW1	27.12.07A
G-CXIP	Thruster T 600N Jab Sprint	1031-T600N-095		17.11.03	R J Howells t/a India Papa Syndicate	Shobdon	25.10.08P
G-CXSM	Cessna 172R Skyhawk II	17280320	G-BXSM	1. 2.07	Airtime Aviation France Ltd	Compton Abbas	25. 4.08E
			N432ES				

G-CYAA - G-CYZZ

G-CYLL	Sequoia F 8L Falco	PFA 100-14572		30.10.06	N J Langrick and A J Newall		
	(Built N J Langrick and A J Newall)				(Holmfirth and Mission, Doncaster)		
G-CYLS	Cessna T303 Crusader	T30300005	N20736	20.12.90	Hangar 8 Ltd	Oxford	18. 5.08E
			G-BKXI, N303CC, (N9355T)				
G-CYMA	Gulfstream GA-7 Cougar	GA7-0083	G-BKOM	15. 8.83	Cyma Petroleum (UK) Ltd	Elstree	22. 8.08E
			N794GA				
G-CYOT	Rans	0507-1810		3.08R	J Middas		
G-CYRA	Kolb Twinstar Mk.3	PFA 205-12434	G-MYRA	30. 1.03	S J Fox	Popham	26. 9.08P
	(Built S J Fox and A P Pickford) (Rotax 503)						
G-CYRS	Bell 206L LongRanger	45030	OH-HOH	16. 6.06	Sky Charter UK Ltd	(Sheffield City)	14. 8.08E
			C-GIIP, N221AM, N66BH, N66LJ, N49770				

G-CZAA - G-CZZZ

G-CZAC	Zenair CH.601XL Zodiac	6-9112		26. 3.04	D Pitt	Roughay Farm, Bishops Waltham	19. 3.08P
	(Built D Pitt - pr.no.PFA 162B-14113) (Tri-cycle u/c)						
G-CZAF	Vickers Supermarine 361 Spitfire FR.IXe		N94141	10. 8.07	Historic Flying Ltd	Duxford	
	(Built as LF.IXb))	CBAF IX.571	Burma AF UB425, (Burma AF UB425), Israel DF 2042, Czech AF JT-10, SL633				
G-CZAG	Sky 90-24 Balloon (Hot Air)	171		5.10.99	S McCarthy	Rothersthorpe, Northampton	7. 5.07
G-CZAW	CZAW Sportcruiser	PFA 338-14542		19. 6.06	Sprite Aviation Services Ltd		
	(Built G Smith)					Inglenook Farm, Maydensole, Dover	
G-CZBE	CFM Streak Shadow SA-M	K 271	G-MZBE	17. 6.03	S Marriott	(Passfield, Liphook)	30.11.08P
	(Built N J Bushell - pr.no.PFA 206-12905) (Rotax 618)						
G-CZCZ	Mudry CAP.10B	54	OE-AYY	28. 7.94	M Farmer	Garston Farm, Marshfield	30. 8.08E
			F-WZCG, HB-SAK, F-BUDT				
G-CZMI	Best Off Sky Ranger 912(2)	SKR0308377		18.11.03	L M Bassett	Longacre Farm, Sandy	14. 1.08P
	(Built T W Thiele - pr.no.BMAA/HB/307)						
G-CZNA	Boeing 767-306ER	27957	C-GZNA	13.12.07	Zoom Airlines Ltd	London Gatwick	
			PH-BZA				
G-CZNE	Pilatus Britten-Norman BN-2B-20 Islander	2301	G-BWZF	27. 7.04	Skyhopper LLP	Gloucestershire	29. 6.08E

G-DAAA - G-DZZZ

G-DAAH	Piper PA-28RT-201T Turbo Arrow IV		N3026U	27. 4.79	R Peplow	Halfpenny Green	29. 6.08E
		28R-7931104					
G-DAAM	Robinson R22 Beta	2043		3. 6.92	J N Plange	(Scunthorpe)	20. 7.08E
G-DAAT	Eurocopter EC.135 T2	0312		4. 5.04	Bond Air Services Ltd	Exeter	13. 7.08E
					(Operated Devon Air Ambulance)		
G-DAAZ	Piper PA-28RT-201T Turbo Arrow IV	28R-7931247	N2896B	17. 1.03	Calais Ltd	Guernsey	29. 3.08E
G-DABS	Robinson R22 Beta II	3083		15. 5.00	BI6 Ltd	Perth	1. 6.08E
G-DACA	Percival P 57 Sea Prince T 1	P57/12	WF118	6. 5.80	P G Vallance Ltd	Charlwood, Surrey	17. 7.81P
					(In Gatwick Aviation Museum 2007 as "WF118")		
G-DACC	Cessna 401B	401B-0112	N77GR	1. 9.86	Niglon Ltd	Wellesbourne Mountford	13.10.07E
			N4488A, G-AYOU, N7972Q				
G-DACF	Cessna 152 II	15281724	G-BURY	13. 6.97	T M and M L Jones	Derby	12.10.07E
			N67285		*(Operated Derby Aero Club)*		
G-DADG	Piper PA-18-150 Super Cub	18-5237	N45498	13.10.04	F J Cox	Eaglescott	12. 5.08P
			IDF/AF 069				
G-DADJ	Glaser-Dirks DG-200	2-43	BGA 2394-DUQ	29. 2.08	A D.Joslin	Wormingford	25. 5.08
G-DAFY	Beech 58 Baron	TH-1591	N5684C	6.10.93	P R Earp	Gloucestershire	3. 1.08E
G-DAGJ	Zenair CH.601XL Zodiac	PFA 162B-14317		28.10.05	D A G Johnson	(Stanford in the Vale, Faringdon)	
	(Built D A G Johnson)						
G-DAIR	Luscombe 8A Silvaire	1474	G-BURK	3.10.97	D F Soul	Emberton	19.10.99P
	(Continental A65)		N28713, NC28713		*(Noted fitted with Diesel Air 100hp 7.03)*		
G-DAIV	Ultramagic H-77 Balloon (Hot Air)	77/184		2.11.00	D Harrison-Morris	Ellesmere	4. 9.07E
G-DAJB	Boeing 757-2T7	23770		26. 2.87	Monarch Airlines Ltd	Luton	13. 5.08E
G-DAJC	Boeing 767-31K	27206	C-GJJC	15. 4.94	Thomas Cook Airlines Ltd t/a MyTravel Airways		
			G-DAJC			Manchester	20. 5.08E
G-DAKK	Douglas C-47A-35-DL Dakota	9798	(G-OFON)	26. 7.94	General Technics Ltd	Lelystad, Netherlands	23. 5.03T
			F-GEOM, French Navy 36, OK-WZB, OK-WDU, 42-23936			*(To Aviodrome Museum 10.06)*	
G-DAKM	Diamond DA.40D Star	D4.222	OE-VPT	21. 9.06	K MacDonald	Blackpool	15.10.08E
			OE-VPU				
G-DAKO	Piper PA-28-236 Dakota	28-7911187	PH-ARW	29. 7.99	Methods Consulting Ltd	Turweston	10.11.07E
			(PH-MFB), D-EECG, PH-ARW, OO-HCX, N29718				
G-DAMY	Europa Aviation Europa	105		21.10.94	R J Kelly and U A Schliessler	Wycombe Air Park	11. 9.08P
	(Built Hart Aviation Ltd - pr.no.PFA 247-12781) (Tri-gear u/c)						
G-DANA	Replica Jodel DR200	PFA 304-13351	G-DAST	2.12.02	F A Bakir tr Cheshire Eagles		
	(Built F A Bakir)					Yew Tree Farm, Lymm Dam	
					(On rebuild 9.05 reportedly a comoosite of an unknown fuselage and wings)		
G-DAND	SOCATA TB-10 Tobago	72		5.12.79	Portway Aviation Ltd	Shobdon	2. 1.09E
G-DANT	Rockwell Commander 114	14298	N4978W	9. 7.96	D P Tierney	Biggin Hill	10. 3.08E
G-DANY	Avtech Jabiru UL	0340		28.12.00	D A Crosbie	(Sudbury)	
	(Built D A Crosbie - pr.no.PFA 274A-13588)						
G-DANZ	Eurocopter AS.355N Ecureuil 2	5658		14. 9.98	Melesey Ltd	Denham	9. 2.08E
G-DAPH	Cessna 180K Skywagon II	18053016	N2620K	29. 1.92	M R L Astor	East Hatley, Tadlow	22.12.07E
G-DARA	Piper PA-34-220T Seneca III	34-8333060	PH-TCT	8.11.88	A J White	Humberside	16. 5.08E
			N83JR, N4297J, N9632N				
G-DARK	CFM Shadow Series DD	K 295		13. 7.00	M W Fitch	North Weald	19. 8.08P
	(Built P M Dewhurst - pr.no.PFA 161-13308) (Rotax 582)					*(New owner 4.07)*	
G-DASH	Rockwell Commander 112A	237	G-BDAJ	31. 3.87	D and M Nelson	Bourn	26. 3.08E
			N1237J				
G-DASS	Comco Ikarus C42 FB100	0509-6758		30. 9.05	D Sempers t/a DAS Services	Wickenby	5.10.08P
G-DASY	Hughes 369E	0574E	N574PP	1. 2.08	R A Roberts t/a Puddleduck Plane Partnership		
	(Hughes 500)					Dunsfold	
G-DATG	Reims Cessna F182P Skylane II	F18200013	D-EATG	8.11.01	Oxford Aeroplane Company Ltd	Oxford	21. 4.08E
G-DATH	Evektor EV-97 Eurostar	PFA 315-13967		8.10.02	D N E D'Ath	Sackville Lodge, Riseley	4. 4.08P
	(Built D N E D'Ath)						
G-DAUF	Aérospatiale AS.365N2 Dauphin 2	6407	N31EH	3. 1.06	Gama Leasing Ltd	Farnborough	22. 3.08E
			XA-SWT, N488FA, JA6676				
G-DAVD	Reims Cessna FR172K Hawk XP	FR17200632	D-EFJT	23.12.99	D M Driver and S Copeland	Spanhoe	6. 4.08E
			(PH-ADL), PH-AXO				
G-DAVE	Jodel D 112	667	F-BICH	16. 8.78	N W Cawley tr Temple Flying Group		
	(Built Etablessement Valladeau)					Griffins Farm, Temple Bruer	23. 8.08P
G-DAVG	Robinson R44 Raven II	10038	G-WOWW	28. 4.03	AG Aviation Ltd	Naas, County Kildare	23. 1.08E

G-DAVO	Gulfstream AA-5B Tiger	AA5B-1226					
G-GAGA				5. 1.96	Douglas Head Consulting Ltd	Elstree	12. 2.08E
			G-BGPG, (G-BGRW)				
G-DAVS	AB Sportine Aviacija LAK-17AT	158	BGA 5171-KKZ	12. 6.06	D Peters tr G-DAVS Syndicate	Burn	18. 5.08
			LY-GIW				
G-DAVV	Robinson R44 Raven II	11079		16. 2.06	D A Gold	(London NW8)	30. 3.08E
G-DAVZ	Cessna 182T Skylane	18281958	N2461C	19.11.07	D Edmondson (Noted 11.07)	Cambridge	
G-DAWG	Scottish Aviation Bulldog Series 120/121		XX522	13. 3.02	R H Goldstone	Barton	2.10.06
		BH120/208			(As "XX522:06" in RAF c/s)		
G-DAWZ	Glasflügel 304 CZ	33	BGA 5232-KNP	5. 5.06	D A Whitley	Parham Park	14. 4.07
	(Built HPH SPOL. Sro).		D-8304		"DA" (Noted 2.08)		
G-DAYS	Europa Aviation Europa	177		9. 5.95	D A Gittins	Sleap	8. 7.08P
	(Built S D, A and A J Hall - pr.no.PFA 247-12810) (Monowheel u/c)						
G-DAYZ	Pietenpol AirCamper	PFA 047-12342		22. 6.01	J G Cronk	(Earnley, Chichester)	
	(Built J G Cronk)						
G-DAZY	Piper PA-34-200T Seneca II	34-7770335	N953A	4. 2.03	Centreline Air Charter Ltd	Bristol	4. 4.08E
			PH-DLM, OE-FGG, N38727		(Operated DHL)		
G-DAZZ	Van's RV-8	PFA 303-14245		20.10.04	D M Hartfree-Bright tr Wishanger RV8		
	(Built D M Hartfree-Bright)				Wishanger Farm, Frensham		23,10.07P
G-DBAT	Lindstrand LBL 56A Balloon (Hot Air)	1001		9. 6.04	G R J Luckett	Fort Collins, Colorado, US	4.10.08A
G-DBCA	Airbus A319-131	2098	D-AVYV	23. 2.04	British Midland Airways Ltd	London Heathrow	22. 2.08E
G-DBCB	Airbus A319-131	2188	D-AVYA	23. 4.04	British Midland Airways Ltd	London Heathrow	22. 4.08E
G-DBCC	Airbus A319-131	2194	D-AVYT	14. 5.04	British Midland Airways Ltd	London Heathrow	13. 5.08E
G-DBCD	Airbus A319-131	2389	D-AVYJ	9. 2.05	British Midland Airways Ltd	London Heathrow	8. 2.08E
G-DBCE	Airbus A319-131	2429	D-AVWG	31. 3.05	British Midland Airways Ltd	London Heathrow	30. 3.08E
G-DBCF	Airbus A319-131	2466	D-AVYA	26. 5.05	British Midland Airways Ltd	London Heathrow	25. 5.08E
G-DBCG	Airbus A319-132	2694	D-AVXD	21. 2.06	British Midland Airways Ltd	London Heathrow	20. 2.08E
G-DBCH	Airbus A319-132	2697	D-AVXE	23. 2.06	British Midland Airways Ltd	London Heathrow	22. 2.08E
G-DBCI	Airbus A319-131	2720	D-AVWC	5. 5.06	British Midland Airways Ltd	London Heathrow	4. 5.08E
G-DBCJ	Airbus A319-131	2981	D-AVXG	9. 1.07	British Midland Airways Ltd	London Heathrow	8. 1.08E
G-DBCK	Airbus A319-131	3049	D-AVYG	2. 3.07	British Midland Airways Ltd	London Heathrow	1. 3.08P
G-DBDB	Magni M-16 Tandem Trainer	PFA G/12-1239	G-IROW	19.10.99	D R Bolsover	RAF Lossiemouth	7. 7.04P
	(Built D R Bolsover) (Rotax 914-UL)		G-DBDB		(Noted 8.07)		
G-DBJD	PZL-Bielsko SZD-9bis Bocian 1D	P-391	BGA 998-BJD	8. 2.08	A D Popple tr Bertie the Bocian Glider Syndicate		
						Lasham	20. 3.08
G-DBLA	Boeing 767-35EER	26063	B-16603	23. 6.06	First Choice Airways Ltd	Manchester	11.10.07E
G-DBLX	Aviat A-1B Husky	2438	N117AA	28. 8.08	Aviat Aircraft (UK) Ltd		
						Lower Grounds Farm, Sherlowe	
G-DBOK	Aerospatiale AS355F2 Ecureuil 2	5463	N620LH	24.10.07	Venturi Capital Ltd (New owner 1.08)	Elstree	
G-DBOY	Agusta A109C	7622	N621MM	29.10.04	Herair Ltd	Wevelgem, Belgium	24.11.07E
			HB-ZEE, OE-XSG, N67SH, 9M-SJI, TUDM M38-03, 9M-TMJ (New owner 2.08)				
G-DBRY	Slingsby T.51 Dart	1434	BGA 1185-BRY	6. 2.08	D J Knights	Kirton-in-Lindsey	18. 6.08
G-DBSA	Slingsby T.51 Dart 15	1405	BGA 1187-BSA	22.10.07	G Burton	Seighford	21. 4.08
G-DBSR	Balony Kubicek BB26Z Balloon (Hot Air)	514		20. 8.07	G J Bell	Petersfield	13.10.08E
G-DBUF	Slingsby T.51 Dart 17R	1469	BGA 1240-BUF	23.11.07	K W Clarke and N G Harrison	Chipping	28. 9.08
G-DBUG	Robinson R44 Clipper	1256	G-OBHI	4. 3.04	Dio (Aviation) Ltd	Welshpool	7.11.07E
G-DBUZ	Schleicher Ka 6CR	6418	BGA 1257-BUZ	4. 1.08	J J Leacroft	Lyveden	24. 5.08
G-DBVB	Schleicher K 7 Rhönadler	7230	BGA 1259-BVB	25. 1.08	Dartmoor Gliding Society Ltd	Brentor	30. 4.08
	(Modified to ASK 13 standard)						
G-DBVH	Slingsby T.51 Dart 17R	1485	BGA 1265-BVH	29. 2.08	P G Addy	(Pudsey)	2. 4.08
G-DBVR	Schleicher 6CR	6441	BGA 1273-BVR	1.11.07	R C Beecroft tr K6CR-BVR Syndicate	Lasham	8. 4.08
G-DBVZ	Schleicher Ka 6CR	6446	BGA 1281-BVZ	12.11.07	L Blair tr G-DBVZ Group	Bellarena	11.11.07
G-DBWJ	Slingsby T.51 Dart 17R	1495	BGA 1290-BWJ	14. 2.08	M F Defendi	Wormingford	20. 8.07
G-DBWM	Slingsby T.51 Dart 17R	1500	BGA 1293-BWM	13. 2.08	P L Poole	Kenley	20. 8.07
G-DBWO	Slingsby T.51 Dart	1505	BGA 1296-BWQ	21. 2.08	G Winch	Wormingford	14. 8.08
G-DBWP	Slingsby T.51 Dart 17R	1501	BGA 1295-BWP	7. 1.08	R.Johnson	Talgarth	21. 4.08
G-DBWS	Slingsby T.51 Dart 17R	1502	BGA 1298-BWS	4.12.07	R D Broome	Hinton-in-the-Hedges	28. 9.08
G-DBXH	Slingsby T.51 Dart 17R	1516	BGA 1313-BXH	14. 2.08	C Rodwell	Husbands Bosworth	15. 5.08
G-DBYL	Schleicher Ka 6CR	6517	BGA 1340-BYL	20.11.07	Channel Gliding Club Ltd	Waldershare Park	2. 2.08
G-DBYM	Schleicher Ka 6CR	6518	BGA 1341-BYM	17.10.07	K S Smith	Wormingford	2. 4.08
			RAFGSA 381, BGA 1341-BYM				
G-DBYU	Schleicher Ka 6CR	6525	BGA 1348-BYU	11. 1.08	G B Sutton	Seighford	28. 3.08
			XW640, BGA 1348-BYU				
G-DBYX	Schleicher Ka 6E	4055	BGA 1351-BYX	19.12.07	J R Dent	Chipping	9. 4.08
G-DBZZ	PZL-Bielsko SZD-24-4A Foka 4	W-308	BGA 1377-BZZ	23. 8.07	A P Benbow	Portmoak	1. 6.08
G-DCAE	Schleicher Ka 6E	4076	BGA 1381-CAE	9.11.07	N Rolfe	Seighford	20. 3.08
G-DCAG	Schleicher Ka 6E	4080	BGA 1383-CAG	28.11.07	S A Farmer tr 715 Syndicate		
					(Hall Green, Birmingham)		30. 4.08
G-DCAS	Schleicher Ka 6E	4029	BGA 1393-CAS	4.10.07	R F Tindall	Gransden Lodge	22. 8.02
			RAFGSA 372				
G-DCAZ	Slingsby T.51 Dart 17R	1611	BGA 1400-CAZ	7. 1.08	J.S.Halford	Eyres Field	7. 6.08
G-DCBA	Slingsby T.51 Dart 17R	1612	BGA 1401-CBA	1. 2.08	M Parsons	Snitterfield	2. 1.08
G-DCBI	Schweizer 269C-1	0295	N86G	10. 7.07	Heli North West Ltd	Barton	
	(Schweizer 300)				(New owner 1.08)		
G-DCBW	Schleicher ASK 13	13034	BGA 1421-CBW	24. 9.07	Stratford on Avon Gliding Club Ltd	Snitterfield	28. 9.08
G-DCCB	Schempp-Hirth SHK-1	52	BGA 1426-CCB	12. 9.07	R M Johnson tr CCB Syndicate	Milfield	17. 9.08
G-DCCE	Schleicher ASK 13	13047	BGA 1429-CCE	25. 2.08	Oxford Gliding Company Ltd		
						RAF Weston-on-the-Green	3. 3.08
G-DCCF	Schleicher ASK 13	13042	BGA 1430-CCF	7. 2.08	Norfolk Gliding Club Ltd	Tibenham	17. 3.08
G-DCCL	Schleicher Ka 6E	4129	BGA 1435-CCL	14. 2.08	J Tayler tr G-DCCL Group	Sutton Bank	30. 3.08
G-DCCP	Schleicher ASK 13	13052	BGA 1438-CCP	4. 2.08	G D Pullen tr Lima 99 Syndicate	Lasham	12. 3.08
G-DCCR	Schleicher Ka 6E	4149	BGA 1440-CCR	16.11.07	A Shaw	Bicester	1. 4.08
G-DCCT	Schleicher ASK 13	13057	BGA 1442-CCT	24. 9.07	Stratford on Avon Gliding Club Ltd	Snitterfield	15. 2.08
G-DCCU	Schleicher Ka 6E	4122	BGA 1443-CCU	5.10.07	J L Hasker	RAF Keevil	11. 4.08
G-DCCV	Schleicher Ka 6E	4160	BGA 1444-CCV	28. 1.08	T M Bell and C H Page	Lasham	17. 8.08

Reg	Type	C/n	Prev ID	Date	Owner	Location	Date
G-DCCW	Schleicher ASK 13	13051	BGA 1445-CCW	20.11.07	Needwood Forest Gliding Club Ltd	Cross Hayes	17. 2.08
G-DCCX	Schleicher ASK 13	13054	BGA 1446-CCX	23. 1.08	Trent Valley Gliding Club Ltd	Kirton-in-Lindsey	30. 5.08
G-DCCY	Schleicher ASK 13	13050	BGA 1447-CCY	30.11.07	Devon & Somerset Gliding Club Ltd	North Hill	29. 3.08
G-DCDC	Lange E1 Antares	25	D-KJWI	15.11.07	J D Williams "Z7"	Portmoak	
G-DCDF	Schleicher Ka 6E	4162	BGA 1454-CDF	5. 2.08	K G Reid tr CDF Syndicate	Rivar Hill	3. 7.08
G-DCDH	Schempp-Hirth HS.2 Cirrus	10	BGA 1456-CDH	6.12.07	A K Moore	Edgehill	25. 3.08
G-DCDW	FFA Diamant 18	033	BGA 1469-CDW	3. 8.07	D R Chapman	Llantisilio	28. 8.08
G-DCEA	Piper PA-34-200T Seneca II	34-8070079	N3567D	13. 2.91	Barnes Olson Aero Leasing Ltd (Operated DHL)	Bristol	16. 7.08E
G-DCEB	PZL-Bielsko SZD-9bis Bocian 1E	P-433	BGA 1474-CEB	5. 2.08	The Bath, Wilts and North Dorset Gliding Club Ltd	Kingston Deverill	1. 8.08
G-DCEM	Schleicher Ka 6E	4212	BGA 1484-CEM	23. 1.08	E W Black	(Newmarket)	23. 3.08
G-DCEX	Schleicher ASK 13	13108	BGA 1494-CEX	19. 2.08	Carlton Moor Gliding Club	Carlton Moor	26. 5.08
G-DCEY	Schleicher Ka 6E	4222	BGA 1495-CEY	12.11.07	R Saunders	Walney Island	11. 2.08
G-DCFA	Schleicher ASK 13	13113	BGA 1497-CFA	21. 2.08	G P Saw	Wycombe Air Park	22. 5.08
G-DCFG	Schleicher ASK 13	13115	BGA 1503-CFG	27. 2.08	Staffordshire Gliding Club Ltd	Seighford	9. 3.08
G-DCFK	Schempp-Hirth Cirrus	38	BGA 1506-CFK	18.10.07	P J Gill tr Cirrus CFK	Seighford	28. 9.08
G-DCFX	Glasflügel H201 Standard Libelle	274	BGA 1518-CFX	17. 9.07	K D Fishenden	Dunstable	28. 9.08
G-DCGB	Schleicher Ka 6E	4247	BGA 1522-CGB	16.11.07	P M Turner and S C Male	Long Mynd	31.10.07
G-DCGE	Schleicher Ka 6E	4246	BGA 1525-CGE	22.11.07	C V Hill and P C Hazlehurst	Bellarena	26. 1.08
G-DCGH	Schleicher K 8B	8772	BGA 1528-CGH	6. 2.08	T G B Hobbis tr K7 (1971) Syndicate	Lasham	24. 5.08
G-DCGO	Schleicher ASK 13	13153	BGA 1535-CGQ	18.12.07	Oxford Gliding Company Ltd	RAF Weston-on-the-Green	4. 1.08
G-DCGS	FFA Diamant 18	055	BGA 1537-CGS	28.11.07	P K Hayward	Parham Park	3. 7.08
G-DCGT	Schempp-Hirth SHK-1	38	BGA 1538-CGT D-1966	23. 1.08	A J Fardoe	Husbands Bosworth	13. 4.08
G-DCGY	Schempp-Hirth Cirrus	51	BGA 1543-CGY	28. 1.08	R A J Jones and G Nevisky	Eaglescott	14. 3.08
G-DCHO	Aquila AT01	AT01-177		18. 2.08	D R Ho	(Market Drayton)	
G-DCHT	Schleicher ASW 15	15013	BGA 1562-CHT	1. 2.08	J N Kelly and L Walker	Hinton-in-the-Hedges	15. 3.08
G-DCJB	Bölkow Phoebus C	919	BGA 1570-CJB	25.10.07	D Clarke and R Idle	Burn	28. 9.08
G-DCJR	Schempp-Hirth Cirrus	87	BGA 1584-CJR	22.12.07	A Rhodes tr CJR Syndicate	AAC Dishforth	5. 4.08
G-DCKD	PZL-Bielsko SZD-30 Pirat	B-327	BGA 1596-CKD	25. 2.08	The Borders (Milfield) Gliding Club Ltd	Milfield	3. 9.08
G-DCKK	Reims Cessna F172N Skyhawk II	F17201589	PH-GRT PH-AXA	19. 5.80	J Maffia	North Weald	20. 8.08E
G-DCKV	Schleicher ASK 13	13253	BGA 1612-CKV	1.12.07	Black Mountains Gliding Club	Talgarth	16. 7.08
G-DCKZ	Schempp-Hirth Standard Cirrus	52	BGA 1616-CKZ F RAFGSA, BGA 1616-CKZ	4.12.07	G I Bustin	Saltby	9. 5.08
G-DCLA	Schempp-Hirth Standard Cirrus	63	BGA 1617-CLA	3.10.07	C Hughes and D J Dye	Nympsfield	28. 9.08
G-DCLP	Glasflügel H201B Standard Libelle	176	BGA 1630-CLP	1.10.07	M Schlotter	Kingston Deverill	28. 9.08
G-DCLT	Schleicher K 7 Rhönadler (Partly modified to ASK 13 standard)	251	BGA 1634-CLT D-5529	15. 2.08	A H Watkins and K W Gardner	(Rhigos)	2. 9.08
G-DCLV	Glasflügel H201B Standard Libelle	180	BGA 1636-CLV	20. 8.07	J M Sherman	Parham Park	29.11.07
G-DCLZ	Schleicher Ka 6E	4056	BGA 1640-CLZ AGA 2	1. 2.08	R M King and T D Fielder	Kenley	29. 8.08
G-DCMF	PZL-Bielsko SZD-32A Foka 5	W-534	BGA 1646-CMF	17. 1.08	D J Linford	Ringmer	21. 6.08
G-DCMG	Schleicher K 7 Rhönadler	462	BGA 1647-CMG D-8116	6. 2.08	T G B Hobbis tr K7 (1971) Syndicate "Fledermaus Zero Five"	Lasham	5. 5.08
G-DCMH	Glasflügel H201B Standard Libelle	224	BGA 1648-CMH	20. 2.08	D Williams	North Hill	20. 1.08
G-DCMI	Mainair Sports Pegasus Quik	7972		7. 8.03	S J E Smith	Eshott	15. 8.08P
G-DCMK	Schleicher ASK 13	13305	BGA 1650-CMK	25. 1.08	The South Wales Gliding Club Ltd	Usk	24. 3.08
G-DCMO	Glasflügel H201B Standard Libelle	233	BGA 1655-CMQ	17. 1.08	E V Todd and L C Wood	Wycombe Air Park	13. 5.08
G-DCMS	Glasflügel H201B Standard Libelle	234	BGA 1657-CMS	28. 1.08	R J Shallcross tr Libelle 602 Syndicate	Challock	17. 6.08
G-DCMV	Glasflügel H201B Standard Libelle	235	BGA 1660-CMV (BGA 1517-CFV)	17. 9.07	E P Lambert	Aston Down	14. 4.08
G-DCNC	Schempp-Hirth Standard Cirrus	167	BGA 1667-CNC	28.11.07	J H Fox tr Cirrus 273 Syndicate	Portmoak	14. 6.08
G-DCNG	Glasflügel H201B Standard Libelle	265	BGA 1671-CNG	5. 9.07	J Mitcheson	Nympsfield	28. 9.08
G-DCNJ	Glasflügel H201B Standard Libelle	272	BGA 1673-CNJ	21.11.07	R Thornley	Crowland	8. 3.08
G-DCNW	Slingsby T.59F Kestrel 19	1791	BGA 1684-CNW	26.10.07	S R Watson	Seighford	13. 3.08
G-DCNY	Glasflügel H201B Standard Libelle	322	BGA 1686-CNY	29.11.07	A D Stevenson tr Libelle 151 Syndicate	Portmoak	14. 4.08
G-DCOJ	Slingsby T.59A Kestrel 17	1727	BGA 1720-CQJ	6.12.07	T W Treadaway	Husbands Bosworth	9. 4.08
G-DCON	Robinson R44 Raven	1646		25. 9.06	D Connelly	Enniskillen	5.10.07E
G-DCOR	Schempp-Hirth Standard Cirrus	220G	BGA 1727-CQR	4. 2.08	S Brown	Wycombe Air Park	30. 5.08
G-DCOY	Schempp-Hirth Standard Cirrus	214	BGA 1734-CQY	12. 9.07	R Farmer	Husbands Bosworth	14. 6.08
G-DCPA	Eurocopter MBB BK-117C-1C	7511	D-HXXL, G-LFBA, D-HECU, D-HMBF		Devon and Cornwall Constabulary	Exeter	16. 6.08E
G-DCPD	Schleicher ASW 17	17026	BGA 1691-CPD	21. 2.08	A J Hewitt	Tibenham	18. 8.08
G-DCPJ	Schleicher Ka 6E	4059	BGA 1696-CPJ OO-ZDA	24. 4.07	E Lowe "CPJ"	Edgehill	24. 5.08
G-DCPM	Glasflügel H201B Standard Libelle	179	BGA 1699-CPM	5. 2.08	K Marsden and P E Jessop Trenchard Lines, Upavon		4. 5.08
G-DCRB	Glasflügel H201B Standard Libelle	243	BGA 1737-CRB	13. 2.08	A I Mawer	Kirton-in-Lindsey	25. 6.08
G-DCRH	Schempp-Hirth Standard Cirrus	233G	BGA 1743-CRH	7. 2.08	P E Thelwall	Gransden Lodge	25. 4.08
G-DCRO	Glasflügel H201B Standard Libelle	326	BGA 1750-CRO	24.10.07	K G Counsell tr G-DCRO Group	Usk	19. 2.08
G-DCRT	Schleicher ASK 13	13396	BGA 1753-CRT	20. 9.07	Bowland Forest Gliding Club Ltd	Chipping	3. 3.08
G-DCRV	Glasflügel H201B Standard Libelle	329	BGA 1755-CRV	18. 1.08	S.Cervantes	Portmoak	23. 5.08
G-DCRW	Glasflügel H201B Standard Libelle	324	BGA 1756-CRW	10.12.07	A Billingham tr 417 Syndicate	Nympsfield	6. 4.08
G-DCSD	Slingsby T.59D Kestrel 19	1800	BGA 1763-CSD	14.11.07	R J Toon	Sutton Bank	11. 4.08
G-DCSE	Robinson R44 Astro	0659		23. 9.99	M P Wilkinson	Sandtoft	16.10.07E
G-DCSF	Slingsby T.59F Kestrel 19	1802	BGA 1765-CSF	15. 1.08	R Birch	Aston Down	9. 2.08
G-DCSG	Robinson R44 Raven	0960	G-TRYG	27. 7.05	Voute Sales Ltd	Wellesbourne Mountford	26. 2.08E
G-DCSK	Slingsby T.59D Kestrel 20	1806	BGA 1769-CSK	1.11.07	H A Torode tr Kestrel CSK Group	Lasham	9. 3.08
G-DCSN	Pilatus B4-PC11AF	21	BGA 1772-CSN	21. 2.08	J S Firth	(Huddersfield)	14. 5.08
G-DCSR	Glasflügel H201B Standard Libelle	368	BGA 1775-CSR	12.11.07	J Eagleton tr Glasgow and West	Portmoak	28. 9.08
G-DCTA	British Aerospace BAe 125 Series 800B	258130	G-OSPG D-CPAS, G-ETOM, G-BVFC, G-TPHK, G-FDSL, G-5-620	15. 1.07	Direct Air Executive Ltd	Oxford	15. 2.08E

G-DCTB	Schempp-Hirth Standard Cirrus	264G	BGA 1785-CTB	19.11.07	I M Young and S McCurdy		
						RAF Weston-on-the-Green	22. 2.08
G-DCTE	Schleicher ASW 17	17012	BGA 1788-CTE	14. 1.08	T Linee	Eyres Field	8. 4.08
G-DCTJ	Slingsby T.59D Kestrel 19	1810	BGA 1792-CTJ	20. 2.08	H B Walrond	(Cockfield, Bury St Edmunds)	10. 9.08
G-DCTM	Slingsby T.59D Kestrel 19	1813	BGA 1795-CTM	20.11.07	C Roney	Gransden Lodge	28.10.07
G-DCTO	Slingsby T.59D Kestrel 19	1816	BGA 1798-CTQ	9. 1.08	K.A.Moules	Trenchard Lines, Upavon	21. 4.08
G-DCTU	Glasflügel H201B Standard Libelle	371	BGA 1802-CTU	20. 2.08	F K Hutchinson and P M Davies	Husbands Bosworth	14. 5.08
G-DCUB	Pilatus B4-PC-11	047	BGA 1809-CUB	7. 9.07	G S Sanderson	Gransden Lodge	22. 2.08
G-DCUJ	Glasflügel H201B Standard Libelle	370	BGA 1816-CUJ	13.11.07	T G B Hobbis	Lasham	2. 5.08
G-DCUT	Pilatus B4 PC-11AF	041	BGA 1823-CUT	1. 6.07	A L Walker	Lasham	19. 8.08
G-DCVB	LET L-13 Blanik	25419	BGA 1831-CVB	22. 2.08	K S Wells and M A Prickett tr Blanik Syndicate		
						Sackville Lodge, Riseley	13. 4.08
G-DCVE	Schempp-Hirth HS.2 Cirrus VTC	127Y	BGA 1834-CVE	13.11.07	H Whybrow	Dunstable	26. 3.08
G-DCVG	Pilatus B4-PC11AF	045	BGA 1836-CVG	29. 1.08	I H Keyser	(Germany)	31. 3.08
G-DCVK	Pilatus B4-PC-11AF	048	BGA 1839-CVK	15.10.07	J P Marriott	Bicester	9. 1.08
G-DCVM	Pilatus B4 PC-11AF	036	BGA 1841-CVM	31. 7.07	J A Mace	Rivar Hill	28. 9.08
G-DCVS	PZL-Bielsko SZD-36A Cobra 15	W-610	BGA 1846-CVS	11. 1.08	I A Burgin tr CVS Group	Darlton	14. 4.08
G-DCVT	PZL-Bielsko SZD-36A Cobra 15	W-609	BGA 1847-CVT	23. 1.08	P Q Benn	Aston Down	30. 3.08
G-DCVV	Pilatus B4-PC-11AF	028	BGA 1849-CVV	17. 9.07	F R Wolff tr Syndicate CVV	North Hill	3. 3.08
G-DCVY	Slingsby T.59D Kestrel 19	1821	BGA 1852-CVY	20. 2.08	D F Catherwood	Chipping	18. 3.07
G-DCWA	Slingsby T.59D Kestrel 19	1825	BGA 1854-CWA	25. 1.08	D J Jeffries	Usk	21. 2.08
G-DCWB	Slingsby T.59D Kestrel 19	1833	BGA 1855-CWB	28.11.07	D J Deacon tr Kestrel 677 Syndicate	Saltby	13. 3.08
G-DCWE	Glasflügel H201B Standard Libelle	482	BGA 1858-CWE	22.11.07	T W J Stoker	Rufforth	3. 4.08
G-DCWF	Slingsby T.59D Kestrel 19	1838	BGA 1859-CWF	18.10.07	P F Nicholson	Hinton-In-the-Hedges	28. 9.08
G-DCWG	Glasflügel H201B Standard Libelle	391	BGA 1860-CWG	28.11.07	G Mitcheson tr Libelle 322 Group	Milfield	10. 7.08
G-DCWH	Schleicher ASK 13	13424	BGA 1861-CWH	16.10.07	York Gliding Centre Ltd	Rufforth	28. 9.08
G-DCWR	Schempp-Hirth Cirrus	133Y	BGA 1869-CWR	14.12.07	P J Concannon tr CWR Group	Thame	23. 6.08
G-DCWX	Glasflügel H201B Standard Libelle	36	BGA 1875-CWX	11. 1.08	C A Weyman	Eyres Field	21. 4.08
			RAFGSA 132				
G-DCXL	SAN Jodel D 140C Mousquetaire III	101	F-BKSM	27. 5.88	A C D Norris	(Caluire Et Cuire, France)	17. 5.08E
G-DCXM	Slingsby T.59D Kestrel 19	1820	BGA 1889-CXM	6.12.07	R P Beck and T Potter	AAC Dishforth	15. 4.08
G-DCYA	Pilatus B4-PC-11	072	BGA 1902-CYA	8.11.07	E J Bromwell tr B4-072 Group	North Hill	2. 2.08
G-DCYG	Glasflügel H201B Standard Libelle	441	BGA 1908-CYG	22.12.07	D Cooke and R Barsby	Husbands Bosworth	14. 1.08
G-DCYM	Schempp-Hirth Standard Cirrus	48	BGA 1913-CYM	26. 9.07	K M Fisher	Husbands Bosworth	28. 9.08
			RAFGSA, D-0578				
G-DCYT	Schempp-Hirth Standard Cirrus	357G	BGA 1919-CYT	25. 9.07	G Royle	Llantisilio	23. 4.08
G-DCZD	Pilatus B4-PC-11	081	BGA 1929-CZD	8. 8.07	S E Marples	Milfield	5. 8.08
G-DCZE	PZL-Bielsko SZD-30 Pirat	S-01.14	BGA 1930-CZE	10.12.07	M R Biddle tr G-DCZE Group	Snitterfield	29. 4.08
G-DCZJ	PZL-Bielsko SZD-30 Pirat	S-01.15	BGA 1934-CZJ	21. 1.08	C L Groves tr Pirat CZJ Group		
						Husbands Bosworth	5. 4.08
G-DCZR	Slingsby T.59D Kestrel 19	1842	BGA 1941-CZR	6.11.07	R P Brisbourne	Rufforth	5. 4.08
G-DDAC	PZL-Bielsko SZD-36A Cobra 15	W-656	BGA 1952-DAC	4 .1.08	R J A Colenso	Husbands Bosworth	6. 5.08
G-DDAJ	Schempp-Hirth Nimbus 2	50	BGA 1958-DAJ	17. 8.07	J D Jones	Nympsfield	28. 9.08
G-DDAK	Schleicher K 7 Rhönadler	893	BGA 1959-DAK	11. 1.08	T J Price tr Vale of Neath Gliding Club	Rhigos	7. 9.08
			D-8851				
G-DDAN	PZL-Bielsko SZD-30 Pirat	S-01.45	BGA 1962-DAN	29. 1.08	J M A Shannon	(Cambridge)	22.11.07
G-DDAP	PZL-Bielsko SZD-30 Pirat	S-01.47	BGA 1963-DAP	13. 2.08	T D Younger tr Delta Alpha Papa Group	Currock Hill	19. 5.08
G-DDAS	Schempp-Hirth Standard Cirrus	378	BGA 1966-DAS	21.11.07	G Goodenough	Burn	2. 4.08
			(BGA1925)				
G-DDAW	Schleicher Ka 6CR	951	BGA 1970-DAW	20. 2.08	P S Holmes and R G Charlesson	Bellarena	14. 9.08
			RAFGSA, D-2025				
G-DDAY	Piper PA-28R-201T Turbo Arrow III		G-BPDO	24.11.88	W G Thompson tr G-DDAY Group	Tatenhill	13. 6.08
		28R-7703112	N3496Q				
G-DDBD	Europa Aviation Europa XS	454		11. 2.03	B Davies	Dunsfoldl	23. 8.08P
	(Built B Davies - pr.no.PFA 247-13569)						
G-DDBN	Slingsby T.59D Kestrel 19	1857	BGA 1986-DBN	11. 1.08	J D Westwood	Nympsfield	4. 5.08
G-DDBP	Glasflügel H205 Standard Club Libelle	51	BGA 1987-DBP	17.10.07	T Forsey tr 551 Syndicate	Wormingford	28. 9.08
G-DDBV	PZL-Bielsko SZD-30 Pirat	S-02.27	BGA 1993-DBV	19. 2.08	A Rasul	Usk	19. 5.08
G-DDBX	PZL-Bielsko SZD-9bis Bocian 1E	P-642	BGA 1995-DBX	13. 2.08	A Veitch tr Highland Bocian Syndicate	Easterton	28. 4.08
G-DDCA	PZL-Bielsko SZD-36A Cobra 15	W-686	BGA 1998-DCA	28.11.07	J R Aylesbury	Upwood	10. 6.07
G-DDCC	Glasflügel H205 Club Libelle	585	BGA 2000-DCC	15.10.07	H J Warbey	Shobdon	7. 3.08
G-DDDA	Schempp-Hirth Standard Cirrus	532G	BGA 2022-DDA	17. 9.07	A J Davis and C G Wrigley	Nympsfield	4. 3.08
G-DDDD	Evektor EV-97 teamEurostar UK	2907		13. 3.07	S Sebastian	East Barling, Essex	12. 3.08E
G-DDDE	PZL-Bielsko SZD-38A Jantar 1	B-641	BGA 2026-DDE	28. 2.08	D W F Gosden tr Jantar One Syndicate	Talgarth	18. 3.08
G-DDDM	Schempp-Hirth Cirrus	164Y	BGA 2033-DDM	11. 1.08	G J W Booth tr DDM Syndicate	Ridgewell	5. 5.08
G-DDDR	Schempp-Hirth Standard Cirrus	531G	BGA 2037-DDR	16.10.07	J D Ewence	Pocklington	28. 9.08
G-DDDY	P&M Quik GT450	8308		23. 8.07	J W Dodson	Leicester	29. 8.08P
G-DDEG	ICA IS-28B2	48	BGA 2051-DEG	7. 9.07	P S Whitehead	Skelling Farm, Penrith	16.11.07
G-DDEO	Glasflügel H205 Club Libelle	97	BGA 2059-DEQ	18.12.07	N J Mitchell	Kingston Deverill	24. 3.08
G-DDEV	Schleicher Ka 6CR	6453	BGA 2064-DEV	7. 1.08	A N and L M Morley	Wormingford	22. 3.08
			RAFGSA 354				
G-DDEW	ICA IS-29D	40	BGA 2065-DEW	30.11.07	G V Prater	(Lower Earley, Reading)	4. 7.07
G-DDEX	LET L-13 Blanik	026348	BGA 2066-DEX	11. 9.07	B A Hutchins tr Blanik DEX Group	Talgarth	24.10.07
			RAFGSA R4, BGA 2066-DEX				
G-DDFK	Molino PIK-20	20039	BGA 2078-DFK	31.10.07	B H and M J Fairclough	North Hill	3. 3.08
			OH-500				
G-DDFL	SZD-38A Jantar-1	B-682	BGA 2079-DFL	9.10.07	P Bellham	Kirton-in-Lindsey	6. 5.08
G-DDFW	PZL-Bielsko SZD-30 Pirat	S-05.45	BGA 2089-DFW	22. 2.08	R G Skerry tr Cloud Nine Syndicate	Strubby	29. 8.07
G-DDGA	Schleicher K 8B	8587	BGA 2093-DGA	11.12.07	The Welland Gliding Club Ltd	Lyveden	1. 5.08
			RAFGSA, BGA 1926-CZA, D-....				
G-DDGE	Schempp-Hirth Standard Cirrus	606	BGA 2097-DGE	9. 1.08	T.E.Snoddy	Bellarena	4. 5.08
G-DDGJ	American Champion 8KCAB Super Decathlon			17. 8.07	T A Mann	(Ballasalla, Isle of Man)	
		1049-2007					
G-DDGK	Schleicher Ka 6CR	6287	BGA 2102-DGK	22.11.07	N Riggott "Betty Blue"	Lasham	9. 5.08

G-DDGY	Schempp-Hirth Nimbus 2	105	BGA 2115-DGY	31.10.07	J.H.Taylor	Nympsfield	15. 1.08
G-DDHC	PZL-Bielsko SZD-41A Jantar Standard 1	B-710	BGA 2119-DHC (BGA 2109)	7. 1.08	M C Burlock and P J Kelly	Rivar Hill	29. 3.08
G-DDHE	Slingsby T.53B	1718	BGA 2132-DHE	13.11.07	J Mattocks tr Aviation Preservation Society of Scotland (APSS) Portmoak		5. 3.08
G-DDHJ	Glaser-Dirks DG-100	48	BGA 2125-DHJ	13.12.07	G E McLaughlin	Bellarena	25. 6.08
G-DDHK	Glaser-Dirks DG-100	50	BGA 2126-DHK	30. 8.07	B J Griffin	Kirton in Lindsey	28. 9.08
G-DDHL	Glaser-Dirks DG-100	52	BGA 2127-DHL	25.10.07	T L Webster tr DHL Syndicate	Challock	24. 2.08
G-DDHM	Schleicher Ka 6E	4124	BGA 2128-DHM RAFGSA 26	19.10.07	J G Heard	Seighford	7. 3.08
G-DDHT	Schleicher Ka 6E	4065	BGA 2134-DHT D-7202	11.12.07	S Foster	Long Mynd	20. 2.08
G-DDIG	Rockwell Commander 114	14397	G-CCDT D-EKGD, OE-KGD, D-EIBC	11. 7.06	D Millard tr Daedalus Flying Group	Lee-on-Solent	16. 5.08E
G-DDJB	Schleicher K 8B	8879	BGA 2142-DJB AGA17	29. 1.08	T World tr Portsmouth Naval Gliding Centre Lee-on-Solent		16. 2.08
G-DDJD	Grob G102 Astir CS	1226	BGA 2144-DJD	16.10.07	P E Gascoigne	Kingston Deverill	28. 9.08
G-DDJE	Schleicher Ka 6CR	6412	BGA2145/DJE, D-3682	13.12.07	E W Russell tr The Friday Syndicate	Wormingford	28. 9.08
G-DDJF	Schempp-Hirth Duo Discus T	121/...	BGA 5182-KLM	21. 4.06	R J H Fack *"JF"*	Long Mynd	14. 5.08
G-DDJL	PZL-Bielsko SZD-41A Jantar Standard 1	B-714	BGA 2151-DJL	14. 9.07	A M Cooper	Llantisilio	28. 9.08
G-DDJN	Eiriavion PIK-20B	20140C	BGA 2153-DJN	20.11.07	M Ireland and S Lambourne	Kingston Deverill	9. 3.08
G-DDJX	Grob G102 Astir CS	1259	BGA 2162-DJX	4. 1.08	P Barnwell	Crowland	13. 4.08
G-DDKD	Glasflügel H206 Hornet	67	BGA 2168-DKD (BGA 2165-DKA)	3. 1.08	B J W Thomas	Eyres Field	28. 4.08
G-DDKE	Schleicher ASK 13	13548	BGA 2169-DKE	25. 1.08	The South Wales Gliding Club Ltd	Usk	13. 4.08
G-DDKL	Schempp-Hirth Nimbus-2	86	BGA 2175-DKL D-2111	1. 2.08	G J Croll	Rattlesden	20. 4.08
G-DDKN	Schleicher Ka 6CR	6456	BGA 2177-DKN D-9358	17. 1.08	A Ciccone	Upwood	2. 4.08
G-DDKT	Eiriavion PIK-20B	20155C	BGA 2182-DKT	29. 2.08	F P Wilson	Pocklington	23. 4.08
G-DDKU	Grob G102 Astir CS	1326	BGA 2183-DKU	12. 9.07	P N Stapleton tr Delta Kilo Unifirm Syndicate North Hill		28. 9.08
G-DDKW	Grob G102 Astir CS	1329	BGA 2185-DKW	8. 2.08	J Friend and R Robertson	Lleweni Parc	30. 3.08
G-DDKX	Grob G102 Astir CS	1331	BGA 2186-DKX	23. 1.08	L R Bennett	Usk	30. 4.08
G-DDLA	Pilatus B4-PC11	149	BGA 2189-DLA RAFGSA	17. 8.07	P R Seddon	Walney Island	3. 6.08
G-DDLB	Schleicher ASK 18	18040	BGA 2190-DLB	28.11.07	The Vale of the White Horse Gliding Centre Ltd Sandhill Farm, Shrivenham		9. 2.08
G-DDLH	Grob G102 Astir CS77	1646	BGA 2196-DLH	28. 1.08	M D and M E Saunders	Lasham	19. 4.08
G-DDLP	Schleicher Ka 6CR	6519	BGA 2202-DLP RAFGSA 355	18. 1.08	J.R Crosse	Crowland	24. 4.08
G-DDLT	ICA IS-28B2	32	BGA 2206-DLT	8. 2.08	M H Simms	Shipdham	3. 7.03
G-DDLY	Eiriavion PIK-20B	20509	BGA 2211-DLY	13.12.07	M Conrad	Bidford	23. 5.08
G-DDMB	Schleicher K 8B	8209	BGA 2214-DMB D-4331	27. 9.07	Crown Service Gliding Club *"Kate"*	Lasham	3. 2.08
G-DDMD	Glaser-Dirks DG-100	75	BGA 2216-DMD	12.12.07	N M Hill	RAF Weston-on-the-Green	24. 2.08
G-DDMG	Schleicher K 8B	8763	BGA 2219-DMG RAFGSA 382	6.11.07	Dorset Gliding Club Ltd	Eyres Field	28. 9.08
G-DDML	Schleicher K 7 Rhönadler	929	BGA 2223-DML D-6194, D-5005	12.12.07	Dumfries and District Gliding Club	Falgunzeon	11. 2.07
G-DDMM	Schempp-Hirth Nimbus 2	125	BGA 2224-DMM	14. 1.08	T.E.Linee	Eyres Field	22. 4.08
G-DDMO	Schleicher Ka 6E	4062	BGA 2227-DMQ RAFGSA 264	23. 1.08	Trent Valley Gliding Club Ltd	Kirton-in-Lindsey	18. 6.08
G-DDMR	Grob G102 Astir CS	1435	BGA 2228-DMR	22.12.07	Mendip Gliding Club Ltd	Halesland	16. 2.08
G-DDMS	Glasflügel H201B Standard Libelle	385	BGA 2229-DMS RNGSA	1.12.07	B I Stoddart	Burn	12. 4.08
G-DDMV	North American T-6G-NF Texan	168-313	N3240N Haitian AF 3209, 49-3209	30. 4.90	C Dabin *(As "493209:ANG" in USAAF "CALIF ANG" yellow c/s)*	Sywell	6. 4.09T
G-DDMX	Schleicher ASK 13	13567	BGA 2234-DMX	25. 1.08	Dartmoor Gliding Society Ltd	Brentor	1. 8.08
G-DDNC	Grob G102 Astir CS	1428	BGA 2239-DNC	18.10.07	K S Wells and R A Lovegrove	Lyveden	27. 6.99
G-DDND	Pilatus B4-PC11AF	136	BGA 2240-DND	7. 2.08	R J Happs tr DND Group	Lasham	21. 4.08
G-DDNE	Grob G102 Astir CS77	1631	BGA 2241-DNE	22.12.07	J Green and M A Wintle tr 621 Astir Syndicate Halesland		26. 3.08
G-DDNG	Schempp-Hirth Nimbus 2	265	BGA 2243-DNG	9.10.07	B H Penfold tr Nimbus 265 Syndicate Trenchard Lines, Upavon		5. 3.08
G-DDNJ	Schleicher ASK 18	18042	BGA 2245-DNJ	17. 1.08	Derbyshire & Lancashire Gliding Club	Camphill	18. 1.08
G-DDNK	Grob G102 Astir CS	1434	BGA 2246-DNK	5.10.07	A Page tr G-DDNK Group	Rattlesden	1. 3.08
G-DDNT	PZL-Bielsko SZD-30 Pirat	S-07.12	BGA 2254-DNT	13.12.07	R A Lashly	Drumshade	27. 4.08
G-DDNW	Schleicher Ka 6CR	829	BGA 2257-DNW	21.11.07	K Marchant and P Carey	Edgehill	23. 4.08
G-DDNX	Schleicher Ka 6CR	6094SI	BGA 2258-DNX D-5107	1.12.07	Black Mountains Gliding Club	Talgarth	28. 9.08
G-DDOA	Schleicher ASK 13	13582	BGA 2285-DQA	12.11.07	Essex & Suffolk Gliding Club Ltd	Wormingford	28. 9.08
G-DDOB	Grob G102 Astir CS77	1653	BGA 2286-DQB	6.12.07	C E Hutson	Kirton-in-Lindsey	1. 4.08
G-DDOF	Schleicher Ka 6CR	6417	BGA 2290-DQF D-5827	6. 2.08	A Graham	(Kirkintilloch, Glasgow)	24. 4.08
G-DDOG	Scottish Aviation Bulldog Series 120/121	BH120/210	XX524	18. 6.01	Deltaero Ltd *(As "XX524:04" in RAF c/s)*	(London SW1)	12. 2.09S
G-DDOK	Schleicher Ka 6E	4341	BGA 2294-DQK D-0541	13. 2.08	R S Hawley and S Y Duxbury	Long Mynd	7. 4.08
G-DDOR	Grob G102 Astir CS77	1667	BGA 2300-DQR	25.10.07	R Wardell-Yerburgh tr The Astir Syndicate Kingston Deverill		28. 9.08
G-DDOX	Schleicher K 7 Rhönadler	743	BGA 2306-DQX D-9127	4. 1.08	The Nene Valley Gliding Club Ltd	Upwood	31. 3.08

(Regd as K 7 but believed modified earlier to ASK 13 standard with fuselage from ASK 13 BGA 1833 and wings from BGA 3331)

G-DDOY	Schleicher K 8B	647	BGA 2307-DQY 22.12.07 D-4375	Mendip Gliding Club Ltd	Halesland	18. 8.08
G-DDPA	Schleicher ASK 18	18044	BGA 2261-DPA 11. 1.08	Rangetour Ltd	Bembridge	4. 3.08
G-DDPL	Eiriavion PIK-20D	20549	BGA 2271-DPL 25. 2.08	H A Schuricht tr 437 Syndicate	Dunstable	22. 1.08
G-DDPO	Grob G102 Astir CS77	1632	BGA 2275-DPQ 9. 1.08	Dorset Gliding Club Ltd	Eyres Field	14. 4.08
G-DDPY	Grob G102 Astir CS77	1652	BGA 2283-DPY 30.10.07	D S Burton	Edgehill	27. 5.08
G-DDRD	Schleicher Ka 6CR	6377SI	BGA 2312-DRD 4.10.07 D-9080	Essex & Suffolk Gliding Club Ltd	Wormingford	28. 9.08
G-DDRM	Schleicher K 7 Rhönadler	7017	BGA 2320-DRM 31.10.07 D-4666	L.G.Cross tr K7 DRM Glider Syndicate	Dunstable	3.10.07
G-DDRT	Eiriavion PIK-20D	20587	BGA 2326-DRT 20.11.07	P F C Fowler tr 688 Syndicate	Long Mynd	4. 4.08
G-DDRU	Grob G102 Astir CS77	1685	BGA 2327-DRU 4.10.07	G Rybak	Lasham	26. 2.08
G-DDRW	Grob G102 Astir CS	1081	BGA 2329-DRW 1. 2.08 D-3311	P A Brooks tr 798 Syndicate	Lasham	1. 5.08
G-DDRZ	Schleicher K 8B	668	BGA 2332-DRZ 18. 1.08 D-4622, D-KANB, D-4622	East Sussex Gliding Club	Ringmer	31. 7.08
G-DDSB	Schleicher Ka 6E	4300	BGA 2334-DSB 12.12.07 D-0263	G B Griffiths	Rattlesden	6. 3.08
G-DDSF	Schleicher K 8B	8220	BGA 2338-DSF 10. 1.08 D-7114	I A McTernan tr Edinburgh University Gliding Club "Snoopy" Portmoak		28. 9.08
G-DDSH	Grob G102 Astir CS77	1696	BGA 2340-DSH 21. 1.08	R B Petrie tr Astir 648 Syndicate	Portmoak	7. 6.08
G-DDST	Schleicher ASW 20L	20059	BGA 2350-DST 17. 9.07	D J Miller	Dunstable	22. 2.08
G-DDSU	Grob G102 Astir CS77	1663	BGA 2351-DSU 21. 9.07	Bowland Forest Gliding Club Ltd	Chipping	28. 9.08
G-DDSV	Pilatus B4-PC11AF	134	BGA 2352-DSV 21. 1.08 RAFGSA 718, RAFGSA 518	G M Drinkell and S J Brunton	Wormingford	1. 6.08
G-DDSX	Schleicher ASW 19B	19188	BGA 2354-DSX 18.10.07	B Ashbourn and G Kamp	Kingston Deverill	28. 9.08
G-DDSY	Schleicher Ka 6CR	561	BGA 2355-DSY 4. 1.08 D-5702	D A Senior "Daisy"	Camphill	14. 3.08
G-DDTA	Glaser-Dirks DG-200	2-27	BGA 2357-DTA 13.12.07	M D Bowman	Rufforth	17. 7.08
G-DDTE	Schleicher ASW 19B	19185	BGA 2361-DTE 7. 2.08	A and G R Purcell	Edgehill	4.12.07
G-DDTK	Glasflügel H303 Mosquito B	109	BGA 2366-DTK 4.12.07	P France	Usk	28. 9.08
G-DDTM	Glaser-Dirks DG-200	2-34	BGA 2368-DTM 18.12.07	R S Skinner	Wormingford	12. 3.08
G-DDTP	Schleicher ASW 20	20078	BGA 2370-DTP 27. 9.07	T S and S M Hills	Lasham	28. 9.08
G-DDTU	Schempp-Hirth Nimbus 2B	167	BGA 2375-DTU 14. 8.07	R E Wooller tr Nimbus Syndicate	Chipping	12. 4.08
G-DDTV	Glasflügel H303 Mosquito B	110	BGA 2376-DTV 4.12.07	S R Evans	Aston Down	14. 9.08
G-DDTX	Glasflügel H303 Mosquito B	111	BGA 2378-DTX 4. 1.08	P T S Nash	Crowland	23. 1.02
G-DDTY	Glasflügel H303 Mosquito B	112	BGA 2379-DTY 6. 2.08	W H L Bullimore	Gransden Lodge	2.11.07
G-DDUF	Schleicher K 8B	8296A	BGA 2386-DUF 24.10.07 D-5294	M Staljan	Nympsfield	6. 7.08
G-DDUK	Schleicher K 8B	752	BGA 2390-DUK 29. 1.08 D-4048	The Bristol Gliding Club Proprietary Ltd	Nympsfield	13. 3.08
G-DDUL	Grob G102 Astir CS77	1720	BGA 2391-DUL 3. 1.08	A Spencer	Kirton-in-Lindsey	2. 4.08
G-DDUR	Schleicher Ka 6CR	6273	BGA 2395-DUR 12.11.07 OY-DLX	B N Bromley and M Whitthread	Strubby	8.12.07
G-DDUX	Grob G102 Astir CS Jeans	2140	BGA 2401-DUX 22.11.07	B T Spreckley (Operated European Soaring Club)	Ontur, Spain	28. 9.08
G-DDVB	Schleicher ASK 13	13596	BGA 2405-DVB 12.11.07	Essex & Suffolk Gliding Club Ltd	Wormingford	2. 2.08
	(Components including c/n plate donated to BGA 3493)					
G-DDVD	LET L-13 Blanik	027021	BGA 2417-DVD 27.11.07 (RNGSA N22)	Vectis Gliding Club Ltd	Bembridge	27.12.08
G-DDVG	Schleicher Ka 6CR	3	BGA 2410-DVG 21.12.07	G Tilley tr G-DDVG Banana Group	Ringmer	20. 2.08
G-DDVL	Schleicher ASW 19	19222	BGA 2414-DVL 17.11.07	A C M Phillips	Lasham	30. 3.08
G-DDVM	Glasflügel H205 Club Libelle	52	BGA 2415-DVM 22. 2.08 RAFGGA 581	M A Field	Wormingford	4. 4.08
G-DDVN	Eiriavion PIK-20D	20641	BGA 2416-DVN 28. 1.08	T P Bassett and A D Butler	Burn	17. 4.08
G-DDVP	Schleicher ASW 19B	19220	BGA 2417-DVP 17. 1.08	P O R Cumming tr VP Syndicate	Wycombe Air Park	29. 1.08
G-DDVS	Schempp-Hirth Standard Cirrus	380'	BGA 2420-DVS 24.10.07 RAFGSA 824	J C and T J Milner	Rufforth	23. 3.08
G-DDVY	Schempp-Hirth Cirrus	52	BGA 2426-DVY 12. 2.08 OO-ZIR	G Martin and M G Ashton	Talgarth	27. 7.08
G-DDWC	Schleicher Ka 6E	4111	BGA 2430-DWC 6.11.07 AGA 11	D E Jones	Ridgewell	12. 4.08
G-DDWG	Schleicher K 8B	165-60	BGA 2434-DWG 31. 1.08 D-5750	Dartmoor Gliding Society	Brentor	12.12.07
G-DDWL	Glasflügel H303 Mosquito B	141	BGA 2438-DWL 1.11.07	H A Stanford	Husbands Bosworth	3. 4.08
G-DDWN	Schleicher K 7 Rhönadler	7101	BGA 2440-DWN 12. 2.08 D-5360	L R and J E Merritt	Saltby	27. 5.08
G-DDWR	Glasflügel H303 Mosquito B	134	BGA 2443-DWR 16.10.07 (BGA 2428-DWA)	C D Lovell	Lasham	11. 3.08
G-DDWT	Slingsby T.65C Vega	1898	BGA 2445-DWT 11.10.07	A P Grimley	(Alderley Edge)	28. 9.08
G-DDWU	Grob G102 Astir CS	1201	BGA 2446-DWU 25.10.07 D-7269	D Evans and I B Cronyn	Hinton-in-the-Hedges	20.12.07
G-DDXB	Schleicher ASW 20	20142	BGA 2453-DXB 25.10.07	J A Timpany tr 81 Syndicate	Nympsfield	28. 9.08
G-DDXD	Slingsby T.65A Vega	1901	BGA 2455-DXD 26 .2.08	M C Rupasinha tr G-DDXD Flying Group	Dunstable	21. 9.08
G-DDXE	Slingsby T.65C Vega	1902	BGA 2456-DXE 16.11.07	H K Rattray	Usk	18. 1.08
G-DDXH	Schleicher Ka 6E	4198	BGA 2459-DXH 25. 1.08 RAFGSA 489, D-4093	B Hughes tr DXH Syndicate	Bicester	22. 3.08
G-DDXJ	Grob G102 Astir CS77	1762	BGA 2460-DXJ 6.12.07	M T Stickland	Portmoak	10. 3.08
G-DDXL	Schempp-Hirth Standard Cirrus	203G	BGA 2462-DXL 17.11.07	C J Button	Aston Down	30. 3.08
G-DDXN	Glaser-Dirks DG-200	2-63	BGA 2464-DXN 9. 1.08	J.A.Johnston	Gransden Lodge	16. 3.08
G-DDXT	Schempp-Hirth Mini-Nimbus C	97	BGA 2469-DXT 10.12.07	H Altmann tr G-DDXT Mini-Nimbus	Wycombe Air Park	4. 3.08

G-DDXW	Glasflügel H303 Mosquito B	142	BGA 2472-DXW	6.12.07	P Newmark	Burn	16. 2.08
G-DDXX	Schleicher ASW 19B	19245	BGA 2473-DXX	14.12.07	B C P Crook	(London SE5)	28. 9.08
G-DDYC	Schleicher Ka 6CR	6390	BGA 2478-DYC	24. 1.08	S S Ryan	Walney Island	22. 4.08
			D-1545				
G-DDYE	Schleicher ASW 20L	20143	BGA 2479-DYE	5. 9.07	T A Sage tr 828 Syndicate	Dunstable	28. 9.08
G-DDYF	Grob G102 Astir CS77	1805	BGA 2480-DYF	29.10.07	York Gliding Centre Ltd	Rufforth	28. 9.08
G-DDYJ	Schleicher Ka 6CR	6583	BGA 2483-DYJ	19. 2.08	Upward Bound Trust	Thame	14. 7.08
			D-5838				
G-DDYU	Schempp-Hirth Nimbus 2C	181	BGA 2491-DYU	12.12.07	K Richards	(Talgarth)	31. 3.05
G-DDZA	Slingsby T.65A Vega 17L	1907	BGA 2496-DZA	21. 9.07	K H Kuntze	Dunstable	2. 3.08
G-DDZG	Schleicher ASW 19B	19267	BGA 2502-DZG	27.11.07	S P Wareham	Kingston Deverill	18. 2.08
G-DDZP	Slingsby T.65A Vega	1911	BGA 2509-DZP	14. 2.08	M T Crews	Milfield	25. 6.08
G-DDZR	ICA IS-28B2	87	BGA 2511-DZR	5.12.07	The Furness Gliding Club Proprietary Ltd t/a Lakes Gliding Club		
						Walney Island	9. 5.08
G-DDZT	Eiriavion PIK-20D	20661	BGA 2513-DZT	31.10.07	A C Garside tr PIK20D 106 Group	Challock	1. 3.08
G-DDZY	Schleicher ASW 19B	19275	BGA 2518-DZY	13. 9.07	M C Fairman	Dunstable	29. 1.08
G-DEAF	Grob G102 Astir CS77	1830	BGA 2525-EAF	25. 2.08	The Borders (Milfield) Gliding Club Ltd	Milfield	29. 9.08
G-DEAH	Schleicher Ka 6E	4085	BGA 2527-EAH	5. 2.08	M Lodge	Lasham	14. 6.08
			D-7542, D-7142				
G-DEAJ	Schempp-Hirth HS.5 Nimbus 2	7	BGA 2528-EAJ	12.11.07	D R Piercey and N Hanney	Eyres Field	31. 3.08
			D-0699				
G-DEAK	Glasflügel H303 Mosquito B	155	BGA 2529-EAK	14. 2.08	T A L Barnes	Aston Down	9. 6.08
G-DEAM	Schempp-Hirth Nimbus 2B	93	BGA 2531-KAM	30.10.07	J Davies tr Alpha Mike Syndicate	Chipping	28. 9.08
			D-2787				
G-DEAN	Solar Wings Pegasus XL-Q	SW-WQ-0123	G-MVJV	30.11.98	Y G Richardson	Damyn's Hall, Upminster	17. 8.05P
	(Trike c/n SW-TE-0117)				*(Noted 1.08)*		
G-DEAR	Eiriavion PIK-20D	20550	BGA 2535-EAR	21. 9.07	D Irwin and R Penman	(Yeovil and Bridport)	28. 9.08
			RAFGSA 16				
G-DEAW	Grob G102 Astir CS77	1831	BGA 2540-EAW	7.11.07	J Cooke tr EAW Syndicate	Camphill	15.11.07
G-DEBR	Europa Aviation Europa	232		31. 1.01	A J Calvert and C T Smallwood	(Buxton/Ripley)	6.11.06P
	(Built A J Calvert and C T Smallwood - pr.no.PFA 247-12922) (Tri-gear u/c)						
G-DEBT	Alpi Pioneer 300	8		5.10.04	N J T Tonks	Shobdon	12. 6.08P
	(Built N J T Tonks - pr.no.PFA 330-14291)						
G-DEBX	Schleicher ASW 20	20058	BGA 2565-EBX	12.11.07	C F Cownden and J P Davies	Gransden Lodge	15. 2.08
			D-7973				
G-DECC	Schleicher Ka 6CR	60/01	BGA 2570-ECC	28. 2.08	G V Higgins tr Redwing	Burn	18. 4.08
			D-5080				
G-DECF	Schleicher Ka 6CR	856	BGA 2573-ECF	23.10.07	S J Daniel tr ECF Group	Aston Down	15. 4.08
			D-5808				
G-DECK	Cessna T210N Turbo Centurion II	21064017	N958MK	29. 2.00	C E Wright	Fenland	24. 4.08E
			D-ERDK, N4834Y				
G-DECL	Slingsby T.65A Vega 17L	1918	BGA 2578-ECL	8.12.07	J Strzebrakowski	Lyveden	19. 6.08
G-DECO	Dyn'Aéro MCR-01 Club	285		15. 9.04	A W Bishop and G Castelli tr G-DECO Flying Group		
	(Built A W Bishop and G Castelli - pr.no.PFA 301A-14246)					Cambridge	24. 5.07P
G-DECP	Rolladen-Schneider LS3-17	3426	BGA 2581-ECP	8.10.07	D Crowhurst and M Ewer	Crowland	17. 3.08
G-DECX	P&M Quik GT450	8263		26. 4.07	D V Lawrence	(Stourbridge)	25. 4.08P
G-DECZ	Schleicher ASK 21	21009	BGA 2591-ECZ	15.10.07	Booker Gliding Club Ltd "ECZ"	Wycombe Air Park	28. 9.08
G-DEDB	CARMAM JP-15/36AR Aiglon	40	BGA 2593-EDB	17. 1.08	R A Putt tr Carmam EDB Group		
						Husbands Bosworth	29. 3.08
G-DEDJ	Glasflügel H303 Mosquito B	185	BGA 2600-EDJ	24. 1.08	D Martin and R Bollow	Camphill	26. 2.08
G-DEDK	Schleicher K 7 Rhönadler	791	BGA 2601-EDK	23. 1.08	North Wales Gliding Club Ltd	Llantisilio	18. 4.08
	(Partly modified to ASK 13 standard)		D-1633				
G-DEDM	Glaser-Dirks DG-200	2-98	BGA 2603-EDM	17. 9.07	A H G St Pierre	Sutton Bank	29. 3.08
G-DEDU	Schleicher ASK 13	13613	BGA 2610-EDU	10. 1.08	Kent Gliding Club Ltd	Challock	28. 2.08
G-DEDY	Slingsby T.65D Vega	1929	BGA 2614-EDY	29.11.07	S J Steadman tr Steadman and Partners		
						Husbands Bosworth	27. 3.08
G-DEEC	Schleicher ASW 20L	20311	BGA 2618-EEC	19.10.07	D M Cushway	Challock	5. 3.08
			(G-BSTS), BGA 2618-EEC				
G-DEEF	Rolladen-Schneider LS3-17	3441	BGA 2621-KEF	27. 9.07	P Morgan tr Echo Echo Foxtrot Group	Rivar Hill	28. 9.08
G-DEEG	Slingsby T.65C Sport Vega	1922	BGA 2622-EEG	21.11.07	G Harris tr Vega Syndicate	Rufforth	2. 5.08
			EI-129, BGA 2622-EEG				
G-DEEK	Schempp-Hirth HS.5 Nimbus 2C	201	BGA 2625-EEK	6.11.07	M N Erlund	Saltby	28. 9.08
G-DEEM	Schleicher K 8B	8688AB	BGA 2627-EEM	25. 1.08	The South Wales Gliding Club Ltd	Usk	28. 5.08
			D-0254				
G-DEEN	Schempp-Hirth Standard Cirrus 75	621	BGA 2628-EEN	22. 2.08	J Hanlon tr G-DEEN Flying Group		
			(BGA 2609-EDT), RAFGSA 87			RAF Weston-on-the-Green	20. 4.08
G-DEEP	Wassmer WA.26P Squale	36	BGA 2629-EEP	15. 2.08	B J Key	Aston Down	15. 4.08
			F-CDSX				
G-DEER	Robinson R22 Beta II	2827		17. 7.98	S R Baber	(Groesfaen, Pontyclun)	7. 8.08E
G-DEES	Rolladen-Schneider LS3-17	3248	BGA 2632	17. 7.98	J Illidge	Camphill	28. 9.08
G-DEEW	Schleicher Ka 6 CR	6188	BGA 2636-EEW	29.11.07	S M Dodds	Saltby	31. 7.08
			RAFGGA, D-6151				
G-DEEX	Rolladen-Schneider LS3-17	3442	BGA 2637-EEX	22. 2.08	M A M Pirie	Aston Down	31. 3.08
G-DEFE	Centrair ASW 20F	20139	BGA 2644-EFE	1. 2.08	D A Mackenzie and W A Horne	Camphill	5. 4.08
G-DEFF	Schempp-Hirth HS.5 Nimbus 2C	208	BGA 2645-EFF	30.11.07	D L Jobbins	Usk	23. 4.08
G-DEFM	British Aerospace BAe 146 Series 200	E2016	G-DEBM	22.10.99	Flightline Ltd	Aberdeen	13 .9.08E
			C-FHAZ		*(Operated IAC)*		
G-DEFT	Flight Design CTSW	07 07 16		4. 9.07	D Arnold	Damyn's Hall, Upminster	3. 9.08P
	(Assembled P&M Aviation Ltd with c/n 8313)						
G-DEFV	Schleicher ASW 20	20041	BGA 2659-EFV	22. 1.08	A R McKillen	Bellarena	13. 5.08
			OE-5162				
G-DEFW	Slingsby T.65C Sport Vega	1938	BGA 2660-EFW	20. 2.08	Darlton Gliding Club Ltd	Darlton	22. 9.08
G-DEFY	Robinson R22 Beta II	3633	N73750	5. 7.04	P M M P Silveira	Cascais-Tires, Portugal	26. 6.08T
G-DEGE	Rolladen-Schneider LS3-a	3465	BGA 2668-EGE	29.10.07	G Szabo-Toth tr EFE Glider Syndicate	Nympsfield	28. 9.08

G-DEGH	Slingsby T.65C Sport Vega	1943	BGA 2671-EGH 26.11.07	K Dykes, M J Davies and R A Starling	Darlton	29. 4.08
G-DEGJ	Slingsby T.65C Sport Vega	1944	BGA 2672-EGJ 4.12.07	M J Heneghan tr 672 Syndicate "672"	Lee-on-Solent	7. 3.08
G-DEGK	Schempp-Hirth Standard Cirrus	542G	BGA 2673-EGK 31.10.07	I Ashdown	Parham Park	28. 9.08
			RAFGSA 569, RAFGSA R2			
G-DEGS	Schempp-Hirth Nimbus 2CS	192	BGA 2680-EGS 29. 1.08	R C Nichols	Pocklington	22. 3.08
			D-2111			
G-DEGX	Slingsby T.65C Sport Vega	1937	BGA 2685-EGX 14. 2.08	C P Raine tr Haddenham Vega Syndicate	Thame	2. 5.07
			RAFGSA R23, BGA 2685-EGX			
G-DEGZ	Schleicher ASK 21	21030	BGA 2687-EGZ 1.12.07	Black Mountains Gliding Club	Talgarth	10. 3.08
G-DEHG	Slingsby T.65C Sport Vega	1940	BGA 2694-EHG 27 .2.08	A E Smith tr Vega Syndicate	Lasham	19. 1.05
G-DEHK	Rolladen-Schneider LS4	4068	BGA 2697-KHK 27. 9.07	R T and G Starling	Nympsfield	28. 9.08
G-DEHL	Rolladen-Schneider LS4	4024	BGA 2698-KHL 25. 9.07	R Theil	Crowland	28. 9.08
G-DEHO	Schleicher ASK 21	21035	BGA 2702-EHQ 18. 1.08	Lasham Gliding Society Ltd	Lasham	20. 2.08
G-DEHP	Schempp-Hirth HS.5 Nimbus 2C	234	BGA 2701-EHP 27.11.07	D J King	Rattlesden	11. 3.08
G-DEHT	Schempp-Hirth Nimbus 2C	235	BGA 2705-EHT 14. 1.08	S.D.Codd	Edgehill	21. 3.08
G-DEHU	Glasflügel 304	209	BGA 2706-EHU 25.10.07	F Townsend	Bidford	28. 9.08
G-DEHV	Schleicher ASW 20 L	20385	BGA 2707-EHV 19. 9.07	M A and B A Roberts	Wormingford	24. 2.08
G-DEHW	ICA IS-28B2	86	BGA 2708-EHW 27. 2.08	P V P V Besouw tr Y6 Group (Dorst, Netherlands)		14. 4.08
G-DEHZ	Schleicher ASW 20L	20388	BGA 2711-EHZ 29.10.07	D Crimmins	Challock	19. 2.08
G-DEJA	ICA IS-28B2	88	BGA 2712-EJA 1. 2.08	M H Simms	Shipdham	19. 4.07
G-DEJC	Slingsby T.65C Sport Vega	1946	BGA 2714-EJC 10. 1.08	D Redfearn and I Powis	Darlton	14. 4.08
G-DEJE	Slingsby T.65C Sport Vega	1947	BGA 2716-EJE 10.12.07	Crown Service Gliding Club	Lasham	24. 2.08
G-DEJH	Eichelsdörfer SB-5E	5041A	BGA 2719-EJH 7. 2.08	B J Dawson and S E Richardson	Pocklington	24. 7.08
			D-5430, D-0087			
G-DEJR	Schleicher ASW 19B	19334	BGA 2727-EJR 1.11.07	M D Thompson tr 193 Syndicate	Nympsfield	28. 9.08
G-DEKA	Cameron Z-90 Balloon (Hot Air)	10665	16.12.04	Sport Promotion SRL La Morra, Piedmont, Italy		15.12.05E
				(Dekalb titles)		
G-DEKC	Schleicher Ka 6E	4079	BGA 2738-EKC 14. 2.08	S L Benn	RAF Cranwell	23. 3.08
			OO-ZDV, OE-0813			
G-DEKD	Schleicher ASK 13	13539	BGA 2739-EKD 10.12.07	Midland Gliding Club Ltd	Long Mynd	19. 4.08
			OH-494			
G-DEKG	Schleicher ASK 21	21067	BGA 2742-EKG 19.11.07	J W Sage tr Army Gliding Association		
			AGA 8, BGA 2742-EKG		Trenchard Lines, Upavon	28. 9.08
				(Operated Wyvern Gliding Club)		
G-DEKJ	Schempp-Hirth Ventus b	36	BGA 2744-EKJ 22.10.07	I J Metcalfe	Nympsfield	28. 9.08
G-DEKS	Scheibe SF27A Zugvögel V	6096	BGA 2752-EKS 31. 1.08	J C Johnson	Parham Park	5. 3.08
			D-8166			
G-DEKU	Schleicher ASW 20L	20384	BGA 2754-EKU 6.11.07	A J Gillson	Sleap	28. 4.08
G-DEKV	Rolladen-Schneider LS4	4102	BGA 2755-EKV 16.11.07	E J Mason and F G Bradney	Lasham	29. 3.08
G-DELA	Schleicher ASW 19B	19346	BGA 2760-ELA 3.12.07	A Stark tr ELA Syndicate	Aboyne	28. 9.08
G-DELD	Slingsby T.65C Sport Vega	1950	BGA 2763-ELD 5. 9.07	N R Skelding tr ELD Syndicate	Snitterfield	21. 2.08
G-DELF	Aero L-29A Delfin	194555	ES-YLM 28. 8.97	B R Green	Manston	26. 9.01P
			Soviet AF 12 (Red)			
G-DELG	Schempp-Hirth Ventus b/16.6	46	BGA 2766-ELG 14.11.07	A G Machin	Burn	17. 4.08
G-DELN	Grob G102 Astir CS Jeans	2024	BGA 2772-ELN 26. 2.08	J M Hughes	Hinton-in-the-Hedges	14. 5.08
G-DELR	Schempp-Hirth Ventus b	45	BGA 2775-ELR 16.10.07	I D Smith	Nympsfield	28. 9.08
G-DELX	Schleicher K 7 Rhönadler	928	BGA 2781-ELX 9. 1.08	The Nene Valley Gliding Club	Upwood	16. 5.08
			D-4023			
G-DELZ	Schleicher ASW 20L	20310	BGA 2783-ELZ 15.10.07	D A Fogden	Wycombe Air Park	28. 9.08
			RAFGGA 569			
G-DEMB	Rolladen-Schneider LS4	4185	BGA 2785-EMB 7. 2.08	R A Hine	Wycombe Air Park	29. 1.08
G-DEME	Glaser-Dirks DG-200/17	2-176CL18	BGA 2788-EME 16. 1.08	E.D.Casagrande	Usk	19. 3.08
G-DEMF	Rolladen-Schneider LS4	4187	BGA 2789-EMF 18. 1.08	M C Oggelsby and R N Johnston		
					Hinton-in-the-Hedges	15. 3.08
G-DEMG	Rolladen-Schneider LS4	4242	BGA 2790-EMG 7.11.07	R C Bowsfield	Aston Down	5. 3.08
G-DEMH	Reims Cessna F172M Skyhawk II	F17201137	G-BFLO 18.11.91	M Hammond	Airfield Farm, Hardwick	15. 6.08E
	(Lycoming O-360)		PH-DMF, (EI-AYO)			
G-DEMJ	Slingsby T.65C Sport Vega	1951	BGA 2792-EMJ 17. 9.07	D J Miles	Seighford	28. 4.08
G-DEMM	Eurocopter AS.350B2 Ecureuil	3741	6.10.03	Abbeyflight Ltd	Redhill	14. 1.08E
G-DEMN	Slingsby T.65D Vega	1935	BGA 2796-EMN 13.12.07	C D Sword	Milfield	23. 7.08
G-DEMP	Slingsby T.65C Sport Vega	1952	BGA 2797-EMP 15.11.07	The Surrey Hills Gliding Club Ltd	Kenley	7. 2.08
G-DEMT	Rolladen-Schneider LS 4	4243	BGA 2801-EMT 28.11.07	M R Fox	Husbands Bosworth	17. 4.08
G-DEMU	Glaser-Dirks DG-200	2-162-1753	BGA 2802-EMU 11.10.07	A Butterfield and N Swinton		
					RAF Weston-on-the-Green	28. 9.08
G-DEMZ	Slingsby T.65A Vega	1891	BGA 2807-EMZ 7. 9.07	F S Smith tr Vega Syndicate	Portmoak	25. 4.08
			G-BGCA			
G-DENB	Cessna F150G	F150-0136	G-ATZZ 14.12.95	M W Sheppardson	Sibson	4. 4.08E
	(Built Reims Aviation SA)					
G-DENC	Cessna F150G	F150-0107	G-AVAP 14.12.95	M Dovey	Conington	11. 5.08E
	(Built Reims Aviation SA)					
G-DEND	Reims Cessna F150M	F15001201	G-WAFC 6. 6.97	R N Tate	Bagby	13.10.07E
			G-BDFI, (OH-CGD)	(Noted 2.08)		
G-DENE	Piper PA-28-140 Cherokee	28-21710	G-ATOS 5. 2.98	D V Magee	Dunkeswell	5. 7.08E
			N11C			
G-DENI	Piper PA-32-300 Cherokee Six	32-7340006	G-BAIA 7.12.95	A Bendkowski	Rochester	3. 6.07T
			N11C			
G-DENO	Glasflügel H201B Standard Libelle	232	BGA 1662-CMX 14.11.07	D M Bland	Burn	6. 3.08
G-DENS	Binder CP.301S Smaragd	121	D-ENSA 20.11.85	I S Leader tr Garston Smaragd Group		
	(Also carries c/n AB.429 denoting completion as Amateur Build)				Garston Farm, Marshfield	2.12.08P
G-DENT	Cameron N-145 Balloon (Hot Air)	4135	8. 4.97	P D Claridge	Treyford, Midhurst	23.11.07T
G-DENV	Schleicher ASW 20L	20554	BGA 2827-ENV 2.11.07	R D Hone	Wycombe Air Park	9. 5.08
G-DENZ	Piper PA-44-180 Seminole	44-7995327	G-INDE 3. 7.97	W J Greenfield	Humberside	23. 6.08E
			G-BHNM, N8077X			
G-DEOA	Rolladen-Schneider LS4	4259	BGA 2856-EQA 10. 1.08	A A Jenkins and R.L.Smith	Wycombe Air Park	15. 4.08

Reg	Type	C/n	Prev ID	Owner	Location	Date
G-DEOJ	Centrair ASW 20FL	20512	BGA 2864-EQJ 15. 2.08	J Sanders and R Grey	Nympsfield	24. 5.08
G-DEON	Schempp-Hirth Nimbus 3-25.5	31	BGA 2868-EQN 8.12.07	R A Lovegrove tr N3 Group	Lyveden	4. 3.08
G-DEOU	Pilatus B4-PC11	201	BGA 2874-EQU 26. 2.08 PH-535	H R E Stott	Chipping	3. 5.08
G-DEOV	Schempp-Hirth Janus C	169	BGA 2875-EQV 14.12.07 ZD974, BGA 2875-EQV	Burn Gliding Club Ltd	Burn	14. 3.08
G-DEOW	Schempp-Hirth Janus C	171	BGA 2876-EQW 8.2.08 ZD975, BGA 2876-EQW	C C Pike tr 383 Syndicate	Rivar Hill	11. 4.08
G-DEPE	Schleicher ASW19B	19335	BGA 2836-EPE 22.11.07 RAFGSA R18, BGA 2836-EPE, RAFGSA R18	P A Goulding	Crowland	15.12.07
G-DEPF	Centrair ASW 20FL	20515	BGA 2837-EPF 23.11.07	D J E Howse tr 323 Syndicate	Gransden Lodge	6. 4.08
G-DEPP	Schleicher ASK 13	1609	BGA 2845-EPP 22.12.07	Mendip Gliding Club Ltd	Halesland	12. 4.08
G-DEPS	Schleicher ASW 20 L	20245	BGA 2848-EPS 1.10.07 RAFGSA 87	C Beveridge	Sandhill Farm, Shrivenham	22. 3.08
G-DEPT	Schleicher K 8B	146/59	BGA 2849-EPT 21.12.07 RAFGGA 504, D-5004	P H Emerton	Lasham	5. 3.08
G-DEPU	Glaser-Dirks DG-101G Elan	E116G85	BGA 2850-EPU 2. 7.07 (BGA 2833)	J F Rogers	Wycombe Air Park	3. 8.08
G-DEPX	Schempp-Hirth Ventus b/16.6	107	BGA 2853-EPX 22.10.07	D L Slobom tr D L Slobom and Partners	Dunstable	28. 9.08
G-DERA	Centrair ASW 20FL	20526	BGA 2880-ERA 14.12.07	R J Lockett	Wormingford	19. 4.08
G-DERB	Robinson R22 Beta	1005	G-BPYH 28. 6.95	S Thompson	Manston	22. 9.07T
G-DERH	Schleicher ASK 21	21147	BGA 2887-ERH 4. 1.08 ZD647, BGA 2887-ERH	Burn Gliding Club Ltd	Burn	5. 5.08
G-DERI	Piper PA-46-500TP Malibu Meridian	4697078	G-PCAR 9.11.03 N51151	Intesa Leasing SpA	(Milan, Lombardy, Italy)	6. 8.08E
G-DERK	Piper PA-46-500TP Malibu Meridian	4697152	N165MA 3. 4.03	D Priestley	Dunkeswell	14. 5.08T
G-DERP	Schleicher ASW 19B	19348	BGA 2893-ERP 23. 1.08 ZD657, BGA 2893-ERP, BGA 2773-ELO	M K Lavender	Bicester	22. 2.08
G-DERS	Schleicher ASW 19B	19383	BGA 2896-ERS 9. 1.08 ZD660, BGA 2896-ERS	J C and C C Marshall	Eyres Field	30. 4.08
G-DERV	Cameron Truck 56 SS Balloon (Hot Air)	1719	21. 3.88	J M Percival Bourton-on-the-Wolds, Loughborough *"Shell UK Truck" (Inflated 4.06)*		22. 2.00A
G-DESB	Schleicher ASK 21	21176	BGA 2905-ESB 23.10.07	A L Garfield tr The Old Boys	Dunstable	8. 3.08
G-DESH	Centrair 101A Pégase	101069	BGA 2911-ESH 9.11.07	J E Moore	Wycombe Air Park	28. 1.08
G-DESJ	Schleicher K 8B	8730	BGA 2912-ESJ 4. 9.07 D-5010	Bowland Forest Gliding Club Ltd	Chipping	16.12.07
G-DESO	DG Flugzeugbau DG-300 Elan	3E10	BGA 2918-ESO 1. 2.08	G R P Brown	Sandhill Farm, Shrivenham	31. 3.08
G-DESP	PZL Bielsko SZD-48-3 Jantar Standard 3	B-1294	BGA 2917-ESP 20.11.07	B Taylor tr Jantar Group RAF Weston-on-the-Green		5. 6.08
G-DEST	Mooney M 20J Mooney 201	24-3429	6.11.98	Allegro Aviation Ltd	(Guernsey)	18. 1.08E
G-DESU	Schleicher ASK 21	21180	BGA 2922-ESU 6.11.07 RAFGSA R40	Aquila Gliding Club Ltd	Hinton-in-the-Hedges	25. 5.08
G-DESW	Centrair 101A Pégase	101068	BGA 2924-ESW 23. 1.08	D A Brown	(Hove)	1. 4.08
G-DETG	Rolladen-Schneider LS4	4349	BGA 2934-ETG 12. 9.07	N P Woods	Gransden Lodge	28. 9.08
G-DETJ	Centrair 101A Pégase	101A0110	BGA 2936-ETJ 14. 1.08	S C Phillips	(Potton, Sandy)	23. 3.08
G-DETM	Centrair 101A Pégase	101A0111	BGA 2939-ETM 8.11.07	B J Darton and J Bone	Wormingford	15. 3.08
G-DETS	Schleicher ASK 13	13635AB	BGA 2944-ETS 12.12.07	Upward Bound Trust	Thame	14. 4.08
G-DETY	Rolladen-Schneider LS4	4368	BGA 2950-ETY 23. 8.07	D T Staff *(Carries "BGA 2350" on fin)*	Wycombe Air Park	7.11.07
G-DETZ	Schleicher ASW 2O CL	20730	BGA 2951-ETZ 28. 1.08	N L Clowes tr The 20 Syndicate	Tibenham	23. 2.08
G-DEUD	Schleicher ASW 20C	20734	BGA 2955-EUD 23.10.07	R Tietema	Husbands Bosworth	15. 2.08
G-DEUF	PZL-Bielsko SZD-50-3 Puchacz	B-1090	BGA 2957-EUF 23. 1.08	A J Pettitt tr uchacz Group	Rivar Hill	26. 8.08
G-DEUH	Rolladen-Schneider LS4	4382	BGA 2959-EUH 4.10.07	A R Turner and F J Parkinson	Nympsfield	13. 4.08
G-DEUJ	Schempp-Hirth Ventus b-16.6	162	BGA 2960-EUJ 13.12.07	M J and A J Millar	Ringmer	18. 4.08
G-DEUK	Centrair ASW 20FL	20530	BGA 2961-KUK 26. 9.07	D S Kershaw	Lasham	26. 2.08
G-DEUS	Schempp-Hirth Ventus b-16.6	192	BGA 2968-EUS 4.10.07	R J Whitaker	Lasham	26. 8.08
G-DEUX	Aérospatiale AS.355F Ecureuil 2	5027	F-GIBI 30. 9.05 D-HAST, F-ODNS	Elmridge Ltd	Kintore	2.11.07E
G-DEUY	Schleicher ASW 20BL	20645	BGA 2974-EUY 16.10.07	D G Roberts tr ASW 20BL - G-DUEY Group	Aston Down	28.12.07
G-DEVF	Schempp-Hirth Nimbus 3T	15/76	BGA 2981-EVF 19.10.07 D-KHIJ	A G Leach	Bembridge	20. 2.08
G-DEVL	Eurocopter EC.120B Colibri	1273	7. 6.02	Eyot (Aviation) Ltd	Compton Abbas	4. 7.08E
G-DEVM	Centrair 101A Pégase	101A0157	BGA 2987-EVM 29.11.07	J G Kosak tr Seahawk Gliding Club RNAS Culdrose		28. 4.08
G-DEVS	Piper PA-28-180 Cherokee B	28-830	G-BGVJ 5. 3.85 D-ENPI, N7066W	B J Hoptroff and J M Whiteley tr 180 Group	Blackbushe	19. 4.08E
G-DEVV	Schleicher ASK 23	23004	BGA 2995-EVV 10.12.07	Midland Gliding Club Ltd	Long Mynd	26. 8.08
G-DEVW	Schleicher ASK 23	23006	BGA 2996-EVW 8. 2.08	London Gliding Club Proprietary Ltd	Dunstable	2. 5.08
G-DEVX	Schleicher ASK 23	23007	BGA 2997-EVX 8. 2.08	London Gliding Club Proprietary Ltd	Dunstable	12. 4.08
G-DEVY	Schleicher ASK 23	23008	BGA 2998-EVY 8. 2.08	London Gliding Club Proprietary Ltd	Dunstable	12. 7.08
G-DEWP	Grob G103A Twin II Acro	33892-K-130	BGA 3013-EWP 11.12.07 ZE523, BGA 3013-EWP	Cambridge Gliding Club Ltd	Gransden Lodge	22. 2.08
G-DEWR	Grob G103A Twin II Acro	33894-K-132	BGA 3015-EWR 8.12.07 RAFGSA R70, ZE525, BGA 3015-EWR	The Bristol Gliding Club (Proprietary) Ltd Nympsfield		26. 8.08
G-DEXA	Grob G103A Twin II Acro	33908-K-143	BGA 3024-EXA 23. 1.08 ZE534, BGA 3024-EXA	Trent Valley Aerotowing Club Ltd	Kirton-in-Lindsey	27. 6.08
G-DEXP	ARV Aviation ARV-1 Super 2 *(Built ARV Aviation - pr.no.PFA 152-11154)*	003	24. 4.85	M J Turner	(Macclesfield)	28. 4.08P
G-DFAF	Schleicher ASW 20L	20214	BGA 3101-FAF 22.11.07 RAFGSA 271, RAFGSA R27	A S Miller	RAF Keevil	21. 4.08
G-DFAR	Glasflügel H205 Club Libelle	58	BGA 3110-FAR 28. 2.08 HB-1262	G Gair	Ringmer	24. 4.08
G-DFAT	Schleicher ASK 13	13528	BGA 3112-FAT 9. 1.08 PH-456	Dorset Gliding Club Ltd	Eyres Field	22. 4.08

G-DFAW	Schempp-Hirth Ventus b/16.6	26	BGA 3115-FAW D-6768	25. 2.08	P R Stafford-Allen	RAF Marham	29. 3.08
G-DFKI	Westland SA.341C Gazelle HT.2	1216	G-BZOT XW907	12. 2.02	Foremans Aviation Ltd	Full Sutton	2. 4.08P
G-DFLY	Piper PA-38-112 Tomahawk	38-79A0450	N9655N	15. 2.79	Ravenair Aircraft Ltd	Liverpool	30. 7.08E
G-DFOG	Rolladen-Schneider LS 7	7050	BGA 3437-FQG D-1712	29.11.07	D W Smith	Sutton Bank	27. 4.08
G-DFOX	Aérospatiale AS.355F1 Ecureuil 2	5203	G-NAAS G-BPRG, G-NWPA, G-NAAS, G-BPRG, N370E	8. 1.07	Venturi Capital Ltd	Redhill	17. 7.08E
G-DFRA	Rolladen-Schneider LS6-b	6151	BGA 3455-FRA D-8081	5.10.07	M Randle tr 79 Syndicate	Aston Down	28. 9.08
G-DFTJ	PZL Bielsko SZD-48 Jantar Standard 2	W-889	BGA 3511-FTJ HB-1472	23.11.07	D Bieniasz and P Nock	Kirton-in-Lindsey	6. 3.08
G-DFUN	Van's RV-6 (Built P R Turner and S Hollingsworth)	PFA 181A-13191		21. 8.06	P R Turner tr G-DFUN Flying Group	(Hook)	
G-DGAW	Schleicher Ka 6CR	61-08	BGA 3688-GAW D-6320	21. 1.08	D Searle & H C Yorke	Snitterfield	13. 3.08
G-DGCL	DG Flugzeugbau DG-800B	8-185B109		27. 3.00	C J Lowrie "102"	Parham Park	19. 4.08E
G-DGET	Bombardier CL-600-2B19 (CL-604 Challenger)	5608	C-FDWU C-GLXQ	21. 2.06	TAG Aviation (UK) Ltd	Farnborough	21. 2.08E
G-DGHD	Robinson R44 Raven II	10436		20. 7.04	Advanced Diesel Engineering Ltd	Walton Wood	24. 8.08E
G-DGHI	Dyn'Aéro MCR-01 Club (Built D G Hall - pr.no.PFA 301A-14128)	275		11.12.03	D G Hall	Pluckley, Ashford	25. 9.08P
G-DGIK	DG Flugzeugbau DG-1000S	10-72T11	BGA 5211-KMU D-3800	5.12.05	R P Davis "460"	(West Mersea, Colchester)	1. 2.08
G-DGIO	Glaser-Dirks DG-100G Elan	E19G7	BGA 2605-EDP	1.10.07	L A Humphries tr EDP Group	North Hill	28. 9.08
G-DGIV	DG Flugzeugbau DG-800B	8-145B69		27.11.98	R Parkin	Kirton-in-Lindsey	12.12.07E
G-DGOD	Robinson R22 Beta II	3889		28.10.05	Astra Helicopters Ltd	Kemble	10.11.07E
G-DGWW	Rand Robinson KR-2 (Built W Wilson) (Hapi Magnum 75)	PFA 129-11044		7. 3.91	W Wilson	Liverpool	30. 9.08P
G-DHAA	Glasflügel H201B Standard Libelle	356	BGA 3777-HAA HB-1090	18.12.07	D J Jones and R N Turner	Gransden Lodge	11.12.07
G-DHAD	Glasflügel H201B Standard Libelle	3	BGA 3780-HAD D-8914	13. 2.08	A Presland	Lasham	24. 5.08
G-DHAH	Aeronca 7BM Champion (Continental C85) (Modified ex 7AC standard)	7AC-4185	G-JTYE N85445, NC85445	12. 7.05	G D Horn (Mappowder, Sturminster Newton) (Damaged Longwood Farm, Southampton 2.8.98)		
G-DHAL	Schleicher ASK 13	13690AB	BGA 3787-HAL	19.10.07	R Birch tr Cotswold Gliding Club	Aston Down	28. 9.08
G-DHAP	Schleicher Ka 6E	4335	BGA 3790-HAP HB-985	22. 2.08	M Fursedon and T Turner	Edgehill	6.10.07
G-DHCC	de Havilland DHC-1 Chipmunk 22	C1/0393	WG321	28. 5.97	Eureka Aviation BVBA (As "WG321:G" in AAC c/s)	Antwerp, Belgium	7. 5.10S
G-DHCE	Schleicher ASW 19B	19305	BGA 3831-HCE D-6527	3.10.07	R T Halliburton	Pocklington	28. 9.08
G-DHCF	PZL-Bielsko SZD-50-3 Puchacz	B-2047	BGA 3832-HCF	17. 1.08	Shalbourne Soaring Society Ltd	Rivar Hill	27. 4.08
G-DHCH	Centrair ASW 20F	20178	BGA 3834-HCH F-CEUL	1.11.07	A C Turk	Bidford	15. 3.08
G-DHCL	Schempp-Hirth Discus B	136	BGA 3837-HCL D-4682	4.12.07	C E Broom and L Chilcot	Usk	7. 3.08
G-DHCO	Glasflügel H201B Standard Libelle	197	BGA 3841-HCQ HB-999	16.11.07	M J Birch	Dunstable	16. 3.08
G-DHCR	PZL-Bielsko SZD-51-1 Junior	B-2003	BGA 3842-HCR	18. 1.08	East Sussex Gliding Club Ltd	Ringmer	16. 3.08
G-DHCU	DG Flugzeugbau DG-300 Club Elan	3E407C66	BGA 3845-HCU	19.12.07	J C A Garland and M S Smith	Kingston Deverill	18. 3.08
G-DHCV	Schleicher ASW 19B	19084	BGA 3846-HCV D-4486	4. 1.08	Novak Consultancy Ltd	Tibenham	4. 5.08
G-DHCW	PZL-Bielsko SZD-51-1 Junior	B-2002	BGA 3847-HCW (BGA 3844-HCT)	21.12.07	Deeside Gliding Club (Aberdeenshire) Ltd	Aboyne	6. 1.08
G-DHCX	Schleicher ASK 21	21541	BGA 3848-HCX	6.11.07	Devon & Somerset Gliding Club Ltd	North Hill	28. 9.08
G-DHCZ	de Havilland DHC-2 Beaver AL.Mk.1	1442	G-BUCJ XP772	2. 3.06	Propshop Ltd (As "XP772" in AAC c/s) (On rebuild 1.07)	Duxford	
G-DHDH	Glaser-Dirks DG-200	2-197	BGA 3858-HDH	26. 2.08	A R Winton	(Witham)	27. 3.08
G-DHDV	de Havilland DH.104 Dove 8	04205	VP981	26.10.98	Air Atlantique Ltd (As "VP981" in "Royal Air Force Transport Command" titles)	Coventry	19. 9.10S
G-DHEM	Schempp-Hirth Discus CS	073CS	BGA 3886-HEM	9. 1.08	G G Lee tr 473 Syndicate	Lasham	28. 9.08
G-DHER	Schleicher ASW 19B	19240	BGA 3890-HER F-CERR	11. 2.08	B Meech	Upwood	17. 5.08
G-DHES	Centrair 101A Pégase	101039	BGA 3891-HES F-CFQF	29. 1.08	C J Cole and S B Lewis	Usk	8. 3.08
G-DHET	Rolladen-Schneider LS6-c18	6263	BGA 3892-HET	22.11.07	M P Brooks	Lasham	28. 2.08
G-DHEZ	Rolladen-Schneider LS6-c	6264	BGA 3898-HEZ	17.10.07	J Cruttenden and J Taylor	Lasham	22. 4.08
G-DHGL	Schempp-Hirth Discus b	431	BGA 3933-HGL	29.10.07	R G Corbin and S E Buckley	Aston Down	16. 3.08
G-DHJH	Airbus A321-211	1238	D-AVZL	7. 6.00	Thomas Cook Airlines Ltd t/a MyTravel Airways	Manchester	6. 6.068E
G-DHKL	Schempp-Hirth Discus bT	120/376	BGA 4004-HKL	17.10.07	M A Thorne	Kingston Deverill	24. 2.08
G-DHLB	Cameron N-90 Balloon (Hot Air)	3261		20. 4.94	B A Bower	Pierantonio, Umbria, Italy	27. 4.08A
G-DHLI	Colt World 90 SS Balloon (Hot Air)	2603		2. 6.94	A D Kent tr Balloon Preservation Flying Group "DHL World" (New owner 6.04)	Petworth	17.12.98A
G-DHMP	Schempp-Hirth Discus b	497	BGA 4050-HMP	1. 2.08	P Charatan tr HMP Discus Syndicate	Challock	31. 5.08
G-DHNX	Rolladen-Schneider LS 4b	4937	BGA 4082-HNX	28.11.07	C S Crocker and K J Screen	Long Mynd	3. 4.08
G-DHOK	Schleicher ASW 20CL	20854	BGA 4118-HQK D-3366	28.11.07	S D Minson	North Hill	1. 4.08
G-DHOX	Schleicher ASW 15B	15326	BGA 4129-HQX D-2315	21.11.07	P Ridgill	Upwood	14. 4.08
G-DHPM	de Havilland DHC-1 Chipmunk 22 (Built OGMA)	55	CS-AZS Portuguese AF FAP1365	28. 3.02	P Meyrick (As "1365" in Portuguese AF c/s)	Sywell	12. 6.08

G-DHPR	Schempp-Hirth Discus b	532	BGA 4100-HPR	23. 8.07	G J Bowser	Nympsfield	18.10.07
G-DHRR	Schleicher ASK 21	21033	BGA 4146-HRR	5.12.07	The Furness Gliding Club Proprietary Ltd t/a Lakes Gliding Club		
			D-7083			Walney Island	30. 1-08
G-DHSJ	Schempp-Hirth Discus b	546	BGA 4163-HSJ	9. 1.08	A.A.Jenkins	Bicester	3. 3.08
G-DHSL	Schempp-Hirth Ventus 2c	1/2	BGA 4165-HSL	29.10.07	H G Woodsend	Aston Down	15. 3.08
	(Incomplete airframe assembled Southern Sailplanes)		(BGA 4154)				
G-DHSR	Sportline Aviacija LAK-12 Lietuva	6178	BGA 4170-HSR	1. 2.08	G Forster	Milfield	7. 6.08
G-DHSS	de Havilland DH.112 Venom FB.50 (FB.1)	836	Swiss AF J-1626	26. 3.99	Aviation and Computer Consultancy Ltd		
	(Built F + W)					(Bournemouth)	22. 4.03P
					(In open store as "WR360" in white RAF c/s 1.08: new owner 2.08)		
G-DHTG	Grob G102 Astir CS	1510	BGA 4185-HTG	23. 1.08	Trent Valley Gliding Club Ltd	Kirton-in-Lindsey	19. 9.08
			RAFGSA R59, RAFGSA R69, RAFGSA 519				
G-DHTM	de Havilland DH.82A Tiger Moth	PFA 157-11095		6. 1.86	E G Waite-Roberts	(Old Basing, Basingstoke)	
	(Built L Causer and E G Waite-Roberts)				*(Believed parts consumed within rebuild of G-APPN qv)*		
G-DHTT	de Havilland DH.112 Venom FB.50 (FB.1)	821	(G-BMOC)	17.10.96	Aviation and Computer Consultancy Ltd		
	(Built F + W)		Swiss AF J-1611			(Bournemouth)	17. 7.99P
					(Noted in Aviation Museum 12.07 as "WR421": new owner 2.08)		
G-DHUM	Rolladen-Schneider LS6-c	6267	BGA 4214-HUM	1. 2.08	A G W Hall	Lasham	30. 3.08
			OO-ZXS, D-4350				
G-DHUU	de Havilland DH.112 Venom FB.50 (FB.1)	749	(G-BMOD)	26. 2.96	Aviation and Computer Consultancy Ltd		
	(Built F + W)		Swiss AF J-1539			(Bournemouth)	24. 5.02P
					(In open store as "WR410" in RAF 6 Sqdn c/s 1.08: new owner 2.08)		
G-DHVM	de Havilland DH.112 Venom FB.50 (FB.1)	752	G-GONE	26.11.03	Aviation Heritage Ltd	Coventry	1. 2.08P
	(Built F + W)		Swiss AF J-1542		*(As "WR470" in RAF 208 Sqdn c/s)*		
G-DHVV	de Havilland DH.115 Vampire T 55	55092	Swiss AF U-1214	5. 9.91	Aviation and Computer Consultancy Ltd		
	(Built F + W) (Reported as built with c/n 974)					(Bournemouth)	5. 6.03P
					(in open store as "XE897" in RAF 54 Sqdn c/s 1.08: new owner 2.08)		
G-DHWW	de Havilland DH.115 Vampire T 55	979	Swiss AF U-1219	5. 9.91	Aviation and Computer Consultancy Ltd		
	(Built F + W) (Reported as built with c/n 974)					(Bournemouth)	23. 4.03P
					(In open store as "XG775" in RN FOFT Yeovilton c/s 1.08: new owner 2.08)		
G-DHXX	de Havilland DH.100 Vampire FB.6	682	Swiss AF J-1173	5. 9.91	Aviation and Computer Consultancy Ltd		
	(Built F + W)					(Bournemouth)	14. 8.02P
					(In open store as "VT871" in RAF 54 Sqdn c/s 1.08: new owner 2.08)		
G-DHYL	Schempp-Hirth Ventus 2a	44	BGA 4310-HYL	6.11.07	Leinster Gliders Ltd	(London W2)	31.10.07
G-DHZF	de Havilland DH.82A Tiger Moth	82309	G-BSTJ	7. 7.99	C A Parker and M R Johnson	Sywell	17. 5.09S
			OO-MEH, OO-GEB, OO-MOR, RNethAF A-13, PH-UFB, A-13, N9192 *(As "N-9192:RCO-N" in RAF c/s)*				
G-DIAL	Cameron N-90 Balloon (Hot Air)	1851		7.11.88	A J Street *"London" (Inflated 8.06)*	Whimple, Exeter	11. 5.00A
G-DIAM	Diamond DA.40D Star	D4.204		23. 5.06	A Overton	Sywell	28. 6.08E
G-DIAT	Piper PA-28-140 Cherokee Cruiser	28-7425322	G-BCGK	19. 7.89	Bristol Flying Centre Ltd	Bristol	22. 8.08T
			N9594N				
G-DICK	Thunder Ax6-56Z Balloon (Hot Air)	159		6. 7.78	R D Sargeant *"Dandag"*	Wollerau, Switzerland	7. 8.07A
G-DIDG	Van's RV-7	LAA 323-14764		15. 2.08	E T and D K Steele	(Sittingbourne)	
	(Built E T Steele)						
G-DIDY	Thruster T600T 450	1052-T600T-116		30. 1.06	D R Sims	Halwell	9. 2.08P
G-DIGG	Robinson R44 Raven II	11904		21. 9.07	Thames Materials Ltd	(London W7)	
G-DIGI	Piper PA-32-300 Six	32-7940224	D-EIES	13.10.98	D Stokes tr Security UN Ltd Group	Stapleford	18.11.07T
			N2947M				
G-DIKY	Murphy Rebel	PFA 232-13182		13. 2.98	R J P Herivel	Alderney	14. 6.08P
	(Built R J P Herivel)						
G-DIMB	Boeing 767-31K	28865		28. 4.97	Monarch Airlines Ltd	Luton	27. 4.08E
G-DIME	Rockwell Commander 114	14123	N49829	9. 3.88	H B Richardson	Badminton	11. 4.08E
G-DINA	Gulfstream AA-5B Tiger	AA5B-1218	N4555Y	27. 2.81	Portway Aviation Ltd	Shobdon	3. 8.08E
G-DING	Colt 77A Balloon (Hot Air)	1862		28. 6.91	G J Bell *"Dingbat"*	Petersfield	16. 4.08A
G-DINK	Lindstrand Bulb SS Balloon (Hot Air)	785		28. 6.01	Dinkelacker-Schwaben Brau AG	Stuttgart, Germany	14.11.07A
G-DINO	Cyclone Airsports Pegasus Quantum 15	7225	G-MGMT	15.12.98	P W Day	(Blidworth, Mansfield)	24. 5.08P
	(Rotax 582)						
G-DINT	Bristol 156 Beaufighter IF	STAN B1 184604	3858M	17. 6.91	T E Moore	Rotary Farm, Hatch	
			X7688		*(On rebuild from various ex Australian components 10.99)*		
G-DIPI	Cameron Tub 80 SS Balloon (Hot Air)	1745		6. 5.88	C G Dobson *(New owner 12.06)*	Streatley, Reading	18. 3.06E
G-DIPM	Piper PA-46-350P Malibu Mirage	4636325	N5350V	20. 2.02	Intesa Leasing SpA	Milan, Lombardy, Italy	1. 3 08E
G-DIRK	Glaser-Dirks DG-400	4-124	D-KEKT	18. 9.86	D G Clews tr G-DIRK Syndicate *"RK"*	Parham Park	27. 4.08E
G-DISA	Scottish Aviation Bulldog Series 100/125		RJordan AF 420	25. 8.04	British Disabled Flying Association	Lasham	21. 7.08E
		BH120/435	RJordan AF 1142, G-31-44				
G-DISK	Piper PA-24-250 Comanche	24-1197	G-APZG	9. 8.89	A Johnston	Guernsey	26. 6.08E
			EI-AKW, N10F				
G-DISO	SAN Jodel D 150 Mascaret	24	9Q-CPK	16.12.86	P F Craven	Wombleton	26. 8.08P
			OO-APK, F-BLDT				
G-DIWY	Piper PA-32-300 Cherokee Six B	32-40731	OY-DLW	26.11.91	IFS Chemicals Ltd	East Winch	13. 9.08E
			D-EHMW, N8931N				
G-DIXY	Piper PA-28-181 Archer III	2843195	N41284	10.12.98	M G Bird	Fowlmere	16.12.07E
			G-DIXY, N41284				
G-DIZI	Reality Escapade 912(1)	JAESC 0012		1. 3.04	N Baumber	(Grantham)	
	(Built N Baumber - pr.no.BMAA/HB/355)						
G-DIZO	Wassmer Jodel D 120A Paris-Nice	326	G-EMKM	30. 5.91	D and E.Aldersea	Breighton	4. 5.08P
			F-BOBG				
G-DIZY	Piper PA-28R-201T Turbo Arrow III		N47570	13.10.88	Calverton Flying Group Ltd	Rochester	2. 9.07T
		28R-7703401					
G-DIZZ	Hughes 369HE	89-0105E	N9029F	19. 2.97	R H Kirke	Redhill	8. 6.08E
	(Hughes 500)						
G-DJAA	Schempp-Hirth Janus B	163	BGA 4348-JAA	16. 1.08	C J Hoare tr Janus B Group (Ashington, Pulborough)		30. 1.08
			D-3147				
G-DJAE	Cessna 500 Citation I	500-0339	G-JEAN	3.11.98	Kenmare Bay Homes Ltd	Dublin	25. 6.08E
			N300EC, N707US, G-JEAN, (N5339J)				

Reg	Type	c/n	Prev id	Date	Owner	Location	Date
G-DJAB	DG Flugzeugbau DG-300 Elan	3E320	BGA 4349-JAB OY-XTC	16.10.07	I G Johnston	Sutton Bank	28. 9.08
G-DJAD	Schleicher ASK 21	21659	BGA 4351-JAD	25 .2.08	The Borders (Milfield) Gliding Club Ltd	Milfield	18. 8.08
G-DJAN	Schempp-Hirth Discus b	575	BGA 4360-JAN	1.10.07	N F Perren	Dunstable	28. 9.08
G-DJAY	Avtech Jabiru UL-450	xxxx		8. 8.00	D J Pearce	(Reading)	15. 5.08P
	(Built D J Pearce - pr.no.PFA 274A-13633)						
G-DJBC	Comco Ikarus C42 FB100	0802-6937		5. 2.08	D Meegan	(Newry)	
G-DJCR	Varga 2150A Kachina	VAC 155-80	EI-CFK G-BLWG, OO-HTD, N8360J	11. 4.96	D J C Robertson	(Clocksbridge, Forfar)	30. 4.99
G-DJET	Diamond DA.42 Twin Star	42.122	OE-VPW	30. 3.06	Papa Bravo Ltd	Bagby	21. 5.08E
G-DJGG	Schleicher ASW 15B	15332	BGA 4498-JGG D-2325	5.12.07	A A Cole	(Ringmer)	19. 3.08
G-DJHP	Valentin Mistral C	MC048/82	BGA 4529-JHP D-4948	21. 1.08	P B Higgs	(Rossett, Wrexham)	22. 2.08
G-DJJA	Piper PA-28-181 Archer II	28-8490014	N4326D	14. 9.87	Interactive Aviation Ltd	(Southall)	19.12.07E
G-DJLL	Schleicher ASK 13	13144	BGA 4598-JLL HB-952	29. 1.08	T World tr Portsmouth Naval Gliding Centre	Lee-on-Solent	16. 2.08
G-DJMD	Schempp-Hirth Discus B	241	BGA 4615-JMD RAFGSA R23	7.12.07	R C Oliver tr Papa 23 Group	Kenley	24. 1.08
G-DJMM	Cessna 172S Skyhawk	172S8482	N227ME	10. 3.05	M Manston	Panshanger	13. 3.08E
G-DJNH	Denney Kitfox Model 3	772		20. 9.90	B D Hanscomb	(Bosbury, Ledbury)	22. 8.08P
	(Built D J N Hall - pr.no.PFA 172-11896)						
G-DJST	Air Création Clipper/iXess 912	xxxxx		12.10.04	D J Stimpson	Sywell	15. 5.08P
	(Buiilt D J Stimpson - pr.no.BMAA/HB/416)						
G-DKBA	DKBA AT 0301-0 Balloon (Hot Air)	013.07.93		15. 5.07	I Chadwick	Patridge Green, Horsham	
G-DKBW	Valentin Mistral C	MC021/79	BGA 4725-JRS D-4921	17.12.07	A Towse	Rattlesden	9. 4.08
G-DKEN	Rolladen-Schneider LS4-a	4172	BGA 5034-KEN OO-ZSM, (OO-ZDG)	15.11.07	H Hay	Wycombe Air Park	10. 2.08
G-DKFU	Schempp-Hirth Ventus -2cxT	114/311	BGA 5064-KFU, D-KOAX	19.11.07	W F Payton	Sutton Bank	23. 3.08
G-DKNY	Robinson R44 Raven II	11651		1. 3.07	D Watson and J Kennedy	Liverpool	22. 3.08E
G-DKDP	Grob G109	6100	(G-BMBD) D-KAMS	9. 7.85	D W and J E Page tr Grob 4	Tibenham	7. 6.08E
G-DKEY	Piper PA-28-161 Warrior II	28-7716084	N1120Q	4. 1.07	B W Gomez	Halfpenny Green	13. 6.08E
G-DKMK	Robinson R44 Raven II	11398		18.12.06	Clear Sky Views Ltd	(Bishopscourt, Straffan, County Kildare)	18. 1.08P
G-DLCB	Europa Aviation Europa	046		16.11.95	K Richards	Talgarth	23. 7.07P
	(Built D J Lockett - pr./no.PFA 247-12652) (Monowheel u/c)						
G-DLCH	Boeing 737-8Q8	30040		22. 4.05	Globespan Airways Ltd t/a Flyglobespan.com	Edinburgh	22. 4.08E
G-DLDL	Robinson R22 Beta	1971		2. 1.92	Airtask Group PLC	Stapleford	2. 5.08E
G-DLEE	SOCATA TB-9 Tampico Club	884	G-BPGX	18. 2.04	D A Lee	Dunkeswell	12. 7.08E
G-DLOM	SOCATA TB-20 Trinidad	1102	N2823Y	13.12.90	J N A Adderley	(Verbier, Switzerland)	2. 9.07
					(Address change 11.07)		
G-DLTR	Piper PA-28-180 Cherokee E	28-5803	G-AYAV N11C	15. 3.96	Light Aircraft Leasing Ltd	(Sheffield City)	4. 8.08E
G-DMAC	Avtech Jabiru UL	0184		15.10.98	C J Pratt	Goodwood	29. 8.08P
	(Built B Macfadden - pr.no.PFA 274-13321 although type prefix should be "274A")						
G-DMAH	SOCATA TB-20 Trinidad GT	2039	F-OILY	2. 4.01	R C and C G Bell	Oxford	9. 4.08T
G-DMCD	Robinson R22 Beta	1201	G-OOLI G-DMCD	14.11.89	Heliair Ltd	Denham	26. 5.08E
G-DMCI	Comco Ikarus C42 FB100	0707-6906		16. 8.07	D McCartan	(Sixmilecross, Omagh)	18.10.08P
G-DMCS	Piper PA-28R-200 Cherokee Arrow II	28R-7635284	G-CPAC PH-SMW, OO-HAU, N75220	29. 5.84	W G Ashton and J Bingley t/a Arrow Associates	Goodwood	19. 4.08E
G-DMCT	Flight Design CT2K	01-04-02-12		10. 7.01	Buha Zajac	(Gloucester)	10.11.08P
	(Assembled Pegasus Aviation Ltd - no c/n issued)						
G-DMND	Diamond DA.42 Twin Star	42.068		4.11.05	MC Air Ltd	Wellesbourne Mountford	8.12.07E
G-DMRA	Robinson R44 Raven II	11802		8. 6.07	D M Richards	(Rock, Kidderminster)	12. 7.08E
G-DMRS	Robinson R44 Raven II	10513		29.10.04	Nottinghamshire Helicopters (2004)Ltd	Tollerton	29.11.07E
G-DMSS	Westland SA.341D Gazelle HT.3	1089	XW858	13. 7.01	Woods of York Ltd	Murton, York	2. 8.06P
					(As "XW858:C" in RAF c/s)		
G-DMVV	Diamond DA.42 Twin Star	42.327		13. 2.08	Diamond Aircraft UK Ltd	Gamston	
G-DMWW	CFM Shadow Series DD	304-DD		12.10.98	Microlight Sport Aviation Ltd Damyns Hall, Upminster		10. 4.08P
G-DNCS	Piper PA-28R-201T Turbo Arrow III	28R-7803024	N47841	3. 1.89	BC Arrow Ltd	Liverpool	9. 7.08E
G-DNGA	Balony Kubicek BB20 Balloon (Hot Air)	235	OK-0235	1. 5.03	G J Bell	Wokingham	14.10.07A
G-DNGR	Colt 31A Balloon (Hot Air)	10162		18.10.01	G J Bell (Inflated 4.06)	Wokingham	13.10.08A
G-DNKS	Comco Ikarus C42 FB80	0606-6822		15. 6.06	D N K and M A Symon	Eshott	27. 7.08P
G-DNOP	Piper PA-46-350P Malibu Mirage	4636302	N4174A	26. 7.00	Campbell Aviation Ltd	Denham	3. 8.08T
G-DOCA	Boeing 737-436	25267		21.10.91	British Airways PLC	London Gatwick	20.12.07E
G-DOCB	Boeing 737-436	25304		16.10.91	British Airways PLC	London Gatwick	15. 2.08E
G-DOCE	Boeing 737-436	25350		20.11.91	British Airways PLC	London Gatwick	6. 8.08E
G-DOCF	Boeing 737-436	25407		9.12.91	British Airways PLC	London Gatwick	9. 7.08E
G-DOCG	Boeing 737-436	25408		16.12.91	British Airways PLC	London Gatwick	15. 8.08E
G-DOCH	Boeing 737-436	25428		19.12.91	British Airways PLC	London Gatwick	18. 8.08E
G-DOCL	Boeing 737-436	25842		2. 3.92	British Airways PLC	London Gatwick	1. 3.08E
G-DOCN	Boeing 737-436	25848		21.10.92	British Airways PLC	London Gatwick	20.10.07E
G-DOCO	Boeing 737-436	25849		26.10.92	British Airways PLC	London Gatwick	15. 8.08E
G-DOCS	Boeing 737-436	25852		1.12.92	British Airways PLC	London Gatwick	30.11.07E
G-DOCT	Boeing 737-436	25853		22.12.92	British Airways PLC	London Gatwick	23.12.07E
G-DOCU	Boeing 737-436	25854		18. 1.93	British Airways PLC	London Gatwick	19. 1.08E
G-DOCV	Boeing 737-436	25855		25. 1.93	British Airways PLC	London Gatwick	24. 1.08E
G-DOCW	Boeing 737-436	25856		2. 2.93	British Airways PLC	London Gatwick	3. 2.08E
G-DOCX	Boeing 737-436	25857		29. 3.93	British Airways PLC	London Gatwick	28. 3.08E

Reg	Type	C/n	Prev id	Date	Owner	Location	Date
G-DOCY	Boeing 737-436	25844	OO-LTQ	17.10.96	British Airways PLC	London Gatwick	17.10.07E
			G-BVBY, TC-ALS, G-BVBY, (G-DOCY)				
G-DOCZ	Boeing 737-436	25858	EC-FXJ	12.12.94	British Airways PLC	London Gatwick	11. 1.08E
			EC-657, G-BVBZ, (G-DOCZ)				
G-DODB	Robinson R22 Beta	0911	N8005R	3. 5.96	L A and G M Evans t/a Helibern Helicopter Services		
					(New owners 10.07)	(Tartwell, Louth)	26. 9.08E
G-DODD	Reims Cessna F172P Skyhawk II	F17202175		5.10.82	K Watts	Moorlands Farm, Farway Common	6. 8.08E
G-DODG	Evektor EV-97A Eurostar	PFA 315-14258		23. 6.04	K L Clarke and R Barton	Keal Cotes,Spilsby	4.10.08P
	(Built R Barton)						
G-DODR	Robinson R22 Beta	1325	N80721	5. 6.96	Exmoor Helicopters Ltd	(Minehead)	27. 4.08E
			(Operated Patriot Aviation) (Struck ground whist hovering Cranfield 14.12.07 and damaged)				
G-DOEA	Gulfstream AA-5A Cheetah	AA5A-0895	G-RJMI	30. 4.96	CJW Holdings Ltd t/a Fairway Flying Services		
			N27170			Sandown, Isle of Wight	6. 9.08T
G-DOFY	Bell 206B-3 JetRanger III	3637	N2283F	26. 8.87	Cinnamond Ltd	Silver Springs, Denham	13. 3.08E
					(Operated Cabair Helicopters)		
G-DOGE	Scottish Aviation Bulldog Series 100/101	BH100/126	G-AZHX	5.12.05	W P Cooper	East Winch	21. 2.72
			SE-LNO, Swedish Army Fv61022, G-AZHX *(Noted 5.07)*				
G-DOGG	Scottish Aviation Bulldog Series 120/121	BH120/308	XX638	3.10.01	P Sengupta	Bourne Park, Hurstbourne Tarrant	26. 3.08T
					(As "XX638" in RAF c/s)		
G-DOGY	Aviat A-1B Husky	2421	N11UK	28. 2.08	Aviat Aircraft (UK) Ltd		
						Lower Grounds Farm, Sherlowe	
G-DOGZ	Rogerson Horizon 1	PFA 241-13129		10. 8.98	J E D Rogerson	Morgansfield, Fishburn	12.10.07P
	(Built J E D Rogerson) (Marked as "Fisher Super Koala") (Rotax 912-UL)						
G-DOIN	Best Off Sky Ranger 912S(1)	SKR0403460		26. 4.04	A G Borer	Stoke, Isle of Grain	8.12.07P
	(Built C D and L J Church - pr.no.BMAA/HB/379)						
G-DOIT	Aérospatiale AS.350B2 Ecureuil	1902	F-GMAZ	10.10.01	FBS Ltd	RAF Shawbury	22.11.07T
			LN-OTA, SE-JAC, LN-OBD, (F-GHYU), LN-OBD, SE-JAC, HB-XPH				
G-DOLF	Eurocopter AS.365N3 Dauphin 2	6779	F-WWPP	25.10.07	Eurocopter UK Ltd	Oxford	
G-DOLY	Cessna T303 Crusader	T30300107	N303MK	20. 7.94	KW Aviation Ltd	Biggin Hill	12. 7.08E
			G-BJZK, (N3645C)				
G-DOME	Piper PA-28-161 Warrior III	2842062	N4160V	12. 1.00	Haimoss Ltd	Old Sarum	31. 1.08T
					(Operated Old Sarum Flying Club)		
G-DOMS	Evektor EV-97A Eurostar	PFA 315-14254		24. 6.04	R K and C A Stewart	Hinton-in-the-Hedges	15. 4.08P
	(Built D J Cross)						
G-DONI	Gulfstream AA-5B Tiger	AA5B-1029	G-BLLT	20. 7.95	W P Moritz	Elstree	20.12.07E
			OO-RTG, (OO-HRS)				
G-DONS	Piper PA-28RT-201T Turbo Arrow IV	28R-8131077	N8336L	22. 4.88	C E Griffiths	Blackbushe	1. 3.08
G-DONT	Zenair CH.601XL Zodiac	PFA 162B-14172		24. 5.04	A C J Butcher	Whaley Farm, New York, Lincoln	18. 6.07P
	(Built N C Butcher)						
G-DOOM	Cameron Z-105 Balloon (Hot Air)	10660		14. 3.05	The Balloon Company Ltd t/a First Flight		
					(Doom Bar titles)	Langford, Bristol	4. 4.08E
G-DOOZ	Aérospatiale AS.355F2 Ecureuil 2	5367	G-BNSX	13. 5.88	Patriot Aviation Ltd	Cranfield	5. 4.08E
G-DORA	Focke-Wulf FW.190-D9	211028	Luftwaffe 211028	21. 5.03	P R Holloway	Old Warden	
					(Completion scheduled for 2009)		
G-DORN	Dornier EKW C-3605	332	HB-RBJ	15. 5.98	R G Gray	Bournemouth	15.11.08P
	(Built F + W)		Swiss AF C-552		*(As "C-552" in Swiss AF c/s)*		
G-DORS	Eurocopter EC.135 T2+	0517		14.12.06	Premier Fund Leasing Ltd	Yeovil	21. 2.08E
					(Operated Dorset and Somerset Air Ambulance)		
G-DOTT	CFM Streak Shadow	xxxx		30.11.04	R J Bell	Movenis, Coleraine	31. 8.08P
	(Built R J Bell - pr.no.PFA 206-13582)						
G-DOVE	Cessna 182Q Skylane II	18266724	N96446	26. 6.80	J Sinclair-Dean	Oxford	23. 7.08E
G-DOVS	Robinson R44 Raven II	11858		8. 8.07	D B Hamilton	(Stonehouse)	29. 8.08E
G-DOWN	Colt 31A Air Chair Balloon (Hot Air)	1570		3. 8.89	M Williams *"Up and Down"*	Wadhurst, Sussex	8. 6.00A
G-DOZI	Comco Ikarus C42 FB100	0606-6824		22. 5.06	D A Izod	Gerpyns Lane, Upminster	7.7.08P
G-DPEP	Aero AT-3 R100	AT3-027		24. 9.07	D C and E P Phillips (Eaton-on-Tern, Market Drayton)		
G-DPHN	Aerospatiale SA.365N1 Dauphin 2	6307	HB-ZBY	11. 4.06	Atlantic Air Ltd	Biggin Hill	17. 1.08E
			LX-HGR, JA9902				
G-DPJR	Sikorsky S-76B	760352	G-JCBA	20. 3.07	Kandahar No.1 Ltd	Oxford	2. 3.08E
			N95UT, N95LT, N120PP, N120PM				
G-DPPF	Agusta A109E Power	11216		26. 6.03	Dyfed-Powys Police Authority		
						(Llangunnor, Carmarthen)	14.. 3.10T
G-DPYE	Robin DR.500-200i Président	14	F-GPDT	26. 8.06	Pye Consulting Group Ltd	Blackpool	7. 9.08E
	(Officially regd as DR.400-500)						
G-DRAG	Cessna 152 II	15283188			L A Maynard and M E Scouller	Old Sarum	30. 8.08E
	(Tail-wheel conversion)		G-REME	27. 4.90	*(Operated Old Sarum Flying Club)*		
			G-DRAG, G-BRNF, N47217				
G-DRAM	Reims FR172F Rocket	FR17200102	OH-CNS	18. 9.98	H R Mitchell and J P Roland tr Clyde River Rats		
	(Floatplane)				*"Spirit of Scotland"*	Lochearnhead	11. 4.08E
G-DRAW	Colt 77A Balloon (Hot Air)	1830		31. 8.90	A G Odell	Macclesfield	29. 8.09A
G-DRAY	Taylor JT.1 Monoplane	PFA 1452		13. 7.78	L J Dray	(Sidmouth)	
	(Built L J Dray)						
G-DRBG	Cessna 172M Skyhawk	17265263	G-MUIL	18. 1.95	Wilkins and Wilkins (Special Auctions) t/a Henlow Flying Club Ltd		
			N64486			RAF Henlow	17. 5.08E
G-DREG	Cosmik Super Chaser	SCH001W		4. 6.07	N R Beale	Deppers Bridge, Southam	
	(Built N R Beale) (Rotax 447)				*(Noted NEC Birmingham 11.07)*		
G-DREX	Cameron Saturn 110 SS Balloon (Hot Air)	4217		28.10.97	LRC Products Ltd	Broxbourne, Hertford	3.11.99A
G-DRFC	Aérospatiale-Alenia ATR 42-320	007	OY-CIB	1. 6.04	Bravo Aviation Ltd	Coventry	9. 8.08E
			F-GFLL, OY-CIB, F-WWEC				
G-DRGN	Cameron N-105 Balloon (Hot Air)	2024		13. 6.91	W I Hooker and C Parker	(Nottingham)	4. 7.01T
G-DRGS	Cessna 182S Skylane	18280375	N2389X	17.11.98	D R G Scott	Edinburgh	3. 3.08E
G-DRID	Reims FR172J Rocket	FR1720434	I-ALGB	19. 9.03	D T J Hoskins, D H Hoskins and G Williams	Cardiff	18. 2.08E
G-DRIV	Robinson R44 Raven II	10126	N75233	19. 9.03	C Reynard	Walton Wood	13.11.07E
			N3624J				
G-DRLH	Eurocopter EC.120B Colibri	1477	F-HFLB	8. 8.07	R L Hartshorn	(Parkhead, Matlock)	15. 8.08E
G-DRMM	Europa Aviation Europa	362		27. 7.98	T J Harrison	(Bristol)	
	(Built M W Mason - pr.no.PFA 247-13201) (Tri-gear u/c)						

Reg	Type	C/n	Prev id	Date	Owner/Operator	Base	Date
G-DRNT	Sikorsky S-76A II Plus	760201	N93WW N3WQ, N3WL, N3121G	5. 4.90	CHC Scotia Ltd	North Denes Heliport	1. 5.08E
G-DROP	Cessna U206C Super Skywagon	U2061230	G-UKNO G-BAMN, 4X-ALL, N71943	7. 8.87	K Brady	Cumbernauld	7. 3.08E
G-DRSV	Robin DR315X Petit Prince	624	F-ZWRS	7. 6.90	R S Voice	Rushett Farm, Chessington	17. 6.08P
	(Officially regd with pr.no.PFA 210-11765 following major rebuild by R S Voice)						
G-DRYI	Cameron N-77 Balloon (Hot Air)	2046		7. 8.89	C A Butter *(Barbour titles)*	Marsh Benham	14. 4.08A
G-DRYS	Cameron N-90 Balloon (Hot Air)	3377		1.12.95	C A Butter *(Barbour titles)*	Marsh Benham	7. 8.08A
G-DRZF	CEA Jodel DR.360 Chevalier	451	F-BRZF	4. 9.91	P K Kaufeler	Earls Colne	7.12.06
G-DSFT	Piper PA-28R-200 Cherokee Arrow II	28R-7335157	G-LFSE G-BAXT, N11C	22.11.00	J Jones	Headcorn	5. 5.08T
G-DSGC	Piper PA-25-260 Pawnee C	25-4890	OY-BDA	3. 5.95	Devon & Somerset Gliding Club Ltd	North Hill	30. 3.08E
G-DSID	Piper PA-34-220T Seneca IV	3447001		21. 7.95	I S Giilbe	(Leigh Woods, Bristol)	5. 7.08E
G-DSKI	Evektor EV-97 Eurostar	PFA 315-14088		25. 6.04	D R Skill	Eshott	15. 8.08P
	(Built D R Skill)						
G-DSLL	Cyclone Airsports Pegasus Quantum 15-912	7836		5. 7.01	R G Jeffery	(Sandbach)	5. 7.07P
	(Marked as "Raven")						
G-DSPI	Robinson R44 Astro	0661		25.10.99	Central Helicopters Ltd	Tollerton	13.12.07T
G-DSPK	Cameron Z-140 Balloon (Hot Air)	10640		7. 1.05	Bailey Balloons Ltd	Pill, Bristol	10. 1.07E
	(D S Smith Packaging titles)						
G-DSPL	Diamond DA.40 Star	40.037		19.11.07	Dynamic Signal Processing Ltd	(Kingsclere, Newbury)	18.10.07E
G-DSPZ	Robinson R44 Raven II	10351		5. 5.04	Focal Point Communications Ltd	(Alresford)	8. 6.08E
G-DSVN	Rolladen-Schneider LS8-18	8079	BGA 4262-HWM	3. 1.08	A R Paul	Dunstable	26. 1.08
G-DTFF	Cessna T182T Turbo Skylane	T18208474	N2196K	25.10.06	Rajair Ltd	Sleap	25.10.07E
G-DTOY	Comco Ikarus C42 FB100	0309-6570		20.10.03	C W Laskey	Upfield Farm, Whitson	23.10.08P
	(Rotax 912-ULS)						
G-DTUG	Wag-Aero Super Sport	PFA 108-14026		13. 5.04	D A Bullock	Bicester	
	(Built D A Bullock)				*(Noted 1.07)*		
G-DTWO	Schempp-Hirth Discus 2A	9	BGA 5217-KNA D-2140	18. 1.06	O Walters tr GW-LL Group "LL"	Bicester	6. 3.08
G-DUAL	Cirrus SR22	1954	N194SR	11.07.06	J P and T M Jones	Denham	12. 7.08E
G-DUBI	Lindstrand LBL 120A Balloon (Hot Air)	1123		4.10.06	A Nimmo	Dubai, United Arab Emirates	12. 9.08E
G-DUDE	Van's RV-8	PFA 303-13246		16. 7.99	W M Hodgkins	Crowfield	15. 6.08P
	(Built W M Hodgkins)				*"Capt Midnight" ("Van's Air Force" and "19" on tail)*		
G-DUDZ	Robin DR.400-180 Régent	2367	G-BXNK	3.12.97	D H Pattison	Lower Upham Farm, Chiseldon	26.12.07E
G-DUGE	Comco Ikarus C42 FB UK	PFA 322-13855		30. 7.02	D Stevenson	Plaistows Farm, St Albans	1. 2.08P
	(Built D Stevenson)						
G-DUGI	Lindstrand LBL 90A Balloon (Hot Air)	562		16. 8.99	J A Folkes	Bulcote, Nottingham	13. 4.08A
G-DUKK	Extra EA.300/L	125	D-EXAC	27.11.00	Extra Aviation Ltd	(Hillam, Leeds)	20. 6.08E
G-DUKY	Robinson R44 Raven	1455		21. 2.05	English Braids Ltd	Gloucestershire	22. 2.08E
G-DUMP	Customflot A25 Balloon (Hot Air)	CC003		19. 5.04	P C Bailey	Over, Cambridge	
G-DUNK	Reims Cessna F172M Skyhawk	F17201402	N90SA PH-TWS, OY-BUL	2. 5.07	Devon and Somerset Flight Training Ltd	Dunkeswell	11. 6.08E
G-DUOD	Bombardier CL-600-2C10	10048	G-MRSH C-GIAI	22. 9.03	A/S Maersk Aviation Holding	Copenhagen, Denmark	16. 4.08E
	(CL-600 Regional Jet 700)						
G-DUOT	Schempp-Hirth Duo Discus T	123/...		3. 8.05	A P Moulang tr G-DUOT Group "666"	Challock	6. 3.07
G-DUOX	Schempp-Hirth Duo Discus	474	BGA 5209-KMS D-4498	3. 4.06	British Gliding Association Ltd "98"	Bicester	14.12.07
G-DURO	Europa Aviation Europa	033		15.11.93	W R C Williams-Wynne	Talybont, Gwynedd	30. 5.08P
	(Built R Swinden - pr.no.PFA 247-12554) (Monowheel u/c)						
G-DURX	Colt 77A Balloon (Hot Air)	1522		25. 5.89	(V Trimble))	(Nuffield, Henley-on-Thames)	26. 6.02A
					(Durex andAvanti titles)		
G-DUSK	de Havilland DH.115 Vampire T 11	15596	XE856	1. 2.99	R M A Robinson and R Horsfield	Bournemouth	
					(Stored unmarked at Aviation Museum 1.07)		
G-DUST	Stolp SA.300 Starduster Too	JP-2	N233JP	28. 4.88	N M Robinson	Compton Abbas	26.11.08P
	(Built J O Perritt) (Lycoming O-360)						
G-DUVL	Reims Cessna F172N Skyhawk II	F17201723	G-BFMU (1)	16. 8.78	I Mackinnon tr G-DUVL Flying Group	White Waltham	7. 8.08E
G-DVBF	Lindstrand LBL 210A Balloon (Hot Air)	188		6. 3.95	Airxcite Ltd t/a Virgin Balloon Flights	Wembley	1. 6.05T
G-DVON	de Havilland DH.104 Devon C 2/2	04201	(G-BLPD) VP955	26.10.84	C L Thatcher tr The 955 Preservation Group		29. 5.96
					(Stored 1.08 as "VP955" in RAF c/s)	Little Rissington	
G-DWCE	Robinson R44 Raven II	11511		17.11.06	G Walters (Leasing) Ltd	(Hirwaun, Aberdare)	30.11.07E
G-DWIA	Chilton DW.1A	PFA 225-12256		25. 1.93	D Elliott	(Brooks Green, Horsham)	
	(Built D Elliott)						
G-DWIB	Chilton DW.1B	PFA 225-12374		22.12.93	J Jennings	(Meldreth, Royston)	
	(Built J Jennings)						
G-DWJM	Cessna 550 Citation II	550-0296	G-BJIR N6888C	19. 5.05	MP Aviation LLP	Biggin Hill	30. 1.08E
G-DWMS	Avtech Jabiru UL-450	0266		21. 6.00	D H S Williams	Sutton Meadows	8.10.08P
	(Built D H S Williams - pr.no.PFA 274A-13491)						
G-DWPF	Tecnam P92-EM Echo	PFA 318-13838		17. 5.02	D J M Williams tr GDWPF Group	Guernsey	20.10.08P
	(Built P I Franklin and D J M Williams)						
G-DWPH	Ultramagic M-77 Balloon (Hot Air)	77/109		17. 3.95	Ultramagic SA *(New owner 12.07)*	Igualada, Spain	15. 7.05
G-DXCC	UltraMagic M-77 Balloon (Hot Air)	77/269		1. 2.06	A Murphy	Dunshaughlin, County Meath	13. 3.08E
G-DYCE	Robinson R44 Raven II	10148		3. 9.03	G Walters (Leasing) Ltd	Kirknewton	29. 9.08T
G-DYKE	Dyke JD-2 Delta	PFA 1331		6. 1.04	M S Bird	Pepperbox, Salisbury	
	(Built P Wilson and M S Bird)						
G-DYMC	Aerospool Dynamic WT9 UK	DY200/2007		6.11.07	D R Stevens	Kemble	29.11.08P
	(Official c/n is "DY200")						
G-DYNA	Aerospool Dynamic WT9 UK	DY135/2006		9. 5.06	Yeoman Light Aircraft Company Ltd	Chiltern Park, Wallingford	1. 3.08P
	(Official c/n is "DY135")						
G-DYNG	Colt 105A Balloon (Hot Air)	1721	G-HSHS	9. 2.98	G J Bell *(New owner 7.07)*	Petersfield	9.10.06A
G-DYNM	Aerospool Dynamic WT9 UK	DY161/2007		30. 5.07	D M Pearson	(Woodcote, Reading)	29. 5.08P
	(Official c/n is "DY161")						

G-EAAA - G-EZZZ (see SECTION 1, PART 1 for original G-EA.. and G-EB..[1919 to 1928] registrations)

Reg	Type	c/n	Prev id	Date	Owner/Operator	Location	Date
G-ECDB	Schleicher Ka 6E	4137	BGA 1450-CDB	13. 2.08	C W R Neve	Currock Hill	7. 5.08
G-EEAD	Slingsby T.65A Vega	1912	BGA 2523-EAD	2.11.07	D S Smith	Sutton Bank	25. 2.08
G-EAGA (2)	Sopwith Dove replica	"3004/1"	(G-BLOO)	22.11.89	A Wood	Old Warden	16. 5.01P
	(80hp Le Rhône)					(On loan to Richard Shuttleworth Trustees)	

(Original Dove G-EAGA c/n 3004/1 to Australia and in use as K-157 by 11.12.19: remains of unregistered Dove, thought to have been K-157
and which crashed Essendon, Victoria 9.3.30, brought to UK circa 1987/88, rebuilt as G-BLOO and subsequently re-registered as above)

Reg	Type	c/n	Prev id	Date	Owner/Operator	Location	Date
G-EAVX (2)	Sopwith Pup	PFA 101-10523	B1807	16. 1.78	K A M Baker	RNAS Yeovilton	
	(Officially regd with c/n "B1807": claimed as rebuild of original Sopwith Pup)				(Noted 3.07 as "B1807:A7" in RFC c/s)		
G-EBJI (2)	Hawker Cygnet replica	PFA 077-10240		9. 8.77	C J Essex	(Coventry)	
	(Built C J Essex)				(Under construction 7.99)		
G-EBZN (2)	de Havilland DH.60X Moth	608	VP-NAA	28.10.88	J Hodgkinson	(Gravesend)	
	(Cirrus I)		VP-YAA, ZS-AAP, G-UAAP		(On rebuild from original components)		
G-ECAC	Alpha Aviation R2120U	120T-0001	ZK-SXY	23. 1.08	Bulldog Aviation Ltd	Earls Colne	
	(Marked as "Alpha 120T")				(Noted 2.08		
G-ECAN	de Havilland DH.84 Dragon	2048	VH-DHX	11. 1.01	A J Norman tr Norman Aeroplane Trust	Rendcomb	25. 6.09S
	(Built de Havilland Aircraft Proprietary Ltd, Australia)		VH-AQU, RAAF A34-59		(Railway Air Services Ltd titles)		
G-ECBH	Reims Cessna F150K	F15000577	D-ECBH	16. 5.85	G Harber tr ECBH Flying Group	Swansea	6. 6.08E
G-ECBI	Schweizer 269C-1	0282	N86G	17. 5.07	Oxford Aviation Services Ltd	Oxford	1. 7.08E
	(Schweizer 300)						
G-ECBO	Eurocopter EC.130 B4	4276		5. 7.07	Hawkrise Aviation LLP	(Sutton Coldfield)	
					(New owner 2.08)		
G-ECDS	de Havilland DH.82A Tiger Moth	86347	N82DS	6.12.07	D A Porter	Griffins Farm, Temple Bruer	
			F-BGFA, NL904				
G-ECDX	de Havilland DH.71 Tiger Moth replica	SP.7		1.11.94	M D Souch and N Parkhouse	Hill Farm, Durley	
	(DH Gipsy I)				(Under build 2.03)		
G-ECGC	Reims Cessna F172N Skyhawk II	F17201850		10.10.79	Cranfield Aviation Leasing Ltd	Cranfield	3. 3.08E
G-ECGO	Bölkow BÖ.208C Junior	599	D-ECGO	24. 8.89	A Flight Aviation Ltd	Prestwick	6. 4.08E
					(Operated Prestwick Flying Club)		
G-ECJI	Dassault Falcon 10	161	I-CREM	21.12.05	Fleet International Aviation and Maritime Finance Ltd		
			F-WWZK, I-CREM, N50SL, N30CN, N230FJ, F-WZGM		(Tortola, Virgin Islands)		15. 2.08E
G-ECJM	Piper PA-28R-201T Turbo Arrow III	28R-7803178	G-FESL	25. 9.90	Regishire Ltd	Bournemouth	16. 5.08
			G-BNRN, N321EC, N3561M				
G-ECKB	Reality Escapade 912	JA ESC 0003		20.12.07	C M and C P Bradford		
	(Built C M Bradford - pr.no:BMAA/HB/533)					Wing Farm, Longbridge Deverill	
G-ECLW	Glasflügel H201 Standard Libelle	174	BGA 1637-CLW	26.11.07	R G Parker	Kirton-in-Lindsey	17. 4.08
G-ECOA	Bombardier DHC-8-402	4180	C-FMUE	14.12.07	Flybe Ltd (Delivered 15.12.08)	Exeter	
G-ECOB	Bombardier DHC-8-402	4185	C-FNEN	18. 1.08	Flybe Ltd (Delivered 19. 1.08)	Exeter	
G-ECOC	Bombardier DHC-8-402	4197		3.08R	Flybe Ltd	Exeter	
G-ECOD	Bombardier DHC-8-402	4201		3.08R	Flybe Ltd	Exeter	
G-ECOE	Bombardier DHC-8-402	4206		4.08R	Flybe Ltd	Exeter	
G-ECOF	Bombardier DHC-8-402			5.08R	Flybe Ltd	Exeter	
G-ECOG	Bombardier DHC-8-402			6.08R	Flybe Ltd	Exeter	
G-ECOH	Bombardier DHC-8-402			7.08R	Flybe Ltd	Exeter	
G-ECOI	Bombardier DHC-8-402			8.08R	Flybe Ltd	Exeter	
G-ECOJ	Bombardier DHC-8-402			9.08R	Flybe Ltd	Exeter	
G-ECOK	Bombardier DHC-8-402			10.08R	Flybe Ltd	Exeter	
G-ECOL	Schempp-Hirth Nimbus 2	11	BGA 1722-CQL	3.12.07	A D F Flintoft and L I Rigby	Crowland	6. 4.08
G-ECON	Cessna 172M Skyhawk II	17264490	G-JONE	18. 9.03	S J Skilton t/a Aviation Rentals	(Bournemouth)	29. 3.08E
	(Thielert TAE 125-01) (3-blade propeller)		N9724V		(Operated Solent School Of Flying) (Diesel engine)		
G-ECOU	Aerospatiale AS.355F2 Ecureuil 2	5464	N4360N	15. 6.07	Rulegate Ltd	(Hamstead Marshall, Newbury)	23. 8.08E
			4X-BJV, N355FT, JA6646				
G-ECOX	Pietenpol AirCamper GN.1	WLAW.1		5.12.78	H C Cox	(Frogland Cross, Bristol)	
	(Built H C Cox - pr.no.PFA 047-10356)				(Under construction 2001)		
G-ECPA	Glasflügel H201B Standard Libelle	328	BGA 1688-CPA	23. 1.08	M J Witton	Long Mynd	6. 4.08
G-ECSW	Pilatus B4-PC11AF	22	BGA 1780-CSW	8. 1.08	I.H.Keyser	Aston Down	9. 4.08
G-ECTF	Comper CLA.7 Swift replica	PFA 103-13078		12. 4.07	P R Cozens	Hinton-in-the-Hedges	
	(Built P R Cozens)						
G-ECUB	Piper PA-18-150 Super Cub	18-6279	G-CBFI	28.11.03	J K Padden	Breighton	6. 3.08E
			SE-FDY, LN-HHA, SE-CTA, N8675D				
G-ECVB	Pietenpol AirCamper	PFA 047-13014		20. 4.00	K S Matcham	Barton Ashes	29 .6.08P
	(Built K S Matcham) (Continental O-200-A)						
G-EDAV	Scottish Aviation Bulldog Series 120/121		XX534	8. 8.01	Historic Helicopters Ltd	Tollerton	6. 8.08
		BH120/220			(As "XX534:B "in RAF c/s)		
G-EDCJ	Cessna 525 CitationJet	525-0105	N305CJ	23. 1.06	Air Charter Scotland (Holdings) Ltd	Prestwick	13. 2.08E
			(D-IAFD), N52081				
G-EDCK	Cessna 525 CitationJet	525-0510	N971DM	19.10.06	Air Charter Scotland (Holdings) Ltd	Glasgow	8.11.07E
			(N278CA), N971DM, N1DM, N5058J				
G-EDCL	Cessna 525A CitationJet CJ2	525A0083	N975DN	14. 8.07	Air Charter Scotland (Holdings) Ltd	Glasgow	
G-EDCS	Raytheon Hawker 400XP	RK-487	N487XP	26. 9.06	Mountain Aviation Ltd	Edinburgh	6.12.07E
G-EDDS	CZAW Sportcruiser	PFA 338-14660		14. 2.08	E H Bishop	(North Duffield, Selby)	
	(Built E H Bishop)						
G-EDEE	Comco Ikarus C42 FB100	0511-6769		15.11.05	Terratrip (UK) Ltd t/a Microavionics	(Horsley, Derby)	25. 1.08P
G-EDEN	SOCATA TB-10 Tobago	66		8. 1.80	N G Pistol tr Group Eden	Elstree	7. 6.08E
G-EDES	Robinson R44 Raven II	10480		8. 9.04	A D Russell	Bourn	10.10.07E
G-EDFS	Pietenpol AirCamper	PFA 047-13206		24. 3.98	D F Slaughter	(Redhill)	
	(Built D F Slaughter)				(New owner 7.07)		
G-EDGA	Piper PA-28-161 Warrior II	28-8516024	D-EDGA	30.8.05	The RAF Halton Aeroplane Club Ltd	RAF Halton	19.10.07E
			N9512N				
G-EDGE	Jodel D 150 Mascaret	111		14. 9.88	A D Edge	RAF Wyton	13. 3.08P
	(Built A D Edge - pr.no.PFA 151-11223) (Continental O-200-A)						

G-EDGI	Piper PA-28-161 Warrior II	28-7916565	D-EBGI N2941R	19. 1.99	R A Forster	Cardiff	28..4.08E
G-EDGY	Zivko Edge 540	0018	N540JN N540SA	16.10.07	C R A Scrope	Little Gransden	
	(Built S K Andeline)						
G-EDHO	Cirrus SR20-G2	1542	N790BH	20. 2.08	Cumulus Aircraft Rentals Ltd	Bournemouth	
G-EDLY	AirBorne XT912-B-Streak III-B	XT912-073		27. 4.05	M and P L Eardley	Tarn Farm, Cockerham	26. 4.08P
		(Wing s/n ST3-058)					
G-EDMC	Cyclone Airsports Pegasus Quantum 15-912	7513		11. 3.99	M W Riley (Noted 9.07)	Longframlington	13. 4.04P
G-EDMV	Eiriavion PIK-20D	20526	BGA 2232-DMV	12.12.07	R Cochrane tr BNA MV	Bellarena	13. 4.08
G-EDNA	Piper PA-38-112 Tomahawk	38-78A0364	OY-BRG	4. 9.84	Top Cat Aviation Ltd	Manchester	5. 1.08E
G-EDRE	Lindstrand LBL 90A Balloon (Hot Air)	1081		17. 3.06	Edren Homes Ltd	Gretton, Corby	4. 5.08E
G-EDRV	Van's RV-6A	PFA 181A-13451		20. 8.99	E A Yates	North Weald	6. 6.08P
	(Built E A Yates)						
G-EDTO	Reims FR172F Rocket	FR17200090	D-EDTQ	21. 3.01	N G Hopkinson	Fenland	30. 5.08E
G-EDVL	Piper PA-28R-200 Cherokee Arrow II		G-BXIN	30. 6.97	J S Develin and Z Islam	Shoreham	15. 8.08E
		28R-7235245	D-EDVL, N1243T		(Operated Sky Leisure)		
G-EDYO	Piper PA-32-260 Cherokee Six	32-415	D-EDYQ (N3529W), N11C	30. 3.07	A L Paton and D Bursey	Guernsey	25. 4.08E
G-EEBB	Sikorsky S-76C	760620	N81027	22. 2.07	Haughey Air Ltd	Belfast City	15. 3.08E
G-EEBD	Scheibe Bergfalke IV	5822	BGA 2547-EBD D-1005	7. 1.08	D A Bell tr Mr D A Bell Syndicate	Burn	10. 7.08
G-EEBF	Schempp-Hirth Mini Nimbus C	138	BGA 2549-EBF	23. 8.07	M Pingel	Talgarth	28. 9.08
G-EEBJ	Cessna 525A CitationJet CJ2	525A0202	N719WP N202CJ	14. 9.07	Skyblue Business Services LLP	(London WC1)	17. 9.08E
G-EEBK	Schempp-Hirth Mini Nimbus C	139	BGA 2553-EBK AGA 2	9.10.07	G Smith and N P Frost	Parham Park	28. 9.08
G-EEBM	Grob G102 Astir CS77	1843	BGA 2555-EBM	17. 1.08	Yorkshire Gliding Club (Proprietary) Ltd	Sutton Bank	30. 1.08
G-EEBR	Glaser-Dirks DG-200/17	2-89-1706	BGA 2559-EBR D-6893	4. 1.08	M D Parsons	Bembridge	10. 6.08
G-EEBZ	Schleicher ASK 13	13614	BGA 2567-EBZ	13.12.07	Booker Gliding Club Ltd "EBZ"	Wycombe Air Park	28. 9.08
G-EECC	Aerospool Dynamic WT9 UK	DY189/2007		6.11.07	Yeoman Light Aircraft Co mpanyLtd		
	(Official c/n recorded as "DY/189")					Manor Farm, Drayton St Leonard	17.12.08P
G-EECH	Robinson R44 Raven II	11922		2.10.07	Select Helicopters Ltd	Aberdeen	
G-EECK	Slingsby T.65A Vega	1917	BGA 2577-ECK	23.10.07	J P Dunnington	Portmoak	19. 1.08
G-EECO	Lindstrand LBL 25A Cloudhopper Balloon (Hot Air)	668		1. 2.00	P A and A J A Bubb	(Storrington, Pulborough)	9. 5.06A
G-EEDE	Centrair ASW 20F	20128	BGA 2596-EDE	4. 1.08	G M Cumner	Aston Down	11. 1.08
G-EEEK	Extra EA.300/200	1034	D-EXTT	31. 5.06	A R Willis	(Earls Colne)	1. 6.08E
G-EEER	Schempp-Hirth Mini Nimbus C	150	BGA 2631-EER	30. 8.07	D J Uren	Culdrose	14. 3.08
G-EEEZ	American Champion 8KCAB Super Decathlon	1034-2007		28. 2.07	Les Wallen Manufacturing Ltd	Rochester	15. 3.08E
G-EEFA	Cameron Z-90 Balloon (Hot Air)	11076		18.12.07	A Murphy	Dunshaughlin, County Meath	
G-EEFK	Centrair ASW 20FL	20140	BGA 2649-EFK F-WFLZ	7.11.07	A P Balkwill and G B Monslow	Snitterfield	21. 2.08
G-EEGL	Christen Eagle II	AES/01/0353	5Y-EGL	14.12.90	M P Swoboda	(Terling, Chelmsford)	1.10.04P
	(Lycoming AEIO-360)				(Noted 3.07)		
G-EEGU	Piper PA-28-161 Warrior II	28-7916457	D-EEGU N2831A	7. 5.02	B C Barber	Norwich	7. 7.08E
G-EEJE	Piper PA-31 Turbo Navajo B	31-825	OH-PNG	18. 5.01	Geeje Ltd	Full Sutton	6. 8.08E
G-EEKA	Glaser-Dirks DG-200/17	2-128-1703	BGA 2736-EKA	4.10.07	M J R Lindsay and P Hayward	Tibenham	5. 3.08
G-EEKY	Piper PA-28-140 Cherokee B	28-25422	OY-DFP LN-BNX, (N8218N)	20. 6.05	W J Hockenhull tr Gauntlet Holdings	RAF Waddington	9. 8.08E
G-EELS	Cessna 208 Grand Caravan	208B0619		3. 3.97	Glass Eels Ltd	Gloucestershire	31. 8.08E
G-EELT	Rolladen-Schneider LS4	4186	BGA 2777-ELT	15. 1.08	K J Wood tr ELT Syndicate	Lasham	9. 3.08
G-EELY	Schleicher Ka 6CR	6536	BGA 2782-ELY D-5172	6.12.07	D Webster tr K6 ELY Group	Bellarena	12. 5.08
	(BGA records for BGA 2782 including de-registration certificate for D-5172 confirms the c/n as 6485/Si: details for c/n 6536 not known))						
G-EENA	Piper PA-32R-301 Saratoga II SP	32R-8013011	C-GBBU	3.10.97	Gamit Ltd	North Weald	17. 9.08E
G-EENE	Rolladen-Schneider LS4	4271	BGA 2812-ENE	9.11.07	A P C Sampson	Dunstable	28. 9.08
G-EENI	Europa Aviation Europa	199		28. 7.98	M P Grimshaw	Milton Keynes	
	(Built M P Grimshaw - pr.no.PFA 247-12831)				(Address change 11.07)		
G-EENK	Schleicher ASK 21	21106	BGA 2817-ENK	18.10.07	W T Alden tr ENK Group	Aston Down	12. 4.08
G-EENN	Schemmp-Hirth Nimbus 3	9	BGA 2820-ENN	14. 8.07	A James and I B Kennedy	Usk	23. 2.08
G-EENW	Schleicher ASW 20L	20567	BGA 2828-ENW	26.11.07	J T A Hunter	Pocklington	13. 3.08
G-EENY	Gulfstream GA-7 Cougar	GA-7-0094	N721G	21. 6.79	Jade Air PLC (Noted 11.04)	Thruxton	20. 7.03T
G-EERH	Ruschmeyer R90-230RG	003	D-EERH	5. 4.01	D Sadler	Perth	2. 5.08E
G-EERV	Van's RV-6	PFA 181-13381	G-NESI	13. 9.01	C B Stirling	Damyn's Hall, Upminster	10. 5 08P
	(Built G Ness, P G Stewart and C B Stirling) (Lycoming O-320)						
G-EERY	Robinson R22 Beta	4128		27. 3.07	EGB (Helicopters) Ltd	Redhill	10. 5.08E
G-EESA	Europa Aviation Europa	025	G-HIIL	9. 4.96	C Deith	(Broadbridge Heath, Horsham)	1. 3.08P
	(Built C B Stirling - pr.no.PFA 247-12535) (NSI EA-81/100) (Monowheel u/c)						
G-EESY	Rolladen-Schneider LS4	4334	BGA 2926-ESY	19.10.07	D A Parkes	Kingston Deverill	23. 6.08
G-EETG	Cessna 172Q Cutlass	17275928	N913AT N913ER, (N65939)	30. 6.05	R W Simpson tr Tango Golf Flying Group	Redhill	5. 9.08E
G-EEUP	SNCAN Stampe SV-4C	451	F-BCXQ	1. 9.78	A M Wajih	Redhill	20. 9.10S
G-EEUX	Schleicher ASK 18	18005	BGA 2973-EUX D-3988	9.11.07	Southdown Gliding Club Ltd	Parham Park	26. 8.08
G-EEWZ	Mainair Sports Pegasus Quik	8101		16. 3.05	A Gillett	Willingale	26. 3.08P
G-EEYE	Mainair Blade 912	1313-0202-7-W1108		13. 5.02	B J Egerton	Ince Blundell	2. 6.07P
G-EEZA	Robinson R44 Raven II	10071	N71959	29. 4.03	Teleology Ltd	(Todmorden)	30. 5.08E
G-EEZR	Robinson R44 Raven II	11391		24. 8.06	Veee Helicopters Ltd	(Twineham, Haywards Heath)	28. 9.07E
G-EEZS	Cessna 182P Skylane	18261338	D-EEZS N63054, D-EEZS, (N20981)	8.11.99	W B Bateson	Blackpool	20. 9.08E

Reg	Type	C/n	Prev id	Date	Owner/Operator	Base	Expiry
G-EEZZ	Zenair CH.601XL Zodiac	PFA 162B-14392		4. 8.05	B Fraser	Latch Farm, Kirknewton	18.12.08P
	(Built B Fraser)						
G-EFAM	Cessna 182S Skylane	18280442	D-EFAM N7269H	7. 6.05	S P Myers tr G-EFAM Flying Group	Barton	7. 7.08E
G-EFBP	Reims Cessna FR172K Hawk XP	FR1720664	D-EFBP PH-AXF	7. 1.04	A Webster	Manston	12. 6.08E
G-EFCM	Piper PA-28-180 Cherokee D	28-4766	SE-FCM	16.11.07	ATC Trading Ltd	Lasham	
G-EFFI	Rotorway Executive 162F	7006		28. 6.06	P D Annison	(Tillingham, Southminster)	
	(Built P D Annison)						
G-EFGH	Robinson R22 Beta	1487	G-ROGG	3. 5.01	Foxtrot Golf Helicopters Ltd	Lower Baads, Peterculter	3. 8.08E
G-EFIR	Piper PA-28-181 Archer II	28-8090275	D-EFIR N8179R	5. 5.99	The Leicestershire Aero Club Ltd	Leicester	4. 8.08E
G-EFLY	Centrair ASW 20FL	20133	BGA 2650-EFL	3. 9.07	I D and J H Atherton	Tibenham	14. 9.08
G-EFOF	Robinson R22 Beta II	3605	N73323	19. 5.04	N T Burton t/a NT Burton Aviation	Costock	17. 6.08E
G-EFRY	Avid Aerobat	PFA 189-12096		22. 3.93	J M Rawles	Ellough, Beccles	21. 7.06P
	(Built J J Donley)				(Noted dismantled at rear of hangar 10.07)		
G-EFSM	Slingsby T 67M-260 Firefly	2072	G-BPLK	16. 7.92	The Cambridge Aero Club Ltd	Cambridge	6. 6.08E
G-EFTE	Bölkow BÖ.207	218	D-EFTE	4. 1.90	R L Earl and B Morris	Landmead Farm, Garford	11. 6.08
G-EFTF	Aérospatiale AS.350B Ecureuil	1847	G-CWIZ	1. 4.03	T J French	(Cumnock)	19. 4.08E
			CS-HDF, G-DJEM, G-ZBAC, G-SEBI, G-BMCU				
G-EGAG	SOCATA TB-20 Trinidad	1675	D-EGAG (3)	29. 8.06	D and E Booth	(Notton, Wakefield)	31. 8.08E
G-EGAL	Christen Eagle II	0042-86	SE-XMU	11. 3.96	J H Penfold tr Eagle Partners	Shoreham	19. 6.08P
	(Lycoming AEIO-360)						
G-EGAN	Enstrom F-28A-UK	103	G-SERA	24. 5.05	Helimove Ltd	Ellough, Beccles	13. 7.08E
			G-BAHU, EI-BDF, G-BAHU				
G-EGBS	Van's RV-9A	PFA 320-14234		13. 4.05	D M Johnstone tr Shobdon RV-9A Group	Shobdon	
	(Built D M Johnstone, A and C Price, M Rowland, M Sweeny and J Turner)						
G-EGEE	Cessna 310Q	310Q0040	G-AZVY	14.11.83	R C Devine	Hawarden	22. 3.08E
			SE-FKV, N7540Q				
G-EGEG	Cessna 172R Skyhawk	17280894	N7262H	4. 7.00	C D Lever	Elstree	20.12.07E
G-EGEL	Christen Eagle II	S 308	N388AG	4. 2.91	P Miny tr G-EGEL Flying Group		
	(Built MLP Aviation Ltd) (Lycoming AEIO-360)		G-EGEL			(Riehen, Switzerland)	3. 8.08P
G-EGGI	Comco Ikarus C42 FB UK	0112-6442?		18. 4.02	A G and G J Higgins	Ashby Lane, Bitteswell	12. 7.07P
	(Built A G and G J Higgins - pr.no.PFA 322-13872) (Kit no.not confirmed)						
G-EGGS	Robin DR.400-180 Régent	1443		15.11.79	R Foot	Lasham	12. 7.08
G-EGGY	Robinson R22 Beta II	3452	G-CCGD	8.11.04	A G and R S Higgins	Ashby Lane, Bitteswell	3. 8.08E
			N75107				
G-EGHB	Ercoupe 415D	1876	N3414G	1. 9.95	P G Vallance	Rochester	29. 9.09S
	(Continental O-200-A)		N99253, NC99253				
G-EGHH	Hawker Hunter F 58	41H-697450	Swiss AF J-4083	4. 7.95	Heritage Aviation Developments Ltd		
					(On rebuild 2007)	(Mursley, Milton Keynes)	
G-EGIL	Christen Eagle II	BOYD-0001	N21SB	7.11.07	J P Nash	Shoreham	
	(Built S F Boyd)						
G-EGJA	SOCATA TB-20 Trinidad	1101	N2807D	13.12.90	D A Williamson	(Potters Bar)	14.12.07E
G-EGLE	Christen Eagle II	F 0053		30. 3.81	D Thorpe tr Eagle Group	North Weald	17. 5.08P
	(Built Airmore Aviation) (Lycoming AEIO-360)						
G-EGLG	Piper PA-31 Turbo Navajo C	31-7812103	N45TY	8. 9.06	H Merkado	Panshanger	8.11.07E
			4X-CCY, N36SG, N27703, G-OATC, G-OJPW, G-BGCC, N27703				
G-EGLL	Piper PA-28-161 Cherokee Warrior II		G-BLEJ	17. 3.06	Airways Aero Associations Ltd	Wycombe Air Park	7. 6.08S
		28-7816257	N2194M		(Operated British Airways Flying Club) (Union Flag c/s)		
G-EGLS	Piper PA-28-181 Archer III	2843348	N4187C	5. 6.00	O Sylvester	(Grantham)	16. 7.08E
G-EGLT	Cessna 310R II	310R1874	G-BHTV	9. 9.93	Reconnaissance Ventures Ltd	Coventry	15. 1.08E
			N1EU, (N3206M)				
G-EGNA	Diamond DA42 Twin Star	42.149		17. 7.06	Egnatia Aviation Ltd	Kavala International, Greece	6. 8.08E
G-EGNR	Piper PA-38-112 Tomahawk	38-79A0233	OY-VIG	6.10.97	R Bestek	City of Derry	3. 7.08E
			SE-KNI, N2570C				
G-EGNS	Gulfstream Aerospace Gulfstream V-SP	5167	N967GA	22. 1.08	Pobedy Corporation	Ronaldsway	
	(Gulfstream 550)						
G-EGPG	Piper PA-18-135 Super Cub	18-3569	N719CS	3. 4.06	G Cormack	Easter Polder Farm, Thornhill	8. 6.08E
			G-BWUC, SX-ASM, EI-181, I-EIYB, MM54-2369, 54-2369				
G-EGSJ	Avtech Jabiru J400	xxx	G-MGRK	29. 8.07	B Greathead tr Seething Jabiru Group	Seething	
	(Built M R Tingle - pr.no.PFA 325-14618)				(Under construction 3.08)		
G-EGTB	Piper PA-28-161 Cherokee Warrior II		G-BPWA	21. 1.04	Airways Aero Association Ltd	Wycombe Air Park	24. 6.08T
		28-7816074	N47450		(Operated British Airways Flying Club)		
G-EGTC	Robinson R44 Raven	1357	G-CCNK	14. 3.05	Beds Heli Services Ltd	Sywell	8. 2.08E
G-EGTR	Piper PA-28-161 Cadet	2841281	G-BRSI	25. 4.98	Stars Fly Ltd	Stapleford	27. 1.08T
			N92001				
G-EGUL	Christen Eagle II	Argence 0001	G-FRYS	19. 1.93	S Shutt	RAF Coningsby	12. 1.07P
	(Built Argence EA) (Lycoming AEIO-360)		N66EA		(Noted 9.07)		
G-EGUR	SAN Jodel D 140B Mousquetaire II	52	D-EGUR	9. 1.04	S H Williams	Hawksbridge Farm, Oxenhope	22. 9.07P
G-EGWN	American Champion 7ECA Citabria Aurora			4.12.07	The Royal Air Force Halton Aeroplane Club Ltd		
		1399-2007			(Noted 12.07)	RAF Halton	
G-EHAV	Glasflügel H201B Standard Libelle	40	BGA 3796-HAV	12.11.07	A Liran and M Truelove	Rivar Hill	3. 5.08
			HB-950				
G-EHBJ	CASA 1-131E Jungmann Series 2000	2150	Spanish AF E3B-550	19. 7.90	E P Howard	Airfield Farm, Hardwick	22. 8.08P
					(Also carries "E 3B-550")		
G-EHCB	Schempp-Hirth Nimbus 3DT	47	BGA 3827-HCB	28. 2.07	H A Torode tr G-EHCB Group "754"	Lasham	7. 5.08
G-EHCZ	Schleicher K 8B	8114	BGA 3850-HCZ	20. 2.08	The Surrey Hills Gliding Club Ltd	Kenley	4. 9.08
			D-4675				
G-EHDS	CASA 1-131E Jungmann Series 2000	2108	G-DUDS	21. 2.05	C W N and A A M Huke	Manor Farm, Dinton	3. 6.00P
	(Enma Tigre G-1V-B)		D-EHDS, Spanish AF E3B-512				
G-EHGF	Piper PA-28-181 Cherokee Archer II		D-EHGF	23.10.00	E Stokes and J Lamb tr Pegasus Flying Group		
		28-7790188	N9534N			Barton	16. 5.08E

Reg	Type	c/n	Prev id	Date	Owner/Operator	Base	Date
G-EHIC	SAN Jodel D 140B Mousquetaire II	53	D-EHIC	20.10.04	M Tolson and D W Smith	RAF Halton	23. 1.08E
G-EHLX	Piper PA-28-181 Archer II	28-8090317	D-EHLX	5.11.99	ASG Leasing Ltd	Guernsey	13. 1.08E
			N8218S				
G-EHMF	Isaacs Fury II	PFA 011-14109		8.10.03	M A Farrelly	(Frodsham)	
	(Built M A Farrelly)						
G-EHMJ	Beech S35 Bonanza	D-7879	D-EHMJ	12. 1.99	A J Daley	Gamston	14. 3.08E
G-EHMM	Robin DR.400-180R Remorqueur	867		10.12.84	Booker Gliding Club Ltd	Wycombe Air Park	26. 4.08E
G-EHMS	MD Helicopters MD.900 Explorer	900-00068	N3212K	12. 7.00	Virgin HEMS (London) Ltd	Denham	12.10.07E
	(All-red Virgin c/s operating London Ambulance Service)						
G-EHUP	Aérospatiale SA.341G Gazelle 1	1407	F-GIJR	3.10.97	M W Helicopters Ltd	Stapleford	22. 3.07T
			N869GT, N869, N49523				
G-EHXP	Rockwell Commander 112A	227	D-EHXP	27. 1.00	A L Stewart	Halfpenny Green	17. 4.08E
			N1227J				
G-EIBM	Robinson R22 Beta	1993	G-BUCL	25. 3.94	HJS Helicopters Ltd	Lower Baads, Peterculter	5. 3.08E
G-EICK	Cessna 172S Skyhawk	172S10426	N12173	13. 7.07	Centenary Flying Group Ltd	Cork, County Cork	5. 8.08E
G-EIER	Margan'ski Swift S-1	119	BGA 4915-JZP	11. 2.08	C Cain and D Poll	(Austria)	6. 8.08
			F-CIAB				
G-EIGG	British Aerospace Jetstream Series 3102	773	SE-LGH	8. 5.07	Highland Airways Ltd	Inverness	14. 5.08E
			OY-SVO, C-FAMK, G-31-773				
G-EIKY	Europa Aviation Europa	054		27. 9.94	J D Milbank tr Europa G-EIKY Group		
	(Built J D Milbank - pr.no.PFA 247-12634) (Monowheel u/c)					Longside, Peterhead	7. 6.07P
G-EIRE	Cessna T182T Turbo Skylane	T18208049	N3500U	24. 7.01	J Byrne	Englefield	26. 4.08T
G-EISG	Beech A36 Bonanza	E-3212	N2533J	2. 4.07	R J and Bridget Howard	Sherburn-in-Elmet	30. 5.08E
			(G-EISG), N326R				
G-EISO	SOCATA MS.892A Rallye Commodore 150	10563	D-EISO	23. 1.01	T E H Simmons tr G-EISO Group		
			F-BNSO			Sandown, Isle of Wight	30. 6.07T
G-EITE	Luscombe 8F Silvaire	3407	N71980	27. 7.88	S R H Martin	Manor Farm, Haddenham	7 12.08P
	(Continental C90)						
G-EIWT	Reims Cessna FR182 Skylane RG II	FR18200052	D-EIWT	28. 1.86	P P D Howard-Johnston	Glenrothes	19. 4.08ET
			OO-BLI				
G-EIZO	Eurocopter EC.120B Colibri	1120	N20GH	31.12.04	R M Bailey	Addiston Mains, Dalmahoy	1. 3.08E
			D-HSUN				
G-EJAE	Glaser-Dirks DG-200	22678	BGA 4352-JAE	7. 2.08	D L P H Waller	RAF Keevil	24. 3.08
			HB-1443				
G-EJAR	Airbus A319-111	2412	D-AVYV	7. 3.05	EasyJet Airline Company Ltd	London Stansted	10. 9.08E
G-EJEL	Cessna 550 Citation II	550-0643	N747CR	19.12.01	A J and E A Elliott	Leeds-Bradford	8. 1.08E
			N643MC, PT-ODW, N13091, (N1259S)				
G-EJGO	Moravan Zlin Z-226T Trener Spezial	199	D-EJGO	7. 8.85	S K T and C M Neofytou	Breighton	3.11.08S
			OK-MHB				
G-EJJB	Airbus A319-111	2380	D-AVWV	1. 2.05	EasyJet Airline Company Ltd	London Stansted	31. 1.08E
G-EJMG	Cessna F150H	F150-0301	D-EJMG	27. 4.98	P R Booth	Durham Tees Valley	20.12.07E
	(Built Reims Aviation SA)						
G-EJJM	P&M Quik 912S	8306		3.08R			
G-EJOC	Aérospatiale AS.350B Ecureuil	1465	G-GEDS	21.12.94	E and S Vandyk t/a Leisure and Retail Helicopters		
			G-HMAN, G-SKIM, G-BIVP			Oxford	8. 7.08E
G-EJRC	Robinson R44 Raven II	11605		29. 1.07	E J R Canvin t/a Perry Farming Company	Conington	22. 2.08E
G-EJRS	Piper PA-28-161 Cadet	2841115	D-EJRS	5. 5.04	Carlisle Flight Training Ltd	Carlisle	2.12.07E
			N9175X				
G-EJTC	Robinson R44 Clipper II	10623		31. 1.05	N Parkhouse	Chelwood Gate, Haywards Heath	23. 3.08E
G-EKEY	Schleicher ASW 20CL	20840	BGA 5044-KEY	11. 1.08	K W Payne	Husbands Bosworth	2. 5.08
			D-3171				
G-EKIM	Alpi Pioneer 300	xxx		11. 5.06	M Langmead and M Elliott	White Waltham	17. 5.08E
	(Built M Langmead and M Elliott - pr.no.PFA 330-14491)						
G-EKIR	Piper PA-28-161 Cadet	2841157	SE-KIR	17. 6.02	Aeros Leasing Ltd	Gloucestershire	11. 8.08E
			(SE-KII)		*(Operated Aeros Flying Club)*		
G-EKKL	Piper PA-28-161 Warrior II	28-8416087	D-EKKL	24. 3.99	Apollo Aviation Advisory Ltd	Shoreham	11. 5.08E
			N43588				
G-EKKO	Robinson R44 Raven	0821		18. 7.00	W A Hawkeswood	(Knowle, Solihull)	11.07.08E
G-EKMN	Moravan Zlin Z-242L	0652	SE-KMN	15. 5.01	R C Poolman	Gloucestershire	23. 9.07T
G-EKOS	Reims Cessna FR182 Skylane RG II	FR18200017	D-EKOS	15. 7.98	S Charlton	Sherburn-in-Elmet	22. 9.08E
G-EKYD	Robinson R44 Raven II	10081		20. 5.03	MDL Air and Leisure Ltd	(Sawston, Cambridge)	12. 6.08E
G-ELAM	Piper PA-30 Twin Comanche B	30-1477	N26PJ	14.10.04	Hangar 39 Ltd	North Weald	20.10.07E
			G-BAWU, (G-BAWV), 9J-RFW, ZS-FAM, N8332Y				
G-ELDR	Piper PA-32-260 Cherokee Six	32-7400027	SE-GBK	21. 1.03	Elder Aviation Ltd	Oxford	21. 3..08E
G-ELEE	Cameron Z-105 Balloon (Hot Air)	4882		11. 7.00	D Eliot	Aberdeen	4. 8.07A
G-ELEN	Robin DR.400-180 Régent	2363		16. 9.97	N R and E Foster	Cannes, France	24. 6.08E
G-ELIS	Piper PA-34-200T Seneca II	34-8070265	G-BOPV	11. 9.03	Bristol Flying Centre Ltd	Bristol	19. 8.08E
			N82323				
G-ELIT	Bell 206L LongRanger	45091	SE-HTK	28. 7.99	Henfield Lodge Aviation Ltd	Goodwood	18. 8.08E
			N2652				
G-ELIZ	Denney Kitfox Model 2	717		19. 7.90	A J Ellis	(Ryde, Isle of Wight)	5.11.93P
	(Built A J Ellis - pr.no.PFA 172-11835)				*(Damaged Brighstone, Isle of Wight 10. 5.93)*		
G-ELKA	Christen Eagle II	0001	N121DJ	18.10.94	J T Matthews	Old Buckenham	22. 5.08P
	(Built A c/n JAMES-0001) (Lycoming AEIO-360)		N1DJ, N99DJ				
G-ELKS	Avid Speed Wing Mk.4	PFA 189-13109		6. 1.98	H S Elkins	(Hebron, Whitland)	9. 7.07P
	(Built H S Elkins) (Jabiru 2200A)						
G-ELLA	Piper PA-32R-301 Saratoga II HP	3246050	N9279Q	13. 8.96	C C W Hart	Old Buckenham	27. 4.08E
			G-ELLA				
G-ELLE	Cameron N-90 Balloon (Hot Air)	4498		11. 1.99	S A Lacey	Norwich Common, Wymondham	15. 6.07A
G-ELLI	Bell 206B-3 JetRanger III	4231	D-HMOF	24. 6.97	Italian Clothes Ltd	Hawarden	16. 7.08E
G-ELMH	North American AT-6D-NT Harvard III	88-16336	FAP1662	22. 7.92	M Hammond	Airfield Farm, Hardwick	31. 5.08P
			EZ341, 42-84555		*"Fools Rush-In" (As "42-84555:EP-H" in USAAC c/s)*		
G-ELMO	Robinson R44 Raven II	10509		7.10.04	Locumlink Associates Ltd	(Ballsbridge, Dublin)	9.11.07E
G-ELNX	Bombardier CL-600-2B19	7508	VH-KXJ	26. 4.02	Eurolynx Corporation	Farnborough	23. 5.08E
	(CL-600 Regional Jet)		C-FMNY				

G-ELOA	Cessna 560XL Citation Excel	560-5106	HB-VND	18. 7.07	TAG Aviation (UK) Ltd	Farnborough	18. 7.08E
			N506AM, N5221Y				
G-ELSE	Diamond DA.42 Twin Star	42.114	OE-VPY	29. 6.06	R Swann	Bournemouth	16. 7.08E
G-ELSI	Air Création Tanarg 912S/iXess 15	FLT.001		19. 1.06	D Daniel	Weston Zoyland	19. 6.08P
	(Built D Daniel - pr.no.BMAA/HB/466 being Flylight kit comprising Trike s/n T05069 and Wing s/n A05146-5134)						
G-ELTE	Agusta A109A II	7269	G-BWZI,	13. 2.06	Henfield Lodge Aviation Ltd	Redhill	5. 3.08E
			OH-HAD, N109AK				
G-ELUN	Robin DR.400-180R Remorqueur	1102	D-ELUN	29. 5.02	P Harper-Little and I A Lane tr Cotswold DR.400 Syndicate		
			I-ALSA			Kemble	5. 5.08E
G-ELUT	Piper PA-28R-200 Cherokee Arrow II		D-ELUT	21.11.03	Green Arrow Europe Ltd	Goodwood	1. 3.08E
		28R-7435009	N56514				
G-ELZN	Piper PA-28-161 Warrior II	28-8416078	D-ELZN	20. 7.99	P A Layzell	Old Buckenham	14. 9.08E
			N9579N				
G-ELZY	Piper PA-28-161 Warrior II	28-8616027	D-ELZY	13. 4.99	Goodwood Road Racing School Ltd	Goodwood	23. 5.08E
			N9095Z, (N163AV), N9641N		(Operated Goodwood Flying Club)		
G-EMAA	Eurocopter EC.135 T2	0448		17. 1.06	Bond Air Services Ltd	Halfpenny Green	26. 3.08E
					(Operated County Air Ambulance)		
G-EMAX	Piper PA-31-350 Navajo Chieftain	31-7952029	N276CT	8.12.98	Atlantic Bridge Aviation Ltd	Lydd	6. 7.08E
			SE-KKP, Swedish Navy 54202 , SE-KKP, LN-PAI				
G-EMBC	Embraer EMB-145EU	145024	PT-SYU	1.10.97	Flybe Ltd	Ronaldsway	8.10.07E
G-EMBD	Embraer EMB-145EU	145039	PT-SZE	7. 1.98	Flybe Ltd	Ronaldsway	11. 1.08E
G-EMBE	Embraer EMB-145EU	145042	PT-SZH	3. 2.98	Flybe Ltd	Ronaldsway	2. 2.08E
G-EMBH	Embraer EMB-145EU	145107		20. 1.99	Flybe Ltd	Birmingham	19. 1.08E
G-EMBI	Embraer EMB-145EU	145126	PT-SDD	23. 4.99	Flybe Ltd	Manchester	22. 4.08E
G-EMBJ	Embraer EMB-145EU	145134	PT-SDL	24. 5.99	Flybe Ltd	Manchester	26. 5.08E
G-EMBK	Embraer EMB-145EU	145167		26. 8.99	Flybe Ltd	Ronaldsway	25. 8.08E
G-EMBL	Embraer EMB-145EU	145177		4.10.99	Flybe Ltd	Ronaldsway	3.10.07E
G-EMBM	Embraer EMB-145EU	145196		22.11.99	Flybe Ltd	Ronaldsway	21.11.07E
G-EMBN	Embraer EMB-145EU	145201		13. 1.00	Flybe Ltd	Ronaldsway	12. 1.08E
G-EMBO	Embraer EMB-145EU	145219		14. 3.00	Flybe Ltd	Ronaldsway	13. 3.08E
G-EMBP	Embraer EMB-145EU	145300	PT-SKR	25. 8.00	Flybe Ltd	Ronaldsway	24. 8.08E
G-EMBU	Embraer EMB-145EU	145458	PT-SVD	22. 6.01	Flybe Ltd	Ronaldsway	21. 6.08E
G-EMBV	Embraer EMB-145EU	145482	PT-SXB	12. 9.01	Flybe Ltd	Ronaldsway	11. 9.08E
G-EMBW	Embraer EMB-145EU	145546	PT-SZJ	19.12.01	Flybe Ltd	Southampton	18.12.07E
G-EMBX	Embraer EMB-145EU	145573	PT-SBJ	21. 3.02	Flybe Ltd	Plymouth	20. 3.08E
G-EMBY	Embraer EMB-145EU	145617	PT-SDF	17. 7.02	Flybe Ltd	Ronaldsway	16. 7.08E
G-EMCA	Commander Aircraft Commander 114B	14661		23. 7.04	S Roberts	Oaksey Park	6. 8.08E
G-EMDM	Diamond DA.40-P9 Star	40009	OE-KPO	7.10.02	D J Munson	Oxford	20.10.07E
			OE-VPO				
G-EMEL	Robinson R44 Raven I	11726		11. 6.07	AGF Aviation Ltd	Welwyn	12. 7.08E
	(Offically regd with c/n 1726 in error)						
G-EMER	Piper PA-34-200 Seneca	34-7350002	N3081T	29. 7.91	Haimoss Ltd	Old Sarum	8. 2.08E
					(Operated Old Sarum Flying Club)		
G-EMHB	Agusta A109E Power	11111	YR-TIA	24. 3.05	Looporder Ltd t/a East Midlands Helicopters		
			HB-ZDL			Costock, Loughborough	6. 4.08E
G-EMHC	Agusta A109E Power	11721		13. 2.08	Looporder Ltd, t/a East Midlands Helicopters		
						Costock, Loughborough	
G-EMHH	Aérospatiale AS.355F2 Ecureuil 2	5169	G-BYKH	3. 8.99	Hancocks Holdings Ltd	Costock, Loughborough	26. 7.08E
			SX-HNP, VR-CCM, N57967				
G-EMHK	MBB BÖ.209 Monsun 150FV	101	G-BLRD	23. 2.06	T A Crone	Cranfield	25. 1.08E
			D-EBOA, (OE-AHM), D-EBOA				
G-EMID	Eurocopter EC.135 P2+	0524		20.12.06	East Midlands Air Support Unit	Sibbertoft	29. 7.08E
G-EMIN	Europa Aviation Europa	083		1. 3.94	S A Lamb	Rochester	24. 9.08P
	(Built G M Clarke and E W Gladstone - pr.no.PFA 247-12673) (Monowheel u/c)						
G-EMJA	CASA 1-131E Jungmann Series 2000	013	(Spanish AF)	2. 9.94	N J Radford	Bicester	4.10.08P
	(Built P J Brand - pr.no.PFA 242-12340) (Enma Tigre G-IV-B) (Composite from Spanish spares imported in 1991)						
G-EMLE	Evektor EV-97 Eurostar	PFA 315-14251		9. 6.04	A R White	Scotland Farm, Hook	18. 7.08P
	(Built A R White)						
G-EMLI	Bombardier CL-600-2B16	5383	N383DT	8. 5.07	Twinjet Aircraft Sales Ltd	Luton	8. 5.08E
	(CL-604 Challenger)		C-GLYK				
G-EMLS	Cessna T210L Turbo Centurion	21060094	D-EMLS	11. 5.07	R D Masters	Standalone Farm, Meppershall	12. 7.08E
			(G-BCJJ), N59107				
G-EMLY	Cyclone Airsports Pegasus Quantum 15-912	7531		30. 6.99	S J Reid	Old Sarum	27. 6.08P
G-EMMI	Robinson R44 Clipper II	10075		6. 6.03	Hub Of The Wheel Ltd	(Offham, West Malling)	27. 6.08E
G-EMMM	Diamond DA.40 Star	40.753		12. 4.07	A J Leigh	Gamston	4. 6.08E
G-EMMS	Piper PA-38-112 Tomahawk	38-78A0526	OO-TKT	14. 9.79	Ravenair Aircraft Ltd	Liverpool	21. 1.08E
			N4414E				
G-EMMY	Rutan VariEze	577		21. 8.78	M J Tooze	Biggin Hill	21. 1.08P
	(Built M J Tooze - pr.no.PFA 074-10222) (Lycoming O-235)						
G-EMSB	Piper PA-22-160 Tri-Pacer	22-7602	G-ARHU	13. 8.03	M S Bird	Pepperbox, Salisbury	10.12.98
			N3726Z				
G-EMSI	Europa Aviation Europa	191		24. 1.95	P W L Thomas	(Askham Bryan, York)	
	(Built P W L Thomas - pr.no.PFA 247-12817) (Tri-gear u/c)						
G-EMSL	Piper PA-28-161 Warrior II	28-8216117	G-TSFT	20. 2.02	Environmental Maintenance Services Ltd	Biggin Hill	7. 3.08E
			G-BLDJ, N9632N				
G-EMSY	de Havilland DH.82A Tiger Moth	83666	G-ASPZ	27. 6.91	B E Micklewright tr G-EMSY Group	Old Sarum	11. 3.10
	(Built Morris Motors Ltd) (Rebuilt with parts ex OO-MOT)		D-EDUM, T7356				
		(Taxied into parked Piper PA-28-161 G-SLYN Old Sarum 15. 8.06 and substantially damaged: noted 2.08)						
G-ENBD	Lindstrand LBL 120A Balloon (Hot Air)	1184		7.11.07	A Nimmo	Dubai, United Arab Emirates	
G-ENCE	Partenavia P68B	141	G-OROY	1. 6.84	J J H and A E Hanna t/a Bicton Aviation	Exeter	25.10.07E
			G-BFSU				
G-ENEE	CFM Streak Shadow	K 280		14. 8.00	T Green	Wombleton	4. 6.04P
	(Built T Green - pr.no.PFA 206-13628) (Rotax 912-UL)						
G-ENES	Bell 206B-3 JetRanger III	4601	C-FFQR	16.10.06	Autogen Bioclear UK Ltd	(Mile End, Calne)	

Reg	Type	C/n	Prev ID	Date	Owner/Operator	Location	Date
G-ENGL	Piper PA-28-140 Cherokee	28-7425151	OY-BGN	19. 7.06	M A English	(Tilney All Saints, King's Lynn)	30. 5.08E
G-ENGO	Steen Skybolt	PFA 064-13429		15.11.00	R G Fulton	Lower Wasing Farm, Brimpton	
	(Built C Docherty and R G Fulton)				(Noted 9.07)		
G-ENHP	Enstrom 480B	5084		17. 8.05	H J Pelham	Cleeves Farm., Chilmark, Salisbury	21. 9.08E
G-ENIE	Nipper T 66 Series 3	PFA 025-10214		17. 3.78	R W Chatterton	Griffins Farm, Temple Bruer	18. 6.08P
	(Built A J Waller) (Volkswagen 1800))						
G-ENII	Reims Cessna F172M Skyhawk II	F17201352	PH-WAG	18. 1.79	J Howley	Fenland	4. 2.08E
			(D-EDQM)				
G-ENNI	Robin R3000/180	128	F-GGJA	5.10.99	I F Doubtfire	Goodwood	24.10.08E
G-ENNK	Cessna 172S Skyhawk SP	172S8538	N72729	15. 9.00	Holden Group Ltd	(Monewden)	10.11.07T
G-ENNY	Cameron V-77 Balloon (Hot Air)	1399		1.12.86	J H Dobson	Streatley, Reading	25.10.05A
G-ENOA	Cessna F172F	F172-0138	G-ASZW	2. 9.81	M K Acors	King's Farm, Thurrock	4.12.07E
	(Built Reims Aviation SA)						
G-ENRE	Avtech Jabiru UL-450	xxxx		28. 6.01	P R Turton	Old Sarum	14.11.08P
	(Built J C Harris - pr.no.PFA 274A-13755)						
G-ENRI	Lindstrand LBL 105A Balloon (Hot Air)	294		4. 8.95	P G Hall	Meanwood, Chard	5. 8.04T
					(Henry Numatic Vacuum Cleaners titles)		
G-ENRY	Cameron N-105 Balloon (Hot Air)	2096		26. 9.89	P G and G R Hall	Petworth	7. 7.94T
					"Henry" (To Balloon Preservation Group 2.04)		
G-ENST	CZAW Sportcruiser	LAA 338-14769		28. 1.08	L M Radcliffe, C Slater and D G Price)		
	(Built L M Radcliffe, C Slater and D G Price)				(Wolverhampton, Milton Keynes and Aylsebury)		
G-ENTS	Van's RV-9A	PFA 320-13917		6. 1.04	L G Johnson	(Washington)	
	(Built L G Johnson)						
G-ENTT	Reims Cessna F152 II	F15201750	G-BHHI	9.11.93	C and A R Hyett	Blackbushe	17. 4.08E
			(PH-CBA)				
G-ENTW	Reims Cessna F152 II	F15201479	G-BFLK	21. 1.93	Firecrest Aviation Ltd	Elstree	30. 9.07E
G-ENVO	MBB BÖ.105CBS-4	S.593	SX-HCK	29. 2.08	F C Owen	(Burnley)	
			D-HDQP, Sweden 73, D-HDQP				
G-ENVY	Mainair Blade	1260-1000-7-W1054		20.12.00	P Millership	Tarn Farm, Cockerham	15.12.07P
	(Rotax 912-UL)						
G-ENZO	Cameron Z-105 Balloon (Hot Air)	10914		21. 9.06	Garelli VI SpA (IVECO Garelli VI titles) Mondovi, Italy		23. 5.08E
G-EODE	Piper PA-46-350P Malibu Mirage	4636217	N45YM	30. 6.06	H J D S Baioes	Cranfield	25. 7.08E
			G-BYLM				
G-EOFF	Taylor JT.2 Titch	PFA 060-10319		6. 7.78	J R Faulkner	Derby	
	(Built G Wylde)				(New owner 7.07)		
G-EOFS	Europa Aviation Europa	296		22. 7.98	G T Leedham	Gunby Lea Farm, Overseal	24. 9.08P
	(Built G T Leedham - pr.no.PFA 247-13033) (Rotax 914-UL) (Tri-gear u/c)						
G-EOFW	Cyclone Airsports Pegasus Quantum 15-912	7582		15.10.99	C D Livingstone t/a G-EOFW Microlight Group		
						Enstone	14.10.08P
G-EOHL	Cessna 182L Skylane	18259279	D-EOHL	4. 3.99	G B Dale and M C Terris	(Armagh)	31. 5.08E
			N70505				
G-EOIN	Zenair CH.701UL STOL	PFA 187-13490		19.11.99	D G Palmer	Mintlaw, Peterhead	23.12.07P
	(Built I M Donnelly) (Verner SVS1400)						
G-EOLD	Piper PA-28-161 Warrior II	28-8516030	D-EOLD	31. 3.00	Goodwood Road Racing Company Ltd	Goodwood	15. 8.08E
			N4390F, N9531N		(Operated Goodwood Flying Club)		
G-EOLX	Cessna 172N Skyhawk II	17269099	G-BOLX	12. 4.06	Westward Airways (Lands End) Ltd	St Just	9.12.07E
			N734TK				
G-EOMA	Airbus A330-243	265	F-WWKU	26. 4.99	Monarch Airlines Ltd	Luton	25. 4.08E
G-EOMK	Robin DR.400-180 Régent	1267	D-EOMK	22.11.07	F Warin	Nympsfield	
G-EORG	Piper PA-38-112 Tomahawk	38-78A0427	N9734N	18. 9.78	P Sharpe	Durham Tees Valley	3. 8.08E
	(Rebuilt with new fuselage: old one stored 9.96)						
G-EORJ	Europa Aviation Europa	347		23. 7.99	P E George	(Sutton Coldfield)	12. 7.07P
	(Built P E George - pr.no.PFA 247-13139) (Monowheel u/c)						
G-EPAR	Robinson R22 Beta II	2781		26. 2.98	J W Ramsbottom t/a Jepar Rotorcraft		
						Higher Barn Farm, Houghton	11. 6.08E
G-EPDI	Cameron N-77 Balloon (Hot Air)	370		25. 1.78	R Moss "Pegasus"	Banchory	29. 6.91A
G-EPIC	Avtech Jabiru UL-450	xxxx		4.11.03	T Chadwick	(Market Weighton)	
	(Built T Chadwick - pr.no.PFA 274A-14125)						
G-EPIM	Cessna R172K Hawk XP	R172-2376	PH-PIM	2.11.07	A H Creaser	(Heckington, Sleaford)	
			N736AQ				
G-EPOC	Avtech Jabiru UL-450	0290		9. 6.04	S Cope	(Laceby)	
	(Built S Cope - pr.no.PFA 274A-13531)						
G-EPOX	Aero Designs Pulsar XP	PFA 202-12355		27. 4.94	M J Whatley	Henstridge	30. 5.08P
	(Built W A Stewart and K F Farey) (Tri-cycle u/c)						
G-EPSN	Ultramagic M-105 Balloon (Hot Air)	105/159		7. 1.08	G Everett	Sandway, Maidstone	
G-EPTR	Piper PA-28R-200 Cherokee Arrow II	28R-7235090	D-EPTR	26. 5.98	Tayflite Ltd	Perth	12. 8.08T
			OH-PTR, (SE-KVF), N4558T				
G-EPZL	PZL-104 Wilga 80	CF14800560	OY-PZL	29. 8.07	J K Houlgrave	Trenchard Farm, Eggesford	30. 8.08E
			SP-KEB				
G-ERBL	Robinson R22 Beta II	2711		26. 6.97	G V Maloney	(Cavan, County Cavan)	28. 8.08E
G-ERCO	Ercoupe 415D	3210	N2585H	7. 4.93	A R and M V Tapp	Manston	31. 8.08S
	(Continental C85)		NC2585H				
G-ERDA	Staaken Z-21A Flitzer	PFA 223-13947		15. 1.03	J Cresswell	Old Sarum	4. 6.07P
	(Built J Cresswell)						
G-ERDS	de Havilland DH.82A Tiger Moth	85028	ZS-BCU	27. 7.94	W A Gerdes	(Florida, US)	11. 7 10
	(Floatplane)		SAAF 2267, T6741				
G-ERFS	Piper PA-28-161 Warrior II	28-8216051	D-EPFS	29.11.02	S Harrison	Lee-on-Solent	7. 3.08E
			N84570				
G-ERIC	Rockwell Commander 112TC	13010	SE-GSA	26. 9.78	Atomchoice Ltd	Cranfield	10. 5.08E
G-ERIK	Cameron N-77 Balloon (Hot Air)	1753		18. 5.88	T M Donnelly "Norsewind"	Sprotbrough, Doncaster	24. 2.00A
G-ERIS	Hughes 369D	11-0871D	G-PJMD	1. 3.96	R J Howard	Leeds	13. 9.07
	(Hughes 500) (Modified to 500E standard)		G-BMJV, N1110S				
G-ERIW	Staaken Z-21 Flitzer	PFA 223-13834		9. 1.04	R I Wasey	Calcot	8. 6.07P
	(Built R I Wasey) (Volkswagen 2180)						

G-ERJA	Embraer EMB-145EP	145229		25. 2.00	Flybe Ltd	Bristol	24. 2.08E
G-ERJB	Embraer EMB-145EP	145237	PT-SIC	13. 3.00	Flybe Ltd	Bristol	12. 3.08E
G-ERJC	Embraer EMB-145EP	145253		25. 4.00	Flybe Ltd	Bristol	25. 4.08E
G-ERJD	Embraer EMB-145EP	145290	PT-SKH	20. 7.00	Flybe Ltd	Bristol	19. 7.08E
G-ERJE	Embraer EMB-145EP	145315	PT-SMG	15. 9.00	Flybe Ltd	Bristol	14. 9.08E
G-ERJF	Embraer EMB-145EP	145325		24.10.00	Flybe Ltd	Bristol	23.10.07E
G-ERJG	Embraer EMB-145EP	145394		8. 3.01	Flybe Ltd	Bristol	7. 3.08E
G-ERMO	ARV Aviation ARV-1 Super 2	018	G-BMWK	7. 1.87	S Vince	(Bradfield, North Walsham)	31. 8.06E
G-ERMS	Thunder AS-33 Airship (Hot Air)	A 1		28.11.78	B R and M.Boyle *"Microbe"*	Budbrooke, Warwick	
G-ERNI	Piper PA-28-181 Archer II	28-8090146	G-OSSY	9.10.91	N F P Hopwood and M Lodge tr The G-ERNI Flying Group		
			N81215			Headcorn	18. 3.08E
G-EROL	Westland SA.341G Gazelle 1	1108	G-NONA	18.10.02	The Coin Group Ltd	Wycombe Air Park	23. 6.08E
			G-FDAV, G-RIFA, G-ORGE, G-BBHU				
G-EROM	Robinson R22 Beta II	3383		19.11.02	Airtask Group PLC	Cambridge	22. 3.08E
G-EROS	Cameron H-34 Balloon (Hot Air)	2296		6. 4.90	A A Brown t/a Reach For The Sky *(Evening Standard titles)*		
					(Active 10.05)	Perry Hill, Worplesdon, Guildford	19. 2.08E
G-ERRI	Lindstrand LBL 77A Balloon (Hot Air)	811		20. 2.02	K J Baxter	Norton, Worcester	23. 8.08A
G-ERRY	Grumman AA-5B Tiger	AA5B-0725	G-BFMJ	20. 3.84	Haniel Aviation Ltd	Turweston	18.10.07E
G-ERTE	Best Off Sky Ranger 912S(1)	SKRxxxx566		27. 4.05	A P Trumper	(Auborm, Lincoln)	12. 7.08P
	(Built A P Trumper - pr.no.BMAA/HB/451)						
G-ERTI	Staaken Z-21A Flitzer	PFA 233-14166		29. 9.06	B S Carpenter	Wycombe Air Park	
	(Built B S Carpenter)						
G-ESCA	Reality Escapade Jabiru(1)	JAESC 0002		25. 4.03	W R Davis-Smith	Sleap	17. 9.08P
	(Built T F Francis - pr.no.BMAA/HB/280)						
G-ESCC	Reality Escapade 912	JAESC 0032		7.10.04	G and S Simons	Jackrell's Farm, Southwater	
	(Built G Simons - pr.no.BMAA/HB/414)				*(Noted 7.07)*		
G-ESCP	Reality Escapade Jabiru(1)	JAESC 0004		19. 1.04	R G Hughes	(Stanford Bridge, Worcester)	27. 6.07P
	(Built R G Hughes - pr.no.BMAA/HB/313)						
G-ESEX	Eurocopter EC.135 T2+	0267	D-HECP	9. 4.03	Essex Police Authority *(Essex Police titles)* Boreham		18. 6.09E
G-ESFT	Piper PA-28-161 Warrior II	28-7916060	G-ENNA	16. 5.97	Falcon Flying Services Ltd	Rochester	11. 5.08E
			N22065				
G-ESGA	Reality Escapade	UK.CKT.010		20. 8.07	T F Francis	Old Sarum	
	(Built T F Francis - pr.no.PFA 345-14706)				*(Noted NEC Birmingham 11.07)*		
G-ESKA	Reality Escapade 912(1)	JAESC 0006		13. 5.04	J H Beard	Buckfast, Buckfastleigh	25. 4.07P
	(Built T F Francis - pr.no.BMAA/HB/371)						
G-ESME	Cessna R182 Skylane RG II	R18201026	G-BNOX	10. 6.03	G C Cherrington	Thruxton	7. 4.08E
			N756AW				
G-ESSL	Cessna 182R Skylane II	18267947	D-EIMP	7.12.06	Euro Seaplane Services Ltd	Cranfield	14. 8.08E
	(Floatplane)		PH-AXP, N9434H		*(Euro Seaplane Services Ltd titles)*		
G-ESSY	Robinson R44 Raven	1281		17. 1.03	EW Guess (Holdings) Ltd	Sibson	9. 5.08E
G-ESTA	Cessna 550 Citation II	550-0127	G-GAUL	24. 6.98	Executive Aviation Services Ltd	Gloucestershire	18. 8.08E
			N550TJ, (N29TG), N29TC, N2631N				
G-ESTR	Van's RV-6	PFA 181A-13638		11. 9.00	R M Johnson	Midlem Farm, Midlem	2. 5.08P
	(Built R M Johnson)				*"Jester"*		
G-ESUS	RotorWay Executive 162F	6169/6724		7.10.96	J Tickner	Street Farm, Takeley	30. 8.08P
	(Built J Tickner) (RotorWay RI 162F)						
G-ETAT	Cessna 172S Skyhawk	172S8674	N747SP	7. 7.05	A D and C Realff t/a ADR Aviation	Shoreham	7. 7.08E
G-ETBY	Piper PA-32-260 Cherokee Six	32-211	G-AWCY	13. 7.89	K Richards-Green and M B Smithson tr G-ETBY Group		
	(Rebuilt with spare Frame No.32-858S)		N3365W			Oxford	25. 9.08E
G-ETCW	Stoddard-Hamilton GlaStar	5627	D-ETCW	12.12.01	P G Hayward	Little Snoring	16. 1.08P
	(Built T Wright) (Tri-cycle u/c)						
G-ETDC	Cessna 172P Skyhawk II	17274690	N53133	4. 5.88	The Moray Flying Club (1990)	RAF Kinloss	29. 7.08E
G-ETFF	Robinson R44 Raven	1747	G-HSLJ	26.10.07	Rajair Ltd	Sleap	13. 9.08E
G-ETFL	Cirrus SR22	2899	N998CT	3.08R		Turweston	
G-ETHI	IAV Bacau Yakovlev Yak-52	899714	LY-AOY	23. 4.03	J S Thrush	(Instow, Bideford)	8. 7.08P
			UR-BFP, Ukraine AF 71 *(yellow)*, DOSAAF 71 *(yellow)*				
G-ETHY	Cessna 208 Caravan I	20800293	N1295M	19.10.98	N A Moore	Movenis, Coleraine	2. 4.08E
			G-ETHY				
G-ETIM	Eurocopter EC.120B Colibri	1387	VH-NZZ	27. 4.05	T R Smith (Agricultural Machinery) Ltd		
						New Lane Farm, North Elmham	9. 6.08E
G-ETIN	Robinson R22 Beta	0853	N9081D	7. 9.88	D I Pointon	Coventry	25. 9.08E
G-ETIV	Robin DR.400-180 Régent	2454		12. 7.00	J Macgilvray	Goodwood	14. 9.08E
G-ETME	Nord 1002 Pingouin	274	N108J	18. 4.00	S H O'Connell and J N Pittock tr 108 Flying Group		
	(Lycoming O-540)		F-BFRV, French AF 274		*(As "KG+EM" in Luftwaffe North Africa c/s)* White Waltham		3. 4.1S0
G-ETNT	Robinson R44 Raven	1479		27. 4.05	P J Tallis	(Freshford, County Kilkenny)	23. 5.08E
G-ETOU	Agusta A109A Grand	22028		19.12.06	P J Ogden	Jetou	3. 1.08E
G-ETPS	Hawker Hunter FGA.9	41H-679959	XE601	15. 9.04	Skyblue Aviation Ltd *(As "XE601" in ETPS c/s)*	Exeter	6. 7.08P
G-EUAB	Europa Aviation Europa XS	xxx		16. 5.07	A D Stephens	(London WC1)	
	(Built A D Stephens - pr.no.PFA 247-13959)						
G-EUAN	Avtech Jabiru UL-D	666		30.11.07	M Wade and M Lusted	(Tonbridge and Rochester)	
G-EUFO	Rolladen-Schneider LS7-WL	7079	BGA 3562-FVQ	10. 1.08	J R Bane and R Hardy	Gransden Lodge	1. 4.08
G-EUJG	Avro 594 Avian IIIA	R3/CN/185	VH-UJG	21. 5.07	R I and D E Souch	Hill Farm, Durley	
			G-AUJG				
G-EUKA	Airbus A320			.08R	British Airways PLC	London Heathrow	
G-EUKB	Airbus A320			.08R	British Airways PLC	London Heathrow	
G-EUKC	Airbus A320			.08R	British Airways PLC	London Heathrow	
G-EUKD	Airbus A320			.08R	British Airways PLC	London Heathrow	
G-EUKE	Airbus A320			.08R	British Airways PLC	London Heathrow	
G-EUKF	Airbus A320			.08R	British Airways PLC	London Heathrow	
G-EUKG	Airbus A320			.08R	British Airways PLC	London Heathrow	
G-EUKH	Airbus A320			.08R	British Airways PLC	London Heathrow	
G-EUKI	Airbus A320			.08R	British Airways PLC	London Heathrow	
G-EUKJ	Airbus A320			.08R	British Airways PLC	London Heathrow	
G-EUKK	Airbus A320			.08R	British Airways PLC	London Heathrow	

Reg	Type	C/n	Prev ID	Date	Owner/Operator	Base	
G-EUKL	Airbus A320			.08R	British Airways PLC	London Heathrow	
G-EUOA	Airbus A319-131	1513	D-AVYE	15. 6.01	British Airways PLC	London Heathrow	14. 6.08E
G-EUOB	Airbus A319-131	1529	D-AVWH	4. 7.01	British Airways PLC	London Heathrow	3. 7.08E
G-EUOC	Airbus A319-131	1537	D-AVYP	16. 7.01	British Airways PLC	London Heathrow	15. 7.08E
G-EUOD	Airbus A319-131	1558	D-AVYJ	16. 8.01	British Airways PLC	London Heathrow	15. 8.08E
G-EUOE	Airbus A319-131	1574	D-AVWF	5. 9.01	British Airways PLC	London Heathrow	4. 9.08E
G-EUOF	Airbus A319-131	1590	D-AVYW	23.10.01	British Airways PLC	London Heathrow	22.10.07T
G-EUOG	Airbus A319-131	1594	D-AVWU	23.10.01	British Airways PLC	London Heathrow	22.10.07T
G-EUOH	Airbus A319-131	1604	D-AVYM	14.12.01	British Airways PLC	London Heathrow	13.12.07E
G-EUOI	Airbus A319-131	1606	D-AVYN	13.11.01	British Airways PLC	London Heathrow	12.11.07T
G-EUPA	Airbus A319-131	1082	D-AVYK	6.10.99	British Airways PLC	London Heathrow	5.10.08E
G-EUPB	Airbus A319-131	1115	D-AVYT	9.11.99	British Airways PLC	London Heathrow	8.11.07E
G-EUPC	Airbus A319-131	1118	D-AVYU	12.11.99	British Airways PLC	London Heathrow	11.11.07E
G-EUPD	Airbus A319-131	1142	D-AVWG	10.12.99	British Airways PLC	London Heathrow	9.12.07E
G-EUPE	Airbus A319-131	1193	D-AVYT	27. 3.00	British Airways PLC	London/Heathrow	26. 3.08E
G-EUPF	Airbus A319-131	1197	D-AVWS	30. 3.00	British Airways PLC	London Heathrow	29. 3.08E
G-EUPG	Airbus A319-131	1222	D-AVYG	25. 5.00	British Airways PLC	London Heathrow	24. 5.08E
G-EUPH	Airbus A319-131	1225	D-AVYK	23. 5.00	British Airways PLC	London Heathrow	22. 5.08E
G-EUPJ	Airbus A319-131	1232	D-AVYJ	30. 5.00	British Airways PLC	London Heathrow	29. 5.08E
G-EUPK	Airbus A319-131	1236	D-AVYO	30. 5.00	British Airways PLC	London Heathrow	29. 5.08E
G-EUPL	Airbus A319-131	1239	D-AVYP	8. 6.00	British Airways PLC	London Heathrow	7. 6.08E
G-EUPM	Airbus A319-131	1258	D-AVYR	30. 6.00	British Airways PLC	London Heathrow	29. 6.08E
G-EUPN	Airbus A319-131	1261	D-AVWA	10. 7.00	British Airways PLC	London Heathrow	9. 7.08E
G-EUPO	Airbus A319-131	1279	D-AVYU	1. 8.00	British Airways PLC	London Heathrow	31. 7.08E
					("Change for Good' titles)		
G-EUPP	Airbus A319-131	1295	D-AVWU	14. 8.00	British Airways PLC	London Heathrow	13. 8.08E
G-EUPR	Airbus A319-131	1329	D-AVYH	9.10.00	British Airways PLC	London Heathrow	8.10.07E
					("Change for Good' titles)		
G-EUPS	Airbus A319-131	1338	D-AVYM	23.10.00	British Airways PLC	London Heathrow	22.10.07E
G-EUPT	Airbus A319-131	1380	D-AVWH	5.12.00	British Airways PLC	London Heathrow	4.12.07E
G-EUPU	Airbus A319-131	1384	D-AVWP	14.12.00	British Airways PLC	London Heathrow	13.12.07E
G-EUPV	Airbus A319-131	1423	D-AVYE	13. 2.01	British Airways PLC	London Heathrow	12. 2.08E
G-EUPW	Airbus A319-131	1440	D-AVYP	6. 3.01	British Airways PLC	London Heathrow	5. 3.08E
G-EUPX	Airbus A319-131	1445	D-AVWB	14.12.01	British Airways PLC	London Heathrow	13.12.07E
G-EUPY	Airbus A319-131	1466	D-AVYK	12. 4.01	British Airways PLC	London Heathrow	11. 4.08E
G-EUPZ	Airbus A319-131	1510	D-AVYY	7. 6.01	British Airways PLC	London Heathrow	6. 6.08E
G-EURT	Eurocopter EC 155 B1	6764	G-EWAT	6. 6.07	William Ewart Properties Ltd	(Belfast)	30. 5.08E
			F-WWOO				
G-EURX	Europa Aviation Europa XS	482		15.12.00	C C Napier	(Newtownards)	
	(Built C C Napier - pr.no.PFA 247-13661) (Tri-gear u/c)						
G-EUSO	Robin DR.400-140 Major	904	F-BUSO	18. 9.03	Weald Air Services Ltd	Headcorn	3.12.07E
G-EUUA	Airbus A320-232	1661	F-WWIH	31. 1.02	British Airways PLC	London Heathrow	30. 1.08E
G-EUUB	Airbus A320-232	1689	F-WWBE	14. 2.02	British Airways PLC	London Heathrow	13. 2.08E
G-EUUC	Airbus A320-232	1696	F-WWIO	28. 2.02	British Airways PLC	London Heathrow	27. 2.08E
G-EUUD	Airbus A320-232	1760	F-WWBN	29. 4.02	British Airways PLC	London Heathrow	28. 4.08E
G-EUUE	Airbus A320-232	1782	F-WWDO	30. 5.02	British Airways PLC	London Heathrow	29. 5 08E
G-EUUF	Airbus A320-232	1814	F-WWIY	29. 7.02	British Airways PLC	London Heathrow	28. 7.08E
G-EUUG	Airbus A320-232	1829	F-WWIU	30. 8.02	British Airways PLC	London Heathrow	29. 8.08E
G-EUUH	Airbus A320-232	1665	F-WWIG	25.10.02	British Airways PLC	London Heathrow	24.10.07E
G-EUUI	Airbus A320-232	1871	F-WWBI	22.11.02	British Airways PLC	London Heathrow	21.11.07E
G-EUUJ	Airbus A320-232	1883	F-WWBQ	25.11.02	British Airways PLC	London Heathrow	24.11.07E
G-EUUK	Airbus A320-232	1899	F-WWDO	20.12.02	British Airways PLC	London Heathrow	19.12.07E
G-EUUL	Airbus A320-232	1708	F-WWIV	20.12.02	British Airways PLC	London Heathrow	19.12.07E
G-EUUM	Airbus A320-232	1907	F-WWDN	23.12.02	British Airways PLC	London Heathrow	22.12.07E
G-EUUN	Airbus A320-232	1910	F-WWDP	31. 1.03	British Airways PLC	London Heathrow	30. 1.08E
G-EUUO	Airbus A320-232	1958	F-WWIT	11. 4.03	British Airways PLC	London Heathrow	10. 4.08E
G-EUUP	Airbus A320-232	2038	F-WWDB	27. 6.03	British Airways PLC	London Heathrow	26. 6.08E
G-EUUR	Airbus A320-232	2040	F-WWID	29. 7.03	British Airways PLC	London Heathrow	28. 7.08E
G-EUUS	Airbus A320-232	3301	F-WWIF	5.12.07	British Airways PLC	London Heathrow	
G-EUUT	Airbus A320-232	3314	F-WWIT	12.12.07	British Airways PLC	London Heathrow	
G-EUUU	Airbus A320-232	3351	F-WW..	3.08R	British Airways PLC	London Heathrow	
G-EUUV	Airbus A320-232	3368	F-WW..	3.08R	British Airways PLC	London Heathrow	
G-EUUW	Airbus A320-232		F-WW..	4.08R	British Airways PLC	London Heathrow	
G-EUUX	Airbus A320-232		F-WW..	5.08R	British Airways PLC	London Heathrow	
G-EUUY	Airbus A320-232		F-WW..	9.08R	British Airways PLC	London Heathrow	
G-EUUZ	Airbus A320-232		F-WW..	10.08R	British Airways PLC	London Heathrow	
G-EUXC	Airbus A321-231	2305	D-AVZE	15.10.04	British Airways PLC	London Heathrow	14.10.07E
G-EUXD	Airbus A321-231	2320	D-AVZO	28.10.04	British Airways PLC	London Heathrow	27.10.07E
G-EUXE	Airbus A321-231	2323	D-AVZP	29.10.04	British Airways PLC	London Heathrow	28.10.07E
G-EUXF	Airbus A321-231	2324	D-AVZQ	4.11.04	British Airways PLC	London Heathrow	3.11.07E
G-EUXG	Airbus A321-231	2351	D-AVZU	2.12.04	British Airways PLC	London Heathrow	1.12.07E
G-EUXH	Airbus A321-231	2363	D-AVZW	17.12.04	British Airways PLC	London Heathrow	16.12.07E
G-EUXI	Airbus A321-231	2536	D-AVZE	5. 8.05	British Airways PLC	London Heathrow	4. 8.08E
G-EUXJ	Airbus A321-231	3081	D-AVZL	17. 4.07	British Airways PLC	London Heathrow	16. 4.08E
G-EUXK	Airbus A321-231	3235	D-AVZI	30. 8.07	British Airways PLC	London Heathrow	29. 8.08E
G-EUXL	Airbus A321-231	3254	D-AVZV	21. 9.07	British Airways PLC	London Heathrow	20. 9.08E
G-EUXM	Airbus A321-231	3290	D-AVZC	21.11.07	British Airways PLC	London Heathrow	
					(Delivered 23.11.07)		
G-EUYA	Airbus A321-232			.08R	British Airways PLC	London Heathrow	
G-EUYB	Airbus A321-232			.08R	British Airways PLC	London Heathrow	
G-EUYC	Airbus A321-232			.09R	British Airways PLC	London Heathrow	
G-EUYD	Airbus A321-232			.09R	British Airways PLC	London Heathrow	
G-EUYE	Airbus A321-232			.09R	British Airways PLC	London Heathrow	
G-EUYF	Airbus A321-232			.09R	British Airways PLC	London Heathrow	

Reg	Type	C/n	Prev id	Date	Owner/Operator	Location	Date
G-EUYG	Airbus A321-232			.09R	British Airways PLC	London Heathrow	
G-EUYH	Airbus A321-232			.10R	British Airways PLC	London Heathrow	
G-EUYI	Airbus A321-232			.10R	British Airways PLC	London Heathrow	
G-EUYJ	Airbus A321-232			.10R	British Airways PLC	London Heathrow	
G-EUYK	Airbus A321-232			.10R	British Airways PLC	London Heathrow	
G-EUYL	Airbus A321-232			.10R	British Airways PLC	London Heathrow	
G-EVAJ	Best Off Sky Ranger Swift 912S(1) SKRxxxx760			22. 2.07	A B Gridley	Sackville Lodge, Riseley	19.11.08P
	(Built A B Gridley - pr.no.BMAA/HB/526)						
G-EVBF	Cameron Z-350 Balloon (Hot Air)	10687		14. 3.05	Airxcite Ltd t/a Virgin Balloon Flights	Wembley	23. 8.08P
G-EVET	Cameron Concept 80 Balloon (Hot Air)	3703		30.10.95	L D and H Vaughan	Wilstone, Tring	30. 5.08A
G-EVEY	Thruster T 600N 450 Sprint	0121-T600N-057		22.11.01	K J Crompton	Newtownards	16.12.08P
G-EVIE	Piper PA-28-161 Warrior II	28-8316043	G-ZULU N4292X	31. 3.04	L Richardson	Dundee	26.10.07T
G-EVIG	Evektor EV-97 teamEurostar UK	2930		9. 3.07	A S Mitchell	Shobdon	8. 3.08E
G-EVII	Schempp-Hirth Ventus 2cT	10/41	BGA 4292-HXS	31.10.07	Active Aviation Ltd	(Urchfont, Devizes)	18. 3.08
G-EVLE	Rearwin 8125 Cloudster	803	G-BVLK N25403, NC25403	10. 4.03	M C Hiscock	Popham	15. 4.08P
G-EVLN	Gulfstream Aerospace Gulfstream G-IV	1175	N18WF VH-CCA, (N1175B), HB-ITJ, N17588	3. 6.02	Metropix Ltd	(London EC4)	5. 9.08E
G-EVPI	Evans VP-1 Series 2 PFA 062-13136			10. 4.03	C P Martyr (Horsted Keynes, Haywards Heath)		21. 3.08P
	(Built C P Martyr) (Volkswagen 1834)						
G-EVRD	Beech 390 Premier 1	RB-172	N7102U	25. 4.07	Commercial Aviation Charters Ltd	(London W1)	25. 4.08E
G-EVRO	Evektor EV-97 Eurostar PFA 315-14137			30. 1.04	J G McMinn	(Lisburn)	9. 1.08P
	(Built R I and D Blain)						
G-EVTO	Piper PA-28-161 Warrior II	28-8016271	N5012V G-EVTO, D-EVTO, N81615	12. 7.05	Redhill Air Services Ltd	Redhill	31. 5.08E
G-EWAN	Protech PT-2C-160 Prostar PFA 249-12425			23. 6.93	C G Shaw	Truleigh Manor Farm, Edburton	15. 3.08P
	(Built C G Shaw) (Lycoming O-320-B2B)						
G-EWAW	Bell 206B-3 JetRanger III	3955	G-DORB SE-HTI, TC-HBN	25. 7.03	D Seymour Ayton Hall, great Ayton, Middlesborough		6. 3.08E
G-EWBC	Avtech Jabiru SK	0249		3.11.00	E W B Comber	White Fen Farm, Ely	3.10.08P
	(Built E W B Comber - pr.no.PFA 274-13457)						
G-EWES	Alpi Pioneer 300	7		24.11.04	R Y Kendal and D A Ions	Morgansfield, Fishburn	12. 6.07P
	(Built R Y Kendal and D A Ions - pr.no.PFA 330-14322)						
G-EWEW	AB Sportine Aviacija LAK-19T	024	BGA 5241-KNZ LY-GNC	22. 5.07	G Paul "KNZ" & "EW2"	Dunstable	21. 5.08
G-EWHT	Robin R2112 Alpha	371		4. 5.04	Ewan Ltd (Operated Cotswold Aero Club)	Gloucestershire	4. 6.08E
G-EWIZ	Pitts S-2S	S18	VH-EHQ	12.11.82	G R J Caunter	Popham	13. 3.08P
	(Built H M Shelvey) (Lycoming AEIO-540)						
G-EWME	Piper PA-28-235 Cherokee Pathfinder 28-7310156		D-EECN N55766	24. 9.04	C J Mewis and E S Ewen	Oaksey Park	29. 9.07E
G-EWRT	Eurocopter EC.135 T2	0347	D-HECF	6.12.04	Eurocopter UK Ltd	Oxford	2. 3.08E
G-EXAM	Piper PA-28RT-201T Turbo Arrow IV 28R-8431003		N45AW N43230	25. 5.05	H S Urquhart t/a Zwetsloot	Inverness	16. 6.08E
G-EXEA	Extra EA.300/L	082		9. 3.99	P J Lawton	Blackbushe	3.11.07E
G-EXEC	Piper PA-34-200 Seneca	34-7450072	(G-EXXC) OY-BGU	11. 5.78	Sky Air Travel Ltd	Stapleford	31. 3.08E
G-EXES	Europa Aviation Europa XS	578		25. 4.03	D Barraclough	Morgansfield, Fishburn	31. 8.08P
	(Built D Barraclough - pr.no.PFA 247-13574)						
G-EXEX	Cessna 404 Titan	404-0037	SE-GZF (N5418G)	3. 5.79	Reconnaissance Ventures Ltd	Lydd	29. 7.08E
	(Coastguard titles, red and white c/s with MCA logo on tail)						
G-EXIT	SOCATA MS.893E Rallye 180GT	12979	F-GARX	22. 9.78	M A Baldwin tr G-EXIT Group Maypole Farm, Chislet		26. 6.08E
G-EXLL	Zenair CH.601XL Zodiac PFA 162B-14205			4. 3.04	B McFadden Mount Airey Farm, South Cave		20. 8.08P
	(Built B McFadden, B Gardner and R Fox) (Tri-cycle u/c)						
G-EXON	Piper PA-28-161 Cadet	2841283	G-EGLD N92007	9.12.03	Plane Talking Ltd	Elstree	26. 1.08E
G-EXPD	Stemme S 10-VT	11-063		5. 7.01	Global Gliding Expeditions Ltd	Rhosgoch	8. 9.07
	(Rotax 914)						
G-EXPL	American Champion 7GCBC Explorer 1220-96			9. 5.96	E J F McEntee	Kirdford	15. 6.08E
G-EXPS	Short SD.3-60 Variant 100	SH3661	EI-SMB	11. 5.99	BAC Group Ltd	Kassel, Hessen, Germany	20. 2.08E
	G-EXPS, TC-AOA, G-BLRT, SE-KRV, G-BLRT, G-14-3661 (BAC Express c/s) "City of Exeter".						
G-EXTR	Extra EA.260	004	D-EDID	10. 8.92	S J Carver	Netherthorpe	28. 3.08P
G-EXXO	Piper PA-28-161 Cadet	2841210	G-CBXP N117ND	22. 1.04	S J Skilton t/a Aviation Rentals	(Lee-on-Solent)	2.12.07E
G-EYAK	Yakovlev Yak-50	801804	RA-01193 DOSAAF?	19. 2.03	P N A Whitehead	Leicester	26. 4.08P
G-EYAS	Denney Kitfox Model 2 PFA 172-11858			3. 3.93	R E Hughes	(Lyme Regis)	7. 9.07P
	(Built E J Young)						
G-EYCO	Robin DR.400-180 Régent	1949		12. 3.90	S J York	Bagby	28. 4.08E
G-EYES	Cessna 402C II	402C0008	SE-IRU G-BLCE, N4648N	16. 7.90	Reconnaissance Ventures Ltd	Coventry	15. 8.08E
	("Air Atlantique" on engine nacelles)						
G-EYNL	MBB BÖ.105DBS-5	S 382	D-HDLR, EC-DSO, D-HDLR	19. 8.96	Sterling Helicopters Ltd	Norwich	11.12.07E
	(Operated East Anglian Air Ambulance)						
G-EYOR	Van's RV-6 PFA 181A-13259			15.10.99	S I Fraser	Henstridge	29. 2.08P
	(Built S I Fraser) (Lycoming O-320)						
G-EYRE	Bell 206L-1 LongRanger	45229	G-STVI N60MA, N5019K	12.11.90	Cardy Construction Ltd	Manston	11. 2.08E
G-EZAA	Airbus A319-111	2677	D-AVYU	10. 2.06	EasyJet Airline Company Ltd	Bristol	9 .2.08E
G-EZAB	Airbus A319-111	2681	D-AVYY	.6. 2.06	EasyJet Airline Company Ltd	London Stansted	5 .2.08E
G-EZAC	Airbus A319-111	2691	D-AVXB	16. 2..06	EasyJet Airline Company Ltd	Bristol	15 .2.08E
G-EZAD	Airbus A319-111	2702	D-AVXI	28. 2.06	EasyJet Airline Company Ltd	London Stansted	27 .2.08E
G-EZAE	Airbus A319-111	2709	D-AVYI	9. 3.06	EasyJet Airline Company Ltd	MIlan, Italy	8 .3.08E
G-EZAF	Airbus A319-111	2715	D-AVYT	16. 3.06	EasyJet Airline Company Ltd	London Stansted	15 .3.08E

G-EZAG	Airbus A319-111	2727	D-AVXG	29. 3.06	EasyJet Airline Company Ltd	Bristol	28 .3.08E
G-EZAH	Airbus A319-111	2729	D-AVXK	30. 3.06	EasyJet Airline Company Ltd	Dortmund, Germany	29 .3.08E
G-EZAI	Airbus A319-111	2735	D-AVXM.	6. 4.06	EasyJet Airline Company Ltd	Liverpool	5 .4.08E
G-EZAJ	Airbus A319-111	2742	D-AVXP	13. 4.06	EasyJet Airline Company Ltd	London Stansted	12. 4.08E
G-EZAK	Airbus A319-111	2744	D-AVXQ	20. 4.06	EasyJet Airline Company Ltd	Milan, Italy	19,4.08E
G-EZAL	Airbus A319-111	2754	D-AVWG	27. 4.06	EasyJet Airline Company Ltd	London Gatwick	26. 4.08E
G-EZAM	Airbus A319-111	2037	HB-JZA	14. 9.04	EasyJet Airline Company Ltd	London Gatwick	15. 8.08E
			G-CCKA, D-AVYS				
G-EZAN	Airbus A319-111	2765	D-AVWL	4.05.06	EasyJet Airline Company Ltd	London Gatwick	3. 5.08E
G-EZAO	Airbus A319-111	2769	D-AVWO	9. 5.06	EasyJet Airline Company Ltd	Glasgow	8. 5.08E
G-EZAP	Airbus A319-111	2777	D-AVYG	16. 5.06	EasyJet Airline Company Ltd	London Gatwick	15. 5.08E
G-EZAR	Mainair Sports Pegasus Quik	7942		18. 3.03	I B Smith and P Thompson	Bakersfield	27. 4.08P
G-EZAS	Airbus A319-111	2779	D-AVYH	.24. 5.06	EasyJet Airline Company Ltd	Edinburgh	23. 5.08E
G-EZAT	Airbus A319-111	2782	D-AVYO	1. 6.06	EasyJet Airline Company Ltd	Glasgow	31. 5.08E
G-EZAU	Airbus A319-111	2795	D-AVWQ	9. 6.06	EasyJet Airline Company Ltd	London Gatwick	8. 6.08E
G-EZAV	Airbus A319-111	2803	D-AVWV	22. 6.06	EasyJet Airline Company Ltd	London Gatwick	21. 6.08E
G-EZAW	Airbus A319-111	2812	D-AVYU	4. 7.06	EasyJet Airline Company Ltd	London Gatwick	3. 7.08E
G-EZAX	Airbus A319-111	2818	D-AVXA	6. 7.06	EasyJet Airline Company Ltd	Glasgow	5. 7.08E
G-EZAY	Airbus A319-111	2827	D-AVXE	12. 7.06	EasyJet Airline Company Ltd	Liverpool	11. 7.08E
G-EZAZ	Airbus A319-111	2829	D-AVXF	20. 7.06	EasyJet Airline Company Ltd	Bristol	19. 7.08E
G-EZBA	Airbus A319-111	2860	D-AVWB	18. 8.06	EasyJet Airline Company Ltd	London Gatwick	17. 8.08E
G-EZBB	Airbus A319-111	2854	D-AVXM	9. 8.06	EasyJet Airline Company Ltd	Liverpool	8. 8.08E
G-EZBC	Airbus A319-111	2866	D-AVWD	5. 9.06	EasyJet Airline Company Ltd	London Gatwick	4. 9.08E
G-EZBD	Airbus A319-111	2873	D-AVWK	13. 9.06	EasyJet Airline Company Ltd	London Gatwick	12 .9.08E
G-EZBE	Airbus A319-111	2884	D-AVXO	28.11.06	EasyJet Airline Company Ltd	Liverpool	15. 8.08E
G-EZBF	Airbus A319-111	2923	D-AVYK	2.11.06	EasyJet Airline Company Ltd	London Gatwick	11. 7.08E
G-EZBG	Airbus A319-111	2946	D-AVXA	24.11.06	EasyJet Airline Company Ltd	Liverpool	21. 8.08E
G-EZBH	Airbus A319-111	2959	D-AVYH	15.12.06	EasyJet Airline Company Ltd	Luton	14.12.07E
G-EZBI	Airbus A319-111	3003	D-AVYB	6. 2.07	EasyJet Airline Company Ltd *"Madrid"*	Luton	5. 2.08E
G-EZBJ	Airbus A319-111	3036	D-AVWJ	21. 2.07	EasyJet Airline Company Ltd	Bristol	20. 2.08E
G-EZBK	Airbus A319-111	3041	D-AVWK	22. 2.07	EasyJet Airline Company Ltd	Berlin, Germany	21. 2.08E
G-EZBL	Airbus A319-111	3053	D-AVYJ	14. 3.07	EasyJet Airline Company Ltd	Berlin, Germany	13. 3.08E
G-EZBM	Airbus A319-111	3059	D-AVWE	22. 3.07	EasyJet Airline Company Ltd	Luton	21. 3.08E
G-EZBN	Airbus A319-111	3061	D-AVWH	23. 3.07	EasyJet Airline Company Ltd	Geneva, Switzerland	22. 3.08E
G-EZBO	Airbus A319-111	3082	D-AVYK	4. 4.07	EasyJet Airline Company Ltd	London Gatwick	3. 4.08E
G-EZBP	Airbus A319-111	3084	D-AVYP	11. 4.07	EasyJet Airline Company Ltd	London Stansted	10. 4.08E
G-EZBR	Airbus A319-111	3088	D-AVYY	26. 4.07	EasyJet Airline Company Ltd	Berlin, Germany	25. 4.08E
G-EZBT	Airbus A319-111	3090	D-AVWM	27. 4.07	EasyJet Airline Company Ltd	London Stansted	26. 4.08E
G-EZBU	Airbus A319-111	3118	D-AVWW	14. 5.07	EasyJet Airline Company Ltd	London Gatwick	13. 5.08E
G-EZBV	Airbus A319-111	3122	D-AVWX	23. 5.07	EasyJet Airline Company Ltd	Bristol	22. 5.08E
G-EZBW	Airbus A319-111	3134	D-AVXE	5. 6.07	EasyJet Airline Company Ltd	London Stansted	5. 6.08E
G-EZBX	Airbus A319-111	3137	D-AVXH	15. 6.07	EasyJet Airline Company Ltd	London Gatwick	14. 6.08E
G-EZBY	Airbus A319-111	3176	D-AVXJ	11. 7.07	EasyJet Airline Company Ltd	Milan, Italy	10. 7.08E
G-EZBZ	Airbus A319-111	3184	D-AVYF	13. 7.07	EasyJet Airline Company Ltd	London Stansted	12. 7.08E
G-EZDA	Airbus A319-111	3413	D-AVYH	21. 2.08	EasyJet Airline Company Ltd	London Gatwick	
G-EZDB	Airbus A319-111	3411	D-AVYF	20. 2.08	EasyJet Airline Company Ltd	Berlin, Germany	
G-EZDC	Airbus A319-111	2043	HB-JZB	20. 9.04	EasyJet Airline Company Ltd	Liverpool	7. 8.08E
			G-CCKB, D-AVYU				
G-EZDD	Airbus A319-111	3442	D-AV..	3.08R	EasyJet Airline Company Ltd		
G-EZDE	Airbus A319-111	3426	D-AVYP	3.08R	EasyJet Airline Company Ltd		
G-EZDF	Airbus A319-111	3432	D-AV..	3.08R	EasyJet Airline Company Ltd		
G-EZDG	Rutan VariEze	002	G-EZOS	1.11.05	D M Gale	Henstridge	4.11.08P
	(Built O Smith - pr.no.PFA 074-10221) (Continental O-200-A)						
G-EZDH	Airbus A319-111	3466	D-AV..	3.08R	EasyJet Airline Company Ltd		
G-EZDI	Airbus A319-111	3537	D-AV..	3.08R	EasyJet Airline Company Ltd		
G-EZDJ	Airbus A319-111	3544	D-AV..	3.08R	EasyJet Airline Company Ltd		
G-EZEA	Airbus A319-111	2119	D-AVWZ	18. 2.04	EasyJet Airline Company Ltd	London Stansted	17. 2.07T
G-EZEB	Airbus A319-111	2120	D-AVYK	25. 3.04	EasyJet Airline Company Ltd	London Stansted	24. 3.08E
G-EZEC	Airbus A319-111	2129	D-AVWR	19. 3.04	EasyJet Airline Company Ltd	London Stansted	18. 3.07T
G-EZED	Airbus A319-111	2170	D-AVWT	7. 4.04	EasyJet Airline Company Ltd	Liverpool	6. 4.08E
G-EZEF	Airbus A319-111	2176	D-AVYS	19. 3.04	EasyJet Airline Company Ltd	London Stansted	15. 3.07T
G-EZEG	Airbus A319-111	2181	D-AVWF	1. 4.04	EasyJet Airline Company Ltd	London Stansted	31 .3.08E
G-EZEJ	Airbus A319-111	2214	D-AVYO	5. 5.04	EasyJet Airline Company Ltd	Liverpool	4. 5.08E
G-EZEK	Airbus A319-111	2224	D-AVYZ	6. 5.04	EasyJet Airline Company Ltd	London Stansted	5. 5.08E
G-EZEL	Westland SA.341G Gazelle 1	1073	(F-GIVQ)	1.12.00	W R Pitcher/Regal Group UK	Leatherhead	30. 4.08E
			I-ATOM, F-BXPG, G-BAZL				
G-EZEO	Airbus A319-111	2249	D-AVYN	17. 6.04	EasyJet Airline Company Ltd	London Stansted	16. 6.08E
G-EZEP	Airbus A319-111	2251	D-AVYQ	1. 7.04	EasyJet Airline Company Ltd	London Stansted	30. 6.08E
G-EZER	Cameron H-34 Balloon (Hot Air)	2366	LX-ROM	31.10.02	D P Tuck	Hinton Charterhouse, Bath	11. 8.06E
G-EZET	Airbus A319-111	2271	D-AVWY	11. 8.04	EasyJet Airline Company Ltd	London Stansted	10. 8.08E
G-EZEU	Airbus A319-111	2283	D-AVYP	5.10.04	EasyJet Airline Company Ltd	London Stansted	4.10.08E
G-EZEV	Airbus A319-111	2289	D-AVYV	9. 9.04	EasyJet Airline Company Ltd	London Stansted	8. 9.08E
G-EZEW	Airbus A319-111	2300	D-AVWH	15.10.04	EasyJet Airline Company Ltd	London Stansted	17. 9.08E
G-EZEZ	Airbus A319-111	2360	D-AVWP	9.12.04	EasyJet Airline Company Ltd	London Stansted	25. 9.08E
G-EZIA	Airbus A319-111	2420	D-AVYL	18. 3.05	EasyJet Airline Company Ltd	London Stansted	17. 3.08E
G-EZIC	Airbus A319-111	2436	D-AVWC	7. 4.05	EasyJet Airline Company Ltd	London Stansted	6. 4.08E
G-EZID	Airbus A319-111	2442	D-AVWT	14. 4.05	EasyJet Airline Company Ltd *(100 titles)*	Liverpool	13. 4.08E
G-EZIE	Airbus A319-111	2446	D-AVWQ	18. 4.05	EasyJet Airline Company Ltd	London Stansted	17. 4.08E
G-EZIG	Airbus A319-111	2460	D-AVYM	3. 5.05	EasyJet Airline Company Ltd	London Stansted	2. 5.08E
G-EZIH	Airbus A319-111	2463	D-AVWV	9. 5.05	EasyJet Airline Company Ltd	London Stansted	8. 5.08E
G-EZII	Airbus A319-111	2471	D-AVYK	25. 5.05	EasyJet Airline Company Ltd	Liverpool	24. 5.08E
G-EZIJ	Airbus A319-111	2477	D-AVYU	2. 6.05	EasyJet Airline Company Ltd	London Stansted	1. 6.08E
G-EZIK	Airbus A319-111	2481	D-AVYV	31. 5.05	EasyJet Airline Company Ltd	London Stansted	30. 5.08E
G-EZIL	Airbus A319-111	2492	D-AVWM	15. 6.05	EasyJet Airline Company Ltd	London Stansted	14. 6.08E

G-EZIM	Airbus A319-111	2495	D-AVYO	17. 6.05	EasyJet Airline Company Ltd	London Stansted	16. 6.08E
G-EZIN	Airbus A319-111	2503	D-AVYZ	28. 6.05	EasyJet Airline Company Ltd	London Stansted	27. 6.08E
G-EZIO	Airbus A319-111	2512	D-AVWP	7. 7.05	EasyJet Airline Company Ltd	London Stansted	6. 7.08E
G-EZIP	Airbus A319-111	2514	D-AVWQ	12. 7.05	EasyJet Airline Company Ltd	London Stansted	11. 7.08E
G-EZIR	Airbus A319-111	2527	D-AVWK	27. 7.05	EasyJet Airline Company Ltd	London Stansted	26. 7.08E
G-EZIS	Airbus A319-111	2528	D-AVWJ	2. 8.05	EasyJet Airline Company Ltd	Liverpool	1. 8.08E
G-EZIT	Airbus A319-111	2538	D-AVYN	11. 8.05	EasyJet Airline Company Ltd	Liverpool	10. 8.08E
G-EZIU	Airbus A319-111	2548	D-AVYF	1. 9.05	EasyJet Airline Company Ltd	London Stansted	31. 8.08E
G-EZIV	Airbus A319-111	2565	D-AVYY	4.10.05	EasyJet Airline Company Ltd	London Stansted	20. 9.08E
G-EZIW	Airbus A319-111	2578	D-AVXE	17.10.05	EasyJet Airline Company Ltd	London Stansted	9. 7.08E
G-EZIX	Airbus A319-111	2605	D-AVXP	17.11.05	EasyJet Airline Company Ltd	London Stansted	25. 9.08E
G-EZIY	Airbus A319-111	2636	D-AVWH	15.12.05	EasyJet Airline Company Ltd	Liverpool	14.12.07E
G-EZIZ	Airbus A319-111	2646	D-AVWQ	12. 1.06	EasyJet Airline Company Ltd	London Stansted	11. 1.08E
G-EZJA	Boeing 737-73V	30235		13.10.00	EasyJet Airline Company Ltd	Luton	24. 9.08E
G-EZJB	Boeing 737-73V	30236	N1787B	22.11.00	EasyJet Airline Company Ltd	Luton	19. 9.08E
G-EZJC	Boeing 737-73V	30237		15.12.00	EasyJet Airline Company Ltd	Luton	13.12.07E
G-EZJF	Boeing 737-73V	30243		15. 8.01	EasyJet Airline Company Ltd	Luton	14. 8.08E
G-EZJG	Boeing 737-73V	30239		28. 9.01	EasyJet Airline Company Ltd	Luton	30. 8.08E
G-EZJH	Boeing 737-73V	30240		15.10.01	EasyJet Airline Company Ltd	Luton	19. 9.08E
G-EZJI	Boeing 737-73V	30241		20.12.01	EasyJet Airline Company Ltd	Luton	19.12.07E
G-EZJJ	Boeing 737-73V	30245		30. 1.02	EasyJet Airline Company Ltd	Luton	29.1.08E
G-EZJK	Boeing 737-73V	30246		7. 2.02	EasyJet Airline Company Ltd	Luton	6. 2.08E
G-EZJL	Boeing 737-73V	30247		12. 2.02	EasyJet Airline Company Ltd	Luton	11. 2.08E
G-EZJM	Boeing 737-73V	30248		24. 4.02	EasyJet Airline Company Ltd	Luton	23. 4.08E
G-EZJN	Boeing 737-73V	30249		8. 5.02	EasyJet Airline Company Ltd	Luton	7. 5.08E
G-EZJO	Boeing 737-73V	30244		6. 6.02	EasyJet Airline Company Ltd	Luton	5. 6.08E
G-EZJP	Boeing 737-73V	32412		11. 6.02	EasyJet Airline Company Ltd	Luton	10. 6.08E
G-EZJR	Boeing 737-73V	32413		20. 8.02	EasyJet Airline Company Ltd	Luton	19. 8.08E
G-EZJS	Boeing 737-73V	32414		23. 9.02	EasyJet Airline Company Ltd	Luton	20. 9.08E
G-EZJT	Boeing 737-73V	32415		19.12.02	EasyJet Airline Company Ltd	Luton	18.12.07E
G-EZJU	Boeing 737-73V	32416	N6046P	21.12.02	EasyJet Airline Company Ltd	Luton	20. 2.08E
G-EZJV	Boeing 737-73V	32417		3. 3.03	EasyJet Airline Company Ltd	Luton	2. 3.08E
G-EZJW	Boeing 737-73V	32418		28. 3.03	EasyJet Airline Company Ltd	Luton	27. 3.08E
G-EZJX	Boeing 737-73V	32419	N1787B	12. 5.03	EasyJet Airline Company Ltd	Luton	11. 5.08E
G-EZJY	Boeing 737-73V	32420		27. 6.03	EazyJet Airline Company Ltd	Luton	26. 6.08E
G-EZJZ	Boeing 737-73V	32421		31. 7.03	EasyJet Airline Company Ltd *"Ray Webstaer"*	Luton	30. 7.08E
G-EZKA	Boeing 737-73V	32422	(G-ESYA)	12. 8.03	EasyJet Airline Company Ltd	Luton	12. 8.08E
G-EZKB	Boeing 737-73V	32423	(G-ESYB)	21. 1.04	EasyJet Airline Company Ltd	Luton	20. 1.07T
G-EZKC	Boeing 737-73V	32424	(G-ESYC)	12. 2.04	EasyJet Airline Company Ltd	Luton	11. 2.07T
G-EZKD	Boeing 737-73V	32425	N1787B	13. 2.04	EasyJet Airline Company Ltd	Luton	12. 2.07T
G-EZKE	Boeing 737-73V	32426	(G-ESYE)	30. 3.04	EasyJet Airline Company Ltd *"Daniel Swaddle"*	Luton	29. 3.08E
G-EZKF	Boeing 737-73V	32427	(G-ESYF)	22. 4.04	EasyJet Airline Company Ltd	Luton	21. 4.07T
G-EZKG	Boeing 737-73V	32428	(G-ESYG)	27. 5.04	EasyJet Airline Company Ltd	Luton	26. 5.07T
G-EZMH	Airbus A319-111	2053	HB-JZD G-CCKD, D-AVYB	24. 9.04	EasyJet Airline Company Ltd	Liverpool	23. 9.07T
G-EZMS	Airbus A319-111	2378	D-AVWS	21. 1.05	EasyJet Airline Company Ltd	Liverpool	20. 1.08E
G-EZNC	Airbus A319-111	2050	HB-JZC G-CCKC, D-AVWF	22. 9.04	EasyJet Airline Company Ltd	London Stansted	17. 9.08E
G-EZNM	Airbus A319-111	2402	D-AVWH	1. 3.05	EasyJet Airline Company Ltd	London Stansted	28. 2.08E
G-EZPG	Airbus A319-111	2385	D-AVYD	15. 2.05	EasyJet Airline Company Ltd	London Stansted	14. 2.06E
G-EZPZ	American Champion 8KCAB Super Decathlon 981-2005			24. 2.05	Decathlon Aviation Ltd	Kemble	7. 7.08E
G-EZSM	Airbus A319-111	2062	HB-JZE G-CCKE, D-AVYD	8.10.04	EasyJet Airline Company Ltd	London Stansted	19. 8.08E
G-EZUB	Zenair CH.601HD Zodiac (Built R A C Stephens)	PFA 162-12765		13. 9.04	R A C Stephens	(Billingshurst)	
G-EZVS	Colt 77B Balloon (Hot Air)	063	SE-ZVS	6. 7.04	A J Lovell	Goteborg, Sweden	17. 2.08A
G-EZXO	Colt 56A Balloon (Hot Air)	421	SE-ZXO	6. 7.04	A J Lovell	Goteborg, Sweden	17. 2.07A
G-EZYU	Piper PA-34-200 Seneca	34-7450110	G-BCDB N41346	4. 7.01	G F Strain	Bournemouth	3.10.07E
G-EZZA	Europa Aviation Europa XS	537		10. 5.02	J C R Davey	(Bicester)	
	(Built J C R Davey - pr.no.PFA 247-13841) (Rotax 914) (Monowheel u/c)						
G-EZZY	Evektor EV-97 Eurostar (Built G Verity)	PFA 315-14533		1. 8.06	G and P M G Verity	Newton Bank, Daresbury	3. 4.08P

G-FAAA - G-FZZZ

G-FABB	Cameron V-77 Balloon (Hot Air)	822	LX-FAB	13.12.89	P Trumper	Axminster	18. 9.07T
G-FABI	Robinson R44 Astro	0325		5. 4.97	R C Hields t/a Hields Aviation	Sherburn in Elmet	12. 5.08T
G-FABM	Beech 95-B55A Baron	TC-2259	G-JOND G-BMVC, N66456	22. 2.91	P E T Price, J E Balmer and F B Miles (Cirencester, Upton-upon-Severn and Hereford)		10. 9.08E
G-FABS	Thunder Ax9-120 Series 2 Balloon (Hot Air) 2399			8. 6.93	R C Corrall (New owner 4.04)	Cretingham, Woodbridge	19.10.02T
G-FACE	Cessna 172S Skyhawk SP	172S9194	N52733	24.10.02	M O Loxton	Parsonage Farm, Eastchurch	28.10.07E
G-FAIR	SOCATA TB-10 Tobago	241		13.10.81	Fairwings Ltd	Stapleford	16. 8.08E
G-FAJC	Alpi Pioneer 300 Hawk (Built F A Cavaciuti - PFA 330A-14639)	xxx		19. 4.07	F A Cavaciuti	Shobdon	6. 6.08P
G-FAKE	Robinson R44 Raven II	10908		18.10.05	P R Holloway	(Southam)	3.11.07E
G-FALC	Aeromere F 8L Falco 3	224	G-AROT	19. 2.81	D M Burbridge	Enstone	19. 6.08E
G-FALO	Sequoia F 8L Falco	1401		10. 5.02	M J and S E Aherne	(Smallford, St Albans)	
G-FAME	CFM Starstreak Shadow SA-II (Built T J Palmer - pr.no.PFA 206A-12973) (Jabiru 2200)	K 273-SA		23. 5.96	B Hawley (New owner 5.07)	(Headington, Oxford)	20.11.04P
G-FAMH	Zenair CH.701 STOL (Built A M Harrhy) (Jabiru 2200A)	PFA 187-13301		26. 6.98	G T Neale	Croft Farm, Defford	26. 9.08P

Reg	Type	C/n	Prev id	Date	Owner/Operator	Location	Date
G-FANL	Cessna R172K Hawk XP	R1722873	N736XQ	7. 6.79	J A Rees	Haverfordwest	6. 7.06T
					(Operated Haverfordwest Air Charter Services)		
G-FANY	Bell 206L-1 LongRanger	45368	G-CCUG	2. 9.05	MB Air Ltd t/a Eagle Helicopters		
			N18UG, N18UC, N13UC, N48ZP, N1075T			Newcastle City Heliport	1. 3.08E
G-FARE	Robinson R44 Raven II	10454		16. 8.04	Toriamos Ltd	(Harolds Cross, Dublin)	7.10.07E
G-FARL	Pitts S-1E	1	N333AB	22.10.03	F L McGee	Liverpool	13. 6.08P
	(Built S C Burgess)				*(Carries "N333AB" also)*		
G-FARM	SOCATA Rallye 235E	12832	F-GARF	10.10.78	Bristol Cars Ltd *(On rebuild 7.06)*	Biggin Hill	27. 6.04
G-FARO	Star-Lite SL-1	PFA 175-11359		19. 6.89	M K Faro	Henstridge	18.11.08P
	(Built M K Faro) (Rotax 447)						
G-FARR	SAN Jodel D 150 Mascaret	58	F-BNIN	21. 7.81	G H Farr	Dairy House Farm, Worleston	19. 5.08P
G-FARY	QAC Quickie Tri-Q	PFA 094A-10951		2. 4.02	F Sayyah	Enstone	15. 6.07P
	(Built J C Simpson and F Sayyah) (Limbach L2000)						
G-FATB	Commander Aircraft Commander 114B	14624	N6037Y	3. 7.96	James D Peace and Co	(Kirkwall)	28. 9.08E
G-FAUX	Cessna 182S Skylane	18280190	D-EWEI	4.12.03	R S Faux	Southend	18. 3.08E
G-FAVC	de Havilland DH.80A Puss Moth	DHC.225	CF-AVC	21.11.03	Liddell Aircraft Ltd	Bournemouth	
	(Built de Havilland Canada)				*(Noted 6.07)*		
G-FBAT	Aeroprakt A22 Foxbat	PFA 317-13591		16. 5.00	J Jordan	Otherton, Cannock	4. 5.08P
	(Built G Faulkner) (Rotax 912-S)						
G-FBEA	Embraer ERJ 190-200 LR	19000029	PT-SGD	1. 9.06	Flybe Ltd	Exeter	31. 8.08E
	(Embraer 195)				*"Wings Of The Community"*		
G-FBEB	Embraer ERJ 190-200 LR	19000057	PT-SII	1.12.06	Flybe Ltd	Exeter	4.12.07E
	(Embraer 195)						
G-FBEC	Embraer ERJ 190-200 LR	19000069	PT-SJI	23. 3.07	Flybe Ltd	Exeter	25. 3.08E
	(Embraer 195)						
G-FBED	Embraer ERJ 190-200 LR	19000084	PT-SNB	4. 6.07	Flybe Ltd	Exeter	6. 6.08E
	(Embraer 195)						
G-FBEE	Embraer ERJ 190-200 LR	19000093	PT-SNN	26. 7.07	Flybe Ltd	Exeter	29. 7.08E
	(Embraer 195)						
G-FBEF	Embraer ERJ 190-200 LR	19000104	PT-SNY	6. 9.07	Flybe Ltd	Exeter	9. 9.08E
	(Embraer 195)						
G-FBEG	Embraer ERJ 190-200 LR	19000120	PT-SQO	1.11.07	Flybe Ltd	Exeter	
	(Embraer 195)				*(Delivered 4.11.07)*		
G-FBEH	Embraer ERJ 190-200 LR	19000128	PT-SQX	23.11.07	Flybe Ltd	Exeter	
	(Embraer 195)				*(Delivered 26.11.07)*		
G-FBEI	Embraer ERJ 190-200 LR	19000143	PT-SYV	10. 1.08	Flybe Ltd	Exeter	
	(Embraer 195)				*(Delivered 14. 1.08)*		
G-FBEJ	Embraer ERJ 190-200 LR	19000150	PT-SAD	.08R	Flybe Ltd	Exeter	
	(Embraer 195)						
G-FBEK	Embraer ERJ 190-200 LR	190000xx	PT-	.08R	Flybe Ltd	Exeter	
	(Embraer 195)						
G-FBEL	Embraer ERJ 190-200 LR	190000xx	PT-	.08R	Flybe Ltd	Exeter	
	(Embraer 195)						
G-FBEM	Embraer ERJ 190-200 LR	190000xx	PT-	.08R	Flybe Ltd	Exeter	
	(Embraer 195)						
G-FBEN	Embraer ERJ 190-200 LR	190000xx	PT-	.08R	Flybe Ltd	Exeter	
	(Embraer 195)						
G-FBII	Comco Ikarus C42 FB100	0310-6574		18.12.03	F Beeson	(Nantwich)	19.12.07P
G-FBMW	Cameron N-90 Balloon (Hot Air)	3019		23. 4.93	K-J Schwer	Erbach-Donaurieden, Germany	10. 9.05A
G-FBOY	Skystar Kitfox Mk.7	PFA 172D-14696		12. 9.07	A Bray	(Brinklow, Rugby)	
	(Built A Bray)						
G-FBPI	Air Navigation and Engineering Co ANEC IV Missel Thrush			19. 1.99	R Trickett	Pendeford, Wolverhampton	
	(Built R Trickett)	PFA 312-13417			*(On loan to Boulton Paul Heritage Project)*		
G-FBRN	Piper PA-28-181 Archer II	28-8290166	D-ERBN	3. 8.98	Herefordshire Aero Club Ltd	Shobdon	28.10.07E
			N82628				
G-FBTT	Aeroprakt A22-L Foxbat	PFA 317A-14743		8. 1.08	G C Ellis	RAF Honington	
	(Built G C Ellis)						
G-FBWH	Piper PA-28R-180 Cherokee Arrow	28R-30368	SE-FCV	23. 8.78	F T Short	Whaley Farm, New York, Lincoln	6. 5.08E
G-FCAB	Diamond DA.42 Twin Star	42.060	OE-VPI	25.10.05	Halfpenny Green Flight Centre Ltd	Halfpenny Green	15.11.08E
G-FCBI	Schweizer 269C-1	0296	N86G	10. 7.07	Oxford Aviation Services Ltd	Oxford	
	(Schweizer 300)				*(Noted 12.07)*		
G-FCDB	Cessna 550 Citation Bravo	550-0985	N5269J	10. 9.01	Eurojet Aviation Ltd	Belfast International	9. 9.08E
G-FCED	Piper PA-31T2 Cheyenne IIXL	31T-8166013	C-FCED	27. 9.04	Air Medical Fleet Ltd	Oxford	8. 2.08E
			N2501Y				
G-FCKD	Eurocopter EC.120B Colibri	1209	PH-ECK	11. 1.06	Heli-Banners Ltd	Denham	16. 2.08E
			ZK-HJD, ZK-HVQ				
G-FCLA	Boeing 757-28A	27621	N1789B	26. 2.97	Thomas Cook Airlines UK Ltd	Manchester	25. 2.08E
G-FCLB	Boeing 757-28A	28164	N751NA	25. 3.97	Thomas Cook Airlines Ltd t/a MyTravel Airways		
			G-FCLB			Manchester	29. 4.08E
G-FCLC	Boeing 757-28A	28166		9. 5.97	Thomas Cook Airlines UK Ltd	Manchester	8. 5.08E
G-FCLD	Boeing 757-25F	28718		25. 4.97	Thomas Cook Airlines UK Ltd	Manchester	26.12.07E
G-FCLE	Boeing 757-28A	28171		24. 5.98	Thomas Cook Airlines Ltd t/a MyTravel Airways		
						Manchester	23. 5.08E
G-FCLF	Boeing 757-28A	28835		24. 3.99	Thomas Cook Airlines Ltd t/a MyTravel Airways		
						Manchester	22. 3.08E
G-FCLG	Boeing 757-28A	24367	N701LF	18.12.98	Thomas Cook Airlines Ltd t/a MyTravel Airways		
			EI-CLM, N381LF, N240LA, C-GTSK, C-GNXI, G-GAWB			Manchester	2. 4.08E
G-FCLH	Boeing 757-28A	26274	N751LF	17. 2.99	Thomas Cook Airlines Ltd t/a MyTravel Airways		
			EI-CLU, N161LF			Manchester	12. 5.08E
G-FCLI	Boeing 757-28A	26275	N651LF	17. 3.99	Thomas Cook Airlines Ltd t/a MyTravel Airways		
			EI-CLV, N151LF			Manchester	1. 6.08E
G-FCLJ	Boeing 757-2Y0	26160	N160GE	26. 4.99	Thomas Cook Airlines UK Ltd	Manchester	25. 4.08E
			EI-CJX, N3519M, N1786B, (B-2830) *(Apple Vacations titles - Apple t/s)*				

G-FCLK	Boeing 757-2Y0	26161	N161GE	6. 4.99	Thomas Cook Airlines UK Ltd	Manchester	5. 4.08E
			EI-CJY, N3521N				
G-FCSP	Robin DR.400-180 Régent	2022		24.10.90	F C Smith t/a FCS Photochemicals	Biggin Hill	28. 3.08E
G-FCUK	Pitts S-1C	02	OH-XPB	9. 8.02	P J Burgess	RAF Cranwell	9. 4.08P
	(Built A Ronnberg)						
G-FCUM	Robinson R44 Raven II	11723		28. 4.07	Solent Projects Ltd	Keyhaven, Lymington	20. 5.08E
G-FDPS	Pitts S-2C	6066	N130PS	11. 2.05	Flights and Dreams Ltd	Cranfield	10. 3.08E
	(Built Aviat Aircraft Inc)						
G-FDZA	Boeing 737-8Q5	35134	N1786B	23. 1.07	Thomsonfly Ltd	Manchester	22. 1.08E
G-FDZB	Boeing 737-8Q5	35131		19. 4.07	Thomsonfly Ltd	Manchester	18. 4.08E
G-FDZD	Boeing 737-8Q5	35132		30. 5.07	Thomsonfly Ltd	Manchester	29. 5.08E
G-FDZE	Boeing 737-8K5	35137	N1786B	16. 1.08	Thomsonfly Ltd *(Delivered 18. 1.08)*	Manchester	
G-FDZF	Boeing 737-8K5	35138	N1786B	4. 2.08	Thomsonfly Ltd *(Delivered 5. 2.08)*	Manchester	
G-FDZG	Boeing 737-8K5	35139		3.08R	Thomsonfly Ltd	Manchester	
G-FDZJ	Boeing 737-8K5	34690	D-ATUI	4.08R	Thomsonfly Ltd	Manchester	
G-FDZO	Boeing 737-8K5	34691	D-ATUA	5.08R	Thomsonfly Ltd	Manchester	
G-FDZP	Boeing 737-8K5	34692	D-ATUB	7.08R	Thomsonfly Ltd	Manchester	
G-FEAB	Piper PA-28-181 Archer III	2843567	N53690	7. 7.04	Feabrex Ltd	Rochester	18. 7.08E
G-FEAR	Robinson R44 Raven II	11610		23. 2.07	Devon Helicopters Ltd	Exeter	8. 3.08E
G-FEBB	Grob G104 Speed Astir IIB	4040	BGA 2545-EBB	3.12.07	A F Grinter tr The Astir Group	Pocklington	27. 4.08
G-FEBE	Cessna 340A II	340A-0345	N405LS	12. 7.88	V Dean	Cranfield	1. 4.08E
			(N37320)				
G-FEBJ	Schleicher ASW 19B	19282	BGA 2552-EBJ	2.11.07	K Teagle and S Hill	Sutton Bank	28. 9.08
G-FECO	Grob G102 Astir CS77	1837	BGA 2582-ECQ	14.12.07	C Peterson	Tibenham	16. 5.08
G-FECR	Embraer EMB-135BJ Legacy	14501020	PT-SVW	12.12.07	London Executive Aviation Ltd	London Stansted	
G-FEDA	Eurocopter EC.120B Colibri	1129	F-WQOD	2. 8.00	Chartergate Aviation LLP	(Liverpool)	22. 8.08E
G-FEES	Eurocopter EC.135 T2	0311		3.12.03	Cairnsilver Ltd c/o Marshall Wace LLP	(London WC2)	27. 5.08E
G-FEET	P&M Pegasus Quik	8133		6.10.05	A N Wilkinson	Headon Farm, Retford	17.10.08P
G-FEFE	Scheibe SF25B Falke	46126	EI-BVZ	11. 4.94	M H Simms	Shipdham	8. 6.06
	(Stark-Stamo MS1500)		D-KADB		*(New owner 1.07)*		
G-FELL	Europa Aviation Europa	372		17. 3.98	N J Wakeling	Leicester	3.12.07P
	(Built J A Fell - pr.no.PFA 247-13208) (Tri-gear u/c)						
G-FELT	Cameron N-77 Balloon (Hot Air)	1174		19. 7.85	Allan Industries Ltd	Aston Rowant, Watlington	27. 3.04A
					"Fuzzy Felt" (New owner 3.07)		
G-FELX	CZAW Sportcruiser	PFA 338-14661		17. 9.07	T F Smith	(Felixstowe)	
	(Built T F Smith)						
G-FERN	Mainair Blade 912	1342-1002-7-W1137		18.10.02	M H Moulai	Sandtoft	4.11.08P
					(Operated Silver Fern Microlights)		
G-FERV	Rolladen-Schneider LS4	4257	BGA 2899-ERV	12. 9.07	R J J Bennett	Long Mynd	20. 9.08
G-FESS	Cyclone Airsports Pegasus Quantum 15-912	7840	G-CBBZ	12. 2.08	P M Fessi	Swinford, Rugby	16. 9.08P
G-FEWG	Fuji FA.200-160 Aero Subaru	FA200-232	G-BBNV	15.10.04	Caseright Ltd *(Noted 1.08)*	Turweston	3.10.07E
G-FEZZ	Agusta-Bell 206B-2 JetRanger II	8317	SU-YAD	16. 9.98	R J Myram	Wycombe Air Park	1.11.07E
			YU-HAT				
G-FFAB	Cameron N-105 Balloon (Hot Air)	4067		20. 2.97	B J Hammond *(Forever Friends titles)*	Chelmsford	25. 5.07A
G-FFAF	Cessna F150L	F15001033	I-FFAF	10. 2.06	M Howells	Barton	11. 5.08E
	(Built Reims Aviation SA)						
G-FFEN	Cessna F150M	F15001204	PH-VGL	25. 8.78	W Stitt and M Fryer	Cherry Tree Farm, Monewden	11. 4.09E
	(Built Reims Aviation SA)						
G-FFFT	Lindstrand LBL 31A Balloon (Hot Air)	705		30. 5.00	J Tyrrell and W Rousell	Wollaston, Wellingborough	27. 9.06A
G-FFIT	P&M Quik	8238		15. 1.07	K A Armstrong *(Noted 12.06)*	Linley Hill, Leven	
G-FFOX	Hawker Hunter T 7B	41H-670788	WV318	10. 1.96	Delta Engineering Aviation Ltd	Kemble	14. 5.06P
	(Composite including components of WV322- see G-BZSE)				*(As "WV318:D" in RAF c/s)*		
G-FFRA	Dassault Falcon 20DC	132	N902FR	28. 5.92	Cobham Leasing Ltd	Durham Tees Valley	20.10.06A
			(N23FR), (N149FE), N2FE, N560L, N4348F, F-WMKG				
G-FFRI	Aérospatiale AS.355F1 Ecureuil 2	5120	G-GLOW	15. 4.93	Sterling Helicopters Ltd	Norwich	23. 5.08E
			G-PAPA, G-CNET, G-MCAH				
G-FFTI	SOCATA TB-20 Trinidad	1065		23. 2.90	R Lenk	Old Buckenham	7.11.07E
G-FFTT	Lindstrand LBL Newspaper SS Balloon (Hot Air)			10. 7.00	P Mason and P Saunders	Brentwood	11.11.06A
		673					
G-FFUN	Cyclone Airsports Pegasus Quantum 15	6655	G-MYMD	9. 6.99	P R Mailer	Longacre Farm, Sandy	25. 1.08P
	(Rotax 503)						
G-FFWD	Cessna 310R II	310R0579	G-TVKE	20. 2.90	T S Courtman	East Midlands	7. 4.07E
			G-EURO, N87468				
G-FGID	Vought FG-1D Corsair	3111	N8297	1.11.91	Patina Ltd	Duxford	20.11.08P
	(Built Goodyear Aircraft Corporation)		N9154Z, Bu.88297		*(As "KD345:130:A" in RN 1850 Sqdn c/s) (Operated The Fighter Collection)*		
G-FGSI	Montgomerie-Bensen B8MR	PGA G/01A-1354		19. 4.07	F G Shepherd	(Leadgate, Alston)	
	(Built F G Shepherd)						
G-FGSK	Cameron Beer Crate-120 SS Balloon (Hot Air)			6. 4.04	Ballon-Sport und Luftwerbung Dresden GmbH		
		10417				Dresden, Germany	12. 5.05A
G-FGAZ	Schleicher Ka 6E	4103	BGA 2651-EFM	21. 9.07	G.S.Foster	Parham Park	17. 4.08
			RAFGSA				
G-FHAS	Scheibe SF25E Super Falke	4359	(D-KOOG)	14. 5.81	Burn Gliding Club Ltd	Burn	18. 7.08E
	(Limbach SL1700)						
G-FIAT	Piper PA-28-140 Cherokee F	28-7425162	G-BBYW	19. 7.89	Demero Ltd and Transcourt Ltd	Oxford	31. 7.08E
			N9622N				
G-FIBS	Aérospatiale AS.350BA Ecureuil	2074	JA9732	14. 6.94	Pristheath Ltd	Denham	8. 8.08E
G-FICS	Flight Design CTSW	07.10.18		17.12.07	R Eve	(Hornchurch)	16.12.08P
	(Assembled P&M Aviation Ltd with c/n 8348)						
G-FIFA	Cessna 404 Titan	404-0644	G-TVIP	24. 5.07	Fly (CI) Ltd	Southend	5. 2.08E
			G-KIWI, G-BHNI, LN-LGM, SE-IFV, G-BHNI, (N5302J) *(Operated Trans Euro Air)*				
G-FIFE	Reims Cessna FA152 Aerobat	FA1520351	G-BFYN	15. 2.95	Tayside Aviation Ltd	Glenrothes	1. 3.08E
G-FIFI	SOCATA TB-20 Trinidad	688	G-BMWS	16. 1.87	F A Saker	Denham	15. 3.08E
G-FIFT	Comco Ikarus C42 FB100	0409-6623		2. 8.04	A R Jones	Carlisle	17.10.08P
G-FIGA	Cessna 152 II	15284644	N6243M	3. 6.87	Central Aircraft Leasing Ltd	Exeter	31. 8.08E

G-FIGB	Cessna 152 II	15285925	N95561	16.11.87	Aerohire Ltd *(Noted 9.07)*	Lee-on-Solent	12. 2.00T
G-FIGP	Boeing 737-2E7	22875	EI-CJI	11. 4.05	European Skybus Ltd	Bournemouth	5. 6.08E
			G-BMDF, (PK-RI.), G-BMDF, 4X-BAB, N4570B *(Stored engineless 1.08)*				
G-FIII	Extra EA.300/L	091	G-RGEE	6.12.04	J S Allison	Andrewsfield	13.12.07E
			D-ESEW				
G-FIJJ	Reims Cessna F177RG Cardinal RG		G-AZFP	29. 4.99	D R Vale	Derby	15. 6.08E
	(Wichita c/n 17700194)	F177RG0031					
G-FIJR	Lockheed L188PF Electra	1138	(EI-HCF)	12. 9.91	Atlantic Airlines Ltd	Coventry	12. 9.08T
			G-FIJR, C-FIJR, CF-IJR, N134US				
G-FIJV	Lockheed L188C Electra	1129	EI-HCE	29. 8.91	Atlantic Airlines Ltd	Coventry	27. 9.07T
			G-FIJV, C-FIJV, CF-IJV, N7143C *(Atlantic Airlines titles)*				
G-FILE	Piper PA-34-200T Seneca II	34-8070108	N8140Z	23. 7.87	A J Warren	Bristol	19.12.07E
G-FILL	Piper PA-31 Navajo C	31-7912069	OO-EJM	28. 6.96	P V Naylor-Leyland	Milton, Peterborough	23. 8.08E
			N3521				
G-FINA	Reims Cessna F150L	F15000826	G-BIFT	12.10.93	A G Freeman	Turweston	16. 2.08E
			PH-CEW				
G-FIND	Reims Cessna F406 Caravan II	F406-0045	OY-PEU	16. 8.90	Reconnaisance Ventures Ltd	Blackpool	5. 5.08E
			5Y-LAN, G-FIND, PH-ALV, F-WZDT *(Operated Ordinance Survey)*				
G-FINK	British Aerospace BAe 125 Series 1000B	259037	XA-RGG	18. 1.07	B T Fink	Southend	1. 2.08E
	(Built Corporate Jets Ltd)		XA-TGK, G-SHEC, G-SCCC, G-5-771				
G-FINZ	III Sky Arrow 650 T	PFA 298-13824		8. 1.03	A G Counsell	Perth	7. 5.08P
	(Built A G Counsell)						
G-FIRM	Cessna 550 Citation Bravo	550-0940	N5263S	29. 9.00	Marshall of Cambridge Aerospace Ltd	Cambridge	2.10.07T
G-FIRS	Robinson R22 Beta II	2807		15. 4.98	Multiflight Ltd	Leeds-Bradford	23. 5.08E
G-FIRZ	Murphy Renegade 912	PFA 188-13494		10.12.99	P J Houtman	Park Farm, Eaton Bray	7. 5.07P
	(Built D M Wood and M Hanley)						
G-FISH	Cessna 310R II	310R1845	N2740Y	8. 5.81	ACS Contracts Ltd	Perth	28.10.07E
G-FITZ	Cessna 335	335-0044	G-RIND	20. 4.95	F L Hunter	(Sheffield City)	5. 5.08E
			N2710L				
G-FIXX	Van's RV-7	PFA 323-14225		31. 8.06	Hambilton Engineering Ltd	(Penwortham, Preston)	
	(Built P C Hambilton)						
G-FIZU	Lockheed L188CF Electra	2014	EI-CHY	6. 4.93	Atlantic Airlines Ltd	Coventry	3. 1.08E
			G-FIZU, SE-IZU, (N857ST), N857U, PH-LLG				
G-FIZY	Europa Aviation Europa XS	384	G-DDSC	16.12.99	R Eyles	(Taunton)	12. 6.08P
	(Built G N Holland - pr.no.PFA 247-13291) *(Jabiru 3300)* *(Tri-gear u/c)*						
G-FIZZ	Piper PA-28-161 Cherokee Warrior II		N2721M	1.12.78	Tecair Aviation Ltd	Shipdham	30. 4.08E
		28-7816301					
G-FJCE	Thruster T 600T	9128-T600T-032		25.11.98	F Cameron	(Craigavon, Belfast)	31. 7.04P
	(Rotax 532)						
G-FJEB	Boeing 757-23A	24290	N290AN	21. 7.03	Flyjet Ltd	London Gatwick	27. 7.08E
			G-OOOJ, N510FP, EC-EMU, EC-248				
G-FJET	Cessna 550 Citation II	550-0419	G-DCFR	7. 7.97	London Executive Aviation Ltd	London City	17. 1.07E
			G-WYLX, VH-JVS, G-JETD, N1217N				
G-FJMS	Partenavia P68B	113	G-SVHA	7. 9.92	J B Randle	Church Farm, Piltdown	15. 8.08E
			OY-AJH				
G-FJTH	Aeroprakt A22 Foxbat	PFA 317-13928		16. 7.03	F J T Hancock	(Berrow, Malvern)	8. 2.08P
	(Built F J T Hancock)						
G-FKNH	Piper PA-15 Vagabond	15-291	CF-KNH	19. 3.97	M J Mothershaw	RAF Woodvale	15. 5.08E
	(Continental C85)		N4517H, NC4517H				
G-FKOS	Piper PA-28-181 Archer II	28-7790591	OE-KOS	27. 3.07	M K Johnson	Shoreham	26. 4.08E
			OY-BTL				
G-FLAG	Colt 77A Balloon (Hot Air)	2000		20. 9.90	B A Williams	Maidstone	18.10.06T
G-FLAK	Beech E55 Baron	TE-1128	N4771M	26. 9.89	D Clark *"Red Baron"*	Great Massingham	29. 7.08E
G-FLAV	Piper PA-28-161 Warrior II	28-8016283	N8171X	7. 4.94	S D E Mills tr The Crew Flying Group	Tollerton	7. 2.08
G-FLBI	Robinson R44 Raven II	10158		10. 9.03	Freshfield Lane Brickworks Ltd		
						Danehill, Haywards Heath	22.10.07E
G-FLCA	Fleet 80 Canuck	068	CS-ACQ	18. 7.90	E C Taylor t/a Tamyco-Oag	Turweston	
			CF-DQP		*(Noted 1.08)*		
G-FLCT	Hallam Fleche	PFA 309-13389		21.10.98	R G Hallam	(Nether Alderley, Macclesfield)	
	(Built R G Hallam)						
G-FLDG	Best Off Sky Ranger 912(2)	SKRxxxx390		21. 4.04	A J Gay	South Wraxall	5. 9.08P
	(Built A J Gay - pr.no.BMAA/HB/328)						
G-FLEA	SOCATA TB-10 Tobago	235	PH-TTP	31. 7.81	R Kilburn tr TB Group	Leicester	8. 8.08E
			G-FLEA				
G-FLEW	Lindstrand LBL 90A Balloon (Hot Air)	586		21. 1.99	A Nimmo	Dubai, United Arab Emirates	13. 9.08A
					(Lindstrand Balloons titles)		
G-FLEX	Mainair Sports Pegasus Quik	7953		15. 5.03	J W McCarthy	Ince Blundell	31. 5.08P
G-FLGT	Lindstrand LBL 105A Balloon (Hot Air)	888		5.12.02	Ballongaventyr I Skane AB	Kävlinge, Sweden	16. 1.08A
G-FLIK	Pitts S-1S	PFA 009-10513		7. 1.81	R P Millinship	Leicester	11. 6.08P
	(Built R P Millinship) *(Lycoming O-320)*						
G-FLIP	Reims Cessna FA152 Aerobat	FA1520375	G-BOES	29.12.80	Cloud 9 Aviation (Leasing) Ltd	(Sheffield City)	16.10.07E
			G-FLIP				
G-FLIT	RotorWay Executive 162F	6324		22.12.98	R S Snell	Phoenix Farm, Lower Upham	10. 8.07P
	(Built R F Rhodes) *(RotorWay RI 162F)*						
G-FLIZ	Staaken Z-21 Flitzer	006		24. 3.97	M A Wood	Shempston Farm, Lossiemouth	13. 2.08P
	(Built G L Brown - pr.no.PFA 223-13115)				*(Also carries "D-694")*		
G-FLKE	Scheibe SF25C Falke	44673		5.10.01	T M Holloway tr RAF Gliding and Soaring Association		
	(Rotax 912S)					RAF Halton	5.12.07E
G-FLKS	Scheibe SF25C Falke	44662	D-KIEQ	16.10.00	London Gliding Club Proprietary Ltd	Dunstable	8. 1.08E
	(Rotax 912S)						
G-FLOA	Cameron O-120 Balloon (Hot Air)	4006		4.10.96	Floating Sensations Ltd	Thatcham	11. 8.08T
G-FLOP	Cessna 152	15282590	N69265	25.11.05	Cloud 9 Aviation (Leasing) Ltd	Full Sutton	20. 2.08E
G-FLOR	Europa Aviation Europa	171		11.11.98	A F C van Eldik	Pent Farm, Postling	2.10.08P
	(Built A F C Van Eldik - pr.no.PFA 247-12793) *(Monowheel u/c)*						

G-FLOW	Cessna 172S Skyhawk	172S9677	N6127S	19. 8.04	M P Dolan	City of Derry	19. 9.08E
G-FLOX	Europa Aviation Europa	129		28. 6.95	T W Eaton tr DPT Group		
	(Built P S Buchan, T W Eaton and B Lewer - pr.no.PFA 247-12732) (Jabiru 2200A) (Monowheel u/c)					Fowle Hall Farm, Laddingford	6. 9.07P
G-FLPI	Rockwell Commander 112A	205	SE-FLP	16. 3.79	H J Freeman	Newcastle	15. 4.08E
			(N1205J)				
G-FLSH	IAV Bacau Yakovlev Yak-52	877409	RA-44550	9. 6.03	M A Wright t/a Boogair "52"	Little Gransden	2. 9.08P
			LY-AKF, DOSAAF 21 (yellow)				
G-FLTA	British Aerospace BAe 146 Series 200	E2048	N189US	25. 2.98	Flightline Ltd	Aberdeen	26. 2.08E
			N365PS		(Operated IAC)		
G-FLTB	British Aerospace BAe 146 Series 200	E2024	EI-CZO	14. 5.02	Flightline Ltd	Aberdeen	30. 1.09E
			G-FLTB, G-CLHA, (G-GNTX), G-DEBC, N168US, N348PS (Operated IAC)				
G-FLTC	British Aerospace BAe 146 Series 300	E3205	G-JEBH	15.12.04	Flightline Ltd	Southend	18.10.07E
			G-BTVO, G-NJID, B-1777, G-BTVO, G-6-205 (Noted 2.08)				
G-FLTG	Cameron A-140 Balloon (Hot Air)	4506		3.11.00	Floating Sensations Ltd	Thatcham	13. 9.06T
G-FLTK	McDonnell Douglas MD-83	49966	OE-LJE	4. 5.07	Flightline Ltd	Paris CDG, France	4. 5.08E
			OH-LPB, SE-DLX, N6204N		(Operated Blue Line)		
G-FLTL	McDonnell Douglas MD-83	49790	OE-LHG	12. 2.07	Flightline Ltd	Milan-Malpensa, Italy	18 .2.08E
			EC-FZC, EC-742, EC-ESJ, EC-307 (Operated Volare.web)				
G-FLTM	McDonnell Douglas MD-83	53052	EC-KBA	1. 6.07	Flightline Ltd	Dublin	
			EC-HGA, N942AS		(Operated Aviajet 12.08)		
G-FLTZ	Beech 58 Baron	TH-1154	G-PSVS	21. 9.93	Flightline Ltd	Southend	21.10.07E
			N5824T, YV-266P		(Noted 1.08)		
G-FLYA	Mooney M 20J Mooney 201	24-3124		8. 6.89	BRF Aviation Ltd	Full Sutton	22. 3.08E
G-FLYB	Comco Ikarus C42 FB100	0309-6572		15. 9.03	C D Back tr G-FLYB Group	Old Sarum	20.11.08P
G-FLYC	Comco Ikarus C42 FB100	0503-6656		7. 4.05	Solent Flight Ltd	Lower Upham	6. 4.08P
G-FLYF	Mainair Blade 912	1371-0305-7-W1166		30. 3.05	Cool Water Direct Ltd	Baxby Manor, Husthwaite	8.11.08P
G-FLYG	Slingsby T 67C	2074	PH-SGA	23. 8.02	G Laden	(North Ferriby)	16. 3.08E
			(PH-SBA)				
G-FLYH	Robinson R22 Beta	1932	CS-HEQ	4.10.02	J R Huggins	Lamberhurst Farm, Faversham	3.10.07E
			G-BXMR, N923FM, N2306E				
G-FLYI	Piper PA-34-200 Seneca	34-7250144	G-BHVO	1. 9.81	S Papi	Southend	10. 8.08E
			SE-FYY		(Operated Willowair Flying Club)		
G-FLYM	Comco Ikarus C42 FB100	0707-6903		30. 7.07	R Stalker	Strathaven	13. 9.08P
G-FLYP	Beagle B 206 Srs 2	B 058	N40CJ	15.10.98	Key Publishing Ltd	Cranfield	7.10.10S
			N97JH, G-AVHO, VQ-LAY, G-AVHO (Noted 1.07)				
G-FLYS	Robinson R44 Astro	0347		5. 6.97	Newmarket Plant Hire Ltd	Cambridge	3. 8.08T
G-FLYT	Europa Aviation Europa	057		15. 5.95	K F and R.Richardson	Wellesbourne Mountford	6. 5.00P
	(Built D W Adams - pr.no.PFA 247-12653) (NSI EA-81/100) (Conventional u/c)				(Noted 11.07)		
G-FLYX	Robinson R44 Raven II	11669		11. 4.07	Sitecrest Aviation LLP	Damyn's Hall, Upminster	19. 4.08E
G-FLYY	British Aircraft Corporation 167 Strikemaster Mk.80A	R Saudi AF 1112		3. 9.01	D T Barber	City of Derry	10. 6.08P
		EEP/JP/163	G-27-31				
G-FLZR	Staaken Z-21 Flitzer	PFA 223-13219		21. 9.01	J F Govan	(East Linton)	
	(Built J F Govan)				(Complete 4.07)		
G-FMAM	Piper PA-28-151 Cherokee Warrior	28-7415056	G-BBXV	7. 6.90	P B Anderson tr Lima Tango Flying Group	Southend	15. 3.08E
			N9603D				
G-FMGG	Maule M-5-235C Lunar Rocket	7260C	G-RAGG	30. 4.02	S Bierbaum	Bodmin	2. 5.08E
			N5632M		(Operated Bodmin Light Aeroplane Services Ltd)		
G-FMKA	Diamond HK 36 TC Super Dimona	36.672		26. 4.00	G P Davis	Kemble	16. 7.08E
G-FMSG	Reims Cessna FA150K Aerobat	FA1500081	G-POTS	4. 1.95	G Owen	Humberside	21. 1.07T
			G-AYUY				
G-FNES	Dassault Falcon 900EX	159	N900SG	12. 6.07	Matrix Aviation Ltd	Paris Le Bourget	26. 6.08E
		N900EX, N959EX, F-WWFR					
G-FNEY	Reims Cessna F177RG Cardinal RG	F177RG0059	F-BTFQ	24. 2.04	F Ney	East Midlands	25 .9.08E
G-FNLD	Cessna 172N Skyhawk II	17270596	(G-BOUG)	3. 8.88	R C Laming and M J Humphrey tr Papa Hotel Flying Group		
			N739KD			Fenland	26. 2.08E
G-FNLY	Reims Cessna F172M	F17200910	G-WACX	20. 3.89	Skytrax Aviation Ltd	Blackbushe	4. 4.08E
			G-BAEX				
G-FNPT	Piper PA-28-161 Warrior III	2842163	N5346Y	2.10.02	Fleetwash Ltd (Cabair titles)	Elstree	17.10.07E
G-FOFO	Robinson R44 Raven II	10320		6. 4.04	P A Williams t/a Towers Aviation	Gamston	24. 5.08E
G-FOGG	Cameron N-90 Balloon (Hot Air)	1365		21.11.86	J P E Money-Kyrle "Phileas Fogg"	Chippenham	25. 9.96A
G-FOGI	Europa Aviation Europa XS	385		29.10.04	B Fogg	Sleap	10. 8.08P
	(Built B Fogg -pr.no.PFA 247-13313)						
G-FOGY	Robinson R22 Beta	1020	N62991	5. 7.99	Aero Maintenance Ltd	Walton Wood	24. 7.08E
			F-GGAI				
G-FOKK	Fokker Dr.1 Triplane replica	PFA 238-14253		18. 1.06	S E and P D Ford	Sywell	
	(Built P D Ford)				(As "477/17" in German military (red) c/s) (Noted 10.07)		
G-FOLI	Robinson R22 Beta II	2813		25. 4.98	G M Duckworth	Halfpenny Green	18. 6.08P
G-FOLY	Pitts S-2A	2213	N31477	26. 7.89	D G Gilmour	Perth	8. 2.08E
	(Built Aerotek Inc)						
G-FONZ	Best Off Sky Ranger 912(2)	SKRxxxx369		15. 9.03	A A Pacitti tr G-FONZ Sky Ranger Group	Strathaven	28. 7.08P
	(Built A A Pacitti - pr.no.BMAA/HB/304)						
G-FOPP	Neico Lancair 320	PFA 191-12319		14. 8.92	Airsport (UK) Ltd	Cranfield	17. 7.08P
	(Built M A Fopp) (Lycoming IO-320)						
G-FORA	Schempp-Hirth Ventus cT	126-400	BGA 4449-JEF	28.11.07	A D Cook	Edgehill	6.12.07
			D-KFWH				
G-FORC	SNCAN Stampe SV-4C	665	(G-BLTJ)	6. 6.85	C C Rollings and F J Hodson	Gloucestershire	12. 6.09T
			F-BDNJ				
G-FORD	SNCAN Stampe SV-4C(G)	129	F-BBNS	7. 2.78	P H Meeson (Noted 5.07)	Rotary Farm, Hatch	24. 5.10S
G-FORR	Piper PA-28-181 Archer III	2843336	N4160Z	20. 4.00	A D Hoy	Jersey	23. 4.08E
			G-FORR, N4160Z				
G-FORZ	Pitts S-1S	PFA 009-13393		3.11.98	N W Parkinson	(High Wycombe)	
	(Built N Parkinson)				(Noted 11.07)		
G-FOSY	SOCATA MS.880B Rallye Club	1304	G-AXAK	7.12.00	A G Foster	Humberside	17. 5.04

Reg	Type	C/n	Prev id	Date	Owner/Operator	Location	Date2
G-FOWL	Colt 90A Balloon (Hot Air)	1198		11. 3.88	The Packhouse Ltd	Farnham	1.10.08A
G-FOWS	Cameron N-105 Balloon (Hot Air)	3995		11.12.96	F R Hart	Bishops Sutton, Bristol	15. 5.08A
G-FOXA	Piper PA-28-161 Cadet	2841240	N9192B	17.11.89	The Leicestershire Aero Club Ltd	Leicester	3. 8.08E
G-FOXB	Aeroprakt A22 Foxbat	PFA 317-13878		15. 3.02	G D McCullough		
	(Buillt M Raflewski)					Slieve Croob, Slievenamoney, Castlewellen	27. 9.07P
G-FOXC	Denney Kitfox Model 3	773		8. 1.91	G Hawkins Newton Peverill Farm, Sturminster Marshall		10. 6.07P
	(Built B W Davis - pr.no.PFA 172-11900)				"Foxc Lady"		
G-FOXD	Denney Kitfox Model 2	PFA 172-11618		22.11.89	P P Trangmar	Deanland	22.10.08P
	(Built D Hanley)						
G-FOXF	Denney Kitfox Model 4	PFA 172-12399		24. 3.00	M S Goodwin	Bridge of Weir	26. 7.08P
	(Built M S Goodwin) (Rotax 912-UL)						
G-FOXG	Denney Kitfox Model 2	452		15. 8.90	J U McKercher	Errol	13. 6.08P
	(Built S M Jackson - pr.no.PFA 172-11886) (Rotax 532)						
G-FOXI	Denney Kitfox Model 2	PFA 172-11508		21. 9.89	I M Walton	Wellesbourne Mountford	21. 8.04P
	(Built I N Jennison) (Rotax 532)				(New owner 11.07)		
G-FOXL	Zenair CH.601XL Zodiac	PFA 162B-14537		11.12.06	M J Lloyd	(Worcester)	
	(Built M J Lloyd)						
G-FOXM	Bell 206B-2 JetRanger II	1514	G-STAK	5. 2.93	R P Maydon t/a Milton Keynes City Air	Oxford	11. 6.08E
			G-BNIS, N35HF, N135VG		(Operated CSE Helicopters - Fox FM Radio)		
G-FOXS	Denney Kitfox Model 2	458		15. 8.90	S P Watkins and C C Rea		
	(Built S P Watkins and C C Rea - pr.no.PFA 172-11571)					Sheepcote Farm, Stourbridge	25. 4.07P
G-FOXX	Denney Kitfox	PFA 172-11509		1.11.89	A W Hodder Belle Vue Farm, Yarnscombe		10. 9.07P
	(Built R O F Harper and P R Skeels) (Struck wire fence on take-off Branscombe 28. 8.07, crashed into line of trees and substantially damaged)						
G-FOXZ	Denney Kitfox	PFA 172-11834		4.12.90	S C Goozee Mapperton Farm, Newton Peverill		17.12.07P
	(Built M Smalley and J C Whittle)						
G-FOZZ	Beech A36 Bonanza	E-2788	N345SF	23. 8.05	Go To Air Ltd	Blackpool	15. 9.08E
			D-EUWR, N82404				
G-FPIG	Piper PA-28-151 Cherokee Warrior	28-7615001	G-BSSR	22. 3.00	G F Strain	Bournemouth	11. 4.08
			N1190X				
G-FPLB	Beech B200 Super King Air	BB-1048	N739MG	3.12.97	Cobham Leasing Ltd	Durham Tees Valley	11. 1.07T
			N223MD, 9Y-TGY		(Operated Flight Precision)		
G-FPLD	Beech B200 Super King Air	BB-1433	N43CE	2.11.01	Flight Precision Ltd	Durham Tees Valley	19.11.07T
			N43AJ, C-GMEV, C-GMEH, N8043K				
G-FPLE	Beech B200 Super King Air	BB-1256	N230DC	12. 9.05	Cobham Leasing Ltd	Durham Tees Valley	18.12.07T
			N1847S, N184JS, N2676M		(Operated Flight Precision)		
G-FPSA	Piper PA-28-161 Warrior II	28-8616038	G-RSFT	28. 2.03	Deep Cleavage Ltd	Exeter	3. 4.08E
			G-WARI, N9276Y				
G-FRAD	Dassault Falcon 20E	304/511	9M-BDK	26.11.86	Cobham Leasing Ltd	Bournemouth	13..6.08E
			G-FRAD, G-BCYF, F-WRQP				
G-FRAF	Dassault Falcon 20E	295/500	N911FR	1. 9.87	Cobham Leasing Ltd	Bournemouth	2. 7.08E
			I-EDIM, F-WRQQ		(Operated FR Aviation)		
G-FRAG	Piper PA-32-300 Six	32-7940284	N3566L	21. 1.80	T A Houghton	Rochester	24. 5.08E
G-FRAH	Dassault Falcon 20DC	223	G-60-01	31. 5.90	Cobham Leasing Ltd	Bournemouth	7.10.07E
			N900FR, (N904FR), N22FE, N4407F, F-WPUX (Operated FR Aviation)				
G-FRAI	Dassault Falcon 20E	270	N901FR	17.10.90	Cobham Leasing Ltd	Durham Tees Valley	3. 6.08E
			N37FE, N4435F, F-WPUZ		(Operated FR Aviation)		
G-FRAJ	Dassault Falcon 20DC	20	N903FR	30. 4.91	Cobham Leasing Ltd	Durham Tees Valley	12.12.07E
			(N25FR), N5FE, (N146FE), N5FE, N367GA, N367, N842F, F-WMKJ (Operated FR Aviation)				
G-FRAK	Dassault Falcon 20DC	213	N905FR	9.10.91	Cobham Leasing Ltd	Bournemouth	13. 4.08E
			N32FE, N4390F, F-WJMM		(Operated FR Aviation)		
G-FRAL	Dassault Falcon 20DC	151	N904FR	17. 3.93	Cobham Leasing Ltd	Durham Tees Valley	22.12.07E
			(N24FR), N3FE, (N148FE), N3FE, N810PA, N810F, N4360F, F-WMK				
G-FRAN	Piper J-3C-65 Cub (L-4J-PI)	12617	G-BIXY	14. 7.86	I Dole tr Essex L-4 Group Rayne Hall Farm, Braintree		7.11.08P
	(Continental C90) (Frame No.12447)		F-BDTZ, 44-80321		(As "480321:H-44" in USAAC c/s)		
G-FRAO	Dassault Falcon 20DC	214	N906FR	23.10.92	Cobham Leasing Ltd	Bournemouth	28. 1.08E
			N33FE, N4400F, F-WNGO		(Operated FR Aviation)		
G-FRAP	Dassault Falcon 20DC	207	N908FR	12. 7.93	Cobham Leasing Ltd	Bournemouth	19.10.07E
			N27FE, N4395F, F-WMKF		(Operated FR Aviation)		
G-FRAR	Dassault Falcon 20DC	209	N909FR	2.12.93	Cobham Leasing Ltd	Bournemouth	15. 2.08E
			N28FE, N4396F, F-WLCX		(Operated FR Aviation)		
G-FRAS	Dassault Falcon 20C	82/418	CAF117501	31. 7.90	Cobham Leasing Ltd	Durham Tees Valley	1.12.07E
			20501, F-WJMM		(Operated FR Aviation)		
G-FRAT	Dassault Falcon 20C	87/424	CAF117502	31. 7.90	Cobham Leasing Ltd	Bournemouth	21. 2.08E
			20502, F-WJMJ		(Operated FR Aviation)		
G-FRAU	Dassault Falcon 20C	97/422	CAF117504	31. 7.90	Cobham Leasing Ltd	Bournemouth	15.12.07E
			20504, F-WJMJ		(Operated FR Aviation)		
G-FRAW	Dassault Falcon 20C	114/420	CAF117507	31. 7.90	Cobham Leasing Ltd	Durham Tees Valley	9. 4.08E
			20507, F-WJMM		(Operated FR Aviation)		
G-FRAY	Cassutt Racer IIIM	PFA 034-11211		24.10.90	C I Fray	(Disley, Stockport)	
	(Built C I Fray)						
G-FRBA	Dassault Falcon 20C	178/459	OH-FFA	16. 7.96	Cobham Leasing Ltd	Bournemouth	16. 5.08E
			F-WPXF		(Operated FR Aviation) "Tornado Trials"		
G-FRCE	Folland Gnat T 1	FL.598	8604M	28.11.89	Airborne Innovations Ltd	North Weald	20. 8.08P
			XS104				
G-FRGN	Piper PA-28-236 Dakota	2811046	N9244N	8. 2.96	P J Vacher	Church Farm, North Moreton	11. 3.08E
G-FRGT	P&M Quik GT450	8341		21.12.07	P J and F S Dodd t/a Peter Dodd Consultants		
						(Chalfont St Peter, Gerrards Cross)	
G-FRIL	Lindstrand LBL 105A Balloon (Hot Air)	1086		19. 9.06	S Travaglia Tavarnelle Val di Pesa, Florence, Italy		18. 9.07E
G-FRNK	Best Off Sky Ranger 912(2)	SKR xxxx528		26. 1.05	M J Burns		
	(Built F Tumelty - pr.no.BMAA/HB/439)					Slieve Croob, Slievenamoney, Castlewellen	26. 7.08P
G-FROM	Comco Ikarus C42 FB100	0309-6554		15. 9.03	Chiltern Airsports Ltd	Chiltern Park, Wallingford	14.10.08P
G-FROS	Piper PA-28R-201 Arrow III	2844118	D-EGXC	7. 2.07	G and P Frost	Shoreham	26. 2.08E
			N3117A				

G-FRYI	Beech 200 Super King Air	BB-210	G-OAVX	15. 3.96	London Executive Aviation Ltd	Stapleford	26. 3.08E
			G-IBCA, G-BMCA, N5657N				
G-FRYL	Raytheon RB390 Premier 1	RB-97	N6197F	11. 8.04	Hawk Air Ltd	Farnborough	17. 8.08E
G-FSEU	Beech 200 Super King Air	BB-331	N87LP	9. 8.06	Air Mercia Ltd	Bristol	20. 9.08E
			N111WA, N400WH, N111JW				
G-FSHA	Denney Kitfox Model 2	PFA 172-11906		20. 9.99	P P Trangmar	(Hailsham)	
	(Built S J Alston)						
G-FTDF	Airbus A320-231	437	C-FTDF	11. 5.05	Thomas Cook Airlines Ltd t/a MyTravel Airways		
			G-FTDF			Manchester	4. 4.08E
	C-FTDF, G-FTDF, C-FTDF, D-AAMS, G-EPFR, G-EPFR, G-BVJV, N437RX, G-BVJV, C-FWOQ, G-BVJV, N427RX, F-WWDM						
G-FTIL	Robin DR.400-180 Régent	1825		10. 3.88	The Pathfinder Flying Club Ltd	RAF Wyton	20. 7.08E
G-FTIM	Robin DR.400-100 Cadet	1829		6. 5.88	C McGee tr Madley Flying Group	Shobdon	5.12.07E
G-FTIN	Robin DR.400-100 Cadet	1830		6. 5.88	G D Clark and M J D Theobald tr YP Flying Group		
						Blackpool	31.10.07E
G-FTSE	Fairey Britten-Norman BN-2A Mk.III-2 Trislander	1053	G-BEPI	23. 5.00	Aurigny Air Services Ltd	Guernsey	18.12.07E
					(Quilter titles)		
G-FTSL	Bombardier CL-600-2B16	5416	N161MD	8.12.04	Farglobe Transport Services Ltd		
	(CL-604 Challenger)		(G-), N161MN, N161MM, N604MG, C-GLXG			(Hamilton, Bermuda)	8.12.07E
G-FTUO	Van's RV-4	926	C-FTUQ	23.12.97	R S Jordan	Shipdham	19. 4.08P
	(Built T Martin) (Lycoming IO-360-B4A)						
G-FUEL	Robin DR.400-180 Régent	1537		15. 5.81	R Darch	East Chinnock, Yeovil	20. 6.08E
G-FUFU	Agusta A109S Grand	22058		20.11.07	Air Harrods Ltd	London Stansted	
G-FUKM	Westland SA.341B Gazelle AH.1	1799	ZA730	18. 8.03	Falcon Aviation Ltd	Deer Park Farm, Babcary	
					(Airframe noted 12.07)		
G-FULL	Piper PA-28R-200 Cherokee Arrow II	28R-7435248	G-HWAY	26.11.84	Stapleford Flying Club Ltd	Stapleford	17.12.07E
			G-JULI, (G-BKDC), OY-POV, CS-AQF, N43128				
G-FULM	Sikorsky S-76C	760583	N7110J	2. 9.05	Air Harrods Ltd	London Stansted	1. 9.08E
G-FUND	Thunder Ax7-65Z Balloon (Hot Air)	376		3.11.81	G Everett	Sandway, Maidstone	21. 8.07A
G-FUNK	Yakovlev Yak-50	852908	RA852908	27. 3.98	Redstar Aero Services Ltd	Tibenham	20.11.08P
			DOSAAF (46 blue ?)				
G-FUNN	Plumb BGP-1 Biplane	PFA 083-12744		16.10.95	J D Anson	(Le Marchais, Fomperron, France)	
	(Built J D Anson)						
G-FUNY	Robinson R44 Raven II	11101		10. 3.06	Concept Group International Ltd	(Coventry)	6. 4.08E
G-FURI	Isaacs Fury II	PFA 011-14467		7. 2.06	S M Johnston	(Brompton on Swale, Richmond)	
	(Built S M Johnston)						
G-FUSE	Cameron N-105 Balloon (Hot Air)	10639		30.11.04	S A Lacey	Norwich Common, Wymondham	11. 7.08E
G-FUZZ	Piper PA-18 Super Cub 95	18-1016	(OO-HMY)	11. 9.80	G W Cline	Gipsy Wood Farm, Warthill	19. 4.08P
	(L-18C-PI) (Frame No.18-1086)		French Army-FMBIT, 51-15319		(As "51-15319:A-319" in USAAF c/s)		
G-FVEL	Cameron Z-90 Balloon (Hot Air)	10580		24. 8.04	Fort Vale Engineering Ltd	Nelson	28. 6.08A
G-FVRY	Colt 105A Balloon (Hot Air)	746	C-FVRY	21. 7.05	R Thompson	(Berry Grove Farm, Liss)	12. 9.06E
			N300NN				
G-FWAB	Flug Werk Focke-Wulf FW190-A8 replica	980554		13. 2.08	Spitfire Ltd	Duxford	
G-FWAY	Lindstrand LBL 90A Balloon (Hot Air)	967		7. 5.04	Harding and Sons Ltd t/a Fairway Furniture		
					(Fairway Furniture titles)	Plymouth	12. 3.08A
G-FWKS	Air Création Tanarg 912S/iXess 15	FLT.xxx	G-SYUT	20.07.07	M A Coffin	(Wrotham, Sevenoaks)	24. 4.08P
	(Built L Cottle - pr.no.BMAA/HB/492 being Flylight kit comprising Trike s/n T05100 and Wing s/n A05188-5195)						
G-FWPW	Piper PA-28-236 Dakota	2811018	N9145L	10.10.88	P A and Franziska.C Winters	Oxford	12.12.08E
G-FXBT	Aeroprakt A22 Foxbat	PFA 317-13787		7. 2.02	R H Jago	Mapperton Farm, Newton Peverill	14. 2.08P
	(Built R Jago)						
G-FYAN	Williams Westwind Balloon (Minimum Lift) MDW-1			6. 1.82	M D Williams	Houghton Regis, Dunstable	
G-FYAO	Williams Westwind Balloon (Minimum Lift) MDW-001			6. 1.82	M D Williams	Houghton Regis, Dunstable	
G-FYAU	Williams Mk.2 Balloon (Minimum Lift) MDW-02			6. 1.82	M D Williams	Houghton Regis, Dunstable	
					(Extant 5.07)		
G-FYAV	Osprey Mk.4E2 Balloon (Minimum Lift) ASC-247			12. 1.82	C D Egan and C Stiles	Hounslow and Feltham	
					(Extant 5.07)		
G-FYBD	Osprey Mk.1E Balloon (Minimum Lift) ASC-136			20. 1.82	M Vincent	St Helier, Jersey	
G-FYBE	Osprey Mk.4D Balloon (Minimum Lift) ASC-128			20. 1.82	M Vincent	St Helier, Jersey	
G-FYBF	Osprey Mk.5 Balloon (Minimum Lift) ASC-218			20. 1.82	M Vincent	St Helier, Jersey	
G-FYBG	Osprey Mk.4G2 Balloon (Minimum Lift) ASC-204			20. 1.82	M Vincent	St Helier, Jersey	
G-FYBH	Osprey Mk.4G Balloon (Minimum Lift) ASC-214			20. 1.82	M Vincent	St Helier, Jersey	
G-FYBI	Osprey Mk.4H Balloon (Minimum Lift) ASC-234			20. 1.82	M Vincent	St Helier, Jersey	
G-FYCL	Osprey Mk.4G Balloon (Minimum Lift) ASC-213			9. 2.82	P J Rogers	Banbury	
G-FYCV	Osprey Mk.4D Balloon (Minimum Lift) ASK-276			19. 2.82	A L Hunter	Luton	
G-FYCZ	Osprey Mk.4D2 Balloon (Minimum Lift) ASC-244			24. 2.82	P Middleton	Colchester	
G-FYDF	Osprey Mk.4D Balloon (Minimum Lift) ASK-278			22. 3.82	K A Jones	Thornton Heath	
G-FYDI	Williams Westwind Two Balloon (Minimum Lift) MDW-005			29. 3.82	M D Williams	Houghton Regis, Dunstable	
G-FYDN	Eaves European 8C Balloon (Minimum Lift) DD34/S 22			5. 4.82	P D Ridout	Eastleigh	
G-FYDO	Osprey Mk.4D Balloon (Minimum Lift) ASK-262			15. 4.82	N L Scallan	Hayes	
G-FYDP	Williams Westwind Three Balloon (Minimum Lift) MDW-006			29. 3.82	M D Williams	Houghton Regis, Dunstable	
					(Extant 5.07)		
G-FYDS	Osprey Mk.4D Balloon (Minimum Lift) ASK-261			15. 4.82	M E Scallan	Hayes	
G-FYEK	Unicorn UE-1C Balloon (Minimum Lift) 82024			2. 7.82	D and D Eaves (Extant 5.07)	Southampton	
G-FYEO	Scallan Eagle Mk.1A Balloon (Minimum Lift) 001			20. 7.82	M E Scallan	Hayes	
G-FYEV	Osprey Mk.1C Balloon (Minimum Lift) ASK-294			10. 8.82	M E Scallan	Hayes	
G-FYEZ	Scallan Firefly Mk.1 Balloon (Minimum Lift) MNS-748			22. 9.82	M E and N L Scallan	Hayes	
G-FYFI	Eaves European E 84PS Balloon (Minimum Lift) S 29			1.12.82	M A Stelling	Barton-le-Clay, Bedford	
					(Extant 5.07)		
G-FYFJ	Williams Westwind Two Balloon (Minimum Lift) MDW-010			14.12.82	M D Williams	Houghton Regis, Dunstable	
					(Extant 5.07)		

G-FYFN	Osprey Saturn 2 DC3 Balloon (Minimum Lift)		17. 2.83	J and M Woods	Bracknell	
	ATC-250-MJS-11					
G-FYFW	Rango NA-55 Balloon (Minimum Lift) NHP-40		8.10.84	A M and N H Ponsford t/a Rango Balloon and Kite Company		
	(Radio controlled)			"Vaughan Williams" (Amended owners 8.07) Leeds		
G-FYFY	Rango NA-55RC Balloon (Minimum Lift) AL-43		28. 2.85	A M Ponsford t/a Rango Balloon and Kite Company		
	(Radio controlled)			"Fifi" (Amended owners 8.07) Leeds		
G-FYGI	Rango NA-55RC Balloon (Minimum Lift) NHP-54		26. 6.90	D K Fish	Manchester	
	(Radio controlled)					
G-FYGJ	Wells Airspeed-300 Balloon (Minimum Lift) 001		8.10.91	N Wells	Paddock Wood, Tunbridge Wells	
G-FYGM	Saffery/Smith Princess Balloon (Minimum Lift)		24.11.97	A and N Smith	Pollington, Goole	
	(Built C Saffery and N Smith) 551					
G-FZIS	Staaken Z-21 Flitzer Type S xxx		3.08R	(V Long)	Not known	
	(Built V Long).			(On build 9.06)		
G-FZZA	General Avia F22-A 018		13. 8.98	APB Leasing Ltd	Sleap	26. 9.08E
G-FZZI	Cameron H-34 Balloon (Hot Air) 2105		30.10.89	Magical Adventures Ltd		
				West Bloomfield, Michigan, US	30. 7.96A	

G-GAAA - G-GZZZ

G-GACA	Percival P 57 Sea Prince T 1	P57/58	WP308	2. 9.80	P G Vallance Ltd	Charlwood, Surrey	4.11.80P
				(In Gatwick Aviation Museum 2007 as "WP308/572")		
G-GACB	Robinson R44 Raven II	10243		9. 1.04	A C Barker Black Bank Farm, Foxt, Stoke-on-Trent	13. 2.08E
G-GAFA	Piper PA-34-200T Seneca II	34-7970218	D-GAFA	12.10.99	Oxford Aviation Training Ltd	Oxford	13.12.07T
			N2247Z				
G-GAFT	Piper PA-44-180 Seminole	4496162	N5324Q	24. 1.03	GT Ventures Ltd	Coventry	28. 1.08E
G-GAII	Hawker Hunter GA.11	HABL-003028	XE685	7.12.94	A G Fowles	Exeter	18. 6.08P
	(Officially regd with c/n 41H-004038)			(As "XE685:861" in RN c/s)		
G-GAJB	Gulfstream AA-5B Tiger	AA5B-1179	G-BHZN	6. 4.87	R Berman and S A Niechcia tr G-GAJB Group		
			N37519			Biggin Hill	8. 2.08E
G-GALA	Piper PA-28-180 Cherokee E	28-5794	G-AYAP	31. 7.89	Flyteam Aviation Ltd	Elstree	10. 5.08E
			N11C				
G-GALB	Piper PA-28-161 Warrior II	28-8616021	D-EHMP	1. 9.00	LB Aviation Ltd	Humberside	25. 7.08E
			N9097E, (N157AV), N9635N				
G-GALL	Piper PA-38-112 Tomahawk	38-78A0025	G-BTEV	1. 6.00	M Lowe and K Hazelwood	Cardiff	30. 5.08E
			N9315T				
G-GALX	Dassault Falcon 900EX	163	F-WWFX	13. 7.06	Charter Air Ltd	Farnborough	16. 7.08E
G-GAME	Cessna T303 Crusader	T30300098	(F-GDFN)	25. 2.83	P Heffron	Swansea	17. 9.08
			N2693C				
G-GAND	Agusta-Bell 206B-2 JetRanger II	8073	G-AWMK	11. 1.00	The Henderson Group	Gollanfield, Nairn	1. 7.08E
			9Y-TFC, G-AWMK, (VR-BCV), G-AWMK				
	(Officially regd with c/n 8073 airframe exchanged with 5N-AQJ [8051] on rebuild 1999: original 5N-AQJ remains as c/n 8051 and became VH-JEF 1.00)						
G-GANE	Sequoia F 8L Falco	906		25. 9.85	S J Gane	Kemble	15. 6.08P
	(Built S J Gane - pr.no.PFA 100-11100) (Lycoming IO-320)						
G-GANG	Bell 206L-4 Long Ranger IV	52352	N70258	6.11.07	The Henderson Group	Gollanfield, Nairn	
G-GAOH	Robin DR.400-2+2 Tri-cycle	1217	F-GAOH	9. 5.05	Exavia Ltd	Exeter	15. 8.08E
G-GAOM	Robin DR.400 2+2 Tri-cycle	1220	F-GAOM	24. 6.05	P M and P A Chapman	(Wadebridge)	1. 9.08E
G-GASP	Piper PA-28-181 Cherokee Archer II	28-7790013	N4328F	15.10.90	M L Robinson tr G-GASP Flying Group	Fairoaks	2. 2.08E
G-GASS	Thunder Ax7-77 Balloon (Hot Air)	1746		19. 4.90	M W Axon tr Servowarm Balloon Syndicate		
					"Travel Gas III"	Brentwood	4. 7.03A
G-GATE	Robinson R44 Raven II	10448		28. 7.04	J W Gate	Stainsby Grange Farm, Thornaby	16. 9.07T
G-GATT	Robinson R44 Raven II	10531		15.11.04	N R Gatt	(Tarporley)	22.11.07E
G-GAZA	Aérospatiale SA.341G Gazelle 1	1187	G-RALE	19. 6.92	The Auster Aircraft Company Ltd	Melton Mowbray	13. 9.07
			G-SFTG, N87712				
G-GAZN	P&M Quik GT450	8271		24. 5.07	G Nicholls	Rufforth	23. 5.08E
G-GAZZ	Aérospatiale SA.341G Gazelle 1	1271	F-GFHD	14. 3.90	Stratton Motor Company (Norfolk) Ltd)		
			YV-242CP, HB-XGA, F-WMHC		(Operated Cheqair Ltd) Tharston, Long Stratton	4. 7.08E
G-GBAB	Piper PA-28-161 Warrior II	28-7816495	HB-PAB	13.12.06	B A Mills	Duxford	24. 5.08E
			D-ELET, N9564N				
G-GBAO	Robin R1180TD Aiglon	277	F-GBAO	9. 9.81	J Toulorge	(Copthorne, Crawley)	25.11.07E
	(Rebuild of R 1180 prototype F-WVKU c/n 01)						
G-GBBB	Schleicher ASH 25	25074	BGA 3532-FUG	15.10.07	M J Wells tr ASH 25 BB Glider Syndicate	Lasham	30. 1.08
			(BGA 3526-FTZ)				
G-GBEE	Mainair Sports Pegasus Quik	8039		21. 5.04	L G White	Finmere	26. 5.08P
G-GBEN	Robinson R44 Raven II	10743	G-CDJZ	20. 6.07	BG(H) Aviation Ltd	(Hednesford, Cannock)	23. 6.08E
G-GBFF	Reims Cessna F172N Skyhawk II	F17201565	F-GBFF	16. 6.99	S J Skilton t/a Aviation Rentals	Bournemouth	14. 9.08E
	(Thielert TAE 125-01) (3-blade propeller)			(Operated Solent School of Flying) (Diesel titles)		
G-GBFR	Reims Cessna F177RG Cardinal RG	F177RG0172	F-GBFR	7. 4.04	Airspeed Aviation Ltd	Derby	
G-GBGA	Scheibe SF25C Falke	44683	D-KIEJ	28. 8.02	British Gliding Association Ltd	Bicester	17. 5.08E
	(Rotax 912S)						
G-GBGB	Ultramagic M-105 Balloon (Hot Air)	105/126		30.12.04	Universal Car Services Ltd	Aldershot	22. 7.07E
G-GBGF	Cameron Dragon SS Balloon (Hot Air)	3016	C-GBGF	23. 8.07	Magical Adventures Ltd	Oswestry	9. 6.97A
			G-BUVH		(New owner 8.07)		
G-GBHI	SOCATA TB-10 Tobago	19	F-GBHI	12.11.97	Robert Purvis Plant Hire Ltd	Glenrothes	21.12.07E
G-GBJP	Mainair Sports Pegasus Quantum 15	8036		16. 8.04	R G Mulford	(Chatham)	15. 8.08P
	(Rotax 582)						
G-GBJS	Robin HR.200-100S Club	73	F-BXJS	4. 5.06	R Bowen	Bodmin	24. 8.08E
G-GBLP	Reims Cessna F172M Skyhawk II	F17201042	G-GWEN	9.11.84	Aviate Scotland Ltd	Glenrothes	20.11.07E
			G-GBLP, N14496				
G-GBLR	Reims Cessna F150L	F15001109	N961L	30. 4.85	Almat Flying Club Ltd	Coventry	4.10.07E
			(D-EDJE)				
G-GBMR	Beech B200 Super King Air	BB-1693	N771SC	29.03.06	M and R Aviation LLP	(Leicester)	30. 3.08E
			N773TP				

G-GBOB	Alpi Pioneer 300 Hawk	PFA 330A-14681		20. 8.07	R E Burgess	(Carmel, Caernarfon)	
	(Built R E Burgess)						
G-GBPP	Rolladen-Schneider LS6-c	6230	BGA 3809-HBJ	24.10.07	G J Lyons and R Sinden	Wycombe Air Park	28. 9.08
G-GBRB	Piper PA-28-180 Cherokee C	28-2583	N8381W	2. 2.00	M S Marsland	Blackbushe	11. 4.08E
G-GBRU	Bell 206B-3 JetRanger III	3997	G-CDGV	15. 2.05	Merlin Estate Management Ltd	Leeds-Bradford	23. 3.08E
			N217PM, XC-PFS				
G-GBSL	Beech 76 Duchess	ME-265	G-BGVG	27. 3.81	M H Cundey *"Dolly"*	Redhill and Alderney	29. 5.08E
G-GBTA	Boeing 737-436	25859	G-BVHA	7. 2.94	British Airways PLC	London Gatwick	31.10.07E
G-GBTB	Boeing 737-436	25860	OO-LTS	23.10.96	British Airways PLC	London Gatwick	28.10.07E
			G-BVHB, OO-LTS, G-BVHB, (G-GBTB)				
G-GBTL	Cessna 172S Skyhawk	172S10322	N1261M	21.11.06	Bohana Technology Ltd		
						Wadswick Manor Farm, Corsham	23.11.07E
G-GBUE	Robin DR.400-120A Petit Prince	1354	G-BPXD	11. 5.89	J A Kane tr G-GBUE Group	Bagby	5.10.07E
			F-GBUE		(Noted 2.08)		
G-GBUN	Cessna 182T Skylane	18281280	N2157P	11.12.03	G M Bunn	Goodwood	2. 2.08E
G-GBVX	Robin DR.400-120A Petit Prince	1419	F-GBVX	2. 3.06	M Patterson	Sorbie Farm, Kingsmuir	6. 6.08E
G-GBXF	Robin HR.200-120 Acrobin	25	HB-EXF	13. 1.06	B A and L.A Mills	Bournemouth	7. 2.08E
					(Operated Dorset Flying Club)		
G-GBXS	Europa Aviation Europa XS	F0005	"G-2000"	1. 4.98	P G Wood	West Throstle Nest Farm, Moorsholm	4. 6.07P
	(Built Europa Aviation Ltd - pr.no.PFA 247-13196)		G-GBXS (Rotax 914-UL) (Monowheel u/c)				
G-GCAC	Europa Aviation Europa XS	559		21. 8.02	J L Gunn	(Hoveton, Norwich)	
	(Built G J Cattermole - pr.no.PFA 247-13940) (Tri-gear u/c)				(New owner 3.04)		
G-GCAT	Piper PA-28-140 Cherokee B	28-26032	G-BFRH	22.10.81	P F Jude tr Group CAT	Sturgate	15.12.07E
			OH-PCA				
G-GCCL	Beech 76 Duchess	ME-322	(G-BNRF)	5. 8.87	Aerolease Ltd	Conington	31. 1.08E
			N6714U				
G-GCEA	P&M Pegasus Quik	8209		12. 9.06	J D Ash	Wickenby	13. 9.08P
G-GCKI	Mooney M 20K Mooney 231	25-0401	N4062H	15. 8.80	B Barr	Seething	16.11.07E
G-GCMW	Grob G102 Astir CS	1112	BGA 5040-KEU	6.11.07	E F Weaver	AAC Wattisham	27. 6.07
			OY-XDE				
G-GCUF	Robin DR.400-160 Chevalier	1504	F-GCUF	19. 4.06	S T Bates	Eddsfield, Octon Lodge Farm, Thwing	22. 5.08E
G-GCYC	Reims Cessna F182Q Skylane II	F18200157	F-GCYC	11. 2.00	A G Dodd	Kemble	18. 9.08E
G-GDAV	Robinson R44 Raven II	10813		12. 7.05	L G Ward	(Bangor Isycoed, Wrexham)	15. 9.08E
G-GDEF	Robin DR.400-120 Petit Prince	1538	F-GDEE	26. 7.07	J M Shackleton	(Oxenhope, Keighley)	25. 7.08E
G-GDER	Robin R1180TD Aiglon II	280	F-GDER	15. 5.97	Berkshire Aviation Services Ltd	Fairoaks	26. 7.08E
G-GDJF	Robinson R44 Raven II	11406	G-DEXT	8. 2.07	Berkley Properties Ltd	(Croft, Skegness)	17.10.07E
G-GDKR	Robin DR.400-140B Major	1623	F-GDKR	12. 6.06	L J Milbank	Sibson	31.10.07E
G-GDMW	Beech 76 Duchess	ME-316	D-GDMW	29.10.04	Apollo Aviation Advisory Ltd	Shoreham	7.12.07E
			LX-DRS, F-GCGB				
G-GDOG	Piper PA-28R-200 Cherokee Arrow II		G-BDXW	17. 4.89	N J Morton tr Mutley Crew Group	Conington	8.11.07E
		28R-7635227	N9235K				
G-GDOV	Robinson R44 Raven	1503		27. 7.05	D B Hamilton	(Stonehouse)	17. 8.08E
G-GDRV	Van's RV-6	21367	C-GDRV	26.11.01	M A Jardim de Queiroz tr G-GDRV Group		
	(Built D Piper) (Lycoming O-320)				"Slavka"	Gloucestershire	24.10.08P
G-GDSG	Agusta A109E Power	11656		16.11.05	Pendley Aviation LLP	Pendley Farm, Aldbury	17.11.07E
G-GDTU	Mudry CAP.10B	193	F-GDTU	27. 5.99	A L Farr and D C Cooper	(Yeovil)	20.12.07E
			(N.....), F-GDTK, F-WZCI				
G-GEBJ	Cessna 525 CitationJet	525-0528	N528CJ	9. 2.08	EBJ Operations Ltd	London Stansted	
G-GEDY	Dassault Falcon 2000	208	F-WWVV	6. 5.04	Victoria Aviation Ltd	(Geneva, Switzerland)	5. 5.08E
G-GEEP	Robin R1180TD Aiglon	266		9. 4.80	C Stratford tr The Aiglon Flying Group	Stapleford	26. 9.07
G-GEES	Cameron N-77 Balloon (Hot Air)	357		8.11.77	N A Carr	Leicester	31. 5.00A
G-GEEZ	Cameron N-77 Balloon (Hot Air)	1159		3. 5.85	Charnwood Forest Turf Accountants Ltd	Leicester	7. 4.96A
					"Tic Tac"		
G-GEHL	Cessna 172S Skyhawk SP	172S8324	N163RA	18. 6.03	Ebryl Ltd	White Waltham	8. 8.08E
G-GEHP	Piper PA-28RT-201 Arrow IV	28R-8218014	F-GEHP	24. 4.98	Aeros Leasing Ltd	Gloucestershire	2. 8.08T
			N82023				
G-GEMM	Cirrus SR20	1138	N241CD	14.12.05	Cumulus Aircraft Rentals Ltd	Blackbushe	7. 3.08E
G-GEMS	Thunder Ax8-90 Series 2 Balloon (Hot Air)	2287	G-BUNP	6.11.92	B Sevenich, Benedikt, S Harren and C Walter		
						Aachen and Bonn, Germany	10. 6.08E
G-GEMX	P&M Quik GT450	8344		31. 1.08	J A Gilchrist (Noted 2.08))	Mendlesham	
G-GENI	Robinson R44 Raven II	11396		13. 9.06	G-GENI LLP	(Hove)	17.10.07E
G-GEOF	Pereira Osprey 2	PFA 070-10384		7. 9.78	G Crossley	(Poulton-le-Fylde)	
	(Built G Crossley)						
G-GEOS	Diamond HK 36 TTC-ECO Super Dimona	36.582	N842WS	19.10.05	University Court of the University of Edinburgh		
			(G-GEOS), N842WS, C-GETC			Glenrothes	9. 3.08E
G-GERT	Van's RV-7	PFA 323-13836		22. 3.04	M Castle-Smith tr Barnstormers	Compton Abbas	
	(M Castle-Smith, B West and A Burroughs)				(Noted 9.06)		
G-GERY	Stoddard-Hamilton GlaStar	PFA 295-13475		6. 7.01	S G Brown	Eddsfield, Octon Lodge Farm, Thwing	17. 8.08P
	(Built G E Collard) (Tailwheel u/c)						
G-GEST	Robinson R44 Clipper II	11159		4. 4.06	Gest Air Ltd	Rennes St Jacques, France	11. 5.08E
G-GEZZ	Bell 206B-2 JetRanger II	1301	N68TJ	16 .2.07	Rivermead Aviation Ltd		
			N59489			(La Tour de Peilz, Vaud, Switzerland)	
G-GFAB	Cameron N-105 Balloon (Hot Air)	2048		4. 8.89	R K Scott	North Perrott, Crewkerne	26. 4.08A
G-GFCA	Piper PA-28-161 Cadet	2841100	N9174X	24. 4.89	Aeros Leasing Ltd	Gloucestershire	4.10.07T
G-GFCB	Piper PA-28-161 Cadet	2841101	N9175X	24. 4.89	A J Warren	Bristol	22. 8.08T
G-GFCD	Piper PA-34-220T Seneca III	34-8133073	G-KIDS	31. 5.90	Stonehurst Aviation Ltd	Blackbushe	28. 4.08E
			N83745				
G-GFEA	Cessna 172S Skyhawk II	172S10214	G-CEDY	27. 9.06	Saltaire Motor Company Ltd t/a Allan Jefferies Barton		7. 9.08E
			N60361				
G-GFEY	Piper PA-34-200T Seneca II	34-7870343	D-GFEY	13. 5.98	Mann Air Ltd	Gloucestershire	24. 2.08E
			D-IFEY, N36599				
G-GFFA	Boeing 737-59D	25038	G-BVZF	10. 2.00	British Airways PLC	London Gatwick	2. 5.08E
			SE-DND, (SE-DNC)				
G-GFFB	Boeing 737-505	25789	LN-BRT	15. 2.00	British Airways PLC	London Gatwick	8. 5.08E

Reg	Type	c/n	Prev id	Date	Owner	Location	Date
G-GFFD	Boeing 737-59D	26419	LY-BFV OY-SEG, G-OBMY, SE-DNI	3. 7.00	British Airways PLC	Manchester	13. 8.08E
G-GFFE	Boeing 737-528	27424	LX-LGR (F-GJNP)	16. 6.00	British Airways PLC	London Gatwick	10. 7.08E
G-GFFF	Boeing 737-53A	24754	G-OBMZ SE-DNC	2. 1.01	British Airways PLC	Manchester	20. 9.08E
G-GFFG	Boeing 737-505	24650	LN-BRC N5573K	20. 9.00	British Airways PLC	Manchester	29.10.08E
G-GFFH	Boeing 737-5H6	27354	VT-JAW 9M-MFG	24.10.00	British Airways PLC	London Gatwick	23. 1.07T
G-GFFI	Boeing 737-528	27425	LX-LGS (F-GJNQ)	9.11.00	British Airways PLC	Manchester	18.12.08E
G-GFFJ	Boeing 737-5H6	27355	VT-JAZ 9M-MFH	19. 1.01	British Airways PLC	Manchester	12. 3.08E
G-GFIA	Cessna 152	15281685	F-GGLI N66950	18. 9.06	Aircraft Grouping Ltd	Barton	18.10.07E
G-GFIB	Reims Cessna F152 II	F15201556	G-BPIO PH-VSO, PH-AXS	14.11.06	Aircraft Grouping Ltd	Blackpool	23. 9.07E
G-GFIC	Cessna 152 II	15281672	G-BORI N66936	12.11.07	Composite Mast Engineering and Technology Ltd (Bacup)		16.10.07E
G-GFKY	Zenair CH.250	34	C-GFKY	23. 4.93	R G Kelsall	RAF Mona	18. 3.08P
	(Built D Koch) (Lycoming O-235)						
G-GFLY	Reims Cessna F150L	F15000822	PH-CES	28. 8.80	Leagate Ltd	Seething	13. 7.08P
G-GFMT	Cessna 172S Skyhawk	172S8258	C-GFMT N341SP	2.11.04	A D Cameron and D Hey tr G-GFMT Flying Group Barton		23.11.07E
G-GFNO	Robin ATL	16	F-GFNO F-WFNO	23. 3.05	D J Watson	Blackpool	12. 5.08E
G-GFOX	Aeroprakt A22 Foxbat	PFA 317-14368		25. 5.05	I A Love and G F Elvis	Mill Farm, Shifnal	14.11.08P
	(Build B J Mould)						
G-GFPA	Piper PA-28-181 Archer III	2843010	N115RT N9256J	13.11.06	Saltaire Motor Company Ltd t/a Allan Jefferies Barton		23.11.07E
G-GFPB	Piper PA-28-181 Archer III	2843409	G-BZHW N4184D, G-BZHW, N4184D	29.10.07	S Viner	Blackpool	11. 3.08E
G-GFRD	Robin ATL	53	F-GFRD	2. 2.05	C Long	Haverfordwest	7. 2.08E
G-GFRO	Robin ATL	64	F-GFRO	28.11.06	B F Walker	Gloucestershire	23. 7.08E
G-GFSA	Cessna 172R Skyhawk	17280221	N410ES	26.10.06	Aircraft Grouping Ltd	Barton	6.11.07E
G-GFTA	Piper PA-28-161 Warrior III	2842047	N4132L G-GFTA, N9525N	1. 4.99	One Zero Three Ltd	Guernsey	21. 4.08E
G-GFTB	Piper PA-28-161 Warrior III	2842048	N4120V G-GFTB, N4120V	7. 5.99	One Zero Three Ltd	Guernsey	6. 5.08E
G-GGCT	Flight Design CT2K	02-08-02-31		18. 2.03	G R Graham	Kirkbride	17. 4.08P
	(Assembled Pegasus Aviation Ltd with c/n 7938)						
G-GGGG	Thunder Ax7-77 Balloon (Hot Air)	162		2. 8.78	T A Gilmour tr Flying G Group	Stockbridge	17. 8.99A
					"Flying G" (Active 9.05)		
G-GGHZ	Robin ATL	123	F-GGHZ	10. 2.05	Modesto's Bakeries Ltd	Barton	18. 5.08E
G-GGJK	Robin DR.400-140B Major 80	1805	F-GGJK	24. 3.05	D Kember tr Headcorn Jodelers	Headcorn	27. 4.08E
G-GGLE	Piper PA-22-108 Colt	22-8914	N5234Z	13. 5.93	K De Dobbelaere	(Wilrijk, Belgium)	10.12.10S
	(Frame No.108-915) (Tail-wheel conversion incorporating parts from G-AROM c/n 22-8805)						
G-GGNG	Robinson R44 Clipper II	11172		25. 5.06	Bburton Helicopters Ltd	(London W1)	19. 6.08E
G-GGOW	Colt 77A Balloon (Hot Air)	1542		19. 6.89	G Everett "Charles Rennie Mackintosh"	Dartford	26. 9.08A
G-GGRR	Scottish Aviation Bulldog Series 120/121	BH120/272	G-CBAM XX614	11. 7.01	M Litherland	Oxford	15.10.08S
					(As "XX614:V" in RAF c/s)		
G-GGTT	Agusta-Bell 47G-4A	2538	F-GGTT I-ANDO	21. 8.97	Phoenix Aviation Refinishers Ltd (Earlsheaton, Dewsbury)		5. 7.10S
G-GHDC	Robinson R44 Raven II	11468		1.11.06	P Mooney	Weston, Leixlip, County Kildare	8.11.07E
G-GHEE	Evektor EV-97 Eurostar	PFA 315-13840		14.12.01	C J Ball	Oxleaze Grange, Hawling, Cheltenham	2.11.08P
	(Built C J Ball)				(Involved in mid-air collision with Cessna 152 G-BNXC near.Moreton-in-Marsh 18.12.05)		
G-GHIA	Cameron N-120 Balloon (Hot Air)	2442		13.11.90	J A Marshall (Active 5.07)	Plaistow, Billingshurst	25. 8.04T
G-GHIN	Thunder Ax7-77 Balloon (Hot Air)	1802		16. 7.90	N T Parry "Pegasus"	Ascot	4. 9.00A
G-GHKX	Piper PA-28-161 Warrior II	28-8416005	N380X G-GHKX, F-GHKX, N4318X	10. 6.99	S J Skilton t/a Aviation Rentals	Halfpenny Green	28.11.07E
	(Thielert TAE 125-01)						
G-GHOW	Reims Cessna F182Q Skylane II	F18200151	OO-MCD F-BJCE	20. 2.01	G How	Top Farm, Croydon, Royston	3. 5.08E
G-GHPG	Cessna 550 Citation II	550-0897	EI-GHP N5079V	22. 2.02	MCP Aviation (Charter) Ltd	Farnborough	18. 3.08E
G-GHRW	Piper PA-28RT-201 Arrow IV	28R-7918140	G-ONAB G-BHAK, N29555	8.12.83	Bonus Aviation Ltd	Cranfield	18. 1.08E
G-GHSI	Piper PA-44-180T Turbo Seminole	44-8107026	SX-ATA N8278Z	2.12.94	M G Roberts t/a Flight Consultancy Services Bournemouth		26. 4.08
G-GHZJ	SOCATA TB-9 Tampico	941	F-GHZJ	4. 3.98	M Haller	Little Snoring	2. 9.08E
G-GIBB	Robinson R44 Raven II	11777		13. 6.07	Tingdene Aviation Ltd	Sywell	4. 7.08E
G-GIDY	Europa Aviation Europa XS	432		18. 2.04	I N Robson tr Gidy Group	(Repton, Derby)	
	(Built I N Robson, P Stewart, R Tuckwell and H Carmichael - pr.no.PFA 247-13467)						
G-GIGI	SOCATA MS.893A Rallye Commodore 180	11637	G-AYVX F-BSFJ	28. 9.81	D J Moore (Noted 3.03)	(Aston Down)	13. 4.00
G-GILI	Robinson R44 Raven	1436		5. 1.05	Twylight Management Ltd	(Douglas, Isle of Man)	13. 1.08E
G-GILT	Cessna 421C Golden Eagle	421C0515	G-BMZC N555WV, N555WW, N885WW, N885EC, N88541 (New owner 5.07)	3. 7.97	Cloud Aviation (Leasing) Ltd	(Sheffield City)	28. 3.07T
G-GIRY	American General AG-5B Tiger	10146	F-GIRY	5. 2.99	F Neefs tr Romeo Yankee Flying Group	Elstree	9. 5.08E
G-GIWT	Europa Aviation Europa XS	463		29. 3.01	A Twigg	(Wootton Bassett)	
	(Built A Twigg - pr.no.PFA 247-13623) (Monowheel u/c)				(Noted incomplete 7.07)		
G-GJCD	Robinson R22 Beta	0966		22. 2.89	J C Lane	Gloucestershire	21.10.07E
G-GJKK	Mooney M 20K Mooney 231	25-1227	F-GJKK	26.11.93	Pergola Ltd	Fairoaks	11. 4.08

G-GKAT	Enstrom 280C Shark	1200	F-GKAT	26. 8.97	D Cummaford	(Wilmslow)	9. 8.08E
			N5694Y				
G-GKFC	TLAC RL5A LW Sherwood Ranger	xxxx	G-MYZI	24.11.98	T R Janaway	(Witney)	23. 7.08P
	(Built K F Crumplin- pr.no. PFA 237-12947) (Jabiru 2200A)						
G-GKKI	Avions Mudry CAP 231EX	02	F-GKKI	23. 1.07	Acro Laser Company Ltd	Hawarden	10. 5.08E
			G-BVXL, F-GKKF, F-WGZC				
G-GKUE	SOCATA TB-9 Tampico	1129	F-GKUE	5. 2.07	I Parkinson	Bagby	3. 5.08E
G-GLAD	Gloster Gladiator II	?	N5903	5. 1.95	Patina Ltd	Duxford	
					((Operated The Fighter Collection as "N5903":in 72 Sqdn RAF c/s) (On rebuild 2008)		
G-GLAK	Sportline Aviacija LAK-12 Lietuva	647	BGA 3717-GCB	15.11.07	L M Middleton	Easterton	5. 4.08
G-GLAW	Cameron N-90 Balloon (Hot Air)	1808		10.10.88	R A Vale	Hurcott, Kidderminster	15. 2.06A
G-GLED	Cessna 150M	15076673	C-GLED	6. 1.89	Firecrest Aviation Ltd	Elstree	26.11.07E
G-GLHI	Best Off Sky Ranger 912S(1)	SKR0403468		30. 6.04	S F Winter	Lower Upham Farm, Chiseldon	9. 6.08P
	(Built G L Higgins - pr.no.BMAA/HB/392)						
G-GLIB	Robinson R44 Raven	1226		12. 6.02	Helisport UK Ltd	Earls Colne	11. 7.08E
G-GLID	Schleicher ASW 28-18E	28723	BGA 5131-KJR	18. 4.06	B A Bateson and P N Marriott	Parham Park	22. 4.08
			D-KEBB, D-KOAB		"E3"		
G-GLII	Great Lakes 2T-1A-2	813	N3613L	8. 8.07	T J Richardson	Popham	
G-GLKE	Robin DR.400-180 Régent	2119	F-GLKE	15. 6.07	Exavia Ltd	Exeter	4 .7.08E
G-GLOC	Extra EA.300/200	1039		30. 3.07	The Cambridge Aero Club Ltd	Cambridge	12. 4.08E
					"cambridgeaeroclub.com"		
G-GLST	Great Lakes 2T-1A Sport Trainer	PFA 321-13646		21. 7.03	D A Graham	(Farnborough)	
	(Built D A Graham)						
G-GLSU	Bücker Bü.181B-1 Bestmann	25071	D-EDUB	21. 7.04	P R Holloway	Old Warden	4.10.10S
	(Built Hagglund and Soner)		Swedish AF Fv25071		(As "GL+SU":6 1 in pseudo Luftwaffe c/s)		
G-GLTT	Piper PA-31-350 Chieftain	31-8452004	N27JV	19. 9.97	Airtime Aviation Ltd	Bournemouth	26. 5.08E
			XA-SVW, XA-SGZ, N606SM, N4115D				
G-GLUC	Van's RV-6	20153	C-GLUC	15.10.99	Speedfreak Ltd	Crosland Moor	11. 4.08P
	(Built L De Sadeleer) (Lycoming O-320)						
G-GLUE	Cameron N-65 Balloon (Hot Air)	390		17. 3.81	L J M Muir and G D Hallett	East Molesey	17. 7.90A
					(Mobile Windscreens titles) "Tacky Jack" and "Jack of Herts"		
G-GLUG	Piper PA-31-350 Chieftain	31-8052077	N2287J	1. 9.94	Champagne-Air Ltd	Newcastle	13. 4.08E
			G-BLOE, G-NITE, N3559A				
G-GMAA	Learjet Model 45	45-167	N5012V	1. 5.02	Gama Aviation Ltd	Farnborough	1. 5.08E
G-GMAB	British Aerospace BAe 125 Series 1000B	259034	N81HH	21.11.01	Gama Aviation Ltd	Farnborough	11. 3.08T
	(Build Corporate Jets Ltd)		N290H, G-BUWX, G-5-761				
G-GMAX	SNCAN Stampe SV-4C	141	G-BXNW	19. 6.87	Glidegold Ltd	(Cookham,, Maidenhead)	29. 8.93T
			F-BBPB		Damaged in crash Booker 3. 6.91: on rebuild 5.96)		
G-GMKD	Robin HR.200-120B	256	F-GMKD	13.11.06	Cardiff Academy of Aviation Ltd	Cardiff	7. 1.08E
G-GMKE	Robin HR.200/120B Club	257	F-GMKE	7.11.07	B A Mills	Bourn	
G-GMPB	Pilatus Britten-Norman BN-2T-4S Defender 4000	4011	G-BWPU	5. 4.02	Greater Manchester Police Authority	Manchester	1. 7.09S
			(9M-TPD), G-BWPU				
G-GMPS	MD Helicopters MD.900 Explorer	900-00081	N7033K	8. 1.01	Greater Manchester Police Authority	Barton	12. 2.10S
G-GMPX	MD Helicopters MD.900 Explorer	900-00122	N9114R	29. 1.08	Greater Manchester Police Authority	Barton	
G-GMSI	SOCATA TB-9 Tampico	145		18. 9.80	M L Rhodes	Halfpenny Green	3. 8.08E
G-GNAA	MD Helicopters MD.900 Explorer	900-00079	PH-RVD	15.12.04	Police Aviation Services Ltd	Durham Tees Valley	14.12.07E
			N70279		(Operated Great North Air Ambulance)		
G-GNJW	Comco Ikarus C42 FB100 VLA	0106-9356		21. 8.01	I R Westrope	(Steeple Bumpstead, Haverhill)	16. 5.08P
	(Built I R Westrope - pr.no.PFA 322-13717) (Kit no unconfirmed - may be 0106-6326)						
G-GNRV	Van's RV-9A	PFA 320-14344		20. 6.05	N K Beavins	Rayne Hall Farm, Braintree	24. 7.08P
	(Built N K Beavins)						
G-GNTB	SAAB-Scania SF.340A	340A-082	HB-AHL	30. 9.91	Loganair Ltd	Glasgow	13. 3.08E
			SE-E82				
G-GNTF	SAAB-Scania SF.340A	340A-113	SE-F13	27.10.94	Loganair Ltd	Glasgow	6. 9.08E
			G-GNTF, HB-AHO, SE-F13				
G-GNTZ	British Aerospace BAe 146 Series 200	E2036	G-CLHB	31. 3.00	Flybe Ltd	Exeter	25.11.07E
			G-GNTZ, HB-IXB, N175US, N355PS (Stored 9.07)				
G-GOAC	Piper PA-34-200T Seneca II	34-7770007	D-GOAC	9.12.03	Oxford Aviation Training Ltd	Oxford	23.11.07E
			N5329F				
G-GOAL	Lindstrand LBL 105A Balloon (Hot Air)	420		18.11.96	I Chadwick tr Balloon Preservation Flying Group		
					(Benfield Reinsurance titles) Partridge Green, Horsham		30. 5.08A
G-GOBD	Piper PA-32R-301 Saratoga II HP	3246193	G-OARW	22. 8.05	B J de'Ath	Southend	29. 9.07E
			EC-IJT, N5339Z		(Noted 1.08)		
G-GOBT	Colt 77A Balloon (Hot Air)	1815		13. 2.91	British Telecommunications PLC "Sky Piper"	Thatcham	18. 3.00A
G-GOCX	Cameron N-90 Balloon (Hot Air)	2619		7. 8.91	R D Parry	Chalford, Stroud	17. 7.08A
G-GOES	Robinson R44 Raven II	10942	EI-KHL	14. 1.08	Rotormotive Ltd	Little Blakenham	
G-GOGB	Lindstrand LBL 90A Balloon (Hot Air)	1011	G-CDFX	20. 1.05	J Dyer	Farnborough	22. 2.06E
G-GOGS	Piper PA-34-200T Seneca II	34-7570228	N1172X	23. 7.03	A Semple	Shoreham	4. 8.06
G-GOGW	Cameron N-90 Balloon (Hot Air)	3304		31. 8.94	S E Carrol	Caversham, Reading	17. 5.05A
					(Great Western titles)		
G-GOLF	SOCATA TB-10 Tobago	250		21.12.81	A C Scamell tr Golf Golf Group	Biggin Hill	14. 9.08E
G-GOLY	Cessna 150L	15075261	SE-KCM	13. 8.07	E Al-Kirkhy	Wycombe Air Park	13. 9.08E
G-GOMO	Learjet Model 45	45-055	G-OLDF	2. 6.05	Air Partner Private Jets Ltd	Biggin Hill	23. 1.08E
			G-JRJR, N45LR, N63MJ				
G-GOOD	SOCATA TB-20 Trinidad	1657	F-GNHJ	4.11.94	T M Sloan and M P Bowcock		
					(Chichester and Haslemere)		12. 2.07T
G-GORE	CFM Streak Shadow	K 138-SA		12. 4.90	M S Clinton	Old Sarum	27. 6.06P
	(Built D N Gore - pr.no.PFA 206-11646) (Rotax 532) (PFA sequence no. duplicates TEAM Mini-MAX G-MWFD)						
G-GOSL	Robin DR.400-180 Régent	1974	G-BSDG	14. 1.02	R M Gosling	Spilstead Farm, Sedlescombe	23. 5.08E
G-GOTC	Gulfstream GA-7 Cougar	GA7-0074	G-BMDY	25. 6.97	Wakelite Ltd	Denham	22. 3.08E
			OO-LCR, OO-HRA				
G-GOTF	Cessna 208B Grand Caravan	208B1175	N208AZ	11.12.06	Trailfinders (Services) Ltd	Oxford	14.12.07E
			N5117U				
G-GOTH	Piper PA-28-161 Warrior III	2842208	N3088U	21. 6.04	J Gosling tr Goose Aviation Syndicate	Barton	24. 6.08E

Reg	Type	C/n	Prev id	Date	Owner/Operator	Location	Expiry
G-GOUP	Robinson R22 Beta	1663	G-DIRE	9. 1.01	Heli Air Ltd	Wellesbourne Mountford	29. 8.08E
G-GPAG	Van's RV-6	PFA 181A-13306		18. 5.01	P A Green	Old Sarum	31. 1.08P
	(Built P A Green) (Lycoming O-320)						
G-GPAS	Avtech Jabiru UL-450	xxxx		15. 1.02	G D Allen	Priory Farm, Tibenham	16.10.08P
	(Built G D Allen - pr.no.PFA 274A-13823)						
G-GPEG	Cameron Sky 90-24 Balloon (Hot Air)	4849		31. 5.00	N T Parrry "Pegasus"	Bracknell	15. 2.08A
G-GPFI	Boeing 737-229	20907	VH-OZQ	31. 7.03	European Skybus Ltd	Bournemouth	2. 4.08E
	G-GPFI, VH-OZQ, G-GPFI, F-GVAC, OO-SDA, LX-LGN, OO-SDA						
	(Op European Aviation in full Ozjet c/s)						
G-GPMW	Piper PA-28RT-201T Turbo Arrow IV	28R-8031041	N3576V	3. 7.89	Calverton Flying Group Ltd	White Waltham	14. 5.08E
G-GPPN	Cameron TR-70 Balloon (Hot Air)	10940		25.10.06	P Lesser	Partille, Sweden	8.11.07E
G-GPSF	Avtech Jabiru J430	0xxx		21. 4.06	P S Furlow	Lodge Farm, Woodham Mortimer	21 10.08P
	(Built P S Furlow - pr.no.PFA 336-14516)						
G-GPST	Phillips St 1 Speedtwin	1		21. 6.90	Speedtwin Developments Ltd	Upper Cae Garw Farm, Trelleck, Monmouth	3.12.03P
	(Built P J C Phillips - pr.no.PFA 207-11645) (Continental O-200-A)						
	(PFA sequence no. duplicates de-registered Kolb Twinstar G-MWWM)						
G-GREY	Piper PA-46-350P Malibu Mirage	4636155	OY-LAR	28.11.03	S T Day and S C Askham	Gloucestershire	10.12.07E
			N1280K, N4129D				
G-GRIN	Van's RV-6	PFA 181-12409		8. 1.98	A Phillips	Boarhunt Farm, Fareham	28. 6.08P
	(Built A Phillips) (Lycoming O-320)						
G-GRMN	Aerospool Dynamic WT9 UK	DY159/2006		2.10.06	R M North	Kimbolton	1. 5.08P
	(Official c/n is "DY/159")						
G-GRND	Agusta A109S Grand	22009		5. 1.06	DFS Trading Ltd	(Doncaster)	4. 1.08E
G-GROE	Grob G115A	8054	I-GROE	22. 6.04	H and E Merkado	Panshanger	30. 9.07E
			(D-EGVV)				
G-GROL	Maule MXT-7-180 Super Rocket	14091C		16. 6.98	D C, C and C Croll (Noted 1.08)	Southend	28.11.07E
G-GRPA	Comco Ikarus C42 FB100	0407-6609		26. 8.04	G R Page	(Waterrow, Taunton)	27 .8.08P
G-GRRC	Piper PA-28-161 Warrior II	2816076	G-BXJX	9. 3.98	Goodwood Road Racing Company Ltd	Goodwood	12.12.07E
			HB-POM, D-EJTB, N9149X		(Operated Goodwood Flying Club)		
G-GRRR	Scottish Aviation Bulldog Series 120/122	BH120/229	G-BXGU	19.10.98	Horizons Europe Ltd	Compton Abbas	31. 5.08E
			Ghana AF G-105				
G-GRVE	Van's RV-6	PFA 181-12566		14. 4.07	R D Carswell	Perranporth	
	(Built R D Carswell)				(Noted 10.07)		
G-GRWL	Lilliput Type 4 Balloon (Minimum Lift) SS Model Bear	L-04		22. 6.06	A E and D E Thomas	Weston, Honiton	
G-GRWW	Robinson R44 Raven II	10382	G-HEEL	6.12.04	G R Williams	Phoenix Farm, Lower Upham	17. 6.08E
G-GRYZ	Beech F33A Bonanza	CE-1668	F-GRYZ	4.10.99	J Kawadri and M Kaveh	Fairoaks	10. 1.08
			D-ESNE, N80011, (OY-GEN), N80011				
G-GSCV	Comco Ikarus C42 FB UK	PFA 322-13939		5. 9.02	G Sipson	(Coventry)	25. 5.07P
	(Built G Sipson)						
G-GSGZ	Mudry CAP.232	08	F-GSGZ	22.11.07	J Paulson	(Frodsham)	
G-GSJH	Bell 206B-3 JetRanger III	3958	G-PENT	15. 3.02	TJ Morris Ltd	Blackpool	10. 6.08E
			G-IIRB, N903CA				
G-GSOO	Hughes 369E	0336E	OE-XHA	6. 9.07	C Springthorpe t/a CS Properties	(Bulcote, Nottingham)	
	(Hughes 500)		D-HABC, F-GGCJ				
G-GSPG	Hughes 369HS	45-0738S	G-GEEE	17. 1.03	S P Giddings t/a S Giddings Aviation		
	(Hughes 500)		G-BDOY			Gowles Farm, Sherrington, Buckingham	4. 1.08E
G-GSPN	Boeing 737-31S	29267	(G-SPAN)	9. 2.04	Globespan Airways Ltd t/a Flyglobespan		
			D-ADBW, N60436, N1787B			Glasgow	28. 3.08E
G-GSPY	Robinson R44 Raven II	10772		31. 8.05	Percy Wood Leaisure Ltd	Sherburn-in-Elmet	21. 9.08E
G-GSRV	Robin DR.500-200i Président	0009	F-GSRV	30.10.07	R G Fairall	Redhill	
	(Officially regd as DR.400-500)						
G-GSSA	Boeing 747-47UF	29256	N495MC	23. 1.02	Global Supply Systems Ltd	London Stansted	27. 1.08E
			(N496MC)				
G-GSSB	Boeing 747-47UF	29252	N491MC	17. 1.03	Global Supply Systems Ltd	London Stansted	20. 1.08E
G-GSSC	Boeing 747-47UF	29255	N494MC	27. 8.03	Global Supply Systems Ltd	London Stansted	28. 8.08E
			OO-TJA, N494MC				
G-GSSO	Gulfstream Aerospace Gulfstream V-SP	5019	SE-RDX	15. 8.06	TAG Aviation (UK) Ltd	Farnborough	16. 8.08E
	(Gulfstream 550)		N919GA				
G-GSST	Grob G102 Astir CS77	1649	BGA 2291-DQG	8.12.07	A G Veitch tr 770 Group	Easterton	13. 4.08
G-GSYJ	Diamond DA.42 Twin Star	42.135	OE-VPI	11. 5.06	Crosby Aviation (Jersey) Ltd	Jersey	1. 6.08E
G-GSYS	Piper PA-34-220T Seneca V	3449363	N60383	8.10.07	Sys (Scaffolding Contractors) Ltd	Gamston	
G-GTEE	P&M Quik GT450	8256		26. 3.07	Fly Hire Ltd	Rufforth	22. 3.08E
G-GTFC	P&M Pegasus Quik	8184		20. 6.06	A J Fell	(Great Cambourne, Cambridge)	25. 7.08P
G-GTGT	P&M Quik GT450	8145		8.12.05	G C Weighell	Enstone	7.12.08P
G-GTHM	Piper PA-38-112 Tomahawk II	38-81A0171	C-GTHM	17.11.86	A B King and T P Powley	Ellough, Beccles	16.11.07E
			N91338				
G-GTJD	P&M Quik GT450	8183		1. 6.06	R D McKellar t/a Robert McKellar Aviation	North Coates	11. 6.08P
G-GTJM	Eurocopter EC.120B Colibri	1428	F-WQDC	20. 7.06	T J Morris Ltd	Blackpool	9.11.07E
G-GTSO	P&M Quik GT450	8164		10. 3.06	J R North	Ince Blundell	7. 3.08P
G-GTTP	P&M Quik GT450	8228		27.11.06	T A H Pollock	Enstone	13.12.08P
G-GTWO	Schleicher ASW 15	15146	BGA 3315-FKE	18.12.07	J M G Carlton	Edgehill	11. 2.08
			D-0794				
G-GUCK	Beech C23 Sundowner 180	M-2221	G-BPYG	9. 4.92	J T Francis	Headcorn	28.10.07E
			N6638R				
G-GUFO	Cameron Saucer 80 SS Balloon (Hot Air)	1641	C-GUFO	10. 6.98	Magical Adventures Ltd		
			G-BOUB			West Bloomfield, Michigan, US	14. 8.05A
G-GULF	Lindstrand LBL 105A Balloon (Hot Air)	320		3.11.95	M A Webb	Meifod, Shrewbury	17. 7.02A
G-GULP	III Sky Arrow 650 T	K130		4.12.00	S Marriott	Old Sarum	14.11.08P
	(Built H R Rotherwick - pr.no.PFA 298-13664) (Rotax 914)						
G-GUMS	Cessna 182P Skylane	18261643	G-CBMN	11.11.02	L W Scattergood	Sandtoft	14. 2.08E
			ZS-KJS, N21458				
G-GUNS	Cameron V-77 Balloon (Hot Air)	2221		9. 5.90	J Pithois	St Urbain, France	2. 4.06E

Registration	Type	Construction No.	Previous ID	Date	Owner/Operator	Base	Expiry
G-GURN	Piper PA-31 Navajo C (Winglets)	31-7912117	G-BHGA N3539M	20. 6.01	Neric Ltd	Fowlmere	23.11.07E
G-GURU	Piper PA-28-161 Warrior II	28-8316018	PH-SVJ N83085	12. 2.02	Fly Guru LLP	Hawarden	7. 4.08E
G-GUSS	Piper PA-28-151 Cherokee Warrior	28-7415497	G-BJRY N43453	16. 8.95	M J Cleaver and J M Newman	Southend	25. 6.08E
G-GUST	Agusta-Bell 206B-2 JetRanger II	8192	G-CBHH F-GALU, G-AYBE	30. 8.96	DNH Helicopters Ltd (Operated Cranfield Helicopters)	Cranfield	27. 5.08E
G-GUYS	Piper PA-34-200T Seneca II	34-7870283	G-BMWT N31984	14. 7.87	Jowett Homes Ltd	Gamston	14.11.07E
G-GVPI	Evans VP-1 Series 2 (Built P A Schafle and G Martin)	PFA 062-10668		9. 8.02	G Martin	Stoke Golding	13. 6.08P
G-GWIZ	Colt Clown SS Balloon (Hot Air)	1369	(G-BPWU)	25. 4.89	Magical Adventures Ltd West Bloomfield, Michigan, US		13. 4.99A
G-GWYN	Reims Cessna F172M Skyhawk II	F17201217	PH-TWN	5. 3.81	C G Tandy tr Magic Carpet Flying Company	Denham	27. 4.08E
G-GYAK	Yakovlev Yak-50	852905	RA-02246 DOSAAF (43 blue ?)	9.12.02	M V Rijske and M W Levy "46"	Wycombe Air Park	23.12.08P
G-GYAT	Sud-Aviation Gardan GY-80-160 Horizon	136	D-EAZZ HB-DCL, F-BMUU	13.12.02	J Luck tr Rochester GYAT Flying Group Club	Rochester	26. 4.08E
G-GYAV	Cessna 172N Skyhawk II	17271362	C-GYAV	26. 8.87	Southport and Merseyside Aero Club (1979) Ltd	Hawarden	15. 5.08E
G-GYBO	Sud-Aviation Gardan GY-80-180 Horizon	228	OY-DTN SE-FGL, OY-DTN	4. 8.98	A L Fogg	Wellesbourne Mountford	15.11.07E
G-GYMM	Piper PA-28R-200 Cherokee Arrow II	28R-7135049	G-AYWW N11C	22. 2.90	MRR Aviation Ltd	Gloucestershire	16.10.07E
G-GYRO	Campbell Cricket replica (Built Howell, Pitcher and J W Pavitt) (Originally registered as Bensen B 8 (c/n 01 and PFA G/01-1046) (Rotax 532)	PFA G/03-1046		26. 2.82	J W Pavitt	St Merryn	19. 6.08P
G-GYTO	Piper PA-28-161 Warrior III	2842082	N160FT N9511N	11. 5.00	Plane Talking Ltd	Elstree	1. 6.08E
G-GZDO	Cessna 172N Skyhawk II	17271826	C-GZDO (N5299E)	11.10.88	G Cambridge and G W J Hall t/a Cambridge Hall Aviation (Operated Firecrest Aviation)	Elstree	19. 8.08E
G-GZIP	Rolladen-Schneider LS8-18	8309	BGA 4784-JUD	14.12.07	D S St J Haughton	Long Mynd	4. 3.08
G-GZLE	Aérospatiale SA.341G Gazelle 1	1145	G-PYOB G-WELA, G-SFTD, G-RIFC, G-SFTD, N641HM, N341BB, F-WKQH	8. 5.01	Gazelle Spares Ltd (New owner 9.07)	Redhill	22.12.06
G-GZRP	Piper PA-42-720 Cheyenne IIIA	42-5501011	C-GZRP N100CS, N888FW, N288FA, PT-OLT, N4116W, (N35DG) N4116W	10. 1.07	Air Medical Fleet Ltd	Oxford	29 .1.08E

G-HAAA - G-HZZZ

Registration	Type	Construction No.	Previous ID	Date	Owner/Operator	Base	Expiry
G-HAAH	Schempp-Hirth Ventus 2cT	52-173	BGA 4776-JTV	6.12.07	C R Lewis tr The V66 Group	Lasham	9. 1.08
G-HAAM	Dassault Mystere Falcon 900	130	F-GKBQ F-WQBN, VP-CID, VR-CID, F-WWFB, F-GOAB, F-WWFC	28. 4.06	Dassault Aviation SA	Paris-Le Bourget, France	4. 5.08E
G-HABI	Best Off Sky Ranger 912S(1) (Built J Habicht - pr.no.BMAA/HB/524)	SKRXxxx738		26. 2.07	J Habicht	(Elsworth, Cambridge)	
G-HABT	Super Marine Spitfire Mk.26 (Built B Trumble)	PFA 324-14487		29. 8.06	B Trumble (Noted 8.07 in RAF c/s with code "A-BT" on starboard side)	Full Sutton	
G-HACE	Van's RV-6A (Built J and S Brennan)	1951	C-GOLZ	22. 5.06	D C McElroy	Perth	30. 7.08P
G-HACK	Piper PA-18-150 Super Cub	18-7168	SE-CSA N10F	20.11.97	S J Harris	Little Rissington	5.12.10S
G-HAEC	Commonwealth CAC-18 Mustang 22 (Composite rebuilt 1974-76 using major components ex Philippine AF P-51D 44-72917) (As "472218:WZ-I" in 78th FG USAAF c/s) "Big Beautiful Doll"	CACM-192-1517	VR-HIU (RP-C651), PI-C651, VH-FCB, A68-192	1. 5.85	R W Davies Little Robhurst Farm, Woodchurch (Operated The Old Flying Machine Company)		14. 6.08P
G-HAFG	Cessna 340A	340A1806	JY-AFG N1230V	5. 8.04	Goldcrest 2001 Ltd	Jersey	13. 8.08E
G-HAFT	Diamond DA.42 Twin Star	42.057		13.10.05	Atlantic Flight Training Ltd	Coventry	31.10.07E
G-HAIB	Aviat A-1B Husky	2255	N53HY	16.11.04	H Brockmueller	Shoreham	9. 3.08E
G-HAIG	Rutan LongEz (Built P N Haig pr.no. PFA 074A-11149) (Lycoming O-235)	1983-L		20. 5.86	C Docherty	RAF Leuchars	5.12.07P
G-HAIR	Robin DR.400-180 Régent	2479		7.12.00	S P Copson	Shotteswell	25. 1.08E
G-HAJJ	Glaser-Dirks DG-400	4-225		15. 2.88	W G Upton and J G Kosak	RNAS Culdrose	21. 6.08E
G-HALC	Piper PA-28R-200 Cherokee Arrow II	28R-7335042	N91253 C-FFQO, CF-FQO	26.11.90	Halcyon Aviation Ltd	Barton	25. 9.08E
G-HALJ	Cessna 140 (Continental C85)	8336	N89308 NC89308	30. 4.96	H A Lloyd-Jennings	Henstridge	5.10.07E
G-HALL	Piper PA-22-160 Tri-Pacer	22-7423	G-ARAH N10F	8.11.79	F P Hall	Clipgate Farm, Denton	27. 3.08E
G-HALP	SOCATA TB-10 Tobago	192	G-BITD	19. 8.81	D Halpern	Wycombe Air Park	25. 9.06T
G-HALT	Mainair Sports Pegasus Quik	8063		1. 9.04	J A Horn	Shotton Colliery, Peterlee	25. 4.08P
G-HAMI	Fuji FA.200-180 Aero Subaru	FA200-188	G-OISF G-BAPT	31. 1.92	K G Cameron, M P Antoniak and Renzacci (UK) PLC	Glebe Farm, Stockton	1.10.07T
G-HAMM	Yakovlev Yak-50	832409	LY-ANG DOSAAF 81	15.10.02	Propeller Studios Ltd	(Hitchin)	10.10.08P
G-HAMP	Aeronca 7ACA Champ	30-72	N9173L	8. 8.88	R J Grimstead (New owner 12.07)	(Tillington, Petworth)	14. 9.05P
G-HAMR	Piper PA-28-161 Warrior II	28-8416077	PH-AMR N4353B	18. 7.06	Electric Scribe 2000 Ltd	Aberdeen	23.10.07E
G-HAMS	P&M Pegasus Quik	8224		1.11.06	P C D Hamilton	(Southwell)	31.10.08P
G-HAMY	Van's RV-6 (Built P W Armstrong)	PFA 181-12305		19. 4.05	P W Armstrong	Spanhoe	10. 9.08P
G-HANG	Diamond DA.42 Twin Star	42.026		7. 6.05	Atlantic Flight Training Ltd	Coventry	23. 6.08E
G-HANS	Robin DR.400 2+2	1384		2. 3.79	J S Russell	Strathaven	14.12.07E
G-HANY	Agusta-Bell 206B-3 JetRanger III	8598	G-JEKP D-HMSF, G-ESAL, G-BHXW	5. 1.01	Eastern Atlantic Helicopters Ltd	Shoreham	17. 9.08E

Regn	Type	C/n	Previous identity	Date	Owner/Operator	Base	Expiry
G-HAPI	Lindstrand LBL 105A Balloon (Hot Air)	669		21. 3.00	Adventure Balloons Ltd	Hartley Wintney, Hook	17. 5.08T
G-HAPR	Bristol 171 Sycamore HC.14	13387	8010M, XG547	15. 6.78	E D ap Rees t/a Helicopters Unlimited	Brussels, Belgium	
	(As "XG547:T-S" in RAF CFS c/s (Transferred to Royal Military Museum 2.08)						
G-HAPY	de Havilland DHC-1 Chipmunk 22	C1/0697	WP803	3. 7.96	Astrojet Ltd	Wycombe Air Park	2.11.08
	(As "WP803" in RAF white and red c/s)						
G-HARD	Dyn'Aéro MCR-01 ULC	PFA 301B-14427		31. 3.06	N A Burnet	Compton Abbas	29. 7.08T
G-HARE	Cameron N-77 Balloon (Hot Air)	1467		12. 3.87	D H Sheryn and C A Buck		
					London SE16 and Widmer End, High Wycombe		25. 8.08A
G-HARI	Raj Hamsa X'Air V2(2)	375?		11. 6.99	S T Welsh	Ince Blundell	12. 3.08P
	(Built D Mahajan - pr.no.BMAA/HB/103)						
G-HARK	Bombardier CL-600-2B16	5646	N646JC, C-GLXD	14. 9.06	Corbridge Ltd	(Guernsey)	14. 9.08E
	(CL-604 Challenger)						
G-HARN	Piper PA-28-181 Archer II	28-8290108	G-DENK, G-BXRJ, HB-PGO	3. 2.00	K Saxton	Coventry	24. 3.08E
G-HARR	Robinson R22 Beta II	3514	N75301	14. 6.04	Unique Helicopters Ltd	Enniskillen	2. 7.08E
G-HART	Cessna 152 II	15279734	(G-BPBF), N757GS	2. 2.89	RVL Aviation Ltd	Coventry	29. 6.08E
	(Tail-wheel u/c conversion)				(Air Atlantique c/s)		
G-HARY	Alon A-2	A 188	G-ATWP	15. 3.93	M B Willis	Bourn	26. 7.10S
G-HASO	Diamond DA.40D Star	D4.070	G-CCLZ	21. 4.04	Diamond Aircraft UK Ltd	Gamston	25. 3.08E
G-HATF	Thorp T-18CW	PFA 076-11481		6.12.01	A T Fraser	(Crowthorne)	
	(Built A T Fraser and GHill)						
G-HATZ	Hatz CB-1	17	N54623	11. 5.89	S P Rollason	Long Marston	16.11.07P
	(Lycoming O-320)				(Carries 'N54623' on tail)		
G-HAUS	Hughes 369HM	52-0214M	G-KBOT, G-RAMM, EI-AVN, N9037F	20. 7.99	J Pulford t/a Pulford Aviation	Hannington, Rushden	1. 8.08E
	(Hughes 500)						
G-HAUT	Schempp-Hirth Mini Nimbus C	149	BGA 2597	8.10.07	L J Kaye tr 530 Syndicate	Shobdon	1. 1.08
G-HAZE	Thunder Ax8-90 Balloon (Hot Air)	989		3. 8.88	T G Church (Tethered 9.05)	Blackburn	23. 6.97T
G-HBBC	de Havilland DH.104 Dove 8	04211	G-ALFM, VP961, G-ALFM, VP961	24. 1.96	BBC Air Ltd	Compton Abbas	23. 3.06
					(Noted 8.07)		
G-HBBH	Comco Ikarus C42 FB100	0608-6835		5. 7.06	B R W Hay	Kemble	22.10.08E
G-HBEK	Agusta A109C	7633	G-DATE, G-RNLD, I-ANAG	31. 1.06	P W Beck t/a Bek Helicopters	(High Legh, Knutsford)	25. 7.08E
G-HBMW	Robinson R22	0170	G-BOFA, N9068D	7. 7.94	Durham Aviation Ltd	Croft Farm, Croft-on-Tees	6. 9.07T
					(Noted 2.08)		
G-HBOS	Scheibe SF25C Falke	44574	D-KTIN	26. 7.01	Coventry Gliding Club Ltd	Husbands Bosworth	29. 9.07E
	(Rotax 912-A)						
G-HBRO	Eurocopter AS.355NP Ecureuil 2	5755	F-HAJE, F-WQDD	7.12.07	Henry Brothers (Magherafelt) Ltd	Redhill	
					(Noted 1.08)		
G-HBUG	Cameron N-90 Balloon (Hot Air)	1991	G-BRCN	21. 6.89	R T and Hilary.Revel	High Wycombe	16.12.07A
					(Thorn-EMI Computeraid titles) (Noted 1.08)		
G-HCAC	Schleicher Ka 6E	4054	BGA 1380-CAC	1. 2.08	M Burridge	Crowland	16. 3.08
G-HCBI	Schweizer 269C-1	0259	N86G	11. 8.06	Plane Talking Ltd	Blackbushe	23.11.07E
	(Schweizer 300)						
G-HCSA	Cessna 525A CitationJet CJ2	525A0334	N52699	20.12.06	Hangar 8 Ltd	Oxford	
G-HCSL	Piper PA-34-220T Seneca III	34-8133237	N84375	9. 5.91	Fly (CI) Ltd	Southend	11.12.07E
					(Operated Trans Euro Air) (Noted 1.08)		
G-HDAE	de Havilland DHC-1 Chipmunk 22	C1/0280	CS-DAE, Portuguese AF 1304	4. 6.03	Airborne Classics Ltd	Enstone	10. 8.09S
G-HDEW	Piper PA-32R-301 Saratoga II SP	3213026	G-BRGZ, N91787	4.12.89	G R Williams	Phoenix Farm, Lower Upham	31. 3.08E
G-HDIX	Enstrom 280FX	2076	N506DH, D-HDIX	19. 2.98	Clovetree Ltd	Hawarden	28. 4.08E
G-HDTV	Agusta A109A II	7266	G-BXWD, N565RJ, I-URIA, D-HEMZ, N109BD	16. 9.04	Castle Air Charters Ltd	Liskeard Heliport	6. 7.08E
G-HEAN	Eurocopter AS.355NP	5747	SE-JJR	29. 8.07	Brookview Developments Ltd	(Maghera, Belfast)	30 .8.08E
G-HEBE	Bell 206B-3 JetRanger III	3745	CS-HDN, N3179A	5. 2.97	M and E Building and Civil Engineering Contractors Ltd	Hawarden	24. 6.08E
G-HEBS	Pilatus Britten-Norman BN-2B-26 Islander	2267	G-BUBJ, N450PM, OY-PHV, JA5318, G-BUBJ	7.12.07	Hebridean Air Services Ltd	Cumbernauld	4. 3.08E
G-HEBZ	Fairey Britten-Norman BN-2A-26 Islander	823	G-BELF, D-IBRA, G-BELF	21. 3.07	Cormack (Aircraft Services) Ltd	Cumbernauld	12. 3.01
					(Noted 3.07)		
G-HECB	Fuji FA.200-160 Aero Subaru	FA200-238	G-BBZO	16. 5.05	H E W E Bailey	(Samois-sur-Seine, France)	24. 8.08E
G-HEDI	Cessna 182T Skylane	18281822	G-CEDU, N6032K	12.12.06	Carpe D Aviation Ltd	Oxford	7. 9.08E
G-HEHE	Eurocopter EC.120B Colibri	1480	EC-KCR	20. 6.07	HE Group Ltd	(Rochester)	23. 7.08E
G-HEJB	Cirrus SR22 GTS	2311	N963SR	23.02.07	G A J Bowles	Carlisle	3. 4.08E
G-HEKK	Rotary Air Force RAF 2000 GTX-SE		G-BXEB	18. 7.07	C J Watkinson	(Great Hekk, Goole)	10. 4.04P
	(Built J S Penny)	PFA G/13-1285			(New owner 7.07)		
G-HEKY	McCulloch J-2	039	G-ORVB, (G-BLGI), (G-BKKL), Bahrain Public Security BPS-3, N4329G	14. 9.07	C J Watkinson	(Great Heck, Goole)	
G-HELA	SOCATA TB-10 Tobago	135	F-GCOF	31.12.03	S J Heller tr Group TB-10	Panshanger	5. 7.08E
G-HELE	Bell 206B-3 JetRanger III	3789	G-OJFR, N18095	21. 2.91	B E E Smith	White Waltham	4. 5.08E
G-HELM	Eurocopter AS.350B2 Ecureuil	4303	(SE-HJE)	23. 8.07	Astro Aviation Ltd	(Middlesborough)	19. 9.08E
G-HELN	Piper PA-18 Super Cub 95	"18-3400"	G-BKDG, MM52-2392, EI-69, EI-141, I-EIWB, MM53-7765, 53-7765	10. 1.86	J J Anziani tr Helen Group	Wycombe Air Park	3. 9.07P
	(L-21B-PI) (Frame No.18-3400)						
G-HELP	Colt 17A Cloudhopper Balloon (Hot Air)	902		16. 2.87	A D Kent tr Balloon Preservation Flying Group		
					"Mondial Cloudhopper"	Petworth	3.10.06A
G-HELV	de Havilland DH.115 Vampire T 55	975	Swiss AF U-1215	17. 9.91	Aviation Heritage Ltd	Coventry	12. 6.08P
	(Built F + W)				(Operated Air Atlantique as "XJ771" in RAF c/s)		
G-HEMS	Aerospatiale SA.365N Dauphin 2	6009	8P-BHD, G-HEMS, F-WYMJ, G-HEMS, N365AM, N365AH	22. 8.88	PLM Dollar Group Ltd	Carlisle	5.12.07E
			(North Cumbria Air Ambulance)				
G-HENT	SOCATA Rallye 110ST Galopin	3210	OO-MBV	28.11.01	R J Patton	City of Derry	31. 3.08E
G-HENY	Cameron V-77 Balloon (Hot Air)	2486		9. 1.91	R S D'Alton "Henny"	Newbury	16. 6.07A

G-HERB	Piper PA-28R-201 Arrow III	28R-7837118	ZS-LAG	5. 6.86	E A Sullivan	Stapleford	19.10.07E
			N3504M				
G-HERC	Cessna 172S Skyhawk SP	172S8985	N5113P	10.12.01	The Cambridge Aero Club Ltd	Cambridge	17. 2.08E
G-HERD	Lindstrand LBL 77B Balloon (Hot Air)	707		31. 7.00	S W Herd	Mold	25. 1.08A
G-HEVN	SOCATA TB-200 Tobago XL	2013	D-EVHN	29.10.03	I K Maclean	Enstone	6.11.07E
G-HEWI	Piper J-3C-65 Cub (L-4J-PI)	12566	G-BLEN	20. 7.84	R Preston tr Denham Grasshopper Flying Group		
	(Continental C90) (Frame No.12396)		D-EBEN, HB-OFZ, 44-80270			Denham	22. 5.09E
G-HEXE	Colt 17A Balloon (Hot Air)	2221		24. 2.04	A Dunnington	Bristol	13. 8.08E
G-HEYY	Cameron Bear 72 SS Balloon (Hot Air)	1244		21. 1.86	Magical Adventures Ltd (Hofmeister Lager Bear)		
					"George"	West Bloomfield, Michigan, US	30.11.98A
G-HFBM	Curtiss Robertson C-2 Robin	352	LV-FBM	24. 4.90	D M Forshaw	High Cross, Ware	15. 2.08P
	(Continental W-670)		NC9279				
G-HFCA	Cessna A150L Aerobat	A1500381	N6081J	30. 8.91	T H Scott	Rayne Hall Farm, Braintree	8.11.07E
	(Texas tail-wheel u/c conversion)						
G-HFCB	Reims Cessna F150L	F15000798	G-AZVR	10. 2.87	P Grace tr G-HFCB Group		
						Cherry Tree Farm, Monewden	12. 6.08E
G-HFCI	Reims Cessna F150L	F15000823	PH-CET	11. 9.80	R S Gunter	(Bristol)	15. 6.08E
G-HFCL	Reims Cessna F152 II	F15201663	G-BGLR	11.10.88	Modi Aviation Ltd	Earls Colne	16. 7.08E
G-HFCT	Reims Cessna F152 II	F15201861		27. 1.81	Stapleford Flying Club Ltd	Stapleford	17. 6.08E
G-HFLY	Robinson R44 Raven II	11876		19.10.07	Helifly (UK) Ltd (Noted 10.07)	Shoreham	
G-HGPI	SOCATA TB-20 Trinidad	851		4. 8.88	M J Jackson and I R Harwood	Bournemouth	14. 5.08
G-HGRB	Robinson R44 Raven	0776		21. 4.06	Hangar 8 Ltd	Oxford	11. 7.06E
G-HGRC	Cessna 525A CitationJet CJ2	525A-0360	N13474	12.10.07	Hangar 8 Ltd	Oxford	
			N52655		(Noted 12.07)		
G-HHAA	Hawker Siddeley Buccaneer S 2B	B3-01-73	9225M	6.12.02	Hawker Hunter Aviation Ltd	RAF Scampton	
	(C/n officially quoted as B3-R-50-67)		XX885		(As "XX885" in RAF c/s) (For airworthy restoration 2006)		
G-HHAB	Hawker Hunter F 58	41H-697439	Swiss AF J-4072	13. 1.03	Hawker Hunter Aviation Ltd	RAF Scampton	
					(Stored as "J-4072" 5.04)		
G-HHAC	Hawker Hunter F 58	41H-691770	G-BWIU	10.12.02	Hawker Hunter Aviation Ltd	RAF Scampton	12. 7.08P
			Swiss AF J-4021		(As "J-4021" in Swiss AF c/s)		
G-HHAF	Hawker Hunter F 58	41H-697448	G-BWKB	13. 1.03	Hawker Hunter Aviation Ltd	RAF Scampton	
			Swiss AF J-4081		(Stored as "J-4081" 5.04)		
G-HHAV	SOCATA MS.894A Rallye Minerva 220	11620	G-AYDG	9.10.02	A Arthur and P Channon tr AV Flying Group		
						Perranporth	12. 8.08E
G-HHHH	Robinson R44 Raven II	11638		8. 3.07	Crown and Cushion Hotel (Chipping Norton) Ltd		
						(Chipping Norton)	22. 3.08E
G-HHII	Hawker Hurricane IIB	CCF/R20023	G-HRLO	5. 4.07	P Teichman t/a Hangar 11 Collection	North Weald	
	(Built Canadian Car and Foundry Co)		RCAF 5403		(On rebuild Moat Farm, Sudbury 8.07: to be "5403" in RCAF c/s)		
G-HHOG	Robinson R44 Clipper II	10584		23.12.04	Fast Helicopters Ltd	Shoreham	1. 2.08E
G-HHUK	Robin HR.200-120B	282	SE-KYN	23. 8.07	S P Elsby	Leeds-Bradford	19. 9.08E
G-HIBM	Cameron N-145 Balloon (Hot Air)	3197		8. 2.94	Alba Ballooning Ltd	Edinburgh	22.10.07T
G-HIEL	Robinson R22 Beta	1120		28. 9.89	Naylors Timber Recovery Ltd	(Sheffield City)	18. 2.08E
G-HIJK	Cessna 421C Golden Eagle	421C-0218	G-OSAL	25. 2.00	Caernarfon Airworld Ltd	Caernarfon	30. 8.08E
			G-HIJK, G-OSAL, OY-BEC, SE-GZI, N5471G				
G-HIJN	Comco Ikarus C42 FB100	0403-6597		19. 5.04	J R North	Ince Blundell	18. 5.08P
G-HILO	Rockwell Commander 114	14224	N4894W	6. 2.98	F H Parkes	Stapleford	6. 5.08E
G-HILS	Cessna F172H	F172-0522	G-AWCH	20.12.88	B F W Lowdon tr Lowdon Aviation Group		
	(Built Reims Aviation SA)					Blackbushe	28. 2.08
G-HILT	SOCATA TB-10 Tobago	298	(G-BMYB)	13. 5.82	S R O'Brien	Crowfield	22. 2.08E
			EI-BOF, G-HILT				
G-HILZ	Van's RV-8	PFA 303-14471		14. 6.06	A G and E A Hill	(Windlesham)	25.11.08P
	(Built A G and E A Hill)						
G-HIND	Maule MT-7-235 Super Rocket	18037C		26. 3.98	M A Ashmole	Perth	29. 4.08E
G-HINZ	Avtech Jabiru SK	xxxx		1. 2.00	B Faupel	Little Staughton	1. 8.07P
	(Built B Faupel - pr.no.PFA 274-13441)						
G-HIPE	Sorrell SNS-7 Hyperbipe	209	N18RS	6. 4.93	B G Ell	Crowfield	24.10.07P
	(Built R Stephen)						
G-HIPO	Robinson R22 Beta	1719	G-BTGB	11. 9.92	SI Plan Electronics (Research) Ltd	Cranfield	24. 4.08E
G-HIRE	Gulfstream GA-7 Cougar	GA7-0091	G-BGSZ	10.12.81	London Aerial Tours Ltd	Rochester	26. 5.08E
			N704G				
G-HISS	Pitts S-2A	2137	G-BLVU	17. 3.92	F L McGee	Liverpool	14.11.07E
	(Built Aerotek Inc)		SE-GTX				
G-HITM	Raj Hamsa X'Air Falcon Jabiru(1)	455		23. 2.00	N J Beale	RNAS Culdrose	2. 8.08P
	(Built D J Hickey - pr.no.BMAA/HB/112)						
G-HIUP	Cameron A-250 Balloon (Hot Air)	4464		16. 4.99	Ladybird Balloons Ltd	Bingham, Nottingham	19. 8.04T
					(New owner 2.08)		
G-HIVA	Cessna 337A Super Skymaster	33700429	G-BAES	28. 3.88	G J Banfield	Gloucestershire	30. 8.08E
			SE-CWW, N5329S				
G-HIVE	Reims Cessna F150M	F15001186	G-BCXT	19. 4.85	M P Lynn	RAF Coltishall	10. 5.08E
G-HIYA	Best Off Sky Ranger 912(2)	SKRxxxx648		30.10.06	R D and C M Parkinson		
	(Built R D Parkinson - pr.no.BMAA/HB/493)					Lower Mountpleasant Farm, Chatteris	19. 9.08P
G-HIZZ	Robinson R22 Beta II	2677	G-CNDY	2. 8.04	S Gallimore and T Hehir t/a Flyfare	Barton	8. 6.08E
			G-BXEW				
G-HJSM	Schempp-Hirth Nimbus 4DM	22/32	G-ROAM	19. 2.01	S H C Marriott tr 60 Syndicate "60"	Lasham	22. 2.08E
G-HJSS	AIA Stampe SV-4C	1101	G-AZNF	7. 9.92	H J Smith	Shoreham	21. 6.09
			F-BGJM, Aeronavale, French AF				
G-HKAA	Schempp-Hirth Duo Discus T	69/364	BGA 5033-KEM	20. 9.07	A Aveling	Lasham	2. 2.08
G-HKHM	Hughes 369D	71-1019D	B-HHM	8. 4.99	Heli Air Ltd	Wellesbourne Mountford	26. 5.08E
	(Hughes 500)		VR-HHM, N50605				
G-HLCF	CFM Starstreak Shadow SA-II	K 256-CD		10. 5.96	G J Chater	Landmead Farm, Garford	22. 6.07P
	(Built S M E Solomon - pr.no.PFA 206-12796) (Rotax 618)						
G-HLEE	Best Off Sky Ranger J2.2(1)	SKRxxxx655		6. 3.07	L Harland	Rochester	
	(Built L Harland - pr.no.BMAA/HB/502)						
G-HMBJ	Commander Aircraft Commander 114B	14636	N6036F	30. 6.97	Bravo Juliet Aviation Ltd	Guernsey	3. 9.08E

Reg	Type	Serial	Prev ID	Date	Owner	Location	Expiry
G-HMED	Piper PA-28-161 Warrior III	2842020	LX-III	21. 7.97	Eglinton Flying Club Ltd	City of Derry	3. 1.08E
G-HMEI	Dassault Mystere Falcon 900	1	F-HOCI F-GIDE, F-WIDE	2. 7.04	Executive Jet Group Ltd	RAF Northolt	15. 7.08E
G-HMEV	Dassault Mystere Falcon 900	5	N905FJ PT-WQM, N905TS, F-GGRH, VH-BGF, N404FJ, F-WWFB	21. 6.06	Maughold Ltd	(Douglas, Isle of Man)	20. 6.08E
G-HMJB	Piper PA-34-220T Seneca III	34-8133040	N8356R	12. 7.89	Cross Atlantic Ventures Ltd *(External storage 10.07)*	Blackpool	10.10.04
G-HMMV	Cessna 525 CitationJet	525-0358	N51564	16. 2.00	EBJ Sales Ltd	Edinburgh	12. 3.08E
G-HMPF	Robinson R44 Astro	0730		8. 3.00	Mightycraft Ltd	White Waltham	20. 3.08E
G-HMPH	Bell 206B-2 JetRanger II	1232	G-BBUY N18090	20. 6.88	Bubnell Ltd	(Sheffield City)	3. 3.08E
G-HMPT	Agusta-Bell 206B-2 JetRanger II	8168	D-HARO	7.11.91	Helicopter Express Ltd Ventfield Farm, Oxfordshire		13. 7.07T
G-HMSS	Bell 206B-2 JetRanger II	1010	ZS-HMS C-GXOI, N58008	7. 5.02	I Valentine t/a Kilrush Aviation Services Kilrush, County Kildare		23.11.07E
G-HNGE	Comco Ikarus C42 FB100	0607-6838		21. 8.06	Haimoss Ltd	Old Sarum	21. 8.07E
G-HOBO	Denney Kitfox Model 4 *(W M Hodgkins)*	PFA 172A-12140		10. 9.92	J P Donovan *"Navy Baby"*	(Milton Keynes)	9.11.08P
G-HOCK	Piper PA-28-180 Cherokee D	28-4395	G-AVSH N11C	15. 5.86	J I Simper tr G-HOCK Flying Group	Goodwood	29. 8.08E
G-HOFM	Cameron N-56 Balloon (Hot Air)	1245		21. 1.86	Magical Adventures Ltd *(Operated Balloon Preservation Group)*	Petworth	30.11.98A
G-HOGS	Cameron Pig 90 SS Balloon (Hot Air)	4121		7. 4.97	Magical Adventures Ltd *"Britannia Piggy Bank"* West Bloomfield, Michigan, US		1. 7.99A
G-HOHO	Colt Santa Claus SS Balloon (Hot Air)	1671		21.12.89	Oxford Promotions (UK) Ltd (Meggen, Switzerland) *(Operated Benno Betschart) (Active 1.06 as "HB-QKC")*		3. 4.03A
G-HOIL	Bombardier Learjet Model 60	60-313	N613H N4003L	3.08R			
G-HOJO	Schempp-Hirth Discus 2a	2	BGA 4533-JHT	12.11.07	R Jones t/a Southern Sailplanes	Lasham	10. 4.08
G-HOLI	Ultramagic M-77 Balloon (Hot Air)	77/294		23. 2.07	G Everett	Sandway, Maidstone	
G-HOLM	Eurocopter EC.135 T2+	0574		20. 8.07	Eurocopter UK Ltd	Oxford	
G-HOLY	SOCATA ST-10 Diplomate	108	F-BSCZ	31. 1.90	M K Barsham *(Noted 10.05)*	Fenland	26. 9.05
G-HOLZ	Agusta-Bell 206B-2 JetRanger II	8038	ZK-IBC G-HOLZ, G-CDBT, R Saudi AF 1206	4. 5.05	D J Raith tr F Raith 1994 Settlement	Gamston	31. 7.08E
G-HOME	Colt 77A Balloon (Hot Air)	032		26. 2.79	G L Barnett t/a Anglia Balloons *"Tardis" (On loan to British Balloon Museum and Library)*	Newbury	27. 5.86A
G-HONG	Slingsby T 67M-200 Firefly	2060	VR-HZR HKG-12, G-7-128	24. 3.94	Jewel Aviation Ltd	Fairoaks	13. 3.08E
G-HONI	Robinson R22 Beta	0871	G-SEGO N9081N	27. 1.00	Patriot Aviation Ltd	Cranfield	2. 1.08E
G-HONK	Cameron O-105 Balloon (Hot Air)	1813		30. 9.88	T G S Dixon *(New owner 3.05)*	Bromsgrove	14. 9.97A
G-HONY	Lilliput Type 1 Series A Balloon (Minimum Lift)	L-01		31. 7.98	A E and D E Thomas	Weston, Honiton	
G-HOOD	SOCATA TB-20 Trinidad GT	2008	F-OILJ	25. 7.00	M J Hoodless	Blackbushe	20. 9.08E
G-HOOV	Cameron N-56 Balloon (Hot Air)	388		2. 3.78	H R Evans *"Hoover"*	Ross-on-Wye	26. 5.89A
G-HOPA	Lindstrand LBL 35A Cloudhopper Balloon (Hot Air)	972		16. 1.04	S F Burden	Munich, Germany	27. 9.08A
G-HOPE	Beech F33A Bonanza	CE-805	N2024Z	27. 2.79	Hope Aviation	Bournemouth	24. 5.08
G-HOPI	Cameron N-42 Balloon (Hot Air)	2724		5.12.91	Ballonverbung Hamburg GmbH	Kiel, Germany	30. 4.05A
G-HOPR	Lindstrand LBL 25A Cloudhopper Balloon (Hot Air)	999		21. 6.04	K C Tanner	Thame	3.10.08A
G-HOPY	Van's RV-6A *(Built R C Hopkinson) (Lycoming O-320-B2B)*	PFA 181-12742		4.12.95	R C Hopkinson	Landmead Farm, Garford	22. 5.08P
G-HORK	Alpi Pioneer 300 Hawk *(Built R Y Kendal - pr.no.PFA 330A-14741)*	xxx		8.12.07	R Y Kendal	(Ewesley Farm, Morpeth)	
G-HOSS	Beech F33A Bonanza	CE-1151	OY-BVT	3. 1.06	T D Broadhurst tr Beech Baron Aviation	Sleap	14. 3.08
G-HOTI	Colt 77A Balloon (Hot Air)	750		13. 7.87	G C Dare *(New owner 9.07)*	Barrington, Ilminster	11. 4.05A
G-HOTT	Cameron O-120 Balloon (Hot Air)	2581		30. 4.91	D L Smith *"Floating Sensations"*	Newbury	17. 5.97T
G-HOTZ	Colt 77B Balloon (Hot Air)	2218		16. 6.92	C J and S M Davies	Castleton, Hope Valley	12. 1.08A
G-HOUS	Colt 31A Air Chair Balloon (Hot Air)	099		7.10.80	The British Balloon Museum and Library *(Barratts titles) "K9" (Inflated 4.06)*	Newbury	3. 5.90A
G-HOWE	Thunder Ax7-77 Balloon (Hot Air)	1340		10. 4.89	M F Howe *"Howie/Howzat"*	Linley Hill, Leven	15. 8.95A
G-HOWL	Rotary Air Force RAF 2000 GTX-SE *(Built M Urbanczyk)*	H2-95-6-164	N4994U	2. 7.01	C J Watkinson	(Great Heck, Goole)	5.10.07P
G-HOXN	Van's RV-9 *(Built F A L Castleden)*	PFA 320-14229		26. 9.06	F A L Castleden tr XRay November Flying Club Horham, Eye		16. 4.08P
G-HPAD	Bell 206B-3 JetRanger III	1997	G-CITZ G-BRTB, N9936K	2. 9.02	Helipad Ltd *(Operated Total Air Management Services (TAMS)*	(Sheffield City)	7. 9.08E
G-HPOL	MD Helicopters MD.900 Explorer	900-00082	N70082	24. 1.01	Humberside Police Authority	Humberside	3. 9.10S
G-HPSB	Commander Aircraft Commander 114B	14678	N6118R	24.10.01	International Employment Services Ltd	Guernsey	5.12.07E
G-HPSE	Commander Aircraft Commander 114B	14638	N6038V	26. 8.97	J C Ferguson	Andrewsfield	27. 9.08E
G-HPSF	Commander Aircraft Commander 114B	14590	N6003F	16.11.04	J Barnett tr Three Foxtrot Group	Guernsey	15.11.07E
G-HPSL	Commander Aircraft Commander 114B	14682	N115KL	26. 8.04	M B Endean	Guernsey	22.10.08E
G-HPUX	Hawker Hunter T 7	41H-693455	8807M XL587	12. 3.99	Hawker Hunter Aviation Ltd *(Stored 5.04 as "XL587/Z")*	RAF Scampton	
G-HRAK	Aérospatiale AS.350B Ecureuil	1749	F-GMPA D-HSAN, SE-HUV, D-HCHL	28. 7.04	R A Kingston	(Stapleford)	11.10.07E
G-HRBS	Robinson R22 Beta II	3537	N75353	11. 3.04	Insight Human Resource and Mangement Consultancy Ltd Goodwood		17. 3.08E
G-HRCC	Robin HR.200-100 Club	18	D-EAWT	1. 2.06	P S Wilson	(Bridge of Feugh, Banchory)	
G-HRDS	Gulfstream Aerospace Gulfstream V-SP *(Gulfstream 550)*	5032	N932GA	14.12.04	Fayair (Jersey) Co Ltd	London Stansted	13.12.07E
G-HRHE	Robinson R22 Beta	1950	G-BTWP	24. 1.97	P Irwin t/a Irwin Plant Sales	(Holywood, Belfast)	7.11.07E
G-HRHI	Beagle B 206 Basset CC.1	B 014	XS770	6. 7.89	M D Lewis *(As "XS770" in Queens Flight c/s) (Noted 1.07)*	Cranfield	20.10.06

G-HRHS	Robinson R44 Astro	0323		15. 4.97	Stratus Aviation Ltd	North Weald	16. 4.08E
G-HRIO	Robin HR.100-210 Safari II	149	F-BTZR	22. 1.87	C D B Cope	Ronaldsway	17.12.07E
G-HRLI	Hawker Hurricane I	41H-136172	V7497	25. 4.02	Hawker Restorations Ltd	Milden	
G-HRLK	SAAB 91D/2 Safir	91376	G-BRZY	6. 3.90	Sylmar Aviation and Services Ltd		
			PH-RLK			Lower Wasing Farm, Brimpton	15. 8.10E
G-HRLM	Brügger MB.2 Colibri	PFA 043-10118		28.12.78	D G Reid	Morgansfield, Fishburn	13. 7.07P
	(Built R A Harris) (Volkswagen 1834)				"Titch"		
G-HRND	Cessna 182T Skylane	18281936	N2252X	31. 5.07	Dingle Star Ltd	Denham	19. 6.08E
G-HRNT	Cessna 182S Skylane	18280395	N2369H	29. 1.99	Rayviation Ltd Eddsfield, Octon Lodge Farm, Thwing		14. 3.06E
					(New owner 2.08)		
G-HROI	Rockwell Commander 112A	326	N1326J	19. 6.89	Intereuropean Aviation Ltd	Jersey	1. 7.08
G-HRPN	Robinson R44 Raven II	10007		26.11.02	Spirit Communications (UK) Ltd	Gamston	22.12.07E
G-HRVD	CCF Harvard 4 (T-6J-CCF Texan)	CCF4-548	G-BSBC	8.12.92	K F Mason and D Featherby t/a Anglia Flight (On rebuild 5.05)		
			Moz PLAF 1741, FAP 1741, WGAF BF+055, WGAF AA+055, 53-4629 Bruntingthorpe					
	(Possibly a composite with rear fuselage of Moz PLAF/FAP 1780/AA+614/53-4622)						
G-HRYZ	Piper PA-28-180 Cherokee Archer	28-7505090	G-WACR	6. 2.06	Lees Avionics Ltd	Fairoaks	9. 7.08E
			G-BCZF, N9517N				
G-HSBC	Lindstrand LBL 69X Balloon (Hot Air)	1153		21. 9.07	A Nimmo	Dubai, United Arab Emirates	
G-HSDW	Bell 206B-2 JetRanger II	1789	ZS-HFC	16.12.85	CI Motors Ltd	(Weeton, Preston)	10.10.07E
G-HSKI	Aviat A-1B Husky	2312		20. 1.06	C J R Flint	(Eastwick, Ellesmere)	22, 6.08E
G-HSLA	Robinson R22 Beta	1130	G-BRTI	22.11.01	Summerline Aviation Ltd	Coventry	1.11.07T
			EI-CDW, (EI-CFJ), G-BRTI, N8044U				
G-HSOO	Hughes 369HE	109-0208E	G-BFYJ	3.11.93	Edwards Aviation Ltd	Walton Wood	27. 9.03T
	(Hughes 500)		F-BRSY		(Noted 10.06)		
G-HSTH	Lindstrand LBL HS-110 Airship (Hot Air)	546		20. 8.98	Ballonsport Helmut Seitz	Kissleg, Germany	26. 5.06A
G-HSXP	Raytheon Hawker 850XP	258827	N7077S	26. 3.07	Fowey Services Ltd	(Cannes, France)	25. 3.08E
G-HTEL	Robinson R44 Raven	1155	N70319	25. 1.02	Forestdale Hotels Ltd	Burley, Ringwood	1. 2.08E
G-HTRL	Piper PA-34-220T Seneca III	34-8333061	G-BXXY	8. 2.00	Air Medical Fleet Ltd	Oxford	29. 3.08E
			PH-TLN, N4295X				
G-HTWE	Rans S-6-116 Coyote II	xxxx,xxx		8. 1.08	H C C Coleridge	(Meysey Hampton, Cirencester)	
	(Built H C C Coleridge - pr.no.PFA 204-14698)						
G-HUBB	Partenavia P68B	194	OY-BJH	27. 5.83	G-HUBB Ltd	Denham	29. 7.04
			SE-GXL				
G-HUCH	Cameron Carrots 80 SS Balloon (Hot Air)	2258	G-BYPS	13. 3.91	Magical Adventures Ltd		
					"Magic Carrots" West Bloomfield, Michigan, US		2. 8.01A
G-HUES	Hughes 369HS	1100270S	G-GASC	1.11.07	A C Richardson	(Hulme Walfield, Congleton)	11. 5.08E
	(Hughes 500)		G-WELD, G-FROG, OO-KAR				
G-HUEW	Europa Aviation Europa XS	592		22. 7.04	C R Wright	Tatenhill	1. 8.08P
	(Built C R Wright - pr.no.PFA 247-14156)						
G-HUEY	Bell UH-1H-BF Iroquois	13560	AE-413	23. 7.85	M Grimshaw t/a G-HUEY Partnership	North Weald	1. 3.08P
			(Argentine Army), 73-22077		(Also coded '"560" in "US Army"' camouflage c/s)		
G-HUFF	Cessna 182P Skylane II	18264076	PH-CAS	31.10.78	A E G Cousins	Southend	11. 7.08E
	(Reims-assembled with c/n F18200033)		N6059F				
G-HUGO	Colt 260A Balloon (Hot Air)	2559		20. 1.94	P G Hall	Meanwood, Chard	5. 8.04T
G-HUGS	Robinson R22 Beta	1455	G-BYHD	27. 2.02	C G P Holden	Gamston	21. 4.08E
			N900AB				
G-HUKA	Hughes 369E	0298E	G-OSOO	12. 2.02	B P Stein	(London WC2)	2. 9.08E
	(Hughes 500)						
G-HULK	Best Off Sky Ranger 912(2)	SKR0207213		16. 1.07	L C Stockman	Plaistow's Farm, St Albans	24. 5.08P
	(Built L C Stockman- pr.no.BAA/HB/238)						
G-HULL	Reims Cessna F150M	F15001255	PH-TGR	19. 1.79	Hull Aero Club Ltd	Linley Hill, Leven	19.10.07T
G-HUMH	Van's RV-9A	PFA 320-14357		15.11.05	H A Daines	Seething	4. 9.08P
	(Built H A Daines)						
G-HUNI	Bellanca 7GCBC Citabria	541-73	OO-IME	21.10.96	The Pilot Centre Ltd	Denham	15.11.10E
			D-EIME				
G-HUPW	Hawker Hurricane I	G5-92301	R4118	21. 8.01	P J and Polly.M A Vacher t/a Minmere Farm Partnership		
	(Built Gloster Aircraft Co Ltd)				(As "R4118:UP-W")	Oxford	21. 3.08P
G-HURI	Hawker Hurricane XIIA (IIB)	72036	RCAF 5711	9. 6.83	Historic Aircraft Collection Ltd	Duxford	12. 7.08P
	(Built Canadian Car and Foundry Co)				(As "Z5140/HA-C" in RAF 126 Sqdn c/s) (Operated The Fighter Collection)		
	(Composite - probably includes parts from c/n 44019 ex RCAF 5424, RCAF 5625 and RCAF 5547)						
G-HURN	Robinson R22 Beta	1441		18. 7.90	Sloane Helicopters Ltd (Noted 10.07)	Sywell	16. 8.07T
G-HURR	Hawker Hurricane XII (IIB)	52024	RCAF 5589	30. 7.90	Spitfire Ltd	Duxford	21. 4.08P
	(Built Canadian Car and Foundry Co)				(As "BD707-AE-C" in 402 Squadron RCAF c/s)		
					(Crashed north of Shoreham near Lancing College 15. 9.07 and destroyed by fire)		
G-HUSK	Aviat A-1B Husky	2214		2. 1.03	P H Yarrow and A T Duke		
						Wisbridge Farm, Reed, Royston	24. 4.08E
G-HUTT	Denney Kitfox Model 2	509		24. 1.90	H D Colliver	Landmead Farm, Garford	23. 2.03P
	(Built M A J Hutt and B Davies - pr.no.PFA 172-11634)				(New owner 10.07)		
G-HUTY	Van's RV-7	PFA 323-14571		26.10.06	S A Hutt	(Angmering, Littlehampton)	
	(Built S A Hutt)						
G-HVAN	TLAC RL5A LW Sherwood Ranger	xxxx		10.12.98	H T H van Neck	Ince Blundell	
	(Built H T H Van Neck - pr.no.PFA 237-13074) (BMW R100)				(Noted 10.06)		
G-HVBF	Lindstrand LBL 210A Balloon (Hot Air)	372		23. 5.96	Airxcite Ltd t/a Virgin Balloon Flights	Wembley	25. 3.07E
G-HVER	Robinson R44 Raven II	11754		29. 5.07	Equation Associates Ltd	Denham	14. 6.08E
G-HVIP	Hawker Hunter T 68	HABL-003215	Swiss AF J-4208	7. 7.95	K G Theurer	Sion, Switzerland	7. 7.07P
			G-9-415, Fv.34080, G-9-56				
G-HVRD	Piper PA-31-350 Navajo Chieftain	31-7305052	G-BEZU	11. 6.87	N Singh	Caernarfon	13. 5.07T
			SE-GDP, N74920, N9666N		(New owner 7.07)		
G-HVRZ	Eurocopter EC.120B Colibri	1338	HB-ZEZ	17. 1. 07	EDM Helicopters Ltd	Elstree	16. 1.08E
G-HWAA	Eurocopter EC.135 T2	0375		21. 2.05	Bond Air Services Ltd	Strensham	6. 4.08E
					(Operated County Air Ambulance)		
G-HXTD	Robin DR.400-180 Régent	2510		24.10.01	Richmond Aviation Ltd	Denham	22.12.07E
G-HYAK	IAV Bacau Yakovlev Yak-52	9011107	LY-ALU	27. 8.02	Goodridge (UK) Ltd	Exeter	12.11.07P
			DOSAAF 124				

| G-HYLT | Piper PA-32R-301 Saratoga II SP | 32R-8213001 | N84588 | 23. 4.86 | T G Gordon | (Castlebar, County Mayo) | 1. 2.08E |
| G-HYST | Enstrom 280FX Shark | 2082 | | 9. 7.98 | S Patten | Barton | 9. 6.08E |

G-IAAA - G-IZZZ

G-IACA	Sikorsky S-92A	920050	N81254	23. 4.07	Bristow Helicopters Ltd	Aberdeen	20. 5.08E
G-IACB	Sikorsky S-92A	920062	N4516G	14.11.07	Bristow Helicopters Ltd	Aberdeen	
G-IACC	Sikorsky S-92A	920063	N45158	15.11.07	Bristow Helicopters Ltd	Aberdeen	
G-IACD	Sikorsky S-92A	920065	N4515G	20.12.07	Bristow Helicopters Ltd	Aberdeen	
G-IACE	Sikorsky S-92A	920066	N45148	20.12.07	Bristow Helicopters Ltd	Aberdeen	
G-IACF	Sikorsky S-92A	920068	N4509G	5. 2.08	Bristow Helicopters Ltd	Aberdeen	
G-IAGD	Robinson R22 Beta	0918	N2018Y G-DRAI, N8808V	16.11.99	E Warren, A Walsh, M Walsh and A Ryan Gorey, County Wexford		5. 2 08E
G-IAJJ	Robinson R44 Raven II	11953		13.11.07	Valley and Vale Properties Ltd *(New owner 2.08)* (Chelford. Macclesfield)		
G-IAJS	Comco Ikarus C42 FB UK	0503-6657		27. 7.05	A J Slater	Dairy House Farm, Worrleston	16. 7.07P
	(Built A J Slater - pr.no.PFA 322-14393)						
G-IAMP	Cameron H-34 Balloon (Hot Air)	2541		11. 3.91	R S Kent tr Balloon Preservation Flying Group *(BPG titles)*	Petworth	15. 5.08A
G-IANB	DG Flugzeugbau DG-808B	8-246B159		12. 3.02	I S Bullock	Sutton Bank	25. 9.08E
G-IANC	SOCATA TB-10 Tobago	150	G-BIAK	15.12.04	I Corbin	Biggin Hill	15. 2.08E
G-IANH	SOCATA TB-10 Tobago	1843	F-OILI	13. 3.00	XD Flight Management Ltd	Goodwood	12. 4.08E
G-IANI	Europa Aviation Europa XS	505		20. 4.01	I F Rickard and Irene.A Watson	Dunsfold	26 11.08P
	(Built I F Rickard and I A Watson - pr.no.PFA 247-13714) (Rotax 914) (Tri-Gear u/c)						
G-IANJ	Reims Cessna F150K	F15000548	G-AXVW	19. 5.98	J A, G M, D T A and J A Rees t/a Messrs Rees of Poyston West	Swansea	20. 9.07T
G-IANN	Kolb Twinstar Mk.3 Extra	PFA 205-14259		7.10.04	I Newman	Sandtoft	26. 2.08P
	(Built I Newman)						
G-IANV	Diamond DA42 Twin Star	42.150	OE-VPI	21. 7.06	TGD Leasing Ltd	(Lapworth, Solihull)	14. 8.08E
G-IANW	Eurocopter AS.350B3 Ecureuil	3447	F-WQPU	18. 9.01	Milford Aviation Services Ltd	(Harrow)	20. 1.08E
G-IARC	Stoddard-Hamilton GlaStar	PFA 295-13261		9.11.99	A A Craig	Prestwick	3. 7.08P
	(Built A A Craig) (Tri-cycle u/c)						
G-IASL	Beech 60 Duke	P-21	G-SING D-IDTA, SE-EXT	18. 4.97	Applied Sweepers Ltd	Perth	8. 3.08E
G-IATU	Cessna 182P Skylane	18261436	G-BIRS G-BBBS, N21131	8. 1.03	Rowena J Bird	Bournemouth	21. 4.08E
G-IBAZ	Comco Ikarus C42 FB100	0409-6622		30. 9.04	B R Underwood Bulkington, Bedworth, Warwickshire,		13.10.08P
G-IBBC	Cameron Sphere 105 SS Balloon (Hot Air)	4082		2. 4.97	R S Kent tr Balloon Preservation Group	Shoreham	17. 7.03A
G-IBBS	Europa Aviation Europa	118		8. 9.94	R H Gibbs	Popham	12. 5.08P
	(Built R H Gibbs - pr.no.PFA 247-12745) (Monowheel u/c)						
G-IBED	Robinson R22 Alpha	0500	G-BMHN	7. 9.93	B C Seedle t/a Brian Seedle Helicopters	(Blackpool)	30. 9.94
G-IBEV	Cameron C-90 Balloon (Hot Air)	10375		10. 4.03	B Drawbridge	Cranbrook	27. 3.08A
G-IBFC	BFC Challenger II Long Wing	CH2-0898-UK-1774		9.11.98	K V Hill	(Baginton, Coventry)	10. 4.08P
	(Built K N Dickinson - pr.no.PFA 177B-13369)						
G-IBFP	Magni M-16 Tandem Trainer	PFA G/12-1240		22. 3.05	B F Pearson	(Eakring, Newark)	4.10.07P
G-IBFW	Piper PA-28R-201 Arrow III	28R-7837235	N31534	22. 1.79	Cinque Ports Aviation Ltd	Lydd	23.11.07E
G-IBHH	Hughes 269C	74-0327	G-BSCD PH-HSH, SE-HFG	20. 8.99	Hughes Helicopter Co Ltd t/a Biggin Hill Helicopters	Biggin Hill	21. 6.07T
	(Hughes 300)						
G-IBIG	Bell 206B-3 JetRanger III	2202	G-BORV C-GVTY, N16763	20. 3.02	Big Heli-Charter Ltd	Manston	28. 7.08E
G-IBLU	Cameron Z-90 Balloon (Hot Air)	4913		4. 8.00	John Aimo Balloons SAS Mondovi, Piedmont, Italy *(Blu titles)*		6. 5.06A
G-IBMS	Robinson R44 Raven II	11287		20. 6.06	Beoley Mill Software Ltd	(Astwood Bank, Redditch)	6. 7.08E
G-IBZS	Cessna 182S Skylane	18280529	N7269A	11.12.99	D C Shepherd	Rochester	5. 1.08
G-ICAB	Robinson R44 Astro	0086		28.11.94	Northumbria Helicopters Ltd	Newcastle	4. 3.07T
G-ICAS	Pitts S-2B	5344	N511P	19. 6.97	J C Smith	Full Sutton	12. 7.08E
	(Built Aviat Inc)						
G-ICBI	Schweizer 269C-1	0272	N86G	14. 3.07	Plane Talking Ltd	Elstree	25. 3.08E
	(Schweizer 300)						
G-ICBM	Stoddard-Hamilton Glasair III Turbine	3337		18.12.00	G V Waters and D N Brown	Deenethorpe	18.10.08P
	(Built G V Waters) (Allison 250-B17B)						
G-ICCL	Robinson R22 Beta	1608	G-ORZZ	25.11.93	A Jahanfar *(Operated The Flight Centre)*	Southend	28. 3.08E
G-ICES	Thunder Ax6-56 SP.1 Balloon (Hot Air)	283		3. 7.80	British Balloon Museum and Library Ltd "Ashfords"	Newbury	3. 6.94A
	(Ice Cream special shape)						
G-ICKY	Lindstrand LBL 77A Balloon (Hot Air)	029		19. 5.93	C J Sanger-Davies	Hawarden	19. 2.08T
G-ICMT	Evektor EV-97 Eurostar	PFA 315-14598		4.12.06	C M Theakstone	Prospect Farm, Wollaston	17. 1.08P
	(Built C M Theakstone)						
G-ICOI	Lindstrand LBL 105A Balloon (Hot Air)	564	(D-O...) G-ICOI	3.11.98	F Schroeder	Mülheim Ruhr, Germany	20. 3.03A
G-ICOM	Reims Cessna F172M Skyhawk II	F17201212	G-BFXI PH-ABA, D-EEVC	25. 4.94	C G Elesmore	Guernsey	25. 7.08E
G-ICON	Rutan LongEz	PFA 074A-11104		29.11.00	S J and M.A Carradice *(Noted 5.06)*	Gamston	
	(Built S J Carradice)						
G-ICRS	Comco Ikarus C42 FB UK	0202-6458		11. 3.02	Ikarus Flying Group Ltd	RAF Halton	11. 4.08P
	(Built A J Whitlock - pr.no.PFA 322-13873)						
G-ICSG	Aérospatiale AS.355F1 Ecureuil 2	5104	G-PAMI G-BUSA	6. 4.93	Stratton Motor Company (Norfolk) Ltd	Southend	7. 8.08E
G-ICWT	Cyclone Airsports Pegasus Quantum 15-912	7632		7. 4.00	C W Taylor	Mill Farm, Shifnal	14. 7.08P
G-IDAB	Cessna 550 Citation Bravo	550-0917	EI-DAB N5100J	16. 3.04	EASSDA Ireland Ltd	(Templepatrick, Ballyclare)	23. 4.08E
G-IDAY	Skyfox CA-25N Gazelle	CA25N-028	VH-RCR	29. 4.96	G G Johnstone	Kingsmuir, Sorbie	26. 6.08E
	(Rotax 912)						
G-IDDI	Cameron N-77 Balloon (Hot Air)	2383		21. 8.90	PSH Skypower Ltd Woodborough, Pewsey *(Allen and Harris - Royal Sun Alliance titles)*		

Reg	Type	C/n	Prev id	Date	Owner/Operator	Location	Status
G-IDER	Schempp-Hirth Discus CS	078CS	BGA 3874-HDS	15.10.07	A J Preston and D B Keith	Bicester	28. 9.08
G-IDII	Dan Rihn DR.107 One Design	PFA 264 12953		16. 6.99	C Darlow	Shacklewell Lodge, Empingham	13.10.07P
	(Built C Darlow) (Lycoming O-360)						
G-IDOL	Evektor EV-97 Eurostar	PFA 315-14549		4. 9.06	T D Baker, J J Lynch and C Moore	Bakersfield	29. 3.08P
	(Built T D Baker, J J Lynch and C Moore)						
G-IDPH	Piper PA-28-181 Archer III	2843585	N3054D	3. 2.04	D Holland	Cambridge	2. 2.08T
G-IDSL	Flight Design CT2K	02-06-02-04		28.10.02	W D Dewey	Wishanger Farm, Frensham	12. 4.08P
	(Assembled Pegasus Aviation Ltd with c/n 7922)						
G-IDUP	Enstrom 280C Shark	1163	G-BRZF N5687D	11. 5.92	Antique Buildings Ltd	Hunterswood Farm, Dunsfold	18. 5.08
G-IDWR	Hughes 369HS	69-0101S	G-AXEJ	26. 5.81	M A and M Gradwell	Barton	5. 1.08E
	(Hughes 500)						
G-IEIO	Piper PA-34-200T Seneca II	34-7670274	EI-EIO N6257J	6.12.02	Jade Air PLC	Thruxton	14. 1.06T
					(Noted 9.06)		
G-IEJH	SAN Jodel D 150A Mascaret	02	G-BPAM F-BLDA, F-WLDA	28. 2.95	A Turner and D Worth	Crowfield	1. 5.08P
G-IEYE	Robin DR.400-180 Régent	2123		29. 1.92	G Wood	Sherburn-in-Elmet	26. 7.08E
G-IFAB	Reims Cessna F182Q Skylane II	F18200127	N61AN G-IFAB, OO-ELM, (OO-HNU)	6. 1.98	Manda Construction Ltd	Inverness	21. 1.08E
G-IFBP	Eurocopter AS.350B2 Ecureuil	9051	F-GTKR (F-GYBR)	27.10.03	F Bird t/a Frank Bird Aviation	Carlisle	2..1.08E
G-IFDM	Robinson R44 Astro	0707		24. 1.00	MFH Helicopters Ltd	Conington	16. 3.08E
G-IFFR	Piper PA-32-300 Cherokee Six	32-7340123	G-BWVO OO-JPC, N55520	1. 4.97	D J D , G D Ritchie and J C Gilbert	RAF Henlow	18. 2.08E
G-IFIF	Cameron TR-60 Balloon (Hot Air)	10811		17.11.05	Cameron Balloons Ltd	Bristol	19. 6.07E
G-IFIT	Piper PA-31-350 Chieftain	31-8052078	G-NABI G-MARG, N3580C	31.12.85	Dart Group PLC	Leeds-Bradford	3. 4.08E
					(Operated Jet2.com)		
G-IFLE	Evektor EV-97 teamEurostar UK	2113		1. 7.04	M R Smith	Otherton, Cannock	10. 7.08P
G-IFLI	Gulfstream AA-5A Cheetah	AA5A-0831	N26948	7. 7.82	C M Petherbridge tr I Fly Group	Linley Hill, Leven	22.12.06
G-IFLP	Piper PA-34-200T Seneca II	34-8070029	N81WS N81149	4. 1.88	Tayflite Ltd	Perth	20. 7.08E
G-IFRH	Agusta A109C	7619	N637CG	7. 1.08	Helicopter Services Ltd	Wycombe Air Park	
G-IFTE	British Aerospace HS 125 Series 700B	257037	G-BFVI G-5-18	16. 5.96	Albion Aviation Management Ltd	Biggin Hill	9. 9.08E
G-IFTF	British Aerospace BAe 125 Series 800B	258021	G-RCEJ VR-CEJ, G-GEIL, G-5-15	21. 1.08	Albion Aviation Management Ltd	Biggin Hill	14. 6.08E
G-IFTS	Robinson R44 Astro	0366		16. 9.97	G P Jones	(Llandeilo)	11.11.06T
G-IFWD	Schempp-Hirth Ventus cT	148	BGA 3575-FWD	8.11.07	R S Maxwell-Fendt	Lasham	1. 4.08
G-IGGL	SOCATA TB-10 Tobago	146	G-BYDC F-GCOL	26. 3.99	G M Richards tr G-IGGL Flying Group	White Waltham	6. 1.08E
G-IGHH	Enstrom 480	5034		1.12.98	Raw Sports Ltd	Gloucestershire	15. 2.08E
G-IGIA	Eurocopter AS.350B3 Ecureuil	3243	I-CFVA	21. 3.07	Faloria Ltd	(Wickford)	23. 7.08E
G-IGIE	SIAI-Marchetti SF.260	2-42	D-EHGB	13. 3.02	D Fletcher and J J Watts	Bournemouth	12. 5.08E
G-IGII	Europa Aviation Europa	011		9. 4.02	C D Peacock	Sywell	3. 7.07P
	(Built W C Walters - pr.no.PFA 247-12506) (NSI EA/81-100) (Conventional u/c)						
G-IGLA	Colt 240A Balloon (Hot Air)	2228		3. 7.92	M L and S M Gabb t/a Heart of England Balloons	Haselor, Alcester	29. 8.03T
					(Barclaycard titles)		
G-IGLE	Cameron V-90 Balloon (Hot Air)	2609		11. 6.91	A A Laing *"Giggle"*	Aberdeen	4. 5.08A
G-IGLZ	American Champion 8KCAB Super Decathlon	914-2003		18. 2.03	Woodgate Aviation (IoM) Ltd	Belfast International	24. 1.08E
G-IGNL	Robinson R44 Clipper II	11208		4. 5.06	Fly Freedom Ltd	(Nicosia, Cyprus)	25. 5.08E
G-IGPW	Eurocopter EC.120B Colibri	1027	G-CBRI	31. 7 99	J Havakin	Middleton One Row, Darlington	21. 7.08E
G-IHOP	Cameron Z-31 Balloon (Hot Air)	10782		28.11.05	N W Roberts	Cardiff	20.10.08P
G-IHOT	Evektor EV-97 teamEurostar UK	2007		1. 4.04	Exodos Airsports Ltd	Plaistows Farm, St Albans	31. 3.07P
					(New owner 1.08)		
G-IIAC	Aeronca 11AC Chief	11AC-169	(G-BTPY) N86359, NC86359	2. 7.91	G R Moore	Black Spring Farm, Castle Bytham	16. 5.08P
	(Continental A65)						
G-IIAI	Mudry CAP.232	7	F-GJGM	22. 1.08	C Butler	(Clowne, Chesterfield)	
G-IIAN	Aero Designs Pulsar	PFA 202-12123		10. 9.91	I G Harrison	(Pentrich, Ripley)	
	(Built I G Harrison)				(Under construction 2000)		
G-IICI	Pitts S-2C	6017	N113PS	20. 5.02	D G Cowen tr Charlie India Group	Redhill	7. 6.08E
	(Built Aviat Inc) (Lycoming AEIO-540)						
G-IICT	Schempp-Hirth Ventus 2cT	72/225	BGA 4921-JZV	12. 7.07	P McLean	RAF Marham	10. 6.08
G-IICX	Schempp-Hirth Ventus 2cxT	171/...	BGA 5199-KMH	3. 4.06	R Jones t/a Southern Sailplanes *"210"*	Lasham	30.11.07
G-IIDI	Extra EA.300/L	047	G-XTRS D-EXJH	5.10.01	Power Aerobatics Ltd	Kemble	13. 3.08E
					(Operated Xtreme Team)		
G-IIDY	Pitts S-2B	5000	G-BPVP N5302M	11.11.02	R P Millinship tr The S-2B Group	Leicester	29.10.07E
	(Built Aerotek Inc)						
G-IIEI	Extra EA.300/S	024	N127DW D-ETXW	3.11.05	Aerobatic Displays Ltd	Wycombe Air Park	17. 1.08E
G-IIEX	Extra EA.300/L	04	JA300L N123EX, D-ETYM, (D-ETYL)	25. 5.05	Extreme Aerobatics Ltd	Shoreham	21. 8.08E
G-IIFR	Robinson R22 Beta II	2841		2. 9.98	R C Hields t/a Hields Aviation	Durham Tees Valley	11. 9.08E
G-IIGI	Van's RV-4	381	N44BZ	7. 4.04	A Darlington tr G-IIGI Flying Club	Popham	28. 8.07P
	(Built R F and C Palmer)						
G-IIID	Dan Rihn DR.107 One Design	PFA 264-12766		6. 7.00	D A Kean	Dunsfold	28. 8.08P
	(Built M A N and A J Newall)						
G-IIIE	Pitts S-2B	5017	N9WQ N9WR	8. 3.04	D Dobson	Little Staughton	18. 8.07T
	(Built Aerotek Inc)						
G-IIIG	Boeing Stearman A75N1 (PT-17) Kaydet	75-4354	G-BSDR N61827, 42-16191	25. 3.91	O Josse and S Bolyn	(Spa, Belgium)	24. 7.09S
	(Continental W670)						
G-IIII	Pitts S-2B	5010	N5330G	6. 1.89	Four Eyes Aerobatics Ltd	Barton	28. 3.08E
	(Built Christen Industries Inc) (Lycoming AEIO-540)						

Reg	Type	C/n	Prev Id	Date	Owner/Operator	Base	Expiry
G-IIIL	Pitts S-1T (Built J L Edwardson)	008	OH-XPT G-IIIL, N15JE	15. 2.89	Empyreal Airways Ltd	Leicester	16.12.08P
G-IIIM	Stolp SA.100 Starduster (Built Starduster Corporation)	4258549	N40D	21. 4.06	H Mackintosh	Old Hay	
G-IIIO	Schempp-Hirth Ventus 2cM	41/73	PH-1110 D-KBBF	10. 8.04	S J Clark	(South Brent)	25. 9.08E
G-IIIR	Pitts S-1S (Built Milam)	604	N27M	21. 1.93	R O Rogers	Hulcote Farm, Salford, Berkshire	18. 6 04P
G-IIIS	Sukhoi Su-26M2	06-07	RA-01321 N626RM, RA-0607, DOSAAF 55 (black) (Red Bull Matadors titles)	7.10.03	Airtime Aerobatics Ltd	Kemble	14. 6.08P
G-IIIT	Pitts S-2A (Built Aerotek Inc)	2222	N7YT	16. 1.89	Aerobatic Displays Ltd (Breitling Angels c/s)	Wycombe Air Park	19. 9.07A
G-IIIV	Pitts Super Stinker 11-260 (Built A N R Houghton) (Lycoming IO-540) (Marked as a "Pitts S1.11B")	PFA 273-13005		4. 2.97	S D Barnard	Leicester	13. 5.08P
G-IIIX	Pitts S-1S (Built J Tarascio)	AJT	G-LBAT G-UCCI, G-BIYN, N455T	22. 5.89	D S T Eggleton	Waits Farm, Belchamp Walter	18.11.08P
G-IIIZ	Sukhoi Su-26M	04-05	RA-44444 DOSAAF 35 (black)	14. 5.03	P M M Bonhomme (Red Bull Matadors titles)	Audley End	14. 6.08P
G-IIMI	Extra EA.300/L	141	D-EXLE	2. 5.01	A Birch	(Blackpool)	31. 5.08T
G-IIMT	Bushby-Long Midget Mustang (Built M J A Trudgill - pr.no.formerly PFA 1327)	PFA 168-1327	G-BDGA	13.11.03	J J Cooke "4"	Hinton-in-the-Hedges	14. 6.08P
G-IINI	Van's RV-9A (Built S Sampson)	PFA 320-13781		6. 8.04	G J Burlington	Oaksey Park	8. 5.08P
G-IIPT	Robinson R22 Beta	2506	G-FUSI N83306	10. 5.01	Milford Garage Ltd t/a Milford Aviation	Cranfield	23. 9.08E
G-IIRG	Stoddard-Hamilton Glasair IIS RG (Built D S Watson) (Lycoming IO-360)	PFA 149-11937		29. 6.93	A C Lang	RNAS Yeovilton	20. 8.07P
G-IIUI	Extra EA.300/S (Exxon Elite titles)	004	G-CCBD OK-XTA, D-EBEW	26.11.03	C W Burkett , J R and M G Jefferies "The Elite Twister" Fullers Hill Farm, Little Gransden		30. 4.08E
G-IIVI	Mudry CAP 232	21	F-GUJM	20. 1.05	Skylane Aviation Ltd	Sherburn-in-Elmet	19. 1.08E
G-IIXF	Van's RV-7	PFA 323-13844		14. 3.07	C A and S Noujaim	(Rendcomb, Chichester)	
G-IIXI	Extra EA.300/L	134	YR-EWG	6. 8.03	B H D H Frere	Higherlands Farm, Branscombe	4.12.07E
G-IIXX	Parsons Two-Place Gyroplane (Built J M Montgomerie) (Rotax 912)	PFA G/8-1225		13.10.93	J M Montgomerie (Noted 11.05)	Kirkbride	
G-IIYK	Yakovlev Yak-50	842706	LY-AFZ DOSAAF 24	15.10.02	D A Hammant	Bere Farm, Warnford	19.10.07P
G-IIZI	Extra EA.300	037	JY-RNB D-ETXA	12.12.96	Power Aerobatics Ltd (Operated Extreme Team)	Kemble	12. 2.08T
G-IJAC	Avid Speed Wing Mk.4 (Built I J A Charlton)	PFA 189-12095		31.12.92	I J A Charlton	(Northchapel, Petworth)	
G-IJAG	Cessna 182T Skylane	18281683	N2284F	7.11.05	R Wicks tr AG Group	Denham	28.11.07E
G-IJBB	Enstrom 480	5010	G-LIVA N900SA, G-PBTT, JA6169	17. 9.99	R P Bateman	Hurley Lodge, Westerham	11.11.07E
G-IJMC	Magni M-16 Tandem Trainer (Arrow GT1000R)	VPM16-UK-106	G-POSA G-BVJM	10. 6.98	P Adams	(Beaconsfield)	25.11.08P
G-IJNK	Robinson R44 Clipper	0780	G-KTOL	28. 9.07	Hi-Range Ltd	(Rough Park., Rugeley)	3. 8.08E
G-IJOE	Piper PA-28RT-201T Turbo Arrow IV	28R-8031178	N8265X N9599N	14. 8.90	J H Bailey tr G-IJOE Group	Sturgate	22. 7.08E
G-IJYS	British Aerospace Jetstream Series 3102	715	G-BTZT N416MX, G-31-715	5.10.92	Avient Ltd	(Amesbury, Salisbury)	18.11.07E
G-IKAP	Cessna T303 Crusader	T30300182	N63SA D-IKAP, N9518C	4. 3.99	T M Beresford (Noted 10.05)	Fowlmere	23. 9.05T
G-IKAT	Diamond DA.20-C1 Katana	C0096	N966CT C-GKAC	14.12.04	S J Phillips	Elstree	12. 1.08E
G-IKBP	Piper PA-28-161 Warrior II	28-8216132	N81762	16. 7.90	K B Page	Goodwood	6. 3 08E
G-IKEA	Cameron IKEA 120 SS Balloon (Hot Air)	10562		14. 6.04	IKEA Ltd (IKEA titles) (Active 5.07)	Bristol	20. 4.08A
G-IKES	Stoddard-Hamilton GlaStar (Built J K Tofte)	5763	N8066A	17. 8.05	M Stow	Newcastle	
G-IKEV	Avtech Jabiru UL-450 (Built K J Bream - pr.no.PFA 274A-14075)	xxxx		29. 6.04	N Grantham	(Godmanchester, Huntingdon)	12. 3.08P
G-IKON	Van's RV-4 (Built S Sampson)	PFA 181-14474		22. 2.06	S Sampson	Ladybank House, Kiplin	
G-IKOS	Cessna 550 Citation Bravo	550-0957	N957PH N51780	27. 5.04	Medox Enterprises Ltd	(Limassol, Cyprus)	9. 6.08E
G-IKRK	Europa Aviation Europa (Built K R Kesterton - pr.no.PFA 247-12903) (Monowheel u/c)	202		16. 4.02	K R Kesterton	Andrewsfield	24. 6.08P
G-IKRS	Comco Ikarus C42 FB UK (Built P G Walton)	PFA 322-13719		1. 8.01	J E Lockwood	(Rugby)	29. 6.07P
G-IKUS	Comco Ikarus C42 FB UK (Built C I Law)	PFA 322-14130		10.10.03	C I Law	Wickenby	1. 5.07P
G-ILBO	Rolladen-Schneider LS3-a	3458	BGA 2639-EEZ	19. 9.07	J P Gilbert	Wormingford	28. 9.08
G-ILDA	Vickers Supermarine 361 Spitfire HF.IX	CBAF.10164	G-BXHZ SAAF???, SM520	11. 7.02	(P W Portelli) (On rebuild 2008 as Tr.IX as "H-99" in R Netherlands AF c/s)	Thruxton	
G-ILEE	Colt 56A Duo Chariot Balloon (Hot Air)	2624		29. 7.94	G I Lindsay "Gillie"	Storrington, Pulborough	16. 4.07A
G-ILET	Robinson R44 Raven II	10789		28. 6.05	Lear Group Ltd	(Stourbridge)	11. 8.08E
G-ILLE	Boeing Stearman E75 (PT-13D) Kaydet (Continental W670)	75-5028	N68979 42-16865, Bu.60906	7. 3.90	A C Ansalt (Also carries "379" in USAAC c/s)	(Ruggell, Liechtenstein)	4.10.08S
G-ILLG	Robinson R44 Raven II	11416		22. 9.06	C B Ellis	(Preston Patrick, Milnthorpe)	17.10.07E
G-ILLY	Piper PA-28-181 Cherokee Archer II	28-7690193	SE-GND	21. 2.80	R A and G.M Spiers (New owners 6.03)	Harpsden Court, Harpsden	19.12.93
G-ILMD	Pilatus PC-12/45	412	N412MD N10778, HB-FSI, N412WC, HB-FRA	11. 8.05	N J Vetch	Goodwood	25. 8.08E
G-ILPY	Cessna 172S Skyhawk	172S8704	N2437B	2. 7.07	D R Turner	Dunkeswell	7. 8.08E
G-ILRS	Comco Ikarus C42 FB UK (Built L R Smith)	PFA 322-13927		19. 6.02	Knitsley Mill Leisure Ltd	(Consett)	13. 5.08P

G-ILSE	Corby CJ-1 Starlet	PFA 134-10818			9. 1.84	S Stride	Halfpenny Green	17. 4.08P
	(Built S Stride) (HAPI Magnum 75)							
G-ILTS	Piper PA-32-300 Six	32-7940217	G-CVOK		28. 3.90	Foremans Aviation Ltd	Full Sutton	26. 5.08E
			OE-DOH, N2941C					
G-ILUA	Alpha Aviation Alpha R2160i	160Ai-07007	ZK-SXY		22. 5.07	A R Haynes	Duxford	13. 6.08E
G-IMAB	Europa Aviation Europa XS	331			1. 2.00	T J Price	Shenstone	21. 2.08P
	(Built A H Brown - pr.no.PFA 247-13128)							
G-IMAC	Bombardier CL-600-2A12	3065	LX-GDC		6.09.05	Gama Aviation Ltd	Farnborough	22. 9.08E
	(CL-601 Challenger)		N601JP, (N45PA), N601JP, N500PE, (N128PE), N1623, N602CC, C-GLYA					
G-IMAN	Colt 31A Sky Chariot Balloon (Hot Air)	2605			23. 6.94	Stratos Ballooning Gmbh and Co KG		
							Ennigerloh, Germany	17. 3.05A
G-IMAR	Agusta A109E Power	11703			14. 5.07	Inishway Properties Ltd	Newtownards	14. 5.08E
G-IMBI	QAC Quickie 1	484	G-BWIT		7.10.02	J D King	Biggin Hill	28. 2.06P
	(Rotax 503)		N4482Z					
G-IMBY	Pietenpol AirCamper	PFA 047-12402			22.12.93	P F Bockh	(Milbourne Port, Sherborne)	
						(New owner 7.06)		
G-IMCD	Van's RV-7	PFA 323-13965			14. 4.04	I G McDowell	RAF Shawbury	18. 2.08P
	(Built I G McDowell)							
G-IMEA	Beech 200 Super King Air	BB-302	G-OWAX		1.11.06	M Magrabi	Bournemouth	6. 9.08E
			N86Y, N300BW, N600CP			*(Operated Airtime Charter)*		
G-IMEC	Piper PA-31 Navajo C	31-7512017	G-BFOM		1.11.06	Airtime Aviation France Ltd	Bournemouth	16. 5.06E
			(F-GJHV), EI-DMI, G-BFOM, HB-LHH, N59933 *(Operated Airtime Charter)*					
G-IMIC	IAV Bacau Yakovlev Yak-52	8910001	RA-02149		21. 8.02	J S and H A Jewell	(Wortwell, Harleston)	19. 7.08P
			DOSAAF 103 *(Yellow)*					
G-IMLI	Cessna 310Q	310Q0491	G-AZYK		3. 4.86	Oakwood Leisure Ltd	Haverfordwest	30. 4.08E
			N4182Q					
G-IMME	Zenair CH.701 STOL	PFA 187-14080			29. 8.03	M Spearman	(Greenhithe)	
	(Built M Spearman)							
G-IMNY	Reality Escapade 912(2)	JAESC 0022			25. 5.04	D S Bremner	Strathaven	23.11.08P
	(Built D S Bremner - pr.no.BMAA/HB/358)							
G-IMOK	Hoffman HK 36R Super Dimona	36317	I-NELI		31. 7.97	A L Garfield	Dunstable	30. 8.08E
			OE-9352					
G-IMPX	Rockwell Commander 112B	512	N1304J		25.10.90	P A Day *(New owner 2.08)*	Old Sarum	1. 6.06
G-IMPY	Avid Flyer C	PFA 189-11439			10. 4.89	T R C Griffin	Haverfordwest	22.10.08P
	(Built T R C Griffin) (Rotax 532)							
G-IMUP	Air Création Tanarg 912S/iXess 15	FLT.005			8. 2.06	P D Hill	Long Marston	30. 7.08P
	(Built P D Hil - pr.no.BMAA/HB/478 being Flylight kit comprising;Trike s/n T05082 and Wing s/n A05150-5145)							
G-INCA	Glaser-Dirks DG-400	4-199			22. 1.87	K D Hook *"320"*	Portmoak	17. 3.08P
G-INCE	Best Off Sky Ranger 912(2)	SKR0302293			12. 3.03	N P Sleigh	Ince Blundell	2. 7.08P
	(Built N P Sleigh - pr.no.BMAA/HB/270)							
G-INDC	Cessna T303 Crusader	T30300122	G-BKFH		28. 6.83	J-Ross Developments Ltd	Welshpool	19. 3.08E
			N4766C					
G-INDX	Robinson R44 Clipper II	10491			20.10.04	Kinetic Avionics Ltd	Elstree	8.11.07E
G-INGA	Thunder Ax8-84 Balloon (Hot Air)	2149			16. 6.92	M L J Ritchie	Weybridge	30. 9.94A
G-INGE	Thruster T 600N Sprint	9039-T600N-033			23. 2.99	R S O'Carroll tr Thruster 1 Group		
							Mullahead, Tandragee	7.10.08P
G-INIT	SOCATA TB-9 Tampico Club	1384	I-IAFS		19. 1.05	P R Shakeshaft	Biggin Hill	30. 1.08E
G-INJA	Comco Ikarus C42 FB100 VLA	PFA 322-14044			24. 4.03	J W G Andrews	Sutton Meadows	29. 2.08P
	(Built J W G Andrews)							
G-INKY	Robinson R22 Beta	1101	G-UDAY		10. 8.05	Saltire Helicopters Ltd	Perth	26. 9.08E
G-INNI	Wassmer Jodel D 112	540	F-BHPU		30. 8.94	S Barry	(Mullinavat, County Kilkenny)	6. 7.08P
G-INNY	Replica Plans SE.5a	PFA 020-10439			18.12.78	M J Speakman	North Coates	15. 5.08P
	(Built R M Ordish) (Continental C90)						*(As "F5459:Y" in RFC c/s)*	
G-INOW	Monnett Moni	223			30. 3.84	W C Brown	(Frimley Green, Camberley)	20. 8.88P
	(Built ARV Aviation Ltd - pr.no.PFA 142-10953) (KEF 107)					*(Stored 8.97)*		
G-INSR	Cameron N-90 Balloon (Hot Air)	4320			23. 4.98	The Smith and Pinching Group Ltd and P Phillips		
							Norwich	21. 8.08A
G-INTO	Pilatus PC-12/45	609	HS-SMC		2. 1. 07	A Colin t/a Into Air (UpperSheringham, Sheringham)		28. 1.08E
			N595PB, HB-FRI					
G-INTS	Van's RV-4	1780			17. 5.06	N J F Campbell	Inverness	7. 8.08P
	(Built N J F Campbell - pr.no.PFA 181-13069)							
G-IOCO	Beech 58 Baron	TH-1783			6. 6.96	Arenberg Consultadoria E Servicos LDA		
							(Madeira, Portugal)	20. 6.08E
G-IOFR	Lindstrand LBL 105A Balloon (Hot Air)	1041			1. 3.05	A I Attwood tr RAF Halton Hot Air Balloon Club		
							Halton Camp, Aylesbury	6. 6.08E
G-IOIA	III Sky Arrow 650 T	P/98/024			20. 3.03	P J Lynch, P G Ward and N J C Ray	Old Sarum	22. 2.08P
	(Built P J Lynch, P G Ward and N J C Ray - pr.no.PFA 298-14008)							
G-IONA	Aérospatiale-Alenia ATR 42-300	017	SP-KEE		19.12.02	Bravo Aviation Ltd	Jersey	19.11.07E
			G-IONA, N971NA, F-WWER			*(New owner 2.08)*		
G-IOOI	Robin DR.400-160 Major 80	1700			31. 5.85	N B Mason	Rendcomb	18. 4.08E
G-IOOP	Christen Eagle II	RUPPERT-0001	N414DE		7. 3.07	A P S Maynard	Shoreham	7. 8.08P
	(Built E J Ruppert)							
G-IOOX	Learjet Model 45	45-243	N4004Q		8. 6.04	Hundred Percent Aviation Ltd	Coventry	7. 6.08E
G-IOPT	Cessna 182P Skylane	18261731	N182EE		9. 6.98	A J Marks and D Madden tr Indy Oscar Group		
			D-ECVM, N21585				Elstree	16. 3.08E
G-IORG	Robinson R22 Beta	1679	OH-HRU		28. 1.00	JLC Aviation Ltd	Hawarden	3. 5.08E
			G-ZAND					
G-IORV	Van's RV-10	PFA 339-14610			26. 3.07	A F S and B L Caldecourt	(Knaphill, Woking)	
G-IOSI	CEA Jodel DR.1050 Sicile	526	F-BLRS		6.10.80	G A Saxby tr Sicile Flying Group		
							(Stratford-upon-Avon)	24. 7.08E
G-IOSO	CEA Jodel DR.1050 Ambassadeur	46	OO-VDV		13. 7.00	A E Jackson	Podington	2.12.06
			F-BJUE					
G-IOWA	Fairey Britten-Norman BN-2A-26 Islander	431	G-BCWO		11.12.06	Isle of Wight Aviation Ltd	Sandown, Isle of Wight	17.12.07E
			SE-LAX, LN-MAC, G-BCWO					

Reg	Type	c/n	Prev id	Date	Owner/Operator	Location	Expiry
G-IOWE	Europa Aviation Europa XS	368		30. 7.99	P A Lowe	Halfpenny Green	2. 8.08P
	(Built P A Lowe - pr.no.PFA 247-13303) (Tri-gear u/c)						
G-IPAL	Cessna 550 Citation Bravo	550-0935	EI-PAL N5264A	21. 1.04	Pacific Aviation Ltd	(Belfast International)	22. 1.07E
G-IPAT	Avtech Jabiru SP-470	xxxx		14. 4.04	G Fleck	Kirkbride	4.11.07P
	(Built M G Thatcher - pr.no.PFA 274B-14227)						
G-IPAX	Cessna 560XL Citation Excel	560-5228	EI-PAX	13. 2.04	Pacific Aviation Ltd	Belfast International	19. 2.08E
G-IPFM	Montgomerie-Bensen B 8MR	PFA G/01-1320	G-BZJR	18.10.05	I P F Meiklejohn	(Forres)	29.11.07P
	(Built N H Collins) (Rotax 582)						
G-IPKA	Alpi Pioneer 300	12		9. 2.05	J R Gibbons	Tibenham	10. 5.07P
	(Built I P King - pr.no.PFA 330-14355)				(Noted 11.07)		
G-IPSI (2)	Grob G109B	6425	G-BMLO	29. 5.86	D G Margetts	Shobdon	12. 6.08E
G-IPSY	Rutan VariEze	1512	(G-IPSI)	19. 6.78	R A Fairclough	Biggin Hill	8. 7.08P
	(Built R A Fairclough - pr.no.PFA 074-10284 (Continental PC60)						
G-IPUP	Beagle B 121 Pup Series 2	B121-036	HB-NAC G-35-036	17. 7.95	R G Hayes	North Weald	23.11.07T
G-IRAF	Rotary Air Force RAF 2000 GTX-SE			17. 6.96	P Robichaud	Henstridge	10. 9.08P
	(Built C D Julian)	PFA G/13-1278					
G-IRAL	Thruster T 600N 450	0035-T600N-083		24. 4.03	J Giraldez	(Burgh Le Marsh, Skegness)	1. 1.08P
	(Official c/n incorrect - date of manufacture [May 2003] indicates correct version should be 0053-T600N-083)						
G-IRAR	Van's RV-9	PFA 320-14106		26. 2.07	J Mapplethorpe	(Compton Martin, Bristol)	
	(Built J Mapplethorpe)						
G-IRIS	Gulfstream AA-5B Tiger	AA5B-1184	G-BIXU N4533N	14.12.87	C Nichol	Bodmin	23. 7.08E
G-IRKB	Piper PA-28R-201 Cherokee Arrow III	28R-7737071	D-EJDS N5814V	7. 3.00	R K Brierley	Earls Colne	1. 6.08E
G-IRLE	Schempp-Hirth Ventus cT	172/562	BGA 3935-HGN	19. 2.08	D J Scholey	Lasham	21. 3.08
G-IRLY	Colt 90A Balloon (Hot Air)	1620		28.12.89	C E R Smart (Maple Leaf symbols)	Waterlooville	4. 9.07A
G-IRLZ	Lindstrand LBL 60X Balloon (Hot Air)	1092		5. 4.06	A M Holly (Sloggi titles)	Breadstone, Berkeley	2. 3.08E
G-IROE	Flight Design CTSW	07.10.11		12.11.07	S Roe	(South Hykeham, Lincoln)	11.11.08P
	(Assembled P&M Aviation Ltd with c/n 8334)						
G-IRON	Europa Aviation Europa XS	583		4. 5.04	T M Clark	(Guildford)	20.11.08P
	(Built T M Clark - pr.no.PFA 247-14235)						
G-IRPC	Cessna 182Q Skylane II	18266039	G-BSKM N559CT, N759JV	15. 5.91	R Warner	Cambridge	17. 7.08E
G-IRTH	Lindstrand LBL 150A Balloon (Hot Air)	772	G-BZTO	20. 6.02	A M Holly	Breadstone, Berkeley	2. 3.08T
					(Cowlin Construction titles)		
G-IRYC	Schweizer 269C-1	0194	N86G	8. 3.05	G Cooper t/a GC Heating	Prees, Shropshire	21. 4.08E
	(Schweizer 300)						
G-ISAX	Piper PA-28-181 Archer III	2843453	N5325G	28. 6.01	M S Kontowtt	Barton	9. 8.08E
G-ISCA	Piper PA-28RT-201 Arrow IV	28R-8118012	N8288Y N9608N	12. 2.91	D J and P Pay	Plymouth	14. 6.08
G-ISDB	Piper PA-28-161 Warrior II	28-7716074	G-BWET SX-ALX, D-EFFQ, N9612N	19. 2.96	Action Air Services Ltd	White Waltham	5. 6.08T
G-ISDN	Boeing Stearman B75N1 (N2S-3) Kaydet	75-1263	N4197X XB-WOV, Bu.3486	6. 2.95	D R L Jones	Rendcomb	2.11.08
	(Officially regd as "A75N1")				(As "14" in US Army c/s)		
G-ISEH	Cessna 182R Skylane II	18267843	G-BIWS N6601N	9.11.90	CSE Bournemouth Ltd	Oxford	2.11.07E
G-ISEL	Best Off Sky Ranger 912(2)	SKRxxxx368		7.11.03	P A Robertson	Sywell	4. 6.08P
	(Built P A Robertson - pr.no.BMAA/HB/312)						
G-ISEW	P&M Quik GT450	8170		20. 4.06	T.W.Lorimer	Strathaven	11. 6.08P
G-ISFC	Piper PA-31 Turbo Navajo B	31-7300970	G-BNEF N7574L	23. 3.94	I M Latiff	Little Staughton	25. 5.08E
G-ISHA	Piper PA-28-161 Cherokee Warrior III	2842211	N3092D	21. 7.04	Clever Clogs (Middleton) Ltd	Barton	13. 8.08E
G-ISHK	Cessna 172S Skyhawk	172S9783	N66116	4. 3.05	Matchpace Ltd	Redhill	4. 4.08E
G-ISKA	WSK-PZL Mielec TS-11 Iskra	1H1018	Polish AF 1018	11. 5.00	P C Harper	Bruntingthorpe	
					(As "1018" in Polish AF c/s) (Noted 3.04)		
G-ISLB	British Aerospace Jetstream Series 3202	871	N871JX N871AE, G-31-871	6. 1.06	Airx Ltd t/a Blue Islands	Jersey	29. 3.08E
G-ISLC	British Aerospace Jetstream Series 3202	873	N873JX N873AE, G-31-873	2. 3.06	Airx Ltd t/a Blue Islands	Jersey	24. 5.08E
G-ISLD	British Aerospace Jetstream Series 3202	915	N915AE G-31-915	24. 7.06	Airx Ltd t/a Blue Islands	Jersey	3. 9.08E
G-ISMA	Van's RV-7A	PFA 323-13875	G-STAF	7.12.07	S Marriott	Old Sarum	
	(Built A F Stafford)						
G-ISMO	Robinson R22 Beta	0870	OH-HOR G-ISMO, N8214T	14.10.88	Moy Motorsport Ltd	Sywell	23. 8.08E
G-ISPH	Bell 206B-3 JetRanger III	4259	G-OPJM D-Balloon (Hot Air)A, C-FOFG	3. 3.06	Blades Aviation (UK) LLP	East Midlands	13. 3.08E
G-ISST	Eurocopter EC.155 B1	6778		13. 6.07	Bristow Helicopters Ltd	Aberdeen	28. 6.08E
G-ISSU	Eurocopter EC.155 B1	6762	F-WWOM	22. 3.07	Bristow Helicopters Ltd	Aberdeen	4. 4.08E
G-ISSV	Eurocopter EC.155 B1	6757	F-WWOG	20.12.06	Bristow Helicopters Ltd	Den Helder, Netherlands	17. 1.08E
G-ISSW	Eurocopter EC.155 B1	6755	F-WWOD	1.12.06	Bristow Helicopters Ltd	Aberdeen	14.12.07E
G-ISSY	Eurocopter EC.120B Colibri	1236	G-CBCG F-WQPT	11.10.01	D R Williams	Stapleford	8.12.07E
G-ITBT	Alpi Pioneer 300 Hawk	xxx		19. 6.07	F Paolini	(Kingswood, Bristol)	7. 8.08P
	(Built F Paolini - pr.no.PFA 330A-14641)						
G-ITFL	Diamond DA.42 Twin Star	42.246	OE-VPY	30. 7.07	Tyrone Fabrication Ltd	Enniskillen	14. 8.08P
G-ITIG	Dassault Falcon 2000EX	102	F-WWMD	1. 3.07	TAG Aviation (UK) Ltd	Farnborough	22. 9.08E
G-ITII	Pitts S-2A	2223	I-VLAT	5. 7.95	Aerobatic Displays Ltd	Wycombe Air Park	31. 1.08E
	(Built Aerotek Inc)						
G-ITOI	Cameron N-90 Balloon (Hot Air)	4785		14. 1.00	A E Lusty	Bourne	2..3.08A
G-ITON	Maule MX-7-235 Super Rocket	10050C	N5670R	11. 9.96	J R S Heaton	Blackpool	20. 9.08E
G-ITPH	Robinson R44 Clipper II	11909		17. 9.07	Island Air Ltd	Newtownards	

G-ITUG	Piper PA-28-180 Cherokee C	28-4121	G-AVNR	14. 8.02	S I Tugwell	Stapleford	25.10.07E
			N11C				
G-ITVM	Lindstrand LBL 105A Balloon (Hot Air)	1017		8.11.04	N C Lindsay	Storrington, Pulborough	16. 4.08E
					(Meridian Tonight titles)		
G-ITWB	de Havilland DHC-1 Chipmunk 22	48	CS-AZO	16. 9.04	I T Whitaker-Bethel	Ellough, Beccles	18. 5.09S
	(Built OGMA)		Portuguese AF FAP 1358				
G-IUAN	Cessna 525 CitationJet	525-0324	N5163C	30. 6.99	RF Celada SpA	Milan-Linate, Lombardy, Italy	23. 3.08E
			(N428PC)				
G-IUII	Aerostar Yakovlev Yak-52	9111604	RA-1281K	28.11.06	W Hanekom	Little Gransden	24. 4.08P
			RA-01281, DOSAAF 69 (grey)				
G-IVAC	Airtour AH-77B Balloon (Hot Air)	012		28.11.89	T D Gibbs	Plaistow, Billingshurst	22. 8.08A
G-IVAL	CAB CAP.10B	307		8. 4.03	I Valentine "307"	Kilrush, County Kildare	6. 7.08E
G-IVAN	Shaw Twin-Eze	PFA 074-10502		11. 9.78	A M Aldridge	Ostend, Belgium	5.10.90P
	(Built I Shaw - c/n 39) (Norton-Wankel)				"Mistress" (Noted 2000)		
G-IVAR	Yakovlev Yak-50	791504	D-EIVI	24. 2.89	A H Soper	Jenkin's Farm, Navestock	16. 5.08P
			(N5219K), DDR-WQT, DM-WQT				
G-IVAS	Bell 206B-3 JetRanger III	3191	G-MCPI	5.12.05	G N Ratcliffe	(Calthwaite, Penrith)	14. 6.08E
			G-ONTB, N3896C				
G-IVDM	Schempp-Hirth Nimbus 4DM	39/55	D-KABV	18.10.02	G W Lynch	Rattlesden	2. 5.08E
G-IVEL	Fournier RF4D	4029	G-AVNY	29. 6.95	V S E Norman	(Rendcomb)	14. 4.01A
G-IVEN	Robinson R44 Raven II	10442		28. 7.04	OKR Group	(Dublin)	13. 9.08E
G-IVER	Europa Aviation Europa XS	486		14. 8.00	I Phillips	(Orpington)	
	(Built I Phillips - pr no.PFA 247-13632) (Convertible u/c)						
G-IVET	Europa Aviation Europa	020		23. 5.97	K J Fraser	(Abingdon)	
	(Built K J Fraser - pr.no.PFA 247-12511) (Conventional u/c)						
G-IVII	Van's RV-7	PFA 323-14222		31. 8.04	M A N Newall	Bagby	
	(Built M A N Newall)						
G-IVIV	Robinson R44 Astro	0016	(N803EH)	2. 8.93	Helitrain Ltd	Shobdon	12.12.07E
G-IVOR	Aeronca 11AC Chief	11AC-1035	EI-BKB	18. 6.82	P R White tr South Western Aeronca Group	Bodmin	3. 6.08P
			G-IVOR, EI-BKB, N9397E				
G-IVYS	Parsons Two-Place Gyroplane	PFA G/8-1275		11. 1.00	R M Harris	(Nottingham)	
	(Built R M Harris) (Mazda RX-7)						
G-IWDB	Raytheon Hawker 800XP	258618	N82GK	2. 3.06	Markoss Aviation UK Ltd	Biggin Hill	15. 3.08E
			N618XP, N896QS, (N895QS)				
G-IWIN	Raj Hamsa X'Air Hawk	xxx		11. 6.07	R Wooldridge	Carlisle	
	(Built R Wooldridge - pr.no.PFA 340-14679)				(Noted 10.07)		
G-IWON	Cameron V-90 Balloon (Hot Air)	2504	G-BTCV	17. 2.92	D P P Jenkinson (Cameron - 21 years titles)	Tring	5. 4.08A
G-IWRB	Agusta A109A II	7386	G-VIPT	10. 8.06	Fuel The Jet LLP	(Wickford)	11. 9.08E
			N109SM, N109AZ, JA9694, N1ZN				
G-IWRC	Eurocopter EC.135 T2	0241	D-HECA	9. 9.02	Hundred Percent Aviation Ltd	Coventry	13.11.07E
G-IXCC	Vickers Supermarine 361 Spitfire IX	????	N644TB	18. 5.88	Spitfire Ltd	(Duxford)	9.12.93P
			G-IXCC, PL344			(New owner 1.08)		
G-IXES	Air Création Clipper/iXess 912	FL.027		3. 3.04	G J Little	Sywell	15. 7.08P
	(Built R Grimwood - pr.no.BMAA/HB/357 being Flylight kit comprising Trike s/n T03027 and Wing s/n 04019-4014) (Trike believed ex French 07-JF)						
G-IXII	Christen Eagle II	T0001	G-BPZI	9. 1.03	R P Marks tr Eagle Flying Group	Dunkeswell	25. 3.08P
	(Built J Trent and R Eicher) (Lycoming IO-360)		N48BB				
G-IYCO	Robin DR.500-200i Président	0031		23. 2.01	Timgee Holdings Ltd	Jersey	1. 4.08E
	(Officially regd as DR.400-500)						
G-IZII	Margan'ski Swift S-1	110	BGA 5240-KNY	9.10.06	G C Westgate	Parham Park	22.10.07
			N110LG				
G-IZIT	Rans S-6-116 Coyote II	0695.841		7. 3.96	A J Best and M Watson	Baxby Manor, Husthwaite	9. 7.08P
	(Built D A Crompton - pr.no.PFA 204A-12965) (Rotax 912-UL) (Tri-cycle u/c)						
	(New frame fitted 1999 after accident 6.9.98 - kit no not known: original frame 841 rebuilt and used to repair G-MWUN qv)						
G-IZOD	Avtech Jabiru UL-450	xxxx		26. 5.00	N J Stillwell	Damyn's Hall, Upminster	26.11.07P
	(Built D A Izod - pr.no.PFA 274A-13541)						
G-IZZI	Cessna T182T Turbo Skylane	T18208100	N51197	19. 3.02	T J and P S Nicholson	Manston	7. 5.08E
G-IZZS	Cessna 172S Skyhawk SP	172S8152	N952SP	1. 7.99	Innovative Aviation Ltd	(Ripon)	12.10.07E
G-IZZY	Cessna 172R Skyhawk	17280419	G-BXSF	7. 9.99	P A Adams and T S Davies	(Llanelli)	11. 7.08E
			N9967F				
G-IZZZ	American Champion 8KCAB Super Decathlon	939-2003		29. 1.04	A M Read	Goodwood	9. 6.07T

G-JAAA - G-JZZZ

G-JAAB	Avtech Jabiru UL-D	655		28. 3.06	E Fogarty	Rochester	13. 5.08P
G-JABB	Avtech Jabiru UL-450	0328		27. 4.00	D J Abbott	Coldharbour Farm, Willingham	13. 4.08P
	(Built D J Royce - pr.no.PFA 274A-13555)						
G-JABE	Avtech Jabiru UL-D	0657	G-CDZX	9.10.06	Alan Developments Ltd	Damyn's Hall, Upminster	1. 8.08P
G-JABI	Avtech Jabiru J400	0xxx		3.10.03	R A Shaw Aviation Ltd	Blackpool	31.12.08P
	(Built R A Shaw - pr.no.PFA 325-14098)						
G-JABJ	Avtech Jabiru J400	0xxx		17.11.03	F H Hancock and L B Watkins	Kemble	3.12.08P
	(Built P G Leonard - pr.no.PFA 325-14126)						
G-JABS	Avtech Jabiru UL-450	xxxx		27. 6.02	P E Todd tr Jabiru Flyer Group	Chilbolton	6. 3.08P
	(Built I R Cook and P E Todd - pr.no.PFA 274A-13704)						
G-JABU	Avtech Jabiru J430	0xxx		9. 1.06	S D Miller	Bourn	2.11.08P
	(Built R J Chapman - pr.no.PFA 336-14515)						
G-JABY	Avtech Jabiru SPL-450	xxxx		2. 2.01	J T Grant	Little Snoring	16.10.07P
	(Built J T Grant - pr.no.PFA 274A-13672)						
G-JABZ	Avtech Jabiru UL-450	xxxx		3. 5.05	A C Barnes	Eshott	2.10.08P
	(Built A C Barnes - pr.no.PFA 274A-14289)						
G-JACA	Piper PA-28-161 Warrior III	2842139	N5328Q	28. 2.02	Channel Islands Aero Club (Jersey) Ltd	Jersey	6. 3.08E
G-JACB	Piper PA-28-181 Archer III	2843278	G-PNNI	23. 7.02	Channel Islands Aero Club (Jersey) Ltd	Jersey	3.11.07E
			N41651			(Noted 1.08)		

Reg	Type	C/n	Prev id	Date	Owner/Operator	Base	Expiry
G-JACC	Piper PA-28-181 Archer III	2843222	G-GIFT	23.12.02	Magnum Holdings Ltd	(St Helier, Jersey)	6.11.07E
			G-IMVA, SE-KIH, N9524N, N4166F				
G-JACK	Cessna 421C Golden Eagle	421C1411	N421GQ	29. 4.97	JCT 600 Ltd	Leeds-Bradford	3. 5.08E
		N125RS, N12028					
G-JACO	Avtech Jabiru UL	0215		14. 4.99	C D Matthews	Kilrush, County Kildare	26. 6.07P
	(Built S Jackson - pr.no.PFA 274A-13371)						
G-JACS	Piper PA-28-181 Archer III	2843078	N9287J	15. 4.97	Vector Air Ltd	Fowlmere	2. 6.08E
			(G-JACS)				
G-JADJ	Piper PA-28-181 Archer III	2843009	N49TP	27. 7.99	Cumulus Aircraft Rentals Ltd	Bournemouth	28. 7.08E
	(Originally intended as c/n 2890240)		N92552				
G-JAEE	Van's RV-6A	PFA 181A-13571		16. 9.02	J A E Edser	(Luton)	
	(Built J A E Edser)						
G-JAES	Bell 206B-2 JetRanger II	1513	G-STOX	13. 1.04	Heli Charter Wales Ltd	Haverfordwest	6. 7.08E
			G-BNIR, N59615				
G-JAGS	Reims Cessna FRA150L Aerobat	FRA1500167	G-BAUY	24.10.01	G Bremer tr RAF Marham Aero Club	RAF Marham	20. 3.08E
			N10633				
G-JAIR	Mainair Blade	1249-0500-7-W1042		11. 7.00	A J Varga	Rufforth	11. 5.06P
	(Rotax 582)				"Joe Loughran"		
G-JAJA	Robinson R44 Raven II	11691		18. 4.07	Jara Aviation Ltd	Jaggards House, Weeley Heath	3. 5.08E
G-JAJB	Grumman American AA-5A Cheetah	AA5A-0590	OY-CJE	30. 4.02	J Bradley	Thruxton	16. 6.08E
			N26434				
G-JAJK	Piper PA-31-350 Chieftain	31-8152014	G-OLDB	16.12.99	Keen Leasing (IoM) Ltd	Belfast International	24. 7.08E
			OY-SKY, G-DIXI, N40717		(Operated Woodgate Executive Air Services)		
G-JAJP	Avtech Jabiru UL-450	0401		1.12.00	J W E Pearson and J Anderson		
	(Built J W E Pearson - pr.no.PFA 274A-13627)					Plaistows Farm, St Albans	21.10.08P
G-JAKF	Robinson R44 Raven II	10866		23. 9.05	J G Froggatt	(Marple Bridge, Stockport)	10.10.07E
G-JAKI	Mooney M 20R Ovation	29-0030		7. 2.95	J M Moss and D M Abrahamson	Dublin	12. 5.08E
G-JAKS	Piper PA-28-160 Cherokee	28-339	G-ARVS	2. 7.99	K Harper	Stapleford	29. 1.07
G-JAMA	Schweizer 269C-1	0165		2. 4.04	JWL Helicopters Ltd	Biggin Hill	12. 6.08E
	(Schweizer 300)						
G-JAME	Zenair CH.601UL Zodiac	6-2818	G-CDFZ	14. 1.05	A Batters	Baxby Manor, Husthwaite	26. 6.08P
	(Built J P Harris, B Yoxall, K Yoxall and N Barnes - pr.no.PFA 162A-14279) (Tri-cycle u/c)						
G-JAMP	Piper PA-28-151 Cherokee Warrior	28-7515026	G-BRJU	3. 4.95	Lapwing Flying Group Ltd	Denham	16. 8.08E
			N44762				
G-JAMY	Europa Aviation Europa XS	449		5. 1.01	J P Sharp	Rayne Hall Farm, Braintree	9. 9.08P
	(Built J P Sharp - pr.no.PFA 247-13557)						
G-JANA	Piper PA-28-181 Archer II	28-7990483	N2838X	12. 2.87	S I van Haaren t/a Vanair Aviation	Stapleford	3. 6.08E
G-JANI	Robinson R44 Astro	0110	N7027W	21. 7.95	JT Helicopters Ltd	(Thruxton)	1.12.07E
			EI-CUI, G-JANI, D-HIMM (2)				
G-JANN	Piper PA-34-220T Seneca III	3433133	N9154W	23. 6.89	MBC Aviation Ltd	Fairoaks	30. 8.07T
					(Operated Synergy Aviation)		
G-JANO	Piper PA-28RT-201 Arrow IV	28R-7918091	SE-IZR	14. 5.98	Nasaire Ltd	Liverpool	9. 9.07T
			N2146X				
G-JANS	Reims FR172J Rocket	FR17200414	PH-GJO	11. 8.78	I G Aizlewood	Rush Green	4. 1.08E
			D-EGJO				
G-JANT	Piper PA-28-181 Archer II	28-8390075	N4297J	23. 2.87	Janair Aviation Ltd	Denham	1. 4.08E
	(Originally built as c/n 28-8290117/N81992/YV-2234P: not delivered and re-manufactured as c/n stated)						
G-JANV	Learjet Model 45	45-124	N124AV	1. 5.07	Jannaire LLP	(Runcorn)	30. 4.08E
			G-OLDL, N4003Q				
G-JARA	Robinson R22 Beta	1837		11. 6.91	Northumbria Helicopters Ltd	Newcastle	14. 9.08E
G-JASE	Piper PA-28-161 Warrior II	28-8216056	N8461R	13. 2.91	Mid-Anglia Flight Centre Ltd t/a Mid-Anglia School of Flying		
						Cambridge	23. 9.08E
G-JAST	Mooney M 20J Mooney 201	24-1010	OO-RYL	1.10.04	S J Tillotson	Elstree	6.12.07E
			(N4004H)				
G-JATD	Robinson R22 Beta	0534	G-HUMF	10. 7.03	Rotormotive Ltd	Little Blakenham	22. 2.08E
			N23743				
G-JAVO	Piper PA-28-161 Warrior II	28-8016130	G-BSXW	17. 9.97	Victor Oscar Ltd	Wellesbourne Mountford	18. 7.08E
			N8119S				
G-JAWC	Cyclone Airsports Pegasus Quantum 15-912	7692		21. 7.00	M H Husey	Damyn's Hall, Upminster	18. 7.08P
G-JAWZ	Pitts S-1S	PFA 009-12846		6.11.95	A R Harding	Leicester	27.11.08P
	(Built S Howes)						
G-JAXS	Avtech Jabiru UL-450	xxxx		10.12.99	J P Pullin	Weston Zoyland	29. 9.08P
	(Built C A Palmer - pr.no.PFA 274A-13548						
G-JAYI	Auster V J/1 Autocrat	2030	OY-ALU	5. 2.93	Aviation Heritage Ltd	Coventry	11. 7.07S
			D-EGYK, OO-ABF				
G-JAYS	Best Off Sky Ranger 912S(1)	SKR0408509		14.12.04	R A Green	Sywell	14.12.07P
	(Built J Williams - pr.no.BMAA/HB/433: kit no.not confirmed - may be SKR0407509)						
G-JBAS	Neico Lancair 200	PFA 191-11465		21.11.03	B A Slater	(West Buckland, Wellington)	
G-JBBZ	Eurocopter AS.350B3 Ecureuil	3580	F-WQDE	13. 1.03	Milford Aviation Services Ltd	(London SW1)	16. 2.08E
			F-WQPV				
G-JBDB	Agusta-Bell 206B-2 JetRanger II	8238	G-OOPS	11. 4.96	Dicksons Van World Ltd	Hawarden	19. 4.08E
			G-BNRD, Oman AF 602				
G-JBDH	Robin DR.400-180 Régent	1901		17. 3.89	W A Clark	Netherthorpe	7. 6.08E
G-JBEN	Mainair Blade 912	1337-0802-7-W1132		13. 9.02	G J Bentley	(Blacon, Chester)	4. 5.07P
G-JBHH	Bell 206B-2 JetRanger II	1129	G-SCOO	26. 4.04	Hughes Helicopter Co Ltd t/a Biggin Hill Helicopters		
			G-CORC, G-CJHI, G-BBFB, N18094			Biggin Hill	27. 5.08E
G-JBII	Robinson R22 Beta	1368	G-BXLA	13. 3.03	Fast Helicopters Ltd	Shoreham	27. 5.08E
			SE-HVX, N4014G				
G-JBIS	Cessna 550 Citation II	550-0447	HB-VIS	11. 1.07	247 Jet Ltd	Southend	1. 3.08E
			(N447CJ), N12482, N1248K				
G-JBIZ	Cessna 550 Citation II	550-0073	VP-CTJ	7.11.05	247 Jet Ltd	Southend	8.12.06E
			F-GBTL, N4621G				
G-JBJB	Colt 69A Balloon (Hot Air)	1274		26. 7.88	Justerini and Brooks Ltd "J & B Jeremy"	London SW1	19. 5.02A
G-JBKA	Robinson R44 Raven	1175		12. 3.02	Bon Accord Glass Ltd	Aberdeen	26. 3.08E

Reg	Type	C/n	Previous identities	Date	Owner	Location	Date
G-JBMC	SOCATA TB-10 Tobago	1230	F-GKVA	10. 5.04	J McCloskey	City of Derry	23. 9.08E
G-JBRE	Rotorsport UK MT-03	RSUK/MT-03/016		23. 7.07	J B R Elliot	Ellough, Beccles	9. 8.08P
G-JBRN	Cessna 182S Skylane	18280029	N432V, G-RITZ, N9872F	11. 6.99	Parallel Flooring Accessories Ltd	Wickenby	14. 6.08E
G-JBSP	Avtech Jabiru SP-470 (Built C R James - pr.no.PFA 274B-13486)	0289		12.10.99	C R James	Ludham	26. 6.08P
G-JBTR	Van's RV-8A (Built R A Ellis)	PFA 303-14562		18. 9.06	R A Ellis	(Haverfordwest)	
G-JBUZ	Robin DR.400-180R Remorqueur	1158	OE-DNW	2. 6.05	D L Saywell	(Pannal, Harrogate)	31. 7.08E
G-JCAP	Robinson R22 Beta II	3415	EI-EWM	25. 6.04	Fly Executive Ltd	(Emberton, Olney)	8. 7.08E
G-JCAR	Piper PA-46-350P Malibu Mirage	4636223	N4148N	17.12.99	Aquarelle Investments Ltd	Shoreham	20. 2.08E
G-JCAS	Piper PA-28-181 Archer II	28-8690036	N9093N, (N170AV), N9648N	12. 6.89	Charlie Alpha Ltd	Jersey	19. 6.08E
G-JCBC	Gulfstream Aerospace Gulfstream V-SP (Gulfstream 550)	5060	N960GA	3. 8.05	J C Bamford Excavators Ltd	East Midlands	3. 8.08E
G-JCBJ	Sikorsky S-76C	760502		9. 7.99	J C Bamford Excavators Ltd	East Midlands	21. 7.08E
G-JCJC	Colt Flying Jeans SS Balloon (Hot Air)	1747	SE-ZHS (New owner 8.07)	8. 6.90	Magical Adventures Ltd	Oswestry	20. 3.97A
G-JCKT	Stemme S 10-VT (Rotax 914)	11-004	D-KSTE	8. 4.98	J C Taylor	Portmoak	15. 5.08E
G-JCMW	Rand Robinson KR-2 (Built M Wildish)	PFA 129-11064		3. 2.99	M Wildish and J Cook	(Gainsborough and Winterton, Scunthorpe)	
G-JCOP	Eurocopter AS.350B3 Ecureuil	4345		8.12.07	Eurocopter UK Ltd	Oxford	
G-JCUB	Piper PA-18-135 Super Cub (L-21B-PI) (Frame No.18-3630)	18-3531	PH-VCH, R Neth AF R-103 , 54-2331	21. 1.82	N Cummins and S Bennett	Weston, Leixlip, County Kildare	28. 7.08E
G-JCWM	Robinson R44 Raven II	11860		17. 9.07	M L J Goff	Old Buckenham	
G-JDBC	Piper PA-34-200T Seneca II	34-7570150	G-BDEF, N33695	9.10.02	Bowdon Aviation Ltd	Manchester	27.10.07E
G-JDEE	SOCATA TB-20 Trinidad	333	G-BKLA, F-BNGX	1. 5.84	M J Wright, M Baker, N Jeffery and E Foers	Leicester	12. 6.08E
G-JDEL	Jodel D 150 Mascaret (Built K F Richardson - pr.no.PFA 151-11276)	112	G-JDLI	19. 9.95	K F and R Richardson (Noted 11.07)	Wellesbourne Mountford	
G-JDIX	Mooney M 20B Mark 21	1866	G-ARTB	28.11.85	A L Hall-Carpenter (Noted 8.05)	Shipdham	16. 1.00
G-JDJM	Piper PA-28-140 Cherokee C	28-26877	(G-HSJM), G-AYIF, N11C	11.10.00	R Jackson-Moore and D J Street tr The Hare Flying Group	Wycombe Air Park	25. 9.08E
G-JEAJ	British Aerospace BAe 146 Series 200	E2099	G-OLCA, G-5-099	20. 9.93	Trident Aviation Leasing Services (Jersey) Ltd (For freighter conversion)	Bucharest, Romania	17. 7.08E
G-JEAM	British Aerospace BAe 146 Series 300	E3128	G-BTJT, HS-TBK, G-11-128	24. 5.93	Flybe Ltd "Pride of Jersey"	London Gatwick	23. 5.08E
G-JEAO	British Aerospace BAe 146 Series 100	E1010	G-UKPC, C-GNVX, N802RW, G-5-512, PT-LEP, G-BKXZ, PT-LEP (Stored 1.07)	19. 9.94	Trident Aviation Leasing Services (Jersey) Ltd	Filton	4. 6.05T
G-JEAS	British Aerospace BAe 146 Series 200	E2020	G-OLHB, G-BSRV, G-OSUN, C-FEXN, N604AW (Stored 9.07)	13. 2.96	Flybe Ltd	Exeter	13. 7.08E
G-JEAX	British Aerospace BAe 146 Series 200	E2136	EI-DNJ, G-JEAX, N136JV, C-FHAP, N136TR, N882DV, (N719TA), N882DV, G-5-136 (Noted 10.07)	16. 2.98	BAE Systems (Operations) Ltd	Bacau, Romania	19. 2.07
G-JEAY	British Aerospace BAe 146 Series 200	E2138	SE-DRL, N138JV, C-FHAA, N138TR, (N719TA), N883DV, G-5-138 (Noted 2.08)	27. 3.01	BAE Systems (Operations) Ltd	Bacau, Romania	26. 3.07T
G-JEBA	British Aerospace BAe 146 Series 300	E3181	HS-TBL, G-6-181, G-BSYR, G-6-181	16. 6.98	Flybe Ltd	London Gatwick	27. 7.08E
G-JEBB	British Aerospace BAe 146 Series 300	E3185	HS-TBK, G-6-185	26. 6.98	Flybe Ltd (Stored 11.07)	Exeter	1.11.07T
G-JEBD	British Aerospace BAe 146 Series 300	E3191	HS-TBJ, G-6-191	14. 7.98	Flybe Ltd	London Gatwick	17. 9.08E
G-JEBE	British Aerospace BAe 146 Series 300	E3206	HS-TBM, G-6-206	28. 5.98	Flybe Ltd	London Gatwick	25. 6.08E
G-JEBF	British Aerospace BAe 146 Series 300	E3202	G-BTUY, G-NJIC, B-17811, B-1781, G-BTUY, G-6-202	25. 6.04	Flybe Ltd	London Gatwick	25. 6.08E
G-JEBG	British Aerospace BAe 146 Series 300	E3209	G-BVCE, G-NJIE, B-1778, G-BVCE, G-6-209 (MANSION.COM titles)	20. 7.04	Flybe Ltd	London Gatwick	13. 7.08E
G-JEBV	British Aerospace Avro 146-RJ100	E3236	G-CDCN, TC-THC, G-6-236	15. 2.05	Trident Jet Leasing (Ireland) Ltd (Stored 8.07)	Kemble	
G-JECE	Bombardier DHC-8-402	4094	C-FDHU	26. 8.04	Flybe Ltd	London Gatwick	2. 9.08E
G-JECF	Bombardier DHC-8-402	4095	C-FDHV	7.10.04	Flybe Ltd	London Gatwick	12.10.07E
G-JECG	Bombardier DHC-8-402	4098	C-FAQH	7. 1.05	Flybe Ltd	London Gatwick	13. 1.08E
G-JECH	Bombardier DHC-8-402	4103	C-FCQC	29. 4.05	Flybe Ltd	London Gatwick	4. 5.08E
G-JECI	Bombardier DHC-8-402	4105	C-FCQK	10. 6.05	Flybe Ltd	London Gatwick	16. 6.08E
G-JECJ	Bombardier DHC-8-402	4110	C-FCVN	16.12.05	Flybe Ltd	London Gatwick	20.12.07E
G-JECK	Bombardier DHC-8-402	4113	C-FDRL	27. 1.06	Flybe Ltd	Birmingham	31. 1.08E
G-JECL	Bombardier DHC-8-402	4114	C-FDRN	27. 1.06	Flybe Ltd "The George Best"	Birmingham	5. 2.08E
G-JECM	Bombardier DHC-8-402	4118	C-FFCE	6. 4.06	Flybe Ltd	Birmingham	10. 4.08E
G-JECN	Bombardier DHC-8-402	4120	C-FFCL	27. 4.06	Flybe Ltd	Birmingham	2. 5.08E
G-JECO	Bombardier DHC-8-402	4126	C-FFPT	4. 7.06	Flybe Ltd	Birmingham	11. 7.08E
G-JECP	Bombardier DHC-8-402	4136	C-FHEL	31.10.06	Flybe Ltd	Birmingham	7.11.07E
G-JECR	Bombardier DHC-8-402	4139	C-FHQM	12.12.06	Flybe Ltd	Birmingham	17.12.07E
G-JECS	Bombardier DHC-8-402	4142	C-FHQV	10.1.07	Flybe Ltd	Birmingham	14. 1.08E
G-JECT	Bombardier DHC-8-402	4144	C-FHQY	30.1.07	Flybe Ltd "Matt Le Tissier"	Birmingham	1. 2.08E
G-JECU	Bombardier DHC-8-402	4146	C-FJKY	1. 2.07	Flybe Ltd	Birmingham	5. 2.08E
G-JECV	Bombardier DHC-8-402	4148	C-FJLE	19. 4.07	Flybe Ltd	Birmingham	23. 4.08E
G-JECW	Bombardier DHC-8-402	4152	C-FJLK	24. 4.07	Flybe Ltd	Birmingham	29. 4.08E
G-JECX	Bombardier DHC-8-402	4155	C-FLKO	13. 6.07	Flybe Ltd	Birmingham	17. 6.08E
G-JECY	Bombardier DHC-8-402	4157	C-FLKV	22. 6.07	Flybe Ltd	Birmingham	27. 6.08E
G-JEDH	Robin DR.400-180 Régent	2343		3. 2.97	J B Hoolahan	Challock	8. 7.08E
G-JEDI	Bombardier DHC-8-402Q (Q400)	4052	C-GFOD	25.10.01	Flybe Ltd	London Gatwick	24.10.07T
G-JEDJ	Bombardier DHC-8-402Q (Q400)	4058	C-FDHZ	23. 1.02	Flybe Ltd	London Gatwick	4. 2.08E

G-JEDK	Bombardier DHC-8-402Q *(Q400)*	4065	C-GEMU	23. 4.02	Flybe Ltd *"Vignoble de Bergerac"*	London Gatwick	30. 4.08E
G-JEDL	Bombardier DHC-8-402Q *(Q400)*	4067	C-GEOZ	17. 6.02	Flybe Ltd	London Gatwick	30. 6.08E
G-JEDM	Bombardier DHC-8-402	4077	C-FGNP	18. 7.03	Flybe Ltd	Exeter	22. 7.08E
G-JEDN	Bombardier DHC-8-402	4078	C-FNGB	31. 7.03	Flybe Ltd	Exeter	7. 8.08E
G-JEDO	Bombardier DHC-8-402	4079	C-GDFT	1. 8.03	Flybe Ltd	Exeter	13. 8.08E
G-JEDP	Bombardier DHC-8-402	4085	C-FDHO	30. 1.04	Flybe Ltd	Exeter	4. 3.08E
G-JEDR	Bombardier DHC-8-402	4087	C-FDHI	5. 3.04	Flybe Ltd	Exeter	15. 3.08E
G-JEDS	Andreasson BA-4B	HA/02	G-BEBT	17.12.02	S B Jedburgh	White Waltham	7.12.07P
	(Built A Horsfall [Hornet Aviation] - pr.no.PFA 038-10158) *(Lycoming O-235-C)*						
G-JEDT	Bombardier DHC-8-402	4088	C-FDHP	19. 3.04	Flybe Ltd	Exeter	23. 3.08E
G-JEDU	Bombardier DHC-8-402	4089	C-GEMU	7. 4.04	Flybe Ltd *"Pride of Exeter"*	Belfast City	13. 4.08E
G-JEDV	Bombardier DHC-8-402	4090	C-FDHX	7. 5.04	Flybe Ltd	Exeter	18. 5.08E
G-JEDW	Bombardier DHC-8-402	4093	C-GFBW	27. 7.04	Flybe Ltd	Exeter	2. 8.08E
G-JEEP	Evektor EV-97 Eurostar	PFA 315-13888	C-CBNK	8.08.06	P A Brigstock	Shacklewell Farm, Empingham	24. 6.08E
	(Built M R M Welch)						
G-JEET	Reims Cessna FA152 Aerobat	FA1520369	G-BHMF	10.12.87	S Papi *(Operated Willowair Flying Club)*	Southend	20. 9.08E
G-JEFA	Robinson R44 Astro	0710		7. 2.00	Simlot Ltd	Denham	11. 6.08T
G-JEJE	Rotary Air Force RAF 2000 GTX-SE			21. 1.03	J W Erswell	(South Brent)	12. 7.07P
	(Built J W Erswell)	PFA G/13-1278					
G-JEMA	British Aerospace ATP	2028	N854AW	24. 2.04	PTB (Emerald) Proprietary Ltd	Blackpool	6. 5.07T
			G-11-028, N5000R)		*(Stored internally 2.08)*		
G-JEMC	British Aerospace ATP	2032	N856AW	29.12.03	PTB (Emerald) Proprietary Ltd	Blackpool	15. 4.07T
			G-11-032		*(Stored externally 2.08)*		
G-JEMD	British Aerospace ATP	2026	S2-ACX	3. 2.04	PTB (Emerald) Proprietary Ltd	Blackpool	
	(Freighter conversion)		(SE-LHX), S2-ACX, G-11-026		*(Stored internally 2.08)*		
G-JEME	British Aerospace ATP	2027	S2-ACY	3. 2.04	PTB (Emerald) Proprietary Ltd		
			(SE-LHY), S2-ACY, G-11-027		*(Stored internally 2.08)*	Blackpool	
G-JEMH	Aérospatiale AS.355F2 Ecureuil 2	5424	G-CDFV	1. 3.06	PJM Helicopters LLP	Costock	25. 9.08E
			RP-C1688, JA9964				
G-JEMI	Lindstrand LBL 90A Balloon (Hot Air)	1189		12.12.07	J A Lawton	Enton, Godalming	
G-JEMX	Short SD.3-60 Variant 100	SH3715	G-SSWX	10. 3.04	BAC Leasing Ltd	Southend	2.12.06E
			N711PM, G-BNDL, G-14-3715		*(In open store 2.08 less engines)*		
G-JENA	Mooney M 20J Mooney 201	24-1304	N1168D	5. 7.82	P Leverkuehn t/a Mooney Partnership		
						Antwerp-Deurne, Belgium	19. 9.08E
G-JENC	Beech B300C Super King Air	FM-14	N814KA	16.10.07	Raytheon Systems Ltd	Hawarden	14.11.08E
					(To become Beech 350C ER "ZZ416" for AAC 2008)		
G-JENI	Cessna R182 Skylane RG II	R18200267	N3284C	17. 9.87	R A Bentley	Stapleford	22. 6.08E
G-JENN	Gulfstream AA-5B Tiger	AA5B-1187	N4533T	7.12.81	M Reed t/a Shadow Aviation	Cranfield	28. 3.08E
					(Operated Cabair)		
G-JENO	Lindstrand LBL 105A Balloon (Hot Air)	916		28. 4.03	S F Redman	Stalbridge, Sturminster Newton	31. 7.08A
G-JERO	Europa Aviation Europa XS	492		13. 6.02	B Robshaw and P Jenkinson	Wombleton	21. 5.07P
	(Built B Robshaw and P Jenkinson - pr.no.PFA 247-13691) *(Rotax 914)* *(Tri-gear u/c)*						
G-JERS	Robinson R22 Beta	1610		21.12.90	Sloane Helicopters Ltd	Sywell	7. 6.08E
G-JESA	Mainair 582 Gemini/Southdown Raven X		G-MNLB	14. 4.04	A E James	Lower Upham Farm, Chiseldon	4. 8.06P
	664-688-6 & SN2232/0117		*(Officially regd as "Southdown Raven X [modified Gemini F2A Trike]")*				
G-JESI	Aérospatiale AS.350B Ecureuil	1205	G-JOSS	16.12.03	Staske Construction Ltd	(Hulcote)	8.11.07E
			F-WQJY, 3A-..., G-WILX, G-RAHM, G-UNIC, G-COLN, G-BHIV				
G-JESS	Piper PA-28R-201T Turbo Arrow III	28R-7803334	G-REIS	18. 9.95	R E Trawicki	Elstree	5. 9.08E
			N36689				
G-JETA	Cessna 550 Citation II	550-0094	G-RDBS	3. 9.79	Icon Two Ltd	Birmingham	10. 9.08E
			G-JETA, (N26630)				
G-JETC	Cessna 550 Citation II	550-0282	G-JCFR	28. 5.81	Interceptor Aviation Ltd	Southend	24. 3.08E
			G-JETC, N68644				
G-JETF	Dassault Falcon 2000EX	078	I-JETF	9. 1.07	TAG Aviation (UK) Ltd	Farnborough	10. 1.08E
			(F-GOTF), F-WWGO				
G-JETH	Hawker Sea Hawk FGA.6	AW-6385	"XE364"	10. 8.83	P G Vallance Ltd	Charlwood, Surrey	
	(Buillt Armstrong-Whitworth Aircraft)		XE489		*(In Gatwick Aviation Museum 2007 as "XE489")*		
	(Composite with WM983, A2511)						
G-JETJ	Cessna 550 Citation II	550-0154	G-EJET	9. 2.93	G-JETJ Ltd	Liverpool	26. 8.08E
			G-DJBE, (N8887N)				
G-JETM	Gloster Meteor T 7	-	VZ638	10. 8.83	P G Vallance Ltd	Charlwood, Surrey	
					(In Gatwick Aviation Museum 2007 as "VZ638" in RN/FRU c/s)		
G-JETO	Cessna 550 Citation II	550-0441	N80LA	9. 1.06	Jet Options Ltd	Birmingham	1. 5.08E
			G-RVHT, N221GA, HB-VKS, VR-CCE, N56PC, N50LM, N1220J				
G-JETU	Aérospatiale AS.355F2 Ecureuil 2	5450	VR-CET	18. 4.96	Arena Aviation Ltd	Redhill	22. 5.08E
			JA6623				
G-JETX	Bell 206B-3 JetRanger III	3208	N3898L	9. 2.88	A Leslie t/a AGL Helicopters	(Crawley)	17. 5.08T
G-JETZ	Hughes 369E	0450E	VR-HJI	26. 3.97	J G Matchett	Sywell	21. 2.08
	(Hughes 500)						
G-JEZZ	Best Off Sky Ranger 582(1)	SKR0402456		6. 4.04	A S Ashton	Phoenix Farm, Lower Upham	13. 4.08P
	(Built J W Barwick - pr.no.BMAA/HB/368)						
G-JFDI	Aerospool Dynamic WT9 UK	DY192/2007		8. 5.07	Yeoman Light Aircraft Company Ltd		
	(Official c/n is "DY192")					Manor Farm, Drayton St Leonard	1.11.08P
G-JFLO	Aerospool Dynamic WT9 UK	DY197/2007		6.11.07	Yeoman Light Aircraft Company Ltd		
	(Official c/n is "DY197")					Manor Farm, Drayton St Leonard	29.11.08P
G-JFMK	Zenair CH.701SP STOL	PFA 187-14264		24. 9.04	J D Pearson	(Uplawmor, Glasgow)	7. 8.08P
	(Built J D Pearson)						
G-JFRV	Van's RV-7A	PFA 323-13851		8.10.03	J H Fisher	Haverfordwest	2. 9.08P
	(Built J H Fisher) *(Tri-cycle u/c)*						
G-JFWI	Reims Cessna F172N Skyhawk II	F17201622	PH-DPA	1. 9.80	Staryear Ltd	Barton	7. 3.08T
			PH-AXY				
G-JGBI	Bell 206L-4 LongRanger IV	52257	N91285	13. 8.01	Dorbcrest Homes Ltd	Blackpool	19. 9.08E
			C-GBUP				

Reg	Type	C/n	Prev identity	Date	Owner/Operator	Location	CofA
G-JGMN	CASA 1-131E Jungmann Series 2000	2011	Spanish AF E3B-407	17. 4.91	P D Scandrett	Rendcomb	20. 6.08P
	(Officially regd as c/n 2011 but carries c/n plate 2104 in rear cockpit - c/n 2011 is regd as N65522)						
G-JGSI	Cyclone Airsports Pegasus Quantum 15-912	7515		19. 4.99	R Leigh	(Middlewich)	30. 7.08P
G-JHAC	Reims Cessna FRA150L Aerobat	FRA1500160	EI-BRX	16. 9.02	J H A Clarke	Oaks Farm, Bromham, Chippenham	19. 7.08E
			G-BACM, EI-BRX, G-BACM				
G-JHEW	Robinson R22 Beta	0672	N23677	20. 7.87	Burbage Farms Ltd	Hinckley	20.12.07
G-JHKP	Europa Aviation Europa XS	536		5.11.03	J D Heykoop	(Pulborough)	
	(Built J D Heykoop - pr.no.PFA 247-13828)						
G-JHNY	Cameron A-210 Balloon (Hot Air)	10487		17. 3.04	Floating Sensations Ltd	Llandeilo	1. 5.08P
G-JHPA	Cessna 172S Skyhawk	172S10419	N1206Y	5. 3.07	JHP Aviation Ltd	(Solihull)	14. 3.08E
G-JHYS	Europa Aviation Europa	314		6. 3.01	S M Dawson	Eshott	2. 8.07P
	(Built J D Boyce and G E Walker - pr.no.PFA 247-13307) (Tri-gear u/c)						
G-JIFI	Schempp-Hirth Duo Discus T	95/420	BGA 5115-KHY	26. 9.05	D K McCarthy	Lasham	30.12.07
	(Officially regd with c/n 95)		D-KOZZ		"620"		
G-JIII	Stolp SA.300 Starduster Too	2-3-12	N9043	27. 5.93	J G McTaggart t/a VTIO Company		
	(Built C S Johnson) (Lycoming IO-360)					Archerfield Estate, Dirleton	9. 8.06P
G-JILL	Rockwell Commander 112TC-A	13304	(OO-HPB)	25. 7.80	D Carlton	Full Sutton	20. 4.08E
			G-JILL, N8070R, HB-NCW				
G-JILS	Van's RV-8	PFA 303-14535		10. 8.06	M R Tingle	Ludham	
	(Built M R Tingle)						
G-JILY	Robinson R44 Raven	0959		5. 1.01	R R Orr	Newtownards	4. 3.08E
G-JIMB	Beagle B 121 Pup Series 1	B121-033	G-AWWF	7. 4.94	P G Fowler	Enstone	26. 5.07T
G-JIMG	Beech B300C Super King Air	FM-17	N817KA	3.08R	(To become Beech 350C ER "ZZ418" for AAC 2008)		
G-JIMH	Reims Cessna F152 II	F15201839	G-SHAH	17. 6.05	S A Edkins and D Howell t/a Emmalin		
			OH-IHA, SE-IHA			Halfpenny Green	7. 6.08E
G-JIMM	Europa Aviation Europa XS	579		13. 7.04	J Riley	(Crays Hill, Billericay)	
	(Built J Riley - pr.no.PFA 247-14071)						
G-JIMZ	Van's RV-4	2488	N30GB	28. 7.06	J W Hale	Netherthorpe	
	(Built J Banks and J Giatrakis 1991)						
G-JINI	Cameron V-77 Balloon (Hot Air)	11025		27. 7.07	I R Warrington	Great Casterton, Stamford	30. 8.08E
G-JIVE	Hughes 369E	0486E	G-DRAR	24. 5.01	Sleekform Ltd	(Sowerby Bridge)	13. 1.08E
	(Hughes 500)		N101LH, N1608Z				
G-JJAB	Avtech Jabiru J400	0xxx		6. 4.05	Propitious Aviation Ltd	Dunsfold	18. 3.08P
	(Built K Ingebrigtsen - pr.no.PFA 325-14339)						
G-JJAN	Piper PA-28-181 Archer II	2890007	N9105Z	28. 3.88	J S Develin and Z Islam	Shoreham	25. 5.08E
G-JJDC	Aviat A-1B Husky	2291	N96HY	31. 8.05	Aerographic Ltd	(Claydon, Ipswich)	15. 3.08E
G-JJEN	Piper PA-28-181 Archer III	2843370	N4190D	25. 8.00	K M R Jenkins	Jersey	24. 8.08E
G-JJFB	Eurocopter EC.120B Colibri	1506		16. 8.07	P A Winslow	(Courteenhall, Northampton)	
					(Noted 12.07)		
G-JJIL	Extra EA 300/L	1270		8.11.07	S French	(Sandon, Buntingford)	
G-JJJL	Agusta A109E Power	11159	G-CEJS	12. 4.07	Brookes Air Charter LLP	Fairoaks	
			RP-C2838				
G-JJSI	British Aerospace BAe 125 Series 800B	258058	G-OMGG	16. 4.04	Gama Aviation Ltd	Farnborough	24.11.07T
			N125JW, G-5-637, N125JW, VH-NMR, ZK-EUI, (ZK-EUR), G-5-510				
G-JKAY	Robinson R44 Raven II	11093		10. 3.06	Jamiroquai Ltd	(London NW6)	6. 4.08E
G-JKMF	Diamond DA.40D Star	D4.033		3. 9.03	A D and C Realff t/a ADR Aviation	Shoreham	17. 2.08E
G-JKMG	Diamond DA.40D Star	D4.202	OE-VPU	11. 5.06	Diamond Aircraft UK Ltd	Gamston	1. 6.08E
	(Carries "DA40TDi Star")						
G-JKMH	Diamond DA.42 Twin Star	42.168		18. 9.06	A D and C Realff t/a ADR Aviation	Shoreham	15.10.07E
G-JKMJ	Diamond DA.42 Twin Star	42.141		23. 6.06	Medox Enterprises Ltd	(Limassol, Cyprus)	16. 7.08E
G-JLAT	Evektor EV-97 Eurostar	PFA 315-14068		14. 5.03	J Latimer	Barton	16. 7.08P
	(Built J Latimer)						
G-JLCA	Piper PA-34-200T Seneca II	34-7870428	G-BOKE	3. 9.97	Tayside Aviation Ltd	Dundee	16. 5.08E
			N21030				
G-JLEE	Agusta-Bell 206B-3 JetRanger III	8588	G-JOKE	10. 2.88	J S Lee	Wycombe Air Park	30.11.07E
			G-CSKY, G-TALY				
G-JLHS	Beech A36 Bonanza	E-2571	N8046U	30.11.90	I G Meredith	Lydd	9. 3.08
G-JLIN	Piper PA-28-161 Cadet	2841013	D-ENXI	24. 8.05	Westmorland Aviation Ltd	Carlisle	22. 9.08E
			N9153X				
G-JLMW	Cameron V-77 Balloon (Hot Air)	1768		23. 6.88	J L M Watkins	Ivybridge	26. 2.99T
G-JLRW	Beech 76 Duchess	ME-165	N60206	4.11.87	Magenta Ltd	Exeter	5. 2.08E
					(Operated Airways Flight Training)		
G-JMAA	Boeing 757-3CQ	32241		24. 4.01	Thomas Cook Airlines UK Ltd	Manchester	23. 4.08E
G-JMAB	Boeing 757-3CQ	32242		14. 5.01	Thomas Cook Airlines UK Ltd	Manchester	13. 5.08E
G-JMAN	Mainair Blade 912S	1290-0601-7-W1085		12. 7.01	J Manuel	(Southport)	15. 7.02P
G-JMAX	Raytheon Hawker 800XP	258456	N41762	13.10.04	J Hargreaves t/a J-Max Air Services	Blackpool	13.10.07E
			N800EM				
G-JMCE	Boeing 757-25F	30758	XA-JPB	24. 6.00	Thomas Cook Airlines UK Ltd	Manchester	25. 4.08E
			G-JMCE				
G-JMCF	Boeing 757-28A	24369	C-FMCF	20. 5.00	Thomas Cook Airlines UK Ltd	Manchester	29. 4.08E
			G-JMCF, C-FOOE				
G-JMCG	Boeing 757-2G5	26278	SX-BLV	27. 4.00	Thomas Cook Airlines Ltd t/a MyTravel Airways		
			G-JMCG, D-AMUQ			Manchester	29. 4.08E
G-JMCW	Bombardier CL600-2B16	5403	D-ADND	27. 2.08	MP Aviation LLP	Biggin Hill	
	(CL-604 Challenger)		N604DC, C-GLWV				
G-JMDI	Schweizer 269C	S 1398	G-FLAT	24. 9.91	J J Potter	Sherburn-in-Elmet	24. 4.08E
	(Schweizer 300)						
G-JMDW	Cessna 550 Citation II	550-0183	HB-VGS	16. 2.04	Phoenix Air Ltd	Biggin Hill	24. 3.08E
			(XC-DUF), N98630				
G-JMJR	Cameron Z-90 Balloon (Hot Air)	10611		17. 1.05	J-M Reck	Evette-Salbert, France	20. 1.08E
	(Lion's Head Shape)						
G-JMKE	Cessna 172S Skyhawk SP	172S9248	N53012	17.12.02	115CR (146) Ltd	Wellesbourne Mountford	23. 2.08E
G-JMMD	Bombardier CL600-2B16	5422	D-ADNE	27. 2.08	MP Aviation LLP	Biggin Hill	
	(CL-604 Challenger)		N605DC, C-GLXU				

Reg	Type	C/n	Prev id	Date	Owner/Operator	Location	Date
G-JMMX	Dassault Falcon 900EX	184	F-WWFN	22.10.07	J Hargreaves t/a J-Max Air Services	Blackpool	21.10.08E
G-JMON	Agusta A109A II	7411	G-RFDS	4. 8.06	Jermon Ltd	(Dungannon)	31. 7.08E
			N1YU, VP-CLA, VR-CLA, G-BOLA, VR-CMP, G-BOLA				
G-JMMP	Bombardier CL-600-2B16	5528	D-AJAG	15. 2.08	MP Aviation LLP	Biggin Hill	
	(CL-604 Challenger)		N528DT, C-GLYO				
G-JMRV	Van's RV-7	PFA 323-14591		16. 5.07	J W Marshall	(Haslingbourne, Petworth)	
	(Built J W Marshall)						
G-JMTS	Robin DR.400-180 Régent	2045		29.11.90	P A Mansbridge	(Upper Basildon, Reading)	13. 7.08E
G-JMXA	Agusta A109E Power Elite	11156		31. 5.02	J Hargreaves t/a J-Max Air Services	Blackpool	30. 5.08E
G-JNAS	Grumman American AA-5A Cheetah	AA5A-0604	SE-GEI	28.11.00	C J Williams	Farley Farm, Romsey	9. 3.07T
			LN-KLE		(On rebuild 10.07)		
G-JNNB	Colt 90A Balloon (Hot Air)	2063		20.12.91	N A P Godfrey	West Leith, Tring	8. 4.07A
					(J & B Rare titles) (Address change 12.07)		
G-JNSC	Schempp-Hirth Janus CT	2-185	BGA 4186-HTH	11.12.07	D S Bramwell tr Janus Syndicate	Thame	13. 7.08
			N137DB, D-KHIE				
G-JNUS	Schempp-Hirth Janus C	215	BGA 4062-HNB	6. 9.07	C Fox	Sleap	27. 3.08
			D-4149				
G-JOAL	Beech B200 Super King Air	BB-1158	N66LM	23. 5.06	South Coast Air Charter LLP	Bournemouth	31. 5.08E
			N419TW, N158EF, N158TJ, N18245, N200KK, (N712PW), N200KK, N200KA				
G-JOBA	P&M Quik GT450	8174		31. 5.06	M B Smith	Tarn Farm, Cockerham	11. 6.08P
G-JOBS	Cessna T182T Turbo Skylane	T18208009	N737RM	27. 9.07	Nortrax Aviation Ltd	(Chester)	8. 7.07T
			G-BZVF, N109LP				
G-JODI	Agusta A109A II	7265	G-BVCJ	27. 2.04	Heli Air (Jersey) Ltd	(St Helier, Jersey)	26.11.07E
			G-CLRL, G-EJCB				
G-JODL	SAN Jodel DR.1050M Excellence	99	F-BJJC	28. 4.86	D Silsbury (Noted 6.04)	Dunkeswell	26.11.99
G-JOEY	Fairey Britten-Norman BN-2A Mk.III-2 Trislander	1016	G-BDGG	27.11.81	Aurigny Air Services Ltd	Guernsey	18. 4.08E
			C-GSAA, G-BDGG		(Aurigny.com titles)		
G-JOIE	American Champion 7GCAA Citabria	502-2005		5.12.05	N Baumber	(Grantham)	27. 2.08E
G-JOJO	Cameron A-210 Balloon (Hot Air)	2674		20. 9.91	A C Rawson and J J Rudoni	Stafford	11. 4.06T
					t/a Wickers World Hot Air Balloon Company		
G-JOKR	Extra EA.300/L	1278		28. 2.08	C Vogelgesang and R Hockey	(London W)	
G-JOLY	Cessna 120	13872	OO-ACE	3. 9.81	B V Meade	Garston Farm, Marshfield	13. 6.08P
	(Continental C85)						
G-JONB	Robinson R22 Beta II	2593		29. 4.96	J Bignall	Mistletoe Farm, Pinner	27. 5.08E
G-JONG	Rotorway Executive 162F	6168	N630GH	27. 4.04	J V George	Street Farm, Takeley	17.12.08P
	(Built S A Foster)						
G-JONH	Robinson R22 Beta	2170		3. 6.93	Eastern Atlantic Helicopters Ltd	Shoreham	15. 9.08E
G-JONI	Reims Cessna FA152 Aerobat	FA1520346	G-BFTU	6. 7.84	R F Poole	Lwr Ground Farm, Shirlowe	23. 1.08E
G-JONM	Piper PA-28-181 Archer III	2843614	OY-PHH	15. 1.08	J H Massey	(Walkeringham, Doncaster)	
G-JONO	Colt 77A Balloon (Hot Air)	1086		22. 6.87	The Sandcliffe Motor Group Ltd	Newbury	17. 9.95A
					"Sandcliffe Ford" (On loan to British Balloon Museum and Library)		
G-JONW	Agusta A109E Power	11624	EI-JON	12. 9.07	Magell Ltd	(Ballymena)	19. 9.08E
G-JONY	Cyclone AX2000 HKS	7503		12. 3.99	K R Matheson (USAF c/s)	Sandtoft	18. 6.08P
G-JONZ	Cessna 172P Skyhawk II	17276233	N97835	28. 9.89	Truman Aviation Ltd	Tollerton	8. 6.08E
G-JOOL	Mainair Blade 912	1262-1000-7-W1056		8.12.00	J R Gibson	Ince Blundell	16. 2.08P
G-JOON	Cessna 182D	18253067	(N....)	9. 6.81	Go Adventure Ireland Ltd		
			G-JOON, OO-ACD, N9967T			Feathard, County Tipperary	29. 1.08E
G-JOPT	Cessna 560 Citation V	560-0159	D-CLEO	26. 1.07	Jet Options Ltd	Birmingham	
			N68MA, (N68854)				
G-JORD	Robinson R44 Raven II	11725		14. 5.07	Overby Ltd	(Ascot)	31. 5.08E
G-JOSH	Cameron N-105 Balloon (Hot Air)	1319		13. 8.86	M White	Cirencester	16. 8.96T
G-JOST	Europa Aviation Europa	234		17. 6.98	A V Orchard and J A Austin	RAF Mona	6.12.07P
	(Built J A Austin - pr.no.PFA 247-12916) (Tri-gear u/c)						
G-JOYD	Robinson R22 Beta II	2769	G-SIMN	17. 6.05	RH Property Services Ltd		
						(Burton-upon-Stather, Scunthorpe)	4. 3.08E
G-JOYT	Piper PA-28-181 Archer II	28-7990132	G-BOVO	13. 2.90	John K Cathcart Ltd	Enniskillen	20. 4.08E
			N2239B				
G-JOYZ	Piper PA-28-181 Archer III	2843018	N9262R	19. 1.96	S W and Joy E Taylor	Biggin Hill	9. 2.08E
			(G-JOYZ)				
G-JPAL	Eurocopter AS.355N Ecureuil II	5692	F-GSJP	9.10.01	JPM Ltd	(Horsham)	6.11.07E
G-JPAT	Robin HR.200-100 Club	76	G-BDJN	13. 9.00	L Girardier and A J McCulloch	Full Sutton	23. 8.08E
G-JPJR	Robinson R44 Raven II	11198		4. 5.06	Longstop Investments Ltd (Pettistree, Woodbridge)		14. 5.08E
G-JPMA	Avtech Jabiru UL	xxxx		24. 5.99	J P Metcalfe	Lydd	19.11.08P
	(Built J P Metcalfe -pr.no.PFA 274A-13399				"Sheila"		
G-JPOT	Piper PA-32R-301 Saratoga II HP	32R-8113065	G-BIYM	1. 8.94	P J Wolstencroft	Duxford	8. 9.08E
			N8385X				
G-JPRO	British Aircraft Corporation BAC 145 Jet Provost T 5A	XW433		10. 8.95	Air Atlantic Ltd	Coventry	19. 3.08P
		EEP/JP/1055			(As "XW433 "in RAF CFS c/s)		
G-JPSX	Dassault Falcon 900EX	132	F-WWFJ	17. 2.04	Sorven Aviation Ltd	Gloucestershire	16. 2.08E
G-JPTT	Enstrom 480	5032	G-PPAH	10. 4.02	P G Lawrence	Gloucestershire	10. 6.07T
G-JPTV	British Aircraft Corporation BAC 145 Jet Provost T 5A	XW355		2. 5.96	S J Davies	Sandtoft	1. 9.07P
	(C/n '...1002' reported)	EEP/JP/1005			(As "XW354" in RAF c/s)		
G-JPVA	British Aircraft Corporation BAC 145 Jet Provost T 5A	XW289	G-BVXT	22. 2.95	H Cooke	RNAS Yeovilton	10. 6.08P
		EEP/JP/953			(As "XW289:73" in RAF 1FTS c/s)		
G-JPWM	Best Off Sky Ranger 912(2)	SKR0412541		24. 3.05	R S Waters and M Pittock	(Etchingham)	21. 5.08P
	(Built R S Waters and M Pittock- pr.no.BMAA/HB/442)						
G-JRED	Robinson R44 Raven II	11286		5. 7.06	J Reddington Ltd	Denham	13. 7.08E
G-JREE	Maule MX-7-180 Super Rocket	11096C	N99MX	13. 4.01	J M P Ree	Church Farm, North Moreton	19. 4.08A
			N30051				
G-JRKD	Jodel D 18	W177	19-3431	7.12.06	R K Davies	Old Sarum	
	(Built J Elari, Australia)				(Wings only noted 4.07)		
G-JRME	Jodel D 140E	444		13.11.02	J E and L L Rex	(Eggborough, Goole)	
	(Built J E and L L Rex - pr.no.PFA 251-13155)				(Under construction 9.07)		
G-JSAK	Robinson R22 Beta II	2959		30. 6.99	J W F and S M Tuke t/a Tukair Aircraft Charter		
						Headcorn	13.10.07E

Reg	Type	C/n	Prev id	Date	Owner	Location	Date
G-JSAR	Eurocopter AS.332L2 Super Puma	2576	F-WQRE	3. 9.02	Bristow Helicopters Ltd	Den Helder, Netherlands	18.12.07E
					(Ditched in North Sea 21.11.06 and washed ashore at Texel)		
G-JSAT	Pilatus Britten-Norman BN-2T Islander	2277	G-BVFK	5. 2.98	P Moore tr Rhine Army Parachute Association		
						Sennelager, Germany	2. 3.08E
G-JSON	Cameron N-105 Balloon (Hot Air)	2933		21. 5.92	Up and Away Ballooning Ltd *"Jason"*	High Wycombe	7. 9.04A
G-JSPL	Avtech Jabiru SPL-450	0358		27.12.00	J A Lord	Knettishall	31. 5.07P
	(Built J A Lord - pr.no.PFA 274A-13604)						
G-JSRV	Van's RV-6	PFA 181A-14407		23. 8.05	J Stringer	Graveley Hall Farm, Graveley	16. 5.08P
	(Built J Stringer)						
G-JTEM	Van's RV-7	PFA 323-14237		30. 4.04	J C Bacon	(Gwehelog, Usk)	
	(Built J C Bacon)						
G-JTNC	Cessna 500 Citation I	500-0264	G-OEJA	9. 1.04	Eurojet Aviation Ltd	Birmingham	11.12.07E
			G-BWFL, F-GLJA, N205FM, N5264J				
G-JTPC	Aeromot AMT-200 Super Ximango	200067		28. 5.97	J T Potter and P G Cowling tr G-JTPC Falcon 3 Group		
						Rufforth	28. 6.08E
G-JTSA	Robinson R44 Raven II	11659		2. 4.07	JTS Aviation Ltd	Denham	11. 4.08E
G-JTWO	Taylor J-2 Cub	1754	G-BPZR	23.10.89	C C Silk Bericote Farm, Blackdown, Leamington Spa		20. 2.08P
	(Built Taylor Aircraft Co Inc) (Continental A65)		N19554, NC19554		*(Carries "NC19554" on tail)*		
G-JUDD	Avtech Jabiru UL-450	0349		9. 8.00	C Judd	Lark Engine Farmhouse, Prickwillow, Ely	11. 9.07P
	(Built C Judd- pr.no.PFA 274A-13570)						
G-JUDE	Robin DR.400-180 Régent	1869		14.10.88	Bravo India Flying Group Ltd	RAF Woodvale	15. 2.07
G-JUDI	North American AT-6D-NT Harvard III	88-14722	FAP 1502	17.11.78	A A Hodgson	Bryn Gwyn Bach	4. 9.08P
	(Regd as c/n "EX915-326165")		SAAF7439, EX915, 41-33888		*(As "FX301:FD-NQ" in RAF c/s)*		
G-JUDY	Grumman AA-5A Cheetah	AA5A-0620	(G-BFWM)	31. 8.78	R Gray t/a Gray Hooper Holt LLP	Biggin Hill	26.11.07E
			N26480				
G-JUGE	Evektor EV-97 teamEurostar UK	1709		7.10.03	L J Appleby	Leicester	12.10.08P
G-JUIN	Cessna T303 Crusader	T30300014	OO-PEN	29. 2.88	M J and J M Newman	Denham	28. 4.08E
			N9401T				
G-JULE	P&M Quik GT450	8219		13.10.06	N A Farrow	(Upper Llandwrog, Caernarfon)	15.10.07P
G-JULL	Stemme S 10-VT	11-039		10. 2.00	J P C Fuchs	Rufforth	22.11.07E
	(Rotax 914)						
G-JULU	Cameron V-90 Balloon (Hot Air)	3611		7. 7.95	N J Appleton	Bristol	4. 4.08A
G-JULZ	Europa Aviation Europa	312		8.10.96	M Parkin	Sandtoft	16. 6.07P
	(Built M Parkin - pr.no.PFA 247-13045) (Rotax 914) (Monowheel u/c)						
G-JUNG	CASA 1-131E Jungmann	1121	Spanish AF E3B-143	23.11.88	K H Wilson	Compton Abbas	29. 5.08P
G-JUPP	Piper PA-32RT-300 Lance II	32R-7885098	G-BNJF	3.10.02	Jupp Air LLP	Halfpenny Green	21. 3.08E
			N31539				
G-JURA	British Aerospace Jetstream Series 3102	772	SE-LDH	21. 5.01	Highland Airways Ltd	Inverness	11. 7.08T
			OY-SVK, C-FAMJ, G-31-772		*"City of Inverness"*		
G-JURG	Rockwell Commander 114A GT	14516	N4752W	19. 9.79	D Wray	Leeds-Bradford	4. 5.08E
	(Laid-down as c/n 14449)						
G-JUST	Beech F33A Bonanza	CE-1165	N334CW	11.10.00	Budge It Aviation Ltd	Elstree	1. 4.08E
G-JVBF	Lindstrand LBL 210A Balloon (Hot Air)	265		5. 6.95	Airxcite Ltd t/a Virgin Balloon Flights	Wembley	19. 6.06E
G-JVBP	Evektor EV-97 teamEurostar UK	2730		31. 5.06	B J Partridge and J A Valentine	Bourn	4. 6.08P
G-JWBI	Agusta-Bell 206B-2 JetRanger II	8435	G-RODS	3. 4.96	J W Bonser	Walsall	26. 9.08E
			G-NOEL, G-BCWN				
G-JWCM	Scottish Aviation Bulldog Series 120/1210		G-BHXB	19.10.99	M L J Goff	Norwich	2. 1.10S
		BH120/408	Botswana DF OD2, G-BHXB				
G-JWDB	Comco Ikarus C42 FB80	0509-6760		24.10.05	J W D Blythe	Swansea	23.10.08P
G-JWDS	Cessna F150G	F150-0216	G-AVNB	15.12.88	G Sayer	(Caerphilly)	29. 9.94T
	(Built Reims Aviation SA)				*(New owner 2.04)*		
G-JWEB	Robinson R44 Raven	1334		3. 9.03	Mastercraft Helicopter Hire Ltd	Hawarden	12. 9.08E
G-JWFT	Robinson R22 Beta	0989		16. 3.89	J P O'Brien	Kintore	19. 4.08E
G-JWIV	CEA Jodel DR.1051 Sicile	431	F-BLMD	6. 9.78	C M Fitton	(Stoke Fleming, Dartmouth)	18. 1.08P
G-JWJW	CASA 1-131E Jungmann Series 2000	419	PH-MRK	15. 5.03	J T and J W Whicher	Breighton	25. 2.08P
			(PH-MRN), D-EDWC, Spanish AF E3B-419				
G-JXTA	British Aerospace Jetstream Series 3103	610	D-CNRY	3. 1.06	Jetstream Executive Travel Ltd	Inverness	12. 6.08E
			SE-KHC, OY-EDB, SE-KHC, D-CONI (2), G-31-50				
G-JXTC	British Aerospace Jetstream Series 3108	690	PH-KJG	21. 6.06	Jetstream Executive Travel Ltd		
			G-LOGT, G-BSFH, PH-KJG, G-31-690			Eindhoven, Netherlands	
					(Noted as "PH-KJG" 8.06 in open storage)		
G-JYAK	Yakovlev Yak-50	853001	RA-01493	26.11.02	J W Stow	North Weald	30.11.07P
			DOSAAF 49 (blue) ?)		*"R-93" (white)*		
G-JYRO	Rotorsport UK MT-03	RSUK/MT-03/006		18.10.06	A Richards	Kirkbride	7. 1.09P

G-KAAA - G-KZZZ

Reg	Type	C/n	Prev id	Date	Owner	Location	Date
G-KAAT	MD Helicopters MD.900 Explorer	900-00056	G-PASS	22. 2.00	Police Aviation Services Ltd	Marden	19. 4.08E
			N9234P		*(Operated Kent Air Ambulance)*		
G-KAEW	Fairey Gannet AEW.Mk.3	F9459	XL500	9. 1.04	T J Manna	North Weald	
	(Built Westland Aircraft Ltd)		A2701, XL500		*(Stored awaiting restoration 6.06)*		
G-KAFT	Diamond DA.40D Star	D4.191	OE-VPU	13. 3.06	Atlantic Flight Training Ltd	Coventry	9. 4.08E
G-KAIR	Piper PA-28-181 Archer II	28-7990176	N3075D	28.12.78	Keen Leasing (IoM) Ltd	Cumbernauld	6.12.07T
					(Operated Cumbernauld Flying School)		
G-KALS	Bombardier BD-100-1A10 Challenger 300	20106	C-FIDX	12.10.06	MCP Continental Ltd	London Stansted	12.10.07E
G-KAMP	Piper PA-18-135 Super Cub	18-3451	D-EDPM	9. 5.97	J R G Furnell	Perth	26. 8.10E
	(L-18C)		96+27, NL+104, AC+502, AS+501, 54-751				
G-KANE	Aérospatiale SA.341G Gazelle 1	1136	G-GAZI	5.12.07	MW Helicopters Ltd	Stapleford	13. 6.08E
			G-BKLU, N32PA, N341VH, N90957				
G-KANZ	Westland Wasp HAS.1	F9664	NZ3909	21.12.05	T J Manna	North Weald	
			XT782		*(Noted 6.07 coded "09")*		
G-KAOM	Scheibe SF25C Falke	4417	D-KAOM	3. 2.98	W T Barnard, G Mckay and J Murdoch	Portmoak	19. 3.08E
	(Limbach SL1700)				tr Falke G-KAOM Syndicate		

Reg	Type	C/n	Prev id	Date	Owner/operator	Location	Date
G-KAOS	Van's RV-7	PFA 323-13956		20. 5.03	A E N Nicholas and D F McGarvey	(Sevenoaks)	
	(Built A E N Nicholas and D F McGarvey)						
G-KAPW	Percival P 56 Provost T 1	PAC/F/311	XF603	22. 9.97	Richard Shuttleworth Trustees	Old Warden	18. 5.08P
					(As "XF603" in RAF c/s)		
G-KARA	Brügger MB.2 Colibri	PFA 043-10980	G-BMUI	1. 6.95	Cara L Reddish	Netherthorpe	21. 8.04P
	(Built Carlton Flying Group) (Volkswagen 1834)						
G-KARI	Fuji FA.200-160 Aero Subaru	FA200-236	G-BBRE	19.12.84	C P Rowley	Prestwick	25. 6.08E
G-KARK	Dyn'Aéro MCR-01 Club	PFA 301A-14010		29.12.03	R Bailes-Brown	Leicester	1. 5.08P
	(Built R Bailes-Brown)						
G-KART	Piper PA-28-161 Warrior II	28-8016088	N8097B	10. 7.91	N Clark (New owner 6.05)	Newcastle	24. 1.04T
G-KASX	Vickers Supermarine 384 Seafire F XVII	FLWA.25488		30.10.03	T J Manna	North Weald	31. 5.08P
	(Built Westland Aircraft Ltd)		A2055, SX336		(As "SX336:105:VL" in RN c/s)		
G-KATG	Bell 206L-1 LongRanger	45783	D-Balloon (Hot Air)B23. 3.07		Lothian Helicopters Ltd	(Pathhead)	2. 5.08E
			N102RD				
G-KATI	Rans S-7 Courier	0795.151		5. 3.96	N Rawlinson Yeatsall Farm, Abbots Bromley		10. 4.07P
	(Built S M Hall - pr.no.PFA 218-12917) (Jabiru 2200A)				(Noted 8.07)		
G-KATS	Piper PA-28-140 Cherokee Cruiser	28-7325022	G-BIRC	26. 8.83	D R A Bott tr G-KATS Group		26. 5.08E
			OY-BGE			(Kingston St Mary, Taunton)	
G-KATT	Cessna 152 II	15285661	G-BMTK	10. 6.93	Central Aircraft Leasing Ltd Halfpenny Green		27.11.07E
			N94387		(Operated RJP Flying School)		
G-KAWA	Denney Kitfox Model 2	PFA 172-11822		11. 3.91	L A James	(Market Bosworth, Nuneaton)	10. 9.07P
	(Built T W C Maton)				(New owner 2.08)		
G-KAXF	Hawker Hunter F 6A	S4/U/3361	8830M	20.12.95	A Offringa	(Ryptsjerk, Netherlands)	3.12.07P
	(Built Armstrong-Whitworth Aircraft)		XF515		(As "XF515:R" in RAF c/s)		
G-KAXT	Westland Wasp HAS.1	F9669	NZ3905	5. 3.02	T J Manna	North Weald	7. 6.08P
			XT787		(As "XT787" in RN c/s)		
G-KAYH	Extra EA.300/L	144		9. 4.02	Integrated Management Practices Ltd		
						Budel, Netherlands	7. 5.08E
G-KAYI	Cameron Z-90 Balloon (Hot Air)	10710		30. 6.05	Snow Business International Ltd	Ebley, Stroud	29. 6.06E
					(Snow Business titles)		
G-KAZA	Sikorsky S-76C	760615	N81085	18. 9.06	Bristow Helicopters Ltd	Kazakhstan	26. 2.08E
G-KAZB	Sikorsky S-76C	760614	N8094S	22. 9.06	Bristow Helicopters Ltd	Kazakhstan	17. 1.08E
G-KAZD	Sikorsky S-76C	760664	N4508N	31. 1.08	Bristow Helicopters Ltd	Kazakhstan	
G-KAZI	P&M Pegasus Quantum 15-912	8120		10. 8.05	Edren Homes Ltd	Deenethorpe	10. 4.08P
G-KBKB	Thunder Ax8-90 Series 2 Balloon (Hot Air)	2089		30.10.91	G Boulden "KB Cars"	Ash, Aldershot	14. 9.03A
G-KBPI	Piper PA-28-161 Cherokee Warrior II		G-BFSZ	21. 5.81	Goodwood Road Racing Company Ltd Goodwood		1. 9.08E
		28-7816468	N9556N		(Operated Goodwood Flying Club)		
G-KCHG	Schempp-Hirth Ventus cT	87/332	BGA 5146-KJW	16. 3.06	D S Jones tr DS Group	North Hill	28. 9.08
			D-KCHG		"DS"		
G-KCIG	Sportavia-Pützer RF5B Sperber	51005	D-KCIG	19. 6.80	J R Bisset tr Deeside Fournier Group	Aboyne	4. 7.06P
G-KCIN	Piper PA-28-161 Cadet	2841102	G-CDOX	3.11.05	G Conrad	Elstree	6.10.07E
			HB-PQC, PH-TED, C-FDYA				
G-KDCC	Europa Aviation Europa XS	452		25. 4.05	K A C Dodd	(Dunmow)	5.12.08P
	(Built K A C Dodd - pr.no.PFA 247-13562)						
G-KDCD	Thruster T 600N	9098-T600N-025	G-MZNW	9.11.05	K J Draper	Stoke, Isle of Grain	13.12.07P
G-KDET	Piper PA-28-161 Cadet	2841158	(SE-KIR)	8. 8.89	Rapidspin Ltd	Perranporth	26. 4.08E
			N9184Z				
G-KDEY	Scheibe SF25E Super Falke	4325	D-KDEY	8. 1.99	D Tucker tr Falke Syndicate	Aston Down	14. 8.08E
	(Limbach SL1700)						
G-KDIX	Jodel D 9 Bébé	PFA 054-10293		23.11.78	P M Bowden	Barton	4. 6.08P
	(Built K Barlow) (Volkswagen 1600)						
G-KDMA	Cessna 560 Citation Ultra	560-0553	N5145V	4. 4.01	Forest Aviation Ltd	Gamston	26. 4.08E
G-KDOG	Scottish Aviation Bulldog Series 120/121		XX624	18. 6.01	Gamit Ltd	North Weald	6. 9.10S
		BH120/289			(As "XX624:E" in RAF c/s)		
G-KEAM	Schleicher ASH 26E	26116	D-KEAM	3. 3.04	D T Reilly "AM"	North Hill	12. 4.08E
G-KEEF	Commander Aircraft Commander 114B	14610	N828DL	17. 6.04	K D Pearse	Fairoaks	18. 7.08E
			VT-PVA, (F-GSDV), VT-PVA, N6025M				
G-KEEN	Stolp SA.300 Starduster Too	800	PH-HAB	19. 7.78	H Sharp tr Sharp Aerobatics		
	(Built R E Ellenbest) (Lycoming IO-540)		(PH-PET), G-KEEN, N800RE		(Cullybacky, Ballymena, County Antrim)		27. 4.04P
					(Under restoration following accident (?) at City of Derry)		
G-KEES	Piper PA-28-180 Cherokee Archer	28-7505025	OO-AJV	29. 5.97	C N Ellerbrook	Wicklewood	15. 9.08E
			OO-HAC, N32102				
G-KEIF	Robinson R44 Raven II	11877	N30675	12.10.07	Flying G Spot Ltd (Noted 11.07)	Shoreham	
G-KEJY	Evektor EV-97 teamEurostar UK	2017		23. 6.04	D Young tr Kemble Eurostar 1	Kemble	22. 6.08P
G-KELI	Robinson R44 Raven II	11040		16. 2.06	Kellys Sales and Service Donegal Ltd		
						(Mountcharles, County Donegal)	30. 3.08E
G-KELL	Van's RV-6	PFA 181-12845		16. 5.95	R G Stephens	Kilrush, County Kildare	10. 6.08P
	(Built J D Kelsall) (Lycoming O-320)						
G-KELS	Van's RV-7	PFA 323-13801		22. 2.02	R G Stephens	Kilrush, County Kildare	27. 3.08P
	(Built J D Kelsall)						
G-KELY	Eurocopter AS350B Ecureuil	2668	G-WKRD	21. 2.07	Kelly Sales and Services Donegal Ltd		
			G-BUJG, G-HEAR, G-BUJG			(Mountcharles, County Donegal)	26.10.07E
G-KELZ	Van's RV-8	PFA 303-13665	G-DJRV	9.11.06	J D Kelsall	Netherthorpe	
	(Built D J Hunt and J D Kelsall)						
G-KELV	Diamond DA.42 Twin Star	42.051	(G-CTCH)	8.11.05	K K Freeman	Plymouth	8.12.07E
			OE-VPI				
G-KEMC	Grob G109	6024	D-KEMC	19.10.84	Norfolk Gliding Club Ltd	Tibenham	12. 7.08E
G-KEMI	Piper PA-28-181 Archer III	2843180	N41493	28.10.98	Modern Air (UK) Ltd	Fowlmere	16.11.07E
G-KEMY	Cessna 182T Skylane	18281206	N53397	27. 8.03	Allen Aircraft Rental Ltd	Cambridge	27. 9.08E
G-KENB	Air Command 503 Commander	PFA G/4-1153		7.11.89	K Brogden	(Heywood)	24. 9.93P
	(Built K Brogden)						
G-KENG	Rotorsport UK MT-03	RSUK/MT-03/011		22. 1.07	K A Graham	RAF Benson	15. 2.08P
G-KENI	RotorWay Executive 152	3599		14. 3.89	A J Wheatley	Street Farm, Takeley	28.11.08P
	(Built K Hassall) (RotorWay RW 152)						

G-KENM	Luscombe 8E Silvaire Deluxe	2908	N21NK	9. 1.91	M G Waters	Ranston Farm, Iwerne Courtney	20.11.08P
	(Continental C90)		N71481, NC71481				
G-KENW	Robin DR.500-200i Président	0039		20. 2.03	K J White	Homefield Farm, Redhill	28. 5.08E
	(Officially regd as DR.400-500)						
G-KENZ	Rutan VariEze	PFA 074-10960	G-BNUI	13. 8.04	K M McConnell	Belfast International	9. 5.08P
	(Built T N F Snead) (Continental O-200-A)						
G-KEPE	Schempp-Hirth Nimbus 3DT	25	BGA 5116-KHZ	14.10.05	T Salter tr Nimbus Syndicate	Lasham	5. 2.08
			D-KEPE		"PE"		
G-KEPP	Rans S-6-ES Coyote II	xxxxx		19.10.04	W Goldsmith	Morgansfield, Fishburn	8. 3.08P
	(Built S Munday -pr.no.PFA 204-14308)						
G-KESS	Glaser-Dirks DG-400	4-257	F-CGRH	15. 8.05	T Flude and N H T Cottrell	Ringmer	16. 8.08E
G-KEST	Steen Skybolt	1	G-BNKG	11. 6.91	B Tempest tr G-KEST Syndicate	Leicester	19.12.08P
	(Built A Todd)		G-RATS, G-RHFI, N443AT				
G-KESY	Slingsby T.59D Kestrel 19	1839	BGA 2902-ERY	1.11.07	A J Whiteman	Halesland	14. 1.08
			EI-125, D-9253				
G-KETH	Agusta-Bell 206B-2 JetRanger II	8418	OO-HOP	14.10.03	DAC Leasing Ltd	(Mannington, Norwich)	2. 6.08E
			PH-HAP, SX-HAP, (HB-XEX)				
G-KEVB	Piper PA-28-181 Archer III	2843098	N9289E	29. 8.97	Palmair Ltd	Elstree	25.10.07E
G-KEVG	Rotorsport UK MT-03	RSUK/MT-03-031		14. 2.08	K J Robinson and R N Bodley	RAF Benson	
G-KEVI	Avtech Jabiru J400	0xxx		19.10.04	K A Allen	Ludham	15. 6.07P
	(Built K A Allen - pr.no.PFA 325-14321)						
G-KEVS	P&M Quik GT450	8311		17. 9.07	K Mallin	Pound Green, Buttonoak, Bewdley	16. 9.08P
G-KEWT	Ultramagic M-90 Balloon (Hot Air)	90/66		27. 5.04	Kew Technik Ltd (Kew Technik titles)	Basingstoke	9. 7.08A
G-KEYS	Piper PA-23-250 Aztec F	27-7854052	N63909	6.10.78	R E Myson	Hardings Farm, Ingatestone	13.11.07E
G-KEYY	Cameron N-77 Balloon (Hot Air)	1748	G-BORZ	14. 6.88	B N Trowbridge	Allestree, Derby	14. 8.05A
G-KFAN	Scheibe SF25B Falke	46301	D-KFAN	14. 5.96	R G and J.A Boyes	Trenchard Farm, Eggesford	29. 5.99
	(Stark-Stamo MS1500)				(Stored 8.07)		
G-KFLY	Flight Design CTSW	06.11.04	G-LFLY	5. 9.07	K L Chorley tr G-KFLY Group	(Long Crendon)	12. 2.08P
	(Assembled P&M Aviation Ltd with c/n 8244)						
G-KFOX	Denney Kitfox Model 2	298		11.10.88	I R Lawrence and R Hampshire	Eaglescott	7. 9.06P
	(Built J Hannibal - pr.no.PFA 172-11447)				(New owners 6.07)		
G-KFRA	Piper PA-32-300 Cherokee Six	32-7840182	G-BGII	9. 9.97	M Drake and W Rankin tr West India Flying Group		
			N20879			Weston, Leixlip, County Kildare	9. 1.08E
G-KFZI	Williams KFZ-1 Tigerfalck	PFA 153-11054		2. 2.89	L R Williams	(Hirwaun, Aberdare)	
	(Built L R Williams - originally laid-down as Kestrel Sport c/n PFA 1530) (Continental C90)						
G-KGAO	Scheibe SF25C-2000 Falke	44386	D-KGAG	30. 7.99	C R Ellis tr Falke 2000 Group	Long Mynd	5. 9.08E
	(Limbach L2000)						
G-KGED	Campbell Cricket Mk.4	PFA G/03-1337		27. 2.04	K G Edwards	(Bridgwater)	
G-KHCC	Schempp-Hirth Ventus bT	34/215	BGA 5224-KNH	3. 4.06	J L G McLane	Sutton Bank	3. 4.08
			D-KHCC		"LM"		
G-KHOM	Aeromot AMT-200 Super Ximango	200091		5. 5.98	P Desmond tr Bowland Ximango Group	Blackpool	28. 6.08E
G-KHOP	Zenair CH.601HDS Zodiac	PFA 162-13561		14. 9.05	K Hopkins	Sleap	24. 9.07P
	(Built K Hopkins)						
G-KHRE	SOCATA Rallye 150SV Garnement	2931	F-GAYR	25. 3.82	D M Gale and K F Crumplin	Henstridge	21. 5.08
G-KICK	Cyclone Airsports Pegasus Quantum 15-912	7679		28. 6.00	Graham van der Gaag	March	12. 7.08P
G-KIDD	Avtech Jabiru J430	0xxx	G-CEBB	26.10.06	R L Kidd	Panshanger	30.10.07P
	(Built K D Pearce - pr.no.PFA 336-14541)						
G-KIII	Extra EA.300/L	1246		2.11.06	Extra 200 Ltd	Goodwood	14.11.07E
G-KIMA	Zenair CH.601XL Zodiac	PFA 162B-14207		21. 3.06	K Martindale	Morgansfield, Fishburn	
	(Built K Martindale) (Tri-cycle u/c)				(Noted 10.07)		
G-KIMB	Robin DR.300-140 Major	470	F-BPXX	23. 3.90	R M Kimbell	Rothwell Lodge Farm, Kettering	2. 6.08E
			F-WPXX				
G-KIMK	Partenavia P68B	27	G-BCPO	23. 2.01	M Konstantinovic	King's Farm, Thurrock	24. 4.08E
G-KIMM	Europa Aviation Europa XS	404		20. 7.99	P A D Clarke	Wadswick Manor Farm, Corsham	28.11.08P
	(Built P A D Clarke - pr.no.PFA 247-13404) (Monowheel u/c)						
G-KIMY	Robin DR.400-140B Major	1401	PH-SRX	7. 6.00	S G Jones (New owner 4.05)	Membury	4. 7.03T
G-KINE	Gulfstream AA-5A Cheetah	AA5A-0896	N27173	20. 7.82	Plane Talking Ltd	Blackbushe	27. 7.08E
G-KIDG	Robinson R44 Raven II	11836		23. 7.07	Skylink UK Ltd	Gamston	29. 7.08E
G-KIPP	Thruster T 600N 450	1031-T600N-094		19.12.03	Compton Abbas Airfield Ltd	Compton Abbas	18.12.07P
G-KIRB	Europa Aviation Europa XS	474	G-OIZI	25.10.06	D E Steade	Croft Farm, Defford	
	(Built K S Duddy - pr.no.PFA 247-13615)				(New owner 11.07)		
G-KIRC	Pietenpol AirCamper	1008	G-BSVZ	20. 3.06	M K Kirk	Barton Ashes	
	(Built H Challis - regd as Pietenpol/Challis Chaffinch)		N3265 (Continental C85)		(Noted 1.07)		
G-KIRK	Piper J-3C-65 Cub	10536	F-BBQC	28. 2.79	M J Kirk	(Barry)	12. 4.06P
	(Regd with Frame No.12490, but		French AF, 43-29245		"Liberty Girl"		
	correct frame actually 10361)		(Ditched in Caribbean 75 miles NW Puerto Plata, Dominican Republic due to engine failure 16. 2.08)				
G-KISS	Rand Robinson KR-2	PFA 129-10899		2. 8.83	E A Rooney	(Whitstable)	
	(Built A C Waller) (Volkswagen 1835)						
G-KITE	Piper PA-28-181 Archer II	28-8490053	N4338X	12. 4.88	A Davis	Bournemouth	1. 5.08T
G-KITF	Denney Kitfox	1156	N156BH	10. 5.89	T Wright	(Christow, Exeter)	2. 9.08P
	(Built J B Hartline) (Rotax 532)						
G-KITH	Alpi Pioneer 300	xxx		22. 9.06	K G Atkinson	Wombleton	
	(Built K G Atkinson - pr.no.PFA 330-14510)						
G-KITI	Pitts S-2E	002	N36BM	21. 6.90	B R Cornes	Kemble	14. 7.08P
	(Built R Jones)				"Super Turkey II"		
G-KITS	Europa Aviation Europa XS	468		13. 6.94	J R Evernden	Wellesbourne Mountford	26. 4.07P
	(Built Europa Aviation Ltd - pr.no.PFA 247-12844) (Mid-West AE.100R) (Tri-gear u/c)						
G-KITT	Curtiss TP-40M Kittyhawk	27490	F-AZPJ	4. 3.98	P A Teichman	North Weald	21. 6.08P
	(Officially regd with c/n 31423)		N1009N, N1233N, RCAF 840, 43-5802 (As "49" in USAAF c/s) "Bengal Tiger"				
	(C/n 31423 was P-40N 43-23484/RCAF 877/N1009N (1) which was scrapped in 1965 when this identity adopted by RCAF 840)						
G-KITY	Denney Kitfox Model 2	456		18. 8.89	J P Jenkins tr Kitfox KFM Group		
	(Built T Ringshaw - pr.no.PFA 172-11565) (IAME KFM 112)					South Lodge Farm, Widmerpool	11. 2.08P
G-KIZZ	Air Création 582(1)/Kiss 450	xxxxx		24. 6.04	J C A Page	(Great Gransden, Sandy)	15. 8.08P
	(Built P David - pr.no.BMAA/HB/388 being Flylight kit comprising Trike s/n T04028 and Wing s/n A04068-4969)						

Reg	Type	C/n	Prev id	Date	Owner	Location	Expiry
G-KKCW	Flight Design CT2K	03-02-04-07		17. 6.03	K C Wigley and Co Ltd	(Shottle, Belper)	4. 4.08P
	(Assembled Mainair Sports Ltd with c/n 7964)						
G-KKER	Avtech Jabiru UL-450	0255		1.10.99	W K Evans	Swansea	9. 5.08P
	(Built K Kerr - pr.no.PFA 274A-13474)						
G-KKES	SOCATA TB-20 Trinidad	1316	G-BTLH	2. 3.92	Island Brokers Ltd	Willey Park Farm, Caterham	18. 5.07T
G-KLAS	Robinson R44 Raven II	11308		11. 7.06	Coates Aviation Ltd	(Ballymount, Dublin)	20. 7.08E
G-KLEM	Klemm Kl.35D	1979	N5050	3.08R	P R Holloway *(Noted 8.07)*	Old Warden	
G-KLYN	Beech B200 Super King Air	BB-1931	G-CLCG N37101	3.10.07	Klyne Air Ltd	Norwich	6.11.07E
G-KMCL	Cessna 152	15281565	N65462	17. 9.07	A A McLellan *(Noted 2.08)*	North Weald	
G-KMRV	Van's RV-9A	PFA 320-14093		17.11.04	G K Mutch	Hawarden	29. 2.08P
	(Built G K Mutch)						
G-KNAP	Piper PA-28-161 Warrior II	28-8116129	G-BIUX N9507N	15. 2.90	Keen Leasing (IoM) Ltd	Belfast International	28. 4.02T
			(Crashed on take off Stevensons Field, Letterkenny, County Donegal 13. 7.99: wreck stored 2.01)				
G-KNEE	Ultramagic M-77C Balloon (Hot Air)	77/234		20. 6.03	M A Green	Rednal	7. 7.08A
G-KNEK	Grob G109B	6437	D-KNEK	22. 5.00	R A Winley tr Syndicate 109	Currock Hill	13. 6.08E
G-KNIB	Robinson R22 Beta II	3145		30.10.00	C G Knibb	Sywell	9. 1.08E
G-KNIX	Cameron Z-315 Balloon (Hot Air)	10728		11. 8.05	Cameron Flights Southern Ltd		
						Woodborough, Pewsey	21. 2.08E
G-KNOB	Lindstrand LBL 180A Balloon (Hot Air)	065		20.12.93	Wye Valley Aviation Ltd	Ross-on-Wye	16. 4.01T
G-KNOW	Piper PA-32-300 Cherokee Six	32-7840111	N9694C	21. 9.88	B R and G E Mullaly	Stapleford	13. 9.08E
G-KNOX	Robinson R22 Beta II	3603		5. 5.04	T/A Knox Shopfitters Ltd	Barton	10 6.08E
G-KNYT	Robinson R44 Astro	0723		13. 3.00	C W and Keeley A M Bootman t/a Aircol	Cranfield	4. 6.08E
G-KOBH	Schempp-Hirth Discus bT	154/549	D-KOBH	23.11.06	C F M Smith and K Neave	Nympsfield	11. 1.08
G-KODA	Cameron O-77 Balloon (Hot Air)	1448		26. 3.87	K Stamurs	Jumprava, Latvia	9. 4.08A
G-KOFM	Glaser-Dirks DG-600/18M	6-66M16	D-KOFM	13. 7.99	A Mossman	Feshiebridge	28. 7.08E
G-KOHF	Schleicher ASK 14	14033	D-KOHF	4. 9.01	J Houlihan	Gowran Grange, Dublin	6. 4.08E
G-KOKL	Hoffmann H 36 Dimona	36276	D-KOKL	4. 3.98	R Smith and R Stembrowicz	Rufforth	18. 4.08E
G-KOLB	Kolb Twinstar Mk.3A	PFA 205-12228		30. 6.93	J L Moar	Wick	29. 9.03P
	(Built P A Akines) (Rotax 912-UL)				*(Noted 5.05)*		
G-KOLI	PZL-110 Koliber 150	03900038		23. 7.90	J R Powell	Poundon, Bicester	31. 8.08
G-KONG	Slingsby T 67M-200 Firefly	2041	VR-HZP HKG-10, G-7-119	24. 3.94	R C Morton	North Weald	29. 1.08E
			"293"				
G-KOOL	de Havilland DH.104 Sea Devon C 2/2	04220	"G-DOVE" VP967	12. 1.82	D S Hunt	Redhill	
					(New owner 1.06)		
G-KORN	Cameron Berentzen Bottle 70 SS Balloon (Hot Air)	1655		10. 5.88	A D, R S Kent, I M Martin and I Chadwick	Petworth	23. 6.00A
					tr Balloon Preservation Flying Group *"Berentzen"*		
G-KOTA	Piper PA-28-236 Dakota	28-8011044	N8130R	23.12.88	D J Fravigar t/a JF Packaging		
						Clough Farm, Croft, Skegness	14. 4.08E
G-KOYY	Schempp-Hirth Nimbus 4T	9	BGA 5205-KMN D-KOYY	28.10.05	R Kalin	Rufforth	21. 5.08
			"Y7"				
G-KPAO	Robinson R44 Astro	0382	G-SSSS	19.11.98	Avonair Ltd	Shobdon	28.11.07E
G-KPLG	Schempp-Hirth Ventus 2cxM	163	BGA 5302-KRK D-KPLG	18.12.07	M F Lassan	Talgarth	
G-KPTT	SOCATA TB-20 Trinidad	1821	F-GRBI	13. 6.01	R W Cooper	East Midlands	17. 6.08E
G-KRES	Stoddard-Hamilton Glasair Super II-SRG	xxxx		12. 6.96	A D Murray	Perth	10. 5.08P
	(Built G Kresfelder - pr.no.PFA 149-12984) (Lycoming IO-360)						
G-KRII	Rand Robinson KR-2	PFA 129-10934		4. 8.89	M R Cleveley (All Saints South Elmham, Halesworth)		
	(Built M R Cleveley)						
G-KRMA	Cessna 425 Corsair	425-0003	D-INGA N98751	21.12.06	Speedstar Holdings Ltd	Wycombe Air Park	22. 3.08P
G-KRNW	Eurocopter EC.135 T2	0175		9. 7.01	Bond Air Services Ltd	RAF St Mawgan	11. 7.08E
					(Operated Cornwall Air Ambulance)		
G-KSIR	Stoddard-Hamilton Glasair IIS RG	2151		15. 4.94	K M Bowen	Upfield Farm, Whitson	10. 6.08P
	(Built R Cayzer - pr.no.PFA 149-12137) (Lycoming IO-360)						
G-KSKS	Cameron N-105 Balloon (Hot Air)	4963		21. 3.01	A Kaye t/a Kiss the Sky Ballooning		
					(New owner 10.07)	Irchester, Wellingborough	6. 9.06T
G-KSKY	Sky 77-24 Balloon (Hot Air)	170		15.10.99	J W Dale	Sinderhope, Hexham	21. 7.07A
G-KSPB	Robinson R44 Raven II	11445		9.10.06	K Sloane and P Burrows t/a Heli2	Leeds-Bradford	15.10.07E
G-KSSH	MD Helicopters MD.900 Explorer	900-00062	G-WMID N3063T	21. 9.07	Police Aviation Services Ltd	(Biggin Hill)	27. 1.09S
					(Operated Surrey Air Ambulance)		
G-KSVB	Piper PA-24-260 Comanche B	24-4657	G-ENIU G-AVJU, N9199P, N10F	8.11.91	S Juggler	Stapleford	7. 6.08E
G-KSWI	Hughes 369E	0204E	G-OOCS G-OTDB, G-BXUR, HA-MSC	19. 4.07	K S Williams	(St Mellion, Saltash)	25. 8.08E
	(Hughes 500)						
G-KTEE	Cameron V-77 Balloon (Hot Air)	2177		28.12.89	D C and N P Bull tr Katie Group	Princes Risborough	13.12.08A
					"Katie"		
G-KTKT	Sky 260-24 Balloon (Hot Air)	110		19. 5.98	T M Donnelly *"Kit Kat"*	Sprotbrough, Doncaster	9. 4.07T
G-KTTY	Denney Kitfox Model 3	PFA 172-12001	G-LESJ	28.11.05	S D Morris	(East Dean, Eastbourne)	16. 7.08P
	(Built L A James)						
G-KTWO	Cessna 182T Skylane	18281742	N282SS	23.11.06	S J G Mole	Droitwich	19.12.07E
G-KUIK	Mainair Sports Pegasus Quik	7990		17.10.03	I A Macadam	Damyn's Hall, Upminster	23.10.07P
G-KUKI	Robinson R22 Beta	1802	G-BTNB N23006	15. 8.02	R D Masters	Standalone Farm, Meppershall	30. 7.08E
G-KULA	Best Off Sky Ranger 912S(1)	SKRxxxx353?		26. 1.04	C R Mason	Sywell	29. 2.08P
	(Built C R Mason - pr.no..BMAA/HB/344)						
G-KUPP	Flight Design CTSW	06.08.21		24.10.06	K D Taylor	(Wigsley, Newark)	23.10.07P
	(Assembled P&M Aviation with c/n 8227)				*(New owner 12.07)*		
G-KUTU	QAC Quickie Q.2	PFA 094A-10758		8. 3.82	J Parkinson and R Nash	Wycombe Air Park	29. 4.86P
	(Built Quick Construction Group) (Limbach L2000)				*(Damaged Cranfield 18.5.85: stored engineless 6.03)*		
G-KUUI	Piper J-3C-65 Cub	17521	N2MD N70515, NC70515	25. 8.05	V S E Norman	Rendcomb	3.10.08E
G-KVBF	Cameron A-340HL Balloon (Hot Air)	4313		6. 4.98	Airxcite Ltd t/a Virgin Balloon Flights	Wembley	2.10.08E
G-KVIP	Beech 200 Super King Air	BB-487	G-CBFS G-PLAT, N8PY, VH-PIL, N198SC, PT-OYR, N40QN, VH-NIC, N40QN, N400N, N243KA	17. 5.02	Capital Trading (Aviation) Ltd	Exeter	29. 5.08E

G-KWAK	Scheibe SF25C Falke (Rotax 912-A)	44581	D-KWAK	8. 1.03	Mendip Gliding Club Ltd	Halesland	6. 2.08E
G-KWAX	Cessna 182E Skylane	18253808	N9902 YV-T-PTS, N2808Y	18. 5.78	D Shaw	Derby	16. 4.06T
G-KWIC	Mainair Sports Pegasus Quik	7962		25. 6.03	T Southwell	(Spalding)	27.10.07P
G-KWIN	Dassault Falcon 2000EX	052	F-WWMA	29. 4.05	Quinn Aviation Ltd	Enniskillen	23. 5.08E
G-KWKI	QAC Quickie Q.200	PFA 094-12158		22.10.91	R Greatrex	Colthrop Manor, Thatcham	28.10.08P
	(Built D G Greatrex and B M Jackson) (Continental O-200-A)						
G-KWLI	Cessna 421C Golden Eagle	421C0168	G-DARR G-BNEZ, N87386	13.11.98	Langley Aviation Ltd	Gamston	8. 2.08E
G-KYAK	SPP Yakovlev Yak C-11	171101	F-AZQI	21.12.78	M Gainza	Little Gransden	2. 1.08P
	G-KYAK, F-AZHQ, G-KYAK, IDF/AF, Egyptian AF 590, Czech AF (As "36" (white) in Soviet AF c/s)						
G-KYLE	Thruster T 600N 450	0053-T600N-113		3. 6.05	W D Kyle	Newtownards	2. 6.08P
G-KYTE	Piper PA-28-161 Warrior II	28-8216043	G-BRRN N84533	20. 1.06	G Whitlow and I C Barlow	Wycombe Air Park	17. 2.08E

G-LAAA - G-LZZZ

G-LAAC	Cameron C-90 Balloon (Hot Air)	10778		27. 1.06	Directorate Army Aviation	AAC Middle Wallop	23. 3.08E
G-LABS	Europa Aviation Europa	049		1. 3.94	C T H Pattinson	Bicester	11. 3.08P
	(Built C T H Pattinson - pr.no.PFA 247-12595) (Monowheel u/c)						
G-LACA	Piper PA-28-161 Cherokee Warrior II	28-7816036	N44883	22. 6.90	Upperstack Ltd t/a LAC Flying School (Operated Lancashire Aero Club)	Barton	11. 4.08E
G-LACB	Piper PA-28-161 Warrior II	28-8216035	N8450A	12. 6.90	Upperstack Ltd t/a LAC Flying School (Operated Lancashire Aero Club)	Barton	9. 7.08E
G-LACD	Piper PA-28-181 Archer III	2843157	G-BYBG N47BK	11.11.98	Central Aircraft Leasing Ltd	Halfpenny Green	25.11.07E
G-LACE	Europa Aviation Europa	256		15. 4.96	J H Phillingham	(Benson, Wallingford)	
	(Built J H Phillingham - pr.no.PFA 247-12962) (Monowheel u/c)						
G-LACI	Cessna 172S Skyhawk	172S9978	N2310C	28.11.05	L Endresz	Blackpool	11.12.07E
G-LACR	Denney Kitfox	PFA 172-11945		4.12.90	C M Rose	(Scone)	
	(Built C M Rose)				(Under construction 2.06)		
G-LADD	Enstrom 480	5037		20. 5.99	R C G Davidson	(Dungannon)	1. 8.08E
G-LADS	Rockwell Commander 114	14314	N4994W (N114XT), N4994W	6.12.90	D F Soul	Emberton, Olney	29. 2.08E
G-LADZ	Enstrom 480	5001	N480E HB-XUX, N480E	31.10.05	Falcon Helicopters Ltd	Barton	21.11.07E
G-LAFT	Diamond DA.40D Star	D4.193		28. 3.06	Atlantic Flight Training Ltd	Coventry	11. 4.08E
G-LAGR	Cameron N-90 Balloon (Hot Air)	1628		25. 1.88	J R Clifton (New owner 3.05)	Nelson, New Zealand	11.10.03A
G-LAID	Robinson R44 Raven II	11377		31. 7.06	Helitech Charter Ltd	Denham	5. 9.08E
G-LAIN	Robinson R22 Beta	1992		7. 2.92	Patriot Aviation Ltd	Cranfield	5. 9.08E
G-LAIR	Stoddard-Hamilton Glasair IIS FT	2106		12. 9.91	A I O'Broin and S T Raby	Grange Farm, Woodwalton	24 .9.08P
	(Built D L Swallow and S T Raby - pr.no.PFA 149-11923)						
G-LAJT	Beech D17S (UC-43-BH)	4885	ZS-AJT	27. 4.05	G W Lynch	New Farm House, Great Oakley	
	ZS-CLM, N1591V, NC60004, CR-LBF, 43-10837 (Noted 9.07)						
G-LAKE	Lake LA-250 Renegade	70	(EI-PJM) G-LAKE, N8415B	12. 7.88	Educational Programmes International Ltd	Biggin Hill	19.12.07E
	(Built Aerofab Inc)						
G-LAKI	CEA Jodel DR.1050 Sicile	534	G-JWBB G-LAKI, F-BLZD	12.11.79	V Panteli	Clipgate Farm, Denton	30. 6.08E
G-LAMA	Aérospatiale SA.315B Lama	2348	SE-HET	17. 3.98	PLM Dollar Group Ltd	Cumbernauld	19. 3.07T
G-LAMM	Europa Aviation Europa	244		20.11.95	S A Lamb	(Paddock Wood, Tonbridge)	
	(Built S A Lamb - pr.no.PFA 247-12941) (Monowheel u/c)						
G-LAMP	Cameron Lightbulb 110 SS Balloon (Hot Air)	4899		21. 7.00	S A Lacey	Norwich Common, Wymondham	21. 6.08A
G-LAMS	Reims Cessna F152 II	F15201431	N54558	23. 6.88	APB Leasing Ltd	Sleap	14.11.07E
G-LANE	Reims Cessna F172N Skyhawk II	F17201853		27. 6.79	G C Bantin	Sproatley	29. 6.08E
G-LANS	Cessna 182T Skylane	18281910	N11827	30. 5.07	AK Enterprises Ltd	(Marlow)	27. 6.08E
G-LAOK	IAV Bacau Yakovlev Yak-52	877404	LY-AOK DOSAAF 16 (yellow)	22. 1.03	I F Vaughan and J P Armitage	Tollerton	20. 9.08P
G-LAOL	Piper PA-28RT-201 Arrow IV	28R-7918211	D-EAOL N2903Y	6.10.99	Goodwood Road Racing Company Ltd "19"	Goodwood	20. 2.08T
G-LAOR	Raytheon Hawker 800XP	258384	N955MC N23455, TC-MDC, N23455	2. 3.04	Select Plant Hire Company Ltd	Southend	26. 3.08E
G-LAPN	Avid Aerobat	PFA 189-12146		4. 3.93	I A P Harper	Croft Farm, Defford	3.10.06P
	(Built R M Shorter)						
G-LAPS	Lindstrand LTL.203T Balloon (Gas Filled)	HF042		13. 4.07	Lindstrand Aeroplatforms Ltd	Leeds Castle	26. 4.08E
G-LARA	Robin DR.400-180 Régent	2050		14. 2.91	K D and C A Brackwell	Goodwood	23. 4.08E
G-LARE	Piper PA-39 Twin Comanche C/R	39-16	N8861Y	20. 2.91	Glareways (Neasden) Ltd	Biggin Hill	26. 4.08E
G-LARK	Helton Lark 95	9517	N5017J	3.12.85	J Fox	Wycombe Air Park	28. 3.08P
G-LARR	Eurocopter AS.350B3 Ecureuil	4137	F-WWXN	15. 1.07	Larsen Manufacturing Ltd	Newtownards	28. 3.08E
G-LARY	Robinson R44 Raven II	10255	(EI-) G-LARY, G-CCRZ	20. 4.07	Michael Fitzgerald and Sons Ltd (Gort, County Galway)		25. 2.08T
G-LASN	Best Off Sky Ranger 912(2)	SKRxxxx479		19. 7.04	L C F Lasne	Derryogue	27. 4.08P
	(Built L C F Lasne - pr.no.BMAA/HB/396)						
G-LASR	Stoddard-Hamilton Glasair Super II-SRG	2027		8. 1.90	G Lewis	(Heswall, Wirral)	
	(Built P Taylor and G Lewis)				(New owner 3.05)		
G-LASS	Rutan VariEze	PFA 074-10209		20. 9.78	J Mellor	Sleap	14. 6.08P
	(Built Calvert, Foreman and O'Hara) (Continental O-200-A)						
G-LASU	Eurocopter EC.135 T2	0228	D-HTSH	3. 9.02	Lancashire Constabulary Air Support Unit	Warton	15.10.08E
G-LAVE	Cessna 172R Skyhawk	17280663	G-BYEV N2377J, N41297	10. 3.99	M L Roland	Southend	10. 5.08E
G-LAXY	Everett Gyroplane Series 3	035		17. 2.94	E J Barton	(Bramley, Tadley)	
	(Built Everett Gyroplanes Ltd - pr.no.PFA G/03-1233)				(New owner 4.06)		

Reg	Type	C/n	Prev id	Date	Owner/Operator	Base	Exp
G-LAZA	Laser Lazer Z200	PFA 123-12682		15. 6.95	D G Jenkins	(Stanton, Bury St Edmunds)	21. 8.08P
	(Built M Hammond) (Lycoming AEIO-360)						
G-LAZL	Piper PA-28-161 Warrior II	28-8116216	D-EAZL	9. 6.99	C P Awdry t/a P and J Awdry and Son	Old Sarum	21. 8.08E
			N9536N				
G-LAZR	Cameron O-77 Balloon (Hot Air)	2240		6. 3.90	Laser Holdings (UK) Ltd	Worcester	10. 6.97A
					(New owner 8.04)		
G-LAZY	Lindstrand LBL Armchair SS Balloon (Hot Air)	129		18. 9.94	The Air Chair Company Ltd-Lindstrand Balloons Ltd "The Chair"	Westville, Indiana, US	27. 4.03A
G-LAZZ	Stoddard-Hamilton GlaStar	PFA 295-13059		31.10.96	A N Evans	Ashcroft Fam, Winsford	18.12.07P
	(Built G K Brunwin and A N Evans) (Tri-cycle u/c)						
G-LBDC	Bell 206B-3 JetRanger III	3806	N206GF	17. 3.06	Fresh Direct Espana Ltd	Turweston	30. 3.08E
			(G-), N509KK, JA9448, N206JG, N3186Z				
G-LBLI	Lindstrand LBL 69A Balloon (Hot Air)	010		4.11.92	N M Gabriel	Kimberley, Nottingham	30. 6.07A
G-LBMM	Piper PA-28-161 Cherokee Warrior II	28-7816440	N6940C	28.11.89	Flexi-Soft Ltd	Wellesbourne Mountford	18. 5.08E
G-LBRC	Piper PA-28RT-201 Arrow IV	28R-7918051	N2245P	20. 7.88	D J V Morgan	Halfpenny Green	28. 3.08E
G-LBUK	Lindstrand LBL 77A Balloon (Hot Air)	922		15. 5.03	Lindstrand Hot Air Balloons Ltd (Lindstrand titles)	Oswestry	31. 7.08A
G-LBUZ	Evektor EV-97A Eurostar	2004-2312		15. 7.05	D P Tassart	Scotland Farm, Hook	14. 8.08P
	(Built D P Tassart - pr.no.PFA 315-14425)						
G-LCGL	Comper CLA.7 Swift replica	PFA 103-11089		1.7.92	J M Greenland	Blackacre Farm, Holt, Trowbridge	25. 4.08P
	(Built J M Greenland) (Pobjoy Niagara 1A)						
G-LCKY	Flight Design CTSW	07.05.04		9. 7.07	I A Gaeten	Chiltern Park, Wallingford	8. 7.08P
	(Assembled P&M Aviation Ltd with c/n 8274)						
G-LCOC	Britten-Norman BN-2A Mk.III-1 Trislander	366	G-BCCU	30. 7.01	Airx Ltd t/a Blue Islands	Alderney	6. 1.08E
			4X-CCK, G-BCCU, 9L-LAR, G-BCCU, (LN-VIV)				
G-LCPL	Aérospatiale AS.365N2 Dauphin 2	6393	PT-YIF	8. 4.05	Charterstyle Ltd	(Kingswinford)	4. 8.08E
			ZS-RAZ, F-WYMI				
G-LCUB	Piper PA-18 Super Cub 95	18-1631	G-AYPR	9. 2.07	The Tiger Club 1990 Ltd	Headcorn	18.12.07E
	(L-18C-PI)		French Army 18-1631, 51-15631				
G-LCYA	Dassault Falcon 900EX	105	F-WWFC	5. 8.02	Airport Management and Investment Ltd	London City	4. 8.08E
G-LCYB	British Aerospace Avro 146-RJ85	E2383	OH-SAH	25. 1.08	BAE Systems (Operations) Ltd (Operated BA Cityflyer)	London City	
G-LDAH	Best Off Sky Ranger 912(2)	SKRxxxx216		8.10.02	P D Brookes and L Dickinson	Long Marston	17. 9.08P
	(Built A S Haslam and L Dickinson - pr.no.BMAA/HB/241)						
G-LDER	Schleicher ASW 22	22027	BGA 3261-FGY	1. 2.08	D Starer and P Shrosbree "527"	Dunstable	19. 3.08
			D-3527				
G-LDFM	Cessna 560XL Citation Excel	560-5242	TC-LMA	17. 2.05	Granard Ltd	Biggin Hill	17. 2.07E
G-LDWS	SAN Jodel D 150 Mascaret	48	G-BKSS	13. 2.04	D H Wilson-Spratt	Ronaldsway	
			F-BMFC		(Noted 10.06)		
G-LDYS	Thunder Ax6-56Z Balloon (Hot Air)	347		18. 5.81	M J Myddelton "Gladys"	Bristol	23. 9.06A
	(Originally regd as Colt 56A)						
G-LEAF	Reims Cessna F406 Caravan II	F406-0018	EI-CKY	7. 3.96	Highland Airways Ltd	Inverness	20. 5.08E
			PH-ALN, OO-TIW, F-WZDX				
G-LEAH	Alpi Pioneer 300	174		11. 1.06	A Bortolan	North Weald	16. 7.08P
	(Built J C Ferguson - pr.no.PFA 330-14497)						
G-LEAI	Cessna 510 Citation Mustang	510-0052		15. 1.08	London Executive Aviation Ltd	London Stansted	
G-LEAM	Piper PA-28-236 Dakota	28-8011061	N35650	1. 7.80	A Incisa tr G-LEAM Group	Elstree	30. 7.08E
G-LEAP	Pilatus Britten-Norman BN-2T Islander	2183	G-BLND	19. 8.87	Skydive Aircraft Ltd	AAC Netheravon	24. 4.08E
G-LEAS	Sky 90-24 Balloon (Hot Air)	158		4. 5.99	C I Humphrey (LNG The Leasing Group titles) (Active 1.06)	Tilehurst, Reading	8. 6.05A
G-LEAU	Cameron N-31 Balloon (Hot Air)	761		5. 8.81	P L Mossman "Perrier"	Trellech, Monmouth	23. 3.08A
G-LEBE	Europa Aviation Europa	237		17. 5.01	P Atkinson	(Carnforth)	
	(Built P Atkinson - pr.no.PFA 247-12927) (Wilksch WAM-120) (Monowheel u/c)						
G-LECA	Aérospatiale AS.355F1 Ecureuil 2	5043	G-BNBK	6. 2.87	Western Power Distribution (South West) PLC	Bristol	24. 7.08E
			C-GBKH				
G-LEDR	Westland SA.341C Gazelle HT.2	1081	G-CBSB	18.12.06	R D Leader	Bourne Park, Hurstbourne Tarrant	4. 4.08P
			XW857		(As "XW857" in RN c/s)		
G-LEED	Denney Kitfox Model 2	450		24. 4.91	S J Walker	(Poole)	20. 3.07P
	(Built G T Leedham - pr.no.PFA 172-11577)						
G-LEEE	Avtech Jabiru UL-450	0293		18. 1.00	L E G Fekete and J P Mimnagh	(Ellesmere Port and Neston)	26. 3.07P
	(Built L E G Fekete - pr.no.PFA 274A-13516)						
G-LEEH	Ultramagic M-90 Balloon (Hot Air)	90/79		3. 8.05	Sport Promotion SRL (Lee titles)	La Morra, Piedmont, Italy	31. 7.08E
G-LEEN	Aero Designs Pulsar XP	PFA 202-12147	G-BZMP	16. 7.01	R B Hemsworth	Eaglescott	12. 6.07P
	(Built D F Gaughan)		G-DESI				
G-LEES	Glaser-Dirks DG-400	4-238		4.10.88	J Bradley	Trenchard Lines, Upavon	9. 4.08E
G-LEEZ	Bell 206L-1 LongRanger	45761	G-BPCT	22. 1.92	Pennine Helicopters Ltd	Oakdene Farm, Saddleworth	27.1.07T
			D-HDBB, N3175G				
G-LEGG	Reims Cessna F182Q Skylane II	F18200145	G-GOOS	26. 6.96	W A L Mitchell	Dunsfold	6. 4.08E
G-LEGO	Cameron O-77 Balloon (Hot Air)	1975		14. 4.89	P M Traviss "Jigsaw II"	Yarm	11. 5.07A
G-LEIC	Reims Cessna FA152 Aerobat	FA1520416		16. 9.86	The Leicestershire Aero Club Ltd	Leicester	31. 8.08E
G-LEKT	Robin DR.400-180 Régent	1181	D-EEKT	1. 2.05	P Bromley	Ronaldsway	2. 3.08E
G-LELE	Lindstrand LBL 31A Balloon (Hot Air)	806		16. 8.01	S A Lacey	Norwich Common, Wymondham	11. 7.08A
G-LEMO	Cessna U206G Stationair 6	U20605407	LN-ALX	15.11.05	Garden House Properties Ltd	East Winch	25. 1.08E
			N6300U				
G-LENF	Mainair Blade 912S	1362-0104-7-W1157		18. 2.04	G D Fuller	North Coates	20. 4.08P
G-LENI	Aérospatiale AS.355F1 Ecureuil 2	5311	G-ZFDB	9. 8.95	Grid Aviation Ltd	(Sheffield City)	21. 4.08E
			G-BLEV				
G-LENN	Cameron V-56 Balloon (Hot Air)	1833		29. 9.88	A Kaye	Wellingborough	4. 5.08A
G-LENS	Thunder Ax7-77Z Balloon (Hot Air)	168		3.11.78	R S Breakwell	Bridgnorth	3.10.08A
G-LENX	Cessna 172N Skyhawk II	17272232	G-BMVJ	15. 2.02	M W Glencross	Cranfield	27. 5.08E
			N9347E				

Reg	Type	C/n		Reg history	Date	Owner/Operator	Location	Date
G-LENY	Piper PA-34-220T Seneca III	34-8233205	N111PS	26. 7.00	Air Medical Fleet Ltd	Oxford	27. 9.08E
			(OK-MKN), PH-SMS, (PH-CCC), D-GAPN, N82396					
G-LEOD	Pietenpol Aircamper	PFA 047-13499		23.11.05	I D McLeod	(Farthing Corner)	
	(Built I D McCleod)				"Dame Flora"		
G-LEOS	Robin DR.400-120 Dauphin 2+2	1884		29.11.88	R J O Walker	Gamston	6. 8.08E
G-LESZ	Skystar Kitfox Model 5	PFA 172C-12822		25.10.02	D A Lord	Shoreham	10. 7.08P
	(Built L A James) (Rotec R2800)						
G-LEVI	Aeronca 7AC Champion	7AC-4001	N85266	17. 4.90	J P A Pumphrey tr G-LEVI Group	White Waltham	13. 5.08P
			NC85266		(Carries "NC85266" on fin)		
G-LEVO	Robinson R44 Raven II	11444		29. 9.06	Leavesley Aviation Ltd	Tatenhill	23.10.07E
G-LEXI	Cameron N-77 Balloon (Hot Air)	438		26.10.78	T Gilbert	Hutton, Weston-super-Mare	3. 8.08A
					(Rolls Royce titles)		
G-LEXX	Van's RV-8	PFA 303-13896		11. 4.02	A A Wordsworth	(Huthwaite, Sutton-in-Ashfield)	1.10.08P
	(Built A A Wordsworth)						
G-LEXY	Van's RV-8	PFA 303-14756		15. 1.08	A A Wordsworth	(Huthwaite, Sutton-in-Ashfield)	
	(Built A A Wordsworth)						
G-LFIX	Vickers Supermarine 509 Spitfire Tr.9		IAC162	1. 2.80	C S Grace	Earls Colne	16. 4.08P
	(C/n is firewall plate no)	CBAF.8463	G-15-175, ML407		"Nicholson Leslie" (As "ML407:OU-V" in RAF 485 Sqdn c/s)		
G-LFOR	Piper J-3C-65 Cub	11876	G-BHZA	11.12.07	A Hoskins and J A Gowdy	(Storrington, Pulborough)	24. 2.84P
			F-BBIN, 44-79580				
G-LFSA	Piper PA-38-112 Tomahawk	38-78A0430	G-BSFC	22.10.90	Liverpool Flying School Ltd	Liverpool	8. 5.08E
			N9739N				
G-LFSB	Piper PA-38-112 Tomahawk	38-78A0072	G-BLYC	20.10.94	Cambrian Flying Club Ltd	Swansea	18. 7.08E
			D-ELID, N9715N				
G-LFSC	Piper PA-28-140 Cherokee Cruiser	28-7425005	G-BGTR	4. 9.95	P A Harvie	Mount Airey Farm, South Cave	6. 7.08E
			OY-BGO, SE-GDS				
G-LFSD	Piper PA-38-112 Tomahawk II	38-82A0046	G-BNPT	21.10.96	Liverpool Flying School Ltd	Liverpool	13. 7.08E
			G-LFSD, N91522				
G-LFSG	Piper PA-28-180 Cherokee E	28-5799	G-AYAA	19. 6.00	Liverpool Flying School Ltd	Liverpool	10.11.07E
			N11C				
G-LFSH	Piper PA-38-112 Tomahawk	38-78A0352	G-BOZM	16. 7.01	Liverpool Flying School Ltd	Liverpool	27. 6.08E
			N6247A				
G-LFSI	Piper PA-28-140 Cherokee C	28-26850	G-AYKV	14. 7.89	M J Green	Humberside	8. 6.08E
			N11C				
G-LFSJ	Piper PA-28-161 Warrior II	28-7916536	G-BPHE	4.11.02	Cloud 9 Aviation (Leasing) Ltd	(Sheffield City)	30. 4.08E
			N2911D				
G-LFSK	Piper PA-28-161 Cherokee Warrior II		SE-IAD	23. 4.04	Cloud 9 Aviation (Leasing) Ltd	(Sheffield City)	6. 9.08E
		28-7816599					
G-LFSM	Piper PA-38-112 Tomahawk	38-78A0449	G-BWNR	21. 9.04	Liverpool Flying School Ltd	Liverpool	23. 6.08E
			N2361E				
G-LFSN	Piper PA-38-112 Tomahawk	38-78A0073	G-BNYV	4.12.06	Liverpool Flying School Ltd	Liverpool	17. 9.08E
			N9364T				
G-LFVB	Vickers Supermarine 349 Spitfire LF.V		8070M	9. 5.94	Patina Ltd "City of Winnipeg"	Duxford	20. 4.08P
		CBAF.2403	5377M, EP120		(As "EP120:AE-A" in 402 Sqdn c/s) (Operated The Fighter Collection)		
G-LFVC	Vickers Supermarine 349 Spitfire L Vc	????	ZK-MKV	28. 9.99	Spitfire Ltd	Duxford	29.11.08P
			A58-178, JG891		(As "JG891:T-B" in RAF 249 Sqdn c/s)		
G-LGAR	Bombardier Learjet Model 60	60-286	N262DB	5. 4.06	TAG Aviation (UK) Ltd	Farnborough	4. 4.08E
			(D-CSIS), N4003K				
G-LGCA	Robin DR.400-180R Remorqueur	1686	HB-KAP	17. 2.04	London Gliding Club Proprietary Ltd	Dunstable	26. 3.08E
G-LGCB	Robin DR.400-180R Remorqueur	1990	D-EHRA	28. 4.05	London Gliding Club Proprietary Ltd	Dunstable	2. 6.08E
G-LGCC	Robin DR.400-180R Remorqueur	1021	G-BNXI	21. 8.07	London Gliding Club Proprietary Ltd	Dunstable	31. 3.08E
			SE-FNI				
G-LGEZ	Rutan Long-EZ	PFA 074A-11361		26. 7.06	P C Elliott	Dunsfold	28 .6.08P
	(Built P C Elliott)				(Noted 9.06)		
G-LGKO	Bombardier CL-600-2B16	5610	C-FEFW	2.11.05	TAG Aviation (UK) Ltd	Farnborough	3.11.07E
	(CL-604 Challenger)		C-GLXU				
G-LGNA	SAAB-Scania SF.340B	340B-199	N592MA	11. 6.99	Loganair Ltd	Glasgow	14. 6.08E
			SE-F99				
G-LGNB	SAAB-Scania SF.340B	340B-216	N595MA	8. 7.99	Loganair Ltd	Glasgow	8. 7.08E
			SE-G16				
G-LGNC	SAAB-Scania SF.340B	340B-318	SE-KXC	9. 6.00	Loganair Ltd	Glasgow	18. 6.08E
			F-GTSF, EC-GMI, F-GMVZ, SE-KXC, SE-C18				
G-LGND	SAAB-Scania SF.340B	340B-169	G-GNTH	7. 9.01	Loganair Ltd	Glasgow	4. 2.08E
			N588MA, SE-F69				
G-LGNE	SAAB-Scania SF.340B	340B-172	G-GNTI	31. 8.01	Loganair Ltd	Glasgow	5. 2.08E
			N589MA, SE-F72				
G-LGNF	SAAB-Scania SF.340B	340B-192	N192JE	8. 8.02	Loganair Ltd	Glasgow	7. 8.08E
			G-GNTJ, N591MA, SE-F92				
G-LGNG	SAAB-Scania SF.340B	340B-327	SE-C27	16.12.02	Loganair Ltd	Glasgow	16.12.07E
			VH-CMH, SE-C27				
G-LGNH	SAAB-Scania SF.340B	340B-333	SE-C33	28. 5.04	Loganair Ltd	Glasgow	30. 5.08E
			VH-XDA, F-GMVX, SE-C33				
G-LGNI	SAAB-Scania SF.340B	340B-160	SE-F60	4. 5.05	Loganair Ltd	Glasgow	3. 5.08E
			ER-SGC, HB-AKA, SE-F60				
G-LGNJ	SAAB-Scania SF.340B	340B-173	SE-F73	27. 5.05	Loganair Ltd	Glasgow	26. 5.08E
			F-GPKD, HB-AKD, SE-F73				
G-LGNK	SAAB-Scania SF.340B	340B-185	SE-F85	7. 7.05	Loganair Ltd	Glasgow	10. 7.08E
			D-CDAU, F-GPKG, (YR-VGT), F-GPKG, HB-AKG, SE-F85				
G-LGNL	SAAB-Scania SF.340B	340B-246	SE-G46	2. 1.08	Loganair Ltd	Glasgow	
			N869DC, XA-TUM, N354BE, SE-G46				
G-LGOC	Aero AT-3 R100	AT3.020	(F-GURG)	9. 3.07	London Transport Flying Club Ltd	Fairoaks	15. 4.08E
G-LGTE	Boeing 737-3Y0	24908	TC-SUP	25. 1.01	British Airways PLC	London Gatwick	26. 3.08E
G-LGTF	Boeing 737-382	24450	N115GB	7. 3.01	British Airways PLC	London Gatwick	30. 4.08E
			TC-IAC, CS-TIE				

G-LGTG	Boeing 737-3Q8	24470	N696BJ	4. 4.01	British Airways PLC	London Gatwick	14. 6.08E
			SX-BFT, N470KB, PK-GWD				
G-LGTH	Boeing 737-3Y0	23924	OO-LTV	4. 4.01	British Airways PLC	London Gatwick	8. 6.08E
			XA-SEM, G-BNGL				
G-LGTI	Boeing 737-3Y0	23925	OO-LTY	2. 4.01	British Airways PLC	London Gatwick	25. 7.08E
			XA-SEO, G-BNGM				
G-LHCA	Robinson R22 Beta II	2947	N299FA	28.10.02	Rotorcraft Ltd	Headcorn	1.12.07E
G-LHCB	Robinson R22 Beta II	3241	G-SIVX	14. 6.04	London Helicopter Centres Ltd	Redhill	1. 8.08E
G-LHCC	Eurocopter EC.120B Colibri	1379	RP-C2579	15. 6.06	MCJ Helicopters Ltd	Redhill	27 .7.08E
			F-OISB, F-WWPC				
G-LHCI	Bell 47G-5	2639	G-SOLH	10.12.07	Leamington Hobby Centre Ltd		
			G-AZMB, CF-NJW			Wellesbourne Mountford	18. 5.08E
G-LHEL	Aérospatiale AS.355F2 Ecureuil 2	5462	N42AT	29. 3.04	Beechview Aviation Ltd	Toome	24. 5.08E
			N70PB				
G-LHMS	Eurocopter EC.120B Colibri	1442	N120CL	9. 5.07	Hadley Helicopters Ltd	Elstree	9. 5.08E
G-LIBB	Cameron V-77 Balloon (Hot Air)	2463		21. 6.91	R J Mercer	Belfast	9. 6.08A
G-LIBL	Glasflügel H201B Standard Libelle	119	BGA 3969-HHY	24.10.07	P A Pearson	(Whyteleafe)	18. 3.08
			SE-TIU				
G-LIBS	Hughes 369HS	43-0469S	N9147F	20. 8.85	R J H Strong	(Vagg Hill, Yeovil)	28. 6.08E
	(Hughes 500)						
G-LIBY	Glasflügel H201B Standard Libelle	175	BGA 1629-CLN	29.11.07	R P Hardcastle	Rufforth	24. 6.08
G-LICK	Cessna 172N Skyhawk II	17270631	N172AG	17. 7.02	Sky Back Ltd	Elstree	13.10.07E
			G-LICK, G-BNTR, N739LQ				
G-LIDA	Hoffman HK 36R Super Dimona	36355		15. 4.92	Bidford Airfield Ltd	Bidford	20. 1.08E
G-LIDE	Piper PA-31-350 Navajo Chieftain	31-7852156	(G-VIDE)	26.10.78	Keen Leasing (IoM) Ltd	Ronaldsway	27.10.07T
			N27800				
G-LIDY	Schleicher ASW 27B	27132	BGA 4791-JUL	25. 9.07	T Stuart	Nympsfield	13.12.07
G-LIFE	Thunder Ax6-56Z Balloon (Hot Air)	135		11. 1.78	D P Hopkins t/a Lakeside Lodge Golf Centre		
					"Golden Delicious"	Pidley, Huntingdon	24. 8.07A
G-LILA	Bell 206L-1 LongRanger	45548	G-NEUF	22. 3.06	Lothian Helicopters Ltd	(Manston)	7.10.07E
			G-BVVV, D-HUGO, OE-KXT, C-GLMM	*(Operated Helicharter?)*			
G-LILP	Europa Aviation Europa XS	487		22. 5.02	G L Jennings	(Shoreham-by-Sea)	
	(Built G L Jennings - pr.no.PFA 247-13802) (Monowheel u/c)						
G-LILY	Bell 206B-3 JetRanger III	4107	G-NTBI	14. 3.95	T S Brown	Goodwood	16. 6.08E
			C-FIJD				
G-LIMO	Bell 206L-1 LongRanger	45476	N5742H	12. 6.03	Heliplayer Ltd	(Sheffield City)	3. 9.08E
			G-LIMO, N5742H				
G-LIMP	Cameron C-80 Balloon (Hot Air)	10391		4. 6.03	T and B Chamberlain	Melborne, York	5. 7.08A
G-LINC	Hughes 369HS	43-0467S	C-FDUZ	14. 5.87	Wavendon Social Housing Ltd	Sywell	28. 2.07T
	(Hughes 500)		CF-DUZ	*(Heavy landing Sywell 2. 1.06 and suffered substantial damage: noted wrecked 10.07)*			
G-LINE	Eurocopter AS.355N Ecureuil 2	5566		22. 3.94	National Grid Company PLC	Oxford	21. 5.08E
G-LINN	Europa Aviation Europa XS	598		20. 8.04	T Pond	Yeatsall Farm, Abbots Bromley	18. 8.08P
	(Built T Pond - pr.no.PFA 247-14118)						
G-LINX	Schweizer 269C-1	0239	N86G	5. 4.06	Heli-Lynx Ltd	Blackpool	11. 5.08E
	(Schweizer 300)						
G-LION	Piper PA-18-135 Super Cub	18-3857	PH-KLB	29. 9.80	J G Jones t/a JG Jones Haulage	Caernarfon	21. 6.08S
	(L-21B-PI) (Frame No.18-3841)		(PH-DKG), R Neth AF R-167, 54-2457 *"Grin'n Bare It"* (As "R-167" in R Neth AF c/s)				
G-LIOT	Cameron O-77 Balloon (Hot Air)	2378		7. 8.90	N D Eliot	London SW19	27. 5.05A
G-LIPE	Robinson R22 Beta	1882	G-BTXJ	23. 1.92	HJS Helicopters Ltd	Lower Baads, Peterculter	4. 4.08E
G-LIPS	Cameron Lips 90 SS Balloon (Hot Air)	4846	G-BZBV	15.11.00	Reach For The Sky Ltd	Worplesdon, Guildford	30. 7.02A
					(New owner 3.04)		
G-LISO	SIAI-Marchetti SM.1019	045	Ital. Army MM57-237	1. 7.04	C Daliso	Vicenza, Italy	
					(Noted 4.06)		
G-LITE	Rockwell Commander 112A	291	OY-RPP	13. 6.80	B G Rhodes	(Henbury, Macclesfield)	1. 2.08E
G-LITZ	Pitts S-1E	PFA 009-11131		3. 3.92	R P Millinship	Leicester	22. 6.06P
	(Built K Eld and J Hughes)				*"Glitz"*		
G-LIVH	Piper J-3C-65 Cub (L-4H-PI)	11529	OO-JAN	31. 3.94	U E Allman	Eaglescott	9. 8.09S
	(Frame No.11354)		OO-AAT, OO-PAX, 43-30238	*(As "330238:A-24" in US Army c/s)*			
G-LIVS	Schleicher ASH 26E	26228		24. 2.05	P O Sturley *"261"*	RAF Wittering	23. 2.08E
G-LIZA	Cessna 340A II	340A1021	G-BMDM	15. 2.90	Tayflite Ltd	Perth	29. 6.08E
			ZS-KRH, N4620N				
G-LIZI	Piper PA-28-160 Cherokee	28-52	G-ARRP	26. 1.89	N F Andrews and A J Kingston tr G-LIZI Group		
			N5050W			Netherthorpe	27. 4.08E
G-LIZZ	Piper PA-E23-250 Aztec E	27-7405268	G-BBWM	26. 7.93	T J Nathan	Biggin Hill	13. 3.08E
			N40532				
G-LJCC	Murphy Rebel	PFA 232-13335		8. 7.98	P H Hyde	(Newton Longville, Milton Keynes)	
	(Built J Clarke)				*(New owner 10.05)*		
G-LJRM	Sikorsky S-76C	760426	D-HBAG	22. 9.05	Ballymore Management Services Ltd	(Dublin)	4. 4.08E
			N101MY, N101MM				
G-LKTB	Piper PA-28-181 Archer III	2843496	N5339X	18.12.01	Top Cat Aviation Ltd	Manchester	12. 1.08E
G-LLAN	Grob G109B	6398	OH-747	19.11.04	J D Scott	Shobdon	6. 1.08E
G-LLEW	Aeromot AMT-200S Super Ximango	200126		15.11.00	N J Watt tr Echo Whiskey Ximango Syndicate		
						Glenrothes	6. 5.07E
G-LLIZ	Robinson R44 Raven II	12140		18. 2.08	Heli Air Ltd	Wellesbourne Mountford	
G-LLLL	Rolladen-Schneider LS8-18	8217	BGA 4657-JNW	25. 9.07	P C Fritche	Parham Park	28. 9.08
G-LLMC	Cessna T310Q II	310Q0914	G-BKSB	16.11.06	Bravo Aviation Ltd	Jersey	11. 9.08E
			VR-CEM, G-BKSB, HB-LMO, OE-FYL, (N69680)				
G-LLMW	Diamond DA.42 Twin Star	42.167	OE-VPY	21. 9.06	M Wai Lau	(London W1)	22.10.07E
G-LLOD	Learjet Model 45	45-236	N66DN	6.11.07	S R Lloyd	Leeds-Bradford	
			N125GW				
G-LLOY	Alpi Pioneer Hawk	xxx		14.11.06	A R Lloyd		
	(Built A R Lloyd and F Cavaciuti - pr.no.PFA 330A-14568)					Orlingbury Hold Farm, Hannington, Northampton	21. 3.08P
G-LMAX	Sequoia F 8L Falco	PFA 100-13423		28.10.02	J Maxwell	(Ascot)	
	(Built J Maxwell)						

Reg	Type	C/n	Prev id	Date	Owner/Operator	Location	Date
G-LMBO	Robinson R44 Raven	1743		8. 8.07	Jewel Aviation and Technology Ltd	Fairoaks	6. 9.08E
G-LMCG	Robinson R44 Raven II	10370	OO-GOW	18. 1.07	Glendale Helicopter Services Ltd		
			D-HALQ			Highfield, Strathaven	1. 2.08E
G-LMLV	Dyn'Aéro MCR-01 Club	82		25.10.99	L and Maddelena La Vecchia	Cambridge	15. 3.08P
	(Built L La Vecchia - pr.no.PFA 301A-13524)						
G-LNAA	MD Helicopters MD.900 Explorer	900-00074	G-76-074	26. 9.00	Police Aviation Services Ltd	RAF Waddington	5.12.07E
			G-LNAA, N7030B		*(Operated Lincolnshire and Nottingham Air Ambulance)*		
G-LNTY	Aérospatiale AS.355F1 Ecureuil 2	5300	G-ECOS	29. 9.03	Sky Select Ltd	(LLanegryn, Tywyn)	26. 2.08T
			G-DOLR, G-BPVB, OH-HAJ, D-HEHN				
G-LNYS	Reims Cessna F177RG Cardinal RG		G-BDCM	30.11.92	D M White	Popham	14. 5.08T
		F177RG0120	OY-BIP				
G-LOAD	Dan Rihn DR.107 One Design	PFA 264-13776		7. 6.02	M J Clark	(Sedgwick Park, Horsham)	
	(Built M J Clark)						
G-LOAN	Cameron N-77 Balloon (Hot Air)	1434		9. 1.87	P Lawman	Northampton	8. 5.01A
	(Newbury Building Society titles)						
G-LOBO	Cameron O-120 Balloon (Hot Air)	3389		3. 1.95	C A Butler t/a Solo Aerostatics	Newbury	26. 7.03A
G-LOCH	Piper J-3C-90 Cub (L-4J-PI)	12687	HB-OCH	10.12.84	J M Greenland Blackacre Farm, Holt, Trowbridge		5.11.08P
	(Frame No.12517)		44-80391				
G-LOCO	Robinson R44 Raven II	11010	G-TEMM	22. 2.06	TJS Hire Co (Humberside) Ltd t/a TJS Self Drive		
						(Scunthorpe)	23. 1.08E
G-LOFB	Lockheed L188CF Electra	1131	N667F	28. 6.94	Atlantic Airlines Ltd	Coventry	8. 2.07T
			N133AJ, CF-IJW, N131US				
G-LOFC	Lockheed L188CF Electra	1100	N665F	15. 6.95	Atlantic Airlines Ltd	Coventry	10. 7.08E
			N289AC, N6123A				
G-LOFD	Lockheed L188CF Electra	1143	LN-FOG	12. 6.97	Atlantic Airlines Ltd	Coventry	15. 6.08E
			LN-MOD, N9745C, (CF-IJC), N9745C				
G-LOFE	Lockheed L188CF Electra	1144	EI-CET	5. 1.99	Atlantic Airlines Ltd	Coventry	19. 3.08E
			(G-FIGF), N668Q, N668F, N24AF, N138US *(Atlantic Airlines titles)*				
G-LOFF	Lockheed L188C Electra	1128	LN-FON (2)	21. 6.00	Atlantic Airlines Ltd	Coventry	
			N342HA, N417MA, OB-R-1138, N417MA, CF-ZST, N7142C				
					(DHL titles and Fred Olsen c/s on tail - stripped - open storage 6.06)		
G-LOFM	Maule MX-7-180A Super Rocket	20027C	N31110	19. 7.95	Air Atlantique Ltd	Coventry	15. 2.08E
G-LOFT	Cessna 500 Citation I	500-0331	LN-NAT	12. 1.95	Fox Tango (Jersey) Ltd	Sleap	25. 3.07E
			EC-FUM, EC-500, LN-NAT, N40AC, N96RE, N86RE, N331CC, (N5331J) *(Noted 10.07)*				
G-LOGO	Hughes 369E	0454E	G-BWLC	4.10.96	Eastern Atlantic Helicopters Ltd	Shoreham	25. 7.05T
	(Hughes 500)		HB-XIJ, SE-JAM		*(Crashed Kensworth, Bedford 2.12.03 and badly damaged)*		
G-LOIS	Avtech Jabiru UL	0144	EI-JAK	14. 9.00	D W Newman	Sackville Lodge, Riseley	29. 5.08P
	(Built S Walshe - pr.no.PFA 274A-0144 (sic): originally built as Irish SAAC pr.no.SAAC-68)						
G-LOKI	Ultramagic M-77C Balloon (Hot Air)	77/260		12. 4.05	L J M Muir and G D Hallett	Montgomery	21. 2.08E
G-LOKM	PZL-110 Koliber 160A	04990080	G-BYSH	26.11.99	PZL International Aviation Marketing and Sales PLC		
			SP-WGH			Earls Colne	16. 1.07T
G-LOKO	Cameron Locomotive 105 SS Balloon (Hot Air)		HB-QBN	19. 9.95	Warsteiner Brauerei Haus Cramer KG		
		3680	G-LOKO			Warstein, Germany	13. 8.08A
G-LOLA	Beech A36 Bonanza	E-2116	N67501	18. 2.02	J H and L F Strutt	Earls Colne	20. 4.08E
G-LOLL	Cameron V-77 Balloon (Hot Air)	2964		4.12.92	R K McCulloch *(New owner 4.06)*	High Wycombe	13. 8.05A
G-LONE	Bell 206L-1 LongRanger	45729	G-CDAJ	5.10.04	Sky Charter UK Ltd	Manston	27.10.07E
			N20AP, N3174W				
G-LOOP	Pitts S-1C	850	5Y-AOX	11. 5.78	D Shutter	Leicester	12. 7.08P
	(Built D Mallinson) (Lycoming O-320) (Marked as "S-1D")						
G-LORC	Piper PA-28-161 Cadet	2841339	D-ESTC	12. 1.99	Sherburn Aero Club Ltd	Sherburn-in-Elmet	12. 4.08E
			N9184W, (N620FT), (SE-KMP)				
G-LORD	Piper PA-34-200T Seneca II	34-7970347	N2908W	6. 5.88	G-LORD Flying Club Ltd	Lee-on-Solent	8. 5.08E
G-LORN	Mudry CAP.10B	282		4. 3.99	J D Gailey	Old Sarum	25. 5.08E
G-LORR	Piper PA-28-181 Archer III	2843037	N9268X	19. 4.96	VA Technology Ltd	Sleap	5. 6.08E
			G-LORR				
G-LORT	Avid Speed Wing Mk.4	1124		12. 2.92	P Mitchell	Long Marston	9. 4.07P
	(Built G E Laucht - pr.no.PFA 189-12219)						
G-LORY	Thunder Ax4-31Z Balloon (Hot Air)	171		28.11.78	A J Moore *"Glory" (Inflated 4.06)*	Northwood	
G-LOSI	Cameron Z-105 Balloon (Hot Air)	10011		15. 1.01	Aeropubblicita Vicenza SRL Caldogno, Veneto, Italy		17. 3.08A
G-LOSM	Gloster Meteor NF.11	S4/U/2342	WM167	8. 6.84	Aviation Heritage Ltd	Coventry	6. 11.08P
	(Built Armstrong-Whitworth Aircraft)				*(As "WM167" in RAF 151 Sqdn c/s: also carries "G-LOSM")*		
G-LOST	Denney Kitfox Model 3	PFA 172-12055		10. 8.95	J H S Booth	Glenrothes	6. 8.01P
	(Built R Baily and H Balfour-Paul) (Rotax 618)				*(Noted 10.07)*		
G-LOSY	Evektor EV-97 Eurostar	PFA 315-14161		22.12.03	J A Shufflebotham	(Stretton)	16. 3.08P
	(Built J A Shufflebotham)						
G-LOTA	Robinson R44 Raven	1232		8. 7.02	Rahtol Ltd	Redhill	10. 7.08E
G-LOTI	Bleriot Type XI replica	PFA 088-10410		21.12.78	Brooklands Museum Trust Ltd	Brooklands	19. 7.82P
	(Built M L Beach) (ABC Scorpion II)				*(On display 2007)*		
G-LOVB	British Aerospace Jetstream Series 3102	622	VH-HSW	12. 8.99	Highland Airways Ltd	Inverness	1. 2.08E
			G-31-622, G-BLCB, G-31-622				
G-LOWS	Sky 77-24 Balloon (Hot Air)	025		19. 3.96	A J Byrne and D J Bellinger *"Dawn Treader"*	Thatcham	15. 4.08
G-LOYA	Reims FR172J Rocket	FR17200352	G-BLVT	4. 8.89	K A D Mitchell	Wellesbourne Mountford	11. 7.08E
			PH-EDI/D-EEDI				
G-LOYD	Aérospatiale SA.341G Gazelle 1	1289	G-SFTC	19. 6.85	I G Lloyd	Ripley, Derbyshire	4. 7.08E
			N47298 *(Rebuilt 1990 with major components of N6957 [c/n 1060])*				
G-LOYN	Robinson R44 Raven II	11599		7. 2.07	Mandarin Aviation Ltd	Redhill	27. 2.08E
G-LPAD	Lindstrand LBL 105A Balloon (Hot Air)	632		5. 8.99	Line Packaging and Display Ltd	Gillingham, Kent	9. 6.08A
G-LROY	Piper PA-28RT-201T Turbo Arrow IV		G-BNTS	23. 3.07	R L West	Norwich	11. 2.08E
		28R-8131024	N8296R				
G-LRBW	Lindstrand HS-110 Airship (Hot Air)	253		2. 8.95	Croymark Ltd	Ottawa, Canada	30. 3.05A
G-LREE	Grob G 109B	6252	D-KEKO	7. 8.07	J T Morgan tr G-LREE Group	Denham	20. 9.08E
G-LRGE	Lindstrand LBL 330A Balloon (Hot Air)	929		31. 7.03	Adventure Balloons Ltd Hartley Wintney, Hook		7 10.08T
					(www.Adventure Balloons.co.uk titles)		
G-LRSN	Robinson R44 Raven	0984		28. 3.01	Kidmane Developments Ltd	Bellaghy	8. 5.08E

G-LSAA	Boeing 757-236	24122	N241CV	17. 5.05	Dart Group PLC	Newcastle	7.10.07E
	TC-FLB, TC-ANM, EC-FFK, EC-744, G-BNSF, (D-AOEB), G-BNSF, EC-ELS, EC-203, G-BNSF						
				"jet 2 Tenerife" (Operated.Jet2.com)			
G-LSAB	Boeing 757-27B	24136	N136CV	17. 5.05	Dart Group PLC	Leeds-Bradford	2. 2.08E
	TC-FLC, TC-ANN, PH-AHF, 4X-EBF, G-OAHF, OY-SHF, PH-AHF						
				"jet 2 Menorca"(Operated.Jet2.com)			
G-LSAC	Boeing 757-23A	25488	N254DG	14. 3.06	Dart Group PLC	Newcastle	22. 5.08E
	G-LSAC, N310FV, C-GTSE, N1792B "jet 2 Lanzarote" (Operated.Jet2.com)						
G-LSAD	Boeing 757-236	24397	SX-BLW	16. 6.06	Dart Group PLC	Leeds-Bradford	1. 8.08E
	G-OOOS, G-BRJD, EC-ESC, EC-349, G-BRJD (Operated.Jet2.com)						
G-LSAE	Boeing 757-27B	24135	OM-SNA	28. 6.06	Dart Group PLC	Leeds-Bradford	11. 9.08E
	N335FV, PH-AHE, OY-SHE, PH-AHE, OY-SHE, PH-AHE "jet2 Murcia" (Operated.Jet2.com)						
G-LSAG	Boeing 757-21B	24014	B-2801	23.11.06	Dart Group PLC	Leeds-Bradford	22. 3.08E
			N1792B		(Operated.Jet2.com)		
G-LSAH	Boeing 757-21B	24015	B-2802	23.11.06	Dart Group PLC	Leeds-Bradford	19. 3.08E
			N5573B		(Operated.Jet2.com)		
G-LSAI	Boeing 757-21B	24016	B-2803	23.11.06	Dart Group PLC	Leeds-Bradford	22. 4.08E
			N5573K		(Operated.Jet2.com)		
G-LSCM	Cessna 172S Skyhawk	172S8445	N612TG	7. 6.04	G A Luscombe	Exeter	4. 7.08T
			N165ME				
G-LSCP	Rolladen-Schneider LS6-18W	6236	BGA 4814-JVK	31. 1.08	L G Blows and M F Collins	Parham Park	4. 8.08
			D-6417				
G-LSED	Rolladen-Schneider LS6-c	6260	BGA 3913-HFQ	17.10.07	G McKnight tr McKnight/Baker Syndicate		
			(BGA 3908-HFK)			RAF Cranwell	28. 9.08
G-LSFB	Rolladen-Schneider LS7-WI	7009	BGA 5042-KEW	31. 1.08	P Thomson	Feshiebridge	28. 5.08
			F-CGYA, F-WGYA, D-1272				
G-LSFI	Gulfstream AA-5A Cheetah	AA5A-0770	G-BGSK	13. 2.84	A D Prothero tr G-LSFI Group		
						North Moor, Scunthorpe	9. 7.06T
G-LSFR	Rolladen-Schneider LS4	4260	BGA 2908-ESE	30.10.07	A Mulder and M Platt	Nympsfield	16. 2.08
G-LSFT	Piper PA-28-161 Warrior II	28-8516008	G-BXTX	10.11.99	Biggin Hill Flying Club Ltd	Biggin Hill	1. 4.08E
			PH-LEH, N130AV, N43682				
G-LSGB	Rolladen-Schneider LS 6b	6184	BGA 3361-FMC	4.12.07	T J Brenton	Wormingford	30. 3.08
G-LSGM	Rolladen-Schneider LS3-17	3346	BGA 5144-KJU	24. 1.06	M W Bewley	Sutton Bank	8. 2.08
			D-6760, OO-ZLD		"GM"		
G-LSHI	Colt 77A Balloon (Hot Air)	1264		20. 7.88	J H Dobson	Streatley, Berkshire	12. 7.95A
					(Lambert Smith and Hampton titles)		
G-LSIF	Rolladen-Schneider LS1-f	383	BGA 4738-JSF	24. 1.08	R C Godden	Wormingford	1. 7.08
			LN-GGE, SE-TOU				
G-LSIV	Rolladen-Schneider LS4	4189	BGA 2806	28. 9.07	D M Bland tr 264 Syndicate	Nympsfield	7. 4.08
G-LSJE	Reality Escapade Jabiru(1)	UK ESC 0006		19. 2.08	L S J Webb	RNAS Culdrose	
	(Built L S J Webb)						
G-LSKV	Rolladen-Schneider LS8-18	8095	BGA 4288-HXN	16.11.07	D Pitman	Bicester	14.12.07
G-LSKY	P&M Pegasus Quik	8119		12. 8.05	G R Hall and P R Brooker		
						Harringe Court, Sellindge, Folkestone	4. 4.08P
G-LSLS	Rolladen-Schneider LS4	4191	BGA 2808-ENA	22.10.07	A M Sanders tr 288 Syndicate	Long Mynd	30. 3.08
G-LSMI	Reims Cessna F152 II	F15201710		1. 2.80	A S Bamrah t/a Falcon Flying Services	Southend	7. 9.08E
					(Operated. Willowair Flying Club)		
G-LSPA	Agusta-Bell 206B-2 JetRanger II	8530	G-INVU	12. 7.06	Heliflight (UK) Ltd	Gloucestershire	12. 6.08E
			G-XXII, G-GGCC, G-BEHG				
G-LSPH	Van's RV-8	PFA 303-13733		3. 9.07	R S Partridge-Hicks		
						Little Haugh Hall, Norton, Bury St. Edmunds	24.10.08P
G-LSTR	Stoddard-Hamilton GlaStar	xxxx		20. 4.98	M G Dovey	Popham	5.11.07P
	(Built R Y Kendal- pr.no.PFA 295-13093) (Tail-wheel u/c)				(New owner 1.08)		
G-LSVI	Rolladen-Schneider LS6-C18	6266	BGA 3910-HFM	12.10.07	F J Sheppard	Wycombe Air Park	1. 7.07
G-LSWL	Robinson R22 Beta	3671	I-JESS	28.11.05	GLS Wales Ltd	Swansea	11.12.07P
G-LTFB	Piper PA-28-140 Cherokee	28-23343	G-AVLU	28. 2.97	C W J Cunningham	Popham	2. 7.08E
			N11C				
G-LTFC	Piper PA-28-140 Cherokee B	28-26259	G-AXTI	8. 6.94	Avon Aviation Ltd t/a The Bristol and Wessex Aeroplane Club		
			N11C			Bristol	4. 2.08E
G-LTMM	Aviat A-1B Husky	2436	N115AA	28. 2.08	Aviat Aircraft (UK) Ltd		
						Lower Grounds Farm, Sherlowe	
G-LTRF	Fournier RF7	7001	G-EHAP	10.12.97	Skyview Systems Ltd	Lavenham	13. 5.08P
			(G-BGVC), D-EHAP, F-WPXV				
G-LTSB	Cameron LTSB 90 SS Balloon (Hot Air)	4483		15. 1.99	ABC Flights Ltd	Clapton in Gordano, Bristol	1. 6.06A
					(Lloyds TSB titles)		
G-LUBE	Cameron N-77 Balloon (Hot Air)	1127		25. 2.85	A C Rawson (Cadbury titles)	Stafford	27. 7.05A
G-LUBY	Avtech Jabiru J430	0xxx		19.12.06	K Luby	(Kearsley, Bolton)	
	(Built K Luby - pr.no.PFA 336-14605)						
G-LUCK	Reims Cessna F150M	F15001238	PH-LEO	13.12.79	Cranfield Aviation Training School Ltd	Cranfield	22. 6.08E
			D-EHRA				
G-LUDM	Van's RV-8	PFA 303-14521		22. 2.06	D F Sargant	Ludham	
	(Built D F Sargant)						
G-LUED	Aero Designs Pulsar	PFA 202-12122		9. 3.92	J C Anderson	Sturgate	14. 3.08P
	(Built J C Anderson)						
G-LUKE	Rutan LongEz	PFA 74A-10978		4. 7.84	R A Pearson	(Knowle, Solihull)	14. 8.03P
	(Built S G Busby) (Lycoming O-235)				(New owner 7.04)		
G-LUKI	Robinson R44 Clipper	0818	G-BZLN	20.10.00	A and D Douglas	(Winchenford, Worcester)	10. 1.08E
G-LUKY	Robinson R44 Astro	0357		10. 7.97	M A Hack t/a Hack Aviation	Gloucestershire	12. 9.08E
G-LULA	Cameron C-90 Balloon (Hot Air)	10833		8. 6.06	S D Davis	Netherbury, Bridport	21. 6.08E
G-LULU	Grob G109	6137		6. 9.82	A P Bowden	Enstone	7. 6.08E
G-LULV	Diamond DA.42 Twin Star	42.313		29. 1.08	Diamond Aircraft UK Ltd	Gamston	
G-LUMB	Best Off Sky Ranger 912(2)	SKRxxxx435		28. 6.05	S Allcock Middle Bank Top Farm, Lumb, Rossendale		
	(Built S Allcock - pr.no.BMAA/HB/378)				(Noted 2007)		
G-LUNA	Piper PA-32RT-300T Turbo Lance II	32R-7987108	N2246Q	19. 3.79	Lance Aviation Ltd	Bagby	31.10.07E

Reg	Type	C/n	Prev ids / Date	Owner / Operator	Base	Expiry
G-LUND	Cessna 340 II	340-0305	G-LAST 27. 3.03	Prospect Developments (Northern) Ltd	Blackpool	17. 9.06T
			G-UNDY, G-BBNR, N69452	*(Noted 10.07)*		
G-LUNE	Mainair Sports Pegasus Quik	8017	18.2.04	D Muir	St Michaels	31. 5.08P
G-LUNG	Rotorsport MT-03	RSUK/MT-03/018	24. 9.07	R H Sawyer and P Krysiak	Kirkbride	3.10.08P
G-LUNY	Pitts S-1S	PFA 009-14757	9. 1.08	R P Millinship tr G-LUNY Group	Leicester	
	(Built C Tector)					
G-LUSC	Luscombe 8E Silvaire Deluxe	3975	D-EFYR 1.11.84	M Fowler	Bruntingthorpe	
			LN-PAT, (NC1248K)	*(On rebuild 9.97)*		
G-LUSH	Piper PA-28-151 Cherokee Warrior	28-7515201	OH-PAB 25. 7.01	S Papi	Southend	4.11.07E
				(Operated Willowair Flying Club) (Noted 1.08)		
G-LUSI	Luscombe 8F Silvaire	6770	N838B 3.10.89	J P Hunt and D M Robinson		
	(Built Temco Engineering) (Continental C85)			Bourne Park, Hurstbourne Tarrant	22. 7.08P	
G-LUST	Luscombe 8E Silvaire Deluxe	6492	N2065B 9.11.89	M Griffiths	Chilbolton	14. 7.05P
	(Continental C85)		NC2065B	*(Noted 11.07)*		
G-LUVY	Aérospatiale AS.355F1 Ecureuil 2	5134	N358E 25. 2.00	DNH Helicopters Ltd	Biggin Hill	31. 8.07T
			ZS-HUA, (G-BPDP), D-HOCH, N358E, N5792M			
G-LUXE	British Aerospace BAe 146 Series 301	E3001	G-5-300 9. 4.87	BAE Systems (Operations) Ltd	Cranfield	5. 5.10S
			G-SSSH, (G-BIAD)	*(Operated Directflight for FAAM [Atmospheric Research])*		
G-LUXY	Cessna 551 Citation II/SP	551-0421	3A-MRB 5.12.06	Mitre Aviation Ltd	Biggin Hill	17.12.07E
			D-IAWA, N550RD, OE-GES, SE-DEF, OO-RJE, (N421CJ), N1217V, (N64735)			
G-LVBF	Lindstrand LBL 330A Balloon (Hot Air)	936	30. 1.04	Airxcite Ltd t/a Virgin Balloon Flights	Wembley	5. 2.06E
G-LVES	Cessna 182S Skylane	18280741	G-ELIE 19. 8.02	R W and A M Glaves	East Midlands	2.10.07T
			N23754			
G-LVLV	Bombardier CL-600-2B16	5372	N314FX 27. 4.04	Gama Aviation Ltd	Farnborough	27. 4.08E
	(CL-604 Challenger)		(N413LV), N314FX, C-GLWR			
G-LVPL	AirBorne XT912-B-Streak III-B	XT912-035	21.12.04	C D Connor	Mill Farm, Shifnal	23. 3.08P
	(Line number "XT912-33" also quoted) (Wing s/n S3-0016)					
G-LWAY	Robinson R44 Raven	1244	N71822 22. 8.02	Glenkerrin Aviation Ltd (Maynooth, County Kildare)		29. 9.07E
				(Operated Lantway Properties Ltd)		
G-LWDC	Canadair CL600-2A12	3031	N54JC 28. 1.08	ISM Aviation Services Ltd	Humberside	
	(CL-601 Challenger))					
G-LWNG	Aero Designs Pulsar	PFA 202-11866	G-OMKF 14.10.02	C Moffat	Eaglescott	15. 9.05P
	(Built M K Faro) (Tri-cycle u/c)			*(Noted 8.07)*		
G-LXRS	Bombardier BD-700-1A10 Global Express	9200	C-FEBX 19.12.06	Profred Partners LLP	(London EC4)	19.12.07E
G-LXUS	Alpi Pioneer 300	xxx	18. 7.05	W C Walters	Spanhoe	20. 3.08P
	(Built W C Walters - pr.no.PFA 330-14390)					
G-LYAK	IAV Bacau Yakovlev Yak-52	822113	LY-AGN 18.12.02	Lee 52 Ltd *(Poke Software titles)*	Lee-on-Solent	13. 2.08P
			Ukraine AF 140 *(yellow)*, DOSAAF 40 *(yellow)*			
G-LYDA	Hoffmann H 36 Dimona	3515	OE-9213 5. 4.94	J W Hagley tr G-LYDA Flying Group		
					Wycombe Air Park	9.10.07E
G-LYDB	Piper PA-31-350 Chieftain	31-8052107	TI-PAI 23. 1.06	Atlantic Bridge Aviation Ltd	Lydd	
			C-GPAI, C-GJLR, N170PA, HI-608CA, N3583C			
G-LYDC	Piper PA-31-350 Navajo Chieftain	31-7652110	N210PM 23. 1.06	Atlantic Bridge Aviation Ltd	Lydd	
			N60FS, N59882, (N79JA), N59882			
G-LYDF	Piper PA-31-350 Navajo Chieftain	31-7952031	N12CD 23. 1.06	Atlantic Bridge Aviation Ltd	Lydd	2.10.07E
			N27784			
G-LYFA	IAV Bacau Yakovlev Yak-52	822608	LY-AFA 31. 3.03	M I Boyd tr Fox Alpha Flying Group	Barton	22. 2.08P
			DOSAAF 110			
G-LYNC	Robinson R22 Beta II	3069	5. 5.00	Traffic Management Services Ltd	Gamston	29. 5.08E
G-LYND	Piper PA-25-235 Pawnee D	"25-6309"	SE-IXU 8. 9.93	York Gliding Centre Ltd	Rufforth	20.12.07E
	(Rebuild of G-ASFZ [25-2246] with new frame)		G-BSFZ, N6672Z			
G-LYNI	Evektor EV-97 Eurostar	PFA 315-14409	14. 9.05	G Evans	Arclid Green, Sandbach	1. 5.08P
	(Built G Evans)					
G-LYNK	CFM Shadow Series DD	303-DD	12.10.98	B J Palfreyman	Watnall	15. 4.08P
G-LYPG	Avtech Jabiru UL-450	0251	6. 7.99	A J Geary	Baxby Manor, Husthwaite	1. 8.07P
	(Built P G Gale - pr.no.PFA 274A-13466)			*(Noted 9.07)*		
G-LYTB	P&M Quik GT450	8204	25. 8.06	B Light	Tarn Farm, Cockerham	5. 9.08P
G-LYTE	Thunder Ax7-77 Balloon (Hot Air)	1113	29. 9.87	G M Bulmer "Crispen"	Hereford	19. 5.91A
G-LZZY	Piper PA-28RT-201T Turbo Arrow IV	28R-8031001	G-BMHZ 8. 5.01	A C Gradidge	Popham	28. 5.08E
			ZS-KII, N8096D			

G-MAAA - G-MZZZ

Reg	Type	C/n	Prev ids / Date	Owner / Operator	Base	Expiry
G-MAAN	Europa Aviation Europa XS	567	7. 1.03	P S Maan	(Desborough)	
	(Built P S Maan - pr.no.PFA 247-14009) (Tri-gear u/c)					
G-MAAV	Eurocopter AS.350B3 Ecureuil	4095	F-GVRR 18. 1.07	Silver Line Aviation LLP	Leeds-Bradford	13. 2.08E
G-MAAX	Bell 206L-1 LongRanger	45232	G-EYLE 14. 3.06	Sky Charter UK Ltd	Manston	26.11.07E
			G-OCRP, V4-AAB, G-OCRP, G-BWCU, N2758A, C-FPET, N2758A, JA9234			
G-MABE	Reims Cessna F150L	F15001119	G-BLJP 20. 6.97	I D McClelland	Popham	26. 4.08E
			N962L			
G-MACA	Robinson R22 Beta	3836	3. 5.05	Helicentre Blackpool Ltd	Blackpool	2. 6.08E
G-MACE	Hughes 369E	0015E	HA-MSA 3. 2.05	West Country Helicopters Ltd	(Chard)	16. 3.08E
	(Hughes 500)		SE-HNA			
G-MACH	SIAI-Marchetti SF.260	1-14	F-BUVY 29.10.80	Cheyne Motors Ltd	Old Sarum	7. 9.08E
			OO-AHR, OO-HAZ, (OO-RAB)			
G-MACK	Piper PA-28R-200 Cherokee Arrow II	28R-7635449	N5213F 18. 8.78	M D Hinge	Old Sarum	18.12.07E
G-MACL	Cirrus SR22	2710	N926SR 3.12.07	Maclaren Asset Management Ltd	Aberdeen	
G-MAFA	Reims Cessna F406 Caravan II	F406-0036	G-DFLT 2. 6.98	Directflight Ltd	Exeter	7. 6.08E
			F-WZDZ	*(Operated DEFRA)*		
G-MAFB	Reims Cessna F406 Caravan II	F406-0080	F-WWSR 27. 5.98	Directflight Ltd	Exeter	28. 9.07T
				(Operated DEFRA - Fisheries Patrol titles)		
G-MAFE	Dornier 228-202K	8009	G-OALF 21.12.92	Cobham Leasing Ltd	Bournemouth	4.11.07E
			G-MLDO, PH-SDO, D-IDON, D-CATI (2), SX-BHB, (PH-HAL), D-IDON *(Operated DEFRA)*			

Reg	Type	C/n	Prev id	Date	Owner/Operator	Location	Expiry
G-MAFF	Pilatus Britten-Norman BN-2T Islander	2119	G-BJED	20. 4.82	Cobham Leasing Ltd *(Operated DEFRA)*	Bournemouth	25. 9.08E
G-MAFI	Dornier 228-202K	8115	D-CAAE	16. 2.87	Cobham Leasing Ltd *(Operated DEFRA)*	Bournemouth	15. 7.08E
G-MAFT	Diamond DA.40D Star	D4.243	OE-VPU (D-EXON)	28. 2.07	Atlantic Flight Training Ltd	Coventry	15. 3.08E
G-MAGC	Cameron Grand Illusion SS Balloon (Hot Air)	4000		19. 1.95	Magical Adventures Ltd	West Bloomfield, Michigan, US	16. 8.03A
G-MAGG	Pitts S-1SE *(Built G C Masterton)*	PFA 009-10873		17. 3.83	O T Elmer	Horsford	9. 4.08P
G-MAGK	Schleicher ASW 20L	20387	BGA 2740-EKE	13.11.07	A G K Mackenzie	Burn	2. 5.08
G-MAGL	Sky 77-24 Balloon (Hot Air)	164		14. 7.99	RCM SARL *(Mag-Lite titles)*	Stuppicht, Luxemburg	28. 5.08
G-MAGZ	Robin DR.500-200i Président *(Officially regd as DR.400-500)*	35	F-GXGC	29. 7.05	T J Thomas	Sywell	2 .2.08E
G-MAIE	Piper PA-32R-301T Saratoga II TC	3257046	N47BK N41283	1.12.00	B R Sennett	Shoreham	9.11.07E
G-MAIK	Piper PA-34-220T Seneca IV	3448078	N73BS	17.11.97	Modern Air (UK) Ltd	Fowlmere	23. 3.08E
G-MAIN	Mainair Blade 912	1202-0699-7-W1005		16. 6.99	D P Pryke	Finmere	7. 8.07P
G-MAIR	Piper PA-34-200T Seneca II	34-7970140	N3029R	15. 2.89	A J Warren *(Operated Bristol Flying Centre)*	Bristol	2. 5.08T
G-MAJA	British Aerospace Jetstream Series 4102 *(Built Jetstream Aircraft Ltd)*	41032	G-4-032	22. 4.94	Air Kilroe Ltd t/a Eastern Airways	Humberside	24. 5.08E
G-MAJB	British Aerospace Jetstream Series 4102 *(Built Jetstream Aircraft Ltd)*	41018	G-BVKT N140MA, G-4-018	1. 6.94	Air Kilroe Ltd t/a Eastern Airways	Humberside	8. 6.08E
G-MAJC	British Aerospace Jetstream Series 4102	41005	G-LOGJ	12. 9.94	Air Kilroe Ltd t/a Eastern Airways	Humberside	20.12.07E
G-MAJD	British Aerospace Jetstream Series 4102	41006	G-WAWR	27. 3.95	Air Kilroe Ltd t/a Eastern Airways	Humberside	2. 3.08E
G-MAJE	British Aerospace Jetstream Series 4102	41007	G-LOGK	12. 9.94	Air Kilroe Ltd t/a Eastern Airways	Humberside	24. 2.08E
G-MAJF	British Aerospace Jetstream Series 4102	41008	G-WAWL	6. 2.95	Air Kilroe Ltd t/a Eastern Airways	Humberside	18. 3.08E
G-MAJG	British Aerospace Jetstream Series 4102	41009	G-LOGL	16. 8.94	Air Kilroe Ltd t/a Eastern Airways	Humberside	30. 3.08E
G-MAJH	British Aerospace Jetstream Series 4102 *(Built Jetstream Aircraft Ltd)*	41010	G-WAYR	4. 4.95	Air Kilroe Ltd t/a Eastern Airways	Humberside	13. 4.08E
G-MAJI	British Aerospace Jetstream Series 4102 *(Built Jetstream Aircraft Ltd)*	41011	G-WAND	20. 3.95	Air Kilroe Ltd t/a Eastern Airways	Humberside	27. 4.08E
G-MAJJ	British Aerospace Jetstream Series 4102 *(Built Jetstream Aircraft Ltd)*	41024	G-WAFT G-4-024	27. 2.95	Air Kilroe Ltd t/a Eastern Airways	Humberside	28.10.07E
G-MAJK	British Aerospace Jetstream Series 4102 *(Built Jetstream Aircraft Ltd)*	41070	G-4-070	27. 7.95	Air Kilroe Ltd t/a Eastern Airways	Humberside	2. 9.08E
G-MAJL	British Aerospace Jetstream Series 4102 *(Built Jetstream Aircraft Ltd)*	41087	G-4-087	1. 4.96	Eastern Airways (UK) Ltd *" "R J Mitchell"*	Humberside	16. 5.08E
G-MAJM	British Aerospace Jetstream Series 4102 *(Built Jetstream Aircraft Ltd)*	41096	G-4-096	23. 9.96	Air Kilroe Ltd t/a Eastern Airways	Humberside	29.10.07E
G-MAJN	British Aerospace Jetstream Series 4102 *(Built Jetstream Aircraft Ltd)*	41014	OY-SVS G-4-014	8. 9.04	Air Kilroe Ltd t/a Eastern Airways	Humberside	8. 9.08E
G-MAJP	British Aerospace Jetstream Series 4101 *(Built Jetstream Aircraft Ltd)*	41039	N550HK (N502TS), G-4-039	14. 9.05	Air Kilroe Ltd t/a Eastern Airways	Humberside	23. 3.08E
G-MAJR	de Havilland DHC-1 Chipmunk 22	C1/0699	WP805	25. 9.96	C Adams tr Chipmunk Shareholders *(As "WP805" in RAF c/s)*	Lee-on-Solent	12.11.09S
G-MAJS	Airbus A300B4-605R	604	F-WWAX	26. 4.91	Monarch Airlines Ltd	Luton	25. 4.08E
G-MAJT	British Aerospace Jetstream Series 4101 *(Built Jetstream Aircraft Ltd)*	41040	N551HK G-4-040	21. 9.05	Air Kilroe Ltd t/a Eastern Airways	Humberside	14. 2.08E
G-MAJU	British Aerospace Jetstream Series 4102 *(Built Jetstream Aircraft Ltd)*	41071	N558HK G-4-071	10. 4.06	Air Kilroe Ltd t/a Eastern Airways	Humberside	26. 6.08E
G-MAJV	British Aerospace Jetstream Series 4102 *(Built Jetstream Aircraft Ltd)*	41074	N557HK G-4-074	10. 4.06	Air Kilroe Ltd t/a Eastern Airways	Humberside	11. 5.08E
G-MAJW	British Aerospace Jetstream Series 4102 *(Built Jetstream Aircraft Ltd)*	41015	N303UE G-4-015	8. 6.06	Air Kilroe Ltd t/a Eastern Airways *(Noted 2.08)*	Humberside	
G-MAJX	British Aerospace Jetstream Series 4102	41098	N330UE G-4-098	8. 6.06	Eastern Airways (Europe) Ltd	Humberside	17. 4.08E
G-MAJY	British Aerospace Jetstream Series 4102	41099	N331UE G-4-099	8. 6.06	Eastern Airways (Europe) Ltd	Humberside	15.10.07E
G-MAJZ	British Aerospace Jetstream Series 4102	41100	N332UE G-4-100	8. 6.06	Eastern Airways (Europe) Ltd	Humberside	14. 1.08E
G-MAKI	Robinson R-44	1752		31. 8.07	Hoe Leasing Ltd	(Hatfield)	13. 9.08E
G-MALA	Piper PA-28-181 Archer II	28-8190055	G-BIIU N82748	6. 3.81	D C and M E Dowell t/a M and D Aviation	Kemble	28. 4.08E
G-MALC	Grumman AA-5 Traveler	AA5-0664	G-BCPM N6170A	19.11.79	B P Hogan	Turweston	7. 6.08E
G-MALS	Mooney M 20K Mooney 231	25-0573	N1061T	16. 8.84	M A Cummings	Old Buckenham	25. 4.08E
G-MALT	Colt Flying Hop SS Balloon (Hot Air)	1447		14. 4.89	P J Stapley *"Hoppie"*	London Colney, St Albans	11. 9.97A
G-MAMC	RotorWay Executive 90 *(Built J Carmichael) (RotorWay RI 162)*	5057		24. 5.94	J R Carmichael *(Damaged landing Cumbernauld 22.9.98)*	(Inverary)	19. 2.99P
G-MAMD	Beech B200 Super King Air	BB-1549	N1069S	16. 7.99	Forest Aviation Ltd	Gamston	16. 7.08E
G-MAMO	Cameron V-77 Balloon (Hot Air)	1616		17.11.87	The Marble Mosaic Company Ltd *"Osprey"*	Weston-super-Mare	27. 8.03A
G-MANH	British Aerospace ATP	2017	G-LOGC	16.11.94	Trident Aircraft Leasing Services (Jersey) Ltd *(Operated Atlantic Airlines))*	Coventry	22. 2.07E
G-MANN	Aérospatiale SA.341G Gazelle 1	1295	G-BKLW N4DQ, N4QQ, N444JJ, N47316, F-WKQH	14. 4.86	N E R Brunt	Panshanger	20. 6.08E
G-MANP	British Aerospace ATP	2023	ES-NBA (PH-MJP),G-MANP, OK-VFO, G-MANP, G-PEEL	28.10.94	Trident Aviation Leasing Services (Jersey) Ltd	Lidköping, Sweden	25.10.06
G-MANS	British Aerospace BAe 146 Series 200	E2088	G-CLHC G-MANS, G-CHSR, G-5-088	22. 5.00	BA Connect Ltd *(Stored 9.07)*	Exeter	25. 4.08E
G-MANW	Tri-R KIS *(Built M T Manwaring)*	PFA 239-12628		12. 9.96	M T Manwaring	(Weston Turville, Aylesbury)	

G-MANX	Clutton FRED Series II	PW.2		31. 5.78	S Styles	(Birmingham)	17. 8.82P
	(Built P Williamson - pr.no.PFA 029-10327) (Ardem 4C02)			(Crashed near Ronaldsway 30.10.81: on rebuild Wellesbourne Mountford 7.90)			
G-MAPL	Robinson R44 Raven	0929	G-BZVP	7. 6.02	Maria G Mazzocchi	(Milan, Lombardy, Italy)	21. 6.08E
G-MAPP	Cessna 402B	402B0583	D-INRH	16. 4.99	Blom Aerofilms Ltd	Cranfield	5.10.07E
			N1445G				
G-MAPR	Beech A36 Bonanza	E-2713	N55916	17. 9.92	Moderandum Ltd	Bournemouth	20. 5.08E
G-MARA	Airbus A321-231	0983	D-AVZB	31. 3.99	Monarch Airlines Ltd	Luton	30. 3.08E
G-MARE	Schweizer 269C	S-1320		12. 8.88	The Earl of Caledon	Caledon Castle, County Tyrone	16. 8.08E
	(Schweizer 300)						
G-MARO	Best Off Sky Ranger J2.2(2)	SKR 0305318		22.12.04	C P Whitford	Middle Pymore Farm, Bridport	3. 9.08P
	(Built E Daleki - pr.no.BMAA/HB/348)						
G-MARX	Van's RV-4	2394-1211	SE-XUU	16.11.04	M W Albery	Enstone	27. 6.08P
	(Built T L Berry)		N42BN				
G-MARZ	Thruster T 600N 450	1031-T600N-093		27. 1.04	S P Warburton	Sandown, Isle of Wight	12. 3.08E
G-MASC	SAN Jodel D 150A Mascaret	37	F-BLDZ	1. 2.91	K F and R.Richardson	Wellesbourne Mountford	5.11.07P
G-MASF	Piper PA-28-181 Cherokee Archer II		OY-EPT	24. 6.97	Mid-Anglia Flight Centre Ltd t/a Mid-Anglia School of Flying		
		28-7790191	LN-NAP			Cambridge	6. 9.08E
G-MASH	Westland-Bell 47G-4A	WA/725	G-AXKU	3.11.89	Kinetic Avionics Ltd	Elstree	12. 3.10
			G-17-10		(US Army c/s)		
G-MASI	P&M Quik GT450	8213		29. 8.06	D M Merritt-Holman	(Benicolet, Spain)	3. 9.08P
G-MASS	Cessna 152 II	15281605	G-BSHN	6. 3.95	MK Aero Support Ltd	Andrewsfield	28. 4.08E
			N65541				
G-MATE	Moravan Zlin Z-50LX	0068		26.10.90	S A W Becker	Goodwood	5 9.08E
G-MATF	Gulfstream Aerospace Gulfstream G-IV	1109	EC-IKP,	23.10.07	Gama Aviation Ltd	Farnborough	
			N101GA, V8-007, V8-SRI, V8-ALI, N1761D				
G-MATS	Colt GA-42 Gas Airship	738	JA1009	11. 6.87	P A Lindstrand	Oswestry	23. 5.90A
			G-MATS		(New owner 6.01)		
G-MATT	Robin R2160	97	G-BKRC	7. 5.85	V P O'Brien	(Durrow, County Laois)	22. 5.08E
			F-BZAC, F-WZAC				
G-MATX	Pilatus PC-12/45	682		20.12.05	Air Matrix Ltd	Lyon-Bron, France	22.12.07E
G-MATY	Robinson R22 Beta II	3686		28.10.04	MT Aviation Ltd	Cambridge	24.11.07E
G-MATZ	Piper PA-28-140 Cherokee Cruiser	28-7325200	G-BASI	11.12.90	R B Walker t/a Midland Air Training School		
			N11C			Coventry	20.12.07E
G-MAUK	Colt 77A Balloon (Hot Air)	901		16. 2.87	B Meeson "Mondial Assistance"	Walsall	4. 6.92A
G-MAUS	Europa Aviation Europa	030		28. 6.05	A P Ringrose	Dunsfold	23.10.08P
	(Built A P Ringrose - pr.no.PFA 247-12651)						
G-MAVI	Robinson R22 Beta	0960		7. 2.89	Northumbria Helicopters Ltd	Carlisle	26. 4.08E
G-MAXG	Pitts S-1S	PFA 009-13233		27. 4.01	Jenks Air Ltd	White Waltham	8. 4.08P
	(Built T P Jenkinson)				"Little Stinger"		
G-MAXI	Piper PA-34-200T Seneca II	34-7670150	N8658C	11. 2.81	Draycott Seneca Syndicate Ltd	Gloucestershire	2. 6.08E
G-MAXR	Ultramagic S-90 Balloon (Hot Air)	90/78		1. 8.05	C F Sanger-Davies	Eveshaml	2. 2.08E
G-MAXS	Mainair Sports Pegasus Quik	8105		16. 3.05	S P Maxwell	North Coates	25. 3.08P
G-MAXV	Van's RV-4	PFA 181-13266		20. 1.00	R S Partridge-Hicks	(Bury St Edmunds)	8.11.07P
	(Built T P Jenkinson) (Lycoming IO-360)						
G-MAYB	Robinson R44 Raven	1429		7.10.04	Highmark Aviation Ltd	(Scunthorpe)	31.10.07T
G-MAYE	Bell 407	53117	F-GLMI	27. 6.05	M Maye	Weston, Leixlip, County Kildare	18. 7.08E
			N14054				
G-MAYO	Piper PA-28-161 Cherokee Warrior II		G-BFBG	20. 2.81	Air Navigation and Trading Company Ltd	Blackpool	8. 7.08E
		28-7716278	N38848				
G-MAZA	Rotorsport UK MT-03	RSUK/MT-03-029		20. 2.08	M Manson and N Crownshaw		
						(Rishworth, Sowerby Bridge)	21. 2.09P
G-MBAA	Hiway Skytrike II/Excalibur	01		23. 4.81	M J Aubrey	Kington, Hereford	
	(Hiro Delta 22)				(Noted 2002)		
G-MBAB	Hovey Whing-Ding II	MA-59		26. 5.81	M J Aubrey	Kington, Hereford	1. 2.98P
	(Built R F Morton - pr.no.PFA 116-10706) (Konig SC340)				(Noted 2002)		
G-MBAW	Pterodactyl Ptraveller	017		14. 7.81	J C K Scardifield	(Lymington)	31. 8.86X
	(Cuyana 430R)						
G-MBBB	Skycraft Scout II	0388W		3. 8.81	A J and B.Chalkley	(Rhoshirwaun, Pwllheli)	
	(Pixie 173)						
G-MBBJ (2)	Hiway Demon	80-00029		15. 2.82	M J Aubrey	Kington, Hereford	X
	(C/n is engine no)				(New owner 11.07)		
G-MBBM	Eipper Quicksilver MX	10960		11. 9.81	J Brown	(Ulverscroft, Markfield)	X
	(Cuyana 430R)				(In storage)		
G-MBCJ	Mainair Tri-Flyer/Solar Wings Typhoon S	JRN-1		30. 9.81	R A Smith	(Harworth, Doncaster)	30. 4.98X
	(Wing c/n T881-225)			(May have replacement Sailwing c/n T382-390L)			
G-MBCK	Eipper Quicksilver MX	GWR-10962		30. 9.81	P Rowbotham	(Hathern, Loughborough)	X
	(Rotax 503)						
G-MBCL	Hiway Skytrike 160/Solar Wings Typhoon			30. 9.81	P J Callis	Halwell	X
		2332 & T1181-307			(New owner 4.04)		
G-MBCU	American Aerolights Eagle Amphibian	3181		5.10.81	J L May	(Drayton, Portsmouth)	9.10.07P
	(Rotax 377)						
G-MBCX	Hornet 250/Airwave Nimrod 165	H090 & 0090 LJH		12.10.81	M Maylor	(Manby, Louth)	31.12.87X
	(Built Airwave Gliders Ltd)						
G-MBDG	Eurowing Goldwing	E 20		19.10.81	B Fussell	(Llanelli)	14.12.94P
	(Konig SC 430)						
G-MBDM	Southdown Trike/Southdown Sigma	SST/001		26.10.81	A R Prentice	(Dartford)	X
	(Fuji-Robin EC-25-PS)						
G-MBET	Micro Engineering (Aviation) Mistral	MEA.103		10.11.81	B H Stephens	Old Sarum	27. 9.98P
	(Fuji-Robin EC-44-PM)				(Noted in trailer 2002)		
G-MBEU	Chargus T 250/Hiway Demon	T 250/06		10.11.81	R C Smith	(Clacton-on-Sea)	31. 5.86X
	(Fuji-Robin EC-25-PS)						
G-MBFK	Hiway Skytrike 250/Hiway Demon 175	LR17D		16.11.81	D W Stamp	(Kidderminster)	X
	(Fuji-Robin EC-25-PS)						
G-MBFO	Eipper Quicksilver MX	MLD-01		17.11.81	J C Larkin	(Flimby, Maryport)	20. 8.93P
	(Cuyuna 430R)						

G-MBFZ	Eurowing Goldwing	MSS-01		25.11.81	D G Palmer	Fetterangus	5. 9.00P
	(Fuji-Robin EC-34-PM)				*(Under active rebuild 2001)*		
G-MBGF	Twamley Trike/Birdman Cherokee	RWT-01		26.11.81	T B Woolley	(Narborough, Leicester)	
	(Built Birdman Enterprises Ltd)						
G-MBGS	Rotec Rally 2B	PCB-1		2.12.81	P C Bell	(Yalding, Maidstone)	
G-MBGX	Southdown Lightning DS	RBDB-1		7.12.81	T Knight	(Kingkerswell, Newton Abbot)	7. 3.92X
	(Sachs-Dolmar 340?) *(Believed now fitted with Ultralight Aviation Systems Storm Buggy Trike ex G-MBKD)*						
G-MBHE	American Aerolights Eagle 430B	4210		18.12.81	R J Osborne	Long Marston	12.10.96P
	(Cuyuna 430R)						
G-MBHK	Mainair Tri-Flyer 330/Flexiform Solo Striker			30.12.81	K T Vinning	(Stratford-upon-Avon)	11. 8.98P
	(Fuji-Robin EC-34-PM)	EB-1 & 036-241181					
	(Original Tri-Flyer 250 Trike c/n 036 replaced by Tri-Flyer 330 c/n 060-382 in 1982)						
G-MBHZ	Pterodactyl Ptraveller	TD-01		6. 1.82	J C K Scardifield	(Milford on Sea, Lymington)	28. 2.86X
	(Cuyuna 430R)						
G-MBIA	Hiway Skytrike/Flexiform Sealander	6172349/336		6. 1.82	I P Cook	(Royton, Oldham)	X
	(Fuji-Robin EC-34-PM)						
G-MBIO	American Aerolights Eagle 215B	E4007-Z		12. 1.82	S Montandon	(Whitbourne, Worcester)	X
					(New owner 5.06)		
G-MBIT	Hiway Skytrike/Demon	2501		18. 1.82	K S Hodgson	(Skutterskelfe, Yarm)	X
	(Fuji-Robin EC-25-PS)						
G-MBIY	Ultrasports Tri-Pacer/Southdown Lightning Phase II 330			19. 1.82	J W Burton	Tarn Farm, Cockerham	18. 4.99P
	(Fuji-Robin EC-34-PM) (Wing c/n L170-439)				*(Stored 2.03)*		
G-MBIZ	Mainair Tri-Flyer 250/Hiway Vulcan			20. 1.82	E F Clapham, W B S Dobi, S P Slade and D M A Templeman		
	(Fuji-Robin EC-25PS)	039-251181 & SD9V				(Bristol)	----
G-MBJD	American Aerolights Eagle 215B	4169		21. 1.82	R W F Boarder	(Tring)	X
	(Zenoah G25B1)						
G-MBJF	Hiway Skytrike II/Vulcan C	80-00099		22. 1.82	C H Bestwick	(Beeston, Nottingham)	X
	(Fuji-Robin EC-25-PS) *(C/n is engine serial no)*						
G-MBJG	Chargus T 250/Airwave Nimrod UP CMT165045			25. 1.82	D H George	Sandown, Isle of Wight	5. 7.05P
	(Fuji-Robin EC-25-PS)						
G-MBJK	American Aerolights Eagle	2742		16. 1.82	B W Olley	(Soham, Ely)	
	(Chrysler 820)				*(Stored 2000)*		
G-MBJL	Hornet 250/Airwave Nimrod	JSRM-01		26. 1.82	A G Lowe	(Dyce, Aberdeen)	20.10.96P
					(Noted at owner's home 4.02)		
G-MBJM	Striplin Lone Ranger	LR-81-00138		26. 1.82	C K Brown	(East Leake, Loughborough)	
	(Built C K Brown) (C/n 81-00138 is engine serial no)						
G-MBKY	American Aerolights Eagle 215B	BF-01		12. 2.82	M J Aubrey	Kington, Hereford	
	(Officially regd with c/n ZFE-15288 which is a corruption of engine type number [Zenoah G25B1 no.15288]) (Noted 2002)						
G-MBKZ	Hiway Skytrike/Super Scorpion	EC25P8-04		12. 2.82	S I Harding	(Mytchett, Camberley)	
	(Fuji-Robin EC-25-PS) *(C/n is corruption of engine type)*						
G-MBLU	Ultrasports Tri-Pacer/Southdown Lightning L195			26. 2.82	C R Franklin	(Landkey, Barnstaple)	X
	(Fuji-Robin EC-25-PS)	L195/191					
G-MBMG	Rotec Rally 2B	RJP-01		3. 3.82	J R Pyper	(Craigavon, County Armagh)	
G-MBMT	Mainair Tri-Flyer/Southdown Lightning 195	TRY-01		8. 3.82	A G Rodenburg and T Abro *(Noted 4.04)*		
	(Fuji-Robin EC-25-PS) *(Wing c/n L195-195?)*				Hillfoots Nurseries and Golf Driving Range, Tillicoultry, Stirling		X
G-MBOF	Pakes Jackdaw	LGP-01		26. 3.82	L G Pakes	(Ryde, Isle of Wight)	
	(Built L G Pakes)				*(Noted dismantled 6.06)*		
G-MBOH	Micro Engineering (Aviation) Mistral	008		29. 3.82	N A Bell	(Broxhill, Fordingbridge)	X
	(Fuji-Robin EC-44-PM)						
G-MBPB (2)	Pterodactyl Ptraveller	PEB-01		7. 4.82	N A Bell	(Broxhill, Fordingbridge)	
	(Built P E Bailey)				*(For rebuild 12.01)*		
G-MBPG	Mainair Tri-Flyer/Solar Wings Typhoon			13. 4.82	S D Thorpe	Otherton, Cannock	14. 6.01P
	(Fuji-Robin EC-25-PS)	189-1983 & T381-105					
	(Original Trike was c/n 067-582 and may have been used for G-MMGT)						
G-MBPJ	Centrair Moto-Delta G 11	001		14. 5.82	J B Jackson	(Mickle Trafford, Chester)	
	(Built Moto Delta)						
G-MBPU	Hiway Skytrike 250/Demon	DSS-01		21. 4.82	D Hines	(Hanklowe, Crewe)	22. 1.04P
G-MBPX	Eurowing Goldwing SP	EW-42		21. 4.82	A R Channon	(Sawston, Cambridge)	6.11.96P
	(Konig SC 430)						
G-MBPY	Ultrasports Tri-Pacer 330/Wasp Gryphon II RKP-01			21. 4.82	D Hawkes and C Poundes	(Milton Keynes)	12. 4.03P
	(Built Wasp) (Fuji-Robin EC-34-PM)						
G-MBRB	Electraflyer Eagle Mk.I	E 2229		9.12.81	R C Bott	(Abergynolwyn, Tywyn)	
G-MBRD	American Aerolights Eagle 215B	E 2635		20. 4.82	R J Osborne	(Cove, Tiverton)	31. 8.85X
	(Fuji-Robin EC-25-PS)						
G-MBRH	Ultraflight Mirage II	83-009 & RALH-01		20. 4.82	R W F Boarder	Field Farm, Oakley	8. 1.01P
G-MBRS	American Aerolights Eagle 215B	RWC.1		23. 4.82	L K Fowler	(Upper Sapey, Worcester)	X
	(Zenoah G25B1)				*(New owner 3.06)*		
G-MBST	Mainair Gemini/Southdown Puma Sprint 141-29383			10. 4.84	G J Bowen	(Llanelli)	25. 5.03P
	(Fuji-Robin EC-44-PM) *(Fitted with Trike from G-MJXA)*						
G-MBSX	Ultraflight Mirage II	240		14. 6.82	C J Draper t/a Medway Microlights		
					(New owner 12.05)	Stoke, Isle of Grain	30. 5.03P
G-MBTF	Mainair Gemini/Southdown Sprint	168-30683		26. 4.82	D E J McVicar	(Antrim, County Antrim)	26. 3.00P
	(Fuji-Robin EC-44-PM)						
G-MBTH	Whittaker MW4	T1081-262L	(G-MBPB (1))	6. 4.82	L Greenfield and M Whittaker tr The MW4 Flying Group		
	(Built M Whittaker - c/n 001) (Fuji-Robin EC-34-PM)					Otherton, Cannock	12. 7.04P
G-MBTJ	Ultrasports Tri-Pacer/Solar Wings Typhoon CSRS-01			2. 4.82	H A Comber	(Poole)	9. 8.06P
	(Fuji-Robin EC-25-PS) *(Wing c/n may be T1081-286L)*						
G-MBTW	Aerodyne Vector 600	1188		10. 5.82	W I Fuller	(Red Lodge, Bury St Edmunds)	X
	(Zenoah G25B1)						
G-MBUZ	Skycraft Scout II	0366		4. 5.82	A C Thorne *(Noted 11.06)*	(Bere Alston, Yelverton)	
G-MBWG	Huntair Pathfinder Mk.1	006		19. 5.82	T Mahmood	Maryculter	14. 7.99P
	(Fuji-Robin EC-34-PM)				*(Noted 1.05)*		
G-MBYI	Ultraflight Lazair IIIE	A464/001		4. 6.82	C M Mackinnon	Strathaven	25. 8.06P
	(Built AMF Microflight Ltd) (Rotax 185 x 2) *(Originally kit no A522 and amended during rebuild C 1982)*						

Reg	Type	C/n	Prev id	Date	Owner/Operator	Location	Status
G-MBYL	Huntair Pathfinder Mk.1	009		4. 6.82	S Porter *(New owner 9.06)*	(Eglinton, Londonderry)	17. 2.02P
G-MBYM	Eipper Quicksilver MX (Cuyuna 430R)	JW-01		4. 6.82	M P Harper and L L Perry	(Priory Farm, Tibenham)	21. 9.96P
G-MBZH	Eurowing Goldwing (Fuji-Robin EC-34-PM)	EW-50		14. 6.82	J Spavins *(Noted 8.05)*	Plaistows Farm, St Albans	31. 3.03P
G-MBZO	Mainair Tri-Flyer/Flexiform Medium Striker (Fuji-Robin EC-34-PM) GRH-01 & 021-101081			15. 6.82	A N Burrows	(Kirk Michael, Isle of Man)	15. 4.98P
G-MBZV	American Aerolights Eagle 215B	4227-Z		16. 6.82	M J Aubrey *(New owner 7.03)*	Kington, Hereford	X
G-MCAI	Robinson R44 Raven II	10423		9. 7.04	M C Allen	Denham	15. 8.08E
G-MCAP	Cameron C-80 Balloon (Hot Air)	10186		30. 7.02	L D Thurgar *(Mencap titles)*	Bristol	23. 9.08A
G-MCCF	Thruster T 600N Sprint	0100-T600N-048		25. 4.01	C C F Fuller	Craysmarsh Farm, Melksham	31. 5.08P
G-MCCG	Robinson R44 Raven	1758		5.10.07	Chris Ford Helicopters Ltd *(Noted 10.07)*	Costock	
G-MCCY	IAV Bacau Yakovlev Yak-52	9011112	LY-AQF UR-BBP, Ukraine AF 129, DOSAAF 129	11.11.04	D P McCoy	Weston, Leixlip, County Kildare	20.11.08P
G-MCDB	Vickers Supermarine 361 Spitfire LF.IX	CBAF IX 401	MA764	27. 2.08	M Collenette	(Sways, Lymington)	
G-MCEL	Cyclone Airsports Pegasus Quantum 15-912 7858			10.10.01	F Hodgson	Sywell	22.10.08P
G-MCJL	Cyclone Airsports Pegasus Quantum 15-912 7497			16. 3.99	Lincoln Enterprises Ltd	North Coates	14. 5.08P
G-MCLY	Cessna 172P Skyhawk	17275597	N61GA SE-IXY, N64643	14. 6.07	McAully Flying Group Ltd	Little Snoring	
G-MCMC	SOCATA TBM-700	261	N181PC	4. 4.06	Sogestao Administraca Gerencia SA	(Cascais, Portugal)	8. 6.08E
G-MCMS	Aero Designs Pulsar PFA 202-11982 (Built M C Manning)			3. 2.93	B R Hunter	Sturgate	10. 9.07P
G-MCOW	Lindstrand LBL 77A Balloon (Hot Air)	1142		13.12.06	S and S Villiers	Donaghadee	8. 6.08E
G-MCOX	Fuji FA.200-180AO Aero Subaru FA200-296		(G-BIMS)	29.12.81	West Surrey Engineering Ltd	Fairoaks	19. 6.08
G-MCOY	Flight Design CT2K (Assembled Pegasus Aviation - no c/n issued)	01-04-01-12		25. 7.01	D Young t/a Pegasus Flight Training (Cotswolds)	Kemble	1. 8.07P
G-MCUB	Reality Escapade UK,CKT.009? (Built A D Janaway - pr.no.PFA 345-14680)			27. 4.07	A D Janaway	Exeter	
G-MCXV	Colomban MC-15 Cri-Cri (Built J P Lorre)	371	F-PYVA	1. 3.00	H A Leek	(Scalford, Melton Mowbray)	25.10.08P
G-MDAC	Piper PA-28-181 Archer II	28-8290154	N8242T	6.11.87	S A Nicklen tr Alpha Charlie Flying Group	Henstridge	18. 6.08E
G-MDAY	Cessna 170B	26350	N2807C	2. 5.03	M Day Bourne Park, Hurstbourne Tarrant (Carries "N2807C" on tail)		29. 6.08
G-MDBC	Cyclone Airsports Pegasus Quantum 15-912 7814			4. 5.01	D B Caiden	East Fortune	26.10.08P
G-MDBD	Airbus A330-243	266	F-WWKG	24. 6.99	Thomas Cook Airlines Ltd t/a MyTravel Airways	Manchester	24. 6.08E
G-MDDT	Robinson R44 Raven II	11474		6.11.06	MT Helicopters Ltd	Chipping Norton	16.11.07E
G-MDGE	Robinson R22 Beta	1475	G-OGOG G-TILL	25. 6.04	Mandarin AviationCLtd	Redhill	16.10.07E
G-MDJE	Cessna 208 Caravan I (Amphibian)	20800336	N208FM XA-TSV, N5263S	13. 6.07	Loch Lomond Seaplanes Ltd Pacific Quay, Glasgow		12. 6.08E
G-MDJN	Beech 95-B55 Baron	TC-1574	G-SUZI G-BAXR	3. 8.04	D J Nock	Gloucestershire	30.11.07E
G-MDKD	Robinson R22 Beta	1247		18. 4.90	D Jones t/a Rotorair	(Johnstown, Carmarthen)	13. 3.08E
G-MDPI	Agusta A109A II	7393	G-PERI G-EXEK, G-SLNE, G-EEVS, G-OTSL	11. 8.04	Langfast Ltd	(Nicholashayne, Wellington)	3. 7.06T
G-MDPY	Robinson R44 Raven II	11582		2. 2.07	McDonnell Aviation Ltd	(Ashford, County Wicklow)	13 .2.08E
G-MEDE	Airbus A320-232	1194	F-WWDY	25. 4.00	British Midland Airways Ltd	London Heathrow	24. 4.08E
G-MEDF	Airbus A321-231	1690	D-AVZX	28. 2.02	British Midland Airways Ltd	London Heathrow	27. 2.08E
G-MEDG	Airbus A321-231	1711	D-AVZK	5. 4.02	British Midland Airways Ltd	London Heathrow	4. 4.08E
G-MEDH	Airbus A320-232	1922	F-WWBX	6. 3.03	British Midland Airways Ltd	London Heathrow	5. 3.08E
G-MEDJ	Airbus A321-231	2190	D-AVZD	8. 4.04	British Midland Airways Ltd	London Heathrow	7. 4.08E
G-MEDK	Airbus A320-232	2441	F-WWBQ	27. 5.05	British Midland Airways Ltd	London Heathrow	26. 5.08E
G-MEDL	Airbus A321-232	2653	D-AVZC	19. 1.06	British Midland Airways Ltd	London Heathrow	18. 1.08E
G-MEDM	Airbus A321-232	2799	D-AVZP	26. 6.06	British Midland Airways Ltd	London Heathrow	25. 6.08E
G-MEDS	Agusta A109E Power	11679		19. 9.06	Sloane Helicopters Ltd	Sywell	18. 9.08E
G-MEEE	Schleicher ASW 20 L	20312	BGA 2620-EEE	11. 9.07	T E Macfadyen	Nympsfield	28. 9.08
G-MEEK	Enstrom 480	5029	N485A	9. 5.06	Rocket Rentals Ltd	Gloucestershire	1. 6.08E
G-MEET	Learjet Model 40	45-2054	N50111	15. 9.06	TAG Aviation (UK) Ltd	Farnborough	19. 9.08E
G-MEGA	Piper PA-28R-201T Turbo Arrow III	28R-7803303	N999JG	13. 2.86	A W Bean	Sandtoft	17. 1.08E
G-MEGG	Europa Aviation Europa XS	358		14. 6.00	M E Mavers	Sleap	8. 6.08P
	(Built M E Mavers - pr.no.PFA 247-13202) (Monowheel u/c)						
G-MEGN	Beech B200 Super King Air	BB-1518	N65LA SU-ZBA, N3218V	30.11.06	Dragonfly Aviation Services LLP	Cardiff	2. 1.08E
G-MELS	Piper PA-28-181 Archer III	2843633	D-EASX N3139C	17. 7.07	Avicorp Ltd	(Ely, Cardiff)	16. 7.08E
G-MELT	Cessna F172H (Built Reims Aviation SA)	F172-0580	G-AWTI	23. 9.83	Falcon Aviation Ltd	Bourne Park, Hurstbourne Tarrant	10. 3.08E
G-MEME	Piper PA-28R-201 Arrow III	2837051	N9219N	17. 8.90	Henry J Clare Ltd	Bodmin	12. 3.08E
G-MENY	Agusta A109 Grand	22059		19.11.07	N Menary	(Portstewart)	
G-MEOW	CFM Streak Shadow (Built S D Hicks - pr.no.PFA 206-12025) (Rotax 582)	K 172		23. 4.93	G J Moor	Craysmarsh Farm, Melksham	12. 4.08P
G-MEPU	Rotorsport UK MT-03	RSUK/MT-03/021		20.10.06	M C Elliott	(Helmdon, Brackley)	19.12.08P
G-MERC	Colt 56A Balloon (Hot Air)	842		11. 6.86	A F and C.D Selby	Loughborough	25. 1.07A
G-MERE	Lindstrand LBL 77A Balloon (Hot Air)	092		7. 4.94	R D Baker	Goodnestone, Canterbury	
G-MERF	Grob G115A	8091	EI-CAB	24. 7.95	G Wylie	White Waltham	16. 6.08E
G-MERL	Piper PA-28RT-201 Arrow IV	28R-7918036	N2116N	27. 6.86	M Giles and W T Jenkins	Cardiff	21. 4.08E
G-METH	Cameron C-90 Balloon (Hot Air)	10841		21. 4.06	A and D Methley	Marshfield, Chippenham	16. 4.08E
G-MEUP	Cameron A-120 Balloon (Hot Air)	2117		5.10.89	Innovation Ballooning Ltd *(Sopwith Aviation Company titles)*	Bath	25. 8.08T
G-MFAC	Cessna F172H (Built Reims Aviation SA)	F172-0387	G-AVBZ	23. 8.01	Ravenair Aircraft Ltd	(Liverpool)	6. 7.08E

Reg	Type	C/n	Prev id	Date	Owner	Location	Expiry
G-MFEF	Reims FR172J Rocket	FR17200426	D-EGJQ	19.10.00	M and E N Ford	Butlers Gyhll, Southwater	26.11.07E
G-MFHI	Europa Aviation Europa	202		14.11.97	P Rees tr Hi Fliers	Rochester	25.12.07P
	(Built M F Howe - pr.no.PFA 247-12841) (Tri-cycle u/c)						
G-MFLI	Cameron V-90 Balloon (Hot Air)	2650		14. 8.91	J M Percival	Bourton-on-the-Wolds, Loughborough	1. 9.08A
	(Mouldform titles) "Mayfly"						
G-MFLJ	P&M Quik GT450	8303		29. 8.07	M F Jakeman	Deenethorpe	28. 8.08P
G-MFLY	Mainair Rapier	1359-1103-7-W1154		30. 3.04	J J Tierney	Chiltern Park, Wallingford	5.10.08P
G-MFMF	Bell 206B-3 JetRanger III	3569	G-BJNJ	4. 6.84	Western Power Distribution (South West) PLC Bristol		3.12.07T
G-MFMM	Scheibe SF25C Falke	4412	(G-MBMM)	20. 4.82	J E Selman	(Ardagh, County Limerick)	16. 7.08P
	(Limbach SL1700)		D-KAEU				
G-MGAA	BFC Challenger II	CH2-0297-1568		18. 8.97	J C Craddock and R J Speight		
	(Built G A Archer and J W E Pearson - pr.no.PFA 177A-13124) (Rotax 582)					(Freshwater, Isle of Wight)	21. 5.08P
G-MGAG	Aviasud Mistral 532GB	0587-045		20. 6.89	M Raj	Otherton, Cannock	27. 6.00P
	(Built Aviasud Engineering - pr.no.BMAA/HB/009)						
G-MGAN	Robinson R44 Astro	0588		10. 5.99	A Taylor	Whitley, Dewsbury	31. 7.08E
G-MGCA	Avtech Jabiru UL	0130		8. 5.98	K D Pearce	Oaklands Farm., Horsham	26. 3.04P
	(Built P A James - pr.no.PFA 274-13228 although type prefix should be "274A")				(New owner 5.06)		
G-MGCB	Solar Wings Pegasus XL-Q	7267		16.10.96	M G Gomez	Headon Farm, Retford	5. 9.05P
	(Trike c/n SW-TE-0344) and ex G-MWUT)						
G-MGCK	Whittaker MW6-S Fatboy Flyer	PFA 164-11262		30. 3.93	M W J Whittaker and L R Orriss		
	(Built M W J Whittaker: offically regd as MW6 Merlin)				(Noted 9.07)	Church Farm, Askern	
G-MGDL	Cyclone Airsports Pegasus Quantum 15	7400		17. 2.98	M J Buchanan	Coldharbour Farm, Willingham	7. 6.08P
	(Rotax 582)						
G-MGEC	Rans S-6-ESD-XL Coyote II	1096.1047		13.10.97	G Clipston	Bakersfield	30. 5.08P
	(Built E Carter - pr.no.PFA 204-13209) (Tri-cycle u/c)						
G-MGEF	Cyclone Airsports Pegasus Quantum 15-912	7261		18. 9.96	G D Castell	Longacre Farm, Sandy	19. 5.08P
G-MGFK	Cyclone Airsports Pegasus Quantum 15-912	7396		2. 2.98	F A A Kay	London Colney	1.10.07P
G-MGGG	Cyclone Airsports Pegasus Quantum 15-912	7377		3.11.97	R A Beauchamp	Shenstone Hall Farm, Shenstone	27. 7.08P
G-MGGT	CFM Streak Shadow SA-M	K 252		3. 6.94	D R Stansfield	Heckington	25.10.08P
	(Built J W V Edmonds - pr.no.PFA 206-12723) (Rotax 618)						
G-MGGV	Cyclone Airsports Pegasus Quantum 15-912	7484		12.10.98	S M Green	Cottage Farm, Norton Juxta	1. 8.08P
G-MGMC	Cyclone Airsports Pegasus Quantum 15-912	7430		28. 4.98	G J Slater	Clench Common	8. 7.08P
G-MGMM	Piper PA-18-150 Super Cub	18-7909189	D-EBRG	1. 6.04	M J Martin	Challock	10. 7.10S
			N9750N				
G-MGND	Rans S-6-ESD-XL Coyote II	1096.1048		27. 6.97	P Vallis	Calton Moor Farm, Ashbourne	10.10.07P
	(Built N N Ducker - pr.no.PFA 204-13152)						
G-MGOD	Medway Raven X	MRB110/106		6. 7.93	A Wherrett, N R Andrew and D J Millward	Doynton	1. 5.00P
					(Noted 1.05)		
G-MGOO	Murphy Renegade Spirit UK	301		14.11.89	P J Dale	(Chesham)	12. 7.08P
	(Built A R Max - pr.no.PFA 188-11580)						
G-MGPA	Comco Ikarus C42 FB100	0412-6635		25. 1.05	S Ashley	Dunkeswell	6. 2.08P
G-MGPD	Solar Wings Pegasus XL-R	6905		9. 1.95	H T Mounfield	Weston Zoyland	4. 5.07P
	(Rotax 462)				(Noted 5.07)		
G-MGPH	CFM Streak Shadow SA-M	286	G-RSPH	27.11.97	V C Readhead	(Saxmundham)	29. 7.00P
	(Built CFM Aircraft Ltd - pr.no.PFA 206-13166) (Rotax 582)				(New owner 3.05)		
G-MGPX	Kolb Twinstar Mk 3 Extra	PFA 205-14701		28. 1.08	S P Garton	(Althorpe, Scunthorpe)	
	(Built S P Garton)						
G-MGRH	Quad City Challenger II	CH2-1189-0482		20. 2.90	M R Brumby	(Gainsborough)	24. 7.06P
	(Built R T Hall) (Hirth 2705.R06)						
G-MGTG	Pegasus Quantum 15-912	7369A	G-MZIO	19.12.97	R B Milton	Plaistows Farm, St Albans	11.11.07P
	(Original c/n 7369 amended after rebuild 11.98)						
G-MGTR	Huntwing/Experience	xxxxx		24. 7.97	A C Ryall	(Cardiff)	
	(Built A C Rydall - pr.no.BMAA/HB/067) (Listed as "Huntwing Avon" in BMAA's records)						
G-MGTV	Thruster T 600N 450 Sprint	0052-T600N-070		14. 3.02	R Bingham and P A Durrans	Mullahead, Tandragee	8.10.08P
G-MGTW	CFM Shadow Series DD	287-DD		23. 1.98	G T Webster	Easter Poldar Farm, Thornhill	24. 3.08P
G-MGUN	Cyclone AX2000	7284		18.12.96	I Lonsdale	Tarn Farm, Cockerham	11. 6.08P
G-MGUY	CFM Shadow Series CD	078		23.11.87	F J Luckhurst and R G M Proost	(Old Sarum)	16. 8.91P
					(Crashed Home Farm, Pontisbury, Shrewsbury 20. 7.91)		
G-MGWH	Thruster T 300	9013-T300-507		8.12.92	J J Hill	Baxby Manor, Husthwaite	26. 9.08P
	(Built Tempest Aviation Ltd) (Rotax 582)						
G-MGWI	Robinson R44 Astro	0663	G-BZEF	4. 5.00	Ed Murray and Sons Ltd	(Bagby)	4. 6.08E
G-MGYB	Embraer EMB-135BJ Legacy	14500972	PT-SFZ	25.10.06	Haughey Air Ltd	Belfast City	24.10.07E
G-MHCB	Enstrom 280C Shark	1031		11.10.95	Springbank Aviation Ltd	Ronaldsway	10. 6.08E
G-MHCD	Enstrom 280C-UK Shark	1112	(SX-...)	12. 7.96	Dayrise EPE	(Thessaloniki, Greece)	6. 6.08E
			G-MHCD, G-SHGG, N627H				
G-MHCE	Enstrom F-28A	150	G-BBHD	22. 8.96	Wyke Commercial Services Ltd	Barton	8.11.07P
G-MHCF	Enstrom 280C-UK Shark	1149	G-GSML	19. 9.96	K, H K and D Collier t/a HKC Helicopter Services		11. 8.07T
			G-BNNV, SE-HIY			Barton	
G-MHCG	Enstrom 280C-UK Shark	1155	G-HAYN	7. 3.97	G L Pritchard	(Capel Coch, Llangefni)	20.10.07E
			G-BPOX, N51776				
G-MHCI	Enstrom 280C Shark	1152	N100WZ	20. 5.97	Charlie India Helicopters Ltd	Hawarden	26. 1.08E
G-MHCJ	Enstrom F-28C-UK	453	N892PT	30. 3.98	P E Toleman t/a Paradise Helicopters	Hawarden	14. 5.08E
G-MHCK	Enstrom 280FX Shark	2006	G-BXXB	5. 6.98	D Shakespeare	(Clent, Stourbridge)	15.11.07E
			ZK-HHN, JA7702				
G-MHCL	Enstrom 280C Shark	1144	N51740	30. 6.98	J A Newton (New owner 3.04)	(Knutsford)	24.11.01T
G-MHCM	Enstrom 280FX Shark	2052	G-IBWF	5. 4.06	Kingswood Bank LLP	Barton	19. 6.08E
			G-ZZWW, G-BSIE, HA-MIN, G-BSIE				
G-MHGS	Stoddard-Hamilton GlaStar	PFA 295-13473		30. 7.03	M Henderson	Cheyne Farm, Stonehaven	20. 2.08P
	(Built M Henderson) (Tri-cycle u/c)						
G-MHJK	Diamond DA.42 Twin Star	42.173	OE-VPY	4. 1.07	JMS Janitorial Supplies Ltd	(Reigate)	8. 2.08E
			OE-VPW				
G-MHMR	Pegasus Quantum 15-912	7969	D-MHMR	19.12.05	L Zivanovic	Halfpenny Green	3. 2.08P
G-MHRV	Van's RV-6A	PFA 181A-13422		28. 7.04	M R Harris	(Luton)	
	(Built M R Harris)						

Reg	Type	C/n	Prev id	Date	Owner	Location	Date
G-MICH	Robinson R22 Beta	0647	G-BNKY	3. 9.87	Tiger Helicopters Ltd	(Shobdon)	10.10.05T
	(Tail rotor struck ground Shobdon 10. 6.03, rolled onto side and substantially damaged)						
G-MICI	Cessna 182S Skylane	18280546	G-WARF N7089F	14. 6.01	S J Parrish t/a Steve Parrish Racing (Douglas, Isle of Man)		18. 8.08E
G-MICK	Reims Cessna F172N Skyhawk II	F17201592	PH-JRA PH-AXB	9. 1.80	S J Gronow tr G-MICK Flying Group	Blackpool	4. 9.08E
G-MICY	Everett Gyroplane Series 1 (Volkswagen 1835)	018	(G-BOVF)	26. 2.90	D M Hughes	(Bartley, Southampton)	2. 5.92P
G-MIDC	Airbus A321-231	835	D-AVZZ	12. 6.98	British Midland Airways Ltd	London Heathrow	11. 6.08E
G-MIDD	Piper PA-28-140 Cherokee Cruiser	28-7325444	G-BBDD N11C	20. 1.97	R B Walker t/a Midland Air Training School	Coventry	5. 6.08E
G-MIDG	Bushby-Long Midget Mustang (Built T Holt) (Lycoming O-320)	385	N11DE N567, N2TH	14. 3.90	C E Bellhouse	Headcorn	17. 6.08P
G-MIDL	Airbus A321-231	1174	D-AVZH	22. 2.00	British Midland Airways Ltd (Star Alliance titles)	London Heathrow	21. 2.08E
G-MIDM	Airbus A321-231	1207	D-AVZR	18. 4.00	British Midland Airways Ltd	London Heathrow	17. 4.08E
G-MIDO	Airbus A320-232	1987	F-WWIR	29. 4.03	British Midland Airways Ltd	London Heathrow	28. 4.08E
G-MIDP	Airbus A320-232	1732	F-WWBK	24. 5.02	British Midland Airways Ltd	London Heathrow	23. 5.08E
G-MIDR	Airbus A320-232	1697	F-WWIQ	22. 4.02	British Midland Airways Ltd	London Heathrow	21. 4.08E
G-MIDS	Airbus A320-232	1424	F-WWBO	21. 3.01	British Midland Airways Ltd	London Heathrow	20. 3.08E
G-MIDT	Airbus A320-232	1418	F-WWBI	14. 3.01	British Midland Airways Ltd	London Heathrow	13. 3.08E
G-MIDU	Airbus A320-232	1407	F-WWDC	27. 2.01	British Midland Airways Ltd	London Heathrow	26. 2.08E
G-MIDX	Airbus A320-232	1177	F-WWDP	21. 3.00	British Midland Airways Ltd (Star Alliance titles)	London Heathrow	20. 3.08E
G-MIDY	Airbus A320-232	1014	F-WWDQ	28. 6.99	British Midland Airways Ltd	London Heathrow	27. 6.08E
G-MIDZ	Airbus A320-232	934	F-WWII	19. 1.99	British Midland Airways Ltd	London Heathrow	18. 1.08E
G-MIFF	Robin DR.400-180 Régent	2076		31. 5.91	J C Harvey tr Westfield Flying Group	Spilstead Farm, Sedlescombe	22. 3.08E
G-MIGG	PZL-Mielec Lim-5	1C1211	G-BWUF Polish AF 1211	17. 1.03	D Miles (At Aviation Museum 2007 for restoration)	Bournemouth	
G-MIII	Extra EA.300/L	013	D-EXFI	5. 9.95	Angels High Ltd	Sywell	2. 8.08E
G-MIKE	Gyroflight Brookland Hornet (Volkswagen 1830)	MG.1		15. 5.78	M H J Goldring	(Newton Abbot)	25. 9.92P
G-MIKI	Rans S-6-ESA Coyote II (Built N R Beale - pr.no.PFA 204-13094) (Rotax 912-UL) (Tri-cycle u/c)	0996.1040		28. 2.97	S P Slade	The Chase, Wickwar	16. 6.07P
G-MILA	Reims Cessna F172N Skyhawk II	F17201686	D-EGHC (2) PH-AYJ	9. 6.98	P J Miller	Cuckoo Tye Farm, Long Melford	16. 9.07A
G-MILD	Scheibe SF25C Falke	44190	D-KDET	20.12.05	The Borders (Milfield) Gliding Club Ltd	Milfield	7. 2.08E
G-MILE	Cameron N-90 Balloon (Hot Air) (Originally regd as N-77: new envelope c/n 10548 fitted 2004)	2411		26. 9.90	Miles Air Ltd (Miles Architectural Ironmongery Ltd titles)	Bristol	28. 6.08A
G-MILI	Bell 206B-3 JetRanger III	2275	C-GGAR 5H-MPV	5.10.94	Westflor (AG) Ltd	Damyn's Hall, Upminster	15. 4.08E
G-MILN	Cessna 182Q Skylane	18265770	N735XQ	9. 7.99	Meon Hill Farms (Stockbridge) Ltd	Thruxton	27. 9.08E
G-MILY	Grumman American AA-5A Cheetah (C/n plate shows maufacturer as Gulfstream American)	AA5A-0672	G-BFXY	2. 9.96	Plane Talking Ltd	Cranfield	17.10.07E
G-MIMA	British Aerospace BAe 146 Series 200	E2079	G-CNMF G-5-079	3. 3.93	Trident Aviation Leasing Services (Jersey) Ltd	Bacau, Romania	25.11.07E
G-MIME	Europa Aviation Europa (Built N W Charles - pr.no.PFA 247-12850) (Monowheel u/c)	203		26. 9.97	N W Charles	Lydeway, Devizes	21. 9.08P
G-MIND	Cessna 404 Titan	404-0004		27. 4.93	Reconnaissance Ventures Ltd (Environment Agency titles + logo on tail)	Coventry	13. 2.08E
G-MINN	Lindstrand LBL 90A Balloon (Hot Air)	883	G-OHUB, SE-GMX, (N3932C)	30.10.02	S M and D Johnson	Bromley	11. 4.08A
G-MINS	Nicollier HN.700 Ménestrel II (Built R Fenion) (Volkswagen 1900)	PFA 217-12354		23.10.92	R Fenion	Kirkbride	16. 5.08P
G-MINT	Pitts S-1S (Built T G Sanderson)	PFA 009-10292		7. 2.83	T G Sanderson	Leicester	11.11.08P
G-MIOO	Miles M.100 Student 2	M1008	G-APLK G-MIOO, G-APLK, XS941, G-APLK, G-35-4	26.10.84	Aces High Ltd (On loan to Museum of Berkshire Aviation and on rebuild as "G-APLK" 2008)	(Woking)	6. 5.86P
G-MIRA	Avtech Jabiru SP-430 (Built B Luyckx - pr.no.PFA 274-13458)	0222	G-LUMA	29. 9.05	C P L Helsen	Balen-Keiheuvel, Belgium	7.12.07P
G-MISH	Cessna 182R Skylane II	18267888	G-RFAB G-BIXT, N6397H	16. 6.95	Graham Churchill Plant Ltd	Finmere	15. 5.08E
G-MISS	Taylor JT.2 Titch (Built A Brenen)	PFA 3234		18.12.78	D Beale (New owner 5.07	Witchford, Ely	
G-MITE	Raj Hamsa X'Air Falcon Jabiru(4) (Built J Jestico - pr.no.BMAA/HB/296)	830		3. 3.04	A Davis	Watnall	1. 5.08P
G-MITC	Robinson R44 Raven II	11884		6. 9.07	HJS Helicopters Ltd (New owner 1.08)	Lower Baads, Peterculter	
G-MITS	Cameron N-77 Balloon (Hot Air)	1115		20. 2.85	G B Davies (Also see G-CCPO) (New owner 8.06)	Thorney, Peterborough	25. 7.99A
G-MIWS	Cessna 310R II	310R1585	G-ODNP N19TP, N2DD, N1836E	1. 2.96	Wilcott Sport and Construction Ltd	Welshpool	15.11.07E
G-MJAE	American Aerolights Eagle	1021		12. 7.82	T B Woolley	(Narborough, Leicester)	
	(C/n not confirmed)						
G-MJAJ	Eurowing Goldwing (Fuji-Robin EC-44-PM)	EW-36		18. 6.82	M J Aubrey (New owner 11.06)	Kington, Hereford	6. 8.03P
G-MJAM	Eipper Quicksilver MX (Cuyuna 430)	JCL-01		18. 6.82	J C Larkin	(Flimby, Maryport)	20. 8.93P
G-MJAN	Hiway Skytrike I/Flexiform Hilander (Valmet)	RPFD-01 & 21U9		21. 6.82	G M Sutcliffe	(Bramhall, Stockport)	4. 3.92X
G-MJAV	Hiway Skytrike II/Demon 175 (Fuji-Robin 250)	817003		23. 6.82	J N J Roberts	(Frizlington)	X
G-MJAY	Eurowing Goldwing (Fuji-Robin EC-34-PM)	EW-58		23. 6.82	M Anthony	(Moreton, Alfreton)	X

G-MJAZ	Aerodyne Vector 627SR Ultravector	1251	PH-1J1	23. 6.82	B Fussell	Swansea	23. 9.93X
	(Konig SC430)		G-MJAZ		(Dismantled 8.06)		
	(Originally regd as Vector 610 but converted 4.88 when PH-1J1)						
G-MJBK	Swallow AeroPlane Swallow B	582007-2		18.11.83	M A Newbould	(Markington, Harrogate)	X
	(Rotax 447)						
G-MJBL	American Aerolights Eagle 215B	2892		25. 6.82	B W Olley	(Soham, Ely)	19. 9.04P
	(Chrysler 820)						
G-MJBS	Ultralight Aviation Systems Storm Buggy/Solar Wings			29. 6.82	G I Sargeant	(Bridgwater)	
			JL814S		(BMAA records show damaged 1982)		
G-MJBV	American Aerolights Eagle 215B	RSP-001		1. 7.82	A W Johnson	(Colwall, Malvern)	11. 8.96P
	(Fuji-Robin EC-25-PS)				(New owner 3.06)		
G-MJBZ	Huntair Pathfinder Mk.1	PK-17		2. 7.82	J C Rose	Eastbach Farm, Coleford	28.12.93P
	(Fuji-Robin EC-34-PM)				(Noted 9.03)		
G-MJCE	Ultrasports Puma/Southdown Sprint X	RGC-01		5. 7.82	L I Bateup	Clench Common	25. 8.01P
	(Fuji-Robin EC-44-PM) (Designation amended by BMAA C 1990)				(Noted 1.07)		
G-MJCU	Tarjani/Solar Wings Typhoon	SCG-01 & T982-610		7. 7.82	J K Ewing	Mapperton Farm, Newton Peverill	X
	(Fuji-Robin EC-25-PS)				(Trike only noted 7.06)		
G-MJDE	Huntair Pathfinder Mk.1	020		9. 7.82	P Rayson	(Holsworthy, Devon)	26.11.07P
	(Fuji-Robin EC-34-PM)						
G-MJDJ	Hiway Skytrike/Demon	VW17D		9. 7.82	A J Cowan	(Billingham)	
G-MJDP	Eurowing Goldwing	GW-001		12. 7.82	B L Keeping tr G-MJDP Flying Group		
	(Fuji-Robin EC-34-PM)				(New owner 1.03)	Davidstow Moor	15.11.92P
G-MJDR	Hiway Skytrike/Demon	PJB-01		14. 7.82	D R Redmile	(Markfield)	
G-MJEB	Southdown Puma Sprint	SN1231/0041		18. 4.85	R J Shelswell	(Budbrooke, Warwick)	1. 5.96P
	(Rotax 447)						
G-MJEE	Mainair Tri-Flyer 250/Solar Wings Typhoon			20. 7.82	M F Eddington	(Wincanton)	11.11.00P
	(Fuji-Robin EC-25-PS)	038-251181					
G-MJEO	American Aerolights Eagle 215B	4562		26. 7.82	A M Shaw	(Alsager, Stoke-on-Trent)	X
	(Zenoah G25B1)						
G-MJER	Ultrasports Tri-Pacer/Flexiform Solo Striker	DSD-01		23. 7.82	D S Simpson	(Graveley Hall Farm, Graveley)	26.12.00P
	(Rotax 447)						
G-MJFB	Ultrasports Tri-Pacer/Flexiform Solo Striker	AJK-01		27. 7.82	B Tetley	(Cowes)	28. 3.06P
	(Fuji-Robin EC-34-PM)						
G-MJFM	Huntair Pathfinder Mk.1	ML-0		12. 9.82	R Gillespie and S P Girr		
	(Fuji-Robin EC-34-PM)				(Killygordon and Balley Bofey, County Donegal)		23. 7.99P
G-MJFX	Skyhook TR1/Sabre	TR1/38		2. 8.82	M R Dean	(Hebden Bridge)	X
	(Hunting HS.525A)						
G-MJFZ	Hiway Skytrike/Demon	JAL-01		29. 7.82	A W Lowrie	(West Rainton, Houghton Le Spring)	X
					(New owner 4.04)		
G-MJHC	Ultrasports Tri-Pacer 330/Southdown Lightning Mk II			9. 8.82	E J Allen	(Fulbourn, Cambridge)	X
	(Fuji-Robin EC-34)	82-00044	(C/n is engine serial no)				
G-MJHR	Mainair Dual Tri-Flyer/Southdown Lightning			12. 8.82	B R Barnes	(Dundrey, Bristol)	
		GNS-01					
G-MJHV	Hiway Skytrike II/Demon	AG-17		13. 8.82	A G Griffiths	(Hyde Heath, Amersham)	
					(New owner 4.05)		
G-MJIA	Ultrasports Tri-Pacer/Flexiform Solo Striker	SE-007		13. 8.82	D G Ellis	Otherton, Cannock	20. 9.96P
	(Rotax 377)				(Noted 1.04)		
G-MJIC	Ultrasports Tri-Pacer/Flexiform Solo Striker	82-00043		13. 8.82	J Curran	(Newry, County Armagh)	15.10.94P
	(Fuji-Robin EC-34-PM)						
G-MJIF	Mainair Tri-Flyer/Flexiform Striker	E-1 EC25PS-04		16. 8.82	R J Payne	(Newmarket)	X
	(Fuji-Robin EC-34-PL) (C/n was original engine type)						
G-MJIR	Eipper Quicksilver MXII	1392		18. 8.82	H Feeney	(Stratford-upon-Avon)	26. 1.95P
	(Rotax 503)				(Stored 8.96)		
G-MJJA	Huntair Pathfinder Mk.1	031		23. 8.82	R D Bateman and J M Watkins		
					(Swimbridge, Barnstaple and Norton, Chichester)		25. 8.02P
G-MJJK	Eipper Quicksilver MXII	3397		25. 8.82	J McCullough	Newtownards	21. 8.06P
	(Rotax 503)				(New owner 8.07)		
G-MJKB	Striplin Skyranger	ST161		2. 9.82	A P Booth	(Winterbourne, Newbury)	
	(Officially quoted as c/n SRI-6-I)						
G-MJKF	Hiway Demon	WGR-01		2. 9.82	S D Hill	(Peppard Common, Henley-on-Thames)	
G-MJKO	Hiway Skytrike/Gold Marque Gyr 188	90030P		7. 9.82	M J Barry	(Nether Stowey, Bridgwater)	X
	(Fuji-Robin EC-25-PS) (Assembled from spares by Windsports)						
G-MJKX	Utralight Flight Phantom	PH.82005		14. 9.82	A P Love	Long Marston	19. 6.04P
	(Fuji-Robin EC-50)				(Noted 7.05)		
G-MJMD	Hiway Skytrike II/Demon 175	OE17D		27. 9.82	T A N Brierley	Baxby Manor, Husthwaite	26. 7.06P
	(Fuji-Robin EC-34-PM)				(Noted 9.07)		
G-MJMN	Mainair Tri-Flyer/Flexiform Striker	087-04882		29. 9.82	K Medd	(Manchester)	22. 7.05P
	(Fuji-Robin EC-34-PM)						
G-MJMR	Mainair Tri-Flyer 250/Solar Wings Typhoon			30. 9.82	J C S Jones	Emlyn's Field, Rhuallt	
		DR-01 & 048-5182			(Stored 12.97)		
G-MJMS	Hiway Skytrike II/Demon 175	EEW-01		30. 9.82	D E Peace	(Rawdon, Leeds)	
G-MJNM	American Aerolights Eagle 430B	702		25.11.82	A W Johnson	(Colwall, Malvern)	19. 9.93P
	(Cuyuna 430R)				(New owner 3.06)		
G-MJNO	American Aerolights Eagle Amphibian	703		24.11.82	R S Martin	(Gosport)	9. 7.06P
	(Rotax 447)						
G-MJNU	Skyhook TR1/Cutlass	TR1/17		19.10.82	R W Taylor	(Wortley, Sheffield)	
G-MJNY	Skyhook TR1/Sabre	TR1/35		3.11.82	P Ratcliffe	(Sheffield)	
G-MJOC	Huntair Pathfinder	048		25.10.82	A J Glynn	Gerpins Lane, Upminster	31. 7.99P
	(Fuji-Robin EC-34-PM)						
G-MJOE	Eurowing Goldwing	EW-55		29.10.82	R J Osborne	(Cove, Tiverton)	X
	(Rotax 377)						
G-MJPA	Rotec Rally 2B	AT-01		5. 1.83	R Boyd	(Armagh, County Armagh)	
G-MJPE	Mainair Tri-Flyer 330/Hiway Demon 175			10.11.82	E G Astin	(Whitby)	7. 8.96P
	(Fuji-Robin EC-34-PM)	117-151282 & OG17D					

G-MJPV	Eipper Quicksilver MX (Cuyuna 430R)	JBW-01		30.11.82	F W Ellis	Water Leisure Park, Skegness 17. 8.04P
G-MJRL	Eurowing Goldwing (Rotax 377)	EW-79 & SWA-5K		30.12.82	M Daniels	(Heanor) 15. 6.00P
G-MJRO	Eurowing Goldwing (Rotax 447)	EW-77 & SWA-04		31.12.82	T B Smith (New owner 8.07)	(Sompting, Lancing) 22. 9.99P
G-MJRR	Reece SkyRanger Series 1	JR-3		26. 4.82	J R Reece	(Liverpool)
G-MJRS	Eurowing Goldwing (Rotax 377)	EW-80 & SWA-6K		5. 1.83	R M Newlands (New owner 3.04)	(East Cowes) 12.10.01P
G-MJRU	MBA Tiger Cub 440	SO.86		6. 1.83	S R Davis	Kemble 31. 1.86X
G-MJSE	Skyrider Airsports Phantom (Fuji-Robin EC-40-PL)	SF-101		24. 1.83	K H A Negal (Noted 5.04)	Red House Farm, Preston Capes 20. 5.02P
G-MJSF	Skyrider Airsports Phantom (Rotax 462)	SF-105	SE-... G-MJSF	24. 1.83	B J Towers (On rebuild 5.00)	(Pershore)
G-MJSL	Dragon Light Aircraft Dragon Series 200 (Rotax 503)	0018		24. 2.83	M J Aubrey (New owner 10.05)	Kington, Hereford 22. 9.99P
G-MJSO	Hiway Skytrike III/Demon 175 (Hiro 22)	SA17D		1. 2.83	D C Read	(Bromsberrow Heath, Ledbury) X
G-MJSP	MBA Romain Super Tiger Cub Special 440	S0.54		7. 2.83	A R Sunley (On rebuild 6.06)	(Chelmsford) X
G-MJST	Pterodactyl Ptraveller	GCS-01		2.12.81	B W Olley (New owner 5.06)	(Soham, Ely) 7. 5.99P
G-MJSY	Eurowing Goldwing (Rotax 377)	EW-63		8. 2.83	A J Rex	(Wrexham) 5. 1.01P
G-MJSZ	Harker DH Wasp (Built D Harker) (Rotax 447)	HA.5		10. 2.83	J J Hill (On overhaul 2004)	Stokesley 24. 3.01P
G-MJTC	Ultrasports Tri-Pacer/Solar Wings Typhoon Medium	T1282-677		14. 2.83	V C Redhead	(Saxmundham)
G-MJTE	Skyrider Airsports Phantom (Fuji-Robin EC-44-PM)	SF-106		15. 2.83	L Zivanovic	Droitwich 27. 4.05P
G-MJTM	Southdown Aerostructure Pipistrelle P2B (KFM-107ER)	019 & SAL/P2B/002		21. 2.83	A M Sirant	Monkswell Farm, Horrabridge 27. 4.08P
G-MJTP	Mainair Tri-Flyer/Flexiform Dual Sealander (Fuji-Robin EC-44-PM)	AJDH-01 & 139-7383		25. 2.83	P Milton (Possibly fitted with Dual Striker Sailwing after accident 29.10.87)	(Bedford) 22. 8.00P
G-MJTR	Southdown Puma DS Mk.1 (Fuji-Robin EC-44-PM)	H362		9. 3.83	A G Rodenburg and T Abro (Noted wrecked 4.04) Hillfoots Nurseries , Tillicoultry, Stirling	15. 7.96P
G-MJTX	Skyrider Aviation Phantom (Fuji-Robin EC-44-PM)	SF-110		1. 3.83	P D Coppin (Noted 9.04)	Lee-on-Solent 22. 4.96P
G-MJTZ	Skyrider Aviation Phantom (Fuji-Robin EC-44-PM) (Engine No.82-00119)	MBS-01		29. 4.83	B J Towers	(Pershore) X
G-MJUC	MBA Tiger Cub 440 (Built Micro Biplane Aviation - pr.no.PFA 140-10908)	RRH-01		7. 3.83	P A Avery (Noted 4.05)	Terrington St John, Wisbech X
G-MJUR	Skyrider Aviation Phantom (Fuji-Robin EC-44-PM)	SF-108		5. 4.83	M J Whiteman-Haywood (New owner 8.06) Pound Green, Buttonoak, Bewdley	20. 9.98P
G-MJUU	Eurowing Goldwing (Fuji-Robin EC-34-PM)	EW-70		28. 3.83	E F Clapham	(Oldbury-on-Severn) 3. 5.97P
G-MJUW	MBA Tiger Cub 440	SO.69		29. 3.83	D G Palmer (Noted 2005)	Mintlaw, Peterhead 7. 6.02P
G-MJUX	Skyrider Aviation Phantom (Built Ultralight Flight Inc) (Fuji-Robin EC-44-PM)	RFF-01 & PH00094		29. 2.84	P J Glover (Noted 8.07 fitted with wings from G-MTTN qv)	North Coates 27. 3.06P
G-MJVE	Medway Hybred 44XL/Solar Wings Typhoon XLII	4483/1 & T483-761XL	(Original Sailwing c/n T283-703XL)	19. 4.83	T A Clark	(Rheda-Wiedenbrueck, Germany) 5. 6.00P
G-MJVF	CFM Shadow Series CD	002		12. 4.83	J A Cook (Stored dismantled 1.08)	Parham 24. 6.04P
G-MJVN	Ultrasports Tri-Pacer/Flexiform Striker (Fuji-Robin EC-44-PM) (Original Trike and engine fitted in G-MJRP)	82-00030-PR1		18. 4.83	R McGookin (Noted 8.05)	Thirdpart Holdings, West Kilbride 5.10.93P
G-MJVP	Eipper Quicksilver MXII (Rotax 503) (Original c/n 1124 became G-MTDO?)	1149		19. 4.83	G J Ward	(Moreton, Dorchester) 10. 7.96P
G-MJVU	Eipper Quicksilver MXII (Rotax 503)	1118		3. 4.84	F J Griffith	(Denbigh) 13. 7.08P
G-MJVX	Skyrider Aviation Phantom (Fuji-Robin EC-44-PM)	JAG-01 & SF-102		27. 4.83	J R Harris	Droppingwell Farm, Bewdley 1. 9.05P
G-MJVY	Dragon Light Aircraft Dragon Series 150 (Rotax 503)	D 150/013		4. 5.83	J C Craddock	(Freshwater, Isle of Wight) 26.10.04P
G-MJWB	Eurowing Goldwing (Fuji-Robin EC-34-PM)	EW-59		24. 5.83	D G Palmer (Noted 7.01)	Fetterangus 25. 8.93P
G-MJWF	MBA Tiger Cub 440	BRH-001 & SO.79		4. 5.83	T and R L Maycock (New owners 6.02)	(Glasgow)
G-MJWK	Huntair Pathfinder 1 (Rotax 447)	JWK-01		1.10.82	D Young tr Kemble Flying Club	Kemble 3. 7.05P
G-MJWW	MBA Super Tiger Cub 440	MU-001		11. 5.83	J J Littler and T J Gayton-Polley (New owner 11.03)	(Chichester) 23. 5.98P
G-MJWZ	Solar Wings Panther XL-S (Originally regd as XL)	T583-781XL		9. 9.85	A L Davies (New owner 10.02)	(Holywell) 27. 1.01P
G-MJXY	Hiway Skytrike 330/Demon 175 (Fuji-Robin EC-34-PM)	KQ17D		31. 5.83	H C Lowther	(Penrith) 25. 7.00P
G-MJYD	MBA Tiger Cub 440	SO.179		1. 6.83	R A Budd (Noted as engineless wreck 4.06)	Darley Moor, Ashbourne 12.11.03P
G-MJYP	Mainair Gemini/Flexiform Dual Striker (Fuji-Robin EC-44-PM)	167-13683		7. 6.83	M S Whitehouse	(Solihull) 23. 7.02P
G-MJYV	Mainair Rapier 1+1/Flexiform Solo Striker (Fuji-Robin EC-34-PM)	175-19783		23.11.83	L H Phillips	(Solihull) X
G-MJYW	Lancashire Micro-Trike Dual 330/Wasp Gryphon III	2/330PM/PGK.6.83/K		28. 6.83	P D Lawrence (Dismantled and Trike used on G-MMPL: parts noted 7.01)	(Munlochy, Ross-shire)
G-MJYX	Mainair Tri-Flyer/Hiway Demon (Fuji-Robin EC-33-PM)	108-251182		9. 6.83	K A Wright (Bagged wings only noted 6.06)	North Coates 7. 9.05P
G-MJZE	MBA Tiger Cub 440	SO.168		14. 6.83	J E D Rogerson tr Fishburn Flying Tigers (Morgansfield, Fishburn)	31. 1.96X

G-MJZK (2)	Southdown Puma Sprint	SN1111/0081		3. 3.86	R J Osborne	(Cove, Tiverton)	18.10.91P
	(Fuji-Robin EC-44-PM)						
G-MJZU	Mainair Gemini/Flexiform Dual Striker			21. 6.83	C G Chambers	Swinford, Rugby	7. 8.04P
	(Fuji-Robin EC-44-PM)	214-41183 & JDR-02	(Trike fitted ex G-MMVX (1))		(New owner 11.04)		
G-MKAA	Boeing 747-2S4F	22169	9G-MKQ	16. 8.06	MK Airlines Ltd	Manston	15. 8.08E
			N713BA, HL7474, LX-TAP, TU-TAP				
G-MKAK	Colt 77A Balloon (Hot Air)	2039		15. 8.91	M Kendrick	Bridgnorth	18. 7.03A
G-MKAS	Piper PA-28-140 Cherokee Cruiser	28-7425338	G-BKVR	30. 4.98	MK Aero Support Ltd	Andrewsfield	16.12.07E
			OY-BGV				
G-MKBA	Boeing 747-2B5F	22481	9G-MKR	29.10.07	MK Airlines Ltd	Manston	
			N778BA, HL7452				
G-MKCA	Boeing 747-2B5B	22482	9K-MKM	30. 1.08	MK Airlines Ltd	Manston	
			N207BA, HL7454				
G-MKDA	Boeing 747-2B5F	22486	9G-MKS	3.10.07	MK Airlines Ltd(	Manston	
			N776BA, HL7459, N8281V				
G-MKEA	Boeing 747-249F	22237	9G-MKU	24.10.07	MK Airlines Ltd	Manston	
			N920FT, VR-HKO, N633FE, (N639FE), N810FT, (N809FT)				
G-MKFA	Boeing 747-245F	21841	9G-MKP	16.11.07	MK Airlines Ltd	Manston	
			N925FT, N638FE, (G-INTL), N638FE, (N633FE), N814FT, N704SW				
G-MKGA	Boeing 747-2R7F	21650	9G-MKL	31.10.07	MK Airlines Ltd	Manston	
			N926FT, N639FE, N809FT, EI-BTQ, LX-DCV				
G-MKHA	Boeing 747-2J6B	23071	B-2446	13.11.07	MK Airlines Ltd	Manston	
			N1781B				
G-MKIA	Vickers Supermarine 300 Spitfire I	6S-30565	P9374	16.11.00	Spitfire Partners LLC	(Castelcucco, Veneto, Italy)	
					(New owners 3.05)		
G-MKII	Eurocopter EC.120B Colibri	1463	F-HAAL	21. 6.07	Focus Ltd	(Cookstown, Belfast)	20. 6.08E
			F-WQDD				
G-MKVB	Vickers Supermarine 349 Spitfire LF.Vb	5718M	2. 5.89	Historic Aircraft Collection Ltd	Duxford	25. 3.08P
		CBAF.2461	BM597		(As "BM597:U-2" in RAF c/s)		
G-MKVI	de Havilland DH.100 Vampire FB.6	676	Swiss AF J-1167	2. 6.92	T C Topen	Hemswell Cliff	14. 9.95P
	(Built F + W)				(Noted as "J-1167" 7.04)		
G-MKXI	Vickers Supermarine 365 Spitfire PR.Mk.XI		N965RF	13.11.89	P A Teichman	North Weald	29. 6.08P
		6S-504719	G-MKXI, R Netherlands AF, PL965		(As "PL965:R" in RAF grey c/s with D-Day stripes)		
G-MLAL	Avtech Jabiru J400	0xxx		23.10.06	M A Scudder	Gloucestershire	30. 5.08P
	(Built M A Scudder - pr.no.PFA 325-14399)						
G-MLAW	P&M Quik GT450	8310		12. 9.07	M Law	Perth	11. 9.08P
G-MLFF	Piper PA-23-250 Aztec E	27-7305194	G-WEBB	31. 1.90	W C Cullinane	Waterford, County Waterford	20. 7.08E
			G-BJBU, N40476				
G-MLHI	Maule MX-7-180 Super Rocket	11073C	G-BTMJ	20. 4.04	L C Gunn tr Maulehigh	White Waltham	4. 9.08E
G-MLJL	Airbus A330-243	254	F-WWKT	15. 6.99	Thomas Cook Airlines Ltd t/a MyTravel Airways		
						Manchester	14. 6.08E
G-MLLA	SOCATA TB-200 Tobago XL	1632	D-EREH	6. 6.05	C E Millar	Goodwood	9. 6.08E
G-MLLE	CEA Jodel DR.200A-B 2+2	136	OY-RVY	16.10.06	A D Evans	Sywell	26. 4.08S
			F-BRVY				
G-MLSN	Hughes 369E	0357E	G-HMAC	12.12.03	Whirlybirds Helicopters Ltd	(Mathern, Chepstow)	16. 6.08E
	(Hughes 500)		HB-XUO				
G-MLTY	Aérospatiale AS.365N2 Dauphin 2	6431	N365EL	4. 6.99	Crosby Enterprises Ltd	Leeds-Bradford	6. 6.08E
			JA6673				
G-MLWI	Thunder Ax7-77 Balloon (Hot Air)	1000		3. 9.86	M L and L P Willoughby	Woodcote, Reading	12. 8.03A
					"Mr Blue Sky"		
G-MLZZ	Best Off Sky Ranger Swift 912S(1) SKRxxx823			6.11.07	D M Robbins	Goodwood	
	(Built D M Robbins - pr.no.BMAA/HB/557)						
G-MMAC	Dragon Light Aircraft Dragon Series 200	003	OY-...	14. 7.82	J F Ashton and J Kirwan	Ince Blundell	X
	(Fuji-Robin EC-44-PM)		G-MMAC		(New owner 6.05)		
G-MMAG	MBA Tiger Cub 440	SO.47		22. 6.83	M J Aubrey (Noted 2002)	Kington, Hereford	14. 9.93P
G-MMAI	Dragon Light Aircraft Dragon Series 150	0032		1. 7.83	G S Richardson	(Cleethorpes)	13. 7.97P
	(Fuji-Robin EC-44-PM)				(Dismantled and parts split between North Coates and owner's home 11.07)		
G-MMAR	Mainair Gemini/Southdown Puma Sprint MS			23. 9.83	A R and J Fawkes	(Leckhampstead, Newbury)	17. 9.98P
	(Fuji-Robin EC-44-PM)	195-11083-2					
G-MMAZ	Southdown Puma Sprint X	MAPB-01		5. 8.83	B E Wagenhauser	(Chew Magna, Bristol)	22. 7.96P
	(Fuji-Robin EC-44-PM)				(New owner 1.08)		
G-MMBL	Ultrasports Puma/Southdown Lightning DS	80-00083		4. 7.83	B J Farrell	(Bilsborrow, Preston)	X
	(Fuji-Robin EC-44-PM) (C/n is engine serial no.)						
G-MMBN	Eurowing Goldwing	EW-89		28. 6.83	E H Jenkins	(Newcastle upon Tyne)	X
	(Rotax 447)						
G-MMBT	MBA Tiger Cub 440	SO.131		19. 7.83	B Chamberlain	(Otley, Ipswich)	X
	(Built Micro Biplane Aviation - pr.no. PFA 140-10924 or 10990: c/n T/A 01 reported also) (Stored 1.91)						
G-MMBU	Eipper Quicksilver MXII	CAL-222		8. 7.83	D A Norwood	Ashcroft Farm, Winsford	13. 7.08P
	(Rotax 503)						
G-MMBV	Huntair Pathfinder	044		8. 7.83	P J Bishop	Tarn Farm, Cockerham	9. 5.07P
	(Originally kit-built by M Philippe) (Fuji-Robin EC-44-PM)						
G-MMBY	Solar Wings Panther XL	T483-759XL		20. 7.83	R M Sheppard and P Huddleston		
						(Malvern and Marlborough)	3. 8.03P
G-MMBZ	Solar Wings Typhoon P	T981-5217		20. 7.83	S C Mann	(Kirkby Malzeard, Ripon)	28. 4.96P
	(Fuji-Robin EC-34-PM)				(New owner 10.00)		
	(Originally thought to have Sailwing c/n T781-217- 5217: possible corruption of S217 for Typhoon Small: rebuilt as c/n T981-228)						
G-MMCI	Ultrasports Puma Sprint X	P 421		28. 9.83	D M Parsons	Gloucestershire	8. 7.06P
	(Fuji-Robin EC-44-PM) (Also c/n DMP-01)				(New owner 12.06)		
G-MMCN	Hiway Skytrike 250/Solar Wings Storm	SMB.8069		19. 7.83	P J Ramsay	(Wrecclesham, Farnham)	X
G-MMCV	Hiway Skytrike II/Solar Wings Typhoon	T583-783		27. 7.83	G Addison	(Kinross)	8. 6.97P
	(Fuji-Robin EC-34-PM)						
G-MMCX	MBA Super Tiger Cub 440	MU.002		8. 8.83	D Harkin	(Johnstone, Renfrew)	
G-MMCZ	Mainair Tri-Flyer/Flexiform Dual Striker	TE-01		10. 8.83	T D Adamson	Wombleton	9. 9.07P
	(Fuji-Robin EC-44-PM) (Mainair Trike c/n 180-6883)						

G-MMDF	Southdown Wild Cat Mk.II/Lightning Phase II	007	24. 8.83	J C Haigh	(Tonbridge)	4.11.03P
	(Fuji-Robin EC-34-PM)					
G-MMDK	Mainair Tri-Flyer/Flexiform Striker	181-16883	7. 9.83	P E Blyth	(Maltby, Rotherham)	30. 5.99P
	(Fuji-Robin EC-34-PM)					
G-MMDN	Mainair Tri-Flyer 330/Flexiform Dual Striker		30. 9.83	M G Griffiths	(Monmouth)	X
	197-983 & RPO.12 *(Mainair c/n not confirmed)*					
G-MMDR	Huntair Pathfinder Mk.II	137	30. 8.83	C Dolling	(Swindon)	
	(Rotax 377)					
G-MMEK	Medway Hybred 44XL	129836	16. 9.83	M G J Bridges	(Exeter)	28. 8.00P
	(Solar Wings Typhoon XLII Sailwing c/n either T883-884XL or T883-887XL)					
G-MMFD	Mainair Tri-Flyer 440	210-31082-2	20. 9.83	M E and W L Chapman		
	(Fuji-Robin EC-44-PM)				(Ashton-under-Lyne and Springhead, Oldham)	6.12.93P
	(Flexiform Dual Striker Sailwing c/n FF/LAI/83/JDR/12: Trike believed to be c/n 210-31083-2)					
G-MMFE	Mainair Tri-Flyer 440	256-784-2	20. 9.83	W Camm	(Wombwell, Barnsley)	16. 6.94P
	(Fuji-Robin EC-44-PM) *(Flexiform Striker Sailwing FF/LAI/83/JDR/13)*					
G-MMFG	Lancashire Micro-Trike 440		20. 9.83	M G Dean and M J Hadland (Tarn Farm, Cockerham)		X
	(Fuji-Robin EC-44-PM) *(Flexiform Dual Striker Sailwing FF/LAI/83/JDR/15)*					
G-MMFS	MBA Tiger Cub 440	SO.64	1.11.83	G S Taylor	Yeatsall Farm, Abbots Bromley	27. 7.01P
				(Noted 8.07)		
G-MMFV	Mainair Tri-Flyer 440/Flexiform Dual Striker		8.12.83	R A Walton	(Slough)	26. 4.97P
	(Fuji-Robin EC-44-PM) 83-00130 & 212-271083			*(New owner 7.03)*		
G-MMFY	Cliff Sims Aztec/Flexiform Dual Striker AZT001CS		14.12.83	K R M Adair and S R Browne (Bognor/Pulborough)		X
				(Amended owner 1.05)		
G-MMGF	MBA Tiger Cub 440	SO.124	18.11.83	J G Boxall	Pittrichie Farm, Whiterashes	22. 8.02P
G-MMGL	MBA Tiger Cub 440	SO.148	23.11.83	H E Dunning	Baxby Manor, Husthwaite	7. 6.06P
	(Built H E Dunning - pr.no.BMAA/HB/050)					
G-MMGS	Solar Wings Panther XL-S	T1283-939XL	28.12.83	R J Hood	London Colney	21. 4.08P
G-MMGT	Huntwing/Pegasus Classic	JAH-7	28.11.83	H Cook	(Newport, Gwent)	24.10.08P
	(Built J A Hunt) (BMW R100) (Currently with Trike c/n SW-TB-1228 ex G-MTOH)					
G-MMGU	SMD Gazelle/Flexiform Sealander	30-4883	1.12.83	A D Cranfield	(Marsh, Wincanton)	X
	(Fuji-Robin EC-44-PM)					
G-MMGV	Whittaker MW5 Sorcerer Series A	001	2.12.83	G N Haffey and M W J Whittaker		
	(Built Microknight Aviation Ltd) (Fuji-Robin EC-34-M)			*(Noted 9.07)*	Church Farm, Askern	1. 9.06P
G-MMHE	Mainair Gemini Sprint	229-184-2	8.12.83	N L Zaman *(New owner 3.06)*	(London Colney)	27. 5.98P
G-MMHK	Hiway Skytrike/Super Scorpion	KSC83	19.12.83	S Davison	(Newcastle upon Tyne)	X
	(Fuji-Robin EC-25-PS)			*(New owner 3.06)*		
G-MMHL	Hiway Skytrike II/Super Scorpion	KSC84	19.12.83	E J Blyth	(Wrelton, Pickering)	X
	(Fuji-Robin EC-44)					
G-MMHN	MBA Tiger Cub 440	SO.136	19.12.83	M J Aubrey *(Noted 2002)*	Kington, Hereford	
G-MMHS	SMD Gazelle/Flexiform Dual Striker	104-11283	21.12.83	C J Meadows	Franklyn's Field, Chewton Mendip	
G-MMIE	MBA Tiger Cub 440	G7-7	3. 1.84	B W Olliver	(Telford)	X
G-MMIW	Southdown Puma Sprint	590	9. 2.84	J Ryland	(Swanley)	26. 9.04P
	(Fuji-Robin EC-44-PM)					
G-MMIX	MBA Tiger Cub 440	MBCB-01	14. 2.84	N J McKain	(Dumfries)	X
				(To Dumfries and Galloway Museum 2007)		
G-MMIZ	Southdown Lightning Mk.II	CB-01	24. 2.84	F E Hall	Prospect Farm, Wollaston	25. 4.05P
				(New owner 3.07)		
G-MMJD	Southdown Puma Sprint	SP/1001	28. 6.83	M P Robertshaw	(Keighley)	20. 7.08P
	(Fuji-Robin EC-44-PM)					
G-MMJF	Solar Wings Panther Dual XL-S		27. 2.84	J Benn	(Sturton-by-Stow, Lincoln)	22. 5.08P
	PXL842-150 & T284-988XL					
G-MMJG	Mainair Tri-Flyer/Flexiform Dual Striker 185-1983		31. 9.83	A Strang	(Ashgill, Larkhall)	10. 9.03P
	(Fuji-Robin EC-44-PM)			*(Under repair 2004)*		
G-MMJT	Mainair Gemini/Southdown Sprint X	JBT-01	20.12.83	D C de la Haye	(Elmley, Sheerness)	21. 7.07P
	(Fuji-Robin EC-44-PM) *(No Mainair identity and probably plans-built by J B Tate)*					
G-MMJV	MBA Tiger Cub 440	SO.195	25. 3.84	D G Palmer	Fetterangus	9. 5.93P
	(Built K Bannister - pr.no.PFA 140-1090)			*(Noted 7.01)*		
G-MMJX	Teman Mono-Fly	01	6. 3.84	M Ingleton	Cripps Barn, Eastchurch	17. 7.04P
	(Built B F J Hope) (Rotax 377)					
G-MMKA	Solar Wings Panther Dual XL	T284-986XL	8. 3.84	R S Wood	(Wallacestone, Falkirk)	X
G-MMKE	Birdman WT-11 Chinook	01817	2. 4.84	D M Jackson	(Belper)	X
	(Rotax 277)					
G-MMKG	Medway Hybred 44XL/Solar Wings Typhoon XLII		9. 3.84	G P Lane	(Bristol)	18. 7.97P
	222847					
	(Sailwing c/n T-?84-1035XL - either '384 or '484) (Reported with Sailwing marked "G-MNYX" 8.96)					
G-MMKL	Mainair Gemini Flash	238-384-2-W11	12. 3.84	D W Cox	(Kenilworth)	29. 9.93P
	(Fuji-Robin EC-44-PM)					
G-MMKM	Mainair Gemini/Flexiform Dual Striker 221-01-84-0002		12. 3.84	S W Hutchinson	(Northallerton)	11. 6.99P
	(Fuji-Robin EC-44-PM)			*(New owner 6.05)*		
	(Originally fitted with Mainair 440 Tri-Flyer Trike [210-1083] and part- exchanged for 440 Gemini as fitted: rebuild of Trike originally exported to US and re-imported)					
G-MMKP	MBA Tiger Cub 440	SO.203	13. 3.84	J W Beaty	(Lowick, Kettering)	
G-MMKR	Mainair Tri-Flyer/Southdown Lightning DS		14. 3.84	C R Madden	(Great Orton)	14. 4.07P
	(Fuji-Robin EC-44-PM) 209-171083 & CM-01 *(Regd as G-MNDK in error and then restored as G-MMKR)*					
G-MMKX	Skyrider Aviation Phantom 330	PH-107R	18. 3.85	G J Lampitt	Pounds Green, Buttonoak, Bewdley	17. 6.01P
	(Fuji-Robin EC-34-PL-02)			*(New owner 10.05)*		
G-MMLE	Eurowing Goldwing SP	EW-81	21. 3.84	M J Aubrey *(New owner 2.07)*	(Kington, Hereford)	
G-MMLH	Hiway Skytrike II 330/Demon PMH-01 & DJL-01		28. 3.84	P M Hendry and D J Lukey		
					(Geneva, Switzerland and Folkestone)	
G-MMMG	Eipper Quicksilver MXL	1383	5. 6.84	J G Campbell	Sandtoft	15. 6.08P
	(Rotax 447)					
G-MMMH	Hadland Willow/Flexiform Striker	MJH 383	9.12.83	M J Hadland	(Ashton-in-Makerfield, Wigan)	6.10.08P
	(BMW R80/7)					
G-MMML	Dragon Light Aircraft Dragon Series 150 D150/002 OY-...		28. 6.83	M J Aubrey	Kington, Hereford	6. 8.00P
	(Fuji-Robin EC-44-PM)	G-MMML		*(New owner 6.07)*		

G-MMMN	Solar Wings Panther Dual XL-S		4. 4.84	C Downton	(Newton Abbot)	16. 7.04P
	PXL 843-150 & T484-105?XL	*(Probably '1059)*				
G-MMNA	Eipper Quicksilver MXII	1046	30. 3.84	J W Dodson	Leicester	2. 1.05P
	(C/n conflicts with Quicksilver G-MMIL)					
G-MMNB	Eipper Quicksilver MX	4286	30. 3.84	J M Lindop	Long Marston	12.10.97P
	(Cuyuna 430R)			*(New owner 6.01)*		
G-MMNC	Eipper Quicksilver MX	4276	30. 3.84	W S Toulmin	(Great Gidding, Huntingdon)	31. 5.96P
				(New owner 2.04)		
G-MMNH	Dragon Light Aircraft Dragon Series 150	D150/42	27. 7.83	T J Barlow	(Dromore, County Down)	X
	(Fuji-Robin EC-44-PM)					
G-MMNN	Sherry Buzzard	1	6. 4.84	E W Sherry	(Stoke-on-Trent)	
	(Built E W Sherry - pr.no.PFA 190-10430)					
G-MMNS	Mitchell U-2 Super Wing	PFA 114-10690	11. 4.84	C Baldwin and J C Lister	(Valley Farm, Winwick)	
	(Built C Baldwin)					
G-MMNT	Flexiform Trike/Flexiform Solo Striker	SSL-1	16. 4.84	C R Thorne	(Lyndhurst, Hampshire)	X
	(Rotax 277)					
G-MMOB	Mainair Gemini/Southdown Sprint		11. 5.84	D Woolcock	St Michaels	25. 6.08P
	(Fuji-Robin EC-44-PM) 244-584-2(K) & EM-01 *(C/n 'K' denotes kit built)*					
G-MMOH	Solar Wings Pegasus XL-R	T484-1054XL	4. 5.84	T H Scott	(Coggeshall, Colchester)	
	(Wing c/n SW-TB-1450)					
	(Trike fitted replacing one formerly on G-MBTT: new Trike now fitted ex G-MYGA)					
G-MMOK	Solar Wings Panther XL-S	T584-1066XL	9. 5.84	R F and A J Foster	(Woodbridge)	17.12.07P
	(Wing c/n PXL844-157)					
G-MMOW	Mainair Gemini Flash	246-684-3-W06	21. 5.84	D P Quaintrell *(Noted 10.06)*	Tarn Farm, Cockerham	3. 6.02P
G-MMPG	Ultrasports Tri-pacer/Lightning Mk.II	NEA-01	8. 6.84	T J Hector	(Guilden Morden, Royston)	15. 4.01P
	(Fuji-Robin EC-34-PM)					
G-MMPH	Southdown Puma Sprint	P 545	20. 6.84	J Siddle	(Alsager, Stoke-on-Trent)	27. 4.05P
	(Fuji-Robin EC-44-PM)			*(New owner 10.05)*		
G-MMPL	Lancashire Micro-Trike 440/Flexiform Dual Striker		5.12.83	P D Lawrence	(Munlochy)	28. 6.07P
	(Fuji-Robin EC-44-PM) PDL-02 & 2/330PM/PGK/683/K *(Trike unit from G-MJYW: maybe flown with exchangeable sailwings)*					
G-MMPO	Mainair Gemini Flash	325-785-3-W65	18. 4.85	M A Feber	Ballinspittle, County Cork	9. 6.06P
	(Fuji-Robin EC-44-PM)					
G-MMPU	R J Heming Trike/Solar Wings Typhoon S4	RJH-01	5. 6.84	J T Halford	(Langham, Holt)	22. 5.96P
	(Fuji-Robin EC-34-PM) *(Wing c/n T782-553L)*					
G-MMPZ	Teman Mono-Fly	JWH-01	2. 7.84	P B Kylo	Glassonby	20. 6.07P
	(Built J W Highton) (Rotax 447)					
G-MMRH	Hiway Skytrike/Demon	JSM-01 & 25R1	20. 6.84	A M Sirant Monkswell Farm, Horrabridge, Yelverton		
				(New owner 5.06)		
G-MMRL	Solar Wings Pegasus XL-R	T684-1102XL	17. 7.84	R J Hood	London Colney	3. 9.05P
	(Trike c/n SW-TB-1233)		*(Trike acquired ex G-MTOM C 2001) (Noted 7.06)*			
G-MMRN	Southdown Puma Sprint	P 544	16. 7.84	D C Read	(Ledbury)	18. 4.01P
	(Fuji-Robin EC-44-PM)					
G-MMRP	Mainair Gemini/Southdown Sprint	259-884-2-P 561	7. 2.85	J C S Jones	Emlyn's Field, Rhuallt	7 .9.08P
	(Fuji-Robin EC-44-PM)					
G-MMRW	Mainair Gemini 440/Flexiform Dual Striker		5. 1.84	M D Hinge	(Hamptworth, Salisbury)	X
	LAI/DS/25 & 216-71283					
G-MMSA	Solar Wings Panther XL-S	T184-1142XL	9. 8.84	T W Thiele and G Savage	(Radwell, Baldock)	27. 5.98P
	(Wing c/n PXL847-189)		*(C/n probably T784-1142XL)*			
G-MMSG	Solar Wings Panther XL-S	T884-1165XL	6. 9.85	R W McKee	(Mancott, Deeside)	4. 6.01P
	(Regd with c/n 8841/65XC)					
G-MMSH	Solar Wings Panther XL-S	T884-1163XL	28. 5.85	I J Drake	(Billericay)	7. 5.90P
	(Wing c/n PXL847-192)					
G-MMSO	Mainair Gemini/Southdown Sprint	255-784-2-P 539	14. 1.86	K A Maughan	Church Farm, Askern	26. 7.99P
	(Fuji-Robin EC-44-PM)			*(Wing only noted 9.07)*		
G-MMSP	Mainair Gemini Flash	265-984-2	17. 8.84	J Whiteford	East Fortune	24. 4.01P
	(Fuji-Robin EC-44-PM) *(Original Sailwing c/n W03 fitted to G-MNGF 1998: current Sailwing identity not known)*					
G-MMTA	Solar Wings Panther XL-R	T884-1164XL	25.10.84	P A McMahon	(Dun Laoghaire, County Dublin)	29. 6.03P
	(Rotax 462HP)	(Sailwing c/n PXL848-194)				
G-MMTC	Solar Wings Pegasus XL-R	T684-1101XL	28. 9.84	T L Moses	(Uplands , Carmarthen)	8. 2.02P
	(Sailwing c/n SW-TB-1037)		*(Original Trike was Ultrasports c/n PXL847-170 and later fitted to G-MNHH) (Dismantled 2.03)*			
G-MMTD	Mainair Tri-Flyer/Hiway Demon 175		16. 8.84	W E Teare	(Ramsey, Isle of Man)	10. 9.03P
	(Fuji-Robin EC-34-PM) 150-30583 & EIA-01		*(Trike originally exported to Denmark)*			
G-MMTG	Mainair Gemini/Southdown Sprint	267-984-2-P577	21. 8.84	J C F Dalton	(St Neots)	13. 8.94P
	(Originally regd as Mainair Tri-Flyer with c/n RPWJ-01)			*(New owner 1.03)*		
G-MMTJ	Southdown Puma Sprint	SN1221/0006	17. 1.85	P J Kirwan	(Geashill, County Offaly)	16. 4.00P
	(Fuji-Robin EC-44-PM)			*(Believed stored 2006)*		
G-MMTL	Mainair Gemini/Southdown Sprint	268-1084-2-P576	3.10.84	K Birkett	Lee-on-Solent	3. 8.05P
	(Fuji-Robin EC-44-PM)					
G-MMTR	Solar Wings Pegasus XL-R	KND-03	27. 9.84	P M Kelsey *(Noted 2.08)*	Yearby	23. 4.08P
	(Originally fitted with Ultrasports Trike/Typhoon Sailwing c/n T984-1211XL: Trike replaced by Solar Wings XL c/n SW-TB-1092 circa 8.86)					
G-MMTS	Solar Wings Panther XL	T784-1157XL	18. 9.84	A E James tr Slow Thrusters		
					Lower Upham Farm, Chiseldon	29. 7.05P
G-MMTV	American Aerolights Eagle 215B Seaplane	SGP-1	25. 9.84	L K Fowler	(Upper Sapey, Worcester)	21.11.96P
	(Fuji-Robin EC-25-PS)			*(New owner 3.06)*		
G-MMTX	Mainair Gemini/Southdown Sprint	275-1284-2-P590	25. 3.85	A Worthington	Tarn Farm, Cockerham	13. 8.05P
	(Fuji-Robin EC-44-PM) *(Originally fitted with Sailwing c/n P 577 from G-MMTG)*					
G-MMTY	Fisher FP.202U	2140	28. 9.84	B E Maggs *(Stored dismantled 6.07)*	Compton Dando	
G-MMTZ	Eurowing Goldwing	EW-60 & SWA-7	28. 9.84	R B D Baker	(Torquay)	15. 7.03P
	(Rotax 447)					
G-MMUA	Southdown Puma Sprint	SN1221/0007	21.12.84	M R Crowhurst	(Ramsey, Isle of Man)	21. 7.05P
	(Fuji-Robin EC-44-PM)					
G-MMUH	Mainair Tri-Flyer/Sprint	270-1084-2-P579	8.11.84	J P Nicklin	(Hayling Island)	20. 9.04P
	(Fuji-Robin EC-44-PM)					
G-MMUM	MBA Tiger Cub 440	SO.019	8. 3.83	Coulson Flying Services Ltd	(Cranfield)	

G-MMUO	Mainair Gemini Flash (Fuji-Robin EC-44-PM)	272-1084-2-W08	29.10.84	B D Bastin and D R Howells	Long Marston	5. 7.07P
G-MMUR	Hiway Skytrike II/Solar Wings Storm (Fuji-Robin EC-25)	SLI.80180	28.12.84	R J Ripley *(Stored at owner's house 1998)*	Field Farm, Oakley	
G-MMUV	Southdown Puma Sprint (Fuji-Robin EC-44-PM)	SN1121/0010	7.11.84	D C Read	(Bromsberrow Heath, Ledbury)	2.11.89P
G-MMUW	Mainair Gemini Flash II (Fuji-Robin EC-44-PM)	60-784-2-W13	17. 1.85	J C K Scardifield	(Milford-on-Sea, Lymington)	23. 3.87P
G-MMUX	Mainair Gemini/Southdown Sprint (Fuji-Robin EC-44-PM) *(Trike c/n confirmed as 284-185-3)*	285-185-3-P587	28.12.84	M D Howe	Priory Farm, Tibenham	8.12.07P
G-MMVA	Southdown Puma Sprint *(Trike c/n P 588)*	SN1121/0011	7.11.84	C E Tomkins *(New owner 5.05)*	(Orlingbury, Kettering)	26. 3.92P
G-MMVH	Southdown Raven X	SN2122/0015	10. 1.85	G, W and K Carwardine (Hadlow Down, Uckfield and Tonbridge)		29. 4.01P
G-MMVI	Southdown Puma Sprint (Fuji-Robin EC-44-PM)	SN1121/0012	28.11.84	G R Williams	(Oakdale, Blackwood)	2.11.97P
G-MMVS	Skyhook TR1 Pixie/Zeus (Solo 210)	TR1/52	28. 2.85	B W Olley	(Soham, Ely)	X
G-MMVX	Southdown Puma Sprint (Fuji-Robin EC-44-PM) *(Wing c/n 41183)*	P452	29.11.83	M P Jones	Haverfordwest	5. 4.03P
G-MMVZ	Southdown Puma Sprint (Fuji-Robin EC-44-PM)	SN1121/0016	15. 1.85	P Whelan *(New owner 5.05)*	(Curragh, County Kildare)	2. 8.04P
G-MMWA	Mainair Gemini Flash II (Fuji-Robin EC-44-PM) *(Trike c/n stamped as "KR271-1184-2")*	271-1184-1-W07	22.11.84	B Olson	(Kirkby-la-Thorpe, Sleaford)	22. 6.07P
G-MMWC	Eipper Quicksilver MXII (Rotax 503)	1041	22.10.84	J S Harris and M Holmes	Old Sarum	27. 7.03P
G-MMWG	P G Greenslade Trike/Flexiform Solo Striker (Rotax 377) *(Registered as Mainair Tri-Flyer Trike but now fitted with Trike from G-MJGN) (Sailwing c/n duplicates G-MMFC)*	FF/LAI/83/JDR/11	17.12.84	C R Green	(Redruth)	26. 6.99P
G-MMWL	Eurowing Goldwing (Rotax 447)	SWA-09 & EW-91	9. 4.85	A D Bales *(New owner 1.06)*	Priory Farm, Tibenham	24. 5.05P
G-MMWS	Ultrasports Tri-Pacer/Flexiform Solo Striker (Rotax 377) *(Originally fitted with Mainair Trike)*	983.SH	21.11.84	P H Risdale	Tower Farm, Wollaston	10. 8.08P
G-MMWX	Southdown Puma Sprint (Fuji-Robin EC-44-PM)	SN1121/0047	10. 4.85	B E Wagenhauser	(Chew Magna, Bristol)	31.10.07P
G-MMXD	Mainair Gemini Flash II (Rotax 447)	282-185-3-W20	28.12.84	W A Bibby *(Noted 2.06)*	Brook Farm, Pilling	13. 8.05P
G-MMXJ	Mainair Gemini Flash II (Rotax 447)	289-185-3-W22	17. 1.85	R Meredith-	(Hardy Radwell, Letchworth)	6. 8.96P
G-MMXL	Mainair Gemini Flash II (Fuji-Robin EC-44-PM)	292-385-3-W36	17. 1.85	G W Warner *(New owner 6.07)*	(Manchester)	16. 5.97P
G-MMXO	Southdown Puma Sprint (Fuji-Robin EC-44-PM)	SN1121/0018	23. 1.85	D J Tasker	Swinford, Rugby	7. 4.08P
G-MMXU	Mainair Gemini Flash II (Fuji-Robin EC-44-PM)	254-784-2-W21	29. 1.85	T J Franklin *(Stored 7.03)*	Graveley Hall Farm, Graveley	14. 7.01P
G-MMXV	Mainair Gemini Flash II (Rotax 503)	298-385-3-W37	29. 1.85	D Roland	(Gamrie, Banff)	30. 9.07P
G-MMXW	Mainair Gemini/Southdown Sprint (Fuji-Robin EC-44-PM)	286-185-3-P597	23. 1.85	A Hodgson	(Milton Keynes)	4. 6.02P
G-MMYA	Solar Wings Pegasus XL-R/Se *(Originally regd as XL)* XL-P Proto & T784-1151XL		30. 1.85	R G Mason	(Aylesbury)	5. 8.06P
G-MMYF	Southdown Puma Sprint (Fuji-Robin EC-44-PM)	SN1121/0026	28. 3.85	M Campbell	(Halifax)	14. 3.05P
G-MMYL	Cyclone 70/Aerial Arts 130SX	CH.01	8. 3.85	E W P van Zeller	(Ashford, Kent)	6. 5.07P
G-MMYN	Solar Wings Pegasus XL-R	T784-1158XL	27. 2.85	H J Long *(Noted 6.07)* Ardenagh Great, Taghmon, County Wexford		17. 7.06P
G-MMYO	Southdown Puma Sprint (Fuji-Robin EC-44-PM) *(Fitted with rainbow Medway Sailwing c3.96 after accident 20.9.95)*	SN1121/0037	11. 4.85	P R Whitehouse	Otherton, Cannock	29. 8.00P
G-MMYT	Southdown Puma Sprint (Fuji-Robin EC-44-PM) SN1121/0046 & T569/P621		15. 4.85	J K Divall	(Chichester)	25. 3.94P
G-MMYU	Southdown Puma Sprint (Rotax 447)	SN1231/0045	11. 6.85	M V Hearns	Glenrothes	21. 4.02P
G-MMYV	Mainair Tri-Flyer/Flexiform Strike *(Built J Webb)* (Rotax 277)	JW-2	22. 3.85	S B Herbert	(Presteigne)	20.12.95P
G-MMYY	Southdown Puma Sprint (Rotax 447)	SN1231/0042	18. 7.85	D J Whittle	(Liverpool)	12. 7.04P
G-MMZA	Mainair Gemini Flash II (Fuji-Robin EC-44-PM)	266-984-3-W60	4. 3.85	G T Johnston	(Craigavon, County Armagh)	30. 6.00P
G-MMZD	Mainair Gemini Flash (Fuji-Robin EC-44-PM)	309-585-3-W49	4. 3.85	P L Dowd	Ince Blundell	24. 7.08P
G-MMZF	Mainair Gemini Flash II (Fuji-Robin EC-44-PM)	299-485-3-W38	4. 3.85	J Tait *(Noted 7.05)*	Eshott	13. 9.03P
G-MMZG	Solar Wings Panther XL-S SW-T/A-1008 & SW-WA-1022		12. 8.85	K A Sutton	(Dartford)	13.10.08P
G-MMZI	Medway Half Pint/Aerial Arts 130SX 2385/1 & 130SX-057		6. 3.85	J Messenger	(Workington)	28. 3.93X
G-MMZJ	Mainair Gemini Flash (Rotax 462)	312-585-3-W51	18. 3.85	R C Bailey	Roddige	25. 4.08P
G-MMZK	Mainair Gemini Flash (Fuji-Robin EC-44-PM) *(Trike ex G-MMEZ: originally regd with Trike c/n 314-585-3 which went to G-MMIR)*	326-785-3-W53	18. 3.85	G Jones and B Lee	(Warrington)	3.11.99P
G-MMZM	Mainair Gemini Flash (Fuji-Robin EC-44-PM)	304-585-3-W44	18. 3.85	H Brown	(Dunbar)	4. 1.04P
G-MMZN	Mainair Gemini Flash II (Fuji-Robin EC-44-PM)	283-185-3-W23	18. 3.85	W K Dalus	(Keyworth, Nottingham)	28. 9.93P

G-MMZV	Mainair Gemini Flash	313-585-3-W52		18. 4.85	R Till	Watnall	6.10.08P
	(Rotax 447)						
G-MMZW	Southdown Puma Sprint			28. 3.85	M G Ashbee	(Cranbrook)	30. 9.00P
	(Fuji-Robin EC-44-PM)	SN1121/0043 & T566/P620			*(Damaged C 8.00)*		
G-MNAC	Mainair Gemini Flash	335-885-3-W72		18. 4.85	I E S Cole	(Llangurig, Llanidloes)	30. 7.06P
	(C/n now verified as 262-884-2 and W04 ex G-MMUT qv)						
G-MNAE	Mainair Gemini Flash	343-885-3-W77		18. 4.85	G C Luddington	(Bletsoe)	29. 7.00P
	(Rotax 447)						
G-MNAI	Solar Wings Panther XL-S	SW-WA-1003		15. 5.85	R G Cameron	Errol	23. 6.98P
	(Trike c/n SW-T/A-1003)				*(Noted stored 8.04)*		
G-MNAR	Solar Wings Pegasus XL-R	SW-WA-1011		6. 8.85	D A Cansdale	(Harlow)	3. 3.03P
	(Trike c/n SW-TB-0014)						
G-MNAW	Solar Wings Pegasus XL-R	SW-WA-1014		16. 8.85	C T H Tenison	(Llanddewi Skirrid, Abergavenny)	25. 5.07P
	(Trike c/n SW-TB-1010)				*(New owner 1.08)*		
G-MNAX	Solar Wings Pegasus XL-R	SW-WA-1015		16. 8.85	B J Phillips	(Beedon, Newbury)	21. 7.96P
	(Trike c/n SW-TB-1011)						
G-MNAY	Solar Wings Pegasus XL-R	SW-WA-1016		6. 8.85	A Seaton	(Sleaford)	11. 9.99P
	(Trike c/n SW-TB-1015)				*(New owner 5.02)*		
G-MNAZ	Solar Wings Pegasus XL-R	SW-WA-1017		6. 8.85	R W Houldsworth	(Rochford)	12. 9.08P
	(Trike c/n SW-TB-1016)						
G-MNBA	Solar Wings Pegasus XL-R	SW-WA-1018		6. 9.85	A J Todd	(Luton)	7. 6.07P
	(Trike c/n SW-TB-1024)						
G-MNBB	Solar Wings Pegasus XL-R	SW-WA-1019		20. 9.85	R Piper	Ince Blundell	3. 8.04P
	(Trike c/n SW-TB-1020)						
G-MNBC	Solar Wings Pegasus XL-R	SW-WA-1020		11.10.85	N Kelly	(Carmarthen)	9. 9.04P
	(Rotax 503)	*(Trike c/n SW-TB-1026)*					
G-MNBD	Mainair Gemini Flash	162-683-W42	G-MMSN	6. 1.86	P Woodcock	Sittles Farm, Alrewas	30.12.03P
	(Fuji-Robin EC-44-PM) *(Originally built as Mainair 440 Tri-Flyer c/n 341-585-3 and W42: unsold and.reworked by Mainair as c/n 162-683 and fitted to G-MMSN. This podded to become a Gemini and used in rebuild of G-MNBD after late 1996 accident)*						
G-MNBE	Southdown Puma Sprint	SN1121/0050		17. 5.85	D Newton	Hunsdon	26. 4.08P
	(Rotax 447)						
G-MNBF	Mainair Gemini Flash	306-585-3-W46		2. 5.85	P Mokryk and S King	(Derby)	25. 5.05P
	(Fuji-Robin EC-44-PM)						
G-MNBG	Mainair Gemini Flash	347-585-3-W66		9. 5.85	T Barnett	Baxby Manor, Husthwaite	15.11.08P
	(Rotax 447)						
G-MNBI	Solar Wings Panther XL-R	T884-1161XL	G-MMVF?	3. 5.85	M O'Connell	(Clonee, Dublin)	3. 6.08P
	(Fuji-Robin EC-44-PM) *(Trike c/n PXL884-178)*						
G-MNBM	Southdown Puma Sprint	SN1231/0058		25. 6.85	C Hall-Gardner	(Nairnside, inverness)	7.10.01P
	(Rotax 447)				*(New owner 2.07)*		
G-MNBN	Mainair Gemini Flash	303-485-3-W43		11. 6.85	I H Gates	Long Marston	28. 5.05P
	(Fuji-Robin EC-44-PM)						
G-MNBP	Mainair Gemini Flash	338-885-3-W75		15. 5.85	G A Harper	Priory Farm, Tibenham	1. 6.08P
	(Fuji-Robin EC-44-PM)						
G-MNBS	Mainair Gemini Flash	308-585-3-W48		15. 5.85	P A Comins	(Nottingham)	20. 6.94P
	(Fuji-Robin EC-44-PM)						
G-MNBT	Mainair Gemini Flash	322-685-3-W62		15. 5.85	R R A Dean	(Chopwell, Newcastle-upon-Tyne)	16. 5.08P
G-MNBV	Mainair Gemini Flash	333-685-3-W70		15. 5.85	J Walshe	(Newtownards)	21. 8.04P
	(Rotax 447)						
G-MNCA	Hunt Avon Sky-Trike/Hiway Demon 175	DA-01		28. 5.85	M A Sirant	Monkswell Farm, Yelverton	26. 3.94X
	(Built Hiway Hang Gliders Ltd and originally regd as Adams Trike)				*(New owner 10.04)*		
G-MNCF	Mainair Gemini Flash	321-685-3-W61		3. 6.85	M R Badminton	(Thorpefield, Thirsk)	4. 5.08P
	(Rotax 447)						
G-MNCG	Mainair Gemini Flash	320-685-3-W59		3. 6.85	I D Mallinson	(Truro)	26.11.07P
	(Rebuilt c2000)						
G-MNCI	Southdown Puma Sprint	SN1231/0059		7. 6.85	R M Wait and N Hewitt	Mill Farm, Shifnal	25. 5.05P
	(Rotax 447)						
G-MNCJ	Mainair Gemini Flash	351-785-3-W83		3. 6.85	R S McLeister	(Accrington)	16.11.93P
	(Fuji-Robin EC-44-PM)	*(Original Trike stolen, new one c/n 282-1284-2 ex G-MMXF fitted c 12.89)*					
G-MNCM	CFM Shadow Series C	006		31. 5.85	K G D Macrae	Drummiard Farm, Bonnybank	19. 6.08P
G-MNCO	Eipper Quicksilver MXII	1045		3. 6.85	S Lawton	(Barnoldswick)	
G-MNCP	Southdown Puma Sprint	SN1231/0071		24. 6.85	D M Lane	(Poole)	10. 4.00P
	(Rotax 447)				*(New owners 8.07)*		
G-MNCS	Skyrider Aviation Phantom	PH.00098		2. 1.86	S P Allen	(Kettering)	25. 7.03P
	(Fuji-Robin EC-44-PM)						
G-MNCU	Medway Hybred 44XL	26485/10		13. 6.85	J E Evans	(Crewe)	24. 6.05P
	(Solar Wings Typhoon Sailwing				*(New owner 12.07)*		
G-MNCV	Medway Hybred 44XL	26485/11		13. 6.85	P D Mickleburgh	Swinford, Rugby	14. 5.08P
	(Pegasus XL-R Sailwing c/n SW-WA-1030)						
G-MNDC	Mainair Gemini Flash	336-885-3-W73		12. 6.85	M Medlock	Popham	21. 6.06P
G-MNDD	Mainair Scorcher	358-685-1-W85		12. 6.85	L Hurman	Enstone	4. 9.08P
G-MNDE	Medway Half Pint/Aerial Arts 130SX	3/8685		19. 6.85	C D Wills	Chilbolton	3.10.03P
	(Wing ex G-MNBZ)				*(Noted 1.07)*		
G-MNDF	Mainair Gemini Flash	327-785-3-W67		25. 6.85	W G Nicol	(Stanley, Perth)	21. 6.08P
	(Rotax 447)						
G-MNDM	Mainair Gemini Flash	324-785-3-W64		11. 7.85	R G Calvert *(New owner 5.07)*	(Keswick)	7. 4.98P
G-MNDO	Solar Wings Pegasus Flash	SW-WF-0001		2. 7.85	G Carr	(Huthwaite, Sutton-in-Ashfield)	26. 7.08P
	(Trike is c/n SW-TB-1012 and Mainair Sailwing c/n W86)						
G-MNDU	Midland Ultralights Sirocco 377GB	MU-011		22. 7.85	M A Collins	Longacre Farm, Sandy	14. 2.04P
	(Rotax 377)						
G-MNDY	Southdown Puma Sprint	DY-01 & P 536		2. 5.84	A M Coupland	(Ashby de la Launde, Lincoln)	19. 6.03P
	(Fuji-Robin EC-44-PM) *(Trike rebuilt c4.99)*				*(New owner 4.06)*		
G-MNEG	Mainair Gemini Flash	360-885-3-W92		8. 7.85	A Sexton	(Nurney, County Kildare)	18.10.99P
	(Rotax 447)				*(New owner 8.04)*		
G-MNEH	Mainair Gemini Flash	361-885-3-W90		8. 7.85	I Rawson	St Michaels	21. 7.08P

G-MNEI	Medway Hybred 44XL	8785/12	9. 7.85	L G Thompson	Long Marston	26. 7.93P
	(Solar Wings Typhoon XLII Sailwing c/n SW-WA-1035)			*(Damaged 28.11.92 and stored 8.96)*		
G-MNEK	Medway Half Pint/Aerial Arts 130S	4/8785	12. 7.85	M I Dougall	(Maidstone)	25. 9.94P
				(Damaged Stoke 6 .7.93)		
G-MNER	CFM Shadow Series CD	008	15. 7.85	F C Claydon	(Wickhambrook, Newmarket)	16. 6.08P
	(Rotax 462)					
G-MNET	Mainair Gemini Flash	349-885-3-W81	23. 7.85	I P Stubbins	North Coates	6. 8.04P
	(Fuji-Robin EC-44-PM)					
G-MNEV	Mainair Gemini Flash	362-1085-3-W108	23. 7.85	M Gardiner	(Farnworth, Bolton)	20. 1.07P
	(Rotax 447)					
G-MNEY	Mainair Gemini Flash	365-1085-3-W94	23. 7.85	D A Spiers	East Fortune	17. 9.04P
	(Rotax 447)					
G-MNFB	Southdown Puma Sprint	SN1231/0077	22. 7.85	C Lawrence	Weston Zoyland	16. 8.05P
	(Rotax 447)					
G-MNFF	Mainair Gemini Flash	371-1185-3-W110	29. 7.85	R P Cook and C H Spencer	St Michaels	24. 5.02P
	(Rotax 447)					
G-MNFG	Southdown Puma Sprint	SN1231/0078	31. 7.85	A C Hing	Longacre Farm, Sandy	12. 6.03P
G-MNFL	AMF Microflight Chevvron 2-32A	CH.002	19. 8.85	P W Wright *(Noted 2.08)*	Saltby	13.12.00P
G-MNFM	Mainair Gemini Flash	366-1085-3-W98	10.10.85	P M Fidell	Wombleton	1. 9.05P
	(Rotax 447)					
G-MNFN	Mainair Gemini Flash	367-1085-3-W99	6.11.85	J R Martin	(Bedale)	13. 8.04P
	(Rotax 447)					
G-MNFP	Mainair Gemini Flash	368-1085-3-W100	23.10.85	S Farnsworth and P Howarth	Tarn Farm, Cockerham	4. 7.06P
	(Rotax 447)					
G-MNGD	Ultrasports Tri-Pacer/Solar Wings Typhoon Medium		13. 8.85	J E Orbell	North Connel, Oban	X
	(Fuji-Robin EC-34-PM)	012 & T681-171		*(New owner 3.07)*		
G-MNGG	Solar Wings Pegasus XL-R	T784-1159XL	21. 8.85	I D Mallinson	Davidstow Moor	9. 8.06P
	(Trike c/n is US.TPR.0002)			*(Noted 9.06)*		
G-MNGK	Mainair Gemini Flash	374-1085-3-W112	5. 9.85	J Pulford	Priory Farm, Tibenham	15. 9.07P
	(Rotax 447)					
G-MNGM	Mainair Gemini Flash	394-1285-3-W109	5. 9.85	R J Webb	Over Farm, Gloucester	22.10.07P
	(Rotax 447) *(Originally supplied with Mainair Trike c/n 377: However this, and Sailwing ex G-MNIO, both stolen from Popham 15/16.3.86: Subsequently, G-MNGM now comprises Trike ex G-MNIO and Sailwing ex G-MNGM)*					
G-MNGT	Mainair Gemini Flash	372-1085-3-W106	30. 9.85	J W Biegus	Arclid Green, Sandbach	7. 6.02P
	(Rotax 447)					
G-MNGU	Mainair Gemini Flash	373-1085-3-W111	30. 9.85	G Macpherson-Irvine	Hunsdon	25. 6.05P
G-MNGW	Mainair Gemini Flash	386-1185-3-W121	30. 9.85	F R Stephens	(Worthing)	23. 4.03P
	(Rotax 447)					
G-MNGX	Southdown Puma Sprint	SN1231/0088	26. 9.85	A J Morris	Sutton Meadows	3. 3.07P
	(Rotax 447)					
G-MNHD	Solar Wings Pegasus XL-R	SW-WA-1047	5.11.85	P D Stiles	(Ashley Down, Bristol)	20. 7.07P
	(Trike c/n SW-TB-1033)					
G-MNHE	Solar Wings Pegasus XL-R/Se	SW-WA-1048	11.12.85	D Stevens	Davidstow Moor	17.10.05P
	(Trike c/n SW-TB-1036)					
G-MNHF	Solar Wings Pegasus XL-R	SW-WA-1049	29.11.85	J E Cox	Shobdon	29. 9.05P
	(Trike c/n SW-TB-1038)					
G-MNHH	Solar Wings Pegasus XL-S	SW-WA-1051	22. 1.86	F J Williams	(Shefford, Bedford)	24. 6.01P
	(Trike is an Ultrasports unit c/n PXL847-170)					
G-MNHI	Solar Wings Pegasus XL-R	SW-WA-1052	8. 1.86	C Council	(Whitstable)	7. 8.07P
	(Trike c/n SW-TB-1042)					
G-MNHJ	Solar Wings Pegasus XL-R	SW-WA-1053	11. 3.86	S J Woodd	(Charlbury, Chipping Norton)	26. 6.93P
	(Trike c/n SW-TB-1056)					
G-MNHK	Solar Wings Pegasus XL-R	SW-WA-1054	9. 7.86	K Buckley	Roddige	2. 6.08P
	(Rotax 462) *(Trike c/n SW-TE-0005)*					
G-MNHL	Solar Wings Pegasus XL-R/Se	SW-WA-1055	9. 7.86	The Microlight School Ltd	Roddige	15.10.08P
	(Rotax 503)*(Trike c/n SW-TB-1077) (Noted with Sailwing (skin only or whole frame?) from G-MTRN and marked "G-MT" under wing 4.06)*					
G-MNHM	Solar Wings Pegasus XL-R	SW-WA-1056	11. 7.86	P A Howell	(Stoke-on-Trent)	31. 8.07P
	(Trike c/n SW-TB-1078)					
G-MNHN	Solar Wings Pegasus XL-R	SW-WA-1057	11. 8.86	Northwest Microlights Ltd	Rochdale	11. 4.07P
	(Trike c/n SW-TB-1079)			*(Noted 11.07)*		
G-MNHR	Solar Wings Pegasus XL-R	SW-WA-1060	7. 8.86	B D Jackson	(Wincanton)	13.11.08P
	(Trike c/n SW-TB-1081)					
G-MNHS	Solar Wings Pegasus XL-R	SW-WA-1061	21. 8.86	M D Packer	Weston Zoyland	12.10.03P
	(Trike c/n SW-TB-1082)			*(Noted 7.04)*		
G-MNHT	Solar Wings Pegasus XL-R	SW-WA-1062	4. 8.86	J W Coventry	Davidstow Moor	4. 9.08P
	(Trike c/n SW-TB-1084)					
G-MNIA	Mainair Gemini Flash	370-1185-3-W105	10.10.85	A E Dix	Long Marston	10. 4.89P
	(Rotax 447)			*(Noted wrecked 1990)*		
G-MNID	Mainair Gemini Flash	369-1185-3-W104	7. 2.86	G Nicholls	(Rotherham)	30. 5.07P
	(Rotax 447) *(Official c/n is incorrect as Trike and Engine no.3706877 stolen from Rufforth 10 or 11.97 so a replacement Trike is fitted. BMAA records show c/n 360-5884-W104: this is a corruption - may be c/n 360-885-3 - but this conflicts with G-MNEG (qv))*					
G-MNIE	Mainair Gemini Flash	388-1185-3-W123	21.11.85	G M Hewer	(Cheltenham)	8. 7.02P
	(Rotax 447)					
G-MNIF	Mainair Gemini Flash	403-286-4-W147	7. 1.86	M Devlin	Dungannon	4. 4.08E
G-MNIG	Mainair Gemini/Flash	391-1285-3-W139	9. 1.86	A B Woods	(Halesworth)	18. 8.08P
	(Rotax 447)					
G-MNIH	Mainair Gemini Flash	379-1185-3-W116	10.12.85	N H S Insall	Dunkeswell	12. 8.08P
	(Rotax 447)					
G-MNII	Mainair Gemini Flash	390-1285-3-W128	6.11.85	R F Finnis	(Guildford)	6. 9.91P
	(Rotax 447)			*(Trike reported at St Michaels 9.96)*		
G-MNIK	Solar Wings Pegasus Photon	SW-WP-0002	29.10.85	J Grotrian	West Knoyle, Warminster	25. 4.07P
	(Trike c/n SW-TP-0002)			*(Operates from Wing Farm, Longbridge Deverill)*		
G-MNIL	Southdown Puma Sprint	SN1231/0094	4.11.85	A Bishop	Ince Blundell	31. 8.05P
	(Rotax 447)					

G-MNIM	Maxair Hummer	PJB-01	29.10.85	K Wood	(Keyham, Leicester)	
G-MNIS	CFM Shadow Series C	014	11.11.85	R W Payne	(Langtoft, Peterborough)	25. 4.92P
G-MNIT	Aerial Arts Alpha Mk.II/130SX	130SX/176	27. 2.86	M J Edmett	(London N3)	15. 8.99
	(Originally regd as Hiway Skytrike II with same c/n)			*(New owner 5.02)*		
G-MNIU	Solar Wings Pegasus Photon	SW-WP-0003	27.11.85	S Ferguson	Cumbernauld	X
	(Fuji-Robin EC-34) (Trike c/n SW-TP-0003)			*(Damaged and stored 3.90: Trike noted 11.06)*		
G-MNIZ	Mainair Gemini Flash	392-1285-3-W130	26. 2.86	A G Power	Higher Barn Farm, Houghton	25. 1.08P
	(Rotax 447)					
G-MNJB	Southdown Raven X	SN2232/0098	10.12.85	W Flood *(New owner 9.05)*	(London SE25)	26. 5.03P
G-MNJD	Mainair Tri-Flyer 440/Sprint	243-10484-2-P 537	2. 4.84	S D Smith	(Rednal, Birmingham)	7. 5.05P
	(Fuji-Robin EC-44-PM)			*(New owner 6.07)*		
G-MNJF	Dragon Light Aircraft Dragon Series 150	0068 (OY) 9-17	2. 1.86	B W Langley	South Wraxall	6. 9.06P
	(Fuji-Robin EC-44-PM)			*(Noted 6.07)*		
G-MNJG	Mainair Gemini/Southdown Puma Sprint MS		29. 9.83	T J Gayton-Polley	(Billingshurst)	20.11.07P
	(Fuji-Robin EC-44-PM) SA.2030 and 251-684-2-P 593					
G-MNJH	Solar Wings Pegasus Flash	SW-WF-0004	22.10.85	C P Course	Church Farm, Wellingborough	18. 8.02P
	(Trike c/n SW-TB-102 & Mainair Sailwing c/n W89)					
G-MNJJ	Solar Wings Pegasus Flash	SW-WF-0006	22.10.85	P A Shelley	(Washbrook, Ipswich)	26.11.96P
	(Trike c/n SW-TB-1029 & Mainair Sailwing c/n W96)					
G-MNJL	Solar Wings Pegasus Flash	SW-WF-0008	21.10.85	S D Thomas	(Bilston)	11.11.94P
	(Trike c/n SW-TB-1028 & Mainair Sailwing c/n W101)					
G-MNJN	Solar Wings Pegasus Flash	SW-WF-0010	19.11.85	D Thorn	Davidstow Moor	5. 7.05P
	(Trike c/n SW-TB-1034 & Mainair Sailwing c/n W103)					
G-MNJR	Solar Wings Pegasus Flash	SW-WF-0013	30.12.85	M G Ashbee	(Cranbrook)	8.10.08P
	(Trike c/n SW-TB-1041 & Mainair Sailwing c/n W133)					
G-MNJS	Southdown Puma Sprint	SN1231/0085	18. 9.85	E A Frost	Sutton Meadows	24. 2.06P
	(Rotax 447)					
G-MNJT	Southdown Raven X	SN2232/0087	20. 9.85	P A Harris	RAF Henlow	7. 3.04P
	(Forced landed east of Exford, Devon 11. 7.03 causing substantial damage)					
G-MNJU	Mainair Gemini Flash	384-1185-3-W119	20. 9.85	H A Taylor	Finmere	3. 6.03P
	(Rotax 447)			*(New owner 1.07)*		
G-MNJX	Medway Hybred 44XL	15885/14	9.12.85	H A Stewart	(Hartlip, Sittingbourne)	23. 7.98P
G-MNKB	Solar Wings Pegasus Photon	SW-WP-0005	14. 1.86	M E Gilbert	Drummaird Farm, Bonnybank	11. 5.06P
	(Trike c/n SW-TP-0005)					
G-MNKC	Solar Wings Pegasus Photon	SW-WP-0006	14. 1.86	K B Woods	(Somersham, Huntingdon)	17. 3.04P
	(Trike c/n SW-TP-0006)			*(New owner 12.07)*		
G-MNKD	Solar Wings Pegasus Photon	SW-WP-0007	14. 1.86	A M Sirant	Davidstow Moor	8. 4.05P
	(Originally allocated Trike c/n SW-TP-0007 but believed exported: current Trike is possibly c/n SW-TP-0016) (New owner 10.07)					
G-MNKE	Solar Wings Pegasus Photon	SW-WP-0008	14. 1.86	M J Olsen	Wombleton	2. 8.04P
	(Trike c/n SW-TP-0008)					
G-MNKG	Solar Wings Pegasus Photon	SW-WP-0010	28. 1.86	T W Thompson	Eshott	11. 6.95P
	(Trike c/n SW-TP-0010)			*(Trike stored 9.97)*		
G-MNKK	Solar Wings Pegasus Photon	SW-WP-0014	28. 1.86	M E Gilbert	(Dalgety Bay, Dunfermline)	7. 5.95P
	(Fuji-Robin EC-34-PM) (Trike c/n SW-TP-0014)					
G-MNKM	MBA Tiger Cub 440	SO.213	30.12.85	A R Sunley *(New owner 11.04)*	(Chelmsford)	17. 2.04P
G-MNKO	Solar Wings Pegasus XL-Q	SW-WX-0001	2. 1.86	T A Goundry	Eshott	29. 9.06P
	(Rotax 447) *(Trike c/n SW-TB-1158)*			*(New owner 1.08)*		
G-MNKP	Solar Wings Pegasus Flash	SW-WF-0014	9. 1.86	I N Miller	Plaistows Farm, St Albans	14. 1.08P
	(Trike c/n SW-TB-1043 & Mainair Sailwing c/n W131)					
G-MNKU	Southdown Puma Sprint	SN1231/0100	29. 1.86	S P O'Hannrachain	(Coolaney, County Sligo)	30. 8.03P
	(Rotax 447)					
G-MNKV	Solar Wings Pegasus Flash	SW-WF-0017	15. 1.86	K S G Lindfield	Dunkeswell	27. 4.06P
	(Trike c/n SW-TB-1047 & Mainair Sailwing c/n W137)					
G-MNKW	Solar Wings Pegasus Flash	SW-WF-0018	28. 1.86	S P Halford	Mill Farm, Hughley, Much Wenlock	29. 7.08P
	(Trike c/n SW-TB-1049 & Mainair Sailwing c/n W140)					
G-MNKX	Solar Wings Pegasus Flash	SW-WF-0019	28. 2.86	P Samal	(Sandy)	3. 8.05P
	(Trike c/n SW-TB-1054 & Mainair Sailwing c/n W139)					
G-MNKZ	Southdown Raven X	SN2232/0102	4. 2.86	G B Gratton	(Amersham)	31. 5.07P
G-MNLH	Romain Cobra Biplane	001	23. 1.86	J W E Romain	(Welwyn)	10. 4.06P
	(Midwest AE50R)					
G-MNLI	Mainair Gemini Flash II	407-286-4-W152	28. 1.86	P M Fessi *(Noted 10.07)*	Swinford, Rugby	28.10.07P
G-MNLM	Southdown Raven X	SN2232/0110	6. 2.86	A P White	(Exmouth)	9. 6.93P
G-MNLN	Southdown Raven X	SN2232/0111	6. 2.86	A S Windley	(Matlock)	27.12.00P
G-MNLT	Southdown Raven X	SN2232/0115	6. 2.86	J L Stachini	Stoke, Isle of Grain	12. 8.01P
G-MNLY	Mainair Gemini Flash	406-386-4-W151	14. 2.86	P D Parry	(Ruthin)	26. 7.05P
G-MNLZ	Southdown Raven X	SN2232/0123	6. 2.86	R Downham *(New owner 6.06)*	(Bacup)	12. 6.02P
G-MNMC	Mainair Gemini/Southdown Puma Sprint MS		20. 3.84	G A Davidson	(Brierfield, Nelson)	18. 6.07P
	222-284-2 & P 524					
G-MNMD	Southdown Raven X	SN2000/0121	10. 2.86	P G Overall	(Crawley)	31. 5.05P
G-MNMG	Mainair Gemini Flash II	419-386-4-W177	11. 2.86	N A M Beyer-Kay	(Southport)	20. 8.94P
	(Rotax 447)					
G-MNMI	Mainair Gemini Flash II	317-685-3-W178	11. 2.86	A D Bales	Priory Farm, Tibenham	12. 6.08P
	(Fuji-Robin EC-44) (Trike and engine ex G-MMZL following accident 8.9.91)					
G-MNMK	Solar Wings Pegasus XL-R	SW-WA-1038	19. 8.85	A F Smallacombe	(Okehampton)	2. 7.00P
	(Trike c/n SW-TB-1021)					
G-MNML	Southdown Puma Sprint	SN1111/0065	4. 8.83	R C Carr	(Boyton, Launceston)	14. 7.97P
	(Fuji-Robin EC-44-PM)					
G-MNMM	Aerotech MW-5(K) Sorcerer	5K-0001-02	11. 2.86	S F N Warnell	(Staines)	17. 8.99P
	(Originally regd as c/n SR101-R4008-01 - now officially regd. as c/n 5K-0001-01) (New owner 9.04)					
G-MNMU	Southdown Puma Raven	SN2232/0127	17. 2.86	M J Curley	(London Colney)	26. 3.06P
G-MNMV	Mainair Gemini Flash	375-1085-3-W113	3. 3.86	S Staig	Tarn Farm, Cockerham	13. 8.06P
	(Rotax 447)					
G-MNMW	Whittaker MW6-1-1 Merlin	PFA 164-11144	16. 4.86	E F Clapham tr G-MNMW Flying Group		
	(Built E F Clapham) (Rotax 582)				Otherton, Cannock	21. 8.08P

G-MNMY	Cyclone 70/Aerial Arts 110SX	CH-02	6. 3.86	N R Beale	Deppers Bridge, Southam	15. 7.05P
G-MNNA	Southdown Raven X	SN2232/0129	4. 3.86	D and G D Palfrey	(Morebath, Tiverton)	20. 7.88P
G-MNNB	Southdown Raven	SN2122/0130	4. 3.86	J F Horn	(Yelverton)	3. 6.03P
	(Fuji-Robin EC-44-PM)					
G-MNNC	Southdown Raven X	SN2232/0131	4. 3.86	S A Sacker	Deenethorpe	5. 8.00P
G-MNNF	Mainair Gemini Flash II	402-286-4-W148	28. 2.86	W J Gunn	Long Marston	8. 4.97P
	(Rotax 447)			*(Stored 1.98)*		
G-MNNG	Squires Lightfly/Solar Wings Photon	SW-WP-0019	25. 2.86	K B Woods	(Somersham, Huntingdon)	X
	(Rotax 277) (Trike may be Mainair Tri-Flyer c/n 032-221181 ex G-MJKY?)			*(Address change 10.07)*		
G-MNNJ	Mainair Gemini Flash II	405-286-4-W150	28. 2.86	H D Lynch	(Fermoy, County Cork)	6. 5.05P
	(ID Plate incorrectly marked as "G-MNNZ")					
G-MNNM	Mainair Scorcher Solo	424-486-1-W182	(G-MNPE)	20. 3.86	S R Leeper and L L Perry	Grove Farm, Needham	9. 2.06P
G-MNNO	Southdown Raven X	SN2232/0133	26. 3.86	M J Robbins	(Tunbridge Wells)	16.12.01P
G-MNNR	Mainair Gemini Flash II	430-586-4-W188	6. 3.86	W A B Hill	Davidstow Moor	9. 6.02P
	(Wing originally quoted as c/n W157)			*(Noted 7.05)*		
G-MNNS	Eurowing Goldwing	EW-74	8. 4.86	J S R Moodie	(Rovie Farm, Rogart)	
	(Rotax 377)			*(Stored 6.06)*		
G-MNNY	Solar Wings Pegasus Flash	SW-WF-0023	14. 3.86	C W Payne	Croft Farm, Defford	20. 3.04P
	(Trike c/n SW-TB-1059 & Mainair Sailwing c/n W161)					
G-MNNZ	Solar Wings Pegasus Flash II	SW-WF-0101	24. 4.86	R D A Henderson	(Carnon Downs, Truro)	1. 4.98P
	(Trike c/n SW-TB-1060 & Mainair Sailwing c/n W162)					
G-MNPA	Solar Wings Pegasus Flash II	SW-WF-0102	18. 4.86	N T Murphy	(Rathangon, County Kildare)	30. 5.98P
	(Rotax 462) (Trike c/n SW-TB-1061) (Original Mainair Sailwing c/n W174 but has now acquired W210 ex G-MNZA) (New owner 9.01)					
G-MNPC	Mainair Gemini Flash II	423-586-4-W181	17. 3.86	M S McGimpsey	Newtownards	2. 5.08P
	(Rotax 462)					
G-MNPG	Mainair Gemini Flash II	437-686-4-W204	20. 3.86	P Kirton	(Braco, Dunblane)	4. 9.06P
	(Rotax 447)					
G-MNPV	Mainair Scorcher Solo	432-586-1-W189	24. 3.86	M L Walsh *(New owner 12.06)*	Mill Farm, Shifnal	21.10.05P
G-MNPY	Mainair Scorcher Solo	452-886-1-W229	25. 3.86	R N O Kingsbury	Miiddle Stoke, Isle of Grain	22. 5.08P
G-MNPZ	Mainair Scorcher Solo	449-886-1-W226	25. 3.86	S Stevens	(Cornhill-on-Tweed)	4. 9.93P
	(Rotax 503) (3-Blade propeller test aircraft)					
G-MNRD	Ultraflight Lazair IIIE	81	17. 6.83	F P Welsh tr Sywell Lazair Group	Sywell	12. 4.05P
				(Noted 10.07)		
G-MNRE	Mainair Scorcher Solo	453-886-1-W230	25. 3.86	A P Pearce	Wickhambrook, Newmarket	27. 6.06P
G-MNRI	Hornet Dual Trainer/Southdown Raven		26. 3.86	R H Goll	(Llansawel, Llandeilo)	2. 8.02P
		HRWA 0051 & SN2000/0119		*(New owner 1.04)*		
G-MNRK	Hornet Dual Trainer/Southdown Raven		26. 3.86	M A H Milne	(Huntly)	30. 7.95P
	(Rotax 447)	HRWA 0053 & SN2000/0183		*(New owner 3.03)*		
G-MNRM	Hornet Dual Trainer/Southdown Raven		26. 3.86	R I Cannan	(Ramsey, Isle of Man)	23. 2.08P
		HRWA 0055 & SN2000/0214				
G-MNRP	Southdown Raven X	SN2232/0135	7. 4.86	C Moore	(Haile, Egremont)	5. 7.95P
G-MNRS	Southdown Raven X	SN2232/0137	7. 4.86	M C Newman	(St Leonards-on-Sea)	29. 7.04P
G-MNRT	Midland Ultralights Sirocco 377GB	MU-016	1. 4.86	R F Hinton	(Mansfield)	18. 8.01P
G-MNRW	Mainair Gemini Flash II	411-486-4-W156	7. 4.86	D Buckthorpe	Clench Common	12.10.04P
	(Rotax 462)			*(Noted 5.05)*		
G-MNRX	Mainair Gemini Flash II	434-686-4-W220	8. 4.86	R Downham	(Bacup)	14. 8.08P
G-MNRZ	Mainair Scorcher Solo	426-586-1-W184	4. 4.86	J Lynch *(New owner 10.07)*	Sandtoft	10. 5.07P
G-MNSA	Mainair Gemini Flash II	442-786-4-W219	18. 4.86	W F G Panayiotiou	(Llanelli)	23. 8.04P
G-MNSD	Ultrasports Tri-Pacer 250/Solar Wings Typhoon S4		23. 4.86	A Strydom	(London WC1)	X
	(Hunting HS.260A)	T182-341L		*(New owner 10.02)*		
G-MNSH	Solar Wings Pegasus Flash II	SW-WF-0104	14. 4.86	D Lee	(Newton Bank Farm, Daresbury)	14. 5.05P
	(Rotax 447) (Trike c/n SW-TB-1063 & Mainair Sailwing c/n W163)					
G-MNSI	Mainair Gemini Flash II	445-786-4-W213	9. 4.86	J-P Trouillard *(New owner 10.06)*	(St Nazaire, France)	9. 6.03P
G-MNSJ	Mainair Gemini Flash II	443-886-4-W223	11. 4.86	G J Cadden	Smithboro, County Monaghan	14. 5.06P
G-MNSL	Southdown Raven X	SN2232/0145	17. 4.86	P B Robinson *(New owner 5.02)*	(Ely)	11. 8.00P
G-MNSX	Southdown Raven X	SN2232/0148	30. 4.86	S F Chave	(Honiton)	18. 7.03P
G-MNSY	Southdown Raven X	SN2232/0149	30. 4.86	L A Hosegood	(Swindon)	8. 3.03P
G-MNTC	Southdown Raven X	SN2232/0150	30. 4.86	D S Bancalari *(New owner 11.01)*	(Norwich)	12.10.92P
G-MNTD	Aerial Arts Chaser/110SX	110SX/255	24. 4.86	B Richardson	(Sunderland)	
	(C/n duplicates G-MTSF)					
G-MNTE	Southdown Raven X	SN2232/0151	30. 4.86	E Foster	Brook Farm, Pilling	27. 6.04P
				(Remains noted 7.07)		
G-MNTI	Mainair Gemini Flash II	447-886-4-W231	8. 5.86	R T Strathie	Nether Huntlywood Farm, Gordon	19. 8.01P
				(Noted 2.06)		
G-MNTK	CFM Shadow Series CD	024	8. 5.86	A B Potts	Eshott	17. 8.04P
G-MNTM	Southdown Raven X	SN2232/0154	19. 5.86	D M Garland	(Atherstone)	24. 7.01P
G-MNTN	Southdown Raven X	SN2232/0155	2. 6.86	J Hall	(Wolverhampton)	25. 1.06P
G-MNTP	CFM Shadow Series C	K 022	19. 5.86	E G White	Landmead Farm, Garford	6. 5.07P
	(Rotax 462)					
G-MNTT	Medway Half Pint/Aerial Arts 130SX	12/1486	7. 4.86	P J Burrow	(Crediton)	20. 6.03P
	(Rotax 462)					
G-MNTU	Mainair Gemini Flash II	460-886-4-W233	9. 7.86	G S Brewer	(Balderton, Newark)	24. 7.06P
	(Rotax 503)					
G-MNTV	Mainair Gemini Flash II	455-886-4-W241	9. 7.86	A M Sirant	Davidstow Moor	17.10.04P
	(Rotax 462)			*(New owner 1.06)*		
G-MNTY	Southdown Raven X	SN2232/0157	29. 5.86	S Phillips	(Snodland)	16. 5.05P
G-MNTZ	Mainair Gemini Flash II	457-886-4-W243	3. 6.86	D E Milner	(Leeds)	4. 1.06P
G-MNUA	Mainair Gemini Flash II	458-886-4-W235	29. 5.86	P Hughes and S Beggan	Newtownards	8.12.07P
	(Rotax 462)					
G-MNUD	Solar Wings Pegasus Flash II	SW-WF-0110	10. 6.86	P G H Milbank	Sutton Meadows	20. 9.03P
	(Rotax 462) Trike c/n SW-TE-0003 & Mainair Sailwing c/n W195)					
G-MNUE	Solar Wings Pegasus Flash II	SW-WF-0108	10. 6.86	R J Saxby	(Dorchester)	24. 7.06P
	(Rotax 462) (Trike c/n SW-TE-0002) (Original Mainair Sailwing c/n W193 but now acquired c/n W209 ex G-MNYA) (New owner 8.07)					
G-MNUF	Mainair Gemini Flash II	472-786-4-W252	13. 6.86	E N Alms	(Crowley, Northwich)	9. 7.08P

G-MNUG	Mainair Gemini Flash II (Rotax 462)	465-986-4-W245		13. 6.86	A S Nader		Ince Blundell	19.10.05P
G-MNUI	Mainair Tri-Flyer/Skyhook Cutlass (Fuji-Robin EC-44-PM)	MH-01		21. 5.86	M Holling		(Pollington, Goole)	28. 2.87X
G-MNUO	Mainair Gemini Flash II (Rotax 462)	421-586-4-W179		9. 7.86	P S Taylor		(Addlestone)	29. 5.06P
G-MNUR	Mainair Gemini Flash II	470-986-4-W250		14. 8.86	J C Greves		(Walton-on-Thames)	30. 3.90P
G-MNUU	Southdown Raven X	SN2232/0162		26. 6.86	P N Jackson *(Noted 8.05)*		Davidstow Moor	10. 9.02P
G-MNUW	Southdown Raven X	SN2232/0163		17. 6.86	B A McDonald		(Cambridge)	19.12.96P
G-MNUX	Solar Wings Pegasus XL-R	SW-WA-1076 *(Trike c/n SW-TB-1072)*		24. 6.86	A M Smith *(Noted 2.08)*		Shotton Colliery, Peterlee	3. 5.03P
G-MNVB	Solar Wings Pegasus XL-R	SW-WA-1077 *(Trike c/n SW-TB-1073)*		7. 7.86	M J Melvin		(Hoddesdon)	10. 4.08P
G-MNVC	Solar Wings Pegasus XL-R	SW-WA-1078 *(Trike c/n SW-TB-1074)*		7. 7.86	M N C Ward		Shobdon	11. 6.00P
G-MNVE	Solar Wings Pegasus XL-R	SW-WA-1079 *(Trike c/n SW-TB-1075)*		19. 6.86	M P Aris		(Welwyn)	11. 8.00P
G-MNVG	Solar Wings Pegasus Flash II (Rotax 447) *(Trike c/n SW-TB-1069 & Mainair Sailwing c/n W194)*	SW-WF-0109		11. 6.86	D J Ward		Low Farm, South Walsham	23. 8.08P
G-MNVH	Solar Wings Pegasus Flash II (Rotax 462) *(Trike c/n SW-TE-0001 & Mainair Sailwing c/n W260)*	SW-WF-0122		23. 6.86	J A Clarke and C Hall		(London N22 and E8)	9. 4.97P
G-MNVI	CFM Shadow Series C	026		17. 6.86	D R C Pugh		(Caersws, Powys)	4. 6.08P
G-MNVJ	CFM Shadow Series CD	028		17. 6.86	V C Readhead		(Saxmundham)	1. 5.08P
G-MNVK	CFM Shadow Series CD	029		17. 6.86	M J Cook		Plaistows Farm, St Albans	16.11.08P
G-MNVL	Medway Half Pint/Aerial Arts 130SX	3/21585 & 130SX-100	G-MNBZ	22. 9.86	B W Austin		Croft Farm, Defford	X
G-MNVN	Southdown Puma Raven (Fuji-Robin EC-44-PM)	SN2132/0165		27. 6.86	R J Styles		(Worcester)	11. 4.08P
G-MNVO	Hovey Whing-Ding II	CW-01		14. 8.86	C Wilson *(New owner 5.02)*		(Basildon)	
G-MNVP	Southdown Raven X	SN2232/0166	(EI- . . .) G-MNVP, (EI- . . .), G-MNVP	23. 6.86	N Furlong	Kilpatrick, Stradbally, County Laois		19.12.03P
G-MNVT	Mainair Gemini Flash II	477-786-4-W258		27. 6.86	A C Barker t/a ACB Hydraulics *(Stored 4.90*		Hinton-in-the-Hedges	28. 7.87P
G-MNVV	Mainair Gemini Flash II	467-986-4-W247		26. 6.86	T Wilbor		Bagby	10. 2.08P
G-MNVW	Mainair Gemini Flash II	466-986-4-W246		26. 6.86	J C Munro-Hunt		(Little Down Farm, Milson)	29. 9.08P
G-MNVZ	Solar Wings Pegasus Photon	SW-WP-0021 *(Trike c/n SW-TP-0021)*		27. 6.86	J J Russ		(Washington)	27. 6.94P
G-MNWD	Mainair Gemini Flash II (Rotax 462)	474-986-4-W254		27. 6.86	M B Rutherford *(Noted 11.07)*		Swinford, Rugby	7. 7.01P
G-MNWG	Southdown Raven X	SN2232/0170		4. 8.86	D Murray		(Clevedon)	9. 5.05P
G-MNWI	Mainair Gemini Flash II	478-986-4-W264		9. 7.86	R N Snook		Strathaven	22. 9.07P
G-MNWL	Arbiter Services Trike/Aerial Arts 130SX	130SX/333		23. 7.86	E H Snook		(Newport Pagnell)	
G-MNWU	Solar Wings Pegasus Flash II (Rotax 462) *(Trike c/n SW-TE-0006 & Mainair Sailwing c/n W196)*	SW-WF-0111		4. 8.86	S P Wass *(Sailwing noted for spares use 4.07)*	Wing Farm, Longbridge Deverill		26. 4.05P
G-MNWW	Solar Wings Pegasus XL Tug (Rotax 462) *(Trike c/n SW-TE-0008)*	SW-WA-1085		8.10.86	N P Chittytr Chiltern Flyers Aero Tow Group		Ginge, Wantage	30. 7.07P
G-MNWY	CFM Shadow Series C *(Built CFM Aircraft Ltd - pr.no.PFA 161-11130)*	K 021		28. 7.86	J Williams *(Noted 8.07)*		Headon Farm, Retford	19. 8.03P
G-MNWZ	Mainair Gemini Flash II	436-686-4-W203	(G-MNXV)	19. 8.86	W T Hume		(Newmilns)	16. 6.98P
G-MNXB	Solar Wings Photon/Mainair Tri-Flyer (Fuji-Robin EC-34-PM) SW-WP-0022 & 016-29981			29. 7.86	G W Carwardine *(Noted 5.07 with Mike Phillips' Trike)*		(Hadlow Down, Uckfield)	16. 6.98P
G-MNXE	Southdown Raven X	SN2232/0202		7. 8.86	A E Silvey		Wilburton, Ely	12. 7.07P
G-MNXF	Southdown Puma Raven	SN2132/0176		2. 9.86	D E Gwenin		(Tring)	13. 5.99P
G-MNXG	Southdown Raven X	SN2232/0181		3. 9.86	M A Williams		(Tonbridge)	22. 7.02P
G-MNXI	Southdown Raven X	SN2232/0179		19. 8.86	P K Morley		Baxby Manor, Husthwaite	30. 9.08P
G-MNXO	Medway Hybred 44XLR	29786/19		3. 9.86	D L Turner		(Chatham)	6. 7.02P
G-MNXP	Solar Wings Pegasus Flash II (Rotax 447) *(Trike c/n SW-TB-1094 & Mainair Sailwing c/n W207)*	SW-WF-0117		16. 9.86	I K Priestley *(New owner 3.04)*		(Thurleigh, Bedford)	6. 8.96P
G-MNXS	Mainair Gemini Flash II (Rotax 462)	480-986-4-W267		8. 9.86	F T Rawlings *(Believed exported to Portugal c1988?)*		(Hereford)	16. 3.89P
G-MNXU	Mainair Gemini Flash II	482-1086-4-W272		18. 8.86	J M Hucker		(Abertillery)	10. 3.98P
G-MNXX	CFM Shadow Series CD	K 027		13. 8.86	R E Williams		(Margam, Port Talbot)	13. 3.08P
G-MNXZ	Whittaker MW5 Sorcerer *(Built P J Cheyney)* (Fuji-Robin EC-34-PM)	PFA 163-11156		13. 8.86	A J Glynn		Gerpins Farm, Upminster	6. 2.08P
G-MNYA	Solar Wings Pegasus Flash II (Rotax 447) *(Trike c/n SW-TB-1098 & Mainair Sailwing c/n W259)*	SW-WF-0119		3. 9.86	C Trollope		Watnall	25. 3.05P
G-MNYC	Solar Wings Pegasus XL-R	SW-WA-1090 *(Trike c/n SW-TB-1097)*		3. 9.86	A N Papworth		Sutton Meadows	16. 7.08P
G-MNYD	Aerial Arts Chaser/110SX (Rotax 377)	110SX/320		19. 8.86	B Richardson		(Eshott)	17.10.04P
G-MNYE	Aerial Arts Chaser/110SX (Rotax 337)	110SX/321		19. 8.86	R J Ripley *(New owner 6.00)*		(Oakley, Bedford)	18.11.99P
G-MNYF	Aerial Arts Chaser/110SX (Rotax 377)	110SX/322		19. 8.86	B Richardson		(Eshott)	12. 5.06P
G-MNYG	Southdown Puma Raven	SN2122/0172		19. 8.86	K Clifford		(Stanmore)	3. 7.00P
G-MNYJ	Mainair Gemini Flash II (Rotax 462)	485-1086-4-W275		8. 9.86	G B Jones		Otherton, Cannock	13. 7.03P
G-MNYK	Mainair Gemini Flash II (Rotax 582)	494-1086-4-W296		11. 9.86	J J Ryan		(Enniscorthy, County Wexford)	4.10.95P
G-MNYL	Southdown Raven X	SN2232/0195		2. 9.86	A D F Clifford *(Noted 5.05)*	Broadmeadow Farm, Hereford		9. 6.98P
G-MNYM	Southdown Raven X	SN2232/0196		2. 9.86	R L Davis		Dunkeswell	11. 6.04P
G-MNYP	Southdown Raven X	SN2232/0207		3. 9.86	A G Davies		(Bristol)	14. 5.01P

G-MNYU	Solar Wings Pegasus XL-R/Se	SW-WA-1092		16. 9.86	G L Turner	Pittrichie Farm, Whiterashes 28. 4.06P
	(Trike c/n SW-TB-1100)					
G-MNYW	Solar Wings Pegasus XL-R	SW-WA-1094		11. 9.86	M P Waldock	(Croydon) 7. 8.98P
	(Trike c/n SW-TB-1102)					
G-MNYX	Solar Wings Pegasus XL-R	SW-WA-1095		19. 9.86	P Mayes and J P Widdowson	(Bridgnorth) 31. 8.08P
	(Rotax 462) (Trike c/n SW-TE-0009)				(See G-MMKG)	
G-MNYZ	Solar Wings Pegasus Flash II	SW-WF-0114		11. 9.86	A C Bartolozzi	(Ely) 7. 8.04P
	(Rotax 462) (Trike c/n SW-TE-0010 & Mainair Sailwing c/n W199)					
G-MNZB	Mainair Gemini Flash II	483-1086-4-W273		8. 9.86	P A Ryde	Mill Farm, Shifnal 25. 3.08P
G-MNZC	Mainair Gemini Flash II	484-1086-4-W274		6. 9.86	C J Whittaker (New owner 11.02)	(Ledbury) 19. 1.89P
G-MNZD	Mainair Gemini Flash II	493-1086-4-W295		8. 9.86	N D Carter (Stored 9.96)	Little Gransden 4. 4.96P
G-MNZF	Mainair Gemini Flash II	496-1186-4-W291		8. 9.86	P C Askew	Tarn Farm, Cockerham 16. 7.08P
G-MNZJ	CFM Shadow Series CD	033		19. 9.86	T E P Eves tr G-MNZJ Shadow Group	Bagby 13. 6.07P
					(Noted 2.08)	
G-MNZK	Solar Wings Pegasus XL-R/Se	SW-WA-1096		24. 9.86	P J Appleby	
					(Foxfield, Carrick-on-Shannon, County Leitrim) 29. 3.04P	
G-MNZP	CFM Shadow Series BD	K 039		19. 9.86	J G Wakeford	Deanland 20. 6.06P
	(Built CFM Aircraft Ltd - pr.no.PFA 161-11206)					
G-MNZR	CFM Shadow Series BD	040		19. 9.86	P J Watson Lower Mountpleasant Farm, Chatteris 20. 7.07P	
G-MNZS	Aerial Arts Alpha/130SX	130SX/376		23. 9.86	N R Beale	Deppers Bridge, Southam 1. 8.00P
	(Rotax 277)					
G-MNZU	Eurowing Goldwing	EW-88		24. 9.86	P D Coppin and P R Millen	
	(Fuji-Robin EC-34-PM)				Colemore Common, Hampshire 5.11.05P	
G-MNZW	Southdown Raven X	SN2232/0220		17.10.86	T A Willcox (Noted 4.06)	Doynton 7. 7.02P
G-MNZX	Southdown Raven X	SN2232/0221		10.10.86	B F Hole	(Warninglid, Haywards Heath) 10.11.07P
G-MNZZ	CFM Shadow Series CD	036		19. 9.86	Shadow Aviation Ltd (New owner 7.06)	Old Sarum 31. 8.05P
G-MOAC	Beech F33A Bonanza	CE-1349	N1563N	25. 5.89	R L Camrass	Le Touquet 30. 5.07
G-MOAN	Aeromot AMT-200S Super Ximango	200.133	PT-PRU	29. 3.04	A E Mayhew	Rochester 30. 4.08E
G-MODE	Eurocopter EC.120B Colibri	1295	F-WQPU	19. 8.02	P A Cripps	(Compton Bassett, Calne) 17.11.07E
G-MOFB	Cameron O-120 Balloon (Hot Air)	4275		13. 1.98	D M Moffat	Chateaux d'Oex, Switzerland 20. 1.08A
G-MOFF	Cameron O-77 Balloon (Hot Air)	2040		27. 7.89	D M Moffat	Alveston, Bristol 7. 9.95A
					"Moff"	
G-MOFZ	Cameron O-90 Balloon (Hot Air)	3350		7. 9.94	D M Moffat	Alveston, Bristol 29. 6.08A
G-MOGI	Grumman AA-5A Cheetah	AA5A-0630	G-BFMU	1. 5.86	J G Stewart tr MOGI Flying Group	Cranfield 12. 1.08E
G-MOGY	Robinson R22 Beta	0899		23.11.88	Northumbria Helicopters Ltd	Newcastle 24. 9.08E
G-MOKE	Cameron V-77 Balloon (Hot Air)	3686		4.10.95	G Moyano tr G-MOKE ASBC Winseler Luxembourg	28. 5.08A
G-MOLE	Taylor JT.2 Titch	PFA 060-10725		20. 1.87	R Calverley	Shobdon 13. 3.08P
	(Buillt S R Mowle)					
G-MOLI	Cameron A-250 Balloon (Hot Air)	3429 (2)		26. 1.95	J J Rudoni and A C K Rawson (Stan Robertson Transport titles)	
	(New envelope fitted 2000 - original c/n retained)				t/a Wickers World Hot Air Balloon Company Stafford 25.10.05T	
G-MOLL	Piper PA-32-301T Turbo Saratoga	32-8024040	N82535	25. 3.91	N A M and R A Brain	Gamston 8. 5.08E
G-MOMA	Thruster T 600N 450 Sprint	0036-T600N-088	G-CCIB	22. 8.03	Turley Farms Ltd	(Dunholme, Lincoln) 25. 8.05P
					(Noted 11.05)	
G-MOMO	Agusta A109E Power Elite	11154		30. 4.02	Air Harrods Ltd	London Stansted 30. 4.08E
G-MONB	Boeing 757-2T7	22780		7. 3.83	Monarch Airlines Ltd	Luton 1. 3.08R
G-MONC	Boeing 757-2T7	22781	PH-AHO	15. 4.83	Monarch Airlines Ltd	Luton 29. 4.08E
			D-ABNY, G-MONC, EC-211, G-MONC			
G-MOND	Boeing 757-2T7	22960	D-ABNZ	28. 4.83	Monarch Airlines Ltd	Luton 13. 5.08E
			G-MOND			
G-MONE	Boeing 757-2T7	23293		27. 2.85	Monarch Airlines Ltd (Renaissance Cruise titles) Luton 25. 2.08E	
G-MONI	Monnett Moni	PFA 142-10925		12. 1.84	R M Edworthy	(Littleover) 16. 4.02P
	(Built ARV Aviation Ltd) (IAME KFM.107)					
G-MONJ	Boeing 757-2T7	24104		26. 2.88	Monarch Airlines Ltd	Luton 23. 1.08E
G-MONK	Boeing 757-2T7	24105		26. 2.88	Monarch Airlines Ltd	Luton 31. 5.08E
G-MONR	Airbus A300B4-605R	540	VH-YMJ	15. 3.90	Monarch Airlines Ltd	Luton 2. 4.08E
			G-MONR, F-WWAT			
G-MONS	Airbus A300B4-605R	556	VH-YMK	17. 4.90	Monarch Airlines Ltd	Luton 3. 5.08E
			G-MONS, F-WWAY			
G-MONX	Airbus A320-212	392	F-WWDR	19. 3.93	Monarch Airlines Ltd	Luton 17. 3.08E
G-MOOO	Learjet Model 40	45-2007	N40PX	5. 8.05	LPC Aviation Ltd	Manchester 9. 8.08E
			N50126		(Operated Northern Executive Aviation Ltd)	
G-MOOR	SOCATA TB-10 Tobago	82	G-MILK	23. 7.91	P D Kirkham	Gamston 4.11.07E
G-MOOS	Hunting Percival P 56 Provost T 1	PAC/F/335	G-BGKA	5. 4.91	H Cooke	RNAS Yeovilton 3. 7.08P
			8041M/XF690		(As "XF690" in RAF c/s)	
G-MOPS	Best Off Sky Ranger Swift 912S	SKRxxxx800		4.10.07	P Stretton	(Littlestone, New Romney)
	(Built P Stretton pr.no.BMAA/HB/547)					
G-MOSS	Beech D55 Baron	TE-548	G-AWAD	12. 6.95	A G E Camisa	Elstree 29. 6.08E
G-MOSY	Cameron O-84 Balloon (Hot Air)	2315	EI-CAO	17. 4.96	P L Mossman	Llanishen, Chepstow 23. 3.08A
					(Budget Traders titles)	
G-MOTA	Bell 206B-3 JetRanger III	4494	N81521	20.10.98	J W Sandle	Runcton Holme, King's Lynn 1.10.07E
G-MOTH	de Havilland DH.82A Tiger Moth	85340	7035M	31. 1.78	P T Szluha	Audley End 9. 6.08
	(Built Morris Motors Ltd)		DE306		(As "K-2567" in RAF c/s)	
G-MOTI	Robin DR.500-200i Président	0006		23.11.98	The Lord Saville of Newdigate tr The Tango India Flying Group	
	(Officially regd as DR.400-500)				Biggin Hill 9. 3.08E	
G-MOTO	Piper PA-24 Comanche	24-3239	G-EDHE	24. 3.87	L T and S Evans	Sandown, Isle of Wight 18.11.07
			N51867, G-ASFH, EI-AMM, N7998P			
G-MOTR	Enstrom 280C Shark	1050	G-BGWS	30. 6.06	Motor Provider Ltd	(Sheffield City) 24. 9.08E
G-MOUL	Maule M-6-235C Super Rocket	7518C		1. 5.90	M Klinge	Prestwick 21. 6.08E
G-MOUN	Beech B200 Super King Air	BB-1734	N123NA	27. 9.02	Real Aero Club de Valencia	Valencia, Spain 7.11.07E
			JA200N, N123NA			
G-MOUR	Folland Gnat T 1	FL.596	8624M	16. 5.90	R F Harvey and M J Gadsby tr Yellowjack Group	
			XS102		(As "XR991" in RAF Yellowjacks c/s) Kemble 28. 4.08P	
G-MOUT	Cessna 182T Skylane	18281315	N2104H	23. 3.04	G Mountain	Leeds-Bradford 4. 7.08E
G-MOVE	Piper PA-60-601P Aerostar	61P-0593-7963263	OO-PKB	5. 1.79	M G Roberts t/a Flight Consultancy Services	
			G-MOVE, N8144J		(Stored engineless 1.08)	Bournemouth 6. 8.05

G-MOVI	Piper PA-32R-301 Saratoga II SP	32R-8313029	G-MARI	6. 2.89	G-BOON Ltd	Wycombe Air Park	12. 4.08E
			N8248H				
G-MOWG	Aeroprakt A22-L Foxbat	PFA 317A-14545		21. 6.06	J Smith	East Winch	14.11.07P
	(Built J Smith)						
G-MOZI	Glasflügel H303 Mosquito	34	BGA 3587-FWR	21. 8.07	J Christensen and P Smith	Weston-on-the-Green	31.10.07
			N77RL				
G-MOZZ	Mudry CAP.10B	256		30.10.90	N Skipworth and J R W Luxton		
						Shrove Furlong Farm, Ilmer	2. 5.08
G-MPAA	Piper PA-28-181 Archer III	2843539	N567SC	17. 6.05	MPFC Ltd	Biggin Hill	29. 6.08E
G-MPAC	Ultravia Pelican PL	PFA 165-12944		6. 4.00	J H Leigh tr The Clipgate Flying Group		
	(Built M J Craven) (Rotax 912-UL)					Clipgate Farm, Denton	2.10.08P
G-MPBH	Reims Cessna FA152 Aerobat	FA1520374	G-FLIC	8.12.88	The Moray Flying Club (1990)	RAF Kinloss	21. 8.08E
			G-BILV				
G-MPBI	Cessna 310R II	310R0584	F-GEBB	21. 7.97	M P Bolshaw	Elstree	13. 3.08E
			HB-LMD, N87473				
G-MPCD	Airbus A320-212	379	C-GZCD	14. 3.94	Monarch Airlines Ltd	Luton	1. 5.08E
			G-MPCD, C-FTDU, G-MPCD, C-FTDU, G-MPCD, C-FTDU, G-MPCD, C-FTDU, G-MPCD, F-WWDY				
G-MPRL	Cessna 210M Centurion	21061892	EC-GKD	5. 8.02	Myriad Public Relations Ltd		
			N732YY			Standalone Farm, Meppershall	19. 8.08E
G-MPSA	Eurocopter MBB BK-117C-2	9065		28.11.05	Metropolitan Police Authority (Metropolitan Police titles)		
	(Eurocopter EC.145)					Lippitts Hill Camp, Chingford	12. 3.08E
G-MPSB	Eurocopter MBB BK-117C-2	9068		28.11.05	Metropolitan Police Authority (Metropolitan Police titles)		
	(Eurocopter EC.145)					Lippitts Hill Camp, Chingford	26.11.08E
G-MPSC	Eurocopter MBB BK-117C-2	9075		19.12.05	Metropolitan Police Authority (Metropolitan Police titles)		
	(Eurocopter EC.145)					Lippitts Hill Camp, Chingford	23. 1.08E
G-MPWI	Robin HR.100-210 Safari II	163	F-GBTY	3. 3.80	P G Clarkson and S King	Bournemouth	9. 5.08E
			F-ODFA, F-BUPD				
G-MPWT	Piper PA-34-220T Seneca III	34-8333068	N4294X	26. 9.88	R L Burt	Fowlmere	20. 5.08E
	(Originally built as c/n 34-8233163)		N888DB, N4294X, N9539N, N8218K "Duke 2"				
G-MRAF	Aeroprakt A22 Foxbat	PFA 317-14370		7. 2.05	M Raflewski	(Dungannon)	
	(Built.M Raflewski)						
G-MRAJ	Hughes 369E	0010E	N51946	19. 3.98	A Jardine	Dundee	10. 6.08E
	(Hughes 500)						
G-MRAM	Mignet HM-1000 Balerit	134		15.11.99	R A Marven	Coleman Green, Hertfordshire	15. 4.07P
G-MRDC	Robinson R44 Raven II	10851	G-ECIL	19. 9.07	D Curran and Sons Ltd	(Bangor)	5.10.07E
G-MRED	Elmwood CA-05 Christavia Mk.1	PFA 185-12935		2. 8.96	E Hewett	Barton Ashes	
	(Built E Hewett) (Continental O-200)					(F/f 6.07)	
G-MRJJ	Mainair Sports Pegasus Quik	7940		16. 4.03	J H Sparks	Doynton	11. 6.08P
G-MRJK	Airbus A320-214	1081	PH-BMC	21. 4.05	Monarch Airlines Ltd	Luton	21. 4.08E
			D-ABLA, F-WQQH, OO-SNF, F-WWIT.				
G-MRKI	Extra EA.300/200	05	N694M	15.12.04	Extra 200 Ltd	Wycombe Air Park	1. 3.08E
G-MRKS	Robinson R44 Raven	0771	G-RAYC	20. 5.03	TJD Trade Ltd	Cranfield	25. 6.08E
G-MRKT	Lindstrand LBL 90A Balloon (Hot Air)	037		7. 6.93	Marketplace Public Relations (London) Ltd	Bristol	27. 7.08A
						"Kaytee"	
G-MRLL	North American P-51D-5-NA Mustang	109-27154	44-13521	22. 8.05	M Hammond	Airfield Farm, Hardwick	
G-MRLN	Sky 240-24 Balloon (Hot Air)	161		4. 8.99	M Wady t/a Merlin Balloons	Hamstreet	3. 5.08T
G-MRMJ	Eurocopter AS.365N3 Dauphin 2	6713		20. 7.05	Whirligig Ltd Aldenham Grange, Letchmore Heath		2. 3.08E
G-MROC	Pegasus Quantum 15-912	7498		22. 1.99	R J Grimwood	Plaistows Farm, St Albans	22. 4.08P
G-MROD	Van's RV-7A	PFA 323-14432		29.11.06	K R Emery	Sittles Farm, Alrewas	17. 5.08P
	(Built M Rhodes)						
G-MROY	Comco Ikarus C42 FB UK	PFA 322-13758		9.10.01	G D Bird	(Bolbeck Park, Milton Keynes)	9. 1.03P
	(Built R Beckham)					(New owner 2.08)	
G-MRRR	Hughes 369E	0473E	YL-HMC	3. 2.06	Estate Air Ltd	Kemble	11. 4.08E
	(Hughes 500)		D-HHMC, (F-GHTX)				
G-MRRY	Robinson R44 Raven II	11780		11. 6.07	Celtic Motorhomes Ltd	Weston, Dublin	5. 7.08E
G-MRSN	Robinson R22 Beta	1654		21. 1.91	M D Thorpe t/a Yorkshire Helicopters	Coney Park, Leeds	20. 6.08E
G-MRST	Piper PA-28RT-201 Arrow IV	28R-7918068	9H-AAU	27.11.86	Calverton Flying Group Ltd	Cranfield	15. 5.08E
			5B-CEC, N3019U				
G-MRTN	SOCATA TB-10 Tobago	62	G-BHET	9. 7.98	P A Gange and M S Colebrook	Thruxton	31. 5.07
					(Noted 1.08)		
G-MRTY	Cameron N-77 Balloon (Hot Air)	1008		24. 4.84	R A, P M G and N T M Vale "Marty" Kidderminster		15. 2.06A
G-MRVL	Van's RV-7	PFA 323-14349		28.10.05	L W Taylor	(Hadleigh, Ipswich)	
	(Built L W Taylor)						
G-MSAL	Morane Saulnier MS.733 Alcyon	143	F-BLXV	16. 6.93	M Isbister tr Alcyon Flying Group	Spanhoe	
			French.Military		(As "143" in Aéronavale c/s) (Noted on rebuild 10.07)		
G-MSCM	Denney Kitfox Model 2	638	G-BSCM	9. 8.07	D J Thomas	Narbonne, France	8. 7.03P
	(Built M Richardson - pr.no.PFA 172-11745)				(Noted 2007)		
G-MSFC	Piper PA-38-112 Tomahawk II	38-81A0067	N25735	11. 5.90	The Sherwood Flying Club Ltd	Tollerton	15.11.07E
G-MSFT	Piper PA-28-161 Warrior II	28-8416093	G-MUMS	2. 4.97	Western Air (Thruxton) Ltd	Thruxton	20. 5.08E
			N118AV				
G-MSIX	DG Flugzeugbau DG-800B	8-156B80		21. 4.99	P Richer tr G-MSIX Group	Dunstable	30. 5.08E
	(New fuselage c/n 274 fitted c 8.02)				"M6"		
G-MSJF	Boeing 737-7Q8	30710		23. 2.07	Globespan Airways Ltd t/a Flyglobespan.com		
						Edinburgh	27. 2.08E
G-MSKY	Comco Ikarus C42 FB UK	PFA 322-13722		3.10.01	J S Mason and P M Yeoman Mullahead, Tandragee		6. 9.08P
	(Built C K Jones)						
G-MSON	Cameron Z-90 Balloon (Hot Air)	11036		22. 6.07	K D Peirce	Hawkhurst, Cranbrook	27. 9.08E
G-MSPT	Eurocopter EC.135 T2	0361		17. 3.05	M Sport Ltd	(Dovenby, Cockermouth)	19. 7.08E
G-MSPY	Pegasus Quantum 15-912	7625		17. 3.00	(J Madhvani) and R K Green		
						Plaistows Farm, St Albans	15. 3.08P
G-MSTC	Gulfstream AA-5A Cheetah	AA5A-0833	G-BIJT	30. 1.95	J Crook tr Association Of Manx Pilots		
			N26950			Andreas, Isle of Man	27. 4.08E
					(Attempted to land downwind Andreas 17. 6.06 and incurred substantial damage)		

Reg	Type	c/n	Prev id	Date	Owner	Location	Expiry
G-MSTG	North American P-51D-25-NT Mustang	124-48271	NZ2427 45-11518	2. 9.97	M Hammond "Janie"	Airfield Farm, Hardwick	19. 8.08P
	(As "414419:LH-F" in USAAF c/s of 350th Fighter Sqdn-353rd Fighter Group)						
G-MSTR	Cameron Monster 110 SS Balloon (Hot Air)	4957	G-OJOB	18. 7.01	ABC Flights Ltd	Clapton in Gordano, Bristol	21. 4.07A
G-MTAA	Solar Wings Pegasus XL-R	SW-WA-1102		15.10.86	M Skrinar	(Feltham)	13. 4.08P
	(Trike c/n SW-TB-1108)						
G-MTAB	Mainair Gemini Flash II	492-1086-4-W290		8.10.86	C Thompson	(Wolverhampton)	5. 6.07P
G-MTAC	Mainair Gemini Flash II	486-1086-4-W278	(YR-...) G-MTAC	15.10.86	R Massey	(Barrowford, Nelson)	2. 5.07P
G-MTAE	Mainair Gemini Flash II	500-1186-4-W302		15.10.86	C E Hannigan	(Bridge of Earrn, Perth)	26. 6.08P
G-MTAF	Mainair Gemini Flash II	499-1186-4-W301		5.10.86	B Eaton	(Chorley)	18..3.07P
G-MTAG	Mainair Gemini Flash II	487-1086-4-W281		15.10.86	M J Cowie and J P Hardy	Ince Blundell	28. 5.04P
G-MTAH	Mainair Gemini Flash II	488-1086-4-W282		16.10.86	G F Atkinson	(Deighton, York)	3. 8.08P
G-MTAI	Solar Wings Pegasus XL-R	SW-WA-1103		14.10.86	S T Elkington	Watnall	1. 2.08P
	(Rotax 503)	*(Trike c/n SW-TB-1109)*					
G-MTAJ	Solar Wings Pegasus XL-R/Se	SW-WA-1104		16.10.86	S Lyman	Deenethorpe	13.12.07P
	(Trike c/n SW-TB-1110)						
G-MTAL	Solar Wings Pegasus Photon	SW-WP-0023		15.10.86	J W Coventry	Davidstow Moor	X
	(Rotax 277?)	*(Trike c/n SW-TP-0023)*			*(New owner 7.07)*		
G-MTAO	Solar Wings Pegasus XL-R	SW-WA-1107		21.10.86	S P Disney	Swinford, Rugby	26. 6.01P
	(Trike c/n SW-TB-1107)				*(New owner 8.03)*		
G-MTAP	Southdown Raven X	SN2232/0225		15.10.86	M C Newman	(St Leonards-on-Sea)	3.11.07P
G-MTAR	Mainair Gemini Flash II	504-1286-4-W307		16.10.86	J B Woolley	(Madrid, Spain)	10. 8.07P
	(Rotax 462)						
G-MTAS	Whittaker MW5 Sorcerer	PFA 163-11166		14.10.86	R J Scott	Popham	12. 8.08P
	(Built E A Henman - may be Model MW5C?) *(Rotax 503)*						
G-MTAV	Solar Wings Pegasus XL-R	SW-WA-1110		21.10.86	S Fairweather and C L Harris	(Nottingham and Warrington)	3.10.08P
	(Trike c/n SW-TB-1115)						
G-MTAW	Solar Wings Pegasus XL-R	SW-WA-1111		21.10.86	M G Ralph	Stour Row, Sturminster Newton	23. 8.08P
	(Trike c/n SW-TB-1116)						
G-MTAX	Solar Wings Pegasus XL-R	SW-WA-1115		27.10.86	G Hawes	Deenethorpe	7. 2.08P
	(Trike c/n SW-TB-1117)						
G-MTAY	Solar Wings Pegasus XL-R	SW-WA-1113		27.10.86	S A McLatchie	Enstone	16.11.05P
	(Trike c/n SW-TB-1118)						
G-MTAZ	Solar Wings Pegasus XL-R	SW-WA-1114		28.10.86	T L Moses	Llansalnt, Carmarthen	25. 3.01P
	(Trike c/n SW-TB-1119)				*(New owner 5.03)*		
G-MTBB	Southdown Raven X	SN2232/0226		16.10.86	A Miller	(Woking)	15.10.02P
G-MTBD	Mainair Gemini Flash II	498-1186-4-W299		16.10.86	J Williams	Oxton	24. 8.05P
	(Wing regd as W229)						
G-MTBE	CFM Shadow Series CD	K 035		16.10.86	S K Brown	Chilbolton	24. 8.08P
	(Rotax 462HP)						
G-MTBH	Mainair Gemini Flash II	524-187-5-W327		28.10.86	T and P Sludds	Newtownards	19.10.08P
	(Rotax 462)						
G-MTBJ	Mainair Gemini Flash II	509-1286-4-W312		27.10.86	R M and P J Perry	Otherton, Cannock	29.10.05P
					(Operated Staffordshire Aero Club)		
G-MTBK	Southdown Raven X	SN2232/0230		28.10.86	G Davies	Deenethorpe	27. 6.99P
	(Rotax 503) *(Officially regd with Rotax 447)*				*(Noted 4.06)*		
G-MTBL	Solar Wings Pegasus XL-R	SW-WA-1117		6.11.86	R N Whiting	Lower Mountpleasant Farm, Chatteris	16. 7.04P
	(Trike c/n SW-TB-1121)						
G-MTBN	Southdown Raven X	SN2232/0227		28.10.86	A J and S E Crosby-Jones	(Rickney, Hailsham)	11. 8.07P
G-MTBO	Southdown Raven X	SN2232/0233		28.10.86	J Liversuch	Doynton	2. 2.08P
G-MTBP	Aerotech MW-5B Sorcerer	SR102-R440B-02		28.10.86	G Bennett	(Caister-on-Sea)	21. 9.94P
	(Fuji-Robin EC-44-PM)						
G-MTBR	Aerotech MW-5B Sorcerer	SR102-R440B-03		20. 1.87	R Poulter	(Peasedown St John, Bath)	4. 8.08P
	(Fuji-Robin EC-44-PM)						
G-MTBS	Aerotech MW-5B Sorcerer	SR102-R440B-04		27.10.86	T B Fowler	(Newent)	5. 4.08P
	(Fuji-Robin EC-44-PM)						
G-MTBU	Solar Wings Pegasus XL-R	SW-WA-1118		13.11.86	R P R Staveley	Watnall	29. 3.06P
	(Trike c/n SW-TB-1122)				*(Noted 10.07)*		
G-MTBV	Solar Wings Pegasus XL-R	SW-WA-1119		6.11.86	T H Scott	(Coggeshall, Colchester)	
					(New owner 6.03)		
G-MTBX	Mainair Gemini Flash II	510-1286-4-W313		6.11.86	B D Hanscomb	(Sudbury)	24. 3.05P
	(Rotax 447)				*(New owner 5.06)*		
G-MTBY	Mainair Gemini Flash II	507-1286-4-W310		6.11.86	D Pearson	(Heywood)	22. 7.05P
	(Rotax 447)						
G-MTBZ	Southdown Raven X	SN2232/0232		10.11.86	K W E Brunnenkant	(Lincoln)	6. 3.05P
G-MTCA	CFM Shadow Series C	K 011		6.11.86	J R L Murray	East Fortune	4. 8.04P
G-MTCE	Mainair Gemini Flash II	511-1286-4-W314		2.12.86	H Shaw	(Woodseaves, Stafford)	9. 8.04P
	(Rotax 462)						
G-MTCH	Solar Wings Pegasus XL-R	SW-WA-1124		28.11.86	M Doyle	(Tullamore, County Offaly)	29.11.95P
	(Trike c/n SW-TB-1126				*(New owner 11.07)*		
G-MTCK	Solar Wings Pegasus Flash II	SW-WF-0127		11.12.86	R H D C Ribeiro	(Leeds)	17. 3.08P
	(Rotax 447) *(Trike c/n SW-TB-1127 & Mainair Sailwing c/n W263)*						
G-MTCM	Southdown Raven X	SN2232/0239		11.12.86	J C Rose *(New owner 9.01)*	Field Farm, Oakley	2. 7.97P
G-MTCN	Solar Wings Pegasus XL-R	SW-WA-1126		16.12.86	S R Hughes	Redlands, Swindon	21. 7.06P
	(Trike c/n SW-TB-1128)						
G-MTCO	Solar Wings Pegasus XL-R	SW-WA-1127		7. 1.87	R Johnson	(Bury St Edmunds)	3. 4.04P
	(Trike c/n SW-TB-1129)						
G-MTCP	Aerial Arts Chaser/110SX	110SX/476		16.12.86	B Richardson	(Eshott)	28. 6.00P
	(Rotax 377)						
G-MTCT	CFM Shadow Series CD	042		16.12.86	R Lawes	(Hayling Island)	19. 9.06P
G-MTCU	Mainair Gemini Flash IIA	451-1286-4-W228		5. 1.87	T J Philip	Ashcroft Farm, Winsford	15. 3.08P
G-MTDD	Aerial Arts Chaser/110SX	110SX/437		26. 1.87	B Richardson	(Eshott)	4. 7.00P
	(Rotax 377)						

G-MTDE	Aerial Arts Chaser/110SX	110SX/438		5. 1.87	M N Hudson	(Alford, Spilsby)	6. 7.08P
	(Rotax 377) *(May now have Rotax 330)*						
G-MTDF	Mainair Gemini Flash II	515-287-5-W319		5. 1.87	P G Barnes *(New owner 2.04)*	(Harwich)	1. 5.03P
G-MTDI	Solar Wings Pegasus XL-R/Se	SW-WA-1132		22. 1.87	R S Mott	(Redditch)	24. 3.08P
	(Trike c/n SW-TB-1134)						
G-MTDK	Aerotech MW-5B Sorcerer	SR102-R440B-06		22. 1.87	C C Wright	Easter Balgillo Farm, Finavon	10. 5.06P
	(Fuji-Robin EC-44-PM) *(To be converted to Rotax 447)*						
G-MTDO	Eipper Quicksilver MXII	1124		27. 2.87	D L Ham	(Feniton, Honiton)	X
	(Rotax 503)						
G-MTDR	Mainair Gemini Flash II	516-287-5-W276		26. 1.87	A L S Routledge and G Bullock		
						Baxby Manor, Husthwaite	19. 6.08P
G-MTDU	CFM Shadow Series CD	K 037		26. 1.87	P G Hutchins	Rufforth	31. 8.08P
G-MTDW	Mainair Gemini Flash II	517-387-5-W212		2. 2.87	S R Leeper	Priory Farm, Tibenham	9. 2.06P
					(Noted dismantled 8.06)		
G-MTDY	Mainair Gemini Flash II	513-187-5-W317		11. 2.87	S Penoyre	(Windlesham)	13.10.00P
	(Rotax 462)						
G-MTEC	Solar Wings Pegasus XL-R	SW-WA-1140		9. 2.87	R W Glover	Kemble	11. 6.94P
	(Trike c/n SW-TB-1142)				*(Trike only noted 2000)*		
G-MTED	Solar Wings Pegasus XL-R	SW-WA-1141		9. 2.87	A A Tollerton	(Stourbridge)	31. 8.01P
	(Trike c/n SW-TB-1143)				*(New owner 11.07)*		
G-MTEE	Solar Wings Pegasus XL-R	SW-WA-1142		13. 2.87	M Worthington	Roddige	7. 8.07P
	(Trike c/n SW-TB-1144) (C/n plate shows SW-WA-1144: new Sailwing fitted ? - see G-MTLG)						
G-MTEK	Mainair Gemini Flash II	523-387-5-W279		3. 3.87	M O'Hearne and G M Wrigley	Rufforth	17. 6.03P
G-MTER	Solar Wings Pegasus XL-R/Se	SW-WA-1144		19. 2.87	M Lowe	Arclid Green, Sandbach	7. 4.02P
	(Trike c/n SW-TB-1146)				*(Noted 3.07)*		
G-MTES	Solar Wings Pegasus XL-R	SW-WA-1145		19. 2.87	N P Read	Davidstow Moor	29. 8.04P
	(Trike c/n SW-TB-1147)						
G-MTET	Solar Wings Pegasus XL-R	SW-WA-1146		19. 2.87	K Gilsenan	(Bedworth)	9.10.07P
	(Trike c/n SW-TB-1148)						
G-MTEU	Solar Wings Pegasus XL-R/Se	SW-WA-1147		19. 2.87	J Rudkin	(Halford, Shipston-on-Stour)	9. 4.01P
	(Trike c/n SW-TB-1149)				*(New owner 11.07)*		
G-MTEW	Solar Wings Pegasus XL-R/Se	SW-WA-1149		19. 2.87	R W and P J Holley	Mill Farm, Shifnal	4. 5.05P
	(Trike c/n SW-TB-1151)						
G-MTEX	Solar Wings Pegasus XL-R	SW-WA-1150		19. 2.87	C M and K M Bradford *(Noted 11.06)*		
	(Trike c/n SW-TB-1152)					Wing Farm, Longbridge Deverill	4. 5.04P
G-MTEY	Mainair Gemini Flash II	518-387-5-W217		20. 2.87	A Wells	(Boroughbridge, York)	27. 3.08P
G-MTFA	Solar Wings Pegasus XL-R	SW-WA-1156		24. 2.87	S Hindle	Tarn Farm, Cockerham	27. 7.07P
	(Rotax 462)	*(Trike c/n SW-TB-1158)*			*(Noted 8.07)*		
G-MTFB	Solar Wings Pegasus XL-R	SW-WA-1157		24. 2.87	S T P Askew	(Melton Mowbray)	24. 9.08P
	(Rotax 462)	*(Trike c/n SW-TE-0015)*					
G-MTFC	Medway Hybred 44XLR	22087/24		23. 3.87	J K Masters	(Hartlip, Sittingbourne)	25. 7.97P
G-MTFG	AMF Microflight Chevvron 2-32C	CH.004		9. 3.87	R Gardner	(Stratford-upon-Avon)	10. 5.07P
G-MTFI	Mainair Gemini Flash II	531-487-5-W289		12. 3.87	L Parker	(Rathconrath, Mullingar)	27. 7.06P
G-MTFM	Solar Wings Pegasus XL-R	SW-WA-1158		13. 3.87	P R G Morley	Newnham, Baldock	26. 4.05P
	(Rotax 462)	*(Trike c/n SW-TE-0016)*					
G-MTFN	Whittaker MW5 Sorcerer	PFA 163-11207		13. 3.87	S M King	Errol	21. 2.05P
	(Built K Southam and D C Britton - may be Model MW5B) (Fuji-Robin EC-44-PM)						
G-MTFP	Solar Wings Pegasus XL-R	SW-WA-1160		18. 3.87	C Rickards	(Swansea)	25. 4.04P
	(Trike c/n SW-TB-1160)						
G-MTFR	Solar Wings Pegasus XL-R/Se	SW-WA-1161		18. 3.87	S Ballantyne	(Larbert)	19. 9.99P
	(Trike c/n SW-TB-1161)						
G-MTFT	Solar Wings Pegasus XL-R	SW-WA-1163		18. 3.87	A T Smith	Mill Farm, Hughley, Much Wenlock	30. 7.00P
	(Trike c/n SW-TB-1163)						
G-MTFU	CFM Shadow Series CD	K 034	EI-DDN	18. 3.87	D Plaster	(Leighton Buzzard)	12. 3.08P
			G-MTFU				
G-MTFZ	CFM Shadow Series CD	053		24. 3.87	R P Stonor	Long Marston	23. 3.08P
G-MTGA	Mainair Gemini Flash II	535-587-5-W293		26. 3.87	B S Ogden	Tarn Farm, Cockerham	25. 5.04P
G-MTGB	Thruster TST Mk.1	837-TST-011		10. 4.87	M J Aubrey *(New owner 11.05)*	Kington, Hereford	11. 9.00P
G-MTGC	Thruster TST Mk.1	837-TST-012		10. 4.87	H Tuvey *(Noted 2.08)*	Gerpins Farm, Upminster	31. 5.04P
G-MTGD	Thruster TST Mk.1	837-TST-013		10. 4.87	C Bayliss tr Golf Delta Group	Ince Blundell	31.10.08P
G-MTGE	Thruster TST Mk.1	837-TST-014		10. 4.87	G W R Swift	(Withyham, Hartfield)	17.10.99P
G-MTGF	Thruster TST Mk.1	837-TST-015		10. 4.87	B Swindon	London Colney	1. 8.08P
G-MTGH	Mainair Gemini Flash II	536-587-5-W294		31. 3.87	J R Gillies	Hunsdon	27. 5.05P
	(Rotax 462)				*(Noted 5.07)*		
G-MTGJ	Solar Wings Pegasus XL-R	SW-WA-1165		1. 4.87	M S Taylor	(Gillingham)	17. 2.02P
	(Trike c/n SW-TB-1165)						
G-MTGK	Solar Wings Pegasus XL-R	SW-WA-1166		1. 4.87	I A Smith	(Canterbury)	1. 8.91P
	(Trike c/n SW-TB-1166)						
G-MTGL	Solar Wings Pegasus XL-R	SW-WA-1167		1. 4.87	P J and R Openshaw	Ince Blundell	9. 6.06P
	(Trike c/n SW-TB-1167)						
G-MTGM	Solar Wings Pegasus XL-R/Se	SW-WA-1168		1. 4.87	D J Barnes tr TGM Syndicate	Roddige	1. 8.08P
	(Original Trike c/n SW-TB-1168 destroyed in gales Roddige 1.98 : now fitted with Trike c/n SW-TB-1099 ex G-MNYT)						
G-MTGN	CFM Shadow Series BD	K 041		31. 3.87	N G Price	Bricket Wood, Radlett	15. 6.03P
G-MTGO	Mainair Gemini Flash IIA	550-587-5-W336		10. 4.87	G Evans	Arclid Green, Sandbach	16. 8.06P
	(Rotax 462)				*(New owner 3.07)*		
G-MTGR	Thruster TST Mk.1	847-TST-017		10. 4.87	M R Grunwell	Gerpins Farm, Upminster	29.11.07P
G-MTGS	Thruster TST Mk.1	847-TST-018		10. 4.87	R J Nelson	Hawksbridge Farm, Oxenhope	23. 7.07P
					(Housed in box trailer at side of hangar)		
G-MTGT	Thruster TST Mk.1	847-TST-019		10. 4.87	B J Gore	(Leeds)	2. 7.08P
G-MTGU	Thruster TST Mk.1	847-TST-020		10. 4.87	J Jordan	Otherton, Cannock	27. 1.06P
G-MTGV	CFM Shadow Series CD	052		8. 4.87	V R Riley	Brook Farm, Pilling	6.11.07P
G-MTGW	CFM Shadow Series CD	054	(I-. . . .)	8. 4.87	A D Grix	(Beccles)	6. 9.05P
			G-MGTW		*(Noted 9.06)*		
G-MTGX	Hornet Dual Trainer/Southdown Raven			13. 4.87	M A Pantling	Weston Zoyland	27.10.07P
	HRWA 0061 & SN2000/0270						

G-MTHB	Aerotech MW-5B Sorcerer	SR102-R440B-08		10. 4.87	K H A Negal	Red House Farm, Preston Capes	6. 4.08P
	(Fuji-Robin EC-44-PM)						
G-MTHG	Solar Wings Pegasus XL-R	SW-WA-1171		13. 4.87	R A Mott	(Redditch)	2. 2.08P
	(Trike c/n SW-TB-1170)						
G-MTHH	Solar Wings Pegasus XL-R	SW-WA-1172		13. 4.87	J Palmer	(Winkleigh)	28.12.98P
	(Trike c/n SW-TB-1171)						
G-MTHI	Solar Wings Pegasus XL-R	SW-WA-1173		13. 4.87	I E Egan	Swinford, Rugby	14.12.08P
	(Trike c/n SW-TB-1172)						
G-MTHJ	Solar Wings Pegasus XL-R	SW-WA-1174		13. 4.87	M R Harrison	(Stratford-upon-Avon)	26. 4.06P
	(Trike c/n SW-TB-1173)				(New owner 7.06)		
G-MTHN	Solar Wings Pegasus XL-R	SW-WA-1178		13. 4.87	M T Seal	(Cilcennin, Lampeter)	28. 3.08P
	(Trike c/n SW-TB-1177)						
G-MTHT	CFM Shadow Series CD	058		22. 4.87	J Kennedy	Mill Farm, Shifnal	10.11.08P
G-MTHV	CFM Shadow Series BD	K 049		7. 5.87	K R Bircher (Noted 7.04)	Over Farm, Gloucester	24. 7.00P
G-MTHW	Mainair Gemini Flash II	540-587-5-W325		14. 5.87	D Parsons	(Bexley)	10. 6.08P
	(Rotax 462)						
G-MTHZ	Mainair Gemini Flash IIA	541-587-5-W329		14. 5.87	A I Kinnear	East Fortune	18. 7.08P
G-MTIA	Mainair Gemini Flash IIA	544-687-5-W332		14. 5.87	G W Jennings	(Llanfairfechan)	3. 4.08P
G-MTIB	Mainair Gemini Flash IIA	545-687-5-W333		14. 5.87	K P Hayes	St Michaels	1. 5.08P
G-MTIE	Solar Wings Pegasus XL-R	SW-WA-1183		18. 5.87	P Wibberley	(Chesterfield)	27.12.07P
	(Rotax 462)	(Trike c/n SW-TE-0019)					
G-MTIH	Solar Wings Pegasus XL-R	SW-WA-1186		18. 5.87	K N Rabey	(Ware)	15. 5.08P
	(Trike c/n SW-TB-118315						
G-MTIJ	Solar Wings Pegasus XL-R/Se	SW-WA-1188		18. 5.87	M J F Gilbody	(Urmston, Manchester)	1. 4.98P
	(Trike c/n SW-TB-1185)						
G-MTIK	Raven Aircraft Raven X	SN2232/0272		19. 5.87	G A Oldershaw	Sutton Meadows	23. 6.08P
G-MTIL	Mainair Gemini Flash IIA	549-687-5-W338		21. 5.87	P G Nolan	Ince Blundell	16. 7.05P
	(Rotax 462)						
G-MTIM	Mainair Gemini Flash IIA	553-687-5-W341		21. 5.87	W M Swan	East Fortune	20. 5.08P
G-MTIN	Mainair Gemini Flash IIA	547-687-5-W335		1. 6.87	S J Firth	(Dallerie, Crieff)	10. 6.08P
G-MTIO	Solar Wings Pegasus XL-R	SW-WA-1190		26. 5.87	A R Wade	(Basildon)	14. 4.07P
	(Trike c/n SW-TB-1187)						
G-MTIP	Solar Wings Pegasus XL-R	SW-WA-1191		26. 5.87	M P Williams	Redlands, Swindon	2. 5.08P
	(Trike c/n SW-TB-1188)						
G-MTIR	Solar Wings Pegasus XL-R/Se	SW-WA-1192		26. 5.87	P Jolley	Watnall	17. 7.08P
	(Trike c/n SW-TB-1189)						
G-MTIS	Solar Wings Pegasus XL-R	SW-WA-1193		26. 5.87	N P Power	(Eastbourne)	25. 7.07P
	(Trike c/n SW-TB-1190)						
G-MTIU	Solar Wings Pegasus XL-R	SW-WA-1194		26. 5.87	D E Pedder	(Hampton)	23. 5.08P
	(Trike c/n SW-TB-1191)						
G-MTIW	Solar Wings Pegasus XL-R	SW-WA-1196		26. 5.87	G S Francis	Weston Zoyland	26.10.08P
	(Trike c/n SW-TB-1193)						
G-MTIX	Solar Wings Pegasus XL-R	SW-WA-1197		26. 5.87	S Pickering	Sutton Meadows	15. 1.01P
	(Trike c/n SW-TB-1194)						
G-MTIY	Solar Wings Pegasus XL-R	SW-WA-1198		26. 5.87	P J Tanner	Weston Zoyland	27. 5.04P
	(Trike c/n SW-TB-1195)						
G-MTIZ	Solar Wings Pegasus XL-R	SW-WA-1199		26. 5.87	S L Blount	Sutton Meadows	22.10.03P
	(Trike c/n SW-TB-1196)						
G-MTJA	Mainair Gemini Flash IIA	551-687-5-W339		15. 6.87	A J Holland and A McJannett-Smith	Finmere	3. 4.05P
					(New owners 10.06)		
G-MTJB	Mainair Gemini Flash IIA	554-687-5-W343		2. 6.87	B Skidmore	Tarn Farm, Cockerham	17. 5.08P
	(Rotax 462)						
G-MTJC	Mainair Gemini Flash IIA	555-687-5-W344		1. 6.87	T A Dockrell	(Kewstoke, Weston-super-Mare)	16. 7.07P
	(808cc Honda BF52) (Now fitted with 788-0590-7-W581 {ex-G-MWHY})						
G-MTJD	Mainair Gemini Flash IIA	552-687-5-W340		5. 6.87	D V A M J Delage	(Prinquiau, France)	10. 3.07P
	(Rotax 462)						
G-MTJE	Mainair Gemini Flash IIA	556-687-5-W345		24. 6.87	M P Tilzey	(Tyldesley, Manchester)	24. 1.08P
G-MTJG	Medway Hybred 44XLR	22587/25		16. 6.87	M A Trodden	(Tupton, Chesterfield)	24. 2.99P
G-MTJH	Solar Wings Pegasus Flash	W342-687-3		17. 6.87	C G Ludgate	(Norwich)	28. 3.04P
	(Trike c/n SW-TB-1050 previously fitted to G-MMUF)						
G-MTJL	Mainair Gemini Flash IIA	548-687-5-W337		17. 6.87	D Allan	Eshott	25. 7.08P
G-MTJS	Solar Wings Pegasus XL-Q	SW-WX-0013		6. 7.87	R J H Hayward	Broadmeadow Farm, Hereford	6. 4.08P
	(Trike c/n SW-TE-0022)						
G-MTJT	Mainair Gemini Flash IIA	558-787-5-W347		16. 7.87	D F Greatbanks	(Lymm)	30.10.08P
	(Rotax 462)						
G-MTJV	Mainair Gemini Flash IIA	562-787-5-W351		16. 7.87	A Taddeo	(Hessle)	18. 5.08P
G-MTJW	Mainair Gemini Flash IIA	563-787-5-W352		16. 7.87	J F Ashton	(Liverpool)	4.10.95P
G-MTJX	Hornet Dual Trainer/Southdown Raven			5. 8.87	J P Kirwan	Ince Blundell	31. 3.99P
	HRWA 0063 & SN2000/0279				(New owner 6.05)		
G-MTJZ	Mainair Gemini Flash IIA	561-787-5-W350		16. 7.87	J G and J A Hamnett	(Stoke-on-Trent)	17. 6.06P
	(Rotax 462)						
G-MTKA	Thruster TST Mk.1	867-TST-021		21. 7.87	C M Bradford and D Marsh	Clench Common	19. 8.08P
G-MTKB	Thruster TST Mk.1	867-TST-022		21. 7.87	M Hanna	Rathfriland, County Down	8. 5.06P
G-MTKD	Thruster TST Mk.1	867-TST-024		21. 7.87	Enda Spain	Kilrush, County Kildare	27. 1.06P
G-MTKE	Thruster TST Mk.1	867-TST-025		21. 7.87	M R Jones	Wing Farm, Longbridge Deverill	27. 8.03P
G-MTKG	Solar Wings Pegasus XL-R/Se	SW-WA-1201		13. 7.87	D J Wilkinson and D H May		
	(Trike c/n SW-TB-1199)					(Babell, Holywell and Cilcain Mold)	11.10.08P
G-MTKH	Solar Wings Pegasus XL-R	SW-WA-1202		13. 7.87	K Brooker	Jackrell's Farm, Southwater	23. 7.08P
	(Trike c/n SW-TB-1200)						
G-MTKI	Solar Wings Pegasus XL-R	SW-WA-1203		13. 7.87	M Wady	Hamstreet, Ashford	18.10.08P
	(Trike c/n SW-TB-1201)						
G-MTKN	Mainair Gemini Flash IIA	566-887-5-W355		15. 7.87	A J Altori	(Colne)	4. 6.03P
G-MTKR	CFM Shadow Series CD	067	9H-ABL G-MTKR	20. 7.87	D P Eichhorn	(Aston Juxta Mondrum,, Nantwich)	21. 6.06P

G-MTKW	Mainair Gemini Flash IIA	569-887-5-W358		13. 7.87	J H McIvor		Newtownards	23. 6.07P
G-MTKX	Mainair Gemini Flash IIA	568-887-5-W357		13. 7.87	G E Jones		(Chorley)	27. 8.00P
G-MTKZ	Mainair Gemini Flash IIA	571-887-5-W360		31. 7.87	I S McNeill		(Longniddry)	23. 8.07P
G-MTLB	Mainair Gemini Flash IIA	573-887-5-W362		31. 7.87	B L Crouch		Rufforth	4. 9.08P
G-MTLC	Mainair Gemini Flash IIA	574-887-5-W363		31. 7.87	R J Alston		(Cromer)	13. 7.02P
G-MTLG	Solar Wings Pegasus XL-R	SW-WA-1211		31. 7.87	G J Simoni		Kemble	17. 8.06P
	(Trike c/n SW-TB-1207)							
G-MTLI	Solar Wings Pegasus XL-R	SW-WA-1213		31. 7.87	M McKay		(Robertsbridge)	3. 9.04P
	(Trike c/n SW-TB-1209)							
G-MTLJ	Solar Wings Pegasus XL-R/Se	SW-WA-1214		31. 7.87	A Brumby	Headon Farm, Retford		30. 7.06P
	(Trike c/n SW-TB-1210)							
G-MTLL	Mainair Gemini Flash IIA	578-987-5-W367		14. 8.87	M S Lawrence		Mill Farm, Shifnal	22. 4.07P
G-MTLM	Thruster TST Mk.1	887-TST-027		5. 8.87	R J Nelson *(New owner 1.06)*		Leicester	24. 6.05P
G-MTLN	Thruster TST Mk.1	887-TST-028		5. 8.87	P W Taylor *(New owner 8.07)*	Priory Farm, Tibenham		17. 9.07P
G-MTLT	Solar Wings Pegasus XL-R	SW-WA-1216		12. 8.87	K M Mayling	Plaistows Farm, St Albans		10.10.03P
	(Trike c/n SW-TB-1212)							
G-MTLV	Solar Wings Pegasus XL-R	SW-WA-1218		12. 8.87	R W Keene	Over Farm, Gloucester		22. 1.04P
	(Trike c/n SW-TB-1214)				*(New owner 8.06)*			
G-MTLX	Medway Hybred 44XLR	20687/26		14. 8.87	D A Coupland	(Ashby-de-la Launde, Lincoln)		2. 3.08P
G-MTLY	Solar Wings Pegasus XL-R	SW-WA-1220		12. 8.87	I Johnston		(Bolton)	5. 7.92P
	(Rotax 462)	*(Trike c/n SW-TE-0026)*						
G-MTLZ	Whittaker MW5 Sorcerer	PFA 163-11241		13. 8.87	J O'Keeffe	(Croom, County Limerick)		15. 8.07P
	(Built E H Gould) (Rotax 377)							
G-MTMA	Mainair Gemini Flash IIA	579-987-5-W368		14. 8.87	R Stafford		Newtownards	16. 9.08P
G-MTMC	Mainair Gemini Flash IIA	581-987-5-W370		14. 8.87	A R Johnson		Brenzett, Kent	1. 7.06P
G-MTME	Solar Wings Pegasus XL-R	SW-WA-1221		18. 8.87	R J Turner	Lower Mountpleasant Farm, Chatteris		7. 9.08P
	(Trike c/n SW-TB-1216)							
G-MTMF	Solar Wings Pegasus XL-R	SW-WA-1222		18. 8.87	J T W Smith		(Mallaig)	4. 8.05P
	(Trike c/n SW-TB-1217)							
G-MTMG	Solar Wings Pegasus XL-R	SW-WA-1223		18. 8.87	C W and Petra E F Suckling		(Rushden)	8.11.04P
	(Trike c/n SW-TB-1218)							
G-MTML	Mainair Gemini Flash IIA	582-1087-5-W371		27. 8.87	J F Ashton		Perth	30. 7.00P
	(Rotax 462)				*(Trike only noted 5.03)*			
G-MTMO	Raven Aircraft Raven X	SN2232/0278	(G-MTKL)	11. 9.87	H Tuvey		(South Ockendon)	3.11.07P
G-MTMP	Hornet Dual Trainer/Southdown Raven			28. 8.87	P G Owen		(York)	6. 8.99P
	(Rotax 462)	HRWA 0064 & SN2000/0288						
G-MTMR	Hornet Dual Trainer/Southdown Raven			28. 8.87	D J Smith		Hucknall	12. 1.06P
	(Rotax 462)	HRWA 0065 & SN2000/0297						
G-MTMT	Mainair Gemini Flash IIA	583-1087-5-W372		3. 9.87	C Pickvance	Tarn Farm, Cockerham		6. 9.04P
	(Rotax 462)				*(Trike only 7.07)*			
G-MTMV	Mainair Gemini Flash IIA	585-1087-5-W374		3. 9.87	G J Small		(Stoke-on-Trent)	23. 4.07P
G-MTMW	Mainair Gemini Flash IIA	587-1087-5-W376		9. 9.87	F Lees		(Walsall)	29. 5.08P
G-MTMX	CFM Shadow Series CD	070		4. 9.87	D R White	Plaistows Farm, St Albans		16.12.07P
G-MTMY	CFM Shadow Series CD	071		4. 9.87	A J Harpley *(Noted 7.05)*		Bagby	1. 2.05P
G-MTNC	Mainair Gemini Flash IIA	588-1087-5-W377		15. 9.87	M G Titmus and M E Cook	Otherton, Cannock		15. 3.08P
G-MTNE	Medway Hybred 44XLR	7987/32		12.10.87	A G Rodenburg		(Tillicoultry)	23. 9.08P
	(Fitted with new Trike as original was transferred to G-MVDC 1988)							
G-MTNF	Medway Hybred 44XLR	1987/31		12.10.87	P A Bedford	Croft Farm, Defford		7. 8.08P
G-MTNG	Mainair Gemini Flash IIA	590-1087-5-W379		21. 9.87	A N Bellis		Shobdon	8. 9.08P
G-MTNH	Mainair Gemini Flash IIA	589-1087-5-W378		17. 9.87	J R Smart	Over Farm, Gloucester		7. 9.05P
	(Rotax 462)							
G-MTNI	Mainair Gemini Flash IIA	595-1187-5-W384		18. 9.87	F J Clarehugh *(Noted 9.07)*		Eshott	25.11.02P
G-MTNJ	Mainair Gemini Flash IIA	593-1187-5-W382		17. 9.87	A D Rickards		(St Helens)	28. 8.08P
	(Rotax 462)							
G-MTNK	Weedhopper JC-24B	1936		28. 9.87	S R Davis		Kemble	X
	(Fuji-Robin EC-34-PM) *(Test flown under "B" Conditions 29.6.00 as "G-???")*				*(Noted 7.05)*			
G-MTNL	Mainair Gemini Flash IIA	591-1187-5-W380		21. 9.87	R A Matthews *(Noted 7.05)*	Otherton, Cannock		14. 1.03P
G-MTNM	Mainair Gemini Flash IIA	592-1187-5-W381		22. 9.87	C J Janson		Shobdon	14.10.08P
G-MTNO	Solar Wings Pegasus XL-Q	SW-WQ-0001		23. 9.87	A F Batchelor	Rayne Hall Farm, Braintree		13. 9.08P
	(Rotax 447)	*(Trike c/n SW-TB-1252)*						
G-MTNP	Solar Wings Pegasus XL-Q	SW-WQ-0002		23. 9.87	G G Roberts	Rayne Hall Farm, Braintree		13. 9.08P
	(Rotax 447)	*(Trike c/n SW-TB-1253)*						
G-MTNR	Thruster TST Mk.1	897-TST-032		1.10.87	A M Sirant	Monkswell Farm, Horrabridge		23. 9.07P
G-MTNT	Thruster TST Mk.1	897-TST-034		1.10.87	S L Biggs tr G-MTNT Aircraft	Mendlesham		1. 6.07P
					(New owner 9.07)			
G-MTNU	Thruster TST Mk.1	897-TST-035		1.10.87	T H Brearley		Dunkeswell	10.12.07P
G-MTNV	Thruster TST Mk.1	897-TST-036		1.10.87	J B Russell *(Stored 7.07)*	Newry Road, Banbridge		11.10.88P
G-MTNY	Mainair Gemini Flash IIA	594-1187-5-W383		2.10.87	R C Granger	(Burnham-on-Crouch)		8. 8.03P
G-MTOA	Solar Wings Pegasus XL-R	SW-WA-1226		15. 9.87	R A Bird	East Hunsbury, Northampton		8. 8.01P
	(Trike c/n SW-TB-1221)				*(Amended owner 5.03)*			
G-MTOB	Solar Wings Pegasus XL-R	SW-WA-1227		15. 9.87	P S Lemm		(Otherton, Cannock)	1.10.97P
	(Trike c/n SW-TB-1222)							
G-MTOD	Solar Wings Pegasus XL-R	SW-WA-1229		15. 9.87	T A Gordon		(Liskeard)	3. 9.00P
	(Trike c/n SW-TB-1224)				*(New owner 3.03)*			
G-MTOE	Solar Wings Pegasus XL-R	SW-WA-1230		15. 9.87	K J Bright		Old Sarum	13. 7.03P
	(Trike c/n SW-TB-1225)							
G-MTOF	Solar Wings Pegasus XL-R/Se	SW-WA-1231		15. 9.87	J C Ettridge	(Hincaster, Milnthorpe)		26. 4.99P
	(Trike c/n SW-TB-1226)				*(Address change 6.07)*			
G-MTOG	Solar Wings Pegasus XL-R	SW-WA-1232		15. 9.87	J M Mclay		(Douglas, Lanark)	5. 5.06P
	(Trike c/n SW-TB-1227)							
G-MTOH	Solar Wings Pegasus XL-R	SW-WA-1233		15. 9.87	H Cook		(Pontypool)	2. 3.02P
	(Trike c/n SW-TB-1228)							
G-MTOJ	Solar Wings Pegasus XL-R/Se	SW-WA-1235		15. 9.87	S Jelley		(Chichester)	20. 6.08P
	(Trike c/n SW-TB-1230)				*"Spirit of Argo"*			

G-MTOK	Solar Wings Pegasus XL-R	SW-WA-1236	2.10.87	W S Davis	Oxton, Nottingham	19.11.04P
	(Trike c/n SW-TB-1231)					
G-MTON	Solar Wings Pegasus XL-R	SW-WA-1239	2.10.87	D J Willett	(Malpas)	30. 5.08P
	(Trike c/n SW-TB-1234)					
G-MTOO	Solar Wings Pegasus XL-R	SW-WA-1240	2.10.87	G Salisbury	(Abercarn, Newport)	29. 7.08P
	(Trike c/n SW-TB-1235)					
G-MTOP	Solar Wings Pegasus XL-R/Se	SW-WA-1241	2.10.87	J Pooler	(Repton, Derby)	9. 4.08P
	(Trike c/n SW-TB-1236)					
G-MTOR	Solar Wings Pegasus XL-R	SW-WA-1242	9.10.87	W F G Panayiotiou	(Llanelli)	28. 7.03P
	(Trike c/n SW-TB-1237)					
G-MTOT	Solar Wings Pegasus XL-R	SW-WA-1244	9.10.87	A J Lloyd	Shobdon	25. 3.04P
	(Noted 11.06)					
G-MTOU	Solar Wings Pegasus XL-R/Se	SW-WA-1245	9.10.87	D T Smith	(Thornaby)	14. 4.04P
	(Trike c/n SW-TB-1240)					
G-MTOY	Solar Wings Pegasus XL-R	SW-WA-1249	19.10.87	C M Bradford tr G-MTOY Group	Yatesbury	15. 8.06P
	(Trike c/n SW-TB-1244)					
G-MTOZ	Solar Wings Pegasus XL-R	SW-WA-1250	19.10.87	I A Macadam	Damyns Hall, Upminster	20. 1.05P
	(Trike c/n SW-TB-1245)			(New owner 9.07)		
G-MTPA	Mainair Gemini Flash IIA	598-1187-5-W394	13.10.87	C J Shorter	(Fareham)	14. 8.07P
	(Rotax 462)					
G-MTPB	Mainair Gemini Flash IIA	599-1187-5-W387	15.10.87	D J Houlding and R Swan		
					(Ashton-on-Ribble, Preston)	13.11.08P
G-MTPC	Raven Aircraft Raven X	SN2232/0309	15.10.87	G W Carwardine	(Hadlow Down, Uckfield)	3.11.90P
	(Rotax 582) (Modified to "Phillips Swphift" standard 1999)					
G-MTPE	Solar Wings Pegasus XL-R	SW-WA-1260	21.10.87	J Basset		
	(Rotax 503) (Trike c/n SW-TB-1258)			Brown Shutters Farm, Norton St Philips, Somerset		9. 6.08P
G-MTPF	Solar Wings Pegasus XL-R	SW-WA-1261	21.10.87	P M Watts and A S Mitchel	Halwell	18.11.05P
	(Trike c/n SW-TB-1259)					
G-MTPG	Solar Wings Pegasus XL-R	SW-WA-1262	21.10.87	J Sullivan	Davidstow Moor	16. 7.03P
	(Trike c/n SW-TB-1260)					
G-MTPH	Solar Wings Pegasus XL-R	SW-WA-1263	30.10.87	G Barker and L Blight		
	(Trike c/n SW-TB-1261)			(Sutton Coldfield and Tamworth)		15.10.08P
G-MTPI	Solar Wings Pegasus XL-R/Se	SW-WA-1264	30.10.87	R J Bullock	Long Marston	6. 8.06P
	(Trike c/n SW-TB-1262)					
G-MTPJ	Solar Wings Pegasus XL-R	SW-WA-1265	30.10.87	D Lockwood	Roddige	9. 6.08P
	(Trike c/n SW-TB-1263)					
G-MTPK	Solar Wings Pegasus XL-R	SW-WA-1266	30.10.87	S H James	Deenethorpe	21.10.01P
	(Trike c/n SW-TB-1264)					
G-MTPL	Solar Wings Pegasus XL-R	SW-WA-1267	30.10.87	C J Jones	(Bath)	31. 1.08P
	(Trike c/n SW-TB-1265)					
G-MTPM	Solar Wings Pegasus XL-R	SW-WA-1268	30.10.87	D K Seal	Roddige	4. 8.04P
	(Trike c/n SW-TB-1266)					
G-MTPN	Solar Wings Pegasus XL-Q	SW-WQ-0004	21.10.87	M J Griffin	Redlands, Swindon	19. 7.06P
	(Rotax 447) (Trike c/n SW-TB-1267)			(Noted 4.07)		
G-MTPP	Solar Wings Pegasus XL-R	SW-WA-1259	21.10.87	P Molyneux	(Southport)	8. 7.05P
	(Trike c/n SW-TB-1257)			(Address change 3.07)		
G-MTPR	Solar Wings Pegasus XL-R	SW-WA-1257	21.10.87	T Kenny	(Ballygar, County Galway)	16. 6.96P
	(Trike c/n SW-TB-1256)					
G-MTPS	Solar Wings Pegasus XL-Q	SW-WX-0011	23.10.87	S P Kyle	Clench Common	3. 1.08P
	(Trike c/n SW-TE-0021)					
G-MTPT	Thruster TST Mk.1	8107-TST-038	23.10.87	G B Gratton tr Chilbolton Thruster Group	Chilbolton	15.12.07P
G-MTPU	Thruster TST Mk.1	8107-TST-039	23.10.87	K J Foxall	Roddige	20. 3.08P
G-MTPW	Thruster TST Mk.1	8107-TST-041	23.10.87	K Hawthorne	(Armagh)	18. 8.05P
G-MTPX	Thruster TST Mk.1	8107-TST-042	23.10.87	T Snook	(Newport Pagnell)	2. 5.93P
G-MTPY	Thruster TST Mk.1	8107-TST-043	23.10.87	C M Bradford	Clench Common	25. 3.08P
G-MTRA	Mainair Gemini Flash IIA	605-1187-5-W395	28.10.87	E N Alms "Yellow Bird"	Guy Lane Farm, Waverton	19. 2.08P
G-MTRC	Midland Ultralights Sirocco 377GB	MU-021	2.11.87	D Thorpe	Grantham	13. 4.03P
G-MTRL	Hornet Dual Trainer/Southdown Raven		4.11.87	J McAlpine	Thirdpart Holdings, West Kilbride	27. 4.05P
	HRWA 0068 & SN2000/0326			(Noted 8.05)		
G-MTRM	Solar Wings Pegasus XL-R	SW-WA-1276	10.11.87	R O Kibble	Deenethorpe	14. 9.08P
	(Rotax 462) (Trike c/n SW-TE-0030)					
G-MTRO	Solar Wings Pegasus XL-R/Se	SW-WA-1270	2.12.87	J Hunter	Eshott	25. 6.08P
	(Trike c/n SW-TB-1271)					
G-MTRS	Solar Wings Pegasus XL-R	SW-WA-1273	2.12.87	J J R Tickle	Llanerchymedd, Gwynedd	13. 6.01P
	(Trike c/n SW-TB-1274)					
G-MTRT	Raven Aircraft Raven X	SN2232/0325	12.11.87	D J Revell	Astwood, Newport Pagnell	16. 4.08P
G-MTRV	Solar Wings Pegasus XL-Q	SW-WX-0010	10.11.87	J C Field	North Coates	6. 6.06P
	(Rotax 477) (Trike c/n SW-TB-1276)			(Dumped following local undershoot 23.7 05)		
G-MTRW	Raven Aircraft Raven X	SN2232/0328	12.11.87	P K J Chun	Rochester	20. 6.06P
G-MTRX	Whittaker MW5 Sorcerer	PFA 163-11202	11.11.87	W Turner	Otherton, Cannock	23. 7.08P
	(Built W Turner)					
G-MTRZ	Mainair Gemini Flash IIA	611-1287-5-W400	17.11.87	D F G Barlow	St Michaels	28. 3.08P
G-MTSC	Mainair Gemini Flash IIA	618-188-5-W407	17.11.87	K Wilson	(Llanddulas, Abergele)	19. 2.08P
G-MTSH	Thruster TST Mk.1	8117-TST-044	3.12.87	R R Orr	Newtownards	13. 4.07P
G-MTSJ	Thruster TST Mk.1	8117-TST-046	3.12.87	R J F Coates tr Sierra Juliet Group	Little Rissington	22. 5.06P
				(Noted 5.07)		
G-MTSK	Thruster TST Mk.1	8117-TST-047	3.12.87	J S Pyke	Clipgate Farm, Denton	24.10.05P
G-MTSM	Thruster TST Mk.1	8117-TST-049	3.12.87	D J Flower	Baxby Manor, Husthwaite	27.10.08P
	(Modified to T300 standard)					
G-MTSN	Solar Wings Pegasus XL-R	SW-WA-1280	14.12.87	G P Lane	Doynton	15. 4.03P
	(Trike c/n SW-TB-1278)					
G-MTSP	Solar Wings Pegasus XL-R	SW-WA-1282	14.12.87	R J Nelson	Swinford, Rugby	11.10.05P
	(Trike c/n SW-TB-1280)			(Noted 10.07)		
G-MTSR	Solar Wings Pegasus XL-R	SW-WA-1283	14.12.87	J Norman	Sackville Lodge, Riseley	24. 8.07P
	(Trike c/n SW-TB-1281)					

G-MTSS	Solar Wings Pegasus XL-R	SW-WA-1284	14.12.87	R J Turner	Lower Mountpleasant Farm, Chatterris	29. 7.08P
	(Rotax 462)	*(Trike c/n SW-TE-0031)*				
G-MTSY	Solar Wings Pegasus XL-R/Se	SW-WA-1289	14. 1.88	N F Waldron	(Loughborough)	24. 5.99P
		(Trike c/n SW-TB-1283)				
G-MTSZ	Solar Wings Pegasus XL-R/Se	SW-WA-1290	14. 1.88	J R Appleton	(Colne)	18. 6.07P
		(Trike c/n SW-TB-1284)				
G-MTTA	Solar Wings Pegasus XL-R	SW-WA-1291	14. 1.88	J J McMennum	Morgansfield, Fishburn	4. 9.00P
	(Rotax 462)	*(Trike c/n SW-TE-0035)*		*(Noted 7.04)*		
G-MTTB	Solar Wings Pegasus XL-R	SW-WA-1292	14. 1.88	P J Soukup	(Winkleigh)	31. 5.07P
	(Rotax 447)	*(Trike c/n SW-TB-1285)*				
G-MTTD	Solar Wings Pegasus XL-Q	SW-WQ-0011	15. 1.88	J P Dilley	Hunsdon	12.10.07P
	(Rotax 447)	*(Trike c/n SW-TB-1286)*				
G-MTTE	Solar Wings Pegasus XL-Q	SW-WQ-0012	15. 1.88	M C Mawson	Rufforth	9. 3.08P
		(Trike c/n SW-TB-1287)				
G-MTTF	Whittaker MW6 Merlin	PFA 164-11273	14.12.87	P Cotton	(Gloucester)	29. 3.95P
	(Built V E Booth) (Rotax 532)					
G-MTTH	CFM Shadow Series BD	K 061	15.12.87	G F Hill and A Y-T Leung *(Noted 8.06)*	Shenstone	6. 9.05P
G-MTTI	Mainair Gemini Flash IIA	620-188-5-W409	14.12.87	S P Maher	(Thornton-Cleveleys)	11. 2.08P
G-MTTM	Mainair Gemini Flash IIA	609-1287-5-W398	5. 1.88	M Anderson	East Fortune	12.10.08P
G-MTTN	Skyrider Aviation Phantom	PH.00100	22. 1.88	T M Weaver	Sywell	20. 6.05P
	(Officially registered as Ultralight Flight Phantom) (Rotax 503)			*(Wings fitted to G-MJUX 8.07 (qv): noted 10.07)*		
G-MTTP	Mainair Gemini Flash IIA	612-188-5-W401	18. 1.88	A Ormson	St Michaels	8. 5.08P
	(Rotax 462)					
G-MTTR	Mainair Gemini Flash IIA	614-188-5-W403	27. 1.88	A Westoby	Hucknall	22. 7.00P
	(Rotax 462)					
G-MTTU	Solar Wings Pegasus XL-R	SW-WA-1294	25. 2.88	A Friend	Weston Zoyland	10. 2.07P
		(Trike c/n SW-TB-1332)		*(Noted 5.07)*		
G-MTTW	Mainair Gemini Flash IIA	622-188-5-W411	15. 1.88	A F Glover	(Woolston, Warrington)	10. 9.06P
	(Rotax 462)					
G-MTTX	Solar Wings Pegasus XL-Q	SW-WQ-0013	15. 2.88	B Richardson	Stanton, Morpeth	21.11.07P
	(Rotax 447)	*(Trike c/n SW-TB-1293)*				
G-MTTY	Solar Wings Pegasus XL-Q	SW-WQ-0014	21. 1.88	G A Tegg	Clench Common	23. 9.06P
G-MTTZ	Solar Wings Pegasus XL-Q	SW-WQ-0015	21. 1.88	J Haskett	(King's Lynn)	17.10.06P
		(Trike c/n SW-TE-0039)				
G-MTUA	Solar Wings Pegasus XL-R/Se	SW-WA-1295	15. 1.88	M D Reardon	(Leeds)	6. 8.05P
		(Trike c/n SW-TB-1294)				
G-MTUB	Thruster TST Mk.1	8018-TST-050	15. 1.88	M Curtin	(Clonmel, County Tipperary)	4. 9.04P
G-MTUC	Thruster TST Mk.1	8018-TST-051	15. 1.88	E J Girling	Davidstow Moor	4. 8.06P
G-MTUD	Thruster TST Mk.1	8018-TST-052	15. 1.88	T Driffield	Baxby Manor, Husthwaite	20.10.08P
	(Modified to T300 standard)					
G-MTUF	Thruster TST Mk.1	8018-TST-054	15. 1.88	P Stark *(Noted dismantled 1.08)*	Strathaven	16. 1.05P
G-MTUI	Solar Wings Pegasus XL-R/Se	SW-WA-1296	21. 1.88	R Green	Long Marston	21. 3.06P
		(Trike c/n SW-TB-1296)				
G-MTUJ	Solar Wings Pegasus XL-R	SW-WA-1297	21. 1.88	R W Pincombe	(Chulmleigh)	31. 5.94P
		(Trike c/n SW-TB-1297)		*(New owner 4.05)*		
G-MTUK	Solar Wings Pegasus XL-R	SW-WA-1298	21. 1.88	N Morgan	Rufforth	19..4.08P
		(Trike c/n SW-TB-1298)				
G-MTUL	Solar Wings Pegasus XL-R/Se	SW-WA-1299	21. 1.88	P J Armitage	(Chichester)	5. 4.08P
		(Trike c/n SW-TB-1299)				
G-MTUN	Solar Wings Pegasus XL-Q	SW-WQ-0016	20. 1.88	M J O'Connor	(Little Budworth, Tarporley)	26. 4.05P
	(Rotax 447)	*(Trike c/n SW-TB-1301)*	*(Fitted with Wing from G-MVUK?)*			
G-MTUP	Solar Wings Pegasus XL-Q	SW-WA-0018	20. 1.88	G Davies	(Market Harborough)	12. 4.08P
	(Rotax 447)	*(Trike c/n SW-TB-1303)*				
G-MTUR	Solar Wings Pegasus XL-Q	SW-WQ-0019	20. 1.88	G Ball	(Tewkesbury)	26. 9.07P
	(Rotax 447)	*(Trike c/n SW-TB-1304)*				
G-MTUS	Solar Wings Pegasus XL-Q	SW-WQ-0020	20. 1.88	A I McPherson	Pratis Farm, Leven	17. 9.08P
	(Rotax 447)	*(Trike c/n SW-TB-1305)*				
G-MTUT	Solar Wings Pegasus XL-Q	SW-WQ-0021	21. 1.88	F A Dimmock	Deenethorpe	10. 5.08P
		(Trike c/n SW-TE-0040)				
G-MTUU	Mainair Gemini Flash IIA	623-288-5-W412	10. 2.88	M Harris	Eshott	23. 2.08P
G-MTUV	Mainair Gemini Flash IIA	624-288-5-W413	28. 1.88	J F Bolton	Plaistows Farm, St Albans	26. 3.08P
	(Rotax 462)					
G-MTUX	Medway Hybred 44XLR	241287/33	2. 2.88	P A R Wilson	(Cloughton, Scarborough)	29. 8.99P
G-MTUY	Solar Wings Pegasus XL-Q	SW-WQ-0022	28. 1.88	H C Lowther	(Eccleston, Chorley)	31. 3.08P
		(Trike c/n SW-TE-0041)				
G-MTVB	Solar Wings Pegasus XL-R	SW-WA-1302	28. 1.88	J Williams	(Worcester)	15.11.03P
		(Trike c/n SW-TB-1307)				
G-MTVG	Mainair Mercury	628-388-6-W417	12. 2.88	C Chapman	(South Witham, Grantham)	14. 2.06P
	(Converted ex Gemini Flash IIA using original Sailwing from G-MTVG and Trike c/n 460-886-4 from G-MNTU) (New owner 1.08)					
G-MTVH	Mainair Gemini Flash IIA	626-288-6-W415	17. 2.88	C Royle	Arclid Green, Sandbach	29. 5.08P
G-MTVI	Mainair Gemini Flash IIA	629-388-6-W416	12. 2.88	R A McDowell	(Slough)	10. 5.92P
G-MTVJ	Mainair Gemini Flash IIA	627-388-6-W418	12. 2.88	D W Buck	Watnall	13. 6.08P
G-MTVK	Solar Wings Pegasus XL-R	SW-WA-1306	15. 2.88	J D MacNamara	(Crediton)	17. 3.98P
		(Trike c/n SW-TB-1311)				
G-MTVL	Solar Wings Pegasus XL-R/Se	SW-WA-1307	15. 2.88	P A Bibby	(Lincoln)	21.10.06P
	(Original Trike c/n SW-TB-1312 but now fitted with Trike c/n SW-TB-1229 ex G-MTOI)					
G-MTVN	Solar Wings Pegasus XL-R	SW-WA-1309	15. 2.88	A I Crighton	Lower Mountpleasant Farm, Chatteris	23. 4.05P
		(Trike c/n SW-TB-1314)				
G-MTVO	Solar Wings Pegasus XL-R	SW-WA-1310	15. 2.88	D A Payne	Long Marston	21. 5.08P
		(Trike c/n SW-TB-1315)				
G-MTVP	Thruster TST Mk.1	8028-TST-056	10. 2.88	J M Evans	Landmead Farm, Garford	13. 1.08P
	(C/n plate marked incorrectly as 8208-TST-056)					
G-MTVR	Thruster TST Mk.1	8028-TST-057	10. 2.88	J A Hindley	Brook Farm, Pilling	30. 7.08P
G-MTVS	Thruster TST Mk.1	8028-TST-058	10. 2.88	J G McMinn	(Craigavon)	20. 6.06P

G-MTVT	Thruster TST Mk.1	8028-TST-059		10. 2.88	M L Walsh and A T Farmer	Mill Farm, Shifnal 29. 6.07P
G-MTVV	Thruster TST Mk.1	8028-TST-061		10. 2.88	M J Payne	(Bath) 9. 6.08P
G-MTVX	Solar Wings Pegasus XL-Q	SW-WQ-0025		3. 3.88	D A Foster	(Melton Mowbray) 29. 6.07P
	(Trike c/n SW-TE-0042)					
G-MTWB	Solar Wings Pegasus XL-R	SW-WA-1312		25. 2.88	R W T Gibbs	(Headington, Oxford) 12. 2.08P
	(Trike c/n SW-TB-1342)					
	(Originally fitted with Trike c/n SW-TB-1318 but damaged, repaired and resold with Sailwing c/n SW-WA-1330 as SE-YOK)					
G-MTWD	Solar Wings Pegasus XL-R	SW-WA-1314		25. 2.88	J C Rawlings	Sywell 6.12.06P
	(Trike c/n SW-TB-1320)				*(Noted 10.07)*	
G-MTWF	Mainair Gemini Flash IIA	630-388-6-W419		25. 2.88	M J J Clutterbuck	
						Broomclose Farm, Longbridge Deverill 12. 9.08P
G-MTWG	Mainair Gemini Flash IIA	631-288-6-W420		25. 2.88	N Mackenzie and P S Bunting Emlyn's Field, Rhuallt	28. 7.00P
					(Noted 1.06)	
G-MTWH	CFM Shadow Series CD	K 064		25. 2.88	A A Ross	Knockbain Farm, Dingwall 23. 9.08P
G-MTWK	CFM Shadow Series CD	073		25. 2.88	J P Batty and J R C Brightman	
						Sackville Lodge, Riseley 21.10.08P
G-MTWL	CFM Shadow Series BD	076		25. 2.88	M J Gray	Manor Farm, Croughton 26.12.03P
G-MTWR	Mainair Gemini Flash IIA	632-388-6-W421		3. 3.88	J B Hodson	Arclid Green, Sandbach 29.10.08P
G-MTWS	Mainair Gemini Flash IIA	633-388-6-W422		3. 3.88	K W Roberts	Church Farm, Askern 22. 8.08P
G-MTWX	Mainair Gemini Flash IIA	634-488-6-W423		11. 3.88	M Rushworth	(Eccleston, Chorley) 24. 3.07P
G-MTWY	Thruster TST Mk.1	8038-TST-062		15. 3.88	J F Gardner *(New owner 6.07)*	(Fulwood, Preston) 25. 2.06P
G-MTWZ	Thruster TST Mk.1	8038-TST-063		15. 3.88	T A Colman	Wing Farm, Longbridge Deverill 11.11.06P
					(Stored 12.06)	
G-MTXA	Thruster TST Mk.1	8038-TST-064		15. 3.88	J Upex	Rufforth 31. 7.08E
G-MTXB	Thruster TST Mk.1	8038-TST-065		15. 3.88	J J Hill	Baxby Manor, Husthwaite 30. 8.03P
G-MTXC	Thruster TST Mk.1	8038-TST-066		15. 3.88	G Carr *(New owner 8.07)*	(Isle of Lewis) 8. 6.04P
G-MTXD	Thruster TST Mk.1	8038-TST-067		15. 3.88	D J Flower	Baxby Manor, Husthwaite 5. 4.08P
	(Modified to T300 standard)					
G-MTXE	Hornet Dual Trainer/Southdown Raven			11. 3.88	F J Marton t/a Charter Systems	Long Marston 22. 5.00P
		HRWA 0070 & SN2000/0332				
G-MTXI	Solar Wings Pegasus XL-Q	SW-WQ-0031		11. 3.88	S A Mallett	(Docking, King's Lynn) 3. 5.08P
	(Rotax 447)	*(Trike c/n SW-TB-1329)*				
G-MTXJ	Solar Wings Pegasus XL-Q	SW-WQ-0032		11. 3.88	E W Laidlaw	(Broom Loan, Kelso) 18. 3.08P
	(Rotax 447)	*(Trike c/n SW-TB-1330)*				
G-MTXK	Solar Wings Pegasus XL-Q	SW-WQ-0033		11. 3.88	J E Borril	Insch 13. 6.07P
	(Rotax 447)	*(Trike c/n SW-TB-1331)*				
G-MTXL	Noble Hardman Snowbird Mk.IV	SB-006		4. 5.88	P J Collins *(Noted 5.06)*	Kilrush, County Kildare 9. 8.05P
G-MTXM	Mainair Gemini Flash IIA	636-488-6-W425		10. 5.88	C Blount, J D Penman and R Tomlinson	
						East Fortune 22. 8.08P
G-MTXO	Whittaker MW6 Merlin	PFA 164-11326		11. 3.88	S J Whyatt	(RAF Brize Norton) 4. 8.98P
	(Built N A Bailes) (Rotax 503)				*(Noted 1.07)*	
G-MTXP	Mainair Gemini Flash IIA	637-488-6-W426		23. 3.88	G S Duerden	St Michaels 27. 4.07P
G-MTXR	CFM Shadow Series CD	K 038		23. 3.88	S A O'Neill	Old Sarum 6.10.08P
G-MTXS	Mainair Gemini Flash IIA	638-488-6-W427		23. 3.88	N O'Brien	Mullinahone, County Tipperary 22. 6.07P
					(New owner 8.07)	
G-MTXU	Noble Hardman Snowbird Mk.IV	SB-007		3. 5.88	J A Rees c/o Haverfordwest Flight Centre	
						(Haverfordwest) 16. 5.89P
G-MTXZ	Mainair Gemini Flash IIA	641-588-6-W430		10. 5.88	P Cave	Upfield Farm, Whitson 19. 7.08P
G-MTYA	Solar Wings Pegasus XL-Q	SW-WQ-0037		29. 3.88	R Howieson	Deenthorpe 10. 2.08P
	(Trike c/n SW-TE-0047)					
G-MTYC	Solar Wings Pegasus XL-Q	SW-WQ-0039		30. 3.88	C I D H Garrison	Sutton Meadows 13.10.07P
	(Trike c/n SW-TE-0049)					
G-MTYD	Solar Wings Pegasus XL-Q	SW-WQ-0040		29. 3.88	R S Colebrook	Redlands, Swindon 3. 6.07P
	(Trike c/n SW-TE-0050)					
G-MTYE	Solar Wings Pegasus XL-Q	SW-WQ-0041		29. 3.88	A J Cook	Enstone 3. 9.08P
	(Trike c/n SW-TE-0051)					
G-MTYF	Solar Wings Pegasus XL-Q	SW-WQ-0042		29. 3.88	M Quarterman Lower Mountpleasant Farm, Chatteris	1. 4.08P
	(Trike c/n SW-TE-0052)					
G-MTYH	Solar Wings Pegasus XL-Q	SW-WQ-0044		7.11.88	I B Currer	(Barmby Moor, York) 17.10.08P
	(Trike c/n SW-TE-0054)					
G-MTYI	Solar Wings Pegasus XL-Q	SW-WQ-0045		30. 3.88	I F Hill	Roddige 24. 7.08P
	(Trike c/n SW-TE-0055)					
G-MTYL	Solar Wings Pegasus XL-Q	SW-WQ-0048		30. 3.88	E T H Cox	(Church Stretton) 20.10.02P
	(Trike c/n SW-TE-0058) (Original Sailwing now replaced by c/n 6412)					
G-MTYP	Solar Wings Pegasus XL-Q	SW-WQ-0052		30. 3.88	J Gray	(Droitwich) 12. 7.05P
	(Trike c/n SW-TE-0062)				*(New owner 10.05)*	
G-MTYR	Solar Wings Pegasus XL-Q	SW-WQ-0053		30. 3.88	M E Grafton	Broadmeadow Farm, Hereford 30. 4.99P
	(Trike c/n SW-TE-0063)				*(Noted 5.05)*	
G-MTYS	Solar Wings Pegasus XL-Q	SW-WQ-0054		30. 3.88	R G Wall	Caerleon 4.10.05P
	(Trike c/n SW-TE-0064)					
G-MTYT	Solar Wings Pegasus XL-Q	SW-WQ-0055		30. 3.88	M G Walsh	Rufforth 13. 9.99P
	(Trike c/n SW-TE-0065)					
G-MTYU	Solar Wings Pegasus XL-Q	SW-WQ-0056		30. 3.88	S East	Baxby Manor, Husthwaite 8. 9.05P
	(Trike c/n SW-TE-0066)				*(Noted 9.07)*	
G-MTYV	Raven Aircraft Raven X	SN2232/0341	(N)	8. 4.88	S R Jones	(Tonyrefail, Porth) 5. 7.07P
			G-MTYV			
G-MTYW	Raven Aircraft Raven X	SN2232/0344		8. 4.88	R Solomans	Stoke, Isle of Grain 28. 7.07P
G-MTYX	Raven Aircraft Raven X	SN2232/0345		8. 4.88	C Rean	(Petersfield) 19. 9.04P
G-MTYY	Solar Wings Pegasus XL-R	SW-WA-1326		6. 5.88	L A Hosegood *(New owner 11.06)*	(Swindon) 24. 1.05P
G-MTZA	Thruster TST Mk.1	8048-TST-068		13. 4.88	J F Gallagher	(Omagh) 13. 5.06P
G-MTZB	Thruster TST Mk.1	8048-TST-069		13. 4.88	L J and J L Eden	Long Marston 2. 6.07P
G-MTZC	Thruster TST Mk.1	8048-TST-070		13. 4.88	R W Marshall	(Armagh) 24. 8.05P
G-MTZD	Thruster TST Mk.1	8048-TST-071		13. 4.88	A Spence	Popham 21. 9.05P
G-MTZF	Thruster TST Mk.1	8048-TST-073		13. 4.88	D C Marsh	Doynton 15. 3.08P

G-MTZG	Mainair Gemini Flash IIA	642-588-6-W431		10. 5.88	P J Bent *(Noted 10.07)*	Swinford, Rugby	21. 7.07P
G-MTZH	Mainair Gemini Flash IIA	643-588-6-W433		9. 6.88	D C Hughes	St Michaels	17.12.01P
	(Rotax 462)						
G-MTZJ	Solar Wings Pegasus XL-R	SW-WA-1328		6. 5.88	W G Harling	(Hedge End, Southampton)	7. 3.08P
	(Trike c/n SW-TB-1335)						
G-MTZK	Solar Wings Pegasus XL-R	SW-WA-1329		6. 5.88	G F Jones	Mill Farm, Shifnal	28. 1.07P
	(Trike c/n SW-TB-1336)						
G-MTZL	Mainair Gemini Flash IIA	645-588-6-W435		10. 5.88	N S Brayn	Popham	13. 4.06P
G-MTZM	Mainair Gemini Flash IIA	646-588-6-W436		3. 5.88	K L Smith	(Leicester)	25.10.08P
G-MTZO	Mainair Gemini Flash IIA	649-688-6-W439		6. 5.88	R C Hinds	(Newnham, Glos)	27. 8.08P
	(Rotax 462)						
G-MTZP	Solar Wings Pegasus XL-Q	SW-WQ-0059		6. 5.88	M J Newman	Sandown, Isle of Wight	23. 6.05P
	(Rotax 447)	*(Trike c/n SW-TB-1337)*			*(Noted 7.05)*		
G-MTZR	Solar Wings Pegasus XL-Q	SW-WQ-0060		6. 5.88	P J Hatchett	(Rhuddlan, Rhyl)	19. 8.98P
	(Rotax 447)	*(Trike c/n SW-TB-1338)*					
G-MTZS	Solar Wings Pegasus XL-Q	SW-WQ-0061		6. 5.88	P A Darling	(Wilmslow)	15. 7.93P
	(Rotax 447)	*(Trike c/n SW-TB-1339)*					
G-MTZV	Mainair Gemini Flash IIA	650-688-6-W440		6. 5.88	A Robinson	Tarn Farm, Cockerham	10. 5.08P
G-MTZW	Mainair Gemini Flash IIA	651-688-6-W441		25. 5.88	J E Rourke	Ince Blundell	13. 4.08P
G-MTZX	Mainair Gemini Flash IIA	652-688-6-W442		23. 6.88	R G Cuckow and J C Thompson	Rufforth	4. 5.08P
G-MTZY	Mainair Gemini Flash IIA	653-688-6-W443		24. 5.88	C N Thornton	Eshott	23. 2.08P
G-MTZZ	Mainair Gemini Flash IIA	654-688-6-W444		14. 6.88	P J Litchfield	Tarn Farm, Cockerham	3. 2.08P
G-MUCK	Lindstrand LBL 77A Balloon (Hot Air)	982		25. 1.05	C J Wootton *(Poppies titles)*	Ormskirk	3. 4.08E
G-MUIR	Cameron V-65 Balloon (Hot Air)	2037		23. 6.89	L J M Muir *"Muriel"*	East Molesey	9. 4.04A
G-MULT	Beech 76 Duchess	ME-396	N810Y	26.10.04	Folada Aero and Technical Services Ltd	Bournemouth	25. 1.08E
G-MUMM	Colt 180A Balloon (Hot Air)	1636	SE-ZES	12. 4.05	D K Hempleman-Adams	Corsham	28. 4.06A
G-MUMY	Van's RV-4	PFA 181-13401		11. 1.05	S D Howes	Durham Tees Valley	14.11.08P
	(Built S D Howes)						
G-MUNI	Mooney M 20J Mooney 201	24-3118		12. 5.89	P R Williams *(Noted 1.08)*	Oxford	1. 9.07
G-MURG	Van's RV-6	PFA 181-12470		22. 6.05	E C Murgatroyd	Sackville Lodge, Riseley	15.12.07P
	(Built E C Murgatroyd)						
G-MURP	Aérospatiale AS.350B Ecureuil	2386	RP-C2388	15.12.04	M Murphy		
			N82632, JA6054, N49GA		Ravensdale, Ravensdale Park, Dundalk, County Louth	19. 4.08E	
G-MURR	Whittaker MW6 Merlin	PFA 164-12502		16. 4.99	D Murray	(Charmy Down, Bath)	
	(Built M Whittaker)				*(Noted 1.05)*		
G-MUSH	Robinson R44 Raven II	10278		18. 2.04	Flightpath Ltd	Costock	10. 3.08E
G-MUSO	Rutan LongEz	PFA 074A-10590		11. 6.83	P A Willis	RAF Coningsby	20. 4.08P
	(Built G B Castle) (Lycoming O-235)						
G-MUTE	Colt 31A Air Chair Balloon (Hot Air)	2099		2.12.91	K Temple	(Tivetshall St Margaret, Norwich)	11.11.99A
					(Address change 10.07)		
G-MUTT	CZAW Sportcruiser	PFA 338-14667		14. 9.07	A McIvor	Brock Farm, Billericay	
	(Built A McIvor)						
G-MUTZ	Avtech Jabiru J430	0xxx		29.12.03	N C Dean	Little Staughton	30. 6.08P
	(Built N C Dean - pr.no.PFA 336-14171)						
G-MVAA	Mainair Gemini Flash IIA	655-688-6-W445		8. 6.88	R M Wigman	Oxton	30.10.08P
G-MVAB	Mainair Gemini Flash IIA	656-688-6-W446		10. 5.88	B Hindley	(Newton Bank Farm, Daresbury)	1. 7.05P
G-MVAC	CFM Shadow Series CD	K 077		12. 5.88	C A S Powell	(Heald Green, Cheadle)	22. 5.07P
G-MVAD	Mainair Gemini Flash IIA	657-688-6-W447		10. 5.88	N D Fox and C I Hemmingway		
						Tarn Farm, Cockerham	20. 7.08P
G-MVAF	Southdown Puma Sprint	P 455	G-MBAF	24. 6.87	J F Horn	Ezenridge Farm, Bere Alston, Yelverton	17. 5.05P
	(Fuji-Robin EC-44-2PM)						
G-MVAG	Thruster TST Mk.1	8058-TST-074		18. 5.88	P Higgins	(Thomastown, Enfield, County Meath)	17. 8.06P
G-MVAH	Thruster TST Mk.1	8058-TST-075		18. 5.88	M W H Henton *"Times Four"*	Popham	18. 8.05P
G-MVAI	Thruster TST Mk.1	8058-TST-076		18. 5.88	A M R Wasse	Mendlesham	7. 5.07P
G-MVAJ	Thruster TST Mk.1	8058-TST-077		18. 5.88	A J Collins *(New owner 12.07)*	Bidford	16. 6.02P
G-MVAK	Thruster TST Mk.1	8058-TST-078		18. 5.88	L A Hosegood *(Noted 11.04)*	Clench Common	24. 8.04P
G-MVAL	Thruster TST Mk.1	8058-TST-079		18. 5.88	G C Brooke	(Elmstead, Colchester)	7. 8.96P
G-MVAM	CFM Shadow Series CD	082		18. 5.88	C P Barber	Brook Farm, Pilling	24. 7.06P
G-MVAN	CFM Shadow Series CD	K 048		18. 5.88	I Brewster	Longacre Farm, Sandy	17.10.08P
	(Built CFM Metal-Fax - pr.no.PFA 161-11219)						
G-MVAO	Mainair Gemini Flash IIA	658-688-6-W448		24. 5.88	S J Robson	Brook Farm, Pilling	9. 4.08P
					(Operated Brook Farm Microlight Centre)		
G-MVAP	Mainair Gemini Flash IIA	659-688-6-W449		24. 5.88	R J Miller	Long Marston	3. 9.08P
G-MVAR	Solar Wings Pegasus XL-R	SW-WA-1331		24. 5.88	A J Thomas	Deenethorpe	24. 1.08P
	(Trike c/n SW-TB-1343)						
G-MVAT	Solar Wings Pegasus XL-R	SW-WA-1333		24. 5.88	R Hickman	Watnall	27.12.07P
	(Trike c/n SW-TB-1345)						
G-MVAV	Solar Wings Pegasus XL-R	SW-WA-1335		24. 5.88	D J Utting	(Bungay)	16. 2.03P
	(Trike c/n SW-TB-1347)						
G-MVAW	Solar Wings Pegasus XL-Q	SW-WQ-0064		24. 5.88	G Sharman	(East Cowes)	3. 4.08P
	(Rotax 447)	*(Trike c/n SW-TB-1348)*					
G-MVAX	Solar Wings Pegasus XL-Q	SW-WQ-0065		24. 5.88	M R Bennett	(West End, Southampton)	8. 6.07P
	(Rotax 447)	*(Trike c/n SW-TB-1349)*			*(New owner 2.08)*		
G-MVAY	Solar Wings Pegasus XL-Q	SW-WQ-0066		24. 5.88	V O Morris	(Kidwelly)	16. 4.97P
	(Rotax 447)	*(Trike c/n SW-TB-1350)*					
G-MVBB	CFM Shadow Series BD	K 051		24. 5.88	R Garrod	(Mickfield, Stowmarket)	8.10.00P
G-MVBC	Mainair Tri-Flyer/Aerial Arts 130SX	130SX-616		24. 5.88	D Beer	(Lee, Ilfracombe)	
	(Believed to be using Mainair Tri-Flyer 250 Trike from G-MJIX)						
G-MVBD	Mainair Gemini Flash IIA	660-688-6-W450		8. 6.88	J Batchelor	(Benfleet)	17.12.03P
	(Rotax 462)						
G-MVBE	Mainair Scorcher	661-688-6-W451		28. 7.88	R Hitchmough	Tarn Farm, Cockerham	29. 7.08P
G-MVBF	Mainair Gemini Flash IIA	662-688-6-W452		14. 6.88	E McCallum	Longframlington	15. 5.08P
	(Rotax 462) *(Original Trike now fitted to G-JESA qv)*						
G-MVBG	Mainair Gemini Flash IIA	663-688-6-W453		25. 5.88	M P Edwards	Mill Farm, Shifnal	16. 7.08P

G-MVBI	Mainair Gemini Flash IIA	665-788-6-W455	7. 6.88	S Irwin	(Morland, Penrith)	30. 9.08P
G-MVBJ	Solar Wings Pegasus XL-R	SW-WA-1338	7. 6.88	R J O Page	(Oupia, France)	4. 8.08P
	(Rotax 462)	*(Trike c/n SW-TE-0033)*				
G-MVBK	Mainair Gemini Flash IIA	666-788-6-W456	7. 6.88	B R McLoughlin	(Liverpool)	8. 8.06P
	(Rotax 462)			*(New owner 10.06)*		
G-MVBL	Mainair Gemini Flash IIA	669-788-6-W459	7. 6.88	S T Cain	(Lathom, Ormskirk)	3. 4.08P
G-MVBM	Mainair Gemini Flash IIA	667-788-6-W457	7. 6.88	A J Graham	Rhedyn Coch Farm, Rhuallt	22. 7.08P
	(Rotax 582) *(Trike reported stolen 8.03 but new Permit issued 5.06 and with new engine suggests replacement Trike)*					
G-MVBN	Mainair Gemini Flash IIA	668-788-6-W458	8. 6.88	M Frankcom	(Astley Park, Darwen)	2. 6.99P
G-MVBO	Mainair Gemini Flash IIA	671-788-6-W461	8. 6.88	J A Brown	(Wheaton Aston, Stafford)	20. 7.07P
G-MVBP	Thruster TST Mk.1	8068-TST-080	14. 6.88	K J Crompton	Newtownards	13. 3.08P
G-MVBT	Thruster TST Mk.1	8068-TST-083	14. 6.88	R Everitt tr TST Group Flying	Ley Farm, Chirk	19.12.07P
	(BMW R100)					
G-MVBY	Solar Wings Pegasus XL-R	SW-WA-1344	17. 6.88	J E Harman tr Pigs R Us Flying Group		
		(Trike c/n SW-TB-1357)			(Napton, Southam)	9. 9.03P
G-MVBZ	Solar Wings Pegasus XL-R	SW-WA-1345	17. 6.88	A G Butler	Shenstone Hall Farm, Shenstone	17. 9.05P
		(Trike c/n SW-TB-1358)				
G-MVCA	Solar Wings Pegasus XL-R	SW-WA-1346	17. 6.88	R Walker	Sutton Meadows	23.11.07P
		(Trike c/n SW-TB-1359)				
G-MVCB	Solar Wings Pegasus XL-R	SW-WA-1347	17. 6.88	L Briscoe	Lower Mountpleasant, Chatteris	8. 5.08P
		(Trike c/n SW-TB-1360)				
G-MVCC	CFM Shadow Series CD	K 045	17. 6.88	G Finney *(New owner 7.07)*	(Brighton)	5. 8.06P
G-MVCD	Medway Hybred 44XLR	MR001/34	14. 6.88	J Thompson	Longacre Farm, Sandy	27. 7.03P
	(Marked as "Raven") (Original Sailwing transferred to G-MVOS: newSailwing c/n not known)					
G-MVCE	Mainair Gemini Flash IIA	672-788-6-W462	23. 6.88	N Ford	(Stockport)	13. 4.06P
G-MVCF	Mainair Gemini Flash IIA	673-788-6-W463	14. 7.88	J S Harris	Old Sarum	1. 6.05P
	(Rotax 462)					
G-MVCI	Noble Hardman Snowbird Mk.IV	SB-011	11.10.88	W L Chapman	(Tarn Farm, Cockerham)	13. 4.95P
G-MVCJ	Noble Hardman Snowbird Mk.IV	SB-012	11.10.88	C W Buxton	Darley Moor, Ashbourne	14. 9.04P
	(Rotax 582) *(Officially regd with Rotax 532)*			*(Noted as engineless wreck 4.06)*		
G-MVCK	Cosmos Trike/La Mouette Profil 19	SDA-01	19. 7.88	S D Alsop	(Midsomer Norton, Bath)	
G-MVCL	Solar Wings Pegasus XL-Q	SW-WQ-0075	27. 6.88	T E Robinson	Insch	5.10.08P
		(Trike c/n SW-TE-0069)				
G-MVCM	Solar Wings Pegasus XL-Q	SW-WQ-0076	27. 6.88	P J Croney	Hunsdon	25. 4.08P
		(Trike c/n SW-TE-0070)				
G-MVCN	Solar Wings Pegasus XL-Q	SW-WQ-0077	27. 6.88	S R S Evans	Rayne Hall Farm, Braintree	14. 5.08P
		(Trike c/n SW-TE-0071)			*(In own trailer)*		
G-MVCP	Solar Wings Pegasus XL-Q	SW-WQ-0079	27. 6.88	J R Fulcher	Deenethorpe	13. 6.08P
		(Trike c/n SW-TE-0073)				
G-MVCR	Solar Wings Pegasus XL-Q	SW-WQ-0080	27. 6.88	P Hoeft	(Stickney, Boston)	1.10.08P
		(Trike c/n SW-TE-0069)				
G-MVCS	Solar Wings Pegasus XL-Q	SW-WQ-0081	27. 6.88	J J Sparrow	Sywell	19. 7.02P
		(Trike c/n SW-TE-0075)				
G-MVCT	Solar Wings Pegasus XL-Q	SW-WQ-0082	27. 6.88	G J Lampitt	Pound Green, Buttonoak, Bewdley	15. 6.06P
		(Trike c/n SW-TE-0076)				
G-MVCV	Solar Wings Pegasus XL-Q	SW-WQ-0084	27. 6.88	M P Williams	Redlands, Swindon	3.11.08P
	(Original Trike c/n SW-TE-0078 damaged and replaced by SW-TE-0108: SW-TE-0078 later repaired and fitted with Sailwing SW-WQ-0105 and regd G-MVHP)					
G-MVCW	CFM Shadow Series BD	084	28. 6.88	D A Coupland	(Ashby-de-la-Launde, Lincoln)	6.10.07P
				(New owner 1.08)		
G-MVCY	Mainair Gemini Flash IIA	674-788-6-W464	14. 7.88	A M Smith	Otherton, Cannock	11.10.05P
G-MVCZ	Mainair Gemini Flash IIA	675-788-6-W465	26. 8.88	P J Devine	(Hindley, Wigan)	14. 5.08P
G-MVDA	Mainair Gemini Flash IIA	676-788-6-W466	13. 7.88	C Tweedley	(Great Orton)	8. 5.06P
	(Rotax 462)					
G-MVDD	Thruster TST Mk.1	8078-TST-086	12. 7.88	D J Love	(Witton, Norwich)	9.11.99P
G-MVDE	Thruster TST Mk.1	8078-TST-087	12. 7.88	R H Davis *(Derelict 2.03)*	Doynton	26. 8.99P
G-MVDF	Thruster TST Mk.1	8078-TST-088	12. 7.88	J Walsh and A R Sunley tr G-MVDF Syndicate		
				(Operated Saxon Microlights)	Rayne Hall Farm, Braintree	12. 4.08P
G-MVDG	Thruster TST Mk.1	8078-TST-089	12. 7.88	D G., P M and A B Smith	Popham	26. 7.00P
				(In open storage in derelict condition 1.06)		
G-MVDH	Thruster TST Mk.1	8078-TST-090	12. 7.88	P E Terrell	(Plymouth)	2. 2.08P
G-MVDJ	Medway Hybred 44XLR	MR010/38	20. 7.88	W D Hutchings	(Nottingham)	8. 9.05P
G-MVDK	Aerial Arts Chaser S	CH.702	5. 8.88	S Adams *(Noted 9.01)*	Leicester	29.11.98P
G-MVDL	Aerial Arts Chaser S	CH.701	11. 8.88	J R Hall	Mapperton Farm, Newton Peverill	26. 4.08P
	(Rotax 462) *(Officially regd with Rotax 377)*			"112"		
G-MVDT	Mainair Gemini Flash IIA	670-788-6-W460	20. 7.88	D C Stephens	(Coleford)	9.11.99P
G-MVDV	Solar Wings Pegasus XL-R	SW-WA-1349	13. 7.88	D Ewing	Roddige	9. 1.08P
		(Trike c/n SW-TB-1362)				
G-MVDW	Solar Wings Pegasus XL-R	SW-WA-1350	13. 7.88	R P Brown	Longacre Farm, Sandy	20. 7.97P
		(Trike c/n SW-TB-1363)			*(Noted wrecked 7.03)*		
G-MVDX	Solar Wings Pegasus XL-R	SW-WA-1351	13. 7.88	C Kett	(Weston Zoyland)	8. 8.98P
		(Trike c/n SW-TB-1364)				
G-MVDY	Solar Wings Pegasus XL-R	SW-WA-1352	13. 7.88	C G Murphy	(Biggin Hill, Westerham)	1. 6.92P
		(Trike c/n SW-TB-1365)				
G-MVDZ	Solar Wings Pegasus XL-R	SW-WA-1353	12. 7.88	A K Pickering	(Robertsbridge)	19. 5.00P
		(Trike c/n SW-TB-1366)				
G-MVEC	Solar Wings Pegasus XL-R	SW-WA-1356	20. 7.88	J A Jarvis	Davidstow Moor	18. 4.03P
		(Trike c/n SW-TB-1369)				
G-MVED	Solar Wings Pegasus XL-R/Se	SW-WA-1357	20. 7.88	P A Sleightholme	Baxby Manor, Husthwaite	28. 9.08P
		(Trike c/n SW-TB-1370)				
G-MVEE	Medway Hybred 44XLR	MR004/35	22. 7.88	D S L Evans	(Gravesend)	4.10.05P
	(Trike c/n same as G-MYMJ and suggests this has a replacement unit)					
G-MVEF	Solar Wings Pegasus XL-R	SW-WA-1358	19. 7.88	A W Leadley *(New owner 8.06)*		
	(Rotax 462)	*(Trike c/n SW-TE-0079)*		(Lismonaghan, Letterkenny, County Donegal)		15.11.93P
G-MVEG	Solar Wings Pegasus XL-R	SW-WA-1359	19. 7.88	A M Shaw	(Alsager, Stoke-on-Trent)	8. 8.08P
	(Rotax 462)	*(Trike c/n SW-TE-0080)*				

G-MVEH	Mainair Gemini Flash IIA	677-788-6-W468		26. 8.88	K Bailey	(Oldham)	18.10.08P
G-MVEI	CFM Shadow Series CD	085		26. 7.88	I G Ferguson *(New owner 1.08)* North Connel, Oban		20.12.07P
G-MVEJ	Mainair Gemini Flash IIA	678-888-6-W469		27. 7.88	E Woods	(Urmston, Manchester)	30. 6.08P
	(Rotax 462)						
G-MVEK	Mainair Gemini Flash IIA	679-888-6-W470		27. 7.88	R M Rea	(Lubenham, Market Harborough)	28. 9.05P
G-MVEL	Mainair Gemini Flash IIA	680-888-6-W471		27. 7.88	M R Starling	(Swafield,, North Walsham)	25. 7.03P
G-MVEN	CFM Shadow Series CD	K 047		26. 7.88	R A Grace *(New owner 8.07)*	(Heathfield)	15. 7.08P
G-MVEO	Mainair Gemini Flash IIA	682-888-6-W472		28. 7.88	K Donaldson	Easter Poldar Farm, Thornhill	17. 3.08P
G-MVER	Mainair Gemini Flash IIA	684-888-6-W474		28. 7.88	J R Davis	(Cheltenham)	18.12.07P
G-MVES	Mainair Gemini Flash IIA	685-888-6-W475		5. 8.88	J Helm	(East Linton)	4. 4.08P
G-MVET	Mainair Gemini Flash IIA	686-888-6-W476		19. 8.88	C Buttery	Bagby	4. 4.08P
G-MVEV	Mainair Gemini Flash IIA	687-888-6-W477		5. 8.88	C Allen	(Alderley Edge)	8. 7.01P
G-MVEX	Solar Wings Pegasus XL-Q	SW-WQ-0088		5. 8.88	D Maher	(Nenagh, CountyTipperary)	5. 3.04P
	(Trike c/n SW-TE-0082)						
G-MVEZ	Solar Wings Pegasus XL-Q	SW-WQ-0090		9. 8.88	P W Millar	(Gorthleck, Inverness)	13. 6.99P
	(Trike c/n SW-TE-0084)						
G-MVFA	Solar Wings Pegasus XL-Q	SW-WQ-0091		9. 8.88	A Johnson	Deenethorpe	24.11.07P
	(Trike c/n SW-TE-0085)						
G-MVFB	Solar Wings Pegasus XL-Q	SW-WQ-0092		9. 8.88	M O Bloy	(King's Lynn)	29.11.07P
	(Trike c/n SW-TE-0086)						
G-MVFC	Solar Wings Pegasus XL-Q	SW-WQ-0093		9. 8.88	D R Joint	Davidstow Moor	31. 5.07P
	(Trike c/n SW-TE-0087)				*(Noted 10.07)*		
G-MVFD	Solar Wings Pegasus XL-Q	SW-WQ-0094		9. 8.88	C D Humphries	Sywell	10. 9.07P
	(Trike c/n SW-TE-0088)						
G-MVFE	Solar Wings Pegasus XL-Q	SW-WQ-0095		9. 8.88	S J Weeks	Kemble	30. 4.00P
	(Trike c/n SW-TE-0089)						
G-MVFF	Solar Wings Pegasus XL-Q	SW-WQ-0096		9. 8.88	A Makepeace	(Guildford)	25. 8.08P
	(Trike c/n SW-TE-0090)						
G-MVFH	CFM Shadow Series CD	086		9. 8.88	G R Read and M D Goad tr G-MVFH Group		
	(Rotax 447)					Mendlesham	19. 5.08P
G-MVFJ	Thruster TST Mk.1	8088-TST-092		11. 8.88	B E Renehan tr Kestrel Flying Group	Popham	20. 4.08P
G-MVFK	Thruster TST Mk.1	8088-TST-093		11. 8.88	C A Gray	Perth	16.11.07P
G-MVFL	Thruster TST Mk.1	8088-TST-094		11. 8.88	E J Wallington Inglenook Farm, Maydensole, Dover		22. 5.02P
					(New owner 10.06)		
G-MVFM	Thruster TST Mk.1	8088-TST-095		11. 8.88	G J Boyer	Weston Zoyland	1. 9.05P
G-MVFO	Thruster TST Mk.1	8088-TST-097		11. 8.88	S R James Humberstone and A L Higgins	Sywell	25. 5.08P
G-MVFP	Solar Wings Pegasus XL-R	SW-WA-1365		9. 8.88	D J Brixton tr Shropshire Tow Group		
	(Trike c/n SW-TB-1371)					Bishops Castle, Shropshire	24. 3.03P
G-MVFS	Solar Wings Pegasus XL-R/Se	SW-WA-1367		9. 8.88	A Cordes	Deenethorpe	25. 6.05P
	(Trike c/n SW-TB-1373)						
G-MVFT	Solar Wings Pegasus XL-R	SW-WA-1368		9. 8.88	S J Whalley	Roddige	16.12.07P
	(Trike c/n SW-TB-1374)						
G-MVFV	Solar Wings Pegasus XL-R	SW-WA-1370		9. 8.88	L R M Grigg	Deenethorpe	25. 6.05P
	(Trike c/n SW-TB-1376)						
G-MVFY	Solar Wings Pegasus XL-R	SW-WA-1373		9. 8.88	T D Bawden	Weston Zoyland	19. 6.04P
	(Trike c/n SW-TB-1379)						
G-MVFZ	Solar Wings Pegasus XL-R	SW-WA-1374		9. 8.88	R K Johnson	Popham	29. 5.05P
	(Trike c/n SW-TB-1380)						
G-MVGA	Aerial Arts Chaser S 508	CH.859		11. 8.88	N R Beale	Deppers Bridge, Southam	31. 5.06P
	(Officially regd with CH.707)						
G-MVGB	Medway Hybred 44XLR	MR011/39		1. 9.88	R Graham *(New owner 5.05)*	(Coulsdon, Surrey)	28. 8.02P
G-MVGC	AMF Microflight Chevvron 2-32C	010		2. 9.88	W Fletcher	Broadmeadow Farm, Hereford	11. 9.08P
G-MVGD	AMF Microflight Chevvron 2-32C	011		5. 9.88	T R James	(Southam)	21. 9.08P
G-MVGE	AMF Microflight Chevvron 2-32C	012		26. 9.88	J Cook	North Moor, Scunthorpe	1. 7.07P
	(Engine lost power on approach North Moor, Scunthorpe 11. 8.07 and forced landed in crops with substantial damage)						
G-MVGF	Aerial Arts Chaser S	CH.720		2. 9.88	P J Higgins	Gedney Dyke, Lutton	11.11.00P
					"The Dingbat" (New owner 4.03)		
G-MVGG	Aerial Arts Chaser S 508	CH.721		2. 9.88	P D Curtis	(Boston Spa, Wetherby)	16. 9.08P
G-MVGH	Aerial Arts Chaser S 447	CH.722		2. 9.88	J E Borrill and J Rochead	North Connel, Oban	5. 6.07P
G-MVGK	Aerial Arts Chaser S	CH.726		2. 9.88	D J Smith *(New owner 10.07)*	Hucknall	1. 9.99P
G-MVGM	Mainair Gemini Flash IIA	691-988-6-W481		25. 8.88	W G Colyer	(Paddock Wood, Tonbridge)	7. 6.07P
G-MVGN	Solar Wings Pegasus XL-R/Se	SW-WA-1377		23. 8.88	M J Smith	(Taunton)	24. 6.05P
	(Trike c/n SW-TB-1381)						
G-MVGO	Solar Wings Pegasus XL-R	SW-WA-1378		23. 8.88	J B Peacock Lower Mountpleasant Farm, Chatteris		14. 9.08P
	(Trike c/n SW-TB-1382)						
G-MVGP	Solar Wings Pegasus XL-R	SW-WA-1379	(EC- . . .)	23. 8.88	J P Cox	Deenethorpe	9. 6.00P
	(Trike c/n SW-TB-1383)		G-MVGP		*(Noted 9.06)*		
G-MVGU	Solar Wings Pegasus XL-Q	SW-WQ-0100		23. 8.88	I A Macadam	Damyns Hall, Upminster	21. 6.04P
	(Trike c/n SW-TB-0092)				*(New owner 10.07)*		
G-MVGW	Solar Wings Pegasus XL-Q	SW-WQ-0102		23. 8.88	M J L de Carvalho and V V P Pedro tr G-MVGW Group		
	(Trike c/n SW-TE-0095)					Lagos, Algarve, Portugal	8. 2.92P
G-MVGY	Medway Hybred 44XLR	MR015/41		31. 8.88	G M Griffiths *(Noted 2.07)*	Perth	16. 8.08P
G-MVGZ	Ultraflight Lazair IIIE	A338	C-?	21.10.88	D M Broom	(Towcester)	25. 3.03P
	(Rotax 185 x 2)						
G-MVHA	Aerial Arts Chaser S-1000	CH.729		24. 8.88	R Meredith-Hardy	Radwell Lodge, Baldock	9. 5.04P
	(Mosler MM CB-38)						
G-MVHB	Powerchute Raider	80105		26. 8.88	A E Askew	(Melton Mowbray)	5. 7.07P
G-MVHC	Powerchute Raider	80106		26. 8.88	G Martin *(New owner 6.06)*	(Lisburn)	10..4.06P
G-MVHD	CFM Shadow Series CD	088		8. 9.88	D Raybould	(New Whittington, Chesterfield)	10. 5.08P
G-MVHE	Mainair Gemini Flash IIA	692-988-6-W482		4.10.88	B R Thomas	Oak Farm, Woodton	27. 3.08P
G-MVHF	Mainair Gemini Flash IIA	693-988-6-W483		4.10.88	M G Nicholson	St Michaels	28. 5.05P
G-MVHG	Mainair Gemini Flash IIA	694-988-6-W484		14.10.88	C A J Elder	(Reddingmuirhead, Falkirk)	10. 6.08P
G-MVHH	Mainair Gemini Flash IIA	607-1187-5-W485		24.10.88	A M Lynch	(Edinburgh)	15.11.06P
	(Original Trike c/n "695.-988-6" replaced by c/n "607-1187-5" ex G-MTSA 1995)						

G-MVHI	Thruster TST Mk.1	8098-TST-100		26. 9.88	L Hurman	Enstone	10. 3.06P
G-MVHJ	Thruster TST Mk.1	8098-TST-101		26. 9.88	S P Macdonald		
						Lower Mountpleasant Farm, Chatteris	19. 4.08P
G-MVHK	Thruster TST Mk.1	8098-TST-102		27. 9.88	D J Gordon	Woodlands Barton Farm, Roche	14. 8.07P
G-MVHL	Thruster TST Mk.1	8098-TST-103		27. 9.88	G Jones	(Llanfairfechan)	16. 7.02P
G-MVHP	Solar Wings Pegasus XL-Q	SW-WQ-0105		23. 9.88	J B Gasson	Lower Mountpleasant Farm, Chatteris	15. 9.07P
	(Trike c/n SW-TE-0078)		*(Damaged Trike from G-MVCV repaired and fitted to Sailwing)*				
G-MVHR	Solar Wings Pegasus XL-Q	SW-WQ-0106		23. 9.88	J M Hucker	Broadmeadow Farm, Hereford	26. 5.04P
	(Trike c/n SW-TE-0099)				*(Noted 5.05)*		
G-MVHS	Solar Wings Pegasus XL-Q	SW-WQ-0107		23. 9.88	C L Lebeter	(Derby)	9. 8.06P
	(Trike c/n SW-TE-0100)						
G-MVHW	Solar Wings Pegasus XL-Q	SW-WQ-0111		23. 9.88	Ultralight Training Ltd	Broadmeadow Farm. Hereford	11. 3.08P
	(Trike c/n SW-TE-0101)						
G-MVHY	Solar Wings Pegasus XL-Q	SW-WQ-0113		23. 9.88	R P Paine	Headon Farm, Retford	17. 8.06P
	(Trike c/n SW-TE-0106)						
G-MVHZ	Hornet Dual Trainer/Southdown Raven			26. 9.88	J M Addison	Insch	11.12.05P
	HRWA 0076 & MHR-101						
G-MVIB	Mainair Gemini Flash IIA	700-1088-4-W490		14.10.88	S, A and Leslie Rosser t/a LSA Systems		
					(Noted 3.07)	Arclid Green, Sandbach	13. 7.06P
G-MVIE	Aerial Arts Chaser S	CH.732		14.10.88	T M Stiles *(Noted 8.03)*	Perth	6. 6.97P
G-MVIF	Medway Raven X	MR020/43		4.10.88	J R Harrison	(Bolsover)	11. 6.07P
	(Originally regd as Hybred 44XLR)						
G-MVIG	CFM Shadow Series B	K 044		5.10.88	M P and P A G Harper	(Priory Farm, Tibenham)	20. 1.94P
	(Rotax 447)				*(Damaged 1993: stored 8.93)*		
G-MVIH	Mainair Gemini Flash IIA	697-1088-6-W487		14.10.88	T M Gilsenan	(Eaton Bray)	15. 8.07P
G-MVIL	Noble Hardman Snowbird Mk.IV	SB-014		6. 2.89	Marine Power (Scotland) Ltd	Kirkbride	9. 8.07P
	(Rotax 582)						
G-MVIM	Noble Hardman Snowbird Mk.IV	SB-015		6. 2.89	W G Goodall *(Noted 7.05)*	Sandtoft	26. 8.91P
G-MVIN	Noble Hardman Snowbird Mk.IV	SB-016		6. 2.89	C P Dawes	Darley Moor, Ashbourne	20. 3.08P
	(Rebuilt to Mk.V standard with Rotax 582)						
G-MVIO	Noble Hardman Snowbird Mk.IV	SB-017		12. 4.89	B Mason-Baker tr Mobility Advice Line		
						Mill Farm, Hughley, Much Wenlock	29. 7.08P
G-MVIP	AMF Microflight Chevvron 2-32C	008		11. 5.88	P C Avery	Lower Mountpleasant Farm, Chatteris	19. 6.07P
G-MVIR	Thruster TST Mk.1	8108-TST-104		21.10.88	T D Gardner	Popham	9. 9.08P
	(C/n plate marked as 8118-TST-104)						
G-MVIT	Thruster TST Mk.1	8108-TST-106	(C-) G-MVIT	21.10.88	A C Bell	Knapthorpe Lodge, Caunton	1.11.08P
					(New owner 11.06)		
G-MVIU	Thruster TST Mk.1	8108-TST-107		21.10.88	M D Reece	Rufforth	31. 7.08P
	(Rebuilt to part T 600 standard)						
G-MVIV	Thruster TST Mk.1	8108-TST-108		21.10.88	G Rainey *(New owner 3.05)*	Weston Zoyland	24. 6.01P
G-MVIX	Mainair Gemini Flash IIA	702-1088-6-W492		14.10.88	R S T MacEwen	East Fortune	20.10.08P
G-MVIY	Mainair Gemini Flash IIA	701-1088-6-W491		14.10.88	J J Valentine	Ince Blundell	15. 9.07P
G-MVIZ	Mainair Gemini Flash IIA	703-1088-6-W493		14.10.88	P R Hutty	(Hessle)	17. 8.08P
G-MVJA	Mainair Gemini Flash IIA	696-988-6-W486		5.12.88	J R Harrison	(Wisbech)	29. 8.06P
G-MVJC	Mainair Gemini Flash IIA	705-1088-6-W495		24.10.88	B Temple	Broadmeadow Farm, Hereford	25. 4.05P
			(Engine failure on take off Priory Farm, Tibenham 15.8.04 and substantially damaged)				
G-MVJD	Solar Wings Pegasus XL-R	SW-WA-1386		24.10.88	B L Prime	Roddige	28. 6.08P
	(Rotax 462)	*(Trike c/n SW-TE-0109)*					
G-MVJE	Mainair Gemini Flash IIA	706-1188-6-W496		21.10.88	G Zuchowski	(Wincham, Northwich)	11. 4.08P
G-MVJF	Aerial Arts Chaser S	CH.743		21.11.88	V S Rudham	Dunkeswell	2. 8.05P
G-MVJG	Aerial Arts Chaser S	CH.749		22.11.88	T H Scott *(Noted 1.07)*	Rayne Hall Farm, Braintree	13. 6.03P
G-MVJH	Aerial Arts Chaser S	CH.751		14.11.88	M van Rompaey	(Scunthorpe)	1. 9.03P
G-MVJI	Aerial Arts Chaser S	CH.752		17.11.88	T Beckham	(Newcastle upon Tyne)	1.11.03P
G-MVJJ	Aerial Arts Chaser S 508	CH.753		14.11.88	C W Potts	Stanton, Morpeth	5. 8.08P
G-MVJK	Aerial Arts Chaser S	CH.754		14.11.88	K J Samuels	(Loughton)	X
G-MVJL	Mainair Gemini Flash IIA	698-1188-6-W488		21.10.88	F Huxley	(Morpeth)	4. 5.06P
G-MVJM	Microflight Spectrum	007		21.10.88	S E Matthews tr Poppy Syndicate	Otherton, Cannock	2. 9.08P
G-MVJN	Solar Wings Pegasus XL-Q	SW-WQ-0116		26.10.88	R A Paintain	Chilbolton	17. 1.06P
	(Trike c/n SW-TE-0110)						
G-MVJO	Solar Wings Pegasus XL-Q	SW-WQ-0117		26.10.88	P Robinson	(Southampton)	22. 9.08P
	(Trike c/n SW-TE-0111)						
G-MVJP	Solar Wings Pegasus XL-Q	SW-WQ-0118		26.10.88	S H Bakowski	Damyn's Hall, Upminster	18. 4.08P
	(Trike c/n SW-TE-0112)						
G-MVJR	Solar Wings Pegasus XL-Q	SW-WQ-0119		26.10.88	A S Wason	Lower Upham Farm, Chiseldon	9. 8.08P
	(Trike c/n SW-TE-0113)						
G-MVJS	Solar Wings Pegasus XL-Q	SW-WQ-0120		26.10.88	S D Morley	Rayne Hall Farm, Braintree	19. 5.08P
	(Trike c/n SW-TE-0114)						
G-MVJT	Solar Wings Pegasus XL-Q	SW-WQ-0121		26.10.88	L A Hosegood	Redlands, Swindon	17. 2.08P
	(Trike c/n SW-TE-0115)						
G-MVJU	Solar Wings Pegasus XL-Q	SW-WQ-0122		26.10.88	J C Longmore	Headon Farm, Retford	8. 2.07P
	(Trike c/n SW-TE-0116)						
G-MVJW	Solar Wings Pegasus XL-Q	SW-WQ-0124		26.10.88	R Dainty and D W Stamp		
	(Trike c/n SE-TE-0118)					Pound Green, Buttonoak, Bewdley	4. 5.06P
G-MVKB	Medway Hybred 44XLR	MR023/45		11.11.88	J Newby	Sandtoft	11. 9.00P
G-MVKC	Mainair Gemini Flash IIA	709-1188-6-W499		16.11.88	R L Bladon	Sittles Farm, Alrewas	28. 3.08P
G-MVKF	Solar Wings Pegasus XL-R	SW-WA-1392		14.11.88	B Shaw	(Prospect Farm, Wollaston)	12. 2.08P
	(Trike c/n SW-TB-1389)						
G-MVKH	Solar Wings Pegasus XL-R	SW-WA-1396		14.11.88	K M Elson	Roddige	15.11.07P
	(Trike c/n SW-TB-1393)						
G-MVKJ	Solar Wings Pegasus XL-R	SW-WA-1398		14.11.88	G V Warner	Croughton	7. 6.02P
	(Rotax 462)	*(Trike c/n SW-TE-0132)*					
	(Officially regd with Rotax 447)						
G-MVKK	Solar Wings Pegasus XL-R	SW-WA-1397		14.11.88	G P Burns	Graveley Hall Farm, Graveley	18. 3.08P
	(Rotax 462)	*(Trike c/n SW-TE-0131)*					

G-MVKL	Solar Wings Pegasus XL-R	SW-WA-1394	14.11.88	J Powell-Tuck	(Mamhilad, Pontypool)	6. 6.91P
	(Trike c/n SW-TB-1391)		*(Pod marked as "XL-Q" but is XL-R model)*			
G-MVKM	Solar Wings Pegasus XL-R	SW-WA-1399	14.11.88	A E Dobson	(Burwod, Craven Arms)	12. 2.05P
	(Original Trike c/n SW-TE-0136 but now uses c/n SW-TB-1152 ex G-MVKM)					
G-MVKN	Solar Wings Pegasus XL-Q	SW-WQ-0126	14.11.88	R A and C A Allen	Siege Cross Farm, Thatcham	7. 9.08P
	(Trike c/n SW-TE-0120)					
G-MVKP	Solar Wings Pegasus XL-Q	SW-WQ-0128	14.11.88	P Mokryk and S King	(Derby)	19. 9.04P
	(Trike c/n SW-TE-0122)					
G-MVKS	Solar Wings Pegasus XL-Q	SW-WQ-0130	14.11.88	K S Wright	Long Marston	13. 5.94P
	(Trike c/n SW-TE-0124)			*(Stored 8.95*		
G-MVKT	Solar Wings Pegasus XL-Q	SW-WQ-0131	14.11.88	P W Ruffle	Enstone	12. 3.08P
	(Trike c/n SW-TE-0125)					
G-MVKU	Solar Wings Pegasus XL-Q	SW-WQ-0132	14.11.88	I K Priestley	Sackville Lodge, Riseley	21.11.08P
	(Trike c/n SW-TE-0126)					
G-MVKV	Solar Wings Pegasus XL-Q	SW-WQ-0152	14.11.88	D R Stansfield	(Sleaford)	4. 6.07P
	(Trike c/n SW-TE-0127: original Sailwing c/n SW-WQ-0133 damaged 14.8.91 and replaced)					
G-MVKW	Solar Wings Pegasus XL-Q	SW-WQ-0134	14.11.88	A T Scott	Walkeridge Farm, Overton	8. 4.08P
	(Trike c/n SW-TE-0128)					
G-MVKZ	Aerial Arts Chaser S	CH.756	5.12.88	T J Barley *(Noted 3.05)* Graveley Hall Farm, Graveley		29. 7.04P
G-MVLA	Aerial Arts Chaser S	CH.762	12.12.88	T Birch	Sittles Farm, Alrewas	23. 7.08P
G-MVLB	Aerial Arts Chaser S	CH.763	5.12.88	R P Wilkinson	Charmy Down, Bath	8. 5.06P
G-MVLC	Aerial Arts Chaser S 447	CH.764	22.11.88	B R Barnes	(Bristol)	10. 5.03P
	(Officially regd with Rotax 377)					
G-MVLD	Aerial Arts Chaser S	CH.765	22.11.88	J Kennedy *(New owner 10.07)*	Mill Farm, Shifnal	10. 6.06P
G-MVLE	Aerial Arts Chaser S	CH.766	5.12.88	R G Hooker	Brunton	29. 1.07P
G-MVLF	Aerial Arts Chaser S 508	CH.767	11. 1.89	I B Smith	Deenethorpe	10.11.07P
G-MVLG	Aerial Arts Chaser S	CH.768	14.11.88	A Strang	East Fortune	26.11.04P
G-MVLJ	CFM Shadow Series CD	092	11.11.88	R S Cochrane	Sutton Meadows	30. 5.07P
G-MVLL	Mainair Gemini Flash IIA	708-1188-6-W498	23.11.88	M I Deeley	(Felthorpe)	15. 5.08P
	(Sailwing c/n now W396 ex G-MTSA)					
G-MVLP	CFM Shadow Series C	095	22.11.88	D Bridgland and D T Moran	Old Sarum	25. 5.08P
	(Rotax 447) (Officially regd with Rotax 503)					
G-MVLR	Mainair Gemini Flash IIA	713-1288-6-W503	30.11.88	P A Louis *(Noted 8.07)*	Tarn Farm, Cockerham	18.11.00P
G-MVLS	Aerial Arts Chaser S 477	CH.773	21. 2.89	T C Brown *(Noted 9.05)*	Mill Farm, Shifnal	20. 4.05P
G-MVLT	Aerial Arts Chaser S	CH.774	5.12.88	B D Searle	(Portsmouth)	19. 7.05P
G-MVLW	Aerial Arts Chaser S	CH.778	28.12.88	E W P van Zeller	(Ashford)	5. 9.99P
G-MVLX	Solar Wings Pegasus XL-Q	SW-WQ-0114	30.11.88	J F Smith	Enstone	22. 6.08P
	(Trike c/n SW-TE-0133)					
G-MVLY	Solar Wings Pegasus XL-Q	SW-WQ-0142	5.12.88	I B Osborn	Manston	2.10.08P
	(Trike c/n SW-TE-0137)					
G-MVMA	Solar Wings Pegasus XL-Q	SW-WQ-0144	5.12.88	G C Winter-Goodwin *(Noted 9.07)*		
				Broomclose Farm, Longbridge Deverill		3. 6.07P
G-MVMC	Solar Wings Pegasus XL-Q	SW-WQ-0146	5.12.88	P Smith and I W Barlow	(Ilkeston)	23. 3.06P
	(Trike c/n SW-TE-0141 & SW-WQ-0146					
G-MVMG	Thruster TST Mk.1	8128-TST-112	12.12.88	A D McCaldin	Mullahead, Tandragee	20. 7.08P
G-MVMI	Thruster TST Mk.1	8128-TST-114	12.12.88	J H Milne	(Norwich)	12. 6.08P
G-MVMK	Medway Hybred 44XLR	MR022/46	12.12.88	D J Lewis	(Grays)	5. 2.94P
G-MVML	Aerial Arts Chaser S	CH.781	28.12.88	G C Luddington	Wilden, Bedford	29. 7.00P
G-MVMM	Aerial Arts Chaser S	CH.792	21. 2.89	D Margereson	(Chesterfield)	30. 7.04P
G-MVMO	Mainair Gemini Flash IIA	715-1288-6-W507	12.12.88	K Austwick	Glassonby	28. 7.08P
G-MVMR	Mainair Gemini Flash IIA	717-1288-6-W509	9. 1.89	P W Ramage	(Rufforth)	20. 9.96P
G-MVMT	Mainair Gemini Flash IIA	718-189-6-W510	22.12.88	R F Sanders *(New owner 4.05)*	Otherton, Cannock	25. 9.98P
G-MVMU	Mainair Gemini Flash IIA	719-189-6-W511	22.12.88	P A Brunt	(Stretford, Manchester)	23. 7.07P
G-MVMV	Mainair Gemini Flash IIA	720-189-6-W512	22.12.88	J M Macdonald	(Pontesbury, Shrewsbury)	24. 3.06P
				(New owner 8.07)		
G-MVMW	Mainair Gemini Flash IIA	710-1188-6-W500	11.11.88	K Downes and B Nock	(Wolverhampton)	31. 7.03P
G-MVMX	Mainair Gemini Flash IIA	721-189-6-W513	23.12.88	D J Rooney	(Rathvilly, County Carlow)	27. 4.08P
	(Rotax 462) (Trike stamped incorrectly as "W512")					
G-MVMY	Mainair Gemini Flash IIA	722-189-6-W514	22.12.88	N G Leteney	(Bury)	21.12.02P
G-MVMZ	Mainair Gemini Flash IIA	723-189-6-W515	22.12.88	S Richards	Otherton, Cannock	24. 5.02P
G-MVNA	Powerchute Raider	81230	12. 7.89	J McGoldrick	Newtownards	6. 7.04P
G-MVNB	Powerchute Raider	81231	12. 7.89	P J Fahie	(Stour Row, Shaftesbury)	11. 8.06P
G-MVNC	Powerchute Raider	81232	12. 7.89	W R Hanley	(Edinburgh)	25. 7.00P
G-MVNJ	Powerchute Raider	81239	12. 7.89	W Kimberlin *(New owner 9.07)*	(Melton Mowbray)	13. 7.90P
G-MVNK	Powerchute Raider	90623	12. 7.89	J Lockyer	(Alsager, Stoke-on-Trent)	16. 7.95P
G-MVNL	Powerchute Raider	90624	12. 7.89	S Penoyre	(Windlesham)	17. 3.01P
G-MVNM	Mainair Gemini Flash IIA	725-189-6-W517	6. 1.89	C D Phillips	Dunkeswell	31. 8.08P
G-MVNN	Whittaker MW5-K Sorcerer	5K-0003-02	28. 3.90	J A T Merino	(Malaga, Spain)	9. 1.06P
	(Built K N Dando - pr.no.BMAA/HB/022)					
G-MVNO	Whittaker MW5-K Sorcerer	5K-0004-02	4. 5.89	R L Wadley	Stoke, Isle of Grain	31. 5.04P
	(Built Aerotech International Ltd)					
G-MVNP	Whittaker MW5-K Sorcerer	5K-0005-02	13. 7.89	A M Edwards	(Wokingham)	30. 6.05P
	(Built Aerotech International Ltd)					
G-MVNR	Whittaker MW5-K Sorcerer	5K-0006-02	4. 5.89	E I Rowlands-Jones	(Mochdre, Newtown)	23. 8.01P
	(Built Aerotech International Ltd)			*(New owner 1.04)*		
G-MVNS	Whittaker MW5-K Sorcerer	5K-0007-02	19. 7.89	A M Sirant	Monkswell Farm, Horrabridge	30.11.07P
	(Built Aerotech International Ltd)					
G-MVNT	Whittaker MW5-K Sorcerer	5K-0008-02	28. 3.90	P E Blyth	Wombleton	5 5.07P
	(Built Aerotech International Ltd)					
G-MVNU	Whittaker MW5-K Sorcerer	5K-0009-02	4. 5.89	J C Rose	Field Farm, Oakley	30. 6.06P
	(Built Aerotech International Ltd)					
G-MVNW	Mainair Gemini Flash IIA	726-189-6-W518	25. 1.89	R J Boydell	Ince Blundell	25. 5.08P
G-MVNX	Mainair Gemini Flash IIA	727-289-6-W519	10. 1.89	I Sidebotham	Barton	13. 5.05P

G-MVNY	Mainair Gemini Flash IIA	724-189-6-W516		11. 1.89	M K Buckland	(Daventry)	29. 7.08P
	(Rotax 462)						
G-MVNZ	Mainair Gemini Flash IIA	728-289-6-W520		11. 1.89	J Howarth	Watnall	11. 7.08P
G-MVOB	Mainair Gemini Flash IIA	729-289-6-W521		16. 1.89	G L Logan	(Great Bourton, Banbury)	23. 7.08P
G-MVOD	Aerial Arts Chaser/110SX	110SX/653		16. 1.89	N R Beale	Deppers Bridge, Southam	9. 4.05P
	(Rotax 377)				*(Noted 6.06)*		
G-MVOF	Mainair Gemini Flash IIA	730-289-6-W522		31. 1.89	P J Nolan	(Coventry)	26 1.08P
G-MVOH	CFM Shadow Series CD	K 090		23. 1.89	D I Farmer	Dunkeswell	2. 9.02P
G-MVOJ	Noble Hardman Snowbird Mk.IV	SB-019		26. 7.89	C D Beetham	Kirkbridge	16. 9.08P
G-MVOL	Noble Hardman Snowbird Mk.IV	SB-021		29. 8.89	E J Lewis tr Swansea Snowbird Fliers	(Swansea)	26. 1.02P
G-MVON	Mainair Gemini Flash IIA	731-289-6-W523		30. 1.89	W R Astbury *(New owner 7.06)*	(Stockport	22.12.05P
G-MVOO	AMF Microflight Chevvron 2-32C	014		10. 1.89	M K Field	Sleap	10. 5.07P
G-MVOP	Aerial Arts Chaser S	CH.787		21. 2.89	D Thorpe *(Noted 3.05)*	Longacre Farm, Sandy	4. 5.03P
G-MVOR	Mainair Gemini Flash IIA	732-289-6-W524	(EC-)	6. 2.89	P T and R M Jenkins	Dunkeswell	5.10.03P
	(Rotax 462)		G-MVOR				
G-MVOT	Thruster TST Mk.1	8029-TST-116		17. 2.89	B L R J Keeping	Davidstow Moor	11.11.07P
G-MVOU	Thruster TST Mk.1	8029-TST-117		17. 2.89	D W Tewson *(New owner 1.07)*	(Marshwood, Bridport)	13. 1.08P
G-MVOV	Thruster TST Mk.1	8029-TST-118		17. 2.89	D J Seymour tr G-MVOV Group	Enstone	18. 6.08P
G-MVOW	Thruster TST Mk.1	8029-TST-119		17. 2.89	J Short and B J Merret	Dunkeswell	17. 7.00P
G-MVOX	Thruster TST Mk.1	8029-TST-120		17. 2.89	J E Davies	Haverfordwest	29. 8.07P
G-MVOY	Thruster TST Mk.1	8029-TST-121		17. 2.89	C Jones	Redlands, Swindon	22. 6.07P
G-MVPA	Mainair Gemini Flash IIA	735-289-7-W527		29. 3.89	J E Milburn	(South Shields)	30. 8.95P
G-MVPB	Mainair Gemini Flash IIA	736-389-7-W528		29. 3.89	O Carter	Baxby Manor, Husthwaite	30. 7.05P
G-MVPC	Mainair Gemini Flash IIA	737-389-7-W529		7. 2.89	W O Flannery	(Scariff, County Clare)	26. 6.07P
	(Mis-stamped with c/n inscription for "740-389-7-W532" which is identity of G-MVPI)						
G-MVPD	Mainair Gemini Flash IIA	738-389-7-W530		7. 2.89	P Thelwell *(Noted 8.07)*	Tarn Farm, Cockerham	16. 2.07P
G-MVPE	Mainair Gemini Flash IIA	739-389-7-W531		7. 2.89	M D Jealous and M Goodrick	(Sandbach)	3.11.08P
G-MVPF	Medway Hybred 44XLR	MR036/52		27. 2.89	G H Crick	Plaistows Farm, St Albans	13. 4.07P
G-MVPH	Whittaker MW6-S Fatboy Flyer	PFA 164-11404		7. 2.89	A K Mascord	(Dolfor, Newtown)	23. 8.99P
	(Built E A Henman) (Rotax 503)				*(New owner 4.06)*		
G-MVPI	Mainair Gemini Flash IIA	740-389-7-W532		9. 2.89	A Shand	(Banchory)	17. 6.08P
G-MVPJ	Rans S-5 Coyote	88.083		15. 2.89	J E D Rogerson	Morgansfield, Fishburn	2. 8.99P
	(Built J Whiting - pr.no.PFA 193-11470)				*(New owner 3.02)*		
G-MVPK	CFM Shadow Series CD	K 091		15. 2.89	P Sarfas	Benson's Farm, Laindon	11. 6.08P
	(Rotax 447) *(Officially regd with Rotax 503)*						
G-MVPL	Medway Hybred 44XLR	MR034/50		1. 3.89	J N J Roberts	(Longacre Farm, Sandy)	30. 4.98P
G-MVPM	Whittaker MW6 Merlin	PFA 164-11272		21. 2.89	K W Curry	(Nantmel, Llandrindod Wells)	30. 4.03P
	(Built S J Field- rReported as Type MW6-T) (Rotax 503)				*(New owner 1.05)*		
G-MVPN	Whittaker MW6 Merlin	PFA 164-11280		21. 2.89	A M Field	(Glastonbury)	18. 5.93P
	(Built A M Field) (Rotax 503)						
G-MVPR	Solar Wings Pegasus XL-Q	SW-WQ-0163		14. 3.89	R S Swift	Finmere	24. 5.08P
	(Trike c/n SW-TE-0149)						
G-MVPS	Solar Wings Pegasus XL-Q	SW-WQ-0140		14. 3.89	R J Hood	London Colney	8. 6.08P
	(Trike c/n SW-TE-0143)						
G-MVPX	Solar Wings Pegasus XL-Q	SW-WQ-0158		28. 3.89	P Gregory and T McLoughlin	Clench Common	24. 6.08P
	(Trike c/n SW-TE-0144)						
G-MVPY	Solar Wings Pegasus XL-Q	SW-WQ-0188		28. 3.89	G H Dawson	Coldharbour Farm, Willingham	23. 6.08P
	(Trike c/n SW-TE-0178)						
G-MVRA	Mainair Gemini Flash IIA	743-489-7-W535		10. 4.89	D P Burgess and P M Ryder		
					(Golcar, Huddersfield and Manchester)		2.10.08P
G-MVRB	Mainair Gemini Flash IIA	747-489-7-W539		29. 3.89	G Callaghan	(Richhill, Armagh)	13. 5.06P
G-MVRC	Mainair Gemini Flash IIA	748-489-7-W540		29. 3.89	M O'Connell	Rufforth	16. 5.03P
G-MVRD	Mainair Gemini Flash IIA	749-489-7-W541		9. 5.89	A R Helm	Altham West, Accrington	25. 3.08P
G-MVRF	Rotec Rally 2B	AIE-01		28. 4.89	A I Edwards	(Hixon, Stafford)	
G-MVRG	Aerial Arts Chaser S	CH.798		14. 4.89	J P Kynaston	(Harlington, Dunstable)	31. 8.99P
G-MVRH	Solar Wings Pegasus XL-Q	SW-WQ-0177		10. 4.89	K Farr	Swinford, Rugby	21. 4.08P
	(Trike c/n SW-TE-0160)						
G-MVRI	Solar Wings Pegasus XL-Q	SW-WQ-0159		10. 4.89	P Martin	Newnham, Baldock	14. 7.08P
	(Trike c/n SW-TE-0145)						
G-MVRJ	Solar Wings Pegasus XL-Q	SW-WQ-0154		10. 4.89	J Goldsmith-Ryan	Eaglescott	3.10.05P
	(Trike c/n SW-TE-0172)						
G-MVRL	Aerial Arts Chaser S 447	CH.801		18. 4.89	C N Beale	Mill Farm, Shifnall	17. 4.07P
G-MVRM	Mainair Gemini Flash IIA	752-489-7-W545		12. 4.89	J S Stevenson	East Fortune	23. 2.08P
	(Rotax 462)						
G-MVRO	CFM Shadow Series CD	K 105		3. 4.89	K H Creed	(Langar, Nottingham)	10.11.08P
G-MVRP	CFM Shadow Series CD	097		7. 4.89	B Barrass *(Noted 10.07)*	Sywell	14. 2.06P
G-MVRR	CFM Shadow Series CD	098		7. 4.89	S Fairweather and S P Christian	Hougham, Lincoln	14. 4.08P
G-MVRT	CFM Shadow Series CD	104		7. 4.89	G M Teasdale	Watnall	2. 2.08P
G-MVRU	Solar Wings Pegasus XL-Q	SW-WQ-0183		12. 4.89	P Copping	(Sackville Lodge, Riseley)	25. 1.08P
	(Trike c/n SW-TE-0166)						
G-MVRV	Powerchute Kestrel	90210		28. 4.89	G M Fletcher	(Chesterfield)	3. 2.97P
G-MVRW	Solar Wings Pegasus XL-Q	SW-WQ-0178		12. 4.89	M A Baldwin	Rochester	10. 8.08P
	(Trike c/n SW-TE-0161)	*(Rebuilt 1999 including new factory supplied Sailwing)*					
G-MVRX	Solar Wings Pegasus XL-Q	SW-WQ-0165		12. 4.89	M Everest	(Hailsham)	18. 6.05P
	(Trike c/n SW-TE-0151)						
G-MVRY	Medway Hybred 44XLR	MR049/56		12. 4.89	K Dodman	(Stowmarket)	4. 3.99P
G-MVRZ	Medway Hybred 44XLR	MR043/57		9. 5.89	I Oswald	(London SE9)	13.11.01P
	(Rotax 503)						
G-MVSB	Solar Wings Pegasus XL-Q	SW-WQ-0193		18. 4.89	M Jennings and D Forde	Rufforth	23.11.02P
	(Trike c/n SW-TE-0184)				*(New owners 3.03)*		
G-MVSD	Solar Wings Pegasus XL-Q	SW-WQ-0195		18. 4.89	D C Maxwell-Grice	Old Sarum	14. 8.08P
	(Trike c/n SW-TE-0186)						
G-MVSE	Solar Wings Pegasus XL-Q	SW-WQ-0196		18. 4.89	L B Richardson	Bagby	17. 2.07P
	(Trike c/n SW-TE-0187)						

G-MVSG	Aerial Arts Chaser S	CH.804		24. 4.89	M Roberts (Melksham)	24. 7.05P
G-MVSI	Medway Hybred 44XLR	MR040/58		18. 4.89	R J Matthews Rochester	17. 7.07P
G-MVSJ	Aviasud Mistral 532GB	072		18. 4.89	P R Hall and J D Hewitson	
	(Built Aviasud Engineering - pr.no.BMAA/HB/013)				(Kirk Bramwith, Doncaster and Hemingbrough, Selby)	20. 4.08P
G-MVSM	Midland Ultralights Sirocco 377GB	MU-023		21. 4.89	C G Benham (Farthingstone, Towcester)	15. 8.04P
					(New owner 9.05)	
G-MVSN	Mainair Gemini Flash IIA	754-589-7-W547		28. 4.89	D W Watson (Noted 9.07) Eshott	30. 7.07P
G-MVSO	Mainair Gemini Flash IIA	755-589-7-W548		27. 4.89	N H Taylor East Fortune	25. 1.08P
G-MVSP	Mainair Gemini Flash IIA	756-589-7-W549		27. 4.89	D R Buchanan Pulborough	4. 4.04P
G-MVST	Mainair Gemini Flash IIA	750-589-7-W543		12. 6.89	I M Watson (Carnforth)	2. 6.08P
	(Rotax 462)					
G-MVSV	Mainair Gemini Flash IIA	757-589-7-W550		11. 5.89	P Shelton St Michaels	12. 9.07P
G-MVSW	Solar Wings Pegasus XL-Q	SW-WQ-0198		17. 5.89	G F Ryland Oxton, Nottingham	10. 3.07P
	(Trike c/n SW-TE-0189)					
G-MVSX	Solar Wings Pegasus XL-Q	SW-WQ-0199		11. 5.89	A R Law Davidstow Moor	2. 9.05P
	(Trike c/n SW-TE-0190)				(Noted 10.07)	
G-MVSY	Solar Wings Pegasus XL-Q	SW-WQ-0200		11. 5.89	G P Turnbull Weston Zoyland	12. 9.04P
	(Trike c/n SW-TE-0191)					
G-MVSZ	Solar Wings Pegasus XL-Q	SW-WQ-0201		11. 5.89	G P Jones (Stoke-on-Trent)	17. 6.08P
	(Trike c/n SW-TE-0192)					
G-MVTA	Solar Wings Pegasus XL-Q	SW-WQ-0202		11. 5.89	P Hanby (Maidstone)	24. 5.08P
	(Trike c/n SW-TE-0193)					
G-MVTC	Mainair Gemini Flash IIA	759-689-7-W552		30. 5.89	P Hocknull (Middlewich)	31. 5.08P
G-MVTD	Whittaker MW6 Merlin	PFA 164-11367		11. 5.89	G J Green (Matlock)	27. 3.04P
	(Built J S Yates) (Rotax 503)					
G-MVTF	Aerial Arts Chaser S 447	CH808		30. 5.89	P Mundy (Prestwich, Manchester)	5. 9.08P
G-MVTI	Solar Wings Pegasus XL-Q	SW-WQ-0206		25. 5.89	D Burdett Sutton Meadows	9.12.05P
	(Trike c/n SW-TE-0217)					
G-MVTJ	Solar Wings Pegasus XL-Q	SW-WQ-0207		25. 5.89	A J Gibbins (Weymouth)	26. 1.08P
	(Trike c/n SW-TE-0197)					
G-MVTK	Solar Wings Pegasus XL-Q	SW-WQ-0208		25. 5.89	N Musgrave (Rhosybol, Amlwch)	12. 5.08P
	(Trike c/n SW-TE-0198)					
G-MVTL	Aerial Arts Chaser S	CH.809		13. 6.89	N D Meer Roddige	30. 7.06P
G-MVTM	Aerial Arts Chaser S 447	CH.810		13. 6.89	G L Davies (Carlton Colville, Lowestoft)	13. 9.06P
	(Officially regd with Rotax 377)					
G-MVUA	Mainair Gemini Flash IIA	760-689-7-W553		14. 6.89	E W Hughes RAF Mona	13. 2.06P
	(Rotax 462)				(Noted 3.07)	
G-MVUB	Thruster T 300	089-T300-373		13. 6.89	S Silk Rochester	26. 6.03P
	(Rotax 532)				(Noted 8.05)	
G-MVUD	Medway Hybred 44XLR	MR037/55		19. 6.89	T W Nelson Carlisle	18. 3.04P
	(Rotax 503)					
G-MVUF	Solar Wings Pegasus XL-Q	SW-WQ-0213		13. 6.89	G and S Simons (Littlehampton)	17. 8.07P
	(Trike c/n SW-TE-0203)					
G-MVUG	Solar Wings Pegasus XL-Q	SW-WQ-0214		13. 6.89	I J Morgan (Bristol)	21. 9.08P
	(Trike c/n SW-TE-0204)					
G-MVUI	Solar Wings Pegasus XL-Q	SW-WQ-0216		13. 6.89	J K Edgecombe Swinford, Rugby	17. 7.08P
	(Trike c/n SW-TE-0206: Sailwing marked incorrectly as c/n SW-TE-0216)					
G-MVUJ	Solar Wings Pegasus XL-Q	SW-WQ-0217		13. 6.89	J H Cooper Field Farm, Oakley	21 9.08P
	(Trike c/n SW-TE-0207)					
G-MVUK	Solar Wings Pegasus XL-Q	SW-WQ-0218		13. 6.89	D Greenslade Redlands, Swindon	27.10.05P
	(Trike c/n SW-TE-0208)					
G-MVUL	Solar Wings Pegasus XL-Q	SW-WQ-0219		13. 6.89	D Hamilton-Brown (Pevensey)	23. 7.07P
	(Trike c/n SW-TE-0209)					
G-MVUM	Solar Wings Pegasus XL-Q	SW-WQ-0220		13. 6.89	S Clay (Falmouth)	11.10.08P
	(Trike c/n SW-TE-0210)					
G-MVUO	AMF Microflight Chevvron 2-32C	015		14. 6.89	P Rawlinson (Sutton, Ely)	4. 6.07P
G-MVUP	Aviasud Mistral 532GB	1087-48	83-CQ	10. 8.89	G R Inston Overseal, Derby	8.10.07P
	(Built Aviasud Engineering - pr.no.BMAA/HB/003)					
G-MVUS	Aerial Arts Chaser S	CH.813		3. 7.89	H Poyzer Eshott	16.12.01P
G-MVUU	Hornet R-ZA	HRWB0061 & ZA110		13. 7.89	K W Warn (Newton Abbot)	27. 7.07P
G-MVVH	Medway Hybred 44XLR	MR047/63		11. 7.89	M S Henson (Portsmouth)	5. 9.08P
G-MVVI	Medway Hybred 44XLR	MR050/64		12. 7.89	J L Ford (Edlesborough, Dunstable)	16. 4.08P
G-MVVK	Solar Wings Pegasus XL-R	SW-WA-1423		11. 7.89	A J Weir (Bath)	2. 2.08P
	(Trike c/n SW-TB-1414)					
G-MVVM	Solar Wings Pegasus XL-R	SW-WA-1425		12. 7.89	A F Cunningham (Sandbach)	15. 7.06P
	(Trike c/n SW-TB-1416)					
G-MVVN	Solar Wings Pegasus XL-Q	SW-WQ-0226		11. 7.89	J R Butler Watnall	20. 5.08P
	(Trike c/n SW-TE-0214)					
G-MVVO	Solar Wings Pegasus XL-Q	SW-WQ-0227		11. 7.89	A L Scarlett Clench Common	29. 7.04P
	(Trike c/n SW-TE-0215)				(Noted 5.05)	
G-MVVP	Solar Wings Pegasus XL-Q	SW-WQ-0228		11. 7.89	M P Wimsey Sutton Meadows	12. 8.08P
	(Trike c/n SW-TE-0216)					
G-MVVR	Medway Hybred 44XLR	MR058/66		20. 7.89	H J Long	
	(Rotax 503)				Ardenagh Great, Taghmon, County Wexford	19.10.08P
G-MVVT	CFM Shadow Series CD	K 101		26. 7.89	W F Hayward (Maud, Peterhead)	7. 9.08P
	(Built CFM Metal-Fax - pr.no.PFA 161-11569)					
G-MVVU	Aerial Arts Chaser S	CH.816		19. 7.89	J T Davies (Loughborough)	27. 6.07P
	(Rotax 462)					
G-MVVV	AMF Microflight Chevvron 2-32C	016	PH-1W9 G-MVVV	11. 5.89	P R Turton Old Sarum	16. 2.08P
G-MVVZ	Powerchute Raider	90628		25. 7.89	J H Cadman (Melton Mowbray)	13. 7.02P
G-MVWJ	Powerchute Raider	90738		25. 7.89	N J Doubek (Stanford-le-Hope)	24. 5.03P
G-MVWN	Thruster T 300	089-T300-374		26. 7.89	T B Reakes tr Whisky November Group	
	(Rotax 503)				Smalls Farm, Charterhouse	12. 7.08P

G-MVWR	Thruster T 300	089-T300-377	26. 7.89	G Rainey	Weston Zoyland	16. 3.08P
	(Rotax 503)					
G-MVWS	Thruster T 300	089-T300-378	26. 7.89	R J Humphries	Walkeridge Farm, Overton	15. 8.95P
	(Rotax 503)				(Stored for spares 3.07)	
G-MVWV	Medway Hybred 44XLR	MR060/69	24. 7.89	H Tuvey	(Aveley, South Ockendon)	17. 8.03P
	(Rotax 447)				(New owner 5.05)	
G-MVWW	Aviasud Mistral 532GB	0389-81	25. 7.89	P S Balmer and B H D Minto	Tarn Farm, Cockerham	25. 1.08P
	(Built Aviasud Engineering - pr.no.BMAA/HB/005)					
G-MVWZ	Aviasud Mistral 532GB	1288-70	2. 8.89	G Gates tr Chilbolton Mistral Group	Chilbolton	16. 4.07P
	(Built Aviasud Engineering - pr.no.BMAA/HB/008)				(Noted11.07)	
G-MVXA	Whittaker MW6 Merlin	PFA 164-11337	17. 8.89	I Brewster	Longacres Farm, Sandy	23. 4.08P
	(Built I Brewster) (Fuji-Robin EC-44-PM)					
G-MVXB	Mainair Gemini Flash IIA	762-789-7-W555	3. 8.89	M E Clennell	Longframlington	14. 8.08P
	(Rotax 462)					
G-MVXC	Mainair Gemini Flash IIA	763-889-7-W556	4. 8.89	D Wood	Arclid Green, Sandbach	31. 5.08P
G-MVXD	Medway Hybred 44XLR	MR061/70	3. 8.89	P R Millen	Lee-on-Solent	9. 6.08P
	(Rotax 503) (Marked as "Raven")					
G-MVXE	Medway Hybred 44XLR	MR063/71	23. 8.89	A M Brittle	Sittles Farm, Alrewas	31. 7.00P
	(Rotax 447)					
G-MVXI	Medway Hybred 44XLR	MR064/72	9. 8.89	T de Landro	Stoke, Isle of Grain	11. 7.05P
	(Rotax 447)					
G-MVXJ	Medway Hybred 44XLR	MR065/73	25. 8.89	P J Wilks	(Edenbridge)	26. 9.90P
	(Rotax 447)					
G-MVXL	Thruster TST Mk.1	8089-TST-122	18. 8.89	A J Smith	(Cardiff)	30. 8.00P
G-MVXM	Medway Hybred 44XLR	MR055/75	17. 8.89	P J Short	(Worcester)	2. 8.04P
	(Rotax 503) (Reported as Medway Raven)					
G-MVXN	Aviasud Mistral 532GB	065	18. 8.89	P W Cade	(New York, Lincoln)	12.10.08P
	(Built Aviasud Engineering - pr.no.BMAA/HB/002)					
G-MVXR	Mainair Gemini Flash IIA	764-889-7-W557	22. 8.89	D M Bayne	East Fortune	7. 8.08P
	(Rotax 462)					
G-MVXS	Mainair Gemini Flash IIA	766-889-7-W559	22. 8.89	J W Wood (Trike only 7.07)	Tarn Farm, Cockerham	25. 7.02P
G-MVXV	Aviasud Mistral 532GB	092	22. 8.89	M F E Chalk	(Shaw, Swindon)	5. 1.03P
	(Built Aviasud Engineering - pr.no.BMAA/HB/004)				(New owner 1.08)	
G-MVXX	AMF Microflight Chevvron 2-32	018	27. 7.89	C K Brown	(Loughborough)	27. 6.05P
G-MVYC	Solar Wings Pegasus XL-Q	SW-WQ-0239	8. 9.89	P E L Street	(Lincoln)	4. 1.08P
		(Trike c/n SW-TE-0224)				
G-MVYD	Solar Wings Pegasus XL-Q	SW-WQ-0240	8. 9.89	T M Wakeley	Shobdon	29. 9.08P
		(Trike c/n SW-TE-0225)				
G-MVYE	Thruster TST Mk.1	8089-TST-123	13. 9.89	M J Aubrey (New owner 1.08)	Kington, Hereford	24. 6.03P
G-MVYK	Hornet R-ZA	HRWB-0076 & ZA117	22. 9.89	P Asbridge	(Llanarmon-yn-Ial, Mold)	22. 7.99P
G-MVYL	Hornet R-ZA	HRWB-0077 & ZA115	22. 9.89	J L Thomas	(Bristol)	28. 3.04P
G-MVYN	Hornet R-ZA	HRWB-0079 & ZA136	22. 9.89	C F Janes	(Lee-on-Solent)	6. 7.08P
G-MVYP	Medway Hybred 44XLR	MR071/77	19. 9.89	J Harmon	Miiddle Stoke, Isle of Grain	12.10.08P
	(Rotax 447)					
G-MVYR	Medway Hybred 44XLR	MR068/76	19. 9.89	K J Clarke	Miiddle Stoke, Isle of Grain	2. 6.08P
	(Rotax 447)					
G-MVYS	Mainair Gemini Flash IIA	770-989-7-W563	19. 9.89	J McGrath (New owner 2.08)	Kirkbride	12. 9.07P
G-MVYT	Noble Hardman Snowbird Mk.IV	SB-022	26. 9.89	D T A Rees	Haverfordwest	8. 6.06P
G-MVYU	Noble Hardman Snowbird Mk.IV	SB-023	7.11.89	B Foster and P Meah	Gerpins Farm, Upminster	29. 7.08P
G-MVYV	Noble Hardman Snowbird Mk.IV	SB-024	21. 8.90	D W Hayden	Swansea	9. 4.08P
G-MVYW	Noble Hardman Snowbird Mk.IV	SB-025	22.10.90	T J Harrison	Upfield Farm, Lllanwern	25. 7.06P
G-MVYX	Noble Hardman Snowbird Mk.IV	SB-026	25.11.91	R McBlain	Kilkerran	10. 5.08P
G-MVYY	Aerial Arts Chaser S 508	CH.824	26. 9.89	C J Gordon and R H Bird	(Laurencekirk)	15. 7.07P
G-MVYZ	CFM Shadow Series BD	121	25. 9.89	C Day	(Salisbury)	15. 8.06P
G-MVZA	Thruster T 300	089-T300-379	26. 9.89	C C Belcher	Walkeridge Farm, Overton	18. 7.07P
G-MVZC	Thruster T 300	089-T300-381	26. 9.89	R A Knight	Chilbolton	20. 6.08P
	(Rotax 532)					
G-MVZD	Thruster T 300	089-T300-382	26. 9.89	T Pearce tr G-MVZD Syndicate	(Twickenham)	3. 5.08P
	(Rotax 532)					
G-MVZG	Thruster T 300	089-T300-385	26. 9.89	R Lewis-Evans	Mapperton Farm, Newton Peverill	10. 4.08P
	(Rotax 532)					
G-MVZI	Thruster T 300	089-T300-387	26. 9.89	R R R Whittern	South Wraxall	19. 8.06P
	(Rotax 503)				(Noted 9.07)	
G-MVZJ	Solar Wings Pegasus XL-Q	SW-WQ-0241	26. 8.89	P Mansfield	Deenethorpe	24.11.07P
		(Trike c/n SW-TE-0226)				
G-MVZK	Quad City Challenger II UK	PFA 177-11498	28. 9.89	D K Maclennan tr G-MVZK Group	Strathaven	23. 9.04P
	(Built K B Tolley) (BMW R 100)				(Noted 8.06)	
G-MVZL	Solar Wings Pegasus XL-Q	SW-WQ-0242	4.10.89	P R Dobson	(Brentwood)	16. 6.05P
		(Trike c/n SW-TE-0227)				
G-MVZM	Aerial Arts Chaser S 447	CH.825	2.11.89	J L Parker	(Maidstone)	19. 5.08P
G-MVZO	Medway Hybred 44XLR	MR072/78	25.10.89	G Drysdale	(Scampton, Lincoln)	30. 7.08P
	(Rotax 503)					
G-MVZP	Murphy Renegade Spirit UK	256	17.10.89	H M Doyle	Lower Mountpleasant Farm, Chatteris	21. 1.05P
	(Built G S Hollingsworth - pr.no.PFA 188-11630)					
G-MVZS	Mainair Gemini Flash IIA	771-1089-7-W564	17.10.89	R L Beese	(Tarporley)	22. 5.08P
G-MVZT	Solar Wings Pegasus XL-Q	SW-WQ-0243	6.10.89	C J Meadows	Franklyn's Field, Chewton Mendip	25. 8.02P
		(Trike c/n SW-TE-0228)				
G-MVZU	Solar Wings Pegasus XL-Q	SW-WQ-0244	6.10.89	M G McMurray	(Farcet, Peterborough)	13. 4.07P
		(Trike c/n SW-TE-0229)				
G-MVZW	Hornet R-ZA	HRWB-0063 & ZA142	27.10.89	K W Warn	Popham	9. 8.02P
G-MVZX	Murphy Renegade Spirit UK	PFA 188-11590	18.10.89	G Holmes	(Pickering)	16. 7.08P
	(Built G Holmes)					
G-MVZZ	AMF Microflight Chevvron 2-32	019	27. 7.89	W A L Mitchell (New owner 1.08)	Deanland	24. 5.07P
G-MWAB	Mainair Gemini Flash IIA	772-1089-7-W565	24.10.89	J E Buckley	(Sandbach)	21. 9.07P

G-MWAC	Solar Wings Pegasus XL-Q	SW-WQ-0260	25.10.89	H Lloyd-Hughes	Emlyn's Field, Rhuallt	10. 5.08P
	(Trike c/n SW-TE-0236)					
G-MWAD	Solar Wings Pegasus XL-Q	SW-WQ-0261	25.10.89	J K Evans	(Brixworth, Northampton)	15. 6.07P
	(Trike c/n SW-TE-0237)					
G-MWAE	CFM Shadow Series CD	130	24.10.89	D J Adams	(Passenham, Milton Kynes)	29. 3.08P
G-MWAF	Solar Wings Pegasus XL-R	SW-WA-1441	30.10.89	J P Bonner	Arclid Green, Sandbach	6. 7.07P
	(Trike c/n SW-TB-1422)					
G-MWAG	Solar Wings Pegasus XL-R	SW-WA-1442	30.10.89	X Norman	(Thame)	11. 8.08P
	(Trike c/n SW-TB-1423)					
G-MWAJ	Murphy Renegade Spirit UK	PFA 188-11438	1.11.89	M Mailey	Blackhill, Draperstown	6. 4.04P
	(Built J Hall) (BMW R 100RS)			*(Noted 2007)*		
G-MWAL	Solar Wings Pegasus XL-Q	SW-WQ-0263	2.11.89	A W Hill	(Bury, Ramsey, Huntingdon)	11. 8.06P
	(Trike c/n SW-TE-0240)			*(Address change 3.07)*		
G-MWAN	Thruster T 300	089-T300-389	14.11.89	E J Girling	Davidstow Moor	7. 7.08P
	(Rotax 532)					
G-MWAP	Thruster T 300	089-T300-391	14.11.89	S F Chave and A G Spurway	(Honiton)	9. 8.04P
	(Rotax 503)			"Wanda"		
G-MWAR	Thruster T 300	089-T300-392	14.11.89	B Cassidy	Dunkeswell	29. 4.08P
	(Rotax 532)					
G-MWAT	Solar Wings Pegasus XL-Q	SW-WQ-0265	13.11.89	D G Seymour	Yatesbury	7. 7.05P
	(Trike c/n SW-TE-0241)					
G-MWAV	Solar Wings Pegasus XL-R	SW-WA-1444	13.11.89	I J Rawlingson	(Stoke-on-Trent)	6. 4.08P
	(Trike c/n SW-TB-1424 appears to have been duplicated with G-MWBL qv)					
G-MWAW	Whittaker MW6 Merlin	PFA 164-11460	10.11.89	J K Buckingham	(Liverpool)	4. 4.08P
	(Built P Palmer) (Rotax 503)					
G-MWBJ	Medway Puma Sprint	MS003/1	21.11.89	C C Strong	(Bures, Cornwall)	14. 7.00P
	(Rotax 447)					
G-MWBK	Solar Wings Pegasus XL-Q	SW-WQ-0271	16.11.89	A W Jarvis	(Motcombe, Shaftesbury)	26. 3.08P
	(Trike c/n SW-TE-0248)					
G-MWBL	Solar Wings Pegasus XL-R/Se	SW-WA-1446	16.11.89	J A Valentine	Eshott	3. 7.04P
	(Trike c/n SW-TB-1424 appears to have been duplicated with G-MWAV qv)			*(Noted 9.07)*		
G-MWBO	Rans S-4 Coyote	89.097	29.11.89	B M Tibenham	Longside, Peterhead	28.11.07P
	(Built L R H d'Ath - pr.no.PFA 193-11583)			*(Crashed on take-off Hatton 9. 6.07 and substantially damaged)*		
G-MWBP	Hornet R-ZA	HRWB-0083/ZA144	29.11.89	S Brader	Tarn Farm, Cockerham	17. 8.05P
G-MWBS	Hornet R-ZA	HRWB-0085/ZA146	29.11.89	P D Jaques	Sandtoft	3.10.08P
	(BMW R100)			"Freedom Hornet"		
G-MWBU	Hornet R-ZA	HRWB-0087/ZA148	29.11.89	J D Nelson	Plaistows Farm, St Albans	12. 9.04P
G-MWBW	Hornet R-ZA	HRWB-0089/ZA150	29.11.89	C G Bentley	(Chesterfield)	15. 5.00P
G-MWBY	Hornet R-ZA	HRWB-0091/ZA152	29.11.89	M Doyle *(New owner 3.05)*	(Tullamore, County Offaly)	19. 6.04P
G-MWCB	Solar Wings Pegasus XL-Q	SW-WQ-0273	1.12.89	J C Whiting	(Lincoln)	25. 9.07P
	(Trike c/n SW-TE-0250)					
G-MWCC	Solar Wings Pegasus XL-R/Se	SW-WA-1447	1.12.89	I K Priestley	Sackville Lodge, Riseley	26. 3.05P
	(Trike c/n SW-TB-1387 ex G-MVKD when latter's Sailwing sold) (Rotax 462)			*(New owner 11.07)*		
G-MWCE	Mainair Gemini Flash IIA	775-1289-7-W568	19.12.89	B A Tooze	Shobdon	6. 9.05P
G-MWCF	Solar Wings Pegasus XL-Q	SW-WQ-0276	13.12.89	R McKie	(Southampton)	29. 9.08P
	(Trike c/n SW-TE-0252)					
G-MWCG	Microflight Spectrum	011	15.12.89	C Ricketts *(New owner 7.07)*	Otherton, Cannock	2. 6.05P
G-MWCH	Rans S-6-ESD Coyote II	0989.067	15.12.89	J G Burns and T Briton tr G-MWCH Group		
	(Built J Whiting - pr.no.PFA 204-11632 - sequence no. duplicates Kitfox G-BSFY)				Morgansfield, Fishburn	17.10.08P
G-MWCI	Powerchute Kestrel	91245	3. 1.90	E G Bray	Clacton	2. 7.05P
G-MWCK	Powerchute Kestrel	91247	3. 1.90	A E Askew *(New owner 12.06)*	(Melton Mowbray)	28.12.04P
G-MWCM	Powerchute Kestrel	91249	3. 1.90	G E Lockyer *(New owner 6.03)*	(Stoke-on-Trent)	17. 6.96P
G-MWCN	Powerchute Kestrel	91250	3. 1.90	J D McKibben *(Noted 7.07)*	Derryrogue	16. 8.04P
G-MWCO	Powerchute Kestrel	91251	3. 1.90	J R E Gladstone (	(Abingdon)	7. 6.08P
G-MWCR	Southdown Puma Sprint	P 516 & SN1121/0070	24. 2.84	S R Hall	Deenethorpe	2. 8.02P
	(Fuji-Robin EC-44-PM)			*(Noted 3.05)*		
G-MWCS	Powerchute Kestrel	91253	3. 1.90	R S McFadyen	(Tamworth)	5. 7.07P
G-MWCU	Solar Wings Pegasus XL-R	SW-WA-1449	27.12.89	T P Noonan	(Dromcollogher, County Limerick)	5. 8.05P
	(Trike c/n SW-TB-1412)					
G-MWCW	Mainair Gemini Flash IIA	776-0190-7-W569	29.12.89	A J Thomas	(Eccleston, Chorley)	11. 8.05P
	(Rotax 462)			*(Bare frame noted 11.06)*		
G-MWCY	Medway Hybred 44XLR	MR077/81	15. 1.90	J K Masters	(Chigwell)	10. 9.04P
	(Rotax 503)					
G-MWCZ	Medway Hybred 44XLR	MR078/82	10. 1.90	A Titcombe	(Aylesford)	22. 6.04P
	(Rotax 503)					
G-MWDB	CFM Shadow Series CD	100	3. 7.89	M D Meade	(Shenley Brook End, MIlton Keynes)	10. 7.04P
G-MWDC	Solar Wings Pegasus XL-R/Se	SW-WA-1450	5. 1.90	S Irwin	Kirkbride	21. 3.08P
	(Rotax 462)	*(Trike c/n SW-TE-0255)*				
G-MWDD	Solar Wings Pegasus XL-Q	SW-WQ-0280	15. 1.90	M Wachowiak	(London W5)	8. 9.08P
	(Trike c/n SW-TE-0258)					
G-MWDE	Hornet RS-ZA	HRWB-0094 & ZA126	10. 1.90	H G Reid	Roddige	13. 6.98P
	(Rotax 532)			*(Trike noted 4.06)*		
G-MWDI	Hornet RS-ZA	HRWB-0098 & ZA158	10. 1.90	R J Perrin	Brook Farm, Pilling	29. 6.05P
	(Rotax 532)					
G-MWDJ	Mainair Gemini Flash IIA	777-0190-7-W570	17. 1.90	M Gardiner	Crosland Moor	27. 6.06P
G-MWDK	Solar Wings Pegasus XL-Q	SW-WQ-0281	17. 1.90	T Wicks	(Rowde, Devizes)	13. 6.08P
	(Trike c/n SW-TE-0259)					
G-MWDL	Solar Wings Pegasus XL-Q	SW-WQ-0282	17. 1.90	S R Isaac	Mapperton Farm, Newton Peverill	17. 6.08P
	(Trike c/n SW-TE-0260)					
G-MWDM	Murphy Renegade Spirit UK	319	18. 1.90	P J Fahie	(Stour Row, Shaftesbury)	13. 7.05P
	(Built M L Smith - pr.no.PFA 188A-11628 which duplicates Streak Shadow G-BRZZ) (Jabiru 2200A) (New owner 10.07)					
G-MWDN	CFM Shadow Series CD	K 102	17. 1.90	A A Duffus	RAF Halton	14. 9.08P
G-MWDS	Thruster T 300	089-T300-395	30. 1.90	A R Elliott	Siege Cross Farm, Thatcham	17. 5.08P
	(Rotax 532)					

G-MWDZ	Eipper Quicksilver MXL II	022		29. 1.90	R G Cook	Cranfield 19. 8.07P
	(Built Eipper Aircraft Inc - originally regd with pr.no.PFA 214-11869) (Rotax 503)					
G-MWEE	Solar Wings Pegasus XL-Q	SW-WQ-0147		12.12.88	R J Sharp Lower Mountpleasant Farm, Chatteris	2. 9.01P
	(Trike c/n SW-TE-0175)				*(Noted 2.08)*	
G-MWEF	Solar Wings Pegasus XL-Q	SW-WQ-0283		30. 1.90	N R Williams	Long Marston 18. 8.08P
	(Rotax 462HP)	*(Trike c/n SE-TE-0261)*				
G-MWEG	Solar Wings Pegasus XL-Q	SW-WQ-0284		30. 1.90	S P Michlig	Long Marston 24. 3.08P
	(Trike c/n SW-TE-0262)					
G-MWEH	Solar Wings Pegasus XL-Q	SW-WQ-0286		7. 2.90	K A Davidson	(Leuchars) 14. 8.07P
	(Trike c/n SW-TE-0264)					
G-MWEK	Whittaker MW5 Sorcerer	PFA 163-11284		20. 2.90	D W and M L Squire	(St Austell) 30. 8.08P
	(Built J T Francis)					
G-MWEL	Mainair Gemini Flash IIA	780-0290-7-W573		13. 2.90	S E Bettley	(Sandbach) 21 6.07P
G-MWEN	CFM Shadow Series CD	K 113		20. 2.90	C Dawn *(New owner 7.03)*	(Market Rasen) 8. 8.01P
G-MWEO	Whittaker MW5 Sorcerer	PFA 163-11263		21. 2.90	J Morton Blackhill, Draperstown	9. 9.04P
	(Built C D Wills) (Fuji-Robin EC-34-PM)				*(Noted 2007)*	
G-MWEP	Rans S-4 Coyote	89.096		21. 2.90	E J Wallington Inglenook Farm, Maydensole, Dover	16. 8.08P
	(Built K E Wedl - pr.no.PFA 193-11616)					
G-MWER	Solar Wings Pegasus XL-Q	SW-WQ-0287		1. 3.90	S P Tkaczyk	(Cardiff) 28. 9.08P
	(Trike c/n SW-TE-0265)					
G-MWES	Rans S-5 Coyote	89.099		1. 2.90	G Scott Lower Mountpleasant Farm, Chatteris	18. 8.04P
	(Built I Fleming and R W Sage - pr.no.PFA 193-11737)			*(Carries "N89099" on tail which matches c/n but is not a p/i) (Noted 8.06)*		
G-MWEY	Hornet R-ZA	HRWB-0104/ZA135		21. 2.90	J Kidd	Tarn Farm, Cockerham 24. 9.00P
G-MWEZ	CFM Shadow Series CD	136		22. 2.90	T D Dawson tr G-MWEZ Group	
					Plaistows Farm, St Albans	2. 6.08P
G-MWFB	CFM Shadow Series CD	K 119		1. 3.90	K W E Brunnenkant	(Lincoln) 21.10.04P
G-MWFC	TEAM Mini-MAX 88	294	G-BTXC	1. 3.90	M Bradley	North Coates 30. 8.08P
	(Built M H D Soltau - pr.no.PFA 186-11648)		G-MWFC			
G-MWFD	TEAM Mini-MAX 88	293		1. 3.90	J T Blackburn	Brook Farm, Pilling 23. 8.06P
	(Built J Riley - pr.no.PFA 186-1164: sequence no. duplicates Shadow G-GORE)					
G-MWFF	Rans S-5 Coyote	89.106		10. 1.90	J S Sweetingham	(Helsby, Frodsham) 27. 1.05P
	(Built M W Holmes - pr.no.PFA 193-11639: originally built as S-4 and converted to S-5 in 2001)					
G-MWFG	Powerchute Kestrel	00358		20. 3.90	R I Simpson	Rochester 18. 5.05P
G-MWFI	Powerchute Kestrel	00360		20. 3.90	R R O'Neill	(Ballygawley, Dungannon) 28. 8.02P
					(New owner 8.03)	
G-MWFL	Powerchute Kestrel	00363		20. 3.90	A Vincent	Fenland 31. 3.02P
G-MWFT	MBA Tiger Cub 440	WFT-02		24.11.83	J R Ravenhill	Chavenage, Tetbury 31. 5.07P
G-MWFU	Quad City Challenger II UK	PFA 177-11654		16. 3.90	M Ellis	North Moor, Scunthorpe 30.10.08P
	(Built K N Dickinson)					
G-MWFV	Quad City Challenger II UK	PFA 177-11655		16. 3.90	P Bowers	(Carlisle) 26. 5.05P
	(Built E G Astin)					
G-MWFW	Rans S-4 Coyote	89.107		16. 3.90	M P Hallam	Jackrell's Farm, Southwater 12. 6.08P
	(Built G R Hillary - pr.no.PFA 193-11662)					
G-MWFX	Quad City Challenger II UK CH2-1189-UK-0485			20. 3.90	I M Walton	Wellesbourne Mountford 13.11.07P
	(Built I M Walton - pr.no.PFA 177-11706) (Rotax 462)					
G-MWFY	Quad City Challenger II UK	PFA 177-11668		20. 3.90	C C B Soden	Weston Zoyland 9. 9.08P
	(Built P J Ladd)					
G-MWFZ	Quad City Challenger II UK CH2-0190-UK-0506			20. 3.90	A Slade	(Enfield)
	(Built A Slade - pr.no.PFA 177-11707)					
G-MWGA	Rans S-5 Coyote	89.092		20. 3.90	A W Lowrie	Eshott 24.11.07P
	(Built M A C Stevenson - pr.no.PFA 193-11810)					
G-MWGC	Medway Hybred 44XLR	MR087/85		26. 3.90	C Spalding	(Hatfield Peverel) 10. 6.06P
	(Rotax 503)				*(Operates from Hunsdon)*	
G-MWGG	Mainair Gemini Flash IIA	785-0390-7-W578		26. 3.90	D Lopez Calton Moor Farm, Ashbourne	26. 4.05P
	(Rotax 462)				*(Noted 7.05)*	
G-MWGI	Whittaker MW5-K Sorcerer	5K-0012-02		28. 3.90	B Barrass	Sywell 21. 7.06P
	(Built Aerotech International Ltd) (Original wings to G-MTBT by 7.96 qv)					
G-MWGJ	Whittaker MW5-K Sorcerer	5K-0014-02		6. 9.90	I Pearson	Bodmin 2.10.08P
	(Built Aerotech International Ltd)					
G-MWGK	Whittaker MW5-K Sorcerer	5K-0015-02	(G-MWLV)	19. 9.90	A A Castleton	The Chase, Wickwar 5. 5.07P
	(Built Aerotech International Ltd)				*(New owner 11.07)*	
G-MWGL	Solar Wings Pegasus XL-Q	SW-WQ-0293		28. 3.90	G D Haimes and A R Campbell	
	(Trike c/n SW-TE-0270)				(Newton Bank Farm, Daresbury)	15. 4.08P
G-MWGM	Solar Wings Pegasus XL-Q	SW-WQ-0294		28. 3.90	G C Christopher Longacre Farm, Sandy	2. 2.08P
	(Trike c/n SW-TE-0271)					
G-MWGN	Rans S-4 Coyote	89.113		26. 3.90	V Hallam	(Torquay) 16. 5.07P
	(Built B H Ashman - pr.no.PFA 193-11709)					
G-MWGO	Aerial Arts Chaser/110SX	110SX/566		28. 3.90	B Nicolson	(Middlesbrough) 28. 4.97P
	(Rotax 377)					
G-MWGR	Solar Wings Pegasus XL-Q	SW-WQ-0296		6. 4.90	A Maskell	Otherton, Cannock 27. 8.08P
	(Trike c/n SW-TE-0272)					
G-MWGU	Powerchute Kestrel	00368	(9H-)	26. 4.90	M Pandolfino	(Luqa, Malta) 19. 7.91P
			G-MWGU			
G-MWGV	Powerchute Kestrel	00369		26. 4.90	G Martin	(Lisburn) 20. 1.00P
				(Collided with hedge on take off Charlemont, Armagh 10. 6.07 with substantial damage)		
G-MWGW	Powerchute Kestrel	00370		26. 4.90	S P Tomlinson	(Leominster) 23. 5.05P
G-MWGZ	Powerchute Kestrel	00373		26. 4.90	L J Lynch	(Ventnor, Isle of Wight) 27. 5.97P
G-MWHC	Solar Wings Pegasus XL-Q	SW-WQ-0304		24. 4.90	P J Lowery Longacre Farm, Sandy	14. 5.99P
	(Trike c/n SW-TE-0274)				*(Stored 7.03)*	
G-MWHF	Solar Wings Pegasus XL-Q	SW-WQ-0305		24. 4.90	N J Troke	Swinford, Rugby 26. 3.05P
	(Trike c/n SW-TE-0275)				*(Noted 10.07)*	
G-MWHG	Solar Wings Pegasus XL-Q	SW-WQ-0306		24. 4.90	I A Lumley	(Great Orton) 4. 2.03P
	(Trike c/n SW-TE-0276)					
G-MWHH	TEAM Mini-MAX 88	326		23. 4.90	I D Worthington	(Raskelf, York) 4. 8.00P
	(Built B F Crick - pr.no.PFA 186-11814)				*(New owner 6.07)*	

G-MWHI	Mainair Gemini Flash IIA 784-0390-5-W577	26. 4.90	P Harwood	Watnall	9.10.08P
	(Rotax 503)				
G-MWHL	Solar Wings Pegasus XL-Q SW-WQ-0308	1. 5.90	S J Reader	Roddige	7. 8.08P
	(Trike c/n SW-TE-0278)				
G-MWHM	Whittaker MW6-S Fatboy Flyer PFA 164-11463	18. 5.90	G H Davies	Otherton, Cannock	2. 8.08P
	(Built D W Squire) (Rotax 532)				
G-MWHO	Mainair Gemini Flash IIA 778-0190-5-W571	10. 5.90	B Epps	Arclid Green, Sandbach	25. 4.08P
G-MWHP	Rans S-6-ESD Coyote II 1089.093	8. 5.90	J F Bickerstaffe	Higher Barn Farm, Houghton	3.12.07P
	(Built J F Bickerstaffe - pr.no.PFA 204-11768) (Rotax 532) (Tri-cycle u/c)				
G-MWHR	Mainair Gemini Flash IIA 787-0590-7-W580	16. 5.90	B Brazier	Brook Farm, Pilling	20.11.08P
G-MWHT	Solar Wings Pegasus Quasar SW-WQQ-0314	15. 5.90	G W F J Dear and K P Byrne		
	(Trike c/n SW-TQ-0005)			Mapperton Farm, Newton Peverill	6. 9.08P
G-MWHU	Solar Wings Pegasus Quasar SW-WQQ-0315	15. 5.90	A F Frost and S J Park	Sywell	13.11.02P
	(Trike c/n SW-TQ-0006)		(Noted 10.07)		
G-MWHX	Solar Wings Pegasus XL-Q SW-WQ-0318	15. 5.90	N P Kelly	Trim, County Meath	17. 7.08P
	(Trike c/n SW-TE-0280)				
G-MWIA	Mainair Gemini Flash IIA 789-0690-7-W582	21. 5.90	M Raj	Otherton, Cannock	26. 9.04P
G-MWIB	Aviasud Mistral 532GB 094	16. 5.90	N W Finn-Kelcey	Weston Underwood, Olney	14. 6.08P
	(Built Aviasud Engineering - pr.no.BMAA/HB/010)		"Weston Belle"		
G-MWIC	Whittaker MW5-C Sorcerer PFA 163-11224	20. 2.90	A M Witt (Bradwell Common, Milton Keynes)		29. 4.05P
	(Built I P Croft)		(Address change 9.07)		
G-MWIE	Solar Wings Pegasus XL-Q SW-WQ-0325	30. 5.90	R Mercer	Long Marston	9. 9.07P
	(Trike c/n SW-TE-0282)				
G-MWIF	Rans S-6-ESD Coyote II 1089.095	30. 5.90	K Kelly (Letterkenny, County Donegal)		7. 5.08P
	(Built M G K Prout - pr.no.PFA 204-11749) (Tri-cycle u/c)				
G-MWIG	Mainair Gemini Flash IIA 790-0690-7-W583	4. 6.90	A P Purbrick	Deenethorpe	15.11.07P
	(Rotax 462)				
G-MWIH	Mainair Gemini Flash IIA 791-0690-5-W584	4. 6.90	J P Norton	Headon Farm, Retford	27. 3.05P
G-MWIL	Medway Hybred 44XLR MR096/90	8. 6.90	P J Bosworth	Otherton, Cannock	7.10.05P
	(Rotax 447)				
G-MWIM	Solar Wings Pegasus Quasar TC SW-WQQ-0326	11. 6.90	R J Styles	Mapperton Farm, Newton Peverill	6. 3.08P
	(Trike c/n SW-TQ-0008)				
G-MWIO	Rans S-4 Coyote 90.117	11. 6.90	S R Davis and G J Simoni	Kemble	26. 4.06P
	(Built G Ferguson - pr.no.PFA 193-11774)				
G-MWIP	Whittaker MW6 Merlin PFA 164-11360	7. 6.90	D Beer and B J Merrett		
	(Built D Beer and B J Merrett) (Rotax 582)			Belle Vue Farm, Yarnscombe	6. 9.08P
G-MWIR	Solar Wings Pegasus XL-Q SW-WQ-0330	8. 6.90	C E Dagless	Yaxham, Dereham	14. 7.03P
	(Trike c/n SW-TE-0283)				
G-MWIS	Solar Wings Pegasus XL-Q SW-WQ-0331	8. 6.90	J P Quinlan	Mapperley	14. 4.08P
	(Trike c/n SW-TE-0284)				
G-MWIU	Solar Wings Pegasus Quasar TC SW-WQQ-0333	8. 6.90	N P Chitty	Lotmead Farm, Wanborough	20. 4.07P
	(Trike c/n SW-TQ-0010)				
G-MWIV	Mainair Gemini Flash 792-0690-5-W585	15. 6.90	P and J Calvert	(Pickering)	14. 7.03P
G-MWIW	Solar Wings Pegasus Quasar SW-WQQ-0334	18. 6.90	T Yates	(Alfreton)	25. 6.04P
	(Trike c/n SW-TQ-0011)				
G-MWIX	Solar Wings Pegasus Quasar TC SW-WQQ-0335	18. 6.90	G Hawes	Deenethorpe	14.10.07P
	(Trike c/n SW-TQ-0012)				
G-MWIY	Solar Wings Pegasus Quasar TC SW-WQQ-0336	22. 6.90	N S Payne	Broadmeadow Farm, Hereford	8. 4.08P
	(Trike c/n SW-TQ-0014)				
G-MWIZ	CFM Shadow Series CD 096	22.11.88	T P Ryan	Plaistows Farm, St Albans	25. 4.08P
	(Rotax 462)				
G-MWJF	CFM Shadow Series CD K 123	26. 6.90	S N White	Chilbolton	27. 4.08P
	(Officially regd as Series "BD") (Rotax 503)				
G-MWJH	Solar Wings Pegasus Quasar SW-WQQ-0340	29. 6.90	S W Walker	Broadmeadow Farm, Hereford	14.12.08P
	(Trike c/n SW-TQ-0017)				
G-MWJI	Solar Wings Pegasus Quasar SW-WQQ-0341	29. 6.90	L Luscombe	Weston Zoyland	13. 7.08P
	(Trike c/n SW-TQ-0018)				
G-MWJJ	Solar Wings Pegasus Quasar SW-WQQ-0342	29. 6.90	R Langham	Oxton	31. 7.05P
	(Trike c/n SW-TQ-0019)				
G-MWJK	Solar Wings Pegasus Quasar SW-WQQ-0343	29. 6.90	M Richardson	(Swansea)	24. 5.07P
	(Trike c/n SW-TQ-0020)				
G-MWJN	Solar Wings Pegasus XL-Q SW-WQ-0344	29. 6.90	J C Corrall Lower Mountpleasant Farm, Chatteris		25. 5.08P
	(Trike c/n SW-TE-0288)				
G-MWJP	Medway Hybred 44XLR MR097/91	29. 6.90	C D Simmons	(Edenbridge)	12. 5.05P
	(Rotax 503)				
G-MWJR	Medway Hybred 44XLR MR098/92	28. 6.90	T G Almond	(Bishops Itchington, Southam)	26. 9.08P
	(Rotax 503)				
G-MWJS	Solar Wings Pegasus Quasar TC SW-WQQ-0349	6. 7.90	R J Milward	Sywell	14. 3.05P
	(Trike c/n SW-TQ-0021)				
G-MWJT	Solar Wings Pegasus Quasar TC SW-WQQ-0350	16. 7.90	N D Townend	Deenethorpe	2. 5.08P
	(Trike c/n SW-TQ-0022)				
G-MWJV	Solar Wings Pegasus Quasar SW-WQQ-0352	6. 7.90	B D Searle	(Hambledon, Waterlooville)	31. 7.08P
	(Trike c/n SW-TQ-0024)				
G-MWJX	Medway Puma Sprint MS009/3	17. 7.90	K Wales	(Gloucester)	22. 9.05P
	(Rotax 447)		(New owner 5.06)		
G-MWJY	Mainair Gemini Flash IIA 797-0790-7-W590	16. 7.90	M D Walton	Longacre Farm, Sandy	19. 7.07P
G-MWKA	Murphy Renegade Spirit UK PFA 188-11864	26. 7.90	C E Neill tr Downlands Flying Group Deanland		8. 4.01P
	(Built Downlands Flying Group and incorporates pr.no.PFA 188-11690)		"Spirit of Lewes"		
G-MWKE	Hornet RS-ZA HRWB-0108 & ZA167	30. 7.90	D R Stapleton	Tarn Farm, Cockerham	4. 5.08P
	(Rotax 532) (Trike c/n overstamped on HRWB-0107)				
G-MWKO	Solar Wings Pegasus XL-Q SW-WQ-0357	31. 7.90	P M Golden	(Theale, Reading)	19.10.08P
	(Trike c/n SW-TE-0290)				
G-MWKP	Solar Wings Pegasus XL-Q SW-WQ-0358	31. 7.90	J D Otter	(Boston)	18. 2.07P
	(Trike c/n SW-TE-0291)				

G-MWKX	Microflight Spectrum	016	3. 8.90	C R Ions	Eshott	14. 5.04P
G-MWKY	Solar Wings Pegasus XL-Q	SW-WQ-0362	3. 8.90	I D Edwards	Roddige	16.12.07P
	(Trike c/n SW-TE-0292)					
G-MWKZ	Solar Wings Pegasus XL-Q	SW-WQ-0363	3. 8.90	T G Burston and I A Fox-Mills	Hunsdon	21. 4.08P
	(Trike c/n SW-TE-0293)					
G-MWLA	Rans S-4 Coyote	89.114	3. 8.90	G J Jones and D C Lees	Andrewsfield	13. 3.08P
	(Built S H Williams - pr.no.PFA 193-11787)					
G-MWLB	Medway Hybred 44XLR	MR104/93	15. 8.90	M W Harmer	Longacre Farm, Sandy	19. 5.08P
	(Rotax 503)					
G-MWLD	CFM Shadow Series CD	106	9. 5.89	R H Cooke	Lee-on-Solent	19. 6.07P
G-MWLE	Solar Wings Pegasus XL-R	SW-WA-1474	9. 8.90	D Stevenson	Plaistows Farm, St Albans	30. 7.06P
	(Trike c/n SW-TB-1425)					
G-MWLF	Solar Wings Pegasus XL-R	SW-WA-1475	9. 8.90	G A McCann	Weston Zoyland	13. 8.08P
	(Trike c/n SW-TB-1426)					
G-MWLG	Solar Wings Pegasus XL-R	SW-WA-1476	9. 8.90	C Cohen	(Birmingham)	16. 6.08P
	(Trike c/n SW-TB-1427)					
G-MWLH	Solar Wings Pegasus Quasar	SW-WQQ-0364	9. 8.90	B Chapman	Hunsdon	3. 8.07P
	(Trike c/n SW-TQ-0030)					
G-MWLJ	Solar Wings Pegasus Quasar	SW-WQQ-0366	9. 8.90	N Khan	(Sutton Coldfield)	21. 9.08P
	(Trike c/n SW-TQ-0032)					
G-MWLK	Solar Wings Pegasus Quasar TC	SW-WQQ-0367	9. 8.90	D J Shippen	(Newton Bank Farm, Daresbury)	3. 1.06P
	(Trike c/n SW-TQ-0033)					
G-MWLL	Solar Wings Pegasus XL-Q	SW-WQ-0338	16. 8.90	J Bacon	Felthorpe	7.10.08P
	(Trike c/n SW-TE-0287)					
G-MWLM	Solar Wings Pegasus XL-Q	SW-WQ-0322	17. 8.90	A A Judge	Hunsdon	28. 6.07P
	(Trike c/n SW-TE-0286)					
G-MWLN	Whittaker MW6-S Fatboy Flyer	PFA 164-11844	16. 8.90	S J Field	(Glastonbury)	5. 6.92P
	(Built S J Field) (Rotax 503)				*"Red Lips"*	
G-MWLO	Whittaker MW6 Merlin	PFA 164-11373	21. 8.90	S P Ganecki tr G-MWLO Flying Group		
	(Built G W Peacock) (Rotax 503)				Church Farm, Askern	29. 8.08P
G-MWLP	Mainair Gemini Flash	801-0990-5-W594	24. 8.90	C Moultrie and C Poziemski	East Fortune	26.10.07P
G-MWLS	Medway Hybred 44XLR	MR081/95	29. 8.90	M A Oliver	Glassonby	4. 8.05P
	(Rotax 503)					
G-MWLT	Mainair Gemini Flash IIA	804-0990-7-W597	31. 8.90	S A Sacker	Black Spring Farm, Castle Bytham	18. 7.03P
				(Noted 2.08)		
G-MWLU	Solar Wings Pegasus XL-R/Se	SW-WA-1478	6. 9.90	T P G Ward	(Great Orton)	14.10.91P
	(Rotax 462)	*(Trike c/n SW-TE-0294)*		*(Stored 9.97)*		
G-MWLW	TEAM Mini-MAX	PFA 186-11717	14. 9.90	L G Horne	Harringe Court, Sellindge, Folkestone	27. 4.08P
	(Built W T Kirk) (Rotax 377)					
G-MWLX	Mainair Gemini Flash IIA	805-0990-7-W598	5.10.90	S D Buchanan	(Edinburgh)	8. 5.08P
G-MWLZ	Rans S-4 Coyote	90.116	8.10.90	B O McCartan	Newry Road, Banbridge	11. 3.05P
	(Built T E G Buckett - pr.no.PFA 193-11887)				*(Noted 7.07)*	
G-MWMB	Powerchute Kestrel	00399	7.11.90	D J Whysall	Ripley, Derbyshire	17. 5.05P
G-MWMC	Powerchute Kestrel	00400	7.11.90	R A Stewart tr Talgarreg Flying Club	(Llandysul)	3.10.05P
G-MWMD	Powerchute Kestrel	00401	7.11.90	D J Jackson	(Melton Constable)	20.11.91P
G-MWMG	Powerchute Kestrel	00404	7.11.90	M D Walton	(Tregaron)	20. 7.06P
G-MWMH	Powerchute Kestrel	00405	7.11.90	E W Potts	(Crymych, Dyfed)	12. 6.04P
G-MWMI	Solar Wings Pegasus Quasar	SW-WQQ-0383	21. 9.90	G Rothery	(Littlehampton)	5. 9.08P
	(Trike c/n SW-TQ-0043)					
G-MWMJ	Solar Wings Pegasus Quasar	SW-WQQ-0384	21. 9.90	M Booth	Kemble	1. 7.07P
	(Trike c/n SW-TQ-0044)					
G-MWMK	Solar Wings Pegasus Quasar	SW-WQQ-0385	21. 9.90	P Adams	(Bristol)	13. 6.05P
	(Trike c/n SW-TQ-0045)					
G-MWML	Solar Wings Pegasus Quasar	SW-WQQ-0386	21. 9.90	S C Key	Deopham Green	18.12.07P
	(Trike c/n SW-TQ-0046)					
G-MWMM	Mainair Gemini Flash IIA	800-0890-7-W593	24. 8.90	R H Church	Croft Farm, Defford	7. 8.08P
	(Rotax 462)					
G-MWMN	Solar Wings Pegasus XL-Q	SW-WQ-0387	2.10.90	N A Rathbone and P A Arnold	Swinford, Rugby	14. 5.08P
	(Trike c/n SW-TE-0297)					
G-MWMO	Solar Wings Pegasus XL-Q	SW-WQ-0388	2.10.90	D S F McNair	(Lochgilphead)	16.10.07P
	(Trike c/n SW-TE-0298)					
G-MWMP	Solar Wings Pegasus XL-Q	SW-WQ-0389	2.10.90	L W Audwell	(Norwich)	9.12.07P
	(Trike c/n SW-TE-0299)					
G-MWMR	Solar Wings Pegasus XL-R	SW-WA-1483	2.10.90	M I Stone	(Barnstaple)	13. 3.00P
	(Rotax 462)	*(Trike c/n SW-TE-0300)*		*(New owner 4.03)*		
G-MWMS	Mainair Gemini Flash	807-1090-5-W600	3.10.90	B A Ritchie	Glenrothes	7. 9.07P
G-MWMT	Mainair Gemini Flash IIA	808-1090-7-W601	3.10.90	R Findlay	Mill Farm, Shifnal	24. 7.08P
G-MWMU	CFM Shadow Series CD	150	2.10.90	A J Thomas	Wickenby	18. 8.08P
	(Manufacturer's records show as c/n 142 with c/n 150 sold to Namibia: plate noted 4.06 shows c/n 150CD)					
G-MWMV	Solar Wings Pegasus XL-R	SW-WA-1484	5.10.90	M A Oakley	Kemble	24. 1.08P
	(Rotax 462)	*(Trike c/n SW-TE-0307)*				
G-MWMW	Murphy Renegade Spirit UK	254	21. 8.89	H Feeney	Priory Farm, Tibenham	20. 7.07P
	(Built M W Hanley -pr.no.PFA 188-11544)				*"Spirit of Cornwall"*	
G-MWMX	Mainair Gemini Flash IIA	810-1090-7-W603	17.10.90	P G Hughes	Newtownards	23. 3.08P
	(Rotax 462)					
G-MWMY	Mainair Gemini Flash IIA	809-1090-7-W602	17.10.90	P J Harrison	Lower Mountpleasant Farm, Chatteris	11.11.08P
	(Rotax 462)					
G-MWMZ	Solar Wings Pegasus XL-Q	SW-WQ-0393	8.10.90	P M Scrivener	Clench Common	14. 8.08P
	(Trike c/n SW-TE-0301)					
G-MWNA	Solar Wings Pegasus XL-Q	SW-WQ-0394	8.10.90	S N Robson	Eshott	17. 1.07P
	(Trike c/n SW-TE-0302)					
G-MWNB	Solar Wings Pegasus XL-Q	SW-WQ-0395	8.10.90	P F J Rogers	(London SW17)	21. 9.08P
	(Trike c/n SW-TE-0303)					

G-MWNC	Solar Wings Pegasus XL-Q	SW-WQ-0396		8.10.90	R G Wyatt tr G-MWNC Group	(Attleborough)	15. 8.08P
	(Trike c/n SW-TE-0304)					
G-MWND	TLAC RL5A LW Sherwood Ranger	001		9.10.90	D A Pike	Brook Farm, Pilling	13. 6.03P
	(Built D A Pike - pr.no.PFA 237-12229) (Rotax 532)					
G-MWNE	Mainair Gemini Flash IIA	803-1090-7-W596		17.10.90	T C Edwards	(Ware)	21. 8.07P
G-MWNF	Murphy Renegade Spirit UK	PFA 188-11853		15.10.90	D J White	Calton Moor Farm, Ashbourne	21. 9.04P
	(Built D J White) (BMW R100)				*(Noted 7.05)*	
G-MWNG	Solar Wings Pegasus XL-Q	SW -WQ-0399		17.10.90	H C Thomson	Easter Balgillo Farm, Finavon	3.11.03P
	(Trike c/n SW-TE-0305)				*(Trike only noted 5.05)*	
G-MWNK	Solar Wings Pegasus Quasar TC	SW-WQQ-0403		1.11.90	G S Lyon	RAF Wyton	1. 8.08P
	(Trike c/n SW-TQA-0054)					
G-MWNL	Solar Wings Pegasus Quasar	SW-WQQ-0404		1.11.90	B J Lyford	Old Sarum	8. 6.08P
	(Trike c/n SW-TQA-0055)					
G-MWNO	AMF Microflight Chevvron 2-32C	025		12.11.90	I K Hogg	Kirkbride	30. 4.05P
G-MWNP	AMF Microflight Chevvron 2-32C	026		31.10.90	M K Field	Sleap	13. 7.08P
G-MWNR	Murphy Renegade Spirit UK	PFA 188-11926		12.11.90	J J Lancaster	Davidstow Moor	13. 7.08P
	(Built J J Lancaster)					
G-MWNS	Mainair Gemini Flash IIA	811-1190-7-W604		6.11.90	J G Hilliard	Deenethorpe	31. 8.08P
G-MWNT	Mainair Gemini Flash IIA	812-1190-7-W605		6.11.90	C G Rodger tr November Tango Group	Glenrothes	23. 7.08P
	(Rotax 582)					
G-MWNU	Mainair Gemini Flash IIA	813-1190-5-W606		6.11.90	C C Muir	Doynton	7. 7.08P
G-MWNV	Powerchute Kestrel	00406		12.11.90	K N Byrne	(Homefield, Isle of Colonsay)	13. 3.92P
G-MWNX	Powerchute Kestrel	00408		12.11.90	J H Greenroyd	(Hebden Bridge)	24. 9.02P
G-MWOC	Powerchute Kestrel	00413		12.11.90	D M F Harvey	(Manorbier, Tenby)	28. 9.08P
G-MWOD	Powerchute Kestrel	00414		12.11.90	T Morgan	(Kidderminster)	4.10.00P
G-MWOE	Powerchute Kestrel	00415		12.11.90	E G Woolnough	(Halesworth)	21. 1.02P
					(New owner 4.04)	
G-MWOF	Microflight Spectrum	018		13.11.90	J E Wright	Biggin Hill	16.12.07P
G-MWOH	Solar Wings Pegasus XL-R/Se	SW-WA-1485		28.11.90	J D Buchanan	Coldharbour Farm, Willingham	7. 6.08P
	(Trike c/n SW-TB-1429)					
G-MWOI	Solar Wings Pegasus XL-R	SW-WA-1486		29.11.90	B T Geoghegan	Roddige	21. 6.07P
	(Trike c/n SW-TB-1430)					
G-MWOJ	Mainair Gemini Flash IIA	814-1290-7-W608		6.12.90	C J Pryce	Ince Blundell	15. 4.07P
G-MWOM	Solar Wings Pegasus Quasar TC	SW-WQQ-0412		1. 3.91	M S Ahmadu	Sackville Lodge, Riseley	9. 9.07P
	(Trike c/n SW-TQ-0060)					
G-MWON	CFM Shadow Series CD	K 128		18.12.90	R E M Gibson-Bevan	Wickenby	14. 7.03P
G-MWOO	Murphy Renegade Spirit UK	318		14. 9.90	R C Wood	Lower Mountpleasant Farm, Chatteris	13. 8.07P
	(Built A Hipkin - pr.no.PFA 188-11811)					
G-MWOP	Solar Wings Pegasus Quasar TC	SW-WQQ-0410		31.12.90	A Baynes	Sywell	23. 8.08P
	(Trike c/n SW-TQC-0059)					
G-MWOR	Solar Wings Pegasus XL-Q	SW-WQ-0411		21.12.90	S E Smith	(North Ride, Welwyn)	1. 6.08P
	(Trike c/n SW-TE-0308)					
G-MWOV	Whittaker MW6 Merlin	PFA 164-11301		9. 1.91	L R Hodgson	Glassonby	1. 8.08P
	(Built C R Melhuish) (Rotax 503)					
G-MWOY	Solar Wings Pegasus XL-Q			7. 1.91	S P Griffin	Sutton Meadows	8. 1.06P
	(Trike c/n SW-TE-0310 & SW-WQ-0414)					
G-MWPB	Mainair Gemini Flash IIA	823-0191-7-W617		3. 1.91	J Fenton	St Michaels	7.10.08P
G-MWPC	Mainair Gemini Flash IIA	826-0191-7-W620		3. 1.91	S J Ware *(New owner 6.07)*	(Woodford, Stockport)	15. 6.05P
G-MWPD	Mainair Gemini Flash IIA	824-0191-7-W618		9. 1.91	P Gazinski	East Fortune	19. 2.08P
G-MWPE	Solar Wings Pegasus XL-Q			9. 1.91	E C R Hudson	Upper Stow, Weedon	2. 6.08P
	(Trike c/n SW-TE-0096 & SW-WQ-0416)		*(Trike ex G-MVGX)*			
G-MWPF	Mainair Gemini Flash IIA	825-0191-7-W619		11. 1.91	G P Taggart	Newtownards	3. 7.08P
G-MWPG	Corbett Farms Spectrum	019		9. 1.91	D Payn tr G-MWPG Group	Eshott	1. 9.08P
G-MWPH	Corbett Farms Spectrum	020		9. 1.91	S Rickett and M J Deacon	Draycott Farm, Chiseldon	11. 9.07P
G-MWPJ	Solar Wings Pegasus XL-Q	SW-WQ-0418		17. 1.91	D S Parker	Carlisle	14. 5.03P
	(Trike c/n SW-TE-0312)					
G-MWPK	Solar Wings Pegasus XL-Q	SW-WQ-0419		17. 1.91	W Parker	Strathaven	12. 7.08P
	(Trike c/n SW-TE-0313)					
G-MWPN	CFM Shadow Series CD	K 147		22. 1.91	W R H Thomas	(Llethtryd, Swansea)	11. 6.99P
G-MWPO	Mainair Gemini Flash IIA	827-0191-7-W621		29. 1.91	G A Johnson	(Liverpool)	11.11.07P
G-MWPP	CFM Streak Shadow M	K 166-SA	G-BTEM	14. 2.91	A J Burton	Wickenby	5. 9.08P
	(Built C A Mortlock - pr.no.PFA 206-11992) (Rotax 582)					
G-MWPR	Whittaker MW6 Merlin	PFA 164-11260		16.10.90	S F N Warnell	(Staines)	
	(Built P J S Ritchie)				*(New owner 10.01)*	
G-MWPS	Murphy Renegade Spirit UK	PFA 188-11931		18. 2.91	M D Stewart	(Husbands Bosworth)	1. 7.98P
	(Built A R Broughton-Tompkins)				*(New owner 6.05)*	
G-MWPU	Solar Wings Pegasus Quasar TC	SW-WQQ-0426		20. 2.91	T A Jennings	(Wilnecote, Tamworth)	6. 7.06P
	(Trike c/n SW-TQC-0062)					
G-MWPW	AMF Microflight Chevvron 2-32C	027		26.11.90	E L T Westman	Broadford, Isle of Skye	26.10.08P
G-MWPX	Solar Wings Pegasus XL-R	SW-WA-1488		27. 2.91	R J Wheeler	Redlands, Swindon	1.10.08P
	(Rotax 462)		*(Trike c/n SW-TE-0315)*			
G-MWPZ	Murphy Renegade Spirit UK	PFA 188-11631		18. 3.91	J Ievers	Rhosgoch	24. 2.99P
	(Built J Ievers)				*(Noted 2.04)*	
G-MWRB	Mainair Gemini Flash IIA	819-0191-7-W613		5. 2.91	R Campbell-Moore *(Noted 8.06)*	Swansea	16. 6.06P
G-MWRC	Mainair Gemini Flash IIA	820-0191-7-W614		5. 2.91	D R Talbot	Chiltern Park, Wallingford	28. 8.08P
G-MWRD	Mainair Gemini Flash IIA	821-0191-7-W615		5. 2.91	L Campbell	(Leamington Spa)	5. 8.08P
	(Motavia?) (Officially regd with Rotax 503)					
G-MWRE	Mainair Gemini Flash IIA	822-0191-7-W616		5. 2.91	A D Dias	Otherton, Cannock	4. 8.08P
G-MWRF	Mainair Gemini Flash IIA	829-0191-7-W623		4. 2.91	N Hay	London Colney	30.10.08P
G-MWRG	Mainair Gemini Flash IIA	830-0191-7-W624		5. 2.91	F J Clarehugh	Eshott	1.12.05P
G-MWRH	Mainair Gemini Flash IIA	831-0191-7-W625		5. 2.91	E G Astin	Eshott	25. 8.08P
G-MWRI	Mainair Gemini Flash IIA	828-0191-7-W622		1. 3.91	J F Booth *(New owner 1.08)*	(Purton, Swindon)	12.12.99P
G-MWRJ	Mainair Gemini Flash IIA	832-0291-7-W626		28. 2.91	R J Lindley	(Crewe)	26. 3.08P

G-MWRL	CFM Shadow Series CD	K 152		13. 2.91	R A and C A Allen	(Midgham, Reading)	18. 8.01P
					(New owners 4.04)		
G-MWRM	Medway Hybred 44XLR	MR086/94/91/S	G-MWLC	26. 2.91	I R M Scott	(Elie, Leven)	6. 4.08P
	(Rotax 503)						
G-MWRN	Solar Wings Pegasus XL-R	SW-WA-1489		5. 3.91	D T MacKenzie	Easter Poldar Farm, Thornhill	28. 3.06P
	(Rotax 462)	*(Trike c/n SW-TE-0316)*			*(Noted 8.07)*		
G-MWRP	Solar Wings Pegasus XL-R	SW-WA-1491		1. 3.91	A R Hughes	Redlands, Swindon	28. 8.08P
	(Rotax 462)	*(Trike c/n SW-TE-0318)*					
G-MWRR	Mainair Gemini Flash IIA	834-0391-7-W628		7. 3.91	J Clark tr G-MWRR Group	Otherton, Cannock	7. 7.08P
G-MWRS	Ultravia Super Pelican	E001-201		9. 5.84	T B Woolley	(Narborough, Leicester)	9. 9.87P
G-MWRT	Solar Wings Pegasus XL-R	SW-WA-1492		15. 3.91	G L Gunnell	Sywell	10. 9.03P
		(Trike c/n SW-TB-1431)					
G-MWRU	Solar Wings Pegasus XL-R	SW-WA-1493		15. 3.91	S W Kettell	Sywell	28. 9.08P
		(Trike c/n SW-TB-1432)					
G-MWRV	Solar Wings Pegasus XL-R	SW-WA-1494		15. 3.91	M S Adams	Roddige	20. 4.05P
		(Trike c/n SW-TB-1433)					
G-MWRW	Solar Wings Pegasus XL-Q	SW-WQ-0431		25. 3.91	L B Hughes	Long Marston	31. 8.07P
		(Trike c/n SW-TE-0320)					
G-MWRX	Solar Wings Pegasus XL-Q	SW-WQ-0432		25. 3.91	W Parkes	Long Marston	17. 9.04P
		(Trike c/n SW-TE-0321)					
G-MWRY	CFM Shadow Series CD	K 162		26. 3.91	A T Armstrong	Davidstow Moor	6. 7.08P
G-MWRZ	AMF Microflight Chevvron 2-32C	028		10. 4.91	P V Prowse	Woodlands Barton Farm, Roche	12. 7.08P
G-MWSA	TEAM Mini-MAX 88	PFA 186-11855		8. 4.91	G J Jones	(Abington, Cambridge)	15. 4.07P
	(Built A N Baumber) (Rotax 377)				*(New owner 2.08)*		
G-MWSB	Mainair Gemini Flash IIA	837-0591-7-W631		30. 4.91	P J Bosworth	Hill Farm, Hughley, Shrewsbury	15. 8.06P
	(Rotax 582)						
G-MWSC	Rans S-6-ESD Coyote II	0191.152		13. 5.91	C J Meadows	Weston Zoyland	27. 8.08P
	(Built B E Francis - pr.no.PFA 204-12019) (Tri-cycle u/c)						
G-MWSD	Solar Wings Pegasus XL-Q	SW-WQ-0430		6. 3.91	A M Harley	Sutton Meadows	16. 7.08P
		(Trike c/n SW-TE-0319)					
G-MWSE	Solar Wings Pegasus XL-R	SW-WA-1496		10. 4.91	Ultra Light Training Ltd	Roddige	11. 3.07P
	(Rotax 462) *(Trike c/n SW-TE-0323 -fitted with Trike from G-MTJR)*						
G-MWSF	Solar Wings Pegasus XL-R	SW-WA-1497		10. 4.91	N A and F W Milne	(Chedburgh, Bury St Edmunds)	13. 7.08P
	(Rotax 462)	*(Trike c/n SW-TE-0324)*					
G-MWSI	Solar Wings Pegasus Quasar TC	SW-WQ-0436		23. 5.91	J A Ganderton	Sywell	30.10.08P
		(Trike c/n SW-TQC-0065)					
G-MWSJ	Solar Wings Pegasus XL-Q	SW-WQ-0437		12. 4.91	R A Barrett	Sutton Meadows	7. 5.08P
		(Trike c/n SW-TE-0326)					
G-MWSK	Solar Wings Pegasus XL-Q	SW-WQ-0438		12. 4.91	J Doogan	(Galashiels)	26. 5.02P
		(Trike c/n SW-TE-0327)			*(New owner 5.05)*		
G-MWSL	Mainair Gemini Flash IIA	835-0491-7-W629		16. 4.91	C W Frost	(Rufforth)	11. 6.98P
G-MWSM	Mainair Gemini Flash IIA	836-0491-7-W630		16. 4.91	R M Wall	(Longacre Farm, Sandy)	19. 4.08P
G-MWSO	Solar Wings Pegasus XL-R	SW-WA-1503		25. 4.91	M A Clayton	(New Romney)	17.11.07P
	(Rotax 462)	*(Trike c/n SW-TE-0329)*					
G-MWSP	Solar Wings Pegasus XL-R	SW-WA-1504		25. 4.91	R Wilkinson	Headon Farm, Retford	22. 5.06P
	(Rotax 462)	*(Trike c/n SW-TE-0330)*			*(Noted 10.06)*		
G-MWSR	Solar Wings Pegasus XL-R	SW-WA-1505		25. 4.91	G P J Davies	Broadmeadow Farm. Hereford	10. 9.08P
	(Rotax 462)	*(Trike c/n SW-TE-0331)*					
G-MWSS	Medway Hybred 44XLR	MR117/97		7. 5.91	C D Hannam and J W Taylor	(Oldcroft, Lydney)	20. 9.03P
	(Rotax 503)				*(New owners 2.07)*		
G-MWST	Medway Hybred 44XLR	MR118/98		8. 5.91	A Ferguson	Broadford, Isle of Skye	3. 8.05P
	(Rotax 503)				*(Noted 8.07)*		
G-MWSU	Medway Hybred 44XLR	MR119/99		1. 5.92	T de Landro	Stoke, Isle of Grain	6. 10.07P
	(Rotax 503)						
G-MWSW	Whittaker MW6 Merlin	PFA 164-11328		15. 2.91	S N F Warnell	(Staines)	
	(Built S N F Warnell)						
G-MWSX	Whittaker MW5 Sorcerer	PFA 163-11549		3. 5.91	D R Drewett	Davidstow Moor	24. 4.08P
	(Built A T Armstrong)						
G-MWSY	Whittaker MW5 Sorcerer	PFA 163-11218		3. 5.91	J E Holloway	Davidstow Moor	21.12.04P
	(Built J E Holloway)				*(Noted 7.05)*		
G-MWSZ	CFM Shadow Series CD	K 158	(G-MWRY)	4. 4.91	D R Drewett and P A Da Silva Turner		
					(Clapham, Worthing and Swanmore,Southampton)		17.10.08P
G-MWTB	Solar Wings Pegasus XL-Q	SW-WQ-0445		8. 5.91	G S Highley	(Corby)	17. 9.04P
		(Trike c/n SW-TE-0333)					
G-MWTC	Solar Wings Pegasus XL-Q	SW-WQ-0446		8. 5.91	M M Chittenden	Lower Road, Hockley	3. 5.08P
		(Trike c/n SW-TE-0334)			*(Operates from Rochester)*		
G-MWTD	Corbett Farms Spectrum	022		13. 5.91	J V Harris *(Noted 10.05)*	Sywell	18. 4.00P
G-MWTE	Corbett Farms Spectrum	023		13. 5.91	T H Evans	(Ammanford)	20. 6.04P
G-MWTG	Mainair Gemini Flash IIA	838-0591-7-W632		16. 5.91	M R Smith	(Oldbury)	27.10.08P
	(Rotax 582)						
G-MWTH	Mainair Gemini Flash IIA	839-0591-7-W633		21. 5.91	A Strang	East Fortune	1. 8.06P
G-MWTI	Solar Wings Pegasus XL-Q	SW-WQ-0274		23. 5.91	O G Johns	Field Farm, Oakley	31. 5.08P
		(Trike c/n SW-TE-0251)					
G-MWTJ	CFM Shadow Series CD	K 167		16. 5.91	T D Wolstenholme	Brook Farm, Pilling	24.11.07P
G-MWTK	Solar Wings Pegasus XL-R/Se	SW-WA-1507		28. 5.91	G Munro	Watnall	21. 5.08P
	(Rotax 462)	*(Trike c/n SW-TE-0335)*					
G-MWTL	Solar Wings Pegasus XL-R	SW-WA-1508		28. 5.91	B Lindsay	(Chipping Sodbury)	13. 7.07P
	(Rotax 462)	*(Trike c/n SW-TE-0336)*					
G-MWTN	CFM Shadow Series CD	K 153		23. 5.91	M J Broom	Buttermilk Farm, Bliswell	3. 7.08P
G-MWTO	Mainair Gemini Flash IIA	840-0591-7-W634		28. 5.91	J Greenhalgh	St Michaels	22. 6.08P
G-MWTP	CFM Shadow Series CD	K 107		23. 5.91	R E M Gibson-Bevan	Wickenby	17. 7.08P
G-MWTR	Mainair Gemini Flash IIA	842-0591-7-W636		31. 5.91	J E Lipinski	Hunsdon	16. 2.08P
	(Rotax 582)						
G-MWTT	Rans S-6-ESD Coyote II	0391.175		30. 4.91	L E Duffin	Insch	28.11.07P
	(Built I K Radcliffe - pr.no.PFA 204-12016) (Tri-cycle u/c)				*"Warrior 2"*		

G-MWTU	Solar Wings Pegasus XL-R	SW-WA-1501		21. 6.91	S Woods	(Banagher, County Offaly)	2. 9.01P
	(Trike c/n SW-TB-1435)						
G-MWTY	Mainair Gemini Flash IIA	843-0691-7-W637		12. 6.91	A McGing and J C Townsend	Ince Blundell	28. 4.04P
					(Noted 8.05)		
G-MWTZ	Mainair Gemini Flash IIA	844-0691-7-W638		12. 6.91	C W R Felce	Riseley, Bedford	14. 9.07P
G-MWUA	CFM Shadow Series CD	K 161		10. 6.91	P A James t/a Cloudbase Aviation G-MWUA	Redhill	21. 6.05P
G-MWUB	Solar Wings Pegasus XL-R	SW-WA-1510		12. 6.91	T R L Bayley	(Edenbridge)	27. 8.08P
	(Rotax 462)	*(Trike c/n SW-TE-0338)*					
G-MWUC	Solar Wings Pegasus XL-R	SW-WA-1511		12. 6.91	M A Hicks	Wickenby	27. 6.05P
	(Rotax 462)	*(Trike c/n SW-TE-0339)*					
G-MWUD	Solar Wings Pegasus XL Tug	SW-WA-1512		12. 6.91	M J Taggart	Clench Common	17. 5.05P
	(Rotax 462)	*(Trike c/n SW-TE-0340)*					
G-MWUH	Murphy Renegade Spirit UK	343		12. 6.91	A I Grant	Washington, Sussex	18. 6.04P
	(Built A I Grant)						
G-MWUI	AMF Microflight Chevvron 2-32C	029		2. 7.91	N D A Graham	North Connel, Oban	12. 4.08P
G-MWUK	Rans S-6-ESD Coyote II	0491.187		1. 7.91	G K Hoult and S J C Pollock	Long Marston	12. 4.08P
	(Built G K Hoult - pr.no.PFA 204-12090) (Tri-cycle u/c)						
G-MWUL	Rans S-6-ESD Coyote II	0391.172		10. 6.91	K W Payne	(Ashford)	26. 8.08P
	(Built K J Lywood - pr.no.PFA 204-12054) (Tri-cycle u/c)						
G-MWUN	Rans S-6-ESD Coyote II	0391-173		10. 6.91	C N Nairn	Nether Huntlywood Farm, Gordon	20. 5.08P
	(Built S Eland - pr.no.PFA 204-12075) (Rebuilt with kit no.0695.841 (ex G-IZIT) c 1994) (Tri-cycle u/c)						
G-MWUO	Solar Wings Pegasus XL-Q	SW-WQ-0379	(ZS-...?)	26. 6.91	A P Slade	Field Farm, Oakley	18. 5.06P
	(Trike c/n SW-TE-0296)						
G-MWUR	Solar Wings Pegasus XL Tug	SW-WA-1518		21. 6.91	A W Buchan tr Nottingham Aerotow Club		
	(Rotax 462)	*(Trike c/n SW-TE-0342)*	*(Officially regd as "XL-R")*			Knapthorpe Lodge, Caunton	19. 8.08P
G-MWUS	Solar Wings Pegasus XL-R	SW-WA-1519		21. 6.91	H R Loxton	Weston Zoyland	29. 8.00P
	(Rotax 462)	*(Trike c/n SW-TE-0343)*					
G-MWUU	Solar Wings Pegasus XL-R	SW-WA-1521		28. 6.91	B R Underwood	Swinford, Rugby	13. 4.08P
	(Rotax 462)	*(Trike c/n SW-TE-0346)*					
G-MWUV	Solar Wings Pegasus XL-R	SW-WA-1522		28. 6.91	C D Baines	Arclid Green, Sandbach	2. 2.07P
	(Rotax 462)	*(Trike c/n SW-TE-0347)*					
G-MWUX	Solar Wings Pegasus XL-Q	SW-WQ-0454		28. 6.91	B D Attwell	Upfield Farm, Whitson	27. 3.03P
	(Originally supplied as a Sailwing only - Trike origin unknown)				*(Noted 8.05)*		
G-MWUY	Solar Wings Pegasus XL-Q	SW-WQ-0455		28. 6.91	M J Sharp	(Kilmarnock)	11. 1.04P
	(Trike c/n SW-TE-0345)						
G-MWUZ	Solar Wings Pegasus XL-Q	SW-WQ-0456		28. 6.91	S R Nanson	(Sittingbourne)	7. 6.06P
	(Trike c/n SW-TE-0350)						
G-MWVA	Solar Wings Pegasus XL-Q	SW-WQ-0457		28. 6.91	G Charles-Jones	Eshott	14. 4.08P
	(Trike c/n SW-TE-0351)						
G-MWVE	Solar Wings Pegasus XL-R	SW-WA-1524		18. 7.91	W A Keel-Stocker	Long Marston	7. 6.07P
	(Trike c/n SW-TB-1441)						
G-MWVF	Solar Wings Pegasus XL-R/Se	SW-WA-1525		18. 7.91	J B Wright	Roddige	8.11.07P
	(Trike c/n SW-TB-1442)						
G-MWVG	CFM Shadow Series CD	151		5. 8.91	Shadow Aviation Ltd	Old Sarum	16.10.08P
G-MWVH	CFM Shadow Series CD	181		5. 8.91	M McKenzie	Insch	25. 8.07P
G-MWVK	Mainair Mercury	849-0891-5-W643		13. 8.91	S B Walters	Swinford, Rugby	31. 7.08P
G-MWVL	Rans S-6 ESD Coyote II	0491-186		13. 8.91	A, A, J T and O D Lewis	Rufforth	25. 7.08P
	(Built J D Hall - pr.no.PFA 204-12118) (Tri-cycle u/c) (Damaged and repaired with frame.no.0892.341: original frame now fitted to G-MZAH)						
G-MWVM	Solar Wings Pegasus Quasar IITC	SW-WX-0020	G-65-8	2. 9.91	J D Jones and A A Edmonds	Mill Farm, Shifnal	2. 6.08P
	(Trike c/n SW-TQ-0031 - Trike c/n duplicates G-MWLI)						
G-MWVN	Mainair Gemini Flash IIA	850-0891-7-W644		19. 8.91	J McCafferty	Rochdale	7. 3.08P
G-MWVO	Mainair Gemini Flash IIA	852-0891-7-W646		27. 8.91	P Webb	(Bristol)	25. 7.05P
	(Rotax 582)						
G-MWVP	Murphy Renegade Spirit UK	345		22. 8.91	P D Mickleburgh	Swinford, Rugby	29. 4.94P
	(Built I E Spencer - pr.no.PFA 188-11735)				*(Noted 5.05)*		
G-MWVR	Mainair Gemini Flash IIA	855-0991-7-W650		30. 8.91	G Cartwright	Northampton	29. 4.07P
G-MWVS	Mainair Gemini Flash IIA	856-0991-7-W651		30. 8.91	S J J Griffiths *(Noted 11.07)*	Ash Farm, Winsford	15. 9.06P
G-MWVT	Mainair Gemini Flash IIA	860-1091-7-W655		2. 9.91	J Barlow and C Osiejuk	Oxton, Nottingham	22. 6.08P
G-MWVY	Mainair Gemini Flash IIA	854-0991-7-W649		4. 9.91	J D Hinton	(Tunbridge Wells)	19. 5.08P
G-MWVZ	Mainair Gemini Flash IIA	863-1091-7-W658		4. 9.91	S N Pryor *(Noted 11.07)*	(Leicester)	1.11.02P
G-MWWB	Mainair Gemini Flash IIA	864-1091-7-W659		18. 9.91	W P Seward	(Chirk, Wrexham)	3.11.08P
G-MWWC	Mainair Gemini Flash IIA	868-1191-7-W663		23. 9.91	A and D Margereson	(Chesterfield)	30. 7.04P
	(Rotax 582)						
G-MWWD	Murphy Renegade Spirit UK	344		23. 9.91	J and A Oswald	Eshott	31.10.08P
	(Built A M Smyth and J M Walter - pr.no.PFA 188-11719)						
G-MWWE	TEAM Mini-Max 88	PFA 186-11925		1.10.91	J Entwistle	Tarn Farm, Cockerham	23. 7.97P
	(Built J C Longmore)				*(Fuselage only 7.07: wings noted 11.06 at Eccleston, Chorley)*		
G-MWWG	Solar Wings Pegasus XL-Q	SW-WQ-0468		3.10.91	A W Guerri tr Form A Q	Rufforth	6. 11.07P
	(Trike c/n SW-TE-0355)						
G-MWWH	Solar Wings Pegasus XL-Q	SW-WQ-0469		3.10.91	A J Alexander	Watnall	5. 9.08P
	(Trike c/n SW-TE-0356)						
G-MWWI	Mainair Gemini Flash IIA	870-1191-7-W665		11.10.91	M A S Nesbitt *(Noted 4.07)*	Strathaven	2.10.03P
G-MWWJ	Mainair Gemini Flash IIA	865-1191-7-W660		22.10.91	I M Ferdinand and A F Glover		
					(Javea, Alicante, Spain and Woolston, Warrington)		17. 2.08P
G-MWWK	Mainair Gemini Flash IIA	866-1191-7-W661		22.10.91	J C Boyd tr JDS Group	Davidstow Moor	31. 7.08P
	(Rotax 582)						
G-MWWN	Mainair Gemini Flash IIA	872-1291-7-W667		22.10.91	F Watts	(Bournemouth)	27. 6.05P
G-MWWP	Rans S-4 Coyote	90.115		21.10.91	R P Cross	(Welton, Lincoln)	1. 8.00P
	(Built R H Braihtwaite - pr.no.PFA 193-12073)				*(New owner 11.04)*		
G-MWWR	Corbett Farms Spectrum	024		23.10.91	K A Wright	North Coates	6. 6.08P
G-MWWS	Thruster T 300	089-T300-370	EI-BYW	4.11.91	S P McCaffrey	Dunkeswell	2. 6.05P
	(Built Tempest Aviation Ltd) (Rotax 532)						
G-MWWV	Solar Wings Pegasus XL-Q	SW-WQ-0470		30.10.91	R W Livingstone	Enniskillen	7. 8.08P
	(Trike c/n SW-TE-0357)						

G-MWWZ	Cyclone Airsports Chaser S 447	CH.829		29.10.91	J F Willoughby *(Noted 9.07)* Shotton Colliery, Peterlee		4. 4.04P
G-MWXA	Mainair Gemini Flash IIA	873-0192-7-W668		30.10.91	M Briongo	Strathaven	28.10.07P
G-MWXB	Mainair Gemini Flash IIA	869-1191-7-W664		6.11.91	N W Barnett	Sittles Farm, Alrewas	3. 1.04P
G-MWXC	Mainair Gemini Flash IIA	874-0192-7-W669		6.11.91	N J Lindsay	Strathaven	4. 8.08P
G-MWXF	Mainair Mercury	867-1191-5-W662		12.11.91	P E Jackson	(Ruthin)	20. 4.07P
G-MWXG	Solar Wings Pegasus Quasar IITC	SW-WQT-0471		7.11.91	J E Moseley	Sutton Meadows	16. 9.08P
	(Trike c/n SW-TQC-0074)						
G-MWXH	Solar Wings Pegasus Quasar IITC	SW-WQT-0472		7.11.91	R P Wilkinson	Charmy Down, Bath	10. 6.06P
	(Trike c/n SW-TQC-0075)						
G-MWXJ	Mainair Mercury	861-1091-5-W656		15.11.91	P J Taylor	Sandtoft	31. 3.06P
G-MWXK	Mainair Mercury	862-1191-5-W657		15.11.91	M P Wilkinson	(Sandtoft)	18. 7.96P
G-MWXL	Mainair Gemini Flash IIA	859-1091-7-W654		12.12.91	S N Catchpole	Thurton	27. 9.08P
	(Rotax 582)						
G-MWXP	Solar Wings Pegasus XL-Q	SW-WQ-0475		26.11.91	A P Attfield	(Sutton Meadows)	18. 8.99P
	(Trike c/n SW-TE-0359)						
G-MWXR	Solar Wings Pegasus XL-Q	SW-WQ-0476		26.11.91	G W Craig	Insch	13. 4.08P
	(Trike c/n SW-TE-0360)						
G-MWXU	Mainair Gemini Flash IIA	882-0192-7-W677		9.12.91	C M Mackinnon	Strathaven	23. 1.03P
	(Rotax 582)					*(Noted dismantled 8.07)*		
G-MWXV	Mainair Gemini Flash IIA	879-1291-7-W674		9.12.91	J Stones	Eshott	3. 6.07P
	(Rotax 582)					*(Noted 9.07)*		
G-MWXW	Cyclone Airsports Chaser S	CH.830		9.12.91	K C Dodd	Roddige	7. 6.07P
	(Rotax 377)						
G-MWXX	Cyclone Airsports Chaser S 447	CH.831	(G-MWEB)	9.12.91	P I Frost	(Guilsborough, Northampton)	21. 7.05P
			(G-MWCD)				
G-MWXY	Cyclone Airsports Chaser S 447	CH.832	(G-MWEC)	19.12.91	B L Dobbs *(New owner 10.07)*	(Dunstable)	16. 8 04P
G-MWXZ	Cyclone Airsports Chaser S 508	CH.836		31.12.91	D L Hadley	(Petham, Canterbury)	4. 6.08P
G-MWYA	Mainair Gemini Flash IIA	886-0292-7-W681		3. 1.92	R F Hunt	St Michaels	30.11.07P
	(Rotax 462)						
G-MWYB	Solar Wings Pegasus XL-Q	SW-WQ-0485		15. 1.92	A D Fowler	(Wroughton, Swindon)	7. 6.08P
	(Trike c/n SW-TE-0364)						
G-MWYC	Solar Wings Pegasus XL-Q	SW-WQ-0486		15. 1.92	M A Collins	Longacre Farm, Sandy	11. 4.07P
	(Trike c/n SW-TE-0365)						
G-MWYD	CFM Shadow Series C	K 179		8. 1.92	D W Hermiston-Hooper	Sandown	8. 8.08P
G-MWYE	Rans S-6-ESD Coyote II	0591.189		10. 1.92	G A M Moffat	(Nantwich)	11. 4.08P
	(Built G A Squires - pr.no.PFA 204-12223) (Tri-cycle u/c)						
G-MWYG	Mainair Gemini Flash IIA	884-0292-7-W679		15. 1.92	P G Fox	Newtownards	13. 4.08P
	(Rotax 582)						
G-MWYH	Mainair Gemini Flash IIA	887-0292-7-W682		15. 1.92	A G Carter and D C Jackson (Giltbrook, Nottingham)		18.11.08P
G-MWYI	Solar Wings Pegasus Quasar IITC	SW-WQT-0488		30. 1.92	T S Chadfield	Graveley Hall Farm, Graveley	20. 7.08P
	(Trike c/n SW-TQC-0083)						
G-MWYJ	Solar Wings Pegasus Quasar IITC	SW-WQT-0489		24. 1.92	J W Edwards	Finmere	19. 5.08P
	(Trike c/n SW-TQC-0084)						
G-MWYL	Mainair Gemini Flash IIA	877-0192-7-W672		17. 1.92	A J Hinks	East Fortune	4. 7.08P
G-MWYM	Cyclone Airsports Chaser S 1000	CH.838		21. 1.92	C J Meadows	(Shepton Mallet)	3.11.07P
	(Mosler MM-CB35) (Reported as rebuild of G-MVJI - perhaps Trike only?)						
G-MWYS	CGS Arrow Flight Hawk I Arrow	H-T-470-R447		17. 2.93	D W Hermiston-Hooper t/a Civilair		
	(Built Arrowflight Ltd - pr.no.BMAA/HB/020) (Rotax 447)					(Ryde, Isle of Wight)		
G-MWYT	Mainair Gemini Flash IIA	881-0392-7-W676		3. 2.92	M A Hodgson	Baxby Manor, Husthwaite	24. 9.08P
G-MWYU	Solar Wings Pegasus XL-Q	SW-WQ-0491		30. 1.92	N Hammerton	(Oxted)	3. 8.07P
	(Trike c/n SW-TE-0364)						
G-MWYV	Mainair Gemini Flash IIA	896-0392-7-W691		3. 2.92	J N Whitworth	Oxton	10. 9.04P
	(Rotax 582)						
G-MWYY	Solar Wings Pegasus XL-Q	SW-WQ-0492		17. 2.92	R D Allard	Deenethorpe	7. 3.08P
	(Trike c/n SW-TE-0365)						
G-MWYZ	Solar Wings Pegasus XL-Q	SW-WQ-0474		20.11.91	A Boston	Sywell	22. 6.07P
	(Trike c/n SW-TE-0358)					*(Noted 10.07)*		
G-MWZA	Mainair Mercury	888-0292-5-W683		7. 2.92	A J Malham	Rufforth	1. 3.08P
G-MWZB	AMF Microflight Chevvron 2-32C	033		10. 2.92	A J Pickup	Membury	7.12.05P
G-MWZC	Mainair Gemini Flash IIA	899-0492-7-W694		7. 2.92	R B Huyshe	(Hinstock, Market Drayton)	17. 4.08P
G-MWZD	Solar Wings Pegasus Quasar IITC	SW-WQT-0494		2. 3.92	J R Burton	Redlands, Swindon	5. 7.07P
	(Trike c/n SW-TQC-0086)						
G-MWZE	Solar Wings Pegasus Quasar IITC	SW-WQT-0495		17. 2.92	H Lorimer	Hunterston Farm, Stair	18. 7.01P
	(Trike c/n SW-TQC-0087)					*(Noted 8.05)*		
G-MWZF	Solar Wings Pegasus Quasar IITC	SW-WQT-0496		17. 2.92	R G T Corney	Clench Common	12. 7.07P
	(Rotax 582) *(Trike c/n SW-TQD-0108 but duplicates G-MYEK)*						
G-MWZG	Mainair Gemini Flash IIA	889-0392-7-W684		7. 2.92	C J O'Sullivan	Newtownards	26. 2.07P
	(Rotax 582)						
G-MWZI	Solar Wings Pegasus XL-R	SW-WA-1533		17. 2.92	K J Slater	Roddige	4.11.07P
	(Rotax 462)	*(Trike c/n SW-TE-0367)*					
G-MWZJ	Solar Wings Pegasus XL-R/Se	SW-WA-1534		17. 2.92	P Kitchen	Shotton Colliery, Peterlee	30. 8.05P
	(Rotax 462)	*(Trike c/n SW-TE-0368)*				*(Noted 2.08)*		
G-MWZL	Mainair Gemini Flash IIA	900-0492-7-W695		17. 2.92	D Renton	East Fortune	5. 7.04P
	(Rotax 582)						
G-MWZM	TEAM Mini-MAX 91	PFA 186-12211	G-BUDD	18. 2.92	C Leighton-Thomas	Charmy Down, Bath	29. 7.02P
	(Built M A J Hutt) (Mosler MM CB-40)		G-MWZM			*"My Buddy" (Noted 1.05)*		
G-MWZN	Mainair Gemini Flash IIA	902-0492-7-W697		25. 2.92	D F Greatbanks	(Lymm)	3. 8.07P
	(Rotax 582)						
G-MWZO	Solar Wings Pegasus Quasar IITC	SW-WQT-0498		26. 2.92	A Robinson	(Ashbourne)	27. 3.06P
	(Trike c/n SW-TQC-0089)					*(New owner 6.06)*		
G-MWZP	Solar Wings Pegasus Quasar IITC	SW-WQT-0499		26. 2.92	C M Lewis	Longacre Farm, Sandy	17. 9.08P
	(Trike c/n SW-TQC-0090)						
G-MWZR	Solar Wings Pegasus Quasar IITC	SW-WQT-0500		26. 2.92	R Veart	Haverfordwest	11. 6.08P
	(Trike c/n SW-TQC-0091)						

G-MWZS	Solar Wings Pegasus Quasar IITC	SW-WQT-0501	EI-CIP	26. 2.92	G Bennett	New Farm House, Great Oakley	9. 4.08P
	(Trike c/n SW-TQC-0092)		G-MWZS				
G-MWZT	Solar Wings Pegasus XL-R	SW-WA-1535		26. 2.92	P J Fahie	(Stour Row, Shaftesbury)	16. 9.07P
	(Rotax 462)	(Trike c/n SW-TE-0370)					
G-MWZU	Solar Wings Pegasus XL-R	SW-WA-1536		26. 2.92	A D Winebloom	Roddige	8. 6.08P
	(Rotax 462)	(Trike c/n SW-TE-0371)					
G-MWZV	Solar Wings Pegasus XL-R	SW-WA-1537		26. 2.92	D J Newby	Clench Common	3.11.08P
	(Rotax 462)	(Trike c/n SW-TE-0372)					
G-MWZW	Solar Wings Pegasus XL-R	SW-WA-1538		26. 2.92	S N Pryor	(Leicester)	14. 6.07P
	(Rotax 462)	(Trike c/n SW-TE-0373)	(Sailwing from cancelled G-MNHB {SW-TE-1045} transferred C 2006)				
G-MWZY	Solar Wings Pegasus XL-R	SW-WA-1540		26. 2.92	S J Barkworth	Rufforth	10. 9.06P
	(Rotax 462)	(Trike c/n SW-TE-0375)					
G-MWZZ	Solar Wings Pegasus XL-R	SW-WA-1541		26. 2.92	The Microlight School (Lichfield) Ltd	Roddige	5. 3.08P
	(Rotax 503)	(Trike c/n SW-TE-0376)					
G-MXPH	British Aircraft Corporation 167 Strikemaster Mk.84		G-SARK	4. 5.07	R S Partridge-Hicks	North Weald	9. 8.08P
		EEP/JP/1931	N2146S, Singapore AF 311, G-27-140 (Also carries "311" in Singapore AF c/s)				
G-MXVI	Vickers Supermarine 361 Spitfire LF.XVIe		6850M	17. 2.89	P M Andrews tr The G2 Trust	Wycombe Air Park	30. 5.02P
		CBAF.IX.4394	TE184		(Noted 11.07)		
G-MYAB	Solar Wings Pegasus XL-R/Se	SW-WA-1542		26. 2.92	A N F Stewart	Long Marston	9. 5.07P
	(Rotax 462)	(Trike c/n SW-TE-0377)					
G-MYAC	Solar Wings Pegasus XL-Q	SW-WQ-0502		26. 2.92	M A Garner	Thetford	24. 7.06P
		(Trike c/n SW-TE-0378)					
G-MYAE	Solar Wings Pegasus XL-Q	SW-WQ-0504		26. 2.92	K J Legg	Redlands, Swindon	11. 8.08P
		(Trike c/n SW-TE-0380)					
G-MYAF	Solar Wings Pegasus XL-Q	SW-WQ-0505		26. 2.92	V Donskovas	Redlands, Swindon	5. 2.08P
		(Trike c/n SW-TE-0381)					
G-MYAG	Quad City Challenger II	PFA 177-12167		25. 2.92	R Shewan	Longside, Peterhead	27. 6.08P
	(Built F Payne)						
G-MYAH	Whittaker MW5 Sorcerer	PFA 163-11233		2. 3.92	V T Betts	Otherton, Cannock	3. 5.08P
	(Built T Knight)						
G-MYAI	Mainair Mercury	892-0392-5-W687		11. 3.92	J Ellerton	(Hazel Grove, Stockport)	6. 5.03P
G-MYAJ	Rans S-6-ESD Coyote II	1291.248		3. 3.92	R M Moulton	Weston Zoyland	27.11.08P
	(Built N J Willmott - pr.no.PFA 204-12227) (Tail-wheel u/c))						
G-MYAK	Solar Wings Pegasus Quasar IITC	SW-WQT-0506	D-M . . .?	5. 3.92	I E Brunning	Ince Blundell	1. 9.03P
	(Trike c/n SW-TQC-0093)		G-MYAK		(Noted 8.05)		
G-MYAM	Murphy Renegade Spirit UK	PFA 188-11907		6. 3.92	A F Reid	Newtownards	14. 9.01P
	(Built S R Groves)						
G-MYAN	Whittaker MW5-K Sorcerer	5K-0017-02	(G-MWNI)	24. 3.92	J Hollings	Comber, County Down	1. 7.03P
	(Built Aerotech International Ltd) (Full Lotus floats)						
G-MYAO	Mainair Gemini Flash IIA	894-0392-7-W689		11. 3.92	J H Livingstone	(Dalmeny, South Queensferry)	9. 8.08P
G-MYAR	Thruster T 300	9022-T300-502		12. 3.92	G Hawkins		2. 9.07P
	(Built Tempest Aviation Ltd) (Rotax 503)			Newton Peverill Farm, Sturminster Marshall			
G-MYAS	Mainair Gemini Flash IIA	895-0392-7-W690		11. 3.92	J R Davis	(Hawling, Cheltenham)	12. 6.04P
				(New owner 2.07)			
G-MYAT	TEAM Mini-Max 88	PFA 186-12017		6. 3.92	A D Bales	Stoke, Holy Cross	13. 6.07P
	(Built D M Couling)			(Force landed 1 mile E of Ditchling Beacon 16. 6.07 with substantial damage)			
G-MYAU	Mainair Gemini Flash IIA	890-0392-7-W685		25. 3.92	P P Allen	(Ely)	20. 6.07P
	(Rotax 462)						
G-MYAY	Corbett Farms Spectrum	027		13. 3.92	P F Craggs (Noted 7.06)	Eshott	21.12.00P
G-MYAZ	Murphy Renegade Spirit UK	PFA 188-12027		16. 3.92	R Smith	Kilkerran	10.10.03P
	(Built R Smith)						
G-MYBA	Rans S-6-ESD Coyote II	1291.247		12. 3.92	A M Hughes	Popham	24.10.08P
	(Built S M Vickers - pr.no.PFA 204-12210) (Tail-wheel u/c)						
	(Now marked "1291.247.0800" and believed to be a re-date following rebuild of frame 800 - not a new one)						
G-MYBB	Maxair Drifter	MD.001		10. 4.92	M Ingleton	Stoke, Isle of Grain	12. 6.92P
	(Built M Ingleton - pr.no.BMAA/HB/014) (Rotax 503) (Initially imported by Medway Microlights: on rebuild 9.05 as "UK Drifter": noted 12.05)						
G-MYBC	CFM Shadow Series CD	K 195		18. 3.92	M E Gilbert	Drummaird Farm, Bonnybank	20. 9.08P
	(Built CFM Metal-Fax - originally pr.no.PFA 206-12221 which type series denotes as Streak Shadow: now shown officially as pr.no.BMAA/HB/047)						
G-MYBD	Solar Wings Pegasus Quasar IITC	SW-WQT-0511		26. 3.92	A Gunn	Abbey Warren Farm, Bucknall	5. 7.07P
	(Trike c/n SW-TQC-0094)						
G-MYBE	Solar Wings Pegasus Quasar IITC	SW-WQT-0512		26. 3.92	N A Cook	(Aughton, Lancaster)	23. 7.08P
	(Trike c/n SW-TQC-0095)						
G-MYBF	Solar Wings Pegasus XL-Q	SW-WQ-0513		26. 3.92	K H Pead	(Ipswich)	25. 4.08P
	(Trike c/n SW-TE-0384)						
G-MYBI	Rans S-6-ESD Coyote II	1291.249		26. 3.92	N C Tambiah	Otherton, Cannock	1. 2.08P
	(Built G A Archer and J A Soilleux - pr.no.PFA 204-12186) (Tri-cycle u/c)						
G-MYBJ	Mainair Gemini Flash IIA	908-0593-7-W706		2. 4.92	G C Bowers	Shipmeadow, Beccles	20. 5.08P
	(Rotax 462)						
G-MYBL	CFM Shadow Series CD	K 194		2. 4.92	A A Castleton and D N Owens	The Chase, Wickwar	5.11.08P
G-MYBM	TEAM Mini-Max 91	PFA 186-12212		3. 4.92	B Hunter	Brook Farm, Pilling	15. 8.08P
	(Built M K Dring) (Mosler MM CB-35)						
G-MYBN	Hiway Skytrike II/Demon 175	BRL-01		14. 4.92	B R Lamming	(Seaton, Hull)	
G-MYBO	Solar Wings Pegasus XL-R	SW-WA-1545		16. 4.92	D Gledhill	(London SW19)	1.11.08P
	(Trike c/n SW-TB-1445)						
G-MYBP	Solar Wings Pegasus XL-R/Se	SW-WA-1546		16. 4.92	S H Williams	(Kidderminster)	2. 8.03P
	(Trike c/n SW-TB-1446)						
G-MYBS	Solar Wings Pegasus XL-Q	SW-WQ-0518		16. 4.92	T Smith	Rochester	9. 7.08P
	(Trike c/n SW-TE-0387)						
G-MYBT	Solar Wings Pegasus Quasar IITC	SW-WQT-0519		16. 4.92	G A Rainbow-Ockwell	Redlands, Swindon	17. 2.08P
	(Trike c/n SW-TQC-0097)						
G-MYBU	Cyclone Airsports Chaser S 447	CH.837	G-69-15	28. 4.92	R L Arscott	Longacre Farm, Sandy	21. 1.00P
			G-MYBU		(Noted 7.03)		
G-MYBV	Solar Wings Pegasus XL-Q	SW-WQ-0522		5. 5.92	P M Langdon	Glassonby	5. 6.08P
	(Trike c/n SW-TE-0393)						

G-MYBW	Solar Wings Pegasus XL-Q	SW-WQ-0523	5. 5.92	J S Chapman	(Knaresborough)	20. 6.08P
	(Trike c/n SW-TE-0394)			(Address change 11.07)		
G-MYBY	Solar Wings Pegasus XL-Q	SW-WQ-0525	5. 5.92	I D A Spanton	Croft Farm, Defford	18. 4.05P
	(Trike c/n SW-TE-0396)			(Noted 2.08)		
G-MYBZ	Solar Wings Pegasus XL-Q	SW-WQ-0526	5. 5.92	A J Blackwell	Long Marston	27. 9.97P
	(Trike c/n SW-TE-0397)			(Noted 7.05)		
G-MYCA	Whittaker MW6-T Merlin	PFA 164-11821	14. 5.92	R A L Harris	(Hove)	23. 6.06P
	(Built N B Morley and E Barfoot) (Rotax 532)					
G-MYCB	Cyclone Airsports Chaser S 447	CH.839	18. 5.92	P Sykes	Mapperton Farm, Newton Peverill	20. 5.08P
G-MYCE	Solar Wings Pegasus Quasar IITC	SW-WQT-0527	14. 5.92	S W Barker	(Scarborough)	23. 7.08P
	(Trike c/n SW-TQC-0098)					
G-MYCJ	Mainair Mercury	906-0592-5-W704	19. 5.92	J Agnew	East Fortune	28.11.04P
G-MYCK	Mainair Gemini Flash IIA	909-0592-7-W707	19. 5.92	J P Hanlon and A C McAllister	Ince Blundell	12. 6.07P
	(Rotax 462)					
G-MYCL	Mainair Mercury	910-0592-5-W708	19. 5.92	Palladium Leisure Ltd	RAF Wyton	13. 9.05P
G-MYCM	CFM Shadow Series CD	196	20. 5.92	T Jones	(London SW6)	20. 5.99P
G-MYCN	Mainair Mercury	901-0492-5-W696	22. 5.92	P Lowham (Noted 1.07)	Newtownards	14. 9.06P
G-MYCO	Murphy Renegade Spirit UK	PFA 188-12020	28. 5.92	S Desormes	(Exeter)	2. 7.07P
	(Built C Slater)					
G-MYCP	Whittaker MW6 Merlin	PFA 164-11505	2. 6.92	A C Jones	Otherton, Cannock	4.11.07P
	(Built R M Clarke) (Rotax 532)					
G-MYCR	Mainair Gemini Flash IIA	875-0192-7-W670	10. 6.92	A P King	Long Marston	21. 7.07P
G-MYCS	Mainair Gemini Flash IIA	911-0592-7-W710	12. 6.92	G Penson tr Husthwaite Alpha Group		
					Baxby Manor, Husthwaite	25.10.07P
G-MYCT	TEAM Mini-MAX 91	PFA 186-12163	30. 3.92	D D Rayment	(Horsham)	17. 6.04P
	(Built M A Curant)					
G-MYCU	Whittaker MW6 Merlin	PFA 164-11627	9. 6.92	R D Thomasson	London Colney	7. 8.07P
	(Built P L Lonsdale and D Shackleton: sequence no.conflicts with Streak Shadow G-ORAF) (Rotax 532)					
G-MYCV	Mainair Mercury	913-0792-5-W712	12. 6.92	G Zuchowski	(Wincham, Northwich)	1. 9.07P
G-MYCX	Powerchute Kestrel	00421	15. 6.92	S J Pugh-Jones (Noted 11.07)	Rufforth	14. 5.05P
G-MYCY	Powerchute Kestrel	00422	15. 6.92	D R M Powell	(Llandysul)	3. 6.06P
G-MYCZ	Powerchute Kestrel	00423	15. 6.92	R R O'Neill	(Ballygawley, Dungannon)	10.10.95P
				(New owner 11.05)		
G-MYDA	Powerchute Kestrel	00424	15. 6.92	K J Greatrix	(Sleaford)	2. 8.07P
G-MYDC	Mainair Mercury	916-0792-5-W715	23. 6.92	G K Thornton	(Radcliffe, Manchester)	10.10.08P
G-MYDD	CFM Shadow Series CD	K 197	22. 6.92	C H Gem	(Marbella, Malaga, Spain)	22.11.95P
G-MYDE	CFM Shadow Series CD	K 187	24. 6.92	D N L Howell	(Upper Colwall, Malvern)	19. 9.06P
G-MYDF	TEAM Mini-MAX 91	PFA 186-12129	24. 6.92	A M Hughes	Popham	23. 5.08P
	(Built L G Horne)					
G-MYDJ	Solar Wings Pegasus XL Tug	SW-WA-1558	1. 7.92	R C Wood and D C Richardson tr Cambridgeshire Aerotow Club		
	(Rotax 462) (Trike c/n SW-TE-0403) (Officially reg as XL-R)				Sutton Meadows	24. 4.08P
G-MYDK	Rans S-6-ESD Coyote II	0392.276	21. 4.92	R W Thompson	Eshott	11.10.08P
	(Built D N Kershaw - pr.no.PFA 204-12239) (Tri-cycle u/c)					
G-MYDM	Whittaker MW6-S Fatboy Flyer	PFA 164-12105	26. 6.92	K Gregan	Kilrush, County Kildare	4. 7.05P
	(Rotax 582)					
G-MYDN	Quad City Challenger II UK	CH2-1091-UK-0736	30. 6.92	T C Hooks	Newtownards	28. 9.08P
	(Built T C Hooks - pr.no.PFA 177-12245) (Rotax 462)					
G-MYDO	Rans S-5 Coyote	89.110	6. 7.92	B J Benton	Long Marston	1.11.08P
	(Built W A Stevens - pr.no.PFA 193-12274)					
G-MYDP	Kolb Twinstar Mk.3	K0002-1291	15. 7.92	E R Howells tr Norberts Flying Group	Leicester	11. 3.08P
	(Built P M Standen - pr.no.PFA 205-12231) (Rotax 503)					
G-MYDR	Thruster T 300	9072-T300-505	21. 7.92	H G Soper	Chiddingley, East Sussex	4.11.08P
	(Built Tempest Aviation Ltd) (Rotax 582)					
G-MYDS	Quad City Challenger II UK	CH2-1289-UK-0500	6. 3.90	L R Graham	Rayne Hall Farm, Braintree	24. 5.07P
	(Built D D Smith - pr.no.PFA 177-11716)					
G-MYDT	Thuster T300	9072-T300-506	21. 7.92	C R Bunce	Redlands, Swindon	10. 1.96P
	(Built Tempest Aviation Ltd) (Rotax 582)				(New owner 8.06)	
G-MYDU	Thruster T 300	9072-T300-504	21. 7.92	S Collins	Killineer, Drogheda, County Louth	16.11.07P
	(Built Tempest Aviation Ltd) (Rotax 582)					
G-MYDV	Mainair Gemini Flash IIA	917-0892-7-W716	29. 7.92	S J Mazilis	(Westhoughton, Bolton)	31. 7.08P
	(Rotax 462)					
G-MYDW	Whittaker MW6 Merlin	PFA 164-12184	27. 7.92	A Chidlow	Church Farm, Askern	2. 9.04P
	(Built W R G West) (Rotax 503)				(Noted dismantled 9.07)	
G-MYDX	Rans S-6-ESD Coyote II	0392.279	27. 7.92	K J Legg and G Cross	Redlands, Swindon	12. 6.08P
	(Built R J Goodburn - pr.no.PFA 204-12238) (Tri-cycle u/c)					
G-MYDZ	Mignet HM-1000 Balerit	66	3. 8.92	D S Simpson	Graveley Hall Farm, Graveley	9.12.07P
G-MYEA	Solar Wings Pegasus XL-Q	SW-WQ-0537	28. 7.92	A M Taylor	Long Marston	13. 4.08P
	(Trike c/n SW-TE-0404)					
G-MYEC	Solar Wings Pegasus XL-Q	SW-WQ-0539	28. 7.92	J I King	(Bath)	2. 6.05P
	(Trike c/n SW-TE-0406)					
G-MYED	Solar Wings Pegasus XL-R	SW-WA-1559	28. 7.92	P K Dale	Bagby	6. 8.07P
	(Rotax 462HP) (Trike c/n SW-TE-0407)					
G-MYEF	Whittaker MW6 Merlin	PFA 164-11327	28. 5.92	R D Thomasson	London Colney	
	(Built S Meadowcroft)				(New owner 9.06)	
G-MYEH	Solar Wings Pegasus XL-R	SW-WA-1561	4. 8.92	P G Strangward tr G-MYEH Flying Group	Roddige	18. 6.08P
	(Trike c/n SW-TB-1448)					
G-MYEI	Cyclone Airsports Chaser S 447	CH.841	18. 8.92	N S Dell	Stanton, Morpeth	17. 9.08P
G-MYEJ	Cyclone Airsports Chaser S 447	CH.842	18. 8.92	S C Reeve	Headon Farm, Retford	15. 3.08P
G-MYEK	Solar Wings Pegasus Quasar IITC	SW-WQT-0540	7. 8.92	M N Dando	Halfpenny Green	2. 9.08P
	(Rotax 582) (Trike c/n SW-TQD-0108 but duplicates G-MWZF)					
G-MYEM	Solar Wings Pegasus Quasar IITC	SW-WQT-0542	7. 8.92	D J Moore	Roddige	22. 4.08P
	(Rotax 582) (Trike c/n SW-TQD-0101)					
G-MYEN	Solar Wings Pegasus Quasar IITC	SW-WQT-0543	7. 8.92	T J Feeney	(Otherton, Cannock)	25. 5.08P
	(Rotax 582) (Trike c/n SW-TQD-0105)					

G-MYEO	Solar Wings Pegasus Quasar IITC SW-WQT-0544		7. 8.92	A G Curtis	Swinford, Rugby	13.10.08P
	(Rotax 582)	(Trike c/n SW-TQD-0106)				
G-MYEP	CFM Shadow Series CD	K 205	13. 8.92	J S Seddon-Harvey	Broadmeadow Farm, Hereford	8. 6.04P
				(Noted 4.05)		
G-MYER	Cyclone AX2000	B 1052901 & CA 001	G-69-27	19. 8.92	T F Horrocks	Wick	28. 8.07P
			G-MYER, G-69-5, 59-GF			
G-MYES	Rans S-6-ESD Coyote II	0392.283	3. 7.92	F J Percival tr Dairy House Flyers		
	(Built G R Pritchard - pr.no.PFA 204-12254) (Tri-cycle u/c)				Dairy House Farm, Worleston	14.10.08P
G-MYET	Whittaker MW6 Merlin	PFA 164-12318	19. 8.92	G Campbell (Noted 3.05)		
	(Built M B Haine) (Rotax 503)				Newton Peverill Farm, Sturminster Marshall	8. 9.04P
G-MYEU	Mainair Gemini Flash IIA	918-0892-7-W718	1. 9.92	C Parry	Ince Blundell	10. 8.08P
G-MYEV	Whittaker MW6 Merlin	PFA 164-11250	25. 8.92	M J Batchelor	The Chase, Wickwar	
	(Built M M Ruck)			(Noted 2.03)		
G-MYEX	Powerchute Kestrel	00426	28. 8.92	R J Watkin (New owner 8.06)	(Melton Mowbray)	6. 6.06P
G-MYFH	Quad City Challenger II UK	CH2-0292-0798	9. 9.92	W I McMillan	RAF Mona	1.12.07P
	(Built C J and R J Lines - pr.no.PFA 177-12282)					
G-MYFI	Cyclone Airsports AX3/503	CA 002	9. 9.92	R Dilkes	(Mitcham)	7. 8.08P
	(C/n C 3093159 also reported)					
G-MYFK	Solar Wings Pegasus Quasar IITC SW-WQT-0553		11. 9.92	C R Cawley	(Broomfield, Chelmsford)	30. 1.08P
	(Rotax 582)	(Trike c/n SW-TQD-0113)				
G-MYFL	Solar Wings Pegasus Quasar IITC SW-WQT-0541/A		11. 9.92	S B Wilkes	Roddige	13. 6.06P
	(Rotax 582)	(Trike c/n SW-TQD-0103)				
	(Originally regd as c/n SW-WQT-0554: replacement Sailwing fitted to Trike G-MYFL after original Sailwing stolen 1. 1.93)					
G-MYFM	Murphy Renegade Spirit UK	PFA 188-12249	9. 9.92	A C Cale	Marley Hall, Ledbury	17. 4.08P
	(Built J M Walsh)					
G-MYFN	Rans S-5 Coyote	89.112	16. 9.92	P Doran	(Monaghan, County Monaghan)	7. 8.03P
	(Built L Kellner - pr.no.PFA 193-12273)					
G-MYFO	Cyclone Airsports Chaser S	CH.843	22. 9.92	D M Broom	Sywell	13. 4.07P
	(Rotax 377)			(Noted 10.07)		
G-MYFP	Mainair Gemini Flash IIA	920-0992-7-W719	2.10.92	R C Reynolds	Arclid Green, Sandbach	26. 9.08P
G-MYFR	Mainair Gemini Flash IIA	921-0992-7-W720	30. 9.92	S B Brady	Arclid Green, Sandbach	28. 8.08P
G-MYFS	Solar Wings Pegasus XL-R	SW-WA-1564	30. 9.92	B J Palfreyman	Watnall	26. 9.08P
		(Trike c/n SW-TB-1453)				
G-MYFT	Mainair Scorcher	922-0992-3-W234	30. 9.92	T Williams	(Hadfield, Glossop)	13. 7.07P
	(Rotax 503)					
G-MYFU	Mainair Gemini Flash IIA	924-1092-7-W722	7.10.92	J Payne	Deenethorpe	5.10.08P
	(Rotax 462)					
G-MYFV	Cyclone Airsports AX3/503	C 2083050	6.10.92	J K Sargent	Stoke, Isle of Grain	28.10.07P
G-MYFW	Cyclone Airsports AX3/503	C 2083051	13.10.92	The Microlight School (Lichfield) Ltd	Roddige	6. 3.08P
G-MYFX	Solar Wings Pegasus XL-Q	SW-WQ-0378	25. 6.93	J R Bluett	(Ware)	24. 8.04P
		(Trike c/n SW-TE-0295)				
G-MYFZ	Cyclone Airsports AX3/503	C 2083048	20.10.92	G Gates	Chilbolton	7. 1.08P
G-MYGD	Cyclone Airsports AX3/503	C 2083049	21.10.92	G J Simoni	Lower Upham Farm, Chiseldon	28. 8.08P
G-MYGE	Whittaker MW6 Merlin	PFA 164-11650	20.10.92	M D and S M North	(Loughton, Milton Keynes)	31.10.07P
	(Built M D North) (Rotax 532)					
G-MYGF	TEAM Mini-MAX 91	PFA 186-12175	22.10.92	R D Barnard	Ley Farm, Chirk	25. 4.08P
	(Built R D Barnard)					
G-MYGH	Rans S-6-ESD Coyote II	0692.318	30.10.92	J R Mosey	(Eccleston, Chorley)	26. 3.08P
	(Built S M Hall - pr.no.PFA 204-12335)					
G-MYGJ	Mainair Mercury	923-0992-7-W721	5.10.92	J R Harnett	(Whitmore, Newcastle)	4. 4.08P
G-MYGK	Cyclone Airsports Chaser S 508	CH.846	3.11.92	P C Collins	(Llanbadoc, Usk)	14.11.95P
G-MYGM	Quad City Challenger II UK CH2-0391-UK-0662		6.11.92	J White and G J Williams	Mill Farm, Shifnall	29. 6.07P
	(Built R Holt - pr.no.PFA 177-12261)					
G-MYGN	AMF Microflight Chevvron 2-32C	034	29.12.92	M F E Chalk	(Shaw, Swindon)	10. 5.08P
G-MYGP	Rans S-6-ESD Coyote II	0992.349	10.11.92	D J Millin	(Newton Abbot)	29. 8.08P
	(Built J S Melville - pr.no.PFA 204-12368) (Tail-wheel u/c)					
G-MYGR	Rans S-6-ESD Coyote II	0992.348	16.11.92	M E Parker	(Irthlingborough, Wellingborough)	17. 5.08P
	(Built D K Haughton - pr.no.PFA 204-12378)					
G-MYGT	Solar Wings Pegasus XL Tug	SW-WA-1569	13.11.92	J J Hoer tr Condors Aerotow Syndicate	Dunkeswell	16. 5.08P
	(Rotax 462)	(Trike c/n SW-TE-0413)	(Officially reg as XL-R)			
G-MYGU	Solar Wings Pegasus XL-R	SW-WA-1570	13.11.92	D R Western	Weston Zoyland	16. 5.05P
	(Rotax 462)	(Trike c/n SW-TE-0414)				
G-MYGV	Solar Wings Pegasus XL Tug	SW-WA-1571	13.11.92	D J Brixton tr Shropshire Tow Group	Leebotwood	9. 4.07P
	(Rotax 462HP)	(Trike c/n SW-TE-0415)	(Officially reg as XL-R)			
G-MYGZ	Mainair Gemini Flash IIA	928-1192-7-W726	18.11.92	P M Reddington	(Ormskirk)	10. 8.08P
	(Rotax 582)					
G-MYHF	Mainair Gemini Flash IIA	929-1092-7-W727	25.11.92	P J Bloor	(Knutsford)	6.10.03P
G-MYHG	Cyclone Airsports AX3/503	C 2103070	27.11.92	C Alsop and N P Thomson	Cumnock	2.12.05P
				(New owners 11.06)		
G-MYHH	Cyclone Airsports AX3/503	C 2103069	30.11.92	D J Harber	(Didcot)	14.11.08P
	(Also c/n CA.006)					
G-MYHI	Rans S-6-ESD Coyote II	0692.312	8.12.92	G F Clews	(Branston, Burton-on-Trent)	16. 9.08P
	(Built L N Anderson - pr.no.PFA 204-12279) (Tailwheel u/c)					
G-MYHJ	Cyclone Airsports AX3/503	C 2103073	11.12.92	J G Campbell	(Barnsley)	21. 9.08P
	(Reported as keel tube c/n C 3093157 - see G-MYME)					
G-MYHK	Rans S-6-ESD Coyote II	0692.311	3.12.92	M R Williamson	Sutton Meadows	18. 6.07P
	(Built J M Longley - pr.no.PFA 204-12349) (Tri-cycle u/c)					
G-MYHL	Mainair Gemini Flash IIA	932-0193-7-W730	21.12.92	B J Riley	(Barnoldswick)	29. 2.08P
G-MYHM	Cyclone Airsports AX3/503	C 2103068	18.12.92	J Walsh tr G-MYHM Group Jenkin's Farm, Navestock		16. 5.08P
	(Also c/n CA.007)					
G-MYHN	Mainair Gemini Flash IIA	933-0193-7-W731	29.12.92	D Avery	Priory Farm, Tibenham	20. 9.07P
	(Rotax 582)			(New owner 12.07)		
G-MYHP	Rans S-6-ESD Coyote II	0892.343	8. 1.93	K E Gair and J G E Lane	East Barling, Essex	21.12.07P
	(Built D A Crompton - pr.no.PFA 204-12406) (Tri-cycle u/c)					

G-MYHR	Cyclone Airsports AX3/503	C.2103071	G-68-8 G-MYHR	15. 1.93	J K Clayton (New owner 1.08)	(Norwich)	27. 6.05P
G-MYHS	Powerchute Kestrel (Frame No.00433, parachute No.931013, engine No.4104716)	00433		26. 1.93	R R O'Neill (New owner 7.05)	(Ballygawley, Dungannon)	6. 4.01P
G-MYIA	Quad City Challenger II UK (Built I J Arkieson)	PFA 177-12400		21. 1.93	I J Arkieson	Ley Farm, Chirk	3.10.00P
G-MYIE	Whittaker MW6-S Fatboy Flyer (Built P A Mercer) (Rotax 532)	PFA 164-11800		26. 1.93	A M Morris	(Winstanley, Wigan)	2. 2.07P
G-MYIF	CFM Shadow Series CD	217		2. 2.93	P J Edwards	(Steart, Bridgwater)	10. 4.08P
G-MYIH	Mainair Gemini Flash IIA (Rotax 582)	937-0293-7-W734		9. 3.93	A N Huggart	Hunsdon	8. 6.08P
G-MYII	TEAM Mini-MAX 91 (Built G W Peacock) (Mosler MM CB-40)	PFA 186-12119		10.11.92	P A Gasson (Address change 3.07)	(Three Mile Cross, Reading)	8. 3.05P
G-MYIJ	Cyclone Airsports AX3/503	C 2103072		8. 2.93	Ultralight Training Ltd	(Coventry)	11. 3.08P
G-MYIK	Kolb Twinstar Mk.3 (Built R P Smith)	PFA 205-12220		13. 1.93	B A Janaway (New owner 2.08)	Dunkeswell	14. 8.07P
G-MYIL	Cyclone Airsports Chaser S 508	CH.849		3. 3.93	R A Rawes "Fricky"	Over Farm, Gloucester	11. 3.08P
G-MYIM	Solar Wings Pegasus Quasar IITC (Rotax 582)	SW-WQT-0579 (Trike c/n SW-TQD-0122)	(EI-...) G-MYIM	22. 2.93	D Forde	Clare Galway, County Galway	9. 9.07P
G-MYIN	Solar Wings Pegasus Quasar IITC (Rotax 582)	SW-WQT-0580 (Trike c/n SW-TQD-0123)		22. 2.93	W P Hughes	RAF Henlow	7. 8.08P
G-MYIO	Solar Wings Pegasus Quasar IITC (Rotax 582)	SW-WQT-0581 (Trike c/n SW-TQD-0124)		22. 2.93	E Foster and J H Peet (Damaged 25. 6.05: engineless wreck noted 6.07)	(Eccleston, Chorley)	19. 8.05P
G-MYIP	CFM Shadow Series CD	K 198		16. 3.93	T Bailey	Otherton, Cannock	3. 3.08P
G-MYIR	Rans S-6-ESD Coyote II (Built J Simpson - pr.no.PFA 204-12458) (Tri-cycle u/c)	0892.344		17. 3.93	P Vergette	North Coates	7.12.07P
G-MYIS	Rans S-6-ESD Coyote II (Built A J Wyatt - pr.no.PFA 204-12382) (Tri-cycle u/c)	0892 346		31.12.92	I S Everett and M Stott	Sackville Lodge, Riseley	22. 8.08P
G-MYIT	Cyclone Airsports Chaser S 508	CH.850		19. 3.93	R Barringer	(Ravensthorpe, Northampton)	28. 3.99P
G-MYIU	Cyclone Airsports AX3/503 (Zanzoterra Z-202) (Officially designated and regd with Rotax 503)	C 3013084		22. 3.93	G R Hill	Mullaghmore, Coleraine	29. 8.06P
G-MYIV	Mainair Gemini Flash IIA (Rotax 582)	938-0393-7-W735		30. 3.93	P S Nicholls	Finmere	9. 4.07P
G-MYIX	Quad City Challenger II UK (Built I M Walton - pr.no.PFA 177-12260)	CH2-0191-UK-0615		5. 1.93	A Studley	Middle Pymore Farm , Bridport	25. 5.06P
G-MYIY	Mainair Gemini Flash IIA	942-0493-7-W737		1. 4.93	I C Macbeth	Arclid Green, Sandbach	22. 6.08P
G-MYIZ	TEAM Mini-MAX 91 (Built J C Longmore)	PFA 186-12347		31. 3.93	J C Longmore	Headon Farm, Retford	15. 1.08P
G-MYJC	Mainair Gemini Flash IIA (Rotax 462)	944-0593-7-W739		7. 4.93	R G Hearsey	(Rye)	16. 7.08P
G-MYJD	Rans S-6-ESD Coyote II (Built D J Dimmer and B Robins - pr.no.PFA 204-12360) (Tail-wheel u/c)	0792.324		23. 4.93	D R Collier	Barton Ashes	6. 8.08P
G-MYJF	Thruster T 300 (Built Tempest Aviation Ltd) (Rotax 582)	9013-T300-509		14. 4.93	P F McConville	(Dungannon)	18. 9.08P
G-MYJJ	Solar Wings Pegasus Quasar IITC (Rotax 582)	SW-WQT-0591 (Trike c/n SW-TQD-0131)		27. 4.93	D Murray	(Clevedon)	1. 9.04P
G-MYJK	Solar Wings Pegasus Quasar IITC (Rotax 582) (Trike c/n SW-TQD-0132 - built with Cyclone c/n 6752)	SW-WQT-0592		27. 4.93	T H Parr	St Michaels	25. 8.08P
G-MYJM	Mainair Gemini Flash IIA (Rotax 582)	945-0593-7-W740		29. 4.93	J T Walker	Newtownards	28. 4.08P
G-MYJO	Cyclone Airsports Chaser S 508	CH.851		30. 4.93	A W Rawlings	Croft Farm, Defford	7.10.08P
G-MYJR	Mainair Mercury	947-0593-7-W742	(EC-) G-MYJR	12. 5.93	D Dreux	(Child Okeford, Blandford Forum)	15. 7.06P
G-MYJS	Solar Wings Pegasus Quasar IITC (Rotax 582)	6581		19. 5.93	P R Saunders	Longacre Farm, Sandy	1. 1.05P
G-MYJT	Solar Wings Pegasus Quasar IITC (Rotax 582)	6582		19. 5.93	H A Duthie	Perth	21. 7.08P
G-MYJU	Solar Wings Pegasus Quasar IITC (Rotax 582)	6573		19. 5.93	P G Penhaligan	Stoke, Isle of Grain	18. 6.07P
G-MYJW	Cyclone Airsports Chaser S 508	CH.856		19. 5.93	A R Mikolajczyk	Church Farm, Askern	25. 8.08P
G-MYJY	Rans S-6-ESD Coyote II (Build G A Clayton - pr.no.PFA 204-12346) (Tri-cycle u/c)	0692.317		24. 5.93	F N Pearson	Linley Hill, Leven	8. 8.06P
G-MYJZ	Whittaker MW5-D Sorcerer (Built J G Beesley)	PFA 163-12385		22. 4.93	P A Aston tr My Jazz Group	(Torquay)	7.11.07P
G-MYKA	Cyclone Airsports AX3/503	C 3013086		25. 5.93	R Nicklin	Otherton, Cannock	29. 2.08P
G-MYKB	Kolb Twinstar Mk.3 (Built J D Holt - pr.no.PFA 205-12398)	K0007-0193		31. 3.93	T Antell (New owner 7.06)	(Watergore, South Petherton)	1. 9.00P
G-MYKC	Mainair Gemini Flash IIA (Rotax 582)	948-0593-7-W743		26. 5.93	R Bricknell	Headon Farm, Retford	3. 9.08P
G-MYKD	Cyclone Airsports Chaser S 508	CH.857		26. 5.93	J B Allan (New owner 7.06)	(Corringham, Stanford-le-Hope)	30.10.05P
G-MYKE	CFM Shadow Series BD	K 031		14. 1.88	M Hughes t/a MKH Engineering (Noted 4.04)	Emlyn's Field, Rhuallt	26.10.96P
G-MYKF	Cyclone Airsports AX3/503	C 3013083		8. 6.93	M A Collins	Longacre Farm, Sandy	24. 7.07P
G-MYKG	Mainair Gemini Flash IIA (Rotax 582)	950-0693-7-W745		21. 6.93	B D Walker	(Sale)	2.11.07P
G-MYKH	Mainair Gemini Flash IIA (Rotax 582)	951-0693-7-W746		21. 6.93	G F Atkinson	Rufforth	9.11.04P
G-MYKJ	TEAM Mini-MAX (Built M Hill) (Rotax 508)	PFA 186-12215		10. 6.93	T De Breffe Gardner	(Kingsclere, Newbury)	8. 5.06P
G-MYKL	Medway Raven X	MRB116/104		6. 7.93	A Williams	Perth	15. 5.08P
G-MYKN	Rans S-6-ESD Coyote II (Built S E Hartles - pr.no.PFA 204-12361) (Tri-cycle u/c)	0892.338		23. 6.93	G C Alderson Lower Mountpleasant Farm, Chatteris		15. 9.06P

G-MYKO	Whittaker MW6-S Fatboy Flyer PFA 164-11919		25. 6.93	K R Challis and C S Andersson		
	(Hirth 2706)				New Farm House, Great Oakley	14. 9.07P
G-MYKP	Solar Wings Pegasus Quasar IITC	6627	7. 7.93	R F Dye and G S B Airth	Perth	22. 2.08P
	(Rotax 582)					
G-MYKR	Solar Wings Pegasus Quasar IITC	6635	7. 7.93	C Stallard	Chase Farm, Little Burstead	6. 8.07P
	(Rotax 582)					
G-MYKS	Solar Wings Pegasus Quasar IITC	6636	7. 7.93	D J Oskis	(Upminster)	29. 4.08P
	(Rotax 582) *(Now fitted with new Trike c/n 6780)*					
G-MYKT	Cyclone Airsports AX3/503	C 3013082	5. 7.93	J D Sanger and J E Seager		
					Stoke, Isle of Grain	2.10.07P
G-MYKV	Mainair Gemini Flash IIA	954-0793-7-W749	13. 7.93	P J Gulliver	Mill Farm, Shifnal	29. 9.05P
G-MYKW	Mainair Mercury	960-0893-7-W755	9. 7.93	J D Hylton	Eshott	9. 11.08P
G-MYKX	Mainair Mercury	961-0893-7-W756	3. 9.93	B W Hunter	(Penicuik)	10. 7.08P
G-MYKY	Mainair Mercury	962-0893-7-W757	6. 8.93	R P Jewit	(York)	22. 7.07P
G-MYKZ	TEAM Mini-MAX 91	PFA 186-11841 G-BVAV	26. 7.93	C Libby	(Teignmouth)	29. 7.05P
	(Built P A Ellis) (Rotax 503)			*(New owner 6.06)*		
G-MYLB	TEAM Mini-MAX 91	PFA 186-12419	2. 8.93	J G Burns	Morgansfield, Fishburn	1. 2.08P
	(Built P Harvey) (Rotax 532)					
G-MYLC	Pegasus Quantum 15	6634	9. 8.93	C McKay	Perth	26. 9.08P
	(Rotax 503)					
G-MYLD	Rans S-6-ESD Coyote II	0892.350	1. 3.93	B Cartwright	Magheralin, Craigavon	27.10.05P
	(Built L R H d'Eath - pr.no.PFA 204-12394) (Tail-wheel u/c)			*(New owner 7.06)*		
G-MYLE	Pegasus Quantum Lite	6609	9. 8.93	S E Powell	Enstone	23. 2.08P
	(Rotax 503) *(Regd as Pegasus Quantum 15)*					
G-MYLF	Rans S-6-ESD Coyote II	0493.483	4. 8.93	A J Spencer	Eagle Moor, Grantham	22. 7.05P
	(Built G R and J A Pritchard - pr.no.PFA 204-12544) (Tri-cycle u/c)			*"Low Flyer"*		
G-MYLG	Mainair Gemini Flash IIA	959-0893-7-W754	6. 8.93	N J Axworthy and C Dunning	(Runcorn)	7. 7.08P
G-MYLH	Pegasus Quantum 15	6632	27. 8.93	J W Atkin	(Stoke-on-Trent)	22. 7.08P
	(Rotax 503)					
G-MYLI	Pegasus Quantum 15	6645	11. 8.93	A M Keyte	(Milton Keynes)	27. 5.08P
	(Rotax 503)					
G-MYLK	Pegasus Quantum 15	6602	27. 8.93	C L Minter tr G-MYLK Group	Deenethorpe	24. 9.04P
	(Rotax 503)					
G-MYLL	Pegasus Quantum 15	6650	31. 8.93	S Hayes	Headon Farm, Retford	28.10.07P
	(Rotax 462HP)					
G-MYLM	Pegasus Quantum 15	6651 (EC-)	31. 8.93	P A Ashton	(Lincoln)	10.11.05P
	(Rotax 582)	G-MYLM				
G-MYLN	Kolb Twinstar Mk.3	K0010-0193	3. 9.93	J F Joyes	Chiltern Park, Wallingford	9. 5.08P
	(Built G E Collard - pr.no.PFA 205-12430)					
G-MYLO	Rans S-6-ESD Coyote II	0692.313	9. 9.93	P Bowers	Perth	28. 9.08P
	(Built J G Dance and P E Lewis - pr.no.PFA 204-12334: frame no.may be 0692.315) (Tri-cycle u/c)					
G-MYLP	Kolb Twinstar Mk.3	K0005-0992 (G-BVCR)	9. 9.93	R Thompson	(Bristol)	27. 5.99P
	(Built D M Stevens - pr.no.PFA 205-12391)					
G-MYLR	Mainair Gemini Flash IIA	964-0993-7-W759	17. 9.93	M D Calder and I J Cleland	(Glasgow)	21.11.07P
	(Rotax 582)					
G-MYLS	Mainair Mercury	966-0993-7-W761	5.10.93	D Burnell-Higgs	Shobdon	6. 9.05P
G-MYLT	Mainair Blade	967-1093-7-W762	23. 9.93	T D Hall	(Long Marston, Tring)	4. 6.08P
	(Rotax 912)					
G-MYLV	CFM Shadow Series CD	220	24. 9.93	R G M-J Proost tr Aviation for Paraplegics and Tetraplegics Trust		
					Old Sarum	24. 3.08P
G-MYLW	Rans S-6-ESD Coyote II	1292.401	4. 8.93	D J Townsend	Priory Farm, Tibenham	29. 9.05P
	(Built J R Worswick - pr.no.PFA 204-12560) (Tri-cycle u/c)			*(New owner 8.07)*		
G-MYLX	Medway Raven X	MRB113/109	6.10.93	T M Knight	(Lower Earley Reading)	23. 9.08P
	(Sailwing c/n also quoted for G-MYVV)					
G-MYLY	Medway Raven X	MRB001/108	23. 9.93	C R Smith	(Stanford-le-Hope)	3.10.94P
	(Sailwing c/n also quoted for G-MYVU)					
G-MYLZ	Pegasus Quantum 15	6672	6.10.93	W G McPherson	(Dunfermline)	30.11.05P
	(Rotax 462)					
G-MYMB	Pegasus Quantum 15	6674	6.10.93	D B Jones	(Bletchley, Milton Keynes)	14.11.08P
	(Rotax 582)					
G-MYMC	Pegasus Quantum 15	6675	6.10.93	D Murray	(Leslie, Glenrothes)	26. 2.08P
	(Rotax 582)					
G-MYME	Cyclone Airsports AX3/503	C 3093157	13.10.93	M K Slaughter tr G-MYME Group	(Earley, Reading)	5.12.04P
	(Officially regd wiith c/n as such but keel tube C 3093157 noted as fitted to G-MYHJ) (New owner 9.07)					
G-MYMH	Rans S-6-ESD Coyote II	0793.520	20.10.93	A R Cattell	Lower Wasing Farm, Brimpton	6.12.07P
	(Built D J Thompsett - pr.no.PFA 204-12576) (Tri-cycle u/c)					
G-MYMI	Kolb Twinstar Mk.3	K0016-0693	21.10.93	F J Brown	(Flitwick, Bedford)	5. 9.05P
	(Built R T P Harris - pr.no.PFA 205-12537)			*(New owner 5.07)*		
G-MYMJ	Medway Raven X	MRB004/110	28.10.93	N Brigginshaw	RAF Wyton	5. 1.08P
	(Sailwing c/n also quoted for G-MYVX)					
G-MYMK	Mainair Gemini Flash IIA	968-1193-7-W763	29.10.93	A Britton	(Rickmansworth)	28. 5.06P
	(Rotax 582)					
G-MYML	Mainair Mercury	969-1193-7-W765	29.10.93	D J Dalley	Stancombe Farm, Askerswell	7. 6.01P
				(Noted 11.06)		
G-MYMM	Air Création 503/Fun 18S GT bis	93/001	30. 9.93	W H Greenwood	Swanborough Farm, Lewes	25. 4.08P
G-MYMN	Whittaker MW6 Merlin	PFA 164-12124	29.10.93	K J Cole	Over Farm, Gloucester	25.11.03P
	(Built K J Cole) (Rotax 582)					
G-MYMO	Mainair Gemini Flash IIA	955-0793-7-W750	24. 6.93	S McCrae	(Eastham, Wirral)	24. 4.08P
G-MYMP	Rans S-6-ESD Coyote II	1291.250 (G-CHAZ)	5.11.93	R L Flowerday	Dunkeswell	11.11.08P
	(Built C H Middleton - pr.no.PFA 204-12436) (Tri-cycle u/c)					
G-MYMR	Rans S-6-ESD Coyote II	0893.529	17.11.93	R J Bentley (Toomevara, Nenagh, County Tipperary)		26. 6.07P
	(Built M J Kay - pr.no.PFA 204-12580) (Tri-cycle u/c)					
G-MYMS	Rans S-6-ESD Coyote II	0893.526	17.11.93	M R Johnson and P G Briscoe	Long Marston	15. 3.08P
	(Built G C Moore - pr.no.PFA 204-12581) (Tri-cycle u/c)					

G-MYMV	Mainair Gemini Flash IIA	971-1193-7-W767	26.11.93	A J Evans	(Pembrey, Burry Port)	8.12.07P
G-MYMW	Cyclone Airsports AX3/503	C 3093156	23.11.93	L J Perring	Field Farm, Oakley	21.5.08P
G-MYMX	Pegasus Quantum 15	6705	1.12.93	N F McKenzie	Insch	21.6.08P
	(Rotax 582)					
G-MYMY	Cyclone Airsports Chaser S 508	CH.860	7.9.93	D L Hadley	(Canterbury)	29.5.07P
G-MYMZ	Cyclone Airsports AX3/503	C 3093154	7.12.93	The Microlight School (Lichfield) Ltd	Roddige	26.2.07P
G-MYNB	Pegasus Quantum 15	6719	14.12.93	S D Powell and R Maude	(Wakefield)	24.1.86P
	(Rotax 582)					
G-MYNC	Mainair Mercury	K973-1293-7-W769	17.12.93	N L Northend	(Newfield, Bishop Auckland)	12.4.08P
G-MYND	Mainair Gemini Flash IIA	841-0591-7-W635	28.5.91	S Wild	Headon Farm, Retford	7.6.08P
G-MYNE	Rans S-6-ESD Coyote II	1292.408	25.6.93	J N W Moss	Enstone	3.12.08P
	(Built G Ferguson - pr.no.PFA 204-12497) (Tail-wheel u/c)					
G-MYNF	Mainair Mercury	974-1293-7-W770	17.1.94	W Gray	(Bonnybank, Leven)	5.3.08P
G-MYNH	Rans S-6-ESD Coyote II	0493.487	30.12.93	E F and V M Clapham	(Oldbury-on-Severn)	29.3.01P
	(Built E F Clapham - pr.no.PFA 204-12616) (Rotax 912-UL) (Tail-wheel u/c)					
G-MYNI	TEAM Mini-MAX 91	PFA 186-12314	22.2.93	I Pearson	(Falmouth)	17.11.99P
	(Built R Barton) (Mosler MM CB-35)			(New owner 11.07)		
G-MYNJ	Mainair Mercury	K972-1293-7-W768	14.1.94	S M Buchan (Noted 9.05)	Deenethorpe	10.8.04P
G-MYNK	Pegasus Quantum 15	6614	17.11.93	J Britton Broomclose Farm, Longbridge Deverill		1.11.07P
	(Rotax 582)			(New owner 2.08)		
G-MYNL	Pegasus Quantum 15	6648	17.11.93	S.J.Whalley	(Stoke-on-Trent)	21.12.07P
	(Rotax 582)					
G-MYNN	Pegasus Quantum 15	6679	17.11.93	V Loy	(North Coates)	12.2.08P
	(Rotax 582)					
G-MYNO	Pegasus Quantum 15	6724	10.1.94	A J Hodson	Sissinghurst, Cranbrook	20.4.08P
	(Rotax 582)					
G-MYNP	Pegasus Quantum 15	6688	17.11.93	K A Davidson	(Dunfermline)	22.7.07P
	(Rotax 582)					
G-MYNR	Pegasus Quantum 15 Super Sport	6692	17.11.93	C A Reynolds	Clench Common	18.4.08P
	(Rotax 582)					
G-MYNS	Pegasus Quantum 15	6694	17.11.93	F J Mcvey	Insch	26.4.08P
	(Rotax 582)					
G-MYNT	Pegasus Quantum 15	6693	17.11.93	C D Arnold	Craysmarsh Farm, Melksham	8.5.08P
	(Rotax 582)					
G-MYNV	Pegasus Quantum 15	6725	10.1.94	J Goldsmith-Ryan	Eaglescott	1.6.07P
	(Rotax 582)					
G-MYNX	CFM Streak Shadow SA-M	K 193-SA-M	15.6.92	T J and M.D Palmer	(Symington, Kilmarnock)	23.10.04P
	(Built P A White - pr.no.PFA 206-12268) (Rotax 618)			(Noted 10.06)		
G-MYNY	Kolb Twinstar Mk.3	K0014-0693	22.11.93	B Alexander	Swinford, Rugby	25.8.98P
	(Built W R C Williams-Wynne - pr.no.PFA 205-12478)			(Noted 5.05)		
G-MYNZ	Pegasus Quantum 15	6709	18.1.94	P W Rogers	(Shawforth, Rochdale)	17.2.07P
	(Rotax 582)					
G-MYOA	Rans S-6-ESD Coyote II	0793.523	23.11.93	R W Trenholm tr Orcas Syndicate		
	(Built H Lang - pr.no.PFA 204-12578) (Tri-cycle u/c)				Otherton, Cannock	30.3.08P
G-MYOB	Mainair Mercury	976-1293-7-W772	8.12.93	P J Higgins (New owner 5.06) Gedney Dyke, Lutton		19.7.05P
G-MYOF	Mainair Mercury	975-1293-7-W771	3.12.93	G Bonnar	Swinford, Rugby	9.3.08P
G-MYOG	Kolb Twinstar Mk.3	K0011-0193	19.1.94	A P de Legh	Redhill	9.9.08P
	(Built A P de Legh - pr.no.PFA 205-12449) (Hirth 2706)					
G-MYOH	CFM Shadow Series CD	K 201	27.1.94	D R Sutton	Brook Farm, Pilling	13.8.08P
G-MYOI	Rans S-6-ESD Coyote II	1292.409	3.2.94	A W Paterson	Strathaven	15.4.08P
	(Built P F Hill - pr.no.PFA 204-12503) (Tailwheel u/c)					
G-MYOL	Air Création/Fun 18S GT bis	94/001	7.2.94	S N Bond	Sywell	29.3.08P
	(Rotax 447)					
G-MYOM	Mainair Gemini Flash IIA	981-0294-7-W777	14.2.94	M A Haughey	Newtownards	18.3.07P
	(Rotax 582)					
G-MYON	CFM Shadow Series CD	240	12.1.94	D W and S E Suttill	(Sykehouse, Goole)	20.12.05P
G-MYOO	Kolb Twinstar Mk.3M	K0004-0192	11.5.92	P D Coppin	Lee-on-Solent	16.11.05P
	(Built P D Coppin and P Watmough - pr.no.PFA 205-12200)					
G-MYOR	Kolb Twinstar Mk.3	PFA 205-12602	16.2.94	J J Littler	Chichester	25.4.08P
	(Built O J and J H Stodhert) (Hirth 2705 RO6)					
G-MYOS	CFM Shadow Series CD	246	18.2.94	E J and C A Bowles	Craysmarsh Farm, Melksham	25.10.08P
G-MYOT	Rans S-6-ESD Coyote II	0893.525	21.2.94	D E Wilson	Davidstow Moor	30.5.08P
	(Built R T Mosforth - pr.no.PFA 204-12668) (Tail-wheel u/c)					
G-MYOU	Pegasus Quantum 15	6726	1.3.94	M Botten and O Kent	Plaistows Farm, St Albans	22.11.08P
	(Rotax 582)					
G-MYOV	Mainair Mercury	K979-0294-7-W775	1.3.94	P Newton	(Buxton)	14.12.03P
G-MYOW	Mainair Gemini Flash IIA	983-0294-7-W779	16.3.94	A J A Fowler	Corn Wood Farm, Adversane	17.9.07P
G-MYOX	Mainair Mercury	K984-0294-7-W780	23.2.94	K Driver	Headon Farm, Retford	6.10.08P
G-MYOY	Cyclone Airsports AX3/503	C 3123191	23.2.94	M R Smith	Otherton, Cannock	16.7.08P
G-MYOZ	BFC Challenger II	UK CH2-1093-1045	24.2.94	A R Thomson	Longside, Peterhead	15.8.08P
	(Built P F Bockh - pr.no.PFA 177A-12640) (Rotax 503)					
G-MYPA	Rans S-6-ESD Coyote II	0893.527	24.2.94	R S McLeister	Tarn Farm, Cockerham	25.1.08P
	(Built E J Garner - pr.no.PFA 204-12509) (Tail-wheel u/c)					
G-MYPC	Kolb Twinstar Mk.3	K0012-0199	2.3.94	J Young and S Hussain	Otherton, Cannock	17.2.07P
	(Built R Pattrick - pr.no.PFA 205-12437)					
G-MYPE	Mainair Gemini Flash IIA	985-0394-7-W781	11.3.94	R Cant	(Musselburgh)	19.2.08P
	(Rotax 582)					
G-MYPG	Solar Wings Pegasus XL-Q	SW-WQ-0176	29.3.89	R D Howie	(Grays)	7.7.08P
G-MYPH	Pegasus Quantum 15	6764	11.3.94	P M J White	Wombleton	8.9.08P
	(Rotax 582)					
G-MYPI	Pegasus Quantum 15	6767	11.3.94	P L Jarvis	Stoke, Isle of Grain	10.9.08P
	(Rotax 582)					
G-MYPJ	Rans S-6-ESD Coyote II	1293.569	18.3.94	K A Eden	Brook Farm, Pilling	9.9.05P
	(Built A W Fish - pr.no.PFA 204-12692) (Tri-cycle u/c)					

G-MYPL	CFM Shadow Series CD	K 213	14. 2.94	G I Madden	(Loughton, Milton Keynes)	11. 7.07P
	(Built CFM Metal-Fax - pr.no.BMAA/HB/080)					
G-MYPM	Cyclone Airsports AX3/503	C 3123188	23. 3.94	Microflight Ireland Ltd	Mullaghmore, Coleraine	26. 6.03P
				(Noted derelict 7.06)		
G-MYPN	Pegasus Quantum 15	6727	12. 4.94	P J S Albon	Sywell	19. 5.08P
	(Rotax 582)					
G-MYPP	Whittaker MW6-S Fatboy Flyer	PFA 164-12413	11. 4.94	G Everett and D Smith	(Maidstone)	1. 4.08P
	(Built D S L Evans)					
G-MYPR	Cyclone Airsports AX3/503	C 3123190	13. 4.94	W R Hibberd	Otherton, Cannock	24. 8.08P
G-MYPS	Whittaker MW6 Merlin	PFA 164-11585	19. 4.94	I S Bishop	Bicester	10. 4.06P
	(Built I S Bishop) (Rotax 503)					
G-MYPT	CFM Shadow Series CD	K 212	22. 4.94	M G and S A Collins	(Oldbury-on-Severn)	13.10.07P
G-MYPV	Mainair Mercury	986-0394-7-W782	18. 3.94	B Donnan	Swinford, Rugby	12. 3.08P
	(Rotax 582)					
G-MYPW	Mainair Gemini Flash IIA	991-0494-7-W787	3. 5.94	T C Edwards	Hunsdon	24. 5.07P
	(Rotax 582)					
G-MYPX	Pegasus Quantum 15	6785	28. 4.94	P J Callis and M Aylett	Swinford, Rugby	23. 6.08P
	(Rotax 582) (Believed to have used "B Conditions" marks "G-69-29" during trials)					
G-MYPY	Pegasus Quantum 15	6786	12. 5.94	C J Johnson	Elm Farm, Wickford	29. 8.08P
	(Rotax 582)					
G-MYPZ	BFC Challenger II UK	CH2-1093-UK-1046	2. 3.94	E G Astin	Whitby	14.10.05P
	(Built E G Astin - pr.no.PFA 177A-12689) (Hirth 2706) (Regd incorrectly as CH2-0194-UK-1046)					
G-MYRB	Whittaker MW5 Sorcerer	PFA 163-11543	14. 4.94	P J Careless	(Little Paxton, St Neots)	
	(Built P J Careless)					
G-MYRC	Mainair Blade	988-0594-7-W784	1. 6.94	T C Brown and J Murphy	Mill Farm, Shifnal	14. 8.08P
	(Rotax 462)					
G-MYRD	Mainair Blade	989-0594-7-W785	20. 5.94	W J Walker	Tarn Farm, Cockerham	21. 2.08P
	(Rotax 582)					
G-MYRE	Cyclone Airsports Chaser S	CH863	10. 5.94	S W Barker	(Scalby, Scarborough)	3. 6.07P
	(Rotax 377)				*(New owner 9.07)*	
G-MYRF	Pegasus Quantum 15	6795	13. 5.94	C Cartwright and B Vincent	Rochdale	22. 5.08P
	(Rotax 462HP)					
G-MYRG	TEAM Mini-MAX 88	PFA 186-11891	17. 5.94	V Grayson	Stoke, Isle of Grain	5. 3.08P
	(Built D G Burrows)					
G-MYRH	BFC Challenger II UK	CH2-1093-1044	10. 3.94	C M Gray	Lee-on-Solent	6. 9.07P
	(Built R T Hall - pr.no.PFA 177A-12690) (Rotax 582)					
G-MYRJ	BFC Challenger II UK	CH2-1093-1042	28. 3.94	C G Trow	Clench Common	21.10.08P
	(Built H F Breakwell and P Woodcock - pr.no.PFA 177A-12658) (Rotax 582)					
G-MYRK	Murphy Renegade Spirit UK	PFA 188-11425	3.10.89	D J Newton	(Cropwell Bishop, Nottingham)	7. 8.08P
	(Built J Brown - c/n 215)					
G-MYRL	TEAM Mini-MAX 91	PFA 186-11967	17. 5.94	J N Hanson	Brook Farm, Pilling	26. 3.08P
	(Built W W Vinten)					
G-MYRM	Pegasus Quantum 15	6800	26. 5.94	G Turner	(Haverhill)	23.10.08P
	(Rotax 582)					
G-MYRN	Pegasus Quantum 15	6801	26. 5.94	G Ferries	Insch	5. 3.07P
	(Rotax 582)				*(Noted 4.07)*	
G-MYRO	Cyclone Airsports AX3/503	C 4043211	6. 6.94	R I Simpson	Clipgate Farm, Denton	22. 8.08P
G-MYRP	Letov LK-2M Sluka	829409x09?	6. 6.94	R M C Hunter	Blue Tile Farm, Hindolveston	7.11.04P
	(Built R L Jones - pr.no.PFA 263-12725) (Rotax 447)					
G-MYRR	Letov LK-2M Sluka	0205	10. 6.94	M Tormey	(Sligo)	18.10.08P
	(Officially regd with c/n 05)					
G-MYRS	Pegasus Quantum 15	6803	13. 6.94	R M Summers	Perth	28. 7.08P
	(Rotax 582)					
G-MYRT	Pegasus Quantum 15	6732	1. 3.94	M C Taylor	Eastbach Farm, Coleford	16. 8.08P
	(Rotax 582)					
G-MYRU	Cyclone Airsports AX3/503	C 4043210	7. 6.94	W A Emmerson	(Newcastle-upon-Tyne)	6. 7.08P
G-MYRV	Cyclone Airsports AX3/503	C 4043209	8. 6.94	M Gardiner	Emlyn's Field, Rhuallt	4. 7.08P
G-MYRW	Mainair Mercury	999-0694-7-W795	17. 6.94	G C Hobson	St Michaels	5. 7.08P
				(Operated Northern Microlight School)		
G-MYRY	Pegasus Quantum Lite	6813	15. 6.94	G M Cruise-Smith	Roddige	20. 1.07P
	(Rotax 582)					
G-MYRZ	Pegasus Quantum 15	6812	15. 6.94	G D Black	Perth	31. 8.08P
	(Rotax 582)					
G-MYSA	Cyclone Airsports Chaser S 508	CH.864	15. 6.94	P Nicholls	Shobdon	13. 4.05P
G-MYSB	Pegasus Quantum 15	6809	22. 6.94	P H Woodward	Roddige	29. 3.07P
	(Rotax 582)					
G-MYSC	Pegasus Quantum 15	6811	22. 6.94	K R White	Dunkeswell	7. 7.08P
	(Rotax 582)					
G-MYSD	BFC Challenger II	CH2-1093-1043	23. 6.94	C E Bell	Spanhoe	6. 8.07P
	(Built C E Bell - pr.no.PFA 177A-12688)					
G-MYSG	Mainair Mercury	K993-0694-7-W790	12. 7.94	N Whitaker	(Whitchurch, Shropshire)	28.12.07P
	(Rotax 582)					
G-MYSI	Mignet HM.14/93	PFA 255-12700	18. 7.94	A R D Seaman	(Dagenham)	
	(Built A R D Seaman)					
G-MYSJ	Mainair Gemini Flash IIA	1001-0894-7-W797	2. 8.94	A Warnock	Newtownards	21. 8.08P
	(Rotax 503)					
G-MYSK	TEAM Mini-MAX 91	PFA 186-12203	25. 7.94	A D Bolshaw	Brook Farm, Pilling	1. 8.02P
	(Built K Worthington)				*(Operated Brook Farm Microlight Centre)*	
G-MYSL	Aviasud Mistral 582GB	066 83-DE	27. 2.92	N W Cawley	Griffins Farm, Temple Bruer	23. 8.08P
	(Built Aviasud Engineering - pr.no..BMAA/HB/007)					
G-MYSM	CFM Shadow Series CD	K 243	22. 3.94	L W Stevens	Black Spring Farm, Castle Bytham	10.10.03P
	(Built CFM Metal-Fax - pr.no.BMAA/HB/049)				*(Noted 2.08)*	
G-MYSO	Cyclone Airsports AX3/503	C 4043215	1. 8.94	N J Stoneman and S Mather	(Stoke, Kent)	22. 3.06P

G-MYSP	Rans S-6-ESD Coyote II	0392-284		26. 5.92	A J Alexander, K G Diamond and B Knight	Redhill	28.11.07P
	(Built S Palmer - pr.no.PFA 204-12265) (Rotax 582) (Tri-cycle u/c)						
G-MYSR	Pegasus Quantum 15	6837		3. 8.94	W G Craig	(Dunfermline)	11.10.07P
	(Rotax 582)						
G-MYSU	Rans S-6-ESD Coyote II	0394.600		5. 8.94	K W Allan	Drummaird Farm, Bonnybank	20. 7.07P
	(Built I Whyte - pr.no.PFA 204-12753)						
G-MYSV	Aerial Arts Chaser S	CH.812	(ex Korea)	24. 8.94	R J Sims and I G Reason	(Salisbury)	22. 7.06P
	(Rotax 377)						
G-MYSW	Pegasus Quantum 15	6834		13. 7.94	C T D Whipps	(Thorrington, Colchester	26. 3.08P
	(Rotax 582)						
G-MYSX	Pegasus Quantum 15	6832		13. 7.94	J L Treves	Longacre Farm, Sandy	7. 6.07P
	(Rotax 503)						
G-MYSY	Pegasus Quantum 15	6864		15. 8.94	B D S Vere	Eaglescott	8. 6.08P
	(Rotax 582)						
G-MYSZ	Mainair Mercury	1006-0894-7-W802		2. 9.94	M A Scholes	Broadmeadow Farm, Hereford	8.12.07P
	(C/n confirmed but see G-MYYY)						
G-MYTB	Mainair Mercury	1004-0894-7-W800		19. 8.94	P J Higgin Red House Farm, Gedney Dyke, Lutton		23. 7.07P
	(Rotax 582)						
G-MYTC	Solar Wings Pegasus XL-Q	SW-WQ-0246	(ex...)	28. 9.94	M J Edmett (New owner 5.02)	(London N3)	
G-MYTD	Mainair Blade	1002-0894-7-W798		18. 8.94	M P Law and B E Warburton	St Michaels	18. 4.08P
	(Rotax 582)						
G-MYTE	Rans S-6-ESD Coyote II	0394.598		22. 7.94	N D Austin	(Borehamwood)	14. 5.07P
	(Built AJ Bourner - pr.no.PFA 204-12718) (Tail-wheel u/c)						
G-MYTG	Mainair Blade	1008-0994-7-W804		16. 9.94	O P Farrell		
	(Rotax 582)				Carstown, Ballymakenny, Drogheda, County Louth		24. 3.08P
G-MYTH	CFM Shadow Series CD	089		7.11.88	H A Leek	Spanhoe	31. 8.08P
G-MYTI	Pegasus Quantum 15	6874		6.10.94	(J Madhvani)	Plaistows Farm, St Albans	26. 2.07P
	(Rotax 582)						
G-MYTJ	Pegasus Quantum 15	6877		29. 9.94	M Jones	Roddige	23. 8.08P
	(Rotax 582)						
G-MYTK	Mainair Mercury	1009-1094-7-W805		29. 9.94	D A Holroyd	Hunsdon	21. 7.08P
G-MYTL	Mainair Blade	1010-1094-7-W807		4.10.94	S Ostrowski	Davidstow Moor	26. 7.05P
	(Rotax 582)						
G-MYTM	Cyclone Airsports AX3/503	C 3123189		13. 4.94	J P Gardiner	(Farnworth)	15.10.07P
G-MYTN	Pegasus Quantum 15	6878		30. 9.94	M Hoggett and M F Ambrose	Sutton Meadows	25. 7.08P
	(Rotax 503)						
G-MYTO	Quad City Challenger II UK	PFA 177-12583		22. 7.94	R W Sage	Priory Farm, Tibenham	16. 4.01P
	(Built K B Tolley and D M Cottingham) (Hirth 2705.R06)				(Noted 2007)		
G-MYTP	CGS Arrow Flight Hawk II	?	N215	6.10.94	R J Turner	Otherton, Cannock	12. 7.05P
	(Built M Whittaker - pr.no.PFA 266-12801: additional c/ns reported ie 215 & H-CGS-489-P but believed former taken from p/i) (Rotax 503)						
G-MYTT	Quad City Challenger II	PFA 177-12761		11.10.94	J Bolton	Pittrichie Farm, Whiterashes	7.11.08P
	(Built P L Fisk - c/n CH2-0394-UK-111)						
G-MYTU	Mainair Blade	1011-1094-7-W808		21.10.94	C J Barker	Watnall	26. 7.07P
	(Rotax 582)				(Noted 10.07)		
G-MYTV	Huntwing Avon	9204010		13.10.94	M Carson	Weston Zoyland	23. 8.08P
	(Built M P Hadden - pr.no.BMAA/HB/029) (Rotax 503)						
G-MYTX	Mainair Mercury	K1003-0894-7-W799		23. 9.94	R Steel	Rufforth	29. 9.08P
G-MYTY	CFM Streak Shadow M	K 242		11. 7.94	K H A Negal	Enstone	6. 6.02P
	(Built N R Beale - pr.no.PFA 206-12607) (Rotax 912-UL)						
G-MYTZ	Air Création 503/Fun 18S GT bis	94/003		7.11.94	B J Curtis	(Todmorden)	15. 9.07P
G-MYUA	Air Création 503/Fun 18S GT bis	94/002		8.11.94	J Leden	Darley Moor, Ashbourne	26. 8.08P
	(To be fitted with Rotax 582 from wrecked Snowbird G-MVCJ)						
G-MYUB	Mainair Mercury	1014-1194-7-W812		14.12.94	T A Ross (Noted 3.06)	Arclid Green, Sandbach	7.10.05P
G-MYUC	Mainair Blade	1015-1294-7-W813		16.11.94	A D Clayton	St Michaels	4.11.08P
	(Rotax 462)						
G-MYUD	Mainair Mercury	1016-1294-7-W814		24.11.94	P W Margetson	Deenethorpe	17. 4.08P
	(Rotax 582)						
G-MYUE	Mainair Mercury	1017-1294-7-W815		22.11.94	G J Digby	(Southend-on-Sea)	20. 5.08P
	(Rotax 582)						
G-MYUF	Murphy Renegade Spirit	PFA 188-12795		16.11.94	F Overall	Whitehall Farm, Wethersfield	6. 2.08P
	(Built C J Dale) (Jabiru 2200A)						
G-MYUH	Solar Wings Pegasus XL-Q	6810		28.11.94	K S Daniels	(London Colney)	14. 9.08P
	(C/n 6810 refers to new Sailwing - Trike unit is ex-G-MVKR (SW-TE-0123)						
G-MYUI	Cyclone Airsports AX3/503	C 4043213		13.12.94	R and M Bailey	Plaistows Farm, St Albans	31. 7.08P
	(C/n carried is C 102822 and probably results from a changed monopole)						
G-MYUK	Mainair Mercury	1020-0195-7-W818		12.12.94	S Lear	Plaistows Farm, St Albans	6. 9.06P
	(Rotax 462)						
G-MYUN	Mainair Blade	1019-0195-7-W817		5.12.94	G A Barratt	(Longridge, Preston)	27. 2.08P
	(Rotax 582)						
G-MYUO	Pegasus Quantum 15	6911		23. 1.95	G R I Tyler	Sutton Meadows	14. 4.08P
	(Rotax 582)						
G-MYUP	Letov LK-2M Sluka	829409x24		20.12.94	J C Dawson	(Oxspring, Sheffield)	29. 8.08P
	(Built F Overall - pr.no.PFA 263-12785 also c/n UK.2) (Rotax 447)						
G-MYUR	Huntwing Avon	9409030		24. 1.95	T C Saltmarsh	Rayne Hall Farm, Braintree	30. 3.05P
	(Built S D Pain - pr.no.BMAA/HB/034) (Rotax 582)				(Noted 1.07)		
G-MYUS	CFM Shadow Series CD	257		26. 1.95	R G M-J Proost tr Aviation for Paraplegics and Tetraplegics Trust		
						Old Sarum	22. 6.08P
G-MYUU	Pegasus Quantum 15	6917		30. 1.95	J A Slocombe	(Backfields, Rochester)	29. 7.08P
	(Rotax 462)						
G-MYUV	Pegasus Quantum 15	6918		6. 2.95	D W Wilson	Mapperley	29.10.08P
	(Rotax 582)						
G-MYUW	Mainair Mercury	1024-0295-7-W822		7. 2.95	G C Hobson	St Michaels	18.11.08P
G-MYUZ	Rans S-6-ESD Coyote II	1293.568		5. 1.95	J E Gattrell and A R Trace	Sittles Farm, Alrewas	19. 6.08P
	(Built D K Ross and B Davies - pr.no.PFA 204-12741) (Rotax 582) (Tri-cycle u/c)						

G-MYVA	Kolb Twinstar Mk.3	PFA 205-12756		13. 2.95	E Bayliss	Ince Blundell	20. 8.08P
	(Built S P Read)						
G-MYVB	Mainair Blade	1021-0195-7-W819		15.12.94	P J Lomax and J A Robinson	St Michaels	24. 4.08P
	(Rotax 582)						
G-MYVC	Pegasus Quantum 15	6904		13. 2.95	R Howes and O Lloyd	Roddige	13.10.07P
	(Rotax 582)						
G-MYVE	Mainair Blade	1027-0295-7-W825		8. 2.95	S Cooke	Tarn Farm, Cockerham	16. 7.08P
	(Rotax 582)						
G-MYVG	Letov LK-2M Sluka	829409x26		15. 2.95	N I Garland	Dunkeswell	28. 9.05P
	(Built L W M Summers - pr.no.PFA 263-12786) (Rotax 447)				*(New owner 2.07)*		
G-MYVH	Mainair Blade	1028-0295-7-W826		21. 2.95	S E Wilks	Knapthorpe Lodge, Caunton	14. 3.08P
G-MYVI	Air Création 503/Fun 18S GT bis	94/004		17. 2.95	P Osborne tr Northampton Aerotow Club	Sywell	14. 6.07P
					(Noted 10.07)		
G-MYVJ	Pegasus Quantum 15	6974		24. 2.95	P W Davidson and A I McPherson		
	(Rotax 582)					Pratis Farm, Leven	7. 4.08P
G-MYVK	Pegasus Quantum 15	6970		27. 2.95	J Thomas	(Burnham-on-Sea)	1. 5.08P
	(Rotax 582)						
G-MYVL	Mainair Mercury	1030-0395-7-W828		1. 3.95	P J Judge	Davidstow Moor	5. 8.07P
	(Rotax 462)						
G-MYVM	Pegasus Quantum 15	6893	G-69-17	9. 3.95	G J Gibson	Perth	27. 4.97P
	(Rotax 582)		G-MYVM		*(Noted 10.07)*		
G-MYVN	Cyclone Airsports AX3/503	C 4043212		16. 3.95	F Watt	Insch	5.10.03P
G-MYVO	Mainair Blade	1013-1194-7-W811		8.11.94	S S Raines	Shobdon	17. 5.08P
	(Rotax 582)						
G-MYVP	Rans S-6-ESD Coyote II	0294.593		27. 3.95	P J Reeves	Walkeridge Farm, Overton	19. 7.08P
	(Built J S Liming - pr.no.PFA 204-12828) (Tri-cycle u/c)						
G-MYVR	Pegasus Quantum 15	6980		21. 3.95	J M Webster	Mapperley	29. 5.07P
	(Rotax 582)				*(Noted 10.07)*		
G-MYVS	Mainair Mercury	1037-0495-7-W835		12. 4.95	P S Flynn	Sandtoft	25. 4.04P
	(Rotax 462)						
G-MYVT	Letov LK-2M Sluka	829409x25		17. 3.95	J P Gardiner	(Newton Bank Farm, Daresbury)	11.11.03P
	(Built J Hannibal - pr.no.PFA 263-12835) (Rotax 447)				*(Noted 11.04)*		
G-MYVV	Medway Hybred 44XLR	MR127/109		3. 4.95	S Perity	(Wisbech)	11. 5.07P
	(Rotax 503) (Sailwing c/n also quoted for G-MYLX)						
G-MYVY	Mainair Blade	1033-0495-7-W831		29. 3.95	G Heeks	Mill Farm, Shifnal	2. 3.08P
	(Rotax 582)						
G-MYVZ	Mainair Blade	1034-0495-7-W832		31. 3.95	R Llewellyn	Landmead Farm, Garford	31. 7.08P
	(Rotax 582)						
G-MYWA	Mainair Mercury	1035-0495-7-W833		30. 3.95	R A Atkinson		
					Ardenagh Great, Taghmon, County Wexford		19.10.08P
G-MYWC	Huntwing Avon	9409038		3. 4.95	M A Coffin	(Wrotham, Sevenoaks)	24. 6.05P
	(Built F J C Binks - pr.no.BMAA/HB/043) (Rotax 503)						
G-MYWD	Thruster T 600N	9035-T600-511	(G-MYOJ)	18. 4.95	M D Kirby	Chase Farm, Little Bursted	16. 8.05P
	(Rotax 582)				*(Substantially damaged after somersaulting during take-off Seething 17. 9.05)*		
G-MYWE	Thruster T 600T	9035-T600-512	(G-MYOK)	18. 4.95	W A Stephenson	(Newry, County Armagh)	1. 8.08P
	(Rotax 503)						
G-MYWG	Pegasus Quantum 15	6998		20. 4.95	S L Greene	Plaistows Farm, St Albans	30. 5.08P
	(Rotax 582)						
G-MYWH	Huntwing/Experience	9409025		20.12.94	R S Sanby	(Eastwood, Nottingham)	
	(Built G N Hatchett - pr.no.BMAA/HB/037)						
G-MYWI	Pegasus Quantum 15	7006		1. 5.95	J R Fulcher	Deenethorpe	14. 6.08P
	(Rotax 582)						
G-MYWJ	Pegasus Quantum 15	6919		24. 1.95	L M Sams	Long Marston	2. 9.08P
	(Rotax 582)						
G-MYWK	Pegasus Quantum 15	7011		1. 5.95	G Hanna	(Drogheda, County Louth)	9. 5.08P
	(Rotax 582)						
G-MYWL	Pegasus Quantum 15	6995		2. 5.95	E Smith	Swinford, Rugby	27. 5.08P
	(Rotax 582)						
G-MYWM	CFM Shadow Series CD	K 227		9. 5.95	N J Mckinley	Plaistows Farm, St Albans	10. 3.07P
	(Built CFM Metal-Fax - pr.no.BMAA/HB/056)						
G-MYWN	Cyclone Airsports Chaser S 508	CH.865		9. 5.95	N R Beale	Deppers Bridge, Southam	21. 7.08P
	(Conceived as Aerial Arts Chaser with c/n CH865, this was built under Cyclone c/n 7016)						
G-MYWO	Cyclone Pegasus Quantum 15	6932		9. 5.95	S Gill and D Hume	Stanton, Morpeth	21.11.07P
	(Rotax 582)						
G-MYWP	Kolb Twinstar Mk.3	K0017-0993		7. 3.95	P R Day	(Southampton)	15. 6.06P
	(Built B Albiston - pr.no.PFA 205-12561)						
G-MYWR	Cyclone Pegasus Quantum 15	7002		10. 5.95	R Horton	(Allestree, Derby)	28. 9.08P
	(Rotax 582)				*(Also carries US Ultralight marks "E032RH")*		
G-MYWS	Cyclone Airsports Chaser S 447	6946 & CH.866		17. 5.95	M H Broadbent	Westfield Farm, Hailsham	6.11.07P
	(Conceived as Aerial Arts Chaser with c/n CH866, this was built under Cyclone c/n 6946)						
G-MYWT	Pegasus Quantum 15	6997		19. 5.95	A G Ransom	Sywell	7.11.06P
	(Rotax 582)						
G-MYWU	Pegasus Quantum 15	7024		25. 5.95	J R Buttle	Dunkeswell	20. 7.08P
	(Rotax 582)						
G-MYWV	Rans S-4C Coyote	93.212		30. 5.95	I D Daniels	Maypole Farm, Chislet	28. 1.08P
	(Built A H Trapp - pr.no.PFA 193-12826)						
G-MYWW	Pegasus Quantum 15	7021		30. 5.95	C W Bailie	Newtownards	3.11.07P
	(Rotax 503)						
G-MYWY	Pegasus Quantum 15	6982		20. 3.95	Annabel Czajka	Stoke, Isle of Grain	11. 4.08P
	(Rotax 582)						
G-MYWZ	Thruster TST Mk.1	8128-TST-115	G-MVMJ	22. 2.93	W H J KNowles	Yundum/Banjul, Gambia	29. 9.04P
	(Rotax 503)						
G-MYXA	TEAM Mini-MAX 91	PFA 186-12266		13. 6.95	D H Clack	Henstridge	5.11.08P
	(Built D S Worman)						

G-MYXB	Rans S-6-ESD Coyote II	1293.567	20. 6.95	V G J Davies and D A Hall	Lee-on-Solent	7.11.07P
	(Built A Aldridge - pr.no.PFA 204-12787) (Tri-cycle u/c)					
G-MYXC	Quad City Challenger II UK CH2-0294-UK-1099		16. 5.95	K N Dickinson	Higher Barn Farm, Houghton	
	(Built K N Dickinson) (Hirth H2706)			*(Noted 6.05)*		
G-MYXD	Solar Wings Pegasus Quasar IITC	7029	21. 6.95	A Cochrane	Longacre Farm, Sandy	21. 4.08P
	(Rotax 582)					
G-MYXE	Pegasus Quantum 15	7061	23. 6.95	W Bowen	Plaistows Farm, St Albans	1. 2.08P
	(Rotax 582)					
G-MYXF	Air Création 503/Fun 18S GT bis	94/005	23. 6.95	T A Morgan	Popham	15. 1.01P
G-MYXG	Rans S-6-ESD Coyote II	0394.599	29. 6.95	G H Lee	Higher Barn Farm, Houghton	20. 6.01P
	(Built G H Lee - pr.no.PFA 204-12879) (Tri-cycle u/c)			*(Noted 6.05)*		
G-MYXH	Cyclone Airsports AX3/503	7028	3. 7.95	S Bayes	Baxby Manor, Husthwaite	13. 3.08P
G-MYXI	Cook Aries 1	xxxx	4. 7.95	H Cook	(Newport, Gwent)	
	(Built H Cook -pr.no. BMAA/HB/048) (Design awaiting finalisation 10.01- planned engine fit is BMW R80)					
G-MYXJ	Mainair Blade	1048-0795-7-W846	17. 7.95	D W Watson	Eshott	9. 1.05P
	(Rotax 582)			*(New owner 10.07)*		
G-MYXK	BFC Challenger II	CH2-1194-1254	11. 7.95	V Vaughan	Kilrush, County Kildare	24. 9.08P
	(Built E G Astin - c/n PFA 177A-12877) (Rotax 503)					
G-MYXL	Mignet HM-1000 Balerit	112	11. 7.95	R W Hollamby	Bardown, Wadhurst	17. 7.08P
G-MYXM	Mainair Blade	1047-0795-7-W845	19. 7.95	S C Hodgson	(Chesterfield)	3.11.07P
	(Rotax 582)					
G-MYXN	Mainair Blade	1046-0795-7-W844	27. 7.95	M R Sands	Shotton Colliery, Peterlee	10. 4.08P
	(Rotax 582)					
G-MYXO	Letov LK-2M Sluka	8295s001	27. 7.95	G W Allport	Mill Farm, Shifnal	27. 7.06P
	(Built K C Rutland - pr.no.PFA 263-12873 (Rotax 447)			*(Noted 11.07)*		
G-MYXP	Rans S-6-ESD Coyote II	0494.605	31. 7.95	R S Amor	Weston Zoyland	1. 9.08P
	(Built K J Lywood - pr.no.PFA 204-12886) (Tail-wheel u/c)					
G-MYXR	Murphy Renegade Spirit UK PFA 188-12755		2. 8.95	S Hooker	(Sellinge, Ashford)	
	(Built S Hooker)					
G-MYXS	Kolb Twinstar Mk.3	K0015-0693	4. 5.94	D Robertson	(Cottam, Preston)	27 9.08P
	(Built M A Smith - pr.no.PFA 205-12528)					
G-MYXT	Pegasus Quantum 15	7073	4. 8.95	P G Hill	(Southwater, Horsham)	8. 4.08P
	(Rotax 582)					
G-MYXU	Thruster T 300	9024-T300-513	16. 8.95	D W Wilson	(Mullahead, Tandragee)	20. 9.08P
	(Built Tempest Aviation Ltd) (Rotax 582)					
G-MYXV	Quad City Challenger II UK CH2-1194-UK-1243		19. 7.95	M L Sumner	(Market Drayton)	14.10.08P
	(Built A Hipkin)					
G-MYXW	Pegasus Quantum 15	7090	24. 8.95	P J Oakey	Lower Mountpleasant Farm, Chatteris	3. 8.08P
	(Rotax 582)					
G-MYXX	Pegasus Quantum 15	7081	25. 8.95	J H Arnold	Milverton, Taunton	3.11.08P
	(Rotax 582)					
G-MYXY	CFM Shadow Series CD	K 245	29. 8.95	A P Watkins and C W J Davis	Roddige	8.12.08P
	(Built CFM Metal-Fax - pr.no.BMAA/HB/059)					
G-MYXZ	Pegasus Quantum 15	7023	21. 6.95	J Ayre	Roddige	1. 1.08P
	(Rotax 582)					
G-MYYA	Mainair Blade	1052-0995-7-W850	1. 9.95	D J Cook	(Northwich)	26. 4.08P
	(Rotax 462)					
G-MYYB	Pegasus Quantum 15 Lite	7079	4. 9.95	A L Johnson	Longacre Farm, Sandy	8.11.07P
G-MYYC	Pegasus Quantum 15	7094	12. 9.95	G F Atkinson	Rufforth	9. 3.08P
	(Rotax 582)					
G-MYYD	Cyclone Airsports Chaser S 447	CH.7099	15. 9.95	K A Armstrong	Linley Hill, Leven	15. 5.07P
G-MYYE	Huntwing Avon 462	9409035	21. 9.95	A J Clarke	(Dunnington, Alcester)	6. 3.08P
	(Built P J Dickinson - pr.no.BMAA/HB/041)					
G-MYYF	Quad City Challenger II UK PFA 177-12811		27. 9.95	J G and J A Smith	Longside, Peterhead	29. 4.08P
	(Built G Ferries)					
G-MYYG	Mainair Blade	1054-0995-7-W852	4.10.95	Angelika Corson	(Beccles)	15.11.03P
	(Rotax 462) (Believed supplied as kit, if so c/n should be K1054-...)					
G-MYYH	Mainair Blade	1056-1095-7-W854	3.10.95	C Nicholson	(Halifax)	2. 8.08P
	(Rotax 582)					
G-MYYI	Pegasus Quantum 15	7101	28. 9.95	M R Rowlands	(Sutton-in-Ashfield)	17.11.04P
	(Rotax 582)					
G-MYYJ	Huntwing Avon	9409033	29. 9.95	R M Jarvis	(Stilton, Peterborough)	
	(Built M J Slatter - pr.no.BMAA/HB/033) (Rotax 503)			*(New owner 11.06)*		
G-MYYK	Pegasus Quantum 15	7100	2.10.95	J D and N G Philp	Lower Upham Farm, Chiseldon	6. 6.08P
	(Rotax 582)					
G-MYYL	Cyclone Airsports AX3/503	7110	4.10.95	D Bedborough	Sywell	13. 9.08P
G-MYYN	Pegasus Quantum 15	7022	3.10.95	J Darby	(Stirling)	13. 2.06P
	(Rotax 582)					
G-MYYP	AMF Microflight Chevvron 2-32C	036	31.10.95	V A L Fahie tr Chevvron Group 1		
					(Stour Row, Shaftesbury)	9. 1.08P
G-MYYR	TEAM Mini-MAX 91	PFA 186-12724	31.10.95	K Stevens	Otherton, Cannock	7.11.05P
	(Built D Palmer)					
G-MYYS	TEAM Mini-MAX	PFA 186-11989	7.11.95	J R Hopkinson	(Chesterfield)	
	(Built J R Hopkinson					
G-MYYU	Mainair Mercury	1062-1295-7-W862	17.11.95	J T and A C Swannick	Ince Blundell	18. 4.06P
G-MYYV	Rans S-6-ESD-XL Coyote II	0896.1026	17.11.95	M B Buttle	Tarn Farm, Cockerham	2. 5.08P
	(Built J Whiting - pr.no.PFA 204-12943: originally kit no.0795.851) (Tri-cycle u/c)					
G-MYYW	Mainair Blade	1051-0895-7-W849	8. 8.95	M D Kirby	Chase Farm, Little Bursted	24. 5.08P
	(Rotax 582)					
G-MYYX	Pegasus Quantum 15	7126	17.11.95	G W Cameron	(Edinburgh)	26. 4.08P
	(Rotax 582)					
G-MYYY	Mainair Blade	1031-0495-7-W829	15. 3.95	E D Locke	Barton	13. 4.08P
	(Rotax 582)					

G-MYYZ	Medway Raven X	MRB135/116	10. 1.96	J W Leaper	Croft Farm, Defford	27. 6.04P
G-MYZA	Whittaker MW6 Merlin	PFA 164-11396	17. 7.95	D C Davies	Over Farm, Gloucester	4. 5.06P
	(Built D C Davies) (Rotax 582)			*(Ground-looped Newent 13.7.05 and substantially damaged)*		
G-MYZB	Pegasus Quantum 15	7124	22.11.95	A Gilruth tr G-MYZB Flying Group	Perth	4. 3.08P
	(Rotax 582)					
G-MYZC	Cyclone Airsports AX3/503	7125	5.12.95	P E Owen *(Noted 7.05)*	Eaglescott	2. 6.04P
G-MYZE	TEAM Mini-MAX 91	PFA 186-12570	28. 9.95	R B M Etherington	Halwell	6. 6.02P
	(Built E H Gould) (Global GMT-35)			*(Noted 11.06)*		
G-MYZF	Cyclone Airsports AX3/503	7133	11.12.95	Microflight (Ireland) Ltd	Mullaghmore, Coleraine	9. 4.08P
G-MYZG	Cyclone Airsports AX3/503	7137	11. 1.96	D S Thomas	(Bishopsteignton, Teignmouth)	27. 7.08P
G-MYZJ	Pegasus Quantum 15	7150	24. 1.96	P Millar	Kirknewton	6. 3.08P
	(Rotax 582)					
G-MYZK	Pegasus Quantum 15	7157	5. 2.96	J D G Welch	(Tweedsmuir, Biggar)	23. 1.08P
	(Rotax 582)					
G-MYZL	Pegasus Quantum 15	7158	5. 2.96	S Jelley	(Chichester)	28. 7.08P
	(Rotax 582)					
G-MYZM	Pegasus Quantum 15	7159	5. 2.96	D Hope	(Uckfield)	11. 5.08P
	(Rotax 582)					
G-MYZO	Medway Raven X	MRB136/115	12. 2.96	M C Arnold	Rochester	26. 7.05P
G-MYZP	CFM Shadow Series DD	249	7. 2.96	R M Davies and P I Hodgson	(Amersham)	31. 5.08P
	(Built D G Cook - pr.no.PFA 161-12914: sequence no.conflicts with G-BXDY)					
G-MYZR	Rans S-6-ESD-XL Coyote II	1295.902	9. 2.96	S E J McLaughlin		
	(Built V R Leggott - pr.no.PFA 204-12958) (Tri-cycle u/c)				Lark Engine Farmhouse, Prickwillow, Ely	15. 8.08P
G-MYZV	Rans S-6-ESD-XL Coyote II	0795.849	26. 2.96	B W Savory	Long Marston	2.10.08P
	(Built H Lammers - pr.no.PFA 204-12946) (Tri-cycle u/c)					
G-MYZY	Pegasus Quantum 15	7156	8. 2.96	N C O Watney	Rochester	25. 6.08P
	(Rotax 582)					
G-MZAA	Mainair Blade	1059-1195-7-W857	24.10.95	A G Butler	Shenstone Hall Farm, Shenstone	23. 6.07P
	(Rotax 462)					
G-MZAB	Mainair Blade	1043-0695-7-W841	26. 5.95	A Meadley	Baxby Manor, Husthwaite	7. 6.05P
	(Rotax 582)					
G-MZAC	BFC Challenger II	CH2-0294-1100	21. 7.95	M N Calhaem	Fradswell, Stafford	26. 3.04P
	(Built M N Calhaem - pr.no.PFA 177A-12716) (Rotax 503)					
G-MZAE	Mainair Blade	1063-1295-7-W863	4.12.95	D J Guild and M R Revelle		
	(Rotax 582)				New Farm House, Great Oakley	19. 5.08P
G-MZAF	Mainair Blade	1045-0795-7-W843	1.12.95	C M Bale	(Newport)	20. 2.08P
	(Rotax 582)					
G-MZAG	Mainair Blade	1042-0695-7-W840	26. 5.95	P W Brewer and D R G Cornwell	St Michaels	16. 5.08P
	(Rotax 582)					
G-MZAH	Rans S-6-ESD Coyote II	0393.470	3. 9.93	C J Collett	Long Marston	18. 8.04P
	(Built A Hipkin- pr.no.PFA 204-12553) (Damaged and repaired with frame.0491-186 [ex G-MWVL]) (Tri-cycle u/c)					
G-MZAJ	Mainair Blade	1067-0196-7-W869	20.12.95	M P Daley	Hunsdon	24. 6.02P
	(Rotax 582)			*(Noted 5.07)*		
G-MZAM	Mainair Blade	1044-0695-7-W842	31. 5.95	B M Marsh and P David	Shobdon	14.10.07P
	(Rotax 582)			*(Noted 12.07)*		
G-MZAN	Pegasus Quantum 15	7188	7. 3.96	P M Leahy	(Exeter)	24. 7.08P
	(Rotax 582)					
G-MZAP	Mainair Blade 912	1036-0495-7-W834	31. 3.95	K D Adams	Ince Blundell	19. 4.08P
G-MZAR	Mainair Blade	1072-0296-7-W874	13. 2.96	C Bayliss	Ince Blundell	4. 4.07P
	(Rotax 582)					
G-MZAS	Mainair Blade	1049-0895-7-W847	15. 8.95	T Carter	Pound Green, Buttonoak, Bewdley	18.10.04P
	(Rotax 582)					
G-MZAT	Mainair Blade	1060-1195-7-W860	29.11.95	M J Moulton	Roddige	21..9.08P
	(Rotax 582)					
G-MZAU	Mainair Blade	1064-0196-7-W864	29.11.95	A F Glover	(Woolston, Warrington)	7. 9.08P
	(Stolen 1999: Sailwing located 2004: new Trike built by P&M Aviation from spare parts: original build numbers retained and replacement Rotax 582 fitted)					
G-MZAV	Mainair Blade	1078-0396-7-W881	11. 3.96	B B Boniface	St Michaels	6. 6.08P
	(Rotax 462)					
G-MZAW	Pegasus Quantum 15	7160	14. 2.96	C A Mackenzie	Sackville Lodge, Riseley	19. 5.08P
	(Rotax 503)					
G-MZAX	Pegasus Quantum 15	7152	11. 3.96	D W Beach	Willingale	30. 3.05P
	(Rotax 582)			*(Noted 8.07)*		
G-MZAY	Mainair Blade	1077-0396-7-W880	15. 3.96	E J Carass	(South Burlingham, Norwich)	15. 6.08P
	(Rotax 462)					
G-MZAZ	Mainair Blade	1040-0595-7-W838	26. 5.95	T Porter and D Whiteley	St Michaels	21. 7.08P
	(Rotax 462)					
G-MZBA	Mainair Blade	1068-0296-7-W870	15. 3.96	S Stone	Over Farm, Gloucester	16. 8.08P
	(Rotax 912-UL)					
G-MZBB	Pegasus Quantum 15	7139	13. 3.96	T Campbell	Glenrothes	27. 8.08P
	(Rotax 582)					
G-MZBC	Pegasus Quantum 15	7077	15. 8.95	B M Quinn	Barlow, Sheffield	18. 7.07P
	(Rotax 582)					
G-MZBD	Rans S-6-ESD-XL Coyote II	0795.850	15. 3.96	C L A Brant	Otherton, Cannock	9. 5.08P
	(Built H W Foster - pr.no.PFA 204-12957) (Tri-cycle u/c)					
G-MZBF	Letov LK-2M Sluka	PFA 263-12881	18. 3.96	V Simpson	Mullahead, Tandragee	25. 3.08P
	(Built C R Stockdale) (Rotax 447)					
G-MZBG	Whittaker MW6-S Fatboy Flyer	PFA 164-12891	20. 3.96	M W Kilvert and I Rowlands-Jones	(Newtown, Powys)	1. 6.01P
	(Built A W Hodder) (Rotax 503)					
G-MZBH	Rans S-6-ESD Coyote II	0392.277	21. 3.96	D Sutherland	Breighton	27. 4.07P
	(Built D Sutherland - pr.no.PFA 204-12244) (Tri-cycle u/c)			*(Noted 12.07)*		
G-MZBI	Pegasus Quantum 15	7189	21. 3.96	A B Sev, A L Bagnall and I W Barlow	Mapperley	8. 8.08P
	(Rotax 582)					
G-MZBK	Letov LK-2M Sluka	8295s002	26. 3.96	G N Holland	(Shoscombe, Bath)	17. 8.06P
	(Built R Painter - pr.no.PFA 263-12872) (Rotax 447)			*(New owner 7.07)*		

G-MZBL	Mainair Blade	1080-0496-7-W883			11. 4.96	C J Rubery	Weston Zoyland	26. 1.08P
	(Rotax 582)						
G-MZBM	Pegasus Quantum 15	7196			12. 4.96	T P Williams	(Penmaenmawr)	13. 6.07P
G-MZBN	CFM Shadow Series CD	K 069	G-MTWP		22. 4.96	P A James	Andrewsfield	9. 6.04P
	(Built CFM Metal-Fax - pr.no.BMAA/HB/073 and issued for rebuild)					(Noted 9.07)		
G-MZBO	Pegasus Quantum 15	7218			3. 5.96	K C Beattie	Perth	15.12.07P
	(Rotax 582)						
G-MZBR	Southdown Raven X	SN2232/0082			24. 5.96	D M Lane	(Stourbridge)	
G-MZBS	CFM Shadow Series D	K 274			14. 5.96	S K Ryan	Plaistows Farm, St Albans	15. 9.06P
	(Built P A White - pr.no.PFA 161-13008)						
G-MZBT	Pegasus Quantum 15-912	7224			22. 5.96	A P Whitmarsh	Jackrell's Farm, Southwater	12. 7.08P
G-MZBU	Rans S-6-ESD-XL Coyote II	0296.938			30. 5.96	C Clark and R S Marriott	Otherton, Cannock	14.10.08P
	(Built J B Marshall - pr.no.PFA 204-12992)						
G-MZBV	Rans S-6-ESD-XL Coyote II	0396.950			30. 5.96	L C Barham and R I Cannan	Andreas, Isle of Man	1. 6.08P
	(Built P F Hill - pr.no.PFA 204-13009) (Rotax 582) (Tri-cycle u/c)						
G-MZBW	Quad City Challenger II UK	CH2-0795-UK-1367			19. 2.96	R T L Chaloner	Dunkeswell	25. 9.07P
	(Built C Bird - pr.no.PFA 177-12971) (Rotax 582)						
G-MZBX	Whittaker MW6-S-LW Fatboy Flyer	PFA 164-12563			16. 5.96	A A Comper	Longacre Farm, Sandy	22. 6.05P
	(Built S Rose and P Tearall) (Rotax 503)					(Noted 9.06)		
G-MZBY	Pegasus Quantum 15	7227			30. 5.96	L G Wray	(Knaresborough)	31. 7.08P
	(Rotax 582)						
G-MZBZ	Quad City Challenger II UK	CH2 0695 UK 1360			11. 3.96	T R Gregory	Dunkeswell	22. 6.05P
	(Built J Flisher - pr.no.PFA 177-12928) (Hirth 2706)						
G-MZCA	Rans S-6-ESD-XL Coyote II	0396.953			31. 5.96	W Scott	Priory Farm, Tibenham	11. 8.07P
	(Built S J Everett, K Kettles and F Williams - pr.no.PFA 204-12997) (Tri-cycle u/c) (Noted 2.08)						
G-MZCB	Cyclone Airsports Chaser S 447	7220			4. 6.96	R W Keene	Over Farm, Gloucester	14. 9.05P
						(New owner 10.07)		
G-MZCC	Mainair Blade	1086-0696-7-W889			7. 6.96	K S Rissmann	(King's Lynn)	18. 5.07P
	(Rotax 912-UL)						
G-MZCD	Mainair Blade	1087-0696-7-W890			10. 6.96	T Charity	(Upton-on-Severn)	27. 1.08P
	(Rotax 582)						
G-MZCE	Mainair Blade	K1088-0696-7-W891			17. 6.96	C T Halliday	Ince Blundell	29. 7.08P
	(Rotax 462)						
G-MZCF	Mainair Blade	1089-0696-7-W892			30. 8.96	C Hannaby	(Wrexham)	9. 8.04P
	(Rotax 462)						
G-MZCG	Mainair Blade	1090-0696-7-W893			17. 6.96	M R Mosley	Headon Farm, Retford	5. 8.08P
	(Rotax 462)						
G-MZCH	Whittaker MW6-S Fatboy Flyer	PFA 164-12131			7. 6.96	J T Moore	Dunkeswell	17. 7.08P
	(Built E J Blake and B G King) (Rotax 503)						
G-MZCI	Pegasus Quantum 15	7231			10. 6.96	P H Risdale	Prospect Farm, Wollaston	6.10.08P
	(Rotax 582)						
G-MZCJ	Pegasus Quantum 15	7233			14. 6.96	F E Hall	Prospect Farm, Wollaston	10. 8.08P
	(Rotax 582)						
G-MZCK	AMF Microflight Chevvron 2-32C	038			11. 7.96	T K Lane	(Symonds Yat, Ross-on-Wye)	19. 6.07P
G-MZCM	Pegasus Quantum Lite	7219			3. 5.96	S G McLachlan	(Stoke-on-Trent)	28. 6.07P
	(Rotax 582)						
G-MZCN	Mainair Blade	1079-0396-7-W882			27. 6.96	P C Williams	(Wallasey)	21. 6.04P
	(Rotax 582)					(New owner 10.05)		
G-MZCO	Mainair Mercury	1091-0796-7-W894			26. 6.96	E Rush	(Congleton)	13.11.06P
	(Rotax 462)						
G-MZCR	Pegasus Quantum 15	7234			28. 6.96	J E P Stubberfield	(Kenley)	23. 7.07P
	(Rotax 503)						
G-MZCS	TEAM Mini-MAX 91	PFA 186-12646			20.12.95	R F Morton	Little Rissington	11. 7.08P
	(Built C S Cox) (Rotax 377)						
G-MZCT	CFM Shadow Series CD	277			11. 7.96	W G Gill	Plaistows Farm, St Albans	21. 8.07P
G-MZCU	Mainair Blade	1082-0496-7-W885			1. 5.96	C E Pearce	Thurton	26. 6.08P
	(Rotax 462)						
G-MZCV	Pegasus Quantum 15	7235			11. 7.96	B S Toole	Guy Lane Farm, Waverton	27. 9.07P
	(Rotax 503)						
G-MZCX	Huntwing Avon Skytrike	9510055			17. 7.96	G R Coghill and W Mccarthy tr Huntwing Group		
	(Built C Harrison - pr.no.BMAA/HB/072) (Rotax 503)						Wick	13. 9.06P
G-MZCY	Pegasus Quantum 15	7236			19. 7.96	J R Appleton and G A Davidson		
	(Rotax 582)						Tarn Farm, Cockerham	4. 9.08P
G-MZDA	Rans S-6-ESD-XL Coyote II	0396.951			29. 7.96	R Plummer and S Day		
	(Built J Dent and W C Lombard - pr.no.PFA 204-13019) (Rotax 582) (Tri-cycle u/c)						Waterstones Farm, Newby Wiske	16. 8.08P
G-MZDB	Pegasus Quantum 15-912	7237			31. 7.96	D T Mackenzie tr Scottish Aerotow Club		
							Easter Poldar Farm, Thornhill	21. 5.08P
G-MZDC	Pegasus Quantum 15	7246			2. 8.96	M T Jones	Enstone	13. 6.06P
	(Rotax 582)						
G-MZDD	Pegasus Quantum 15	7114	G-69-23		11. 7.96	C D Reeves	Weston Zoyland	3.12.07P
	(Rotax 503)						
G-MZDE	Pegasus Quantum 15	7238			12. 7.96	R G Hedley	(High Lane, Stockport)	21. 3.08P
	(Rotax 582)						
G-MZDF	Mainair Blade	1093-0896-7-W896			15. 8.96	M Liptrot	Glassonby	22. 5.08P
	(Rotax 462)						
G-MZDG	Rans S-6-ESD-XL Coyote II	0696.1002			7. 8.96	J M Coffin	Darley Mor, Ashbourne	6. 7.07P
	(Built R Rhodes - pr.no.PFA 204-13030) (Tri-cycle u/c)						
G-MZDH	Pegasus Quantum 15-912	7248			12. 8.96	R C Reynolds	Arclid Green, Sandbach	11.11.06P
						(New owner 9.07)		
G-MZDJ	Medway Raven X	MRB138/119			19. 8.96	R Bryan (Noted 1.05)	Doynton	11. 8.04P
G-MZDK	Mainair Blade	1084-0596-7-W887			9. 5.96	B L Cook	Sandtoft	24. 1.08P
	(Rotax 582)	(C/n reported as 1084-0696-7)					
G-MZDL	Whittaker MW6-S Fatboy Flyer	PFA 164-12412			19. 8.96	J P S Ixer and M F Frost	(Braintree)	10. 5.08P
	(Built C D Wills) (Rotax 582)						

G-MZDM	Rans S-6-ESD-XL Coyote II	0396.954		2. 9.96	M E Nicholas	Kemble	18. 9.06P
	(Built M E Nicholas - pr.no..PFA 204-13022) Rotax 503) *(Tri-cycle u/c)*						
G-MZDN	Pegasus Quantum 15	7255		5. 9.96	P G Ford	(Ely)	12. 7.07P
	(Rotax 582)						
G-MZDP	AMF Microflight Chevvron 2-32C	020		3. 4.90	F Overall	Whitehall Farm, Wethersfield	16. 3.96P
					(Damaged mid 1995: stored 2001) (New owner 6.02)		
G-MZDR	Rans S-6-ESD-XL Coyote II	0396.592		8. 8.96	J D Gibbons	(Newry, County Armagh)	21. 3.04P
	(Built R Pyper and P McGill - pr.no.PFA 204-13012)						
G-MZDS	Cyclone Airsports AX3/503	7253		16. 9.96	M P James	(Burton Joyce, Nottingham)	16.12.07P
G-MZDT	Mainair Blade	1096-0996-7-W899		19. 9.96	T J Williams	Barton	8. 7.06P
	(Rotax 582)				*(Noted 6.07)*		
G-MZDU	Pegasus Quantum 15-912	7260		19. 9.96	G A Breen	Portimão, Faro, Portugal	26.10.07P
G-MZDV	Pegasus Quantum 15	7199		9. 4.96	P M Wilkinson	(Great Orton)	5. 6.01P
	(Rotax 582)						
G-MZDX	Letov LK-2M Sluka	8295s004		30. 9.96	J L Barker	Priory Farm, Tibenham	11.12.06P
	(Built T J T Dorricott - pr.no.PFA 263-12882) (Rotax 447)				*(Noted 2007)*		
G-MZDY	Pegasus Quantum 15	7263		2.10.96	R Bailey	Sutton Meadows	7.10.04P
	(Rotax 462HP)						
G-MZDZ	Hunt Avon/Huntwing	9501042		23.10.96	E W Laidlaw	(Turriff)	
	(Built E W Laidlaw - pr.no.BMAA/HB/072)				*(Under construction 2001)*		
G-MZEA	Quad City Challenger II	CH2-0294-1101		22. 4.96	G S Cridland	Wymeswold	29. 8.08P
	(Built G S Cridland - pr.no.PFA 177A-12728) (Hirth 2706)						
G-MZEB	Mainair Blade	1074-0396-7-W876		22. 7.96	G Todd	(Clotton, Tarporley)	13. 7.05P
	(Rotax 462)				*(New owner 11.05)*		
G-MZEC	Pegasus Quantum 15 Super Sport	7278		24.10.96	A B Godber	Bradley Ashbourne, Derby	28. 3.08P
	(Rotax 582)						
G-MZED	Mainair Blade	1092-0796-7-W895		3. 7.96	C W Potts	Eshott	5. 6.08P
	(Rotax 582)						
G-MZEE	Pegasus Quantum 15	7245		9. 8.96	J L Brogan	Stoke, Isle of Grain	1. 6.08P
	(Rotax 582)						
G-MZEG	Mainair Blade	1095-0896-7-W898		8. 8.96	R and A Soltysik	Otherton, Cannock	12.10.08P
	(Rotax 582)						
G-MZEH	Pegasus Quantum 15	7259		19. 9.96	P S Hall	Rushden	16.10.08P
	(Rotax 582)						
G-MZEJ	Mainair Blade	1097-0996-7-W900		8.10.96	P G Thomas	St Michaels	29. 4.07P
	(Rotax 462)						
G-MZEK	Mainair Mercury	1098-1096-7-W901		14.10.96	M Whiteman-Heywood	Arclid Green, Sandbach	2. 4.08P
	(Rotax 462)						
G-MZEL	Cyclone Airsports AX3-503	7250		30.10.96	R I Simpson *(New owner 2.08)*	Rochester	18. 4.04P
G-MZEM	Pegasus Quantum 15-912	7277		8.11.96	L H Black	Newtownards	5. 3.07P
G-MZEN	Rans S-6-ESD Coyote II	1294.705		9. 7.96	I Fernihough	Bradley	6. 4.08P
	(Built P Bottomley - pr.no.PFA 204-12823) (Tri-cycle u/c)						
G-MZEO	Rans S-6-ESD-XL Coyote II	0696.1001		19.11.96	R W Lenthall	Headon Farm, Retford	17. 8.06P
	(Built J A A Dungey - pr.no.PFA 204-13046)						
G-MZEP	Mainair Rapier	1103-1296-7-W906		13.12.96	B O'Connor	Eddsfield, Octon Lodge Farm, Thwing	10. 9.06P
G-MZER	Cyclone AX2000	7251	G-69-28	4.12.96	J H Keep	Henstridge	16. 4.08P
			G-MZER				
G-MZES	Letov LK-2M Sluka	8296K10		5.12.96	J L Self	Priory Farm, Tibenham	15. 8.08P
	(Built C Parkinson - pr.no.PFA 263-13064) (Rotax 447)						
G-MZEU	Rans S-6-ESD-XL Coyote II	0296.939		23.12.96	N Grugan	Eshott	26. 3.08P
	(Built J E Holloway - pr.no.PFA 204-13023) (Tri-cycle u/c)						
G-MZEV	Mainair Rapier	1101-1296-7-W904		7. 1.97	W T Gardner	Tarsan Lane, Portadown	23. 8.08P
G-MZEW	Mainair Blade	1105-0197-7-W908		13. 1.97	S J Meehan	Sittles Farm, Alrewas	7. 6.08P
	(Rotax 462)						
G-MZEX	Pegasus Quantum 15	7292		19.11.96	G Redfern and B Woolley	Mapperley	22. 4.08P
	(Rotax 582)						
G-MZEY	Micro Aviation B 22S Bantam	96-002	ZK-TII	7. 1.97	K T Bettington and D Harris	Priory Farm, Tibenham	14.10.07P
G-MZEZ	Pegasus Quantum 15-912	7285		8.11.96	M G Evans	Finmere	5. 9.08P
G-MZFA	Cyclone AX2000	7301		17.12.96	R S Mcmaster	Sackville Lodge, Riseley	20. 3.08P
G-MZFB	Mainair Blade	1108-0197-7-W911		7. 1.97	A J Plant	(Manchester)	17.10.08P
	(Rotax 462)						
G-MZFC	Letov LK-2M Sluka	8296K009		7. 1.97	P W Maddocks	Stoke, Isle of Grain	31.10.07P
	(Built G Johnson - pr.no.PFA 263-13063) (Rotax 447)						
G-MZFD	Mainair Rapier	1109-0197-7-W912		24. 1.97	R Gill	Knapthorpe Lodge, Caunton	2. 9.06P
	(Rotax 462)						
G-MZFE	Huntwing Avon	9507049		16. 1.97	G J Latham	Sittles Farm, Alrewas	15. 6.05P
	(Built G J Latham - pr.no.BMAA/HB/061) (Rotax 503)						
G-MZFF	Huntwing Avon 503	9604058		22. 1.97	B J Adamson	Ince Blundell	16. 1.03P
	(Built B J Adamson - pr.no.BMAA/HB/074)				*(Noted 8.05)*		
G-MZFG	Pegasus Quantum 15	7305		21. 1.97	A M Prentice	Yundum/Banjul, Gambia	23. 3.05P
	(Rotax 582)						
G-MZFH	AMF Microflight Chevvron 2-32C	039		27. 3.97	P J Tyler	Sleap	8. 5.08P
G-MZFI	Lorimer Iolaire	xxxxx		30. 1.97	H Lorimer	Hunterston Farm, Stair	
	(Built H Lorimer - pr.no.BMAA/HB/035) (BMW)				*"Iolaire" (Stored 11.06)*		
G-MZFK	Whittaker MW6 Merlin	PFA 164-11626		10. 2.97	G J Chadwick tr G-MZFK Flying Group		
	(Built K Worthington) (Rotax 532)					Tarn Farm, Cockerham	9.12.02P
G-MZFL	Rans S-6-ESD-XL Coyote II	0696.999		12. 2.97	H Adams	Kirkbride	15. 8.08P
	(Built G A Clayton - pr.no.PFA 204-13041) (Tri-cycle u/c)						
G-MZFN	Rans S-6-ESD Coyote II	1195.894		26. 2.97	C J and W R Wallbank	Ley Farm, Chirk	16. 4.08P
	(Built C R Wallbank - pr.no.PFA 204-12977)						
G-MZFO	Thruster T 600N	9037-T600N-001		4. 3.97	J Berry	Barton	24. 8.07P
	(Rotax 503)						
G-MZFR	Thruster T 600N	9047-T600N-003		4. 3.97	M Firman tr Blue Bird Syndicate	Dunkeswell	28. 7.08P
	(Rotax 503)						

G-MZFS	Mainair Blade	1110-0297-7-W913	8. 1.97	P Bailey	(Perth)	18. 9.06P
	(Rotax 582) *(Officially regd with Trike c/n 1010-0297-7)*			*(Noted 2.07)*		
G-MZFT	Pegasus Quantum 15-912	7264	2.10.96	R T Anderson	Hunsdon	24. 8.08P
G-MZFU	Thruster T 600N 450 Jab	9047-T600N-004	4. 3.97	G J Slater	Clench Common	13. 2.08P
G-MZFV	Pegasus Quantum 15-912	7324	13. 3.97	B Cook	Hunsdon	22. 4.08P
G-MZFX	Cyclone AX2000	7322	14. 3.97	Flylight Airsports Ltd	Sywell	7. 6.07P
G-MZFY	Rans S-6-ESD-XL Coyote II	0696.1003	17. 3.97	L G Tserkezos	Popham	23. 3.08P
	(Built L G Tserkezos - pr.no.PFA 204-13043) (Tri-cycle u/c)					
G-MZFZ	Mainair Blade	1119-0497-7-W922	2. 4.97	D C Keeble Lower Mountpleasant Farm, Chatteris		21.12.07P
	(Rotax 582)			*(Noted 1.08)*		
G-MZGA	Cyclone AX2000	7303	17.12.96	T K Duffy	Ellough, Beccles	1.11.08P
G-MZGB	Cyclone AX2000	7302	28. 1.97	P Hegarty	Lower Mountpleasant Farm, Chatteris	19. 5.08P
G-MZGC	Cyclone AX2000	7304	20.12.96	C E Walls Stonewalls, Victoria Bridge, Strabane		16. 6.07P
G-MZGD	Rans S-5 Coyote	89.095	1. 4.97	M J Olsen	Wombleton	14. 8.08P
	(Built A G Headford - pr.no.PFA 193-13096))					
G-MZGF	Letov LK-2M Sluka	8296K008	8. 4.97	G Lombardi and R C Hinkins	RAF Wyton	3.10.07P
	(Built R J Cook - pr. no. PFA 263-13073) (Rotax 447)					
G-MZGG	Pegasus Quantum 15	7327	10. 4.97	R W Partington	Sywell	5. 5.08P
	(Rotax 503)					
G-MZGH	Huntwing Avon 462	9406021	20.10.96	J H Cole	Otherton, Cannock	8.11.08P
	(Built G C Horner - pr.no.BMAA/HB/070)					
G-MZGI	Mainair Blade	1117-0397-7-W920	11. 4.97	H M Roberts	Caernarfon	8. 8.08P
	(Rotax 912-UL)					
G-MZGJ	Kolb Twinstar Mk.3	K0008-0193	16. 4.97	S J Pugh-Jones	Haverfordwest	16. 9.08P
	(Built P Coppock - pr.no.PFA 205-12421) (Hirth 2705 R06)					
G-MZGK	Pegasus Quantum 15	7331	30. 4.97	C D Cross and S H Moss	Sywell	13. 1.08P
	(Rotax 582)					
G-MZGL	Mainair Rapier	1104-0197-7-W907	18.12.96	V J Noonan	(Wybunbury, Nantwich)	27. 7.07P
G-MZGM	Cyclone AX2000	7334	1. 5.97	W G Dunn	Winkleigh, Devon	9. 7.08P
G-MZGN	Pegasus Quantum 15	7332	2. 5.97	B J Youngs	Sutton Meadows	23. 5.08P
	(Rotax 503)					
G-MZGO	Pegasus Quantum 15	7320	20. 3.97	S F G Allen	Long Marston	25. 8.07P
	(Rotax 582)					
G-MZGP	Cyclone AX2000	7333	7. 5.97	D G Palmer tr Buchan Light Aeroplane Club		
					Mintlaw, Peterhead	14. 6.07P
G-MZGS	CFM Shadow Series DD	K 284	8. 5.97	P Bayliss	Ince Blundell	20. 2.07P
	(Built M J McChrystal - pr.no.PFA 161-13050) (Rotax 447)					
G-MZGT	Roger Hardy RH7B Tiger Light PFA 230-13013		10. 3.97	P J Fahie	(Stour Row, Shaftesbury)	21. 1.05P
	(Built J B McNab)			*(Noted 12.06)*		
G-MZGU	Arrowflight Hawk II (UK) PFA 266-13075		8. 5.97	J N Holden	Mullaghmore, Coleraine	3. 5.02P
	(Built Arrowflight Aviation Ltd) (Rotax 503)			*(Noted 7.06)*		
G-MZGV	Pegasus Quantum 15	7339	12. 6.97	R E Kilby tr G-MZGV Syndicate	Dunkeswell	20 7.08P
	(Rotax 582)					
G-MZGW	Mainair Blade	1112-0297-7-W915	19. 2.97	R Almond	Wickhambrook, Newmarket	2.11.08P
	(Rotax 462)					
G-MZGY	Thruster T 600N	9057-T600N-006	28. 4.97	R V Horlock	Wing Farm, Longbridge Deverill	18. 9.07P
	(Rotax 503) *(Type change to T600N-430)*					
G-MZGZ	Thruster T 600N	9057-T600N-007	28. 4.97	R P Stonor tr Golf Zulu Group	Long Marston	30.11.07P
	(Rotax 503)					
G-MZHA	Thruster T 600T	9057-T600T-008	28. 4.97	R V Buxton	Feshiebridge	10. 8.05P
	(Rotax 503)					
G-MZHB	Mainair Blade	1114-0297-7-W917	19. 2.97	A Szczepanek	Guy Lane Farm, Waverton	13. 4.08P
	(Rotax 462)					
G-MZHD	Thruster T 600T	9067-T600T-010	13. 5.97	B E Foster	(Tain)	12. 6.08P
	(Rotax 503)					
G-MZHE	Thruster T 600N	9067-T600N-011	13. 5.97	R Bellew	(Collon, County Meath)	26. 6.08P
	(Rotax 503)					
G-MZHF	Thruster T 600N Spriint	9067-T600N-012	13. 5.97	R Benner and K Harmston	Watnall	4.10.08P
	(Rotax 582)					
G-MZHG	Whittaker MW6-T	PFA 164-11420	16. 6.97	R Hatton	Andreas, Isle of Man	24. 6.06P
	(Built M G Speers) (Rotax 532)			*(New owner 12.06)*		
G-MZHI	Pegasus Quantum 15	7337	27. 5.97	F P MacDonald	(Boothlands Farm, Newdigate)	12. 7.08P
	(Rotax 582)					
G-MZHJ	Mainair Rapier	1123-0697-7-W926	17. 6.97	G Standish and R Jones		
	(Rotax 462)				(Lowton, Warrington and Manchester)	22. 6.08P
G-MZHK	Pegasus Quantum 15	7352	24. 6.97	O Goodwin	(York)	16. 5.08P
	(Rotax 582)					
G-MZHL	Mainair Rapier	1126-0797-7-W929	30. 6.97	A Bryant	North Coates	2. 9.08P
G-MZHM	TEAM Hi-MAX 1700R PFA 272-12912		8. 1.97	M H McKeown	(Gorey, County Wexford)	28. 3.08P
	(Built M H McKeown) (Robin 440) (Officially regd with Rotax 447)					
G-MZHN	Pegasus Quantum 15	7351	27. 6.97	F W Frerichs	Sackville Lodge, Riseley	3. 6.08P
	(Rotax 462HP)					
G-MZHO	Quad City Challenger II PFA 177-12936		15. 7.97	J Pavelin	East Barling, Essex	21. 8.08P
	(Built J Pavelin)					
G-MZHP	Pegasus Quantum 15	7353	15. 7.97	P C J Coidan	(Garboldisham, Diss)	10. 2.08P
	(Rotax 582)					
G-MZHR	Cyclone AX2000	7307	7. 3.97	J Leden and C P Dawes	Darley Moor, Ashbourne	3. 8.08P
G-MZHS	Thruster T 600T	9077-T600T-013	4. 7.97	D Mahajan	Damyn's Hall, Upminster	29.10.07P
	(Rotax 582) *(Officially regd with Rotax 503)*					
G-MZHT	Whittaker MW6 Merlin	PFA 164-11244	12. 6.97	G J Chadwick	Tarn Farm, Cockerham	18. 8.05P
	(Built P Mogg) (Hirth 2706)					
G-MZHU	Thruster T 600N Sprint	9077-T600T-019	4. 7.97	E Lewis	Weston Zoyland	8.11.08P
	(Rotax 582) *(Originally built as "T 600T")*					

G-MZHV	Thruster T 600N Sprint	9077-T600T-018		4. 7.97	H G Denton	Leicester	14. 8.08P
	(Rotax 582) *(Originally built as "T 600T")*						
G-MZHW	Thruster T 600N	9077-T600N-017		4. 7.97	K H Smalley	Wickenby	26. 9.08P
	(Rotax 503)						
G-MZHY	Thruster T 600N	9077-T600N-015		4. 7.97	G Jones	Emlyn's Field, Rhuallt	6. 4.08P
	(Rotax 503)						
G-MZIA	TEAM Hi-MAX 1700R	PFA 272-13020		25. 4.97	I J Arkieson	(Meols, Wirral)	
	(Built I J Arkieson)						
G-MZIB	Pegasus Quantum 15	7354		15. 7.97	S Murphy	Trim, County Meath	3. 7.08P
	(Rotax 582)						
G-MZIC	Pegasus Quantum 15	7348		24. 6.97	H M Squire and C F Two t/a Swansea Airsports Services		
	(Rotax 503)					(Clapham, Bedford)	6. 8.03P
G-MZID	Whittaker MW6 Merlin	PFA 164-11383		15. 7.97	C P F Sheppard	(Grange Mill, Matlock)	24. 8.06P
	(Built M G A Wood) (Rotax 503)						
G-MZIE	Pegasus Quantum 15	7359		6. 8.97	Flylight Airsports Ltd	Sywell	11. 2.08P
	(Rotax 582)						
G-MZIF	Pegasus Quantum 15	7355		16. 7.97	D Parsons	(Bexley)	3.10.08P
	(Rotax 582)						
G-MZIH	Mainair Blade	1128-0797-7-W931		16. 7.97	L C Wellington-Graham	Baxby Manor, Husthwaite	9. 8.08P
	(Rotax 462)						
G-MZII	TEAM Mini-MAX 88	PFA 186-11842		19. 3.97	M J Kirk	Haverfordwest	10. 4.04P
	(Built G F M Garner)						
G-MZIJ	Pegasus Quantum 15	7362		14. 8.97	D L Wright	Sywell	31. 5.08P
	(Rotax 582)						
G-MZIK	Pegasus Quantum 15	7368		8. 9.97	L A Read	Eaglescott	8.10.08P
	(Rotax 582)						
G-MZIL	Mainair Rapier	1132-0897-7-W935		1. 9.97	G S Highley	Deenethorpe	11.11.07P
	(Rotax 462)						
G-MZIM	Mainair Rapier	1124-0697-7-W927		9. 6.97	M J McKegney	Newtownards	1. 9.08P
	(Rotax 462)						
G-MZIR	Mainair Blade	1134-0997-7-W937		18. 9.97	S Connor	Rhedyn Coch Farm, Rhuallt	29. 7.08P
	(Rotax 582)						
G-MZIS	Mainair Blade	1115-0397-7-W918		17. 2.97	M K Richings	(Scarborough)	26. 4.08P
	(Rotax 462)						
G-MZIT	Mainair Blade	1129-0897-7-W932		16. 7.97	P M Horn	Shotton Colliery, Peterlee	25. 4.08P
	(Rotax 912-UL)						
G-MZIU	Pegasus Quantum 15	7371		15.10.97	S Timperley	Rufforth	5. 4.08P
	(Rotax 582)						
G-MZIV	Cyclone AX2000	7372		21.10.97	C J Tomlin	Knapthorpe Lodge, Caunton	29. 9.08P
G-MZIW	Mainair Blade	1127-0797-7-W930		16. 7.97	M J Lea	Tarn Farm, Cockerham	3. 2.08P
G-MZIX	Mignet HM-1000 Balerit	130		23. 9.97	P E H Scott	(Stockbridge)	10. 6.08P
G-MZIY	Rans S-6-ESD-XL Coyote II	1096.1050		29. 9.97	P A Bell	Tarn Farm, Cockerham	20.12.07P
	(Built P A Bell - pr.no.PFA 204-13184) (Tri-cycle u/c) *(Rebuilt with new fuselage frame C 1998)*						
G-MZIZ	Murphy Renegade Spirit UK	257	G-MWGP	21.10.92	R B Hawkins	Davidstow Moor	13. 6.07P
	(Built B Bayley - pr.no.PFA 188-11701)						
G-MZJA	Mainair Blade	1135-0997-7-W938		30. 9.97	R C McArthur	Ince Blundell	1.10.07P
	(Rotax 582)						
G-MZJB	Aviasud Mistral	047	(ex ?)	30. 9.97	J M Whitham (Delves Farm, Delves, Huddersfield)		
					(New owner 3.04)		
G-MZJD	Mainair Blade	1130-0897-7-W933		7. 8.97	P Barkert and R W Neal		
	(Rotax 503)				(Fulwood, Preston and Hindley, Wigan)		3.10.08P
G-MZJE	Mainair Rapier	1136-1097-7-W939		17.10.97	J E Davies	(Southport)	5. 8.04P
G-MZJF	Cyclone AX2000	7378		2.12.97	P W Hastings *(Noted 4.06)*	Long Marston	21.12.04P
G-MZJG	Pegasus Quantum 15	7335		2. 5.97	P D Myer	Upfield Farm, Whitson	18. 7.08P
	(Rotax 462)						
G-MZJH	Pegasus Quantum 15	7350		25. 6.97	P Copping	Deenethorpe	15. 2.08P
	(Rotax 503)						
G-MZJI	Rans S-6-ESD-XL Coyote II	1096.1046		3.11.97	M A Newbould and C Topp	Baxby Manor, Husthwaite	22. 9.06P
	(Built J Whiting - pr.no.PFA 204-13221) (Tri-cycle u/c)						
G-MZJJ	Murphy Maverick	PFA 259-13016		5.11.97	R J Collins	Belle Vue Farm, Yarnscombe	29.11.08P
	(Built M F Cottam) (Jabiru 2200A)						
G-MZJK	Mainair Blade	1100-1196-7-W903		19.11.96	P G Angus	Higher Barn Farm, Houghton	7. 12.07P
	(Rotax 582)						
G-MZJL	Cyclone AX2000	7363		11. 8.97	M H Owen	Weston Zoyland	5. 6.08P
G-MZJM	Rans S-6-ESD-XL Coyote II	1096.1049		19.11.97	K A Hastie	Popham	25. 4.08P
	(Built R J Hopkins - pr.no.PFA 204-13215)						
G-MZJN	Pegasus Quantum 15	7376		11.11.97	J Nelson	Mapperley	24. 8.08P
	(Rotax 582)						
G-MZJO	Pegasus Quantum 15	7338		17. 6.97	D J Cook	Eaglescott	7. 6.08P
	(Rotax 582)						
G-MZJP	Whittaker MW6-S Fatboy Flyer	PFA 164-13049		21.10.97	D J Burton and C A J Funnell	(Brighton)	
	(Built D J Burton and C A J Funnell)						
G-MZJR	Cyclone AX2000	7385		11.11.97	N A Martin tr Marlborough Aerotow Group		
	(HKS 700E)					Clench Common	8. 3.08P
G-MZJS	Murphy Maverick 430	PFA 259-13017		12.12.97	P C E Roberts	(Truro)	18. 9.08P
	(Built R D Bernard) (Jabiru 2200A)						
G-MZJT	Pegasus Quantum 15-912	7399		23.12.97	N Hammerton	(Oxted)	15. 7.08P
G-MZJV	Mainair Blade	1141-0198-7-W944		7. 1.98	M A Roberts	West Malling	13. 6.04P
G-MZJW	Pegasus Quantum 15-912	7390		27. 1.98	W H J Knowles	Yundum/Banjul, Gambia	8.10.04P
G-MZJX	Mainair Blade	1139-0198-7-W942		9. 1.98	A D Taylor	Glassonby	25. 5.08P
	(Rotax 503)						
G-MZJY	Pegasus Quantum 15-912	7394	(EI-)	23.12.97	M F Turff	Longacre Farm, Sandy	18. 7.08P
			G-MZJY				
G-MZJZ	Mainair Blade	1121-0597-7-W924		23. 6.97	P McParlin *(Noted 8.05)*	Ince Blundell	16. 7.05P

G-MZKA	Pegasus Quantum 15	7380		1.12.97	A S R McSherry	West Kilbride	25. 4.05P
G-MZKC	Cyclone AX2000	7398		22. 1.98	D Cioffi tr Broad Farm Flyers		
						Broad Farm, Eastbourne	24. 2.08P
G-MZKD	Pegasus Quantum 15	7404		19. 3.98	S J M Morling	(Fivehead, Taunton)	20. 8.08P
G-MZKE	Rans S-6-ESD-XL Coyote II	0797.1142		19. 1.98	M S J Bateman	North Coates	30. 5.07P
	(Build I Findlay - pr.no.PFA 204-13248)						
G-MZKF	Pegasus Quantum 15	7407		21. 1.98	C Lamb and P J Cragg	Northiam, Rye	6. 8.08P
G-MZKG	Mainair Blade	1145-0198-7-W948		23. 1.98	N S Rigby	Ince Blundell	18. 7.08P
	(Rotax 582)						
G-MZKH	CFM Shadow Series DD	292-DD		23. 1.98	S P H Calvert	Deanland	26. 9.06P
G-MZKI	Mainair Rapier	1147-0298-7-W950		12. 2.98	D L Aspinall	North Connel, Oban	30. 5.08P
G-MZKJ	Mainair Blade	1039-0595-7-W837		19. 5.95	L G M Maddick	Leicester	1. 5.05P
	(Rotax 582)					(Noted 10.07)	
G-MZKK	Mainair Blade	1140-0198-7-W943		12. 2.98	D I Lee	Finmere	7. 3.08P
G-MZKL	Pegasus Quantum 15	7360		18. 8.97	G Williams	(Ilkeston)	5. 4.08P
	(Rotax 582)						
G-MZKM	Mainair Blade	1133-0897-7-W936		15. 8.97	G F J Field	Headon Farm, Retford	29. 6.08P
G-MZKN	Mainair Rapier	1138-1297-7-W941		12.12.97	G Craig (Noted 1.07)	Newtownards	13. 4.08P
G-MZKR	Thruster T 600N	9038-T600N-021		27. 1.98	R J Arnett	(Albufeira, Portugal)	1 .3.03P
	(Rotax 582UL)						
G-MZKS	Thruster T 600N	9038-T600N-022		27. 1.98	P J Hepburn	Stoke, Isle of Grain	13.10.08P
	(HKS 700E) (Officially regd with Rotax 582)						
G-MZKT	Thruster T 600N Sprint	9038-T600T-023		27. 1.98	M J O'Connor	Cottage Farm, Norton Juxta	21. 4.08P
	(Rotax 582UL) (Originally built as "T 600T")						
G-MZKU	Thruster T 600T	9038-T600T-024		27. 1.98	A S Day	Ginge, Wantage	25. 9.08P
	(Rotax 582UL) (Officially regd with Rotax 503)						
G-MZKV	Mainair Blade	1144-0198-7-W947		28. 1.98	J D Harriman	(Dudley)	24. 4.08P
G-MZKW	Quad City Challenger II	PFA 177-12518		22. 3.94	K W Warn	Siege Cross Farm, Thatcham	16.10.05P
	(Built K W Warn) (Hirth 2705 R06)						
G-MZKY	Pegasus Quantum 15	7403		16. 1.98	P S Constable	Redlands, Swindon	16. 8.06P
	(HKS 700E)						
G-MZKZ	Mainair Blade	K1137-0298-7-W940		18. 2.98	R P Wolstenholme	Arclid Green, Sandbach	7. 8.04P
	(Rotax 582)					(Noted 3.07)	
G-MZLA	Pegasus Quantum 15	7415		27. 2.98	D W C Beer tr G-MZLA Quantum Syndicate		
	(Rotax 582)					Trenchard Farm, Eggesford	23. 5.08P
G-MZLC	Mainair Blade	1146-0298-7-W949		26. 2.98	P A Kershaw	Ince Blundell	6. 4.08P
G-MZLD	Pegasus Quantum 15-912	7416		24. 3.98	D Hamilton	Strathaven	27. 8.08P
G-MZLE	Murphy Maverick 430	PFA 259-12955	G-BXSZ	27. 2.98	J S Hill	Castle Kennedy, Stranraer	17. 6.08P
	(Built A A Plumridge) (Jabiru 2200A)						
G-MZLF	Pegasus Quantum 15	7417		30. 3.98	S Seymour	Deenethorpe	13. 5.04P
	(Rotax 503)					(Noted 3.05)	
G-MZLG	Rans S-6-ESD-XL Coyote II	0897.1143		3. 3.98	F Y Allery	(Warboys, Huntingdon)	6. 8.07P
	(Built R H J Jenkins - pr.no.PFA 204-13192) (Tri-cycle u/c)					(New owner 1.08)	
G-MZLI	Mignet HM-1000 Balerit	133		5. 3.98	A G Barr (Noted 4.05)	Otherton, Cannock	17.10.04P
G-MZLJ	Pegasus Quantum 15	7421		20. 3.98	J H Bradbury	Arclid Green, Sandbach	13. 7.08P
	(Rotax 503)						
G-MZLK	Ultrasports Tri-Pacer/Solar Wings Typhoon T285-1471			9. 3.98	M D Harris	(Earls Barton, Northampton)	16.11.08P
	(Fuji-Robin EC-34-PM) (Trike unit ex G-MJEC and Sailwing is Typhoon S4+ (ex-hanglider) s/n T785-1471M)						
G-MZLL	Rans S-6-ESD-XL Coyote II	0696.998		23. 9.97	J A Willats and G W Champion		
	(Built J A Willats and G W Champion - pr.no.PFA 204-13067)					Maypole Farm, Chislet	20. 5.08P
G-MZLM	Cyclone AX2000	7425		22. 4.98	P E Hadley	Swinford, Rugby	6. 4.08P
	(Modified to tug version)						
G-MZLN	Pegasus Quantum 15	7431		14. 4.98	P A Greening	(Leighton Buzzard)	14. 1.06P
	(Rotax 503)					(New owner 11.07)	
G-MZLP	CFM Shadow D Series SS	K 299-D		1. 4.98	D J Gordon	Woodlands Barton Farm, Roche	1.1.08P
G-MZLR	Solar Wings Pegasus XL-Q	7441		28. 5.98	B Lorraine	Eshott	4. 8.08P
	(Trike c/n SW-TB-1040 ex G-MNJP fitted with new Sailwing c/n 7441)						
G-MZLS	Cyclone AX2000	7428		6. 7.98	A C A Hayes	Otherton, Cannock	15.12.07P
	(HKS 700E V3)						
G-MZLT	Pegasus Quantum 15-912	7438		24. 4.98	M H Colin	Otherton, Cannock	1. 5.08P
G-MZLU	Cyclone AX2000	7439		28. 7.98	E Pashley	Popham	9. 3.08P
	(HKS 700E V3)						
G-MZLV	Pegasus Quantum 15	7437		29. 4.98	A Armsby	Weston Zoyland	16. 2.08P
	(Rotax 503)						
G-MZLW	Pegasus Quantum 15	7440		28. 4.98	G Cunliffe and R W R Crevel	Sywell	11. 7.08P
	(Rotax 582)						
G-MZLX	Micro Aviation B 22S Bantam	97-013	ZK-JIV	9.12.97	D L Howell	Longacre Farm, Sandy	26. 9.05P
G-MZLY	Letov LK-2M Sluka	PFA 263-13065		20. 4.98	W McCarthy	Wick	21. 3.07P
	(Built B G M Chapman) (Rotax 447 1V)						
G-MZLZ	Mainair Blade	1154-0498-7-W957		21. 4.98	P J Hopkins	Deenethorpe	11. 4.08P
G-MZMA	Solar Wings Pegasus Quasar IITC	6611		1. 9.93	S Dixon	Longframlington	30. 6.07P
	(Rotax 582)						
G-MZMC	Pegasus Quantum 15-912	7206		10. 5.96	J J Baker	Deenethorpe	1. 6.08P
G-MZMD	Mainair Blade	1148-0398-7-W951		5. 3.98	T Gate	(Clitheroe)	30. 4.08P
G-MZME	Medway EclipseR	151/129E	G-582	8. 4.98	T Bowles	North Connel, Oban	20. 1.08P
	(Jabiru 2200A)						
G-MZMF	Pegasus Quantum 15	7387		30. 4.98	A J Tranter	Perth	17.10.07P
	(HKS)						
G-MZMG	Pegasus Quantum 15 Super Sport	7446		27. 5.98	I Abraham	Weston Zoyland	6.11.08P
	(Rotax 503)						
G-MZMH	Pegasus Quantum 15-912	7402		27. 1.98	M Hurtubise	(Leamington Spa)	4. 7.07P
G-MZMJ	Mainair Blade	1155-0598-7-W958		8. 5.98	T F R Calladine	Oxton	23. 6.08P
G-MZMK	AMF Microflight Chevvron 2-32C	040		19. 5.98	K D Calvert	Park Farm, Eaton Bray	20. 9.03P
G-MZML	Mainair Blade	1158-0698-7-W961		19. 5.98	W Russell	Easter Poldar Farm, Thornhill	14.11.08P

G-MZMM	Mainair Blade	1162-0698-7-W965		19. 5.98	J Lynch	Sturgate	3. 4.08P
	(Rotax 462)						
G-MZMN	Pegasus Quantum 15-912	7445		21. 5.98	L A Hosegood	Redlands, Swindon	5. 5.08P
G-MZMO	TEAM Mini-MAX 91	PFA 186-12951		20. 5.98	K R Mason	(Kings Heath, Birmingham)	25. 9.08P
	(Built I M Ross)						
G-MZMP	Mainair Blade	1160-0698-7-W963		20. 5.98	A Munro	Willingale	5. 2.07P
	(Rotax 582)						
G-MZMS	Rans S-6-ES Coyote II	1298.1203		26. 5.98	D G Matthews	Long Marston	9.10.07P
	(Built J G Dungey - pr.no.PFA 204-13294: rebuilt with kit no 0897.1145 ex G-MZMU c9.03) (Rotax 582) (Tri-cycle u/c)						
G-MZMT	Pegasus Quantum 15	7449		18. 6.98	B J Kitson	Sutton Meadows	20. 1.07P
	(Rotax 582)						
G-MZMU	Rans S-6-ESD-XL Coyote II	0897.1145		5. 6.98	J P Lamb and J Willcox	(Wotton-under-Edge)	23. 1.08P
	(Built S Cox - pr.no.PFA 204-13242: rebuilt with kit no.0298.1203 c2003) (Rotax 582)						
G-MZMV	Mainair Blade	1152-0496-7-W955		30. 3.98	J Mayer	Otherton, Cannock	22.12.07P
	(Rotax 462)						
G-MZMW	Mignet HM-1000 Balerit	125		2.10.96	M E Whapham	Corn Wood Farm, Adversane	10.10.08P
G-MZMX	Cyclone AX2000	7451		8. 9.98	L A Lacy	Roddige	9. 9.07P
	(HKS 700E V3)						
G-MZMY	Mainair Blade	1153-0498-7-W956		16. 3.98	C J Millership	St Michaels	29. 6.08P
	(Rotax 462)						
G-MZMZ	Mainair Blade	1081-0496-7-W884		22. 4.96	W A Stacey	(Rayleigh)	2. 7.07P
G-MZNA	Quad City Challenger II UK	CH2-0894-UK-1193	EI-CLE	19. 3.98	S Hennessy	(Dublin)	14. 4.08P
	(Built M Tormey)						
G-MZNB	Pegasus Quantum 15-912	7456		17. 7.98	F Gorse	Caernarfon	10. 8.06P
G-MZNC	Mainair Blade	1161-0698-7-W964		22. 6.98	K Medd	(Manchester)	14. 7.08P
G-MZND	Mainair Rapier	1170-0898-7-W973		24. 6.98	D W Stamp	Pound Green, Buttonoak, Bewdley	24 8.07P
G-MZNE	Whittaker MW6-S Fatboy Flyer	PFA 164-13120		26. 6.98	M B Horan	(Uttoxeter)	5. 6.07P
	(Built V E Booth) (Rotax 582)						
G-MZNG	Pegasus Quantum 15-912	7457		11. 8.98	S B Wilkes	Halfpenny Green	14. 4.08P
G-MZNH	CFM Shadow Series DD	K 297-DD		30. 6.98	P A James tr Cloudbase Aviation G-MZNH	Redhill	25. 6.08P
G-MZNI	Mainair Blade	1163-0698-7-W966		3. 7.98	A Joyce	(Ashbourne, County Meath)	31. 3.08P
G-MZNJ	Mainair Blade	1168-0798-7-W971		6. 7.98	S J Taft	Sturgate	16. 8.07P
	(Rotax 462)				(New owner 9.07)		
G-MZNL	Mainair Blade	1165-0798-7-W968		6. 7.98	M A Williams	Stowting Russ, Folkestone	1. 7.06P
					(Stolen from Stowting overnight 2.10.05)		
G-MZNM	TEAM Mini-MAX 91	PFA 186-12304		10. 7.98	P Stark	Strathaven	1.10.08P
	(Built N P Thomson) (Fuji-Robin EC-44) (Open cockpit)						
G-MZNN	TEAM Mini-MAX 91	PFA 186-13125		10. 7.98	D M Dronsfield	Brook Farm, Pilling	17. 6.02P
	(Built D M Dronsfield)				(Noted dismantled 7.07)		
G-MZNO	Mainair Blade	1167-0798-7-W970		9. 6.98	R C Colclough	Arclid Green, Sandbach	9. 9.08P
	(Rotax 462)						
G-MZNP	Pegasus Quantum 15-912	7466	G-69-55	22. 7.98	G J McNally	Strathaven	13. 9.08P
G-MZNR	Pegasus Quantum 15	7465		17. 8.98	E S Wills	(Paignton)	16. 4.08P
	(Rotax 503)						
G-MZNS	Pegasus Quantum 15-912 Super Sport	7473		31. 7.98	M J Robbins	Rochester	26.11.08P
G-MZNT	Pegasus Quantum 15-912 Super Sport	7470		25. 9.98	R V Barber	Hunsdon	25.10.08P
G-MZNU	Mainair Rapier	174-0898-7-W977		5. 8.98	G G Wilson and R Winstanley	Eshott	10. 8.08P
G-MZNV	Rans S-6-ESD-XL Coyote II	1294.704		7. 8.98	A P Thomas	Barton Ashes	8. 5.08P
	(Built D E Rubery - pr.no.PFA 204-12884) (Tri-cycle u/c)						
G-MZNX	Thruster T 600N	9098-T600N-026		10. 8.98	B S Beacroft	(Barnetby)	7.10.08P
	(Rotax 503)						
G-MZNY	Thruster T 600N	9098-T600N-027		10. 8.98	L O Partington and G Price	Barton	26. 9.08P
	(Rotax 582)						
G-MZNZ	Letov LK-2M Sluka	8295s015		21. 4.98	B F Crick	Long Marston	25.11.05P
	(Built K T Vinning - pr.no.PFA 263-13274) (Rotax 447)						
G-MZOC	Mainair Blade	1172-0898-7-W975		10. 8.98	R A Carr (Noted 7.06)	Eshott	5.12.05P
G-MZOD	Pegasus Quantum 15-912	7435		28. 4.98	J W Mann	Enstone	13. 5.08P
G-MZOE	Cyclone AX2000	7472		17. 9.98	R J Cook	Cumbernauld	28. 4.08P
	(HKS 700E V3)						
G-MZOF	Mainair Blade	1122-0697-7-W925		5. 6.97	R M Ellis	Long Marston	15. 5.08P
	(Rotax 462)						
G-MZOG	Pegasus Quantum 15	7471		12.10.98	E Nicoliello	(Crook)	14. 6.08P
	(Rotax 503)						
G-MZOH	Whittaker MW5-D Sorcerer	PFA 163-13060		14. 8.98	M Field	Higher Barn Farm, Houghton	27. 9.07P
	(Built D M Precious) (Fuji-Robin EC-44) (Officially recorded as Rotax 377)						
G-MZOI	Letov LK-2M Sluka	8296s012		17. 8.98	B S P Finch	Kemble	16. 7.08P
	(Built K P Taylor - pr.no.PFA 263-13238) (Rotax 447 1V)						
G-MZOJ	Pegasus Quantum 15	7478		9.11.98	A C Lane	Dunkeswell	25. 6.08P
	(Rotax 582)						
G-MZOK	Whittaker MW6 Merlin	PFA 164-11568		24. 8.97	R E Arnold tr G-MZOK Syndicate		
	(Built R K Willcox) (Rotax 582)					Otherton, Cannock	16. 7.08P
G-MZOM	CFM Shadow Series DD	302-DD		8. 9.98	P S Winteron and P Tidd tr Side-Stick Syndicate		
						Lower Mountpleasant Farm, Chatteris	18.11.06P
G-MZOP	Mainair Blade	1178-0998-7-W981		11. 9.98	M Gardiner (Noted 8.07)	Rhedyn Coch Farm, Rhuallt	23.10.05P
G-MZOR	Mainair Blade	1173-0898-7-W976		21. 9.98	D L Foxley	Ince Blundell	2. 3.08P
G-MZOS	Pegasus Quantum 15-912	7458		6.10.98	R J Field	Sandown, Isle of Wight	5. 4.08P
G-MZOV	Pegasus Quantum 15	7512		9. 3.99	C S Garrett tr Pegasus XL Group	Enstone	13. 6.08P
	(Rotax 503) (Badged as a "Quantum Super Sport")						
G-MZOW	Pegasus Quantum 15-912	7502		9. 3.99	J C Kitchen (Noted 2.08)	Stoke, Isle of Grain	3.12.07P
G-MZOX	Letov LK-2M Sluka	PFA 263-13415		15. 2.99	C M James	Maypole Farm, Chislet	1. 6.06P
	(Built C M James) (Rotax 447)						
G-MZOY	TEAM Mini-MAX 91	PFA 186-12526		29. 3.99	P R and S E Whitehouse	(Cold Norton, Stone)	
	(Built E F Smith)				(New owners 11.06)		
G-MZOZ	Rans S-6-ESD-XL Coyote II	1096.1052		20. 5.98	D C and S G Emmons	Englefield	21. 9.08P
	(Built D C and S G Emmons - pr.no.PFA 204-13168) (Rotax 912) (Officially recorded with Rotax 503) (Tri-cycle u/c)						

G-MZPB	Mignet HM-1000 Balerit	124		4.10.96	J K Evans	Chiltern Park, Wallingford	18.12.07P
G-MZPD	Pegasus Quantum 15 (Rotax 582)	7013		9. 5.95	P M Dewhurst	Sywell	24. 1.08P
G-MZPH	Mainair Blade (Rotax 582)	1177-0998-7-W980		26. 8.98	J D Hoyland	Chilbolton	8.12.07P
G-MZPJ	TEAM Mini-MAX 91 (Built P R Jenson) (Rotax 503)	PFA 186-12277		23.11.92	P R Jenson	Sittles Farm, Alrewas	25. 7.08P
G-MZPW	Solar Wings Pegasus Quasar IITC (Rotax 582)	6892		26.10.94	T J Walsh	(Hereford)	30. 6.07P
G-MZRC	Pegasus Quantum 15 (Rotax 582)	7482		25.11.98	M Hopkins (Noted 11.07)	Rufforth	23. 2.03P
G-MZRH	Pegasus Quantum 15 (Rotax 582)	7269		11.10.96	R J Ware	Roddige	20. 7.07P
G-MZRM	Pegasus Quantum 15-912	7455		10. 7.98	A J Coton	(Balsall Common, Coventry)	1.11.08P
G-MZRS	CFM Shadow Series CD	141		4. 4.90	P C Hancox	Croft Farm, Defford	22. 6.08P
G-MZSC	Pegasus Quantum 15-912	7370		3.10.97	J A Lockert	(Hereford)	29. 5.08P
G-MZSD	Mainair Blade	1179-0998-7-W978		21. 8.98	M D Vearncombe	Weston Zoyland	1. 4.08P
G-MZSM	Mainair Blade (Rotax 582)	1000-0794-7-W796		15. 7.94	P R Anderson	Oxton, Nottingham	20.12.08P
G-MZTA	Mignet HM-1000 Balerit	120		14. 5.96	A Fusco tr Sky Light Group	(Burwash)	8. 5.01P
G-MZTS	Aerial Arts Chaser S 447	CH703	G-MVDM	19. 3.96	D G Ellis	(Tamworth)	7. 6.08P
G-MZUB	Rans S-6-ESD-XL Coyote II (Built B O Dowsett - pr.no.PFA 204-13244) (Tri-cycle u/c)	0897.1144		30. 4.98	B O Dowsett	Little Gransden	9. 8.08P
G-MZZT	Kolb Twinstar Mk.3 (Built P I Morgans - pr.no.PFA 205-12596)	K0006-0992		1. 5.98	D E Martin	Plaistows Farm, St Albans	26. 6.08P
G-MZZY	Mainair Blade	1050-0895-7-W848		13.11.95	A Mucznik	Oxton	22. 6.08P

G-NAAA - G-NZZZ

G-NAAA	MBB BÖ.105DBS-4 (Rebuilt with new pod S 912 C 1993)	S 34/912	G-BUTN	6. 4.99	Bond Air Services Ltd	Blackpool	21. 2.08E
			G-AZTI, EI-BTE, G-AZTI, EC-DRY, G-AZTI, D-HDAN (Operated Lancashire Air Ambulance)					
G-NAAB	MBB BÖ.105DBS-4	S 416	D-HDMO	23. 3.99	Bond Air Services Ltd	Thruxton	8. 4.08T
			D-HSTP, D-HDMO		(Operated Hampshire Ambulance Trust)		
G-NACA	Norman NAC-2 Freelance 180	2001		23.11.87	B E Norman	Little Rissington	
					(Stored 1.08)		
G-NACI	Norman NAC-2 Freelance 180	NAC.001	G-AXFB	20. 6.84	L J Martin and D G French	Sandown, Isle of Wight	1.10.08P
G-NADS	TEAM Mini-MAX 91 (Built G Evans and P M Spencer)	PFA 186-12995		8. 2.99	J P Harris	Church Farm, Askern	27. 4.08P
G-NADZ	Van's RV-4 (Built AE Tolle) (Lycoming O-360)	3	G-BROP N19AT	21. 6.07	J K Cook (Noted 8.07)	Hill Farm, Nayland	3.11.05P
G-NAGG	Rotorsport UK MT-03	RSUK/MT-03/012		18. 5.07	C A Clements	Bourne Park, Hurstbourne Tarrant	31. 5.08P
G-NANI	Robinson R44 Clipper II	11537		9. 1.07	MOS GmbH	Ahrensburg, Germany	18. 1.08E
G-NANO	Avid Speed Wing (Built T M C Handley)	PFA 189-12094		23. 1.08	T M C Handley	(Wood Street Village, Guildford)	
G-NAPO	Pegasus Quantum 15-912	7799		6. 4.01	A W Rodman	(West Kilbride)	26. 6.08P
G-NAPP	Van's RV-7 (Built R J Napp)	PFA 323-14115		3. 9.03	R J Napp	Brock Farm, Billericay	29.10.08P
G-NARG	Air Création Tanarg 912S/iXess 15	FLT.xxx		24. 6.05	K Kirby	Sywell	13. 1.08P
	(Built Flylight Airsports Ltd - pr.no.BMAA/HB/450 being Flylight kit comprising Trike s/n T05020 and Wing s/n A05040-5041)						
G-NARO	Cassutt Racer (Built P Musso) (aka Musso Racer Original)	M 14372	G-BTXR N68PM	14. 4.98	D A Wirdnam	Redhill	7.10.00P
G-NARR	Stolp SA300 Starduster Too (Built G J D Thomson)	PFA 035-14674		16.11.07	G J D Thomson	(West Lothian)	
G-NATT	Rockwell Commander 114A	14538	N5921N	14. 1.80	Northgleam Ltd	Liverpool	2.11.07E
G-NATX	Cameron O-65 Balloon (Hot Air)	1681		3. 3.88	A G E Faulkner	Willenhall	5. 5.91T
					(National Express Rapide titles)		
G-NATY	Folland Gnat T 1	FL.548	8642M XR537	19. 6.90	Drilling Systems Ltd	Bournemouth	
					(F/f 9. 8.07 after rebuild as "XR537" in Red Arrows c/s)		
G-NBDD	Robin DR.400-180 Régent	1103	F-BXVN	26. 9.88	B and S E Chambers	(Harringworth, Corby)	7. 3.08E
G-NCCI	Comco Ikarus C42 FB80	0708-6910		10.10.07	Fly42 Ltd	(Wootton Bassett, Swindon)	9.10.08P
G-NCFC	Piper PA-38-112 Tomahawk II	38-81A0107	N737V G-BNOA, N23272	14. 1.99	J D Yorke	Plymouth	6. 7.08E
G-NCFE	Piper PA-38-112 Tomahawk	38-80A0081	8642M G-BKMK OO-GME, (OO-HKD), N9676N	1. 7.99	R M Browes	Norwich	19. 8.07T
G-NCUB	Piper J-3C-65 Cub (L-4H-PI)	11599	G-BGXV F-BFQT, AO-GAB, 43-30308	6. 7.84	E V Moffatt and R E Nerou	Woodlow Farm, Bosbury	28.10.08P
G-NDAA	MBB BÖ.105DBS-4	S 914	G-WMAA G-PASB, VH-LSA, G-BDMC, D-HDEC (Operated North Devon Air Ambulance)	1. 2.06	Bond Air Services Ltd	Eaglescott	27. 9.08E
	(Rebuilt 1994 with new airframe: original frame c/n S 135 to The Helicopter Museum, Weston-super-Mare as "G-PASB" - see SECTION 4, Part 1						
G-NDGC	Grob G109	6150		7. 4.83	J E Bedford and M Mathieson	Rougham	23.11.07E
G-NDOL	Europa Aviation Europa (Built G K Brunwin - pr.no.PFA 247-12594) (NSI EA-81) (Monowheel u/c)	044		30.11.93	S Longstaff	Yew Tree Farm, Lymm Dam	29.10.07P
G-NDOT	Thruster T 600N 450	0052-T600N-066		18. 6.02	P C Bailey	Hill Farm, Over, Cambridge	10. 7.07P
G-NDPA	Comco Ikarus C42 FB UK (Built R O'Malley-White)	PFA 322-14056	G-OOMW	1.12.05	C K Jones	Sywell	28.10.08P
G-NEAL	Piper PA-32-260 Cherokee Six	32-1048	G-BFPY N5588J	7.11.83	V Walker tr VSD Group	Shobdon	2. 8.07
G-NEAT	Europa Aviation Europa (Built M Burton - pr.no.PFA 247-12642) (Tri-cycle u/c)	065		28. 6.94	M Burton	Sleap	21. 5.08P
G-NEAU	Eurocopter EC.135 T2	0333	D-HECB	13. 9.04	Northumbria Police Authority	Durham Tees Valley	15. 3.08T
G-NEEL	RotorWay Executive 90 (Built P N Haigh) (RotorWay RI 162)	5002		7. 8.90	C Bedford	(Skegness)	6. 7.08P
G-NEEN	MD Helicopters MD.500N Notar	LN018	G-NOTR N520MD	17.11.05	Otus Associates Ltd	Shoreham	27. 3.08E

Reg	Type	c/n	Prev id	Date	Owner/Operator	Location	Expiry
G-NEGG	EAA Acrosport II *(Built R S Challis)*	844	N715RJ	16. 1.04	D K Keays and R S Goodwin	Bidford	23. 8.08P
G-NEGS	Thunder Ax7-77 Balloon (Hot Air)	1059		18. 3.87	M Rowlands *"Hot-Shot"*	Ashton-in-Makerfield	15 5.05A
G-NEIL	Thunder AX3/503 Maxi Sky Chariot Balloon (Hot Air)	379		2.12.81	N A Robertson *"Neil" (Operated A Moore)*	Great Missenden	6. 4.08A
G-NELI	Piper PA-28R-180 Cherokee Arrow	28R-31011	OH-PWW D-EMWE, N7693J	9. 2.01	A Jahanfar	Southend	17. 4.08E
G-NELY	MD Helicopters MD.600N	RN018	N958SD	26.10.05	Eastern Atlantic Helicopters Ltd	Shoreham	1.11.07E
G-NEMO	Raj Hamsa X'Air Jabiru *(Built D G Smith - pr.no.BMAA/HB/158)*	602		11. 3.04	D G Smith *(Noted 4.04)*	Rochester	
G-NEON	Piper PA-32-300B Cherokee Six	32-40683	D-EMKW N4246R	7. 4.00	S C A Lever	Fairoaks	24. 5.08E
G-NERC	Piper PA-31-350 Navajo Chieftain	31-7405402	G-BBXX N66869	26. 4.94	Natural Environment Research Council *(Operated Air Atlantique)*	Coventry	19. 7.08E
G-NERO	Cameron Z-105 Balloon (Hot Air)	11042		20. 9.07	Tavolera SRL	Cuneo, Italy	9. 8.08E
G-NESA	Europa Aviation Europa XS *(Built K G and V E Summerhill - pr.no.PFA 247-13544) (Tri-gear u/c)*	450		17. 4.01	A M Kay *(New owner 2.08)*	Nuthampstead	
G-NESE	Tecnam P2002-JF	039		9. 6.06	N and S Easton *(Badly damaged 30. 9.07 in accident Blair Atholl and on repair 11.07)*	(Perth)	5. 7.08E
G-NESH	Robinson R44 Clipper II	11609		8. 2.07	M Tancock	(Hong Kong, PRC)	11. 3.08E
G-NEST	Christen Eagle II *(Built M Shay)*	SHAY 0001	N23MS	14. 9.06	P R Cox	Compton Abbas	12. 4.08P
G-NESV	Eurocopter EC.135 T1	0067		4. 2.99	Northumbria Police Authority *(Operated North East Police)*	Newcastle	30. 3.08E
G-NESW	Piper PA-34-220T Seneca III	34-8233072	D-GAMO N8064M	13.12.02	G C U Guida	Jersey	2. 2.08E
G-NESY	Piper PA-18 Super Cub 95	18-7482	N124SA SE-CUG	18. 8.00	V Fisher	North Side, Thorney	26 .3.08E
G-NETB	Cirrus SR22	1548	N226TS	10. 7.06	Cirrusnet Ltd	Turweston	11. 7.08E
G-NETR	Aérospatiale AS.355F1 Ecureuil 2	5164	G-JARV G-OGHL, N5796S	4.04.06	PLM Dollar Group Ltd *(Operated Network Rail)*	Cumbernauld	27. 5.08E
G-NETY	Piper PA-18-150 Super Cub	1809108	N4159K	8. 9.95	N B Mason	Rendcomb	3. 7.08E
G-NEWR	Piper PA-31-350 Navajo Chieftain	31-7952129	N35251	23. 8.79	MAS Airways Ltd	Biggin Hill	2.11.07E
G-NEWT	Beech 35 Bonanza *(Continental E-185 = C35 status)*	D-1168	G-APVW EI-BIL, G-APVW, N9866F, 4X-ACI, IDF/AF 0604, ZS-BTE	28. 2.90	J S Allison	RAF Halton	21. 7.08E
G-NEWZ	Bell 206B-3 JetRanger III	4475	C-GBVZ	28. 1.98	Guay Tulliemet Aviation Ltd	(Eastleigh)	1. 4.07
G-NFLA	British Aerospace Jetstream Series 3102	637	G-BRGN G-BLHC, G-31-637	15. 2.06	Cranfield University *(Operated National Flying Laboratory Centre)*	Cranfield	16. 7.08E
G-NFLY	Tecnam P2002-EA Sierra *(Built C N Hodgson)*	PFA 333-14613		28. 3.07	C N Hodgson	(London W5)	
G-NFNF	Robin DR.400-180 Régent	2047	VP-BNU VR-BNU, G-BTDU	15.11.02	N French	Lower Wasing Farm, Brimpton	3.12.07
G-NGRM	Spezio DAL-1 Tuholer *(Built R Mitchell) (Lycoming O-290-G)*	134	N6RM	14. 8.90	S H Crook *(Crashed near Le Touquet 24. 7.99 following engine failure: noted 12.03)*	Roughay Farm, Bishops Waltham	7. 2.00P
G-NHRH	Piper PA-28-140 Cherokee	28-22807	OY-BIC SE-EZP	19. 5.82	C J Milsom	Compton Abbas	19. 8.08E
G-NHRJ	Europa Aviation Europa XS *(Built D A Lowe - pr.no.PFA 247-13112) (Tri-gear u/c)*	333		30. 9.99	D A Lowe *(Noted 3.03)*	Lower Grounds Farm, Sherlowe	
G-NICC	Evektor EV-97 teamEurostar UK	1913		1. 3.04	Pickup and Son Property Maintenance Ltd	Leicester	9. 8.08P
G-NICI	Robinson R44 Raven II	10854		31. 8.05	David Fishwick Vehicles Sales Ltd	Coal Aston	10.10.07E
G-NICY	Beech B300C Super King Air	FM-16	N816KA	21.11.07	Raytheon Systems Ltd *(To become Beech 350C ER "ZZ417" for AAC 2008)*	Hawarden	27.11.10S
G-NIDG	Evektor EV-97 Eurostar *(Built N R Beale - pr.no.PFA 315-13580) (Also identified as Evektor 99 Eurostar)*	990609		29. 2.00	Skydrive Ltd	Church Farm, Shotteswell	30.11.05P
G-NIEN	Van's RV-9A *(Built G R Pybus)*	PFA 320-14419		19. 4.06	G R Pybus	Morgansfield, Fishburn	
G-NIFE	SNCAN Stampe SV-4A	156	F-BBBL French AF/CEV, F-BFCE, French AF/CEV	27. 5.05	C C Rollings and F J Hodson t/a Tiger Airways *(As "156" in French AF c/s)* Gloucestershire		6. 7.08T
G-NIGC	Avtech Jabiru UL-450 *(Built N Creeney - pr.no.PFA 274A-13703)*	xxxx		3. 5.01	R Holt	Mill Farm, Shifnal	15. 8.08P
G-NIGE	Luscombe 8E Silvaire Deluxe *(Continental C85)*	3525	G-BSHG N72098, NC72098	6. 6.90	Gardan Party Ltd	Popham	7. 5.08P
G-NIGL	Europa Aviation Europa *(Built N M Graham - pr.no.PFA 247-12775) (Conventional u/c)*	147		6. 7.95	N M Graham	(Chandlers Ford, Eastleigh)	
G-NIGS	Thunder Ax7-65 Balloon (Hot Air)	1663		30. 1.90	Sophie D Annett	Palestine, Andover	15. 4.06A
G-NIJM	Piper PA-28R-180 Arrow	28R-30644	D-EDTM N4923J	27. 8.04	A P Thorne	Shipdham	13.10.07E
G-NIKE	Piper PA-28-181 Cherokee Archer II	28-8390086	N4315N	4. 7.89	Key Properties Ltd	White Waltham	26.10.07E
G-NIKK	Diamond DA.20-C1 Katana	C0109	N909CT C-FDVP	5.12.05	Cubair Flight Training Ltd *(Nose-leg failed during landing Redhill 5. 6.06 and substantially damaged)*	Redhill	30. 1.08E
G-NIKO	Airbus A321-211	1250	D-AVZA	21. 6.00	Thomas Cook Airlines Ltd t/a MyTravel Airways	Manchester	20. 6.08E
G-NIMA	Balony Kubicek BB30Z Balloon (Hot Air)	458		16.10.06	C Williamson	Goudhurst, Cranbrook	16.10.07E
G-NIMB	Schempp-Hirth Nimbus 2C	180	BGA 2495-DYZ	3.10.07	M J Slade	Eyres Field	3. 4.08
G-NINA	Piper PA-28-161 Cherokee Warrior II	28-7716162	G-BEUC N3507Q	29. 7.88	A P Gorrod *(Noted 11.07)*	Tibenham	16.10.07E
G-NINB	Piper PA-28-180 Cherokee Challenger	28-7305234	SE-KHR OY-DLR, CS-AHY, N11C	16. 7.99	P A Layzell *(Seriously damaged in gales at Old Buckenham 1.07)*	Old Buckenham	21. 8.08E
G-NINC	Piper PA-28-180 Cherokee G	28-7205016	SE-KVH N2166T	2. 2.00	P A Layzell	Old Buckenham	12. 4.08E
G-NIND	Piper PA-28-180 Cherokee Challenger	28-7305420	SE-GAT	6. 6.07	P A Layzell	Old Buckenham	20. 9.08E

G-NINE	Murphy Renegade 912	448		16. 6.93	R F Bond	Garston Farm, Marshfield	6. 6.08P
	(Built R F Bond - pr.no.PFA 188-12191						
G-NIOG	Robinson R44 Clipper II	10471		1. 9.04	Alu-Fix Contracts Ltd	(Belfast)	27. 9.07E
G-NIOS	Piper PA-32-301 Saratoga II SP	32R-8513004	N4381Z	28. 9.90	D J Everett and R R Alderslade t/a Plant Aviaton		
			N105DX, N4381Z			Stapleford	19. 5.08E
G-NIPA	Nipper T 66 RA.45 Series 3	S 120	G-AWDD	7. 6.96	R J O Walker	North Lopham	13. 4.04P
	(Built Slingsby Aircraft Co Ltd as c/n 1627 for Nipper Aircraft Ltd) (Volkswagen 1834 (Acro))						
G-NIPP	Nipper T 66 RA.45 Series 3	S 103	G-AVKJ	17. 1.00	R J Porter	Insch	21. 8.97P
	(Volkswagen 1834)				*(Noted 4.07)*		
	(Originally built Avions Fairey SA as c/n T66/32: rebuilt Slingsby Aircraft Co Ltd as c/n 1587 for Nipper Aircraft Ltd)						
G-NIPR	Nipper T 66 RA.45 Series 3	S 108	G-AVXC	15. 7.05	P A Gibbs	Inverness	28.10.08P
	(Built Slingsby Aircraft Co Ltd as c/n 1605 for Nipper Aircraft Ltd) (Ardem 4C02)						
G-NITA	Piper PA-28-180 Cherokee C	28-2909	G-AVVG	16. 1.84	T Clifford	Cranfield	17.11.97T
	(Used spare Frame No.28-3807S)		N7517W		*(Wreck noted 1.06)*		
G-NIVA	Eurocopter EC.155B1	6642	N84AZ	2. 9.05	Lanthwaite Aviation Ltd	Cambridge	1. 9.08E
G-NIVT	Schempp-Hirth Nimbus 4T	3	BGA 4546-JJG	8.10.07	M Clarke and P G Sheard	Lasham	26. 2.08
			D-KIXL				
G-NJAG	Cessna 207 Skywagon	20700093	D-EMDN	2. 8.78	G H Nolan	Biggin Hill	21. 6.08E
			(N91152)				
G-NJBA	Rotorway Executive 162F	6927		10. 3.05	BWP (TV) Ltd t/a British Waterproofing		
					(Noted 2.08)	Street Farm, Takeley	
G-NJET	Schempp-Hirth Ventus cT	161/521	BGA 4461-JET	15. 1.08	J Hudson	Lasham	8. 3.08
			RAFGSA R38				
G-NJIM	Piper PA-32R-301T Turbo Saratoga		D-EHDL	19. 9.05	J L Rivers	Coventry	29.11.07E
		32R-8229035	N8147H				
G-NJPW	P&M Quik GT450	8150		2. 2.06	N J P West	Landmead Farm, Garford	2. 2.08P
G-NJSH	Robinson R22 Beta	0780		19. 4.88	A J Hawes	Sywell	29. 6.08E
G-NJSP	Avtech Jabiru J430	0xxx		6. 4.06	N J S Pitman	Brock Farm, Billericay	21. 9.07P
	(Built N J S Pitman - pr.no.PFA 336-14514)						
G-NJTC	Aeroprakt A22-L Foxbat	PFA 317A-14565		6. 9.06	B Jackson and T F Casey	Carlisle	15. 2.08P
	(Built B Jackson and T F Casey)						
G-NLEE	Cessna 182Q Skylane II	18265934	G-TLTD	1.12.93	G Hall	Compton Abbas	12. 6.08
			N759EL				
G-NLYB	Cameron N-105 Balloon (Hot Air)	10012		19. 4.01	P H E van Overwalle	Nazareth, Belgium	12. 4.08A
	(Pink Elephant Head Shape)						
G-NMAK	Airbus A319-115	2550	D-AVYH	27. 9.05	Twinjet Aircraft Sales Ltd	Luton	26. 9.08E
					(Operated Al Kharafi Group)		
G-NMBG	Avtech Jabiru J400	0xxx		15. 2.06	D K Shead	(Chattis Hill, Stockbridge)	
	(Built D K Shead - pr.no.PFA 325-14461)						
G-NMID	Eurocopter EC.135 T2	0300		29. 9.03	Derbyshire Constabulary	(Butterley Hall, Ripley)	29. 3.10S
					(Operated North Midlands Police)		
G-NMOS	Cameron C-80 Balloon (Hot Air)	4966		5. 1.01	C J Thomas and M C East	Farnham	17. 7.08A
					(Riversoft titles)		
G-NNAC	Piper PA-18-135 Super Cub	18-3820	PH-PSW	19. 5.81	PAW Flying Services Ltd	Bagby	31. 5.10S
	(L-21B-PI) (Frame No.18-3820)		R Neth AF R-130, 54-2420				
G-NNON	Mainair Blade	1318-0302-7-W1113		24. 4.02	D R Kennedy *(New owner 3.07)*	(Bathgate)	7. 6.06P
G-NOBI	Spezio HES-1 Tuholer Sport	162	N1603	28.11.90	T N J Cuypers	(Brecht, Belgium)	15. 8.07P
	(Built H E Stidham) (Continental C125)						
G-NOCK	Reims Cessna FR182 Skylane RG II	FR18200036	G-BGTK	18. 1.94	F J Whidbourne	Park Farm, East Worldham, Alton	14. 5.08
			(D-EHZB)				
G-NODE	Gulfstream AA-5B Tiger	AA5B-1182	N4533L	22. 5.81	Strategic Telecom Networks Ltd	Blackbushe	20. 7.08T
G-NODY	American General AG-5B Tiger	10076	N1194C	3.10.91	Abraxas Aviation Ltd *(Operated Cabair)*	Elstree	12. 3.08E
G-NOIR	Bell 222	47031	G-OJLC	9. 8.91	Goodman Real Estate Developments 2003		
			G-OSEB, G-BNDA, A40-CG			Blackbushe	31. 5.08E
G-NOIZ	Yakovlev Yak-55M	910104	RA-44537	5. 2.04	S C Cattlin	White Waltham	19. 7.08P
			HA-JAM, DOSAAF 04 *(blue)*				
G-NOMO	Cameron O-31 Balloon (Hot Air)	241		31.10.00	Tim Balloon Promotion Airships Ltd		
						Ceva, Piedmont, Italy	11.10.08A
G-NONE	Dyn'Aéro MCR-01 ULC	PFA 301B-14238		2. 7.04	J Flisher	Dunkeswell	30. 5.07P
	(Built J Flisher)						
G-NONI	Grumman AA-5 Traveler	AA5-0383	G-BBDA	1. 8.88	P J Evans tr November India Flying Group	Exeter	4. 7.08T
			(EI-AYL), G-BBDA				
G-NOOK	Mainair Blade 912S	1281-0401-7-W1076		11. 6.01	P M Knight	Elm Farm, Wickford	29. 9.08P
G-NOOR	Commander Aircraft Commander 114B	14656		6. 2.98	As-Al Ltd	Lausanne-La Blecherette, Switzerland	9. 6.08E
G-NORA	Comco Ikarus C42 FB UK	0504-6676		13. 7.05	N A Rathbone	Swinford, Rugby	29. 8.08P
	(Built N A Rathbone - pr.no.PFA 322-14420)						
G-NORB	Air et Aventure Saturne S11OK	SC981482		28.11.05	R N Pearce	(Halesowen)	
G-NORD	SNCAC NC.854	7	F-BFIS	20.10.78	W J McCollum	Coagh, County Londonderry	27. 5.82P
					(Remains noted 11.01 - new owner 2.06)		
G-NORT	Robinson R22 Beta	3404		7. 1.03	Plane Talking Ltd	Rochester	23. 2.08E
G-NOSE	Cessna 402B	402B0823	N98AR	23. 4.96	Reconnaissance Ventures Ltd	Coventry	7. 1.08E
			G-MPCU, SE-IRL, OO-TAT, (OO-SEL), N3946C *(Atlantic titles)*				
G-NOSY	Robinson R44 Astro	0064	G-LATK	6. 3.03	R C Hields t/a Hields Aviation	Hawarden	30. 5.08T
			G-BVMK				
G-NOTE	Piper PA-28-181 Archer III	2843082	D-ESPI	19. 9.97	J Beach	Elstree	26.10.07E
			N9282N				
G-NOTS	Best Off Sky Ranger 912S(1)	SKR0401433		24. 6.05	P M Dewhurst	Sywell	1. 8.08P
	(Built P M Dewhurst - pr.no.BMAA/HB/352)						
G-NOTT	Nott ULD2 Balloon (Hot Air)	06		11. 6.86	J R P Nott	London NW8	
G-NOTY	Westland Scout AH.1	F9630	XT624	5.11.97	R P Coplestone	Thruxton	23. 4.08P
G-NOUS	Cessna 172S Skyhawk	172S10649	N1733L	23. 1.08	Flyglass Ltd	(Beaconsfield)	
G-NOWW	Mainair Blade 912	1227-1299-7-W1020		10.12.99	C Bodill	Oxton	23. 2.06P
G-NPKJ	Van's RV-6	PFA 181-13138		12. 2.98	M R Turner	Sturgate	5. 3.08P
	(Built K Jones) (Lycoming IO-360)						

G-NPPL   Comco Ikarus C42 FB100   0306-6543
          (Officially regd as 0307-6543)
G-NROY   Piper PA-32RT-300 Lance II   32R-7985070
G-NRRA   SIAI-Marchetti SF.260W   116
G-NRSC   Piper PA-23-250 Aztec E   27-7305142
G-NRYL   Mooney M 20R Ovation   29-0303
G-NSBB   Comco Ikarus C42 FB100 VLA   PFA 322-14162
          (Built B Bayes and N E Sams)
G-NSEW   Robinson R44 Astro   0615
G-NSJS   Cessna 680 Citation Sovereign   680-0161
G-NSOF   Robin HR.200-120B   334
G-NSTG   Cessna F150F   F150-0058
          (Built Reims Aviation SA) (Wichita c/n 15063499) (Tail-wheel conversion)
G-NSUK   Piper PA-34-220T Seneca V   3449256
G-NTWK   Aérospatiale AS.355F2 Ecureuil 2   5347
G-NUFC   Best Off Sky Ranger Swift 912S(1) SKRxxxx768
          (Built C R Rosby - pr.no.BMAA/HB/529)
G-NUGC   Grob G103A Twin II Acro   34040-K-271
G-NUKA   Piper PA-28-181 Archer II   28-8290134
G-NULA   Flight Design CT2K   02-05-05-04
          (Assembled Pegasus Aviation as c/n 7913)
G-NUNI   Lindstrand LBL 77A Balloon (Hot Air) 1181
G-NUTA   Christen Eagle II   0471
          (Built D Sondermann)
G-NUTS   Cameron Mr Peanut 35 SS Balloon (Hot Air) 711
G-NUTT   Mainair Sports Pegasus Quik   8114
G-NUTY   Aérospatiale AS.350B Ecureuil   1490
G-NVBF   Lindstrand LBL 210A Balloon (Hot Air) 249
G-NWAA   Eurocopter EC.135 T2   0427
G-NWAR   Agusta A109S Grand   22019
G-NWDC   Robinson R22 Beta   3929
G-NWFC   Cessna 172P Skyhawk   17276305
G-NWFG   Cessna 172P Skyhawk   17274192
G-NWPR   Cameron N-77 Balloon (Hot Air)   1181
          (Rebuilt with new envelope c/n 1667)
G-NWPS   Eurocopter EC.135 T1   0063
G-NXUS   Miller Nexus Mustang   PFA 341-14578
          (Built G W Miller)
G-NYLE   Robinson R44 Raven II   11407
G-NYMB   Schempp-Hirth Nimbus 3dT   63
G-NYMF   Piper PA-25-235 Pawnee D   25-7556112
G-NYZS   Cessna 182G Skylane   18255135
G-NZGL   Cameron O-105 Balloon (Hot Air)   1361
G-NZSS   Boeing Stearman E75 (N2S-5) Kaydet 75-8611
          (Lycoming R-680)

G-90-1   2. 9.03   D C Jarman tr Papa Lima Group   Old Sarum 14.10.08P
G-LYNN   26.11.93   B Nedjati-Gilani   White Waltham 29. 2.08E
  G-BGNY, N3024L
F-GOBF   29.11.00   G Boot   Lydd   7. 6.08P
  Philippines AF BF8431, OO-SMB   *(As "BF8431:31" in Burkina Faso Defence Force c/s)*
N250MC   23. 6.00   Geminair Services Ltd   Bournemouth 11. 9.08A
  (N244AR), N250MC, EI-BXP, G-BSFL, PH-NOA, 9M-AUS, PH-NOA, N40378
N10391   10. 3.04   Deltamood Ltd   Wevelgem, Belgium   7. 4.08T
                     15. 1.04   B Bayes and N E Sams
                                          Orlingbury Hold Farm, Orlingbury 29. 5.08P
                      6. 7.99   Captive Audience (UK) Ltd   Denham 11. 7.08E
                     26. 9.07   Ferncroft Ltd   Jersey 26. 9.08E
                      4. 6.99   Modi Aviation Ltd   Sibson 28. 6.08E
G-ATNI   16. 8.89   Westair Flying Services Ltd   Sleap 26. 8.08E
N126RB (2)   27. 2.03   Genus Plc   Blackbushe   6. 3.08E
G-FTWO   16. 5.06   PLM Dollar Group Ltd   Inverness 18. 4.08E
  G-OJOR, G-FTWO, G-BMUS   *(Network Rail titles)*
                     22. 2.07   C R Rosby   (Belford)
BGA 4729-JRW   17. 1.08   M G Barnes tr University of Nottingham Glidng Club
  RAFGSA R15, RAFGGA 556   RAF Cranwell 17. 2.08
OY-CJI   9. 1.04   N Ibrahim   Panshanger 15. 5.08E
  N8209A
                     17.10.02   R C Skidmore tr G-NULA Flying Group
                                                      Norton, Daventry 30. 4.08P
                     15. 1.08   J A Folkes   Bulcote, Nottingham
D-ECCA   15. 8.06   R A Pugh tr Blue Eagle Group   Henstridge   7.11.08P
                     18. 2.81   Balloon Flights International Ltd   Bristol   7. 4.86A
                                "Mr Peanut II" (Inflated 4.06)
                     29. 4.05   G P Nutter   Bagby 31. 7.08P
G-BXKT   20. 7.98   J A Ruck   Shobdon 16.10.08E
  F-GXRT, N333FH, N5797V
                     19. 5.95   Airxcite Ltd t/a Virgin Balloon Flights   Wembley   4. 9.04T
                     10.10.05   Bond Air Services Ltd   Blackpool 30.11.07E
                                "Katie" (Operated North West Ambulance Authority)
                     21. 8.06   JJB Sports PLC   (Martland Mill, Wigan)   4.10.07E
                                (New owner 2.08)
G-SBAR   6.11.07   Heli-4-Charter LLP   Manchester 21. 9.08E
N98523   4. 7.07   North Weald Flying Group Ltd   North Weald
N6396K   31. 7.07   North Weald Flying Group Ltd   North Weald
                     15. 8.85   D B Court   Ormskirk 30. 6.93A
                                (New owner 4.02)
                     15.10.98   North Wales Police Authority   Boddelwydden 11. 2.08E
                     20. 9.06   G W Miller   (London N15)
                     14. 9.06   N O'Farrell   Weston, Leixlip, County Kildare   5.10.07E
BGA 4008-HKQ   9.11.07   A J Rees tr Nimbus Syndicate   Nympsfield 15. 2.08
OO-PAL   8. 2.02   The Bristol Gliding Club Proprietary Ltd Nympsfield 30. 5.08E
  N267JW, N9799P
                      8. 4.04   P Ragg   Portiamo, Portugal 26. 7.08E
G-ASRR   3. 9.86   R A., P M G and N T M Vale *"Nazgul"* Kidderminster 19. 9.07A
  (G-CBIL), EI-ATF, G-ASRR, N3735U
N4325   31. 1.89   D L H Barrell   Cherry Tree Farm, Monewden 27. 6.05T
  Bu.43517, 42-109578   *(As "343251:27" in USAAC c/s)*

G-OAAA - G-OZZZ

G-OAAA   Piper PA-28-161 Warrior II   2816107
G-OAAF   British Aerospace ATP   2029
G-OABB   SAN Jodel D 150 Mascaret   01
G-OABC   Colt 69A Balloon (Hot Air)   1159
G-OABO   Enstrom F-28A   097
G-OABR   American General AG-5B Tiger   10124
G-OACA   Piper PA-44-180 Seminole   44-7995202
G-OACE   Valentin Taifun 17E   1017
G-OACF   CAB Robin DR.400-180   2534
G-OACG   Piper PA-34-200T Seneca II   34-7870177
G-OACI   SOCATA MS.893E Rallye 180GT   13086
G-OACP   de Havilland DHC-1 Chipmunk 22   35
          (Built OGMA) (Lycoming O-360)
G-OADY   Beech 76 Duchess   ME-56
G-OAER   Lindstrand LBL 105A Balloon (Hot Air) 359
G-OAFF   Cessna 208 Caravan I   20800415

N9142N   8. 9.93   Central Aircraft Leasing Ltd   Halfpenny Green 22. 9.08E
G-JEMB   27. 2.07   Atlantic Airlines Ltd   Coventry 11. 7.08E
  N855AW, G-11-029
F-BJST   21. 1.97   K Manley   Swanborough Farm, Lewes 21. 3.08E
  F-WJST
                     17.11.87   P A C Stuart-Kregor   Newbury 26. 6.00A
G-BAIB   10. 7.98   C R Taylor   (Wacton, Norwich) 12. 7.08E
                     15. 4.98   Vulcan House Management UK Ltd   Biggin Hill   9. 8.07E
  N256ER
G-GSFT   31. 7.02   D Coplowe t/a Lenham Motorsport   Elstree 20. 1.08E
  EI-BYZ, N2193K
D-KCBA   22. 1.87   D R Piercy   Eyres Field 31. 5.08E
                     30.10.03   A C Fletcher   Sherburn-in-Elmet 22.12.07E
G-BUNR   10. 3.94   Cega Aviation Ltd   Goodwood   9.12.07E
  EI-CFI, N9245C
G-DOOR   5. 5.98   A M Quayle   Alderney   6. 4.08E
  EI-BHD, F-GBCF
(CS-DAO)   20. 8.96   Aeroclub de Portugal   Spanhoe 10. 3.07
  Portuguese AF FAP 1345   *(Noted 10.07)*
N5022M   27.10.86   Multiflight Ltd   Leeds-Bradford   1. 3.08E
                      4. 3.96   T M Donnelly *"Aero"*   Sprotbrough, Doncaster 25. 6.01A
N5265N   26. 6.07   R Durie tr Army Parachute Association
                                                          AAC Netheravon   4. 7.08E

Reg	Type	C/n	Prev id	Date	Owner/Operator	Location	Status
G-OAFR	Cameron Z-105 Balloon (Hot Air)	11018		30. 5.07	PSH Skypower Ltd	Woodborough, Pewsey	19. 7.08E
G-OAFT	Cessna 152 II	15285177	G-BNKM	19. 4.88	Evensport Ltd	Walton Hall Farm, Purleigh	18.11.02T
			N6161Q		*(Stored 1.07)*		
G-OAGI	FLS Aerospace Sprint 160	001	G-FLSI	30.11.06	Black Art Composites Ltd-British Light Aircraft Company Ltd		
	(Marketed as British Aircraft Company Redwing 160")					Thruxton	10. 9.08P
G-OAHC	Beech F33C Bonanza	CJ-133	G-BTTF	2. 9.91	Cirrus Aviation Ltd	Clacton	5. 8.08E
			PH-BND				
G-OAJB	Cyclone AX2000	7281	G-MZFJ	16. 2.99	T A Lipinski	(Ilford)	21. 5.07P
G-OAJC	Robinson R44 Raven	1381		12. 5.04	Adare International Transport Ltd		
						(Roscrea, County Tipperary)	29. 5.08E
G-OAJL	Comco Ikarus C42 FB100	0403-6589		18. 5.04	T Collins	Dunkeswell	20. 5.08P
G-OAJS	Piper PA-39 Twin Comanche C/R	39-15	G-BCIO	9. 3.94	Go-AJS Ltd	Sherburn-in-Elmet	21. 3.08E
			N49JA, N57RG, G-BCIO, N8860Y				
G-OAKR	Cessna 172S Skyhawk	172S9643	N21738	10. 6.04	A K Robson	Oaksey Park	23. 6.07
G-OALD	SOCATA TB-20 Trinidad	490	N54TB	17. 3.88	D A Grief t/a Gold Aviation	Biggin Hill	24. 5.08E
			F-GBLL				
G-OALH	Tecnam P92-EA Echo	PFA 318-13675		12. 6.01	L Hill	(Ulverston)	20. 3.07P
	(Built L Hill)						
G-OAMF	Pegasus Quantum 15-912	7764		20.12.00	P J Kilshaw	Graveley Hall Farm, Graveley	28. 3.08P
G-OAMG	Bell 206B-3 JetRanger III	2901	G-COAL	25. 2.86	Alan Mann Helicopters Ltd	Fairoaks	19. 6.08E
G-OAMI	Bell 206B-2 JetRanger II	464	G-BAUN	15. 3.01	Techno Solutions Ltd	Goodwood	2. 3.08E
			5N-BAY, G-BAUN, 5N-AOU, VR-BIA, G-BAUN, N2261W				
G-OAML	Cameron AML-105 Balloon (Hot Air)	3881		4.12.96	Stratton Motor Company (Norfolk) Ltd		
						Long Stratton, Norwich	9. 8.08A
G-OAMP	Reims Cessna F177RG Cardinal RG		G-AYPF	30.11.93	G D Boulger	(RAF Woodvale)	9.11.07E
	(Wichita c/n 17700098)	F177RG0006					
G-OANI	Piper PA-28-161 Warrior II	28-8416091	N43570	8. 1.91	J F Mitchell	Oxford	8. 9.97
					(Damaged Upton Farm, Dover 16.6.96: wreck noted 9.96)		
G-OANN	Zenair CH.601HDS Zodiac	PFA 162-12932		2. 2.96	I J M Donnelly	Stonehaven	26. 7.06P
	(Built P Noden) (Rotax 912-UL)						
G-OAPE	Cessna T303 Crusader	T30300245	N303MF	3. 2.99	C Twiston-Davies and P L Drew	Jersey	27. 2.08E
			D-INKA, N9960C, M303HW, N9960C				
G-OAPR	Brantly B 2B	446	(G-BPST)	21. 4.89	E D ap Rees t/a Helicopter International Magazine		
			N2280U			Weston-super-Mare	1. 7.07
G-OAPW	Glaser-Dirks DG-400	4-268		17. 4.90	P L Poole	(Acton Beauchamp, Worcester)	27. 6.08E
G-OARA	Piper PA-28R-201 Arrow III	2837002	N802ND	28.10.98	Obmit Ltd	(Albourne, Hassocks)	30. 5.08T
			N9622N				
G-OARC	Piper PA-28RT-201 Arrow IV	28R-7918009	EC-HXO	17. 8.99	Plane Talking Ltd	Elstree	4.11.07E
			G-OARC, EC-JAE, EC-HXO, G-OARC, G-BMVE, N3071K				
G-OARG	Cameron C-80 Balloon (Hot Air)	3379		20.10.94	G and R Madelin *"Argent"*	Farnham/London SW15	14.11.06A
G-OARI	Piper PA-28R-201 Arrow III	2837005	N170ND	14.10.02	Plane Talking Ltd	Denham	12.11.07E
G-OARO	Piper PA-28R-201 Arrow III	2837006	N171ND	30.10.01	Plane Talking Ltd	Bournemouth	5.11.07T
G-OART	Piper PA-23-250 Aztec D	27-4293	G-AXKD	26.11.93	A N and S L Palmer	Old Buckenham	3. 5.08E
			N6936Y				
G-OARU	Piper PA-28R-201 Arrow III	2837026	N174ND	24. 5.02	Plane Talking Ltd *(Operated Cabair)*	Bournemouth	16. 8.08E
G-OARV	ARV Aviation ARV-1 Super 2	008		18. 6.84	N R Beale	(Sproughton, Ipswich)	12.10.87P
	(Built ARV Aviation Ltd - pr.no.PFA 152-11060) (Originally kit no 001 and rebuilt with kit no.008 C 1986) (Stored 1.91)						
G-OASG	Schleicher ASW 27-18	29015	BGA 5235-KNT	13. 2.08	P F Brice	Wycombe Air Park	
			D-7429		*"629"*		
G-OASH	Robinson R22 Beta	0761	N2627Z	13. 6.88	J C Lane *(Operated Heliflight (UK))*	Gloucestershire	22. 6.08E
G-OASJ	Thruster T 600N 450 Sprint	0037-T600N-090		13.10.03	A S Johnson	Mapperton Farm, Newton Peverill	14.11.08P
G-OASP	Aérospatiale AS.355F2 Ecureuil 2	5479	F-GJAJ	3. 8.95	Helicopter Services Ltd	Wycombe Air Park	26. 1.08E
			F-WYMH				
G-OASW	Schleicher ASW 27	27227	BGA 5160-KKL	10. 3.06	M P W Mee *"MM"*	Wycombe Air Park	14. 3.07
					(Crashed into trees Lasham 8. 8.06 and substantially damaged)		
G-OATE	Pegasus Quantum 15-912	8064		27. 8.04	S J Goate	Sywell	26. 8.08P
G-OATV	Cameron V-77 Balloon (Hot Air)	2149		14. 2.90	W G Andrews	Plymouth	23.10.93A
G-OAVA	Robinson R22 Beta II	3303		8. 3.02	B W Faulkner		
						(Twentyways Farm, Ramsdean, Petersfield)	2. 4.08E
G-OAWD	Aérospatiale AS.350B Ecureuil	1790	G-IIPM	7. 2.06	Helicopter Ltd	Walton Wood	12. 3.08E
			G-GWIL				
G-OAWS	Cameron Colt 77A Balloon (Hot Air)	4340		23. 4.98	E A and H A Evans	Walton, Chesterfield	6. 7.05A
					(Active 5.07)		
G-OBAK	Piper PA-28R-201T Turbo Arrow III		D-EKOR	27. 8.02	D R Freeth t/a DP Group Aviation	Fairoaks	11.10.07
		28R-7703054	N1146Q				
G-OBAL	Mooney M 20J Mooney 201	24-1601	N56569	27.11.86	Thomsonfly Ltd *(Operated Britannia Flying Club)*Luton	25. 4.08E	
G-OBAM	Bell 206B-3 JetRanger III	4511	N6379U	25. 5.99	Cherwell Tobacco Ltd	(Whitchurch, Shropshire)	13. 7.08E
G-OBAN	SAN Jodel D 140B Mousquetaire II	80	G-ATSU	20. 2.92	Shauna R Cameron	North Connel, Oban	13. 6.07
			F-BKSA				
G-OBAX	Thruster T 600N 450 Jab Sprint	0051-T600N-053		12. 7.01	J Northage and M E Hutchinson		
						Baxby Manor, Husthwaite	14. 7.08P
G-OBAZ	Best Off Sky Ranger 912(2)	SKR0310391		17.11.03	B J Marsh	Plaistows Farm, St Albans	30. 6.08P
	(Built B J Marsh - pr.no.BMAA/HB/322)						
G-OBBC	Colt 90A Balloon (Hot Air)	1358		11. 5.89	R A and Maxine.A Riley	Bromsgrove	23. 2.07A
					(BBC in the Midlands titles) "Beeb"		
G-OBBO	Cessna 182S Skylane	18280534	N7274Z	8. 6.99	A E Kedros	Oxford	29. 6.08E
G-OBBY	Robinson R44	0939		4.12.00	Holdsmart Ltd	(London E18)	29.10.08E
G-OBCC	Cessna 560 Citation Ultra	560-0497	OE-GCD	8.12.06	MP Aviation LLP	(Horley)	11. 1.08E
			N497TA, TC-MET, N5161J				
G-OBDA	Diamond DA.20-A1 Katana	10260	C-FDVT	2. 7.98	Oscar Papa Ltd	Halfpenny Green	30. 7.08E
G-OBDM	Europa Aviation Europa XS	572		16.12.03	B D McHugh	(Orpington)	
	(Built B D McHugh - pr.no.PFA 247-14048)						
G-OBDN	Piper PA-28-161 Warrior III	2842177	N53586	10. 7.03	R M Bennett	(Tadworth)	15. 8.08E

Regn	Type	C/n	Prev id	Date	Owner/Operator	Base	Cert
G-OBEE	Boeing Stearman A75N1 Kaydet (N2S-3 Kaydet)	75-1174	N5580S N6734S, BuA3397	21. 2.05	P G Smith (As "3397:174" in US Navy c/s)	Old Buckenham	16. 6.08T
G-OBEI	SOCATA TB-200 Tobago XL (Carries Tobago GT titles)	2096	F-OIUX	26. 6.02	Rapido Aviation Ltd Weston, Leixlip, County Kildare		29. 6.08E
G-OBEN	Cessna 152 II	15281856	G-NALI G-BHVM, N67477	16. 8.93	Flying Time Ltd (Operated Airbase Flying Club)	Shoreham	29. 3.08E
G-OBET	Sky 77-24 Balloon (Hot Air)	178		22. 2.00	P M Watkins and S M Carden	Chippenham	12. 9.07A
G-OBEV	Europa Aviation Europa (Built M B Hill - pr.no.PFA 247-12813) (Monowheel u/c)	188		3. 2.98	M B Hill and N I Hill	(Dursley)	
G-OBFC	Piper PA-28-161 Warrior III	2816118	N9252X	15. 7.96	Bflying Ltd (Went off runway landing Henstridge 15. 4.07 and badly damaged: to Ringwood for possible rebuild)	Bournemouth	16. 8.08E
G-OBFE	Sky 120-24 Balloon (Hot Air)	167	D-OBFE	28. 4.03	H Schmidt	Siegen, Germany	23. 7.08
G-OBFS	Piper PA-28-161 Warrior III	2842039	N41274	4.12.98	Plane Talking Ltd	Denham	3.12.07E
G-OBGC	SOCATA TB-20 Trinidad	1898		13. 5.99	Bidford Airfield Ltd	Bidford	11. 7.08E
G-OBHD	Short SD.3-60 Variant 100	SH3714	G-BNDK G-OBHD, G-BNDK, G-14-3714	20. 1.87	BAC Leasing Ltd (New owner 11.06)	(Southend-on-Sea)	5. 3.06E
G-OBIB	Colt 120A Balloon (Hot Air)	4229		9. 1.98	M W A Shemilt (New owner 12.05) Henley-on-Thames		25. 1.02A
G-OBIL	Robinson R22 Beta	0792		10. 5.88	Aerolease Ltd	Sywell	24. 8.08E
G-OBIO	Robinson R22 Beta	1402	N7724M	29. 6.98	Heli Air Ltd	Denham	25. 8.08E
G-OBJB	Lindstrand LBL 90A Balloon (Hot Air)	640		12.11.99	Beaulah J Bower	Perugia, Umbria, Italy	27 4.08A
G-OBJH	Colt 77A Balloon (Hot Air)	2569		11. 3.94	Hayrick Ltd	Cranbrook	1. 9.07
G-OBJP	Pegasus Quantum 15-912	7847		29. 8.01	S J Baker	Sutton Meadows	22. 8.08P
G-OBJT	Europa Aviation Europa (Built J T Grant - pr.no.PFA 247-12623) (Rotax 912ULS) (Tri-gear u/c)	055	G-MUZO	16.11.00	B J Tarmar	Old Sarum	11. 9.08P
G-OBKS	Bell 407	53531	ZS-HCF C-GLZM	21. 3.07	Alard Properties Ltd	Blackpool	4. 6.08E
G-OBLC	Beech 76 Duchess	ME-249	N6635R	3. 6.87	Pridenote Ltd	Sturgate	17. 5.08E
G-OBLU	Cameron H-34 Balloon (Hot Air)	4914		4. 8.00	John Aimo Balloons SAS Mondovi, Piedmont, Italy (Blu titles)		19. 8.07A
G-OBMI	Mainair Blade	1289-0601-7-W1084		19. 6.01	I G Webster and P Clark Ashcroft Farm, Winsford		26. 7.08P
G-OBMP	Boeing 737-3Q8	24963		8. 1.92	British Midland Airways Ltd "Robin Hood Baby" (Operated bmiBaby)	East Midlands	19. 3.08E
G-OBMS	Reims Cessna F172N Skyhawk II	F17201584	OO-BWA (OO-HWA), D-EBYX	16. 4.84	D Beverley, A J and A P Ransome Sherburn-in-Elmet		7. 7.08E
G-OBMW	Grumman AA-5 Traveler	AA5-0805	G-BDFV	4. 7.79	Fretcourt Ltd	Leeds-Bradford	13. 6.08E
G-OBNA	Piper PA-34-220T Seneca V	3449002	N9281D (N338DB)	25. 5.00	Palmair Ltd	Elstree	14. 8.08E
G-OBNC	Britten-Norman BN-2B-20 Islander	3000		9. 2.05	Britten-Norman Aircraft Ltd	Bembridge	
G-OBNL	Britten-Norman BN-2A-21 Islander	523	G-BDVX Belgian Army B-07, G-BDVX	21. 5.07	B-N Group Ltd	Bembridge	9. 5.08E
G-OBNW	Piper PA-31-350 Navajo Chieftain	31-7305103	OY-EBE EI-BYE, G-BFDA, SE-GDR, N9684N (New owner 2.08)	4. 4.03	D A Hoyle	Blackpool	5. 5.07T
G-OBRA	Cameron Z-315 Balloon (Hot Air)	10729		11. 8.05	Cameron Flights Southern Ltd Woodborough, Pewsey		21. 2.08E
G-OBRY	Cameron N-180 Balloon (Hot Air)	3010		1. 3.93	A C K Rawson and J J Rudoni t/a Wickers World Hot Air Balloon Company (Bryant Homes titles)	Stafford	21. 8.08T
G-OBSM	Robinson R44 Raven	1030	G-CDSE N43861, C-FAEP	15.12.05	Flight Solutions Ltd	Panshanger	26. 1.08E
G-OBTS	Cameron C-80 Balloon (Hot Air)	3589		18. 4.95	C F Cushion	Petersfield	21. 9.07A
G-OBUN	Cameron A-250 Balloon (Hot Air)	4711		29. 2.00	A C K Rawson and J J Rudoni t/a Wickers World Hot Air Balloon Company	Stafford	16.11.05T
G-OBUP	Glaser-Dirks DG-800B	8-381B280X42		31.10.07	J D Montagu	Lasham	
G-OBUU	Comper CLA.7 Swift replica (Built J A Pothecary and R H Hunt)	PFA 103-12165		25. 1.07	J A Pothecary and R H Hunt	(Old Sarum)	
G-OBUY	Colt 69A Balloon (Hot Air)	2031		7. 8.91	A D Kent tr Balloon Preservation Flying Group Petworth		5. 5.07A
G-OBYB	Boeing 767-304ER	28040		17. 5.96	Thomsonfly Ltd	Luton	16. 5.08E
G-OBYD	Boeing 767-304ER	28042	SE-DZG G-OBYD	4. 3.97	Thomsonfly Ltd	Luton	2. 5.08E
G-OBYE	Boeing 767-304ER	28979	D-AGYE G-OBYE	26. 2.98	Thomsonfly Ltd "Bill Travers"	Luton	28.10.07E
G-OBYF	Boeing 767-304ER	28208	D-AGYF G-OBYF	8. 6.98	Thomsonfly Ltd	Luton	30. 4.08E
G-OBYG	Boeing 767-304ER	29137		13. 1.99	Thomsonfly Ltd	Luton	12. 1.08E
G-OBYH	Boeing 767-304ER	28883	SE-DZO D-AGYH, G-OBYH	4. 2.99	Thomsonfly Ltd	Luton	24. 4.08E
G-OBYI	Boeing 767-304ER	29138		1. 2.00	Thomsonfly Ltd	Luton	31. 1.08E
G-OBYJ	Boeing 767-304ER	29384		20. 2.00	Thomsonfly Ltd	Luton	18. 2.08E
G-OBYT	Agusta-Bell 206A JetRanger	8237	G-BNRC Oman AF 601	30. 1.95	R J Everett	(Sproughton, Ipswich)	12. 7.03T
G-OCAD	Sequoia F 8L Falco (Built C W Garrard) (Lycoming IO-320)	PFA 100-12114		8. 6.92	I R Court tr Falco Flying Group	Leicester	23. 1.08P
G-OCAM	Gulfstream AA-5A Cheetah	AA5A-0741	G-BLHO OO-RTJ, OO-HRN	24. 3.94	I H Seach-Allen Standalone Farm, Meppershall		10. 9.08E
G-OCAR	Colt 77A Balloon (Hot Air)	1099		6. 8.87	S C J Derham "Toyota"	Bridgnorth	25. 8.00A
G-OCBI	Schweizer 269C-1 (Schweizer 300)	0139	N86G	14. 8.02	JWL Helicopters Ltd	Biggin Hill	10.10.07E
G-OCBS	Lindstrand LBL 210A Balloon (Hot Air)	602		21. 7.99	G Binder	Sonnenbuhl, Germany	4. 9.08A
G-OCBT	IAV Bacau Yakovlev Yak-52	9011011	LY-AQH HA-HUZ, LY-AMC, DOSAAF 103 (yellow)	30. 3.05	W M Burnett t/a Cambridge Business Travel Little Gransden		16. 5.08P
G-OCCD	Diamond DA.40D Star	D4.225		21. 9.06	Plane Talking Ltd (Operated Cabair)	Elstree	22.10.07E
G-OCCE	Diamond DA.40D Star	D4.226	OE-VPU	22 9.06	Plane Talking Ltd (Operated Cabair)	Cranfield	7.12.07E
G-OCCF	Diamond DA.40D Star	D4.229	OE-VPU	2 10.06	Plane Talking Ltd (Operated Cabair)	Cranfield	31.10.07E
G-OCCG	Diamond DA.40D Star	D4.230	OE-VPU	9.10.06	Plane Talking Ltd (Operated Cabair)	Cambridge	20.11.07E

G-OCCH	Diamond DA.40D Star	D4.233		9.10.06	Venturi Capital Ltd *(Operated Cabair)*		Cranfield	20.11.07E
G-OCCK	Diamond DA.40D Star	D4.234	OE-VPT	23.11.06	Venturi Capital Ltd *(Operated Cabair)*		Cranfield	16. 1.08E
G-OCCL	Diamond DA.40D Star	D4.237		17.10.06	Venturi Capital Ltd *(Operated Cabair)*		Cranfield	20.11.07E
G-OCCM	Diamond DA.40D Star	D4.238		16.11.06	Plane Talking Ltd *(Operated Cabair)*		Cranfield	12.12.07E
G-OCCN	Diamond DA.40D Star	D4.241	OE-VPU (G-OCCT)	23.11.06	Venturi Capital Ltd *(Operated Cabair)*		Cranfield	29. 1.08E
G-OCCO	Diamond DA.40D Star	D4.242		29.11.06	Plane Talking Ltd *(Operated Cabair)*		Cranfield	16. 1.08E
G-OCCP	Diamond DA.40D Star	D4.245	OE-VPU (G-OCCU)	7.12.06	Plane Talking Ltd *(Operated Cabair)*		Elstree	28. 1.08E
G-OCCR	Diamond DA.40D Star	D4.246	OE-UDV	5. 1.07	Gamich LLP		(London SW1)	8. 2.08E
G-OCCS	Diamond DA.40D Star	D4.249	OE-VPU	15.12.06	Plane Talking Ltd *(Operated Cabair)*		Elstree	16. 1.08E
G-OCCT	Diamond DA.40D Star	D4.250	OE-UDP	14.12.06	Plane Talking Ltd *(Operated Cabair)*		Stapleford	28. 1.08E
G-OCCU	Diamond DA.40D Star	D4.252		18.12.06	Plane Talking Ltd *(Operated Cabair)*		Elstree	8. 2.08E
G-OCCV	Diamond DA.42 Twin Star	42.010	F-GSIM	22.11.07	Chalrey Ltd		Cranfield	
G-OCCW	Diamond DA.42 Twin Star	42.154	OE-VPY	3. 8.06	Plane Talking Ltd *(Operated Cabair)*		Cranfield	6. 9.08E
G-OCCX	Diamond DA.42 Twin Star	42.155	OE-VPW	3. 8.06	Plane Talking Ltd *(Operated Cabair)*		Cranfield	10. 9.08E
G-OCCY	Diamond DA.42 Twin Star	42.158		3. 8.06	Venturi Capital Ltd *(Operated Cabair)*		Cranfield	6. 9.08E
G-OCCZ	Diamond DA.42 Twin Star	42.161		23. 8.06	Venturi Capital Ltd *(Operated Cabair)*		Cranfield	10. 9.08E
G-OCDP	Flight Design CTSW	06.08.22		23.10.06	M A Beadman	Armshold Farm, Kington		31. 8.08P
	(Assembled P&M Aviation Ltd as c/n 8226)							
G-OCDW	Avtech Jabiru UL-450	xxxx		31. 3.04	H Burroughs		Henstridge	3. 1.08P
	(Built C D Wood - pr.no.PFA 274A-14122)							
G-OCEG	Beech 200 Super King Air	BB-588	N578BM	11. 9.07	Cega Aviation Ltd	Wycombe Air Park		
					(Noted 10.07)			
G-OCFC	Robin R2160	374		21. 6.02	Cornwall Flying Club Ltd		Bodmin	24. 7.08T
G-OCFD	Bell 206B-3 JetRanger III	3165	G-WGAL	10. 6.04	Cranfield Helicopters Ltd		Sywell	29. 4.08E
			G-OICS, N678TM, N678TW					
G-OCFM	Piper PA-34-200 Seneca	34-7350021	G-ELBC	20. 4.04	Stapleford Flying Club Ltd		Stapleford	27.12.07T
			G-BANS, N15110		*(Operated Capital Radio)*			
G-OCHM	Robinson R44 Raven	1055		4. 5.01	Westleigh Developments Ltd			
						Whetstone, Leicestershire		6. 5.08E
G-OCJK	Schweizer 269C	S 1294	N69A	10.12.87	P Crawley		Shipley	27. 5.00
	(Schweizer 300)				*(New owner 5.02)*			
G-OCJT	Cessna 525A CitationJet CJ2	525A0113	N525VV	12. 6.07	Standard Aviation Ltd		Newcastle	11. 6.08E
G-OCLC	Aviat A-1B Husky *(Floatplane)*	2380	N440HY	8. 6.07	Caledonian Seaplanes Ltd	St Fillans, Loch Earn		10. 6.08E
G-OCMM	Agusta A109A II	7347	G-BXCB	20. 3.01	Meade Air LLP	(Sherston, Malmesbury)		13. 8.08E
			F-GJSH, G-ISEB, G-IADT, G-HBCA					
G-OCMT	Evektor EV-97 teamEurostar UK	1701		14. 7.03	P Crowhurst		Sywell	3. 8.08P
G-OCON	Robinson R44 Raven	1608		12. 5.06	Conwell Contracts (UK) Ltd		Enniskillen	31. 5.08E
G-OCOV	Robinson R22 Beta II	3217		23. 5.01	Flight Training Ltd		Coventry	5. 6.08T
G-OCPC	Reims Cessna FA152 Aerobat	FA1520343		20. 1.78	Westward Airways (Lands End) Ltd		St Just	12. 8.08E
G-OCRI	Colomban MC-15 Cri-Cri	524		24. 6.92	M J J Dunning	(Bredbury, Stockport)		
	(Built M J J Dunning - pr.no.PFA 133-12288)							
G-OCSC	Bombardier CL-600-2B16	5505	N655TS	4. 9.06	Ocean Sky (UK) Ltd		East Midlands	21. 9.08E
	(CL-604 Challenger)		VP-BHS, N505JD, C-GLYK					
G-OCSD	Bombardier CL-600-2B16	5591	N604CD	4. 9.06	Ocean Sky (UK) Ltd		East Midlands	5. 9.08E
	(CL-604 Challenger)		C-GLYA					
G-OCST	Agusta-Bell 206B-3 JetRanger III	8694	N39AH	14.12.94	Lift West Ltd		Liskeard Heliport	31. 1.08E
			VR-CDG, G-BMKM					
G-OCTI	Piper PA-32-260 Cherokee Six	32-288	G-BGZX	26. 7.88	D G Williams	(Dinan, France)		2. 9.08E
			9XR-MP, 5Y-ADH, N3427W					
G-OCTU	Piper PA-28-161 Cadet	2841282	EC-IHB	16.11.89	S J Skilton t/a Aviation Rentals		Denham	24. 7.08E
			G-OCTU, N91997					
G-OCUB	Piper J-3C-90 Cub (L-4J-PI)	13248	OO-JOZ	21. 4.81	C A Foss and P A Brook tr Florence Flying Group *"Florence"*			
	(Frame No.13078)		PH-NKC, PH-UCH(1), 45-4508		*(Operated Zebedee Flying Group)*	Shoreham		19. 8.08P
	(Officially regd with c/n 13215, f/n 13045, but this was 45-4475/PH-UCW and rebuilt as PH-UCH(2))							
G-ODAC	Reims Cessna F152 II	F15201824	G-BITG	19.12.96	T M and M L Jones		Derby	15. 9.07T
	(Rebuilt with cockpit/front fuselage of G-BITG 6.96)				*(Operated Derby Aero Club)*			
G-ODAD	Colt 77A Balloon (Hot Air)	2001		20. 2.91	K Meehan *"Odyssey"*		Much Wenlock	12.10.08A
G-ODAF	Lindstrand LBL 105A Balloon (Hot Air)	1042		10. 3.05	T J Horne	North Crawley, Newport Pagnell		23. 5.08E
					(LDV and Brian Currie titles)			
G-ODAK	Piper PA-28-236 Dakota	28-7911162	D-EXMA	29. 2.00	Airways Aero Associations Ltd	Wycombe Air Park		8. 4.08E
			OH-SMO, N386WT, N22328		*(Operated British Airways Flying Club) (Union Flag c/s)*			
G-ODAT	Aero L-29 Delfin	194227	ES-YLV	28. 7.99	Graniteweb Ltd		North Weald	15. 3.06P
			Estonian AF, Soviet AF					
G-ODAY	Cameron N-56 Balloon (Hot Air)	551		16. 7.79	The British Balloon Museum and Library Ltd			
						Southampton		9. 7.07A
G-ODBN	Lindstrand Flowers SS Balloon (Hot Air)	389		22. 5.96	Magical Adventures Ltd *"Sainsbury's Flowers"*			
						West Bloomfield, Michigan, US		12.10.03A
G-ODCC	Bell 206L-3 LongRanger III	51070	N206LS	7. 2.07	D Chisnall t/a DCC Aviation			
						(Blackfield, Southampton)		3. 7.08E
G-ODCS	Robinson R22 Beta II	2828		19. 5.98	L Crevatin		(London NW8)	29. 9.07T
G-ODDS	Pitts S-2A	2225	N31486	31. 8.05	A C Cassidy		White Waltham	17.10.07E
	(Built Aerotek Inc)							
G-ODDY	Lindstrand LBL 105A Balloon (Hot Air)	042		15. 7.93	P and T.Huckle		Oakwood, Derby	25. 5.08A
G-ODEE	Van's RV-6	PFA 181A-13173	PH-RVM	14. 4.00	D Cook	(Middleton, Tamworth)		27. 3.08P
	(Built D Powell)		G-ODEE					
G-ODEN	Piper PA-28-161 Cadet	2841282	N92004	22.11.89	S J Skilton t/a Aviation Rentals		Denham	12.12.07E
G-ODGS	Avtech Jabiru UL-450	0247		2. 8.99	D G Salt		(Ashbourne)	11. 6.08P
	(Built D G Salt - pr.no.PFA 274A-13472)							
G-ODHB	Robinson R44 Raven II	10985		5.12.05	A J Mossop		Gloucestershire	17. 1.09E
					(Operated Rise Helicopters)			
G-ODIN	Mudry CAP.10B	192	F-GDTH	16.12.93	T W Harris		Wycombe Air Park	7. 8.08T
G-ODJB	Robinson R22 Beta II	3463		10. 7.03	N T Burton		Costock	29. 8.08E

Reg	Type	C/n	Prev id	Date	Owner/Operator	Location	Date
G-ODJD	Raj Hamsa X'Air 582(7)	559		25. 4.01	M Bastin	Lower Upham Farm, Chiseldon	19.10.07P
	(Built D J Davis - pr.no.BMAA/HB/151)						
G-ODJF	Lindstrand LBL 90B Balloon (Hot Air)	1075		11. 4.06	Helena Dos Santos SA	Corroios, Portugal	21. 6.08E
G-ODJG	Europa Aviation Europa	167		3. 5.96	C S Andersson and K R Challis *(New owners 1.08)*		
	(Built D J Goldsmith - pr.no.PFA 247-12889) (Monowheel u/c)					New House Farm, Great Oakley	9.11.07P
G-ODJH	Mooney M 20C Mark 21	690083	G-BMLH	19. 1.93	A P Howells	(Pontypridd)	13. 9.08E
			N9293V				
G-ODLY	Cessna 310J	310J0077	G-TUBY	21. 3.88	R Himmelein	Blackbushe	21. 6.08
			G-ASZZ, N3077L				
G-ODMC	Aérospatiale AS.350B1 Ecureuil	2200	G-BPVF	17.10.89	D M Coombs t/a DM Leasing Company	Denham	26.10.08E
G-ODNH	Schweizer 269C-1	0112	N41S	5. 9.00	DNH Helicopters Ltd	Turweston	25. 9.08E
	(Schweizer 300)						
G-ODOC	Robinson R44 Astro	0372		27. 8.97	Gas and Air Ltd	Wycombe Air Park	21. 1.07T
G-ODOG	Piper PA-28R-200 Cherokee Arrow II	28R-7235197	EI-BPB	2. 8.96	Advanced Investments Ltd	Sibson	8.10.07E
			G-BAAR, N11C				
G-ODPJ	Magni M-16 Tandem Trainer	VPM16-UK-111	G-BVWX	4. 4.03	K J Robinson and S Palmer	RAF Benson	9. 9.08P
	(Built M L Smith) (Arrow GT1000R)						
G-ODRY	Evektor EV-97 teamEurostar UK	2316		28. 4.05	C Prince and P Maddox	Halfpenny Green	27. 4.08P
G-ODSK	Boeing 737-37Q	28537		23. 7.97	British Midland Airways Ltd	East Midlands	27. 7.08E
					"Baby Dragon fly" (Operated bmiBaby)		
G-ODTW	Europa Aviation Europa	215		7. 9.95	D T Walters	(Meopham, Gravesend)	
	(Built D T Walters - pr.no.PFA 247-12890) (Monowheel u/c)						
G-ODUD	Piper PA-28-181 Cherokee Archer II	28-7790107	G-IBBO	15. 3.04	G-ODUD Aviation Ltd	(Ardingly, Haywards Heath)	13. 3.08E
			D-EPCA, N5389F				
G-ODUO	Schempp-Hirth Duo Discus	29	BGA 4113-HQE	26.11.07	A J Eddie tr 3D Syndicate	Aboyne	25. 4.08
G-ODVB	CFM Shadow Series DD	300-DD	G-MGDB	3.11.98	R J Slatter	Newnham, Baldock	29. 7.07P
G-OEAC	Mooney M 20J Mooney 201	24-1636	N57656	16. 6.88	S Lovatt	Tollerton	5. 4.08E
G-OEAT	Robinson R22 Beta	0650	G-RACH	8. 1.98	C Y O Seeds Ltd	Wycombe Air Park	17. 3.08E
G-OEBJ	Cessna 525 CitationJet	525-0423	N292SG	8. 8.06	European Business Jets Syndicate GNS LLP		
			N62SH, N5201J			Cambridge	23. 8.08E
G-OECM	Commander Aircraft Commander 114B	14627	N6107Y	4. 3.04	ECM (Vehicle Delivery Service) Ltd	Carlisle	6. 4.08E
G-OEDB	Piper PA-38-112 Tomahawk	38-79A0167	G-BGGJ	9. 5.89	M A Petrie	Hawarden	8. 3.08E
			N9694N				
G-OEDP	Cameron N-77 Balloon (Hot Air)	2189		28.12.89	M J Betts *"Eastern Counties Press"*	Norwich	12. 6.01A
G-OEGG	Cameron Egg 65 SS Balloon (Hot Air)	2140		4.12.89	A D Kent t/a Calorie Watch Balloon Team	Petworth	22. 6.08A
G-OEGL	Christen Eagle II	001	N46JH	12. 1.98	R Dauncey tr The Eagle Flight Syndicate	Shoreham	30. 4.08P
	(Lycoming IO-360)						
G-OEJC	Robinson R44 Clipper *(Floats)*	1469		4. 4.05	A J Cain	Sywell	21. 4.08E
G-OELD	Pegasus Quantum 15-912	7765		20.12.00	R P Butler	Newtownards	17. 3.08P
G-OELZ	Wassmer WA.52 Europa	66	F-BTLO	10. 8.05	J A Simms tr G-OELZ Group	Breighton	22. 3.08E
G-OEMT	Eurocopter MBB BK-117C-1	7538	D-HMEC	13. 2.06	Sterling Helicopters Ltd	RAF Wyton	26. 3.08E
					(Operated East Anglia Air Ambulance)		
G-OERR	Lindstrand LBL 60A Balloon (Hot Air)	469		30. 6.97	P C Gooch	Alresford	4. 5.08E
G-OERS	Cessna 172N Skyhawk II	17268856	G-SSRS	24. 5.94	E R Stevens	Leicester	27. 9.08E
			N734HA				
G-OERX	Cameron O-65 Balloon (Hot Air)	4004		23. 1.96	R Roehsler	(Vienna, Austria)	27. 2.97A
G-OESY	Reality Easy Raider Jab22	0005		16.11.01	G C Long	Plaistows Farm, St Albans	16. 6.08P
	(Built T F Francis - pr.no.BMAA/HB/193)						
G-OETI	Bell 206B-3 JetRanger III	2533	G-RMIE	23. 7.02	AIM Racing Ltd	Manston	27. 2.08E
			G-BPIE, N327WM				
G-OETV	Piper PA-31-350 Navajo Chieftain	31-7852073	N27597	16. 6.04	Skydrift Ltd	Norwich	30. 6.08E
G-OEVA	Piper PA-32-260 Cherokee Six	32-219	G-FLJA	13. 3.03	M G Cookson	North Weald	22. 3.08E
	(Rebuilt using spare Frame No.32-860S)		G-AVTJ, N3373W				
G-OEWD	Raytheon RB390 Premier 1	RB-126	N3726G	3. 6.05	Bookajet Aircraft Management Ltd	Farnborough	9. 6.08E
G-OEZI	Reality Easy Raider Jab22	0007		31. 5.02	J R Moore	Baxby Manor, Husthwaite	16. 5.08P
	(Built M A Claydon - pr.no.BMAA/HB/216) (Replacement fuselage fitted as original noted Westfield Farm, Hailsham 2004)						
	(Stalled during touch-and-go Staindrop, County Durham 20.10.07, struck ground and extensively damaged)						
G-OEZY	Europa Aviation Europa	042		8. 8.95	A W Wakefield	Conington	19. 7.07P
	(Built A W Wakefield - pr.no.PFA 247-12590) (Monowheel u/c)						
G-OFAA	Cameron Z-105 Balloon (Hot Air)	10886		9. 8.06	D J Constant "Royal Navy".	Queen Camel, Yeovil	5. 8.08E
G-OFAS	Robinson R22 Beta	0559		17. 6.86	Fast Helicopters Ltd	Thruxton	25. 4.08E
G-OFBJ	Thunder Ax7-77A Balloon (Hot Air)	2050		2. 9.91	J C Harris *(New owner 2.08)*	Newbury	25. 9.99A
G-OFBU	Comco Ikarus C42 FB UK	0301-6328		28. 8.01	J Pearce tr Old Sarum C42 Group	Old Sarum	31. 1.08P
	(Built Fly Buy Ultralights Ltd - pr.no.PFA 322-13653)						
G-OFCH	Agusta-Bell 206B-2 JetRanger II	8337	HB-XUI	15. 5.00	Fleet Coast Helicopters Ltd	Shoreham	11. 7.03T
			G-BKDA, LN-OQX	*(Rolled over, struck ground Morn Farm, Chickerell 4. 1.02 and badly damaged)*			
G-OFCM	Reims Cessna F172L	F17200839	G-AZUN	21.10.81	J R Wright	Jersey	27. 6.08E
			(OO-FCB)				
G-OFDT	Mainair Pegasus Quik	8320		9.11.07	D Bardsley	(Hyde)	2.12.08P
G-OFER	Piper PA-18-150 Super Cub	18-7709058	N83509	29.12.89	M S W Meagher	Shenington	20. 2.08
G-OFFA	Pietenpol AirCamper	PFA 047-13181		3.11.98	D J Street tr Offa Group	Bicester	14. 2.08P
	(Built Offa Group)				*"Sweet FA"*		
G-OFFO	Extra EA.300/L	1226		10. 3.06	2 Excel Aviation Ltd *(2 Excel Aviation titles)*	Sywell	23. 3.08E
G-OFIL	Robinson R44 Astro	0555		15. 1.99	B J North t/a North Helicopters	Redhill	21. 4.08E
G-OFIT	SOCATA TB-10 Tobago	938	G-BRIU	11. 9.89	G M Richards tr GFI Aviation Group	White Waltham	26. 5.08E
G-OFLY	Cessna 210M Centurion II	21061600	(D-EBYM)	13.10.79	A P Mothew	Southend	30. 7.08E
			N732LQ				
G-OFMC	British Aerospace Avro 146-RJ100	E3264	G-CDUI	11. 4.07	Flightline Ltd	Southend	7.12.07E
			TC-THM, G-6-264		*(Operated Ford Motor Company) (Noted 1.08)*		
G-OFOA	British Aerospace BAe 146 Series 100	E1006	G-BKMN	3. 3.98	Formula One Adminstration Ltd	Biggin Hill	14. 7.08E
			EI-COF, SE-DRH, G-BKMN, G-ODAN				
G-OFOM	British Aerospace BAe 146 Series 100	E1144	N3206T	16. 3.00	Formula One Management Ltd	Biggin Hill	6.10.07E
			PK-DTA, G-BSLP, (PK-DTA), G-6-144, G-11-144, (G-BRLM)				

G-OFOX	Denney Kitfox	PFA 172-11523		1.11.89	P R Skeels	(Sandbach)	
	(Built P R Skeels)						
G-OFRB	Everett Gyroplane Series 2	006	(G-BLSR)	7. 8.85	C Gilholm	(Selkirk)	18. 2.08P
	(Rotax 582)						
G-OFRY	Cessna 152 II	15281420	G-BPHS	8. 2.93	Devon and Somerset Flight Training Ltd	Dunkeswell	5. 4.08E
			N49971				
G-OFST	Bell 206L-3 LongRanger III	51300	5B-CJW	2.11.06	Heron Helicopters Ltd	(Herne Bay)	6.11.08E
			G-BXIB, EC-EQQ				
G-OFTI	Piper PA-28-140 Cherokee Cruiser	28-7325201	G-BRKU	11. 6.90	G S A Spencer	Andrewsfield	16.10.07E
			N15926				
G-OGAN	Europa Aviation Europa	100		28. 7.94	J R Malpass	Henstridge	18. 9.07P
	(Built M A Jackson, M P Gogan and R S Cullum - pr.no.PFA 247-12734) (Tri-gear u/c)						
G-OGAR	PZL-Bielsko SZD-45A Ogar	B-601	SP-0004	29. 1.90	P Rasmussen tr Perranporth Ogar Flying Group		
						Perranporth	5. 6.08E
G-OGAY	Balony Kubicek BB26 Balloon (Hot Air)	337	OK-0337	16. 2.05	J W Soukup	Bristol	21. 2.06E
G-OGAZ	Aérospatiale SA.341G Gazelle 1	1274	G-OCJR	12. 1.94	I M and Sheena.M Graham t/a Killochries Fold		
			G-BRGS, F-GEQA, N341SG, (N341P), N341SG, N47295			Linlithgow	10. 5.08E
G-OGBD	Boeing 737-3L9	27833	OY-MAR	16. 3.98	British Midland Airways Ltd	East Midlands	12. 3.08E
			D-ADBJ, OY-MAR		(Operated bmiBaby)		
G-OGBE	Boeing 737-3L9	27834	OY-MAS	24.11.98	British Midland Airways Ltd	East Midlands	17.12.07E
					"Derby's baby pride" (Operated bmiBaby)		
G-OGBR	Mudry CAP.232	20	N232MG	7. 2.08	G C J Cooper (Owmby-on-Spital, Market Rasen)		
G-OGCE	Bell 206L-3 LongRanger III	51206	N140JW	4. 8.06	Beechview Aviation Ltd	Newtownards	14.10.08E
			EI-LHD, D-HKLW, N3025J				
G-OGEM	Piper PA-28-181 Archer II	28-8190226	N83816	10. 3.88	GEM Rewinds Ltd	Coventry	8.11.07E
G-OGEO	Aérospatiale SA.341G Gazelle 1	1417	G-BXJK	28. 1.02	MW Helicopters Ltd	Falkirk	4.10.07E
			F-GEHC, N341AT, N49536				
G-OGES	Enstrom 280FX Shark	2078	G-CBYL	15.11.02	G N Ratcliffe	Barton	2. 3.08E
			HB-XAJ				
G-OGET	Piper PA-39 Twin Comanche C/R	39-87	G-AYXY	14. 3.83	D Saxton	Lee-on-Solent	12. 9.05
			N8930Y		(Noted 9.07)		
G-OGGY	Aviat A-1B Husky Pup	NF0005	N144HP	27. 2.04	Chris Irvine Aviation Ltd	Perranporth	25. 9.08E
G-OGJM	Cameron C-80 Balloon (Hot Air)	4869		21.11.00	G J Madelin	Farnham	6.11.08A
G-OGJP	Hughes 369E	0512E	N685F	23. 1.01	MJ Church Plant Ltd	Gloucestershire	11. 4.08T
	(Hughes 500)		N5223X				
G-OGJS	Rutan Cozy	PFA 159-11169		27. 1.89	G J Stamper	(Carlisle)	14. 9.98P
	(Built G J Stamper) (Lycoming O-360)				(Stored 2003)		
G-OGKB	Sequoia F 8L Falco	PFA 100-12153		3. 1.07	G K Brothwood	Liverpool	
	(Built A Powell and G K Brothwood)				(Noted 1.07)		
G-OGOH	Robinson R22 Beta II	2738	G-IPDM	25.11.02	E K Richardson	(Manchester)	31. 5.08E
			G-OMSG				
G-OGOS	Everett Gyroplane	004	7Q-YES	30. 7.84	N A Seymour	(Norwich)	12. 9.90P
	(Volkswagen 1834)		G-OGOS				
G-OGSA	Avtech Jabiru UL-450	0299		10. 2.00	M M Danek	Redlands, Swindon	10 1.07P
	(Built G J Slater - pr.no.PFA 274A-13540)						
G-OGSS	Lindstrand LBL 120A Balloon (Hot Air)	683		19. 5.00	R Klarer	Erbach, Germany	21. 2.08A
G-OGTS	Air Command 532 Elite	0432		19.12.88	GTS Engineering (Coventry) Ltd t/a GTS Cars		
	(Built G E Heritage - pr.no.PFA G/104-1125)					(Coventry)	1.10.90P
G-OHAC	Reims Cessna F182Q Skylane II	F18200048	D-ENCM	11. 7.01	The RAF Halton Aeroplane Club	RAF Halton	18. 7.08T
G-OHAL	Pietenpol AirCamper	PFA 047-12840		25.11.96	J F Morris	Old Warden	
	(Built H C Danby)				(New owner 2.08)		
G-OHCP	Aérospatiale AS.355F1 Ecureuil 2	5249	G-BTVS	14. 3.94	AJJ Developments Ltd	Elstree	21. 8.08T
			G-STVE, G-TOFF, G-BKJX				
G-OHGC	Scheibe SF25C Falke	44695	D-KBLC	26. 7.04	D J Marpole tr Heron Gliding Club	RNAS Yeovilton	18. 9.08E
	(Rotax 912-S)						
G-OHHI	Bell 206L-1 LongRanger	45552	G-BWYJ	30. 4.98	Sky Charter UK Ltd	Southend	14. 5.08E
			D-HOBD, D-HGAD				
G-OHIO	Dyn'Aéro MCR-01	AGA4-181-20-MA0173	N3085Q	19. 1.07	J M Keane	Deanland	
	(Built P Ghiles)						
G-OHJV	Robinson R44 Raven	1722	N457R	16. 8.07	HJV Ltd	Church Farm, North Moreton	
G-OHKS	Pegasus Quantum 15(HKS)	7505		24. 3.99	S J Farr	Newtonards	26. 5.08P
	(HKS 700E s/n 99030A)						
G-OHLI	Robinson R44 Clipper II	10832		8. 8.05	K C McCarthy, D R Smith and D Keene t/a NCS Partnership		
	(Officially regd as "Raven II")					Denham	7. 9.08E
G-OHIY	Van's RV-10	PFA 339-14730		8.12.07	M A Hutton	(Haxby, York)	
	(Built M A Hutton)						
G-OHMS	Aérospatiale AS.355F1 Ecureuil 2	5194	N367E	15. 6.90	Western Power Distribution (South West) PLC	Bristol	24. 8.08E
G-OHNO	Yakovlev Yak-55	901104	OY-TLL	24. 4.07	R Graham, E Mason and S Whatmough	Shoreham	
			SE-LOO, RA-07777, DOSAAF 97 (blue)				
G-OHOV	Rotorway Executive 162F	6885		14. 9.04	M G Bird	(Royston)	
	(Built M G Bird)						
G-OHSA	Cameron N-77 Balloon (Hot Air)	4269		2. 2.98	D N and L.J Close	Chute Forest, Andover	15. 4.01A
					(HSA Healthcare titles)		
G-OHSL	Robinson R22 Beta	0967	G-BPNF	4. 7.01	Tiger Helicopters Ltd	Shobdon	24. 8.08E
			N8029H				
G-OHVA	Mainair Blade 912	1189-0199-7-W992		6.11.98	M C Metatidj	(La Baule, France)	27. 3.04P
G-OHVR	Robinson R44 Raven II	10212	G-STOT	15. 8.05	NMC Developments Ltd	Newtownards	22.12.07E
G-OHWV	Raj Hamsa X'Air 582(4)	474		18.11.99	H W Vasey	Woodlands Barton Farm, Roche	8. 6.08P
	(Built H W Vasey - pr.no.BMAA/HB/121)						
G-OHYE	Thruster T 600N 450 Sprint	0042-T600N-098	G-CCRO	9. 3.04	P J Read tr G-OHYE Group	Enstone	17. 3.08P
G-OIBM	Rockwell Commander 114	14295	G-BLVZ	14.10.88	E J Percival	Blackbushe	22. 7.08
			SX-AJO, N4957W				
G-OIBO	Piper PA-28-180 Cherokee C	28-3794	G-AVAZ	21. 1.87	Thomsonfly Ltd	Wellesbourne Mountford	26. 6.08E
			N11C				

Reg	Type	C/n	Prev ID	Date	Owner/Operator	Location	Expiry
G-OIBU	Bell 412EP	36433	N6587U C-FMQI	27. 7.07	Bristow Helicopters Ltd	Mauritania	5. 9.08E
G-OICO	Lindstrand LBL 42A Balloon (Hot Air)	566	(F-) G-OICO	3.11.98	B Esposito (New owner 3.05)	London N10	12.11.99A
G-OIDW	Cessna F150G (Built Reims Aviation SA)	F150-0188	N70163 D-EGTI	24. 4.90	A Naish (As "00195700" in pseudo-USAF c/s) "Lil' Baby Doll"	Perth	3. 8.08E
G-OIFM	Cameron Dude 90 SS Balloon (Hot Air) (Radio One FM DJ's Head and Earphones)	2841		18. 6.92	Magical Adventures Ltd "Cool Dude" West Bloomfield, Michigan, US		29. 5.99A
G-OIHC	Piper PA-32R-301 Saratoga II SP	3246163	N237TB	6.12.06	N J Lipczynski	Biggin Hill	21.10.07E
G-OIIO	Robinson R22 Beta	2444	G-ULAB N8311Z	27. 3.02	Un Pied Sur Terre Ltd t/a Whizzard Helicopters	Welshpool	17. 7.08E
G-OIMC	Cessna 152 II	15285506	N93521	15. 5.87	East Midlands Flying School Ltd	East Midlands	8. 9.08E
G-OINK	Piper J-3C-65 Cub (L-4J-PI) (Frame no.12613)	12613	G-BILD G-KERK, F-BBQD, 44-80317	22. 3.83	A R Harding	Newton Farm, Sudbury	19. 7.99P
G-OINV	British Aerospace BAe 146 Series 300	E3171	VH-EWI G-6-171, VH-EWI, G-6-171	17. 2.00	Flybe Ltd	Inverness	15. 5.08E
G-OIOB	Mudry CAP.10B	194	N501DW	30. 1.08	A L Hall-Carpenter (Noted 2.08)	Old Buckenham	
G-OIOZ	Thunder AX9-120 Series 2 Balloon (Hot Air)	4434		17.11.98	M G Barlow	Skipton	2. 3.08T
G-OISO	Reims Cessna FA150 Aerobat (Built as FRA150L)	FRA1500213	G-BBJW	3. 4.90	L A and B A Mills	Duxford	26. 8.08E
G-OITV	Enstrom 280C Shark	1038	G-HRVY G-DUGY, G-BEEL	9. 4.96	C W Brierley Jones	(Warrington)	25. 4.08E
G-OIVN	Liberty XL-2	0008	N511XL	17. 5.07	I Shaw	Wombleton	
G-OJAB	Avtech Jabiru SK (Built K D Pearce - pr.no.PFA 274-13031)	0088		19. 9.96	S D Athalye and J Berger	Elstree	22. 5.08P
G-OJAC	Mooney M 20J Mooney 201	24-1490	N5767E	20. 8.90	Hornet Engineering Ltd	Biggin Hill	16. 2.08E
G-OJAE	Hughes 269C (Hughes 300)	90-0966	N1101W	12. 2.90	D P Wring	Dunkeswell	30. 1.08E
G-OJAG	Cessna 172S Skyhawk	172S9794	N66124	4. 4.05	Wycombe Air Centre Ltd	Wycombe Air Park	12. 5.08E
G-OJAJ	Dassault Falcon 2000EX	132	F-WWGN	30.11.07	BG Aviation Ltd	(London W1)	
G-OJAN	Robinson R22 Beta	2012	G-SANS G-BUHX	22. 5.01	Heliflight (UK) Ltd	Gloucestershire	5. 9.08E
G-OJAS	Auster J/1U Workmaster	3501	F-BJAS F-WJAS, (F-OBHT)	21. 3.00	D S Hunt (Noted in "Wings'" Museum 1.04: new owner 1.06)	Redhill	
G-OJAV	Fairey Britten-Norman BN-2A Mk.III-2 Trislander	1024	G-BDOS (4X-CCI), G-BDOS	6. 6.90	Lyddair Ltd (Noted 5.07)	Lydd	29. 1.07T
G-OJAZ	Robinson R44 Raven II	11216		2. 5.06	M Crocker and R Sweet	Kemble	25. 5.08E
G-OJBB	Enstrom 280FX	2084		14. 6.99	Pendragon (Design and Build) Ltd	Gloucestershire	1. 7.08E
G-OJBM	Cameron N-90 Balloon (Hot Air)	2899		28. 9.92	P Spinlove	Chalfont St Giles	23. 9.93A
G-OJBS	Cameron N-105 Balloon (Hot Air)	4733		8. 3.00	Up and Away Ballooning Ltd	High Wycombe	5. 4.08T
G-OJBW	Lindstrand J & B Bottle SS Balloon (Hot Air)	436		26. 8.97	N A P Godfrey (Address change 12.07)	West Leith, Tring	20. 5.02A
G-OJCW	Piper PA-32RT-300 Lance II	32R-7985062	N3016K	9. 1.80	P G Dobson	Blackbushe	11. 8.07
G-OJDA	EAA Acrosport II (Built D B Almey) (Lycoming O-360-A4A) (Project type no.should be 072A)	PFA 072-11067		1. 4.98	D B Almey	Fenland	2. 6.08P
G-OJDC	Thunder Ax7-77 Balloon (Hot Air)	875		9. 1.89	A Heginbottom	Cheadle Hulme, Cheadle	23. 9.06A
G-OJDS	Comco Ikarus C42 FB80	0411-6633		26.11.04	J D Smith	Baxby Manor, Husthwaite	1. 2.08P
G-OJEG	Airbus A321-231	1015	D-AVZN	14. 5.99	Monarch Airlines Ltd	Luton	13. 5.08E
G-OJEH	Piper PA-28-181 Archer II	28-8690051	D-EDPA N9125Y	17.12.02	P C and M A Greenaway	Biggin Hill	2. 2.08E
G-OJEN	Cameron V-77 Balloon (Hot Air)	3302		26. 5.94	C Westwood	Clayton West, Huddersfield	6.12.08A
G-OJGT	Maule M-5-235C Lunar Rocket	7285C	LN-AEL (LN-BEK), N5635V	30. 6.98	J G Townsend	Lower Upham Farm, Chiseldon	22. 7.08E
G-OJHB	Colt Flying Ice Cream Cone SS Balloon (Hot Air)	2591		23. 6.94	Stratos Ballooning Gmbh and Co KG	Ennigerloh, Germany	16. 4.04A
G-OJHC	Cessna 182P Skylane	182-64535	N86AD	21. 8.07	Stapleford Flying Club Ltd	Stapleford	28. 8.08P
G-OJHL	Europa Aviation Europa (Built J H Lace - pr.no.PFA 247-13039) (Monowheel u/c)	311		12. 5.97	J H Lace "Lady Lace"	Prestwick	16. 8.08P
G-OJIB	Boeing 757-23A	24292	G-OOOG C-GOOG, G-OOOG, C-FOOG, G-OOOG, C-FOOG, G-OOOG, C-FOOG, G-OOOG, C-FOOG, G-OOOG, C-FOOG, G-OOOG	31. 3.06	Astraeus Ltd	London Gatwick	1. 4.08E
G-OJIL	Piper PA-31-350 Navajo Chieftain	31-7652175	OY-BTP	28. 5.97	Redhill Aviation Ltd (Operated Redhill Charters)	Blackbushe	26. 6.08E
G-OJIM	Piper PA-28R-201T Turbo Arrow III	28R-7703200	N38299	4. 8.86	Grey Fox Investigations Ltd	Biggin Hill	5. 2.08E
G-OJJB	Mooney M 20K Mooney 231	25-1161		12. 8.88	G Italiano	Roma-Urbe, Lazio, Italy	2. 8.08
G-OJJF	Druine D 31 Turbulent (Built J J Ferguson) (Volkswagen 1300)	378 & 31	OO-30	6. 1.97	J J Ferguson (Noted 4.04)	Belle Vue Farm, Yarnscombe	
G-OJJV	P&M Pegasus Quik	8276		7. 6.07	J J Valentine	Ince Blundell	6. 6.08P
G-OJKM	Rans S-7 Courier (Built M Jackson - pr.no.PFA 218-12982)	1095.158		5. 3.01	M J Hasker	(Stockcross, Newbury)	22.10.08P
G-OJLH	TEAM Mini-MAX 91 (Built J L Hamer)	PFA 186-12164	G-MYAW	12.12.01	J L Hamer	Hartpury	13. 4.08P
G-OJMB	Airbus A330-243	427	F-WWYH	8.11.01	Thomas Cook Airlines UK Ltd	Manchester	8.11.07E
G-OJMC	Airbus A330-243	456	F-WWKI	5. 3.02	Thomas Cook Airlines UK Ltd	Manchester	4. 3.08E
G-OJMF	Enstrom 280FX	2086	G-DDOD	12. 6.01	JMF Ltd	Ballymoney, County Antrim	11. 5.08E
G-OJMR	Airbus A300B4-605R	605	F-WWAY	3. 5.91	Monarch Airlines Ltd	Luton	2. 5.08E
G-OJMS	Cameron Z-90 Balloon (Hot Air)	10860		28. 9.06	Joinerysoft Ltd (Joinery Soft titles)	Chipping Norton	26 .9.08E
G-OJMW	Cessna 550 Citation Bravo	550-1042	G-ORDB N51869	16.12.05	Horizon Air Charter LLP	Gloucestershire	12.12.07E
G-OJNB	Lindstrand LBL 21A Balloon (Hot Air)	085		14. 2.94	N A P Godfrey (J & B titles) (Address change 12.07)	West Leith, Tring	17. 4.04A

G-OJNE	Schempp-Hirth Nimbus 3T	22-88	BGA 4344-HZW	27.11.07	J N Ellis	Sutton Bank	19. 7.08
			D-KILO				
G-OJOD	Jodel D 18	PFA 169-12774		20. 6.02	D Hawkes and Charmaine.Poundes (Milton Keynes)		
	(Built D Hawkes)						
G-OJON	Taylor JT.2 Titch	PFA 3208		6.10.78	A Donald	Netherthorpe	18. 2.08P
	(Built J H Fell) (Continental C90)						
G-OJPS	Bell 206B-2 JetRanger II	1484	G-UEST	30.10.06	Milford Garage Ltd t/a Milford Aviation	Cranfield	23. 7.08E
			G-ROYB, G-BLWU, ZS-PAW				
G-OJRH	Robinson R44 Astro	0321		11. 4.97	Holgate Construction Ltd	Emley Moor, Huddersfield	20. 6.08
G-OJRM	Cessna T182T Turbo Skylane	T18208007	N72778	19. 7.01	Colne Airways Ltd	Earls Colne	22. 8.08E
G-OJRO	Beech B90 King Air	LJ-327	OY-JRO	13. 9.07	Fly (CI) Ltd	Southend	13. 9.08E
			N827K, (N507M), N827K				
G-OJSA	British Aerospace Jetstream Series 3102	711	OY-SVJ	20. 6.06	JS Airlines Ltd	Inverness	5. 7.08E
			G-BTYG, N415MX, G-31-711				
G-OJSH	Thruster T 600N 450	0061-T600N-052		29. 5.01	S A Lewis tr November Whiskey Flying Club	Shobdon	23. 9.08P
G-OJVA	Van's RV-6	PFA 181-12292		6. 9.96	J A Village	Moorgreen Farm, Barlow	6. 2.08P
	(Built J A Village) (Lycoming O-320)						
G-OJVH	Cessna F150H	F150-0356	G-AWJZ	27. 3.81	A W Cairns	RAF Brize Norton	14. 6.08T
	(Built Reims Aviation SA)				"Blue Too"		
G-OJVL	Van's RV-6	PFA 181-12441		28.10.02	S E Tomlinson	(Bournemouth)	
	(Built S E Tomlinson)				(Under construction at owners home 7.07)		
G-OJWB	Hawker 800XP	258674	N841WS	2.11.07	Hangar 8 Ltd	Oxford	
			N674XP		(Noted 12.07)		
G-OJWS	Piper PA-28-161 Cherokee Warrior II		N6377C	13. 7.88	P J Ward	Denham	7.12.07E
		28-7816415					
G-OKAG	Piper PA-28R-180 Cherokee Arrow	28R-30075	N3764T	15. 4.88	B.R Green	Oxford	4. 5.08E
G-OKAY	Pitts S-1E Special	12358	N35WH	27. 5.80	J L Bellamy	Fenland	19.10.06P
	(Built W D Henline)				(Address change 11.07)		
G-OKBT	Colt 25A Sky Chariot Mk.II Balloon (Hot Air)			10.11.92	British Telecommunications PLC	Thatcham	18. 4.03A
		2301			"Skypiper II"		
G-OKCC	Cameron N-90 Balloon (Hot Air)	1741		6. 5.88	D J Head	Newbury	25. 7.00A
G-OKCP	Lindstrand LBL Battery SS Balloon (Hot Air)	621	OO-BXY	9. 5.05	A M Holly	Breadstone, Berkeley	19. 9.07E
			G-MAXX		(New owner 1.08)		
G-OKED	Cessna 150L	15074250	N19223	29.1.93	L J Pluck	Clipgate Farm, Denton	3. 4.08E
G-OKEM	Mainair Sports Pegasus Quik	8047		23. 7.04	G R F Daniel	Eaglescott	15. 7.08P
G-OKEN	Piper PA-28R-201T Turbo Arrow III		N47518	20.10.87	K Woodcock	(Huddersfield)	19. 8.08E
		28R-7703390					
G-OKER	Van's RV-7	PFA 323-14233		11. 5.04	R M Johnson	(Selkirk)	
	(Built R M Johnson)						
G-OKEV	Europa Aviation Europa	328		11. 6.97	K A Kedward	Halfpenny Green	14 12.07P
	(Built K A Pilcher - pr.no.PFA 247-13091) (Tri-gear u/c)				"Freedom"		
G-OKEY	Robinson R22 Beta	2004		14. 1.92	Fast Helicopters Ltd	Shoreham	7. 5.08E
G-OKIM	Best Off Sky Ranger 912(2)	SKR0310395		23.12.03	K P Taylor	RAF Henlow	25. 9.08P
	(Built K P Taylor - pr.no.BMAA/HB/333)						
G-OKIS	Tri-R KIS	PFA 239-12248		15. 6.92	M R Cleveley	Tibenham	20. 5.08P
	(Built B W Davies) (Canadian Air Motive CAM.100)						
G-OKLL	Schempp-Hirth Discus b	404	BGA 3856-HDF	23. 1.08	K L Mcfarland	Bellarena	28.12.07
G-OKMA	Tri-R KIS	PFA 239-12808		22.11.95	K Miller	(Coventry)	30. 9.08P
	(Built K Miller) (Continental IO-240) (Tri-cycle u/c)						
G-OKPW	Tri-R KilS	PFA 239-12359		17. 8.93	K P Wordsworth	Lydd	20.11.07P
	(Built K P Wordsworth) (Continental O-200-A) (Tri-cycle u/c)						
G-OKTI	Aquila AT01	AT01-172		12.10.07	P H Ferdinand (Noted 11.07)	North Weald	
G-OKYA	Cameron V-77 Balloon (Hot Air)	1259		4. 3.87	R J Pearce	Doagh, Ballyclare	8. 6.08E
	(Replacement envelope c/n 3331)						
G-OKYM	Piper PA-28-140 Cherokee	28-23303	G-AVLS	10. 5.88	Hi-Fliers Aviation Ltd	Bagby	26. 4.08E
			N11C				
G-OLAA	Alpi Pioneer 300 Hawk	xxx		4.10.07	G G Hammond	Sorbie Farm, Kingsmuir	
	(Built G G Hammond - pr.no.PFA 330A-14719)				(Noted NEC Birmingham 11.07)		
G-OLAU	Robinson R22 Beta	1119		5. 9.89	Thistle Aviation Ltd	Oxford	21. 7.08E
G-OLAW	Lindstrand LBL 25A Cloudhopper Balloon (Hot Air)			9.12.94	George Law Plant Ltd	Kidderminster	21. 9.08A
		170			"Law Hopper"		
G-OLCP	Eurocopter AS.355N Ecureuil 2	5580	G-CLIP	18. 2.02	Charterstyle Ltd	Blackbushe	11. 4.08E
G-OLDD	British Aerospace BAe 125 Series 800B	258106	PK-RGM	11. 3.99	Air Partner Private Jets Ltd	London Stansted	22. 8.08E
			PK-WSJ, G-5-580				
G-OLDG	Cessna T182T Turbo Skylane	T18208127	G-CBTJ	17.10.02	Gold Aviation Ltd	London Stansted	22. 8.08E
			N5170R				
G-OLDH	Aérospatiale SA.341G Gazelle 1	1307	G-UTZY	10. 3.04	Gold Aviation Ltd	Biggin Hill	21. 2.08E
			G-BKLV, N341SC				
G-OLDK	Learjet Model 45	45-311	N40078	2.10.06	Air Partner Private Jets Ltd	Stansted	1.10.07E
G-OLDM	Pegasus Quantum 15-912	7589		10.12.99	A P Watkins	Roddige	9. 4.08P
G-OLDN	Bell 206L LongRanger	45077	G-TBCA	2.10.84	Sky Charter UK Ltd	Balado	30. 7.08E
			G-BFAL, N64689, A6-BCL				
G-OLDO	Eurocopter EC.120B Colibri	1489	G-HIGI	29.11.07	Gold Aviation Ltd	Biggin Hill	4. 9.08E
G-OLDP	Mainair Sports Pegasus Quik	7957		28. 5.03	M J Wilson and G Lace	Ince Blundell	30. 7.08P
G-OLDT	Learjet Model 45	45-265	N5017J	30. 6.05	Air Partner Private Jets Ltd	London Stansted	30. 6.08E
G-OLDW	Learjet Model 45XR	45-294	N5014E	10. 4.06	Air Partner Private Jets Ltd	Biggin Hill	10. 4.08E
G-OLEE	Reims Cessna F152 II	F15201797		11. 9.80	Redhill Air Services Ltd	Redhill	8. 4.08E
G-OLEM	Jodel D 18	PFA 169-11613	G-BSBP	11. 2.02	G E Roe	Garston Farm, Marshfield	28.11.07P
	(Built R T Pratt) (Revmaster R2100)						
G-OLEO	Thunder Ax10-210 Series 2 Balloon (Hot Air)			9. 1.97	M W A Shemilt	Henley-on-Thames	11. 6.03T
		3974			(New owner 7.07)		
G-OLEZ	Piper J-3C-65 Cub	18432	G-BSAX	8. 8.01	L Powell	(Canterbury)	
			N98260, NC98260		(For restoration)		
G-OLFA	Eurocopter AS.350B3 Ecureuil	3108	N64AD	11. 5.05	Heliaviation Ltd	Blackbushe	20.12.07E

Reg	Type	C/n	Prev id	Date	Owner/Operator	Location	Expiry
G-OLFB	Pegasus Quantum 15-912	7767		2. 3.01	A J Boyd	Newtownards	9. 4.08P
G-OLFC	Piper PA-38-112 Tomahawk	38-79A0995	G-BGZG N9658N	6.12.85	M W Glencross	Cranfield	21. 4.08E
G-OLFO	Robinson R44 Raven	1305		6. 6.03	Crinstown Aviation Ltd	(Cloghran, County Dublin)	25. 7.08E
G-OLFT	Rockwell Commander 114	14274	G-WJMN N4954W	28. 3.85	D A Tubby	Liverpool	16. 5.08E
G-OLFZ	P&M Quik GT450	8354		15. 2.08	A J Boyd *(Noted 2.08)*	Newtownards	
G-OLGA	CFM Starstreak Shadow SA-II	K 288		15.10.97	N F Smith	Halstead, Essex	1.11.08P
	(Built N F Smith - pr.no.PFA 206-13164) (Rotax 618)						
G-OLJT	Mainair Gemini Flash IIA	570-887-5-W359	G-MTKY	16. 9.98	A Wraith	Sandtoft	14. 3.04P
G-OLLI	Cameron O-31 Balloon (Hot Air)	196		11. 5.76	N A Robertson	Newbury	9. 1.07A
	(Golly Special shape)				*"Golly III" (Loaned British Balloon Museum and Library 2002)*		
G-OLLS	Cessna T206H Turbo Stationair 6	T20608401	N5361L	8. 3.04	Loch Lomond Seaplanes Ltd	Luss, Loch Lomond	8. 3.07T
	(Floatplane)				*(Noted 5.07)*		
G-OLMA	Partenavia P68B	159	G-BGBT	15. 4.85	C M Evans	Plymouth	14. 9.08E
G-OLNT	Aerospatiale SA.365N1 Dauphin 2	6309	N111EP G-POAV, G-BOPI	24. 8.06	LNT Aviation Ltd	Leeds-Bradford	25. 9.08E
G-OLOW	Robinson R44 Astro	0100		3.10.94	G-OLOW LLP	(Harrogate)	14. 6.08E
G-OLRT	Robinson R22 Beta	1378	N4014R	21. 5.90	The Henderson Group	Gollanfield, Inverness	9.10.07E
G-OLSF	Piper PA-28-161 Cadet	2841284	G-OTYJ G-OLSF, N92008	23.11.89	Bflying Ltd	Bournemouth	27. 1.08E
					(Operated Bournemouth Flying Club)		
G-OLTT	Pilatus PC-12/45	648	HB-FSU	27. 7.05	H Nathanson	Goodwood	1. 8.08E
G-OLUG	Cameron Z-120 Balloon (Hot Air)	10349	D-OLUG	13. 6.07	K-H Gruenauer	Schwabish Hall, Germany	28. 6.08E
G-OMAF	Dornier 228-202K	8112	D-CAAD	16. 2.87	Cobham Leasing Ltd	Bournemouth	20.11.07E
					(Operated DEFRA (Fisheries Patrol))		
G-OMAG	Cessna 182B Skylane	52214	F-BJEC N7214E	13. 5.05	Bodmin Light Aeroplane Services Ltd	Perranporth	22. 5.08E
G-OMAL	Thruster T 600N 450	0061-T600N-050		16. 5.01	M Howland	Wickenby	16. 6.08P
G-OMAP	Rockwell Commander 685	12036	F-GIRX F-OCGX, F-ZBBU, N6525V	4.11.94	Cooper Aerial Surveys Ltd	Wickenby	1. 6.07E
G-OMAT	Piper PA-28-140 Cherokee D	28-7125139	G-JIMY G-AYUG, N11C	27. 8.87	R B Walker t/a Midland Air Training School	Leicester	16.11.07E
G-OMAX	Brantly B 2B	473	G-AVJN	7. 8.87	P D Benmax *(Noted 6.05)*	Gaminglay	16.11.03
G-OMCC	Aérospatiale AS.350B Ecureuil	1836	G-JTCM G-HLEN, G-LOLY, JA9897, N5805T, HP-1084P, HP-1084, N5805T	26.03.03	Michael Car Centres Ltd	(Kirk Michael, Isle of Man)	29. 5.08E
G-OMCD	Robinson R44 Clipper II	10249		21. 1.04	J G M and H D McDiarmid t/a McDiarmid Partnership	Callington, Plymouth	26. 2.08E
G-OMDB	Van's RV-6A	25735		14. 8.02	D A Roseblade	(Dubai, United Arab Emirates)	
	(Built D A G Roseblade)						
G-OMDD	Thunder Ax8-90 Series 2 Balloon (Hot Air)	4345		2. 4.98	M D Dickinson	Old Sodbury, Bristol	17. 4.08A
G-OMDG	Hoffmann H 36 Dimona	3510	OE-9215	19.11.98	D Coulson tr Ards Dimona Group *(Noted 9.06)*	Strandhill, Sligo, County Sligo	9. 1.05
G-OMDH	Hughes 369E	0293E		14.11.88	Stiltgate Ltd	Wycombe Air Park	16. 4.08T
	(Hughes 500)						
G-OMDR	Agusta-Bell 206B-3 JetRanger III	8610	G-HRAY G-VANG, G-BIZA	8.12.97	Interceptor Properties Ltd	Southend	28.11.07E
					(Noted 1.08)		
G-OMEA	Cessna 560XL Citation XLS	560-5610	LX-GDX N52613	16.11.07	The Cambridge Aero Club Ltd t/a Marshall Executive Aviation	Cambridge	
G-OMEL	Robinson R44 Astro	0073	G-BVPB	30. 9.96	Helitrain Ltd	Bristol	23. 1.08E
G-OMEN	Cameron Z-90 Balloon (Hot Air)	10614		25. 6.04	MRC Howard Ltd	Timperley, Altrincham	21. 8.07T
					(Manchester Evening News titles)		
G-OMEX	Zenair CH.701UL STOL	PFA 187-13556		11.12.01	S J Perry	(Bucknall, Woodhall Spa)	6.11.08P
	(Built S J Perry)						
G-OMEZ	Zenair CH.601HDS Zodiac	PFA 162-13552		16. 7.01	C J Gow	Perth	21. 2.08P
	(Built C J Gow)						
G-OMFG	Cameron A-120 Balloon (Hot Air)	4965		7. 2.01	M F Glue	Hertford	5. 4.08T
G-OMGH	Robinson R44 Clipper II	10259		29. 1.04	Universal Energy Ltd	Wycombe Air Park	26. 2.08T
G-OMGI	Beech B200 Super King Air	BB-1259	N800MG D-IDSM, N734P	19. 6.06	MGI Aviation Ltd	Durham Tees Valley	18. 7.08E
G-OMHC	Piper PA-28RT-201 Arrow IV	28R-7918105	N3072Y	10. 2.81	Tatenhill Aviation Ltd	Tatenhill	9. 6.08E
G-OMHD	English Electric Canberra PR.Mk.9	SH.1724	XH134	15. 8.06	Midair SA	Kemble	
	(Built Short Brothers and Harland Ltd)				*(Noted 8.06)*		
G-OMHI	Mills MH-1	MH.001		8.10.97	J P Mills	(Stockport)	
	(Built J P Mills)				*(Noted 7.05)*		
G-OMHP	Avtech Jabiru UL	xxxx		23. 5.00	J Livingstone	(Whitburn, Bathgate)	25. 8.07P
	(Built M H Player - pr.no.PFA 274A-13584)						
G-OMIA	SOCATA MS.893A Rallye Commodore 180	12074	D-ENME F-BUGE, (D-ENMH)	21. 7.98	(P W Portelli)	Not known	5. 1.08E
G-OMIK	Europa Aviation Europa	270		12. 1.98	M J Clews tr Mikite Flying Group	White Waltham	29. 9.08P
	(Built M J Clews - pr.no.PFA 247-12991) (Rotax 914-UL) (Monowheel u/c)						
G-OMIW	P&M Quik	8232		24. 1.07	M I Woodward	(Shipston-on-Stour)	11. 2.08P
G-OMJA	Piper PA-28-181 Archer II	28-7690328	A6-DXB N75319	26.10.07	C A Patter	North Coates	
					(Noted 8.07)		
G-OMJC	Raytheon RB390 Premier 1	RB-88	N4488F	17. 6.04	Manhattan Jet Charter Ltd	Farnborough	17. 6.08E
G-OMJT	Rutan LongEz	968		14.10.92	M J Timmons	Prestwick	20.12.07P
	(Built M J Timmons - pr.no.PFA 074A-10703) (Lycoming O-235)						
G-OMKA	Robinson R44 Clipper II	11533		15.12.06	MK Airlines Ltd	Redhill	19.12.07E
	(Officially regd as "Raven II")				*(Noted 1.08)*		
G-OMLC	EAA Acrosport II	PFA 072-12151		7.11.05	M A C Chapman *(Noted 1.06)*	(Guildford)	
G-OMLS	Bell 206B-2 JetRanger II	1957	N80367 G-OMLS, D-HAFN, N9909K	2. 2.04	M L Scott	Bagby	4. 4.08E
G-OMMG	Robinson R22 Beta	1041	G-BPYX	25. 2.94	Preston Associates Ltd	Yearby	18. 6.08T
G-OMMM	Colt 90A Balloon (Hot Air)	2328		20. 1.93	(V Trimble)	(Nuffield, Henley-on-Thames)	19. 4.06A
					(Avient Cargo titles)		

Reg	Type	Serial	Prev ids	Date	Owner	Location	Expiry
G-OMNI	Piper PA-28R-200 Cherokee Arrow II	28R-7335130	G-BAWA N11C	3. 1.84	Cotswold Aviation Services Ltd	Gloucestershire	8. 6.08E
G-OMOL	Maule MX-7-180C Super Rocket *(Floatplane)*	28012C		15. 8.00	Highland Seaplanes Ltd	North Connell, Oban	18. 7.08E
G-OMOO	Ultramagic T-150 Balloon (Hot Air)	150/06		4. 6.07	Robert Wiseman Dairies PLC	Skirling, Biggar	6. 7.08E
G-OMPW	Mainair Sports Pegasus Quik	8088		12. 1.05	MPW Decorators Ltd	Strubby	9. 2.08P
G-OMRB	Cameron V-77 Balloon (Hot Air)	2184		29. 8.90	I J Jevons *"Harlequin"*	Bristol	8. 8.08A
G-OMRH	Cessna 550 Citation Bravo	550-1086	N58HK N52446	12.12.06	McAir Services LLP	Hawarden	18.12.07E
G-OMSS	Best Off Sky Ranger 912(2) *(Built M S Schofield - pr.no.BMAA/HB/425)*	SKR0409523		6. 1.05	J T James	Sutton Meadows	13. 3.08P
G-OMST	Piper PA-28-161 Warrior III	2842121	G-BZUA N53363	1. 8.01	Mid-Sussex Timber Co Ltd	Biggin Hill	11. 6.08E
G-OMUM	Rockwell Commander 114	14067 (PH-MMM), N4737W	PH-JJJ	24. 1.97	C E Campbell	Blackbushe	18. 3.08E
G-OMWE	Zenair CH.601HD Zodiac *(Built P J Roy) (Mid West AE100R)*	PFA 162-12740	(N) G-OMWE, G-BVXU	21. 3.97	G Cockburn	(Hawick)	19. 7.07P
G-OMYA	Airbus A320-214	716	G-BXKB N716AW, G-BXKB, F-WWIZ	5. 3.07	Thomas Cook Airlines Ltd t/a MyTravel Airways	Manchester	5. 5.08E
G-OMYJ	Airbus A321-211	677	G-OOAF G-UNID, G-UKLO, D-AVZO	26. 4.07	Thomas Cook Airlines Ltd t/a MyTravel Airways	Manchester	6. 5.08E
G-OMYT	Airbus A330-243	301	G-MOJO F-WWYE	14. 5.03	Thomas Cook Airlines Ltd t/a MyTravel Airways	Manchester	7.11 07E
G-ONAF	Naval Aircraft Factory N3N-3 *(Wright Whirlwind R 760)*	xxxx	N45192 Bu.4406	31. 1.89	J P Birnie tr N3N-3 Group *(As "4406:12" in US Navy c/s)*	Sandown, Isle of Wight	31. 8.09S
G-ONAL	Beech 200 Super King Air *(To Model B200 status + 4-blade propellers 1999)*	BB-30	G-HAMA N244JB, N211JB, N3090C, N3030C, N200CA	16. 1.06	Northern Aviation Ltd	Durham Tees Valley	1. 2.08E
G-ONAT	Grob G102 Astir CS77	1804	BGA 5296-KRE HB-1459	23.10.07	N A Toogood	RAF Weston-on-the-Green	
G-ONAV	Piper PA-31 Navajo C	31-7812004	G-IGAR D-IGAR, N27378	29. 1.93	Panther Aviation Ltd	Elstree	18. 6.08E
G-ONCB	Lindstrand LBL 31A Balloon (Hot Air)	393		4. 6.96	S J Hunphreys *New owner 6.07)*	Prestwood, Great Missenden	5. 4.05A
G-ONCL	Colt 77A Balloon (Hot Air)	1637		4. 4.90	T J Gouder	Thornbury, Bristol	2. 8.08A
G-ONCS	Tipsy Nipper T 66 Series 3B *(Built E Shouler) (Volkswagen 1834)*	PFA 1390	G-AZBA	18.12.06	N C Spooner tr Ardleigh Flying Group	Bounds Farm, Ardleigh	14. 5.08P
G-ONEC	Cirrus SR22	2488	N686SR	22. 6.07	One Charter PLC	Farnborough	12. 7.08E
G-ONED	Dan Rihn DR.107 One Design *(Built A Bickmore)*	PFA 264-14746		26.11.07	A Bickmore	(High Wycombe)	
G-ONEL	Agusta A109C	7630	G-JBEK VH-LUI, Malaysian AF M38-06	11. 6.07	Cheshire Helicopters Ltd	(Wilmslow)	29. 6.08E
G-ONEP	Robinson R44 Raven II	11363		4. 8.06	Neptune Property Developments Ltd	Dreemore Road, Dungannon	17. 8.08E
G-ONER	Van's RV-8 *(Built J A Hawkins)*	80563	N563JH	3.10.06	S L Morris	Compton Abbas	
G-ONES	Slingsby T 67M-200 Firefly	2046	SE-LBB LN-TFB, G-7-122	12.11.01	E P Lambert	Exeter	26. 6.06T
G-ONET	Piper PA-28-180 Cherokee E	28-5802	G-AYAU N11C	3. 6.98	Hatfield Flying Club Ltd	Elstree	28. 9.07E
G-ONEZ	Glaser-Dirks DG-200/17	2-143/1738	BGA 4878-JYB D-1086	17. 1.08	R M Nuza tr One Zulu Group	Rufforth	21. 5.08
G-ONFL	Murphy Maverick *(Built K Godfrey and G Lockwood - pr.no.PFA 259-12750) (Rotax 503)*	402	G-MYUJ	27.11 98	M J Whiteman-Haywood *(New owners 8.06)*	Pound Green, Buttonoak, Bewdley	20.12.05P
G-ONGA	Robinson R44 Raven II	10479		5.10.04	Silvergate Leisure Ltd	Sywell	30. 1.08E
G-ONGC	Robin DR.400-180R Remorqueur	1385	EI-CKA SE-GHM	11.11.98	Norfolk Gliding Club Ltd	Tibenham	25. 5.08E
G-ONHH	Forney F-1A Aircoupe	5725	G-ARHA N3030G	13.12.89	R D I Tarry *"Easy Rider"*	Pytchley Grange, Kettering	12. 6.10S
G-ONIG	Murphy Elite *(Built N Smith - pr.no.PFA 232-14042)*	745E?		29. 4.03	N S Smith	(Derby)	
G-ONIX	Cameron C-80 Balloon (Hot Air)	4411		12. 8.98	D J Griffin *(New owner 10.06)*	Bowerhill, Melksham	10.11.07A
G-ONKA	Aeronca K *(Lycoming O-145)*	K283	N19780 NC19780	21.10.91	N J R Minchin *"Aggnes"*	Hill Top Farm, Hambledon	12. 6.08P
G-ONMT	Robinson R22 Beta II	2963		20. 7.99	R C Hayward and J H Garrioch t/a Polar Helicopters	Manston	5.10.07E
G-ONON	Rotary Air Force RAF 2000 GTX-SE *(Built M S R Allen)* PFA G/13-1313			13. 8.99	M P Lhermette *(Marked as "RAF 2000 GTX SE Fi")*	(Faversham)	22. 8.08P
G-ONPA (2)	Piper PA-31-350 Navajo Chieftain	31-7952110	N89PA N35225	6. 5.98	Synergy Aircraft Leasing Ltd	Fairoaks	15.10.07T
G-ONSO	Pitts S-1S *(Built T D McNamara)*	TM-1	G-BRRS N18TM	24. 7.06	A P S Maynard	(Pulborough)	25. 6.93P
G-ONTV	Agusta-Bell 206B-3 JetRanger III	8733	D-HUNT TC-HKJ, (D-HSAV), I-GPFP, I-PIEF	1. 4.98	Castle Air Charters Ltd	Liskeard Heliport	12. 4.08E
G-ONUN	Van's RV-6A *(Built R E Nunn) (Lycoming O-360)*	PFA 181-12976		20. 2.96	R E Nunn	Clipgate Farm, Denton	25. 2.08P
G-ONUP	Enstrom F-28C	348	G-MHCA G-SHWW, G-SMUJ, G-BHTF	18. 1.00	North Wales Military Aviation Services Ltd *(New owner 10.07)*	Hawarden	20. 6.02
G-ONYX	Bell 206B-3 JetRanger III	4160	G-BXPN N18EA, D-HOBA, (D-HOBE)	22. 1.98	Kenrye Developments Ltd	Newtownards	30. 7.08E
G-ONZO	Cameron N-77 Balloon (Hot Air)	1089		13.11.84	K Temple *"Gonzo" (Address change 10.07)*	Tivetshall St Margaret, Norwich	19. 7.99A
G-OOAE	Airbus A321-211	852	(G-UNIF) D-AVZG	14. 7.98	First Choice Airways Ltd *(To be re-regd G-OOPE by 5.08)*	Manchester	13. 7.08E

G-OOAN	Boeing 767-39H	26256	G-UKLH	26. 1.99	First Choice Airways Ltd *"Caribbean Star"*	Manchester	4. 4.08E
					(To be re-regd G-OOPN by 5.08)		
G-OOAR	Airbus A320-214	1320	F-WWDT	3.11.00	First Choice Airways Ltd	Manchester	2.11.07E
G-OOAU	Airbus A320-214	1637	F-WWDM	10. 1.02	First Choice Airways Ltd	Manchester	9. 1.08E
					(To be re-regd G-OOPU by 5.08)		
G-OOAV	Airbus A321-211	1720	D-AVXA	29. 4.02	First Choice Airways Ltd	Manchester	28. 4.08E
G-OOAW	Airbus A320-214	1777	F-WWDM	27. 5.02	First Choice Airways Ltd	Manchester	26. 5.08E
					(To be re-regd G-OOPW by 5.08)		
G-OOBA	Boeing 757-28A	32446	C-GUBA	9. 2.01	First Choice Airways Ltd	Manchester	20. 4.08E
			G-OOBA, N446GE, (N558NA)				
G-OOBC	Boeing 757-28A	33098		28. 3.03	First Choice Airways Ltd	Manchester	27. 3.08E
G-OOBD	Boeing 757-28A	33099		31. 3.03	First Choice Airways Ltd	Manchester	30. 3.08E
G-OOBE	Boeing 757-28A	33100		19. 5.03	First Choice Airways Ltd	Manchester	18. 5.08E
G-OOBF	Boeing 757-28A	33101		19. 4.04	First Choice Airways Ltd	Manchester	18. 4.08E
G-OOBI	Boeing 757-2B7	27146	N615AU	29. 6.04	First Choice Airways Ltd	Manchester	9.10.07E
G-OOBJ	Boeing 757-2B7	27147	N616AU	21. 5.04	First Choice Airways Ltd	Manchester	5.12.07E
G-OOBK	Boeing 767-324	27392	VN-A762	18.11.04	First Choice Airways Ltd	Manchester	17. 2.08E
			S7-RGV, EI-CMD, N1785B, (N48901)				
G-OOBL	Boeing 767-324	27393	VN-A764	4. 4.05	First Choice Airways Ltd	Manchester	7. 4.08E
			S7-RGW, EI-CME, N1794B, (N58902)				
G-OOBM	Boeing 767-324ER	27568	VN-A765	10.11.05	First Choice Airways Ltd	Manchester	15. 1.08E
			S7-RGU, EI-CMH, N47904				
G-OOCH	Ultramagic H-42 Balloon (Hot Air)	42-03		6. 9.07	P C Gooch	Alresford	
G-OODE	SNCAN Stampe SV-4C	500	G-AZNN	9. 5.77	A R Radford	Redhill	17.11.08S
			F-BDGI, French AF				
G-OODI	Pitts S-1D	KH.1	G-BBBU	23.12.80	R M Buchan	Leicester	7. 5.07P
	(Built Etheridge and Lincs Aerial)				*"Little Bumble"* (Noted 10.07		
G-OODM	Cessna 525A CitationJet CJ2	525A0190	N680JB	8.12.06	Hangar 8 Ltd	Oxford	7.12.07E
			N5141F				
G-OODW	Piper PA-28-181 Archer II	28-8490031	N4332C	14. 7.87	Goodwood Road Racing Company Ltd	Goodwood	19.12.07E
					(Operated Goodwood Flying Club)		
G-OOER	Lindstrand LBL 25A Cloudhopper Balloon (Hot Air)			15. 8.94	Airborne Adventures Ltd	Skipton	6. 5.05P
		125					
G-OOFE	Thruster T 600N 450 Sprint	0036-T600N-087		8. 7.03	Rochester Microlights Ltd	Damyn's Hall, Upminster	27. 7.08P
G-OOFR	Robinson R44 Raven II	11928		9.10.07	Beechview Aviation Ltd	Toome	
					(New premises 11.07)		
G-OOFT	Piper PA-28-161 Warrior III	2842083	N170FT	25. 5.00	Plane Talking Ltd	Elstree	22. 6.08E
G-OOGA	Gulfstream GA-7 Cougar	GA7-0111	SE-IEA	3. 2.86	B Robinson	Denham	25.11.07E
	(C/n correct but duplicates that for YV-1334P)		N758G				
G-OOGI	Gulfstream GA-7 Cougar	GA7-0077	G-PLAS	16. 1.95	Plane Talking Ltd	Cranfield	13.10.07E
			G-BGHL, N789GA		(Operated Cabair)		
G-OOGL	Hughes 369E	0234E	ZS-HVH	21.11.06	Eastern Atlantic Helicopters Ltd	Shoreham	
	(Hughes 500)		N1603S				
G-OOGO	Grumman American GA-7 Cougar	GA7-0049	N762GA	12.11.97	J Prus-Wisniewski	Elstree	13. 1.08E
G-OOGS	Gulfstream GA-7 Cougar	GA7-0105	G-BGJW	19. 6.98	Cloud 9 Aviation (Leasing) Ltd	Leeds-Bradford	27. 3.08E
			N737G				
G-OOIO	Eurocopter AS.350B3 Ecureuil	3463		17.10.01	Hovering Ltd	Elstree	19.11.07E
G-OOJC	Bensen B 8MR	PFA G/101-1303		4.12.98	J R Cooper	Henstridge	
	(Built J R Cooper) (Converted ex Air Command)				(Noted 8.05)		
G-OOJP	Commander Aircraft Commander 114B	14567	N92JT	24.12.99	R J Rother	Kirknewton	5. 3.08E
			D-EYCA				
G-OOLE	Cessna 172M Skyhawk II	17266712	G-BOSI	25. 8.89	P S Eccersley	Humberside	3. 4.08E
			N80714				
G-OOLL	Air Création Tanarg 912S/iXess 15	FLT.xxx		27. 4.06	R R Celentano	Strathaven	21. 8.08P
	(Built J W McCarthy - pr.no.BMAA/HB/487 being Flylight kit comprising Trike s/n T05083 and Wing s/n A05151-5142)						
G-OOMF	Piper PA-18-150 Super Cub	18-8560	N45554	13. 4.06	R C and C G Bell	Enstone	14. 5.08E
			Israeli DF 020				
G-OONA	Robinson R44 Clipper II	10907		18.10.05	Honeybee Aviation Ltd	Elstree	6.11.07E
G-OONE	Mooney M 20J Mooney 201	24-3039		31. 7.87	Go One Aviation Ltd	Welshpool	19. 9.08E
G-OONI	Thunder Ax7-77 Balloon (Hot Air)	1534		9. 3.90	Fivedata Ltd *"Bridesnightie"*	Todmorden	31. 3.01A
G-OONK	Cirrus SR22	1230	N202NK	3.11.06	Heathfield Rentals Ltd	Exeter	16.11.07E
G-OONY	Piper PA-28-161 Warrior II	28-8316015	N83071	26. 7.89	D A Field	Compton Abbas	4.11.07E
G-OOOK	Boeing 757-236	25054	C-FLOK	9.10.02	First Choice Airways Ltd	Manchester	7. 5.08E
			G-OOOK, C-FLOK, G-OOOK, SE-DUK, (G-JOEM), SE-DUK, N100FS, EI-CMA, XA-MMX, N3502P, N5002K, (EC-668), (G-BSNB)				
					(To be re-regd G-OOPK by 5.08)		
G-OOON	Piper PA-34-220T Seneca III	34-8533024	N822CB	8. 1.03	Synergy Aircraft Leasing Ltd	Fairoaks	1. 3.08E
			ZS-LWI, N2431Q, N9513N				
G-OOOX	Boeing 757-2Y0	26158		24. 2.93	First Choice Airways Ltd	Manchester	22. 3.08E
G-OOPE	Airbus A321-211	852	G-OOAE	5.08R	First Choice Airways Ltd	Manchester	13. 7.08E
			(G-UNIF), D-AVZG				
G-OOPH	Airbus A321-211	781	G-OOAH	4. 2.08	First Choice Airways Ltd	Manchester	2. 3.08E
			G-UNIE, D-AVZK				
G-OOPK	Boeing 757-236	25054	G-OOOK	5.08R	First Choice Airways Ltd	Manchester	7. 5.08E
			C-FLOK, G-OOOK, C-FLOK, G-OOOK, SE-DUK, (G-JOEM), SE-DUK, N100FS, EI-CMA, XA-MMX, N3502P, N5002K, (EC-668), (G-BSNB)				
G-OOPN	Boeing 767-39H	26256	G-OOAN	5.08R	First Choice Airways Ltd	Manchester	4. 4.08E
			G-UKLH		*"Caribbean Star"*		
G-OOPU	Airbus A320-214	1637	G-OOAU	5.08R	First Choice Airways Ltd	Manchester	9. 1.08E
			F-WWDM				
G-OOPW	Airbus A320-214	1777	G-OOAW	5.08R	First Choice Airways Ltd	Manchester	26. 5.08E
			F-WWDM				
G-OOPX	Airbus A320-214	2180	G-OOAX	24. 1.08	First Choice Airways Ltd	Manchester	6. 4.08E
			F-WWDY				
G-OORV	Van's RV-6	24319	N120XK	21.12.06	T I Williams	Shoreham	17. 5.08P
	(Built C and D Henwood)						

Reg	Type	C/n	Prev ID	Date	Owner/Operator	Location	Expiry
G-OOSE	Rutan VariEze	1536		7.12.78	B O Smith and J A Towers	Yearby	
	(Built J A Towers - pr.no.PFA 074-10326)				(Stored dismantled 2.08)		
G-OOSH	Zenair CH.601UL Zodiac	PFA 162A-14022		18.11.05	D J Paget	Dunkeswell	31. 5.07P
G-OOSI	Cessna 404 Titan	404-0855	VT-DAT	31. 1.03	Cooper Aerial Surveys Ltd	Blackpool	1. 5.08E
			N404N, F-WQFV, F-ZBDB, F-BRGN, N68104 (Ordnance Survey titles)				
G-OOSY	de Havilland DH.82A Tiger Moth	85831	F-BGFI	6. 9.94	M Goosey tr Flying Tigers (Frame noted Woburn 8.03)		
	(Composite rebuild)		French AF, DE971		(Top Farm, Ecclesall, Stafford)		
G-OOTB	SOCATA TB-20 Trinidad GT	2180	D-EADS	11. 5.04	A T Paton	(London SW18)	7. 6.08T
G-OOTC	Piper PA-28R-201T Turbo Arrow III	28R-7703086	G-CLIV	18. 1.94	D G and C M King	Turweston	5. 7.08E
			N3011Q				
G-OOTT	Eurocopter AS.350B3 Ecureuil	3953		20. 7.05	Libertas (UK) Ltd	Southend	16. 3.08E
G-OOTW	Cameron Z-275 Balloon (Hot Air)	10380		6. 6.03	Airborne Balloon Management Ltd	Tonbridge	5. 9.08T
G-OOXP	Aero Designs Pulsar XP	PFA 202-11915		25.10.90	K A O'Neill	Plaistows Farm, St Albans	1.11.08P
	(Built G W Associates Ltd)						
G-OPAG	Piper PA-34-200 Seneca	34-7250348	N506DM	16.10.90	A H Lavender	Biggin Hill	11. 5.08E
			G-BNGB, F-BTQT, F-BTMT				
G-OPAM	Reims Cessna F152 II	F15201536	G-BFZS	5. 9.86	PJC (Leasing) Ltd "Little Red Rooster"	Stapleford	26. 6.08E
G-OPAT	Beech 76 Duchess	ME-304	G-BHAO	6.12.82	R D J Axford	Wycombe Air Park	8. 8.08E
G-OPAZ	Pazmany PL-2	PFA 069-10673		20. 3.98	K Morris	Haverfordwest	15. 8.08P
	(Built K Morris) (Lycoming O-235)				"Y Myddryg Bach Melyn"		
G-OPCG	Cessna 182T Skylane	18280948	N2451Y	18. 2.02	P L Nolan	Fairoaks	21. 3.08E
G-OPCS	Hughes 369E	0333E	CS-HBN	31. 1.01	Eastern Atlantic Helicopters Ltd	Shoreham	12. 7.08E
	(Hughes 500)		N500AH				
G-OPDG	Robinson R44 Raven II	11815		27. 7.07	Heli Air Ltd	Wellesbourne Mountford	21. 8.08E
G-OPDS	Denney Kitfox Model 4	PFA 172A-12259		8. 1.93	P Madden	Strathaven	11. 8.07P
	(Built P D Sparling)						
G-OPEJ	TEAM Mini-Max 91	PFA 186-14388		5. 1.07	P E Jackson	(Ruthin)	10. 9.08P
	(Built P E Jackson)						
G-OPEN	Bell 206B-3 JetRanger III	4300	N743BT	20. 1.05	Gazelle Aviation LLP	(Wetherby)	6. 1.08E
			N206AJ, N2155K, C-GFNP				
G-OPEP	Piper PA-28RT-201T Turbo Arrow IV	28R-7931070	OY-PEP	3.12.97	S A F Elliott t/a Sam Aviation	Cranfield	24. 9.08E
			N2217Q				
G-OPET	Piper PA-28-181 Cherokee Archer II	28-7690067	OH-PET	3. 1.02	Cambrian Flying Group Ltd	Cardiff	23. 3.08E
			OY-BLC				
G-OPFA	Alpi Pioneer 300	6		23.11.04	S Eddison and R Minett	Gloucestershire	5.10.07P
	(Built S Eddison and R Minett - pr.no.PFA 330-14298)						
G-OPFR	Diamond DA.42 Twin Star	42.077	OE-VPI	5.12.05	P F Rothwell	Cranfield	23. 1.08E
G-OPFT	Cessna 172R Skyhawk	17280316	N9491F	11. 3.98	Northern Aviation Ltd	Durham Tees Valley	23. 2.08E
G-OPFW	Hawker Siddeley HS.748 Series 2A/266	1714	G-BMFT	1. 7.98	PTB (Emerald) Proprietary Ltd	Blackpool	16. 2.07T
			VP-BFT, VR-BFT, G-BMFT, 5W-FAO, G11-10 (Stored externally 2.08)				
G-OPHA	Robinson R44 Astro	0359	PH-WBW	17. 7.97	H W Euridge	(Redlynch, Salisbury)	14. 6.08E
			G-OPHA, CS-HDW, G-OPHA				
G-OPHT	Schleicher ASH 26E	26105		6. 2.97	P Turner "T1"	Nympsfield	21. 9.08E
G-OPIC	Reims Cessna FRA150L Aerobat	FRA1500234	G-BGNZ	20. 6.95	A V Harmer	(Shotesham All Saints, Norwich)	23. 1.08E
			PH-GAB, D-EIQE				
G-OPIK	Eiriavion PIK-20E	20233	PH-651	27. 1.82	A J McWilliam	Aston Down	12. 3.08E
G-OPIT	CFM Streak Shadow	K 126-SA		22.11.89	I Sinnett	Bodmin	8. 7.03P
	(Built L W Opit - pr.no.PFA 161A-11624) (Rotax 532)						
G-OPJB	Boeing 757-23A	24924	N924AW	19. 3.05	Astraeus Ltd	London Gatwick	24. 3.08E
			TJ-CAH, N924AW, C-FXOK, (5Y-BHG)				
G-OPJC	Cessna 152 II	15282280	N68354	7. 6.88	PJC (Leasing) Ltd	Stapleford	17.10.07E
G-OPJD	Piper PA-28RT-201T Turbo Arrow IV	28R-8231028	N8097V	2.10.89	J M McMillan	Thruxton	7. 3.08E
G-OPJK	Europa Aviation Europa	017		29. 4.93	F D Hollinshead	Sleap	29. 4.08P
	(Built P J Kember - pr.no.PFA 247-12487) (Monowheel u/c)						
G-OPJS	Pietenpol AirCamper	PFA 047-12834		10.11.00	P J Shenton	Sywell	
	(Built P J and J W Shenton)				(Noted 1.05)		
G-OPKF	Cameron Bowler 90 SS Balloon (Hot Air)	2314		12. 6.90	D K Fish	Manchester	2. 8.03A
G-OPLC	de Havilland DH.104 Dove 8	04212	G-BLRB	10. 1.91	W G T Pritchard	Redhill	15. 5.08S
			VP962		(Operated Mayfair Dove)		
G-OPME	Piper PA-23-250 Aztec D	27-4099	G-ODIR	31. 3.94	Portway Aviation Ltd	Shobdon	14.10.07T
			G-AZGB, N878SH, N9...N				
G-OPMT	Lindstrand LBL 105A Balloon (Hot Air)	052		30. 9.93	K R Karlstrom	Northwood	29.10.08A
G-OPNH	Stoddard-Hamilton Glasair Super II-SRG	2364	G-CINY	14.10.98	J L Mangelschots	Balen-Keiheuvel, Belgium	26. 5.08P
	(Built P N Haigh - pr.no.PFA 149-13011) (Lycoming IO-360)						
G-OPPL	Gulfstream AA-5A Cheetah	AA5A-0867	G-BGNN	11.10.85	Plane Talking Ltd	Blackbushe	8. 8.08E
G-OPRC	Europa Aviation Europa XS	378		22. 6.01	M J Ashby-Arnold	Wombleton	8. 3.08P
	(Built I Chaplin - pr.no.PFA 247-13281) (Tri-gear u/c)						
G-OPSF	Piper PA-38-112 Tomahawk	38-79A0998	EI-BLT	13.10.82	Panshanger School of Flying Ltd	High Cross, Ware	29. 1.08E
			G-BGZI, N9664N				
G-OPSL	Piper PA-32R-301 Saratoga II SP	32R-8013085	G-IMPW	4. 1.99	P R Tomkins	(Robertsbridge)	10. 7.08E
			N8186A				
G-OPSS	Cirrus SR20-G2	1458	N410CD	28.10.04	Cumulus Aircraft Rentals Ltd	Lee-on-Solent	13.12.07E
G-OPST	Cessna 182R Skylane II	18267932	OO-HFF	16. 6.88	M J G Wellings and Welmacs Ltd	Shoreham	1. 5.08E
			N9317H				
G-OPTF	Robinson R44 Raven II	10235		9. 1.04	Franks Helicopter Leasing Ltd	Wycombe Air Park	6. 2.08T
G-OPTI	Piper PA-28-161 Warrior II	28-7716210	N5888V	29. 9.06	A K Hulme	Andrewsfield	26.10.07E
G-OPUB	Slingsby T 67M-160 Firefly	2002	G-DLTA	18.10.96	P M Barker	Leeds-Bradford	9. 9.07T
			G-SFTX				
G-OPUK	Piper PA-28-161 Warrior III	2842288	N30904	29.08.07	GEFA Gesellschaft fur Absatzfinanzierung mbH	(Wuppertal, Germany)	
G-OPUP	Beagle B 121 Pup Series 2	B121-062	G-AXEU	31.10.84	F A Zubiel	White Waltham	12. 6.08E
			(5N-AJC)				

G-OPUS	Avtech Jabiru SK	0194			16. 7.98	K W Whistance	(Much Dewchurch, Hereford)	26. 9.08P
	(Built S Percy - pr.no.PFA 274-13343)							
G-OPVM	Van's RV-9A	PFA 320-14351			8. 8.05	P Mather	Andrewsfield	5.12.08P
	(Built P Mather)							
G-OPWK	Grumman AA-5A Cheetah	AA5A-0663	G-OAEL		26. 5.92	J H Sandham t/a Sandham Aviation	Carlisle	6. 9.02T
			N26706			(New owner 9.07)		
G-OPWS	Mooney M 20K Mooney 231	25-0663	N1162W		12. 4.91	A R Mills	Fowlmere	7.11.07
G-OPYE	Cessna 172S Skyhawk SP	172S8059	N653SP		19. 2.99	Far North Aviation	Wick	25. 2.08E
G-ORAC	Cameron Van 110 SS Balloon (Hot Air)	4577			22. 6.99	A G Kennedy (RAC titles)	Nelson	7. 6.08A
G-ORAE	Van's RV-7	PFA 323-14016			20. 3.03	R W Eaton tr G-ORAE Group	(Chesterfield)	
	(Built R W Eaton)							
G-ORAF	CFM Streak Shadow	K 134-SA			18. 5.90	A P Hunn	(George Town, Cayman Isles)	1.11.00P
	(Built G A Taylor - pr.no.PFA 161A-11627: sequence no.conflicts with MW6 G-MYCU) (Rotax 532) (Dismantled 5.00)							
G-ORAL	Hawker Siddeley HS.748 Series 2A/334	1756	G-BPDA		13. 8.99	PTB (Emerald) Proprietary Ltd	Blackpool	12.11.07E
			G-GLAS, 9Y-TFS, G-11-8			"John J Goodall" (Stored externally 2.08)		
G-ORAM	Thruster T600N 450	0071-T600N-117			13. 6.07	J A Ward	(Greetwell, Lincoln)	12. 6.08P
G-ORAR	Piper PA-28-181 Archer III	2890224	N9255G		6. 6.95	P N and S M Thornton	Goodwood	8. 7.07
G-ORAS	Clutton FRED Series II	PFA 029-11002			14. 6.01	A I Sutherland	Fearn	22.11.08P
	(Built A I Sutherland)							
G-ORAU	Evektor EV-97A Eurostar	PFA 315A-14655			4. 6.07	W R C Williams-Wynne	Talybont, Gwynedd	19.12.08P
	(Built W R C Williams-Wynne)							
G-ORAY	Reims Cessna F182Q Skylane II	F18200132	G-BHDN		18. 3.94	Unicorn Consultants Ltd	(Douglas, Isle of Man)	18. 1.08E
G-ORBK	Robinson R44 Raven II	10213	G-CCNO		28.11.03	GTC (UK) Ltd	Wycombe Air Park	22.12.07E
G-ORBS	Mainair Blade	1336-0802-7-W1131			19. 8.02	J W Dodson	Leicester	11.10.07P
	(Rotax 582)							
G-ORCA	Van's RV-4	PFA 181-12924			25.11.04	M R H Wishart	Tingwall	29. 7.08P
	(Built M R H Wishart) (Superior XP-IO-360-B1A2)							
G-ORCW	Schempp-Hirth Ventus 2cT	134/...	BGA 5108-KHQ		21.11.05	R C Wilson "A39"	Aboyne	7.12.07
G-ORDH	Eurocopter AS.355N Ecureuil 2	5744	F-WWXS		11. 7.06	Harpin Ltd	Leeds-Bradford	5.10.07E
G-ORDS	Thruster T 600N 450	0042-T600N-100			14. 1.04	Thruster Air Services Ltd	Ginge, Wantage	6. 4.08P
G-ORED	Pilatus Britten-Norman BN-2T Islander	2142	G-BJYW		10. 1.85	Fly BN Ltd	(London SE16)	26. 2.08A
G-OREV	Revolution Helicopters Mini-500	0112			8. 8.96	R H Everett	(Lee-on-Solent)	
G-ORGY	Cameron Z-210 Balloon (Hot Air)	10320			9. 7.02	Cameron Flights Southern Ltd		
							Woodborough, Pewsey	22. 2.08T
G-ORHE	Cessna 500 Citation I	500-0220	(N619EA)		25. 3.96	EASSDA Ireland Ltd	(Templepatrick, Ballyclare)	24. 7.08E
			G-OBEL, G-BOGA, N932HA, N93WD, N5220J					
G-ORIG	Glaser-Dirks DG-800A	8-39-A29	BGA 4972-		5. 4.94	I Godfrey	Lasham	14. 5.08E
			G-ORIG					
G-ORIX	ARV K1 Super 2	034	G-BUXH		16. 9.93	T M Lyons	(Newcastle)	9. 4.07P
	(Built P M Harrison - pr.no.PFA 152-12424)		(G-BNVK) (Mid West AE.100R)					
G-ORJA	Beech B200 Super King Air	BB-1570	N1120Z		5.06.03	Airwest Ltd	Bristol	4. 6.08E
			N50PM, N1120Z					
G-ORJW	Laverda F 8L Falco Series 4	403	(PH-...)		2.12.85	Viking BV	Standalone Farm, Meppershall	13. 9.10S
			G-ORJW, D-ELDV, D-ELDY					
G-ORKY	Aérospatiale AS.350B2 Ecureuil	2153	N66NN		3. 1.08	MCJ Helicopters Ltd	Redhill	
			JA9791					
G-ORLA	P&M Pegasus Quik	8268			21. 5.07	J Summers	Redlands, Swindon	21. 5.08P
G-ORLE	Agusta A109A	7163	G-USTB		22. 6.07	Oracle Aviation LLP	Redhill	18. 7.08E
			D-HEEG, D-HEEF, VR-CKN, HB-XKM					
G-ORMA	Aérospatiale AS.355F1 Ecureuil 2	5192	G-SITE		9.11.98	MW Helicopters Ltd	Stapleford	15. 6.07T
			G-BPHC, N365E			(Sky News titles)		
G-ORMB	Robinson R22 Beta	1607			14.12.90	CHC Scotia Ltd	Cumbernauld	19.10.07E
G-ORMG	Cessna 172R Skyhawk	17280344	N9518F		25. 9.98	J R T Royle	Andrewsfield	5. 4.08E
G-ORMW	Comco Ikarus C42 FB100	0501-6653			11. 4.05	A Boswell tr C42 Dodo Syndicate		
							(Corfe Mullion, Wimborne)	5. 4.08P
G-OROD	Piper PA-18-150 Super Cub	18-7856	SE-CRD		27. 6.89	B W Faulkner	(Petersfield)	13. 3.08E
G-OROO	Cessna 560XL Citation XLS	560-5724			30. 8.07	Rooney Air Ltd	Edinburgh	29. 8.08E
G-OROS	Comco Ikarus C42 FB80	0509-6759			7.10.05	R I Simpson	Clipgate Farm, Denton	29.10.08P
G-ORPC	Europa Aviation Europa XS	443			5. 2.04	P W Churms	(Farnborough)	
	(Built P W Churms - pr.no.PFA 247-13521)					(Noted unmarked at PFA Kemble 7.05)		
G-ORPR	Cameron O-77 Balloon (Hot Air)	2341			26. 6.90	S R Vining	Puxey, Sturminster Newton	6. 4.08A
G-ORRG	Robin DR.400-180 Régent	1216	OO-VPI		6. 2.08	P G Folland tr Radley Robin Group		
							(Chilton Foliat, Hungerford)	
G-ORRI	Eurocopter AS.350B3 Ecureuil	4182	F-GKLF		28. 3.07	Sable Air ApS	(Copenhagen, Denmark)	1. 4.08E
			F-WWXM					
G-ORTH	Beech E90 King Air	LW-136	G-DEXY		12.11.03	P A and C J Crowther	Biggin Hill	12. 2.08E
			N750DC, N30CW, N84GA, N328TB, TR-LTT					
G-ORUG	Thruster T 600N 450 Sprint	0033-T600N-080			2. 9.03	Lincoln Enterprises Ltd	North Coates	18. 9.08P
G-ORVE	Van's RV-6	21710	N2084J		16. 7.07	F M Sperryn and R J F Swain	(Ellenhall, Stafford)	10. 9.08P
	(Built M R Spiller)							
G-ORVG	Van's RV-6	PFA 181A-13509			2. 1.01	J T M Ball tr RV Group	Biggin Hill	15. 3.08P
	(Built R J Fry) (Lycoming O-360)							
G-ORVR	Partenavia P68	115	G-BFBD		2.10.95	Ravenair Aircraft Ltd	Liverpool	7. 4.08E
	(Officially regd as "P68B")							
G-ORVS	Van's RV-9	PFA 320-13999			10. 9.07	C J Marsh	Binstead, Isle of Wight	
	(Built C J Marsh)							
G-ORZA	Diamond DA.42 Twin Star	42.062	G-FCAC		4. 8.06	M J Hill	Bournemouth	6. 2.08E
			OE-VPI					
G-OSAT	Cameron Z-105 Balloon (Hot Air)	10564			18. 6.04	Lotus Balloons Ltd	Broughton, Stockbridge	7. 8.07A
						(Astra titles)		
G-OSAW	QAC Quickie Q.2	2443	G-BVYT		17. 9.04	S A Wilson	RNAS Yeovilton	2. 9.00P
	(Built N A Evans)		N3797S			(Noted 3.06)		
G-OSCC	Piper PA-32-300 Cherokee Six	32-7540020	G-BGFD		27.11.84	BG and G Airlines Ltd	Jersey	17. 4.08E
			D-EOSH, N32186					

Reg	Type	C/n	Prev id	Date	Owner/Operator	Base	Expiry
G-OSCO	TEAM Mini-MAX 91 (Built PJ Schofield)	PFA 186-12878		24.12.96	M A Perry	Benson's Farm, Laindon	13. 6.08P
G-OSDI	Beech 58 Baron	TH-1111	G-BHFY	27. 7.84	A W Eldridge and J A Heard	Guernsey	18.12.07E
G-OSEA	Pilatus Britten-Norman BN-2B-26 Islander	2175	G-BKOL	27. 8.85	W T Johnson and Sons (Huddersfield) Ltd	Crosland Moor	23. 3.08E
G-OSEE	Robinson R22 Beta	0917		11. 1.89	M Jones	Manston	13. 2.08E
G-OSEP	Mainair Blade 912	1340-0902-7-W1135		29.10.02	J D Smith	Baxby Manor, Husthwaite	19.10.08P
G-OSFA	Diamond HK 36 TC Super Dimona	36.649		15. 6.99	Oxfordshire Sportflying Ltd	Enstone	8. 8.08E
G-OSFS	Reims Cessna F177RG Cardinal RG	F177RG0082	F-BUMP	26. 1.04	Cardinal Sin Ltd t/a Staverton Flying School	Gloucestershire	24. 5.08E
G-OSGB	Piper PA-31-350 Navajo Chieftain	31-7952155	G-YSKY N3529D	25. 1.99	Scankort A/S	(Taastrup, Denmark)	20. 6.08E
G-OSHL	Robinson R22 Beta	1000		19. 4.89	Sloane Helicopters Ltd	Sywell	24. 5.08E
G-OSIC	Pitts S-1C (Built R Hendry) (Lycoming O-320)	1921-77	G-BUAW N29DH	7.10.02	J A Dodd	White Waltham	13. 8.07P
G-OSII	Cessna 172N Skyhawk II	17267768	G-BIVY N73973	17.10.95	R A Kehoe tr India India Flying Group	Andrewsfield	7. 4.08E
G-OSIS	Pitts S-1S (Built C Butler)	PFA 009-12043		19. 9.94	C Butler	(Stanfree, Chesterfield)	
G-OSIT	Pitts S-1T (Built Pitts Aerobatics)	1023	N96JD	7.12.01	P J Tomlinson	Kemble	5. 1.08E
G-OSIX	Piper PA-32-260 Cherokee Six	32-499	G-AZMO SE-EYN	5. 8.86	J T Le Bon	Lee on Solent	2. 6.08E
G-OSJF	Piper PA-23-250 Aztec F	27-8054041	G-SFHR G-BHSO, N2527Z	25. 7.05	S J Fawley	Blackpool	26.10.07E
G-OSJL	Robinson R44 Raven II	11452		23.10.06	Darlo Air Ltd	(Maynooth, County Kildare)	16.11.07E
G-OSJN	Europa Aviation Europa XS (Built S J Nash - pr.no.PFA 247-13687)	495		3. 6.03	S J Nash	St Peter Port, Guernsey	18.11.08P
G-OSKP	Enstrom 480	5002	F-GSOT G-OSKP, N480EN	6. 6.94	C C Butt	Hawarden	18. 3.08E
G-OSKR	Best Off Sky Ranger 912(2) (Built Sky Ranger UK Ltd - pr.no.BMAA/HB/249)	SKR0201162		14. 1.03	Sky Ranger UK Ltd	Sywell	15. 6.08P
G-OSKY	Cessna 172M Skyhawk II	17267389	A6-KCB N73343	27. 2.79	Skyhawk Leasing Ltd	Wellesbourne Mountford	8. 7.08E
G-OSLD	Europa Aviation Europa XS (Built S C Percy - pr.no.PFA 247-13641) (Rotax 914-UL) (Tri-gear u/c)	485		23. 8.00	Opus Software Ltd	Black Spring Farm, Castle Bytham	21. 3.08P
G-OSLO	Schweizer 269C (Schweizer 300)	S 1360	N7507L	15. 3.89	AH Helicopter Services Ltd	Dunkeswell	21. 3.08E
G-OSMD	Bell 206B-2 JetRanger II	2034	G-LTEK G-BMIB, ZS-HGH	12. 2.99	Stuart Aviation Ltd	White Waltham	17. 5.08E
G-OSND	Reims Cessna FRA150M Aerobat	FRA1500272	G-BDOU	16.10.84	Wilkins and Wilkins (Special Auctions) Ltd t/a Henlow Flying Club	RAF Henlow	2. 3.08E
G-OSOE	Hawker Siddeley HS.748 Series 2A/275	1697	G-AYYG ZK-MCF, C-GRCU, ZK-MCF, G-AYYG, ZK-MCF, G-AYYG, ZK-MCF, G-AYYG, G-11-9	17.11.97	PTB (Emerald) Proprietary Ltd	Blackpool *(Stored externally 2.08)*	10.11.07E
G-OSOH	Cessna 525 CitationJet	525-0271	HB-VNK N860DB, N860DD	11. 2.08	Hangar 8 Ltd	Oxford	
G-OSPD	Evektor EV-97 teamEurostar UK	1708		3. 9.03	V C Garwood	Rochester	14. 9.08P
G-OSPK	Cessna 172S Skyhawk II	172S10261	N6069D	22. 9.06	Kenward Orthopaedic Ltd	Leeds-Bradford	18.10.07E
G-OSPS	Piper PA-18 Super Cub 95 (L-18C-PI) (Frame No.18-1527)	18-1555	OO-SPS G-AWRH, OO-HMI, French Army 51-15555	9. 7.92	J P Morrissey	Weston, Leixlip, County Kildare	27. 6.10E
G-OSPY	Cirrus SR20 GTS	1546	N81706	9. 9.05	Cumulus Aircraft Rentals Ltd	Bournemouth	22. 9.08E
G-OSSA	Cessna TU206B Super Skywagon B	U2060824	4X-CHT C-GDTO, N139LA, (N3824G)	17.11.03	Skydive St Andrews Ltd	Sorbie Farm, Kingsmuir	16. 5.08E
G-OSSF	Gulfstream AA-5A Cheetah	AA5A-0863	G-MELD G-BHCB	1. 2.00	The Burnett Group Ltd	Kemble	6. 4.07T
G-OSSI	Robinson R44 Raven II	10470		27. 8.04	Goss Air Ltd	Leeds-Bradford	22. 9.07P
G-OSST	Colt 77A Balloon (Hot Air)	737		28.10.85	British Airways PLC *"Concorde II" (Noted 9.05)*	West Drayton	10.10.96A
G-OSTC	Gulfstream AA-5A Cheetah	AA5A-0848	N26967	22. 4.91	5th Generation Designs Ltd	White Waltham	10. 2.07T
G-OSTL	Comco Ikarus C42 FB100	0503-6661		30. 3.05	S T Ling	Dunkeswell	3. 4.07P
G-OSTU	Gulfstream AA-5A Cheetah	AA5A-0807	G-BGCL	18. 4.95	The Burnett Group Ltd	Kemble	31. 7.08E
G-OSTY	Cessna F150G (Built Reims Aviation SA)	F150-0129	G-AVCU	21. 3.97	R F Newman	Stapleford	31. 5.08E
G-OSUP	Lindstrand LBL 90A Balloon (Hot Air)	098		17. 3.94	T J Orchard tr British Airways Balloon Club *(British Airways Clubs titles)*	Wycombe Air Park	27. 8.08T
G-OSUS	Mooney M 20K Mooney 231	25-0429	OY-SUS (N3597H)	7.11.94	J B and M O King	Goodwood	12. 2.08E
G-OSUT	Scheibe SF25C Rotax-Falke	44588	D-KTIK	24. 4.06	Yorkshire Gliding Club (Proprietary) Ltd	Sutton Bank	18 .5.08E
G-OSZA	Pitts S-2A (Built Aerotek Inc)	2134	N60CP N80058	22. 7.05	P J Heilbron	(Guildford)	8. 9.08E
G-OSZB	Pitts S-2B (Built Christen Industries Inc) (Lycoming AEIO-540)	5200	G-OGEE OH-SKY	10. 2.04	P M Ambrose	Popham	25. 4.08E
G-OTAL	ARV Aviation ARV-1 Super 2 (Rotax 914-UL)	024	G-BNGZ	10. 9.87	N R Beale	Church Farm, Shotteswell	2. 5.08P
G-OTAM	Cessna 172M Skyhawk II	17264098	N29060	13. 2.89	G V White	Shipdham	11. 5.08E
G-OTAN	Piper PA-18-135 Super Cub (L-21B-PI) (Frame No.18-3850)	18-3845	OO-TAN (OO-DPD), R Neth AF R-155, 54-2445	28.10.96	S D Turner *(As "54-2445:A-445 in US Army c/s)"*	Audley End	25. 6.09E
G-OTBA	Hawker Siddeley HS.748 Series 2A/242	1712	A3-MCA ZK-MCA, G-11-7	14. 3.01	PTB (Emerald) Proprietary Ltd *(Stored externally 2.08)*	Blackpool	3. 5.07T
G-OTBY	Piper PA-32-300 Six	32-7940219	N2932G	14. 2.91	M J Willing	Jersey	5. 4.08
G-OTCH	CFM Streak Shadow (Built H E Gotch - pr.no.PFA 206-12401) (Rotax 582)	K 207		28.10.93	H E Gotch *(New owner 3.05)*	(Brigstock, Kettering)	3. 9.02P
G-OTCS	Beech B300C Super King Air	FM-18	N818KA	3.08R	*(To become Beech 350C ER "ZZ419" for AAC 2008)*		

Reg	Type	Serial	Prev id	Date	Owner	Location	Date
G-OTCV	Best Off Sky Ranger 912S(1)	SKR0407511		13.12.04	T C Viner	Wolvey	27. 4.08P
	(Built T C Viner - pr.no.BMAA/HB/436)				"Terry Viner"		
G-OTCZ	Schempp-Hirth Ventus 2cT	137/352	BGA 5147-KJX	7.12.05	D H Conway tr CZ Group	Nympsfield	31.12.07
			D-KAAQ		"CZ"		
G-OTDA	Boeing 737-31S	29266	D-ADBV	5. 2.04	Globespan Airways Ltd t/a Flyglobespan.com		
			N1786B			Glasgow	8. 3.08E
G-OTDI	Diamond DA.40D Star	D4.031		10. 9.03	Atrium Ltd	Denham	21.11.07E
G-OTEL	Thunder Ax8-90 Balloon (Hot Air)	1790		13. 6.90	D N Belton	Chard	31. 7.03A
G-OTFL	Eurocopter EC.120B Colibri	1073	G-IBRI	6. 7.05	Tyrone Farbrication Ltd	(Dungannon)	13.12.07E
			LX-HCR				
G-OTFT	Piper PA-38-112 Tomahawk	38-78A0311	G-BNKW	14. 3.97	P Tribble	Panshanger	30.10.07E
			N9274T				
G-OTGA	Piper PA-28R-201 Arrow III	28R-7837281	ZS-KFI	21. 2.01	TG Aviation Ltd	Manston	1. 4.07E
G-OTHE	Enstrom 280C-UK Shark	1226	G-OPJT	22. 9.87	G E Heritage (Breach Oak Farm, Corley, Coventry)		22.12.07E
			G-BKCO				
G-OTIB	Robin DR.400-180R Remorqueur	1545	D-EGIA	26. 4.00	Norfolk Gliding Club Ltd	Tibenham	29. 5.08E
G-OTIG	Gulfstream AA-5B Tiger	AA5B-0996	G-PENN	28. 7.00	D H Green	Elstree	30. 9.07E
			(I-TIGR), N3756L				
G-OTIM	Bensen B 8MV	PFA G/101-1084		5. 6.90	T J Deane	(Tilehurst, Reading)	
	(Built T J Deane)						
G-OTIV	Aerospool Dynamic WT9 UK	DY194/2007		6.11.07	Yeoman Light Aircraft Company Ltd	Bagby	5.11.08P
	(Official c/n is "DY194")						
G-OTJB	Robinson R44 Raven	0813		4. 8.00	D N and J Farrell	Liverpool	7. 9.08E
G-OTJH	Pegasus Quantum 15-912	7791		20. 3.01	L R Gartside	Newnham, Baldock	12. 4.08P
G-OTNA	Robinson R44 Raven II	11092		7. 2. 06	Abel Developments Ltd		
						(Little Cressingham, Thetford)	6. 4.08E
G-OTOE	Aeronca 7AC Champion	7AC-4621	G-BRWW	2. 4.90	J M Gale Coombe Farm, Spreyton, Crediton		10. 5.95P
			N1070E, NC1070E		(Damaged Coombe Farm 31.5.95)		
G-OTOO	Stolp SA.300 Starduster Too	PFA 035-13352		26. 8.98	I M Castle	Spanhoe	
	(Built I M Castle)				(Noted 10.07?)		
G-OTOY	Robinson R22 Beta	0888	G-BPEW	5. 9.97	Heli Air Ltd	Wellesbourne Mountford	19.10.07E
G-OTRV	Van's RV-6	PFA 181-13302		27. 5.98	A Burani	(London SW5)	27. 3.08P
	(Built W R C Williams-Wynne) (Lycoming O-360) (Tailwheel u/c)						
G-OTRY	Schleicher ASW 24	24023	BGA 3372-FMP	18. 1.08	A.R.Harrison and G.Pursey	Dunstable	8. 7.08
G-OTSP	Aérospatiale AS.355F1 Ecureuil 2	5177	G-XPOL	31. 3.98	MW Helicopters Ltd	Stapleford	17. 4.08E
			G-BPRF, N363E				
G-OTTI	Cameron OTTI 34 SS Balloon (Hot Air)	3490		23. 3.95	Ballonwerbung Hamburg GmbH	Kiel, Germany	30. 4.05A
G-OTTO	Cameron Katalog 82 SS Balloon (Hot Air)	2843		15. 6.92	Ballonwerbung Hamburg GmbH	Kiel, Germany	6. 7.03A
	(New envelope 1999 - c/n 4382)				"Otto Versand Katalog"		
G-OTTZ	Robinson R44 Raven II	11779		22. 6.07	Glenmore Helicopters Ltd		
						(Ballybofey, County Donegal)	5. 7.08E
G-OTUG	Piper PA-18-150 Super Cub	18-5352	(G-BKNM)	17. 2.83	A J Lewis	Gloucestershire	3. 4.08E
	(Frame No.18-5424)		PH-MBA, French Army 18-5352, N10F				
G-OTUI	SOCATA TB-20 Trinidad	1096	G-KKDL	7. 3.03	D J Taylor and J T Flint	Cranfield	21.12.07E
			G-BSHU		(Noted 2.08)		
G-OTUN	Evektor EV-97 Eurostar	PFA 315-13865		15. 5.02	S P Slater	Bodmin	24. 7.07P
	(Built E O Otun)				(New owner 2.08)		
G-OTUP	Lindstrand LBL 180A Balloon (Hot Air)	111		28. 3.94	Westcountry Ballooning Ltd Queen Camel, Yeovil		17. 4.08T
G-OTVI	Robinson R44 Raven II	10833		9. 9.05	R C Hields t/a Hields Aviation	Sherburn-in-Elmet	4.10.07E
G-OTVR	Piper PA-34-220T Seneca V	3449279	N53497	25. 7.05	Bladerunner Aviation Ltd	Barton	24. 7.08E
G-OTWO	Rutan Defiant	114		24. 6.87	B Wronski	Gloucestershire	27. 8.08P
	(Built D G Foreman) (Lycoming O-320)						
G-OTYE	Evektor EV-97 Eurostar	PFA 315-13858		15. 4.02	A B Godber and J Tye "Ali Minimum"		
	(Built A B Godber and J Tye)				(Hulland Ward, Ashbourne and Holloway, Matlock)		29. 5.08P
G-OTYP	Piper PA-28-180 Cherokee Challenger		F-BTYP	13. 1.04	I R Chaplin	Cambridge	31. 5.08E
		28-7305166	N11C)				
G-OUCH	Cameron N-105 Balloon (Hot Air)	4830		3. 5.00	Flying Pictures Ltd	Chilbolton, Stockbridge	26. 3.03A
					(Elastoplast titles)		
G-OUHI	Europa Aviation Europa XS	488		7. 6.01	Airplan Flight Equipment Ltd	Barton	
	(Built D R Philpott - pr.no.PFA 247-13684) (Tri-gear u/c)				(New owner 8.04)		
G-OUIK	Mainair Sports Pegasus Quik	7983		22. 8.03	M C Shortman Broadmeadow Farm, Hereford		25. 8.08P
G-OUMC	Lindstrand LBL 105A Balloon (Hot Air)	724		14. 9.00	A M Holly t/a Executive Ballooning		
					(Uphill Motor Company titles) Breadstone, Berkeley		2. 4.08T
G-OURO	Europa Aviation Europa	016		13.12.93	M Crunden	Damyn's Hall, Upminster	10. 7.07P
	(Buillt D Dufton - pr.no.PFA 247-12522) (NSI EA-81/100) (Tri-gear u/c)				(Noted 9.07)		
G-OUVI	Cameron O-105 Balloon (Hot Air)	1766		4. 5.89	P Spellward tr Bristol University Hot Air Ballooning Society		
					"Uvistat II" (Inflated 5.06)	Bristol	31. 3.94A
G-OVAA	Colt Jumbo SS Balloon (Hot Air)	1426		11. 5.89	I Chadwick tr Balloon Preservation Flying Group		
	(Conventional Balloon (Hot Air) with nose/wings and tail of Virgin Boeing 747)				(Inflated 4.06) Partridge Green, Horsham		5. 5.08A
G-OVAG	Tipsy Nipper T 66 Series 1	T66/15	OO-VAG	7. 4.04	L D Johnston	Perth	20. 6.08P
	(Built Avions Fairey SA)		OO-LYS				
G-OVAL	Comco Ikarus C42 FB100	0407-6608		18. 8.04	N G Tomes	Dunkeswell	14. 8.08P
G-OVAX	Colt AS-105 GD Mk II Airship (Hot Air)	1501		3. 7.89	Fly In Balloons SRL	Villafalletto, Italy	21. 3.07E
					(Liu-Jo titles)		
G-OVBF	Cameron A-250 Balloon (Hot Air)	3494		1. 3.95	Airxcite Ltd t/a Virgin Balloon Flights	Wembley	18. 3.07E
					"Virgin Oscar"		
G-OVET	Cameron O-56 Balloon (Hot Air)	3939		25. 6.96	A R Hardwick and E Fearon	Bristol	21. 5.08A
G-OVFM	Cessna 120	14720	N2119V	29. 4.88	A Sutherland and A P Bacon	Wick	10. 4.08P
	(Continental O-200-A)		NC2119V				
G-OVFR	Reims Cessna F172N Skyhawk II	F17201892		23. 5.79	Marine and Aviation Ltd	Lee-on-Solent	13. 7.08E
G-OVIA	Lindstrand LBL 105A Balloon (Hot Air)	1002		9. 7.04	N C Lindsay	Pulborough	16. 4.08A
G-OVIC	Cameron A-250 Balloon (Hot Air)	4409	SE-ZKA	29.10.04	M E White	Templeogue, Dublin	13. 7.08E
G-OVID	Avid Flyer	NMFC 11760	N879UP	31. 5.91	W J Lister	Strathaven	7. 5.08P
	(Built J Pelafigue) (Rotax 532)						

G-OVII	Van's RV-7	PFA 323-14100		30. 9.04	T J Richardson	(Hook)	12. 2.08P
	(Built T J Richardson)						
G-OVIN	Rockwell Commander 112TC	13090	OY-DVN	19.11.04	G-OVIN Aviation Ltd	Southend	16. 2.08E
			D-EIXN, N4585W				
G-OVLA	Comco Ikarus C42 FB UK	0303-6550		4. 2.03	B C and P A Webb t/a Webb Plant Sales		
	(Built N Sams and B Bayes - pr.no.PFA 322-14028)					Dunkeswell	2.11.08P
G-OVMC	Reims Cessna F152 II	F15201667		29. 5.79	Atlantic Flight Training Ltd	Coventry	19. 8.07T
G-OVNR	Robinson R22 Beta	1634		24.12.90	Beechview Aviation Ltd	Newtownards	16. 9.08E
G-OVOL	Best Off Sky Ranger 912S(1)	SP012		2. 6.05	A S Docherty	Graveley Hall Farm, Graveley	21. 6.08P
	(Built Sky Ranger UK Ltd - pr.no.BMAA/HB/447)						
G-OVON	Piper PA-18-95 Super Cub	18-1596	OY-ELG	1. 6.05	Veronica F A Stanley	Gloucestershire	27. 7.08E
			D-ECXO, French Army 51-15596				
G-OWAC	Reims Cessna F152 II	F15201678	G-BHEB	25. 2.80	Aviation South West Ltd	Exeter	10. 4.08E
			(OO-HNW)				
G-OWAK	Reims Cessna F152 II	F15201677	G-BHEA	25. 2.80	A S Bamrah t/a Falcon Flying Services	Rochester	12.12.07E
G-OWAL	Piper PA-34-220T Seneca III	3448030	D-GAPN	7. 7.98	R G and W Allison	Gamston	9.11.07E
			N9163K				
G-OWAN	Cessna 210D Centurion	21058321	N672P	11.06.07	G Owen	Leeds-Bradford	19. 6.08E
			HB-CII, D-EDEG, OE-DEG, N3821Y				
G-OWAP	Piper PA-28-161 Cherokee Warrior II		G-BXNH	13. 6.05	Airways Aero Association Ltd	Wycombe Air Park	21.12.07E
		28-7816314	N2828M		(Operated British Airways Flying Club) (Union Flag c/s)		
G-OWAR	Piper PA-28-161 Warrior II	28-8616054	TF-OBO	18. 2.88	Bickertons Aerodromes Ltd	Denham	19. 2.08E
			N9521N		(Operated The Pilot Centre)		
G-OWAZ	Pitts S-1C	43JM	G-BRPI	22.11.94	P E S Latham	Sleap	20. 3.08P
	(Built J Magueri) (Lycoming O-320)		N199M		"Tiny Dancer"		
G-OWCS	Cessna 182J Skylane	18257009	D-EFSA	25.11.02	P Ragg	(Weerberg, Austria)	15. 1.06
			N2909F		(Operates in Africa)		
G-OWEL	Colt 105A Balloon (Hot Air)	1773		18. 5.90	S R Seager	Aylesbury	16. 3.98T
G-OWEN	K & S Jungster 1	PFA 044-10124		13.11.78	R C Owen	(Danehill, Haywards Heath)	
	(Built R C Owen) (Continental C90)						
G-OWET	Thurston TSC-1A2 Teal	037	C-FNOR	28. 9.94	D Nieman	Ventfield Farm, Oxfordshire	18. 7.07
			(N1342W)				
G-OWFS	Cessna A152 Aerobat	A1520805	G-DESY	21. 5.02	Westair Flying Services Ltd	Blackpool	24. 4.08E
			G-BNJE, N7386L				
G-OWGC	Slingsby T 61F Venture T 2	1875	XZ555	14. 8.91	Wolds Gliding Club Ltd	Pocklington	21. 1.07
G-OWLC	Piper PA-31 Turbo Navajo	31-679	G-AYFZ	13. 6.91	Channel Airways Ltd	Guernsey	30. 5.08E
			N6771L				
G-OWMC	Thruster T 600N 450	0122-T600N-076		5. 3.03	A R Hughes t/a Wiltshire Microlight Centre		
						Yatesbury	19. 4.08P
G-OWND	Robinson R44 Astro	0644		26. 8.99	R E Todd	Sandtoft	15. 9.08E
G-OWOW	Cessna 152 II	15283199	G-BMSZ	10. 5.95	Plane Talking Ltd	Wycombe Air Park	22.12.07E
			N47254		(Operated Wycombe Flying Centre)		
G-OWRD	Agusta A109C	7649	G-USTC	21. 2.05	Wickford Development Company Ltd		
			JA6695, (G-LAXO)			Wickford House, Hatfield Peverel	2. 6.08E
G-OWRT	Cessna 182G Skylane	18255077	G-ASUL	24. 8.00	Blackpool and Fylde Aero Club Ltd	Blackpool	18. 6.08E
			N3677U				
G-OWST	Cessna 172S Skyhawk	172S8163	G-WABH	17. 6.05	Manx Aero Marine Management Ltd)	Blackpool	7. 5.08E
			N961SP				
G-OWWW	Europa Aviation Europa XS	051		9. 6.94	R F W Holder tr Whisky Group	High Cross, Ware	16. 5.08P
	(Built W R C Williams-Wynne and R F W Holder - pr.no.PFA 247-12683) (Tri-gear u/c)						
G-OWYE	Lindstrand LBL 240A Balloon (Hot Air)	645		27. 4.00	Wye Valley Aviation Ltd	Bridstow, Ross-on-Wye	5.10.08T
G-OWYN	Aviamilano F 14 Nibbio	208	HB-EVZ	2. 2.87	R Nash	Shoreham	3. 9.08P
			I-SERE				
G-OXBC	Cameron A-140 Balloon (Hot Air)	4981		2. 2.01	J E Rose "Oxford Balloon Company"	Abingdon	18.12.08A
G-OXBY	Cameron N-90 Balloon (Hot Air)	1993	PH-DUM	9. 6.94	C A Oxby "The Zit"	(Doncaster)	
G-OXKB	Cameron Jaguar XK8 Sports Car 110 SS Balloon (Hot Air)			9. 7.96	D M Moffat	Bristol	5.10.07A
		3941			"Jaguar XK8"		
G-OXLC	Boeing 737-8BK/W	33029	5B-DCE	1.12.06	XL Airways UK Ltd	London Gatwick	20.12.07E
			N1786B				
G-OXLS	Cessna 560XL Citation XLS	560-5675	N5266F	18. 1.07	GO XLS Ltd	Guernsey	18.1.08E
G-OXOM	Piper PA-28-161 Cadet	2841285	G-BRSG (2)	9.12.03	S J Skilton t/a Aviation Rentals	Elstree	4. 1.08E
			N92011				
G-OXTC	Piper PA-23-250 Aztec D	27-4344	G-AZOD	31. 5.89	A S Bamrah t/a Falcon Flying Services	Biggin Hill	15. 6.98T
			N697RC, N6976Y		(Noted 6.05)		
G-OXVI	Vickers Supermarine 361 Spitfire LF.XVIe		7246M	22. 8.89	Spitfire Ltd	Duxford	7. 7.08P
		CBAF.IX.4262	TD248		(As "TD248:CR-S" in RAF 74 Sqdn c/s)		
G-OYAK	SPP Yakovlev Yak C-11	171205	EAF 705	25. 2.88	A H Soper	Little Gransden	22.12.07P
	(C/n quoted as 1701139 and or 690120 also)		OK-KIH		(As "9" (white) in Russian AF c/s)		
G-OYES	Mainair Blade 912	1186-1198-7-W989		12.11.98	B Mcadam and A Hatton	(Dalkeith and Loanhead)	10. 5.08P
G-OYIO	Robin DR.400-120 Dauphin 2+2	2038	OO-YIO	16. 2.07	Bustard Flying Club Ltd	Boscombe Down	17. 5.08
	(Offiicially regd as DR.400-120 Petit Prince)						
G-OYST	Agusta-Bell 206B-2 JetRanger II	8440	G-JIMW	9.10.02	Adroit Services Corporation	Southend	14. 5.08E
			G-UNIK, G-TPPH, G-BCYP				
G-OYTE	Rans S-6-ES Coyote II	0404 1563		21. 7.04	I M Vass	Morgansfield, Fishburn	4. 2.08P
	(Built I M Vass - pr.no.PFA 204-14263) (Tri-cycle u/c)						
G-OZAC	Bell 407	53062	OY-HMM	8. 5.07	Narragansett LLP t/a Helilux	(Pontprenn, Cardiff)	4. 6.08E
			OE-XWG, D-HASI, C-GFNM				
G-OZAR	Enstrom 480	5007	G-BWFF	31. 7.95	Benham Helicopters Ltd	Gloucestershire	22.12.07E
G-OZBB	Airbus A320-212	389	C-GZUM	21. 3.94	Monarch Airlines Ltd	Luton	29. 4.08E
	G-OZBB, C-GZUM, G-OZBB, G-GXBB, G-OZBB, C-FTDW, G-OZBB, G-FTDW, G-OZBB, C-FTDW, G-OZBB, C-FTDW, G-OZBB, F-WWDI						
G-OZBE	Airbus A321-231	1707	D-AVZH	27. 3.02	Monarch Airlines Ltd	Luton	26. 3.08E
G-OZBF	Airbus A321-231	1763	D-AVZB	20. 6.02	Monarch Airlines Ltd	Luton	19. 6.08E
G-OZBG	Airbus A321-231	1941	D-AVXC	20. 3.03	Monarch Airlines Ltd	Luton	19. 3.08E
G-OZBH	Airbus A321-231	2105	D-AVXB	17. 3.04	Monarch Airlines Ltd	Luton	16. 3.08E

G-OZBI	Airbus A321-231	2234	D-AVZV	4. 6.04	Monarch Airlines Ltd	Luton	3. 6.08E
G-OZBJ	Airbus A320-212	0446	N446AN	16. 2.05	Monarch Airlines Ltd	Luton	15. 2.08E
			I-PEKR, N446AN, G-MONZ, C-FTDI, G-MONZ, C-FTDI, G-MONZ, C-FTDI, G-MONZ, F-WWDJ				
G-OZBK	Airbus A320-214	1370	PH-BMD	28. 4.05	Monarch Airlines Ltd	Luton	27. 4.08E
			D-ABLB, F-WQQI, OO-SNG, F-WWIL.				
G-OZBL	Airbus A321-231	864	G-MIDE	12. 5.06	Monarch Airlines Ltd	Luton	13. 8.08E
			D-AVZB				
G-OZBM	Airbus A321-231	1045	G-MIDJ	14. 3.07	Monarch Airlines Ltd	Luton	15. 7.08E
			D-AVZO				
G-OZBN	Airbus A321-231	1153	G-MIDK	2. 4.07	Monarch Airlines Ltd	Luton	11. 1.08E
			D-AVZF				
G-OZBO	Airbus A321-231	1207	G-MIDM	14. 5.07	Monarch Airlines Ltd	Luton	17. 4.08E
			D-AVZR				
G-OZBP	Airbus A321-231	1433	G-TTIB	6. 2.08	Monarch Airlines Ltd	Luton	26. 2.08E
			D-AVZC				
G-OZBR	Airbus A321-231	1794	N586NK	3.08R	Monarch Airlines Ltd	Luton	
G-OZBS	Airbus A321-231	1428	G-TTIA	8.08R	Monarch Airlines Ltd	Luton	
			D-AVZA				
G-OZEE	Avid Speed Wing Mk.4	PFA 189-12308		18. 4.94	G D Bailey	Old Sarum	18.12.07P
	(Built S C Goozee)						
G-OZEF	Europa Aviation Europa XS	538		23.12.03	Z M Ahmad	(Southall)	
	(Built Z M Ahmad - pr.no.PFA 247-14041)						
G-OZIE	Avtech Jabiru J400	0xxx		30. 6.05	S A Bowkett	Sleap	23. 1.08P
	(Built S A Bowkett - pr.no.PFA 325-14284)						
G-OZOI	Cessna R182 Skylane RG II	R18201950	G-ROBK	31. 5.85	J R and F.L Gibson Fleming t/a Ranston Farms		
						Ranston Farm, Iwerne Courtney	30. 7.08
G-OZOO	Cessna 172N Skyhawk II	17267663	G-BWEI	17.11.99	R A Brown	(Clowne, Chesterfield)	27. 8.07T
			N73767		(New owner 2.08)		
G-OZOZ	Schempp-Hirth Nimbus 3dT	6	BGA 4458-JEQ	27.11.07	C M Hawkes tr OZ Syndicate	Ringmer	22. 9.08
			OO-ZOZ, HB-1921, D-7695				
G-OZRH	British Aerospace BAe 146 Series 200	E2047	(EI-DDF)	29. 1.96	Flightline Ltd	Zurich, Switzerland	1. 2.08E
			N188US, N364PS		(Operated IAC)		
G-OZZI	Avtech Jabiru SK	0157		15. 8.97	A H Godfrey	(Weston-super-Mare)	22. 6.08P
	(Built A H Godfrey and E J Stradling - pr.no.PFA 274-13176)						
G-OZZY	Robinson R22 Beta II	2982	EI-RZZ	2. 9.03	London Helicopter Centres Ltd	Redhill	2. 9.08E
			G-PWEL				

G-PAAA - G-PZZZ

G-PACE	Robin R1180T Aiglon	218		16.10.78	T C Wise and M T Fitzpatrick	(Codicote, Hitchin)	18. 4.08E
G-PACL	Robinson R22 Beta	1893	N2314S	17.12.91	R Wharam	(Rotherham)	3.10.07E
G-PACT	Piper PA-28-181 Archer III	2843546	N5368F	25. 3.03	A Parsons	(London SW6)	25. 3.08E
G-PADD	Gulfstream AA-5A Cheetah	AA5A-0780	G-ESTE	27.10.03	Caseright Ltd	Turweston	8.12.04T
			G-GHNC, N26877		(Noted 1.08)		
G-PADE	Reality Escapade Jabiru(3)	JAESC 0027		2. 6.04	C L G Innocent	(Worthing)	27. 6.08P
	(Built C L G Innocent - pr.no.BMAA/HB/369) (Tailwheel u/c)						
G-PADI	Cameron V-77 Balloon (Hot Air)	1809		18. 8.88	R F Penney "Padiwac"	Watford	23. 4.06A
G-PAFR	DG Flugzeugbau DG-300 Elan	3E344	BGA 3500-FSX	5.10.07	P Morgan	Parham Park	17. 1.08
G-PAIZ	Piper PA-12 Super Cruiser	12-2018	N3215M	11. 4.94	B R Pearson	Eaglescott	16. 8.07T
			NC3215M		(Carries "NC3215M" on tail)		
G-PALY	Piper PA-28-181 Archer III	2843039	PH-AEC	8. 8.07	Innovative Aviation Ltd	(Ripon)	19. 9.08P
G-PAMY	Robinson R44 Clipper II	11641		6. 3.07	Batchelor Aviation Ltd	(Caterham)	15. 3.08E
G-PARG	Pitts S-1S	19528-1	N18FW	30. 6.03	R C Pargeter	Sorbie Farm, Kingsmuir	12. 3.08P
	(Built F G Weaver)						
G-PARI	Cessna 172RG Cutlass II	172RG0010	N4685R	19.11.79	Applied Signs Ltd	Tatenhill	30. 5.08E
G-PART	Partenavia P68	62	F-GMPT	19.12.84	Ravenair Aircraft Ltd	Liverpool	21. 1.08E
	(Officially regd as "P68B")		G-PART, OY-CEY, D-GATE, PH-EEO, (N718R)				
G-PASG	MBB BÖ.105DBS-4	S 819	G-MHSL	7.12.92	Police Aviation Services Ltd	Leeds-Bradford	13. 5.08E
			D-HFCC		(Operated Yorkshire Air Ambulance)		
G-PASH	Aérospatiale AS.355F1 Ecureuil 2	5040	F-GHLI	17. 5.96	Diamond Aviation Ltd	(Sheffield City)	23. 5.08E
			LX-HUG, F-GHLI, N356E				
G-PASN	Enstrom F-28F	427	G-BSHZ	19. 4.05	Passion 4 Health International Ltd	(Chertsey)	30.12.07E
			N51702				
G-PASV	Pilatus Britten-Norman BN-2B-21 Islander	2157	G-BKJH	26. 2.92	Police Aviation Services Ltd	Gloucestershire	18. 7.08E
			HC-BNR, G-BKJH				
G-PASX	MBB BÖ.105DBS-4	S 814	D-HDZX	20.12.89	Police Aviation Services Ltd	Gloucestershire	13. 2.08E
G-PATF	Europa Aviation Europa	107		5. 1.99	E P Farrell	(Beaconsfield)	
	(Built E P Farrell - pr.no.PFA 247-12757) (Monowheel u/c)						
G-PATG	Cameron O-90 Balloon (Hot Air)	3856		13. 3.96	Bath University Students Union	Claverton Down, Bath	7. 6.06A
G-PATN	SOCATA TB-10 Tobago	307	G-LUAR	25. 3.97	M D Booth tr G-PATN Owners Group	Humberside	29. 2.08E
G-PATO	Zenair CH.601UL Zodiac	PFA 162A-14328		2. 3.05	D L Walker	(Plumpton Green, Lewes)	16. 8.08P
	(Built D L Walker) (Tri-cycle u/c)						
G-PATP	Lindstrand LBL 77A Balloon (Hot Air)	471		8. 7.97	P Pruchnickyj	Weston Turville, Buckingham	19. 7.08
G-PATS	Europa Aviation Europa	216		19. 7.95	D J G Kesterton tr G-PATS Flying Group		
	(Built N Surman - pr.no.PFA 247-12888)				(New owner 4.05)	(Milton Keynes)	
G-PATX	Lindstrand LBL 90A Balloon (Hot Air)	778		19. 6.01	P C Gooch	Alresford	9. 7.08A
G-PATZ	Europa Aviation Europa	069		2. 6.98	H P H Griffin tr G-PATZ Group	Denham	1. 8.07P
	(Built H P H Griffin - pr.no.PFA 247-12625) (Monowheel u/c)						
G-PAVL	Robin R3000/120	170		22.11.96	Autogas Worldwide Ltd	(Newport)	20. 3.08T
G-PAWL	Piper PA-28-140 Cherokee	28-24456	G-AWEU	8. 9.82	A E Davies tr G-PAWL Group	Barton	7. 9.07
			N11C				
G-PAWN	Piper PA-25-260 Pawnee C	25-5207	G-BEHS	12. 3.01	A P Meredith	Lasham	25. 6.93A
			OE-AFX, N8755L		(New owner 3.01)		

G-PAWS	Gulfstream AA-5A Cheetah	AA5A-0806	N2623Q	8. 2.82	M J Patrick	Goodwood	11.10.07E
G-PAWZ	Best Off Sky Ranger Swift 912S(1) SKRxxxx758			23. 7.07	S D McMurran	(Norton, Daventry)	
	(Built S D McMurran - pr.no.BMAA/HB/528)						
G-PAXX	Piper PA-20-135 Pacer	20-1107	N135XX	20. 5.83	D W Grace	Landmead Farm, Garford	4.10.10SE
			G-PAXX, (G-ARCE), F-BLLA, CN-TDJ, F-DADR				
G-PAYD	Robin DR.400-180 Régent	847	D-EAYD	14. 1.03	A Head	Bicester	27. 3.08E
G-PAZY	Pazmany PL-4A	PFA 017-10378	G-BLAJ	20.11.89	M Richardson	(Durrington, Salisbury)	3.10.95P
	(Built J D Le Pine) (Continental A65)				(New owner 11.05)		
G-PBEC	Van's RV-7	72125		21. 8.07	P G Reid	Derby	16.12.08P
	(Built P G Reid- pr.no.PFA 323-14382)						
G-PBEE	Robinson R44 Clipper	0829		11. 9.00	P Barnard	Guernsey	21. 9.08T
G-PBEK	Agusta A109A	7135	G-BXIV	20.12.04	Castle Air Charters Ltd	Liskeard Heliport	10. 3.08E
			F-GERU, HB-XOK, D-HFZF				
G-PBEL	CFM Shadow Series DD	305-DD		27.10.98	P Richardson	(New Balderton, Newark)	19.10.08P
G-PBRL	Robinson R22 Beta	4053		15. 6.06	Barley Mo Ltd	Headcorn	6. 7.08E
G-PBUS	Avtech Jabiru SK	0164		18. 8.98	J F Heath	Carlisle	7. 5.08P
	(Built G R Pybus - pr.no.PFA 274-13269)						
G-PBYA	Consolidated PBY-5A Catalina	CV-283	C-FNJF	19.11.04	Catalina Aircraft Ltd	Duxford	26. 4.09S
	(Built Canadian Vickers Ltd)		CF-NJF, F-ZBBD, CF-NJF, F-ZBAY, CF-NJF, RCAF 11005 (As "433915" in USAAF c/s)				
	(Originally built for RCAF as Canso A: new c/s represents OA-10A Catalina 44-33915 of 5th Emergency Rescue Squadron, 8th Air Force)						
G-PBYY	Enstrom 280FX Shark	2077	G-BXKV	15. 8.97	B Morgan	Gloucestershire	31. 5.08E
			D-HHML				
G-PCAF	Pietenpol AirCamper	PFA 047-12433		1. 6.94	C C and F M Barley	Manor Farm, Tongham	10. 9.08P
	(Built C C and F M Barley)						
G-PCAM	Fairey Britten-Norman BN-2A Mk.III-2 Trislander		G-BEPH	26. 9.01	Aurigny Air Services Ltd	Guernsey	14. 6.04T
		1052	S7-AAG, G-BEPH		(ABN AMRO Bank titles) (Stored 1.06)		
G-PCAT	SOCATA TB-10 Tobago	60	G-BHER	17. 7.03	Lortell Ltd	Oxford	13. 5.08T
			4X-AKK, G-BHER				
G-PCCC	Alpi Pioneer 300	112		31. 3.04	R Pidcock	Fenland	24. 5.08P
	(Built F A Civaciuti - pr.no.PFA 330-14220)						
G-PCDP	Moravan Zlin Z-526F Trener	1163	SP-CDP	24.10.94	J Mann	Brock Farm, Billericay	23. 4.08E
	(Walter M137A)				"Ticker"		
G-PCOP	Beech B200 Super King Air	BB-1860	N6200G	7.10.05	Albert Bartlett and Sons (Airdrie) Ltd	Glasgow	22.11.07E
G-PDGE	Eurocopter EC.120B Colibri	1211	F-WQPD	20. 7.01	A J Wicklow	Cumbernauld	10. 9.08E
G-PDGF	Eurocopter AS.350B2 Ecureuil	9024	G-FROH	25. 5.07	PLM Dollar Group Ltd	Inverness	24. 1.08E
G-PDGG	Aeromere F 8L Falco Series 3	208	OO-TOS	6. 1.98	P D G Grist	Sibson	31. 5.10S
			I-BLIZ				
G-PDGN	Aérospatiale SA.365N Dauphin 2	6074	PH-SSU	5. 4.01	PLM Dollar Group Ltd	Inverness	19. 7.08E
			5N-ATX, PH-SSU, (G-BLDR), G-TRAF, G-BLDR				
G-PDGR	Aérospatiale AS.350B2 Ecureuil	2559	G-RICC	26. 1.07	PLM Dollar Group Ltd	Inverness	23. 3.08E
			G-BTXA				
G-PDGT	Aérospatiale AS.355F2 Ecureuil 2	5374	N325SC	27.11.07	PLM Dollar Group Ltd t/a PDG Helicopters	Inverness	27.11.06T
			G-BOOV		(Noted 11.07)		
G-PDHJ	Cessna T182R Turbo Skylane II	T18268092	N6888H	3. 1.85	P G Vallance Ltd	Redhill	22. 8.08E
G-PDOC	Piper PA-44-180 Seminole	44-7995090	G-PVAF	17.12.85	T White t/a Medicare	Newcastle	22.10.07E
			N2242A				
G-PDOG	Cessna O-1E Bird Dog	24550	F-GKGP	25. 9.98	J D Needham	Old Manor Farm, Anwick	12. 5.08
	(Regd as Cessna 305C)		French Army		(As "24550:GP" in USAF c/s)		
G-PDSI	Cessna 172N Skyhawk II	17270420	N739BU	4. 1.88	A J Clements and C I Bateman tr DA Flying Group		
						Blackbushe	19. 4.08E
G-PEAK	Agusta-Bell 206B-2 JetRanger II	8242	G-BLJE	7. 3.94	Techanimation Ltd	(Stansted)	4. 6.08E
			SE-HBW				
G-PEAR	P&M Pegasus Quik	8309		20. 9.07	C D Hayle	(Balby, Doncaster)	2.10.08P
G-PECK	Piper PA-32-300 Cherokee Six D	32-7140008	G-ETAV	22. 4.03	H Peck	Gamston	26. 4.08E
			G-MCAR, G-LADA, G-AYWK, N8616N				
G-PEGA	Pegasus Quantum 15-912	7700		14. 8.00	B A Showell	Maypole Farm, Chislet	21. 8.07P
G-PEGE	Best Off Sky Ranger 912(2)	SKR 0511640		31. 1.06	A N Hughes	Weston Zoyland	26.10.08P
	(Built A N Hughes - pr.no.BMAA/HB/479) (C/n possibly SKR0508640)						
G-PEGG	Colt 90A Balloon (Hot Air)	1550		28. 6.89	Ballon Vole Association	Fontaine les Dijon, France	2. 3.08A
G-PEGI	Piper PA-34-200T Seneca II	34-7970339	N2907A	27.11.89	Tayflite Ltd	Perth	9. 9.08T
G-PEGY	Europa Aviation Europa	096		16. 5.00	M T Dawson	Leeds-Bradford	5. 4.08P
	(Built M T Dawson - pr.no.PFA 247-12713) (Rotax 914-UL) (Tri-gear u/c)						
G-PEGZ	Centrair 101A Pégase	101A0179	BGA 3871-HDW	16.10.07	J A P Eldem	Walney Island	3. 5.06
			F-CGEE				
G-PEJM	Piper PA-28-181 Archer III	2843355	N41860	28. 6.00	I Harris	(Bishop's Cannings, Devizes)	9. 7.08E
G-PEKT	SOCATA TB-20 Trinidad	532	N24AS	28. 7.89	A J Dales	Mount Airey Farm, South Cave	30. 3.08E
G-PELS	Agusta-Bell 206A JetRanger	8185	G-DNCN	6.11.06	M P May	(Ossett)	24. 5.08E
			9H-AAJ, Libyan Arab Rep AF 8185, 5A-BAM				
G-PENH	Ultramagic M-90 Balloon (Hot Air)	90-98		10.12.07	G Holtham	Heage, Belper	
G-PEPA	Cessna 206H Stationair	20608181	G-MGMG	15. 6.04	R D Lygo	Goodwood	16.11.07E
			N5076D				
G-PEPL	MD Helicopters MD.600N	RN047	N3047L	5. 2.01	Blue Anchor Leisure Ltd	(ingoldmells, Skegness)	26. 4.07
G-PEPS	Robinson R44 Astro	0722	G-LFBW	13. 9.06	Hopkinsons Fair Deals Ltd		
			G-ODES			(East Hardwick, Pontefract)	16. 3.08E
G-PERC	Cameron N-90 Balloon (Hot Air)	10127		29. 8.01	P A Foot and I R Warrington	Stamford	2. 3.08A
					(Stanton Marris titles)		
G-PERE	Robinson R22 Beta II	3382	N70881	24. 2.03	Central Helicopters Ltd	Tollerton	6. 3.08E
G-PERZ	Bell 206B-3 JetRanger III	4411	N6272T	7. 1.97	Alpha Air Ltd	(Gravesend)	5. 4.08T
G-PEST	Hawker Tempest II	12202	HA604	9.10.89	Tempest Two Ltd	Hemswell	
	(Built Bristol Aeroplane Co Ltd) (Regd with c/n "1181")		Indian AF, MW401		(On rebuild 2008)		
G-PETH	Piper PA-24-260 Comanche C	24-4979	N9469P	15.10.04	S H Petherbridge	Gamston	12.12.07E
G-PETR	Piper PA-28-140 Cherokee Cruiser	28-7425320	G-BCJL	23. 9.85	A A Gardner	Ronaldsway	25. 1.08T
			N9591N				
G-PETS	Diamond DA.42 Twin Star	42.169		2.10.06	Airways Aircraft Leasing Ltd	Newcastle	31.10.07E

G-PEYO	Gefa-Flug AS 105 GD Airship (Hot Air)	0047		12.12.07	International Merchandising Promotion and Services SA		
						Genval, Belgium	
G-PFAA	EAA Biplane Model P2	PEB/03		19. 9.78	R J Marshall	Watchford Farm, Yarcombe	1. 2.08P
	(Built P E Barker pr.no.PFA 1338) (Continental PC90)						
G-PFAF	Clutton FRED Series II	PFA 029-10310		30.10.78	M S Perkins	Stoke Golding	13.11.08P
	(Built K Fern and M S Perkins)						
G-PFAG	Evans VP-1	PFA 7022		13.11.78	D Pope	(Attleborough)	30. 6.89P
	(Built N S Giles-Townsend) (Volkswagen 1600)				(Stored 1.06)		
G-PFAH	Evans VP-1	PFA 7004		23.11.78	J A Scott	Chestnut Farm, Tipps End	24. 4.08P
	(Built J A Scott) (Volkswagen 1834)						
G-PFAL	Clutton FRED Series II	PFA 029-10243		7.12.78	J M Robinson	Derrytrasna Glen, Bannfoot	27. 7.88P
	(Built H Pugh) (Volkswagen 1600)				(Noted 8.07)		
G-PFAO	Evans VP-1	PFA 7008		12.12.78	P W Price	(Cheadle)	
	(Built P W Price)						
G-PFAP	Phoenix Currie Wot	PFA 058-10315		12.12.78	J H Seed	Black Spring Farm, Castle Bytham	17.12.96P
	(Built P G Abbey as an SE.5a replica) (Continental O-200-A)				(As "C1904:Z" in RFC c/s) (Noted 2.08)		
G-PFAR	Isaacs Fury II	PFA 011-10220		18.12.78	G Edwards	Roughay Farm, Bishops Waltham	9. 6.07P
	(Built C J Repik) (Continental O-200-A)				(As "K2059" in RAF 25 Sqdn c/s)		
G-PFAT	Monnett Sonerai II	PFA 015-10312		26.10.78	H B Carter	(St Clement, Jersey)	24.10.92P
	(Built H B Carter) (Volkswagen 1834)				(Stored Newcastle 5.93)		
G-PFAW	Evans VP-1	PFA 062-10183		18.12.78	R F Shingler	Forest Farm, Welshpool	28. 6.07P
	(Built R F Shingler) (Volkswagen 1834)						
G-PFAY	EAA Biplane	1525		18.12.78	A K Lang and A L Young (Address change 3.07)		
	(Built A K Lang and A L Young - pr.no.PFA 1525)				(Ilton, Ilminster and Henstridge)		
G-PFCI	Piper PA-34-220T Seneca IV	3447014	N401JC	17. 5.06	Offshore Nautical CI Ltd	Jersey	20. 8.08E
			G-PFCI, N35AL, D-GLPE, N9267L				
G-PFCL	Cessna 172S Skyhawk SP	172S9330	N53287	19. 3.03	Critical Simulations Ltd	Elstree	10. 4.08E
G-PFFN	Beech 200 Super King Air	BB-456	N456CD	7. 4.00	The Puffin Club Ltd	Leicester	17. 4.08E
			N861D, N124BB, C6-BFP, C6-CAA, N80NF, N80NE, N100FB				
G-PFML	Robinson R44 Astro	0082		9. 9.94	D J Parker t/a Skyscraper Aviation		
						Hanover Farm, Addington, Buckingham	6.11.06T
G-PFSL	Reims Cessna F152	F15201746	PH-TWF	30. 8.00	P A Simon	Headcorn	3. 4.08T
			D-ENAX				
G-PGAC	Dyn'Aéro MCR-01 Club	48		27. 1.99	D T S Walsh and G A Coatesworth	Cambridge	26. 7.07P
	(Built G A Coatesworth - pr.no.PFA 301-13186)						
G-PGFG	Tecnam P92-EM Echo	PFA 318-13772		30.10.01	P G Fitzgerald	Franklyn's Field, Chewton Mendip	26. 6.07P
	(Built P G Fitzgerald) (Rotax 912S)				"Charlie's Angel"		
G-PGGY	Robinson R44 Clipper II	11115		3. 4.06	Linic Consultants Ltd	(Sutton)	27. 4.08E
G-PGHM	Air Création 582(1)/Kiss 450	FL024		4. 2.04	P G H Millbank	Sutton Meadows	22. 7.08P
	(Built P G H Millbank - pr.no.BMAA/HB/341 being Flylight kit comprising Trike s/n T03111 and Wing s/n xxxx)						
G-PGSA	Thruster T 600N	0080-T600N-046		11. 8.00	A J A Hitchcock	Popham	15. 2.08P
	(Rotax 582)						
G-PGSI	Robin R2160 Alpha Sport	309	F-GSAF	9. 3.00	M A Spencer	North Weald	12. 7.08E
G-PGUY	Sky 70-16 Balloon (Hot Air)	131	G-BXZJ	13.12.99	J L Guy t/a Black Sheep Balloons	Skipton	17. 6.04
G-PHAA	Reims Cessna F150M	F15001159	G-BCPE	19. 6.97	P H Archard t/a PHA Aviation	Elstree	19. 6.08T
G-PHIL	Gyroflight Brooklands Hornet	17		7. 7.78	A J Philpotts	St Merryn	11. 8.89P
	(Volkswagen 1600)				(Stored 5.90)		
G-PHLB	Rotary Air Force RAF 2000 GTX-SE			11. 3.04	P R Bell	(Lower Apperley, Gloucester)	23. 5.05P
	(Built P R Bell)	PFA G/13-1359					
G-PHLY	Reims Cessna FRA150L Aerobat	FRA1500214	G-BBKU	24. 3.06	M Bonsall	Netherthorpe	25. 6.08E
G-PHNX	Schempp-Hirth Duo Discus xT	157	BGA 5248-KOG	14. 3.07	J L Birch and R Maskell "KOG"	Gransden Lodge	4. 3.08
G-PHOR	Reims Cessna FRA150L Aerobat	FRA1500157	G-BACC	19.10.06	M Bonsall	Netherthorpe	29. 2.08E
G-PHOX	Aeroprakt A22-L Foxbat	PFA 317A-14635		8. 5.07	J D Webb	Rhosgoch	
	(Built J D Webb)						
G-PHSI	Colt 90A Balloon (Hot Air)	2181		12. 5.92	P H Strickland (New owner 5.03)	Bedford	21. 7.01A
G-PHTG	SOCATA TB-10 Tobago	1008		15.11.89	A J Baggarley	Shoreham	14.10.07E
G-PHTO	Beech 390 Premier 1	RB-125	N312SL	26. 4.06	Bookajet Aircraft Management Ltd	Farnborough	16. 5.08E
			N3725F				
G-PHUN	Reims Cessna FRA150L Aerobat	FRA1500177	G-BAIN	27. 6.06	M Bonsall	Netherthorpe	4. 8.08E
G-PHVM	Van's RV-8	PFA 303-14609		16.10.07	G Howes and V Millard	Crowfield	
	(Built G Howes and V Millard)						
G-PHXS	Europa Aviation Europa XS	523		22. 7.02	P Handford	(Wellingborough)	
	(Built P Handford - pr.no.PFA 247-13876) (Tri-gear u/c)						
G-PHYL	Denney Kitfox Model 4	PFA 172A-12189		14. 9.98	J Dunn	Siege Cross Farm, Thatcham	28. 6.08P
	(Built J Dunn)						
G-PHMG	Van's RV-8	PFA 303-13639		27. 4.07	M Gibson and P R Hall	(Goole and Doncaster)	
	(Built M Gibson and P R Hall)						
G-PHYS	Avtech Jabiru SP-470	xxxx		19. 2.03	P C Knight	Halfpenny Green	26.11.08P
	(Built P C Knight - pr.no.PFA 274B-13926)						
G-PIAF	Thunder Ax7-65 Balloon (Hot Air)	1885		19.11.90	L Battersey "No Regrets/La Vie en Rose"	Newbury	24. 3.94A
G-PIDG	Robinson R44 Astro	0678		23.11.99	P J Rogers	Sywell	21.12.07E
G-PIEL	Menavia Piel CP.301A Emeraude	218	G-BARY	17.11.88	P R Thorne	Cublington	16.10.08P
			F-BIJR				
G-PIES	Thunder Ax7-77Z Balloon (Hot Air)	263		13. 2.80	S J Hollingsworth and M K Bellamy		
					(Pork Farms titles) Bleasby and Ironville, Nottngham		21. 9.08A
G-PIET	Pietenpol AirCamper	PFA 047-12267		1. 4.93	A R Wyatt	(Cottered, Buntingford)	14. 5.05P
	(Built N D Marshall) (Continental C90)				(New owner 9.07)		
G-PIGG	Lindstrand Flying Pig SS Balloon (Hot Air)	473		18. 8.97	Iris Heidenreich	Remscheid, Germany	25. 3.08A
G-PIGI	Evektor EV-97 teamEurostar UK	2315		23. 2.05	P A Aston tr Pigs Might Fly Group	Exeter	22. 2.08P
G-PIGS	SOCATA Rallye 150ST	2696	G-BDWB	13. 6.88	D Hodgson tr Boonhill Flying Group	Wombleton	14. 8.08E
G-PIGY	Short SC.7 Skyvan 3A Variant 100	SH1943	LX-JUL	21.12.95	Invicta Aviation Ltd	Sibson	11. 4.08E
			5T-MAM, (G-14-111)				
G-PIIT	Pitts S-2AE	1984	N3QQ	14. 2.07	Mansfield Property Consultancy Ltd	Leicester	27. 8.08P
	(Built R S McGlashon)						

Reg	Type	C/n	Prev ID	Date	Owner	Location	Expiry
G-PIIX	Cessna P210N Pressurized Centurion II	P21000130	G-KATH (N4898P)	12. 6.95	D L Harrisberg and R Dennis	Elstree	21. 3.08E
G-PIKD	Eiriavion PIK-20D	20638	BGA 2412-DVJ	21. 5.07	M C Hayes "DVJ" and "869	Shobdon	22. 3.08
G-PIKK	Piper PA-28-140 Cherokee	28-22932	G-AVLA N11C, (N9509W)	19. 8.88	A S McBain tr Coventry Aviators Flying Group	Coventry	10.11.07E
G-PILE	RotorWay Executive 90 (Built J B Russell) (RotorWay RI 162)	5143		27. 7.93	J B Russell	Magheramorne, County Antrim	5.11.98P
G-PILL	Avid Flyer Mk.4 (Built D R Meston) (Rotax 912-UL)	PFA 189-12333		12. 8.97	D R Meston	Old Sarum	8. 8.08P
G-PILY	Pilatus B4-PC-11	138	BGA 2296-DQM RAFGSA 506	12.11.07	N Frost	(Buxton)	11. 2.08
G-PILZ	Rotorsport UK MT-03	RSUK/MT-03/013		21. 6.07	Specialsalvia Ltd	Kirkbride	12. 7.08E
G-PIMM	Ultramagic M-77 Balloon (Hot Air)	77/263		1. 3.05	G Everett	Sandway, Maidstone	26. 9.08E
G-PIMP	Robinson R44 Raven	12123		5. 2.08	Heli Air Ltd	Wellesbourne Mountford	
G-PINC	Cameron Z-90 Balloon (Hot Air)	10441		23. 9.03	M Cowling	Dubai, United Arab Emirates	30. 7.08A
G-PING	Gulfstream AA-5A Cheetah	AA5A-0878	G-OCWC G-WULL, N27153	6.12.95	P J Kirkpatrick	Standalone Farm, Meppershall	3. 7.08E
G-PINT	Cameron Barrel 60 SS Balloon (Hot Air) (Wells Brewery Beer Barrel shape)	794		4. 1.82	D K Fish "Charles Wells"	Manchester	27. 6.08A
G-PINX	Lindstrand Pink Panther SS Balloon (Hot Air)	032		23. 4.93	Magical Adventures Ltd	West Bloomfield, Michigan, US	30. 5.99A
G-PION	Alpi Pioneer 300 (Built F A Cavaciuti - pr.no.PFA 330-14294)	xxx		7. 6.05	P F J Burton	Henstridge	27. 7.08P
G-PIPR	Piper PA-18 Super Cub 95 (Frame No.18-832)	18-826	G-BCDC 4X-ANQ, IDF/AF, 4X-ADE	11.10.96	D S Sweet	Dunkeswell	19.10.07E
G-PIPS	Van's RV-4 (Built C J Marsh) (Lycoming O-320-D1A)	PFA 181-11836		3. 8.90	F W Hardiman	(Purley)	20. 5.08P
G-PIPY	Cameron Scottish Piper 105 SS Balloon (Hot Air)	3815		30. 1.96	Cameron Balloons Ltd "Pipy" (Operated M Moffat)	Bristol	29. 6.08A
G-PIRO	Cameron TR-70 Balloon (Hot Air)	10789		28. 4.05	A C Booth	Bristol	24. 5.08E
G-PITS	Pitts S-2AE (Built B Bray)	PFA 009-11001		4. 7.85	P N A and S N Whithead (New owners 6.06)	Leicester	5. 8.04P
G-PITZ	Pitts S-2A (Built Razorback Air Services)	100ER	N183ER	2.10.87	J A Coutts	Nut Tree Farm, Redenhall	22. 3.08P
G-PIXE	Colt 31A Balloon (Hot Air)	4883		11. 7.00	N D Eliot	London SW19	4. 8.07A
G-PIXI	Pegasus Quantum 15-912	7557		27. 8.99	K J Rexter	Cumbernauld	19. 9.08P
G-PIXL	Robinson R44 Clipper II	11221		28. 6.06	Flying TV Ltd	Denham	6. 7.08E
G-PIXX	Robinson R44 Raven II	10263		16. 4.04	Flying TV Ltd	Denham	10. 5.08E
G-PIXY	Super Marine Spitfire Mk.26 (Built R Collenette)	PFA 324-14477		13. 2.06	R Collenette	(Boldre, Lymington)	
G-PIZZ	Lindstrand LBL 105A Balloon (Hot Air)	629		27. 7.99	HD Bargain SRL (Runner Pizza titles)	Florence, Italy	27. 8.06A
G-PJCC	Piper PA-28-161 Warrior II	2816043	OY-ODN SE-IUI	30. 3.04	PJC (Leasing) Ltd	Stapleford	20. 4.08E
G-PJLO	Boeing 767-35EER	26064	B-16605	7. 8.06	First Choice Airways Ltd	Manchester	1. 4.08P
G-PJMT	Neico Lancair 320 (Built P J and M T Holland) (Lycoming IO-320-D) (Tri-cycle u/c)	PFA 191-12348		8. 5.98	V Hatton and P Gilroy	(Churston Ferrers, Brixham and Lindridge, Teignmouth)	14. 6.08P
G-PJNZ	Commander Aircraft Commander 114B	14618	N6033Z	7. 9.04	P D Jackson	Biggin Hill	12. 9.08E
G-PJSY	Van's RV-6 (Built P J York)	PFA 181-13107		19. 7.04	P J York	Leicester	26. 3.08P
G-PJTM	Reims Cessna FR172K Hawk XP	FR17200611	EI-CHJ G-BFIF	13.10.98	P J McNamara t/a Jane Air	Haverfordwest	23.11.07E
G-PKPK	Schweizer 269C (Schweizer 300)	S 1454	EI-CAR N69A	3. 8.93	C H Dobson	(South Elkington, Louth)	26. 9.08E
G-PKRG	Cessna 560XL Citation XLS	560-5613	N613XL N5265B	22. 9.06	Parkridge (Aviation) Ltd	(Shirley, Solihull)	21. 9.08E
G-PLAC	Piper PA-31-350 Chieftain	31-8052038	G-OLDA G-BNDS, N131PP, N3550N	23.12.98	Y Leysen	Biggin Hill	27. 2.08E
G-PLAD	Kolb Twinstar Mk.3 Extra (Built P J Ladd)	PFA 205-14350		25. 1.05	P J Ladd	(Holt , Trowbridge)	16. 5.07P
G-PLAJ	British Aerospace Jetstream Series 3102	738	N2274C C-GJPH, N331QB, G-31-738	30. 3.00	Jetstream Executive Travel Ltd	Inverness	13.10.07E
G-PLAL	Eurocopter EC.135 T2	0407		26. 6.06	Pure Leisure Air Ltd	(Yealand Redmayne, Carnforth)	1.10.07E
G-PLAN	Reims Cessna F150L	F15001066	PH-SPR	11. 8.78	D A Johnson tr G-PLAN Flying Group	Barton	30. 1.08E
G-PLAY	Robin R2112	170	F-ODIT	1. 8.79	A M and Gay F Granger tr Alpha Flying Group	Cranfield	10. 8.08E
G-PLAZ	Rockwell Commander 112A	345	G-RDCI G-BFWG, ZS-JRX, N1345J	15. 4.04	I Hunt	Cardiff	16.11.08E
G-PLBI	Cessna 172S Skyhawk SP	172S8822	N35368	8. 5.01	G Greenall	(Ledbury)	30. 6.07T
G-PLEE	Cessna 182Q Skylane II	18266570	N95538	4.12.87	Sunderland Parachute Centre Ltd t/a Peterlee Parachute Centre	Shotton Colliery, Peterlee	24. 5.08E
G-PLIV	Pazmany PL-4A (Built B P North) (Continental A65-8)	PFA 017-10155		19.12.78	B P North	RAF Halton	31 7.08P
G-PLMB	Aérospatiale AS.350B Ecureuil	1207	G-BMMB C-GBEW, (N36033)	26. 3.86	PLM Dollar Group Ltd	Inverness	15. 2.08E
G-PLMH	Eurocopter AS.350B2 Ecureuil	2156	F-WQDJ G-PLMH, HB-XTE, F-WQPK, HB-XTE	9. 1.95	PLM Dollar Group Ltd	Inverness	25. 2.08E
G-PLMI	Aérospatiale SA.365C1 Dauphin 2	5001	F-GFYH F-WZAE	19. 6.95	PLM Dollar Group Ltd	Cumbernauld	8. 7.08E
G-PLOD	Tecnam P92-EM Echo (Built S P Pearson)	PFA 318-14152		23. 6.04	G M and J Jupp	Conington	18. 8.08P
G-PLOW	Hughes 269B (Hughes 300)	67-0317	G-AVUM	13. 9.83	C Walton Ltd t/a Sulby Aerial Surveys (New owner 8.04)	Sibbertoft	29.11.92
G-PLPC	Schweizer 269C (Schweizer 300)	S 1558	G-JMAT	14. 4.97	Power Lines, Piper and Cables Ltd	(Carluke)	2. 8.08E

G-PLPL	Agusta A109E Power	11168	G-TMWC	4. 6.07	BG Aviation Ltd	Fairoaks	27. 4.08E
			VH-BQR, VH-FOX				
G-PLPM	Europa Aviation Europa XS	383		17. 5.00	P L P Mansfield	(Hartley Wintney)	
	(Built P L P Mansfield - pr.no.PFA 247-13287) (Monowheel u/c)						
G-PLSA	Aero Designs Pulsar XP	PFA 202-12283	G-NEVS	20.12.04	C A Yardley	Gamston	2 .8.08P
	(Built N Warrener)						
G-PLXI	British Aerospace ATP	2001	G-MATP	26. 8.94	BAE Systems (Operations) Ltd	Woodford	2.12.92P
	(Development a/c with PW 127D engines)		(G-OATP)		(Stored 3.06)		
G-PMAM	Cameron V-65 Balloon (Hot Air)	1155		29. 5.85	P A Meecham "Tempus Fugit		
					Milton-under-Wychwood, Chipping Norton		28. 1.08A
G-PMHT	SOCATA TBM-850	440		29. 2.08	Ewan Ltd	(Thrupp, Stroud)	
	(Officially regd as TBM-700N)						
G-PMNF	Vickers Supermarine 361 Spitfire HF.IX		SAAF??	29. 4.96	P R Monk	Biggin Hill	6. 2.09P
		CBAF.10372	TA805		(As "TA805/FX-M" in 234 Sqn RAF c/s)		
G-PNGC	Schleicher ASK 21	21770	BGA 5078-KGJ	24. 1.06	Portsmouth Naval Gliding Club "N3"	Lee-on-Solent	28. 9.08
G-PNEU	Colt Bibendum 110 SS Balloon (Hot Air)	4223		5. 1.98	A M Holly	Breadstone, Berkeley	26. 6.02A
	(Built Cameron Balloons Ltd)				(Michelin titles) (New owner 7.07)		
G-PNIX	Reims Cessna FRA150L Aerobat	FRA1500205	G-BBEO	2.11.04	D C Bonsall t/a Dukeries Aviation	Netherthorpe	21. 6.08E
					(Operated Phoenix Flying Club)		
G-POCO	Cessna 152	15283956	N6592B	8.10.04	K M Watts	Shobdon	8. 3.08E
			G-POCO, N6592B				
G-POGO	Flight Design CT2K	01-06-02-12		30. 7.01	L I Bailey	Norton, Daventry	16. 8.08P
	(Assembled Pegasus Aviation - no c/n issued)						
G-POLL	Best Off Sky Ranger 912S(1)	SKR0305313?		26. 2.04	D L Pollitt	Tarn Farm, Cockerham	12. 7.08P
	(Built D L Pollitt - pr.no.BMAA/HB/290)						
G-POLY	Cameron N-77 Balloon (Hot Air)	428		13. 7.78	D M Barnes, N.F Biggs, D J Thornley, J L Hinton and M A C Life		
					tr The Empty Wallets Balloon Group "Polywallets" Bristol		14. 9.08E
G-POND	Oldfield Baby Lakes	01	N87ED	2.10.90	U Reichert	(Fehrbellin, Germany)	30. 7.08P
	(Built G E Davis) (Continental A80)						
G-POOH	Piper J-3C-65 Cub	6932	F-BEGY	17.10.79	P Robinson		
	(Frame No.7015)		NC38324		Upper Harford Farm, Bourton-on-the-Water		9. 8.10S
G-POOL	ARV Aviation ARV-1 Super 2	025	G-BNHA	28. 8.87	P A Dawson	(St Denis du Pin, France)	9. 9.90T
G-POOP	Dyn'Aéro MCR-01 Club	81		5.11.97	E and K Nicholson t/a Eurodata Computer Supplies		
	(Built P Bondar - pr.no.PFA 301-13190)					Leicester	21.10.08P
G-POPA	Beech A36 Bonanza	E-2177	N7007F	20. 5.92	C J O'Sullivan	Southend	18. 1.08E
			N7204R				
G-POPE	Eiriavion PIK-20E	20257		5. 3.80	J C Mills	(Haywards Heath)	25. 8.08E
G-POPI	SOCATA TB-10 Tobago	315	G-BKEN	20. 4.90	C J Earle tr G-POPI Flying Group	Seething	27. 3.07
			(G-BKEL)				
G-POPP	Colt 105A Balloon (Hot Air)	1776		1. 3.91	R Ashford "Mercier"	Petworth	31. 7.08A
G-POPS	Piper PA-34-220T Seneca III	34-8133150	N8407H	11. 6.90	Mallard Homes Ltd	Gloucestershire	31. 5.08E
G-POPW	Cessna 182S Skylane	18280204	N9451F	10. 7.98	Cider Press Investment Company Ltd	Conington	21. 8.08E
G-POPY	Best Off Sky Ranger Swift 912S(1)	SKRxxxx737		6. 3.07	C D and L J Church		
	(Built C D and L J Church - pr.no.BMAA/HB/519)				Newton Peverill Farm, Sturminster Marshall		25. 6.08P
G-PORK	Grumman AA-5B Tiger	AA5B-0625	EI-BMT	28. 2.84	D Thomas and C M M Grange tr Tiger Touring Group		
			G-BFHS			Bournemouth	3. 2.08E
G-PORT	Bell 206B-3 JetRanger III	2784	N37AH	23. 8.89	J Poole	East Wellow, Romsey	19. 8.08E
			N39TV, N397TV, N2774R				
G-POSH	Colt 56A Balloon (Hot Air)	822	N-BMPT	10. 6.86	B K Rippon	Didcot	12. 8.08A
G-POUX	Pou du Ciel-Bifly	JBMD-01	59-ABT	29. 6.07	G D Priest	(Redditch)	
	(Built J Bierinx and M Dugourd)						
G-POWB	Beech B300 Super King Air	FL-506	N7106L	8. 2.07	Hagondale Ltd	London Stansted	8. 2.08E
					(Operated Titan Airways)		
G-POWC	Boeing 737-33AQC	25402	SE-DPB	3. 4.07	Titan Airways Ltd	London Stansted	2. 4.08E
			N33AW				
G-POWL	Cessna 182R Skylane II	18267813	N9070G	11.11.82	Powell Print Ltd	Manston	4. 6.08E
			D-EOMF, N6265N				
G-POZA	Reality Escapde Jabiru ULP(1)	JAESC 0014		5. 2.04	M R Jones	Wing Farm, Longbridge Deverill	
	(Built M R Jones - pr.no.BMAA/HB/347) (UL260i)				(On buildd 10.07)		
G-PPLC	Cessna 560 Citation V	560-0059	F-GKHL	18. 2.05	Sterling Helicopters Ltd t/a Sterling Aviation		
			N2687L			Biggin Hill	9. 3.08E
G-PPLG	Rotorsport UK MT-03	RSUK/MT-03/010		9. 1.07	J E Butler	Kirkbride	5. 2.08P
G-PPLL	Van's RV-7A	PFA 323-14240		28. 6.04	P G Leonard	Damyn's Hall, Upminster	20. 3.08P
	(Built P G Leonard)						
G-PPPP	Denney Kitfox Model 3	771		9. 1.91	R Powers	Otherton, Cannock	12. 7.07P
	(Built P Eastwood - pr.no.PFA 172-11830)						
G-PPTS	Robinson R44 Clipper	0664		14.10.99	J and L Prowse	(Coleshill, Birmingham)	18.12.07E
G-PRAG	Brügger MB.2 Colibri	PFA 043-10362		29.11.78	D Frankland tr Colibri Flying Group	RAF Mona	26. 2.04P
	(Built P Russell) (Volkswagen 1835)						
G-PRAH	Flight Design CT2K	01-06-01-12		31. 7.01	P R A Hammond	London Colney	4. 5.07P
	(Assembled Pegasus Aviation - no c/n issued)						
G-PREI	Raytheon RB390 Premier 1	RB-60	LX-PRE	13.10.05	Craft Air SA	Farnborough	13.10.07E
			N6160D				
G-PRET	Robinson R44 Astro	0381		8.10.97	J A Wilson		
					Folly Farm, Cop Hill, Slaithwaite, Huddersfield		29.10.06T
G-PREY	Pereira Osprey 2	88	G-BEPB	28. 9.99	N S Dalrymple	(Dunoon)	8. 6.98P
	(Built J J and A J C Zwetsloot - pr.no.PFA 070-10193) (Lycoming IO-320)				(New owner 12.05)		
G-PREZ	Robin DR.500-200i Président	0038		26. 7.02	C Morris tr Régent Group	Bidford	23. 8.08E
	(Officially regd as DR.400-500)						
G-PRII	Hawker Hunter PR.11	41H-670690	N723WT	14. 7.99	Stick and Rudder Aviation Ltd	Exeter	5. 9.03P
			A2616, WT723		(As "WT723:866" in RN c/s and noted 1.07)		
G-PRIM	Piper PA-38-112 Tomahawk	38-78A0669	N2398A	28. 1.87	Braddock Ltd (Noted derelict 11.07)	Chilbolton	25.12.01T

Reg	Type	C/n	Previous identity	Date	Owner / Operator	Location	Expiry
G-PRKR	Bombardier CL-600-2B16 (CL-604 Challenger)	5617	C-FEYU, C-GLXB	10. 1.06	TAG Aviation (UK) Ltd	Farnborough	9. 1.08E
G-PRLY	Avtech Jabiru SK (Built N J Bond - pr.no.PFA 274-13385)	0219	G-BYKY	11. 3.02	N C Cowell	City of Derry	2. 4.08P
G-PRNT	Cameron V-90 Balloon (Hot Air)	2819		23. 3.92	Shaun Bradley Project Services Ltd	Stockbridge	6. 9.07A
G-PROB	Eurocopter AS.350B2 Ecureuil	2825	G-PROD	25. 6.01	Irvine Aviation Ltd	Denham	26. 4.08E
G-PROF	Lindstrand LBL 90A Balloon (Hot Air) (Professional Financial Services titles)	740		14. 2.01	S J Wardle	Thrapston, Kettering	31. 8.08A
G-PROJ	Robinson R44 Raven II	11695		24. 4.07	Project Racing Team Ltd	Bournemouth	24. 5.08E
G-PROM	Aérospatiale AS.350B Ecureuil (Noted 1.07)	1486	G-MAGY, G-BIYC	11.10.96	P Hughes t/a General Cabins and Engineering	Newtownards	23.10.05T
G-PROS	Van's RV-7A (Built S A Jarret)	PFA 323-14146		27. 4.06	S A Jarrett	(Clevedon)	
G-PROV	Hunting Percival P 84 Jet Provost T 52A (T 4) (As "104" in SAAF (S Yemen) AF c/s)	PAC/W/23905	Singapore AF 352, SAAF (S Yemen) AF 104, G-27-7, XS228	13.12.83	Hollytree Management Ltd tr Provost Group	North Weald	12. 7.08P
G-PROW	Evektor EV-97 Eurostar (Built G M Prowling)	PFA 315-13968		30.10.02	G M Prowling	Baxby Manor, Husthwaite	15. 3.08P
G-PRSI	Pegasus Quantum 15-912	7492		17.12.98	S I Laurence	Hunsdon	8. 2.08P
G-PRTT	Cameron N-31 Balloon (Hot Air)	1374		6.11.86	J M Albury "Baby Pritt"	Cirencester	13.11.00A
G-PRXI	Vickers Supermarine 365 Spitfire PR.XI (As "PL983:JV-F" in RAF 4 Sqdn, 2 TAF c/s) (On rebuild 6.06)	6S/583003	PL983, G-15-109, N74138, PL983	6. 6.83	Propshop Ltd	Sandown, Isle of Wight	11. 6.01P
G-PSAX	Lindstrand LBL 77B Balloon (Hot Air)	960		8.10.03	M V Farrant	Loxwood, Billingshurst	14. 5.08A
G-PSFG	Robin R2160i (Noted 12.07)	337	G-COVD, G-BYOF	5.12.07	Mardenair Ltd	Goodwood	15.12.06T
G-PSGC	Piper PA-25-260 Pawnee C	25-5324	G-BDDT, CS-AIX, N8820L	29. 4.04	Peterborough and Spalding Gliding Club Ltd	Crowland	16. 1.08E
G-PSHR	Agusta-Bell 206B-3 JetRanger III	8690	G-HSLB, F-GUJR, SX-HEN, F-GRCY, I-ELEP	22. 8.05	Sky Select Ltd	(Tywyn)	2. 6.08E
G-PSKY	Best Off Sky Ranger 912S(1) (Built S Ivell - pr.no.BMAA/HB/430)	SKR0409524		3. 2.05	G Mills tr Sky Ranger Flying Group G-PSKY	Crosland Moor	5. 9.08P
G-PSNI	Eurocopter EC.135 T2	0337		26. 7.04	Police Service of Northern Ireland	Belfast International	20. 4.08T
G-PSON	Colt Cylinder One SS Balloon (Hot Air) (Panasonic Battery shape) (Panasonic Battery titles)	1780	PH-SON	14. 3.95	R S and A D Kent tr Balloon Preservation Group	Petworth	1. 5.08A
G-PSRT	Piper PA-28-151 Cherokee Warrior (Noted 2.08)	28-7615225	G-BSGN, N9657K	18. 3.99	P A S Dyke	RAF Waddington	30. 9.07E
G-PSST	Hawker Hunter F 58A "Miss Demeanour"	HABL-003115	Swiss AF J-4104, G-9-317, A2568, XF947	12. 2.97	Heritage Aviation Developments Ltd	Exeter	23.11.08P
G-PSUE	CFM Shadow Series CD	K 139	G-MYAA	1. 4.99	D A Crosbie (New owner 3.04)	(Sudbury)	19. 5.03P
G-PSUK	Thruster T 600N 450	0044-T600N-101		26. 5.04	A J Dunlop	Longacre Farm, Sandy	30. 7.08P
G-PTAG	Europa Aviation Europa (Built R C Harrison - pr.no.PFA 247-13121) (Rotax 914) (Tri-gear u/c) (Noted 8.08)	337		14.12.98	R C Harrison	Wickenby	17. 4.07P
G-PTAR	Best Off Sky Ranger 912S(1) (Built A C Aiken - pr.no.BMAA/HB/509) (Ran away on engine-start Plaistows 3.11.07, nose-leg collapsed and overturned with substantial damage)	SKRxxxx687		6. 7.06	A C Aiken	(Harrow)	11. 1.08P
G-PTDP	Bücker Bü.133C Jungmeister	1018	G-AEZX (2), N5A, PP-TDP	31. 8.05	T J Reeve	North Lopham, Diss	27. 7.00P
G-PTRE	SOCATA TB-20 Trinidad	762	G-BNKU	14. 6.88	Trantshore Ltd	Lydd	14. 6.08E
G-PTTS	Pitts S-2A (Built Aerotek Inc)	2179	N555JR, N32TP, N31450	9. 5.03	N D Voce	Leicester	19. 3.08T
G-PTWO	Pilatus P 2-05 (As "U-110" in Swiss AF c/s)	600-30	Swiss AF U-110, Swiss AF A-110	26. 2.81	R G Meredith	Rochester	25. 5.08P
G-PTYE	Europa Aviation Europa (Built J Tye - pr.no.PFA 247-12496) (Monowheel u/c) (Failed to gain height on take-off Carltonmoor 16. 3.03, struck stone wall and substantially damaged)	001		22. 1.96	P J Carnes t/a Hitech International	Derby	1. 9.03P
G-PUDL	Piper PA-18-150 Super Cub	18-7292	SE-CSE	24. 2.98	R A Roberts (Noted 2.08)	Audley End	16. 6.07
G-PUDS	Europa Aviation Europa (Built I Milner - pr.no.PFA 247-12999) (Rotax 914-UL) (Tri-gear u/c)	253		9.10.97	M J Riley	(Binfield, Bracknell)	14.11.07P
G-PUFF	Thunder Ax7-77 Bolt Balloon (Hot Air) "Puffin II"	165		17.11.78	C A Gould tr Intervarsity Balloon Club	Ipswich	26. 7.08A
G-PUFN	Cessna 340A II	340A0114	N532KG, N532KC, N5477J	4.12.96	G R Case	Guernsey	27. 9.08E
G-PUGS	Cessna 182H Skylane	18256480	SE-ESM, N8380S	15. 5.00	N C and M F Shaw	Great Massingham	15. 6.08E
G-PUKA	Avtech Jabiru J400 (Built D P Harris - pr.no.PFA 325-14120)	0130		11. 9.03	D P Harris	(Stanton Drew, Bristol)	1.11.08P
G-PUKB	Piper PA-28-181 Archer III	2843660	N31144	17. 9.07	GEFA Gesellschaft fur Absatzfinanzierung mbH	(Wuppertal, Germany)	25. 9.08E
G-PUMA	Aérospatiale AS.332L Super Puma	2038	F-WMHB	31. 1.83	CHC Scotia Ltd	Aberdeen	12. 4.08E
G-PUMB	Aérospatiale AS.332L Super Puma	2075		31. 1.83	CHC Scotia Ltd	Aberdeen	15. 5.08E
G-PUMD	Aérospatiale AS.332L Super Puma	2077	F-WXFD	31. 1.83	CHC Scotia Ltd	Aberdeen	23. 8.08E
G-PUME	Aérospatiale AS.332L Super Puma	2091		3. 8.83	CHC Scotia Ltd	Aberdeen	6. 9.08E
G-PUMN	Eurocopter AS.332L2 Super Puma	2484	LN-OHF	16. 7.99	CHC Scotia Ltd	Aberdeen	26. 7.08E
G-PUMO	Eurocopter AS.332L2 Super Puma	2467		30. 9.98	CHC Scotia Ltd	Aberdeen	25.10.08E
G-PUMS	Eurocopter AS.332L2 Super Puma	2504		18. 8.00	CHC Scotia Ltd	Aberdeen	30. 1.08E
G-PUNK	Thunder AX8-105 Balloon (Hot Air)	1719		28. 3.90	S C Kinsey	Amersham	15. 5.99T
G-PUPP	Beagle B 121 Pup Series 2	B121-174	G-BASD, (SE-FOG), G-BASD	23.11.93	A D Wood and B R Hunter	Sturgate	25. 5.08
G-PUPY	Europa Aviation Europa XS (Built P G Johnson - pr.no.PFA 247-13694) (Monowheel u/c) (New owner 10.07)	499		10. 9.02	V F Flett	(Lhanbryde, Elgin)	
G-PURL	Piper PA-32R-301 Saratoga II HP	3213078	N620PL, N92434	30.11.05	I Blamire	Lee-on-Solent	7.12.07E
G-PURR	Gulfstream AA-5A Cheetah	AA5A-0794	G-BJDN, N26893	22. 2.82	N Bass t/a Nabco Retail Display	Elstree	1. 9.08E

G-PURS	RotorWay Executive	3827		19. 1.90	J E Houseman	Headlinks Farm, Clitheroe	5. 6.96P
	(Built J E Houseman) (RotorWay RW 152)				*(Noted 2007)*		
G-PUSH	Rutan LongEz	PFA 074A-10740		11. 7.83	E G Peterson	(Woodthorpe, Nottingham)	
	(Built E G Peterson)						
G-PUSI	Cessna T303 Crusader	T30300273	N3479V	26. 7.88	A J Beck t/a Crusader Craft	Henstridge	9. 7.08E
G-PUSS	Cameron N-77 Balloon (Hot Air)	1577		6.10.87	L D Thurgar *"Dick Whittington"*	Bristol	18. 6.01A
G-PUSY	TLAC RL5A LW Sherwood Ranger	xxxx	G-MZNF	25. 6.99	S C Briggs	(Santa Luce, Pisa, Italy)	13. 7.06P
	(Built B J Chester-Master - pr.no.PFA 237-12964)		(Rotax 582)		*(Address change 10.06)*		
G-PUTT	Cameron Golfball 76 SS Balloon (Hot Air)	2060	LX-KIK	8. 8.95	D P Hopkins t/a Lakeside Lodge Golf Centre		
						Pidley, Huntingdon	
G-PVBF	Lindstrand LBL 260S Balloon (Hot Air)	504		7. 4.98	Virgin Balloon Flights Ltd	London SE16	15. 2.07E
G-PVCV	Robin DR.400-140 Major	919	F-BVCV	19.10.06	Leonie M Poor and P N Bevan	Perth	19.10.07E
G-PVET	de Havilland DHC-1 Chipmunk 22	C1/0017	WB565	23. 5.97	Connect Properties Ltd	Kemble	7. 2.010S
					(As "WB565:X" in AAC c/s)		
G-PVIP	Cessna 421C Golden Eagle	421C0118	G-RLMC	30. 6.04	Passion 4 Health International Ltd	(Chertsey)	22. 1.07E
			PH-SBI, D-IMAZ, I-CCNN, N3849C				
G-PVML	Robin DR.400-140B Major	972	F-BVML	28. 2. 06	Weald Air Services Ltd	Headcorn	18. 7.08E
G-PVPC	Pilatus PC-12/45	632	HB-FPV	27. 6.05	GE Capital Corporation (Leasing) Ltd	Bournemouth	7. 7.08E
G-PVSS	P&M Quik GT450	8302		8. 8.07	P V Stevens	Field Farm, Oakley	7. 8.08P
G-PVST	Thruster T 600N 450 Sprint	0122-T600N-074		29.10.02	R J Davey	Anwick	15. 5.08P
G-PWBE	de Havilland DH.82A Tiger Moth	LES.1	VH-KRW	23. 7.99	P W Beales	White Waltham	8. 1.07P
	(Built Lawrence Engineering and Sales Proprietary Ltd., Camden, NSW, Australia ex-RAAF spares)						
G-PWIT	Bell 206L-1 LongRanger	45193	D-HHSW	18. 5.00	A R King	Gloucestershire	19. 7.08E
			G-DWMI, N18092				
G-PWNS	Cessna 525 CitationJet	525-0153	VP-CNF	30. 3.07	Hangar 8 Ltd	Oxford	15. 4.08E
			N551Q, N551G, N5090V				
G-PWUL	Van's RV-6	PFA 181-12773		3. 7.02	D Stephens and S King	Damyn's Hall, Upminster	31. 7.08P
	(Built P C Woolley)						
G-PYNE	Thruster T 600N 450	0072-T600N-067		27. 8.02	R Dereham	Shipmeadow, Beccles	19.11.07P
G-PYPA	Robinson R44 Raven II	11668		30. 3.07	Heli Air Ltd	Wellesbourne Mountford	3. 5.08E
G-PYPE	Van's RV-7	PFA 323-14398		12. 9.06	R and L Pyper	Newtownards	16. 4.08P
	(Built R Pyper)						
G-PYRO	Cameron N-65 Balloon (Hot Air)	567		8. 1.80	A C Booth	Bristol	30.12.04A
					"Pyromania" (Active 9.05)		
G-PZAZ	Piper PA-31-350 Navajo Chieftain	31-7405214	G-VTAX	18. 1.95	Air Medical Fleet Ltd	Oxford	24. 5.08E
			(G-UTAX), N54266				
G-PZIZ	Piper PA-31-350 Navajo Chieftain	31-7405429	G-CAFZ	30.10.98	Air Medical Fleet Ltd	Oxford	18. 4.08E
			G-BPPT, N54297, N9655N				

G-RAAA - G-RZZZ

G-RABA	Reims FR172H Rocket	FR17200292	D-ECSE	14.12.04	Air Ads Ltd	Blackpool	8. 2.08E
G-RABS	Alpi Pioneer 300	xxx		31. 8.06	J Mullen	(Lanark)	
	(Built J Mullen - pr.no.PFA 330-14563)						
G-RACI	Beech C90 King Air	LJ-819	G-SHAM	10. 4.03	E Flight SRL	(Milan, Italy)	1. 8.08E
			N2063A				
G-RACO	Piper PA-28R-200 Cherokee Arrow II		N1498X	12. 9.91	Graco Group Ltd	Barton	8. 7.08E
		28R-7535300					
G-RACR	Ultramagic M-65C Balloon (Hot Air)	65/143		8. 4.05	R A Vale	Kidderminster	26. 4.08E
G-RACY	Cessna 182S Skylane	18280588	N7273Y	19.10.99	N J and P.D Fuller	Cambridge	29.12.07
G-RADA	Soko P-2 Kraguj	024	Yugoslav AF 30140	25. 9.96	M G Roberts t/a Flight Consultancy Services		
						Biggin Hill	5. 9.05P
G-RADI	Piper PA-28-181 Archer II	28-8690002	N2582X	6. 5.98	M Ruter	White Waltham	5. 7.08E
			N9608N				
G-RADR	Douglas AD-4NA Skyraider	7722	G-RAID	30.10.03	T J Manna	North Weald	31. 5.08P
	(SFERMA c/n 42)		F-AZED, TR-K.., French AF 42, Bu.126922				
					(As "26922:AK 402" of USN VA-176 Sqdn,:USS Intrepid c/s)		
G-RAEM	Rutan LongEz	557		15. 3.82	G F H Singleton tr Easy Group	(Matlock)	18. 6.93P
	(Built G F H Singleton - pr.no.PFA 074A-10638) (Lycoming O-235)						
G-RAES	Boeing 777-236	27491	(G-ZZZN)	10. 6.97	British Airways PLC	London Heathrow	9. 6.08E
G-RAFA	Grob G115A	8081	D-EGVV	2. 3.89	RAF College Flying Club Ltd	RAF Cranwell	2. 7.08E
G-RAFB	Grob G115A	8079	D-EGVV	2. 3.89	RAF College Flying Club Ltd	RAF Cranwell	19. 4.07T
G-RAFC	Robin R2112 Alpha	192		19. 5.80	J E Churchill tr RAF Charlie Group	Conington	16. 7.08E
G-RAFE	Thunder Ax7-77 Bolt Balloon (Hot Air)	176		18.12.78	L P Hooper tr Giraffe Balloon Syndicate	Bristol	21. 5.08A
					"Giraffe"		
G-RAFG	Slingsby T 67C Firefly	2076		2.11.89	Arrow Flying Ltd	Popham	24. 5.08E
G-RAFH	Thruster T 600N 450	0032-T600N-063		10. 4.02	M E Howard tr RAF Microlight Flying Association (FH)		
						RAF Halton	20. 4.08P
G-RAFI	Hunting Percival P 84 Jet Provost T 4	8458M		18.12.92	R J Everett	(Spoughton, Ipswich)	11. 3.00P
		PAC/W/17641	XP672				
					(As "XP672:03" in RAF c/s)		
G-RAFO	Beech B200 Super King Air	BB-1836	N60476	11. 3.04	Serco Ltd *(Allocated "ZK455")*	RAF Cranwell	18. 3.08E
G-RAFP	Beech B200 Super King Air	BB-1837	N61037	11. 3.04	Serco Ltd *(Allocated "ZK456")*	RAF Cranwell	18. 3.08E
G-RAFR	Best Off Sky Ranger J2.2(1)	SKR0404487		8.10.04	M E Howard tr RAF Microlight Flying Association (FR)		
	(Built P Waters - pr.no.BMAA/HB/410)					RAF Halton	4. 9.07P
G-RAFS	Thruster T 600N 450	0041-T600N-097		5. 4.04	M E Howard tr RAF Microlight Flying Association (FS)		
						RAF Halton	4. 4.08P
G-RAFT	Rutan LongEz	PFA 074A-10734		9. 8.82	B Wronski	Gloucestershire	16. 7.07P
	(Built D G Foreman) (Continental O-240-A)				*"A Craft of Graft"*		
G-RAFV	Avid Speed Wing	PFA 189-11738	G-MOTT	28. 7.04	A F Vizoso	RAF Halton	4. 4.08P
	(Built M D Ott)						
G-RAFW	Mooney M 20E Super 21	805	G-ATHW	14.11.84	Vinola (Knitwear) Manufacturing Co Ltd	Leicester	7. 4.08E
			N5881Q				
G-RAFY	Best Off Sky Ranger Swift 912S(1)	SKRxxxx757		7. 3.07	M E Howard tr RAF Microlight Flying Association		
	(Built J Kumela and P Waters - pr.no.BMAA/HB/523)					RAF Halton	23 .8.08P

Reg	Type	C/n	Prev identity	Date	Owner/Operator	Location	Expiry
G-RAFZ	Rotary Air Force RAF 2000 GTX-SE			7. 5.02	John Pavitt (Engineers) Ltd	(Torrington)	
	(Built J W Pavitt)	PFA G/13-1295					
G-RAGE	Wilson Cassutt IIIM	PFA 034-10241	G-BEUN	17.10.06	R S Grace	Duxford	7. 7.97P
	(Built M S Crossley) (Continental C90)						
G-RAGS	Pietenpol AirCamper	PFA 047-11551		8. 6.94	R F Billington	(Kenilworth)	
	(Built R F Billington)						
G-RAGT	Piper PA-32-301FT 6x	3232038	N3116F	3. 6.05	Oxhill Aviation	Wellesbourne Mountford	5. 6.08E
G-RAIG	Scottish Aviation Bulldog Series 100/101	BH100/146	SE-LLI Fv61037, G-AZMR	12. 9.03	Power Aerobatics Ltd	Kemble	12. 7 10T
G-RAIL	Colt 105A Balloon (Hot Air)	1434		31. 3.89	Ballooning World Ltd *"Railfreight"*	London NW1	4. 1.04A
G-RAIN	Maule M-5-235C Lunar Rocket	7262C	N5632J	26. 7.79	N M Humphries	(Crickham, Wedmore)	2.12.07E
G-RAIR	Schleicher ASH 25	25095	BGA 3623-FYD	31.10.07	P T Reading and Viscount Cobham	Lasham	30. 1.08
G-RAIX	CCF Harvard 4 (T-6J-CCF Texan)	CCF4...	G-BIWX MM53-846, RM-22/51-17	16. 2.98	M R Paul	Lee-on-Solent	25. 9.08P
	(Possibly c/n CCF4-409 ex 51-17227)				*(As "KF584:RAI-X'" in RAF c/s)*		
G-RAJA	Raj Hamsa X'Air 582(2)	456		13. 9.99	M D Gregory	Belle Vue Farm, Yarnscombe	29. 1.08P
	(Built S R Roberts - pr.no.BMAA/HB/118)						
G-RALA	Robinson R44 Clipper II	10788		12. 7.05	Rala Aviation Ltd	Cambridge	11. 8.08E
G-RALD	Robinson R22HP	0218	G-CHIL (G-BMXI), N9074K	25. 1.96	Heli Air Ltd	Hawarden	11. 1.08E
G-RAMA	Cameron C-70 Balloon (Hot Air)	10939		23.11.06	Poppies (UK) Ltd	Wootton Fitzpaine, Bridport	25. 8.08E
G-RAMI	Bell 206B-3 JetRanger III	2955	N1080N	18.10.90	M D Thorpe t/a Yorkshire Helicopters	Coney Park, Leeds	4.10.07E
G-RAMP	Piper J-3C-65 Cub	6658	N35941 NC35941	5. 7.90	R N Whittall	Frogland Cross	31. 8.01P
					(New owner 3.04)		
G-RAMS	Piper PA-32R-301 Saratoga II SP	32R-8013134	N8271Z	17.10.80	Air Tobago Ltd	Gamston	21. 7.08E
G-RAMY	Bell 206B-2 JetRanger II	1401	N59554	22. 9.95	Lincair Ltd	Humberside	21.11.07E
G-RANS	Rans S-10 Sakota	0489.049		17. 8.89	J D Weller	(Sutton Coldfield)	23. 6.00P
	(Built J D Weller - pr.no.PFA 194-11537) (Rotax 532)						
G-RAPH	Cameron O-77 Balloon (Hot Air)	1673		21. 3.88	P A Sweatman	Coventry	16. 4.08T
G-RAPI	Lindstrand LBL 105A Balloon (Hot Air)	998		16. 7.04	M White t/a Rapido Balloons	Cirencester	16. 8.08A
					(Rapido titles)		
G-RARB	Cessna 172N Skyhawk II	17272334	G-BOII N4702D	4. 6.96	Cristal Air Ltd	Deanland	16. 7.08E
					(Operated Ace Aviation)		
G-RASA	Diamond DA.42 Twin Star	42.144	OE-VPY	30. 6.06	C D Hill	North Weald	6. 8.08E
G-RASC	Evans VP-2	V2-1178		14.12.78	A L Hall-Carpenter	Shipdham	14.12.06P
	(Built R A Codling - pr.no.PFA 063-10422) (Continental A65)				*(New owner 5.07)*		
G-RASH	Grob G109B	6217	OH-686	24. 6.04	C Kaminski tr G-RASH Syndicate	Eaglescott	2. 9.08E
G-RATA	Robinson R22 Beta	3875		24. 6.05	Itervolo Ltd	Sywell	14. 7.08P
G-RATC	Van's RV-4	PFA 181-13996		30. 5.06	A F Ratcliffe	(Whaston, Richmond)	
	(Built A F Ratcliffe)						
G-RATE	Gulfstream AA-5A Cheetah	AA5A-0781	G-BIFF (G-BIBR), N26879	11. 6.84	B P Robinson	Blackbushe	25.11.07E
G-RATH	Rotorway Executive 162F	6886		12.10.04	M S Cole	Street Farm, Takeley	
	(Built M S Cole)				*(Noted 12.08)*		
G-RATI	Reims Cessna F172M Skyhawk II	F17201311	G-PATI G-WACZ, G-BCUK	22.12.05	The Howells Group PLC	Barton	26. 5.08E
G-RATV	Piper PA-28RT-201T Turbo Arrow IV	28R-8431005	G-WILS PH-DPD, N4330W	20. 6.05	Redapple Ltd	Fairoaks	22. 5.08E
G-RATZ	Europa Aviation Europa	037		16. 6.95	W Goldsmith	Morgansfield, Fishburn	23. 8.08P
	(Built R Muller - pr.no.PFA 247-12582) (Monowheel u/c)						
G-RAVE	Mainair Mercury 582/Southdown Raven X	538-0487 & SN2232/0219	G-MNZV	22.12.98	M J Robbins	Rochester	20. 3.04P
	(Sailwing is ex G-MNCV [SN2000/0219])						
G-RAVN	Robinson R44 Raven	1022		23. 3.01	A and L Smith t/a Brambledown Aircraft Hire	(Bradley Green, Redditch)	12. 4.08E
G-RAWS	RotorWay Executive 162F	6492/6978		14.11.00	Raw Sports Ltd	Street Farm, Takeley	3. 1.08P
	(Built B W Grindle)						
G-RAYA	Denney Kitfox Model 4	PFA 172A-12403		14.12.92	R M Cornwell	Redlands, Swindon	20. 3.08P
	(Built A K Ray)						
G-RAYB	P&M Quik GT450	8237		19. 2.07	R Blatchford	Dunkeswell	18. 2.08P
G-RAYE	Piper PA-32-260 Cherokee Six	32-460	G-ATTY N11C	30. 5.96	A P Adshead	(Newcastle)	27. 9.08E
G-RAYH	Zenair CH.701UL STOL	PFA 187-13583		7. 7.03	R Horner	Baxby Manor, Husthwaite	11.11.08P
	(Built R Horner)						
G-RAYO	Lindstrand LBL 90A Balloon (Hot Air)	949		13.10.03	R Owen	Standish, Wigan	15. 4.08A
G-RAYS	Zenair CH.250 Zenith	RED.001		26.10.78	M J Malbon	Derby	6. 7.07P
	(Built R E Delves - originally pr.no.PFA 024-10460 - completed MJ Malbon as pr.no.PFA 113-10460) (Lycoming O-320) (Noted 8.07)						
G-RAYZ	Tecnam P2002-EA Sierra	PFA 333-14567		5. 2.07	R Wells	Morgansfield, Fishburn	
	(Built R Wells)						
G-RAZY	Piper PA-28-181 Archer II	28-8090102	G-REXS N8093Y	11. 2.04	S Empson	Wycombe Air Park	16. 6.08E
G-RAZZ	Maule MX-7-180 Super Rocket	11050C	N266MM D-EOLW, N6118L	10.11.04	C D Baird	Roughay Farm, Bishops Waltham	24.11.07E
G-RBBB	Europa Aviation Europa	073		6. 5.94	T J Hartwell	Sackville Lodge, Riseley	12. 8.05P
	(Built W M Goodman and I H McCleod - pr.no.PFA 247-12664) (Monowheel u/c)						
G-RBCI	Fairey Britten-Norman BN-2A Mk.III-2 Trislander	1035	G-BDWV 8P-ASF, G-BDWV	16. 3.01	Aurigny Air Services Ltd	Guernsey	6. 7.08T
G-RBCT	Schempp-Hirth Ventus 2cT	03/10	BGA 4505-JGP N200EE, D-KHIA	27. 7.07	R Brown	Aston Down	2. 4.08
G-RBJW	Europa Aviation Europa XS	473		15. 7.04	J Worthington and R J Bull	(Kinloss, Foress and Nairn)	
	(Built J Worthington and R J Bull - pr.no.PFA 247-13600)						
G-RBMS	Cirrus SR22	2781	N837SR	19.12.07	D J Bowie *(Noted 12.07)*	Sleap	
G-RBMV	Cameron O-31 Balloon (Hot Air)	4658		27. 7.99	P D Griffiths	Totton, Southampton	3. 7.05A
					(Address change 3.07)		

Reg	Type	C/n	Prev id	Date	Owner/Operator	Location	Date
G-RBOW	Thunder Ax7-65 Balloon (Hot Air)	1439		24. 4.89	R S Mcdonald *"Rain-Beau-Lune"*	Burcott, Leighton Buzzard	2. 8.08A
					(Address change 10..07)		
G-RBRO	Embraer EMB-135BJ Legacy	14500982	PT-SHV	12.12.07	Platinum Associates Ltd	London Stansted	
G-RBSN	Comco Ikarus C42 FB80	0407-6610		23. 8.04	P B and M Robinson	Sutton Meadows	25. 8.08P
G-RCED	Rockwell Commander 114	14241	VR-CED	19. 6.92	D G Welch	Tollerton	16. 5.08E
			N4917W				
G-RCHY	Evektor EV-97 Eurostar	PFA 315-14187		30. 3.04	N McKenzie	Kirkbride	6. 7.07P
	(Built N McKenzie)				*(Noted 8.07)*		
G-RCKT	Harmon Rocket II	PFA 314-13536		10.10.03	K E Armstrong	Armshold Farm, Kington	24. 9.08P
	(Built K E Armstrong: type is a modified Van's RV-4 taildragger) (Lycoming O-540)						
G-RCMC	Murphy Renegade 912	485		1. 2.93	R C M Collisson	Bicester	30. 6.05P
	(Built B D Godden - pr.no.PFA 188-12483)				*(Noted 1.07)*		
G-RCMF	Cameron V-77 Balloon (Hot Air)	1618		23.11.87	J M Percival Bourton-on-the-Wolds, Loughborough		19. 8.97A
G-RCML	Sky 77-24 Balloon (Hot Air)	148		9. 3.99	RCM SARL	Stuppicht, Luxembourg	29. 5.07
G-RCNB	Eurocopter EC.120B Colibri	1333	F-WQPX	20. 3.03	D N Brown tr Furbs Pension Fund	Deenethorpe	28. 4.08E
G-RCOM	Bell 206L-3 LongRanger III	51599	TC-HZT	24.10.02	3GRComm Ltd	(Hereford)	14. 2.08E
G-RCRC	P&M Pegasus Quik	8252		9. 3.07	R Stalker	Easter Poldar Farm, Thornhill	22. 3.08P
G-RCST	Avtech Jabiru J430	0xxx		18. 4.06	G R Cotterell	White House Farm, Southery	27. 6.08P
	(Built G R Cotterell - pr.no.PFA 336-14513)						
G-RCWK	Cessna 182T Skylane	18281982	N11603	2.11.07	R C W King	Filton	
G-RDCO	Avtech Jabiru J400	0xxx		15. 4.03	RDCO (International) LLP	Sleap	20.12.05P
	(Built J M Record - pr.no.PFA 325-14052)						
G-RDDT	Schempp-Hirth Duo Discus T	116/448	BGA 5150-KKA	5. 4.06	R Witter *"DDT"*	Lleweni Parc	12. 4.08
G-RDEL	Robinson R44 Raven	1071		5. 6.01	Isaonas SL	(Palma de Mallorca, Spain)	27. 6.08E
G-RDHS	Europa Aviation Europa XS	549		31. 5.02	R D H Spencer	Earls Colne	5. 9.07P
	(Built R D H Spencer - pr.no.PFA 247-13887) (Tri-gear u/c)						
G-RDMV	Raytheon Hawker 800XP	258496	N175TM	7. 6.06	Clearwater Aviation Ltd	(Antrim)	7. 6.08E
			N125TM				
G-RDNS	Rans S-6-S Super Six Coyote	xxxx		2.11.04	P G Cowling and J S Crofts	Rufforth	24. 5.08P
	(Built G J McDill - pr.no.PFA 204-14307) (Tailwheel u/c)						
G-READ	Colt 77A Balloon (Hot Air)	1158	EI-BYI	16.11.87	C A Gould tr Intervarsity Balloon Club	Ipswich	25. 9.06A
			G-READ		*(New owner 7.07)*		
G-REAL	Eurocopter AS.350B2 Ecureuil	3032	G-DRHL	26. 8.04	Imagine Leisure Ltd	Dunsfold	29. 4.08E
G-REAN	Enstrom 480B	5087		21. 2.06	Toure International Ltd	Oxford	27. 3.08E
G-REAP	Pitts S-1S	PFA 009-11557		7. 2.90	R Dixon	Netherthorpe	22.10.08P
	(Built S D Howes)				*"The Grim Reaper"*		
G-REAR	Lindstrand LBL 69X Balloon (Hot Air)	977		12. 2.04	A M Holly *(Sloggi titles)*	Breadstone, Berkeley	2. 3.08A
G-REAS	Van's RV-6A	PFA 181-12188		16. 8.94	T J Smith	Sleap	17. 8.08P
	(Built D W Reast) (Lycoming O-320)						
G-REBB	Murphy Rebel	376R	N13BN	23. 8.05	M Stow	(Blaydon-on-Tyne)	
	(Built W W Newkirk)						
G-RECE	Cameron C-80 Balloon (Hot Air)	10435		16. 6.03	M Kotsageridis	Thessaloniki, Greece	16. 6.04A
G-RECK	Piper PA-28-140 Cherokee B	28-25656	G-AXJW	17. 3.88	R J Grantham	Clutton Hill Farm, Clutton	26. 8.07E
			N11C				
G-RECO	Jurca MJ.5-L2 Sirocco	96	F-PYYD	30. 9.91	J D Tseliki	(Douglas, Isle of Man)	
	(Built J Y Guillou)		F-WYYD		*(Stored 11.07)*		
G-RECS	Piper PA-38-112 Tomahawk II	38-81A0118	N5824H	23. 4.02	S H and Claire.L Maynard	(Middlesbrough)	2. 5.05T
			D-EFFX, N23138				
G-REDB	Cessna 310Q	310Q0811	G-BBIC	17. 6.93	Red Baron Haulage Ltd	Full Sutton	11. 9.08E
			N69600				
G-REDC	Pegasus Quantum 15-912	7572		30. 9.99	R F Richardson	Little Snoring	18. 9.08P
G-REDD	Cessna 310R II	310R1833	G-BMGT	2.10.96	G Wightman	Blackpool	25. 3.05
			ZS-KSY, (N2738X)		*(Noted 10.07)*		
G-REDI	Robinson R44 Clipper	0817		2. 8.00	Redeye.com Ltd	(Sheffield City)	14. 9.08E
G-REDJ	Eurocopter AS.332L2 Super Puma II	2608	F-WWOJ	19. 5.04	International Aviation Leasing Ltd	Aberdeen	20. 5.08E
G-REDK	Eurocopter AS.332L2 Super Puma II	2610	F-WWOM	2. 6.04	International Aviation Leasing Ltd	Aberdeen	6. 6.08E
G-REDL	Eurocopter AS.332L2 Super Puma II	2612	F-WWOD	30. 6.04	International Aviation Leasing Ltd	Aberdeen	5. 7.08E
G-REDM	Eurocopter AS.332L2 Super Puma II	2614	F-WWOF	26. 7.04	International Aviation Leasing Ltd	Aberdeen	29.7.08E
G-REDN	Eurocopter AS.332L2 Super Puma II	2616	F-WQDH	20. 8.04	International Aviation Leasing Ltd	Aberdeen	22. 8.08E
G-REDO	Eurocopter AS.332L2 Super Puma II	2622	F-WWOH	12. 9.05	International Aviation Leasing Ltd	Sumburgh	15. 9.08E
G-REDP	Eurocopter AS.332L2 Super Puma II	2634	F-WWOB	17.11.05	International Aviation Leasing Ltd	Sumburgh	14.11.07E
G-REDS	Cessna 560XL Citation Excel	560-5167	N250SM	10.10.02	Bridge Aviation Ltd	Hawarden	9.10.07E
			N5188N				
G-REDX	Experimental Aviation Berkut	002		27. 1.95	G V Waters	RAF Coltishall	23. 6.08P
	(Built G V Waters - pr.no.PFA 252-12481) (Lycoming O-360-A1A)						
G-REDY	Robinson R22 Beta II	3402	G-CBXO	28. 7.03	Plane Talking Ltd	Blackbushe	1. 4.08E
			N71909				
G-REDZ	Thruster T 600N 450 Sprint	0037-T600N-091		5. 8.03	M R Jones Broomclose Farm, Longbridge Deverill		4. 8.07P
	(While practising simulated engine-failure on take-off Redlands, Swindon 15. 7.07 failed to respond to corrective actions and impacted nose-down,						
	insurance wreck bought by Galaxy Microlights new owner 11.07)						
G-REEC	Sequoia F 8L Falco	654	LN-LCA	2. 7.96	J D Tseliki	Kittyhawk Farm, Deanland	22. 7.08P
	(Lycoming IO-320)						
G-REED	Mainair Blade 912S	1282-0501-7-W1077		11. 6.01	I C Macbeth	Arclid Green, Sandbach	12. 4.08P
G-REEF	Mainair Blade 912S	1285-0501-7-W1080		15. 6.01	G Mowll	Caerrnarfon	2. 7.08P
G-REEK	Grumman AA-5A Cheetah	AA5A-0429	N7129L	12. 9.77	J and A Pearson	(Dundee)	10.12.01
G-REEM	Aérospatiale AS.355F1 Ecureuil 2	5175	G-EMAN	9. 3.98	Heliking Ltd	Denham	24. 6.08T
			G-WEKR, G-CHLA, N818RL, C-FLXH, N818RL, N818R, N5798U				
G-REEN	Cessna 340	340-0063	G-AZYR	2. 2.84	R D Cornish	North Weald	6.11.07E
			N5893M				
G-REER	Centrair 101A Pégase	101A033	BGA 3593-FWX	15.10.07	P M Greer	Nympsfield	11. 4.08
			F-CFRZ				
G-REES	SAN Jodel D 140C Mousquetaire III	156	F-BMFR	23. 4.80	C C Rea tr G-REES Flying Group		
						Sheepcote Farm, Stourbridge	5. 9.10
G-REET	Grumman American AA-5B Tiger	AA5B-0706	G-BFPB	2. 9.05	Tiger AA-5B Ltd	(Leamington Spa)	12. 7.07E

Reg	Type	C/n	Prev id	Date	Owner/Operator	Location	
G-REGE	Robinson R44 Raven	1517		20.10.05	Rege Aviation LLP	(Hull)	3.11.07E
G-REGS	Thunder Ax7-77 Balloon (Hot Air)	1812		4. 7.90	M E Gregory	Hascot Hill, Stowmarket	30. 8.95A
					(New owner 2.08)		
G-REJP	Europa Aviation Europa XS	xxxx		31. 8.06	A Milner	(Hauxton, Cambridge)	14 .8.08P
	(Built A Milner - pr.no.PFA 247-14086)						
G-REKO	Solar Wings Pegasus Quasar IITC	SW-WQT-0467	G-MWWA	14.11.01	M Sims	Haverfordwest	12. 7.07P
	(Trike c/n SW-TQC-0073)						
G-RELL	Druine D 62B Condor	RAE 619	G-OPJH	14. 8.07	P S Grellier	Barton Ashes	23.10.07P
	(Built Rollason Aircraft and Engines)		G-AVDW				
G-RENO	SOCATA TB-10 Tobago	249		10.12.81	Lamond Ltd	Coventry	24. 5.08E
G-REPH	Pegasus Quantum 15-912	7785		6. 2.01	R S Partridge-Hicks	(Bury St Edmunds)	3. 5.03P
G-RESC	Eurocopter MBB BK-117C-1C	7504	D-HELW	6. 7.07	Sterling Helicopters Ltd	RAF Wyton	2. 8.08E
			I-BKBS, D-HOTZ, X-..., D-HOTZ, D-HECA, D-HMBF				
G-RESG	Dyn'Aéro MCR-01 Club	237		10. 4.03	R E S Greenwood	Newmarket	29.11.08P
	(Built R E S Greenwood - pr.no.PFA 301A-13994)						
G-REST	Beech P35 Bonanza	D-7171	G-ASFJ	14.12.82	C R E S Taylor	North Weald	27.10.07E
G-RETA	CASA 1-131E Jungmann Series 2000	2197	Spanish AF E3B-305	24. 3.80	Richard Shuttleworth Trustees	Old Warden	10. 4.08P
					(As "4477:GD+EG" in Luftwaffe WW2 c/s)		
G-REVE	Van's RV-6	PFA 181-12945		29. 8.07	R C Dyer	(Felixstowe)	
	(Built R C Dyer)						
G-REVO	Best Off Sky Ranger 912(2)	SKRxxxx408		2. 2.04	M McCall	(Moira, Craigavon)	21. 8.08P
	(Built R T Henry - pr.no.BMAA/HB/346)						
G-REYS	Bombardier CL-600-2B16	5467	N467RD	17. 9.01	Greyscape Ltd	Farnborough	16. 9.08E
	(CL-604 Challenger)		C-GLWX				
G-RFIO	Aeromot AMT-200 Super Ximango	200048		6. 3.95	M D Evens	Kirkbride	30. 6.08E
G-RFOX	Denney Kitfox Model 3	PFA 172-12029		5. 9.05	L G G Faulkner and R Nicklin	Otherton, Cannock	
	(Built L G G Faulkner and R Nicklin)						
G-RFSB	Sportavia-Pützer RF5B Sperber	51045	N55HC	2.12.88	J F McAulay tr G-RFSB Group	RAF Cranwell	19. 9.08P
			D-KEAO				
G-RFUN	Robinson R44 Raven	1239		17. 7.02	Watchbrick Ltd	(Sheffield)	11. 8.08E
G-RGAP	Cessna 172S Skyhawk	172S10421	N1216Z	18. 1.07	Certrain Ltd	Wycombe Air Park	8. 2.08E
G-RGEN	Cessna T337D Super Skymaster	3371062	G-EDOT	24. 5.96	Legoprint SpA	Bergamo Valbrembo, Italy	11. 6.06
			G-BJIY, 9Q-CPF, PH-JWL, N86056 *(Noted 9.07)*				
G-RGNT	Robinson R44 Raven II	10514	G-DMCG	26. 1.05	P R Nott t/a Regent Aviation	(Frating, Colchester)	31.10.07E
G-RGTS	Schempp-Hirth Discus b	140	BGA 4301-HYB	29.11.07	G R Green	Wormingford	28. 2.08
			D-4684				
G-RGUS	Fairchild 24R-46A Argus III	1145	(PH-)	16. 9.86	P J and J L Bryan	Sibson	21. 4.08
	(UC-61K-FA)		G-RGUS, ZS-UJZ, ZS-BAY, KK527, 44-83184 *(As "44-83184:7" in USAAF c/s)*				
G-RHAM	Best Off Sky Ranger 582(1)	SKR0509647		9. 1.06	G Eden	Eshott	25. 9.08P
	(Built G Eden - pr.no.BMAA/HB/482)						
G-RHCB	Schweizer 269C-1	0036	N201WL	20. 3.98	Helicopter One Ltd	Bournemouth	9. 4.07T
	(Schweizer 300)				*(Noted 11.07)*		
G-RHHT	Piper PA-32RT-300 Lance II	32R-7885190	N36476	3. 7.78	M R Boutel	Sywell	23. 5.08E
G-RHOP	Fairey Britten-Norman BN-2A Mk.III-2 Trislander	1042	G-WEAC	11. 3.04	Airx Ltd t/a Blue Islands	Alderney	18. 3.08E
			5H-AZD, G-BEFP, (4X-CCL), G-BEFP, N30WA, JA6401, G-BEFP				
G-RHYM	Piper PA-31 Turbo Navajo B	31-815	G-BJLO	24. 4.02	ATC Trading Ltd	Lasham	30. 1.08E
			F-BTQG, (F-BTDV), N7428L				
G-RHYS	RotorWay Executive 90	5140		8.11.93	A K Voase	(Hornsea)	21. 7.04P
	(Built B Williams) (RotorWay RI 162)				*(New owner 5.05)*		
G-RIAT	Robinson R22 Beta II	2684		27. 5.97	HJS Helicopters Ltd	Lower Baads, Peterculter	29. 6.08E
G-RIAM	SOCATA TB-10 Tobago	85	F-GFLA	31. 1.07	H Varia	Leicester	18. 7.08E
			F-ZVLA				
G-RIBA	P&M Quik GT450	8217		21.11.06	R J Murphy	East Fortune	20.11.08P
G-RIBZ	Enstrom 480B	5055		14. 8.03	Premiair Aviation Group Ltd	Blackbushe	17. 9.08E
G-RICK	Beech 95-B55 Baron	TC-1472		23. 5.84	James Jack Lifting Services Ltd	Inverness	18.10.07E
G-RICO	American General AG-5B Tiger	10162	G-BAAG	14. 5.99	I J Ward	Blackbushe	12. 7.08E
G-RICS	Europa Aviation Europa	125	N130U	19. 3.96	R G Allen t/a The Flying Property Doctor		
	(Built R G Allen - pr.no.PFA 247-12747) (NSI EA81) (Conventional u/c)					Wellcross Grange, Slinfold	29. 5.08P
G-RIDA	Eurocopter AS.355NP Ecureuil 2	5754	F-WQDE	7.12.07	Eurocopter UK Ltd	Oxford	
G-RIDD	Robinson R22 Beta II	3685		14.10.04	KTWO Ltd	(Abridge, Romford)	28.10.07E
G-RIDE	Stephens Akro	111	N81AC	10. 8.78	R Mitchell t/a Mitchell Aviation	Sleap	13. 8.92P
	(Built N Mardis) (Lycoming AIO-360)		N55NM		*(Noted 10.06)*		
G-RIDG	Van's RV-7A	PFA 323-14449		4. 1.06	B A Ridgway	Rhigos	
	(Built B A Ridgway)						
G-RIDL	Robinson R22 Beta II	3194		30. 3.01	Corserve International Ltd	(Stockport)	16. 7.08E
G-RIEF	DG Flugzeugbau DG-1000T	10-85T23	BGA 5239-KNC	19. 7.06	J T Hitchcock *"EF"*	Parham Park	17. 7.08
G-RIET	Hoffmann H 36 Dimona	36224	I-RIET	6. 8.02	L J McKelvie tr Dimona Gliding Group	Bellarena	22.12.07E
G-RIEV	Rolladen-Schneider LS8-18	8039	BGA 4192-HTP	4..1.08	R D Grieve	(North Lopham, Diss)	9. 5.08
			D-3175				
G-RIFB	Hughes 269C	116-0562	N7428F	17. 5.90	R A Roberts t/a Puddleduck Plane Partnership		
	(Hughes 300)					Dunsfold	4. 4.08E
G-RIFN	Mudry CAP.10B	276		6. 6.96	D E Starkey and R A J Spurrell	White Waltham	8. 8.08E
G-RIFS	Rotorsport UK MT-03	RSUK/MT-03/020		18.10.07	B Griffiths	Charity Farm, Baxterley	25.10.08P
G-RIGB	Thunder Ax7-77 Balloon (Hot Air)	1201		16. 3.88	N J Bettin	Farnham	2. 2.08A
G-RIGH	Piper PA-32R-301 Saratoga II HP	3246123	N41272	23.12.98	Right Aviation Ltd	Fowlmere	27. 1.08E
			G-RIGH, N41272				
G-RIGS	Piper PA-60-601P Aerostar	61P-0621-7963281	N8220J	18. 5.79	G G Caravatti and P G Penati	Milan-Bresso, Italy	25 .2.08
					"Marilyn"		
G-RIHN	Dan Rihn DR.107 One Design	PFA 264-14201		18. 5.04	J P Brown	White Waltham	26. 9.08P
	(Built J P Brown)						
G-RIIN	PZL-104M Wilga 2000	00010010	SP-WEI	27. 6.01	E A M Austin	North Weald	22. 7.07E
G-RIIV	Van's RV-4	1340	N24EL	20. 2.08	C Baldwin	(Timperley, Altrincham)	
	(Built E C Lorr)						
G-RIKI	Mainair Blade 912	1280-0401-7-W1075		29. 8.01	R Cook	Easter Poldar Farm, Thornhill	22.11.07P

G-RIKS	Europa Aviation Europa XS	393		18.10.01	R Morris	Benington	17.10.08P
	(Built R Morris - pr.no.PFA 247-13329) (Tri-gear u/c)						
G-RIKY	Mainair Sports Pegasus Quik	8007		17.12.03	P J Bent	Swinford, Rugby	28. 1.08P
G-RILA	Flight Design CTSW	06.08.11		29. 9.06	P Mahony	(Middle Wallop, Stockbridge)	5.10.07P
	(Assembled P&M Aviation Ltd as c/n 8182)						
G-RIMB	Lindstrand LBL 105A Balloon (Hot Air)	827		15. 3.02	D Grimshaw	Leyland	11. 4.08T
					(Parkinson's of Leyland titles)		
G-RIME	Lindstrand LBL 25A Cloudhopper Balloon (Hot Air)			9.12.03	N Ivison	Barton Seagrave, Kettering	26. 6.08A
		954			(Poppies titles)		
G-RIMM	Westland Wasp HAS.1	F9605	NZ Navy NZ3907	11. 3.99	G P Hinkley	Green Barn Farm, Badwell Green	24. 9.08P
			XT435		(As "XT435:430" in RN c/s)		
G-RINN	Mainair Blade	1261-1000-7-W1055		2. 1.01	J P Lang	Guy Lane Farm, Waverton	9. 2.08P
	(Rotax 582)						
G-RINO	Thunder Ax7-77 Balloon (Hot Air)	975		24. 6.87	D J Head "Cerous"	Newbury	5. 3.94T
G-RINS	Rans S-6-ESD Coyote II	0498.1220		15. 3.99	D Watt	Ladthwaite Farm, Kirkby Steven	18. 5.08P
	(Built D G Watts - pr.no.PFA 204-13361) (Rotax 582)						
G-RINT	CFM Streak Shadow	K 199-SA		7.12.93	D and J S Grint	Shoreham	12.12.07P
	(Built D Grint- pr.no.PFA 206-12251) (Rotax 582)						
G-RIOT	Silence Twister	PFA 329-14700		11.10.07	Zulu Glasstek Ltd	Baileys Farm, Long Crendon	
	(Built P M Wells)						
G-RISE	Cameron V-90 Balloon (Hot Air)	2395		21. 9.90	D L Smith "Rise N' Shine"	Newbury	18. 9.05T
G-RISH	Rotorway Executive 162F	6926		15. 3.05	C S Rische	(Felmingham, North Walsham)	
	(Built C S Rische)						
G-RISK	Hughes 369E	0157E	SE-HNZ	28. 6.06	Wavendon Social Housing Ltd	Sywell	12. 9.08E
	(Hughes 500)		LN-OMV				
G-RIST	Cessna 310R II	310R1294	G-DATS	28. 4.81	R Jessop	Bournemouth	17. 3.08E
			(N6128X)				
G-RISY	Van's RV-7	PFA 323-14320		10. 2.05	A J A Weal	(Worthing)	
	(Built A J A Weal)						
G-RITT	P&M Quik GT450	8230		8.12.06	S B Williams	(Headcorn, Ashford)	4. 2.08P
G-RIVE	Jodel D 153	PFA 235-12856		14. 7.04	P Fines	(Benniworth, Market Rasen)	12.12.08P
	(Built P Fines)						
G-RIVR	Thruster T 600F	9029-T600N-031		3.12.99	Thruster Air Services Ltd	Ginge, Wantage	7.12.00P
	(Hirth H2706) (Officially regd as "T 600N" with Rotax 582 and noted 1.05 in float configuration)						
G-RIVT	Van's RV-6	PFA 181-12743		31. 7.95	N Reddish	Netherthorpe	25. 4.08P
	(Built N Reddish) (Lycoming O-320)						
G-RIXA	Piper J-3C Cub	18711	7Q-YDF	19. 1.07	A J Rix	(Pent Farm, Postling)	
			5Y-KEV, VP-KEV, VP-NAE, ZS-AZT				
G-RIXS	Europa Aviation Europa XS	533		2. 7.02	R Iddon	Blackpool	19. 6.07P
	(Built R Iddon - pr.no.PFA 247-13822) (Tri-gear u/c)						
G-RIXY	Cameron Z-77 Balloon (Hot Air)	10788		23. 1.06	Rix Petroleum Ltd	Hull	26. 1.08P
G-RIZE	Cameron O-90 Balloon (Hot Air)	3163		13.12.93	S F Burden	Noordwijk, Netherlands	27. 9.08A
G-RIZI	Cameron N-90 Balloon (Hot Air)	3080	(F-GXIL)	12. 5.93	R Wiles	Durgates, Wadhurst	25. 5.04A
			G-RIZI		(Address change 10.07)		
G-RIZZ	Piper PA-28-161 Cherokee Warrior II		D-EMFW	11. 2.99	Modi Aviation Ltd	Sibson	21. 3.08E
		28-7816494	N9563N				
G-RJAH	Boeing Stearman D75N1 (PT-27BW) Kaydet	75-4041	N75957	6. 4.90	R J Horne	Little Rissington	11. 4.04
	(Continental W670)		RCAF FJ991, 42-15852		(As "44" in US Army Air Corps c/s: noted 1.08)		
G-RJAM	Sequoia F 8L Falco	PFA 100-11665		26. 7.00	R J Marks	Dunkeswell	
	(Built R J Marks)				(Noted 11.04)		
G-RJCC	Cessna 172S Skyhawk	172S10525	OE-DAN	21.12.07	R J Chapman (Noted 1.08)	North Weald	
G-RJMS	Piper PA-28R-201 Arrow III	28R-7837059	N6223H	19. 1.88	M G Hill	Crosland Moor	21. 6.08E
G-RJRJ	Aerotechnik EV-97A Eurostar	LAA 315A-14763		29. 1.08	D P Myatt tr G-RJRJ Flying Group		
	(Built D P Myatt and J Patterson)				(Old Marston, Oxford)		
G-RJWW	Maule M-5-235C Lunar Rocket	7250C	G-BRWG	6.10.87	PAW Flying Services Ltd	Full Sutton	21.10.06T
			N5632H				
G-RJWX	Europa Aviation Europa XS	359		11. 9.00	J R Jones	Sleap	20. 1.08P
	(Built J R Jones - pr.no.PFA 247-13197) (Monowheel u/c)						
G-RJXA	Embraer EMB-145EP	145136	PT-SDN	18. 6.99	British Midland Airways Ltd	East Midlands	17. 6.08E
					(Operated bmi Regional)		
G-RJXB	Embraer EMB-145EP	145142	PT-SDS	23. 6.99	British Midland Airways Ltd	East Midlands	27. 6.08E
					(Operated bmi Regional)		
G-RJXC	Embraer EMB-145EP	145153	PT-SEE	15. 7.99	British Midland Airways Ltd	East Midlands	14. 7.08E
					(Operated bmi Regional)		
G-RJXD	Embraer EMB-145EP	145207		4. 2.00	British Midland Airways Ltd	East Midlands	3. 2.08E
					(Operated bmi Regional)		
G-RJXE	Embraer EMB-145EP	145245	PT-SIJ	10. 4.00	British Midland Airways Ltd	East Midlands	9. 4.08E
					(Operated bmi Regional)		
G-RJXF	Embraer EMB-145EP	145280	PT-SJW	29. 6.00	British Midland Airways Ltd	East Midlands	28. 6.08E
					(Operated bmi Regional)		
G-RJXG	Embraer EMB-145EP	145390		20. 2.01	British Midland Airways Ltd	East Midlands	19. 2.08E
					(Operated bmi Regional)		
G-RJXH	Embraer EMB-145EP	145442	PT-SVD	1. 6.01	British Midland Airways Ltd	East Midlands	31. 5.08E
					(Operated bmi Regional)		
G-RJXI	Embraer EMB-145EP	145454	PT-SVD	22. 6.01	British Midland Airways Ltd	East Midlands	21. 6.08E
					(Operated bmi Regional) (Star Alliance titles)		
G-RJXJ	Embraer EMB-135ER	145473		23. 7.01	British Midland Airways Ltd	East Midlands	22. 7.08E
					(Operated bmi Regional)		
G-RJXK	Embraer EMB-135ER	145494	PT-SXN	14. 9.01	British Midland Airways Ltd	East Midlands	13. 9.08E
					(Operated bmi Regional) (Star Alliance titles)		
G-RJXL	Embraer EMB-135ER	145376	PT-SQA	20.12.04	British Midland Airways Ltd	East Midlands	19.12.07E
			(EI-LCY), PT-SQA, (CN-RLF), PT-SQA				
G-RJXM	Embraer EMB-145MP	145216	PH-RXA	23.12.05	British Midland Airways Ltd	East Midlands	22.12.07E
			PT-SHC				

Reg	Type	C/n	Prev id	Date	Owner/Operator	Base	Expiry
G-RJXN	Embraer EMB-145MP	145336	SP-LGI PT-SNC	19.10.06	British Midland Regional Ltd	Aberdeen	18.10.07E
G-RJXO	Embraer EMB-145MP	145339	SP-LGK PT-SNF	31.10.06	British Midland Regional Ltd	Aberdeen	30.10.07E
G-RKEL	Agusta-Bell 206B-3 JetRanger III	8617	HB-XPR F-GCVE	2. 8.01	Nunkeeling Ltd	(Brough)	12. 6.08E
G-RKET	Taylor JT.2 Titch (Built P A Dunley)	PFA 3223	G-BIBK	25. 8.99	P A Dunley (New owner 12.05)	(Castle Donington, Derby)	
G-RLEF	Hawker Hurricane XII (Built Canadian Car and Foundry Co)	42020	RCAF 5385	5. 3.07	P J Lawton	Thruxton	
G-RLFI	Reims Cessna FA152 Aerobat	FA1520340	G-DFTS	17. 1.90	Tayside Aviation Ltd	Glenrothes	15.11 07E
G-RLMW	Tecnam P2002-EA Sierra (Built J S Melville and R O'Malley-White - pr.no.PFA 333-14536)	162		1. 6.06	R O'Malley-White	Clench Common	21.11.07P
G-RLON	Fairey Britten-Norman BN-2A Mk.III-2 Trislander	1008	G-ITEX G-OCTA, VR-CAA, (G-OLPL), VR-CAA, DQ-FCF, G-BCXW	26. 4.02	Aurigny Air Services Ltd (Royal London Asset Management titles)	Guernsey	16 12.07E
G-RMAC	Europa Aviation Europa (Built P J Lawless - pr.no.PFA 247-12717) (Monowheel u/c)	109		3. 7.97	P J Lawless	Kemble	16. 6.08P
G-RMAN	Aero Designs Pulsar (Built M B Redman)	PFA 202-13071		6. 6.97	M B Redman	Old Sarum	15. 8.08P
G-RMBM	Robinson R44 Raven II	11049		8. 2.06	R and B Moseley t/a Bramble Developments	Hannington, Rushden	22. 2.08E
G-RMIT	Van's RV-4 (Built J P Kloos) (Lycoming O-320)	PFA 181-12207 24..6.08P		4. 9.96	J P Kloos	Truleigh Manor Farm, Edburton	13. 6.08P
G-RMHE	Aerospool Dynamic WT9 UK (Official c/n is "DY155")	DY155/2006		2.10.06	R M Hughes-Ellis	(Tregynon, Newtown)	24. 6.08P
G-RMMT	Europa Aviation Europa XS (Built N Schmitt) (Rotax 914) (Tri-cycle u/c)	A260	N929N (N29N reported)	28. 1.05	N Schmitt "Grommit"	Tollerton	18. 8.08P
G-RMPY	Evektor EV-97 Eurostar (Built N R Beale)	PFA 315-14139		4. 2.04	N R Beale	Church Farm, Shotteswell	2. 8.08P
G-RMRV	Van's RV-7A (Built R Morris)	PFA 323-14434		25. 5.07	R Morris	Cambridge	
G-RMUG	Cameron Nescafe Mug 90 SS Balloon (Hot Air)	3450		3. 5.95	Nestle UK Ltd "Nescafe"	Croydon	12. 7.03A
G-RNAC	IAV Bacau Yakovlev Yak-52	888912	RA-44463 DOSAAF 99	25. 7.03	M Hynett tr RNAEC Group "23"	RNAS Yeovilton	22.11.08P
G-RNBW	Bell 206B-2 JetRanger II	2270	F-GQFH F-WQFH, HB-XUF, F-GFBP, N900JJ, N16UC	9. 1.98	Rainbow Helicopters Ltd	Whimple	24. 3.08E
G-RNCH	Piper PA-28-181 Archer II	28-8190141	HB-PHR D-EIFP, N83235	19. 4.06	Carlisle Flight Training Ltd	Carlisle	11. 5.08E
G-RNDD	Robin DR.500-200i Président (Officially regd as DR.400-500)	0037		2. 5.03	Witham (Specialist Vehicles) Ltd (New owner 4.07)	(Colsterworth, Grantham)	26. 5.08E
G-RNGO	Robinson R22 Beta II	3035		19. 1.00	Janabeck Investments Ltd	Gloucestershire	13. 3.08T
G-RNHF	Hawker Sea Fury T 20	"ES.3615"	N281L N8476W, G-BCOW, D-CACO, G-9-64, VX281 (In "Royal Navy" c/s coded "281": dismantled.6.07)	1. 6.07	Royal Navy Historic Flight	North Weald	23. 6.80P
G-RNIE	Cameron Ball 70 SS Balloon (Hot Air)	2333		3. 8.90	N J Bland "Schwarzenegger"	Didcot	8. 6.06A
G-RNLI	Vickers Supermarine 236 Walrus 1	S2/5591	W2718	13.12.90	Solent Sky Ltd (New owner 11.06) (As "W2718/AA5Y" in 751 Sqdn RN c/s:)	Southampton	
G-RNRM	Cessna A185F Skywagon	185-02541	N1826R	20. 1.87	Skydive St Andrews Ltd "Thunderchild"	Sorbie Farm, Kingsmuir	6. 3.08E
G-RNRS	Scottish Aviation Bulldog Series 100/101	BH100/132	SE-LLF Fv61026, G-AZIT	12. 9.03	Power Aerobatics Ltd	Kemble	3. 6.10T
G-ROAD	Robinson R44 Raven II	11589		29. 1.07	Ainscough Ltd	(Ince, Wigan)	13. 2.08E
G-ROBD	Europa Aviation Europa (Built R D Davies - pr.no.PFA 247-12671) (Monowheel u/c)	078		23. 2.94	R D Davies	(Cowbridge)	
G-ROBN	Robin R1180T Aiglon	220		16. 8.78	N D Anderson	Old Sarum	26.11.07T
G-ROBT	Hawker Hurricane I (Built Gloster Aircraft Co Ltd)	---	P2902	19. 9.94	R A Roberts (On rebuild by Hawker Restorations Ltd from remains salvaged 1988 at Dunkirk Beach: to be "P2902/DX-X")	Moat Farm, Milden	
G-ROBZ	Grob G109B	6442	I-BREM	19. 6.07	J D Huband tr Bravo Zulu Group	(Cricklade, Swindon)	19. 7.08E
G-ROCH	Cessna T303 Crusader	T30300129	N4962C	29. 3.90	R S Bentley	Cambridge	7. 6.08E
G-ROCK	Thunder Ax7-77 Balloon (Hot Air)	781		25. 2.86	M A Green "Rocky"	Rednal	28. 7.05A
G-ROCR	Schweizer 269C (Schweizer 300)	S 1336	N219MS	14. 6.90	C J Williams	Sandown, Isle of Wight	23. 4.08T
G-ROCT	Robinson R44 Raven II	11854		10. 8.07	C R Turton t/a Marketwatch	Headcorn	30. 8.08E
G-RODC	Steen Skybolt (Built R H Williams)	4568	N10624	20. 2.02	J W Teesdale and S Yelland (Thornton Le Clay, York and Ferrensby, Knaresborough)		4. 3.08P
G-RODD	Cessna 310R II	310R0544	G-TEDD G-MADI, N87396, G-MADI, N87396	2.10.89	R J Herbert Engineering Ltd	Marshland, Wisbech	22. 5.08E
G-RODG	Avtech Jabiru UL (Built I M Donnelly - pr.no.PFA 274A-13379)	xxxx		14. 4.99	P C Appleton (Noted 7.05)	Davidstow Moor	9. 5.04P
G-RODI	Isaacs Fury (Built D C J Summerfield) (Lycoming O-290)	PFA 011-10130		22.12.78	C J Riley (As "K3731" in RAF 43 Sqdn c/s)	(Middle Rasen, Market Rasen)	4. 3.08P
G-RODJ	Comco Ikarus C42 FB80	0709-6912		2.10.07	R K Jenkins t/a Swansea Sport Flying	Swansea	28.10.08P
G-RODZ	Van's RV-3A (Built T F Hinckley)	10622	N68AR	4. 7.07	R M Laver	Shoreham	
G-ROEI	Avro Roe 1 replica (Built Brooklands Museum)	PFA 344-14629		6. 2.08	Brooklands Museum Trust Ltd	Brooklands	
G-ROGE	Robinson R44 Raven II	11462		1.11.06	Phil Rogerson Ltd	Yeoland Conyers, Carnforth	16.11.07E
G-ROGY	Cameron Concept 60 Balloon (Hot Air)	3055		11. 5.93	S A Laing	Banchory	20. 9.08A
G-RODJ	Comco Ikarus C42 FB80	0709-6912		2.10.07	R K Jenkins tr Swansea Sport Flying	Swansea	28.10.08P
G-ROKT	Reims FR172E Rocket	FR1720046	N261SA D-ECLY	1.05.03	Sylmar Aviation and Services Ltd	Lower Wasing Farm, Brimpton	20. 12.07E
G-ROLF	Piper PA-32R-301 Saratoga II SP	32R-8113018	N83052	7. 1.81	P F Larkins	Panshanger	19. 5.08

G-ROLL	Pitts S-2A	2175	N31444	20. 2.80	Aerobatic Displays Ltd		Wycombe Air Park	17. 7.07A
	(Built Aerotek Inc)				"Breitling Angels" (yellow) c/s			
G-ROLY	Reims Cessna F172N Skyhawk II	F17201945	G-BHIH	1.12.04	R B A Stones tr G-ROLY Group		Gamston	12. 9.07E
G-ROME	III Sky Arrow 650 TC	C011		26. 5.99	Sky Arrow (Kits) UK Ltd		Old Sarum	26. 8.08E
	(Built Iniziative Industriali Italiane)							
G-ROMP	Extra EA.230H	001	S5-MBP	13. 1.05	G G Ferriman		Jericho Farm, Lambley	18. 5.08P
	(Built W Hawickhorst)		OO-JVD, D-EIWH					
G-ROMS	Lindstrand LBL 105G Balloon (Hot Air)	401		13. 9.96	T D Donnelly tr Gromit Balloon Group			
					"Gromit"		Sprotbrough, Doncaster	13. 9.00A
G-ROMW	Cyclone AX2000	7486		4. 2.99	K V Falvey		Sackville Lodge, Riseley	8. 7.08P
	(HKS 700E V3)							
G-RONA	Europa Aviation Europa	043		17. 1.95	C M Noakes	Shenstone Hall Farm, Shenstone		22.10.08P
	(Built C M Noakes - pr.no.PFA 247-12588) (Monowheel u/c)				"Mr Jake"			
G-ROND	Short SD.3-60 Variant 100	SH3604	EI-CWG	1.11.01	BAC Leasing Ltd		Edinburgh	26.11.06E
			G-OLAH, G-BPCO, G-RMSS, G-BKKU (Noted 12.07)					
G-RONG	Piper PA-28R-200 Cherokee Arrow II		N16451	14. 6.90	E Tang		(London W1)	2.11.07E
		28R-7335148						
G-RONI	Cameron V-77 Balloon (Hot Air)	2349		27. 7.90	R E Simpson "Roni"		Great Missenden	15. 8.02A
G-RONS	Robin DR.400-180 Régent	2088		17. 7.91	R and K Baker		Swansea	24.10.08E
G-RONW	Clutton FRED Series II	PFA 029-10121		18.12.78	F J Keitch		(Clayhidon, Cullompton)	29. 3.04P
	(Built P Gronow)				(New owner 8.07)			
G-ROOK	Reims Cessna F172P Skyhawk II	F17202081	PH-TGY	12. 1.81	Rolim Ltd		Aberdeen	7.12.07E
			G-ROOK		(Operated Bon Accord Flying Group)			
G-ROOV	Europa Aviation Europa XS	354		16. 7.98	P W Hawkins and K Siggery		Biggin Hill	20. 6.08P
	(Built D Richardson - pr.no.PFA 247-13214) (Rotax 914-UL) (Tri-gear u/c)							
G-RORI	Folland Gnat T 1	FL.549	8621M	18.10.93	Swept Wing Ltd		North Weald	18. 6.08P
			XR538		(As "XR538:01" in RAF c/s)			
G-RORY	Focke-Wulf Piaggio FWP.149D	014	G-TOWN	2. 8.88	M Edwards		Barton	7. 1.08
	(Piaggio c/n 338)		D-EFFY, 90+06, BB+394 7					
G-ROSI	Thunder Ax7-77 Balloon (Hot Air)	1284		29. 6.88	J E Rose "Rosi"		Abingdon	21. 9.96A
G-ROSS	Practavia Pilot Sprite	132		28. 2.80	A D Janaway		Exeter	
	(Built F M T Ross - pr.no.PFA 005-10404)				(New owner 6.04)			
G-ROTF	Robinson R22 Beta	3928	EI-DKO	27.11.06	Rotorflight Ltd		Bristol	1.11.07E
G-ROTG	Robinson R44 Raven II	11553		30. 1.07	Rotorflight Ltd		Bristol	1. 3.08E
G-ROTI	Luscombe 8A Silvaire	2117	N45590	18. 4.89	R Ludgate and A L Chapman			
	(Continental A65)		NC45590		(Stored 7.05)		Old Hay, Paddock Wood	9.10.97P
G-ROTR	Brantly B 2B	403	N2192U	9.12.91	P G R Brown		(Crediton)	17.11.02
G-ROTS	CFM Streak Shadow	K 120-SA		21.12.89	A G Vallis and C J Kendal		Barton	8. 8.07P
	(Builtt H R Cayzer - pr.no.PFA 161A-11603) (Rotax 582)							
G-ROUP	Reims Cessna F172M Skyhawk II	F17201451	N8068U	23. 5.84	Perranporth Flying School Ltd		Perranporth	16. 3.08E
G-ROUS	Piper PA-34-200T Seneca II	34-7870187	(G-BFTB)	26. 4.78	Oxford Aviation Training Ltd		Oxford	23. 4.08E
			N9412C					
G-ROUT	Robinson R22 Beta	1241	N8068U	23. 1.90	Preston Associates Ltd		(Guisborough)	19. 8.07T
G-ROVE	Piper PA-18-135 Super Cub	18-3846	PH-VLO	6. 5.82	S J Gaveston		Headcorn	1. 6.08
	(L-21B-PI) (Frame No.18-3853)		(PH-DKF), R Neth AF R-156, 54-2446 (As "R-156" in R Netherlands AF c/s and also carries '54-2446')					
G-ROVY	Robinson R22 Beta II	2957		9. 7.99	Plane Talking Ltd		Blackbushe	23. 9.08E
G-ROWA	Aquila AT01	AT01-174		31.10.07	Chicory Crops Ltd		Gloucestershire	
G-ROWE	Reims Cessna F182P Skylane II	F18200007	OO-CNG	18.12.95	D Rowe		St Just	2. 5.06E
G-ROWI	Europa Aviation Europa XS	435		16. 6.99	R M Carson		(Cheltenham)	
	(Built R M Carson - pr.no.PFA 247-13482) (Wilksch WAM-120) (Monowheel u/c)							
G-ROWL	Grumman AA-5B Tiger	AA5B-0595	(N28410)	26.10.77	T A Timms	Standalone Farm, Meppershall		26. 6.08E
G-ROWR	Robinson R44 Raven	1036		17. 4.01	R A Oldworth		(Petworth)	27. 4.08T
G-ROWS	Piper PA-28-151 Cherokee Warrior	28-7715296	N8949F	15. 9.78	S Goodchild	Eddsfield, Octon Lodge Farm, Thwing		27. 3.08E
G-ROYC	Avtech Jabiru UL-450	xxxx		24. 4.03	M Daleki		Field Farm, Oakley	20.12.07P
	(Built R Clark - pr.no.PFA 274A-13990)							
G-ROZI	Robinson R44 Astro	0252		26. 3.96	Rotormotive Ltd		(Sproughton, Ipswich)	29. 4.08E
				(Made heavy landing York Racecourse 16. 6.06, extensively distorting the airframe)				
G-ROZY	Cameron R-36 Gas/Balloon (Hot Air)	1141		20. 5.85	J W Soukup (New owner 12.05)		Bristol	18. 9.96A
G-ROZZ	Comco Ikarus C42 FB80	0407-6607		19. 8.04	A J Blackwell		Long Marston	19.10.08P
G-RPAF	Europa Aviation Europa XS	605		26. 1.05	R P Frost		(Woolley, Wakefield)	
	(Built R P Frost - pr.no.PFA 247-14202)							
G-RPBM	Cameron Z-210 Balloon (Hot Air)	10230		6. 3.02	The Balloon Company Ltd t/a First Flight			
					(Robert Price Builders Merchants titles) Langford, Bristol			2.10.08T
G-RPCC	Europa Aviation Europa XS	PFA 247-14615		10. 1.07	R P Churchill-Colman	(Curdridge, Southampton)		
	(Built R P Churchill-Colman)				(Address change 7.07)			
G-RPEZ	Rutan LongEz	PFA 074A-10746		3. 4.84	D G Foreman		(Swanley)	
	(Built B A Fairston and D Richardson)				(New owner 7.03)			
G-RPRV	Van's RV-9A	PFA 320-13936		17.10.03	G R Pybus		Morgansfield, Fishburn	16. 6.07P
	(Built G R Pybus)				(Noted 10.07)			
G-RRAZ	Embraer EMB-135BJ Legacy	14500954	G-RUBN	26. 9.07	Raz Air Ltd		London Stansted	12.12.07E
			PT-SFC					
G-RRCU	CEA Jodel DR.221B Dauphin	129	F-BRCU	9.12.99	Merlin Flying Club Ltd		Hucknall	12. 2.08E
G-RRFC	SOCATA TB-20 Trinidad GT	2053	F-OILV	9. 5.01	C A Hawkins		Blackbushe	24. 7.08E
G-RRGN	Vickers Supermarine 390 Spitfire PR.XIX		G-MXIX	23.12.96	Rolls-Royce PLC		Filton	3. 9.08P
		6S/594677	PS853		(As "PS853:C" in RAF 2nd TAF/PRU c/s)			
G-RROB	Robinson R44 Raven II	10011		6.12.02	Something Different Charters LLP		Stapleford	27. 2.08E
G-RROD	Piper PA-30 Twin Comanche B	30-1221	G-SHAW	20. 6.00	R P Coplestone		Thruxton	5. 8.08T
			LN-BWS, N10F					
G-RROW	Lindstrand LBL 105A Balloon (Hot Air)	1118		30. 6.06	Lindstrand Hot Air Balloons Ltd		Oswestry	20. 8.07E
					(REDROW titles)			
G-RRSR	Piper J-3C-65 Cub	12905	N1315V	7. 9.05	R W Roberts		Duxford	7. 3.09S
			44-80609		"Special Delivery" (As "480173:H-57" in USAAC c/s)			
G-RRVX	Van's RV-10	PFA 339-14601		5.12.06	R E Garforth		(Hockley)	
	(Built R E Garforth)				(Under construction 1.08)			

Reg	Type	c/n	Prev id	Date	Owner	Base	Exp
G-RSAF	British Aircraft Corporation 167 Strikemaster Mk.80A	EEP/JP/3687	R Saudi AF 1120 G-27-231	8. 4.05	M A Petrie and J E Rowley *(To be "417" in RAF of Oman c/s) (Noted 3.06)*	Hawarden	
G-RSHI	Piper PA-34-220T Seneca V	3449077	D-GMGM N9265Q	4. 2.08	A G Hill t/a R S Hill and Sons	Bournemouth	
G-RSKR	Piper PA-28-161 Warrior II	28-7916181	G-BOJY N3030G	27. 4.95	Transport Command Ltd	Shoreham	4.12.07E
G-RSKY	Best Off Sky Ranger 912(2) *(Built C G Benham - pr.no.BMAA/HB/382)*	SKR0403452		12.10.04	C G Benham	Red House Farm, Preston Capes	20. 9.08P
G-RSMC	Medway SLA 100 Executive	131106		24. 8.07	Nene Valley Microlights Ltd	Sackville Farm, Riseley	10. 9.08P
G-RSMT	Rotorsport UK MT-03	RSUK/MT-03/015		1. 5.07	Rotorsport UK Ltd	Poplar Farm., Prolly Moor, Wentor, Bishops Castle	12. 6.08P
G-RSSF	Denney Kitfox Model 2 *(Built R W Somerville)*	PFA 172-12125		9.10.92	R W Somerville *(Noted 10.03)*	Comber, County Down	15. 5.97P
G-RSVP	Robinson R22 Beta II	2788		5. 2.98	Plane Talking Ltd	Blackbushe	21. 3.08E
G-RSWO	Cessna 172R Skyhawk	17280206	N9401F	25. 2.98	AC Management Associates Ltd	Kemble	4. 4.08E
G-RSWW	Robinson R22 Beta	1775	N40815	16. 5.91	R S Weston-Woods t/a Woodstock Enterprises	Rochester	8. 8.08E
G-RSXL	Cessna 560 Citation XLS	56-5699	N5148M	16. 5.07	Aircraft Leasing Overseas Ltd	(Horley)	16 .5.08E
G-RTBI	Thunder Ax6-56 Balloon (Hot Air)	2584		19. 4.94	P J Waller *(Address change 9.07)*	Wymondham	8. 7.02A
G-RTFM	Avtech Jabiru J400 *(Built I A Macphee - pr.no.PFA 325-14463)*	xxxx		28. 2.08	I A Macphee	(Norwich)	
G-RTHS	Rans S-6-ES Coyote II *(Built T Harrison-Smith - pr/no.PFA 204-14753)*	xxxx.xxxx		17. 1.08	T Harrison-Smith	Brock Farm, Billericay	
G-RTMS	Rans S-6-ES Coyote II *(Built C J Arthur - pr.no.PFA 204-14149) (Tri-cycle u/c)*	1202.1470		19. 8.04	C J Arthur	Eshott	4. 7.08P
G-RTMY	Comco Ikarus C42 FB100	0502-6655		11. 4.05	R F Learney tr Mike Yankee Group	Redhill	10. 4.08P
G-RTRT	PZL-104MA Wilga 2000	00060021	SP-WHO	8. 6.06	Erica A M Austin	Oaksey Park	26. 7.08E
G-RTUG	Robin DR.400-180 Régent	1208	D-ELHI	14.10.05	R Feakes tr Windrushers Robin Syndicate	Bicester	16.10.07E
G-RTWO	Robinson R44 Raven II	10618		21. 1.05	Stanley Air Ltd	(Rathcoole, County Dublin)	24. 2.08E
G-RTWW	Robinson R44 Astro	0438		20. 3.98	R Woods t/a Rotorvation	(Fawkham, Longfield)	7. 5.08E
G-RUBB	Gulfstream AA-5B Tiger	AA5B-0928	(G-BKVI) OO-NAS, (OO-HRC)	20. 9.83	D E Gee	Blackbushe	23.11.07E
G-RUBY	Piper PA-28RT-201T Turbo Arrow IV	28R-8331037	G-BROU N4306K	5. 1.90	R Harman tr Arrow Aircraft Group	Tatenhill	30. 6.08E
G-RUDD	Cameron V-65 Balloon (Hot Air)	844		19. 5.82	N A Apsey *(Kodak titles)* "Smilie"	High Wycombe	20. 5.00A
G-RUES	Robin HR.100-210 Safari II	185	F-BVCH	31. 7.02	R H R Rue	Turweston	23. 9.08E
G-RUFF	Mainair Blade 912	1203-0799-7-W1006		18. 6.99	M Chambers and A Scott	Crosland Moor	17. 6.08P
G-RUFS	Avtech Jabiru UL *(Built J W Holland - pr.no.PFA 274A-13359)*	0200		19.11.99	S Richens	Lower Upham Farm, Chiseldon	9. 7.08P
G-RUGS	Campbell Cricket Mk.4 *(Built J L G Mclane)*	PFA G/103-1307		11. 2.99	J L G Mclane	(Gilling East, York)	
G-RUIA	Reims Cessna F172N Skyhawk II	F17201856	PH-AXA (3)	4.10.79	Knockin Flying Club Ltd	Knockin, Shropshire	6. 9.08E
G-RULE	Robinson R44 Raven II	11039		3. 2.06	Wiksy Charter Ltd	Hawarden	7. 2.08E
G-RUMI	Noble Hardman Snowbird Mk.IV	SB-018	G-MVOI	9. 9.02	G Crossley *(Noted 8.04)*	(Anglesey)	13. 6.02P
G-RUMM	Grumman F8F-2P Bearcat	D 1088	NX700HL NX700H, N1YY, N4995V, Bu.121714	20. 3.98	Patina Ltd *(As "21714:201B" in USN c/s) (Operated The Fighter Collection)*	Duxford	5. 7.08P
G-RUMN	American AA-1A Trainer	AA1A-0086	N87599 D-EAFB, (N9386L)	30. 5.80	M T Manwaring	Fenland	26. 5.08E
G-RUMW	Grumman FM-2 Wildcat	5765	N4845V BuA.86711	15. 4.98	Patina Ltd *(As "F" in FAA c/s) (Operated The Fighter Collection)*	Duxford	1. 7.08P
G-RUNT	Cassutt Racer IIIM *(Built N A Brendish - pr.no.PFA 034-10860) (Lycoming O-235)*	161149		12. 4.83	R S Grace "Nemesis" & "1" *(Noted 10.07)*	Audley End	16. 7.08P
G-RUSI	SOCATA TB-9 Tampico	1095	I-ODTZ	8.12.05	Aviation Sales and Leasing Ltd	Caernarfon	30. 3.08E
G-RUSL	Van's RV-6A *(Built G Russell)*	PFA 181-13522		22.10.01	G R Russell *(Noted 10.05)*	Middle Pymore Farm , Bridport	
G-RUVI	Zenair CH.601UL Zodiac *(Built P G Depper) (Tri-cycle u/c)*	PFA 162A-13933		8.11.02	P G Depper "Indulgence"	Pound Green, Buttonoak, Bewdley	15. 5.07P
G-RUVY	Van's RV-9A *(Built R D Taylor)*	PFA 320-13807		4. 1.02	R Taylor	Henstridge	4. 6.08P
G-RUZZ	Robinson R44 Raven II	10082		20. 5.03	Russell Harrison PLC	(Chipping Norton)	20. 6.08T
G-RVAB	Van's RV-7 *(Built I M Belmore)*	PFA 323-14005		20. 9.04	I M Belmore and A T Banks	(Horsham)	
G-RVAC	Van's RV-7 *(Built A F S and B Caldecourt)*	PFA 323-14445		7. 9.05	A F S and B Caldecourt *(Under construction 1.08)*	Popham	
G-RVAL	Van's RV-8 *(Built R N York)*	PFA 303-13532		23. 7.01	R N York	Dunsfold	18.11.08P
G-RVAN	Van's RV-6 *(Built D Broom) (Lycoming IO-320)*	PFA 181-12657		25. 4.97	D Broom	Benington	22. 4.07P
G-RVAW	Van's RV-6 *(Built A A Wordsworth) (Lycoming IO-320-A1A)*	PFA 181-13234		24.11.97	P E Bates tr High Flatts RV Group	High Flatts Farm, Chester-le-Street	16. 8.08P
G-RVBA	Van's RV-8A *(Buillt S Hawksworth)*	PFA 303-13309		26.10.99	D P Richard *(New owner 3.05)*	(London SW16)	
G-RVBC	Van's RV-6A *(Built T G Gibbs)*	PFA 181-12618		16. 2.00	T G Gibbs	(Faukland, Radstock)	
G-RVBF	Cameron A-340 Balloon (Hot Air)	10493		23. 2.04	Airxcite Ltd t/a Virgin Balloon Flights	Wembley	10. 9.08E
G-RVCE	Van's RV-6A *(Built M D Barnard and C Voelger)*	PFA 181-13372		28. 6.01	M D Barnard and C Voelger	Glebe Farm, Southam	23. 7.08E
G-RVCG	Van's RV-6A *(Built C J Griffin)*	PFA 181A-13602		26. 4.01	G C Calder	Shoreham	29. 4.08P
G-RVCH	Van's RV-8A *(Built C R Harrison)*	PFA 303-14116		9.11.07	C R Harrison	Dunkeswell	
G-RVCL	Van's RV-6 *(Built C Lamb)*	PFA 181A-13439		18. 2.99	R Manning	Netherthorpe	23 .8.08P

G-RVDG	Van's RV-9A	PFA 320-14310		6. 1.05	D M Gill	Bicester	16. 4.08P
	(Built D M Gill)						
G-RVDJ	Van's RV-6	PFA 181-12938		8. 2.99	J D Jewitt	(Cliffe, Selby)	3.10.07P
	(Built J D Hewitt) (Lycoming O-360)						
G-RVDP	Van's RV-4	PFA 181-13416		10. 5.00	P White	(Fethard, County Tipperary)	12. 4.08P
	(Built D H Pattison)						
G-RVDR	Van's RV-6A	PFA 181-13098		15. 5.00	P R Redfern	Breighton	31. 7.08P
	(Built D E Reast) (Lycoming IO-320)						
G-RVEE	Van's RV-6A	PFA 181-12262		16. 2.93	J C A Wheeler	Perth	23. 5.08P
	(Built J C A Wheeler) (Lycoming O-360) (Tri-cycle u/c)						
G-RVET	Van's RV-6	PFA 181-12852		9. 3.98	D R Coleman	Rochester	11. 2.08P
	(Built D R Coleman) (Lycoming O-300)						
G-RVGA	Van's RV-6A	PFA 181-13079		11. 5.98	D P Dawson	RAF Henlow	20. 4.08P
	(Built D P Dawson) (Lycoming IO-320)						
G-RVIA	Van's RV-6A	PFA 181-12289		13. 8.97	S Wells, tr G-RVIA Group	Belle Vue Farm, Yarnscombe	11.11.08P
	(Built A J Rose) (Lycoming O-320)						
G-RVIB	Van's RV-6	PFA 181-13220		22. 6.99	K Martin and P Gorman	Kilrush, County Kildare	2. 5.08P
	(Built I M Belmore) (Lycoming O-320)						
G-RVIC	Van's RV-6A	PFA 181-13319		11. 6.04	I T Corse	(Laurencekirk)	
	(Built I T Corse)						
G-RVII	Van's RV-7	PFA 181A-13576		13. 9.01	P H C Hall	Popham	
	(Built P H Hall) (Project conceived originally as a RV-6, hence the '181A type prefix) (Noted 5.07)						
G-RVIN	Van's RV-6	PFA 181-13236		28.11.97	R G Jones	Rednal	13. 4.08P
	(Built N Reddish) (Lycoming O-320)						
G-RVIO	Van's RV-10	PFA 339-14547		14. 7.06	R C Hopkinson	Langmead Farm, Garford	
	(Built R C Hopkinson)						
G-RVIS	Van's RV-8	PFA 303-14031		17. 6.03	I V Sharman	(Horley)	
	(Built I V Sharman)						
G-RVIT	Van's RV-6	PFA 181-12422		1. 5.95	P J Shotbolt		
	(Built K F Crumplin) (Lycoming O-360)					Ingthorpe Farm, Ingthorpe, Great Casterton, Stamford	7. 9.07P
G-RVIV	Van's RV-4	PFA 181-12366		31.12.97	G S Scott	(Truleigh Manor Farm, Edburton)	18. 4.08P
	(Built G S Scott) (Lycoming O-320)						
G-RVIX	Van's RV-9A	90243		11. 9.01	R E Garforth	Southend	19.11.08P
	(Built R E Garforth - pr.no.PFA 320-13779)						
G-RVJM	Van's RV-6	PFA 181A-13861		4.12.02	M D Challoner	(Stalbridge, Sturminster Newton)	
	(Built M D Challoner)						
G-RVJO	Van's RV-9A	PFA 320-13778		5. 1.07	J E Singleton	(Moreton Pinkney, Daventry)	16. 1.09P
	(Built J E Singleton)						
G-RVJP	Van's RV-9A	PFA 320-14364		28.10.05	R M Palmer	Cambridge	27. 3.08P
	(Built R M Palmer)						
G-RVJW	Van's RV-4	PFA 181-12987		26. 8.05	J M Williams	(Winsford)	
	(Built J M Williams)						
G-RVLC	Van's RV-9A	PFA 320-13780		27. 4.07	L J Clark	(Broom, Alcester)	
	(Built L J Clark)						
G-RVMB	Van's RV-9A	PFA 320-14324		16. 6.06	M James and R W Littledale	(Hinton-in-the-Hedges)	12. 9.08P
	(Built M James and R W Littledale)						
G-RVMC	Van's RV-7	PFA 323-13897		9. 5.03	M R McNeil	(Selby)	22. 9.08P
	(Built M R McNeil)						
G-RVMJ	Van's RV-4	PFA 181-13433		16. 2.99	M J de Ruiter	(Aghalee, Craigavon)	
	(Built M J de Ruiter)					(Under construction 2006)	
G-RVMT	Van's RV-6	PFA 181A-13644		30. 1.01	M J Aldridge	Rougham	9. 7.08P
	(Built M R Tingle) (Lycoming O-360)						
G-RVMZ	Van's RV-8	PFA 303-13395		12.11.99	A E Kay Parsons Farm, Waterperry Common, Oakley		4. 1.09P
	(Built M W Zipfell) (Lycoming O-360)						
G-RVNH	Van's RV-9A	PFA 320-13952		20. 7.06	N R Haines	(Lea, Malmesbury)	
	(Built N R Haines)						
G-RVNS	Van's RV-4	PFA 181-12443	G-CBGN	12.10.07	N P D Smith	(Upper Caldecote, Biggleswade)	26. 3.08P
	(Built G A Nash) (Lycoming O-320)						
G-RVPH	Van's RV-8	PFA 303-13906		25. 5.04	J C P Herbert	(Saffron Walden)	
	(Built J C P Herbert)						
G-RVPL	Van's RV-8	PFA 303-13885		6. 8.04	A P Lawton	Great Massingham	11. 1.08P
	(Built A P Lawton)						
G-RVPM	Van's RV-4	PFA 181-12270	G-RVDS	20. 2.06	P J McMahon	Ludham	22. 4.08P
	(Built D F Sargant) (Lycoming O-320)						
G-RVPW	Van's RV-6A	PFA 181A-13481		9. 6.03	P Waldron	Netherthorpe	8.11.08P
	(Built P Waldron)						
G-RVRA	Piper PA-28-140 Cherokee Cruiser	28-7625038	G-OWVA N4459X	14. 1.97	Mona Aviation Ltd /a Mona Flying Club	RAF Mona	19. 4.08E
G-RVRB	Piper PA-34-200T Seneca II	34-7970440	G-BTAJ N22MJ, N45113	24. 2.97	Ravenair Aircraft Ltd	Liverpool	2. 9.08E
G-RVRC	Piper PA-23-250 Aztec E	27-7405336	G-BNPD N101VH, N40591	14.10.97	West-Tec Ltd	Wellesbourne Mountford	7. 5.08E
G-RVRD	Piper PA-23-250 Aztec E	27-4634	G-BRAV G-BBCM, N14021	16. 3.98	Ravenair Aircraft Ltd	Liverpool	7. 2.08E
G-RVRE	Partenavia P68B	57	D-GIFR (N4412H), D-GIFR, LN-LMS	8.12.03	Ravenair Aircraft Ltd	Liverpool	14. 2.08E
G-RVRF	Piper PA-38-112 Tomahawk	38-78A0714	G-BGEL N9723N	21.11.97	Ravenair Aircraft Ltdr	Liverpool	26. 6.08E
G-RVRG	Piper PA-38-112 Tomahawk	38-79A1092	G-BHAF N9703N	3. 8.98	Ravenair Aircraft Ltd	Liverpool	15. 8.08E
G-RVRH	Van's RV-3B	PFA 099-10821		17. 2.03	R Hodgson	(Bramley, Guildford)	
	(Built R Hodgson)						
G-RVRI	Cessna 172H Skyhawk	17255822	G-CCCC SE-ELU, N2622L	26. 9.05	Ravenair Aircraft Ltd	Liverpool	12. 5.07E

Reg	Type	C/n	Prev ID	Date	Owner/Operator	Base	Expiry
G-RVRJ	Piper PA-E23-250 Aztec E	27-7305004	G-BBGB N40206	12.10.04	Ravenair Aircraft Ltd	Liverpool	27. 4.08E
G-RVRK	Piper PA-38-112 Tomahawk	38-79A1068	G-BGZW N9674N	9. 8.05	Ravenair Aircraft Ltd	Liverpool	10. 1.08E
G-RVRL	Piper PA-38-112 Tomahawk	38-78A0711	G-BGBY N9689N	9.8.05	Ravenair Aircraft Ltd	Liverpool	13. 3.08E
G-RVRM	Piper PA-38-112 Tomahawk	38-78A0525	G-BGEK N9662N	20.10.05	Ravenair Aircraft Ltd	Liverpool	7. 6.08E
G-RVRN	Piper PA-28-161 Warrior II	28-7916325	G-BPID N2137V	12.12.05	Ravenair Aircraft Ltd	Liverpool	11. 7.08E
G-RVRO	Piper PA-38-112 Tomahawk II	38-82A0017	G-BOUD N91365	14. 6.06	Ravenair Aircraft Ltd	Ronaldsway	11. 7.08E
G-RVRP	Van's RV-7 (Built R C Parris)	PFA 323-14085		16. 7.03	R C Parris (Address change 10.07)	(Leighton Buzzard)	
G-RVRR	Piper PA-38-112 Tomahawk	38-79A0199 N2474C	G-BRHT	20. 8.07	Ravenair Aircraft Ltd	Liverpool	10. 3.08E
G-RVRT	Piper PA-28-140 Cherokee C	28-26933	G-AYKX N11C	13. 9.06	Ravenair Aircraft Ltd	Liverpool	31. 5.08E
G-RVRV	Van's RV-4 (Built P Jenkins)	PFA 181-13024		29. 9.98	P Jenkins (Amended owner 8.02)	(Inverness)	
G-RVRW	Piper PA-23-250 Aztec E	27-7305045	G-BAVZ N40241	17.12.04	Ravenair Aircraft Ltd	Liverpool	11. 7.08E
G-RVSA	Van's RV-6A (Buil W H Knott)	PFA 181A-12574		19. 5.99	W H Knott	Dornoch	19.11.07P
G-RVSD	Van's RV-9A (Built S W Damarell)	PFA 320-14092		23. 5.06	S W Damarell	(Peatmor, Swindon)	
G-RVSG	Van's RV-9A (Built S Gerrish)	PFA 320-14265		10.11.04	S Gerrish (Under construction 1.08)	Lasham	
G-RVSH	Van's RV-6A (Built S J D Hall)	PFA 181A-13026		20. 9.02	S J D Hall	Blackbushe	11. 8.06P
G-RVSR	Van's RV-8 (Built S W and R K Elders)	PFA 303-14470		4. 6.07	S W and R K Elders	(Branston, Lincoln)	
G-RVSX	Van's RV-6 (Built R L West)	PFA 181-13090		18. 9.97	R L and V A West	Shoreham	25. 7.08P
G-RVTE	Van's RV-6 (Buit E McShane and T Feeny)	PFA 181A-13523		23. 1.08	E McShane and T Feeny	Strabane and Eglinton, Londonderry	
G-RVTN	Van's RV-10 (Built C I Law)	PFA 339-14602		15. 5.07	C I Law	Wickenby	
G-RVTT	Van's RV-7 (Built A Phillips)	PFA 323-13852		9.11.07	A Phillips	Boarhunt Farm, Fareham	
G-RVUK	Van's RV-7 (Built R J Fray)	PFA 323-14441		8. 6.06	R J Fray	Furze Farm, Peterborough	15.11.08P
G-RVVI	Van's RV-6 (Built J E Alsford and J N Parr) (Lycoming AEIO-360)	PFA 181-12418		26. 1.93	J E Alsford and J N Parr	Wycombe Air Park	9. 7.08P
G-RVVY	Van's RV-10 (Built P R Marskell)	PFA 339-14599		16. 3.07	P R Marskell	(Chippenham)	
G-RWAY	Rotorway Executive 162F (Built D L Urch and S Andrews) (RotorWay RI 162F)	6414	G-URCH	18.11.04	A G Rackstraw (New owner 3.06)	Tollerton	
G-RWEW	Robinson R44 Clipper II	11148		5. 4.06	R Williamson t/a Northern Heli Charters	Leeds-Bradford	7. 5.08E
G-RWGS	Robinson R-44 II	11963		29.10.07	Heli Air Ltd	Wellesbourne Mountford	
G-RWGW	Learjet Model 45	45-213	G-MUTD D-CEWR, N50126	1. 2.07	Woodlands Air LLP	Manchester	12.11.07E
G-RWHC	Cameron A-180 Balloon (Hot Air)	2700		16. 4.92	J J Rudoni and A C K Rawson t/a Wickers World Hot Air Balloon Company	Stafford	13. 4.00T
G-RWIA	Robinson R22 Beta	0753	G-BOEZ	26.11.07	R W I'Anson	(Wilmslow)	26. 3.06T
G-RWIN	Rearwin 175 Skyranger (Continental A75)	1522	N32391 NC32391	12. 9.90	A B Bourne and N D Battye	RAF Henlow	18. 7.05P
G-RWLA	Eurocopter EC.135 T2+	635		11. 2.08	Eurocopter UK Ltd	Oxford	
G-RWLY	Europa Aviation Europa XS (Built C R Arkle - pr.no.PFA 247-13701) (Tri-gear u/c)	469		22. 3.01	C R Arkle	(Ascot)	
G-RWMW	Zenair CH.601XL Zodiac (Built A G Campbell)	PFA 162B-14231	G-DROO	16. 8.06	R W H Watson and M Whyte	Maybole	15. 8.08P
G-RWRW	Ultramagic M-77 Balloon (Hot Air)	77/221		11.11.02	Flying Pictures Ltd	Chilbolton, Stockbridge	
G-RWSS	Denney Kitfox Model 2 (Built R W Somerville)	PFA 172-12008		16. 4.91	R W Somerville (Under rebuild 2006?)	(Larne)	14. 6.93P
G-RXUK	Lindstrand LBL 105A Balloon (Hot Air)	232		29. 3.95	Zebedee Balloon Service Ltd	Newtown, Hungerford	22.10.08A
G-RYAL	Avtech Jabiru UL (Built A C Ryall - pr.no.PFA 274A-13365)	0212		6. 7.99	A C Ryall	Upfield Farm, Whitson, Llanwern	15. 8.08P
G-RYNS	Piper PA-32-301FT 6x	3232071	N30970	14. 9.07	D A Earle	Dunkeswell	17. 9.08E
G-RYPH	Mainair Blade 912	1248-0500-7-W1041		8. 6.00	I A Cunningham	Easter Poldar Farm, Thornhill	10. 4.08P
G-RYZZ	Robinson R44 Raven II	11418	N31448	15.11.06	Rivermead Aviation Ltd	Gloucestershire	11. 1.08E

G-SAAA - G-SZZZ

Reg	Type	C/n	Prev ID	Date	Owner/Operator	Base	Expiry
G-SAAA	Flight Design CTSW (Assembled P&M Aviation Ltd as c/n 8161)	05.12.09		17. 2.06	D J Collier t/a Sunfun Group	Lower Mountpleasant Farm, Chatteris	15. 7.08P
G-SAAB	Rockwell Commander 112TC	13002	G-BEFS N1502J	5.12.79	J B Barbour	(Rattray, Blairgowrie)	2. 4.08E
G-SAAM	Cessna T182R Turbo Skylane II	T18268200	G-TAGL G-SAAM, N2399E	23. 5.84	Sound Power Ltd	Perth	25.11.07E
G-SAAW	Boeing 737-8Q8	30619		16. 5.05	Globespan Airways Ltd t/a Flyglobespan.com	Edinburgh	11. 5.08E

Reg	Type	C/n	Prev id	Date	Owner/Operator	Base	Expiry
G-SABA	Piper PA-28R-201T Turbo Arrow III	28R-7703268	G-BFEN N38745	22. 8.79	C A Burton	Sherburn-in-Elmet	23. 5.08E
G-SABR	North American F-86A-5NA Sabre (Regd with c/n 151-083)	151-43547	N178 N68388, 48-178	6.11.91	Golden Apple Operations Ltd (As "8178:FU-178" in 4th Fighter Wing USAF c/s) (Operated The Old Flying Machine Company)	Duxford	20. 6.08P
G-SACB	Reims Cessna F152 II	F15201501	G-BFRB	7. 3.84	P Wilson	Liverpool	20. 5.08E
G-SACD	Cessna F172H (Built Reims Aviation SA)	F172-0385	G-AVCD	13. 6.83	Northbrook College (Sussex) (Noted as instructional airframe 11.05)	Shoreham	27. 7.00T
G-SACH	Stoddard-Hamilton GlaStar (Built R S Holt) (Tailwheel u/c)	PFA 295-13088		27. 8.99	R S Holt	Croft Farm, Defford	29.10.08P
G-SACI	Piper PA-28-161 Warrior II	28-8216123	N81535	26. 7.89	PJC (Leasing) Ltd	Stapleford	2. 5.08E
G-SACK	Robin R2160	316		2. 5.97	Sherburn Aero Club Ltd	Sherburn-in-Elmet	19. 6.08E
G-SACO	Piper PA-28-161 Warrior II	28-8416085	N4358Z	1. 6.89	Stapleford Flying Club Ltd	Stapleford	7. 9.08E
G-SACR	Piper PA-28-161 Cadet	2841046	N91618	6. 2.89	Sherburn Aero Club Ltd	Sherburn-in-Elmet	20. 2.08E
G-SACS	Piper PA-28-161 Cadet	2841047	N91619	6. 2.89	Sherburn Aero Club Ltd	Sherburn-in-Elmet	14. 3.08E
G-SACT	Piper PA-28-161 Cadet	2841048	N9162D	6. 2.89	Sherburn Aero Club Ltd	Sherburn-in-Elmet	25. 2.08E
G-SACX	Aero AT-3 R100	AT3-028		7.11.07	Sherburn Aero Club Ltd (Delivered 2.08)	Sherburn-in-Elmet	
G-SACY	Aero AT-3 R100	AT3-029		12.12.07	Sherburn Aero Club Ltd (Delivered 2.08)	Sherburn-in-Elmet	
G-SAFE	Cameron N-77 Balloon (Hot Air)	511		14. 2.79	P J Waller "The High Flyer" (Address change 9.07)	Wymondham	21. 4.91A
G-SAFI	Piel CP.1320 (Built C S Carleton-Smith)	PFA 183-12103		23. 7.01	C S Carleton-Smith	(Great Missenden)	
G-SAFR	SAAB 91D Safir	91-382	PH-RLR	10.10.95	Sylmar Aviation and Services Ltd (Lower Wasing Farm, Brimpton)		
G-SAGA	Grob G109B	6364	OE-9254	28. 6.90	G-GROB Ltd	Wycombe Air Park	16. 7.08E
G-SAGE	Luscombe 8A Silvaire (Continental A65)	2581	G-AKTL N71154, NC71154	15. 8.90	C D Howell	Higherlands Farm, Branscombe	9. 7.08P
G-SAHI	FLS Aerospace Sprint 160 (Lycoming O-235) (Built Trago Mills Ltd as type SAH-1)	001		21.10.80	M J A Trughill	RAF Henlow	13. 7.07P
G-SAIG	Robinson R44 Raven II	11364		4. 8.06	Torfield Aviation Ltd	Headcorn	21. 9.08E
G-SAIX	Cameron N-77 Balloon (Hot Air)	626	N386CB	14. 1.99	B Sevenich, Benedikt, S Harren and C Walther	Aachen and Bonn, Germany	21. 2.00A
G-SAJA	Schempp-Hirth Discus 2c	22	BGA 5243-KOB	22..1.07	J Arnold "KOB"	RAF Keevil	25. 1.08
G-SALA	Piper PA-32-300 Six	32-7940106	(G-BHEJ) N2184Z	17.10.79	Stonebold Ltd	White Waltham	16. 2.08E
G-SALE	Cameron Z-90 Balloon (Hot Air)	10944		15.12.06	R D Baker	Rowling, Goodnestone, Canterbury	18.12.07E
G-SALL	Reims Cessna F150L	F15000682	PH-LTY D-ECPH	19. 1.79	D and P A Hailey	Lower Wasing Farm, Brimpton	20. 9.08
G-SAMG	Grob G109B	6278		16. 5.84	T M Holloway tr RAF Gliding and Soaring Association	RAF Henlow	16. 4.08E
G-SAMJ	Partenavia P68B (C/n indicates P68 model)	101	D-GERA CS-AYB, D-GERA	27. 4.01	Ravenair Aircraft Ltd	Liverpool	26. 7.08E
G-SAMM	Cessna 340A II (RAM-conversion)	340A0742	N37TJ N2671A	7. 3.88	Calverton Flying Group Ltd	Coventry	12. 6.08E
G-SAMP	Agusta A109E Power	11673		30. 6.06	Bulbourne Insurance Services Ltd	Gamston	29. 6.08E
G-SAMY	Europa Aviation Europa (Built K R Tallent and P Vallis - pr.no.PFA 247-12901) (Tri-gear u/c)	221		17. 8.95	P Vallis (New owner 4.04)	(Alfreton)	
G-SAMZ	Cessna 150D	15060536	G-ASSO N4536U	19. 4.84	F A Bakir	Yew Tree Farm, Lymm Dam	12. 1.08E
G-SAOC	Schempp-Hirth Discus 2cT	54		29. 6.07	T M Holloway tr RAF Gliding and Soaring Association "R6" (Operated Chilterns Gliding Centre)	RAF Halton	4. 7.08
G-SAPM	SOCATA TB-20 Trinidad	1009	G-EWFN G-BRTY	8.12.04	G-SAPM Ltd	Filton	7. 4.08E
G-SARA	Piper PA-28-181 Archer II	28-7990039	N21270	6. 4.81	Apollo Aviation Advisory Ltd	Shoreham	23. 5.08E
G-SARB	Sikorsky S-92A	920045	N80562	18. 9.07	CHC Scotia Ltd (Operated HM Coastguard)	(Aberdeen)	18. 9.08E
G-SARC	Sikorsky S-92A	920052	N45168	30.11.07	CHC Scotia Ltd (Operated HM Coastguard)	(Aberdeen)	
G-SARD	Agusta AW139			4.08R	CHC Scotia Ltd (Operated Marine and Coastguard Agency)		
G-SARH	Piper PA-28-161 Warrior II	28-8216173	N8232Q	18. 2.91	Sussex Flying Club Ltd	Shoreham	18. 2.08E
G-SARM	Comco Ikarus C42 FB100	0504-6674		13. 5.05	S Birt tr G-SARM Group	Old Sarum	18. 5.08E
G-SARO	Saro Skeeter AOP.12	S2/5097	XL812	17. 7.78	B Chamberlain (Operated Historic Aircraft Flight as "XL812" in AAC c/s)	AAC Middle Wallop	30.10.06
G-SARV	Van's RV-4 (Built S N Aston) (Lycoming O-320)	PFA 181-12606		2.10.00	J E Singleton tr Hinton Flying Group	Hinton-in-the-Hedges	28. 5.08P
G-SASA	Eurocopter EC.135 T1	0147		12.10.00	Bond Air Services Ltd (Operated Scottish Air Ambulance)	Iverness	22.10.07E
G-SASB	Eurocopter EC.135 T2	0151		29. 9.00	Bond Air Services Ltd (Operated Scottish Air Ambulance)	Glasgow City Heliport	5.10.07E
G-SASC	Beech B200C Super King Air	BL-150	N6178D	30.12.05	Gama Aviation Ltd (Operated Scottish Air Ambulance)	Glasgow	4. 1.07E
G-SASD	Beech B200C Super King Air	BL-151	N6178F	4. 1.06	Gama Aviation Ltd (Operated Scottish Air Ambulance)	Aberdeen	29. 1.08E
G-SASG	Schleicher ASW 27-18E	29530		16.11.07	F B Jeynes	Bidford	
G-SASH	MD Helicopters MD.900 Explorer	900-00080	PH-SHF N7008Q	10. 6.05	Yorkshire Air Ambulance Ltd	Leeds-Bradford	21. 6.08E
G-SASI	CZAW Sportcruiser (Built F Sayyah and J C Simpson)	PFA 338-14651		9. 7.07	F Sayyah and J C Simpson	(Crawley)	
G-SATL	Cameron Sphere 105 SS Balloon (Hot Air)	2696		5.12.91	Ballonverbung Hamburg GmbH	Kiel, Germany	29. 4.97A

G-SATN	Piper PA-25-260 Pawnee C	25-5179	N8722L	10. 8.05	T M Holloway tr RAF Gliding and Soaring Association RAF Halton		
G-SAUF	Colt 90A Balloon (Hot Air)	1497		25. 5.89	K H Medau	Baden, Germany	21. 6.04A
	(New envelope c/n 2492 c1990/1)						
G-SAUK	Rans S-6-ES Coyote II	0904.1611		5. 1.05	M D Tulloch	Pittrichie Farm, Whiterashes	26. 4.07P
	(Built D A Smith and E Robshaw - pr.no.PFA 204-14346) (Tri-cycle u/c)						
G-SAWI	Piper PA-32RT-300T Turbo Lance II	32R-7887069	OY-CJJ N36719	23. 6.99	Regularity Ltd	Exeter	15. 6.08E
G-SAXC	Cameron N-105 Balloon (Hot Air)	3864	G-SAXO	6. 1.06	The Altitude Balloon Company Ltd	Thame	25. 5.00A
					(New owner 8.06)		
G-SAXN	Beech 200 Super King Air	BB-108	G-OMNH N108BM, RP-C1979, TR-LWC	23. 5.06	Saxonair Ltd	Norwich	20. 8.08E
G-SAXT	Schempp-Hirth Duo Discus xT	158	BGA 5242-KOA D-KIIH	15. 3.07	T M Holloway tr RAF Gliding and Soaring Association "KPH-26"	RAF Halton	13. 3.08
					(Operated Chilterns Gliding Centre)		
G-SAYS	Rotary Air Force RAF 2000 GTX-SE			4. 9.00	The Aziz Corporation Ltd (West Stratton, Winchester)		10. 7.07P
	(Built K Aziz)	PFA G/13-1322					
G-SAZY	Avtech Jabiru J400	0xxx		16. 4.03	J E Howe	Henstridge	12. 2.08P
	(Built N J Bond - pr.no.PFA 325-14057)						
G-SAZZ	Piel CP.328 Super Emeraude	PFA 216-11940		4. 7.01	D J Long	Gloucestershire	11.12.08P
	(Built D J Long)						
G-SBAE	Reims Cessna F172P Skyhawk II	F17202200	D-EOCD (3)	3. 6.98	BAE Systems (Operations) Ltd	Blackpool	7. 8.08E
G-SBHH	Schweizer 269C	S 1314	G-XALP N41S	7. 5.02	C S, H C S and J W Padield t/a S and J Padfield and Partners	(Great Warley, Brentwood)	13. 5.08E
	(Schweizer 300)						
G-SBIZ	Cameron Z-90 Balloon (Hot Air)	10348		12.12.02	Snow Business International Ltd	Stroud	8. 6.08A
					(Snow Business titles)		
G-SBKR	SOCATA TB-10 Tobago	1077	D-EAGG	10. 3.04	S C M Bagley	Duxford	29. 4.08E
G-SBKS	Cessna 206H Stationair	20608290	N22188	21. 6.07	Alard Properties Ltd	Sleap	1. 7.08E
G-SBLT	Steen Skybolt	MH-01		14. 4.92	S D Arnold tr Skybolt Group	(Coventry)	
	(Built M A McCallum and N Workman)						
G-SBMM	Piper PA-28R-180 Cherokee Arrow	28R-30877	G-BBEL SE-FDX	8. 2.02	K S Kalsi	Cambridge	18. 6.08E
G-SBMO	Robin R2160i	116	EI-BMO SE-GSZ	12. 2.99	D Henderson, U Simpson and M Mannion Weston, Leixlip, County Kildare		24. 3.06T
G-SBOL	Steen Skybolt	PFA 064-14453		6.12.07	K R H Wingate	Halwell	
	(Built K R H Wingate)						
G-SBRA	Robinson R44 Raven II	10233		17.12.03	Airpoint Aviation Ltd	(Dublin)	18. 3.08T
G-SBRK	Aero AT-3 R100	AT3-021	(F-GURH)	14. 3.07	Sywell Aerodrome Ltd	Sywell	26. 4.08P
G-SBUS	Britten-Norman BN-2A-26 Islander	3013	G-BMMH RP-C578	31.10.86	Isles of Scilly Skybus Ltd	St Just	17. 4.08E
	(Built PADC)						
G-SBUT	Robinson R22 Beta II	2739	G-BXMT	18. 5.98	Fast Helicopters Ltd	Shoreham	29. 1.08T
G-SCAN	Vinten Wallis WA-116 Series 100/R	001		5. 7.82	K H Wallis	Reymerston Hall, Norfolk	14. 2.06P
	(Rotax 532)						
G-SCBI	SOCATA TB-20 Trinidad	1908	F-OIGV	10. 8.99	S C Brown t/a Ace Services	Enstone	17. 8.08E
G-SCFO	Cameron O-77 Balloon (Hot Air)	1131		3. 5.85	M K Grigson	Petworth	24. 5.95A
					"Southern Counties" (Operated Balloon Preservation Group)		
G-SCHI	Eurocopter AS.350B2 Ecureuil	3337	F-WQOQ	5. 2.01	Patriot Aviation Ltd	Cranfield	6. 4.08E
G-SCHO	Robinson R22 Beta	3833		3. 5.05	Blades Aviation (UK) LLP	East Midlands	23. 5.08E
G-SCII	Agusta A109C	7628	G-JONA VP-CWA, JA6610	18. 8.06	C and M Coldstores (Carrickmacross, County Monaghan)		6. 4.08E
G-SCIP	SOCATA TB-20 Trinidad GT	2014	F-OILO	19. 9.00	The Studio People Ltd	Welshpool	17.10.07E
G-SCLX	FLS Aerospace Sprint 160	002	G-PLYM	14. 7.94	E J F McEntee	Kirdford	25. 4.08E
	(Marketed by British Light Aircraft Company as "Redwing 160")						
G-SCNN	Schempp-Hirth Standard Cirrus	173	BGA 1677-CNN	22.12.07	G C Short	Keiheuvel, Belgium	13. 4.08
G-SCOI	Agusta A109E Power	11051	G-HPWH G-HWPH	16. 8.02	Trustair Ltd	Euxton, Chorley	23. 6.08E
G-SCOL	Gippsland GA-8 Airvan	GA8-05-088	VH-FNG	28. 3.06	Sunderland Parachute Centre Ltd Shotton Colliery, Peterlee		4. 5.08E
G-SCPD	Reality Escapade 912(1)	JAESC 0015		30. 1.04	R W L Breckell	Ince Blundell	23.10.08P
	(Built R Gibson - pr.no.BMAA/HB/319)						
G-SCPL	Piper PA-28-140 Cherokee Cruiser	28-7725160	G-BPVL N1785H	4. 5.89	Aeros Leasing Ltd	Gloucestershire	23. 9.07T
G-SCRZ	CZAW Sportcruiser	PFA 338-14684		29. 8.07	P M Grant	(Horncastle)	
	(Built P M Grant)						
G-SCTA	Westland Scout AH.1	F9701	XV126	18.12.95	G R Harrison	(Guildford)	26. 4.08P
G-SCUB	Piper PA-18-135 Super Cub	18-3847	PH-GAX R Neth AF R-157, 54-2447	13.12.78	M E Needham	Old Manor Farm, Anwick	31. 5.10S
	(L-21B-PI) (Frame No.18-3849)				*(As "54-2447" in US Army c/s)*		
	(Collided with power cables landing Old Manor Farm, Alnwick 6.10.07, struck the ground and extensively damaged)						
G-SCUD	Montgomerie-Bensen B 8MR	PFA G/101-1294		18. 8.97	D Taylor	(Fritchley, Belper)	
	(Built D Taylor)						
G-SCUL	Rutan Cozy	PFA 159-13212		28. 5.98	K R W Scull	(Trostrey, Usk)	
	(Built K R W Scull)						
G-SDAT	Flight Design CTSW	07.03.21		23. 7.07	A R Wade	Damyn's Hall, Upminster	22. 7.08P
	(Assembled P&M Aviation Ltd with c/n 8312)						
G-SDCI	Bell 206B-2 JetRanger II	925	G-GHCL G-SHVV, N72GM, N83106	24. 2.00	S D Coomes	(Auldhouse, East Kilbride)	29. 6.08E
G-SDCT	Agusta A109E Power	11045	VP-BIL G-SOHI	14. 5.07	Church Island Aviation Ltd	(Toomebridge, Antrim)	13. 5.08E
G-SDEV	de Havilland DH.104 Sea Devon C 20	04472	XK895	29. 3.90	Aviation Heritage Ltd	Coventry	17. 9.01
					(As "XK895:CU-19" in RN 771 Sqdn c/s) (New owner 6.05)		
G-SDFM	Evektor EV-97 Eurostar	PFA 315-13884		23. 8.02	M J Miles tr G-SDFM Eurostar Group Priory Farm, Tibenham		28. 2.08P
	(Built A K Paterson)						
G-SDLW	Cameron O-105 Balloon (Hot Air)	2460		11. 3.91	S P Watkins *(New owner 9.05)*	Bristol	4. 6.05A
G-SDOB	Tecnam P2002-EA Sierra	PFA 333-14529		26. 4.06	S P S Dornan	Kirknewton	15. 2.08P
	(Built G E Collard and S P S Dornan)						

G-SDOI	Aeroprakt A22 Foxbat	PFA 317-14064		26. 6.03	S A Owen	Kirknewton	22. 8.07P
	(Built S P S Dornan)						
G-SDOZ	Tecnam P92-EA Echo-Super	PFA 318A-14287		9. 9.04	D M Stewart tr Cumbernauld Flyers G-SDOZ		
	(Built S P S Dornan)					Cumbernauld	1. 5.08P
G-SEAI	Cessna U206G Stationair II	U20604059	N756FQ	20. 3.92	K O'Connor	Weston, Leixlip, County Kildare	12. 6.08T
	(Amphibian)						
G-SEAJ	Cessna 525 CitationJet	525-0113	N111AM	13. 2.08	CJ 525 Ltd	Bristol	
			N5214K				
G-SEAT	Colt 42A Balloon (Hot Air)	817		28. 5.86	D G Such and M Tomlin	Barkway, Royston	7. 4.95A
					(New owners 2.08)		
G-SEBY	Ultramagic M-105 Balloon (Hot Air)	105/144		19. 3.07	Prestige Milano Group SRL	Ferrara, Italy	3. 6.08A
G-SEDO	Cameron N-105 Balloon (Hot Air)	10388		28. 3.03	Wye Valley Aviation Ltd	Bridstowm Ross-on-Wye	10. 6.08A
					(New owner 7.07)		
G-SEED	Piper J-3C-90 Cub (L-4H-PI)	11098	EI-BAP	28. 1.80	J H Seed	Black Spring Farm, Castle Bytham	15. 8.08P
	(Frame No.10932)		F-BFBZ, 44-80203, 43-29807				
	(Official identity is c/n 12499/44-80203 and probably rebuilt 1945)						
G-SEEE	P&M Quik GT450	8235		22. 1.07	R Meredith-Hardy	(Baldock)	28. 1.08P
G-SEEK	Cessna T210N Turbo Centurion II	21064579	N9721Y	14.10.83	A Hopper	Little Shelford	22. 3.08E
G-SEFC	Boeing 737-7Q8	30687	N1787B	1. 5.07	Globespan Airways Ltd t/a Flyglobespan.com		
						Glasgow	1. 5.08E
G-SEFI	Robinson R44 Raven II	10147	N75271	2.10.03	Kermann Avionics Sales Ltd (Noted 4.07)	Denham	27.11.06T
G-SEGA	Cameron Sonic 90 SS Balloon (Hot Air)	2896		16. 9.92	A D Kent tr Balloon Preservation Flying Group		
	(Sonic The Hedgehog shape)				"Sonic" (New owner 6.04)	Petworth	29. 6.00A
G-SEIL	Pilatus Britten-Norman BN-2B-26 Islander	2103	G-BIIP	7.12.07	Highland Airways Ltd	North Connel, Oban	26. 3.08E
			6Y-JQJ, 6Y-JKJ, N411JA, G-BIIP				
G-SEJW	Piper PA-28-161 Cherokee Warrior II		N9557N	19. 4.78	Keen Leasing Ltd	Perth	18. 6.08E
		28-7816469					
G-SELC	Diamond DA.42 Twin Star	42.032		30. 6.05	Stapleford Flying Club Ltd	Stapleford	20. 7.08E
G-SELF	Europa Aviation Europa	279		10. 8.01	N D Crisp, A H Lames and E J Hatcher	Rochester	18. 3.08P
	(Built N D Crisp, A H Lames and E J Hatcher - pr.no.PFA 247-12996) (Jabiru 3300) (Monowheel u/c)						
G-SELL	Robin DR.400-180 Régent	1153	D-EEMT	7. 3.85	J A Warters	Kirkbride	15. 2.08E
G-SELX	Pilatus Britten-Norman BN-2T Turbine Islander		G-BJEC	2.06.06	Fly BN Ltd	Bembridge	1.11.07E
	(Originally regd as a BN-2B)	2118	UAE AF 318, UAE AF 411, G-BJEC				
G-SELY	Agusta-Bell 206B-3 JetRanger III	8740		26. 7.96	CT Rental Ltd	Cumbernauld	15. 9.08E
G-SEMI	Piper PA-44-180 Seminole	44-7995052	G-DENW	23. 2.99	M Djukic and J Benfell	Halfpenny Green	23. 3.08E
			N21439		"Lady Gabriella II"		
G-SEMR	Cessna T206H Turbo Stationair	T20608669	N11347	6. 2.07	Semer LLP	Poplar Hall Farm, Elmsett	10. 2.08E
G-SENA	Rutan LongEz	1325	F-PZSQ	11.11.96	G Bennett	(Caister-on-Sea, Great Yarmouth)	
	(Built R Bazin)		F-WZSQ				
G-SEND	Colt 90A Balloon (Hot Air)	2100		2.12.91	Air du Vent (New owner 12.06)	Paris, France	27. 7.08T
G-SENE	Piper PA-34-200T Seneca II	34-8170069	N797WA	20.11.03	M O'Hara	Halfpenny Green	26.11.06T
			N8314P		(Noted 10..07) (centralaviation.co.uk titles)		
G-SENX	Piper PA-34-200T Seneca II	34-7870356	G-DARE	15. 5.95	First Air Ltd	Cardiff	15. 7.07T
			G-WOTS, G-SEVL, N36742				
G-SEPA	Eurocopter AS.355N Ecureuil 2	5525	G-METD	25. 7.96	Metropolitan Police Authority		
			G-BUJF, F-WYMF			Lippitts Hill Camp, Chingford	1. 9.08S
G-SEPB	Eurocopter AS.355N Ecureuil 2	5574	G-BVSE	1. 2.95	Metropolitan Police Authority		
						Lippitts Hill Camp, Chingford	14. 5.08E
G-SEPC	Eurocopter AS.355N Ecureuil 2	5596	G-BWGV	29.11.95	Metropolitan Police Authority		
						Lippitts Hill Camp, Chingford	22. 3.08T
G-SEPT	Cameron N-105 Balloon (Hot Air)	1880		22.11.88	P Gooch	Alresford	26. 8.07A
					(Septodont - Dentist`s Supplies titles)		
G-SERC	Beech B300 Super King Air	FL-438	N61638	22. 6.05	Bridgtown Plant Ltd	Gamston	20. 7.08E
G-SERE	Diamond DA.42 Twin Star	42.314		19.12.07	Diamond Aircraft UK Ltd	Belfast International	
					(Noted 2.08)		
G-SERL	SOCATA TB-10 Tobago	109	G-LANA	28. 5.92	R J Searle	Rochester	10. 7.08E
			EI-BIH				
G-SERV	Cameron N-105 Balloon (Hot Air)	10382		16. 4.03	PSH Skypower Ltd	Woodborough, Pewsey	28. 2.07A
					(Servo Connectors titles)		
G-SETI	Cameron Sky 80-16 Balloon (Hot Air)	4853		25. 9.00	R P Allan	Aston Rowant, Watlington	30. 6.08A
G-SEVA	Replica Plans SE.5a	PFA 020-10955		19. 6.85	I D Gregory	Boscombe Down	1. 1.08P
	(Built I D Gregory) (Continental C90)				(As "F-141:G" in RFC 141 Sqdn c/s)		
G-SEVE	Cessna 172N Skyhawk II	17269970	N738GR	10. 1.90	MK Aero Support Ltd	Netherthorpe	15. 6.08E
					(Operated Sheffield Aero Club)		
G-SEVN	Van's RV-7	PFA 323-13795		13. 9.01	N Reddish	Netherthorpe	28. 8.08P
	(Built N Reddish)						
G-SEWP	Aérospatiale AS.355F2 Ecureuil 2	5480	G-OFIN	14. 8.00	Veritair Ltd	Cardiff Heliport	14. 6.08T
			G-DANS, G-BTNM		(Operated South East Wales Police)		
G-SEXE	Scheibe SF25C-2000 Falke	44396	N716SF	31. 7.03	Repulor Ltd	Sleap	13. 3.08T
	(Limbach L 2000)		(D-KNII)				
G-SEXI	Cessna 172M Skyhawk II	17263806	N1964V	21. 4.92	Willowair Flying Club (1996) Ltd	(Southend)	5. 9.04T
					(Bounced landing Nayland 2. 02 and overran, struck hedge and substantially damaged)		
G-SEXX	Piper PA-28-161 Cherokee Warrior II		SE-GVD	12.05.03	Weald Air Services Ltd	Headcorn	1. 6.08E
		28-7816196					
G-SFAR	Comco Ikarus C42 FB100	0704-6883		27. 3.07	S Farrow	Barton	21. 5.08P
G-SFCJ	Cessna 525 CitationJet	525-0245	N33CJ	21. 7.04	Sureflight Aviation Ltd	Oxford	30. 7.08E
			N5124J				
G-SFLA	Comco Ikarus C42 FB80	0701-6867		15. 6.07	Solent Flight Ltd	Phoenix Farm, Lower Upham	17. 6.08P
G-SFLB	Comco Ikarus C42 FB80	0709-6914		13.11.07	Solent Flight Ltd	Phoenix Farm, Lower Upham	12.11.08P
G-SFLY	Diamond DA.40 Star	40362		31. 3.04	L and Nathalie.P L Turner	Sleap	1. 7.08E
G-SFOX	RotorWay Executive 90	5059	G-BUAH	11.10.93	Magpie Technology Ltd Crabtree Farm, Crowborough		19.12.07P
	(Built I L Griffith) (RotorWay RI 162)						
G-SFPA	Reims Cessna F406 Caravan II	F406-0064		11.11.91	Secretary of State for Scotland per Dept of Agriculture and Fisheries		
					(Operated Highland Airways for Scottish Fisheries Protection Agency)	Inverness	25. 2.08E

G-SFPB	Reims Cessna F406 Caravan II	F406-0065		11.11.91	Secretary of State for Scotland per Dept of Agriculture and Fisheries	Inverness	26. 4.08E
					(Operated Highland Airways for Scottish Fisheries Protection Agency)		
G-SFRY	Thunder Ax7-77 Balloon (Hot Air)	1667		23. 1.90	M Rowlands	Wigan	8. 9.08A
G-SFSL	Cameron Z-105 Balloon (Hot Air)	10308		31. 7.02	B A Benjamin tr Somerfield Staff Lottery Fund	Bristol	20. 2.07T
					(Somerfield Supermarkets titles)		
G-SFTZ	Slingsby T 67M-160 Firefly	2000		7. 2.83	Western Air (Thruxton) Ltd	Thruxton	7. 3.08E
G-SGEC	Beech B200 Super King Air	BB-1747	N214FW	19. 8.03	Keypoint Aviation LLP	Gamston	26. 8.08E
G-SGEN	Comco Ikarus C42 FB80	0407-6611		27. 8.04	G A Arturi	Old Sarum	10. 1.08P
G-SGSE	Piper PA-28-181 Cherokee Archer II		G-BOJX	2.12.96	U Patel	Barton	7. 6.08E
		28-7890332	N3774M				
G-SHAA	Enstrom 280C-UK Shark	1011	N280Q	8. 7.88	C J and D Whitehead t/a ELT Radio Telephones		
						(Read, Burnley)	8.11.07E
G-SHAF	Robinson R44 Raven II	10892		20.10.05	Tresillian Leisure Ltd	Denham	10.11.08E
G-SHAK	Cameron Cabin SS Balloon (Hot Air)	2820	SE-ZHO	23. 8.07	Magical Adventures Ltd	Oswestry	23. 5.97A
			G-ODIS				
G-SHAN	Robinson R44 Clipper II	10617		28. 1.05	Interguide Investment Holdings Ltd		
						(Damyn's Hall, Upminster)	3. 3.08E
G-SHAR	Cessna 182T Skylane	18281636	N1968L	11.11.05	S Harding	Denham	4.12.07E
G-SHAY	Piper PA-28R-201T Turbo Arrow III		G-JEFS	17. 9.01	R Rudderham tr Alpha Yankee	Earls Colne	27.10.07E
		28R-7703365	G-BFDG, N47381				
G-SHED	Piper PA-28-181 Cherokee Archer II		G-BRAU	12. 6.89	D R Allard tr G-SHED Flying Group	Gloucestershire	28. 6.08
		28-7890068	N47411				
G-SHEE	P&M Quik GT450	8284		31. 7.07	L Cottle	Baxby Manor, Husthwaite	12. 8.08P
G-SHEZ	Mainair Sports Pegasus Quik	7993		28.10.03	C Surman	(Cranleigh)	8.11.08P
G-SHIM	CFM Streak Shadow	K 228-SA		19. 5.93	J A Weston	Shobdon	12.11.07P
	(Built E G Shimmin - pr.no.PFA 206-12501) (Rotax 582)						
G-SHMI	Evektor EV-97 teamEurostar UK	3013		3.10.07	Poet Pilot (UK) Ltd	Gloucestershire	2.10.08P
					(Operated Skytime Flight Training)		
G-SHMS	Agusta Bell 206B-2 JetRanger II	8739	EI-GWT	29.10.07	S H Moore and Sons Ltd	(Pomeroy, Dungannon)	2. 8.08E
			G-CORT				
G-SHOG	Colomban MC-15 Cri-Cri	001	G-PFAB	3.10.96	C R Thompson	Popham	31. 3.08P
	(Built G Nappez) (JPX PUL-212)		F-PYPU				
G-SHPP	Hughes 269A (TH-55A)	36-0481	N80559	24. 7.89	Helirouge Ltd	(Newcastle)	23. 4.08T
	(Hughes 300)		64-18169				
G-SHRK	Enstrom 280C-UK Shark	1173	N373SA	6. 1.97	Flighthire Ltd	Henstridge	27. 6.08E
			G-SHRK, G-BGMX, EI-CCS, G-SHXX, G-BGMX, EI-BHR, G-BGMX, (F-GBOS)				
G-SHRT	Robinson R44 Raven II	10473		14. 9.04	Overby Ltd	(Ascot)	16. 9.07T
G-SHSH	Europa Aviation Europa	113		7. 4.98	S G Hayman and J Price	(Sevenoaks)	8. 8.08P
	(Built D G Hillam - pr.no.PFA 247-12722) (Monowheel u/c)						
G-SHSP	Cessna 172S Skyhawk SP	172S8079	N6535P	25. 3.99	Shropshire Aero Club Ltd	Sleap	27. 4.08E
			N9552Q				
G-SHUF	Mainair Blade	1241-0200-7-W1034		10. 3.00	R G Bradley	(Newton Bank Farm, Daresbury)	27. 3.07P
	(Rotax 582)						
G-SHUG	Piper PA-28R-201T Turbo Arrow III		N1026Q	17. 5.88	G-SHUG Ltd	Wycombe Air Park	10. 7.08E
G-SHUU	Enstrom 280C-UK-2 Shark	1221	G-OMCP	16.10.89	D Ellis	Hawarden	11.12.07E
			G-KENY, G-BJFG, N8617N				
G-SHUV	Aerosport Woody Pusher	PFA 007A-13960		20. 9.02	J R Wraight	(Chatham)	
	(Built J R Wraight)						
G-SHWK	Cessna 172S Skyhawk	172S9642	N21733	2. 6.04	The Cambridge Aero Club Ltd	Cambridge	19. 6.08E
G-SIAI	SIAI-Marchetti SF.260W	361/31-005	F-GVAB (2)	15. 1.01	D Gage	Wycombe Air Park	29. 3.08P
			OO-XCP, FAB-184		*(As "FAB-184" in Bolivian AF c/s)*		
G-SIAL	Hawker Hunter F 58	41H-697457	Swiss AF J-4090	2.10.95	Classic Aviation Ltd	Exeter	21. 3.01P
					(Fuselage noted as "J-4090" 7.06)		
G-SIAM	Cameron V-90 Balloon (Hot Air)	4096	G-BXBS	7. 3.01	M V Farrant	(Loxwood, Billingshurst)	24. 7.07A
G-SICA	Britten-Norman BN-2B-20 Islander	2304	G-SLAP	19. 7.06	Shetland Leasing and Property Development Ltd		
						Tingwall	17.12.07E
G-SICB	Pilatus Britten-Norman BN-2B-20 Islander	2260	G-NESU	12. 6.06	Shetland Islands Council	Tingwall	3. 4.08E
			G-BTVN		*(www.shetland.gov.uk titles)*		
G-SIGN	Piper PA-39 Twin Comanche C/R	39-8	OY-TOO	9. 2.78	D Buttle	Blackbushe	18. 5.08
			N8853Y				
G-SIIB	Pitts S-2B	5218	G-BUVY	24. 3.93	M Zikes	(Prague, Czech Republic)	30. 4.08E
	(Built Aviat Inc) (Lycoming AEIO-540)		N6073U		*(Noted damaged Oloumuc, Czech Republic 9.07)*		
G-SIID	Sukhoi Su-26M2	01-04	RA-44531	17.11.03	R N Goode	Bggin Hill	31. 5.08P
			PK-SDM		*(Honda titles)*		
G-SIIE	Pitts S-2B	5057	G-SKYD	6. 2.04	J and T J Bennett	(Hareby, Spilsby)	17. 6.08E
	(Built Christen Industries Inc) (Lycoming AEIO-540)		N5331N				
G-SIII	Extra EA.300	058	D-ETYE	10. 1.95	Fun Flight Ltd	White Waltham	21.12.07E
					(Fun Flight titles) "61"		
G-SIIS	Pitts S-1S	PFA 009-13485	G-RIPE	3. 7.02	I H Searson	Leicester	12.11.08P
	(Built J A Harris)						
G-SIJJ	North American P-51D-20-NA Mustang	122-31894	F-AZMU	20.03.03	P A Teichman "Jumpin' Jacques"	North Weald	15. 7.08P
			N5306M, HK-2812P, HK-2812X, N5411V, 44-72035		*(As "472035" in USAF c/s)*		
G-SIJW	Scottish Aviation Bulldog Series 120/121		XX630	31. 3.00	M Miles	Shenington	15. 3.08S
		BH120/295			*(As "XX630:25" in RAF c/s)*		
G-SILC	Boeing 767-204	24736	G-BRIF	14. 9.07	Flyjet Ltd	Luton	18.11.07E
			(PH-AHM), G-BRIF		*(Operated Silverjet)*		
G-SILS	Pietenpol AirCamper	PFA 047-13331		29. 6.98	D Silsbury	Dunkeswell	
	(Built D Silsbury -single-seat version of Aircamper designated Pietenpol Skyscout) (On build 3.07)						
G-SILY	Pegasus Quantum 15	8074		17.12.04	J I Smith	St Michaels	15. 1.08P
G-SIMI	Cameron A-315 Balloon (Hot Air)	3391		10. 3.95	Balloon School (International) Ltd t/a Balloon Safaris		
						Colhook Common, Petworth	11. 7.08T
G-SIMM	Comco Ikarus C42 FB100 VLA	PFA 322-14286		6. 9.04	D Simmons	(Newmarket)	21. 9.07P
	(Built D Simmons)						
G-SIMP	Avtech Jabiru UL-450	xxxx		4. 1.02	E Bentley	Morgansfield, Fishburn	15. 2.08P
	(Built J C Simpson - pr.no.PFA 274B-13794)						

Reg	Type	C/n	Prev id	Date	Owner/Operator	Location	Date2
G-SIMS	Robinson R22 Beta	1596	N7800R LV-RBZ	14. 6.04	HS (Holdings) Ltd t/a Heli-One	Durham Tees Valley	24. 7.08E
G-SIMY	Piper PA-32-300 Cherokee Six	32-7640082	G-OCPF G-BOCH, N9292K	22. 3.04	I Simpson	Kirkbride	26. 9.08E
G-SINK	Schleicher ASH 25	25139	BGA 5009-KDM F-CHAY	17. 9.07	A F W Watson tr G-SINK Group	Cranwell	25. 3.08
G-SIPA	SIPA 903	63	G-BGBM F-BGBM	31. 5.83	A C Leak and J H Dilland *(On restoration 2007)*	(Southampton)	14. 2.89P
G-SIRA	Embraer EMB-135BJ Legacy	14500832	OE-IAS (N832SG), PT-SIL	19.10.05	Amsair Aircraft Ltd	London Stansted	27.10.07E
G-SIRD	Robinson R44 Raven II	11745		21. 5.07	Peglington Productions Ltd	Wycombe Air Park	31. 5.08E
G-SIRE	Best Off Sky Ranger Swift 912S(1) SKRxxxx740 *(Built P Rigby- pr.no.BMAA/HB/531)*			26. 3.07	P Rigby	Flint Farm, Norfolk	18.12.08P
G-SIRO	Dassault Falcon 900EX	172	F-WWFL	16. 5.07	Condor Aviation LLP	Leeds-Bradford	16. 5.08E
G-SIRS	Cessna 560XL Citation Excel	560-5185	N51042	1. 8.01	London Executive Aviation Ltd	London Stansted	1. 8.08E
G-SISI	Schempp-Hirth Duo Discus	193	BGA 5002-KDE PH-1141	17. 8.07	R N John tr Glider Sierra India	Dunstable	19.11.07
G-SISU	P&M Quik GT450	6215		29. 8.06	Executive and Business Aviation Support Ltd	Oxford	28. 8.07P
G-SITA	Pegasus Quantum 15-912	7797		18. 6.01	A D Curtin	Newnham, Baldock	15. 6.08P
G-SIVJ	Westland SA.341C Gazelle HT.2	2012	G-CBSG	26. 6.02	Skytrace (UK) Ltd	Halfpenny Green	11. 3.08P
G-SIVN	MD Helicopters MD.500N Notar	LN089	N9RU G-SIVN, (HB-ZBS), (XA-), N3234D	2.11.04	Cumbrian Seafoods Ltd	(Hexham)	17. 2.08E
G-SIVR	MD Helicopters MD.900 Explorer	900-00102	N7002S	20. 8.02	Mandarin Aviation Ltd	Redhill	5. 9.08E
G-SIVW	Lake LA-250 Renegade *(Built Aerofab Inc)*	233	N8553T	6. 2.03	C J Siva-Jothy	Redhill	24. 5.08E
G-SIXC	Douglas DC-6B	45550	N93459 N90645, B-1006, XW-PFZ, B-1006 *(Atlantic c/s with Air Atlantique titles) (New owner 7.07)*	20. 3.87	Air Atlantique Ltd	Coventry	4. 4.05T
G-SIXD	Piper PA-32-300 Cherokee Six D	32-7140007	HB-OMH N8615N	25. 3.98	M B Payne and I Gordon	King's Farm, Thurrock	28.12.07E
G-SIXS	Whittaker MW6-S Fatboy Flyer	PFA 164-12521		27. 8.03	P E Young *(Address change 11.07)*	Peat Inn, Cupar	
	(Built R H Braithwaite)						
G-SIXT	Piper PA-28-161 Warrior II	2816056	G-BSSX N9141H	22. 2.08	Airways Aero Associations Ltd *(Operated British Airways Flying Club) (Union Flag c/s)*	Wycombe Air Park	14.11.07E
G-SIXX	Colt 77A Balloon (Hot Air)	1327		21.10.88	M Dear and M Taylor	Marlow and Aylesbury	19. 4.08A
G-SIXY	Van's RV-6 *(Built C J Hall and C R P Hamlett)*	PFA 181-13368		9. 3.99	C J Hall and C R P Hamlett	(Cambridge)	
G-SIZZ	Avtech Jabiru J400 *(Built K J Betterley - pr.no.PFA 325-14483)*	0xxx		13. 2. 06	K J Betterley	(Shanklin, Isle of Wight)	16. 4.08P
G-SJCH	Pilatus Britten-Norman BN-2T-4S Islander	4006	G-BWPK	18.11.99	Hampshire Police Authority *"Sir John Charles Hoddinott"*	Lee-on-Solent	26. 2.08E
G-SJEN	Comco Ikarus C42 FB80 *(Built M C Henry)*	0405-6602		1. 7.04	C M Mackinnon	Strathaven	2. 4.08P
G-SJES	Evektor EV-97 teamEurostar UK	2918		15. 6.07	Purple Aviation Ltd	Eshott	14. 6.08P
G-SJET	Boeing 767-216ER	23624	G-FJEC N769BC, TJ-AAC, N769BC, 5R-MFE, N151LF, PT-TAH, CC-CJV, N4528Y, (N4529T)	29.11.06	Flyjet Ltd *(Silverjet c/s) "Silver Spirit"*	Luton	11. 4.08E
G-SJKR	Lindstrand LBL 90A Balloon (Hot Air)	756		26. 1.01	S J Roake *"Smarthouse"*	Frimley, Camberley	22. 8.07A
G-SKAN	Reims Cessna F172M Skyhawk II	F17201120	G-BFKT F-BVBJ	8. 7.85	J Williams and M Richardson	Boscombe Down	16. 4.08T
G-SKCI	Rutan VariEze *(Built S K Cockburn)*	PFA 074-12081		30. 3.01	A Levitt *(New owner 1.07)*	(Blackshaw Edge, Hebden Bridge)	
G-SKEW	Mudry CAP.232	11	F-GXRB F-GRRG, F-GKCK, French Army	28.11.03	J H Askew	Wickenby	15. 2.08E
G-SKIE	Steen Skybolt *(Built D Axe)*	AACA-357	ZK-DEN	29. 8.97	P G Kavanagh	Barton	25. 3.08P
G-SKII	Agusta-Bell 206B-3 JetRanger III	8562	EI-BKT D-HAFD, HB-XIC	22. 4.03	K Toner t/a K P Toner (Developments)	(Milford, Armagh)	13. 5.08E
G-SKKY	Cessna 172S Skyhawk	172S9850	N14897	30. 6.05	Skyquest Ltd	White Waltham	1. 8.08E
G-SKNT	Pitts S-2A *(Built Aerotek Inc)*	2048	G-PEAL N81LF, N48KA	31. 3.03	T G Lloyd *(On rebuild 3.07)*	Oaksey Park	21. 2.92T
G-SKOT	Cameron V-42 Balloon (Hot Air)	4813		27. 6.00	S A Laing	Banchory	20. 9.08A
G-SKPG	Best Off Sky Ranger 912(2) *(Built P Gibbs - pr.no.BMAA/HB/400)*	SKRxxxx483		11.11.04	P Gibbs	Plaistows Farm, St Albans	13.12.08P
G-SKPH	Yakovlev Yak-50	853010	G-BWWH LY-ABL, LY-XNI, DOSAAF	15. 3.05	R S Partridge-Hicks and I C Austin *(As "853010")* Little Haugh Hall, Norton,. Bury St Edmunds		9. 1.09P
G-SKRA	Best Off Sky Ranger 912(2) *(Built P A Banks- pr.no.BMAA/HB/458)*	SKR0504599		21.11.05	P A Banks	Finmere	10. 7.08P
G-SKRG	Best Off Sky Ranger 912(2) *(Built R W Goddin - pr.no.BMAA/HB/298)*	SKR0307352		2. 9.03	R W Goddin	Longacres Farm, Sandy	13.12.08P
G-SKSW	Best Off Sky Ranger Swift 912S(1) SKRxxxx804 *(Built M D and S M North - pr.no.BMAA/HB/553)*			3.10.07	M D and S M North	(Milton Keynes)	
G-SKUA	Stoddard-Hamilton GlaStar *(Built L A James) (Tri-cycle u/c)*	PFA 295-13241	G-LEZZ	30. 8.07	F P Smiddy	Rochester	27. 7.08P
G-SKYC	Slingsby T 67M Firefly	2009	G-BLDP	13. 6.97	T W Cassells *(Noted 2.08)*	Bagby	26.10.07E
G-SKYE	Cessna TU206G Turbo Stationair 6 II	U20604568	(G-DROP) N9783M	1. 8.79	S M C Harvey	Hinton-in-the-Hedges	19. 8.07
G-SKYF	SOCATA TB-10 Tobago	1589	VH-YHG	1. 5.01	W L McNeil	Oxford	21. 6.08E
G-SKYJ	Cameron Z-315 Balloon (Hot Air)	10964		14. 6.07	Cameron Flights Southern Ltd	Woodborough, Pewsey	17. 6.08E
G-SKYK	Cameron A-275 Balloon (Hot Air)	4879		31. 7.00	Cameron Flights Southern Ltd *(Cameron Balloons titles)*	Woodborough, Pewsey	22. 2.08T
G-SKYL	Cessna 182S Skylane	18280176	N4104D	19. 6.98	Skylane Aviation Ltd	Sherburn-in-Elmet	19. 9.08E
G-SKYN	Aérospatiale AS.355F1 Ecureuil 2	5185	G-OGRK G-BWZC, (G-MOBZ), N107KF, N5799R *(Operated Sky News)*	21.11.03	Arena Aviation Ltd	Redhill	24. 4.08T

Reg	Type	C/n	Prev ID	Date	Owner/Operator	Base	Date
G-SKYO	Slingsby T 67M-200 Firefly	2264		20. 9.00	R H Evelyn	White Waltham	26. 2.08E
G-SKYR	Cameron A-180 Balloon (Hot Air)	2826		31. 3.92	Cameron Flights Southern Ltd		
					"Candy Floss"	Woodborough, Pewsey	29. 4.00T
G-SKYT	III Sky Arrow 650 TC	C004		6. 9.96	W M Bell and S J Brooks	Bicester	11. 6.08
	(Built Iniziative Industriali Italian)						
G-SKYU	Cameron A-210 Balloon (Hot Air)	10129		28. 8.01	Cameron Flights Southern Ltd		
					(Evening Advertiser titles)	Woodborough, Pewsey	22. 2.08T
G-SKYV	Piper PA-28RT-201T Turbo Arrow IV		G-BNZG	20. 9.04	P Ashley	(Port Soderick, Isle of Man)	18. 3.02
		28R-8031132	N82376		(Noew owner 3.07)		
G-SKYW	Aérospatiale AS.355F1 Ecureuil 2	5261	G-BTIS	17. 1.05	Skywalker Aviation Ltd	Elstree	8. 7.08E
			G-TALI				
G-SKYX	Cameron A-210 Balloon (Hot Air)	4613		22. 6.99	Cameron Flights Southern Ltd		
					(Whitely Village titles)	Woodborough, Pewsey	7. 8.08T
G-SKYY	Cameron A-250 Balloon (Hot Air)	3402		9. 3.95	Cameron Flights Southern Ltd		
					"City of Southampton"	Woodborough, Pewsey	9. 3.01T
G-SLAC	Cameron N-77 Balloon (Hot Air)	2295		7. 6.90	B L Alderson (New owner 10.07)	Southport	20. 4.97A
G-SLCE	Cameron C-80 Balloon (Hot Air)	4022		24. 2.97	A M Holly	Breadstone, Berkeley	1. 6.07A
G-SLCT	Diamond DA.42 Twin Star	42.031		30. 6.05	Stapleford Flying Club Ltd	Stapleford	20. 7.08E
G-SLEA	Mudry CAP.10B	124		19.12.80	M J M Jenkins	RAF Wittering	14. 8.08E
G-SLII	Cameron O-90 Balloon (Hot Air)	2388		20. 9.90	R B and A MHarris "Mad Dash"	Buckden, St Neots	17. 8.03A
G-SLIP	Reality Easy Raider BMW R100	0004		21. 5.02	D R Squires	(Wokingham)	
	(Built J S Harris - pr.no.BMAA/HB/215)						
G-SLMG	Diamond HK 36 TTC Super Dimona	36.727	N267JP	5. 8.04	P R Thody and A R Morley tr G-SLMG Syndicate		
						Nympsfield	8. 2.08E
G-SLNT	Flight Design CTSW	06.10.02		28. 2.07	S Munday	Longacre Farm, Sandy	5. 3.08E
	(Assembled P&M Aviation Ltd with c/n 8254)						
G-SLNW	Robinson R22 Beta II	3524	G-LNIC	7. 4.06	Heli-4-Charter LLP	Barton	5. 2.08E
G-SLOK	Robinson R44 Raven II	10752		23. 5.05	Heli-4-Charter LLP	Manchester	23. 6.08E
G-SLTN	SOCATA TB-20 Trinidad	763	HB-KBR	6. 8.99	Oceana Air Ltd	Elstree	27. 8.08E
G-SLVR	Boeing 767-204	24757	G-BRIG	8. 5.07	Flyjet Ltd	Luton	17. 4.08E
			(PH-AHN), G-BRIG		(Operated Silverjet)		
G-SLYN	Piper PA-28-161 Warrior II	28-8116204	N161WA	12. 4.89	Airtime Aviation France Ltd	Bournemouth	8. 6.07T
			N8373K				
G-SMAC	MD Helicopters MD.500N Notar	LN020	N8330F	21.12.05	R A Roberts t/a Puddleduck Plane Partnership		
			N5200R			Dunsfold	11. 1.08E
G-SMAN	Airbus A330-243	261	F-WWKR	26. 3.99	Monarch Airlines Ltd	Luton	25. 3.08E
G-SMAS	British Aircraft Corporation 167 Strikemaster Mk.80A	EEP/JP/149	R Saudi AF 1104	25. 4.05	M A Petrie	Hawarden	
			G-27-23		(As ""1104" in Royal Saudi AF c/s) (Noted 3.06)		
G-SMBM	Pegasus Quantum 15-912 Super Sport	7602		24. 1.00	N Charles and P A Henretty	Swinford, Rugby	20. 3.08P
G-SMCL	Cessna 150M	15077385	N63546	17. 9.07	A A McLellan (Noted 2.08)	North Weald	
G-SMDH	Europa Aviation Europa XS	403		8.10.98	S W Pitt	Blackbushe	21.11.08P
	(Built S W Pitt - pr.no.PFA 247-13367) (Tri-gear u/c)						
G-SMDJ	Eurocopter AS.350B2 Ecureuil	3187		21. 4.99	M Ziani de Ferranti	(Llanfairfechan)	12. 8.09E
G-SMIG	Cameron O-65 Balloon (Hot Air)	922		6. 6.83	R D Parry (San Miguel titles) (Active 5.05)	Stroud	28. 7.87A
G-SMJJ	Cessna 414A Chancellor II	414A0425	N2694H	24. 3.81	Gull Air Ltd	Guernsey	1. 6.08E
G-SMKM	Cirrus SR20	1662	N50910	27. 7.06	K Mallet	Jersey	31. 7.08E
G-SMRS	Cessna 172F Skyhawk	17252558	N8656U	17. 3.06	M R Sarlin "The Missus"	Andrewsfield	3. 7.08E
G-SMRT	Lindstrand LBL 260A Balloon (Hot Air)	1034		2. 6.05	M E White	Templeogue, Dublin	13. 7.08E
G-SMTH	Piper PA-28-140 Cherokee C	28-26916	G-AYJS	28. 9.90	R W Harris and A Jahanfar	Southend	6.12.07E
			N11C		(Noted 1.08)		
G-SMTJ	Airbus A321-211	1972	D-AVXG	15. 5.03	Thomas Cook Airlines Ltd t/a MyTravel Airways		
						Manchester	14. 5.08E
G-SNAK	Lindstrand LBL 105A Balloon (Hot Air)	404		23. 9.96	Ballooning Adventures Ltd	(Hexham)	3. 4.07T
G-SNAP	Cameron V-77 Balloon (Hot Air)	1217		29.11.85	C J S Limon "Snapshot"	Great Missenden	19. 9.04A
G-SNEV	CFM Streak Shadow SA	K 283		17. 9.96	J D Reed	Henstridge	25. 7.08P
	(Built N G Smart - pr.no.PFA 206-13042) (Rotax 582)						
G-SNIF	Cameron A-300 Balloon (Hot Air)	10658		14. 4.05	A C K Rawson and J J Rudoni	Stafford	18. 4.08E
G-SNOG	Air Création 582(1)/Kiss 400	FL011		2. 5.02	P S Wesley	Sywell	4. 4.08P
	(Built B H Ashman - pr.no.BMAA/HB/219 being Flylight kit comprising Trike s/n T02033 and Wing s/n A02048-2045)						
G-SNOP	Europa Aviation Europa	040	G-DESL	3. 1.07	Bob Crowe Aircraft Sales Ltd	Cranfield	10.11.98P
	(Built W R C Williams-Wynne - pr.no.PFA 247-12597)		G-WWWG , "G-DSEL", G-WWWG (Monowheel u/c)				
G-SNOW (2)	Cameron V-77 Balloon (Hot Air)	2050		21. 6.79	G G Cannon and P Haworth	Foulridge, Colne	25. 5.08A
	(Officially regd with c/n 541 but ftted with replacement envelope 1989)						
G-SNOZ	Europa Aviation Europa	032	G-DONZ	7.10.04	P O Bayliss	(Porthcawl)	
	(Built D J Smith and D McNicholl - pr.no.PFA 247-12545)				(New owner 2.07)		
G-SNUZ	Piper PA-28-161 Warrior II	28-8416021	G-PSFT	19.12.01	JCOA Ltd	Fairoaks	10.12.06T
			G-BPDS, N4328P				
G-SOAF	British Aircraft Corporation 167 Strikemaster Mk.82A	PS.376	Omani AF 425	21. 2.05	Strikemaster Flying Club	Hawarden	30. 9.08P
					(As "425" in RAF of Oman c/s)		
G-SOAR	Eiriavion PIK-20E	20214		21. 6.79	R I Huttlestone	Bidford	7. 6.02
					(New owner 7.06)		
G-SOBI	Piper PA-28-181 Cherokee Archer II	28-7690212	D-EAQL	3. 5.00	Northern Aviation Ltd	Durham Tees Valley	13. 8.08E
G-SOCK	Mainair Sports Pegasus Quik	8041		25. 5.04	J F Shaw and K R McCartney		
						Baxby Manor, Husthwaite	31. 7.08P
G-SOCT	Yakovlev Yak-50	842804	LY-XCD	17. 3.04	C R Turton	Headcorn	5. 6.08P
			DOSAAF 32		(Also carries "CT304:RB-A" in pseudo-RAF scheme)		
G-SOEI	Hawker Siddeley HS.748 Series 2A/242	1689	ZK-DES	25. 2.98	PTB (Emerald) Proprietary Lt	Blackpool	17. 4.07T
					(Stored externally 2.08)		
G-SOFT	Thunder Ax7-77 Balloon (Hot Air)	1339		5.12.88	A J Bowen	Aberdour, Burntisland	11. 9.99A
					"Enterprise Software" (Noted 8.06)		
G-SOHO	Diamond DA.40D Star	D4.079		12. 2.04	Soho Aviation Ltd	Stapleford	24. 4.08E
G-SOKO	Soko P-2 Kraguj	033	G-BRXK	6. 1.94	A L Tuttle	Spanhoe	14. 6.06P
			Yugoslav Army 30149		(As "30149:149" in Yugoslav AF c/s) (New owner 7.07)		

G-SOLA	Star-Lite SL-1	203TG			9. 6.88	G P Thomas	(Furnace, Llanelli)	31. 3.93P
	(Built P Clifton and A Clarke - pr.no.PFA 175-11311) (Rotax 447)					"A Star Is Born" (New owner 6.06)		
G-SONA	SOCATA TB-10 Tobago	151	G-BIBI		24.10.80	H Poulson tr G-SONA Group	(Harrogate)	7. 9.08E
G-SOOC	Hughes 369HS	111-0354S	G-BRRX		6.10.93	R J H Strong	Vagg Hill, Yeovil	23. 2.06
	(Hughes 500)		N9083F			(Noted 12.07)		
G-SOOM	Glaser-Dirks DG-500M	5E42M20	BGA 4907		14. 5.92	G W Kirton	(Lamassara, Andorra)	5.10.06
			G-SOOM					
G-SOOS	Colt 21A Cloudhopper Balloon (Hot Air)	1263			7. 6.88	P J Stapley	Redcar	25. 3.95A
G-SOOT	Piper PA-28-180 Cherokee C	28-4033	G-AVNM		19. 8.88	A G Branch	Exeter	23. 9.08E
			N11C					
G-SOOZ	Rans S-6-ESN Coyote II	0899.1335			27. 4.01	S N Lawrence	(Driffield)	27.11.08P
	(Built A Batters - pr.no.PFA 204-13543) (Rotax 582) (Tri-cycle u/c)							
G-SOPH	Best Off Sky Ranger 912(2)	SKR0212286			25. 2.03	G E Reynolds	Sackville Lodge, Riseley	1. 9.08P
	(Built N A Read - pr.no.BMAA/HB/259)							
G-SOPP	Enstrom 280FX	2024	G-OSAB		23.10.97	F P M Sopp and L A Moore		
			N86259				Jefferies Farm, Billingshurst	1. 6.08E
G-SORA	DG Flugzeugbau DG-500/22 Elan	5E35S7	BGA 5269-KPC		23. 2.07	C A Boyle, C P Arthur, B Douglas and R Jackson		
			PH-1082, D-5219			"KPC"	Rufforth	19. 3.08
G-SORT	Cameron N-90 Balloon (Hot Air)	2878			13. 7.92	A Brown "Streamline"	Bristol	8. 7.04A
G-SOUL	Cessna 310R II	310R0140	N5020J		27. 6.88	Reconnaissance Ventures Ltd	Coventry	27. 6.08E
						(Atlantic Reconnaissance titles, red/white c/s)		
G-SOVA	Cessna 550 Citation II	550-0649	N649DA		11.12.06	Mitre Aviation Ltd	Biggin Hill	19.12.07E
			HB-VMH, N44LQ, N44LC, N4320P, I-ATSE, (N1310Z)					
G-SOVB	Learjet Model 45	45-138	N138AX		12. 9.06	Sovereign Air Ltd	Doncaster-Sheffield	11. 9.08E
			G-OLDJ, N5018G					
G-SOVC	Learjet Model 45	45-161	N161AV		25. 9.07	Cumulus Investment Holdings Ltd		
							Doncaster-Sheffield	24. 9.08E
G-SPAM	Avid Aerobat	829			9. 5.91	Full Sutton Flying Centre Ltd	Full Sutton	19. 7.02P
	(Built C M Hicks - pr.no.PFA 189-12074)					(New owner 1.07)		
G-SPAO	Eurocopter EC.135 T2+	0546			19. 4.07	Bond Air Services Ltd	Glasgow City Heliport	4. 9.08E
						(Operated Strathclyde Police)		
G-SPAT	Aero AT-3 R100	AT3.008	SP-EAR		20.10.04	S2T Aero Ltd	North Weald	25.10.07E
			(SP-ERM)					
G-SPDR	de Havilland DH.115 Sea Vampire T 35	15641	VH-RAN		19. 5.00	M J Cobb	(Hungary)	
			Royal Australian Navy N6-766, XG766 (As "N6-766": for overhaul 2007)					
G-SPDY	Raj Hamsa X'Air Hawk	xxxx			27. 4.07	G H Gilmour-White	(Thorverton, Exeter)	
	(Built G H Gilmour-White - pr.no.PFA 340-14678)					(Noted part built NEC Birmingham 11.07)		
G-SPEE	Robinson R22 Beta	0939	G-BPJC		20. 7.94	Verve Systems Ltd	Shobdon	6. 2.08E
G-SPEL	Sky 220-24 Balloon (Hot Air)	045			26. 7.96	T G Church t/a Pendle Balloon Company		
						(Pendle titles)	Clayton le Dale, Blackburn	20.10.08T
G-SPEY	Agusta-Bell 206B-3 JetRanger III	8608	G-BIGO		1. 4.81	G Elliott	(Luton)	28. 9.07E
G-SPFX	Rutan Cozy	PFA 159-13113			30. 4.97	B D Tutty	(Gillingham)	
	(Built B D Tutty)							
G-SPHU	Eurocopter EC.135 T2	0245	D-HKBA		12.11.02	Bond Air Services Ltd	(Boreham)	27. 2.08E
						(Operated Essex Air Ambulance)		
G-SPIN	Pitts S-2A	2110	N5CQ		13. 3.80	S D Judd	Wycombe Air Park	30. 4.08T
	(Built Aerotek Inc)					"Breitling Angels" (navy blue) c/s		
G-SPIT	Vickers Supermarine 379 Spitfire FR.XIVe		(G-BGHB)		2. 3.79	Patina Ltd	Duxford	20. 4.08P
		6S/649205	Indian AF T-20, MV293			(As "MV268:JE-J") (Operated The Fighter Collection)		
G-SPMM	Best Off Sky Ranger Swift 912S(1) SKRxxxx773				1. 6.07	S M Pink and M J Milne	Titsey, Oxted	
	(Built S M Pink and M J Milne - pr.no.BMAA/HB/539)							
G-SPOG	SAN Jodel DR.1050 Ambassadeur	155	G-AXVS		25. 9.95	P D Thomas and T J Bates (		
			F-BJNL				Dairy House Farm, Worlston	13. 6.77S
			(Damaged Stoneacre Farm, Bredhurst 17. 2.91: on rebuild 1995: new owners 2.07)					
G-SPOR	Beech B200 Super King Air	BB-1557	N57TL		3. 9.99	Select Plant Hire Company Ltd	Southend	19. 9.08E
			N57TS					
G-SPJE	Robinson R44 Raven II	12026			4.12.07	Heli Air Ltd (Noted 12.07)	Leicester	
G-SPUR	Cessna 550 Citation II	550-0714	N593EM		27.10.98	London Executive Aviation Ltd	London Stansted	15.11.07E
			N12035					
G-SPVK	Eurocopter AS.350B3 Ecureuil	4301	G-CERU		24. 9.07	Eurocopter UK Ltd	Oxford	
			F-WWXL					
G-SPYS	Robinson R44 Raven II	11274			14. 6.06	SKP Partnerships LLP	Wycombe Air Park	6. 7.08E
G-SRAW	Alpi Pioneer 300	xxx			3. 6.05	A R Lloyd and M Clare		
	(Built B W Grindle - pr.no.PFA 330-14292)					Orlingbury Hold Farm, Hannington, Northampton		1.11.08P
G-SRII	Reality Easy Raider 503	10			2. 3.01	R J Creasey tr Sierra Romeo India India Group		
	(Built T F Francis - pr.no.BMAA/HB/163: originally regd as Sky Raider II 503 until 8.01)						Maypole Farm, Chislet	12.11.04P
G-SROE	Westland Scout AH.1	F9508	XP907		26.10.95	Bolenda Engineering Ltd)	Ipswich	20. 3.06P
						(As "XP907" in AAC c/s)		
G-SRVA	Cirrus SR20	1513	N60986		31. 8.05	Aero GB Ltd	Gloucestershire	26. 9.08E
G-SRVO	Cameron N-90 Balloon (Hot Air)	3551			10. 4.95	Servo and Electronic Sales Ltd (Servo titles)	Lydd	29. 7.04A
G-SRWN	Piper PA-28-161 Warrior II	28-8116284	G-MAND		30. 7.02	S Smith	(Alton)	3.12.01T
			G-BRKT, N8082Z					
G-SRYY	Europa Aviation Europa XS	530			19. 9.02	S R Young	Nortom Malreward	31. 5.08P
	(Built S R Young - pr.no.PFA 247-13806) (Jabiru 3300A) (Tri-gear u/c)					(Noted 6.07)		
G-SSCL	Hughes 369E	0491E	N684F		25. 4.98	Stevens Construction Ltd	Rochester	21. 2.08E
	(Hughes 500)							
G-SSEA	Aérospatiale-Alenia ATR 42-300	196	OY-CIT		29. 8.03	Air Wales Ltd	Guernsey	25. 1.08E
			C-FZVZ, C-GITI, F-WWEK			(Stored 4.06)		
G-SSEX	Rotorway Executive 162F	6809			21. 3.06	M Middleby	(Killyleagh, Downpatrick)	
	(Built J Donnon)							
G-SSIX	Rans S-6-116 Coyote II	0394.602			5. 9.94	R I Kelly	Wellesbourne Mountford	14. 7.05P
	(Built J V Squires - pr.no.PFA 204A-12749) (Frame rebuilt and remarked as "0899.1335.800ES") (Rotax 582) (Tailwheel u/c)							
G-SSJP	Robinson R44 Clipper II	10574			7. 1.05	Global Helicopters Ltd	Southend	23. 1.08E
G-SSKY	Pilatus Britten-Norman BN-2B-26 Islander	2247	G-BSWT		11. 5.92	Isles of Scilly Skybus Ltd	St Just	31. 3.08E

G-SSLF	Lindstrand LBL 210A Balloon (Hot Air)	649		29. 2.00	High On Adventure Balloons Ltd *(Somerfield titles)*		
					(Address change 11.07)	West Clandon, Guildford	28. 5.08T
G-SSSC	Sikorsky S-76C	760408		26.10.93	CHC Scotia Ltd	Aberdeen	13. 1.07T
G-SSSD	Sikorsky S-76C	760415		26.10.93	CHC Scotia Ltd	Aberdeen	22.12.07E
G-SSSE	Sikorsky S-76C	760417		23.11.93	CHC Scotia Ltd	Aberdeen	2. 2.08E
G-SSTI	Cameron N-105 Balloon (Hot Air)	3238		30. 3.94	British Airways PLC *"Concorde"*	West Drayton	4. 9.08T
G-SSWV	Sportavia-Pützer RF5B Sperber	51032	N55WV	31. 5.90	N Fisher and D Athey	Camphill	14.12.06P
			D-KEAI				
G-SSXX	Eurocopter EC.135 T2	0270	G-SSSX	31. 3.03	Bond Air Services Ltd	Boreham	27. 5.08E
					(Operated Essex Air Ambulance)		
G-STAA	Robinson R44 Astro	0492	G-HALE	11. 4.06	Walker Plant Services Ltd	Gamston	24. 9.08E
G-STAT	Cessna U206F Stationair II	U20603485	A6-MAM	20. 2.79	K Brady tr Scottish Parachute Club		
			N8732Q			East Leys Farm, Grindale	17.10.05
					(Force landed 8.03: fuselage noted 8.07)		
G-STAV	Cameron O-84 Balloon (Hot Air)	2913		29. 9.92	F Horsfall	Chipping Camden	1. 7.07A
G-STAY	Reims Cessna FR172K Hawk XP	FR17200620	D-EOVX	15.12.00	J M Wilkins	Haverfordwest	25. 3.08E
			OE-DVX				
G-STCC	Bombardier CL-600-2B16	5623	N623HA	9. 1.08	Private Jet Holding Ltd	London Stanstedl	
	(CL-604 Challenger)						
G-STCH	Fieseler Fi 156A-1 Storch	2088	Luftwaffe 2088	21. 5.03	P R Holloway	Old Warden	
	(Argus AS10C)				*(New owner 1.07)*		
G-STDL	Phillips ST2 Speedtwin	PFA 207-12674	G-DPST	21. 6.06	Speedtwin Developments Ltd	Old Sarum	
	(2 x 140hp Walter LOM M332B)				*(Noted 5.07)*		
	(Developed from original Speedtwin Developments design by late P Phillips: assets and company acquired by M Ducker)						
G-STEA	Piper PA-28R-200 Cherokee Arrow II		HB-OIH	18. 6.02	P J Alderton	Fairoaks	7.11.07E
		28R-7235096	N4569T				
G-STEM	Stemme S 10-V	14-027	D-KSTE	2. 7.97	J Abbess tr G-STEM Group	Tibenham	4. 4.08E
G-STEN	Stemme S 10	10-32	D-KGCH	9. 1.92	J P Lyell tr G-STEN Syndicate *"4"*	Lasham	18. 5.08E
G-STEP	Schweizer 269C	S 1494		1.10.90	M Johnson	Neath	1. 3.08T
	(Schweizer 300)						
G-STER	Bell 206B-3 JetRanger III	4116	OO-EGA	23. 3.94	Maintopic Ltd	Hawarden	23. 6.08E
G-STEU	Rolladen-Schneider LS6-18W	6362	BGA 4153-HRY	24. 1.08	F K Russell	Dunstable	4. 4.08
G-STEV	CEA Jodel DR.221 Dauphin	61	F-BOZD	9. 3.82	S W Talbot	Croft Farm, Defford	26. 5.08
G-STGR	Agusta A109S Grand	22027	ZS-BAX	24.10.07	WA Developments International Ltd	Carlisle	
					(Noted 11.07)		
G-STHA	Piper PA-31-350 Chieftain	31-8052077	G-GLUG	29. 5.07	Skydrift Ltd	Shoreham	13. 4.08E
			N2287J, G-BLOE, G-NITE, N3559A *(SkySouth.co.uk titles).*				
G-STIG	Focke-Wulf FW.44J Stieglitz	183	OO-JKT (2)	16. 2.04	P R Holloway	Old Warden	26. 7.10S
			D-EHDH (2), LV-YYX		*(As "D2692" in Luftwaffe c/s)*		
G-STME	Stemme S 10-VT	11-115		17. 1.08	R A Roberts *(Noted 2.08)*	Lasham	
G-STMP	SAN Stampe SV-4A	241	F-BCKB	11. 3.83	A C Thorne	Bere Alston, Yelverton	
					(Noted dismantled 11.06)		
G-STNS	Agusta A109A II	7324	N716HA	26. 4.06	Heliflight (UK) Ltd	Gloucestershire	14. 6.08E
			N4RP, N109WS, D-HOOC, N1YB, N109KA				
G-STOB	Raytheon Hawker 400XP	RK-502	N502XP	20. 2.07	STA (2006) LLP	Carlisle	2. 4.08E
G-STOK	Cameron Colt 77B Balloon (Hot Air)	4791		4. 5.00	J.E Wetters and M H Read	Timperley, Altrincham	22. 3.08A
					"Hollybush"		
G-STON	Eurocopter AS.355N Ecureuil 2	5663	VP-BCE	1.12.05	Narragansett LLP	(Cardiff)	26. 2.08E
G-STOO	Stolp SA.300 Starduster Too	PFA 035-13870		30. 1.03	K F Crumplin	Henstridge	
	(Built K F Crumplin)				*(Noted 4.07)*		
G-STOP	Robinson R44 Raven II	10852		5. 9.05	Cartis Ltd H O'Kelly and L Denning	(Dublin)	15. 9.08E
G-STOW	Cameron Wine Box 90 SS Balloon (Hot Air)			2.10.98	I Martin and D Groombridge t/a Flying Enterprises Partnership		
		4420			*(Stowells of Chelsea titles)* Alveston and Portishead, Bristol		23. 7.08A
G-STPH	Robinson R44 Raven	1613		14. 6.06	Westrock Aviation Ltd		
						(Manorhamilton, County Leitrim)	3. 7.08E
G-STPI	Cameron A-250 Balloon (Hot Air)	4102		26. 2.97	The Ballooning Business Ltd	Walcote, Alcester	9. 3.07T
G-STRF	Boeing 737-76N	29885	EI-CXD	1. 4.04	Astraeus Ltd	London Gatwick	31. 3.07T
G-STRG	Cyclone AX2000	7837		24. 7.01	D Young tr Pegasus Flight Training (Cotswolds)		
	(HKS 700E V3)					Kemble	10.10.08P
G-STRH	Boeing 737-76N	32737	EI-CXE	17. 5.04	Astraeus Ltd	London Gatwick	16. 5.08E
G-STRI	Boeing 737-33A	25011	SX-BBT	10. 5.05	Astraeus Ltd	Goteborg, Sweden	9. 5.08E
			F-GRSA, OO-LTO, VH-OAN, OO-LTO, N227AW, PP-SOF *(Operated FlyMe)*				
G-STRJ	Boeing 737-33A	25119	ZK-JNE	22. 4.05	Astraeus Ltd	Goteborg, Sweden	22. 4.08E
			VH-JNE, PT-SER, PP-SOL		*(Operated FlyMe)*		
G-STRK	CFM Streak Shadow SA	K 143-SA		4. 4.90	E J Hadley	(Arch, Switzerland)	21. 4.04P
	(Built M E Dodd - pr.no.PFA 161-11762: project series should be "161A")) (Rotax 582)						
G-STRL	Eurocopter AS.355N Ecureuil 2	5733		14.12.04	Harrier Enterprises Ltd	(Douglas, Isle of Man)	3. 7.08E
G-STRM	Cameron N-90 Balloon (Hot Air)	3568		3. 7.95	A Brown	Winscombe	6. 9.06E
G-STRX	Boeing 757-28A	25621	N459AX	5. 2.08	Astraeus Ltd	London Gatwick	
			N551NA, N25621, C-FXOO				
G-STRY	Boeing 757-28A	28161	N369AX,	16.12.07	Astraeus Ltd	London Gatwick	
			N543NA, N161KB, C-FOON				
G-STRZ	Boeing 757-258	27622	4X-EBI	1. 4.07	Astraeus Ltd	London Gatwick	4. 4.08E
G-STUA	Pitts S-2A	2164	N13GT	6. 3.91	P J G Margetson-Rushmore tr G-STUA Group		
	(Built Aerotek Inc)					Stapleford	21. 3.08E
G-STUB	Pitts S-2B	5163	N260Y	5. 5.94	P T Borchert	Old Sarum	13. 8.08T
	(Built Christen Industries Inc) (Lycoming AEIO-540)						
G-STUE	Europa Aviation Europa	xxxx		20.11.06	S Philp	(Worcester)	
	(Built S Philp) - pr.no.PFA 247-12869)						
G-STUF	Learjet Model 40	45-2074	N40012	27. 4.07	Air Partner Private Jets Ltd	Biggin Hill	26. 4.08E
G-STUY	Robinson R44 Raven II	10508		8.10.04	S Mayers	Redhill	16.11.07E
G-STWO	ARV Aviation ARV-1 Super 2	002		24. 4.85	P M Paul	Draycott Farm, Chiseldon	29. 6.07P
	(Built ARV Aviation Ltd - pr.no.PFA 152-11048)						

Reg	Type	C/n	Prev id	Date	Owner	Location	Exp
G-STYL	Pitts S-1S	GJSN-1P	N665JG	26. 1.88	C R Hampson	(Knowle, Fareham)	30. 1.08P
	(Built G Harben and G Smith) (Lycoming-O-320)						
G-SUCH	Cameron N-77 Balloon (Hot Air)	676	G-BIGD	3. 9.01	D G Such	Barkway, Royston	4. 1.84A
G-SUCK	Cameron Z-105 Balloon (Hot Air)	10280		16. 5.02	R P Wade	Shevington, Wigan	25. 5.08A
G-SUCT	Robinson R22 Beta	4078		29. 9.06	P Irwin t/a Irwin Plant Sales	Enniskillen	11.10.07E
G-SUEA	Diamond DA.42 Twin Star	42.256		26. 6.07	S D Coxen t/a Sue Air	Stapleford	11. 7.08E
G-SUEB	Piper PA-28-181 Archer III	2843466		18. 7.01	Saxon Logistics Ltd	Elstree	18. 2.08E
			N495AF				
			G-SUEB, N5330M				
G-SUED	Thunder Ax8-90 Balloon (Hot Air)	1546	G-PINE	22.10.02	E C Lubbock and S A Kidd	Billericay	6. 3.07A
G-SUEL	P&M Quik GT450	8301		23. 7.07	J M Ingram	(Hardwicke, Gloucester)	19. 7.08P
G-SUEY	Bell 206L-1 LongRanger	45612	C-GCET	5. 3.04	Aerospeed Ltd	Manston	26. 9.08E
			N300CS, N3901Q				
G-SUEZ	Agusta-Bell 206B-2 JetRanger II	8319	SU-YAE	16. 9.98	Aerospeed Ltd	Manston	5. 7.08E
			YU-HAZ				
G-SUFF	Eurocopter EC.135 T1	0118		1. 2.00	Suffolk Constabulary Air Support Unit		
						Ellough, Beccles	23. 8.09S
G-SUKI	Piper PA-38-112 Tomahawk	38-79A0260	G-BPNV	22. 5.91	Ravenair Aircraft Ltd	Liverpool	7. 7.08E
			N2313D				
G-SUMX	Robinson R22 Beta II	3274		1.11.01	J A Bickerstaffe	Blackpool	16.11.07T
G-SUMZ	Robinson R44 Raven II	10490		11.11.04	Frankham Brothers Ltd	Bruntingthorpe	11.11.07E
G-SUNN	Robinson R44 Clipper	1367	N7531L	16. 7.04	C Wilkins	(Thruxton)	15. 8.07T
G-SUPA	Piper PA-18-150 Super Cub	18-5395	PH-BAJ	13.12.78	D Sutton tr G-SUPA Owners Group	Headcorn	22.12.07E
	(Frame no.18-5512)		PH-MBF, French Army 18-5395, N10F				
G-SURG	Piper PA-30 Twin Comanche B	30-1424	G-VIST	18. 6.90	A R Taylor	Turweston	26. 5.08E
			G-AVHZ, N8287Y				
G-SURY	Eurocopter EC.135 T2	0283		17. 6.03	Surrey Police Authority	Fairoaks	12. 2.10T
G-SUSE	Europa Aviation Europa XS	554		25. 6.02	P R Tunney	(Sale)	
	(Built P R Tunney - pr.no.PFA 247-13905) (BMW1100RS)						
G-SUSI	Cameron V-77 Balloon (Hot Air)	1133		22. 7.85	J H Dyden "Susi"	Okehampton	9. 8.04A
G-SUSX	MD Helicopters MD.900 Explorer	900-00065	N3065W	19. 1.00	Sussex Police Authority	Shoreham	18. 2.10S
G-SUTD	Avtech Jabiru UL-D	662		14. 8.06	E Bentley	(Stockton-on-Tees)	13.12.07P
	(On start up Wickenby 18. 2.07 moved off, collided with portacabin and weighbridge and incurred substantial damage)						
G-SUTN	III Sky Arrow 650 TC	C007		27. 8.98	D J Goldsmith	Headcorn	1.12.07P
	(Built Iniziative Industriali Italian)						
G-SUZN	Piper PA-28-161 Warrior II	28-8016187	N3573C	16. 1.91	E Reed t/a St George Flight Training		
			N9540N			Durham Tees Valley	4. 5.08E
G-SUZY	Taylor JT.1 Monoplane	PFA 055-10395		1.12.78	N Gregson	Ashcroft Farm, Winsford	27. 1.04P
	(Built S A Kaniok)						
G-SVDG	Avtech Jabiru SK	xxxx		5.12.05	R Tellegen	Old Sarum	14. 1.08P
	(Built R Tellegen - pr.no.PFA 274-13442)						
G-SVEA	Piper PA-28-161 Warrior II	28-7916082	N30299	16.12.98	E-C V Dunning tr G-SVEA Group	Oxford	19.12.07E
G-SVEN	Centrair 101A Pégase	101A0262	BGA 4329-HZF	15. 1.08	A J Cronshaw	Gransden Lodge	13. 2.08
			PH-796				
G-SVET	Yakovlev Yak-50	822210	RA-44459	16. 9.03	Yak-52 Ltd	Compton Abbas	9.11.07P
			LY-AGG, DOSAAF 107		"Svetlana"		
G-SVIP	Cessna 421B Golden Eagle	421B0820	G-BNYJ	12. 3.97	T Stone-Brown	(Henfield)	26.12.03T
			N4686Q, D-IMVB, N1590G		(New owner 1.05)		
G-SVIV	SNCAN Stampe SV-4C	475	N65214	7. 8.90	R Taylor	Plymouth	24. 8.08
			F-BDBL				
G-SVNC	Rolladen-Schneider LS4	4190	BGA 3552-FVE	13.11.07	M C Jenkins	Dunstable	15. 3.08
			RAFGSA 232, RAFGSA R30, D-4542				
G-SVPN	Piper PA-32R-301T Saratoga II TC	3257310	N48HB	24. 8.05	Caspian Air Services Ltd	Oxford	29. 8.08E
			N164MA, N9529N				
G-SVSB	Cessna 680 Citation Sovereign	680-0094	N5263D	27. 9.06	Ferron Trading Ltd	Jersey	27. 9.08E
G-SWAK	Oldfield Baby Lakes	88	N4287X	2.11.07	J P Nash	(Brighton)	
	(Built R W Hunt)						
G-SWAT	Robinson R44 Raven II	10041	N75097	24. 2.03	J S Corr	Weston, Leixlip, County Kildare	12. 4.08T
G-SWCT	Flight Design CTSW	xx.xx.xx		31. 1.08	J A Shufflebotham	(Marton. Macclesfield)	30. 1.09P
	(Assembled P&M Aviation Ltd with c/n 8364)						
G-SWEE	Beech 95-B55 Baron	TC-1406	G-AZDK	16. 4.03	Orman (Carrolls Farm) Ltd	Great Massingham	17. 5.08E
G-SWEL	Hughes 369HS	61-0328S	G-RBUT	18. 7.96	M A Crook and A E Wright	Barton	27. 7.08E
	(Hughes 500)		C-FTXZ, CF-TXZ				
G-SWLL	Aero AT-3 R100	AT3.012	SP-KAC	24.10.05	Sywell Aerodrome Ltd	Sywell	24.11.07P
G-SWON	Pitts S-1S	093	N522H	14. 7.05	S L Goldspink	(Northill, Biggleswade)	15.11.08P
	(Built R Heverling)						
G-SWOT	Phoenix Currie Super Wot	PFA 3011		10. 9.80	D A Porter	Griffin Farm, Temple Bruer	6.11.08P
	(Built G Chittenden) (Continental O-200-A)				(As "C3011:S" in RAF c/s [SE.5a guise])		
G-SWPR	Cameron N-56 Balloon (Hot Air)	829		16. 3.82	A Brown "Post Code"	Bristol	5. 7.95A
G-SWSW	Schempp-Hirth Ventus bT	61/273	BGA 4562-JJY	17. 8.07	S R Way	Parham Park	19. 1.08
			PH-981, D-KMIH				
G-SWWM	Westland SA.341C Gazelle HT.2	1033	XW853	6. 5.03	M S Beaton "53"	Deer Park Farm, Babcary	7. 5.08P
G-SXTY	Bombardier Learjet Model 60	60-280	OE-GKP	21. 6.07	TAG Aviation (UK) Ltd	Farnborough	26. 6.08E
			N50127				
G-SYCO	Europa Aviation Europa	031		27.11.95	P J Tiller	(Northampton)	23. 1.06P
	(Built J W E de Frayssinet - pr.no.PFA 247-12540) (NSI EA-81/118) (Conventional u/c) (New owner 5.07)						
G-SYDE	Piper PA-32R-301T Saratoga II TC	3257380	N31064	5. 7.05	J Cottrell and J D Richardson	Earls Colne	7. 7.08E
G-SYEL	Aero AT-3 R100	AT3.019		21. 8.06	Sywell Aerodrome Ltd	Sywell	13. 9.08E
G-SYFW	WAR Focke-Wulf FW190 replica	269		28. 2.83	R P Cross	Wickenby	10.11.05P
	(Built M R Parr - pr.no.PFA 081-10584) (Continental O-200-A)				(As W/Nr "7334/2+1" in Luftwaffe c/s)		
G-SYGA	Beech B200 Super King Air	BB-1044	G-BPPM	15.11.07	Synergy Aircraft Leasing Ltd	Fairoaks	17.10.07E
			N7061T, C-GJJT, N815CE, (N815CF), N815CE, N62895 (Noted 1.08)				
G-SYLJ	Embraer EMB-135BJ Legacy	14500937	(PT-SCI)	12.12.05	TAG Aviation (UK) Ltd	Farnborough	18.12.07E
			G-SYLJ, PT-SCI				

G-SYPA	Aérospatiale AS.355F2 Ecureuil 2	5193	LV-WHC	25. 9.96	Veritair Ltd t/a British International	(Sherborne)	2. 4.08T
			F-WYMS, G-BPRE, N366E				
G-SYPS	MD Helicopters MD.900 Explorer	900-00104		3. 7.03	South Yorkshire Police Authority	(Sheffield City)	3. 7.10S
			N7034X, (PH-PXF)				
G-SYWL	Aero AT-3 R100	AT3.011	SP-KOT	24.10.05	Sywell Aerodrome Ltd	Sywell	24.11.07P

G-TAAA - G-TZZZ

G-TAAA	Cirrus SR20 GTS	1562	N81283	3.11.05	TAA UK Ltd	Denham	3.11.07E
G-TAAB	Cirrus SR22	1769	N944CD	10. 7.06	TAA UK Ltd	Denham	11. 7.08E
G-TAAC	Cirrus SR20	1694	N997SR	14. 9.06	TAA UK Ltd	Denham	21. 9.08E
G-TABI	Cirrus SR20	1705	N950SR	4. 9.06	N Carter	Jersey	7. 9.08E
G-TABS	Embraer EMB-110P1 Bandeirante	110212	G-PBAC	18. 8.98	Skydrift Ltd	Southend	10.11.06E
			F-GCLA, F-OGME, F-GCLA, PT-GME *(Stored 1.08)*				
G-TACK	Grob G109B	6279		30. 5.84	A P Mayne	Exeter	23. 5.08E
G-TADC	Aeroprakt A22 Foxbat	PFA 317-13883		16. 4.02	R J Sharp	Rochester	7. 8.08P
	(Built R J Sharp)						
G-TAFC	Maule M-7-235B Super Rocket	23062C	N210SA	11. 1.05	The Amphibious Flying Club Ltd	Enniskillen	7. 8.08E
	(Floatplane)		G-TAFC, N210SA, N9164M, C-GFVX				
G-TAFF	CASA 1-131E Jungmann	1129	G-BFNE	7. 9.84	A J E Smith	Breighton	22. 7.05P
			Spanish AF E3B-148		*(On rebuild 12.07)*		
G-TAFI	Bücker Bü.133C Jungmeister	24	N2210	27. 1.93	R J Lamplough	Manor Farm, East Garston	5. 7.01P
	(Built Dornier-Werke AG)		HB-MIF, Swiss AF U-77				
G-TAGA	Bombardier CL-600-2B16	5659	C-FJCB	30. 4.07	TAG Aviation (UK) Ltd	Farnborough	30. 4.08E
	(CL604 Challenger)		C-GLYK				
G-TAGG	Eurocopter EC.135 T2	0341		3. 9.04	Taggart Homes Ltd	(Londonderry)	1.12.07E
G-TAGH	Beech B200 Super King Air	BB-1720	N208CW	13. 3.06	Taggart Aviation Ltd		
			N608TA			Weston, Leixlip, County Kildare	23. 3.08
G-TAGR	Europa Aviation Europa	317		23. 8.02	C G Sutton	(Kenilworth)	5. 4.07P
	(Built A G Rackstraw - pr.no.PFA 247-13061)				*(New owner 9.07)*		
G-TAGT	Robinson R22 Beta	4015	N74385	6.04.06	Taggart Aviation Ltd	City of Derry	11. 4.08E
G-TAIL	Cessna 150J	15070152	N60220	21. 4.89	T N Ashworth	Blackpool	12. 7.08E
G-TAJF	Lindstrand LBL 77A Balloon (Hot Air)	905		28. 4.03	T A J Fowles	Chester	14. 8.08A
G-TAKE	Aérospatiale AS.355F1 Ecureuil 2	5088	G-OITN	18. 8.05	Arena Aviation Ltd	Redhill	14. 2.08E
			N400HH, N5788B				
G-TALA	Cessna 152 II	15285134	G-BNPZ	6. 3.07	Tatenhill Aviation Ltd	Tatenhill	22. 2.08E
			N6109Q				
G-TALB	Cessna 152 II	15283767	G-BORO	6. 3.07	Tatenhill Aviation Ltd	Tatenhill	27. 3.08E
			N5130B				
G-TALC	Cessna 152 II	15284941	G-BPBG	24. 4.07	Tatenhill Aviation Ltd	Tatenhill	22. 7.08E
			N5418P				
G-TALD	Reims Cessna F152 II	F15201718	G-BHRM	5. 4.07	Tatenhill Aviation Ltd	Tatenhill	25. 4.08E
			F-GCHR				
G-TALE	Piper PA-28-181 Archer II	28-8290048	G-BJOA	30.10.07	Tatenhill Aviation Ltd	Tatenhill	21.11.07E
			N8453H				
G-TALF	Piper PA-24-250 Comanche	24-1094	G-APUZ	27.11.07	Tatenhill Aviation Ltd	Tatenhill	30. 9.07E
			N6000P				
G-TALG	Piper PA-28-151 Cherokee Warrior	28-7715219	G-BELP	14. 2.08	Tatenhill Aviation Ltd	Tatenhill	17. 8.07T
			N9543N				
G-TAMA	Schweizer 269D	0051A	N86G	10. 3.05	Total Air Management Services Ltd	(Sheffield City)	12. 6.08E
	(Schweizer 333)						
G-TAMB	Schweizer 269D	0052A	N86G	6. 6.05	Total Air Management Services Ltd	(Sheffield City)	21. 7.08E
	(Schweizer 333)						
G-TAMC	Schweizer 269D	0054A	N86G	2. 8.05	Total Air Management Services Ltd	(Sheffield City)	13. 9.08E
	(Schweizer 333)						
G-TAMD	Schweizer 269D	0056A	N86G	1.12.05	Total Air Management Services Ltd	(Sheffield City)	13. 6.08E
	(Schweizer 333)						
G-TAME	Schweizer 269D	0035A	N2119S	10. 1.05	Total Air Management Services Ltd	(Sheffield City)	24. 1.08E
	(Schweizer 333)						
G-TAMF	Bell 206B-3 JetRanger III	2734	G-BXDS	15. 2.07	Total Air Management Services Ltd	Perth	24. 7.08E
			G-OVBJ. G-BXDS, OY-HDK, N661PS				
G-TAMR	Cessna 172S Skyhawk SP	172S8480	N2458J	7. 6.00	Apem Ltd	(Manchester)	31. 7.08E
G-TAMS	Beech A23-24 Musketeer Super	MA-190	OY-DKF	30. 6.00	Aerograde Ltd	Old Buckenham	26..4.08E
G-TANA	Air Création Tanarg 912S(2)/iXess 15	FLT.xxx		17. 1.06	A P Marks	Naseby, Northampton	12. 9.08P
	(Built A Marks - pr.no.BMAA/HB/485 being Flylight kit comprisiing Trike s/n T05099 and Wing s/n A05187-5194)						
G-TAND	Robinson R44 Astro	0478		12. 6.98	Global Air Charter Ltd	Blackbushe	6. 9.08E
G-TANI	Gulfstream GA-7 Cougar	GA7-0107	G-VJAI	18. 5.95	S Spier	Elstree	6. 3.08E
			G-OCAB, G-BICF, N8500H, N29707				
G-TANJ	Raj Hamsa X'Air 582(5)	629		21. 6.01	R Thorman	Perth	22. 5.08P
	(Built R Thorman - pr.no.BMAA/HB/171)						
G-TANK	Cameron N-90 Balloon (Hot Air)	3625		20. 6.95	A M, A H and D J Mercer	Belfast	7. 9.08A
G-TANS	SOCATA TB-20 Trinidad	1870	F-GRBX	25. 9.98	K P Threlfall	Halfpenny Green	1.12.07E
G-TANY	EAA Acrosport II	PFA 072A-13821		19. 2.04	P J Tanulak	Sleap	17.12.08P
	(Built P J Tanulak)						
G-TAPE	Piper PA-23-250 Aztec D	27-4054	G-AWVW	7.10.83	D J Hare	Fairoaks	10. 5.08T
			OY-RPF, G-AWVW, N6799Y, N9654N *(Operated Merlix Air)*				
G-TAPS	Piper PA-28RT-201T Turbo Arrow IV		HB-PLV	2. 6.04	P G Doble	Fairoaks	5. 7.08E
		28R-8131080	N83423				
G-TARG	Air Création Tanarg 912S/iXess 15	FLT.xxx		12. 6.06	B Thompson	(Rouffignac, France)	31. 7.08P
	(Built P M Dewhurst - pr.no.BMAA/HB/501 being Flylight kit comprising Trike s/n xxxx and Wing s/n xxxx)						
G-TARN	Pietenpol AirCamper	PFA 047-13349		3. 8.98	P J Heilbron	(Guildford)	
	(Built P J Heilbron)						
G-TARR	P&M Pegasus Quik	8264		27. 4.07	M J Tarrant	(Devizes)	26. 4.08P

Reg	Type	c/n	Prev identities	Date	Owner / Operator	Base	Expiry
G-TART	Piper PA-28-236 Dakota	28-7911261	N2945C	18.12.90	Prescot Planes Ltd	Goodwood	18. 6.08E
G-TASH	Cessna 172N	17270531	PH-KOS, N739GL	4.11.98	Flight Academy (Gyrocopters) Ltd	Barton	30.11.07E
G-TASK	Cessna 404 Titan	404-0829	PH-MPC, SE-IHL, N6806Q	10. 3.93	Reconnaissance Ventures Ltd *(Red and white Coastguard c/s)*	Coventry	8. 7.08E
G-TATO	Robinson R22 Beta	3418	EI-OBJ	8. 5.07	Mullahead Property Company Ltd	(Mullahead, Tandragee)	15. 5.08E
G-TATS	Aérospatiale AS.350BA Ecureuil	1905	F-GHSN, N37AW	14. 5.01	T J Hoare	(Hollycombe, Liphook)	7. 6.08T
G-TATT	Gardan GY-20 Minicab *(Built L Tattershall)*	PFA 056-10347		30.11.78	P W Tattershall tr Tatt's Group *(Noted 2007)* Smelthwaites Farm , Newton in Bowland, Clitheroe		
G-TAXI	Piper PA-23-250 Aztec E	27-7305085	N40270	6. 4.78	M Roberts	Bagby	26. 6.08E
G-TAYC	Gulfstream Aerospace Gulfstream IV-X	4060	N460GA	18. 1.07	TAG Aviation (UK) Ltd	Farnborough	17. 1.08E
G-TAYI	Grob G115	8008	(D-ENFT), G-TAYI, G-DODO, D-ENFT	12. 9.90	K P Widdowson and K Hackshall	Sandtoft	9. 8.08E
G-TAYS	Reims Cessna F152 II	F15201697	G-LFCA	28.10.91	Tayside Aviation Ltd	Glenrothes	8. 7.07T
G-TAZZ	Dan Rihn DR.107 One Design *(Built C J Gow)*	PFA 264-14038		20. 2.06	C J Gow	(Broughty Ferry, Dundee)	
G-TBAE	British Aerospace BAe 146 Series 200	E2018	G-JEAR, G-HWPB, G-6-018, G-BSRU, G-OSKI, N603AW	6. 1.03	BAE Systems (Corporate Air Travel) Ltd	Warton	7. 4.08E
G-TBAG	Murphy Renegade 912 *(Built M Tetley)*	PFA 188-11912		11.12.90	M R Tetley	Newton-on-Rawcliffe, Yorkshire	24.10.08P
G-TBAH	Bell 206B-2 JetRanger II	2051	G-OMJB, N315JP, N712WG, N712WC, N9989K	10.12.01	RB Helicopters Ltd	Ballyclare	19. 1.08E
G-TBBC	Pegasus Quantum 15-912	7583		6.12.99	J Horn	Eshott	25. 4.08P
G-TBEA	Cessna 525A CitationJet CJ2	525A-0191	N776LB	19. 5.06	Xclusive Jet Charter Ltd	Bournemouth	31. 5.08E
G-TBGL	Agusta A109A II	7412	G-VJCB, G-BOUA	6. 1.99	Bulford Holdings Ltd *(Noted 12.07)*	Fairoaks	22. 3.07T
G-TBGT	SOCATA TB-20 Trinidad GT	2027	F-OILF	1.12.00	A J Maitland-Robinson	(St Lawrence, Jersey)	11. 2.08E
G-TBHH	Aérospatiale AS.355F2 Ecureuil 2	5346	G-HOOT, G-SCOW, ZS-HSW, G-POON, G-MCAL	1.12.06	Hughes Helicopters Ltd t/a Biggin Hill Helicopters	Biggin Hill	23. 2.08E
G-TBIC	British Aerospace BAe 146 Series 200	E2025	N167US, N349PS	15. 1.97	NEX Aviation Aircrafts Ltd *(Operated IAC)*	Aberdeen	16. 1.08E
G-TBIO	SOCATA TB-10 Tobago	340	F-BNGZ	10. 2.83	Delta Bird Aviation Ltd	Barton	16. 5.08E
G-TBJP	Mainair Sports Pegasus Quik	8071		29. 9.04	R Rajkowski	(Stratford-upon-Avon)	6.10.08P
G-TBLB	P&M Quik GT450	8188		1. 6.06	B L Benson	(Egerton, Malpas)	4. 6.08P
G-TBLY	Eurocopter EC.120B Colibri	1192	F-WQOV	12. 3.01	A D Bly Aircraft Leasing Ltd	Panshanger	28. 2.08E
G-TBMW	Murphy Renegade Spirit *(Built J R Peters and S J Spavins)*	PFA 188A-11725	(G-MYIG)	20.10.98	S J and M J Spavins *(Stalled and spun in Brooklands Farm, Alconbury 2. 7.06 and substantially damaged)*	Longacre Farm, Sandy	8. 2.07P
G-TBOK	SOCATA TB-10 Tobago	1111	SX-ABF, F-GKUA	26. 6.02	TB10 Ltd	Dunkeswell	27.10.07E
G-TBSV	SOCATA TB-20 Trinidad GT	2169	N403MS, F-HKJT, F-WWRB	10.10.06	Condron Concrete Ltd *(Noted 2006)*	Ballyduff, Tullamore, County Offaly	
G-TBTB	Robinson R44 Raven	1559	G-CDUN	24. 3.06	A R Banks t/a ARB Helicopters *"Balhousie Care Group"*	Perth	18. 3.08E
G-TBTN	SOCATA TB-10 Tobago	322	G-BKIA	7. 8.03	Airways International Ltd	Perth	20.10.07E
G-TBXX	SOCATA TB-10 Tobago	276		16. 3.82	Aeroplane Ltd	Headcorn	27. 4.08E
G-TBZI	SOCATA TB-21 Trinidad TC	871	N21HR	25. 7.96	PMM Management Ltd	Biggin Hill	25. 1.08E
G-TBZO	SOCATA TB-20 Trinidad	444		8. 8.84	R P Lewis and D L Clarke	Shoreham	27. 4.08E
G-TCAL	Robinson R44 Raven II	11628		13. 3.07	C M Gough-Cooper	Barton	27. 3.08E
G-TCAN	Colt 69A Balloon (Hot Air)	1996		19. 7.91	H C J Williams *"Toucan"*	Bristol	24. 5.08A
G-TCAS	Cameron Z-275 Balloon (Hot Air)	10343		28. 2.03	The Ballooning Business Ltd *(Central Auto Supplies titles)*	Walcote, Alcester	27. 3.08T
G-TCBA	Boeing 757-28A	28203	G-OOOY	22. 5.06	Thomas Cook Airlines UK Ltd	Manchester	20. 5.08E
G-TCCA	Boeing 767-31K	27205	G-SJMC, C-GLMC, G-SJMC, N6038E	11. 2.08	Thomas Cook Airlines Ltd t/a MyTravel Airways	Manchester	22.11.07E
G-TCEE	Hughes 369HS *(Hughes 500)*	61-0326S	G-AZVM, N9091F	6.09.05	Aviation Styling Ltd	Phoenix Farm, Lower Upham	22. 5.08E
G-TCMM	Agusta-Bell 206B-3 JetRanger III	8560	EI-BXX, G-JMVB, G-OIML	24. 3.04	Transair (UK) Ltd	Goodwood	30. 4.08E
G-TCNM	Tecnam P92-EA Echo *(Built J Quaife)*	PFA 318-13922		12. 8.02	F G Walker	(Hawarden, Deeside)	21.10.08P
G-TCNY	Mainair Sports Pegasus Quik	8037		13. 5.04	T Butler	Enstone	13. 5.08P
G-TCOM	Piper PA-30 Twin Comanche C	30-1967	N555JC, N8810Y	29. 1.96	Commair Ltd	(Jersey)	24. 5.08E
G-TCTC	Piper PA-28RT-201T Turbo Arrow IV *(Originally built as N9524N [28R-8631006])*	2831001	N9130B	1.12.89	M-D Lopez	(Brussels, Belgium)	12. 4.08E
G-TCUB	Piper J-3C-65 Cub *(Frame No.13805)*	13970	N9039Q, N67666, NC67666, Bu.29684, 45-55204	31. 7.87	C Kirk	Whaley Farm, New York, Lincoln	8. 7.07
G-TCXA	Airbus A330-243	795	F-WWKR	16.11.06	Thomas Cook Airlines UK Ltd	Manchester	15.11.07E
G-TDOG	Scottish Aviation Bulldog Series 120/121	BH120/230	XX538	17. 9.01	G S Taylor *(As "XX538:O" in RAF c/s)*	Shobdon	26. 5.08E
G-TDRA	Cessna 172S Skyhawk	172S9848	N1539T	26. 7.05	TDR Aviation Ltd	Newtownards	7. 8.08E
G-TDVB	Dyn'Aéro MCR-01 ULC *(Built D Brunt - pr.no.PFA 301B-14015)*	242		23. 1.03	D V Brunt	Plaistows Farm, St Albans	26. 9.08P
G-TDYN	Aerospool Dynamic WT9 UK *(Official c/n is "DY147")*	DY147/2006		2.10.06	L J and A A Rice	Quebec Farm, Knook, Warminster	1. 5.08P
G-TEAS	Air Création Tanarg 912S/iXess 15 *(Built G C Teasdale - pr.no.BMAA/HB/489 being Flylight kit comprising Trike s/n T05081 and Wing s/n A05149-5143)*	FLT.xxx		30. 1.06	G C Teasdale	Old Sarum	27 .6.08P
G-TEBZ	Piper PA-28R-201 Cherokee Arrow III	28R-7737050	N105CC	7. 1.00	Bowen-Air Ltd	(Stretton, Burton-on-Trent)	14. 9.08E
G-TECC	Aeronca 7AC Champion	7AC-5269	N1704E, NC1704E	26. 6.91	N J Orchard-Armitage	Waldershare Park	14. 8.08P
G-TECH	Rockwell Commander 114	14074	G-BEDH, N4744W	8. 8.85	P A Reed and S Rae	Elstree	14. 8.08E

G-TECK	Cameron V-77 Balloon (Hot Air)	625		21. 3.86	M W A Shemilt	Henley-on-Thames	5. 8.02A
G-TECM	Tecnam P92-EM Echo	PFA 318-13667		1.12.00	N G H Staunton	Draycott Farm, Chiseldon	15.10.08P
	(Built D A Lawrence)						
G-TECO	Tecnam P92-EA Echo	PFA 318-13830		16. 2.05	A N Buchan	(Calton Moor Farm, Ashbourne)	16. 5.08P
	(Built A N Buchan)						
G-TECS	Tecnam P2002-EA Sierra	PFA 333-14325		16. 6.04	D A Lawrence	Draycott Farm, Chiseldon	24. 4.07P
	(Built D A Lawrence) (Originally regd as pr.no.PFA 318A-14250)						
G-TEDB	Reims Cessna F150L	F15000772	G-AZLZ	20. 1.05	E L Bamford	Haverfordwest	16. 3.08T
G-TEDF	Cameron N-90 Balloon (Hot Air)	2634		8. 8.91	Fort Vale Engineering Ltd	Nelson	10. 7.05A
G-TEDI	Best Off Sky Ranger J2.2(1)	SKR0207217		1. 5.03	K Lorenzen	Sywell	25.12.08P
	(Built D A Smith and E Robshaw - pr.no.BMAA/HB/243)				(Noted 1.07)		
G-TEDS	SOCATA TB-10 Tobago	57	G-BHCO	29. 3.83	M Camp tr G-TEDS Group Aviation	Bruntingthorpe	16. 5.08E
G-TEDW	Air Création 582(2)/Kiss 450	FL026		21. 1.04	F P Welsh	(Troutbeck, Windermere)	28. 5.08P
	(Built D J Wood - pr.no.BMAA/HB/343 being Flylight kit comprising Trike s/n T03103 and Wing s/n A03184-3179)						
G-TEDY	Evans VP-1	PFA 062-10383	G-BHGN	4.10.90	N K Marston	(Harrow)	1. 7.97P
	(Built A Cameron) (Volkswagen 1834)				"The Plank"		
G-TEFC	Piper PA-28-140 Cherokee F	28-7325088	OY-PRC	18. 6.80	I A P Harper and C J Watson tr Foxtrot Charlie Flyers		
			N15530			Halfpenny Green	18. 4.08E
G-TEGS	Bell 206B-3 JetRanger III	4622	C-FLZN	17. 4.07	E Drinkwater	(Barton)	31. 5.08P
G-TEHL	CFM Streak Shadow M	185	G-MYJE	20.11.98	J Anderson	Plaistows Farm, St Albans	18. 7.07P
	(Built A K Paterson - pr.no.PFA 206-13412) (Rotax 503)						
G-TELC	Rotorsport UK MT-03	RSUK/MT-03-028		23. 1.08	A J Turner	(Writtle, Chelmsford)	
G-TELY	Agusta A109A II	7326	N1HQ	10. 3.89	Castle Air Charters Ltd	Liskeard Heliport	24. 7.08E
			N200SH				
G-TEMB	Tecnam P2002-EA Sierra	PFA 333-14593		29.11.06	M B Hill	Nympsfield	
	(Built M B Hill)						
G-TEMP	Piper PA-28-180 Cherokee E	28-5806	G-AYBK	15. 5.89	F Busch International Ltd	Andrewsfield	6. 9.08E
			N11C				
G-TEMT	Hawker Tempest II	420	HA586	9.10.89	Tempest Two Ltd	Wickenby	
			(RIAF), MW763		(To be "MW763:HF-A" in RAF 183 Sqdn c/s: noted 10.06)		
G-TENG	Extra EA.300/L	172		8.12.03	10G Aerobatics Ltd	North Weald	29.12.06T
G-TENS	HOAC DV.20 Katana	20148	G-BXBW	28. 2.01	D C Wellard	Croft Farm, Defford	26. 7.08E
			D-ESHM				
G-TENT	Auster J/1N Alpha	2058	G-AKJU	1. 2.90	R C Callaway-Lewis	(South Mundham, Chichester)	30.10.08S
			TW513				
G-TERN	Europa Aviation Europa	106		18. 7.97	J Smith	(York)	13. 5.08P
	(Built J E G Lundesjo - pr.no.PFA 247-12780) (NSI EA-81/100) (Monowheel u/c)						
G-TERR	Cyclone Airsports Pegasus Quik	7925		6. 1.03	T R Thomas	Kemble	13. 1.08P
G-TERY	Piper PA-28-181 Archer II	28-7990078	G-BOXZ	13. 1.89	J R Bratherton	Bagby	31. 5.08E
			N22402				
G-TESI	Tecnam P2002-EA Sierra	PFA 333-14481		23.11.05	C C Burgess	White Waltham	5. 6.07P
	(Built P J Mitchell)				(New owner 1.08)		
G-TESR	Tecnam P2002-RG Sierra	PFA 333A-14758		4. 1.08	Tecnam UK Ltd	Hinton-in-the-Hedges	
	(Built P J Mitchell)						
G-TEST	Piper PA-34-200 Seneca	34-7450116	OO-RPW	28. 7.89	Stapleford Flying Club Ltd	Stapleford	23.12.07E
			G-BLCD, PH-PLZ, N41409				
G-TETI	Cameron N-90 Balloon (Hot Air)	2877	D-OBMW	9. 2.00	Teti SpA	Firenze, Italy	
G-TEWS	Piper PA-28-140 Cherokee B	28-25128	G-KEAN	23. 5.88	P M Ireland	South Lodge Farm, Widmerpool	4.11.07E
			G-AWTM, N11C				
G-TEXN	North American T-6G-NT Texan	168-176	G-BHTH	22. 6.05	Thunderprop Ltd	Shoreham	5 12.08E
			N2807G, 49-3072		(As "3072:72 in US Navy c/s)		
G-TEXS	Van's RV-6	23830	N996SF	28.10.04	D McCann	(Clonaslee, County Laois)	1. 3.08P
	(Built S Formhals)						
G-TEXT	Robinson R44 Raven II	10577		7.12.04	Sunken Ltd	(Dublin)	13. 1.08E
G-TFCI	Reims Cessna FA152 Aerobat	FA1520358		25.10.79	Tayside Aviation Ltd	Glenrothes	25. 2.08E
G-TFIN	Piper PA-32RT-300T Turbo Lance II	32R-7887012	N221RT	23.4.03	M D Parker	Bourn	9. 5.08E
			D-ELAL				
G-TFIX	Pegasus Quantum 15-912	8048		21. 7.04	T G Jones	Caernarfon	8. 7.08P
G-TFLY	Air Création 582(2)/Kiss 450	FL029		28. 6.05	A J Ladell	Sutton Meadows	22.11.07P
	(Built A J Ladell - pr.no.BMAA/HB/438 being Flylight kit [actually FL030 as FL027 duplicated] comprising Trike s/n T040843 and Wing s/n D065015)						
G-TFOG	Best Off Sky Ranger 912(2)	SKR0511661		2. 3.06	T J Fogg	Tarn Farm, Cockerham	3. 7.08P
	(Built T J Fogg - pr.no.BMAA/HB/494)						
G-TFOX	Denney Kitfox Model 2	PFA 172-11817		3. 6.91	D C Lugg	RNAS Culdrose	4. 7.07P
	(Built F A Roberts)				(New owner 9.07)		
G-TFUN	Valentin Taifun 17E	1011	D-KIHP	28.12.83	G F Wynn tr North West Taifun Group	Blackpool	23. 1.08E
					(Hangared in Container)		
G-TFYN	Piper PA-32RT-300 Lance II	32R-7885128	N5HG	28. 4.00	R C Poolman	Gloucestershire	5. 7.03T
			D-ELAE, N31740		(Noted 1.06)		
G-TGDL	Robinson R44 Raven II	11746		21. 5.07	Enable International Ltd	Wellesbourne Mountford	21. 6.08E
G-TGER	Gulfstream AA-5B Tiger	AA5B-0952	G-BFZP	20. 2.86	L J Haldenby	Rochester	3. 9.08E
G-TGGR	Eurocopter EC.120B Colibri	1224	SE-JMF	22. 7.04	Winterburn and Son Ltd	(Gomersal, Cleckheaton)	1. 8.07T
					(New owner 1.08)		
G-TGRA	Agusta A109A	7201	D-HEED	15. 2.01	Tiger Helicopters Ltd	Shobdon	14. 5.08E
			N3983N, HB-XNF, I-PATZ				
G-TGRD	Robinson R22 Beta II	2712	G-OPTS	16. 6.04	Tiger Helicopters Ltd	Shobdon	17. 8.08E
G-TGRE	Robinson R22 Alpha	0471	G-SOLD	11. 9.03	Tiger Helicopters Ltd	Shobdon	17. 6.06T
			N8559X				
G-TGRS	Robinson R22 Beta	1069	G-DELL	5.11.97	Tiger Helicopters Ltd	Shobdon	23. 8.08E
			N80466				
G-TGRZ	Bell 206B-2 JetRanger II	2288	G-BXZX	15. 6.00	Tiger Helicopters Ltd	Shobdon	21.11.07E
			N27EA, N286CA, N93AT, N16873				
G-TGTT	Robinson R44 Raven II	10023	G-STUS	8. 1.08	London Helicopter Centres Ltd	Redhill	4. 2.06E
			N369SB, G-STUS				
G-THAT	Raj Hamsa X'Air Falcon 912(1)	613		27. 5.02	A N Green	Stoke, Isle of Grain	5. 7.08P
	(Built M G Thatcher - pr.no.BMAA/HB/221)						

G-THEA	Boeing Stearman E75 (N2S-5) Kaydet (Lycoming R-680)	75-5736A	(EI-RYR) N1733B, USN Bu.38122	18. 3.81	C M Ryan *"Spirit of Tipperary'"*	Weston, Leixlip, County Kildare	18.12.08E
G-THEO	TEAM Mini-MAX 91 (Built T Willford) (Built up rear fuselage)	PFA 186-13099		9. 2.99	D W Melville	Dunkeswell	7. 8.08P
G-THIN	Reims FR172E Rocket	FR17200016	G-BXYY OY-AHO, F-WLIP	4.12.02	C A Ussher	New Laithe Farm, Harewood	24. 6.08E
G-THLA	Robinson R22 Beta II	3462		18. 7.03	Thurston Helicopters Ltd	Headcorn	8. 8.08E
G-THMB	Van's RV-9A (Built C H P Bell)	PFA 320-14266		26. 6.06	C H P Bell Eddsfield, Octon Lodge Farm, Thwing		
G-THOC	Boeing 737-59D	24694	G-BVKA SE-DNA, (SE-DLA)	28. 4.04	Thomsonfly Ltd *"Spirit of Doncaster"*	Doncaster-Sheffield	28. 2.08E
G-THOD	Boeing 737-59D	24695	G-BVKC SE-DNB, (SE-DLB)	30. 6.04	Thomsonfly Ltd *"The Three Spires"*	Coventry	15. 5.08E
G-THOE	Boeing 737-3Q8	26313	G-BZZH N14384	9.12.04	Thomsonfly Ltd	Bournemouth	19. 3.08E
G-THOF	Boeing 737-3Q8	26314	G-BZZI N73385	9.12.04	Thomsonfly Ltd	Bournemouth	27. 3.08E
G-THOG	Boeing 737-31S	29057	D-ADBM	1. 4.05	Thomsonfly Ltd	Bournemouth	7. 4.08E
G-THOH	Boeing 737-31S	29058	D-ADBN	22. 4.05	Thomsonfly Ltd	Coventry	21. 4.08E
G-THOI	Boeing 737-36Q	29327	G-OFRA	27. 5.05	Thomsonfly Ltd	Doncaster-Sheffield	17. 5.08E
G-THOJ	Boeing 737-36Q	28659	G-ODUS D-ADBX	4. 4.06	Thomsonfly Ltd	Doncaster-Sheffield	15. 4.08E
G-THOK	Boeing 737-36Q	28660	G-IGOB EC-GNU	20. 4.06	Thomsonfly Ltd	Doncaster-Sheffield	24. 1.08E
G-THOL	Boeing 737-36N	28594	G-IGOK N1786B	27. 4.06	Thomsonfly Ltd	Coventry	23. 4.08E
G-THOM	Thunder Ax6-56 Balloon (Hot Air)	366		14. 7.81	T H Wilson *"Macavity"*	Shieldaig, Strathcarron	14. 8.07A
G-THON	Boeing 737-36N	28596	G-IGOL N1015X	27. 6.06	Thomsonfly Ltd	Doncaster-Sheffield	25. 6.08E
G-THOO	Boeing 737-33V	29335	HA-LKT G-EZYK	30. 1.07	Thomsonfly Ltd	Coventry	30. 1.08E
G-THOP	Boeing 737-3U3	28740	N335AW N1790B, N1787B, (PK-GGM), (PK-GGK)	28. 2.07	Thomsonfly Ltd	(Luton)	22. 5.08E
G-THOS	Thunder Ax7-77 Balloon (Hot Air)	769		20. 2.86	C E A Breton *"Tohskcub"*	Saltford, Bristol	14. 3.01A
G-THOT	Avtech Jabiru SK (Built N V Cook - pr.no.PFA 274-13159)	xxxx		16. 9.97	S G Holton	Poplar Hall Farm, Elmsett	26.11.08P
G-THRE	Cessna 182S Skylane	18280454	N2391A	6. 5.99	C Malet	Roques sur Garonne, France	22. 2.08E
G-THRM	Schleicher ASW 27	27142	G-CJWC BGA 4831-JWC	26.10.07	C G Starkey	Lasham	28.12.07
G-THSL	Piper PA-28R-201 Arrow III	28R-7837278	N36396	11. 9.78	D M Markscheffel	Southend	3. 4.08E
G-THZL	SOCATA TB-20 Trinidad	534	F-GJDR N65TB	9. 5.96	Thistle Aviation Ltd	Oxford	16. 4.08E
G-TICH	Taylor JT.2 Titch (Built A J House, C J Wheeler and R Davitt - pr.no.originally allocated as PFA 3213)	PFA 060-3213		12. 2.01	R Davitt (New owner 1.06)	(Thatcham)	
G-TIDS	SAN Jodel D 150 Mascaret	44	OO-GAN	15. 4.86	M R Parker	Sywell	26.11.08P
G-TIGA	de Havilland DH.82A Tiger Moth (Built Morris Motors Ltd)	83547	G-AOEG T7120	5. 6.85	D E Leatherland	Tollerton	2. 5.10S
G-TIGC	Aérospatiale AS.332L Super Puma	2024	G-BJYH F-WTNJ	14. 4.82	Bristow Helicopters Ltd *"Royal Burgh of Montrose"*	Aberdeen	17. 5.08E
G-TIGE	Aérospatiale AS.332L Super Puma	2028	G-BJYJ F-WTNM	15. 4.82	Bristow Helicopters Ltd *"City of Dundee"*	Aberdeen	7. 6.08E
G-TIGF	Aérospatiale AS.332L Super Puma	2030	F-WKQJ	15. 4.82	Bristow Helicopters Ltd *"Peterhead"*	Aberdeen	27. 6.08E
G-TIGG	Aérospatiale AS.332L Super Puma	2032	F-WXFT	15. 4.82	Bristow Helicopters Ltd *"Macduff"*	Aberdeen	1. 8.08E
G-TIGJ	Aérospatiale AS.332L Super Puma	2042	VH-BHT G-TIGJ	15. 4.82	Bristow Helicopters Ltd *"Rosehearty"*	(Mauritania)	29. 6.08E
G-TIGO	Aérospatiale AS.332L Super Puma	2061	PP-MIM G-TIGO, F-WMHH	18. 2.83	Bristow Helicopters Ltd *"Royal Burgh of Arbroath"*	Aberdeen	22. 8.08E
G-TIGS	Aérospatiale AS.332L Super Puma	2086		6. 5.83	Bristow Helicopters Ltd *"Findochty"*	Aberdeen	27. 6.08E
G-TIGV	Aérospatiale AS.332L Super Puma	2099	LN-ONC G-TIGVS, LN-ONC, G-TIGV, LN-OPF, G-TIGV *"Burghead"*	12. 1.84	Bristow Helicopters Ltd	Aberdeen	25. 6.08E
G-TIII	Pitts S-2A (Built Aerotek Inc)	2196	G-BGSE N947	27. 2.89	S B Janvrin tr Treble India Group	Redhill	1. 5.08E
G-TILE	Robinson R22 Beta	1100		4. 8.89	Fenland Helicopters Ltd	Cranfield	27. 6.08E
G-TILI	Bell 206B-2 JetRanger II	2061	F-GHFN N7037A, XC-BOQ	6. 3.96	TLC Handling Ltd	Sandtoft	30. 1.08E
G-TIMB	Rutan VariEze (Built B Wronski) (Continental O-200-A)	PFA 074-10795	G-BKXJ	11. 6.85	P G Kavanagh *"Kitty"*	Barton	15. 8.07P
G-TIMC	Robinson R44 Raven II	11102	G-CDUR	30. 3.06	T Clark Aviation LLP	Wycombe Air Park	6. 4.08E
G-TIMG	Beagle Terrier 3 (Built T J Goodwin to comprise Auster 6 fuselage frame and wing of VF505 unused in rebuild of Terrier G-ASOM - noted 8.03)	"PFA 00-318"		7. 3.01	T J Goodwin	(Manningtree)	
G-TIMH	Robinson R22	4108	N3158D	19. 2.07	HP Rentals Ltd	(Old Brampton, Chesterfield)	27. 2.08E
G-TIMK	Piper PA-28-181 Archer II	28-8090214	OO-TRT PH-EAS, OO-HLN, N8142H	25. 8.81	T Baker	Halfpenny Green	23. 8.08E
G-TIML	Cessna 172S Skyhawk	172S10187	N6031F	31. 7.06	Tim Leacock Aircraft Sales Ltd	Bournemouth	8. 8.08E
G-TIMM	Folland Gnat T 1	FL.519	8618M XP504	19. 2.92	T J Manna t/a Kennet Aviation (As *"XS111"* in RAF c/s)	North Weald	20. 5.08P
G-TIMP	Aeronca 7BCM Champion (Continental C85)	7AC-3392	N84681 NC84681	14. 8.92	R B Valler	Goodwood	19. 9.07P
G-TIMS	Falconar F-12A Cruiser (Built T Sheridan)	PFA 022-12134		1.10.91	T Sheridan	Wellingborough	
G-TIMY	Sud-Aviation Gardan GY-80-160 Horizon	36	I-TIKI	17. 1.00	R G Whyte	Dunstable	28. 7.08E
G-TINA	SOCATA TB-10 Tobago	67		30.10.79	A Lister	Shipdham	10. 3.08E
G-TING	Cameron O-120 Balloon (Hot Air)	4007		4.10.96	Floating Sensations Ltd	Thatcham	11. 8.06T
G-TINK	Robinson R22 Beta	0937	G-NICH	22. 5.01	Helicentre Liverpool Ltd	Walton Wood	22.12.07E

Reg	Type	c/n	Prev id	Date	Owner	Location	Date
G-TINS	Cameron N-90 Balloon (Hot Air)	1626		27. 1.88	J R Clifton	Nelson, New Zealand	11.10.03A
					(Carling Black Label titles)		
G-TINT	Evektor EV-97A Eurostar	PFA 315-14394		8. 8.05	I A Cunningham	Perth	11. 1.08P
	(Built I A Cunningham)						
G-TINY	Moravan Zlin Z-526F Trener	1257	OK-CMD	10. 5.95	D Evans	Little Gransden	6. 2.08E
	(Walter M137A)		G-TINY, YR-ZAD				
G-TIPS	Nipper T 66 Series 3	T66/50	OO-VAL	27. 3.95	R F L Cuypers and F V Neefs	Denham	10. 8.06P
			9Q-CYJ, 9O-CYJ, (OO-CYJ), (OO-CCD)				
	(Built Avions Fairey SA: rebuilt R F L Cuypers - pr.no.PFA 025-12696) (Jabiru 2200A)						
G-TIVS	Rans S-6-ES Coyote II	1203.1536		10. 5.04	D Kay	Little Gransden	29.10.08P
	(Built S Hoyle - pr.no.PFA 204-14236) (Tri-cycle u/c)						
G-TIVV	Evektor EV-97 Eurostar	PFA 315-14435		4. 8.05	I Shulver	Baxby Manor, Husthwaite	13.11.08P
	(Built S Hoyle)						
G-TJAL	Avtech Jabiru SPL-430	0210		21. 2.03	D W Cross	Wickenby	6. 2.08P
	(Built T J Adams-Lewis - pr.no.PFA 274A-13360)						
G-TJAV	Mainair Sports Pegasus Quik	8070		23. 9.04	B Robertson	Black Isle, Cromarty	23.12.07P
G-TJAY	Piper PA-22-135 Tri-Pacer	22-730	N730TJ	11. 5.93	D Pegley	(Wisborough Green, Billingshurst)	28. 9.08E
			N2353A				
G-TJDM	Van's RV-6A	PFA 181-13370		21. 9.07	J D Michie	(Lightwater)	
	(Built J D Michie)						
G-TKAY	Europa Aviation Europa	179		2. 6.99	A M Kay	Nuthampstead	14. 8.07P
	(Built A M Kay - pr.no.PFA 247-12804) (Monowheel u/c)						
G-TKGR	Lindstrand Racing Car SS Balloon (Hot Air) 380			28. 8.96	Brown and Williamson Tobacco Corporation (Export) Ltd		
					"Team Green"	Louisville, Kentucky, US	20. 8.99A
G-TKIS	Tri-R KIS	029		23.12.93	J L Bone	Biggin Hill	28. 4.06P
	(Built J L Bone - pr.no.FA 239-12358) (Lycoming O-290-D2) (Tail-wheel u/c)						
G-TKPZ	Cessna 310R II	310R1225		19. 3.90	Aircraft Engineers Ltd	Prestwick	1. 4.08E
			N1909G				
G-TLDK	Piper PA-22-150 Caribbean	22-4726	N6072D	27. 1.97	A M Thomson	(Cheriton, Alresford)	
	(Tailwheel u/c)				*(Noted 2006)*		
G-TLDL	Medway SLA 100 Executive	290906		29. 3.07	D T Lucas	Stoke, Isle of Grain	28. 3.08E
G-TLEL	American Blimp Corp A-60+ Airship	003	I-TIRE	17. 5.02	Lightship Europe Ltd	(Chilbolton, Stockbridge)	26. 5.05T
			N2017A		*(New owner 8.05)*		
G-TLET	Piper PA-28-161 Cadet	2841259	G-GFCF	25. 8.04	A D and C Realff t/a ADR Aviation	Shoreham	10. 3.08E
	(Thielert TAE 125-01)		G-RHBH, N9193J				
G-TLTL	Schempp-Hirth Discus CS	257CS	BGA 4679-JPU	11. 1.08	E K.Armitage	Camphill	27. 2.08
G-TMAN	Ozone/Adventure Roadster-Funflyer Quattro			22. 2.08	P A Mahony	(Derriford, Plymouth)	
		MAG-J-03B100/1070108					
G-TMCB	Best Off Sky Ranger 912(2)	SKR0309378		23.10.03	A H McBreen	(Woolscott, Rugby)	3.12.08P
	(Built A H McBreen - pr.no.BMAA/HB/310)						
G-TMCC	Cameron N-90 Balloon (Hot Air)	4327		30. 3.98	Prudential Assurance Company Ltd	Bristol	7. 6.02A
					(The Mall-Cribbs Causeway titles)		
G-TMKI	Percival P 56 Provost T 1	PAC/F/268	WW453	1. 7.92	B L Robinson	(Barrington, Ilminster)	
G-TMOL	SOCATA TB-20 Trinidad	2103	F-OJBQ	24.12.01	Blackbrooks LLP	Belfast International	20. 1.08E
G-TMRA	Short SD.3-60 Variant 100	SH3686	G-SSWC	5.11.06	HD Air Ltd	(Sutton Courtenay, Abingdon)	14.11.07E
			SE-LGE, G-BMHX, G-14-3686 *(New owner 1.08)*				
G-TMRB	Short SD.3-60 Variant 100	SH3690	G-SSWB	14.12.06	HD Air Ltd	Luton	10. 1.08E
			C6-BFT, N690PC, G-BMLE, G-14-3690 *(Noted 2.08)*				
G-TMRO	Short SD.3-60 Variant 100	SH3712	EI-SMA	15. 7.05	BAC Group Ltd	Rennes, France	21. 7.06E
			G-OBLK, G-BNDI, G-OBLK, G-BNDI, G-14-3172 *(Noted 10.06)*				
G-TMUR	Agusta A109A II	7289	G-CEPO	14. 5.07	Castle Air Charters Ltd	Liskeard Heliport	9.10.08E
			RP-C2400, I-MIIT, N109BB				
G-TNRG	Air Création Tanarg 912S(2)/iXess 15	FLT002		2.11.05	C M Saysell	Plaistows Farm, St Albans	25 10.08P
	(Built C M Saysell - pr.no.BMAA/HB/468 being Flylight kit comprising Trike s/n T05070 and Wing s/n A05147-5129)						
G-TNTN	Thunder Ax6-56 Balloon (Hot Air)	1991		25. 4.91	H M Savage and J F Trehern *"Tintin"*	Edinburgh	4 5.08A
G-TOAD	SAN Jodel D 140 Mousquetaire	27	F-BIZG	27. 9.88	J H Stevens	Headcorn	24. 7.08E
G-TOAK	SOCATA TB-20 Trinidad	468	N83AV	5.12.89	K Kane and A Marshall tr Phoenix Group		
						Enniskillen	11. 1.08E
G-TOBA	SOCATA TB-10 Tobago	625	N600N	4. 4.91	E J Downing	Lee-on-Solent	15. 5.08E
G-TOBI	Reims Cessna F172K	F17200792	G-AYVB	5. 1.84	A P Brisley tr The TOBI Group	Leicester	14. 7.08E
G-TODG	Flight Design CTSW	07.04.06		26. 4.07	M G Titmus	Otherton, Cannock	26. 4.08P
	(Assembled P&M Aviation Ltd with c/n 8288)						
G-TOFT	Thunder and Colt 90A Balloon (Hot Air)	1693		8. 3.90	C S Perceval *"Bumble"*	Great Missenden	20. 5.03A
G-TOGO	Van's RV-6A	PFA 181A-13447		6. 4.99	I R Thomas	Shoreham	13. 5.08P
	(Built G Schwetz)				*"Gernot"*		
G-TOHS	Cameron V-31 Balloon (Hot Air)	10267		4.11.02	J P Moore	Great Missenden	7. 4.08
G-TOIL	Enstrom 480B	5082		4. 7.05	Toughers Oil Distributors Ltd		
					Tougher Business Park, Newhall, Naas, County Kildare		10. 8.08E
G-TOLI	Robinson R44 Raven II	12009		17.11.07	JNK 2000 Ltd	(Thornbury, Bromyard)	
G-TOLL	Piper PA-28R-201 Arrow III	28R-7837025	N52HV	12.10.00	Arrow Aircraft Ltd	Tatenhill	4. 1.08E
			D-ECIW, N9007K				
G-TOLY	Robinson R22 Beta II	2809	G-NSHR	8. 2.01	HelicopterServices Ltd	Wycombe Air Park	13. 3.08T
G-TOMC	North American AT-6D Texan	88-14602	French AF 114700	22. 4.02	A A Marshall tr Texan Restoration	Bruntingthorpe	
			42-44514		*(On rebuild 5.05)*		
G-TOMJ	Flight Design CT2K	03-04-01-14		28. 7.03	J Fleming	Perth	21. 8.07P
	(Assembled Mainair Sports Ltd with c/n 7975)						
G-TOMM	Robinson R22 Beta II	3384		5.11.02	EBG (Helicopters) Ltd	Redhill	2.12.07E
G-TOMS	Piper PA-38-112 Tomahawk	38-79A0453	N9658N	22. 1.79	A J Hutchinson tr G-TOMS Group	Swansea	25.10.08T
G-TOMZ	Denney Kitfox Model 2	PFA 172-11977		15.11.00	G G Ansell	Kimbolton	22. 5.08P
	(Built P T Knight and L James) (Rotax 912)						
G-TONN	Mainair Sports Pegasus Quik	7954		28. 5.03	P C Bishop	Dunkeswell	21. 6.08P
G-TONS	Slingsby T 67M-200 Firefly	2045	LN-TFA	22. 7.03	D I Stanbridge	(Taverham, Norwich)	28. 1.08E
			SE-LBA, LN-TFA, G-7-121				
G-TOOL	Thunder Ax8-105 Balloon (Hot Air)	1670		29. 3.90	D V Howard *(Toolmaster Hire titles)*	Bath	7. 6.08A

Reg	Type	C/n	Prev ID	Date	Owner/Operator	Location	Status
G-TOOT	Dyn'Aéro MCR-01 Club PFA 301-13542			1. 3.01	S W Hosking	Newton Peverill, Sturminster Marshall	23. 9.08P
	(Built E K Griffin)						
G-TOPC	Aérospatiale AS.355F1 Ecureuil 2	5313	I-LGOG	29. 7.97	Kinetic Avionics Ltd	Elstree	6.11.07E
			3A-MCS, D-HOSY, OE-BXV, D-HOSY				
G-TOPK	Europa Aviation Europa XS	1000		16. 3.04	P J Kember	Fowle Hall Farm, Laddingford	20. 6.07P
	(Built P J Kember - pr.no.PFA 247-14193) (Tri-Gear u/c)						
G-TOPO	Piper PA-23-250 Turbo Aztec E	27-4587	G-BGWW	23. 1.07	Keen Leasing (IoM) Ltd	Ronaldsway	7. 6.08E
			OO-ABH, N13971				
G-TOPS	Aérospatiale AS.355F1 Ecureuil 2	5151	G-BPRH	7. 5.91	Sterling Helicopters Ltd	Hawarden	24. 1.08E
			N360E, N5794F				
G-TOPZ	Aérospatiale SA.342J Gazelle	1473	F-GGTJ	20.12.06	Top Yachts Ltd	(Exeter)	11. 1.08E
			F-WXFX, C-GVWC				
G-TORC	Piper PA-28R-200 Cherokee Arrow II		OE-DIU	18. 7.03	Solo Leisure Ltd	Old Sarum	25. 9.08T
		28R-7535036	N32236				
G-TORK	Cameron Z-105 Balloon (Hot Air)	10968		5. 1.07	M E Dunstan-Sewell	St Andrews, Bristol	16. 1.08E
					(Rotork titles)		
G-TORN	Flight Design CTSW	06.05.04		1. 2.07	D J Haygreen	(Rhos-on-Sea, Colwyn Bay)	31. 1.08P
	(Assembled P&M Aviation Ltd with c/n 8189)						
G-TORS	Robinson R22 Beta II	3021		4. 1.00	IW Aviation Ltd	Wellesbourne Mountford	23. 3.08E
G-TOSH	Robinson R22 Beta	0933	N2629S	14. 3.97	J T Helicopters Ltd	Thruxton	3.10.07E
			LV-RBD, N8012T				
G-TOTN	Cessna 210M Centurion II	21061674	G-BVZM	15. 7.04	K Bettoney	(Laxey, Isle of Man)	21. 6.08E
			OO-CNJ, N732PV				
G-TOTO	Reims Cessna F177RG Cardinal RG		G-OADE	29. 8.89	A S C Richardson	(London W12)	5. 8.08E
		F177RG0049	G-AZKH				
G-TOUR	Robin R2112	187		9.10.79	Mardenair Ltd	Goodwood	28. 3.08E
					(Operated Plessey Flying Group)		
G-TOWS	Piper PA-25-260 Pawnee C	25-4853	PH-VBT	17. 7.91	Lasham Gliding Society Ltd	Lasham	3. 4.08E
	(Hoffman 4 -blade propeller)		D-EAVI, N4370Y, N9722N				
G-TOYA	Boeing 737-3Q8	26310	G-BZZE	13.12.04	British Midland Airways Ltd	East Midlands	17.12.07E
			N14381		"Brummie Baby" (Operated BMI Baby)		
G-TOYB	Boeing 737-3Q8	26311	G-BZZF	24.11.04	British Midland Airways Ltd	East Midlands	21. 7.06E
			N19382		(Operated BMI Baby)		
G-TOYC	Boeing 737-3Q8	26312	G-BZZG	13.12.04	British Midland Airways Ltd	Birmingham	3. 3.08E
			N14383		(Operated BMI Baby)		
G-TOYD	Boeing 737-3Q8	26307	G-EZYT	13. 6.05	British Midland Airways Ltd	East Midlands	27. 6.08E
			HB-IIE, N721LF, (HB-IIE)		(Operated BMI Baby)		
G-TOYE	Boeing 737-33A	27455	OO-LTU	4. 5.05	British Midland Airways Ltd	East Midlands	12. 5.08E
					(Operated BMI Baby)		
G-TOYF	Boeing 737-36N	28557	G-IGOO	28.11.05	British Midland Airways Ltd	East Midlands	20. 3.08E
			G-SMDB		"Rainbow Baby" (Operated BMI Baby)		
G-TOYG	Boeing 737-36N	28872	G-IGOJ	13. 1.06	British Midland Airways Ltd	East Midlands	20.11.07E
			N1795B, (N968WP)		"Butterfly Baby" (Operated BMI Baby)		
G-TOYH	Boeing 737-36N	28570	G-IGOY	22.12.05	British Midland Airways Ltd	East Midlands	10. 4.08E
			CS-TGQ		"Baby of the North" (Operated BMI Baby)		
G-TOYI	Boeing 737			3.08R	British Midland Airways Ltd	East Midlands	
G-TOYJ	Boeing 737-36M	28332	PK-GGW	10. 4.07	British Midland Airways Ltd	East Midlands	10. 4.08E
			YR-BGY, OO-VEA, (OO-EBZ)				
G-TOYK	Boeing 737-33R	28870 N870GX	PP-VPX	31. 5.07	British Midland Airways Ltd	East Midlands	31. 5.08E
			N965WP		(Operated BMI Baby)		
G-TOYZ	Bell 206B-3 JetRanger III	3949	G-RGER	21.11.96	Potter Aviation Ltd	Welshpool	28. 2.08E
			N75EA, JA9452, N32018				
G-TPSL	Cessna 182S Skylane	18280398	N23700	11.12.98	A N Purslow	Blackbushe	16. 3.08E
G-TPWL	P&M Quik GT450	8187		16. 5.06	P W Lupton	Arclid Green, Sandbach	9. 5.08E
G-TRAC	Robinson R44 Astro	0598		10. 5.99	C Sharples	Thruxton	24. 5.08E
G-TRAM	Pegasus Quantum 15-912 Super Sport	7552		29. 7.99	L M Courtney, P Smith and T Clifton		
						Mapperley, Nottingham	11.10.08P
G-TRAN	Beech 76 Duchess	ME-408	G-NIFR	15. 3.93	Multiflight Ltd	Leeds-Bradford	25. 9.07T
			N1808A				
G-TRAT	Pilatus PC-12/47	710	HB-FQX	18. 4.06	D J Trathen "t4"	Bournemouth	18. 4.08E
G-TRAX	Reims Cessna F172M Skyhawk F172O1081		D-EIQU	22.11.06	Skytrax Aviation Ltd	Blackbushe	14. 1.08E
	(Thielert TAE 125-01)						
G-TRBO	Schleicher ASW 28-18E	28743	BGA 5238-KNW	18. 7.06	C J Davison and A Closkey	Saltby	22. 1.08
G-TRCW	Robinson R44 Clipper	1217	N844PR	31. 8.06	Leus Aviation Ltd	Nicosia, Cyprus	30.10.07E
G-TRCY	Robinson R44 Astro	0668		22.10.99	Sugarfree Air Ltd	Nicosia, Cyprus	19. 1.08E
G-TREC	Cessna 421C Golden Eagle	421C0838	G-TLOL	2. 7.96	Sovereign Business Integration PLC	Cranfield	6. 3.08E
			(N2659K)				
G-TREE	Bell 206B-3 JetRanger III	2826	N2779U	15. 6.87	R B Eaton t/a Bush Woodlands	Halfpenny Green	12. 3.08T
G-TREK	Jodel D 18	182		1. 5.92	R H Mole	Leicester	30. 8.08P
	(Built R H Mole - pr.no.PFA 169-11265) (JPX4TX @ 65hp)						
G-TREX	Alpi Pioneer 300	9		6. 1.05	R K King	Gloucestershire	1. 2.08P
	(Built R K King - pr.no.PFA 330-14305)						
G-TRIB	Lindstrand HS-110 Airship (Hot Air)	174	(N....)	23. 1.95	J Addison	Melton Mowbray	17. 8.05A
G-TRIC	de Havilland DHC-1 Chipmunk 22A	C1/0080	G-AOSZ	18.12.89	A A Fernandez Ocana, Castilla, La Mancha, Spain		2.11.09S
			WB635		(As "18013:013" in RCAF c/s)		
G-TRIG	Cameron Z-90 Balloon (Hot Air)	10446		28. 7.03	Trigger Concepts Ltd	Swallowfield, Reading	12. 8.08A
					(Intel Inside/Centrino titles)		
G-TRIM	Monnett Moni	00258T		16. 2.84	E A Brotherton-Ratcliffe	(London SW6)	
	(Built Monnett Aircraft- pr.no.PFA 142-11012)				(New owner 1.05)		
G-TRIN	SOCATA TB-20 Trinidad	1131		25. 6.90	D P Boyle	Leeds-Bradford	9. 3.08E
G-TRIO	Cessna 172M Skyhawk II	17266271	G-BNXY	30. 7.91	C M B Reid	Rochester	29. 1.08E
			N9621H				
G-TRNT	Robinson R44 Raven II	10293	OE-XHW	17. 9.04	Charles Trent Ltd	Bournemouth	23. 9.07T
G-TROP	Cessna T310R II	310R1381	N4250C	31.12.86	D E Carpenter	Shoreham	19. 5.08E

G-TROY	North American T-28A Trojan	142/174-545	F-AZFV	21. 4.99	S G Howell and S Tilling	Duxford	12.12.08P
			French AF 142, 51-7692		(As "517692:142" in French AF c/s)		
G-TRTM	DG Flugzeugbau DG-808C	8-378B277X39		23. 8.07	ATSI Ltd	(Chalfont St Giles)	
G-TRUD	Enstrom 480	5022	XT-BOK	27. 2.01	Sussex Aviation Ltd	Shoreham	25. 3.08E
G-TRUE	Hughes 369E	0490E	N6TK	12. 9.94	N E Bailey	(Ogbourne Maizey, Marlborough)	10. 6.08T
	(Hughes 500)		ZK-HFP				
G-TRUK	Stoddard-Hamilton Glasair RG	575R		23. 7.84	M P Jackson	Fairoaks	26. 6.08P
	(Built M P Jackson - pr.no.PFA 149-11015) (Lycoming O-320)						
G-TRUX	Colt 77A Balloon (Hot Air)	1860		13.11.90	J B R Elliot	Gorleston, Great Yarmouth	10. 2.06P
G-TRYK	Air Création 582(2)/Kiss 450	FL004		31.10.01	S Elsbury and S van Straten (Noted 9.07)		
	(Built S Elsbury - pr.no.BMAA/HB/191 being Flylight kit comprising Trike s/n T01098 and Wing s/n A01157-1163)					Damyn's Hall, Upminster	25. 6.06P
G-TRYX	Enstrom 480B	5083		15. 7.05	Atryx Aviation LLP	North Weald	10. 8.08E
G-TSAC	Tecnam P2002-EA Sierra	PFA 333-14611		19.12.07	A G Cozens	Goodwood	
	(Built A G Cozens)						
G-TSDS	Piper PA-32R-301 Saratoga II SP	32R-8013132	N145AV	3.10.05	I R Jones	Liverpool	17.11.07E
			EC-HHM, G-TRIP, G-HOSK, PH-WET, OO-HKN, N8261X				
G-TSGA	Piper PA-28R-201 Cherokee Arrow III		G-ONSF	3. 7.07	TSG Aviation Ltd	(Bourne)	4. 4.08E
		28R-7737082	G-EMAK, D-EMAK, N38180				
G-TSGJ	Piper PA-28-181 Archer II	28-8090109	N8097W	12. 9.88	J O Elliott and G White tr Golf Juliet Flying Group		
						Durham Tees Valley	1. 2.07
G-TSIX	North American AT-6C-1-NT Harvard IIA	88-9725	FAP1535	19. 3.79	S J Davies	Sandtoft	29.11.08P
			SAAF7183, EX289, 41-33262		(As "111836/JZ:6" in USN c/s)		
G-TSKD	Raj Hamsa X'Air Falcon Jabiru(2)	633		8. 5.01	T Sexton and K B Dupuy	Southend	2.11.08P
	(Built T Sexton and K B Dupuy - pr.no.BMAA/HB/165)						
G-TSKY	Beagle B 121 Pup Series 2	B121-010	OE-CFM	6. 4.98	R G Hayes	North Weald	31. 5.08E
			HB-NAA, G-AWDY, HB-NAA, G-AWDY				
G-TSLC	Schweizer 269C-1	0246	(G-CDYV (1))	22. 6.06	TSL Contractors Ltd	Glenforsa, Isle of Mull	25. 7.08E
	(Schweizer 300)		N86G				
G-TSOB	Rans S-6-ES Coyote II	1202.1471		28. 6.04	S Luck	Audley End	14. 1.08P
	(Built S C Luck - pr.no.PFA 204-14066)(Tri-cycle u/c)				"The Spirit of Brooklands"		
G-TSOL	EAA Acrosport	PFA 072-11391	G-BPKI	18. 7.00	A G Fowles	(Shrewsbury)	31. 3.00P
	(Built J Sykes) (Lycoming O-320)						
G-TSUE	Europa Aviation Europa	048		15. 8.05	A L and S Thorne	White Waltham	
	(Built A L Thorne - pr.no.PFA 247-12612)						
G-TSWI	Lindstrand LBL 90A Balloon (Hot Air)	1149		5. 2.07	Dylan Harvey Group Ltd	Salford	12. 3.08E
G-TTDD	Zenair CH.701 STOL	PFA 187-13106		1. 9.97	D B Dainton and V D Asque	Little Staughton	12. 3.08P
	(Built B E Trinder and D B Dainton) (Jabiru 2200A)						
G-TTFG	Colt 77B Balloon (Hot Air)	1993	G-BUZF	5. 2.08	M J and T J Turner (Wellingborough-Southampton)		3. 9.08A
G-TTHC	Robinson R22 Beta	1196		21.12.89	Multiflight Ltd	Leeds-Bradford	23. 6.08E
G-TTHL	Ruschmeyer R90-230RG	016	G-TODE	1. 5.07	H Loll	(Mechtersen, Germany)	26. 5.08E
			D-EEAX				
G-TTIA	Airbus A321-231	1428	D-AVZA	19. 2.01	GB Airways Ltd "Mons Teide"	London Gatwick	18. 2.08E
					(To become G-OZBS with Monarch 8.08)		
G-TTIC	Airbus A321-231	1869	D-AVZZ	12.12.02	GB Airways Ltd	London Gatwick	11.12.07E
G-TTID	Airbus A321-231	2462	D-AVZB	12. 5.05	GB Airways Ltd	London Gatwick	11. 5.08E
			(G-EUXI)				
G-TTIE	Airbus A321-231	2682	D-AVZD	23. 5.06	GB Airways Ltd	London Gatwick	22. 5.08E
			(G-EUXJ)				
G-TTIF	Airbus A321-231	3106	D-AVZC	25. 5.07	GB Airways Ltd	London Gatwick	24. 5.08E
			(G-EUXL)				
G-TTIG	Airbus A321-231	3382	D-AVZL	21. 2.08	GB Airways Ltd	London Gatwick	
G-TTIH	Airbus A321-231		D-AV..	.08R	GB Airways Ltd	London Gatwick	
G-TTII	Airbus A321-231		D-AV..	.08R	GB Airways Ltd	London Gatwick	
G-TTMB	Bell 206B-3 JetRanger III	947	G-RNME	26. 6.03	Sky Charter UK Ltd	(Sheffield City)	23. 8.08E
			G-CBDF, N211KR, JA9119, N58064				
G-TTOB	Airbus A320-232	1687	F-WWIM	11. 2.02	GB Airways Ltd "Mons Calpe"	London Gatwick	13. 2.08E
G-TTOC	Airbus A320-232	1715	F-WWDB	6. 3.02	GB Airways Ltd "Mons Veleta"	London Gatwick	5. 3.08E
G-TTOD	Airbus A320-232	1723	F-WWBH	14. 3.02	GB Airways Ltd "Mons Estrela"	London Gatwick	13. 3.08E
G-TTOE	Airbus A320-232	1754	F-WWDH	11. 4.02	GB Airways Ltd	London Gatwick	10. 4.08E
					"Mons Cruz De Tejeda"		
G-TTOF	Airbus A320-232	1918	F-WWIS	13. 2.03	GB Airways Ltd	London Gatwick	12. 2.08E
G-TTOG	Airbus A320-232	1969	F-WWDZ	10. 4.03	GB Airways Ltd	London Gatwick	9. 4.08E
G-TTOH	Airbus A320-232	1993	F-WWDO	2. 5.03	GB Airways Ltd	London Gatwick	1. 5.08E
G-TTOI	Airbus A320-232	2137	F-WWBN	11.12.03	GB Airways Ltd	London Gatwick	10.12.07E
G-TTOJ	Airbus A320-232	2157	F-WWDE	30. 3.04	GB Airways Ltd	London Gatwick	29. 3.07T
G-TTOK	Airbus A320-232			3.08R	GB Airways Ltd	London Gatwick	
G-TTOY	CFM Streak Shadow SA	K 233		15. 4.96	J Softley	(Newbury)	11.12.07P
	(Built D A Payne - pr.no.PFA 206-12805) (Rotax 618)						
G-TTRL	Van's RV-9A	PFA 320-14248		11.12.07	J E Gattrell	Sittles Farm, Alrewas	
	(Built J E Gattrell)						
G-TUBB	Avtech Jabiru UL-450	0256		1.10.99	A H Bower	Chavenage, Tetbury	17. 2.08P
	(Built A H Bower and A Silvester - pr.no.PFA 274A-13484)						
G-TUCK	Van's RV-8	81534		25. 9.03	M A Tuck	Oxford	18. 8.08P
	(Built M A Tuck - pr.no.PFA 303-13706)						
G-TUDR	Cameron V-77 Balloon (Hot Air)	1135		20. 5.85	J W Soukup	Bristol	29. 9.04A
					"Tudor Rose and HVIIIR" (New owner 12.05)		
G-TUGG	Piper PA-18-150 Super Cub	18-8274	PH-MAH	10. 1.83	Ulster Gliding Club Ltd	Bellarena	2. 9.10S
	(Lycoming O-360-A3) (Frame No.18-8497)		N5451Y				
G-TUGS	Piper PA-25-235 Pawnee D	25-7756062	G-BFEW	31. 7.06	J A Stephen	Aboyne	26. 4.07E
			N82553				
G-TUGY	Robin DR.400-180 Régent	2052	D-EPAR	27. 4.98	J M Airey tr Buckminster Gliding Club Group	Saltby	19. 5.08E
G-TULP	Lindstrand LBL Tulips SS Balloon (Hot Air)	662	(PH-AJT)	16.10.00	Oxford Promotions (UK) Ltd	(Kentucky, US)	3. 4.03A
			(PH-TLP), PH-ORA)		(Operated F Prell)		

G-TUNE	Robinson R22 Beta	0818	N60661	12. 1.99	D T Carslaw t/a HR Helicopters	Kintore	6. 2.08E
			G-OJVI, (G-OJVJ)				
G-TURF	Reims Cessna F406 Caravan II	F406-0020	PH-FWF	17.10.96	Reconnaisance Ventures Ltd	Coventry	20. 1.08E
			(EI-CND), PH-FWF, F-WZDS *(COASTGUARD titles, red/white c/s with MCA logo on tail)*				
G-TUSA	Pegasus Quantum 15-912	7841		9. 8.01	N J Holt	Weston Zoyland	27. 4.08P
	(Veered to right on take-off Weston Zoyland 31. 7.07, struck fence and susbstantially damaged)						
G-TUTU	Cameron O-105 Balloon (Hot Air)	10659		17. 1.05	A C K Rawson and J J Rudoni	Stafford	18.12.07E
G-TVAM	MBB BÖ.105DBS-4	S 392	G-SPOL	26. 6.03	Bond Air Services Ltd	White Waltham	5. 6.08E
			VR-BGV, D-HDLH		*(Operated Thames Valley Air Ambulance)*		
G-TVBF	Lindstrand LBL 310A Balloon (Hot Air)	439		2. 4.97	Airxcite Ltd t/a Virgin Balloon Flights	Wembley	7 .7.08E
G-TVCO	Gippsland GA-8 Airvan	GA8-06-101		1.11.06	Zyox Ltd	Oxford	6.12.07P
G-TVEE	Hughes 369HS	14-0557S	N45457	26. 1.05	M Webb	Elstree	10. 5.08E
	(Hughes 500)		ZK-HCM, N22352, C-GCXK, N500AH, N500WH				
G-TVHD	Aérospatiale AS.355F2 Ecureuil 2	5449	ZK-ILN	7. 2.08	Arena Aviation Ltd	Redhill	
			JA6638				
G-TVII	Hawker Hunter T 7	41H-693834	XX467	8.12.97	G R Montgomery tr G-TVII Group	Exeter	
			R Jordanian AF 836, RSAF 70-617, G-9-214, XL605 *(As "XX467:86" 1.07)*				
G-TVIJ	CCF Harvard 4 (T-6J-CCF Texan)	CCF4-442	G-BSBE	10.12.93	R W Davies	Little Robhurst Farm, Woodchurch	23. 7.07P
			Moz PLAF 1730, FAP 1730, WGAF AA+652, 52-8521 *(As "28521:TA-521" in USAF yellow c/s)*				
G-TVTV	Cameron TV 90SS Balloon (Hot Air)	2357		14. 9.90	J Krebs	Erfstadt, Germany	19. 8.02A
G-TWEL	Piper PA-28-181 Archer II	28-8090290	N81963	12. 6.80	IAE Ltd	Cranfield	25. 5.08E
G-TWEY	Colt 69A Balloon (Hot Air)	700		24. 7.85	N Bland	Didcot	12. 1.02A
G-TWIN	Piper PA-44-180 Seminole	44-7995072	N30267	6.11.78	Bonus Aviation Ltd	Cranfield	21. 5.08E
G-TWIZ	Rockwell Commander 114	14375	SE-GSP	9. 5.90	B C and P M Cox	Biggin Hill	23. 6.08E
			N5808N				
G-TWOA	Schempp-Hirth Discus 2a	82	BGA 4843-JWQ	31.10.07	A J McNamara	Wycombe Air Park	22.11.07
G-TWOC	Schempp-Hirth Ventus 2cT	141/369	BGA 5165-KKS	6. 3.06	D Heslop "2C"	Wormingford	27. 3.08
G-TWOT	Schempp-Hirth Discus 2T	14/127	BGA 5156-KKG	31. 8.06	S G Lapworth	Lasham	4. 4.08
			OY-XSY, D-KKAH		"2T"		
G-TWSR	Silence Twister	PFA 329-14385		24. 3.05	J A Hallam	New Farm, Felton	5. 4.08P
	(Built J A Hallam)						
G-TWST	Silence Twister	PFA 329-14211		7. 9.04	Zulu Glasstek Ltd	Baileys Farm, Long Crendon	15.11.08P
	(Built P M Wells)						
G-TWTW	Denney Kitfox Model 2	PFA 172-11730		24. 3.04	T Willford	Spetisbury, Blandford Forum	22.10.87P
	(Built T Willford)						
G-TXSE	Rotary Air Force RAF 2000 GTX-SE			1. 3.96	A Levitt	(Blackshaw Head, Hebden Bridge)	1. 1.98P
	(Built P Green)	PFA G/113-1271			*(New owner 11.05)*		
G-TYAK	IAV Bacau Yakovlev Yak-52	899907	RA-01038	23.12.02	S J Ducker	Breighton	15.11.08P
			LY-AIE, DOSAAF 94 *(yellow)* *(Noted 12.07)*				
G-TYCN	Agusta A109E Power	11123	G-VMCO	30. 7.03	A J Walter (Aviation) Ltd	(Horsham)	30. 7.08E
G-TYER	Robin DR.500-200i Président	0021	F-GTZB	25. 4.00	Chartfleet Ltd	Northorpe, Bourne, Lincoln	22. 6.08E
	(Officially regd as DR.400-500)						
G-TYGA	Gulfstream AA-5B Tiger	AA5B-1161	G-BHNZ	22. 2.82	D H and R J Carman	Rochester	29. 1.08E
			(D-EGDS), N4547L				
G-TYGR	Best Off Sky Ranger 912S(1)	SKRxxxx498		8.11.04	M J Poole	(Barnsley)	4. 7.08P
	(Built M J Poole - pr.no.BMAA/HB/420)						
G-TYKE	Avtech Jabiru UL-450	xxxx		8. 6.01	R Rhodes and J Rochead	North Connel, Oban	12. 7.08P
	(Built A Parker - pr.no.PFA 274A-13739)						
G-TYMS	Cessna 172P Skyhawk	17275815	N65674	9. 2.07	ESS Land Management	(Hailsham)	19..6.08E
G-TYNE	SOCATA TB-20 Trinidad	1523	F-GRBM	6.11.97	N V Price	Newcastle	30.11.07E
			F-WWRW, CS-AZH, F-OHDE				
G-TYRE	Reims Cessna F172M Skyhawk II	F17201222	OY-BIA	16. 2.79	S C Moss	Gloucestershire	31. 8.08E
G-TZEE	SOCATA TB-10 Tobago	727	F-GFQG	9. 1.03	Zytech Ltd	Earls Colne	29. 2.08E
G-TZII	Thorp T 211B	PFA 305-13285		2. 6.99	M J Newton Frandley	Northwich	29. 8.08P
	(Built AD Aerospace Ltd) (Wilksch WAM-120)						

G-UAAA - G-UZZZ

G-UACA	Best Off Sky Ranger R100(2)	SKRxxxx384		25. 6.04	R G Openshaw Harringe Court, Sellindge, Folkestone		
	(Built R Openshaw - pr.no.BMAA/HB/324)				*(Noted 1.07)*		
G-UAKE	North American P-51D-5-NA Mustang	109-27587	44-13954	17. 2.04	P S Warner	(Dumbleton, Evesham)	
					(New owner 10.06)		
G-UANO	de Havilland DHC-1 Chipmunk Mk.20	57	G-BYYW	18.10.06	N Rhind tr Gooney Bird Group	White Waltham	
	(Built OGMA)		CS-DAQ, Portuguese AF FAP 1367 *(As "1367" in Portuguese AF c/s)*				
G-UANT	Piper PA-28-140 Cherokee F	28-7325568	OO-MYR	12. 4.02	Air Navigation and Trading Company Ltd	Blackpool	9.11.07E
			N56084				
G-UAPA	Robin DR.400-140B Major	2213	F-GMXC	11. 1.95	Carlos Saraiva Lda	(Alges, Portugal)	20.10.07E
G-UAPO	Ruschmeyer R90-230RG	019	D-EECT	2. 3.95	P Randall	Sturgate	23. 7.08E
G-UAVA	Piper PA-30 Twin Comanche B	30-1413	D-GLDU	16. 6.03	M D Northwood	Enstone	22.11.07E
			HB-LDU, N8279Y				
G-UCCC	Cameron Sign 90 SS Balloon (Hot Air)	3918		5. 7.96	B Conway	Wheatley, Oxford	6. 9.99A
G-UDGE	Thruster T600N Sprint	9099-T600N-037	G-BYPI	17. 9.99	A P Scott tr G-UDGE Syndicate	Shobdon	16.12.07P
	(Rotax 582)						
G-UDOG	Scottish Aviation Bulldog Series 120/121		XX518	24. 1.02	Gamit Ltd	North Weald	15. 8.10S
		BH.120/204			*(As "XX518:S" in RAF c/s)*		
G-UFAW	Raj Hamsa X'Air 582(5)	582		24. 7.01	P Batchelor	(Sedgewick Park, Horsham)	12. 9.10P
	(Built J H Goddard - pr.no.BMAA/HB/167)						
G-UFCB	Cessna 172S Skyhawk SP	172S8318	N455SP	25. 1.00	The Cambridge Aero Club Ltd	Cambridge	23 .3.08E
G-UFCC	Cessna 172S Skyhawk SP	172S8611	N2466X	8. 1.01	Skypix Aviation Ltd	Thruxton	11. 4.08E
G-UFCD	Cessna 172S Skyhawk SP	172S8443	G-OYZK	4. 1.01	Iolar Ltd	Cambridge	28. 9.08E
			N7262C				
G-UFCE	Cessna 172S Skyhawk SP	172S9305	N5318Y	20. 2.03	Ulster Flying Club (1961) Ltd	Newtownards	21 3.08E
G-UFCF	Cessna 172S Skyhawk SP	172S9306	N5320Y	20. 2.03	Global Traffic Network UK Ltd	(London WC1)	4. 3.08E

Reg	Type	C/n	Prev id	Date	Owner/Operator	Location	
G-UFCG	Cessna 172S Skyhawk SP	172S9450	N2154T	28. 7.03	Ulster Flying Club (1961) Ltd	Newtownards	7. 8.08E
G-UFCH	Cessna 172S Skyhawk SP	172S9507	N53551	4.11.03	Ulster Flying Club (1961) Ltd	Newtownards	12.11.08E
G-UFCI	Cessna 172S Skyhawk	172S10508	N21946	12. 2.08	Ulster Flying Club (1961) Ltd	Newtownards	
G-UFCJ	Cessna 172S Skyhawk	172S10485	G-RMIN N2246T	25. 2.08	Ulster Flying Club (1961) Ltd	Newtownards	
G-UFCx.	Cessna 172S Skyhawk	172S10505	N21927	3.08R	Ulster Flying Club (1961) Ltd	Newtownards	
G-UFLY	Cessna F150H	F150-0264	G-AVVY	29. 9.89	Westair Flying Services Ltd	Blackpool	4. 5.08E
	(Built Reims Aviation SA)						
G-UHIH	Bell UH-1H Iroquois	13208	NX41574 72-21509	14.12.05	MSS Holdings Ltd Wesham House Farm, Kirkham		12. 3.08P
	(As "72-21509:129" in US Army c/s) "Miss Jo"						
G-UILA	Aquila AT01	AT01-165		18. 4.07	Aquila Sport Aeroplanes LLP (Kilndown, Cranbrook)		24. 5.08E
G-UILD	Grob G109B	6419		28. 1.86	M H Player Wing Farm, Longbridge Deverill		26. 5.08E
G-UILE	Neico Lancair 320	PFA 191-12538		17. 1.94	R J Martin	Limoges, France	10. 9.08P
	(Built R J Martin)						
G-UILT	Cessna T303 Crusader	T30300280	G-EDRY N4817V	3. 7.00	W J Forrest tr G-UILT Group	Blackpool	11.10.07E
G-UINN	Stolp SA.300 Starduster Too	HB.1980-1	EI-CDQ C-GTLJ	16. 3.98	J D H Gordon	Charterhall	2. 1.08P
	(Built Haakon Baaken) (Lycoming O-360)						
G-UIST	British Aerospace Jetstream Series 3102	750	N190PC	15. 3.02	Highland Airways Ltd	Inverness	27. 5.08E
	(N331QH), N840JS, G-31-750						
G-UJAB	Avtech Jabiru UL	0193		27. 1.99	C A Thomas Top Farm, Croydon, Royston		10. 7.08P
	(Built C A Thomas - pr.no.PFA 274A-13373)						
G-UJGK	Avtech Jabiru UL-450	0329		17. 4.00	W G Upton and J G Kosak	RNAS Culdrose	1. 6.08P
	(Built W G Upton and J G Kosak - pr.no.PFA 274A-13558)						
G-UKAT	Aero AT-3	PFA 327-14107		14. 4.04	T Archer tr G-UKAT Group	North Weald	14. 9.08P
	(Built T Archer)						
G-UKAW	Agusta A109E	11003	I-VRGT	21.12.07	Westland Helicopters Ltd	Yeovil	
G-UKOZ	Avtech Jabiru SK	0190		16. 6.99	D J Burnett White House Farm, Southery		30.10.08P
	(Built D J Burnett - pr.no.PFA 274-13310)						
G-UKUK	Head Ax8-105 Balloon (Hot Air)	248	N8303U	1. 9.97	P A George *"Union Jack"* Princes Risborough		6. 7.08A
G-UKZM	Boeing 767-3Q8ER	27686	EC-HKS	22.05.07	Zoom Airlines Ltd	London Gatwick	3. 6.08E
					"City of London"		
G-ULAS	de Havilland DHC-1 Chipmunk 22	C1/0554	WK517	14. 6.96	ULAS Flying Club Ltd)	RAF Benson	10. 9.08S
	(As "WK517" in RAF c/s)						
G-ULES	Aérospatiale AS.355F2 Ecureuil 2	5364	G-OBHL G-HARO, G-DAFT, G-BNNN	6. 3.03	Select Plant Hire Company Ltd	Southend	20. 1.08E
G-ULHI	Scottish Aviation Bulldog Series 100/101	BH100/148	G-OPOD SE-LLK, Fv61038, G-AZMS	30. 9.03	Power Aerobatics Ltd	Kemble	28.1.11T
G-ULIA	Cameron V-77 Balloon (Hot Air)	2860		20. 5.92	J M Dean	High Littleton, Bath	24. 7.08A
G-ULPS	Everett Gyroplane Series 1	007	G-BMNY	13. 7.93	C J Watkinson	(Goole)	10. 7.01P
	(Volkswagen 1835)						
G-ULSY	Comco Ikarus C42 FB80	0405-6603		26. 7.04	P J Fahie tr Ikarus 1 Flying Group *(Operated Swallow Aviation)* (Stour Row, Shaftesbury)		25. 7.08P
G-ULTR	Cameron A-105 Balloon (Hot Air)	4100		24. 2.97	P Glydon *(Ultrafilter titles)*	Bristol	19. 7.07T
G-UMAS	Rotorsport UK MT-03	RSUK/MT-03/024		12.11.07	BAE Systems (Operations) Ltd	Warton	8. 1.09P
G-UMMI	Piper PA-31 Navajo C	31-7912060	G-BGSO N3519F	11. 8.92	J A, G M, D T A and J A Rees t/a Messrs Rees of Poynston West	Haverfordwest	14. 8.08E
G-UMMY	Best Off Sky Ranger J2.2(1)	SKR0409521		25. 7.05	A R Williams	Damyn's Hall, Upminster	15. 2.08P
	(Built A R Williams - pr.no.BMAA/HB/437)						
G-UNDD	Piper PA-23-250 Aztec E	27-4832	G-BATX N14271	22. 3.00	G J and D P Deadman	Goodwood	27. 9.07E
G-UNER	Lindstrand LBL 90A Balloon (Hot Air)	895		16. 4.03	St Dunstans *(St Dunstans titles)*	London W1	9. 6.08A
G-UNGE	Lindstrand LBL 90A Balloon (Hot Air)	122	G-BVPJ	6.12.96	M T Stevens tr Silver Ghost Balloon Club (Warwick)		21. 5.08A
G-UNGO	Pietenpol AirCamper	PFA 047-13951		16. 9.02	A R Wyatt	(Buntingford)	23. 3.08
	(Built A R Wyatt and P Thody)						
G-UNIN	Schempp-Hirth Ventus b	135	BGA 4378-JBG OE-5315	8.11.07	W R Longstaff tr U9 Syndicate	Feshie Bridge	
G-UNIV	Montgomerie-Parsons Two-Place Gyroplane		G-BWTP	3. 8.99	Department of Aerospace Engineering, University of Glasgow		
	(Built J M Montgomerie) (Rotax 618) PFA G/8-1276					(Glasgow)	18. 1.05P
G-UNIX	VPM M16 Tandem Trainer PFA G/12-1349		ZU-AHX	10. 3.06	A P Wilkinson	Melrose Farm, Melbourne	28. 8.08P
	(Built A P Wilkinson)						
G-UNNA	Jabiru UL-450	xxxx		13. 4.07	N D A Graham	North Connel, Oban	
	(Built N D A Graham - pr.no.PFA 274A-14442)				*(On build 2007)*		
G-UPFS	Waco UPF-7	5660	N32029	27. 8.04	D N Peters and N R Finlayson	Little Gransden	11.11.07
G-UPHI	Best Off Sky Ranger Swift 912S(1) SKRxxxx629			2.10.06	Flylight Airsports Ltd	Sywell	5. 2.08P
	(Built P M Dewhurst - pr.no.BMAA/HB/480)						
G-UPHL	Cameron Concept 80 Balloon (Hot Air)	3002		23. 2.93	CSM (Weston) Ltd t/a Uphill Motor Company *(Uphill Motors titles)* Weston-super-Mare		20. 4.06T
G-UPPP	Colt 77A Balloon (Hot Air)	852		4. 8.86	D Michel Neuves Maisons, Meurthe-et-Moselle, France		17. 2.05A
G-UPTA	Best Off Sky Ranger 912(1)	SKRxxxx645?		15. 2.06	D Minnock	(Navan	20. 8.08P
	(Built P E Tait - pr.no.BMAA/HB/488)						
G-UPUP	Cameron V-77 Balloon (Hot Air)	1828		21. 7.89	S R Burden *"Fantasia"* Noordwijk, Netherlands		9. 5.04T
G-UPUZ	Lindstrand LBL 120A Balloon (Hot Air)	969		26. 1.04	C J Sanger-Davies	Hawarden, Deeside	15. 4.08A
G-UROP	Beech 95-B55 Baron	TC-2452	N64311	17. 9.90	Pooler International Ltd	Sleap	12.10.07E
G-URRR	Air Command 582 Sport	0630		13. 6.90	L Armes	(Basildon)	
	(Built L Armes - pr.no.PFA G/4-1200)						
G-URUS	Maule MX-7-180B Super Rocket	22014C	N611BH	28. 6.04	Broomco Ltd	Thruxton	15.12.07E
G-USAM (2)	Cameron Uncle Sam SS Balloon (Hot Air)	1120		20. 5.85	Corn Palace Balloon Club Ltd	(US)	27. 6.00A
	(Uncle Sam head shape) (New envelope c/n 4526 C 3.99)				*(Active Albuquerque, New Mexico, US 10.06)*		
G-USIL	Thunder Ax7-77 Balloon (Hot Air)	1587		22. 8.89	Window on the World Ltd *"Mantis"*	London SE1	18. 1.07A
G-USKY	Aviat A-1B Husky	2261		8. 4.04	B Walker and Co (Dursley) Ltd	Gloucestershire	2. 7.08E
G-USMC	Cameron Chestie 90 SS Balloon (Hot Air)	1251		24. 4.86	J W Soukup	Bristol	15. 6.00A
	(US Marine Corps Bulldog shape)				*(Noted Albuquerque, New Mexico, US 10.06)*		

Reg	Type	Serial	Prev ID	Date	Owner/Operator	Location	Expiry
G-USRV	Van's RV-6 (Built F M Carter)	23771	N200HC	9. 7.04	M P Comley and N Horseman (Orpington) and Oxted		11.10.07P
G-USSI	Stoddard-Hamilton Glasair III (Built H R Rotherwick)	3380		30.12.03	Lord Rotherwick	Oxford	
G-USSR	Cameron Doll 90SS Balloon (Hot Air) (Russian Doll shape)	2273		29. 3.90	Corn Palace Balloon Club Ltd (US) "Matrioshka" (Noted Albuquerque, New Mexico, US 10.06)		9. 6.00A
G-USSY	Piper PA-28-181 Archer II	28-8290011	N8439R	7.11.88	Western Air (Thruxton) Ltd	Thruxton	19. 2.08E
G-USTH	Agusta A109A II	7304	N109UK	12. 9.05	Stratton Motor Company (Norfolk) Ltd		
			F-GKGV, (F-GUHS), F-GKGV, N109PS, N109FM			Long Stratton, Norwich	1.12.07E
G-USTS	Agusta A109A II	7275	G-MKSF	24.11.03	MB Air Ltd t/a Eagle Helicopters		
			N18SF, F-GDPR			Newcastle City Heliport	21. 2.08E
G-USTY	Clutton FRED Series III (Built S Styles)	PFA 029-10390		11.10.78	R G Hallam	Netherthorpe	8.12.05P
G-UTSI	Rand Robinson KR-2 (Built K B Gutridge - pr.no.PFA 129-10966)	KBG-01		2.10.89	K B Gutridge	Biggin Hill	21. 8.08P
G-UTSY	Piper PA-28R-201 Cherokee Arrow III	28R-7737052	N3346Q	29. 8.86	Arrow Aviation Ltd	Southend	14. 3.08E
G-UTTS	Robinson R44 Raven	0865	G-ROAP	20.10.00	Celtic Motorhomes Ltd	Weston, Leixlip, County Kildare	21.12.07E
G-UTZI	Robinson R44 Raven II	10590		24.12.04	S K Miles (Sant Feliu Guixols, Girona, Spain)		1. 2.08E
G-UURO	Evektor EV-97 Eurostar (Built E M Middleton)	PFA 315-14480		4. 1.06	E M Middleton	Broadmeadow Farm, Hereford	20. 2.08P
G-UVBF	Lindstrand LBL 400A Balloon (Hot Air)	1051		19. 8.05	Airxcite Ltd t/a Virgin Balloon Flights	Wembley	15. 4.08E
G-UVIP	Cessna 421C Golden Eagle	421C0603	G-BSKH N88600	23.11.98	MMAir Ltd	North Weald	18. 9.08E
G-UVNR	British Aircraft Corporation 167 Strikemaster Mk.87 EEP/JP/2876 & PS.168 (or PS.174?)		G-BXFS Botswana DF OJ10, Kenyan AF 605, G-27-195	4. 5.01	Global Aviation Services Ltd	Hawarden	24. 5.08P
G-UYGB	Bombardier BD-100-1A10 Challenger 300	20169	C-FOAT	10. 1.08	Air Partner Private Jets Ltd	London Stansted	
G-UZEL	Aérospatiale SA.341G Gazelle 1	1413	G-BRNH YU-HBO	21.11.89	Fairalls of Godstone Ltd	Redhill	9. 6.08E
G-UZLE	Colt 77A Balloon (Hot Air)	2021		1. 8.91	Flying Pictures Ltd "John Courage"	Chilbolton, Stockbridge	25. 5.00A
G-UZUP	Evektor EV-97A Eurostar (Built S A Woodhams)	PFA 315A-14528		21. 6.06	S A Woodhams "Serenity"	Netherthorpe	22.11.07P
G-UZZL	Van's RV-7 (Built P Chaplin)	PFA 323-13982		22. 8.06	P Chaplin	(Ridgmont, Bedford)	
G-UZZY	Enstrom 480	5013	G-BWMD (F-GOTA), G-BWMD	29.10.04	Shoreham Helicopters Ltds.	Shoreham	13. 8.08E

G-VAAA - G-VZZZ

Reg	Type	Serial	Prev ID	Date	Owner/Operator	Location	Expiry
G-VAAC	Piper PA-28-181 Archer III	2843398	G-CCDN HB-PQA, N4176W	11. 9.07	A J Catzelfis	Elstree	8. 5.08E
G-VAIR	Airbus A340-313	164	F-WWJA	21. 4.97	Virgin Atlantic Airways Ltd "Maiden Tokyo"	London Gatwick	20. 4.08E
G-VALI	Cessna 182S Skylane	18280757	N238ME	2. 3.07	Valley Flying Company Ltd	Valley Farm, Stafford	24. 5.08E
G-VALS	Pietenpol AirCamper (Built J R D Bygraves)	PFA 047-13157		30. 7.97	J R D Bygraves (Noted 10.05)	Little Gransden	
G-VALV	Robinson R44 Raven	1421		9. 9.04	Valve Train Components Ltd	(Matlock)	4.10.07E
G-VALY	SOCATA TB-21 Trinidad	2081	N246SS (N717TB)	30. 3.04	R J Thwaites and Westflight Aviation Ltd	Gloucestershire	27. 4.08E
G-VALZ	Cameron N-120 Balloon (Hot Air)	4998		9. 1.01	D Ling	Nottingham	20 11.07T
G-VANA	Gippsland GA-8 Airvan	GA8-04-046	VH-KLN	20.12.05	P Marsden (Noted 2.08)	Cranfield	21.12.07E
G-VAND	Gippsland GA-8 Airvan	GA8-07-114		19. 9.07	IAE Ltd	Cranfield	20. 9.08E
G-VANN	Van's RV-7A (Built D N and J A Carnegie)	PFA 323-14034		5. 7.04	D N and J A Carnegie	Kirkbride	23. 5.08E
G-VANS	Van's RV-4	355	N16TS	7. 9.92	M Swanborough and D Jones "Betsy"	Breighton	12.12.08P
G-VANZ	Van's RV-6A (Built S J Baxter)	PFA 181-12531		15. 7.93	S J Baxter	(Macclesfield)	
G-VARG	Varga 2150A Kachina	VAC 157-80	OO-RTY N80716	14. 5.84	J Denton	Sandtoft	22. 9.08E
G-VART	Rotorway Executive 90 (Built N J Bethell) (RotorWay RI 162)	5003	G-BSUR	11. 8.03	I R Brown and K E Parker	(Sittingbourne)	1. 8.08P
G-VAST	Boeing 747-41R	28757		17. 6.97	Virgin Atlantic Airways Ltd "Ladybird"	London Heathrow	16. 6.08E
G-VATL	Airbus A340-642	376	F-WWCC	31.10.03	Virgin Atlantic Airways Ltd "Miss Kitty"	London Heathrow	30.10.07E
G-VBCA	Cirrus SR22	2656	N967SR	11.10.07	C A S Atha	Bagby	17.10.08P
G-VBFA	Ultramagic N-250 Balloon (Hot Air)	250/44		6. 4.06	Airxcite Ltd t/a Virgin Balloon Flights	Wembley	29. 2.08E
G-VBFB	Ultramagic N-355 Balloon (Hot Air)	355/09		5. 5.06	Airxcite Ltd t/a Virgin Balloon Flights	Wembley	22. 8.08E
G-VBFC	Ultramagic N-250 Balloon (Hot Air)	250/45		5. 5.06	Airxcite Ltd t/a Virgin Balloon Flights	Wembley	16. 3.08E
G-VBFD	Ultramagic N-250 Balloon (Hot Air)	250/46		20. 6.06	Airxcite Ltd t/a Virgin Balloon Flights	Wembley	12. 3.08E
G-VBFE	UltraMagic N-355 Balloon (Hot Air)	355/10		7. 7.06	Airxcite Ltd t/a Virgin Balloon Flights	Wembley	8. 7.08E
G-VBFF	Lindstrand LBL 360A Balloon (Hot Air)	1116		8. 8.06	Airxcite Ltd t/a Virgin Balloon Flights	Bagby	5. 2.08E
G-VBFG	Cameron Z-350 Balloon (Hot Air)	10984		8. 3.07	Airxcite Ltd t/a Virgin Balloon Flights	Wembley	8. 3.08E
G-VBFH	Cameron Z-350 Balloon (Hot Air)	10985		8. 3.07	Airxcite Ltd t/a Virgin Balloon Flights	Wembley	8. 3.08E
G-VBFI	Cameron Z-350 Balloon (Hot Air)	10986		8. 3.07	Airxcite Ltd t/a Virgin Balloon Flights	Wembley	8. 3.08E
G-VBFJ	Cameron Z-350 Balloon (Hot Air)	11006		8. 3.07	Airxcite Ltd t/a Virgin Balloon Flights	Wembley	29. 4.08E
G-VBFK	Cameron Z-350 Balloon (Hot Air)	11007		8. 3.07	Airxcite Ltd t/a Virgin Balloon Flights	Wembley	5. 6.08E
G-VBIG	Boeing 747-4Q8	26255		10. 6.96	Virgin Atlantic Airways Ltd "Tinker Belle"	London Gatwick	9. 6.08E
G-VBLU	Airbus A340-642	723	F-WWCS	30. 1.06	Virgin Atlantic Airways Ltd "Soul Sister"	London Heathrow	29. 1.08E

Reg	Type	C/n	Prev id	Date	Owner	Location	Expiry
G-VBUG	Airbus A340-642	804	F-WWCV	28. 2.07	Virgin Atlantic Airways Ltd "Lady Bird"	London Heathrow	27. 2.08E
G-VCED	Airbus A320-231	0193	OY-CNI F-WWIX	21. 1.97	Thomas Cook Airlines Ltd t/a MyTravel Airways	Birmingham	30. 1.08E
G-VCIO	EAA Acrosport II (Built F Sharples, V Millard and R F Bond) (Lycoming O-360)	PFA 072A-12388		9.10.97	C M Knight	Batwell Farm, Gillingham	27. 5.08P
G-VCJH	Robinson R22 Beta	1569		26.10.90	ACS Aviation Ltd (New owner 5.07)	(East Kilbride, Glasgow)	13. 1.00T
G-VCML	Beech 58 Baron	TH-1346	N2289R	31.10.97	St Angelo Aviation Ltd	Lydd	18. 4.08E
G-VCXT	Schempp-Hirth Ventus 2cT	144/..	BGA 5158-KKJ D-KOZZ	4.11.05	R F Aldous "RA"	Kirchheim-Hahnwide, Germany	30. 4.08
G-VDOG	Cessna 305C Bird Dog (L-19E)	24582	F-BIFB French Army	18. 8.06	E P Morrow (As "24582" in US Army c/s)	Newtownards	31. 5.10E
G-VECD	Robin R1180T Aiglon II	234	F-GCAD	22. 6.00	B Lee	Eddsfield, Octon Lodge Farm, Thwing	22. 7.08E
G-VECG	Robin R2160 Alpha Sport	322	F-GSRD	6. 2.02	Mistral Aviation Ltd (Operated Vectair)	Dunsfold	1. 3.08E
G-VEGA	Slingsby T.65A Vega	1889	BGA 2729-EJT G-VEGA, (G-BFZN)	20.10.78	W A M Sanderson	Wormingford	16. 2.08
G-VEIL	Airbus A340-642	575	F-WWCK	8. 4.04	Virgin Atlantic Airways Ltd "Queen of the Skies"	London Heathrow	7. 4.08E
G-VEIT	Robinson R44 Raven II	10091		11. 6.03	Field Marshall Helicopters Ltd	Wycombe Air Park	3. 8.08E
G-VELA	SIAI-Marchetti S 208 (Officially regd as "S 205-22R")	4-149	N949W	30.10.89	Broadland Flyers Ltd	Norwich	18. 7.08E
G-VELD	Airbus A340-313	214	F-WWJY	16. 3.98	Virgin Atlantic Airways Ltd "African Queen-We Are Better By Four'"	London Gatwick	15. 3.08E
G-VENC	Schempp-Hirth Ventus 2c	9/21	BGA 4249-HVY	17. 9.07	J B Giddins	Hinton-in-the-Hedges	9. 3.08
G-VENI	de Havilland DH.112 Venom FB.50 (FB.1) (Built F + W)	733	Swiss AF J-1523	8. 6.84	Aviation and Computer Consultancy Ltd (In open store as "VV612" in RAF silver c/s 1.08: new owner 2.08)	(Bournemouth)	25. 7.01P
G-VENM	de Havilland DH.112 Venom FB.50 (FB.1) (Built F + W)	824	G-BLIE Swiss AF J-1614	16. 6.99	T J Manna (As "WK436" in RAF 11 Sqdn c/s)	North Weald	11. 6.08P
G-VENT	Schempp-Hirth Ventus 2cM	3/17	BGA 4918 D-KBTL	25. 9.01	P D Barker tr G-VENT Syndicate	(Haywards Heath)	28. 4.08E
G-VERA	Gardan GY-201 Minicab (Built D K Shipton)	PFA 056-12236		7. 6.94	D K Shipton	(Peterborough)	
G-VERN	Piper PA-32R-300 Cherokee Lance	32R-7680151	G-BVBG N19BP, N8363C	16. 4.03	D J Whitcombe	Cardiff	27. 9.08E
G-VETA	Hawker Hunter T 7	41H-693751	G-BVWN A2729, XL600	2. 7.96	Skyblue Aviation Ltd	Exeter	27. 6.08P
G-VETS	Enstrom 280C-UK Shark	1015	G-FSDC G-BKTG, OY-HBP	11. 9.95	A J Warburton (Noted 4.06)	Barton	28. 7.02
G-VEYE	Robinson R22	0140	G-BPTP N9056H	8. 2.00	Manor PC's Ltd	Tatenhill	31. 3.08E
G-VEZE	Rutan VariEze (Built S D Brown, S Evans and M Roper)	PFA 074-10285		2. 9.77	S D Brown, S Evans and M Roper	Biggin Hill	30. 5.08P
G-VFAB	Boeing 747-4Q8	24958		28. 4.94	Virgin Atlantic Airways Ltd "Lady Penelope"	London Gatwick	27. 4.08E
G-VFAR	Airbus A340-313X	225	(G-VPOW) F-WWJ	12. 6.98	Virgin Atlantic Airways Ltd "Diana"	London Gatwick	11. 6.08E
G-VFAS	Piper PA-28R-200 Cherokee Arrow II	28R-7435104	G-MEAH G-BSNM, N46PR, G-BSNM, N46PR, N54439	15. 1.08	P Wood	Wendens Ambo, Saffron Walden	14. 9.08E
G-VFIT	Airbus A340-642	753	F-WWCG	24. 5.06	Virgin Atlantic Airways Ltd "Dancing Queen"	London Heathrow	23. 5.08E
G-VFIZ	Airbus A340-642	764	F-WWCB	19. 7.06	Virgin Atlantic Airways Ltd "Bubbles"	London Heathrow	18. 7.08E
G-VFOX	Airbus A340-642	449	F-WWCM	23.12.02	Virgin Atlantic Airways Ltd " "Silver Lady"	London Heathrow	22.12.07E
G-VFUN	Airbus A340-642		F-WW..	,08R	Virgin Atlantic Airways Ltd " "Party Girl"	London Heathrow	
G-VGAG	Cirrus SR20 GTS	1572	N54149	25.10.05	Alfred Graham Ltd (Noted 1.08)	Southend	3.11.07E
G-VGAL	Boeing 747-443	32337	(EI-CVH)	26. 4.01	Virgin Atlantic Airways Ltd "Jersey Girl"	London Gatwick	25. 4.08E
G-VGAS	Airbus A340-642	639	F-WWCI	9. 5.05	Virgin Atlantic Airways Ltd "Varga Girl"	London Heathrow	8. 5.08E
G-VGMB	Eurocopter EC.135 P2+	0550	N643LH	8. 6.07	Finlay (Holdings) Ltd	Enniskillen	19. 7.08E
G-VGMC	Eurocopter AS.355N Ecureuil 2	5693	G-HEMH F-WQPV	2. 3.04	E A and A Jackson t/a Eassda Aviation (Noted 1.08)	Redhill	20.12.07E
G-VGOA	Airbus A340-642	371	F-WWCB	30. 8.03	Virgin Atlantic Airways Ltd "Indian Princess"	London Heathrow	29. 8.08E
G-VGVG	ICP MXP-740 Savannah VG Jabiru(1) (Built M F Cottam - pr.no.BMAA/HB/542)	xx.07-51-588		22. 6.07	M F Cottam tr Savannah Flying Group	Wickenby	
G-VHOL	Airbus A340-311	002	F-WWAS	30. 5.97	Virgin Atlantic Airways Ltd "Jetstreamer"	London Gatwick	29. 5.08E
G-VHOT	Boeing 747-4Q8	26326		12.10.94	Virgin Atlantic Airways Ltd" "Tubular Belle"	London Gatwick	11.10.07E
G-VIBA	Cameron DP-80 Airship (Hot Air)	1729		28. 5.91	J W Soukup (New owner 12.05)	Bristol	3. 2.99A
G-VICC	Piper PA-28-161 Warrior II	28-7916317	G-JFHL N2249U	3. 3.92	Freedom Aviation Ltd	RAF Lyneham	19. 8.08E
G-VICE	Hughes 369E (Hughes 500)	0365E	D-HLIS	16. 5.95	M W A Dunn	(Longdown, Exeter)	2.12.07E
G-VICI	de Havilland DH.112 Venom FB.50 (FB.1) (Built F + W)	783	HB-RVB (G-BMOB), Swiss AF J-1573	6. 2.95	Aviation and Computer Consultancy Ltd (In open store as "J-1573" in Swiss AF c/s 1.08: new owner 2.08)	(Bournemouth)	24.11.99P
G-VICM	Beech F33C Bonanza	CJ-136	PH-BNG	3. 7.91	Velocity Engineering Ltd	Elstree	20. 5.08E
G-VICS	Commander Aircraft Commander 114B	14655	N655V	3. 2.98	Millennium Aviation Ltd	Guernsey	17. 4.08E

G-VICT	Piper PA-31 Turbo Navajo B	31-7401211	G-BBZI N7590L	10. 9.99	Aircraft Leasing APS	(Esbjerg, Denmark)	13. 8.08E
G-VIEW	Vinten Wallis WA-116/L (Limbach L2000)	002		5. 7.82	K H Wallis (Stored 8.01)	Reymerston Hall, Norfolk	6.10.85P
G-VIIA	Boeing 777-236	27483	N5022E (G-ZZZF)	3. 7.97	British Airways PLC	London Gatwick	2. 7.08E
G-VIIB	Boeing 777-236	27484	N5023Q (G-ZZZG)	23. 5.97	British Airways PLC	London Gatwick	30. 1.08E
G-VIIC	Boeing 777-236	27485	N5016R (G-ZZZH)	6. 2.97	British Airways PLC	London Gatwick	20. 8.08E
G-VIID	Boeing 777-236	27486	(G-ZZZI)	18. 2.97	British Airways PLC	London Gatwick	15. 9.08E
G-VIIE	Boeing 777-236	27487	(G-ZZZJ)	27. 2.97	British Airways PLC	London Gatwick	23. 9.08E
G-VIIF	Boeing 777-236	27488	(G-ZZZK)	19. 3.97	British Airways PLC	London Gatwick	1.11.08E
G-VIIG	Boeing 777-236	27489	(G-ZZZL)	9. 4.97	British Airways PLC	London Gatwick	8. 4.08E
G-VIIH	Boeing 777-236	27490	(G-ZZZM)	7. 5.97	British Airways PLC	London Gatwick	6. 5.08E
G-VIIJ	Boeing 777-236	27492	(G-ZZZP)	29.12.97	British Airways PLC	London Gatwick	21. 8.08E
G-VIIK	Boeing 777-236	28840		3. 2.98	British Airways PLC	London Gatwick	2. 2.07T
G-VIIL	Boeing 777-236	27493		13. 3.98	British Airways PLC	London Gatwick	12. 3.08E
G-VIIM	Boeing 777-236	28841		26. 3.98	British Airways PLC	London Heathrow	13. 9.08E
G-VIIN	Boeing 777-236	29319		21. 8.98	British Airways PLC	London Heathrow	20. 8.08E
G-VIIO	Boeing 777-236	29320		26. 1.99	British Airways PLC	London Gatwick	25. 1.08E
G-VIIP	Boeing 777-236	29321		9. 2.99	British Airways PLC	London Gatwick	8. 2.08E
G-VIIR	Boeing 777-236	29322		18. 3.99	British Airways PLC	London Gatwick	17. 3.08E
G-VIIS	Boeing 777-236	29323		1. 4.99	British Airways PLC	London Heathrow	31. 3.08E
G-VIIT	Boeing 777-236	29962		26. 5.99	British Airways PLC	London Heathrow	25. 5.08E
G-VIIU	Boeing 777-236	29963		28. 5.99	British Airways PLC	London Heathrow	27. 5.08E
G-VIIV	Boeing 777-236	29964		29. 6.99	British Airways PLC	London Gatwick	28. 6.08E
G-VIIW	Boeing 777-236	29965		30. 7.99	British Airways PLC	London Gatwick	29. 7.08E
G-VIIX	Boeing 777-236	29966		11. 8.99	British Airways PLC	London Gatwick	10. 8.08E
G-VIIY	Boeing 777-236	29967		22.10.99	British Airways PLC	London Gatwick	21.10.07E
G-VIIZ	CZAW Sportcruiser (Built N I G Hart)	PFA 338-14672		4. 9.07	Skyview Systems Ltd (Noted 1.08)	Waits Farm, Sudbury	
G-VIKE	Bellanca 17-30A Super Viking 300A	79-30911	N302CB	8. 7.80	S J Doughty	Halfpenny Green	10. 6.08E
G-VIKY	Cameron A-120 Balloon (Hot Air)	3068		27. 4.93	P J Stapley	London Colney	26.10.06A
G-VILA	Avtech Jabiru UL (Built D Cassidy - pr.no.PFA 274A-13364)	0213	G-BYIF	18. 7.02	G T Clipstone	(Ipswich)	19. 7.08P
G-VILL	Laser Lazer Z200 (Built M G Jefferies) (Lycoming AEIO-360)	10	G-BOYZ	10. 6.96	J Owczarek	(Hochdahl, Germany)	11. 8.08P
G-VINH	Flight Design CTSW (Assembled P&M Aviation Ltd with c/n 8190)	06.05.16		28. 7.06	Aardbus Ltd	Damyn's Hall, Upminster	2. 7.08P
G-VINO	Sky 90-24 Balloon (Hot Air)	102		25. 2.98	Fivedata Ltd (Lambrini Bianco titles)	Todmorden	4. 6.06A
G-VIPA	Cessna 182S Skylane	18280720	N148ME	13. 9.00	Rollright Aviation Ltd	Oxford	23.11.07E
G-VIPH	Agusta A109C	7643	EI-CUV G-BVNH, G-LAXO	21. 9.01	Cheqair Ltd	Tharston, Long Stratton	26. 7.08E
G-VIPI	British Aerospace BAe 125 Series 800B (Build Corporate Jets Ltd)	258222	G-5-745	27. 7.92	Yeates of Leicester Ltd	Farnborough	28. 9.07E
G-VIPP	Piper PA-31-350 Navajo Chieftain	31-7952244	G-OGRV G-BMPX, N3543D	6. 8.93	Capital Trading Aviation Ltd	Exeter	28. 8.08E
G-VIPR	Eurocopter EC.120B Colibri	1049	F-GRAE	8.12.05	Amey Aviation LLP	(Milton Keynes)	21.12.07E
G-VIPU	Piper PA-31-350 Navajo Chieftain	31-8152115	G-MOHS G-BWOC,N40898,(CP-1665)	8.11.07	Capital Trading (Aviation) Ltd	Exeter	19.10.07E
G-VIPV	Piper PA-31-350 Navajo Chieftain	31-7952092	G-MRMR OH-PRE, G-WROX, G-BNZI, N3517T	13.11.07	Capital Trading (Aviation) Ltd	Exeter	6. 2.08E
G-VIPX	Piper PA-31-350 Navajo Chieftain	31-7305006	G-PMAX G-GRAM, G-BRHF, N7679L	3. 9.07	Capital Trading (Aviation) Ltd	Exeter	19. 9.08E
G-VIPY	Piper PA-31-350 Navajo Chieftain	31-7852143	EI-JTC G-POLO, (EI-...), G-POLO, N27750	10.10.97	Capital Trading Aviation Ltd	Exeter	12.10.07E
G-VIPZ	Sikorsky S-61N Mk.II	61-824	G-DAWS G-LAWS, G-BHOF, LN-ONK, G-BHOF, LN-ONK, G-BHOF	3. 5.06	Veritair Ltd t/a British International	Penzance Heliport	10. 7.08E
G-VITE	Robin R1180T Aiglon	219		16.10.78	D T Scrutton and N B Rolfe tr G-VITE Flying Group	Stapleford	1.10.07E
G-VITL	Lindstrand LBL 105A Balloon (Hot Air)	720		24. 8.00	Vital Services Group Ltd t/a Vital Resources (Vital Resources titles)	Salford	21. 8.08A
G-VIVA	Thunder Ax7-65 Bolt Balloon (Hot Air)	190		28.11.78	R J Mitchener (Inflated 4.02)	Andover	18. 3.99A
G-VIVI	Taylor JT.2 Titch (Built D G Tucker)	PFA 060-12405		4.11.96	D G Tucker	New Farm House, Great Oakley	21. 2.06P
	(Departed from runway on take-off New Farm House, Great Oakley 2. 7.05 and badly damaged: noted 5.06)						
G-VIVM	Hunting Percival P 84 Jet Provost T 5	PAC/W/23907	G-BVWF XS230	25. 3.96	The Skys The Ltd (International Test Pilots School titles)	North Weald	10.12.08P
G-VIVO	Nicollier HN.700 Ménestrel II (Built D G Tucker)	PFA 217-14039		5. 7.05	D G Tucker	Hill Farm, Nayland	
G-VIVS	Piper PA-28-151 Cherokee Warrior	28-7615377	LN-NAL	31. 3.06	S J Harrison and Vivienne A Donnelly	Carlisle	7.11.08P
G-VIXN	de Havilland DH.110 Sea Vixen FAW.2 (TT)	10145	8828M XS587	5. 8.85	P G Vallance Ltd (In Gatwick Aviation Museum 2007 as "XS587" in RN c/s)	Charlwood, Surrey	
G-VIXX	Alpi Pioneer 300 (Built K P O'Sullivan - pr.no.PFA 330-14465)	xxx	G-CESE G-CERJ	20. 7.07	K P O'Sullivan	(Gilcombe, Bruton)	
G-VIZA	Lindstrand LBL 260A Balloon (Hot Air)	792	A6-XEV	8.12.06	A Nimmo	Dubai, United Arab Emirates	
G-VIZZ	Sportavia RS.180 Sportsman	6018	D-EFBK	25.10.79	J D Howard and S J Morris tr Exeter Fournier Group	Exeter	31. 5.08
G-VJAB	Avtech Jabiru UL	0142		25. 6.98	A Thornton	(Southport)	31. 8.08P
	(Built S T Aviation Ltd - pr.no.PFA 274-13322 although type prefix should be "274A")						
G-VJET	Avro 698 Vulcan B 2	Not known	XL426	7. 7.87	R J Clarkson tr The Vulcan Restoration Trust (Noted as "XL426" and "G-VJET" 2.08)	Southend	
G-VJIM	Thunder and Colt Jumbo SS Balloon (Hot Air) (Registered as Colt Jumbo-2)	1298	(G-BPJI)	7. 8.89	Magical Adventures Ltd (Virgin Atlantic titles) "Jumbo Jim"	West Bloomfield, Michigan, US	14.10.02A

G-VKIT	Europa Aviation Europa	163		11. 6.01	T H Crow	Bicester	10. 4.08P
	(Built T H Crow - pr.no.PFA 247-12783) (Monowheel u/c)						
G-VKNG	Boeing 767-3Z9ER	23765	OE-LAU	10. 9.04	XL Airways UK Ltd	London Gatwick	25.11.07E
			N6009N, (OE-LAA), N767PW				
G-VKNI	Boeing 767-383ER	24358	TF-ATT	27. 6.06	XL Airways UK Ltd	London Gatwick	27. 6.07E
			OY-KDH, (SE-DOF), OY-KDH, I-AEJB				
G-VKUP	Cameron Z-90 Balloon (Hot Air)	10803		10. 5.06	Global Brands Ltd	Clay Cross, Chesterfield	8. 4.07E
					(VK VODKA KICK titles)		
G-VKVK	Eurocopter AS.350B3 Ecureuil	3362	G-XMEN	30. 6.05	GBL Aviation LLP	(Clay Cross, Chesterfield)	4. 7.08E
			F-WQDG, G-ZWRC, F-GPNE				
G-VLCC	Schleicher ASG 29E	29511	BGA 5270-KPD	3.08R	Viscount Cobham	Lasham	
			D-KLCC		*"CC"*		
G-VLCN	Avro 698 Vulcan B 2		XH558	6. 2.95	Vulcan to the Sky Trust Ltd	Bruntingthorpe	
					(First post restoration flight 18.10.07 as "XH558")		
G-VLIP	Boeing 747-443	32338	(EI-CVI)	15. 5.01	Virgin Atlantic Airways Ltd	London Gatwick	14. 5.08E
					"Hot Lips"		
G-VMCG	Piper PA-38-112 Tomahawk	38-79A0950	G-BSVX	12. 9.03	W G E James	Aberporth	29. 6.08E
			N2336P				
G-VMDE (2)	Cessna P210N Pressurized Centurion II		(N4717P)	20. 7.78	S J Davies	(Sandtoft)	3. 7.08E
		P21000088					
G-VMEG	Airbus A340-642	391	F-WWCK	5.10.02	Virgin Atlantic Airways Ltd	London Heathrow	3.10.07E
					"Mystic Maiden-4 Engines 4 Longhaul""		
G-VMJM	SOCATA TB-10 Tobago	1361	G-BTOK	21. 4.92	Cardonstar Ltd	Enstone	7. 6.08E
G-VMSL	Robinson R22 Alpha	0483	G-KILY	5. 2.98	L L F Smith	Wycombe Air Park	26.12.03T
			N8561M				
					(Force landed and rolled over near Turweston 4. 6.01)		
G-VNAP	Airbus A340-642	622	F-WWCE	24. 2.05	Virgin Atlantic Airways Ltd	London Heathrow	23. 2.08E
					"Sleeping Beauty"		
G-VNOM	de Havilland DH.112 Venom FB.50 (FB.1)	842	Swiss AF J-1632	13. 7.84	T J Manna	Salisbury Hall, London Colney	
	(Built F + W)			*(Unmarked pod only 5.04) (On loan to de Havilland Heritage Museum)*				
G-VNON	Reality Escapade Jabiru(3)	JAESC 0008		4.10.05	P A Vernon	Craysmarsh Farm, Melksham	19. 9.08P
	(Built P A Vernon -pr.no.BMAA/HB/325)						
G-VNTS	Schempp-Hirth Ventus bT	46/240	BGA 4400-JCE	14. 8.07	A G Reid tr 911 Syndicate	Bidford	28. 1.08
			D-KFMS				
G-VNUS	Hughes 269C	122-0175	G-BATT	20. 9.00	Enable International Ltd	Wellesbourne Mountford	14. 1.07T
	(Hughes 300)						
G-VOAR	Piper PA-28-181 Archer III	2843011	N9256Q	3.11.95	Solent Flight Ltd	Fairoaks	7. 1.08E
G-VOCE	Robinson R22 Beta	1249	G-BSCL	30. 7.07	J J Voce	(Guiseley, Leeds)	11. 8.02P
G-VODA (1)	Cameron N-77 Balloon (Hot Air)	2208		8. 2.90	I Harris	Bishops Cannings, Devizes	29. 9.08A
	(Crown ring removed and fitted to new envelope G-VODA (2) c/n 4164 12.97 by Cameron Balloons: original envelope rebuilt by						
	Zebedee Balloon Service with new crown ring 1.07 and registered G-CEJC as c/n 4164 qv)						
G-VOGE	Airbus A340-642	416	F-WWCF	29.11.02	Virgin Atlantic Airways Ltd	London Heathrow	28.11.07E
					"Cover Girl"		
G-VOID	Piper PA-28RT-201 Arrow IV	28R-8118049	ZS-KTM	17. 8.87	B R Green	Stapleford	2. 4.08E
			(G-GCAA), ZS-KTM, N83232				
G-VOIP	Westland SA.341G Gazelle HT.3	1792	G-HOBZ	15.11.05	Q.Milne	(Echt, Westhill, Aberdeen)	5. 6.08P
			G-CBSJ, ZA802				
G-VOLO	Alpi Pioneer 300	xxx		21. 6.05	J W Clark and J Buglass	Sleap	
	(Built J W Clark and J Buglass - pr.no.PFA 330-14389)			*(Noted 8.05)*				
G-VONA	Sikorsky S-76A	760086	G-BUXB	15. 4.03	Von Essen Aviation Ltd	Blackbushe	16. 8.08E
			(F-GSJG), G-BUXB, VR-CCZ, N399BB, N39RP				
G-VONB	Sikorsky S-76B	760399	G-POAH	8.10.03	Von Essen Aviation Ltd	Blackbushe	17. 5.08E
G-VONC	Sikorsky S-76B	760354	N966PR	29.11.06	Von Essen Aviation Ltd	Blackbushe	2. 5.08E
			N24PL, N421MK				
G-VOND	Bell 222	47041	G-OWCG	17.11.03	Von Essen Aviation Ltd	Denham	12. 3.08E
			G-VERT, G-JLBZ, G-BNDB, A40-CH				
G-VONE	Eurocopter AS.355N Ecureuil 2	5572	G-LCON	11. 3.04	Von Essen Aviation Ltd	Denham	27. 6.08E
G-VONF	Aérospatiale AS.355F1 Ecureuil 2	5262	G-BXBT	3. 2.05	Von Essen Aviation Ltd	Hawarden	26. 9.08E
			G-TMMC, G-JLCO				
G-VONG	Aérospatiale AS.355F1 Ecureuil 2	5327	G-OILX	4. 5.06	Von Essen Aviation Ltd	Denham	19. 2.08E
			ZH141, G-OILX, ZH141, G-OILX, G-RMGN, G-BMCY				
G-VONH	Aérospatiale AS.355F1 Ecureuil 2	5303	G-BKUL	12. 5.06	Von Essen Aviation Ltd	Denham	12. 4.08E
			ZJ140, G-FFHI, G-GWHH, G-BKUL				
G-VONJ	Raytheon RB390 Premier 1	RB-66	N931BR	4.11.05	Von Essen Aviation Ltd	Farnborough	8.11.06E
			VP-BAE, N50586				
G-VONK	Aérospatiale AS.355F1 Ecureuil 2	5325	G-BLRI (2)	15. 1.07	Von Essen Aviation Ltd	Denham	18. 4.08E
			ZJ139, G-NUTZ, G-BLRI				
G-VONS	Piper PA-32R-301T Saratoga II TC	3257155	N602MA	28. 7.03	W S Stanley	Gloucestershire	19.12.07E
G-VOOM	Pitts S-1S	PFA 009-12989		8. 4.03	P G Roberts	(Maidenhead)	
	(Built P G Roberts)						
G-VORN	Evektor EV-97 Eurostar	20042126	G-ODAV	2. 5.07	A Vaughan	Eshott	9..11.07P
	(Built B R Davies - pr.no.PFA 315-14299)						
G-VPAT	Evans VP-1 Series 2	PFA 062-13907		11. 2.04	A P Twort	Kittyhawk Farm, Deanland	
	(Built A P Twort)				*(Under construction 2004)*		
G-VPCB	Evans VP-1 Series 2	PFA 062-13901		28. 2.03	CI A Bloom	Kittyhawk Farm, Deanland	
	(Built C Bloom)				*(Under construction 2004)*		
G-VPSI	Cameron Z-1600 Balloon (Hot Air)	10704		22. 7.05	JK (England) Ltd	London W1	
					(Believed written off following altitude record at Mumbai, India 26.11.05)		
G-VPSJ	Europa Aviation Europa	023		29. 7.93	J D Bean	(Oxford)	
	(Built J D Bean - pr.no.PFA 247-12520) (Monowheel u/c)						
G-VRED	Airbus A340-642	768	F-WWCH	19.10.06	Virgin Atlantic Airways Ltd	London Heathrow	18.10.07E
					"Scarlet Lady"		
G-VROC	Boeing 747-41R	32746		22.10.03	Virgin Atlantic Airways Ltd	London Heathrow	21.10.07E
					"Mustang Sally"		

G-VROD	Aeroprakt A22 Foxbat	PFA 317-13991		18. 3.03	S E Kearney	Derryogue	17. 7.08P
	(Built P A Sanders)						
G-VROE	Avro 652A Anson T 21	3634	G-BFIR	3. 3.98	Air Atlantique Ltd	Coventry	31.10.08P
			7881M, WD413		(As "WD413" in RAF c/s)		
G-VROM	Boeing 747-443	32339	(EI-CVJ)	29. 5.01	Virgin Atlantic Airways Ltd	London Gatwick	28. 5.08E
					"Barbarella"		
G-VROS	Boeing 747-443	30885	(EI-CVG)	22. 3.01	Virgin Atlantic Airways Ltd	London Heathrow	21. 3.08E
					"English Rose"		
G-VROY	Boeing 747-443	32340	(EI-CVK)	18. 6.01	Virgin Atlantic Airways Ltd	London Gatwick	17. 6.08E
					"Pretty Woman"		
G-VRTX	Enstrom 280FX Shark	2044	G-CBNH	8. 7.02	Bladerunner Aviation Ltd	Barton	3. 4.08E
			Chilean Army H-180				
G-VRVI	Cameron O-90 Balloon (Hot Air)	2522		27. 2.91	SNT Property Ltd	Bristol	5. 8.05A
G-VSEA	Airbus A340-311	003	F-WWDA	7. 7.97	Virgin Atlantic Airways Ltd	London Gatwick	6. 7.08E
					"Plane Sailing"		
G-VSGE	Cameron O-105 Balloon (Hot Air)	2382	I-VSGE	14. 8.02	G Aimo	Mondovi, Italy	2. 4.05A
			G-BSSD				
G-VSHY	Airbus A340-642	383	F-WWCD	26. 7.02	Virgin Atlantic Airways Ltd	London Heathrow	25. 7.08E
					"Madam Butterfly"		
G-VSIX	Schempp-Hirth Ventus 2cT	102/293	BGA 5006-KDJ	13.11.07	M Nash-Wortham tr V6 Group	Lasham	11. 2.08
G-VSSH	Airbus A340-642	615	F-WWCZ.	31. 1.05	Virgin Atlantic Airways Ltd	London Heathrow	30. 1.08E
					"Sweet Dreamer"		
G-VSUN	Airbus A340-313	114	F-WWJI	30. 4.96	Virgin Atlantic Airways Ltd	London Heathrow	29. 4.08E
			(F-GLZJ)		"Rainbow Lady"		
G-VTAL	Beech V35 Bonanza	D-7978	HB-EJB	27. 2.03	R Chamberlain tr Wellesbourne Bonanza Group		
			D-EFTH			Wellesbourne Mountford	27. 4.08E
G-VTCT	Schempp-Hirth Ventus 2cT	90/266	BGA 4976-KCC	9. 1.08	J B Hoolahan tr V26 Syndicate	Challock	9. 5.08
G-VTII	de Havilland DH.115 Vampire T 11	15127	WZ507	9. 1.80	M B Hooton tr Vampire Preservation Group		
					(As "WZ507:74" in RAF c/s)	North Weald	1. 9.08P
G-VTOP	Boeing 747-4Q8	28194		28. 1.97	Virgin Atlantic Airways Ltd	London Gatwick	17. 3.08E
					"Virginia Plain"		
G-VTUS	Schempp-Hirth Ventus 2cT	64/199	BGA 4886-JYJ	19.10.07	P G Myers tr Ventus 02 Syndicate	Chipping	2. 4.08
G-VTWO	Schempp-Hirth Ventus 2c	28/75	BGA 5084-KGQ	13. 4.06	F and B Birlison	Aston Down	3.12.07
			D-0602		"565"		
G-VUEA	Cessna 550 Citation II	550-0671	G-BWOM	20. 6.02	AD Aviation Ltd	Liverpool	21. 5.08E
			N671EA, 9M-TAA, (N6761L)				
G-VUEM	Cessna 501 Citation I	501-0178	G-FLVU	24. 4.06	Frandley Aviation Partnership LLP	Liverpool	12. 7.08E
			N83ND, N4246A, LV-PML, N67749				
G-VUEZ	Cessna 550 Citation II	550-0008	N70XA	21. 4.05	AD Aviation Ltd	Liverpool	12. 6.08E
			N70X, N550JF, (N108AJ), OE-GIW, N575W, N98840				
G-VVBF	Colt 315A Balloon (Hot Air)	4058		3. 3.97	Airxcite Ltd t/a Virgin Balloon Flights	Wembley	17. 8.05T
G-VVBK	Piper PA-34-200T Seneca II	34-7570303	G-BSBS	26. 1.89	Ravenair Aircraft Ltd	Liverpool	1. 9.07T
			G-BDRI, SE-GLG				
G-VVBL	Robinson R44 Raven II	11606		31. 1.07	Valley View Building and Engineering Services Ltd		
						Southend	1. 3.08E
G-VVIP	Cessna 421C Golden Eagle	421C0699	G-BMWB	7. 7.92	My Sky Air Charter Ltd	Cranfield	30. 4.07T
			N2655L		(Noted 2.08)		
G-VVPA	Bombardier CL600-2B16	5612	OE-IPK	29. 2.08	TAG Aviation (UK) Ltd	Farnborough	
	(CL-604 Challenger))		C-FEPN, C-GLXY				
G-VVTV	Diamond DA.42 Twin Star	42.170	OE-VPY	18. 9.06	A D R R Northeast and S A Cook	Wycombe Air Park	8.11.07E
G-VVVV	Best Off Sky Ranger 912(2)	SKR0407510		15.12.04	J Thomas	Weston Zoyland	22. 3.07P
	(Built J Thomas and J B Hobbs - pr.no.BMAA/HB/427)				(Noted 5.07)		
G-VVWW	Enstrom 280C Shark	2056	N7802J	22.10.03	P J Odendaal	Southend	10. 1.08E
			JA7822				
G-VWEB	Airbus A340-642	787	F-WWCZ	20.12.06	Virgin Atlantic Airways Ltd	London Gatwick	19.12.07E
					"Surfer Girl"		
G-VWIN	Airbus A340-642	736	F-WWCL	28. 2.06	Virgin Atlantic Airways Ltd	London Heathrow	27. 2.08E
					"Lady Luck"		
G-VWKD	Airbus A340-642	706	F-WWCQ	28.11.05	Virgin Atlantic Airways Ltd	London Heathrow	27.11.07E
					"Miss Behavin"		
G-VWOW	Boeing 747-41R	32745		31.10.01	Virgin Atlantic Airways Ltd	London Heathrow	12.12.07E
					"Cosmic Girl"		
G-VXLG	Boeing 747-41R	29406		30. 9.98	Virgin Atlantic Airways Ltd	London Heathrow	29. 9.07T
					"Ruby Tuesday"		
G-VYGR	Colt 120A Balloon (Hot Air)	2479		24. 9.93	H van Hoesel	S'Hertogenbosch, Netherlands	20. 5.08E
G-VYOU	Airbus A340-642	765	F-WWCK	23. 8.06	Virgin Atlantic Airways Ltd	London Heathrow	22. 8.08E
					"Emmeline Heansy"		

G-WAAA - G-WZZZ

G-WAAC	Cameron N-56 Balloon (Hot Air)	492		14. 2.79	N P Hemsley tr Whacko Balloon Group	Crawley	26. 6.97A
					"Whacko"		
G-WAAN	MBB BÖ.105DB	S 20	G-AZOR	14.11.03	PLM Dollar Group Ltd	(Penrith)	26. 7.08E
			EC-DOE, G-AZOR, D-HDAC		"Pride of Cumbria"		
G-WAAS	MBB BÖ.105DBS-4	S 138/911	G-ESAM	26. 6.03	Bond Air Services Ltd	Swansea	24. 6.08E
	(Remanufactured with new pod c/n S 911 C 2003)		G-BUIB, G-BDYZ, D-HDEF		(Operated Welsh Air Ambulance)		
G-WACB	Reims Cessna F152 II	F15201972		16. 9.86	Wycombe Air Centre Ltd	Wycombe Air Park	2. 3.08E
G-WACE	Reims Cessna F152 II	F15201978		16. 9.86	Wycombe Air Centre Ltd	Wycombe Air Park	2. 5.08E
G-WACF	Cessna 152 II	15284852	N628GH	20. 1.87	Wycombe Air Centre Ltd	Wycombe Air Park	24.11.07T
			(LV-PMB), N628GH				
G-WACG	Cessna 152 II	15285536	ZS-KXY	4.11.86	Wycombe Air Centre Ltd	Wycombe Air Park	10. 4.08E
			(N93699)				
G-WACH	Cessna FA152 Aerobat	FA1520425		18. 6.87	Wycombe Air Centre Ltd	Wycombe Air Park	7. 8.08E
	(Built Reims Aviation SA)						

Reg	Type	C/n	Prev ID	Date	Owner	Location	Date
G-WACI	Beech 76 Duchess	ME-289	N6703Y	26. 7.88	Wycombe Air Centre Ltd	Wycombe Air Park	20.11.07T
G-WACJ	Beech 76 Duchess	ME-278	N6700Y	3. 1.89	Wycombe Air Centre Ltd	Wycombe Air Park	7. 5.08E
G-WACL	Reims Cessna F172N Skyhawk II	F17201912	G-BHGG	19. 6.89	A G Arthur	Perranporth	22. 4.08E
G-WACO	Waco UPF-7	5400	N29903	28. 1.87	R F L Cuypers	Antwerp, Belgium	13. 5.90
			NC29903		*(Damaged Liverpool 15. 4.89: under restoration 2006)*		
G-WACT	Reims Cessna F152 II	F15201908	G-BKFT	24. 6.86	N Clark	Eshott	12. 7.08E
G-WACU	Reims Cessna FA152 Aerobat	FA1520380	G-BJZU	10. 7.86	Wycombe Air Centre Ltd	Wycombe Air Park	9. 6.08T
G-WACW	Cessna 172P Skyhawk II	17274057	N5307K	16. 5.88	The Exeter Flying Club Ltd	Exeter	28. 6.08T
G-WACY	Reims Cessna F172P Skyhawk II	F17202217	F-GDOZ	3.10.86	Wycombe Air Centre Ltd	Wycombe Air Park	21. 1.08E
G-WADI	Piper PA-46-350P Malibu Mirage	4636205		8. 5.99	Air Malibu AG	(Triesen, Liechtenstein)	2. 6.08E
G-WADS	Robinson R22 Beta	1224	G-NICO	25. 4.96	Un Pied Sur Terre Ltd t/a Whizzard Helicopters	Welshpool	12. 4.08E
G-WAFU	Robinson R44 Raven	1364		25. 2.04	D O'Gorman t/a Midland Crane Hire	Weston, Leixlip, County Kildare	3. 4.08E
G-WAGG	Robinson R22 Beta II	2960		7. 7.99	J B Wagstaff t/a N J Wagstaff Leasing	Costock	15. 9.08E
G-WAGN	Stinson 108-3 Voyager	108-4216	N6216M	22. 6.05	S E H Ellcome	Cumbernauld	25. 4.10S
	(Built Consolidate Vultee Aircraft)		NC6216M				
G-WAGS	Robinson R44 Raven II	10891		7.10.05	Wagstaff Homes Ltd	Gamston	31.10.07E
G-WAHL	QAC Quickie	PFA 094-10619		20. 9.00	A A M Wahlberg	Lee-on-Solent	
	(Built A A M Wahlberg)				*(Noted 9.04)*		
G-WAIN	Cessna 550 Citation Bravo	550-1100	N110BR	24. 3.06	Ferron Trading Ltd	Jersey	23. 3.08E
			N5203S				
G-WAIR	Piper PA-32-301 Saratoga	32-8506010	N2607X	14. 1.91	P J Hopkins tr Finningley Aviation	(Cookswood)	13. 5.06
			N9577N		*(Noted 10.07)*		
G-WAIT	Cameron V-77 Balloon (Hot Air)	2390		20.11.90	C P Brown	Ely	24. 7.99A
G-WAKE	Mainair Blade 912	1244-0300-7-W1037		6. 3.00	B W Webster *(Noted 11.07)*	Rochdae	3. 5.07P
G-WAKY	Cyclone AX2000	7890		5. 4.02	York Microlight Centre Ltd	Rufforth	18. 8.08P
	(HKS 700E V3)						
G-WALI	Robinson R44 Raven II	10849		30. 8.05	Casdron Enterprises Ltd Phoenix Farm, Lower Upham		29. 9.07E
G-WALY	Maule MX-7-180 Super Rocket	11028C	N5668H	23. 1.03	A J West (Long Last Farm, East End, Pavenham)		14. 7.06T
G-WAMS	Piper PA-28R-201 Arrow	2844050	N491A	29. 4.04	Stapleford Flying Club Ltd	Stapleford	20. 5.08E
			N5328Q				
G-WARA	Piper PA-28-161 Warrior III	2842021	EC-HXU	3. 9.97	S J Skilton t/a Aviation Rentals	White Waltham	6. 4.08E
			G-WARA, N9289N, (G-WARA), N9289N				
G-WARB	Piper PA-28-161 Warrior III	2842034	N41286	4. 9.98	Muller Aircraft Leasing Ltd	Biggin Hill	9. 9.08E
			(G-WARB), N41286				
G-WARD	Taylor JT.1 Monoplane	WB.VI		1.12.80	R P J Hunter	Redhill	22. 2.00P
	(Built G Ward - pr.no.PFA 1407) (Volkswagen 1834)				*(Damaged Redhill 17. 9.99)*		
G-WARE	Piper PA-28-161 Warrior II	28-8416080	N4357L	21. 7.89	W B Ware	Filton	28. 4.08E
			("N4354Z")				
G-WARH	Piper PA-28-161 Warrior III	2842063	N4177Y	4. 2.00	Central Aircraft Leasing Ltd	Fairoaks	13. 3.08E
			G-WARH				
G-WARK	Schweizer 269C	S 1354		13.11.89	A R Baker	(Seamer, Scarborough)	3. 7.08E
	(Schweizer 300)						
G-WARO	Piper PA-28-161 Warrior III	2842015	EC-HVT	24.10.97	S J Skilton t/a Aviation Rentals	Exeter	17. 3.08E
			G-WARO, N92946, (G-WARO), N92946 *(Operated Exeter Flying School)*				
G-WARP	Cessna 182F	18254633	G-ASHB	6. 6.95	R D Fowden	Haverfordwest	16. 4.08E
			N3233U		*(New owner 7.05)*		
G-WARR	Piper PA-28-161 Warrior II	28-7916321	N3074U	15. 9.88	T J and G M Laundy	RAF Halton	13. 3.08E
					(Operated RAF Halton Aeroplane Club)		
G-WARS	Piper PA-28-161 Warrior III	2842022	N9281X	7.11.97	Blaneby Ltd	Biggin Hill	12.11.07T
			(G-WARS), N9281X				
G-WARU	Piper PA-28-161 Warrior III	2842023	EC-HVU	6.11.97	S J Skilton t/a Aviation Rentals	Blackpool	1. 6.08E
			G-WARU, N92880		*(Operated Flight Acadeny)*		
G-WARV	Piper PA-28-161 Warrior III	2842036	N41247	9.10.98	Plane Talking Ltd	Biggin Hill	21.10.07T
			(G-WARV), N41247		*(Noted 2.08)*		
G-WARW	Piper PA-28-161 Warrior III	2842037	N41254	17.11.98	Lomac Aviators Ltd	Liverpool	2. 3.08E
			(G-WARW), N41254				
G-WARX	Piper PA-28-161 Warrior III	2842038	N4126D	15.12.98	C M A Clark	Shobdon	17. 4.08E
			(G-WARX), N4126D				
G-WARY	Piper PA-28-161 Warrior III	2842024	N9287X	13.11.97	Transport Command Ltd	Shoreham	4.12.07E
			(G-WARY), N9287X				
G-WARZ	Piper PA-28-161 Warrior III	2842025	EC-IBI	26.11.97	S J Skilton t/a Aviation Rentals	Blackpool	6. 2.08T
			G-WARZ, N92944		*(Operated Flight Academy)*		
G-WATJ	Beech B200GT Super King Air	BY-14	N43004	3. 1.08	Saxonhenge Ltd	(Llandygai, Bangor)	
G-WATR	Christen A-1 Husky *(Floatplane)*	1040	N2941W	2. 4.03	S N Gregory	Lochearnhead	17. 6.08E
G-WAVA	Robin HR.200-120B	352		10. 7.00	Plane Talking Ltd	Elstree	11. 1.08E
G-WAVE (2)	Grob G109B	6381		1. 8.85	C G Wray	Park Farm, Eaton Bray	14. 5.08E
G-WAVI	Robin HR.200-120B	346	G-BZDG	8. 5.01	Plane Talking Ltd	Elstree	12. 4.08E
G-WAVN	Robin HR.200-120B	344	G-VECA	2. 5.02	Plane Talking Ltd	Elstree	20. 2.08E
G-WAVS	Piper PA-28-161 Warrior III	2842035	G-WARC	1.11.05	Oldromway Aviation Ltd	Wellesbourne Mountford	17. 9.08E
			N41244, (G-WARC), N41244				
G-WAVT	Robin R2160I	375	G-CBLG	7.12.04	Plane Talking Ltd	Elstree	25. 5.08E
G-WAVV	Robin HR.200-120B	291	G-GORF	6. 3.06	Oldromway Aviation Ltd	Wellesbourne Mountford	12. 3.08E
			F-GORF				
G-WAVY	Grob G109B	6374	F-CAQP	5. 5.05	G M Brightman and T Donovan tr G-WAVY Group	Shenington	26. 5.08E
			F-WAQP				
G-WAZP	Best Off Sky Ranger 912(2)	SKR0212288		10. 6.04	L V McClune	Hunsdon	12.10.08P
	(Built K H A Negal - pr.no.BMAA/HB/273)						
G-WAZZ	Pitts S-1S	7-0332	G-BRRP	17. 6.94	D T Knight	White Waltham	19. 8.04P
	(Built T H Decarlo)		N3TD				
G-WBAT	Wombat Gyrocopter	CJ-001	G-BSID	31. 5.90	M R Harrison	(Guernsey)	
	(Built C D Julian) (Rotax 532)						
G-WBEV	Cameron N-77 Balloon (Hot Air)	4376	G-PVCU	15.12.04	T J and M Turner Southampton and Wellingborough		27. 6.08E
					"Beverley's"		

G-WBHH	Bell 206B-3 JetRanger III	2410	N5001N	16. 4.07	Hughes Helicopter Co Ltd t/a Biggin Hill Helicopters		
						Biggin Hill	
G-WBLY	Mainair Sports Pegasus Quik	8057		30. 7.04	A J Lindsay "Coastbuster"	Newtownards	29. 7.08P
G-WBMG	Cameron N Ele 90SS Balloon (Hot Air)	3086	(G-BUYV)	5. 7.93	P H E van Overwalle	Nazareth, Belgium	22. 6.02A
G-WBTS	Falconar F-11W-200	PFA 32-10070	G-BDPL	22.10.90	W C Brown	Chilbolton	26. 7.08P
	(Built A J Watson) (Continental O-200-A)						
G-WBVS	Diamond DA.40D Star	D4.060		23.10.03	G W Beavis	Durham Tees Valley	17. 1.08E
G-WCAO	Eurocopter EC.135 T2	0204	D-HECU	8. 4.02	Avon and Somerset Constabulary and Gloucestershire Constabulary		
					(Operated Western Counties Police)	Filton	13. 6 08E
G-WCAT	Colt Flying Mitt SS Balloon (Hot Air)	1744		30. 5.90	I Chadwick tr Balloon Preservation Flying Group		
					"Washcat"	Petworth	28.11.03A
G-WCCI	Embraer EMB-135BJ Legacy	145505	G-REUB	7. 8.07	Altarello Ltd	London Stansted	7.12.07E
			PT-SAF				
G-WCCP	Beech B200 Super King Air	BB-1295	N295CP	16.10.06	William Cook Aviation Ltd	(Sheffield)	27.11.07E
			N95MW, N3079S				
G-WCEI	SOCATA MS.894E Rallye 220GT	12141	G-BAOC	28. 5.85	R A L Lucas	Bagby	18.10.07E
G-WCRD	Aérospatiale SA.341G Gazelle	1390	F-GEHD	25.10.02	Wickford Development Company Ltd		
			N6KT, N49527			Wickford House, Hatfield Peverel	18.12.07E
G-WCUB	Piper PA-18-150 Super Cub	18-8278	HB-OLR	11. 5.01	P A Walley	Croft Farm, Defford	13.11.10E
			N5514Y				
G-WDEB	Thunder Ax7-77 Balloon (Hot Air)	1606		26. 9.89	A Heginbottom	Cheadle	4. 8.07A
G-WDEV	Westland SA.341G Gazelle 1	1098	G-IZEL	30. 9.98	Mentorvale Construction Ltd	(Balgriffin, Dublin)	3. 4.08E
			G-BBHW				
G-WDGC	Rolladen-Schneider LS8-18	8395	G-CEWJ	8. 2.08	W D G Chappel	(Pewsey)	21. 3.08
			BGA 4904-JZC				
G-WDKR	Aérospatiale AS.355F2 Ecureuil 2	5115	ZJ635	24. 7.95	Cheshire Helicopters Ltd	(Sharcott, Wilmslow)	19. 3.08E
			G-NEXT, G-WDKR, G-NEXT, I-NEXT, G-NEXT, G-OMAV, G-NEXT				
G-WEBS	American Champion 7ECA Citabria Aurora			30. 1.06	P J Webb	Andrewsfield	4. 5.08E
		1395-2005					
G-WEEK	Best Off Sky Ranger 912(2)	SKRxxxx628		19. 1.06	D J Prothero and R J Brown	RNAS Culdrose	28. 9.08P
	(Built D J Prothero and R J Brown - pr.no.BMAA/HB/476)						
G-WEGO	Robinson R44 Raven II	10325		28. 4.04	A and E Fire Equipment Ltd	Gloucestershire	13. 5.08E
G-WELI	Cameron N-77 Balloon (Hot Air)	1078		26. 9.84	M A Shannon "Wellie"	Southampton	5. 7.04A
G-WELS	Cameron N-65 Balloon (Hot Air)	1297		7. 4.86	K J Vickery "Talisman"	Billingshurst	26. 6.92A
G-WELY	Agusta A109E Power	11710		9. 8.07	Titan Airways Ltd	London Stansted	8. 8.08E
G-WENA	Aérospatiale AS.355F2 Ecureuil 2	5260	G-MOBI	19. 4.04	Kensington and Chelsea Aviation Ltd	Redhill	3. 5.08E
			G-MUFF, G-CORR				
G-WEND	Piper PA-28RT-201 Arrow IV	28R-8118026	PH-SYL	8.11.82	Tayside Aviation Ltd	Glenrothes	14. 6.08E
			N8296L				
G-WERY	SOCATA TB-20 Trinidad	305		2. 4.82	G L Appleyard and C Hawkesworth tr WERY Flying Group		
						Sherburn-in-Elmet	18. 5.08E
G-WESX	CFM Streak Shadow	K 116-SA		2. 2.90	M Catania	(Mold)	22. 5.08P
	(Built N Ramsey - pr.no.PFA 161A-11561) (Rotax 582)						
G-WETI	Cameron N-31 Balloon (Hot Air)	449		27.11.78	C A Butter and J J T Cooke	Marsh Benham	11. 9.00A
G-WFFW	Piper PA-28-161 Warrior II	28-8116161	N8342A	26.10.93	S Letheren and D Jelly		
						(Sutton Benger, Chippenham)	2. 2.08E
G-WFLY	Mainair Sports Pegasus Quik	8073		8.10.04	D E Lord	Crosland Moor	17.10.08P
G-WFOX	Robinson R22 Beta II	2826		2. 6.98	G Kenna	Tatenhill	23. 7.08E
G-WGCS	Piper PA-18 Super Cub 95	18-1528	(G-BLSV)	21.12.84	S C Thompson	Newells Farm, Bolney	10. 8.08P
	(L-18C-PI) (Frame No.18-1500)		French Army, F-MBCH, French Army 51-15528				
G-WGHB	Canadair CL-30 (T-33AN) Silver Star Mk.3		CF-EHB	9. 5.74	R H and G C Cooper	Mendlesham	13. 6.77P
		T33-640	CAF 133640, RCAF 21640		(On rebuild 8.06)		
G-WGSC	Pilatus PC-6/B2-H4 Turbo-Porter	848	(G-BRVM)	2. 1.90	D M Penny	(France)	29. 3.08E
			OE-ECS				
G-WHAM	Eurocopter AS.350B3 Ecureuil	3494		18. 1.02	B M Christie t/a Horizon Helicopter Hire	Goodwood	21. 4.08E
G-WHAT	Colt 77A Balloon (Hot Air)	1911		15. 3.91	M A Scholes "Chad"	London SE25	15..5.08T
G-WHEE	Pegasus Quantum 15-912	7510		26. 3.99	Airways Airsports Ltd	Darley Moor, Ashbourne	8..3.07P
G-WHEN	Tecnam P92-EM Echo	PFA 318-13679		7. 2.01	E Windle	Popham	
	(Built C D Marsh)				(Noted 1.08)		
G-WHIM	Colt 77A Balloon (Hot Air)	1476		10. 4.89	D L Morgan	Ilford	28. 7.04A
G-WHIN	Eurocopter EC.135 T2	0394		21.12.05	P Neill	(Ballinderry Upper, Lisburn)	27. 4.08E
G-WHOG	CFM Streak Shadow	K 253-SA		21. 9.94	B R Cannell	Old Sarum	21. 5.08P
	(Built B R Cannell - pr.no.PFA 206-12776) (Rotax 618)				"Wart Hog"		
G-WHOO	RotorWay Executive 162F	6495		5. 6.01	C A Saul	(Canvey Island)	10. 8.08P
	(Built C A Saull) (RotorWay RI 162F)						
G-WHRL	Schweizer 269C	S 1453	EC-GGX	19. 4.90	M Gardiner	Henstridge	11. 9.08E
	(Schweizer 300)		CS-HDG, G-WHRL, N41S				
G-WHST	Eurocopter AS.350B2 Ecureuil	2915	G-BWYA	9. 8.96	Keltruck Ltd	(West Bromwich)	26. 9.08E
G-WIBB	Jodel D 18	PFA 169-11640		18. 6.96	M N Martin	Leicester	26. 9.06P
	(Built J Wibberley) (Subaru EA81)				(Noted 10.07)		
G-WIBS	CASA 1-131E Jungmann Series 2000	2005	Spanish AF E3B-401	25. 3.99	C Willoughby	(Ashford)	
G-WIDZ	Staaken Z-21 Flitzer	PFA 223-14314		26. 8.05	T F Crossman	(Loddon, Norwich)	
	(Built T F Crossman)						
G-WIEZ	Cameron C-80 Balloon (Hot Air)	3265	PH-WIE	5. 4.07	J M Stables t/a Blue Sky Balloons		
						Arkendale, Knaresborough	17. 4.08E
G-WIFE	Cessna R182 Skylane RG II	R18200244	G-BGVT	11.12.01	A L Brown tr Wife 182 Group	Glenrothes	10. 5.08E
			N3162C				
G-WIFI	Cameron Z-90 Balloon (Hot Air)	10624		9. 9.04	Trigger Concepts Ltd	Swallowfield, Reading	12. 8.08A
					(Centrino titles)		
G-WIGY	Pitts S-1S	7-0115	G-ITTI	31. 5.07	M J Wright	Leicester	6. 3.08P
	(Built S Eisenberger)		N91VA				
G-WIIZ	Agusta-Bell 206B-2 JetRanger II	8111	G-DBHH	28.10.03	B J Green t/a Helicopters R Go		
			G-AWVO, VH-BHI, PK-HCA, G-AWVO, 9Y-TDN, PK-HBG, G-AWVO Draycott Farm, Chiseldon				9. 7.08T

G-WIKY	Cessna 208B Grand Caravan	208B1024	EC-JGQ	17. 4.03	Provident Partners Ltd	Oxford	1. 4.08E
			G-WIKY, N5117U				
G-WILD	Pitts S-1T	1017	ZS-LMM	6.12.85	N J Wakefield	Shobdon	15. 6.08E
	(Built Pitts Aerobatics)						
G-WILG	PZL-104 Wilga 35A	62153	G-AZYJ	15. 4.97	M H Bletsoe-Brown *(Noted 10.07)*	Sywell	20. 9.07
G-WILT	Comco Ikarus C42 FB100	0506-6687		14. 7.05	M A Curtis	(Witcombe, Martock)	30. 8.08P
G-WIMP	Colt 56A Balloon (Hot Air)	755		13. 2.86	T and B Chamberlain	Melbourne, York	5. 7.08A
G-WINA	Cessna 560XL Citation Excel	560-5343	N5145V	17.12.03	Inclination 1 LLP	Stepleford	21.12.07E
G-WINI	Scottish Aviation Bulldog Series 120/121		G-CBCO	23. 9.03	A Bole	Conington	15. 6.09E
		BH120/238	XX546		*(As "XX546:03" in RAF c/s)*		
G-WINK	Grumman AA-5B Tiger	AA5B-0327	N74658	14.12.90	B S Cooke tr Wing Group	Elstree	1. 5.08E
G-WINN	Stolp SA.200 Starduster Too	615	N6275	15. 1.08	J C and R D P Cadle (Blockley, Moreton-in-Marsh)		
	(Built B Scofield)						
G-WINS	Piper PA-32-300 Cherokee Six	32-7640065	N8476C	24. 4.91	Cheyenne Ltd	Jersey	19. 3.08E
G-WINT	Pilatus PC-12/47	830		12. 7.07	Air Winton Ltd	Oxford	18. 7.08E
G-WIRE	Aérospatiale AS.355F1 Ecureuil 2	5312	G-CEGB	22. 1.90	National Grid Company PLC	Oxford	18. 6.08E
			G-BLJL				
G-WIRL	Robinson R22 Beta	0671		27. 7.87	Rivermead Aviation Ltd	Gloucestershire	2. 8.08E
G-WISE	Piper PA-28-181 Archer III	2843658	N30910	17. 8.07	M Arnold	Old Sarum	23. 9.08P
G-WISH	Lindstrand Cake SS Balloon (Hot Air)	006		14.12.92	Oxford Promotions (UK) Ltd	(Kentucky, US)	3. 4.03A
	(Birthday Cake shape)				*(Operated F Prell)*		
G-WIXI	Akrotech Europe CAP.10B	279		27. 1.98	P A Willmington	(Dartford)	16. 6.08E
G-WIZA	Robinson R22 Beta	0861	G-PERL	16.11.94	Patriot Aviation Ltd	Cranfield	29. 1.08E
			N90815				
G-WIZD	Lindstrand LBL 180A Balloon (Hot Air)	066		12.11.93	Wizard Balloons Cambridge Ltd		
					Barningham, Bury St Edmunds		18. 6.07E
G-WIZI	Enstrom 280FX	2040	Chilean Army H-177	8. 7.02	D I Wadsworth	Hawarden	11 12.07E
G-WIZR	Robinson R22 Beta II	2799		9. 3.98	Aerolease Ltd	Conington	13. 5.08E
G-WIZS	Mainair Sports Pegasus Quik	8019		17. 3.04	G R Barker	Bourn	26. 4.08P
G-WIZY	Robinson R22 Beta	0566	G-BMWX	26. 8.97	Fancy Plates Ltd	Enniskillen	22. 6.08E
			N24196				
G-WIZZ	Agusta-Bell 206B-2 JetRanger II	8540		7.12.77	Rivermead Aviation Ltd	(Reading)	23. 5.08E
G-WJAC	Cameron TR-70 Balloon (Hot Air)	10694		29. 4.05	S J and J A Bellaby	Nottingham	8. 4.08E
G-WJCJ	Eurocopter EC.155 B1	6748	F-WWOO	31.10.06	Starspeed Ltd	Blackbushe	5.11.07E
G-WLAC	Piper PA-18-150 Super Cub	18-8899	G-HAHA	2. 6.98	White Waltham Airfield Ltd	White Waltham	12. 8.08E
			G-BSWE, N9194P				
G-WLDN	Robinson R44 Raven	1507		16. 9.05	Fly Executive Ltd	Cranfield	5.10.07E
G-WLGC	Piper PA-28-181 Archer III	2843484	G-FLUX	16. 4.07	Staircase 8 Ltd	Goodwood	17. 4.08E
			N5339U				
G-WLKI	Lindstrand LBL 150A Balloon (Hot Air)	1140		27. 3.07	C Wilkinson	Akeld Steads, Wooler	4. 4.08E
G-WLLS	Rolladen-Schneider LS8-18	8038	BGA 4189-HTL	6.11.07	A and L Wells	Nympsfield	22.11.07
G-WLMS	Mainair Blade 912	1223-0999-7-W1016		23. 9.99	I D Smart and M Holman	Finmere	7 12.07P
G-WLSN	Best Off Sky Ranger 912S(1)	SKRxxxx639		24.11.05	A., A R and A R Wilson	Darley Moor, Ashbourne	26. 7.08P
	(Built A., A R and A R Wilson - pr.no.BMAA/HB/474)						
G-WMAO	Eurocopter EC.135 P2+	0501		22. 8.06	West Midlands Police Authority	Birmingham	17. 7.08E
G-WMAS	Eurocopter EC.135 T2	0174		18. 6.01	Bond Air Services Ltd	RAF Cosford	26. 6.08E
					(Operated County Air Ambulance)		
G-WMBT	Robinson R44 Raven II	10353		5. 5.04	K G Ward	(Bangor-on-Dee, Wrexham)	13. 3.08E
G-WMLT	Cessna 182Q Skylane II	18266689	G-BOPG	23. 4.02	G Wimlett	Blackpool	1. 5.08E
			N95962				
G-WMTM	Gulfstream AA-5B Tiger	AA5B-1035	N4517V	8. 1.91	G Hance tr Falcon Flying Group		
					(Bridge of Don, Aberdeen)		25. 8.08E
G-WMWM	Robinson R44 Raven	0767		27. 4.00	MMAIR Ltd		
					Yew Tree Farm, Ford End, Clavering, Saffron Walden		3. 8.08E
G-WNAA	Agusta A109E Power	11090	G-TVAC	28. 5.03	Sloane Helicopters Ltd	Coventry	10. 4.08E
					(Operated Warwickshire and Northampton Air Ambulance)		
G-WNGS	Cameron N-105 Balloon (Hot Air)	4385		15. 7.98	R M Horn	Chelmsford	6.12.07A
G-WNTR	Piper PA-28-161 Cherokee Warrior II		G-BFNJ	13. 1.06	D M Jarman tr Fleetlands Flying Group Lee-on-Solent		6. 6.08E
		28-7816281	N9520N		*(Fleetlands Flying Group titles and "NJ" from previous registration on nose)*		
G-WOCO	Waco YMF-5C	F5C091	N770MM	10. 1.05	Flight Management Solutions Ltd	Gloucestershire	13. 4.08E
	(Built Waco Classic Aircraft Corporation 2000)						
G-WOFM	Agusta A109E Power	11678	G-NWRR	29. 8.06	Quinnasette Ltd	Oxford	8. 8.08E
G-WOLF	Piper PA-28-140 Cherokee Cruiser	28-7425439	OY-TOD	20. 3.80	M W Fitch tr The Yak Group	Elstree	30. 5.08E
G-WONE	Schempp-Hirth Ventus 2cT	55/179	BGA 4795-JUQ	11. 9.07	J P Wright	Lasham	26. 4.08
G-WONN	Eurocopter EC.135 T2+	0597		30. 8.07	Eurocopter UK Ltd	Oxford	
G-WOOD	Beech 95-B55A Baron	TC-1283	SE-GRC	17. 9.79	M A Rooney	Sturgate	6. 3.08E
			G-AYID, SE-EXK				
G-WOOF	Enstrom 480	5027		3. 3.98	Netcopter.co.uk Ltd and Curvature Ltd	Hawarden	23. 7.08E
G-WOOL	Colt 77A Balloon (Hot Air)	2044		23. 2.93	T G, C L Pembrey and N P Helmsley	Steyning	15. 5.08
					tr Whacko Balloon Group		
G-WORM	Thruster T 600N 450 Sprint	9109-T600N-039		5.10.99	S and M Rickett	Redlands, Swindon	12. 4.08P
	(Rotax 582 UL)						
G-WOWA	de Havilland DHC-8-311	296	C-GZOF	23.10.03	Air South West Ltd	Plymouth	22.10.07T
			G-BRYS, PH-SDG, D-BKIS, C-GFQL				
G-WOWB	de Havilland DHC-8-311	334	C-GZOU	29.10.03	Air South West Ltd	Plymouth	28.10.07T
			G-BRYT, D-BKIR, C-GFEN				
G-WOWC	de Havilland DHC-8-311	311	N784BC	29.10.04	Air South West Ltd	Plymouth	11.11.07E
			G-BRYO, N434AW, C-GEVP				
G-WOWD	de Havilland DHC-8-311	286	C-FDIY	6. 5.05	Air South West Ltd	Plymouth	5. 5.08E
			N547DS, JY-RWA, C-FXGF, N432AW, C-GFCF, N432AW, C-GFCF				
G-WOWE	de Havilland DHC-8-311	256	C-FFBG	3. 3.06	Air South West Ltd	Plymouth	3. 3.08E
			G-BRYI, C-GEOA		*"Cloud Surfer"*		
G-WPAS	MD Helicopters MD.900 Explorer	900-00053		1. 7.98	Police Aviation Services Ltd	Devizes	9.11.10S
					(Operated Wiltshire Police)		

Reg	Type	C/n	Prev ID	Date	Owner/Operator	Location	Status
G-WRBI	Agusta A109E Power	11017	G-CRST N709AT, HB-XQM	22.11.07	Fuel The Jet LLP	(Dukinfield)	24. 7.08E
G-WREN	Pitts S-2A (Built Aerotek Inc)	2229	N9472	8. 1.81	Modi Aviation Ltd	Sibson	27. 4.08E
G-WRFM	Enstrom 280C-UK Shark	1202	G-CTSI G-BKIO, (G-BKHN), SE-HLB	21. 4.89	A J Clark	(Codnor, Ripley)	25. 8.07
G-WRIT	Colt 77A Balloon (Hot Air)	1328		15. 9.88	G Pusey "Legal Eagle"	Seville, Spain	11. 7.08A
G-WRSY	Enstrom 480B	5077		19. 4.05	Pietas Ltd	Denham	7. 5.08E
G-WRWR	Robinson R22 Beta II	2964		20. 7.99	MFH Helicopters Ltd	(London W1)	22. 8.08E
G-WSKY	Enstrom 280C-UK-2 Shark	1037	G-BEEK	25. 7.83	M I Edwards	Brandon, Suffolk	15. 7.08E
G-WSSX	Comco Ikarus C42 FB100	0608-6837		31.10.06	Haimoss Ltd	Old Sarum	1.11.08P
G-WTAV	Robinson R44 Raven II	11449		29. 9.06	William Taylor Aviation Ltd (Operated The Flight Centre) (Noted 1.08)	Southend	23.10.07E
G-WTEC	Cirrus SR22	2627	N819SR	29. 8.07	B J White	Goodwood	2. 9.08E
G-WTWO	Aquila AT01	AT01-176		9. 1.08	J P Wright	(Ellisfield, Basingstoke)	
G-WUFF	Europa Aviation Europa (Built M A Barker - pr.no.PFA 247-12942) (Monowheel u/c)	235		19. 1.99	M A Barker (Noted 12.07)	Breighton	10. 8.07P
G-WULF	WAR Focke-Wulf FW190 replica (Built SBV Aeroservices Ltd - pr.no.PFA 081-10328) (Continental O-200-A)	204		24. 2.78	A Howe (As "8+-" in Luftwaffe c/s)	(Birmingham)	22. 6.01P
G-WUSH	Eurocopter EC.120B Colibri	1290		15. 5.02	Bridgestock Ltd	(Ballyhaunis, County Mayo)	15. 8.08E
G-WVBF	Lindstrand LBL 210A Balloon (Hot Air)	312		6.12.95	Airxcite Ltd t/a Virgin Balloon Flights	Wembley	22. 4.04T
G-WVIP	Beech B200 Super King Air	BB-625	N869AM N8SZ, N8SP, N18BH, N302EC, N6682U	18.08.04	Capital Trading (Aviation) Ltd	Exeter	19. 8.08E
G-WWAL	Piper PA-28R-180 Cherokee Arrow	28R-30461	G-AZSH N4612J	23.10.98	White Waltham Airfield Ltd	White Waltham	30.11.07E
G-WWAY	Piper PA-28-181 Archer II	28-8690031	D-ELCX N165AV, N9643N	30. 3.04	R A Witchell	Andrewsfield	14. 3.08T
G-WWBB	Airbus A330-243	404	F-WWKP	30. 5.01	British Midland Airways Ltd	London Heathrow	29. 5.08E
G-WWBC	Airbus A330-243			3.08R	British Midland Airways Ltd	London Heathrow	
G-WWBD	Airbus A330-243	401	F-WWKN	9. 5.01	British Midland Airways Ltd (Star Alliance titles)	London Heathrow	8. 5.08E
G-WWBM	Airbus A330-243	398	F-WWKL	27. 4.01	British Midland Airways Ltd	London Heathrow	26. 4.08E
G-WWIZ	Beech 58 Baron	TH-429	G-GAMA G-BBSD	18.10.96	F R M Harding	(Doddinghurst, Brentwood)	5. 7.08E
G-WWOW	Robinson R44 Raven I	1724		11. 6.07	Capital Helicopters Ltd	Kirknewton	10. 7.08E
G-WYAT	CFM Streak Shadow SA (Built M G Whyatt - pr.no.PFA 206-12993) (Rotax 618)	K 279		9. 6.97	J C Carter (New owner 2.08	Cambridge	21.11.04P
G-WYCH	Cameron Witch 90SS Balloon (Hot Air)	1330		30. 9.86	Corn Palace Balloon Club Ltd "Hilda" (Active Albuquerque, New Mexico, US 10.06)	(US)	13. 7.99A
G-WYKD	Air Création Tanarg 912S(2)/iXess 15 (Built D C Dewey - pr.no.BMAA/HB/559 being Flylight kit comprising Trike s/n xxxxx and Wing s/n xxxxx)	FLT.xxx		4. 1.08	D C Dewey Lower Mountpleasant Farm, Chatteris		
G-WYLE	Rans S-6-ES Coyote II (Built A and R W Osborne - pr.no.PFA 204-14330)	0904.1610		26.11.04	A and R W Osborne	Priory Farm, Tibenham	12. 6.08P
G-WYND	Wittman W.8 Tailwind (Built R S Marriott and C Clark)	PFA 031-12407		2. 8.99	R S Marriott and C Clark tr Forge Group	(Scunthorpe)	
G-WYNE	British Aerospace BAe 125 Series 800B (Built Corporate Jets Ltd)	258240	G-CJAA G-HCFR, HB-VLT, G-SHEA, G-BUWC, G-5-772	17.10.06	Mercury Air Ltd	Biggin Hill	15. 1.08E
G-WYNT	Cameron N-56 Balloon (Hot Air)	1038		3. 4.84	S L G Williams "Gwyntoedd Dros Cymru" and "Winds over Wales"	Bristol	24. 5.08A
G-WYPA	MBB BÖ.105DBS-4	S 815	D-HDZY	27.10.89	Police Aviation Services Ltd	Dunsfold	27. 1.08E
G-WYSP	Robinson R44 Astro	0657		17. 9.99	Clear Aviation Ltd	Durham Tees Valley	29. 9.07E
G-WYVN	DG Flugzeugbau DG-1000T	10-63T5	BGA 5179-KLH	10. 2.06	J W Sage tr Army Gliding Association "12" (Operated Wyvern (Army) Gliding Club)	Trenchard Lines, Upavon	17. 3.08
G-WZOL	TLAC RL5B LWS Sherwood Ranger (Built G W F Webb - pr.no.PFA 237-12887) (Jabiru 2200A)	xxxx	G-MZOL	20. 1.99	S J Spavins	Longacre Farm, Sandy	29. 2.08P
G-WZOY	Rans S-6-ES Coyote II (Built S P Read - pr.no.PFA 204-14735)	0707-1821		29.11.07	M H Wise and S P Read	(Weston Zoyland)	
G-WZRD	Eurocopter EC.120B Colibri	1455		3.11.06	Conductia Enterprises Ltd	(Nicosia, Cyprus)	25. 2.08E

G-XAAA - G-XZZZ

Reg	Type	C/n	Prev ID	Date	Owner/Operator	Location	Status
G-XALT	Piper PA-38-112 Tomahawk	38-79A0801	PH-ALT OO-TLT, N9651N	9.10.06	D Shew (Noted 1.08)	Thruxton	3.12.07E
G-XARV	ARV Aviation ARV-1 Super 2 (Rotax 912-S)	010	G-OPIG G-BMSJ	8.11.95	D J Burton	Shoreham	6. 6.08P
G-XATS	Pitts S-2A (Built Pitts Aerobatics)	2147	CS-AZE N338BD	29. 3.01	Air Training Services Ltd (Operated "Black Formation")	Wycombe Air Park	17.11.07E
G-XAVI	Piper PA-28-161 Warrior II	28-7916258	G-SACZ N2098N	12. 6.06	J R Santamaria	Guernsey	5. 6.08E
G-XAXA	Fairey Britten-Norman BN-2A-26 Islander	530	G-LOTO G-BDWG, (N90255), (C-GYUF), G-BDWG (Noted 1.08)	22. 8.00	Airx Ltd t/a Blue Islands	Jersey	28.11.07E
G-XAYR	Raj Hamsa X'Air 582(2) (Built M J Kaye - pr.no.BMAA/HB/122)	471		4. 1.00	D L Connolly and R V Barber	Little Gransden	30. 4.08P
G-XBCI	Bell 206B-3 JetRanger III	4466	N206EE RP-C1778, N80706, C-GAJH	17. 6.04	BCI Helicopter Charters Ltd	(Thruxton)	15. 7.08E
G-XBEL	Cessna 560XL Citation XLS	560-5698	N5091J	2. 5.07	Aviation Beauport Ltd	Jersey	2. 6.08E
G-XBGA	Glaser-Dirks DG-500-22 Elan	5E71S12	BGA 3955-HHJ	13. 2.08	N Kelly	Bicester	27. 5.08
G-XBLU	Cessna 680 Citation Sovereign	680-0143	N1318X	15. 8.07	Datel Holdings Ltd	(Stone)	14. 8.08E
G-XBOX	Bell 206B-3 JetRanger III	3370	G-OOHO G-OCHC, G-KLEE, G-SIZL, G-BOSW, N2063T	31. 1.05	Mainstream Digital Ltd	Shobdon	24. 8.08E
G-XCBI	Schweizer 269C-1 (Schweizer 300)	0301		7. 8.07	B Durkan & B McKevitt	Enniskillen	23. 8.08E
G-XCCC	Extra EA.300/L	142		20. 8.01	P T Fellows	Rochester	18. 9.08E

G-XCIT	Alpi Pioneer 300	4		16. 9.04	A Thomas	Shobdon	15. 8.08P
	(Built A Thomas - pr.no.PFA 330-14296)						
G-XCIV	Rolladen-Schneider LS4-a	4355	BGA 3709-GBT N220BB	6.11.07	S M Platt tr IV Group	Long Mynd	21. 3.08
G-XCUB	Piper PA-18-150 Super Cub	18-8109036	N9348T	1. 5.81	M C Barraclough	(East Tisted, Alton)	23. 5.08
G-XDUO	Schempp-Hirth Duo Discus xT	162	BGA 5247-KOF	8. 3.07	F B Jeynes tr G-XDUO Group "KOF"	Bidford	6. 3.08
G-XDWE	P&M Quik GT450	8242		15. 2.07	D Ewing	Roddige	14. 2.08P
G-XELA	Robinson R44 Raven II	11378		26. 8.06	A Yew	(Bordean, Petersfield)	21. 9.08E
G-XENA	Piper PA-28-161 Cherokee Warrior II	28-7716158	N3486Q	29. 6.98	P Brewer	Shoreham	16. 5.08E
G-XFLY	Lambert Aircraft Mission M212-100 PFA 306-13380			3. 2.00	Lambert Aircraft Engineering BVBA	Kortrijk, Wevelgem, Belgium	30. 6.07P
G-XHOT	Cameron Z-105 Balloon (Hot Air)	10999		5. 1.07	S F Burden	Noordwijk ,Netherlands	7. 1.08E
G-XIII	Van's RV-7	PFA 323-14165		20. 2.04	G Wright tr G-XIII Group	Sherburn-in-Elmet	17. 8.08P
	(Built G Wright)						
G-XINE	Piper PA-28-161 Cherokee Warrior II	28-7716112	G-BPAC N2567Q	14.10.03	P Tee	Denham	22. 5.08E
G-XIOO	Raj Hamsa X'Air 133(1)	681		27. 1.03	B J Fallows	(Ammanford)	5.11.08P
	(Built R Paton and A Start - pr.no.BMAA/HB/247)						
G-XIXI	Evektor EV-97 teamEurostar UK	2938		12. 7.07	J A C Cockfield	RNAS Culdrose	30. 6.08P
G-XJCB	Sikorsky S-76C+	760616	N8093J	29. 1.07	J C Bamford Excavations Ltd	East Midlands	14. 2.08E
G-XJJM	P&M Pegasus Quik	8306		23. 8.07	J J Murtagh	Barton	22. 8.08P
G-XJON	Schempp-Hirth Ventus 2b	114	BGA 4895-JYT (BGA 4895)	17. 9.07	J C Bastin	Lasham	1. 3.08
G-XKEN	Piper PA-34-200T Seneca II	34-7970003	N3036A	5. 9.01	Beresford Pumps Ltd	(Saltly, Birmingham)	26.10.07E
G-XKKA	Diamond HK 36 TTC Super Dimona	36.677	S5-KKA	16. 2.07	S M Godleman tr G-XKKA Group Gransden Lodge		15. 3.08E
					(Noted 2.08)		
G-XLAA	Boeing 737-8Q8/W	28226	G-OKDN	13. 3.01	XL Airways UK Ltd	London Gatwick	26. 7.08E
G-XLAB	Boeing 737-8Q8/W	28218	G-OJSW	14. 5.01	XL Airways UK Ltd	London Gatwick	10.12.07E
G-XLAD	Boeing 737-81Q	29052	N906MA	27. 2.01	XL Airways UK Ltd	London Gatwick	18. 4.08E
			G-XLAD, G-ODMW, N1786B, (N8254Q)				
G-XLAI	Boeing 737-8Q8/W	30702		25. 5.06	XL Airways UK Ltd	London Gatwick	24. 5.08E
G-XLAJ	Boeing 737-8Q8/W	30703		13. 6.06	XL Airways UK Ltd	London Gatwick	12. 6.08E
G-XLAK	Boeing 737-8FH/W	35092		26. 1.07	XL Airways UK Ltd	London Gatwick	25. 1.08E
G-XLAM	Best Off Sky Ranger 912S(1)	SKR0504609		19.12.05	D M Broom tr X-LAM Sky Ranger Syndicate Sywell		25. 9.08P
	(Built D M Broom - pr.no.BMAA/HB/460)						
G-XLAN	Boeing 737-86N/W	32685		20. 2.07	XL Airways UK Ltd	London Gatwick	19. 2.08E
G-XLAO	Boeing 737-86N/W	32690		2. 5.07	XL Airways UK Ltd	London Gatwick	1. 5.08E
G-XLIV	Robinson R44 Raven	0810		11. 7.00	Rotorcraft Ltd	Redhill	14.11.07T
G-XLLL	Aérospatiale AS.355F1 Ecureuil 2	5033	G-PASF	14. 2.06	Sharpness Dock Ltd	(Victoria Wharf, Plymouth)	6. 4.08E
			G-SCHU, N915EG, N5777H				
G-XLMB	Cessna 560XL Citation Excel	560-5259	N52526	25. 6.02	Aviation Beauport Ltd	Jersey	25. 6.08E
G-XLNT	Zenair CH.601XL Zodiac	PFA 162B-14182		27. 1.04	P H Ronfell tr Zenair G-XLNT Group	Tarn Farm, Cockerham	10. 4.08P
	(Built P H and S J Ronfell)						
G-XLTG	Cessna 182S Skylane	18280234	N9571L	17. 7.98	D H Morgan Standalone Farm, Meppershall		5. 8.08E
G-XLXL	Robin DR.400-160 Knight	813	G-BAUD	3. 1.92	L R Marchant	Rochester	3. 8.08E
G-XMGO	Aeromot AMT-200S Super Ximango	200127		18. 4.01	R P Beck and G McLean	Rufforth	11. 6.08E
G-XMII	Eurocopter EC.135 T2	0215		15. 4.02	Merseyside Police Authority	RAF Woodvale	6. 8.08E
G-XOAR	Schleicher ASG 29E	29518	BGA 5285 D-KPRB	3.08R	R Browne	RAF Cranwell	
					"XS"		
G-XOIL	Eurocopter AS.355N Ecureuil 2	5627	G-LOUN	5. 3.03	Firstearl Marine and Aviation Ltd	Denham	15. 6.08E
G-XOXO	Extra EA.300/L	1234		27. 7.06	Skyhigh Aerobatics Ltd	Sywell	28. 8.08E
G-XPBI	Letov LK-2M Sluka	PFA 263-13341		4.12.98	K Harness	North Coates	14. 8.06P
	(Built P Bishop) (Rotax 447)						
G-XPDA	Cameron Z-120 Balloon (Hot Air)	11038		6. 8.07	ABC Flights Ltd Clapton in Gordano, Bristol		30. 7.08E
					(Expediia.co.uk titles)		
G-XPII	Cessna R172K Hawk XP	R1723071	G-DIVA N758FX	6.11.06	A M Deacon tr The Hawk Flying Group	Leicester	10.10.07E
G-XPSS	Short SD.3-60 Variant 100	SH3713	EI-CPR	2. 5.01	BAC Group Ltd	Edinburgh	22. 8.07E
			G-OBOH, G-BNDJ, G-14-3713 "City of Derby"				
G-XPXP	Aero Designs Pulsar XP	218		30. 3.92	B J Edwards Belle Vue Farm, Yarnscombe		20. 7.08P
	(Built B J Edwards - pr.no.PFA 202-11958) (Tail-wheel u/c)						
G-XRAF	Raj Hamsa X'Air 582(2)	513		7. 4.00	S Marathe Sackville Lodge, Riseley		21.11.08P
	(Built M E Howard and S Stockill - pr.no.BMAA/HB/132)						
G-XRAY	Rand Robinson KR-2	PFA 129-11227		30. 4.87	R S Smith	Barthol Chapel	
	(Built R S Smith)				(Under construction 2001)		
G-XRED	Pitts S-1C	338H	G-SWUN	28.11.05	J E Rands	Wickenby	8. 7.07P
	(Built R Merrick) (Lycoming O-320)		G-BSXH, N14RM				
G-XRLD	Cameron A-250 Balloon (Hot Air)	4820		25. 4.00	J A B Gray Daglingworth, Cirencester		8. 3.08T
					(Red Letter Days titles)		
G-XRXR	Raj Hamsa X'Air 582(5)	431		13. 9.99	R J Philpotts Pound Green, Buttonoak, Bewdley		19. 5.08P
	(Built I S Walsh - pr.no.BMAA/HB/102)						
G-XRVX	Van's RV-10	PFA 339-14592		24.11.06	N K Lamping	(Weaverham, Northwich)	
	(Built N K Lamping)						
G-XSAM	Van's RV-9A	PFA 320-13797		18. 9.02	D G Lucas	Plymouth	
	(Built D G Lucas)				(Under construction 10.07)		
G-XSDJ	Europa Aviation Europa XS	402		3. 2.99	D N Joyce	Gloucestershire	21. 6.87P
	(Built D N Joyce - pr.no.PFA 247-13378) (Rotax 914-UL) (Monowheel u/c)						
G-XSEA	Van's RV-8	PFA 303-14228		15. 8.05	H M Darlington	High Easter	19. 1.08P
	(Built N I Hart)						
G-XSEL	Silence Twister	PFA 329-14594		3.10.07	Skyview Systems Ltd	Lavenham	
	(Built N I G Hart)						
G-XSFT	Piper PA-23-250 Aztec F	27-7754103	G-CPPC G-BGBH, N63773	18. 6.86	T L B Dykes	Carlisle	1. 6.08E

Reg	Type	C/n	Prev ID	Date	Owner/Operator	Location	Date
G-XSKY	Cameron N-77 Balloon (Hot Air)	2508		26. 3.91	D Hempleman-Adams	Corsham	7. 8.08A
G-XTEE	AirBorne XT912-B-Streak III-B	XT912-026	T2-2252	25. 8.04	G J Webster t/a Airborne Australia In UK		
	(Wing s/n S3B-051)					Mill Farm, Shifnal	8. 3.08P
G-XTEK	Robinson R44 Astro	0647		11. 8.99	R C Hields t/a Hields Aviation	Sherburn-in-Elmet	11.10.07E
G-XTHT	AirBorne XT912-B-Streak III-B	XT912-200		4.12.07	H A Taylor	Bicester	16.12.08P
	(Wing s/n SB3-212)						
G-XTNI	AirBorne XT912-B-Streak III-B	XT912-067		10. 5.05	A J Parry	Tarsan Lane, Portadown	9. 5.07P
	(Wing s/n ST3-043)				*(Noted 7.07)*		
G-XTNR	AirBorne XT912-B-Streak III-B	XT912-050	T2-2283	21. 7.06	N Rose	Old Sarum	2. 7.07P
	(Wing s/n ST3-26-XT)						
G-XTOR	Fairey Britten-Norman BN-2A Mk.III-2 Trislander		G-BAXD	1. 4.96	Aurigny Air Services Ltd	Guernsey	5. 7.08E
	(Fuselage ex N3266G [1065] fitted 2.96)	359					
G-XTRA	Extra EA.230	12A	SE-XVB	21. 1.87	Xtra Aerobatics Ltd	Sherburn-in-Elmet	26. 6.08P
			G-XTRA, D-EDLF				
G-XTRM	Robinson R44 Raven II	11923		3.10.07	Anglian Helicopters Ltd	Norwich	
G-XTUN	Westland-Bell 47G-3B1	WA/382	G-BGZK	11. 5.99	P A Rogers	(Betws yn Rhos, Abergele)	10.11.11S
			XT223		*(As "XT223" in AAC c/s)*		
G-XVBF	Lindstrand LBL 330A Balloon (Hot Air)	966		30. 1.04	Airxcite Ltd t/a Virgin Balloon Flights	Wembley	26. 4.08T
G-XVOM	Van's RV-6	PFA 181-12894		6. 4.01	A Baker-Munton	Leicester	3. 7.08P
	(Built A Baker-Munton)						
G-XWEB	Best Off Sky Ranger 912(2)	SKR0411539		13. 4.05	K B Woods	(Somersham, Huntingdon)	28. 3.08P
	(Built K B Woods and T J Hector - pr.no.BMAA/HB/443)						
G-XWON	Rolladen-Schneider LS8-18	8305	BGA 4783-JUC	7. 1.08	P K Carpenter and S M Godleman	Challock	1. 4.08
G-XXEA	Sikorsky S-76C	760492		21.12.98	T C Hewlett, Director of Royal Travel	Blackbushe	4. 1.07E
					(Operated Queen's Flight)		
G-XXIV	Agusta-Bell 206B-3 JetRanger III	8717		27. 4.89	Bart Fifty Nine Ltd	(Portbury, Bristol)	5. 7.08E
G-XXIX	Schleicher ASG 29E	29514	BGA xxxx	3.08R	R and A Pentecost	Lasham	
			D-KPRA		*"630"*		
G-XXRS	Bombardier BD-700-1A10 Global Express	9169	C-FCSR	24. 1.06	Tag Aviation (UK) Ltd	Farnborough	23. 1.08E
G-XXTR	Extra EA.300/L	126	G-ECCC	13. 8.02	A C Fletcher	Sherburn-in-Elmet	7. 4.08E
			D-EDGE				
G-XXVB	Schempp-Hirth Ventus B	32	BGA 2743-EKH	28.11.07	R Johnson	Parham Park	29.11.07
G-XXVI	Sukhoi Su-26M	04-10	RA-0410	2. 4.93	A N Onn *(As "39")*	Headcorn	2. 5.08P
G-XYAK	IAV Bacau Yakovlev Yak-52	899413	RA-44469	6. 3.03	M G F di Prima	Duxford	19. 7.08P
			LY-AFX, DOSAAF 69 *(blue)*		*"69"*		
G-XYJY	Best Off Sky Ranger 912(2)	SKRxxxxxxx		20.10.03	A V Francis	Little Gransden	21. 6.08P
	(Built A V Francis - pr.no.BMAA/HB/309)						

G-YAAA - G-YZZZ

Reg	Type	C/n	Prev ID	Date	Owner/Operator	Location	Date
G-YAAK	Yakovlev Yak-50	812003	G-BWJT	23. 3.05	R J Luke	Lee-on-Solent	20.11.08P
			RA-01385, DOSAAF50				
G-YACB	Robinson R22 Beta II	3092	G-VOSL	24. 1.02	J Chapman t/a Property Network		
						(Inchmarlo, Banchory)	27. 6.08E
G-YADA	Comco Ikarus C42 FB100	0707-6901		29. 6.07	D F Hughes	Halfpenny Gren	19. 9.08P
G-YAKA	Yakovlev Yak-50	822303	LY-ANJ	10.11.94	M Chapman	Stewton, Louth	1.10.08P
			DOSAAF 80				
G-YAKB	Aerostar Yakovlev Yak-52	9211517	RA-44491	25.11.02	Kemble Air Services Ltd	Kemble	21. 6.07P
			LY-AOB				
G-YAKC	IAV Bacau Yakovlev Yak-52	867212	LY-AKC	25. 6.02	T J Wilson	Andrewsfield	25. 6.08P
			DOSAAF 153 *(yellow)*?				
G-YAKD	IAV Bacau Yakovlev Yak-52	845002	LY-AQQ	18.10.07	P Doggett	Andrewsfield	4.11.08P
			DOSAAF 152 *(red)* ?				
G-YAKF	Aerostar Yakovlev Yak-52	9111205	ZU-IAK	25.10.07	A B Taylor-Roberts	(Amesbury, Salisbury)	
			RA02090, DOSAAF10				
G-YAKH	IAV Bacau Yakovlev Yak-52	899915	RA-01948	24.12.02	Plus 7 Minus 5 Ltd	White Waltham	4. 1.08P
			LY-AFV, DOSAAF 102 *(white)*		*(As "33" (white) in Soviet AF c/s))*		
G-YAKI	IAV Bacau Yakovlev Yak-52	866904	LY-ANM	20. 9.94	Yak One Ltd	Popham	16. 5.08P
			DOSAAF 100		*(As "100" in DOSAAF c/s)*		
G-YAKK	Yakovlev Yak-50	853104	RA-01293	5.11.02	J A Heanen	(Grantham)	11. 7.08P
G-YAKM	Yakovlev Yak-50	842710	RA-44461	6. 2.04	Airborne Services Ltd	Compton Abbas	11. 4.08P
			Ukraine 28 *(blue)*		*(As "61" (red) in Soviet AF c/s)*		
G-YAKN	IAV Bacau Yakovlev Yak-52	855905	RA-44466	6. 2.04	Airborne Services Ltd	Compton Abbas	23. 5.08P
			DOSAAF 105 *(blue)*		*(As "66" (red) in Soviet AF c/s)*		
G-YAKO	IAV Bacau Yakovlev Yak-52	822203	RA-01493 (1)	8. 5.99	M K Shaw	Norwich	30. 4.08P
G-YAKP	Yakovlev Yak-9	01-35	DOSAAF	3. 1.08	M V Rijkse and N M R Richards	Wycombe Air Park	
G-YAKR	IAV Bacau Yakovlev Yak-52	899803	LY-AOV	15.11.02	R A Alexander tr G-YAKR Group	North Weald	5.12.07P
			Ukraine AF 75 *(yellow)*, DOSAAF 75		*(Also carries "03" (yellow))*		
G-YAKT	IAV Bacau Yakovlev Yak-52	8910302	RA-01564	21. 1.03	S Wilkinson tr G-YAKT Group	White Waltham	11. 6.08P
			DOSAAF 149 *(yellow)*		*(As '01564')*		
G-YAKU	Yakovlev Yak-50	822305	RA-44549	6.11.03	D J Hopkinson	Compton Abbas	7. 5.08P
			G-BXNO, LY-ASD, DOSAAF 82 *(yellow)*		*(As "49" (red) in Soviet AF c/s)*		
G-YAKV	Aerostar Yakovlev Yak-52	9111311	RA-02209	8. 7.03	P D Scandrett	Rendcomb	14. 9.08P
			RA-9111311, DOSAAF 31		*(As "31" in Soviet AF c/s)*		
G-YAKX	Aerostar Yakovlev Yak-52	9111307	RA-44473	13. 3.96	The X-Fliers Ltd	Popham	7. 1.08P
			G-YAKX, RA-9111307, DOSAAF 27		*(As "27" (red) in Soviet AF c/s)*		
G-YAKY	IAV Bacau Yakovlev Yak-52	844109	LY-AKX	26. 2.96	W T Marriott	(Wickenby)	7. 3.02P
			DOSAAF 24 *(red)*		*(On rebuild 2005)*		
G-YAKZ	Yakovlev Yak-50	853206	RA-44533	7.11.03	Airborne Services Ltd	Compton Abbas	10. 5.08P
					(As "33" in Soviet AF c/s)		
G-YANK	Piper PA-28-181 Archer II	28-8090163	N81314	19. 3.93	J A Millar-Craig tr G-YANK Flying Group	Tatenhill	11. 7.08E
G-YARR	Mainair Rapier	1255-0700-7-W1049		14. 8.00	D Yarr	St Michaels	28. 3.08P

G-YARV	ARV Aviation ARV-1 Super 2	K 004	G-BMDO	15.10.01	A M Oliver	(Market Lavington, Devizes)	16. 8.08P
	(Built Hornet Aviation Ltd - pr.no.PFA 152-11127)		(Rotax 914)				
G-YAWW	Piper PA-28RT-201T Turbo Arrow IV		N2929Y	15.11.90	Barton Aviation Ltd	Liverpool	9. 7.08E
		28R-8031024					
G-YBAA	Reims FR172J Rocket	FR17200579	5Y-BAA	15.11.84	A Evans	Bourn	21. 6.08E
G-YCII	LET Yakovlev C-11	25III/08	F-AZPA	13. 1.00	R W Davies	(Woodchurch, Ashford)	14. 6.05P
			Egyptian AF		(As "11" (yellow) in Soviet AF c/s)		
					(Clipped tree on final approach North Weald 1. 6.05 and damaged)		
G-YCUB	Piper PA-18-150 Super Cub	1809077	N4993X	23. 8.96	F W Rogers Garage (Saltash) Ltd	Bodmin	29. 3.08E
			N4157T				
G-YEAH	Robinson R44 Raven II	10453		3. 8.04	Turboprop Leasing LLP	(Manor Park, Runcorn)	13. 9.07T
G-YELL	Murphy Rebel	PFA 232-12381		1. 5.95	A H Godfrey	(Lympsham, Weston-super-Mare)	
	(Built A D Keen)				(New owner 11.07)		
G-YEOM	Piper PA-31-350 Chieftain	31-8352022	N41108	3. 1.89	Foster Yeoman Ltd	Bristol	8. 6.08E
G-YEWS	RotorWay Executive	3850		22. 6.89	R Turrell and P Mason	(Wickford)	17. 6.93E
	(Built D G Pollard - c/n DGP-1) (RotorWay RW 152)						
G-YFLY	Magni M-16 Tandem Trainer	VPM16-UK114	G-BWGI	14.10.96	A J Unwin	Kemble	13.10.06P
	(Built Arrow Engines UK) (Arrow GT1000R)						
G-YFUT	IAV Bacau Yakovlev Yak-52	888410	LY-FUT	6. 2.03	R Oliver	Swansea	12. 7.08P
			Ukraine AF 22 (yellow), DOSAAF 22				
G-YFZT	Cessna 172S Skyhawk	172S9587	N20974	24. 2.04	AB Integro Ltd	Wycombe Air Park	10. 4.08T
G-YHPV	Cessna 310N	310N0054	N510PS	1.12.04	P O Hayes and V E Young		4. 5.08E
			G-YHPV, N510PS, G-AWTA, EI-ATB, N4154Q			Waterford, County Waterford	
G-YIII	Reims Cessna F150L	F15000827	PH-CEX	5. 6.80	Merlin Flying Club Ltd	Hucknall	10.10.07T
G-YIIK	Robinson R44 Astro	0640		9. 8.99	South West Air Charter Ltd	Truro	4. 9.08E
G-YIPI	Reims Cessna FR172K Hawk XP	FR1720616	OY-IPI	9. 1.03	A J G Davis	St Mary's, Isles of Scilly	2. 3.08E
			D-EIPI				
G-YJET	Montgomerie-Bensen B 8MR	PFA G/01-1072	G-BMUH	25. 9.96	A Shuttleworth	Barton	7. 5.07P
	(Built J M Montgomerie) (Rotax 582)						
G-YKCT	Aerostar Yakovlev Yak-52	9010307	LY-ATI	29. 5.02	A Fergusson tr G-YKCT Group	Carlisle	13. 6.08P
			Ukraine AF 04, DOSAAF 04				
G-YKSO	Yakovlev Yak-50	791506	LY-APT	8. 4.02	Classic Displays Ltd	North Weald	23. 5.08P
G-YKSS	Yakovlev Yak-55	901103	RA-44525	1. 7.03	I D Trask	Headcorn	2. 8.08P
			DOSAAF 96 (blue)				
G-YKSZ	Aerostar Yakovlev Yak-52	9311709		16.12.93	N Rhind tr Tzarina Group	White Waltham	20. 9.08P
					(As "01" (yellow) in Soviet AF c/s)		
G-YKYK	Aerostar Yakovlev Yak-52	9812106	LY-AHB	16. 6.03	K J Pilling	North Weald	14. 8.08P
G-YLYB	Cameron N-105 Balloon (Hot Air)	4482		15. 1.99	P L N Dowlen tr Blackhorse Balloon Club		
					(Lloyds TSB titles)	High Wycombe	6. 7.08A
G-YMBO	Robinson R22 Mariner	2054M	OY-HFR	21. 8.95	Helicentre Blackpool Ltd	Blackpool	18. 9.08E
G-YMFC	Waco YMF	F5033	N90B	6. 4.04	S J Brenchley	Coventry	24. 8.08E
	(Built Classic Aircraft Corporation, 1990)						
G-YMMA	Boeing 777-236	30302	N5017Q	7. 1.00	British Airways PLC	London Heathrow	6. 1.08E
G-YMMB	Boeing 777-236	30303		18. 1.00	British Airways PLC	London Heathrow	17. 1.08E
G-YMMC	Boeing 777-236	30304		4. 2.00	British Airways PLC	London Heathrow	3. 2.08E
G-YMMD	Boeing 777-236	30305		19. 2.00	British Airways PLC	London Heathrow	17. 2.08E
G-YMME	Boeing 777-236	30306		16. 4.00	British Airways PLC	London Heathrow	14. 4.08E
G-YMMF	Boeing 777-236	30307		17. 5.00	British Airways PLC	London Heathrow	16. 5.08E
G-YMMG	Boeing 777-236	30308		28. 9.00	British Airways PLC	London Heathrow	28. 7.08E
G-YMMH	Boeing 777-236	30309		14.10.00	British Airways PLC	London Heathrow	13.10.07E
G-YMMI	Boeing 777-236	30310		2.11.00	British Airways PLC	London Heathrow	1.11.07E
G-YMMJ	Boeing 777-236	30311		8.12.00	British Airways PLC	London Heathrow	7.12.07E
G-YMMK	Boeing 777-236	30312		8.12.00	British Airways PLC	London Heathrow	2.10.07E
G-YMML	Boeing 777-236	30313		10. 4.01	British Airways PLC	London Heathrow	13. 4.08E
G-YMMM	Boeing 777-236	30314		31. 5.01	British Airways PLC	London Heathrow	30. 5.08E
					(Incurred heavy landing London Heathrow 17. 1.08 and substantially damaged)		
G-YMMN	Boeing 777-236	30316		15. 6.01	British Airways PLC	London Heathrow	14. 6.08E
G-YMMO	Boeing 777-236	30317		17. 9.01	British Airways PLC	London Heathrow	13. 9.08E
G-YMMP	Boeing 777-236	30315		30.10.01	British Airways PLC	London Heathrow	29.10.07E
G-YMMR	Boeing 777-236			1.09R	British Airways PLC	London Heathrow	
G-YMMS	Boeing 777-236			3.09R	British Airways PLC	London Heathrow	
G-YMMT	Boeing 777-236			3.09R	British Airways PLC	London Heathrow	
G-YMMU	Boeing 777-236			4.09R	British Airways PLC	London Heathrow	
G-YNOT	Druine D 62B Condor	RAE 649	G-AYFH	10.11.83	A Littlefair	Thruxton	4. 9.03P
	(Built Rollason Aircraft and Engines)				(Noted 6.05)		
G-YNYS	Cessna 172S Skyhawk	172S8725	N835SP	23.11.05	T V Hughes	Caernarfon	7. 3.08
G-YODA	Schempp-Hirth Ventus 2cT	82/249	BGA 4943-KAT	6.11.07	P C Naegeli	Lasham	15. 3.08
G-YOGI	Robin DR.400-140B Major	1090	G-BDME	1.10.86	M M Pepper	Sibson	30. 4.08E
G-YOHO	Glasflügel H201B Standard Libelle	597	BGA 3750-GDM	27.11.07	M P Theo	Waldershare Park	23. 1.08
			D-6666				
G-YORK	Reims Cessna F172M Skyhawk II	F17201354	PH-LUY	14.12.78	H-R A E Waetjen	(Athboy, County Meath)	23. 8.08E
			F-WLIT				
G-YOTS	Aerostar Yakovlev Yak-52	9010308	LY-AOW	4. 5.03	G S Jones tr YOTS Group Wellcross Grange, Slinfold		3. 6.08P
			Ukraine AF 105, DOSAAF 05 (yellow)				
G-YOYO	Pitts S-1E	PFA 009-10885	G-OTSW	22. 5.96	J D L Richardson	Exeter	2. 8.08P
	(Built W R Penaluna)		G-BLHE				
G-YPOL	MD Helicopters MD.900 Explorer	900-00078	N7038S	4.10.00	West Yorkshire Police Authority	Wakefield	25. 1.10S
G-YPSY	Andreasson BA-4B	PFA 038-10352		7. 6.78	D J Howell	Halfpenny Green	30. 3.08P
	(Built H P Burrill) (Continental O-200-A)						
G-YRAF	Rotary Air Force RAF 2000 GTX-SE			1. 6.01	J R Cooper	(Maritime Quarter, Swansea)	22. 5.08P
	(Built C V King and J R Cooper) PFA G/13-1289						
G-YRIL	Luscombe 8E Silvaire Deluxe	5945	N1318B	3. 2.92	C Potter	North Weald	7.12.08P
	(Continental O-200-A)		NC1318B				
G-YROE	ELA Aviacion ELA 07R	01050510712		26. 3.07	J P R MacLaren	(Glasgow)	

G-YROI Air Command 532 Elite 0002 N532CG 3. 9.87 W B Lumb (Manchester) 17.12.90P
(Built Air Command Manufacturing Inc)
G-YROJ Rotary Air Force RAF 2000 GTX-SE   26.11.04 J R Mercer (Formby, Liverpool)
(Built J R Mercer) PFA G/13-1343
G-YROM Rotorsport UK MT-03 RSUK-MT-03-019 21. 9.07 M W King (Etchingham) 8.10.08P
G-YROO Rotary Air Force RAF 2000 GTX-SE   27.11.01 K D and C S Rhodes Henstridge 24. 4.08P
(Built K D Rhodes and C S Oakes) PFA G/13-1341
G-YROX Rotorsport UK MT-03 RSUK/MT-03/005 21. 8.06 C A M Holmes-Surplus and N F Surplus (Larne) 23. 9.08P
G-YROY Montgomerie-Bensen B 8MR PFA G/101A-1145 12. 9.89 S S Wilson Melrose Farm, Melbourne 14.11.07P
(Built R D Armishaw) (Rotax 532)
G-YRUS Jodel D 140E PFA 251-14090 G-YRNS 8. 9.03 W E Massam (Blagdon, Bristol)
(Built W E Massam)
G-YSMO Mainair Sports Pegasus Quik 8049   12. 7.04 W J Byrd and I G Harban Long Marston 6. 7.08P
G-YSPY Cessna 172Q Cutlass II 17275932 N917AT 4. 2.03 J Henderson Deanland 2. 7.06T
N917ER, (N65957)
G-YSTT Piper PA-32R-301 Saratoga II HP 3246056 N848T 4. 8.97 A W Kendrick Halfpenny Green 26. 3.08
N9282D
G-YULL Piper PA-28-180 Cherokee E 28-5603   30. 3.79 G Watkinson-Yull (La Massana, Andorra) 2.11.07E
9H-AAC, N2390R
G-YUMM Cameron N-90 Balloon (Hot Air) 2723   12.12.91 H Stringer Scalby, Scarborough 7. 7.08A
G-YUPI Cameron N-90 Balloon (Hot Air) 1602   12. 1.88 MCVH SA Brussels, Belgium 22.11.98A
G-YVBF Lindstrand LBL 317S Balloon (Hot Air) 505   2. 4.98 Airxcite Ltd t/a Virgin Balloon Fights Wembley 9. 3.06E
G-YVES Alpi Pioneer 300 2   7.12.04 M C Birchall Upfield Farm, Whitson 20. 7.08P
(Built M C Birchall - pr.no.PFA 330-14290)
G-YVET Cameron V-90 Balloon (Hot Air) 3182   11.10.93 J A Hibberd Rotterdam, Netherlands 31. 7.07A
G-YYAK IAV Bacau Yakovlev Yak-52 878101 LY-AOM 18. 4.02 J Armstrong and D W Lamb Durham Tees Valley 26. 7.08P
DOSAAF 118
G-YYYY Max Holste MH.1521C1 Broussard 208 F-GDPZ 10. 3.00 P F Burrow tr Eggesford Heritage Flight
French Air Force   Trenchard Farm, Eggesford 8. 8.09S
(As "208: IR" in French A/F c/s)
G-YZYZ Mainair Blade 912 1357-0803-7-W1152   14. 8.03 P G Eastlake Hunsdon 16. 8.08P

G-ZAAA - G-ZZZZ

G-ZAAP CZAW Sportcruiser PFA 338-14663   31. 1.08 L A Seers (Penenden Heath, Maidstone)
(Built L A Seers)
G-ZAAZ Van's RV-8 PFA 303-13279   2. 7.02 P A Soper (Layham, Ipswich) 1. 6.08P
(Built P A Soper)
G-ZABC Sky 90-24 Balloon (Hot Air) 062   10. 4.97 P Donnelly Maghera 27.10.07A
G-ZACE Cessna 172S Skyhawk SP 172S8808 F-HAMC 3. 9.02 Sywell Aerodrome Ltd Sywell 7. 9.08E
N3527P
G-ZACH Robin DR.400-100 Cadet 1831 G-FTIO 20.10.92 A P Wellings Sandown, isle of Wight 12.10.07E
G-ZADA Best Off Sky Ranger 912S(1) SKRxxxx547   11.10.06 B Bisley Stoke, Isle of Grain 20. 8.08P
(Built D F Hughes - pr.no.BMAA/HB/446)   (New owner 6.07)
G-ZADY Eurocopter EC.120B Colibri 1316 N127DF 6. 6.05 Cambridge Aviation Ltd Cambridge 20. 9.08E
F-WQDZ
G-ZAIR Zenair CH.601HD Zodiac PFA 162-12194   21. 2.92 J R Standring Crosland Moor 29. 7.08P
(Built B E Shaw) (Tri-cycle u/c)
G-ZANG Piper PA-28-140 Cherokee E 28-7225178 SE-FYT 29. 7.04 W J Hockenhull tr Gauntlet Holdings
RAF Waddington 26. 2.08E
G-ZANY Diamond DA.40D Star D4.040   23.10.03 Altair Aviation Ltd Stapleford 7.12.07E
(Suffered engine failure over Hanningfield Reservoir 30.12.06 and made forced landing in field: fuselage to Wing Farm, Longbridge Deverill for repair 2007)
G-ZAPH Bell 206B-3 JetRanger III 4401 G-DBMW 6. 2.01 Northern Flights Ltd Fairoaks 30. 5.08E
C-GAJH
G-ZAPK British Aerospace BAe 146 Series 200QC E2148 G-BTIA 25. 4.96 Titan Airways Ltd London Stansted 17. 4.08E
ZS-NCB, G-BTIA, G-6-148, G-PRIN
G-ZAPN British Aerospace BAe 146 Series 200QC E2119 ZK-NZC 20. 9.99 Titan Airways Ltd London Stansted 15.11.07E
G-BPBT
G-ZAPO British Aerospace BAe 146 Series 200QC E2176 F-GMMP 28. 7.00 Titan Airways Ltd London Stansted 3. 8.08E
G-BWLG, VH-NJQ, G-PRCS
G-ZAPR British Aerospace BAe 146 Series 200QT E2114 VH-JJZ 19.12.03 Titan Airways Ltd London Stansted 15. 1.07T
G-BOXE
G-ZAPU Boeing 757-2Y0 26151 EI-MON 22. 4.03 Titan Airways Ltd London Stansted 29. 4.08E
4X-BAY, SE-DUL, SX-BBY, XA-KWK, XA-SCB
G-ZAPV Boeing 737-3Y0 24546 G-IGOC 27. 2.04 Hagondale Ltd Exeter 9. 5.08E
EI-BZH (Operated Titan Airways in Royal Mail c/s)
G-ZAPW Boeing 737-3L9 24219 G-IGOX 11. 2.05 Titan Airways Ltd Bournemouth 20. 3.08E
N219TY, PH-TSW, OY-MMO, G-BOZB, OY-MMO, N1786B "Crystal Holidays"
G-ZAPX Boeing 757-256 29309 EC-HIS 17. 5.06 Titan Airways Ltd London Stansted 16. 5.08E
G-ZAPY Robinson R22 Beta 0788 G-INGB 8. 7.98 Heli Air Ltd Wellesbourne Mountford 5. 2.08E
G-ZAPZ Boeing 737-33A(QC) 25401 SE-DPA 22.12.06 Hagondale Ltd Leeds-Bradford 16.1.08E
TF-ELA, SE-DPA, N1786B (Operated Jet 2)
G-ZARI Grumman AA-5B Tiger AA5B-0845 G-BHVY 7. 3.86 ZARI Aviation Ltd Biggin Hill 23. 2.08E
N28835
G-ZARV ARV Aviation ARV-1 Super 2 PFA 152-13035   26. 2.97 P R Snowden Higham, Bury St Edmunds 21. 6.08P
(Built P R Snowden) (Rotax 914-UL)
G-ZAVI Comco Ikarus C42 FB100 0601-6777   25. 1.06 J King Damyn's Hall, Upminster 19. 3.08P
G-ZAZA Piper PA-18 Super Cub 95 18-2041 D-ENAS 1. 5.84 Airborne Taxi Services Ltd (Operated Adrian Swire)
(L-18C-PI) R Neth AF R-66, 52-2441   (Lambourn Gallops, Lambourne) 10. 5.08P
G-ZBED Robinson R22 Beta 1684 N63993 18.11.99 P D Spinks Stream Farm, Sherburn-in-Elmet 3. 1.08E
F-GHHM
G-ZBLT Cessna 182S Skylane 18280910 (EI-) 6. 7.01 K Dardis tr Cessna 182S Group
G-ZBLT, N72764   Abbeyshrule, County Longford 12. 9.08E

Reg	Type	Serial	Prev ID	Date	Owner	Location	Date
G-ZEBO	Thunder Ax8-105 Series 2 Balloon (Hot Air)	2197		22. 5.92	S M Waterton *"Gazebo"*	Borehamwood	22. 3.08
G-ZEBY	Piper PA-28-140 Cherokee F	28-7325240	G-BFBF EI-BMG, G-BFBF, PH-SRF	7.04.04	G Gee	Full Sutton	24. 5.08E
G-ZECH	CZAW Sportcruiser (Built P J Reilly)	PFA 338-14685		11. 1.08	P J Reilly	Old Sarum	
G-ZEIN	Slingsby T 67M-260 Firefly	2234		19. 7.95	R C P Brookhouse	Manston	22. 8.08E
G-ZELE	Westland SA.341C Gazelle HT.2	1007	G-CBSA XW845	27. 5.03	A Cook t/a C3 Consulting *"47" (RAF c/s)*	Crookfoot Farm, Elwick	9.11.08P
G-ZENA	Zenair CH.701UL STOL (Built A N Aston)	PFA 187-13637		16.10.00	A N Aston	(Wolverhampton)	
G-ZENI	Zenair CH.601HD Zodiac (Built P P Plumley)	PFA 162-14366		17. 8.06	P P Plumley	(Newport Pagnell)	
G-ZENN	Schempp-Hirth Ventus 2cT	136/348	BGA 5148-KJY D-KOZX	11.11.05	Z Marczynski *"304"*	Lasham	22. 2.08
G-ZEPI	Colt GA-42 Gas Airship (RR Continental O-200B)	878	G-ISPY (G-BPRB)	9. 4.92	P A Lindstrand	Oswestry	12. 5.93A
G-ZERO	Grumman AA-5B Tiger	AA5B-0051	OO-PEC	3. 9.80	Emery-Little Insurance Brokers Ltd *(Stored 11.07)*	Compton Abbas	26. 3.08E
G-ZETA	Lindstrand LBL 105A Balloon (Hot Air)	952		27. 1.04	S Travaglia *(Lindstrand titles)*	Tavarnelle Val di Pesa, Florence, Italy	2. 9.08A
G-ZEXL	Extra EA.300/L	1225		10. 3.06	2 Excel Aviation Ltd *(2 Excel Aviation titles)*	Sywell	23. 3.08E
G-ZGZG	Cessna 182T Skylane	18282036	N12722	20.12.07	J Noble *(Noted 12.07)*	Shoreham	
G-ZHKF	Reality Escapade 912(1) (Built C D Wills - pr.no.BMAA/HB/415)	JAESC 0045		26.11.04	C D and C M Wills	Chilbolton	14.12.07P
G-ZHWH	RotorWay Executive 162F (Built B Alexander) (RotorWay RI 162F)	6596		19.11.01	B Alexander	(Canterbury)	
G-ZIGI	Robin DR.400-180 Régent	2107		19.11.91	D C R Writer	Rochester	5. 7.08E
G-ZIGY	Europa Aviation Europa XS (Built K D Weston - pr.no.PFA 247-13693)	497		25. 2.05	K D Weston	(Gosport)	
G-ZIII	Pitts S-2B (Built Christen Industries Inc)	5151	G-CDBH SE-LVI, F-GMOV, OO-MOV, N10ZX, (N71ZX), N10ZX	3. 5.05	J W Sullivan	Maypole Farm, Chislet	24.11.07E
G-ZINT	Cameron Z-77 Balloon (Hot Air)	10488		17. 9.03	Film Production Consultants SRL	Rome, Italy	31. 3.07A
G-ZIPA	Rockwell Commander 114A (Originally laid down as c/n 14436)	14505	G-BHRA N5891N	3. 9.98	C M McLeod and E I Atkin t/a C and E Procurements	Durham Tees Valley	19. 6.08E
G-ZIPI	Robin DR.400-180 Régent	1557		22. 2.82	H U and D C Stahlberg	Rochester	2. 6.08E
G-ZIPY	Wittman W.8 Tailwind (Built M J Butler) (Lycoming O-235)	PFA 031-11339		29. 5.91	K J Nurcombe	Spanhoe	20. 2.08P
G-ZITZ	Aérospatiale AS.355F2 Ecureuil 2	5135	N596SJ 9M-BDA, F-GIFR, F-WZKZ	26. 4.04	Heli Aviation Ltd	Blackbushe	20. 9.07T
G-ZIZI	Cessna 525 CitationJet	525-0345	N5185V	10.11.99	Ortac Air Ltd	Guernsey	17.11.07E
G-ZIZZ	Agusta A109A II	7390	N109AR	16.11.07	Fortis Property Investment LLP *(Noted 2.08)*	Southend	
G-ZLIN	Moravan Zlin Z-526 Trener Master (Modified from Z-326 standard)	916	G-BBCR OH-TZF *(C/n confirmed but duplicates I-ETRM)*	30. 6.81	N J Arthur	Bicester	15. 9.08S
G-ZLLE	Aérospatiale SA.341G Gazelle 1	1012	N504KH JA9098	4.10.01	MW Helicopters Ltd	Stapleford	6.11.07E
G-ZLOJ	Beech A36 Bonanza	E-1677	ZS-LOJ N6748J	11. 9.98	W D Gray *(Operated Bournemouth Flying Club)*	Bournemouth	24. 1.08E
G-ZMAM	Piper PA-28-181 Cherokee Archer II	28-7890059	G-BNPN N47379	3.11.00	Z Mahmood	Elstree	9.10.07E
G-ZODY	Zenair CH.601UL Zodiac (Built B H Stephens and Partners - pr.no.PFA 162A-14239) (Tri-cycle u/c)	6-2354?		26. 5.04	B H Stephens tr Sarum AX2000 Group	Old Sarum	21.11.07P
G-ZONX	Sonex Aircraft Sonex (Built A Carter)	PFA 337-14689		15. 5.07	A Carter	(Holmfirth)	
G-ZOOL	Reims Cessna FA152 Aerobat	FA1520357	G-BGXZ	11.11.94	W J D Tollett	Turweston	9. 5.08E
G-ZOOT	Robinson R44 Clipper II	11924		9. 1.08	C Evans	(Chiddingfold, Godalming)	
G-ZORO	Europa Aviation Europa (Built N T Read - pr.no.PFA 247-12672) (Monowheel u/c)	074		20. 6.95	N T Read	(Gillingham)	
G-ZOSA	American Champion 7GCAA Citabria	509-2006		30.11.06	R McQueen	(Mauchline)	12. 7.10S
G-ZRZZ	Cirrus SR22	2020	N634SR	30. 3.07	Computerised Training Systems Ltd	Humberside	15. 5.08E
G-ZSKD	Cameron Z-90 Balloon (Hot Air)	10749		16. 2.06	M J Gunston	(Blackwater, Camberley)	21 8.07E
G-ZSKY	Best Off Sky Ranger Swift 912S(1) (Built N R Henry and J J C Scott - pr.no.BMAA/HB/543)	SKR0703771		20. 6.07	N R Henry and J J C Scott	(Nuneaton and Coalville)	20. 9.08P
G-ZTED	Europa Aviation Europa (Built J J Kennedy and E W Gladstone - pr.no.PFA 247-12492) (Monowheel u/c)	015		30. 4.96	J J Kennedy and E W Gladstone	Perth	30. 7.07P
G-ZUMI	Van's RV-8 (Built P M Wells)	PFA 303-13527		6. 3.02	S E Leach *(New owner 1.08)*	Perth	19. 8.07P
G-ZUMO	Pilatus PC-12/47	732	HB-FRQ	20. 7.06	Breckenridge Ltd	(Jersey)	20. 7.08E
G-ZVBF	Cameron A-400 Balloon (Hot Air)	4280		21. 1.98	Airxcite Ltd t/a Virgin Balloon Flights	Wembley	30.10.06E
G-ZVKO	Edge 360 (Built C Huey)	1	N360CH	14. 2.06	C Butler	Netherthorpe	19. 6.07P
G-ZWAR	Eurocopter EC.120B Colibri	1024	D-HVIP	14. 4.00	Hedgeton Trading Ltd	Lower Baads, Peterculter	3. 8.08E
G-ZXCL	Extra EA.300/L	1223		27. 2.06	2 Excel Aviation Ltd *(2 Excel Aviation titles)*	Sywell	15. 3.08E
G-ZXEL	Extra EA.300/L	1224		27. 2.06	2 Excel Aviation Ltd *(2 Excel Aviation titles)*	Sywell	15. 3.08E
G-ZXZX	Learjet Model 45	45-005	N455LJ	16. 1.04	Gama Aviation Ltd	Farnborough	18. 1.08E
G-ZYAK	IAV Bacau Yakovlev Yak-52	877415	LY-AFK DOSAAF 27	14. 2.03	J A H van Rossom	(Brussels, Belgium)	9. 5.08P
G-ZZAC	Evektor EV-97 Eurostar (Built S A Ivell)	PFA 315-14642		10. 5.07	S A Ivell	Crosland Moor	2. 7.08P
G-ZZAJ	Schleicher ASH 26E	26232		15. 7.05	A T Johnstone	Wycombe Air Park	26. 7.08E
G-ZZAP	American Champion 8KCAB Super Decathlon	871-2000	N900JF	28. 7.04	L Maikowski, E Mason, S Hipwell and J Pothecary	Shoreham	10.10.07E
G-ZZDG	Cirrus SR20	1733	N985SR	19.12.06	D M Green	Halfpenny Green	19.12.07E

G-ZZEL	Westland SA.341B Gazelle AH.1	1152	G-BZYJ XW885	25.11.02	Tregenna Castle Hotel Ltd	RAF Shawbury	12. 2.08P
G-ZZLE	Westland SA.341C Gazelle HT.2	1402	G-CBSE XX436	29. 4.05	Estates (UK) Management Ltd (As "XX436:CU-39" in RN c/s)	(Hull)	23. 8.08P
G-ZZOE	Eurocopter EC.120B Colibri	1196	F-WQOX	21. 3.01	J F H James	Banbury	9. 7.08E
G-ZZOW	Medway EclipseR	178/156		31. 8.06	P J Croney	Retreat Farm, Little Baddow	30. 8.08P
G-ZZSA	Eurocopter EC.225LP Super Puma	2603	F-WWOJ	21. 7.05	Bristow Helicopters Ltd	Aberdeen	27. 7.08E
G-ZZSB	Eurocopter EC.225LP Super Puma	2615	F-WWOG	11. 8.05	Bristow Helicopters Ltd	Aberdeen	15. 8.08E
G-ZZSC	Eurocopter EC.225LP Super Puma	2654	F-WWOG	13. 9.06	Bristow Helicopters Ltd	Aberdeen	14.10.07E
G-ZZSD	Eurocopter EC.225LP Super Puma	2658	F-WWOQ	5.12.06	Bristow Helicopters Ltd	Aberdeen	18.12.07E
G-ZZSE	Eurocopter EC.225LP Super Puma	2660	F-WWOT	14. 2.07	Bristow Helicopters Ltd	Aberdeen	25. 2.08E
G-ZZSF	Eurocopter EC.225LP Super Puma	2662	F-WWOR	5. 4.07	Bristow Helicopters Ltd	Aberdeen	15. 4.08E
G-ZZXX	P&M Quik GT450	8177		19. 4.06	Nature First Ltd	Gloucestershire	25. 6.08P
G-ZZZA	Boeing 777-236	27105	N77779	20. 5.96	British Airways PLC	London Heathrow	19. 5.08E
G-ZZZB	Boeing 777-236	27106	N77771	28. 3.97	British Airways PLC	London Heathrow	3.12.07E
G-ZZZC	Boeing 777-236	27107	N5014K	11.11.95	British Airways PLC	London Heathrow	10.11.07E
G-ZZZG	Alpi Pioneer 300 (Built C K Parsons - pr.no.PFA 330-14373)	xxx		9. 3.05	J D Clabon and J Reed	Shobdon	
G-ZZZS	Eurocopter EC.120B Colibri	1321	OO-WER F-WQDI	26.11.07	R E S and D Medway (Noted 1.08)	Redhill	

PART 3 – DE-REGISTERED EXTANT AIRCRAFT

The following have been noted since 2000 and are still considered to be extant.

Registration	Type	Construction No	Previous Identity Reg.Date	Registered Owner(Operator)	(Unconfirmed) Base	CofA Expy
G-ABTC	Comper CLA.7 Swift	S 32/1	1. 1.32	P Channon	Porthtowan	18. 7.84P
				(Cancelled 22. 2.99 by CAA: noted 6.04)		
G-ACGT	Avro 594B Avian IIIA	R3/CN/171	EI-AAB 8. 5.33	Yorkshire Light Aircraft	(Yorkshire)	21. 7.39
	(Originally regd as Avro 594A)			*(Cancelled xx.xx.xx by CAA: under restoration 11.04)*		
G-ADGZ	de Havilland DH.82A Tiger Moth	3344	23. 5.35	Not known	Hill Farm, Durley	
				(Cancelled 17. 9.40: to RAF as BB700 9.40) (Reported 5.02)		
G-ADXS	Mignet HM.14 Pou-Du-Ciel	CLS.1	18.11.35	C L Storey.	Breighton	
	(Built C L Storey)			*(Cancelled 1.12.36 as WFU: on display 12.07) "The Fleeing Fly"*		
G-AEFG	Mignet HM.14 Pou-du-Ciel	JN.1	BAPC.75 27. 3.36	A M and N H Ponsford	Selby	
	(Built J Nolan)			*(Cancelled in 31. 3.38 census: under restoration 2.04)*		
G-AEWU	Aeronca 100	AB.116	3.37	(B Cox)	Frogland Cross	4. 8.39
				(DBR when portable hangar collapsed Farnborough 2.55: stored 2003)		
G-AFGD	BA L 25c Swallow II	469	BK897 4. 4.38	A T Williams, B Arden, C A Cook, J Hughes and M Barmby		
	(Pobjoy Cataract 3)		G-AFGD	tr South Wales Swallow Group	Shobdon	9. 4.01P
				(Cancelled 6. 4.01 by CAA: noted 11.06 for restoration)		
G-AFIU	Parker CA-4 Parasol	CA-4	19.10.82	S P Connatty	Barton	
	(Built C F Parker) (Luton Minor components with registration reserved in 1938)			*(Cancelled 31. 3.99 by CAA: stored 4.06)*		
G-AFLW	Miles M.17 Monarch	792	2.11.38	N I Dalziel	White Waltham	30. 7.98
				(Cancelled 3. 5.01 by CAA: noted 6.06)		
G-AFVN	Tipsy Trainer 1	12	15. 7.39	D F Lingard	Fenland	2. 1.03P
	(Walter Mikron 2)			*(Cancelled 20.11.06 as WFU)*		
G-AGOY	Miles M.38 Messenger 3	4690	EI-AGE 5. 6.45	P A Brook	(West Chiltington, Pulborough)	25.11.53
			G-AGOY, HB-EIP, G-AGOY, U-0247 *(On rebuild 4.92: as "U-0247" :cancelled 20.12.06 by CAA)*			
G-AHAV	Auster J/1N Alpha	1863	(HB-EOM) 13. 2.46	J S Antrum	Headcorn	21. 6.75
	(Built Taylor Aeroplanes)			*(Stored 10.04?) (Cancelled 28. 3.06 by CAA)*		
G-AHHK	Auster J/1 Autocrat	2014	11. 5.46	C J Baker	Carr Farm, Thorney, Newark	22. 3.70
				(Cancelled 3. 4.89 as WFU: derelict frame noted 1.05)		
G-AHUJ	Miles M.14A Hawk Trainer 3	1900	R1914 6. 6.46	W J D Roberts tr Strathallan Aircraft Collection		
					Strathallan	9. 7.98P
				(Cancelled 19.11.99 as WFU: stored as "R1914" 6.07)		
G-AIDN	Vickers Supermarine 502 Spitfire T.8		N32 22. 8.46	Not known	not known	
		6S/729058	MT818	*(Cancelled 3. 7.86 - to N58JE: believed returned to UK 2007)*		
G-AIJI	Auster J/1N Alpha	2307	15. 4.47	C J Baker	Carr Farm, Thorney, Newark	
	(Originally regd as J/1 Autocrat)	*(Damaged in gales Humberside 12. 1.75: cancelled 12. 3.75 as WFU: dismantled frame and tail section noted 1.05)*				
G-AIJS	Auster V J/4 Archer	2074	13.11.46	Not known	Not known	14.12.71
				(Cancelled 1. 9.81 as WFU: fuselage noted 12. 9.06 anti-clockwise on M25 near M1 junction)		
G- AIRI	de Havilland DH.82A Tiger Moth	3761	N5488 22.10.46	E R Goodwin	Little Gransden	9.11.81
				(Cancelled 3. 4.89 as WFU: stored 10.05)		
G-AJBJ	de Havilland DH.89A Dragon Rapide	6765	NF894 20. 1.47	John Pierce Aviation Ltd	Ley Farm, Chirk	14. 9.61T
				(Cancelled 16.12.91 by CAA: noted 5.05 without marks)		
G-AJCL (2)	de Havilland DH.89A Dragon Rapide	6722	NF851 7. 9.48	John Pierce Aviation Ltd	Ley Farm, Chirk	
				(WFU Shobdon 1.71: cancelled 24. 5.71: noted 5.05 without marks)		
G-AJOA	de Havilland DH.82A Tiger Moth	83167	T5424 29. 4.47	Aero Antiques	Hill Farm, Durley	22. 5.03
		(Badly damaged landing Lotmead Farm, Wanborough, Swindon 13. 5.01: sold 10.01 for rebuild: cancelled 19. 3.03 as WFU)				
G-AJUD	Auster V J/1 Autocrat	2614	5. 6.47	C L Sawyer	(Bromham, Bedford)	18. 5.74
				(On rebuild 12.97: cancelled 31. 3.99 by CAA: noted for sale 2000)		
G-AJVH	Fairey Swordfish II	?	LS326 28. 5.47	Royal Navy Historic Flight	RNAS Yeovilton	
				*(Cancelled 30. 4.59 as restored to RN) *"As "LS326:L2" in RN 836 Sqdn c/s -"City of Liverpool"*		
G-AKBO	Miles M.38 Messenger 2A	6378	15. 7.47	P R Holloway	Enstone	3. 8.03
				(Cancelled 24. 8.04 by CAA: under restoration 5.06)		
G-AKOE	de Havilland DH.89A Dragon Rapide 4	6601	X7484 3.12.47	J E Pierce	Ley Farm, Chirk	25. 7.82
				(Cancelled 18. 6.02 by CAA: noted 5.05 in BEA c/s)		
G-AKUG (2)	Luscombe 8A Silvaire	3689	N77962 21. 7.88	(R S Bird)	Glebe Farm, Stockton	16. 3.05P
	(Continental A65)		NC77962			
		(Damaged on take off Stockton, Wiltshire 17. 7.04: cancelled 18. 2.05 by CAA: under repair 2007)				
G-AKWT	Taylorcraft J Auster 5	998	MT360 1. 4.48	C J Baker	Carr Farm, Thorney, Newark	22. 7.49
				(Crashed Tollerton 7.8.48: derelict frame stored 1.05)		
G-AKZN	Percival Proctor III	K 386	8380M 24. 5.48	Royal Air Force Museum Reserve Collection	RAF Stafford	29.11.63
			Z7197	*(Cancelled 27 .9.63 as WFU and reverted to military marks as "Z7197": noted 2.04)*		
G-ALNV	Taylorcraft J Auster 5	1216	RT578 21. 4.49	C J Baker	Carr Farm, Thorney, Newark	4. 7.50
				(WFU and silver frame stored 1.05)		
G-ALVP	de Havilland DH.82A Tiger Moth	82711	R4770 26. 9.49	D and R Leatherland	Tollerton	15. 2.61
				(Cancelled as WFU 2.61 and stored: noted dismantled 11.04)		
G-AMKL	Auster B 4	2983	XA177 3. 7.51	C J Baker	Carr Farm, Thorney, Newark	
			G-AMKL, G-25-2	*(Dismantled Rearsby 1956: cancelled 24. 9.58: new fuselage 1.05)*		
G-AMTD	Auster J/5F Aiglet Trainer	2783	EI-AVL 24. 5.52	The Leicestershire Aero Club Ltd	Leicester	8.12.93
			G-AMTD			
		(Damaged landing Hayrish Farm, Okehampton 7. 8.93: cancelled 15. 1.99 as WFU: wings noted 10.07)				
G-AMYL	Piper PA-17 Vagabond	17-30	N4613H 24. 4.87	P J Penn-Sayer t/a The Fun Airplane Co		
	(Continental C75)		NC4613H	*"Yankee Lady"* Scaynes Hill, Haywards Heath		20. 6.89P
				(Stored 2004: cancelled 27. 4.06 by CAA)		
G-ANHW	Taylorcraft J Auster 5D	1396	TJ320 5.12.53	D J Baker	Carr Farm, Thorney, Newark	9. 3.70
	(Originally regd as Auster 5)			*(Forced landed Carlton Manor, Norfolk 1970: WFU 15.12.71: derelict fuselage noted stored 1.05)*		
G-ANPK	de Havilland DH.82A Tiger Moth	3571	L6936 5. 4.54	A D Hodgkinson	Thruxton	10. 7.97T
				(Damaged Jaywick Sands, Clacton-on-Sea 18.8.96: on rebuild 2002: cancelled 7.1.03 by CAA)		
G-ANUW	de Havilland DH.104 Dove 6	04458	16. 5.55	Jet Aviation Preservation Group	Long Marston	22. 7.81
				(Cancelled 5. 6.96 as WFU: noted 2.04)		

G-ANWX   Auster J/5L Aiglet Trainer   3131   25.11.54   M F Frost tr Nayland Aiglet Group   Maypole Farm, Chislet   2. 5.94
(Overturned landing Fenland 1. 8.93 and substantially damaged: cancelled 24. 9.93 as WFU: noted dismantled 8.05)

G-AOAI   Blackburn Beverley C 1   1002   XB259   15. 3.55   Fort Paull Armouries   Paull, Yorkshire
(Cancelled 30.3.55) (As "XB259")

G-AOCP (2)   Taylorcraft J Auster 5   1800   W462   25. 5.56   C J Baker   Carr Farm, Thorney, Newark
(Composite using G-AKOT)   *(WFU 22. 6.68: fuselage frame noted 1.05)*

G-AOGE   Percival Proctor III   H 210   BV651   24.11.55   N I Dalziel   Biggin Hill   21. 5.84
(Cancelled 19. 1.99 by CAA: stored 4.04)

G-APDF   de Havilland DH.106 Comet 4   6407   2. 2.57   M Painter   (Chipping Campden)
(To RAE 3.67 as XV814 and cancelled: nose only preserved)

G-APFG   Boeing 707-436   17708   N5094K   7. 8.59   G Spoors   Cove, Farnborough   24. 5.81T
(Cancelled 11.68 as WFU: nose only 5.03)

G-APKM   Auster J/1N Alpha   3385   27. 1.58   C J Baker   Carr Farm, Thorney, Newark   9. 1.89
(Cancelled 9.10.91 as temporary WFU: noted dismantled 1.05)

G-APOD   Tipsy Belfair   536   (OO-TIF)   16. 7.58   L F Potts   (Culloden)   23. 8.88P
(Walter Mikron 2)   *(Cancelled 6. 9.00 by CAA: under restoration 2.01)*

G-APOL   Druine D 31 Turbulent   PFA 439   31. 7.58   A Gregori and S Tinker   (Morpeth)   18. 6.94P
(Built P J Houston) (Ardem 4C02)   *(Damaged Charterhall 24. 7.93: cancelled 13. 9.00 as WFU: stored 2.03)*

G-APRF   Auster Alpha 5   3412   VR-LAF   8.12.58   W B Bateson   Blackpool   14.11.00
      G-APRF   *(Cancelled 14. 6.05 by CAA: stored 10.07)*

G-APRJ   Avro 694 Lincoln B 2   -   RF342   29.12.58   ?   Martham, Great Yarmouth
      G-36-3, G-29-1, G-APRJ, RF342
(Cancelled 22. 2.05 by CAA: airframe noted 12.05: nose, as "G-29-1", stored 2.06)

G-APSO   de Havilland DH.104 Dove 5   04505   (N1046T)   16. 2.59   (Devonair Ltd)   Little Rissington   8. 7.78T
      G-APSO
(Cancelled 2. 5.01 as WFU: wings fitted to G-BWWC: forward fuselage only fitted with stub wings as engine test-bed 1.08)

G-APSY   Bensen B7MC   02   22. 2.59   J Howell   (Copthorne, Sussex)
(Built J Howell - c/n JH/001)   *(Cancelled 13. 4.73 as WFU: stored 10.03)*

G-APSZ   Cessna 172   46472   N6372E   21. 5.59   Not known   Ronaldsway   4. 6.84
(Damaged Barton 2. 3.84 and cancelled: stored 10.06)

G-APYW   Piper PA-22-150 Caribbean   22-4994   N7131D   3. 3.60   ?   Midden Zeeland, Netherlands   6. 7.88
(Cancelled 12. 7.93 by CAA: frame noted 10.05)

G-ARAP   Champion 7FC Tri-Traveler   7FC-394   12. 9.60   (J McGonagal)   Bellarena   26. 6.82P
(Originally regd as a 7EC))   *(Damaged in crash 9. 81 Eglington: cancelled xx.x.xx: fuselage noted 9.07)*

G-ARBF   Bensen B 7M   004   6. 5.60   (D R Shepherd)   (Prestwick)
(Built J S Sproule)   *(Crashed Tangmere 29. 4.61 and cancelled xx.x.xx: airframe stored at home 2003)*

G-ARBM   Auster V J/1B Aiglet   2792   EI-AMO   8. 6.60   A D Hodgkinson   Dunkirk Farm, Canterbury   6. 6.03
      G-ARBM, VP-SZZ, VP-KKR   *(Cancelled 30. 7.04 by CAA)*

G-ARCI   Cessna 310D   39266   N6966T   21.10.60   Sandtoft Air Services Ltd   Blackpool   25. 4.84
(Damaged Sandtoft 22. 8.86: cancelled 3. 1.89 by CAA: in open store less tail 11.05)

G-ARDG   Lancashire Aircraft EP-9 Prospector 2   47   14. 7.60   G Pearce   Redhill
(Cancelled 28. 5.82 as WFU: noted 6.05)

G-ARDZ   SAN Jodel D 140A Mousquetaire   49   10.11.60   M J Wright   Cherry Tree Farm, Monewden   29.11.91
(Cancelled 26. 2.99 by CAA: noted 2.06)

G-ARGB   Auster 6A Tugmaster   2593   VF635   12.10.60   C J Baker   Carr Farm, Thorney, Newark   21. 6.74
(Cancelled 21. 6.74(?): dismantled fuselage noted 1.05)

G-BRKX   Air Command 532 Elite   0619   8. 9.89   K Davis   Church Farm, Askern   10.12.90
(Built K Davis - pr.no PFA G/04-1150)   *(Cancelled 28. 2.02 by CAA: noted stored 9.07)*

G-ARLY   Auster J/5P Autocar   3271   (VH-...)   14. 4.61   (G Green and P J Eliott)   (Switzerland)   6. 6.71
(Sold Switzerland 11.87 and cancelled 25. 2.99 by CAA: on rebuild 2003 to D 6/180 standard using parts ex Airedale G-ARNR and wings ex J/5R G-APAA)

G-AROJ   Beagle A 109 Airedale   B 508   HB-EUC   17. 5.61   C J Baker   Carr Farm, Thorney, Newark   8. 1.76
(Originally regd with c/n A 109-1)   G-AROJ   *(Cancelled 21. 1.80: noted dismantled 1.05)*

G-ARPO (2)   de Havilland DH.121 Trident 1C   2116   (G-ARPP)   23. 3.64   International Fire Training Centre   Durham Tees Valley   12. 1.86T
(WFU 12.12.83: noted 2.08)

G-ARTJ   Bensen B 8M   7   22. 9.61   M A Stewart   (Wilkieston Farm, Peat Inn)
(Volkswagen 1600) (Originally regd with c/n 8-104-100)   *(Cancelled 6. 6.75 as WFU: stored 2003?)*

G-ARTM   Beagle A 61 Terrier 1   3723   WE536   9.10.61   C J Baker   Carr Farm, Thorney, Newark   13.11.71
(Crashed Priory Farm, Turvey, Bedford 28. 5.70 and cancelled 12. 9.73 as WFU: fuselage, part rebuilt. noted 1.05)

G-ARUO   Piper PA-24 Comanche   24-2427   N7251P   16. 1.62   Not known   Farley Farm, Romsey   22. 8.00
(Cancelled 18. 7.00 by CAA: stored derelict 10.07

G-ARXC   Beagle A 109 Airedale   B 510   EI-ATD   9. 4.62   C J Baker   Carr Farm, Thorney, Newark   27. 6.76
(Originally regd with c/n A 109-3)   G-ARXC   *(Cancelled 12. 4.89 as WFU: fuselage on rebuild 1.05)*

G-ARXN   Tipsy Nipper T 66 Series 3   T66/77   3. 7.62   C E Pickton and I Wood tr The Griffon Flying Group   Hucknall   19. 8.90P
((Built Cobelavia SA) (Volkswagen 1800)   *(Cancelled 12. 4.89 by CAA: on rebuild 6.06)*

G-ASCJ   Piper PA-24-250 Comanche   24-2368   5N-AEB   2. 8.62   ?   Walton New Road Business Park, Bruntingthorpe   2.10.88
      N7197P   *(DBR landing Bournemouth 10.9.86: cancelled 8.1.87 as WFU: fuselage in scrapyard 2.04)*

G-ASDF   Edwards Gyrocopter   NAFE.1   17.10.62   M J Aubrey   Kington, Hereford
(Built N A F Edwards) (Triumph T110) (Mod. Adams-Wilson XH-1 Hobbycopter)   *(Cancelled in 1963 as not completed: noted 2002)*

G-ASEF   Auster 6A Tugmaster   ?   VW985   17.12.62   (M Thomason)   ?   19.12.66
(Damaged Bicester 1966 and cancelled 13. 1.67: stored 10.03)

G-ASER   Piper PA-23-250 Aztec B   27-2283   28. 1.63   Not known   Bournemouth   17. 8.74
(Crashed into Nigg Bay, Cromarty, Aberdeen 14. 9.72: cancelled 24.11.72 as WFU: stored Aviation Musuem 12.07)

G-ASIP   Auster 6A Tugmaster   2549   VF608   22. 5.63   (C Applegarth)   ?   19. 7.73
(Damaged by fire Nympsfield 7. 5.73: on rebuild 9.03)

G-ASJZ   SAN Jodel D 117A   826   F-BITD   5. 7.63   W J Siertsema   Chilbolton   12. 7.06P
(Swung to left landing Old Buckenham 10. 6.06, undercarriage collapsed and substantially damaged: cancelled 10.10.06 as TWFU)

G-ASLP   Bensen B 7   11   3. 9.63   R Light and T Smith   (Stockport)
(Cancelled 4. 9.73 as WFU: parts only stored 8.06)

G-ASLR   Agusta-Bell 47J-2 Ranger   2057   3. 9.63   Flamingo Club and Harleys American Diner
      Avenida Espana, Adeje, Playa de Las Americas, Tenerife, Spain   7. 3.96T
(Damaged on take-off Bristol 31.1.96: cancelled 28. 2.97 as WFU: noted 2.04 minus tail rotor: no marks but regn on c/n plate in canopy)

G-ASNY   Campbell Bensen B8   RCA203   15. 1.64   (D L Wallis)   (Stockport)   16. 3.70P
(Built Campbell Aircraft Ltd) (McCulloch O-100-1)   *(Cancelled 17.12.91 by CAA) (With R Light complete 8.06)*

G-ASSB	Piper PA-30 Twin Comanche	30-432	N10F	22. 4.64	Brooklands Technical College	Weybridge	11. 3.93T
					(Cancelled 25. 8.92 as WFU: instructional airframe 10.03)		
G-ASWF	Beagle A 109 Airedale	B 537		26. 8.64	(C J Baker)	Spanhoe	24. 7.83
					(Cancelled 3. 2.89 by CAA: noted dismantled 10.07)		
G-ASXC	SIPA 903	8	G-DWEL	6.10.64	B L Procter	Dunkeswell	
	(Continental C90)		G-ASXC, F-BEYK		*(Wide-track sprung-steel undercarriage)*		
G-ASXF	Brantly 305	1014		7.10.64	?	Amen Corner, Binfield, Bracknell	16 .2.79
					(Cancelled 24. 5.82 as WFU: in open storage 12.07)		
G-ASYK	Piper PA-30 Twin Comanche	30-573	N7543Y	6.11.64	? Walton New Road Business Park, Bruntingthorpe		28. 7.97T
					(Crashed on take-off from Sandown, IoW 11. 5.96: cancelled 30.10.96 as WFU: noted 2.04)		
G-ATEP	EAA Biplane	PFA 1301		28. 5.65	E L Martin	Sausmarez Park, Guernsey	18. 6.73
	(Built E L Martin) (Continental C75)				*(Cancelled 14. 7.86 by CAA: frame stored 5.03)*		
G-ATFK	Piper PA-30 Twin Comanche	30-721	N7642Y	17. 6.65	? Walton New Road Business Park, Bruntingthorpe		22.11.90
					(Damaged landing White Waltham 12. 6.89: cancelled 21.10.92 by CAA: noted 2.04)		
G-ATHN	SNCAN 1101 Noralpha	84	F-BFUZ	5. 8.65	E L Martin	St Peter Port, Guernsey	27. 6.75S
			French.Military		*(Cancelled 16.12.91 by CAA: stored 5.03)*		
G-ATIG	Handley Page HPR.7 Dart Herald	214	PP-SDI	25. 8.65	Nordic Oil Services Ltd	Norwich	14.10.97T
		177	G-ATIG		*(Cancelled 29.10.96 as WFU: instructional use 2.06)*		
G-ATKG	Hiller UH-12B	496	RThai.AF103	21.10.65	?	Eshott	28.11.89T
					(Cancelled 21.1.80 as WFU: noted 2005)		
G-ATLH	Fewsdale Tigercraft Gyroplane	F T5		6.12.65	R Light	(Stockport)	
					(Cancelled 10. 2.82 as WFU: reported complete 8.06)		
G-ATMI	Hawker Siddeley HS.748 Series 2A/225	1592	VP-LIU	4. 1.66	Emerald Airways Ltd	Blackpool	18. 5.00T
			G-ATMI, VP-LIU, G-ATMI, VP-LIU, G-ATMI, VP-LIU, G-ATMI				
					(Cancelled 30. 7.01 as WFU: fuselage on fire dump 1.04)		
G-ATMN (2)	Cessna F150F	F150-0060	(G-ATNE)	6. 1.66	C R Hardiman	(Blaenannarch, Cardigan)	2. 7.84T
	(Built Reims Aviation SA) (Wichita c/n 15063526)				*(Cancelled 21.10.04 as WFU: noted roadrunning southbound on M1 north of Luton 30. 8.07)*		
G-ATMW	Piper PA-28-140 Cherokee	28-21486		11. 1.66	Bencray Ltd	Blackpool	6. 8.08E
					(Operated Blackpool Air Centre) (Cancelled 16.11.07 as PWFU)		
G-ATPD	Hawker Siddeley HS.125 Series 1B/522	25085	5N-AGU	11. 2.66	Wessex Air (Holdings) Ltd	Bournemouth	14.10.98T
			G-ATPD		*(WFU 1997 and cancelled 2.12.03 as WFU: noted with Fire Section 6.05)*		
G-ATRP	Piper PA-28-140 Cherokee	28-21885	N11C	4. 3.66	JRB Aviation Ltd	Southend	20. 9.84.
					(Damaged Boughton Monchelsea 16.10.81: cancelled 10.11.86 as WFU: wreck stored dismantled 1.08)		
G-ATWE	Morane-Saulnier MS.892A Rallye Commodore 150	10634		13. 6.66	(D I Murray)	Upfield Farm, Whitson	15. 2.82
	(Badly damaged in forced landing west of Taunton 29. 3.81: cancelled 3. 4.89 by CAA, restored 24. 4.89 for rebuild: cancelled 17. 2.99 by CAA: noted 8.06)						
G-ATWR	Piper PA-30 Twin Comanche B	30-1134	N8025Y	30. 6.66	? Walton New Road Business Park, Bruntingthorpe		22.12.94T
					(Damaged in crash Crosland Moor 14. 9.93: cancelled 18. 4.95 as TWFU: fuselage in scrapyard compound 3.04)		
G-ATWS	Phoenix Luton LA-4A Minor	1195		30. 6.66	W M Grant	(Tain)	26. 3.69P
	(Built D H Handley - Phoenix pr.no.PAL 1195) (Incorporates c/n PFA 818)				*(Cancelled 8. 2.82: noted 2003)*		
G-ATWT	Bensen B 8M	21102	G-29-3	5. 7.66	Not known	Bere Alston, Yelverton	
	(Buit Napier Aircraft Co)				*(WFU 10.70 and cancelled 31. 1.77 as WFU: noted dismantled 11.06)*		
G-AVCY	Piper PA-30 Twin Comanche B	30-1367	N8241Y	16.12.66	? Walton New Road Business Park, Bruntingthorpe		26. 7.93
					(Crashed on take-off Cardiff 9. 3.91 and cancelled 17. 7.91 as WFU: noted 2.04)		
G-AVDF	Beagle B 121 Pup Series 100	B 121-001		28.12.66	D Collings	Lower Wasing Farm, Brimpton	22. 5.68
	(Originally registered as B 121C c/n B 151, became B 121 Series 100 2.69)				*(Cancelled 22. 5.68 as WFU: noted 1.03)*		
G-AVDS	Beech 65-B80 QueenAir	LD-337	A40-CS	5. 1.67	City of Bristol College	Filton	26. 8.77
			G-AVDS		*(Cancelled 1. 3.89 as WFU: dumped 2.04)*		
G-AVEZ	Handley Page HPR.7 Dart Herald 210	169	PP-ASW	31. 1.67	?	Norwich	
			G-AVEZ, HB-AAH		*(WFU on 5. 1.81 and cancelled 4. 1.83: on fire dump 2.06)*		
G-AVFE	Hawker Siddeley HS.121 Trident 2E	2144		1. 2.67	Belfast Airport Fire Service	Belfast International	6. 5.85T
					(WFU 20. 3.85: noted 2.04)		
G-AVFG	Hawker Siddeley HS.121 Trident 2E	2146		1. 2.67	Fire Station	Manchester	2. 7.85T
					(WFU 24. 5.85: noted as "G-SMOKE" 10.05)		
G-AVFJ	Hawker Siddeley HS.121 Trident 2E	2149		1. 2.67	International Fire Training Centre Durham Tees Valley		18. 9.83T
					(WFU 6.82: cancelled 9. 7.82: front fuselage noted 2.04)		
G-AVGJ	SAN Jodel DR.1050 Ambassadeur	265	F-BJYJ	31. 1.67	(D J Kirkwood and S T Gilbert)	Enstone	22. 4.85P
					(WFU 1985 with glue failure cancelled 10. 6.93 by CAA: noted 5.05)		
G-AVJH	Druine D 62 Condor	PFA 603		31. 3.67	R Chapman	London Gatwick	4.11.83P
	(Built J Norton)				*(Crashed Nefyn, Gwynedd 31. 7.83: cancelled 5. 1.89: as spares 5.05 for rebuild of G-AXGU qv)*		
G-AVKL	Piper PA-30 Twin Comanche B	30-1418	OY-DHL	25. 4.67	Northbrook College (Sussex)	Shoreham	27. 6.08E
			G-AVKL, N8284Y		*(Cancelled 28.9.07 as WFU)*		
G-AVKT	Tipsy Nipper T 66 Series 3	T66/70	OO-HEL	1. 5.67	?	Yearby	
	(Built Cobelavia SA)		OO-DEL				
	(Crashed Constable Burton, Paull, Yorkshire 19. 9.72: cancelled 14. 2.73 as destroyed: frame possibly noted 12.06)						
G-AVLH	Piper PA-28-140 Cherokee	28-23368		8. 5.67	(M B Rothschild)	(Kent)	18. 8.00
					(Cancelled 23. 4.02 by CAA: for possible rebuild 1.05)		
G-AVMJ	British Aircraft Corporation One-Eleven 510ED	BAC.138		11. 5.67	(Not known)	Horton, Wimborne	17.11.94T
					(WFU 6.94 and cancelled 11. 5.01 by CAA: noted 2007)		
G-AVMT	British Aircraft Corporation One-Eleven 510ED	BAC.147		11. 5.67	European Aviation Air Charter Ltd	Cardiff	5.12.03T
					(Cancelled 17.12.04 as WFU: fuselage with Fire Section 2.05)		
G-AVNP	Piper PA-28-180 Cherokee C	28-4113	N11C	26. 5.67	(Southend Airport Fire Services)	Southend	21.10.01T
					(Force landed near Nayland 28. 4.01: cancelled 27.11.01 as destroyed: wreck used for rescue training 1.07)		
G-AVPH	Cessna F150G	F150-0197		20. 6.67	The Zero 9 Flight Academy Ltd	Ellough, Beccles	9. 4.86T
	(Built Reims Aviation SA)				*(Cancelled 26. 3.02 by CAA: fuselage stored 10.07)*		
G-AVPS	Piper PA-30-160 Twin Comanche B	30-1548	N8393Y	27. 6.67	(J M Bisco)	Farley Farm, Romsey	11.11.05
					(Damaged 2004: cancelled 6. 7.05 by CAA: stored derelict 10.07)		
G-AVTT	Ercoupe 415D	4399	SE-BFZ	21. 8.67	Wright Farm Eggs Ltd Cherry Tree Farm, Monewden		20. 1.86
	(Continental C85)		NC3774H		*(Cancelled 12. 4.02 as temporarily WFU: stored 2.06)*		
G-AVVI	Piper PA-30 Twin Comanche B	30-1613	EI-AVD	5.10.67	? Walton New Road Business Park, Bruntingthorpe		7. 3.94
			G-AVVI, N8454Y		*(Cancelled as WFU 29. 9.97: fuselage in scrapyard 2.04)*		
G-AVWE	Piper PA-28-140 Cherokee	28-23720	N11C	19.10.67	W C C Never	Blackpool	22. 4.82T
					(WFU and cancelled 8. 6.89 by CAA: fuselage stored 10.07)		
G-AVYP	Piper PA-28-140 Cherokee	28-24211	N11C	4.11.67	K Hobbs t/a Aldergrove Flight Training Centre		
					(Cancelled 3. 7.03 by CAA)	Belfast International	14. 2.04T

G-AWBT   Piper PA-30 Twin Comanche B   30-1668   N8508Y   22. 1.68   Cranfield University   Cranfield   25. 3.89
(Damaged Humberside 10. 3.88: cancelled 15. 7.88 as WFU: derelict airframe 1.07)

G-AWGA   Beagle A 109 Airedale   B 535   EI-ATA   3. 4.68   (J R Bowden)   (Headcorn)
  G-AWGA, D-ENRU   *(Cancelled 30. 9.86 as WFU: stored for spares 2004?)*

G-AWJA   Cessna 182L Skylane   18258883   N1658C   3. 5.68   D M Penny tr Wild Geese School of Adventure Flying
(Cancelled as destroyed 29.11.88: wreck noted 8.05)   Movenis, Coleraine   21. 4.85

G-AWJF   Nipper T 66 RA.45 Series 3   S 122   8. 5.68   S Maric   (Stewarton)   7. 6.88P
(Built Slingsby Aircraft Co Ltd as c/n 1629 for Nipper Aircraft Ltd)   *(Cancelled 17. 9.91 by CAA: stored 2004)*

G-AWKM   Beagle B 121 Pup Series 1   B121-017   11. 6.68   (D M G Jenkins)   Bourne Park, Hurstbourne Tarrant   29. 6.84
(Damaged Swansea 7.91: cancelled 28. 5.02 by CAA: fuselage stored 5.06)

G-AWKP   CEA Jodel DR.253 Régent   130   14. 6.68   G R W Wright   Blackpool   1.10.98
(Forced landed SE Waterford 8. 6.98: cancelled 13.10.98 by CAA: fuselage noted 10.07)

G-AWKX   Beech A65 Queen Air   LC-303   21. 6.68   (Northbrook College)   Shoreham   25.10.88T
(Cancelled 19 12 90 as PWFU: as instructional airframe 3.06)

G-AWMZ   Cessna F172H   F172-0554   2. 8.68   ?   Cark-in-Cartmel   22. 4.77
(Built Reims Aviation SA)   *(Hit ground Bucknarrowbridge, Bootle 18. 1.76: cancelled 1. 9.81 as WFU: used as parachute club training aid 4.05)*

G-AWOX   Westland Wessex 60 Series 1   WA/686   G-17-2   28. 8.68   Paintball Adventure West   Bristol   13. 1.83
  G-AWOX, 5N-AJO, G-AWOX, 9Y-TFB, G-AWOX, VH-BHE (3), G-AWOX, VR-BCV, G-AWOX, G-17-1
(Cancelled 23.11.82 as TWFU: noted 2.06)

G-AWUA   Cessna P206D Super Skylane   P206-0550   N8750Z   21.11.68   J E Ball and R W F Marsh   Blackpool   4.12.87
(Damaged Thruxton 16.10.87: cancelled 11. 8.88 as destroyed: wreck stored 10.07)

G-AWUH   Cessna F150H   F150-0307   25.11.68   H D Hounsell   Phoenix Farm, Lower Upham   16. 7.94
(Built Reims Aviation SA)   *(Cancelled 8. 7.97 as WFU: fuselage dumped 8.06)*

G-AWUK   Cessna F150H   Caernarfon, Wales

G-AWWO   CEA Jodel DR.1050 Ambassadeur   552   F-BLOI   8. 1.69   A R Grimshaw and A A Macleod   (Spalding)   15. 5.06
(Cancelled 29 .3.05 as PWFU: noted 10.05)

G-AWYV   British Aircraft Corporation One-Eleven 501EX   11. 2.69   ?   Alton   24. 6.04T
  BAC.178   *(Cancelled 17.12.04 as WFU: front fuselage preserved as "The Departure Lounge Café" 12.05)*

G-AWZR   Hawker Siddeley HS.121 Trident 3B Series 101   14. 1.69   International Fire Training Centre   Durham Tees Valley   9. 4.86T
  2318   *(WFU 27. 9.85 and cancelled 26. 3.86 as WFU: noted 11.03)*

G-AWZS   Hawker Siddeley HS.121 Trident 3B Series 101   14. 1.69   International Fire Training Centre   Durham Tees Valley   9. 9.86T
  2319   *(WFU 5.12.85 and cancelled 18. 3.86 as WFU: noted 2.08)*

G-AWZU   Hawker Siddeley HS.121 Trident 3B Series 101   14. 1.69   (British Airways PLC)   (Basingstoke)   3. 7.86T
  2321   *"Tina" (Cancelled 18. 3.86 as WFU: nose only noted 9.03)*

G-AXAU   Piper PA-30 Twin Comanche   30-1753   N8613Y   15. 3.99   Bartcourt Ltd   Bournemouth   8. 3.86T
(Cancelled 2. 5.02 by CAA: noted minus tail 6.05)

G-AXDU   Beagle B 121 Pup Series 2   B121-048   G-35-048   18. 4.69   R G Hayes   Near Parish Hall, Bennington, Stevenage   14. 5.98T
(Damaged North Weald 20. 9.97: cancelled 12. 1.98 as destroyed: battered fuselage noted 1.04)

G-AXEI   Ward P 45 Gnome   P 45   25. 4.69   A J E Smith and N H Ponsford   Breighton
(Built M Ward)   *(Cancelled 30. 5.84 as WFU: noted 12.07)*

G-AXGU   Druine D 62B Condor   RAE 640   3. 6.69   R Chapman   London Gatwick   22. 5.76
(Built Rollason Aircraft and Engines)   *(Crashed near Godalming, Surrey 31. 3.75: cancelled 8. 3.88 as WFU: stored 5.05)*

G-AXIY   Bird Gyrocopter   GB.001   3. 7.69   G Bird   (Stockport)
(Built G Bird)   *(Cancelled 9 8.91 by CAA: with R Light dismantled 8.06)*

G-AXMD   Omega O-20 Balloon (Hot Air)   06   7. 8.69   (P F Smart)   Oakley, Basingstoke
(Acquired second envelope c/n 07 c 1969 or 1970)   *"Nimble" (Cancelled 7.12.89 as WFU: extant 2007)*

G-AXTH   Piper PA-28-140 Cherokee B   28-26283   N11C   26.11.69   West London Aero Services Ltd   Blackpool   27.10.90T
(Damaged in forced landing near Compton Abbas 28. 2.88: .cancelled by CAA 13. 7.95) (Wreck stored 10.07)

G-AXYZ   WHE Airbuggy   1005   10. 3.70   (R Light)   Stockport   22.12.92P
(Volkswagen 1600) (Originally regd as McCandless M 4)   *(Complete 8.06: cancelled 8. 9.06 by CAA)*

G-AXZB   WHE Airbuggy   1007   10. 3.70   (R Light)   Stockport   18.11.86P
(Volkswagen 1834) (Originally regd as McCandless M 4)   *(Complete 8.06: cancelled 8. 9.06 by CAA)*

G-AYDW   Beagle A 61 Terrier 2   B 646   G-ARLM (1)   20. 5.70   Stick & Rudder Associates   Trenchard Farm, Eggesford   1. 7.73
(Conversion of Auster 6 c/n 1936)   TW568   *(Cancelled 1. 7.85 by CAA: noted 2.06)*

G-AYGB   Cessna 310Q   310Q0111   N7611Q   2. 7.70   Perth College   Perth   23.10.87T
(Cancelled 23. 6.94 by CAA: instructional airframe 1.06)

G-AYHI   Campbell Cricket   CA-341   21. 7.70   J F MacKay   (North Kessock)   19. 8.86P
(Volkswagen 1600)   *(Cancelled 2. 3.99 by CAA: noted 2003)*

G-AYJZ   Cameron (Ax8) O-84 Balloon (Hot Air)   16   30. 9.70   Briitish Balloon Museum and Library   Newbury
(Original canopy replaced by c/n 433)   *"Godolphin" (Cancelled 21. 5.75 - to EI-BAY) (As "EI-BAY" (1))*

G-AYKG   SOCATA St -10 Diplomate   117   30. 9.70   ?   Tulley's Farm, Crawley
(Damaged Crowland 4. 3.75: cancelled 27. 6.75 as WFU: noted 10.03)

G-AYSK   Phoenix Luton LA-4A Minor   PFA 832   17. 2.71   S R Smith tr Luton Minor Group   Barton   24. 5.05P
(Built L Plant) (Continental A65)
(After being hand-swung Barton 8. 9.06 moved off unmanned and crashed inverted with severe damage: noted 12.06: cancelled 16. 1.07 as PWFU)

G-AYWA   Avro 19 Series 2   1361   OO-VIT   14. 4.71   Air Atlantic Historic Flight   (Coventry)
  OO-DFA, OO-CFA   *(Cancelled 22. 8.73 as PWFU: on long term restoration 3.02)*

G-AYXW   Evans VP-1   PFA 1544   30. 4.71   M Howe   Netherthorpe   15. 8.01P
(Built J S Penny) (Ardem 4C02)   *(Cancelled 7. 6.02 by CAA: noted 4.04)*

G-AZDF (2)   Cameron O-84 Balloon (Hot Air)   24   18. 8.71   K L C M Busemeyer   London W2
(Cancelled 22. 4.88 as WFU: noted 2006)

G-AZDZ   Cessna 172K Skyhawk   17258501   5N-AIH   25. 8.71   The Fire Service College   Moreton-in-Marsh   25. 2.83
  N1647C, N84508
(Forced landing Delapre Golf Course, Northampton 19. 9.81 and extensively damaged: cancelled 5.12.83 as destroyed: frame noted 8.03)

G-AZLP   Vickers 813 Viscount   346   ZS-CDT   4. 1.72   International Fire Training Centre   Durham Tees Valley   3. 4.82T
  (ZS-SBT), ZS-CDT   *(Cancelled 19.12.86 as WFU) (Fire services fuselage only 2.08)*

G-AZLS   Vickers 813 Viscount   348   ZS-CDV   4. 1.72   International Fire Training Centre   Durham Tees Valley   9. 6.83T
  (ZS-SBV), ZS-CDV   *(Cancelled 19.12.86 as WFU) (Fire services fuselage only 2.08)*

G-AZMN   AESL Airtourer T5 (Super 150)   A 550   28. 1.72   I Young and W Crozier   Oaksey Park   7. 5.89
(Crashed near Glasgow 23. 6.87: cancelled 14. 9.88 by CAA: stored 9.03)

G-AZMX   Piper PA-28-140 Cherokee D   28-24777   SE-FLL   7. 2.72   Mooney Aviation Ltd   Ley Farm, Chirk   24.10.83
  LN-LMK (3)   *(Cancelled 9. 1.84 as PWFU: airframe noted 9.04)*

G-AZNC   Vickers 813 Viscount   352   (G-AZLW) (1)   8. 2.72   Britsh Aerospace PLC   Durham Tees Valley   18. 5.83T
  ZS-CDZ, (ZS-SBZ), ZS-CDZ   *(Cancelled 27.10.88 as WFU).(Used by Fire Services 2.08)*

| G-AZRV | Piper PA-28R-200 Cherokee Arrow II | N2309T | 4. 4.72 | General Airline Ltd | Compton Abbas | 25. 8.02T |
| | | 28R-7135191 | | | | |

(Crashed on take-off Compton Abbas 30.12.00: cancelled 20. 6.01 as destroyed: fuselage for training 1.06)

| G-AZRX | Sud-Aviation Gardan GY-80-160 Horizon | 14 | F-BLIJ | 4. 4.72 | Adventure Island Pleasure Ground | Southend-on-Sea | 20. 2.92 |

(Damaged Sandtoft 14. 8.91: cancelled 21.10.91 by CAA: on display Crazy Golf Course, Marine Parade 2.08)

| G-AZXG | Piper PA-23-250 Aztec D | 27-4328 | N6963Y | 23. 6.72 | Cranfield University | Cranfield | 18. 9.94 |

(Crashed Little Snoring 25.10.91: cancelled 6. 5.93 by CAA: airframe dumped 1.07)

| G-AZZX | Reims Cessna FRA150L Aerobat | FRA1500152 | | 27. 7.72 | M Hewison | Plaistows Farm, St Albans | 16. 8.88 |

(Overturned landing Newtownards 28. 2.87: on rebuild 12.93: cancelled 14.12.94 by CAA , restored 28. 8.97: cancelled 9. 5.01 by CAA: stored 5.04)

| G-BAAX | Cameron O-84 Balloon (Hot Air) | 50 | | 8. 8.72 | The New Holker Estates Company Ltd | | |
| | | | | | Cark-in-Cartmel, Grange-over-Sands | 31. 5.85A |

(Cancelled 11. 5.93 as WFU: stored 2006)

| G-BADL | Piper PA-34-200-2 Seneca | 34-7250247 | N5307T | 4. 9.72 | (K Smith and M Corbett) Willey Park Farm, Caterham | | |

(Damaged on landing Turnhouse 21.10.95: cancelled 15. 8.96 as WFU: fuselage noted 2.04)

| G-BADZ | Pitts S-2A | 2038 | | 21. 9.72 | (D Richardson) | Exeter | 5. 6.00 |
| | *(Built Aerotek Inc)* | | | | | | |

(Cancelled 4. 4.02 by CAA: noted in hangar roof 12.05)

| G-BAGO | Cessna 421B Golden Eagle | 421B0356 | N7613Q | 24.10.72 | (M S Choksey) | Coventry | 7. 3.07 |

(Cancelled 15. 4.05 as sold to US: noted 6.05 as "G-BAGO")

| G-BAIL | Reims FR.172J Rocket | FR17200370 | | 22.11.72 | R H Blair tr Gloucestershire Flying Club Bournemouth | | 7. 7.00 |

(Overturned on landing 6. 3.99 Farley Farm, Romsey: cancelled 6. 7.99 by CAA: stored 11.06)

| G-BAOM | SOCATA MS.880B Rallye Club | 2255 | | 6. 2.73 | P J D Feehan | Exeter | 17. 4.03 |

(Cancelled 27.11.03 as PWFU: noted 12.05)

| G-BAPF | Vickers 814 Viscount | 338 | SE-FOY | 12. 2.73 | The Fire Service College | Moreton-in-Marsh | 13. 6.90 |
| | | | G-BAPF, D-ANUN | | "Marilyn Monroe" | | |

(Cancelled 17. 6.92 by CAA: airframe extant 9.07 in Hot Air c/s)

| G-BAPM | Fuji FA.200-160 Aero Subaru | FA200-172 | | 13. 2.73 | Oakfleet Ltd | Glebe Farm, Stockton | 28. 5.01 |

(Cancelled 6.11.98 by CAA: noted 9.06)

| G-BASL | Piper PA-28-140 Cherokee F | 28-7325195 | N11C | 13. 3.73 | Justgold Ltd | Blackpool | 11. 5.08E |

(Cancelled 25. 2.08 by CAA)

| G-BASU | Piper PA-31-350 Navajo Chieftain | 31-7305023 | N7693L | 15. 3.73 | Keystart Ltd t/a Streamline Aviation | | |
| | | | | | Trenchard Farm, Eggesford | 3.11.87T |

(Crashed on take-off Duonreay 12. 5.87 and badly damaged: cancelled 24. 7.89 as destroyed: fuselage noted 2.06)

| G-BAUA | Piper PA-23-250 Aztec D | 27-4048 | N6718Y | 26. 3.73 | David Parr & Associates Ltd | Shoreham | 27. 7.92 |

(Cancelled 15. 9.00 by CAA: stored dismantled 3.06)

| G-BAUI | Piper PA-23-250 Aztec D | 27-4335 | LN-RTS | 29. 3.73 | (Gloucester University) | Gloucestershire | 5.12.88 |

(Cancelled 26. 1.89 by CAA: noted as Instructional airframe 1.06)

| G-BAUJ | Piper PA-23-250 Aztec E | 27-7304986 | N14390 | 29. 3.73 | (S Bramwell) | Cranfield | 25. 7.94T |

(Cancelled 31.10.02 by CAA: dumped 1.07)

| G-BAUR | Fokker F-27 Friendship 200 | 10225 | PH-FEP | 5. 4.73 | (Jersey European Airways Ltd) | Exeter | |
| | | | 9V-BAP, 9M-AMI, (VR-RCZ), PH-FEP *(Cancelled 25. 1.96 as WFU: fuselage on fire dump 12.05)* | | | | |

| G-BAVS | Grumman AA-5 Traveler | AA5-0349 | | 12. 4.73 | (V J Peake) | Bournemouth | 8.11.94 |

(Cancelled 31.10.96 by CAA: noted 6.05)

| G-BAWN | Piper PA-30 Twin Comanche C | 30-1948 | N8790Y | 24. 4.73 | ? Walton New Road Business Park, Bruntingthorpe | | 3. 5.98 |

(Cancelled as WFU 23. 6.98: fuselage in scrapyard 8.03)

| G-BAYL | SNCAN Nord 1203 Norecrin VI | 161 | F-BEQV | 18. 5.73 | J E Pierce | Ley Farm, Chirk | |

(Cancelled 14.11.91 by CAA: fuselage outside 5.05)

| G-BAZJ | Handley Page HPR.7 Dart Herald 209 | 183 | 4X-AHR | 30. 5.73 | Guernsey Airport Fire Service | Guernsey | 24.11.84T |
| | | | G-8-1 | | | | |

(Cancelled 4. 1.85 as WFU: in open storage 2.04)

| G-BBBX | Cessna 310L | 310L0134 | OY-EGW | 28. 6.73 | Atlantic Air Transport Ltd | Coventry | 30.10.07E |
| | | | N3284X | | | | |

(Cancelled 18. 4.07 as PWFU)

| G-BBEV | Piper PA-28-140 Cherokee D | 28-7125340 | LN-MTM | 8. 8.73 | (Comed Schedule Services Ltd) | Blackpool | 9. 9.01T |

(Cancelled as PWFU 16. 5.07: noted 6.07)

| G-BBFC | Grumman AA-1B Trainer | AA1B-0245 | (N9945L) | 14. 8.73 | (I J Hiatt tr G-BBFC Flying Club) | Bournemouth | 25.12.96 |

(Damaged Perranporth 9. 6.96: cancelled as temporarily unregd 14.10.96: fuselage noted 6.05)

| G-BBHE | Enstrom F-28A | 153 | EI-BSD | 3. 9.73 | Clarke Aviation Ltd | Waterford, County Waterford | 24. 4.08E |
| | | | G-BBHE | | | | |

(Cancelled 22.. 2.06 as PWFU)

| G-BBNO | Piper PA-23-250 Aztec | 27-4656 | N964PA | 22.10.73 | A S Bamrah t/a Falcon Flying Services | Biggin Hill | 18. 1.92 |

(Cancelled 13. 3.01 as PWFU: noted 6.07)

| G-BBRZ | Grumman AA-5 Traveler | AA5-0471 | (EI-AYV) | 15.11.73 | C P Osborne | Movenis, Coleraine | 30. 4.99 |
| | | | G-BBRZ | | | | |

(Cancelled 10. 2.05 by CAA: fuselage only noted 4.05)

| G-BBSC | Beech B24R Sierra 200 | MC-217 | | 15.11.73 | I Millar and G H Emerson | Belfast International | 3. 6.99 |

(Cancelled 27. 7.01 by CAA: noted 1.04)

| G-BBYO | Fairey Britten-Norman BN-2A Mk.III-1 Trislander | ZS-KMH | 27. 2.74 | (Aurigny Air Services Ltd) | Guernsey | 1. 5.92T |
| | | 362 | G-BBYO, G-BBWR | *(WFU 2.92 and cancelled 23. 2.95: fuselage for Airport Fire Service 3.03)* | | | |

| G-BCEO | Grumman AA-5 Traveler | 7. 5.74 | AA5-0575 | | W Bateson | Blackpool | |

(Crashed near Selby Farm, Stanton, Morpeth 28. 4.02: cancelled 11. 7.02 as destroyed: wreck noted 10.07)

| G-BCGA | Piper PA-34-200-2 Seneca | 34-7450166 | N41975 | 4. 6.74 | Not known | Ronaldsway | 15. 7.78 |

(Crashed and DBR landing RAF Waddington 18.12.77: fuselage stored 10.06)

| G-BCGP | Gazebo Ax6-65 Balloon (Hot Air) | 1 | | 13. 6.74 | Briitish Balloon Museum and Library | Newbury | |
| | | | | | "Aries" *(Cancelled 18.12.79 as WFU)* | | |

| G-BCGX | Bede BD-5 | 4916 | | 18. 6.74 | R Hodgson | (Cumbernauld) | |
| | *(Built R Hodgson - pr.no.PFA 014-10063)* | | | | | | |

(No Permit issued: cancelled 4.12.96 as WFU: noted road-running 9.05)

| G-CCIC | Thruster T 600N 450 Sprint | 0036-T600N-086 | | 25. 7.03 | M L Smith | Popham | 6.10.05P |

(Cancelled 26. 3.07 as PWFU: noted 5.07)

| G-BCIE | Piper PA-28-151 Cherokee Warrior | 28-7415405 | N9588N | 3. 7.74 | Perth College | Perth | 19.12.99T |

(Extensively damaged Perth 27. 5.99: cancelled 15. 9.99 as destroyed: dumped 1.06)

| G-BCJH | Mooney M 20F Executive | 670126 | N9549M | 11. 7.74 | P J Bossard | Bourn | 30. 6.91 |

(Cancelled 26. 9.00 by CAA: derelict 10.05)

| G-BCKF | K & S SA 102.5 Cavalier | 71055 | | 29. 7.74 | K Fairness | (Eyemouth) | |
| | *(Built K Fairness - pr.no.PFA 1594)* | | | | | | |

(No Permit issued and.cancelled 8. 7.91 by CAA: stored 2001)

| G-BCMF | Levi Go-Plane RL.6 Series 1 | EAA.3678 | | 5. 9.74 | R Levi | (Porchfield, Isle of Wight) | |
| | *(Built R Levi)* | | | | | | |

(DBR on first flight Bembridge 16.11.74: cancelled 5.12.83 by CAA: stored 6.06)

| G-BCSM | Bellanca 8GCBC Scout | 108-74 | | 29.11.74 | The Furness Gliding Club Propietary Ltd | | |
| | | | | | Eastbach Farm, Coleford | 30. 4.04 |

(Swung to right landing Walney Island 12. 5.02: struck ground causing extensive damage: cancelled 2.12.02: for potential rebuild 8.03)

G-BCTA	Piper PA-28-151 Cherokee Warrior	28-7515113		6.12.74	T G Aviation Ltd	Fairoaks	28. 6.00T

G-BCTA Piper PA-28-151 Cherokee Warrior 28-7515113 6.12.74 T G Aviation Ltd Fairoaks 28. 6.00T
(Cancelled 16. 7.98 as WFU: on scrap-heap as "G-OOAT" 3.06 - see G-BDKV)

G-BCTU Reims Cessna FRA150M Aerobat FRA1500268 30.12.74 J S Rees Willey Park Farm, Caterham 11. 1.00
(Cancelled 17. 1.00 as WFU: nted 3.06)

G-BCUP Scottish Aviation Bulldog Series 120/122 Ghana AF G-108 9. 1.75 Aerofab Restorations Bourne Park, Hurstbourne Tarrant
BH120/372 G-BCUP *(Cancelled 9. 6.76 - to Ghana AF as G-108: stored as "G-108" 5.03)*

G-BCUW Reims Cessna F177RG Cardinal RG SE-GKL 10.1.75 S J Westley Cranfield 12. 5.00T
F177RG0119 *(Cancelled 18. 8.04 by CAA: noted 1.07)*

G-BCVE Evans VP-2 V2-1015 16. 1.75 North Western PFA Strut Barton
(Built G Bentley - pr.no.PFA 7210) *(Cancelled 6. 6.93 as TWFU: noted 1.07)*

G-BCWR Fairey Britten-Norman BN-2A-20 Islander 433 OY-RPZ 13. 2.75 Defence Aviation Repair Agency RAF St Athan
(OY-RPH), G-BCWR
(Cancelled 21.4.75 - to (OY-RPH), OY-RPZ , restored 8.5.86: front fuselage for technical mock-up as "OY-RPZ" 1994: cancelled 26.10.94 as WFU: noted 5.03)

G-BCXZ Cameron O-56 Balloon (Hot Air) 154 4. 3.75 Olives from Spain Ltd Firenze, Italy 11.12.98A
(Cancelled 19. 5.93 by CAA: noted inflated 10.03)

G-BDCC de Havilland DHC.1 Chipmunk 22 C1/0258 WD321 25. 4.75 Coventry Gliding Club Ltd Husbands Bosworth 24. 3.02
(Written off 29. 8.99 and cancelled 8. 4.04 as WFU: fuselage dumped 5.05: wings only noted 10.07)

G-BDCE Cessna F172H F172-0704 PH-EHB 5. 5.75 Copperplane Ltd Bournemouth 26. 4.01T
(Built Reims Aviation SA) *(Damaged by gales Bournemouth: cancelled 12.11.02 by CAA: stored 11.06)*

G-BDGY Piper PA-28-140 Cherokee 28-23613 N3536K 5. 8.75 S J Willcox Compton Dando
(Cancelled 4. 1.05 as PWFU: stored dismantled 6.07)

G-BDHJ Pazmany PL-1 PFA 3604 5. 8.75 L J Greenhough Sleap 5.11.97P
(Built H Jones and originally regd as Jones-Pazmany PL-1) *(Cancelled 11. 5.01 by CAA: noted 3.04)*

G-BDIN Scottish Aviation Bulldog Series 100/125 R Jordan AF 408 20. 8.75 R D Dickson tr British Disabled Flying Association
BH120/377 JY-BAI, G-BDIN Lasham 4. 7.76S
(Noted less engine 2006: cancelled 1.8.07 as WFU)

G-BDKV Piper PA-28R-200 Cherokee Arrow II EI-AYE 29.10.75 (Bravo Juliet Whiskey Flying Ltd) Fairoaks 8. 4.95
28R-7335297 (G-BBEH), N55837 *(Cancelled 25. 5.94 as destroyed : dumped as "G-OOAT" 5.06 - see G-BCTA)*

G-BDMM Jodel D 11 PFA 901 5.11.75 P N Marshall Barton
(Built D M Metcalf) *(Cancelled 27. 1.97 by CAA: noted 11.04)*

G-BDNZ Cameron O-77 Balloon (Hot Air) 203 8. 1.76 D G Such Barkway, Royston 15. 6.96A
(Tethered 9.05: cancelled 24. 5.06 by CAA)

G-BDRB Grumman AA-5B Tiger AA5B-0175 6. 2.76 Dorset Air Ltd Bournemouth 23. 8.96
(Crashed on take-off Wing Farm, Longbridge Deverill 16. 5.94: cancelled 3.10.94 as WFU: fuselage noted 1.07)

G-BDRL Stits SA-3A Playboy P-689 N730GF 12. 2.76 O C Bradley Mullaghmore, Coleraine 17. 6.98P
(Built D R Fisher) (Continental C85) *(Cancelled 11. 5.01 by CAA: stored 4.03)*

G-BDXF Boeing 747-236B 21351 23. 3.78 European Skybus Ltd Kemble 30. 4.06T
(Cancelled 9. 1.07 as WFU: stored minus two engines 1.07)

G-BDXG Boeing 747-236B 21536 16. 6.78 European Skybus Ltd Bournemouth 30. 6.06T
(Cancelled 29. 3.06 as WFU: fuselage stored 1.07)

G-BDXH Boeing 747-236B 21635 23. 2.79 European Skybus Ltd Bournemouth 2. 5.04T
(Cancelled 7. 3.06 as WFU: fuselage stored 1.07)

G-BEDB SNCAN Nord 1203 Norecrin II 117 F-BEOB 5. 8.76 (B F G Lister) Ley Farm, Chirk 11. 6.80P
(Cancelled 14.11.91 by CAA: noted stripped 5.05)

G-BENF Cessna T210L Turbo Centurion II 21061356 N732AE 17. 2.77 ? Cherry Tree Farm, Monewden 24. 5.82
D-EIPY/N732AE *(Crashed Ipswich 29. 5.81: cancelled 25. 3.85 as destroyed: in open storage 2.06)*

G-BEPS Short SC.5 Belfast C 1 SH1822 G-52-13 6. 4.77 Heavylift Aviation Holdings Ltd Southend 31. 8.02T
XR368 *(Cancelled 8. 5.03 by CAA: under gradual refurbishment 2.08)*

G-BERW Rockwell Commander 114 14214 N4884W 6. 5.77 Romeo Whiskey Ltd Lee-on-Solent 5. 5.07
(Cancelled 27. 7.07 as PWFU: noted 9.07)

G-BETO Morane-Saulnier MS.885 Super Rallye 34 F-BKED 18. 5.77 (A J and A Hawley) Farley Farm, Romsey 11.12.04
(Cancelled 27.10.06 as PWFU: stored derelict 10.07)

G-BEUK Fuji FA.200-160 Aero Subaru FA200-284 24. 5.77 C B Mellor ta BM Aviation Glebe Farm, Stockton 2.11.00T
(Overran runway on take-off Glebe Farm 8. 1.99 and badly damaged: cancelled 25. 6.02 by CAA) (Noted 9.06)

G-BEVR Fairey Britten-Norman BN-2A Mk.III-2 Trislander 6Y-JQE 10. 6.77 Cormack (Aircraft Services) Ltd Cumbernauld 6. 7.82S
1056 G-BEVR, XA-THE (2), G-BEVR *(Cancelled 20. 3.03 by CAA: noted 5.03)*

G-BEVV Fairey Britten-Norman BN-2A Mk.III-2 Trislander 6Y-JQK 10. 6.77 Cormack (Aero Club Services) Ltd Cumbernauld
1059 G-BNZD, G-BEVV *(On rebuild but stored by 2.03: cancelled 20. 3.03 by CAA)*

G-BEWP Reims Cessna F150M F15001426 13. 6.77 Perth College Perth 12. 8.85
(Crashed Aboyne 4.10.83 and cancelled 5.12.83 as destroyed:instructional use 1.06)

G-BEYN Evans VP-2 V2-3167 1. 8.77 C D Denham tr East Fortune Flying Group
(Built C D Denham - pr.no.PFA 063-10271) *(Cancelled 2. 9.91 by CAA: noted 2006)* (Musselborough)

G-BEZS Reims FR172J Rocket FR17200562 (I-CCAJ) 11. 8.77 B A Wallace Bourn 22. 9.79
(Damaged near Stapleford 15. 6.79: front fuselage stored 2.02)

G-BFDV Westland WG.13 Lynx HC.28 WA/028 TAD.013 3.10.77 School of Electrical and Aeronautical Engineering
(Originally regd as "Lynx 02F") Qatar AF 1, G-17-20 Princess Marina College, Arborfield
(Cancelled 6.78: as Instructional airframe "QP-30" 9.05)

G-BFHX Evans VP-1 PFA 062-10283 2.12.77 A D Bohanna and D I Trussler Popham 7. 4.99P
(Built D F Gibson) (Volkswagen 1600) *(Cancelled 21. 4.05 by CAA: stored 10.05)*

G-BFKG Reims Cessna F152 II F15201463 26. 1. 78 Luton Flight Training Ltd Biggin Hill 25.11.90T
(Blown over by jet blast Luton 11.11.89: cancelled 16. 3.92 as WFU: fuselage noted 6.07)

G-BFNU Britten-Norman BN-2B-21 Islander 877 16. 3.78 Isles of Scilly Skybus Ltd St Just 18. 89T
(Built IRMA) *(Cancelled 28. 1.94 as WFU: fuselage only 3.07)*

G-BFWK Piper PA-28-161 Cherokee Warrior II N9589N 23. 6.78 Marham Investments Ltd Belfast International 8.12.99T
28-7816610 *(Cancelled 26. 5.98 as WFU: wrecked fuselage stored 1.06)*

G-BFWL Reims Cessna F150L F15000971 PH-KDC 4.10.78 P Maher tr G-BFWL Flying Group Barton 27. 3.00
(Cancelled 21. 2.00 as WFU: fuselage noted 1.04)

G-BFZR Gulfstream American AA-5B Tiger AA5B-0979 EI-BJS 3.11.78 P C Morrissey Oxford 24. 5.07
G-BFZR
(Force-landed after take-off Oxford 15.10.04: cancelled 3.11.05 by CAA: remnants noted 8.07)

G-BGAY Cameron O-77 Balloon (Hot Air) 446 4.12.78 P C A and S W C Hall Uxbridge 16.12.91A
(Cancelled 4. 8.98 by CAA: extant 2007)

G-BGBF Druine D 31A Turbulent PFA 1658 24.10.78 K Pullen tr Eaglescott Turbulent Group Eaglescott 25. 3.04P
(Built L Davies) (Volkswagen 1600) *(Noted in hangar roof 3.06: cancelled 10. 9.07 by CAA)*

G-BGBV	Slingsby T.65A Vega	1890	BGA 2800-EMS	25.10.78	M P Day tr Vega Syndicate BGA2800	Tibenham	27. 5.08
G-BGCX	Taylor JT.2 Titch	PFA 3221		23.11.78	(G M R Walters)	Lower Wasing Farm, Brimpton	

(Built G M R Walters)
(No Permit issued and cancelled 27. 3.99 as PWFU: noted 6.05)

G-BGEA	Reims Cessna F150M	F15001396	OY-BJK	22. 3.79	C J Hopewell	Sibson	8 .7.06T

(Cancelled 4. 2.05 as PWFU: fuselage stored externally 7.07)

G-BGFK	Evans VP-1	PFA 062-10343		20.12.78	Not known	Waterstones Farm, Newby Wiske	

(Built I N M Cameron)
(Cancelled 7. 4.99: stored 2.08)

G-BGGG	Piper PA-38-112 Tomahawk	38-79A0163	N9675N	10. 1.79	CMV Ltd	Bagby	28. 6.04T

(Cancelled 6.10.05 by CAA: stored 2.08)

G-BGHW	Thunder Ax8-90 Balloon (Hot Air)	175		30. 1.79	W G Johnston	Edinburgh	

(Cancelled 19. 5.93 by CAA: stored 2001)

G-BGRN	Piper PA-38-112 Tomahawk	38-79A0897	N9684N	25. 4.79	(Goodwood Road Racing Company Ltd)	Goodwood	12. 2.00T

(Cancelled 30. 8.01 as WFU: noted derelict 6.06)

G-BGZS	Keirs Heated Air Tube Balloon (Minimum Lift)			7. 8.79	M N J Kirby	Manchester	
		01					

(Built K J Faulkner)
(Cancelled 2.12.93 by CAA: extant 5.07)

G-BHEH	Cessna 310G	310G-0016	N1720	14. 4.80	F J Shevill	Shoreham	9.12.96
			N8916Z				

(Cancelled 24. 8.00 as WFU: fuselage dumped 1.06)

G-BHGP	SOCATA TB-10 Tobago	100		17. 1.80	D Suleyman	Stapleford	29. 5.05

(Cancelled 21. 3.07 as temporarily wfu)

G-BHIC	Reims Cessna F182Q Skylane II	F18200135		18.12.79	Oxford Aviation Services Ltd	Alton	3. 8.08E
	(SMA SR305-230-diesel)						

(Cancelled 4. 5.07 as destoyed: noted Air Salvage International 8.07)

G-BHJA	Cessna A152 Aerobat	A1520835	N4954A	11. 3.80	Cornwall Flying Club Ltd	Biggin Hill	9. 4.92T

(Damaged in heavy landing Bodmin 21. 7.90: cancelled 8.4.02 by CAA: fuselage noted 6.07)

G-BHKE	Bensen B 8MS	VW.1		7. 1.80	N B Gray	Kirkbride	

(Built V C Whitehead - pr.no.G/01-1009)
(Cancelled 3. 2.04 by CAA: noted 8.07)

G-BHMH	Reims Cessna FA152 Aerobat	FA1520367		16. 5.80	Flairhire Ltd t/a Redhill Flying Club	Biggin Hill	13. 8.89T

(Damaged when wing struck tree Hale Farm, Chiddingstone 22. 9.86: cancelled as WFU 9. 8.89: fuselage noted 6.07)

G-BHMM	Avenger T 200-2112 Balloon (Minimum Lift)			29. 1.80	M Murphy	Herne Bay	
		MM2					

(Built M Murphy)
(Cancelled 4. 8.98 by CAA: extant 5.07)

G--BHPN	Colt 14A Cloudhopper Balloon (Hot Air)	081	(SE-..)	6. 3.80	Lindtstrand Technologies Ltd	Oswestry	29. 1.06E
			G-BHPN				

(Cancelled 24. 8.06 by CAA: active 1.07)

G-BHSA	Cessna 152 II	152-83693	(N4889B)	1. 5.80	D Copley	Sturgate	

(Cancelled 18. 5.04 as PWFU: noted 8.05 in bare metal)

G-BHSL	CASA 1131E Jungmann	1117	Spanish AF E3B-236	18. 6.80	H I Taylor	Gloucestershire	19. 7.96P

(Damaged on take off Cranfield 6. 7.96. cancelled 23. 8.00 by CAA: stored dismantled 1.06)

G-BHUP	Reims Cessna F152 II	F15201773		2. 5.80	Stapleford Flying Club Ltd	Stapleford	9.10.89T

(Damaged near Barton 17. 5.89 and cancelled 15. 2.95 by CAA) (Gutted fuselage noted 11.06)

G-BICY	Piper PA-23-160 Apache	23-1640	OO-AOL	26. 9.80	A M Lynn c/o Busy Bee Engineering	Sibson	15. 7.07
			5N-ACL, VR-NDF, PH-ACL, N4010P	(Cancelled 1. 8.06 as PWFU: noted 7.07 in external storage)			

G-BIFN	Bensen B 8MR	KW.1		7.10.80	(R Light)	Stockport	

(Built K Willows - pr.no.PFA G/01-1010)
(Dismantled 8.06: cancelled 8. 9.06 by CAA)

G-BIGM	Avenger T 200-2112 Balloon (Minimum Lift)			6.10.80	M Murphy	Herne Bay	
		MM3					

(Built M Murphy)
(Cancelled 4. 8.98 by CAA: extant 5.07)

G-BIGU	Bensen B 8MR	JRM.1		5.11.80	I B Pitt-Steele	Felthorpe	18. 9.03P

(Built C G Ponsford - pr.no.PFA G/01-1032) (Rotax 532)
(Cancelled 19. 4.04 as WFU)

G-BIIF	Fournier RF4D	4047		25.11.80	J A Taylor and J A Bridges	Biggin Hill	18. 3.93A

(Cancelled 24. 9.92 by CAA: fuselage noted 6.05)

G-BIJX	Reims Cessna F152 II	F15201829		29.12.80	A S Bamrah t/a Falcon Flying Services	Biggin Hill	3 .6.05

(Cancelled 28.11.03 as PWFU: fuselage noted 6.07)

G-BILK	Reims Cessna FA.152 Aerobat	FA1520372		9. 1.81	Exeter Flying Club Ltd	Exeter	13. 5.02T

(Forced landed and overturned in field near Exeter 18.4.01 and substantially damaged: cancelled 10.8.01 as destroyed: noted 12.05)

G-BINZ	Rango NA-8 Balloon (Minimum Lift)	SBG-14		9. 2.81	M O Davies and T J Sweeting t/a Stansted Balloon Group	Bishops Stortford	

(Cancelled 2.12.93 by CAA: extant 5.07)

G-BIOS	Morris Scruggs BL2B Balloon (Minimum Lift)			5. 2.81	D Eaves	Southampton	
		81220					

(Cancelled 27.10.88 as PWFU: extant 5.07)

G-BIRB	SOCATA MS.880B Rallye 100T	2460	F-BVAQ	30. 3.81	(E Smith) (Cancelled 13. 7.92 by CAA: noted 6.06)		
					Jungle Jim's adventure playground, Shanklin, Isle of Wight	16. 6.90	

G-BIRY	Cameron V-77 Balloon (Hot Air)	715		12. 3.81	(P G Bish)	Hungerford	15. 5.99A

(Cancelled 10.12.02 by CAA: noted 1.05)

G-BIUL	Cameron Bellows 60SS Balloon (Hot Air)	703		27. 3.81	(J Haydon)	Abingdon	12. 5.91A
	(Expansion Joint Shape)						

(Cancelled 26. 6.98 by PWFU: stored intact 2007))

G-BIVL	Bensen B 8M	TED-01		10. 4.81	R Gardiner	Bere Alston, Yelverton	29. 4.87P

(Built T E Davies - pr.no.PFA G/01-1011)
(Cancelled 3. 4.97 by CAA: noted 11.06)

G-BIVS	Stansted Featherlight Mk.2 Balloon (Minimum Lift)			15. 4.81	J M J Roberts and S R Rushton		
		002				Rayne, Braintreee and Castle Donington, Derby	

(Cancelled 13.12.88 by CAA: extant 5.07)

G-BIWD	Morris Scruggs RS.5000 Balloon (Minimum Lift)			26. 6.81	D Eaves	Southampton	
		81545					

(Cancelled 30.11.01 as PWFU: extant 5.07)

G-BJAA	Unicorn UE-1A Balloon (Minimum Lift)	81007		2. 6.81	K H Turner t/a Hot Air Cold Ash	Cold Ash, Newbury	

(Cancelled 30.11.88 by CAA: extant 5.07)

G-BJDV	Kingram 01 Balloon (Minimum Lift)	TS-01		4. 8.81	S Ingram and T J King	Eastleigh and Southampton	
	(Bullt T King)						

(Cancelled 12.12.88 by CAA: extant 5.07)

G-BJDY	Unicorn UE-4A Balloon (Minimum Lift)	81012		28. 7.81	I Chadwick tr Unicorn Group		
						Partridge Green, Horsham	

(Cancelled 19. 7.82 as WFU: extant 5.07)

G-BJEN	Morris Scruggs RS.5000 Balloon (Minimum Lift)			5. 8.81	N J Richardson	Eastleigh	
		81548					

(Cancelled 14.1.02 as PWFU: extant 5.07)

G-BJES	Morris Scruggs RS.5000 Balloon (Minimum Lift)			5. 8.81	J E Christopher	Eastleigh	
		81551					

(Cancelled 2.12.93 by CAA: extant 5.07)

G-BJFW	Windsor Mk V Balloon (Minimum Lift)	402		11. 8.81	S E Meagher tr The Windsor Balloon Group		
						London SW15	

(Cancelled 18.10.88 as PWFU: extant 5.07)

G-BJGF	Eaves Dodo Mk.1 Balloon (Minimum Lift)	DD.1		19. 8.81	D and D Eaves	Southampton	

(Cancelled 30.11.01 as PWFU: extant 5.07)

G-BJGG	Eaves Dodo Mk.2 Balloon (Minimum Lift) DD.2	19. 8.81	D and D Eaves	Southampton
			(Cancelled 30.11.01 as PWFU: extant 5.07)	
G-BJGN	Morris Scruggs RS.5000 Balloon (Minimum Lift)	21. 8.81	K H Turner t/a Hot Air Cold Ash	Cold Ash, Newbury
	81554		*(Cancelled 30.11.88 by CAA: extant 5.07)*	
G-BJHI	Chown Osprey Lizzieliner Mk.1B Balloon (Minimum Lift)	9. 9.81	A P and K E Chown	Southampton
	04		*(Cancelled 10. 1.83 by CAA: extant 5.07)*	
G-BJHJ	Chown Osprey Lizzieliner Mk.1C Balloon (Minimum Lift)	9. 9.81	D Eaves	Southampton
	07		*(Cancelled 27.10.88 as PWFU: extant 5.07)*	
G-BJHN	Chown Osprey Lizzieliner Mk.1B Balloon (Minimum Lift)	9. 9.81	J E Christopher	Eastleigh
	14		*(Cancelled 2.12.93 by CAA: extant 5.07)*	
G-BJHO	Chown Osprey Lizzieliner Mk.1C Balloon (Minimum Lift)	9. 9.81	G G Kneller	Southampton
	15		*(Cancelled 2.12.93 by CAA: extant 5.07)*	
G-BJHP	Chown Osprey Lizzieliner Mk.1C Balloon (Minimum Lift)	9. 9.81	N J Richardson	Eastleigh
	16		*(Cancelled 14.1.02 as PWFU: extant 5.07)*	
G-BJHR	Chown Osprey Lizzieliner Mk.1B Balloon (Minimum Lift)	9. 9.81	M Christopher	Eastleigh
	17		*(Cancelled 8.12.88 by CAA: extant 5.07)*	
G-BJHW	Chown Osprey Lizzieliner Mk.1C Balloon (Minimum Lift)	9. 9.81	N J Richardson	Eastleigh
	19		*(Cancelled 14.1.02 as PWFU: extant 5.07)*	
G-BJHY	Chown Osprey Lizzieliner Mk.1B Balloon (Minimum Lift)	9. 9.81	S Ingram and T J King Eastleigh and Southampton	
	21		*(Cancelled 12.12.88 by CAA: extant 5.07)*	
G-BJHZ	Chown Osprey Lizzieliner Mk.1B Balloon (Minimum Lift)	9. 9.81	M Christopher	Eastleigh
	27		*(Cancelled 8.12.88 by CAA: extant 5.07)*	
G-BJIK	Chown Osprey Lizzieliner Mk.1B Balloon (Minimum Lift)	9. 9.81	A P and K E Chown	Southampton
	23		*(Cancelled 2. 6.83 as WFU: extant 5.07)*	
G-BJJD	Eaves Dodo Mk 1 Balloon (Minimum Lift) DD.6	9. 9.81	A P Chown and K R Bundy	Southampton
			(Cancelled 2. 6.83 as WFU: extant 5.07)	
G-BJJE	Eaves Dodo Mk 3 Balloon (Minimum Lift) DD.7	9. 9.81	D Eaves	Southampton
			(Cancelled 30.11.01 as PWFU: extant 5.07)	
G-BJJF	Eaves Dodo Mk 4 Balloon (Minimum Lift) DD.8	9. 9.81	D Eaves	Southampton
			(Cancelled 27.10.88 as PWFU: extant 5.07)	
G-BJJG	Eaves Dodo Mk 5 Balloon (Minimum Lift) DD.9	9. 9.81	D Eaves	Southampton
			(Cancelled 27.10.88 as PWFU: extant 5.07)	
G-BJJM	Rooke & Hounsell Bitterne Mk.1 Balloon (Minimum Lift)	9. 9.81	A P and K E Chown	Southampton
	RH.06		*(Cancelled 10. 1.83 by CAA: extant 5.07)*	
G-BJKV	Chown Osprey Mk.1F Balloon (Minimum Lift) 30	17. 9.81	B Diggle	Cheadle
			(Cancelled 8.12.88 by CAA: extant 5.07)	
G-BJKZ	Chown Osprey Mk.1F Balloon (Minimum Lift) 31	17. 9.81	M N J Kirby	Manchester
			(Cancelled 17.11.88 as PWFU: extant 5.07)	
G-BJLE	Chown Osprey Lizzieliner Mk.1B Balloon (Minimum Lift)	21. 9.81	I Chadwick	Partridge Green, Horsham
	32		*(Cancelled 21. 4.98 as PWFU: extant 5.07)*	
G-BJLN	Stansted Mk.3 Balloon (Minimum Lift) 301	23. 9.81	A P Newman and T J Sweeeting t/a Stansted Balloon Group	
			Braintree and Bishops Stortford	
			(Cancelled 29.11.88 by CAA: extant 5.07)	
G-BJLP	Stansted Mk.3 Balloon (Minimum Lift) 302	23. 9.81	M O Davies and N P Kemp t/a Stansted Balloon Group	
			Little Hallingbury, Bishops Stortford and Braintree	
			(Cancelled 12.12.88 by CAA: extant 5.07)	
G-BJMG	Eaves European E 26C Balloon (Minimum Lift)	25. 9.81	A P Chown and D Eaves	Southampton
	S 4		*(Cancelled 15.10.98 by CAA: extant 5.07)*	
G-BJMH	Chown Osprey Mk.3A Balloon (Minimum Lift) 37	9. 9.81	D Eaves	Southampton
			(Cancelled 27.10.88 as PWFU: extant 5.07)	
G-BJMT	Chown Osprey Mk.1E Balloon (Minimum Lift)	2.10.81	M J Sheather	Southampton
	AKC-45		*(Cancelled 29.11.88 by CAA: extant 5.07)*	
G-BJNB	WAR Vought F-4U Corsair replica PFA 118-10711	13.10.81	A V Francis	Beeches Farm, South Scarle
	(Built A V Francis)		*(Cancelled 8.11.89 by CAA: under slow rebuild 8.05)*	
G-BJNI	Chown Osprey Mk.1C Balloon (Minimum Lift)	9.10.81	M J Sheather	Southampton
	AKC-49		*(Cancelled 29.11.88 by CAA: extant 5.07)*	
G-BJPT	Chown Osprey Mk.3G Balloon (Minimum Lift)	16.10.81	A P Chown	Southampton
	AKC-79		*(Cancelled xxxxxxx by CAA: extant 5.07)*	
G-BJRB	Eaves European E 254 Balloon (Minimum Lift)	23.10.81	D Eaves	Southampton
	S 5		*(Cancelled 30.11.01 by CAA: extant 5.07)*	
G-BJRC	Eaves European E 84R Balloon (Minimum Lift)	23.10.81	D Eaves	Southampton
	S 7		*(Cancelled 30.11.01 by CAA: extant 5.07)*	
G-BJRD	Eaves European E 84R Balloon (Minimum Lift)	23.10.81	D Eaves	Southampton
	S 8		*(Cancelled 30.11.01 by CAA: extant 5.07)*	
G-BJRL	Chown Osprey Mk.4B Balloon (Minimum Lift)	28.10.81	G G Kneller	Southampton
	AKC-67		*(Cancelled 2.12.93 by CAA: extant 5.07)*	
G-BJRO	Chown Osprey Mk.4D Balloon (Minimum Lift)	28.10.81	M Christopher	Eastleigh
	AKC-82		*(Cancelled 8.12.88 by CAA: extant 5.07)*	
G-BJSC	Chown Osprey Mk.4D Balloon (Minimum Lift)	12.11.81	N J Richardson	Eastleigh
	AKC-84		*(Cancelled 14. 1.02 as PWFU: extant 5.07)*	
G-BJSD	Chown Osprey Mk.4D Balloon (Minimum Lift)	12.11.81	N J Richardson	Eastleigh
	AKC-83		*(Cancelled 14. 1.02 as PWFU: extant 5.07)*	
G-BJSF	Chown Osprey Mk.4B Balloon (Minimum Lift)	9.11.81	J E Christopher	Eastleigh
	AKC-66		*(Cancelled 2.12.93 by CAA: extant 5.07)*	
G-BJSI	Chown Osprey Mk.1E Balloon (Minimum Lift)	9.11.81	N J Richardson	Eastleigh
	AKC-43		*(Cancelled 14. 1.02 as PWFU: extant 5.07)*	
G-BJSK	Chown Osprey Mk.1E Balloon (Minimum Lift)	9.11.81	J E Christopher	Eastleigh
	AKC-65		*(Cancelled 2.12.93 by CAA: extant 5.07)*	
G-BJSX	Unicorn UE-1C Balloon (Minimum Lift) 82023	10.11.81	N J Richardson	Eastleigh
			(Cancelled 14. 1.02 as PWFU: extant 5.07)	
G-BJTZ	Chown Osprey Mk.4A Balloon (Minimum Lift)	27.11.81	M J Sheather	Southampton
	AKC-38		*(Cancelled 29.11.88 by CAA: extant 5.07)*	
G-BJUO	Unicorn UE-4B Balloon (Minimum Lift) 81022	2.11.81	I Chadwick tr Unicorn Group	
			Partridge Green, Horsham	
			(DBF 12.4.82 Alton Towers: cancelled 19.7.82 as WFU: extant 5.07)	

G-BJVM	Cessna 172N Skyhawk II	17269374	N737FA	14.12.81	I C Maclennan Gunton Hall, Somerton	1. 8.08E
					(Cancelled 18.12.07 by CAA)	
G-BJZX	Grob G109	6109	(D-KGRO)	3. 9.82	Oxfordshire Sport Flying Ltd Blackpool	4. 9.00
					(Cancelled 18. 3.02 as WFU: fuselage noted 10.07)	
G-BKIE	Short SD.3-30 Variant100	SH3005	G-SLUG	15. 9.82	International Fire Training Centre Durham Tees Valley	22. 8.93T
			G-BKIE, G-METP, G-METO, G-BKIE, C-GTAS, G-14-3005		(Cancelled 16.9.97 as PWFU).(Fire services use 2.08)	
G-BKHR	Luton LA-4A Minor PFA 051-10228			24. 8.82	C B Buscombe and R Goldsworthy	
	(Built R J Parkhouse) (Volkswagen 1834)				(St Austell and Probus, Truro)	6. 1.04P
					(Cancelled 30. 8.05 by CAA)	
G-BKRU	Crossley Racer PFA 131-10797				(M S Crossley) (Peterborough)	24. 1.90P
	(Built M S Crossley) (Continental C90-14F)				(Cancelled 2. 3.99 by CAA: noted 5.05)	
G-BKRV	Hovey Beta Bird PFA 135-10875			30. 3.83	M J Aubrey Kington, Hereford	25.6.97P
	(Built A V Francis) (Rotax 503)				(Cancelled 18. 6.98 by CAA: noted 2002) .	
G-BLDC	K & S Jungster 1 PFA 044-10701			29.12.83	(A W Brown) Longside, Peterhead	6. 3.90P
	(Built C A Laycock)				(No Permit issued - cancelled 6. 3.99 by CAA: on build 2007)	
G-BLLM	Piper PA-23-250 Aztec E	27-4619	G-BBNM	18. 1.84	C and M Thomas t/a Ammanford Trade Sales Alton	21. 8.98
			OY-POR, G-BBNM, N14001		(Cancelled 8. 4.02 by CAA: noted Air Salvage International 8.07)	
G-BLPK	Cameron V-65 Balloon (Hot Air)	1069		24. 9.84	A J and C P Nicholls t/a Bernard Hunter and Bristol Cine Sales	
					(Cancelled 19. 1.99 by CAA: noted 5.07) Ashton, Bristol	9. 8.96A
G-BLRJ	CEA Jodel DR.1051 Sicile	502	F-BLRJ	8. 2.78	M P Hallam Deenethorpe	17. 7.00
					(Cancelled 6. 3.02 as WFU: noted 6.03)	
G-BLSD	de Havilland DH.112 Venom FB.54	928	N203DM	20. 5.85	Aces High Ltd Grove Technology Park, Wantage	
	(Built F + W)		G-BLSD, Swiss AF J-1758		(Cancelled 5.. 6.96 as WFU: as gate guardian.in RAF c/s 10.07)	
G-BLTU	Slingsby T 67B Firefly	2024		16. 1.85	(RAF Wyton Flying Club Ltd)	
					Chiltern Park, Wallingford	4. 4.07T
					(Cancelled 26. 6.06 as PWFU: noted 6.07)	
G-BLVY	Colt 21A Cloudhopper Balloon (Hot Air)	634		18. 2.85	Colt Balloons Ltd (US)	13. 2.86A
					(Cancelled 7. 5.91 on sale to Holland) (Active Albuquerque, New Mexico, US 10.03 without marks)	
G-BLWW	Aerocar Taylor Mini-Imp Model C PFA 136-10880			1. 3.85	M K Field tr The Brize Group Sleap	4. 6.87P
	(Built W E Wilks) (Continental O-200-A)				(Cancelled 13.10.00 by CAA: noted 8.07)	
G-BLYJ	Cameron V-77 Balloon (Hot Air)	408		1. 5.85	E E Clark and J A Lomas Melton Mowbray	15. 6.89A
					(Cancelled 7. 5.93 as destroyed: inflated 4.06)	
G-BMFN	QAC Quickie Tri-Q 200	EMK 017		27. 9.85	A H Hartog Thruxton	1. 5.02P
	(Built EMK Aeroplane Ltd - pr.no.PFA 094A1-11062) (Continental O-200-A)				(Cancelled 30. 3.05 by CAA: noted 8.06)	
G-BMGC	Fairey Swordfish II	?-	RCan Navy W5856 23.10.85		Royal Navy Historic Flight RNAS Yeovilton	
	(Built Blackburn Aeroplane and Motor Company Ltd)		W5856		(Cancelled 2. 9.91 by CAA) (As "W5856:A2A" in RN 810 Sqdn c/s-"City of Leeds")	
G-BMIR (2)	Westland Wasp HAS.1	F9670	XT788	24. 1.86	Park Aviation Supplies	
					(Little Glovers Farm, Charlwood, Surrey)	
	(Cancelled 22.12.95 by CAA) (Exhibited in Flightaid's travelling roadshow as "XT788/474" in Royal Navy c/s 9.07)					
G-BMJB	Cessna 152 II	15280030	N757VD	3. 2.86	Bobbington Air Training School Ltd Lee-on-Solent	16. 6.00
					(Cancelled 12. 6.00 as WFU: fuselage noted 9.07 - wings stored Halfpenny Green 10.07)	
G-BMJG	Piper PA-28R-200 Cherokee Arrow	28R-35046	ZS-TNS	23.12.85	Western Air (Thruxton) Ltd Blackpool	4. 2.99T
			ZS-FYC, N9345N		(Damaged Thruxton 11.10.98: cancelled 15. 4.99 by CAA: fuselage noted 10.07)	
G-BMKW	Cameron V-77 Balloon (Hot Air)	608		29. 1.86	M H Redman Stalbridge, Sturminster Newton	21. 9.00A
					(Noted 8.06: cancelled 1. 2.08 by CAA)	
G-BMLC	Short SD.3-60 Variant 100	SH3688	SE-LDA	18. 2.86	BAC Leasing Ltd (Coventry)	24. 5.05T
			G-BMLC, G-14-3688		(Cancelled 6. 6.07 as WFU)	
G-BMOO	Clutton FRED SeriesII PFA 029-10770			11. 4.86	(N Purllant) Saltby	8. 8.91P
	(Built N Purllant) (Webster Whirlwind radial)				(Cancelled 22. 2.99 by CAA: noted 6.07 less wings or tailplane in pseudo-RAF c/s)	
G-BMUJ	Colt Drachenfisch SS Balloon (Hot Air)	835		3. 6.86	(Virgin Airship and Balloon Company Ltd) Telford	27. 7.91A
	(Futuristic special shape)				"Drachenfisch" ("Dragon Fish") (Cancelled 4.11.03 as WFU: stored in good condition 2004)	
G-BMUK	Colt UFO SS Balloon (Hot Air)	836		3. 6.86	(Virgin Airship and Balloon Company Ltd) Telford	26. 4.95A
	(Futuristic special shape)				"UFO" and "Dream Station" (Cancelled 4.11.03 as WFU: stored in good condition 2004)	
G-BMUL	Colt Kindermond SS Balloon (Hot Air)	837		3. 6.86	(Virgin Airship and Balloon Company Ltd) Telford	26. 9.91A
	(Futuristic special shape)				"Kindermond" ("Childrens' Moon") (Cancelled 4.11.03 as WFU: stored in good condition 2004)	
G-BMYA	Colt 56A Balloon (Hot Air)	864		13. 8.86	(J Haydon) Abingdon	2.12.92A
					(Cancelled 29. 4.97 as PWFU: stored intact 2007)	
G-BNCX	Hawker Hunter T 7	41H/695454	XL621	9. 1.87	FLS Aerospace (Lovaux) Ltd Dunsfold	28. 3.87P
					(Cancelled 1. 3.93 as PWFU) (As Gate guardian "XL621")	
G-BNJA	Wag Aero Wag-a-Bond PFA 137-10886			3. 4.87	B E Maggs Willey Park Farm, Caterham	3. 8.03P
	(Built R A Yates) (Continental O-200-A)				(Cancelled 17. 2.04 by CAA: noted 3.06)	
G-BNKF	Colt AS-56 Airship (Hot Air)	899		20. 5.87	Formtrack Ltd London SE16	14. 9.98A
					(Cancelled 20.10.00 by CAA: noted 5.07)	
G-BNMI	Colt Black Knight Balloon (Hot Air)	1096		1. 6. 87	Virgin Airship and Balloon Company Ltd (Telford)	26. 9.91A
					(Cancelled 4.11.03 as WFU: stored in good condition 2004)	
G-BNNC	Cameron N-77 Balloon (Hot Air)	1523		16. 6.87	T M C McCoy Peasedown St John, Bath	9.10.96
					(Cancelled 2. 6.98 as WFU: noted 2007)	
G-BNPL	Piper PA-38-112 Tomahawk	38-79A0524	N2420G	28. 7.87	Cardiff-Wales Flying Club Gloucestershire	30. 1.03T
					(Cancelled 24. 3.05 by CAA: fuselage noted 7.05 in outside storage)	
G-BNXG	Cameron DP-70 Airship (Hot Air)	1558		23. 9.87	Rexstyle Ltd (US)	23.10.88A
					(Cancelled 18. 6.93 by CAA: noted 8.06)	
G-BOAM	Robinson R22 Beta	0717		10.12.87	Plane Talking Ltd Quatro Vientos, MadridI	27. 1.08E
					(Cancelled 17. 2.07 by CAA: noted 5.07)	
G-BOBZ	Piper PA-28-181 Archer II	28-8090257	N81671	21.12.87	Trustcomms International Ltd Biggin Hill	9. 3.98
					(Cancelled 29. 4.05 by CAA: noted 6.07)	
G-BODH	Slingsby Cadet III Motor Glider PFA 042-10108		BGA 474	5. 1.88	M M Bain "Fochinell" Wick	13. 8.02P
	(Re-built C D Denham believed from Slingsby T 8 Tutor G-ALNK {MHL/RT.13}) (Volkswagen 1834) (Cancelled 1. 3.05 by CAA: stored 6.07)					
G-BOJD	Cameron N-77 Balloon (Hot Air)	1653		11. 3.88	P A Sweatman Birmingham	3. 9.05
					"Bluebird" (Cancelled 29. 6.06 as WFU: extant 5.07)	
G-BOKK	Piper PA-28-161 Warrior II	28-8116300	N8427L	6. 4.88	Gosky Aviation Ltd Blackpool	7. 6.97T
					(Damaged Hamgreen, Redditch 18. 5.95: cancelled 8. 9.95 as WFU: wreck noted 10.07)	
G-BORM	Hawker Siddeley HS.748 Series 2B/217	1670	RP-C1043	29. 7.88	(Parkhouse Aviation) Wycombe Air Park	
			V2-LAA, VP-LAA, 9Y-TDH		(Cancelled 18. 6.92 by CAA: cockpit only 12.05)	

G-BOVG	Cessna F172H	F172-0627	OO-ANN	2. 8.88	No.1476 Squadron, ATC		RAF Halton	14. 9.91
	(Built Reims Aviation SA)		D-ELTR	*(Damaged Southend 1991: cancelled 26. 9.95 as WFU: instructional fuselage 9.07)*				
G-BOWC	Cessna 150J	15070458	N60626	24.10.88	(C J Moore and M R Wilson)		Croft Farm, Defford	16. 9.94
	(Forced landed near Barton 10. 7.94: cancelled as WFU 16. 9.94) (To Missionary Aviation Fellowship as "G-BMAF" for fund-raising events - noted 6.04)							
G-BOWK	Cameron N-90 Balloon (Hot Air)	1764		1. 8.88	S R Bridge (*Cavendish Loans titles*)		Grantham	
	(Cancelled 8.11.01 as WFU: inflated 4.06)							
G-BOXB	Piper PA-28-161 Warrior II	2816064	N9142H	12. 8.88	First Class Ltd		Willey Farm, Caterham	6. 2.03T
	(Failed to gain height on take-off from Little Bredy 19. 3.03 and badly damaged: cancelled 26. 8.03 by CAA: wreck noted 5.03 for scrap)							
G-BOXH	Pitts S-1S	MP4	N8LA	29. 7.88	E Mason and R Graham		Not known	16. 5.07P
	(Built B Halstock and J Mills)							
	(Damaged in accident Oving near Chichester 10.12.06: cancelled 17. 3.07 as destroyed: wreck noted 9. 3.07 northbound on M40 between Junctions 9 and 10)							
G-BPAD	Piper PA-34-200T Seneca II	34-7870431	N21208	`23. 8.88	Liverpool Flying School Ltd		Cranfield	
	(Destroyed in crash Saddle Hill, Bowland, Lancashire 15. 7.92: cancelled 20. 2.97 as destroyed: wreck noted 1.06)							
G-BPAO	Air Command 503 Commander	0424		8. 9.88	D J A L Sagar		Croft Farm, Defford	8. 8.91P
	(Built D J Sagar - pr.no.PFA G/04-1097)				*(Cancelled 23. 2.99 as PWFU: noted 1.02)*			
G-BPAV	Clutton FRED series 2	PFA 029-12074		21.11.78	P A Valentine		Wycombe Air Park	
	(Built P A Valentine)				*(Cancelled 12. 8.03 by CAA: unfinished fuselage noted 5.06)*			
G-BPCJ	Cessna 150J	15070797	N61096	26. 9.88	B E Simpson and C R Hughes			
						Amen Corner, Binfield, Bracknell		
	(Badly damaged in gales Compton Abbas 25. 1.90: cancelled 4. 7.90 by CAA: in open storage 12.07)							
G-BPDK	Sorrell SNS-7 Hyperbipe	242	N85BL	6.10.88	A J Cable		Barton	23. 6.95P
					(Cancelled 17. 2.99 by CAA: wings only noted 10.06)			
G-BPEL	Piper PA-28-151 Cherokee Warrior	28-7415172	C-FEYM	10.10.88	R W Harris and A Jahanfar		Southend	8. 2.92T
					(Cancelled 28. 2.02 as WFU: dismantled wreck stored 1.08)			
G-BPGM	Cessna 152	15284932	N5380P	14.11.88	J D Peace and Co		Glenrothes	14. 4.05T
					(Cancelled 5.10.04 as PWFU: noted dumped 6.06)			
G-BPIY	Cessna 152 II	15284073	N5249H	19.12.88	A S Bamrah t/a Falcon Flying Services		Biggin Hill	19.11.97
					(Badly damaged landing Earls Colne 12. 8.97: cancelled as PWFU 13. 3.01)			
G-BPLF	Cameron V-77 Balloon (Hot Air)	1903		16. 1.89	I R Warrington and R Macmillan		Stamford	
					(Cancelled 22. 9.04 by CAA: inflated 4.06)			
G-BPMM	Champion 7ECA Citabria	498	N5132T	22. 3.89	J Murray	(Ballymena, County Antrim)		25. 2.97P
					(Noted 1.04: cancelled 29. 4.05 by CAA)			
G-BPOA	Gloster Meteor T 7	?-	WF877	16. 3.89	(Aces High Ltd)		Duxford	
					(Cancelled 5. 6.96 as WFU: noted 4.06)			
G-BPRP	Cessna 150E	15061269	N3569J	10. 3.89	P A Griffin		Shoreham	3. 5.98
	(Badly damaged by gales 12.97 Shoreham: cancelled 22.10.99 as WFU: noted fire dump 9.02)							
G-BPUY	Cessna 150K	15071427	N5927G	25. 4.89	M Hewison		Plaistows Farm, St Albans	
	(No UK CofA issued: cancelled 22.12.95 by CAA: unmarked fuselage under plastic 5.04)							
G-BPYI	Cameron O-77 Balloon (Hot Air)	1988		9. 5.89	N J Logue		Pembroke Dock	9. 7.05A
					(Cancelled 10. 5.05 by CAA: inflated 4.06)			
G-BRBF	Cessna 152 II	15281993	N67748	8. 6.89	G Jackson t/a Jacksons Tool and Plant Hire		Bagby	5. 7.98T
					(Cancelled 17. 5.01 by CAA: noted stored 2.08)			
G-BRCI	Pitts S-1C	4668	N351S	6. 7.89	G L A Vandormael		Sint-Truiden, Belgium	2. 8.08P
	(Built J Ballentyne) (Lycoming O-320)				*(Cancelled 25. 2.08 by CAA)*			
G-BREA	Bensen B 8MR	PFA G/01-1006		6. 7.89	P Robichaud		Henstridge	6. 9.06P
	(Built R Firth) (Rotax 503)				*(Cancelled 25. 9.06 as TWFU)*			
G-BREZ	Cessna 172M Skyhawk II	17266742	N80775	14. 7.89	Not known		Fenland	
					(Cancelled 16. 4.93 - to EI-CHS: under restoration 2.08)			
G-BRFN	Piper PA-38-112 Tomahawk	38-79A0397	N2326F	23.10.89	Light Aircraft Leasing (UK) Ltd		Exeter	10.12.03T
					(Cancelled 25. 9.03 by CAA: noted 12.05)			
G-BRGP	Colt Flying Stork SS Balloon (Hot Air)	1409		25. 7.89	T and C Realisations Ltd		(US)	11.10.94A
	"Great Eggspectations" (Cancelled 10. 3.95 by CAA: active Albuquerque, New Mexico, US 10.06 as "G-BRGP")							
G-BRHB	Boeing Stearman B75N1 (N2S-3) Kaydet	75-6508	EC-AID	10. 8.89	P R Bennett and R Sage	Priory Farm, Tibenham		
			N67955, Bu.05334		*(Noted 3.05: cancelled 3. 8.05 as WFU)*			
G-BRML	Piper PA-38-112 Tomahawk	38-79A1017	N2510P	3.10.89	P H Rogers		Wellesbourne Mountford	3. 6.02T
					(Cancelled 5. 4.05 by CAA: dumped 8.05)			
G-BRTC	Cessna 150G	15065996	N3296J	1. 3.90	Thorpe Air Ltd		Kirknewton	
	(Blown over by gales Bournemouth 23.12.91 and badly damaged: cancelled 3. 2.99 as PWFU: wreck noted 3.06)							
G-BRUA	Cessna 152 II	15281212	N49267	11. 1.90	BBC Air Ltd		Exeter	5. 11.05T
					(Cancelled 21.11.05 as PWFU: fuselage noted 1.07)			
G-BRUE	Cameron V-77 Balloon (Hot Air)	2183		15.12.89	B J Newman and P L Harrison		Rushden	26. 7.99A
					(Cancelled 13. 3.01 as PWFU: noted 8.05)			
G-BRVH	Smyth Model S Sidewinder	PFA 092-11251		19.12.89	I C White		Abbeville, France	10. 5.02P
	(Built I Bellamy) (Lycoming O-290)				*(Cancelled 24. 7.02 by CAA: noted 6.07)*			
G-BSET	Beagle B 206 Basset CC.1	B 006	XS765	3.12.86	IAE Ltd		Cranfield	28. 7.98
					(Cancelled 25. 3.04 as WFU: spares source as "XS765" 7.05)			
G-BSGR	Boeing Stearman E75 (PT-17) Kaydet	75-4721	N75864	19. 6.90	A G Dunkerley		Kemble	
			EC-ATY, N55050, 42-16558		*(Cancelled 10. 3.99 by CAA: noted unmarked 2.04)*			
	(Composite rebuild of EC-AMD {75-4721} and EC-ATY {75-6714} and also reported as (ex?) N126SE)							
G-BSHR	Reims Cessna F 172N Skyhawk II	F17201616	G-BFGE	23.10.84	Deep Cleavage Ltd		Exeter	24. 4.03T
					(Cancelled 21. 2.02 as WFU: on fire dump 2.06)			
G-BSOV	Piper PA-38-112 Tomahawk II	38-81A0031	N25637	20. 8.90	A Dodd		Cranfield	1. 3.98T
	(Damaged Panshanger 7.10.95: cancelled 5. 6.01 by CAA: noted dismantled 1.06)							
G-BSPC	SAN Jodel D 140C Mousquetaire III	150	F-BMFN	2.11.81	B E Cotton		Rufforth	31.10.85
					(Cancelled 15. 8.94 by CAA: noted derelict 9.07)			
G-BSPF	Cessna T303 Crusader	T30300100	OY-SVH	31. 7.90	K P Gibben tr G-BSPF Crusader Group		Blackpool	28.10.99
			N3116C		*(Crashed Burton Joyce, Nottingham 16. 7.98: cancelled 25. 8.98 as WFU: wreck noted 10.07)*			
G-BSUH	Cessna 140	8092	N89088	15.10.90	K J O'Brien		Abbeyshrule, County Longford	2. 5.94
	(Continental C85)		NC89088		*(Damaged Gowran Grange 6.93: cancelled 28. 4.95 by CAA: airframe stored 5.06)*			
G-BSUT	Rans S-6-ESA Coyote II	0990.138		2.10.90	N J Hancock and S J Mathison		Barton	8. 2.07P
	(Built P Clegg - pr.no.PFA 204-11897) (Rotax 582) (Tri-cycle u/c)							
	(Had accident 7. 8.06 Warrington (Cheshire) strip: noted in workshops near Leyland 12.07 on rebuild with Jabiru 2200B) (Cancelled 21. 1.08 by CAA)							
G-BSXP	Air Command 532 Elite	0633		5.11.90	(R Light)		Stockport	
	(Built B J West)				*(Cancelled 8.12.00 as PWFU: reported dismantled 8.06)*			

G-BSYK	Piper PA-38-112 Tomahawk II	38-81A0143	N23449	23. 1.91	Flychoice Ltd	Halfpenny Green	

(No CofA issued: cancelled 10. 3.99 by CAA: stored 10.07)

G-BSYL	Piper PA-38-112 Tomahawk II	38-81A0172	N91333	23. 1.91	Flychoice Ltd	Halfpenny Green	

(No CofA issued: cancelled 10. 3.99 by CAA: stored 10.07)

G-BSYM	Piper PA-38-112 Tomahawk II	38-82A0072	N2507V	30. 1.91	Flychoice Ltd	Wellesbourne Mountford	4. 9.94T

(Damaged 27. 7.94: cancelled 26.10.00 by CAA: dumped 5.05)

G-BTAR	Piper PA-38-112 Tomahawk	38-79A0383	N2584D	13. 2.91	Aerohire Ltd	Blackpool	12. 3.00T

(Damaged Liverpool 19. 6.98: cancelled 9. 4.02 by CAA: noted 10.07)

G-BTBN	Denney Kitfox Model 2	686		31.12.90	R C Bowley	Croft Farm, Defford	19. 8.04P

(Built Valley Avon Flying Group - pr.no.PFA 172-11859)　　　　　　　*(Cancelled 21. 7.05 as WFU)*

G-BTEI	Everett Campbell Cricket Series3	023		31. 1.91	R A Jarvis	(Lisbellow, Inniskillen)	21.12.98P

(Built J W Highton)　　　*(Damaged in forced landing nr.Great Orton 15. 8.95: stored 8.98) (Cancelled 23. 5.01 by CAA) (Reported 2004)*

G-BTFP	Piper PA-38-112 Tomahawk	38-78A0340	N6201A	17. 4.91	CMV Ltd	Bagby	6. 8.00T

(Cancelled 10.10.05 by CAA: stored 2.08)

G-BTIG	Montgomerie-Bensen B 8MR	PFA G/01-1093		21. 3.91	K Jarvis	Kirkbride	10. 4.04P

(Built N Beale and D Beevers) (Rotax 532)　　　*(Cancelled 13. 4.04 by CAA: noted 8.07)*

G-BTIN	Cessna 150C	15059905	N7805Z	26. 3.91	Perth Technical College	Perth	17. 4.00

(Overturned by gales Edinburgh 23.12.99 and cancelled 10. 5.01 as WFU: as instructional airframe 1.06)

G-BTLL	Pilatus P 3-03	323-5	A-806	18. 4.91	D L Masters	Headcorn	23. 6.94P

(Cancelled 27.10.95 by CAA: stored as "A-806" in Swiss AF c/s 6.05)

G-BTPB	Cameron N-105 Balloon (Hot Air)	1536		6. 7.87	D J Farrar	Collingham, Wetherby	14. 8.05A

(Cancelled 8. 7.05 by CAA)

G-BTRE	Reims Cessna F172H	F17200657	N10657	3. 7.91	S Clark	(London SW4)	18.10.07E

(Cancelled 24. 1.05 as Destroyed: noted 3.05 on trailer Northbound on M20 near Aylesford, Kent)

G-BTRX	Cameron V-77 Balloon (Hot Air)	1143	VH-HIH	12. 7.91	R P Jones and N P Hemsley	Horsham and Crawley	16. 4.97A

(Cancelled 2. 5.97 as WFU: inflated 6.02)

G-BTSC	Evans VP-2	PFA 063-10342		20.10.78	G B O'Neill	(Upwood, Cambridge)	13. 2.96P

(Built D J Keam- Truro SChool) (Arrow GT500)　　　*(Stored 6.00: cancelled 20. 1.03 by CAA)*

G-BTUD	CFM Image	IM-01	G-MWPV	21. 8.91	D G Cook	(Aldringham, Leiston)	21. 1.95P

(Built D G Cook - pr.no.PFA 222-12012)　　　*(Cancelled 5. 2.99 as PWFU: noted 2007)*

G-BTVG	Cessna 140	12350	N2114N	30. 8.91	V C Gover	Kirknewton	15. 4.99P

(Cancelled 18. 5.01 by CAA: noted 3.06)

G-BTYX	Cessna 140	11004	N76568 NC76568	27.11.91	J R H Willis and A Coulson tr G-BTYX Group	Rochester	23. 2.98T

(Cancelled 10. 4.01 by CAA: stored 6.05)

G-BUBR	Cameron A-250 Balloon (Hot Air)	2779		5. 5. 92	Balloon Flights International Ltd	Bristol	2. 9.01T

(Cancelled 24. 6.03 as WFU: stored 2004)

G-BUDY	Colt 17A Cloudhopper Balloon (Hot Air)	413		28. 6. 82	Bondbaste Ltd	(France)	19. 1.94A

(Cancelled 19. 5.93 by CAA: active 1.07)

G-BUEZ	Hawker Hunter F 6A	S4/U/3275	8736M XF375	3. 4.92	The Old Flying Machine (Air Museum) Company Ltd		

(Built Armstrong-Whitworth Aircraft Ltd　　　　　　　　　　　　*Spanhoe　(Cancelled 28. 8.01 as WFU: noted 10.07)*

G-BUFF	Wassmer Jodel D 112	1302	F-BMYD	9. 8.78	(M Mold)	Watchford Farm, Yarcombe	

(Cancelled 29. 8.91 by CAA - no CofA or Permit issued: fuselage noted 8.07)

G-BUGI	Evans VP-2	PFA 7201		16. 4.92	J A Rees	Long Marston	12. 1.04P

(Built D Silsbury) (Continental A65-8)　　　*(Cancelled 24. 7.06 by CAA: noted 12.06)*

G-BUOC	Cameron A-210 Balloon (Hot Air)	2924		5.10.92	(C Bailey)	Not known	12. 6.03T

(Cancelled 7. 1.05 by CAA: extant 1.07)

G-BURF	Rand Robinson KR-2	PFA 129-11345		30.11.92	P J H Moorhouse and B L Hewart	Green St, Sunbury	

(Built P J H Moorhouse and B L Hewart) (Volkswagen 1834)　　　*(Cancelled 14. 8.02 by CAA - no PtoF issued: noted 12.05)*

G-BURR	Auster AOP.9	xxxx	7851M WZ706	28. 9.92	R P D Folkes	AAC Middle Wallop	

(Cancelled 18. 3.99 by CAA: as "WZ706" - on rebuild 9.05)

G-BUSD	Airbus A320-111	0011	(G-BRAC) F-WWDF	21. 7.88	British Airways PLC	Lasham	21. 7.07T

"Isle of Mull" (Cancelled 5.12.06 as WFU: for scrapping 11.06)

G-BUWJ	Pitts S-1C	2002	N110R	25. 3.93	G Breen tr G-BUWJ Flying Group		

(Built J T Griffins) (Lycoming O-320)　　　*(Cancelled 8.12.05 by CAA) Portimão, Faro, Portugal 14. 4.06P*

G-BUZL	Magni M-16 Tandem Trainer	VPM16-UK-105		18. 6.93	C M Jones	Kirkbride	22. 4.08P

(Rotax 914)　　　*(Cancelled 20.11.07 by CAA)*

G-BVBF	Piper PA-28-151 Cherokee Warrior	28-7515206	N31JM N32633	22. 7.93	R K Spence	Cardiff	

(No CofA issued: cancelled 18. 3.99 by CAA: noted 1.06)

G-BVBN	Cameron A-210 Balloon (Hot Air)	2904		2. 8.93	S M and M L Gabb t/a Heart of England Balloons		

Alcester 10.10.01T　　　(Cancelled 13. 5.03 by CAA)

G-BVBP	Avro 683 Lancaster B 10	?	RCAF KB994	4. 8.93	(D Copley)	North Weald	

(Built Victory Aircraft, Canada as Lancaster B X)　　　*(Forward fuselage noted 8.01: cancelled 22. 2.05 by CAA)*

G-BVHY	Pilatus Britten-Norman BN-2T-4R Defender 4000	4004		21. 1.94	B N Group Ltd	Bembridge	

(Stored 11.00: cancelled 6. 4.04 as WFU)

G-BVIG	Cameron A-250 Balloon (Hot Air)	3213		26. 1.94	Balloon Flights International Ltd	Bristol	2. 9.01T

(Cancelled 24. 6.03 as WFU: stored 2004)

G-BVKV	Cameron N-90 Balloon (Hot Air)	3236		24. 3.94	Pringle of Scotland Ltd	Hawick	3. 2.97A

(Cancelled 24. 9.01 as PWFU: stored 2006)

G-BVMG	Bensen B 80V	PFA G/01-1056		25. 4.94	D Moffat	Lochview House, Limerigg	

(Built D Moffat)　　　*(Cancelled 11.12.00 by CAA - no PtoF issued: stored 2.03)*

G-BVOD	Montgomerie-Parsons Two-Place Gyroplane	G/08-1238		8. 6.94	J M Montgomerie	Crosshill	

(Cancelled 23.11.00 as WFU - no PtoF issued: noted hung in rafters 8.05)

G-BVWK	Air and Space 18A Gyroplane	18-14	SE-HID N6108S	19.12.94	Whisky Mike (Aviation) Ltd	(Kinnetties, Forfar)	

(Cancelled 18.10.00 as temporarily WFU: noted 2004 on road)

G-BVWL	Air and Space 18A Gyroplane	18-63	SE-HIE N90588, N6152S	19.12.94	Whisky Mike (Aviation) Ltd	(Kinnetties, Forfar)	

(Cancelled 18.10.00 as temporarily WFU: noted 2004 on road)

G-BVXC	English Electric Canberra B(I).8	6649	WT333	9. 1.95	Classic Aviation Projects Ltd	Bruntingthorpe	

(Cancelled 22. 4.03 as PWFU: as "WT333" 3.06)

G-BWAE	Rotary Air Force RAF 2000	PFA G/13-1252		27. 2.95	D P Kearns	(Lichfield)	23. 7.03P

(Built B J Crockett)　　　*(Damaged Kemble 30. 7.96: cancelled 1. 9.03 as WFU: noted on M25 Westbound 1.06)*

G-BWBC	Cameron N-90AS Balloon (Hot Air)	3574		12. 6.95	Wetterauer Montgolfieren EV	Budingen, Germany	16. 3.06A

"Zeppelin" (Cancelled 31. 1.06 by CAA)

G-BWCW	Barnett Rotorcraft J4B	PFA G/14-1256		5. 5.95	S H Kirkby	Farley Farm, Romsey	

(Built S H Kirkby)　　　*(Cancelled 2. 3.05 as PWFU: stored 10.07)*

G-BWLX	Westland Scout AH.1	F9709	XV134	29.12.95	JM Helicopters Ltd	Oaksey Park	13. 8.04P
	(As "XV134:P" in AAC c/s: cancelled 7. 9.04 by CAA: stored 6.05)						
G-BWNL	Europa Aviation Europa	068		27. 2.96	H Smith	Morgansfield, Fishburn	
	(Built H Smith - pr.no.PFA 247-12675) (Tri-gear u/c)		*(Damaged Fishburn 14.12.97: cancelled 11.12.00 by CAA - no PtoF issued: on rebuild 2002)*				
G-BWNX	Thunder Ax10-180 Series2 Balloon (Hot Air)		G-OWBC	2. 1.96	MJN Balloon Management Ltd	London SW1	2. 4.01T
		2352			*(Cancelled 26. 2.02 by CAA: noted 3.05)*		
G-BWOL	Hawker Sea Fury FB.11	ES.3617 & 61631	D-CACY (2)	18. 3.96	The Old Flying Machine (Air Museum) Company Ltd		
			G-9-603, WG599			Catfield, Norfolk	
					(Cancelled 4. 1.01 by CAA: on restoration 8.02)		
G-BWTF	Lindstrand Bear SS Balloon (Hot Air)	375		3. 6.96	Free Enterprise Balloons Ltd	London SE16	31.10.06A
					(Cancelled 9.10.06 by CAA: active Albuquerque, New Mexico, US 10.06 as "G-BWTF")		
G-BWTU	Lindstrand LBL 77A Balloon (Hot Air)	376		17. 6.96	Virgin Airship and Balloon Company Ltd	Telford	14. 1.02A
					(Cancelled 31. 1.03 as PWFU: noted active Tavistock 8.06)		
G-BWUW	British Aircraft Corporation BAC 145 Jet Provost T 5A	XW423	18. 7.96	North East Wales Institute		
		EEP/JP/1045			Deeside College, Connah's Quay, Deeside 14. 2.02P		
					(Cancelled 29. 6.06 as PWFU: to Instructional airframe.as "XW423:14" in RAF c/s)		
G-BWVL	Cessna 150M	15077229	N50NA	13. 8.96	A D Shaw	Kemble	18. 1.03T
			N63286		*(Cancelled 26. 4.05 by CAA: stored 8.06)*		
G-BWWJ	Hughes 269C	113-0256	G-BMYZ	25. 2.87	Dave Nieman Models Ltd	Oxford	26.10.96
	(Hughes 300C)		N8996F		*(Cancelled 25. 6.02 by CAA: stored 8.07)*		
G-BXBB	Piper PA-20 Pacer	20-959	EC-AOZ	24. 1.97	M.E.R.Coghlan	Farley Farm, Romsey	
			N1133C		*(Cancelled 22. 4.03 by CAA: stored as "EC-AOZ")*		
G-BXBH	Hunting Percival P 84 Jet Provost T 3A	PAC/W/9241	XM365	29. 1.97	G-BXBH Provost Ltd	North Weald	31. 8.01P
					(Cancelled 10.10.02 by CAA: noted as "XM365" 6.07)		
G-BXDD	Rotary Air Force RAF 2000 GTX-SE			9. 1.97	A Wane	Kirkbride	4. 7.00P
	(Built R M Savage)	PFA G/13-1284			*(Noted 5.07: cancelled 25. 9.07 by CAA)*		
G-BXMW	Cameron A-275 Balloon (Hot Air)	4247		19. 2.98	Ballooning Network Ltd	Bristol	23. 9.04T
					(Cancelled 23. 9.04 as PWFU: noted 2006)		
G-BXSB	Cameron PM-80 Balloon (Hot Air)	4298		11. 3.98	Flying Pictures Ltd	(US)	13.10.02A
	(Coca Cola bottle)				*(Cancelled 31. 1.02 by CAA: active 2006)*		
G-BXYU	Reims Cessna F152 II	F15201804	OH-CKD	31. 7.98	Exeter Flying Club Ltd	Exeter	24. 8.01T
			SE-IFY		*(Cancelled 16.10.99 as destroyed Whiddon Down, Okehampton 2. 8.99,*		
					unmarked fuselage noted 12.05)		
G-BYDX	American General AG-5B Tiger	10051	N374SA	6. 1.99	A J Watson tr Bibit Group	Farley Farm, Romsey	5. 5.08
			G-BYDX, F-GKBH, N1191Y		*(Damaged 2005: cancelled 29.11.05 as destroyed: on rebuild 10.07)*		
G-BYED	British Aircraft Corporation BAC 145 Jet Provost T 5A	N166A	23.11.98	M A Petrie and J E Rowley	Hawarden	23. 5.01P
		EEP/JP/966	XW302		*(Cancelled 30.12.04 as WFU: noted 5.05)*		
G-BYFK	Cameron Printer 105 SS Balloon (Hot Air) 4522			4. 3.99	Flying Pictures Ltd	Chilbolton, Stockbridge	26. 5.03A
					(Samsung Printers titles) (Cancelled 29. 9.03 as WFU)		
G-BYIW	Cameron PM-80 Balloon (Hot Air)	4596		14. 5.99	A Schneider	Borken, Germany	27. 4.05A
	(Coca Cola bottle)				*(Cancelled 28. 1.05 by CAA)*		
G-BYKR	Piper PA-28-161 Warrior II	2816061	HB-PLM	22. 6.99	Oxford Aviation Services Ltd	Oxford	11. 8.08E
		(Engine failed on take off Oxford 30. 8.06 and substantially damaged: cancelled 22. 8.07 as destroyed: noted 8.07)				
G-BYKX	Cameron N-90 Balloon (Hot Air)	4657		10. 8.99	G Davis	Reading	9. 6.08A
					"Knowledgepool" (Cancelled 1.8.07 by CAA)		
G-BYOV	Cyclone Airsports Pegasus Quantum 15-912 7554			17. 8.99	Microlight Hire Ltd	Wickenby	14.11.07P
					(Cancelled 3. 1.08 by CAA)		
G-BYOY	Canadair CL-30 (T-33AN) Silver Star Mk.3	N36TH	8. 2.00	K K Gerstorfer	North Weald	
		T33-231	N333DV, N134AT, N10018, N134AT, RCAF 21231				
					(Cancelled 8. 6.05 by CAA: noted as "N36TH" in USAF c/s 6.07)		
G-BYYK	Boeing 737-229C	20916	OO-SDK	11. 1.00	European Aviation Air Charter Ltd	Bournemouth	
					(Cancelled 24. 4.06 as PWFU: fuselage stored as "OO- SDK" 1.07)		
G-BZAJ	WSK PZL-110 Koliber 160A	04990082	SP-WGK	10. 2.00	Koliber (No1) Ltd	North Weald	
			(Crashed Clayton 26.10.05 with extensive damage: cancelled 9. 5.06 as destroyed: fuselage dumped 6.07 as "AJ")				
G-BZBD	Westland Scout AH.1	F 9638	XT632	7. 3.00	Military Helicopters Ltd	North Weald	10. 7.01P
					(Cancelled 5.10.00 as PWFU: to Kennet Aviation for spares or restoration 1.06)		
G-BZDT	Maule MXT-7-180 Super Rocket	14099C		11. 8.00	Strongcrew Ltd	East Winch	2 .8.06
					(Cancelled 1.12.05 as destroyed: noted wrecked 8.06)		
G-BZFG	Sky 105-24 Balloon (Hot Air)	4842		27. 4.00	Virgin Airship and Balloon CompanyLtd	Telford	28. 4.03A
					(Cancelled 12.11.03 as PWFU: inflated 4.06)		
G-BZRC	de Havilland DH.115 Vampire T 11	15143	WZ584	26. 3.01	(D Copley)	Armthorpe, Doncaster	
					(Cancelled 22. 2.05 by CAA: dismantled as "WZ584:K" 12.05)		
G-BZRD	de Havilland DH.115 Vampire T 11	15687	XH313	27. 3.01	(D Copley)	(Godstone, Surrey)	
					(Dismantled as "XH313:E" 1.05: cancelled 22. 2.05 by CAA)		
G-BZRE	Hunting Percival P 56 Provost T 1	PAC/F/265	7689M?	15. 5.01	(Parkhouse Aviation)	Bournemouth	
			WW450		*(Cancelled 22. 2.05 by CAA: fuselage stored as "WW421:P-B" 2007*		
	(Officially regd with c/n PAC/F/234 as fitted with wings from 7688M? ex WW421)						
G-BZRF	Hunting Percival P 56 Provost T 1	PAC/F/062	7698M	15. 5.01	(Parkhouse Aviation)	Exeter	
			WV499		*(Cancelled 22. 2.05 by CAA: dismantled as "WV499:P-G" 1.07)*		
G-BZSR	Hawker Hunter T 7	41H-693832	A2617	15. 2.01	Stick and Rudder Aviation Ltd	(Meetkerke, Belgium)	
			XL601		*(On rebuild 2002 in red and white livery of 4 FTS: cancelled 14. 5.04 as WFU)*		
G-BZTU	Mainair Blade 912	1272-0201-7-W1066		8. 2.01	I Johnson	Ellough, Beccles	24. 3.05P
			(Had accident Waldringfield, Suffolk 31. 5.04 and cancelled 25.11.04 as destroyed: noted 12.04)				
G-BZVL	Aero-Vodochody L-39C Albatros	730932	ES-YLB	22. 4.02	Rocket Seat Ltd	Alton	25. 4.03P
			Soviet AF		*(Cancelled 8. 1.03 as PWFU: noted Air Salvage International 8.07)*		
G-BZWR	Mainair Rapier	1275-0301-7-W1070		7. 3.01	R J Swann	Carlisle	24. 8.04P
					(Cancelled 22. 9.04 by CAA: noted 2.07)		
G-CBCU	BAe.Harrier GR.3	FL/41H-0250295	ZD668	9.11.01	Y Dumortier Hannants Model Warehouse, Oulton Broad		
	(C/n officially quoted as 41H-0250295)				*(Cancelled 14. 3.05 as sold to USA: noted 2.07)*		
G-CBFD	Westland Gazelle HT.Mk.2	1158	XW887	24.10.01	Aerocars Ltd	Deer Park Farm, Babcary	20.12.04P
					(Cancelled 4. 8.04 by CAA: cab and frame noted 12.07)		
G-CBGK	BAe.Harrier GR.3	FL/41H-0150252	9220M	13.12.01	Y Dumortier Hannants Model Warehouse, Oulton Broad		
	(C/n officially quoted as 41H-712218)		XZ995		*(Cancelled 14. 3.05 as sold to USA: noted 2.07)*		
G-CCBI	Raj Hamsa X'Air R100(2)	600		4. 2.03	H Adams	Kirkbride	14. 9.06P
	(Built H Adams - pr.no.BMAA/HB/192)				*(Cancelled 6. 3.06 by CAA)*		

G-CCGJ	Raj Hamsa X'Air 582(6)		604		30. 6.03	M C Rangeley North Coates
	(Built M C Rangeley - pr.no.BMAA/HB/188)					(Noted 4.04: cancelled 1. 7.04 as WFU - no PtoF issued)
G-CCJS	Reality Easy Raider		0002		2. 9.03	K Wright Andreas, Isle of Man
	(Built K Wright - pr.no.BMAA/HB/293)					(Noted 10.07: cancelled 7. 1.08 by CAA)
G-CCNL	Raj Hamsa X'Air Falcon 133(1)		909		24.12.03	G A J Salter Longacre Farm, Sandy 20. 7.06P
	(Built S Rance and A Davis - pr.no.BMAA/HB/326)					(Cancelled 31. 7.06 by CAA) (Noted 9,06)
G-CCOA	Scottish Aviation Bulldog Series 120/122		Ghana AF G-111	4. 9.96		Cranfield University (Isle of Wight)
		BH120/375	G-BCUU			(Damaged Cranfield 22. 8.01: cancelled 11. 6.02 as WFU)
	(Fuselage noted 2004 as "G-AXEH" to represent prototype Bulldog for proposed Beagle museum)					
G-CDCZ	Mainair Pegasus Quantum 15-912		8072		1.10.04	Light Flight Ltd Lower Mountpleasant Farm, Chatteris 3.10.06P
						(Cancelled - sold as ZU- ECB 26. 1.06: noted as "G-CDCZ" 3.06)
G-CEXP	Handley Page HPR.7 Dart Herald 209		195	I-ZERC	29.10.87	British Airports Authority London Gatwick 7.11.96T
				G-BFRJ, 4X-AHO		(WFU 8.3.96: cancelled 22. 3.96 by CAA: stored 10,05)
G-CFLY	Cessna 172F		17252635	PH-SNO	25. 8.78	I Hughes and B T Williams tr Cee-Fly Blackpool 13. 7.95
				N8731U		(Cancelled 5. 6.95 by CAA: stored 10.07)
G-CHTT	Varga 2150A Kachina		VAC-162-80		7. 9.84	H W Hall Southend 6. 9.87
	(Damaged near Hatherleigh, Devon 27. 4.86 and cancelled 9. 8.94 by CAA: wreck stored dismantled 2.08)					
G-CONV	Convair 440-54 Metropolitan		484	CS-TML	19. 7.01	Atlantic Air Transport Ltd Coventry
	(Built General Dynamics Corporation)			N357SA, N28KE, N28KA, N4402		
	(Atlantic c/s with Air Atlantique titles - minus engines - in open store 6.06: cancelled 20.12.06 as WFU)					
G-DADS	Hughes 369HS		22-0369S	N888SS	11. 6.90	Executive Aviation Services Ltd Sywell 2. 8.02T
	(Hughes 500)			N9101F		(Cancelled 31.10.02 as destroyed : noted stored 7.07)
G-DAJW	K & S Jungster I		PFA 1517		20.11.78	A J Walters (Tranent)
						(Cancelled 2. 9.91 by CAA: reported as stored 2004)
G-DESS	Mooney M 20J Model 201		24-1272	N11598	20.10.87	R M Hitchin Stock 18. 5.06
	(Badly damaged landing 14.11.04 Wadswick Manor Farm, Corsham : cancelled 17. 3.05 as destroyed: wreckage noted 1.07)					
G-DKGF	Viking Dragonfly Mk.1	PFA 139-10898			16.10.86	P C Dowbor Enstone
	(Built K G Fathers) (Volkswagen 1834)					(Cancelled 29. 3.01 by CAA: derelict 5.05)
G-DNHI	Agusta A109A		7154	N754AM	11. 4.05	DNH Helicopters Ltd Redhill 13. 6.08E
				I-AVJJ, I-CELB, N33SV, N59340, (N43BL), N59340 (Cancelled 7. 6.07 by CAA)		
G-DRCI	Avtech Jabiru UL		xxxx		20. 9.04	D R Calo (Chipperfield, Kings Langley)
	(Built D R Calo - pr.no.PFA 274A-14301)					(Cancelled 19. 1.05 by CAA no PtoF yet issued)
G-ECAT	Fokker F-27 Friendship 500		10672	G-JEAI	14. 4.00	Euroceltic Airways Ltd Strandhill, Sligo, County Sligo 16.12.02T
				VH-EWZ, PH-EXS		
	(Skidded off end of runway landing in heavy rain Sligo 3.11.02, badly danaged and cancelled 12. 8.03 by CAA: fuselage with Fire Service 6.07)					
G-EESE	Cessna U206G Stationair 6		U20603883	OO-DMA	28. 2.85	D M Penny tr Wild Geese School of Adventure Flying
				N7344C		Movenis, Coleraine 1. 4.91
	(Crashed Magilligan, County Londonderry 31.12.88: cancelled 17. 7.90 as destroyed: fuselage noted 8.06)					
G-EGGG	Lindstrand LBL 90A Balloon (Hot Air)		269		14. 6.95	S M Edwards Houston. Texas, US
	(Humpty Dumpty shape)					(Cancelled 26.2.97 by CAA: to N912HD 5.97: active Albuquerque, NM, US 10.03 as "G-EGGG")
G-EIIR	Cameron N-77 Balloon (Hot Air)		358		16.11.77	D V Howard Bath 14. 5.93A
						(Cancelled by CAA 23.10.01: stored 1.07)
G-EMIL	Messerschmitt Bf109E-3		1983	Luftwaffe 1983?	11.12.03	G R Lacey Fairoaks
	(Fuselage complete with wings and engine work under way 2007: cancelled 11.1.07 by CAA)					
G-FANC	Fairchild 24R-46 Argus		R46-347	N77647	16.10.89	A T Fines Priory Farm, Tibenham 26. 5.03T
				NC77647		(Cancelled 30. 7.03 by CAA after arson attack Felthorpe 18. 2.03: fuselage noted 2007)
G-FAYE	Reims Cessna F150M		F15001252	PH-VSK	24. 1.80	Cheshire Air Training Services Ltd Sibson 29. 7.07T
						(Withdrawn for spares 8.06: cancelled 8.1.07 by CAA: noted 7.07)
G-FBIX	de Havilland DH.100 Vampire FB.9		22100	7705M	24. 7.91	D G Jones Bournemouth
				WL505		(Cancelled 17. 5.05 by CAA: stored unmarked in Aviation Museum 1.07)
G-FISK	Pazmany PL-4A	PFA 017-10129			14.12.88	K S Woodard Little Snoring 11. 4.96P
	(Built K S Woodard) (Volkswagen 1834)					(Cancelled 8.11.00 by CAA: noted stored 8.05)
G-FLAP	Cessna A152 Aerobat		A1520856	G-BHJB	14. 6.02	JN Leasing Ltd Sandtoft 18. 9.08E
				N4662A		(Cancelled 20.10.06 by CAA)
G-FLTY	Embraer EMB-110P1 Bandeirante		110215	G-ZUSS	28. 8.92	Skydrift Ltd Southend 5. 8.05T
				G-REGA, N711NH, PT-GMH		(Cancelled 11. 4.06 by CAA: in open store, engineless 1.08)
G-FTAX	Cessna 421C Golden Eagle		421C0308	N8363G	23. 8.84	Gold Air International Ltd Cambridge 16. 5.01T
				G-BFFM, N8363G		(Cancelled 8. 7.03 as WFU: noted in open store minus various parts 9.03)
G-FUJI	Fuji FA.200-180 Aero Subaru		FA200-156	D-EMMI	14. 9.79	R Gizzi Glebe Farm, Stockton 29. 6.92
						(Damaged landing in field Newton, Powys 5. 5.92: cancelled 1.3.94 as WFU: noted 9.06)
G-FXII	Vickers Supermarine 366 Spitfire F XIIE		EN224		4.12.89	(P R Arnold) Not known
		6S/197707				(Cancelled 9. 5.02 as temporarily WFU: in store 2006)
G-FYAP	Williams Mk.2 Balloon (Minimum Lift)	MDW-03			6. 1.82	G E Clarke Luton
						(Cancelled 8.12.88 by CAA: extant 5.07))
G-FYBB	Chown Portswood Mk.16 Balloon (Minimum Lift)				15. 1.82	A P Chown Southampton
		ASK-151				(Cancelled 15.10.84 as PFU: extant 5.07)
G-FYBO	Chown Osprey Mk.4B Balloon (Minimum Lift)				29. 1.82	D Eaves Southampton
		AKC-94				(Cancelled 27.10.88 as PWFU: extant 5.07)
G-FYBP	Eaves European E 84PW Balloon (Minimum Lift)				29. 1.82	D Eaves Southampton
		S 20				(Cancelled 30.11.01 as PWFU: extant 5.07)
G-FYBX	Chown Portswood Mk.16 Balloon (Minimum Lift)				1. 2.82	I Chadwick Partridge Green, Horsham
		ASK-161				(Cancelled 21. 4.98 as PWFU: extant 5.07)
G-FYCT	Solent Osprey Mk.4D Balloon (Minimum Lift)				18. 2.82	S T Wallbank Luton
		ASK-277				(Cancelled 2.12.93 by CAA: extant 5.07)
G-FYDB	Eaves European E 84EL Euroliner Balloon (Minimum Lift)				17. 3.82	D Eaves Southampton
		S 23				(Cancelled 27.10.88 as PWFU: extant 5.07)
G-FYDC	Eaves European EDH.1 Balloon (Minimum Lift)				17. 3.82	D Eaves and H W Davies Southampton
		S 24				(Cancelled 2. 1.02 as PWFU: extant 5.07)
G-FYDG	Solent Osprey Mk.4D Balloon (Minimum Lift)				29. 3.82	M D Williams Houghton Regis, Dunstable
		ASK-270				(Cancelled 8.11.88 as PWFU: extant 5.07)
G-FYDU	Solent Osprey Mk-4D Balloon (Minimum Lift)				23. 4.82	J R Moody Sandown, Isle of Wight
		ASK-267				(Cancelled 18.10.88 as PWFU: extant 5.07)
G-FYFA	Eaves European E 84LD Balloon (Minimum Lift)				12.10.82	D Goddard and D Eaves Southampton
		S 26				(Cancelled 2. 1.02 as PWFU: extant 5.07)

G-FYFG	Eaves European E 84DE Balloon (Minimum Lift)	S 28			26.11.82	D Eaves	Southampton	
	(Cancelled 30.11.01 as PWFU: extant 5.07)							
G-FYFH	Eaves European E 84DS Balloon (Minimum Lift)	S 30			26.11.82	D Eaves	Southampton	
	(Cancelled 30.11.01 as PWFU: extant 5.07)							
G-FYGH	Busby Buz-B20N Balloon (Minimum Lift)	DSD-01N			8. 6.89	D P Busby	Southampton	
	(Cancelled 18.10.95 by CAA: extant 5.07)							
G-GCJL	British Aerospace Jetstream Series 4100	41001			5. 2.91	BAE Systems (Operations) Ltd	Humberside	29. 4.95S
	(Cancelled 15.11.02 as WFU: stored 6.05)							
G-GCNZ	Cessna 150M Commuter	15075933	C-GCNZ		8.11.88	Firecrest Aviation Ltd	Elstree	27. 3.98T
	(Cancelled 8. 6.99 as destroyed: fuselage noted 2.04)							
G-GEGE	Robinson R-22 Beta	2994			19.10.99	S and C Hewgill tr CSL International		
	(Cancelled 2. 7.01 by CAA) Wellesbourne Mountford							28.10.02T
	(Stored in damaged condition 6.04)							
G-GRAY	Cessna 172N Skyhawk II	17272375	N4859D		3.12.79	Truman Aviation Ltd	Tollerton	13. 2.95
	(Damaged ditching Firth of Forth, Musslelurgh 2. 4.93: cancelled 27. 9.00 as WFU: stored 10.05)							
G-GREG	CEA Jodel DR.220 2+2	47	F-BOKR		3.10.84	J T Wilson	Crosland Moor	19. 2.91
	(Cancelled 1. 4.97 by CAA: noted 9.07)							
G-HEAD	Colt Flying Head Balloon (Hot Air)	304			18. 8.81	E K Nyberg	(Stockholm, Sweden)	
	(Cancelled 4.12.01 by CAA: extant 5.07)							
G-HMES	Piper PA-28-161 Warrior II	28-8126070	OY-CSN N8471N		21. 4.89	Cleveland Flying Scholl Ltd	Bagby	20. 8.01T
	(Cancelled. 5.5.04 as wfu/: noted dismantled 2.08)							
G-IBRO	Reims Cessna F152	F15201957	EI-BRO		11.10.95	East Midlands Aircraft Hire Ltd	Leicester	14. 3.05T
	(Engine failed during landing 1 m N Leicester 3. 3.05 and substantially damaged: cancelled 29. 6.05 as destroyed: bare fuselage and wings noted 10.07)							
G-IJMI	Extra EA.300/L	1193			16. 2.05	Aerobatiques LLP	Hawarden	31. 3.08E
	(Cancelled 21. 1.08 by CAA)							
G-IOIT	Lockheed L1011-385-1 Tristar 200	193N-1145	G-CEAP SE-DPM, G-BEAL		6. 5.98	Classic Airways Ltd	London Stansted	
	(Cancelled 1.10.98 by CAA: noted 8.06)							
G-IXTI	Extra EA.300/L	121			15. 9.00	J C Merry	(East Coker, Yeovil)	22.10.06T
	(Cancelled 12. 9.05 by CAA)							
G-JABO	WAR Focke-Wulf FW190-A3 replica				23. 8.01	S P Taylor	Clench Common	
	(Built S P Taylor) PFA 081-11786					*(Cancelled 19. 7.07 by CAA: noted 1.08)*			
G-JEAT	British Aerospace BAe 146 Series 100	E1071	N171TR J8-VBB, G-BVUY, B-2706, G-5-071		11.10.96	Jersey European Airways (UK) Ltd	Exeter	23.10.05T
				(Cancelled 4. 8.04 as WFU: on fire dump 1.07)				
G-JSCL	Rans S-10 Sakota	1289.075			12. 4.90	D L Davies	Emlyns Field, Rhuallt	
	(Built J D Bedford - pr.no PFA 194-11781)					*(Crashed Emlyns Field 16. 7.91: cancelled 16.12.97 as WFU: remains noted 4.04)*			
G-KNOT	Hunting Percival P 84 Jet Provost T 3A	PAC/W/13893	G-BVEG XN629		9. 6.99	R S Partridge-Hicks	North Weald	10.10.07P
				(Cancelled 21. 6.07 as WFU: noded as "XN629:49" in RAF c/s 6.07)				
G-LEZE	Rutan LongEz	PFA 074A-10702			31. 3.82	K G M Loyal, A J Draper, J R J Giesler and C McGeachy		
	(Built K G M Loyal) (Wilksch Diesel)					*(Cancelled 22. 9.03 by CAA: on rebuild 2006)* Nympsfield			5.11.01P
G-LOFA	Lockheed L188CF Electra	2002	N359Q F-OGST, N359AC, TI-LRM, N359AC, HC-AVX, N359AC, VH-ECA		10. 2.94	Atlantic Air Transport Ltd	Coventry	9. 2.00T
				(Cancelled 29. 7.98 as WFU: with Fire Section 11.02)				
G-LOFG	Lockheed L188C Electra	1116	LN-FOL (2) N669F, N404GN, N6126A		21. 6.00	Atlantic Air Transport Ltd	Coventry	
	(Cancelled 16.6.04 as destroyed: airframe, minus starboard outer wing, on fire dump as "LN-FOL" 6.06:							
G-LOWE	Monnett Sonerai I	367	16.11.78			R M Kinch	Shenington	12. 8.97P
	(Built J A Lowe - pr.no.PFA 15-10344) (Volkswagen 1834)					*(Cancelled 16. 9.97 as Temporarily WFU: noted 3.06)*			
G-LYDD	Piper PA-31 Turbo Navajo	31-537	N6796L		8. 5.89	Janes Aviation Ltd	Blackpool	12. 5.89T
				(Damaged Lydd 17. 7.91: cancelled 30. 3.93 as WFU: fuselage on fire dump 11.05)				
G-MALK	Reims Cessna F172N Skyhawk II	F17201886	PH-SVS PH-AXF (3)		1. 7.81	Edinburgh Airport Fire Service	Edinburgh	
				(Crashed near Lochgilphead 23. 7.97: cancelled 23.12.97 as destroyed: fuselage for instructional use 2.06)				
G-MANT	Cessna 210L Centurion II	21060970	G-MAXY N550SV		22. 5.85	Sea-Front Crazee Golf	Great Yarmouth	2.10.94
				(Damaged near Oxford 16. 2.92: cancelled 3. 4.92 by CAA: noted 9.05)				
G-MAPS	Sky Flying Map SS Balloon (Hot Air)	105			20. 7.98	The Balloon Advertising Company Ltd	Petworth	28. 2.01A
	"OS Map" *(Cancelled 31. 7.01 as WFU: on loan to Balloon Preservation Group)*							
G-MBFS	American Aerolights Eagle	RF-01			19.11.81	M J Aubrey	Kington, Hereford	
	(Fuji-Robin EC-25-PS)					*(Cancelled 24. 5.90 as WFU: noted 2002)*			
G-MBJX	Hiway Skytrike I/Hiway Super Scorpion						East Fortune, Scotland	
G-MBLK	Ultrasports Tri-Pacer/Southdown Lightning DS	DS-390			18. 2.82	M J Aubrey	Kington, Hereford	
	(Fuji-Robin EC-44)					*(Cancelled 23. 6.97 as WFU: noted 2002).*			
G-MBPM	Eurowing Goldwing						East Fortune, Scotland	
G-MBTG	Mainair Gemini/Southdown Sprint	064-19482 & P 431			26. 4.82	D M Pearson	Roddige	15.10.94P
	(Originally regd as Mainair Tri-Flyer Dual)					*(Cancelled 31. 3.00 by CAA: noted 4.06)*			
G-MBUE	MBA Tiger Cub 440						Newark, Nottinghamshire	
G-MBWE	American Aerolights Eagle	2937			18. 5.82	M J Aubrey	Kington, Hereford	
	(Fuji-Robin EC-25-PS)					*(Cancelled 24. 3.99 as WFU: noted 2002)*			
G-MBWH	Jordan Duet Series 1	D82001			20. 5.82	Designability Ltd	Kemble	
	(Cancelled 22. 3.02 as WFU: noted 2004)							
G-MBWI	Lafayette Hi-Nuski Mk.1	30680			8. 6.82	M J Aubrey	Kington, Hereford	
	(Cancelled 13. 6.90 as WFU: noted 11.03)							
G-MBYH	Maxair Hummer	001			4. 6.82	T T Parr	Doynton	31.12.87P
	(Cancelled 19. 5.97 by CAA: noted derelict 2.03)							
G-MBYK	Huntair Pathfinder Mk.1	012			4. 6.82	R C Barnett	Letterkenny, County Donegal	17. 6.97P
	(Cancelled 30. 5.01 by CAA: noted 4.04)							
G-MESS	SNCAN 1101 Noralpha	87	F-BEEV F-WZBI, French AF 87		21. 5.03	G Spooner	Earls Colne	
				(Cancelled 25. 1.07 as WFU: noted dismantled 2007)				
G-METE	Gloster Meteor F8						Temora, New South Wales, Australia	
G-MGFO	Pegasus Quantum 15	7410			24. 3.98	A Gulliver	Clench Common	19. 3.00P
	(Cancelled 10. 5.99 as WFU: stored 5.06)							
G-MHBD	Cameron O-105 Balloon (Hot Air)	1021			23. 2.84	P A Sweatman	Birmingham	25. 7.90A
	(Dawsons Toys titles) (Cancelled as WFU 17. 4.98: extant 5.07)							
G-MIKS	Robinson R44 Clipper II	10314			15. 4.04	Direct Timber Ltd	(Coalville)	6. 5.07T
	(Cancelled 11.10.07 by CAA)							

G-MJAL	Wheeler Scout Mk.III/3/R	0433 R/3	18. 6.82	G W Wickington	(Hamble, Southampton)	
	(Built Ron Wheeler Aircraft Sales Proprietary)			(Cancelled 22. 8.00 by CAA: displayed Popham 5.04)		
G-MJBN	American Aerolights Eagle Rainbow	3132		(A Smith)	Sibsey	
				(Cancelled 6. 9.94 by CAA: stored 1.07)		
G-MJBT	Eipper Quicksilver MX II	DJ/NBII & 3662	30. 6.82	G A Barclay	Letterkenny, County Donegal	X
	(Cuyana 430R)			(Cancelled 24. 1.95 by CAA: noted 4.04)		
G-MJCF	Maxair Hummer	SMC-01	5. 7.82	R G Banfield	Doynton	X
	(Fuji-Robin EC-25-PS)			(Cancelled 24. 1.95 by CAA: noted derelict 2.03)		
G-MJDH	Huntair Pathfinder Mk.1	015	9. 7.82	T Mahmood	Insch	12. 8.01P
	(Fuji-Robin EC-44-PM)			(Cancelled 10. 6.02 as WFU: noted wrecked 3.07)		
G-MJLK	Squires Dragonfly 250-II	D 105	10. 9.82	G Carter	Breighton	
	(Built G A Squires)			(Cancelled 18. 4.90 as WFU: wreck stored 12.07)		
G-MJMB	Weedhopper JC-24	846	23. 9.82	M J Aubrey	Kington, Hereford	
	(Chotia 460)			(Cancelled 7. 9.94 by CAA: noted 2002)		
G-MJOI	Ultrasports Tri-Pacer/Hiway Demon	817003	1.11.82	S J Walker	Biggin Hill	
				(Cancelled 1.11.89 as WFU: noted 6.05)		
G-MJVR	Ultrasports Panther/Flexiform Dual Striker LAH		20. 4.83	D J Evans	Longacre Farm, Sandy	11. 6.93P
	(Fuji-Robin EC-44-PM) (Originally regd as a Tripacer)			(Cancelled 28.11.95 by CAA: Trike noted 7.03)		
G-MJXD	MBA Tiger Cub 440	011/061	16. 5.83	(W L Rogers)	Halwell	
				(Cancelled 3. 4.02 as WFU: noted 5.05)		
G-MJXF	MBA Tiger Cub 440	EJH-01	1. 6.83	N P Day	Jackrells Farm, Southwater	
				(Cancelled 5. 9.94 by CAA: stored 8.03)		
G-MJYE	Popplewell Trike/Southdown Lightning	GP-02	1. 6.83	J A Hindley Lower Mountpleasant Farm, Chatteris		X
	(Fuji-Robin EC-44-PM)			(Cancelled 4.10.90 as destroyed: wreck noted 5.05)		
G-MMAE	Dragon Light Aircraft Dragon Series 200	005	7. 9.82	P J Sheehy and K S Matcham	Lee-on-Solent	1. 5.08P
	(Fuji-Robin EC-44-PM)			(Cancelled 27.10.07 by CAA)		
G-MMAO	Southdown Puma Sprint X	HS.549	28.12.83	P A Kershaw	Ince Blundell	14. 3.00P
				(Cancelled 31. 5.01 by CAA: stored 6.03)		
G-MMBE	MBA Tiger Cub 440	SO.74	30. 6.83	R W Pearce and R J B Jordan		
				(Alderley Edge and Hest Bank, Lancaster)		
				(Cancelled 4. 2.92 by CAA: noted 2007)		
G-MMFZ	Striplin (AES) Skyranger	HAW-01	18.11.83	M J Aubrey	Kington, Hereford	
	(Cuyana 430)			(Cancelled 3.10.01.by CAA: noted 2002)		
G-MMHG	Hiway Skytrike 250/Solar Wings Storm DRB-01		13.12.83	M J Aubrey	Kington, Hereford	
	(Fuji-Robin EC-25-PM)			(Cancelled 22. 9.93 by CAA: noted 2002)		
G-MMIH	MBA Tiger Cub 440	SO.130	25. 4.84	R A Davis	Kemble	19. 8.93P
				(Cancelled 3. 3.05 by CAA: noted 3.06)		
G-MMKY	Jordan Duet Series 1	CHS-01	19. 3.84	C H Smith	Field Farm, Oakley	
	(Rotax 503)			(Cancelled 1. 9.95 by CAA: fuselage stored 1.06)		
G-MMLV	Southdown Puma 330/Lightning	P3-84-164	29.11.84	C L Newcombe	RNAS Yeovilton	31. 5.97P
	(Officially regd as Southdown Lightning/Tri-Pacer) (Fuji-Robin EC-34-PM)			(Cancelled 30. 4.01 by CAA as PWFU: noted 3.06)		
	(C/n also quoted as NOP 3-84-164)					
G-MMNV	Weedhopper JC-24	NLR-01	17. 4.84	N L Rice	Strathaven	
				(Cancelled 4. 6.90 as WFU: noted 6.06)		
G-MMOG	Huntair Pathfinder Mk.I	011	9. 5.84	E C Jarvis	Letterkenny, County Donegal	5. 5.95P
				(Cancelled 26. 7.95 on sale to Ireland: noted 4.04)		
G-MMPI	Pterodactyl Ptraveler	108	23. 5.84	M J Aubrey	Kington, Hereford	
	(Fuji-Robin EC-25)			(Cancelled 24. 8.94 as WFU: noted 2002)		
G-MMPJ	Mainair Gemini/Southdown Sprint		10. 8.84	Mainair Ltd	Rochdale	
	(Orig regd as Tri-Flyer 440) MSB-01, 264-884-2 & P 567			(Cancelled 24. 4.92 by CAA: stored 12.04)		
G-MMPR	Dragon Light Aircraft Dragon Series 150	0011	18. 4.83	P N B Rosenfeld	Letterkenny, County Donegal	28. 2.07P
				(Cancelled 8.10.93 by CAA: noted 4.04)		
G-MMUL	Ward Elf	E-47	16.10.84	N H Ponsford	Breighton	
	(Built M Ward)			(Cancelled 12. 4.89 by CAA: noted 12.07)		
G-MMUT	Mainair Gemini Flash II	235-484-2 -W04	5.10.84	S C Briggs	Rochdale	5. 7.01P
	(Fuji-Robin EC-44-PM) (Original c/n 62-484-2-W04)			(Cancelled as PWFU 14. 1.05: noted 11.06 for trials)		
	(Fitted with new Trike first used on G-MMFC (3) and Sailwing c/n W73 6.98 - also see G-MNAC)					
G-MMVP	Mainair Gemini Flash II	76-1284-2-W12	17.12.84	S C McGowan	Longacre Farm, Sandy	24. 1.05P
	(Fuji-Robin EC-44-PM)			(Cancelled 7. 9.04 by CAA: noted 7.05)		
G-MMYZ	Southdown Puma Sprint	SN1231/0034	28. 2.85	M Bodill	Roddige	19. 2.99P
	(Rotax 447)			(Damaged in gales Roddige 1.98: cancelled 31. 5.01 by CAA: Trike noted in poor state 1.04)		
G-MMZB	Mainair Gemini Flash	319-685-3-W58	4. 3.85	M A Nolan	(Eccleston, Chorley)	23. 5.02P
	(Fuji-Robin EC-44-PM)			(Cancelled 24. 2.05 by CAA: engineless wreck noted 6.07)		
G-MMZZ	Maxair Hummer	0010	8. 4.82	M J Aubrey	Kington, Hereford	
	(Fuji-Robin EC-25-)			(Cancelled 12. 6.00 by CAA: noted 2002)		
G-MNAK	Solar Wings Panther XL-S	SW-WA-1005	15. 5.85	F J McVey	Insch	15. 8.04P
		(Trike c/n SW-T/A-1005)		(Cancelled 16. 1.04 as WFU)		
G-MNBR	Mainair Gemini Flash	345-985-3-W79	15. 5.85	N A P Gregory	Long Marston	5. 2.94P
	(Rotax 447)			(Cancelled 31. 5.00 by CAA: stored 7.05)		
G-MNBW	Mainair Gemini Flash	332-685-3-W69	15. 5.85	G A Brown and N S Brotherton	Weston Zoyland	10. 9.03P
	(Rotax 447) (C/n now SW-WF-0005-W95 ex G-MNJI)			(Cancelled 21. 6.04 by CAA)		
G-MNFA	Mainair Tri-Flyer/Solar Wings Typhoon		29.12.83	R S Lee Mill Farm, Hughley, Much Wenlock		10.10.92P
	(Trike ex G-MJFA) DRJ-01 & GWW-01			(Cancelled 4. 5.01 by CAA: noted 9.04)		
G-MNFX	Southdown Puma Sprint	SN1231/0079	14. 8.85	A M Shaw	(Eccleston, Chorley)	6. 9.04P
	(Rotax 447)			(Cancelled 15. 2.05 as PWFU: engineless wreck noted 6.07)		
G-MNGO	Hiway Skytrike/Solar Wings Storm	21U8	5. 9.85	S Adams	(Gaddesbry)	
				(Cancelled 20. 3.89 by CAA: stored 2005)		
G-MNJO	Solar Wings Pegasus Flash	SW-WF-0011	19.11.85	S Clarke	Swinford, Rugby	21. 7.07P
	(Trike c/n SW-TB-1035 & Mainair Sailwing c/n W126)			(Cancelled 12. 4.07 by CAA)		
G-MNKN	Wheeler Scout Mk.III/3/R	410	6. 1.86	M J Aubrey	Kington, Hereford	
	(Built Skycraft (UK) Ltd) (Fuji-Robin EC-25)			(Cancelled 19. 2.99 as WFU: noted 2002)		
G-MNME	Hiway Skytrike/Demon WTP-01 & 3535009		12. 2.86	M J Aubrey	Kington, Hereford	10. 6.93
	(Rotax 377)			(Cancelled 28. 4.00 by CAA: noted 2002) .		

G-MNMN	Medway Hybred 44XLR	8286/16	7. 3.86	D S Blofeld	Stoke, Isle of Grain	31. 8.06P
				(Cancelled 29. 9.07 by CAA)		
G-MNMO	Mainair Gemini Flash II	398-186-4-W141	27. 2.86	P D Hawkesworth and G Wigglesworth		
	(Rotax 447)				Bere Alston, Yelverton	28. 5.99P
				(Cancelled 10. 3.00 by CAA: Trike noted 11.06)		
G-MNNL	Mainair Gemini Flash II	429-486-4-W186	28. 2.86	D Wilson	Oxton, Nottingham	21.11.05P
				(Noted 9.07: cancelled 13.11.07 by CAA)		
G-MNTS	Mainair Gemini Flash II	450-886-4-W227	3. 4.86	C G Lomas	(Brotherton, Boston)	16. 1.02P
	(Rotax 462)			*(New owner 3.07: cancelled 18. 9.07 by CAA)*		
G-MNYV	Solar Wings Pegasus XL-R/Se	SW-WA-1093	11. 9.86	(B J Green)	Sywell	30.11.99P
	(Trike c/n SW-TB-1101)			*(Cancelled 23. 8.02 by CAA: noted 2.07)*		
G-MOSI	de Havilland DH.98 Mosquito TT.35			Dayton, Ohio, US		
G-MTBA	Solar Wings Pegasus XL-R	SW-WA-1115	27.10.86	R J W Franklin and M C Buffery	Redlands, Swindon	24. 6.93P
	(Trike c/n SW-TB-1120)			*(Cancelled 19. 4.05 by CAA: noted as wreck 8.05)*		
G-MTBT	Aerotech MW.5B Sorcerer	SR102-R440B-05	10. 4.87	N W Finn-Kelcey	Weston Underwood, Olney	19. 5.92P
	(Fuji-Robin EC-44-PM) *(pr.no BMAA/HB/027 allocated for rebuild after accident 12.10.91 using wings of G-MWGI (qv)*					
				(Cancelled 7. 8.96 by CAA: noted 9.07)		
G-MTBW	Mainair Gemini Flash II	520-187-5-W322	6.11.86	J Sharman	Otherton, Cannock	21. 9.97P
				(Cancelled 23. 2.98 by CAA: noted 7.05)		
G-MTCW	Mainair Gemini Flash II	502-1186-4-W304	5. 1.87	E W Hughes	(Eccleston, Chorley)	21. 4.07P
	(Rotax 462)			*(Cancelled 19.12.06 by CAA: noted 6.07)*		
G-MTDH	Solar Wings Pegasus XL-R	SW-WA-1131	22. 1.87	J Packman	Long Marston	23. 1.07P
	(Trike c/n SW-TB-1133) (Rebuilt 5.04 with Sailwing c/n SW-WA-1005 ex G-MNAK) (Cancelled 29.10.06 by CAA)					
G-MTDV	Solar Wings Pegasus XL-R	SW-WA-1136	3. 2.87	S J Adcock	Rufforth	28. 8.94P
				(Cancelled 8. 6.00 by CAA: noted 11.07))		
G-MTEI	Mainair Gemini Flash II	440-287-5-W269	18. 2.87	B F Levy and R E Symonds		
					(Guildford and Send, Woking)	26. 1.08P
				(Cancelled 25. 2.08 by CAA)		
G-MTEJ	Mainair Gemini Flash II	522-387-5-W277	18. 2.87	M Atkinson	Tarn Farm, Cockerham	17. 3.06P
	(Rotax 462)			*(Noted 11.06: cancelled 21. 2.07 as wfu)*		
G-MTSO	Solar Wings Pegasus XL-R/Se	SW-WA-1281	14.12.87	P Wibberley	(Chesterfield)	20. 5.03P
	(Trike c/n SW-TB-1279)			*(Cancelled 4. 5.04 as WFU)*		
G-MTTL	Ultrasports Tri-Pacer 330/Excalibur	EXS-872	23. 3.88	M J Aubrey	Kington, Hereford	7. 9.92P
	(Fuji-Robin EC-34-PM)			*(Cancelled 20.11.95 by CAA: noted 2002)*		
G-MTUE	Thruster TST Mk.1	8018-TST-053	15. 1.88	J P McVitty	Gort, Derrykee	11. 6.94P
				(Cancelled 23. 5.00 by CAA: noted 7.04)		
G-MTOS	Solar Wings Pegasus XL-R	SW-WA-1243	9.10.87	C McKay	Perth	15.12.07P
	(Trike c/n SW-TB-1238)			*(Cancelled 15. 3.07 as PWFU)*		
G-MTXH	Solar Wings Pegasus XL-Q	SW-WQ-0030	11. 3.88	J Rhodes	Church Farm, Askern	21. 7.97P
	(Rotax 447)	*(Trike c/n SW-TB-1328)*		*(Cancelled 12. 5.05 by CAA: wing only noted 9.07)*		
G-MVDR	Aerial Arts Chaser S 447	CH.708	11. 8.88	S B Walters	Deenethorpe	8. 3.07P
	(Officially regd with Rotax 377)	*(Overturned landing Long Marston 17.6.06 when nosewheel moved off centreline: cancelled 7.9.06 as TWFU)*				
G-MVDS	Hiway Skytrike/Demon 175	PB-01	30. 6.88	P Butler	Broadmeadow Farm, Hereford	
				(Cancelled 24. 1.95 by CAA: stored 11.06)		
G-MVGI	Aerial Arts Chaser S	CH.723	1. 9.88	J Bagnall	Mill Farm, Hughley, Much Wenlock	13. 7.97P
				(Cancelled 6. 1.03 as sold to Ireland but noted stored as "G-MVGI" 9.04)		
G-MVHN	Aerial Arts Chaser S	CH.728	9. 8.88	J E Sweetingham	Benson's Farm, Laindon	10. 6.01P
				(Cancelled 4. 2.05 as PWFU: noted 1.08)		
G-MVKO	Solar Wings Pegasus XL-Q	SW-WQ-0127	14.11.88	G Beaven	Yatesbury	25 4.07P
	(Trike c/n SW-TE-0121)			*(Cancelled 7. 8.07 by CAA)*		
G-MVME	Thruster TST Mk.1	8128-TST-110	12.12.88	S J Payne	Wing Farm, Longbridge Deverill	10. 4.06P
				(Cancelled 21. 8.06 as WFU: noted for spares 4.07)		
G-MVRS	CFM Shadow Series BD			Doncaster, Yorkshire		
G-MVSU	Microflight Spectrum	008	4. 5.89	M W Shepherd	Otherton, Cannock	21. 5.04P
				(Cancelled 22. 4.04 as destroyed: noted 5.07)		
G-MVUR	Hornet RS-ZA	HRWA-0050 & ZA107	3. 7.89	M J Moulton	Roddige	4. 4.08P
	(Rotax 532) *(Originally regd with Trike c/n HRWA-0076 but now confirmed with HRWA-0050 [ex G-MVLK] (Cancelled 13.11.07 by CAA)*					
G-MVZR	Aviasud Mistral 532GB	090	9.10.89	S E and J A Robinson	Crosland Moor	7. 6.01P
	(Built Aviasud Engineering - pr.no.BMAA/HB/011)			*(Cancelled 14. 3.05 by CAA: noted 9.07)*		
G-MVZV	Solar Wings Pegasus XL-Q	SW-WQ-0245	6.10.89	C R Cawley	Rochester	25. 4.07P
	(Trike c/n SW-TE-0230)			*(Cancelled 12. 5.07 by CAA)*		
G-MWBR	Hornet RS-ZA	HRWB-0084/ZA145	29.11.89	I A Clark	Longacre Farm, Sandy	4. 9.06P
				(Cancelled 18. 6.07 by CAA: noted 7.07)		
G-MWCP	Powerchute Kestrel	91252	3. 1.90	Iris Fraser	Insch	20.10.01P
				(Cancelled 10. 5.05 by CAA: stored 11.05)		
G-MWHS	AMF Chevvron 2-32C	021	18. 5.90	Airshare Flying Club Ltd	Kirkbride	
				(Cancelled 22.11.00 by CAA: noted 5.07)		
G-MWJW	Whittaker MW5 Sorcerer	JDW-02	11. 5.90	S Badby	Shenington	20. 7.06P
	(Built J D Webb - pr.no.PFA 163-11186) (Fuji-Robin EC-44-PM)			*(Cancelled 17. 5.07 by CAA)*		
G-MWJZ	CFM Shadow Series CD	K 132	19. 7.90	D Mahajan	Lower Mountpleasant Farm, Chatteris	23. 7.99P
	(Severely damaged Chatteris during 1999: cancelled 24.12.01 as WFU: engine and wings removed and stored 5.05)					
G-MWFS	Solar Wings Pegasus XL-Q	SW-WQ-0289	14. 3.90	C P Hughes	Emlyn's Field, Rhuallt	10. 6.08P
	(Trike c/n SW-TE-0267)			*(Cancelled 20. 2.08 by CAA)*		
G-MWUF	Solar Wings Pegasus XL-R	SW-WA-1514	13. 6.91	J G Jackson	Enstone	27. 7.05P
	(Trike c/n SW-TB-1439)			*(Cancelled 21. 1.05 as WFU)*		
G-MWUP	Solar Wings Pegasus XL-R	SW-WA-1517	21. 6.91	G R Hall and P R Brooker *(Cancelled 21. 6.06 by CAA)*		
	(Rotax 462)	*(Trike c/n SW-TE-0341)*			(Petham. Canterbury and Smarden, Ashford)	5. 9.06P
G-MWWM	Kolb Twinstar Mk.2	PFA 205-11645	(G-BTXC)	17.10.91	D Jordan	RAF Brize Norton	21. 6.04P
	(Built D Jordan) (Rotax 503) (PFA pr.no.duplicates G-GPST)			*(Cancelled 11. 6.05 by CAA)*		
G-MWXN	Mainair Gemini Flash IIA	878-0192-7-W673	20.11.91	A P Martin	(Nottingham)	30. 5.06P
	(Rotax 582)			*(Cancelled 7. 7.06 by CAA)*		
G-MYBG	Solar Wings Pegasus XL-Q	SW-WQ-0514	26. 3.92	M Aylett and P A Henretty	Swinford, Rugby	9. 7.03P
	(Trike c/n SW-TE-0385)			*(Cancelled 2..6.06 by CAA: noted damaged 10.07)*		

G-MYEG	Solar Wings Pegasus XL-R	SW-WA-1560		4. 8.92	I D Nuttall	(Coughton, Ross-on-Wye)	27. 4.06P
	(Trike c/n SW-TB-1447)				(Cancelled 20..3.07 by CAA)		
G-MYUL	Quad City Challenger II UK	CH2-1293-UK-1063		10. 1.95	P Knott	Crosland Moor	24. 5.02P
	(Built A G Easson - pr.no.PFA 177-12687)				(Cancelled 24. 5.05 by CAA: noted 9.07)		
G-MYWB	Edel Corniche-Scorpion	004		31. 3.95	P F Funnell	Rufforth	
	(Built Edel - pr.no.BMAA/HB/071)				(Cancelled 7. 8.98 by CAA: noted 11.07)		
G-MYWF	CFM Shadow Series CD	K 248		18. 4.95	M A Newman	(Benhall, Saxmundham)	10. 7.07P
	(Built CFM Metal-Fax - pr.no.BMAA/HB/068)				(Cancelled 22. 1.08 by CAA)		
G-MYZN	Whittaker MW6-S-LW Fatboy Flyer			31. 1.96	M K Shaw	RAF Halton	28. 6.07P
	(Built M K Shaw) (Rotax 582)	PFA 164-12431			(Cancelled 23. 6.07 as PWFU)		
G-MZAK	Mainair Mercury	1070-0296-7-W872		15. 1.96	M J Taylor	Rochdale	16. 5.05P
	(Cancelled 30. 6.05 as transferred to South Africa: trike stored at P&M 2.08)						
G-MZFM	Pegasus Quantum 15	7310		21. 2.97	G A Ratcliffe	(Newcastle)	8. 5.08P
	(Rotax 582)				(Cancelled 25. 2.08 by CAA)		
G-MZGX	Thruster T 600N	9057-T600N-005		28. 4.97	G E Norton	(Lincoln)	2. 9.08P
	(Rotax 503)				(Cancelled 15. 1.08 by CAA)		
G-NAAT	Folland Gnat T 1	FL.507	XM697	27.11.89	Hunter Flying Club	Exeter	
					(Cancelled 10..4.95 as WFU: noted 12.05)		
G-NBSI	Cameron N-77 Balloon (Hot Air)	427		3. 8.78	(D S Dunlop and A J Matthews)	Nottingham	21. 4.91A
					tr Nottingham Hot Air Balloon Club		
					(Cancelled 14. 6.93 as WFU: active 9.05)		
G-NFLC	Handley Page HP137 Jetstream 1	222	G-AXUI	12.12.95	Air Service Training	Perth	3. 6.04T
			G-8-9		(Cancelled 3.8.04 as WFU: used as instructional airframe 1.06)		
G-NOVO	Colt AS-56 Airship (Hot Air)	1067		20. 5.87	J R Huggins	Dover	29. 4.97A
	(Konig SC430)				(Noted 2004: cancelled 14.10.05 by CAA)		
G-NRDC	NDN Aircraft NDN-6 Fieldmaster	004		8. 6.81	EPA Aircraft Company Ltd	Sandown, Isle of Wight	17.10.87P
					(Cancelled 3. 2.95 by CAA: wreck noted 4.06)		
G-OEWA	de Havilland DH.104 Dove 8	04528	G-DDCD	10. 6.98	D.C.Hunter	Little Rissington	AC
			G-ARUM		(Cancelled 24. 5.05 by CAA: stored 1.08 as "G-DDCD")		
G-OFMB	Rand-Robinson KR-2	7808	N5337X	29. 4.97	F M and S I Burden	Gloucestershire	
	(Built M A Shepard)				(Cancelled 10. 1.06 as PWFU: on fire dump 2.08)		
G-OFRT	Lockheed L188CF Electra	1075	N347HA	29.10.91	Dart Group PLC	Coventry	28.10.01T
			N423MA, N23AF, N64405, SE-FGC, N5537F		(Cancelled 12. 5.03 by CAA: stored 5.03)		
G-OHEA	Hawker Siddeley HS 125 Series 3B/RA	25144	G-AVRG	25.11.86	Cranfield University	Cranfield	7. 8.92T
			G-5-12		(Cancelled 23. 6.94 as WFU: fuselage dumped 2.08)		
G-OICV	Robinson R22 Beta	0991	G-BPWH	11. 2.93	Helicentre Ltd	Blackpool	18. 3.01
					(Damaged Blackpool 18. 7.99: cancelled 19.11.99 as WFU: shell only 10.07)		
G-OLPG	Colt 77A Balloon (Hot Air)	2568		11. 3.94	D J Farrar	Collingham, Wetherby	16. 2.03
					(Cancelled 9. 3.04 by CAA)		
G-OMOG	Gulfstream AA-5A Cheetah	AA5A-0793	G-BHWR	4. 3.88	Solent Flight Aircraft Ltd Phoenix Farm, Lower Upham		15. 4.02T
			N26892		(Cancelled 23. 7.01 by CAA: fuselage noted 10.05)		
G-ONOW	Bell 206A JetRanger	605	G-AYMX	8. 8.88	J Lucketti	Walton Wood	27. 4.00T
					(Cancelled 24. 5.05 by CAA: noted 11.06)		
G-OPDM	Enstrom 280FX Shark	2021	N8627Q	7. 1.98	(Lamindene Ltd)	Seething	15. 5.04T
			PH-GBL, N650PG	(Crashed County Kerry 7. 6.03: cancelled 12.. 2.04 by CAA: cockpit noted 5.05)			
G-ORJX	BAE Systems Avro 146-RJX85	E2376		16. 2.00	BAE Systems (Operations) Ltd	Woodford	
					(Cancelled 12.12.02 as WFU: stored 3.06)		
G-OVNE	Cessna 401A	401A-0036	N401XX	11. 3.88	M A Billings	Norwich	8.10.92.
			(N171SF), N71SF, N6236Q	(Cancelled 8.. 2.94 by CAA: noted 10.05)			
G-PIPI	Mainair Sports Pegasus Quik	8109		30. 3.05	R D Kay	Sleap	29. 3.08P
					(Cancelled 25. 2.08 by CAA)		
G-RACA	Percival P 57 Sea Prince T 1	P57/49	WM735	2. 9.80	D A Cotton	Long Marston	4.11.80P
					"Gods Kitchen" (Cancelled 28.11.95 by CAA: derelict 7.05)		
G-RANZ	Rans S-10 Sakota	0589.050		2.11.89	O M C Dismore	Popham	27. 6.03P
	(Built B A Philips - pr.no.PFA 194-11536) (Rotax 532)				(Cancelled 22. 9.05 by CAA: stored 10.05)		
G-RAVL	Handley Page 137 Jetstream 200	208	G-AWVK	2.12.86	Cranfield University	Cranfield	26. 2.94
			N1035S, G-AWVK	(Cancelled 30. 1.01 as WFU: for Instructional use 1.07)			
G-REID	Rotorway Scorpion 133	1147	G-BGAW	7.12.81	Not known	?	18.3.91P
					(Cancelled 19. 4.99 by CAA: noted 8.06 southbound on A34 near Winchester)		
G-RMAX	Cameron C-80 Balloon (Hot Air)	4705		6.12.99	M Quinn and D Curtain Athlone, County Westmeath		4. 7.06A
					(Cancelled 23. 6.07 by CAA)		
G-SADE	Reims Cessna F150L	F15000752	G-AZJW	28. 5.91	N E Sams	Cranfield	21. 9.97T
					(Cancelled 24. 5.05 by CAA: stored 1.06)		
G-SHIV	Gulfstream GA-7 Cougar	GA7-0092	N713G	22.11.84	Wesley Aircraft Ltd	Cranfield	18.1.98T
					(Cancelled 16. 9.04 by CAA: dumped 1.07)		
G-SION	Piper PA-38-112 Tomahawk II	38-81A0146	N23661	30. 1.91	F D Dunstan t/a Naiad Air Services	Enstone	
					(Cancelled 9. 9.02 by CAA: dumped 5.06)		
G-SMHK	Cameron D-38 Airship (Hot Air)	697		5. 1.81	San Miguel Brewery Ltd	Hong Kong	
					(Cancelled 14. 7.93 as PWFU: active 4.06)		
G-SSWA	Short SD.3-30 Variant 100	SH3042	D-CTAG	15.10.99	Emerald Airways Ltd	Blackpool	14.12.06T
			G-BHHU, OY-MUC, G-BHHU, N181AP, N332MV, G-BHHU, G-14-3042				
					(Cancelled 13.12.06 as PWFU: fuselage only 10.07)		
G-SSWE	Short SD.3-60 Variant 100	SH3705	SE-IXE	15. 7.02	BAC Leasing Ltd	Coventry	22. 8.05T
			(G-BNBA), G-14-3705		(Cancelled 6. 6.07 as PWFU)		
G-SSWM	Short SD.3-60 Variant 100	SH3648	SE-KCI	28. 9.01	BAC Leasing Ltd	Coventry	14.10.06E
			G-OAAS, OY-MMB, G-BLIL, G-14-3648 (Cancelled 6. 6.07 as PWFU)				
G-SSWO	Short SD.3-60 Variant 100	SH3609	SE-KLO	8.10.01	BAC Leasing Ltd	Blackpool	4.12.04T
			N343MV, (G-BKMY), G-14-3609 (Cancelled 6. 6.07 as PWFU: stored externally 10.07)				
G-SSWR	Short SD.3-60 Variant 100	SH3670	SE-KGV	2.10.01	BAC Leasing Ltd	Coventry	13.11.06E
			HR-IAQ, N108PS, B-3603, G-BLWJ, G-14-3670 (Cancelled 6. 6.07 as PWFU)				
G-STOR	Fieseler Fi 156D-0 Storch	110451	Luftwaffe 110451	21. 5.03	G R Lacey	Fairoaks	
			(Cancelled 25. 1.07 as WFU: to Robert Blanchard, Miami, Florida for completion 9.07)				
G-STUK	Junkers Ju 87/R4	6234	Luftwaffe 6234	19.12.03	G R Lacey	Fairoaks	
			(Scheduled rebuild to start 2006 and be complete by 2009/2010: cancelled 11. 1.07 by CAA)				

G-THUG   MD Helicopters MD.600N   RN026   G-RHUG   4. 7.00   Helidirect UK Ltd   Shoreham   17.11.00
                                                   N92088
                    (Substantially damaged landing Peplow Hall, Shropshire 27. 8.00: .cancelled 22.11.00 as destroyed: wreck stored 11.05)
G-TIGH   Aérospatiale AS.332L Super Puma   2034   F-WXFL   15. 4.82   Bristow Helicopters Ltd   Aberdeen   24. 8.92T
                    (Damaged 100m NE of Shetland Isles 14. 3.92: cancelled 3. 8.92 as destroyed: for instruction use 3.06)
G-TOBY   Cessna 172B   47852   G-ARCM   8. 4.81   J A Kelman   Shoreham   28. 4.85
                                                   N6952X   *(Damaged Sandown, IoW 15.10.83: cancelled 27. 2.90 by CAA: instructional airframe 11.05)*
G-TORE   Hunting Percival P 84 Jet Provost T 3A   PAC/W/9212   XM405   14. 6.91   (R J Everett)   Islington, London EC1   5. 5.95P
                    (Cancelled 24. 2.04 by CAA: to City University as instructional airframe 9.03)
G-UPPY   Cameron DP-80 Airship (Hot Air)   2274   29. 3.90   Jacques W Soukup Enterprises Ltd   Bristol   27. 8.94A
                    (Cancelled 15. 9.05 by CAA: active 9.05)
G-VDIR   Cessna 310R II   310R0211   N5091J   31. 1.91   J Driver   North Weald   21. 6.07T
                    (Landed on grass North Weald 4. 9.05 and severely damaged: cancelled 3. 3.06 as destroyed: noted damaged 6.07)
G-VIBA   Cameron DP-80 Airship (Hot Air)   1729   28. 5.91   Jacques W Soukup Enterprises Ltd   Bristol   3. 2.99A
                    (Cancelled 15. 9.05 by CAA: active 9.05)
G-VTEN   Vinten-Wallis WA-117 Venom   UMA-01 & 003   22. 4.85   K H Wallis   Reymerston Hall, Norfolk   3.12.85P
          (Continental O-200-B)   *(Cancelled 12. 6.89 as WFU: stored unmarked 8.03)*
G-VULC   Avro 698 Vulcan B 2A   ?   N655AV   27. 2.84   Radarmoor Ltd   Wellesbourne Mountford
                                                   G-VULC, XM655   *(Cancelled 25. 3.02 as WFU: noted 3.06 as "XM655")*
G-WHDP   Cessna 182S Skylane II   18280178   N178TC   12. 5.98   Heatherford Ltd   Farnborough
                    (Crashed on landing St Mawgan 23. 6.01: cancelled 31.12.01 as destroyed: noted 4.04)
G-WOLV   Comco Ikarus C42 FB100 VLA   0601-6784   25. 1.06   Solent Flight Ltd   Lee-on-Solent   6. 7.07P
          (Built S Du Boulay - pr.no.PFA 322-14499)   *(Cancelled 17.12.07 by CAA)*
G-WSEC   Enstrom F-28C   398   G-BONF   19.12.88   D A Weldon   Kilrush, County Kildare   28. 6.08E
                                                   N51661   *(Cancelled 16. 8.07 as PWFU)*
G-YROS   Bensen B 8M   PFA G/101-1004   29. 1.81   Flight Acadamy (Gyrocopters) Ltd   Kirkbride   6. 6.97P
          (Built J M Montgomerie) (HAPI 60-6M)   *(Noted 7.06) (Cancelled 15. 5.07 by CAA)*
G-YUGO   Hawker Siddeley HS.125 Series 1B/R-522   25094   25. 5.88   RCR Aviation Ltd   Biggin Hill   19. 4.91
                    (Cancelled 29. 3.93 as PWFU: noted 6.05)
G-YURO   Europa Aviation Europa   001   6. 4.92   Europa Management (International) Ltd   Wombleton   9. 6.95P
          (Built Europa Aviation Ltd - pr.no.PFA 220-11981)   *(Cancelled 22. 4.98 as WFU: noted incomplete 4.05)*

The following preserved balloons and airships are held in the British Balloon Museum and Library collection based in Newbury.

Registration	Type	Construction No	Previous Identity	Reg.Date	Remarks	CofA Expy
G-ATGN	Thorn K-800 Coal Gas Balloon (Gas Filled) *(Built J Thorn)*	2		12. 7.65	Cancelled 23. 6.81 as WFU "Eccles"	
G-ATXR	Abingdon Spherical Free Balloon (Hot Air) *(Built RAF Abingdon Free Balloon Club)*	AFB-1		22. 7.66	Cancelled 14. 7.86 by CAA *(Basket only)*	1. 9.76
G-AVTL	Brighton Ax7-65 Balloon (Hot Air)	01		17. 8.67	Cancelled 11. 9.81 as WFU	
	(Built Hot-Air Group and originally regd as Hot-Air Group ¼ Free Balloon with c/n 1)					
G-AWCR	Piccard Ax6 Balloon (Hot Air)	6204		29. 1.68	Cancelled 24. 5.78 as WFU "London Pride 1")	
G-AWJB	Brighton MAB-65 Balloon (Hot Air)	MAB-3		3. 5.68	Cancelled 4.12.70 on sale to Italy (ntu) *(Regd HB-BOU (1) 2.73) (As "HB-BOU")*	
G-AWMO	Omega O-84 Balloon (Hot Air) *(Built Omega Aerostatics Ltd)*	01		31. 7.68	Cancelled 13. 5.69 to OY-BOB "Blue Strike"	
G-AWOK	Sussex Gas Balloon (Gas Filled) *(Built University of Sussex Ballooning Society)*	SARD.1		7. 8.68	Cancelled 29. 2.84 as WFU "Sardinia" (Withdrawn 1970)	
G-AXVU	Omega 84 Balloon (Hot Air)	09		7. 1.70	Cancelled 22. 8.89 as WFU "Henry VIII"	28. 4.77S
G-AXXP	Bradshaw 76 (Ax7) Balloon (Hot Air) *(Built R F D Bradshaw)*	RB.001		20. 2.70	Cancelled 9. 9.81 "Ignis Volens" (WFU 2.77)	
G-AYAJ	Cameron O-84 Balloon (Hot Air) *(Built D A Cameron)*	11		31. 3.70	Cancelled 1. 2.90 as PWFU "Flaming Pearl"	
G-AYAL	Omega 56 Balloon (Hot Air)	10		2. 4.70	Cancelled 18.10.84 by CAA "Nimble II"	25. 8.76S
G-AZBH	Cameron O-84 Balloon (Hot Air)	23		8. 7.71	Cancelled 30. 8.85 as WFU "Serendipity"	31. 3.85A
G-AZER	Cameron O-42 (Ax5) Balloon (Hot Air)	26		9. 9.71	Cancelled 25. 3.92 by CAA "Shy Tot"	15. 5.81A
G-AZJI	Western O-65 Balloon (Hot Air)	007		2.12.71	Cancelled 19. 5.93 by CAA "Peek-A-Boo"	
G-AZSP	Cameron O-84 Balloon (Hot Air)	43		18. 4.72	Cancelled 11. 1.82 as WFU "Esso"	22. 3.82A
G-AZUV	Cameron O-65 Balloon (Hot Air)	41		12. 5.72	Cancelled 6. 1.82 by CAA "Icarus" (Damaged Rendharn Green, Suffolk xx.xx.xx)	23. 6.83A
G-AZUW	Cameron A-140 Balloon (Hot Air)	45		12. 5.72	Cancelled 7. 6.73 - to F-WTVO 6.73, to F-BTVO and 5Y-SIL "Cumulonimbus"	
G-AZYL	Portslade Free Balloon (Hot Air) *(Built Portslade School)*	MK 17		10. 7.72	Cancelled 25. 4.85 as PWFU	
G-BAMK	Cameron D-96 Airship (Hot Air)	72		11. 1.73	Cancelled 16. 8.00 by CAA "Isibidbi"	24. 4.90A
G-BAXF	Cameron O-77 Balloon (Hot Air)	74		3. 5.73	Cancelled 5. 9.95 by CAA "Granna"	20. 7.86A
G-BAXK	Thunder Ax7-77 Balloon (Hot Air)	005		9. 5.73	Cancelled 7. 9.01 as WFU "Jack O'Newbury"	2. 7.91A
G-BAVU	Cameron A-105 Balloon (Hot Air)	66		11. 4.73	Cancelled 6.12.01 by CAA	5.10.84A
G-BBFS	Vandem-Bemden K-460 (Gasfilled) Balloon *(Built F Vandem-Bemden - pr/no.VDB-16)*	75	OO-BGX	10. 8.73	Cancelled 19. 5.93 by CAA "Le Tomate"	
G-BBLL	Cameron O-84 Balloon (Hot Air)	84		2.10.73	Cancelled 19. 5.93 by CAA "Boadicea"	25. 5.81A
G-BBYU	Cameron O-56 Balloon (Hot Air)	96		19. 2.74	Cancelled 9. 8.89 as WFU "Chieftain"	28. 2.82A
G-BCAR	Thunder Ax7-77 Balloon (Hot Air)	019		5. 3.74	Cancelled 2. 4.92 by CAA "Marie Antoinette"	
G-BCFD	West Ax3-15 Balloon (Hot Air) *(Built J West)*	JW.1		16. 5.74	Cancelled 30. 1.87 by CAA "Hellfire"	
G-BCFE	Byrne Odyssey 4000 Balloon (Minimum Lift) *(Built A J Byrne)*	AJB-2		20. 5.74	Cancelled 19. 9.85 as WFU "Odyssey"	
G-BDVG	Thunder Ax6-56A Balloon (Hot Air)	067		2. 4.76	Cancelled 3. 4.92 by CAA "Argonaut"	26. 5.95A
G-BEEE	Thunder Ax6-56A Balloon (Hot Air)	070		20. 8.76	Cancelled 19. 5.93 by CAA "Avia"	11. 5.84A
G-BEPO	Cameron N-77 Balloon (Hot Air)	279		1. 4.77	Cancelled 14. 5.98 as WFU "Sungas"	27. 6.94A
G-BEPZ	Cameron D-96 Airship (Hot Air)	300		13. 4.77	Cancelled 28. 4.94 as WFU) "Zanussi" *(Damaged Warren Farm, Savernake Forest 8. 1.94 and DBR during recovery)*	12. 2.90A

G-BETF	Cameron Champion 35 SS Balloon (Hot Air) 280		17. 5.77	Cancelled 24. 1.92 as WFU	6. 4.84A
	(Champion Spark Plug shape)			"Champion"	
G-BETH	Thunder Ax6-56A Balloon (Hot Air)	113	27. 5.77	Cancelled 11. 5.93 as WFU "Debenhams"	31. 5.78
G-BEVI (3)	Thunder Ax7-77A Balloon (Hot Air)	125	30. 5.77	Cancelled 8. 1.92 as WFU "Prime Bang"	
G-BFAB	Cameron N-56 Balloon (Hot Air)	297	15. 8.77	Cancelled 21. 4.92 by CAA "Phonogram"	10. 8.92A
G-BFOZ	Thunder Ax6-56 Plug Balloon (Hot Air)	144	20. 3.78	Cancelled 16. 4.92 by CAA "Motorway"	10. 9.89A
G-BGAS	Colting Ax8-105A Balloon (Hot Air)	001	27. 6.78	Cancelled xx.xx.xx	12. 9.82A
				(Destroyed Flims, Switzerland 20. 9.8 J · basket only)	
G-BGOO	Colt Flame 56SS Balloon (Hot Air)	039	27. 4.79	Cancelled 19. 5.93 by CAA	
	(Smiling Flame shape)			"Mr Gas"	
G-BGPF	Thunder Ax6-56Z Balloon (Hot Air)	206	13. 7.79	Cancelled 21.11.89 as WFU "Pepsi"	27. 6.82A
G-BHKN	Colt 14A Cloudhopper Balloon (Hot Air)	068	17. 1.80	Cancelled 5.12.89 as WFU	
	(Officially regd as Colt 12A)			"Green Ice 2"	
G-BHKR	Colt 14A Cloudhopper Balloon (Hot Air)	071	17. 1.80	Cancelled 5.12.89 as WFU	
	(Officially regd as Colt 12A)			"Green Ice 5"	
G-BIAZ	Cameron AT-165 Balloon (Hot-Air)	400	7. 2.78	Cancelled 27. 5.80 as destroyed "Zanussi"	3. 4.80
	(Used for 1978 Atlantic attempt:: hot air envelope destroyed Trubenbuch, Austria 14. 1.80: inner helium cell envelope only)				
G-BIDV	Colt 17A Cloudhopper Balloon (Hot Air)	789	29. 1.79	Cancelled 20. 5.93 by CAA	19.12.89A
	(Originally was Colt 14A c/n 034)			"Smirnoff"	
G-BIGT	Colt 77A Balloon (Hot Air)	078	28. 2.80	Cancelled 4. 2.87 by CAA	20. 2.83A
				"Big T" (Damaged Belton Hall, Grantham 23. 8.81?)	
G-BKES	Cameron Bottle 57 SS Balloon (Hot Air)	846	25. 6.82	Cancelled 1. 5.90 by CAA	13. 5.87A
	(Robinsons Barley Water Bottle)			"Robinsons Barley Water"	
G-BKMR	Thunder Ax3 Maxi Sky Chariot Balloon (Hot Air) 497		12. 1.83	Cancelled 23. 4.98 as WFU	31. 8.90A
				"The Weasel "	
G-BLIO	Cameron R-42 Balloon (Gas & Hot Air)	1015	17. 4.84	Cancelled 24. 1.90 as destroyed	17. 5.84P
G-BMEZ	Cameron DP-70 Airship (Hot Air)	1130	18. 9.85	Cancelled 20. 6.91 as sold as EC-FUS	4. 5.89A
	(Originally regd as D-50)			(Envelope only)	
G-BNHN	Colt Ariel Bottle SS Balloon (Hot Air)	1045	30. 3.87	Cancelled 24. 1.92 as WFU "Ariel"	5. 5.89A
G-BOGR	Colt 180A Balloon (Hot Air)	1183	11. 5.88	Cancelled 28. 4.97 as WFU "Britannia"	13. 3.92T
G-BOTL	Colt 42A SS Balloon (Hot Air)	466	23.11.82	Cancelled 21.11.89 as WFU "Bottle"	
G-BPKN	Colt AS-80 Mk.II Airship (Hot Air)	1297	11. 1.89	Cancelled 7. 1.91 by CAA "Fuji"	14. 3.91A
G-BPLD	Thunder and Colt AS-261 Airship (Hot Air)	1380	25. 1.89	Cancelled 13. 6.89 - to F-WGGM, F-GHRI 5.91, to F-WGGM	
G-BRZC	Cameron N-90 Balloon (Hot Air)	2227	8. 2.90	Cancelled 29. 4.97 as WFU "Unipart II"	2.12.92A
G-BUBL	Thunder Ax8-105 Balloon (Hot Air)	1147	10.12.87	Cancelled 16. 6.98 as WFU	16. 9.91T
				"Mercier" and "L'Espit d'Adventure"	
G-BUUU	Cameron Bottle 77 SS Balloon (Hot Air)	2980	11. 2.93	Cancelled 22.10.01 by CAA	4. 3.94A
	(Bells Whisky Bottle shape)			"Bells Whisky"	
G-BVBJ	Colt Flying Coffee Jar 1 SS Balloon (Hot Air)		27. 7.93	Cancelled 29. 4.97 as WFU	21.11.96A
	(Maxwell House Jar)	2427		"Maxwell House I"	
G-BVBK	Colt Flying Coffee Jar 2 SS Balloon (Hot Air)		27. 7.93	Cancelled 29. 4.97 as WFU	14. 2.97A
	(Maxwell House Jar)	2428		"Maxwell House II"	
G-BVBX	Cameron N-90M Balloon (Hot Air)	3102	10. 8.93	Cancelled 10. 2.97 as temporarily WFU "Mercury"	27. 9.95A
G-BVFY	Colt 210A Balloon (Hot Air)	2493	DQ-BVF	30. 9.93	Cancelled 14. 3.06 by CA	11. 5.00T
			G-BVFY		"Scotair"	
G-BVIO	Colt Flying Drinks Can SS Balloon (Hot Air)		4. 2.94	Cancelled 6.11.01 as WFU	9. 6.00A
	(Budweiser Can shape)	2538		"Budweiser Can II"	
G-BVWH	Cameron N-90 Lightbulb SS Balloon (Hot Air)		8.12.94	Cancelled 17.12.01 as WFU	2. 9.98A
		3404		"Phillips Light Bulb"	
G-CHUB	Colt Cylinder Two N-51 Balloon (Hot Air)	1720	11. 4.90	Cancelled 12.12.01 as WFU	19.12.95A
	(Fire Extinguisher shape)			"Chubb Fire Extinguisher"	
G-FTFT	Colt Financial Times 90 SS Balloon (Hot Air)		14. 1.88	Cancelled 13. 5.98 as WFU	5. 6.95A
		1163		"Financial Times"	
G-FZZZ	Colt 56A Balloon (Hot Air)	507	23. 2.83	Cancelled 29. 4.97 as WFU "Alka Seltzer 1'"	
G-LCIO	Colt 240A Balloon (Hot Air)	1381	23. 1.89	Cancelled 25 .5.94 as WFU	7. 3.91A
				"Star Flyer 2" (Damaged landing after first overflight Mt Everest by hot air balloon 21.10.91)	
G-LOAG	Cameron N-77 Balloon (Hot Air)	359	10.11.77	Cancelled 31. 3.93 as destroyed	6. 4.84A
				"Famous Grouse" (Envelope only)	
G-OBUD	Colt 69A Balloon (Hot Air)	698	26. 6.85	Cancelled 29. 4.97 as WFU "Budweiser"	1. 2.90A
G-OFIZ	Cameron Can 80 SS Balloon (Hot Air)	2106	30.10.89	Cancelled 10. 2.97 as temporarily WFU	2.12.91A
				"Andrews Can"	
G-PARR	Colt Bottle 90 SS Balloon (Hot Air)	1953	15. 3.91	Cancelled 10. 2.97 as temporarily WFU	29. 9.94A
	(Old Parr Whisky bottle shape)			"Old Parr"	
G-PERR	Cameron Bottle 60 SS Balloon (Hot Air)	699	28. 1.81	Cancelled 24. 1.92 as WFU "Perrier"	3. 6.84A
G-PLUG	Colt 105A Balloon (Hot Air)	1958	17. 4.91	Cancelled 23. 7.96 by CAA	14. 8.95T
G-PUBS	Colt Beer Glass 56 SS Balloon (Hot Air)	037	7. 6.79	Cancelled 1.12.95 by CAA	30.11.90A

The following preserved, balloons and airships are held in the Balloon Preservation Group collection based in Petworth.

Registration	Type	Construction No	Previous Identity Reg.Date		Remarks	CofA Expy
G-AYVA	Cameron O-84 Balloon (Hot Air)	17		30. 3.71	Cancelled 19. 5.93 by CAA "April Fool"	6. 9.76
G-BAKO	Cameron O-84 Balloon (Hot Air)	57		18.12.72	Cancelled 19. 5.93 by CAA "Pied Piper"	12. 7.76
G-BAND	Cameron O-84 Balloon (Hot Air)	52		22. 1.73	Cancelled 17. 4.98 as PWFU "Clover"	
G-BAOW	Cameron O-65 Balloon (Hot Air)	59		6. 2.73	Cancelled 15.10.01 by CAA "Winslow Boy"	9. 5.74S
G-BAST	Cameron O-84 Balloon (Hot Air)	70		15. 3.73	Cancelled 19. 5.93 by CAA "Honey"	2. 5.84A
G-BAYC	Cameron O-65 Balloon (Hot Air)	68	(HB-BOU)	17. 5.73	Cancelled 15. 5.98 as WFU	25. 5.78S
			G-BAYC		'Viva Verdi'	
G-BBYL	Cameron O-77 Balloon (Hot Air)	89		8. 2.74	Cancelled 19. 5.93 by CAA "Jammy"	19. 6.77S
G-BBYR	Cameron O-65 Balloon (Hot Air)	97		14. 2.74	Cancelled 30. 1.87 by CAA "Phoenix"	15. 7.81
G-BCAP	Cameron O-56 Balloon (Hot Air)	92		5. 3.74	Cancelled 30. 3.93 as WFU "Honey Child"	1. 5.88A
G-BCAS	Thunder Ax7-77 Balloon (Hot Air)	018		5. 3.74	Cancelled 30.11.01 by CAA "Drifter"	9. 4.91A
G-BCCH	Thunder Ax6-56A Balloon (Hot Air)	024		4. 4.74	Cancelled 15.11.82 as sold Belgium - NTU "Wrangler"	11. 4.81A

G-BCNR	Thunder Ax7-77A Balloon (Hot Air)	028		13. 9.74	Cancelled 19. 5.93 by CAA "Howdy"	15. 5.81A
G-BCRE	Cameron O-77 Balloon (Hot Air)	128		30.10.74	Cancelled 19. 5.93 by CAA "Snapdragon"	6.10.83A
G-BDGO	Thunder Ax7-77 Balloon (Hot Air)	048		16. 7.75	Cancelled 12. 6.02 by CAA "J & B"	2. 2.82A
G-BDMO	Thunder Ax7-77A Balloon (Hot Air)	053	(EC-...)	25.11.75	Cancelled 8. 3.95 as WFU	16. 8.86A
			G-BDMO		"Flash Harry"	
G-BEJB	Thunder Ax6-56A Balloon (Hot Air)	096		31.12.76	Cancelled 10. 5.02 by CAA	21. 5.87A
	(Original canopy destroyed by fire Latimer 4. 9.77: replacement c/n not known)				"Baby J & B"	
G-BGST	Thunder Ax7-65 Bolt Balloon (Hot Air)	217		14. 5.79	Cancelled 7.12.01 by CAA "Black Fred"	23. 3.91A
G-BHAT	Thunder Ax7-77 Bolt Balloon (Hot Air)	250		17. 3.80	Cancelled 29. 4.93 as WFU "Witter"	14. 6.92A
G-BHYO	Cameron N-77 Balloon (Hot Air)	659		30. 6.80	Cancelled 3. 1.08 by CAA "Alcock and Sissons"	8. 5.97A
G-BJZC	Thunder Ax7-65Z Balloon (Hot Air)	416		5. 3.82	Cancelled 8. 7.98 as WFU Greenpeace Trinity"	17. 6.94A
G-BKIY	Thunder Ax3 Sky Chariot Balloon (Hot Air)	464		7.10.82	Cancelled 15.11.01 as WFU "Michaelangelo"	
G-BKOW	Colt 77A Balloon (Hot Air)	505		6. 9.84	Cancelled 29. 4.97 as WFU "Lady Di" (Elle titles))	14. 2.88A
G-BKIK	Cameron DG-19 Airship (Gas Filled)	776		23. 8.82	Cancelled 5. 9.00 as WFU	4. 9.88A
	(Rotax 400)				"B & Q"	
G-BLDL	Cameron Truck 56 SS Balloon (Hot Air)	990		10. 1.84	Cancelled 21.10.96 by CAA "Europa"	
G-BLGX	Thunder Ax7-65 Balloon (Hot Air)	551		16. 4.84	Cancelled 19. 5.93 by CAA)	23. 9.05A
G-BLIP	Cameron N-77 Balloon (Hot Air)	1031		17. 4.84	Cancelled 23. 6.98 as WFU "Systems 80"	26. 3.94A
G-BLJF	Cameron O-65 Balloon (Hot Air)	1041		14. 5.84	Cancelled 17.11.05 as PWFU	16. 8.00A
G-BLKJ	Thunder Ax7-65 Balloon (Hot Air)	580		18. 7.84	Cancelled 25. 5.97 as PWFU "Up & Coming"	3. 2.96A
G-BLSH	Cameron V-77 Balloon (Hot Air)	1085		7.12.84	Cancelled 30. 3.98 as WFU "Compass Rose"	14. 1.95A
G-BLUE	Colting Ax7-77A Balloon (Hot Air)	77A-011		2. 5.78	Cancelled 30.11.01 by CAA	20. 9.99A
	(Officially regd as Colt 77A c/n 11)					
G-BLZB	Cameron N-65 Balloon (Hot Air)	1164		21. 5.85	Cancelled 22.11.01 as WFU "Pro-Sport"	25. 4.90A
G-BMKX	Cameron Elephant 77 SS Balloon (Hot Air)	1196		6. 2.86	Cancelled 21.10.96 as WFU "Benjamin I"	19. 2.89A
G-BMST	Cameron N-31 Balloon (Hot Air)	1317		4. 6.86	Cancelled 1. 5.92 as WFU	16. 2.90A
					"B&Q" (Badly damaged and for spares 12.01)	
G-BMUR	Cameron Zero 25 Airship (Gas Filled)	1169		11. 6.86	Cancelled 21.10.96 as WFU "Zero 25"	
G-BNCH	Cameron V-77 Balloon (Hot Air)	1398		11.12.86	Cancelled 25. 6.02 as WFU "Sapper II"	19. 6.92A
G-BNHL	Colt Beer Glass 90 SS Balloon (Hot Air)	1042		24 .3.87	Cancelled 22. 6.98 as WFU "Gatzweiler"	4. 3.97A
G-BOCF	Colt 77A Balloon (Hot Air)	1178		4. 1.88	Cancelled 6.10.03 as WFU	25. 7.94T
G-BOGT	Colt 77A Balloon (Hot Air)	1212		21. 3.88	Cancelled 9. 5.97 as WFU "British Gas	2.12.94A
G-BONK	Colt 180A Balloon (Hot Air)	1167		14.12.87	Cancelled 28.11.01 as WFU "Bonkette"	2.11.94T
G-BONV	Colt 17A Cloudhopper Balloon (Hot Air)	1238		3. 5.88	Cancelled 22.11.01 as WFU "Bryant Group"	1. 4.93A
G-BOOP	Cameron N-90 Balloon (Hot Air)	1702	(G-BOMX)	11. 5.88	Cancelled 31.10.95 by CAA	28. 9.95A
					"Betty Boop" (Unipart titles)	
G-BORA	Colt 77A Balloon (Hot Air)	1233		19. 5.88	Cancelled 17. 9.98 as WFU "Carla"	24. 8.94A
G-BOTE	Thunder Ax8-90 Balloon (Hot Air)	555		14. 6.88	Cancelled 12.12.95 as WFU "Barge Fox"	16. 2.95T
G-BPAH	Colt 69A Balloon (Hot Air)	512		2. 6.83	Cancelled 13. 5.02 by CAA "J & B Phil"	15. 8.88A
G-BPDF	Cameron V-77 Balloon (Hot Air)	1806		6.10.88	Cancelled 17. 3.05 by CAA	31. 7.00A
G-BPFJ	Cameron Can 90 SS Balloon (Hot Air)	1834		14.11.88	Cancelled 9. 5.97 as WFU	10.12.93A
	(Budweiser Beer Can shape)				"Budweiser Can I"	
G-BPFX	Colt 21A Cloudhopper Balloon (Hot Air)	1348		7.11.88	Cancelled 23.12.98 as WFU "Budweiser Hopper"	21.11.96T
G-BPSZ	Cameron N-180 Balloon (Hot Air)	1911		14. 3.89	Cancelled 9. 5.01 as WFU) "Park Furnishers"	30. 4.01T
G-BRFR	Cameron N-105 Balloon (Hot Air)	2042		14. 7.89	Cancelled 9. 5.97 as WFU	6.12.93A
					"Rover" (Badly damaged, spares use only)	
G-BRLX	Cameron N-77 Balloon (Hot Air)	2095		13. 9.89	Cancelled 23.10.01 by CAA "National Power"	1. 6.96A
G-BSBM	Cameron N-77 Balloon (Hot Air)	2229		8. 3.90	Cancelled 15. 7.98 as WFU "Nuclear Electric 1"	21.11.96A
G-BTML	Cameron Rupert Bear 90 SS Balloon (Hot Air)			16. 5.91	Cancelled 29. 4.97 as WFU	31.12.94A
		2533			"Rupert Bear"	
G-BTJF	Thunder Ax10-180 Series 2 Balloon (Hot Air)			28. 3.91	Cancelled 4. 8.03 as destroyed	4. 5.01T
		1952			"Yorkshire Lad"	
G-BUET	Colt Flying Drinks Can SS Balloon (Hot Air)	2162		30. 3.92	Cancelled 29. 4.97 as WFU	10.12.93A
	(Budweiser Can shape)				"Bud King Can"	
G-BUEU	Colt 21A Cloudhopper Balloon (Hot Air)	2163		30. 3.92	Cancelled 29. 4.97 as WFU "Bud King Hopper"	2.12.94A
G-BUKC	Cameron A-180 Balloon (Hot Air)	2870		3. 7.92	Cancelled 11.10.99 as WFU "Cloud Nine"	2. 3.00T
G-BUXA	Colt 210A Balloon (Hot Air)	2400		28. 4.93	Cancelled 20.12.01 as WFU "Buxam"	7. 4.99T
G-BWPL	Airtour AH-56 Balloon (Hot Air)	011	G-OAFC	19. 3.96	Cancelled 17. 9.01 as WFU	
					"Paul J Donnellan" (As "G-OAFC")	
G-BWUR	Thunder Ax10-210 Series 2 Balloon (Hot Air)			11. 7.96	Cancelled 14. 3.06 by CAA	7. 4.01T
		3910			"Kinetic"	
G-BWZP	Cameron Home Special 105 SS Balloon (Hot Air)			6.12.96	Cancelled 15. 1.04 as WFU	10. 4.02A
		4051			(Barclays Mortgages titles)	
G-BXAX	Cameron N-77 Balloon (Hot Air)	2010		25. 5.89	Cancelled 31. 1.02 as WFU "Citroën"	21.11.96A
G-BXHM	Lindstrand LBL 25A Cloudhopper Balloon (Hot Air)			30. 5.97	Cancelled 6.11.01 as WFU	7. 5.00A
		466			"Bud Ice and Michelob"	
G-BXND	Cameron Thomas the Tank Engine 110 SS Balloon (Hot Air)			23. 2.00	Cancelled 19.11.02 by CAA	25. 6.02A
		4254				
G-COLR	Colt 69A Balloon (Hot Air)	780		8. 4.86	Cancelled 21. 5.93 as WFU "Bubble"	1. 4.93A
G-COMP	Cameron N-90 Balloon (Hot Air)	1564		24. 9.87	Cancelled 18.12.01 by CAA "Computacentre I"	20. 5.97A
G-CURE	Colt 77A Balloon (Hot Air)	1424		3. 7.89	Cancelled 29. 4.97 as WFU	21.11.96A
	(Standard shape plus Tablet blisters)				"Alka Seltzer III"	
G-DHLZ	Colt 31A Air Chair Balloon (Hot Air)	2604		2. 6.94	Cancelled 9. 4.99 as WFU "DHL Parcel"	23. 7.99A
G-ETFT	Colt Financial Times SS Balloon (Hot Air)	1792	G-BSGZ	11. 1.91	Cancelled 10.12.02 by CAA "Financial Times II"	14.10.00A
G-FZZY	Colt 69A Balloon (Hot Air)	779		19. 2.86	Cancelled 29. 4.97 as WFU "Alka-Seltzer II"	16. 2.90A
G-GEUP	Cameron N-77 Balloon (Hot Air)	880		8.12.82	Cancelled 9. 5.01 as WFU "Gee-Up"	19. 7.96
G-GRIP	Cameron Colt Bibendum 110 SS Balloon (Hot Air)			5. 1.98	Cancelled 7. 9.05 as WFU	25. 1.02A
		4224			(Michelin titles)	
G-GURL	Cameron A-210 Balloon (Hot Air)	2387		3. 9.90	Cancelled 2.12.98 as WFU "Hot Airlines"	9. 8.96T
G-HENS	Cameron N-65 Balloon (Hot Air)	740		8. 7.81	Cancelled 8. 4.93 by CAA "Free Range"	16. 7.90A
G-HLIX	Cameron Helix Oilcan 61 SS Balloon (Hot Air)			20. 9.85	Cancelled 29. 4.97 as WFU	25. 4.90A
	(Originally regd as 80 SS)			1192	"Helix Oil Can"	
G-IGEL	Cameron N-90 Balloon (Hot Air)	2726		7. 4.92	Cancelled 18.12.01 by CAA "Computacentre II"	12. 5.97A

G-IMAG	Colt 77A Balloon (Hot Air)	1718		9. 3.90	Cancelled 31. 1.02 as WFU	19. 1.00A

G-IMAG   Colt 77A Balloon (Hot Air)   1718   9. 3.90   Cancelled 31. 1.02 as WFU   19. 1.00A
            (Second envelope c/n 2254 as original DBF 6.92)   *"Agfa"*
"G-OAFC"   Airtour AH-56 Balloon (Hot Air)   011   23. 5.90   Cancelled 17. 1.96 as PWFU - re-regd as G-BWPL qv
G-OCND   Cameron O-77 Balloon (Hot Air)   1020   6. 2.84   Cancelled 19. 5.95 by CAA *"CND Airborne"*   6.11.93A
G-OHDC   Colt Film Cassette SS Balloon (Hot Air) 2633   8. 8.94   Cancelled 31.1.02 as WFU   26. 8.99A
            (Agfa Film Can shape)   *"Agfa HDC Can"*
G-JANB   Colt Flying Bottle SS Balloon (Hot Air) 1643   16. 2.90   Cancelled 20.12.01 by CAA   30. 9.96A
            (J & B Whisky Bottle shape)   *"J & B Bottle"*
G-LLAI   Colt 21A Cloudhopper Balloon (Hot Air)   519   (G-BKTX)   18. 7.83   Cancelled 16. 7.90 by CAA
                                                                                          "Llama" (Lowndes Laing Insurance titles)
G-MAAC   Advanced Airship Corporation ANR-1 Airship (Gas Filled)   16. 1.89   Cancelled 15.11.00 by CAA
                                                    01   *"ANR-1"*
G-NPWR   Cameron RX-100 Balloon (Hot Air)   2849   13. 7.92   Cancelled 15. 7.98 as WFU *"Nuclear Rozier"*   21.11.96A
G-NWPB   Thunder Ax7-77Z Balloon (Hot Air)   278   13. 5.80   Cancelled 27. 4.90 by CAA *"Post Office"*   17.10.89A
G-OLDV   Colt 90A Balloon (Hot Air)   2592   5. 5.94   Cancelled 29. 6.99 as WFU *"LDV"*   10.11.98A
G-OSVY   Sky 31-24 Balloon (Hot Air)   104   28. 5.98   Cancelled 31. 7.01 as WFU *"OS Hopper"*   11. 3.00A
G-OXRG   Colt Film Can SS Balloon (Hot Air)   2138   17. 1.92   Cancelled 29. 4.97 as WFU   21.11.96A
            (Agfacolor Film Can shape)   *"Agfa XRG Can"*
G-PONY   Colt 31A Air Chair Balloon (Hot Air)   434   23. 8.82   Cancelled 19. 5.95 by CAA *"Neddie"*
G-PURE   Cameron Can 70 SS Balloon (Hot Air)   1913   18. 1.89   Cancelled 29. 4.97 as WFU   10.12.93A
            (Guinness Can)   *"Guinness Can"*
G-PYLN   Cameron Pylon 80 SS Balloon (Hot Air) 2958   G-BUSO   18. 1.93   Cancelled 6.11.01 as WFU   25. 4.97A
            (Electricity Pylon shape)   *"Essex Girl"*
G-RARE   Thunder Ax5-42 SS Balloon (Hot Air)   266   20. 2.80   Cancelled 14. 5.02 by CAA   7. 4.95A
            (J & B Rare Whisky Bottle shape)   *"J & B Hamish"*
G-RIPS   Cameron Action Man-Parachutist 110 SS Balloon (Hot Air)   29. 4.97   Cancelled 23. 7.02 as WFU   25. 5.00A
                                                    4092   *"Action Man"*
G-SCAH   Cameron V-77 Balloon (Hot Air)   788   18. 1.82   Cancelled 30.11.01 by CAA *"Orpheus"*   24. 7.87A
G-SEUK   Cameron TV 80 Balloon (Hot Air)   3810   12. 4.96   Cancelled 31. 1.02 as WFU   24. 3.00A
            (Samsung Computer shape)   *"Samsung Monitor"*
G-SGAS   Colt 31A Balloon (Hot Air)   2073   31.10.91   Cancelled 23. 6.07 as destroyed *(Shell Gas titles)* 26. 4.01A
G-TTWO   Colt 56A Balloon (Hot Air)   087   14. 5.80   Cancelled 14.11.95 as WFU *"Tea 4 Two"*   1. 9.87A
G-UNIP   Cameron Oil Container SS Balloon (Hot Air)   15. 3.91   Cancelled 31.1.02 as WFU   7.11.96A
            (Unipart Sureflow Oil Can)   2532   *"Unipart Can"*
G-VOLT   Cameron N-77 Balloon (Hot Air)   2157   8.11.89   Cancelled 23.10.01 as WFU *"National Power II"*   25. 4.97A
G-WATT   Cameron Cooling Tower SS Balloon (Hot Air)   8.11.89   Cancelled 23.10.01 as WFU *"Cooling Tower"*   22. 8.96A
G-WINE   Thunder AX7-77Z Balloon (Hot Air)   472   25.11.82   *Cancelled 10. 4.02 by CAA "Gemini"*   17. 6.97A
G-WORK   Thunder Ax10-180 Series 2 Balloon (Hot Air)   DQ-PBF   12. 5.93   Cancelled 3.11.97 - sold as DQ-PBF   26. 5.97A
                                                    2396   G-WORK   *(Paradise Balloon Flights titles) (As "DQ-PBF")*
G-ZUMP   Cameron N-77 Balloon (Hot Air)   377   18. 1.78   Cancelled 8. 4.98 as WFU   3. 5.91A
            (Rebuilt 1985 with new canopy c/n 1107)   *"Gazump"*

The following are preserved in Museums and available private collections. Full details are shown in SECTION 4, Part 1.

Registration	Type	Location
G-EACN	BAT FK.23 Bantam 1	Schiphol, Netherlands
G-EACQ	Avro 534 Baby	Brisbane, Australia
G-EAML	Airco DH.6	Pretoria, South Africa
G-EAOU	Vickers FB.27A Vimy IV	Adelaide, Australia
G-EAQM	Airco DH.9	Canberra, Australia
G-EBIB	Royal Aircraft Factory SE.5a	South Kensington, London
G-EBIC	Royal Aircraft Factory SE.5a	Hendon, London
G-EBJE	Avro 504K	Hendon, London
G-EBJG	Parnall Pixie III	Coventry, Warwickshire
G-EBMB	Hawker Cygnet I	RAF Cosford, Shropshire
G-EBNO	de Havilland DH.60 Moth	Halmstad, Sweden
G-EBNU	Avro 504K	Jyväskylä, Finland
G-EBOV	Avro 581E Avian	South Brisbane, Queensland, Australia
G-EBUB	Westland Widgeon III	Wangaratta, Victoria, Australia
G-EBYY	Cierva C 8L Mk.2	Paris Le Bourget, France
G-EBZM	Avro 594A Avian IIIA	Manchester
G-AAAH	de Havilland DH.60G Moth	Santa Paula, California, US
G-AACN	Handley Page HP.39 Gugnunc	Wroughton, Wiltshire
G-AAHD	Avro 594 Avian IV	Stockholm, Sweden
G-AAMX (2)	American Moth Corporation DH.60GM Moth	Hendon, London
G-AAMZ (2)	de Havilland DH.60G Moth	Santa Paula, California, US
G-AANJ (2)	Luft-Verkehrs Gesellschaft C VI	Hendon, London
G-AARO (2)	Arrow Sport A2-60	Chantilly, Virginia, US
G-ABAA	Avro 504K	Manchester
G-ABBB	Bristol 105A Bulldog IIA	Hendon, London
G-ABDW	de Havilland DH.80A Puss Moth	East Fortune, Scotland
G-ABIH	de Havilland DH.80A Puss Moth	Rhinebeck, New York, US
G-ABLF	Avro 616 Avian Sport	Salisbury, Australia
G-ABLK	Avro 616 Avian V	South Brisbane, South Australia
G-ABLM	Cierva C 24	Salisbury Hall, London Colney, Hertfordshire
G-ABMR	Hawker Hart	Hendon, London
G-ABOI	Wheeler Slymph	Coventry, Warwickshire
G-ABUU	Comper CLA.7 Swift	Madrid, Spain
G-ABXH	Cierva C 19 Mk.IVP	Madrid, Spain
G-ACGO	Saunders-Roe A 19 Cloud	Prague, Czech Republic
G-ACGR	Percival Type D Gull Four IIA	Brussels, Belgium
G-ACIT	de Havilland DH84 Dragon 1	Wroughton, Wiltshire

G-ACPP	de Havilland DH.89 Dragon Rapide	Wetaskiwin, Alberta, Canada
G-ACUP	Percival Type D Gull Six	Wangaratta, Victoria, Australia
G-ACUU	Cierva C 30A	Duxford, Cambridgeshire
G-ACUX	Short S 16 Scion 1	Belfast, Northern Ireland
G-ACVA	Kay Gyroplane 33/1	East Fortune, Scotland
G-ACWM	Cierva C 30A	Weston-super-Mare, Somerset
G-ACWP	Cierva C 30A	South Kensington, London
G-ACXA	Cierva C 30A	Milan, Italy
G-ACXK	de Havilland DH.60G-III Moth Major	Madrid, Spain
G-ACYK	Spartan Cruiser III	East Fortune, Scotland
G-ACYR	de Havilland DH.89 Dragon Rapide	Madrid, Spain
G-ADAH	de Havilland DH.89 Dragon Rapide	Manchester
G-ADLS	Miles M.3C Falcon Six	Madrid, Spain
G-ADMW	Miles M.2H Hawk Major	RAF Stafford, Staffordhire
G-ADOT	de Havilland DH.87B Hornet Moth	Salisbury Hall, London Colney, Hertfordshire
G-ADPR	Percival Type D Gull Six	Auckland, New Zealand
G-ADWO	de Havilland DH.82A Tiger Moth	Southampton, Hampshire
G-AEEH	Mignet HM.14 Pou-Du-Ciel	RAF Cosford, Shropshire
G-AEGV	Mignet HM.14 Pou-Du-Ciel	Coventry, Warwickshire
G-AEHM	Mignet HM.14 Pou-Du-Ciel	Wroughton, Wiltshire
G-AEJZ	Mignet HM.14 Pou-Du-Ciel	Hemswell, Lincolnshire
G-AEKR	Mignet HM.14 Pou-Du-Ciel	Doncaster, Yorkshire
G-AEKV	Kronfeld (BAC) Drone de luxe	Brooklands, Surrey
G-AEKW	Miles M.12 Mohawk	RAF Cosford, Shropshire
G-AERD	Percival Type D Gull Six	Canberra, Australia
G-AERN	de Havilland DH.89A Dragon Rapide	Madrid, Spain
G-AETA	Caudron G III	Hendon, London
G-AEVZ	BA L 25c Swallow II	Madrid, Spain
G-AEYF	General Aircraft Monospar St 25 Ambulance	Egeskov, Denmark
G-AFBS	Miles M.14A Hawk Trainer 3	Duxford, Cambridgeshire
G-AFDX	Hanriot HD.1	Hendon, London
G-AFGK	Miles M.11A Whitney Straight	Wetaskiwin, Alberta, Canada
G-AFJR	Tipsy Trainer 1	Brussels, Belgium
G-AFNJ	de Havilland DH.94 Moth Minor	La Ferté-Alais, Essonne, France
G-AFOR	de Havilland DH.94 Moth Minor	Caboolture, Queensland, Australia
G-AFOW	de Havilland DH.94 Moth Minor	Albury, New South Wales, Australia
G-AFRV	Tipsy Trainer I	Brussels, Belgium
G-AFTN	Taylorcraft Plus C2	Coalville, Leicestershire
G-AFVH	Tipsy S 2	Brussels, Belgium
G-AFWN	Auster J/1 Autocrat	Stauning, Denmark
G-AGBN	General Aircraft GAL.42 Cygnet 2	East Fortune, Scotland
G-AGCN	Lockheed 18-56 Lodestar II (C-56D-LO)	Auckland, New Zealand
G-AGIJ	Lockheed 18-56 Lodestar II (C-60A-5-LO)	Stockholm, Sweden
G-AGNV	Avro 685 York C 1	RAF Cosford, Shropshire
G-AGOS	Reid and Sigrist RS.4 Desford Trainer	Coalville. Leicestershire
G-AGPG	Avro 652A Anson 19 Series 2	Hooton Park, Cheshire
G-AGRU	Vickers 657 Viking 1	Brooklands, Surrey
G-AGRW	Vickers 639 Viking 1	Vienna, Austria
G-AGTB	Percival Proctor V	Kogarah, New South Wales, Australia
G-AGXS	Auster V J/1 Autocrat	Sils-Girona, Spain
G-AGYX	Douglas C-47A-10-DK Dakota 3	Hendon, London
G-AGZI	Consolidated-Vultee CV.32-3 (LB-30) Liberator II	Anchorage, Alaska, US
G-AHAT	Auster J/1N Alpha	Dumfries, Scotland
G-AHAY	Auster V J/1 Autocrat	Beersheba, Israel
G-AHDI	Percival Proctor I	Melbourne, Victoria, Australia
G-AHED	de Havilland DH.89A Dragon Rapide 6	RAF Stafford, Staffordhire
G-AHHE	Auster V J/1 Autocrat	Hamilton East, New Zealand
G-AHJR (2)	Short S 25 Sunderland MR.5	Auckland, New Zealand
G-AHKO	Taylorcraft Plus D	Stauning, Denmark
G-AHKY	Miles M.18 Series 2	East Fortune, Scotland
G-AHLO	de Havilland DH.80A Puss Moth	Rockcliffe, Ottawa, Ontario, Canada
G-AHLX	Douglas C-47A-30-DK Dakota	Belgrade, Serbia
G-AHMJ	Cierva C 30A	Polk City, Florida ,US
G-AHOT	Vickers 498 Viking 1A	Johannesburg, South Africa
G-AHRI	de Havilland DH.104 Dove 1B	Newark, Nottinghamshire
G-AHTW	Airspeed AS.40 Oxford 1	Duxford, Cambridgeshire
G-AHVG	Percival Proctor II	Alice Springs, Australia
G-AHZY	Percival Proctor V	Brussels, Belgium
G-AIBE	Fairey Fulmar 2	RNAS Yeovilton, Somerset
G-AICH	Bristol 170 Freighter Mk.1A	Buenos Aires, Argentina
G-AIJK	Auster V J/4 Archer	Coalville. Leicestershire
G-AIKR	Airspeed AS.65 Consul	Rockcliffe, Ottawa, Ontario, Canada
G-AIMI	Bristol 170 Freighter 21E	Point Cook, Victoria, Australia
G-AINT	Bristol 170 Freighter 31MNZ	Christchurch, New Zealand
G-AIPE	Taylorcraft J Auster 5	Rosendaal, Netherlands
G-AIPW	Taylorcraft Auster 5A Series 160	Amman, Jordan
G-AISU	Vickers Supermarine 349 Spitfire LF.VB	RAF Coningsby
G-AITB	Airspeed AS.40 Oxford 1	Hendon, London
G-AITF	Airspeed AS.40 Oxford 1	Pretoria, South Africa
G-AIWY	de Havilland DH.89A Dragon Rapide	Helsingør, Denmark
G-AIXA	Taylorcraft Plus D	Hendon, London
G-AIYT	Douglas C-47A-10-DK Dakota	Beersheba, Israel
G-AIZE	Fairchild F 24W-41A Argus II	RAF Cosford, Shropshire
G-AIZG	Vickers Supermarine 236 Walrus 1	RNAS Yeovilton, Somerset

G-AIZW	Auster V J/1 Autocrat	Halmstad, Sweden
G-AJAV	Douglas C-47A-5-DK Dakota	Aragua, Maracay, Venezuela
G-AJEB	Auster J/1N Alpha	Hooton Park, Cheshire
G-AJEC	Auster V J/1 Autocrat	Wanaka, New Zealand
G-AJHW	Sikorsky S-51	Point Cook, Victoria, Australia
G-AJJP	Fairey FB.2 Jet Gyrodyne	Woodley, Berkshire
G-AJKF (2)	de Havilland DH.84 Dragon III	Point Cook, Victoria, Australia
G-AJKG (2)	Miles M.38 Messenger 2A	Melbourne, Victoria, Australia
G-AJLR	Airspeed AS.65 Consul	Singapore
G-AJMC	Bristol 156 Beaufighter TF.X	Beersheba, Israel
G-AJOC	Miles M.38 Messenger 2A	BBelfast, Northern Ireland
G-AJOZ	Fairchild 24W-41A Argus 1	Elvington, Yorkshire
G-AJPC	Fairchild F 24W-41A Argus II	Helsinki, Finland
G-AJRH	Auster J/1N Alpha	Loughborough, Leicestershire
G-AJTI	Miles M.65 Gemini 1A	Pretoria, South Africa
G-AJVL	Miles M.38 Messenger 2A	Caboolture, Queensland, Australia
G-AKAA	Piper J-3C-65 Cub (L-4H-PI)	Madrid, Spain
G-AKAO	Miles M.38 Messenger 2A	Halmstad, Sweden
G-AKCO	Short S 25 Sandringham 7	Paris Le Bourget, France
G-AKDK	Miles M.65 Gemini 1A	Helsingør, Denmark
G-AKEE	de Havilland DH.82A Tiger Moth	Ratamalana, Sri Lanka
G-AKEL	Miles M.65 Gemini 1A	Belfast, Northern Ireland
G-AKGE	Miles M.65 Gemini 3C	Belfast, Northern Ireland
G-AKGV	de Havilland DH.89A Dragon Rapide	Sault Sainte Marie, Ontario, Canada
G-AKIS	Miles M.38 Messenger 2A	Brussels, Belgium
G-AKIZ	Fairchild F 24R-41A Argus II	Helsinki, Finland
G-AKKA	Miles M 65 Gemini 1A	Stavangar, Norway
G-AKKR	Miles M.14A Hawk Trainer 3	AAC Middle Wallop, Hampshire
G-AKKY	Miles M.14A Hawk Trainer 3	Woodley, Berkshire
G-AKLL	Douglas C-47A-30-DK Dakota	Sinsheim, Germany
G-AKLS	Short SA.6 Sealand 1	Belgrade, Serbia
G-AKLW	Short SA.6 Sealand 1	Belfast, Northern Ireland
G-AKNP	Short S.45 Solent 3	Oakland, California, US
G-AKNV	de Havilland DH.89A Dragon Rapide	Brussels, Belgium
G-AKOW	Taylorcraft J Auster 5	AAC Middle Wallop, Hampshire
G-AKRS	de Havilland DH.89A Dragon Rapide	Beersheba, Israel
G-AKVD	Chrislea CH.3 Series 2 Super Ace	Tokyo, Japan
G-AKZY	Messerschmitt Bf.108D-1 Taifun	Albuquerque, New Mexico, US
G-ALBN	Bristol 173 Mk.1	Kemble, Gloucestershire
G-ALBP	Miles M.38 Messenger 4A	Wangaratta, Victoria, Australia
G-ALCK	Percival Proctor III	Duxford, Cambridgeshire
G-ALCS (2)	Miles M.65 Gemini 3C	Leitrim, County Leitrim, Ireland
G-ALCU	de Havilland DH.104 Dove 2B	Coventry, Warwickshire
G-ALDG	Handley Page HP.81 Hermes IV	Duxford, Cambridgeshire
G-ALFO	Douglas C-47A-90-DL Dakota	Addison, Dallas, Texas, US
G-ALFT	de Havilland DH.104 Dove 6	Caernarfon, Wales
G-ALFU	de Havilland DH.104 Dove 6	Duxford, Cambridgeshire
G-ALGB	de Havilland DH.89A Dragon Rapide	Paris Le Bourget, France
G-ALIS	Percival Proctor III	Bull Creek, Western Australia
G-ALJZ	EoN AP.5 Olympia 2B	Woodley, Berkshire
G-ALMB	Westland-Sikorsky S-51 Dragonfly Mk.1A	Vigna di Valle. Italy
G-ALMN	EoN AP.7 Primary	Woodley, Berkshire
G-ALNH	Slingsby T 6 Kite 1	AAC Middle Wallop, Hampshire
G-ALRX	Bristol 175 Britannia Series 101	Kemble, Gloucestershire
(G-ALSP)	Bristol 171 Sycamore 3	Rochester, Kent
G-ALSX	Bristol 171 Sycamore 3	Weston-super-Mare, Somerset
G-ALUA	Winter LF-1 Zaunkönig	Munich, Germany
G-ALWC	Douglas C-47A-25-DK Dakota	Toulouse, France
G-ALWF	Vickers 701 Viscount	Duxford, Cambridgeshire
G-ALXT	de Havilland DH.89A Dragon Rapide	Wroughton, Wiltshire
G-ALYB	Taylorcraft J Auster 5	Doncaster, Yorkshire
G-ALZE	Britten-Norman BN-1F	Southampton, Hampshire
G-ALZF	de Havilland DH.89A Dragon Rapide	La Ferté-Alais, Essonne, France
G-ALZL	de Havilland DH.114 Heron Series 1	Bull Creek, Western Australia
G-ALZO (2)	Airspeed AS.57 Ambassador 2	Duxford, Cambridgeshire
G-AMAU	Hawker Hurricane IIc	RAF Coningsby, Lincolnshire
G-AMCA	Douglas C-47B-30-DK Dakota 3	Lelystad, Netherlands
G-AMDA	Avro 652A Anson 1	Duxford, Cambridgeshire
G-AMDD	de Havilland DH.104 Dove 6	Leitrim, County Leitrim, Ireland
G-AMFU	de Havilland DH.104 Dove 6	Lelystad, Netherlands
G-AMHB	Westland-Sikorsky S-51 Dragonfly Mk.1B	Bebeduoro, Brazil
G-AMHJ	Douglas C-47A-25-DK Dakota 6	RAF Shawbury, Shropshire
G-AMJD	de Havilland DH.82A Tiger Moth	Brussels, Belgium
G-AMJR	de Havilland DH.82A Tiger Moth	Jyväskylä, Finland
G-AMJT	Westland-Sikorsky S-55 Whirlwind HAR.1	Elvington, Yorkshire
G-AMJW	Westland-Sikorsky S-51 Mk.1A	Bangkok, Thailand
G-AMJY	Douglas C-47B-40-DK Dakota	Ratamalana, Sri Lanka
G-AMLF	de Havilland DH.82A Tiger Moth	Santa Paula, California, US
G-AMLZ	Percival P 50 Prince 6E	Caernarfon, Wales
G-AMMA	de Havilland DHC-1 Chipmunk 21	Stauning, Denmark
G-AMMC	Miles M.14A Hawk Trainer 3	Auckland, New Zealand
G-AMNL	Douglas C-47B-35-DK Dakota	Montevideo, Uruguay
G-AMOG (2)	Vickers 701 Viscount	East Fortune, Scotland
G-AMOI	Vickers 701 Viscount	Bebeduoro, Brazil

G-AMOU	de Havilland DH.82A Tiger Moth	Bangkok, Thailand
G-AMPM	de Havilland DH.82A Tiger Moth	Mackay, Queensland, Australia
G-AMPO	Douglas C-47B-30-DK Dakota 3	RAF Lyneham, Wiltshire
G-AMRM	de Havilland DH.82A Tiger Moth	Auckland, New Zealand
G-AMSM	Douglas C-47B-20-DK Dakota	Brenzett
G-AMTL	de Havilland DH.82A Tiger Moth	Zaventem, Belgium
G-AMWI	Bristol 171 Sycamore 4	Kogarah, New South Wales, Australia
G-AMXR	de Havilland DH.104 Dove 6	Salisbury Hall, London Colney, Hertfordshire
G-AMXS	de Havilland DH.104 Dove 2A	Maracay, Venezuela
G-AMXX	de Havilland DH.104 Dove 2A	Hermeskeil, Trier, Germany
G-AMYA(2)	Zlin Z.381 Bestmann	Polk City, Florida, US
G-AMYJ	Douglas C-47B-25-DK Dakota 6	Elvington, Yorkshire
G-AMZH	Douglas C-47B-20-DK Dakota	Port Moresby, Papua-New Guinea
G-AMZO	de Havilland DH.87B Hornet Moth	Stauning, Denmark
G-AMZW	Douglas C-47B-20-DK Dakota	Johannesburg, South Africa
G-ANAV	de Havilland DH.106 Comet 1A	Wroughton, Wiltshire
G-ANCF	Bristol 175 Britannia Series 308F	Liverpool, Merseyside
G-ANCN	de Havilland DH.82A Tiger Moth	Dayton, Ohio, US
G-ANCY	de Havilland DH.82A Tiger Moth	Stauning, Denmark
G-ANEJ	de Havilland DH.82A Tiger Moth	Kuala Lumpur, Malaysia
G-ANFH	Westland WS.55 Whirlwind 1	Weston-super-Mare, Somerset
G-ANFU	Taylorcraft J Auster 5	Newcastle upon Tyne, Northumberland & Tyneside
G-ANFW	de Havilland DH.82A Tiger Moth	Ta'Qali, Malta
G-ANGV	Auster V J/1B Aiglet	Queenstown, New Zealand
G-ANHD	Vickers 701C Viscount	Bebeduoro, Brazil
G-ANHM	Taylorcraft G Auster 4	Murwillumbah, New South Wales, Australia
G-ANIU	Taylorcraft J Auster 5	Stockholm, Sweden
G-ANIZ	de Havilland DH.82A Tiger Moth	Galveston, New Mexico, US
G-ANJG	de Havilland DH.82A Tiger Moth	La Ferté-Alais, Essonne, France
G-ANJV	Westland WS-55 Whirlwind 3	Weston-super-Mare, Somerset
G-ANKV	de Havilland DH.82A Tiger Moth	Croydon, London
G-ANLW	Westland WS-51 Series 2 Widgeon	Flixton, Bungay, Suffolk
G-ANNC	de Havilland DH.82A Tiger Moth	Santa Teresa, New Mexico, US
G-ANNW	Auster J/5F Aiglet Trainer	Kuwait City, Kuwait
G-ANOS	de Havilland DH.82A Tiger Moth	Brandon, Manitoba, Canada
G-ANOV	de Havilland DH.104 Dove 6	East Fortune, Scotland
G-ANPV (2)	de Havilland DH.114 Heron 2D	Melbourne, Victoria, Australia
G-ANRX	de Havilland DH.82A Tiger Moth	Salisbury Hall, London Colney, Hertfordshire
G-ANSG	de Havilland DH.82A Tiger Moth	La Ferté-Alais, Essonne, France
G-ANSO	Gloster Meteor T 7	Halmstad, Sweden
G-ANTK	Avro 685 York C 1	Duxford, Cambridgeshire
G-ANUO	de Havilland DH.114 Heron 2D	Croydon, London
G-ANVU	de Havilland DH.104 Dove 1B	Linköping, Sweden
G-ANXB	de Havilland DH.114 Heron 1B	Newark, Nottinghamshire
G-ANXP	Piper J-3C-65 Cub (L-4H-PI)	Liorac-sur-Louyre, Dordogne, France
G-ANZS	de Havilland DH.82A Tiger Moth	Yering, Victoria, Australia
G-AODA	Westland WS-55 Whirlwind 3	Weston-super-Mare, Somerset
G-AOEL	de Havilland DH.82A Tiger Moth	East Fortune, Scotland
G-AOFR	de Havilland DH.82A Tiger Moth	Egeskov, Denmark
G-AOFX (2)	Vickers 701C Viscount	Sao Paulo, Brazil
G-AOGA	Miles M.75 Aries 1	Leitrim, County Leitrim, Republic of Ireland
G-AOGJ	de Havilland DH.82A Tiger Moth	La Ferté-Alais, Essonne, France
G-AOGW	de Havilland DH.114 Heron 2E	Sault Sainte Marie, Ontario, Canada
G-AOHD (2)	Hunting Percival P 84 Jet Provost T 2	Point Cook, Victoria,Australia
G-AOIE	Douglas DC-7C	Leitrim, County Leitrim, Republic of Ireland
G-AOJG	Hunting-Percival P 66 President 1	Helsingør, Denmark
G-AOJT	de Havilland DH.106 Comet IXB	Salisbury Hall, London Colney, Hertfordshire
G-AOJX	de Havilland DH.82A Tiger Moth	Brussels, Belgium
G-AOKO	Percival P 40 Prentice 1	Doncaster, Yorkshire
G-AOKZ	Percival P 40 Prentice 1	Coventry, Warwickshire
G-AOMF	Percival P 40 Prentice 1	Wanaka, New Zealand
G-AOPL	Percival P 40 Prentice 1	Pretoria, South Africa
G-AOPO	Percival P 40 Prentice 1	Brussels, Belgium
G-AOSP	de Havilland DHC-1 Chipmunk 22	Scone, New South Wales, Australia
G-AOTI	de Havilland DH.114 Heron 2D	Salisbury Hall, London Colney, Hertfordshire
G-AOUF	de Havilland DH.104 Dove 6	Helsingør, Denmark
G-AOUJ	Fairey Ultralight Helicopter	Weston-super-Mare, Somerset
G-AOUR	de Havilland DH.82A Tiger Moth	Belfast, Northern Ireland
G-AOVF	Bristol 175 Britannia Series 312F	RAF Cosford, Shropshire
G-AOVT	Bristol 175 Britannia Series 312	Duxford, Cambridgeshire
G-AOXG	de Havilland DH.82A Tiger Moth	RNAS Yeovilton, Somerset
G-AOVU	de Havilland DH.106 Comet 4C	Seattle, Washington, US
G-AOXL	de Havilland DH.114 Heron 1B	Stavangar, Norway
G-AOYU	de Havilland DH.82A Tiger Moth	Wetaskiwin, Alberta, Canada
G-AOZE	Westland WS-51/2 Widgeon	Weston-super-Mare, Somerset
G-AOZZ	Armstrong-Whitworth 650 Argosy Series 100	Belleville, Michigan, US
G-APAD	Edgar Percival EP.9	Greenock, South Australia
G-APAS	de Havilland DH.106 Comet 1A	RAF Cosford, Shropshire
G-APCN	Boulton Paul P 108 Balliol T 2	Negombo, Sri Lanka
G-APDB	de Havilland DH.106 Comet 4	Duxford, Cambridgeshire
G-APEJ	Vickers 953C Vanguard Merchantman	Brooklands, Surrey
G-APEP	Vickers 953C Vanguard Merchantman	Brooklands, Surrey
G-APES	Vickers 953C Vanguard Merchantman	East Midlands
G-APFJ	Boeing 707-436	East Fortune, Scotland

G-APHV	Avro 652A Anson C 19 Series 2	East Fortune, Scotland
G-APHY	Scottish Aviation Twin Pioneer Series 1	Quesnel, British Columbia, Canada
G-APIM	Vickers 806 Viscount	Brooklands, Surrey
G-APIT	Percival P 40 Prentice 1	Lasham, Hampshire
G-APIY	Percival P 40 Prentice 1	Newark, Nottinghamshire
G-APJJ (2)	Fairey Ultralight Helicopter	Coventry, Warwickshire
G-APJP	de Havilland DH.82A Tiger Moth	Helsingør, Denmark
G-APJT	Scottish Aviation Twin Pioneer Series 1	Kuala Lumpur, Malaysia
G-APLG	Auster J/5L Aiglet Trainer	Carlisle, Cumbria
G-APMY	Piper PA-23-160 Apache	Doncaster, Yorkshire
G-APNJ	Cessna 310	Newark, Nottinghamshire
G-APNV	Saunders-Roe P 531-1	RNAS Yeovilton, Somerset
G-APPT	de Havilland DH.82A Tiger Moth	Brussels, Belgium
G-APRL	Armstrong-Whitworth 650 Argosy Series 101	Coventry, Warwickshire
G-APTS	de Havilland DHC-1 Chipmunk 22A	Adelaide, South Australia
G-APTW	Westland WS-51/2 Widgeon	Sunderland, Northumberland and Tyneside
G-APUD	Bensen B-7MC	Manchester
G-APUP	Sopwith Pup replica	Hendon, London
G-APVV	Mooney M 20A	Newark, Nottinghamshire
G-APWA	Handley Page HPR.7 Dart Herald 100	Woodley, Berkshire
G-APWJ	Handley Page HPR.7 Dart Herald 201	Duxford, Cambridgeshire
G-APWN	Westland WS-55 Whirlwind 3	Coventry, Warwickshire
G-APWY	Piaggio P 166	Wroughton, Wiltshire
G-APXA	Westland-Sikorsky S-55 Whirlwind Series 2	Kuwait City, Kuwaitt
G-APXB	Westland-Sikorsky S-55 Whirlwind Series 2	Kuwait City, Kuwait
G-APXG	de Havilland DH.114 Heron 2D	Winnipeg, Manitoba, Canada
G-APXW	Lancashire Aircraft EP-9 Prospector	AAC Middle Wallop, Hampshire
G-APXX	de Havilland DHA.3 Drover 2	Lasham, Hampshire
G-APYD	de Havilland DH.106 Comet 4B	Wroughton, Wiltshire
G-ARAD	Phoenix Luton LA-5A Major	Sunderland, Northumberland & Tyneside
G-ARCX	Gloster Meteor NF.14	East Fortune, Scotland
G-ARDE	de Havilland DH.104 Dove 6	Sharjah, United Arab Emirates
G-AREA	de Havilland DH.104 Dove 8	Salisbury Hall, London Colney, Hertfordshire
G-ARGI (2)	Auster 6A Tugmaster	Doncaster, Yorkshire
G-ARHX	de Havilland DH.104 Dove 8	Doncaster, Yorkshire
G-ARLU (2)	Cessna 172B	Baldonnel, Northern Ireland
G-ARPH	de Havilland DH.121 Trident 1C	East Fortune, Scotland
G-ARRM	Beagle B 206X	Shoreham, West Sussex
G-ARTZ (1)	McCandless M 2 Gyroplane	Belfast, Northern Ireland
G-ARUE (2)	de Havilland DH.104 Dove 7	Sinsheim, Germany
G-ARVF	Vickers VC-10 Series 1101	Hermeskeil, Trier, Germany
G-ARVM (2)	Vickers VC-10 Series 1101	Brooklands, Surrey
G-ARVN (2)	Servotec CR LTH 1 Grasshopper 1	Weston-super-Mare, Somerset
G-ARYB	de Havilland DH.125 Series 1	Coventry, Warwickshire
G-ARYC	de Havilland DH.125 Series 1	Salisbury Hall, London Colney, Hertfordshire
G-ARYD	Auster AOP.6	AAC Middle Wallop, Hampshire
G-ASCB	Beagle A 109 Airedale	Alverca, Portugal
G-ASCD	Beagle A 61 Terrier 2	Elvington, Yorkshire
G-ASCF	Beagle A 61 Terrier 2	Gardemoen, Norway
G-ASCT	Bensen B 7MC	Weston-super-Mare, Somerset
G-ASCX	de Havilland DH.114 Heron 2D	Launceston, Tasmania, Australia
G-ASCY	Phoenix Luton LA-4A Minor	Miami, Florida, US
G-ASDS	Vickers 843 Viscount	Beijing, China
G-ASFI	de Havilland DH.114 Heron 2D	Bankstown, New South Wales, Australia
G-ASGC	Vickers Super VC-10 Series 1151	Duxford, Cambridgeshire
G-ASHD	Brantly B 2A	Weston-super-Mare, Somerset
G-ASIX	Vickers VC-10 Series 1103	Brooklands, Surrey
G-ASJD	British Aircraft Corporation One-Eleven 201AC	Boscombe Down, Wiltshire
G-ASKB	de Havilland DH.98 Mosquito TT.35	Miami, Florida, US
G-ASKC	de Havilland DH.98 Mosquito TT.35	Duxford, Cambridgeshire
G-ASKK	Handley Page HPR.7 Dart Herald 211	Norwich, Norfolk
G-ASOF	Beagle B.206 Series.1	Birmingham, Alabama, US
G-ASOL	Bell 47D-1	Sunderland, Northumberland & Tyneside
G-ASRF	Gowland GWG.2 Jenny Wren	Flixton, Bungay, Suffolk
G-ASRL	Beagle A 61 Terrier 2	Krugersdorp, South Africa
G-ASSM	Hawker Siddeley HS.125 Series 1/522	South Kensington, London
G-ASSZ	Cessna 310A	Helsingør, Denmark
G-ASTL	Fairey Firefly 1	RNAS Yeovilton, Somerset
G-ASTP	Hiller UH-12C	Weston-super-Mare, Somerset
G-ASUG	Beech E18S-9700	East Fortune, Scotland
G-ASVC	de Havilland DH.114 Heron 2D	Caloundra, Queensland, Australia
G-ASVO	Handley Page HPR.7 Dart Herald 214	Inverness, Scotland
G-ASWJ	Beagle B 206C Series 1	(Coventry, Warwickshire)
G-ASXM	Armstrong-Whitworth 650 Argosy Series 222	Marlborough, New Zealand
G-ASXN	Armstrong-Whitworth 650 Argosy Series 222	Marlborough, New Zealand
G-ASXX	Avro 683 Lancaster B VII	East Kirkby, Lincolnshire
G-ASYD	British Aircraft Corporation One-Eleven 475AM	Brooklands, Surrey
G-ATBZ	Westland WS-58 Wessex 60 Series 1	Weston-super-Mare, Somerset
G-ATDD	Beagle B 206 Series 1	Kemble, Gloucestershire
G-ATFG	Brantly B 2B	Weston-super-Mare, Somerset
G-ATGJ	de Havilland DH.104 Riley Dove 5	Ballarat, Victoria, Australia
G-ATGK	de Havilland DH.104 Riley Dove 400	Amman, Jordan
G-ATJJ	de Havilland DHC.1 Chipmunk 22	Brooklands, Surrey
G-ATKV	Westland WS-55 Whirlwind 3	Weston-super-Mare, Somerset

G-ATOY	Piper PA-24-260 Comanche B	East Fortune, Scotland
G-ATTN	Piccard Balloon (Hot Air) (62,000 cu ft)	Wroughton, Wiltshire
G-ATVP	Vickers FB.5 Gunbus replica	Hendon, London
G-ATXL	Avro 504K replica	Rhinebeck, New York, US
G-ATXX	McCandless M 4	Belfast, Northern Ireland
G-AVAA	Cessna F150G	Doncaster, Yorkshire
G-AVAV	Vickers Supermarine 509 Spitfire Tr.9	Oshkosh, Wisconsin, US
G-AVFH	Hawker Siddeley HS.121 Trident 2E	Salisbury Hall, London Colney, Hertfordshire
G-AVFB	Hawker Siddeley HS.121 Trident 2E	Duxford, Cambridgeshire
G-AVHE	Vickers 812 Viscount	Stuttgart, Germany
G-AVJB	Vickers 815 Viscount	Hillerstorp, Sweden
G-AVKE	Gadfly HDW-1	Weston-super-Mare, Somerset
G-AVLP	Beagle B.206 Series.2	Birmingham, Alabama, US
G-AVMO	British Aircraft Corporation One-Eleven 510ED	East Fortune, Scotland
G-AVMU	British Aircraft Corporation One-Eleven 510ED	Duxford, Cambridgeshire
G-AVNE	Westland WS-58 Wessex 60 Series 1	Weston-super-Mare, Somerset
G-AVPC	Druine D 31 Turbulent	East Fortune, Scotland
G-AVPN	Handley Page HPR.7 Dart Herald 213	Elvington, Yorkshire
G-AVVO	Avro 652A Anson 19 Series 2	Newark, Nottinghamshire
G-AVVR	Avro 652A Anson 19 Series 2	Pendeford, Wolverhampton, West Midlands
G-AVXV	Bleriot XI	La Baule, Loire-Atlantique, France
G-AVZB	LET Z-37 Cmelak	Wroughton, Wiltshire
G-AWAU	Vickers FB.27A Vimy replica	Hendon, London
G-AWAW	Cessna F150F	South Kensington, London
G-AWFM	de Havilland DH.104 Dove 6	Johannesburg, South Africa
G-AWHA	CASA 2111D	Munich, Germany
G-AWHB	CASA 2111D	Seattle, Washington, US
G-AWHE	Hispano HA.1112-MIL Buchon	Midland, Texas, US
G-AWHJ	Hispano HA.1112-MIL Buchon	Kalamazoo, Michigan, US
G-AWHL	Hispano HA.1112-MIL Buchon	Seattle, Washington, US
G-AWHN	Hispano HA.1112-MIL Buchon	Tillamook, Oregon, US
G-AWHO	Hispano HA.1112-MIL Buchon	Oshkosh, Wisconsin, US
G-AWHS	Hispano HA.1112-MIL Buchon	Sinsheim, Germany
G-AWID	Britten-Norman BN-2A Islander	Khlong Luang, Thailand
G-AWIJ	Vickers Supermarine 329 Spitfire IIA	RAF Coningsby, Lincolnshire
G-AWJV	de Havilland DH.98 Mosquito TT.35	Salisbury Hall, London Colney, Hertfordshire
G-AWON	English Electric Lightning F 53	Norwich, Norfolk
G-AWRP	Servotech CR.LTH.1 Grasshopper II	Weston-super-Mare, Somerset
G-AWRS	Avro 652A Anson C 19 Series 2	Sunderland, Northumberland & Tyneside
G-AWSA	Avro 652A Anson C 19/2	Flixton, Bungay, Suffolk
G-AWTD	Percival P 56 Provost T 1	Gweru, Zimbabwe
G-AWYY	Slingsby T 57 Sopwith Camel F 1 replica	RNAS Yeovilton, Somerset
G-AWZI	Hawker Siddeley HS.121 Trident 3B Series 101	Farnborough, Hampshire
G-AWZJ	Hawker Siddeley HS.121 Trident 3B Series 101	Dumfries, Scotland
G-AWZK	Hawker Siddeley HS.121 Trident 3B Series 101	Manchester
G-AWZM	Hawker Siddeley HS.121 Trident 3B Series 101	Wroughton, Wiltshire
G-AWZP	Hawker Siddeley HS.121 Trident 3B Series 101	Manchester
G-AXDN	British Aircraft Corporation Concorde	Duxford, Cambridgeshire
G-AXEE	English Electric Lightning F 53	Kuwait City, Kuwait
G-AXEF	British Aircraft Corporation 167 Strikemaster Mk.81	Santa Rosa, California , US
G-AXEH	Beagle B 125 Bulldog 1	East Fortune, Scotland *(See G-CCOA below)*
G-AXFM	Servotec CR.LTH.1 Grasshopper II	Weston-super-Mare, Somerset
G-AXKS	Westland-Bell 47G-4A	AAC Middle Wallop, Hampshire
G-AXOM	Penn-Smith Gyroplane	Lower Stondon, Bedfordshire
G-AYAG	Boeing 707-321	Leitrim, County Leitrim, Republic of Ireland
G-AYAZ	Britten-Norman BN-2A-7 Islander	Hong Kong, China
G-AYBX	Campbell Cricket	Alexandria, Egypt
G-AYFA	Scottish Aviation Twin Pioneer Mk.3	Carlisle, Cumbria
G-AYFO	Bücker Bü.133 Jungmeister	Polk City, Florida, US
G-AYHS	British Aircraft Corporation 167 Strikemaster Mk.84	Olympia, Washington, US
G-AYTA	SOCATA MS.880B Rallye Club	Manchester
G-AYUK	Western-Brighton M-B65 Balloon (Hot Air)	Munich, Germany
G-AYXT	Westland WS-55 Whirlwind HAS.7 (Series 2)	Weston-super-Mare, Somerset
G-AYZJ	Westland WS-55 Whirlwind HAS.7	Newark, Nottinghamshire
G-AYZM	Scottish Aviation Bulldog Series 101	Halmstad, Sweden
G-AZAK	Scottish Aviation Bulldog Series 101 (SK-61)	Linköping, Sweden
G-AZAU	Servotec CR.LTH.1 Grasshopper II	Weston-super-Mare, Somerset
G-AZAZ	Bensen B 8M	RNAS Yeovilton, Somerset
G-AZBV	Britten-Norman BN-2A-2 Islander	Beersheba, Israel
G-AZCM	Beagle B 121 Pup Series 150	Manston
G-AZFW	Hawker Siddeley HS.121 Trident 2E Series 102	Guangzou, China
G-AZJO	Scottish Aviation Bulldog Series 101 (SK-61)	Linköping, Sweden
G-AZLM	Reims Cessna F172L	Flixton, Bungay, Suffolk
G-AZMF	British Aircraft Corporation One-Eleven 530FX	Bournemouth, Dorset
G-AZPH	Pitts S 1S	South Kensington, London
G-AZWO	Scottish Aviation Bulldog Series 101 (SK-61)	Linköping, Sweden
G-AZYB	Bell 47H-1	Weston-super-Mare, Somerset
G-BACK	de Havilland DH.82A Tiger Moth	Santiago, Chile
G-BAGJ	Westland SA.341G Gazelle 1	Sunderland, Northumberland & Tyneside
G-BAHB	de Havilland DH.104 Dove 5	Port Adelaide, South Australia
G-BAMH	Westland S-55 Whirlwind Series 3	East Midlands
G-BAJJ	Hawker Siddeley HS.121 Trident 2E Series 108	Beijing, China
G-BAPS	Campbell Cougar Gyroplane	Weston-super-Mare, Somerset
G-BAVN	Boeing Stearman A75N-1 Kaydet	Västerås, Sweden

G-BBBV	Handley Page HP.137 Jetstream	East Fortune, Scotland
G-BBDG	British Aircraft Corporation Concorde Type 1 Variant 100	Brooklands, Surrey
G-BBGN	Cameron A-375 Balloon (Hot Air)	Wroughton, Wiltshire
G-BBMI	Dewoitine D 26	Polk City, Florida, US
G-BBNC	de Havilland DHC-1 Chipmunk T 10	Salisbury Hall, London Colney, Hertfordshire
G-BBVF	Scottish Aviation Twin Pioneer 3	East Fortune, Scotland
G-BBVU	Hawker Siddeley HS.121 Trident 2E Series 109	Guangzou, China
G-BBVV	Hawker Siddeley HS.121 Trident 2E Series 109	Nanjing, China
G-BBVW	Hawker Siddeley HS.121 Trident 2E Series 109	Guangzou, China
G-BBVZ	Hawker Siddeley HS.121 Trident 2E Series 109	Beijing, China
G-BBWG	Hawker Siddeley HS.121 Trident 2E Series 109	Beijing, China
G-BBZL	Westland-Bell 47G-3B1	Stavangar, Norway
G-BBYM	Handley Page HP.137 Jetstream 200	RAF Cosford, Shropshire
G-BCOH	Avro 683 Lancaster Mk.10 AR	Polk City, Florida, US
G-BCWL	Westland Lysander IIIA	Polk City, Florida, US
G-BCXO	MBB BÖ.105DD	Land's End
G-BCYK	Avro (Canada) CF-100 Canuck Mk.IV	Duxford, Cambridgeshire
G-BCZS	Fairey Britten-Norman BN-2A-21 Islander	Stavangar, Norway
G-BDBS	Short SD.3-30 UTT	Langford Lodge, Belfast, Northern Ireland
G-BDBZ	Westland WS-55 Whirlwind 2 (HAR.10)	Elvington, Yorkshire
G-BDDX	Whittaker MW2B Excalibur	Trago Mills, Newton Abbot
G-BDFU	PMPS Dragonfly MPA Mk.1	East Fortune, Scotland
G-BDIW	de Havilland DH.106 Comet 4C	Hermeskeil, Trier, Germany
G-BDIX	de Havilland DH.106 Comet 4C	East Fortune, Scotland
G-BDVO	Short SC.7 Skyvan 3 Variant 100	Caracas, Venezuela
G-BDPU	Fairey Britten-Norman BN-2A-21 Islander	Brussels, Belgium
G-BDUP	Bristol 175 Britannia Series 253	Kemble, Gloucestershire
G-BDVS	Fokker F 27 Friendship 200	Flixton, Bungay, Suffolk
G-BDYG	Percival P 56 Provost T 1	East Fortune, Scotland
G-BEBC	Westland WS-55 Whirlwind HAR.10	Norwich, Norfolk
G-BECL	CASA 352L	La Ferté-Alais, Essonne, France
G-BECE	Aerospace Developments AD500 Series B.1 Airship	Doncaster, Yorkshire
G-BEDV	Vickers 668 Varsity T 1	Duxford, Cambridgeshire
G-BEED	Fairey Britten-Norman BN-2A-21 Islander	Grace Hollogne, Belgium
G-BEEX	de Havilland DH.106 Comet 4C	Sunderland, Northumberland & Tyneside
G-BEOX	Lockheed 414 Hudson IIIA	Hendon, London
G-BEOZ	Armstrong-Whitworth AW.650 Argosy 101	East Midlands
G-BESY	British Aircraft Corporation 167 Strikemaster Mk.80A	Duxford, Cambridgeshire
G-BEWT	Short SD.3-30 Variant 100	Millville, New Jersey, US
G-BEYB	Fairey Flycatcher replica	RNAS Yeovilton, Somerset
G-BEYF	Handley Page HPR.7 Dart Herald 401	Bournemouth, Dorset
G-BFBP	Piper PA-25-235 Pawnee D	Wainfleet, Lincolnshire
G-BFCZ	Sopwith Camel F 1 replica	Brooklands, Surrey
G-BFDE	Sopwith Tabloid Scout replica	Hendon, London
G-BFEY	Piper PA-25-235 Pawnee D	Wainfleet, Lincolnshire
G-BFHD	CASA 352L	Washington, US
G-BFHE	CASA 352L	Johannesburg, South Africa
G-BFHG	CASA 352L	Polk City, Florida, US
G-BFIP	Wallbro Monoplane replica	Flixton, Bungay, Suffolk
G-BFOO	British Aircraft Corporation 167 Strikemaster Mk.80A	Dhahran, Saudi Arabia
G-BFTZ	SOCATA MS.880B Rallye Club	Newark, Nottinghamshire
G-BFXL	Williams Albatross D Va replica	RNAS Yeovilton, Somerset
G-BFYO	SPAD XIII replica	Duxford, Cambridgeshire
G-BGCF	Douglas C-47A-90-DL Dakota	Barksdale AFB, Louisiana, US
G-BGGR	North American AT-6A Harvard	Stuttgart, Germany
G-BGHF	Westland WG.30 Series 100-60	Weston-super-Mare, Somerset
G-BGLB	Bede BD.5B	Wroughton, Wiltshire
G-BGSB	Hunting-Percival P 56 Provost T 1	Bait al Falaj, Muscat, Oman
G-BGWZ	Eclipse Super Eagle	RNAS Yeovilton, Somerset
G-BHDK	Boeing TB-29A-45-BN Superfortress	Duxford, Cambridgeshire
G-BHMY	Fokker F 27 Friendship 600	Norwich, Norfolk
G-BHNG	Piper PA-23-250 Aztec E	Filching Manor, Wannock, Sussex
G-BHUB	Douglas C-47A-85-DL Dakota	Duxford, Cambridgeshire
G-BHUW	Boeing Stearman A75N1 (N2S-5) Kaydet	Munich, Germany
G-BIAT	Sopwith Pup replica	Christchurch, New Zealand
G-BIAU	Sopwith Pup replica	RNAS Yeovilton, Somerset
G-BIDN	Percival P.57 Sea Prince T.1	New York, Ontario, Canada
G-BIDW	Sopwith 1½ Strutter replica	Hendon, London
G-BIHN	Airship Industries Skyship 500	Millom, Cumbria
G-BIRW	Morane Saulnier MS.505 Criquet	East Fortune, Scotland
G-BJAD	Clutton FRED Series II	Newark, Nottinghamshire
G-BJCL	Morane Saulnier MS.230 Parasol	Polk City, Florida, US
G-BJHS	Short S 25 Sandringham	Polk City, Florida, US
G-BJHV	Voisin Scale replica	Brooklands, Surrey
G-BJSG	Vickers Supermarine 361 Spitfire LF.IXc	Chino, California, US
G-BJWY	Sikorsky S-55 (HRS-2) Whirlwind HAR.21	Carlisle, Cumbria
G-BKBR (2)	Cameron Chateau 84SS Balloon (Hot Air)	Balleroy, Calvados, France
G-BKDT	Royal Aircraft Factory SE.5a replica	Elvington, Yorkshire
G-BKFD	Westland WG.30 Series 100	Weston-super-Mare, Somerset
G-BKFF	Westland WG.30 Series 100	Weston-super-Mare, Somerset
G-BKGD	Westland WG.30 Series 100	Weston-super-Mare, Somerset
G-BKLZ	Vinten Wallis WA-116MC	Hermeskeil, Trier, Germany
G-BKMW	Short SD.3-30 Sherpa Variant 100	Belfast, Ireland
G-BKNN	Cameron Minar-E-Pakistan Balloon (Hot Air)	Balleroy, Calvados, France

G-BKPG	Luscombe P3 Rattler Strike	Newark, Nottinghamshire
G-BKPY	SAAB 91B/2 Safir	Newark, Nottinghamshire
G-BKRG	Beech C-45G-BH	Lelystad, Netherlands
G-BKRL	Chichester-Miles Leopard	Bournemouth, Dorset
G-BLFE	Cameron Sphinx 72 SS Balloon (Hot Air)	Balleroy, Calvados, France
G-BLFL	Douglas C-47B-45-DK Dakota	Berlin, Germany
G-BLKA	de Havilland DH.112 Venom FB.Mk.54	Salisbury Hall, London Colney, Hertfordshire
G-BLKU	Colt Flame 56 SS Balloon (Hot Air)	Manchester
(G-BLMC)	Avro 698 Vulcan B 2A	East Midlands
G-BLRW	Cameron Elephant 77 SS Balloon (Hot Air)	Balleroy, Calvados, France
G-BLWM	Bristol 20 M 1C replica	Hendon, London
(G-BLXI (1))	Bleriot Type XI replica	Cannes, France
(G-BLZW)	Republic P-47D-30-RA Thunderbolt	Palm Springs, California, US
G-BMEW	Lockheed 18-56 Lodestar	Gardemoen, Norway
G-BMFB	Douglas Skyraider AEW.1 (AD-4W)	Tillamook, Oregon, US
G-BMUN	Cameron Harley 78 SS Balloon (Hot Air)	Balleroy, Calvados, France
G-BMWN	Cameron Temple 80 SS Balloon (Hot Air)	Balleroy, Calvados, France
G-BMYP	Fairey Gannet AEW.3	Elvington, Yorkshire
G-BMZF	Aero-Vodochody SBLim-2A	RNAS Yeovilton, Somerset
G-BNFK	Cameron Egg 89 SS Balloon (Hot Air)	Balleroy, Calvados, France
G-BNPG	Percival P 66 Pembroke C 1	Västerås, Sweden
G-BNJU	Cameron Bust 80 SS Balloon (Hot Air)	Balleroy, Calvados, France
G-BOAA	British Aircraft Corporation Concorde Type 1 Variant 102	East Fortune, Scotland
G-BOAB	British Aircraft Corporation Concorde Type 1 Variant 102	London Heathrow
G-BOAC	British Aircraft Corporation Concorde Type 1 Variant 102	Manchester
G-BOAD	British Aircraft Corporation Concorde Type 1 Variant 102	New York, US
G-BOAE	British Aircraft Corporation Concorde Type 1 Variant 102	Barbados Grantley Adams
G-BOAF	British Aircraft Corporation Concorde Type 1 Variant 102	Filton, Bristol
G-BOAG	British Aircraft Corporation Concorde Type 1 Variant 102	Seattle, Washington, US
G-BOCB	Hawker Siddeley HS.125 Series 1B/522	Doncaster, Yorkshire
G-BOOM	Hawker Hunter T 7 (T 53)	Amman, Jordan
G-BPLT	Bristol 20 M 1C replica	Los Cerillos, Santiago, Chile
G-BPOV	Cameron Magazine 90 SS Balloon (Hot Air)	Balleroy, Calvados, France
G-BPSP	Cameron Ship 90 SS Balloon (Hot Air)	Balleroy, Calvados, France
G-BRAM	Mikoyan MiG-21PF	RAF Cosford, Shropshire
G-BRDV	Replica Viking Spitfire prototype	Southampton, Hampshire
G-BRMA	Westland-Sikorsky S-51 Dragonfly HR.5	Weston-super-Mare, Somerset
G-BRMB	Bristol 192 Belvedere HC.1	Weston-super-Mare, Somerset
G-BRMC	Stampe et Renard SV-4B	Antwerp, Belgium
G-BRNM	Chichester-Miles Leopard	Bournemouth, Dorset
G-BRXM	Colt GA-42 Gas Airship.	Helsinki, Finland
G-BSKS	Nieuport 28C-1	Fort Rucker, Alabama, US
G-BSST	British Aircraft Corporation Concorde 002	RNAS Yeovilton, Somerset
G-BSSY	CSS-13 Aeroklubowy	Old Warden
G-BTHD	Yakovlev Yak-3U	Chino, California, US
G-BTSY	English Electric Lightning F 6	Binbrook
G-BTUC	Embraer EMB-312 Tucano	Langford Lodge, Belfast, Northern Ireland
G-BUCF	Grumman F8F-1B Bearcat	Chino, California, US
G-BURM	English Electric Canberra TT.18	Temora, New South Wales, Australia
G-BUWA	Vickers Supermarine 349 Spitfire F Vc	Seattle, Washington, US
G-BVLM	de Havilland DH.115 Vampire T 55	Amman, Jordan
G-BVOL	Douglas C-47B-40-DL Dakota	Lelystad, Netherlands
G-BVPO	de Havilland DH.100 Vampire FB.6	Amman, Jordan
G-BVWG	Hawker Hunter T 8C	Cape Town, South Africa
G-BVWV	Hawker Hunter F 6A	Cape Town, South Africa
G-BWGR	North American TB-25N-NC Mitchell	Brussels, Belgium
G-BWJZ	de Havilland DHC-1 Chipmunk 22	Manston
G-BWKA	Hawker Hunter F 58	Amman, Jordan
G-BWKC	Hawker Hunter F 58	Amman, Jordan
G-BXSL	Westland Scout AH.Mk.1	Hermeskeil, Trier, Germany
G-BXYA	Lotnicze Zaklady Naprawcz CSS-13	Polk City, Florida, US
G-BYDR	North American B-25D Mitchell	Seattle, Washington, US
G-BYDS	Messerschmitt Bf.109E-3	Seattle, Washington, US
G-BYKV	Avro 504K replica	Point Cook, Victoria, Australia
G-BZNL	North American F-86A Sabre	Seattle, Washington, US
G-CBEP	British Aerospace Jetstream Series 3200	Bankstown, New South Wales, Australia
G-CCMV	Vought FG-1D Corsair	Addison, Dallas, Texas, US
G-CCVV	Vickers Supermarine 379 Spitfire FR.XIVe	Polk City, Florida, US
G-CONI	Lockheed 749A-79 Constellation	Wroughton, Wiltshire
G-DELB	Robinson R22 Beta	Doncaster, Yorkshire
G-DUCK	Grumman G 44 Widgeon (OA-14)	Biscarrosse, Landes, France
G-DEVN	de Havilland DH.104 Devon C 2/2	Merseburg, Germany
G-DMCA	McDonnell Douglas DC-10-30	Manchester International
G-EHIL	EH Industries EH-101	Weston-super-Mare, Somerset
G-ELEC	Westland WG.30 Series 200	Weston-super-Mare, Somerset
G-EFIS	Westland WG.30 Series 100	Weston-super- Mare
G-FIST	Fieseler Fi.156C-3 Storch	Vigna di Valle, Italy
G-FIRE	Vickers Supermarine 379 Spitfire FR.XIVc	Palm Springs, California, US
G-FOKW	Focke-Wulf Fw.190A-5	Seattle, Washington, US
G-FORT	Boeing 299-O (B-17G-95-DL) Fortress	Galveston, New Mexico, US
G-FRJB	Aircraft Designs Sheriff SA-1	East Midlands
G-FSIX	English Electric Lightning F 6	Cape Town, South Africa
G-FXIV	Vickers Supermarine 379 Spitfire FR.XIVc	Hannover, Germany
G-HAUL	Westland WG.30-300	Weston-super-Mare, Somerset

G-HELI	Saro Skeeter AOP.12	Gatow, Berlin, Germany
G-HNTR	Hawker Hunter T 7	Elvington, Yorkshire
G-HUNN	Hispano HA.1112-M1L Buchon	Addison, Dallas, Texas, US
G-HUNT	Hawker Hunter F 51	Oshkosh, Wisconsin, US
G-IRJX	BAE Systems Avro 146-RJX100	Manchester
G-JMAC	British Aerospace Jetstream Series 4100	Liverpool, Merseyside
G-JSSD	Handley Page HP.137 Jetstream 1	East Fortune, Scotland
G-LANC	Avro 683 Lancaster B X	Duxford, Cambridgeshire
G-LIOA	Lockheed 10A Electra	South Kensington, London
G-LIZY	Westland Lysander III	Duxford, Cambridgeshire
G-LTNG	English Electric Lightning T 5	Cape Town, South Africa
G-LYNX	Westland WG.13 Lynx 800	Weston-super-Mare, Somerset
G-MBBZ	Volmer VJ.24W	Newark, Nottinghamshire
G-MBDL	Striplin (AES) Lone Ranger	Sunderland, Northumberland & Tyneside
G-MBEP	American Aerolights Eagle 215B	Caernarfon, Wales
G-MJDW	Eipper Quicksilver MXII	Newark, Nottinghamshire
G-MJKP	Hiway Skystrike/Super Scorpion	Doncaster, Yorkshire
G-MJPB	Manuel Ladybird	Brooklands, Surrey
G-MJRA	Mainair Tri-Flyer 250/Hiway Demon	Elvington, Yorkshire
G-MJSU	MBA Tiger Cub 440	Flixton, Bungay, Suffolk
(G-MJWH)	Chargus Vortex 120	Coventry
G-MJWS	Eurowing Goldwing	Langford Lodge, Belfast, Northern Ireland
G-MJXE	Mainair Tri-Flyer 330/Hiway Demon 175	Manchester
G-MMCB	Huntair Pathfinder II	Wroughton, Wiltshire
G-MMLI	Mainair Tri-Flyer 250/Solar Wings Typhoon S	East Fortune, Scotland
G-MTFK	Moult Trike/Flexiform Striker	Flixton, Bungay, Suffolk
G-MURY	Robinson R44 Astro	Chantilly, Virginia, US
G-OGIL	Short SD.3-30 Variant.100	Sunderland, Northumberland & Tyneside
G-OIOI	EH Industries EH-101 Heliliner	Hendon, London
G-OMIG	Aero-Vodochody SBLim-2A	San Carlos, Brazil
G-OTED	Robinson R22HP	Weston-super-Mare, Somerset
G-OTHL	Robinson R22 Beta	Hendon, London
G-OPAS	Vickers 806 Viscount	Bournemouth, Dorset
G-OPIB	English Electric Lightning F 6	Cape Town, South Africa
G-PASB	MBB BÖ.105D	Weston-super-Mare, Somerset
G-RBOS	Colt AS 105 Airship (Hot Air)	Wroughton, Wiltshire
G-RENT	Robinson R22 Beta	Langford Lodge, Belfast, Northern Ireland
G-RWWW	Westland WS-55 Whirlwind HCC.12	Weston-super-Mare, Somerset
G-SALY	Hawker Sea Fury FB.X	Midland, Texas, US
G-SEXY	American AA-1 Yankee	Liverpool, Merseyside
G-SFTA	Westland SA.341G Gazelle 1	Sunderland, Northumberland & Tyneside
G-SWIF	Vickers Supermarine 552 Swift F 7	Southampton, Hampshire
G-SXVI	Vickers Supermarine 361 Spitfire LF.XVIe	McMinnville, Oregon, US
G-TFRB	Air Command 532 Elite Sport	Elvington, Yorkshire
G-THUN	Republic P-47D-40RA Thunderbolt	Millville, New Jersey, US
G-TURK	Cameron Sultan 80 SS Balloon (Hot Air)	Balleroy, Calvados, France
G-TURP	Aérospatiale SA341G Gazelle 1	Charlwood, Surrey
G-USTV	Messerschmitt Bf.109G-2/Trop	Hendon, London
G-USUK	Colt 2500A Balloon (Hot Air)	Duxford, Cambridgeshire
G-VIII	Vickers Supermarine 359 Spitfire LF.VIII	Addison, Dallas, Texas, US
G-VTOL	Hawker Siddeley Harrier T 52	Brooklands, Surrey
G-WWII	Vickers-Supermarine 379 Spitfire F.XIVe	Chino, California, US
G-XVIB	Vickers Supermarine 361 Spitfire LF.XVIe	Polk City, Florida, US

PART 4 – AIRCRAFT REGISTERED and CANCELLED in 2007 and 2008

Registration	Type	Construction Number	Previous Identity	Date	Registered Owner (Operator)	Cancellation details	Date
G-BGLJ	Bell 212	30548	ZJ969	4. 6.07	FB Heliservices Ltd	To ZJ969	8. 6.07
	G-BGLJ, ZJ969, G-BGLJ, ZJ969, G-BGLJ, EC-HCZ, (EC-HCP), G-BGLJ, (EC-GHP), EC-295, G-BGLJ, 9Y-TIJ, G-BGLJ, 5N-AJX, G-BGLJ						
	5N-AJX, G-BGLJ, EP-HBZ, VR-BEJ, N2956W				*(Also restored 24. 9.07 and cancelled to MOD 1.10.07 as ZJ969)*		
G-BTLC	Aérospatiale AS.365N2 Dauphin 2	6406	ZJ164	22. 4.91	Veritair Ltd	To ZJ164	12.10.07
			G-BTLC, ZJ164		*(Restored 12.10.07)*		
G-CBPO	Yakovlev Yak-50	853101	LY-AOT	29. 1.07	R A Cayless	To VH-xxx	13. 6.07
			RA-44476, DOSAAF 59 *(blue)*				
G-CECN	Rockwell Commander 690B	11482	HS-TFG	13. 7.07	FM-International OY	To N95590	20. 2.08
			N745T, N4224U, YV-212CP, (N81805)				
G-CEHA	British Aerospace Avro 146-RJ85	E2333	N515XJ	6. 3.07	BAE Systems (Funding One) Ltd	To EI-RJC	6.12.07
			G-6-333				
G-CEHB	British Aerospace Avro 146-RJ85	E2344	N519XJ	28. 6.07	BAE Systems (Funding One) Ltd	To EI-RJG	18.12.07
			G-6-344				
G-CEIJ	British Aerospace BAe 146 Series 200	E2204	I-FLRU	6. 2.07	Trident Jet (Dublin) Ltd	To PK-LNI	8.11.07
			I-FLRA, G-6-204, G-OSAS, G-6-204				
G-CEJH	ELA Aviacion ELA 07S	09061140724		23. 1.07	M C Woodhouse	Cancelled by CAA	5.10.07
G-CEJS	Agusta A109E Power	11159	RP-C2838	4. 1.07	Castle Air Charters Ltd	To G-JJJL	12. 4.07
G-CEKN	Robinson R44 Raven II	11600		13. 3.07	Heli Air Ltd	To EI-DVX	15. 3.07
G-CEKP	Sikorsky S-76C+	760641	N875AL	11. 4.07	Bristow Helicopters Ltd	To 9M-SPS	6. 7.07
G-CEKR	Sikorsky S-76C+	760645	N878AL	11. 4.07	Caledonian Helicopters Ltd	To 9M-SPT	9. 8.07
G-CEOA	Bell 407	53331	EI-DBN	19. 6.07	Magell Ltd	To C-FTJU-	18. 2.08
			N8268T				
G-CEOR	Sikorsky S-76C+	760654	N45003	22. 6.07	Caledonian Helicopters Ltd	To 9M-Sxx	1.10.07
G-CEPO	Agusta A109A II	7289	RP-C2400	30. 4.07	Castle Air Charters Ltd	To G-TMUR	14. 5.07
			I-MIIT, N109BB				
G-CERJ	Alpi Pioneer 300	xxx		30. 4.07	K P O'Sullivan	To G-CESE	11. 5.07
	(Built K P O'Sullivan - pr.no.PFA 330-14465)						
G-CERU	Eurocopter AS.350B3 Ecureuil	4301	F-WWXL	7. 8.07	McAlpine Helicopters Ltd	To G-SPVK	24. 9.07
G-CESE	Alpi Pioneer 300	xxx	G-CERJ	11. 5.07	K P O'Sullivan	To G-VIXX	20. 7.07
	(Built K P O'Sullivan - pr.no.PFA 330-14465)						
G-CESF	Evektor EV-97 teamEurostar UK	3008		14. 8.07	R Joy tr Eurostar Group	Cancelled as PWFU	14.12.07
G-CEVR	H and E Revolution-R120 Paramotor	0106231		15.11.07	N Flint	Cancelled as PWFU	24. 1.08
G-CEWJ	Rolladen-Schneider LS8-18	8395	BGA 4904-JZC	13.11.07	M H Patel	To G-WDGC	8. 2.08
G-CJMC	Bombardier Learjet Model 60	60-300	OH-AEM	5. 3.07	Corporate Jet Management Ltd	To EI-xxx	21.12.07
			N40081				
G-CJWC	Schleicher ASW 27	27142	BGA 4831-JWC	19.10.07	C G Starkey	To G-THRM	26.10.07
G-CKFU	Schempp-Hirth Ventus 2cxT	114/311	BGA 5064-KFU	31.10.07	W F Payton	To G-DKFU	19.11.07
			D-KOAX				
G-CKOS	Letov LF-107 Lunak	45	BGA 5258-KOS	5. 3.07	J Rehousek	Cancelled by CAA	18. 2.08
			OK-0829		*"KOS"*		
G-CRST	Agusta A109E Power	11017	N709AT	27. 4.07	Castle Air Charters Ltd	To G-WRBI	22.11.07
			HB-XQM				
G-DASO	Dassault Mystere Falcon 50EX	268	G-ITIH	4. 4.07	Bramptonia Ltd	To M-DASO	14. 1.08
			F-WQBL, N268FJ, F-WQBL, PH-JNL, CS-TMS, EC-GTR, F-WWHS				
G-DDBR	Slingsby T.59D Kestrel 19	1858	BGA 1989-DBR	29.11.07	P L Poole	To OK-xxx	5. 2.08
G-EWAT	Eurocopter EC.155 B1	6764	F-WWOO	30. 5.07	McAlpine Helicopters Ltd	To G-EURT	6. 6.07
G-HIGI	Eurocopter EC.120B Colibri	1489		9. 5.07	McAlpine Helicopters Ltd	To G-OLDO	29.11.07
G-HSLJ	Robinson R44 Raven	1747		16. 8.07	Homewood Developments Ltd	To G-ETFF	26.10.07
G-IIOJ	Schempp-Hirth Nimbus 4M	3	D-KLXX	6. 3.07	S G Jones *(Noted Lasham 2.08)*	To D-KIOJ	29. 8.07
G-JEAD	Fokker F 27 Friendship 500	10627	I-FWXB	14.11.90	BAC Group Ltd	To 5Y-xxx-	8.11.07
			G-JEAD, VH-EWU, PH-EXL		*(Restored 18. 7.07)*		
G-KKAZ	Airbus A320-214	2003	C-FZAZ	23. 5.03	MyTravel Airways Ltd	To C-FZAZ	5.11.07
			G-KKAZ, C-FZAZ, G-KKAZ, C-FZAZ, G-KKAZ, G-FZAZ, G-KKAZ, F-WWBN *(Restored 19..4.07)*				
G-LFLY	Flight Design CTSW	06.11.04		24. 1.07	I A Gaetan	To G-KFLY	5. 9.07
	(Assembled P&M Aviation Ltd with c/n 8244)						
G-LHCL	Eurocopter AS.355N Ecureuil 2	5644	N604AZ	14. 9.07	Lloyd Helicopters Europe Ltd	To F-xxxx	6.12.07
			N605DS				
G-MGRK	Avtech Jabiru J400	xxx		30. 5.07	M R Tingle	To G-EGSJ	29. 8.07
	(Built M R Tingle -pr.no.PFA 325-14618)						
G-NTOO	Aérospatiale AS.365N2 Dauphin 2	6372	ZJ165	19.10.90	Veritair Ltd	To ZJ165	12.10.07t
			G-NTOO, ZJ165		*(Restorexd 12.10.07)*		
G-OCLE	Pilatus PC-12-47	867	HB-FSY	17.12.07	Pilatus PC-12 Centre UK Ltd	To N867PP	28. 2.08
G-OOOZ	Boeing 757-236	25593	C-GOOZ	5. 4.02	First Choice Airways Ltd	To C-GOOZ	27.11.07
			G-OOOZ, C-GOOZ, G-OOOZ, C-GOOZ, G-OOOZ, N593RA, C-GRYX, N593KA, SE-DSL, N593KA, G-BUDZ, C-FNXY, G-BUDZ *(Restored 30. 3.07)*				
G-RMIN	Cessna 172S Skyhawk	172S10485	N2246T	13. 7.07	Ulster Flying Club (1961) Ltd	To G-UFCJ	25. 2.08
G-SETH	de Havilland DHC-1 Chipmunk 22	30	CS-DAI	26. 7.07	C C W Hart	Cancelled as PWFU	24. 1.08
	(Built OGMA)		Portuguese AF 1340				
G-SUEC	Piper PA-32-301XTC Saratoga	3255029	D-EGTC	10. 1.07	H L Chan	To M-SUEC	15. 2.08
			N30908				
G-XLAL	Boeing 737-8FH/W	35093		13 2.07	XL Airways UK Ltd	To D-AXLD	26. 4.07

SECTION 2

PART 1 – REPUBLIC OF IRELAND REGISTER

No official C of A data is available and it is difficult to determine the status of aircraft. We are grateful, therefore, for the few reports, which find their way into the "Round and About" section of Air-Britain News. This year we are indebted to the excellent monthly Irish Air Letter - journal of Current and Historical Irish Aviation - and the Editors and Publishers Paul Cunniffe, Karl E Hayes and Eamon C Powers - email: *ial.magazine@upcmail.ie*.

Other information has come from Ian Burnett's monthly Overseas Register section published in Air-Britain News and other important data has been supplied by Richard Cawsey, Ken Parfitt and Tony Pither. We have also received updated information from Ian Thompson and Hugo Wilhare on some elderly examples. Those aircraft still listed on the official Irish Aviation Authority's website Register are retained even if there have not been any recent positive sightings. In fact several aircraft known to have been broken up remain on the current register (January 2008). A reminder that the Status decode indiicates that N = paperwork change date or non-active specimen sighted and A = indicates some activity, hopefully! Official cancellations which are still noted as extant are contained in Part 2 below.

Just a remnder: the Aer Lingus names are in English on the port side and Gaellic on the starboard side. Many thanks to all contributors this year.

Registration	Type	Construction No	Previous Identity	Date	Registered Owner*(Operator)*	(Unconfirmed) Base	Status
EI-ABI (2)	de Havilland DH.84 Dragon 2	6105	EI-AFK	12. 8.85	Aer Lingus Ltd	Dublin	A2005
			G-AECZ, AV982, G-AECZ		*"Iolar"*		
(EI-ABU)	Spartan 3-Seater II				See G-ABYN - details in SECTION 4, Part 1		
						Mandeville, Gore, New Zealand	
EI-ADV	Piper PA-12 Super Cruiser	12-3459	NC4031H	11. 5.48	R E Levis	Not known	N2006
	(Lycoming O-235)				*(Badly damaged in force landing Maynooth, Weston 8. 7.99: on rebuild)*		
EI-AFE	Piper J-3C-90 Cub	16687	OO-COR	11. 3.49	J Conlan	Whitesland House, Kildare	A2006
			D-ELAB, N9954F, EI-AFE, NC79076				
EI-AFF	BA L.25C Swallow II	406	G-ADMF	18. 5.49	J Molloy, J J Sullivan and B Donoghue		N 6.07
	(Pobjoy Cataract II)					Ardenagh Great, Taghmon	
EI-AGD	Taylorcraft Plus D	108	G-AFUB	26. 5.53	B and K O'Sullivan	(Abbeyshrule)	N 4.96
			HL534, G-AFUB		*(Current status unknown)*		
EI-AGJ	Auster V J/1 Autocrat	2208	G-AIPZ	3.11.53	T G Rafter	Seven Parks Farm, Balbriggan	N2005
					(Suffered damage as result of hangar collapse Ballyboghil)		
EI-AHI (2)	de Havilland DH.82A Tiger Moth	85347	G-APRA	17. 9.93	High Fidelity Flyers	Monasterevin	A 4.06
			DE313				
EI-AKM	Piper J-3C-65 Cub	15810	N88194	17.11.58	J A Kent	Kilmoon, Ashbourne	N11.07
			NC88194		*(New owner)*		
EI-ALH	Taylorcraft Plus D	106	G-AHLJ	5. 5.60	N Reilly	Ballyjamesduff	N 9.05
	(Built Auster Aircraft Ltd)		HH987, G-AFTZ				
EI-ALP	Avro 643 Cadet	848	G-ADIE	12. 9.60	J C O'Loughlin	Seven Parks Farm, Balbriggan	N2006
	(Genet Major)				*(Engine seizure 12. 6.77: awaiting spares and stored)*		
EI-AMK	Auster V J/1 Autocrat	1838	G-AGTV	19. 9.62	J J O'Sullivan	(Newcastle, Dublin)	N1998
					(WFU after engine failure 5.79: sold 4.95: stored for Irish Air Corps Museum: current status unknown)		
EI-AMY	Auster J/1N Alpha	2634	G-AJUW	9. 4.63	T Lennon *(Current status unknown)*	(Maynooth)	N 4.92
EI-ANT	Champion 7ECA Citabria	7ECA-38		13. 1.65	T Croke, H Sydner, D Foley and E Lennon	Gorey	A 4.06
EI-ANY	Piper PA-18 Super Cub 95	18-7152	G-AREU	18.11.64	The Bogavia Group	Kilrush	A 5.06
			N3096Z				
EI-AOB	Piper PA-28-140 Cherokee	28-20667		28. 4.65	Knock Flying Group	Waterford	A 9.04
EI-AOS	Cessna 310B	35578	G-ARIG	1.11.65	Southair Ltd		
			EI-AOS, G-ARIG, N5378A		*(WFU and completely scrapped 1992)*		
EI-APS (2)	Schleicher ASK14	14008	(EI-114)	24.11.69	E Shiel, P Ward and P Finlay		
			G-AWVV, D-KOBB			(Gowran Grange, Naas)	N10.04
EI-ARH (2)	Slingsby T.56 SE5 rep	1590	G-AVOT	22. 6.67	L Garrison	(Flabob, California, US)	N 5.96
	(Lycoming O-235)				*(Current status unknown)*		
EI-ARM	Slingsby T.56 SE5 rep	1594	G-AVOX	22. 6.67	M L Putman	Sanger, Texas. US	N10.99
	(Lycoming O-235) *(Regd with c/n 1595 ex G-AVOY)*				*(Registered in US as N912AC)*		
EI-ARW	Jodel DR.1050	118		14. 8.67	J Davy	Moyne	N 2.03
EI-ASR (2)	McCandless M.4 Gyroplane	M.4-5	G-AXHZ	29. 9.69	G J J Fasenfeld	Sion Mills, Strabane	N 4.96
	(Built R and W McCandless) (Volkswagen)				*(Reported as sold to R.McGregor: current status unknown)*		
EI-AST	Cessna F150H	F150-0273		30. 1.68	Ormand Flying Club Ltd	Birr	A 5.06
	(Built Reims Aviation SA)						
EI-ATJ	Beagle B.121 Pup Series 2	B121-029	G-35-029	10. 2.69	L.O'Leary	Waterford	A 4.06
EI-ATK	Piper PA-28-140 Cherokee	28-24120	G-AVUP	18.10.68	Mayo Flying Club	Abbeyshrule	N 5.06
			N11C		*(Damaged Connaught 14. 2.87: noted wrecked)*		
EI-ATL	Aeronca 7AC Champion	7AC-4674	N1119E	22. 9.69	Kildare Flying Club	(Abbeyshrule)	
					(Damaged Weston 26.11.75: used for spares in restoration of EI-AVB) (Current status unknown)		
EI-ATS	SOCATA MS.880B Rallye Club	1582		20. 4.70	ATS Group	(Abbeyshrule)	N 4.96
					(Stored: current status unknown)		
EI-AUB	de Havilland DH.82A Tiger Moth				See SECTION 4, Part 1	Stayner, Ontario, Canada	
EI-AUG	SOCATA MS.894A Rallye Minerva 220	11080		17. 6.70	K O'Leary *(Fuselage only)*	Haverfordwest	N 6.06
EI-AUM	Auster V J/1 Autocrat	2612	G-AJRN	11. 9.70	T G Rafter	Seven Parks Farm, Balbriggan	N2005
					(Wings noted Monastervin 4.06)		
EI-AUO	Reims Cessna FA150K Aerobat	FA1500074		2. 3.70	S Burke	Spanish Point	N 9.06
EI-AUS	Auster J/5F Aiglet Trainer	2779	G-AMRL	17.11.70	T Stevens and T Lennon	(Powerscourt)	N2002
					(Current status unknown)		
EI-AUT	Forney F-1A Aircoupe	5731	G-ARXS	21.12.70	Southair Ltd	(Cork)	N 8.97
			D-EBSA, N3037G		*(Current status unknown)*		
EI-AUY	Morane-Saulnier MS.502 Criquet	338	F-BCDG	30.11.70	Historical Aircraft Preservation Group	Duxford	A 9.05
	(Argus AS.10)		French Military		*(As "CF+HF" in Luftwaffe c/s)*		
EI-AVB	Aeronca 7AC Champion	7AC-1790	7P-AXK	14. 6.71	T Brett	Thonotosassa, Florida, US	N10.99
	(Continental A65)		ZS-AXK				
EI-AVE (2)	Piper PA-18-95 Super Cub	18-7375	G-ARCT	9. 1.73	P.J.Gallagher	Strandhill, Sligo	
			EI-AVE, G-ARCT, N10F		*(New owner 8.07)*		

Reg	Type	C/n	Prev id	Date	Owner	Location	Status
EI-AVM	Reims Cessna F150L	F15000745		3. 3.72	Tojo Air Leasing Ltd	Abbeyshrule	A 8.06
EI-AWD	Piper PA-22-160 Tri-Pacer	22-6411	G-APXV	17. 1.73	J P Montcalm	Clonkeen, Emyvale	N2005
			N9437D		*(Blown over in gales Cork 12.81: stored)*		
EI-AWH	Cessna 210J Centurion	21059067	G-AZCC	19. 1.73	Rathcoole Flying Club	Rathcoole	A 4.05
			(EI-AWH), G-AZCC, 5N-AIE, N1734C, (N6167F)				
EI-AWP	de Havilland DH.82A Tiger Moth	85931	F-BGCL	4. 7.72	A P Bruton	Abbeyshrule	A 5.06
	(Regd with c/n 19577)		French AF, DF195				
EI-AWR	Malmö MFI-9 Junior	010	LN-HAG	12. 6.73	A Szorfy	Abbeyshrule	A 5.06
			(SE-EBW)				
EI-AWU	SOCATA MS.880B Rallye Club	880	G-AVIM	12. 1.74	Longford Aviation Ltd	Milford	N 7.05
					(Fuselage to Strains scrapyard 8.02)		
EI-AYA	SOCATA MS.880B Rallye Club	2256	G-BAON	27. 7.73	Limerick Flying Club (Coonagh) Ltd	Coonagh	A 8.02
EI-AYB	Gardan GY-80-180 Horizon	156	F-BNQP	5.10.73	J B Smith	Abbeyshrule	A 8.06
EI-AYD	Grumman-American AA-5 Traveler	0380	G-BAZE	9. 7.73	V O'Rourke, P Howick and H Martini		
			N5480L		*(Written off after forced landing Castlehayestown, Taghmon 21. 8.94)*		
EI-AYF	Reims Cessna FRA150L Aerobat	FRA1500218		26. 3.74	S Bruton	Abbeyshrule	A 8.06
EI-AYI	Morane MS.880B Rallye Club	189	F-OBXE	21.11.73	J McNamara	Cloncarmeel	20062
EI-AYK	Reims Cessna F172M Skyhawk II	F17201092		25. 3.74	D Gallagher	Trim	A 5.06
EI-AYN	Britten-Norman BN-2A-8 Islander	704	G-BBFJ	26. 3.74	Galway Aviation Services Ltd	Connemara	A 7.05
	(Built IRMA)				*"Inis-Mor" (Operated Aer Arann Islands)*		
EI-AYR	Schleicher ASK 16	16022	(EI-119)	5. 4.74	B O'Broin	Kilrush	A 5.06
EI-AYT (2)	SOCATA MS.894A Rallye Minerva 220	11065	G-AXIU	6. 8.74	K A O'Connor	Abbeyshrule	N 5.00
					(Damaged Palklasmore 12.11.89: wreck only)		
EI-AYY	Evans VP-1	MD01		18. 8.75	R Dowd and P O'Rourke	Kilrush	A 5.06
	(Built M Donoghue as SAAC pr.no.003)						
EI-BAJ	SNCAN Stampe SV-4C	171	F-BBPN	17.10.74	Dublin Tiger Group *(On rebuild)*	Trim	N 4.06
EI-BAR	Thunder Ax8-105 Balloon (Hot Air)	014	G-BCAM	26. 2.75	J Burke and V Hourihane	Cahir	
					"Rockwell" (WFU: current status unknown)		
EI-BAT	Reims Cessna F150M	F15001196		2. 5.75	K A O'Connor	Weston, Dublin	A 5.06
					(Operated National Flight Centre)		
EI-BAV	Piper PA-22-108 Colt	22-8347	G-ARKO	30. 4.75	E Finnamore and J Deegen	Birr	A 1.03
EI-BAY (1)	Cameron (Ax8) O-84 Balloon (Hot Air)				See G-AYJZ in SECTION 1, Part 2		
EI-BBC	Piper PA-28-180 Cherokee B	28-1049	G-ASEJ	18. 6.75	Vero Beach Ltd	Strandhill, Sligo	A 4.06
EI-BBD	Evans VP-1	VP-1-No.2		13. 8.76	Volksplane Group	Celbridge	N2006
	(Built B Feeley and D Goss as SAAC pr.no.002) (Volkswagen 1600)				*(Damaged 12. 9.81: on rebuild)*		
EI-BBE	Champion 7FC Tri-Traveller	7FC-393	G-APZW	7. 9.75	R McNally and C Carey	Abbeyshrule	A 8.06
	(Tail-wheel conversion to 7EC Traveller status)						
EI-BBG	SOCATA Rallye 100ST	2592		27.10.75	Weston Ltd *(Believed probably scrapped)*		
EI-BBI	SOCATA Rallye 150ST	2663		13.10.75	Kilkenny Airport Ltd	Kilkenny	N 6.07
EI-BBJ	SOCATA MS.880B Rallye 100S	2361	F-BUVX	7.11.75	Weston Ltd *(Derelict)*	Weston, Dublin	N 5.06
EI-BBO	SOCATA MS.893E Rallye 180GT	12522	F-BVNM	8. 3.76	G P Moorhead	Hacketstown	A 1.03
EI-BBV	Piper J-3C-65 Cub (L-4J-PI)	13058	D-ELWY	14. 6.76	F Cronin	Kilrush	A 8.06
	(Frame No.12888)		F-BEGB, 44-80762		*(As "480762" in USAAF c/s)*		
EI-BCE	Britten Norman BN-2A-26 Islander	519	G-BDUV	14. 9.76	Galway Aviation Services Ltd	Connemara	A 7.05
					"Inis-Meain" (Operated Aer Arann Islands)		
EI-BCF	Bensen B-8M Gyrocopter	47941	N....	24. 8.76	P Flanagan	(Kilrush)	N1997
	(McCulloch.AF O-100)				*(Stored: current status unknown)*		
EI-BCJ (2)	Aeromere F.8L Falco 3	204	G-ATAK	19. 1.77	M P McLoughlin	(Naas)	N 1.03
			D-ENYB		*(On rebuild)*		
EI-BCK	Reims Cessna F172N Skyhawk II	F17201543		22.11.76	K A O'Connor	Weston, Dublin	A 5.06
EI-BCL	Cessna 182P Skylane II	18264300	N1366M	22.11.76	L Burke	Carnmore, Galway	A 7.06
	(Reims assembled with c/n F1820045)						
EI-BCM	Piper J-3C-65 Cub (L-4H-PI)	11983	F-BNAV	26.11.76	Kilmoon Flying Group	Abbeyshrule	A 5.06
			N9857F, 44-79687 ??				
EI-BCN	Piper J-3C-65 Cub (L-4H-PI)	12335	F-BFQE	26.11.76	H Diver	Kilrush	A 5.06
			OO-PIE, 44-80039				
EI-BCO	Piper J-3C-65 Cub	"1"	F-BBIV	26.11.76	J Molloy	Kilmoon, Ashbourne	
					(Believed still stored as unconverted "F-BBIV")		
EI-BCP	Druine D.62B Condor	RAE 618	G-AVCZ	27. 1.77	A Delaney	Dolla	A 7.02
	(Built Rollason Aircraft and Engines)						
EI-BCS	SOCATA MS.880B Rallye 100T	2550	F-BVZV	4. 2.77	Organic Fruit and Vegetables of Ireland Ltd Kilkenny		A 8.04
EI-BCU	SOCATA MS.880B Rallye 100T	2595	F-BXTH	10. 2.77	Weston Ltd *(Derelict)*	Weston, Dublin	N 5.06
EI-BCW	SOCATA MS.880B Rallye Club	1783	G-AYKE	18. 4.77	Kilkenny Flying Club *(Believed probably scrapped during 1998)*		
EI-BDH	SOCATA MS.880B Rallye Club	1270	G-AWOB	18. 7.77	Munster Wings Ltd		
					(Damaged Cork 5.12.78: stored for repair but used as spare source and scrapped during late 1980s)		
EI-BDK	SOCATA MS.880B Rallye 100T	2561	F-BXMZ	10. 8.77	Limerick Flying Club (Coonagh) Ltd	(Abbeyshrule)	N 9.99
					(Airframe stored: current status unknown)		
EI-BDL	Evans VP-2	V2-2101		7. 9.77	P Buggle	Kilrush	A 5.06
	(Built J Duggan as PFA 7213 and then SAAC pr.no.004) (Volkswagen)						
EI-BDM	Piper PA-23-250 Aztec D	27-4166	G-AXIV	10.10.77	G A Costello	Dromod	N 4.06
			N6826Y		*(Dismantled)*		
EI-BDR	Piper PA-28-180 Cherokee C	28-3980	G-BAAO	8.12.77	Cherokee Group	Waterford	N 8.06
			LN-AEL, SE-FAG				
EI-BEA	SOCATA Rallye 100ST	3007		28. 2.78	Weston Ltd	Weston, Dublin	N 4.01
					(Dismantled fuselage hangared)		
EI-BEN	Piper J-3C-65 Cub (L-4J-PI)	12546	G-BCUC	28. 4.78	J J O'Sullivan	Weston, Dublin	A 7.03
	(Frame No.12376)		F-BFMN, 44-80250				
EI-BEP	SOCATA MS.892A Rallye Commodore 150	11947	F-BTJT	14. 4.78	H Lynch and J O'Leary		N 1.03
					(Stripped hulk noted)	Abbeyshrule	
EI-BFE	Cessna F150G	F150-0158	G-AVGM	3. 8.78	Southair Ltd	(Cork)	N 1.02
	(Built Reims Aviation SA)				*(Current status uinknown)*		
EI-BFF	Beech A23-24 Musketeer Super III	MA-352	G-AXCJ	20. 8.78	J Lankfer	(Limerick)	A 8.05
EI-BFI	SOCATA Rallye 100ST	2618		10. 8.78	J O'Neill	Abbeyshrule	N 5.06
					(Crashed 14.12.85 and wrecked)		

EI-BFO	Piper J-3C-90 Cub (L-4J-PI)	12701	F-BFQJ	11. 9.78	D Gordon	Trim	N 4.06
	(Frame No.12531) (Regd as c/n 8911)		N79856, NC79856, 44-80405 *(Frame stored)*				
EI-BFP	SOCATA Rallye 100ST	2942	F-GARR	6.10.78	Limerick Flying Club (Coonagh) Ltd	Coonagh	N10.06
EI-BFR	SOCATA Rallye 100ST	2429	F-OCVK	9.11.78	Wexford Flying Group Ardenagh Great, Taghmon		A 6.07
EI-BGA	SOCATA Rallye 100ST	2549	G-BCXC	23.11.78	J F Frew	Mullaghmore	A 6.06
			F-OCZQ				
EI-BGB	SOCATA MS.880B Rallye Club	1913	G-AZKB	22. 1.79	Limerick Flying Club (Coonagh) Ltd	Lisburn	N2003
					(Believed scrapped 1998 but remnant seen as garden ornament!)		
EI-BGC	SOCATA MS.880B Rallye Club	1265	F-BRDC	22.12.78	P Moran	Roscommon	
					(WFU and cannibalised: current status unknown)		
EI-BGD	SOCATA MS.880B Rallye Club	2287	F-BUJI	18.12.78	N Kavanagh	Abbeyshrule	N 1.03
					(Stripped hulk:: current status unknown)		
EI-BGJ	Reims Cessna F152 II	F15201664		14. 5.79	Sligo Aeronautical Club Ltd	Strandhill, Sligo	A 5.06
EI-BGS	SOCATA MS.893E Rallye 180GT	12675	F-BXTY	25. 4.79	M Farrelly		
	(Badly damaged in gales Millicent, Clane 3.91 and stored as spares source: believed probably scrapped)						
EI-BGT	Colt 77A Balloon (Hot Air)	041		14. 5.79	M J Mills	Navan	N 9.01
	(New envelope c/n 1092 - original fitted to EI-BBM)				*"Spirit of Ireland" (Ryan Air titles)*		
EI-BGU	SOCATA MS.880B Rallye Club	875	F-BONM	9. 5.79	M F Neary	Abbeyshrule	N 9.99
					(Wreck stored: current status unknown)		
EI-BHC	Reims Cessna F177RG Cardinal RG	F177RG0010	G-AYTG	11. 7.79	L Gavin	Weston, Dublin	A 5.06
	(Wichita c/n 17700117)				*"Hot Chocolate"*		
EI-BHF	SOCATA MS.892A Rallye Commodore 150	10742	F-BPBP	10. 7.79	B Mullen		
					(WFU Strandhill 1987: engine to EI-BYL: scrapped c.1989)		
EI-BHI	Bell 206B-2 JetRanger II	906	G-BAKX	14. 8.79	G Tracey	Tallaght, Dublin	A 8.06
EI-BHM	Reims Cessna F337E Super Skymaster	F33700004	OO-PDC	1.11.79	City of Dublin VEC	Bolton St, Dublin	N 9.01
	(Wichita c/n 33701217)		OO-PDG		*(With College of Technology as instructional airframe)*		
EI-BHN	SOCATA MS.893A Rallye Commodore 180	11422	F-BRRO	11.10.79	T Garvan *(On overhaul)*	Hacketstown	N 1.03
EI-BHP	SOCATA MS.893A Rallye Commodore 180	11459	F-BSAA	12.10.79	Spanish Point Flying Club	(Spanish Point)	
					(Current status unknown)		
EI-BHT	Beech 77 Skipper	WA-77		17.10.79	M Casey	Galway	N11.07
EI-BHV	Aeronca 7EC Traveler	7EC-739	G-AVDU	30.10.79	P O'Donnell and Partners Ballyboe, Kilsheelan		A2006
			N9837Y				
EI-BHW	Cessna F150F	F150-0013	G-ATMK	22.11.79	R Sharpe	(Weston, Dublin)	
	(Built Reims Aviation SA) (Wichita c/n 15062671)				*(Current status unknown)*		
EI-BHY	SOCATA Rallye 150ST	2929	F-GARL	19.11.79	Limerick Flying Club (Coonagh) Ltd	Coonagh	A10.06
EI-BIB	Reims Cessna F152 II	F15201724		30.11.79	Galway Flying Club Ltd	Carnmore, Galway	A 7.06
EI-BID	Piper PA-18 Super Cub 95 (L-18C-PI)	18-1524	D-EAES	30.11.79	S Coghlan and P Ryan	Carnmore, Galway	A 4.06
			French Army 18-1524, 51-15524				
EI-BIG	Moravan Zlin 526 Trener Master	1086	D-EBUP	7.12.79	P V Lonkhuyzen *(Damaged 9.91 and acquired for spares?)*		
			OO-BUT		Luxters Farm, Hambleden, Henley-on-Thames		N2002
EI-BIJ	Agusta-Bell 206B-2 JetRanger II	8432	G-BCVZ	29. 1.80	Medavia Properties Ltd	Dublin Heliport	A 6.06
					(Operated Celtic Helicopters Ltd)		
EI-BIK	Piper PA-18-150 Super Cub	18-7909088	N82276	1. 2.80	Dublin Gliding Club Ltd Gowran Grange, Naas		A 4.06
	(Modified to 180hp)						
EI-BIM	Morane MS.880B Rallye Club	305	F-BKYJ	28. 3.80	D Millar	Abbeyshrule	N 6.97
					(Stored: current status unknown)		
EI-BIO	Piper J-3C-65 Cub (L-4J-PI)	12657	F-BGXP	27. 5.80	H Duggan	Kilrush	A 6.06
			OO-GAE, 44-80361				
EI-BIR	Reims Cessna F172M Skyhawk II	F17201225	F-BVXI	24. 3.80	Figile Flying Group	Clonbullogue	N 1.07
EI-BIS	Robin R1180TD Aiglon	268		14. 5.80	The Robin Aiglon Group	City of Derry	A 3.07
EI-BIT	SOCATA MS.887 Rallye 125	2169	F-BULQ	18. 3.80	Spanish Point Flying Club *(Derelict)*	Kilrush	N 8.04
EI-BIV	Bellanca 8KCAB Super Decathlon	464-79	N5032Q	3. 6.80	Aerocrat Pilots Ltd	Weston, Dublin	A 5.06
EI-BIW	SOCATA MS.880B Rallye Club	1144	F-BPGB	19. 5.80	E J Barr		
	(Crashed take off Rosnakil, Fanad 10. 8.86 , substantially damaged and scrapped although rear section of fuselage used as display item in nightclub at Intercounty Hotel, Lifford from 1988 until fire destroyed the hotel about 1991)						
EI-BJB	Aeronca 7DC Champion	7AC-925	G-BKKM	16. 4.80	W Kennedy	Killenaule	N12.00
	(Continental C85)		EI-BJB, N82296, NC82296		*(Stored incomplete)*		
EI-BJC	Aeronca 7AC Champion	7AC-4927	N1366E	2. 4.80	E Griffin	Blackwater	N 8.04
	(Continental A65)		NC1366E, SE-FBW, OY-DKN		*(Crashed Edenderry 9.82)*		
EI-BJI	Reims FR172E Rocket	FR17200040	G-BAAS	23. 5.80	Irish Parachute Club Ltd		
			SE-FBW, OY-DKN		*(Crashed Edenderry 9.82: probably scrapped pre 1990)*		
EI-BJJ	Aeronca 15AC Sedan	15AC-226	(G-BHXP)	6. 6.80	O Bruton	Abbeyshrule	N 3.98
			EI-BJJ, N1214H		*(Stored: current status unknown)*		
EI-BJK	SOCATA Rallye 110ST	3226	F-GBKY	8. 7.80	M Keenan	Kilrush	A 4.06
EI-BJM	Cessna A152 Aerobat	A1520936	N761CC	18. 9.80	K A O'Connor	Weston, Dublin	A 5.06
EI-BJO	Cessna R172K Hawk XP II	R1723340	N758TD	6. 8.80	Merlin Manufacturing (Galway) Ltd	Carnmore, Galway	A 7.06
EI-BJT	Piper PA-38-112 Tomahawk	38-78A0818	G-BGEU	16.10.80	S Corrigan and W Lennon	Abbeyshrule	A 5.06
			N9650N				
EI-BKC	Aeronca 15AC Sedan	15AC-467	N1394H	5.11.80	G Hendrick, M Farrell and J Keating	Birr	A 1.03
EI-BKF	Cessna F172H	F172-0476	G-AVUX	4.12.80	D Darby	Haverfordwest	N 6.06
	(Built Reims Aviation SA)						
EI-BKK	Taylor JT.1 Monoplane	PFA 1421	G-AYYC	2. 2.81	J Sullivan	Waterford	N 1.06
	(Built S B Sharp) (Volkswagen 1500)						
EI-BKN	SOCATA Rallye 100ST	3035	F-GBCK	18. 2.81	Weston Ltd *(Stored)*	Weston, Dublin	N 8.02
EI-BKU	SOCATA MS.892A Rallye Commodore 150	10990	F-BRLG	21. 5.81	Limerick Flying Club (Coonagh) Ltd	Abbeyshrule	N 5.99
					(Operateden stored: current status unknown)		
EI-BLB	SNCAN Stampe SV-4C	323	F-BCTE	27. 7.81	J E Hutchinson and R A Stafford	(Dolla)	N2006
	(Hit overhead cables and crashed Albert Lock Jamestown Canal 1. 6.97 and substantially damaged: remains stored)						
EI-BLD	MBB BÖ.105DB	S.381	D-HDLQ	21. 7.81	Irish Helicopters Ltd		
					Trevet Airfield, Dunshaughlin, County Meath		A 5.06
EI-BLE	Eipper Quicksilver	IMA-003		20. 8.81	R P St.George-Smith		
	(Yamaha KT100SP)				*(Severely damaged in accident near Kilkenny (airfield?), 8.81: believed scrapped)*		
EI-BLN	Eipper Quicksilver MX	MX.01		26. 8.81	O J Conway and B Daffy	(Ennis)	
	(Cuyana 340)				*(Believed scrapped)*		

EI-BMA	SOCATA MS.880B Rallye Club	1965	F-BTJR	26. 1.82	W Rankin and M Kelleher	Abbeyshrule	N 1.03
					(Wings only noted)		
EI-BMB	SOCATA MS.880B Rallye 100T	2505	G-BJCO	5. 1.82	Glyde Court Developments Ltd	Weston, Dublin	N 5.06
			F-BVLB				
EI-BMF	Laverda F.8L Super Falco Series IV	416	G-AWSU	28. 1.82	M Slazenger	Powerscourt	A 8.05
EI-BMH	SOCATA MS.880B Rallye Club	1277	(G-BIDS)	19. 2.82	N J Bracken		
			F-BSTJ				
	(To Abbeyshrule 1982 with "EI-BMH" chalked on tail: found to have severe corrosion, removed to private house in Lifford and scrapped in early 1990s. Did not carry Irish marks officially and remained as "G-BIDS")						
EI-BMI	SOCATA TB-9 Tampico	203	F-GCOV	12. 5.82	D Pratt	Weston, Dublin	A 5.06
EI-BMJ	SOCATA MS.880B Rallye 100T	2594	F-BXTG	10. 3.82	Limerick Flying Club (Coonagh)Ltd	Coonagh	A10.06
EI-BMM	Reims Cessna F152 II	F15201899		10. 3.82	P Redmond	Weston, Dublin	A 5.06
EI-BMN	Reims Cessna F152 II	F15201912		10. 3.82	K A.O'Connor	Weston, Dublin	A 4.06
EI-BMU	Monnett Sonerai IIL	01224		19. 5.82	A Fenton	Strandhill, Sligo	N 9.06
	(Built D Connaire and P Ford as SAAC pr.no.014) (Volkswagen 2100)						
EI-BMV	American Aviation AA-5 Traveler	AA5-0200	G-BAEJ	28. 7.82	K A H E Tierney	Abbeyshrule	N 1.03
					(Damaged Brittas Bay 3.93: stripped hulk noted)		
EI-BMW	Skytrike/Hiway Vulcan	LM-100		1. 6.82	L Maddock	(Carlow)	
	(Built L Maddock) (Fuji-Robin)				*(Current status unknown)*		
EI-BNF	Eurowing Goldwing	xxxx		22. 9.82	T Morelli		
	(Fuji-Robin)				*(Scrapped 1985)*		
EI-BNH	Hiway Skytrike	AS.09		18.10.82	M Martin	Tullamore	
	(Fuji-Robin EC-25-PS)				*(Current status unknown)*		
EI-BNJ	Evans VP-2	xxxx		24. 1.83	G A Cashman		
	(Volkswagen 2000)				*(Believed scrapped 1996)*		
EI-BNK	Cessna U206F Stationair	U20601706	G-HILL	23.12.82	Irish Parachute Club Ltd	Clonbullogue	A 4.06
			PH-ADN, D-EEXY, N9506G				
EI-BNL	Rand Robinson KR-2	xxxx		13. 1.83	K Hayes		
	(Volkswagen 2000)				*(Reported construction abandoned and destroyed pre 2006)*		
EI-BNP	Rotorway Executive 145	xxxx		1. 3.83	R L Renfroe		
	(Rotorway 145)				*(Not completed 1989)*		
EI-BNT	Cvjetkovic CA-65	xxxx		23. 3.83	B Tobin and P G Ryan	(Tallagh)	N 1.03
	(Lycoming O-290)				*(Under construction)*		
EI-BNU	SOCATA MS.880B Rallye Club	1204	F-BPQV	7. 4.83	P A Doyle	Coonagh	N 1.03
EI-BOA	Pterodactyl	xxxx		3. 5.83	A Murphy		
	(Cuyana 430)				*(Believed dismantled and probably scrapped 1985)*		
EI-BOE	SOCATA TB-10 Tobago	301	F-GDBL	12. 9.83	Tobago Group	Weston, Dublin	A 5.07
EI-BOH	Eipper Quicksilver	xxxx		8. 9.83	J Leech		
	(Yamaha 970cc)				*(Believed dismantled and probably scrapped 1980s)*		
EI-BOV	Rand Robinson KR-2	xxxx		7. 5.84	G O'Hara and G Callan	(Strandhill, Sligo)	
	(Built G O'Hara and G Callan as SAAC pr.no.011) (Volkswagen 1835)				"Kitty Hawk"		
					(Damaged Carnmore 3.91 on re-build 1999: current status unknown)		
EI-BOX	Box Duet	xxxx		12.10.84	K Riccius	(Newcastle)	
	(Rotax 503)				*(Current status unknown)*		
EI-BPE	Viking Dragonfly	xxxx		15.10.84	G G Bracken	(Westport)	N 1.01
	(Built G G Bracken as SAAC pr.no.016) (HAPI Volkswagen 1835)				*(Not completed and stored)*		
EI-BPL	Reims Cessna F172K	F17200758	G-AYSG	28. 3.85	Phoenix Flying Ltd	Shannon	A 5.07
EI-BPN	Flexiform Striker	xxxx		12. 3.85	P H Collins	(Dunlaoghaire)	
	(Fuji Robin 50cc)				*(Current status unknown)*		
EI-BPO	Southdown Puma	1923		12. 3.85	A Channing	Millicent Farm, Clane	A2006
	(Fuji-Robin EC-44-PM - s/n.82-00108) (C/n also reported as 1924)						
EI-BPP	Eipper Quicksilver MX	3207		12. 3.85	J A Smith	Abbeyshrule	N 1.03
	(Cuyana 430)				*(Stored)*		
EI-BPT	Skyhook Sabre	xxxx		26. 3.85	T M McGrath	(Glounthane)	
	(Rowena Solo 210)				*(Believed dismantled)*		
EI-BPU	Hiway Demon	xxxx		26. 3.85	A Channing	Abbeyshrule	A 5.00
	(Fuji-Robin EC-25-PS)						
EI-BRK	Flexiform Trike	LM.102		17. 6.85	L Maddock		
	(Built L Maddock) (Fuji Robin)			*(Damage to propeller taxiing Clonmore on pre 1994: WFU and scrapped during 1994)*			
EI-BRS	Cessna P172D	P17257173	G-WPUI	2. 9.85	P Mathews	Waterford	N 8.06
			G-AXPI, 9M-AMR, N11B, (N8573X) *(In poor condition)*				
EI-BRU	Evans VP-1	V-12-84-CQ		5.11.85	Home Bru Flying Group	Weston, Dublin	A 6.02
	(Built C Quinn as SAAC pr.no.018)) (Volkswagen 1600)						
EI-BRV	Hiway Demon Skytrike	xxxx		5.11.85	M Garvey and C Tully	Rockfield, Kells	A2006
	(Fuji-Robin EC-25-PS)						
EI-BRW	Hovey Delta Bird	xxxx		5.11.85	A & E Aerosport		
	(Built A & E Aerosport) (Volkswagen 1300)						
	(Originally regd as Ultra-Lite Deltabird but is a Bimax Osprey: dismantled after crash near Fermoy 1986 and scrapped)						
EI-BSB	Wassmer Jodel D.112	1067	G-AWIG	23. 6.87	Estartit Ltd	Ardenagh Great, Taghmon	A 7.06
	(Re-built W Kennedy as SAAC pr.no.025)		F-BKAA				
EI-BSC	Reims Cessna F172N Skyhawk II	F17201651	G-NIUS	10.12.85	S Phelan	Weston, Dublin	A 8.06
EI-BSG	Bensen B-80 Gyrocopter	HB		30. 1.86	J Todd	(Riverstick)	N 3.90
	(McCullough 4318)				*(Stored: current status unknown)*		
EI-BSK	SOCATA TB-9 Tampico	618		9. 4.86	T Drury	Weston, Dublin	A 5.06
EI-BSL	Piper PA-34-220T Seneca III	34-8233041	N8468X	27. 6.86	P Greenan	Weston, Dublin	A 5.06
EI-BSN	Cameron O-65 Balloon (Hot Air)	1278		14. 4.86	C O'Neill and T Hooper "Erin-Go-Bragh"	Cavan	A 6.06
EI-BSO	Piper PA-28-140 Cherokee B	28-25449	C-GOBL	16. 4.86	H M Hanley	Waterford	A 4.06
			N8241N				
EI-BSW	Solar Wings Pegasus XL-R	SW-WA-1122		22. 6.87	E Fitzgerald	(Ballycashin)	A2006
	(Rotax 447) (Trike c/n SW-TB-1124)						
EI-BSX	Piper J-3C-65 Cub	8912	G-ICUB	25. 3.86	J and T O'Dwyer	(Gowran Grange, Naas)	
	(Frame No.8999)		F-BEGT, NC79805, 45-4515, 42-36788 *(Current status unknown)*				
	(Official c/n 13255 is incorrect as a/c probably rebuilt c.1945)						
EI-BUA	Cessna 172M Skyhawk II	17265451	N5458H	8. 8.86	K A O'Connor	Weston, Dublin	A 5.06

EI-BUC	Jodel D.9 Bébé	PFA 929	G-BASY	20. 1.87	B Lyons and M Blake	Thurles, Moyne	A 4.06
	(Built R L Sambell) (Volkswagen 1500)						
EI-BUF	Cessna 210N Centurion II	21063070	G-MCDS	18.12.86	210 Group	Abbeyshrule	A 6.07
			G-BHNB, N6496N				
EI-BUG	SOCATA ST-10 Diplomate	125	G-STIO	4. 2.87	J Cooke	Weston, Dublin	N 1.03
			OH-SAB		*(Derelict)*		
EI-BUH	Lake LA-4-200 Buccaneer	543	G-PARK	27. 5.87	P Redden	Weston, Dublin	A.6.04
			G-BBGK, N39779				
EI-BUJ	SOCATA MS.892A Rallye Commodore 150	10737	G-FOAM	27. 2.87	T Cunniffe		
			G-AVPL		*(Damaged pre 1992: stored and probably scrapped)*		
EI-BUL	Whittaker MW.5 Sorcerer	1		4. 3.87	J Culleton	(Mountmellick)	
	(Built Aerotech and J Greene) (Citröen 602cc)				*(Current status unknown)*		
EI-BUN	Beech 76 Duchess	ME-371	(EI-BUO)	26. 6.87	K A O'Connor	Weston, Dublin	A 5.07
			N37001		*(Operated National Flight Centre)*		
EI-BUT	GEMS MS.893A Rallye Commodore 180	10559	SE-IMV	30. 7.87	T Keating	Weston, Dublin	A 4.06
			F-BNBU		*(Galerien c/s)*		
EI-BVB	Whittaker MW.6 Merlin	1		14. 9.87	R England	(Watergrasshill)	N 9.00
	(Built R England as SAAC pr.no.051) (Rotax 503)				*(Current status unknown)*		
EI-BVJ (2)	AMF Microflight Chevvron 2-32	009		16. 2.88	S.J.Dunne	(Bolybeg, Ballymore Eustace)	
	(Konig SD570)				*(Current status unknown)*		
EI-BVK	Piper PA-38-112 Tomahawk	38-79A0966	OO-FLG	2. 3.88	M Martin	Trim	A 5.06
			OO-HLG, N9705N				
EI-BVT	Evans VP-2	V2-2129	G-BEIE	29. 4.88	P Morrison	(Cobh)	N 1.01
	(Regd F G Morris as PFA 7221 and then J J O'Sullivan as SAAC pr.no.020) (Volkswagen 1834) (Under construction: current status unknown)						
EI-BVY	Heintz Zenith CH.200AA-RW	2-582		7. 6.88	J Matthews and M Skelly	(Abbeyshrule)	A 7.01
	(Built M Skellly and J Mathews as SAAC pr.no.026) (Lycoming O-320)				*(Current status unknown)*		
EI-BWH	Partenavia P.68C	212	G-BHJP	11.12.87	K Buckley	Cork	A 6.04
EI-BXL	Polaris FIB (Flying Inflatable Boat)	M.561628		27. 6.91	M McKeon	(Roslevan, Ennis)	
	(Rotax 503)				*(Presumed stored at owner's home)*		
EI-BXO	Fouga (Valmet) CM-170 Magister	213	N18FM	21.11.88	G W Connolly	(Swords)	N 4.96
			Finnish AF FM-28		*(Stored: current status unknown)*		
EI-BXT	Druine D.62B Condor	RAE 626	G-AVZE	24. 8.88	The Condor Group	Abbeyshrule	A 5.06
	(Built Rollason Aircraft and Engines)						
EI-BYA	Thruster TST Mk.1	8504	G-MNDA	1. 2.89	E Fagan	(Killykeen, Kilnaleck)	
	(Rotax 503)				*(Current status unknown)*		
EI-BYF	Cessna 150M Commuter	15076654	N3924V	20.11.89	The High Kings Flying Group Ltd	Abbeyshrule	A 8.06
EI-BYG	SOCATA TB-9 Tampico Club	928		23. 8.89	M McGinn	Weston, Dublin	A 5.06
EI-BYJ	Bell 206B-2 JetRanger II	1897	N49725	23. 6.89	Medeva Properties Ltd	Dublin Heliport	A 1.03
EI-BYL (1)	Heintz Zenith CH-250	2866	(EI-BYD (1))	14. 6.89	M McLoughlin	Kilrush	A 5.06
	(Built A Corcoran as SAAC pr.no.020) (Lycoming O-320)						
EI-BYO	Aérospatiale-Alenia ATR 42-310	161	OY-CIS	20.12.02	Nordic Aviation Contractors (Ireland) Ltd	Dublin	A 6.06
			EI-BYO, F-WWEH		*(Operated Aer Arann Express)*		
EI-BYR	Bell 206L-3 LongRanger III	51284	(EI-LMG)	15. 8.89	H.S.S	Dublin	N 9.07
			EI-BYR, D-HBAD				
EI-BYX	Champion 7GCAA Citabria	7GCAA-40	N546DS	4. 4.90	P J Gallagher	Coonagh	A10.06
EI-BYY	Piper J-3C-85 Cub	12494	EC-AQZ	12. 4.90	The Cub Club	Galway	A12.01
	(Frame No.12322)		HB-OSG, 44-80198				
	(Regd with c/n 22288 and officially ex G-AKTJ, N3595K, NC3595K)						
EI-CAC	Grob G-115A	8092		22.10.89	G Tracey	Weston, Dublin	A 5.06
EI-CAD	Grob G-115A	8104	G-WIZB	22. 8.03	Flightwise Training Services Ltd	Weston, Dublin	N 4.07
			EI-CAD				
EI-CAE	Grob G-115A	8105		5. 4.90	O O'Reilly	Cork	N 6.07
EI-CAN	Aerotech MW.5(K) Sorcerer	5K-0011-02	(G-MWGH)	15. 6.90	V Vaughan	Glountha, Kilkenny	N 6.07
	(Rotax 447)						
EI-CAP	Cessna R182 Skylane RGII	R18200056	G-BMUF	27. 4.90	M J Hanlon	Weston, Dublin	A 8.02
			N7342W				
EI-CAU	AMF Microflight Chevvron 2-32C	022		14.11.90	J Tarrant	Rathcoole	A 7.05
	(Konig SD32)						
EI-CAW	Bell 206B-2 JetRanger II	780	N2947W	11. 7.90	Celtic Helicopters (Maintenance Services) Ltd		
					(Dismantled)	Dublin Heliport	A 5.00
EI-CAX	Cessna P210N Pressurized Centurion II		(EI-CAS)	9. 7.90	K A O'Connor	Weston, Dublin	N 5.06
		P21000215	G-OPMB, N4553K		*(Stored)*		
EI-CAY	Mooney M.20C Ranger	690074	N9272V	14.11.90	Ranger Flights Ltd *(Stored dismantled)*　Hacketstown		N 1.03
EI-CBK	Aérospatiale-Alenia ATR 42-310	199	F-WWEM	25. 7.90	Nordic Aviation Contractors (Ireland) Ltd	Dublin	A 6.06
					(Operated Aer Arann Express)		
EI-CBQ	Boeing 737-3YO	24907	9M-AAA	19. 3.91	Airplanes Holdings Ltd *(Operated Kras Air)*		
			UR-GAE, EI-CBQ			Krasnoyarsk-Yemilianovo, Russia	A2008
EI-CBR	McDonnell-Douglas MD-83	49939		3.12.90	Airplanes 111 Ltd	Bogota-Eldorado, Colombia	A2008
					(Operated Avianca) "Ciudad de Bucaramanga"		
EI-CBS	McDonnell-Douglas MD-83	49942		10.12.90	GECAS Technical Services Ltd *"Ciudad de Cucuta"*		
						Medellin-Olaya Herrara, Colombia	A2008
					(Operated Sociedad Aeronautica de Medellin Consolida)		
EI-CBY	McDonnell-Douglas MD-83	49944		30. 7.91	GE Transportation Finance (Ireland) Ltd *"Ciudad de Barranquilla"*		
					(Operated Avianca)	Bogota-Eldorado, Colombia	A2008
EI-CBZ	McDonnell-Douglas MD-83	49945		13. 8.91	GE Transportation Finance (Ireland) Ltd *(Operated Avianca)*		
					"Ciudad de Santiago de Cali"	Bogota-Eldorado, Colombia	A2008
EI-CCC	McDonnell-Douglas MD-83	49946		27. 9.91	Airplanes 111 Ltd	Bogota-Eldorado, Colombia	A2008
					(Operated Avianca) "Ciudad de Pereira"		
EI-CCD	Grob G-115A	8108	D-EIUD	15. 8.90	Kal Aviation Ltd	Weston, Dublin	A 5.06
			(P/i may be D-EIWD)				
EI-CCE (2)	McDonnell-Douglas MD-83	49947		19. 9.91	GE Transportation Finance (Ireland) Ltd *"Ciudad de Medelin"*		
					(Operated Avianca)	Bogota-Eldorado, Colombia	A2008
EI-CCF	Aeronca 11AC Chief	11AC-S-40	N3826E	10. 1.91	G McGuinness	Trim	N 3.07
	(Continental A65)		NC3826E				

EI-CCJ	Cessna 152 II	15280174	N24251	9.10.90	M P Cahill	Dublin	N 2.95
					(Stored: current status unknown)		
EI-CCK	Cessna 152 II	15279610	N757BM	9.10.90	M P Cahill	(Newcastle, Dublin)	
					(Damaged pre 1995: current status unknown)		
EI-CCL	Cessna 152 II	15280382	N24791	9.10.90	M P Cahill	Dublin	
					(Damaged Bray Head 4. 5.93: current status unknown)		
EI-CCM	Cessna 152 II	15282320	N68679	9.10.90	E Hopkins	Newcastle, Dublin	A 5.07
EI-CCV	Cessna R172K Hawk XPII	R1723039	N758EP	2. 3.91	Kerry Aero Club Ltd	(Farranfore, Kerry)	
					(Current status unknown)		
EI-CDD	Boeing 737-548	24989	EI-BXH	3. 7.91	Castle 2003-2 Ireland Ltd *(Operated Rossiya Russian Airlines)*		
						St Petersburg-Pulkovo, Russia	A2008
EI-CDE	Boeing 737-548	25115	PT-SLM	21. 5.91	Castle 2003-2 Ireland Ltd *(Operated Rossiya Russian Airlines)*		
			EI-CDE, (EI-BXJ)			St Petersburg-Pulkovo, Russia	A2008
EI-CDF	Boeing 737-548	25737		23. 3.92	Jetscape Aviation Ireland Ltd		
					(Operated Rossiya Russian Airlines) St Petersburg-Pulkovo, Russia		A2008
EI-CDG	Boeing 737-548	25738		7. 4.92	Nordic Aviation Contractors (Ireland) Ltd		
					(Operated Rossiya Russian Airlines) St Petersburg-Pulkovo, Russia		A2008
EI-CDH	Boeing 737-548	25739		14. 4.92	Jetscape Aviation Ireland Ltd		
					(Operated Rossiya Russian Airlines) St Petersburg-Pulkovo, Russia		A2008
EI-CDP	Cessna 182L	18258955	G-FALL	20. 5.91	Irish Parachute Club Ltd	Clonbullogue	A 4.06
			OY-AHS, N4230S				
EI-CDV	Cessna 150G	15066677	N2777S	17. 7.91	K A O'Connor	Weston, Dublin	A 5.06
EI-CDX	Cessna 210K Centurion	21059329	G-AYGN	14. 8.91	Falcon Aviation Ltd	Waterford	A 4.06
			N9429M				
EI-CDY	McDonnell-Douglas MD-83	49948		27. 9.91	GE Transportation Finance (Ireland) Ltd *"Ciudad de Santa Maria"*		
					(Operated Sociedad Aeronautica de Medellin Consolida) Medellin-Olaya Herrara, Colombia		A2008
EI-CEG	SOCATA MS.893E Rallye 180GT	13083	SE-GTS	31.10.91	M Jarrett	Powerscourt	N 3.07
EI-CEN	Thruster T.300	9012-T300-500		2. 3.92	P J Murphy	(Antville, Macroom)	
	(Rotax 582)				*(Current status unknown)*		
EI-CEP	McDonnell-Douglas MD-83	53122		14. 4.92	GE Transportation Finance (Ireland) Ltd *"San Andres Isla"*		
					(Operated Avianca) Bogota-Eldorado, Colombia		A2008
EI-CEQ	McDonnell-Douglas MD-83	53123		14. 4.92	GE Transportation Finance (Ireland) Ltd *"Ciudad de Leticia"*		
					(Operated Avianca) Bogota-Eldorado, Colombia		A2008
EI-CER	McDonnell-Douglas MD-83	53125	N9017P	20. 5.92	Airplanes 111 Ltd *"Ciudad de Monteria"*		
					(Operated Avianca) Bogota-Eldorado, Colombia		A2008
EI-CES	Taylorcraft BC-65	2231	G-BTEG	25. 3.92	B J Douglas	(Thomastown)	A 7.06
			N27590, NC27590				
EI-CEY	Boeing 757-2Y0ER	26152		10. 8.92	Aero Ireland Ltd	Bogota-Eldorado, Colombia	A2008
					(Operated Avianca)		
EI-CEZ	Boeing 757-2Y0ER	26154		18. 9.92	Airplanes Holdings Ltd	Bogota-Eldorado, Colombia	A2008
					(Operated Avianca)		
EI-CFE	Robinson R22 Beta	1709	G-BTHG	15. 5.91	Millicent Golf and Country Club	Clane	A 9.02
EI-CFF	Piper PA-12 Super Cruiser	12-3928	N78544	23. 5.91	J and T O'Dwyer	Kilrush	A 5.06
	(Lycoming O-235)		NC78544				
EI-CFG	Rousseau Piel CP.301B Emeraude	112	G-ARIW	1. 6.91	F Doyle	Murntown, Taghmon	N 1.02
			F-BIRQ		*(Stored as "G-ARIW")*		
EI-CFH	Piper PA-12 Super Cruiser	12-3110	(EI-CCE)	1. 6.91	G Treacy	Shinrone	A 6.06
	(Lycoming O-320)		N4214M, NC4214M				
EI-CFO	Piper J-3C-65 Cub (L-4H-PI)	11947	OO-RAZ	13. 5.92	J Mathews and Partners Derrytrasna Glen, Bannfoot		N 8.07
			OO-RAF, 44-79651		*((As "479651" in USAAF c/s)*		
EI-CFP	Cessna 172P Skyhawk II	17274428	N52178	15. 7.91	K A O'Connor	Weston, Dublin	A 5.06
					(Operated National Flight Centre)		
EI-CFX	Robinson R22 Beta	0793	G-OSPI	16. 6.92	B O'Sullivan	Thurles	A 8.02
EI-CFY	Cessna 172N Skyhawk II	17268902	N734JZ	18. 6.92	K A O'Connor	Weston, Dublin	A 4.06
EI-CFZ	McDonnell-Douglas MD-83	53120	N6206F	29. 7.92	Airplanes 111 Ltd	Bogota-Eldorado, Colombia	A2008
					"Ciudad de San Juan de Pasto" (Operated Avianca)		
EI-CGB	TEAM Mini-MAX	xxxx		20. 8.92	M Garvey	(Abbeyshrule)	
	(Built M Garvey as SAAC pr.no.036)				*(Current status unknown)*		
EI-CGC	Stinson 108-3 Station Wagon	108-5243	OO-IAC	17. 7.92	D A Weldon	(Dublin)	A 1.03
			OO-JAC, N3B				
EI-CGD	Cessna 172M Skyhawk II	17262309	OO-BMT	30. 7.92	G Cashman	Weston, Dublin	A 5.07
			N12846				
EI-CGF	Phoenix Luton LA-5 Major	PAL-1124	G-BENH	31. 7.92	J Duggan	Ardenagh Great, Taghmon	N 6.07
	(Regd C D McCartney as PFA 1208 then F Doyle as SAAC pr.no.019)						
EI-CGG	Ercoupe 415C	3147	N2522H	10. 9.92	Irish Ercoupe Group	Weston, Dublin	N 5.06
	(Continental C75)		NC2522H		*(Derelict)*		
EI-CGH	Cessna 210N Centurion II	21063524	N6374A	16.11.92	J Smith	Abbeyshrule	A 5.06
EI-CGJ	Solar Wings Pegasus XL-R	SW-WA-1506	G-MWTV	5. 4.93	P Hearty		
	(Rotax 447)				*(Crashed Portarlington late 1995 and scrapped)*		
EI-CGM	Solar Wings Pegasus XL-R	SW-WA-1502	G-MWVC	14.11.92	Microflight Ltd	(Ballyfore, Daingean)	
	(Rotax 447)				*(Current status unknown)*		
EI-CGN	Solar Wings Pegasus XL-R	SW-WA-1529	G-MWXM	14.11.92	V Power	Donamore, New Ross	A 8.00
	(Rotax 447)						
EI-CGP	Piper PA-28-140 Cherokee C	28-26928	G-MLUA	25.11.92	L A Tattan	Cork	A 5.07
			G-AYJT, N11C		*(Operated Euroair Training)*		
EI-CGT	Cessna 152 II	15282331	G-BPBL	10.12.92	J Rafter	(Naul)	
			N16SU, N68715		*(Current status unknown)*		
EI-CGV	Piper J-5A Cub Cruiser	5-624	G-BPKT	11.12.92	B Reilly	Trim	N12.07
			N35372, NC35372				
EI-CHH (2)	Boeing 737-317	23177	(N302AL)	15. 1.93	Airplanes Finance Ltd Kaliningrad-Khrabovo, Russia		A2008
			EI-CHH, (EI-CGX), PT-WBG, PP-SNU, C-FCPL *(Operated KD Avia)*				
EI-CHK	Piper J-3C-65 Cub Special	23019	C-FHNS	10. 3.93	N Higgins	(Longwood)	A 7.99
			CF-HNS, N1492N, NC1492N *(Current status unknown)*				

Reg	Type	C/n	Previous identity	Date	Owner/Operator	Location	Status
EI-CHM	Cessna 150M Commuter	15079288	G-BSZX, N714MU	2. 3.93	K A O'Connor *(Operated National Flight Centre)*	Weston, Dublin *(Crashed 25. 5.06 near Mullingar)*	A 5.06
EI-CHR	CFM Shadow Series BD *(Rotax 447)*	063	G-MTKT	20. 5.93	B Kelly	Ardclough, Straffan	N 5.04
EI-CHS	Cessna 172M Skyhawk II	17266742	G-BREZ, N80775	26. 4.93	B A Mills *(On restoration to G-BREZ)*	Fenland	N 2.08
EI-CHT	Solar Wings Pegasus XL-R	SW-WA-1568	G-BZXU	27. 3.02	J Grattan	Hawkfield, Newbridge	N 5.04
EI-CHV	Agusta A109A II	7149	VR-BMM, HB-XTJ, D-HASV	10. 6.93	Celtic Helicopters Ltd	Celtic Heliport, Knocksedan, Dublin Airport	A 5.07
EI-CIA	SOCATA MS.880B Rallye Club	1218	G-MONA, G-AWJK	26. 4.93	G Hackett and C Mason	Thurles, Moyne	N 6.07
EI-CIF	Piper PA-28-180 Cherokee C *(Rebuilt 1967 with spare frame c/n 28-3808S)*	28-2853	G-AVVV, N8880J	12. 6.93	AA Flying Group	Waterford	A 8.06
EI-CIG	Piper PA-18-150 Super Cub *(Frame No.18-7360)*	18-7203	G-BGWF, ST-AFJ, ST-ABN	12. 6.93	K A O'Connor	Weston, Dublin	A 5.06
EI-CIH	Ercoupe 415CD	4834	G-BZKS, EI-CIH, OO-AIA, (PH-NDO), N94723, NC94723	25. 6.93	R D Harper	Galway	N 2.07
EI-CIJ	Cessna 340	3400304	G-BBVE, N69451	2. 7.93	Airlink Airways Ltd	Liverpool	A 7.06
EI-CIM	Avid Flyer Model IV *(Built P Swan as SAAC pr.no.041)*	1125D		17. 8.93	P Swan	Weston, Dublin	A 6.04
EI-CIN	Cessna 150K	15071728	G-OCIN, EI-CIN, G-BSXG, N6228G	6. 9.93	K A.O'Connor	Weston, Dublin	A 5.07
EI-CIR (2)	Cessna 551 Citation II *(Built as Cessna 550 EI-CIR (1) c/n 550-0128)*	551-0174	N60AR, EI-CIR (1), F-WLEF, 9A-BPU, RC-BPU, YU-BPU, N220LA, N536M, N2631V	29.11.93	Aircraft International Renting Ltd	Dinard, France	N 5.06
EI-CIV	Piper PA-28-140 Cherokee Cruiser	28-7725232	G-BEXY, N9648N	20.11.93	L A Tatton	Abbeysrule	N 6.07
EI-CIW	McDonnell-Douglas MD-83	49785	HL-7271	30.12.93	Aergo Leasing 113 Ltd *"Isola Tremiti" (Operated Meridiana)*	Olbia, Italy	A2008
EI-CIZ	Steen Skybolt *(Built B J Counts) (Lycoming IO-360)*	001	G-BSAO, N303BC	12.12.93	J Keane *(Crashed near Ard Fert, County Kerry 29. 7.07 and substantially damaged)*	Coonagh	
EI-CJJ	Slingsby T-31M Motor Tutor *(Built J J Sullivan as SAAC pr.no.40?) (Volkswagen VW1600)*	907	XE794	19. 1.06	J J Sullivan	Gorey	
EI-CJR	SNCAN Stampe SV-4A	318	G-BKBK, OO-CLR, F-BCLR	28. 2.94	P McKenna	Carnmore, Galway	A 4.06
EI-CJS	Jodel Wassmer D.120A Paris-Nice	339	F-BOYF	28. 2.94	A Flood	Birr	A 1.03
EI-CJT	Slingsby T.31 Cadet III *(Built P C Williams - c/n PCW-001) (Volkswagen 1835)*	830	G-BPCW, XA288	25. 2.94	J Tarrant *(Stored)*	Rathcoole	N2006
EI-CJV	Konsuprod Moskito 2 *(Rotax 582)*	004	D-MBGM	12. 3.94	Messrs Peril, Kingston, Hanly and Fitzgerald *(Dismantled)*	Coonagh	N 8.04
EI-CJZ	Whittaker MW-6S Fatboy Flyer *(Built D M Precious) (Rotax 503)*	PFA 164-11493	G-MWTW	24. 3.94	M McCarthy	Watergrasshill	A 9.00
EI-CKF	Hunt Avon/Hunt Wing *(Built J Hunt- pr.no. BMAA/HB/015)*	JAH-8	G-MWPT, EI-CKF, G-MWPT	3. 6.94	M Leyden *(New owner 1.07)*	(Ennis)	
EI-CKG	Hunt Avon *(Built J Hunt) (Rotax 447)*	92009013		2. 7.94	B Kenny *(Current status unknown)*	(Clara)	
EI-CKH	Piper PA-18 Super Cub 95	18-7248	G-APZK, N10F	3. 6.94	G Brady	Kilrush	A 5.06
EI-CKI	Thruster TST Mk.1 *(Rotax 503)*	8078-TST-091	G-MVDI	3. 6.94	D.Baker	(Brannockstown)	N 9.07
EI-CKJ	Cameron N-77 Balloon (Hot Air)	3305		6. 7.94	F Meldon "Goodfellas"	Blackrock	A 9.06
EI-CKM	McDonnell-Douglas MD-83	49792	TC-INC, EI-CKM, (D-ALLW), EI-CKM, XA-RPH, EC-FFP, EC-733, XA-RPH	10. 8.94	Airplanes Finance Ltd *"Isola dell'Asinara" (Operated Meridiana)*	Olbia, Italy	A2008
EI-CKN	Whittaker MW-6S Fatboy Flyer *(Built Aero-Tech International) (Rotax 462)*	BCA.8942		29. 7.94	F Byrne and M O'Carroll *(Current status unknown)*	(Kilrush)	
EI-CKT	Mainair Gemini/Flash *(Fuji-Robin EC-44-PM)*	307-585-3- W47	G-MNCB	27. 9.94	C Burke *(Current status unknown)*	(Darrary, Clonakilty)	
EI-CKU	Solar Wings Pegasus XL-R *(Rotax 447) (Trike c/n SW-TB-1434)*	SW-WA-1500	G-MWVB	14.10.94	M O'Regan *(Current status unknown)*	(Edenderry)	
EI-CKZ	Jodel D.18 *(Volkswagen 1834)*	229		5. 4.95	J O'Brien *(Under construction?)*	(Glen of Imal)	
EI-CLA	HOAC DV-20 Katana	20106		24. 3.95	Weston Ltd	Weston, Dublin	A 5.06
EI-CLL	Whittaker MW-6S Fatboy Flyer *(Built Aero-Tech International) (Rotax 503)*	1069		2. 4.95	F Stack *(Stored?)*	(Midleton)	
EI-CLQ	Reims Cessna F172N Skyhawk II	F17201653	G-BFLV	26. 5.95	Just Having Fun 172 Group	Limetree, Portarlington	A 6.06
EI-CLW	Boeing 737-3Y0	25187	XA-SAB	10. 6.95	Airplanes Finance Ltd *(Operated Kras Air)*	Krasnoyarsk-Yemilianovo, Russia	A2008
EI-CLZ	Boeing 737-3Y0	25179	XA-RJR, N3521N	27. 7.95	Airplanes Finance Ltd *(Operated Kras Air)*	Krasnoyarsk-Yemilianovo, Russia	A2008
EI-CMB	Piper PA-28-140 Cherokee Cruiser	28-7725094	G-BELR, N9541N	5. 9.95	Dublin Flyers Ltd	Dublin	A 5.06
EI-CMK	Eurowing Goldwing ST *(Built M Garrigan as SAAC pr.no.57) (Fuji-Robin EC-PM-34)*	76		22.12.95	M Garrigan *(Under construction?)*	(Clondara,)	
EI-CML	Cessna 150M	15076786	G-BNSS, N45207	5. 1.96	K A O'Connor	Weston, Dublin	A 5.06
EI-CMN	Piper PA-12 Super Cruiser *(Lycoming O-235)*	12-1617	N2363M, NC2363M	26. 1.96	A McNamee and Partners	Birr	A 5.06
EI-CMR	Rutan LongEz *(Built F O'Caoimh as SAAC pr.no.028) (Lycoming O-235)*	1716		2. 5.96	F and C.O'Caoimh	Waterford	A 4.06
EI-CMS	British Aerospace BAe 146 Series 200A	E2044	N184US, N361PS	24. 4.96	CityJet Ltd *(Operated Air France Regional)*	Paris CDG, France	A2008
EI-CMT	Piper PA-34-200T Seneca II	34-7870088	G-BNER, N2590M	23. 4.96	Atlantic Flight Training Ltd	Cork	A 5.07

Reg	Type	c/n	Prev id	Date	Owner/Operator	Location	Code
EI-CMU	Mainair Mercury (Rotax 462)	1071-0296-7 and W873		3. 5.96	L Langan and L Laffan	Wexford and Waterford	N 8.01
EI-CMV	Cessna 150L	150-72747	G-MSES N1447Q	17. 5.96	K A O'Connor	Weston, Dublin	A 5.06
EI-CMW	Rotorway Executive (Rotorway RW 162D)	3550		13. 5.96	B McNamee (Current status unknown)	(Dunboyne)	
EI-CMY	British Aerospace BAe 146 Series 200A	E2039	N177US N356PS	19. 6.96	CityJet Ltd (Operated Air France Regional)	Paris CDG, France	A2008
EI-CNA	Letov LK-2M Sluka (Built G Doody as SAAC pr.no.059) (Rotax 447)	8295S005		28. 6.96	G Doody	(Portlaoise)	A 7.00
EI-CNB	British Aerospace BAe 146 Series 200A	E2046	(EI-CMZ) N187US, N363PS	3. 8.96	CityJet Ltd (Operated Air France Regional)	Paris CDG, France	A2008
EI-CNC	Team Mini-Max 1600 (Built A M S Allen as SAAC pr.no.042) (Rotax 447)	514		10. 9.96	A M S.Allen	Enniskillen	A 7.01
EI-CNG	Air and Space 18-A Gyroplane	18-75	G-BALB N6170S	10. 9.96	P Joyce	Waterford	A 8.06
EI-CNL	Sikorsky S-61N Mk.II	61746	G-BDDA ZS-RBU, G-BDDA, N91201, G-BDDA (IMES Rescue titles)	19.12.96	CHC Ireland Ltd	Waterford	A 5.07
EI-CNQ	British Aerospace BAe 146 Series 200	E2031	G-OWLD N173US, N353PS	2. 7.97	CityJet Ltd (Operated Air France Regional)	Paris CDG, France	A2008
EI-CNR	McDonnell-Douglas MD-83	53199	N531LS PK-FED, N531LS, SU-BMF, EI-CNR, SE-DLU, N13627 (Operated Meridiana)	10. 4.97	Aircraft Finance Trust Ireland Ltd	Olbia, Italy	A2008
EI-CNU	Pegasus Quantum 15-912	7326		10. 4.97	M Ffrench	Donamore, New Ross,	A 6.01
EI-COE	Europa Aviation Europa (Built F Flynn as SAAC pr.no.060) (Jabiru 2200) (Monowheel u/c)	286		29. 5.97	F Flynn (Under construction)	(Urlanmore)	N 1.01
EI-COG	Gyroscopic Rotorcraft Gyroplane (Subaru AE81) (Official c/n G.120 may be type designation)	G.120		11. 3.98	R C Fidler and D D Bracken (Current status unknown)	(Letterkenny)	A 8.98
EI-COH	Boeing 737-430	27001	D-ABKB (VT-S..), D-ABKB	6. 6.97	ACS Aircraft Leasing (Ireland) Ltd (Operated Air One)	 Rome -Fiumicino, Italy	 A2008
EI-COI	Boeing 737-430	27002	D-ABKC	13.11.97	Challey Ltd (Operated Air One)	Rome -Fiumicino, Italy	A2008
EI-COJ	Boeing 737-430	27005	D-ABKK (D-ABKF)	13.11.97	Challey Ltd (Operated Air One)	Rome -Fiumicino, Italy	A2008
EI-COK	Boeing 737-430	27003	F-GRNZ EI-COK, D-ABKD	22. 4.02	ACS Aircraft Leasing (Ireland) Ltd (Operated Air One)	 Rome -Fiumicino, Italy	 A2008
EI-COM	Whittaker MW-6S Fatboy Flyer (Built M Watson as SAAC pr.no.064) (Rotax 582)	1		10.10.97	M Watson (Under construction)	Clonbullogue	N 1.01
EI-COO	Carlson Sparrow II (Rotax 532)	302		13. 8.97	D Logue (Current status unknown)	(Weston, Dublin)	
EI-COT	Reims Cessna F172N Skyhawk II	F17201884	D-EIEF	24.11.97	Tojo Air Leasing Ltd	Abbeyshrule	A 8.06
EI-COY	Piper J-3C-65 Cub Special (Continental A65-8) (Floatplane).	22519	N3319N NC3319N	5.11.97	W Flood	Abbeyshrule	N 1.07
EI-COZ	Piper PA-28-140 Cherokee C	28-26796	G-AYMZ N11C	5.11.97	L A Tattan	Cork	N 5.07
EI-CPC	Airbus A321-211	815	D-AVZT	8. 5.98	Aer Lingus Ltd "St.Fergus/Feargus"	Dublin	A2008
EI-CPD	Airbus A321-211	841	D-AVZA	19. 6.98	Aer Lingus Ltd "St.Davnet/Damhnat"	Dublin	A2008
EI-CPE	Airbus A321-211	926	D-AVZQ	11.12.98	Aer Lingus Ltd "St.Enda/Eanna"	Dublin	A2008
EI-CPF	Airbus A321-211	991	D-AVZE	9. 4.99	Aer Lingus Ltd "St.Ida/Ide"	Dublin	A2008
EI-CPG	Airbus A321-211	1023	D-AVZR	28. 5.99	Aer Lingus Ltd "St.Aidan/Aodhan"	Dublin	A2008
EI-CPH	Airbus A321-211	1094	F-WWDD D-AVZA	22.11.99	Aer Lingus Ltd "St.Dervilla/Dearbhile"	Dublin	A2008
EI-CPI	Rutan LongEz (Lycoming O-235)	17		18.12.97	D J Ryan "Lady Elizabeth"	Waterford	A 4.06
EI-CPN	Auster J/4	2073	G-AIJR	1. 4.98	E Fagan	Abbeyshrule	A12.00
EI-CPO	Robinson R.22B2 Beta	2775	G-BXUJ	23. 9.98	D Byrne	Weston, Dublin	N 1.07
EI-CPP	Piper J-3C-65 Cub (L-4H-PI) (Rebuilt Glasthule, Dublin 1994/1998)	12052	G-BIGH F-BFQV, OO-GAS, OO-GAZ, 44-79756	23. 3.98	E Fitzgerald Ardenagh Great, Taghmon		A 8.06
EI-CPT	Aérospatiale-Alenia ATR 42-300	191	C-GIQS (ZS-NYP), C-GIQS, F-WWEA (Operated Aer Arann Express)	12. 6.98	Nordic Aviation Contractors (Ireland) Ltd	Dublin	A 6.06
EI-CPX	III Sky Arrow 650T (Built M McCarthy as SAAC pr.no.67)	K.122		24. 6.98	M McCarthy	Watergrasshill	A.8.00
EI-CRB	Lindstrand LBL 90A Balloon (Hot Air)	550		23. 9.98	J and C Concannon (Current status unknown)	(Tuam)	
EI-CRD	Boeing 767-31BER	26259	B-2565	29.10.98	ILFC Ireland Ltd (Operated Alitalia)	Rome-Fiumicino, Italy	A2008
EI-CRE	McDonnell-Douglas MD-83	49854	D-ALLL	11.12.98	AAR Ireland Ltd "Tavolara-Punta Coda Cavallo" (Operated Meridiana)	Olbia, Italy	A2008
EI-CRF	Boeing 767-31B	25170	B-2566	4.12.98	ILFC Ireland Ltd (Operated Alitalia)	Rome-Fiumicino, Italy	A2008
EI-CRG	Robin DR400/180 Régent	2021	D-EHEC	11.12.98	D and B Lodge	Waterford	A 4.06
EI-CRH	McDonnell-Douglas MD-83	49935	HB-IKM G-DCAC, N3004C	10. 2.99	Airplanes 111 Ltd "Torre Guaceto" (Operated Meridiana)	Olbia, Italy	A2008
EI-CRK	Airbus A330-301	070	(EI-NYC) F-WWKV	18.11.94	Aer Lingus Ltd "St Brigid/Brighid"	Dublin	A2008
EI-CRL	Boeing 767-343ER	30008	(I-DEIB)	22. 3.99	GECAS Technical Services Ltd Rome-Fiumicino, Italy "Leonardo da Vinci" (Operated Alitalia)		A2008
EI-CRM	Boeing 767-343	30009		8. 4.99	GECAS Technical Services Ltd Rome-Fiumicino, Italy "Amerigo Vespucci" (Operated Alitalia)		A2008
EI-CRO	Boeing 767-3Q8ER	29383		16. 4.99	ILFC Ireland Ltd "Francesco de Pinedo" (Operated Alitalia)	Rome-Fiumicino, Italy	A2008
EI-CRR	Aeronca 11AC Chief	11AC-1605	OO-ESM (OO-DEL), OO-ESM	13. 4.99	L Maddock and Partners	Killamaster	A 1.03
EI-CRU	Cessna 152	15285621	G-BNSW N94213	21. 9.99	W Reilly	Inis Mor	A 5.04

Reg	Type	C/n	Prev id	Date	Owner/Operator	Base	Status
EI-CRV	Hoffman H.36 Dimona	3674	OE-9319 HB-2081	2. 6.99	The Dimona Group	Waterford	A 4.06
EI-CRW	McDonnell-Douglas MD-83	49951	HB-IKN G-GMJM, N13627	8. 4.99	Airplanes IAL Ltd *"Portofino" (Operated Meridiana)*	Olbia, Italy	A2008
EI-CRX	SOCATA TB-9 Tampico	1170	F-GKUL	21. 5.99	The Hotel Bravo Flying Club Ltd	Weston, Dublin	A 5.06
EI-CRY	Medway EclipseR	160/138		2. 6.99	G A Murphy *(Current status unknown)* (Rathcoole)		
EI-CRZ	Boeing 737-36E	26322	EC-GGE EC-798	14. 4.99	ILFC Ireland Ltd *(Operated Air One)*	Rome -Fiumicino, Italy	A2008
EI-CSF	Boeing 737-8AS/W	29921	N1786B	24. 5.00	Ryanair Ltd *(Dites Non a la Surcharge Kerosene D'Air France titles)*	Dublin	A2008
EI-CSG	Boeing 737-8AS	29922	N1786B	31. 5.00	Ryanair Ltd	Dublin	A2008
EI-CSH	Boeing 737-8AS	29923	N1787B	9. 6.00	Ryanair Ltd *(Auf Wiedersehen Lufthansa titles)*	Dublin	A2008
EI-CSI	Boeing 737-8AS	29924	N1796B	12. 6.00	Ryanair Ltd *(Frankfurt-Hahn logo)*	Dublin	A2008
EI-CSJ	Boeing 737-8AS	29925	N1786B	20. 6.00	Ryanair Ltd	Dublin	A2008
EI-CSM	Boeing 737-8AS	29926	N...	7.12.00	Ryanair Ltd	Dublin	A2008
EI-CSN	Boeing 737-8AS	29927	N...	11.12.00	Ryanair Ltd	Dublin	A2008
EI-CSO	Boeing 737-8AS/W	29928	N...	11. 1.01	Ryanair Ltd	Dublin	A2008
EI-CSP	Boeing 737-8AS	29929	N...	25. 1.01	Ryanair Ltd	Dublin	A2008
EI-CSQ	Boeing 737-8AS/W	29930	N...	26. 1.01	Ryanair Ltd	Dublin	A2008
EI-CSR	Boeing 737-8AS	29931	N...	5.12.01	Ryanair Ltd	Dublin	A2008
EI-CSS	Boeing 737-8AS	29932	N...	14.12.01	Ryanair Ltd	Dublin	A2008
EI-CST	Boeing 737-8AS/W	29933	N...	19.12.01	Ryanair Ltd	Dublin	A2008
EI-CSU	Boeing 737-36E	27626	EC-GGZ EC-799	14. 4.99	ILFC Ireland Ltd *(Operated Air One)*	Rome -Fiumicino, Italy	A2008
EI-CSV	Boeing 737-8AS/W	29934		18. 1.02	Ryanair Ltd *(Nyköping titles)*	Dublin	A2008
EI-CSW	Boeing 737-8AS	29935		4. 2.02	Ryanair Ltd *(Catalunya Costa Brava Pirineu de Girona titles)*	Dublin	A2008
EI-CSX	Boeing 737-8AS/W	32778		21. 5.02	Ryanair Ltd	Dublin	A2008
EI-CSY	Boeing 737-8AS/W	32779		25. 6.02	Ryanair Ltd	Dublin	A2008
EI-CSZ	Boeing 737-8AS/W	32780		15. 7.02	Ryanair Ltd *(Arrivederci Alitalia titles)*	Dublin	A2008
EI-CTA	Boeing 737-8AS/W	29936		19.11.02	Ryanair Ltd	Dublin	A2008
EI-CTB	Boeing 737-8AS/W	29937		19.11.02	Ryanair Ltd *(Say No To BA Fuel Levy titles)*	Dublin	A2008
EI-CTC	Medway EclipseR	158/137		2. 6.99	P A McMahon	Dunlaoghaire	A 1.03
EI-CTG	Stoddard-Hamilton SH-2R Glasair RG	721R	N721WR	3. 6.99	K Higgins	Carnmore, Galway	A 6.07
EI-CTI	Reims Cessna FRA150L	FRA1500261	G-BCRN	29. 4.99	J Logan and T Bradford *(Wings only noted Clonbullogue 4.06)*	Ballynacarigy	A 1.03
EI-CTL	Aerotech MW-5B Sorcerer SR102-R440B-07 (Fuji-Robin EC-44-PM)		G-MTFH	21. 5.99	M Wade	Kilrush	A 1.03
EI-CTT	Piper PA-28-161 Cherokee Warrior II	28-7716305	N38974	14. 7.99	Conair Group	Knock	A12.01
EI-CUA	Boeing 737-4K5	24901	D-AHLR	29. 9.99	Aerco Ireland Ltd *(Operated Blu Express)*	Rome-Fiumicino, Italy	A2008
EI-CUD	Boeing 737-4Q8	26298	TC-JEI	13. 3.00	Castle 2003-2 Ireland Ltd *(Operated Blu Express)*	Rome-Fiumicino, Italy	A2008
EI-CUE	Cameron N-105 Balloon (Hot Air)	4683		16. 9.99	Eircom Ltd *"Eircom"*	Celbridge	A12.03
EI-CUG	Bell 206B-2 JetRanger II	4177	N248BC N118GC	21.10.99	Avatar Aviation Ltd	Dublin	A2003
EI-CUJ	Cessna 172N Skyhawk II	17271985	G-BJGO N6038E	19.11.99	M Nally	Abbeyshrule	A 5.06
EI-CUM	Airbus A320-232	542	N721LF S7-RGL, PK-AWE, N542LF, EI-CUM, OO-COF. F-WWIH *(Operated Windjet)*	24. 3.05	ILFC Ireland Ltd	Catania, Italy	A2008
EI-CUN	Boeing 737-4K5	27074	D-AHLS (D-AHLG)	13. 4.00	Aerco Ireland Ltd *(Operated Blu Express)*	Rome-Fiumicino, Italy	A2008
EI-CUP	Cessna 335	335-0018	N2706X	5. 5.00	J Greany	Kerry	A 6.04
EI-CUS	Agusta-Bell 206B-3 JetRanger III	8721	(EI-...), G-OONS, G-LIND, G-OONS	24. 8.00	Doherty Quarries and Waste Management.	Carryduff	A 7.01
EI-CUT	Maule MX 7-180A (Nosewheel u/c)	21080C		6. 4.01	Cosair Ltd	Trim	A 4.06
EI-CUW	Pilatus Britten-Norman BN-2B-20 Islander	2293	G-BWYW	8.11.00	Galway Aviation Services Ltd *(Operated Aer Arann Islands)*	Connemara	A 5.07
EI-CVA	Airbus A320-214	1242	F-WWIT	22. 6.00	Aer Lingus Ltd *"St Schira/Scire"*	Dublin	A2008
EI-CVB	Airbus A320-214	1394	F-WWIV	8. 2.01	Aer Lingus Ltd *"St Mobhi/Mobhi"*	Dublin	A2008
EI-CVC	Airbus A320-214	1443	F-WWBG	6. 4.01	Aer Lingus Ltd *"St Kealin/Caoilfhionn"*	Dublin	A2008
EI-CVD	Airbus A320-214	1467	F-WWDK	10. 5.01	Aer Lingus Ltd *"St Kevin/Caoimhin"*	Dublin	A2008
EI-CVL	Ercoupe 415CD	4754	G-ASNF PH-NCF, NC94647	15. 3.01	B Lyons and J Hackett	Thurles, Moyne	N 6.07
EI-CVM	Schweizer 269C (Schweizer 300)	S1328	G-GIRO N41S	7.11.00	B Moloney	Tralee	A 1.03
EI-CVR	Aérospatiale-Alenia ATR 42-310	022	F-GGLK OH-LTB, F-WWEI	17. 1.01	Nordic Aviation Contractor (Ireland) Ltd *(Operated Aer Arann Express)*	Dublin	A2008
EI-CVS	Aérospatiale-Alenia ATR 42-310	033	F-GIRC F-WIAF, OH-LTC, F-WWEO	16. 3.01	Nordic Aviation Contractors (Ireland) Ltd *(Operated Aer Arann Express)*	Dublin	A2008
EI-CVW	Bensen B8M Gyrocopter (Built F Kavanagh)	FK-199801		26. 5.05	F Kavanagh	Kilrush	A 5.06
EI-CVY	Brock KB-2 Gyrocopter	074		7. 8.03	G Smyth	(Swords)	
EI-CWE	Boeing 737-42C	24232	N941PG PH-BPE, G-UKLD	18. 5.01	Rockshaw Ltd *(Operated Air One)*	Rome -Fiumicino, Italy	A2008
EI-CWF	Boeing 737-42C	24814	PH-BPG G-UKLG	16. 5.01	Rockshaw Ltd *(Operated Air One)*	Rome -Fiumicino, Italy	A2008
EI-CWH	Agusta A109E Power	11106		17. 7.01	Lochbrea Aircraft Ltd	Carnmore, Galway	A 6.07
EI-CWL	Robinson R22 Beta	0885	G-BXCX G-MFHL	19. 9.01	J McLoughlin *(Current status unknown)*	(Dunboyne)	
EI-CWR	Robinson R22 Beta II	3234	G-CBDB	2.11.01	Eirecopter Helicopters Ltd	Weston, Dublin	A10.06

EI-CWW	Boeing 737-4YO	24906	EC-GAZ EC-850, 9M-MJO	19.12.01	Airplanes Holdings Ltd (Operated Air One)	Rome -Fiumicino, Italy	A2008
EI-CWX	Boeing 737-4YO	24912	EC-GBN EC-851, 9M-MJQ	6.12.01	Airplanes Holdings Ltd (Operated Air One)	Rome -Fiumicino, Italy	A2008
EI-CXC	Raj Hamsa X'Air 502T	333	(44 SU)	6. 9.02	T McDevitt	(Glencar)	A 8.06
EI-CXJ	Boeing 737-4Q8	25164	G-BUHJ N164LF	22. 3.02	Castle 2003-1 Ireland Ltd (Operated Central Wings)	Warsaw-Okecie, Poland	A2008
EI-CXK	Boeing 737-4S3	25596	G-OGBA G-OBMK	9. 4.02	Bravo Aircraft Management Ltd (Operated Transaero Airlines) 	Moscow-Domodedovo, Russia	A2008
EI-CXM	Boeing 737-4Q8	26302	VH-VOZ TC-JEM	17. 5.02	ILFC Ireland Ltd (Operated Central Wings)	Warsaw-Okecie, Poland	A2008
EI-CXN	Boeing 737-329	23772	OO-SDW N506GX, OO-SDW	1. 5.02	Embarcadero Aircraft Securitization Trust Ireland Ltd (Operated Transaero Airlines)	Moscow-Domodedovo, Russia	A2008
EI-CXO	Boeing 767-3GS	28111	N581LF D-AMUJ	12. 4.02	ILFC Ireland Ltd (Operated Blue Panorama Airlines)	Rome-Fiumicino, italy	A2008
EI-CXR	Boeing 737-329	24355	OO-SYA (OO-SQA)	31. 5.02	Embarcadero Aircraft Securitization Trust Ireland Ltd (Operated Transaero Airlines)	Moscow-Domodedovo, Russia	A11.05
EI-CXS	Sikorsky S.61N	61816	IAC257 EI-CXS, C-GBKZ, LN-OQU	14.10.04	CHC Ireland Ltd (IMES Rescue titles)	Strandhill, Sligo	A2008
EI-CXV	Boeing 737-8CX	32364		3. 7.02	MASL Ireland (14) Ltd "Khubelai Khaan" (Operated MIAT Mongolian Airlines)	Ulan Bator, Mongolia	A2008
EI-CXY	Evektor EV-97 Eurostar	2000-0701	OK-FUR	31. 10.02	G Doody, E McEvoy and S Pallister	Portlaoise	A 7.05
EI-CXZ	Boeing 767-216ER	24973	N502GX VH-RMM, N483GX, CC-CEF (Operated Transaero Airlines)	25. 7.02	Embarcadero Aircraft Securitization Trust Ireland Ltd 	Moscow-Domodedovo, Russia	A2008
EI-CZA	ATEC Zephyr 2000 (Built M Higgins)	Z580602A		17. 7.03	P Whitehouse-Tedd	(Carnmore, Galway)	N 8.06
EI-CZC	CFM Streak Shadow	K269SA11	G-BWHJ	16. 7.02	M Culhane and D Burrows (Current status unknown)	(Rathcoole)	
EI-CZD	Boeing 767-216ER	23623	N762TA CC-CJU, N4529T	2. 9.02	Capablue Ltd (Operated Transaero Airlines)	Moscow-Domodedovo, Russia	A2008
EI-CZG	Boeing 737-4Q8	25740	VH-VGB N257BR, SU-PTA, EC-HAN, TC-JED (Operated Central Wings))	8.10.02	ILFC Ireland Ltd 	Warsaw-Okecie, Poland	A2008
EI-CZH	Boeing 767-3G5ER	29435	D-AMUO	9. 8.02	ILFC Ireland Ltd (Operated Blue Panorama Airlines)	Rome-Fiumicino, Italy	A2008
EI-CZK	Boeing 737-4YO	24519	N519AP TC-ACA, VR-CAB	10. 1.03	Aergo Leasing 113 Ltd (Operated Transaero Airlines)	Moscow-Domodedovo, Russia	A2008
EI-CZL	Schweizer 269C-1 (Schweizer 300)	0147	G-CDTW EI-CZL, N86G	19.12.02	Cahir Oil Ltd	(Tipperary)	N 7.07
EI-CZM	Robinson R.44 Raven II	10054		24. 4.03	M I C A D Developments Ltd	Oranmore, Galway	A 6.07
EI-CZN	Sikorsky S.61N	61740	G-CBWC OY-HDO, LN-OSU	15. 4.03	CHC Ireland Ltd (IMES Rescue titles)	Dublin	A2008
EI-CZP	Schweizer 269C-1 (Schweizer 300)	0149		2. 5.03	NG Kam Tim (Operated European Helicopter Academy)	Weston, Dublin	A 5.06
EI-DAA	Airbus A330-202	397	F-WWKX	17. 4.01	Aer Lingus Ltd "St Keeva/Caoimhe"	Dublin	A2008
EI-DAC	Boeing 737-8AS/W	29938		2.12.02	Ryanair Ltd	Dublin	A2008
EI-DAD	Boeing 737-8AS/W	33544		3.12.02	Ryanair Ltd (Nein Zum Lufthansa Kerosinzuschlag titles)	Dublin	A2008
EI-DAE	Boeing 737-8AS	33545		9.12.02	Ryanair Ltd	Dublin	A2008
EI-DAF	Boeing 737-8AS	29939		9. 1.03	Ryanair Ltd (City of Nyköping titles)	Dublin	A2008
EI-DAG	Boeing 737-8AS	29940		17. 1.03	Ryanair Ltd	Dublin	A2008
EI-DAH	Boeing 737-8AS/W	33546		22. 1.03	Ryanair Ltd	Dublin	A2008
EI-DAI	Boeing 737-8AS/W	33547		3. 2.03	Ryanair Ltd	Dublin	A2008
EI-DAJ	Boeing 737-8AS	33548		4. 2.03	Ryanair Ltd	Dublin	A2008
EI-DAK	Boeing 737-8AS/W	33717		17. 4.03	Ryanair Ltd	Dublin	A2008
EI-DAL	Boeing 737-8AS/W	33718		22. 4.03	Ryanair Ltd	Dublin	A2008
EI-DAM	Boeing 737-8AS	33719		23. 4.03	Ryanair Ltd	Dublin	A2008
EI-DAN	Boeing 737-8AS/W	33549		2. 9.03	Ryanair Ltd	Dublin	A2008
EI-DAO	Boeing 737-8AS/W	33550	N1800B	5. 9.03	Ryanair Ltd (Pride of Scotland titles)	Dublin	A2008
EI-DAP	Boeing 737-8AS/W	33551	N6066U	18. 9.03	Ryanair Ltd	Dublin	A2008
EI-DAR	Boeing 737-8AS/W	33552	(EI-DAQ)	11. 9.03	Ryanair Ltd	Dublin	A2008
EI-DAS	Boeing 737-8AS/W	33553	(EI-DAR)	12. 9.03	Ryanair Ltd	Dublin	A2008
EI-DAT	Boeing 737-8AS/W	33554		5.12.03	Ryanair Ltd	Dublin	A2008
EI-DAV	Boeing 737-8AS/W	33555		9. 1.04	Ryanair Ltd	Dublin	A2008
EI-DAW	Boeing 737-8AS/W	33556		8. 1.04	Ryanair Ltd	Dublin	A2008
EI-DAX	Boeing 737-8AS/W	33557		23. 1.04	Ryanair Ltd	Dublin	A2008
EI-DAY	Boeing 737-8AS/W	33558		2. 2.04	Ryanair Ltd	Dublin	A2008
EI-DAZ	Boeing 737-8AS/W	33559		3. 2.04	Ryanair Ltd	Dublin	A2008
EI-DBF	Boeing 767-3Q8	24745	F-GHGF	23. 4.03	ACG Acquisition Ireland Ltd (Operated Transaero Airlines) 	Moscow-Domodedovo, Russia	A2008
EI-DBG	Boeing 767-3Q8	24746	F-GHGG	14 .5.03	Charlie Aircraft Management Ltd (Operated Transaero Airlines) 	Moscow-Domodedovo, Russia	A2008
EI-DBH	CFM Streak Shadow SA-11	K.278		14. 4.03	M O'Mahony (Stored?)	(Ballyskerdane, Carrignavar)	
EI-DBI	Raj Hamsa X'Air Mk.2 Falcon (Jabiru 2200)	671		16. 4.03	E Hamilton	Kilrush	A 5.06
EI-DBJ	Huntwing Pegasus XL Classic (Built C Kiernan - pr.no.BMAA/HB/039)	xxxxx	G-MZCZ	19. 5.03	P A McMahon	Clonbullogue	A 5.06
EI-DBK	Boeing 777-243ER	32783		10.10.03	GECAS Technical Services Ltd "Ostuni" (Operated.Alitalia)	Rome-Fiumicino, Italy	A2008
EI-DBL	Boeing 777-243ER	32781		14. 11.03	GECAS Technical Services Ltd "Sestriere" (Operated.Alitalia)	Rome-Fiumicino, Italy	A2008
EI-DBM	Boeing 777-243ER	32782		12.12.03	GECAS Technical Services Ltd "Argentario" (Operated.Alitalia)	Rome-Fiumicino, Italy	A2008
EI-DBO	Air Création 582(1)/Kiss 400 (Wing s/n A03034-3033)	xxxx		13. 5.03	E Spain	(Monasterevin)	A 6.07

EI-DBP	Boeing 767-35H	26389	C-GGBJ	23. 5.03	CIT Aerospace International	Rome-Fiumicino, Italy	A2008
			(VH-BZN), ZK-NCM, N800CZ, N60659 *"Duca degli Abruzzi" (Operated.Alitalia)*				
EI-DBU	Boeing 767-37E	25077	F-GHGH	8. 7.03	Pegasus Aviation Ireland Ltd *(Operated Transaero Airlines)*		
						Moscow-Domodedovo, Russia	A2008
EI-DBV	Rand Kar X'Air 602T	516	44-AEE	13. 8.03	S Scanlon	Emlagh, Lispole	A2006
	(Rotax 582)						
EI-DBW	Boeing 767-201	23899	N647US	10. 9.03	Orix Aircraft Management Ltd *(Operated Transaero Airlines)*		
			N607P			Moscow-Domodedovo, Russia	A2008
EI-DBX	Magni M-18 Spartan	18-032181		3. 7.03	M Concannon	Abbeyshrule	A 8.06
EI-DCA	Raj Hamsa X'Air	742		18. 7.03	S Cahill	Ferskill, Granard	A2006
	(Jabiru 2200)						
EI-DCB	Boeing 737-8AS/W	33560		10. 2.04	Ryanair Ltd	Dublin	A2008
EI-DCC	Boeing 737-8AS/W	33561		11. 3.04	Ryanair Ltd	Dublin	A2008
EI-DCD	Boeing 737-8AS	33562		12. 3.04	Ryanair Ltd *(Pride of Scotland titles)*	Dublin	A2008
EI-DCE	Boeing 737-8AS/W	33563		25. 3.04	Ryanair Ltd	Dublin	A2008
EI-DCF	Boeing 737-8AS	33804		1. 7.04	Ryanair Ltd	Dublin	A2008
EI-DCG	Boeing 737-8AS	33805		2. 7.04	Ryanair Ltd	Dublin	A2008
EI-DCH	Boeing 737-8AS	33566		3. 8.04	Ryaniar Ltd	Dublin	A2008
EI-DCI	Boeing 737-8AS	33567		3. 8.04	Ryanair Ltd	Dublin	A2008
EI-DCJ	Boeing 737-8AS/W	33564		1. 9.04	Ryanair Ltd	Dublin	A2008
EI-DCK	Boeing 737-8AS/W	33565		1. 9.04	Ryanair Ltd	Dublin	A2008
EI-DCL	Boeing 737-8AS/W	33806		1.10.04	Ryanair Ltd	Dublin	A2008
EI-DCM	Boeing 737-8AS/W	33807		1.10.04	Ryanair Ltd	Dublin	A2008
EI-DCN	Boeing 737-8AS/W	33808	N60436	1.11.04	Ryanair Ltd	Dublin	A2008
EI-DCO	Boeing 737-8AS/W	33809		1.11.04	Ryanair Ltd	Dublin	A2008
EI-DCP	Boeing 737-8AS/W	33810		1.11.04	Ryanair Ltd *(City of Nyköping titles)*	Dublin	A2008
EI-DCR	Boeing 737-8AS/W	33811		2.12.04	Ryanair Ltd	Dublin	A2008
EI-DCS	Boeing 737-8AS/W	33812		3.12.04	Ryanair Ltd	Dublin	A2008
EI-DCT	Boeing 737-8AS/W	33813		11.12.04	Ryanair Ltd	Dublin	A2008
EI-DCV	Boeing 737-8AS/W	33814		14.12.04	Ryanair Ltd	Dublin	A2008
EI-DCW	Boeing 737-8AS/W	33568		13. 1.05	Ryanair Ltd	Dublin	A2008
EI-DCX	Boeing 737-8AS/W	33569		21. 1.05	Ryanair Ltd	Dublin	A2008
EI-DCY	Boeing 737-8AS/W	33570		25. 1.05	Ryanair Ltd	Dublin	A2008
EI-DCZ	Boeing 737-8AS/W	33815		26. 1.05	Ryanair Ltd	Dublin	A2008
EI-DDA	Robinson R44 Raven II	10105	G-CCIP	26. 9.03	J O'R Security Ltd	Weston, Dublin	A 5.06
EI-DDB	Eurocopter EC.120B Colibri	1341	G-CCIL	30.12.03	J Cuddy	Weston, Dublin	A 5.06
EI-DDC	Reims Cessna F.172M	1082	G-BCEC	15.10.03	Trim Flying Club Ltd	Trim	A 5.07
EI-DDD	Aeronca 7AC Champion	7AC-2895	G-BTRH	27. 4.04	J Sullivan and M Quinn	Coonagh	A10.06
			N84204, NC84204				
EI-DDH	Boeing 777-243ER	32784		15. 5.04	GECAS Technical Services Ltd	Rome-Fiumicino, Italy	A2008
					"Tropea" (Operated.Alitalia)		
EI-DDI	Schweizer S.269C-1	0156	OO-SAC	6.11.03	B Hade	Weston, Dublin	A 5.06
	(Schweizer 300CBi)		N86G		*(Operated European Helicopter Academy)*		
EI-DDJ	Raj Hamsa X'Air 582	863		24. 9.03	P J McHugh	Haugh, Donegal Town	A2006
EI-DDK	Boeing 737-4S3	24165	N758BC	3.12.03	Boeing Capital Leasing Ltd *(Operated Transaero Airlines)*		
			VT-SIH, VT-JAI, N690MA, G-BPKC			Moscow-Domodedovo, Russia	A2008
EI-DDO	Montgomerie Merlin	0072		21. 5.04	C Condell *(Current status unknown)*	(Celbridge)	
EI-DDP	Southdown Puma Sprint	1121/0031	G-MMYJ	27. 5.04	M Mannion	(Kilrush)	N 4.07
EI-DDR	Bensen B.8V Gyrocopter	xxxx		2. 6.05	P MacCabe and K Reynolds	Kilrush	A 5.06
	(Built P MacCabe and K Reynolds as SAAC pr.no.037) (VW/Limbach SL1700)						
EI-DDW	Boeing 767-3S1ER	26608	N979PG	9. 1.04	Pegasus Aviation Ireland Ltd	Rome-Fiumicino, Italy	A2008
			C-GGBI, (N769TA)		*"Sebastiano Caboto" (Operated.Alitalia)*		
EI-DDX	Cessna 172S	172S8313	G-UFCA	19. 2.04	Flight Training Ltd	Cork	A 5.07
			N2461P				
EI-DDY	Boeing 737-4YO	24904	HA-LEV	6. 5.04	Aerco Ireland Ltd	Moscow-Domodedovo, Russia	A2008
			TC-JDE		*(Operated Transaero Airlines)*		
EI-DDZ	Piper PA-28-181Cherokee Archer II	28-7690211	PH-PDW	4. 6.04	Ardnari Ltd	Weston, Dublin	A 8.05
			OO-HAT, N8882E				
EI-DEA	Airbus A320-214	2191	F-WWBX	30. 4.04	Aer Lingus Ltd	Belfast International	A2008
					"St Fidelma/Fiedeilme"		
EI-DEB	Airbus A320-214	2206	F-WWBP	19. 5.04	Aer Lingus Ltd *"St Nathy/Nathi"*	Dublin	A2008
EI-DEC	Airbus A320-214	2217	F-WWBH	4. 6.04	Aer Lingus Ltd *"St Fergal/Fearghal"*	Dublin	A2008
EI-DEE	Airbus A320-214	2250	F-WWBE	27. 8.04	Aer Lingus Ltd *"St Ultan/Ultan"*	Dublin	A2008
EI-DEF	Airbus A320-214	2256	F-WWBK	2. 9.04	Aer Lingus Ltd *"St Declan/Deaglan"*	Dublin	A2008
EI-DEG	Airbus A320-214	2272	F-WWIB	10. 9.04	Aer Lingus Ltd *"St Fachtna/Fachtna"*	Dublin	A2008
EI-DEH	Airbus A320-214	2294	F-WWDF	20.10.04	Aer Lingus Ltd *"St Conleth/Connlaodh"*	Dublin	A2008
EI-DEI	Airbus A320-214	2374	F-WWDU	14.2.05	Aer Lingus Ltd	Dublin	A2008
					"St Oliver Plunkett/Oilibhear Pluinceid"		
EI-DEJ	Airbus A320-214	2364	F-WWDI	3.2.05	Aer Lingus Ltd *"St Kilian/Cillian"*	Dublin	A2008
EI-DEK	Airbus A320-214	2399	F-WWIZ	24 3.05	Aer Lingus Ltd *"St Eunan/Eunan"*	Dublin	A2008
EI-DEL	Airbus A320-214	2409	F-WWDE	13.4 05	Aer Lingus Ltd *"St Ibar/Ibhar"*	Dublin	A2008
EI-DEM	Airbus A320-214	2411	F-WWDG	7.4.05	Aer Lingus Ltd *"St Canice/Cainneach"*	Dublin	A2008
EI-DEN	Airbus A320-214	2432	F-WWBK	13. 5.05	Aer Lingus Ltd *"St Kieran/Ciaran"*	Dublin	A2008
EI-DEO	Airbus A320-214	2486	F-WWIV	6. 7.05	Aer Lingus Ltd *"St Senan/Seanan"*	Dublin	A2008
EI-DEP	Airbus A320-214	2542	F-WWIU	7. 10.05	Aer Lingus Ltd *"St Eugene/Eoghan"*	Dublin	A2008
EI-DER	Airbus A320-214	2583	F-WWDE	3. 11.05	Aer Lingus Ltd *"St Mel/Mel"*	Dublin	A2008
EI-DES	Airbus A320-214	2635	F-WWDZ	22.12.05	Aer Lingus Ltd *"St Pappin/Paipan"*	Dublin	A2008
EI-DET	Airbus A320-214	2810	F-WWIP	28. 6.06	Aer Lingus Ltd *"St Brendan/Breandan"*	Dublin	A2008
EI-DEW	British Aerospace BAe 146 Series 300	E3142	G-UKAC	20 5.04	CityJet Ltd	Paris CDG, France	A2008
			G-5-142		*(Operated Air France Regional)*		
EI-DEX	British Aerospace BAe 146 Series 300	E3157	G-UKID	11. 6.04	CityJet Ltd	Paris CDG, France	A2008
			G-6-157		*(Operated Air France Regional)*		
EI-DEY	Airbus A319-112	1102	D-ANDA	6. 5.04	Olbia Ltd	Olbia, Italy	A2008
			F-WQQE, OO-SSD, D-AVYI		*"Capo Rizzuto" (Operated Meridiana)*		

Reg	Type	C/N	Prev id	Date	Owner/Operator	Location	Code
EI-DEZ	Airbus A319-112	1283	D-ANDE F-WQQF, OO-SSI, D-AVYI	25. 2.04	Olbia Ltd *"Capo Gallo" (Operated Meridiana)*	Olbia, Italy	A2008
EI-DFA	Airbus A319-112	1305	D-ANDI F-WQQG, OO-SSJ, D-AVWX	30. 3.04	Olbia Ltd *"Capo Carbonara" (Operated Meridiana)*	Olbia, Italy	A2008
EI-DFD	Boeing 737-4S3	24163	G-BVNM G-BPKE, 9M-MJJ, G-BPKA	4. 8.04	Orix Aircraft Management Ltd *(Operated Air One)*	Naples, Italy	A2008
EI-DFE	Boeing 737-4S3	24164	G-BVNN G-BPKB, 9M-MLA, G-BPKB	27. 4.04	Orix Aircraft Management Ltd *(Operated Air One)*	Naples, Italy	A2008
EI-DFF	Boeing 737-4S3	24167	G-BVNO G-BPKE, 9M-MLB, G-BPKE	6. 5.04	Orix Aircraft Management Ltd *(Operated Air One)*	Naples, Italy	A2008
EI-DFG	Embraer EMB-170-100LR *(Embraer 170)*	17000008	(I-EMCX) PT-SKA	24. 3.04	GECAS Technical Services Ltd *Via Appia" (Operated Alitalia Express)*	Rome-Fiumicino, Italy	A2008
EI-DFH	Embraer EMB-170-100LR *(Embraer 170)*	17000009	PT-SKB	20. 4.04	GECAS Technical Services Ltd *Via Aurélia" (Operated Alitalia Express)*	Rome-Fiumicino, Italy	A2008
EI-DFI	Embraer EMB-170-100LR *(Embraer 170)*	17000010	PT-SKC	20. 5.04	GECAS Technical Services Ltd *"Via Cassia" (Operated Alitalia Express)*	Rome-Fiumicino, Italy	A2008
EI-DFJ	Embraer EMB-170-100LR *(Embraer 170)*	17000011	PT-SKD	30. 6.04	GECAS Technical Services Ltd *"Via Flaminia" (Operated Alitalia Express)*	Rome-Fiumicino, Italy	A2008
EI-DFK	Embraer EMB-170-100LR *(Embraer 170)*	17000032	PT-SUA	30. 6.04	GECAS Technical Services Ltd *"Via Salaria" (Operated Alitalia Express)*	Rome-Fiumicino, Italy	A2008
EI-DFL	Embraer EMB-170-100LR *(Embraer 170)*	17000036	PT-SUF	16. 7.04	GECAS Technical Services Ltd *"Via Tiburtina Valeria" (Operated Alitalia Express)*	Rome-Fiumicino, Italy	A2008
EI-DFM	Evektor EV-97 Eurostar	2003-1706		8. 3.04	M O'Connell	Enniskillen,	N10.06
EI-DFN	Airbus A.320-211	0204	F-GJVC	3.08R	AerCap *(Operated Windjet)*	Catania, Italy	
EI-DFO	Airbus A.320-211	0371	A6-ABX C-FTDD, SU-LBA, TC-OND, N531LF, C-FLSJ, F-WWIQ *(Operated Windjet)*	20. 4.04	Triton Aviation Ireland Ltd	Catania, Italy	A2008
EI-DFP	Airbus A.319-112	1048	F-OHJV F-WIHE, OO-SSA, D-AVYT	11. 5.04	Wilmington Trust SP Services (Dublin) Ltd *"Capo Caccia" (Operated Meridiana)*	Olbia, Italy	A2008
EI-DFS	Boeing 767-33A	25346	ET-AKW V8-RBE	31. 5.04	Jeritt Ltd *(Operated Transaero Airlines)*	Moscow-Domodedovo, Russia	A2008
EI-DFW	Robinson R44 Raven	1377	G-CCUM N7536G	3. 6.04	Blue Star Helicopters Ltd	Cork	A 6.07
EI-DFX	Air Création 582(1)/Kiss 400 *(Wing s/n A04007-4007)*	xxxx		13. 5.04	H Eoghan	Tullamore	A 9.06
EI-DFY	Raj Hamsa X'Air R100(2) *(Built P McGirr and R Gillespie - pr/no BMAA/HB/096)*	430	G-BYLN	13. 5.04	P McGirr and R Gillespie	Drumavish Killygordon	A2006
EI-DGA	Urban Air UFM-11UK Lambada	16/11		16. 4.04	P and D Dunkin	Abbeyshrule	A 8.06
EI-DGG	Raj Hamsa X'Air 133	899		9. 6.04	N Geh	Ferskill, Granard	A10.04
EI-DGH	Raj Hamsa X'Air 582	861		9. 6.04	M Garvey and T McGowan	Clonmellon, Devlin	A2006
EI-DGI	ICP MXP740 Savannah Jabiru 03-10-51-2365 *(Built N Farrell - pr.no.BMAA/HB/34)*		G-CCPR	7. 9.04	N Farrell *(Crashed and destroyed Ferskill 2. 4.05)*	(Ferskill, Granard)	
EI-DGJ	Raj Hamsa X'Air 582(11) *(Built R Morelli - pr.no.BMAA/HB/210)*	707	G-CCEV	9. 6.04	N Brereton	Granard	A12.06
EI-DGK	Raj Hamsa X'Air 133	856		9. 6.04	B Chambers	(Castlefinn)	
EI-DGL	Boeing 737-46J	27171	SX-BMA D-ABAE	6. 7.04	Olbia Ltd *(Operated Air One)*	Rome -Fiumicino, Italy	A10.07
EI-DGM	Boeing 737-4C9	26437	LX-LGG (2)	15. 7.04	Lux Aircraft Leasing One Ltd *(For Op Ukraine International as UR-GAV 2007).*	Shannon	
EI-DGP	Urban Air UFM-11UK Lambada	15/11	OK-IUA-68	24.11.04	M Tormey	Abbeyshrule	A 8.06
EI-DGR	Urban Air UFM-11UK Lambada	17/11		21. 7.04	M Tormey	Abbeyshrule	N 1.05
EI-DGS	ATEC Zephyr 2000	861003A		20.10.04	O Williams	(Galway)	N12.06
EI-DGT	Urban Air UFM-11UK Lambada	14/11	OK-FUA-09	12. 8.04	A and P Aviation Ltd	Carnmore, Galway	A 7.06
EI-DGV	ATEC Zephyr 2000	Z509702A		8. 9.05	M Donoghue	Carnmore, Galway	A 8.04
EI-DGW	Cameron Z-90 Balloon (Hot Air)	10607		15. 9.04	J Leahy	Navan	N 1.07
EI-DGX	Cessna 152	15281296	G-BPJL N49473	19.10.04	K A O'Connor	Weston, Dublin	A 5.06
EI-DGY	Urban Air UFM-11 Lambada	10/11	OK-EUU-55	15.10.04	D McMorrow	Abbeyshrule	N12.06
EI-DGZ	Boeing 737-86N/W	28624	EC-HMK N1786B	27.10.04	Celestial Aviation Trading 18 Ltd *(Operated Ryanair International)* Wichita-Mid Continent, Kansas, US		A2008
EI-DHA	Boeing 737-8AS/W	33571		1. 2.05	Ryanair Ltd	Dublin	A2008
EI-DHB	Boeing 737-8AS	33572		23. 2.05	Ryanair Ltd	Dublin	A2008
EI-DHC	Boeing 737-8AS/W	33573		17. 2.05	Ryanair Ltd	Dublin	A2008
EI-DHD	Boeing 737-8AS/W	33816		25. 2.05	Ryanair Ltd	Dublin	A2008
EI-DHE	Boeing 737-8AS	33574		2. 3.05	Ryanair Ltd	Dublin	A2008
EI-DHF	Boeing 737-8AS/W	33575		3. 3.05	Ryanair Ltd	Dublin	A2008
EI-DHG	Boeing 737-8AS/W	33576		18. 3.05	Ryanair Ltd	Dublin	A2008
EI-DHH	Boeing 737-8AS	33817		29. 3.05	Ryanair Ltd	Dublin	A2008
EI-DHI	Boeing 737-8AS	33818		11. 4.05	Ryanair Ltd	Dublin	A2008
EI-DHJ	Boeing 737-8AS/W	33819		20. 4.05	Ryanair Ltd	Dublin	A2008
EI-DHK	Boeing 737-8AS	33820		28. 4.05	Ryanair Ltd	Dublin	A2008
EI-DHM	Boeing 737-8AS	33821		28. 4.05	Ryanair Ltd	Dublin	A2008
EI-DHN	Boeing 737-8AS	33577		1. 9.05	Ryanair Ltd	Dublin	A2008
EI-DHO	Boeing 737-8AS	33578		14.10.05	Ryanair Ltd	Dublin	A2008
EI-DHP	Boeing 737-8AS	33579		21.10.05	Ryanair Ltd	Dublin	A2008
EI-DHR	Boeing 737-8AS	33822		24.10.05	Ryanair Ltd	Dublin	A2008
EI-DHS	Boeing 737-8AS	33580		7.11.05	Ryanair Ltd	Dublin	A2008
EI-DHT	Boeing 737-8AS	33581		14.11.05	Ryanair Ltd	Dublin	A2008
EI-DHV	Boeing 737-8AS	33582		14.11.05	Ryanair Ltd	Dublin	A2008
EI-DHW	Boeing 737-8AS	33823	N1786B	23.11.05	Ryanair Ltd	Dublin	A2008
EI-DHX	Boeing 737-8AS	33585		5.12.05	Ryanair Ltd	Dublin	A2008
EI-DHY	Boeing 737-8AS	33824	N1781B	6.12.05	Ryanair Ltd	Dublin	A2008
EI-DHZ	Boeing 737-8AS/W	33583		19.12.05	Ryanair Ltd	Dublin	A2008
EI-DIA	Solar Wings Pegasus XL-Q *(Trike c/n SW-TE-0379)*	SW-WQ-0503	G-MYAD	15. 9.04	P Byrne *(Current status unknown)*	(Hacketstown)	

Reg	Type	Serial	Prev ID	Date	Owner/Operator	Location	CofA
EI-DIB	Air Création 582(1)/Kiss 400	xxxx		10. 9.04	E Redmond	(Ferns	
	(Wing s/n A04117-4123)				*(Current status unknown)*		
EI-DIF	PA.31-350 Navajo Chieftain	31-7752105	G-OAMT	4. 2.05	Wrenair Ltd (Visionair)	Weston, Dublin	N 1.08
			G-BXKS, N350RC, EC-EBN, N27230				
EI-DIY	Van's RV-4	3254		16. 3.05	J A Kent	(Pinecroft, Dunshaughlin)	
	(Built J A Kent)				*(Under construction?)*		
EI-DIZ	Robinson R22 Beta II	3684	G-PPLA	23.12.04	Blue Star Helicopters Ltd	(Cork)	
			N74327				
EI-DJH	Airbus A.320-232	814	I-PEKW	20.12.04	ILFC Ireland Ltd	Bergamo-Orio al Serio, Italy	A2008
			N471LF, SU-LBB, F-WWII		*(Operated Myway)*		
EI-DJI	Airbus A.320-232	1757	I-PEKQ	20.12.04	ILFC Ireland Ltd	Bergamo-Orio al Serio, Italy	A2008
			F-WWIR		*(Operated Myway)*		
EI-DJJ	British Aerospace BAe 146 Series 200	E.2040	VH-YAF	4. 5.05	CityJet Ltd	Exeter	N2008
			G-DEBG, N178US, N357PS				
EI-DJK	Boeing 737-382	24365	9H-ADM	9. 1.05	Triton Aviation Ireland Ltd *(Operated KD Avia)*		
			CS-TIB		*"Yuri Ternirkanov"*	Kaliningrad-Khrabovo, Russia	A2008
EI-DJM	Piper PA-28-161 Warrior II	28-8316106	HB-POV	21. 2.05	Waterford Aero Club	Waterford	A 4.06
			N4314K				
EI-DJO	Agusta A109E	11158	D-HIRL	14. 2.05	Tandrelle Ltd	Dublin	A 5.06
			N32GH, D-HOME				
EI-DJR	Boeing 737-3YO	23927	G-IGOG	7. 7.05	Larrett Ltd	Kaliningrad-Khrabovo, Russia	A2008
			F-GLLE, PT-TEK		*"Alexander Marinesko" (Operated KD Avia)*		
EI-DJS	Boeing 737-3YO	23926	G-IGOH	13. 7.05	Wodell Ltd	Kaliningrad-Khrabovo, Russia	A2008
			F-GLLD, PT-TEJ		*"Viktor Geraschchenko" (Operated KD Avia)*		
EI-DJT	Boeing 737-86N/W	28592	N975RY	16. 4.05	Lift Ireland Leasing Ltd *(Operated Ryan International)*		
			EC-IEN, CN-RNN, N1779B, N1768B			Prague-Ruzyne, Czech Republic	A2008
EI-DJU	Boeing 737-86N/W	28619	N255RY	28. 4.05	Celestial Aviation Trading 17 Ltd *(Operated Futura International)*		
			EC-HLN. N1786B			Palma de Mellorca, Spain	A2008
EI-DJW	Robinson R44 Raven	1498		14. 6.05	Horizon Helicopters Ltd	Weston, Dublin	
EI-DJX	Farrington Twinstarr	98016	N234MJ	22. 6.05	F Kavanagh	Shipdham	A 8..06
	(Built S Howell)						
EI-DJY	Grob G.115	8048	D-EFFX (2)	29. 4.05	Atlantic Flight Training Ltd	Cork	A 5.07
EI-DJZ	Lindstrand LBL-31A Cloudhopper	1035		7. 7.05	M E White	Dublin	N 1.07
EI-DKB	ICP MXP740 Savannah Jabiru	04-11-51-343		6. 5.05	B Gurnett and Partners	(Ardfert)	N 10.06
	(Built N Farrell)						
EI-DKC	Pegasus Quasar	SVV-WQQ-0351	G-MWJU	22. 4.05	K Daly	Abbeyshrule	A 8.06
EI-DKD	Boeing 737-86N/W	28617	N974RY	27. 4.05	OH Aircraft III (Ireland) Ltd *(Operated Ryan International)*		
			EC-HJJ, N1787B			Wichita-Mid Continent, Kansas, US	A2008
EI-DKE	Air Création 582(1)/Kiss 400	xxxx		12. 5.05	J Bennett	Kilrush	A 4.06
	(Wing s/n AO4172-4187)						
EI-DKI	Robinson R22 Beta II	3882	N74703	29. 7.05	P Gilboy	Weston, Dublin	N 4.07
EI-DKJ	Thruster T600N	0047-T600N-105	G-CDBN	11. 5.05	C Brogan	Kilrush	A 4.06
EI-DKK	Raj Hamsa X'Air Jabiru 3(5)	857		11. 5.05	M Tolan	Tandragee	A 5.06
	(Built M Tolan)						
EI-DKL	Boeing 757-231	28482	N714P	21. 6.05	Pegasus Palls 99 Ireland Ltd	Rome-Fiumicino, Italy	A2008
					(Operated Blue Panorama Airlines)		
EI-DKM	Agusta Bell 206B Jetranger	8623	F-GCVY	7. 7.05	Stelbury Ltd	Weston, Dublin	A 6.07
EI-DKN	ELA Aviacion ELA-07	00045		31. 5.05	S Brennan	Kilrush	A 5.06
EI-DKT	Raj Hamsa X'Air 582(11)	798		22. 6.05	I Brereton	Clonbullogue	A 5.06
EI-DKU	Air Création 582(1)/Kiss 400	xxxx		22. 6.05	J Doran	Shinglis, Ballymore	A2006
	(Wing s/n A05036-5040)						
EI-DKV	Boeing 737-505	24272	G-GFFC	28. 6.05	Brookdell Ltd	Tijuana, Mexico	A2008
			LN-BRG		*(Operated Aerovolar)*		
EI-DKW	Evektor EV-97 Eurostar	2005-2513		28. 6.05	Ormond Flying Club Ltd	Birr	A 5.06
EI-DKY	Raj Hamsa X'Air 582	720	G-CBTY	27. 7.05	M Clarke	(Clonsilla, Dublin)	N11.07
	(Buit K Quigley - pr.no.BMAA/HB/222)						
EI-DKZ	Reality Escapade 912(1)	JAESC0040	G-CDFH	29. 7.05	J Deegan	Limetree, Portarlington	A 4.06
	(Built J Deegan - pr.no.BMAA/HB/423)						
EI-DLB	Boeing 737-8AS	33584	N1786B	19.12.05	Ryanair Ltd	Dublin	A2008
EI-DLC	Boeing 737-8AS	33586	N1786B	13. 1.06	Ryanair Ltd	Dublin	A2008
EI-DLD	Boeing 737-8AS	33825		13. 1.06	Ryanair Ltd	Dublin	A2008
EI-DLE	Boeing 737-8AS/W	33587		9 .2.06	Ryanair Ltd	Dublin	A2008
EI-DLF	Boeing 737-8AS/W	33588		13..2.06	Ryanair Ltd *"Bye Bye SkyEurope"*	Dublin	A2008
EI-DLG	Boeing 737-8AS/W	33589	N1786B	14 .2.06	Ryanair Ltd *"ZEGNAMY PLL LOT !"*	Dublin	A2008
EI-DLH	Boeing 737-8AS/W	33590		6. 3.06	Ryanair Ltd	Dublin	A2008
EI-DLI	Boeing 737-8AS/W	33591	N1786B	22. 3.06	Ryanair Ltd	Dublin	A2008
EI-DLJ	Boeing 737-8AS/W	34177		28. 3.06	Ryanair Ltd	Dublin	A2008
EI-DLK	Boeing 737-8AS/W	33592	N1786B	29. 3.06	Ryanair Ltd	Dublin	A2008
EI-DLL	Boeing 737-8AS/W	33593		10. 4.06	Ryanair Ltd	Dublin	A2008
EI-DLM	Boeing 737-8AS/W	33594		20. 4.06	Ryanair Ltd *"Bye Bye Latehansa"*	Dublin	A2008
EI-DLN	Boeing 737-8AS/W	33595		24. 4.06	Ryanair Ltd *"Bye Bye Baby"*	Dublin	A2008
EI-DLO	Boeing 737-8AS/W	34178		25. 4.06	Ryanair Ltd *"Bye Bye EasyJet"*	Dublin	A2008
EI-DLR	Boeing 737-8AS/W	33596		25. 9.06	Ryanair Ltd	Dublin	A2008
EI-DLS	Boeing 737-8AS/W	33621		26. 9.06	Ryanair Ltd	Dublin	A2008
EI-DLT	Boeing 737-8AS/W	33597		27. 9.06	Ryanair Ltd	Dublin	A2008
EI-DLV	Boeing 737-8AS/W	33598		28. 9.06	Ryanair Ltd	Dublin	A2008
EI-DLW	Boeing 737-8AS/W	33599		17.10.06	Ryanair Ltd	Dublin	A2008
EI-DLX	Boeing 737-8AS/W	33600		18.10.06	Ryanair Ltd	Dublin	A2008
EI-DLY	Boeing 737-8AS/W	33601		26.10.06	Ryanair Ltd	Dublin	A2008
EI-DLZ	Boeing 737-8AS/W	33622		8.11.06	Ryanair Ltd	Dublin	A2008
EI-DMA	SOCATA MS892E-150	12376	G-BVAN	22.12.05	Curly Cale Ltd	Farranfore, Kerry	N 6.07
			F-BVAN				
EI-DMB	Best Off Sky Ranger 912S(1)	SKR0503588		19. 8.05	Fun 2 Fly Ltd	Kilpatrick, Stradbally	A 8.06
	(Built N Furlong amd E Spain)						

Reg	Type	C/n	Prev id	Date	Owner/Operator	Location	
EI-DMC	Schweizer S.269C-1 *(Schweizer 300CBi)*	0205	N86G	18. 8.05	B Hade	Weston, Dublin	A 5.06
EI-DMG	Cessna 441 Conquest	441-0165	N140MP N27214	4. 7.01	Dawn Meats Group Ltd	Waterford	A 5.07
EI-DMH	Boeing 767-260	23106	N271SW ET-AIE, N1792B	25.10.05	Woodrow Leasing Ltd *(Operated Kras Air)* Krasnoyarsk-Yemilianovo, Russia		A2008
EI-DMJ	Boeing 767-306	27958	PH-BZB	7. 10.05	ILFC Ireland Ltd Milan-Malpensa, Italy *(Operated NEOS)*		A2008
EI-DMK	British Aerospace BAe 146 Series 200	E2022	G-DEBE N163US, N346PS	18. 1.06	(Flightline Ltd) Southend *(To revert to G-DEBE 2008)*		A2008
EI-DML	Bell 206B JetRanger	2914	CS-HEK N6280J, (C-....), N1078Q	29. 9.05	Morrissey Fencing Ltd	Durrow	A 5.07
EI-DMM	Boeing 737-33A	24092	G-IGOI G-OBMD	30.11.05	GAIF II Ireland Two Ltd *(Operated KD Avia)* "Valery Gergiev" Kaliningrad-Khrabovo, Russia		A2008
EI-DMN	Boeing 737-3K2	23411	N550FA	2. 12.05	Pegasus Palls.99 Ireland Ltd "Lidor Samiev"		
			TC-ESA, N943PG, PH-HVF, XA-STM, PH-HVF, XA-STM, PH-HVF, XA-STM, PH-HVF, XA-STM, PH-HVF, CS-TIR, PH-HVF *(Operated KD Avia)* Kaliningrad-Khrabovo, Russia					A2008
EI-DMP	Boeing 767-2Q8	24448	N330LF	22.12.06	ILFC Ireland Ltd Krasnoyarsk-Yemilianovo, Russia		
			OB-1765-P, OB-1765, CC-CJR, N201LF, N264MT, S7-AAS, (S7-1HM) *(Operated Kras Air)*					
EI-DMR	Boeing 737-436	25851	G-DOCR	27.10.05	Dillondell Ltd Rome -Fiumicino, Italy *(Operated Air One)*		A2008
EI-DMS	Robinson R22 Beta	1248	(EI-DRS (1)) G-MUFY, D-HICH	13.10.05	Tarmacadam Paving Services Ltd Weston, Dublin		A 6.06
EI-DMT	Agusta A109C	7623	F-GTRJ I-CRBM, I-CRBN	14.10.05	Dasbar Ltd Dublin *(Operated Celtic Helicopters)*		
EI-DMU	Whittaker MW6S *(Built G Maher)*	PFA 164-12235		13.12.05	G Maher (Loughlinstown) *(Stored?)*		
EI-DMX	Boeing 737-752/W	34297	(XA-XAM)	16.11.05	Celestial Aviation Trading 66 Ltd *(Operated AeroMexico)* Mexico City-Benito Juarez, Mexico		A2008
EI-DMY	Boeing 737-752/W	34298	(XA-YAM)	29.11.05	Celestial Aviation Trading 66 Ltd *(Operated AeroMexico)* Mexico City-Benito Juarez, Mexico		A2008
EI-DMZ	Boeing 737-8FH/W	29671	EC-JGE	16.12.05	Airspeed Ireland Leasing 17 Ltd *(Operated Garuda-Indonesia)* Jakarta-Soekarno Hatta, Indonesia		A2008
EI-DNA	Boeing 757-231	28483	N715TW	8. 12.05	Rockshaw Ltd Rome-Fiumicino, Italy *(Operated Blue Panorama Airlines)*		A2008
EI-DNB	Boeing 737-752/W	34299		.16. 1.06	CIT Aerospace International *(Operated AeroMexico)* Mexico City-Benito Juarez, Mexico		A2008
EI-DNC	Boeing 737-752/W	34300		21. 2.06	CIT Aerospace International *(Operated AeroMexico)* Mexico City-Benito Juarez, Mexico		A2008
EI-DND	Boeing 737-86N/W	28612	EC-IUC TC-SUA, N1786B	3. 1.06	Celestial Aviation Trading 18 Ltd *(Operated Ryanair International)* Palma de Mellorca, Spain		
EI-DNH	Boeing 737-3Y5	25614	9H-ABS	21.12.05	Boeing Capital Leasing Ltd *(Operated Kras Air)* Krasnoyarsk-Yemilianovo, Russia		A2008
EI-DNL	Bensen B.8M Gyrocopter *(Built J Henry and H O'Driscoll)*	B8M-073		10. 1.06	J Henry and H O'Driscoll (Blessington) *(Under construction?)*		
EI-DNM	Boeing 737-4S3	24166	EC-JHX VT-SIY, N768BC, VT-SII, VT-JAJ, N691MA, G-BPKD	1. 3.06	Boeing Capital Leasing Ltd *(Operated Transaero Airlines)* Moscow-Domodedovo, Russia		A2008
EI-DNN	Bede BD-5G *(Built H J Cox)* (Midwest AE110RA)	HJC.4523	G-BCOX	7. 2.07	H J and E.M Cox (Waterford)		N2007
EI-DNO	Bede BD-5A *(Built R A Gardner - pr.no.PFA 14-10074)* (Hirth 2706E)	4885	G-BCLV	14. 2.07	R A Gardiner (Waterford)		N2007
EI-DNP	Airbus A320-212	421	A4O-EF F-WWIO	1. 4.05	Ovenstone Ltd Catania, Italy *(Operated Windjet)*		A2008
EI-DNR	Raj Hamsa X'Air 582(5) *(Built N Farrell - pr.no.BMAA/HB/251)*	791	G-CCAX	27. 2.06	N Furlong and J Grattan Kilpatrick, Stradbally		A2008
EI-DNS	Boeing 737-329	23771	F-GUYH F-WQUE, CN-RDB, OO-SDV	4. 4.06	Embarcadero Aircraft Securitization Trust Ireland Ltd Krasnoyarsk-Yemilianovo, Russia *(Operated Kras Air)*		A2008
EI-DNT	Boeing 737-329	24356	F-GRNV F-WQUE, CN-RDA, OO-SYB, (OO-SQB)	14. 6.06	Embarcadero Aircraft Securitization Trust Ireland Ltd Krasnoyarsk-Yemilianovo, Russia *(Operated.Kras Air)*		A2008
EI-DNU	Schweizer 269C-1 *(Schweizer 300CBi)*	0233	N86G	12. 5.06	NG Kam Tim Weston, Dublin		A 5.06
EI-DNV	Urban Air UFM-11 Lambada	12/11	OK-EUU 56	27. 2.06	F Maughan *(Stored?)* (Ardclogh, Straffan)		
EI-DNW	Best Off Sky Ranger J2.2(1) *(Built M Kerrisson - pr.no.BMAA/HB/373)*	SKRxxxx453	G-CCUC	31. 3.06	M Kerrisson Coonagh		A10.06
EI-DNX	Boeing 737-31S	29055	VT-SAW VT-SIX, D-ADBK	13. 4.06	Osprey Aviation Ireland Ltd Rome -Fiumicino, Italy *(Operated Air One)*		A2008
EI-DNY	Boeing 737-3TO	23360	N17309	4. 4.06	BCI Aircraft Leasing Ireland Ltd Tijuana, Mexico *(Operated Aerovolar)*		A2008
EI-DNZ	Boeing 737-3TO	23363	N60312	4. 4.06	BCI Aircraft Leasing Ireland Ltd Tijuana, Mexico *(Operated Aerovolar)*		A2008
EI-DOB	Zenair CH.701	7-9272		13. 2.07	D O'Brien (Mullagh)		N2007
EI-DOD	Airbus A320-231	0444	G-FHAJ D-ACAF, N444RX, TC-ONF, N444RX, F-WWBY	11. 4.06	Hannover Leasing Aircraft Ireland Ltd *(Operated Myair)* Bergamo-Orio al Serio, Italy		A2008
EI-DOE	Airbus A320-211	215	F-GJVE	9. 6.06	ALS Irish Aircraft Leasing MSN 215 Ltd *(Operated Windjet)* Catania. Italy		A2008
EI-DOF	Boeing 767-306ER	27610	PH-BZD	24. 4.06	ILFC Ireland Ltd Tel Aviv-Ben Gurion, Israel *(Operated Israir)*		A2008
EI-DOH	Boeing 737-31S	29056	VT-SAX VT-SIW, D-ADBL	30. 6.06	Challey Ltd Rome -Fiumicino, Italy *(Operated Air One)*		A2008
EI-DOI	Evektor EV-97 Eurostar	20062708		30. 3.06	E.McEvoy Eyne		
EI-DOM	Boeing 737-3G7	24011	N370WL N304AW	4. 8.06	CIT Capital Finance Ireland Ltd *(Operated KD Avia)* "Sergey Prisekin" Kaliningrad-Khrabovo, Russia		A2008

Reg	Type	c/n	Prev ID	Date	Owner/Operator	Location	
EI-DON	Boeing 737-3Y0	23812	N375PA	28.12.06	CIT Capital Finance Ireland Ltd (Operated KD Avia)		
			N238CT, PT-TEI			Kaliningrad-Khrabovo, Russia	A2008
EI-DOO	Boeing 737-35B	23917	N222DZ	28.12.06	CIT Capital Finance Ireland Ltd (Operated KD Avia)		
			D-AGEB		"Yuriy Antonov"	Kaliningrad-Khrabovo, Russia	A2008
EI-DOP	Airbus A320-232	816	B-HSF	22. 6.06	ILFC Ireland Ltd	Catania. Italy	A2008
			F-WWIT		(Operated Windjet)		
EI-DOR	Boeing 737-4YO	24689	EC-IOU	5. 5.06	Futura GAEL	Dublin	A2008
			PK-MBK, EC-GVB, PT-TDD, EC-EXY, EC-403				
EI-DOS	Boeing 737-49R	28881	PK-GWZ	21. 4.06	Celestial Aviation Trading 37 Ltd		
			N460PR, N1790B		(Operated Air One)	Rome -Fiumicino, Italy	A2008
EI-DOT	Bombardier CL-600-2D24	15066		23. 5.06	Challey Ltd	Rome -Fiumicino, Italy	A2008
	(CRJ 900 Regional Jet)				(Operated Air One Cityliner)		
EI-DOU	Bombardier CL-600-2D24	15068		23. 5.06	Challey Ltd	Rome -Fiumicino, Italy	A2008
	(CRJ 900 Regional Jet)				(Operated Air One Cityliner)		
EI-DOV	Boeing 737-48E	27632	HL-7512	21. 6.06	ILFC Ireland Ltd	Rome -Fiumicino, Italy	A2008
					(Operated Air One)		
EI-DOW	Mainair Blade 912	1361-0104-7-W1156	G-CCPB	1. 6.06	D G Fortune	Kilrush	A 5.06
EI-DOX	Solar Wings Pegasus XL-R	SW-WA-1089	G-MNYB	12. 5.06	T Noonan	Fermoy	
		(Trike c/n SW-TB-1096)					
EI-DOY	PZL Koliber			3.08R	Limerick Flying Club (Coonagh) Ltd	Coonagh	N10.06
EI-DPA	Boeing 737-8AS/W	33602		16.11.06	Ryanair Ltd	Dublin	A2008
EI-DPB	Boeing 737-8AS/W	33603	N1787B	20.11.06	Ryanair Ltd	Dublin	A2008
EI-DPC	Boeing 737-8AS/W	33604	N1786B	6.12.06	Ryanair Ltd	Dublin	A2008
EI-DPD	Boeing 737-8AS/W	33623	N1786B	6.12.06	Ryanair Ltd	Dublin	A2008
EI-DPE	Boeing 737-8AS/W	33605		21.12.06	Ryanair Ltd	Dublin	A2008
EI-DPF	Boeing 737-8AS/W	33606		23. 1.07	Ryanair Ltd	Dublin	A2008
EI-DPG	Boeing 737-8AS/W	33607		26. 1.07	Ryanair Ltd	Dublin	A2008
EI-DPH	Boeing 737-8AS/W	33624		1. 2.07	Ryanair Ltd	Dublin	A2008
EI-DPI	Boeing 737-8AS/W	33608		7. 2.07	Ryanair Ltd	Dublin	A2008
EI-DPJ	Boeing 737-8AS/W	33609		13. 2.07	Ryanair Ltd	Dublin	A2008
EI-DPK	Boeing 737-8AS/W	33610		16. 2.07	Ryanair Ltd	Dublin	A2008
EI-DPL	Boeing 737-8AS/W	33611		23. 2.07	Ryanair Ltd	Dublin	
EI-DPM	Boeing 737-8AS/W	33640	N1786B	5. 3.07	Ryanair Ltd	Dublin	
EI-DPN	Boeing 737-8AS/W	35549	N1787B	7. 3.07	Ryanair Ltd	Dublin	
EI-DPO	Boeing 737-8AS/W	33612		14. 3.07	Ryanair Ltd	Dublin	
EI-DPP	Boeing 737-8AS/W	33613		20. 3.07	Ryanair Ltd	Dublin	
EI-DPR	Boeing 737-8AS/W	33614	N1786B	28. 3.07	Ryanair Ltd	Dublin	
EI-DPS	Boeing 737-8AS/W	33641		29. 3.07	Ryanair Ltd	Dublin	
EI-DPT	Boeing 737-8AS/W	35550	N1787B	4. 4.07	Ryanair Ltd	Dublin	
EI-DPV	Boeing 737-8AS/W	35551	N1779B	13. 4.07	Ryanair Ltd	Dublin	
EI-DPW	Boeing 737-8AS/W	35552		15. 5.07	Ryanair Ltd	Dublin	
EI-DPX	Boeing 737-8AS/W	35553		30. 5.07	Ryanair Ltd	Dublin	
EI-DPY	Boeing 737-8AS/W	33615		11. 9.07	Ryanair Ltd	Dublin	
EI-DPZ	Boeing 737-8AS/W	33616		12. 9.07	Ryanair Ltd	Dublin	
EI-DRA	Boeing 737-852/W	35114	N1779B	6. 9.06	Mexican Aircraft Leasing II Ltd (Operated AeroMexico)		
						Mexico City-Benito Juarez, Mexico	A2008
EI-DRB	Boeing 737-852/W	35115		10.10.06	Mexican Aircraft Leasing II Ltd (Operated AeroMexico)		
						Mexico City-Benito Juarez, Mexico	A2008
EI-DRC	Boeing 737-852/W	35116		19.10.06	Mexican Aircraft Leasing II Ltd (Operated AeroMexico)		
						Mexico City-Benito Juarez, Mexico	A2008
EI-DRD	Boeing 737-752/W	35117	N1786B	5.12.06	Mexican Aircraft Leasing II Ltd (Operated AeroMexico)		
						Mexico City-Benito Juarez, Mexico	A2008
EI-DRE	Boeing 737-752/W	35787	N1786B	21.11.06	Mexican Aircraft Leasing II Ltd (Operated AeroMexico)		
						Mexico City-Benito Juarez, Mexico	A2008
EI-DRG	Airbus A320-231	0338	G-GTDK	14. 6.06	Male Lease One (Dublin) Ltd (Operated Myway)		
			C-GTDK, D-AFTI, N302ML, N338RX, F-WWIM			Bergamo-Orio al Serio, Italy	A2008
EI-DRH	Mainair Blade	1320-0402-7-W1115	G-CBOL	8. 6.06	J McErlain	Newtownards	A 4.06
EI-DRI	Bombardier CL-600-2D24	15075		19. 6.06	Challey Ltd	Rome-Fiumicino, Italy	A2008
	(CRJ 900 Regional Jet)				(Operated Air One Cityliner)		
EI-DRJ	Bombardier CL-600-2D24	15077		21. 7.06	Challey Ltd	Rome-Fiumicino, Italy	A2008
	(CRJ 900 Regional Jet)				(Operated Air One Cityliner)		
EI-DRK	Bombardier CL-600-2D24	15076		22. 6.06	Challey Ltd	Rome-Fiumicino, Italy	A2008
	(CRJ 900 Regional Jet)				(Operated Air One Cityliner)		
EI-DRL	Raj Hamsa X'Air Jabiru	1005		23. 6.06	C Kiernan	Granard	
EI-DRM	Urban Air UFM-10 Samba	3/10	OK-FUU-31	7. 7.06	M Tormey	Abbeyshrule	A 8.06
EI-DRN	Robinson R44 Raven	1607		19. 7.06	Blue Star Helicopters Ltd	Cork	A 6.07
EI-DRO	Tecnam P20021-JF	044		3. 8.06	Ossory Flying and Gliding Club Ltd	Kilkenny	N 6.07
EI-DRR	Boeing 737-347	23181	N3301	14. 9.06	BCI Aircraft Leasing Ireland B Ltd	Tijuana, Mexico	A2008
					(Operated Aerovolar)		
EI-DRT	Air Création Tanarg 912S`iXess 15	A060826078		1. 8.06	L Daly	Tullamore	
EI-DRU	Tecnam P92/EM Echo	543	I-6351	29.12.06	P Gallogly	Abbeyshrule	
EI-DRW	Evektor EV-97R Eurostar	20062709		31. 7.06	Eurostar Flying Club Ltd	Coonagh	A10.06
EI-DRX	Raj Hamsa X'Air 582(5)	1048		21 .8.06	M Sheelan and D McShane	Granard	
EI-DSA	Airbus A320-216	2869	F-WWBE	14. 9.06	Aircraft Purchase Company No.1 Ltd		
					(Operated Air One)	Rome -Fiumicino, Italy	A2008
EI-DSB	Airbus A320-216	2932	F-WWBX	9.11.06	Aircraft Purchase Company No.1 Ltd		
					(Operated Air One)	Rome -Fiumicino, Italy	A2008
EI-DSC	Airbus A320-216	2995	F-WWIY	18. 1.07	Aircraft Purchase Company No.2 Ltd		
					(Operated Air One)	Rome -Fiumicino, Italy	A2008
EI-DSD	Airbus A320-216	3076	F-WWIP	22. 3.07	Aircraft Purchase Company No.3 Ltd		
					(Operated Air One)	Rome -Fiumicino, Italy	A2008
EI-DSE	Airbus A320-216	3079	F-WWIL	29. 3.07	Aircraft Purchase Company No.3 Ltd		
					(Operated Air One)	Rome -Fiumicino, Italy	A2008
EI-DSF	Airbus A320-216	3080	F-WWIV	4. 4.07	Aircraft Purchase Company No.4 Ltd		
					(Operated Air One)	Rome -Fiumicino, Italy	A2008

Reg	Type	C/n	Prev id	Date	Owner/Operator	Location	
EI-DSG	Airbus A320-216	3115	F-WWIZ	26. 4.07	Aircraft Purchase Company No 4 Ltd *(Operated Air One)*	Rome -Fiumicino, Italy	A2008
EI-DSH	Airbus A320-216	3178	F-WWDS	12. 7.07	Aircraft Purchase Company No 5 Ltd *(Operated Air One)*	Rome -Fiumicino, Italy	A2008
EI-DSI	Airbus A320-216	3213	F-WWIU	27. 9.07	Aircraft Purchase Company No 6 Ltd *(Operated Air One)*	Rome -Fiumicino, Italy	A2008
EI-DSJ	Airbus A320-216	3295	F-WWDV	9.11.07	Aircraft Purchase Company No 6 Ltd *(Operated Air One)*	Rome -Fiumicino, Italy	A2008
EI-DSK	Airbus A320-216	3328	F-WWIX	4.12.07	Aircraft Purchase Company No 6 Ltd *(Operated Air One)*	Rome -Fiumicino, Italy	A2008
EI-DSL	Airbus A320-216	3343	F-WWBO	18.12.07	Aircraft Purchase Company No 6 Ltd *(Operated Air One)*	Rome -Fiumicino, Italy	A2008
EI-DSM	Airbus A320-216	3362	F-WWIR	22. 1.08	Aircraft Purchase Company No 7 Ltd *(Operated Air One)*	Rome -Fiumicino, Italy	A2008
EI-DTP	Boeing 737-347	23182	N302WA	10.11.06	BCI Aircraft Leasing B Ltd *(Operated Aerovolar)*	Tijuana, Mexico	A2008
EI-DTR	Robinson R44 Raven	1652		20.12.06	Loughoran Properties Ltd	Galway	
EI-DTS	Piper PA18-95 Super Cub	18-5822	OO-VIK N7484D	4.10.06	P.Dunne, K Synott and M Murphy	(Drogheda, County Louth	N11.07
EI-DTT	ELA Aviacion ELA 07 R100	04061050722		6.10.06	N Steele	Kilrush	
EI-DTU	Boeing 737-5Y0	25175	B-2546	24.10.06	Celestial Aviation Trading Ltd *(Operated Transaero Airlines)*	Moscow-Domodedovo, Russia	A2008
EI-DTV	Boeing 737-5Y0	25183	B-2549	10.11.06	Airplanes Holdings Ltd Moscow-Domodedovo, Russia *(Operated Transaero Airlines)*		A2008
EI-DTW	Boeing 737-5Y0	25188	B-2550-	6.12.06	Airplanes Holdings Ltd Moscow-Domodedovo, Russia *(Operated Transaero Airlines)*		A2008
EI-DTX	Boeing 737-5Y8	28052	LY-AZX PT-SSE	5.10.06	ILFC Ireland Ltd Moscow-Domodedovo, Russia *(Operated Transaero Airlines)*		A2008
EI-DTY	Boeing 737-3M8	25017	G-IGOV N250GE, LZ-BOF, N250GE, 9V-TRD, N760BE, N35030, (OO-LTH)	8.12.06	Celestial Aviation Trading 36 Ltd *(Operated KD Avia)* Kaliningrad-Khrabovo, Russia		
EI-DUA	Boeing 757-256	26247	N241LF PP-VTQ, EC-GZY, N1795B	16.11.06	ILFC Ireland Ltd Krasnoyarsk-Yemilianovo, Russia *(Operated Kras Air)*		A2008
EI-DUB	Airbus A330-301ER	055		6. 5.94	Aer Lingus Ltd *"St.Patrick/Padraig"*	Dublin	A2008
EI-DUC	Boeing 757-256	26248	N263LF PP-VTR, EC-GZZ	16.11.06	ILFC Ireland Ltd Krasnoyarsk-Yemilianovo, Russia *(Operated Kras Air)*		A2008
EI-DUD	Boeing 757-256	26249	N271LF PP-VTS, EC-HAA, N1786B	20.12.06	ILFC Ireland Ltd Krasnoyarsk-Yemilianovo, Russia *(Operated Kras Air)*		A2008
EI-DUE	Boeing 757-256	26250	N272LF PP-VTT, EC-HDM	18. 1.07	ILFC Ireland Ltd Krasnoyarsk-Yemilianovo, Russia *(Operated Kras Air)*		A2008
EI-DUF	Aérospatiale SA.365N Dauphin 2	6315	PR-YOF F-WQEX, JA9932, F-WQAZ	13.11.07	Dauphin 2 Aviation Ltd	Trevet	
EI-DUH	Scintex CP.1310-C3 Super Emeraude	921	F-BJMK	12.12.06	W Kennedy	Killenaule	A 5.07
EI-DUI	Gulfstream-American GA-7 Cougar	GA7-0114	G-GENN G-BNAB, G-BGYP	11. 5.07	D O'Toole	Waterford	
EI-DUJ	Evektor EV-97 Eurostar	20062814		9. 3.07	E Fitzpatrick	(Ballyliffin)	
EI-DUK	Bombardier CL-600-2D24 *(CRJ 900 Regional Jet)*	15104		28.11.06	Challey Ltd Rome-Fiumicino, Italy *(Operated Air One Cityliner)*		A2008
EI-DUL	Alpi Aviation Pioneer *(Built J Hackett)*	181-UK		21. 5.07	J Hackett	(Mountrath)	N12.07
EI-DUM	Bombardier CL.600-2D24 *(CRJ 900 Regional Jet)*	15103		24. 1.07	Al Waha Lease (Ireland No 2) Ltd *(Operated Myair)* Bergamo-Orio al Serio, Italy		A2008
EI-DUO	Airbus A330-203	0841	F-WWYT	25 .5.07	Aer Lingus Ltd *"St.Columba/Column"*	Dublin	A2008
EI-DUS	Boeing 737-3M8	24021	TF-ELM F-GIXP, 9V-SQZ, N40495, N315FL, OO-LTB, (F-GKTE), OO-ITB, (F-ODSU), (OO-BTB)	12. 1.07	Aerco Ireland Ltd *"Maestrale"* Rome-Ciampino, Italy *(Operated Mistral Air)*		A2008
EI-DUT	Bell 206B-3 JetRanger III	4551	G-CRLH G-RJTT, C-GRJE	23. 3.07	AV-8 Helicopters Ireland Ltd	(Craugwell)	A 6.07
EI-DUU	Bombardier CL.600-2D24 *(CRJ 900 Regional Jet)*	15102		24. 1.07	Al Waha Lease (Ireland No 2) Ltd *(Operated Myair)* Bergamo-Orio al Serio, Italy		A2008
EI-DUV	Beech 95 B55 Baron	TC-1618	N3045W	13. 3.07	J Given	Weston, Dublin	
EI-DUX	Bombardier CL.600-2D24 *(CRJ 900 Regional Jet)*	15110		31. 1.07	Al Waha Lease (Ireland No 2) Ltd *(Operated Myair)* Bergamo-Orio al Serio, Italy		A2008
EI-DUY	Bombardier CL.600-2D24 *(CRJ 900 Regional Jet)*	15112		31. 1.07	Al Waha Lease (Ireland No 2) Ltd *(Operated Myair)* Bergamo-Orio al Serio, Italy		A2008
EI-DUZ	Airbus A330-203	0847	F-WWKM	26. 6.07	Aer Lingus Ltd *"St.Aoife/Aoife"*.	Dublin	A2008
EI-DVA	Boeing 737-36E	25159	F-GIXM F-WIXM, (F-GLXO), N315FL, EC-703)	9. 2.07	Celestial Aviation Trading 19 Ltd *(Operated Mistral Air* Rome-Ciampino, Italy		A2008
EI-DVC	Boeing 737-33A	25426	SE-DPC N34AW	9. 2.07	Ansett Worldwide Aviation Ireland Ltd *"Libeccio"* *(Operated Mistral Air)* Rome-Ciampino, Italy		A2008
EI-DVD	Airbus A319-113	0647	F-GPMH D-AVYD	7. 2.07	Castle 2003-1 Ireland Ltd Catania, Italy *(Operated Windjet)*		A2008
EI-DVE	Airbus A320-214	3129	F-WWBJ	18. 5.07	Aer Lingus Ltd *"St.Aideen/Etaion"*	Dublin	A2008
EI-DVF	Airbus A320-214	3136	F-WWDF	17. 5.07	Aer Lingus Ltd *"St.Jarlath/Iarflaith"*	Belfast International	A2008
EI-DVG	Airbus A320-214	3318	F-WWIV	28.11.07	Aer Lingus Ltd *"St.Flannan/Flannan"*	Dublin	A2008
EI-DVH	Airbus A320-214	3345	F-WWBP	14.12.07	Aer Lingus Ltd *"St.Clare/Ciara"*	Dublin	A2008
EI-DVO	Barnett J4B2	227	C-FRKB	9. 3.07	T Brennan	(Castleconnell)	
EI-DVP	Bombardier CL-600-2D24 *(CRJ 900 Regional Jet)*	15116		9. 3.07	Aircraft Purchase Company No.2 Ltd *(Operated Air One Cityliner)* Rome -Fiumicino, Italy		A2008
EI-DVR	Bombardier CL-600-2D24 *(CRJ 900 Regional Jet)*	15118		16. 4.07	Aircraft Purchase Co No.3 Ltd/ *(Operated Air One Cityliner)* Rome -Fiumicino, Italy		A2008
EI-DVS	Bombardier CL-600-2D24 *(CRJ 900 Regional Jet)*	15119		30. 4.07	Aircraft Purchase Co No.3 Ltd/ *(Operated Air One Cityliner)* Rome -Fiumicino, Italy		A2008
EI-DVT	Bombardier CL-600-2D24 *(CRJ 900 Regional Jet)*	15123		30. 4.07	Aircraft Purchase Co No.4 Ltd/ *(Operated Air One Cityliner)* Rome -Fiumicino, Italy		A2008

EI-DVU	Airbus A319-113	660	F-GPMI D-AVYC	9. 3.07	Castle 2003-2 Ireland Ltd (Operated WindJet)	Catania, Italy	A2008
EI-DVX	Robinson R44 Raven II	11600	G-CEKD	20. 3.07	Aceville Developments Ltd Clogheen Business Park, Cork		A 6.07
EI-DVY	Boeing 737-31S	29059	LZ-BOM D-ADBO	10. 7.07	DSF Aircraft Leasing (Ireland) Ltd "Città di Palermo" (Operated Blu-Express) Rome -Fiumicino, Italy		A2008
EI-DVZ	Robinson R44 Raven II	11629		7. 3.07	D.Mcauliffe	Cork	A 6.07
EI-DWA	Boeing 737-8AS/W	33617		12. 9.07	Ryanair Ltd	Dublin	A2008
EI-DWB	Boeing 737-8AS/W	36075		18. 9.07	Ryanair Ltd	Dublin	A2008
EI-DWC	Boeing 737-8AS/W	36076		20. 9.07	Ryanair Ltd	Dublin	A2008
EI-DWD	Boeing 737-8AS/W	33642		25. 9.07	Ryanair Ltd	Dublin	A2008
EI-DWE	Boeing 737-8AS/W	36074		27. 9.07	Ryanair Ltd	Dublin	A2008
EI-DWF	Boeing 737-8AS/W	33619		3.10.07	Ryanair Ltd	Dublin	A2008
EI-DWG	Boeing 737-8AS/W	33620		3.10.07	Ryanair Ltd	Dublin	A2008
EI-DWH	Boeing 737-8AS/W	33637		19.10.07	Ryanair Ltd	Dublin	A2008
EI-DWI	Boeing 737-8AS/W	33643		19.10.07	Ryanair Ltd	Dublin	A2008
EI-DWJ	Boeing 737-8AS/W	36077		.22.10.07	Ryanair Ltd	Dublin	A2008
EI-DWK	Boeing 737-8AS/W	36078		27.10.07	Ryanair Ltd	Dublin	A2008
EI-DWL	Boeing 737-8AS/W	33618		26.10.07	Ryanair Ltd	Dublin	A2008
EI-DWM	Boeing 737-8AS/W	36080		7.11.07	Ryanair Ltd	Dublin	A2008
EI-DWO	Boeing 737-8AS/W	36079		19.11.07	Ryanair Ltd	Dublin	A2008
EI-DWP	Boeing 737-8AS/W	36082		21.11.07	Ryanair Ltd	Dublin	A2008
EI-DWR	Boeing 737-8AS/W	36081	N1786B	29.11.07	Ryanair Ltd	Dublin	A2008
EI-DWS	Boeing 737-8AS/W	33625		7. 1.08	Ryanair Ltd	Dublin	A2008
EI-DWT	Boeing 737-8AS/W	33626		18. 1.08	Ryanair Ltd	Dublin	A2008
EI-DWV	Boeing 737-8AS/W	33627		22. 1.08	Ryanair Ltd	Dublin	A2008
EI-DWW	Boeing 737-8AS/W	33629		.2.08	Ryanair Ltd (Delivered 8. 2.08)	Dublin	A2008
EI-DWX	Boeing 737-8AS/W	33630		.2.08	Ryanair Ltd (Delivered 9. 2.08)	Dublin	A2008
EI-DWY	Boeing 737-8AS/W	33638		2.08	Ryanair Ltd (Delivered 20. 2.08)	Dublin	A2008
EI-DWZ	Boeing 737-8AS/W	33628		2.08	Ryanair Ltd (Delivered 22. 2.08)	Dublin	A2008
EI-DXA	Comco Ikarus C42	0604-6809		26. 1.07	M.Kirrane	(County Galway)	
EI-DXB	Boeing 737-31S	29060	LZ-BON D-ADBP, N1786B	20. 6.07	DSF Aircraft Leasing (Ireland) Ltd "Città di Roma" (Operated Blu Express) Rome-Fiumicino, Italy		A2008
EI-DXC	Boeing 737-4Q8	26300	TC-JKA SX-BFA, TC-JEL	22. 6.07	Castle 2003-1 Ireland Ltd Rome-Fiumicino, Italy (Operated Air One)		A2008
EI-DXG	Boeing 737-4Q8	25376	TC-JEN	9. 5.07	ILFC Ireland Ltd Rome-Fiumicino, Italy (Operated Air One)		A2008
EI-DXH	Robinson R44 Raven	1699		2. 5.07	Gannon Brothers (Keelogues) Ltd	Oranmore	A 6.07
EI-DXI	Robinson R22 Beta II	4117	N3013G	19. 4.07	CNW Helicopters Ltd	Cork	N 7.07
EI-DXJ	Robinson R22 Beta II	4120	N3015F	19. 4.07	Montague Aviation (Sales and Leasing) Ltd	(Gorey)	
EI-DXK	Robinson R44 Raven II	11621		19. 4.07	Ashdown Park Hotel Ltd	(Gorey)	
EI-DXL	CFM Shadow Series CD	K.232	PH-2S5	15.10.07	F Lynch	Fermoy	
EI-DXM	Raj Hansa X'Air 582(4)	402	G-BYTT	11. 5.07	B P Nugent	(Tallaght, Dublin)	
	(Built R P Reeves - pr.no.BMAA/HB/100)						
EI-DXN	Zenair CH.601HD	9-9095		30. 5.07	N Gallagher	Wexford	
EI-DXO	Boeing 737-46J	27826	EC-KDZ N826BG, D-AYAA, D-ABAH	10. 7.07	Constitution Aircraft Leasing (Ireland) 3 Ltd Palma de Mallorca, Spain (Operated Futura International)		A2008
EI-DXP	Cyclone AX3/503	7252	G-MZDO	29. 6.07	J McCann	Limetree	
EI-DXS	CFM Shadow Series C	K.023	G-MYNA	4.10.07	R.W.Frost	Mallow, County.Cork	
EI-DXT	Urban Air UFM-10 Samba	10/10	OK-GUA 19	14.12.07	N Irwin	(Femoy, County Cork)	
EI-DXU	ELA Aviacion ELA 07 R115	100612307		11.12.07	R.Savage	(Kildare)	
EI-DXW	Bombardier Learjet Model 60	60-300	G-CJMC OH-AEM, N40081	24.12.07	Airlink Airways Ltd	Shannon	A2008
EI-DXX	Raj Hamsa X'Air 582(6)	685	G-CBFT	20.12.07	S.J.MacSweeney	Birr	
	(Built T Collins - pr,no.BMAA/HB/190)						
EI-DXZ	Urban Air UFM-10 Samba	20/10	OK-GUA 27	14.12.07	D.O'Leary	Kilrush	
EI-DYA	Boeing 737-8AS/W	33631		3.08R	Ryanair Ltd	Dublin	
EI-DYB	Boeing 737-8AS/W	33633		3.08R	Ryanair Ltd	Dublin	
EI-DYC	Boeing 737-8AS/W	36567		3.08R	Ryanair Ltd	Dublin	
EI-DYD	Boeing 737-8AS/W	33632		3.08R	Ryanair Ltd	Dublin	
EI-DYE	Boeing 737-8AS/W	36568		3.08R	Ryanair Ltd	Dublin	
EI-DYF	Boeing 737-8AS/W	36569		3.08R	Ryanair Ltd	Dublin	
EI-DYG	Boeing 737-8AS/W	33639		3.08R	Ryanair Ltd	Dublin	
EI-DZA	Colt 21A Balloon (Hot Air)	527	G-MLGL	11.12.07	P Baker	Abbeyview, Trim	
	(Sean's Bar-Ireland's Oldest Pub titles)						
EI-DZB	Colt 14A Cloudhopper Balloon (Hot Air)	2580	G-BVKX	11.12.07	P Baker	Abbeyview, Trim	
EI-DZE	Urban Air UFM-10 Samba	14/10	OK-GUA 24	18.12.07	M.Tormey	Abbeyshrule	
EI-DZC	Boeing 737-7Q8	30037	5T-CLM	12.10.07	ILFC Ireland Ltd Paris-Orly, France (Stored in Air Mauritanie c/s)		N 2.08
EI-DZI	Robinson R44 Raven	1522	G-CDLX	25. 1.08	P.Reynolds and T.Kelly	Letterkenny	
EI-EAZ	Cessna 172R	17281146	N74LU	9. 8.07	Atlantic Flight Training Ltd	Cork	
EI-EBJ	Robinson R44 Raven	1358		18. 5.04	Gibbons Developments Ltd	Oranmore	N 3.07
EI-ECA	Agusta A109A II	7387	N109RP JA9662	28. 2.97	Blue Star Helicopters Ltd (Operated Premier Helicopters)	Cork	A2008
EI-EDR	Piper PA-28R-200 Cherokee Arrow II 28R-7435265		G-BCGD N9628N	19.11.87	Dublin Flyers Ltd	Dublin	A 4.06
EI-EGG	Robinson R44 Raven	1344	G-CCLI	10.12.03	In-Flight Aviation Ltd	Weston, Dublin	A 5.06
EI-EGR	Robinson R44 Raven II	11078		30. 3.06	J C Southern Copters Ltd	(Cork)	
EI-EHB	Robinson R22 Beta II	3569		18. 5.04	Blue Star Helicopters Ltd	(Cork)	
EI-EHE	Robinson R22 Beta II	3654		1.10.04	Blue Star Helicopters Ltd	Cork	A 4.06
EI-EHG	Robinson R22 Beta	3509	N75302	16. 4.04	G Jordan	(Legan, Killglass)	A 8.06
EI-EJR	Robinson R44 Raven	1504		8. 9.05	Gerair Ltd	(Edenderry)	
EI-ELL	Medway EclipseR	157/136		2. 6.99	Microflex Ltd	Kilrush	A 1.03

Reg	Type	C/n	Prev id	Date	Owner/Operator	Location	
EI-EMG	Robinson R22 Beta II	3809		8. 6.05	M Brennan	Oranmore Heliport, Galway	A 7.06
EI-ESK	Robinson R44 Raven II	11484	G-CEFR	6.11.07	Esker Bus and & Coach Ltd		
						(Kilbeggan, County Westmeath)	
EI-EUR	Eurocopter EC.120B Colibri	1138	G-BZMK	14.12.00	Atlantic Helicopters Ltd	Dublin	A 6.07
			F-WQOE				
EI-EWR	Airbus A330-202	330	F-WWKV	9. 5.00	Aer Lingus Ltd	Dublin	A2008
					"St Laurence O'Toole/Lorcan O Tuathail"		
EI-EXC	Robinson R44 Raven	1312		24. 6.03	S Keaney	(Carrigtwohill)	N 2.05
EI-EXG	Robinson R22 Beta II	3698	N7337F	18.11.04	21st Century Aviation Ltd		
						Oranmore Heliport, Galway	A 4.06
EI-EXH	Robinson R44 Raven	1730		9.10.07	Executive Helicopter Maintenance Ltd	Oranmore	
EI-EXM	Robinson R44 Raven	1700	N30607	27. 7.07	Executive Helicopter Maintenance Ltd	Oranmore	
EI-FAB	Eurocopter EC.120B Colibri	1155	F-HIAN	10. 7.07	Billy Jet Ltd	(Rathangane)	
			VP-BRD, F-WQDK				
EI-FAR	Robinson R44 Raven II	11305		23. 8.06	Fardolan Ltd	(Corrofin, Tuam, Galway)	A 6.07
EI-FBG	Reims Cessna F182Q Skylane	F18200032	D-EFBG	4. 7.00	J Paxton	Weston, Dublin	A 5.06
			(F-GAGU)				
EI-FGL	Eurocopter EC.120B Colibri	1492	PH-ECM	5.12.07	Fanning Machine Rentals Ltd	(Arklow)	
			F-WWXM				
EI-FOX	Robinson R44 Raven	1693		17. 4.07	Trotfox Ltd	Farranfore, Kerry	
EI-FPL	Bell 206L-3 Long Ranger	51040	HA-FLY	10. 4.07	Fernwave Ireland Ltd	Dublin	A 5.07
			D-HAPY (2), D-HBBZ (3)				
EI-FXA	Aérospatiale-Alenia ATR 42-300	282	N282AT	22. 4.05	Air Contractors (Ireland)Ltd *(Operated Fedex)*		
			(N281AE), N282AT, F-WWLI			Memphis-International, Tennessee, US	A2008
EI-FXB	Aérospatiale-Alenia ATR 42-300	243	(N927FX)	12. 5.05	Air Contractors (Ireland) Ltd *(Operated Fedex)*		
			N246AE, N243AT, F-WWEQ			Memphis-International, Tennessee, US	A2008
EI-FXC	Aérospatiale-Alenia ATR 42-300	273	N310DK	25. 8.05	Air Contractors (Ireland)Ltd *(Operated Fedex)*		
			(N925FX), N271AT, N273AT, F-WWEC			Memphis-International, Tennessee, US	A2008
EI-FXD	Aérospatiale-Alenia ATR 42-300	273	N271AT	29. 6.05	Air Contractors (Ireland)Ltd *(Operated Fedex)*		
			N273AT, F-WWEQ			Memphis-International, Tennessee, US	A2008
EI-FXE	Aérospatiale-Alenia ATR 42-320	327	N327AT	21.10.05	Air Contractors (Ireland) Ltd *(Operated Fedex)*		
			(N926FX), N327AT, F-WWLM			Memphis-International, Tennessee, US	A2008
EI-FXG	Aérospatiale-Alenia ATR 72-202	224	(N814FX)	9. 8.05	Air Contractors (Ireland) Ltd *(Operated Fedex)*		
			D-ANFA, F-WWEQ			Memphis-International, Tennessee, US	A2008
EI-FXH	Aérospatiale-Alenia ATR 72-212	229	N815FX	2. 2.06	Air Contractors (Ireland) Ltd *(Operated Fedex)*		
			D-ANFB, F-WWEX			Memphis-International, Tennessee, US	A2008
EI-FXI	Aérospatiale-Alenia ATR 72-202F	294	N818FX	18.10.06	Air Contractors (Ireland) Ltd*(Operated Fedex)*		
			D-ANFE, F-WWLS			Memphis-International, Tennessee, US	A2008
EI-FXJ	Aérospatiale-Alenia ATR 72-202F	292	N813FX	17. 5.07	Air Contractors (Ireland) Ltd*(Operated Fedex)*		
			D-ANFF, F-WWLT			Memphis-International, Tennessee, US	A2008
EI-FXK	Aérospatiale-Alenia ATR 72-202F	256	N817FX	10. 8.07	Air Contractors (Ireland) Ltd *(Operated Fedex)*		
			D-ANFD, F-WWEE			Memphis-International, Tennessee, US	A2008
EI-GAA	Boeing 767-266ER	23179	N567KM	25. 5.04	Arbor Finance Ltd Krasnoyarsk-Yemilianovo, Russia		A2008
			ZS-SRB, N573SW, SU-GAI, N1788B *(Operated.Krask Air)*				
EI-GAN	Bell 407	53551	N20446	13. 6.03	Robswall Property Ltd	Dublin	A 6.04
			C-GFNR				
EI-GAV	Robinson R22 Beta II	3485	N75264	17.10.03	Weston Davinci Services Ltd	Weston, Dublin	A 5.07
EI-GBA	Boeing 767-266ER	23180	N573JW	25. 5.04	Arbor Finance Ltd Krasnoyarsk-Yemilianovo, Russia		A2008
			ZS-SRC, N575SW, SU-GAJ, N1789B *(Operated.Kras Air)*				
EI-GCE	Sikorsky S-61N	61817	LN-ORC (4)	30. 4.07	CHC Ireland Ltd	Shannon	A2008
			(LN-OQU)			*(IMES Rescue titles)*		
EI-GDL	Gulfstream Aerospace Gulfstream V-SP	5068	N968GA	10. 8.05	Westair Aviation Ltd	Shannon	
	(Gulfstream 550)						
EI-GER	Maule MX-7-180A Star Rocket	20006C		7. 1.94	P J L.Ryan	Trim	A 4.06
	(Tail-wheel u/c)						
EI-GFC	SOCATA TB-9 Tampico	141	G-BIAA	9.10.93	B McGrath, J Ryan and D O'Neill	Waterford	A 4.06
EI-GHT	Bell 206B JetRanger III	3565	G-JAHL	14. 3.06	Dunican High Reach Equipment Ltd	(Garristown)	A 4.06
			N666ST				
EI-GKL	Robinson R22 Beta II	3570		19. 5.04	Eamon Duffy (Rosemount) Ltd	Oranmore	N 6.07
EI-GLA	Schleicher ASK 21	21002	EI-150	28. 3.07	Dublin Gliding Club Ltd	Kilkenny	N 6.07
			D-6957			*"ICS"*		
EI-GLB	Schleicher ASK 21	21060	EI-164	28. 3.07	Dublin Gliding Club Ltd	Bellarena	N 7.07
			D-4089					
EI-GLC	Centrair 101A Pégase	101-102	EI-163	28. 3.07	Dublin Gliding Club Ltd	Gowran Grange, Naas	
			PH-738			*"ZC"*		
EI-GLD	Schleicher ASK 13	13131	EI-112	28. 3.07	Dublin Gliding Club Ltd	Gowran Grange, Naas	
EI-GLF	Schleicher K 8B	8468	EI-108	28. 3.07	Dublin Gliding Club Ltd *"08"*	Gowran Grange, Naas	
EI-GLG	Schleicher Ka 6CR	662	EI-127	3.08R		Gowran Grange, Naas	
			PH-259				
EI-GLH	Sportine Aviacija LAK-17A	136	EI-169	28. 3.07	S Kinnear	Gowran Grange, Naas	
			HA-4511			*"T8"*		
EI-GLI	Schempp-Hirth Duo Discus T	106/435	EI-159	28. 3.07	B Ramseyer *"BR"*	Gowran Grange, Naas	
EI-GLJ	Glaser-Dirks DG-200	2-88	EI-145	28. 3.07	M A Kelly	Gowran Grange, Naas	
			PH-930, D-7610					
EI-GLK	Schempp-Hirth Standard Cirrus	304	EI-148	28. 3.07	P Conran and D McKenna	Gowran Grange, Naas	
			BGA 4334, D-2060			*"HZL"*		
EI-GLL	Glaser-Dirks DG-200	2-22	EI-147	28. 3.07	P Denman and C Craig	Gowran Grange, Naas	
			D-6780			*"DS"*		
EI-GLM	Schleicher Ka 6CR	6565	EI-111	28. 3.07	P Denman and C Craig	Gowran Grange, Naas	
			IGA 9			*"11"*		
EI-GLN	Glasflügel H201 Standard Libelle	267	EI-165	28. 3.07	D McMahon	Gowran Grange, Naas	
			BGA 1693-CPF			*"T15"*		
EI-GLO	Scheibe Zugvogel IIIB	1085	EI-146	28. 3.07	M J Walsh, J Murphey and N Shortt		
			D-4096			*"TK"*	Gowran Grange, Naas	

Reg	Type	C/n	Previous identity	Date	Owner/Operator	Location	CofA
EI-GLP	EoN AP.5 Olympia 2B	EoN/O/155	EI-115, BGA 1097	28. 3.07	J Cashin	Kilkenny	
EI-GLR	Schleicher ASW 20L	20054	EI-167, BGA 2371	28. 3.07	K Commins "189"	Gowran Grange, Naas	
EI-GLT	Schempp-Hirth Discus b	219	EI-149, BGA 3320-FKK	4. 5.07	D Thomas	Gowran Grange, Naas	
EI-GLS	Rolladen-Schneider LS7-WL	7135	EI-177, 3A-MCD (2)	28. 3.07	M McHugo	Gowran Grange, Naas	
EI-GLU	Schleicher Ka 6CR	808	EI-161, BGA 3536-FUM, D-6289	28. 3.07	K Commins, R Woods and S Kinnear	Kilkenny	N 6.07
EI-GLV	Schleicher ASW 19B	19316	EI-153, BGA 4274-HWZ, HB-1524	28. 3.07	C Sinclair and B O'Neill "53"	Gowran Grange, Naas	
EI-GLW	Schleicher Ka 6CR	6649	EI-128, D-1393	28. 3.07	J Murphy and Partners	Bellarena	N 7.07
EI-GMB	Schleicher ASW 17	17031	EI-132, D-2365	28. 3.07	D O'Hogan, C M and D M Begley "TK"	Gowran Grange, Naas	
EI-GMC	Schleicher ASK 18	18007	EI-136, BGA 2945-ETT, D-6868	20. 9.07	D O'Hogan, K Reynolds, M and D M Begley	Gowran Grange, Naas	
EI-GMD	Bölkow Phoebus C	908	EI-158, BGA 4202-HTZ, OO-ZDJ, BGA 1573	28. 3.07	F McDonnell and B de Tourtoulon	Gowran Grange, Naas	
EI-GME	Eiriavion PIK-20D	20603	OH-562	18. 5.07	P McKenzie-Brown	Kilkenny	N 6.07
EI-GMF	Schleicher ASK 13	13189	EI-113	28. 3.07	Ossory Flying and Gliding Club Ltd	Kilkenny	N 6.07
EI-GPT	Robinson R22 Beta II	3317	N70637	8.11.04	Treaty Plant and Tool (Hire and Sales) Ltd	(Limerick)	A 6.04
EI-GPZ	Robinson R44 Raven	1388		5. 8.04	G and P Transport Ltd	Castlebar	A 6.07
EI-GSE	Reims Cessna F.172M	F17201105	D-EDXO	12. 4.02	K A O'Connor (Operated National Flight Centre)	Weston, Dublin	A 5.06
EI-GSM	Cessna 182S	18280188	N9541Q	17. 6.98	Westpoint Flying Group Ltd	Weston, Dublin	A 6.06
EI-GTY	Robinson R22 Beta II	3808		17. 6.05	Executive Helicopter Maintenance Ltd	Oranmore	A 6.07
EI-GWY	Cessna 172R Skyhawk	17280162	N9497F	31.12.97	Atlantic Flight Training Ltd	Cork	A 5.07
EI-GYM	Agusta A109S Grand	22046		5. 7.07	Barkisland (Developments) Ltd	Weston, Dublin	A 7.07
EI-HAM	Light-Aero Avid Flyer (Built H Goulding as SAAC pr.no.034) (Rotax 582)	1072-90		18.11.96	H Goulding (Current status unknown)	(Bray)	
EI-HAZ	Robinson R44 Raven	1558		3. 5.06	Forestbrook Developments Ltd	Cork	
EI-HCS	Grob G-109B	6414	G-BMHR	18. 8.95	H Sydner	Gorey	A 4.06
EI-HER	Bell 206B-3 JetRanger III	3408	G-HIER, G-BRFD, N2069N	1. 7.94	S L Ryan	Thurles	A 6.07
EI-HHH	Agusta A109E Power	11208	D-HPWR	8. 5.06	F Gormley and Partners	Weston, Dublin	A 2.07
EI-HOK.	Eurocopter EC.130B4	4034	G-CDVW, F-WQVY, F-WQDA	30. 5.06	Heli Leasing Partnership (L O' Kane and J Hegarty)	Weston, Dublin	A 6.07
EI-HXM	Bell 206B-2 JetRanger II	4105	ZS-HXM, N7131J	28. 7.00	Premier Star Equipment Ltd	Manston	A2008
EI-IAN	Pilatus PC-6/B2-H4 Turbo Porter	810	HB-FGI	30. 8.05	Irish Parachute Club Ltd	Clonbullogue	A 4.06
EI-IAW	Bombardier Learjet Model 60	218	N8084J, N50157	14. 6.01	Voltage Plus Ltd	Shannon	A 5.05
EI-IGA	Boeing 757-230	24748	I-AIGA, D-ABJW, N298BA, PH-DBH, D-ABND	20.10.06	Constitution Aircraft Leasing (Ireland) 3 Ltd (Operated Air Italy)	Milan-Malpensa, Italy	A2008
EI-IGB	Boeing 757-230	24738	I-AIGB, N248BA, PH-DBB, D-ABNB	21.11.06	Constitution Aircraft Leasing (Ireland) 3 Ltd (Operated Air Italy) "Citta de Somma Lombardo"	Milan-Malpensa, Italy	A2008
EI-IGC	Boeing 757-230	24747	I-AIGC, D-ABSG, N723BA, (SP-FVK), N723BA, PH-DBA, D-ANBC	20. 9.06	Constitution Aircraft Leasing (Ireland) 3 Ltd (Operated Air Italy Polska)	Warsaw-Okecie, Poland	A2008
EI-IHL	Aérospatiale AS.350B1 Ecureuil	1963	G-BWFY, N518R	27. 5.04	Irish Helicopters Ltd	Trevet Airfield, Dunshaughlin, County Meathn	A 5.06
	(Crashed near Ballynacally, Kildysert, County Clare 12. 7.07 and substantially damaged)						
EI-ING	Reims Cessna F172P	F17202084	G-BING	19. 8.05	21st Century Flyers Ltd	Dublin	A 9.07
EI-IRE	Bombardier CL-600-2B16 (CL-604 Challenger)	5515	N515DM, C-GLXF	20. 8.02	Starair (Ireland)Ltd	Dublin	A 1.03
EI-IRV	Aérospatiale AS.350B Ecureuil	1713	D-HENY	14.10.03	S Harries	Weston, Dublin	A 6.07
EI-HUM	Van's RV-7 (Built G Humphreys)	70588-1		8. 2.07	G Humphreys	Coonagh	
EI-JAC	Bell 206B JetRanger	3594	G-CCLY, G-TILT, G-BRJO, N2295Z	26. 5.05	Aerial Explorations	Weston, Dublin	A 6.07
EI-JAL	Robinson R44 Raven II	10329	N7530N	5. 8.04	D Doherty	City of Derry	A 7.07
EI-JAR	Robinson R44 Raven	1523		8.12.05	J Coleman	Cork	A 6.07
EI-JBC	Agusta A109A	7126	F-GATN	24. 7.97	Medeva Properties Ltd	Dublin Heliport	A10.06
EI-JFC	Agusta A109S	22021	N84RE	21.11.06	J J Fleming Contstruction Co	(Bandon, Cork)	
EI-JFD	Robinson R44 Raven	0969		13. 3.01	New World Plant Ltd	Galway	A 6.04
EI-JFK	Airbus A330-301	086	F-GMDE	11. 7.95	Aer Lingus Ltd "St.Colmcille/Colmcille"	Dublin	A2008
EI-JIM	Urban Air UFM-10 Samba XLA	43		21.12.06	J Smith	(Laytown)	
EI-JIV	Lockheed L.382G Hercules	4673	ZS-JIV, D2-THE, ZS-JIV	15.11.02	Air Contractors (Ireland) Ltd (ORSL titles)	Dublin	A2008
EI-JWP	Robnson R44 Raven II	11653	N3017B	11. 6.07	Joyce Walker Aviation Ltd	Enniskillen	A.7.07
EI-KDH	Piper PA-28-181 Archer III	2843422	N301PA, N41870	1. 6.05	K O'Driscoll and D Harris	Weston, Dublin	A 5.06
EI-KEO	Agusta A109S	22004	G-DACN	10. 9.07	Clear Skies Aviation Ltd (Operated Premier Helicopters)	Lifford, County.Donegal	A 5.07
EI-KEV	Raj Hamsa X'Air 133(1) (Built C Blackburn)	567	G-BZLD	21. 5.04	K Glynn	Birr	A 5.06
EI-KEY	Robinson R44 Raven	1649		20.12.06	Gerry Keyes Ltd	(Limerick)	
EI-KHR	Robinson R22 Beta II	3849	N74572	8. 6.05	Billy Jet Ltd (Operated Kildare Helicopters)	Weston, Dublin	A 5.06
EI-KJC	Hawker 850XP	258805	N71025	24. 1.07	Skypro Executive Jets Ltd (Operated Airlink Airways)	(Dublin)	A 5.07
EI-LAF	Bell 206B-3 JetRanger III	4090	N47LM, N62AJ, G-DPPA, C-FHPA	13. 4.04	Shamrock Helicopters Ltd	Weston, Dublin	A 5.06

Reg	Type	C/n	Prev ID	Date	Owner/Operator	Location	Ref
EI-LAJ	Robinson R44 Raven II	11200		26. 7.06	Heliwest Ltd	Galway	
EI-LAL	Agusta A109E	11118	G-JERL	19. 8.05	Lalco Development Co Ltd	Galway	A 6.07
EI-LAX	Airbus A330-202	269	F-WWKV	29. 4.99	Aer Lingus Ltd "St.Mella/Mella"	Dublin	A2008
EI-LFC	Tecnam P.2002-JF	63		10. 7.07	Limerick Flying Club (Coonagh) Ltd	Coonagh	
EI-LIT	MBB BÖ.105S	S.434	A6-DBH	20. 2.96	Irish Helicopters Ltd		
			Dubai 105, D-HDMH		Trevet Airfield, Dunshaughlin, County Meath		A 5.06
EI-LKS	Eurocopter EC.130B4	3643	F-WQDQ	20. 1.03	WIGAF Leasing Co Ltd	Dublin	A 6.07
					(Operated Premier Helicopters)		
EI-LMK	Agusta A109S	22061		29.11.07	Skyheli Ltd	Dublin	
EI-LNX	Eurocopter EC.130B4	3498	N460AE	10. 6.02	WIGAF Leasing Co Ltd	Dublin	A2008
					(Operated Premier Helicopters)		
EI-LOC	Robinson R44 Raven	1620		26. 7.06	Donville Heli's Ltd	Galway	A 6.07
EI-LTO	Boeing 757-23N	30232	N523AT	5. 12.05	Fastway Leasing Ltd Ufa, Bashkortostan, Russia		A2008
					(Operated Air Bashkortostan)		
EI-LTY	Boeing 757-23N	30735	N526AT	22. 2.06	City Leasing Ltd Moscow-Domodedovo, Russia		A2008
					(Operated VIM Airlines)		
EI-LVA	Airbus A321-231	1950	I-LIVA	2.10.07	AWAS Aviation Trading Ltd Milan-Malpensa, Italy		A2008
			D-AVXE]		(Operated Livingston)		
EI-LVB	Airbus A321-231	1970	I-LIVB	10. 5.07	AWAS Aviation Trading Ltd Milan-Malpensa, Italy		A2008
			D-AVZK		(Operated Livingston)		
EI-LVD	Airbus A321-231	792	I-LIVD	10. 5.07	S.A.L.E Ireland Ltd Milan-Malpensa, Italy		A2008
			F-WQST, D-ALAH, D-AVZM		(Operated Livingston)		
EI-MAG	Robinson R22 Beta	2592	G-DHGS	3. 8.01	J Smyth and Sons Ltd	Oranmore	N12.06
EI-MAX	Learjet Model 31A	31A-233	N233BX	26. 4.04	Airlink Airways	Westport	A12.05
			LX-PAT, N5005X				
EI-MCC	Robinson R44 Raven II	10507	G-CDAU	1.12.04	Coates Aviation Ltd	Dublin	
EI-MCF	Cessna 172R Skyhawk	17280799	N2469D	20. 1.00	Galway Flying Club Ltd	Carnmore, Galway	A 6.06
EI-MCP	Agusta A109C	7634	VH-NBX	13. 7.06	Quarry and Mining Equipment Ltd	(Navan)	
			VH-XNB, N109CW, N7LQ, VP-CHJ, VP-CEC, VR-CEC, 3A-MSG				
EI-MED	Bell 222A	47061	N40EA	3.08R	Executive Helicopters	Galway	
			(D-HAAD				
EI-MEJ	Bell 206B-3 JetRanger III	4582	N909WB	6. 4.05	Gaelic Helicopters Ltd	Mallow	A 6.07
EI-MEL	Agusta A109C	7672	LV-WXA	20. 6.00	M.Walsh Celtic Heliport, Knocksedan, Dublin		N 8.07
			N27ET, LV-WXA, N4NM				
EI-MEN	Agusta A109S	22017		5. 7.06	Men-Entirl Ltd	Weston, Dublin	A 7.07
EI-MER	Bell 206B JetRanger	4513	N60507	28. 9.99	Gaelic Helicopters Ltd	Westpoint	A 5.07
EI-MES	Sikorsky S-61N	61776	G-BXAE	27. 3.97	CHC Ireland Ltd	Dublin	A2008
			LN-OQO		(IMES Rescue titles)		
EI-MIK	Eurocopter EC.120B Colibri	1104	G-BZIU	22. 6.01	Executive Helicopter Maintenance Ltd	Oranmore	N 7.07
EI-MIP	Aérospatiale SA.365N Dauphin 2	6119	G-BLEY	20. 3.96	CHC Ireland Ltd	Cork	A 6.04
			F-WTNM				
EI-MIT	Agusta A109E Power Elite	11162		17. 1.03	Mercury Engineering Ltd		
					Celtic Heliport, Knocksedan, Dublin Airport		A 5.07
EI-MJR	Robinson R44 Raven	1391	N72603	5. 8.04	M Melville	Oranmore	
EI-MLN	Agusta A109E	11115	G-ECMM	23. 9.05	Earthquake (IRL)Ltd	Dublin	
			G-SIVC				
EI-MMO	Robinson R44 Raven	1389	G-CDRE	9. 1.08	Tallis Windfield Construction Ltd	Kilkenny	
			EI-MMO, (EI-EHF)				
EI-MOR	Robinson R44 Raven	1392		5. 8.04	Blue Star Helicopters Ltd	Cork	A 5.07
EI-MPW	Robinson R44 Raven	1554		14. 2.06	Connacht Helicopters Ltd	Ballina	A 4.06
EI-MSG	Agusta A109E	11692		27. 2.07	Beckdrive Ltd	Dublin	A 5.07
EI-MUL	Robinson R44 Clipper	1074		29. 8.01	Cotton Box Design Group Ltd	Galway	A 6.07
EI-MVK	Robinson R44 Raven II	10583	N74461	22. 4.05	Ashleypark International Ltd	Weston, Dublin	A 5.07
EI-NBD	Robinson R44 Raven	1571		10. 3.06	N B Property Developments Ltd	Oranmore Heliport	A 6.07
EI-NBG	Agusta A109S	22047		30. 8.07	A Logue and W Moffet	Ballinderry	A 8.07
EI-NBP	Robinson R44 Raven	1728		10. 8.07	N.B.Property Developments Ltd	Oranmore	
EI-NFW	Cessna 172S Skyhawk	172S9861	G-CDOU	28. 2.06	Galway Flying Club Ltd	Carnmore, Galway	A 7.06
			N1538W				
EI-NJA	Robinson R44 Raven II	11945	N155N.	21.12.07	Nojo Aviation Ltd	Weston	
EI-NVL	Jora Jora	C129		25 7.03	N Van Lonkhuyzen	Abbeyshrule	A 8.06
EI-NZO	Eurocopter EC.120B Colibri	1257	G-CBJF	6. 2.04	Billy Jet Ltd	(Rathangan)	N 3.06
EI-ODD	Bell 206B-3 JetRanger III	3627	G-CDES	25.11.05	Zero Altitude Ltd	Dublin	A11.05
			N22751				
EI-OFM	Reims Cessna F172N	F17201988	G-EOFM	6. 5.05	21st Century Flyers Ltd	Dublin	A10.06
			D-EDFM				
EI-OLI	Robinson R44 Raven	1698		20. 6.07	Alcock and Brown Aviation Ltd	Oranmore	
EI-ORD	Airbus A330-301	059	(EI-USA)	6. 6.97	Aer Lingus PLC	Dublin	A2008
			F-GMDD		"St.Maeve/Maedbh"		
EI-OZB	Airbus A300B4-103F	184	F-GOZB	5. 4.02	Air Contractors (Ireland) Ltd Paris CDG, France		A2008
			SX-BEH, F-WZMA		(Operated Europe Airpost)		
EI-OZC	Airbus A300B4-103F	189	F-GOZC	8. 2.02	Air Contractors (Ireland) Ltd Paris CDG, France		A2008
			SX-BEI, F-WZMF		(Operated DHL)		
EI-PAT	British Aerospace BAe.146 Series 200	E2030	G-ZAPL	11.10.99	Brimstage Ltd Paris CDG, France		A2008
			G-WLCY, N172US, N352US		((Operated Air France Regional for CityJet)		
EI-PCI	Bell 206B-3 JetRanger III	4072	N208M	6. 2.03	Malcove Ltd	Dublin	A 6.07
			JA9850, C-GAJN				
EI-PDG	Aérospatiale AS.350B Ecureuil	1089	G-BMAV	19.10.07	Irish Helicopters Ltd		
					Trevet Airfield, Dunshaughlin, County Meath		
EI-PEC	Robinson R44 Raven II	10354		2. 6.04	P Sexton Carrickwood, Lough Ennel, Mullingar		A2006
EI-PEL	Agusta A109E	11071	HB-ZBK	16.11.06	P Elliott and Company Ltd	(Dunshaughlin)	
			D-HGHI, N50GH, 5B-CJS				
EI-PJD	Aérospatiale AS.350B Ecureuil	3594	SE-JGY	15.10.03	New World Plant Ltd	Weston, Dublin	A 5.07
EI-PJW	Eurocopter EC.120B Colibri	1111	D-HUAD	23.12.03	P White	Oranmore	A 9.05
			F-WQDT				

Reg	Type	C/n	Prev id	Date	Owner/Operator	Location	Ref
EI-PKS	Bell 206B-3 JetRanger III	4480	OE-XAC D-HFIS	7.11.03	Hawk Springs Ltd (Operated Premier Helicopters)	Dublin	N11.07
EI-PMI	Agusta-Bell 206B-3 JetRanger III	8614	EI-BLG G-BIGS	19. 9.96	Ping Golf Equipment Ltd (Current status unknown)	Dublin	A 8.99
EI-POD	Cessna 177B	17702729	N1444C	3. 8.95	Trim Flying Club Ltd	Trim	A 4.06
EI-POP	Cameron Z-90 Balloon (Hot Air)	10753		23. 9.05	The Travel Department Ltd	Dublin	A 1.07
EI-PRI	Bell 206B-3 JetRanger III	4523	N6389V C-GLZM	29. 2.00	Brentwood Properties Ltd	Castleknock	A10.02
EI-RAV	Robinson R44 Raven	1581		31. 5.06	Executive Helicopters Maintenance Ltd	Oranmore	
EI-RCG	Sikorsky S-61N	61807	G-BZSN LN-OQB	25. 9.01	CHC Ireland Ltd (IMES Rescue titles)	Shannon	A2008
EI-REA	Aérospatiale-Alenia ATR 72-201	441	F-WQNC G-BWTL, F-WWLG	30. 5.02	Comhfhorbairt (Gaillimh) (Operated Aer Arann Express)	Dublin	A2008
EI-REB	Aérospatiale-Alenia ATR 72-201	470	F-WONH F-WQOL, F-WQOF, G-BWTM, F-WWED (Operated Aer Arann Express)	17. 5.02	Comhfhorbairt (Gaillimh)	Dublin	A2008
EI-RED	Aérospatiale-Alenia ATR 72-202	373	F-GJRX HS-PGA, F-WQAK, F-GKOL, F-WWEU (Operated Aer Arann Express)	5. 6.03	Comhfhorbairt (Gaillimh)	Dublin	A2008
EI-REF	Aérospatiale-Alenia ATR 72-202	201	F-GKOA	23. 6.04	Comhfhorbairt (Gaillimh) (Operated Aer Arann Express)	Galway	A2008
EI-REG	Aerospatiale-Alenia ATR 72-202	367	F-WQRK (2) EC-IMH, F-GJRQ, HS-PGB, F-WQAJ, F-GKOK, F-WWEX (Operated Aer Arann Express)	29. 4.05	Comhfhorbairt (Gaillimh)	Galway	A2008
EI-REH	Aérospatiale-Alenia ATR 72-202	260	OY-RTA F-WQNF, EC-FIV, EC-873, F-WWEH (Operated Aer Arann Express)	14. 2.06	Comhfhorbairt (Gaillimh)	Galway	A2008
EI-REI	Aérospatiale-Alenia ATR 72-201	267	OY-RTB F-WQNI, EC-JFX, EC-874, F-WWEM (Operated Aer Arann Express)	19.11.05	Comhfhorbairt (Gaillimh)	Galway	A2008
EI-REJ	Aérospatiale-Alenia ATR 72-201	126	ES-KRA OH-KRA, F-WWEM	18. 5.06	Comhfhorbairt (Gaillimh) (Operated Air Atlantique)	Coventry	A2008
EI-REL	Aérospatiale-Alenia ATR 72-212	748	F-WWEI	25. 5.07	Comhfhorbairt (Gaillimh) Teo Helsinki-Vantaa, Iceland (Operated Finncomm Airlines)		A2008
EI-REM	Aérospatiale-Alenia ATR 72-212A	760	F-WWEW	25.10.07	Comhfhorbairt (Gaillimh) Teo (Operated Aer Arann Express)	Galway	A2008
EI-REN	Aérospatiale-Alenia ATR 72-2xx			3.08R	Comhfhorbairt (Gaillimh) Teo (Operated Aer Arann Express)	Galway	
EI-REO	Aérospatiale-Alenia ATR 72-2xx			3.08R	Comhfhorbairt (Gaillimh) Teo (Operated Aer Arann Express)	Galway	
EI-REP	Aérospatiale-Alenia ATR 72-2xx			5.08R	Comhfhorbairt (Gaillimh) Teo (Operated Aer Arann Express)	Galway	
EI-RER	Aérospatiale-Alenia ATR 72-2xx			9.08R	Comhfhorbairt (Gaillimh) Teo (Operated Aer Arann Express)	Galway	
EI-RES	Aérospatiale-Alenia ATR 72-2xx			13.08R	Comhfhorbairt (Gaillimh) Teo (Operated Aer Arann Express)	Galway	
EI-RET	Aérospatiale-Alenia ATR 72-2xx			1.09R	Comhfhorbairt (Gaillimh) Teo (Operated Aer Arann Express)	Galway	
EI-REU	Aérospatiale-Alenia ATR 72-2xx			2.09R	Comhfhorbairt (Gaillimh) Teo (Operated Aer Arann Express)	Galway	
EI-REV	Bombardier Learjet Model 60	60-149	N260CA VP-BEZ, SU-EZI, SU-BNI, (ZS-JRM), N149LY	25.11.05	Airlink Airways Ltd	Dublin	A2005
EI-REW	Aérospatiale-Alenia ATR 72-500			4.09R	Comhfhorbairt (Gaillimh) Teo (Operated Aer Arann Express)	Galway	
EI-RHM	Bell 407	53137	G-DCDB C-FCDB	19. 1.06	Euro Jet Ireland Ltd	Dublin	A2008
EI-RJA	British Aerospace Avro 146-RJ85	E2329	G-CDYK N513XJ, G-6-329	23.10.07	CityJet Ltd Paris CDG, France "Rathlin Island" (Operated Air France)		A2008
EI-RJB	British Aerospace Avro 146-RJ85	E2330	G-CEBS N514XJ, G-6-330	8. 6.07	CityJet Ltd Paris CDG, France "Bere Island" (Operated Air France)		A2008
EI-RJC	British Aerospace Avro 146-RJ85	E2333	G-CEHA N515XJ, G-6-333	6.12.07	CityJet Ltd Paris CDG, France "Achill Island" (Operated Air France)		A2008
EI-RJD	British Aerospace Avro 146-RJ85	E2334	G-CEFL N516XJ, G-6-334	10. 8.07	CityJet Ltd Paris CDG, France "Valentia Island" (Operated Air France)		A2008
EI-RJE	British Aerospace Avro 146-RJ85	E2335	G-CEBU N517XJ, G-6-335	9. 3.07	CityJet Ltd Paris CDG, France "St MacDara's Island" (Operated Air France)		A2008
EI-RJF	British Aerospace Avro 146-RJ85	E2337	G-CEFN N518XJ, G-6-337	24. 8.07	CityJet Ltd Paris CDG, France "Great Blasket island" (Operated Air France)		A2008
EI-RJG	British Aerospace Avro 146-RJ85	E2344	G-CEHB N519XJ, G-6-344	18.12.07	CityJet Ltd Paris CDG, France "Sherkin Island" (Operated Air France)		A2008
EI-RJH	British Aerospace Avro 146-RJ85	E2345	N520XJ G-6-345	3.08R	CityJet Ltd Cologne, Germany "inishturk" (Currently registered as G-CEIC)		N12.06
EI-RJI	British Aerospace Avro 146-RJ85	E2346	N521XJ G-6-346	2. 5.07	CityJet Ltd Paris CDG, France "Skellig Michael" (Operated Air France)		A2008
EI-RJJ	British Aerospace Avro 146-RJ85	E2347	G-CEIF N522XJ, G-6-347	3.08R	CityJet Ltd Paris CDG, France "Hare Island" (Operated Air France)		A2008
EI-RJK	British Aerospace Avro 146-RJ85	E2348	N523XJ G-6-348	20. 9.07	CityJet Ltd Paris CDG, France "Collanmore Island" (Operated Air France)		A2008
EI-RJL	British Aerospace Avro 146-RJ85	E2349	N524XJ G-6-349	20. 9.07	CityJet Ltd Norwich "Inishmurray"		N11.07
EI-RJM	British Aerospace Avro 146-RJ85	E2350	N525XJ G-6-350	13. 7.07	CityJet Ltd Norwich "Caher Island"		N11.07
EI-RJN	British Aerospace Avro 146-RJ85	E2351	N526XJ G-6-351	11. 1.07	CityJet Ltd Paris CDG, France "Lake Isle of Inisheer" (Operated Air France)		A2008
EI-RJO	British Aerospace Avro 146-RJ85	E2352	N527XJ G-6-352	11. 1.07	CityJet Ltd Paris CDG, France "Inis Mor" (Operated Air France)		A2008
EI-RJP	British Aerospace Avro 146-RJ85	E2363	N529XJ G-6-363	18. 8.06	CityJet Ltd Paris CDG, France "Clare island" (Operated Air France)		A2008

Reg	Type	C/n	Prev id	Date	Owner/Operator	Location	Code
EI-RJR	British Aerospace Avro 146-RJ85	E2364	N530XJ G-6-364	27.11.06	CityJet Ltd "Tory Island" (Operated Air France)	Paris CDG, France	A2008
EI-RJS	British Aerospace Avro 146-RJ85	E2365	N531XJ G-6-365	16. 4.07	CityJet Ltd "Dursey Island" (Operated Air France)	Paris CDG, France	A2008
EI-RJT	British Aerospace Avro 146-RJ85	E2366	N532XJ G-6-366	.16. 4.07	CityJet Ltd "Inishbofin" (Operated Air France)	Paris CDG, France	A2008
EI-RJU	British Aerospace Avro 146-RJ85	E2367	N533XJ G-6-367	.24. 5 07	CityJet Ltd "Cape Clear" (Operated Air France)	Paris CDG, France	A2008
EI-RJV	British Aerospace Avro 146-RJ85	E2370	N534XJ G-6-370	24. 5.07	CityJet Ltd "Lambay Island" (Operated Air France)	Paris CDG, France	A2008
EI-RJW	British Aerospace Avro 146-RJ85	E2371	N535XJ G-6-371	13. 7.07	CityJet Ltd "Garinish Island" (Operated Air France)	Paris CDG, France	A2008
EI-RJX	British Aerospace Avro 146-RJ85	E2372	N536XJ G-6-372	20. 9.07	CityJet Ltd "Scattery Island" (Operated Air France)	Paris CDG, France	A2008
EI-RMC	Bell 206B-3 JetRanger III	488	G-BWLO N2290W	16.12.99	Westair Aviation Ltd	Shannon	A 7.01
EI-ROB	Robin R.1180TD	270	PH-AIG	30. 3.05	Extras Ltd	Waterford	A 8.06
EI-RON	Robinson R44 Raven	1606		19. 7.06	Atlantic Distributors Ltd	Galway	
EI-SAC	Cessna 172P Skyhawk	17276263	N98149	22. 9.00	Sligo Aeronautical Club Ltd	Strandhill, Sligo	A 6.07
EI-SAM	Extra EA.300/200	031	(D-EDGE (5))	19. 7.01	D Bruton	Abbeyshrule	A 5.06
EI-SAR	Sikorsky S-61N (Mitsubishi c/n M61-001)	61-143	G-AYOM N4585, JA9506, N94565	26. 6.98	CHC Ireland Ltd (IMES Rescue titles)	Waterford	A2008
EI-SAT	Steen Skybolt (Built D Hall)	1	N52DH	22.10.99	B O'Sullivan	Abbeyshrule	A 5.06
EI-SBM	Agusta A109E	11174		1. 5.04	Ballymore Management Services Ltd Celtic Heliport, Knocksedan, Dublin Airport		A 6.07
EI-SBP	Cessna T206H Stationair TC	T20608159	N2354M N4234H	16. 8.00	P Morrissey	Oxford	N 1.08
EI-SEA	Progressive Aerodyne Searey Amphibian (Built J Brennan)	1DK359C		19. 4.06	J Brennan	Strandhill, Sligo	A 1.07
EI-SGF	Robinson R44 Raven	1401	N74108	1.10.04	M Reilly and S Filan	Carraroe	
EI-SGN	Robinson R44 Raven	1648		18.10.06	M Reilly and S Filan	Carraroe	A 6.07
EI-SKB	PIper PA-44-180 Seminole	44-7995112	G-BGJB G-ISFT, EI-CHF, G-BGJB, N3046B	17.12.07	Shemburn Ltd	Waterford	
EI-SKE	Robin DR.400-140B Earl	2630	D-ERAA (PH-ASG), (PH-NEW), (PH-NFW)	20.12.07	Shemburn Ltd	Weston, Dublin	
EI-SKG	Robin DR.400-135CDi	2610		30.11.06	Shemburn Ltd	Weston, Dublin	
EI-SKL	Robin DR.400-135CDi	2611		30.11.06	Shemburn Ltd	Weston, Dublin	
EI-SKP	Reims Cessna F172P	F17202101	PH-VSZ D-EOFR	16. 2.06	Shemburn Ltd	Waterford	A 4.06
EI-SKR	Piper PA-44-180 Seminole	44-7995008	G-BOHX N36814	3.08R	Shemburn Ltd	Waterford	
EI-SKS	Robin R.2160	307	OO-OBC	13. 7.04	Shemburn Ltd	Weston, Dublin	A 5.06
EI-SKT	Piper PA-44-180 Seminole	44-7995004	G-BGSG N36538	27.11.02	Shemburn Ltd	Weston, Dublin	A 5.06
EI-SKU	Piper PA28RT-201 Arrow IV	28R-7918145	G-BXYS PH-SBS, N29561	14. 2.03	Shemburn Ltd	Waterford	A 4.06
EI-SKV	Robin R.2160D	171	PH-BLO	28. 3.03	Shemburn Ltd	Weston, Dublin	A 5.06
EI-SKW	Piper PA-28-161 Warrior II	28-8216115	D-EIBV N9630NJ	18. 2.04	Shemburn Ltd	Weston, Dublin	A 5.06
EI-SLA	Aerospatiale-Alenia ATR 42-300	149	SE-LST F-WQNP, G-WFEP, N4210G, F-WWEV (Operated Linkair Express)	4. 3.05	Air Contractors (Ireland)Ltd	Milan-Linate, Italy	A2008
EI-SLC	Aérospatiale-Alenia ATR 42-300	082	OY-CIE D-BATB, F-WWEH	27. 8.04	Air Contractors (Ireland) Ltd (Operated Linkair Express)	Milan-Linate, Italy	A2008
EI-SLF	Aérospatiale-Alenia ATR 72-202	210	OY-RUA B-22703, F-WWEH	26.11.02	Air Contractors (Ireland) Ltd	Dublin	A2008
EI-SLG	Aérospatiale-Alenia ATR 72-201	183	F-WQNI EC-EYK, EC-515, F-WWES	18. 4.05	Air Contractors (Ireland) Ltd	Dublin	A2008
EI-SLH	Aérospatiale-Alenia ATR 72-202	157	OY-RTG F-WQNH, EC-EUJ, EC-384, F-WWEL	12. 8.05	Air Contractors (Ireland)Ltd	Dublin	A2008
EI-SMK	Zenair CH.701 (Built S King)	7-3551		15.10.03	S King	(County Kildare)	
EI-SNJ	Bell 407	53442	N407J PP-MSJ, N6096D, C-GFNR	17.12.03	Moriam Ltd	Dublin	A 6.07
EI-SPB	Cessna T206H Stationair TC	T20608753	N2321V	4.10.07	P Morrissey	Dublin	
EI-SQG	Agusta A109E Power	11084		1. 8.00	Quinn Group Ltd (Operated Premier Helicopters)	Dublin	A 5.07
EI-STR	Bell 407	53282	N44504	19. 5.00	G and H Homes Ltd	(Listowel)	N 1.03
EI-STT	Cessna 172M	17266228	D-EVBB N9557H	30 .8.00	Trim Flying Club Ltd	Trim	A 7.06
EI-SUB	Robinson R44 Raven	1535		17. 1.06	EI-SUB Ltd	Killarney	A 6.07
EI-SWD	Robinson R44 Raven	1633		30. 8.06	New World Plant Ltd	Galway	A 6.07
EI-TAB	Airbus A320-233	1624	F-WWIZ	27. 6.02	CIT Aerospace International Ltd "Mensajero de Esperanza" (Operated TACA) San Salvador-Comalapa, El Salvador		A2008
EI-TAC	Airbus A320-233	1676	F-WWBX (N486TA), F-WWBX	18.10.02	CIT Aerospace International (Operated TACA) San Salvador-Comalapa, El Salvador		A2008
EI-TAD	Airbus A320-233	2301	F-WWDF	6.12.05	Alvi Leasing Ltd (Operated TACA) San Salvador-Comalapa, El Salvador		A2008
EI-TAF	Airbus A320-233	1374	N465TA F-WWIM	24. 3.06	Alix Leasing Ltd (Operated Martinair) San Salvador-Comalapa, El Salvador		A2008
EI-TAG	Airbus A320-233	2791	(N495TA) F-WWBY	1. 6.06	CIT Aerospace International (Operated TACA) San Salvador-Comalapa, El Salvador		A2008
EI-TBM	SOCATA TBM.700	232		3. 7.02	Folens Management Services Ltd	Weston, Dublin	A 4.06

Reg	Type	C/n	Prev id	Date	Owner/Operator	Location	Notes
EI-TGF	Robinson R22 Beta II	3855		1. 7.05	Skyexpress Ltd	Oranmore Heliport, Galway	A 4.06
EI-TIP	Bell 430	49074	N430MK	12. 6.02	Starair (Ireland) Ltd	Dublin	A 5.07
			N9151Z, C-GAHJ				
EI-TKI	Robinson R22 Beta	1195	G-OBIP	22. 8.91	J McDaid	(Slavary, Buncrana)	A10.00
EI-TMH	Robinson R44 Raven	1402		26. 8.04	Architectural Construction Ltd	Weston, Dublin	A 6.07
EI-TOM	Bell 407	53744	N5080N	31. 7.07	Tougher's Oil Distributors Ltd	(Newhall, County Clare)	
			C-FLVT				
EI-TON	Raj Hamsa X'Air 582(5)	718	G-CCCZ	9. 2.06	R A Merrigan	Birr	
	(Built M B Cooke - pr.no.BMAA/HB/200)						
EI-TOY	Robinson R44 Raven	1294		2. 4.03	Metroheli Ltd	Weston, Dublin	A10.05
EI-TWO	Agusta A109E	11131	D-HARY (3)	17. 2.05	Alburn Transport Ltd	Dublin	A 3.06
			B-7770				
EI-UFO	Piper PA-22-150 Tri-Pacer	22-4942	G-BRZR	12. 2.94	W Treacy	Trim	A 4.06
	(Tail-wheel conversion)		N7045D				
EI-UNB	Boeing 767-3P6ER	26234	A4O-GY	16. 1.08	Capablue Ltd	Moscow-Domodedovo, Russia	A2008
					(Operated Transaero Airlines)		
EI-UNI	Robinson R-44 Raven II	11498		8.12.06	Unipipe (Ireland) Ltd	Weston, Dublin	A 6.07
EI-UPA	McDonnell-Douglas MD-11F	48426	I-DUPA	11. 7.05	Pegasus Aviation MD-11-1 Ltd	Rome, Italy	A2008
			N9020Z		*"Gioacchino Rossini" (Operated Alitalia Cargo)*		
EI-UPE	McDonnell-Douglas MD-11F	48427	I-DUPE	27.10.05	Pegasus Aviation MD-11-3 Ltd	Rome, Italy	A2008
					"Giuseppe Verdi" (Operated Alitalia Cargo)		
EI-UPI	McDonnell-Douglas MD-11F	48428	I-DUPI	31. 8.05	Pegasus Aviation MD-11-2 Ltd	Rome, Italy	A2008
			N9020U		*"Giacomo Puccini" (Operated Alitalia Cargo)*		
EI-UPO	McDonnell-Douglas MD-11F	48429	I-DUPO	28. 9.05	Pegasus Aviation MD-11-4 Ltd	Rome, Italy	A2008
					"Nicolo Paganini" (Operated Alitalia Cargo)		
EI-UPU	McDonnell-Douglas MD-11C	48430	I-DUPU	25. 7.06	Pegasus Aviation MD-11-5 Ltd	Rome, Italy	A2008
					"Antonio Vivaldi" (Operated Alitalia Cargo)		
EI-VIC	Robinson R44 Raven II	11644		3. 4.07	Aeroglen Ltd	Dublin	A 6.07
EI-VIV	Bombardier Learjet Model 60	60-305	OH-VIV	18. 7.07	Airlink Airways Ltd	Shannon	A 7.07
			N40050				
EI-VLN	Piper PA-18A-150 Super Cub	18-6797	G-ASCU	17.10.07	D O'Mahoney	(Kilrush)	
			VP-JBL				
EI-WAC	Piper PA-23-250 Aztec E	27-4683	G-AZBK	26. 5.95	Westair Aviation Ltd	Shannon	A 7.01
			N14077				
EI-WAV	Bell 430	49028	N4213V	24.12.97	Westair Aviation Ltd	Shannon	A 5.07
EI-WIG	Best Off Sky Ranger 912(2)	SKR0504608		29. 6.07	M Brereton	Limetree	
	(Built M Brereton)						
EI-WJN	Hawker Siddeley HS.125 Series 700A	257062	N416RD	30. 5.00	Westair Aviation Ltd	Shannon	A 5.07
			N26EA, RA02809, G-5-708, RA02809, (G-BWJX), G-5-708, N7062B, HB-VGF, G-5-708, HB-VGF, G-5-16					
EI-WMN	Piper PA-23-250 Aztec F	27-7954063	G-ZSFT	12.10.00	Westair Aviation Ltd	Shannon	A 5.07
			G-SALT, G-BGTH, N2551M, N9731N					
EI-WRN	Piper PA-28-151 Cherokee Warrior	28-7615212	G-BDZX	5.10.99	Waterford Aero Club Ltd	Waterford	A 4.06
			N9559N				
EI-WWI	Robinson R44 Raven	11799		17. 7.07	Talger Developments Ltd		
						(Baltinglass, County Wicklow)	
EI-WXP	Hawker 800XP	258382	SE-DYE	9.11.07	Westair Aviation Ltd	Shannon	
			N23451				
EI-XLA	Urban Air UFM-10 Samba XLA	XXLA 35		28. 3.06	K.Dardis	Abbeyshrule	N 1.08
EI-YBZ	Robinson R44 Raven	1468		15. 4.05	ILH Enterprises Ltd	Limerick	
EI-YLG	Robin HR200/120B	336	G-BYLG	28.11.05	The Leinster Aero Club Ltd	Weston, Dublin	A 9.07

Registrations awaited 2008:

EI-...	Aerial Arts Chaser S	CH.723	G-MVGI	3.08R	Not known	Mill Farm, Hughley, Much Wenlock
			(Officially transferred from UK to Republic of Ireland 6.1.03 but noted stored as "G-MVGI" 9.04)			
EI-...	Bensen B.8M	PFA G/01-1196	G-BTAH	3.08R	Not known	
	(Built T B Johnson)		*(Officially transferred from UK to Republic of Ireland 25. 4.06)*			
EI-...	Raven Aircraft Raven X	SN2232/0257	G-MTHC	3.08R	*(Officially transferred from UK to Republic of Ireland 25. 4.06)*	
EI-...	Rotary Air Force RAF 2000 GTX-SE	PFA G/13-1302	G-BYDW	3.08R	(R.I.Young)	(Kilrush)
	(Built M T Byrne)		*(Officially transferred from UK to Republic of Ireland 15. 5.06)*			
EI-...	Rans S-4 Coyote	89.098	G-MVXW	3.08R	Not known	
	(Built D Hedley-Goddard - pr.no.PFA 193-11545)		*(Officially transferred from UK to Republic of Ireland 6. 2.07)*			
EI-.	Solar Wings Pegasus XL-Q	SW-WQ-0576	G-MZCP	3.08R	*(Officially transferred from UK to Republic of Ireland 6. 9.07)*	
EI-...	Thruster T.600NT	9067-T600T-009	G-MZHC	3.08R	*(Officially transferred from UK to Republic of Ireland 25.10.07)*	
EI-...	Robinson R44	0822	G-RDWD	3.08R	Redwood Properties Ltd	Weston
			G-EUGN		*(Officially transferred from UK to Republic of Ireland 6.12.07)*	
EI-...	Robinson R44 Raven II	10551	G-CDCA	3.08R	L Behan and Sons Ltd (Rathcoole, County Dublin)	
			(Officially transferred from UK to Republic of Ireland 17. 1.08)			
EI-...	Cessna 172R Skyhawk	17280781	G-TAIT	23. 7.02	(L A Tattan)	(Carrigtwonill, County Cork) 6.12.07E
			G-DREY, N23726		*(Officially transferred from UK to Republic of Ireland 5. 2.08)*	
EI-..	Aérospatiale SA.315B Lama	2489	I-LOGI	3.08R		
			(F-GEEK), N49521			
EI-...	Aérospatiale SA.315B Lama	2568	I-ELPA	3.08R		
			F-GCFO			
EI-...	Aérospatiale SA.315B Lama	2661	I-EPEP	3.08R		
EI-...	Boeing 737-3Q8	23507	N327AW	3.08R	Not known	Kaliningrad-Khrabovo, Russia
			N398US, N348AU, N751L		*(Operated KD Avia)*	
EI-...	Boeing 737-301	23260	N325AW	3.08R	Not known	Kaliningrad-Khrabovo, Russia
			N582US, N309P		*(Operated KD Avia)*	
EI-...	Boeing 737-301	23261	N324AW	3.08R	Not known	Kaliningrad-Khrabovo, Russia
			N583US, N312P		*(Operated KD Avia)*	
EI-...	MBB BK.117B-2	7164	I-HBHG	3.08R		
			D-HBHG, Abu Dhabi Police S-716, D-HBHG			
EI-...	McDonnell Douglas MD-82	49112	9A-CDC	3.08R	Eir Jet Ltd	Shannon
			PK-ALI, PK-IMD, N14814, N814NY, N480AC			
EI-...	Piper J-5A Cub Cruiser	5-36	N27151	3.08R		
			NC27151			
EI-...	Wassmer WA.81 Piranha	804	F-GAIF	3.08R	Not known	Abbeyshrule A 6.07

PART 2 – DE-REGISTERED EXTANT AIRCRAFT

The following have been reported since 2000 and are believed to be extant.

Registration	Type	Construction No	Previous Identity	Reg.Date	Registered Owner (Operator)	(Unconfirmed) Base	CofA Expy
EI-ACY	Auster V J/1 Autocrat	2146	G-AIBK	20. 5.47	Not known	(Dublin)	N 11.07
	(Crashed Oughterard 5. 4.67 and cancelled xx.xx.xx?: noted 11.07 en route Dromore, County.Down to Dublin for rebuild)						
EI-ALU	Avro 643 Cadet	657	G-ACIH		(B Cox) *(Cancelled xx.xx.xx:)*	Frogland Cross	N 9.01
EI-AMF	Taylorcraft Plus D	157	G-ARRK	26. 4.62	C J Baker	Carr Farm,Thorney, Newark	N 1.05
	(Built Auster Aircraft Ltd)		G-AHUM, LB286		*(Cancelled 3.4.70 as WFU: fuselage partly restored)*		
EI-ANA	Taylorcraft Plus D	206	G-AHCG	29.8 .63	N Reilly	Ballyjamesduff	N 9.05
	(Built Auster Aircraft Ltd)		LB347		*(Cancelled as WFU c.1972)*		
EI-APF	Cessna F150G	F150-0112		6. 3.66	Sligo Aero Club Ltd	Kirknewton	N 3.06
	(Built Reims Aviation SA)				*(Cancelled 16.1.06: noted wrecked)*		
EI-ASU	Beagle A.61 Terrier 2	B.633	G-ASRG	10. 1.68	C Lebroda and Partners	Trim	N 1.03
			WE599		*(Cancelled 15.6.77 as "sold abroad" but stored in container)*		
EI-AVC	Reims Cessna F.337F Super Skymaster	0032	N4757	26. 8.71	Not known	Castlerock	N 7.07
	(Wichita c/n 33701355)				*(Cancelled)*		
EI-AYL (2)	Beagle A.109 Airedale				Details in SECTION 1, Part 2	Spanhoe	N 4.03
EI-BAS	Reims Cessna F172M	F17201262		2. 5.75	(Iona National Airways)	Bournemouth	N 6.05
					(Cancelled 6.3.03 as beyond repair: dismantled)		
EI-BBK	Beagle A.109 Airedale				Details in SECTION 1, Part 2	Spanhoe	N 4.03
EI-BGG	SOCATA MS.892E Rallye 150GT	12824	F-GAFS	30. 1.79	M Martin *(Cancelled 31.1.06)*	Abbeyshrule	A 6.04
EI-BHK	SOCATA MS.880B Rallye Club	1307	F-BRJE	20. 8.79	Not known	Kilkenny	N 6.06
					(Cancelled 8.9.00 as WFU: derelict)		
EI-BIC	Reims Cessna F172N Skyhawk II	F17201965	(OO-HNZ)	15. 2.80	Oriel Flying Group Ltd	Abbeyshrule	N 6.04
					(Damaged Castlebar 13.4.95: cancelled 18.11.02: wreck in open storage)		
EI-BKE	Morane MS.885 Super Rallye	278	F-BKUN	9. 2.81	Not known	Abbeyshrule	N 5.06
			F-WKUN		*(Crashed Ballyclumack, Wexford 5.4.81: stripped hulk stored)*		
EI-BKM	Zenith CH.200-RW-AA	2-471		2. 2.81	D van de Braam	Clonkeen, Emyvale	N2002
	(Built Dr McGann)				*(Cancelled 28.2.94 as "sold (spares) UK": stored)*		
EI-BNR	American Aviation AA-5 Traveler	AA5-0203	N9992Q	1. 3.83	Not known	Abbeyshrule	N 5.06
	(Regd with c/n 202 in error)		CS-AHJ		*(DBR on 21.2.88: cancelled 22.7.88: soted wrecked)*		
EI-BSF	Avro 748 Series 1/105	1544	EC-DTP	28. 5.86	Ryanair Ltd *"Spirit of Tipperary"*	Dublin	N 1.04
			G-BEKD, LV-HHF, LV-PUM		*(Fuselage used as cabin trainer for fire training in all-white c/s)*		
EI-CAA	Reims FR172J Rocket	FR17200486	17. 8.89		O.Bruton	Abbeyshrule	N 5.06
			5Y-ATO		*(Damaged 1993/94: cancelled 27.11.98 as WFU: noted wrecked)*		
EI-CAZ	Fairchild-Hiller FH-227D	519	SE-KBR	23. 9.91	Norwich Airport Fire Service	Norwich	N 2.06
			C-FNAK, CF-NAK, (N701U, N2735R *(Cancelled 15.12.94: dumped*				
EI-CFV	SOCATA MS.880B Rallye Club	1850	G-OLFS	13. 5.92	Not known	Abbeyshrule	N.5.06
			G-AYYZ		*(Cancelled 15.11.00 as scrapped: noted wrecked)*		
EI-CHN	SOCATA MS.880B Rallye Club	901	G-AVIO	22. 2.93	Limerick Flying Club (Coonagh) Ltd	Abbeyshrule	N 5.06
					(Cancelled 3.7.03 as scrapped: noted wrecked)		
EI-CJD	Boeing 737-204ADV	22966	G-BKHE	18. 2.94	Dublin Airport Authority	Dublin	N 1.05
			(G-BKGU)		*(Cancelled 29.10.04 as WFU: used for tug practice and other duties)*		
EI-CJE	Boeing 737-204ADV	22639	G-BJCU	10. 3.94	(Ryanair Ltd) *(Jaguar titles)*	Prestwick	N10.04
			EC-DVE, G-BJCU		*(Cancelled 16.11.04 as WFU: stored engineless)*		
EI-CJF	Boeing 737-204ADV	22967	G-BTZF	24. 3.94	(Ryanair Ltd)	Prestwick	N10.04
			G-BKHF, (G-BKGV)		*(Cancelled 25.11.04 as WFU: stored)*		
EI-CKQ	Boeing 737-2K2ADV	22906	PH-TVS	7.10.94	Ryanair Ltd	Bournemouth	N 7.05
					(Canceled 29.10.04 as WFU: fuselage stored)		
EI-CKR	Boeing 737-2K2ADV	22025	PH-TVR	4. 5.95	Ryanair Ltd	(Moston, Manchester)	N12.06
			C-FICP, PH-TVR, (D-AJAA), PH-TVR *(Cancelled 19.10.04 as WFU: fuselage only)*				
EI-CKS	Boeing 737-2T5ADV	22023	PH-TVX	1. 6.95	Ryanair Ltd	Prestwick	N10.04
			OE-ILE, PH-TVX, G-BGTW		*(Cancelled 1.12.04 as WFU: stored)*		

The following are preserved in Museums and available private collections. Full details are shown in SECTION 4, Part 1.

Registration	Type	Base
("EI-ABH")	HM.14 Pou-du-Ciel replica	Meath
EI-AKA	Fokker F-27 Friendship 100	Lelystad, Netherlands
EI-ALR	Douglas C-47-DL Dakota	Nimes-Garons, Gard, France
EI-ALT	Douglas C-47A-10-DK Dakota	Paris Le Bourget, France
EI-APT (2)	Fokker D.VII/65 replica	Antwerp, Belgium
EI-APU (2)	Fokker D.VII/65 replica	Marlborough, New Zealand
EI-APV	Fokker D.VII/65 replica	Birmingham, Alabama, US
EI-ARC	Pfalz D.III replica	Marlborough, New Zealand
EI-ARD	Pfalz D.III replica	Marlborough, New Zealand
EI-ARS (2)	Douglas C-54E-5-DO Skymaster	Rhein-Main Air Force Base, Frankfurt, Germany
EI-ATP	Phoenix Luton LA-4A Minor	Stauning, Denmark
EI-AYO (2)	Douglas DC-3A-197	Wroughton, Wiltshire
EI-BAG	Cessna 172A	Langford Lodge, Belfast, Northern Ireland
EI-BUO	Aero Composites Sea Hawker	Langford Lodge, Belfast, Northern Ireland

PART 3 – AIRCRAFT REGISTERED and CANCELLED in 2007 and 2008

EI-DUW	ABS Aerolight Xenon R	CAK177OR		18. 1.07	S Brennan	To F-xxxx	2.11.07
EI-DVV	Embraer EMB-170-200LR (ERJ-175)	17000154	PT-SET	28. 2.07	Celestial Aviation Trading 20 Ltd	To SP-LIF	xx.3.07
EI-DVW	Embraer EMB-170-200LR (ERJ-175)	17000153	PT-SER	27. 2.07	Celestial Aviation Trading 20 Ltd	To SP-LIE	xx.3.07
EI-DZD	Boeing 737-7Q8	28210	5T-CLK	12.10.07	Castle 2003-2 Ireland Ltd (Operated Sterling Airlines)		
	N341LF, LV-YYC, N801LF, (HB-III), N5573P					Reserved as OY-MRS	1.08
EI-GMA	Schleicher ASW 27B	27174	EI-151	28. 3.07	K Houlihan	To G-CKRM	6 .2.08
EI-ICE	Raytheon Hawker 400A	RK-521	N521XP	27. 6.07	Airlink Airways Ltd	To N521XP	10.12.07
EI-SLI	Aérospatiale-Alenia ATR 472-320	115	CS-TLR	28. 9.07	Air Contractors (Ireland) Ltd	To 5Y-BVD	18.10.07
	PT-MTO, HK-4205, HK-4205X, XA-TPZ, XA-MAR, F-WWEL						

SECTION 3

PART 1 – ISLE OF MAN IRELAND REGISTER

The Isle of Man civil aircraft register came into existence on 1st May.2007. The Isle of Man is a self-governing British Crown Dependancy and not part of the UK or the European Union. Unlike the UK register it is possible to transfer existing registrations to other aircraft. At present there are no plans to include public commercial transport aircraft on this register. Our thanks go to Brian Johnson, Alan Johnson and Paul Hewins.

Only one registration was cancelled in 2007 (M-ANSL) details of which we have included below rather than allocating a separate Part 2 to it this year.

Registration	Type	Construction No	Previous Identity	Date	Registered Owner (Operator)	(Unconfirmed) Base	Status
M-AGIC	Cessna 680 Citation Sovereign	680-0138	N51984	20. 6.07	Trustair Ltd	Blackpool	A12.07
M-AJDM	Cessna 525A CitationJet CJ2	525A-0009	F-HAPP	22. 1.08	Mazia Investments Ltd		
			N525LC, N5235G			(Tortola, British Virgin Islands)	
M-ALAN	Piper PA-30 Twin Comanche C	30-1982	G-BKCL	18.12.07	A Burrows	Ronaldsway	A 1.08
			G-AXSP, N8824Y				
M-ANIN	SOCATA TB-20 Trindad GT	2161	N882	3. 8.07	Harland Aviation Ltd	Ronaldsway	A10.07
			F-OIMA				
M-ANSL	Cessna 560 Citation Encore	560-0773	N5207A	29.10.07	ITTUR AB	Cancelled. To SE-RIT 12.07	xx
M-AZDA	Piper PA-28			3.08R			
M-BIGG	Bombardier CL-600-2B16	5722	C-FOGE	24. 1.08	Signal Aviation Ltd	(Jersey)	
	(CL-600 Challenger)						
M-BONO	Cessna 172N Skyhawk II	17270299	G-BONO	19.11.07	J D McCandless	Newtownards	A12.07
			C-GSMF, N738WS				
M-BWFC	Cessna 560 Citation XLS+	560-5690	N560FC	1. 5.07	Bakewell Industries Ltd	Ronaldsway	A 1.08
			(VP-BWC), N5130J				
M-CHEM	Dassault Falcon 2000EX EASy	128	N628SA	1.11.07	INEOS Aviation LLP	Bournemouth	A 1.08
			(VP-BOE), F-WWGS				
M-DASO	Dassault Falcon 50	268	G-DASO	15. 1.08	Bramptonia Ltd	Coventry	A 1.08
			G-ITIH, F-WQBL, N268FJ, F-WQBL, PH-JNL, CS-TMS, EC-GTR, F-WWHS				
M-EDIA	Piper PA-34-200T Seneca	34-7970055	G-TAIR	18.12.07	Nigel Kenny Aviation Ltd	Ronaldsway	
			N3059H				
M-ELON	Cessna 525B CitationJet CJ3	525B-0148	N148CJ	1. 5.07	Sleepwell Aviation Ltd	Ronaldsway	A 1.08
			N52397				
M-ERIT	Agusta-Westland AW139	31102		13.12.07	Merit Engineering Ltd	Enniskillen	A 1.08
M-FALC	Dassault Falcon 900EX	31	HZ-OFC4	31.10.07	Noclaf Ltd	Luton	
			F-GSAI, F-WWFC				
M-FOUR	Beech A36 Bonanza	E-3541	N68MR	13.12.07	Larvotto LP	Kemble	A 1.08
			N5111Y, (N566C), N5111Y				
M-GINZ	SOCATA TB-20 Trinidad GT	2140	N565G	18. 7.07	Whitesand Investments Ltd	Blackpool	A11.07
M-GULF	Gulfstream Aerospace Gulfstream IV	1082	N1082A	17. 8.07	Earth One Ltd	Ronaldsway	A 1.08
			(N82BR), N1082A				
M-HAWK	Hawker 800XP	258494	VP-BXP	15.11.07	INEOS Aviation LLP	Bournemouth	A 1.08
			N808TA				
M-HDAM	British Aerospace BAe 125 Series 800B	258037	7O-ADC	3. 8.07	ABG Air Ltd	(Farnborough)	A 1.08
			4W-ACN, G-5-501, G-5-15				
M-ICKY	Pilatus PC-12/45	508	N508DL	19.10.07	Saxon Logistics Ltd	Goodwood	A 1.08
			(N118CD), N508DL, ZS-KAL				
M-ICRO	Cessna 525A CitationJet CJ2+	525A-0347	N5262X	2. 5.07	Pektron Group Ltd	Gamston	A12.07
M-IDAS	Agusta A109E Power	11112	N555GS	16.10.07	Trustair Ltd	(Euxton, Chorley)	A10.07
			N109LF				
M-LLGC	Bombardier BD-700-1A11 Global 5000	9227	C-FJNZ	31.10.07	LL Avia Management SA	(Limassol, Cyprus)	A 1.08
M-MANX	Cessna 425 Conquest	425-0044	N425HS	16. 8.07	Mastercraft Ltd	Wycombe Air Park	A10.07
			N555BE, VH-PTH, N6774L				
M-NEWT	Bombardier BD-100-1A10 Challenger 300	20151	C-FLQX	13.11.07	Sterling Aviation Properties LLP	Luton	A12.07
M-NINE	Beech G58 Baron	TH-2203	N220Q	13.12.07	Larvotto LP	Kemble	A12.07
M-ONTY	Sikorsky S-76B	760356	G-BWDO	15. 5.07	Trustair Ltd	Blackpool	A 1.08
			VR-CPN, N9HM				
M-OORE	Beech 350 Super King Air	FL-569	N569KA	14. 1.08	Byecross (IOM) Ltd	Ronaldsway	A 1.08
M-OTOR	Beech C90A King Air	LJ-1733	N590PS	29.11.07	Pektron Group Ltd	Gamston	A12.07
M-PHML	American General AG-5B Tiger	10141	G-PHML	19.12.07	I J Ross and J R Shannon	Ronaldsway	A 1.08
			PH-MLB				
M-RAVA	LET L.200D Morava	171402	OK-RHJ	24. 1.08	R H Jowett	(Derbyhaven, Isle of Man)	
			(OK-MAL), SP-NXY, SP-NAC				
M-RURU	Dassault Falcon 900B	140	N900UT	31.10.07	Opus Nominees Ltd	Luton	A 1.08
			N70HS, VR-CES, F-WWFL				
M-SAIR	Dassault Falcon 900B	141	C-GHML	21. 9.07	W A Developments International Ltd	Carlisle	A12.07
			XA-OVA, XA-OVR, N141FJ, F-WWFK (Operated Stobart Air)				
M-SUEC	Piper PA-32-301XTC Saratoga	3255029	G-SUEC	3.08R	(H L Chan)	Ronaldsway	A 2.08
			D-EGTC, N30908				
M-TAGB	Bombardier BD-100-1A10 Challenger 300	20172	C-FPMU	30. 1.08	TAG Aviation (UK) Ltd	Farnborough	
M-XONE	Cessna 525 CitationJet CJ2	525A-0031	VP-BFC	20. 6.07	Newshore Ltd	Jersey	A 1.08
			N312CJ, N5204D				
M-YAKW	Cessna 208B Grand Caravan	208B1059	G-OAKW	1.11.07	A K Webb	Wellesbourne Mountford	A 1.08
			N4024W, N5075K				
M-YJET	Dassault Falcon 2000LX			7.08R			
M-YNJC	Embraer EMB-135BJ Legacy	14500961	G-ONJC	31. 8.07	Newjetco (Europe) Ltd	London Stansted	A10.07
			PT-SFI				
M-YSKY	Raytheon 390 Premier 1A	RB-209	N209BP	6.11.07	RB209 IOM Ltd	Ronaldsway	A 1.08

SECTION 4

PART 1 – UK & EIRE CIVIL REGISTERED AIRCRAFT IN MUSEUMS AND PRIVATE COLLECTIONS

The publication of Bob Ogden's *"Museum and Collections of North America"* by Air-Britain in 2007 has allowed another opportunity to update the North American entries below. Details are only shown fro collections which are readily accessible to public viewing. Some Museums and collections also hold aircraft which have current Certificates of Registration and these entries remain pertinent to SECTION 1 therefore. Full access details to the all the North American museums, and a great deal more information, can be found in Bob Ogden's book.

Thanks to Bryan Foster (South Africa), Dave Hughes (New Zealand), Bernard Martin and Bob Ogden for updates. Other updating details have been taken from Museum websites.

Registration	Type	Construction No	Previous Identity	Date	Remarks	CofA Expy

ENGLAND

BEDFORDSHIRE
Stondon Transport Museum, Lower Stondon SG16 JN (www.transportmuseum.co.uk)

G-AXOM	Penn-Smith Gyroplane	DJPS.1		26. 9.69	Cancelled 11.10.74 as WFU	24. 2.71P
	(Volkswagen 1600)					
BAPC.77	Mignet HM.14 Pou-Du-Ciel	xxxx			*(As "G-ADRG")*	
	(Citroën 425cc) *(Modern reproduction)*					

Richard Shuttleworth Trustees, Old Warden SG18 9EP (www.shuttleworth.org)

G-AHKX	Avro 19 Series 2				Details in SECTION 1, Part 2	
G-BSSY	CSS-13 Aeroklubowy	0094	YU-CLJ	6.11.90	Cancelled 23. 6.94 by CAA - sold as N588NB 7.94	
	(Licence built Polikarpov Po-2?) *(The quoted c/n is suspect)*				*(As fictitious "ZK-POZ" 7.03)*	
G-KAPW	Percival P.56 Provost T.1				Details in SECTION 1, Part 2	
G-RETA	CASA 1-131E Jungmann Series 2000				Details in SECTION 1, Part 2	
BAPC.1	Roe Triplane IV reconstruction				See G-ARSG in SECTION 1, Part 2	
BAPC.2	Bristol Boxkite reconstruction				See G-ASPP in SECTION 1, Part 2	
BAPC.3	Bleriot Type XI				See G-AANG (2) in SECTION 1, Part 2	
BAPC.4	Deperdussin Monoplane				See G-AANH (2) in SECTION 1, Part 2	
BAPC.5	Blackburn Monoplane				See G-AANI (2) in SECTION 1, Part 2	
BAPC.8	Dixon Ornithopter reconstruction	xxxx				
BAPC.11	English Electric Wren composite				See G-EBNV in SECTION 1, Part 2	
BAPC.271	Messerschmitt Me 163B Komet fsm	xxxx			*(As "191454")*	
	(Walter HWK 509A-2 rocket motor) *(Wingless)*					

BERKSHIRE
Museum of Berkshire Aviation/Royal Berkshire Aviation Society and The Herald Society (+) ,Woodley RG5 4UF

G-AJJP	Fairey FB.2 Jet Gyrodyne	F.9420 & FB.2		1. 3.47	Cancelled 9.11.50 - to RAF as XD759 @ 11.50	
					(As "XJ389")	
G-AKKY	Miles M.14A Hawk Trainer 3	2078	T9841	23. 6.48	Cancelled 12. 4.73 as WFU	6.11.64
	(Also allocated BAPC.44 to reflect rebuild status from various parts)				*(WFU 11.60) (As "L6906")*	
G-APWA	Handley Page HPR.7 Dart Herald 100 (+)	149	PP-SDM	28. 9.59	Cancelled 29. 1.87 as WFU	6. 4.82T
			G-APWA, PP-SDM, PP-ASV, G-APWA *(BEA titles)*			
G-MIOO	Miles M.100 Student 2	M1008	G-APLK	26.10.84	See SECTION 1. Part 2	
			G-MIOO, G-APLK, XS941, G-APLK, G-35-4 *(On rebuild as "G-APLK" 3.02)*			
BAPC.233	Broburn Wanderlust sailplane	---			*Built 1946*	
BAPC.248	McBroom Hang Glider	---			*Built 1974*	
BGA 562	EoN AP.5 Olympia 2B	EoN/O/037	G-ALJZ			
			BGA 562			
BGA 589	EoN AP.7 Primary	EoN/P/012	G-ALMN			
			BGA 589			

BRISTOL
City Museum and Art Gallery, Clifton BS8 1RL (www.bristol-city.gov.uk/museums)

BAPC.40	Bristol Boxkite reconstruction	BOX 3 & BM.7281			*(Built for "Those Magnificent Men in Their Flying Machines" film)*	
	(Gnome)					

Bristol Aero Collection, Filton *(also see Gloucestershire and Kemble)*

G-BOAF	British Aircraft Corporation Concorde Type 1 Variant 102	216 & 100-016	G-N94AF 12. 6.80 G-BFKX		Cancelled 4. 5.04 as WFU	11. 6.04T

CAMBRIDGESHIRE
Imperial War Museum, Duxford CB2 4QR (www.iwm.org.uk)

G-ACUU	Cierva C.30A	726	(G-AIXE)	26. 6.34	Cancelled 14.11.88 as WFU	30. 4.60
	(Avro 671) (AS Civet)		HM580, G-ACUU		*(WFU 4.60) (As "HM580:KX-K")*	
G-AFBS	Miles M.14A Hawk Trainer 3	539	(G-AKKU)	17. 9.37	Cancelled 22.12.95 by CAA	25. 2.63
			BB661, G-AFBS		*(Dismantled and unmarked 4.03)*	
G-AHTW	Airspeed AS.40 Oxford 1	3083	V3388	6. 6.46	Cancelled 3. 4.89 by CAA *(As "V3388")*	15.12.60
G-ALCK	Percival Proctor III	H.536	LZ766	18. 6.48	WFU *(As "LZ766")*	19. 6.63
G-AMDA	Avro 652A Anson 1	xxxx	N4877	20. 7.50	Cancelled 9. 9.81 by CAA *(As "N4877:MK-V")*	14.12.62
G-ASKC	de Havilland DH.98 Mosquito TT.35	xxxx	TA719	8. 7.63	Crashed 27. 7.64 *(As "TA719:6 T")*	18. 1.64
G-BCYK	Avro (Canada) CF-100 Canuck Mk.IV	xxxx	RCAF 18393	18. 3.75	Cancelled 15. 9.81 as WFU	
					(As "18393" in RCAF c/s)	
G-BEDV	Vickers 668 Varsity T.1	xxxx	WJ945	26. 7.76	Cancelled 15. 6.89 by CAA *(As "WJ945:21")*	15.10.87P
G-BESY	British Aircraft Corporation 167 Strikemaster Mk.80A G-27-299	PS.364	Saudi AF 1133, G-27-299	26. 4.77	British 7.77 *(As "1133" in Saudi c/s)*	
	(Officially regd as Mk.88)					
G-LANC	Avro 683 Lancaster B.X	xxxx	RCAF KB889	31. 1.85	Cancelled 2. 9.91 by CAA	
	(Built Victory Aircraft, Canada)				*(As "KB889:NA-I" in RAF 428 Sqdn c/s)*	

G-LIZY   Westland Lysander III   "504/39" RCAF 1558 20. 6.86 Cancelled 18. 4.89 as WFU
      (C/n also quoted as "Y1351")   V9300   (As "V9673:MA-J" in RAF 161 Sqdn c/s)
G-USUK   Colt 2500A Balloon (Hot Air)   1100   1. 6.87 Cancelled 21. 8.90 as WFU "Virgin Atlantic Flyer"   19. 8.87P
                     (On loan from Virgin Atlantic Airways Ltd) (Gondola displayed - remainder stored)
EI-AUY   Morane-Saulnier MS.502 Criquet   338   F-BCDG 30.11.70 Cancellation details not known
      (Argus AS.10)   French Military   (On loan from G Warner) (As "CF+HF" in Luftwaffe c/s)
BAPC.93   Fieseler Fi 103 (V-1)   xxxx   (BAPC identity unconfirmed)
BAPC.209   Supermarine Spitfire LF.IXC fsm   xxxx   (As "MJ751:DU-V" in RAF 321 Sqdn c/s) (Built for "Piece of Cake" TV series)
BAPC.267   Hawker Hurricane fsm   xxxx   (As "P2954:WX-E" in RAF c/s)

American Air Museum, Duxford
G-BFYO   SPAD XIII replica   0035   D-EOWM 16.11.78 Cancelled 14.10.86 as WFU   21. 6.82P
      (Built Williams Flugzeugbau) (Lycoming AIO-360)   (As "1 4513 S" in 3rd Escadrille French AF c/s)
G-BHDK   Boeing TB-29A-45-BN Superfortress   11225   44-61748 27. 9.79 Cancelled 29. 2.84 as WFU "Hawg Wild"
                             (As "461748:Y" in USAF c/s)
G-BHUB   Douglas C-47A-85DL Dakota   19975   "G-AGIV" 30. 4.80 Cancelled 19.10.81 as WFU
                  Spanish AF T3-29, N51V, N9985F, SE-BBH, 43-15509 (As "315509:W7-S" in USAAF c/s)
BAPC.255   North American P-51D Mustang fsm   xxxx   (As "463209:WZ-S" in 78th FG c/s)
      (Built Rialto, CA, US 1990)

Duxford Aviation Society, Duxford
G-ALDG   Handley Page HP.81 Hermes IV   HP.81/8   27.10.49 WFU 9.62   9. 1.63
                           (BOAC titles) "Horsa" (Unmarked fuselage only)
G-ALFU   de Havilland DH.104 Dove 6   04234   14.12.48 Cancelled 14.11.72 as WFU   4. 6.71
G-ALWF   Vickers 701 Viscount   5   2. 1.50 Cancelled 18. 4.72 as WFU   16. 4.72
G-ALZO (2)   Airspeed AS.57 Ambassador 2   5226   R Jordan AF 108 5. 4.50 Cancelled 10. 9.81 as WFU   14. 5.71
                      G-ALZO, (G-AMAD)   (Unmarked 4.03)
G-ANTK   Avro 685 York C.1   xxxx   MW232   23. 7.54 WFU Lasham 30. 4.64 (Dan Air titles)   29.10.64T
G-AOVT   Bristol 175 Britannia 312   13427   23. 6.58 Cancelled 21. 9.81 as WFU (Monarch titles)   11. 3.75T
G-APDB   de Havilland DH.106 Comet 4   6403   9M-AOB   2. 5.57 Cancelled 18. 2.74 as WFU   7.10.74
                      G-APDB   (Dan-Air titles)
G-APWJ   Handley Page HPR.7 Dart Herald 201   158   28. 9.59 Cancelled 10. 7.85 as WFU (Air UK titles)   21.12.85
G-ASGC   Vickers Super VC-10 Series 1151   853   11. 4.63 WFU 15.4.80 (BOAC-Cunard titles)   20. 4.80
G-AVFB   Hawker Siddeley HS.121 Trident 2E 2141   5B-DAC   1. 2.67 Cancelled 9. 7.82   30. 9.82
                      G-AVFB   (WFU 27.3.82) (BEA titles)
G-AVMU   British Aircraft Corporation One-Eleven 510ED   11. 5.67 Cancelled 12. 7.93 as WFU   8. 1.95T
                  BAC.148   (British Airways titles) "County of Dorset"
G-AXDN   British Aircraft Corporation Concorde   01   16. 4.69 Cancelled 10.11.86 as WFU   30. 9.77
      (Officially regd with Bristol c/n 13522)

CHESHIRE
Hooton Park Trust and Griffin Trust (&), Hooton Park L65 1BQ
G-AGPG   Avro 652A Anson 19 Series 2   1212   15. 6.45 Cancelled 5.11.75   13. 2.71
      (Originally regd as Anson XII, to Anson XIX - 1.47 and to Avro 19 Series.2 - 5.52) (On loan from The Aeroplane Collection)
G-AJEB   Auster J/1N Alpha   2325   14. 3.47 Cancelled 9. 6.81 as WFU   27. 3.69
                            (On loan from The Aeroplane Collection)
BAPC.68   Hawker Hurricane fsm (&)   xxxx   "P3975"   (Built for "Battle of Britain" film) (As "H3426")
BAPC.204   McBroom Hang Glider   xxxx

CORNWALL
Land's End Theme Park, Land's End TR19 7AA
G-BCXO   MBB BÖ.105DD   S.80   D-HDCE 27. 2.75 Cancelled 4. 3.92 as WFU
      (C/n S.80 is the original pod, replaced @1992 and subsequently rebuilt as display piece "G-CDBS")
"G-CDBS"   MBB BÖ.105DD   See above
BAPC.137   Sopwith Baby Floatplane replica   xxxx   Ex Leisure Sport
      (Built FEM Displays Ltd 1978)

CUMBRIA
Solway Aviation Museum and Edward Haughey Aviation Heritage Centre, Carlisle CA6 4NW (www.solway-aviation-museum.org.uk)
G-APLG   Auster J/5L Aiglet Trainer   3148   4. 3.58 Cancelled 11. 2.99 by CAA   26.10.68
G-AYFA   Scottish Aviation Twin Pioneer Mk.3 538   G-31-15 15. 6.70 Cancelled 16. 5.91 as WFU   24. 5.82
      (Originally regd as a CC.2)   XM285   (Nose only)
G-BJWY   Sikorsky S-55 (HRS-2) Whirlwind HAR.21 55xxx A2576   25. 1.82 Cancelled 23. 2.94 by CAA
                      WV198, Bu.130191   (As "WV198:K") (On loan from D.Charles)

RAF Millom Museum, Haverigg LA18 4NA
G-BIHN   Airship Industries Skyship 500 Airship (Gas Filled)   2.11.80 Cancelled 31. 1.91 by CAA   1. 4.79
                  1214/02   (Destroyed San Francisco, Ca, US 1985: gondola only)
BAPC.231   Mignet HM.14 Pou-Du-Ciel   xxxx   (On loan from South Copeland Aviation Group)
      (Thought originally built @ Ulverston 1936 with Anzani engine)   (As "G-ADRX")
BAPC.260   Mignet HM.280   xxxx

Windermere Steamboat Centre, Windermere LA23 1BN (www.steamboat.co.uk)
BGA 266   Slingsby T.1 Falcon 1 Waterglider   237A   29. 5.36

DEVON

Trago Mills Shopping Mall, Newton Abbot

G-BDDX	Whittaker MW2B Excalibur	PFA 041-10106		28. 5.75	WFU 1976
	(Built M W Whittaker - c/n 001) (Volkswagen 1500)				

DORSET

Bournemouth Aviation Museum, Bournemouth BH23 6SE (www.aviation-museum.co.uk)

G-AZMF	British Aircraft Corporation One-Eleven 530FX		7Q-YKJ	14. 1.72	Cancelled 10. 3.06 as WFU	Bournemouth	22. 1.04T
		BAC.240	G-AZMF, PT-TYY, G-AZMF		*(European VIP First c/s) "The European Express"*		
G-BEYF	Handley Page HPR.7 Dart Herald 401	175	FM1022	13. 7.77	Cancelled 18.11.99 as WFU		11. 3.01T
					(On loan from Dart Group PLC)		
G-BKRL	Chichester-Miles Leopard	001		21. 3.83	Cancelled 25. 1.99 as WFU		14.12.91P
	(Noel Penny 301)						
G-BRFC	Percival P.57 Sea Prince T.1				Details in SECTION 1, Part 2		
G-BRNM	Chichester-Miles Leopard	002		17.10.89	Cancelled 31. 1.05 as WFU		
G-BWAF	Hawker Hunter F 6A	S4/U/3393	8831M	24. 2.95	Details in SECTION 1, Part 2		
G-DHTT	de Havilland DH.112 Venom FB.50 (FB.1)				Details in SECTION 1, Part 2		
G-MIGG	PZL-Mielec Lim-5				Details in SECTION 1, Part 2		
G-OPAS	Vickers 806 Viscount	263	G-AOYN	5.10.94	Cancelled 28. 7.97 as destroyed		26. 3.97T
					(WFU 6.96 Southend and broken up) (Parcelforce titles) (Nose only)		

NB: Museum closed 12.07, exhibits may be re-located.

GLOUCESTERSHIRE

Jet Age Museum, Gloucestershire (*Awaiting permanent home*)

BAPC.72	Hawker Hurricane fsm	xxxx			*(Built for "Battle of Britain" film)*
					(As "V6799:SD-X" of RN 501 Sqdn c/s)
BAPC.259	Gloster Gamecock	xxxx			*(Under construction 2.04)*

Bristol Aero Collection, Kemble GL7 6BA(www.bristolaero.com) (*To move to Bristol Filton 2006/7*)

G-ALBN	Bristol 173 Mk.1	12871	7648M	22. 7.48	Cancelled - to RAF as XF785 in 1953
			XF785		*(As "XF785")*
G-ALRX	Bristol 175 Britannia Series 101	12874	(WB473)	25. 6.51	Cancelled 5. 4.54 as Withdrawn
			(VX447)		*(DBR landing Littleton-upon-Severn 4.2.54)*
					(Nose only - on loan from Britannia Aircraft Preservation Trust)
G-ATDD	Beagle B.206 Series 1	B.013	(VH-...)	27. 4.65	U/c collapsed Sherburn 6.73 and cancelled
	(Originally regd as Beagle B.206R - to Series 1 1966)				G-ATDD *(Nose only)*
BAPC.87	Bristol 30/46 Babe III reconstruction	1			*(As "G-EASQ")*
	(Built W.Sneesby)				

Britannia Aircraft Preservation Trust, Kemble

G-BDUP	Bristol 175 Britannia Series .253	13508	EL-WXA	31. 3.76	Cancelled 9. 8.84 to CU-T120 @ 8.84.
			CU-T120, G-BDUP, XM496		*(As "XM496" in RAF c/s)*

HAMPSHIRE

Farnborough Air Sciences Trust (FAST Museum) Farnborough GU16 6DH

G-AWZI*	Hawker Siddeley HS.121 Trident 3B Series 101			14. 1.69	Cancelled 9. 7.87 as destroyed	5. 8.85T
		2310			*(WFU 1.5.85: cockpit only)*	
G-9-449	Hawker Hunter FGA.9	xxxx	XE650		*(Front fuselage only)*	

Whittle Memorial, Ively, Farnborough

BAPC.285	Gloster E28/39 fsm	xxxx			
	(Built Sir Frank Whittle Commemorative Trust)				

Prince's Mead Shopping Centre, Farnborough

BAPC.208	Royal Aircraft Factory SE.5A	xxxx			*(As "D276:A")*
	(Built AJD Engineering)				

Second World War Aircraft Preservation Society, Lasham

G-APIT	Percival P.40 Prentice 1	PAC-016	VR192	28.11.57	Cancelled 8.11.79 as WFU *(As "VR192")*	7. 9.67
G-APXX	de Havilland DHA.3 Drover 2	5014	VH-EAS	15.12.59	Cancelled 26.11.73 as WFU - regn not taken up	
			VH-EAZ		*(As "VH-FDT")*	

Museum of Army Flying, AAC Middle Wallop SO20 8DY (www.flying-museum.org.uk)

G-ABOX (2)	Sopwith Pup				Details in SECTION 1, Part 2	
G-AKKR	Miles M.14A Hawk Trainer 3	1995	"T9967"	23. 6.48	Cancelled 16. 7.69 as PWFU	10. 4.65
	(May be T9967 [2160] from 1943 rebuild)		8378M, G-AKKR, T9708		*(As "T9707")*	
G-AKOW	Taylorcraft J Auster 5	1579	PH-NAD (2)	23.12.47	Cancelled 5. 8.87 as WFU	26. 6.82
	(Regd as c/n TJ569A after rebuild in Holland)		PH-NEG, G-AKOW, TJ569		*(As "TJ569")*	
G-APOI	Saunders-Roe Skeeter Series 8				Details in SECTION 1, Part 2	
G-APXW	Lancashire Aircraft EP-9 Prospector	43		22.12.59	Cancelled 20. 5.82	22. 5.76
					(Composite rebuild ex G-APWZ and others) (As "XM819" in Army c/s)	
G-ARYD	Auster AOP.6	xxxx	WJ358	8. 3.62	Cancelled 5. 8.87 as WFU *(Conversion abandoned 9.63) (As "WJ358")*	
G-AXKS	Westland-Bell 47G-4A	WA.723	G-17-8	22. 7.69	Cancelled 22. 4.82 as WFU	21. 9.82
G-SARO	Saro Skeeter AOP.12				Details in SECTION 1, Part 2	
BAPC.80	Airspeed AS.58 Horsa II				*(Composite from LH208, TL659 and 8569M) (As "KJ351")*	
BAPC.163	AFEE 10/42 Rotachute Rotabuggy reconstruction				*(On loan from Wessex Aviation Society) (As "B-415")*	
BAPC.185	WACO CG-4A Hadrian Glider	xxxx			*(Fuselage only) (As "243809")*	
BAPC.261	General Aircraft Hotspur replica	xxxx			*(As "HH379")*	
	(Composite from anonymous cockpit of Mk.1 and rear of Mk.II, HH379)					
BGA 285	Slingsby T.6 Kite 1	247A	G-ALNH		*(As "G-2-4" in 1 GTS RAF c/s)*	
			BGA 285			

Solent Sky, Southampton SO1 1FR (www.spitfireonline.co.uk)

| G-ADWO | de Havilland DH.82A Tiger Moth | 3455 | BB807 | 9.12.35 | Cancelled 15. 9.58 as destroyed | |
| | | | G-ADWO | | (As "BB807") | |

(Restored 3.51 and overhauled with fuselage of BB860 (ex G-ADXT): damaged landing Christchurch 31. 7.58 and WFU: fuselage/parts ex G-AOAC and parts ex G-AOJJ used in composite rebuild 1987/90: completed to static condition 1990)

G-ALZE	Britten-Norman BN-1F	1		16. 3.50	Cancelled 8. 6.89 as WFU	
G-BRDV	Replica Viking Spitfire prototype	PFA 130-10796		3. 7.89	Cancelled 19.5.00 as WFU	18. 2.95P
	(Built Viking Wood Products - c/n HD36/001) (Jaguar V-12 350hp)				*(As "K5054" in RAF c/s) (On loan from Replica Spitfire Ltd)*	
G-SWIF	Vickers Supermarine 552 Swift F.7	VA.9597	XF114	1. 6.90	Cancelled 19. 7.04 as WFU	
BAPC.7	Southampton University Man Powered Aircraft (SUMPAC)					
BAPC.164	Wight Quadraplane Type 1 fsm	xxxx			*(As "N248")*	
BAPC.210	Avro 504J	xxxx			*(As "C4451")*	
	Built AJD Engineering) (Gnome Monosoupape 100hp)					
BAPC.215	Airwave Hang Glider	xxxx				
BAPC.253	Mignet HM.14 Pou-Du-Ciel replica	xxxx			*(Built 1990s) (As "G-ADZW") (On loan from H.Shore)*	

HERTFORDSHIRE
Galleria Shopping Mall, Hatfield

| BAPC.257 | de Havilland DH.88 Comet fsm | xxxx | | | *(As "G-ACSS") "Grosvenor House"* |

de Havilland Aircraft Heritage Centre, Salisbury Hall, London Colney AL2 1BU (www.dehavillandmuseum.co.uk)

G-ABLM	Cierva C.24	710		22. 4.31	Cancelled as WFU 12.34	16. 1.35
	(DH Gipsy III)				(On loan from Science Museum)	
G-ADOT	de Havilland DH.87B Hornet Moth	8027	X9326	?.11.35	Cancelled as WFU	15.10.59
			G-ADOT			
G-AMXR	de Havilland DH.104 Dove 6	04379	D-CFSB	21. 1.53	Cancelled 22. 7.54 - to D-CFSB 7.54	
			G-AMXR, N4280V		(Subsequently and as D-IFSB (1))	
G-ANRX	de Havilland DH.82A Tiger Moth	3863	N6550	25. 5.54	WFU 23. 9.74 as WFU	20. 6.61
G-AOJT	de Havilland DH.106 Comet IXB	06020	F-BGNX	11. 5.56	Cancelled 9. 7.56 as WFU	5. 7.56
					(Fuselage only) (As "F-BGNX" in Air France titles)	
G-AOTI	de Havilland DH.114 Heron 2D	14107	G-5-19	25. 7.56	Cancelled 17.10.95 as WFU (Unmarked)	24. 6.87T
G-AREA	de Havilland DH.104 Dove 8	04520		3. 8.60	Cancelled 19. 9.00 by CAA	18. 9.87
G-ARYC	de Havilland DH.125 Series 1	25003		1. 3.62	Cancelled 31. 3.76 as WFU (WFU 1.8.73)	1. 8.73
G-AVFH	Hawker Siddeley HS.121 Trident 2E	2147		1. 2.67	Cancelled 12. 5.82	18. 5.83T
					(WFU 24.10.81) (Forward fuselage only)	
G-AWJV	de Havilland DH.98 Mosquito TT.35	xxxx	TA634	21. 5.68	Cancelled 19.10.70 as WFU (As "TA634:8K-K" in RAF 571 Sqdn c/s)	
G-BBNC	de Havilland DHC-1 Chipmunk T.10	C1/0682	WP790	12.10.73	Cancelled 23. 9.74 as WFU (As "WP790:T")	
G-BLKA	de Havilland DH.112 Venom FB.Mk.54 (FB.4)	960	(G-VENM (1))	13. 7.84	Cancelled 13.10.00 by CAA	14. 7.95P
	(Built F + W) (Officially regd as c/n 431)		Swiss AF J-1790		(Unmarked pod only)	
G-VNOM	de Havilland DH.112 Venom FB.50 (FB.1)	842	Swiss AF J-1632	13. 7.84	Details in SECTION 1 Part 2	
BAPC.186	de Havilland DH.82B Queen Bee composite		"K3584"		(As "LF789:R2-K")	
		xxxx	(Original p/i not known)			
BAPC.216	de Havilland DH.88 Comet fsm	xxxx			(As "G-ACSS")	
BAPC.232	Airspeed AS.58 Horsa I/II Glider composite				(Composite airframe from unidentified components)	
		xxxx				

KENT
Brenzett Aeronautical Museum Trust, Brenzett TN29 0EE

| G-AMSM | Douglas C-47B-20-DK Dakota | 15764/27209 | KN274 | 28. 4.52 | Cancelled 11. 9.78 as WFU | |
| | | | 43-49948 | | (Ground-looped on take-off Lydd 17. 8.78) (Nose only) | |

Dover Museum, Dover (www.dovermuseum.co.uk)

| BAPC.290 | Fieseler Fi.104 flying-bomb fsm |

Battle of Britain Memorial, Capel Le Ferne, Folkestone

BAPC.291	Hawker Hurricane I fsm	xxxx		(As "P2970:US-X" in RAF 56 Sqdn c/s)
	(Built GB Replicas)			"Little Willie"
BAPC.299	Supermarine Spitfire I fsm	xxxx		(As "R6775:YT-J" in RAF 72 Sqdn c/s))'
	(Built GB Replicas)			

Kent Battle of Britain Museum, Hawkinge CT18 7AG (www.kbobm.org)

BAPC.36	Fieseler Fi 103 (V-1) fsm	xxxx		(Built for "Operation Crossbow" film)
BAPC.63	Hawker Hurricane fsm	xxxx	"L1592"	(Built for "Battle of Britain" film)
				(As "P3208:SD-T" in RAF 501 Sqdn c/s)
BAPC.64	Hawker Hurricane fsm	xxxx		(Built for "Battle of Britain" film)
				(As "P3059:SD-N" in RAF 501 Sqdn c/s)
BAPC.65	Supermarine Spitfire fsm	xxxx		(Built for "Battle of Britain" film)
				(As "N3289:DW-K" in RAF 610 Sqdn c/s)
BAPC.66	Messerschmitt Bf109 fsm	1480		(Built for "Battle of Britain" film) (As "480/6")
BAPC.67	Messerschmitt Bf109 fsm	xxxx		(Built for "Battle of Britain" film) (As "14" in JG52 c/s)
BAPC.69	Supermarine Spitfire fsm	xxxx		(Built for "Battle of Britain" film)
				(As "N3313:KL-B" in RAF 54 Sqdn c/s)
BAPC.74	Messerschmitt Bf109 fsm	6357		(Built for "Battle of Britain" film) (As "6357:6")
BAPC.133	Fokker Dr.1 fsm	xxxx		(As "425:17")
BAPC.272	Hawker Hurricane fsm	xxxx		(As "N2532:GZ-H" in RAF 32 Sqdn c/s)
BAPC.273	Hawker Hurricane fsm	xxxx		(As "P2921:GZ-L" in RAF 32 Sqdn c/s)
BAPC.278	Hawker Hurricane fsm	xxxx		(As "P3679:GZ-K" in RAF 32 Sqdn c/s)
BAPC.297	Supermarine Spitfire reproduction	xxxx		
BAPC.298	Supermarine Spitfire IX fsm	xxxx		

Lashenden Air Warfare Museum, Headcorn TN27 9HX

| BAPC.91 | Fieseler Fi.103R-IV Reichenberg | xxxx | | (Under restoration 4.03) |

RAF Manston History Museum, Manston CT12 5DF (www.raf-manston.fsnet.co.uk)
G-AZCM	Beagle B.121 Pup Series .150	B121-155	G-35-155	30. 7.71	Cancelled 4. 5.72 as sold abroad *(To HB-NAV 5.72)*
G-BWJZ	de Havilland DHC-1Chipmunk 22	C1/0653	WK638	23.11.95	Cancelled as WFU 4.4.00

Medway Aircraft Preservation Society, Rochester ME5 9TX
(G-ALSP)	Bristol 171 Sycamore 3	12900		17.11.50	Regn NTU and cancelled 26. 3.52 - *to RAF as WV783 @ 4.52*
					(As "WV783")
G-36-1	Short SB.4 Sherpa	SH.1604	G-14-1		Cancelled - WFU 5.66
	(Short & Harland Experimental & Research Aircraft)				*(Fuselage only)*

LEICESTERSHIRE
Snibston Discovery Park, Coalville LE67 3LN
G-AFTN	Taylorcraft Plus C2	102	HL535	2. 5.39	Cancelled 13. 1.99 by CAA	1.11.57
			G-AFTN			
G-AGOS	Reid and Sigrist RS.4 Desford Trainer	3	VZ728	?. 5.45	Cancelled 9.11.81 as WFU	28.11.80P
			G-AGOS		*(As "VZ728")*	
G-AIJK	Auster V J/4 Archer	2067		13.11.46	CofA expired and WFU	24. 8.68

Charnwood Museum, Loughborough LE11 3QU
G-AJRH	Auster J/1N Alpha	2606		12. 5.47	Cancelled 18. 1.99 by CAA	5. 6.69

Whittle Memorial A426, Lutterworth
BAPC.284	Gloster E28/39 fsm	xxxx	
	(Built Sir Frank Whittle Commemorative Trust)		

East Midlands Aeropark, East Midlands Airport
G-APES	Vickers 953C Vanguard Merchantman	721		9. 9.57	Cancelled 28. 2.97 as WFU *(Nose only)* "Swiftsure"	2.10.95T
G-BAMH	Westland S-55 Whirlwind Series 3	WA.83	VR-BEP	10. 1.73	Cancelled 31.10.73 - to VR-BEP 10.73	
			G-BAMH, XG588		*(As "XG588 in SAR c/s)*	
G-BEOZ	Armstrong-Whitworth AW.650 Argosy 101	6660	N895U	28. 3.77	Cancelled 19.11.87 as WFU	28. 5.86T
			N6502R, G-1-7		*(Elan titles)* "Fat Albert"	
G-BHDD	Vickers 668 Varsity T.1	xxxx	WL626	18.10.79	Details in SECTION 1, Part 2	
(G-BLMC)	Avro 698 Vulcan B.2A		XM575	R	Reservation @ 8.84 not taken up *(As "XM575")*	
G-FRJB	Aircraft Designs Sheriff SA-1	0001		18. 5.81	Cancelled 6. 2.87 by CAA	
					(Not completed: unfinished airframe without marks)	

Stanford Hall and Percy Pilcher Museum, Stanford Hall, Stanford LE17 6DH (www.stanfordhall.co.uk)
BAPC.45	Pilcher Hawk Glider reconstruction	xxxx	
	(Built Armstrong-Whitworth Aviation apprentices 1957/58)		

Thorpe Camp Visitor Centre, Woodhall Spa (www.thorpecamp.org.uk)
"G-AJOZ"	Fairchild F,21W-41A Argus 1		*(Full-scale replica)* **(Original at Elvington qv)**
BAPC.294	Fairchild Argus fsm		

LINCOLNSHIRE
Lightning Association, Binbrook LN8 6DR
G-BTSY	English Electric Lightning F.6	95207	XR724	25. 7.91	Cancelled 26. 5.92 as TWFU - no Permit issued
					(As "XR724")

Battle of Britain Memorial Flight, RAF Coningsby LN4 4SY
G-AISU	Vickers Supermarine 349 Spitfire LF.VB	AB910		25.10.46	Cancelled as transferred to Military Marks
		CBAF.1061			*(As "AB910:IR-G" in RAF 222 Sqdn c/s)*
G-AMAU	Hawker Hurricane IIc	xxxx	PZ865	1. 5.50	Cancelled 19.12.72 as transferred to Military Marks
	(12,780th and final Hurricane built)				*(As "PZ865:JX-E" in RAFSEAC c/s)*
G-AWIJ	Vickers Supermarine 329 Spitfire IIA	CBAF.14	P7350	25. 4.68	Cancelled 29. 2.84 to MOD "Blue Peter"
					(Returned to RAF) (As "P7350:XT-D" in RAF 603 Sqdn c/s)

Royal Air Force Cranwell
BAPC.225	Supermarine Spitfire IX fsm	xxxx	*(As "P8448:"UM-D" in RAF 52 Sqdn c/s)*

Royal Air Force Digby
BAPC.229	Supermarine Spitfire IX fsm	xxxx	"L1096"	*(As "MJ832:DN-Y" in RAF 416 Sqdn c/s) "City of Oshawa"*

Lincolnshire Aviation Heritage Centre, East Kirkby (www.lincsaviation.co.uk)
G-ASXX	Avro 683 Lancaster B.VII	xxxx	(8375M)	22.10.64	Cancelled 16.2.79 as WFU
			French Navy WU-15, NX611		
	(As "NX611:LE-C" in RAF 630 Sqdn c/s "City of Sheffield" [starboard] and "NX611:DX-C" in RAF 57 Sqdn c/s "Just Jane" [port])				

Bomber County Aviation Musem, Hemswell (www.lineone.net/~bcam)
G-AEJZ	Mignet HM.14 Pou-Du-Ciel	TLC.1	G-AEJZ	9. 6.36	Cancelled 31.12.38 in census
	(Built T L Crosland)				*(Allocated "BAPC.120") (As "G-AEJZ") (Stored 3.04)*

Aerial Application Collection, Wainfleet
G-BFBP	Piper PA-25-235 Pawnee D	25-7756033		7. 9.77	Cancelled 21. 6.78 as destroyed
					(Crashed near Comberton, Cambridge 11.5.78) (Cockpit only)
G-BFEY	Piper PA-25-235 Pawnee D	25-7756039		20.10.77	Cancelled 17. 7.90 as WFU *(Fuselage frame only)*	19.1.87

LONDON
Croydon Airport Visitor Centre, Croydon (www.croydon.gov.uk/airport-soc/)
G-ANKV	de Havilland DH.82A Tiger Moth	84166	T7793	30.12.53	Cancelled 9.56 - not converted	
	(Provenance uncertain)				*(As "T7793" in RAF c/s)*	
G-ANUO	de Havilland DH.114 Heron 2D	14062		27. 9.54	Cancelled 9. 8.96 as WFU	12. 9.86T
					(As "G-AOXL" in Morton Air Services c/s) (Note original G-AOXL below)	

"G-AOXL"   de Havilland DH.114 Heron 2D   See above
                                                                                 (Note original G-AOXL at Flyhistorick Museum Sola, Stavangar-Lufthavn)
BAPC.168   DH.60G Moth reconstruction   8058   *"Jason" (As "G-AAAH")*

British Airports Authority, Heathrow
G-BOAB   British Aircraft Corporation Concorde Type 1 Variant 102 G-N94AB   3. 4.74   Cancelled 4. 5.04 as WFU   19. 9.01T
             208 & 100-008   G-BOAB

Royal Air Force Memorial Chapel, Biggin Hill
BAPC.219   Hawker Hurricane I fsm   xxxx   *(As "L1710:AL-D" in RAF 79 Sqdn c/s)*
BAPC.220   Supermarine Spitfire I fsm   xxxx   *(As "N3194:GR-Z" in RAF 92 Sqdn c/s)*

Royal Air Force Museum, Hendon NW9 5LL (www.rafmuseum.org.uk)
G-EBIC   Royal Aircraft Factory.SE.5A   688/2404   "B4563"   26. 9.23   Cancelled 31.12.38   3. 9.30
             (Wolseley Viper 200hp) *(Regd with c/n 687/2404)*   9208M, G-EBIC, F937   *(WFU 9.30) (As "F938")*
G-EBJE   Avro 504K   927   (9205M)   ?. 7.24   Cancelled ?.12.34   29. 9.34
             (Includes components of Avro 548A G-EBKN ex E449)   *(As "E449")*
G-AAMX (2)   American Moth Corporation DH.60GM Moth   125   NC926M   11. 9.86   Cancelled 19. 8.95 as WFU   7. 5.94P
             (DH Gipsy II)
G-AANJ (2)   Luft-Verkehrs Gesellschaft C.VI   4503   9239M   29.10.81   Cancelled 11.12.03 as WFU   16. 5.03P
             (Benz @ 230hp)   C7198, 18, "1594", C7198, 18 *(As "7198:18" in German Air Force c/s)*
             (Composite aircraft including parts from LVG 1594: captured 1916/17 and allotted RFC serial "XG7")
G-ABBB   Bristol 105A Bulldog IIA   7446   "K2227"   12. 6.30   Cancelled 22. 9.61 as PWFU
                                                      G-ABBB, R-11, G-ABBB   *(As "K2227")*
G-ABMR   Hawker Hart   H.H-1   "J9933"   28. 5.31   Cancelled 2. 2.59 - to "J9933" and later "J9941")
                                                      G-ABMR   *(As "J9941" in RAF 57 Sqdn c/s)*   11. 6.57
G-AETA   Caudron G.III   7487   O-BELA   29. 1.37   Sold to RAF 1972
             (Anzani 90hp) *(Also reported as c/n 5019 or 5021)*   O-BELA, (9203M)   *(As "3066" in RNAS c/s)*
G-AFDX   Hanriot HD.1   "HD.1" OO-APJ   4. 5.38   Cancellation details not known
                                                      Belgian AF H-1, Belgian AF N75 *(As "HD-75")*
             (DBR landing Old Warden 17.6.39: wings destroyed in air raid Brooklands 1940, fuselage survived and rebuilt 1968)
G-AGYX   Douglas C-47A-10DK Dakota 3   12472   5N-ATA   15. 1.46   Cancelled 1.7.65 - to PH-MAG 7.65
                                                      PH-MAG, G-AGYX, (OD-...), G-AGYX, KG437, 42-9264 *(Subsequently N9050T) (Nose only)*
G-AITB   Airspeed AS.40 Oxford 1   xxxx   MP425   1.11.46   WFU *(As "MP425" in RAF 1536 BATF c/s)*   24. 5.61
G-AIXA   Taylorcraft Plus D   134   LB264   13. 1.47   Cancelled 13.12.02 by CAA *(As "LB264")*   21. 2.02P
G-APUP   Sopwith Pup replica   B.5292 & PFA 1582   9213M   13. 2.59   Cancelled 4.10.84 by CAA   28. 6.78
             (Built K C D St Cyrien) Le Rhone)   G-APUP, N5182   *(As "N5182")*
G-ATVP   Vickers FB.5 Gunbus replica   VAFA-01 & FB.5   31. 5.66   Cancelled 27. 2.69 as WFU   6. 5.69
             (Built Vintage Aircraft and Flying Association) (Gnome Monosoupape 100 hp)   *(As "2345" in RFC c/s)*
G-AWAU   Vickers FB.27A Vimy replica   VAFA-02   "H651"   8. 1.68   Cancelled 19. 7.73 as WFU *"Triple First" (As "F8614")*   4. 8.69
G-BEOX   Lockheed 414 Hudson IIIA   414-6464   VH-AGJ   25. 3.77   Cancelled 22.12.81 as WFU
             (A-29A-LO)   VH-SMM, R.Australian AF A16-199, FH174, 41-36975 *(As "A16-199: SF-R")*
G-BFDE   Sopwith Tabloid Scout replica   168   "168"   22. 9.77   Cancelled 8.12.86 as WFU   4. 6.83P
             (Built D M Cashmore - pr.no.PFA 067-10186) (Continental PC.60)   *(As "168" in RNAS c/s)*
G-BIDW   Sopwith "1½" Strutter replica   WA/5   "9382"   24. 9.80   Cancelled 4. 2.87 by CAA   29.12.80P
             (Built Westward Airways (Lands End) Ltd) (Le Clerget)   *(As "A8226" in RFC 45 Sqdn c/s)*
G-BLWM   Bristol 20 M.1C replica   -------   "C4912"   12. 3.85   Cancelled 12. 5.88 by CAA   12. 8.87P
             (Built D M Cashmore - pr.no.PFA 112-10862) (110 hp Gnome)   *(As "C4994" in RFC c/s)*
G-OIOI   EH Industries EH-101 Heliliner   50008   23.11.88   Cancelled 1. 4.96 - to MOD   5. 5.94P
             (Airframe No.PP8)   *(To RAF as "ZJ116")*
G-OTHL   Robinson R22 Beta   0738   G-DSGN   28.11.94   Cancelled 8. 2.00 as WFU *(As "G-RAFM")*   27. 4.03T
G-USTV   Messerschmitt Bf.109G-2/Trop   xxxx   8478M   26.10.90   Cancelled as PWFU 24. 9.98   30. 5.98P
             (Built Erla Maschinenwerk GmbH)   10639   RN228, Luftwaffe   *(As "10639/6" in Luftwaffe III/JG77 c/s)*
BAPC.83   Kawasaki Type 5 Model 1b (Ki 100)   xxxx   8476M   *(As "24")*
BAPC.92   Fieseler Fi 103 (V-1)   xxxx
BAPC.100   Clarke TWK   xxxx   *(On loan from Science Museum)*
BAPC.106   Bleriot Type XI   xxxx   9209M   *(As "164")*
             (1910 original) (Anzani 40hp)
BAPC.107   Bleriot Type XXVII   xxxx   9202M
             (1911 original)
BAPC.165   Bristol F.2b Fighter   xxxx   *(As "E2466" in RAF 22 Sqdn c/s)*
             (RR Falcon replica)
BAPC.181   Royal Aircraft Factory BE.2b reconstruction   xxxx   *(As "687")*
             (Renault V8) *(Restoration from original components)*
BAPC.205   Hawker Hurricane IIc fsm   xxxx   *(As "BE421:XP-G" in RAF 174 Sqdn c/s)*
BAPC.206   Supermarine Spitfire IX fsm   xxxx   *(As "MH486:FF-A" in RAF 132 Sqdn c/s)*
BAPC.292   Eurofighter Typhoon fsm   xxxx
BAPC.293   Supermarine Spitfire fsm   xxxx
             (Built Concepts and Innovations)
BAPC.296   Army Balloon Factory Nulli reproduction xxxx

Royal Air Force, Bentley Priory, HQ 11/18 Groups
BAPC.217   Supermarine Spitfire I fsm   xxxx   *(As "K9926:JH-C" in RAF 317 Sqdn c/s)*
BAPC.218   Hawker Hurricane IIc fsm   xxxx   "P3386"   *(As "BN230:FT-A"in RAF 43 Sqdn c/s)*

Royal Air Force, Northolt
BAPC.221   Supermarine Spitfire LF.IX fsm   xxxx   *(As "EN526:SZ-G" in RAF 316 Sqdn c/s)*

Royal Air Force, Uxbridge
BAPC.222   Supermarine Spitfire IX fsm   xxxx   *(As "BR600:SH-V" in RAF 64 Sqdn c/s)*

Science Museum, South Kensington, London SW7 2DD (www.sciencemuseum.org.uk)
G-EBIB   Royal Aircraft Factory SE.5A   687/2404   "F939"   26. 9.23   Cancelled 1.12.46   8. 8.35
             (Regd with c/n 688/2404)   G-EBIB, F937   *(WFU)*

G-AAAH	de Havilland DH.60G Moth	804		30. 8.28	Cancelled 12.31	23.12.30

(Original but note two BAPC.reproductions depicted as "G-AAAH" exist –see below) "Jason"

G-ACWP	Cierva C.30A	728	AP507	24. 7.34	Cancelled 1. 6.40 on sale *(Impressment)*	6. 3.41

(Avro 671)   G-ACWP   *(As "AP507:KX-P" in RAF 529 Sqdn c/s)*

G-ASSM	Hawker Siddeley HS.125 Series 1/522	25010	5N-AMK	5. 5.64	Cancelled 28. 5.80 as sold in Nigeria	

      G-ASSM

G-AWAW	Cessna F150F	F150-0037	OY-DKJ	5. 1.68	Cancelled 16. 5.90 as WFU	8. 6.92T

(Built Reims Aviation SA) (Wichita c/n 15063167)

G-AZPH	Pitts S.1S	S1S-001-C	N11CB	13. 3.72	Cancelled 8. 1.97 as WFU	4. 9.91P

(Lycoming IO-360)   *"Neil Williams" (Ground-looped landing Little Snoring 10.5.91)*

G-LIOA	Lockheed 10A Electra	1037	N5171N	6. 5.83	Cancelled 26. 4.02 as WFU	

      NC243, NC14959   *(As "NC5171N")*

G-RNLI	Vickers Supermarine 236 Walrus 1				Details in SECTION 1, Part 2	

BAPC.50	Roe Triplane Type I	xxxx				

(1909 original) (JAP 9hp)

BAPC.51	Vickers FB.27 Vimy IV	13				

(Rebuild of 1919 original) (RR Eagle VIII 360hp)

BAPC.53	Wright Flyer reconstruction	xxxx				

(Built Hatfield)

BAPC.54	JAP/Harding Monoplane	xxxx				

(Built J.A.Prestwich & Co 1910) (Modified Bleriot XI (JAP Anzani 45hp)

BAPC.55	Levasseur-Antoinette Developed Type VII Monoplane					

(1909 original) (Antoinette V8 50hp)   xxxx

BAPC.56	Fokker E.III	xxxx			*(Captured @ Somme, France 4.1916)*	

(Oberusal 100hp)   *(As "210:16") (Skeletal airframe)*

BAPC.62	Cody Type V Biplane	xxxx				

(1912 original) (Austro-Daimler 120hp)   *(As "304")*

BAPC.124	Lilienthal Glider Type XI reconstruction				*(Display reproduction of BAPC.52 qv)*	

      xxxx

BAPC.199	Fieseler Fi 103 (V-1)	xxxx			*(As "442795")*	

BGA 2091	Schempp-Hirth HS.4 Standard Cirrus	396	AGA...		*(As "DFY")*	9. 5.02

Imperial War Museum, South Lambeth, London SE1 6HZ (www.iwm.org.uk)

BAPC.90	Colditz Cock replica	xxxx			*(Built for BBC "The Colditz Story" film)*	

BAPC.198	Fieseler Fi 103 (V-1)	xxxx				

MANCHESTER

Museum of Science and Industry in Manchester, Castlefield, Manchester M3 4JP (www.msim.org.uk)

G-EBZM	Avro 594A Avian IIIA	R3/CN/160		?.7.28	Cancelled 1.12.46 by Secretary of State	20. 1.38

(ADC Cirrus) (Fitted with parts from G-ABEE)   *(On loan from The Aeroplane Collection)*

G-ABAA	Avro 504K	xxxx	9244M	11. 9.30	Cancelled 1939?	11. 4.39

      "H2311", G-ABAA

G-ADAH	de Havilland DH.89 Dragon Rapide	6278		30. 1.35	WFU 1969 *"Pioneer"*	9. 6.47

(Allied Airways (Gandar Dower) titles) (On loan from The Aeroplane Collection)

G-APUD	Bensen B-7Mc	1		11. 5.59	Cancelled 27. 2.70 as WFU	27. 9.60

(On loan from The Aeroplane Collection)

G-AWZP	Hawker Siddeley HS.121 Trident 3B Series 101			14. 1.69	Cancelled 27. 6.86 as destroyed	14. 3.86T

      2317   *(Nose section only)*

G-AYTA	SOCATA MS.880B Rallye Club	1789		19. 2.71	Cancelled 12. 5.93 as WFU	7.11.88

G-BLKU	Colt Flame 56 SS Balloon (Hot Air)	572		17. 7.84	Cancelled 1. 5.92 as WFU *"Mr.Wonderfuel II"*	

G-MJXE	Mainair Tri-Flyer 330/Hiway Demon 175			17. 5.83	Cancelled 19.10.00 as TWFU	21. 3.95P

      102-131082 & HS-001   *(On loan from The Aeroplane Collection)*

BAPC.6	Roe Triplane Type I	xxxx			*"Bullseye Avroplane" (As "14")*	

(JAP @ 9hp)

BAPC.12	Mignet HM.14 Pou-Du-Ciel	xxxx				

(Scott A2S)

BAPC.98	Yokosuka MXY-7 Ohka II	xxxx	8485M		*(As "997")*	

BAPC.175	Volmer VJ-23 Swingwing Powered Hang Glider ---					

(McCulloch @ 9hp)   xxxx

BAPC.182	Wood Ornithopter	xxxx			*(Stored 3.04)*	

BAPC.251	Hiway Spectrum Hang-Glider	xxxx			*(Stored 3.04)*	

(Built 1980)

BAPC.252	Flexiform Wing Hang-Glider	xxxx			*(Stored 3.04)*	

(Built 1982)

BGA 1156	EoN AP.10 460 Series 1	EoN/S/007	BGA 2666	26. 1.64	*(On loan from J.H.May)*	18. 4.97

      AGA.6, BGA 1156   *(As "BQT")*

Aviation Viewing Park, Manchester International Airport

G-AWZK	Hawker Siddeley HS.121 Trident 3B Series 101			14. 1.69	Cancelled 29. 5.90 as WFU	14.10.86T

      2312   *(BEA Quarter Union Jack titles)*

G-BOAC	British Aircraft Corporation Concorde Type 1 Variant 102		G-N81AC	3.4.74	Cancelled 4. 5.04 as WFU	16. 5.05T

      204 & 100-004   G-BOAC

G-DMCA	McDonnell Douglas DC-10-30	48266	N3016Z	12. 3.96	Cancelled 3.11.03 as destroyed	11. 3.03T

(Forward 60 feet of fuselage, including flight deck and 70 seats, retained for use an education classroom)

G-IRJX	BAE SYSTEMS Avro 146-RJX100	E3378		24. 5.00	Cancelled 20. 2.03 as wfu)	

MERSEYSIDE

Wirral Aviation Society, Liverpool Marriott Hotel South, Liverpool-John Lennon Airport (www.jetstream-club.org)

G-ANCF	Bristol 175 Britannia Series 308F	12922	5Y-AZP	3. 1.58	Cancelled 21. 2.84 as WFU	12. 1.81

(Originally regd as Series 305)   G-ANCF, LV-GJB, LV-PPJ, (G-ANCF), G-14-1, G-18-4, G-ANCF, (N6597C)

      (On loan from Britannia Aircraft Preservation Trust) (Fuselage only)

G-JMAC	British Aerospace Jetstream Series 4100	41004	G-JAMD	12. 6.92	Cancelled 21. 5.03 by CAA	6.10.97A

      G-JXLI

G-SEXY	American AA-1 Yankee	AA1-0442	G-AYLM	30. 6.81	Cancelled 15.11.00 by CAA	17. 3.95
	(Regd incorrectly as c/n AA1-0042)				*(Badly damaged in forced landing Burscough, Lancashire 11.2.94)*	
BAPC.280	de Havilland DH.89 Dragon Rapide fsm	xxxx			*"Neptune" (As "G-AEAJ" in Railway Air Services c/s)*	

WEST MIDLANDS
Boulton Paul Aircraft Heritage Project, Pendeford, Wolverhampton WV8 1EU

G-AVVR	Avro 652A Anson 19 Series 2	"34530"	VP519	6.10.67	Cancelled by CAA 16. 9.72 - not converted	
					(On loan from The Aeroplane Collection) (Cockpit only as "VP519")	
G-BPIP	Slingsby T.31 Motor Cadet III				Details in SECTION 1, Part 2	
G-FBPI	Air Navigation and Engineering Co ANEC IV Missel Thrush				Details in SECTION 1, Part 2	
BAPC.274	Boulton & Paul P.6 fsm	xxxx			*(As "X-25")*	
BAPC.281	Boulton Paul Defiant recreation	xxxx			*(As "L7005:PS-B" in RAF 264 Sqdn c/s)*	
BGA 1759	Slingsby T.8 Tutor	xxxx	RAFGSA.178	10.72		
BGA 1992	Hirth Go IV Goevier 3	557	D-5233	13. 7.74	*(As "DBU")*	19. 7.87

NORFOLK
Royal Air Force Coltishall

BAPC.223	Hawker Hurricane I fsm	xxxx			*(As "V7467:LE-D" in RAF 242 Sqdn c/s)*	

City of Norwich Aviation Museum, Norwich Airport NR10 3JE

G-ASKK	Handley Page HPR.7 Dart Herald 211	161	PP-ASU	17. 7.63	Cancelled 29. 4.85 as WFU	19. 5.85T
			G-ASKK, PI-C910, CF-MCK			
G-AWON	English Electric Lightning F.53	95291	G-27-56	9. 8.68	Cancelled 9.68 - to R.Saudi AF as 53-686 4.69	
					(Subsequently RSAF 201, 203 and 1305) (As "ZF592")	
G-BEBC	Westland WS-55 Whirlwind HAR.10	WA.371	8463M	25. 6.76	Cancelled 5.12.83 as WFU	
			XP355		*(Not converted) (As "XP355:A")*	
G-BHMY	Fokker F.27 Friendship 600	10196	F-GBDK (2)	6. 5.80	Cancelled as PWFU 22. 3.03	22. 5.99T
			(F-GBRV), PK-PFS, JA8606, PH-FDL		*(Donated by KLM (UK) Ltd - less engines)*	

NORTHAMPTONSHIRE
Sywell Aviation Museum, Sywell, Northampton (www.sywellaerodrome.co.uk/history)

BAPC.234	Vickers FB.5 Gunbus fsm	xxxx			*(Built 1985 for "Gunbus" film) (As "GBH-7")*	

NORTHUMBERLAND and TYNESIDE
Military Vehicle Museum, Newcastle upon Tyne NE2 4PZ (www.military-museum.org.uk)

G-ANFU	Taylorcraft J Auster 5	1748	TW385	31.10.53	Cancelled 3. 8.76 as WFU	17. 2.71
					(On rebuild with frame of un-identified Auster 5.93) (As "NJ719" with starboard wing ex G-AKPH)	

North East Aircraft Museum, Usworth, Sunderland SR5 3HZ

G-APTW	Westland WS-51/2 Widgeon	WA/H/150		27. 4.59	Cancelled 24. 8.77 as WFU	26. 9.75
G-ARAD	Phoenix Luton LA-5A Major PAL/1204 & PFA 836			29. 4.60	Cancelled 16.10.02 as WFU - completed but not flown	
G-ASOL	Bell 47D-1	4	N146B	31. 1.64	Cancelled 5.12.83 as WFU	6. 9.71
G-AWRS	Avro 652A Anson C.19 Series 2	"33785"	TX213	14.10.68	Cancelled 30. 5.84 as PWFU (WFU 5. 2.73)	10. 8.73
G-BEEX	de Havilland DH.106 Comet 4C	6458	SU-ALM	10. 9.76	Cancelled 19. 5.83	
					(Not converted and broken up Lasham 8.77: nose section only)	
G-MBDL	Striplin (AES) Lone Ranger	109		21.10.81	Cancelled 13. 6.90 by CAA	
G-OGIL	Short SD.3-30 Var.100	SH.3068	G-BITV	23. 1.89	Cancelled 12.11.92 as WFU	21. 4.93T
			G-14-3068		*(Damaged Newcastle 1.7.92)*	
G-SFTA	Westland SA.341G Gazelle 1	1039	G-SFTA	10. 9.82	Cancelled 21. 5.86 as WFU	24. 2.86
			HB-XIL, G-BAGJ, (XW858)		*(Crashed near Alston, Cumbria 7. 3.84) (As "G-BAGJ")*	
BAPC.96	Brown Helicopter	xxxx				
BAPC.97	Luton LA.4 Minor	xxxx			*(As "G-AFUG")*	
	(JAP J99)					
BAPC.119	Bensen B.7 Gyroglider	xxxx				
BAPC.211	Mignet HM.14 Pou-Du-Ciel replica	xxxx			*(As "G-ADVU")*	
	(Built Ken Fern/Vintage and Rotary Wing Collection 1993)					
BAPC.228	Olympus Hang Glider	xxxx				

NOTTINGHAMSHIRE
Wonderland Pleasure Park, Farnsfield, Mansfield

BAPC.288	Hawker Hurricane fsm				*(As "V7467:LE-D" in RAF 242 Sqdn c/s)*	

Newark Air Museum, Winthorpe, Newark NG24 2NY (www.newarkairmuseum.co.uk)

G-AHRI	de Havilland DH.104 Dove 1B	04008	4X-ARI	11. 7.46	Cancelled 18. 5.72 as WFU	
			G-AHRI			
G-ANXB	de Havilland DH.114 Heron 1B	14048	G-5-14	3.12.54	Cancelled 2.11.81 as PWFU	25. 3.79
					(BEA Scottish Airways titles) "Sir James Young Simpson"	
G-APIY	Percival P.40 Prentice 1	PAC-075	VR249	28.11.57	Cancelled 19. 4.73	18. 3.67
					(WFU 18.3.67) (As "VR249:FA-EL" in RAFC c/s)	
G-APNJ	Cessna 310	35335	EI-AJY	2. 6.58	Cancelled 5.12.83 as WFU　　　　　　Newark	28.11.74
			N3635D			
G-APVV	Mooney M.20A	1474	N8164E	30. 7.59	Cancelled 3. 4.89 by CAA *(Crashed at Barton 11.1.81)*	19. 9.81
G-AVVO	Avro 652A Anson 19 Series 2	34219	VL348		Cancelled 16. 9.72 by CAA *(As "VL348")*	6.10.67
G-AYZJ	Westland WS-55 Whirlwind HAS.7	WA.263	XM685	24. 5.71	Cancelled 29.12.80 as WFU	
	(Also c/n WAG/34)				*(As "XM685/PO-513")*	
G-BFTZ	SOCATA MS.880B Rallye Club	1269	F-BPAX	2. 6.78	Cancelled 14.11.91 by CAA	19. 9.81
					(On loan from The Aeroplane Collection)	
G-BJAD	Clutton FRED Series II				Details in SECTION 1, Part 2	
G-BKPG	Luscombe P3 Rattler Strike	003		7. 3.83	Cancelled 31. 7.91 by CAA *(No Permit issued)*	
G-BKPY	SAAB 91B/2 Safir	91321	R NorAF 56321	23. 3.83	Cancelled 8. 2.02 as WFU *(As "56321" in R.NorAF c/s)*	
G-MBBZ	Volmer VJ-24W	7		23. 9.81	Cancelled 29.11.95 as WFU	
G-MBUE	MBA Tiger Cub 440	MBA-001		29. 4.82	Cancelled 6. 9.94 by CAA *(Originally regd as Micro-Bipe c/n 001)*	

G-MJDW	Eipper Quicksilver MXII	RI-01		15. 7.82	Cancelled 13. 2.08 as PWFU	5. 5.07P
	(Cuyuna 430)	*(C/n noted as 3506)*				
BAPC.43	Mignet HM.14 Pou-Du-Ciel replica	xxxx				
	(Scott A2S)					
BAPC.101	Mignet HM.14 Pou-Du-Ciel replica	xxxx				
BAPC.183	Zurowski ZP-1 Helicopter	xxxx			*(Polish AF c/s)*	
	(Panhard 850cc)					

OXFORDSHIRE
Royal Air Force Benson

BAPC.226	Supermarine Spitfire XI fsm	xxxx			*(As "EN343" in PRU c/s)*	

SHROPSHIRE
Royal Air Force Cosford Museum including Michael Beetham Conservation Centre ($), Cosford TF11 8UP (www.rafmuseum.com)

G-EBMB	Hawker Cygnet I **($)**	1	No.14 (Lympne 1924)	29. 7.25	Cancelled 30.11.61	30.11.61
	(Bristol Cherub III)					
G-AEEH	Mignet HM.14 Pou-Du-Ciel	EGD.1		13. 3.36	Cancelled 8.46 in census - WFU 15. 5.38	15. 5.38
	(Built E G Davis)					
G-AEKW	Miles M.12 Mohawk **($)**	298	HM503	14. 7.36	Crashed Spain 1. 1.50	1. 3.50
			G-AEKW, "G-AEKN"			
"G-AFAP"	CASA 352L	163	Spanish AF T2B-272		*(Original British Airways titles)* **(Not original G-AFAP)**	
	(Junkers Ju 52/3m)					
G-AGNV	Avro 685 York C.1	1223	"MW100"	20. 8.45	WFU 9.10.64	6. 3.65
			"LV633", G-AGNV, TS798		*(As "TS798")*	
G-AIZE	Fairchild F.24W-41A Argus II	565	N9996F	18.12.46	Cancelled 6. 4.73	6. 8.66
	(UC-61A-FA)		G-AIZE, 43-14601		*(WFU) (As "FS628")*	
"G-AJOV"	Westland WS-51 Dragonfly HR.3	WA/H/80	WP495		*(BEA titles)* **(Not original G-AJOV)**	
G-AOVF	Bristol 175 Britannia Series 312F	13237	9Q-CAZ	13. 2.57	Cancelled 21.11.84 as WFU	
			G-AOVF		*(BOAC titles)*	
G-APAS	de Havilland DH.106 Comet 1A	06022	8351M	23. 5.57	Cancelled 22.10.58	
			XM823, G-APAS, G-5-23, F-BGNZ		*(BOAC titles)*	
G-BBYM	Handley Page HP.137 Jetstream 200	243	G-AYWR	13. 2.74	Cancelled 7. 6.00 as WFU	20. 9.98A
			G-8-13			
G-BRAM	Mikoyan MiG-21PF	xxxx	Hungarian AF 503	22. 5.89	Cancelled 16. 4.99 by CAA	
					(As "503" in Russian AF c/s)	
BAPC.82	Hawker Afghan Hind	41H/81899			*(R.Afghan AF c/s)*	
	(RR Kestrel)					
BAPC.84	Mitsubishi Ki 46 III (Dinah)	xxxx	8484M		*(As "5439")*	
BAPC.94	Fieseler Fi 103 (V-1)	xxxx	8483M			
BAPC.99	Yokosuka MXY-7 Ohka II	xxxx	8486M			
BGA 572	Slingsby T.21B Sedbergh TX.1 **($)**	539	8884M		*(As "VX275")*	
			VX275, BGA 572			

Assault Glider Association, RAF Shawbury (www.assaultgliderproject.co.uk)

G-AMHJ*	Douglas C-47A-25DK Dakota 6	13468	SU-AZI	6. 2.51	Cancelled 23. 1.03 as wfu	5.12.00A
			G-AMHJ, ZS-BRW, KG651, 42-108962			
BAPC.279	Airspeed AS.58 Horsa reconstruction				*(As "LH291")*	

Wartime Aircraft Recovery Group Aviation Museum, Sleap (www.wargroup.homestead.com)

BAPC.148	Hawker Fury II fsm	xxxx			*(As "K7271" in RAF 1 Sqdn c/s)*	

SOMERSET
The Helicopter Museum, Weston-super-Mare BS24 8PP (www.helicoptermuseum.co.uk)

G-ACWM	Cierva C.30A	715	(G-AHMK)	24. 7.34	Cancelled 17. 3.59 as WFU	13. 7.40
	(Avro 671)		AP506, G-ACWM		*(On loan from E.D.ap Rees) (No external marks)*	
G-ALSX	Bristol 171 Sycamore 3	12892	G-48-1	17.11.50	Cancelled as WFU	24. 9.65
			G-ALSX, VR-TBS, G-ALSX		*(On loan from E.D.ap Rees)*	
G-ANFH	Westland WS.55 Whirlwind Series 1	WA.15		27.10.53	Cancelled 2. 9.77 as WFU	17. 7.71
					(On loan from E.D.ap Rees) (No external marks)	
G-ANJV	Westland WS-55 Whirlwind Series 3	WA.24	VR-BET	14.12.53	Cancelled 8. 1.74 on sale in Bermuda	
			G-ANJV		*(On loan from E.D.ap Rees) (No external marks) (Stored 3.02)*	
G-AODA	Westland WS-55 Whirlwind Series 3	WA.113	9Y-TDA	13. 5.55	Cancelled 23. 9.93 by CAA	23. 8.91A
			EP-HAC, G-AODA		*(Bristow Helicopters c/s) "Dorado"*	
G-AOUJ	Fairey Ultralight Helicopter	F.9424	XJ928	1. 8.56	Cancelled 26. 2.69 as Destroyed	29. 3.59
					(WFU) (On loan from E.D.ap Rees)	
G-AOZE	Westland WS-51/2 Widgeon	WA/H/141	5N-ABW	11. 1.57	Cancelled 20. 6.62 on sale in Nigeria	
			G-AOZE		*(On loan from E.D.ap Rees)*	
G-ARVN (2)	Servotec CR LTH1 Grasshopper 1	1		16. 2.63	Cancelled 14. 3.77 as WFU	18. 5.63
					(On loan from E.D.ap Rees)	
G-ASCT	Bensen B.7Mc	DC.3		14. 8.62	Cancelled 20. 9.73 as PWFU	11.11.66P
	(McCulloch 4318E)				*(Built D.Campbell) (Stored 3.02)*	
G-ASHD	Brantly B.2A	314		2. 4.63	Cancelled 22. 6.67 as Destroyed	5. 6.67
					(Crashed into River Colne, Brightlingsea, Essex 19. 2.67) (Stored 3.02)	
G-ASTP	Hiller UH-12C	1045	N9750C	4. 6.64	Cancelled 24.1.90 by CAA	3. 7.82
G-ATBZ	Westland WS-58 Wessex 60 Series 1	WA/461		22. 3.65	Cancelled as TWFU 23.11.82	15.12.81
					(WFU 5.12.81 - to G-17-4) (Stored 3.02)	
G-ATFG	Brantly B.2B	448		16. 6.65	Cancelled 25. 9.87 as WFU	25. 3.85
	(Composite with parts from G-ASLO and G-AXSR)					
G-ATKV	Westland WS-55 Whirlwind 3	WA/493	VR-BEU	11.11.65	Cancelled 8. 1.74	
			G-ATKV, EP-HAN (1), G-ATKV		*(To VR-BEU 1.74) (Stored 3.02)*	
G-AVKE	Gadfly HDW-1	HDW-1		19. 4.67	Cancelled 12.10.81 as WFU	
	(Continental IO-340A)				*(On loan from E.D.ap Rees)*	

G-AVNE	Westland WS-58 Wessex 60 Series 1	WA.561	G-17-3	15. 5.67	Cancelled 23.11.82 as TWFU	7. 2.83
			G-AVNE, 5N-AJL, G-AVNE, 9M-ASS, VH-BHC, PK-HBQ, G-AVNE, (G-AVMC) (As "G-AVNE" & "G-17-3")			
G-AWRP	Servotec CR.LTH.1 Grasshopper II	GB.1		14.10.68	Cancelled 5.12.83 as WFU	12. 5.72P
G-AXFM	Servotec CR.LTH.1 Grasshopper II	GB.2		19. 5.69	Cancelled 5.12.83 as WFU	
					(Completed as Ground-Running Rig) (Stored 3.02)	
G-AYXT	Westland WS-55 Whirlwind HAS.7 (Series .2	WA.167	XK940	28. 4.71	Cancelled 8. 8.00 by CAA	4. 2.99P
					(As "XK940")	
G-AZAU	Servotec CR.LTH.1 Grasshopper II	GB.3		21. 6.71	Cancelled 5.12.83 as WFU (Incomplete Rig) (Stored 3.02)	
G-AZYB	Bell 47H-1	1538	LN-OQG	4. 7.72	Cancelled 22. 4.85 as destroyed	8. 9.84
			SE-HBE, OO-SHW		(Crashed St.Mary Bourne, Thruxton 21. 4.84)	
					(On loan from E.D.ap Rees) (As "OO-SHW")	
G-BAPS	Campbell Cougar Gyroplane	CA/6000		14. 2.73	Cancelled 21. 1.87 by CAA	20. 5.74
	(Continental O-240-A)				(On loan from A.M.W.Curzon-Howe-Herrick)	
G-BGHF	Westland WG.30 Series 100-60	WA.001.P		4. 1.79	Cancelled 29. 3.89 as WFU	1. 8.86
G-BKFD	Westland WG.30 Series.100	004	G-17-28	22. 6.82	Cancelled 6.12.82 (To N5820T) (Stored 3.02)	
G-BKFF	Westland WG.30 Series.100	006	G-17-30	22. 6.82	Cancelled 6.12.82 (To N5840T) (Stored 3.02)	
G-BKGD	Westland WG.30 Series.100	002	(G-BKBJ)	15. 7.82	Cancelled 15. 4.93 as WFU	6. 7.93
G-BRMA	Westland-Sikorsky S-51 Dragonfly HR.5	WA/H/50	WG719	15. 6.78	Cancelled 30. 3.89 as WFU	
					(On loan from E.D.ap Rees) (As "WG719")	
G-BRMB	Bristol 192 Belvedere HC.1	13347	7997M	15. 6.78	Cancelled 3. 7.96 as WFU	
			XG452		(On loan from E.D.ap Rees) (As "XG452")	
G-EFIS	Westland WG.30 Series 100	014	G-17-18	24. 6.84	Cancelled 27.11.84 (To N114WG 11.84) (As "N114WG")	
G-EHIL	EH Industries EH-101	50003	ZH647	9. 7.87	Cancelled 28.4.99 as PWFU	9. 7.87
	(Airframe No.PP3)				(To MoD as ZH647 9.93 and restored 8.98)	
G-ELEC	Westland WG.30 Series 200	007	G-BKNV	17. 6.83	Cancelled 27. 2.98 as WFU	28. 6.95P
G-HAUL	Westland WG.30 Series 300	020	G-17-22	3. 7.86	Cancelled 22. 4.92 as WFU	27.10.86P
G-LYNX	Westland WG.13 Lynx 800	WA/102	ZA500	6.11.78	Cancelled 27. 2.98 as WFU	
			G-LYNX, ZB500		(As "ZB500")	
G-OTED	Robinson R-22 HP	0209	G-BMYR	17. 1.96	Andrews Heli-Lease Ltd	17. 2.02T
			ZS-HLG		(Cancelled 26. 3.02 as PWFU)	
G-PASB	MBB BÖ.105D	S.135	VH-LSA	2. 3.89	Cancelled 9. 8.94 as WFU	
			G-BDMC, D-HDEC		(Original pod from 1994 rebuild)	
G-RWWW	Westland WS-55 Whirlwind HCC.12	WA/418	8727M	21. 6.90	Cancelled 10. 7.00 as WFU	25. 8.96P
			XR486		(As "XR486" in Queens Flight c/s)	
BAPC.10	Hafner R-11 Revoplane	xxxx				
	(Salmson 45hp)					
BAPC.60	Murray M.1 Helicopter	xxxx				
	(JAPJ99 @ 36hp)					
BAPC.128	Watkinson CG-4 Cyclogyroplane Man Powered Gyroplane Mark IV					
BAPC.153	Westland WG-33 Mock-up	xxxx			(Engineering mock-up)	
BAPC.212	Bensen B.6 Gyrocopter	xxxx			(Stored 3.04)	
BAPC.213	Cranfield Vertigo Man Powered Helicopter				(Stored 3.04)	
		xxxx				
BAPC.264	Bensen B.8M	xxxx			(Built 1984)	
BAPC.289	Gyro-Boat	xxxx				

Fleet Air Arm Museum/FAAM Cobham Hall ($), RNAS Yeovilton BA22 8HT (www.fleetairarm.com)

G-AIBE	Fairey Fulmar 2	F.3707	N1854	29. 7.46	Cancelled 30. 4.59 - to N1854	6. 7.59
			G-AIBE, N1854		(As "N1854")	
G-AIZG	Vickers Supermarine 236 Walrus 1	6S/21840	EI-ACC	20.12.46	Cancelled 1963	
			IAC N-18, L2301		(As "L2301")	
G-AOXG	de Havilland DH.82A Tiger Moth ($)	83805	XL717	3.10.56	Cancelled as sold as XL717 @ 10.56	
			G-AOXG, T7291		(As "G-ABUL")	
G-APNV	Saunders-Roe P.531-1	S2/5268		24. 6.58	Cancelled 1.10.59 - to XN332 @ 10.59 (As "XN332: 759")	
G-ASTL	Fairey Firefly 1	F.5607	SE-BRD	1. 6.64	WFU 3. 2.82	
			Z2033		(As "Z2033: 275 N" in RN 1771 Sqdn c/s)	
G-AWYY	Slingsby T.57 Sopwith Camel F.1 replica	1701	"C1701"	14. 2.69	Cancelled 25.11.91 as WFU	1. 9.85P
	(Clerget)		N1917H, G-AWYY		(As "B6401")	
G-AZAZ	Bensen B.8M ($)	RNEC.1		2. 7.71	Cancelled 19. 9.75 as WFU	
	(Built T E Davies)					
G-BEYB	Fairey Flycatcher replica	WA/3		11. 7.77	Cancelled 12. 7.96 as WFU	
	(Built Westward Airways (Lands End) Ltd)				(As "S1287:5" in FAA c/s)	
G-BFXL	Albatros D.Va replica	0034	D-EGKO	24. 8.78	Cancelled 10. 3.97 as WFU	5.11.91P
	(Built Williams Flugzeugbau) (Ranger 6-440-C5)				(As "D5397:17" in German c/s and "D-EGKO"on lower fuselage)	
G-BGWZ	Eclipse Super Eagle ($)	ESE.007		29. 6.79	Cancelled 5.12.83 as WFU (No external marks)	
G-BIAU	Sopwith Pup replica	EMK 002		4. 1.83	Cancelled 10. 3.97 as WFU	13. 9.89P
	(Built Skysport Engineering) (Le Rhone 80hp)				(As "N6452" in RNAS c/s)	
G-BMZF	WSK-Mielec LIM-2	1B-01420	Polish AF 01420	18.12.86	Cancelled 23. 2.90 as WFU	
	(MiG-15bis)				(In North Korean c/s but with no marks)	
G-BSST	British Aircraft Corporation Concorde 002	002		6. 5.68	Cancelled 21. 1.87 as WFU	31.10.74P
	(Officially regd with Bristol c/n 13520)				(WFU 4. 3.76) (On loan from Science Museum)	
BAPC.58	Yokosuka MXY-7 Ohka II	xxxx			(As "15-1585") (On loan from Science Museum)	
BAPC.88	Fokker Dr.1 5/8th scale model	xxxx			(As "102:17")	
	(Modified Lawrence Parasol airframe)					
BAPC.111	Sopwith Triplane fsm	xxxx			"Black Maria" (As "N5492:B" in Royal Navy Air Service c/s)	
BAPC.149	Short S.27 replica ($)	xxxx				

STAFFORDSHIRE

Royal Air Force Museum Reserve Collection, RAF Stafford

G-ADMW	Miles M.2H Hawk Major	177	DG590	30. 7.35	Cancelled 16. 9.86 by CAA	30. 7.65
			8379M, G-ADMW			
G-AHED	de Havilland DH.89A Dragon Rapide 6	6944	RL962	27. 2.46	Cancelled 3. 3.69 (WFU)	17. 4.68
BAPC.108	Fairey Swordfish IV				(As "HS503")	
BAPC.237	Fieseler Fi 103 (V-1)					

SUFFOLK

Norfolk and Suffolk Aviation Museum, Flixton, Bungay NR35 1NZ (www.aviationmuseum.net)

G-ANLW	Westland WS-51 Series 2 Widgeon	WA/H/133	"MD497"	23. 3.54	Cancelled 15.11.02 as WFU	27. 5.81A
			G-ANLW		(On loan from Sloane Helicopters Ltd)	
G-ASRF	Gowland GWG.2 Jenny Wren	PFA 1300		18. 3.64	Cancelled 11.12.96 by CAA	4. 6.71P
	(Built G W Gowland - c/n GWG.2 using modified Luton Minor wings once fitted to G-AGEP)					
G-AWSA	Avro 652A Anson C.19/2	"293483"	(N5054)	21.10.68	Cancelled 18. 8.69 as sold in US	
			G-AWSA, VL349		(Not delivered) (As "VL349:V7-Q")	
G-AZLM	Cessna F172L	F17200842		31.12.71	Cancelled 15. 4.91 as destroyed	
	(Built Reims Aviation SA)				(Crashed on take off Badminton 23.3.91) (Fuselage only)	
G-BDVS	Fokker F.27 Friendship 200	10232	S2-ABK	20. 4.76	Cancelled 19.12.96 as WFU	
			PH-FEX, PH-EXC, 9M-AMM, PH-FEX (Scrapped 12.96 - nose only) "Eric Gandar Dower"			
G-BFIP	Wallbro Monoplane replica	WA-1		16.12.77	Cancelled 28. 3.01 as TWFU	22. 4.82P
	(McCulloch/Wallis)				(On loan from K.H.Wallis) (No external marks)	
G-MJSU	MBA Tiger Cub 440	SO.75/1		2. 2.83	Cancelled 23. 6.93 by CAA	31. 1.86E
G-MTFK	Moult Trike/Flexiform Striker	DIM-01		23. 3.87	Cancelled 13. 6.90 by CAA	
	(Officially regd with c/n SO.175)					
BAPC.71	Supermarine Spitfire fsm	xxxx	"P9390"		(Built for "Battle of Britain" film)	
			"N3317"		(As "P8140:ZP-K" in RAF 74 Sqdn c/s) "Nuflier"	
BAPC.115	Mignet HM.14 Pou-Du-Ciel replica	xxxx			(On loan from I Hancock)	
	(Douglas 500cc)					
BAPC.147	Bensen B.7 Gyroglider	xxxx			(As "LHS-1")	
BAPC.239	Fokker D.VIII 5/8th scale model	xxxx			(As "694")	
BGA 1461	EoN AP.7 Primary	xxxx	(CDN)		(As "CDN")	5.69*
BGA 2384	Grunau Baby III	xxxx	BGA 2074	7. 6.78	(As "DUD")	29. 3.92
			RAFGSA.374, D-9142			
BGA 4002	Penrose Pegasus 2 replica	001	HKJ	7.93	(As "HKJ")	15. 9.98
BGA 4757	Colditz Cock replica	xxxx	"JTA"	1.00	(As "JTA")	20. 2.00
	(Built Southdown Aero Services and J.Lee)				"Spirit of Colditz"	

Wings Of Liberty Memorial Park, USAF Lakenheath

BAPC.269	Supermarine Spitfire V fsm	xxxx			(As "BM631:XR-C" in RAF 71 Sqdn c/s)	

SURREY

Brooklands Museum, Brooklands, Weybridge KT13 0QN (www.motor-software.co.uk/brooklands)

G-AEKV	Kronfeld (BAC) Drone de luxe	30		13. 1.37	Cancelled 14. 1.99 as WFU	6.10.60P
					(On loan from M.L.Beach) (Allocated BGA 2510 5.79)	
G-AGRU	Vickers 657 Viking 1	112	VP-TAX	8. 5.46	WFU 9.63	9. 1.64
			G-AGRU		"Vagrant" (BEA titles)	
G-APEJ	Vickers 953C Vanguard Merchantman	713		9. 9.57	Cancelled 15.11.96 as WFU	
					"Ajax" (WFU 24.12.92: broken up 1. 6.95: nose section only)	
G-APEP	Vickers 953C Vanguard Merchantman	719		9. 9.57	Cancelled 28. 2.97 as WFU	1.10.98T
					"Superb" (Hunting Cargo Airlines titles)	
G-APIM	Vickers 806 Viscount	412		19.11.57	Cancelled "Viscount Stephen Piercey"	19. 7.88T
					(DBR struck by Short SD.3-30 G-BHWT on 11. 1.88) (British Air Ferries titles)	
G-ARRM	Beagle B.206X	B.001		23. 6.61	WFU 1965? and cancelled 9. 4.74 as PWFU	23.12.64
	(Originally regd as Beagle B.206 Series 1 [B2/1010]: re-designated 9.61)				(On loan to Shoreham Airport Historical Association, Shoreham 5.05	
G-ARVM (2)	Vickers VC-10 Series 1101	815	(G-ARVJ)	16. 1.63	WFU 22.10.79 (Nose only)	5. 8.80
G-ASIX	Vickers VC-10 Series 1103	820		29. 5.63	Cancelled 10.10.74 - to A40-AB @ 10.74) (As "A40-AB")	
G-ASYD	British Aircraft Corporation One-Eleven 475AM			9.11.64	Cancelled 25. 7.94 as WFU	13. 7.94
		BAC.053				
	(Originally regd as Series 400AM: converted to prototype Serie 500 1967: to Series 475EM 1970)					
G-ATJJ	de Havilland DHC.1 Chipmunk 22	C1/0797	WP921	21. 9.65	Restored to RAF as WP921 1.68: cancelled ???	
					(Cockpit section only as "WP921")	
G-BBDG	British Aircraft Corporation Concorde Type 1 Variant 100			7. 8.73	Cancelled 12.81 as WFU	. 3.82P
		13523 & 100-02				
G-BFCZ	Sopwith Camel F.1 replica	WA/2		12.10.77	Cancelled 23. 1.03 as WFU	23. 2.89P
	(Built Westward Airways (Lands End) Ltd) (Clerget 9B)				(As "B7270")	
G-BJHV	Voisin Scale replica	MPS-1		1. 9.81	Cancelled 4. 7.91 by CAA	
	(Built M P Sayer)				(On loan from M.P.Sayer)	
G-MJPB	Manuel Ladybird	WLM-14		9.11.82	Cancelled 13. 6.90 by CAA (On loan from Estate of W.L.Manuel)	
G-VTOL	Hawker Siddeley Harrier T.52	B3/41H/735795	ZA250	27. 7.70	Cancelled 3.90 by CAA	2.11.86S
			G-VTOL, (XW273)			
BAPC.29	Mignet HM.14 Pou-Du-Ciel replica	---			(As "G-ADRY")	
	(Built P.D.Roberts, Swansea 1960/78) (Anzani "V")					
BAPC.114	Vickers Type 60 Viking IV reconstruction	xxxx-	"R4"		(As "G-EBED") (Built for "The Land Time Forgot" film)	
BAPC.177	Avro 504K fsm	xxxx	"G1381"		(As "G-AACA" in Brooklands School of Flying c/s)	
	(Clerget 130hp)					
BAPC.187	Roe Type I Biplane reconstruction	xxxx				
	(Built M.L.Beach) (ABC 24hp)					
BAPC.249	Hawker Fury I fsm	xxxx			(As "K5673" in RAF 1 Sqdn 'A' Flight c/s)	
	(Built Brooklands 1990s)					
BAPC.250	Royal Aircraft Factory SE.5a replica	xxxx			(As "F5475:A") "1st Battalion Honourable Artillery Company"	
	(Built Brooklands 1990s)					
BAPC.256	Santos Dumont Type 20 Demoiselle reconstruction					
	(Built J Aubot 1996/97)	xxxx				
BGA 162	Manuel Willow Wren	xxxx		9.34	"The Willow Wren"	
BGA 643	Slingsby T.15 Gull III	364A	TJ711	11.49	((On loan from M L Beach) (As "ATH")	20. 6.04
BGA 3922	Abbott-Baynes Scud I replica	001		R	(As "HFZ")	

Gatwick Aviation Museum, Charlwood RH6 0BT (www.gatwick-aviation-museum.co.uk)

G-BLID	de Havilland DH.112 Venom FB.50 (FB.1)	Details in SECTION 1, Part 2
G-DACA	Percival P.57 Sea Prince T.1	Details in SECTION 1, Part 2

Reg	Type	c/n	Prev id	Date	Fate	
G-GACA	Percival P.57 Sea Prince T.1				Details in SECTION 1, Part 2	
G-JETH	Hawker Sea Hawk FGA.6				Details in SECTION 1, Part 2	
G-JETM	Gloster Meteor T.7				Details in SECTION 1, Part 2	
G-TURP	Aérospatiale SA341G Gazelle 1	1445	G-BKLS	21. 1.88	Cancelled 17. 8.92 as WFU	2.12.91T
			N17MT, N14MT, N49549		*(No external marks)*	
			(Damaged Stanford-le-Hope 9. 9.91: restored as G-BKLS 5.11.91 for rebuild but cancelled)			
G-VIXN	de Havilland DH.110 Sea Vixen FAW.2 (TT)				Details in SECTION 1 Part 2	

Redwing Presrvation Trust, Redhill RH1 5JY

G-ABNX	Robinson Redwing 2				Details in SECTION 1 Part 2	

Wings Museum, Redhill RH1 5JY

G-AIUA	Miles M.14A Hawk Trainer 3				Details in SECTION 1 Part 2	
G-KOOL	de Havilland DH.104 Sea Devon C.2/2				Details in SECTION 1 Part 2	
G-OJAS	Auster J/1U Workmaster				Details in SECTION 1 Part 2	

SUSSEX

Shoreham Airport Historical Association, Shoreham Airport BN43 5FF (www.thearchiveshoreham.co.uk)

G-ARRM	Beagle B.206				On loan from Brooklands Museum, Surrey *(qv)*	
BAPC.20	Lee-Richards Annular Biplane replica	xxxx			*(Built for "Those Magnificent Men in Their Flying Machines" film)*	
BAPC.300	Piffard Hummingbird reproduction	xxxx				

Trailer Visitor Centre, Shoreham Airport BN43 5FF (www.thearchiveshoreham.co.uk)

BAPC.277	Mignet HM.14 Pou-Du-Ciel replica	xxxx			*"L'Autre Aviation" on tail*	

Tangmere Military Aviation Museum, Tangmere PO20 6ES (www.tangmere-museum.org.uk)

BAPC.214	Supermarine Spitfire prototype fsm	xxxx			*(As "K5054")*	
BAPC.241	Hawker Hurricane I fsm	xxxx			*(As "L1679:JX-G" in RAF 1 Sqdn c/s)*	
	(Built Aerofab 1994)					
BAPC.242	Supermarine Spitfire VB replica	xxxx			*(As "BL924:AZ-G" in RAF 234 Sqdn c/s)*	
	(Built TDL Reps 1994)				*"Valde Maar Atterdag"*	

Foulkes-Halbard Collection, Filching Manor, Wannock BN26 5QA

G-BHNG	Piper PA-23-250 Aztec E	27-7405432	N54125	13. 5.80	Cancelled 12.12.86 by CAA	
	(Badly damaged following collision with Cessna F152 G-BFRB on take-off Shoreham 19.12.81) *(Fuselage only)*					
BAPC.127	Halton Man Powered Aircraft Group Jupiter					
		xxxx				
IAHC.2	Aldritt Monoplane replica	xxxx				

WARWICKSHIRE

Midland Air Museum, Coventry CV8 3AZ (www.midlandairmuseum.org.uk)

G-EBJG	Parnall Pixie III	xxxx	No.17/18*	. 9.24	Cancelled 1.12.46 by Sec of State	2.10.36
			("Lympne 1924?)		*(Components only 2.05)*	
G-ABOI	Wheeler Slymph	AHW.1		17. 7.31	Cancelled 1.12.46 by Sec of State	
					(On loan from A.H.Wheeler) (Dismantled components only 2.05)	
G-AEGV	Mignet HM.14 Pou-Du-Ciel	EMAC.1		22. 4.36	Cancelled 12.37 *(WFU 26.5.37)*	26. 5.37
	(Built East Midlands Aviation Company)					
G-ALCU	de Havilland DH.104 Dove 2B	04022	VT-CEH	3. 8.48	Cancelled 8. 9.78 as WFU	16. 3.73
					(Displayed as "G-ALVD" in 'Dunlop Aviation Division' c/s)	
"G-ALVD"	de Havilland DH.104 Dove 2B				See above	
G-AOKZ	Percival P.40 Prentice 1	PAC-238	VS623	20. 4.56	Not converted *(Became instructional airframe)*	
					((As "VS623" with wings from G-AONB - No wheel spats)	
G-APJJ (2)	Fairey Ultralight Helicopter	F.9428		4.12.57	Cancelled 2. 3.73 as WFU *(Royal Navy' c/s)*	1. 4.59
G-APRL	Armstrong-Whitworth 650 Argosy Series 101		N890U	2. 1.59	Cancelled 19.11.87 as WFU	23. 3.87T
		AW.6652	N602Z, N6507R, G-APRL		*(Elan titles) "Edna"*	
G-APWN	Westland WS-55 Whirlwind 3	WA.298	VR-BER	8. 9.59	Cancelled 25. 6.81 as WFU	17. 5.78
			G-APWN, 5N-AGI, G-APWN		*(Bristow Helicopters titles) "Skerries"*	
G-ARYB	de Havilland DH.125 Series.1	25002		1. 3.62	Cancelled 4. 3.69 *(Mounted wingless on plinths)*	22. 1.68
G-ASWJ	Beagle B.206C Series 1	B.009		9. 9.64	Cancelled 9. 9.75 as WFU	
	(To RAF Halton as 8449M in 1976: on loan to City of Bristol College, Ashley Down, Bristol as "8449M")					
(G-MJWH)	Chargus Vortex 120	xxxx		R		
	(Regn reserved 1983 for Chargus T.250 and engine: fitted to 1974 Vortex hang glider: abandoned and only wing on display)					
BAPC.9	Humber-Bleriot XI Monoplane reconstruction				*(No markings)*	
	(Humber)		xxxx			
BAPC.32	Crossley Tom Thumb	xxxx			*(Not completed Banbury 1937) (Stored 2.04)*	
BAPC.126	Rollason-Druine D.31 Turbulent	xxxx			*(Static airframe) (Yellow c/s, no markings)*	
BAPC.179	Sopwith Pup fsm	xxxx			*(As "A7317")*	
"BGA 804"	Slingsby Cadet TX.1	xxxx			*(As "BAA") (Also see SECTION 5, Part 1)*	

WILTSHIRE

Boscombe Down Aviation Collection, Boscombe Down

G-ASJD	British Aircraft Corporation One-Eleven 201AC			6. 6.63	Cancelled 1.10.71 - *to RAF as XX105 in 10.71*	
		BAC.008				

Royal Air Force Lyneham

G-AMPO	Douglas C-47B-30DK Dakota 3	16437/33185	LN-RTO	25. 2.52	Cancelled 18.10.01 as WFU	29. 3.97A
	(Regd as c/n 16438/33186)		G-AMPO, KN566, 44-76853		*(As "FZ625")*	

National Museum of Science & Industry, Wroughton SN4 9NS (www.sciencemuseum.org.uk/wroughton)

G-AACN	Handley Page HP.39 Gugnunc	1	K1908	2.11.28	Cancelled 12.30 on transfer to RAF	19.9.30
			G-AACN			
G-ACIT	de Havilland DH84 Dragon 1	6039		24. 7.33	Cancelled 26. 4.02 as WFU	25. 5.74
G-AEHM	Mignet HM.14 Pou-Du-Ciel	HJD.1		30. 4.36	Cancelled in 3.39 census	
	(Built H J Dolman) (ABC Scorpion @ 35 hp)				*"Blue Finch"*	

G-ALXT	de Havilland DH.89A Dragon Rapide	6736	4R-AAI	24. 1.50	Cancelled 5. 7.51 - to CY-AAI		
			CY-AAI, G-ALXT, NF865		*(Railway Air Service titles) "Star of Scotia"*		
G-ANAV	de Havilland DH.106 Comet 1A	06013	CF-CUM	15. 8.53	Cancelled 1. 7.55 as WFU		
					(Broken up RAE Farnborough 1955: nose section)		
G-APWY	Piaggio P.166	362		16.12.59	Cancelled 20.10.00 by CAA	14. 3.81	
G-APYD	de Havilland DH.106 Comet 4B	6438	SX-DAL	21. 1.60	Cancelled 23.11.79 as WFU	3. 8.79T	
			G-APYD		*(Dan-Air titles)*		
G-ATTN	Piccard Balloon (Hot Air) (62,000 cu ft) 15 & 1352			27. 4.66	Cancelled 5.12.77 as PWFU		
					(Envelope and basket stored 6.94) "The Red Dragon"		
G-AVZB	LET Z-37 Cmelak	04-08	OK-WKQ	30.11.67	Cancelled 21.12.88 as WFU	5. 4.84A	
G-AWZM	Hawker Siddeley HS.121 Trident 3B Series 101			14. 1.69	Cancelled 18. 3.86 as WFU	13.12.85T	
		2314			*(WFU 13.12.85) (British Airways titles)*		
G-BBGN	Cameron A-375 Balloon (Hot Air)	90		23. 8.73	Cancelled 22. 8.89 as WFU		
G-BGLB	Bede BD.5B 3796 & PFA 14-10085			2. 3.79	Cancelled 21.11.91 by CAA	4.8.81P	
	(Hirth 230R)						
G-CONI	Lockheed 749A-79 Constellation	2553	N7777G	12. 5.82	Cancelled 13. 6.84 as WFU		
			(N173X), N7777G, TI-1045P, PH-LDT, PH-TET *(As "N7777G" in TWA c/s)*				
G-MMCB	Huntair Pathfinder II	136		13. 7.83	Cancelled 23.11.88 as WFU		
G-RBOS	Colt AS-105 HA Airship	390		9. 2.82	Cancelled 3. 4.97 by CAA	6. 3.87A	
EI-AYO (2)	Douglas DC-3A-197	1911	N655GP	5.3.76	Cancelled 28.11.78 as sold to UK Science Museum		
			N65556, N255JB, N8695E, N333H, NC16071				
BAPC.52	Lilienthal Glider Type XI	xxxx					
	(1895 original)						
BAPC.162	Goodhart Man Powered Aircraft Newbury Manflier						
		xxxx					
BAPC.172	Chargus Midas Super E Hang Glider	xxxx					
BAPC.173	Birdman Promotions Grasshopper	xxxx					
BAPC.174	Bensen B.7 Gyroglider	xxxx					
BAPC.188	McBroom Cobra 88 Hang Glider	xxxx					
BAPC.276	Hartman Ornithopter	xxxx					

YORKSHIRE

AeroVenture - South Yorkshire Air Museum , Doncaster DN4 5EP (www.aeroventure.org.uk/mainexhibits.php)

G-ALYB	Taylorcraft J Auster 5	1173	RT520	3. 2.50	Cancelled 29. 2.84 by CAA *(Fuselage only)*	26. 5.63	
G-AOKO	Percival P.40 Prentice 1	PAC-234	VS621	13. 4.56	Cancelled 9.10.84 as WFU	23.10.72	
					(On loan from Atlantic Air Transport Ltd)		
G-APMY	Piper PA-23-160 Apache	23-1258	EI-AJT	15. 5.58	WFU 1.11.81 *(On loan from W.Fern)*	1.11.81	
G-ARGI (2)	Auster 6A Tugmaster	2299	VF530	8.12.60	WFU at Heathfield in 7.73 *(Fuselage stored)*	4.7.76	
G-ARHX	de Havilland DH.104 Dove 8	04513		11. 1.61	WFU 8. 9.78	8. 9.78	
G-AVAA	Cessna F150G	F150-0164		14.10.66	Cancelled 16. 4.96 by CAA	5. 7.96	
	(Built Reims Aviation SA)				*(Fuselage only)*		
G-BECE	Aerospace Developments AD500 Series B.1 Airship (Hot Air)			14. 7.76	Cancelled xx.xx.xx by CAA	1. 4.79P	
	(2 x Porsche 930/03/AD11)	1214/1			*(Badly damaged in gales Cardington 9.3.79: gondola only)*		
G-BOCB	Hawker Siddeley HS.125 Series 1B/522	25106	G-OMCA	14. 9.87	Cancelled as WFU 22. 2.95 *(WFU Luton 1994 for spares)*	16.10.90	
			G-DJMJ, G-AWUF, 5N-ALY, G-AWUF, HZ-BIN *(Cockpit only)*				
G-DELB	Robinson R22 Beta	0799	N26461	18. 5.88	Cancelled 20. 4.95 by CAA *(DBR Sherburn-in-Elmet 27.12.94)*		
G-MJKP	Hiway Skystrike-Super Scorpion	PEB-01		7. 9.82	Cancelled 9.12.94 as WFU		
	(Fuji-Robin EC-25)						
G-MVRS	CFM Shadow Series BD	099		7. 4.89	Cancelled 5. 7.90 as destroyed	4. 6.90P	
					(Engineless fuselage shell in Storage Shed 4.04)		
EI-JWM	Robinson R22 Beta	1386	G-BSLB	21.11.92	Cancelled 28. 5.07		
BAPC.207	Austin Whippet fsm	xxxx			*(As "K.158")*		
	(Built Ken Fern/Vintage and Rotary Wing Collection c.1993)				*(On loan from D Charles)*		
BGA .2036	Slingsby T.21B	630	RAFGSA 247	3.75			
			WB969				
BGA 2517	Slingsby T.30B Prefect TX.1	577	WE987	6.79	*(As "WE987")*		
BGA 3239	Slingsby T.31B	708	WT913	26.10.86	*(On loan from J.M.Brookes and Partners) (As "WT913")*	21. 7.96	

Eden Camp Modern History Theme Museum, Malton YO17 6RT (www.edencamp.co.uk)

BAPC.230	Supermarine Spitfire fsm	xxxx	"AA908"		*(As "AB550:GE-P" in RAF 349 Sqdn c/s)*	
	(Built TDL Replicas 1993)					
BAPC.235	Fieseler Fi 103 (V-1) fsm	xxxx				
	(Built TDL Replicas 1993)					
BAPC.236	Hawker Hurricane fsm	xxxx			*(As "P2793:SD-M" in RAF 501 Sqdn c/s)*	
	(Built G B Moulders, Norfolk 1993)					

Fort Paull Armouries, Hedon HU12 8FP (www.fortpaull.com)

G-AOAI	Blackburn Beverley C.1	1002	XB259	15. 3.55	Cancelled 30. 3.55 *(Restored as XB259)*	

Museum and Art Gallery, Doncaster DN1 2AE (www.doncaster.gov.uk)

G-AEKR	Mignet HM.14 Pou-Du-Ciel	CAC.1		26. 6.36	WFU and cancelled 31. 7.38	22. 6.37
	(Buit E Claybourne & Co)			*(Stored Doncaster 1938/1960: dbf RAF Finningley 4.9.70: rebuilt and and allocated "G-AEKR" (BAPC.121)*		
BAPC.275	Bensen B.7	xxxx				
	(Built S J R Wood, Warmsworth) (Volkswagen 1600)					

Street Life Museum, High Street, Hull

BAPC.287	Blackburn Lincock fsm	xxxx			*(As "G-EBVO")*	
	(Built BAE, Brough c 2002)					

Yorkshire Air Museum, Elvington YO41 4AU (www.yorkshireairmuseum.co.uk)

G-AJOZ	Fairchild 24W-41A Argus 1	347	FK338	21. 4.47	Cancelled	15.12.63
	(UC-61-FA)		42-32142		*(Crashed Rennes, France 16. 8.62)*	
G-AMJT	Westland-Sikorsky S-55 Whirlwind HAR.1 WA/1		G-17-1	25. 5.51	Cancelled 13. 3.53 - to RN as XA862 3.53 *(Front fuselage)*	

G-AMYJ	Douglas C-47B-25DK Dakota 6	15968/32716	SU-AZF	23. 2.53	Cancelled 12.12.01 as WFU	4. 4.97A
	G-AMYJ, XF747, G-AMYJ, KN353, 44-76384					
G-ASCD	Beagle A.61 Terrier 2	B.615	PH-SFT	23. 7.62	Cancelled 5.10.89 as WFU	26. 9.71
			(PH-SCD), G-ASCD, VW993		(As "TJ704:JA")	
G-AVPN	Handley Page HPR.7 Dart Herald 213	176	I-TIVB	22. 6.67	Cancelled 8.12.97 as WFU	14.12.99T
			G-AVPN, D-BIBI, (HB-AAK)		(Channel Express titles)	
G-BDBZ	Westland WS-55 Whirlwind 2 (HAR.10)	WA.62	XJ398	23. 4.75	Cancelled 28. 3.85 by CAA (Not converted)	
	(Regd with c/n WA.386)		(XD768)		(As "XJ398") (On loan from Yorkshire Helicopter Preservation Group)	
G-BKDT	Royal Aircraft Factory SE.5A replica	278		26. 5.82	Cancelled 11. 7.91 by CAA (No Permit issued)	
	(Built J A Tetley - pr.no.PFA 080-10325)				(As "F943" - these marks carried by G-BIHF also)	
G-BMYP	Fairey Gannet AEW.3	F.9461	8610M	19. 9.86	Cancelled 22. 2.05 by CAA)	
	(Built Westland Aircraft Ltd)		XL502		(As "XL502" in 849 Sqdn:B" Flight RN c/s)	
G-HNTR	Hawker Hunter T.7	HABL-003311	8834M	7. 7.89	Cancelled 11.10.91 as WFU	
			XL572		(As "XL571:V" in "Blue Diamonds" c/s)	
G-MJRA	Mainair Tri-Flyer 250/Hiway Demon	PRJM-01		21.12.82	Cancelled 24. 1.95 by CAA	28. 6.91
G-TFRB	Air Command 532 Elite Sport	PFA G/04-1167		26. 4.90	Cancelled 7. 6.01 by CAA	6. 8.98P
	(Built F R Blennerhasset - kit no.0628)					
BAPC.28	Wright Flyer fsm	xxxx				
BAPC.41	Royal Aircraft Factory BE.2c replica	xxxx			(As "6232")	
	(Built RAF Halton apprentices)					
BAPC.42	Avro 504K fsm	xxxx			(As "H1968")	
BAPC.76	Mignet HM.14 Pou-Du-Ciel replica	xxxx			(As "G-AFFI")	
	(Modern reproduction) (Scott)					
BAPC.89	Cayley Glider fsm	xxxx				
BAPC.130	Blackburn (1911) Monoplane fsm	xxxx			"Mercury" (Built for TV Series."The Flambards")	
BAPC.157	WACO CG-4A Hadrian Glider	xxxx			(As "237123") (Fuselage frame section only and tail pieces ex 456476)	
BAPC.240	Messerschmitt Bf.109G fsm	xxxx				
	(Built D.Thorton 1994)					
BAPC.254	Supermarine Spitfire 1 fsm	xxxx			(As "R6690:PR-A" in RAF 609 Sqdn c/s)	
BAPC.265	Hawker Hurricane fsm	xxxx			(As "P3873:YO-H" in RCAF 1 Sqdn c/s)	
BAPC.270	de Havilland DH.60 Moth fsm	xxxx			(As "G-AAAH") "Jason"	

SCOTLAND

Dumfries and Galloway Aviation Museum, Dumfries DG2 9PS (www.members.xoom.com/dgamuseum)

G-AHAT	Auster J/1N Alpha	1849	(HB-EOK)	11. 2.46	Cancelled 7. 7.75 as WFU (Crashed 31. 8.74) (Frame only)	6. 2.75
G-AWZJ	Hawker Siddeley HS.121 Trident 3B Series 101			14. 1.69	Cancelled 7. 3.86 as WFU	12. 9.86T
		2311			(Forward fuselage only)	
G-MMIX	MBA Tiger Cub 440	MBCB-01		14. 2.84	Details in SECTION 1, Part 2	

National Museums of Scotland - Museum of Flight, East Fortune EH39 5LF (www.nms.ac.uk/flight)

G-ABDW	de Havilland DH.80A Puss Moth	2051	VH-UQB	23. 8.30	Cancelled 12.33 WFU and 21. 1.82 PWFU	
			G-ABDW		(To VH-UQB 27. 5.31 and restored 25. 3.77) (As "VH-UQB")	
G-ACVA	Kay Gyroplane 33/1	1002		26. 6.34	Cancelled 9.58	
	(Built Oddie Bradbury and Cull Ltd) (Pobjoy R 75hp)				(On loan from Glasgow Museum of Transport)	
G-ACYK	Spartan Cruiser III	101		2. 5.35	Crashed Largs, Ayrshire 14.1.38 (Fuselage only)	2. 6.38
G-AGBN	General Aircraft GAL.42 Cygnet 2	111	ES915	4.10.40	Cancelled 15.11.88 as WFU	28.11.80P
			G-AGBN			
G-AHKY	Miles M.18 Series 2	4426	HM545	26. 4.46	Cancelled 19. 3.92 as WFU	20. 9.89P
			U-0224, U-8			
G-AMOG (2)	Vickers 701 Viscount	7	(G-AMNZ)	23. 5.52	Cancelled 17. 5.76 as WFU	14. 6.77
					(BEA titles) "RMA Robert Falcon Scott"	
G-ANOV	de Havilland DH.104 Dove 6	04445	G-5-16	11. 3.54	Cancelled 6. 7.81 as WFU (Civil Aviation Authority titles)	31. 5.75
G-AOEL	de Havilland DH.82A Tiger Moth	82537	N9510	27. 9.55	WFU 18. 7.72	18. 7.72
G-APFJ	Boeing 707-436	17711		7. 8.59	WFU 12. 6.81 (Nose only)	16. 2.82T
G-APHV	Avro 652A Anson C.19 Series 2	xxxx	VM360	19. 9.57	Cancelled 21. 1.82 as PWFU (As "VM360")	15. 6.73
G-ARCX	Gloster Meteor NF.14	AW.2163	WM261	8. 9.60	Cancelled 25.10.73 as WFU	20. 2.69S
	(Built Armstrong-Whitworth Aircraft)				(WFU 2.69)	
G-ARPH	de Havilland DH.121 Trident 1C	2108		13. 4.61	WFU 26. 3.82 (Nose only)	8. 9.82T
G-ASUG	Beech E18S-9700	BA-111	N575C	7. 3.64	WFU 12. 5.75	23. 7.75
			N555CB, N24R		(Loganair c/s)	
G-ATOY	Piper PA-24-260 Comanche B	24-4346	N8893P	7. 2.66	Crashed near Elstree 6. 3.79 "Myth Too" (Fuselage only)	
G-AVMO	British Aircraft Corporation One-Eleven 510ED			11. 5.67	Cancelled 12. 7.93 as WFU	3. 2.95T
		BAC.143			(British Airways titles) "Lothian Region"	
G-AVPC	Druine D.31 Turbulent	PFA 544		15. 6.67	Cancelled 13. 9.02 as PWFU	28. 9.99P
	(Built J Sharp)					
G-AXEH	Beagle B.125 Bulldog 1	B.125-001		25. 4.69	Cancelled 15. 1.77 as WFU	15. 1.77
G-BBBV	Handley Page HP.137 Jetstream	234	N14234	26. 6.73	Cancelled 21. 8.74 (To N200SE 8.74)	
			N102SC, N1BE, (N200SE), G-BBBV, G-8-12 (Fuselage used by BAe as Jetstream 31 mock-up)			
G-BBVF	Scottish Aviation Twin Pioneer 3	558	7978M	17.12.73	Cancelled 8.8.83	14. 5.82
			XM961			
G-BDFU	PMPS Dragonfly MPA Mk.1	01		14. 7.75	Cancelled 12.83 as WFU	
	(Built Prestwick MPA Group)				(On loan from R.J.Hardy and R.Churcher)	
G-BDIX	de Havilland DH.106 Comet 4C	6471	XR399	1. 9.75	Cancelled 2. 9.91 by CAA (Dan-Air titles)	11.10.81T
G-BDYG	Percival P.56 Provost T.1	PAC/F/056	7696M	25. 5.76	Cancelled 4.11.91 by CAA	28.11.80P
			WV493		(As "WV493:29 A-P")	
G-BIRW	Morane-Saulnier MS.505 Criquet	695/28	OO-FIS	10. 4.81	Cancelled 15.11.88 as WFU	3. 6.83P
			F-BDQS, French AF 695		(As "FI+S" in Luftwaffe c/s)	
G-BOAA	British Aircraft Corporation Concorde Type 1 Variant 102		G-N94AA	3. 4.74	Cancelled 4. 5.04 as WFU	24. 2.01T
		206 & 100-006	G-BOAA			
G-JSSD	Handley Page HP.137 Jetstream 1	227	N510F	14. 6.79	Cancelled 4. 1.96 by CAA	9.10.90
	(Conv to BAe Jetstream Series 3001 prototype.1979/80)		N510E, N12227, G-AXJZ			

G-MBJX	Hiway Skytrike I/Hiway Super Scorpion	MM-01			2. 2.82	Cancelled 13. 6.90 by CAA	
	(Valmet SM160 s/n 15108)						
G-MBPM	Eurowing Goldwing	EW-21			14. 4.82	Cancelled 30. 8.00 as WFU	21. 8.98P
	(Fuji-Robin EC-34-PM)						
G-MMLI	Mainair Tri-Flyer 250/Solar Wings Typhoon S	BAPC.244			26. 3.84	Cancelled 7. 9.94 by CAA	
	RPAT-01 & T484-423L					(Originally regd as Hiway Skytrike Mk.II 250)	
BAPC.49	Pilcher Hawk Glider	xxxx					
	(1896 original) (Rebuilt after fatal crash Stanford Hall, Leicester 30.9.1899)						
BAPC.59	Sopwith F1 Camel fsm	xxxx	"D3419"			(As "B5577:W")	
			"F1921"				
BAPC.70	Auster AOP.5	TAY/33153	"GALES"			(As "TJ398") (On loan from Aircraft Preservation Society of Scotland)	
BAPC.85	Weir W-2	xxxx				(As "W-2") (On loan)	
	(Weir Dryad II 50hp)						
BAPC.160	Chargus 18/50 Hang Glider	xxxx					
BAPC.195	Birdman Sports Moonraker 77 Hang Glider						
	(Built c.1977)	xxxx					
BAPC.196	Southdown Sailwings Sigma 2m Hang Glider						
	(Built c.1980)	xxxx					
BAPC.197	Scotkites Cirrus III Hang Glider	xxxx					
	(Built 1977)						
BAPC.245	Electraflyer Floater Hang Glider	xxxx				(Wing only)	
	(Built 1979)						
BAPC.246	Hiway Cloudbase Hang Glider	xxxx					
	(Built 1978)						
BAPC.247	Albatros ASG.21 Hang Glider	xxxx					
	(Built 1977)						
BAPC.262	Catto CP-16	xxxx					
BGA 852	Slingsby T.8 Tutor	xxxx	TS291		2. 7.58	(As "TS291")	
BGA 902	Slingsby T.12 Gull I	xxxx			15. 5.59	(As "BED") "G-ALPHA"	
BGA 1014	Slingsby T.21B	556	SE-SHK		1.62	(As "BJV")	

City of Edinburgh Council, Edinburgh Airport

| BAPC.227 | Supermarine Spitfire IA fsm | xxxx | | | | (As "L1070:XT-A" in RAF 603 Sqdn c/s) | |

Museum of Transport, Kelvin Hall, Glasgow G3 8DP

| BAPC.48 | Pilcher Hawk glider replica | xxxx | | | | (Stored 3.04) | |
| | (Built No.2175 Sqdn ATC, Glasgow 1966) | | | | | | |

Highland Aviation Museum, Dalcross, Inverness

| G-ASVO | Handley Page HPR.7 Dart Herald 214 | 185 | PP-SDG | | 13. 8.64 | Cancelled 25. 9.01 by CAA | 14. 1.00T |
| | | | G-ASVO, G-8-3 | | | (WFU after collision Hurn 8.4.97: front fuselage only) | |

WALES

Caernarfon Air Museum, Caernarfon, Gwynedd LL54 5TP (www.caeairparc.com)

G-ALFT	de Havilland DH.104 Dove 6	04233			14.12.48	Cancelled 11. 2.77 as WFU	13. 6.73
G-AMLZ	Percival P.50 Prince 6E	P.46	(VR-TBN)		23.11.51	Cancelled 9.10.84 as WFU	18. 6.71
G-AWUK	Cessna F150H	F150-0344			25.11.68	Cancelled 13. 4.73 as WFU	3. 9.73
	(Built Reims Aviation SA)					(Crashed Shoreham 4. 9.71) (Cockpit only)	
G-MBEP	American Aerolights Eagle 215B	2877			9.11.81	Cancelled 16. 5.96 as WFU	8. 4.96E
	(Chrysler 820)						
BAPC.201	Mignet HM.14 Pou-Du-Ciel replica	xxxx					
BAPC.286	Mignet HM.14 Flea	xxxx					
	(Scott A2S)						

National Industrial Museum, Swansea

| BAPC.47 | Watkins CHW Monoplane | xxxx | | | | | |
| | (Watkins 40hp) | | | | | | |

Maes Artro Village, Llanbedr, Harlech

| BAPC.202 | Supermarine Spitfire V fsm | xxxx | | | | (Built for "Piece of Cake" TV series) | |
| | | | | | | (As "MAV467:R-O") | |

IRELAND

Irish Aer Corps Museum, Baldonnel, Dublin

| G-ARLU (2) | Cessna 172B | 17248502 | N8002X | | 14. 6.61 | Cancelled 6. 8.80 as WFU | 6.10.78 |
| | | | | | | (DBR Biggin Hill 30.10.77: fuselage only as "IAC 98") | |

Nutgrove Shopping Centre, Churchtown, Dublin

| EI-124 | Grob G.102 Astir Standard CS 77 | 1761 | D-... | | .80 | | |

Meath Aero Museum, Ashbourne, County Meath

("EI-ABH")	HM.14 Pou-du-Ciel replica	1				Under construction - fuselage complete 5.01	
IGA.6	Slingsby T.8 Tutor	xxxx	IAC.6		.56		
			VM657				

South East Aviation Enthusiasts Group c/o Cavan and Leitrim Railway, Dromod, Leitrim, County Leitrim

G-ALCS (2)	Miles M.65 Gemini 3C	WAL/C/1001			7.11.49	Cancelled 30. 5.84 by CAA	
	(Originally regd as Series 3A with c/n 6534)					(WFU 1983)	
	(Cockpit only remains and the provenance was suspect but now thought to be from Miles M.65 Gemini 1A G-AKEL when transferred						
	to Ulster Folk & Transport Museum: components only noted 4.96 and was for rebuild with G-AKGE)						
G-AMDD	de Havilland DH.104 Dove 6	04292			8. 8.50	Cancelled 26. 9.68 (As "IAC 176")	
	(Originally regd as Series.2, then Series 2B)					(To VQ-ZJC 9.68, 3D-AAI, VP-YKF and IAC 176)	
G-AOGA	Miles M.75 Aries 1	75/1007	EI-ANB		9.11.55	Cancelled 30. 5.84	10.10.69
			G-AOGA			(To EI-ANB 18. 5.63, restored 10. 9.65: damaged Cork 8. 8.69)	

G-AOIE	Douglas DC-7C	45115	PH-SAX	27. 8.56	Cancelled 31. 3.70 as WFU	
			G-AOIE		(To PH-SAX 10. 4.67, restored 18.11.69: scrapped 10.97: fuselage only)	
G-AYAG	Boeing 707-321	18085	N759PA	26. 3.70	Cancelled 8.12.72 (	
					(To G-41-2-72, (CS-BDG) (N435MA) and VP-BDF 12.72) As "VP-BDF") (Nose only)	
IAHC.1	Mignet HM.14 Pou-Du-Ciel	xxxx			"St.Patrick" (Noted 4.04)	
BGA 1410	Grunau Baby III		RAFGSA 378	5. 9.67	(As "CBK")	
	(Built Sfg.Schaffin)		D-4676			
BGA 1424	Slingsby T.8 Tutor	SSK/FF27	RAFGSA 214	10.67	(As "CBZ")	

Ulster Folk and Transport Museum, Holywood, Belfast BT18 0EU (www.nidex.com/uftm)

G-ACUX	Short S.16 Scion 1	S.776	VH-UUP	26. 6.34	Cancelled 2.38 and 7.81	
			G-ACUX		(To VH-UUP 2.10.35 and restored 25.3.77) (Stripped frame)	
G-AJOC	Miles M.38 Messenger 2A	6370		23. 4.47	Cancelled 5. 1.82 as WFU	18. 5.72
					(Rear fuselage)	
G-AKEL	Miles M.65 Gemini 1A	6484		8. 9.47	Cancelled 30. 5.84 as WFU	29. 4.72
					(Centre section) (But see entry for South East Aviation Enthusiasts Group above)	
G-AKGE	Miles M.65 Gemini 3C	6488	EI-ALM	18.10.47	Cancelled 30. 5.84	7. 6.74
			G-AKGE			
G-AKLW	Short SA.6 Sealand 1	SH.1571	(USA)	26.11.47	Sold abroad 8.51	
			R Saudi AF, SU-AHY, G-AKLW (On display dismantled 6.05)			
G-AOUR	de Havilland DH.82A Tiger Moth	86341	NL898	14. 8.56	Crashed Newtownards 6. 6.65	19.11.66
G-ARTZ (1)	McCandless M.2	M2/1		?.10.61	Replaced by G-ARTZ (2) – see SECTION 1, Part 2	
	(Triumph 650cc)					
G-ATXX	McCandless M.4	M4/3		27. 7.66	Cancelled 9. 9.70 as WFU	
	(Volkswagen 1600)					
G-BKMW	Short SD.3-30 Sherpa Var.100	SH3094	G-14-3094	13.12.82	Cancelled 14.11.96 as WFU (Broken up 3.96) (Cockpit only)	14. 9.90
BGA 470	Short Nimbus	S.1312		.47	(Stored 1.04)	8.75
IAHC.6	Ferguson monoplane replica	xxxx				
	(Built Capt J.Kelly Rogers 1974) (Original engine)					
IAHC.9	Ferguson monoplane replica	xxxx			(Stored 1.04)	
	(Built L.Hannah 1980)					

Ulster Aviation Heritage, Langford Lodge, Belfast BT16 1WQ (www.ulsteraviationsociety.co.uk)

G-BDBS	Short SD.3-30 UTT	SH.1935 & SH.3001	G-14-3001	21. 4.75	Cancelled 1. 7.93 as WFU	28. 9.92S
	(Airframe originally laid down as SC.7 Skyvan c/n SH.1935)					
G-BTUC	Embraer EMB-312 Tucano	312007	G-14-007	19. 6.86	Cancelled 20.12.96 as WFU	11. 9.93
			PP-ZTC			
G-MJWS	Eurowing Goldwing	EW-22		16. 5.83	Cancelled 23. 6.97 by CAA	
	(Fuji-Robin EC-34-PM)					
G-RENT	Robinson R22 Beta	0758	N2635M	17. 3.88	Cancelled 11.12.03 as WFU	12. 6.94T
					(Damaged Newtownards 30.9.92)	
EI-BAG	Cessna 172A	47571	G-ARAV	7. 8.74	(Damaged 3.10.76)	26. 6.79
			N9771T			
EI-BUO	Aero Composites Sea Hawker	80		25. 8.87		
	(Aka Glass S.005E)					
BAPC.263	Chargus Cyclone	xxxx				
	(Built 1979)					
BAPC.266	Rogallo Hang Glider	xxxx				

ARGENTINA

Museo Nacional de Aeronatica, Buenos Aires

| G-AICH | Bristol 170 Freighter Mk.1A | 12751 | | 26. 8.46 | Cancelled 19.12.46 - to LV-XIM 2.47 | |
| | | | | | (Subsequently LV-AEY, Argentine AF T-30 and TC-330) | |

AUSTRALIA

Australian War Memorial, Canberra, Australian Capital Territory

| G-EAQM | Airco DH.9 | --- | F1278 | 31.12.19 | Cancelled 8. 1.20 | 1. 1.21 |
| | (AS Puma) | | | | (NTU and to Australia 1920 as "G-EAQM") | |

National Museum of Australia, Canberra, Australian Capital Territory

| G-AERD | Percival Type D Gull Six | D.65 | HB-OFU | 16. 9.77 | Cancelled 28.11.86 on sale to Australia | |

Camden Museum of Aviation, Kogarah, New South Wales

G-AGTB	Percival Proctor V	Ae.8		8.12.45	Cancelled 5.11.47 - to VH-BCM 11.47	
	(C/n reported as changed to Ae.9)				(Subsequently VH-SST and VH-BCM) (As "NP336")	
G-AMWI	Bristol 171 Sycamore 4	13070		1.12.52	Cancelled 1958 - to RN as "XN635"	
					(Subsequently VH-BAW) (As "XR592")	

Donald and Robert Bunn Collection, Albury, New South Wales

| G-AFOW | de Havilland DH.94 Moth Minor | 94047 | | 16. 5.39 | Cancelled 16. 5.39 - to R.Australia AF 10.39 but NTU | |
| | | | | | (Subsequently VH-ACS 23.1.40) | |

Australian Aviation Museum, Bankstown, New South Wales (www.aamb.com.au)

G-ASFI	de Havilland DH.114 Heron 2D	14108	(N4661T)	4. 3.63	Cancelled 15. 9.64 - to CR-GAT	
	(Converted to Riley Heron)		G-ASFI, West German AF CA+001, G-5-15			
					(Subsequently VH-CLW, T3-ATA, DQ-FDY, VH-CLW and DQ-FDY) (As "DQ-FDY")	
G-CBEP	British Aerospace Jetstream Series 3200	980	(SE-LJB)	23.11.01	Cancelled 20.10.06 - to VH-OTE	
	(Built Jetstream Aircraft Ltd)		F-GMVN, G-31-980		(As "VH-OTE")	

Greg and Nick Challinor Collection, Murwillumbah Airfield, Murwillumbah, New South Wales

| G-ANHM | Taylorcraft G Auster 4 | 846 | MT137 | 5.12.53 | Cancelled 12.10.54 - to VH-AZO 11.54 | |
| | | | | | (Subsequently VH-ILS and VH-HPM) | |

Pay's Flying Museum, Scone Aerodrome, Scone, New South Wales

G-AOSP	de Havilland DHC-1 Chipmunk 22	C1/0174	WB722	26. 6.56	Cancelled - *to VH-BTL* *(Subsequently VH-BWF and VH-AMV)*

Temora Aviation Museum, Temora, New South Wales

G-BURM	English Electric Canberra TT.18 *(Built Handley Page Ltd)*	xxxx	WJ680	11.12.92	Cancelled 3. 7.02 - *to VH-ZQN 7.02* *(As "A84-234" in RAAF 77 Sqdn c/s)*	2.12.02P
G-METE	Gloster Meteor F.8	G5/361641	VZ467	5.11.91	Cancelled 26.10.01 - *to VH-MBX* *"Halestorm" (As "A77-851" in RAAF 77 Sqdn c/s)*	20.6.02P

Central Australian Aviation Museum, Alice Springs, Northern Territory

G-AHVG	Percival Proctor II	H.224	BV658	17. 6.46	Cancelled 25. 3.57 - *to VH-AVG 5.58*

Queensland Air Museum, Caloundra Airfield, Queensland

G-ASVC	de Havilland DH.114 Heron 2D *(Converted to Riley Heron)*	14123	EC-AOF	31. 7.64	Cancelled 1.10.64 - *to VQ-FAF* *(Subsequently VH-KAM -noted 2007)*

Queensland Museum, South Brisbane, Queensland

G-EACQ	Avro 534 Baby	534/1	VH-UCQ G-AUCQ, G-EACQ, K-131	29. 5.19	Sold 6.21 - *to G-AUCQ 12.7.21* *(Subsequently VH-UCQ 10.30) (As "G-EACQ")*	
G-EBOV	Avro 581E Avian *(Originally regd as Avro 581, to 581A in 1927 and modified to 581E)*	5116	No 9 (Lympne 1926) 7. 7.26		Cancelled 14. 1.30 as sold in Australia	30. 1.29
G-ABLK	Avro 616 Avian V	R3/CN/523	VH-UQG G-ABLK	4.31	Cancelled - *to VH-UQG 16.9.31* *(Restored 16. 8.32 and crashed south Reggane, Sahara 12.4.33)*	

Caboolture Warplane Museum Trust, Caboolture Airfield, Caboolture, Queensland

G-AFOR	de Havilland DH.94 Moth Minor	9404		29. 8.39	Cancelled - *to VH-AGL 1939* *(Subsequently R.Australian AF A21-14 @ 2.40 and VH-AGO) (As "A21-14")*
G-AJVL	Miles M.38 Messenger 2A	6372		30. 5.47	Cancelled 1.12.49 - *to VH-BJM 11.49* *(Subsequently VH-BJH)*

Mackay Tiger Moth Museum, Mackay, Queensland

G-AMPM	de Havilland DH.82A Tiger Moth	86128	EM945	23. 2.52	Cancelled 31. 3.52 - *to ZK-BBF 4.52* *(Subsequently VH-IVN)*

Classic Jets Fighter Museum, Parafield Airport, Adelaide, South Australia

G-APTS	de Havilland DHC-1 Chipmunk 22A *(Originally regd as Mk.22)*	C1/0683	WP791	21. 4.59	Cancelled 1. 7.93 - *to VH-ZIZ 7.94*

Sir Ross and Sir Keith Smith War Memorial, Adelaide, South Australia

G-EAOU	Vickers FB.27A Vimy IV	---	(A5-1) G-EAOU/F8630	23.10.19	Cancelled 1920 *(As "G-EAOU")*	31.10.20

Lincoln Nitschke's Military and Historical Aircraft Collection, Greenock, South Australia

G-APAD	Edgar Percival EP.9	27	(VH-SSW) G-43-6	18. 3.57	Cancelled 1. 8.58 - *to VH-SSX 8.9.58*

South Australian Aviation Museum, Port Adelaide, South Australia

G-BAHB	de Havilland DH.104 Dove 5	04107	CS-TAC	31.10.72	Cancelled 14. 3.74 - *to VH-CLD (2) 3.74*

Geoff Davis Collection, Salisbury, South Australia

G-ABLF	Avro 616 Avian Sport	R3/CN/522		. 4.31	Cancelled 8.36 - *to VH-UVX 2.36* *(Rebuilt with parts of, and flew as, VH-UQE) (As "VH-UVX")*

Queen Victoria Museum, Launceston, Tasmania

G-ASCX	de Havilland DH.114 Heron 2D *(Converted to Riley Heron)*	14124	West German AF 30. 8.62 CA+002		Cancelled 7.5.70 -*to VH-CLV*

Ballarat Aviation Museum, Ballarat, Victoria

G-ATGJ	de Havilland DH.104 Riley Dove 5 *(Originally registered as DH.104 Dove 5B)*	04113	R.Jordanian AF D-101 12. 7.65 TJ-ACB, YI-ABL		Cancelled 1.11.65 as TWFU *(Restored 9.10.69: cancelled 20.3.74 - sold as VH-ABK)*

The Australian National Aviation Museum, Moorabbin, Melbourne, Victoria (www.aarg.com.au)

G-AHDI	Percival Proctor I	K.253	P6194	26. 2.46	Cancelled 1. 6.51 - *to VH-AUC 6.51* *(As "VH-AUC" and "A75-1")*
G-AJKG (2)	Miles M.38 Messenger 2A	6373		30. 5.47	Cancelled 17. 8.53 - *to VH-AVQ* *(Stored)*
G-ANPV(2)	de Havilland DH.114 Heron 2D *(Converted to Riley Heron)*	14098	G-5-24 (G-ANPV)	20.11.56	Cancelled 5. 1.71 - *to VH-CLX.* *(As "VH-CLX"*

Clyde North Aeronautical Preservation Group, Mount Waverley, Victoria

"G-ACSS"	de Havilland DH.88 Comet replica	---	"G-ACSP"		

Royal Australian Air Force Museum, Point Cook, Victoria (www.defence.gov.au/RAAF/raafmuseum)/

G-AIMI	Bristol 170 Freighter 21E	12799		3.12.46	Cancelled 24. 1.49 - *to RAF as WB482 30. 3.49* *(Subsequently R.Australian AF A81-1 on 14. 4.49 and VH-SJG) (As "A81-1")*
G-AJHW	Sikorsky S-51	51-17	WB220 G-AJHW	27. 2.47	Cancelled 22. 5.57 - *to CF-JTO 6.57* *(Subsequently R.Australian AF A80-374)*
G-AJKF (2)	de Havilland DH.84 Dragon III *(Built de Havilland Aircraft Pty Ltd, Australia)*	2081	RAAF A34-92	28. 3.47	Cancelled 19. 8.48 as NTU - *to VH-BDS 28. 4.48* *(Subsequently VH-AML) (As "VH-AML and "A34-92")*
G-AOHD (2)	Hunting Percival P.84 Jet Provost T.2	P.84/12	RAAF A99-001 G-AOHD	26. 3.56	Cancelled - *to RAAF as A99-001 8.61* *(Restored to UK but subsequently A99-001)*
G-BYKV	Avro 504K replica *(Built Hawker Restorations Ltd)*	0015		27. 5.99	Cancelled 16. 8.02 as transferred to VH- *(Subsequently "A3-17") (As "E3747")*

Airworld, Wangaratta, Victoria

G-EBUB	Westland Widgeon III	WA.1695		12. 3.28	Cancelled 8.28 - *to G-AUHU 30. 7.28*	
					(Subsequently VH-UHU)	
G-ACUP	Percival Tyoe D Gull Six	D.46		. 7.34	Cancelled 5.39 - *to VH-ACM 31. 7.39*	
					(Subsequently VH-CCM)	
G-ALBP	Miles M.38 Messenger 4A	---	RH376	18. 6.48	Cancelled 7. 7.55 - *to VH-WYN 4.55*	
	(Originally regd as Messenger 1)					

Nelson Wilson Collection, Yering, Victoria

G-ANZS	de Havilland DH.82A Tiger Moth	85082	T6813	4. 3.55	Cancelled 18. 6.59 - *to VH-DCH 2.60.*	

RAAF Association Aviation Heritage Museum, Bull Creek, Western Australia (www.raafawa.org.au/wa/museum)

G-ALIS	Percival Proctor III	K.392	Z7203	21. 2.49	Cancelled 21. 2.52 - *to VH-BQR 2.52*	
					(Subsequently VH-GAS) (As "VH-BQR")	
G-ALZL	de Havilland DH.114 Heron Series 1	10903	LN-BDH	30. 3.50	Cancelled 25. 4.54 - *to LN-BDH*	
			G-ALZL		*(Restored 21.5.54: cancelled 2.12.66 - to OY-DGS and subsequently and as "VH-CJS")*	
BGA 334	Slingsby T.12 Gull I	293A		4.38	Cancelled - *to VH-GHL (As "VH-GHL")*	

AUSTRIA

McDonald's Restaurant, Vienna-Schwechat Airport, Vienna

G-AGRW	Vickers 639 Viking 1	115	XF640	8. 5.46	WFU 8.64	9. 7.68
	(Originally registered as 498 Viking 1A)		G-AGRW		*(No markings)*	

BARBADOS

Grantly Adams Airport

G-BOAE	British Aircraft Corporation Concorde Type 1 Variant 102	G-N94AE	9. 5.75	Cancelled 4. 5.04 as WFU	18. 7.05T
	212 & 100-012	G-BOAE			

BELGIUM

Stampe and Vertongen Museum, Antwerp

G-BRMC	Stampe et Renard SV-4B	1160	SLN-03	17. 3.78	Cancelled 2. 9.93 - *to OO-GWD*	
			Belgium AF V-18		*(As "OO-GWD")*	
EI-APT (2)	Fokker D.VII/65 replica	02	EI-APU	2. 6.67	Cancelled 28. 5.85 - *to N903AC*	
	(Built Rousseau Aviation)		F-BNDG-		*(As "O-BOBE")*	

Koninklijk Leger Museum/Musée Royal de l'Armée, Brussels (www.klm-mra.be/klm-new/engels/main01.php?id=collecties/virtueel)

G-ACGR	Percival Tyoe D Gull Four IIA	D.29		11. 5.33	Cancelled 12.34 - crashed Waterloo, Belgium 12.34	20. 6.35
	(DH Gipsy Major I) *(Originally regd as P.1B)*				*(As "G-ACGR")*	
G-AFJR	Tipsy Trainer 1	2		20. 8.38	Cancelled 12. 4.89 as TWFU	10. 9.64
	(Converted to Belfair)				*(As "G-AFJR")*	
G-AFRV	Tipsy Trainer I	10		15. 7.39	Cancelled 10. 2.87 by CAA	
					(As "G-AFRV")	
G-AFVH	Tipsy S.2	29	OO-ASB	7. 6.39	Cancelled 27. 7.49 - *to OO-TIP*	
					(As "OO-TIP")	
G-AHZY	Percival Proctor V	Ae.84		14. 8.46	Cancelled 25. 7.57 - *to OO-ARM*	
					(As "OO-ARM")	
G-AKIS	Miles M.38 Messenger 2A	6725		19. 9.47	Cancelled 24. 2.70 as WFU	5. 8.70
					(As "G-AKIS")	
G-AKNV	de Havilland DH.89A Dragon Rapide	6458	G-AKNV	2.12.47	Cancelled 27. 9.55 - *to OO-AFG 9.55*	
			EI-AGK, G-AKNV, R5922		*(Subsequently OO-CNP 4.64) (As OO-CNP)*	
G-AMJD	de Havilland DH.82A Tiger Moth	83728	T7238	9. 4.51	Cancelled 11.11.52 - *to OO-SOI 10.52*	
					(As "T-24:UR-!")	
G-AMTP	de Havilland DH.82A Tiger Moth	84875	T6534	17. 7.52	Cancelled 29. 8.52 - *to OO-ETP 7.53*	
					(As "OO-ETP")	
G-AOJX	de Havilland DH.82A Tiger Moth	3272	K4276	18. 4.56	Cancelled 5. 6.56 - *to OO-EVS 7.56*	
					(As "OO-EVS")	
G-AOPO	Percival P.40 Prentice 1	PAC-215	VS613	30. 5.56	Cancelled 11. 9.58 - *to OO-OPO 4.58*	
					(As "OO-OPO")	
G-APPT	de Havilland DH.82A Tiger Moth	84567	T6100	24.10.58	Cancelled 2. 1.59 - *to OO-SOK*	
					(Subsequently OO-SOW) (As "OO-SOW")	
G-BDPU	Fairey Britten-Norman BN-2A-21 Islander	510		5. 2.76	Cancelled 19.11.76 - *to Belgium Army as B-06:OTA-LF 8.76*	
	(Originally regd as BN-2A-26)				*(As "B-06")*	
G-BWGR	North American TB-25N-NC Mitchell	108-34200	N9494Z	18. 8.95	Cancelled 22. 2.05 by CAA - no UK CofA issued:	
	(Official c/n 108-30925 - corruption of USAAF serial)		44-30925		*(As "151632")*	
G-HAPR	Bristol 171 Sycamore HC.14				See SECTION 1 ,Part 2	
BAPC.19	Bristol F2b Fighter fuselage frame	---			*(As "66")*	
	(Rebuilt to static condition by Skysport Engineering 6.89 with parts from J8264)					

Musée de la Base de Bierset, Grace Hollogne

G-BEED	Fairey Britten-Norman BN-2B-21 Islander	549		25. 8.76	Cancelled 25. 8.77 - *to Belgium Army as B-11:OTA-LK 7.77*	
					(As "B-11")	

BRAZIL

Museu de Armas, Veiculos Motorizados e Avioes Antigos "Eduardo Andreia Matarazzo", Bebeduoro

G-AMHB	Westland-Sikorsky S-51 Dragonfly Mk.1B	WA/H/030	18. 1.51	Cancelled 12. 5.51 - *to OO-CWA 5.51*	
				(Subsequently XB-JUQ and PT-HAL)	
G-AMOI	Vickers 701 Viscount	22	23. 5.52	Cancelled 23. 3.63 - *to (PP-SRK), PP-SRL 10.62*	
G-ANHD	Vickers 701C Viscount	64	12.12.53	Cancelled 23. 4.63 - *to PP-SRO 8.62*	

TAM Museum, San Carlos

G-OMIG	WSK SBLim-2A	622047	PLW-6247	10.11.92	Cancelled 1. 8.00 by CAA as sold to Brazil	
	(MiG-15UTI)		(Polish AF)		*(Stored dismantled 10.02 as "PLW-6247")*	
	(Built Aero Vodochody as S.103/MiG 15bis; later rebuilt in Poland)					

Fundacao Museu de Technologia de Sao Paulo, Sao Paulo
G-AOFX (2)   Vickers 701C Viscount   182   20.12.55   Cancelled 25. 7.63 - to PP-SRS 8.63

CANADA

Reynolds-Alberta Museum, Wetaskiwin, Alberta (http://machinemuseum.net)
G-ACPP   de Havilland DH.89 Dragon Rapide   6254   20. 2.35   Cancelled - sold as CF-PTK 6.61
                                                                            (As "CF-PTK")

G-AFGK   Miles M.11A Whitney Straight   509   U-1   6. 4.38   Cancelled 13.9.77 - to N72511 9.77
                                                                       (Subsequently and as "CF-FGK")

G-AOYU   de Havilland DH.82A Tiger Moth   82270   N9151   27.12.56   Cancelled 14. 7.71 on sale to US
                                                                        (Subsequently and as "C-GABB")

Quesnel Heritage Aircraft Museum, Richbar Store, Quesnel, British Columbia
G-APHY   Scottish Aviation Twin Pioneer Series.1   508   9K-ACC   2.10.57   Cancelled 16. 8.74 - to C-FSTX 8.74
                                                          G-APHY, VR-OAF   *(Subsequently and as "C-GSTX") (Front fuselage only)*

Commonwealth Air Training Plan Museum, Brandon Municipal Airport, Brandon, Manitoba
G-ANOS   de Havilland DH.82A Tiger Moth   85461   DE465   4. 3.54   Cancelled 31. 8.72 - to CF-JNF 8.72
                                                                       (Subsequently C-FNJF) (As "4188")

Western Canada Aviation Museum, Winnipeg, Manitoba (www.wcam.mb.ca)
G-APXG   de Havilland DH.114 Heron 2D   14137   20.11.59   Cancelled 25. 6.60 - to Kuwait AF 303 1.60
         (Converted to Saunders ST-27 [008])   *(Subsequently 9K-BAA and CF-CNX) (As "C-FCNX")*

National Air Force Museum of Canada, CFB Trenton, Astra, Ontario (www.airforcemuseum.ca)
BAPC.224   Supermarine Spitfire V fsm   *(As "ML380")*
           (Built TDL Replicas)

Canada Aviation Museum, Rockcliffe, Ottawa, Ontario (http://aeroweb.brooklyn.cuny.edu/museums/ont/cnam.htm)
G-AANM (2)   Bristol F 2b Fighter composite   Details at SECTION 1, Part 2
                                                                       (As "D7889")

G-AHLO   de Havilland DH.80A Puss Moth   2187   HM534   1. 5.46   Cancelled 26. 9.69 - to CF-PEI 10.69
                                                  (DR630), Bu.A8877   *(As "CF-PEI")*

G-AIKR   Airspeed AS.65 Consul   4338   PK286   25. 9.46   WFU *(As "G-AIKR")*   14. 5.65

Canadian Bushplane Heritage Centre, Sault Sainte Marie, Ontario (www.bushplane.com)
G-AKGV   de Havilland DH.89A Dragon Rapide   6796   F-BFPU   9.10.47   Cancelled 25. 7.50 - sold as F-BFPU
                                                      G-AKGV, NR697   *(Restored 7.11.75: cancelled 21. 6.76 - sold as (C-GXFJ)*
                                                                             (Subsequently and as "C-FAYE")

G-AOGW   de Havilland DH.114 Heron 2E   14095   2. 2.56   Cancelled 14. 2.73 - to C-GCML 9.72
         (Converted to Saunders ST-27 [009])   *(As "C-GCML")*

Collingwood Clasic Aircraft Foundation Stayner, Ontario (www.classicaircraft.ca)
EI-AUB   de Havilland DH.82A Tiger Moth   86509   F-BGCP   26. 8.69   Cancelled 7.10.75 - sold as N82JS 10.75
                                                   French AF, NM201   *(Subsequently and as "C-GSTP" - registered as c/n 86508 (ex NM200))*

Toronto Aerospace Museum, North York, Ontario (http://torontoaerospacemuseum.com)
G-BIDN   Percival P.57 Sea Prince T.1   P57/31   WF133   22. 9.80   Cancelled 13.11.84 - to N57AW 10.84.   19. 2.98P
         (Originally regd with c/n P57/27)   *(Subsequently and as "C-GJIE")*

CHILE

Museo Nacional deAeronautica de Chile, Los Cerillos, Santiago
G-BACK   de Havilland DH.82A Tiger Moth   85879   F-BDOB   4. 9.72   Cancelled 25. 1.89 as sold to Chilean AF Museum in 12.87
                                                   French AF, DF130   *(Subsquently CC-DMC)*

G-BPLT   Bristol 20 M.1C replica   AJD-1   18. 1.89   Cancelled by CAA 22. 6.89 - to CC-DMA
         (Built AJD Engieering Ltd)   *(As "C4988")*

CHINA (PEOPLES REPUBLIC)

Military Museum of China, Beijing
G-BBVZ   Hawker Siddeley HS.121 Trident 2E Series.109   3. 1.74   Cancelled 30. 8.77 - to China as B-294 8.77
                                                2182   *(Subsequently B-2207)*

China Aviation Museum, Chiangping, Beijing (www.china.org.cn)
G-ASDS   Vickers 843 Viscount   453   8.11.62   Cancelled 19. 9.63 - to China as 84303 8.63
                                                            (Subsequently 406 and B-406) (As "50258")

G-BAJJ   Hawker Siddeley HS.121 Trident 2E Series 108   28.11.72   Cancelled 1. 6.76 - to China as 276 6.76
                                                2173   *(Subsequently B-276 and B-2213) (As "50051")*

G-BBWG   Hawker Siddeley HS.121 Trident 2E Series 109   3. 1.74   Cancelled 22. 5.78 - to China as 269 4.78
                                                2188   *(Subsequently B-269) (As "50055")*

Guangzou Technical Institute Museum, Guangzou
G-AZFW   Hawker Siddeley HS.121 Trident 2E Series 102   29. 9.71   Cancelled 6. 9.73 - to China as 246 9.73
                                                2160   *(Subsequently B-2219)*

G-BBVU   Hawker Siddeley HS.121 Trident 2E Series 109   3. 1.74   Cancelled 7. 2.77 - to China as 284 2.77
                                                2177   *(Subsequently B-284 and B-2116)*

G-BBVW   Hawker Siddeley HS.121 Trident 2E Series 109   3. 1.74   Cancelled 1. 4.77 - to China as 288 4.77
                                                2179   *(Subsequently B-288 and B-2117)*

Hong Kong Historic Aviation Association, Chek Lap Kok Airport, Hong Kong
G-AYAZ   Britten-Norman BN-2A-7 Islander   615   9V-BDW   6. 4.70   Cancelled - to R.Hong Kong AuxAF as HKG-7 12.71
                                                   G-AYAZ

Nanjing Hangkong Xueyan, Nanjing

G-BBVV	Hawker Siddeley HS.121 Trident 2E Series 109		3. 1.74	Cancelled 7. 2.77 - *to China as B-286 2.77*
	2178			*(Subsequently B-2210)*

CZECH REPUBLIC
Historicky Ustav Armady Ceske Republicky - Letecke Muzeum Kbely, Prague

G-ACGO	Saunders-Roe A.19 Cloud	A.19/5	8. 5.33	Cancelled - *to OK-BAK 7.34*
				(As "OK-BAK")

DENMARK
Danmarks Flyvemuseum, Helsingør

G-AIWY	de Havilland DH.89A Dragon Rapide	6775	NR676	22.11.46	Cancelled 7. 1.47 - *to OY-AAO*	
					(As "OY-AAO")	
G-AKDK	Miles M.65 Gemini 1A	6469		22. 8.47	Cancelled 5.11.73 as WFU	27. 3.70
					(As "G-AKGE")	
G-AOJG	Hunting-Percival P.66 President I HPAL/PEM/79			27. 3.56	Cancelled 4. 7.59 - *to Danish AF as 69-697 7.59*	
	(Originally regd as Prince 5) (Also c/n P66/79)				*(Subsequently Danish AF M-697 and OY-AVA) (As "OY-AVA")*	
G-AOUF	de Havilland DH.104 Dove 6	04476		19. 7.56	Cancelled 23. 4.68 - *to D-IBYW*	
					(Subsequently OY-DHZ) (As "OY-DHZ")	
G-APJP	de Havilland DH.82A Tiger Moth	82869	(G-AOCV)	30. 7.57	Cancelled 30.10.79 - *to SE-GXO 7.80*	
			R4961		*(As "S-16")*	
G-ASSZ	Cessna 310A	35407	N5207A	12. 5.64	Cancelled 2. 2.69 - *to OY-DRH 4.69*	
	(Riley 65 conversion)				*(As "OY-DRH")*	

Egeskov Veteranmuseum, Egeskov

G-AEYF	General Aircraft Monospar ST.25 Ambulance			31. 5.37	Cancelled - *to Denmark as OY-DAZ 3.39*
		GAL/ST25/95			*(As "OY-DAZ")*
G-AOFR	de Havilland DH.82A Tiger Moth	86425	NL913	27.10.55	Cancelled 20.11.60 - *to SE-COX 9.61*
					(Subsequently OY-BAK and "S-11") (As "NL913")

Dansk Veteranflysamlung, Stauning

G-AFWN	Auster J/1 Autocrat	124		1. 8.39	Cancelled 23. 7.56 - *to D-EKOM 9.56*
	(Originally regd as Taylorcraft Plus D, converted in 1945)				*(As "OY-...")*
G-AHKO	Taylorcraft Plus D	228	LB381	24. 4.46	Cancelled 10. 3.56 - *to D-ECOD 3.56*
					(Subsequently OY-DSH) (As "LB381")
G-AMMA	de Havilland DHC-1 Chipmunk 21	C1/0470		21. 9.51	Cancelled 23. 4.69 - *to OY-DHJ 7.69.*
					(As "OY-AHJ")
G-AMZO	de Havilland DH.87B Hornet Moth	8040	SE-ALD	15. 5.53	Cancelled 14. 2.74 - *restored as OY-DEZ 5.74*
			OY-DEZ, VR-RAI		*(As "OY-DEZ")*
G-ANCY	de Havilland DH.82A Tiger Moth	85234	DE164	12. 9.53	Cancelled 1. 3.55 - *to OO-DLA 5.55*
					(As "OY-ECH")
EI-ATP	Phoenix Luton LA-4A Minor	PAL 1124	G-ASCY	29. 8.69	Cancelled as sold USA 7.73
	(Built Cornelius Bros)				*(Subsequently N924GB) (No marks - not confirmed)*

EGYPT
Military Museum, Alexandria

G-AYBX	Campbell Cricket	CA/331	20. 4.70	Cancelled 1. 9.70 - *to Kuwait*
				(As "G-AYBX")

FINLAND
Keski-Suomen Ilmailumuseo, Tikkakoski, Jyväskylä

G-EBNU	Avro 504K	xxxx---	E448	19. 3.26	Cancelled - *to Finnish AF as 1H49 9.26*
					(As "AV-57")
G-AMJR	de Havilland DH.82A Tiger Moth	85167	T6958	23. 5.51	Cancelled 20. 9.51 - *to OH-ELA*
					(As "OH-XLA")
GN-101	Folland Fo.141 Gnat F.1	FL-8	G-39-6		*(As "G-39-6")*

Suomen Ilmailumuseo, Tietotie, Helsinki

G-AJPC	Fairchild F.24W-41A Argus II	324	FK315	21. 4.47	Cancelled 11. 1.52 - *to OH-FCJ*
	(UC-61-FA)		42-32119		*(As "OH-FCJ")*
G-AKIZ	Fairchild F.24R-41A Argus II	287	EV779	23. 9.47	Cancelled 10. 1.52 - *to OH-FCK.*
	(UC-61-FA)		41-38843		*(As "OH-FCK")*
G-BRXM	Colt GA-42 Gas Airship	1152	31. 1.90		Cancelled 14. 9.90 - *to OH-ITA.*
					(As "OH-KTA") (Gondola only)

FRANCE
Musée des Ballons, Chateau de Balleroy, Balleroy, 14 Calvados

G-BKBR (2)	Cameron Chateau 84SS Balloon (Hot Air)	743	11. 5.82	Cancelled 29. 4.93 as WFU	
	(Forbes Chateau de Balleroy shape)				
G-BKNN	Cameron Minar-E-Pakistan Balloon (Hot Air)	900	7. 2.82	Cancelled 29. 4.93 as WFU	
	(240ft Moslem National Monument shape)				
G-BLFE	Cameron Sphinx 72SS Balloon (Hot Air)	1011	22. 2.84	Cancelled 29. 4.93 as WFU	
	(Egyptian Sphinx shape)				
G-BLRW	Cameron Elephant 77SS Balloon (Hot Air)	1074	14.12.84	Cancelled 14.11.02 by CAA *"Great Sky Elephant"*	1.10.00A
G-BMUN	Cameron Harley 78SS Balloon (Hot Air)	1188	10. 6.86	Cancelled 12.11.01 as WFU	23. 5.99
	(Harley Davidson Motorcycle shape)				
G-BMWN	Cameron Temple 80SS Balloon (Hot Air)	1211	9. 7.86	Cancelled 14.11.02 by CAA *"Temple"*	17. 6.96A
G-BNFK	Cameron Egg 89SS Balloon (Hot Air)	1436	20. 2.87	Cancelled 14.11.02 by CAA	15. 7.02A
	(Faberge Rosebud Egg shape)			*"Faberge Easter Egg"*	
G-BNJU	Cameron Bust 80SS Balloon (Hot Air)	1324	13. 5.87	Cancelled 1.5.03 as WFU	19. 1.03A
				"Ludwig von Beethoven"	

G-BPOV	Cameron Magazine 90SS Balloon (Hot Air) 1890			10. 3.89	Cancelled 14.11.02 by CAA	5. 7.01A
	(Forbes Magazine shape)				*"Forbes Capitalist Tool"*	
G-BPSP	Cameron Ship 90SS Balloon (Hot Air)	1848		10. 3.89	Cancelled 14.11.02 by CAA	17. 6.94
	(Columbus Santa Maria shape)				*"Santa Maria"*	
G-BRWZ	Cameron Macaw 90SS Balloon (Hot Air)				Details in SECTION 1, Part 2	
G-BTCZ	Cameron Chateau-84SS Balloon (Hot Air)				Details in SECTION 1, Part 2	
G-TURK	Cameron Sultan 80SS Balloon (Hot Air)	1711		12. 4.88	Cancelled 28. 8.02 by CAA	18. 6.00A

Musée Aéronautique Presq'île Côte D'Amour, La Baule-Escoublac Aerodrome, La Baule 44 Loire-Atlantique

| G-AVXV | Bleriot XI | 225 | | 2.11.67 | Cancelled 16. 7.92 - *to F-AZIN* |
| | | | | | *(As "F-AZIN")* |

Musée Historique de l'Hydraviation, Biscarrosse, 40 Landes

| G-DUCK | Grumman G.44 Widgeon (OA-14) | 1218 | N3103Q | 15.11.88 | Cancelled 24. 3.93 on transfer to France |
| | | | N58337, 42-38217, NC28679 | | *(As "G-DUCK")* |

Amicale Jean-Baptiste Salis, La Ferté-Alais, 91 Essonne

G-AFNJ	de Havilland DH.94 Moth Minor	94038	AW113	15. 5.39	Impressed as AW113 9. 6.40, restored 6.4.46
			G-AFNJ		Cancelled 17. 7.54 - *sold as F-BAOG 7.54*
					(Subsequently F-PAOG) (As "F-PAOG")
G-ALZF	de Havilland DH.89A Dragon Rapide	6541	X7381	24. 3.50	Cancelled - sold as F-BGON 9.52
					(Subsequently F-AZCA) (As "F-AZCA")
G-ANJG	de Havilland DH.82A Tiger Moth	83875	T7349	12.12.53	Cancelled 26. 5.54 - *sold as F-BGZT 6.54.*
					(As "F-BGZT")
G-ANSG	de Havilland DH.82A Tiger Moth	85569	DE615	2. 6.54	Cancelled: crashed near Caen, France 15.6.57
					(As "G-ANSG")
G-AOGJ	de Havilland DH.82A Tiger Moth	83283	T7025	15.12.55	Cancelled 16. 1.56 - *to OO-SOB 3.56. .*
	(C/n 83285 also quoted)				*(As "OO-SOB")*
G-BECL	CASA 352L	24	Spanish AF T2B-212	27. 7.76	Cancelled 19. 6.90 - *sold as F-AZJU*
	(Junkers Ju.52/3M) (C/n also reported as 103)				*(As "N9+AA")*

Association des Cages à Poules d'Acquitaine, Liorac-sur-Louyre, 24 Dordogne

| G-ANXP | Piper J3C-65 Cub (L-4H-PI) | 12192 | N79819 | 13.12.54 | Cancelled 14.10.55 - *sold as D-EGUL 10.55.* |
| | | | 44-79896 | *(Subsequently PH-CMS, (OO-LSD), OO-GMS - to F-GLMS 12.91) (As "F-GLMS")-* | | |

Collection de la Base Aéronavale de Nimes-Garons, 30 Gard

| EI-ALR | Douglas C-47-DL Dakota | 4579 | EI-ACG | 2. 1.61 | Cancelled 14. 1.61 - *sold to French Navy as 8487/87* |
| | | | 41-18487 | | *(Call sign F-YFGC later F-YGGB) (As "87")* |

Musée de l'Air et de l'Espace, Le Bourget, 93 Seine-Saint-Denis, Paris (www.mae.org)

G-EBYY	Cierva C.8L Mk.2	---		21. 6.28	Sold 4.30 abroad?	13. 7.29
	(Avro 617) (AS Lynx @ 180hp)				*(As "G-EBYY")*	
G-AKCO	Short S.25 Sandringham 7	SH57C	JM719	29. 7.47	Cancelled 10. 5.55	
	(Sunderland GR.3 c/n SB2022 conversion)				*(To VH-APG 10.54 subsequently F-OBIP) (As "F-OBIP")*	
G-ALGB	de Havilland DH.89A Dragon Rapide	6706	HG721	17.12.48	Cancelled - sold as F-BHCD 10.54 (As "F-BHCD")	
EI-ALT	Douglas C-47A-10-DK Dakota	12471	EI-ACT	2. 1.61	Cancelled in 2. 1.61 - *to French Navy as 12471:71*	
			KG436, 42-92647		*(As "12471:71")*	

Musée de L'Automoiliste, Aire de Breguieres, Mougins, Cannes, 06 Alpes-Maritimes

(G-BLXI) (1)	Bleriot Type XI replica	EMK 010		3.85R	NTU - to BAPC.132
	(Built L.D.Goldsmith - pr.no PFA 88-10864 @ 1976 from original components: rebuilt Skysport Engineering @ 1982 - possibly same a/c as BAPC.189)				
	(Anzani 25hp)				*(No markings)*

Ailes Anciennes Toulouse, Blagnac, Toulouse, 31 Haute-Garonne

G-ALWC	Douglas C-47A-25-DK Dakota	13590	KG723	10. 1.50	Cancelled 11. 82 - *to F-GBOL but NTU:*	6. 2.83
			42-93654		cancelled 29. 2.84 by CAA, restored 1. 5.84, cancelled 3. 4.89 by CAA	
					(As G-ALWC")	

GERMANY

Deutches Tecknikmuseum, Berlin

G-BLFL	Douglas C-47B-45-DK Dakota	16954, 34214	N951CA	14. 3.84	Cancelled 12.8.85 - to N951CA: restored 5.11.85:
			G-BLFL, Spanish AF T3-54, N73856, 45-951 cancelled 27. 8.86 - to N951CA (As "45-0951")		
BAPC.194	Santos Dumont Type 20 Demoiselle	PPS/DEM/1	24 bis		*(Built for "Those Magnificent Men in Their Flying Machines" film)*
	(Built Personal Plane Services) (ABC Scorpion 30hp)				*(As "BAPC.194")*

Luftwaffen Museum, Gatow, Berlin

| G-HELI | Saro Skeeter AOP.12 | S2/5110? | | 15. 6.78 | Cancelled 22. 3.95 on sale to Germany. |
| | *(Composite of cabin 7870M/XM556 and boom 7979M/XM529 [S2/5105])* | | | | *(As "XM556")* |

Luftbrückengedenkanlage, Rhein-Main Air Force Base, Frankfurt

EI-ARS (2)	Douglas C-54E-5-DO Skymaster	27289	N88887	9.12.69	Cancelled 22. 6.77 - restored as N88887 8.77
			EL-ALP, N88887, ZS-LMH, N88887, FAR-91, N88887, EI-ARS, LN-TUR, EI-ARS, HB-ILU, N88887, NC88887, 44-9063		
					(As "44-9063")

Luftfahrt Museum, Laatzen- Hannover, Hannover

| G-FXIV | Vickers Supermarine 379 Spitfire FR.XIVc | xxx | Indian AF T44 | 11. 4.80 | Cancelled 5. 2.85 as WFU |
| | | | Indian AF HS..., MV370 | | *(As "MV370")* |

Flugausstellung Junior, Hermeskeil, Trier (www.flugaustellung.de)

G-AMXX	de Havilland DH.104 Dove 2A	04406		22. 1.53	Cancelled 21.10.54 - *to RN as Sea Devon C.20 XJ348 10.54:*
					restored as G-NAVY 6. 1.82: cancelled 2. 7.91 as WFU. (As "XJ348")
G-ARVF	Vickers VC-10-1101	808		16. 1.63	Cancelled as WFU 11. 4.83	23. 7.81
					(As "G-ARVF" in UAE titles)

G-BDIW	de Havilland DH.106 Comet 4C	6470	XR398	1. 9.75	Cancelled 23. 2.81 to Germany	8.6.81
					(As "G-BDIW" in Dan-Air titles)	
G-BKLZ	Vinten Wallis WA-116MC	UMA-01		8.12.82	Cancelled as destroyed 8. 6.89	16.12.83P
	(Aka Vinten VJ-22 Autogyro)				(As "G-55-2")	
G-BXSL	Westland Scout AH.Mk.1	F.9762	XW799	17. 2.98	Cancelled 7. 5.02 by CAA	19. 8.02P
					(As "G-BXSL")	

Luftfahrt Museum Merseburg, Merseburg Sud

G-DEVN	de Havilland DH.104 Devon C.2/2	04269	WB533	26.10.84	Cancelled 16.11.90 by CAA	4.2.85P
					(As "WB533")	

Deutsches Museum, Oberschleisseim, Munich (www.deutsches-museum.de)

G-ALUA	Winter LF-1 Zaunkönig	V-2	VX190	28. 6.49	Cancelled 16. 4.74 - to EI-AYU 5.74	
			D-YBAR		(Subsequently D-EBCQ) (As "D-EBCQ")	
G-AWHA	CASA 2111D	025	Spanish AF B2I-77 14. 5.68		Cancelled 15. 8.70 - to D-CAGI 8.70	
	(He.111H-16)				(As "B2I-77)"	
G-AYUK	Western-Brighton M-B65 Balloon (Hot Air)	003		17. 3.71	Cancelled 10.12.73 - to D-Westfalen II 12.73	
					(As "D-Westfalen II")	
G-BHUW	Boeing-Stearman A75N1 (N2S-5) Kaydet	75-3475	N474	16. 5.80	Cancelled 7.12.83 - to D-EFTX 4.92	
			N64639, BuA.30038		(As "D-EFTX")	

Auto und Technik Museum, Sinsheim (www.tecknik.museum.de)

G-AKLL	Douglas C-47A-30-DK Dakota	14005/25450	KG773	18.11.47	Cancelled 6. 6.50 - to EC-AEU	
			43-48189		(Subsequently Spanish AF T.3-62, N8041A and "D-CORA") (As "D-CADE")	
G-ARUE (2)	de Havilland DH.104 Dove 7	04530	Irish Air Corps 194	7.10.80	Sold as D-IKER 10.83 and cancelled 17.7.86 by CAA	
			(G-ARUE)		(No markings)	
G-AWHS	Hispano HA.1112-MIL Buchon	228	Spanish AF C4K-170 14. 5.68		Cancelled 17. 2.69 on sale to Spain	
	(Messerschmitt Bf.109G) (Daimler-Benz.605D)				(Subsequently N170BG) (As "4+-" in Luftwaffe c/s)	

Albatros Flugmuseum, Stuttgart Airport, Stuttgart

G-AVHE	Vickers 812 Viscount	363	(G-AVGY)	20. 2.67	Cancelled 14. 2.73 as destroyed	
			N251V		(WFU 30. 3.70 and broken up 8.72)	
					(Forward fuselage only as "G-AVHE")	
G-BGGR	North American AT-6A Harvard	77-4176	Portuguese AF	17. 1.79	Cancelled 20. 4.79 - D-FOBY reserved 4.79)	
			1608, 41-217		(As "D-FOBY")	

Deutsches Segelfligzeugmuseum, Wassererkuppe

BGA 1711	Aachen FVA.10B Rheinland	xxxx	CPZ	4.72	(As "D-12-354")	
			RAFGGA521			
BGA 3277	Lippisch Hols-der-Teufel replica	xxxx-	FHQ	6.87	(As "BGA .3277")	

ISRAEL

Israeli Air Force Museum, Hatzerim Air Force Base, Beersheba

G-AHAY	Auster V J/1 Autocrat	1956		12. 3.46	Cancelled - to Israel 10. 3.83 for preservation	
					(Subsequently "VQ-PAS" and "1948") (As "13")	
G-AIYT	Douglas C-47A-10-DK Dakota	12486	KG451	20.12.46	Cancelled 12. 3.47 - to ZS-BCJ 4.47	
			42-92661			
G-AJMC	Bristol 156 Beaufighter TF.X	---	RD448	10. 4.47	Cancelled 28. 5.49 - to Israeli DF/AF	
					(As "171")	
G-AKRS	de Havilland DH.89A Dragon Rapide	6952	RL981	21. 1.48	Cancelled 29. 2.84 - to Israeli DF/AF Museum as 4X-970/002 @ 5.78	
					(As "VQ-PAR:002")	
G-AZBV	Britten-Norman BN-2A-2 Islander	285	(EI-AVO)	16. 7.71	Cancelled 16. 3.72 - to 4X-AYK 5.72	
			G-AZBV, G-51-285		(Subsequently 4X-FNP) (As "004:4X-FMD")	

ITALY

Museo Nazionale della Scienza e della Tecnica, Milan

G-ACXA	Cierva C.30A	753		4. 4.35	Cancelled - to I-CIER 8.35	
	(Avro 671)				(As "I-CIER")	

Museo Storico dell'Aeronautica Militaire Italiana, Vigna di Valle

G-ALMB	Westland-Sikorsky S-51 Dragonfly Mk.1A	WA/H/006		29. 3.49	Cancelled 13. 4.51 - to I-MCOM 4.51	
					(As "MM80118")	
G-FIST	Fieseler Fi.156C-3 Storch	156-5802	D-EDEC	23.11.83	Cancelled 4.12.90 by CAA: restored 25.2.91:	
			I-FAGG, MM12822		cancelled 24. 4.95 on sale to Italy)	
					(As "MM12822/20")	

JAPAN

Tokyo Metropolitan College of Aeronautical Engineering "Fame " Gallery, Tokyo

G-AKVD	Chrislea CH.3 Series 2 Super Ace	112	(VH-BRP)	8. 3.48	Cancelled 10. 2.53 - to JA3062 2.53	
			G-AKVD			

JORDAN

Royal Jordanian Air Force Historic Flight, King Abdulla Air Base, Amman

G-AIPW	Taylorcraft Auster 5A Series 160	2204		9. 1.47	Cancelled 13.11.95 on sale to Jordan	
	(Originally regd as J/1 Autocrat)				(As "A-410" in Arab Legion AF c/s)	
G-ATGK	de Havilland DH.104 Riley Dove 400	04288	F-BORJ	12. 7.65	Cancelled 7. 3.67 - sold as F-BORJ	
	(Originally regd as DH.104 Dove 5B)		G-ATGK, R.Jordanian AF D-102, TJ-ACC, (TJ-ABG) (As "JY-AEU")			
					(Restored 21. 2.75: cancelled 19.12.75 - sold as JY-AEU)	
G-BOOM	Hawker Hunter T.7 (T.53)	41H/693749	G-9-432	6.10.80	Cancelled 23.6.97 on sale to Jordan.	
			R.Danish AF ET-274, R.Netherlands AF N-307 (As Jordan AF "800")			
G-BVLM	de Havilland DH.115 Vampire T.55	976	ZH563	6. 4.94	Cancelled 23. 6.97 on sale to Jordan	
	(Built F + W)		Swiss AF U-1216		(As Jordan AF "209")	

G-BVPO	de Havilland DH.100 Vampire FB.6	615	HB-RVO	11. 7.94	Cancelled 23. 6.97 *on sale to Jordan.*	
	(Built F + W)		Swiss AF J-1106		*(As Jordan AF "109")*	
G-BWKA	Hawker Hunter F.58	41H-697442	Swiss AF J-4075	12.10.95	Cancelled 23. 6.97 *on sale to Jordan.*	
					(As Jordan AF "843")	
G-BWKC	Hawker Hunter F.58	41H-697394	Swiss AF J-4025	12.10.95	Cancelled 29. 9.99 *on sale to Jordan*	
					(As Jordan AF "712:E")	

KUWAIT
Kuwait Air Force Collection, Kuwait International Airport

G-ANNW	Auster J/5F Aiglet Trainer	3120		15. 2.54	Cancelled 25. 6.60 - *to K-AAAE 8.60*	
					(Subsequently 9K-AAE) (As "K-AAAE ")	
G-APXA	Westland-Sikorsky S-55 Whirlwind Series.2			28.10.59	Cancelled 25. 6.60 - *to 9K-BHA 5.60*	
	(Originally regd as Series 1)	WA/318			*(Subsequently Kuwait AF 312)*	
G-APXB	Westland-Sikorsky S-55 Whirlwind Series.2			28.10.59	Cancelled 25. 6.60 - *to 9K-BHB 6.60*	
	(Originally regd as Series 1)	WA/319			*(Subsequently Kuwait AF 313)*	

Museum of Science and Industry, Kuwait City

| G-AXEE | English Electric Lightning F.53 | 95311 | G-27-86 | 24. 4.69 | Cancelled 10. 6.69 - *to Kuwaiti AF as 418* | |
| | | | | | *(As "53-418")* | |

MALTA
Malta Aviation Museum Foundation, Ta'Qali

| G-ANFW | de Havilland DH.82A Tiger Moth | 85660 | DE730 | 5.11.53 | Cancelled 10. 3.00 by CAA | 21. 7.01 |
| | *(Built Morris Motors) (Regd with Fuselage No.3737)* | | | | *(As G-"ANFW")* | |

MALAYSIA
Muzium Tentera Udara Diraja Malaysia, Sungai Besi Airfield, Kuala Lumpur

G-ANEJ	de Havilland DH.82A Tiger Moth	85592	DE638	1.10.53	Cancelled as WFU 10. 9.73 - DBR landing Owstwich, Yorkshire 15. 5.65	
					(Sold R.Malaysian AF 2.89) (As "T7245")	
G-APJT	Scottish Aviation Twin Pioneer Series.1	529		18.12.57	Cancelled 18. 4.58 - *to Malaysian AF as FM1001 4.58*	

NETHERLANDS
Aviodrome Museum, Lelystad Airfield, Lelystad

G-EACN	BAT FK.23 Bantam	FK23/15	K-123	22. 7.19	Cancelled .7.19 - NTU and no CofA issued	
	(ABC Wasp)		F1654		*(Originally regd as K-123 @ 29. 5.19) (As "K-123")*	
G-AMCA	Douglas C-47B-30DK Dakota 3	16218/32966	KN487	1. 6.50	Cancelled 16.10.03 as WFU	10.12.00A
			44-76634		*(As "PH-ALR" in KLM orange prewar c/s Holland titles)*	
G-AMFU	de Havilland DH.104 Dove 6	04117	VP-KDE	30.10.50	Cancelled 7. 8.69 - *to OO-SCD.*	
	(Originally regd as a Dove 1)				*(Front fuselage only as "OO-SCD")*	
G-BKRG	Beech C-45G-BH	AF-222	N75WB	5. 5.83	Cancelled 27. 4.98 as WFU	
	(Regd as C-45H)		N9072Z, 51-11665		*(As "G-BKRG")*	
G-BVOL	Douglas C-47B-40-DL Dakota	9836	ZS-NJE (2)	14. 6.94	Cancelled 16. 5.96 on sale to the Netherlands for spares	
			SAAF 6867, FD938, 42-23974		*(As "PH-TCB" in postwar KLM c/s)*	
EI-AKA	Fokker F-27 Friendship 100	10105	PH-FAA	10. 9.57	Cancelled 6.66 - *to PH-FSF.*	
					(Subsequently ZK-NAH, VH-NLS) (As "PH-FHF")	
BAPC.22	Mignet HM.14 Pou-Du-Ciel replica	WM.1			*(As "G-AE0F")*	
	(Scott A2S)					
BAPC.105	Bleriot Type XI	54				
	(Composite from original components including c/n 54: built L.D.Goldsmith @ 1976 at RAF Colerne) (Anzani "V" 25hp)					

Vliegend Museum Seppe, Seppe Airfield, Rosendaal

| G-AIPE | Taylorcraft J Auster 5 | 1416 | TJ347 | 17.12.46 | Cancelled 22. 5.52 - *to PH-NET (2) 6.52* | |
| | | | | | *(As "PH-NET")* | |

NEW ZEALAND
Jean Batten Memorial, Terminal Building, Auckland International Airport, Auckland

| G-ADPR | Percival Type D Gull Six | D.55 | AX866 | 29. 8.35 | Cancelled 14. 3.95 - *to ZK-DPR* | 1. 8.95P |
| | | | G-ADPR | | | |

Museum of Transport, Technolgy and Social History, Point Chevalier, Auckland

G-AGCN	Lockheed 18-56 Lodestar II (C-56D-LO)	2020	AX756	29. 9.41	Cancelled 19.11.47 - *restored as AX756 @ 11.47*	
	(Originally regd as 18-08 Lodestar I; converted 1944)		42-53504, NC25630			
					(Subsequently EC-Axx 12.48, Spanish AF T.4-? @ 1.49, N9933F and ZK-BVE)	
G-AHJR (2)	Short S.25 Sunderland MR.5	SH1552	SZ584	27. 6.46	Cancelled 15. 5.48 - *restored as SZ584 @ 4.48*	
					(As "NZ4115")	
G-AMMC	Miles M.14A Hawk Trainer 3	779	L8353	15. 9.51	Cancelled 1.10.53 - *to ZK-AYW 11.53*	
					(As "L8353")	
G-AMRM	de Havilland DH.82A Tiger Moth	83513	T7106	18. 4.52	Cancelled 3. 6.52 - *to ZK-BBI 8.52*	

Air Force World - Royal New Zealand Air Force Museum, RNZAF Wigram, Christchurch

G-AINT	Bristol 170 Freighter 31MNZ	12834	G-18-100	27. 1.47	Cancelled 17. 4.52 - *to R.New Zealand AF as NZ5903 2.52*	
G-BIAT	Sopwith Pup replica	001		3.12.82	Cancelled 9. 8.89 - *to Australia - NTU - to New Zealand as "N6460"*	
	(Built Skysport Engineering Ltd)					

New Zealand Vintage Aero Club, Hamilton Airport, Hamilton East

G-AHHE	Auster V J/1 Autocrat	1994		9. 4.46	Cancelled as NTU - *to G-AERO 5.46*	
					(Subsequently ZK-AWX)	
BGA 787	Slingsby T.42B Eagle	1091			Cancelled - *to ZK-GBG*	

Argosy Trust, Woodborne, Woodbourne Airfield, Marlborough

| G-ASXM | Armstrong-Whitworth 650 Argosy Series 222 | | | 14.10.64 | Cancelled 22. 6.70 - *sold as CF-TAG* | |
| | | AW.6801 | | | *(Subsequently EI-AVJ, CF-TAG and ZK-SAF) (Fuselage only)* | |

| G-ASXN | Armstrong-Whitworth 650 Argosy Series .222 | | | 14.10.64 | Cancelled 31. 1.70 - sold as CF-TAJ. |
| | | AW.6802 | | | (Subsequently ZK-SAE) |

New Zealand Sport and Vintage Aviation Society, Hood Airport, Masterton

G-AFSH	de Havilland DH.82A Tiger Moth	82139	X5106	20. 4.39	Cancelled - to X5106 5.1.40, restored 4.1.52
			G-AFSH		cancelled 23. 3.52 - to ZK-BAT 3.52
G-ANSJ	de Havilland DH.82A Tiger Moth	85071	T6802	10. 6.54	Cancelled 7.10.56 - to ZK-BLV 10.55
G-ANSU	de Havilland DH.82A Tiger Moth	85768	DE883	29. 6.54	Cancelled 15. 8.54 - to ZK-BGY 11.54
					(Subsequently ZK-BVN)
G-AOAF	de Havilland DH.82A Tiger Moth	82812	R4895	14. 3.55	Cancelled 16. 5.55 - to ZK-BLK 8.55

Omaka Heritage Aviation Centre, Marlborough

EI-APU (2)	Fokker D.VII/65 replica	01	F-BNDG	2. 6.67	Cancelled 28. 5.85 - to N902AC - now ZK-FOD
	(Built Rousseau Aviation)				
EI-ARC	Pfalz D.III replica	PPS/PFLZ/1	G-ATIF	29. 5.67	Cancelled 28. 5.85 - to N906AC - now ZK-FLZ
	(Built Personal Plane Services)				
EI-ARD	Pfalz D.III replica	PT.16	G-ATIJ	29. 5.67	Cancelled 28. 5.85 - to N905AC - now ZK-JPI
	(Built Hampshire Aeroplane Club)				

Queenstown Museum, Queenstown

| G-ANGV | AusterV J/1B Aiglet | 3122 | | 30.11.53 | Cancelled 23. 3.54 - to ZK-BDX 3.54 |

Wanaka Transport Museum, Wanaka Airport, Wanaka

G-AJEC	Auster V J/1 Autocrat	2327		14. 3.47	Cancelled 18.11.54 - to ZK-BJL 1.55
G-AOMF	Percival P.40 Prentice 1	PAC-252	(VH-...)	3. 5.56	Cancelled - to ZK-DJC 6.72
	(Officially regd with c/n 5820/1)		G-AOMF, VS316		

NORWAY

Forsvarsmuseet Flysamlingen, Gardemoen

G-ASCF	Beagle A.61 Terrier 2	B.617	WE548	23. 7.62	Cancelled 10. 4.67 - to SE-ELO 9.67
					(As "RT514")
G-BMEW	Lockheed 18-56 Lodestar	18-2444	OH-SIR	30. 9.85	Cancelled 15. 7.86 on sale to "Canada"
	(C-60A-5-LO) (Gulfstar conversion c.4.59)		(N283M), OH-MAP, N283M, N9223R, N105G, N69898 ,NC69898, 42-55983		
					(As "G-AGIH")

Flyhistorick Museum Sola, Stavangar-Lufthavn

G-AKKA	Miles M.65 Gemini 1A	6528		21.10.47	Cancelled 27. 4.48 - to LN-TAH
					(As "LN-TAH")
G-AOXL	de Havilland DH.114 Heron 1B	14015	(LN-BFY)	5. 4.57	Cancelled 13. 9.71 - to LN-BFY: NTU and restored 21.9.71
			G-AOXL, PK-GHB		Cancelled 11.10.71 - to LN-BFY 2.72
					(As "LN-PSG" in Braathens- SAFE c/s)
G-BBZL	Westland-Bell 47G-3B1	WA/583	S Yemen AF 404	26. 2.74	Cancelled 2. 6.82- to SE-HME 6.82
					(Subsequently "LN-ORB") (As "LN-ORB")
G-BCZS	Fairey Britten-Norman BN-2A-21 Islander	441		1. 4.75	Cancelled 19. 8.77 - to LN-MAF 5..57
					(As "LN-MAF"")

OMAN

Sultanate of Oman Armed Forces Museum, Bait al Falaj Airfield, Muscat

| G-BGSB | Hunting-Percival P.56 Provost T.1 | PAC/F/057 | 7922M | 21. 5.79 | Cancelled 11.12.87 by CAA - to Oman AF 1982 |
| | (C/n officially quoted as 886391) (Also c/n P56/57) | | WV494 | | (As "XF868") |

PAPUA - NEW GUINEA

Air Nuigini Collection, Jackson Airport, Port Moresby

| G-AMZH | Douglas C-47B-20-DK Dakota | 15665/27110 | KN421 | 2. 5.53 | Cancelled 20. 5.65 - to VH-SBW 22.5.65 |
| | | | 43-49849 | | (Subsequently P2-SBW 1.6.74 and P2-ANQ 3.12.75). |

PORTUGAL

Museu do Ar, Alverca (www.emfa.pt/museu)

G-ASCB	Beagle A.109 Airedale	B.527		23. 7.62	Crashed into River Douro, Barqueiros do Douro, Portugal
					26. 7.64: rebuilt as CS-AIB 6.68 and cancelled
					(As "CS-AIB")
BGA 619	Slingsby T.21B	551		10.48	Sold as CS-PAI 1.51
					(As "CS-PAI")

SAUDI ARABIA

Dhahran Air Force Base Collection, King Abdul-al-Azix Air Base, Dhahran

| G-BFOO | British Aircraft Corporation 167 Strikemaster Mk.80A | G-27-312 | | 22..3.78 | Cancelled xx 5.78 - to R.Saudi AF as 1135 |
| | | PS.366 | | | |

SERBIA and MONTENEGRO

Muzej Yugoslovenskog Vazduhplovsta, Surcin Airport, Belgrade

G-AHLX	Douglas C-47A-30-DK Dakota	14035/25480	KG803	8. 5.46	Cancelled 23.12.47 - to YU-ABG 12.47
			43-48219		(As "YU-ABG")
G-AKLS	Short SA.6 Sealand 1	SH1567	G-14-2	26.11.47	Cancelled 7. 3.51 - to YU-CFK 9.51
			G-AKLS, (VP-TBC), G-AKLS		(As "0662")
11601	Folland Fo.141 Gnat F.1	FL-14	G-39-8		(As "11601")

SINGAPORE

Singapore Science Centre, Singapore

| G-AJLR | Airspeed AS.65 Consul | 5136 | R6029 | 25. 5.47 | Cancelled 26. 2.73 as WFU | 23. 4.63 |
| | | | | | (As "VR-SCO") (Noted wrecked 2.03) | |

REPUBLIC of SOUTH AFRICA

Classic Jets South Africa, Cape Town International Airport, Cape Town

G-BVWG	Hawker Hunter T.8C	41H-693836	XL598	8.12.94	Cancelled 12. 6.95 - to ZU-ATH	
	(Officially regd with c/n 41H-695320)				"880"	
G-BVWV	Hawker Hunter F.6A	41H-679991	8829M	22.12.94	Cancelled 30. 8.95 - to ZU-AUJ 9.95	
	(Officially regd with c/n 41H-674112)		XE653		(All yellow - no marks carried)	
G-FSIX	English Electric Lightning F.6	95116	XP693	31.12.92	Cancelled 13. 2.97 - to ZU-BEY 2.97	
					(As "XP693")	
G-LTNG	English Electric Lightning T.5	B1/95011	8503M	8.11.89	Cancelled 13. 2.97 - to ZU-BEX 2.97	
			XS451		(As "XS451")	
G-OPIB	English Electric Lightning F.6	95238	XR773	31.12.92	Cancelled 13. 2.97 - to ZU-BEW 2.97	
					(As "XR773")	

South African Airways Museum and Historic Flight, Jan Smuts International Airport, Johannesburg (www.historicflight.co.za)

G-AHOT	Vickers 498 Viking 1A	121	XD635	27. 6.46	Cancelled 26. 9.54 - to ZS-DKH 10.54
			G-AHOT		
G-AWFM	de Havilland DH.104 Dove 6	04079	9J-RHX	27. 3.68	Cancelled 26. 8.81 - to ZS-BCC 10.78
			VP-YLX, VP-RCL, ZS-BCC, (G-AJOU)		
G-BFHE	CASA 352L	164	Spanish AF T2B-273 23.11.77		Cancelled 12. 5.81 - to ZS-UYU 8.81
	(Junkers Ju 52/3m)				(Subsequently ZS-AFA)

Caesar's Place Casino, Jan Smuts International Airport, Johannesburg

G-AMZW	Douglas C-47B-20-DK Dakota	15654/27099	KN231	29. 5.53	Cancelled 1. 7.53 - to SN-AAH 7.53
			43-49838		(Subsequently ST-AAH, Sudan AF 424, ST-AAH) (As SAAF 6850 and/or ZS-BMF)

Wings and Wheels Museum , Jack Taylor Airfield, Krugersdorp

G-ASRL	Beagle A.61 Terrier 2	B.631	WE609	18. 3.64	Cancelled as WFU 18. 9.69 - crashed Kota, Malawi 18.4.69
					(Repaired as VP-WDN 1970)

South African Air Force Museum, Pretoria

G-EAML	Airco DH.6	---	C9449	8. 9.19	Cancelled 19. 9.19 - to South Africa	18. 9.20
					(Components only preserved as "G-EAML")	
G-AITF	Airspeed AS.40 Oxford 1	---	ED290	1.11.46	Cancelled 31.10.61 as PWFU	8. 6.60
					(As "G-AITF")	
G-AJTI	Miles M.65 Gemini 1A	6444		2. 6.47	Cancelled 8.10.47 - to ZS-BRV 10.47	
G-AOPL	Percival P.40 Prentice 1	PAC-207	VS609	30. 5.56	Cancelled 24. 4.67 - to ZS-EUS 5.67	

SPAIN

Col-Lecccio d'Automobils de Salvador Claret, Sils-Girona

G-AGXS	Auster V J/1 Autocrat	1967		24. 1.46	Cancelled 12. 5.55 - to EC-ALD 8.55.
					(As "EC-ALD")

Fundación Infante de Orleans, Cuatro-Vientos, Madrid

G-ABUU	Comper CLA.7 Swift	S.32/5		7. 3.32	Cancelled 18.1.99 - to EC-HAM 2.99	
					(As "EC-AAT")	
G-ACXK	de Havilland DH.60G-III Moth Major	5095		18. 8.34	Abandoned Bucharest, Romainia on German invasion 9.39:	
					cancelled 11.45 (As EC-INK)	
G-ADLS	Miles M.3C Falcon Six	231		15. 7.35	Cancelled 8.36 - to EC-ACB	
	(Provenance not confirmed)				(As "EC-ACB")	
G-AEVZ	BA L.25c Swallow II	475		19. 3.37	Cancelled 7.9.01 as sold to Spain as EC-IMP	15. 6.01P
	(Blackburn Cirrus Minor)				(As EC-IMP)	
G-AFAX	BA Eagle 2				Details in SECTION 1, Part 2	
					(As G-AFAX)	
G-AKAA	Piper J3C-65 Cub (L-4H-PI)	10780	43-29489	23. 6.47	Cancelled 31.10.96 - to EC-GQE 10.96	
					(As "EC-GQE")	

Museo del Aire, Cuatro-Vientos, Madrid

G-ABXH	Cierva C.19 Mk.IVP	5158		1. 6.32	Cancelled - to EC-W13 and EC-ATT 12.32	
	(Avro 620)				(Subsequently Spanish AF 30-62, EC-CAB and EC-AIM)	
					(As "EC-AIM'")	
G-ACYR	de Havilland DH.89 Dragon Rapide	6261		15.10.34	WFU (Olley Air Services titles)	23. 8.47
					(As "G-ACYR")	
G-AERN	de Havilland DH.89A Dragon Rapide	6345		13. 1.37	Cancelled - sold as EC-AKO 12.54	
					(As "40-1")	
BGA 1402	Slingsby HP-14C	1637			To EC-BOL 5.68 (As "EC-BOL")	

SRI LANKA

Katunayake-Negombe Base Collection, Negombo

G-APCN	Boulton Paul P.108 Balliol T.2	BPA.10C	WG224	12. 5.57	Cancelled 13. 8.57 - to Ceylon AF as CA310 8.57
	(Second issue of c/n)				

Sri Lanka Air Force Musem, Ratamalana Air Force Base, Ratamalana

G-AKEE	de Havilland DH.82A Tiger Moth	---	"T7179"	18. 8.47	Cancelled 25. 9.47 - to VP-CAW 9.47
					(Subsequently CY-AAW) (As "CX-123")
G-AMJY	Douglas C-47B-40-DK Dakota	16808/33556	KP254	2. 6.51	Cancelled 11.11.59 - to 4R-ACI 11.59
			44-77224		(As "CR-822")

SWEDEN

Svedinos Bil Och Flygmuseum, Slöinge, Halmstad

G-EBNO	de Havilland DH.60 Moth	261		19. 2.26	Cancelled 26. 7.28 - to S-AABS
	(Cirrus I)				(Subsequently SE-ABS) (As "Fv5555")
G-AIZW	Auster V J/1 Autocrat	2230		31. 1.47	Cancelled 14. 8.58 - to SE-CGR
					(As "SE-CGR")

G-AKAO   Miles M.38 Messenger 2A   6703   27. 6.47   Cancelled 7. 9.53 - *to SE-BYY*
                                                                                      (As "SE-BYY")
G-ANSO   Gloster Meteor T.7   G5/1525   G-7-1   12. 6.54   Cancelled 11. 8.59 - *to SE-DCC*
                                                                                      (As "WS774:4")
            (Originally built and regd 19. 6.50 as Meteor F.8 G-AMCJ {G5/1210}: to R.Danish AF as 490, then Egyptian AF as 1424, then rebuilt as G-ANSO)
G-AYZM   Scottish Aviation Bulldog Serie 101 BH.100-105   25. 5.71   Cancelled 2. 9.71 - *to Swedish Army as Fv61005 8.71.*
                                                                                      (As "Fv61005")

High Chapperal Park, Hillerstorp
G-AVJB   Vickers 815 Viscount   375   (LX-LGD)   21. 3.67   Cancelled 28.10.86 - *to SE-IVY*
                                                        G-AVJB, AP-AJF   *"Big Airland" (As "SE-IVY")*

Flyvapenmuseum, Malmslatt, Linköping
G-ANVU   de Havilland DH.104 Dove 1B   04082   VR-NAP   12.11.54   WFU 1977: cancelled 20. 6.85 by CAA: 14. 9.77T
            (Originally regd as Series.1)   restored 15.4.86: cancelled 16. 9.86 *on sale to Sweden)*
                                                                                      (As "G-ANVU")
G-AZAK   Scottish Aviation Bulldog Series 101 (SK-61)   18. 6.71   Cancelled 17. 9.71 - *to Swedish Army as Fv61006*
                                                BH.100/106   *(As "Fv61006")*
G-AZJO   Scottish Aviation Bulldog Series 101 (SK-61)   8.12.71   Cancelled 7. 2.72 - *to Swedish Army as Fv61030*
                                                BH.100/137   *(As "Fv61030")*
G-AZWO   Scottish Aviation Bulldog Series 101 (SK-61)   8. 6.72   Cancelled 19.10.72 - *to Swedish Army as Fv61068*
                                                BH.100/186   *(As "Fv61068")*

Arlanda Flygmuseum, Arlanda Airport, Stockholm
G-AAHD   Avro 594 Avian IV   R3/CN/318   5.29   Cancelled - *to Sweden as SE-ADT 8.33*
                                                                                      (As "SE-ADT" in nearby shopping complex)
G-AGIJ   Lockheed 18-56 Lodestar II   2593   43-16433   4. 3.44   Cancelled 9. 7.45 - *to R.Norwegian AF as 2593:T-AE*
            (C-60A-5-LO)   *(Subsequently OH-VKP and SE-BZE)*
                                                                                      (As "SE-BZE")
G-ANIU   Taylorcraft J Auster 5   841   MS977   5.12.53   Cancelled 12.10.55 - *to LN-BDU 2.55.(Subsequently SE-CBT)*
                                                                                      (As "SE-CBT")

Västerås Flygmuseum, Hässlo Airfield, Västerås
G-BAVN   Boeing-Stearman A75N-1 Kaydet   75-5659 4X-AMT   13. 4.73   Cancelled 22.10.84 - *to SE-AMT 8.84*
            (Regd with c/n "3250-2606", which is a part number) N5367N, 42-17496   *(As "SE-AMT")*
G-BNPG   Percival P.66 Pembroke C.1   PAC/66/082 XK884   30. 6.87   Cancelled 4. 5.88 - *to SE-BKH*
                              (Also c/n K66/045)   *(As "SE-BKH"")*

THAILAND
Foundation for the Preservation and the Development of Thai Aircraft, Don Muang Air Force Base, Don Muang, Bangkok
G-AMOU   de Havilland DH.82A Tiger Moth   84695   N200D   5. 2.52   Cancelled 18.11.93 on sale to Thailand.
                                                        9M-ALJ, VR-RBZ, G-AMOU, T6269 *(As "21")*

Royal Thai Air Force Museum, Don Muang Air Force Base, Don Muang, Bangkok
G-AMJW   Westland-Sikorsky S-51 Mk.1A   WA/H/120 G-17-2   9. 1.52   Cancelled 22. 5.53 - *to R.Thailand AF as 305-53 5.53*

Golden Jubilee Museum of Agriculture, Khlong Luang
G-AWID   Britten-Norman BN-2A Islander   26   17. 4.68   Cancelled - *to R.Thailand AF as 501 10.68*

UNITED ARAB EMIRATES
Al Mahata Museum, The Sharjah Aviation Museum, Sharjah
G-ARDE   de Havilland DH.104 Dove 6   04469   I-TONY   15.11.60   Cancelled 30. 5.01 by CAA)   25. 8.91
                                                                                      (As "G-AJPR" in Gulf Air c/s

UNITED STATES
Southern Museum of Flight, Birmingham, Alabama (www.southernmuseumofflight.org/
G-ASOF   Beagle B.206 Series.1   B.007   28. 1.64   Cancelled 29.12.80 - *to N163 (As "N163")*
G-AVLK   Beagle B.206 Series 2   B.059   8. 5.67   Cancelled 16. 4.74 - *to N15JP (As "N15JP")*
EI-APV   Fokker D.VII/65 replica   03   F-BNDH   2. 6.67   Cancelled 28. 5.85 - *to N904AC(As "N904AC").*
            (Built Rousseau Aviation)

United States Army Aviation Museum, Fort Rucker, Alabama (www.armyavnmuseum.org)
G-BSKS   Nieuport 28C-1   6531   "N5246"   27. 6.90   Cancelled 1. 4.93 on sale to US
                                                        US Navy   *(As "17-6531:5" in 94 Aero Sqn AEF c/s)*

Alaska Aviation Heritage Museum, Anchorage, Alaska (www.alaskaairmuseum.org)
G-AGZI   Consolidated-Vultee CV.32-3 (LB-30) Liberator II   55   AL557   11. 1.46   Cancelled 24. 2.48 - *to SX-DAA 2.48*
                                                                                      (Subsequently N9981F, N68735 and N92MK) (As "N92MK")

Planes of Fame Air Museum, Chino, California (www.planesoffame.org)
G-BJSG   Vickers Supermarine 361 Spitfire LF.IXc   HS543   29. 1.81   Cancelled 3.12.01 - *to NX2TF*
            (Also firewall No.6S/730116)   6S/735188   Indian AF, G-15-11, ML417   *(As "NX2TF")*
G-BTHD   Yakovlev Yak-3U   170101   (France)   7. 3.91   Cancelled 14. 3.05 - *to N.....*
            (Conversion of LET Yak C.11)   Egypt AF 533   *(As "30")*
G-WWII   Vickers-Supermarine 379 Spitfire F.XIVe   F-AZSJ   9. 7.79   Cancelled 6. 2.98 - *to F-AZSJ., restored 19. 3.92*   5. 6 04P
                                               6S/663452   G-WWII, F-AZSJ, Indian AF, SM832   - *cancelled 16. 2.04 - to N54SF (As "NX54SF")*
BAPC.110   Fokker D.VIIF fsm   *(As "5125:18")*
BAPC.136   Deperdussin 1913 Monoplane fsm   *(As "19")*
BAPC.140   Curtiss 42A (R3C2) fsm   *(As "3" in US Army c/s)*
BAPC.141   Macchi M.39 fsm   *(As "5")*
            (Gipsy Queen)
BAPC.156   Supermarine S.6B fsm   *(As "S1595")*

Yanks Air Museum, Chino, California (www.yanksair.com)

G-BUCF	Grumman F8F-1B Bearcat	D.779	R.Thai AF 122095	18. 2.92	Cancelled 12.11.92 - to N2209 8.93
			BuA.122095		(As "N2209")

Palm Springs Air Museum, Palm Springs, California (www.palmspringsairmuseum.org)

G-BLZW	Republic P-47D-30-RA Thunderbolt	399-55744	N47DE	15. 7.85	Cancelled 4.11.85 - to NX47RP 3.86. .
			Peruvian AF 122, Peruvian AF 547, 45-49205 (Subsequently N47DE 6.86) (As "228473""")		
G-FIRE	Vickers Supermarine 379 Spitfire FR.XIVc		Belgium AF SG128	21. 3.79	Cancelled 13. 2.89 -to N8118J 2.89. .
		6S/648206	G-15-1, NH904		(Subsequently N114BP)

Western Aerospace Museum, Oakland, California (www.westernaerospacemuseum.org/

G-AKNP	Short S.45 Solent 3	S.1295	NJ203	2.12.47	Cancelled 20. 3.51 - to VH-TOB 1.51
					(Subsequently N9946F) (As "NJ203")

Aviation Museum of Santa Paula, Santa Paula, California (www.amszp.org/

G-AAMZ (2)	de Havilland DH.60G Moth	1293	EC-ABX	13. 7.87	Cancelled 4. 9.98 - to N60MZ
			EC-BAU, Spanish AF 30-52, EC-NAN, M-CNAN, MW-134 (As "G-AAMZ")		
G-AMLF	de Havilland DH.82A Tiger Moth	86572	PG675	18. 8.51	Cancelled 21. 7.71 - to N675LF (As "G-ADGV").

Pacific Coast Air Museum, Santa Rosa, California (pacificcoastairmuseum.org)

G-AXEF	British Aircraft Corporation 167 Strikemaster Mk.81 G-27-35			24. 4.69	Cancelled 10. 6.69 - to South Yemen AF as 503
	EEP/JP/165 & PS.128				(Subsequently Singapore AF 322 and N167SM (As "N167M")

Church Street Collection, Orlando, Florida

BAPC.139	Fokker Dr.1 Triplane fsm				(As "102/17")

Fantasy of Flight, Polk City, Florida (www.fantasyofflight.com)

G-AHMJ	Cierva C.30A	R3/CA/43	K4235	8. 5.46	Cancelled 9. 2.50 as WFU
	(Avro 671) (Rota I) (Official c/n quoted incorrectly as 774 - which was a Danish Avro 621)				(Restored 8. 4.93: cancelled 12.11.98 - to US) (As "K4235")
G-AMYA(2)	Zlin Z.381 Bestmann	461	OO-AVC	17. 6.87	Cancelled by CAA 31.10.96 - to NX181BU 21. 2.96P
	(Czech-built Bücker Bü.181 Bestmann)		OK-AVC		(As "AM+YA")
G-ASKB	de Havilland DH.98 Mosquito TT.35	xxxx	N35MK	8. 7.63	Cancelled 17. 6.83 - to N35MK and restored 16.3.87:
			G-ASKB, N35MK, G-ASKB, RS712 cancelled 20.10.87 - to N35MK 3.88 (As " NX35MK")		
					(Used in film "Mosquito Squadron" 6.68 as "HJ690: HT-N")
			(On loan to Experimental Aircraft Association Air Adventure Museum, Witttman Field, Oshkosh, Wisconsin)		
G-AYFO	Bücker Bü.133 Jungmeister	4	HB-MIO	24. 6.70	Cancelled 28. 4.71 - to N40BJ
	(Built Dornier)		Swiss AF U-57		(As "YR-PAX")
G-BBMI	Dewoitine D.26	10853	HB-RAA	11.10.73	Cancelled 30. 5.84 - to N282DW
	(Built EKW)		Swiss AF 282		(As "N282DW")
G-BCOH	Avro 683 Lancaster Mk.10 AR	277	CF-TQC	24. 9.74	Cancelled 23. 2.93
	(Built Victory Aircraft, Canada)		RCAF KB976		(As "G-BCOH")
G-BCWL	Westland Lysander IIIA	1244	RCAF	9. 9.75	Cancelled 3. 6.99 - to N.....(As "V9281").
	(Built National Steel Car Corporation Ltd.) (Composite - main airframe possibly RCAF 2403, parts from RCAF 2341, 2349, 2391)				
G-BFHG	CASA 352L	153	Spanish AF T2B-262 23.11.77		Cancelled 27. 9.94 - to US
	(Junkers Ju 52/3m) (C/n reported as 155)				(Subsequently "D2+60" and "D-TABX") (As "VK-NZ")
G-BJCL	Morane Saulnier MS.230 Parasol	1049	EI-ARG	22. 7.81	Cancelled 27. 1.88 - to N230MS
			F-BGMR, French Military		(As "N230MS")
G-BJHS	Short S.25 Sandringham	SH.55C	(EI-BYI)	11. 9.81	Cancelled 12. 8.93 - to N814ML
	(Sunderland GR.3 c/n SH974 conversion)		G-BJHS, N158J, VH-BRF, R.NZ AF NZ4108, ML814 (Carries "N814ML, G-BJHS and ML814")		
G-BXYA	CSS-13 Aeroklubowy	0365	SP-ACP (3)	3. 7.98	Cancelled 13.11.98 - to US
	(Licence built Polikarpov Po-2)		(SP-FCN), SP-ACN (3), PLW-...(As "N50074")		
G-CCVV	Vickers Supermarine 379 Spitfire FR.XIVe		Indian AF "42"	18. 5.88	Cancelled 6. 1.93 as TWFU
		6S/649186	MV262		(As "G-CCVV")
G-XVIB	Vickers Supermarine 361 Spitfire LF.XVIe		N476TE	3. 7.89	Cancelled 1. 2.90 - to N476TE: restored 3.5.94:
		CBAF.IX.4610	G-XVIB, 8071M, 7451M, TE476 cancelled 21. 9.95 and restored 1.96 as N476TE)		

Eighth Air Force Museum, Barksdale Air Force Base, Louisiana (www.mightyeighth.org)

G-BGCF	Douglas C-47A-90-DL Dakota	20596	Spanish AF T3-3320.11.78		Cancelled 30. 1.80 - to N3753C 4.80
			N86453, 43-16130		(As "43-16130")

Air Zoo, Kalamazoo, Michigan (www.airzoo.org)

G-AWHJ	Hispano HA.1112-MIL Buchon	171	Spanish AF C4K-100 14.5.68		Cancelled 20. 2.69 - to N90605 2.69 subsequently N76GE
	(Messerschmitt Bf.109G)				("As C4.K-19")

Yankee Air Museum, Belleville, Michigan (www,yankeeairmuseum.org)

G-AOZZ	Armstrong-Whitworth 650 ArgosySeries.100			12. 3.57	Cancelled 1.10.68 - to G-11-1 11.68 and N896U 12.68.
		AW.6651			(As "N896U")

Millville Army Airfield Museum, Millville, New Jersey (www.p47millville.org)

G-BEWT	Short SD.3-30 Variant 100	SH3011	G-14-3011	20. 6.77	Cancelled 28.10.77 - to N331GW (As "82-25343")
G-THUN	Republic P-47D-40RA Thunderbolt	399-55731	N47DD	18. 6.99	Cancelled 21. 7.06 - to NX47DD 7. 7.07P
			Peruvian AF 119, Peruvian AF 545, 45-49192 (As "226671")		
	(Composite rebuild from wreck of original N47DD plus an unidentified P-47N fuselage)				

Southwest Soaring Museum, Moriaty, New Mexico (www.swsoaringmuseum.org)

BGA.3219	Slingsby T.21B Seburgh TX.1	606	WB941	7.87	To N941B (As "N941B")

War Eagles Museum, Santa Teresa, New Mexico (www.war-eagles-air-museum.com)

G-ANNC	de Havilland DH.82A Tiger Moth	84569	T6102	22. 1.54	Cancelled 9. 4.58 - to OO-SOM (2) 4.58
					(Subsequently N7158N)

Lone Star Flight Museum, Galveston Airport, New Mexico (www.lsfm.org)

G-FORT	Boeing 299-O (B-17G-95-DL) Fortress	8627	F-BEEC	11. 4.84	Cancelled 2. 7.87 - to N900RW
			ZS-EEC, F-BEEC, 44-85718 (As "238050")		
G-ANIZ	de Havilland DH.82A Tiger Moth	83896	T7467	7.12.53	Cancelled 6.12.67 - to N9714. (As "N9714")

Intrepid Air and Space Museum, Manhattan, New York (www.intrepidmuseum.org/pages/concorde)
G-BOAD	British Aircraft Corporation Concorde Type 1 Variant 102	210 & 100-010	G-N94AD G-BOAD	9. 5.75	Cancelled 4. 5.04 as WFU 3.12.04T (As "G-BOAD")

Rhinebeck Aerodrome Museum, Rhinebeck, New York (www.oldrhinebeck.org)
G-ABIH	de Havilland DH.80A Puss Moth	2140		17. 2.31	Cancelled 11.31 - to NC770N (Subsequently N770N and NC770N) (As "N770N")
G-ATXL	Avro 504K replica (Built Hampshire Aero Club)	HAC-1		19. 7.66	Cancelled 6. 8.71 - to N2929 (As "E2939")

National Museum of United States Air Force, Wright-Patterson Air Force Base, Dayton, Ohio (www.nationalmuseum.af.mil)
G-ANCN	de Havilland DH.82A Tiger Moth (Officially regd with c/n 85521)	85674	DE744	4. 9.53	Cancelled xx.4..55 - to OO-NCN subsequently N39DH. 21. 6.55 (As "N39DH)"
G-MOSI	de Havilland DH.98 Mosquito TT.35	xxxx	N98DH N9797, G-ASKA, RS709	10.11.81	Cancelled 21. 1.87 by CAA 17.12.84P (Subsequently to USA (As "NS519")

Evergreen Aviation Museum, McMinnville, Oregon (www.sprucegoose.org)
G-SXVI	Vickers Supermarine 361 Spitfire LF.XVIe	7001M CBAF-11470	6709M, TE356	25. 2.87	Cancelled 15. 1.90 - to N356V - subsequently N356TE (As "N356TE")

Tillamook Naval Air Station Museum, Tillamook, Oregon (www.tillamookair.com)
G-AWHN	Hispano HA.1112-MIL Buchon (Messerschmitt Bf.109G)	193	Spanish AF C4K-130 14. 5.68		Cancelled 20. 2.69 - to N90602 (As "N90602")
G-BMFB	Douglas Skyraider AEW.1 (AD-4W)	7850	SE-EBK G-31-12, WV181, BuA.126867	24. 9.85	Cancelled 1.5.90 - to N4277N (As "NX4277N")

Cavanaugh Flight Museum, Addison Airport, Dallas, Texas (www.cavanaughflightmuseum.com)
G-ALFO	Douglas C-47A-90-DL Dakota	20401	N20DH N700E, N300A, N94529, VH-BHC, 43-15935	30.12.48	Cancelled 22.12.50 - to N94529. (As "32585")
G-HUNN	Hispano HA.1112-M1L Buchon (Messerschmitt Bf.109G)	235	G-BJZZ N48157, Spanish AF C4K-172	29. 4.87	Cancelled 9.10.91 - to N109GU 31. 5.92P (As "N100GU")
G-VIII	Vickers Supermarine 359 Spitfire LF.VIII	6S/479770	I-SPIT Indian AF T17, MT719	27. 4.89	Cancelled 9. 7.93 - to N719MT 18. 6.93A (As *NX719MT")
G-CCMV	Vought FG-1D Corsair (Built Goodyear Aircraft Corporation)	3660	N448AG N4717C, Bu.92399	21.11.00	Cancelled 5. 9.02 - to N451FG 13. 5.03P (As "N451FG")

Commemorative Air Force American Airpower Heritage Museum, Midland, Texas (www.commemorativeairforce.org)
G-SALY	Hawker Sea Fury FB.XI	41H-696792	WJ288	12. 7.83	Cancelled 2.1.91 - to N15S (As "WJ288:153:P in RN c/s) (On loan from Memphis, Tennessee)
G-AWHE	Hispano HA.1112-MIL Buchon (Messerschmitt Bf.109G) (Regd incorrectly as c/n 64)	67	Spanish AF C4K-31 14. 5.68		Cancelled 20. 2.69 - to N109ME (As "N109ME")
G-AKZY	Messerschmitt Bf.108D-1 Taifun	3059	Luftwaffe D-ERPN	7. 6.48	Cancelled - to HB-DUB 1.50 - subsequently N2231) (As "N2231") (On loan from Hobbs, New Mexico)
G-MXIV	Vickers Supermarine 379 Spitfire FR.XIVc	6S/583887	Indian AF T3 NH749	11. 4.80	Cancelled 15. 5.85 - to NX749DP 19. 7.85P (As "NX749DP") (On loan from Camarillo, California)

National Air and Space Museum, Steven F.Udvar-Hazy Centre, Chantilly, Virginia (www.nasm.si.edu)
G-AARO (2)	Arrow Sport A2-60	341	N932S NC932S	17. 9.79	Cancelled in 6.83 - to N280AS 18. 2.83P (Subsequently N9325) (As "G-AARO" @ Paul E Garber Facility)
G-BFHD	CASA 352L (Junkers Ju 52/3m)	146	Spanish AF T2B-255 23.11.77 Spanish AF "721-8"		Cancelled 21. 1.88 on sale to West Germany (Subsequently to NASM) (As "N8+AA" in Lufthansa c/s - displayed Dulles international Airport, Washington, DC)
G-MURY	Robinson R44 Astro	0201		19. 7.95	Cancelled 9.10.03 as sold to US 17. 5.04T (As "G-MURY")

Museum of Flight, Boeing Field, Seattle, Washington (www.museumofflight.org)
G-AOVU	de Havilland DH.106 Comet 4C	6424	(G-APMD) (G-APDN)	22.10.59	Cancelled 25. 3.60 - to XA-NAR, subsequently N888WA (As "N888WA")
G-AVAV	Vickers Supermarine 509 Spitfire Tr.9	CBAF/7269	Irish Air Corps 159 8.11.66 G-15-172, MJ772		Cancelled 18. 5.75 - to N8R. subsequently N8R (As "N8R") (On loan from Museum of Flight)
G-AWHL	Hispano HA.1112-MIL Buchon (Messerschmitt Bf.109G)	186	Spanish AF C4K-122 14. 5.68		Cancelled 17. 2.69 on sale to Spain, subsequently NX109J (As "N109J")
G-BOAG	British Aircraft Corporation Concorde Type 1 Variant 102	214 & 100-014	G-BFKW	9. 2.81	Cancelled 4. 5.04 as WFU 3. 4.05T (As "G-BOAG")

Olympic Flight Museum, Olympia, Washington (www.olympicflightmuseum.com)
G-AYHS	British Aircraft Corporation 167 Strikemaster Mk.84	G-27-143 EEP/JP/1934 & PS.151		22. 7.70	Cancelled 28. 9.70.- to Singapore AF as 314 - subsequently N121463 and N72445 (As "XR366")

Flying Heritage Collection, Seattle, Washington (www.flyingheritage.com)
G-AWHB	CASA 2111D (Heinkel 111H-16) (Officially quoted as c/n 167 ex Spanish AF B2I-37)	049	Spanish AF B2I-57 14. 5.68		Cancelled as WFU 11. 9.74, restored 16.10.89 cancelled 27. 4.01 as sold US:(As "G-AWHB")
G-BUWA	Vickers-Supermarine 349 Spitfire F.Vc (Built Westland Aircraft Ltd 1942) WASP/20/288		C-FDUY 7555M, 5378M, AR614	19. 3.93	Cancelled 12.1 .00 as PWFU 1. 7.00 (To N614VC 2.00)
G-BYDS	Messerschmitt Bf.109E-3	1342	Luftwaffe	24.11.98	Cancelled 16.11.04 as transferred to US (To N342FH 11.04
G-BYDR	North American B-25D Mitchell	100-20644	N25644 N88972, CF-OGQ, KL161, 43-3318		Cancelled 15. 4.04 - to N25644 (As "N25644")
G-BZNL	North American F-86A Sabre	161-211	49-1217	14.11.00	Cancelled 20.12.01 to N4912 (As "N4912")
G-FOKW	Focke-Wulf Fw.190A-5	0151227)	Luftwaffe DG+HO 6. 3.96		Cancelled 8. 2.01 - to N19027 (As "N19027")

Experimental Aircraft Association Air Adventure Museum, Witttman Field, Oshkosh, Wisconsin (http://museum.eaa.org/)
G-ASKB	de Havilland DH.98 Mosquito TT.35		On loan from Fantasy of Flight, Polk City, Florida qv
G-AVAV	Vickers Supermarine 509 Spitfire Tr.		On loan from Museum of Flight, Seattle, Washington

G-AWHO	Hispano HA.1112-MIL Buchon (Messerschmitt Bf.109G)	199	Spanish AF C4K-127 14.5.68	Cancelled 20. 2.69 - *to N90601, subsequently N109BF)* (As "N109BF")
G-HUNT	Hawker Hunter F.51	41H-680277	G-9-440 5. 7.78	Cancelled 10.12.87 - *to N50972, subsequently N611JR*
			Danish AF E-418, Danish AF 35-418	*(As "WB188")*

URUGUAY
Museo Aeronautico, San Gabriel, Montevideo

| G-AMNL | Douglas C-47B-35-DK Dakota | 16644/33392 | XF767 30.11.51 | Cancelled 23.11.61 - *to I-TAVO 1.62* |
| | | | G-AMNL, KN682, 44-77060 | *(Subsequently CX-BDB)* |

VENEZUELA
Museo del Transporte, Caracas

| G-BDVO | Short SC.7 Skyvan 3-100 | SH1949 | G-14-117 20. 4.76 | Cancelled - *to YV-O-MC-9 8.76* |
| | | | | *(Subsequently YV-O-MTC-9)* |

Escaudron Legendario, Base Area el Libertador, Palo Negro, Aragua, Maracay

| G-AJAV | Douglas C-47A-5-DK Dakota | 12386 | KG377 9. 1.47 | Cancelled 6. 9.50 - *to N19E 9.50.* |
| | | | 42-92571 | *(Subsquently N70, N70F N40G, YV-P-EPO and YV-T-RTC)* |

Museo Aeronautica de la Fuerza Aerea Venezolana, Maracay (caminosdevenezuela.com/contenidos/destinos/museo_aeronautico/index)

| G-AMXS | de Havilland DH.104 Dove 2A | 04382 | (N4281C) 21. 1.53 | Cancelled 28. 8.53 - *to YV-T-FTQ* |
| | | | | *(Subsequently 3C-R1) (As "2531")* |

ZIMBABWE
Zimbabwe Military Museum, Gweru

| G-AWTD | Percival P.56 Provost T.1 | P56/285 *(Also c/n PAC/F/285)* | (D-....) XF554 8.11.68 | Cancelled - *to Rhodesian AF as 3614 1973* |

PART 2 – BRITISH AVIATION PRESERVATION COUNCIL REGISTER

The British Aviation Preservation Council (BAPC) was formed in 1967 and is the national body for the preservation of aviation related items. It is a voluntary staffed body which undertakes a representation, co-ordination and enabling role. BAPC membership includes national, local authority, independent and service museums, private collections, voluntary groups and other organisations involved in the advancement of aviation preservation in the UK. A number of overseas aircraft preservation organisations have affiliated membership.

The BAPC Register of Anonymous Airframes was started in the 1980s as a way of flagging up aircraft which had not managed to be given a formal method of identification, for example a civilian registration, a military serial or a construction number for one reason or another. Such examples include "pioneer" aircraft built and flown before registration systems were devised, unfinished projects, deliberate omissions and Hang gliders and similar devices. Additionally, the register allows other airframes and smilar items which would not normally need an formal identity such as man-powered aircraft, full scale models for use as "gate guardians" or other display purposes and non flying reproductions intended only for display purposes. Most exhibits held in Museums are usually on display.

Register No	Type	Construction No	Previous Identity	Remarks	Location
BAPC.1	Roe Triplane IV reconstruction			Details in SECTION 4, Part 1	Old Warden
BAPC.2	Bristol Boxkite reconstruction	BOX.1 & BM.7279		Details in SECTION 4, Part 1 *(As "12A")*	Old Warden
BAPC.3	Bleriot Type XI			Details in SECTION 4, Part 1	Old Warden
BAPC.4	Deperdussin Monoplane			Details in SECTION 4, Part 1	Old Warden
BAPC.5	Blackburn Monoplane			Details in SECTION 4, Part 1	Old Warden
BAPC.6	Roe Triplane Type I			Details in SECTION 4, Part 1 *(As "14")*	Manchester
BAPC.7	Southampton University Man Powered Aircraft (SUMPAC)			Details in SECTION 4, Part 1	Southampton
BAPC.8	Dixon Ornithopter reconstruction			Details in SECTION 4, Part 1	Old Warden
BAPC.9	Humber-Bleriot XI Monoplane reconstruction			Details in SECTION 4, Part 1	Coventry
BAPC.10	Hafner R-11 Revoplane			Details in SECTION 4, Part 1	Weston-super-Mare
BAPC.11	English Electric Wren composite			Details in SECTION 4, Part 1 *(As "4")*	Old Warden
BAPC.12	Mignet HM.14 Pou-Du-Ciel			Details in SECTION 4, Part 1	Manchester
BAPC.13	Mignet HM.14 Pou-Du-Ciel			Brimpex Metal Treatments Ltd	Sheffield
	(Douglas 600cc)			*(Under restoration 3.98)*	
BAPC.14	Addyman Standard Training Glider			Ponsford Collection	Selby
BAPC.15	Addyman Standard Training Glider	YA2		Ponsford Collection	Wigan
	(Rebuilt Yorkshire Aeroplanes)			*(Stored 2.04)*	
BAPC.16	Addyman Ultralight			Ponsford Collection	Selby
BAPC.17	Woodhams Sprite			BB Aviation	Bossingham, Canterbury
BAPC.18	Killick Man Powered Gyroplane			Ponsford Collection	Selby
BAPC.19	Bristol F2b Fighter fuselage frame			Details in SECTION 4, Part 1	Brussels, Belgium
				(As "66" in Belgian AF c/s)	
BAPC.20	Lee-Richards Annular Bi-plane reconstruction			Details in SECTION 4, Part 1	Shoreham
BAPC.21	Thruxton Jackaroo			M.J.Brett	-----
	(Used as spares in rebuild of G-APAL)			*(Conversion abandoned)*	
BAPC.22	Mignet HM.14 Pou-Du-Ciel			Details in SECTION 4, Part 1 Schiphol, Netherlands	
				(As "G-AE0F")	
BAPC.23	*Allocated in error – originally used by 1/2th scale SE.5 replica at Newark Air Museum*				
BAPC.24	*Allocated in error – originally used by 2/3rd scale Currie Wot replica at Newark Air Museum*				
BAPC.25	Nyborg TGN.III Sailplane			P Williams	Warwick
BAPC.26	Auster AOP.9			*Fuselage frame only - scrapped Swansea*	
BAPC.27	Mignet HM.14 Pou-Du-Ciel reconstruction			M J Abbey	-----
	(Under construction 1988 - presumably abandoned)				
BAPC.28	Wright Flyer fsm			Details in SECTION 4, Part 1	Elvington
BAPC.29	Mignet HM.14 Pou-Du-Ciel			Details in SECTION 4, Part 1	
				(As "G-ADRY")	Brooklands
BAPC.30	DFS Grunau Baby			Destroyed by fire Swansea 1969	
BAPC.31	Slingsby T.7 Tutor			Believed scrapped Swansea	
BAPC.32	Crossley Tom Thumb			Details in SECTION 4, Part 1	Coventry
BAPC.33	DFS 108-49 Grunau Baby IIB		BGA 2400 VN148, LN+ST	*(To Denmark for rebuild 2003)*	
BAPC.34	DFS 108-49 Grunau Baby IIB	030892	RAFGSA.281 RAFGGA GK.4/LZ+AR	D.Elsdon Hazlemere, Buckingham *(Originally on rebuild as BGA 2362: possibly used for spares)*	
BAPC.35	EoN AP.7 Primary	EoN/P/063		ex Russavia Collection	Pocklington
				(On rebuild as BGA 2493: current status unknown)	
BAPC.36	Fieseler Fi 103 V1 fsm			Details in SECTION 4, Part 1	Hawkinge
BAPC.37	Blake Bluetit			See G-BXIY - details in SECTION 1, Part 2	
BAPC.38	Bristol Scout D fsm			K Williams and M Thorn	Solihull
	(Gnome 80 hp)			*(As "A1742")*	
BAPC.39	Addyman Zephyr Sailplane			Ponsford Collection	Selby
				(Parts held for eventual rebuild)	
BAPC.40	Bristol Boxkite reconstruction	BOX 3 & BM.7281		Details in SECTION 4, Part 1	Bristol
BAPC.41	Royal Aircraft Factory BE.2c replica			Details in SECTION 4, Part 1 *(As "6232")*	Elvington
BAPC.42	Avro 504K fsm			Details in SECTION 4, Part 1 *(As "H1968")*	Elvington
BAPC.43	Mignet HM.14 Pou-Du-Ciel			Details in SECTION 4, Part 1	Newark
BAPC.44	Miles M.14A Magister			Details in SECTION 4, Part 1 *(As "L6906")*	Woodley
BAPC.45	Pilcher Hawk Glider reconstruction			Details in SECTION 4, Part 1	Stanford Hall
BAPC.46	Mignet HM.14 Pou-Du-Ciel			Probably scrapped	
BAPC.47	Watkins CHW monoplane			Details in SECTION 4, Part 1	Swansea
BAPC.48	Pilcher Hawk Glider reconstruction			Details in SECTION 4, Part 1	Glasgow
BAPC.49	Pilcher Hawk Glider			Details in SECTION 4, Part 1	East Fortune
BAPC.50	Roe Triplane Type I			Details in SECTION 4, Part 1	
					South Kensington, London
BAPC.51	Vickers FB.27 Vimy IV			Details in SECTION 4, Part 1	
					South Kensington, London
BAPC.52	Lilienthal Glider Type XI			Details in SECTION 4, Part 1	Wroughton
BAPC.53	Wright Flyer reconstruction			Details in SECTION 4, Part 1	
					South Kensington, London

BAPC.54	JAP/Harding Monoplane			Details in SECTION 4, Part 1
				South Kensington, London
BAPC.55	Levasseur-Antoinette Developed Type VII Monoplane			Details in SECTION 4, Part 1
				South Kensington, London
BAPC.56	Fokker E.III			Details in SECTION 4, Part 1
				(As "210:16") South Kensington, London
BAPC.57	Pilcher Hawk Glider reconstruction			E Littledike St Albans
	(Built Martin and Miller, Edinburgh 1930)			
BAPC.58	Yokosuka MXY-7 Ohka II			Details in SECTION 4, Part 1 RNAS Yeovilton
				(As "15-1585")
BAPC.59	Sopwith F1 Camel fsm			Details in SECTION 4, Part 1 East Fortune
				(As "B5577:W")
BAPC.60	Murray M.1 Helicopter			Details in SECTION 4, Part 1 Weston-super-Mare
BAPC.61	Stewart Man Powered Ornithopter			A Smith *"Bellbird II"* Sibsey
BAPC.62	Cody Type V Biplane			Details in SECTION 4, Part 1
				(As "304") South Kensington, London
BAPC.63	Hawker Hurricane fsm			Details in SECTION 4, Part 1 Hawkinge
				(As "P3208:SD-T" in RAF 501 Sqdn c/s)
BAPC.64	Hawker Hurricane fsm			Details in SECTION 4, Part 1 Hawkinge
				(As "P3059:SD-N" in RAF 501 Sqdn c/s)
BAPC.65	Supermarine Spitfire fsm			Details in SECTION 4, Part 1 Hawkinge
				(As "N3289:DW-K" in RAF 610 Sqdn c/s)
BAPC.66	Messerschmitt Bf109 fsm			Details in SECTION 4, Part 1 Hawkinge
BAPC.67	Messerschmitt Bf109 fsm			Details in SECTION 4, Part 1 Hawkinge
				(As "14" in JG52 c/s)
BAPC.68	Hawker Hurricane fsm			Details in SECTION 4, Part 1 Hooton Park
BAPC.69	Supermarine Spitfire fsm			Details in SECTION 4, Part 1 Hawkinge
				(As "N3313:KL-B" in RAF 54 Sqdn c/s)
BAPC.70	Auster AOP.5			Details in SECTION 4, Part 1 East Fortune
				(As "TJ398")
BAPC.71	Supermarine Spitfire fsm			Details in SECTION 4, Part 1 Flixton
				(As "P8140:ZP-K" in RAF 74 Sqdn c/s)
BAPC.72	Hawker Hurricane fsm			Details in SECTION 4, Part 1 Gloucestershire
				(As "V6799:SD-X" of RAF 501 RAAF Sqdn c/s)
BAPC.73	Hawker Hurricane fsm			Not known *(Current status unknown)*
				(Was displayed "Queens Head" Public House, Bishops Stortford)
BAPC.74	Messerschmitt Bf109 fsm			Details in SECTION 4, Part 1 Hawkinge
BAPC.75	Mignet HM.14 Pou-Du-Ciel			See G-AEFG - details in SECTION 1, Part 2 Selby
BAPC.76	Mignet HM.14 Pou-Du-Ciel			Details in SECTION 4, Part 1 Elvington
				(As "G-AFFI")
BAPC.77	Mignet HM.14 Pou-Du-Ciel			Details in SECTION 4, Part 1 Lower Stondon
				(As "G-ADRG")
BAPC.78	Hawker Afghan Hind			See G-AENP - details in SECTION 1, Part 2
BAPC.79	Fiat G.46-4b	71	FHE	Not known La Ferte Alais, France
			MM53211	*(Stored as "MM53211:ZI-4")*
BAPC.80	Airspeed AS.58 Horsa II			Details in SECTION 4, Part 1 AAC Middle Wallop
				(Fuselage only: as "KJ351")
BAPC.81	Hawkridge Nacelle Dagling	10471	BGA 493	Russavia Collection *(On rebuild)* Hemel Hempstead
BAPC.82	Hawker Afghan Hind			Details in SECTION 4, Part 1 RAF Cosford
BAPC.83	Kawasaki Type 5 Model 1b (Ki 100)			Details in SECTION 4, Part 1 *(As "24")* Hendon
BAPC.84	Mitsubishi Ki 46 III (Dinah)			Details in SECTION 4, Part 1 RAF Cosford
				(As "5439")
BAPC.85	Weir W-2			Details in SECTION 4, Part 1 East Fortune
BAPC.86	DH.82A Tiger Moth			*(Current status unknown)*
BAPC.87	Bristol 30/46 Babe III reconstruction			Details in SECTION 4, Part 1 *(As "G-EASQ")* Kemble
BAPC.88	Fokker Dr.1 5/8th scale model			Details in SECTION 4, Part 1 RNAS Yeovilton
				(As "102:17")
BAPC.89	Cayley Glider fsm			Details in SECTION 4, Part 1 Elvington
BAPC.90	Colditz Cock Glider reconstruction			Details in SECTION 4, Part 1 South Lambeth
BAPC.91	Fieseler Fi 103R-IV (V-1)			Details in SECTION 4, Part 1 Headcorn
BAPC.92	Fieseler Fi 103 (V-1)			Details in SECTION 4, Part 1 Hendon
BAPC.93	Fieseler Fi 103 (V-1)			Details in SECTION 4, Part 1 Duxford
BAPC.94	Fieseler Fi 103 (V-1)			Details in SECTION 4, Part 1 RAF Cosford
BAPC.95	Gizmer Autogyro			F.Fewsdale *(Current status unknown)* Darlington
BAPC.96	Brown Helicopter			Details in SECTION 4, Part 1 Sunderland
BAPC.97	Luton LA.4 Minor			Details in SECTION 4, Part 1 Sunderland
				(As "G-AFUG")
BAPC.98	Yokosuka MXY-7 Ohka II			Details in SECTION 4, Part 1 *(As "997")* Manchester
BAPC.99	Yokosuka MXY-7 Ohka II			Details in SECTION 4, Part 1 RAF Cosford
BAPC.100	Clarke TWK			Details in SECTION 4, Part 1 Hendon
BAPC.101	Mignet HM.14 Pou-Du-Ciel			Details in SECTION 4, Part 1 Newark
BAPC.102	Mignet HM.14 Pou-Du-Ciel			Not constructed - parts to BAPC.75
BAPC.103	Pilcher Hawk reconstruction			Personal Plane Services Ltd Wycombe Air Park
	(Built E.A.S.Hulton, London 1969)			
BAPC.104	Bleriot Type XI		G-AVXV	Not known *(Sold as F-AZIN 1992)*
BAPC.105	Bleriot Type XI		54	Details in SECTION 4, Part 1 Lelystad, Netherlands
BAPC.106	Bleriot Type XI			Details in SECTION 4, Part 1 RAF Cosford
BAPC.107	Bleriot Type XXVII			Details in SECTION 4, Part 1 Hendon
BAPC.108	Fairey Swordfish IV			Details in SECTION 4, Part 1 RAF Stafford
				(As "HS503")
BAPC.109	Slingsby T.7 Cadet TX.1	28	8599M	Not known
			BGA 679	*(Current status unknown)*
BAPC.110	Fokker D.VIIF fsm			Details in SECTION 4, Part 1 Chino, CA, USA
				(As "5125:18")

BAPC.111	Sopwith Triplane fsm			Details in SECTION 4, Part 1 RNAS Yeovilton
				(As "N5492")
BAPC.112	AirCo DH.2 fsm			See G-BFVH - deatils in SECTION 1, Part 2
				(As "5964")
BAPC.113	Royal Aircraft Factory SE.5A fsm			Ex Leisure Sport *(As "B4863": current status unknown)*
BAPC.114	Vickers Type 60 Viking IV reconstruction			Details in SECTION 4, Part 1 Brooklands
				(As "G-EBED")
BAPC.115	Mignet HM.14 Pou-Du-Ciel			Details in SECTION 4, Part 1 Flixton
BAPC.116	Santos-Dumont Demoiselle XX reconstruction			Ex Flambards Theme Park
	(JAP J99)			*(Current status unknown)*
BAPC.117	Royal Aircraft Factory BE.2c fsm			P Smith Hawkinge
	(Built Ackland and Shaw 1976) (Gipsy Major)			*(Built for BBC TV "Wings")*
BAPC.118	Albatros D.Va fsm			Not known *(As "C19/15": current status unknown)*
BAPC.119	Bensen B.7 Gyroglider			Details in SECTION 4, Part 1 Sunderland
BAPC.120	Mignet HM.14 Pou-Du-Ciel			Details in SECTION 4, Part 1 *(As G-AEJZ)* Hemswell
BAPC.121	Mignet HM.14 Pou-Du-Ciel			Details in SECTION 4, Part 1 Doncaster
				(As "G-AEKR")
BAPC.122	Avro 504 fsm			Not known
	(Built Personal Plane Services 1976) (Ford 1300)			*(Built for BBC TV "Wings")* *(As "1881": current status unknown)*
BAPC.123	Vickers FB.5 Gunbus fsm	1186/2	ZS-UHN	A.Topen Cranfield
	(Built IES Projects Ltd 1975)			*(As "P641")* *(Built for "Shout at the Devil" film)*
				(Small components only)
BAPC.124	Lilienthal Glider Type XI reconstruction			Details in SECTION 4, Part 1
				South Kensington, London
BAPC.125	Clay Cherub ground trainer			Not known (Coventry)
BAPC.126	Rollason-Druine D.31 Turbulent			Details in SECTION 4, Part 1 Coventry
BAPC.127	Halton Man Powered Aircraft Group Jupiter			Details in SECTION 4, Part 1
				Filching Manor, Wannock
BAPC.128	Watkinson CG-4 Cyclogyroplane Man Powered Gyroplane Mark IV			Details in SECTION 4, Part 1 Weston-super-Mare
BAPC.129	Blackburn (1911) Monoplane fsm			Not known *(Built for TV Series."The Flambards")*
				"Mercury" (Sold 1993: current status unknown)
BAPC.130	Blackburn (1911) Monoplane fsm			Details in SECTION 4, Part 1 Elvington
BAPC.131	Pilcher Hawk Glider reconstruction			C.Paton London E
	(Built C.Paton 1972 for film)			*(Current status unknown - probably stored)*
BAPC.132	Bleriot Type XI	PFA 88- 10864		Details in SECTION 4, Part 1
				Mougins, Cannes, France
BAPC.133	Fokker Dr.1 fsm			Details in SECTION 4, Part 1 Hawkinge
				(As "425:17")
BAPC.134	Aerotek Pitts S.2A		"G-RKSF"	Toyota Cars (Northampton)
BAPC.135	Bristol 20 M.1C Monoplane fsm			Ex Leisure Sport
				(As "C4912": sold 10.87: current status unknown)
BAPC.136	Deperdussin 1913 Monoplane fsm			Details in SECTION 4, Part 1 Chino, CA, USA
				(As "19")
BAPC.137	Sopwith Baby Floatplane fsm			Ex Leisure Sport Lands End
	(Built FEM Displays Ltd 1978)			
BAPC.138	Hansa Brandenberg W.29 fsm			Ex Leisure Sport
	(Ford 1300)			*(As "2292": sold prior to 10.87: current status unknown)*
BAPC.139	Fokker Dr.1 Triplane fsm			Details in SECTION 4, Part 1 Orlando, Florida, US
				(As "102/17")
BAPC.140	Curtiss 42A R3C2 fsm			Details in SECTION 4, Part 1 Chino, Califronia, USA
				(As "3" in US Army c/s)
BAPC.141	Macchi M.39 fsm			Details in SECTION 4, Part 1 Chino, California, USA
				(As "5")
BAPC.142	Royal Aircraft Factory SE.5A fsm			Not known Switzerland
				(As "F5459:Y") *(Sold 1.5.93: current status unknown)*
BAPC.143	Paxton Man Powered Aircraft			R.A.Paxton Gloucestershire
				(Current status unknown: presumed stored)
BAPC.144	Weybridge Man Powered Aircraft Group Mercury			Not known RAF Cranwell
	(Previously "Dumbo" rebuilt)			*"Mercury" (Current status unknown)*
BAPC.145	Oliver Man Powered Aircraft			Not known Warton
				(Current status unknown: possibly scrapped)
BAPC.146	Pedals Aeronauts Man Powered Aircraft Toucan			Not known *(Current status unknown)*
				"Toucan" (Centre section/power train only)
BAPC.147	Bensen B.7 Gyroglider			Details in SECTION 4, Part 1 *(As "LHS-1")* Flixton
BAPC.148	Hawker Fury II fsm			Details in SECTION 4, Part 1 Sleap
				(As "K7271" in 1 Sqdn c/s)
BAPC.149	Short S.27 fsm			Details in SECTION 4, Part 1 RNAS Yeovilton
BAPC.150	Sepecat Jaguar GR.1 fsm		"XX718"	RAF Exhibition Production and Transportation Team
			"XX732"	*(As "XX725:GU" in RAF 54 Sqdn c/s)* Oman
BAPC.151	Sepecat Jaguar GR.1A fsm		"XX824"	RAF Exhibition Production and Transportation Team
				(As"XZ363:A") RAF Cranwell
BAPC.152	BAe Hawk T.1A fsm		"XX262"	RAF Exhibition Production and Transportation Team
			"XX162"	*(As "XX226:74" in RAF 74 Sqdn c/s)* RAF Cranwell
BAPC.153	Westland WG-33 Mock-up			Details in SECTION 4, Part 1 Weston-super-Mare
BAPC.154	Druine D.31 Turbulent	PFA 1654		Lincolnshire Aviation Society East Kirkby
				(Unfinished: stored 3.96)
BAPC.155	Panavia Tornado GR.1 fsm		"ZA368"	RAF Exhibition Production and Transportation Team
			"ZA446","ZA600", "ZA322"	*(As "ZA556")* RAF Cranwell
BAPC.156	Supermarine S.6B fsm			National Air Race Museum Chino, Cakifornia, USA
				(As "S1595")
BAPC.157	WACO CG-4A Hadrian Glider			Details in SECTION 4, Part 1 Elvington
				(As "237123")
BAPC.158	Fieseler Fi 103 (V1)			Defence Explosives Ordnance Disposal School
				Chattenden

BAPC.159	Yokosuka MXY-7 Ohka II	Defence Explosives Ordnance Disposal School	
			Chattenden
BAPC.160	Chargus 18/50 Hang Glider	Details in SECTION 4, Part 1	East Fortune
BAPC.161	Stewart Man Powered Ornithopter	Not known	(Louth)
	(Built A Stewart)	*"Coppelia" (Stored 8.98: current status unknown)*	
BAPC.162	Goodhart Man Powered Aircraft Newbury Manflier	Details in SECTION 4, Part 1	Wroughton
BAPC.163	AFEE 10/42 Rotachute Rotabuggy reconstruction	Details in SECTION 4, Part 1	AAC Middle Wallop
		(As "B-415")	
BAPC.164	Wight Quadraplane Type 1 fsm	Details in SECTION 4, Part 1	Southampton
		(As "N248")	
BAPC.165	Bristol F.2b Fighter	Details in SECTION 4, Part 1	Hendon
		(As "E2466" in RAF 22 Sqdn c/s)	
BAPC.166	Bristol F.2b Fighter composite	See G-AANM - details in SECTION 1, Part 2	
BAPC.167	Royal Aircraft Factory SE.5A fsm	Exported 12.97	(US)
	(Built TDL Replicas Ltd)		
BAPC.168	DH.60G Moth reconstruction 8058	Details in SECTION 4, Part 1 *(As "G-AAAH")* Croydon	
BAPC.169	Sepecat Jaguar GR.1 fsm	RAF (No.1 School of Technical Training)	
	(Engine systems static demonstration airframe)	*(As "XX110")*	RAF Cosford
BAPC.170	Pilcher Hawk Glider reconstruction	A Gourlay	Strathallan
	(Built A.Gourlay 1983)	*(Built for "Kings Royal" BBC film)*	
BAPC.171	BAe Hawk T.1 fsm "XX297"	RAF Exhibition Production and Transportation Team	
	"XX262"	*(As "XX253")*	RAF Cranwell
BAPC.172	Chargus Midas Super E Hang Glider	Details in SECTION 4, Part 1	Wroughton
BAPC.173	Birdman Promotions Grasshopper	Details in SECTION 4, Part 1	Wroughton
BAPC.174	Bensen B.7 Gyroglider	Details in SECTION 4, Part 1	Wroughton
BAPC.175	Volmer VJ-23 Swingwing Powered Hang Glider	Details in SECTION 4, Part 1	Manchester
BAPC.176	Royal Aircraft Factory SE.5A scale model	Details in SECTION 4, Part 1 *(As "A485")*	Not known
BAPC.177	Avro 504K fsm	Details in SECTION 4, Part 1	Brooklands
		(As "G-AACA" in Brooklands School of Flying c/s)	
BAPC.178	Avro 504K fsm "E373"	By-gone Times Antique Warehouse *(German c/s)*	
		(Current status unknown)	Eccleston, Leyland
BAPC.179	Sopwith Pup fsm	Details in SECTION 4, Part 1 *(As "A7317")*	Coventry
BAPC.180	McCurdy Silver Dart reconstruction	Reynolds Pioneer Museum (?)	
			Wetaskiwin, Alberta, Canada
BAPC.181	Royal Aircraft Factory BE.2b reconstruction	Details in SECTION 4, Part 1 *(As "687")*	Hendon
BAPC.182	Wood Ornithopter	Details in SECTION 4, Part 1	Manchester
BAPC.183	Zurowski ZP-1 Helicopter	Details in SECTION 4, Part 1	Newark
BAPC.184	Supermarine Spitfire IX fsm	Rolls Royce Heritage Trust	Derby
	(Built Specialised Mouldings Ltd 1985)	*(As "EN398)*	
BAPC.185	WACO CG-4A Hadrian Glider	Details in SECTION 4, Part 1	AAC Middle Wallop
		(As "243809")	
BAPC.186	de Havilland DH.82B Queen Bee composite	Details in SECTION 4, Part 1	London Colney
		(As "LF789:R2-K")	
BAPC.187	Roe Type I Biplane reconstruction	Details in SECTION 4, Part 1	Brooklands
BAPC.188	McBroom Cobra 88 Hang Glider	Details in SECTION 4, Part 1	Wroughton
BAPC.189	Bleriot Type XI replica	See BAPC.132 *(Current status unknown)*	
	(Anzani) (Some original parts ex Goldsmith Trust)	*(Sold @ Christies 31.10.86, probably to France)*	
BAPC.190	Supermarine Spitfire fsm	P Smith *(As "K5054")*	Hawkinge
BAPC.191	BAe Harrier GR.7 fsm "ZD472"	RAF Exhibition Production and Transportation Team	
		(As "ZH139:01")	RAF Cranwell
BAPC.192	Weedhopper JC24	M J Aubrey	Kington, Hertford
BAPC.193	Hovey WDII Whing Ding	M J Aubrey	Kington, Hertford
BAPC.194	Santos Dumont Type 20 Demoiselle	Details in SECTION 4, Part 1	Berlin, Germany
BAPC.195	Birdman Sports Moonraker 77 Hang Glider	Details in SECTION 4, Part 1	East Fortune
BAPC.196	Southdown Sailwings Sigma 2m Hang Glider	Details in SECTION 4, Part 1	East Fortune
BAPC.197	Scotkites Cirrus III Hang Glider	Details in SECTION 4, Part 1	East Fortune
BAPC.198	Fieseler Fi 103 (V-1)	Details in SECTION 4, Part 1 South Lambeth, London	
BAPC.199	Fieseler Fi 103 (V-1)	Details in SECTION 4, Part 1	
		(As "442795")	South Kensington, London
BAPC.200	Bensen B.7 Gyroglider	Not known	Leeds
	(Composite of three airframes)	*(Current status unknown)*	
BAPC.201	Mignet HM.14 Pou-Du-Ciel	Details in SECTION 4, Part 1	Caernarfon
BAPC.202	Supermarine Spitfire V fsm	Details in SECTION 4, Part 1	Llanbedr
		(As "MAV467:"RO")	
BAPC.203	Chrislea LC.1 Airguard replica	The Aeroplane Collection	Wigan
		(As "G-AFIN") (Current status unknown: burnt 1998?)	
BAPC.204	McBroom Hang Glider	Details in SECTION 4, Part 1	Hooton Park
BAPC.205	Hawker Hurricane IIc fsm	Details in SECTION 4, Part 1	Hendon
		(As "BE421:XP-G" in RAF 174 Sqdn c/s)	
BAPC.206	Supermarine Spitfire IX fsm	Details in SECTION 4, Part 1	Hendon
		(As "MH486:FF-A" in RAF 132 Sqdn c/s)	
BAPC.207	Austin Whippet fsm	Details in SECTION 4, Part 1 *(As "K.158")*	Doncaster
BAPC.208	Royal Aircraft Factory SE.5A	Details in SECTION 4, Part 1	Farnborough
BAPC.209	Supermarine Spitfire LF.IXC fsm	Details in SECTION 4, Part 1	
			Niagara Falls, Ontario, Canada
		(Built for "Piece of Cake" TV series) (As "MH415:FU-N")	
BAPC.210	Avro 504J	Details in SECTION 4, Part 1	Southampton
	(Built AJD Engineering)	*(As "C4451")*	
BAPC.211	Mignet HM.14 Pou-Du-Ciel	Details in SECTION 4, Part 1	Sunderland
		(As "G-ADVU")	
BAPC.212	Bensen B.6 Gyrocopter	Details in SECTION 4, Part 1	Weston-super-Mare
BAPC.213	Cranfield Vertigo Man Powered Helicopter	Details in SECTION 4, Part 1	Weston-super-Mare
BAPC.214	Supermarine Spitfire Prototype fsm	Details in SECTION 4, Part 1 *(As "K5054")*	Tangmere
BAPC.215	Airwave Hang Glider	Details in SECTION 4, Part 1	Southampton

BAPC.216	de Havilland DH.88 Comet fsm	Details in SECTION 4, Part 1	London Colney
		(As "G-ACSS")	
BAPC.217	Supermarine Spitfire I fsm	Details in SECTION 4, Part 1	RAF Bentley Priory
		(As "K9926:JH-C" in RAF 317 Sqdn c/s)	
BAPC.218	Hawker Hurricane IIc fsm	Details in SECTION 4, Part 1	RAF Bentley Priory
		(As "BN230:FT-A"in RAF 43 Sqdn c/s)	
BAPC.219	Hawker Hurricane I fsm	Details in SECTION 4, Part 1	Biggin Hill
		(As "L1710:AL-D" in RAF 79 Sqdn c/s)	
BAPC.220	Supermarine Spitfire I fsm	Details in SECTION 4, Part 1	Biggin Hill
		(As "N3194:GR-Z" in RAF 92 Sqdn c/s)	
BAPC.221	Supermarine Spitfire LF.IX fsm	Details in SECTION 4, Part 1	RAF Northolt
		(As "EN526SZ-G" in RAF 316 Sqdn c/s)	
BAPC.222	Supermarine Spitfire IX fsm	Details in SECTION 4, Part 1	RAF Uxbridge
		(As "BR600:SH-V" in RAF 64 Sqdn c/s)	
BAPC.223	Hawker Hurricane I fsm	Details in SECTION 4, Part 1	RAF Coltishall
		(As "V7467:LE-D"in RAF 242 Sqdn c/s) (See BAPC.288)	
BAPC.224	Supermarine Spitfire V fsm	Details in SECTION 4, Part 1	
		(As "ML380")	Trenton, Ontario, Canada
BAPC.225	Supermarine Spitfire IX fsm	Details in SECTION 4, Part 1	RAF Cranwell
		(As "P8448:"UM-D" in RAF 52 Sqdn c/s)	
BAPC.226	Supermarine Spitfire XI fsm	Details in SECTION 4, Part 1	RAF Benson
		(As "EN343" in PRU c/s)	
BAPC.227	Supermarine Spitfire IA fsm	Details in SECTION 4, Part 1	Edinburgh
		(As "L1070:XT-A" in RAF 603 Sqdn c/s)	
BAPC.228	Olympus Hang Glider	Details in SECTION 4, Part 1	Sunderland
BAPC.229	Supermarine Spitfire IX fsm	Details in SECTION 4, Part 1	RAF Digby
		(As "MJ832:DN-Y" in RAF 416 Sqdn c/s)	
BAPC.230	Supermarine Spitfire fsm	Details in SECTION 4, Part 1	Malton
		(As "AB550:GE-P" in RAF 349 Sqdn c/s)	
BAPC.231	Mignet HM.14 Pou-Du-Ciel	Details in SECTION 4, Part 1	RAF Millom
		(As "G-ADRX")	
BAPC.232	Airspeed AS.58 Horsa I/II Glider composite	Details in SECTION 4, Part 1	London Colney
BAPC.233	Broburn Wanderlust sailplane	Details in SECTION 4, Part 1	Woodley
BAPC.234	Vickers FB.5 Gunbus fsm	Details in SECTION 4, Part 1 *(As "GBH-7")*	Sywell
BAPC.235	Fieseler Fi 103 (V-1) fsm	Details in SECTION 4, Part 1	Malton
BAPC.236	Hawker Hurricane fsm	Details in SECTION 4, Part 1	Malton
		(As "P2793:SD-M" in RAF 501 Sqdn c/s)	
BAPC.237	Fieseler Fi 103 (V-1)	Details in SECTION 4, Part 1	RAF Stafford
BAPC.238	Waxflatter Ornithopter replica	Personal Plane Services Ltd	Compton Abbas
	(Built Personal Plane Services)	*(Built for "Young Sherlock Holmes")*	
BAPC.239	Fokker D.VIII 5/8th scale model	Details in SECTION 4, Part 1 *(As "694")*	Flixton
BAPC.240	Messerschmitt Bf.109G fsm	Details in SECTION 4, Part 1	Elvington
BAPC.241	Hawker Hurricane I fsm	Details in SECTION 4, Part 1	Tangmere
		(As "L1679:JX-G" in 1 Sqdn c/s)	
BAPC.242	Supermarine Spitfire VB fsm	Details in SECTION 4, Part 1	Tangmere
		(As "BL924:AZ-G" in RAF 234 Sqdn c/s)	
BAPC.243	Mignet HM.14 Pou-Du-Ciel "A-FLEA"	P.Ward	Malvern Wells
	(Built Bill Francis) (Scott A2S)	*(As "G-ADYV")*	
BAPC.244	Mainair Tri-Flyer 250/Solar Wings Typhoon S	Details in SECTION 4, Part 1	East Fortune
		(As "G-MMLI)"	
BAPC.245	Electraflyer Floater Hang Glider	Details in SECTION 4, Part 1	East Fortune
BAPC.246	Hiway Cloudbase Hang Glider	Details in SECTION 4, Part 1	East Fortune
BAPC.247	Albatros ASG.21 Hang Glider	Details in SECTION 4, Part 1	East Fortune
BAPC.248	McBroom Hang Glider	Details in SECTION 4, Part 1	Woodley
BAPC.249	Hawker Fury I fsm	Details in SECTION 4, Part 1	Brooklands
		(As "K5673" in 1 Sqdn 'A' Flight c/s)	
BAPC.250	Royal Aircraft Factory SE.5A replica	Details in SECTION 4, Part 1	Brooklands
		(As "F5475:A")	
BAPC.251	Hiway Spectrum Hang Glider	Details in SECTION 4, Part 1	Manchester
BAPC.252	Flexiform Wing Hang Glider	Details in SECTION 4, Part 1	Manchester
BAPC.253	Mignet HM.14 Pou-Du-Ciel replica	Details in SECTION 4, Part 1	Southampton
		(As "G-ADZW")	
BAPC.254	Supermarine Spitfire 1 fsm	Details in SECTION 4, Part 1	Elvington
		(As "R6690:PR-A" in RAF 609 Sqdn c/s)	
BAPC.255	North American P-51D Mustang fsm	Details in SECTION 4, Part 1	Duxford
BAPC.256	Santos Dumont Type 20 Demoiselle reconstruction	Details in SECTION 4, Part 1	Brooklands
BAPC.257	de Havilland DH.88 Comet model	Details in SECTION 4, Part 1 *(As "G-ACSS")* Hatfield	
BAPC.258	Adams RFD-GQ Balloon (5,000 cu.ft) xxxx	British Balloon Museum and Library	Newbury
	(Built RFD-GQ Parachutes)		
BAPC.259	Gloster Gamecock	Details in SECTION 4, Part 1	Gloucestershire
BAPC.260	Mignet HM.280	Details in SECTION 4, Part 1	RAF Millom
BAPC.261	General Aircraft Hotspur replica	Details in SECTION 4, Part 1	AAC Middle Wallop
		(As "HH379")	
BAPC.262	Catto CP-16	Details in SECTION 4, Part 1	East Fortune
BAPC.263	Chargus Cyclone	Details in SECTION 4, Part 1 Langford Lodge, Belfast	
BAPC.264	Bensen B8M	Details in SECTION 4, Part 1	Weston-super-Mare
BAPC.265	Hawker Hurricane fsm	Details in SECTION 4, Part 1	Elvington
		(As "P3873:YO-H" in RCAF 1 Sqdn c/s)	
BAPC.266	Rogallo Hang Glider	Details in SECTION 4, Part 1 Langford Lodge, Belfast	
BAPC.267	Hawker Hurricane fsm	Details in SECTION 4, Part 1	Duxford
		(As "R4115:LE-X")	
BAPC.268	Supermarine Spitfire fsm	B Wallond	St Mawgan
		(Built for "Dark Blue World") (As "N3317:AI-A")	
BAPC.269	Supermarine Spitfire V fsm	Details in SECTION 4, Part 1	USAF Lakenheath
		(As "BM631:XR-C" in RAF 71 Sqdn c/s)	

BAPC.270	de Havilland DH.60 Moth fsm	Details in SECTION 4, Part 1	Elvington
		(As "G-AAAH")	
BAPC.271	Messerschmitt Me 163B Komet fsm	Details in SECTION 4, Part 1	Old Warden
		(As "191454")	
BAPC.272	Hawker Hurricane fsm	Details in SECTION 4, Part 1	Hawkinge
		(As "N2532:GZ-H" in RAF 32 Sqdn c/s)	
BAPC.273	Hawker Hurricane fsm	Details in SECTION 4, Part 1	Hawkinge
		(As "P2921:GZ-L" in RAF 32 Sqdn c/s)	
BAPC.274	Boulton & Paul P.6 fsm	Details in SECTION 4, Part 1	Wolverhampton
		(As "X-25")	
BAPC.275	Bensen B.7	Details in SECTION 4, Part 1	Doncaster
BAPC.276	Hartman Ornithopter	Details in SECTION 4, Part 1	Wroughton
BAPC.277	Mignet HM.14 Pou-Du-Ciel	Details in SECTION 4, Part 1	Shoreham
BAPC.278	Hawker Hurricane fsm	Details in SECTION 4, Part 1	Hawkinge
		(As "P3679:GZ-K" in RAF 32 Sqdn c/s)	
BAPC.279	Airspeed AS.58 Horsa reconstruction	Details in SECTION 4, Part 1	RAF Shawbury
BAPC.280	de Havilland DH.89 Dragon Rapide fsm	Details in SECTION 4, Part 1	Liverpool
		(As "G-AEAJ" in Railway Air Services c/s)	
BAPC.281	Boulton Paul Defiant fsm	Details in SECTION 4, Part 1	Wolverhampton
		(As "L7005:PS-B" in RAF 264 Sqdn c/s)	
BAPC.282	Manx Eider Duck	Not known	Ronaldsway
BAPC.283	Supermarine Spitfire fsm	A Saunders	Jurby
	(Built F Brown)	(Built for "Piece of Cake" TV series)	
BAPC.284	Gloster E28/39 fsm	Details in SECTION 4, Part 1	Lutterworth
BAPC.285	Gloster E28/39 fsm	Details in SECTION 4, Part 1	Farnborough
BAPC.286	Mignet HM.14 Flea	Details in SECTION 4, Part 1	Cardiff
	(Scott A2S)		
BAPC.287	Blackburn F2 Lincock fsm	Details in SECTION 4, Part 1 (As "G-EBVO")	Hull
BAPC.288	Hawker Hurricane fsm	Details in SECTION 4, Part 1	Farnsfield
		(As "V7467:LE-D" in RAF 242 Sqdn c/s) (see BAPC.223)	
BAPC.289	Gyro-Boat	Details in SECTION 4, Part 1	Weston-super-Mare
BAPC.290	Fieseler Fi.104 flying-bomb fsm	Details in SECTION 4, Part 1	Dover
BAPC.291	Hawker Hurricane I fsm	Details in SECTION 4, Part 1	
			Capel Le Ferne, Folkestone
		(As "P2970:US-X" in RAF 56 Sqdn c/s)	
BAPC.292	Eurofighter Typhoon fsm	Details in SECTION 4, Part 1	Hendon
BAPC.293	Supermarine Spitfire fsm	Details in SECTION 4, Part 1	Hendon
BAPC.294	Fairchild Argus	Details in SECTION 4, Part 1	Woodhall Spa
BAPC.295	Leonardo Da Vinci hang-glider reproduction	Skysport Engineering	Hatch
	(Built Skysport Engineering)	(Built for Channel 4 TV documentary "Leonardo's Dream Machines")	
BAPC.296	Army Balloon Factory Nulli reproduction		Hendon
BAPC.297	Supermarine Spitfire reproduction	Details in SECTION 4, Part 1	Hawkinge
BAPC.298	Supermarine Spitfire IX fsm	Details in SECTION 4, Part 1	Hawkinge
BAPC.299	Supermarine Spitfire I fsm	Details in SECTION 4, Part 1	
			Capel le Ferne .Folkestone
		(As "P9338" in RAF 72 Sqdn c/s)	
BAPC.300	Piffard Hummingbird reproduction	Details in SECTION 4, Part 1	Shoreham

PART 3 – IRISH AVIATION HISTORICAL COUNCIL REGISTER

The IAHC Register came into existence with similar objectives to the BAPC.

Register No.	Type	Construction No	Previous Identity	Remarks	Location
IAHC.1	Mignet HM.14 Pou-Du-Ciel			Details in SECTION 4, Part 1	Dromod, County Leitrim
IAHC.2	Aldritt Monoplane replica			Details in SECTION 4, Part 1	
					Filching Manor, Wannock
IAHC.3	Mignet HM.14 Pou-Du-Ciel			M.Donohoe	Delgany
	(Built 1937 but unflown)				
IAHC.4	Hawker Hector		IAAC....	D.McCarthy	Not known
				(Believed components on rebuild Florida, USA)	
IAHC.5	Not known			Not known	
IAHC.6.	Ferguson Monoplane replica			Details in SECTION 4, Part 1	Belfast
IAHC.7	Sligo Concept			G.O'Hara	Sligo
				(Was stored incomplete 8.91: current status unknown)	
IAHC.8	O'Hara Autogyro			G.O'Hara	Sligo
				(Was stored incomplete 8.91: current status unknown)	
IAHC.9	Ferguson Monoplane replica			Details in SECTION 4, Part 1	Belfast

SECTION 5

PART 1 – OVERSEAS CIVIL REGISTERED AIRCRAFT LOCATED IN UK AND IRELAND

A further batch of aircraft has been removed from this edition where no recent sightings have been recorded. Several others are in danger of suffering a similar fate and your contributions are invited if you can provide an update on their current status either to the Editor or to paul.hewins@virgin.net.

Although a few aircraft have transferred to the new Isle of Man register its inception is unlikely to have a major effect on this Section as the Isle of Man's Department of Trade and Industry do not propose registering aircraft below 5,700 kg other than for residents or businesses operating from there. As in previous editions leased and stored airliners are omitted unless there is a reasonable likelihood they will still be present when this reaches the reader. Underlining indicates a significant change to previously published information while an asterisk in Part 1 denotes the registration no longer appears on the relevant country register.

This Section could not have been produced without the assistance of the following to whom due credit is acknowledged: Jeff Bell (Sywell), Tony Broadhurst, Peter Budden, Nigel Burch (Biggin Hill), Richard Cawsey, Mike Cain and Kevin Dupuy (Southend), Terry Dann, Bryan Foster, Dave Haines (Gloucestershire), Phil and Nigel Kemp (North Weald), Bob Kent (Shoreham), Andy Mac (Stapleford), Bernard Martin, Nigel Ponsford (Breighton), Bob Sauvary (Jersey), Andy Smith (Guernsey), Martin Steggalls (Crowfield), Mike Stroud, Paul Sweatman, Bill Teasdale, John Tietjen (Andrewsfield and Rayne) and Barrie Womersley plus the numerous contributors to the AB-Sightings, Airfields, CAE and Helicopters mailing lis

Registration	Type	Construction No	Previous Identity	Owner(Operator)	(Unconfirmed) Base	Last noted
UNITED ARAB EMIRATES						
A6-ESH	Airbus A319-133X	910		Ruler of Sharjah	Farnborough and Sharjah	1.08
A6-HEH	Boeing 737-8AJ	32825		Dubai Air Wing	Farnborough and Dubai	1.08
A6-HRS	Boeing 737-7EO	29251		Dubai Air Wing	Farnborough and Dubai	7.07
A6-MRM	Boeing 737-8EC	32450		Dubai Air Wing	Farnborough and Dubai	1.08
CANADA						
C-FQIP	Lake LA-4-200 Buccaneer	679	N1068L	P J Molloy	Elstree	12.07
C-GWJO*	Boeing 737-2A3	20299	HR-SHO	Newcastle Aviation Academy	Newcastle	11.07
			HR-TNR, CX-BHM, N1797B, N1787B (For instructional use)			
PORTUGAL						
CS-ARI	Robin HR.100-210 Safari	159	F-BUHV	Not known	Cranfield	2.07
GERMANY						
D-ASDB	VFW-Fokker VFW-614	G-019	OY-RRW	Not known	RAF St Athan	7.05
			D-ASDB, German AF 17+03 (Instructional Airframe)			
D-CALM	Dornier Do 228-101	7051		Deutsches Zentrum fur Luft und Raumfahrt	Oxford	1.08
D-EAAH	Bölkow BÖ.209 Monsun 160RV	168		Not known	Farley Farm, Romsey	10.07
D-EAAW	Bölkow BÖ.209 Monsun 160RV	181		Not known	Farley Farm, Romsey	10.07
D-EAGC	Cessna F172H	F172-0637	(D-EBEB)	Not known	Liverpool	10.07
D-EAMB	Bölkow BÖ.208C Junior	597	OE-AMB	Not known	Wolverhampton	10.07
			D-ECGE			
D-EANS	Mooney M.20G Statesman	680008	N586MA	Not known	Lee-on-Solent	1.08
D-EAOB	Piper PA-28-181 Archer II	2890082	N9147X	Not known	Cavan, County Meath	4.07
D-EAPF	Robin DR.400-180R Remorqueur	1630		P Fink	Lasham	9.07
D-EAWW	Piper PA-28R-201 Arrow III	28R-7837199	N9469C	Not known	Oxford	1.08
D-EBLI	Bölkow BÖ.207	223		Not known	Farley Farm, Romsey	10.07
D-EBLO	Bölkow BÖ.207	224		Not known	Gamston	9.06
D-EBWE*	Piper PA-28-235 Cherokee	28-10431	N8874W	Not known	Manston	1.07
D-EBWS	Cessna T210N Turbo Centurion II	21064341	N6339Y	S Jack	Sherburn-in-Elmet	10.07
D-EBXR	Reims FR172K Hawk XP	FR17200597	HB-CXO	Not known	Waterford	7.07
D-ECFE	Oberlerchner JOB 15-150	060	OE-CAO	Not known	Barton	12.07
D-ECGI	Bölkow BÖ.208C Junior	598		Not known	Little Rissington	1.08
D-EDEL	Piper PA-32-300 Cherokee Six D	32-7140009	N8617N	Not known	Fairoaks	1.08
D-EDEQ	Beech B24R Sierra 200	MC-239		C Jones	Shoreham	2.08
D-EDNA	Bölkow BÖ.208C Junior	578		C Hampson	Dunkeswell	5.07
D-EEAH	Bölkow BÖ.208C Junior	658	(D-EJMH)	J Webb	Bourne Park, Hurstbourne Tarrant	11.07
D-EEHW	Cessna P210N Pressurized Centurion II	P21000455	N731FX	Not known	Exeter	8.07
D-EEPI	Wassmer WA.54 Atlantic	151		R Hunter	Stapleford	6.07
D-EEVY	Cessna 170A	19537	D-ELYC	Not known	Andrewsfield	12.07
			N5503C			
D-EFDL	Grumman AA-5 Traveler	AA5-0645		Not known	(Kilkenny)	5.07
D-EFFA	Ruschmeyer R90-230RG	018	D-ELVY (2)	K Cropp	Southend	2.08
			(D-EEBY (2))			
D-EFJG	Bölkow BÖ.209 Monsun 160RV	129		R.Truesdale	Newtownards	7.07
D-EFQE	Bölkow BÖ.207	266		J Webb	Popham	1.08
D-EFTI	Bölkow BÖ.207	219		M Hayles	Turweston	1.08
D-EFVS	Wassmer WA.52 Europa	22		M Hales	Sandown, Isle of Wight	1.08
D-EFZC	SIAI-Marchetti S.208	2-18		Not known	Brimpton	9.07
D-EFZO	Cessna F172F	F172-0156		Not known	Stapleford	6.07
D-EGDC	Grumman AA-5B Tiger	AA5B-0728		Not known	Guernsey	1.08
D-EGEU*	Piper PA-22-108 Colt	22-9055	EL-AEU	Not known	Derby	8.06
			5N-AEH	(Badly damaged by storms 27.10.02 Farley Farm, Romsey)		
D-EGHW	Bölkow BÖ.209 Monsun 150FV	170	HB-UER	Not known	(Thruxton)	11.07
			D-EAAJ			
D-EGKE	SOCATA Rallye 180TS Galerien	3325		Suffolk Soaring Club	Rougham	8.07
D-EGLW*	Piper PA-38-112 Tomahawk	38-80A0105	N9694N	Not known (Fire and Rescue trainer)	Old Warden	4.07
D-EGVA	Piper PA-28R-200 Cherokee Arrow II	28R-7635229	N9255K	M Williams	Wellesbourne Mountford	1.08

Reg	Type	S/N	Prev ID	Owner/Operator	Location	Date
D-EHJL	Piaggio FWP.149	045	90+31 AC+441, AS+441, GA+394, D-EGEW, GA+394	C A Tyers *(Windmill Aviation)*	Spanhoe	10.07
D-EHKY	Bölkow BÖ.207	272		Not known	Haverfordwest	4.07
D-EHLA	Bölkow BÖ.207	273		J Webb	Lodge Farm, St Osyth	7.07
D-EHOP	Bölkow BÖ.207	206		Not known	Hill Farm, Nayland	9.07
D-EHUQ	Bölkow BÖ.207	207		J Kempton *(Spares source for G-EFTE)*	Landmead Farm, Garford	8.07
D-EHYX*	Bölkow BÖ.207	209		Not known	Spalding	6.05
				(Crashed landing 27. 8.04 Coetir Bach Farm, Maesybont: damaged fuselage for sale with Skycraft)		
D-EIAR	CEA DR.250-160 Capitaine	98		D G Holmann	Leicester	8.07
D-EIIP	Reims Cessna F182Q Skylane	F18200091		Not known *(N90DJ reserved)*	Guernsey	1.08
D-EIKR	Robin DR.400-180 Regent	1839	F-ODSI	Not known	(Cambridge)	4.07
D-EIVF	PZL-110 Koliber 150	03930051		Not known	Kilrush	11.07
D-EJBI	Bölkow BÖ.207	242	G-EJBI D-EJBI	J O'Donnell	Biggin Hill	7.07
D-EJLY	Cessna 182K Skylane	18257879	N2679Q	Not known	Stoodleigh	7.07
D-EKDN	Beech A36 Bonanza	E-2353	N7241Y	Not known	North Weald	1.08
D-EKHW	Piper PA-28RT-201T Turbo Arrow IV	28R-8031094		Not known	Hawarden	10.07
D-EKJD	Reims FR172J Rocket	FR17200582		T Paravicini	Bourn	10.07
D-ELSR (2)	Robin DR.400-180R Remo 180	2012		R Taggart	Kilrush	1.08
D-EMUH	Bölkow BÖ.208C Junior	623		N Beavins	Rayne Hall Farm, Rayne	6.06
D-EMZC*	Reims FR172G Rocket	FR17200154		Not known	Cork	3.05
D-ENTO	American General AG-5B Tiger	10166	N1198T	Not known	Elstree	12.07
D-EOAJ	Piaggio FWP.149D	028	90+18 AC+409, DE+394	Not known	Goodwood	12.07
D-EQXD	Klemm Kl.35D	1979	(G-KLEM) N5050, N505Q, SE-BGD, Fv5050 *(As "NQ+NR" in Luftwaffe c/s)*	P Holloway	Old Warden	10.07
D-ETTO	Extra EA.300/L	1174		Not known	Panshanger	9.07
D-EWAT	Commander Aircraft Commander 114B	14564		Not known	Blackbushe	2.08
D-EXGC	Extra EA.200	027		Not known	Andrewsfield	12.07
D-FBPS	Cessan 208B Grand Caravan	208B0494	LV-YJC N208BA, N1219G	Not known *(Operated British Parachute School)*	Langar	7.07
D-FLOH	Cessna 208B Grand Caravan	208B0576	N1041F	Not known) *(Operated British Parachute School)*	Langar	7.07
D-GEWU *	Beech 76 Duchess	ME-398		Not known *(Cancelled 5.07)*	Perranporth	1.08
D-GPEZ	Piper PA-30 Twin Comanche C	30-1871	N8798Y N9703N	Not known	RAF Wittering	10.07
D-HCKV	Agusta A109A-II	7345	N109HC N2GN	University Technical School	Gloucestershire	1.05
				(Damaged near Newby Bridge, Cumbria 2.1.00: hulk marked "G-OPAS")		
D-IBPN	Beech 58P Baron	TJ-424	N6526S	Small World Aviation	North Weald	9.07
D-KAAD *	Schleicher ASG 29E	29519		A Darlington *"7" (Reserved as G-CKOO)*	Lasham	7.07
D-KBJG *	Schleicher ASG 29E	29512		J Gorringe *"XE" (To be BGA 5255)*	Lasham	8.07
D-KEEJ *	Schleicher ASG 29E	29513		E Johnston *"G9" (Reserved as G-CKOZ*	Dunstable	8.07
D-KGLM	Grob G.109B	6237		Not known	Wing Farm, Longbridge Deverill	10.07
D-KIFF	SFS-31 Milan	6604		N Grayson	Boscombe Down	7.06
D-KKAM	Schleicher ASW 22BLE	22065	D-KBJL	D Taylor *"499"*	Sutton Bank	.07
D-KLCC *	Schleicher ASG 29E	29511		Viscount Cobham *"CC" (Reserved as G-VLCC)*	Lasham	8.07
D-KMDP	Fournier RF-3	37	F-BMDP	Not known	Carnmore, Galway	9.07
D-KNZG *	Schleicher ASG 29E	29510		P Wells *"Z" (Reserved as G-CKOY)*	Wycombe Air Park	5.07
D-KPRA *	Schleicher ASG 29E	29514		R and A Pentecost *"630" (Reserved as G-XXIX)*	Lasham	1.08
D-KPRB *	Schleicher ASG 29E	29518		R Browne *"XS" (Reserved as G-XOAR)*	RAF Cranwell	7.07
D-KPRC *	Schleicher ASG 29E	29501	D-2529	R Cheetham *"E1" (To be BGA 5236)*	Husbands Bosworth	10.07
D-1155 *	Schleicher K.8B	8589		Not known *(Stored)*	Edgehill	8.07
D-2782 *	Schempp-Hirth Cirrus VTC	163Y		M Cuming *"PC" (Derelict)*	Edgehill	8.07
D-7429 *	Schleicher ASG 29	29015		P Brice *"629" (Reserved as G-OASG)*	Wycombe Air Park	7.06
D-9729 *	Schleicher ASG 29	29024		D Strange and R C Bromwich *"290" (Reserved as G-CKOE)*	RAF Keevil	11.07
D-MBRG	Aerostyle Breezer	47		Not known *(Also carries "G-90-2")*	Wolverhampton	5.06
D-MDMM	Impulse 100	Not known		Not known	Damyns Hall, Upminster	8.06

SPAIN

Reg	Type	S/N	Prev ID	Owner/Operator	Location	Date
EC-CFA*	Boeing 727-256	20811	N907RF EC-AFA	Not known *(Stored)*	Shannon	5.06
EC-DDX*	Boeing 727-256A	21779		Directions Finningley *(Fuselage used as training aid)*	Sheffield-Doncaster	11.07
EC-EP6	ELA Aviacion ELA-07	03060940724		Not known	Kirkbride	10.07

FRANCE

Reg	Type	S/N	Prev ID	Owner/Operator	Location	Date
F-BBSO*	Taylorcraft Auster 5	1792	G-AMJM TW452	D.J.Baker *(Dismantled frame)*	Carr Farm, Thorney, Newark	6.05
F-BMCY*	Potez 840	02		Not known *(Stored dismantled)*	North Roe, Shetland	12.05
F-BMHM	Piper J-3C-65 Cub	11907	N840HP F-BJSU, F-WJSU Fr Military 44-79611	A R Capel *(Damaged Sumburgh 29. 3.81)*	(Milton Keynes)	11.05
F-BPFP	Sud-Aviation SA.315B Lama	2006/15		I Clark	(Sandy)	2.07
F-BRHN*	Bölkow BÖ.208C Junior	688	D-EEAK	B Parant *(Stored)*	Farley Farm, Romsey	4.07

Reg	Type	c/n	Prev ids	Owner	Location	Date
F-BROC	CEA DR.360 Chevalier	379		P. O'Donnell	North Weald	10.07
F-BSPQ	Robin DR.300-120 Petit Prince	621		E J Horsfall	Blackpool	10.06
F-BTKO*	Robin HR.100-210 Safari	142		Fly Ltd (Stored dismantled)	Turweston	1.08
F-BXCP	Max Holste MH.1521M Broussard	149	ALAT	Giles & Charles English	White Waltham	8.07
F-GAIF *	Wassmer WA.81 Pirana	804		Not known (Cxashed 6.07)	Abbeyshrule	10.07
F-GCTU*	Piper PA-38-112 Tomahawk	38-80A0085	N9694N	Not known (Stripped fuselage)	Sandford Holiday Park, Dorset	9.07
F-GFGH	SOCATA Rallye 235E Gabier	13337	F-ODNQ	I Watts	Bagby	2.08
F-GFOR	Robin ATL	42		M Godsell	Haverfordwest	11.06
F-GIBU	Aérospatiale SA.342J Gazelle	1470	HB-XMU, N9000A	Global Aviation Services Ltd	Hawarden	11.07
F-GJPB *	SOCATA TB-9 Tampico	896		Northbrook College (Instructional airframe)	Shoreham	12.06
F-GJQI	Robin ATL L	133		C Fox	Weston Zoyland	8.05
F-GKGN	Grumman-American AA-5B Tiger	AA5B-0089	G-BGDN, N6147A	B Moran	Kilrush	10.07
F-GKMZ	Mudry CAP.232	09		FCP Ltd	Headcorn	9.07
F-GLAO	SOCATA TB-9 Tampico Club	1106		Aero Club de Bigorre (Dismantled)	Bournemouth	8.05
F-GLTR	Cessna 172R	17280833		Citicapital Societe par Actions Simplifiee (Crashed Sainte-Hélène-sur-Isère 3. 1.03: stored)	Andrewsfield	1.08
F-GMHH*	Robin HR.100-210 Safari	155	3A-MUZ, F-BUHH	Fly Ltd (Stored dismantled)	Turweston	1.08
F-GODZ	Pilatus PC-6/340 Porter	340	(N340N), ST-AFR, HB-FAR	SARL Fly High Icarius (Operated Black Knights Parachute Club)	Bank End Farm, Cockerham	10.07
F-GOTC	Mudry CAP.232	15	OO-CXD	T Cassells	Bagby	2.08
F-GOXD	Robin DR.400-180RP Remorquer	1817	HB-KBU, D-EAJD	G Richardson	Little Staughton	8.07
F-GOZO	Mudry CAP.231	8	F-WQOM, CN-ABK	R Buchan	White Waltham	11.07
F-GPBF	Piper PA-31T Cheyenne II	31T-7920094	OH-PYE, SE-ICS	F Michienzi	Elstree	12.07
F-GXDB	Mudry CAP.232	33		D Britten "Diana"	Fairoaks	9.07
F-GXFP	Sud-Aviation SA.318C Alouette Astazou	2152	French Army	F Cilliers	(Bury St Edmunds)	6.06
F-GYRO	Mudry CAP.232	25		A Cassidy (Securicor titles) (Current status unknown)	White Waltham	9.04
F-JITM	Funk FK-14 Polaris	Not known		Not known	Lasham	8.06
F-PYOY	Heintz Zenith 100	52		B L Featherstone (In open store)	Southend	1.08
21YV	Dyn'Aéro MCR-01	314		Not known	(Highclere)	8.06
31WI	Farrington Twinstarr Gyrocopter	TS97013		W de Saar (Current status unknown)	Shipdham	8.06
95MR	Power Assist Swift	Not known		Not known	Easter Poldar Farm, Thornhill	2.07

HUNGARY

Reg	Type	c/n	Prev ids	Owner	Location	Date
HA-ACL	Dornier Do.28D-2 Skyservant (Walter M-601 turbo conversion)	4125	D-IDRC, 58+50	Trener Kft (Operated Wingglider Ltd)	Hibaldstow	8.07
HA-ACO	Dornier Do.28D-2 Skyservant (Walter M-601 turbo conversion)	4335	G-BWCN, 5N-AYE, D-ILID, 9V-BKL, D-ILID	Trener Kft (Operated Wingglider Ltd)	RAF Weston-on-the-Green	7.07
HA-HUA	Yakovlev Yak-18T	01-32	LY-AQG	Kobo-Coop 96 Kft	White Waltham	9.07
HA-HUB	Yakovlev Yak-12M	210999	G-PFKD, LY-FKD, SP-FKD, SP-AAD, PLW85	Kobo-Coop 96 Kft (Operated R Bade)	Dunsfold	10.07
HA-HUD	Sukhoi Su-29	"76021"		Kobo-Coop 96 Kft	North Weald	1.08
HA-HUE	Yakovlev Yak-18T	12-33		Kobo-Coop 96 Kft	Rochester	1.08
HA-IDL	Sud Aviation Alouette II	1388	75+48, QW+233, QW+738, PA+139, PG+137	Kobo-Coop 96 Kft	Spilstead Farm, Sedlescombe	7.07
HA-JAB	Yakovlev Yak-18T	22202023842	FLARF-02160, CCCP-44420	Kobo-Coop 96 Kft	Spilstead Farm, Hastings	11.07
HA-JAC	Yakovlev Yak-18T	22202034139	RA-44506, HA-JAC, FLA-02159	Kobo-Coop 96 Kft (Current status unknown)	(Sleap)	6.04
HA-LAQ	LET L-410UVP-E4	841332	HAF-332, HA-YFB	Farnair Hungary Kft	South Cerney	8.07
HA-LFB	Aérospatiale SA.341G Gazelle	1074	N223DP, N90778	Not known	Not known	11.07
HA-LFH	Aérospatiale SA.342J Gazelle	1775	RP-C5131	Not known	(Breighton)	12.06
HA-LFM	Aerospatiale SA.341G Gazelle	1301	G-OCMJ, G-HTPS, G-BRNI, YU-HBI	Hidroplan Nord Kft (Operated A Parker)	(Tadcaster)	1.08
HA-LFQ	Aérospatiale SA.342L Gazelle	1854	IAC241	Not known	(Tadcaster)	11.07
HA-LFZ	Sud-Aviation SA318C Alouette II	2043	French Army	Hidroplan Nord Kft	Brierley	9.07
HA-MKE	WSK-PZL Antonov An-2R	1G158-34	UR-07714, CCCP-07714	Trener Kft (Left by road 2005- current status unknown)	Popham	4.05
HA-MKF	Antonov An-2	1G233-43	OM-248, OM-UIN, OK-UIN	Trener Kft	Popham	1.08
HA-NAH	Technoavia SMG-92 Finist	00-003	RA-44484	Not known (Op Wingglider Ltd)	Hibaldstow	2.08
HA-PPC	Sud Aviation SE.3130 Alouette II	1500	G-UGLY, G-BSFN, XP967, F-WIEQ	Not known	(Hull)	6.07
HA-PPY	SOKO SO341 Gazelle (Aerospatiale c/n 1118)	021	HA-LFR, HA-VLA, YU-HDN, JRV12653	J R Saul	Brierley	7.05
HA-SMD	Yakovlev Yak-18T	13-35	LZ-TCC	Not known	North Weald	1.08
HA-TVA	Scottish Aviation Bulldog Series 100	BH100/134	Fv61028, G-AZIV	Not known	Old Sarum	1.08
HA-VOC	Dornier Do.28D-2 Skyservant (Walter M-601 turbo conversion?)	4331	TC-FBC, D-IDWM, CN-85, D-IDWM	Trener Kft (Operated Wingglider Ltd)	Hibaldstow	11.06
HA-YAB	Yakovlev Yak-18T	12-35	RA-44777	Kobo-Coop 96 Kft	Rendcomb	9.07
HA-YAD	Yakovlev Yak-18T	22202054812	RA-81584	Kobo-Coop 96 Kft	Elstree	12.07
HA-YAE	Yakovlev Yak-18T	11-35	RA-44000	Kobo-Coop 96 Kft	Shobdon	12.07

Reg	Type	c/n	Prev id	Owner/Operator	Location	Date
HA-YAF	Yakovlev Yak-18T	08-34	RA-44480	Kobo-Coop 96 Kft	Dunsfold	2.08
HA-YAG	Yakovlev Yak-18T	05-36	RA-01555	Kobo-Coop 96 Kft	Compton Abbas	1.08
				(Operated R McGuire)		
HA-YAH	Technoavia Yak-18T	18-33	RA-44470	Kobo-Coop 96 Kft	Oaksey Park	4.07
HA-YAJ	Yakovlev Yak-18T	01-33	LY-APP	Kobo-Coop 96 Kft	Wycombe Air Park	12.07
			LY-AOG			
HA-YAK	Yakovlev Yak-18T	22202044785	LY-AFS	Kobo-Coop 96 Kft	Stoke Golding	9.07
			DOSAAF			
HA-YAM	Yakovlev Yak-18T	22202047812	RA-44504	Kobo-Coop 96 Kft	New Farm House, Great Oakley	8.05
			LY-AMJ , DOSAAF, CCCP-81558			
HA-YAN	Yakovlev Yak-18T	10-34	RA-44465	Kobo-Coop 96 Kft	White Waltham	8.07
			LY-AOL			
HA-YAO	Sukhoi Su-29	N1001.001	RA-44479	Kobo-Coop 96 Kft (Operated D Barke)	Southend	2.08
HA-YAP	Yakovlev Yak-18T	22202034023	RA-44545	Kobo-Coop 96 Kft	White Waltham	1.08
			LY-AIH, ES-FYE			
HA-YAR	Sukhoi Su-29	75-03	RA-01609	Kobo-Coop 96 Kft	White Waltham	12.07
			RA-7503			
HA-YAU	Yakovlev Yak-18T	15-35	RA-44527	Kobo-Coop 96 Kft	White Waltham	12.07
HA-YAV	Yakovlev Yak-18T	22202047817	RA-01153	Kobo-Coop 96 Kft	Eaglescott	1.08
				(Operated M Robinson)		
HA-YAW	Sukhoi Su-29	74-05	N229JD	Kobo-Coop 96 Kft	Fairoaks	1.08
HA-YAZ	Yakovlev Yak-18T	7201413	CCCP44311	Kobo-Coop 96 Kft	Goodwood	12.07
HA-YDF	Technoavia SMG-92 Finist	01-0005		G-92 Kereskedelmi.Kft	Hibaldstow	4.06
				(Operated Wingglider Ltd)		
HA-YFC	LET L-410-FG	851528		Farnair Hungary	Sibson	11.07

SWITZERLAND

Reg	Type	c/n	Prev id	Owner/Operator	Location	Date
HB-DFT	Mooney M.20J	24-0837		Air Link AG	Andrewsfield	1.08
HB-ITF	Gulfstream Aerospace Gulfstream IV	1202	N369XL	Credit Suisse	Farnborough	8.07
			JY-RAY, V8-009, V8-MSB, N432GA (Operatederate GAMA Aviation)			
HB-IVR	Bombardier CL-600-2B-16	5318	HB-IKQ	Interline SA	Luton	1.08
	(CL-604 Challenger)		(TC-DHE), C-FYYH, C-GLXO (Operated Execujet Charter AG)			
HB-OBP *	Piper J-3C-65 Cub	11709	43-30418	Not known	Dunsfold	4.07
HB-OLP	Piper PA-28-140 Cherokee	28-20495	N6425W	A Krapf	Seething	2.08

SAUDI ARABIA

Reg	Type	c/n	Prev id	Owner/Operator	Location	Date
HZ-AB3	Boeing 727-2U5AR	22362	V8-BG1	Al Anwa Establishment	Lasham	8.06
			V8-HM2, V8-HM1, V8-UB1, V8-HM1, JY-HNH			
HZ-ARK	Gulfstream Aerospace Gulfstream V-SP	5074	N574GA	Mawarid Ltd	Farnborough	1.08
	(Gulfstream 550)					
HZ-OFC5	Dassault Falcon 900EX/EASy	180	F-WWFD	Olayan Finance Co	Luton	1.08
HZ-SJP3	Bombardier CL-600-2B-16	5346	N604JP	Jouannou and Parskevaides		
	(CL-604 Challenger)		C-GLXS		Farnborough and Larnaca	12.07

ITALY

Reg	Type	c/n	Prev id	Owner/Operator	Location	Date
I-EIXM*	Piper PA-18-135 Super Cub	18-3572	MM54-2372	Not known	Kesgrave, Ipswich	12.06
			54-2372	(In open store as "EI-184")		
I-LELF	SIAI-Marchetti SF.260C	568/41-004		Not known	Elstree	5.06
I-TERB	British Aerospace BAe.146 Series 200	E2012	EI-DBY	Not known	Southend	2.08
			G-DEFK, G-DEBK, C-FHAV, N601AW (Being parted out)			
I-TERV	British Aerospace BAe.146 Series 200	E-2014	EI-DBZ	Not known	Southend	2.08
			G-DEFL, G-DEBL, C-FHAX, N602AW (In store in Club Air c/s)			
I-TOMI*	Nardi FN.305D	Not known		Not known (Stored)	Wycombe Air Park	5.05
I-6929	Aeropro Eurofox	Not known		Not known	Kilrush	10.07
I-6943	Pegasus Quantum 914	Not known	G-59-7	R Meredith-Hardy	Barton	10.07

NORWAY

Reg	Type	c/n	Prev id	Owner/Operator	Location	Date
LN-AMY	North American AT-6D Harvard	88-16849	(LN-LCS)	T Manna	North Weald	9.07
			(LN-LCN), N10595, 42-85068	"Amy" (As "8084" in Breitling Fighter Team titles)		
LN-KKA*	Fokker F.27-050	20117	PH-DLT	Air Salvage International	Alton	5.06
			D-AFKY, PH-DLT, OE-LFZ, (VH-FNL), PH-EXA (Fuselage only)			

ARGENTINA

Reg	Type	c/n	Prev id	Owner/Operator	Location	Date
LV-AZF	Boeing 747-267B	23048	N230AL	Southern Winds	Manston	11.07
			LV-AZF, N230AL, G-VRUM, (ZS-PJI), (G-CCMB), G-VRUM, TF-ATV, G-VRUM, B-HIF, VR-HIF, N6066U (Stored)			
LV-RIE	Nord 1002 Pingouin	240		R.J.Lamplough (Stored)	East Garston	12.05
LV-WTY	McDonnell-Douglas MD-81	48011	LV-PMJ	Not known	Shannon	10.06
			N532MD, HB-INM	(Stored unmarked)		

LUXEMBOURG

Reg	Type	c/n	Prev id	Owner/Operator	Location	Date
LX-FTA	Dassault Falcon 900C	201	N210FJ	Northgate SARL	Farnborough	1.08
			F-WWFA	(Operated Global Jet Luxembourg SA)		
LX-TRE	Tecnam P2002JF Sierra	003		Tredex Senc	Kilrush	11.07

LITHUANIA

Reg	Type	c/n	Prev id	Owner/Operator	Location	Date
LY-AHD	Yakovlev Yak-12	30119	SP-CXW	Not known	Little Gransden	12.04
			PLW....	(Current status unknown)		
LY-ALT	Yakovlev Yak-52	822704	DOSAAF 121	Titan Airways Ltd (Current status unknown)	Elmsett	8.04
LY-BIG	Antonov An-2T	1G236-23	Ukraine AF 48 (red)	Air Unique "Baltic Bear"	Tatenhill	1.08
LY-MHC	Antonov An-2R	1G215-33	LY-AVK	Lietuvos Svedijos UAB	Blackpool	12.07
			CCCP40896	"103"		

BULGARIA

Registration	Type	C/N	Previous Identity	Owner/Operator	Location	Date
LZ-TIM	British Aerospace BAe 146 Series 100	E1258	EI-CPJ	TIM Holdings	Southend	2.08
			9H-ACN, (9H-ABX), G-6-258	(Stored) (In open store)		

UNITED STATES

Registration	Type	C/N	Previous Identity	Owner/Operator	Location	Date
N1FD	SOCATA TB-200 XL Tobago	1614		Siek Aviation Inc	Blackbushe	2.08
N1FY	Cessna 421C Golden Eagle I	421C1067	N345TG	LME Aviation (Operated Estate Air)	Kemble	5.07
N2CL	Piper PA-28RT-201T Turbo Arrow IV	28R-8131054	N8333S	Southern Aircraft Consultancy Inc	Frensham	10.07
			N9649N	(Under repair Stapleford)		
N2FU	Learjet Model 31	31-027	N30LJ	Wilmington Trust Company	Biggin Hill	1.08
			N91201	(Operated Formula One Administration)		
N2NR	Agusta A109A-II	7350	N800AH	N2NR Inc	Oxford	6.07
N2RK	Lockheed L.188PF Electra	2010	N178RV	Electra Aero Inc (Stored)	Coventry	10.07
			C-GNWC, N178RV, N63AJ, CF-NAX, N33506, ZK-TEB, (ZK-BMQ)			
N3HK	Cessna 340 II	340-0538	G-VAUN	Southern Aircraft Consultancy Inc	North Weald	1.08
			D-IOFW, N5148J			
N4HG	Lockheed L.188PF Electra	1140	G-LOFH	Electra Airways	Coventry	10.07
			N9744C	(Stored unmarked)		
N4VQ	Beech A36 Bonanza	E-3014	SP-FNK	VIP Transport Inc	Not known	11.06
			N3263W	(Overran runway Fenland 30.10.06)		
N5LL	Piper PA-31 Navajo C	31-7812041	N27495	Southern Aircraft Consultancy Inc	Leeds-Bradford	2.08
N6NE	Lockheed Jetstar 731	5006/40	(VR-CCC)	Aerospace Finance Leasing Inc	Southampton	2.07
			N6NE, N222Y, N731JS, N227K, N12R, N9280R (Damaged Southampton 27.11.92: on fire dump)			
N7EY	Piper PA-30 Twin Comanche	30-571	F-BNFH	Charnwood Aviation	White Waltham	9.07
			F-OCDS, N7508Y			
N8MZ	Piper PA-30 Twin Comanche B	30-1648	G-ORDO	Francis Aviation	Lee-on-Solent	9.07
			N8485Y			
N8UF	Agusta A109A-II	7268	N1RN	Eastern Atlantic Helicopters	(Gamston)	11.07
			N109AX			
N8YG	Piper PA-32R-301T Saratoga II TC	3257151	OY-LAA	Normac Aviation	Lydd	9.07
N9AY	Cessna 421C Golden Eagle III	421C0844	G-NSGI	Sooty Aviation Inc	Cranfield	2.08
			N421EL, XA-RAE, N421EB, (N21MW), N421EB, N2659Z			
N9FJ	Aérospatiale AS.350B-2 Ecureuil	3148		Boultbee Aviation	Denham	1.08
N9SZ	Cirrus SR22-GTS	1232		Vision ISS Inc	Cambridge	1.08
N10MC	Cirrus SR22	1084		La Luisa Aviation (Operated M Collett)	Jersey	9.07
N11FV	Cessna T303 Crusader	T30300133	G-BXRI	Auster Aviation	Guernsey	1.08
			HB-LNI, (N5143C)			
N12AB	Ruschmeyer R90-230RG	027		Cremair Inc	Elstree	8.07
N12AG	Pilatus PC-12/47	854	HB-FSK	Aircraft Guaranty Corporation	(Fairoaks)	1.08
N12SJ	Cirrus SR22–G3 Turbo	2740		Johnson Airways	(Turweston)	1.08
N12ZX	Mooney M.20J	24-3227		S Ames	Oxford	1.08
N13DT	Robinson R44 Raven I	1651		MCR Aviation	(Republic of Ireland)	1.08
N14AF	Rockwell Commander 112TC-A	13258	G-GRIF	Southern Aircraft Consultancy	Burnham on Crouch	9.07
			G-BHXC, N1005C			
N14HF	Maule MT-7-235 Star Rocket	18084C		Hamilton-Fairley Aviation	Bramshill	1.08
N14MT	Cessna TR182 Skylane RG	R18201227		Southern Aircraft Consultancy Inc	North Weald	1.08
N17UK	Cirrus SR22	0200	N7UK	Southern Aircraft Consultancy Inc	Rochester	11.07
N18GH	McDonnell Douglas MD.520N	LN014	N317PC	Adrian Raymond Aviation	(Radstock)	11.07
			N16113			
N18V	Beech UC-43-BH Traveler	6869	NC18	R.J.Lamplough (As "DR828:PB1")	East Garston	8.04
			Bu 32898, FT507, 44-67761			
N19F	Cessna 337A Super Skymaster (Robertson STOL conversion)	33700289	N6289F	Southern Aircraft Consultancy Inc	Wadswick Manor Farm, Corsham	8.07
N19GL	Brantly B.2B	2004		Southern Aircraft Consultancy Inc	Hill Top Farm, Hambledon	5.07
N20AG	SOCATA TB-20 Trinidad	2003	N29KF	Archway International Inc	Jersey	11.07
N20UK	Mooney M.20F Executive	22-1380	N9155J	E-Plane Inc	Biggin Hill	1.08
			G-BDVU			
N21UH	United Helicopter Corp UH-12C	UH2001		Southern Aircraft Consultancy Inc	Shipmeadow, Beccles	3.07
N22CG	Cessna 441 Conquest II	441-0119		Jubilee Airways Inc (Operated M.Klinge)	Prestwick	7.07
N22NN	Cessna 182P Skylane	18263497	OE-DGU	Southern Aircraft Consultancy Inc	Elstree	12.07
			N5717J			
N23KY	Cessna P210N Centurion	P21000447	N731ER	Southern Aircraft Consultancy Inc (Operated Pacnet Europe)	Fairoaks	1.08
N25KB	Piper PA-24-250 Comanche	24-3034	F-BKRK	Southern Aircraft Consultancy Inc (Operated K Bettoney)	Farley Farm, Romsey	4.07
			N7814P			
N25PR	Piper PA-30-160 Twin Comanche B	30-1511	G-AVPR	PSL Aviation	Gloucestershire	5.07
			N8395Y			
N25XZ	Cessna 182G	18255388	HB-CST	Southern Aircraft Consultancy Inc	Bodmin	10.07
			OE-DDM, N2188R			
N26HE	Cessna 421C Golden Eagle II (Winglets)	421C0687		Wells Fargo Bank Northwest NA (Operated Springhurst Ltd)	Biggin Hill	1.08
N27BG	Cessna 340A	340A0656		Traca Inc (Operated B Gregory)	Cranfield	5.07
N27HK	Beech 200 Super King Air	BB-1350	A7-AHK	Aircraft Guaranty Trust LLC	Weston, Dublin	1.08
			N1570F, N147VC, N1570F			
N27MW	Beech B58 Baron	TH-995	ZS-MTG	B58 Aviation Inc	Fairoaks	1.08
N28TE	Raytheon 58 Baron	TH-1951		Ecosse Aviation Inc	Blackbushe	2.08
N30FL	Beech C90 King Air	LJ-741	(N90FL)	Keep Holdings Inc	Southend	2.08
			F-GFLD, HB-GGW, I-AZIO	(Operated Flightline)		
N30NW	Piper PA-30-160 Twin Comanche	30-312	G-ASON	R S Barnett	Shipmeadow, Beccles	11.07
			N7273Y			
N31GN	Cessna 310R II	310R-1541	N410RS	J A Keim	Kirknewton	11.07
			G-BTGN, N410RS, N5331C			

N31NB	Piper PA-31 Turbo Navajo B	31-7401239
N31RB	Grumman-American AA-5B Tiger	AA5B-0156
N32LE	Piper PA-32R-301T Turbo Saratoga SP	
		32R-8329016
N33EW	Mitsubishi MU-2B-60	1519SA
N33NW	SOCATA TB-20 Trinidad	1073
N34FA	SOCATA TB-20 Trinidad	866
N34RF	Beech C90B King Air	LJ-1371
N35AD	Piper PA-30 Twin Comanche B	30-1121
N35AG	Agusta A109S Grand	22050
N35AL	Diamond DA 42 Twin Star	42.147
N35SN	Beech 35-33 Debonair	CD-207
N36NB	Beech A36 Bonanza	E-2274
N36SU	Beech A36 Bonanza	E-3034
N36TH*	Canadair CL-30 (T-33AN) Silver Star Mk.3	
N37EL	SOCATA TB-20 Trinidad	378
N37LP	Bell 407	53049
N37LW	Piper PA-23-250 Aztec	27-134
N37US	Piper PA-34-200T Seneca II	34-8070111
N37VB	Cessna 421C	421C-0418
N39SE	Diamond DA.40 Star	40.299
N39TA	Beech B24R Sierra 200	MC-230
N40EA	Bell 222A	47061
N40GD	Cirrus SR22	0473
N40XR	Bombardier Learjet 40	45-2028
N41AK	Beech F90 King Air	LA-188
N41FT	Piper PA-39 Twin Comanche C/R	39-59
N42FW*	Beech E33 Bonanza	CD-1199
N43GG	Piper PA-34-200T Seneca II	34-7670066
N43SV	Boeing-Stearman PT-13D Kaydet	75-5541
N45PJ	Piper PA-46-500TP Malibu Meridian	4697031
N46BM	Beech E90 King Air	LW-198
N46WK	Piper PA-46-500TP Malibu Meridian	4697090
N46PJ	Cessna 551 Citaion II/SP	551-0027
N46PL	Piper PA-46-500TP Malibu Meridian	4697054
N48CA	Piper PA-32R-301 Saratoga II HP	3246232
N48NS	Cessna 550 Citation Bravo	550-0939
N49BH	Aviat A-1B Husky	2315
N50AY	Rockwell Commander 114	14527
N50VC	Cessna 525 CitationJet CJ1+	525-0609
N51AH	Piper PA-32R-301 Saratoga SP	32R-8413017
N51ER	American Champion 7GCAA	484-2004
N51WF	Rockwell 690C Turbo Commander	11684
N54EW	Britten-Norman BN-2T Islander	2145
N55BN	Beech 95-B55 Baron	TC-1572
N55EN	Beech E55 Baron	TE-942
N56GH	Bell 206B-3 JetRanger III	4281
N57CR	Hiller UH-12C	909
N57MT	Cessna T303 Crusader	T30300211
N58GT	Beech B58 Baron (Winglets)	TH-1090
N58YD	Beech 58 Baron	TH-1427
N59SD	McDonnell Douglas MD.369E	0019E
N59GG	Beech C90A King Air	LJ-1734

G-OSFT		Athole Aviation Inc	Deenethorpe	4.07
G-MDAS, 5N-AEP, G-BJCZ, N61427 (Operated N Brown)			
		Southern Aircraft Consultancy Inc	Bournemouth	12.07
		(Operated T Cromber t/a Echo Echo Group)		
		Southern Aircraft Consultancy (Operated Light into Europe)		
		New Farm House, Great Oakley		5.06
N331W		Florida Express Corp	Southend	2.08
N33TW, N434MA		(Operated King Aviation)		
N666HM		Southern Aircraft Consultancy Inc	Nottingham	1.08
OO-PDV, F-GLAC				
G-BPFG		Southern Aircraft Consultancy Inc	Elstree	2.08
VT-PPC		Roflec Inc	Guernsey	1.08
N696WW, C-FSGZ				
HB-LDE		Southern Aircraft Consultancy Inc	Jersey	7.07
N8014Y				
		Aircraft Guaranty Management LLC	Fairoaks	12.07
OE-VPY		Able Liston Aviation	Jersey	11.07
D-EKOW		Plane Fun Inc	Old Sarum	1.08
F-GKTZ		Minute Aviation Inc	Biggin Hill	3.07
N7249H				
OY-TFE		Zoomair Inc	Fairoaks	1.08
N1096Y				
		See G-BYOY in SECTION 1, Part 3	North Weald	
G-GDGR		Southern Aircraft Consultancy Inc	Stapleford	12.07
F-GDGR				
		Aircraft Guaranty Title LLC	Weston, Dublin	12.07
G-EEVA		Southern Aircraft Consultancy Inc		
G-ASND, N4800P			Morgansfield, Fishburn	11.07
G-PLUS		Southern Aircraft Consultancy Inc	Jersey	7.07
N81406		(Operated Skycabs)		
EC-IFT		Lowndes Aviation	Bournemouth	1.08
G-FWRP, N3919C				
		Southern Aircraft Consultancy Inc	Bodmin	1.08
G-BBVJ		Southern Aircraft Consultancy Inc	Sturgate	12.07
SE-HTN		Anglo Services Inc	Oranmore	9.07
G-DMAF, G-BLSZ, D-HCHS, (D-HHAD) (Reserved as EI-MED)			
		Aircraft Guaranty Trust LLC	Leeds-Bradford	2.08
		Wells Fargo Bank Northwest NA	Bournemouth	1.08
		(Operated Jet-Care International)		
N41CK		I and S Graham Aviation	Glasgow	12.07
N6429M				
G-BZLW		Southern Aircraft Consultancy Inc		
ZS-NLF, ZS-MRH, ZS-IKG, N8904Y			Farley Farm, Romsey	9.07
N7682N		Southern Aircraft Consultancy Inc	Kirknewton	3.06
		(Operated Feroz Wadia) (Cx 1.07)		
G-ROLA		Southern Aircraft Consultancy Inc	Shoreham	10.07
N4537X, G-ROLA, N4537X				
		A de Cadenet "796" (Current status unknown) Oxford		5.04
		Billings Flying Service	Weston, Dublin	1.08
G-WELL		Sherborne Aviation	Bournemouth	1.08
N202CC, (N7PB), N202CC				
SE-LTM		Skypark Holding	Gloucestershire	11.07
N189DB, N46WK, N46WE, N5343C				
N522CC		Aircraft Guaranty Trust LLC	Cranfield	2.08
N552CC, N44GT, N552CC, N98753				
D-FKAI		AvCorp Leasing	Gloucestershire and Jersey	8.05
N53263, (D-FKAI), N53263, (PH-EPS)				
		Southern Aircraft Consultancy Inc	Panshanger	11.07
VP-BNS		Tower House Investments	Jersey	9.07
(N939BB), N5076K				
G-USKI		Southern Aircraft Consultancy Inc	Hunts Green	9.07
		(Operated B Hill)		
HB-NCZ		Stronghold Aviation	Rochester	8.07
G-BGTE, N5910N				
		Mistral Aviation	Guernsey	1.08
G-REAH		Southern Aircraft Consultancy Inc	Panshanger	9.07
G-CELL, (G-BLRI), N4361D				
		Southern Aircraft Consultancy Inc	Abbeyshrule	8.07
N5936K		Aviation Air Services	Fairoaks	1.08
G-BOBC		BN Aircraft Sales Inc	Bembridge	6.07
G-BJYZ				
G-KCAS		Snowadam Inc	Tatenhill	1.08
G-KCEA, N2840W		(Operated C.Butler)		
		Monckton Byng Inc	Elstree	12.07
		Aircraft Guaranty Trust LLC	Dublin	11.07
		(Operated Hennessy Aviation)		
		Pulse Helicopter Corp	Sywell	12.07
D-IEEG		Flying Dog Inc	Guernsey	1.08
N9748C				
HB-GIK		Swiftair Inc	Finmere	9.07
G-OLYD		Southern Aircraft Consultancy Inc	Gamston	6.07
N7255H, ZS-LYC, N7255H				
		Sky Dock Helicopter Holdings	(Faldingworth)	10.07
		Glasdon Aviation	Blackpool	1.08

Reg	Type	Serial
N59VT	Beech K35 Bonanza	D-5897
N60GM	Cessna 421C Golden Eagle III	421C0828
N60LW	Cessna 550 Citation Bravo	550-1129
N60NZ	Beech 60 Duke	P-339
N61DE	Piper PA-32-300 Six	32-7940030
N61FD	SIAI-Marchetti SF.260C	719
N61FM	Agusta A.109A	7197
N61HB	Piper PA-34-220T Seneca V	3449217
N61MF *	Mooney M.20J	24-0847
N61PS	Pitts S-2B	5230
N64GG	Beech B300 King Air	FL-274
N64JG	Bell 206B-2 Jet Ranger	1507
N64LA	Cessna 421C Golden Eagle	421C1064
N64VB	Beech 58 Baron	TH-305
N65JF	Piper PA-28-181 Archer II	28-7990140
N65MJ	Beech 58P Baron	TJ-487
N65TG	Agusta A119	14529
N66SG	Bombardier Learjet 45	45-073
N66SW*	Cessna 340	340-0011
N69LJ	Bombardier Learjet 60	60-027
N60LP	Piper PA 61P Aerostar 601P	61P 0611 230
N70AA	Beech 70 Queen Air	LB-35
N70QJ	Sikorsky S-76A	760284
N70VB	Ted Smith Aerostar 600A	60-0446-150
NX71MY	Vimy 19/94 Inc Vimy FB-27	01
N71VE	Rockwell Commander 690A	11043
N71WZ	Piper PA-46-350P Malibu Mirage	4636275
N72GD	Raytheon RB390 Premier 1A	RB-163
N73AE	Mudry CAP.10B	278
N73GR	Piper PA-28-181 Archer III	2843586
N73MW	Beech B200 Super King Air	BB-22
N74DC	Pitts S-2A Special	2228
N74PM	Agusta A109C	7636
N75CY	Partenavia AP.68TP300 Spartacus	8001
N75FW	Cessna 421C Golden Eagle	421C0706
N75TC	Cessna 172N	17268913
N77YY	Piper PA-32R-301T Saratoga II TC	3257120
N78GG	Beech F33A Bonanza	CE-699
N78HB	Aviat A-1B Husky	2066
N78XP	Reims FR172K Hawk XP II	FR17200603
N79AP	Beech 58P Baron	TJ-206
N79EL	Beech 400A Beechjet	RK-214
N79HR	Lancair Columbia LC41-550FG	41017
N80BA	Pitts S-1A	648-4
N80HB	Cessna 525B CitationJet CJ3	525B0163
N80HQ	Cessna 510 Citation Mustang	510-0021
N80JN*	Mitsubishi MU-2J	626
N80MC	Mudry CAP.10B	221
N80N	Cessna T337G Super Skymaster	P3370197
N80NS	Cirrus SR22-G3	2839
N84VK	Piper PA-24-180 Comanche	24-1492
N85LB	Cessna 340A II	340A0486
N85WS	Pitts S-1T	1028
N88NA	Piper PA-32R-301T Turbo Saratoga SP	32R-8529005
N90BE	Mooney M.20K	25-1143
N90YA	Cessna 425 Corsair	425-0090
N91ME	SOCATA TB-20 Trinidad	2152

Reg	Owner	Location	Date
D-EMEF	Southern Aircraft Consultancy Inc	White Waltham	12.07
	Southern Aircraft Consultancy Inc	Gamston	10.07
N52029	PIHL Delaware Inc	Luton	12.07
	International Air Services	Haverfordwest	11.06
	(Operated D F Keedy)		
G-LADE	Southern Aircraft Consultancy Inc	Andrewsfield	12.07
N3008L			
	Aerial Obsessions Inc "35"	North Weald	2.08
D-HANS	Eastern Atlantic Helicopters	Shoreham	1.08
G-CBAA	HBC Aviation Inc	Thurrock and Guernsey	1.08
N53445			
G-BYDD	M Flynn	Bournemouth	9.05
D-EIWM	*(Overran runway landing Fairoaks 8. 5.05: cancelled 6.06 by FAA: wreck stored)*		
	D J Swartz	Wickenby	10.06
	Specsavers Aviation	Guernsey	1.08
N589LB	Celtic Aircraft Inc *(Stored)*	Hawarden	5.07
G-MUVG	421C-1064 Inc	Fairoaks	1.08
N421DD, N6865P			
N273TB	Galv-Aero Flight Center	Sleap	1.08
N2087C	Southern Aircraft Consultancy Inc	Nottingham	6.07
	Grange Aviation	Donegal, County Donegal	11.07
	Milltown Helicopter Inc	(Ireland)	8.07
N65U	Woolsington Wunderbus Inc	Newcastle	12.07
	(Operated Sagesoft)		
N5035Q	Not known	Gamston	4.06
	(Cancelled 5.03 by FAA as sold in UK)		
	Wilmington Trust Co	Biggin Hill	1.08
C TIME	Southern Aircraft Consultancy Inc	Bournemouth	1.00
N8058J			
G-REXP	ST Aviation	Wellesbourne Mountford	1.08
N70AA, G-KEAA, G-REXP, G-AYPC			
N700J	Shannon Helicopters	Shannon	12.07
C-GVHQ	Southern Aircraft Consultancy Inc	Blackbushe	2.08
N9805Q			
	Brooklands Vimy Inc *(Stored)*	Dunsfold	8.07
N71VT	Airbourne Inc	Wickenby	1.08
N2VQ, N2VA			
	(Operated Cooper Aerial Surveys)		
C-FLER	Arlington Aviation	Bournemouth	12.07
N7163E	Stallion Enterprises	Bournemouth	11.07
	Cole Aviation	Spilstead Farm, Sedlescombe	11.07
N586SE	Southern Aircraft Consultancy Inc	Kirknewton	11.07
N7300R	Royal Palm Air Lease	Plymouth	5.05
	(Current status unknown)		
I-ALAT	H J Seery *(Operated D.Cockburn)*	Rush Green	9.07
D-HOFP	Ortac Inc	(Whitegate)	7.07
I-SEIN	*(Operated Huktra UK Ltd)*		
	My Spartacus Inc *(Operated D Clarkson)*	Southend	2.08
G-OSCH	Forward Aviation	Cranfield	2.08
G-SALI, N26552			
	Aircraft Guaranty Title & Trust LLC	Tibenham	2.08
G-LLYY	Flying Start Aviation Inc	Guernsey	1.08
N4165C			
	(Operated M J Start)		
G-ENSI	Southern Aircraft Consultancy Inc	Blackbushe	2.08
D-ENSI			
	(Operated G Garnett)		
N115BB	HBC Aviation Inc	King's Farm, Thurrock	1.06
G-FOFF, N115BB			
	(Operated T Holding)		
G-BFFZ	Blackburn Aeroplane Co	Menheniot, Liskeard	4.07
F-WZDU			
VH-ORP	Aircraft Guaranty Title LLC	Enstone	12.07
ZK-TML, N6648Z			
	(Operated R & B Services Ltd)		
	Edra Lauren Leasing Corporation	East Midlands	9.07
	(Operated DFS Furniture)		
	Rotherwick Inc	Oxford	1.08
	Thomas D Stronge	(Belfast)	1.06
	(Crashed 7.11.99 - stored)		
N5267K	HBC Aviation	Guernsey	2.08
	Jane Air Inc	Southampton	9.07
EC-GLU	Aircraft Guaranty Title Corp	Waterford	7.07
OY-ATZ, SE-GHY, N476MA	*(Cancelled 6.07 by FAA: derelict)*		
	Cole Aviation	Spilstead Farm, Sedlescombe	11.07
	Marks Parks Inc	Wolverhampton	8.07
	Bonus Aviation	Newcastle	1.08
D-EINS	N84VK Inc	Tatenhill	1.08
N6382P			
G-OPLB	*(Operated L Darcy)*		
	Southern Aircraft Consultancy Inc		
G-FCHJ, G-BJLS, (N6315X)	*(Operated A Ruff)*	Newcastle and Eshott	3.07
	Southern Aircraft Consultancy Inc	Shoreham	2.08
G-PAPS	Southern Aircraft Consultancy Inc	Gamston	9.07
F-GELX, N4385D	*(Operated Nicol Aviation)*		
G-MOON	Southern Aircraft Consultancy Inc	Enstone	9.05
N252BT			
N90GA	Southern Aircraft Consultancy Inc	Donegal	2.08
G-BHNY, (N68476)			
	Carr Aviation	Wellesbourne Mountford	1.08

Reg	Type	Serial				
N91TH	Agusta A109E Power	11651		Agusta Holding Inc	(Republic of Ireland)	9.07
N94SA	Champion 7ECA Citabria	227	OY-AUG	International Air Services	Blockmoor Farm, Soham	5.07
			D-EFLO	*(Operated J Surbey)*		
N95D	Piper PA-34-220T Seneca V	3449060	N9506N	Zeta Aviation Inc	Welshpool	11.07
N95TA	Piper PA-31 Turbo Navajo B	31-7300971	N7576L	High Flyers Aviation	Newcastle	12.07
N96HC	Bell 206L-1 Long Ranger II	45285		Southern Aircraft Consultancy Inc	Cork, County Cork	7.06
N96MR	Cessna 525B CitationJet CJ3	525B0067		CJ3 Holding Inc	Bournemouth	1.08
N96XW *	Farrington Twinstarr Gyrocopter	TS-008		Not known	Shipdham	10.07
				(Cancelled 8.04 by FAA: noted as "96XW")		
N97GP	SOCATA TB-20 Trinidad	1837	G-WASI	Air Touring Inc	Goodwood	8.07
			D-EVHV			
N98AG	Partenavia AP.68TP-300 Spartacus	8011	I-VULE	Aircraft Guaranty Trust LLC	Alscot	2.08
N99ET	SOCATA TB-10 Tobago	226	G-BJDG	E.A.Terris	Wycombe Air Park	6.06
			F-BNGR			
N100JS	Cessna 525B CitationJet CJ3	525B-0095	N5214K	Jato Aviation	RAF Northolt	1.08
N101DW	Piper PA-32R-300 Cherokee Lance			Southern Aircraft Consultancy Inc	Panshanger	10.07
		32R-7680399				
N101UK	Mooney M.20K	25-0631		Southern Aircraft Consultancy Inc	(Sheffield City)	11.07
N105SK	Reims Cessna F150L	F15000877	G-IAWE	Aerospace Trust Management LLC	Sleap	7.07
			EI-AWE			
N108SR	Cirrus SR22	1868		Gardiner Aircraft Inc	Stapleford	7.07
N109AB	Agusta A109E Power	11015		Airabco Inc	Rhyader	5.07
N109AG	Agusta A109A-II	7260	N20RQ	JLC Aviation	Shoreham	9.07
			N20RG			
N109AN	Agusta A109A-II	7348		MW Helicopters Inc	Stapleford	1.08
N109MJ	Agusta A109E Power	11617	N606SR	Newshore Holding Inc	Ronaldsway	10.07
N109NL	Agusta A109A-II	7415		Hirecopter Inc	(Shobdon)	11.07
N109TD	Agusta A109E Power	11011	5N-BGX	Carlyle Aviation	Bournemouth	11.07
			N108WP, N27BV, N27BD, N1ZL			
N109TF	Agusta A109A-II	7328	VH-NWD	Chestham Park Inc	Goodwood	11.07
			VH-DMR, (VH-MRS)	*(Operated Castle Helicopters Inc)*		
N109TK	Agusta A109C	7650	N109TW	Botany Aviation	(Botany Bay)	11.07
			D-HCKM			
N109WF	Agusta A109A-II	7298	N109BC	Agusta 109 LLC	Stapleford	1.08
				(Operated Lenham Racing)		
N112JA	Rockwell Commander 112TC-A	13182	5Y-MBK	Southern Aircraft Consultancy Inc		
					Sandown, Isle of Wight	11.07
N112SR	Cirrus SR22-GTS	1869		Saratoga Facilities Inc	Redhill	1.08
N112WM	Piper PA-32-300 Cherokee Six D	32-7140001	G-AZTD	Southern Aircraft Consultancy Inc	Full Sutton	8.07
			N8611N			
N113AC	SOCATA TB-20 Trinidad GT	2121	G-TTAC	Southern Aircraft Consultancy Inc	Shoreham	10.07
			F-OIMD, (N212GT)			
N114ED	Commander Aircraft Commander 114B	14637	G-PADS	Southern Aircraft Consultancy Inc	Guernsey	1.08
			N60987			
N115MD	Commander Aircraft Commander 114TC	20039		Southern Aircraft Consultancy Inc	Fairoaks	1.08
N115TB	Commander Aircraft Commander 114TC	20031		Aircraft Guaranty Corporation	Oxford	9.06
N116HS	Bell UH-1L	6171	Bu154949	Yorkshire Helicopters USA Inc	Coney Park, Leeds	10.07
				(Stored dismantled)		
N116WG	Westland WG-30-100	016	(G-BLLG)	Cogent PLC	Montrose	7.03
				(Operated Oil Petroleum Training Industry Board)		
N119BM	Agusta A119 Koala	14016		HSS (USA) Ltd	Dublin	6.07
				(Operated The Mansfield Group)		
N120HH	Bell 407	53661		407 Holding Inc	Peldon, Colchester	2.08
				(Operated Oyster Leasing Ltd)		
N121EL*	Gates Learjet 25	25-010	(N121GL)	Kingston University	Roehampton, Surrey	10.06
			(N82UH), (N10BF), N102PS, N671WM, N846HC, N846GA *(For instructional use)*			
N121HT	Cirrus SR22	0794		Aircraft Guaranty Title LLC	Gloucestershire	10.07
N121JF	Beech F33A Bonanza	CE-1578	OO-PMK	Aero Algarve Ltd	Elstree	2.08
			F-GJGA, N81701			
N121MT	Britten-Norman BN-2T Turbine Islander	880	N200LQ	Swiftair Inc	Finmere	6.07
	(Build IRMA)		USAF 88-0916, N5097R, N73413, (YV-2173P), N413JA, G-BFNX			
N122MG	Cirrus SR22-GTS	1250		122MG Inc	Turweston	1.08
N122SM	Cessna 525A CitationJet CJ2	525A-0151		Fegotila Inc	Gloucestershire	10.07
N123AX	Piper PA-32R-301 Saratoga II HP	3246060	G-LLTT	Axis Aircraft Leasing Inc	Gloucestershire	7.06
			N9283P			
N123DU	Piper PA-28-161 Cherokee Warrior II		G-BPDU	Fletcher Aviation	Guernsey	1.08
		28-7716195	N5672V	*(Southern Flight Centre titles)*		
N123DV	Cirrus SR22-GTS	1313		Fletcher Aviation	Guernsey	1.08
N123NN	Piper PA-34-220T Seneca V	3449273	G-MDCA	Eagle Power Aviation	(Coventry)	2.08
			N53643			
N123SA	Piper PA-18-150 Super Cub	18-1372	French Army	Southern Aircraft Consultancy Inc	Glenforsa	7.06
			51-15372	*(Operated B Walsh)*		
N123UK	Mooney M.20J	24-3167	G-ZZIP	Southern Aircraft Consultancy Inc	Southend	2.08
			N1086N	*(Operated H T El-Kasaby)*		
N125AV	Beech 58 Baron	TH-1341	5B-CJV	Sav Air Inc	RAF Shawbury	7.07
			N6342U	*(Impounded)*		
N125MM	Rockwell Turbo Commander 690C	11605	HB-GPB	Xentrapharm Aviation	Weston, Dublin	12.07
			D-ILAN, N5856K			
N127BU	Cessna 551 Citation II/SP	551-0179	N203BE	Dolphin Express	Biggin Hill	2.08
			HZ-ZTC, HZ-AAI, N2635D			
N129SC	Piper PA-32-300 Cherokee Six	32-7440057		Manx Orthopaedic Services	Ronaldsway	4.07
N131CD	Cirrus SR20	1031		N90TK Inc	Elstree	2.08
N132CK	Cessna 421A	421A0038	EI-TCK	Southern Aircraft Consultancy Inc	Weston, Dublin	6.07
			G-AXAW, (EI-TCK), G-AXAW, N2238Q			

N132LE	Piper PA-32-300 Cherokee Six	32-40038
N134TT	Cessna 305C Bird Dog	24541
N136SA	American General AG-5B	10164
N141HT	Cirrus SR22 Turbo	2219
N142TW	Beech 58 Baron	
N145DF	Cessna S550 Citation II	S550-0018
N145DR	Piper PA-34-220T Seneca V	3449240
N146FL	Beech F90 King Air	LA-59
N147CD	Cirrus SR20	1043
N147DC	Douglas C-47A-75-DL Dakota	19347
N147GT	Cirrus SR22-G2	1069
N147KA	Cirrus SR22-GTS	1944
N147LD	Cirrus SR22	0937
N147LK	Cirrus SR22-GTS	1687
N147VC	Cirrus SR22	0689
N150JC	Beech A35 Bonanza	D-2084
N150ZZ	Cirrus SR22-G3	2609
N151CG	Cirrus SR22	0344
N153H	Bell 222B	47138
N154DJ	Cessna T303 Crusader	T30300230
N160SR	Cirrus SR22-GTS	2161
N161FF	Piper PA-28-161 Cherokee Warrior II	28-7716097
N164SR	Cirrus SR20	1763
N170AZ	Cessna 170A	19674
N171JB	Piper PA-28R-180 Cherokee Arrow	28R-30756
N171JJ	Bombardier BD-700 Global 5000	9209
N171WM	Piper PA-23-250 Aztec C	27-3498
N172AM	Cessna 172M Skyhawk II	17264993
N173RG	Velocity 173RG	3RE052
N177MA	Piper PA-46-350P Malibu Mirage	4622177
N177SA	Reims Cessna F177RG Cardinal RG	F177RG0171
N180BB	Cessna 180K	18053103
N180FN	Cessna 180K	18053201
N180LK	Piper PA-28-180 Cherokee F	28-7105121
N181WW	Beagle B.206 Series 1	B.018
N182GC	Reims Cessna F182Q Skylane II	F18200068
N184CD	Cirrus SR20	1087
N186CB	Piper PA-46-350P Malibu Mirage	4622085
N187SA	Piper PA-28R-200 Cherokee Arrow II	28R-7235139
N188S	Agusta A109A-II	7349
N188WS	Cessna 560XL Citation XL	560-5179
N189SA	Piper PA-31-325 Navajo C/R	31-7512045
N191ME	Cessna T206H Turbo Stationair	T20608188
N192JM	Mooney M.20R Ovation	29-0337
N192SR	Cirrus SR22-GTS G3 Turbo	2467
N195NJ	Agusta A109E Power	11043
N198JH	Cessna 525 CitationJet	525-0265
N199PS	Piper PA-34-220T Seneca V	3449108
N199ZZ	Cirrus SR22-GTS-G3	2542
N200GK	Piper PA-28R-200 Cherokee Arrow II	28R-7335287
N200RE	Beech E90 King Air	LW-164
N200UP	Dassault Falcon 50	55
N201W	Bell 47D-1	83
N201YK	Mooney M.20J	24-0518
N202AA	Cessna 421C Golden Eagle	421C1015
N203CD	Cirrus SR20-G2	1451
N203SA	Piper AE-1 Cub Cruiser	5-1477
N206CF	Cessna TU206G Turbo Stationair 6	U20605128

G-AVFS	Southern Aircraft Consultancy (Operated Light into Europe)		
		New Farm House, Great Oakley	2.08
F-GFVE	Southern Aircraft Consultancy Inc		
F-WFVE, French Army	(US Marines c/s)	Belle Vue Farm, Yarnscombe	10.07
G-RICA	Southern Aircraft Consultancy Inc	(Dunkeswell)	12.07
	Aircraft Guaranty Management LLC	Gloucestershire	1.08
TH-1841	Specialized Aircraft Services Inc	Fairoaks	2.07
N1AF	Wells Fargo Bank Northwest NA	Luton	5.07
N814CC, N501NB, (N1259K)			
	Cleevewood Aviation Inc	Gloucestershire	11.07
G-FLTI	Keep Holdings	Guernsey and Southend	2.08
N7P	(Operated Flightline)		
	Free Flight Aviation	Blackbushe	2.08
G-DAKS	Aces High US Inc	North Weald	9.07
TS423, "108841", "KG374", "G-AGHY", TS423, 42-100884 (As "2100884:L4" in US AF c/s)			
	Free Flight Aviation	Denham	2.08
N174SR	Free Flight Aviation	Shoreham	1.08
N23AM	Free Flight Aviation	Denham	1.08
N745CD	Free Flight Aviation	Blackbushe	2.08
	Free Flight Aviation	Wycombe Air Park	2.08
N8674A	R.M.Hornblower (Stored on trailer)	Southend	1.08
	Alexander Fitzgibbons	Denham	1.08
	N151CG Inc	Old Sarum	1.08
	Kea Lew Inc	Castleknock, County Dublin	6.07
F-GGLJ	N154DJ Inc	Cranfield	2.08
N9891C			
	Southern Aircraft Consultancy Inc	Weston, Dublin	1.08
G-BYXU	Southern Aircraft Consultancy Inc	(Waterford)	5.07
EI-BXU, G-BNUP, N2282Q	(Operated F McGovern & F O'Sullivan)		
	Lisa Hall	Cambridge	11.07
HB-CAZ	Southern Aircraft Consultancy Inc	Strathallan	6.07
N5720C	(Operated A Gregori)		
N7414J	J A Henson	Kirknewton	11.07
C-FIIG	Aircraft Guaranty Corp	Luton	1.08
	(Operated MBI International)		
G-BXPS	International Air Services	Biggin Hill	5.07
G-AYLY, N6258Y	(Operated W Moore marked "G-BXPS")		
G-BXHG	Southern Aircraft Consultancy Inc		
N64057			
		Coonagh, Co Limerick	10.07
	Aircraft Guaranty Title & Trust LLC	North Weald	7.07
	Southern Aircraft Consultancy Inc	Weston, Dublin	7.04
	(Current status unknown)		
F-GBFI	Southern Aircraft Consultancy Inc	Southend	1.08
	(Operated A Jahanfar)		
	Southern Aircraft Consultancy Inc	Humberside	11.07
	Rivet Inc	Fordham, Newmarket	10.07
	Boston Commercial Corporation	Henstridge	8.07
G-BCJF	International Air Services	Biggin Hill	5.07
N181WW, G-BCJF, XS773	(Operated G Nolan)		
G-BFOD	Southern Aircraft Consultancy Inc	Alderney	9.07
	(Operated G Clarke)		
	R F Aviation	Crowfield	1.08
D-EXCC	Aircraft Guaranty Holdings & Trust LLC	Liverpool	10.07
N9188D			
G-BOJH	Southern Aircraft Consultancy Inc	Cumbernauld	4.07
N2821T	"Knight of the Thistle"		
	JSJ Aviation	Leeds-Bradford	2.08
N86TW	Beacon Eire Inc	Weston, Dublin	1.08
N512DR, N51984	(Reserved as "N186WS")		
G-BMGH	Southern Aircraft Consultancy Inc	Southend	2.08
ZS-LEU, N8493, A2-CAT	(Operated J Jacques)		
	Low Desert Aviation	Bagby	2.08
	Southern Aircraft Consultancy Inc	Plymouth	1.08
	Hazelhurst Aircraft Inc	Goodwood	1.08
	Thornridge Services	Weston, Dublin	1.08
	(Operated Emerald Helicopters)		
	Aircraft Guaranty Management LLC	Bournemouth	10.07
	(Operated Enex Aviation)		
	Veryord Inc	Elstree	2.08
	November Zulu Ltd	Stapleford	2.08
G-BBIA	Southern Aircraft Consultancy Inc	Stapleford	2.08
N11C	(Operated G H Kilby)		
	J G Villon	Cranfield	2.08
N96UH	Wells Fargo Bank Northwest NA	Farnborough	12.07
N300CR, N625CR, N332MQ, N332MC, N1CN, (N30N), N839F, N73FJ, F-WZHU			
48-0803	Southern Aircraft Consultancy Inc	Lower Upham	10.07
	(Stored dismantled)		
	J McTaggart	Dirleton, Archerfield	12.06
	Simply Living Ltd	Biggin Hill	9.07
	Mustarrow Inc	Manchester	11.07
G-BWUG	Southern Aircraft Consultancy Inc	Eggesford	9.07
(ZK-USN), N62073, NC62073, Bu30274 (As "Bu30274" in US Navy c/s)			
	Southern Aircraft Consultancy Inc		
		Navan, County Meath	6.07

Reg	Type	C/n
N206HE	Bell 206B JetRanger	2880
N206MF	Bell 206B-3 JetRanger III	4488
N208B	Cessna 208B Grand Caravan	208B1023
N208ER	Bell 206B Jet Ranger	4527
N208NJ	Cessna 208B Grand Caravan	208B1051
N209DW	Lancair Columbia LC41-550FG	41504
N209SA	Piper PA-22-108 Colt	22-8448
N210AD	Cessna 210G Centurion	21058835
N210CP	Cessna 210M Centurion	21062034
N210EU	Cessna T210L Turbo Centurion	21061152
N210NM	Cessna 210K Centurion	21059255
N212MZ	Mooney M.20F	22-1332
N212W	Hiller UH-12A	237
N214AE	Aérospatiale AS.350B2 Ecureuil	4019
N216GC	Piper PA-28R-200 Cherokee Arrow B	28R-7135151
N216HK *	CGS Hawk IIA	HT468R447
	(C/n on plate H-CGS-490P)	
N218BA	Boeing 747-245F	20827
N218SA	Piper PA-24-250 Comanche	24-1877
N218Y	Cessna 310Q	310Q0507
N220RJ	Cirrus SR22	1775
N221CH	Cirrus SR22-GTS-G3 Turbo	2672
N222ED	Cirrus SR22-G2	1103
N222LB	Bell 407	53229
N222SW	Cirrus SR22-G2	0977
N222WX	Bell 222A	47021
N223JG	SOCATA TBM-850	406
N224CJ	Cessna 525 CitationJet	525-0224
N228CX	SOCATA TBM-700	84
N228TM	Raytheon Hawker 800XP	258458
N230MJ	Piper PA-30 Twin Comanche B	30-1302
N234RG	Pilatus PC-12/45	520
N235PF	Piper PA-28-235 Cherokee Pathfinder	28-7410083
N239MY	Hughes OH-6A	49-1132
N242ML	Cessna 525 CitationJet	525-0506
N243SA	Piper PA-22-108 Colt	22-8376
N245CB	Piper PA-34-220T Seneca III	34-8333007
N249SP	Cessna 210L Centurion	21060990
N249SR	British Aerospace BAe125 Series 800A	258249
N250AC	Piper PA-31 Navajo C	31-7612040
N250BW	Piper PA-23-250 Aztec C	27-3799
N250CC	Piper PA-24-250 Comanche	24-1931
N250MD	Piper PA-31 Turbo Navajo B	31-742
N250TB	Piper PA-23-250 Aztec D	27-4577
N250TM	Beech 200 Super King Air	BB-822
N250TP	Beech A36TP Bonanza	E-2408
	(Allison 250-B17)	
NX251RJ	North American TP-51 Mustang	124-44703
N252JP	Hughes 369E	0346E
	(Hughes 500)	
N257JM	SOCATA TBM-850	356
N257SA	Piper PA-32-300 Cherokee Six B	32-40755
N258RP	Beech 58 Baron	TH-1737
N259BK	Hughes OH-6A	30-1376
N259SA	Cessna F172G	F172-0278
	(Built Reims Aviation SA)	
N260AP	SIAI-Marchetti SF.260D	839
N262BM	Cirrus SR20	1143
N262J	SOCATA TBM-700	292

Reg	Operator	Location	Date
N316JP	Southern Aircraft Consultancy Inc	(Weymouth)	1.08
	Southern Aircraft Consultancy Inc	Republic of Ireland	8.07
N208ST	Aircraft Guaranty Title & Trust LLC	Strathallan	8.07
	(Operated B Munro) (Undercarriage damaged in Iceland 8. 8.07)		
	Aircraft Guaranty Holdings & Trust LLC	Weston, Dublin	11.07
	Dolphin Aviation Group	Wellesbourne Mountford	1.08
	White Columbia Inc	Oxford	1.08
EI-AYS	Southern Aircraft Consultancy Inc	Abbeyshrule	3.06
G-ARKT			
OE-DES	Uniplane Inc	Guernsey	1.08
	Robert Helmstetter	(Coventry)	4.07
SP-FWK	International Air Services	Elstree	1.08
(N103AG), D-EAWO, N2191S (Operated A Miller)			
D-ECAL	Alpine Air Leasing	Standalone Farm, Meppershall	11.07
N8255M			
	Marc Zuccaro	Biggin Hill	12.07
51-4015	Southern Aircraft Consultancy Inc	Henstridge	8.07
	Axle Heli Inc	(Republic of Ireland)	11.07
G-EVVA	American Flight Academy	Elstree	12.07
G-BAZU, EI-AVH, N11C			
	CGS Aviation Inc	Castlerock, County Londonderry	7.07
	(Cancelled 11.91 by FAA: stored)		
G-GAFX	Wilmington Trust Co	Manston	10.07
N641FE, VP-BXP, N641FE, (N632FE), N812FT, N702SW (Stored)			
G-OJOK	Southern Aircraft Consultancy Inc		
PH-DZE, D-EIEI, N6749P		Boonhill Farm, Fadmoor	11.07
G-AZYM	Southern Aircraft Consultancy Inc	Guernsey	10.06
N218Y, G-AZYM, N5893M, N4592L			
	CD Aero	Gloucestershire	11.07
	Rift Valley Flying Co	Elstree	1.08
	Engdev Inc	Coventry	10.07
N222BX	Wells Fargo Bank Northwest NA	Shannon	9.07
	Staywhite Inc	Cork	2.08
EI-BOR	Newtown Aviation		
LN-OSB	Ashgrove House, Newtown, Tramore, County Waterford		7.07
	Jag Aviation	Guernsey	1.08
N52038	Janabeck Aviation	Gloucestershire	12.07
	Turbine Aviation Inc (Operated B.Holmes)	Southend	1.08
	Wells Fargo Bank Northwest NA	Cork, County Cork	3.07
	(Operated EMC Corporation)		
G-AVCX	Cabledraw Inc	Standalone Farm, Meppershall	7.07
N8185Y			
	Wells Fargo Bank Northwest NA	Belfast City	1.08
OO-DDC	Southern Aircraft Consultancy Inc	Southend	2.08
	(Operated Pathfinder Group)		
N910GD	Southern Aircraft Consultancy Inc	(Kilrush)	11.07
68-17172			
	Branksome Aviation	Bournemouth	1.08
G-ARKR	Southern Aircraft Consultancy Inc	Henstridge	1.08
	Universal Aviation Corp	Biggin Hill	9.07
4X-CGU	Alpine Air Leasing	Standalone Farm, Meppershall	1.08
N500HF	N800SR Aviation	Dublin	12.07
(N826SU), N326SU, N933H, G-5-786			
G-NWAC	North West Air Inc	Liverpool	10.07
G-BDUJ, N59814			
N6602W	Southern Aircraft Consultancy Inc	Seething	9.07
G-AYSA, N6509Y			
N957JK	Aerodynamics Worldwide	Gloucestershire	2.08
OE-DEU, N6798P			
D-ICHY	Oilsearch Aviation	Gloucestershire	1.06
F-BTCK, N7222L			
G-VHFA	Motor City Aviation LLC	Prestwick	8.07
G-BZFE, G-AZFE, EI-BPA, G-AZFE, N13962 (Stored)			
F-GIND	Richard Lewis Aviation	Cranfield	12.07
N3FH, N3844E			
N416HC	Minster Enterprises Inc	Tatenhill	5.05
N600TT, N3107K			
44-84847	S Hinton	Duxford	10.07
(As "44-84847:CY-D in USAAF c/s) "Miss Velma")			
N121JP	Eastern Atlantic Helicopters	(Waterford)	10.07
	Blackbrook Aviation	Filton	1.08
OY-PCF	Southern Aircraft Consultancy Inc	Wadswick	12.07
OH-PCF			
G-BWRP	Aradian Aviation	Guernsey	1.08
VR-BVB, N3217H			
69-16006	Aircraft Guaranty Management LLC		
	(Operated Ocean Helicopters)	(Republic of Ireland)	12.07
EI-BAO	Southern Aircraft Consultancy Inc	North Coates	9.07
G-ATNH			
	(On rebuild for Humberside Flying Club)		
I-ISAK	Pauls Airplane Inc	Old Sarum	11.07
	Southern Aircraft Consultancy Inc	Eglinton	9.07
	Sales Force Management Inc	Southend	2.08

Registration	Type	C/N	Owner	Location	Date
N276SA	Brantly B.2B	474	G-AXSR Southern Aircraft Consultancy Inc	(Stevenage)	6.07
			G-ROOF, G-AXSR, N2237U		
N277CD	Cessna 210L Centurion	21059663	SE-IGY Bonner-Davies Aviation Inc	Headcorn	12.07
			N1163Q		
N277DS	Cessna R182	R18201871	Schuybroek Aviation	Fairoaks	1.08
N277SA	Piper PA-28-140 Cherokee	28-21661	SE-EYG C M McCoole	Coonagh, County Limerick	2.08
N278DB	Mooney M.20R Ovation	29-0301	Aircraft Guaranty Management & Trust LLC	Blackpool	11.07
N278SA	Cessna 177RG Cardinal RG	177RG0571	OO-ALT Southern Aircraft Consultancy Inc	Gloucestershire	7.07
			N2171Q		
N280SA	Maule MX-7-180 Star Rocket	11070C	G-BSKT Southern Aircraft Consultancy Inc	Kirknewton	11.07
N288GS	Beech 200 Super King Air	BB-1555	N98DA Avtrade Inc	Shoreham	11.07
N289CW	Cessna T303 Crusader	T30300032	F-GJDP T303 Holding Inc	Perranporth	2.08
			N19HK, N45526, C-GNTK, (N9636T)		
N295S	Piper PA-46-350P Malibu Mirage	4636174	N295SS Convergence Aviation	Biggin Hill	11.07
	(Jetprop DLX conversion)				
N297CJ	SNCASE SE.313B Alouette II	1847	F-GLPI Southern Aircraft Consultancy Inc	Redhill	1.08
			(FAP9214), 77+00		
N297GT	SOCATA TB-21 Trinidad	2197	Fab Aircraft Inc	Jersey	11.07
N297SR	Cirrus SR22-GTS	2058	JJE Airplane Inc	Wellesbourne Mountford	1.08
N300AQ	Bombardier Learjet 45	45-211	Boultbee Aviation	Luton	1.08
			N300AA N50490, N50145		
N305RD	Mooney M20K	25-0844	Southern Aircraft Consultancy Inc	Dunkeswell	12.07
N305SE	Mooney M20K	25-0377	N231RH Navajo Aviation	Deenethorpe	8.07
N309CJ	Cessna 525A CitationJet CJ2+	525A-0309	CJ Airways Inc	Guernsey	1.08
N309LJ*	Learjet Inc Learjet 25	25-034	N309AJ City of Bristol College	Gloucestershire	6.06
			N19FN, N17AR, N3UC, N6GC, N242WT, N954FA, N954GA *(For ground instructional use)*		
N310QQ	Cessna 310Q	310Q0695	G-BAUE Veryord Inc	Elstree	5.06
			N8048Q *(Operated H Gold)*		
N310WT	Cessna 310R II	310R1257	G-BGXK Southern Aircraft Consultancy Inc	Perth	9.07
			N6070X *(Still marked "G-BGXK")*		
N320MR	Piper PA-30 Twin Comanche C	30-1917	G-CALV (2) N320MR Inc	Elstree	12.07
	(Modified to PA-39 C/R status)		G-AZFO, N8761Y		
N321KL	Mooney M.20J (201)	24-1102	G-BPKL International Air Services	Stapleford	12.07
			N1008K *(Operated London Link Flying Ltd)*		
N322MC	MD Helicopters MD 369E	0224E	AAA Flight Inc *(Operated Jepar Rotorcraft)*	Blackpool	10.07
N322RJ	Beech 60 Duke	P-322	Southern Aircraft Consultancy Inc	Leeds-Bradford	12.07
N324JC	Cessna 500 Citation I	500-0324	N52TC Foxdale Aviation	Ronaldsway	1.08
			N324C, (N5324J)		
N324JS	SOCATA TBM-700	230	Sunlit Beacon Inc	Luton	11.07
N327BM	Cirrus SR22 Turbo	2355	SR Turbo Air Inc	Coventry	1.08
N337UK	Reims/Cessns F337G Skymaster	F33700084	G-BOWD E-Plane Inc	Biggin Hill	2.08
			N337BC, G-BLSB, EI-BET, D-INAI, (N53697)		
N338DB	Piper PA-46-500TP Malibu Meridian	4697155	N53677 Oakfield Aviation	Jersey	11.07
N340AJ	Bell 206L-4 Long Ranger	52132	N98867 Yorkshire Helicopters (USA) Inc	Coney Park, Leeds	11.07
			5Y-BKR, N98867		
N340DW	Cessna 340A-II	340A0497	G-BISJ Southern Aircraft Consultancy Inc	Coventry	10.07
			OO-LFK, N6328X		
N340GJ	Cessna 340A	340A0637	Bee Bee Aviation	Elstree	1.08
N340SC	Cessna 340	340-0363	Hastingwood Management Inc	North Weald	10.07
N340YP	Cessna 340A II	340A0990	VR-CHR ILEA Inc	Biggin Hill	1.08
			G-OCAN, D-ICIC, (N3970C)		
N343RR	Piper PA-46-500TP Malibu Meridian	4697197	Herb Aviation	Leeds-Bradford	2.08
N345TB	SOCATA TB-20 Trinidad	1914	Monty 345TB LLC	Biggin Hill	10.07
			(Reserved as N268DS)		
N346X	Maule M5-210C Strata Rocket	6156C	E S Miserey	Biggin Hill	9.06
N350AY	Aérospatiale AS.350B3 Ecureuil	4267	Glenkerrin Aviation	(Republic of Ireland)	9.07
N350DG	Lancair Columbia LC42-550FG	42074	Skypartners Worldwide Inc	Blackpool	1.08
N350PB	Piper PA-31-350 Chieftain	31-8252028	PFB Self Drive Inc	Coventry	7.07
	(Panther II conversion and winglets)		HP-1309 N3548S		
N350UK	Aérospatiale AS.350B Ecureuil	1244	F-GJYG M W Helicopters Inc	(Canterbury)	11.07
N352CD	Cirrus SR22-GTS	1367	Rosenblum Enterprises	Bournemouth	1.08
N352CM	Piper PA-46-350P Malibu Mirage	4636019	G-DODI Continental Capital Markets Aviation	Bournemouth	9.07
N352F	Farnborough F1C3 Kestrel	0001	Farnborough Aircraft Inc	Redhill	1.08
N355GW	Cessna 172S	172S9355	Southern Aircraft Consultancy Inc	Rochester	11.07
N357PS	Dassault Falcon 20F-5	357	N342KF Falcon Acquisitions LLC	Farnborough	1.08
			N342K, N435TP, N435T, N4469F, F-WMKI		
N359DW	Piper PA-30 Twin Comanche	30-770	G-ATET L W Durrell	Jersey	7.07
			N230ET		
N364AB	Beech B36TC Bonanza	EA-519	Andair Inc	Gloucestershire	2.08
N365WA	Cessna 550 Citation II	550-0333	N123GM Wrenair Inc	Weston, Dublin	1.08
			N313CE, PT-LCW, N67990 *(Operated Visionair)*		
N369AN	Cessna 182S	18280696	Air View Ltd	Jersey	8.07
N369HL	Hughes 369D	117-0220D	G-CCUN Southern Aircraft Consultancy Inc	Redhill	11.07
			N644WA, N58169		
N370SA	Piper PA-23-250 Aztec F	27-8054005	G-BKVN Southern Aircraft Consultancy Inc	Southend and Guernsey	1.08
			N6959A		
N373DJ	Cessna 650 Citation III	650-0038	N366GE MacBeth Aviation	Dublin	1.08
			N366G		
N375SA	Piper PA-34-200T Seneca II	34-7670002	G-BMWP Southern Aircraft Consultancy Inc	Gamston	8.07
			N3946X		
N376SR	Cirrus SR22	2736	Caseright Inc	Turweston	1.08
N380CA	Piper PA-32R-301T Saratoga IITC	3257080	Continental Capital Aviation	Durham Tees Valley	6.05
			(Current status unknown)		

Reg	Type	c/n	Reg	Owner	Base	Date
N380CR	Cessna 525 CitationJet CJ1+	525-0643	N5228Z	50 North Aviation	Leeds-Bradford	2.08
N382AS	Reims Cessna F182Q Skylane	F1820049	D-EAAF	Southern Aircraft Consultancy Inc	Bagby	2.08
N382RW*	Vickers-Supermarine 361 Spitfire LFXVIe		G-XVIA	Airframe Assemblies	Sandown, Isle of Wight	2.07
		CBAF.IX4640	RW382	*(Crashed 3. 6.98 in California, US: as "RW382" on rebuild)*		
N393N	Robinson R44 Raven I	1467	G-CDHV	Pelmont Aviation	(Gamston)	5.07
N395TC	Commander Aircraft Commander 114TC	20003		AQZ Aviation Inc	Bembridge	12.07
N399BH	Sikorsky S.76B	760311	N89WC	Barrack Aviation	Dublin	1.08
N400HF	Lancair Columbia LC41-550FG	41577		Feggair Inc	Biggin Hill	9.07
N400UK	Lancair Columbia LC41-550FG	41062		Lucy in the Sky Corp	White Waltham	12.07
N400YY	Extra EA400	019		Bas Aviation	Leeds-Bradford	10.07
N401JN	Cessna 401	401-0166	G-ROAR	Special Scope Inc	Blackpool	12.07
			G-BZFL, G-AWSF, N4066Q			
N402BL	Beech F90 King Air	LA-130	N81SD	Hastingwood Management	North Weald	2.08
				Aircraft Guaranty Holdings & Trust LLC		
N407AG	Bell 407	53559			Weston, Dublin	12.07
N407CG	Bell 407	53731	N3009Y	Relar Inc	(Galway)	6.07
N407CL	Bell 407	53597		N407CL Inc	Dublin	1.08
N407WD	Bell 407	53694	HP-1609	Newtown Aviation	(Waterford, County Waterford)	9.07
N409SA	Reims Cessna FR182 Skylane RG		G-BJDI	Southern Aircraft Consultancy Inc	Ronaldsway	10.07
		FR18200046	N8062H			
N411BC	Piper PA-28-181 Archer III	2843339		Southern Aircraft Consultancy Inc	Elstree	12.07
N411DP	Commander Aircraft Commander 114A	14517	D-EGGB	Southern Aircraft Consultancy Inc	Fairoaks	9.07
N414AK	Cessna 414A Chancellor II	414A-0321	D-IAAU	N414AK Aviation	Southend	2.08
			(N2686Y)			
N414FZ	Cessna 414RAM	414-0175	G-AZFZ	Lizard Aviation Inc	Jersey	1.08
			N8245Q			
N414MB	Pitts S-2A	2236		LME Aviation	Wycombe Air Park	12.07
N418WS	Beech 58 Baron	TH-1967	N4467N	Millburn World Travel Services Two Inc	Edinburgh	9.07
				(Operated W Scott & Partners Ltd)		
N421CA*	Cessna 421C Golden Eagle III	421C0153	XA-RYC	Golden Eagle Haulage Inc	Wycombe Air Park	10.05
			N115JH, N5263J	*(Cancelled 2.07 by FAA)*		
N421DD	Cessna 421C Golden Eagle	421C0315		Fidair Corporation	Fairoaks	1.08
N421EA	Cessna 421C Golden Eagle	421C1079		Nielaster Inc	Biggin Hill	5.07
N423RS	Consolidated-Vultee PBY-5A Catalina	1785	C-FJJG	Southern Aircraft Consultancy Inc	Lee-on-Solent	12.07
			CF-JJG, N4002A, BuAer48423			
				(Operated Super Catalina Restoration as "JV828" in RAF 210 Sqdn c/s)		
N425DR	Cessna 425 Conquest I	425-0199	VP-BDR	Intercity Co Inc	Wycombe Air Park	10.07
N425SL	Cessna 425 Corsair	425-0236	G-BNDY	Aircraft Guaranty Title & Trust LLC	Leeds-Bradford	2.08
			N1262T	*(Operated Standard Aviation Ltd)*		
N434A	Cirrus SR22-GTS	1382		Amsair Executive Aviation	Stapleford	2.08
N438DD	Cessna 310D	39278		C Koscso	Bourn	10.07
N440GC	Piper PA-44-180T Turbo Seminole	44-8107065	G-GISO	Lucon Chasnais Flying Inc	Coventry	10.07
			D-GISO, N82112, N9602N			
N442BJ	Reims Cessna F177RG Cardinal RG		F-BVBC	Southern Aircraft Consultancy Inc	Kirknewton	11.07
		F177RG0094				
N449J	Agusta A109E Power	11056	G-RCMS	Jay Industries	Weston, Dublin	12.07
			G-BZEI	*(Operated Emerald Helicopters)*		
N449TA	Piper PA-31 Turbo Navajo	31-480	G-CCRY	William L Shoufler	Elstree	12.07
			F-BTMM, N449TA			
N454CC	Bell UH-1E	6199	Bu155344	Southern Aircraft Consultancy Inc		
					Howth, County Dublin	7.05
				(Operated Independent Helicopters Ltd)		
N456MS	Bombardier BD-700 Global 5000	9149	C-FAIY	Wells Fargo Bank Northwest NA	Farnborough	1.08
				(Operated TAG Aviation)		
N456PP	Beech C90A King Air	LJ-1699		Air Montgomery Inc	Fairoaks	1.08
N456TL	Reims Cessna FT337GP Super Skymaster		SX-PBA	CCC Aviation	Coventry	10.07
		FP3370019	F-ODFY, F-BUDU			
N458BG	de Havilland DHC.1 Chipmunk 22	C1/0508	WG458	BG Chipmunks Inc *(As "WG458:2")*	Breighton	9.07
N468DB	Beech G58 Baron	TH-2161		Wells Fargo Bank Northwest NA	Guernsey	10.07
N470RD	Cirrus SRV-G2	1636		CD1636 Inc	Weston, Dublin	1.08
N473DC	Douglas C-47A Dakota III	19345	N5831B	Dakota Heritage Inc	Liverpool	12.07
			C-FKAZ, CF-KAZ, TS422, 42-100882	*(As "2100882/P-3X" in USAF c/s)*		
N477KA	Bell 407	53579		Wilmington Trust Co	Not known	12.06
				(Operated Samar Air)		
N480BB	Enstrom 480B	5056		N480BB Inc	Shoreham	7.07
N480DD	Enstrom 480	5017	G-HADA	DWM International	Shoreham	10.07
N480JB	Enstrom 480B	5108		Eastern Atlantic Helicopters	Shoreham	6.07
N480KP	Enstrom 480B	5053		Eastern Atlantic Helicopters	North Weald	8.07
N482CD	Cirrus SR22-GTS	1482		Heritage Aviation	Sleap	9.07
N485ED	Piper PA-23-250 Aztec C	27-3864	G-BAED	Southern Aircraft Consultancy Inc	Waterford	8.07
			N6567Y			
N485LT	Hawker 800XP	258485	A7-AAL	Surewings Inc	Luton	1.08
			(HZ-KSRD), N44515	*(Operated Ambrion Aviation)*		
N497XP	Hawker 400XP	RK-497		Aircraft Guaranty Management & Trust LLC		
				(Operated V & P Midlands Ltd)	East Midlands	11.07
N498YY	Cessna 525 CitationJet	525-0498	N5201J	John Mills Aviation	Blackpool	10.07
			N498YY, N5223K	*(Fuselage on low loader Le Bourget 23.10.07 after ground accident at Avignon)*		
N499AG	Piper PA-30 Twin Comanche	30-1415	F-GALF	N499AG Inc	Bournemouth	1.08
			G-AVJT, N8281Y			
N499MS	Piper PA-28-181 Archer III	2843166	G-EPJM	MS Aviation	Jersey	7.07
			N41268			
N500AV	Piper PA-24-260 Comanche C	24-4805	OO-SAP	Southern Aircraft Consultancy Inc	Welshpool	8.07
N500CS	Beech B200 Super King Air	BB-773	N83JE	FML Beech Inc	Bournemouth	1.08
			N3913U, OY-BEH			

Reg	Type	Serial
N500LN	Howard 500	500-113
	(Lockheed PV-1 Ventura [5560] conversion)	
N500RK	Hughes 369HS	73-0502S
	(Hughes 500)	
N500SY	McDonnell Douglas MD.369E	0007E
N500TY	McDonnell Douglas MD.369E	0086E
N500UK	Eclipse Aviation EA500	000051
N500XV	Hughes 369D	120-0881D
	(Hughes 500)	
N501DW	Mudry CAP.10B	194
N502TC	Piper PA-30 Twin Comanche	30-881
N503DW	Mudry CAP.10B	202
N505HA	Aérospatiale SA.341G Gazelle	1022
N510W	Bell 222B	47133
N511TC	Cessna 525 CitationJet	525-0074
N515SC	Piper PA-32R-301T Saratoga II TC	3257315
N517TS	Agusta A109E Power	11057
N518XL	Liberty Aerospace XL-2	0013
N519MC	Piper PA-28-140 Cherokee Cruiser	28-7325519
N520DR	Cirrus SR20	1491
N521CD	Cirrus SR22-G3	2441
N521LB	Beech E90 King Air	LW-249
N524SF	Cessna 525 CitationJet	525-0240
N525DB	Reims Cessna F172H	F172-0484
N525PM	Cessna 525A CitationJet CJ2	525A-0067
N527EW	Cessna 501 Citation 1	501-0322
N531RM	Pitts S.2C	6018
	(Built Aviat)	
N535CE	Cessna 560 Citation Ultra	560-0635
N535TK	Maule MXT-7-180	14025C
N542CD	Cirrus SR22	1186
N550LD	Cessna 550 Citation II	550-0323
N550PD	Cessna 550 Citation Bravo	550-0995
N551TT	Piper PA-32R-301T Saratoga II TC	3257026
N554RB	Beech E55 Baron	TE-1141
N555WA	MD Helicopters MD.900	900-00010
N556MA *	Beagle B.121 Pup 1	B121-013
N559C	Piper PA-34-220T Seneca V	3449238
N560TH	Cessna 560XL Citation Excel	560-5215
N562RR	Piper PA-32-301FT 6x	3232021
N565F	Aérospatiale SA.341G Gazelle	1182
N566N	Cessna U206G Turbo Stationair	U20605745
N569DM	Cessna 525A CitationJet CJ2	525A0088
N573VE	Cirrus SR22-G2	1078
N575GM	SOCATA TB-20 Trinidad	1872
N575NR	Cessna 560XLS Citation Excel	560-5759
N581AF	Beech 58 Baron	TH-2063
N582C	SOCATA TBM-700	274
N588CD	Cirrus SR22-GTS	1758
N590CD	Cirrus SR22-G2	0957
N591JM	Agusta A109C	7609
N593CD	Cirrus SR22	1809
N601AR	Piper Aerostar 601P	61P-0569-7963247
N604FD	Eurocopter EC.155B	6580
N606AT	Cessna 650 Citation VI	650-0225
N613F	Piper PA-39 Twin Comanche C/R	39-45
N629RS	Piper PA-44-180T Turbo Seminole	44-8207005
N638DB	Piper PA-46-350P Malibu Mirage	4636248
N642P	Piper PA-31 Turbo Navajo B	31-761
N646JR	Piper PA-32RT-300T Turbo Lance II	32R-7987019
N652NR	Cessna 560 Citation Encore	560-0652
N652P	Piper PA-18-150 Super Cub	18-7809098
N656JM	Reims Cessna FR182 Skylane RGII	FR1820049
N660WB	Pilatus PC-12/47	760

Reg	Operator	Location	Date
N381RD	Western Aviation Leasing Inc	Exeter	12.05
N206G, N200G, N539N, SAAF 6417, FP579, Bu.34670 (Operated Baker Petroleum)			
N901WJ	Southern Aircraft Consultancy Inc		
XC-UHF		Top Farm, Croydon, Royston	9.07
N5144Q	0454E Inc	Shoreham	11.07
C-GRVV	Eastern Atlantic Helicopters	Shoreham	11.07
	EA51 Inc	Blackpool	1.08
OO-LVK	Southern Aircraft Consultancy Inc	Blackpool	6.07
OE-XBB, N190CA, N5293E, C-GHVK			
	Cole Aviation	Spilstead Farm, Sedlescombe	11.07
G-BMSX	Southern Aircraft Consultancy Inc (Current status unknown)		
N502TC, N7802Y		Standalone Farm, Meppershall	11.03
	Kennard Aviation	Rochester	9.07
JA9164	Southern Aircraft Consultancy Inc	Breighton	1.08
N7040Z	Wells Fargo Bank Northwest NA		
	(Operated Renault Ireland)	Naas, County Kildare	6.07
N26581	Eagle III LLC	Cambridge	11.07
	Southern Aircraft Consultancy Inc	Cardiff	4.07
	M Solomon (Operated Eastern Helicopters)	Southend	1.08
	W Roberts	Biggin Hill	1.08
G-BBID	R Lobell	Elstree	12.07
N120SR	N120SR Aviation	North Weald	11.07
G-SRZO, N60524			
	Assegai Aviation	Denham	2.08
N68CC	Monckton Byng Inc	Elstree	11.07
(N28CC), N30KC			
N525GM	C P Lockyer Inc	Coventry	11.07
G-AWGR	Southern Aircraft Consultancy Inc	Sleap	5.07
N525DB, G-AWGR			
N5141F	Wells Fargo Bank Northwest NA	Oxford	1.08
(N769EW)	Rockville Aero Inc	Jersey	1.08
(N669DM), N314GS, N374GS, N2663J			
	Southern Aircraft Consultancy Inc	Panshanger	1.08
	Latium Jet Services (IOM)	Gloucestershire	1.08
	R S Barnett	Shipmeadow, Beccles	9.07
	Siek Aviation	Elstree	12.07
VP-CLD	Pan Maritime US Inc	Filton	10.07
N323AM, TC-YZB, TC-FMB, TC-FAL, OE-GCP, (N5703C)			
	Ravenheat Aviation	Leeds-Bradford	2.08
G-GOTO	Southern Aircraft Consultancy Inc	Blackbushe	2.08
N92965, G-GOTO, N92965			
G-BNRH	E Hilvert	Coventry	10.07
N7855E			
N9208V	N555WA Inc (Operated Stobart Air)	(Crick)	1.08
G-AWEB	G V Crowe	Norwich	7.05
(Forced landed short of Thurrock 14. 7.05 due to engine failure: cancelled 7.06 by FAA: current status unknown)			
	Chiswell Aviation Inc	Guernsey and Alderney	1.08
VP-CPC	N560TH Inc	Blackpool	1.08
N5091J, N560TH			
N30614	Countrywide Aviation	Fadmoor	1.08
	Skyrunner Aviation	Manor Farm, Binham	9.07
	American King Air Ferries Inc	Clonbullogue	12.07
	(Operated Irish Parachute Club)		
	Euro Exec Aviation	Cranfield	12.07
	Flanes Ltd	Biggin Hill	12.07
	Wedd Aviation	Cambridge	2.08
	Cross Jet Inc	Kerry, Co Kerry	2.08
	N581AF Inc	Sleap	11.07
	Islander Aviation	Ronaldsway	1.08
	Southern Aircraft Consultancy Inc	Rochester	11.07
	(Reserved as N95GT))		
	Loch Ard Air LLC	Perth	9.06
N109KH	Gateway Aviation	Stapleford	7.07
N133H, N1NQ			
	Hannah Aviation	Manchester	9.07
N3839H	Southern Aircraft Consultancy Inc (Operated The Fabric Factory)		
F-GKCL , N3839H, G-RACE, N8083J		Jersey and Southend	2.08
	Wells Fargo Bank Northwest NA	Denham	1.08
(N225CV)	Longborough Aviation	Weston, Dublin	1.08
N1301Z	(Operated CityWest Hotel)		
N8887Y	Southern Aircraft Consultancy Inc	Stapleford	7.07
4X-CCU	International Air Services	Ronaldsway	8.07
	(Operated R J Schreiber)		
N500UD	Corporate Air (Ireland) Inc	(Belfast)	1.08
G-EEAC, G-SKKA, G-FOAL, G-RMAE, N7239L			
PH-LFD	Southern Aircraft Consultancy Inc	Gloucestershire	3.07
N3032A			
	Cross Jet Inc	Kerry, County Kerry	1.08
G-BTDX	Southern Aircraft Consultancy Inc	(Ireland)	6.07
N62595			
G-BHEO	JM Aviation (Europe) Inc	Old Sarum	1.08
HB-FSO	Newtown Aviation	Waterford	1.08

Reg	Type	C/n	Prev regs	Owner / Operator	Base	Date
N661KK	Piper PA-28-181 Archer II	2890028	HB-PKN, N9104F	Southern Aircraft Consultancy Inc	Fairoaks	2.08
N662KK	Piper PA-18-150 Super Cub	18-8209023	N45490, IDF/AF112	Southern Aircraft Consultancy Inc	Fairoaks	2.08
N663CD	Cirrus SR22	1847		Phantom Air	Sleap	7.07
N665CH	Cessna 525 CitationJet	525-0504		Volante Aviation	Coventry	8.07
N666AW	Piper PA-31 Navajo C	31-7612061		Atlantic International Air Charter Inc	Biggin Hill	7.07
N666BM	Pitts S-1T (Built Aviat)	1057		International Air Services *"Devil Poo" (Operated S P Johnson)*	Enstone	10.07
N666GA	Gulfstream AA-5B Tiger	AA5B-1136		Southern Aircraft Consultancy Inc	Thruxton	1.08
N669MM	Bellanca 8KCAB-180 Super Decathlon	825-99		Red Kite Inc	White Waltham	10.07
N671B	Raytheon A36 Bonanza	E-3409		N671B Inc	Leeds-Bradford	2.08
N672LE	Eurocopter EC.155B1	6652	F-WQEP	HEC01 LLC *(Operated TAG Aviation)*	Blackbushe	1.08
N673SA	Piper PA-24-250 Comanche	24-2240	G-ARFH, N7087P	Southern Aircraft Consultancy Inc	East Winch	5.07
N674BW	Grumman AA-5A Cheetah	AA5A-0674	G-BXOO, N26721	Go Aviation UK Inc	Elstree	8.07
N675BW	Beech V35B Bonanza	D-10134	D-ENCA	Southern Aircraft Consultancy Inc	Cranfield	2.08
N680GG	Cessna 680 Sovereign	680-0104		Wells Fargo Bank Northwest NA *(Operated Countrywide Coventry Ltd)*	East Midlands	1.08
N681EW	Reims Cessna F182Q Skylane II	F18200039	G-BLEW, F-GAQD	Southern Aircraft Consultancy Inc	Henstridge	12.07
N683GW	Beech C90A King Air	LJ-1683		Copart Inc *(Operated Userve Ltd)*	Cranfield	2.08
N686RH	Bell 407	53714		Trans Air Inc *(Operated R L Hartshorn)*	Greenisland, Co Antrim	11.07
N690CL	Rockwell 690A Turbo Commander	11153	N46663, N53RF, N57074	Centerline Aerospace Inc	Norwich	1.08
N691J	Piper PA-28RT-201T Turbo Arrow IV	28R-8631003	N473BS, G-BNYY, N25WA, N77860, G-BNYY, N9129X, N9517N	Piper Arrow Inc *(Operated I Jacobs t/a Chatham Glyn Fabrics)*	Southend	2.08
N696XX	McDonnell Douglas MD.369E	0544E	N90DE	696 Heli Inc *(Operated Kuki Helicopters)*	Gamston	8.07
N697RB	Pitts S-1T	1042		Aerospace Trust Management	Dunsfold	8.07
N700EL	SOCATA TBM-700	209	N701AR	Air Twinlite Inc	Weston, Dublin	1.08
N700GY	SOCATA TBM-700C2	302	D-FBFT	N700VB Inc	Guernsey	1.08
N700KV	SOCATA TBM-700C2	296		Shephard Aviation	(Goodwood)	11.07
N700S	SOCATA TBM-700	193		Stonehedge Aviation	Fairoaks	11.07
N700VA	SOCATA TBM-700	233	F-OIKI	Wells Fargo Bank Northwest NA *(Overran runway into River Tay, Dundee 24.10.03: fuselage with Recovair)*	Fairoaks	7.07
N700VB	SOCATA TBM-700	237	F-OIKJ	Paul Castle Inc	Biggin Hill	12.07
N702MB	SOCATA TBM-700	314		TBM 700 Inc	Bournemouth	11.07
N702SR	Cirrus SR22-GTS	2198		N702SR Inc	Kemble	11.07
N707BM	Bell 206L-1 Long Ranger	45533		Billy Moloney Inc	Cork	12.07
N707QJ	Boeing 707-368C	21261	A20-261, N7486B, HZ-ACI	T M Vaughan	Manston	11.07
N707TJ	Boeing-Stearman A75N1 (N2S-1) Kaydet (Pratt & Whitney R-985 450hp)	75-950	N9PK, N50057, Bu.3173	M G Plaskett *(Team Guinot) (Operated V.S.E.Norman t/a Aerosuperbatics Ltd)*	Rendcomb	9.07
N707XJ	Cessna 177A Cardinal	17701340	SE-FKO, (LN-FAK), (OY-AGM), N30579	Southern Aircraft Consultancy Inc *(Operated I A Quereshi)*	Shoreham	6.07
N708SP	Bombardier Learjet 45	45-014		Tappeto Magico Inc	Cranfield	1.08
N709AM	SOCATA TB-21 Trinidad	2101		AMC Aviation	Sherburn-in-Elmet	11.07
N709EL	Beech 400A Beechjet	RK-52	(N709EW), N709JB	GAL Air Inc *(Operated DFS Furniture)*	East Midlands	1.08
N711TL	Piper PA-60 Aerostar 700P	60-8423017	N700SX, N15GK, XB-EXQ, N6906Y	Southern Aircraft Consultancy Inc	Biggin Hill	1.08
N712DB	Beech 65-A90 King Air	LJ-311	F-GNBA, HB-GIN, F-GIGP, N114SV, N10XL, N909K *(Operated Skyclad)*	Metro Air Inc	Weston, Dublin	7.07
N715BC	Beech A36 Bonanza	E-782	F-BXOZ	N715BC Inc	Denham	1.08
N717HL	Beech 58P Baron	TJ-160		Dawson Lion Inc	Weston, Dublin	10.07
N719CD	Cirrus SR22	0051		Southern Aircraft Consultancy Inc	Plymouth	9.07
N719EL	Hawker 400XP	RK-488		Edra Lauren Leasing Corp *(Operated DFS Furniture)*	East Midlands	11.07
N720B	Bell 206L-1 LongRanger II	45452	G-DALE, G-HBUS	Omega Air Inc	Dublin	6.07
N730WF	Cirrus SR22	1147		R & R Flying Inc	Abbeyshrule	11.07
N731	Boeing Stearman A75N-1	75-045		Wings Venture Ltd "352"	Gloucestershire	9.07
N735BZ	Cessna 182Q Skylane	18265307		L Underhill	RAF Wyton	7.06
N735CX	Cessna 182Q Skylane II (Modified to Advanced Lift 260 STOL)	18265329		Wilmington Trust Company *(Operated B.Holmes)*	Barnard Farm, Thurrock	10.07
N737M	Boeing 737-8EQ	33361	N737SP, N737M	Wells Fargo Bank Northwest NA *(Operated EIE Eagle Inc Establishment)*	Luton	1.08
N741CD	Cirrus SR22	0137		Staveley Aviation	Blackpool	2.08
N745HA	Agusta A109A-II	7413	G-CBDR	Heli Holding Inc	Liskeard Heliport	11.07
N747MM	Piper PA-28R-200 Cherokee Arrow II	28R-7335445	PH-MLP, N56489	N747MM Aviation	Denham	10.07
N747WW	Piper PA-23-250 Aztec D	27-4330	G-AXOG, N6965Y	International Air Services *(Operated A Mattacks)*	Biggin Hill	6.07
N747YK	Cessna 310R II	310R0138	G-BTYK, N200VC, N5018J	YK Inc	Jersey	1.08
N748D	Avro 748 Series 1	1559	G-ASJT, XW750, G-ASJT	Aerospace Trust Management *(Used as instructional airframe)*	Sheffield-Doncaster	11.07
N750GF	Cessna 750 Citation X	750-0244	N52655	S'porter Air Inc	Gloucestershire	11.07
N750NS	Cessna 750 Citation X	750-0172	N5066U	Aircraft Guaranty Holdings & Trust LLC *(Operated Aviation Beauport)*	Jersey	5.07
N753TW	Cirrus SR22-GTS	1413		N753TW Inc	Denham	1.08

Reg	Type	C/N	Prev ID	Owner/Operator	Location	Date
N761JU	Cessna T210M Centurion	21062300		International Air Services	Wycombe Air Park	8.07
	(Operated A W Chesters) (Ha wheels up landing 7. 8.07)					
N766AM	Aérospatiale AS.355N Ecureuil 2	5601		Beacon Aviation	Beacon Farm, Leicestershire	9.06
	(Operated Beacon Energy (Aviation) Ltd)					
N767CM	Beech A36 Bonanza	E-2723	G-ORSP N56037	Makins Aviation	Cranfield	2.08
N770RM	SOCATA TB-9 Tampico	131	PH-CAG	M P Sandell	Bournemouth	1.08
N771SR	Cirrus SR22-GTS G3 Turbo	2771		H K DeCarlucci	Denham	2.08
N775RG	Maule M5-210C Strata Rocket	6048C	G-CBVW A2-WNP, ZS-LVB	Southern Aircraft Consultancy Inc	Great Massingham	5.06
N775SB	Bell 407	53705		N775SB Inc	Leeds-Bradford	2.08
N780ND	World Helicopters Hiller UH-12C	WH6003		Southern Aircraft Consultancy Inc	Rochester	10.07
N781CD	Cirrus SR20-G2	1423		Cirrus Group Inc	Carnmore, Galway	10.07
N784F	Bell 206B-3 JetRanger III	2508	N16LT	Southern Aircraft Consultancy Inc	Oaksey Park	11.07
N799CD	Cirrus SR22-GTS	1543		GPA Inc	Kilrush	11.07
N799JH	Piper PA-28RT-201T Turbo Arrow IV	28R-8231051	HB-PNE PH-HJM, N8206B	Southern Aircraft Consultancy Inc (Operated J Havers)	North Weald	7.07
N800BN	Bombardier CL-600-2B19 (CL-604 Challenger)	5600	C-GLWZ	Wilmington Trust Co	Luton	1.08
N800C	Cirrus SR22	0367		Rozelle Aviation	Blackpool	12.07
N800FR	Raytheon RB390 Premier 1A	RB-165	N7165X	Wells Fargo Bank Northwest NA (Operated White and Cope Aviation)	Luton	1.08
N800HL	Bell 222	47054	N800HH N8140A, N37VA	Yorkshire Helicopters USA Inc	Coney Park, Leeds	11.06
N800UK	Raytheon Hawker 800XP	258577	N51027	Wells Fargo Bank Northwest NA (Operated Liberty Aviation)	Leeds-Bradford	2.08
N800VM	Beech 76 Duchess	ME-318	G-BHGM	Southern Aircraft Consultancy Inc	Gloucestershire	11.07
N800WK	Agusta A109A-II	7341	N500WK	Ottoman Empire Inc	Shoreham	1.00
N808CA	Piper PA-32R-301 Saratoga II HP	3246240		Buchanan Aviation	(Kirknewton)	10.07
N808NC	Gulfstream 695B Commander 1200	96085		Wilmington Trust Co (Operated Coopers Aerial Surveys)	Gamston	11.05
N808VT	Piper PA-28R-201 Cherokee Arrow III	28R-7737051		Southern Aircraft Consultancy Inc	Panshanger	10.07
N814WS	Cessna 510 Citation Mustang	510-0032	N4107D	Millburn World Travel Services Four Inc (Operated Walter Scott & Partners Ltd)	Edinburgh	1.08
N816RL	Beech E90 King Air	LW-187	N66BP N816EP, N900MH, N2187L	Springair Inc (Operated English Braids Ltd)	Gloucestershire	12.04
N818MJ	Piper PA-23-250 Aztec B	27-2486	G-ASNH	Retail Management Associates	Charlton Park, Malmesbury	1.08
N818Y	Piper PA-30 Twin Comanche B	30-1458	ZS-CAO ZS-EYB, A2-ZFE, ZS-EYB, VQ-ZIY, ZS-EYB, N8318Y	One Eighty Yankee Aviation Inc	Guernsey	1.08
N820CD	Cirrus SR22	0180		Southern Aircraft Consultancy Inc	Guernsey	1.08
N831M	Hiller UH-12B	330	51-16170	Southern Aircraft Consultancy Inc	Shipmeadow, Beccles	3.07
N834CD	Cirrus SR22	0168		Southern Aircraft Consultancy Inc	Seething	9.07
N836TP	Beech A36TP Bonanza	E-2124	N6770M	Hastingwood Aviation Inc (Operated Velcourt East PLC)	Tatenhill	7.07
N840CD	Cirrus SR20-GTS	1535		Weston Flyers	Weston, Dublin	1.08
N840PN	Rockwell 690C Turbo Commander	11679	ZS-SLL N840VB, (N5931K), N840VB, N5931K	Southern Aircraft Consultancy Inc	Fairoaks	11.07
N840TC	Rockwell 690C Turbo Commander	11688	XC-HAB (N5940K)	Aircraft Guaranty Title Corp (Operated Select Interiors)	North Weald	1.08
N841WS (2)	Gulfstream Aerospace Gulfstream 450	4099	N199GA	Milburn World Travel Services Five Inc (Operated Walter Scott & Partners Ltd)	Edinburgh	1.08
N843SR	Cirrus SR22-G3	2790		XYZ Aviation	Denham	1.08
N846MA	Cessna 560 Citation V	560-0046	G-CJAE G-CZAR, (N26656)	Pan Maritime Inc	Filton	1.08
N850LH	SOCATA TBM-850	374	F-WWRR	Liton Services	Biggin Hill	1.08
N851WA	SOCATA TBM-850	394		WA Aviation	Cambridge	1.08
N852CD	Cirrus SR22	0219		Southern Aircraft Consultancy Inc	Guernsey	1.08
N852FT*	Boeing 747-122F	19757	N4712U	PIK Ltd (Unmarked in fire service use)	Prestwick	5.07
N866C	Cirrus SR22	0397		Aircraft Guaranty Trust LLC	Turweston	1.08
N866LP	Piper PA-46-350P Malibu Mirage	4636130	N666LP N92928	TLP Aviation Inc	(Fairoaks)	12.07
N877SW	Agusta A109A-II	7283	N8772W N877SW	N877SW Inc	Shoreham	9.07
N882JH	Maule M.7-235B	23056C		Everbright Aviation Inc	Exeter	11.06
N883DP	Cessna R182Skylane RGII	R18201883	G-GOZO G-BJZO, (G-BJYE), N5521T	Southern Aircraft Consultancy Inc (Operated D Pelling)	Mount Airey Farm, Hull	6.07
N888MY	Cessna 182T	18281957		Jet Force Inc	Panshanger	10.07
N889VF	Cessna T303 Crusader	T30300102	D-ILEI N3141C	Southern Aircraft Consultancy Inc	Liverpool	10.07
N897US	Fokker F.28-0100	11392	PH-EZD	Aircraft Finance Services Inc (Stored)	Norwich	11.07
N898US	Fokker F.28-0100	11398	PH-EZJ	Aircraft Finance Services Inc (Stored)	Norwich	11.07
N900CB	Cessna 421C Golden Eagle III	421C0837	VP-CPR VR-CPR, N2659F	Lancaster Aviation (Operated Fifty North)	Leeds-Bradford	2.08
N900NS	Dassault Falcon 900EX/EASy	150	F-WWFI	Aircraft Guaranty Title LLC (Operated Aviamax Aviation)	Farnborough	1.08
N900RK	Mooney M.20J	24-3402		Romeo Kilo Flying Group	Cranfield	2.08
N900UK	Cirrus SR22	1463		Annas Flight Services	Turweston	1.08
N901RL	Bell 430	49078		Aircraft Guaranty Holdings & Trust LLC	Dublin	11.07
N902JW	MD Helicopters MD.902	9000086	N7006X	Blue Anchor Leisure (Operated John Woodward Property Developments)	Gamston	11.07
N902SR	Cirrus SR22	2356		Lucy Lu Inc	Liverpool	1.08

Reg	Type	c/n	Prev id	Owner/Operator	Location	Date
N908W	Sikorsky S-92	920007		Laws Helicopter LLC *(Operated Air Harrods)*	London Stansted	1.08
N909PS	Cessna 501 Citation I/SP	501-0008	N900PS	Silversteel America Inc	Jersey	11.07
			(N501DB), N6HT, N362CC, N5362J			
N911DN	Bell UH-1H Iroquois	9624	67-17426	Yorkshire Helicopters USA Inc	Coney Park, Leeds	4.07
N916CD	Cirrus SR22	0318		Farnborough Aircraft Inc	Redhill	11.07
N918Y	Piper PA-30 Twin Comanche	30-736	ZS-NLH	Southern Aircraft Consultancy Inc	Shobdon	12.07
			N31RK, ZS-NLH, ZS-FZR, CR-AJR, ZS-EIU, VQ-ZIS, N7658Y			
N922CE	Cirrus SR22-G3	2521		Eden Aviation	Blackbushe	1.08
N937BP	Mooney M.20J	24-3046	G-OOOO	Southern Aircraft Consultancy Inc	Wycombe Air Park	10.07
			N205EE			
N937DR	Cessna 172R	17280217		Southern Aircraft Consultancy Inc	Donegal	6.07
N950H	Dassault Falcon 50EX	307		Island Aviation Inc	Farnborough	1.08
N951SF	Beech 56TC Baron	TG-83	N23PB	Timcar Inc	Elstree	12.07
N955SH	Piper PA-46-350P Malibu Mirage *(DLX conversion)*	4636339		Southern Aircraft Consultancy Inc	North Weald	2.08
N956CD	Cirrus SR22	1844		Aircraft Guaranty Title & Trust LLC	Denham	2.07
N957T	Piper PA-32R-301 Saratoga II HP	3246176		Severn Valley Aviation	Shobdon	12.07
N971RJ	Piper PA-39 Twin Comanche C/R	39-111	G-AZBC	Aircraft Guaranty Corporation	Biggin Hill	6.07
			N8951Y			
N973BB	Mitsubishi MU-2B-60 Marquise	1509SA		Romeo Aviation Inc	Jersey	9.07
N980HB	Rockwell Commander 695	95006		HBC Aviation Inc	Thurrock	12.07
N982CD	Cirrus SR22-GTS	1853		November CD Inc	Denham	2.08
N983AJ	Beech B200 Super King Air	BB-983	D-ISAZ	Aircraft Guaranty LLC	Lydd	2.08
			N983EB, D-ILTO, N87FE, N6JE, (D-IKFC), N6JE, N6JL *(Op Lyddair)*			
N988SR	Cirrus SR22-GTS	2038		Aircraft Guaranty Title & Trust LLC	Jersey	10.07
N989Y	Piper PA-24-260 Comanche B	24-4306	G-UVNA	Southern Aircraft Consultancy Inc	Great Oakley	11.07
			G-BAHG, 5Y-AFX, N8831P			
N994K	Hughes 269A (TH-55A)	0840	67-16733	Southern Aircraft Consultancy Inc	Perranporth	1.08
N994SR	Cirrus SR20-G2	1669		Ashpitel Aviation	Thruxton	1.08
N997JM	SOCATA TBM-700	244	LX-JFG	Sunwave Aviation	Dunkeswell	8.06
			F-GLBQ			
N999BE (2)	Dassault Falcon 7X	8	F-WWUE	Wilmington Trust Co *(Operated B Eccleston)*	Biggin Hill	1.08
N999F	Beech F33A Bonanza	CE-1282	OO-OVB	N T N Fox Systems Inc	Newcastle	11.07
N999MH	Cessna 195B	7168	OH-CSE	E Detiger	Compton Abbas	1.08
N999PD	Waco YMF-F5C	F5C108		Airpark Aviators	Coventry	10.07
N999RL	Robinson R44 Raven II	10614	G-CDEZ	Heli Twinlite	Kilrush	3.07
N1024L	Beech 60 Duke	P-78	C-FOPH	Southern Aircraft Consultancy Inc *(Operated R.Ogden)*	North Weald	7.07
			CF-OPH, N1024L, CF-OPH			
N1027G	Maule M.7-235B	23032C		Southern Aircraft Consultancy Inc *(Operated T Clark)*	Elstree	12.07
N1092H	Beech C90A King Air	LJ-1454		Park Close Aviation Inc	Blackbushe	11.07
N1196R	Raven S-40A Balloon (Hot Air)	S40A-141		P Sweatman *"Froggy"*	Birmingham	4.07
N1262K	Cessna 425 Corsair	425-0234		Goldsteel Inc	Jersey	12.07
N1320S	Cessna 182P Skylane II	18264884		Hamilton-Fairley Avn	Hatch Gate Farm, Bramshill	11.07
N1325M	Boeing Stearman E75(N2S-5) Kaydet	75-8484	Bu43390	Eastern Stearman Inc *(Operated Blackbarn Aviation) (Frame only)*	Priory Farm, Tibenham	10.07
NC1328	Fairchild F24R-46KS Argus	3310		Eastern Stearman Inc *(Operated Blackbarn Aviation) (Frame only)*	Priory Farm, Tibenham	3.07
N1329T	Cessna T182T Turbo Skylane	T18208667		Denston Hall Inc *(Reserved as N148RM)*	Appleacre Farm, Stradishall	12.07
N1344	Ryan PT-22-RY Recruit	2086	41-20877	Flying Heritage Inc *(Operated Mrs.H.Mitchell t/a PT Flight)*	Sleap	10.06
N1350J	Rockwell Commander 112B	516		Fish Associates Inc	Elmsett	1.08
N1376C	Lancair Columbia LC41-550FG	41656		GP Aviation Inc	Goodwood	11.07
N1407J	Rockwell Commander 112A	407		Blue Lake Aviation Inc	Blackbushe	1.08
N1417W	Lancair Columbia LC42-550FG	42523		My Columbia Inc	Biggin Hill	7.07
N1424C	Cessna 182T Skylane	18281610		Glendoe Inc	(Bowldown)	11.07
N1551D	Cessna 190	7773		Southern Aircraft Consultancy Inc	Old Buckenham	11.07
N1554E	Cessna 172N	17271044		International Air Services *(Operated S Turton)*	(Barnstaple)	5.05
N1569C	Cirrus SR22	0581		Southern Aircraft Consultancy Inc	(Turweston)	1.08
N1604K*	Luscombe 8A Silvaire			See G-BSOE - details in SECTION 1, Part 2 Sturgate		
N1711G	Cessna 340	340-0516		Air Touring Inc	(Biggin Hill)	11.06
N1731B	Boeing A75N-1 Stearman	75-5716	42-17553	Eastern Stearman Inc *(As "42-17553:716")*	Bidford	10.07
N1745M	Cessna 182P Skylane II	18264424		D Thomas	Cardiff	10.07
N1757H	Cessna 310C	35857		Southern Aircraft Consultancy Inc	Panshanger	10.07
N1778X	Cessna 210L Centurion	21060798		Central Investment Corporation	Denham	7.07
N1835W	Beech 95-B55 Baron	TC-1513	ZS-ING	Southern Aircraft Consultancy Inc	Bournemouth	11.07
			N1835W			
N1937Z	Cessna 172RG Cutlass RG	172RG0908	EI-BVS	Air Twinlite Inc	Ronaldsway	6.07
N1944A	Douglas DC-3C-47A-80-DL	19677	(N5211A)	Wings Venture Ltd	Oxford	1.08
			N3239W, RDanAF K-683, RNorAF 43-15211 *(As "315211:J8-Z")*			
N2061K	Beech 58P Pressurised Baron	TJ-161		R Wagstaff	Oxford	1.08
N2086P	Piper PA-23 Apache	23-674	N286GB	Southern Aircraft Consultancy Inc	Blackpool	9.07
			N2086P			
N2105J*	Bell 222	47066		Anglo Services Inc Oranmore Heliport, Galway *(Damaged in hangar fire 9.4.06: cancelled 8.06 by FAA)*		7.07
N2121T	Gulfstream AA-5B Tiger	AA5B-1031		J.Siebols	Southend	2.08
N2136E	Piper PA-28RT-201 Arrow IV	28R-7918002		Southern Aircraft Consultancy Inc	(Sheffield City)	11.07
N2216X	Cessna 337 Super Skymaster	3370116		Southern Aircraft Consultancy Inc	Belfast	7.07
N2231F	Cessna 182T	18281925		Southern Aircraft Consultancy Inc	Perth	1.08

Registration	Type	c/n	Other regs	Owner/Operator	Location	Date
N2273Q	Piper PA-28-181 Cherokee Archer II	28-7790389		Southern Aircraft Consultancy Inc	Panshanger	10.07
N2299L	Beech F33A Bonanza	CE-677		Stafford W Freeborn	Thruxton	12.07
N2341S	Beech B300 King Air	FL-241		Specsavers Aviation Inc	Guernsey	1.08
N2366D	Cessna 170B	20518		Southern Aircraft Consultancy Inc	Turweston	1.08
N2379C	Cessna R182 Skylane RG	R18200170		West Country Aviation Inc	(Bromsberrow)	1.08
N2401Z	Piper PA-23-250 Aztec F	27-8054034		Pan Maritime US Inc	Filton	3.07
N2405Y	Piper PA-28-181 Archer II	28-8590070		Southern Aircraft Consultancy Inc	Panshanger	10.07
N2445V	Cessna 182S	18280699		N2445V Inc	Gloucestershire	1.08
N2454Y	Cessna 182S	18280918		Seima Aviation	Great Massingham	5.07
N2480X	Piper PA-31T1 Cheyenne I	31T-8104026		Jane Air	Southampton	11.06
N2500	Beech D.18S	A-558	N50W, N8614A, N66W, N5V, N5297C	J and V Barnum	Bruntingthorpe	1.08
N2536Y	Britten-Norman BN-2T Islander	2303	G-CDCJ	Islander Aviation	Ronaldsway	12.07
N2548T	Navion Model H Rangemaster	NAV-4-2548		Navion Airways Inc	Guernsey	1.08
NC2612	Stinson Junior R	8754		A.L.Young (Stored)	Henstridge	8.07
N2652P	Piper PA-22-135 Tri-Pacer (Tailwheel conversion)	22-2992		Southern Aircraft Consultancy Inc "Lil Red"	Taghmon, County Wexford	9.06
N2742Y	Hughes 369HS	62-0389S		Crestband Inc	(Trewen)	6.07
N2923N	Piper PA-32-300 Cherokee Six	32-7940207		Southern Aircraft Consultancy Inc	Jersey	11.07
N2929W	Piper PA-28-151 Cherokee Warrior	28-7415457	OO-GPE, N9619N	Funair Inc *(Operated M Gorlow)*	Elstree	12.07
N2943D	Piper PA-28RT-201 Arrow IV	28R-7918231	G-BSLD, N2943D	Southern Aircraft Consultancy Inc *(Operated E.Gawronek)*	Liverpool	10.07
N2967N	Piper PA-32-300 Six	32-7940242		Aerotechnics Aviation Inc	Guernsey	1.08
N2989M	Piper PA-32-300 Six	32-7840062		International Air Services *(Operated Mark Johnston Racing)*	Bagby	2.08
N3023W	Beech V35B Bonanza	D-9517		M A Cargent	Fowlmere	11.07
N3044B	Piper PA-34-200T Seneca II	34-7970012		Aerotechnics Aviation Inc	Alderney	7.07
N3084F	Reims Cessna F150L	F1500670		MRC Aviation	Lower Mountpleasant, Chatteris	9.07
N3103L	Beech 200 Super King Air	BB-1933		Wells Fargo Bank Northwest NA	Oxford	2.08
N3109X	Cessna 150F	15064509		Southern Aircraft Consultancy Inc *(Operated The Lucy Flying Group)*	Kilrush	10.07
N3400W	Piper PA-32-260 Cherokee Six	32-261		L R Harville	Coventry	7.05
N3586D	Piper PA-31-325 Navajo C/R	31-8012065		L. W.Durrell	Jersey	7.07
N3596T	Aero Commander 500	500-752	N359CT, N8437C, (N3821C)	Rt Barnett	Norwich	10.07
N3669D	Beech 60 Duke	P-544	G-CBYK, N3669D	Vetch Aviation	Goodwood	1.08
N3864	Ryan Navion B	NAV-4-2285B		Southern Aircraft Consultancy Inc *(Operated G Spooner)*	Earls Colne	2.08
N3922B	Boeing-Stearman E75 (PT-17) Kaydet (Continental W670)	75-5805	42-17642	Eastern Stearman Inc *(Operated P Hoffmann)*	Priory Farm, Tibenham	12.07
N4085E	Piper PA-18-150 Super Cub	18-7809059		R N Hall	Goodwood	3.06
N4102D	Reims Cessna FR182 Skylane RG	FR18200029	PH-CTM, SE-IBB	Alpine Air Leasing	Seething	9.07
N4168D	Piper PA-34-220T Seneca V	3449158		AAL Inc	Shoreham	10.07
N4173T	Cessna 320D Skyknight	320D0073		N4173T Inc *(Operated J.Irwin)*	Cranfield	11.07
N4178W	Piper PA-32R-301T Saratoga IITC	3257178		Mistress Two Inc	Blackbushe	2.08
N4238C	Mudry CAP.10B	155		Southern Aircraft Consultancy Inc *(As "52" in Mexican AF c/s)*	Rotary Farm, Hatch	6.06
N4297A	Piper PA-39 Twin Comanche C/R	39-114	G-AZBW, N8954Y	Southern Aircraft Consultancy Inc *(Operated T Norman)*	Kirkwall	12.07
N4305H	Mooney M.20J	24-0788		Southern Aircraft Consultancy Inc	Elmsett	10.07
N4337K	Cessna 150K	15071583	G-BTSA, N6083G	T L Crook	Coleman Green	1.08
N4422P	Piper PA-23-160 Geronimo	23-1936		W J Armstrong Inc	Thruxton	1.08
N4514X	Piper PA-28-181 Cherokee Archer II	28-7690027		Baxter 4514X Holdings Inc	Cambridge	8.07
N4519U (1)	Head AX9-118 Balloon (Hot Air)	184		P Sweatman "Ground Hog"	Birmingham	4.07
	(Original envelope- replacement in use with Northern Light Balloon Expeditions)					
NC4531H	Piper PA-15 Vagabond	15-305		E A Terris	Wycombe Air Park	7.06
N4575C	Grumman G.21A Goose	B-120		Aerofloat G21A Inc	Weston, Dublin	12.07
N4596N	Boeing-Stearman E75 (PT-13D) Kaydet (Lycoming R680-7)	75-5945	42-17782	Phil Dacy Aviation *(US Mail c/s) (Current status unknown)*	Shoreham	11.04
N4599W	Rockwell Commander 112TC	13089		N4599W Inc	Conington	2.08
N4698W	Rockwell Commander 112TC-A	13274		M P Sandell	Bournemouth	1.08
N4712V	Boeing Stearman PT-13D Kaydet	75-5094	42-16931	Southern Aircraft Consultancy Inc *(As "W:104" in USAAC c/s)*	Hardwick	6.07
N4770B	Cessna 152	15283626		N R Coplow	Panshanger	10.07
N4779B*	Cessna 152	15283630		Not known *(Cancelled 9.04 by FAA)*	Shobdon	10.07
N4806E	Douglas B-26C Invader	27451	44-34172	A26 Europe Inc (Catfield, Great Yarmouth) *(Stored with Hull Aero)*		2.06
N5020A	Cessna T182T	T18208097		Tancred Aviation	Sherburn-in-Elmet	8.07
N5025J	Hiller UH-12B	726		Hiller Inc (Stored)	Henstridge	8.07
N5043X	Cessna 172C	17249424	G-BWJP	International Air Services *(Operated T W Case)* Moorlands Farm, Farway Common		7.06
N5052P	Piper PA-24-180 Comanche	24-56	G-ATFS, N5052P	T A G Randell *(Under restoration)*	Farley Farm, Romsey	5.05
N5057V	Boeing-Stearman PT-13D Kaydet	75-5598	42-17435	M G Plaskett *(Team Guinot) (Operated V.S.E.Norman)*	Rendcomb	9.07
N5084V	Cirrus SR22-G2	0831		SR22 Holding Inc	Denham	2.08
N5113S	Cessna 750 Citation X	750-0013	N5113, N5241Z	Inter Air Leasing LLC	Luton	11.06

Reg	Type	Serial	Prev regs	Owner/Operator	Location	Date
N5120	Bell 430	49095		Wells Fargo Bank Northwest NA (Operated JJB Sports)	Blackpool	1.08
N5240H	Piper PA-16 Clipper	16-44		Southern Aircraft Consultancy Inc (Operated D.Hillier)	Wellcross Grange, Slinfold	2.06
N5264Q	MD Helicopters MD.369E	0126E		Southern Aircraft Consultancy Inc	Donegal, County Donegal	6.07
N5277T	Piper PA-32-260 Cherokee Six E	32-7200031		K R Denman	Goodwood	1.08
N5315V	Hiller UH-12C	757		Southern Aircraft Consultancy Inc	Lower Upham	3.07
N5317V	Hiller UH-12C	768		Canaan Helicopters (Operated Pulse Helicopters)	(Sherbourne)	2.06
N5320N	Piper PA-46-500TP Malibu Meridian	4697153		Bridgelink Finance Inc	Bournemouth	9.07
N5336Z	Cirrus SR20	1413		Southern Aircraft Consultancy Inc	Perth	1.08
N5428C	Cessna 170A	19462		Southern Aircraft Consultancy Inc (Operated P.Norman)	Audley End	10.07
N5632R	Maule M-5-235C Lunar Rocket	7244C		Southern Aircraft Consultancy Inc (Operated RD Group)	Stowes Farm, Tillingham	4.06
N5647S	Maule M-5-235C Rocket	7345C		Virginia Aircraft Trust Corp	Yeatsall Farm, Abbotts Bromley	8.07
N5730H	Piper PA-16 Clipper	16-342		Southern Aircraft Consultancy Inc	Yeatsall Farm, Abbotts Bromley	8.07
N5736	Raytheon Hawker 800XP2	258471	N43642	Hawker Partnership Inc (Operated Howard Holdings plc)	Cork and Luton	1.08
N5834N*	Rockwell Commander 114	14383		W F Chmura (Crashed 23.10.98 - cancelled 7.99 by FAA - hulk only)	Peterstone, Cardiff	11.04
N5839P	Piper PA-24-180 Comanche	24-920		Aircraft Guaranty Management LLC	Blackbushe	2.08
N5880T	Westland WG-30-100	009	G-17-31	Offshore Fire & Survival Training Centre	Norwich	4.07
N5900H	Piper PA-16 Clipper	16-520		Southern Aircraft Consultancy Inc	Shenstone	7.06
N5915V	Piper PA-28-161Cherokee Warrior II	28-7716215		Southern Aircraft Consultancy Inc	North Weald	11.07
N6010Y	Commander Aircraft Commander 114B	14589		Camrose Inc	Biggin Hill	2.08
N6024V	Commander Aircraft Commander 114B	14609		Hinsby Inc	Guernsey	1.08
N6039X	Commander Aircraft Commander 114B	14639		Little Beetle Inc	Guernsey	1.08
N6078T	Cessna T182T	T18208621		Aircraft Guaranty Title Corp LLC	Shobdon	5.07
N6081F	Commander Aircraft Commander 114B	14681		DSS Inc	Kemble	11.07
N6088F (2)	Commander Aircraft Commander 114TC	20043	N948PW	Turnberry Holdings Inc	Blackbushe	2.08
N6088Z	Commander Aircraft Commander 114B	14662	N6088F (1)	Southern Aircraft Consultancy Inc	Guernsey	1.08
N6095A	Commander Aircraft Commander 114B	14635		Bonbois Aviation	Guernsey	1.08
N6130X	Maule M6-235C Super Rocket	7497C		Pelmont Aviation	Chilbolton	4.07
N6182G	Cessna 172N Skyhawk II	17273576		Southern Aircraft Consultancy Inc	Cambridge	1.08
N6302W	Government Aircraft Factory N22B Nomad	F-159	VH-HWB	Chatteris Aviation Inc (Operated London Parachute Centre) Lower Mount.Pleasant, Chatteris		5.07
N6339U	Piper PA-28-236 Dakota	28-8011089	OO-JFD F-GCMU, OO-HLM, N8152S)	Southern Aircraft Consultancy Inc	Wickenby	10.07
N6438C	Stinson L-5C Sentinel	1428		Eastern Stearman Inc (Operated P Bennett and N Nice as "298177:R-8")	Priory Farm, Tibenham	12.07
N6498V	Cessna T303 Crusader	T30300313	G-CRUS N6498V	Southern Aircraft Consultancy Inc	Guernsey	1.08
N6593W	Cessna P210N Centurion (Silver Eagle Allison turboprop conversion)	P210-00801		Southern Aircraft Consultancy Inc "Rose Anne" (Operated Pacific Network Air)	Brittas House, Limerick	1.08
N6601Y	Piper PA-23-250 Aztec C	27-3905	XC-DAZ N6601Y	3 Greens Aviation	Blackpool	11.05
N6602Y	Piper PA-28-140 Cherokee	28-21943	G-ATTG N11C	Southern Aircraft Consultancy Inc	Seething	10.07
N6620W	Alon A-2 Aircoupe	A-110		Southern Aircraft Consultancy Inc	Plymouth	10.07
N6632L	Beech C23 Musketeer	M-2188		W J Forrest	Ventfield Farm, Oxford	8.06
N6819F	Cessna 150F	15063419		W J Davis (On fire dump)	Shoreham	5.03
N6830B	Piper PA-22-150 Tri-Pacer	22-4128		Southern Aircraft Consultancy Inc	Crowfield	1.08
N6907E	Cessna 175A Skylark	56407		Southern Aircraft Consultancy Inc (Operated C Webb)	Popham	1.08
N6920B	Piper PA-34-220T Seneca III	34-8533025		Southern Aircraft Consultancy Inc	Blackbushe	2.08
N6954J	Piper PA-32R-300 Cherokee Lance	32R-7680394		Matrix Aviation Inc	Norwich	2.08
N7027E	Hawker Tempest V	Not known	EJ693	K Weeks (Stored)	Wycombe Air Park	7.06
N7070A	Cessna S550 Citation II	S550-0068	N4049 N404G, N1272Z	Omega Air Inc	Dublin	12.07
N7098V	North American TF-51D Mustang	122-40411	IDF/AF RCAF9245, 44-73871	Mustang Air Inc (Stored)	(Greenham Common)	2.04
N7148R	Beech B55 Baron	TC-2028	N2198L C-GWFD, N2198L, D-IGRW, N2198L	Air Services Holdings Corp	Exeter	9.07
N7172Z	Hughes 369C	122-0438S		Southern Aircraft Consultancy Inc	Fairoaks	1.08
N7205T	Beech A36 Bonanza	E-2182		Minster Enterprises	Tatenhill	1.08
N7219L	Beech B55 Baron	TC-717	HB-GBX OE-FDF, HB-GBX	Southern Aircraft Consultancy Inc	Elstree	12.07
N7223Y	Beech 58 Baron	TH-1456		Southern Aircraft Consultancy Inc	Elstree	2.08
N7238X	Piper PA-18-95 Super Cub	18-1629	G-BWUO OO-MEU, OO-HNG, French Army, 51-15629 (Operated J Surbey)	International Air Services	Blockmoor Farm, Soham	4.06
N7242N	Agusta A109A-II	7355	ZK-HJC	Cannon Air	Liskeard Heliport	10.07
N7251Y	Beech A36 Bonanza	E-2277		Turbo Arrow Inc	Elstree	1.08
N7263S	Cessna 150H	15067963		Cesna Inc (Stored)	Plaistows Farm, St Albans	10.07
N7348P	Piper PA-24-250 Comanche	24-2526		Southern Aircraft Consultancy Inc (Operated J.Bown)	Netherthorpe	9.07
N7374A	Cessna A150M Aerobat 135 (Tail-wheel conversion)	A1500726		Southern Aircraft Consultancy Inc "Turnin' Tricks"	Branscombe	10.05

Reg	Type	Serial	Reg 2	Owner/Operator	Location	Date
N7423V	Mooney M.20E Chapparal	21-1163		Southern Aircraft Consultancy Inc		
					Hinton in the Hedges	10.07
N7456P	Piper PA-24-250 Comanche	24-2646		Southern Aircraft Consultancy Inc	Gamston	9.07
N7600E	Bellanca 14-19-2 Cruisemaster	4102		Egmond Aircraft LLC Westover Farm, Sheepwash		8.07
N7640F	Piper PA-32R-300 Cherokee Lance		ZS-OGX	Southern Aircraft Consultancy Inc		
		32R-7780069	N7640F		Wellesbourne Mountford	6.07
N7801R	Bell 47G-5	7801		Skyman Logistics	Beckley, Oxford	8.04
N7832P	Piper PA-24-250 Comanche	24-3052		Three Two Papa Inc	Enstone	1.08
N7976Y	Piper PA-30 Twin Comanche B	30-1075		Southern Aircraft Consultancy Inc	Guernsey	1.08
N8010M	Bell 407	53728		Dempsey 407 Inc (Republic of Ireland)		9.07
				(Reserved as N407MD)		
N8105Z	Piper PA-28RT-201T Turbo Arrow IV			Southern Aircraft Consultancy Inc	Elstree	11.07
		28R-8031007				
N8153E	Piper PA-28RT-201T Turbo Arrow IV		N9561N	P B Payne	RAF Mona	4.07
		28R-8131185	N84205			
N8159Q	Cirrus SR20	1388		DSL Corporation	Swansea	11.07
N8225Y	Cessna 177RG Cardinal RG	177RG1247		International Air Services Upper Hill Farm, Hughley		10.07
				(Operated D J Knight Cardinal Group)		
N8241Z	Piper PA-28-161 Warrior II	28-8316079		Pett Air Inc	Henstridge	1.08
N8258F	Beech B36TC Bonanza	EA-513		Millfore Aviation Inc	Gloucestershire	8.07
N8412B	Piper PA-28RT-201T Turbo Arrow IV			Sweepline Inc Bourne Park, Hurstbourne Tarrant		1.08
		28R-8131164				
N8523Y	Piper PA-30 Twin Comanche	30-1684		Leadbolt Inc	Gloucestershire	5.07
N8702K	Cessna 340A	340A0623		Southern Aircraft Consultancy Inc	Goodwood	1.08
N8754J	Aviat A-1 Husky	1160		Southern Aircraft Consultancy Inc	Guernsey	1.08
	(Built Christen Industries)			(Operated A.Febrache)		
N8829P	Piper PA-24-260 Comanche	24-4285		J Melville	(Dunkeswell)	12.07
N8862V	Bellanca 17-31ATC Turbo Super Viking	31022		S B Barber	Popham	1.08
N8911Y	Piper PA-39 Twin Comanche C/R	39-66	G-AYFT	Southern Aircraft Consultancy Inc		
			N8911Y	(Stored) Farley Farm, Romsey		10.07
N8990F	Hughes 269C	64-0313		Southern Aircraft Consultancy Inc	Kilrush	10.07
N9057F	Hughes 369HS	129-0230S		Southern Aircraft Consultancy Inc	Kilrush	11.07
N9070L	British Aerospace BAe 146 Series 300	E3147	ZK-NZJ	T S Whetter	Bournemouth	1.08
			G-6-147, G-5-147, G-11-147	(Stored)		
N9086L	British Aerospace BAe 146 Series 300	E3135	ZK-NZG	T S Whetter	Bournemouth	1.08
			G-5-135	(Stored)		
N9089Z	North American TB-25N Mitchell	108-35186	(G-BKXW)	Aero Associates Inc	Wycombe Air Park	1.07
			N9089Z, 44-30861	(Stored dismantled with Parkhouse Aviation)		
N9122N	Piper PA-46-310P Malibu	4608097		Air Libra Inc	Oxford	1.08
N9123X	Piper PA-32R-301T Turbo Saratoga SP			Vector Sky Service Inc Shoreham and Hilversum		10.07
		3229003				
N9133D	Bell 407	53648		Duignan & McCarthy Inc (Republic of Ireland)		10.07
N9146N	Cessna 401B	401B0010		A J Air Ltd Inc	Weston, Dublin	10.07
	(RAM conversion)			(In derelict condition)		
N9275Y	Piper PA-46-310P Malibu	46-8608026		International Air Services	Haverfordwest	8.07
				(Operated D F Keedy)		
N9325N	Piper PA-28R-200 Cherokee Arrow	28R-35025		Southern Aircraft Consultancy Inc	Panshanger	2.08
	(Lopresti version)			(Operated H Mercado)		
N9362	Sud-Aviation SA316B Alouette III	1739		Southern Aircraft Consultancy Inc		
					Halton Moor, Leeds	5.07
N9381P	Piper PA-24-260 Comanche C	24-4882		Southern Aircraft Consultancy Inc	Elstree	2.08
N9533Y	Cessna T.210N Centurion	21064539		Simply Living Ltd	Liverpool	7.05
N9680Q	Cessna 172M	17265764		Aircraft Guaranty Holdings & Trust LLC	Jersey	7.07
				(Operated Jersey Aero Club)		
N9838Z	Beech B90 King Air	LJ-435	D-IHCH	Skydive Midwest Aviation	Dunkeswell	12.07
			D-ILVW			
N9861M	Maule M.4-210C	1058C		Southern Aircraft Consultancy Inc	Fairoaks	1.08
N9870C	Cessna T303 Crusader	T30300227		Aircraft Guaranty Holdings & Trust LLC	Liverpool	10.07
N9950	Curtiss P-40N Warhawk	33723	44-7983	Sky Fire Corp (Greenham Common)		2.04
				(Stored in container)		
N10053	Boeing Stearman A75N1	75-4986	XB-XIH	Eastern Stearman	Bagby	2.08
				(Under restoration for R Knights)		
N11824	Cessna 150L	15075652		Southern Aircraft Consultancy Inc	Turweston	1.08
N13253	Cessna 172M Skyhawk	17262613		Anglia Aviation Inc Plaistows Farm, St Albans		10.07
				(Stored)		
N14113	North American T-28B Trojan	174-398	Haiti AF 1236	Radial Revelations Ltd	Duxford	11.07
			N14113, FrAF 119, 51-7545	"Little Rascal" (As "51-7545:119" in French AF c/s)		
NC16403*	Cessna C.34 Airmaster	322		Alan House Lower Wasing Farm, Brimpton		9.07
				(Cancelled 5.99 by FAA and stored)		
N17596	Schweizer S269C-1	0300		Magell Aviation USA Inc	(Ballymena)	1.08
NC18028	Beech D17S	147	NC18028	P.H.McConnell	Popham	1.08
N19753	Cessna 172L	17260723		Aircraft Guaranty Title & Trust Llc	Elstree	2.08
N20981	Cessna 172M	17263885		Aircraft Guaranty Title & Trust LLC	(Abbeyshrule)	7.07
N21381	Piper PA-34-200 Seneca	34-7350274	F-BUTM	Tickton Inc	Dunkeswell	12.07
			F-ETAL			
N21419	British Aircraft Corporation 167 Strikemaster Mk.81		R Singapore AF 323	NW MAS Ltd	Hawarden	10.07
		EEP/JP/168	South Yemen AF 504, G-AXFX	(Stored at Hawarden Air Services)		
N21927	Cessna 172S Skyhawk	172S10505		CSE Aviation	Belfast International	2.08
				(For Ulster Flying Club 2008 as G-UFCx)		
N23659	Beech B58 Baron	TH-893		International Air Services	Guernsey	1.08
				(Operated M G Williams)		
N24136	Beech A36 Bonanza	E-1233		Dickens Aviation Inc	North Weald	8.07
N24730*	Piper PA-38-112 Tomahawk			See G-BTIL - detail in SECTION 1, Part 2 Eaglescott		

Reg	Type	c/n	Prev id	Operator	Location	Date
N25644	North American B-25D Mitchell	100-20644		Vulcan Warbirds Inc	North Weald	6.07
			N88972, CF-OGQ, KL161, 43-3318	*"Grumpy" (As "KL161/VO-B" in RAF 98 Sqn c/s)*		
N26634	Piper PA-24-250 Comanche	24-3551		Atlanticair Inc	Slinfold	10.07
			PH-BUS, D-ELPY, N8306P			
N29566	Piper PA-28RT-201 Arrow IV	28R-7918146	D-EJLH	Southern Aircraft Consultancy Inc	Denham	1.08
N30562	Bell 407	53750		Air Move Partnership	Weston, Dublin	12.07
N30593	Cessna 210L Centurion	21059938		Southern Aircraft Consultancy Inc	Cranfield	11.07
N31008	Piper PA-32R-301 Saratoga IIHP	3246229		China Saratoga Airline	Elstree	1.08
N31356	Douglas DC-4-1009	42914		Aces High US Inc	North Weald	6.07
			C-FTAW	*(As "44-42914")*		
			EL-ADR, N6404			
N32625 *	Piper PA-34-200T Seneca II	34-7570039	G-PALM	(Fire Section)	Guernsey	1.08
			SE-LAN, N32625			
N33514	Hiller UH-12B	661	51-16408	Pulse Helicopter Corporation	(Sherbourne)	2.06
				(Damaged 18.11.04 - stored)		
N33870	Fairchild M62A (PT-19-FA) Cornell	T40-237	G-BTNY	Ice Strike Corp	(Suffolk)	2.06
			N33870, US Army	*(As "02538" in US Army c/s)*		
NC33884	Aeronca 65CA Chief	CA.14101		P W & J M Brewer	Bodmin	10.07
N36362	Cessna 180 Skywagon	31691	G-BHVZ	Southern Aircraft Consultancy Inc *(Operated W Burgess)*		
			F-BHMU, N4739B		Bourne Park, Hurstbourne Tarrant	9.07
N36665	Beech A36 Bonanza	E-1696		M Flynn	Fairoaks	1.08
N37172	Beech B300 King Air	FL-472		Wells Fargo Bank Northwest NA	Biggin Hill	1.08
N37379	Cessna 421C Golden Eagle	421C0654	G-DJEA	Bettany Aircraft	Jersey	7.07
			TC-AAA, N37379, (N24BS), N37379	*(Reserved as N339TB)*		
N38273	Piper PA-28R-201 Cherokee Arrow III			S W Freeborn	Blackbushe	2.08
		28R-7737086		*(Operated L.Slater)*		
N38763	Hiller UH-12B	497	G-ATZB	M Elkins	Elstree	12.07
			102 R Thai AF			
N38940	Boeing-Stearman A75N1 (PT-17) Kaydet		(G-BSNK)	Eastern Stearman Inc	Priory Farm, Tibenham	12.07
	(Continental R670)	75-1822	N38940, N55300, 41-8263	*(Operated P Bennett as "18263/822" in US Army c/s)*		
N38945	Piper PA-32R-300 Cherokee Lance			Southern Aircraft Consultancy Inc	Stapleford	2.08
		32R-7780490				
N39605	Piper PA-34-200T Seneca II	34-7870397		Fly Horizon US Inc	Swansea	2.08
N41098	Cessna 421B Golden Eagle	421B0448		Hughston Aircraft Corp	Elstree	12.07
N42527	Bell 407	53384		Aircraft Guaranty Title & Trust LLC	Shannon	7.07
				(Operated Rollico Aviation)		
N44914	Douglas C-54D Skymaster	10630	Bu56498	Aces High US Inc	North Weald	6.07
			42-72525	*(As "56498" in US c/s)*		
N45458	Piper PA-18-150 Super Cub	18-8553	IDF/AF012	Palace Aviation Investment *(Stored)*	Steventon	4.07
N45462	Piper PA-18-150 Super Cub	18-8309015	IDF/AF134	Palace Aviation Investment *(Stored)*	Steventon	1.08
N45477	Piper PA-18-150 Super Cub	18-8309003	IDF/AF122	Palace Aviation Investment *(Stored)*	Steventon	1.08
N45507	Piper PA-18-150 Super Cub	18-8566	IDF/AF024	Palace Aviation Investment *(Stored)*	Steventon	4.07
N45526	Piper PA-18-150 Super Cub	18-8309014	IDF/AF133	Palace Aviation Investment *(Stored)*	Steventon	1.08
N45531	Piper PA-18-150 Super Cub	18-8209022	IDF/AF111	Palace Aviation Investment *(Stored)*	Steventon	4.07
N45543	Piper PA-18-150 Super Cub	18-8109034	IDF/AF103	Palace Aviation Investment *(Stored)*	Steventon	1.08
N45552	Piper PA-18-150 Super Cub	18-8563	IDF/AF027	Palace Aviation Investment	Popham	1.08
N47351*	Cessna 152	15283219		Not known	Hill Farm, Nayland	3.05
				(Cancelled 4.91 by FAA as destroyed: derelict fuselage stored)		
N47494	Piper PA-28R-201 Cherokee Arrow III			M R Horwitz Inc	Panshanger	10.07
		28R-7737166				
N49272	Fairchild M.62C/PT-23A-HO Cornell	437HO	42-49413	Flying Heritage Inc	Sleap	11.07
	(Continental W670)			*(Operated R.E.Mitchell t/a PT Flight as "23" in USAAC c/s)*		
N50029	Cessna 172	28807	LX-AIB	Southern Aircraft Consultancy Inc	Exeter	3.07
			N6707A	*(Operated E.Byrd)*		
N52485	Boeing-Stearman A75N1 (PT-17) Kaydet			Roland Stearman Aviation *(As "169" in US Navy c/s)*		
		75-4494			Cherry Tree Farm, Monewden	9.06
N53103	Cessna 177RG Cardinal RG	177RG1347		Vectis Aircraft	Sandown, Isle of Wight	9.07
N54105	Cirrus SR22-G2	1139		Gopub Aviation	Leeds-Bradford	2.08
N54211	Piper PA-23-250 Aztec E	27-7554006	G-ITTU	Southern Aircraft Consultancy Inc	Elstree	8.07
			D-IKLW, G-BCSW, N54211	*(Noted road running on M25 (S) 6. 8.07)*		
N54922	Boeing-Stearman A75N1 (PT-17) Kaydet		Bu.30054	M G Plaskett	Rendcomb	9.06
	(Pratt & Witney 985-14B)	75-3491		*(Team Guinot) (Operated V.S.E.Norman)*		
N56421	Ryan PT-22-RY Recruit	1539	41-15510	Flying Heritage Inc	Sleap	10.06
				(Operated R.E.Mitchell t/a PT Flight as "855" in US Army c/s)		
N56462	Maule M.6-235 Rocket	7409C		Avocet (US) Inc	East Winch	8.07
N56643	Maule M.5-180C	8086C		Southern Aircraft Consultancy Inc (Boscombe Down)		8.06
				(Operated C Schofield)		
N57783	Stinson L-5 Sentinel	76-511	42-98270 ?	J F Tillman	Priory Farm, Tibenham	10.07
				(Frame - spares for N6438C)		
N58283	Aerospatiale SA.341G Gazelle	1015		D B Pearce	Bourne Park	8.07
N58566	Consolidated-Vultee BT-15-VN Valiant	10670	42-41882	Flying Heritage Inc	Sleap	11.06
				(Operated R.E.Mitchell t/a PT Flight in US Army c/s)		
N59269	Boeing Stearman A75L3	75-3867		R W Hightower	Stock	7.04
				"817" (Current status unknown)		
N60256	Beech C35 Bonanza	D-3346	OO-DOL	R.M.Hornblower	Southend	2.08
			OO-JAN	*(Nosewheel collapsed landing 28. 1.05 - in open store with no propeller 2.08)*		
N60526	Beech E55 Baron	TE-1159		E Walsh	Elstree	12.07
N61787	Piper J-3C-65 Cub	13624	45-4884	Gypsy Fliers Draycott Farm, Chiseldon		8.06
				(As "54884/57-D")		
N61970	Piper PA-24-250 Comanche	24-3364	OO-GOE	Southern Aircraft Consultancy Inc	Gamston	8.07
			F-OCBM, 5R-MVA, N8198P, N10F *(Operated Nunn & Green)*			
N62171	Hiller Felt UH-12C	GF-2		Southern Aircraft Consultancy Inc	Tuam, Galway	12.04
N62842	Boeing-Stearman PT-17 Kaydet	75-3851		Eastern Stearman Inc	Priory Farm, Tibenham	10.07
				(Frame stored)		
N63590	Boeing-Stearman N2S-3 Kaydet	75-7143	Bu.07539	Eastern Stearman Inc	Brock Farm, Brentwood	8.07
				(Operated I Stockwell as "07539/143" in US Navy c/s)		

Reg	Type	C/n	Prev id	Owner/Operator	Location	Date
N65200	Boeing-Stearman D75N1 Kaydet	75-3817	FJ767	Eastern Stearman Inc	Goodwood	12.07
N65565	Boeing Stearman B75N1 Kaydet	75-7463		Ortac Inc	Sywell	11.07
N68427	Boeing-Stearman A75N1 (N2S-4) Kaydet	75-5000	Bu 55771	Eastern Stearman Inc Priory Farm, Tibenham		10.07
	(Operated Blackbarn Aviation) (Frame only)					
N70844	Piper PA-23-250 Aztec D	27-4194	G-AZSZ	International Air Services	Biggin Hill	6.07
			N6851Y	*(Operated A A Mattacks)*		
N71763	Cessna 180K	18053191		China Pilot Inc	(Newmarket)	5.07
N74189	Boeing Stearman PT-17	75-717		M G Plaskett	Rendcomb	9.07
				(Team Guinot) (Operated Aerosuperbatics Ltd)		
N75048	Piper PA-28-181 Cherokee Archer II	28-7690286		Southern Aircraft Consultancy Inc		
				(Operated I Sibley) St Marys, Isle of Scilly		4.07
N75822	Cessna 172N	17267979		Hercmar Inc	Crowfield	1.08
N76402*	Cessna 140	10828	NC76402	(C.Murgatroyd)	Blackpool	11.05
	(Crashed near Meppershall 9.8.98 : cancelled 4.99 by FAA) (Wreck stored)					
N77342	Cessna 120	11783		Southern Aircraft Consultancy Inc		
					(Republic of Ireland)	4.07
N80035	Pitts S-2A	2070		Southern Aircraft Consultancy Inc	Panshanger	7.07
N80056	Cessna 421B Golden Eagle	421B0654	G-HASI	CB Aviation Inc	Hawarden	10.07
			G-BTDK, OY-BFA, N1558G			
N80364	Cessna 500 Citation I	500-0299	OY-TKI	Wells Fargo Bank Northwest NA Weston, Dublin		1.08
	N80364, (OY-EBD), N80364, PT-OZX, YV-940CP, N5133K, ZS-MGH, N55AK, N66TR, N3JJ, HB-VEO, N5299J *(Operated National Flight Centre)*					
N80533	Cessna 172M Skyhawk	17266640		Southern Aircraft Consultancy Inc	Alderney	11.07
N81188	Piper PA-28-236 Dakota	28-8211026		Retail Management Associates		
					Charlton Park, Malmesbury	8.07
N84142	Lake LA-250 Buccaneer	69		Plane Fun Inc	Bournemouth	4.07
N84718	Piper PA-28RT-201T Turbo Arrow IV	28R-8231013		Southern Aircraft Consultancy Inc East Midlands		9.07
N90011	MD Helicopters MD.902	900-00115		Latium Helicopter Charters UK Inc	Shoreham	10.07
N90724	Hiller UH-12C	810	55-4106	Southern Aircraft Consultancy Inc *(Current status unknown)*		
					Lower Botrea Farm, Sancreed	11.03
N91384	Rockwell Commander 690A	11118	SE-FLN	Airbourne Inc	Wickenby	9.07
N92001	MD Helicopters MD.900	900-00040		Aradian Aviation	Not known	2.07
N92562	Piper PA-46-350P Malibu Mirage	4636010		Trevair Inc	Ronaldsway	11.07
N93938	Erco 415C	1261		Merkado Holdings	Panshanger	12.06
N95409	Cessna 172R	17280424		Southern Aircraft Consultancy Inc	Not known	6.06
				(Current status unknown)		
N96240	Beech D18S (3TM)	CA-159	G-AYAH	Edwards Worldwide Aviation	North Weald	6.07
			N6123, RCAF 1559			
N97121*	Embraer EMB-110P1 Bandeirante	110.334	PT-SDK	Guernsey Airport Fire Service *(Hulk only)* Guernsey		1.08
N97821	Mooney M.20J	24-1080		Southern Aircraft Consultancy Inc	Panshanger	11.07
			OO-LFK, N6328X			

AUSTRIA

Reg	Type	C/n	Prev id	Owner/Operator	Location	Date
OE-IFB	Bombardier CL-600-2B16	5704	(D-AFIB)	Vista Jet Gmbh	Oxford	1.08
	(CL-605 Challenger)		C-FLKC			
OE-KKC	Diamond DA 40D Star	D4.036	(OM-HLH)	Diamond Aircraft Industries GmbH	Gamston	10.07
			OE-DDC			
OE-LRE	Bombardier CL-600-2B19	7059	(JA02J)	Air Salvage International	Alton	2.07
	(CL-600 Regional Jet)		OE-LRE, C-FMND	*(Fuselage stored)*		
OE-XBA	Agusta-Bell AB206B-3 JetRanger III	8557	HB-XPW	Belair-Helicopter Luftverkehrs	Strathallan	8.06
			G-TKHM, G-MKAN, G-DOUG			

CZECH REPUBLIC

Reg	Type	C/n	Prev id	Owner/Operator	Location	Date
OK-DUA 14	Jora sro Jora	Not known		Not known	Abbeyshrule	10.06
OK-DUU 15	Urban Air UFM-11 Lambada	3/11		M.Tormey	Kilkenny	7.06
OK-FUA 05	Urban Air UFM-11 Lambada	13/11	OK-EUU-02	T Mackey	Abbeyshrule	10.06
OK-GUA 16	Urban Air UFM-10 Samba	Not known		Not known	Minnistown, County Mear	10.07
OK-GUA 28	Urban Air UFM-10 Samba	21/10		Not known *(Current status unknown)* Abbeyshrule		8.04
OK-IUA 69	TL Ultralight TL 2000 Sting RG	Not known		Not known Tarn Farm, Cockerham		9.06
OK-JUA 03	Urban Air Samba XXL	Not known		Not known	Willingale	10.07
OK-KUA 16	Urban Air Samba XXL	Not known		Not known	Abbeyshrule	10.07
OK-KUA 26	Urban Air Samba XXL	Not known		Not known	Kilkenny	6.07
OK-LUA 36	Urban Air Samba XXL	Not known		Not known	Abbeyshrule	6.07

BELGIUM

Reg	Type	C/n	Prev id	Owner/Operator	Location	Date
OO-AJK	Nord 1203 Norecrin	261	F-BFJE	Not known *(Stored unmarked)*	Exeter	1.07
OO-DFS	Piper PA-18 Super Cub 95	18-1637	French Army	A Alderdice Kilkeel, County Down		7.07
			51-15637	*(Under restoration)*		
OO-DHN*	Boeing 727-31	20113	N260NE	European Air Transport-DHL	Lasham	1.08
			N97891	*(Stored: acquired false marks "N9748C" for film 6.06)*		
OO-DHR*	Boeing 727-35F	19834	N932FT	European Air Transport-DHL	Lasham	1.08
			(N526FE), N932FT, N1958	*(Stored)*		
OO-EII	Bücker Bü.133C Jungmeister	51	D-EIII (2)	RLM Aviation	Fairoaks	8.05
			Spanish. AF	*(Stored)*		
OO-GCO	Grumman-American AA-5A Cheetah	AA5A-0526	OO-HGB	N Foden	Broughton	1.07
				(Converted to flight simulator)		
OO-MEL*	Focke-Wulf Piaggio FWP.149D	113	90+93	Not known Draycott Farm, Chiseldon		5.07
			AC+470, JC+394, AS+428	*(Stored dismantled)*		
OO-MHB*	Piper PA-28-236 Dakota	28-8011143	G-BMHB	R W H Watson	Blackpool	12.05
			D6-PAD, N81321, N9593N	*(Damaged Southend 20.10.90 : wreck stored:)*		
OO-NAT	SOCATA MS.880B Rallye Club	2253	G-BAOK	R W H Watson Grimmet Farm, Maybole		7.05
				(Fuselage stored)		

OO-SDK*	Boeing 737-229C			See G-BYYK - details in SECTION 1, Part 3		
					Bournemouth	1.07
OO-TND*	Boeing 737-301F	23515	N346US	Air Salvage International	Lasham	6.07
			N325P	*(Fuselage stored)*		
OO-WIO*	Reims Cessna FRA150L Aerobat	FRA1500183	F-BUMG	Department of Engineering, Salford University Salford		8.03
				(Used as instructional airframe)		
OO-A95	CFM Shadow C-D	200CD		Not known	Old Sarum	1.06

DENMARK

OY-BTZ	Piper PA-31-350 Navajo Chieftain	31-7752031	SE-GPM	Company Flight K/S	East Midlands	9.07
OY-DFD	Mooney M.20F Executive	670327	N2968L	M Hales	Little Staughton	12.07
OY-DRS	Reims Cessna F172K	F17200786	LN-LJY	U Odlund *(Stored dismantled)*	Old Buckenham	11.07
OY-EGZ	Cessna F172H	F172-0324	N17013	P and C Bak	Alderney	1.07
OY-FAA	Taylor J-2 Cub	964	LN-EAP	J Hansen	Croft Farm, Defford	1.08
OY-HGB*	Hughes 369D	1146D	CS-HCI	Biggin Hill Helicopters	Biggin Hill	6.07
	(Hughes 500)		G-ONTA	*(Cabin in outside storage)*		
OY-ILG	Bombardier BD-700 Global Express	9163	C-FCPH	Graff Aviation Ltd	Luton	1.08
OY-MUB*	Short SD.3-30 Variant 200	SH.3069	G-BITX	Wolds Gliding Club	Pocklington	8.07
			G-14-3069	*(Fuselage used as mobile briefing room)*		
OY-NMH	Government Aircraft Factory N-24A Nomad		ZK-NMH	Airlog	Old Buckenham	11.07
		74FA	N870US, PH-HAG, (PH-DHL), N5579K, VH-PNF			
OY-OCV	Bombardier Learjet 45	45-306	N5009T	Aviation Partnership Denmark ApS	Dublin	12.07
OY-PBH	LET L-410UVP-E20	972736	OK-DDC	Alebco Corporation	Inverness	1.08
				(Op Benair A/S)		

NETHERLANDS

PH-DUC	Stoddard-Hamilton Glasair IIRG-S	2069	N51DA	R S van Dijk	Little Gransden	7.07
PH-KRC	Cessna 180K	18052799	SE-KRC	S J Beaty	Wold Lodge, Finedon	12.07
			N61790			
PH-NLK*	Piper PA-23-160 Apache	23-1694	OY-DCG	Not known	Water Leisure Park, Skegness	5.06
			SE-CKW, N10F	*(Wreck stored for spares)*		
PH-PAB*	Neico Lancair 360	766		D C Ratcliffe *(Cancelled 8.07)*	Shoreham	6.05
PH-PWA	Van's RV-8	80836		W Moore	Membury	1.08
PH-TMH	Piper PA-38-112 Tomahawk	38-79A0261	N2314D	A Breslin	Kilrush	11.07
PH-TWR	Ken Brock KB-2 Gyroplane	1006		A G W Davis	Shipdham	7.06
PH-ZZY	SOCATA MS893E Rallye 180GT	12074		M L B Warriner	Trevethoe Farm, Lelant	10.07
			OO-AON			
			F-GACN			
PH-3P3 *	WDL Fascination D4BK	106		R Simpson	(Longhope, Gloucestershire)	7.06
PH-3W6	CZAW CH-601XL Zodiac	6-9666		O C D Masters	Kilrush	11.07

INDONESIA

PK-MTV	British Aerospace ATP		See G-BTZG - details in SECTION 1, Part 2		
				Woodford	3.06

ARUBA

P4-HEC	Eurocopter EC.155B	6600	LX-HEC	Not known	Blackbushe	1.08
			F-WQPX			
P4-LJG	Cessna 750 Citation X	750-0228	N5267J	Venair	Dublin	1.08
P4-MMG	Boeing 727-30	18368	VP-CMM	MMG Aviation	Southend	2.08
			VR-CMM, N841MM, N728JE, N72700, N9234Z, D-ABIM *(Stored with no markings)*			

RUSSIA

FLARF01035	Yakovlev Yak-52	8910106	LY-AIG	Not known	Haverfordwest	7.07
			Ukraine AF 23 *(yellow)*	*(Spares use)*		
FLARF02089	Polikarpov I-15bis	4439		The Fighter Collection *"19"*	Duxford	9.07
RA-01274	Yakovlev Yak-55	910103	DOSAAF 03	Not known *"03"*	Wolverhampton	10.07
RA01370	Yakovlev Yak-18T	22202032912	CCCP-44478	Not known	White Waltham	1.08
				(Damaged fuselage stored as "LY-AOO")		

THE PHILIPPINES

RP-C2900	Agusta A109A	7228	I-DEKO	Castle Helicopters	Liskeard Heliport	3.07
			N9047C	*(Stored)*		
RP-C8023*	Conroy CL-44-O	16	9G-LCA	Transglobal Airways Corporation	Bournemouth	1.08
			(P4-GUP), 4K-GUP, EI-BND, N447T			

SWEDEN

SE-BOG	Boeing Stearman B75N1	75-7128	N59085	V S Norman	Rendcomb	9.07
			BuA07524	*(Team Guinot)*		
SE-BRG*	Fairey Firefly TT.1	F.6071	DT989	ARCO *(Stored dismantled)*	Duxford	9.07
SE-DRB*	British Aerospace BAe 146 Series 200			See G-CBAE - details in SECTION 1, Part 2	Exeter	1.07
SE-EOS	Piper PA-28-180 Cherokee C	28-2533		G Nichols	Phoenix Farm, Lower Upham	1.08
SE-GPU	Piper PA-28-161 Cherokee Warrior II			Ljungbyheds Flygklubb	East Winch	10.04
		28-7716200		*(Current status unknown)*		
SE-GVH	Piper PA-38-112 Tomahawk	38-78A0053		Not known *(In open store)*	Little Staughton	12.07
SE-HXF*	Rotorway Scorpion	SE-1		Not known *(Stored)*	Earls Colne	4.06
SE-IFB	Reims/Cessna F172N	F17202005		Not known	Little Snoring	10.07
SE-IIV	Piper PA-24-260 Comanche C	24-4970	HB-OHZ	Not known	Gamston	10.07
			N9462P			
SE-KBU	Christen A-1 Husky	1038		A Allan	Lochearnhead	8.06
SE-LTE	Cessna P337H Pressurized Skymaster		N73S	Not known	Sleap	12.07
		P337-0352	N6MQ			
SE-UCF	Slingsby T.61F Venture	1983	ZA664	Goteborgs Segelflygklubb	Shenington	5.07

POLAND
SP-CHD*	PZL-101A Gawron	74134		(T Wood) *(Stored in container)*	North Weald	5.07

SUDAN
ST-AHZ	Piper PA-31 Turbo Navajo	31-473	G-AXMR	Not known	Elstree	8.04
			N6558L	*(Fire practice use: burnt-out fuselage noted)*		

GREECE
SX-AJM	Piper PA-28R-200 Cherokee Arrow II		F-BVRC	Not known	Sandtoft	10.07
		28R-7435174	F-ETBI			
SX-BFM*	Piper PA-31-350 Chieftain	31-8052204	N4504J	Not known	(Ringwood)	2.06
				(Fuselage stored unmarked and derelict)		
SX-BLX	Airbus A320-211	029	LZ-BHA	Greece Airways	Glasgow	12.07
			N290SE, VH-HYG, F-WWDF	*(Impounded all white)*		
SX-BNL	Embraer EMB.110P2 Bandeirante	110224	N614KC	Not known	Kemble	7.07
			PT-GMQ	*(EuroAir titles) (Fire dump as "G-FIRE")*		
SX-HCF	Agusta A109A-II	7207	N71PT	Castle Air Charters Ltd	Liskeard Heliport	2.06
			N4263A	*(Cabin stored)*		
SX-122*	Glasflügel H303 Mosquito	94		Skycraft *(Crashed 8. 6.79: stored)*	Spalding	6.05

SLOVENIA
S5-HPC*	Agusta A109A	7129	SL-HPC	Castle Helicopters	Liskeard Heliport	3.07
				(Slovenian Police titles) (Stored)		

TURKEY
TC-ALM*	Boeing 727-230	20431	TC-IKO	Fire Services	East Midlands	9.07
			TC-JUH, TC-ALB, N878UM, D-ABDI *(Used as trainer)*			
TC-MBE	Fokker F.27 Friendship 500	10639	D-ACCT	MNG Airlines	Coventry	11.07
			G-JEAG, D-ADAP, G-JEAG, VH-EWX, PH-EXG *(Stored – wfu)*			

ICELAND
TF-ELL	Boeing 737-210C	20138	N41026	Ardennes Epsilon Ltd	Southend	2.08
			F-GGFI, N4906	*(ATA Brasil c/s: was to become PR-CMA)*		

UKRAINE
UR-VTV	LET L-410UVP Turbolet	810705	CCCP67069	Ukrainian Pilot School	Headcorn	10.07
				(Op Headcorn Parachute Club)		

AUSTRALIA
VH-AHL	Hawker Siddeley HS.748 Series 2/228	1606	A10-606	Clewer Aviation *(In open store)*	Southend	2.08
VH-AMQ	Hawker Siddeley HS.748 Series 2/228	1603	A10-603	Clewer Aviation	Southend	2.08
				"Wg.Cdr.Grant 'Bing' Kelly" (In open store)		
VH-AYS	Hawker Siddeley HS.748 Series 2/228	1608	A10-608	Clewer Aviation *(In open store)*	Southend	2.08
VH-JRQ	Jabiru Aircraft Pty J160-C	069		Jabiru Aircraft Pty Ltd	Southery	9.06
VH-JVL	Piper PA-18-150 Super Cub	18-6615	ZS-JVX	J S Machura	Bagby	2.08
		(C/n reported as 18-6038)	TR-LPC, TN-ABK, F-OBKU			
VH-PSR	Agusta A119 Koala	14037		Silver Rook Ltd	(Douglas, Isle of Man)	6.07

BERMUDA (Current series)
VP-BAA	Boeing 727-51	19123	N727AK	Marbyia Investments	Southend	2.08
			TP-05, TP-01, N477US			
VP-BAB	Boeing 727-76	19254	N682G	Marbyia Investments	Southend	2.08
			N10XY, N8043B, VH-TJD, (N8043B), VH-TJD			
VP-BAM	Bombardier BD-700 Global 5000	9157	C-FBQD	Theberton Inc	London Stansted	1.08
VP-BAT	Boeing 747SP-21	21648	VR-BAT	Worldwide Aircraft Holding (Bermuda)	Bournemouth	1.08
			N148UA, N539PA			
VP-BBW	Boeing 737-7BJ	30076	N737BF	Altitude 41 Ltd	Farnborough and Moscow	12.07
			P4-CZT, VP-CZT, N737MC, D-AXXL, N374MC, N1784B, N1786B *(Operated GAMA Aviation)*			
VP-BBX	Gulfstream Aerospace Gulfstream V-SP	622	N806AC	Altitude 50 Ltd	Farnborough and Moscow	1.08
	(Gulfstream G-550)		N304K, N622GA	*(Operated GAMA Aviation)*		
VP-BCC	Bombardier CL-600-2B19	7717	C-GZSQ	CCC (Bermuda) Inc	Farnborough and Athens	8.07
	(CL-600 Regional Jet)		C-FMNX			
VP-BCI	Bombardier CL-600-2B19	7351	N351BA	CCC (Bermuda) Ltd	Farnborough and Athens	12.07
	(CL-600 Regional Jet)		ZS-OGH, N351EJ, C-FMLF			
VP-BCL	Bombardier CL-600-2C10	10247	N710TS	Global Jet Charters	Farnborough and Athens	1.08
	(CRJ-700 Regional Jet)		C-FHMG	*(Operated Consolidated Contracters)*		
VP-BCT	Rockwell 695B Turbo Commander	96208	N695BE	Control Techniques (Bermuda) Ltd	Welshpool	1.08
			VH-PJC, VH-LTM, N230GA			
VP-BDL	Dassault Falcon 2000	111	F-WWVF	Sioux Corporation	Luton	1.08
VP-BEP	Gulfstream Aerospace Gulfstream V	636	N910V	British Petroleum Plc	Farnborough	1.08
			N556GA			
VP-BGE	Cessna 500 Citation I	500-0287	N287AB	Ross Aviation	Filton	1.08
			PT-WHZ, N31LH, OY-CGO, N57MB, N73LL, N287CC, (N5287J)			
VP-BGN	Gulfstream Aerospace Gulfstream V-SP	5011	N991GA	Rockfield Holdings	Luton	1.08
	(Gulfstream 550)		(N522QS)			
VP-BGO	Bombardier CL-600-2B19	5404	C-GLYO	Sun International Management Ltd	Farnborough	1.08
	(CL-604 Challenger)					
VP-BJA	Bombardier CL-600-2B19	5639	C-FGYI	Jetsteff Aviation	Biggin Hill	1.08
	(CL-604 Challenger)					
VP-BKI	Gulfstream Aerospace Gulfstream IVSP	1255	N934DF	Not known	Farnborough and Moscow	1.08
			VP-BNN, N600PM, N437GA *(Operated GAMA Aviation)*			

Reg	Type	Serial
VP-BKK	Hawker Siddeley HS.125 Series.400A/731	25238
VP-BKQ	Bell 430	49008
VP-BKZ	Gulfstream Aerospace Gulfstream V	602
VP-BLA	Gulfstream Aerospace Gulfstream V-SP (Gulfstream 550)	5024
VP-BLR	Gulfstream Aerospace Gulfstream V-SP (Gulfstream 550)	5059
VP-BLS	Pilatus PC-XII	176
VP-BLW	Gulfstream Aerospace Gulfstream V-SP (Gulfstream 550)	5129
VP-BMP	Dassault Falcon 50EX	345
VP-BMZ	Rockwell Turbo Commander 690D (Built Gulfstream Aerospace)	15033
VP-BNI	Sikorsky S76C	760506
VP-BNK	Hawker 800XP	258625
VP-BNL	Gulfstream Aerospace Gulfstream V	607
VP-BNM	Sikorsky S-76B	760333
VP-BNO	Gulfstream Aerospace Gulfstream V-SP (Gulfstream 550)	5050
VP-BNZ	Boeing 737-7HD	35959
VP-BOW	Bombardier BD-700 Global Express	9141
VP-BPS*	Consolidated 28-5ACF (PBY-5A) Catalina	1997
VP-BUL	Aérospatiale AS.365N2 Dauphin 2	6492
VP-BUS	Gulfstream Aerospace Gulfstream IV	1127
VP-BWR	Boeing 737-79T	29317

CAYMAN ISLANDS

Reg	Type	Serial
VP-CAP	Bombardier CL-600-2B19 (CL-604 Challenger)	5415
VP-CAT	Cessna 501 Citation I	501-0232
VP-CBX	Gulfstream Aerospace Gulfstream V	511
VP-CEB	Bombardier BD.700 Global Express	9083
VP-CED	Cessna 550 Citation Bravo	550-0870
VP-CEO	Bombardier CL-600-2B19 (CL-604 Challenger)	5539
VP-CFF	Gulfstream Aerospace Gulfstream IVSP	1265
VP-CFS	Hawker 800XP	258582
VP-CFT	Bombardier CL-600-2B16 (CL-601-3A Challenger)	5067
VP-CGN	Gulfstream Aerospace Gulfstream V-SP (Gulfstream 550)	5149
VP-CHU	Bombardier CL-600-2B19 (CL-604 Challenger)	5510
VP-CIC	Bombardier CL-600-2B16 (CL-601-3A Challenger)	5011
VP-CJI	Cessna 525 CitationJet	525-0526
VP-CKA	Boeing 727-82	20489
VP-CLA	Gulfstream Aerospace Gulfstream IV	1402
VP-CLV	Bombardier BD-100 Challenger 300	20041
VP-CMD	Dassault Falcon 2000EX/EASy	82
VP-CMR	Gulfstream Aerospace Gulfstream IV	1117
VP-COD	Hawker 850XP	258816
VP-COM	Cessna 500 Citation I	500-318
VP-COP	Bombardier CL-600-2B19 (CL-604 Challenger)	5552
VP-CPT	British Aerospace BAe 125 Series 1000B	259004
VP-CRB	Bombardier Learjet 60	60-125
VP-CRC	Bombardier BD-700 Global Express	9196
VP-CSF	Gulfstream Aerospace Gulfstream IV	1390

Reg	Operator	Location	Date
VR-BKK	Jetsteff Aviation	Bournemouth	5.07
N808V, N125GC, G-TOPF, G-AYER, 9K-ACR, G-AYER			
N62833	Arkesden Aviation	Blackbushe	10.07
N602GV	Dennis Vanguard International (Switchgear)	Birmingham	12.07
N538GA			
N924GA	ISPAT Aviation	Luton	1.08
N959GA	AC Executive Aircraft	Dublin	1.08
	(Operated International Jet Club)		
N176BS	B.L.Schroeder	Fairoaks	1.08
VP-BLS, HB-FSL			
N529GA	Specialised Transportation Bermuda Ltd	Biggin Hill	9.07
F-WWHA	Tower House Consultants Ltd	Jersey and Southampton	11.07
VR-BMZ	Aviatica Trading Co Ltd - Marlborough Fine Art Ltd		
G-MFAL, N49GA, (N5925N)		Fairoaks	1.08
N7686S	Not known	(Weybridge)	4.07
TC-HRT, N728TP			
N305JA	Nebula III Ltd	Farnborough and Moscow	6.07
N625XP	*(Operated GAMA Aviation)*		
N303K	Nebula Ltd	Farnborough	12.07
N559GA	*(Operated GAMA Aviation)*		
N595JS	Nebula II Ltd	Blackbushe	1.08
N595ST, N5AY			
N950GA	Cloud Air Services	Farnborough	12.07
	Dennis Vanguard International (Switchgear)	Birmingham	12.06
C-GAGS	Express Aviation	Luton	1.08
VR-BPS	PS (Bermuda) Ltd	Weston, Dublin	1.08
G-BLSC, C-FMIR, N608FF, CF-MIR, N10023, Bu.46633 *(Stored)*			
N914K	Regal Aviation	London Stansted	11.07
VR-BUS	A E C International Ltd	Farnborough	1.08
VR-BLR, N427GA	*(Op U Schwarzenbach)*		
N1787B	Bel Air Ltd	London Stansted	1.08
N318FX	Thunder Air	Farnborough	1.08
C-GLWT			
VR-CAT	Kestrel Aviation/Aviation Jet	Guernsey	1.07
VR-CHF, N35TL, N853KB, N2616C, (N2616G)			
N511GA	Aravco	Farnborough	1.08
C-GKLF	Silver Arrows SA	Luton	12.07
N700AU, C-GHYT			
N50612	Myair	Manchester	1.08
VP-BDY	Not known	Farnborough	12.07
PP-BIA, N539AB, C-GLXK			
N540W	Meral Holdings Ltd	Farnborough	10.07
N465GA			
XA-JMS	Not known	Farnborough	12.07
(N170SK), N50182			
HB-IUF	Not known	North Weald	1.08
N220TW, 9A-CRT, 9A-CRO, N603CC, C-GLXF			
N649GA	Adams Trust Appointed Fund/Millican Trustees SARL	Luton	12.07
N610SA	Avijet Ltd	Farnborough	12.07
B-7696, N511SC, C-GLWV			
VR-CIC	TGC Aviation Ltd - Fakhar Ltd	Farnborough	1.08
N602UK, N611MH, JA8283, N603CC, C-GLXD			
SP-KCL	Not known	Farnborough	1.08
N526LC			
VR-CKA	Samco Aviation	Southend	2.08
N727FH, N727KS, N46793, CS-TBP *(Operated Executive Air Transport: In open store)*			
N602PL	International Jet Club	Farnborough	8.07
N602PM, N479GA			
N141LJ	Czar Aviation	London Stansted	1.08
C-GZED			
F-WWGS	M Mosely	Biggin Hill	1.08
N105BH	Fitzwilton PLC	Luton	1.08
G-HARF, N1761J			
(N850ZH)	Iceland Foods Ltd	Hawarden	1.08
N74166			
VR-COM	Rapid 3864 Ltd	Biggin Hill	1.08
N944B, N518CC, N5318J			
N552TS	Not known	Farnborough	1.08
ZS-ALT, N552CC, C-GLWR			
VR-CPT	Reno Investments Inc	Biggin Hill	1.08
G-LRBJ, G-5-779	*(Operated Avtec)*		
N60LR	Lisane Ltd	Guernsey	1.08
C-FEBQ	International Jet Club	Luton	1.08
N1874M	MSF Aviation	Luton	1.08
N490GA			

VP-CSN	Cessna 560 Citation Ultra	560-0401	N401CV	Scottish & Newcastle Breweries Ltd	Edinburgh	1.08
			N5197A			
VP-CSP	British Aerospace BAe 125 Series 800B	258210	HB-VMI	Not known	Hawarden	12.07
			G-RAAR, G-5-705			
VP-CXP	Hawker 800XPi	258728	N110DD	Scottish & Newcastle Breweries PLC	Edinburgh	1.08
			N728XP			

BERMUDA (Old series)

VR-BEB*	British Aircraft Corporation One-Eleven 527FK		RP-C1181	European Aviation Ltd	Bournemouth	1.08
		BAC.226	PI-C1181	(Fire Compound - all white and no marks)		

INDIA

VT-EKE *	Westland WG.30-160	021	G-BLPR	Turbine World	Honeycrock Farm, Redhill	12.07
			G-17-17			
VT-EKK *	Westland WG.30-160	025	G-17-13	Turbine World	Honeycrock Farm, Redhil	
VT-EKL *	Westland WG.30-160	028	G-17-14	Turbine World	Honeycrock Farm, Redhil	
VT-EKM *	Westland WG.30-160	027	G-17-15	Turbine World	Honeycrock Farm, Redhil	
VT-EKT *	Westland WG.30-160	035	G-17-23	Turbine World	Honeycrock Farm, Redhil	
VT-EKW *	Westland WG.30-160	038	G-17-26	Turbine World	Honeycrock Farm, Redhil	
VT-EKX *	Westland WG.30-160	039	G-17-27	Turbine World	Honeycrock Farm, Redhil	
	("Nine" WG.30s reported as "under secure lock and key" 12.07 but not sighted - probably including VT-EKK to VT-EKX reported earlier)					
VT-UBG	Hawker Siddeley HS.125 Series F400B	25254	G-5-624	United Breweries (Holdings) Ltd	Hawarden	10.07
			VT-UBG, G-VJAY, G-5-624, G-AYLG, 3D-AVL, G-AYLG (Stored stripped)			

MEXICO

XB-RIY	Boeing- Stearman N2S-3 Kaydet	75-7275	N52093	Not known	Rendcomb	4.04
			BuA 07671	(Stored - composite)		

LATVIA

YL-CBJ*	Yakovlev Yak-52	790404	DOSAAF	Hawarden Air Services ("20 blue")	Hawarden	1.05
YL-LEU*	WSK-PZL Antonov An-2R	1G-165-45	CCCP19731	Hawarden Air Services	Hawarden	10.07
			SP-ZFP, CCCP19731	(As "CCCP-19731") (Dismantled)		
YL-LEV*	WSK-PZL Antonov An-2R	1G-148-29	CCCP07268	Hawarden Air Services	Hawarden	10.07
				(As "CCCP07268")		
YL-LEW*	WSK-PZL Antonov An-2R	1G-182-28	CCCP56471	Hawarden Air Services	Hawarden	10.07
				(As "CCCP56471")		
YL-LEX*	WSK-PZL Antonov An-2R	1G-187-58	CCCP54949	Hawarden Air Services	Hawarden	10.07
				(As "CCCP54949")		
YL-LEY*	WSK-PZL Antonov An-2R	1G-173-11	CCCP40784	Hawarden Air Services	Hawarden	10.07
				(As "CCCP40784")		
YL-LEZ*	WSK-PZL Antonov An-2R	1G-165-47	CCCP19733	Hawarden Air Services	Hawarden	10.07
				(As "CCCP19733")		
YL-LFA*	WSK-PZL Antonov An-2R	1G-172-20	CCCP40748	Hawarden Air Services	Hawarden	10.07
				(As "CCCP40748")		
YL-LFB*	WSK-PZL Antonov An-2R	1G-173-12	CCCP40785	Hawarden Air Services	Hawarden	10.07
				(As "CCCP40785")		
YL-LFC*	WSK-PZL Antonov An-2R	1G-206-44	CCCP17939	Hawarden Air Services	Hawarden	10.07
				(As "CCCP17939")		
YL-LFD*	WSK-PZL Antonov An-2R	1G-172-21	CCCP40749	Hawarden Air Services	Hawarden	10.07
				(As "CCCP40749")		
YL-LHN*	Mil Mi-2	524006025	CCCP20320	Hawarden Air Services	Hawarden	10.07
				(As "CCCP20320")		
YL-LHO*	Mil Mi-2	535025126	CCCP20619	Hawarden Air Services	Hawarden	10.07
				(As "CCCP20619")		
YL-MIG*	Aviatika MAI-890	037		Hawarden Air Services ("37 yellow")	Hawarden	10.07
YL-PAF*	Aero Vodochody L-29S Delfin	591771	Soviet AF 18 red	Hawarden Air Services	Hawarden	10.07
				(Stored dismantled)		
YL-PAG*	Aero Vodochody L-29 Delfin	491273	Soviet AF 51 red	Not known (Stored unmarked)	Breighton	9.07

SERBIA and MONTENEGRO

YU-DLG	UTVA 66	0812 ?	JRV51109	Shuttle Air	Biggin Hill	6.07
YU-HEH	Soko Aérospatiale SA.341G Gazelle	011	JRV12619	Kestrel Shipping	(Bickerstaffe)	11.07
YU-HEI	Soko Aérospatiale SA.341G Gazelle	012	JRV12620	Not known (Honister.com titles)	(Mosser, Cumbria)	10.07
YU-HES	Aérospatiale SA.342J Gazelle	1057	F-GOSO	Not known	(Brookmans Park)	1.08
			EC-EQU, C-GEJE, (N341NA), N9042U, C-FGCE, CF-GCE			
YU-HET	Aérospatiale SA.342 Gazelle	1204	F-GFDG	Not known	Darwen	10.07
			TG-KOV			
YU-HEV	Aérospatiale SA.342J Gazelle	1393	F-GCCZ	Not known	(Republic of Ireland)	6.07
			(KAF-401)			
YU-HEY	Aérospatiale SA.341G Gazelle	1320	F-GEHF	Not known	Stapleford	9.06
			N905XX, N905X, N49508			
YU-MAN	Aérospatiale SA.341G Gazelle	1277	G-WMAN	(J Wightman)	(Ballyclare, County Antrim)	9.07
			ZS-HUR, N4491L, YV-54CP			
YU-PJB	Aérospatiale SA.341G Gazelle	1392	G-BZLA	P J Brown	Redhill	1.08
			N2TV, N49534			
YU-YAB	SOKO G-2A Galeb	Not known	JRV23170	Shuttle Air	Biggin Hill	5.07

NEW ZEALAND

ZK-AGM*	de Havilland DH.83 Fox Moth	"4085"		Not known	Denford Manor, Hungerford	12.03
	(Composite of parts of ZK-ADH c/n 4085 with fuselage produced by de Havilland Technical School apprentices: provenance uncertain as					
	ZK-AGM "destroyed by fire" 27. 4.63 after crash near Wanaka)			(Unmarked fuselage)		
ZK-BMI*	Auster B.8 Agricola Series 1	B.101	(G-ANYG)	D.J.Baker	Carr Farm, Thorney, Newark	1.05
			G-25-3	(Rear fuselage frame - new fin constructed 2004)		

ZK-CCU*	Auster B.8 Agricola	B.105	ZK-BMM	D J Baker	Carr Farm, Thorney, Newark	1.05
	(Composite rebuild by Airepair as c/n AIRP/850 after crash)			*(Centre section stored in container)*		
ZK-GIL	Schempp Hirth Discus 2a	41		B J Flewett	Wycombe Air Park	6.07
ZK-JQK	Pacific Aerospace PAC 750XL	118		Pacific Aerospace Corporation	Hinton in the Hedges	2.08
				(Operated Hinton Skydiving Centre)		
ZK-KAY	Pacific Aerospace PAC 750XL	107		Pacific Aerospace Corporation	Cranfield	2.08
	(Operated North West Parachute Centre: damaged during mid air collision with Luscombe G-AKUI 16.12.07: fuselage only)					
ZK-PCI	Pilatus PC-6/B1-H2	523	HB-FBA	Highland Air Ltd *(Operated Skydive)*	Grindale	8.07

REPUBLIC of SOUTH AFRICA

ZS-MBI	Rockwell Commander 114	14361		F W A Engelbrecht	Oxford	1.08
ZS-MRU	Douglas DC-3	4363	N234Z	Nationwide Charter Pty Ltd	Dunsfold	12.07
			HZ-TA3, N234Z, N1699M, N69D, N1699M, BuAe4703			
				"Spirit of Adventure" (Reserved as TF-AVN)		
ZS-ODJ	Hawker Siddeley HS.748 Series 2A/263			See G-BPNJ - details in SECTION 1, Part 2		
					Blackpool	6.06
ZU-DCX *	Chayair Sycamore Mk 1	SYCA0043		Not known	Kilrush	11.07

NIGERIA

5N-AAN*	British Aerospace BAe 125 Series.F3B/RA		F-GFMP	Newcastle Aviation Academy	Newcastle	11.07
		25125	G-AVAI, LN-NPA, G-AVAI	*(For instructional use)*		
5N-AGV	Grumman G-1159 Gulfstream II	177	N17587	Federal Republic of Nigeria *(Stored)*	Luton	1.08
5N-AJT*	Bell 212	30636	G-BCLG	Bristow Helicopters Ltd	Redhill	1.04
			EP-HBY, VR-BFK, G-BCLG, 9M-ATV, VR-BFK, G-BCLG, N18091 *(Current status unknown)*			
5N-AJU*	Bell 212	30632	G-BFDJ	Bristow Helicopters Ltd	Redhill	1.04
			EP-HCA, VR-BGP, G-BFDJ, 9V-BGE, B-2309, 9V-BGE *(Current status unknown)*			
5N-AJV*	Bell 212	30868	G-BGMK	Bristow Helicopters Ltd	Redhill	1.04
			EP-HCC, VR-BGR, N18096	*(Current status unknown)*		
5N-AJW*	Bell 212	30601	G-BGML	Bristow Helicopters Ltd	Redhill	1.04
			EP-HBL, VR-BEX	*(Current status unknown)*		
5N BDA	Aérospatiale AS365N Dauphin 2	6077	PH-SST	Not known	Aberdeen	10.07
			8P-BHM, PH-SST, EC-EEP, PH-SST, F-WYME *(Stored outside)*			
5N BET	Aérospatiale AS365N Dauphin 2	6087	TJ-DEM	Not known	Aberdeen	10.07
			5N-ATP, PH-SSR, F-ODQG, F-WXFB *(Stored outside)*			
5N-BHN*	Bell 212	32135	G-BJJP	Bristow Helicopters Ltd	Redhill	1.04
		)	N5736D	*(Current status unknown)*		
5N-HHH*	British Aircraft Corporation One-Eleven 401AK		HZ-NB2	Airport Fire Service	Southend	2.08
		BAC.064	N5024	*(For rescue training as "G-FIRE")*		

GHANA

9G-BOB	Westland Wessex HC.2	WA/624	G-HANA	Not known	Honeycrock Farm,Redhil	12.07
			XV729	*(Africa Gateway titles)*		
9G-MKA	Douglas DC-8F-55	45804	N855BC	MK Airlines	Manston	10.07
			CX-BLN, C-GMXP, N855BC, HP-927, PH-DCZ, OY-KTC *(Stored)*			

ZAMBIA

9J-RBC	Piper PA-28-140 Cherokee	28-20693	N11C	N Livni	North Weald	2.08
			N6602W	*"Namakau"*		

SIERRA LEONE

9L-LSA	Sud Aviation SA330L Puma	1506	Chilean Army H261	Not known	Not known	8.06
				"301" (Road running SW @ Horsham 14.8.06)		
9L-LSG	Sud Aviation SA330F Puma	1242	Chilean Army H259	Not known *(Stored in wharehouse)*	(Kirkby)	11.04

MALAYSIA

9M-BCR	Dassault Falcon 20C	35	N809P	Everett Aero	Sproughton	3.06
			(N1777R), N809F, F-WMKG			

PART 2 – OVERSEAS CIVIL REGISTERED AIRCRAFT LOCATED IN MUSEUMS AND PRIVATE COLLECTIONS.

Registration	Type	Construction No	Previous Identity	Owner(Operator)	Location
MUSCAT and OMAN					
A40-AB	Vickers VC-10 Series 1103			See G-ASIX - details in SECTION 4, Part 1	Brooklands
CANADA					
CF-BXO	Vickers-Supermarine 304 Stranraer	CV-209	RCAF 920	RAF Museum *(As "920:QN-" in RCAF c/s)*	Hendon
CF-EPV	Aviation Traders ATL.98 Carvair	10448/8	EI-AMR	56th Fighter Group Museum	Halesworth
			N88819, 42-72343	*(Cockpit section only)*	
CF-EQS	Boeing-Stearman A75N1 (PT-17-BW) Kaydet		75-1728	American Air Museum	Duxford
		41-8169		*(As "217786:25" in USAAF c/s)*	
CF-KCG	Grumman TBM-3E Avenger AS.3	2066	RCN326	American Air Museum	Duxford
			Bu.69327	*(As "46214::X-3" in USN c/s)*	
C-GYZI	Cameron O-77 Balloon (Hot Air)	269		Balloon Preservation Group "Aeolus"	Middle Rasen
GERMANY					
D-CATA	Hawker Sea Fury T.20S	ES.8503	D-FATA	Royal Naval Historic Flight	RNAS Yeovilton
			G-9-30, VZ345	*(As "VZ345": crashed 19.4.85 and stored)*	
D-HGBX	Enstrom F.280	1189	SE-HKX	Aces High Flying Museum *(Gutted pod)*	North Weald
D-HMQV	Bolkow Bö.102 Helitrainer		6216	The Helicopter Museum	Weston-super-Mare
				(Development aircraft)	
D-HOAY	Kamov Ka.26	7001309	DDR-SPY	The Helicopter Museum	Weston-super-Mare
			DM-SPY	*(As "DDR-SPY")*	
D-IFSB	de Havilland DH.104 Dove 6			See G-AMXR - details in SECTION 4, Part 1	
					Salisbury Hall, London Colney
D-Opha	Fire Balloons 3000 Balloon (Hot Air)	057	D-TALCID	Balloon Preservation Group "Talcid"	Middle Rasen
D-Pamgas	Cameron N-90 Balloon (Hot Air)	1288		Balloon Preservation Group "Pamgas"	Middle Rasen
DDR-SPY	Kamov Ka.26			See D-HOAY above	Weston-super-Mare
FRANCE					
F-BDRS	Boeing B-17G-95DL Flying Fortress	--	N68269	American Air Museum "Mary Alice"	Duxford
			32376, NL68269, 44-83735	*(As "231983:IY-G" in 401st BG/615th BS USAAF c/s)*	
F-BGEQ	de Havilland DH.82A Tiger Moth	86305	French AF	Brooklands Museum	Denford Manor, Hungerford
			NL846	*(Stored two-thirds restored)*	
F-BGNR	Vickers 708 Viscount	35	(OY-AFO)	Midland Air Museum	Coventry
			(OY-AFN), F-BGNR		
F-BGNX	de Havilland DH.106 Comet 1XB			See G-AOJT - details in SECTION 4, Part 1	
					Salisbury Hall, London Colney
F-BTGV	Aero Spacelines 377SGT Super Guppy 201 001		N211AS	British Aviation Heritage-Cold War Jets Collection	
				(As "1")	Bruntingthorpe
F-BTRP	Sud-Aviation SA.321F Super Frelon	01	F-WMHC	The Helicopter Museum	Weston-super-Mare
	(Converted from SA.321 c/n 116)		F-BTRP, F-WKQC, F-OCZV, F-RAFR, F-OCMF, F-BMHC, F-WMHC		
				(As "F-OCMF" in Olympic Airways c/s)	
F-WGGM	Thunder & Colt AS-261 HA Airship			See G-BPLD - details in SECTION 1, Part 3	Newbury
F-WQAP	Aérospatiale SA365N Dauphin 2	6001	F-WZJJ	The Helicopter Museum	Weston-super-Mare
F-HMFI	Farman F.40	6799	9204M	RAF Museum	RAF Cosford
	(Modified to F141 Status)			*(At Conservation Centre: no markings)*	
SWITZERLAND					
HB-BOU	Brighton MAB-65 Balloon (Hot Air)			See G-AWJB - details in SECTION 4 Part 2	Newbury
HB-NAV	Beagle B.121 Pup Series 150			See G-AZCM - details in SECTION 4, Part 1	Dover
NORWAY					
LN-BNM	Noorduyn AT-16-ND Harvard IIB	14-639	31-329	RAF Museum	Hendon
			R.Dan AF, FE905, 42-12392	*(As "FE905" in RAF/RCAF c/s)*	
ARGENTINA					
LQ-BLT	MBB BÖ.105-CBS	S.863		North East Aircraft Museum	Usworth, Sunderland
	(Non-airworthy pod is original airframe which crashed 13.6.96: shipped to UK and rebuilt with airframe c/n S.915)				
UNITED STATES					
N7SY	Hunting Percival P.57 Sea Prince			See G-BRFC - details in SECTION 4, Part 1	Bournemouth
N18E	Boeing 247D	1722	NC18E	National Museum of Science & Industry	Wroughton
			NC18, NC13340		
N46EA	Percival P.66 Pembroke C.1	P66/83	8452M	P.G.Vallance Ltd	Charlwood, Surrey
	(Regd with c/n K66-046)		XK885	*(Gatwick Aviation Museum)*	
N47DD	Republic P47D-30-RA Thunderbolt	399-55731	N47DD	Imperial War Museum Collection-American Air Museum	
			Peru AF FAP119, 45-49192	"Oregon's Britannia" *(As "226413:ZU-N")*	Duxford
N51RT	North American F-51D Mustang	122-40949	N555BM	R C Tullius *(Loaned to RAF Museum)*	Hendon
			YV-508CP, N555BM, N4409, N6319T, RCAF9235, 44-74409		
				"The Duck" (As "413317:VF-B in 336FS-4th FG c/s)	
N112WG	Westland WG-30-100	012		The Helicopter Museum	Weston-super-Mare
N114WG	Westland WG-30-100			See G-EFIS - details in SECTION 4, Part 1	Weston-super-Mare
N118WG	Westland WG-30-100	018		The Helicopter Museum	Weston-super-Mare
N196B	North American F-86A-5-NA Sabre	151-43611	48-0242	Midland Air Museum	Coventry
				(As "8242:FU-242" in USAF c/s)	
NC285RS	North American Navion	NAV-4-119		South East Aviation Enthusiasts Group	Dromod,County.Leitrim
				"My Way" (Crashed 11. 6.79:cockpit section and tailplane only)	
N413JB	Cameron O-84 Balloon (Hot Air)	723		Balloon Preservation Group "Autumn Fall"	Middle Rasen

N588NB	CSS-13			See G-BSSY - details in SECTION 4 Part 2	Old Warden
N2138J	English Electric Canberra TT.18		WK126	S D Picatti	Gloucestershire
	(Built A V Roe & Co)	EEA/R3/EA3/6640		(Stored: loaned to Gloucestershire Aviation Collection as "WK126:843")	
N2700	Fairchild C-119G-FA	10689	3C-ABA	Wings Museum	Redhill
			Belgian AF CP-9, 51-2700	(Nose only)	
N3188H	ERCO 415C Ercoupe	3813	NC3188H	AeroVenture	Doncaster
				(Damaged c7.89: fuselage suspended from roof)	
N4519U	Head AX9-118 Balloon (Hot Air)	184		Northern Light Balloon Expeditions	Middle Rasen
				"Ground Hog" (Operated Balloon Preservation Group)	
N4565L	Douglas DC-3-201A	2108	(N3TV)	Aero Venture	Doncaster
			LV-GYP, LV-PCV, N129H, N512, N51D, N80C, NC21744		
N4990T	Thunder Ax7-65B Balloon (Hot Air)	123		British Balloon Museum & Library "Stormy Weather"	Newbury
N5023U	Avian Magnum IX Balloon (Hot Air)	169		Balloon Preservation Group "Tumbleweed"	Middle Rasen
NC5171N	Lockheed 10A Electra			See details in SECTION 4, Part 1	South Kensington
N5237V	Boeing B-17G-95-DL Flying Fortress	32509		RAF Museum	Hendon
			N5237V, Bu.77233, 44-83868	(As "44-83868:N" in 94th BG USAAF c/s)	
N5419	Bristol Scout D replica	01		FAA Museum	RNAS Yeovilton
	(Built Leo Opdycke 1983)			(Frame only)	
N5820T	Westland WG-30-100			See G-BKFD - details in SECTION 4, Part 1	Weston-super-Mare
N5840T	Westland WG-30-100			See G-BKFF - details in SECTION 4, Part 1	Weston-super-Mare
N6526D	North American P-51D-25NA Mustang		RCAF 9289	RAF Museum	RAF Cosford
	(Composite)	122-39874	44-73415	"Little Friend" (As "413573:B6-K" in 361st FS-357th FG USAAF c/s)	
N6699D	Piasecki HUP-3 Retriever	51	RCN 622	Not known	Weston-super-Mare
			USN/51-16622	(Loaned to The Helicopter Museum as "622" in RCN c/s)	
N7614C	North American B-25J/PBJ-1J Mitchell		44-31171	Imperial War Museum/American Air Museum	Duxford
		108-37246		(As "31171" in US Marines c/s)	
N7777G	Lockheed L.749A-79 Constellation			See G-CONI - details in SECTION 4, Part 1	Wroughton
N9050T	Douglas C-47A-10DK Dakota 3			See G-AGYX - details in SECTION 4, Part 1	Hendon
N9115Z	North American TB-25N-20NC Mitchell		(8838M)	RAF Museum	Hendon
		108-32641	44-29366	"Hanover Street" and "Catch 22" (As "34037" in USAAF c/s)	
N12006	Raven S.50A Balloon (Hot Air)	111		R Higbie "Cheers"	Newbury
				(On loan to British Balloon Museum & Library)	
N14234	Handley Page HP.137 Jetstream			See G-BBBV - details in SECTION 4, Part 1	East Fortune
N16676	Fairchild F.24CR-C8F Argus	3101	NC16676	A Langendal	Flixton
				(Frame only) (On loan to Norfolk & Suffolk Aviation Museum)	
N33600	Cessna L-19A-CE Bird Dog	22303	51-11989	Museum of Army Flying	AAC Middle Wallop
				(As "111989" in US Army c/s)	
N66630	Schweizer TG-3A	63	42-52983	Imperial War Museum	Duxford
			(P/i not confirmed)	(As "252983" in USAAC c/s)	
N70457	MD Helicopters MD.600N	RN-057		Aces High	Pinewood Studios
				(Cancelled 10.01: stored as "511" for film)	
N99153	North American T-28C Trojan	252-52	Zaire AF FG-289	W R Montague	Flixton
	(FAA quote c/n 226-93)		Congo AF FA-289, Bu.146289 (Crashed Limoges, France 14.12.77)		
				(On loan to Norfolk & Suffolk Aviation Museum: fuselage only as "146289:2W")	

BELGIUM

OO-BFH	Piccard Gas Balloon	xxxx		National Museum of Science & Industry	Wroughton
				(Gondola only)	
OO-BRM	Thunder Ax7-77 Balloon (Hot Air)	1111		Balloon Preservation Group	Middle Rasen
OO-JAT	Cameron Zero 25 Airship	1407		Balloon Preservation Group	Middle Rasen
OO-SHW	Bell 47H-1			See G-AZYB - details in SECTION 4, Part 1	Weston-super-Mare

DENMARK

OY-BOB	Omega O-80 Balloon (Hot Air)			See G-AWMO - details in SECTION 1, Part 3	Newbury
OY-BOW	Colting 77A Balloon (Hot Air)	77A-014	SE-ZVB	British Balloon Museum & Library "Circus"	Newbury

RUSSIA

RA-01378	Yakovlev Yak-52	833004	DOSAAF 14	Wellesbourne Wartime Museum	Wellesbourne Mountford
	(Composite with c/n 833805/DOSAAF 134 which is now N54GT)				
RA-01641	Antonov An-2R	1G-190-47		Staffordshire Aircraft Restoration Team	Sleap
				"3":(Crashed Milton 2.11.99: forward fuselage preserved)	

SWEDEN

SE-AZB	Cierva C.30A Autogiro	R3/CA.954	K4232	RAF Museum	Hendon
	(Avro 671)			(As "K4232")	

POLAND

SP-SAY	Mil Mi-2	529538125		The Helicopter Museum	Weston-super-Mare

GREECE

SX-OAD	Boeing 747-212B	21684	9V-SQI	Cold War Jets Collection "Olympic Flame"	Bruntingthorpe
				(Carried false marks "G-ASDA" 8.06 for ASDA promotion)	

ICELAND

TF-ABP	Lockheed L.1011-385-100 Tristar	1045	VR-HOG	Aces High Flying Museum	North Weald
			N323EA	(Nose only)	
TF-SHC	Miles M.25 Martinet TT.1	xxxx	MS902	Museum of Berkshire Aviation	Woodley
				(Crashed 18.7.51: on rebuild with Master components)	

AUSTRALIA

VH-ALB	Vickers-Supermarine 228 Seagull V	xxxx	A2-4	RAF Museum (As "A2-4")	Hendon

VH-ASM	Avro 652A Anson I	72960	W2068	RAF Museum (As "W2068::68" in RAF c/s)	Hendon
VH-AYY	Kavanagh D-77 Balloon (Hot Air)	KB136		Balloon Preservation Group "Carlsberg"	Middle Rasen
VH-BRC	Short S.24 Sandringham IV	SH.55C	N158C	Science Museum "Beachcomber"	Southampton
			VP-LVE, N158C, VH-BRC, ZK-AMH, JM715 (On loan to Hall of Aviation) (Ansett c/s)		
"VH-FDT"	de Havilland DHA.3 Drover			See G-APXX –details in SECTION 4, Part 1	Lasham
VH-SNB	de Havilland DH.84A Dragon	2002	VH-ASK	National Museums of Scotland/Museum of Flight	East Fortune
			A34-13		
VH-UQB	de Havilland DH.80A Puss Moth			See G-ABDW - details in SECTION 4, Part 1	East Fortune
VH-UTH	General Aircraft Monospar ST-12	ST12/36		Newark Air Museum	Innsworth
				(On rebuild by Cotswold Aircraft Restoration Group)	
VH-UUP	Short S.16 Scion 1			See G-ACUX - details in SECTION 4, Part 1	Belfast

BERMUDA (New series)

| VP-BDF | Boeing 707-312 | | | See G-AYAG - details in SECTION 4, Part 1 | |
| | | | | | Leitrim, County Leitrim |

FALKLAND ISLANDS

| 'VP-FAK' | de Havilland Canada DHC-3 Otter | 294 | (VP-FAI) | de Havilland Aircraft Heritage Centre | |
| | | | | (As '294') | Salisbury Hall, London Colney |

BERMUDA (Old series)

| VR-BEU | Westland WS-55 Whirlwind 3 | | | See G-ATKV - details in SECTION 4, Part 1 | Weston-super-Mare |

KENYA

| 5Y-SIL | Cameron A-140 Balloon (Hot Air) | | | See G-AZUW - details in SECTION 1, Part 2 | Newbury |

SENEGAL

| 6W-SAF | Douglas C-47A-65-DL | 19074 | F-GEFU | Aces High Flying Museum | Pinewood Studios |
| | | | 42-100611 | (As "42-100766") "Lilly Belle" (Nose section only stored) | |

PART 3 – OVERSEAS-REGISTERED ENTRIES REMOVED FROM 2007 EDITION

Registration	Type	C/n	Reason for removal
GERMANY			
D-EDYQ	Piper PA-32-260 Cherokee Six	32-415	To G-EDYO 3.07
D-EFQR	Robin DR.400-180 Regent	1369	To G-CETB 7.07
D-EGVY	Piper PA-28-161 Warrior III	2842244	To G-CEJD 2.07
D-EGXC	Piper PA-28R-201 Arrow	2844118	To G-FROS 2.07
D-EMLS	Cessna T210L Turbo Centurion	21060094	To G-EMLS 5.07
D-EOMK	Robin DR.400-180 Regent	1267	To G-EOMK 11.07
D-EXCC	Piper PA-46-350P Malibu Mirage	4622085	To N186CB 12.06 – see SECTION 5 Part 1
D-KOOL	Schleicher ASH 25EB 28	25258	Stolen 10.12.07 from Dunstable in trailer. Engine and cockpit area cut off when trailer recovered.
D-MVMM	WDL Fascination	Not known	No reports since 2.03
LIBERIA (Old series)			
EL-AKJ*	Boeing 707-321C	19375	See N2NF below
EL-AKL*	Boeing 707-351C	18922	No reports since 7.03 – broken up ?
ESTONIA			
ES-YLK*	Aero L-29A Delfin	194521	No reports since 8.03
FRANCE			
F-GFLD	Beech C90 King Air	LJ-741	To N30FL 2.07 – see SECTION 5 Part 1
F-GKKI	Avions Mudry CAP.231EX	02	To G-GKKI 1.07
F-GSGZ	Mudry CAP.232	08	To G-GSGZ 11.07
F-PAGD*	Auster V J/1 Autocrat	2218	No reports since 8.02
THAILAND			
HS-TFG	Rockwell 690B Turbo Commander	11482	To G-CECN 7.07
SAUDI ARABIA			
HZ-OFC4	Dassault Falcon 900EX	31	To M-FALC 10.07
ITALY			
I-TERK	British Aerospace BAe.146-200	E2066	Restored as G-CCJP 7.07
I-6351	Tecnam P.92 Echo	543	To EI-DRU 12.06
LUXEMBOURG			
LX-POO *	Raytheon RB390 Premier	RB-18	To N23WA 12.07
LX-TLB	Douglas DC-8-62F	45925	Broken up Manston by 9.06
LITHUANIA			
LY-AFO	Antonov An-2R	1G-211-42	No reports since 4.03
UNITED STATES			
N2NF	Boeing 707-321C	19375	Scrapped Southend 4.07
N7AG	Agusta A109A Mk.II	7436	Sold New York, USA 11.07
N8JX	Extra EA300/S	021	Sold in Austria to Red Bull
N13PF	Piper PA-39 Twin Comanche C/R	39-80	Crashed Vannes, France 25. 8.07
N14EP	SOCATA TB-20 Trinidad GT	2061	To PH-NCW 9.07
N15CK	Maule MX-7-235 Star Rocket	10012C	To Casarrubios, Spain by 6.07
N55CJ	Cessna 525 CitationJet	525-0298	To USA 29.3.07 – sold in Nebraska
N60B	Rockwell 690A Turbo Commander	11172	To N60BM 1.07
N66DN	Bombardier Learjet 45	45-236	To G-LLOD 11.07
N80HC	Beech 58 Baron	TH-672	Sold in the Netherlands 10.07
N85VK	Partenavia P.68C	279	To SE-LYG 5.07
N89WC	Sikorsky S-76B	760311	To N399BH 7.07 – see SECTION 5 Part 1
N90DE	McDonnell Douglas MD.369E	0544E	To N696XX 1.07 – see SECTION 5 Part 1
N90FL	Beech C90 King Air		See F-GFLD above
N90SA	Reims Cessna F172M	F17201402	To G-DUNK 5.07
N90U	Piper PA-46-350P Malibu Mirage	4622106	Sold in Germany 2006
N109AR	Agusta A109A	7390	To G-ZIZZ 11.07
N125ZZ	Hawker 800XP	258630	Returned to USA by 10.07
N160TR	Piper PA-31T Cheyenne II	31T-7920036	Crashed Rieschweiler, Germany 12.2.07
N176AF	Cessna 650 Citation III	650-0176	To N504RP 1.07
N208EC	Cessna 208B Grand Caravan	208B1153	Crashed near Connemara Airport, Ireland 5.7.07
N230FT	Piper PA-28-161 Cadet	2841224	To G-CEJF 11.07
N231CM	Piper PA-46-500TP Malibu Meridian	4697146	To Texas, USA by 9.07
N250JF	Neico Lancair 360	644-320-389FB	Returned to New York(?), USA 2007
N313CF	Bell UH-1H Iroquois	5657	No reports since 10.06. Believed exported to new owners in Washington, USA ?
N325SC	Aérospatiale AS.355F2 Ecureuil 2	5374	To G-PDGT 9.07
N326SC	Aérospatiale AS.355F2 Ecureuil 2	5409	Sold in Ohio, USA 8.07
N328BX	Bombardier CL-600-2B19	5328	To LN-BWG 10.07
N340CD	Cirrus SR22	1354	Sold in California, USA 8.07
N357J	Cessna 525A CitationJet CJ2	525A-0184	To USA 26.4.07 – sold in Georgia
N369SB	Robinson R.44 Raven II	10023	Restored as G-STUS 11.07
N400RG	Boeing 727-22	19149	Returned to USA 6.07

N425HS	Cessna 425 Corsair	425-0044	To M-MANX 8.07
N425RR	Rockwell Commander 690A	11259	To ZS-PXR 9.07
N476D	Pilatus PC-12/45	476	Sold in Georgia, USA 10.07
N500ZW	Hughes 369D	570139D	To ZS-HTX 1.07
N502DW	Mudry CAP.10B	195	To G-CPDW 4.07
N529M	Hawker 800XP	258446	Sold in Michigan, USA 12.07
N555GS	Agusta A109E Power	11112	To M-IDAS 10.07
N565G	SOCATA TB-20 Trinidad	2140	To M-GINZ 7.07
N598MT	Bombardier CL-600-2B19	5502	Sold Nevada, USA 2.07
N614AW	British Aerospace BAe 146 Series 300A	E3132	Scrapped Southend 4.07
N620LH	Aérospatiale AS.355F Twin Squirrel 2	5463	To G-DBOK 10.07
N637CG	Agusta A109C	7619	To G-IFRH 1.08
N634SR	Cirrus SR22-GTS	2020	To G-ZRZZ 3.07
N650DR	Cessna 650 Citation III	650-0181	Sold in New York, USA 11.07
N672P	Cessna 210D Centurion	21058321	To G-OWAN 6.07
N702AR	SOCATA TBM-700	275	Sold in Mississippi 5.07
N709AT	Agusta A109E Power	11017	To G-CRST 4.07 then G-WRBI 11.07
N726RP	Cessna 525A CitationJet CJ2	525A0114	Sold in Colorado, USA 5.07
N737RM	Cessna T182T Turbo Skylane	T18208009	To G-JOBS 9.07
N753RT	Hughes 369D	80-0753D	To ZK-IKL 9.07
N777FC	Dassault Falcon 200	508	Sold in Texas, USA 10.07
N778MA	Cessna 525A CitationJet CJ2	525A-0222	To VT-DOV 3.07
N790BH	Cirrus SR20-G2	1542	To G-EDHO 2.08
N810BW	Cessna 402C	402C0279	Sold in Massachusetts, USA 9.07
N841WS	Hawker 800XP	258674	To G-OJWB 11.07. Replaced by G-450 with same registration
N882	SOCATA TB-20 Trinidad GT	2161	To M-ANIN 8.07
N959JB	Piper PA-23-250 Aztec F	27-7754115	Restored as G-BSVP 4.07
N999BE	Dassault Falcon 2000EX/EASy	032	To N377GM 7.07
N1298C	Cirrus SR20	1315	To G-CMLS 4.07
N2195B	Piper PA-34-200T Seneca II	34-7970006	Written off Gresse-en-Vercours, France 10. 2.07
N2326Y	Beech 58P Baron	TJ-83	Crashed in sea 7 miles off Cherbourg 23. 1.08
N2437B	Cessna 172S	172S8704	To G-ILPY 7.07
N5000S	Beech 58 Baron	TH-2041	To G-CIZZ 1.08
N5050*	Klemm Kl.35D	1979	To D-EQXD 8.07 – see SECTION 5 Part 1
N6088F (1)	Commander Aircraft Commander 114B	14662	To N6088Z 2.07 – see SECTION 5 Part 1
N9606H *	Fairchild M-62A-4 Cornell	T43-4361	To G-CEVL 11.07
N9727G	Cessna 180H	18052227	Sold in Germany 11.07
N32180	Bell 407	53598	To VT-…12.07
N45490	Piper PA-18-150 Super Cub	18-8209023	To N662KK 10.07
N56608	Boeing-Stearman A75N1 Kaydet	75-2888	Sold in Belgium 10.07
N67548	Cessna 152	15281906	To G-CEUS 1.08
N90704	Grumman AA-5A Cheetah	AA5A-0301	To Morocco 12. 5.07

CZECH REPUBLIC

OK-GUA 19	Urban Air UFM-10 Samba	10/10	To EI-DXT 12.07
OK-GUA 24	Urban Air UFM-10 Samba	14/10	To EI-DZE 12.07
OK-GUA 27	Urban Air UFM-10 Samba	20/10	To EI-DXZ 12.07

BELGIUM

| OO-YIO | Robin DR.400-120 Dauphin 2+2 | 2038 | To G-OYIO 2.07 |

DENMARK

OY-JRO	Beech 65-B90 King Air	LJ-327	To G-OJRO 9.07
OY-JRR	de Havilland DHC.2 Turbo Beaver III		Crashed Headcorn 11.3.07
		1632/TB-18	
OY-PBI	LET L-410UVP-E20	871936	Replaced by OY-PBH 2007

NETHERLANDS

| PH-2S5 * | CFM Shadow Series CD | K232 | To EI-DXL 10.07 |

RUSSIA

| RA-44476 | Yakovlev Yak-50 | 853101 | To G- CBPO 1.07 |
| RA-44515 | Yakovlev Yak-52 | 9111515 | No reports since2.03 |

SWEDEN

| SE-FCM | Piper PA-28-180 Cherokee D | 28-4766 | To G-EFCM 11.07 |
| SE-IRI | Cessna A185F Skywagon | 18503177 | To ZK- … 6.07 |

UKRAINE

| UR-67439 | LET L-410UVP Turbolet | 841204 | Replaced at Headcorn in 2007 by UR-VTV |

BERMUDA (New series)

VP-BFC	Cessna 525A CitationJet CJ2	525A0031	To M-XONE 6.07
VP-BIE	Canadair CL-601 Challenger 1A	3016	To N388DB 1.07
VP-BKH	Gulfstream Aerospace Gulfstream IV	1029	To N44ZF 4.07

CAYMAN ISLANDS

VP-CBM	Cessna 550 Citation II	550-0729	To N38NA 7.07
VP-CCO	Cessna 550 Citation II	550-0321	To YU-FCS 2.07
VP-CGE	Cessna 650 Citation VII	650-7077	To N603HD 3.07
VP-CGL	Cessna 550 Citation Bravo	550-0884	To D-CSWM 8.07

VP-CJP	Canadair CL-601-3A Challenger	5022		To N655TH 12.07
VP-CJR	Cessna 550 Citation II	550-0354		To SE-RBD 12.07
VP-CLD	Cessna 550 Citation II	550-0323		To N550LD 2.07 – see SECTION 5 Part 1
VP-CME	Boeing 767-231ER	22567		To Garons 21.12.06. Stored Chateauroux by 5.07
VP-CNF	Cessna 525 CitationJet	525-0153		To G-PWNS 3.07
VP-COU	Bombardier BD-700 Global Express	9084		To EC-KKN 10.07

SERBIA and MONTENEGRO

| YU-HEW | Aérospatiale SA.341G Gazelle | 1491 | G-SKUL | Crashed near Harrogate 26.1.08 |

ISRAEL

| 4X-BJO* | Bell 206L-1 Long Ranger | 45361 | | Sold in USA – crated out from Southend 8.07 |

SECTION 6

PART 1 – BRITISH GLIDING ASSOCIATION

The BGA glider register follows the same format as the main aircraft registers in this book, except that each glider can have up to four different identities.
Column 1 shows either the G- registration in the case of gliders which are registered with the CAA or the three-letter Trigraph (Tg) issued by the BGA.
Column 2 shows the BGA number - the Certificate of Airworthiness (CofA) number issued by the British Gliding Association. This is the primary reference and can usually be found on the fin or rear fuselage in small characters.
Column 3 shows the markings actually carried on the glider, which is usually either the trigraph or a BGA-allocated competition number. Occasionally ex-military or civil markings are carried. - an index to these marks is in Part 2 below and a dash indicates that no code is worn.

The official BGA list is extended by including non-current gliders and those with recently lapsed CofAs for which no cancellation details are known but which may survive. We include the complete expiry dates for CofA and the complete date for the first issue where known. Where a BGA CofA number has been reserved for future use, the reservation date is shown prefixed by the letter 'R'. Most entries with a CofA expiry before the year 2003 have been deleted if there is no news on their fate or continued existence. The non-current gliders include examples known to be in storage or under restoration in the ownership of members of the Vintage Glider Club *(www.vintagegliderclub.org)*. Similar entries, where a reason for the non-renewal of CofA is known, that are accident details or sale abroad, have been retained but these will be removed in the next edition. There is no official record held of bases, so information in the "(Unconfirmed) Base" column is largely related to owners' addresses and feedback we receive from readers, as well as information given on gliding club websites and in the BGA magazine "Sailplane & Gliding".

The continuing influence of the European Aviation Safety Agency (EASA) means major cha nges to UK glider certification this year. Until September 2007 only newly imported gliders had to be registered, but now the majority of existing gliders are having to be issued with G- registrations and an EASA CofA. This process is due to be completed for the UK glider fleet by September 2008. The BGA are currently issuing these aircraft with interim CofAs expiring on 28 September 2008 so that they can still fly pending transition to the EASA system. The only exceptions to the process are a number of vintage designs which are exempted under the EASA Regulation 1592/2002 "New Annex II" list dated 12 September 2007 and should remain unregistered and under BGA control.

The BGA register has been updated by Richard Cawsey. Special thanks are due to the BGA for their support, in particular to their Chief Executive Pete Stratten, and to Technical Administrator Terry Eato. Information is current to February 2008.

Reg/Tg	BGA	Code	Type	Construction No	Previous Identity	Date	Owner(*Operator*)	(Unconfirmed) Base	CofA Expy
-	162	-	Manuel Willow Wren	-		9.34	Brooklands Museum	Brooklands	*
AAA	231	-	Abbott-Baynes Scud II	215B	G-ALOT	8.35	L P Woodage	Dunstable	1. 6.06
			(Completed Slingsby)		BGA 231				
-	236	-	Slingsby T.6 Kirby Kite	27A	G-ALUD	14.11.35	P Underwood	Eaton Bray	*
					BGA 236, BGA 222		*(For rebuild 2007)*		
AAX	251	-	Slingsby T.6 Kirby Kite	227A	(ex RAF)	30. 3.36	R Boyd	Rivar Hill	29. 5.08
					BGA 251				
ABG	260	-	Schweyer Rhönsperber	35/22		4. 5.36	F K Russell tr Rhönsperber Syndicate	Dunstable	18. 7.08
-	266	-	Slingsby T.1 Falcon I Waterglider	237A		29. 5.36	Windermere Steamboats & Museum	Windermere	*
ABZ	277	-	Grunau Baby II	-	RAFGSA 270	25. 8.36	J R Furnell	Portmoak	18. 6.08
			(Built F.Coleman)		BGA 277, G-ALKU, BGA 277				
G-ALJR	283	ACF	Abbott-Baynes Scud III	2	G-ALJR	18.12.36	L. P Woodage	Dunstable	4. 3.06
					BGA 283				
ACH	285	E	Slingsby T.6 Kirby Kite	247A	G-ALNH	30.12.36	Museum of Army Flying	AAC Middle Wallop	5.99*
					BGA 285		*(As "G285" in 1 GTS RAF c/s)*		
ADJ	310	-	Slingsby T.6 Kirby Kite	258B	RAFGSA 182	9. 2.37	A M Maufe	Tibenham	26. 8.08
					VD218, BGA 310		*(Rebuilt 1982 with components ex BGA 327 c/n 285A)*		
AEM	337	-	Schleicher Rhönbussard	620	RAFGSA 265	25. 4.38	C Wills and S White	Lasham	14. 9.08
					BGA 337, G-ALME, BGA 337, TK710, BGA 337				
-	370		Grunau Baby II	1		11.10.38	N Scully	Saltby	8. 6.77*
			(Built S Hobson)				*(Stored 2003)*		
AGE	378	900	Slingsby T.12 Gull	312A	G-ALPJ	14. 9.38	M L Beach	Halton	16. 8.04
					BGA 378				
AHC	400	F	Slingsby T.6 Kirby Kite	336A	VD165	6. 5.39	P J Underwood	(Eaton Bray)	21. 8.01
			(Uses wings from Special T.6 c/n 355A)		BGA 400		*(In 1 GTS RAF c/s)*		
AHU	416	-	Scott Viking I	114	G-ALRD	19. 6.39	W den Baars	Haamstede, Netherlands	28. 5.07
					BGA 416				
AJW	442	AJW	Slingsby T.8 Tutor	MHL/RC/8	G-ALMX	8.46	M Hodgson	Dunstable	14. 8.98
			(Built by Martin Hearn Ltd)		BGA 442				
-	448	-	Jacobs Schweyer Weihe	000348	G-ALJW	6.47	D Phillips	(Snitterfield)	*
					BGA 448, LO+WQ		*(Damaged Thun, Switzerland 20. 7.79)*		
AKD	449		DFS Olympia-Meise	227	LF+VO	7.47	T Bolt *(For restoration)*	(Plymouth)	5.85*
AKW	466		Slingsby T.8 Tutor	MHL/RT/7		11.46	D Kitchen	Tibenham	6. 7.96
-	470	-	Short Nimbus	S.1312		.47	Ulster Folk & Transport Museum	Holywood, Belfast	8.75*
							(Stored 2004)		
ALR	485	-	Slingsby T.8 Tutor	513	G-ALPE	11.46	R van Aalst	Asperden, Germany	26. 7.08
					BGA 485				
ALW	490	G-ALRK	Hütter H.17	-	G-ALRK	13. 8.48	N I Newton	Wycombe Air Park	13. 5.08
			(Built D.Campbell)		BGA 490				
-	491		Hawkridge Dagling	08471		2.47	N H Ponsford *(Stored 2006)*	(Selby)	*
-	493	-	Hawkridge Nacelle Dagling	10471		7.47	P J Underwood	Eaton Bray	*
			(Also allotted BAPC.81)				*(Last known on rebuild 2004)*		
AMK	503	AMK	EoN AP.5 Olympia 2	EoN/O/003	G-ALJP	5.47	R Maxfield	(Burn)	28. 5.95
					BGA 503		*(For restoration 2.06)*		
AMM	505	AMM	EoN AP.5 Olympia 2	EoN/O/006	G-ALJV	5.47	J R Furnell	Portmoak	14. 4.08
					BGA 505				
AMR	509	AMR	EoN AP.5 Olympia 2	EoN/O/011	G-ALLA	5.47	K J Nurcombe	Husbands Bosworth	23. 7.08
					BGA 509				
-	521		Slingsby T.26 Kite 2	MHL/RK.5		.	Not known *(Stored)*	Chalfont St.Giles	20. 6.80
ANW	538	ANW	EoN AP.5 Olympia 2	EoN/O/040	G-ALNE	7.47	Midland Air Museum	Baginton	9. 3.04
					BGA 538				

Reg	BGA	Trigraph	Type	c/n	History	Date	Owner	Location	Date
APC	544	APC	EoN AP.5 Olympia 2	EoN/O/046	G-ALMJ BGA 544	9.47	R D Bryce-Smith	Gransden Lodge	23. 4.08
-	562	-	EoN AP.5 Olympia 2	EoN/O/037	G-ALJZ BGA 562	7.47	Museum of Berkshire Aviation (Crashed 20. 7.58; wreck on display 8.04)	Woodley	*
APZ	565	-	Slingsby T.25 Gull 4 (Rebuilt with Kite 2 fuselage no MHL/210)	505	G-ALPB BGA 565	.	A Fidler	Crowland	27. 6.08
AQN	578	AQN	Grunau Baby IIB (Built by Hawkridge)	G.3348	G-ALSO BGA 578	27. 7.48	G D Pullen	Lasham	11. 6.08
-	580		EoN AP.7 Primary	EoN/P/003	G-ALPS BGA 580	.	Shuttleworth Collection (Under restoration 2006)	Old Warden	*
-	588		EoN AP.7 Primary	EoN/P/011		.	N H Ponsford (Stored 2006)	(Selby)	*
-	589	G-ALMN	EoN AP.7 Primary	EoN/P/012	G-ALMN BGA 589	19. 5.48	Museum of Berkshire Aviation (Stored 2006)	Woodley	4.51*
G-ALLF	599	ARK / G-ALLF	Slingsby T.30A Prefect	548	PH-1 BGA 599, G-ALLF, BGA 599	.	K M Fresson	Parham	15. 8.04
ARM	601	ARM	Slingsby T.21B	543	G-ALKX BGA 601	8.48	South London Gliding Centre	Kenley	23. 8.05
ASB	614	ASB	Slingsby T.21B	549	RNGSA BGA 614, G-ALLT, BGA 614	9.48	R A Robertson and Partners	Talgarth	7. 8.08
ASC	615		Grunau Baby IIB (Built by Hawkridge)	G-4848		2.49	M Diller (Under restoration 2006)	Burgheim, Germany	13. 8.94
ASN	625		Slingsby T.30B Prefect	567	G-ALPC BGA 625	1.49	J Kosak (Stored 2007)	Culdrose	24. 5.99
-	628	-	EoN AP.8 Baby	EoN/B/004	(BGA 645) G-ALRU, BGA 628	3.49	R Kent (Crashed Bardney 28. 5.71; on rebuild 9.07)	Shoreham	*
AST	629	G-ALRH	EoN AP.8 Baby	EoN/B/005	G-ALRH BGA 629	3.49	EoN Baby Syndicate "Liver Bird" (Last known extant 2000)	Chipping	1. 9.96
ATH	643	-	Slingsby T.15 Gull III	364A	TJ711	7.11.49	Brooklands Museum	Brooklands	20. 6.04
ATL	646	-	Slingsby T.21B	536	G-ALKS	6.50	G Markham (Stored 3.07)	Enstone	12. 7.96
ATR	651	-	Slingsby T.13 Petrel	361A	EI-101 IGA 101, IAC 101, BGA 651, G-ALPP	7.50	G P Saw	Wycombe Air Park	29. 4.08
ATV	655	OK-8592	Zlin 24 Krajanek	101	G-ALMP OK-8592	4.50	J M Dredge	Wycombe Air Park	5. 5.07
AUD	663	663	Slingsby T.26 Kite 2B	727		1.52	F G Bradney and E Mason	Lasham	22. 4.08
AUF	665	-	Slingsby T.21B	653		4.51	R.Harvey (Stored 8.06)	Kemble	4.86*
AUG	666	AUG	Slingsby T.21B	643		15. 6.51	Cambridge Gliding Club	Gransden Lodge	8. 7.08
AUP	673	N21	Slingsby T.21B	636		26. 7.51	T21 Group	Lee-on-Solent	3.12.08
AUU	678	AUU	EoN AP.5 Olympia 2	EoN/O/076		10. 4.52	B Lee	Parham	15. 7.04
AUW	680	-	Avia 40P	117		5. 9.52	F Ragot (Reserved as F-AZQP 7.07)	St.Auban, France	5. 8.07
AVA	684	-	Abbott-Baynes Scud III	3		10. 1.53	E A Hull	Dunstable	27. 5.08
AVB	685	AVB	Slingsby T.34A Sky	644	G-644	10. 2.53	R Moyse	Lasham	5. 3.07
AVC	686	AVC	Slingsby T.34A Sky	670		3.53	P J Teagle "Kinder Scout II"	Camphill	5. 8.07
AVF	689	AVF	Slingsby T.26 Kite 2A	728	RAFGSA 294 BGA 689	8. 4.53	C P Raine	Thame	29. 8.08
AVL	694		Slingsby T.34A Sky	671	G-671	15. 5.53	M P Wakem	Long Mynd	6. 8.08
AVQ	698	G46	Slingsby T.34A Sky	645	G-645	9. 9.53	L M Middleton "Gertie"	Easterton	16. 9.08
AVT	701	-	Slingsby T.30B Prefect	857		14. 2.54	K Schickling	Aschaffenburg, Germany	19. 5.08
AWD	711	AWD	Slingsby T.21B	950		30. 9.54	D B Brown tr T.21 Syndicate	Chipping	19. 9.04
AWS	724	AWS	Slingsby T.41 Skylark 2S	997		31. 7.56	D MCornelius	Dunstable	29. 8.06
AWT	725		Slingsby T.37 Skylark	879		23. 6.55	P FWoodcock (For restoration 2006)	(South Yorkshire)	25. 6.89
AWU	726	AWU	EoN AP.5 Olympia 2	EoN/O/082		20. 5.55	M J Riley	Sackville Lodge, Riseley	11. 5.08
AWX	729	AWX	Slingsby T.41 Skylark 2	946		27. 1.56	A G Leach (Stored 6.07)	Bembridge	24. 4.01
AWZ	731	AWZ	Slingsby T.7 Cadet	SSK/FF169	RA847	8. 1.57	R Moyse	Lasham	27. 4.08
AXB	733	AXB	Slingsby T.41 Skylark 2	926		24. 2.56	A L Shaw	Lyveden	30. 6.02
AXD	735	AXD	Slingsby T.43 Skylark 3	1014		.	A P Stacey (Badly damaged Aston Down 11. 7.03; new owner 2.08)	RAF Keevil	5. 6.04
AXE	736	AXE	Slingsby T.43 Skylark 3	1029		27. 3.56	C J Bushell (Noted 2003)	Snitterfield	21. 8.01
AXJ	740	AXJ	Slingsby T.42A Eagle 2	994		.56	A Kendall	Pocklington	19. 1.08
AXL	742	AXL	Slingsby T.43 Skylark 3	1030		7. 6.56	D J Mills and Partners	Kingston Deverill	19. 1.08
AXP	745	AXP	Slingsby T.41 Skylark 2	949		5. 4.56	I McHardy	Not known	16. 3.08
AXV	751	-	Slingsby T.26 Kite 2A	-		16. 4.56	R.Wilgoss	Wycombe Air Park	25. 8.08
AYD	759	AYD	Slingsby T.41 Skylark 2	1048		21. 7.56	R Milligan (Under restoration 6.07)	Falgunzeon	11. 9.03
AYF	761	AYF	Slingsby T.43 Skylark 3B	1058		8. 9.56	D.Chisholm (Noted 9.07)	Rufforth	28. 8.05
AYH	763	AYH	Slingsby T.43 Skylark 3B	1066		11.10.56	A.D.Griffiths	Upwood	19. 6.08
-	765	-	Slingsby T.21B	1080		31.10.56	Not known (Fuselage for use in repair of BGA 3324 @ 8.04)	AAC Wattisham	4.70*
AYY	778	33	Slingsby T.41 Skylark 2C	1073		1. 2.57	A.C.Cummins	Llantisilio	8. 6.08
AZA	780	AZA	Slingsby T.42B Eagle 3	1085	RNGSA 2-08 BGA 780	18. 4.57	Not known (Extant 2003)	Not known	23. 7.01
AZC	782	782	Slingsby T.21B	1096		27. 5.57	M Schima	Wiener Neustadt West, Austria	19. 5.08
-	791	VM684	Slingsby T.8 Tutor	-	VM684	20. 1.57	Hooton Park Trust (On loan from P Storrar)	Hooton Park	2.71*
AZP	793		Slingsby T.41 Skylark 2	999		13. 1.57	R Milligan (Under restoration 6.07)	Falgunzeon	13. 8.97
AZQ	794	VM687	Slingsby T.8 Tutor	-	VM687	.57	D.Gibbs	Lee-on-Solent	22. 4.06
AZR	795	AZR	EoN AP.5 Olympia 2	EoN/O/101		3. 6.58	Not known (Under restoration)	Syerston	28. 7.95
AZX	801	AZX	Slingsby T.41 Skylark 2	995	BGA 1909 AGA 4, BGA 801	9. 4.57	B.J.Griffin	Saltby	23. 4.08
AZY	802		Slingsby T.41 Skylark 2 (Mod.)	963		16. 4.57	A J Jackson (Stored 2006)	(Burn)	29. 6.97
BAA	804	BAA	Slingsby T.8 Tutor	931	XE761, VM589	10. 5.57	A P Stacey (Under restoration 5.06) (Cadet TX.1 "BGA 804 ex VM589" is at Midland Air Museum, Coventry)	RAF Keevil	9. 3.97
BAC	806	BAC	Slingsby T.43 Skylark 3B	1101	RNGSA CU19 BGA 806	17. 7.57	F K Hutchinson	Husbands Bosworth	24. 4.04

BAL	813	BAL	Slingsby T.43 Skylark 3B	1111		12.11.57	D.A Wilson	Milfield	13. 5.06
BAM	814	BAM	Slingsby T.41 Skylark 2	1108		1. 2.58	R.G.Boyton	Wormingford	2. 6.02
BAN	815	BAN	Slingsby T.30B Prefect	1120		3. 1.58	J.S.Allison	Bicester	3. 7.07
BAV	822	BAV	Slingsby T.41 Skylark 2B	1113		22. 2.58	M.H.Simms	Shipdham	16. 4.02
BAW	823	BAW	Slingsby T.43 Skylark 3B	1126		14. 2.58	R.Joy and Partner	Halesland	16. 3.07
BAY	825	BAY	Slingsby T.42B Eagle 3	1116		28. 3.58	M.Lodge (Stored 9.07)	Ringmer	15. 8.00
BAZ	826	BAZ	Slingsby T.41 Skylark 2	1112		26. 3.58	A Wilson	Sutton Bank	16. 6.08
BBB	828	BBB	Slingsby T.42B Eagle 3	1118		11. 4.58	I.K.Mitchell	North Hill	22.10.03
-	830		Slingsby T.42B Eagle 3	1119		21. 6.58	D Williams and M Lodge (Stored 9.07)	Ringmer	7.79*
BBG	833	BBG	Slingsby T.8 Tutor	-	VW535	3. 9.57	J Bennett	Upwood	26. 7.07
BBH	834	BBH	EoN Olympia 2	EoN/O/041	(BGA 539)	22. 8.57	L P Woodage	Dunstable	17. 4.08
BBQ	841	BBQ	Slingsby T.42B Eagle 3	1115		14. 5.58	L Adamson and Partners	Milfield	3.10.05
BBT	844	BBT	Slingsby T.43 Skylark 3B	1134	RAFGSA 234 BGA 844	6. 6.58	J P Gilbert	Wormingford	4. 5.08
BBU	845	BBU	Slingsby T.41 Skylark 2B	1135		13. 6.58	D A Bullock	Bicester	12.10.08
-	852	TS291	Slingsby T.8 Tutor	SSK/FF250	TS291	2. 7.58	Museum of Flight	East Fortune	12.66*
BCF	856		Slingsby T.21B (Built Leighton Park School)	1		10.10.58	P Underwood	Eaton Bray	5. 81*
			(Blown over Haddenham 14. 6.80: to Poland 10.05)						
BCH	858	BCH	Slingsby T.8 Tutor	SSK/FF489	VM547	30. 9.58	K.van Rooy	Weelde, Belgium	24. 1.05
BCP	864	BCP	Slingsby T.43 Skylark 3B	1140		1.11.58	J Gilbert (Stored 11.07)	(Essex)	13. 4.02
BCS	867	549	Slingsby T.43 Skylark 3B	1144		5.12.58	A P Stacey	RAF Keevil	16. 4.05
BCU	869	2	Slingsby T.21B	1148		1.59	C Mioni	Thionville-Yutz, France	5.86*
			(Under restoration 10.07)						
BCV	870	155	Slingsby T.43 Skylark 3B	1195		6. 4.59	J Turner (Kent Vintage Glider Group)	Challock	15. 9.07
BCW	871	BCW	Slingsby T.43 Skylark 3B	1147		12. 3.59	G Walker	Parham	28. 2.07
BCY	873	T45	Slingsby T.45 Swallow	1198		10. 4.59	T Wilkinson (Stored 7.06)	Sackville Lodge, Riseley	19. 5.05
BDA	875	BDA	Slingsby T.21B	1205	AGA 7 BGA 875	22. 6.59	J F Forster	Venlo, Netherlands	26.10.08
BDF	880	BDF	Slingsby T.42B Eagle 3	1213		28. 9.59	D.C.Phillips	Snitterfield	14. 8.04
BDR	890	BDR	Slingsby T.45 Swallow	1243		11. 6.60	J.M.Turner	Waldershare Park	19. 6.08
BDW	895		Slingsby T.8 Tutor	-	VM637	30. 4.59	Newark Air Museum	Winthorpe	6.93
BDX	896	BDX	Slingsby T.41 Skylark 2 (Built C Hurst)	CH.095/1		10. 6.59	H D Maddams	Ridgewell	8. 8.08
BEA	899	BEA	Slingsby T.41 Skylark 2	1194		1. 7.59	M.L.Ryan	RAF Keevil	26. 8.06
-	902	-	Slingsby T.12 Gull	Not known		15. 5.59	Museum of Flight	East Fortune	*
BEF	904	-	Slingsby T.8 Tutor	SSK/FF934		29. 10.59	J Szladowski (Stored 6.06)	Camphill	2. 5.96
BEL	909	BEL	EoN AP.5 Olympia 2B	EoN/O/126		21.12.59	J.G.Gilbert and Partners	Wormingford	11. 5.05
BEM	910	BEM	Slingsby T.45 Swallow	1221		5. 2.60	J M Muir	Halesland	11. 5.08
BET	916		Slingsby T.43 Skylark 3B	1227		9. 3.60	A C.Robertson and Partners (Stored 7.05)	Feshiebridge	31. 5.98
BEX	920	G91	Slingsby T.43 Skylark 3F	1229		8. 4.60	S Barber	Rivar Hill	27. 9.03
BEY	921	BEY	Slingsby T.45 Swallow	1230		14. 4.60	G.P.Hayes	Kenley	30. 7.08
BEZ	922	BEZ	Slingsby T.43 Skylark 3F	1232		29. 4.60	T.L.Cook	Feshiebridge	6. 5.08
BFC	925	BFC	Slingsby T.43 Skylark 3F	1239		20. 5.60	Strathclyde Gliding Club	Strathaven	9. 4.03
BFE	927	BFE	Slingsby T.43 Skylark 3F	1244		24. 6.60	I Dunkley	New Zealand	4. 6.03
BFG	929	BFG	Slingsby T.43 Skylark 3F	1245		8. 7.60	T.J.Wilkinson	Sackville Lodge, Riseley	14. 6.06
BFP	936	D1	Schleicher K7	702		30. 5.60	Dartmoor Gliding Society (Stored 2005)	Brentor	28. 4.96
BFY	945	BFY	Slingsby T.21B	1251	RAFGGA 515 RAFGSA 286, BGA 945	9.60	M Wood	Sutton Bank	11. 6.08
BGB	948	-	Slingsby T.21B (Robin EC-44PM)	1274	RAFGSA 282 BGA 948	11.60	J Elliott and H Bosworth	Strubby	25. 8.05
BGD	950	BGD	Slingsby T.43 Skylark 3F	1276		26.11.60	Essex University Gliding Club	AAC Wattisham	21. 5.05
BGL	957	BGL	Slingsby T.43 Skylark 3F	1296		1. 3.61	P.A Rose	Walney Island	9. 3.08
BGP	960	R83	Slingsby T.21B	1297	RAFGSA 283 BGA 960	1.61	K.Ueyama	Tocumwal, Australia	21. 5.06
			(Cancelled 5.12.06; to VH-GUC 12.06)						
BGR	962	BGR	EoN AP.5 Olympia 2B	EoN/O/124		4. 6.60	M.H.Gagg	RAF Cosford	5. 1.05
BHC	973	BHC	EoN AP.5 Olympia 2B	EoN/O/138		9. 1.61	M.Pedwell	Bidford	1. 5.06
BHQ	985	BHQ	Slingsby T.43 Skylark 3F	1304		15. 4.61	T.Wiseman	Andreas	14. 5.08
BHT	988	BHT	Slingsby T.43 Skylark 3F	1306		19. 4.61	A P Stacey	RAF Keevil	17. 8.07
BJB	996	BJB	Slingsby T.43 Skylark 3F (Built Jones, Pentelow and Saint)	SSK/JPS/1		19. 4.61	C J Ferrier	Falgunzeon	19. 1.08
BJC	997	BJC	EoN AP.5 Olympia 2B	EoN/O/135		15. 4.61	P.J.Devey	Lyveden	29. 9.04
G-DBJD	998	BJD	SZD-9bis Bocian 1D	P-391		6. 5.61	G.Pullen (Bocian Syndicate)	Lasham	20. 3.08
BJF	1000	BJF	Slingsby T.21B	1309		16. 6.61	Sedbergh Syndicate	Wormingford	31. 5.08
BJJ	1003	-	Slingsby T.45 Swallow	1310		23. 6.61	A P Stacey (Stored 5.06)	RAF Keevil	8.82*
BJK	1004	BJK	Slingsby T.43 Skylark 3F	1311		14. 7.61	R.Skinner	Wormingford	7. 8.08
BJP	1008	BJP	Slingsby T.45 Swallow	1316		4. 9.61	G Williams	Seighford	5. 6.07
BJQ	1009	BJQ	Slingsby T.49A Capstan	1314		23. 2.62	Bidford Gliding Centre	Bidford	1. 6.08
-	1013	113	Slingsby T.43 Skylark 3G	1320		12.61	J McIver (For restoration 1.07)	(Dumfries)	7.77*
BJV	1014	-	Slingsby T.21B	556	SE-SHK	1.62	Museum of Flight (Stored)	East Fortune	*
BJY	1017	BJY	Slingsby T.45 Swallow	1324		1. 3.62	D.A Wiseman	Andreas	14. 5.08
BJZ	1018		Slingsby T.45 Swallow	1325		17. 3.62	J.P.Marshall (Stored 2005)	North Connel	20.11.96
BKA	1019	BKA	Slingsby T.50 Skylark 4	1326	EI-117 BGA 1019	28. 5.62	Mendip Gliding Club	Halesland	31.10.08
BKC	1021	BKC	Jacobs Schweyer Weihe (Built AB Flygindustri)	231	SE-SNE Fv.8312	15. 4.61	B.Briggs	RAF Cranwell	19. 8.07
BKE	1023	BKE	Slingsby T.43 Skylark 3F (Built C Ross)	1715/CR/1		13. 7.61	A Honnor	Eyres Field	8. 7.07
BKH	1026	BKH	Schleicher Ka 2B	1028		26. 7.61	T J Wilkinson	Sackville Lodge, Riseley	7. 4.08
BKJ	1027	BKJ / 270	Schleicher Ka 6CR	565	9G-AAR	7.61	Vale of White Horse Gliding Centre Sandhill Farm, Shrivenham		24. 3.06
BKL	1029	BKL	EoN AP.5 Olympia 2B	EoN/O/134		18. 6.61	J E Herring	Lasham	21. 5.08
BKN	1031	BKN	Schleicher K7	1091		23. 9.61	P.Hibbard	Wormingford	4. 8.04
BKS	1035	BKS	EoN AP.5 Olympia 2B	EoN/O/144		11. 11.61	N W Woodward	Wycombe Air Park	8. 5.08

BGA	No	Reg	Type	c/n	Prev ID	Date	Owner	Location	Date
BKU	1037	BKU	EoN AP.5 Olympia 2B	EoN/O/153		1.62	D.N.MacKay	Aboyne	14. 5.08
BKW	1039	BKW	Schleicher Ka 6 Rhönsegler	295	OH-RSA	10.9. 62	P.J.Montgomery *(Under restoration)*	(W.Sussex)	2. 5.01
BKX	1040	BKX	EoN AP.5 Olympia 2B	EoN/O/148		19. 3.62	D.J.Allibone	Eyres Field	5.11.06
BLA	1043	BLA	Slingsby T.50 Skylark 4	1331		5. 5.62	I.Russell	Milfield	17. 2.08
BLE	1047	BLE	Slingsby T.50 Skylark 4	1335	RNGSA 1-228 BGA 1047	28. 6.62	S.Frank	Easterton	3. 4.08
BLH	1050	BLH	Slingsby T.50 Skylark 4	1338	RAFGSA BGA 1050	10. 7.62	D Wakefield	Rufforth	14. 6.08
BLJ	1051	BLJ	EoN AP.6 Olympia 419X	EoN/4/009		10. 1.62	I D Walton and Syndicate *"Big Bird"*	Long Mynd	25. 9.07
BLK	1052	67	EoN AP.6 Olympia 419X	EoN/4/007	G-APSX	13. 3.62	G T Bowes *"Wild Goose"*	Seighford	16. 9.08
BLL	1053	BLL	Slingsby T.34A Sky	821	PH-203	6. 4.62	H Stubbe	Lemelerveld, Netherlands	16. 7.07
BLN	1055	BLN	EoN AP.5 Olympia 2B	EoN/O/152		7. 3.62	M.R.Derwent	RAF Cranwell	1. 4.08
BLP	1056	BLP	EoN AP.5 Olympia 2B	EoN/O/149		7. 3.62	R.E.Wooller and Partners	Chipping	14. 4.08
BLQ	1057	BLQ	EoN AP.5 Olympia 2 Special	EoN/O/042	RAFGSA 145 (BGA 540)	27. 7.62	K.Wood and Partners	Winthorpe	12. 7.06
BLS	1059		EoN AP.5 Olympia 2B *(EoN rebuild of BGA 897 [EoN/O/128])*	EoN/O/151		14. 7.62	R Andrews	Long Mynd	7. 7.07
BLU	1061	BLU	Slingsby T.45 Swallow	1340		27. 7.62	J.M.Brookes	Strubby	26. 4.08
BLW	1063	BLW	Slingsby T.50 Skylark 4	1342		8.62	S.R.A Trusler	RAF Weston-on-the-Green	20. 6.08
BLZ	1066	1066	Slingsby T.50 Skylark 4	1346		26.11.62	M S Radice	Kingston Deverill	24. 3.08
BMM	1078	BMM	SZD-9bis Bocian 1D	P-397		10.62	E.W.Burgess *(Stored 4.07)*	Currock Hill	19. 6.05
BMQ	1081	BMQ	Slingsby T.21B	1351		16.11.62	W.E.Masterton	Blenheim, Jamaica	25. 1.04
BMU	1085		Slingsby T.21B (T) *(Rotax 503)*	1355	9G-ABD BGA 1085	9.11.62	D.Woolerton and Partners *"Spruce Goose" (Fuselage stored 2.07)*	North Coates	27. 9.97
BMW	1087	BMW	Slingsby T.50 Skylark 4	1357		1. 1.63	M.Williams	Lasham	5. 2.08
BMX	1088	739	Slingsby T.50 Skylark 4	1358	RAFGSA 308 BGA 1088	4. 1.63	S Stanwix *(739 Syndicate)*	Eyres Field	28. 5.08
BMY	1089	163	Slingsby T.50 Skylark 4	1361		26. 1.63	M H Simms *(Stored 2006)*	Shipdham	7. 4.98
BNA	1091	-	Shenstone Harbinger Mk.2	1		12.12.62	S.Edyvean *(Noted 7.07)*	Bicester	7. 5.04
BNC	1093	BNC	Jacobs Schweyer Weihe *(Built AB Kockums Flygindustri)*	1	SE-SHU	11. 3.63	K.S.Green	Lasham	22. 9.08
BND	1094	BND	Schleicher Ka 6CR	1157		12. 3.63	E Richards	Strubby	25. 5.08
BNE	1095	BNE	Slingsby T.50 Skylark 4	1375		7. 4.63	D.Kershaw	Lasham	19. 1.08
BNH	1098	BNH	Schleicher Ka 6CR	6115		28. 3.63	Bath, Wilts and North Dorset Gliding Club	Kingston Deverill	29. 7.08
BNK	1100	BNK	Slingsby T.50 Skylark 4	1362		2. 2.63	E.D.Weekes and Partners	RAF Weston-on-the-Green	26. 4.08
BNM	1102	"BMN"	Slingsby T.50 Skylark 4	1367		28. 2.63	D.Hertzberg	Ridgewell	7. 9.07
BNN	1103	BNN	Slingsby T.50 Skylark 4	1366		22. 2.63	A.A Jenkins	Bicester	8. 6.08
BNP	1104	653	Slingsby T.50 Skylark 4	1368		8. 3.63	A R Worters	North Connel	22. 7.01
BNR	1106	BNR	Slingsby T.49B Capstan	1370		8.63	A Walford	Gransden Lodge	20. 4.08
BNS	1107	XS652	Slingsby T.45 Swallow	1373	XS652 BGA 1107	20. 3.63	P.N.Ling and Partner	Rufforth	2. 8.08
BNU	1109		Slingsby T.45 Swallow	1377		5.63	P.Cammish *(Stored 2.06)*	North Connel	15. 6.02
BPA	1115	BPA	Slingsby T.50 Skylark 4	1383		5.63	A P Stacey	RAF Keevil	3. 1.06
							(Overshot field landing 9. 6.05 Halesland; under restoration 2007)		
BPC	1117	BPC	Slingsby T.50 Skylark 4	1389		19. 7.63	J L.Grayer and Partner	Ringmer	8. 8.08
BPD	1118	N55	Slingsby T.49B Capstan	1390		22. 7.63	J G Kosak	RNAS Culdrose	29. 7.08
BPE	1119	BPE	Slingsby T.50 Skylark 4	1391		6.63	M.H.Simms	Shipdham	25. 5.03
BPG	1121	741	Slingsby T.50 Skylark 4	1393		7.63	P Orchard	Long Mynd	16. 4.08
BPK	1124	BPK	Slingsby T.50 Skylark 4	1381		22. 6.63	Y Marom	Crowland	10.11.06
BPN	1127	BPN	Standard Austria	003	OE-0496	6.63	R.K.Avery and Partners	Eaglescott	10. 1.06
BPS	1131	BPS	Slingsby T.49B Capstan	1399		9.63	Deeside Capstan Group	Aboyne	8. 6.08
BPT	1132		Slingsby T.49B Capstan	1400		10.63	Not known *(Fuselage stored 2004)*	Bicester	11. 2.95
BPU	1133		Slingsby T.49B Capstan	1402		11.63	J Hailey tr Capstan Syndicate *(Under repair 2004)*	Dunstable	17. 3.98
BPV	1134	BPV	Slingsby T.49B Capstan	1404		20.12.63	G.L.Barrett	RAF Weston-on-the-Green	15. 4.08
BPW	1135	BPW	Slingsby T.49B Capstan	1408		1.64	Ulster Gliding Club	Bellarena	26. 1.06
BPX	1136	859	Slingsby T.45 Swallow	1397	XS859 BGA 1136	1. 1.64	N R Antcliffe	Pocklington	14. 1.08
BPZ	1138	BPZ	Slingsby T.50 Skylark 4	1406		3.64	T Smith (Stored 2006)	Swindon	10. 7.00
BQE	1143	RA905	Slingsby T.7 Cadet	-	RAFGSA 273 RA905	8.63	Trenchard Museum	RAF Halton	14. 3.00
BQF	1144	1	Slingsby T.21B	1168	XN189	10.63	C Mioni *(Under restoration 10.07)*	Thionville-Yutz, France	13. 4.02
-	1147		DFS Kranich II *(Built Schleicher)*	821	RAFGSA 215	11.63	M.C.Russell *(To Bad Tolz Vintage Gliding Club, Germany for restoration 7.02)*	Bishops Stortford	11.66*
BQP	1152	BQP	Slingsby T.30B Prefect	646	RAFGSA 159	2.64	R J Brimfield	Dunstable	2. 6.08
BQQ	1153	-	EoN AP.5 Olympia 2B *(Rebuilt 1993 using wings from BGA 678)*	EoN/O/121	RAFGSA 244	8. 2.64	I D Smith *"Dopey"*	Nympsfield	23. 8.08
BQT	1156	BQT	EoN AP.10 460 Series 1	EoN/S/007	BGA 2666 AGA 6, BGA 1156	26. 1.64	Museum of Science & Industry	Manchester	18. 4.97
BQU	1157	BQU	Schleicher K7	7141	RNGSA AR66 BGA 1157	15. 4.64	W Hoekstra	Haamstede, Netherlands	31. 3.04
BRA	1163	BRA	Slingsby T.49B Capstan	1417		4.64	I.Pattingale	RAF Odiham	29. 5.04
BRB	1164	T51	Slingsby T.51 Dart 15	1423	RAFGSA 334 BGA 1164	27. 4.64	M.Sansom	North Hill	16. 6.08
BRC	1165	BRC	Slingsby T.45 Swallow 1	1407		1. 5.64	J.R.Smalley	Kirton in Lindsey	20. 4.06
BRE	1167	BRE	Slingsby T.45 Swallow 2	1415		8. 5.64	A.Swannack and Partners *(Stored 9.07)*	Shipdham	19. 5.01
BRG	1169	-	Slingsby T.45 Swallow	1410		5.64	A.W.F.Edwards	Gransden Lodge	2.11.07
BRJ	1171	426	EoN AP.10 460 Series 1	EoN/S/011		18. 3.64	T J Wilkinson	Sackville Lodge, Riseley	24. 5.08
G-APWL	1172	243	EoN AP.10 460 Series 1A	EoN/S/001	G-APWL BGA 1172, G-APWL, RAFGSA 268, G-APWL	26. 4.64	J W Williams	Eaglescott	26. 4.00

BRM	1174	BRM	Schleicher K7	776	D-4635		5.64	D.S.Driver	Lleweni Parc	21.10.07
BRQ	1177	BRQ	EoN AP.10 460 Series 1C	EoN/S/003	G-ARFU		6.64	J.Steel and Partners (Stored 2004)	Falgunzeon	4. 8.96
BRT	1180	BRT	Slingsby T.51 Dart 15	1430			19. 6.64	C.Logue	RAF Marham	8. 7.07
BRU	1181	BRU	Slingsby T.51 Dart 15	1429			11. 6.64	M.H.Simms	Shipdham	3. 4.07
BRW	1183	BRW	Slingsby T.49B Capstan	1413			25. 6.64	D A Sinclair	Lasham	30. 1.08
G-DBRY	1185	BRY	Slingsby T.51 Dart 15	1434			7.64	D J Knights	Kirton in Lindsey	18. 6.08
G-DBSA	1187	BSA	Slingsby T.51 Dart 15	1405			7.64	G Burton	Seighford	21. 4.08
BSC	1189	BSC	Slingsby T.50 Skylark 4	1422			25. 8.64	P.Pain	Bidford	20. 3.08
BSE	1191	BSE	Slingsby T.49B Capstan	1414			11. 9.64	Windrushers Gliding Club	Bicester	28. 9.08
BSG	1193	BSG	Slingsby T.50 Skylark 4	1436			9.64	North Wales Gliding Club	Llantisilio	23. 6.07
BSH	1194	BSH	Slingsby T.50 Skylark 4	1444			3.11.64	J M Verrill	Lee-on-Solent	19. 9.07
BSK	1196	BSK	Slingsby T.49B Capstan	1418			10.64	S.Whitaker	Parham	16. 4.08
BSL	1197	BSL	Slingsby T.51 Dart 17	1445			10.64	C.J.Owles	Tibenham	11. 9.07
BSM	1198	597	Slingsby T.51 Dart 15	1439			10.64	D.Tait	Cross Hayes	29. 5.06
BSQ	1201	463	EoN AP.10 460 Series 1	EoN/S/014			1. 5.64	K.G.Ashford	Husbands Bosworth	10. 5.05
BSR	1202	BSR	Slingsby T.50 Skylark 4	1443			17.12.64	A J Young	Challock	15.10.08
BSS	1203	T49	Slingsby T.49B Capstan	1449			12.64	M Tomlinson	Talgarth	20. 8.08
BST	1204	J13	Slingsby T.49B Capstan	1451			1.65	B.Bullimore and J.N.Gale	Gransden Lodge	5.11.05
								(To N42727 12.07)		
BSW	1207	BSW	Slingsby T.51 Dart 15	1459			19. 2.65	B L Owen	Tibenham	25. 9.08
BSZ	1210	BSZ	Slingsby T.50 Skylark 4	1460			26. 4.65	G P Hayes	Kenley	17. 8.08
BTA	1211	BTA	Slingsby T.45 Swallow	1473			6.65	A P Stacey	RAF Keevil	7. 5.06
BTE	1215	BTE	Slingsby T.21B	557	OH-KSA		1.65	J.Assmann	Borkenberge, Germany	5. 9.07
					SE-SHL			"Buttercup"		
BTG	1217	BTG	EoN AP.10 460 Series 1	EoN/S/024			25. 2.65	C Shepherd	RAF Weston-on-the-Green	17. 5.08
BTH	1218	BTH	Slingsby T.21B	JHB/2			3.65	P Gilmore	Aston Down	14. 9.08
			(Built J.Hulme: restored 1995 with wings from BGA 3238)							
BTJ	1219	BTJ	Schleicher Ka 6CR	6367			3.65	D.Keith	Rivar Hill	17. 7.08
BTK	1220	BTK	Slingsby T.50 Skylark 4	1364	SE-SZW		3.65	J.M.Hall	Long Mynd	27. 8.03
BTM	1222	211	Schleicher Ka 6CR	6174			25. 3.65	G.A.Childs	Strubby	24. 3.07
BTN	1223	BTN	EoN AP.10 460 Series 1	EoN/S/022	AGA 15		21. 3.65	S.C.Thompson	Parham	21. 8.08
					BGA 1223					
BTQ	1225	BTQ	EoN AP.10 460 Series 1	EoN/S/029			4. 4.65	D.Street	Burn	19. 7.08
BTV	1230	BTV	Jacobs Schweyer Weihe	000358	RAFGGA		7. 5.65	I Dunkley	New Zealand	11. 8.07
BUC	1237	A23	Slingsby T.49B Capstan	1472			27. 6.65	P R Redshaw	Walney Island	10. 2.08
BUE	1239	BUE	Slingsby T.50 Skylark 4	1468			7.65	G J Jones	Seighford	1. 5.08
G-DBUF	1240	366	Slingsby T.51 Dart 17R	1469			7.65	K W Clarke and N G Harrison	Chipping	28. 9.08
BUR	1249	BUR	Slingsby T.49B Capstan	1482			11.65	R J Playle	Edgehill	13. 6.08
BUT	1251	BUT	Slingsby T.43 Skylark 3F	VRT.1			7.65	I.Bannister tr Sky Syndicate	Chipping	5. 6.08
			(Built V and R Tull)							
BUU	1252	BUU	EoN Baby	EoN/B/047	RAFGSA 255		9. 4.65	R H Short	Lyveden	21. 7.08
BUV	1253	BUV	EoN AP.10 460 Series 1	EoN/S/030			7.65	T.Edwards	Camphill	1.11.07
BUW	1254	BUW	Slingsby T.21B	Not known	RAFGSA 242		8.65	J.N.Wardle "Lucy"	Lasham	9. 8.06
G-DBUZ	1257	BUZ	Schleicher Ka 6CR	6418			14. 8.65	R.Leacroft	Lyveden	24. 5.08
G-DBVB	1259	BVB	Schleicher K7	7230			11. 9.65	Dartmoor Gliding Society	Brentor	30. 4.08
			(Modified to ASK 13 standard)							
BVE	1262	61	Slingsby T.51 Dart 17R	1483			11.65	K.Hale and Partner	Sandhill Farm, Shrivenham	31. 3.08
BVF	1263	BVF	Slingsby T.45 Swallow	1481			12.11.65	J S Morgan (Stored 1.08)	Pershore	13. 8.03
G-DBVH	1265	BVH	Slingsby T.51 Dart 17R	1485			10.12.65	D.J.Simpson	Halesland	2. 4.08
BVJ	1266	BVJ	Slingsby T.51 Dart 17R	1486			1.66	A P Stacey	RAF Keevil	14. 6.07
								(Hit hedge on field landing,Chedworth, Gloucestershire.5. 5.07; for rebuild)		
BVL	1268	404	Slingsby T.51 Dart 15	1487			1.66	D Stabler (Noted 2007)	Shipdham	16. 8.99
BVM	1269	150	Slingsby T.51 Dart 17R	1492			1.66	N.H.Ponsford (Stored 2006)	(Selby)	5.89*
BVN	1270	BVN	EoN AP.10 460 Series 1	EoN/S/023			3.65	C Heide	North Hill	19. 8.08
G-DBVR	1273	BVR	Schleicher Ka 6CR	6441			5.10.65	R C Beecroft and Partners	Lasham	8. 4.08
BVW	1278		EoN AP.6 Olympia 403	EoN/4/001	RAFGSA 306		8.65	Not known	Lasham	29. 5.01
					G-APEW			(Noted 2007)		
BVX	1279	BVX	Schleicher Ka 6CR	6439			10.65	R Lynch	Kingston Deverill	2. 9.08
BVY	1280	BVY	LET L-13 Blanik	173121			17.10.65	D G Coats	Portmoak	3. 2.08
G-DBVZ	1281	BVZ	Schleicher Ka 6CR	6446			29.10.65	L Blair and Partners	Bellarena	11.11.07
BWB	1283	B96	EoN AP.10 460 Series 1	EoN/S/036			28.11.65	S Metcalfe	Tibenham	17.12.03
BWC	1284	BWC	Schleicher Ka 6CR	6449			15.12.65	R Maksymowicz	Snitterfield	3. 6.08
BWE	1286	BWE	EoN AP.10 460 Series 1	EoN/S/035			30.12.65	C.Hughes	Talgarth	14. 9.08
BWG	1288	465	EoN AP.10 465 Series 2	EoN/S/038			7.12.65	R Kent (Preserved 2006)	Shoreham	27. 4.97
G-DBWJ	1290	317	Slingsby T.51 Dart 17R	1495			10. 2.66	M F Defendi	Wormingford	20. 8.07
BWK	1291		Slingsby T.45 Swallow	1493			8. 2.66	K.Hubbard and Partners	Brentor	5. 6.03
G-DBWM	1293	182	Slingsby T.51 Dart 17R	1500			4.66	P L Poole	Kenley	20. 8.07
G-DBWP	1295	17R	Slingsby T.51 Dart 17R	1501			3.66	R.Johnson	Talgarth	21. 4.08
G-DBWO	1296	BWO	Slingsby T.51 Dart 15	1505			3.66	G.Winch	Wormingford	14. 8.08
G-DBWS	1298	517	Slingsby T.51 Dart 17R	1502			4.66	R D Broome	Hinton-in-the-Hedges	28. 9.08
BWT	1299	BWT	Slingsby T.51 Dart 15R	1508			4.66	D White	Aboyne	23. 9.08
BWU	1300	BWU	EoN AP.10 460 Series 1	EoN/S/034			21. 1.66	S H Gibson	Ridgewell	16. 4.08
BWX	1303	BWX	EoN AP.5 Olympia 2B	101			2. 2.66	P Bendrey and M Deittert	Aston Down	19. 7.05
			(Built from spares)							
BXB	1307		EoN AP.10 460 Series 1	EoN/S/040			3.66	I Pattingale (Stored 2007)	(RAF Odiham)	30.10.02
BXE	1310	BXE	Slingsby T.51 Dart 15R	1509			5.66	S.Briggs	Currock Hill	9. 2.08
BXG	1312	686	Slingsby T.51 Dart 17R	1512			5.66	J.M.Whelan	Saltby	25. 5.08
G-DBXH	1313	BXH	Slingsby T.51 Dart 17R	1516			6.66	C.Rodwell	Husbands Bosworth	15. 5.08
BXK	1315		Slingsby T.21B	1510			6.66	Not known	Rufforth	*
								(Damaged Falgunzeon 18. 5.80)		
BXL	1316	121	Slingsby T.51 Dart 17R	1517			24. 6.66	W.R.Longstaff and Partner	Feshiebridge	27. 9.04
BXM	1317	9A	Slingsby T.51 Dart 17R	1521			6. 7.66	P.R.Davie	Dunstable	20. 7.08
BXP	1319		Slingsby T.45 Swallow 2	1522			19. 7.66	Carlton Moor Gliding Club	Carlton Moor	10. 6.06
BXR	1321		LET L-13 Blanik	173301	G-ATPX		5.66	Not known (Stored 2006)	Shipdham	12.92

BXT	1323	BXT	Schleicher Ka 6CR	6492		30. 4.66	C Knowles	Dunstable	6. 7.08
BXW	1326	BXW	LET L-13 Blanik	173305	RAFGSA 337	16. 6.66	R Chapman	Bidford	6. 3.07
					BGA 1326, G-ATRB				
BXY	1328	BXY	EoN AP.10 460 Series 1	EoN/S/042		20. 6.66	G.K.Stanford	Brentor	26. 7.03
BYA	1330	BYA	Slingsby T.51 Dart 17R	1518		7.66	G Ward	Not known	18. 5.05
							(Damaged Easterton 15. 8.04; under restoration 2006)		
BYC	1332	BYC	Slingsby T.51 Dart 17R	1526		16. 8.66	N A Jaffray	Snitterfield	21. 2.08
BYE	1334	643	EoN AP.10 460 Series 1	EoN/S/044		22. 9.66	G Bartle	Ringmer	7. 7.08
BYG	1336	225	Slingsby T.51 Dart 17R	1535	RAFGSA	11.66	W.T.Emery	Rufforth	13. 6.05
					BGA 1336				
G-DBYL	1340	BYL	Schleicher Ka 6CR	6517		17. 7.66	Channel Gliding Club	Waldershare Park	2. 2.08
G-DBYM	1341	558	Schleicher Ka 6CR	6518	RAFGSA 381	7.66	K.S.Smith	Wormingford	2. 4.08
					BGA 1341				
-	1346		Slingsby T.31B	Not known	RAFGSA 297	8.66	Not known *(Noted 6.07)*	Halfpenny Green	1.79*
G-DBYU	1348	350	Schleicher Ka 6CR	6525	XW640	9.66	G B Sutton	Seighford	28. 3.08
					BGA 1348				
G-DBYX	1351	BYX	Schleicher Ka 6E	4055		12.66	J R Dent	Chipping	9. 4.08
BZA	1354	BZA	Slingsby T.21B	1162	RAFGSA 318	28.11.66	Bicester T21 Syndicate	Bicester	14. 6.08
					XN183				
BZB	1355	BZB	EoN AP.10 460 Series 1	EoN/S/047		10.66	D.C.Ratcliffe Syndicate	Parham	21. 5.04
BZC	1356	BZC	Slingsby T.51 Dart 17R	1563		2.67	A.N.Ely	Strubby	28. 3.04
BZF	1359	311	Slingsby T.51 Dart 17R	1570		5. 4.67	D C Charles	Ridgewell	22. 5.08
BZG	1360	BZG	Slingsby T.49B Capstan	1581		28. 4.67	Dorset Gliding Club	Eyres Field	7. 7.08
BZH	1361	406	Slingsby T.51 Dart 17R	1580		20. 4.67	G Polkinghorne *(Stored 8.07)*	North Hill	19.12.00
BZL	1364	BZL	Slingsby T.45 Swallow	1596		7.67	Cairngorm Swallow Syndicate	Feshiebridge	14. 8.00
							(Stored 6.06)		
BZM	1365	BZM	Slingsby T.45 Swallow	1597		7.67	F.Webster *(Stored 7.06)*	Easterton	4. 6.05
BZP	1367	F4	SZD-24-4A Foka 4	W-301		1.67	J H Atherton	Edgehill	3. 6.06
BZV	1373	BZV	EoN AP.10 460 Series 1	EoN/S/046		15. 2.67	P J Chaisty	Usk	4. 8.08
BZX	1375	BZX	Schleicher Ka 6CR	6571		3.67	Leeds University Gliding Club	AAC Dishforth	7.10.07
BZY	1376	BZY	Slingsby T.31B	SSK/FF1817	BGA 1175	3.67	D Bramwell tr The Blue Brick Syndicate	Thame	4. 5.08
			(Rebuild of BGA 1175)						
G-DBZZ	1377	77	SZD-24-4A Foka 4	W-308		3.67	A P Benbow	Portmoak	1. 6.08
G-HCAC	1380	994	Schleicher Ka 6E	4054		3.67	M.Burridge	Crowland	16. 3.08
G-DCAE	1381	578	Schleicher Ka 6E	4076		8. 4.67	N.Rolfe	Seighford	20. 3.08
CAF	1382	CAF	EoN AP.5 Olympia 2B	EoN/O/131	RAFGSA 254	5. 4.67	B.Kozuh	Ljubljana, Slovenia	17. 7.05
G-DCAG	1383	715	Schleicher Ka 6E	4080		4.67	H G Williams and Partners	Snitterfield	30. 4.08
CAK	1386	117	EoN AP.5 Olympia 2B	EoN/O/122	RAFGSA 246	1. 4.67	K.Ueyama	Tocumwal, Australia	9. 8.06
							(Cancelled 5.12.06; to VH-GVO 12.06)		
CAN	1389	CAN	EoN AP.10 460 Series 1	EoN/S/050		3.67	B.Kozuh	Ljubljana, Slovenia	14. 8.08
CAQ	1391	812	Schempp-Hirth SHK	37		3.67	M Entwistle	(Llandrindod Wells)	17. 8.08
CAR	1392	422	Schempp-Hirth SHK-1	40		4.67	P.Gentil	Aston Down	26. 5.08
G-DCAS	1393	372	Schleicher Ka 6E	4029	RAFGSA 372	5.67	R.F.Tindall	Gransden Lodge	22. 8.02
CAT	1394	CAT	EoN AP.10 460 Series 1	EoN/S/051		5.67	D.C.Phillips and Partners	Snitterfield	9. 7.08
CAV	1396	CAV	Schleicher ASK 13	13015		5.67	M.F.Cuming	Edgehill	18. 9.08
CAX	1398	CAX	Slingsby T.45 Swallow	1598		7.67	G.M.Hicks *(Stored 2005)*	Waldershare Park	17. 8.02
G-DCAZ	1400	500	Slingsby T.51 Dart 17WR	1611		7.68	J.S.Halford	Eyres Field	7. 6.08
G-DCBA	1401	679	Slingsby T.51 Dart 17WR	1612		7.68	M Parsons	Snitterfield	2. 1.08
CBK	1410	-	Grunau Baby III	-	RAFGSA 378	5. 9.67	P Bedford	Dromod, County Leitrim	4.83*
			(Built Sfg.Schaffin)		D-4676		*(Preserved at Cavan and Leitrim Railway 6.07)*		
CBM	1412	CBM	Schleicher Ka 6CR	6607		7.67	F Ballard	Nympsfield	9. 6.05
CBR	1416	CBR	Avionautica RIO M.100S	044		8. 7.67	G Viglione	Rattlesden	28. 7.06
G-DCBW	1421	CBW	Schleicher ASK 13	13034		8.67	Stratford on Avon Gliding Club	Snitterfield	28. 9.08
CBY	1423	475	Schleicher Ka 6CR	960	RAFGSA 322	10.67	G Martin	Talgarth	10. 7.08
					D-3222				
-	1424	-	Slingsby T.8 Tutor	SSK/FF27	RAFGSA 214	10.67	P Bedford	Dromod, County Leitrim	4.78*
					RA877		*(Preserved at Cavan and Leitrim Railway 6.07)*		
CCA	1425	CCA	Schleicher Ka 6E	4126		10.67	R K Forrest	Feshiebridge	21. 4.08
G-DCCB	1426	CCB	Schempp-Hirth SHK-1	52		7.67	R M Johnson and Partners	Milfield	17. 9.08
CCC	1427	CCC	Schleicher ASK 13	13035	RAFGSA R83	11.67	Shenington Gliding Club	Edgehill	28. 9.08
					BGA 1427				
CCD	1428	373	Schleicher Ka 6E	4127		12.67	M.H.Phelps	Edgehill	18. 9.06
G-DCCE	1429	CCE	Schleicher ASK 13	13047		12.67	Oxford Gliding Club	RAF Weston-on-the-Green	3. 3.08
							(See BGA 1501)		
G-DCCF	1430	CCF	Schleicher ASK 13	13042		12.67	Norfolk Gliding Club	Tibenham	17. 3.08
CCG	1431	CCG	Schleicher Ka 6E	4125		31.12.67	C Hughes	Nympsfield	14. 9.08
CCJ	1433	878	Schleicher Ka 6CR	6145	RAFGSA 323	10.67	S Badby	Edgehill	4. 6.05
G-DCCL	1435	47	Schleicher Ka 6E	4129		3.68	J Tayler and Partners	Sutton Bank	30. 3.08
CCM	1436	CCM	Schleicher ASK 13	13053		2.68	Burn Gliding Club	Burn	11.12.07
G-DCCP	1438	L99	Schleicher ASK 13	13052		2.68	G D Pullen and Partners	Lasham	12. 3.08
G-DCCR	1440	CCR	Schleicher Ka 6E	4149		2.68	A.Shaw	Bicester	1. 4.08
CCS	1441	CCS	Slingsby T.41 Skylark 2	1008	PH-230	3.68	Nottingham University Gliding Club	RAF Cranwell	1. 3.08
G-DCCT	1442	CCT	Schleicher ASK 13	13057		3.68	Stratford on Avon Gliding Club	Snitterfield	15. 2.08
G-DCCU	1443	CCU	Schleicher Ka 6E	4122		3.68	J L Hasker	RAF Keevil	11. 4.08
G-DCCV	1444	CCV	Schleicher Ka 6E	4160		3.68	T M Bell and C H Page	Kingston Deverill	17. 8.08
G-DCCW	1445	CCW	Schleicher ASK 13	13051		3.68	Needwood Forest Gliding Club	Cross Hayes	17. 2.08
G-DCCX	1446	CCX	Schleicher ASK 13	13054		3.68	Trent Valley Gliding Club	Kirton in Lindsey	30. 5.08
G-DCCY	1447	CCY	Schleicher ASK 13	13050		3.68	Devon & Somerset Gliding Club	North Hill	29. 3.08
CCZ	1448	CCZ	Schleicher ASK 13	13070		3.68	Windrushers Gliding Club	Bicester	29. 8.08
CDA	1449	CDA	Schleicher Ka 6E	4136		3.68	CDA Syndicate	Aboyne	10. 9.08
G-ECDB	1450	CDB	Schleicher Ka 6E	4137		3.68	C W R Neve	Currock Hill	7. 5.08
CDD	1452	CDD	Schleicher Ka 6E	4165		26. 3.68	C D Sterritt	Lasham	1. 9.06
G-DCDF	1454	683	Schleicher Ka 6E	4162		3.68	K G Reid and Partners	Rivar Hill	3. 7.08
CDG	1455	CDG	FFA Diamant 18	35		19. 5.68	S Cashin	Kilkenny, Ireland	11. 5.08

G-DCDH	1456	619	Schempp-Hirth Cirrus	10		4.68	A.K.Moore	Edgehill	25. 3.08
CDK	1458	CDK	Schleicher K 8B	8747		5.68	Burn Gliding Club	Burn	5. 2.07
-	1461	-	EoN AP.7 Primary	Not known		30. 5.68	Norfolk & Suffolk Aviation Museum	Flixton	29. 5.69
CDQ	1463		Grunau Baby III	R161		14. 6.68	Not known (Under repair 2000)	Not known	14. 9.91
CDR	1464	CDR	Scheibe Bergfalke III	5625		8.68	N.M Neil	Eaglescott	2. 4.04
CDU	1467	PH	Schempp-Hirth SHK-1	V.1	D-8441	15. 3.68	P Hibbard	Wormingford	26. 3.08
G-DCDW	1469	CDW	FFA Diamant 18	033		31. 8.68	D Chapman	Llantisilio	28. 8.08
CDX	1470	CDX	SZD-30 Pirat	W-392		4. 6.68	Newark Air Museum	Winthorpe	6. 1.07
CDZ	1472	CDZ	Schleicher Ka 6E	4177		5.68	J R Minnis	Wormingford	27. 7.08
CEA	1473	CEA	Schempp-Hirth Cirrus	21	XZ405 BGA 1473, D-8437	8.68	M Greenwood	Long Mynd	11. 5.08
G-DCEB	1474	CEB	SZD-9bis Bocian 1E	P-433		5.68	Bath, Wilts and North Dorset Gliding Club	Kingston Deverill	1. 8.08
CEC	1475	18	Schempp-Hirth Cirrus	22		7.68	C.R.Ellis	Long Mynd	23. 9.08
CEH	1480	CEH	Wassmer WA-22 Super Javelot	68	F-OTAN-C6 F-CCLU	7.68	N.A.Mills	Wycombe Air Park	19. 8.08
CEK	1482		Slingsby T.21B (T) (Fuji-Robin EC-34PM s/n 82-00391)	1151	RAFGSA 369 XN147	19. 7.68	D.Woolerton (Stored 2.07)	North Coates	7. 5.05
CEL	1483	JD	Schleicher Ka 6E	4174		2. 8.68	Essex & Suffolk Gliding Club	Wormingford	27. 9.08
G-DCEM	1484	CEM	Schleicher Ka 6E	4212		2. 8.68	E W Black	(Newmarket)	23. 3.08
CEN	1485	CEN	SZD-30 Pirat	W-393	SP-2520	7.68	A Spencer	Kirton in Lindsey	19. 4.08
CEQ	1487	458	Schleicher Ka 6E	4230		10. 8.68	C.L.Lagden and Partners	Wormingford	15. 8.08
CEW	1493	CEW	Schleicher Ka 6E	4209		8.68	A Gait	Dunstable	8. 6.08
CEX	1494	CEX	Schleicher ASK 13	13108		9.68	Carlton Moor Gliding Club	Carlton Moor	26. 5.08
G-DCEY	1495	CEY	Schleicher Ka 6E	4222		8.68	R Saunders	Walney	11. 2.08
G-DCFA	1497	CFA	Schleicher ASK 13	13113		10.68	G P Saw	Wycombe Air Park	22. 5.08
CFC	1499	CFC	Schleicher K7	470	F-OTAN-C1	11.68	P.Barnes	Dunstable	10. 9.07
CFE	1501	"CCE"	Schleicher ASK 13	13112	EI-143 BGA 1501	10.68	Loughborough Students' Union Gliding Club	RAF Wittering	24. 5.08
CFF	1502	CFF	Schleicher K 8B	8765		10.68	Denbigh Gliding Club	Lleweni Parc	26. 9.08
G-DCFG	1503	CFG	Schleicher ASK 13	13115		10.68	Staffordshire Gliding Club	Seighford	9. 3.08
G-DCFK	1506	CFK	Schempp-Hirth Cirrus	38		11.68	P J Gill and Partners	Seighford	28. 8.08
CFL	1507	CFL	Schleicher Ka 6E	4215		10.68	B Roberts	Camphill	6. 4.08
CFM	1508	CFM	Schleicher ASK 13	13121		7.12.68	Vale of White Horse Gliding Centre (Undershot and crashed, Sandhill Farm 24.11.07) Sandhill Farm, Shrivenham		17. 2.08
CFS	1513	CFS	Glasflügel Standard Libelle	83		4.70	P.G.F.Steele and Partner	Shipdham	7. 9.08
CFT	1514	62	Slingsby T59A Kestrel 17	1729		29. 3.73	J.A.Kane	Sutton Bank	30. 6.05
CFW	1517		Glasflügel Standard Libelle	275		17. 2.72	D J Edwards	Rhigos	3. 9.08
G-DCFX	1518	CFX	Glasflügel Standard Libelle 201B	274		28. 2.72	K D Fishenden	Dunstable	28. 9.08
CFY	1519	862	Glasflügel Standard Libelle	270		17. 3.72	C.W.Stevens	Pocklington	16. 8.08
G-DCGB	1522	CGB	Schleicher Ka 6E	4247		12.68	P M Turner and S C Male	Long Mynd	31.10.07
CGD	1524	CGD	Schleicher Ka 6E	4202		1.69	I F Smith	Lasham	17. 9.08
G-DCGE	1525	CGE	Schleicher Ka 6E	4246		1.69	P C Hazlehurst and C V Hill	Bellarena	26. 1.08
G-DCGH	1528	153	Schleicher K 8B	8772		23. 2.69	I G Brice and Partners	Lasham	24. 5.08
CGJ	1529	CGJ	Schleicher K 8B	8773		2.69	Nene Valley Gliding Club	Upwood	2. 5.08
CGM	1532	CGM	FFA Diamant 18	053		4. 4.69	J.G.Batch	Hinton-in-the-Hedges	29. 6.08
CGN	1533	309	Schleicher Ka 6E	4173		3.69	R.H.Targett	Nympsfield	18. 4.01
G-DCGO	1535	CGO	Schleicher ASK 13	13153		7. 4.69	Oxford Gliding Club	RAF Weston-on-the-Green	4. 1.08
G-DCGS	1537	CGS	FFA Diamant 18	055		20. 7.69	P K Hayward	Parham	3. 7.08
G-DCGT	1538	449	Schempp-Hirth SHK-1	38	D-1966	4.69	A.J.Fardoe	Husbands Bosworth	17. 2.08
CGU	1539		EoN Olympia 2B	EoN/O/115	RAFGSA 228	4.69	A Levitt	.	24. 5.08
CGV	1540	CGV	PIK-16C Vasama	48		4.69	D.J.Osborne and Partners	Currock Hill	29. 8.08
CGX	1542	CGX	Bölkow Phoebus C	869		4.69	T Coldwell	Sackville Lodge, Riseley	3. 7.08
G-DCGY	1543	CGY	Schempp-Hirth Cirrus	51		18. 4.69	R A Jones and G Nevisky	Brentor	14. 3.08
CGZ	1544	CGZ	Schempp-Hirth SHK	39		2. 5.69	R Fretwell	RAF Keevil	20. 8.08
CHB	1546	577	Schleicher Ka 6E	4235		5.69	D.L.Jones	RAF Weston-on-the-Green	16. 6.08
CHC	1547		Bölkow Phoebus C	858		5.69	D Garner	Rhigos	25. 9.08
CHE	1549	CHE	Slingsby T.41 Skylark 2 (Built Doncaster Sailplane Services)	DSS.002		6.69	M.S.Howey	Burn	30. 5.05
CHG	1551	N52	SZD-30 Pirat	B-294		27. 6.69	Seahawk Gliding Club	RNAS Culdrose	1. 9.08
CHK	1554	CHK	EoN AP.5 Olympia 2B	EoN/O/130	RAFGSA 253	6.69	R W Sheffield	Halesland	17. 9.08
CHL	1555	CHL	SZD-30 Pirat	B-295		6.69	T.A.Sage	Dunstable	25. 9.06
CHQ	1559		Slingsby T.31B	1186	RAFGSA 316 XN247	6.69	N H Ponsford (Stored 2006)	Wigan	7.82*
G-DCHT	1562	846	Schleicher ASW 15	15013		8.69	J N Kelly and L Walker	Hinton-in-the-Hedges	15. 3.08
CHU	1563	CHU	Schleicher K 8B	8794		10. 8.69	H B Chalmers (Highland Gliding Club Syndicate)	Easterton	19. 7.06
CHW	1565	CHW	Schleicher ASK 13	13187		8.69	B J Thomas	Eyres Field	18. 9.08
CHZ	1568	857	Schleicher Ka 6E	4153	N6916	9.69	V Harrington	Ridgewell	21. 9.07
G-DCJB	1570	CJB	Bölkow Phoebus C	919		12.69	D Clarke and R Idle	Burn	28. 9.08
CJF	1574	474	Schleicher K 8B	8803		29.11.69	Surrey & Hants Gliding Club	Lasham	20.11.06
CJG	1575	CJG	Wassmer WA-21 Javelot II	38	F-OTAN-C4 F-CCEZ	7. 1.70	R S Hanslip	Burn	11. 5.04
CJJ	1577	CJJ	Bölkow Phoebus C	913		15. 1.70	P Maddocks	Portmoak	10. 4.07
CJK	1578	CJK	Schempp-Hirth SHK	35	RAFGSA	7. 2.70	R.H.Short	Lyveden	19. 5.08
CJL	1579	222	Schempp-Hirth SHK-1	42	OO-ZLG	2.70	M.F.Brook	RAF Wittering	29. 6.06
CJM	1580	CJM	Schleicher K 8B	8814		8. 3.70	Surrey & Hants Gliding Club	Lasham	28. 4.06
CJN	1581	CJN	Schempp-Hirth SHK-1	55		3.70	R.Makin	Camphill	25. 6.05
CJP	1582	CJP	Schleicher ASW 15	15041		3.70	C.Paine	Ridgewell	20. 7.07
G-DCJR	1584	CJR	Schempp-Hirth Cirrus	87		3.70	J Brown and Partners	AAC Dishforth	5. 4.08
-	1588		Slingsby T.21B	1167	XN188	3.70	V Meers	Wolverhampton	*
CJY	1591	CJY	Schleicher Ka 6CR	555	RAFGSA	4.70	K J Hartley	Bicester	20.10.07
CKC	1595	595	Bölkow Phoebus C	936	(BGA 1590)	21. 4.70	S.W.Bennett	Milfield	27. 1.07

Reg	BGA	Code	Type	c/n	Prev id	Date	Owner	Location	Last
G-DCKD	1596	CKD	SZD-30 Pirat	B-327		4.70	Borders Gliding Club	Milfield	3. 9.08
CKF	1598	961	Glasflügel Standard Libelle	101		4.70	S.M.Turner	Crowland	20. 5.06
-	1599		Slingsby T.8 Tutor	JHB5/SSK/FF918	VW506	5.70	M H Simms (Under restoration 6.07)	Shipdham	5.79*
CKJ	1601		Slingsby T.30B Prefect	740	PH-197	4.71	Not known (Stored 2006)	Crosshill	14. 4.90
CKL	1603	CKL	Schleicher Ka 6E	4336		4.70	I.Lowes and Partners	Milfield	15. 9.08
CKN	1605	CKN	SZD-9bis Bocian 1E	P-496		5.70	G Morris (Stored 4.05)	Strubby	26. 6.04
CKP	1606	CKP	Schleicher ASW 15	15058		7.70	M.G.Shaw and Partners	Portmoak	3. 5.07
CKR	1608	CKR	Schleicher ASK 13	13247		7.70	Essex Gliding Club	Ridgewell	24. 7.08
CKU	1611	CKU	Schleicher ASK 13	13243		11. 8.70	Essex Gliding Club	Ridgewell	28. 9.08
G-DCKV	1612	T10	Schleicher ASK 13	13253		12. 8.70	Black Mountains Gliding Club	Talgarth	16. 7.08
CKY	1615	743	Glasflügel Standard Libelle	139		22. 8.70	G.Herbert	Edgehill	13. 5.03
G-DCKZ	1616	724	Schempp-Hirth Standard Cirrus	52	RAFGSA BGA 1616	20. 8.70	G I Bustin	Saltby	9. 5.08
G-DCLA	1617	CLA	Schempp-Hirth Standard Cirrus	63		8.11.70	C Hughes and D J Dye	Nympsfield	28. 9.08
-	1625	-	EoN AP.7 Primary	EoN/P/035	WP267	8. 2.71	T Akerman	Poitiers, France	7. 2.72
							(Last known on rebuild 2004)		
CLK	1626	CLK	Schleicher K7	607	D-5714	1. 2.71	Cornish Gliding Club	Perranporth	20. 8.08
			(Partly modified to ASK 13 standard)						
CLM	1628	535	Glasflügel Standard Libelle	178		12. 2.71	C Heide	North Hill	27. 6.08
G-LIBY	1629		Glasflügel Standard Libelle 201B	175		12. 4.71	R P Hardcastle	Rufforth	24. 6.08
G-DCLP	1630	948	Glasflügel Standard Libelle 201B	176		2.71	M Schlotter	Kingston Deverill	28. 9.08
CLQ	1631	CLQ	Schempp-Hirth Cirrus	99		29. 1.71	M H Simms	Shipdham	6. 5.08
CLR	1632	284	Glasflügel Standard Libelle 201B	173		15. 4.71	R.A.Christie	Easterton	27. 4.07
G-DCLT	1634	CLT	Schleicher K7	251	D-5529	6. 4.71	R.Spencer tr The Syndicate	Rhigos	2. 9.08
			(Partly modified to ASK 13 standard)						
G-DCLV	1636	CLV	Glasflügel Standard Libelle 201B	180		13. 3.71	J.M.Sherman	Parham	29.11.07
G-ECLW	1637	937	Glasflügel Standard Libelle 201B	174		12. 3.71	R G Parker	Kirton in Lindsey	17. 4.08
CLY	1639	"CYL"	Schempp-Hirth Gö 3 Minimoa	378	PH-390 D-5076	20. 3.72	F K Russell	Dunstable	7. 9.08
G-DCLZ	1640	799	Schleicher Ka 6E	4056	AGA 2	2. 4.71	R M King and T D Fielder	Kenley	29. 8.08
G-DCMF	1646	CMF	SZD-32A Foka 5	W-534		7.71	D J Linford	Ringmer	21. 6.08
G-DCMG	1647	CMG	Schleicher K7	462	D-8116	14. 7.71	T G Hobbis "Fledermaus Zero Five"	Lasham	5. 5.08
G-DCMH	1648	165	Glasflügel Standard Libelle 201B	224		12. 7.71	D Williams	North Hill	20. 1.08
G-DCMK	1650	CMK	Schleicher ASK 13	13305		28. 8.71	South Wales Gliding Club	Usk	24. 3.08
CMN	1653	CMN	Schleicher K 8B	8870		23. 8.71	Bristol & Gloucestershire Gliding Club	Nympsfield	18. 6.08
G-DCMO	1655	CMO	Glasflügel Standard Libelle 201B	233		13. 8.71	E V Todd and L C Wood	Wycombe Air Park	13. 5.08
CMR	1656	CMR	Glasflügel Standard Libelle	225		15. 8.71	J.A.Dandie and Partners	Portmoak	31. 8.08
G-DCMS	1657	602	Glasflügel Standard Libelle 201B	234		10. 8.71	R I Lloyd and Partners	Challock	17. 6.08
G-DCMV	1660	184	Glasflügel Standard Libelle 201B	235		11. 8.71	E P Lambert	Aston Down	28. 9.08
CMW	1661	CMW	Glasflügel Standard Libelle 201B	242		28. 9.71	T E Rose	Wycombe Air Park	4. 5.08
G-DENO	1662	226	Glasflügel Standard Libelle 201B	232		11. 9.71	D M Bland	Burn	6. 3.08
CMY	1663	-	Grunau Baby IIIC	1	RAFGSA 373 D-1090	1.72	J S Morgan	Pershore	*
			(Built by LSV Füssen)				(Under restoration 2006)		
CMZ	1664	CMZ	Schleicher K7	323	D-5589	11. 6.72	Cornish Gliding Club	Perranporth	28. 7.06
			(Partly modified to ASK 13 standard)						
G-DCNC	1667	273	Schempp-Hirth Standard Cirrus	167		3.12.71	J.H.Fox and Partners	Portmoak	14. 6.08
CND	1668	CND	SZD-9bis Bocian 1E	P-428	RAFGSA 392	30. 1.72	Angus Gliding Club	Drumshade	17. 9.08
CNE	1669	525	Glasflügel Standard Libelle	266		9. 1.72	E.T.Melville	Portmoak	6. 7.08
CNF	1670	709	Glasflügel Standard Libelle 201B	271		16. 1.72	T J Mottershead	Pocklington	14. 5.08
G-DCNG	1671	622	Glasflügel Standard Libelle 201B	265		24. 2.72	J Mitcheson	Nympsfield	28. 9.08
G-DCNJ	1673	CNJ	Glasflügel Standard Libelle 201B	272		9. 2.72	R Thornley	Crowland	8. 3.08
CNK	1674	CNK	SZD-30 Pirat	B-459		16. 3.72	D L Hyde	Portmoak	26. 4.08
CNM	1676	CNM	SZD-9bis Bocian 1E	P-551		13. 2.72	G.Morriss	Crowland	5. 4.08
G-SCNN	1677	CNN	Schempp-Hirth Standard Cirrus	173		26. 2.72	G C Short	Keiheuvel, Belgium	13. 4.08
CNP	1678	CNP	Glasflügel Standard Libelle	264		9. 3.72	I G Carrick	Camphill	24. 9.08
CNS	1681	CNS	Slingsby T.59A Kestrel 17	1724		21. 4.72	J R Greenwell	Carlton Moor	8. 9.08
CNV	1683	229	Slingsby T..59F Kestrel 19	1790		22. 6.72	R.Birch	Aston Down	25. 3.07
G-DCNW	1684	625	Slingsby T..59F Kestrel 19	1791		13. 7.72	S.R.Watson	Seighford	13. 3.08
CNX	1685	818	Slingsby T..59F Kestrel 20	1792		27. 7.72	M L Boxall	Rufforth	30. 6.08
G-DCNY	1686	151	Glasflügel Standard Libelle 201B	322		22. 9.72	A D Stevenson and Partners	Portmoak	14. 4.08
G-ECPA	1688	466	Glasflügel Standard Libelle 201B	328		1. 9.72	M J Witton	Long Mynd	6. 4.08
CPB	1689	858	Slingsby T..59D Kestrel 19	1796		28.10.72	A.T.Vidion	Tibenham	26. 5.07
G-DCPD	1691	401	Schleicher ASW 17	17026		8. 3.74	D.A.Johnstone	Tibenham	18. 8.08
CPG	1694	CPG	Schleicher K7	7036	D-4029	15. 4.72	P Emerton	Lasham	28. 7.08
G-DCPJ	1696	CPJ	Schleicher Ka 6E	4059	OO-ZDA	9. 4.72	E E Lown	Edgehill	24. 5.08
CPL	1698		Slingsby T.8 Tutor	SSK/FF477	RAFGSA 183	26. 4.72	A P Stacey	RAF Keevil	17. 3.08
G-DCPM	1699	CPM	Glasflügel Standard Libelle	179		12. 4.72	K Marsden & P E Jessop	Trenchard Lines, Upavon	4. 5.08
CPQ	1702	695	Torva Sprite Series 2	003		.	McLean Aviation (Stored 6.03)	Rufforth	6.84*
CPU	1706	761	Schempp-Hirth Standard Cirrus	194		15. 4.72	J.P.J.Ketelaar	Feshiebridge	19. 8.08
CPV	1707	P19	SZD-30 Pirat	B-470		31. 3.72	G Francis	Portmoak	1. 7.08
CPX	1709	CPX	SZD-30 Pirat	B-460		7. 4.72	M.Codd	Talgarth	26. 6.08
CPZ	1711	*	Aachen FVA.10B Rheinland	Not known	RAFGGA 521	4.72	Deutsches Segelflugmuseum	Wasserkuppe, Germany	24. 8.96
							(On display as "D-12-354" 2006)		
CQC	1714	CQC	SZD-30 Pirat	B-472		15. 4.72	N White	Crowland	20. 4.08
CQG	1718	CQG	EoN AP.5 Olympia 2B	EoN/O/044	RAFGSA 206 (BGA 542)	24. 4.72	A Wilson and C Jakuba	Sutton Bank	10.11.07
G-DCOJ	1720	17K	Slingsby T..59A Kestrel 17	1727		20. 5.72	T W Treadaway	Husbands Bosworth	9. 4.08
G-ECOL	1722	339	Schempp-Hirth Nimbus-2	11		25. 5.72	A D F Flintoft and L I Rigby	Crowland	6. 4.08
CQM	1723	234	Slingsby T..59F Kestrel 19	1765		22. 5.72	A G Truman	Lasham	9. 9.07
CQN	1724	CQN	Schempp-Hirth Standard Cirrus	204G		19. 5.72	M.G.Sankey and Partners	Lasham	5. 6.08
G-CEWE	1725	918	Schempp-Hirth Nimbus-2	4		4.72	D.Caunt and Partners	Wycombe Air Park	8. 1.08
COO	1726	139	Schempp-Hirth Nimbus-2	5		4.72	I R Duncan	Portmoak	22. 3.08
G-DCOR	1727	703	Schempp-Hirth Standard Cirrus	220G		28. 5.72	S Brown	Wycombe Air Park	30. 5.08

CQW	1732	342	SZD-36A Cobra 15	W-572		6.72	P Zelazowski	Rivar Hill	3.11.07
							(Under restoration 2003)		
-	1759	-	Slingsby T.8 Tutor	-	RAFGSA 178	10.72	Boulton Paul Association	Wolverhampton	7.77*
CSB	1761	CSB	Slingsby T..59F Kestrel 19	1798		17.11.72	W Fischer	Eyres Field	13. 9.08
G-DCSD	1763	53	Slingsby T..59D Kestrel 19	1800		1.12.72	R J Toon	Sutton Bank	11. 4.08
G-DCSF	1765	34Z	Slingsby T..59F Kestrel 19	1802		1.73	R Birch	Aston Down	9. 2.08
CSJ	1768	CSJ	Glasflügel Standard Libelle 201B	372		26. 1.73	A Deacon	Usk	19. 7.08
G-DCSK	1769	387	Slingsby T..59D Kestrel 20	1806		3.73	H A Torode and Partners	Lasham	3. 3.08
CSL	1770		Slingsby T.8 Tutor	928	XE758 VF181	15.10.72	W.den Baars	Haamstede, Netherlands	19. 9.00
G-DCSN	1772	CSN	Pilatus B4-PC11	021		7. 3.73	D E Brummitt and Partrner	(Doncaster)	14. 5.08
CSP	1773	CSP	Pilatus B4-PC11	027		3.73	I.Pendlebury	Chipping	19. 9.08
G-DCSR	1775	808	Glasflügel Standard Libelle 201B	368		14. 1.73	W.G.Miller and Partners	Portmoak	28. 9.08
CSV	1779	CSV	SZD-30 Pirat	B-515		3.12.72	M P Flanagan	Darlton	20. 3.06
G-ECSW	1780	CSW	Pilatus B4-PC11AF	022		12.72	I.H.Keyser	Aston Down	9. 4.08
G-DCTB	1785	579	Schempp-Hirth Standard Cirrus	264G		1.73	I Young & S McCurdy	RAF Weston-on-the-Green	22. 2.08
G-DCTE	1788	74	Schleicher ASW 17	17012		1.73	T E Linee	Eyres Field	8. 4.08
CTF	1789		Schleicher Rhönlerche II	1	D-3574	26. 1.73	M.Goodman	Lleweni Parc	24. 1.04
			(Built LSC Wermelskirchen) (Owner quotes p/i D-4346, but unconfirmed)					*(Stored 2005)*	
G-DCTJ	1792	CTJ	Slingsby T..59D Kestrel 19	1810		14. 3.73	W.Waldren and Partners	Dunstable	10. 9.08
CTL	1794	CTL	Slingsby T..59D Kestrel 19	1812		28. 3.73	P Hibbard	Wormingford	12. 5.08
G-DCTM	1795	254	Slingsby T..59D Kestrel 19	1813		3.73	C Roney	Gransden Lodge	28.10.07
CTP	1797	49	Slingsby T..59D Kestrel 19	1815		14. 4.73	D.C.Austin	Sutton Bank	1. 7.08
G-DCTO	1798	CTO	Slingsby T..59D Kestrel 20	1816		27. 4.73	K.A.Moules	Trenchard Lines, Upavon	21. 4.08
CTR	1799	402	Slingsby T..59D Kestrel 19	1817		5.73	D.J.Marpole	RNAS Yeovilton	27. 4.08
CTS	1800	CTS	EoN AP.5 Olympia 2B	EoN/O/157	RNGSA	13. 1.73	J R Rolfe	Upwood	21. 5.08
CTT	1801	873	Schempp-Hirth Standard Cirrus	277G		17. 2.73	S.K.Ancsell	Lasham	16. 8.08
G-DCTU	1802	501	Glasflügel Standard Libelle 201B	371		2.73	F.Davies	Husbands Bosworth	14. 5.08
CTV	1803		SZD-30 Pirat	B-528		18. 2.73	B.Fantham	Rhigos	25. 7.08
CTX	1805	CTX	SZD-30 Pirat	B-527		2.73	P.Goulding	Crowland	8. 9.08
CTZ	1807	CTZ	Schleicher K 8B	8035/B5	D-KOCU D-5203	3. 4.73	Scottish Gliding Union Ltd	Portmoak	12. 9.07
G-DCUB	1809	CUB	Pilatus B4-PC11	047		31. 3.73	G S Sanderson	Gransden Lodge	22. 2.08
CUC	1810	678	Pilatus B4-PC11	003	HB-1102	5.73	R Burghall	(Rotherham)	21. 6.08
CUD	1811	CUD	Yorkshire Sailplanes YS-53 Sovereign	02		7.72	E C Murgatroyd	Sackville Lodge, Riseley	11. 5.08
			(Built from Slingsby T.53B XV951 [1574] w/o 11.4.72)						
G-DCUJ	1816	706	Glasflügel Standard Libelle 201B	370		13. 2.73	T G B Hobbis	Lasham	2. 5.08
CUM	1819	CUM	SZD-30 Pirat	B-534		24. 2.73	E.Hughes	Pocklington	4. 4.06
CUQ	1821	CUQ	Pilatus B4-PC11	040		2.73	Cotswold Gliding Club	Aston Down	29. 7.08
CUS	1822	842	Schempp-Hirth Cirrus VTC	126Y		3.73	G.F.Wearing	Chipping	5. 7.08
G-DCUT	1823	B4	Pilatus B4-PC11AF	041		3.73	A L Walker	Lasham	19. 8.08
CVA	1830	CVA	LET L-13 Blanik	025418		3.73	Andreas Gliding Club	Andreas	14. 5.08
							"Boggles the Blanik"		
G-DCVB	1831	CVB	LET L-13 Blanik	025419		3.73	K S Wells	Sackville Lodge, Riseley	13. 4.08
CVC	1832	CVC	SZD-30 Pirat	B-535		3.73	T.Wilkinson	Sackville Lodge, Riseley	20. 7.08
G-DCVE	1834	BZ	Schempp-Hirth Cirrus VTC	127Y		15. 3.73	H Whybrow	Dunstable	26. 3.08
G-DCVG	1836	565	Pilatus B4-PC11AF	045		19. 3.73	I H Keyser and D Poll	Germany	31. 3.08
CVH	1837	CVH	Schempp-Hirth SHK	34	N6524A	30. 3.73	J.C.Fletcher *(Stored 7.07)*	Bicester	27. 7.06
G-DCVK	1839	92	Pilatus B4-PC11AF	048		22. 3.73	J P Marriott	Bicester	9. 1.08
CVL	1840	253	Glasflügel Standard Libelle 201B	369		2.73	J Williams	Kirton in Lindsey	22. 2.08
G-DCVM	1841	CVM	Pilatus B4-PC11 (Powered)	036		23. 3.73	J.A.Mace	Rivar Hill	28. 9.08
CVP	1843	CVP	SZD-9bis Bocian 1E	P-597		17. 3.73	Not known *(Stored 4.07)*	Aboyne	3. 8.04
CVQ	1844	428	Glasflügel Standard Libelle 201B	374		23. 3.73	C.J.Taunton and Partners	Dunstable	29. 4.04
CVR	1845	CVR	SZD-30 Pirat	B-538		27. 3.73	J.R.Hornby	Darlton	26. 6.04
G-DCVS	1846	CVS	SZD-36A Cobra 15	W-610		3.73	I A Burgin and Partners	Darlton	14. 4.08
G-DCVT	1847	CVT	SZD-36A Cobra 15	W-609		27. 3.73	P Q Benn	Aston Down	30. 3.08
G-DCVV	1849	CVV	Pilatus B4-PC11AF	028		27. 3.73	F.R.Wolff and Partners	North Hill	3. 3.08
CVW	1850	423	Slingsby T..59D Kestrel 19	1818		29. 5.73	P.B.Hogarth	Halesland	28. 7.08
G-DCVY	1852	355	Slingsby T..59D Kestrel 19	1821		4. 7.73	A B Dickinson	Chipping	18. 3.07
G-DCWA	1854	539	Slingsby T..59D Kestrel 19	1825		28. 9.73	D J Jeffries	Usk	21. 2.08
G-DCWB	1855	677	Slingsby T..59D Kestrel 19	1833		9. 1.74	D J Deacon and Partners	Saltby	13. 3.08
CWD	1857	CWD	Slingsby T..59D Kestrel 19	1835		29. 1.74	G K Holloway	Aboyne	27. 9.08
G-DCWE	1858	468	Glasflügel Standard Libelle 201B	482		31. 1.74	T W J Stoker	Rufforth	3. 4.08
G-DCWF	1859	CWF	Slingsby T..59D Kestrel 19	1838		2.74	P.F.Nicholson	Hinton-In-The-Hedges	28. 9.08
G-DCWG	1860	322	Glasflügel Standard Libelle 201B	391		7. 4.73	G Mitcheson and Partners	Milfield	10. 7.08
G-DCWH	1861	CWH	Schleicher ASK 13	13424		12. 4.73	York Gliding Centre	Rufforth	28. 9.08
CWJ	1862	CWJ	Schleicher K7	630	D-6057 D-5723	27. 4.73	Angus Gliding Club	Drumshade	8.10.08
G-DCWR	1869	917	Schempp-Hirth Cirrus VTC	133Y		4.73	P J Concannon and Partners	Thame	23. 6.08
CWS	1870	CWS	Schempp-Hirth Cirrus VTC	129Y		19. 4.73	R.W.Cassels and Partners	Ridgewell	11. 5.08
CWT	1871	978	Glasflügel Standard Libelle 201B	384		4.73	S W Swan	Parham	18. 5.08
-	1872	D-5627	Schleicher Rhönlerche II	390	D-5627	22. 4.73	Sailplane Preservation Group	Shoreham	11.76*
							(Stored 9.07)		
CWV	1873	Z	Schleicher Rhönlerche II	123	D-8226	22. 4.73	11th Bristol (Headley Park) Scouts	Aston Down	5.94*
							(Stored 1.08)		
G-DCWX	1875	832	Glasflügel Standard Libelle	36	RAFGSA 132	4.73	C.A.Weyman	Eyres Field	21. 4.08
CWY	1876	146	Glasflügel Standard Libelle 201B	387		14. 4.73	S J Taylor	Portmoak	9. 7.08
CWZ	1877	CWZ	Glasflügel Standard Libelle 201B	392		30. 4.73	K Hopkinson	Camphill	16. 4.08
CXH	1885	CXH	SZD-36A Cobra 15	W-619		10. 6.73	C D Street	Parham	11. 9.04
CXK	1887	CXK	Glasflügel Standard Libelle 201B	383		6.73	C.A.Turner	Cross Hayes	23. 4.08
CXL	1888	CXL	SZD-30 Pirat	B-548		6.73	A K Holden	Rivar Hill	1. 6.07
G-DCXM	1889	532	Slingsby T..59D Kestrel 19	1820		7.73	R.P.Beck and T Potter	AAC Dishforth	15. 4.08
CXP	1891		Yorkshire Sailplanes YS-55 Consort	07	BGA 1892	10. 5.76	A.D.Coles	North Hill	23. 4.06
CXV	1897	CXV	Yorkshire Sailplanes YS-53 Sovereign	03		7.74	P G Myers	Chipping	19. 5.08

Reg	No.	Tri	Type	c/n	Prev id	Date	Owner	Location	Date
G-DCYA	1902	503	Pilatus B4-PC11	072		7.73	E.J.Bromwell and Partners	North Hill	2. 2.08
CYC	1904	CYC	Pilatus B4-PC11	029	N47247	7.73	D.F.Barley	Ringmer	24.10.07
CYD	1905	CYD	SZD-30 Pirat	B-559		25. 7.73	I.Johnston	Milfield	19. 6.06
G-DCYG	1908	YG	Glasflügel Standard Libelle 201B	441		8.73	D J Cooke and R Barsby	Husbands Bosworth	14. 1.08
CYJ	1910	CYJ	Grunau Baby IIB	031000	D-6021	11. 8.73	C.Bird	Dunstable	1.90*
			(Built Petera 1943)				(Under restoration 2000)		
CYK	1911	248	Pilatus B4-PC11	078		8.73	I.M.Trotter tr Pilatus Soaring Syndicate	Portmoak	31. 3.07
G-DCYM	1913	299	Schempp-Hirth Standard Cirrus	48	D-0578	9.73	K M Fisher	Husbands Bosworth	28. 9.08
CYN	1914	N4	Slingsby T..59D Kestrel 19	JP/054		10.74	S.J.Cooke and Partners	Gransden Lodge	18. 2.08
			(Built D Jones and T Pentelow)						
CYQ	1916	477	Schempp-Hirth Standard Cirrus	364		27. 9.73	B.M.Reeves	Nympsfield	1. 4.08
G-DCYT	1919	CYT	Schempp-Hirth Standard Cirrus	357G		9.73	G.Royle	Llantisilio	23. 4.08
CYV	1921	CYV	Birmingham Guild BG-135	5		9.73	E J Gunner	Kingston Deverill	7.11.08
CYZ	1925	CYZ	Schleicher K 8B	8882	RAFGSA	8. 9.74	Oxford Gliding Club	RAF Weston-on-the-Green	3. 7.08
G-DCZD	1929	CZD	Pilatus B4-PC11	081		12.73	S.E.Marples	Milfield	5. 8.08
G-DCZE	1930	CZE	SZD-30 Pirat	S-01.14		23.12.73	M R Biddle tr G-DCZE Group	Snitterfield	29. 4.08
CZG	1932	CZG	SZD-30 Pirat	S-01.16		31.12.73	J.T.Pajdak	Kenley	11. 6.06
G-DCZJ	1934	CZJ	SZD-30 Pirat	S-01.15		29.12.73	C.L Groves and Partners	Husbands Bosworth	5. 4.08
CZM	1937	CZM	München Mü 13D III	10/52	D-1488	9.74	H.Chapple	Bicester	2. 6.08
CZN	1938	CZN	Schleicher ASW 15B	15329		13. 3.74	P.C.Tuppen and Partners	Bembridge	8. 7.08
CZQ	1940	CZQ	Slingsby T..59D Kestrel 19	1840		5. 4.74	M Allen	Husbands Bosworth	16. 8.08
G-DCZR	1941	CZR	Slingsby T..59D Kestrel 19	1842		4.74	R.P.Brisbourne	Rufforth	5. 4.08
CZU	1944	826	Slingsby T..59D Kestrel 19	1849		14. 6.74	K.R.Merritt and P.F.Croote	Halesland	28. 9.08
CZV	1945	415	Slingsby T..59D Kestrel 19	1850		16. 7.74	V.F.G.Tull	Dunstable	15. 6.03
CZW	1946	A3	Slingsby T..59D Kestrel 20	1846		17.10.76	C.D Berry	Bidford	21. 4.04
G-DDAC	1952	DAC	SZD-36A Cobra 15	W-656		3.74	R J A Colenso	Husbands Bosworth	6. 5.08
G-DDAJ	1958	14	Schempp-Hirth Nimbus-2	50		21. 3.74	J.D.Jones	Nympsfield	28. 9.08
G-DDAK	1959	DAK	Schleicher K7	893	D-8851	26. 3.74	Vale of Neath Gliding Club	Rhigos	7. 9.08
DAL	1960	DAL	EoN AP.6 Olympia 419	EoN/4/010	RAFGSA 301	4.74	B Kozuh	Ljubljana, Slovenia	19. 5.08
G-DDAN	1962		SZD-30 Pirat	S-01.45		23. 3.74	J M A Shannon	(Cambridge)	22.11.07
G-DDAP	1963	DAP	SZD-30 Pirat	S-01.47		4.74	T D Younger and Partners	Currock Hill	19. 5.08
DAR	1965	DAR	Slingsby T.21B	SSK/FF1200	RAFGSA 404	1. 6.74	P T Nash	Crowland	6. 7.08
G-DDAS	1966	DAS	Schempp-Hirth Standard Cirrus	378	(BGA 1925)	4.74	G.Goodenough	Burn	2. 4.08
DAU	1968	DAU	SZD-30 Pirat	S-01.50		27. 4.74	J Sentance	Darlton	26. 9.08
DAV	1969	240	SZD-38A Jantar-1	B-608		4.74	S A Lewis	Brentor	17. 9.08
G-DDAW	1970	DAW	Schleicher Ka 6CR	951	RAFGSA D-2025	8. 6.74	P.S.Holmes	Bellarena	14. 9.08
DBA	1974	207	EoN AP.5 Olympia 2B	EoN/O/156	RNGSA 208	25. 5.74	W.R.Williams	RAF Halton	20. 6.04
DBB	1975	DBB	Slingsby T.51 Dart 17R	DG/51/01		5. 2.76	M Ladley	Shipdham	11. 1.08
			(Built Greenfly Aviation)						
DBC	1976	851	Pilatus B4-PC11	135		6.74	J.H.France and Partners	Shobdon	27. 7.08
DBD	1977	DBD	SZD-30 Pirat	S-02.02		6.74	E W Burgess	Lyveden	9. 6.08
DBG	1980	DBG	ICA-Brasov IS-29D	31		6.74	P.S.Whitehead	Walney	13. 4.07
DBJ	1982	691	Slingsby T..59D Kestrel 19	1856	BGA 1892 BGA 1982	19.10.74	T.Barr-Smith	Kenley	10. 4.06
DBK	1983	523	Slingsby T..59D Kestrel 19	1861		2.12.74	523 Syndicate	North Hill	25. 9.08
G-DDBN	1986	575	Slingsby T..59D Kestrel 19	1857		25. 3.75	J D Westwood	Nympsfield	4. 5.08
G-DDBP	1987	551	Glasflügel Club Libelle 205	51		1. 5.75	T Forsey and Partners	Wormingford	28. 9.08
G-CETJ	1988	DBQ	Slingsby T..59D Kestrel 19	1863		17. 4.75	S M Sanderson	Sutton Bank	12. 9.08
G-DDBR	1989	182	Slingsby T..59D Kestrel 19	1858		22. 4.75	P.L.Poole	Kenley	10. 6.08
							(Cancelled 28. 1.08 - to Czech Republic)		
DBS	1990	DBS	Slingsby T..59D Kestrel 19	1864		24. 4.75	G M Barratt	Darlton	16. 9.08
DBU	1992	-	Schempp-Hirth Gö 4 Goevier II	557	D-5233	13. 7.74	Boulton Paul Association	Wolverhampton	19. 7.87
G-DDBV	1993	DBV	SZD-30 Pirat	S-02.27		1. 7.74	G Robertson	Usk	19. 5.08
DBW	1994	DBW	SZD-9bis Bocian 1E	P-641		12. 7.74	Sackville Gliding Club	Sackville Lodge, Riseley	3. 4.99
							(Stored 2.08)		
G-DDBX	1995	DBX	SZD-9bis Bocian 1E	P-642		20. 7.74	A.G.Veitch tr Highland Bocian Syndicate	Easterton	28. 4.08
G-DDCA	1998	DCA	SZD-36A Cobra 15	W-686		18. 9.74	R J Aylesbury and J Young	Upwood	10. 6.07
G-DDCC	2000	324	Glasflügel Standard Libelle 201B	585		11.74	H J Warbey	Shobdon	28. 9.08
DCE	2002	DCE	Slingsby T.41 Skylark 2B	1003	RAFGGA 540 PH-225	11.74	J Salvin	Darlton	5. 9.07
DCN	2010		Slingsby T.21B	1250	RAFGGA 501 RAFGSA 287, BGA 943	1.75	M R Dawson (New owner 1.07)	(Vinax, France)	16. 7.95
DCZ	2021	DCZ	King-Elliott-Street Osprey 2	1470		10.75	P Hardman	Dunstable	6.11.07
			(Believed to be converted Slingsby T.51 Dart but c/n conflicts with BGA 1245)						
G-DDDA	2022	DDA	Schempp-Hirth Standard Cirrus	532G		2.75	C G Wrigley and A J Davis	Nympsfield	4. 3.08
DDB	2023	DDB	Schleicher ASK 13	13493		2.75	Shenington Gliding Club	Edgehill	28. 9.08
DDC	2024	DDC	Slingsby T.21B	1157	RAFGSA 313 XN153	3.75	J S Shaw and Partners	Perranporth	22. 4.08
DDD	2025	695	Schempp-Hirth Nimbus-2	84	G-BKPM BGA 2025	3.75	C A Mansfield	Lasham	3. 9.08
G-DDDE	2026		SZD-38A Jantar-1	B-641		4.75	K Richards	Talgarth	18. 3.08
DDK	2031	DDK	SZD-30 Pirat	S-04.08		4.75	P Jennings	Bembridge	15.10.05
DDL	2032	DDL	Schleicher K 8B	218/61	D-5156	4.75	York Gliding Centre	Rufforth	30. 4.08
G-DDDM	2033	959	Schempp-Hirth Cirrus VTC	164Y		3.75	G J Booth and Partners	Ridgewell	5. 5.08
DDN	2034	DDN	SZD-9bis Bocian 1E	P-429	RAFGSA 393	3.75	Bath, Wilts and North Dorset Gliding Club	Kingston Deverill	5. 8.05
DDQ	2036	-	Slingsby T.21B	630	RAFGSA 247 WB969	3.75	AeroVenture	Doncaster	*
							(Damaged 24. 8.80; frame on display 2007)		
G-DDDR	2037	680	Schempp-Hirth Standard Cirrus	531G		3.75	J D Ewence	Pocklington	28. 9.08
DDW	2042	DDW	SZD-30 Pirat	S-04.33		4.75	D P O'Flanagan	Parham	12. 5.08
DDY	2044	DDY	Schleicher Ka 6CR	678	D-8841	4.75	D Bowden	Cross Hayes	3. 6.08
DEB	2047	DEB	Slingsby T..59D Kestrel 19	1866		24.10.75	J L Smoker	RAF Weston-on-the-Green	19. 6.05
DEF	2050	DEF	ICA-Brasov IS-28B2	49		8.77	Not known (Stored 2007)	Shipdham	*

G-DDEG	2051	DEG	ICA-Brasov IS-28B2	48		.	P S Whitehead	Skelling Farm, Penrith	16.11.07
DEP	2058	DEP	Schleicher Ka 6CR	6452	AGA .	4.75	M D Brooks	Saltby	9.11.08
					BGA 2058, RAFGSA 350				
G-DDEO	2059	716	Glasflügel Club Libelle 205	97		4.75	N J Mitchell	Kingston Deverill	28. 9.08
G-DDEV	2064	DEV	Schleicher Ka 6CR	6453	RAFGSA 354	9. 6.75	L and N Morley	Wormingford	22. 3.08
G-DDEW	2065	DEW	ICA-Brasov IS-29D	40		12. 6.75	G V Prater	Lasham	4. 7.07
G-DDEX	2066	DEX	LET L-13 Blanik	026348	RAFGSA R4	1. 7.75	B A Hutchins	Talgarth	24.10.07
					BGA 2066				
DEY	2067	DEY	LET L-13 Blanik	026352	RAFGSA R12	10. 7.75	Eight Ball Soaring Association	Shipdham	9. 9.03
					BGA 2067		(Broken up for spares)		
DFC	2071	128	Schempp-Hirth Standard Cirrus	592G		7.75	I Helme	Usk	18. 3.08
DFE	2073	DFE	Eiriavion PIK-20B	20052		7.75	M Roff-Jarrett	Lasham	15. 7.08
G-DDFK	2078	DFK	Molino PIK-20	20039	OH-500	14. 9.75	M J and B H Fairclough	North Hill	3. 3.08
G-DDFL	2079	DFL	SZD-38A Jantar-1	B-682		9.75	P Bellham	Kirton in Lindsey	6. 5.08
DFN	2081	959	Glaser-Dirks DG-100	30		9.75	D.J Clarke	Wormingford	8. 3.08
DFP	2082	DFP	Aeromere M.100S	029	I-LSUO	9.75	D.and J Lee	Pocklington	23. 2.03
DFR	2084	DFR	Grob G102 Astir CS	1038		10.75	Windrushers Gliding Club	Bicester	12. 3.08
DFV	2088		SZD-38A Jantar-1	B-684		7.12.75	G Bambrook	Edgehill	15.12.01
G-DDFW	2089	DFW	SZD-30 Pirat	S-05.45		26.11.75	R Skerry	Strubby	29. 8.07
DFX	2090	767	SZD-41A Jantar-Standard	B-691		10.75	J C Tait and Partners	Easterton	23. 4.08
DFY	2091	DFY	Schempp-Hirth Standard Cirrus	396	AGA .	5.11.75	Science Museum (On display)	South Kensington	3. 3.92
G-DDGA	2093	DGA	Schleicher K 8B	8587	RAFGSA 334	11.75	Welland Gliding Club	Lyveden	1. 5.08
					BGA 1926, RAFGSA 334				
G-DDGE	2097	DGE	Schempp-Hirth Standard Cirrus 75	606		12.75	T E Snoddy	Bellarena	4. 5.08
DGG	2099	DGG	Schleicher Ka 6E	4061	RAFGSA 263	15.12.75	N F Holmes and Partners	Long Mynd	22. 9.08
DGH	2100	DGH	SZD-30 Pirat	B-533	RNGSA	12.75	T Bell and V Turner	Kingston Deverill	10. 3.07
G-DDGK	2102	DGK	Schleicher Ka 6CR	6287	D-3224	21.12.75	IBM Gliding Club "Betty Blue"	Lasham	9. 5.08
DGP	2106	DGP	LET L-13 Blanik	026560		26. 5.76	B Kozuh	Ljubljana, Slovenia	30. 6.06
DGV	2112	-	Breguet 905S Fauvette	2	HB-632	6. 7.76	P Oldfield	(N Yorkshire)	27. 9.08
DGX	2114	610	Schempp-Hirth Standard Cirrus 75	619	AGA 3	11. 5.76	G R Seaman and Partners	Lasham	3. 6.08
					BGA 2114				
G-DDGY	2115	195	Schempp-Hirth Nimbus-2B	105		11. 5.76	J H Taylor and Partners	Nympsfield	15. 1.08
DHA	2117	DHA	Schleicher K 8B	1055	D-8848	23. 6.76	Booker Gliding Club	Wycombe Air Park	1. 2.07
			(C/n conflicts with D-8616)		D-5148				
G-DDHC	2119	811	SZD-41A Jantar-Standard	B-710	(BGA 2109)	9. 6.76	M C Burlock	Rivar Hill	29. 3.08
DHG	2123	DHG	Schleicher Ka 6CR	1131	D-5170	23. 6.76	Angus Gliding Club	Drumshade	20. 9.08
DHH	2124	116	Eiriavion PIK-20B	20124		5.76	D.M Steed	Sackville Lodge, Riseley	8.12.07
G-DDHJ	2125	DHJ	Glaser-Dirks DG-100	48		1.76	G E McLaughlin	Bellarena	25. 6.08
G-DDHK	2126	A30	Glaser-Dirks DG-100	50		1.76	B J Griffin	Kirton in Lindsey	28. 9.08
G-DDHL	2127	DHL	Glaser-Dirks DG-100	52		1.76	T L Webster and Partners	Challock	24. 2.08
G-DDHM	2128	DHM	Schleicher Ka 6E	4124	RAFGSA 26	6. 2.76	J G Heard	Seighford	7. 3.08
DHN	2129	824	Eiriavion PIK-20B	20082		1.76	G J Bass	Challock	15. 8.08
G-DDHE	2132	DHE	Slingsby T.53B	1718		15. 7.76	E L Pole	Portmoak	5. 3.08
							(Aviation Preservation Society of Scotland)		
G-DDHT	2134	DHT	Schleicher Ka 6E	4065	D-7202	2.76	S Foster	Long Mynd	20. 2.08
DHV	2136	P20	Eiriavion PIK-20B	20111		3.76	M Parker	Nympsfield	13. 6.08
DHW	2137	951	Schempp-Hirth Nimbus-2	106		23. 4.76	A J Bauld	Portmoak	3. 6.06
DHX	2138	7V	Schempp-Hirth Standard Cirrus	"635"		3.76	J Franke	Lasham	7. 6.08
			(Rebuilt 6.05 with airframe from D-3264 (533G))						
DHY	2139	DHY	Schleicher K7	1137	RAFGSA 266	14. 4.76	G Whittaker	Chipping	21. 1.07
					D-5162				
DHZ	2140	DHZ	SZD-30 Pirat	S-06.41		23. 4.76	Peterborough & Spalding Gliding Club	Crowland	29. 6.08
DJA	2141	DJA	SZD-30 Pirat	S-06.42		23. 4.76	J Young	Milfield	18. 5.03
G-DDJB	2142	N11	Schleicher K 8B	8879	AGA 17	7. 4.76	Portsmouth Naval Gliding Club	Lee-on-Solent	16. 2.08
					BGA 2142, RAFGSA 397				
G-DDJD	2144	DJD	Grob G102 Astir CS	1226		5. 8.76	P E Gascoigne	Kingston Deverill	28. 9.08
G-DDJE	2145	DJE	Schleicher Ka 6CR	6412	D-3682	15. 7.76	E W Russell	Wormingford	28. 9.08
DJF	2146	500	Halford JSH Scorpion	001		7.77	R G Greenslade	(Doncaster)	*
							(Previously at South Yorkshire Air Museum - for restoration)		
DJK	2150	DJK	Schleicher ASK 18	18030		15. 7.76	Booker Gliding Club	Wycombe Air Park	20. 6.08
G-DDJL	2151	DJL	SZD-41A Jantar-Standard	B-714		16. 7.76	A M Cooper	Llantisilio	28. 9.08
DJM	2152	DJM	SZD-41A Jantar-Standard	B-715		17. 8.76	G B Dennis	Talgarth	28. 6.08
G-DDJN	2153	407	Eiriavion PIK-20B	20140C		16. 7.76	S Lambourne and M Ireland	Kingston Deverill	9. 3.08
DJP	2154	DJP	Schleicher K 8B	8588	RAFGSA 335	21. 7.76	Sackville Vintage Gliding Club (Stored 2.08)		17. 6.03
								Sackville Lodge, Riseley	17. 6.03
G-CEWP	2155	214	Grob G102 Astir CS	1258		17.10.76	R D Slater	Usk	27. 2.08
DJR	2156	"FGT"	Schleicher Ka 6CR	680	D-8423	4. 8.76	Cornish Gliding Club	Perranporth	20. 8.08
DJS	2157	DJS	Schempp-Hirth SHK-1	51	SE-TNF	16. 7.76	J S S Selman	Limerick, Ireland	3. 8.05
					OY-MFX, HB-898				
DJT	2158	DJT	Schleicher K7	Not known	RAFGSA	7.76	Denbigh Gliding Club	Lleweni Parc	3. 6.06
							(Note: BGA 4271 is marked "DJT" also)		
DJW	2161	-	Manuel Condor	1		7.76	C V and R C Inwood (Stored 2005)	Lasham	18. 5.98
G-DDJX	2162	614	Grob G102 Astir CS	1259		17.11.76	P Barnwell and R Duke	Crowland	13. 4.08
DJZ	2164	989	Eiriavion PIK-20B	20144		4. 8.76	P Collin	Shipdham	13. 4.08
DKB	2166	DKB	Schempp-Hirth Standard Austria S	32	F-CCPR	4. 8.76	J R Parr	Burn	25.10.03
DKC	2167	DKC	Schleicher K 8B	8261	D-1431	8.76	Yorkshire Gliding Club	Sutton Bank	23. 4.08
G-DDKD	2168	759	Glasflügel Hornet	67	(BGA 2165)	8.76	B J W Thomas and Partners	Eyres Field	28. 4.08
G-DDKE	2169	DKE	Schleicher ASK 13	13548		28. 9.76	South Wales Gliding Club	Usk	13. 4.08
DKG	2171	DKG	Schleicher Ka 6CR	6233	D-4327	8.76	L Footring and Partners	Wormingford	9. 5.08
DKH	2172	769	LET L-13 Blanik	026644		8. 9.76	T Wiltshire	Shipdham	11. 9.04
							(To Thailand as HS-CMU 2007)		
G-DDKL	2175	444	Schempp-Hirth Nimbus-2B	86	D-2111	8. 9.76	G J Croll	Rattlesden	20. 4.08
DKM	2176	DKM	Glasflügel Hornet	49	(BGA 2213)	9.76	S Lee	Rattlesden	14. 4.08
					BGA 2176, D-7816				

G-DDKN	2177	DKN	Schleicher Ka 6CR	6456	D-9358	12. 3.77	A Ciccone	Upwood	2. 4.08
	DKR	2180	DKR	Grob G102 Astir CS	1327		9.76	Oxford Gliding Club	RAF Weston-on-the-Green	18. 6.08
	DKS	2181	788	Grob G102 Astir CS	1330		23.12.76	C K Lewis	Lasham	9. 5.04
G-DDKT	2182	DKT	Eiriavion PIK-20B	20155C		4.11.76	S Wilson	Rufforth	23. 4.08
G-DDKU	2183	DKU	Grob G102 Astir CS	1326		11.76	P N Stapleton and Partners	North Hill	28. 9.08
G-DDKW	2185	DKW	Grob G102 Astir CS	1329		9.76	J H C Friend and R Robertson	Lleweni Parc	30. 3.08
G-DDKX	2186	353	Grob G102 Astir CS	1331		9.76	L R and J M Bennett	Usk	30. 4.08
	DKY	2187	DKY	Schleicher K7	7187	RAFGSA 342	4.11.76	Defford Aero Club (Stored 2005)	Challock	14. 8.02
G-DDLA	2189	DLA	Pilatus B4-PC11	149	RAFGSA	17.10.76	P R Seddon	Walney Island	3. 6.08
G-DDLB	2190	DLB	Schleicher ASK 18	18040		17.10.76	Vale of White Horse Gliding Centre		
								Sandhill Farm, Shrivenham	9. 2.08
	DLC	2191	C	Schleicher ASK 13	13549		4.11.76	Lasham Gliding Society	Lasham	17. 5.08
	DLD	2192	DLD	Schleicher K 8B	8766	RAFGSA 383	17.11.76	Shalbourne Soaring Society	Rivar Hill	7. 8.06
	DLE	2193	433	Schleicher Ka 6E	4074	AGA 8	4.11.76	D.C Unwin	Darlton	9. 5.08
					RAFGSA				
	DLG	2195	DLG	Schempp-Hirth Standard Cirrus	579	AGA 2	17.10.76	S Naylor	Burn	24. 9.08
G-DDLH	2196	378	Grob G102 Astir CS77	1646		2.77	M D and M E Saunders	Lasham	19. 4.08
	DLJ	2197	DLJ	Eiriavion PIK-20B	20157		16.12.76	M S Parkes	Milfield	9. 8.08
	DLM	2200	266	Grob G102 Astir CS	1260	(BGA 2163)	1.12.76	I A Davison	North Hill	26. 9.08
G-DDLP	2202	DLP	Schleicher Ka 6CR	6519	RAFGSA 355	11.76	J R Crosse	Crowland	24. 4.08
	DLS	2205	DLS	Schleicher K 8B	8650	D-5718	1.12.76	North Devon Gliding Club	Eaglescott	26. 6.07
G-DDLT	2206	IS28	ICA-Brasov IS-28B2	32		12.76	M H Simms	Shipdham	3. 7.03
	DLU	2207	R93	ICA-Brasov IS-28B2	33	RAFGSA R93	12.76	RAFGSA	Kingsfield, Cyprus	2.12.06
					NEJSGSA 3, EI-141, BGA 2207				
	DLW	2209	DLW	SZD-30 Pirat	B-467	PH-433	12.76	G F Bryce and Partners	North Connel	29. 4.96
							(Stored 2.06)		
G-DDLY	2211	DLY	Eiriavion PIK-20D	20509		5. 1.77	M Conrad	Bidford	23. 5.08
	DLZ	2212	456	Swales SD3-15T	03		12.76	R E Harris	Rivar Hill	25. 5.05
G-DDMB	2214	831	Schleicher K 8B	8209	D-4331	18. 1.77	Crown Service Gliding Club "Kate"	Lasham	3. 2.08
G-DDMD	2216	251	Glaser-Dirks DG-100	75		12.76	N M Hill	RAF Weston-on-the-Green	24. 2.08
	DMF	2218	DMF	Schleicher K7	7073	D-4313	2. 3.77	J S Morgan	Bidford	22. 9.08
G-DDMG	2219	DMG	Schleicher K 8B	8763	RAFGSA 382	19. 3.77	Dorset Gliding Club	Eyres Field	28. 9.08
	DMH	2220	DMH	Grob G102 Astir CS	1511		23. 4.77	Oxford Gliding Club	RAF Weston-on-the-Green	21. 6.08
	DMJ	2221	DMJ	Schleicher K 8B	8077	PH-290	19. 3.77	Not known (Stored 10.04)	Strathaven	23. 9.93
	DMK	2222	593	Schempp-Hirth SHK	25	D-5401	5. 4.77	P Gray	Aston Down	3. 6.08
G-DDML	2223	DML	Schleicher K7	929	D-6194, D-5005	4. 2.77	Dumfries & District Gliding Club	Falgunzeon	11. 2.07
G-DDMM	2224	74	Schempp-Hirth Nimbus-2	125		4. 2.77	T E Linee	Eyres Field	24. 4.08
	DMN	2225	DMN	Glasflügel Mosquito	20		2.77	R P Brecknock	Dunstable	27. 3.03
	DMP	2226	233	Grob G102 Astir CS	1239	ZS-GKF	1. 3.77	P Miles	Dunstable	3. 5.08
G-DDMO	2227	DMO	Schleicher Ka 6E	4062	RAFGSA 264	12. 3.77	Trent Valley Gliding Club	Kirton in Lindsey	18. 6.08
G-DDMR	2228	511	Grob G102 Astir CS	1435		19. 3.77	Mendip Gliding Club	Halesland	16. 2.08
G-DDMS	2229	259	Glasflügel Standard Libelle 201B	385	RNGSA 259	19. 3.77	B I Stoddart	Burn	12. 4.08
	DMU	2231	392	Eiriavion PIK-20D	20524		3.77	J Mjels	Sutton Bank	2. 5.08
G-EDMV	2232	"DVM"	Eiriavion PIK-20D	20526		12. 4.77	R Cochrane	Bellarena	13. 4.08
G-DDMX	2234	DMX	Schleicher ASK 13	13567		5. 4.77	Dartmoor Gliding Society	Brentor	1. 8.08
	DNB	2238		Grunau Baby IIB	2	RAFGSA 380	2.77	P Underwood	Eaton Bray	*
					D-5766		(On rebuild 2000; to be in Luftwaffe c/s)		
G-DDNC	2239		Grob G102 Astir CS	1428		13. 4.77	R A Lovegrove and K S Wells	Lyveden	27. 6.99
G-DDND	2240	DND	Pilatus B4-PC11AF	136		19. 3.77	R J Happs and Partners	Lasham	3. 2.08
G-DDNE	2241	DNE	Grob G102 Astir CS77	1631		15. 7.77	J J Green and Partners	Halesland	26. 3.08
	DNF	2242	DNF	SZD-9bis Bocian 1D	P-354	HB-657	23. 4.77	M G Shaw	Portmoak	24. 2.08
G-DDNG	2243	265	Schempp-Hirth Nimbus-2	126		5. 4.77	B H Penfold	Trenchard Lines, Upavon	5. 3.08
G-DDNJ	2245	DNJ	Schleicher ASK 18	18042		13. 4.77	Derbyshire & Lancashire Gliding Club	Camphill	18. 1.08
G-DDNK	2246	745	Grob G102 Astir CS	1434		3. 5.77	A C Page and Partners	Rattlesden	1. 3.08
G-AXZH	2247	123	Glasflügel Standard Libelle	82	RAFGSA 742	23. 4.77	M C Gregorie	Gransden Lodge	6. 6.08
					RAFGSA 16, G-AXZH				
G-CEVV	2251	307	Rolladen-Schneider LS3	3035		1.77	M C Cooper and Partners	Challock	8. 3.08
G-DDNT	2254	DNT	SZD-30 Pirat	S-07.12		25. 5.77	R K Lashly	Drumshade	27. 4.08
	DNU	2255	DNU	SZD-42-1 Jantar 2A	B-783		4.77	C D.Rowland and Partners	Wycombe Air Park	26. 5.08
	DNV	2256	DNV	Schleicher ASK 13	13568		4.77	Channel Gliding Club	Waldershare Park	7. 6.08
G-DDNW	2257	DNW	Schleicher Ka 6CR	829	??	5.77	K F Marchant and P Carey	Edgehill	23. 4.08
G-DDNX	2258	DNX	Schleicher Ka 6CR	6094Si	D-5107	14. 6.77	Black Mountains Gliding Club	Talgarth	28. 9.08
	DNZ	2260	DNZ	Schleicher K 8B	8095	D-1711	5.77	Southampton University Gliding Club	Bicester	28. 8.08
G-DDPA	2261	DPA	Schleicher ASK 18	18044		25. 5.77	Rangetour Ltd	Bembridge	4. 3.08
	DPG	2267	DPG	München Mü 13D III	005	D-1327	14. 6.77	G J Moore	Dunstable	3. 6.08
	DPH	2268	287	Schempp-Hirth Mini Nimbus	9		5.77	J W Murdoch	Portmoak	30. 4.08
	DPJ	2269	DPJ	Grob G102 Astir CS77	1641		8. 7.77	G Chaplin	Lasham	26. 4.05
	DPK	2270	DPK	Glasflügel Mosquito	27		6.77	G Lawley	Cross Hayes	11. 9.08
G-DDPL	2271	437	Eiriavion PIK-20D	20549		26. 6.77	H A Schuricht	Dunstable	22. 1.08
	DPP	2274	DPP	Scheibe Ka 2B Rhönschwalbe	105	D-1880	1. 7.77	B G Hoekstra	Breda, Netherlands	8. 7.02
G-DDPO	2275	DPO	Grob G102 Astir CS77	1632		8. 7.77	Dorset Gliding Club	Eyres Field	14. 4.08
	DPR	2276	D-1265	Scheibe L-Spatz	05	D-1265	8. 7.77	C P Raine "Sparrowfahrt"	Thame	25. 7.01
	DPT	2278	DPT	Scheibe L-Spatz 55	01	RAFGSA	25. 8.77	B V Smith (Stored 9.07)	Rufforth	12. 7.98
	DPU	2279	DPU	EoN AP.5 Olympia 2B	EoN/O/142	RAFGSA 274	6. 9.77	J M Turner	Challock	12. 5.07
	DPX	2282	RZ	Schleicher ASW 19B	19126		7.77	R A Johnson	Long Mynd	19. 6.08
G-DDPY	2283	375	Grob G102 Astir CS77	1652		8.77	D S Burton	Edgehill	27. 5.08
	DPZ	2284	DPZ	Slingsby T.34A Sky	822	HB-561	9. 8.77	J S Morgan (Under restoration 2005)	Pershore	3. 7.00
G-DDOA	2285	DOA	Schleicher ASK 13	13582		8.77	Essex & Suffolk Gliding Club	Wormingford	28. 9.08
G-DDOB	2286	844	Grob G102 Astir CS77	1653		8.77	C E Hutson	Kirton in Lindsey	1. 4.08
	DQC	2287	DQC	Schleicher Ka 6CR	6373Si	D-5725	26. 9.77	P Morant	Lasham	15. 9.08
	DQD	2288	DQD	Slingsby T.8 Tutor	-		25. 8.77	K J Nurcombe	Husbands Bosworth	10.10.03
					(Assembled F Breeze from parts)				
	DQE	2289	480	Grob G102 Astir CS77	1636		8.77	Heron Gliding Club	RNAS Yeovilton	25. 7.08
G-DDOF	2290	DOF	Schleicher Ka 6CR	6417	D-5827	9.77	A Graham	(Kirkintilloch)	24. 4.08

G-GSST	2291	770	Grob G102 Astir CS77	1649		6. 9.77	A G Veitch and Partners	Easterton	13. 4.08
G-DDOK	2294	542	Schleicher Ka 6E	4341	D-0541	15.10.77	S Y Duxbury and R S Hawley	Long Mynd	7. 4.08
G-PILY	2296	DQM	Pilatus B4-PC11	138	RAFGSA 506	15.10.77	N Frost	(Buxton)	11. 2.08
DQP	2298	DQP	Schleicher K 8B	1181	??	15.11.77	V W Jennings	RAF Wittering	1.10.06
G-DDOR	2300	556	Grob G102 Astir CS77	1667		10.77	R Yerburgh and Partners	Kingston Deverill	28. 9.08
G-CEWO	2301	DQS	Schleicher Ka 6CR	1065	D-5144	23.11.77	J M Robinson	North Hill	9. 2.08
DQU	2303	DQU	Eiriavion PIK-20D-78	20579		10.77	E L Pole	Portmoak	5. 8.08
G-DDOX	2306	DOX	Schleicher K7	743	D-9127	15.11.77	Nene Valley Gliding Club	Upwood	31. 3.08
			(Modified to ASK 13 standard, with fuselage from ASK 13 BGA 1833; wings now from BGA 3331)						
G-DDOY	2307	DOY	Schleicher K 8B	647	D-4375	11.77	Mendip Gliding Club	Halesland	18. 8.08
DRA	2309	904	Schleicher Ka 6CR	1118	D-9011	11.77	904 Syndicate	Shobdon	27. 7.08
DRB	2310	86	Glaser-Dirks DG-100	31	PH-532	11.77	J D.Peck	Bicester	5. 4.08
G-DDRD	2312	DRD	Schleicher Ka 6CR	6377Si	D-9080	11.77	Essex & Suffolk Gliding Club	Wormingford	28. 9.08
DRE	2313	DRE	Schleicher Ka 6CR	6197	D-8558	25. 1.78	J H Jowett	North Hill	27. 8.08
DRJ	2317	D	Schleicher ASK 13	13583		11. 1.78	Lasham Gliding Society	Lasham	11. 4.08
DRK	2318	NT	Grob G102 Astir CS77	1686		12.77	N Toogood	RAF Weston-on-the-Green	24. 4.07
DRL	2319	DRL	Scheibe SF 26A Standard	5040	D-7073	15.12.77	D King	Strubby	21. 9.08
G-DDRM	2320	DRM	Schleicher K7	7017	D-4666	1. 2.78	L G Cross and Syndicate	Dunstable	3.10.07
DRN	2321	821	Glasflügel Mosquito	82		11. 2.78	A Roberts	Cross Hayes	1. 6.08
DRP	2322	DRP	Pilatus B4-PC11	080	RAFGSA BGA 1927	5. 1.78	M C Moxon	RAF Weston-on-the-Green	18. 4.08
DRQ	2323	258	Grob G103 Twin Astir	3027		25. 1.78	J S Catmur	Sleap	26. 4.08
DRR	2324	DRR	Schleicher Ka 2 Rhönschwalbe	49	D-8108	11. 1.78	Dumfries and District Gliding Club	Falgunzeon	28. 7.08
G-DDRT	2326	688	Eiriavion PIK-20D-78	20587		5. 1.78	P F C Fowler and Partners	Long Mynd	4. 4.08
G-DDRU	2327	334	Grob G102 Astir CS77	1685		5.1.78	G Rybak	Lasham	26. 2.08
G-DDRV	2328	DRV	Schleicher K 8B	8026	D-6169	1.78	P G Clayton	Portmoak	25. 9.08
G-DDRW	2329	798	Grob G102 Astir CS	1081	D-3311	23. 2.78	P A Brooks and Partners	Lasham	1. 5.08
DRY	2331		Schleicher Ka 6BR	370	D-5553	11. 2.78	S Urry	Tibenham	25. 9.08
G-DDRZ	2332	DRZ	Schleicher K 8B	668	D-4622 D-KANB, D-4622	1. 2.78	East Sussex Gliding Club	Ringmer	31. 7.08
DSA	2333	DSA	Slingsby T.30B Prefect	575	WE985	11. 2.78	J M Turner	Challock	14. 6.08
G-DDSB	2334	DSB	Schleicher Ka 6E	4300	D-0263	15. 3.78	B Griffith	Rattlesden	6. 3.08
DSE	2337	227	Schempp-Hirth Mini Nimbus	36		2.78	G J Binnie	Bicester	4. 8.08
G-DDSF	2338	DSF	Schleicher K 8B	8220	D-7114	2.78	Edinburgh University Gliding Club "Snoopy"	Portmoak	28. 9.08
DSG	2339		Schleicher Ka 6CR	6393	D-5696	13. 4.78	R N Boddy	Wycombe Air Park	29. 8.07
G-DDSH	2340	648	Grob G102 Astir CS77	1696		13. 4.78	R B Petrie and Partners	Portmoak	7. 6.08
DSJ	2341	DSJ	Grob G103 Twin Astir	3050		8. 3.78	Herefordshire Gliding Club	Shobdon	24. 8.08
DSL	2343	DSL	Grob G103 Twin Astir	3041		2. 3.78	Shenington Gliding Club	Edgehill	28. 9.08
DSM	2344	-	Fauvel AV.22S	3	F-CCGM	4.78	I Dunkley	Jezow, Poland	1. 8.95
							(Under restoration 2006)		
DSP	2346	270	Schempp-Hirth Mini Nimbus	33		9. 3.78	R I Hey and Partners	Nympsfield	5. 4.08
G-DDST	2350	972	Schleicher ASW 20L	20059		24. 8.78	D J Miller	Dunstable	22. 2.08
G-DDSU	2351	DSU	Grob G102 Astir CS77	1663		19. 4.78	Bowland Forest Gliding Club	Chipping	28. 9.08
G-DDSV	2352	DSV	Pilatus B4-PC11AF	134	RAFGSA 718 RAFGSA 518	23. 3.78	S J Brenton and G M Drinkell	Wormingford	1. 6.08
G-DDSX	2354	877	Schleicher ASW 19B	19188		13. 4.78	B Ashbourn and G Kamp	Kingston Deverill	28. 9.08
G-DDSY	2355	DSY	Schleicher Ka 6CR	561	D-5702	28. 4.78	D A Senior and Partners "Daisy"	Camphill	14. 3.08
G-DDTA	2357	699	Glaser-Dirks DG-200	2-27		9. 5.78	M Bowman	Rufforth	17. 7.08
DTC	2359	DTC	Schempp-Hirth Janus B	63	RAFGSA R9 RAFGSA 16, BGA 2359	4.78	Dukeries Gliding Club	Darlton	16. 6.08
G-DDTE	2361	DTE	Schleicher ASW 19B	19185		28. 4.78	G R and A Purcell	Edgehill	4.12.07
DTG	2363	DTG	Schempp-Hirth SHK-1	012	D-2034	9. 5.78	J P Dean	AAC Wattisham	24. 6.08
G-DDTK	2366	760	Glasflügel Mosquito B	109		17. 5.78	P France	Usk	28. 9.08
G-DDTM	2368	DTM	Glaser-Dirks DG-200	2-34		31. 5.78	R S Skinner	Wormingford	12. 3.08
DTN	2369	DTN	Schleicher K 8B	117/58	D-	1. 6.78	F McKeegan	AAC Wattisham	24. 8.08
G-DDTP	2370	915	Schleicher ASW 20	20078		4. 5.78	T S and S M Hills	Lasham	28. 9.08
DTR	2372	DTR	EoN AP.6 Olympia 401	EoN/4/005		31. 5.78	P Blackman	(Ringmer)	15. 5.02
					NEJSGSA 7 RAFGSA 252, G-APSI		(Stored 2006)		
G-DDTU	2375	DTU	Schempp-Hirth Nimbus-2B	167		9. 5.78	R E Wooller	Chipping	28. 9.08
G-DDTV	2376	704	Glasflügel Mosquito B	110		7. 6.78	S R Evans	Aston Down	5. 4.08
DTW	2377	DTW	SZD-30 Pirat	S-07.11		7. 6.78	C Kaminski	Eaglescott	30. 7.05
G-DDTX	2378	DTX	Glasflügel Mosquito B	111		18. 5.78	P T S Nash	Crowland	23. 1.02
G-DDTY	2379	766	Glasflügel Mosquito B	112		18. 5.78	W H L Bullimore	Gransden Lodge	2.11.07
DTZ	2380	S30	Slingsby T.30B Prefect	573	WE983	21. 6.78	D.Gibbs	Lee-on-Solent	14.12.06
DUB	2382	912	Glasflügel Mosquito B	113		31. 5.78	F B Reilly and Partners	Portmoak	9. 6.08
DUC	2383	-	CARMAM M.100S Mésange	012	F-CCSA	7. 6.78	Not known (Stored 1.05)	Carlton Moor	5.88*
DUD	2384	-	Grunau Baby III	Not known	BGA 2074 RAFGSA 374, D-9142	7. 6.78	Norfolk & Suffolk Aviation Museum	Flixton	29. 3.92
DUE	2385	A11	Schleicher ASK 13	13591	AGA 15 BGA 2385	4. 7.78	Anglia Gliding Club	AAC Wattisham	4. 5.08
G-DDUF	2386	DUF	Schleicher K 8B	8296A	D-5294	11. 7.78	M Staljan	Nympsfield	6. 7.08
DUH	2388	DUH	Scheibe L-Spatz 55	760	??	28. 7.78	R J Aylesbury	Upwood	14. 7.08
G-DDUK	2390	DUK	Schleicher K 8B	752	D-4048	21. 6.78	Bristol & Gloucestershire Gliding Club	Nympsfield	13. 3.08
G-DDUL	2391	642	Grob G102 Astir CS77	1720		21. 6.78	A Spencer	Kirton in Lindsey	2. 4.08
G-DADJ	2394	DUQ	Glaser-Dirks DG-200	2-43		4. 7.78	A D.Joslin	Wormingford	25. 5.08
G-DDUR	2395	DUR	Schleicher Ka 6CR	6273	OY-DLX	15. 8.78	B N Bromley and M Whitthread	Strubby	8.12.07
DUS	2396	638	Schleicher Ka 6E	4263	OY-XCB HB-948	8.78	R Bartlett	Tibenham	10.11.05
DUT	2397	T34	Schleicher ASW 20	20089		24. 8.78	M E Doig	Portmoak	11. 6.08
G-DDUX	2401	DUX	Grob G102 Astir CS Jeans	2140		25. 9.78	B T Spreckley	Ontur, Spain	28. 9.08
DUY	2402	652	Glaser-Dirks DG-100	24	PH-525	13.10.78	A C Saxton and Partners	Currock Hill	26. 7.05
G-DDVB	2405	DVB	Schleicher ASK 13	13596		8.78	Essex & Suffolk Gliding Club	Wormingford	2. 2.08
			(Components including c/n plate donated to BGA 3493)						

DVC	2406	DVC	Schleicher ASK 13	13597		31. 8.78	Staffordshire Gliding Club	Seighford	5. 6.08
G-DDVD	2407	DVD	LET L-13 Blanik	027021		9. 9.78	Vectis Gliding Club	Bembridge	27.12.08
G-DDVG	2410	DVG	Schleicher Ka 6CR	003	D-1916	22.11.78	G Tilley and Partners	Ringmer	20. 2.08
			(Built Holzmann Diespeck)						
DVH	2411	DVH	Schleicher Ka 6E	4117	RAFGSA 315	31. 8.78	R A J Jones	Brentor	23. 9.08
G-PIKD	2412	869	Eiriavion PIK-20D-78	20638		9. 9.78	M C Hayes	Shobdon	22. 3.08
DVK	2413	732	SZD-48 Jantar-Standard 2	W-868		22. 9.78	G P Nuttall	Wycombe Air Park	30. 6.08
G-DDVL	2414	X96	Schleicher ASW 19	19222		10.10.78	A C M Phillips	Lasham	30. 3.08
G-DDVM	2415	DVM	Glasflügel Club Libelle 205	52	RAFGGA 581	12. 9.78	M A Field *(See BGA 2232)*	Wormingford	4. 4.08
G-DDVN	2416	DVN	Eiriavion PIK-20D-78	20641		22.11.78	T P Bassett and A D Butler	Burn	17. 4.08
G-DDVP	2417	971	Schleicher ASW 19B	19220		23. 9.78	P Cumming and Partners	Wycombe Air Park	29. 1.08
G-DDVS	2420	VS	Schempp-Hirth Standard Cirrus	"380"	RAFGSA 824	26. 9.78	T J and J C Milner	Rufforth	23. 3.08
			(C/n duplicates VH-GGC)						
DVV	2423	810	Schleicher ASW 20L	20100		9.78	A Hooper	Usk	8. 8.08
DVX	2425	S13	Schleicher ASK 13	13598		5.10.78	Shenington Gliding Club	Edgehill	28. 9.08
G-DDVY	2426	272	Schempp-Hirth Cirrus	52	OO-ZIR	10.78	M G Ashton and G Martin	Talgarth	27. 7.08
DVZ	2427	Z25	Glasflügel Mosquito B	133		31.10.78	B H Shaw	Husbands Bosworth	25. 6.08
DWB	2429	733	Glasflügel Mosquito B	135		10.11.78	T Edwards	(Derby)	9. 4.08
G-DDWC	2430	DWC	Schleicher Ka 6E	4111	AGA 11	24.10.78	D E Jones	Ridgewell	12. 4.08
DWE	2432	DWE	Schleicher K7	7132	D-5427	3.11.78	N T Large	Lleweni Parc	5. 1.04
DWF	2433	-	Grunau Baby IIB	-	AGA 16	11.78	D Shrimpton	RAF Keevil	9. 1.02
			(Built RNAY Fleetlands)		RNGSA 1-13, VW743		*(Stored 5.06)*		
G-DDWG	2434	DWG	Schleicher K 8B	165/60	D-5750	11.78	Dartmoor Gliding Society	Brentor	12.12.07
DWJ	2436	191	Glaser-Dirks DG-200	2-59		11.78	P R Desmond	Chipping	22. 3.08
G-DDWL	2438	DWL	Glasflügel Mosquito B	141		2.12.78	H A Stanford	Husbands Bosworth	3. 4.08
G-DDWN	2440	DWN	Schleicher K7	7101	D-5360	12.78	L R Merritt	Saltby	27. 5.08
DWP	2441	447	Glasflügel Mosquito B	136		15.12.78	R H Yarney	Lasham	23. 8.08
G-CEWW	2442	DWQ	Grob G102 Astir CS77	1758		9. 1.79	M R Woodiwiss	Sleap	14. 4.08
G-DDWR	2443	P9	Glasflügel Mosquito B	134	(BGA 2428)	23. 1.79	C D.Lovell	Lasham	11. 3.08
DWS	2444	728	Eiriavion PIK-20D-78	20652		7. 3.79	D.G Slocombe	Burn	6. 5.08
G-DDWT	2445	886	Slingsby T.65A Vega	1898		1.79	A P Grimley	(Cheshire)	28. 9.08
G-DDWU	2446	DWU	Grob G102 Astir CS	1201	D-7269	30. 1.79	D Evans and I B Cronyn	Hinton-in-the-Hedges	20.12.07
DWW	2448	DWW	Slingsby T.65A Vega	1896		2. 3.79	C J Pennycuick	Usk	18. 5.08
DXA	2452	483	Glasflügel Mosquito B	137		14. 2.79	K S Whiteley	Gransden Lodge	19. 4.08
G-DDXB	2453	81	Schleicher ASW 20	20142		.79	J A Timpany and Partners	Nympsfield	28. 9.08
G-DDXD	2455	132	Slingsby T.65A Vega 17L	1901		20. 4.79	P Stammell	Dunstable	21. 9.08
G-DDXE	2456	DXE	Slingsby T.65A Vega	1902		16. 5.79	H K Rattray	Usk	18. 1.08
DXF	2457	DXF	Slingsby T.65A Vega	1903		16. 5.79	B A Walker	Crowland	8. 6.08
DXG	2458	DXG	Slingsby T.65A Vega 17L	1906		2. 6.79	A D Morrison	Feshiebridge	18. 7.08
G-DDXH	2459	DXH	Schleicher Ka 6E	4198	RAFGSA 489	28. 3.79	B Hughes and Partners	Bicester	22. 3.08
					D-4093				
G-DDXJ	2460	DXJ	Grob G102 Astir CS77	1762		2. 3.79	M T Stickland	Portmoak	3.10.08
DXK	2461	160	Centrair ASW 20F	20108		15. 5.79	A Townsend	Nympsfield	17. 7.08
G-DDXL	2462	DXL	Schempp-Hirth Standard Cirrus	203G	AGA 1	6. 3.79	C J Button	Aston Down	30. 3.08
DXM	2463	DXM	Schleicher K7	626	RAFGGA 551	20. 3.79	Vale of Neath Gliding Club	Shipdham	26. 4.04
			(Partly modified to ASK 13 standard)		D-5707				
G-DDXN	2464	267	Glaser-Dirks DG-200	2-63		17. 3.79	J A Johnston	Gransden Lodge	16. 3.08
DXQ	2466	147	Schempp-Hirth Mini Nimbus C	96		13. 3.79	T Lamb and P Hawkin RAF Weston-on-the-Green		10. 7.08
G-DDXT	2469	286	Schempp-Hirth Mini Nimbus C	97		14. 3.79	J M Beattie and Partners	Wycombe Air Park	4. 3.08
G-BDWZ	2470	DXU	Slingsby T..59J Kestrel 22	1867	G-BDWZ	11. 4.79	T J Wilkinson	Sackville Lodge, Riseley	29. 4.08
G-DDXW	2472	354	Glasflügel Mosquito B	142		7. 4.79	P Newmark and R G Baines	Burn	16. 2.08
G-DDXX	2473	580	Schleicher ASW 19B	19245		17. 3.79	B C P Crook	(London)	28. 9.08
DXY	2474	HB-474	Müller Moswey III	Not known	HB-474	20. 4.79	B Pearson	Eaglescott	9. 8.04
DYB	2477	"DYN"	Schleicher K7	167/59	D-5775	29. 3.79	South London Gliding Centre	Kenley	9. 5.04
G-DDYC	2478	DYC	Schleicher Ka 6CR	6390	D-1545	20. 3.79	S S Ryan	Walney	22. 4.08
G-DDYE	2479	828	Schleicher ASW 20L	20143		27. 3.79	T A Sage and Partners	Dunstable	28. 9.08
G-DDYF	2480	850	Grob G102 Astir CS77	1805		7. 4.79	York Gliding Centre	Rufforth	28. 9.08
G-BDZG	2481	592	Slingsby T..59H Kestrel 22	1868	G-BDZG	31. 3.79	S P Wareham	Kingston Deverill	18. 2.08
DYH	2482	DYH	Glaser-Dirks DG-200	2-75		5. 4.79	P Johnson	Milfield	23. 9.08
G-DDYJ	2483	DYJ	Schleicher Ka 6CR	6583	D-5838	15. 5.79	R M Morris	Dunstable	14. 7.08
DYL	2485	DYL	CARMAM JP 15-36A Aiglon	37		4.79	P A Pickering	Crowland	17. 5.08
DYN	2486	DYN	Schleicher Ka 6CR	6129Si	D-8458	1. 5.79	J Hunneman *(See BGA 2477)*	Rivar Hill	24. 4.03
DYR	2489	DYR	Schleicher K7	766	D-5220	12. 4.79	UWE Gliding Club	Aston Down	1. 6.07
			(Partly modified to ASK 13 standard)						
G-DDYU	2491	742	Schempp-Hirth Nimbus-2C	181		18. 4.79	K Richards	Talgarth	31. 3.05
DYX	2494	M5	Schleicher ASW 20	20135		23. 6.79	J L Bugbee	North Hill	24. 9.08
G-NIMB	2495	943	Schempp-Hirth Nimbus-2C	180		24. 4.79	M J Slade	Eyres Field	3. 4.08
G-DDZA	2496	DZA	Slingsby T.65A Vega 17L	1907		26. 6.79	K-H Kuntze	Dunstable	2. 3.08
DZB	2497	639	Slingsby T.65A Vega	1908		10. 7.79	A A Black	Drumshade	5. 9.08
DZC	2498		Scheibe L-Spatz 55	642	RAFGGA 502	4. 5.79	G A Ford	(Aston Down)	23.10.98
					D-5629		*(Stored 2006)*		
DZF	2501	152	Schempp-Hirth Standard Cirrus	421G	RAFGSA 27	15. 5.79	L S Hood	Bicester	31. 5.08
G-DDZG	2502	909	Schleicher ASW 19B	19267		10. 5.79	S P Wareham	Kingston Deverill	18. 2.08
DZJ	2504	576	Grob G102 Club Astir	2230		11. 5.79	D.W Bassett and Partners	Halesland	30. 6.08
DZM	2507	DZM	Slingsby T.65A Vega	1909		10. 7.79	D.G MacArthur	Long Mynd	17. 5.08
DZN	2508	990	Slingsby T.65A Vega 17L	1910		13. 7.79	D.A White	Aboyne	30. 7.07
G-DDZP	2509	DZP	Slingsby T.65A Vega	1911		17.11.79	M T Crews	Milfield	25. 6.08
G-DDZR	2511	DZR	ICA-Brasov IS-28B2	87		13. 6.79	Lakes Gliding Club	Walney Island	9. 5.08
DZS	2512	DZS	SZD-8bis-0 Jaskolka	183	HB-583	30. 5.79	R A Wilgoss	Wycombe Air Park	28. 8.08
G-DDZT	2513	106	Eiriavion PIK-20D-78	20661		9. 6.79	A C Garside and Partners	Challock	1. 3.08
DZU	2514	DZU	Grob G102 Astir CS	1076	D-3308	6. 6.79	P F Clarke	Wycombe Air Park	30. 4.08
DZV	2515	839	Scheibe SF 27A Zugvogel V	6065	D-5839	17. 7.79	N Newham	Usk	8. 5.05
DZW	2516	DZW	Schleicher Ka 6CR	6628	D-1045	11. 7.79	A Wildman	Husbands Bosworth	18. 7.03
DZX	2517	-	Slingsby T.30B Prefect	577	WE987	6.79	AeroVenture *(On loan)*	Doncaster	17. 7.89

Reg	BGA	Code	Type	c/n	Prev id	Date	Owner	Location	Date
G-DDZY	2518	757	Schleicher ASW 19B	19275		13. 6.79	M C Fairman	Dunstable	29. 1.08
EAC	2522	367	Grob G102 Astir CS77	1803		14. 6.79	I Pickering	Aston Down	27. 7.06
G-EEAD	2523	EAD	Slingsby T.65A Vega	1912		30.11.79	D S Smith	Sutton Bank	25. 2.08
EAE	2524	107	Schleicher ASW 20L	20224		20. 6.79	A Smith	Challock	11. 3.08
G-DEAF	2525	EAF	Grob G102 Astir CS77	1830		12. 7.79	J Bell	Milfield	29. 9.08
EAG	2526	EAG	Slingsby T.65A Vega	1913		4. 9.79	D King	Usk	4. 9.08
G-DEAH	2527	EAH	Schleicher Ka 6E	4085	D-7542, D-7142	12. 7.79	M Lodge	Lasham	14. 6.08
G-DEAJ	2528	EAJ	Schempp-Hirth Nimbus-2	7	D-0699	28. 6.79	D R Piercy and N Hanney	Eyres Field	31. 3.08
G-DEAK	2529	594	Glasflügel Mosquito B	155		29. 6.79	T A L Barnes	Aston Down	9. 6.08
G-DEAM	2531	EAM	Schempp-Hirth Nimbus-2B	93	D-2787	10. 7.79	J Davies (Alpha Mike Syndicate)	Chipping	28. 9.08
G-DEAR	2535	EAR	Eiriavion PIK-20D	20550	RAFGSA 16	28. 7.79	D Irwin and R Penman　　(Yeovil and Bridport)		28. 9.08
EAT	2537	786	Eiriavion PIK-20D-78	20664		22. 8.79	M J Crawley and Partners	Lasham	5. 9.08
EAU	2538	EAU	Schleicher K7	7092	PH-304	29. 1.80	Welland Gliding Club	Lyveden	8. 9.07
			(Partly modified to ASK 13 standard)						
EAV	2539	360	Schempp-Hirth Mini Nimbus C	136		31. 7.79	G D.Crawford	RAF Weston-on-the-Green	22. 4.06
G-DEAW	2540	EAW	Grob G102 Astir CS77	1831		21. 7.79	J Cooke and Partners	Camphill	15.11.07
EBA	2544	EBA	Slingsby T.65A Vega 17L	1914		1.11.79	M W Dickson	Portmoak	16. 5.08
G-FEBB	2545	881	Grob G104 Speed Astir IIB	4040		28. 7.79	A F Grinter and Partners	Pocklington	27. 4.08
EBC	2546	EBC	Slingsby T.30B Prefect	583	RAFGSA 33	1. 8.79	K R Reeves	RAF Syerston	16. 5.04
			(Built from parts ex BGA 808 and BGA 1618?)　WE993				"Jonathan Livingstone Prefect"		
G-EEBD	2547	EBD	Scheibe Bergfalke IV	5822	D-1005	4. 9.79	D A Bell and Partners	Burn	10. 7.08
EBE	2548	EBE	Issoire E78 Silene	07		20.11.79	B A Burgess	Husbands Bosworth	22. 4.08
G-EEBF	2549	EBF	Schempp-Hirth Mini Nimbus C	138		17. 8.79	M Pingel	Talgarth	28. 9.08
EBG	2550	EBG	Eiriavion PIK-20D-78	20662		4. 9.79	P F Woodcock	Camphill	23.11.07
G-FEBJ	2552	h11	Schleicher ASW 19B	19282		21. 8.79	S J Hill and K Teagle	Sutton Bank	28. 9.08
G-EEBK	2553	552	Schempp-Hirth Mini Nimbus C	139	AGA 2 BGA 2553	17. 8.79	G Smith and N P Frost	Parham	28. 9.08
EBL	2554	EBL	Schleicher ASK 13	13610		7. 9.79	Derbyshire & Lancashire Gliding Club	Camphill	4.11.07
G-EEBM	2555	EBM	Grob G102 Astir CS77	1843		7. 2.80	Yorkshire Gliding Club	Sutton Bank	30. 1.08
EBN	2556	37	Centrair ASW 20FL	20118		22. 8.79	S MacArthur	Camphill	6. 7.08
EBP	2557	EBP	Allgaier Geier I	3/4	D-9025	4. 9.79	R A Earnshaw-Fretwell (Stored 4.07)	RAF Keevil	21. 7.01
G-EEBR	2559	EBR	Glaser-Dirks DG-200/17	2-89/1706	D-6893	6. 9.79	M D.Parsons	Bembridge	10. 6.08
EBS	2560	EBS	Scheibe Zugvogel IIIA	1054	LX-CAF D-8363	21.11.79	I D.McLeod	Challock	27. 8.08
							"Schwarzhornfalke"		
G-DEBX	2565	644	Schleicher ASW 20	20058	D-7973	21. 9.79	J P Davies and C Cownden	Gransden Lodge	15. 2.08
G-EEBZ	2567	EBZ	Schleicher ASK 13	13614		15. 1.80	Booker Gliding Club	Wycombe Air Park	28. 9.08
G-DECC	2570	ECC	Schleicher Ka 6CR	60/01	D-5080	10.10.79	G Higgins	Burn	18. 4.08
G-DECF	2573	ECF	Schleicher Ka 6CR	856	D-5808	24. 4.80	S J Daniell and Partners	Aston Down	15. 4.08
ECG	2574	ECG	Schempp-Hirth SHK	19	D-5359, D-1329	10.10.79	J L Williams	Trenchard Lines, Upavon	27. 4.08
ECH	2575	ECH	Glasflügel Mosquito B	173		24. 1.80	A Walker and Partners	Rattlesden	9. 8.08
ECJ	2576	ECJ	Slingsby T.65A Vega	1916		21.12.79	J E B Hart and Partners	Sutton Bank	27. 4.08
G-EECK	2577	ECK	Slingsby T.65A Vega	1917		13.12.79	J P Dunnington	Portmoak	19. 1.08
G-DECL	2578	ECL	Slingsby T.65A Vega 17L	1918		2. 2.80	J B Strzebrakowski	Lyveden	19. 6.08
ECM	2579	ECM	Slingsby T.65A Vega	1919		15. 1.80	F L Wilson	Aston Down	23. 9.08
G-DECP	2581	ECP	Rolladen-Schneider LS3-17	3426		26. 3.80	D Crowhurst and M Ewer	Crowland	17. 3.08
G-FECO	2582	ECO	Grob G102 Astir CS77	1837		25.10.79	C Peterson	Tibenham	16. 5.08
ECR	2583	WE990	Slingsby T.30B Prefect	580	WE990	10.79	D Ladley (Under restoration 2007)	Norfolk	7.84*
ECS	2584	955	Glasflügel Mosquito B	166		26.10.79	K L Fixter	Llantisilio	17. 8.08
ECT	2585	604	Glasflügel 604	2	I-FEVG, D-0279	4.10.79	P T Nash (Cancelled 1.12.07)	Crowland	1. 6.08
ECW	2588	ECW	Schleicher ASK 21	21008		2. 3.80	Norfolk Gliding Club	Tibenham	22. 6.08
G-DECZ	2591	ECZ	Schleicher ASK 21	21009		26. 4.80	Booker Gliding Club	Wycombe Air Park	28. 9.08
EDA	2592	647	Slingsby T.65A Vega 17L	1888	G-BFYW	30.11.79	S Whitaker	Parham	9. 9.08
G-DEDB	2593	EDB	CARMAM JP 15-36AR Aiglon	40		1. 2.80	R A Putt and Partners	Husbands Bosworth	29. 3.08
EDC	2594	-	Schleicher K7	244	D-8527	13. 2.80	J C Shipley (Stored 8.07)	Camphill	8. 7.04
EDD	2595	W17	Schleicher ASW 17	17043	D-6865	23. 4.80	M D.Etherington	Saltby	14.12.05
G-EEDE	2596	750	Centrair ASW 20F	20128		27. 2.80	G M Cumner	Aston Down	11. 1.08
G-HAUT	2597	530	Schempp-Hirth Mini Nimbus C	149		8. 1.80	L J Kaye and Partners	Shobdon	1. 1.08
EDG	2598	EDG	Schleicher Ka 6CR	6512	RAFGSA	9. 1.80	M Wood	RAF Cranwell	20. 7.08
EDH	2599	EDH	Glasflügel Mosquito B	184		25. 3.80	D.G Cooper	Tibenham	24. 7.05
G-DEDJ	2600	EDJ	Glasflügel Mosquito B	185		4. 4.80	D H Martin and R Bollom	Camphill	26. 2.08
G-DEDK	2601	EDK	Schleicher K7	791	D-1633	13. 2.80	North Wales Gliding Club	Llantisilio	18. 4.08
			(Partly modified to ASK 13 standard)						
EDL	2602	-	Focke-Wulf Weihe 50	4	D-0893 HB-555	26. 1.80	F K Russell	Dunstable	14.10.96
							(Being restored during 2000)		
G-DEDM	2603	EDM	Glaser-Dirks DG-200	2-98		17. 2.80	A H G St Pierre	Sutton Bank	29. 3.08
EDN	2604	820	Glaser-Dirks DG-100G Elan	E12G6		14. 2.80	A P Scott and Partners	Currock Hill	6. 7.08
G-DIGIO	2605	EDP	Glaser-Dirks DG-100G Elan	E19G7		12. 2.80	L Humphries and Partners	North Hill	28. 9.08
G-DEDU	2610	EDU	Schleicher ASK 13	13613		22. 3.80	Kent Gliding Club	Challock	28. 2.08
EDV	2611	541	Slingsby T.65A Vega 17L	1893	G-BGCU	8. 2.80	K Challinor	Long Mynd	24. 7.07
EDW	2612	EDW	Schleicher ASK 21	21010		5. 4.80	UCLU Gliding Club	RAF Halton	11. 7.08
EDX	2613	EDX	Slingsby T.65D Vega	1928		20. 5.80	G Kirkham	Camphill	27. 4.08
G-DEDY	2614	EDY	Slingsby T.65D Vega	1929		23. 5.80	C J Steadman and Partners	Husbands Bosworth	27. 3.08
EDZ	2615	EDZ	Slingsby T.65C Sport Vega	1931		18. 6.80	R C Copley	Walney Island	12. 6.08
EEA	2616	337	Slingsby T.65C Sport Vega	1932		27. 6.80	L Dent	Milfield	28. 9.08
G-DEEC	2618	EEC	Schleicher ASW 20L	20311	G-BSTS BGA 2618	27. 6.80	D M Cushway	Challock	5. 3.08
EED	2619	EED	Schleicher K 8B	590	RAFGSA R91 NEJSGSA, BGA 2619, D-5703	1. 3.80	A Twigg	Bicester	9. 8.08
G-MEEE	2620	EEE	Schleicher ASW 20L	20312		4. 4.80	T E Macfadyen	Nympsfield	28. 9.08
G-DEEF	2621	EEF	Rolladen-Schneider LS3-17	3441		13. 6.80	P Morgan and Partners	Rivar Hill	28. 9.08
G-DEEG	2622	EEG	Slingsby T.65C Sport Vega	1922	EI-129 BGA 2622	25. 2.80	G Harris and Partners	Rufforth	2. 5.08
EEH	2623	166	Schleicher ASW 19	19042	RAFGGA 166	27. 2.80	K Kiely	AAC Dishforth	24. 7.08
EEJ	2624	EEJ	Schleicher ASW 20L	20314		20. 9.80	R R Stoward	Dunstable	25. 7.04

G-DEEK	2625	996	Schempp-Hirth Nimbus-2C	201		23. 2.80	M N Erlund	Saltby	28. 9.08
G-DEEM	2627	EEM	Schleicher K 8B	8688AB	D-0254	28. 2.80	South Wales Gliding Club	Usk	28. 5.08
G-DEEN	2628	EEN	Schempp-Hirth Standard Cirrus 75	621	(BGA 2609) RAFGSA 87	1. 3.80	J Hanlon	RAF Weston-on-the-Green	20. 4.08
G-DEEP	2629	EEP	Wassmer WA-26P Squale	36	F-CDSX	30. 6.80	B J Key and Partners	Aston Down	15. 4.08
EEO	2630	EEO	Grob G102 Standard Astir II	5015S		3.80	P A Jewell	Lleweni Parc	18.11.07
G-EEER	2631	EER	Schempp-Hirth Mini Nimbus C	150		14. 3.80	D.J Uren	Culdrose	14. 3.08
G-DEES	2632	50	Rolladen-Schneider LS3-17	3248		26. 3.80	J Illidge	Camphill	28. 9.08
EEV	2635	BW	Centrair ASW 20FL	20145		15. 5.80	R Baez	Wittstock-Berlinchen, Germany	28. 9.08
G-DEEW	2636	EEW	Schleicher Ka 6CR	6188	RAFGGA D-6151	26. 3.80	S Dodds	Saltby	31. 7.08
G-DEEX	2637	EEX	Rolladen-Schneider LS3-17	3442		5. 7.80	W A Dallimer and Partner	Aston Down	31. 3.08
G-ILBO	2639	157	Rolladen-Schneider LS3-a	3458		10. 6.80	J P Gilbert	Wormingford	28. 9.08
EFA	2640	470	Schleicher ASW 20L	20326		2. 7.80	R G Cooper	Dunstable	29. 5.08
EFB	2641	EFB	Schempp-Hirth Nimbus-2C	216		3. 4.80	N Revell and Partners	Saltby	23. 7.07
EFC	2642	EFC	Siebert Sie 3	3018	D-0811	3. 4.80	M S A Skinner	Cross Hayes	25. 5.08
G-DEFE	2644	586	Centrair ASW 20F	20139		1. 5.80	W A Horne and D A Mackenzie	Camphill	5. 4.08
G-DEFF	2645	737	Schempp-Hirth Nimbus-2C	208		10. 4.80	D.L Jobbins	Usk	23. 4.08
EFG	2646	EFG	Schleicher K 8B	Not known	RAFGGA	10. 4.80	Essex Gliding Club	Ridgewell	27. 4.08
EFJ	2648	EFJ	Centrair ASW 20F	20127		12. 4.80	D.E Ball	Wycombe Air Park	26. 5.06
G-EEFK	2649	643	Centrair ASW 20FL	20140	F-WFLZ	15. 5.80	G B Monslow and A P Balkwill	Snitterfield	21. 2.08
G-EFLY	2650	LY	Centrair ASW 20FL	20133		15. 5.80	I D and J H Atherton	Tibenham	14. 9.08
G-FGAZ	2651	GAZ	Schleicher Ka 6E	4103	RAFGSA	4. 6.80	G S Foster	Parham	17. 4.08
EFN	2652	EFN	Scheibe L-Spatz 55	635	D-1617	17. 5.80	J A Halliday	Aston Down	6. 7.08
EFS	2656	LS3	Rolladen-Schneider LS3	3022	HB-1356	14. 5.80	S Carmichael	Dunstable	29. 8.07
EFT	2657	EFT	Schempp-Hirth Nimbus-2B	26	HB-1160	23. 4.80	S A Adlard	Long Mynd	17. 5.08
G-DEFV	2659	EFV	Schleicher ASW 20	20041	OE-5162	12. 6.80	A R McKillen	Bellarena	13. 5.08
G-DEFW	2660	EFW	Slingsby T.65C Sport Vega	1938		18. 7.80	Darlton Gliding Club	Darlton	22. 9.08
EFZ	2663	EFZ	Rolladen-Schneider LS3-a	3273		21. 7.80	D.H Gardner	Aston Down	9. 6.08
EGD	2667	827	Schleicher ASW 17	17028	D-2343	25. 6.80	C J Teagle	Sutton Bank	31. 5.08
G-DEGE	2668	EGE	Rolladen-Schneider LS3-a	3465		31. 7.80	G Szabo-Toth and Partners	Nympsfield	28. 9.08
EGF	2669	EGF	Slingsby T.65C Sport Vega	1936		28. 6.80	P Aitken	Lee-on-Solent	24. 2.08
EGG	2670	JH	Slingsby T.65C Sport Vega	1939		23. 9.80	R Robbins	Usk	22.12.05
G-DEGH	2671	EGH	Slingsby T.65C Sport Vega	1943		28.11.80	M J Davies and Partners	Darlton	29. 4.08
G-DEGJ	2672	672	Slingsby T.65C Sport Vega	1944		12.12.80	M J Heneghan and Partners	Lee-on-Solent	7. 3.08
G-DEGK	2673	569	Schempp-Hirth Standard Cirrus	542G	RAFGSA 569 RAFGSA R2	1. 7.80	I Ashdown	Parham	28. 9.08
EGN	2676	EGN	Grob G103 Twin II	3542		19. 8.80	Staffordshire Gliding Club "Stone Eagle"	Seighford	19. 9.08
EGP	2677	BS1	Schleicher ASW 20L	20336		17. 9.80	B K Scaysbrook	Husbands Bosworth	25. 7.08
EGR	2679	EGR	Breguet 905SA Fauvette	18	F-CCGT	22. 8.80	P Parker	Dunstable	15. 2.03
G-DEGS	2680	2CS	Schempp-Hirth Nimbus-2CS	192	D-2111	21. 7.80	R C Nichols	Pocklington	22. 3.08
EGT	2681	EGT	Slingsby T.65D Vega	1933		28. 7.80	D.M Badley and Partners	Sleap	28. 4.08
EGU	2682	EGU	Slingsby T.65A Vega 17L	1921		28. 7.80	M N Bishop (W/o 2006)	Challock	17. 8.06
EGW	2684	EGW	Schempp-Hirth Mini Nimbus B (Modified to Mini Nimbus C?)	78	HB-1447	1. 8.80	I F Barnes	Ridgewell	21. 7.08
G-DEGX	2685	EGX	Slingsby T.65C Sport Vega	1937	RAFGSA R23 BGA 2685	15.10.80	C P Raine and Partners	Thame	2. 5.07
G-DEGZ	2687	EGZ	Schleicher ASK 21	21030		28.10.80	Black Mountains Gliding Club	Talgarth	10. 3.08
EHA	2688	D-5084	Schleicher K 8B	136/59	D-5084	2. 9.80	Not known (Stored 6.04)	Fairwood Common	2. 9.81
EHB	2689	K3	Schleicher Ka 3	3	RAFGGA 559	23.10.80	L S Hood	RAF Cranwell	28. 5.05
EHC	2690	EHC	Akaflieg Braunschweig SB-5B	5017	D-9310	14. 8.80	R I Davidson	Husbands Bosworth	12. 5.05
EHD	2691	891	Schleicher ASW 20L	20386		21. 4.81	B Lumb	Sutton Bank	22. 5.08
EHE	2692	WE992	Slingsby T.30B Prefect	582	WE992	29. 9.80	A P Stacey (Stored 4.07)	RAF Keevil	5. 3.98
G-DEHG	2694	453	Slingsby T.65C Sport Vega	1940		21.10.80	A Smith and Partners	Lasham	19. 1.05
EHH	2695	V7	Schempp-Hirth Ventus a	07		5.11.80	J A White	Wycombe Air Park	2. 8.08
G-DEHK	2697	490	Rolladen-Schneider LS4	4068		15. 3.81	R T and G Starling	Nympsfield	28. 9.08
G-DEHL	2698	435	Rolladen-Schneider LS4	4024		24. 4.81	R Theil	Crowland	28. 9.08
EHM	2699	EHM	Schleicher Ka 6E	4118	RAFGSA 318	28. 3.81	J Symonds	Kingston Deverill	9. 8.08
EHN	2700	EHN	Slingsby T.65C Sport Vega	1942	G-BILH BGA 2700	17.12.80	A A Hampshire	Shipdham	9. 8.08
G-DEHP	2701	EHP	Schempp-Hirth Nimbus-2C	234		2. 7.81	D.J King	Rattlesden	11. 3.08
G-DEHO	2702	431	Schleicher ASK 21	21035		21.11.80	Lasham Gliding Society	Lasham	20. 2.08
EHS	2704	EHS	ICA-Brasov IS-28B2	89		3.12.80	M Terry	Darlton	24. 3.08
G-DEHT	2705	EHT	Schempp-Hirth Nimbus-2C	235		15. 8.81	S D.Codd	Edgehill	21. 3.08
G-DEHU	2706	849	Glasflügel 304	209		5.11.80	F Townsend	Bidford	28. 9.08
G-DEHV	2707	481	Schleicher ASW 20L	20385		6. 1.81	M A and B A Roberts	Wormingford	24. 2.08
G-DEHW	2708	EHW	ICA-Brasov IS-28B2	86		9. 1.81	P Van Besouw	(Netherlands)	14. 4.08
EHX	2709		Grunau Baby IIB	134	D-1128	12.80	J A Knowles	.	17. 2.08
EHY	2710	EHY	Slingsby T.65D Vega	1941		8. 1.81	B G Skilton	Ringmer	2. 5.07
G-DEHZ	2711	413	Schleicher ASW 20L	20388		29. 1.81	D Crimmins	Challock	19. 2.08
G-DEJA	2712	EJA	ICA-Brasov IS-28B2	88		16. 1.81	M H Simms	Shipdham	19. 4.07
EJB	2713	EJB	Slingsby T.65C Sport Vega	1945		23. 1.81	D Tait	Cross Hayes	11. 6.08
G-DEJC	2714	EJC	Slingsby T.65C Sport Vega	1946		9. 2.81	D Redfearn and I Powis	Darlton	14. 4.08
EJD	2715	261	Slingsby T.65D Vega 17L	1930	RAFGGA 510 BGA 2715	29. 6.81	A J French	Rufforth	28. 5.97
							(Damaged Dunstable 28.3.97: wreck noted 2006)		
G-DEJE	2716	EJE	Slingsby T.65C Sport Vega	1947		16. 2.81	Crown Service Gliding Club	Lasham	24. 2.08
EJF	2717	EJF	Schleicher K 8B	8966	D-2328	15. 1.81	Shalbourne Soaring Society	Rivar Hill	15. 7.08
G-DEJH	2719	"EHJ"	Akaflieg Braunschweig SB-5E	5041A	D-5430 D-0087	14. 1.81	B J Dawson and S E Richardson	Pocklington	24. 7.08
EJJ	2720	"WJ306"	Slingsby T.21B	618	RAFGSA 120 BGA 662, WB957	1. 3.81	A C Jarvis	Parham	2. 5.08
			(See BGA 3240 for the real WJ306)						
EJM	2723	385	Schempp-Hirth Janus C	112	BGA 4168 RAFGSA R1, BGA 2723, D-7013	2.81	H A Torode	Lasham	16. 4.08

G-CEVZ	2726	EJQ	Centrair ASW 20FL	20184		20. 4.81	J R Rayner and J R Matthews	Parham	4. 4.08
G-DEJR	2727	193	Schleicher ASW 19B	19334		12. 4.81	M D Thompson and Partners	Nympsfield	28. 9.08
EJS	2728	319	Slingsby T.65C Sport Vega	1948		20. 3.81	A D.McLeman	Portmoak	19. 9.08
G-VEGA	2729	AS	Slingsby T.65A Vega	1889	G-VEGA (G-BFZN)	5. 3.81	W A M Sanderson	Wormingford	16. 2.08
EJY	2734	EJY	SZD-9bis Bocian 1D	P-351	D-1587	13. 4.81	J A Stephen	Aboyne	29. 3.08
EJZ	2735	EJZ	Scheibe SF 26A Standard	5020	D-8473	3.81	M H Simms (New owner 6.07)	Shipdham	7.92
G-EEKA	2736	EKA	Glaser-Dirks DG-202/17	2-128/1730		3. 8.81	M J Lindsay and P Hayward	Tibenham	5. 3.08
G-DEKC	2738	EKC	Schleicher Ka 6E	4079	OO-ZDV OE-0813	18. 6.81	S L Benn	RAF Cranwell	23. 3.08
G-DEKD	2739	EKD	Schleicher ASK 13	13539	OH-494	21. 4.81	Midland Gliding Club	Long Mynd	19. 4.08
G-MAGK	2740	20L	Schleicher ASW 20L	20387		15. 4.81	A G K Mackenzie	Burn	2. 5.08
EKF	2741	EKF	Grob G102 Club Astir III	5519C		14. 6.81	Bristol & Gloucestershire Gliding Club	Nympsfield	17. 5.08
G-DEKG	2742	EKG	Schleicher ASK 21	21067	AGA 8 BGA 2742	24.11.81	Wyvern Gliding Club	Trenchard Lines, Upavon	28. 9.08
G-XXVB	2743	714	Schempp-Hirth Ventus b	32		1. 5.81	R G Johnson	Parham	29.11.07
G-DEKJ	2744	EKJ	Schempp-Hirth Ventus b	36		7. 5.81	I J Metcalfe	Nympsfield	28. 9.08
EKK	2745	EKK	SZD-48 Jantar-Standard 2	W-853		9. 5.81	P Scott	Gransden Lodge	25.12.06
							(Hit tree landing on ridge, near Lleweni Parc 14. 3.07)		
EKM	2747	-	Schleicher K 8B	657	PH-258	28. 5.81	Not known (Wreck stored 2.08)	Aston Down	2.89
EKP	2749	EKP	Glaser-Dirks DG-101G Elan	E71G46		3.10.81	P J Masson	Lasham	22. 6.08
EKR	2751	117	Schempp-Hirth Nimbus-2C	195	D-4904	25. 6.81	K S Walters and Partners	Lyveden	14. 4.08
							(Crashed on launch, Lyveden 2. 9.07)		
G-DEKS	2752	EKS	Scheibe SF 27A Zugvogel V	6096	D-8166	28. 4.81	J C Johnson	Ringmer	5. 3.08
EKT	2753	EKT	Wassmer WA-30 Bijave	241	F-CDML	11. 5.81	D.C Reynolds	AAC Dishforth	31. 8.08
G-DEKU	2754	408	Schleicher ASW 20L	20384		19. 5.81	A J Gillson	Sleap	28. 4.08
G-DEKV	2755	EKV	Rolladen-Schneider LS4	4102		12. 7.81	F G Bradney and E J Mason	Lasham	29. 3.08
EKW	2756	300	Schempp-Hirth Nimbus-2B	111	D-7245	7. 6.81	R S Jobar	Lasham	31. 5.08
EKX	2757	EKX	Schleicher Ka 6E	4027	D-1221	20. 6.81	A Coatsworth	Eyres Field	25. 8.08
G-DELA	2760	ELA	Schleicher ASW 19B	19346		28. 7.81	A G Stark and Partners	Aboyne	28. 9.08
ELC	2762	ELC	Slingsby T.45 Swallow	1474	AGA RAFGSA 346	25. 5.81	J Povall	AAC Dishforth	24.11.08
G-DELD	2763	ELD	Slingsby T.65C Sport Vega	1950		17. 8.81	N R Skelding and Partners	Snitterfield	21. 2.08
ELE	2764	ELE	Schleicher ASK 21	21065		1. 7.81	Midland Gliding Club	Long Mynd	29. 6.07
G-DELG	2766	ELG	Schempp-Hirth Ventus b/16.6	46		19. 8.81	A G Machin	Burn	17. 4.08
ELH	2767	ELH	Slingsby T.21B	Not known	RAFGSA 314 RAF	16. 9.81	Not known	Enstone	10. 7.91
			(Possibly ex WB966 [627])				(Stored 2005)		
ELL	2770	L01	Vogt Lo 100 Zwergreiher	25	HB-591	27. 7.81	LO100 Syndicate	RAF Halton	13. 9.08
G-DELN	2772	ELN	Grob G102 Astir CS Jeans	2024	??	12. 8.81	I Hammond Syndicate	Hinton-in-the-Hedges	14. 5.08
ELQ	2774	ELQ	Slingsby T.65D Vega	1934		3. 9.81	I Sim and Partners	Milfield	28. 8.08
G-DELR	2775	188	Schempp-Hirth Ventus b	45		19. 8.81	I D.Smith	Nympsfield	28. 9.08
ELS	2776	ELS	EoN AP.10 460 Series1	EoN/S/020	RAFGGA 530	7. 2.82	D.G Shepherd	Easterton	28. 4.08
G-EELT	2777	ELT	Rolladen-Schneider LS4	4186		20. 1.82	M Buckland and Partners	Lasham	9. 3.08
ELU	2778	696	Schleicher ASW 20L	20462		15. 4.82	G Fryer	Aston Down	30. 4.06
ELV	2779	ELV	Scheibe Zugvogel IIIB	1088	F-CCPX	5. 9.81	C R W Hill	Upwood	20. 4.08
G-DELX	2781	ELX	Schleicher K7	928	D-4023	18. 9.81	Nene Valley Gliding Club	Upwood	16. 5.08
G-EELY	2782	ELY	Schleicher Ka 6CR	6485Si	D-5172	28. 9.81	P F Richardson and Partners	Bellarena	12. 5.08
G-DELZ	2783	719	Schleicher ASW 20L	20310	RAFGGA 569	4.10.81	D.A Fogden	Wycombe Air Park	28. 9.08
G-DEMB	2785	RH	Rolladen-Schneider LS4	4185		1. 4.82	R A Hine	Wycombe Air Park	29. 1.08
G-DEME	2788	515	Glaser-Dirks DG-202/17C	2-176CL18		20. 5.82	E D.Casagrande	Usk	19. 3.08
G-DEMF	2789	452	Rolladen-Schneider LS4	4187		6. 3.82	R N Johnston	Hinton-in-the-Hedges	15. 3.08
G-DEMG	2790	EMG	Rolladen-Schneider LS4	4242		8. 5.82	R C Bowsfield	Aston Down	5. 3.08
G-DEMJ	2792	EMJ	Slingsby T.65C Sport Vega	1951		1. 2.82	D J Miles	Seighford	28. 4.08
EMK	2793	EMK	Slingsby T.45 Swallow	Not known	RAFGGA 545	14. 4.82	P T Pollard-Wilkins	Ringmer	22. 8.08
EML	2794	EML	Slingsby T.65A Vega	1892	G-BGCB	8.12.81	J W Williams	Brentor	24. 4.07
G-DEMN	2796	EMN	Slingsby T.65D Vega	1935		25. 1.82	C D Sword	Milfield	23. 7.08
G-DEMP	2797	EMP	Slingsby T.65C Sport Vega	1952		2. 2.82	Surrey Hills Gliding Club	Kenley	7. 2.08
EMR	2799	EMR	Slingsby T.65C Sport Vega	1954		10. 2.82	D A Woodforth	Strubby	7. 8.08
G-BGBV	2800	T65	Slingsby T.65A Vega 17L	1890	G-BGBV	26. 1.82	M P Day and Partners	Tibenham	27. 5.08
G-DEMT	2801	MF	Rolladen-Schneider LS4	4243		10. 6.82	M R Fox	Husbands Bosworth	17. 4.08
G-DEMU	2802	616	Glaser-Dirks DG-202/17	2-162/1753		1. 7.82	N Swinton and A Butterfield		
								RAF Weston-on-the-Green	28. 9.08
EMV	2803	EMV	Schleicher K7	Not known	AGA 13	1. 1.82	Shalbourne Soaring Society	Rivar Hill	11. 7.04
							(Wfu with glue failure)		
EMW	2804	17	Grunau Baby III	Not known	D-1373	5. 7.89	M T Sands	Santo Tome del Puerto, Spain	2. 7.08
G-LSIV	2806	264	Rolladen-Schneider LS4	4189		15. 4.82	D M Bland	Nympsfield	7. 4.08
G-DEMZ	2807	EMZ	Slingsby T.65A Vega	1891	G-BGCA	5. 2.82	F S Smith and Partners	Portmoak	25. 4.08
G-LSLS	2808	288	Rolladen-Schneider LS4	4191		31. 5.82	A M Sanders	Long Mynd	30. 3.08
G-EENE	2812	281	Rolladen-Schneider LS4	4271		1. 6.82	A P C Sampson	Dunstable	28. 9.08
ENG	2814	ENG	Focke-Wulf Kranich III	79	D-5420	8. 3.82	P R Davie and Partners	Germany	17. 8.04
							(To D-9666 2007)		
ENJ	2816	771	Schempp-Hirth Ventus b	62		25. 3.82	S J Boyden	Lasham	28. 8.08
G-EENK	2817	ENK	Schleicher ASK 21	21106		12. 4.82	W T Alden and Partners	Aston Down	12. 4.08
G-EENN	2820	345	Schempp-Hirth Nimbus-3/25.5	9		5. 4.83	I B Kennedy and A James	Usk	23. 2.08
ENP	2821	295	Schempp-Hirth Nimbus-3/25.5	10		12.11.82	D.Hayen	Goetsenhoven, Belgium	2. 3.08
							(To OO-YAF 7.07)		
ENT	2825	902	Glasflügel 304	210		13. 5.82	M J Hastings and Partners		
								RAF Weston-on-the-Green	28. 6.08
ENU	2826	435	Glaser-Dirks DG-101G Elan	E108G78		8. 8.82	R D.Platt	Long Mynd	7. 4.08
G-DENV	2827	181	Schleicher ASW 20L	20554		27. 5.82	R D.Hone	Wycombe Air Park	9. 5.08
G-EENW	2828	ENW	Schleicher ASW 20L	20567		28. 5.82	J T A Hunter	Pocklington	13. 3.08
ENX	2829	276	SZD-48 Jantar-Standard 2	W-857	(BGA 2746)	24. 6.82	J M Hire	Currock Hill	9. 4.08
ENY	2830	ENY	Schleicher ASK 13	13606	RAFGSA R17	22. 7.82	Aquila Gliding Club	Hinton-in-the-Hedges	2. 6.04
							(Stored 8.07)		

ENZ	2831	RNT	Schleicher ASW 19B	19366		29. 6.82	O Pugh	Wycombe Air Park	29. 4.08
EPD	2835	EPD	Schleicher ASK 21	21119		29. 8.82	J E Ashcroft	Chipping	9. 7.08
G-DEPE	2836	EPE	Schleicher ASW 19B	19335	RAFGSA R18	29. 6.82	P A Goulding	Crowland	15.12.07
					BGA 2836, RAFGSA R18				
G-DEPF	2837	323	Centrair ASW 20FLP	20515		1. 7.82	D.J Howse and Partners	Gransden Lodge	6. 4.08
EPJ	2840	EPJ	Nord 2000	10399/69	F-CACX	26. 8.92	S Dijkstra & Partners	Woensdrecht, Netherlands	9. 6.07
EPM	2843	EPM	Scheibe SF 34	5115		22.10.82	Angus Gliding Club	Drumshade	29. 8.05
G-DEPP	2845	EPP	Schleicher ASK 13	1609		28.12.82	Mendip Gliding Club	Halesland	12. 4.08
			(Rebuild of PH-368 [13064]: c/n is spare fuselage no.)						
EPR	2847	EPR	Hütter H.17	Not known	(Kenya)	30. 9.82	A C Jarvis	Parham	5. 5.08
					PH-269				
G-DEPS	2848	765	Schleicher ASW 20L	20245	RAFGSA 87	5. 7.85	C Beveridge	Sandhill Farm, Shrivenham	22. 3.08
G-DEPT	2849	EPT	Schleicher K 8B	146/59	RAFGGA 504	14. 9.82	P H Emerton	Lasham	5. 3.08
			(Built Aero-Club Minden)		D-5004				
G-DEPU	2850	EPU	Glaser-Dirks DG-101G Elan	E116G85	(BGA 2833)	31.10.82	J F Rogers	Wycombe Air Park	3. 8.08
EPV	2851	EPV	Schleicher K7	7148	D-5468	8.10.82	South London Gliding Centre	Kenley	11. 5.08
EPW	2852	EPW	Schleicher Ka 6CR	6537	(Kenya)	21. 3.83	J Kitchen	Kirton in Lindsey	7. 2.05
G-DEPX	2853	EPX	Schempp-Hirth Ventus b/16.6	107		20.10.82	D L Slobom and Partners	Dunstable	28. 9.08
EPZ	2855		Scheibe Bergfalke II/55	370	D-4012	15. 1.83	G W Sturgess	Trenchard Lines, Upavon	11. 8.96
							(Being refurbished 2000)		
G-DEOA	2856	279	Rolladen-Schneider LS4	4259		24. 6.83	R L Smith and A A Jenkins	Wycombe Air Park	15. 4.08
EQB	2857	EQB	SZD-30 Pirat	S-06.48	D-2702	31.10.82	R Firman	Wycombe Air Park	6. 2.08
EQD	2859	EQD	Grob G102 Astir CS77	1614	PH-570	14. 1.83	D.S Fenton and Partners	Usk	18. 8.08
EQE	2860	EQE	Schleicher ASK 13	13627AB		14. 4.83	Essex Gliding Club	Ridgewell	13.11.07
EQF	2861	EQF	Schleicher ASK 13	13626AB		8. 3.85	Essex Gliding Club	Ridgewell	27. 2.08
G-CEXY	2862	239	Schleicher ASW 19B	19265	PH-665	16.12.82	B A Tansley and Partners	Challock	28. 9.08
G-DEOJ	2864	968	Centrair ASW 20FL	20512		21. 1.83	R Grey and J Sanders	Nympsfield	24. 5.08
EQK	2865	EQK	Centrair 101A Pégase	101054		30. 5.83	L J Desmet	Pocklington	7. 6.08
EQM	2867	EQM	CARMAM M.100S Mésange	81	F-CDKQ	20. 3.83	S C Renfrew	Usk	4.11.07
G-DEON	2868	D5	Schempp-Hirth Nimbus-3/24.5	31		21. 2.83	R A Lovegrove and Partners	Lyveden	4. 3.08
EQP	2869	158	Glaser-Dirks DG-202/17	2-187/1761		10. 3.83	Not known *(Wreck noted 2.08)*	Aston Down	22.10.92
G-CEVK	2870	451	Schleicher Ka 6CR	6541	AGA 24	6. 3.83	C R Reese and Partners	Challock	28. 9.08
					BGA 1353				
G-CEWC	2871	EQR	Schleicher ASK 21	21157		25. 4.83	London Gliding Club	Dunstable	28. 9.08
EQT	2873	EQT	Grob G103A Twin II Acro	3787-K-65	RAFGSA R58	15. 4.83	R Tyrell	Edgehill	12. 2.08
					BGA 2873				
G-DEOU	2874	EQU	Pilatus B4-PC11	201	PH-535	2. 4.83	H Stott	Chipping	3. 5.08
G-DEOV	2875	EOV	Schempp-Hirth Janus C	169	ZD974	8. 3.83	Burn Gliding Club	Burn	14. 3.08
					BGA 2875				
G-DEOW	2876	383	Schempp-Hirth Janus C	171	ZD975	24. 4.83	G R Seaman and Partners	Rivar Hill	11. 4.08
					BGA 2876				
EQX	2877	EQX	CARMAM M 200 Foehn	54	F-CDKR	11. 4.83	R Pettifer and Partners	Chipping	12. 7.08
EQY	2878	-	BAC.VII rep	01		8. 9.91	D Rogers	(Middlesex)	21. 5.96P
			(Rebuild of BAC Drone using wings of G-AEJR and new fuselage)				*(Being refurbished as powered aircraft)*		
EQZ	2879	EQZ	Schleicher K 8B	8113A	D-8763	13. 4.83	Cotswold Gliding Club *(Stored 12.07)*	Aston Down	1. 5.05
G-DERA	2880	283	Centrair ASW 20FL	20526		4.83	R J Lockett	Wormingford	19. 4.08
ERB	2881	ERB	Slingsby T.50 Skylark 4 Special	001		25. 4.83	B V Smith	Sutton Bank	14. 8.08
			(Built C.Almack)						
G-DERH	2887	ERH	Schleicher ASK 21	21147	ZD647	28. 4.83	Burn Gliding Club	Burn	5. 5.08
					BGA 2887				
ERJ	2888	R35	Schleicher ASK 21	21148	RAFGSA R35	28. 4.83	RAFGSA Four Counties Gliding Club	Wittering	5. 4.08
					ZD648, BGA 2888				
G-DERP	2893	ML	Schleicher ASW 19B	19348	ZD657	28. 4.83	M K Lavender	Bicester	22. 2.08
					BGA 2893, BGA 2773				
ERQ	2894	298	Schleicher ASW 19B	19381	(BGA 4849)	28. 4.83	L O'Grady	Seighford	23. 4.07
					ZD658, BGA 2894		*(To VH-LLU 3.07)*		
ERR	2895	ERR	Schleicher ASW 19B	19382	ZD659	28. 4.83	D M Hook	Lasham	27. 9.08
					BGA 2895				
G-DERS	2896	ERS	Schleicher ASW 19B	19383	ZD660	28. 4.83	J C Marshall	Eyres Field	30. 4.08
					BGA 2896				
ERU	2898	NX	Schempp-Hirth Nimbus-3	13	RAFGSA R26	4. 5.83	L Urbani	Roitzschjora, Germany	11. 4.08
					D-6330				
G-FERV	2899	854	Rolladen-Schneider LS4	4257		19. 5.83	R J J Bennett	Long Mynd	20. 9.08
ERW	2900	ERW	Slingsby T.21B	1130	RAFGSA 237	24. 5.83	N Jardine	Sebring, Florida	11. 6.05
					BGA 842		*"The Spruce Goose"*		
ERX	2901	180	Centrair 101A Pégase	101058		3. 8.83	C N Harder	Rivar Hill	14. 4.08
G-KESY	2902	983	Slingsby T..59D Kestrel 19	1839	EI-125, D-9253	14. 6.83	A J Whiteman	Halesland	14. 1.08
ERZ	2903	-	Oberlerchner Mg 19a Steinadler	015	OE-0324	1. 6.83	C Wills	Wycombe Air Park	6. 4.06
ESA	2904	ESA	SZD-9bis Bocian 1E	P-750		21. 6.83	F C Wevers	Amersfoort, Netherlands	17.10.03
G-DESB	2905	ESB	Schleicher ASK 21	21176		2. 9.83	A L Garfield and Partners	Dunstable	8. 3.08
ESC	2906	379	Rolladen-Schneider LS4	4261		25. 6.83	J Crawford	Bicester	24. 8.08
G-LSFR	2908	LS4	Rolladen-Schneider LS4	4260		26. 6.83	M F Platt and A Mulder	Nympsfield	28. 9.08
G-DESH	2911	118	Centrair 101A Pégase	101069		2. 7.83	J E Moore	Wycombe Air Park	28. 1.08
G-DESJ	2912	ESJ	Schleicher K 8B	8730	D-5010	13. 7.83	Bowland Forest Gliding Club	Chipping	28. 9.08
ESK	2913	ESK	Schleicher Ka 2B	697	RAFGGA 594	23. 7.83	W R Williams	RAF Halton	20. 5.00
					D-5947		*(Noted 4.07)*		
ESM	2915	ESM	Breguet 905SA Fauvette	30	F-CCJA	14.10.83	J Doppelbauer	Gunzenhausen, Germany	6. 7.08
G-DESP	2917	ESP	SZD-48-3 Jantar-Standard 3	B-1294		19. 4.84	B Taylor and Partners	RAF Weston-on-the-Green	5. 6.08
G-DESO	2918	231	Glaser-Dirks DG-300 Elan	3E10		23. 4.84	G R P Brown	Sandhill Farm, Shrivenham	31. 3.08
G-DESU	2922	ESU	Schleicher ASK 21	21180	RAFGSA R40	12.11.83	Banbury Gliding Club	Hinton-in-the-Hedges	25. 5.08
			(Composite with RAFGSA R28 (c/n 21154)		BGA 2922				
G-DESW	2924	590	Centrair 101A Pégase	101068		20. 3.84	D A Brown	Usk	1. 4.08
ESX	2925	ESX	Schleicher K 8B	8805	RAFGGA 553	10. 9.83	Not known	Aston Down	31.12.96
							(W/o Pocklington 2. 2.96; stored dismantled 1.08)		

G-EESY	2926	ESY	Rolladen-Schneider LS4	4334		4. 2.84	D A Parkes	Kingston Deverill	23. 6.08
ETA	2928	ETA	Schleicher ASK 21	21181		19.11.83	R Stone	Hinton-in-the-Hedges	29. 4.08
ETB	2929	ETB	Schleicher Ka 6E	4365	HB-1021	20.11.83	A J Padgett	RAF Marham	27. 9.08
ETD	2931	ETD	Schleicher K 8B	8918	RAFGSA R44	30.12.83	Cotswold Gliding Club	Aston Down	24. 8.08
					BGA 2931, RAFGSA 244				
ETE	2932	-	Fauvel AV.36CR	214	RAFGSA R53	8.87	Shuttleworth Collection	Old Warden	7. 6.98
					D-5353, D-8259		"The Budgie" (On display 2006)		
G-DETG	2934	NW	Rolladen-Schneider LS4	4349		7. 2.84	N P Woods	Gransden Lodge	28. 9.08
ETH	2935	ETH	Schleicher K 8B	120	D-5755	23. 3.84	North Wales Gliding Club	Llantisilio	3. 9.03
G-DETJ	2936	223	Centrair 101A Pégase	101A0110		8. 8.84	S C Phillips	(Potton)	23. 3.08
ETK	2937	215	SZD-48 Jantar-Standard 2	W-876	OY-XJO	14. 2.84	M H Jones	Portmoak	3. 8.07
G-DETM	2939	M7	Centrair 101A Pégase	101A0111		11. 4.84	J Bone and B J Darton	Wormingford	15. 3.08
ETP	2941	WB943	Slingsby T.21B	610	WB943	16. 6.84	P Hepworth tr Ouse T.21 Syndicate	Rufforth	9. 7.07
ETR	2943	S7	Schleicher K7	3	D-8339	21. 2.84	Shenington Gliding Club	Edgehill	26. 7.04
G-DETS	2944	ETS	Schleicher ASK 13	13635AB		3. 3.84	Upward Bound Trust	Thame	14. 4.08
ETU	2946	ETU	Schleicher K7	Not known	RAFGSA R8	24. 3.84	M J Libell	Strubby	25. 5.04
					BGA 2607				
ETV	2947	ETV	Rolladen-Schneider LS4	4314	(BGA 2919)	23. 3.84	T A Meaker	Lasham	13. 3.08
G-DETY	2950	249	Rolladen-Schneider LS4	4368		16. 4.84	D T Staff	Wycombe Air Park	7.11.07
G-DETZ	2951	20	Schleicher ASW 20CL	20730		20. 3.84	N L Clowes and Partners	Tibenham	23. 2.08
EUC	2954	EUC	Schleicher ASK 13	13104	AGA 12	15. 4.84	Bristol & Gloucestershire Gliding Club	Nympsfield	6. 6.08
G-DEUD	2955	X56	Schleicher ASW 20C	20734		3. 6.84	R Tietema	Husbands Bosworth	15. 2.08
EUE	2956	EUE	Scheibe SF 27A Zugvogel V	6106	D-5342	6. 4.84	Newark & Notts Gliding Club	Darlton	8. 4.07
G-DEUF	2957	EUF	SZD-50-3 Puchacz	B-1090		30. 5.84	A J Pettitt and Syndicate	Rivar Hill	26. 8.08
G-DEUH	2959	446	Rolladen-Schneider LS4	4382		14. 4.84	A R Turner and F J Parkinson	Nympsfield	13. 4.08
G-DEUJ	2960	217	Schempp-Hirth Ventus b/16.6	162		9. 4.84	M J and A J Millar	Ringmer	18. 4.08
G-DEUK	2961	992	Centrair ASW 20FL	20530		20. 5.84	D S Kershaw	Lasham	26. 2.08
EUN	2964	-	Slingsby T.21B	588	RAFGSA R92	20. 4.84	N I Newton	Wycombe Air Park	20. 6.08
					RAFGSA 212, WB925				
EUQ	2966	EUQ	Schleicher K7	863	D-4639	8. 5.84	J Marsden	Wormingford	1. 3.07
G-DEUS	2968	443	Schempp-Hirth Ventus b/16.6	192		19. 5.84	R J Whitaker	Lasham	28. 9.08
G-EEUX	2973	EUX	Schleicher ASK 18	18005	D-3988	28. 5.84	Southdown Gliding Club	Parham	28. 9.08
G-DEUY	2974	88	Schleicher ASW 20BL	20645		8. 6.84	D G Roberts and Partners	Aston Down	28.12.07
EUZ	2975		Slingsby T.21B	620	WB959	24. 6.84	Dartmoor Gliding Association	Brentor	31. 8.04
EVB	2977	EVB	Schleicher K7	7004	D-5109	12. 6.84	Channel Gliding Club	Waldershare Park	11. 5.05
EVC	2978	EVC	CARMAM M.200 Foehn	55	F-CDKT	6. 4.08	W Young and Partners	Pocklington	6. 4.08
G-CEVD	2979	382	Rolladen-Schneider LS3	3024	N63LS, D-7914	11. 8.84	C H Appleyard and Partners	Lasham	14. 2.08
G-CEVE	2980	491	Centrair 101A Pégase	101A0141		19. 6.84	J W North and T Newham	Lasham	28. 9.08
G-DEVF	2981	90	Schempp-Hirth Nimbus-3T	15/76	D-KHIJ	19. 3.85	A G Leach	Bembridge	20. 2.08
EVG	2982	EVG	Schleicher K7	396	D-0018	17. 7.84	Derbyshire & Lancashire Gliding Club	Camphill	16. 4.08
EVH	2983	EVH	Schleicher Ka 10	10008	HB-791	26. 5.86	J W Bolt	Brentor	21. 8.03
EVJ	2984	H	Schleicher ASK 13	13637AB		14. 7.84	Lasham Gliding Society	Lasham	4. 9.08
EVK	2985	EVK	Grob G102 Astir CS	1397	PH-546	20.12.86	Peterborough & Spalding Gliding Club	Crowland	17. 4.08
EVL	2986	SA1	Grob G102 Astir CS77	1638	PH-575	26. 7.84	J R Bates	Lasham	18. 7.08
G-DEVM	2987	N51	Centrair 101A Pégase	101A0157		17. 8.84	Seahawk Gliding Club	RNAS Culdrose	28. 4.08
EVN	2988		Monnett Monerai	312	BGA 3190	7.11.87	Not known	Bellarena	6.11.88
					(BGA 2988)		(Noted 5.07)		
EVP	2989	K	Schleicher ASK 13	13638AB		23. 8.84	Lasham Gliding Society	Lasham	27. 9.08
EVQ	2990	EVQ	Centrair 101A Pégase	101A0149		19. 8.84	K Sleigh	Rattlesden	3. 7.08
EVR	2991	EVR	LET L-13 Blanik	172604	G-ASVS	30. 8.84	N A Mills	Hinton-in-the-Hedges	3. 7.07
					OK-3840				
EVS	2992	EVS	SZD-50-3 Puchacz	B-1091		6. 9.84	Deeside Gliding Club	Aboyne	7. 8.08
G-DEVV	2995	EVV	Schleicher ASK 23	23004		21.11.84	Midland Gliding Club	Long Mynd	28. 9.08
G-DEVW	2996	EVW	Schleicher ASK 23	23006		4. 1.85	London Gliding Club	Dunstable	2. 5.08
G-DEVX	2997	EVX	Schleicher ASK 23	23007		7. 1.85	London Gliding Club	Dunstable	12. 4.08
G-DEVY	2998	EVY	Schleicher ASK 23	23008		31. 1.85	London Gliding Club	Dunstable	12. 7.08
EWG	3006	VE	Grob G103A Twin II Acro	33885-K-123	ZE501	25.10.84	J Ryan	Lyveden	11. 6.08
					BGA 3006				
G-DEWP	3013	EWP	Grob G103A Twin II Acro	33892-K-130	ZE523	3.11.84	Cambridge Gliding Club	Gransden Lodge	22. 2.08
					BGA 3013				
G-DEWR	3015	P70	Grob G103A Twin II Acro	33894-K-132	RAFGSA R70	9.11.84	Bristol & Gloucestershire Gliding Club	Nympsfield	28. 9.08
					ZE525, BGA 3015				
G-DEXA	3024	EXA	Grob G103A Twin II Acro	33908-K-143	ZE534	3.12.84	Trent Valley Gliding Club	Kirton in Lindsey	27. 6.08
					BGA 3024				
EYS	3064	R71	Grob G103A Twin II Acro	33961-K-194	RAFGSA R71	9. 3.85	RAFGSA Fenland Gliding Club	RAF Marham	18. 5.08
					ZE612, BGA 3064				
EZE	3076	EZE	Grob G103A Twin II Acro	33981-K-214	ZE634	3. 5.85	T R Dews	Kingston Deverill	17. 9.08
					BGA 3076				
G-DFAF	3101	271	Schleicher ASW 20	20214	RAFGSA 271	5.10.84	A S Miller	RAF Keevil	21. 4.08
					RAFGSA R27				
G-CFAJ	3103	FAJ	Glaser-Dirks DG-300 Elan	3E50		3.10.84	B A Brown	Milfield	11. 3.08
G-CFAM	3106	J15	Schempp-Hirth Nimbus-3/24.5	79		16. 3.85	K J Hartley and Partners	Bicester	11. 6.08
FAN	3107	202	Centrair 101A Pégase	101A0161		25.10.84	J Rayner	Parham	15.12.07
						(Groundlooped on field landing Chanctonbury 23. 1.07)			
G-CFAO	3109	631	Rolladen-Schneider LS4	4465		9. 3.85	C A Meir	Seighford	9. 3.08
G-DFAR	3110	FAR	Glasflügel Club Libelle 205	58	HB-1262	5. 6.85	G A Gair	Ringmer	24. 4.08
G-DFAT	3112	FAT	Schleicher ASK 13	13528	PH-456	22. 1.85	Dorset Gliding Club	Eyres Field	22. 4.08
FAV	3114	FAV	ICA-Brasov IS-32A	05		27.12.84	Black Mountains Gliding Club	Talgarth	6. 8.08
G-DFAW	3115	333	Schempp-Hirth Ventus b/16.6	26	D-6768	23. 3.85	P R Stafford-Allen	RAF Marham	29. 3.08
G-CFBA	3119	178	Schleicher ASW 20BL	20665		23. 1.85	A A Docherty	Long Mynd	31. 3.08
G-CFBB	3120	822	Schempp-Hirth Standard Cirrus	327G	RAFGGA 312	10.12.84	R Andrewartha and B F R Smyth	Nympsfield	28. 9.08
G-CFBC	3121	FBC	Schleicher ASW 15B	15356	OH-439	19. 5.85	C Knock & J Myrdal Sandhill Farm, Shrivenham		28. 9.08
FBD	3122	FBD	Schleicher ASW 15B	15407	OH-445	19. 5.85	D A Wilson	Milfield	15. 5.08
FBE	3123	1	Rolladen-Schneider LS6	6028	D-9384	2. 6.85	T J Wills	New Zealand	28. 8.08

Reg	BGA	Trigraph	Type	c/n	Prev ID	Date	Owner	Location	Date
FBF	3124	175	Glaser-Dirks DG-300 Elan	3E9	BGA 2952	16. 1.85	P J Machacek	Saltby	25. 9.08
G-CFBH	3126	177	Glaser-Dirks DG-101G Elan	E156G123		1. 4.85	IBM Gliding Club	Lasham	22. 3.08
FBJ	3127	FBJ	Schleicher K 8B	8221	D-6340	18. 2.85	Bidford Gliding Centre	Bidford	20. 6.07
FBM	3130	727	Schempp-Hirth Nimbus-3/24.5	73		28. 2.85	D K Gardiner	Aboyne/Portmoak	14. 7.08
G-CFBN	3131	FBN	Glasflügel Mosquito B	167	D-6364	1. 5.85	S R and J Nash	Sandhill Farm, Shrivenham	28. 9.08
FBQ	3133	464	Schleicher ASW 20BL	20669		16. 4.85	R A Robertson	Talgarth	19. 4.08
FBR	3134	773	Grob G102 Astir CS77	1701	SE-TSV	5. 3.89	R Robinson	Wormingford	23. 4.08
G-CFBT	3136	488	Schempp-Hirth Ventus bT	35/218		12. 3.85	S H Gibson and Partners	Gransden Lodge	18.12.07
G-CFBV	3138	FBV	Schleicher ASK 21	21223		2. 5.85	London Gliding Club	Dunstable	8. 3.08
G-CFBW	3139	395	Glaser-Dirks DG-101G Elan	E174G140		11. 4.85	G N Phillips and Partners	Lasham	9. 2.08
FBY	3141	780	Schempp-Hirth Discus b	20		12. 4.85	D Latimer	Sutton Bank	16. 7.08
G-CFBZ	3142	D-4667	Schleicher Ka 6CR	6016	D-4667	12. 5.85	R H Martyn and R E Branch	Wycombe Air Park	10. 2.08
					D-KIMN, D-4667				
G-CFCB	3144	FCB	Centrair 101 Pégase	10100178	F-CGEA	15. 4.85	N Stratton and M Forster	Portmoak	7. 2.08
FCC	3145	XN243	Slingsby T.31B	1182	XN243	6. 5.85	R Linde	Emmerich, Germany	7. 4.08
FCD	3146	641	Centrair 101A Pégase B	101A0207		1. 5.85	G J Bass	Challock	26. 6.08
FCF	3148	993	Slingsby T.21B	MHL/017	WB990	12. 5.85	G Pullen	Lasham	24. 4.08
FCG	3149	WT871	Slingsby T.31B	681	WT871	5. 5.85	C Wevers	Amersfoort, Netherlands	21. 2.04
G-CFCJ	3151	571	Grob G102 Astir CS	1231	D-4205	19. 5.85	M Levitt and I Ashby	Aston Down	28. 9.08
FCK	3152	671	Schempp-Hirth Ventus b/16.6	241		6. 5.85	L J Scott	Sleap	21. 6.05
FCM	3154	411	Glaser-Dirks DG-300 Elan	3E94		17. 5.85	I Roberts and A J Davis	Cross Hayes	12.11.08
G-CFCN	3155	920	Schempp-Hirth Standard Cirrus	131	D-0191	18. 6.85	S M Robinson	Nympsfield	3. 3.08
G-CFCP	3156	721	Rolladen-Schneider LS6-a	6030		2. 7.85	R E Robertson	Dunstable	1. 4.08
G-CFCR	3158	113	Schleicher Ka 6E	4223	OH-375	10. 6.85	R F Whittaker	Lasham	27. 2.08
					OH-REC				
G-CFCS	3159	2R	Schempp-Hirth Nimbus-2C	233	D-5993	7. 7.85	P J Dolling and J Luck	Hinton-in-the-Hedges	13.12.07
FCT	3160	WB944	Slingsby T.21B	611	WB944	16.12.86	D C Perkins	Bicester	30. 4.08
FCV	3162	FCV	Schleicher ASW 20	20076	RAFGSA R24	7. 6.85	M J Davis and Partners	RAF Cosford	24.10.05
FCW	3163	L	Schleicher ASK 13	13642AB		27. 6.85	Lasham Gliding Society	Lasham	21. 8.08
FCY	3165	FCY	Schleicher ASW 15	15122	D-0748	29. 6.85	M Shaw	Ridgewell	9. 4.08
FCZ	3166	-	Slingsby T.1 Falcon 1 replica	Not known		9. 7.85	D D Knight	RAF Halton	3. 5.08
			(Built Southdown Aero Services)						
G-CFDA	3167	7D	Schleicher ASW 15	15050	D-0511	2. 7.85	N I Newton and Partners	Wycombe Air Park	13.11.07
FDC	3169	FDC	Pottier JP 15-34 Kit Club	TAH.50/60		10. 3.87	T A Hollings	Rufforth	18. 9.08
FDD	3170	FDD	Schleicher K 8B	8972	AGA 5	11. 7.85	Shalbourne Soaring Society	Rivar Hill	3. 3.07
G-CFDE	3171	510	Schempp-Hirth Ventus bT	53/256		26. 8.85	P Clay	Sutton Bank	27. 3.08
FDF	3172	FDF	Grob G102 Astir CS	1321	D-7338	2. 9.85	R H Davies	Nympsfield	27. 8.08
FDK	3176	FDK	Slingsby T..59D Kestrel 19	1832	(BGA 4927)	28. 8.85	T Gauder	Speyer, Germany	8. 5.08
					BGA 3176, G-BBVC				
FDP	3180	IS30	ICA-Brasov IS-30	08		24. 5.86	M H Simms	Shipdham	18. 9.04
FDQ	3181	FDQ	Slingsby T.31B	710	WT915	19. 9.85	J F Forster "Chris Wills"	Hilversum, Netherlands	18. 5.08
G-CFDR	3182	FDR	Schleicher Ka 6CR	6119	D-8456	18.11.85	Dartmoor Gliding Society	Brentor	1. 8.08
G-CFDM	3185	H20	Schempp-Hirth Discus b	87		23. 5.86	J L Whiting	Edgehill	8. 3.08
FDV	3186	D-5826	LET L-13 Blanik	173333	D-5826	4.86	T Wiltshire	Shipdham	4. 7.98
					D-KOEB, D-5826		(Sold Thailand 2007)		
FDW	3187	438	Glaser-Dirks DG-300 Elan	3E143		26. 1.86	C Hadley	Brentor	16. 8.08
FDX	3188	FDX	SZD-48-1 Jantar-Standard 2	B-1251	(BGA 2916)	22.12.85	R Simpson	Ringmer	30. 9.08
FDY	3189	FDY	Slingsby T.21B	MHL 020	WB978	26. 1.86	R Lloyd	Challock	11. 9.08
FEA	3191	FEA	Grob G103 Twin Astir	3151	RAFGSA R83	6.12.85	M Woodcock	Rufforth	23. 5.08
					RAFGSA 833				
FEB	3192	SH8	Grob G102 Club Astir III	5643C		15.11.85	Surrey & Hants Gliding Club	Lasham	7. 5.08
FED	3194	WT914	Slingsby T.31B	709	WT914	8. 2.86	Not known (Stored 2007)	Tibenham	7. 2.87
FEE	3195	-	Slingsby T.21B	MHL 016	WB989	20. 1.86	K Schickling	Aschaffenburg, Germany	10. 8.08
G-CFEF	3196	FEF	Grob G102 Astir CS	1164	OY-XGC	9. 2.86	Oxford University Gliding Club	Bicester	4. 3.08
G-CFEG	3197	120	Schempp-Hirth Ventus b/16.6	279		12. 2.86	K F Moorhouse and R W Partridge	Lasham	27. 3.08
G-CFEH	3198	318	Centrair 101A Pégase	10100268		1. 5.86	Booker Gliding Club	Wycombe Air Park	21. 3.08
			(Rebuilt with new fuselage c/n 01304: original fuselage rebuilt as BGA 3560)						
G-CFEJ	3199	LC	Schempp-Hirth Discus b	76		22. 2.86	L Coles	Wycombe Air Park	4. 2.08
FEL	3201	FEL	Schleicher K7	7231	RAFGGA 575	22. 9.86	Dukeries Gliding Club	Darlton	19.11.05
					D-5 . . .				
G-CFEN	3203	FEN	SZD-50-3 Puchacz	B-1326		24. 3.86	Northumbria Gliding Club	Currock Hill	23. 9.08
FEQ	3205	M	Schleicher ASK 13	13650AB		7. 4.86	Lasham Gliding Society	Lasham	28.11.07
FER	3206	370	Schempp-Hirth Discus b	75		27. 3.86	J P Whitehead	Aston Down	19. 2.08
G-CFES	3207	564	Schempp-Hirth Discus b	88		4. 4.86	P W Berridge	Sandhill Farm, Shrivenham	2. 2.08
FEX	3212	FEX	Grob G102 Astir CS77	1660	D-7492	6. 4.86	J Taylor	Upwood	19. 9.08
FEZ	3214	-	EoN AP.7 Primary	EoN/P/037	RAFGSA R13	19. 9.86	A P Stacey	RAF Keevil	3. 6.01
					RAFGSA 113, WP269		(For restoration)		
FFA	3215	FFA	Schleicher ASK 13	13651AB		15. 5.86	Staffordshire Gliding Club	Seighford	13. 2.07
G-CFFB	3216	R9	Grob G102 Astir CS	1123	RAFGSA R9	10. 6.86	RAFGSA Chilterns Gliding Centre	RAF Halton	28. 9.08
					RAFGSA R97, BGA 3216, D-6977				
G-CFFC	3217	FFC	Centrair 101A Pégase	101A0255		30. 5.86	B Douglas	Rufforth	16. 4.08
FFG	3221	WB920	Slingsby T.21B	559	WB920	2. 6.86	J H Wisselink	Woensdrecht, Netherlands	16. 6.08
FFH	3222	FFH	Schleicher ASW 20	20037	D-7947	4. 4.87	C Leverkuehn (To VH-GVN 10.07)	Dunstable	17. 9.07
G-CFFK	3224	128	Schempp-Hirth Nimbus-3/24.5	87		11. 4.87	I Ashdown	Parham	28. 9.08
FFL	3225	FFL	Slingsby T.21B	MHL.020	WB993	28. 6.87	B van Aalst	Asperden, Germany	17. 5.08
FFP	3228	93	Schleicher ASW 19B	19317	RAFGSA R19	12. 6.86	J M Hutchinson	Wycombe Air Park	21. 4.08
FFQ	3229	FFQ	Slingsby T.31B	913	XE800	18. 8.86	K J Grosse	RAF Odiham	26. 3.03
G-CFFS	3231	FFS	Centrair 101A Pégase	101A0265		27. 6.86	W Murray	Gransden Lodge	3. 4.08
G-CFFT	3232	FFT	Schempp-Hirth Discus b	110		30. 6.86	R Maskell	Gransden Lodge	4. 4.08
G-CFFU	3233	FFU	Glaser-Dirks DG-101G Elan	E200G166		11. 1.87	K T Tutthill and Partners	Chipping	31. 3.08
G-CFFV	3234	FFV	SZD-51-1 Junior	B-1616	F-WGJA	26. 8.86	Herefordshire Gliding Club	Shobdon	5. 4.08
FFW	3235	FFW	Slingsby T.21B	1155	XN151	2.10.87	R Schmid	Aalen-Elchingen, Germany	19. 6.08
G-CFFX	3236	627	Schempp-Hirth Discus b	109		12. 7.86	P J Tiller	Husbands Bosworth	5. 4.08
G-CFFY	3237	FFY	SZD-51-1 Junior	W-938		24.11.86	Scottish Gliding Union	Portmoak	2. 4.08

FFZ	3238	WB981	Slingsby T.21B	MHL.008	WB981	21. 8.86	A P Stacey	RAF Keevil	24. 4.08
FGA	3239	WT913	Slingsby T.31B	708	WT913	26.10.86	AeroVenture (On loan)	Doncaster	21. 7.96
FGB	3240	WJ306	Slingsby T.21B	654	WJ306	23. 8.86	Oxford Gliding Club RAF Weston-on-the-Green		27. 8.08
							"Daisy" (BGA 2720 also carries "WJ306")		
FGC	3241	WT918	Slingsby T.31B	713	WT918	24. 8.86	K Litek	Jena, Germany	4. 8.08
FGE	3243	-	Slingsby T.21B	619	WB958	9.87	Not known (Stored 11.06)	Edgehill	21. 4.93
G-CFGF	3244	141	Schempp-Hirth Nimbus-3T	25/91		16. 8.86	R E Cross	Lasham	14. 1.08
FGG	3245	WG498	Slingsby T.21B	665	WG498	29. 9.86	G A Ford and Partners	Aston Down	14. 6.07
FGJ	3247	FGJ	Schleicher Ka 6CR	6634	D-1041	22. 9.86	F Spaargaren	Lleweni Parc	24. 9.08
G-CFGK	3248	FGK	Grob G102 Astir CS	1323	RAFGSA R61	6. 2.93	P Allingham	Eyres Field	15. 4.08
					RAFGSA 316				
FGM	3250	"F-GM"	Slingsby T.21B	1160	XN156	19. 7.87	R B Petrie	Portmoak	24. 1.08
G-CFGP	3252	FGP	Schleicher ASW 19	19121	C-GJXG	1.11.86	A E Prime and Partners	Tibenham	20. 3.08
G-CFGR	3254	N29	Schleicher ASK 13	13655AB		24.10.86	Portsmouth Naval Gliding Club	Lee-on-Solent	10. 8.07
			(Built Jubi)						
FGS	3255	"XN419"	Slingsby T.21B	1161	XN157	11.10.86	D W Cole	Long Mynd	8. 8.08
FGT	3256	FGT	Glaser-Dirks DG-300 Elan	3E217		6. 3.87	S C Williams (See BGA 2156)	Wycombe Air Park	6.12.07
FGU	3257	806	Schempp-Hirth Standard Cirrus	147	D-0193	27. 4.87	L E Ingram	Snitterfield	23. 9.08
FGV	3258	FGV	Schleicher K7	Not known	OO-...	15.12.86	Nene Valley Gliding Club	Upwood	9. 4.03
			(Hybrid using ex Belgian Ka 7 fuselage and wings from Ka 2 BGA 2662)						
G-CFGW	3259	701	Centrair 101A Pégase	101A0275		23. 6.87	L P Smith	Kingston Deverill	18. 3.08
G-LDER	3261	527	Schleicher ASW 22	22027	D-3527	3.12.86	P Shrosbree and D Starer	Dunstable	19. 3.08
FGZ	3262	FGZ	Schleicher K7	7238	D-5376	1.87	Dartmoor Gliding Society (Stored 2005) Brentor		9.10.99
FHB	3264		Slingsby T.21B (T)	MHL.018	WB991	17. 2.87	G Traves	East Kirkby	12. 9.04
			(Fuji-Robin EC-34PM)						
G-CFHD	3266	196	Schleicher ASW 20BL	20694	RAFGGA	15. 2.87	P Brown and Partners	Bicester	30. 4.08
G-CFHF	3268	FHF	SZD-51-1 Junior	W-952		20. 3.87	Black Mountains Gliding Club	Talgarth	30. 4.08
G-CFHG	3269	187	Schempp-Hirth Mini Nimbus C	140	(BGA 3213)	22. 3.87	R W and M P Weaver	Usk	21.12.06
					ZS-GNI				
FHJ	3271	987	Centrair 101A Pégase	101A0278		13. 5.87	Booker Gliding Club	Wycombe Air Park	3. 4.08
FHK	3272	WT900	Slingsby T.31B	695	WT900	22. 4.87	A Hepburn and Partners	Lee-on-Solent	6. 5.06
G-CFHL	3273	136	Rolladen-Schneider LS4	4633		17. 4.87	I P Hicks and R Puritz	Dunstable	19. 2.08
G-CFHM	3274	P	Schleicher ASK 13	13662AB		7. 6.87	Lasham Gliding Society	Lasham	13.12.07
FHN	3275	FHN	Schleicher K 8B	Not known	RAFGSA R85	5. 6.87	B F Cracknell	Upwood	16. 3.08
					RAFGSA 385, RAFGSA 360				
FHQ	3277	-	Hols der Teufel rep	001		21. 3.90	Deutsches Segelflugmuseum		N/E
			(Built M L Beach)				(On display 2006) Wasserkuppe, Germany		
G-CFHR	3278	Q5	Schempp-Hirth Discus b	152		8. 6.87	J Jervis and Partners	Edgehill	8. 2.08
FHS	3279	154	Schempp-Hirth Ventus cT	82/326		11. 6.87	R Andrews	Long Mynd	25. 9.08
G-CFHT	3280	FHT	Grob G102 Astir CS	1234	D-4208	12. 6.87	E K Sharp	Bicester	9. 5.08
FHU	3281	FHU	Schleicher K7	629	RAFGSA R15	17. 6.87	Dartmoor Gliding Society	Brentor	4. 3.05
			(Modified to ASK 13 standard)		RAFGGA, D-5722				
G-CFHV	3282	FHV	SZD-48-1 Jantar-Standard 2	B-1036	D-4516	25. 6.87	R A Williams and Partners	Long Mynd	10. 5.08
G-CFHW	3283	698	Grob G102 Astir CS	1087	D-6987	30. 6.87	P R J Halliday and Partners	Lasham	18. 2.08
FHY	3285	H5	Scheibe SF 27A Zugvogel V	6045	D-1868	28. 6.87	J M Pursey	North Hill	27. 9.08
FHZ	3286	FHZ	Schleicher Ka 6CR	949	D-4661	20. 8.87	G D Leatherland	Husbands Bosworth	24. 5.08
FJA	3287	FJA	Slingsby T.21B	1152	XN148	8. 7.87	M Steiner	Lachen-Speyerdorf, Germany	11. 5.08
FJB	3288	FJB	Slingsby T.21B	MHL.002	WB975	8. 7.87	Angus Gliding Club (As "WB975")	Drumshade	16. 6.07
FJD	3290	T21	Slingsby T.21B	MHL.007	WB980	29. 8.87	K W Payne and Partners	Husbands Bosworth	14. 5.08
G-CFJE	3291	744	Schleicher ASW 20BL	20953		1. 8.87	A Groves	Lee-on-Solent	28. 9.08
FJF	3292	FJF	Slingsby T.21B	586	WB923	7. 9.87	R L Horsnell	Snitterfield	15. 5.08
FJH	3294	FJH	Grob G102 Astir CS77	1763	AGA 7	11. 7.87	Shalbourne Soaring Society	Rivar Hill	3. 4.08
G-CFJK	3296	FJK	Centrair 101A Pégase	101070	N4429W	30. 4.88	T J Parker and A W McKee	Bicester	26. 4.08
G-CFJM	3298	143	Rolladen-Schneider LS4-a	4665	D-1431	4.12.87	K Woods and S Hill	Dunstable	22. 6.08
FJN	3299	903	Slingsby T.31B	698	WT903	17. 2.88	B Kozuh	Ljubljana, Slovenia	19. 7.06
FJQ	3301	FJQ	Schempp-Hirth Ventus cT	104/365		24. 3.88	B Rood	Hinton-in-the-Hedges	29. 8.06
G-CFJR	3302	950	Glaser-Dirks DG-300 Club Elan			12. 2.88	W J Palmer and H Smith	France	11. 3.08
				3E270C2					
G-CFJS	3303	257	Glaser-Dirks DG-300 Club Elan			28. 5.88	K L Goldsmith	Rattlesden	9. 4.08
				3E271C3					
FJT	3304	997	Centrair 101A Pégase	101A0284		20. 2.88	D M Smith and A Marlow	Wycombe Air Park	21. 5.08
FJV	3306	FJV	Schleicher ASW 15	15109	D-0710	3.11.87	R Abercrombie	Milfield	22.10.07
G-CFJW	3307	FJW	Schleicher K7	980	OH-241	15.11.88	A J Pettitt and Syndicate	Rivar Hill	9. 6.08
					OH-KKF				
G-CFJX	3308	FJX	Glaser-Dirks DG-300 Elan	3E261		6. 2.88	Crown Service Gliding Club	Lasham	4. 2.08
G-CFJZ	3310	-	Schempp-Hirth SHK	14	D-9330	2. 4.88	R H Hanna and B C Irwin	Bellarena	24. 6.08
FKA	3311	FKA	Schleicher Ka 6CR	6239	D-7037, D-5435	21. 2.88	E Drake	Kingston Deverill	15. 6.06
FKB	3312	FKB	Glaser-Dirks DG-600	6-8		10.88	J A Watt	Dunstable	7. 4.08
G-GTWO	3315	G2	Schleicher ASW 15	15146	D-0794	6. 3.88	J M G Carlton and R Jackson	Edgehill	11. 2.08
G-CFKG	3317	125	Rolladen-Schneider LS4-a	4673		18. 5.88	D A Smith and Partners	Kingston Deverill	16. 3.08
FKH	3318	FKH	Schleicher Ka 6CR	6343	EI-109	31. 3.88	Ulster Gliding Club	Bellarena	14. 9.08
					IGA 106				
G-CFKL	3321	159	Schleicher ASW 20BL	20954		21. 3.88	J M Ley	Wormingford	18.12.07
FKM	3322	SH3	Schempp-Hirth Discus b	212		19. 3.88	Surrey & Hants Gliding Club	Lasham	31. 5.08
FKP	3324	WB971	Slingsby T.21B	632	WB971	28. 2.88	M Powell	AAC Wattisham	13. 6.05
							(Damaged Camphill 1. 7.04; for rebuild with fuselage of BGA 765)		
FKT	3328	FKT	Schleicher K 8B	8382	D-5366	8. 5.88	A R Bushnell	Lyveden	7. 6.08
G-CFKY	3329	FKY	Schleicher Ka 6CR	822	D-0025	6. 4.88	J A Timmis	Camphill	25. 6.08
FKX	3332	FKX	Schleicher Ka 6CR	6433	D-4316	30. 4.88	J Bates and Partners	Lasham	1. 7.05
FLB	3336	XA295/D	Slingsby T.31B	837	XA295	23. 8.88	R Birch	Aston Down	14. 9.08
G-CFLC	3337	368	Glaser-Dirks DG-300 Elan	3E310		26. 9.88	J L Hey	Rufforth	19. 3.08
G-CFLE	3339	314	Schempp-Hirth Discus b	207		7. 5.88	Booker Gliding Club	Wycombe Air Park	28. 9.08
FLF	3340	Z4	Rolladen-Schneider LS4-a	4694		20. 3.88	D E Lamb	Wycombe Air Park	14. 4.08
G-CFLH	3342	FLH	Schleicher K 8B	22	OH-361	12. 5.88	South Wales Gliding Club	Usk	14. 4.08
			(Built KK Lehtovaara O/Y)		OH-RTW				

FLK	3344	FLK	Schleicher K7	985	D-5047	12. 1.89	Darlton Gliding Club *(Cancelled 21.1.08)*	Darlton	14. 9.08
FLL	3345	FLL	SZD-9bis Bocian 1D	F-877	OH-336	30. 7.88	Bath, Wilts and North Dorset Gliding Club		
					OH-KBP			Kingston Deverill	21. 5.08
FLQ	3349	FLQ	Schleicher K 8B	8195A	D-8887	15. 8.88	F J Glanville	Long Mynd	26. 5.07
FLS	3351	FLS	Schleicher Ka 6CR	6180	D-4001	16.11.88	P B Arms	RAF Halton	22. 6.07
FLT	3352	FLT	Glasflügel Standard Libelle 201B	41	D-0211	11.12.88	C Glover	Husbands Bosworth	5. 6.08
G-CFLW	3355	51	Schempp-Hirth Std Cirrus 75	656	F-CEMT	3. 7.88	J K Pack	Lasham	28. 9.08
G-CFLX	3356	FLX	Glaser-Dirks DG-300 Club Elan			19.10.88	R Emms and Partners	Upwood	16. 3.08
				3E304C19					
FLZ	3358	FLZ	Scheibe SF 27A Zugvogel V	6061	D-5378	14. 7.88	M F Frost	Ridgewell	19. 1.08
FMA	3359	-	Slingsby T.38 Grasshopper	793	WZ797	8. 8.88	Not known *(Stored 2005)*	Upwood	7. 8.89
G-LSGB	3361	6B	Rolladen-Schneider LS6-b	6184		27. 7.88	T J Brenton	Wormingford	30. 3.08
FME	3363	927	Schleicher ASW 15	15164	D-0825	1. 8.88	T J Stanley	Sutton Bank	3. 1.07
FMG	3365	969	Schempp-Hirth Discus b	242		3. 8.88	J Melvin	Dunstable	12. 4.08
G-CFMH	3366	B	Schleicher ASK 13	13673AB		22. 8.88	Lasham Gliding Society	Lasham	28. 9.08
G-CFMK	3368	Z	Centrair 101 Pégase Club	10100293		20. 1.90	D Hatch	Nympsfield	28. 1.08
G-CFML	3369	FML	Schleicher ASW 15B	15294	F-CEGR	21.11.89	G H Macmillan and Partners	Snitterfield	6. 1.08
FMM	3370	FMM	Schleicher Ka 6CR	6328	D-1260	20.10.88	D Hall	Burn	21. 5.05
G-CFMN	3371	FMN	Schempp-Hirth Ventus cT	123/397		12. 9.88	R E Matthews and Partners	Lasham	1. 2.08
G-OTRY	3372	328	Schleicher ASW 24	24023		21. 1.89	A R Harrison and G Pursey	Dunstable	8. 7.08
G-CFMO	3373	158	Schempp-Hirth Discus b	243		1.10.88	P D Bagnall	Nympsfield	5. 4.08
FMR	3374	FMR	Neukom Standard Elfe S-2	05	HB-801	8.11.88	M Powell and Partners	Camphill	11. 2.08
G-CFMS	3375	519	Schleicher ASW 15	15061	N111SP	13.10.89	A F Brind	Rivar Hill	22. 6.08
G-CFMT	3376	FMT	Schempp-Hirth Standard Cirrus	249	N2HM	9. 2.89	S R Westlake	North Hill	20. 6.08
G-CFMU	3377	FMU	Schempp-Hirth Standard Cirrus	236	N3LB	14. 7.90	A R Harrison and J Gammage	Aston Down	16. 2.08
G-CFMY	3381	371	Rolladen-Schneider LS7	7004	D-1256	18.12.88	M Newman and Partners	Camphill	17. 4.08
FMZ	3382	FMZ	Schleicher K7	7018	D-0635	22.11.88	Nene Valley Gliding Club	Upwood	17. 7.04
G-CFNA	3383	FNA	Schleicher K 8B	8499	D-5670	13.11.88	Bowland Forest Gliding Club	Chipping	28. 9.08
FNC	3385	-	Slingsby T.21B	601	WB934	5.11.88	G Follmann	Oberschleissheim, Germany	1. 5.08
G-CFND	3386	FND	Schleicher Ka 6E	4069	PH-366	14.11.88	T Barton	Talgarth	12. 2.08
FNE	3387	FNE	SZD-38A Jantar-1	B-612	HB-1215	20.12.88	J Murray	Rivar Hill	5.10.07
FNF	3388	461	Schleicher ASW 22BL	22053		20.12.88	461 Syndicate	Wycombe Air Park	1. 4.08
G-CFNG	3389	163	Schleicher ASW 24	24015		10. 5.89	P H Pickett	Snitterfield	28. 9.08
G-CFNH	3390	A19	Schleicher ASW 19	19174	D-7969	9. 2.89	S N Longland	Gransden Lodge	8. 4.08
FNK	3392	FNK	Slingsby T.65A Vega	1897	N9023H	10.12.88	I P Goldstraw and Partner	Dunstable	6. 6.06
G-CFNL	3393	705	Schempp-Hirth Discus b	253		28.11.88	P Musto and A S Ramsay	Long Mynd	31. 1.08
G-CFNM	3394	FNM	Centrair 101B Pégase	101B0289	F-CGSE	30. 3.89	D T Hartley	Husbands Bosworth	28. 9.08
G-CFNN	3395	109	Schempp-Hirth Ventus cT	130/407		8.12.88	D G Every	Eyres Field	6.12.07
FNP	3396	FNP	Schleicher Ka 6CR	567	D-4657	16. 1.89	P T Pollard-Wilkins	Ringmer	21. 8.06
FNQ	3397	282	Schempp-Hirth Discus b	259		18.12.88	C E Fernando	Aston Down	17. 3.08
G-CFNR	3398	330	Schempp-Hirth Discus b	255		20. 3.89	R A Amor	Nympsfield	13. 4.08
G-CFNS	3399	FNS	Glaser-Dirks DG-300 Club Elan			2. 4.89	P E Williams and Partners	Portmoak	2. 7.08
				3E314C23					
G-CFNT	3400	674	Glaser-Dirks DG-600	6-12		12.88	M R Johnson and Partners	Sutton Bank	29. 3.08
G-CFNU	3401	190	Rolladen-Schneider LS4-a	4732	D-1376	9. 4.89	R J Simpson	Nympsfield	6. 1.08
FNX	3404	FNX	Wassmer WA-30 Bijave	84	F-CCTJ	2. 1.89	8 Ball Soaring Association	Shipdham	17. 1.05
FPB	3408	FPB	Schleicher ASW 15B	15243	D-2068	18.12.88	R C Tatlow	Darlton	6. 7.08
FPD	3410	973	Rolladen-Schneider LS7	7033	D-5178	14. 1.89	S Wilson	Pocklington	13.12.07
G-CFPE	3411	238	Schempp-Hirth Ventus cT	131/408		14. 1.89	R Palmer	Bidford	5. 4.08
G-CFPH	3414	GB2	Centrair ASW 20F	20132	F-CFFX	29. 1.89	G R Burkert	Bidford	11. 3.08
G-CFPL	3417	242	Schempp-Hirth Ventus c	409		27. 1.89	R V Barrett	Nympsfield	28. 9.08
G-CFPM	3418	FPM	SZD-51-1 Junior	B-1788		6. 3.89	Kent Gliding Club	Challock	28. 9.08
G-CFPN	3419	HD	Schleicher ASW 20	20376	RAFGGA 545	5. 3.89	M Rayner	Lasham	19. 8.08
					D-8780				
FPP	3420	N2	Schempp-Hirth Nimbus-2B	142	D-6779, D-2111	26. 3.89	R Jones	Walney Island	23. 6.08
FPQ	3421	FPQ	Schleicher K7	EB180/61	D-5184	15. 2.89	East Sussex Gliding Club	Ringmer	24. 2.05
FPS	3423	FPS	Slingsby T.21B	MHL.001	OH-914X	3. 2.89	J Holland	Brandenburg-Mühlenfeld, Germany	15. 6.08
					LN-GAO, BGA 3423, WB974				
FPT	3424	574	Schleicher ASW 20	20007	D-7574	18. 2.89	L Hornsey and Partners	RAF Halton	15. 3.08
FPU	3425	FPU	Schleicher Ka 2B Rhönschwalbe	-	HB-698	17. 2.89	T J Wilkinson	Sackville Lodge, Riseley	4. 4.06
			(Built Segelfluggruppe Zwingen)						
FPV	3426	FPV	Schleicher Ka 6E	4123	N29JG	10. 3.89	A McLean	Bembridge	7. 9.08
					G-AWTP, RAFGSA 29				
FPW	3427	606	Glaser-Dirks DG-600	6-17		13. 4.89	P B Gray	Camphill	3. 5.08
G-CFPX	3428	FPX	Schleicher ASK 13	13325	F-CDYR	21. 6.89	R B Witter	Lleweni Parc	17. 8.07
G-CFOB	3432	FOB	Schleicher ASW 15B	15340	D-2345	10. 8.89	A Maitland	Drumshade	16. 3.08
FQC	3433	201	Glaser-Dirks DG-202/17C	2-178CL19	HB-1645	8. 3.89	C Nunn	Wormingford	24. 2.08
FQD	3434	FQD	Schleicher K 8B	8289	D-1908	6. 3.89	Kent Gliding Club	Challock	7. 1.05
FQE	3435	FQE	Schleicher K 8B	3	D-6329	3. 4.89	Cotswold Gliding Club *(Stored 1.08)*	Aston Down	9. 4.01
G-CFOF	3436	FOF	Scheibe SF 27A Zugvogel V	6025	D-0009	19. 2.89	S Maddex	Darlton	6. 5.08
G-DFOG	3437	952	Rolladen-Schneider LS7	7050	D-1712	4. 6.89	D W Smith	Sutton Bank	27. 4.08
G-CEVN	3438	A98	Rolladen-Schneider LS7	7029	D-1316	15. 4.89	B C Toon and N Gaunt	Sutton Bank	28. 9.08
G-CFOK	3440	FOK	Grob G103C Twin III Acro	34123		15. 8.89	York Gliding Centre	Rufforth	28. 9.08
FQL	3441	772	Schleicher Ka 6CR	6235	HB-772	18. 3.89	P R Alderson	Lasham	12. 5.08
FQM	3442	FQM	Scheibe SF 27A Zugvogel V	6098	D-9421	19. 2.89	R D Noon	Darlton	6. 6.08
FQR	3446	FQR	Schleicher K 8B	8537	PH-349	9. 3.89	Dorset Gliding Club	Eyres Field	16. 6.06
G-CFOT	3448	484	SZD-48-3 Jantar-Standard 3	B-1891	(BGA 3409)	28. 3.90	T H Greenwood	Rivar Hill	18. 5.08
G-CFOU	3449	FOU	Schleicher K7	1139	D-8614, HB-709	13. 3.89	Channel Gliding Club	Waldershare Park	3. 3.08
G-CFOY	3453	785	Schempp-Hirth Discus b	274		16. 4.89	J W Slater and B W Mills	Dunstable	4. 8.08
G-CFOZ	3454	L51	Rolladen-Schneider LS1-f	391	F-CEKH	12. 6.89	A G Wallace and Partners	Bidford	26. 2.08
G-DFRA	3455	79	Rolladen-Schneider LS6-b	6151	D-8081	20. 4.89	M Randle and Partners	Aston Down	28. 9.08
G-CFRB	3456	FRB	Schempp-Hirth Ventus c	404		4. 3.89	C J Ratcliffe	Seighford	14. 3.08
FRC	3457	998	Schempp-Hirth Nimbus-2B	151	D-4980	15. 5.89	T J Lean	Lasham	14. 6.08
FRE	3459	FRE	Schleicher Ka 6E	4349	F-CDTL	13. 4.89	D J Stewart	Parham	3. 7.08

FRG	3461	FRG	Siebert Sie 3	3009	D-0739	7. 4.89	A Cridge	Talgarth	11. 1.09
FRH	3462	634	Schleicher ASW 20CL	20740	D-9229	2. 4.89	J N Wilton and Partner	Husbands Bosworth	6. 4.08
FRJ	3463	RJ	Schempp-Hirth Standard Cirrus	103	HB-1041	23. 4.89	K R Kay	Tibenham	31. 3.08
G-CFRK	3464	FRK	Schleicher ASW 15B	15214	D-0941	21. 3.89	M Hill	Edgehill	21.10.07
G-CFRL	3465	FRL	Grob G102 Astir CS	1373	D-7402	22. 4.89	South Wales Gliding Club	Usk	13. 4.08
FRQ	3469	XT653	Slingsby T.45 Swallow	1420	XT653	27. 4.89	D Shrimpton	RAF Keevil	3. 7.03
G-CFRR	3470	495	Centrair 101A Pégase	101034	(BGA 3451) F-CFQA	16. 4.89	P A Lewis	Walney Island	4. 6.08
G-CFRS	3471	FRS	Scheibe Zugvogel IIIB	1097	D-2171 HB-749	27. 4.89	S W Vallei and R C Theobald	Rivar Hill	26. 4.08
G-CFRV	3474	FRV	Centrair 101A Pégase	101A0325		28.10.89	P J Britten	Wycombe Air Park	14. 9.08
G-CFRW	3475	268	Schleicher ASW 20L	20202	D-5981	5. 5.89	S R Jarvis	Lasham	4. 3.08
G-CFRX	3476	FRX	Centrair 101A Pégase	101A0315		30. 5.89	S Woolrich	Portmoak	13. 2.08
FRZ	3478	FRZ	Schempp-Hirth Standard Cirrus	348G	HB-1194 D-2172	15. 5.89	S Lapworth	Lasham	6. 6.08
FSA	3479	498	Grob G102 Astir CS	1277	D-7371	9. 4.89	J R Carpenter	Lasham	19. 8.08
FSB	3480	-	Slingsby T.38 Grasshopper	1269	XP492	R	Not known *(Stored 2005)*	Eyres Field	
FSC	3481	WZ755	Slingsby T.38 Grasshopper	751	WZ755	27. 4.90	Boulton Paul Heritage Project	Wolverhampton	30. 4.93
G-CFSD	3482	N28	Schleicher ASK 13	13367	D-0863	24. 5.89	Portsmouth Naval Gliding Club	Lee-on-Solent	16. 8.08
FSE	3483	FSE	Schleicher Ka 6CR	6021	D-1946	19. 8.89	G W Lobb	North Hill	28. 7.04
G-CFSH	3486	FSH	Grob G102 Astir CS Jeans	2090	D-7532	9. 5.89	Buckminster Gliding Club	Saltby	7. 7.08
FSJ	3487	WT908	Slingsby T.31B	703	WT908	22. 5.89	R J Abrahams	Dunstable	8. 1.99
FSK	3488	FSK	Slingsby T.38 Grasshopper	791	WZ795	26. 6.89	E Janssen	Lemelerveld, Netherlands	27. 5.08
G-CFSR	3494	FSR	Glaser-Dirks DG-300 Elan	3E343		24. 8.89	A P Montague and J E May	Nympsfield	22. 1.08
FSS	3495	FSS	Schleicher Ka 6E	4019	D-5260	19. 8.89	P R Robey	Lasham	6. 8.08
G-CFST	3496	FST	Schleicher ASH 25E	25073	(BGA 3530)	12.10.89	K H Lloyd and D Tucker	Aston Down	18. 3.08
FSU	3497	FSU/55	Scheibe Zugvogel IIIA	1060	D-9055	30. 6.89	F Dobbs	Bellarena	13. 6.07
FSV	3498	WZ819	Slingsby T.38 Grasshopper	800	WZ819	26. 6.89	P D Mann	RAF Halton	6. 6.04
G-PAFR	3500	405	Glaser-Dirks DG-300 Elan	3E344		11. 7.89	P Morgan	Parham	17. 1.08
G-CFSZ	3502	FSZ	Grob G102 Astir CS77	1841	D-2908	29. 7.89	N Greenwood	Aston Down	17. 1.08
G-CFTB	3504	FTB	Schleicher Ka 6CR (Built Bitz)	019	D-8900	22. 7.89	P J F Blair	Snitterfield	24. 1.08
G-CFTC	3505	N56	SZD-51-1 Junior	B-1860		23. 7.89	Seahawk Gliding Club	RNAS Culdrose	20. 3.08
G-CFTD	3506	FTD	Schleicher ASW 15B	15191	D-0872	23. 8.89	E Stephenson	Milfield	29. 4.08
FTF	3508	FTF	Schleicher Ka 6CR	6294	D-6081	5. 9.89	T Delap	Parham	12. 6.06
G-CFTH	3510	FTH	SZD-50-3 Puchacz	B-1881		24. 8.89	Buckminster Gliding Club	Saltby	17.12.07
G-DFTJ	3511	"FTI"	SZD-48 Jantar-Standard 2	W-889	HB-1472	25. 8.89	D P Bieniasz and P Nock	Kirton in Lindsey	6. 3.08
G-CFTK	3512	518	Grob G102 Astir CS Jeans	2059	OE-5152	17.10.89	Ulster Gliding Club	Bellarena	8. 9.07
G-CFTL	3513	FTL	Schleicher ASW 20CL	20751	D-3564	2. 9.89	J S and S V Shaw	Perranporth	22. 4.08
FTM	3514	-	Schleicher K 8B	513	D-5708	30. 8.89	Vale of Neath Gliding Club	Rhigos	9. 4.06
FTN	3515	853	Schleicher K 8B	996	D-8539 D-KAEL, D-8539	11. 3.89	C B Hogarth Syndicate	Halesland	15.11.07
G-CFTP	3516	332	Schleicher ASW 20CL	20733	D-3640	4. 1.90	M S Hawkins	Kingston Deverill	31. 5.08
G-CFTR	3518	FTR	Grob G102 Astir CS77	1606	D-4807	6.10.89	Lakes Gliding Club	Walney Island	9. 3.08
G-CFTS	3519	FTS	Glaser-Dirks DG-300 Club Elan	3E349C38		12.10.89	A J E Taylor and Partners	Parham	23. 5.08
FTU	3521	FTU	Schleicher K7	302	HB-599	25. 9.89	Dartmoor Gliding Society *(Stored 2005)*	Brentor	25. 3.03
G-CFTV	3522	944	Rolladen-Schneider LS7-WL	7073		9.10.89	D Hilton	Wycombe Air Park	3. 3.08
G-CFTW	3523	230	Schempp-Hirth Discus b	292		4.10.89	P A Startup	North Hill	28. 9.08
			(Rebuilt with new fuselage after accident 21. 6.91; original fuselage rebuilt as BGA 3879)						
G-CFTY	3525	753	Rolladen-Schneider LS7-WL	7075		8.10.89	A M Burgess and J A Thompson	Easterton	4. 4.08
FUB	3528	-	Schleicher Ka 6CR	6007	D-8573	6.11.89	D E Hooper	Brentor	4. 9.08
FUD	3529	2	SZD-9bis Bocian 1E	P-689	SP-2807	2.11.89	Mendip Gliding Club *(Stored 12.07)*	Halesland	16. 4.04
FUF	3531	FUF	Scheibe SF 27A Zugvogel V	6089	D-6068	30. 9.89	East Sussex Gliding Club	Ringmer	22. 4.04
G-GBBB	3532	BB	Schleicher ASH 25	25074	(BGA 3526)	20.10.89	M J Wells and Partners	Lasham	30. 1.08
G-CFUH	3533	192	Schempp-Hirth Ventus c	438		12.10.89	M A Gale and Partners	Eyres Field	28. 9.08
G-CFUJ	3534	FUJ	Glaser-Dirks DG-300 Elan	3E353		5.12.89	R S Jones and Partners	Portmoak	4. 3.08
G-CFUL	3535	803	Schempp-Hirth Discus b	293		14. 3.90	P J Warner and Partners	Dunstable	22. 2.08
G-CFUN	3537	FUN	Schleicher ASW 20CL	20813	D-3432	5. 4.91	W H Parker and S Economou	Booker	6. 3.08
FUP	3538	SH4	Schempp-Hirth Discus b	291		18.10.89	Surrey & Hants Gliding Club	Lasham	17. 6.08
FUQ	3539	FUQ	Scheibe SF 27A Zugvogel V	6090	D-5196	1. 4.90	G Elliott and Partners	Ringmer	10. 5.03
FUR	3540	256	Schempp-Hirth Ventus cT	145/446		15. 3.90	K Martin	Shobdon	3. 4.08
G-CFUS	3541	FUS	SZD-51-1 Junior	B-1912		20.11.89	Scottish Gliding Union Ltd	Portmoak	28. 9.08
FUT	3542	612	Glaser-Dirks DG-300 Club Elan	3E350C39		11. 3.90	M J Barnett	Gransden Lodge	14. 6.08
G-CFUU	3543	FUU	Glaser-Dirks DG-300 Club Elan	3E360C45		4. 3.90	D Penny	Perranporth	28. 9.08
G-CFUV	3544	194	Rolladen-Schneider LS7-WL	7068		4.11.89	E Alston	North Hill	28. 9.08
FUW	3545	XE807	Slingsby T.31B Cadet TX.3	920	XE807	20.11.89	G Tischler	Germany	27. 7.08
G-CFUY	3546	FUY	SZD-50-3 Puchacz	B-1983		30.11.89	Bath, Wilts and North Dorset Gliding Club	Kingston Deverill	6. 5.08
FVA	3548	N15	Schleicher K 8B	1051	D-5117	13. 4.90	Portsmouth Naval Gliding Club	Lee-on-Solent	18.10.06
FVB	3549	228	Schempp-Hirth Ventus cT	144/445		13. 1.90	R J Harraway	Parham	4. 3.08
							(Cancelled 16. 7.07; to PH-1397 8.07)		
G-CFVC	3550	FVC	Schleicher ASK 13 (Built Jubi)	13682AB		11.12.89	Mendip Gliding Club	Halesland	25. 1.08
G-SVNC	3552	7C	Rolladen-Schneider LS4	4190	RAFGSA 232 RAFGSA R30, D-4542	12. 1.90	M C Jenkins	Dunstable	15. 3.08
G-CFVE	3553	FVE	Schempp-Hirth Nimbus-2C	202	D-2880	3. 3.90	L C Mitchell	Chipping	19. 6.08
G-CFVH	3555	246	Rolladen-Schneider LS7	7067	(BGA 3527)	18.12.89	B R Forrest	Wycombe Air Park	11. 4.08
FVL	3558	FVL	Scheibe Zugvogel IIIB	1082	D-5224	29.12.89	T G Homan	Darlton	8. 8.08
G-CFVM	3559	369	Centrair 101A Pégase	101A0345		15. 3.90	S H North	Kingston Deverill	11. 4.08
G-CFVN	3560	FVN	Centrair 101A Pégase	101A0268/2		16. 1.90	G G Butler	Snitterfield	1. 2.08
			(Rebuild of BGA 3198 and carries c/n 10100268)						

G-CFVP	3561	FVP	Centrair 101A Pégase	101A0350		22. 4.90	J R Parry and Partners	Long Mynd	25. 9.08
G-EUFO	3562	FVQ	Rolladen-Schneider LS7-WL	7079		18. 1.90	R Hardy and J R Bane	Gransden Lodge	1. 4.08
G-CFVS	3564	FVS	Schempp-Hirth Standard Cirrus	359G	D-2168	25. 3.90	P A Clark	Lasham	24. 1.08
G-CFVU	3566	FVU	Schleicher ASK 13	13062	D-1348	17. 4.90	Vale of White Horse Gliding Centre		
								Sandhill Farm, Shrivenham	28. 9.08
G-CFVV	3567	FVV	Centrair 101A Pégase	101A0353		27. 4.90	Cambridge Gliding Club	Gransden Lodge	1. 7.08
G-CFVW	3568	FVW	Schempp-Hirth Ventus bT	51/252	D-KORN	26. 1.90	I C Champness and R F Barber	Lasham	28. 9.08
G-CFVZ	3571	PS	Schleicher Ka 6E	4007	D-4104	27. 2.90	R C Fisher	Kingston Deverill	21. 6.08
G-CFWA	3572	FWA	Schleicher Ka 6CR	6227	D-1062	26. 3.90	D Cousins and A Parker	Usk	5.10.07
G-CFWB	3573	FWB	Schleicher ASK 13	13224	HB-989	2. 4.90	Cotswold Gliding Club	Aston Down	19. 1.08
G-CFWC	3574	609	Grob G103C Twin III Acro	34154		5. 4.90	South Wales Gliding Club	Usk	17. 3.08
G-IFWD	3575	FWD-888	Schempp-Hirth Ventus cT	148/468		10. 5.90	R S Maxwell-Fendt	Lasham	1. 4.08
G-CFWE	3576	FWE	SZD-50-3 Puchacz	B-1984	(BGA 3547)	5. 2.90	Deeside Gliding Club	Aboyne	28. 9.08
FWF	3577	L57	Rolladen-Schneider LS7	7097		28. 2.90	G P Hibberd	Husbands Bosworth	8. 7.08
FWH	3579	FWH	Scheibe SF 27A Zugvogel V	6024	D-4733	10. 2.90	M D Smith	Aston Down	8. 6.08
FWJ	3580	S3	Rolladen-Schneider LS7-WL	7078		22. 3.90	J P Popika	Gransden Lodge	1. 8.08
G-CFWK	3581	29	Schempp-Hirth Nimbus-3DT	32		22. 3.90	A J Dibdin and Partners	Gransden Lodge	27. 3.08
G-CFWL	3582	FWL	Schleicher K 8B	106/58	D-7151	24. 2.90	M Staniscia	(Kettering)	3. 8.08
G-CFWM	3583	FWM	Glaser-Dirks DG-300 Club Elan			15. 6.90	S A Gunn-Russell and Partners	Long Mynd	28. 9.08
				3E373C50					
G-CFWP	3585	980	Schleicher ASW 19B	19262	D-5980	4. 4.90	B Spriggs	Dunstable	17. 3.08
G-MOZI	3587	277	Glasflügel Mosquito	34	N77RL	26. 3.90	P Smith and J Christensen		
								RAF Weston-on-the-Green	19. 9.08
G-CFWS	3588	662	Schleicher ASW 20C	20765	D-6623	18. 2.90	G W Martin and Partners	Ridgewell	3. 4.08
G-CFWT	3589	FWT	SZD-50-3 Puchacz	B-1988		24. 3.90	The Gliding Centre	Husbands Bosworth	11. 1.08
G-CFWU	3590	768	Rolladen-Schneider LS7-WL	7080		19. 3.90	G E Thomas	Husbands Bosworth	29. 9.08
G-CFWW	3592	FWW	Schleicher ASH 25E	25093		19. 6.90	A T Farmer	Bicester	28. 2.08
G-REER	3593	FWX	Centrair 101A Pégase	101033	F-CFRZ	27. 3.90	P M Greer	Nympsfield	11. 4.08
G-CFWY	3594	FWY	Centrair 101A Pégase	101071	F-CFXE	23. 3.90	R Johnson and Partners	Lasham	5. 4.08
G-CFWZ	3595	FWZ	Schleicher ASW 19B	19342	D-2603	14. 4.90	C Grey	Camphill	15.12.07
G-CFXA	3596	567	Grob G104 Speed Astir IIB	4083	D-2671	16. 4.90	C M Hawkes	Ringmer	22. 9.08
FXB	3597	FXB	Schleicher K 8B	8193/A	D-5597	29. 3.90	R J Morris	Brentor	1. 4.08
FXC	3598	FXC	Schleicher Ka 6E	4268	RAFGGA 150	9. 8.90	J Wilson and A K Bailey	Kingston Deverill	31. 5.08
					D-0150				
G-CFXD	3599	285	Centrair 101A Pégase	101A0346	(BGA 3563)	31. 3.90	The Gliding Centre	Husbands Bosworth	27.12.07
FXE	3600	35	Rolladen-Schneider LS7	7090		23. 3.90	J C Kingerlee	RAF Weston-on-the-Green	28. 9.05
FXF	3601	FXF	Slingsby T.50 Skylark 4	1455	HB-812	7. 5.90	A J Hewitt	Shipdham	5. 5.08
G-CFXH	3603	-	Schleicher K7	353	D-4040	10. 4.90	Vale of Neath Gliding Club	Rhigos	6. 9.08
G-CFXJ	3604	247	Schleicher ASW 24	24086		4. 5.90	A K Laylee and G Dale	Lasham	28. 9.08
FXL	3606	108	Schleicher ASH 25	25088		11. 4.90	C Simpson and Partners	Husbands Bosworth	13. 4.08
FXM	3607	173	Schempp-Hirth Discus bT	16/301	D-KHIA	12. 4.90	R Bottomley	Pocklington	23. 7.08
FXP	3609	FXP	LET L-23 Super Blanik	907609		17. 7.90	Cambridge University Gliding Club	Gransden Lodge	28. 6.07
G-CFZO	3610	954	Schempp-Hirth Nimbus-3DT	31		21. 4.90	D G Tanner	Lasham	28. 9.08
FXR	3611	L12	Sportine Aviacija LAK-12	6162		4. 9.90	S R Blackmore	Hinton-in-the-Hedges	23. 4.05
FXS	3612	FXS	Schleicher Ka 6E	4228	D-0073	7. 5.90	R Woodhouse and B C Wade	Tibenham	27. 6.07
FXT	3613		Centrair 101A Pégase	101056	F-CFQV	4.90	K Ludlow	Viterbo, Italy	4. 8.02
G-CFXU	3614	FXU	Schleicher Ka 6E	4071	OH-343	8. 6.90	J Wright	Lasham	14. 3.08
					OH-RSY				
G-CFXW	3616	FXW	Schleicher K 8B	8651	D-7203	5. 4.90	South Wales Gliding Club	Usk	24. 3.07
					D-KOLA, D-7203				
FXY	3618	EC	Schleicher ASW 15B	15348	F-CEJL	21. 5.90	P W Armstrong	Husbands Bosworth	13. 6.08
G-CFYA	3620	FYA	SZD-50-3 Puchacz	B-2022		9. 5.90	Cairngorm Gliding Club	Feshiebridge	25. 3.08
G-CFYB	3621	779	Rolladen-Schneider LS7	7102		2. 5.90	V P Haley and A T Macdonald	Wormingford	28. 9.08
G-CFYC	3622	V10	Schempp-Hirth Ventus b	83	F-CEDR	2. 5.90	K Fear	Crowland	20. 4.08
					F-WEDR				
G-RAIR	3623	942	Schleicher ASH 25	25095		19. 5.90	Viscount Cobham and P T Reading	Lasham	30. 1.08
FYE	3624	FYE	Scheibe Zugvogel IIIB	1067	OY-MHX	20. 5.90	G Pearce and Partners	Brentor	7. 9.08
					SE-TCE, OY-EFX, D-1814				
FYF	3625	FYF	Schleicher ASK 21	21470		4. 8.90	London Gliding Club	Dunstable	10. 5.08
FYG	3626	FYG	Glasflügel Club Libelle 205	22	OH-545	13. 5.90	L Ballard	Talgarth	23. 8.08
FYH	3627	224	Rolladen-Schneider LS4-a	4804		4. 7.90	G W Craig	RAF Weston-on-the-Green	28. 9.08
G-CFYJ	3628	FYJ	Schempp-Hirth Standard Cirrus	581G	D-8931	12. 7.90	S A Gibson and Partners	Pocklington	29.12.07
G-CFYK	3629	7R	Rolladen-Schneider LS7-WL	7108		1. 6.90	R R Ward	Gransden Lodge	26. 1.08
G-CFYL	3630	FYL	SZD-50-3 Puchacz	B-1990		21. 6.90	Deeside Gliding Club	Aboyne	28. 9.08
G-CFYM	3631	326	Schempp-Hirth Discus bT	31/328		1. 6.90	B F Laverick-Smith	Challock	28. 9.08
G-CFYN	3632	J3	Schempp-Hirth Discus b	179	N75J	14. 7.90	P R Foulger and N White	Wormingford	21. 3.08
FYR	3635	FYR	LET L-23 Super Blanik	917816		2. 7.92	A M Cooper	Lleweni Parc	31. 5.07
G-CFYU	3638	DG	Glaser-Dirks DG-101 Elan	E111	OY-XMR	28. 6.90	I Shepherd	RAF Weston-on-the-Green	5. 7.08
					SE-TYO				
G-CFYV	3639	FYV	Schleicher ASK 21	21468		25. 7.90	Bristol & Gloucestershire Gliding Club	Nympsfield	28. 9.08
G-CFYW	3640	KC	Rolladen-Schneider LS7-WL	7111		6. 6.90	D S Lodge	Pocklington	19. 1.08
FYX	3641	FYX	Schempp-Hirth Discus bT	32/333		3. 7.90	D A Salmon	Camphill	4. 4.08
FYY	3642	S	Schleicher ASK 13	13685AB		9. 7.90	Lasham Gliding Society	Lasham	7. 3.08
FYZ	3643	171	Schleicher ASH 25	25097		18. 7.90	M G Thick	Sutton Bank	3. 7.08
G-CFZA	3644	FZA	SZD-51-1 Junior	B-1913		23. 7.90	Booker Gliding Club	Wycombe Air Park	29. 1.08
G-CFZB	3645	669	Glasflügel Standard Libelle 201B	112	OH-388	31. 7.90	J C Meyer	Nympsfield	2. 1.08
					OH-GLA				
FZC	3646	FZC	Schempp-Hirth SHK-1	58	OH-357	30. 8.91	J F Mills	RAF Cranwell	22. 6.06
					OH-SHA				
G-CFZF	3649	FZF	SZD-51-1 Junior	B-1861		21. 7.90	Devon & Somerset Gliding Club	North Hill	28. 9.08
FZG	3650	FZG	SZD-9bis Bocian 1D	F-859	SP-2450	24. 9.90	J H Nash	Shipdham	14.10.06
G-CFZH	3651	FZH	Schempp-Hirth Ventus c	455		26. 7.90	G D Clack and Partners	Lasham	22. 1.08
FZK	3653	FZK	Schempp-Hirth Standard Cirrus	81	HB-967	2. 9.90	R S Burgoyne and S Lucas	Aston Down	27. 9.08
G-CFZL	3654	Z6	Schleicher ASW 20CL	20764	D-5937	12. 7.90	A L and R M Housden	Aboyne	8.11.07

FZM	3655	FZM	Scheibe SF 27A Zugvogel V	6103	D-1772	7. 8.90	N Dickenson	Chipping	31. 8.08
G-CFZN	3656	K13	Schleicher ASK 13	13045	D-5759	9. 8.90	Black Mountains Gliding Club	Talgarth	16. 5.08
G-CFZP	3657	N16	SZD-51-1 Junior	B-1926		9. 8.90	Portsmouth Naval Gliding Club	Lee-on-Solent	19. 6.08
G-CFXO	3658	FXQ	SZD-50-3 Puchacz	B-2024	(BGA 3637)	9. 8.90	The Gliding Centre	Husbands Bosworth	29. 3.08
FZR	3659	FZR	Schleicher Ka 6CR	6136	D-8459	17.12.90	D Albasiny	North Hill	18. 9.08
FZU	3662		Slingsby T.38 Grasshopper	761	WZ765	8. 8.91	Luftwaffenmuseum	Berlin-Gatow	26.12.96
							(On display 2006)		
G-CFZV	3663	480	Rolladen-Schneider LS7	7116		16.12.90	R N Boddy	Wycombe Air Park	8. 3.08
G-CFZW	3664	FZW	Glaser-Dirks DG-300 Club Elan			23. 9.90	D O'Flanagan and Partners	Parham	7. 3.08
				3E378C53					
FZZ	3667	FZZ	LET L-33 Solo	940220		28. 4.95	D A Wiseman	Andreas	14. 5.08
GAB	3669	GAB	Sportine Aviacija LAK-12	6170		12. 1.91	M J Wilshere	RAF Halton	9. 9.08
GAC	3670	GAC	Schleicher Ka 6CR	6301	(BGA 3647)	11.90	McLean Aviation	Rufforth	2. 2.99
					RAFGGA 557, D-5572		*(W/o 25.11.98; stored 2006)*		
GAD	3671	L5	Rolladen-Schneider LS3	3032	HB-1363	19.11.90	P B Turner	Challock	9. 8.08
G-CGAF	3673	778	Schleicher ASK 21	21152	ZD652	8.11.90	Lasham Gliding Society	Lasham	15. 3.08
					BGA 2892				
G-CGAG	3674	GAG	Schleicher ASK 21	21143	ZD645	24. 1.91	Stratford on Avon Gliding Club	Snitterfield	28. 9.08
G-CGAH	3675	GAH	Schempp-Hirth Standard Cirrus	572	HB-1240	3.12.90	J W Williams	(Bideford)	30. 3.08
GAJ	3676	GAJ	Glaser-Dirks DG-300 Club Elan			10.12.90	S M Lewis	Long Mynd	9. 6.08
				3E385C56					
GAK	3677	GAK	LET L-13 Blanik	174522	2-84 (Lithuania)	5. 7.97	North Wales Gliding Club	Llantisilio	27. 1.07
G-CGAM	3679	GAM	Schleicher ASK 21	21144	ZD646	21.11.90	Oxford University Gliding Club	Bicester	24. 2.08
					BGA 2886				
GAN	3680	83	Glasflügel H 301 Libelle	8	D-4111	12.12.90	L Roberts	Nympsfield	26. 8.08
GAP	3681	GAP	Schempp-Hirth Ventus bT	14/150	OH-774	28. 4.91	J R Greenwell	Milfield	25. 8.08
					N416DP				
GAQ	3682	GAQ	Schleicher K7	3	PH-788	19. 4.91	Channel Gliding Club	Waldershare Park	24. 7.06
					D-5550		*(Wfu 2006)*		
GAR	3683	AW	Rolladen-Schneider LS6-c	6205		2.11.90	A Warbrick	Feshiebridge	25. 6.08
G-CGAS	3684	GAS	Schempp-Hirth Ventus cT	157/509		30. 5.91	M W Edwards	Kingston Deverill	28. 9.08
GAT	3685	GAT	Grob G102 Astir CS	1130	D-4176	23.11.90	C Smales	Cross Hayes	13. 7.08
GAU	3686	725	Glasflügel Standard Libelle 201B	498	F-CELA	11. 6.93	D R Pickett	Crowland	12. 4.08
G-CGAV	3687	GAV	Scheibe SF 27A Zugvogel V	6073	D-5287	18.11.90	R A Kempton and Partners	Darlton	1. 9.08
G-DGAW	3688	GAW	Schleicher Ka 6CR	61/08	D-6320	30.12.90	H C Yorke and D Searle	Snitterfield	13. 3.08
GAX	3689	302	SZD-55-1	551190008		30. 4.91	P Gold	Rougham	5. 4.08
GBA	3692	GBA	Schleicher ASK 13	13417	D-2114	4.12.90	Burn Gliding Club	Burn	6. 5.08
G-CGBB	3693	GBB	Schleicher ASK 21	21073	D-3239	11.12.90	Edinburgh University Gliding Club	Portmoak	17. 3.08
G-CGBD	3695	GBD	SZD-50-3 Puchacz	B-2028		27. 4.91	Northumbria Gliding Club	Currock Hill	17. 6.08
GBE	3696	-	Schleicher Ka 6CR-Pe	6133A	D-4085	23.12.90	S Simpson	Darlton	9.10.08
G-CGBF	3697	GBF	Schleicher ASK 21	21142	ZD644	3. 2.91	BBC Gliding Group	Wycombe Air Park	28. 9.08
					BGA 2883				
G-CGBG	3698	521	Rolladen-Schneider LS6-c	6214		12.12.90	C M Greaves	Rufforth	7. 2.08
G-CGBJ	3700	GBJ	Grob G102 Astir CS	1107	D-4167	5. 1.91	Banbury Gliding Club	Hinton-in-the-Hedges	16. 4.08
G-CGBK	3701	GBK	Grob G102 Astir CS	1461	D-7451	5. 1.91	B J and A R Griffiths	Saltby	28. 9.08
G-CGBL	3702	720	Rolladen-Schneider LS7-WL	7119		12.11.90	M J Aldridge	Rougham	2. 3.08
GBM	3703	GBM	Scheibe SF 27A Zugvogel V	6060	RAFGGA	2. 1.91	G Cook tr BFMT Syndicate	North Hill	12.12.07
					D-5409				
G-CGBN	3704	843	Schleicher ASK 21	21141	ZD643	14. 3.91	Essex & Suffolk Gliding Club	Wormingford	1. 3.08
					BGA 2884				
G-CGBO	3706	C30	Rolladen-Schneider LS6	6082	D-3725	6. 2.91	G D Sutherland and Partners	Wycombe Air Park	17. 3.08
G-CGBR	3707	218	Rolladen-Schneider LS6-c	6196	D-3482	25.11.90	V L Brown	Snitterfield	12. 9.08
GBS	3708	206	Glaser-Dirks DG-300 Club Elan			15. 3.91	S M Tilling	Long Mynd	27. 9.08
				3E389C58					
G-XCIV	3709	IV	Rolladen-Schneider LS4-a	4355	N220BB	8. 4.91	S M Platt and Partners	Long Mynd	21. 3.08
G-CGBU	3710	922	Centrair 101A Pégase 90	101A0394		3. 4.91	S I Ross and Partners	Parham	15. 2.08
G-CGBV	3711	GBV	Schleicher ASK 21	21149	ZD649	23. 4.91	Wolds Gliding Club	Pocklington	27. 3.08
					BGA 2889				
G-CGBX	3713	52	Schleicher ASW 22	22029	D-4325	27. 2.91	D A Ashby	Sutton Bank	26. 2.08
GBY	3714	425	Rolladen-Schneider LS7	7121		21. 1.91	W J Morecraft and Partners	Saltby	17. 9.08
G-CGBZ	3715	GBZ	Glaser-Dirks DG-500 Elan Trainer			10. 8.91	Needwood Forest Gliding Club	Cross Hayes	11. 5.08
				5E34T10					
G-CGCA	3716	GCA	Schleicher ASW 19B	19281	D-3179	2. 3.91	Deeside Gliding Club	Aboyne	30. 1.08
G-GLAK	3717	236	Sportine Aviacija LAK-12	647	??	29. 3.91	L M Middleton	Dunstable	5. 4.08
G-CGCC	3718	GCC	SZD-51-1 Junior	B-1928		10. 3.91	The Gliding Centre	Husbands Bosworth	31. 3.08
GCD	3719	507	Schempp-Hirth Standard Cirrus	476	PH-507	21. 2.91	W G Anderson	Feshiebridge	23. 4.08
G-CWLC	3720	8	Schleicher ASH 25	25105		19. 2.91	C L Withall	Dunstable	1. 4.08
G-CGCF	3721	GCF	Schleicher ASK 23	23010	AGA 9	8. 2.91	Needwood Forest Gliding Club	Cross Hayes	18. 2.08
GCG	3722	S81	Schleicher K 8B	8186	D-5227	5. 2.91	Shenington Gliding Club *(Stored 8.07)*	Edgehill	24.10.04
GCJ	3724	GCJ	Sportine Aviacija LAK-12	626	??	30. 3.91	P Crowhurst	Crowland	27. 5.05
			(New wings with reconditioned 1982-built fuselage)						
GCK	3725	GCK	SZD-50-3 Puchacz	B-2025	G-BTJV	8. 3.91	Kent Gliding Club	Challock	6. 4.08
G-CGCL	3726	GCL	Grob G102 Astir CS	1194	D-7311	10. 3.91	A J Williams	Parham	18. 5.08
G-CGCM	3727	347	Rolladen-Schneider LS6-c	6216		12. 3.91	G R Glazebrook	Dunstable	28. 9.08
G-CGCP	3729	GCP	Schleicher Ka 6CR	6416	D-6369	3. 5.91	D and B Clarke	Burn	28. 5.08
GCQ	3730	GCQ	Schempp-Hirth Cirrus VTC	135Y	D-2945	2. 4.91	Dumfries and District Gliding Club	Falgunzeon	23. 1.07
G-CGCR	3731	748	Schleicher ASW 15B	15447	D-6887	23. 3.91	R C Page	Nympsfield	17. 3.08
GCS	3732	H12	Glasflügel Club Libelle 205	159	F-CEQL	7. 7.91	D G Coats	Portmoak	31. 8.08
G-CGCT	3733	TB2	Schempp-Hirth Discus b	360		22. 3.91	D A White	Dunstable	17. 2.08
G-CGCU	3734	GCU	SZD-50-3 Puchacz	B-2023	(BGA 3619)	19. 3.91	Buckminster Gliding Club	Saltby	27. 2.08
GCX	3736	N6	Schleicher ASW 15	15034	D-0420	21. 5.91	P T Collier and Partner	Snitterfield	9. 2.08
GCY	3737	GCY	Centrair 101A Pégase 90	101A0392		22. 4.91	J E Jervis	Edgehill	9. 3.08
G-CGDA	3739	546	Rolladen-Schneider LS3-17	3448	RAFGGA 546	20. 5.91	A R Fish	Saltby	1. 2.08
G-CGDB	3740	GDB	Schleicher K 8B	8152	HB-738	23. 3.91	Welland Gliding Club	Lyveden	7. 8.08

Reg	No	Comp	Type	Serial	Prev ID	Date	Owner	Location	Date
G-CGDE	3743	GDE	Schleicher Ka 6CR	6570Si	D-5306	26. 4.91	P D Rowlands	North Hill	23. 9.08
GDF	3744	GDF	Schleicher Ka 6BR	389	D-8544	17. 4.91	M A Sheehan	Cross Hayes	22. 9.08
GDJ	3747	450	Rolladen-Schneider LS4-a	4832		27. 4.91	A Clark	Lee-on-Solent	11. 7.08
G-CGDK	3748	GDK	Schleicher K 8B	8240	D-5381	15. 4.91	Vale of Neath Gliding Club	Rhigos	24. 7.08
					D-KANU, D-5381				
G-YOHO	3750	668	Glasflügel Standard Libelle 201B	597	D-6666	29. 4.91	M P Theo	Waldershare Park	23. 1.08
GDN	3751	294	Rolladen-Schneider LS3-17	3291	D-6932	28. 4.91	S J Pepler	Sandhill Farm, Shrivenham	15. 5.08
G-CGDO	3753	GDO	Grob G102 Astir CS	1145	D-7229	11. 5.91	P Lowe and R Bostock	Seighford	28. 9.08
GDR	3754	GDR	Schempp-Hirth Discus CS	016CS		5. 5.91	A J Limb	Husbands Bosworth	15. 6.08
G-CGDS	3755	GDS	Schleicher ASW 15B	15205	D-0902	20. 6.91	B Birk and P A Crouch	Ringmer	17. 2.08
G-CGDT	3756	T54	Schleicher ASW 24	24120		10. 5.91	R D McVean	Chipping	4. 4.08
G-CGDU	3757	801	Schleicher ASW 24	24118		8. 6.91	G J Moore	Dunstable	28. 9.08
GDV	3758	GDV	Schleicher Ka 6E	4099	OO-ZWQ	20. 6.91	P Hardman	Dunstable	7. 6.08
					I-NEST, OE-0807				
GDW	3759	GDW	Scheibe SF 27A Zugvogel V	6116	D-1997	16. 5.91	M W Hands	Saltby	26. 7.06
G-CGDX	3760	HB2	Schempp-Hirth Discus CS	023CS		2. 7.91	The Gliding Centre	Husbands Bosworth	28. 9.08
G-CGDY	3761	914	Schleicher ASW 15B	15220	D-0947	6. 5.91	G A Stewart and Partners	Bidford	20. 2.08
G-CGDZ	3762	524	Schleicher ASW 24	24116		17. 5.91	J M Norman and Partners	Pocklington	1. 4.08
GEA	3763	GEA	Schleicher Ka 6CR	849	(BGA 3605)	7. 6.91	C Deane	Rufforth	7. 6.08
					D-5801				
GEB	3764	GEB	Grob G102 Astir CS77	1628	PH-576	7. 6.91	T R Dews	Kingston Deverill	17. 9.08
GEE	3767	928	Glasflügel Standard Libelle 201B	94	D-0928	6. 6.91	C Metcalfe	Darlton	2. 4.08
GEG	3769	GEG	Schleicher K 8B	689	HB-639	27. 4.91	Darlton Gliding Club	Darlton	25. 9.08
GEH	3770	219	Schleicher ASW 15B	15276	D-2124	9. 7.91	C J Ireland	Challock	4. 5.08
G-CGEL	3772	GEL	SZD-50-3 Puchacz	B-2030		29. 5.91	Northumbria Gliding Club	Currock Hill	7. 5.08
GEM	3773	GEM	Schleicher Ka 6CR	6249	D-8486	4. 6.91	D C Perkins and Partners	Thame	20. 7.08
GEN	3774	GEN	Slingsby T.21B	1154	RAFGGA 550	16. 5.92	A Harris	Germany	11. 6.08
					XN150				
G-CGEP	3775	GEP	Schempp-Hirth Standard Cirrus	205G	D-0917	10. 6.91	D J Bundock	Wycombe Air Park	30. 3.08
GEQ	3776	2001	SZD-12A Mucha 100A	462	D-0921	6. 6.91	R A Earnshaw-Fretwell	Trenchard Lines, Upavon	10. 7.08
G-DHAA	3777	263	Glasflügel Standard Libelle 201B	356	HB-1090	20. 6.91	D J Jones and R N Turner	Gransden Lodge	11.12.07
G-CHAB	3778	HAB	Schleicher Ka 6CR	6596	D-1596	31. 7.91	P Saunders	Usk	18. 1.08
HAC	3779	HAC	SZD-50-3 Puchacz	B-2035		29. 6.91	Peterborough & Spalding Gliding Club	Crowland	14. 5.08
G-DHAD	3780	429	Glasflügel Standard Libelle	3	D-8914	5. 7.91	A Presland	Lasham	24. 5.08
HAE	3781	HAE	Glasflügel Club Libelle 205	75	D-8687	5. 7.91	S R Morgan	Lee-on-Solent	11. 9.08
G-CHAF	3782	HAF	SZD-50-3 Puchacz	B-2031		4. 7.91	Seahawk Gliding Club	RNAS Culdrose	13. 3.08
HAG	3783	HAG	Schleicher K7	834	D-5795	21. 5.92	Denbigh Gliding Club	Lleweni Parc	24. 3.07
HAJ	3785	391	Schempp-Hirth Ventus c	517		19. 7.91	Surrey & Hants Gliding Club	Lasham	18. 2.08
HAK	3786	XA302	Slingsby T.31B	844	XA302	17. 8.91	RAF Museum (On display 9.07)	Hendon	24. 5.96
G-DHAL	3787	HAL	Schleicher ASK 13	13690AB		7. 9.91	Cotswold Gliding Club	Aston Down	4. 4.08
			(Built Jubi)						
HAN	3789	278	Schempp-Hirth Standard Cirrus	130	D-0326	14. 8.91	I Ashdown	Parham	8. 4.05
G-DHAP	3790	HAP	Schleicher Ka 6E	4335	HB-985	29. 8.91	M W Fursedon	Edgehill	6.10.07
HAR	3792	HAR	Schleicher K 8B	8151	D-8453	4. 9.91	G Weale (For restoration)	Brentor	4. 7.97
G-CHAO	3791	114	Rolladen-Schneider LS6-b	6150	D-8079	2. 9.91	A R J Hughes	Wycombe Air Park	13. 4.08
HAS	3793	HAS	SZD-50-3 Puchacz	B-2043		17. 8.91	The Gliding Centre	Husbands Bosworth	19. 2.08
HAT	3794	HAT	Glaser-Dirks DG-200/17	2-93/1709	D-6843	26. 8.91	G K Holloway	Aboyne	13. 4.08
G-EHAV	3796	J34	Glasflügel Standard Libelle 201B	40	HB-950	25. 8.91	M Truelove and A Liran	Rivar Hill	3. 5.08
G-CHAX	3798	HAX	Schempp-Hirth Standard Cirrus	2	ZS-GHZ	10.10.91	R Jarvis and C Keating	Rivar Hill	11. 8.08
					ZS-TIM, ZS-GGR, D-0302				
G-CHAY	3799	HAY	Rolladen-Schneider LS7	7154		15.10.91	N J Leaton and Partners	Gransden Lodge	19. 3.08
G-CHBA	3801	729	Rolladen-Schneider LS7	7156	D-6041	12.10.91	P O'Donald	Gransden Lodge	28. 9.08
G-CHBB	3802	HBB	Schleicher ASW 24	24132		19. 9.91	London Gliding Club	Dunstable	28. 9.08
G-CHBC	3803	HBC	Rolladen-Schneider LS6-c	6209	D-....	20. 9.91	A Crowden	Talgarth	28. 9.08
G-CHBD	3804	HBD	Glaser-Dirks DG-200	2-12	HB-1384	5.10.91	D A Clempson	Portmoak	28. 9.08
G-CHBE	3805	356	Glaser-Dirks DG-300 Elan	3E237	SE-UFB	21. 5.92	M Weston and Partners	Aston Down	6. 4.08
HBF	3806	2CK	Schempp-Hirth Nimbus-2C	191	D-3369	5.10.91	J A Clark	Talgarth	12. 7.08
G-CHBG	3807	96	Schleicher ASW 24	24133		10.12.91	Imperial College Gliding Club	Lasham	25. 3.08
G-CHBH	3808	496	Grob G103C Twin III	36006		14.10.91	Imperial College Gliding Club	Lasham	3. 3.08
G-GBPP	3809	949	Rolladen-Schneider LS6-c18	6230		26. 9.91	G J Lyons and R Sinden	Wycombe Air Park	28. 9.08
HBK	3810	HBK	Grob G103 Twin Astir	3254-T-31	RAFGGA 550	29. 9.91	A G Machin	Burn	1. 4.08
					D-2389				
HBL	3811	HBL	Grob G102 Astir CS77	1626	RAFGSA R78	17.10.91	Bidford Gliding Club	Bidford	13. 6.08
					RAFGSA 778				
HBM	3812	755	Grob G102 Astir CS77	1633	RAFGSA R65	3.12.91	S W Bradford	Bicester	16. 3.08
					RAFGSA R66, RAFGSA 546				
HBP	3814	522	Glaser-Dirks DG-500/22 Elan	5E36S8		15.11.91	A Taverna	Borgo San Lorenzo, Italy	30. 6.08
HBQ	3815	HBQ	Schleicher Ka 6CR	6611	D-5616	22.11.91	P A Shuttleworth	Long Mynd	21. 5.08
HBS	3817	HBS	SZD-41A Jantar-Standard	B-852	D-4160	2.12.91	G A King	Talgarth	11. 7.08
G-CHBT	3819	HBT	Grob G102 Club Astir	2235	PH-675	9. 2.92	M D Evans and Partners	Darlton	23. 3.08
G-CHBU	3820	605	Centrair ASW 20F	20527	F-CFSI	22.11.91	R Williams	Ringmer	28. 4.08
G-CHBV	3821	667	Schempp-Hirth Nimbus-2B	143	D-7850	1.12.91	G Evison and Partners	Sutton Bank	11. 4.08
HBX	3823	HBX	Slingsby T.45 Swallow	1386	8801M, XS650	16. 5.93	J P Ben David	Lasham	17. 6.08
HBZ	3825	HBZ	Slingsby T.15 Gull III rep	-		28. 6.92	P R Philpot	Chipping	3. 8.08
HCA	3826	HCA	Grob G103 Twin Astir	3289	D-0094	24.12.91	D Munroe and Partners	Rougham	26. 4.08
					OO-ZOH, D-3063				
G-EHCB	3827	754	Schempp-Hirth Nimbus-3DT			24.12.91	H A Torode and Partners	Lasham	7. 5.08
HCC	3829	HCC	SZD-50-3 Puchacz	B-2048		4. 1.92	Heron Gliding Club	RNAS Yeovilton	21. 6.08
G-DHCE	3831	346	Schleicher ASW 19B	19305	D-6527	6. 1.92	R T Halliburton	Pocklington	28. 9.08
G-DHCF	3832	HCF	SZD-50-3 Puchacz	B-2047		20.12.91	Shalbourne Soaring Society	Rivar Hill	27. 4.08
HCG	3833	HCG	Maupin Woodstock One	Not known		7.10.92	R Harvey	Tibenham	28. 1.08
			(Built R Harvey)						
G-DHCH	3834	355	Centrair ASW 20F	20178	F-CEUL	20. 3.92	A C Turk	Bidford	15. 3.08
HCJ	3835	HCJ	Grob G103 Twin II	3709	RAFGGA 611	24. 1.92	Peterborough & Spalding Gliding Club	Crowland	27. 7.08
					D-2611				

HCK	3836	WB962	Slingsby T.21B	623	RAFGGA WB962	2. 1.92	V Mallon	Kleve-Wisseler Dünen, Germany	13. 4.08
G-DHCL	3837	HCL	Schempp-Hirth Discus b	136	D-4682	13. 3.92	C E Broom and L Chicot	Usk	7. 3.08
HCM	3838	HCM	Schleicher K7	498	D-5669	4. 3.92	M P Barnard (Stored 8.07)	Edgehill	29. 8.02
HCN	3839	HCN	CARMAM M.200 Foehn	24	F-CDDR	21.12.92	8 Ball Soaring Association	Shipdham	28. 6.05
HCP	3840	HCP	Avialsa A.60 Fauconnet	123K	F-CDLA	19. 2.93	C Kaminski (Being refurbished)	Eaglescott	31. 7.95
G-DHCO	3841	HCO	Glasflügel Standard Libelle 201B	197	HB-999	28. 1.92	M J Birch	Dunstable	16. 3.08
G-DHCR	3842	394	SZD-51-1 Junior	B-2003		28. 4.92	East Sussex Gliding Club	Ringmer	16. 3.08
G-DHCU	3845	78	Glaser-Dirks DG-300 Club Elan	3E407C66		7. 2.92	M S Smith and J C A Garland	Kingston Deverill	18. 3.08
G-DHCV	3846	X19	Schleicher ASW 19B	19084	D-4486	14. 5.93	J A Novak	Tibenham	4. 5.08
G-DHCW	3847	HCW	SZD-51-1 Junior	B-2002	(BGA 3844)	1. 2.92	Deeside Gliding Club	Aboyne	6. 1.08
G-DHCX	3848	HCX	Schleicher ASK 21	21541		16. 5.92	Devon & Somerset Gliding Club	North Hill	28. 5.08
HCY	3849	HCY	Glaser-Dirks DG-300 Club Elan	3E413C67		10. 5.94	S T Dry	RAF Keevil	28. 8.05
G-EHCZ	3850	HCZ	Schleicher K 8B	8114A	D-4675	21. 2.92	South London Gliding Centre	Kenley	4. 9.08
G-CHDA	3851	HDA	Pilatus B4-PC11AF	017	D-0964	18. 3.92	F P and C M E Bois	Lasham	5. 6.08
G-CHDB	3852	HDB	SZD-51-1 Junior	B-1997		4. 3.92	Stratford on Avon Gliding Club	Snitterfield	12. 1.08
HDC	3853	HDC	Schleicher ASK 13	13308	D-0750	19. 3.93	Derbyshire & Lancashire Gliding Club	Camphill	14. 5.08
G-CHDD	3854	591	Centrair 101B Pégase 90	101B0425		5. 4.92	P M Weston and Partners	Gransden Lodge	28. 9.08
G-CHDE	3855	HDE	Pilatus B4-PC11AF	223	VH-XOZ VH-WQP	12. 4.92	A A Jenkins	Wycombe Air Park	5. 5.08
G-OKLL	3856	910	Schempp-Hirth Discus b	404		21. 2.92	K Loughrey	Bellarena	28.12.07
G-DHDH	3858	991	Glaser-Dirks DG-202/15	2-197	??	24. 5.92	A J Millson (See BGA 3862)	Trenchard Lines, Upavon	27. 3.08
G-CHDJ	3859	HDJ	Schleicher ASW 20CL	20828	D-8442	4. 3.92	G E Lambert	Weelde, Belgium	30. 4.08
G-CHDL	3861	137	Schleicher ASW 20	20082	D-1617 OH-495	13. 4.92	C R Faulkner and Partners	Currock Hill	21. 5.08
HDM	3862	"HDH"	SZD-12A Mucha 100A	448	SP-1987	15. 4.92	T J Wilkinson	Sackville Lodge, Riseley	19. 5.05
G-CHDN	3863	HDN	Schleicher K 8B	2	D-8017	17. 3.92	Upward Bound Trust	Thame	28. 4.08
G-CHDP	3864	N36	SZD-50-3 Puchacz	B-2050		6. 3.92	Heron Gliding Club	RNAS Yeovilton	30. 3.08
G-CHDR	3866	467	Glaser-Dirks DG-300 Elan	3E95	RAFGSA R30	14. 3.92	R Robins	Pocklington	22. 1.08
G-CHDU	3869	HDU	SZD-51-1 Junior	B-1996		25. 3.92	Cambridge Gliding Club	Gransden Lodge	28. 9.08
HDV	3870	882	Schleicher ASW 19B	19345	D-2876	20. 4.92	882 Syndicate	Long Mynd	16. 4.08
G-PEGZ	3871	HDW	Centrair 101A Pégase	101A0179	F-CGEE	21. 3.92	J P Eldem	Walney	3. 5.06
G-CHDX	3872	A2	Rolladen-Schneider LS7-WL	7161		27. 3.92	R T Halliburton and D Holborn	Pocklington	15. 3.08
G-CHDY	3873	HDY	Schleicher K 8B	8277	D-4094	24. 3.92	V Mallon	Kleve-Wisseler Dünen, Germany	13. 4.08
G-IDER	3874	W4	Schempp-Hirth Discus CS	078CS		7. 7.92	D B Keith and A J Preston	Bicester	28. 9.08
HEB	3876	HEB	Schleicher Ka 6CR	6289	HB-773	6. 5.92	J Burrow	North Hill	26. 9.08
G-CHEC	3877	308	SZD-55-1	551191019		10. 5.92	D C Pye	Challock	24. 4.08
HED	3878	840	Schempp-Hirth Ventus a	17	D-2524	18. 4.92	S D Foster	RAF Keevil	14. 7.08
HEE	3879	AH	Schempp-Hirth Discus b	292		14. 4.92	A Henderson	Wycombe Air Park	22. 2.08
			(Rebuild of BGA 3523 after accident 21. 6.91 but see BGA 4047)						
G-CHEF	3880	HEF	Glaser-Dirks DG-500 Elan Trainer	5E53T20		24. 5.92	Yorkshire Gliding Club	Sutton Bank	20. 3.08
HEG	3881	HEG	Sportine Aviacija LAK-12	6206		27. 6.92	R Kmita and Partners	Kirton in Lindsey	9. 9.08
G-CHEH	3882	795	Rolladen-Schneider LS7-WL	7163	D-6078	24. 6.92	P D Candler	Dunstable	30. 1.08
G-CHEJ	3883	HEK	SZD-51-1 Junior	B-2009	BGA 3893 (BGA 3884)	29. 5.94	Cambridge Gliding Club	Gransden Lodge	16. 3.08
HEL	3885	DZ	Rolladen-Schneider LS4	4027	(BGA 3896) D-6431	26. 5.92	D G MacArthur	Long Mynd	16. 4.08
G-DHEM	3886	473	Schempp-Hirth Discus CS	073CS		22. 5.92	G G Lee and Partners	Lasham	28. 9.08
G-CHEN	3887	735	Schempp-Hirth Discus b	422		5. 6.92	P K Carpenter and Partners	Challock	8. 3.08
G-CHEP	3888	HEP	SZD-50-3 Puchacz	B-2057		30. 5.92	Peterborough & Spalding Gliding Club	Crowland	5. 4.08
G-CHEO	3889	611	Schleicher ASW 20L	20410	D-6747	6. 6.92	M Chant and Partners	North Hill	27. 2.08
G-DHER	3890	HER	Schleicher ASW 19B	19240	F-CERR	1. 4.93	B Meech	Upwood	17. 5.08
G-DHES	3891	HES	Centrair 101A Pégase	101039	F-CFQF	13. 2.93	C J Cole and S B Lewis	Usk	8. 3.08
G-DHET	3892	335	Rolladen-Schneider LS6-18W	6263		26. 5.92	M P Brooks	Lasham	28. 2.08
HEV	3894	HEV	Schempp-Hirth Cirrus	41	OO-ZXY (OO-ZOZ), D-0104	26. 5.92	K Mosset	Portmoak	23. 9.08
HEW	3895	486	Rolladen-Schneider LS6-18W	6250		29. 4.92	H Stone	RAF Weston-on-the-Green	2. 3.08
			(Fitted with new wings after an accident in 1996 and new fuselage after another accident 11. 7.99 - see BGA 4952)						
G-DHEZ	3898	607	Rolladen-Schneider LS6-c	6264		16. 7.92	J E Cruttenden and J Taylor	Lasham	22. 4.08
HFA	3899	65	Schempp-Hirth Ventus b/16.6	251	RAFGSA R24	26. 6.92	A Lincoln	Lasham	11. 9.08
G-CHFB	3900	HFB	Schleicher Ka 6CR	6344Si	D-5825	13. 7.92	P J Galloway	Rhigos	1. 9.08
HFC	3901	WB924	Slingsby T.21B	587	WB924	25. 7.92	T Rose and Partners	Dunstable	10. 7.08
HFE	3903	XN187	Slingsby T.21B	1166	XN187	23. 6.92	A Hill and Partners	RAF Halton	27. 8.08
G-CHFF	3904	870	Schempp-Hirth Standard Cirrus	539	D-8916	14. 2.93	R S Morrisroe and Partners	Upwood	4. 4.08
HFG	3905	HFG / XN186	Slingsby T.21B	1165	XN186	28. 6.92	M H Simms	RAF Watton	28. 8.05
G-CHFH	3906	HFH	SZD-50-3 Puchacz	B-2059		4. 8.92	Trent Valley Gliding Club	Kirton in Lindsey	6. 3.08
HFL	3909	925-SSC	Schleicher ASH 25	25147		18. 7.92	Scottish Gliding Association (Crashed Tomintoul 2. 9.07)	Portmoak	22. 2.08
G-LSVI	3910	747	Rolladen-Schneider LS6-c18	6266		8. 7.92	F J Sheppard	Wycombe Air Park	14. 8.08
G-LSED	3913	126	Rolladen-Schneider LS6-c	6260	(BGA 3908)	23. 6.92	G McKnight and Partners	RAF Cranwell	28. 9.08
G-CHFV	3918	F21	Schempp-Hirth Ventus b/16.6	204	D-5235	1.10.92	A Cliffe and B Pearson	Seighford	4. 4.08
HFW	3919	HFW	Schleicher K 8B	8108	HB-705	24. 9.92	Oxford Gliding Club	RAF Weston-on-the-Green	7. 9.08
G-CHFX	3920	82	Schempp-Hirth Nimbus-4T	12		3. 7.92	R Jones	Lasham	26. 3.08
G-CHFY	3921	940	Schempp-Hirth Ventus cT	168/554	(BGA 3916) (BGA 3867)	21. 7.92	M T Day and D J Ellis	Lasham	28. 9.08
HFZ	3922	-	Abbott-Baynes Scud replica (Built M L Beach)	001		R	Brooklands Museum	Brooklands	
HGA	3923	HGA	Wassmer WA-26P Squale	43	F-CDUH	30. 3.93	E C Murgatroyd	Sackville Lodge, Riseley	15. 5.04
G-CHGB	3924	509	Grob G102 Astir CS	1356	D-7386	16.11.92	P J Hollamby and Partners	Lee-on-Solent	11. 9.08
			(Rebuilt with wings and components from RAFGGA 507)						

Reg	BGA	Code	Type	C/n	Prev ID	Date	Owner	Location	Date
HGF	3928	HGF	Schleicher ASW 15B	15264	D-2128	25. 8.92	P Mylett	Camphill	12. 5.08
G-CHGG	3929	HGG	Schempp-Hirth Standard Cirrus	362	HB-1172	31.12.92	N P Holifield	Bicester	21. 3.08
HGH	3930	HGH	Schleicher ASW 19B	19351	D-1199	26. 8.92	A Wood	North Hill	19. 1.04
G-CHGK	3932	HGK	Schempp-Hirth Discus bT	96/435		30.10.92	C C Redrup and Partners	Lasham	28. 9.08
G-DHGL	3933	583	Schempp-Hirth Discus b	431		30. 7.92	R G Corbin and S E Buckley	Aston Down	16. 3.08
G-IRLE	3935	D9	Schempp-Hirth Ventus cT	172/562		18. 9.92	D J Scholey	Lasham	21. 3.08
HGP	3936	HGP	Rolladen-Schneider LS6-c	6270		3.11.92	D Elrington	Camphill	30. 5.08
HGQ	3937	637	Sportine Aviacija LAK-12	6208		1.12.92	D M Cornelius	Dunstable	24. 9.08
G-CHGR	3938	HGR	Sportine Aviacija LAK-12	6186		22. 3.93	F R and R G Stevens	Husbands Bosworth	28. 9.08
G-CHGS	3939	730	Schempp-Hirth Discus b	439		6.11.92	S J Bryan and P J Bramley	Lasham	28. 9.08
G-CHGT	3940		FFA Diamant 16.5	40	HB-929	12. 4.94	R W Collins and E Gibson	Burn	30. 4.08
G-CHGV	3942	HGV	Glaser-Dirks DG-500/22 Elan	5E70S11		26. 2.93	A J Hulme and Partners	Gransden Lodge	14. 1.08
G-CHGW	3943	HGW	Centrair ASW 20F	20102	F-CFFB	1. 1.93	M Dixon	Nympsfield	3.11.07
HGX	3944	783	Sportine Aviacija LAK-12	6201		3. 5.93	M Jenks	Kingston Deverill	23. 5.08
HGY	3945		SZD-24C Foka	W-180	SP-2385	16.12.92	Peterborough & Spalding Gliding Club	Crowland	27. 6.07
G-CHGZ	3946	502	Schempp-Hirth Discus bT	95/434		18.12.92	G D Coppin and Partners	Lasham	6. 3.08
HHD	3950	HHD	SZD-51-1 Junior	B-2010		19. 3.93	Derbyshire & Lancashire Gliding Club	Camphill	7. 1.07
			(Cancelled 19. 2.07; to PH-1393 4.07)						
G-CHHE	3951	HHE	SZD-51-1 Junior	B-2008		30. 6.93	Bowland Forest Gliding Club	Chipping	28. 9.08
HHG	3953	WT910	Slingsby T.31B	705	WT910	9. 1.93	N J Jardine	Sebring, Florida	5. 8.06
G-CHHH	3954	963	Rolladen-Schneider LS6-c	6289		11.12.92	P H Rackham	Dunstable	28. 9.08
G-XBGA	3955	X97	Glaser-Dirks DG-500/22 Elan	5E71S12		9. 2.93	N A Kelly	Bicester	27. 5.08
G-CHHK	3956	838	Schleicher ASW 19B	19384	ZD661 BGA 2897	14. 3.93	M Walker	Burn	11. 5.07
G-CHHM	3958	HM	Sportine Aviacija LAK-12	6195		9. 8.93	D Martin Bordeaux Léognan Saucats, France		17. 1.08
HHN	3959	979	Schempp-Hirth Ventus b/16.6	205	RAFGSA R27	6. 2.93	N A C Norman	Feshiebridge	11. 5.08
HHP	3960	KL	Schempp-Hirth Discus b	399	SE-UKL	12. 2.93	F R Knowles	Aboyne	21. 9.08
G-CHHO	3961	97Z	Schempp-Hirth Discus bT	106/453		12. 2.93	P J Tratt and Partners	Parham	27. 3.08
G-CHHR	3962	100	SZD-55-1	551191020		18. 4.93	R T and G Starling	Nympsfield	28. 9.08
G-CHHS	3963	HHS	Schleicher ASW 20	20008	SE-TTU	3. 3.93	P J Rocks and D Britt	Kirton in Lindsey	1. 4.08
G-CHHT	3964	855	Rolladen-Schneider LS6-c	6292		18. 7.93	G O Humphries	Kingston Deverill	1. 3.08
G-CHHU	3965	445	Rolladen-Schneider LS6-c	6296		15. 2.93	J S Weston	Bellarena	28. 9.08
G-CHHW	3967	237	Sportine Aviacija LAK-12	6212		19. 3.93	A J Dibdin	Gransden Lodge	4. 3.08
HHX	3968	HHX	Wassmer WA-26P Squale	14	F-CDQJ	27. 2.93	M H Gagg	Chauvigny, France	9. 3.08
G-LIBL	3969	RT	Glasflügel Standard Libelle 201B	119	SE-TIU	1. 4.93	P A Pearson	Husbands Bosworth	18. 3.08
G-CHJA	3971	HJA	VFW-Fokker FK-3	0008	D-0409	9. 8.93	M A Johnson Sackville Lodge, Riseley		17. 3.08
G-CHJC	3973	25	Rolladen-Schneider LS6-c	6290		17. 3.93	F J Davies & I C Woodhouse	Husbands Bosworth	28. 9.08
HJD	3974	HJD	Schleicher Ka 6E	4141	D-.... OH-505, SE-TFM	4. 2.94	J P Stafford	Edgehill	30. 8.07
HJE	3975	HJE	Schleicher K 8B	8259	(BGA 3926) RAFGGA 505, RAFGGA 971	16. 4.93	Denbigh Gliding Club	Lleweni Parc	15.12.07
G-CHJF	3976	245	Rolladen-Schneider LS6-c	6291		29. 4.93	J L Bridge	Gransden Lodge	28. 9.08
G-CHJH	3978	HJH	Schempp-Hirth Discus bT	65/391	N224WT	22. 4.93	J C Leonard and Partners	Bembridge	25. 4.08
HJJ	3979		Slingsby T.38 Grasshopper	797	WZ816	R	J Wilkins *(Stored 2003)*	Redhill	
HJK	3980	HJK	Schleicher K7	795	RAFGSA R5 D-5791	14. 6.93	Leeds University Gliding Club	AAC Dishforth	1. 5.03
G-CHJL	3981	516	Schempp-Hirth Discus bT	105/451		3. 5.93	M J Huddart	Saltby	28. 9.08
HJM	3982	HJM	Hütter H.28 III replica *(Built E R Duffin)*	ED 02		25. 5.93	B Pearson *(Being refurbished)*	Eaglescott	12. 6.99
HJN	3983	HJN	Schempp-Hirth Standard Cirrus	440G	HB-1206	2. 6.93	A Fidler	Crowland	13. 9.08
G-CHJP	3985		Schleicher Ka 6CR	616	OH-210 OH-RSB	6. 5.07	D M Cornelius	Dunstable	5. 5.08
G-CHJR	3986	B9	Glasflügel Standard Libelle 201B	102	SE-TIO	26. 5.95	B Magnani and B O Marcham	Tibenham	29. 5.08
HJT	3988	292	Centrair ASW 20F	20115	F-CFFL	3. 6.93	M O Breen	Wycombe Air Park	27. 8.08
HJV	3990	HJV	Grob G102 Astir CS	1007	D-7000	7. 6.93	Cotswold Gliding Club	Aston Down	11. 8.08
HJX	3991	203	Rolladen-Schneider LS6-c	6271		28. 5.93	R S Hatwell and M Haynes	Tibenham	16. 9.08
G-CHJY	3992	HJY	Schempp-Hirth Standard Cirrus	459	HB-1207	23. 6.93	J Hogbin and Partners	Currock Hill	28. 7.08
HJZ	3993	865	Schleicher ASW 15B	15190	OH-408	15. 5.94	R R Beezer	Camphill	29. 9.05
G-CHKA	3994	860	Schempp-Hirth Discus CS	120CS		20. 5.93	M P and R W Weaver	Usk	20.12.08
G-CHKB	3995	HKB	Grob G102 Astir CS77	1658	D-7491	26.10.93	R Peach	RAF Keevil	5. 4.08
G-CHKC	3996	HKC	Schempp-Hirth Standard Cirrus	520G	D-3268	28. 8.93	Welland Gliding Club	Lyveden	1. 5.08
G-CHKD	3997	C34	Schempp-Hirth Standard Cirrus	576G	F-CEMF	7. 7.93	M Truelove and A Liran	Rivar Hill	24. 4.08
HKJ	4002	-	Penrose Pegasus 2 *(Built J M Lee)*	001		14. 7.93	Norfolk & Suffolk Aviation Museum	Flixton	15. 9.98
G-CHKK	4003	HKK	Schleicher K 8B	8886	D-0866	16. 1.94	W Rossmann and Partners	Drumshade	3. 4.08
G-DHKL	4004	919	Schempp-Hirth Discus bT	120/476		27. 7.93	M A Thorne	Kingston Deverill	28. 9.08
HKM	4005	HKM	Grob G102 Astir CS Jeans	2108	D-7636	25. 3.94	Essex & Suffolk Gliding Club	Wormingford	17. 8.08
HKP	4007	HKP	Schleicher ASK 23B	23100	D-2935 HB-1935	9. 8.93	Midland Gliding Club	Long Mynd	30. 1.07
G-NYMB	4008	970	Schempp-Hirth Nimbus-3DT	63		7. 8.93	T Stuart and Syndicate	Nympsfield	15. 2.08
G-CHKR	4009	985	Jastreb Standard Cirrus G/81	276	OH-663	15.10.93	S E Crozier and N White	Crowland	30. 5.08
HKS	4010	HKS	Jastreb Standard Cirrus G/81	361	SE-TZS	11.11.93	A S Edlin	Saltby	1. 4.08
HKT	4011	HKT	Schleicher ASW 19	19168	D-7958	4.10.93	P Clayton	Burn	26. 8.06
			(C/n conflicts with OE-5174 but believed correct)						
HKU	4012	C29	Schempp-Hirth Standard Cirrus	513G	F-CEMA	5.12.93	T J Wheeler and Partner	Hinton-in-the-Hedges	2. 6.08
G-CHKV	4013	HKV	Scheibe Zugvogel IIIA	1034	D-8294	6.10.93	Dartmoor Gliding Society	Brentor	11. 9.08
HKW	4014	HKW	Marco J 5 *(Built D Austin - regd with c/n 001)*	009	G-BSBO	2. 6.94	G K Owen *"Flying Penguin II"*	Bidford	19. 3.04
G-CHKX	4015	HKX	Rolladen-Schneider LS4-b	4933		18.12.93	D J Hughes and Partners	Long Mynd	19. 2.08
G-CHKY	4016	HKY	Schempp-Hirth Discus b	461		14.10.93	O J Anderson and C V Hill	Bellarena	3. 4.08
HKZ	4017	P31	CARMAM JP 15-36AR Aiglon	31	F-CFGA	27. 9.93	R Borthwick	Milfield	19. 6.07
HLB	4019	365	Rolladen-Schneider LS4-b	4935		27. 4.94	E G Leach	Wormingford	7. 9.08
G-CHLC	4020	HLC	Pilatus B4-PC11AF	177	F-CFGA OH-455 SE-UFX	10. 3.94	E A Lockhart	Lasham	2. 5.08

HLH	4025	HLH	Schleicher K 8B	8637	RAFGGA 569 D-5691	26. 2.94	R Das		Edgehill	28. 9.08
HLK	4027	HLK	Glasflügel H 301 Libelle	85	SE-TFS	11. 4.95	G L Barrett	RAF Weston-on-the-Green		8. 7.08
G-CHLM	4029	819	Schleicher ASW 19B	19269	OH-538	10. 2.94	R A Colbeck		Dunstable	24. 5.05
G-CHLN	4030	805	Schempp-Hirth Discus CS	143CS		18. 1.94	Portsmouth Naval Gliding Club	Lee-on-Solent		6. 4.07
G-CHLP	4031	HLP	Schleicher ASK 21	21597		24. 3.94	Southdown Gliding Club		Parham	25. 3.08
G-CEWZ	4032	381	Schempp-Hirth Discus bT	128/490		22.12.93	J F Goudie		Portmoak	28. 9.08
HLR	4033	XE786	Slingsby T.31B	899	XE786	18.12.93	D Thomson (Stored 2006)		Arbroath	15. 4.04
G-CHLS	4034	V5	Schempp-Hirth Discus b	114	RAFGSA R11	28. 1.94	R A Lennard		Dunstable	8. 1.08
HLU	4036	HLU	Scheibe SF 27A Zugvogel V	6101	SE-TGP	22. 2.94	.. King		Halesland	8. 5.08
G-CHLV	4038	HLV	Schleicher ASW 19B	19325	D-8799	3. 4.94	P J Belcher and R I Brickwood	Gransden Lodge		15. 1.08
G-CHLX	4039	26Q	Schleicher ASH 25	25124	D-3988	27. 2.94	P W Armstrong	Husbands Bosworth		9. 3.08
G-CHLY	4040	Z45	Schempp-Hirth Discus CS	161CS		15. 6.94	T Barton		Talgarth	14. 4.08
HLZ	4041	S20	Schleicher ASW 20BL	20951	D-8188	19. 3.94	B A Fairston	Husbands Bosworth		17. 7.08
						(Crashed near Husbands Bosworth 6. 8.07)				
G-CHMA	4042	HMA	SZD-51-1 Junior	B-2132		30. 3.94	The Gliding Centre	Husbands Bosworth		15. 1.08
G-CHMB	4043	HMB	Glaser-Dirks DG-300 Elan	3E105	D-4676	31. 3.94	A D Langlands		Edgehill	31. 1.08
HMG	4044	HMG	ICA-Brasov IS-28B2	353		20. 4.94	A Sutton and Partners		Snitterfield	15. 3.08
HMH	4045	HMH	Schleicher K 8B	5	D-5735	15. 4.94	Shenington Gliding Club		Edgehill	31. 3.08
			(Built by Bayer; officially regd as c/n 2330)							
G-CHMK	4046	122	Rolladen-Schneider LS6-18W	6324	D-1245	18. 3.94	A S Decloux	Gransden Lodge		11. 3.08
HML	4047	38	Schempp-Hirth Discus CS	114CS	OO-ZTU	16. 3.94	I D Bateman		Parham	25. 8.08
			(Composite with wings from BGA 3879)							
G-CHMM	4048	D19	Jastreb Glasflügel 304B	322	SE-UGZ D-1005	31. 3.94	S I Hogg and Partners	Husbands Bosworth		20.12.07
G-DHMP	4050	HMP	Schempp-Hirth Discus b	497		13. 3.94	P Charatan and Partners		Challock	31. 5.08
G-CHMO	4051	364	Schempp-Hirth Discus CS	099CS	D-7160	8. 3.94	S Barter		Ringmer	28. 9.08
HMS	4053	HMS	Glaser-Dirks DG-100	40	D-2579	8. 4.94	D A Fall		(Stourbridge)	7. 6.08
G-CHMT	4054	380	Glasflügel Mosquito B	153	F-CEDY	20. 3.94	R J Pirie and J Taberham		Eaglescott	28. 9.08
G-CHMU	4055	HMU	CARMAM JP 15-36AR Aiglon	22	F-CETT	7. 5.94	J R Holmes and Partners	Kingston Deverill		9. 3.08
HMV	4056	HMV	Schleicher ASK 13	13177	D-0268	9. 5.94	Windrushers Gliding Club		Bicester	15. 6.08
G-CHMX	4058	PZ	Rolladen-Schneider LS4-b	4230	OO-ZNN F-CEIO	14. 5.94	P Shuttleworth and J M Hall		Long Mynd	16. 4.08
G-CHMY	4059	HMY	Schempp-Hirth Standard Cirrus	121	HB-1034	29. 4.94	D G Nisbet	RAF Weston-on-the-Green		2. 5.08
HMZ	4060	469	Fedorov Me-7 Mechta	M.004		12. 4.94	R Ellis (Stored 2003)		(Wales)	12. 2.96
G-CHNA	4061	HNA	Glaser-Dirks DG-500/20 Elan	5E128W3		14. 7.94	M S Armstrong and Partners		Camphill	28. 9.08
G-JNUS	4062	563	Schempp-Hirth Janus C	215	D-4149	16. 4.94	C M Fox		Sleap	29. 9.08
G-CHNC	4063	HNC	Schleicher ASW 19B	19297	OH-515	18. 4.94	T Highton		Tibenham	4. 4.08
HND	4064	HND	Scheibe Zugvogel IIIA	1044	HB-735 D-9119	23. 5.94	M Y Kiteley	Sackville Lodge, Riseley		13. 7.08
HNE	4065	708	Schempp-Hirth Nimbus-2B	91	D-2786	10. 5.94	P Uden		Saltby	7. 5.08
G-CHNF	4066	315	Schempp-Hirth Duo Discus	11		11. 5.94	Booker Gliding Club	Wycombe Air Park		28. 9.08
HNG	4067	HNG	Schleicher K 8B	132/59	D-8378	5. 5.94	Bidford Gliding Centre		Bidford	19. 9.08
						(Also carries "8378")				
G-CHNH	4068	Z99	Schempp-Hirth Nimbus-2C	187	D-2830	31. 3.94	R J Hart		Tibenham	6. 2.08
HNJ	4069	HNJ	Schleicher K7	7031	D-1667 RAFGGA ??, D-6233	6. 5.94	N J Orchard-Armitage	Waldershare Park		5. 4.05
G-CHNK	4070	HNK	SZD-51-1 Junior	B-1496	SP-3299 (SP-3290)	20. 5.94	Booker Gliding Club	Wycombe Air Park		28. 9.08
G-CHNM	4072	55	Jastreb Standard Cirrus G/81	360	SE-TZT	2. 7.94	N C Harrison and Partners	Husbands Bosworth		9. 4.08
HNN	4073	HNN	Schempp-Hirth Duo Discus	21		15. 9.94	B T Spreckley		(France)	23. 9.08
HNS	4077	XN185	Slingsby T.21B	1164	8942M XN185	21. 6.94	RAF Museum	RAF Stafford		12. 4.04
						(Stored 2007)				
HNT	4078	105	Schleicher ASW 15	15167	F-CEAQ	27. 4.94	S Lintott	Waldershare Park		25. 6.08
G-CHNU	4079	48	Schempp-Hirth Nimbus-4DT	3/5	D-KHIA	25. 5.94	D E Findon		Bidford	28. 9.08
G-CHNV	4080	692	Rolladen-Schneider LS4-b	4960		11.12.94	S K Armstrong and P H Dixon	Kirton in Lindsey		2. 5.08
G-CHNW	4081	220	Schempp-Hirth Duo Discus	25		21.11.94	A R Head and Partners	Gransden Lodge		21. 3.08
G-DHNX	4082	585	Rolladen-Schneider LS4-b	4937		6. 7.94	C S Crocker and K J Screen		Long Mynd	3. 4.08
HNY	4083	HNY	Centrair 101A Pégase	101020	F-CFRP	12.10.95	M O Breen	Wycombe Air Park		30. 8.08
G-CHNZ	4084	RY	Centrair 101A Pégase	101032	F-CFRY	14. 7.94	R H Partington		Milfield	19. 2.08
HPA	4085		Issoire E78 Silene	04	F-CFEA	25. 6.94	P Woodcock		Burn	2. 4.08
G-CHPC	4087	HPC	Schleicher ASW 20CL	20787	D-3424	20 .7.94	B L Liddiard and P J Williams		(Sussex)	27. 3.08
G-CHPD	4088	62	Rolladen-Schneider LS6-c18	6331	D-1054	24.10.94	J A Kane and S A Hughes		Sutton Bank	28. 9.08
G-CHPE	4089	HPE	Schleicher ASK 13	13510	D-3992	2.10.94	Dumfries & District Gliding Club	Falgunzeon		13. 7.08
HPF	4090	"HPH"	SZD-9bis Bocian 1E	P-740	OH-508	3. 8.94	Bath, Wilts and North Dorset Gliding Club			
						(Overshot landing 24. 4.00 - stored 2.08)		Kingston Deverill		23. 2.01
HPG	4091	HPG	Maupin Woodstock	551	VR-HKI	14. 7.96	J M Stockwell	Boonah, Australia		10. 9.08
			(Built J M Stockwell)							
G-CHPH	4092	DS	Schempp-Hirth Discus CS	174CS		21. 9.94	A D Johnson and J E Kelk		Wormingford	8. 5.08
G-CHPL	4095	HPL	Rolladen-Schneider LS4-b	4959	(BGA 4071)	28. 7.94	Southdown Gliding Club		Parham	30. 1.08
HPM	4096	HPM	Grob G102 Astir CS	1072	D-3304	21.11.94	M Ogbe		Halesland	14. 6.08
HPP	4098		Slingsby T.38 Grasshopper	863	XA230	5. 2.95	E Fowkes	Gransden Lodge		3. 9.08
G-CHPO	4099	HPO	Schleicher Ka 6CR	6200	D-1933	5.10.94	M and A Ewer		Crowland	23. 3.08
G-DHPR	4100	K9	Schempp-Hirth Discus b	532		20. 2.95	G J Bowser		Nympsfield	27. 9.08
G-CHPT	4102	HPT	Fedorov Me7 Mechta	M006		29. 3.96	A E Griffiths		Long Mynd	4. 4.08
G-CHPV	4104	HPV	Schleicher ASK 21	21608		13.10.94	Scottish Gliding Union		Portmoak	28. 9.08
G-CHPW	4105	HPW	Schleicher ASK 21	21609		25.11.94	Scottish Gliding Union		Portmoak	28. 9.08
G-CHPX	4106	693	Schempp-Hirth Discus CS	177CS		12. 4.95	M A Whitehead and Partners	Gransden Lodge		28. 9.08
HQB	4110	WB935	Slingsby T.21B	602	WB935	1.10.94	C E Anson	Hahnweide, Germany		13. 4.08
			(Officially regd with c/n 1099 which is a corruption of fuselage no. SSK/FF1099)							
HQC	4111	HQC	Scheibe Bergfalke II/55	322	D-9004	20.12.94	S H Gibson	Gransden Lodge		5.10.06
HQD	4112	A20	Schleicher ASW 20	20288	SE-ULA OH-548	1.11.94	S E Archer-Jones		Bicester	29. 4.08
G-ODUO	4113	3D	Schempp-Hirth Duo Discus	29		19. 2.95	3D Syndicate		Aboyne	25. 4.08

HQF	4114	HQF	CARMAM M.100S Mésange	26	F-CCSO	3.11.94	M Farrelly	Long Mynd	8.10.07
HQG	4115	HQG	Sportine Aviacija LAK-12	6222		30. 4.95	J M Pursey	North Hill	11. 9.08
G-CFCA	4117	762	Schempp-Hirth Discus b	336	D-1762	10. 2.95	M R Hayden	Dunstable	23. 3.07
G-DHOK	4118	S2	Schleicher ASW 20CL	20854	D-3366	18. 1.95	S D Minson	North Hill	1. 4.08
HQL	4119	LS6	Rolladen-Schneider LS6-18W	6352	D-0794	3. 3.95	D P Masson	Lasham	26. 5.08
G-CHOM	4120	HOM	Schempp-Hirth Discus b	44	RAFGSA R10	23. 1.95	Cambridge Gliding Club	Gransden Lodge	28. 9.08
HQN	4121	D64	Schempp-Hirth Nimbus-2B	139	D-6494	29. 1.95	A J Nurse	Nympsfield	10. 3.05
G-CHOR	4123	T19	Schempp-Hirth Discus b	531		26. 4.95	A Twigg	Bicester	31. 3.08
HQS	4124	HQS	Grob G103 Twin Astir	3155	OO-ZEG	26. 2.95	Essex & Suffolk Gliding Club	Wormingford	28. 8.08
HQT	4125	A77	Grob G102 Astir CS77	1678	RAFGGA 561	12. 2.95	E Beckmann	Lasham	10. 3.06
G-CHOV	4127	HOV	SZD-51-1 Junior	B-2139		20. 3.95	The Gliding Centre	Husbands Bosworth	26. 7.08
G-CHOW	4128	MH	Schempp-Hirth Discus b	538		9. 3.95	M H Hardwick	Wycombe Air Park	28. 9.08
G-DHOX	4129	HOX	Schleicher ASW 15B	15326	D-2315	13. 3.95	P Ridgill and R Sibley	Upwood	14. 4.08
G-CHOY	4130	HOY	Schempp-Hirth Mini Nimbus C	113	D-3364	14. 3.95	A H Sparrow	Rivar Hill	26. 2.08
G-CHOZ	4131	U2	Rolladen-Schneider LS6-18W	6353	D-1486	6. 3.95	R E Scott	Parham	21. 1.08
G-CHRA	4132	N19	Grob G102 Astir CS	1109	D-4169	21. 4.95	Portsmouth Naval Gliding Club	Lee-on-Solent	29. 3.08
G-CHRB	4133	HRB	Sportine Aviacija LAK-12	6223		4.11.95	J E Nevill	Aboyne	23. 9.08
G-CHRC	4134	390	Glaser-Dirks DG-500/20 Elan	5E136W5		15. 5.95	D Rhys-Jones and Partners	Parham	24. 4.08
HRD	4135	-	Slingsby T.21B	634	WB973	18. 3.95	C Langenau	Aukrug, Germany	15. 6.08
G-CHRG	4138	HRG	SZD-51-1 Junior	B-2013		25. 4.95	Scottish Gliding Union Ltd	Portmoak	3. 6.08
HRJ	4139	HRJ	Schleicher K 8B	8093Ei	D-5048	26. 4.95	Shenington Gliding Club	Edgehill	28. 9.08
HRK	4140	HRK	Centrair 101A Pégase	101048	F-CFQJ	16. 5.95	P T Bushill	Dunstable	6. 6.08
HRL	4141	HRL	Schempp-Hirth Standard Cirrus	525	D-3099	26. 4.95	A Smurthwaite	Camphill	8. 5.08
G-CHRN	4143	HRN	Schleicher ASK 18	18026	HB-1308	7. 4.95	Stratford on Avon Gliding Club	Snitterfield	9. 3.08
HRQ	4145	169	Schempp-Hirth Mini Nimbus C	123	(BGA 4122) SE-TVB	17. 4.95	C Buzzard	Husbands Bosworth	4. 4.07
G-DHRR	4146	D70	Schleicher ASK 21	21033	D-7083	2. 2.95	Lakes Gliding Club	Walney Island	30. 1.08
G-CHRS	4147	B33	Schempp-Hirth Discus CS	100CS	D-5100	1. 5.95	M E Hughes	Husbands Bosworth	4. 4.08
HRT	4148	HRT	Schleicher K 8B	8390A	D-5599	9. 3.96	Heron Gliding Club	RNAS Yeovilton	20. 6.04
G-CHRW	4151	802	Schempp-Hirth Duo Discus	43	(BGA 4160)	22. 6.95	A J Davis and Partners	Nympsfield	28. 9.08
G-CHRX	4152	P5	Schempp-Hirth Discus a	545		24. 5.95	N Worrell and G S Bird	Lasham	15. 2.08
G-STEU	4153	L8	Rolladen-Schneider LS6-18W	6362		2. 6.95	F K Russell	Dunstable	4. 4.08
G-CHSA	4155	A1	Rolladen-Schneider LS6-18W	6361		8. 8.95	D A Benton	Snitterfield	11.10.07
HSB	4156	HSB	Glaser-Dirks DG-303 Elan	3E461		20. 7.95	A Kerwin-Nye	Ringmer	30. 3.07
G-CHSC	4157	99	SZD-50-3 Puchacz	B-2079		15. 8.95	British Gliding Association	Husbands Bosworth	5. 4.08
G-CHSD	4158	D15	Schempp-Hirth Discus b (Rebuild of BGA 3406 [258])	258/1	(BGA 4142)	19. 6.95	J R Reed and Partners (W/o 26.8.94)	Dunstable	27. 3.08
G-CHSE	4159	HSE	Grob G102 Astir CS77	1635	RAFGSA R68 RAFGSA 548	2. 9.95	A Mutch	Portmoak	8. 3.08
HSG	4161	HSG	Scheibe SF 27A Zugvogel V	1705/E	D-7827 OE-0827	11. 7.95	C T Oliver	Lyveden	22. 4.08
HSH	4162	HSH	Scheibe Zugvogel IIIB	7/1041	D-6558	12. 7.95	K S Smith	Wormingford	18.12.05
G-DHSJ	4163	D54	Schempp-Hirth Discus b	546		3. 7.95	A A Jenkins	Bicester	3. 3.08
HSK	4164	751	Schleicher ASW 20CL	20827	D-3499	18. 7.95	C Ramshorn	Gransden Lodge	1. 5.08
G-DHSL	4165	213	Schempp-Hirth Ventus-2c (Incomplete airframe assembled Southern Sailplanes)	1/2	(BGA 4154)	4. 7.95	H G Woodsend	Aston Down	28. 9.08
G-CHSM	4166	HSM	Schleicher ASK 13	13145	D-0168	18. 7.95	Stratford on Avon Gliding Club	Snitterfield	2. 3.08
G-CHSN	4167	HSN	Schleicher Ka 6CR	6218	OO-ZZF D-8546	1. 8.95	Needwood Forest Gliding Club	Cross Hayes	16. 2.08
HSP	4168	385	Schempp-Hirth Janus C	112	RAFGSA R1 BGA 2723, D-7013	9. 5.04	H A Torode (Reverted to BGA 2723 -4.07)	Lasham	9. 2.06
G-CHSO	4169	493	Schempp-Hirth Discus b	99	D-2943	8. 8.95	Midland Gliding Club	Long Mynd	28. 9.08
G-DHSR	4170	313	Sportine Aviacija LAK-12	6178		3. 8.95	G Forster	Milfield	7. 6.08
HSU	4173		Schleicher ASK 18	18025	AGA 16	R	Booker Gliding Club (Being refurbished)	Wycombe Air Park	
G-CHSV	4174	HSV	Schempp-Hirth Standard Cirrus	195	D-0785	14. 3.96	C D Morrow	Rivar Hill	27. 4.06
G-CHSW	4175	777	Schempp-Hirth Duo Discus	48		25. 8.95	M P S Roberts	Gransden Lodge	28. 9.08
G-CHSX	4176	HSX	Scheibe SF 27A Zugvogel V	6031	SE-TDT	26. 9.95	C B Downes and G M Wright	Wormingford	7. 2.08
HSZ	4178	497	Rolladen-Schneider LS8-a	8030		11.11.95	I G Garden	Wycombe Air Park	15. 3.08
G-CHTB	4180	HTB	Schempp-Hirth Janus	07	D-3114	27. 7.95	J B Maddison	Kirton-in-Lindsey	1. 5.08
HTC	4181	HTC	Schleicher ASW 15B	15188	OE-0930	26.10.95	C I Knapp	Camphill	25. 6.08
G-CHTD	4182	HTD	Grob G102 Astir CS	1012	D-6508	20. 5.96	C R Little and Partners	Halesland	8. 3.08
G-CHTE	4183	HTE	Grob G102 Astir CS77	1716	RAFGSA R82 RAFGSA 882	23.11.95	P R Crabb and Partners	Challock	9. 4.08
G-CHTF	4184	HTF	Sportine Aviacija LAK-12	6180	??	1. 6.96	S Pozerskis & N C Harrison	Husbands Bosworth	30. 4.08
G-DHTG	4185	HTG	Grob G102 Astir CS	1510	RAFGSA R59 RAFGSA R69, RAFGSA 519	30.10.95	Trent Valley Gliding Club	Kirton-in-Lindsey	19. 9.08
G-JNSC	4186	C4	Schempp-Hirth Janus CT	2/185	N137DB D-KHIE	13.11.95	D S Bramwell and Partners	Thame	13. 7.08
HTJ	4187	HTJ	Schleicher ASK 13	13125	D-6048 PL62 (Belgian Air Cadets)	2.12.95	Queens University Gliding Club	Bellarena	14. 9.08
G-WLLS	4189	LS	Rolladen-Schneider LS8-18	8038	D-3156	23.10.95	A and L M Wells	Nympsfield	28. 9.08
G-CHTM	4190	Z8	Rolladen-Schneider LS8-18	8036		5. 3.96	M J Chapman	Seighford	28. 9.08
G-CHTN	4191	S22	Schleicher ASW 22	22013	ZS-GLN	16. 4.96	R C Hodge	Dunstable	22. 9.08
G-RIEV	4192	L58	Rolladen-Schneider LS8-18	8039	D-3175	11.95	R D Grieve	(Diss)	9. 5.08
G-CHTR	4194	HTR	Grob G102 Astir CS	1190	D-7307	20.11.95	I P and D M Wright	Kingston Deverill	11. 3.08
G-CHTS	4195	H8	Rolladen-Schneider LS8-18	8040		22.11.95	A R Head and P Rowden	Gransden Lodge	27. 3.08
HTT	4196	HTT	Schleicher ASW 20CL	20627	D-2410	24.11.95	J S Hogarth	Camphill	17. 4.08
G-CHTU	4197	HTU	Schempp-Hirth Cirrus	88	D-0478	29.12.95	R Salmon	Burn	12. 4.08
G-CHTV	4198	HTV	Schleicher ASK 21	21624	D-8355	3. 3.96	Cambridge Gliding Club	Gransden Lodge	20. 3.08
G-CHTY	4201	HTY	LET L-13 Blanik	026318	LY-GDT DOSAAF	1. 4.96	North Devon Gliding Club	Eaglescott	8. 6.08
G-CHUA	4203	HUA	Schleicher ASW 19B	19091	D-3840	29.12.95	G D Vaughan	(Pontefract)	5. 5.07
HUB	4204	HUB	SZD-48-3 Jantar-Standard 3	B-1527	DOSAAF	17. 3.96	C Chatburn	Portmoak	11. 4.08

Reg	No	Code	Type	Serial	Prev ID	Date	Owner	Location	Date
G-CHUD	4206	HUD	Schleicher ASK 13	13018	D-9203	21. 2.96	London Gliding Club	Dunstable	28. 9.08
HUE	4207	N5	Schleicher ASW 27	27022		12. 7.96	M J Smith	Sutton Bank	15. 3.08
G-CHUF	4208	HUF	Schleicher ASK 13	13109	OO-ZWE	10. 3.96	Welland Gliding Club	Lyveden	25. 3.08
G-CHUH	4210	D31	Schempp-Hirth Janus	15	D-3116	9. 5.96	D M Abbey and Partners	Husbands Bosworth	1. 4.08
G-CHUJ	4211	X70	Centrair ASW 20F	20170	F-CFLY	5. 3.96	M Manning and Partners	Rattlesden	4. 4.08
HUK	4212	HUK	Schleicher Ka 6CR	6385	SE-TCN	15. 4.96	T J Donovan and Partner	Lyveden	13. 9.08
HUL	4213	624	Schempp-Hirth Cirrus	V3	HB-900	26. 2.96	I Ashton and Partners	Chipping	1. 5.05
G-DHUM	4214	241	Rolladen-Schneider LS6-c	6267	OO-ZXS D-4350	25. 3.96	A G W Hall	Lasham	30. 3.08
G-CHUN	4215	HUN	Grob G102 Astir CS Jeans	2089	D-7531	27. 2.96	Staffordshire Gliding Club	Seighford	12. 3.08
HUP	4216	WK	Schempp-Hirth Ventus-2cT	4/11		16. 2.96	W Kos	Bielsko-Biala, Poland	6. 4.08
G-CHUO	4217	DP	Fedorov Me7 Mechta	M007		21. 6.96	E A Hull	Dunstable	9. 4.08
G-CHUR	4218	HUR	Schempp-Hirth Cirrus	12	HB-927	20. 4.96	M Rossiter and A F Thomas	Talgarth	23. 4.08
HUS	4219	HUS	Scheibe SF 27A Zugvogel V	6010	D-1035	6. 8.97	D M Le Maistre	Edgehill	15. 2.08
G-CHUT	4220	HUT	Centrair ASW 20F	20187	F-CEUQ	14. 4.96	G A Macfadyen	Nympsfield	28. 9.08
G-CHUU	4221	HUU	Schleicher ASK 13	AB13527	D-7506 D-8945	15. 4.96	Upward Bound Trust	Thame	21. 9.08
G-CHUV	4222	64	Rolladen-Schneider LS8-18	8056	D-3823	2. 4.96	C P A Jeffery	Gransden Lodge	22. 3.08
G-CHUW	4223	S8	Rolladen-Schneider LS8-a	8058		11. 6.96	S E Bort and Partners	Challock	17. 3.08
G-CHUY	4225	HUY	Schempp-Hirth Ventus cT	84/329	D-KILZ	3. 4.96	M A and M N Challans	Lasham	28. 9.08
G-CHUZ	4226	200	Schempp-Hirth Discus bT	158/559		2. 3.96	P A Gelsthorpe	Nympsfield	1. 3.08
HVB	4228	HVB	Slingsby T.31B	850	(BGA 3249) XA308	27. 4.96	M Hoogenbosch "Top Less"	Hilversum, Netherlands	18. 5.08
HVC	4229	HVC	Slingsby T.38 Grasshopper	765	WZ769	4. 5.01	J F Forster	Hilversum, Netherlands	21. 9.05
HVD	4230	KO	SZD-55-1	551193052		23. 4.96	K Ostromecki (Cancelled 6.12.07)	Poland	4. 3.08
G-CHVE	4231	W54	Schempp-Hirth Ventus-2cT	8/19	D-KHIA	28. 3.96	R B Witter	Lleweni Parc	28. 9.08
G-CHVF	4232	B8	Rolladen-Schneider LS8-18	8059	D-1683	16. 4.96	J Haigh and R B Coote	Parham	28. 9.08
HVG	4233	RP1	Schleicher ASK 21	21062	D-2606	17. 4.96	Rattlesden Gliding Club	Rattlesden	28. 4.08
HVH	4234	HVH	Pilatus B4-PC11AF	067	D-2156	21. 5.96	London Gliding Club	Dunstable	31. 5.08
HVJ	4235	962	Scheibe SF 27A Zugvogel V	6012	OE-0762	1. 6.96	C P Bleaden	Kirton-in-Lindsey	27. 7.04
G-CHVK	4236	HVK	Grob G102 Astir CS	1161	D-4182	26. 4.96	P G Goulding	Crowland	7. 5.08
G-CHVL	4237	LS8	Rolladen-Schneider LS8-18	8060		16. 4.96	M W Durham and Partners	Bicester	30. 3.08
HVM	4238	393	Glaser-Dirks DG-300 Elan	3E177	D-4314	17. 5.96	Surrey & Hants Gliding Club	Lasham	29.11.07
G-CHVP	4240	930	Schleicher ASW 20	20374	D-1961 BGA 4076, EC-DLN	3. 5.96	E J Smallbone and Partners	Lasham	13. 2.08
HVQ	4241	HVQ	Schleicher ASK 13	13251	D-0605	27. 4.96	R B Brown	Bidford	18. 9.08
HVR	4242	HVR	Schempp-Hirth Discus b	560		3. 5.96	Yorkshire Gliding Club	Sutton Bank	3. 4.08
G-CHVT	4244	A9	Schempp-Hirth Ventus-2b	37		10. 5.96	G Alison and Partners	Wycombe Air Park	28. 9.08
G-CHVU	4245	59	Rolladen-Schneider LS8-18	8066		30. 4.96	European Soaring Club	(France)	20. 3.08
G-CHVV	4246	HVV	Rolladen-Schneider LS4-b	41009		5. 1.97	A J Bardgett	Milfield	28. 9.08
G-CHVW	4247	HVW	Schleicher ASK 13	13431	D-2140	14. 4.96	Rattlesden Gliding Club	Rattlesden	17.12.07
G-CHVX	4248	F20	Centrair ASW 20F	20528	F-CFSJ	13. 6.96	J A Castle	(Leicester)	8. 4.08
G-VENC	4249	584	Schempp-Hirth Ventus-2c	9/21		17. 5.96	J B Giddins	Hinton-in-the-Hedges	28. 9.08
G-CHVZ	4250	HVZ	Schempp-Hirth Standard Cirrus	567G	HB-1269	5. 6.96	P H V Alexander and Partners	Upwood	6. 4.08
HWA	4251	31	Schempp-Hirth Ventus-2c	8/20		7. 6.96	C Garton	Lasham	11. 9.08
HWB	4252	775	Schempp-Hirth Duo Discus	84		25. 5.96	Lasham Gliding Society	Lasham	8. 9.08
G-CHWC	4253	L18	Glasflügel Standard Libelle 201B	310	HB-1076	7. 7.96	J C R Rogers and Partners	RAF Cranwell	24. 8.08
HWD	4254	HWD	Schempp-Hirth Standard Cirrus	97	HB-987	3. 6.96	M R Hoskins	Rivar Hill	8. 5.06
HWE	4255	HWE	Schempp-Hirth Standard Cirrus	1151	HB-700	31. 5.96	J P Brady (Wreck stored 2004)	Brentor	9. 2.04
HWF	4256	2ZC	Jastreb Standard Cirrus G/81	281	SE-TZC	12. 6.96	M D Langford and Partner	Talgarth	25. 5.08
HWG	4257	HWG	Glasflügel Standard Libelle 201B	259	HB-1051	19. 6.96	M Kalweit	Dunstable	28. 8.08
G-CHWH	4258	712	Schempp-Hirth Ventus cT	182/599	RAFGGA 506	7. 6.96	H R Browning	Lasham	28. 9.08
G-CHWL	4261	84	Rolladen-Schneider LS8-a	8076		15. 6.96	W M Coffee	Snitterfield	9. 2.08
G-DSVN	4262	D7	Rolladen-Schneider LS8-18	8079		23. 7.96	A R Paul	Dunstable	26. 1.08
HWN	4263	598	Schempp-Hirth Nimbus-3T	8/60	D-KHIF	5. 7.96	H Hampel	Michelbach,Germany	4. 7.08
HWP	4264	HWP	Glaser-Dirks DG-100G Elan	E24G13	D-3772	12. 7.96	M Procter	Pocklington	26. 6.08
HWQ	4265	HWQ	Scheibe L-Spatz 55	607	D-6195	12. 7.96	A Gruber "Heisse Kartoffel"	Usk	6. 8.08
G-CHWS	4267	Z5	Rolladen-Schneider LS8-18	8080		14. 2.97	G A Chalmers	Easterton	15. 2.08
HWT	4268	S83	Schleicher K 8B	8780	HB-958	13. 7.96	A K Bailey	Edgehill	31. 5.08
G-CHWW	4271	DJT	Grob G103A Twin II Acro	3658-K-27	OE-5285	23. 8.96	Crown Service Gliding Club	Lasham	27. 3.08
G-CHWX	4272	HWX	SZD-59 Acro	B-2170		3. 9.96	D W F Gosden	Talgarth	10. 8.08
HWY	4273	168	Jastreb Standard Cirrus G/81	359	LN-GAL	6. 9.96	D D Copeland	Lasham	7. 5.08
HXA	4275	Z33	Scheibe Zugvogel IIIB	1107	D-2005	17. 3.97	P Kent	Saltby	29. 5.08
HXB	4276	HXB/52	Grob G102 Astir CS77	1819	D-6755	29. 9.96	T S Miller	Lyveden	14. 7.07
G-CHXC	4278	M8	Rolladen-Schneider LS8-18	8094		24. 2.97	S M Smith	Gransden Lodge	28. 9.08
G-CHXD	4279	HXD	Schleicher ASW 27	27030		8. 3.97	M Jerman and J Quartermaine	Sutton Bank	28. 9.08
G-CHXE	4280	Y4	Schleicher ASW 19B	19053	D-6699	25. 9.96	V Bettle and M Hargreaves	Wormingford	29. 5.08
G-CHXH	4283	HXH	Schempp-Hirth Discus b	573	BGA 4375 (BGA 4283)	28. 6.98	Deeside Gliding Club	Aboyne	28. 9.08
G-CHXJ	4284	HXJ	Schleicher ASK 13	13216	D-0417	29.11.96	Cotswold Gliding Club	Aston Down	28. 9.08
HXL	4286	OK-0927	Letov LF-107 Lunak	39	OK-0927 OK-0827	1.11.96	G P Saw "Czech Mate"	Wycombe Air Park	5. 4.08
HXM	4287	HXM	Grob G102 Astir CS	1272	D-7367	15.11.96	Bristol University Gliding Club	Nympsfield	3. 7.08
G-LSKV	4288	KV	Rolladen-Schneider LS8-18	8095		28. 1.97	D S Pitman	Bicester	28. 9.08
G-CHXP	4289	856	Schleicher ASK 13	13023	D-3656	19.11.96	Vale of White Horse Gliding Centre Sandhill Farm, Shrivenham		7. 3.08
G-CHXO	4290	711	Schleicher ASH 25B	25187	OH-874	23.11.96	M Chant and Partners	North Hill	13. 3.08
G-CHXR	4291	560	Schempp-Hirth Ventus cT	88/333	D-KESH	20. 2.97	J W a'Court and M Benson	Lasham	28. 9.08
G-EVII	4292	V11	Schempp-Hirth Ventus-2cT	10/41		27.11.96	I R Cook	Lasham	18. 3.08
G-CHXT	4293	S4	Rolladen-Schneider LS4-a	4325	ZS-GNV	21. 3.97	European Soaring Club	(France)	5. 4.08
G-CHXU	4294	HXU	Schleicher ASW 19B	19359	SE-TXN	14. 4.97	D P Binney	Pocklington	7. 9.08
G-CHXV	4295	HXV	Schleicher ASK 13	13080	D-5462	5.12.96	Banbury Gliding Club	Hinton-in-the-Hedges	20. 1.08
G-CHXW	4296	325	Rolladen-Schneider LS8-18	8097		7. 3.97	W Aspland	Wycombe Air Park	23. 3.08
HXX	4297	HXX	Schempp-Hirth Standard Cirrus	154G	D-0363	29. 1.97	J F Anscomb	Lasham	6. 2.08

G-CHXY	4298	HXY	Grob G102 Astir CS 77	1781	D-7689	8.12.96	G W Powell	Edgehill	25. 3.08
G-CHXZ	4299	S5	Rolladen-Schneider LS4	4249	SE-TXF	30. 3.97	E J Foggin	Sandhill Farm, Shrivenham	8. 2.08
G-CHYA	4300	DD	Rolladen-Schneider LS6-c18	6349	D-2162	28. 2.97	R H Dixon	Kingston Deverill	2. 3.08
G-RGTS	4301	T5	Schempp-Hirth Discus b	140	D-4684	19. 4.97	G R Green	Wormingford	28. 2.08
G-CHYD	4303	HYD	Schleicher ASW 24	24039	OE-5460	13. 2.97	S A Adlard	Long Mynd	5. 2.08
G-CHYE	4304	913	DG Flugzeugbau DG-505 Elan Orion	5E167X22		22.12.96	Bristol & Gloucestershire Gliding Club	Nympsfield	9. 4.08
G-CHYF	4305	660	Rolladen-Schneider LS8-18	8106		15. 3.97	R E Francis	Nympsfield	28. 9.08
HYH	4307	HYH	Rolladen-Schneider LS3-17	3186	D-6650	18. 1.97	B Silke	Bellarena	26. 6.08
HYJ	4308	HYJ	Schleicher ASK 21	21066	D-2724	17. 1.97	Highland Gliding Club	Easterton	3. 5.08
HYK	4309	HYK	Centrair ASW 20FLP	20176	F-CEUN	25. 9.97	J C Riddell	Rufforth	15. 5.08
G-DHYL	4310	K4	Schempp-Hirth Ventus-2a	44		31. 5.97	N J Passmore	Parham	28. 9.08
HYM	4311	PW5	PZL-Swidnik PW-5 Smyk	17.06.020		28. 2.97	P Jones "Iceman"	Lasham	8. 4.08
HYN	4312	HYN / 1018	Schleicher K 8B	8310A	D-1018	9.11.97	G Brook	Upwood	9. 4.05
HYP	4313	HYP	SZD-50-3 Puchacz	B-2082		22. 2.97	Rattlesden Gliding Club	Rattlesden	9. 3.08
G-CHYR	4315	432	Schleicher ASW 27	27013	D-8733	11. 3.97	A R Hutchings and A P Brown	Dunstable	21. 2.07
HYS	4316	A14	Schleicher ASK 21	21519	RAFGGA 514	14. 4.98	Anglia Gliding Club	AAC Wattisham	19. 5.08
G-CHYT	4317	HYT	Schleicher ASK 21	21568	AGA 20 RAFGGA 515	23.1.99	Wyvern Gliding Club	Trenchard Lines, Upavon	7. 2.08
HYU	4318	A61	Schempp-Hirth Discus CS	192CS	AGA ?? RAFGGA 561	29. 6.99	Anglia Gliding Club	AAC Wattisham	27. 5.08
G-CHYW	4320	HYW	Schleicher K 8B	8163A	D-5316 D-3202	13. 3.97	Lincolnshire Gliding Club	Strubby	5. 4.08
G-CHYX	4321	HYX	Schleicher K 8B	686	D-5742	24. 1.98	Oxford University Gliding Club	Bicester	2. 2.08
G-CHYY	4322	A26	Schempp-Hirth Nimbus-3DT	21	RAFGSA R26 D-KAFA	1. 3.97	A C Broadbridge and Partners	Bidford	28. 9.08
G-CHZA	4324	374	Schempp-Hirth Nimbus-3/24.5	94	SE-UFO	27. 4.97	P J Kite	Lasham	13.12.07
HZB	4325	HZB	PZL-Swidnik PW-5 Smyk	17.06.021		28. 2.97	Burn Gliding Club	Burn	6. 5.08
HZC	4326	216	Grob G102 Astir CS	1092	D-6991	24. 3.97	K G Laws	Lasham	15.12.05
G-CHZD	4327	HZD	Schleicher ASW 15B	15327	D-2191	20. 3.97	C P Ellison and W C Davis	Rivar Hill	13. 4.08
G-CHZE	4328	HZE	Schempp-Hirth Discus CS	121CS	D-6946	24. 3.97	S B Marshall	Portmoak	28. 9.08
G-SVEN	4329	G7	Centrair 101A Pégase	101A0262	PH-796	6. 5.97	A J Cronshaw	Gransden Lodge	13. 2.08
G-CHZG	4330	X8	Rolladen-Schneider LS8-18	8118		10. 3.97	M J and T J Webb	RAF Halton	22. 3.08
HZH	4331	HZH	Schleicher Ka 6CR	6461	HB-836	1. 6.97	M E de Torre	Darlton	30. 5.04
G-CHZJ	4332	HZJ	Schempp-Hirth Standard Cirrus	23	HB-981	18. 3.97	R H D Adams and P Fletcher	Edgehill	28. 3.08
G-CHZM	4335	U1	Rolladen-Schneider LS4-a	4762	D-1394	14. 4.97	J M Bevan and B Toulson	Husbands Bosworth	17. 3.08
HZN	4336	D-6173	Schleicher Ka 2B Rhönschwalbe	195	D-6173	28. 3.97	R A Willgoss	Wycombe Air Park	26. 8.08
HZP	4337	56	Rolladen-Schneider LS8-18	8117		12. 3.97	S J Redman	Gransden Lodge	25. 4.05
G-CHZO	4338	LZ	Schleicher ASW 27	27018	D-4499	10. 3.97	A A Gilmore	Husbands Bosworth	6. 4.08
G-CHZR	4339	HZR	Schleicher ASK 21	21079	D-4491	1. 5.97	D J Brookman and Partners	Aston Down	29. 3.08
HZS	4340	K1	Schempp-Hirth Ventus-2a	43		27. 3.97	A E Kay (To PH-1401 10.07)	Wycombe Air Park	17. 7.08
HZT	4341	X50	Centrair ASW 20F	20150	F-CFLL	19. 8.97	T J Banks	Ringmer	24. 3.08
G-CHZU	4342	B11	Schempp-Hirth Standard Cirrus	366	HB-1258 N71KW	30. 4.97	N S Murning	Eyres Field	31. 1.08
HZV	4343	P61	Schempp-Hirth Standard Cirrus	305	VH-GFZ BGA 4343, HB-1457, D-2061	30. 4.97	S Sheard	Pocklington	11. 6.08
G-OJNE	4344	112	Schempp-Hirth Nimbus-3T	22/88	D-KILO	1. 6.97	J N Ellis	Sutton Bank	19. 7.08
HZX	4345	476	Schleicher K 8B	8257	D-8476	12. 4.97	T I Taylor-Peach	Upwood	25. 7.08
G-CHZY	4346	EN	Rolladen-Schneider LS4-a	4479	D-3458	19. 4.97	N P Wedi	Wycombe Air Park	28. 9.08
G-CHZZ	4347	LD	Schleicher ASW 20L	20353	HB-1691 D-1153, N20EE	27. 4.97	C M Davey and Partners	RAF Wittering	31. 5.08
G-DJAA	4348	JAA	Schempp-Hirth Janus B	163	D-3147	18. 4.97	I Ashdown and Partners	Parham	30. 1.08
G-DJAB	4349	JAB	Glaser-Dirks DG-300 Elan	3E320	OY-XTC	24. 4.97	I G Johnston	Sutton Bank	28. 9.08
JAC	4350	JAC	Schempp-Hirth Duo Discus	128		24. 5.97	R Bottomley	Pocklington	20. 6.08
G-DJAD	4351	JAD	Schleicher ASK 21	21659		1.10.97	Borders Gliding Club	Milfield	18. 8.08
G-EJAE	4352	N8	Glaser-Dirks DG-200/17C	2-62	HB-1443	21. 4.97	D L P H Waller	RAF Keevil	24. 3.08
JAH	4355	921	Schempp-Hirth Discus b	572		30. 5.97	K Neave	Nympsfield	3. 7.08
JAK	4357		Schleicher Ka 6E	4301	F-CDRJ	R	Not known	Not known	
JAL	4358	JAL	Schleicher Ka 6E	4360	F-CDTX	19. 6.97	N Gilkes	Lee-on-Solent	27. 5.08
JAM	4359	777	Schleicher ASW 15B	15353	D-2360	29.5.97	T J Beckwith	Sackville Lodge, Riseley	23. 7.06
G-DJAN	4360	603	Schempp-Hirth Discus b	575		6.10.97	N F Perren	Dunstable	28. 9.08
JAP	4361	-	Slingsby T.38 Grasshopper (Believed to be ex WZ818 [799])	779	WZ783	R	R H Targett	Nympsfield	
G-CJAO	4362	823	Schempp-Hirth Discus b	190	D-0960	2. 6.97	A W Lyth and J Weddell	Ringmer	18. 3.08
JAR	4363	P3	Schempp-Hirth Discus bT	83/417	D-KHEI	16. 5.97	D G Maddicks	Nympsfield	4. 5.08
G-CJAS	4364	7Q	Glasflügel Standard Libelle 201B	109	SE-TIS	29. 5.97	M J Collett	Wycombe Air Park	21.12.07
G-CJAT	4365	JAT	Schleicher K 8B	8150	D-4390	6. 6.97	Wolds Gliding Club	Pocklington	11. 8.08
JAU	4366	WB922	Slingsby T.21B	585	WB922	27. 5.97	A Clarke	RAF Hullavington	19. 7.08
G-CJAV	4367	JAV	Schleicher ASK 21	21662		1.12.97	Wolds Gliding Club	Pocklington	1. 2.08
G-CJAW	4368	M4	Glaser-Dirks DG-202/17	2-180/1759	D-5618	12. 6.97	T McKinley and J P Kirby	Bembridge	21. 3.08
G-CJAX	4369	JAX	Schleicher ASK 21	21665		21. 1.98	Wolds Gliding Club	Pocklington	28. 9.08
JAZ	4371	JAZ	Grob G102 Astir CS Jeans	2073	D-7586	28. 8.97	Bath, Wilts and North Dorset Gliding Club	Kingston Deverill	16. 9.08
JBA	4372	JBA / XP463	Slingsby T.38 Grasshopper (Assembled from components; p/i is starboard wing only)	1262	XP463	8. 6.98	C Pullen	Lasham	22. 5.07
JBB	4373	P8	Rolladen-Schneider LS8	8003	D-8023	22. 8.97	C Bruce	(Sussex)	3. 5.08
JBE	4376	LX	ISF Mistral-C	MC020/79	OY-XLX PH-667	4. 7.97	R R Penman	RNAS Yeovilton	13. 8.08
JBF	4377	JBF	Glasflügel Standard Libelle	246	F-CDPV	22. 7.97	KJohnson	Wycombe Air Park	10. 5.07
G-UNIN	4378	U9	Schempp-Hirth Ventus b	135	OE-5315	20. 7.97	W R Longstaff and Partners	Feshiebridge	23. 3.08
G-CJBH	4379	537	Eiriavion PIK-20D-78	20621	OH-529	6. 7.97	537 Syndicate	Parham	29. 1.08
JBJ	4380	G81	Jastreb Standard Cirrus G/81	280	SE-TZD	8. 7.97	S Dutton	Lasham	2. 7.08

G-CJBK	4381	L3	Schleicher ASW 19B	19204	D-4099, PH-602	4.11.97	P M Sharpe and D Caielli	Dunstable	9. 1.08
G-CJBM	4383	JBM	Schleicher ASK 21	21089	D-6391	26. 7.97	Midland Gliding Club	Long Mynd	5. 6.08
JBP	4385	B2	Rolladen-Schneider LS6-18W	6378		25. 7.97	L E Garcia-Castillo	Ocana, Spain	2. 6.08
							(Cancelled 22. 1.08)		
JBQ	4386	L7	Rolladen-Schneider LS8-18	8148		24. 9.97	C C Watt	Dunstable	21. 9.08
G-CJBR	4387	AC	Schempp-Hirth Discus b	90	F-CGGD	8. 8.97	M R C Corrance and Partners	Kenley	20. 9.08
					F-WGGD				
G-CJBS	4388	JBS	ESAG LAK-12	6115	??	10. 8.97	I G Smith and Partners	Ringmer	14. 3.08
G-CJBT	4389	JBT	Schleicher ASW 19B	19075	D-4477	2. 8.97	C Braithwaite	Kingston Deverill	29. 7.08
JBU	4390	HL	Rolladen-Schneider LS6-18W	6350	D-0462	23. 9.97	J Gorringe (To ZK-GHL 8.07)	Lasham	2. 8.07
G-CJBW	4392	710	Schempp-Hirth Discus bT	34/337	D-KBJR	8. 8.97	N C Pringle and Partners	Lasham	23. 1.08
G-CJBX	4393	JBX	Rolladen-Schneider LS4-a	4293	D-9111	26. 4.98	P W Lee and Partner	Nympsfield	27. 3.07
G-CJBY	4394	JBY	Sportine Aviacija LAK-12	6185		12. 8.97	P Steggles	Rattlesden	25. 7.08
JBZ	4395	JBZ	Grob G102 Astir CS	1492	D-4794	30. 8.97	S J Harris	(Welshpool)	17. 9.08
JCA	4396	JCA	Schleicher ASW 15B	15202	(BGA 4049)	11. 9.97	S Briggs and Partners	Currock Hill	6. 4.08
					OH-410				
G-CJCD	4399	HS	Schleicher ASW 24	24101	D-6091	16.10.97	M D Evershed	Gransden Lodge	1. 3.08
G-VNTS	4400	911	Schempp-Hirth Ventus bT	46/240	D-KFMS	15. 9.97	A G Reid	Bidford	28. 9.08
G-CJCF	4401	JCF	Grob G102 Astir CS77	1705	PH-1012	23. 9.97	Northumbria Gliding Club	Currock Hill	2. 6.08
					D-7634				
G-CJCG	4402	JCG	PZL-Swidnik PW-5 Smyk	17.09.003		29. 9.97	J O Lavery	Bellarena	28. 9.08
G-CJCJ	4404	C7	Schempp-Hirth Standard Cirrus	434G	SE-TNC	7. 5.98	R P Carter and R Johnson	Husbands Bosworth	18. 4.08
G-CJCK	4405	DC	Schempp-Hirth Discus bT	92/430	D-KIDE	9.10.97	D C Coppin	Lasham	28. 9.08
JCL	4406	T2	Rolladen-Schneider LS8-18	8147		29.10.97	T W Slater (To OY-XDB 5.07)	Aboyne	31. 8.07
G-CJCM	4407	W27	Schleicher ASW 27	27064		11.12.97	K E Singer and J R Klunder	Camphill	4. 5.08
G-CJCN	4408	JA9	Schempp-Hirth Standard Cirrus 75	646	D-7247	20.10.97	S C J Barker	Pocklington	28. 9.08
G-CJCP	4409	F2	Rolladen-Schneider LS8-18	8146		29.10.97	D P Francis	Bicester	28. 9.08
G-CEWI	4410	W19	Schleicher ASW 19B	19086	PH-562	5.12.97	S R Edwards and K Steele	Gransden Lodge	28. 9.08
JCR	4411	JCR	Grob G102 Astir CS	1181	OE-5188	28.10.97	B Harrison	Kingston Deverill	11.11.05
JCS	4412	WT898	Slingsby T.31B	693	BGA 3284	23.10.97	G Schwab	Graz, Austria	28. 6.04
					WT898				
G-CJCT	4413	176	Schempp-Hirth Nimbus-4T	21	D-KKKL	4.10.97	D S Innes	Lasham	8. 5.08
G-CJCU	4414	JCU	Schempp-Hirth Standard Cirrus B	688	D-6604	29.10.97	R A Davenport	Aston Down	13. 3.08
JCV	4415	IM	Schleicher ASH 25E	25069	D-KAIM	14.11.97	R C Verdier	Gransden Lodge	6. 7.08
JCW	4416	JCW	Grob G102 Astir CS77	1612	PH-573	1.10.97	N G Smith	Nympsfield	26. 4.08
G-CJCX	4417	JCX	Schempp-Hirth Discus bT	93/432	D-KJOB	30.10.97	R Starmer	Bidford	27. 3.08
JCY	4418	F3	Rolladen-Schneider LS8-18	8171		9.12.97	R Zaccour	Alzate Brianza, Italy	30. 6.08
JCZ	4419	JCZ	Schleicher Ka 6CR	6108	D-7152	15.11.97	R Monk	Eyres Field	12. 4.08
JDA	4420	GR	Schempp-Hirth Nimbus-3/24.5	8	D-1788	9.11.97	G R Ross	Lasham	7. 3.06
JDB	4421	WZ828	Slingsby T.38 Grasshopper	809	WZ828	6.11.97	A Clarke	RAF Hullavington	2. 8.08
G-CJDC	4422	A27	Schleicher ASW 27	27010	D-6209	13.12.97	J J Marshall	Dunstable	28. 9.08
JDD	4423	JDD	Glaser-Dirks DG-202/17C	2-171CL17	PH-717	31.12.97	D A Littler	Chipping	4. 3.08
G-CJDE	4424	543	Rolladen-Schneider LS8-18	8151		1. 5.98	M N Davies and B Kerby	Snitterfield	16. 4.08
JDF	4425	907	Schleicher ASH 25E	25150	D-KPAS	24.11.97	W Young	Pocklington	17. 5.08
G-CJDG	4426	KW	Rolladen-Schneider LS6-b	6145	D-5675	7. 2.98	A Moss	Nympsfield	2. 3.08
G-CJDJ	4428	434	Rolladen-Schneider LS3	3010	D-7729	18.11.97	J C Burdett	Walney Island	10. 2.08
G-CJDK	4429	841	Rolladen-Schneider LS8-18	8153		3. 3.98	G K Drury	Challock	28. 9.08
JDL	4430	SR	Schempp-Hirth Discus bT	165/578		12. 4.98	S Robinson	Chipping	1. 6.08
G-CJDM	4431	WE	Schleicher ASW 15B	15280	F-CEGL	22. 1.98	W Ellis	Wormingford	20. 4.08
JDN	4432	JDN	DG Flugzeugbau DG-505 Elan Orion	5E180X31		20. 3.98	Devon & Somerset Gliding Club	North Hill	7. 3.08
							(Crashed on landing North Hill 22. 4.07)		
G-CJDP	4433	JDP	Glaser-Dirks DG-202/17	2-134/1732	D-6545	3.12.97	R Fielding and Partners	Camphill	28. 9.08
G-CJDR	4435	JDR	Schleicher ASW 15	15053	D-6910	5. 2.98	M Waters "Rocinante"	Waldershare Park	2. 4.08
G-CJDS	4436	JDS	Schempp-Hirth StD Cirrus 75	638	D-4057	7. 3.98	S Holland	Rivar Hill	16. 3.08
					OY-XCZ				
G-CJDT	4437	232	Rolladen-Schneider LS8-a	8172		23. 1.98	R J Rebbeck	Dunstable	14. 5.08
G-CJDU	4438	JDU	LET L-13 Blanik	026303	D-8919	22.12.97	Herefordshire Gliding Club	Shobdon	27. 7.08
G-CJDV	4439	JH	DG Flugzeugbau DG-303 Elan Acro	3E481A24		21. 3.98	J Herman and S C Williams	Wycombe Air Park	6.12.07
JDW	4440	JDW	PZL-Swidnik PW-5 Smyk	17.09.018		23.12.97	Burn Gliding Club *(Stored for spares 9.07)*	Burn	14.12.00
G-CJDX	4441	JDX	Wassmer WA28F Espadon	101	F-CDZU	29.12.97	K J Woods	(Cambridge)	10. 5.08
JDY	4442	P2	Rolladen-Schneider LS8-18	8173		8. 2.98	P O Paterson	Lasham	29. 3.08
JDZ	4443	N1	Schempp-Hirth Nimbus-4T	18	D-KOLF	9. 1.98	P Harvey	Lasham	26. 3.08
G-CJEA	4444	D4	Rolladen-Schneider LS8-18	8159	D-2411	9. 3.98	R I Davidson and D J Westwood	Husbands Bosworth	25. 4.08
G-CJEB	4445	JEB	Schleicher ASW 24	24172	D-9344	10. 2.98	M A Taylor and S L Barnes	Rattlesden	28. 2.08
G-CJEC	4446	JEC	SZD-50-3 Puchacz	B-2197		6. 4.98	Cambridge Gliding Club	Gransden Lodge	28. 9.08
JED	4447	JED	Schleicher ASW 15B	15427	D-3976	23. 1.98	J T Leppanen (See BGA 4822)	(Portugal)	16. 3.08
G-CJEE	4448	JEE	Schleicher ASW 20L	20073	(BGA 4456)	9. 2.98	J C Baldock	Nympsfield	28. 9.08
					D-7666				
G-FORA	4449	4A	Schempp-Hirth Ventus cT	126/400	D-KFWH	28. 1.98	A D Cook	Edgehill	28. 9.08
G-CTAG	4450	C1	Rolladen-Schneider LS8-18	8150		24. 1.98	C Tagg	Pocklington	28. 9.08
G-CJEH	4451	KE	Glasflügel Mosquito B	172	OY-XKE	15. 2.98	M J Vickery	Lasham	22. 3.08
JEJ	4452	WA2	Rolladen-Schneider LS7-WL	7074	OE-5477	23. 3.98	S Derwin	Portmoak	23. 9.08
G-CJEL	4453	JEL	Schleicher ASW 24	24044	PH-866	14. 2.98	D Robson	Milfield	12. 5.08
G-CJEM	4455	572	Schempp-Hirth Duo Discus	146		13. 3.98	D W Briggs and Partners	Aston Down	28. 9.08
G-CJEP	4457	JEP	Rolladen-Schneider LS4-b	41021		1. 8.98	C F Carter and N Backes	Long Mynd	16. 4.08
G-OZOZ	4458	OZ	Schempp-Hirth Nimbus-3DT	6	OO-ZOZ	13. 2.98	C M Hawkes and Partners	Ringmer	24.11.07
					HB-1921, D-7695				
G-CJER	4459	JER	Schempp-Hirth Standard Cirrus 75	654	D-6475	6. 4.98	S R Brown and Partners	Snitterfield	7. 4.08
					OO-ZBM				
G-NJET	4461	JET	Schempp-Hirth Ventus cT	161/521	RAFGSA R38	20. 2.98	J Hudson	Lasham	8. 3.08
G-CJEU	4462	JEU	Glasflügel Standard Libelle	55	SE-TIC	6. 4.98	D B Johns	Aston Down	30. 3.08
G-CJEV	4463	JEV	Schempp-Hirth Standard Cirrus B	650	OE-5072	24. 2.98	G F C King and E Perrin	North Hill	22. 1.08

G-CJEW	4464	D41	Schleicher Ka 6CR	6493	D-4116	22.2.98	S Blundell	Bidford	1. 3.08
G-CJEX	4465	DW	Schempp-Hirth Ventus-2a	64		9.3.98	D S Watt	Bicester	21. 2.08
JEZ	4467	274	Glaser-Dirks DG-100	3	PH-792, D-3721	14.3.98	G F Prior	Wycombe Air Park	19. 8.08
G-CJFA	4468	JFA	Schempp-Hirth Standard Cirrus	225	D-0974	15.4.98	P M Sheahan	Lasham	21. 3.08
G-CJFC	4470	R55	Schempp-Hirth Discus CS	054CS	RAFGSA R55	11.3.98	RAFGSA Fenland Gliding Club	RAF Marham	21. 9.08
JFD	4471	R8	Grob G102 Astir CS	1379	RAFGSA R8	12. 3.98	RAFGSA Centre	Bicester	30.10.03
					OY-XG				
G-CJFE	4472	16	Schempp-Hirth Janus CT	21/299	RAFGSA R16	12.3.98	RAFGSA Bannerdown Gliding Club	RAF Keevil	30.10.07
G-CJFF	4473	JFF	Schempp-Hirth Duo Discus	131	RAFGSA R26	11.3.98	RAFGSA Chilterns Gliding Centre	RAF Halton	28. 9.08
G-CJFH	4475	R1	Schempp-Hirth Duo Discus	118	RAFGSA R1	12.3.98	RAFGSA Fulmar Gliding Club	Easterton	4. 4.08
G-CJFJ	4476	JFJ	Schleicher ASW 20CL	20830	D-8307, F-CGCS	7.4.98	R J Stirk	Burn	1. 4.08
G-CJFK	4477	JFK	Schleicher ASW 20L	20201	D-5979	15.4.98	D Holt	Llantisilio	16. 5.08
G-CJFL	4478	42	Rolladen-Schneider LS8-18	8178		12.3.98	G N Smith and N Hoare	Dunstable	28. 9.08
JFM	4479	JFM	Schleicher ASK 13	13222	D-0396	27.3.98	Darlton Gliding Club	Darlton	10. 7.08
JFN	4480	M25	Schleicher ASH 25E	25060	D-KCOH	20. 6.98	C Smithers	Gransden Lodge	26. 4.08
G-CENK	4482	651	Schempp-Hirth Nimbus-4DT	9/40		9. 5.98	P Whitt	Shobdon	9. 7.08
G-CJFR	4483	221	Schempp-Hirth Ventus cT	170/560	RAFGSA R24	20.12.97	J G Allen	Bicester	9. 1.08
G-CJFT	4485	JFT	Schleicher K 8B	8451	D-1883	23.3.98	Surrey Hills Gliding Club	Kenley	31. 8.06
G-CJFU	4486	JFU	Schleicher ASW 19B	19038	D-4531	23.3.98	M T Stanley	Sutton Bank	9. 3.08
JFV	4487	WA1	Schleicher ASK 21	21675		29.6.98	Scottish Gliding Union	Portmoak	19. 6.08
JFW	4488	JFW	Sportine Aviacija LAK-12	6192	LX-CDM	4.4.98	E W Burgess	Lyveden	8. 5.08
G-CJFX	4489	144	Rolladen-Schneider LS8-a	8174		27.3.98	P E Baker	Gransden Lodge	28. 9.08
JFY	4490	JFY	Fedorov Me7b Mechta	8		16.10.98	D S Adams	Rivar Hill	22. 1.04
JGA	4492	JGA	Fedorov Me7b Mechta	10		16.10.98	N Wilkinson	Challock	14. 8.08
JGB	4493	CU	Schleicher K 8B	AB.02	D-8868	16. 5.98	Cambridge University Gliding Club Gransden Lodge		1. 3.08
G-CJGD	4495	JGD	Schleicher K 8B	8214A-SH	D-....	17.4.98	R E Pettifer and C A McLay	Chipping	21. 4.08
JGE	4496	K21	Schleicher ASK 21	21068	RAFGSA R21	14.4.98	R Wall and Partners	Bidford	26. 5.05
JGF	4497	JGF	Neukom Elfe S4D	416	BGA 3316	13.5.98	C V Inwood	Lasham	29. 4.06
					D-4820				
G-DJGG	4498	JGG	Schleicher ASW 15B	15332	D-2325	3. 4.98	A A Cole	Ringmer	19. 3.08
JGH	4499	JGH	Schempp-Hirth Nimbus-2C	188	OO-ZZM	12.4.98	J Swannack	Darlton	16. 7.08
					D-2834				
G-CJGJ	4500	JGJ	Schleicher ASK 21	21039	RAFGSA R22	14.4.98	Midland Gliding Club	Long Mynd	28. 9.08
G-CJGK	4501	JGK	Eiriavion PIK-20D-78	20571	OO-ZDL, D-6707	7.4.98	R Cassidy and W Stephen	Milfield	20. 4.08
G-CJGL	4502	27	Schempp-Hirth Discus CS	148CS	RAFGSA R27	4.98	RAFGSA Chilterns Glding Centre	RAF Halton	28. 9.08
G-CJGM	4503	R53	Schempp-Hirth Discus CS	036CS	RAFGSA R53	4.98	RAFGSA Fulmar Gliding Club	Easterton	6. 5.08
G-CJGN	4504	867	Schempp-Hirth Standard Cirrus	554	D-8674	4.98	P A Shuttleworth	(Tadcaster)	21. 5.08
G-RBCT	4505	E8	Schempp-Hirth Ventus-2cT	3/10	N200EE, D-KHIA	4.98	R Brown	Aston Down	28. 9.08
G-CJGR	4507	BT	Schempp-Hirth Discus bT	10/275	D-KGPS, D-5461	5.98	D A Sinclair	Lasham	19. 3.08
G-CJGS	4508	L2	Rolladen-Schneider LS8-18	8180		5.98	M D Allan	Shobdon	28. 9.08
JGU	4510	JGU	Schempp-Hirth Mini Nimbus B	69	HB-1427	5.98	M Burrows	Darlton	7. 9.08
JGV	4511	LGC	Schempp-Hirth Duo Discus	173	(D-4020)	4.00	London Gliding Club	Dunstable	16. 5.08
G-CJGW	4512	JGW	Schleicher ASK 13	13146	D-0169	5.98	Darlton Gliding Club	Darlton	3. 2.08
JGX	4513	JGX	Schleicher K 8B	753	D-1878	5.98	J Fisher	Andreas	14. 5.08
JGY	4514	C3	Schempp-Hirth Standard Cirrus	333	SE-TMU	5.98	P Short	Husbands Bosworth	29. 4.08
JGZ	4515	JGZ	Glasflügel Standard Libelle 201B	193	D-0697	15. 5.98	J H Edwards	Pocklington	19. 4.07
JHA	4516	EU	Schempp-Hirth StD Cirrus 75	645	D-4240	5.98	G Carruthers	Pocklington	2. 4.07
JHB	4517	JHB	Scheibe L-Spatz 55	552	D-1618	8.98	A Gruber	Usk	6. 8.08
G-CJHD	4519	JHD	Schleicher Ka 6E	4307	OY-XGS, D-0272	5.98	M A King	Lyveden	25. 3.08
JHE	4520	JHE	Grob G102 Astir CS Jeans	2189	CS-PBI	5.98	Aero Club de Portugal	Sintra	17. 4.08
					BGA 3977, D-7764				
JHG	4522	513	Grob G102 Astir CS	1084	D-6984	5.98	P L Zelazowski	Edgehill	20. 9.08
JHH	4523	986	Schempp-Hirth Standard Cirrus	349G	D-3006	5.98	R J Lodge	Dunstable	13. 2.08
G-CJHJ	4524	JHJ	Glasflügel Standard Libelle 201B	495	HB-1187	30.6.01	M E Hahnefeld and Partners	Parham	9. 2.08
G-CJHK	4525	JHK	Schleicher K 8B	Not known	AGA 21	8.98	Stratford on Avon Gliding Club	Snitterfield	12. 4.08
					(BGA 4319), RAFGGA 558				
G-CJHL	4526	JHL	Schleicher Ka 6E	4073	SE-TFB	6.98	M R Doran	Wormingford	4. 4.08
G-CJHM	4527	JHM	Schempp-Hirth Discus b	373	OO-ZGZ	6.98	J H May	Cosford	13. 3.08
JHN	4528	JHN	Grob G102 Astir CS Jeans	2110	D-7638	5.98	A M Percival	Kingston Deverill	11. 2.08
G-DJHP	4529	JHP	Valentin Mistral-C	MC048/82	D-4948	6.98	P B Higgs	(Wrexham)	22. 2.08
G-CJHO	4530	R43	Schleicher ASK 18	18021	RAFGSA R43	9.98	RAFGSA Wrekin Gliding Club	RAF Cosford	5. 3.08
					RAFGSA 713, RAFGSA 113				
G-CJHR	4531	A34	Centrair SNC-34C Alliance	34026		6.98	Borders Gliding Club	Milfield	21. 6.08
JHS	4532	JHS	Schleicher ASW 19B	19047	D-6716	3.99	B Crow	Usk	12. 6.08
G-HOJO	4533	6	Schempp-Hirth Discus-2a	2		5.98	R Jones	Lasham	10. 4.08
JHU	4534	868	Rolladen-Schneider LS8-18	8197		7.98	S P Ball and Partners	Sutton Bank	17. 5.08
JHW	4536	JHW	Glaser-Dirks DG-200	2-19	HB-1400	6.98	A Thornhill	Burn	6. 2.05
JHX	4537	JHX	Bölkow Phoebus C	930	OO-ZYN	6.98	M Dunlop	Shipdham	19. 2.03
					F-CDON		(Noted 2007)		
G-CJHY	4538	LT	Rolladen-Schneider LS8-18	8181	D-9988	18.6.98	L E N Tanner and N H Wall	Nympsfield	10. 2.08
G-CJHZ	4539	G41	Schleicher ASW 20	20313	D-6532	6.98	T J Stanley	Sutton Bank	28. 9.08
G-CJJB	4541	615	Rolladen-Schneider LS4	4542	D-2397	6.98	M Tomlinson	Talgarth	3. 4.08
JJD	4543	K11	Schempp-Hirth Discus bT	5/262	D-KIHS	7.98	D Wilson	Burn	23. 9.08
JJE	4544	JO1	Schempp-Hirth Discus a	379	OE-5530	7.98	N Braithwaite	Walney Island	12. 7.08
					VH-XQT				
G-CJJF	4545	G1	Schleicher ASW 27	27086		6.98	G F Read	Wycombe Air Park	28. 9.08
G-NIVT	4546	V1	Schempp-Hirth Nimbus-4T	3	D-KIXL	7.98	P G Sheard and M Clarke	Lasham	26. 2.08
G-CJJH	4547	899	DG Flugzeugbau DG-800S	8-137S30		4.99	W R Brown	Husbands Bosworth	15. 5.08
G-CJJJ	4548	JJJ	Schempp-Hirth Standard Cirrus	284	D-2946	7.98	F R and R G Stevens	Husbands Bosworth	9. 2.08
G-CJJK	4549	K8	Rolladen-Schneider LS8-18	8199		6.8.98	J E C White	Dunstable	28. 9.08
JJL	4550	JJL	Schleicher ASW 19B	19302	D-4227	4.99	M Bacic and Partners	Bicester	1. 3.08
JJM	4551	JJM	Schempp-Hirth Standard Cirrus	403G	D-2933	7.98	Skycraft	Spalding	12. 7.05
JJN	4552	JJN	Slingsby T.38 Grasshopper	1267	XP490	7.98	611 VGS	RAF Watton	21. 7.99
			(Regd as '2067" from Frame no.SSK/FF/2067)						

G-CJJP	4553	494	Schempp-Hirth Duo Discus	180		7.98	N Clements and Partners	Long Mynd	28. 9.08
G-CJJR	4555	R73	Schleicher ASK 21	21054	RAFGGA 513	8.98	RAFGSA Chilterns Gliding Centre	RAF Halton	28. 9.08
JJS	4556	XA240	Slingsby T.38 Grasshopper	873	XA240	R	A Stacey (Stored 4.07)	RAF Keevil	
G-CJJT	4557	933	Schleicher ASW 27	27070	D-6209	8.98	T M World	Lee-on-Solent	5. 5.08
JJU	4558	H2	Rolladen-Schneider LS8-a	8200		8.98	A J French	Dunstable	13. 8.07
G-CJJX	4561		Schleicher ASW 15B	15323	D-2312	9.98	M D Brooks	Saltby	26. 3.08
G-SWSW	4562	SW	Schempp-Hirth Ventus bT	61/273	PH-981	9.98	S R Way	Parham	28. 9.08
					D-KMIH				
G-CJJZ	4563	15	Schempp-Hirth Discus bT	156/556	OO-ZQX	9.98	S J C Parker	Nympsfield	28. 9.08
G-CJKA	4564	JKA	Schleicher ASK 21	21059	D-8835	10.98	East Sussex Gliding Club	Ringmer	14. 6.08
JKB	4565	JKB	PZL-Swidnik PW-5 Smyk	17.10.008		9.98	J C Gibson	Chipping	25. 5.08
G-CFOX	4566	JKC	Marganski MDM-1 Fox	224	SP-P632	9.98	M Newman and Partners	Parham	28. 9.08
G-CJKD	4567	P1	Rolladen-Schneider LS8-18	8215		10.98	D Abbey and G Glover	Husbands Bosworth	29. 4.08
JKE	4568	JKE	PZL-Swidnik PW-5 Smyk	17.11.025		10.98	Burn Gliding Club	Burn	2. 9.06
JKF	4569	JKF	Glaser-Dirks DG-200	2-35	D-6069	10.98	M J Barrett (See BGA 4659)	North Hill	12. 6.07
G-CJKG	4570	R48	Schleicher ASK 18	18036	RAFGSA R48	3.99	RAFGSA Chilterns Gliding Centre	RAF Halton	10.12.07
					RAFGSA 448				
JKH	4571	P30	Schempp-Hirth Ventus cT	174/566	RAFGSA R30	10.98	J F Fitzgerald	Usk	11. 4.08
G-CJKJ	4572	R21	Schleicher ASK 21	21679		10.98	RAFGSA Chilterns Gliding Centre	RAF Halton	7. 1.08
JKK	4573	A7	Schleicher ASK 21	21182	AGA 11	10.98	British Army (Germany) Gliding Centre		
							Javelin Barracks, Elmpt Station, Germany		28. 9.08
G-CJKL	4574	W8	Rolladen-Schneider LS8-18	8218		4.99	R J Welford	Gransden Lodge	26. 3.08
G-CJKM	4575	Z10	Glaser-Dirks DG-202/17	2-148/1746	D-4155	10.98	E W Russell	Wormingford	28. 9.08
G-CJKN	4576	790	Rolladen-Schneider LS8-18	8214		10.98	D A Booth	Husbands Bosworth	28. 9.08
G-CJKP	4577	PH1	Rolladen-Schneider LS4-b	41000	PH-1089	12.98	D M Hope	Wycombe Air Park	18. 2.08
G-CJKO	4578	R20	Schleicher ASK 21	21098	RAFGSA R20	1.99	RAFGSA Four Counties Gliding Club	Wittering	20. 7.07
G-CJKR	4579	JKR	Schempp-Hirth Discus b	151	RAFGSA R12	11.98	T Wright	Husbands Bosworth	4. 3.08
G-CJKS	4580	S19	Schleicher ASW 19B	19362	D-1273	11.98	D M Brown and P D F Adshead	Dunstable	19. 6.08
JKT	4581	R7	Schleicher ASK 13	13615	RAFGSA R7	8.99	RAFGSA Clevelands Gliding Club	AAC Dishforth	31. 5.08
G-CJKU	4582	R33	Schleicher ASK 18	18022	RAFGSA R33	6.99	RAFGSA Clevelands Gliding Club	AAC Dishforth	28. 9.08
					RAFGSA 223				
G-CJKV	4583	JKV	Grob G103A Twin II Acro	34042-K-273	RAFGSA R52	5.99	Welland Gliding Club	Lyveden	13. 6.08
G-CJKW	4584	JKW	Grob G102 Astir CS 77	1666	RAFGSA R60	1.99	Bath, Wilts and North Dorset Gliding Club		
					RAFGSA 560			Kingston Deverill	24. 6.08
G-CJKX	4585	JKX	Schempp-Hirth Discus b	247	RAFGSA R17	8.99	A R Armstrong	RAF Keevil	13. 4.08
G-CJKY	4586	243	Schempp-Hirth Ventus cT	181/597	RAFGSA R24	11.98	M P Osborn and G V Matthews	RAF Cosford	28. 9.08
					RAFGSA 557				
G-CJKZ	4587	R25	Schleicher ASK 21	21123	RAFGSA R25	12.98	RAFGSA Chilterns Gliding Centre	RAF Halton	19. 2.08
G-CJLA	4588	JLA	Schempp-Hirth Ventus-2cT	26/94	PH-1129	11.98	E C Neighbour	Camphill	28. 9.08
G-CJLC	4590	R10	Schempp-Hirth Discus CS	193CS	RAFGSA R10	11.98	RAFGSA Four Counties Gliding Club	Wittering	25. 3.08
JLE	4592	JLE	Schleicher ASK 13	13245	RAFGSA R90	10.98	British Army (Germany) Gliding Centre		
					NEJSGSA 1			Javelin Barracks, Elmpt Station, Germany	17. 3.07
JLF	4593	JLF	Schleicher ASK 13	13150	AGA 14	12.98	Wyvern Gliding Club	Trenchard Lines, Upavon	7. 7.07
G-CJLG	4594	JLG	SZD-51-1 Junior	B-1933	AGA 5	2.99	Wyvern Gliding Club	Trenchard Lines, Upavon	17. 2.08
					(BGA 3699)				
G-CJLH	4595	JLH	Rolladen-Schneider LS4	4256	AGA 1	3.99	C A Sorace and Partners	Dunstable	19. 4.08
G-CJLJ	4596	A8	Rolladen-Schneider LS4-b	4997	AGA 2	12.98	Wyvern Gliding Club	Trenchard Lines, Upavon	9. 5.08
G-CJLK	4597	LS7	Rolladen-Schneider LS7	7112	AGA 3	10.4.99	D N Munro and S G Hamilton	Nympsfield	5. 5.08
G-DJLL	4598	N25	Schleicher ASK 13	13144	HB-952	11.98	Portsmouth Naval Gliding Club	Lee-on-Solent	16. 2.08
G-CJLN	4600	R4	Rolladen-Schneider LS8-18	8169	RAFGSA R4	3.99	RAFGSA Cranwell Gliding Club	RAF Cranwell	28. 9.08
G-CJLP	4601	R39	Schempp-Hirth Discus CS	034CS	RAFGSA R39	4.99	RAFGSA Cranwell Gliding Club	RAF Cranwell	7. 2.08
G-CJLO	4602	JLO	Schleicher ASK 13	13608	RAFGSA R40	4.99	Bowland Forest Gliding Club	Chipping	28. 9.08
					RAFGSA R4				
G-CJLR	4603	R57	Grob G102 Astir CS	1509	RAFGSA R57	2.99	RAFGSA Cranwell Gliding Club	RAF Cranwell	28. 9.08
					RAFGSA 507				
G-CJLS	4604	R75	Schleicher K 8B	8950	RAFGSA R75	3.99	RAFGSA Crusaders Gliding Club		
					RAFGSA 285			Kingsfield, Cyprus	1.12.07
JLU	4606	11	Schempp-Hirth Ventus-2cT	37/126		3.99	R L Fox and P M Kirschner	Bicester	21. 4.08
JLV	4607	JLV	Schleicher Ka 6E	4192	OY-XEU, D-4424	1.99	J C Cooper	Lyveden	27. 8.08
G-CJLW	4608	87	Schempp-Hirth Discus CS	033CS	RAFGSA R87	12.98	RAFGSA Wrekin Gliding Club	RAF Cosford	17. 3.08
JLX	4609	JLX	Schempp-Hirth Standard Cirrus	279G	OO-ZGL, D-1985	11.98	M W Fisher	Talgarth	30. 3.07
G-CJLY	4610	JLY	Schleicher ASW 27	27111		6.99	P C Piggott and L M Astle	Husbands Bosworth	16. 5.08
G-CJLZ	4611	21	Grob G103A Twin II Acro	3633-K-15	D-7912	12.98	B L Eppy and Partners	Lasham	28. 3.08
JMA	4612	R36	Schleicher ASK 18	18038	RAFGSA R36	6.99	RAFGSA Four Counties Gliding Club	Wittering	27. 8.08
					RAFGSA 236				
JMC	4614	R22	Schleicher ASK 21	21681		12.98	RAFGSA Wrekin Gliding Club	RAF Cosford	11. 6.08
G-DJMD	4615	P23	Schempp-Hirth Discus b	241	RAFGSA R23	3.4.99	R C Oliver and Partners	Kenley	24. 1.08
JME	4616	JME	Schleicher K7	5	D-8867	12.98	W E Masterton	Blenheim, Jamaica	25. 1.04
JMG	4618	JMG	SZD-51-1 Junior	B-2192		4.99	Kent Gliding Club	Challock	9. 3.08
G-CJMH	4619	JMH	Schempp-Hirth Standard Cirrus	571	HB-1263	12.98	J G Walker	Pocklington	28. 4.08
JMJ	4620	R46	Schleicher ASK 13	13616	RAFGSA R46	9.99	RAFGSA Fenland Gliding Club	RAF Marham	21. 9.08
					RAFGSA R16				
G-CJMK	4621	R49	Schleicher ASK 18	18023	RAFGSA R49	1.99	RAFGSA Crusaders Gliding Club		
					RAFGSA 318			Kingsfield, Cyprus	2. 8.07
JML	4622	R63	Grob G102 Astir CS 77	1718	RAFGSA R63	1.99	RAFGSA Kestrel Gliding Club	RAF Odiham	28. 9.08
					RAFGSA 883				
G-CJMN	4624	636	Schempp-Hirth Nimbus-2	38	D-1129	12.98	R A Holroyd	Pocklington	28. 9.08
					HB-1159				
G-CJMO	4625	781	Rolladen-Schneider LS8-18	8225		12.98	D J Langrick	Husbands Bosworth	20. 4.08
G-CJMP	4626	JMP	Schleicher ASK 13	13436	D-2984	1.99	East Sussex Gliding Club	Ringmer	11. 3.08
JMR	4628	628	Rolladen-Schneider LS8-18	8198	D-0280	12.98	R J Rebbeck	Dunstable	7. 5.08
JMS	4629	R23	Schleicher ASK 21	21212	RAFGGA 521	11.98	RAFGSA Kestrel Gliding Club	RAF Odiham	28. 9.08
G-CJMT	4630	301	Rolladen-Schneider LS8-18	8223		2.99	D P and K M Draper	Lasham	28. 9.08
G-CJMU	4631	JMU	Rolladen-Schneider LS8-18	8246		3.99	J G Guy	Portmoak	27. 2.08

Reg	No	Trigraph	Type	c/n	Prev ID	Date	Owner	Location	Date2
G-CJMV	4632	EW	Schempp-Hirth Nimbus-2C	179	D-6738	1.99	K R Walton and G Tucker	Lee-on-Solent	10. 3.08
G-CJMW	4633	R61	Schleicher ASK 13	13688AB	RAFGGA R61 RAFGGA 567	1.99	RAFGSA Bannerdown Gliding Club	RAF Keevil	11. 4.08
JMX	4634	JMX	Schleicher ASK 13	13107	RAFGSA R86 RAFGGA 386	2.99	Shalbourne Soaring Society	Rivar Hill	22. 3.08
G-CJMY	4635	JMY	SZD-51-1 Junior	W-959	OO-ZRH	3.99	Highland Gliding Club	Easterton	27. 8.08
G-CJMZ	4636	R37	Schleicher ASK 13	13099	RAFGSA R37 RAFGGA 378	1.99	RAFGSA Bannerdown Gliding Club	RAF Keevil	27. 4.08
JNA	4637	JNA	Grob G102 Astir CS Jeans	2160	D-4556	2.99	Shenington Gliding Club	Edgehill	5. 6.08
JNB	4638	D1	Rolladen-Schneider LS8-18	8227		2.99	P M Shelton	Husbands Bosworth	3. 6.08
G-CJNE	4641	W10	Schempp-Hirth Discus-2a	18	D-4499	2. 3.99	R Priest	Wycombe Air Park	19. 4.08
JNF	4642	80	Schempp-Hirth Discus-2a	12		2.99	A J Davis	Nympsfield	29. 4.08
G-CJNG	4643	JNG	Glasflügel Standard Libelle 201B	6	SE-TFU	3.99	C A Willson	Rivar Hill	12. 8.08
G-CJNJ	4645	198	Rolladen-Schneider LS8-18	8226		2.99	A B Laws	Crowland	15. 3.08
JNK	4646	676	Rolladen-Schneider LS8-18	8244		2.99	Wyvern Gliding Club	Trenchard Lines, Upavon	21. 4.08
JNL	4647	DR7	Schempp-Hirth Janus	25	HB-1313	2.99	D M Ruttle	Strubby	29. 4.04
			(Crashed on field landing near Brimham Rocks, North Yorkshire 1. 8.03; wreck to New Zealand for rebuild)						
JNM	4648	P4	Rolladen-Schneider LS8-18	8232	(BGA 4617) D-8217	3.99	P Onn	Dunstable	28. 3.08
G-CJNN	4649	JNN	Schleicher K 8B	8744	D-8583	3.99	Buckminster Gliding Club	Saltby	28. 9.08
G-CJNP	4650	EF	Rolladen-Schneider LS6-b	6109	D-5853	20. 7.03	P S Fink	Lasham	21. 4.08
G-CJNO	4651	441	Glaser-Dirks DG-300 Elan	3E341	SE-UHO	30. 4.99	R Friend	Husbands Bosworth	24. 4.08
G-CJNR	4652	JNR	Glasflügel Mosquito B	159	D-5908	3.99	I H Agutter and B R Smith	Wormingford	2. 3.08
G-CJNT	4654	SC	Schleicher ASW 19B	19371	D-2233	4.99	M D Borrowdale	Lasham	18. 3.08
G-LLLL	4657	L4	Rolladen-Schneider LS8-18	8217		3.99	P C Fritche	Parham	28. 9.08
G-CJNX	4658	JNX	LET L-13A Blanik	827408	OK-2712	5.99	Vectis Gliding Club	Bembridge	28. 9.08
JNY	4659	661	Schempp-Hirth Discus-2b	17	D-4498	3.99	J R W Kronfeld	Lasham	19. 9.08
			(Carries "BGA 4569" on fin)						
G-CJNZ	4660	813	Glaser-Dirks DG-100	70	(D-7324) HB-1324	3.99	R Jones and T Tordoff	Rufforth	4. 8.08
G-CJPA	4661	HB1	Schempp-Hirth Duo Discus	201		3.99	The Gliding Centre	Husbands Bosworth	20. 3.08
JPC	4663	JPC	Schleicher ASK 13	13256	RAFGSA R51	31. 3.99	Shalbourne Soaring Society	Rivar Hill	16. 7.08
G-CVZT	4664	V2T	Schempp-Hirth Ventus-2cT	39/129		3.99	M W Conboy and C D Sterritt	Lasham	17. 1.08
JPF	4666	PF	Glaser-Dirks DG-100	22	D-3735	5.99	D C W Sanders	Parham	9. 9.08
G-CJPH	4668	CB	Rolladen-Schneider LS8-18	8259		7.99	J P Ben-David	Lasham	6. 4.08
JPJ	4669	JPJ	Grob G104 Speed Astir IIB	4089	OE-5352	4.99	R J Maisonpierre	Rougham	23. 5.08
JPK	4670	-	Slingsby T.34A Sky	672	RAFGSA 876 XA876, G-672	5.99	J Tournier	Wycombe Air Park	2. 6.07
G-CJPL	4671	RW	Rolladen-Schneider LS8-18	8249	D-2562	4.99	I A Reekie	Dunstable	28. 8.08
JPM	4672	JPM	Grob G102 Astir CS Jeans	2209	D-3825	5.99	J Thorpe	Camphill	11. 4.08
G-CJPP	4674	388	Schempp-Hirth Discus b	206	AGA 4	4.99	Scottish Gliding Union	Portmoak	28. 9.08
G-CJPO	4675	R32	Schleicher ASK 18	18002	RAFGSA R32 RAFGGA 213, D-3978	5.99	RAFGSA Bannerdown Gliding Club	RAF Keevil	16. 3.08
G-CJPR	4676	161	Rolladen-Schneider LS8-18	8245		4.99	D M Byass & J A McCoshim	Wycombe Air Park	5. 4.08
G-CJPS	4677	CL	Schleicher ASW 27	27108		5.99	P T and E W Healy	Lasham	28. 9.08
G-CJPT	4678	JPT	Schleicher ASW 27	27113		10.99	R C and W Willis-Fleming	North Hill	16. 4.08
G-TLTL	4679	TL2	Schempp-Hirth Discus CS	257CS		4.99	E K Armitage	Camphill	27. 2.08
G-CJPV	4680	R88	Schleicher ASK 13	13312	RAFGSA R88 RAFGSA 186	5.99	RAFGSA Crusaders Gliding Club	Kingsfield, Cyprus	5. 6.08
JPW	4681	JPW	Glaser-Dirks DG-200	2-48	D-2201	5.99	J R Parr	Burn	10. 8.08
G-CJPX	4682	JPX	Schleicher ASW 15	15160	D-0823	5.99	P F Daly and R Hayden	Upwood	14. 4.08
G-CJPY	4683	R59	Schleicher ASK 13	13653AB	RAFGSA R59 RAFGGA 509	5.99	RAFGSA Cranwell Gliding Club	RAF Cranwell	5. 1.08
G-CJPZ	4684	R56	Schleicher ASK 18	18027	RAFGSA R56 RAFGGA 563	4.99	RAFGSA Cranwell Gliding Club	RAF Cranwell	19. 1.08
G-CJOA	4685	547	Schempp-Hirth Discus b	265	BGA 4535 RAFGGA 547, RAFGGA 500	4.99	Bannerdown Gliding Club	RAF Keevil	28. 9.08
JQB	4686	JQB	Schleicher K 8B	8880	RAFGSA R98 RAFGGA 398	5.99	T R Edwards	Edgehill	19. 5.08
G-CJOC	4687		Schempp-Hirth Discus bT	127/488	D-KITT	28.5.99	D S Cooper and Partners	Wycombe Air Park	2.12.07
			(Rebuilt with new fuselage after accident 25. 6.99 - see BGA 4838)						
G-CJOD	4688	R3	Rolladen-Schneider LS8-18	8224		5.99	RAFGSA Bannerdown Gliding Club	RAF Keevil	28. 9.08
JQE	4689	JQE	Schempp-Hirth Standard Cirrus	25	OO-ZRS, D-0483	6.99	R J Nunn	Wormingford	19. 4.08
G-CEYC	4690	5GC	DG Flugzeugbau DG-505 Elan Orion	5E194X38	S5-7516	6.99	Scottish Gliding Union	Portmoak	28. 2.08
G-CJOG	4691	P50	Grob G103A Twin II Acro	33964-K-197	RAFGSA R50	5.99	R G Tait and Partners	Easterton	25. 5.08
JQH	4692	JQH	Sportine Aviacija LAK-12	6188		24. 5.99	D J Lee	Pocklington	9. 8.07
G-CJOJ	4693	JOJ	Schleicher K 8B	8795	RAFGSA R47 BGA 1564	28. 5.99	P W Burgess	Seighford	27. 5.08
G-CEUN	4694	506	Schempp-Hirth Discus CS	075CS	RAFGGA 501	5.99	RAFGSA Chilterns Gliding Centre	RAF Halton	15. 1.08
G-CEUG	4696	Z9	Schleicher ASW 27	27114		6.99	R J Smith	Wycombe Air Park	28. 9.08
JQN	4697	R67	Grob G102 Astir CS 77	1634	RAFGSA R67 RAFGSA 547	6.99	RAFGSA Fulmar Gliding Club	Easterton	25. 9.08
JOP	4698	eb	Centrair 101A Pégase	101066	F-CFQY	6.99	R H Moss	Nympsfield	5. 4.08
G-CJOO	4699	185	Schempp-Hirth Duo Discus	227		3.00	KG Reid and Partners	Rivar Hill	10. 3.08
G-CJOR	4700	JOR	Schempp-Hirth Ventus-2cT	49/152		10.99	N A MacLean and A M George	Lasham	28. 9.08
G-CJOS	4701	JQS	Schempp-Hirth Standard Cirrus	251G	D-1147	6.99	R K Arkley and Partners	Milfield	7. 7.08
JQT	4702	JQT	Grob G102 Astir CS Jeans	2076	D-7589	6.99	East Sussex Gliding Club	Ringmer	4. 4.07
							(Crashed on undershoot, Ringmer 31. 3.07)		
G-CJOU	4704	Z12	Schleicher ASW 27	27112		7.99	J W White	Wycombe Air Park	22. 9.08
G-CJOW	4705	GS	Schempp-Hirth Cirrus 18	47	D-0186	7.99	G Smith and G Stilgoe	Parham	19. 1.08
G-CJOX	4706	JOX	Schleicher ASK 21	21702		9.99	Southdown Gliding Club	Parham	28. 9.08
JQY	4707	R92	Slingsby T.21B Sedbergh	666	RAFGSA R92 NEJSGSA 4, WG499	6.99	RAFGSA Crusaders Gliding Club	Kingsfield, Cyprus	31. 8.08

JQZ	4708	JQZ	Schleicher K 8B	8854	RAFGSA R42 RAFGSA 323	7.99	Derbyshire & Lancashire Gliding Club	Camphill	8. 8.08
G-CJRA	4709	253	Rolladen-Schneider LS8-18	8263		24.7.99	J Williams	Kirton-in-Lindsey	28. 9.08
G-CJRB	4710	S33	Schleicher ASW 19B	19227	D-2713	7.99	J W Baxter	Lasham	12. 3.07
G-CJRC	4711	JRC	Glaser-Dirks DG-300 Elan	3E20	HB-1718	8.99	P J Sillett	Tibenham	3.11.07
JRD	4712	JRD	Grob G102 Astir CS	1487	RAFGGA 540, D-4791	27.6.99	A Hadwin	(Reading)	13. 9.08
G-CJRE	4713	RS	Schleicher ASW 15	15048	LN-GGL OH-391, OH-RWA	8.99	R A Starling	Darlton	28. 9.08
G-CJRF	4714	JRF	SZD-50-3 Puchacz	B-1395	OO-ZTX D-8213, SP-3285	8.99	Wolds Gliding Club	Pocklington	11. 8.08
G-CJRG	4715	JRG	Schempp-Hirth Standard Cirrus	146	D-0297	8.99	DP and K M Draper	Lasham	28. 9.08
G-CJRH	4716	T27	Schleicher ASW 27	27118		8.99	P C Jarvis and C Jackson	Lasham	28. 9.08
G-CJRJ	4717	JRJ	SZD-50-3 Puchacz	503199327		8.99	Bidford Gliding Centre	Bidford	18. 7.08
JRK	4718	618	Rolladen-Schneider LS8-18	8267		9.99	D King	Snitterfield	24. 9.08
G-CJRL	4719	JRL	Glaser-Dirks DG-101G Elan	E185G151	D-1246	2.00	P Lazenby	Aston Down	20. 2.08
JRM	4720	212	Grob G102 Astir CS	1332	BGA 4314 AGA 6	21.9.99	Anglia Gliding Club	AAC Wattisham	6. 4.08
JRN	4721	PT	Glaser-Dirks DG-202/17C	2-118CL04	D-7267	1.10.99	T G Roberts (Cancelled 22. 1.08)	Lasham	6. 9.08
JRP	4722	JRP	Grob G102 Astir CS Jeans	2244	D-5951	9.99	Borders Gliding Club	Milfield	30.10.07
JRQ	4723	PM3	Pfenninger-Markwalder Elfe PM3	001	N6351U N63514, HB-526	11.99	G McLean	Lleweni Parc	23. 8.08
G-CJRR	4724	LA	Schempp-Hirth Discus bT	50/367	PH-1087 D-KBHM	3.00	M W Cater and J P Walker	Husbands Bosworth	17. 5.08
G-DKBW	4725	AT	Valentin Mistral-C	MC021/79	D-4921	3.00	A Towse	Rattlesden	9. 4.08
G-CJRT	4726	JRT	Schempp-Hirth Standard Cirrus	99	D-0734	10.99	J A Tipler	Husbands Bosworth	28. 9.08
G-CJRU	4727	SK	Schleicher ASW 24	24168	D-7085	1.00	S A Kerby	Snitterfield	28. 9.08
JRV	4728	B19	Schleicher ASW 19B	19233	D-2644	10.99	M Roome	Lasham	21. 1.08
G-NUGC	4729	JRW	Grob G103A Twin II Acro	34040-K-271	RAFGSA R15 RAFGGA 556	10.99	Nottingham University Gliding Club	RAF Cranwell	17. 2.08
JRX	4730	R41	Schleicher ASK 13	13375	RAFGSA R41 RAFGSA 241	10.99	RAFGSA Chilterns Gliding Centre	RAF Halton	24. 5.08
JRZ	4732		Colditz Cock replica (Under construction M Francis)	-		R	R M Francis	Camphill	
JSB	4734	UWE	Rolladen-Schneider LS4	4424	D-4541	2.00	H Vare	Speyer, Germany	16. 2.08
JSC	4735	44	Schempp-Hirth Nimbus-3DT	10	F-CFUE F-WFUE, D-KFUE	11.99	M J Aldridge (Crashed Lasham 11. 8.07)	Rougham	6. 3.08
G-CJSD	4736	R77	Grob G102 Astir CS	1133	RAFGSA R77 D-4177	2.00	RAFGSA Fenland Gliding Club	RAF Marham	16. 2.08
G-CJSE	4737	296	Schempp-Hirth Discus b	365	PH-918	3.00	Imperial College Gliding Club	Lasham	9. 3.08
G-LSIF	4738	414	Rolladen-Schneider LS1-f	383	LN-GGE SE-TOU	3.00	R C Godden	Wormingford	1. 7.08
G-CJSG	4739	36	Schleicher Ka 6E	4248	D-0090	2.00	A J Emck	Lasham	17. 1.07
JSH	4740	SH9	Grob G102 Club Astir IIIB	5504CB	D-6470	11.99	Surrey & Hants Gliding Club	Lasham	12. 4.08
G-CJSJ	4741	7X	Rolladen-Schneider LS7-WL	7058	D-5774	10.99	S P Woolcock	Gransden Lodge	28. 9.08
G-CJSK	4742	JSK	Grob G102 Astir CS	1521	D-7455	11.99	P T Pearce and J D Hanton	Brentor	16. 3.08
G-CJSL	4743	JSL	Schempp-Hirth Ventus cT	121/395	D-KIFL	11.99	P Jackson and R H Gisby	Bidford	30.12.07
JSN	4745	JSN	Schleicher K 8B	8916	RAFGSA R45 RAFGSA 245	11.99	Cotswold Gliding Club	Aston Down	13.10.08
JSP	4746	JSP	Slingsby T.31B (Restoration using wings of XE798)	1189	BGA 2724 XN250	4.7.04	R Wulfers (Carries "BGA 4756" which is now G-CJSZ)	Deelen, Netherlands	4. 5.08
JSQ	4747	F1	Rolladen-Schneider LS8-b	8301	D-KKAF	5.00	I Mountain	RAF Cranwell	19.11.08
JSR	4748	JSR	SZD-50-3 Puchacz	B-1386	OY-XRV SP-3283	3.00	Bidford Gliding Centre (Spun in Bidford 7.7.07)	Bidford	7. 3.08
G-CJSS	4749	JB	Schleicher ASW 27B	27121		12.99	J H Belk	Dunstable	28. 2.08
G-CJST	4750	X5	Rolladen-Schneider LS1-c	86	OO-ZPA, D-0766	1.00	M W Hands	Saltby	5. 4.08
G-CJSU	4751	95	Rolladen-Schneider LS8-18	8297	D-0543	3.00	J G Bell	Lasham	17. 1.08
JSV	4752	R80	Schleicher ASK 13	13127	RAFGSA R80 BGA 1509	1.00	RAFGSA Chilterns Gliding Centre	RAF Halton	21. 9.08
G-CJSW	4753	IH4	Rolladen-Schneider LS4-a	4262	ZS-GOP	10.00	European Soaring Club	Ontur, Spain	28. 9.08
JSX	4754	JSX	AMS-Flight DG-505 Elan Orion	5E200X44		5.00	Oxford Gliding Club	RAF Weston-on-the-Green	5. 6.08
G-CJSZ	4756	JSZ	Schleicher ASK 18	18012	D-6878	4.00	C J N Weston (See BGA 4746)	Challock	1. 5.08
JTA	4757	-	Colditz Cock rep (Built by Southdown Aero Services and John Lee)	SA3		1.00	Norfolk & Suffolk Aviation Museum	Flixton	20. 2.08
G-CJTB	4758	V17	Schleicher ASW 24	24017	D-3465	2.00	M E Knell and Partners	RAF Keevil	28. 9.08
JTC	4759	JTC	Glaser-Dirks DG-100G	84G5	(BGA 4744) HB-1335	25.5.00	A Burger	(Neustadt, Germany)	5. 7.05
JTE	4761	JTE	Schempp-Hirth Standard Cirrus	470G	D-3718	2.00	P W Symonds	Ringmer	6. 4.08
JTF	4762	Z3	Schleicher ASW 27B	27125		3.00	T J Scott	Wycombe Air Park	9. 4.08
JTG	4763	D55	SZD-55-1	551197100	N4364R	13.3.00	A Kobus (Cancelled 10.7.07 to N95AK)	(US)	24. 4.08
G-CJTH	4764	L24	Schleicher ASW 24	24218	D-7681	3.00	R J Lodge	Dunstable	9. 4.08
G-CJTJ	4765	JTJ	Schempp-Hirth Mini Nimbus B	73	D-7620	4.3.00	A Richards	Culdrose	6. 4.08
G-CJTK	4766	JTK	AMS-Flight DG-303 Elan Acro	3E487A28		11.5.00	A Jorgensen	Wycombe Air Park	6. 3.08
JTL	4767	352	Rolladen-Schneider LS8-18	8317		26.3.00	L S Hood	Wycombe Air Park	13. 6.08
G-CJTM	4768	418	Rolladen-Schneider LS8-18	8268		16.2.00	A D Holmes	Nympsfield	26. 2.08
G-CJTN	4769	E5	Glaser-Dirks DG-300 Elan	3E19	HB-1717	3.00	I P McKavney	Nympsfield	24. 2.08
G-CJTP	4770	JTP	Schleicher ASW 20L	20569	D-4688	3.00	C A Sheldon	Pocklington	4. 5.08
G-CJTO	4771	JTO	Glasflügel Mosquito	88	OO-ZYL	4.00	I Hamilton and Partners	Chipping	20. 4.08
G-CJTR	4772	D-53	Rolladen-Schneider LS7	7104	D-5309	3.00	G W Howarth and Partners	RAF Halton	14. 1.08
JTS	4773	JTS	Schempp-Hirth Cirrus VTC	108	S5-3059 SL-3059, YU-4200	3.00	S M N Skinner	Kenley	15. 7.08
G-CJTU	4775	377	Schempp-Hirth Duo Discus T	4/234		3.00	R Starmer (377 Syndicate)	Bidford	30. 3.08

G-HAAH	4776	V66	Schempp-Hirth Ventus-2cT	52/173		3.00	C R Lewis and Partners	Lasham	9. 1.08
JTW	4777	AV8	Glasflügel Mosquito B	199	F-CELX	4.00	M Wright	Tibenham	4. 4.08
JTX	4778	JTX	Start+Flug H101 Salto	47	D-9260	3.00	C Schneeberger	Maxdorf, Germany	4. 1.08
G-CJTY	4779	JTY	Rolladen-Schneider LS8-a	8102	SE-USA	4.00	BBC Gliding Group	Wycombe Air Park	28. 9.08
JUB	4782	894	Schempp-Hirth Discus CS	268CS		4.00	D F Wass	Darlton	6. 9.08
G-XWON	4783	X1	Rolladen-Schneider LS8-18	8305		4.00	S M Godleman and P K Carpenter	Challock	1. 4.08
G-GZIP	4784	Z19	Rolladen-Schneider LS8-18	8309		3.00	D S Haughton	Long Mynd	4. 3.08
G-CJUE	4785	X15	Rolladen-Schneider LS8-18	8295		3.00	G Goudie and S Waterfall	Gransden Lodge	28. 9.08
JUF	4786	46	Schempp-Hirth Ventus-2cT	53/174		4.00	M H Pope	Bidford	28. 9.08
JUG	4787	FE	Issoire E78 Silene	9	F-CFED	7.00	J Sanders	Ringmer	24. 9.08
JUH	4788	Z2	Schleicher ASW 27B	27129		4.00	B Flewett	Wycombe Air Park	28. 9.08
JUJ	4789	Z1	Schleicher ASW 27B	27127		4.00	P M Wells	Wycombe Air Park	22. 9.08
JUK	4790	554	Grob G102 Astir CS	1430	PH-552	10. 6.00	P G Freer	Wycombe Air Park	16. 4.08
G-LIDY	4791	621	Schleicher ASW 27B	27132		4.00	T Stuart	Nympsfield	28. 9.08
G-CJUM	4792	2UP	Schempp-Hirth Duo Discus T	5/243		4.00	B A Bateson and Partners	Parham	25. 3.08
JUN	4793	M19	Schleicher ASW 19B	19096	D-3844	8. 5.00	M P Roberts	Gransden Lodge	17. 5.08
G-CJUP	4794	183	Schempp-Hirth Discus-2b	60		5.00	P J Ward	Aston Down	29. 3.08
G-WONE	4795	W1	Schempp-Hirth Ventus-2cT	55/179		5.00	J P Wright	Lasham	29. 9.08
JUR	4796	JUR	Valentin Mistral-C	MC042/81	HB-1596	5.00	Essex Gliding Club	Ridgewell	18. 5.08
G-CJUS	4797	JUS	Grob G102 Astir CS	1403	(BGA 4774) D-4269	5.00	East Sussex Gliding Club	Ringmer	25. 5.08
G-CJUU	4799	JUU	Schempp-Hirth Standard Cirrus	450	PH-500	5.00	H R Fraser	Milfield	14. 5.08
G-CJUV	4800	SH2	Schempp-Hirth Discus b	551	D-8257	6.00	Surrey & Hants Gliding Club	Lasham	29. 3.08
JUW	4801	4T	Schleicher ASW 19B	19074	D-4476	5.00	P D Griffiths and Partners	RAF Keevil	4. 8.08
JUX	4802	CD1	AviaStroitel AC-4c	051		5.00	R J Walton	Saltby	9. 2.08
JUY	4803	JUY	Valentin Mistral-C	MC041/81	D-4941	25. 5.00	M S F Wood	Lee-on-Solent	5. 3.08
			(Overshot landing Talgarth 27. 3.07)						
G-CJUZ	4804	M80	Schleicher ASW 19B	19146	D-7932	6.00	D Heaton	Seighford	28. 9.08
G-CJVA	4805	JVA	Schempp-Hirth Ventus-2cT	66/203		8. 2.01	M S Armstrong	Camphill	28. 9.08
G-CJVB	4806	DF	Schempp-Hirth Discus bT	111/462	D-KUNK	5.00	C J Edwards	Nympsfield	28. 9.08
G-CJVC	4807	JVC	SZD-51-1 Junior	B-1799	SP-3434	6.00	York Gliding Centre	Rufforth	28. 9.08
G-CJVE	4809	JVE	Eiriavion PIK-20D-78	20631	OY-XJC	6.00	S R Wilkinson	Kirton-in-Lindsey	1. 5.08
JVF	4810	JH1	Schempp-Hirth Discus CS	271CS		6.00	J Hodgson	Wormingford	5. 6.08
JVG	4811	420	Schempp-Hirth Discus bT	121/477	D-KSOP	6.00	D J Tagg	Lasham	15. 6.08
G-CJVJ	4813	JS	Sportine Aviacija LAK-17A	108		6.00	J A Sutton	Milfield	6. 3.08
G-LSCP	4814	CP	Rolladen-Schneider LS6-c18	6236	D-6417	1. 7.00	M F Collins and L G Blows	Parham	4. 8.08
G-CJVL	4815	JVL	Glaser-Dirks DG-300 Elan	3E158	HB-1833	7.00	A T Vidion and A Griffiths	Tibenham	11. 1.08
G-CJVM	4816	GP	Schleicher ASW 27B	27138		6.00	G KPayne	Dunstable	28. 9.08
G-CJVP	4818	D8	Glaser-Dirks DG-200	2-1	D-8200	7.00	M S Howey and S Leadbeater	Burn	1. 4.08
JVQ	4819	68	Schleicher ASW 27B	27136		7.00	B L Cooper	Wycombe Air Park	20. 9.08
JVR	4820	540	Schempp-Hirth Discus-2b	72		10. 7.00	M F Evans	Lasham	6. 7.08
G-CJVS	4821	S1	Schleicher ASW 28	28003	D-4008	9.00	S J Kelman	Gransden Lodge	28. 9.08
G-CJED	4822	JED	Schempp-Hirth Nimbus-3/25.5	37	D-3176	7.00	J R Edyvean	Bicester	23. 5.08
G-CJVU	4823	C74	Lanaverre CS11/75L Std Cirrus	28	F-CEVT	7.12.00	C R Coates and Partners	Snitterfield	14. 1.08
JVV	4824	J50	Schempp-Hirth Janus C	176	D-4150	8.00	G R Jenkins	Lasham	16. 4.08
G-CJVW	4825	15A	Schleicher ASW 15	15042	HB-992	20. 2.01	J M Taylor	Dunstable	12.10.07
G-CJVX	4826	988	Schempp-Hirth Discus CS	087CS	D-0263	12. 8.00	M P Kemp and Partners	Challock	26. 3.08
JVY	4827	F6	Schempp-Hirth Discus b	175	RAFSGA R6	8.00	M R Garwood	Husbands Bosworth	29. 9.08
G-CJVZ	4828	JVZ	Schleicher ASK 21	21721		12.00	Yorkshire Gliding Club "Sharpe's Classique"	Sutton Bank	28. 9.08
G-CJWA	4829	C6	Schleicher ASW 28	28005		10.00	M J Taylor and P R Porter	Lyveden	28. 9.08
G-CJWB	4830	JWB	Schleicher ASK 13	13671AB	D-1066	12.00	East Sussex Gliding Club	Ringmer	8. 5.08
G-THRM	4831	900	Schleicher ASW 27B	27142		10.00	C G Starkey	Lasham	28.12.07
G-CJWD	4832	JWD	Schleicher ASK 21	21724		16. 2.01	London Gliding Club	Dunstable	27. 3.08
JWE	4833	JWE	Slingsby T.21B	1159	XN155	1. 7.00	M Selss	Bad Tolz, Germany	19. 6.08
JWF	4834	S27	Schleicher ASW 27B	27144		11.00	B A Fairston	Husbands Bosworth	30. 9.08
G-CJWG	4835	880	Schempp-Hirth Nimbus-3DT	11	D-KMGD	11. 2.01	T P Browning and Partners	Lasham	28. 9.08
G-CTWO	4836	C2	Schempp-Hirth Standard Cirrus	256	SE-TMZ	14. 6.01	R J Griffin	Edgehill	28. 9.08
G-CJWJ	4837	R38	Schleicher ASK 13	13599	RAFSGA R38 RAFSGA R3	11.00	RAFSGA Wrekin Gliding Club	RAF Cosford	13. 1.08
G-CJWK	4838	722	Schempp-Hirth Discus bT	453/1		11.00	R Thompson and Partners	Nympsfield	14. 2.08
			(Composite rebuild including parts from BGA 4687 [127/488] and BGA 3961 [106/453])						
JWL	4839		Schempp-Hirth Ventus b/16.6	125	D-6667	11.00	S Weber (To D-6667 2007)	Dettingen,Germany	29.10.07
G-CJWM	4840	T12	Grob G103 Twin II	3536	D-8730	11.00	Norfolk Gliding Club	Tibenham	17. 4.08
JWN	4841	UY	Rolladen-Schneider LS4-a	4728	D-7008	24. 2.01	D Bartek	Dannstadt, Germany	16. 2.08
JWP	4842		Bölkow Phoebus B1	875	D-0128	15. 7.02	P Sheard	Lasham	5. 8.04
G-TWOA	4843	310	Schempp-Hirth Discus-2a	82		11.00	A J McNamara	Wycombe Air Park	28. 9.08
G-CJWR	4844	NJ1	Grob G102 Astir CS	1271	D-7366	1.01	G J Hunter and Partners	Portmoak	20. 1.08
JWS	4845	JWS	Schleicher ASW 15B	15098S	D-4656	14. 4.01	B Pridgeon	Kirton-in-Lindsey	3. 7.08
G-CJWT	4846	JWT	Glaser-Dirks DG-200	2-42	D-6560 D-6660	11.00	K R Nash	Kingston Deverill	28. 9.08
JWU	4847	GA	Schempp-Hirth Ventus bT	19/159	ZS-GOW	10.00	G Tabbner	Wycombe Air Park	13. 9.08
G-CJWV	4848	S60	Glasflügel Standard Libelle 201B	411	OY-XBG	14. 3.01	A Beatty	Challock	28. 9.08
G-CJWX	4850	63	Schempp-Hirth Ventus-2cT	63/198		20.12.00	S G Olender	Santo Tome del Puerto, Spain	28. 9.08
G-CJWZ	4852	W22	Schleicher ASW 22	22037	D-3422	22. 1.01	D Prosolek	Saltby	7.12.07
G-CJXA	4853	Y44	Schempp-Hirth Nimbus-3DT	9	D-KKYY D-4444	3. 2.01	B C Morris and Partners	Lasham	17. 2.08
G-CJXB	4854	JXB	Centrair 201B Marianne	201015	F-CGMN	27. 1.01	C A Sheldon and Partners	Pocklington	27. 3.08
G-CJXC	4855	JXC	Wassmer WA28 Espadon	102	F-CDZV	27. 3.01	A P Montague	Nympsfield	5. 6.08
JXD	4856	WB961	Slingsby T.21B	622	WB961	20. 1.01	F Brune	Eudenbach, Germany	26. 6.06
JXE	4857	JXE	SZD-22C Mucha Standard	F-717	SP-2330	12. 8.01	C E Harwood	Wormingford	11. 6.05
G-CJXG	4859	W5	Eiriavion PIK-20D-78	20660	PH-670	23. 2.01	S Ingason and Partners	Lee-on-Solent	21. 4.08
JXH	4860	DH2	Schleicher ASW 20L	20067	D-7657	17. 2.01	D Heath	Edgehill	2. 5.05
JXJ	4861	W7	Schleicher ASW 28	28012		29. 1.01	E W Johnston	Dunstable	26. 3.07

JXK	4862	W3	Schempp-Hirth Ventus bT	49/247	D-KLOE	25. 1.01	P Turner	Halesland	25. 6.08
G-CJXL	4863	SO1	Schempp-Hirth Discus CS	278CS		5. 4.01	M J Hasluck and J Hall	Parham	23. 1.08
G-CJXM	4864	JXM	Schleicher ASK 13	13542	RAFGSA R34	25. 2.01	Windrushers Gliding Club	Bicester	23. 3.08
					F-CERF				
G-CJXN	4865	Z35	Centrair 201B Marianne	201A035	F-CBLI	21. 2.01	R D Trussell	(Ilkeston)	24. 3.08
G-CJXP	4866	JXP	Glaser-Dirks DG-100	18	PH-520	16. 5.01	R M Wootten	Eyres Field	19. 3.08
G-CJXR	4868	DM	Schempp-Hirth Discus b	540	D-9152	8. 4.01	Cambridge Gliding Club	Gransden Lodge	25. 3.08
JXS	4869	JXS	Schleicher K 8B	8778	RAFGSA R95	7. 3.04	Stratford on Avon Gliding Club	Snitterfield	20. 3.08
					RAFGSA 395				
G-CJXT	4870	CT	Schleicher ASW 24B	24233	D-6706	9. 3.01	P McAuley	Snitterfield	10.12.07
JXU	4871	646	Rolladen-Schneider LS8-18	8354		10. 3.01	C J Alldis	Long Mynd	3. 5.08
G-CJXW	4873	871	Schempp-Hirth Duo Discus T	7/250	D-KOZX	11. 5.01	C Bainbridge	Wormingford	7. 6.08
G-CJXX	4874	JXX	Pilatus B4-PC11AF	013	HB-1112	28. 5.01	N H Buckenham	Rattlesden	6. 6.08
JXY	4875	JXY	Neukom Elfe S4A	68	HB-1267	29. 5.01	D V Wilson	Ringmer	20. 4.08
G-CJXZ	4876	27B	Schleicher ASW 27B	27152		16. 3.01	P R H Starey	Wycombe Air Park	28. 9.08
JYA	4877	WB988	Slingsby T.21B	MHL.015	WB988	31. 3.01	C Bravo	Santo Tome del Puerto, Spain	8. 3.08
G-ONEZ	4878	1Z	Glaser-Dirks DG-202/17	2-143/1738	D-1086	1. 5.01	R M Nuza (1Z Syndicate)	Rufforth	21. 5.08
G-CJYC	4880	JYC	Grob G102 Astir CS	1429	RAFGSA R19	9. 4.01	R A Christie	Easterton	4.11.07
					RAFGSA 742, D-7425				
G-CJYD	4881	T6	Schleicher ASW 27B	27155		25. 3.01	J E Gatfield	Wycombe Air Park	28. 9.08
G-CJYE	4882	JYE	Schleicher ASK 13	13191	D-0347	11. 4.01	North Wales Gliding Club	Llantisilio	15. 5.08
G-CJYF	4883	N55	Schempp-Hirth Discus CS	281CS		11. 4.01	R D Stroud	Wycombe Air Park	17. 3.08
JYG	4884	OK-0833	Letov LF-107 Lunak	49	OK-0833	21. 9.02	M Launer	Rossfeld, Germany	17. 9.08
G-VTUS	4886	2	Schempp-Hirth Ventus-2cT	64/199		1. 5.01	P G Myers and Partners	Chipping	2. 4.08
JYL	4888		Sportine Aviacija LAK-12	6197	(Slovenia)	9. 5.01	A Camerotto	Udine, Italy	27. 6.08
					ROSTO				
G-CJYN	4890	RB1	Schempp-Hirth Discus-2b	94		9. 5.01	R Brigliadori	Alzate Brianza, Italy	27. 6.08
G-CJYP	4891	B12	Grob G102 Club Astir II	5018C	D-8743	19. 5.01	Norfolk Gliding Club	Tibenham	25. 9.08
JYQ	4892	485	Glaser-Dirks DG-101G Elan	E181G147	D-1485	15. 6.02	A M Booth	Wormingford	26. 8.08
JYR	4893	B20	Schempp-Hirth Duo Discus T	16/267	D-KOZX	3. 7.01	R Starmer	Bidford	4. 5.08
G-CJYS	4894	878	Schempp-Hirth Mini Nimbus C	106	HB-1437	6. 6.01	A Jenkins	Shobdon	5. 7.08
G-XJON	4895	E4	Schempp-Hirth Ventus-2b	114	(BGA 4885)	15. 6.01	J C Bastin	Lasham	1. 3.08
G-CJYU	4896	R11	Schempp-Hirth Ventus-2cT	70/216		15. 6.01	RAFGSA Chilterns Gliding Centre	RAF Halton	3. 4.08
JYV	4897	JYV	Schleicher K 8B	133	D-8395	18. 6.01	European Soaring Club	Le Blanc, France	4. 7.04
JYW	4898	JYW	Schleicher K 8B	8432A	D-5682	18. 6.01	European Soaring Club	Le Blanc, France	4. 7.04
JYX	4899	JYX	Rolladen-Schneider LS3-17	3289	D-3517	18. 6.01	B Spreckley	Ontur, Spain	16. 6.08
G-CJZB	4903	JZB	AMS-Flight DG-505 Elan Orion			28. 7.01	J I May and Partners	Bicester	28. 9.08
				5E223X61					
G-WDGC	4904	M9	Rolladen-Schneider LS8-18	8395		11. 3.02	W D G Chappel	(Pewsey)	21. 3.08
JZD	4905	JZD	Dittmar Condor IV	018	(D-0125)	7. 3.02	J Kruse	Uetersen, Germany	16. 7.06
					LV-DHV				
G-CJZE	4906	JZE	Schleicher ASK 13	13433	OY-XPJ	11.11.01	Needwood Forest Gliding Club	Cross Hayes	16. 3.08
					D-2125				
G-CJZG	4908	SM	Schempp-Hirth Discus bT	9/272	D-KISM	9. 7.01	R Acreman	North Hill	2. 5.08
G-CJZH	4909	JZH	Schleicher ASW 20CL	20754	D-5932	10. 7.01	C P Gibson	Lasham	28. 9.08
G-CJZK	4911	JZK	AMS-Flight DG-505 Elan Orion			1. 9.01	Devon & Somerset Gliding Club	North Hill	29. 7.08
				5E225X63					
G-CJZL	4912	BS	Schempp-Hirth Mini Nimbus B	92	HB-1453	25. 8.01	S J Aldridge	Saltby	16. 5.08
G-CJZM	4913	LE	Schempp-Hirth Ventus-2ax	117		24. 8.01	M D Wells	Nympsfield	28. 9.08
G-CJZN	4914	JZN	Schleicher ASW 28	28038		19.12.01	P J Coward	Husbands Bosworth	8.12.07
JZP	4915	JZP	Marganski Swift S-1	119	F-CIAB	26. 9.01	C Cain	Lasham	6.8.07
G-IICT	4921	V2C	Schempp-Hirth Ventus-2cT	72/225		14. 9.01	P McLean	RAF Marham	10. 6.08
G-CJZX	4923	P10	Schleicher ASW 27B	27166		22. 9.01	P R Barley and D M Jones	RAF Halton	28. 9.08
JZY	4924	SH7	Grob G102 Standard Astir III	5600S	D-6951	2.10.01	Surrey & Hants Gliding Club	Lasham	17.12.07
G-CJZZ	4925	JZZ	Rolladen-Schneider LS7-WL	7128	SE-UIU	28. 3.02	J H Tucker	Crowland	22. 3.08
KAA	4926	XE790 / KAA	Slingsby T.31B	903	XE790	14. 9.02	N Stalpers	Castricum, Netherlands	5.10.08
G-CKAC	4928	KAC	Glaser-Dirks DG-202	2-159	HB-1611	3.10.01	C Morton-Fincham	Saltby	18. 9.08
KAE	4930	KAE	Centrair 101A Pégase	101A0152	F-CGBN	4. 6.02	Rattlesden Gliding Club	Rattlesden	17. 4.08
KAF	4931	DD2	Schempp-Hirth Duo Discus T	49/330		24. 7.02	M R Smith	Aboyne	28. 9.08
KAG	4932	EE	Schempp-Hirth Nimbus-3T	23/89	D-KMHF	15.11.01	K Engelhardt	Lüsse, Germany	8. 9.08
G-CKAH	4933	KAH	Schempp-Hirth Discus bT	112/464	D-KNZZ	13.11.01	R M Brown	Bicester	28. 9.08
G-CKAJ	4934	KAJ	Schempp-Hirth Ventus-2cT	86/...		18. 5.02	A N Redington	RNAS Culdrose	23. 4.08
KAK	4935	J1	Schleicher ASW 28	28032		1.11.01	R A Johnson	Husbands Bosworth	30. 3.08
G-CKAL	4936	A28	Schleicher ASW 28	28031		13.11.01	D A Smith and P A Ivens	Nympsfield	16. 2.08
G-CKAM	4937	KAM	Glasflügel Club Libelle 205	83	D-8928	10.12.02	P A Cronk and R C Tallowin	Lyveden	9.12.07
G-CKAN	4938	KAN	SZD-50-3 Puchacz	B-2106	PH-1104	10.12.01	Bath, Wilts and North Dorset Gliding Club Kingston Deverill		28. 2.08
G-CKAP	4939	KAP	Schempp-Hirth Discus CS	290CS		16. 2.02	A A Stewart and Partners	Portmoak	28. 9.08
KAR	4941	977	Schempp-Hirth Duo Discus T	35/309	D-KHAF	3.12.01	J Giacopazzi and Partners	Portmoak	9. 5.08
G-CKAS	4942	KAS	Schempp-Hirth Ventus-2cT	93/271	(BGA 4995)	2. 7.02	R E Fletcher and Partners	Lasham	29. 8.08
G-YODA	4943	520	Schempp-Hirth Ventus-2cT	82/249		22. 3.02	P C Naegeli	Lasham	28. 9.08
KAU	4944	KAU	AMS-Flight DG-303 Elan Acro			20. 4.02	G Earle	Talgarth	19. 5.08
				3E500A35					
G-CKAV	4945	535	Rolladen-Schneider LS4-a	4696	D-1055	11. 2.02	A J Cockerell	Aston Down	28. 9.08
G-CKAW	4946	KAW	AMS-Flight DG-505 Elan Orion			10. 3.02	Midland Gliding Club	Long Mynd	16. 9.08
				5E228X66					
G-CKAX	4947	KAX	AMS-Flight DG-505 Elan Orion			12. 4.02	York Gliding Centre	Rufforth	7. 5.08
				5E229X67					
G-CKAY	4948	KAY	Grob G102 Astir CS	1452	D-7433	7. 2.02	Lincolnshire Gliding Club	Strubby	17. 2.08
KAZ	4949	J2	Glaser-Dirks DG-600/18	6-5	VH-GHS	19. 3.02	M Geisen	Mönchsheide, Germany	11. 2.08
					D-1666				
G-CKBA	4950	KBA	Centrair 101A Pégase 90	101A0435	HB-3096	28. 3.02	C J N Weston	Challock	18. 4.08
KBB	4951	KBB	Schempp-Hirth Mini Nimbus C	147	HB-1508	12. 2.02	K E Ballington	Cross Hayes	13. 7.04

Reg	BGA	Code	Type	Serial	Prev ID	Date	Owner	Location	Date
KBC	4952	066	Rolladen-Schneider LS6-c	6250-1		9. 2.03	A P Hatton	Husbands Bosworth	24. 9.08
			(Rebuilt using original fuselage and wings of BGA 3895)						
G-CKBD	4953	NU	Grob G102 Astir CS	1217	D-7290	4. 4.02	R A Morriss	Crowland	3. 3.07
G-CKBF	4955	AG1	AMS-Flight DG-303 Elan	3E498		10. 4.02	A L Garfield	Dunstable	28. 9.08
G-CKBG	4956	71	Schempp-Hirth Ventus-2cT	83/250		15. 3.02	J F D'Arcy and Partners	Lasham	7. 4.08
G-CKBH	4957	H1	Rolladen-Schneider LS6	6072	D-7798	4. 4.02	F C Ballard and P Walker	Nympsfield	5. 5.07
G-CKBK	4959	409	Schempp-Hirth Ventus-2cT	79/244		15. 4.02	D Rhys-Jones	Parham	4. 3.08
G-CKBL	4960	N12	Grob G102 Astir CS	1464	D-7436	13. 4.02	Norfolk Gliding Club	Tibenham	9. 2.08
G-CKBM	4961	73	Schleicher ASW 28	28046	D-0001	29. 3.02	M E Newland-Smith and M Poole	Dunstable	28. 9.08
G-CKBN	4962	NH	SZD-55-1	551190004	SE-ULV	26. 3.02	N D Pearson	Ringmer	15. 3.08
KBP	4963	XA310	Slingsby T.31B	852	XA310	20. 4.02	A P Stacey	RAF Keevil	17. 6.07
G-CKBS	4966	MS	Glaser-Dirks DG-600	6-42	OO-YPH	20. 4.02	M S Szymkowicz	Bicester	21. 2.08
					D-4882				
KBT	4967	633	Schempp-Hirth Standard Cirrus	561G	D-4755	3. 6.02	P R Johnson	Wormingford	2. 6.04
G-CKBU	4968	104	Schleicher ASW 28	28040		18. 4.02	G C Metcalfe	Lasham	28. 9.08
G-CKBV	4969	H4	Schleicher ASW 28	28045		24. 4.02	P Whipp	Dunstable	6. 9.08
KBW	4970	OM-0973	Letov LF-107 Lunak	22	OM-0973	9. 6.02	P Walsh	Saltby	19. 8.08
					OK-0973				
KBX	4971	421	Schleicher ASW 27	27092	PH-1146	11. 5.02	M Wright	Rattlesden	3. 4.08
KBZ	4973	C64	Rolladen-Schneider LS8-b	8425	D-3229	12. 5.02	P G Crabb	Husbands Bosworth	28. 9.08
KCA	4974	C65	Rolladen-Schneider LS8-b	8424	D-9503	3. 5.02	S J Crabb	Wroclaw, Poland	28. 9.08
G-CKCB	4975	MY	Rolladen-Schneider LS4-a	4776	PH-887	7. 6.02	Bristol & Gloucestershire Gliding Club	Nympsfield	28. 9.08
					PH-1597				
G-VTCT	4976	V26	Schempp-Hirth Ventus-2cT	90/266		13. 5.02	J B Hoolahan and Partners	Challock	9. 5.08
KCD	4977	410	Schempp-Hirth Ventus-2cT	91/267		20. 5.02	R S Jobar	Lasham	9. 9.08
KCE	4978	24	Schempp-Hirth Ventus-2cT	85/256		28. 5.02	RAFGSA Clevelands Gliding Club	AAC Dishforth	2. 3.08
KCG	4980	T99	Schleicher ASW 27B	27182		31. 5.02	T N McGee	Dunstable	15.12.06
G-CKCH	4981	EA	Schempp-Hirth Ventus-2cT	56/186	PH-1191	12. 7.02	L R Marks and J J Pridal	Lasham	24. 4.08
G-CKCJ	4982	V8	Schleicher ASW 28	28051		16. 7.02	S L Withall	Dunstable	3. 4.08
KCL	4984	KCL	Rolladen-Schneider LS4	4123	D-4239	12. 7.02	R L Fox	Pocklington	2. 5.08
KCM	4985	J8	Glasflügel Standard Libelle	104	HB-968	17. 7.02	G A Cox	Eyres Field	15. 7.08
G-CKCN	4986	700	Schleicher ASW 27B	27188	D-0001	11. 7.02	W J Head and A Walford	Gransden Lodge	28. 9.08
KCP	4987	NG1	Grob G102 Astir CS	1094	OY-XDB	7. 8.02	Norfolk Gliding Club	Tibenham	16. 8.08
G-CEUP	4988	L10	PZL-Swidnik PW-5 Smyk	17.04.010	OY-XYE	4. 1.03	P H Young	Chipping	27. 3.08
G-CKCR	4989	RB	Sportine Aviacija LAK-17A	132		3. 6.02	L Bertoncini	Alzate Brianza, Italy	29. 6.08
G-JAPK	4990	PK	Grob G103A Twin II Acro	3691-K-42	D-6940, OH-645	7. 7.02	Cairngorm Gliding Club	Feshiebridge	23. 3.08
G-CKCT	4991	KCT	Schleicher ASK 21	21751		14.12.02	Kent Gliding Club	Challock	28. 9.08
G-CKCV	4993	WE4	Schempp-Hirth Duo Discus T	54/339	D-KOZZ	7. 8.02	A J Buchanan and Partners	Parham	28. 9.08
KCW	4994	KCW	Glaser-Dirks DG-202/17	2-137/1735	D-6539	6. 9.02	R W Adamson	Portmoak	9. 5.08
G-CKCY	4996	AV	Schleicher ASW 20	20068	PH-597	14.11.02	A J Wilson and S R Tromans	Nympsfield	3. 3.08
					(OY-XTM), PH-597				
G-CKCZ	4997	KCZ	Schleicher ASK 21	21749		9. 8.02	Booker Gliding Club	Wycombe Air Park	21. 3.08
G-CKDA	4998	406	Schempp-Hirth Ventus-2bx	138	(BGA 5008)	21. 2.03	D J Eade	Lasham	28. 9.08
					D-4999				
G-CKDB	4999	KDB	Schleicher Ka 6CR	6431	HB-805	20. 9.02	Banbury Gliding Club	Hinton-in-the-Hedges	20. 1.08
G-CKDC	5000	5K	Centrair ASW 20F	20524	F-CFSF	16. 3.03	A R Blanchard and D J Graham	Rattlesden	9. 4.08
G-SISI	5002	Si	Schempp-Hirth Duo Discus	193	PH-1141	29.10.02	R N John	Dunstable	28. 9.08
G-CKDF	5003	E7	Schleicher ASK 21	21006	D-6539	29. 9.02	Portsmouth Naval Gliding Club	Lee-on-Solent	28. 9.08
KDG	5004	6S	Glasflügel Club Libelle 205	119	OO-YHL	22.10.02	Not known	Perth	21.10.03
					D-2473		*(Crashed Advie Bridge 27. 7.03; wreck on fire dump 2.07)*		
G-CKDH	5005	KDH	Schleicher K 8B	E4	D-8428	3. 1.03	Midland Gliding Club	Long Mynd	29. 9.08
G-VSIX	5006	V6	Schempp-Hirth Ventus-2cT	102/293		21. 3.03	M Nash-Wortham and Partners	Lasham	28. 9.08
G-CKDK	5007	KDK	Rolladen-Schneider LS4-a	4352	D-4106	9.11.02	M C and P A Ridger	Long Mynd	13. 4.08
G-SINK	5009	RC	Schleicher ASH 25	25139	F-CHAY	15. 2.03	A F Watson	RAF Cranwell	25.11.08
G-CKDN	5010	150	Schleicher ASW 27B	27208		3. 1.03	J S McCullagh	Lasham	28. 9.08
KDP	5011	KDP	Schleicher ASK 21	21760		23. 5.03	Kent Gliding Club	Challock	4. 5.08
G-CKDO	5012	808	Schempp-Hirth Ventus-2cT	97/...		29.11.02	A R Milne	Kingston Deverill	6.12.07
KDR	5013	KDR	SZD-48-3 Jantar-Standard 3	B-1642	DOSAAF	22.10.03	S J Kochanowski	Gamston	11.12.05
G-CKDS	5014	172	Schleicher ASW 27B	27202		20.2.03	G D Morris and A W Gillett	Nympsfield	28. 9.08
KDT	5015	OK-0975	Letov LF-107 Lunak	12	OK-0975	29.9.02	D Poll	Switzerland	13. 8.08
G-CKDU	5016	KDU	Glaser-Dirks DG-202/17	2-161/1752	D-6000	10.3.03	P G Noonan	Edgehill	28. 3.08
G-CKDV	5017	KDV	Schempp-Hirth Ventus b/16.6	224	HB-1770	1.2.03	M A Codd	Talgarth	28. 9.08
G-CKDW	5018	292	Schleicher ASW 27B	27196		28.3.03	C Colton	Gransden Lodge	16. 3.08
G-CKDX	5019	KDX	Glaser-Dirks DG-200	2-11	D-7218	5.2.03	A Miles-Bailey	Aston Down	21. 3.08
G-CKDY	5020	503	Glaser-Dirks DG-100	78	D-2591	21.3.03	P T Claiden and Partners	Dunstable	27.11.07
KDZ	5021	C75	Schempp-Hirth StD Cirrus 75	696	OO-ZKE	2.2.03	D F Bromley and Partners	RAF Cranwell	13. 7.08
G-CKEA	5022	KEA	Schempp-Hirth Cirrus 18	11	D-8807, HB-911	11.3.03	C M Reed	Rattlesden	5. 1.08
G-CKEB	5023	N	Schempp-Hirth Standard Cirrus	436G	F-CEFN	13.3.03	P Smith	Rivar Hill	27. 3.08
G-CKEC	5024	PF	Rolladen-Schneider LS4-a	4469	D-5170	13.3.03	European Soaring Club	Ontur, Spain	28. 9.08
G-CKED	5025	MB	Schleicher ASW 27B	27203	D-0001	14.2.03	M H Bull	Crowland	28. 9.08
G-CKEE	5026	KEE	Grob G102 Astir CS	1135	D-4179	30.3.03	Essex & Suffolk Gliding Club	Wormingford	17. 1.08
KEJ	5030	KEJ	Schleicher ASK 21	21765		23.7.03	London Gliding Club	Dunstable	26. 4.08
G-CKEK	5031	KEK	Schleicher ASK 21	21767		12.9.03	Devon & Somerset Gliding Club	North Hill	28. 9.08
G-CKEL	5032	SK1	Rolladen-Schneider LS8-18	8454		16.3.03	P D Kaye and C W Nicolson	Gransden Lodge	16. 4.08
G-HKAA	5033	570	Schempp-Hirth Duo Discus T	69/364		13.3.03	H Kindell and A Aveling	Lasham	28. 9.08
G-DKEN	5034	CH	Rolladen-Schneider LS4-a	4172	OO-ZSM	20.3.03	H R Hay	Wycombe Air Park	10. 2.08
					(OO-ZDG)				
KEP	5035	KEP	Rolladen-Schneider LS6-b	6188	F-CGUI	31.3.03	P J Coward	Husbands Bosworth	28. 9.08
					F-WGUI, D-5017				
G-CKER	5037	KER	Schleicher ASW 19B	19224	OY-XJI	6.5.03	B Van Woerden and Partners	Feshiebridge	15. 4.08
G-CKES	5038	KES	Schempp-Hirth Cirrus 18	46	D-6955	6.5.03	N Hawley and D M Judd	RAF Cosford	30. 5.08
					HB-955				
KET	5039	456	Rolladen-Schneider LS8-b	8459		29.4.03	M B Jefferyes	Dunstable	16. 7.08
G-GCMW	5040	ED	Grob G102 Astir CS	1112	OY-XDE	30.4.03	E F Weaver	AAC Wattisham	28. 9.08

Reg	No.	Code	Type	c/n	Prev ID	Date	Owner	Location	Date
G-CKEV	5041	R2	Schempp-Hirth Duo Discus	368		15. 4.03	RAFGSA Cranwell Gliding Club	RAF Cranwell	28. 9.08
G-LSFB	5042	FB	Rolladen-Schneider LS7-WL	7009	F-CGYA	22. 5.03	P Thomson	Feshiebridge	28. 5.08
					F-WGYA, D-1272				
G-CKEX	5043	KEX	Schleicher ASW 19B	19115	I-IUUH	18. 5.03	E D Johnson	Lyveden	28. 9.08
					D-7551				
G-EKEY	5044	KEY	Schleicher ASW 20CL	20840	D-3171	23. 5.03	K W Payne	Husbands Bosworth	2. 5.08
G-CKEZ	5045	EZ	Rolladen-Schneider LS8-t	8464	D-KSAB	20. 5.03	D A Jesty	Brentor	19. 6.08
G-CKFA	5046	S75	Schempp-Hirth Standard Cirrus 75	644	D-2124	9. 5.03	C F Jordan	Aboyne	23. 5.08
					F-CEMQ				
G-CKFB	5047	BK	Schempp-Hirth Discus-2T	30/179	D-KOZZ	7. 5.03	P A G and P L Holland	Kirton-in-Lindsey	23. 9.08
G-CKFC	5048	M2	Schempp-Hirth Ventus-2cT	105/...	D-KOZZ	17. 5.03	M R Emmett	Wycombe Air Park	28. 9.08
G-CKFD	5049	906	Schleicher ASW 27B	27211		12. 5.03	W T Craig	Dunstable	14. 2.08
G-CKFE	5050	61	Eiriavion PIK-20D	20520	D-8103	19. 7.03	M J McSorley	Bellarena	8. 4.07
					OE-5103				
G-CKFG	5052	KFG	Grob G103A Twin II Acro	3771-K-57	D-1339	25. 6.03	South London Gliding Centre	Kenley	23. 6.08
G-CKFH	5053	134	Schempp-Hirth Mini Nimbus	15	D-4819	12. 7.03	T Beck	Aston Down	16. 4.07
G-CKFJ	5054	KFJ	Schleicher ASK 13	13136	PH-383	15. 7.03	York Gliding Centre	Rufforth	11. 3.08
G-CKFK	5055	2W	Schempp-Hirth Std Cirrus 75-VTC	203	S5-3058	8. 7.03	R J Clarke	North Hill	29. 3.08
					SL-3058, YU-4295				
G-CKFL	5056	Y11	Rolladen-Schneider LS4	4080	HB-1619	1. 8.03	D A O'Brien and D R Taylor	Tibenham	23. 2.08
G-CKFM	5057	149	Rolladen-Schneider LS8-18	8475	D-9502	28. 6.03	A J H Smith	Rougham	13. 7.08
G-CKFN	5058	DS2	DG Flugzeugbau DG-1000S	10-29S28		5. 7.03	Yorkshire Gliding Club	Sutton Bank	28. 9.08
G-CKFP	5059	124	Schempp-Hirth Ventus-2cxT	110/304	D-KKAH	18. 6.03	C Sutton	Saltby	28. 9.08
G-CEUR	5060	250	Schempp-Hirth Ventus-2cxT	109/303	D-KKAO	3. 7.03	P R Hamblin	Lasham	6. 9.08
KFR	5061	KFR	Schleicher ASK 13	13433	D-3536	15. 9.03	European Soaring Club	(France)	27. 9.08
					RAFGGA 535, D-3535				
G-CKFT	5063	UP2	Schempp-Hirth Duo Discus T	77/...	D-KIIH	31. 7.03	L R Merritt and Partners	Saltby	4. 4.08
G-DKFU	5064	X11	Schempp-Hirth Ventus-2cxT	114/311	D-KOAX	4. 8.03	W F Payton	Sutton Bank	23. 3.08
G-CKFV	5065	KFV	Rolladen-Schneider LS8-t	8476	D-KOBP	19. 8.03	G A Rowden and K I Arkley	Sutton Bank	16. 4.08
KFW	5066	KFW	Grunau Baby IIB	5	D-6932	9.9.07	R Slade	Kingston Deverill	8. 9.08
					D-1932				
KFX	5067	T11	Centrair 101AP Pégase	101029	HB-1664	18.11.03	A McNicholas	Sandhill Farm, Shrivenham	28. 1.08
G-CKFY	5068	KFY	Schleicher ASK 21	21776		20. 3.04	Cambridge Gliding Club	Gransden Lodge	28. 9.08
KFZ	5069		Grob G103A Twin II Acro	34012-K-245	ZE659	8. 9.03R	T Dews	Wing Farm, Longbridge Deverill	
					BGA 3089		*(Stored 2005)*		
G-CKGA	5070	370	Schempp-Hirth Ventus-2cxT	115/312	D-KIBL	13. 4.04	D R Campbell	Wycombe Air Park	28. 9.08
G-CKGB	5071	T3	Schempp-Hirth Ventus-2cxT	117/...	D-KDAH	4. 1.04	D R Irving	Portmoak	28. 9.08
G-CKGC	5072	J6	Schempp-Hirth Ventus-2cxT	118/317	D-KMAF	19.12.03	C P Jeffery	Gransden Lodge	20. 9.08
G-CKGD	5073	V9	Schempp-Hirth Ventus-2cxT	119/318	D-KEAD	27. 2.04	C Morris and H Bosworth	Bidford	28. 9.08
KGE	5074		Slingsby T.38 Grasshopper	'785'	WZ789 ??	11. 9.03R	W den Baars	Haamstede, Netherlands	
			[Possibly c/n 778 ex WZ782 reported with W den Baars]						
G-CKGF	5075	233	Schempp-Hirth Duo Discus T	84/397		11. 2.04	J P McNamee	Gransden Lodge	7.12.07
KGG	5076		Schleicher Ka 6CR	6646	HB-924	22. 9.03R	K Ballington	(Burton-on-Trent)	
G-CKGH	5077	KGH	Grob G102 Club Astir II	5057C	OO-ZVS	8.10.03	I M Gavan	Kenley	22.11.07
G-PNGC	5078	N3	Schleicher ASK 21	21770		2.11.03	Portsmouth Naval Gliding Club	Lee-on-Solent	28. 9.08
							(Carries "BGA 5978" on fin)		
G-CKGK	5079	R28	Schleicher ASK 21	21766		24.10.03	RAFGSA Clevelands Gliding Club	AAC Dishforth	28. 9.08
G-CKGL	5080	X4	Schempp-Hirth Ventus-2cT	88/263	EI-152	6. 3.04	W D Inglis	Bidford	26. 4.08
KGM	5081	B55	Centrair 101A Pégase	101055	F-CFQR	15. 4.05	S France	Shobdon	19. 4.07
G-CKGN	5082	KGN	Schleicher ASW 28-18	28505	D-3063	15. 3.05	M Jerman	Sutton Bank	17. 3.07
					D-0001				
G-VTWO	5084	565	Schempp-Hirth Ventus-2c	28/75	D-0602	19. 1.04	F G T Birlison	Aston Down	28. 9.08
G-CKGT	5087	41	Jastreb Standard Cirrus 75-VTC	294	HA-4283	12.12.03	R del Moro	Enemonzo, Italy	1. 7.08
G-CKGU	5088	690	Schleicher ASW 19B	19208	PL68	10. 4.04	D M Ruttle	Chipping	22. 4.07
					(Belgian Air Cadets)				
G-CKGV	5089	KGV	Schleicher ASW 28-18	28512	D-7062	4.11.04	A H Reynolds	Long Mynd	30. 3.08
G-CKGX	5091	KGX	Schleicher ASK 21	21782		2. 7.04	The Gliding Centre	Husbands Bosworth	4. 5.08
G-CKGY	5092	KGY	Scheibe Bergfalke IV	5839	SE-TLL	9. 4.04	North Devon Gliding Club	Eaglescott	23. 6.07
G-DIIA	5093	57	Schempp-Hirth Discus-2a	196	D-1117	18. 3.04	M J Young	Grenoble-Le Versoud, France	13. 2.07
							(To D-2691 2007)		
G-CKHA	5094	KHA	SZD-51-1 Junior	B-1918	(SP-3691)	16. 6.04	Devon & Somerset Gliding Club	North Hill	28. 9.08
					D-2843, DDR-2803				
G-CKHB	5095	-	Rolladen-Schneider LS3	3316	D-2635	7. 5.04	P Dunthorne	Nympsfield	13. 4.08
G-CKHC	5096	KHC	DG Flugzeugbau DG-505/20 Elan	5E178W11	D-6401	22. 5.04	T J Donovan	Edgehill	23. 3.08
G-CKHD	5097	T4	Schleicher ASW 27B	27222		7. 4.04	N D Tillett	Dunstable	28. 9.08
G-CKHE	5098	X17	Sportine Aviacija LAK-17A	122	OM-0118	9. 5.04	N J Gough and A J Garrity	RAF Wittering	25. 5.08
G-CKHF	5099	XD2	Schleicher ASW 20	20229	D-3162	16. 5.04	C H Brown	AAC Dishforth	14. 5.08
G-CKHG	5100	K5	Schleicher ASW 27B	27223		7. 5.04	R A King	Bicester	7. 2.08
G-CKHH	5101	KHH	Schleicher ASK 13	13171	LN-GAX	4. 4.04	Lincolnshire Gliding Club	Strubby	6. 3.08
G-CDDB	5102	KM	Schempp-Hirth Standard Cirrus	577G	F-CEMG	16. 5.04	K D Barker	(St Nicolas de la Grave, France)	5. 2.08
G-CKHK	5103	KHK	Schempp-Hirth Duo Discus T	100/426	D-KKAO	28. 8.04	I Ashton and Partners	Chipping	23. 6.08
KHL	5104		Rolladen-Schneider LS1-f	452	F-CEKZ	17. 5.04R	K Sleigh	Rattlesden	
G-CKHM	5105	KHM	Centrair 101A Pégase 90	101A0359	F-CHDE	29. 4.05	A Bland	Lasham	4. 4.08
G-CKHN	5106	KHN	SZD-51-1 Junior	B-2142	OE-5614	10. 6.04	Nene Valley Gliding Club	Upwood	13. 7.08
					SP-3612				
G-CKHP	5107	70	Rolladen-Schneider LS8-18	8337	N818FD	2. 6.04	A D May	Dunstable	2. 5.08
G-ORCW	5108	A39	Schempp-Hirth Ventus-2cxT	134/...		16.12.04	R C Wilson	Aboyne	28. 9.08
G-CKHR	5109	KHR	SZD-51-1 Junior	B-1775	HB-1928	27. 6.04	Wolds Gliding Club	Pocklington	19. 3.08
G-CKHS	5110	KO	Rolladen-Schneider LS7-WL	7043	PH-862	26.10.04	G F Coles and E W Russell	Wormingford	15. 3.08
					D-5157				
G-CKHT	5111	424	Schempp-Hirth Standard Cirrus	259G	D-1139	1. 9.04	M Holden	Lasham	8. 3.08
G-CKHV	5112		Glaser-Dirks DG-100	77	HB-1331	26. 7.04	M J Brown	RAF Weston-on-the-Green	29. 7.08
G-CKHW	5113	KHW	SZD-50-3 Puchacz	503.A.004.001		17. 8.04	Derbyshire & Lancashire Gliding Club	Camphill	17. 8.08

Reg	BGA	Comp	Type	Serial	Prev ID	Date	Owner	Location	Date
G-CKHX	5114	6X	Schleicher ASW 28-18E	28720	D-KAMF	13. 4.05	M C Foreman and P J O'Connell	Lasham	11. 4.08
G-JIFI	5115	620	Schempp-Hirth Duo Discus T	95/420	D-KOZZ	9. 7.04	D K McCarthy	Lasham	28. 9.08
G-KEPE	5116	PE	Schempp-Hirth Nimbus-3DT	25	D-KEPE	11. 8.04	T Salter and Partners	Lasham	5. 2.08
G-CKJA	5117	28E	Schleicher ASW 28-18	28712	D-6051 D-0001	21. 3.05	J Vella-Grech	Sleap	7. 2.08
G-CKJB	5118	LW	Schempp-Hirth Ventus bT	26/191	D-KBST	15. 9.04	J Sorrell	Usk	21. 7.08
G-CKJC	5119	617	Schempp-Hirth Nimbus-3T	6/57	D-KUPA OY-KHX, D-KHXB	14. 9.04	A C Wright	Sutton Bank	9. 2.08
G-CKJD	5120	GX	Schempp-Hirth Std Cirrus 75-VTC	241	F-CDOZ	5. 2.05	J N Rebbeck	Wycombe Air Park	4. 5.08
G-CKJE	5121	321	DG Flugzeugbau LS8-18	8498		24.11.04	M D Wells	Bidford	28. 9.08
G-CKJF	5122	GW	Schempp-Hirth Standard Cirrus	414G	OY-XGW D-9247	5. 2.05	J G Wilson and Partners	Bicester	23. 3.08
G-CKJG	5123	901	Schempp-Hirth Cirrus VTC	153Y	EC-CKO	22. 3.05	S J Wright	Rattlesden	23. 3.08
G-CKJH	5124	KJH	AMS-Flight DG-303 Elan	3E506		8.12.04	Yorkshire Gliding Club	Sutton Bank	28. 9.08
G-CKJJ	5125	KJJ	AMS-Flight DG-505 Elan Orion	5E249X79	S5-AMS01	12.12.04	Ulster Gliding Club	Bellarena	28. 9.08
G-CKJK	5126	C66	Schempp-Hirth Janus Ce	283	D-3666	7. 1.05	Janus Syndicate	Pocklington	25. 4.08
G-CKJL	5127	KJL	Schleicher ASK 13	13468	D-2338	8. 9.04	Lincolnshire Gliding Club	Strubby	21. 9.08
G-CKJM	5128	7A	Schempp-Hirth Ventus cT	120/394	D-KAHE OH-781	5.11.04	J C Ferguson	Portmoak	28. 9.08
G-CKJN	5129	9E	Schleicher ASW 20	20052	D-7964	15.12.04	R Logan	Bellarena	17.11.07
G-CKJP	5130	R12	Schleicher ASK 21	21783	D-0001	9.11.04	RAFGSA Bannerdown Gliding Club	RAF Keevil	28. 9.08
G-GLID	5131	E3	Schleicher ASW 28-18E	28723	D-KEBB D-KOAB	13. 4.05	B A Bateson and P N Marriott	Parham	28. 9.08
G-CKJS	5132	JW	Schleicher ASW 28-18E	28713	D-KHJW BGA 5132, D-KHJW	6.11.04	J R Warren and A Hegner	Wycombe Air Park	15. 3.08
G-CTAA	5133	AA	Schempp-Hirth Janus	16	N2AA	11.12.04	D P Catt	Bicester	27. 1.08
G-LSGM	5144	GM	Rolladen-Schneider LS3-17	3346	D-6760 OO-ZLD	13.2.05	M W Bewley	Sutton Bank	8. 2.08
G-CKJV	5145	AP	Schleicher ASW 28-18E	28725	D-KFAP D-KOAB	13. 4.05	A Price	Nympsfield	19. 3.08
G-KCHG	5146	DS	Schempp-Hirth Ventus cT	87/332	D-KCHG	6.12.04	D S Jones	North Hill	28. 9.08
G-OTCZ	5147	CZ	Schempp-Hirth Ventus-2cxT	137/352	D-KAAQ	11. 2.05	D H Conway and D R Zarb	Nympsfield	28. 9.08
G-ZENN	5148	304	Schempp-Hirth Ventus-2cxT	136/348	D-KOZX	21. 2.05	Z Marczynski	Lasham	22. 2.08
G-CKJZ	5149	E17	Schempp-Hirth Discus bT	75/403	OE-9367	10. 4.05	A I Mawer	Kirton-in-Lindsey	13. 2.08
G-RDDT	5150	DDT	Schempp-Hirth Duo Discus T	116/448		1. 4.05	R B Witter	Lleweni Parc	12. 4.08
G-CKKB	5151	KKB	Centrair 101A Pégase	101A0209	SE-TZU	2. 5.05	M Rushton	Lyveden	9. 6.08
G-CKKC	5152	KKC	AMS-Flight DG-303 Elan Acro	3E509A41		15. 5.05	M P Elllis and Partners	Burn	14. 5.08
G-CKKD	5153	AP1	Schleicher ASW 28-18E	28734		3. 6.05	A Palmer	Dunstable	29. 3.08
G-CKKE	5154	F94	Schempp-Hirth Duo Discus T	103/429	D-KOZZ	23. 2.05	M Powell-Brett and T Moyes	Bicester	29. 3.08
G-CKKF	5155	306	Schempp-Hirth Ventus-2cxT	139/364		23. 2.05	A R McGregor	Kingston Deverill	28. 9.08
G-TWOT	5156	2T	Schempp-Hirth Discus-2T	14/127	OY-XSY D-KKAH	1. 4.05	S G Lapworth	Lasham	4. 4.08
G-CKKH	5157	AG	Schleicher ASW 27B	27231	D-0001	9. 3.05	P L Hurd	Dunstable	28. 9.08
G-VCXT	5158	RA	Schempp-Hirth Ventus-2cxT	144/...	(BGA 5166) D-KOZZ	22. 4.05	R F Aldous	Kirchheim-Hahnweide, Germany	28. 9.08
G-CKKK	5159	960	Sportine Aviacija LAK-17A	161	LY-GGF	22. 3.05	C J Nicholas	Ridgewell	13. 4.08
G-OASW	5160	MM	Schleicher ASW 27B	27227		15. 3.05	M P Mee	Wycombe Air Park	14. 3.07
							(Crashed into trees 8.8.06 Lasham and substantially damaged)		
G-CKKM	5161	B3	Schleicher ASW 28-18	28502	D-9004, D-0001	18.3.05	R F Thirkell	Lasham	17. 3.07
G-CKKN	5162	GB1	Schempp-Hirth Duo Discus	165	D-8215	18. 3.05	M J Jordy	Husbands Bosworth	22. 2.08
G-CKKP	5163	BF1	Schleicher ASK 21	21795		1. 7.05	Bowland Forest Gliding Club	Chipping	23. 6.08
G-CKKR	5164	KKR	Schleicher ASK 13	13065	PH-391	25. 4.05	Banbury Gliding Club	Hinton-in-the-Hedges	26. 4.08
G-TWOC	5165	2C	Schempp-Hirth Ventus-2cxT	141/369		20. 4.05	D Heslop	Wormingford	27. 3.08
G-CKKV	5167	776	DG Flugzeugbau DG-1000S	10-57T2		28. 4.05	Lasham Gliding Society	Lasham	14. 5.08
KKW	5168	KKW	Allstar PZL SZD-51-1 Junior	511.A.05.010		27. 7.05	Scottish Gliding Union	Portmoak	26. 7.06
							(Hit power cable 17. 5.06 landing near Glenrothes; stored 1.08)		
G-CKKX	5169	449	Rolladen-Schneider LS4-a	4827	PH-928 D-3529	14. 5.05	B W Svenson	Pocklington	2. 2.08
G-CKKY	5170	440	Schempp-Hirth Duo Discus T	124/...		25. 7.05	P D Duffin	Wormingford	29. 3.08
G-DAVS	5171	-	Sportine Aviacija LAK-17AT	158	LY-GIW	7. 4.05	D Peters	Burn	18. 5.08
G-CKLA	5172	KLA	Schleicher ASK 13	13363	PH-1084 D-0857	19. 5.05	Booker Gliding Club	Wycombe Air Park	14. 6.07
G-CKLB	5173	Z27	Schleicher ASW 27B	27234		11. 5.05	S J Riddington and C Curtis	Husbands Bosworth	28. 9.08
G-CKLC	5174	KLC	Glasflügel Hornet	39	SE-TPL	14. 6.05	P R Thomas	Dunstable	9. 6.08
G-CKLD	5175	797	Schempp-Hirth Discus-2cT	1/2	D-KDCC	27. 5.05	J P Galloway	Portmoak	28. 9.08
KLE	5176	-	SZD-22B Mucha Standard	524	OO-ZIS	30. 8.07	B Stephenson	(Grantham)	29. 8.08
G-CKLF	5177	08	Schempp-Hirth Janus	59	D-2170 I-ANUS	10. 6.05	T J Edmunds	RAF Marham	21. 9.08
G-CKLG	5178	KLG	Rolladen-Schneider LS4	4264	F-CAEQ D-5530	20. 8.05	J Heath & Partners	Sandhill Farm, Shrivenham	29. 8.08
G-WYVN	5179	12	DG Flugzeugbau DG-1000T	10-63T5	D-3800	7. 6.05	Wyvern Gliding Club	Trenchard Lines, Upavon	17. 3.08
G-DUOT	5180	666	Schempp-Hirth Duo Discus T	123/466		10. 8.05	A P Moulang	Challock	28. 9.08
G-DDJF	5182	JF	Schempp-Hirth Duo Discus T	121/...		20. 6.05	R J Fack	Long Mynd	14. 5.08
G-CKLN	5183	M11	Rolladen-Schneider LS4-a	4791	D-2823	6. 7.05	K E Jenkinson	Husbands Bosworth	5. 7.08
G-CKLP	5184	205	Schleicher ASW 28-18E	28737	D-KOAB	28. 6.05	J T Birch	Gransden Lodge	28. 9.08
G-CKLR	5185	Z55	SZD-55-1	551193056	F-CHSP F-WHSP	24. 9.05	A N Gibson and D T King	Trenchard Lines, Upavon	22. 4.08
G-CKLS	5186	KLS	Rolladen-Schneider LS4	4637	D-6786	20. 7.05	Wolds Gliding Club	Pocklington	16. 6.08
G-CKLT	5187	GT	Schempp-Hirth Nimbus-3/25.5	1	D-5052 EC-EBP, D-2111	23. 7.05	G N Thomas	AAC Wattisham	5. 4.08
G-CKLV	5188	KLV	Schempp-Hirth Discus-2cT	20/27	D-KKFC	27. 1.06	J Iglehart	Lasham	15. 3.08
G-CKLW	5189	KLW	Schleicher ASK 21	21799		22.12.05	Yorkshire Gliding Club	Sutton Bank	28. 9.08

Reg	No	Code	Type	Serial	Prev ID	Date	Owner	Location	Date
G-CKLX	5190		Bölkow Phoebus B1	757	OE-0851	16. 5.07	D R Poleck	Germany	15. 5.08
G-CKLY	5191	D6	DG Flugzeugbau DG-1000T	10-66T6	D-KAAD	1.10.05	R J Large	Husbands Bosworth	8. 5.08
G-CKMA	5192	GR8	DG Flugzeugbau LS8-st	8510		1.12.05	G Rizk	Saltby	30.11.06
G-CKMB	5193	KMB	Sportine Aviacija LAK-19T	018	LY-GJE	15. 3.07	D J McKenzie	Camphill	14. 3.08
G-CKMC	5194	KMC	Grob G102 Astir CS 77	1625	LN-GBA D-4799	11.11.05	L Gregoire	Lasham	20. 9.08
G-CKMD	5195	V12	Schempp-Hirth Standard Cirrus	31	SE-TIX D-0528	3.10.05	C Roberts	Snitterfield	13. 3.08
G-CKME	5196	DB	DG Flugzeugbau LS8-st	8504		22. 1.06	D Bradley	Sutton Bank	16. 2.08
G-CKMF	5197	KMF	Centrair 101A Pégase	101038	F-CFQE	1. 5.06	D Jamin	Dunstable	29. 4.08
G-CKMG	5198	AD	Glaser-Dirks DG-101G Elan	E159G126	HB-1733	4. 2.06	A W Roberts	Dunstable	4. 4.08
G-IICX	5199	210	Schempp-Hirth Ventus-2cxT	171/...		31. 3.06	Southern Sailplanes	Lasham	30.11.07
G-CKMI	5200	-	Schleicher K 8C	81006	RAFGGA 562	28. 9.05	V Mallon	Kleve-Wisseler Dünen, Germany	28. 8.08
G-CKMJ	5201	-	Schleicher Ka 6CR	6109	RAFGGA 555 D-8455	28. 9.05	V Mallon	Kleve-Wisseler Dünen, Germany	27. 9.06
G-LYDR	5202	1F	Schempp-Hirth Discus-2cT	21/29	(D-KABC)	1. 3.06	A Firmin *(To C-GYDR 11.07)*	Lasham	4. 4.08
G-CKML	5203	KA	Schempp-Hirth Duo Discus T	52/336	PH-1256	12. 4.06	J J Pridal and Partners	Lasham	12. 4.08
G-CKMM	5204	RM	Schleicher ASW 28-18E	28742		2.12.05	R Munro	Wycombe Air Park	18.12.07
G-KOYY	5205	Y7	Schempp-Hirth Nimbus-4T	9	D-KOYY	22.12.05	R Kalin	Rufforth	21. 5.08
G-CKMO	5206	L7	Rolladen-Schneider LS7-WL	7007	PH-861 D-1264	11. 1.06	G Turpin	RAF Keevil	5. 4.08
G-CKMP	5207	KMP	Sportine Aviacija LAK-17A	173	LY-GMZ	18. 1.06	J L McIver	Portmoak	28. 9.08
G-CKMR	5208	-	Letov LF-107 Lunak	54	OK-0838	13. 4.06	W Seitz	Pohlheim, Germany	10. 4.08
G-DUOX	5209	98	Schempp-Hirth Duo Discus x	474	D-4498	24. 3.06	British Gliding Association	Bicester	14.12.07
G-CKMT	5210	-	Grob G103C Twin III Acro	34157	PH-1151 D-0659	17. 1.06	Borders Gliding Club	Milfield	14. 1.08
G-DGIK	5211	460	DG Flugzeugbau DG-1000S	10-72T11	D-3800	6. 1.06	R P Davis	(Colchester)	1. 2.08
G-CKMV	5212	KMV	Rolladen-Schneider LS3-17	3329	D-6931	5.12.05	F C Roles	Husbands Bosworth	28. 9.08
G-CKMW	5213	R18	Schleicher ASK 21	21798		3.12.05	RAFGSA Cranwell Gliding Club	RAF Cranwell	28. 9.08
KMX	5214		Sportine Aviacija LAK-19T	020	LY-GMV	16.11.05R	Baltic Sailplanes	Husbands Bosworth	
							(Not taken up; to BGA 5267)		
G-CKMY	5215	W81	Schleicher ASW 20L	20392	PH-803 D-8833	4. 2.06	C M Davey	RAF Wittering	18. 4.08
G-CKMZ	5216	J5	Schleicher ASW 28-18E	28716	D-KBJM	17. 2.06	J R Martindale	Walney Island	7. 2.08
G-DTWO	5217	LL	Schempp-Hirth Discus-2a	9	D-2140	3. 2.06	O J Walters	Bicester	6. 3.08
G-CKNB	5218	505	Schempp-Hirth Standard Cirrus	222	S5-3056 SL-3056, YU-4209	1. 5.06	D S Kershaw and A Booker	Lasham	16. 4.08
G-CKNC	5219	NC	Caproni Vizzola Calif A-21S	240	F-CEUE	1. 4.06	J J Pritchard	Lasham	19. 5.08
G-CKND	5220	KND	DG Flugzeugbau DG-1000T	10-76T15		12. 6.06	S Heaton	Sutton Bank	11. 6.08
G-CKNE	5221	KNE	VTC-75 Standard Cirrus	199	S5-3057 SL-3057, YU-4293	8. 2.06R	G MacDonald	Lasham	30. 7.08
G-CKNF	5222	KNF	DG Flugzeugbau DG-1000T	10-81T20	D-KTOA	11. 7.06	C R Thomas and Partners	Lasham	9. 7.08
G-CKNG	5223	209	Schleicher ASW 28-18E	28747	D-KOAB	7. 8.06	M Brockington	Talgarth	21. 8.08
G-KHCC	5224	LM	Schempp-Hirth Ventus bT	34/215	D-KHCC	5. 4.06	L McLane	Sutton Bank	3. 4.08
KNI	5225	W9	Glasflügel Club Libelle 205	150	F-CEQG	7. 3.06R	K Sleigh *(Carries "G-CKNI")*	Rattlesden	
G-CKNJ	5226	D11	Schempp-Hirth Duo Discus xT	142/491		28. 6.06	P L Hurd and Partners	Dunstable	28. 9.08
G-CKNK	5227	-	Glaser-Dirks DG-500 Elan Trainer	5E116T48	D-5661	5. 5.06	Cotswold Gliding Club	Aston Down	1. 5.08
G-CKNL	5228	KNL	Schleicher ASK 21	21811	D-0001	9. 4.06	Buckminster Gliding Club	Saltby	29. 4.08
G-CKNM	5229	K18	Schleicher ASK 18	18037	PH-908 D-4539	3. 6.06	I L Pattingale	RAF Odiham	28. 9.08
G-CKNN	5230	-	Slingsby T.21B	MHL.012	OY-XSI SE-SMA, WB985	4.06	R Wassermann	Donzdorf, Germany	26. 4.08
G-CKNO	5231	KNO	Schempp-Hirth Ventus-2cxT	179/429	D-KOZZ	20. 6.06	C McEwen	Aston Down	28. 9.08
G-DAWZ	5232	DA	HpH Glasflügel 304CZ-17	33	D-8304	15. 4.06	D Whitley	Parham	14. 4.07
G-CKNR	5233	KNR	Schempp-Hirth Ventus-2cxT	181	D-KIIH	24. 7.06	R Nicholls	Husbands Bosworth	19. 7.08
G-CKNS	5234	-	Rolladen-Schneider LS4-a	4398	SE-UEP OH-714	8. 6.06	I R Willows	Husbands Bosworth	6. 6.08
G-OASG	5235	629	Schleicher ASG 29	29015	D-7429	16. 5.06R	P Brice	Wycombe Air Park	
KNU	5236	E1	Schleicher ASG 29E	29501	D-KPRC D-2529	16. 5.06R	R Cheetham	Husbands Bosworth	
G-CKNV	5237	KNV	Schleicher ASW 28-18E	28749	D-KOAB	23. 7.06	D Brain	Dunstable	28. 9.08
G-TRBO	5238	28T	Schleicher ASW 28-18E	28743		4. 8.06	A Cluskey and C Davison	Saltby	28. 9.08
G-RIEF	5239	EF	DG Flugzeugbau DG-1000T	10-85T23	D-KTOA	20. 7.06	J T Hitchcock	Parham	17. 7.08
G-IZII	5240	-	Marganski Swift S-1	110	N110LG	23.10.06	G C Westgate	Parham	28. 9.08
KNZ	5241		Sportine Aviacija LAK-19T	024	LY-GNC	22. 8.06R	G Paul *(Not taken up; to BGA 5284)*		
KOA	5242		Schempp-Hirth Duo Discus xT	158		23. 8.06R	J Arnold *(Not taken up; to BGA 5274)*		
G-SAJA	5243	JA	Schempp-Hirth Discus-2c	22		26. 1.07	J G Arnold	RAF Keevil	28. 9.08
KOC	5244		Schempp-Hirth Discus-2c	Not known		23. 8.06R	J Arnold *(For RAFGSA)*		
G-CKOD	5245	OD	Schempp-Hirth Discus bT	11/282	HB-2157 D-KECC	15.12.06	A L Harris and M W Talbot	Nympsfield	28. 9.08
KOE	5246	290	Schleicher ASG 29	29024	D-9729	8. 9.06R	R C Bromwich *(Reserved as G-CKOE)*	RAF Keevil	
G-XDUO	5247	DUO	Schempp-Hirth Duo Discus xT	162/519		7. 3.07	F Jeynes	Bidford	28. 9.08
G-PHNX	5248	72	Schempp-Hirth Duo Discus xT	157	D-KIIH	5. 3.07	J Birch	Gransden Lodge	28. 9.08
G-CKOH	5249	45	DG Flugzeugbau DG-1000T	10-87T25		23.11.06	Lasham Gliding Society	Lasham	22.11.07
G-CKOI	5250	170	Sportine Aviacija LAK-17AT	183	LY-GQF	21.12.06	C G Corbett	Dunstable	28. 9.08
G-CKOJ	5251	W2	Schempp-Hirth Duo Discus	188	OE-5583	17. 2.07	M R Dawson	Saintes, France	28. 9.08
G-CKOK	5252	X9	Schempp-Hirth Discus-2cT	50	D-KOZZ	13. 4.07	B D Scougall	Portmoak	14. 4.08
G-CKOL	5253	OL	Schempp-Hirth Duo Discus xT	164	D-KIIH	23. 4.07	P Harmer and Partners	North Hill	22. 4.08
G-CKOM	5254	LE	Schleicher ASG 29	29023	D-9529 D-0001	10.11.06R	L Wells	Nympsfield	28. 9.08
KON	5255	XE	Schleicher ASG 29E	29512	D-KBJG	14.11.06R	J Gorringe *(Reserved as G-CKON)*	Lasham	
KOO	5256	7	Schleicher ASG 29E	29519	D-KAAD	15.11.06R	A Darlington *(Reserved as G-CKOO)*	Lasham	
G-KOBH	5257		Schempp-Hirth Discus bT	154/549	D-KOBH	12. 1.07	K Neave	Nympsfield	28. 9.08

Reg	No	Code	Type	Serial	Prev ID	Date	Owner	Location	Last
G-CKOS	5258		Letov LF-107 Lunak	45	OK-0829	21. 4.07	J Rehousek	Germany	20. 4.08
G-CKOR	5259	KOR	Glaser-Dirks DG-300 Elan	3E110	PH-768	16.12.06	J A Sparrow	Gransden Lodge	15.12.07
G-CKOT	5260	-	Schleicher ASK 21	21818	D-0001	30. 5.07	Ulster Gliding Club	Bellarena	29. 5.08
G-CKOU	5261	1UP	Sportine Aviacija LAK-19T	027		5. 6.07	R Walker and Partners	Parham	4. 6.08
G-CKOV	5262		Issoire E78B Silene	05	F-CFEB	27. 4.07	I Stork	Portugal	26. 4.08
G-CKOW	5263	KOW	AMS-Flight DG-505 Elan Orion	5E260X89		16. 5.07	Southdown Gliding Club	Parham	15. 5.08
G-CKOX	5264		AMS-Flight DG-505 Elan Orion	5E258X87		2. 9.07	Seahawk Gliding Club	Culdrose	1. 9.08
KOY	5265	Z	Schleicher ASG 29E	29510	D-KNZG	7. 1.07R	P Wells (Reserved as G-CKOY)	Wycombe Air Park	
KOZ	5266	G9	Schleicher ASG 29E	29513	D-KEEJ	15. 1.07R	E Johnston (Reserved as G-CKOZ)	Dunstable	
G-CKPA	5267	L19	Sportine Aviacija LAK-19T	020	(BGA 5214) LY-GMV	9. 3.07	R Bridges (Baltic Sailplanes)	Husbands Bosworth	28. 9.08
G-CKPB	5268	FE	Schempp-Hirth Discus b	166	LN-GFE SE-UFE	8. 5.07	M Cuming	Edgehill	7. 5.08
G-SORA	5269		Glaser-Dirks DG-500/22 Elan	5E35S7	PH-1082 D-5219	20. 3.07	M Boyle	Rufforth	19. 3.08
KPD	5270	CC	Schleicher ASG 29E	29511	D-KLCC	19. 2.07R	Viscount Cobham (Reserved as G-VLCC)	Lasham	
G-CKPE	5271	2S	Schempp-Hirth Duo Discus	56	HB-3088	10. 4.07	M Cuming	Edgehill	9. 4.08
KPF	5272		DG Flugzeugbau DG-808C	8-377B276	D-KBTM	8. 3.07R	T Meaker	Lasham	
G-CKPG	5273	KPG	Schempp-Hirth Discus-2cT	59	D-KOZZ	27. 7.07	G Knight and R Baker	Gransden Lodge	26. 7.08
G-SAXT	5274	26	Schempp-Hirth Duo Discus xT	158/513	(BGA 5242) D-KIIH	14. 3.07	RAFGSA Chilterns Gliding Centre	RAF Halton	13. 3.08
G-CFHO	5275	T40	Grob G103 Twin II	3566	F-CFHO	28. 4.07	Surrey Hills Gliding Club	Kenley	27. 4.08
G-CKPJ	5276		Neukom Elfe S4D	411AB	D-4598	21. 3.07R	J Szladowski	Camphill	
G-CKPK	5277		Schempp-Hirth Ventus-2cxT	197	D-KIHH	18. 7.07	I C Lees	Pocklington	17. 7.08
G-CKPL	5278	KPL	Schempp-Hirth Standard Cirrus 75	649	F-CEMS	29. 9.07	L Roberts (Cancelled 27.10.07)	North Hill	28. 9.08
G-CKPM	5279	8T	DG Flugzeugbau LS8-st	8517		20. 5.07	J Bayford	Gransden Lodge	19. 5.08
G-CKPN	5280		SZD-51-1 Junior	B-1927	HB-3036	13. 9.07	Rattlesden Gliding Club	Rattlesden	12. 9.08
G-CKPO	5281	BW	Schempp-Hirth Duo Discus xT	171	D-KOZZ (D-KDWF)	16. 7.07	B Walker	Nympsfield	15. 7.08
G-CKPP	5282	KPP	Schleicher ASK 21	21824	D-0001	20. 7.07	The Gliding Centre	Husbands Bosworth	19. 7.08
KPR	5283		Slingsby T.31B	915	XE802	8. 5.07R	K Ballington	Abbots Bromley	
G-EWEW	5284	EW2	Sportine Aviacija LAK-19T	024	(BGA 5241) LY-GNC	22. 5.07	G Paul	Dunstable	21. 5.08
KPT	5285	XS	Schleicher ASG 29E	29518	D-KPRB	11. 5.07R	R Browne (Reserved as G-XOAR)	RAF Cranwell	
KPU	5286	293	Schleicher ASG 29	Not known		22. 5.07R	J Kellerman	Gransden Lodge	
G-CKPV	5287		Schempp-Hirth Mini Nimbus B	63	PH-607	29. 5.07R	C Pollard	Rougham	
G-SAOC	5288	R6	Schempp-Hirth Discus-2cT	54	D-KOZZ	5. 7.07	RAFGSA Chilterns Gliding Centre	RAF Halton	4. 7.08
G-CKPX	5289	KPX	ZS Jezow PW-6U	78.04.03		11. 7.07R	J C Gibson and Partners	Chipping	
G-CKPY	5290		Schempp-Hirth Duo Discus xT	174		12. 7.07R	C Marren & Partners	Trenchard Lines, Upavon	
G-CKPZ	5291	T9	Schleicher ASW 20	20360	D-4090	8. 9.07	T J Davies	RAF Cranwell	7. 9.08
KRA	5292		DG Flugzeugbau DG-1000T	10-113T35		26. 7.07R	K McLean	Rufforth	
G-CKRB	5293	KRB	Schleicher ASK 13	13292	D-0220	13. 9.07	Derbyshire & Lancashire Gliding Club	Camphill	12. 9.08
G-CKRC	5294		Schleicher ASW 28-18E	28735	D-KUPC	27. 9.07	M Woodcock	(Chester)	26. 9.08
KRD	5295		Schleicher ASG 29E	29537		11. 8.07R	R Thirkell	Lasham	
G-ONAT	5296		Grob G102 Astir CS77	1804	HB-1459	20. 9.07R	K Sleigh	Rattlesden	
G-CKRF	5297		Glaser-Dirks DG-300 Elan	3E392	PH-923	23.10.07	G A King	Talgarth	
KRG	5298	DS	Schempp-Hirth Nimbus-3T	4/51	D-KTFP HB-2147, D-KAPE, VH-GAA	25.10.07R	D Smith	Bidford	
G-CKRH	5299		Grob G103 Twin II	2596	F-CFYJ D-3963	14.11.07R	Staffordshire Gliding Club	Seighford	
KRI	5300		Schleicher ASK 21	21835		20.11.07R	Kent Gliding Club	Challock	
KRJ	5301		Schleicher ASG 29E	29544		29.11.07R	J Thompson	(Watford)	
G-KPLG	5302		Schempp-Hirth Ventus-2cxM	163	D-KPLG	18.12.07R	M Lassan	Talgarth	
KRL	5303		Schleicher ASG 29E	29562		21.12.07R	J Clarke	Not known	
G-CKRM	5304		Schleicher ASW 27B	27174	EI-GMA EI-151	14. 1.08R	C Luton	Husbands Bosworth	
G-CKRN	5305		Grob G102 Astir CS	1261	D-7356	15. 1.08R	P Sallis	(Northampton)	
KRO	5306		Schempp-Hirth Duo Discus XLT	185		17. 1.08R	B Morris	Lasham	
KRP	5307		Schleicher ASG 29E	29532		28. 1.08R	S Ell	Sutton Bank	
G-CKRR	5308		Schleicher ASW 15B	15393	D-9288	29. 1.08R	S Day	(Cheshire)	
KRS	5309		FFA Diamant 16.5	038	OO-ZII BGA 1471	11. 2.08R	K Burns	Edgehill	

PART 2 (i) – BGACOMPETITION NUMBER INDEX

BGACompetition Numbers are issued to pilots and not to individual gliders. They change frequently. There is no formal list of Competition Numbers or control over other gliders wearing similar or previous numbers or other (tail) codes- see Part 2 (ii) below. Therefore, this listing is a composite one based on BGAinformation and reported sightings. Identities marked with an asterisk indicate where gliders have been observed with the numbers shown although not listed in the current BGArecord. In some cases because joint (syndicate) ownership is common this means that the Competition Number belongs to a member of a syndicate other than the one whose name appears as owner in the BGA's records. The member's name is shown where the glider concerned is not identified or the number is reserved for future use. The missing numbers are not allocated.

No.	BGANo.	No.	BGANo.	No.	BGANo.	No.	BGANo.
1	1144*, 3123	76	R O Linee	157	2639	239	2862
2	869*, 3529*, 4886	77	1377	158	2869*, 3373	240	1969*
3	J D Bally	78	3845	159	3321	241	1737*, 4214
4	G-STEN	79	3455	160	2461	242	3417
5	G D A Green	80	4642	161	4676	243	1172*, 4586
6	4533	81	J R Upton, 2453*	163	1089*, 3389	244	S G Olender
7	5256	82	3920	165	1648	245	3976
8	3720	83	3680	166	2623	246	3555
08	5177	84	4261	167	V L Brown	247	3604
9	R C Ellis	85	D J Robertson	168	4273	248	1911
10	L G Watts	86	2310	169	4145	249	2950*
11	4606	87	4608	170	5250	250	5060
12	5179	88	2974	171	3643	251	2216
13	D-KOOL	89	J A Millar	172	5014	253	1840, 4709
14	1958	90	R A Foot, 2981*	173	3607*	254	1795
15	4563	92	1839	175	3124	256	D S Towson, 3540*
16	4472	93	3228	176	4413	257	3303
17	2804	94	G-BZYG	177	3126	258	2323
18	1475	95	4751	178	3119	259	2229
19	M P Roberts	96	3807	180	2901	260	G-CDPX
20	2951	97	B.G.A.	181	2827	261	2715*, G-LIVS
21	4611	98	5209	182	1293, 1989	262	D W Allison
22	J Zealley	99	4157	183	4794*	263	R N Turner, 3777*
23	G-BYEC	100	3962	184	1660	264	2806
24	4978	101	L Hepworth	185	4699	265	2243
25	3973	102	G-DGCL	187	3269	266	2200
26	5274	104	4968	188	2775	267	2464
27	4502	105	4078	190	3401	268	3475*
28	D S McKay	106	2513	191	2436	270	1027*, 2346
29	3581	107	G O Avis, 2524*	192	3533	271	3101
31	4251	108	3606	193	J C Baldock, 2727*	272	2426
33	778	109	3395	194	3544	273	1667
34	T J Murphy	110	R Jones	195	2115	274	4467
35	3600	111	M F Lassan	196	R C Sharman, 3266*	276	2829
36	4739	112	4344	198	4645	277	3587
37	2556	113	1013*, 3158	199	G-JULL	278	3789*
38	4047	114	3791	200	4226	279	2856
39	W S Stephen	115	G-BZEM	201	3433*	281	2812
40	B Fitchett	116	2124	202	3107	282	3397
41	R F Aldous, 5087*	117	1386*, 2751	203	3991	283	2880
42	4478	118	2911	205	5184	284	1632
44	4735	119	E W Richards	206	3708	285	3599
45	5249	120	3197	207	1974*	286	J M Beattie, 2469*
46	4786	121	1316	208	4687	287	2268
47	1435	122	4046	209	5223	288	2808
48	4079	123	2247	210	5199	290	5246
49	1797	124	5059	211	1222	292	3988*, 5018
50	2632	125	3317	212	4720*	293	5286
51	3355	126	3913	213	4165	294	3751
52	3713, 4276*	128	3224	214	2155	295	2821
53	1763	129	2071	215	2937	296	4737
54	R Jones	130	R Lemin	216	4326	297	J C Bailey
55	3497*, 4072	131	W J Dean	217	2960	298	2894
56	4337	132	2455	218	3707	299	1913*
57	5093	134	5053	219	3770	300	2756
58	J F D'Arcy	136	3273	220	4081	301	4630
59	4245	137	3861	221	4483	302	3689*
60	G-HJSM	138	R Theil	222	1579	303	S G Olender
61	1262*, 5050	139	1726	223	2936	304	5148
62	1514, 4088*	140	R D Payne	224	3627	306	5155
63	4850	141	3244	225	1336	307	2251
64	4222	143	3298	226	1662	308	3877
65	3899	144	4489	227	A T Farmer, 2337*	310	4843
66	J Delafield	146	1876	228	3549	311	1359
066	4952	147	2466	229	1683	313	4170*
67	1052*	148	S Burton	230	3523	314	3339
68	4819	149	5057	231	2918	315	4066
69	E C Wright	150	1269*, 5010	232	4437	317	1290
70	5107	151	1686	233	2226*, 5075	318	3198
71	4956	152	2501	234	1723	319	2728
72	5248	153	1528	236	3717	320	G-INCA
73	4961	154	3279	237	3967	321	5121
74	1788*, 2224	155	870	238	3411	322	1860*

No.	BGANo.	No.	BGANo.	No.	BGANo.	No.	BGANo.
323	2837	425	3714	532	1889	637	3937*
324	2000	426	1171*	535	1628*, 4945	638	2396
325	4296	428	1844	537	4379	639	2497*
326	3631	429	3780	538	3199*	640	H C Evans
328	3372	431	2702	539	1854	641	3146
330	3398	432	4315	540	4820	642	2391
332	3516	433	2193	541	2611	643	1334*, 2649
333	3115	434	4428	542	2294	644	2565
334	2327	435	2698*, 2826	543	4424	646	4871
335	3892	437	W A Coates, 2271*	546	3739	647	2592*
337	2616	438	3187	547	4685	648	2340
339	1722	440	5170	549	867	651	4482
341	I R Willows	441	4651	550	L G Watts	652	2402*
342	1732	443	2968	551	1987	653	1104*
345	2820	444	2175	552	2553	656	M B Jefferyes
346	3831	445	3965	554	4790	660	4305
347	3727	446	2959	555	R S Maxwell-Fendt	661	4659
350	1348	447	R H Yarney, 2441*	556	2300	662	3588
351	1741	449	1538*, 5169	558	1341	663	663
352	4767	450	3747	560	4291	665	J B Dalton
353	2186	451	2870	561	J A Hallam	666	5180
354	2472	452	2789	563	4062	667	3821*
355	1852*, 3834	453	2694*	564	3207	668	3750
356	3805	456	2212*, 5039	565	1836*, 5084	669	3645
357	M P Brooks	458	1487	566	1748	671	3152
360	2539	460	5211	567	3596	672	2672
361	K A Hale	461	3388	569	2673	674	3400
363	D K Gardiner	463	1201*	570	5033	676	4646
364	4051	464	3133	571	3151	677	1855
365	4019	465	1288*	572	4455	678	1810
366	1240	466	1688	574	3424	679	M Parsons, 1401*
367	2522	467	3866	575	1986	680	2037
368	3337	468	1858	576	2504	683	1454
369	3559	469	4060*	577	1546	685	J R Luxton
370	3206*, 5070	470	2640*	578	1381	686	1312
371	3381	473	3886	579	1785	687	3883
372	1393	474	1574	580	B Crook, 2473*	688	2326
373	1428*	475	1423	581	P S Worth	690	5088
374	4324	476	4345*	583	3933	691	1982*
375	2283	477	1916	584	4249	692	4080
376	C J Short	480	2289*, 3663	585	4082	693	4106*
377	4775	481	2707	586	2644	695	1702*, 2025
378	2196	483	2452	590	2924	696	2778
379	2906	484	3448	591	3854	698	3283
380	4054	485	4892	592	2481	699	2357
381	4032	486	3895	593	2222	700	4986
382	2979*	488	3136*	594	2529	701	3259
383	2876	490	2697	595	1595	703	1727
385	A Groves, 2723*	491	2980	597	1198	704	2376
386	G-ORIG	492	D A White	598	4263*	705	3393
387	1769	493	4169	601	J D Spencer	706	1816
388	4674*	494	4553	602	M G Miller, 1657*	707	1752
390	4134*	495	3470	603	4360	708	4065
391	3785	496	3808	604	2585	709	1670
392	2231	497	4178	605	3820	710	J D Atkinson, 4392*
393	4238	498	3479	606	3427	711	4290
394	3842	499	D-KKAM	607	3898	712	4258
395	3139*	500	1400, 2146*	609	3574	714	2743
400	G-BLRM	501	1802	610	2114	715	1383
401	A J Hewitt, 1691*	502	3946	611	3889	716	2059
402	1799	503	1902*, 5020	612	3542	719	2783
403	G-BSOM*	505	5218	614	2162*	720	3702
404	1268	506	4694	615	4541	721	3156
405	3500	507	3719	616	2802	722	4838
406	1361*, 4998	509	3924	617	5119	724	1616
407	2153	510	3171	618	4718	725	3686
408	2754	511	2228*	619	1456	727	3130*
409	4959	513	4522	620	5115	728	2444
410	R Jones, 4977*	515	2788	621	4791	729	3801
411	3154	516	3981	622	1671	730	3939
413	2711	517	1298	624	4213	732	2413
414	4738	518	3512*	625	1684	733	2429*
415	1945	519	3375	626	G-BZSP*	734	F G Bradney
417	1756	520	4943	627	3236	735	3887
418	4768	521	3698	628	4628	737	2645
419	M L Boxall	522	3814	629	5235	739	1088
420	4811	523	1983*	630	D-KPRA	741	P Orchard, 1121*
421	4971	524	3762	631	3109	742	2491*
422	1392	525	1669	633	4967	743	1615
423	1850	527	3261	634	3462	744	3291
424	5111	530	A A Maitland, 2597*	636	4624	745	2246

No.	BGANo.	No.	BGANo.	No.	BGANo.
747	3910	858	A M Griffiths, 1689*	992	2961
748	3731	859	1136*	993	3148
750	2596	860	3994	994	1380
751	4164	862	1519	996	2625
753	3525	865	3993*	997	3304
754	3827*	867	4504	998	3457
755	3812	868	4534	1018	4312*
757	2518	869	2412	1066	1066*
758	J Nash	870	3904	2001	3776*
759	2168*	871	4873	8378	4067*
760	2366	873	1801		
761	1706	877	2354		
762	4117	878	1433*, 4894		
765	2848*	880	4835		
766	2379	881	2545		
767	2090	882	3870*		
768	3590	886	2445		
769	2172*	888	3575		
770	2291	891	2691		
771	2816	894	4782		
772	3441	899	4547		
773	3134	900	378*, 4831		
775	4252	901	5123		
776	5167	902	2825		
777	4175, 4359*	903	3299*		
778	3673	904	2309*		
779	C Villa, 3621*	906	5049		
780	3141	907	4425		
781	4625	909	2502		
782	782*	910	3856		
783	3944	911	4400		
785	3453	912	2382		
786	2537	913	4304		
787	C J Pollard	914	3761		
788	2181	915	2370		
790	4576	917	1869		
791	S R Bruce	918	1725		
795	3882	919	4004		
797	5175	920	K Neave, 3155*		
798	2329	921	4355		
799	1640	922	3710		
800	G-LEES	925	A G Veitch, 3909*		
801	3757	927	3363		
802	4151	928	3767		
803	3535*	930	4240		
805	4030	933	4557		
806	3257	937	1637		
808	1775*, 5012	940	3921		
810	2423*	942	3623		
811	2119	943	2495		
812	1391	944	3522		
813	4660	948	1630		
818	1685	949	3809		
819	4029	950	3302		
820	S J Gooch, 2604*	951	2137*		
821	2321	952	3437		
822	3120	954	3610		
823	4362*	955	2584		
824	2129	959	L A Mundy, 2033, 2081*		
826	1944	960	5159		
827	2667	961	1598		
828	2479	962	4235*		
831	2214	963	3954		
832	1875	968	2864		
837	D S Carter	969	3365*		
838	3956	970	4008		
839	2515*	971	2417		
840	3878	972	2350*		
841	4429	973	3410		
842	1822	977	4941		
843	3704	978	1871		
844	2286	979	3959		
846	1562*	980	N F Perren, 3585*		
849	2706	983	2902		
850	2480	985	4009		
851	1976*	986	4523*		
853	3515*	987	3271		
854	2899	988	4826		
855	3964	989	2164		
856	4289	990	2508		
857	1568	991	3858		

PART 2 (ii) – BGA ALPHA-NUMERIC TAIL CODE INDEX

Code	Value	Code	Value	Code	Value	Code	Value
1F	5202	B2	4385	DJT	4271*	HD	3419
1UP	5261	B3	5161	DM	4868	HDH	3862*
1Z	4878	B4	1823	DP	4217	HJT	4187*
2C	5165	B8	4232	DR7	4647	HL	4390
2CK	3806	B9	B O Marcham, 3986*	DS	4092*, 5146*, 5298	HPH	4090*
2CS	2680	B11	4342	DS2	5058	HS	4399
2R	3159	B12	4891	DUO	5247	IM	4415*
2S	5271	B19	4728	DV8	1743	IV	3709
2T	5156	B20	4893	DVM	2232*	IH4	4753
2UP	4792	B33	4147	DW	4465	IS28	2206
2W	5055	B55	5081*	DYN	2477*	IS30	3180
2ZC	4256	B96	1283*	DZ	3885	J1	4935
3D	4113	BB	3532	E	285*	J2	4949
4A	4449	BF1	5163	E1	5236	J3	3632
4Q	S Menges	BJ	G-BMBJ	E3	5131	J4	P G Sheard
4T	4801	BK	5047	E4	4895	J5	5216
5GC	4690	BMN	1102*	E5	4769	J6	5072
5K	5000	BS	4912	E7	5003	J7	J P Eldem
6B	3361	BS1	2677	E8	4505	J8	4985
6S	5004*	BT	4507	E11	S R Ell	J13	1204*
6X	5114	BW	2635*, 5281	E17	5149	J15	3106
7A	5128	BZ	1834	EA	4981	J34	3796
7C	3552	C	2191	EB	4698	J50	4824
7D	3167*	C1	4450	EC	3618	JA	5243
7Q	4364	C2	4836	ED	5040*	JA9	4408
7R	3629	C3	D A Rose, 4514*	EE	4932*	JB	4749
7V	2138	C4	4186	EF	4650*, 5239	JD	1483
7X	4741	C6	4829	EHJ	2719*	JED	4822*
8T	5259	C7	4404	EN	4346	JF	5182
9A	1317	C29	4012	EU	4516*	JG	J P Gorringe
9E	5129	C30	3706	EW	4632	JH	2670*, 4439
9W	K J Sleigh	C34	3997	EW2	5284	JH1	4810
15A	4825	C64	4973*	EZ	5045	JO1	4544
17K	1720	C65	4974*	F	400*	JS	4813
17R	1295	C66	5126	F1	4747	JW	5132
20L	2740	C74	4823	F2	4409	K	2989
26E	G-CCLR	C75	5021*	F3	4418*	K1	4340
26Q	4039	CB	4668	F4	1367	K3	2689*
27B	4876	CC	5270	F6	4827	K4	4310
28E	5117	CD1	4802	F20	4248	K5	5100
28T	5238	CH	5034	F21	3918	K8	4549
29E	G-SASG	CJ	M Wright	F94	5154*	K9	4100
34Z	1765	CL	4677	FB	5042	K11	4543
97Z	3961	CP	4814	FE	4787*, 5268	K13	3656
A1	4155	CS	C D Sterritt	FGT	2156*	K18	5229
A2	3872	CT	4870	FKY	3329*	K19	K Millar
A3	1946*	CU	4493	FLN	3348*	K21	4496
A7	4573	CYL	1639*	FTI	3511*	KA	5203*
A8	4596	CZ	5147	FXQ	3658*	KC	3640
A9	4244	D	2317	G1	4545	KE	4451*
A11	2385	D1	936*, 4638	G2	3315	KL	3960
A14	4316*	D2	I D Smith	G7	4329*	KM	5102
A19	3390	D3	W J Dean	G9	5266	KO	4230*, 5110
A20	4112	D4	4444	G41	4539	KR	4627
A23	1237	D5	2868*	G46	698	KT	1744*
A26	4322	D6	5191	G81	4380	KV	4288
A27	4422	D7	4262	G91	920*	KW	4426
A28	4936	D8	4818	GA	4847	L	3163
A30	2126	D9	3935	GAZ	2651*	L01	2770
A34	4531	D11	5226	GB1	5162*	L2	4508
A39	5108	D15	4158	GB2	3414	L3	4381
A61	4318	D19	4048*	GM	5144	L4	4657
A77	4125*	D31	S A Young, 4210*	GP	4816	L5	3671
A98	3438	D41	4464*	GR	4420	L7	4386, 5206*
AA	5133	D53	4772	GR8	5192	L8	4153
AC	4387	D54	4163	GS	4705*	L10	4988
AC4	G Bowser	D55	4763	GT	5187	L12	3611
AD	5198	D64	4121*	GW	5122	L17	4703
AG	5157	D70	4146	GX	5120	L18	4253
AG1	4955*	DA	5232	H	2984	L19	5267
AH	3879	DB	5196	H1	4957	L24	4764
AJ	G-ZZAJ	DC	4405	H2	4558	L51	3454
AM	A Magenis	DD	4300	H4	4969	L57	3577
AP	5145	DD2	4931	H5	3285*	L58	4192
AP1	5153	DDT	5150*	H8	4195	L99	1438*
AS	2729	DF	4806	H11	2552	LA	4724
AT	4725	DG	3638	H12	3732	LC	3199
AV	4996	DG3	D N Mackay	H17	2847	LD	4347
AV8	4777	DH2	4860	H20	3185	LE	4913, 5254
AW	3683	DHG	2132*	HB1	4661	LGC	4511*
B	3366	DI	A W Roberts	HB2	3760	LL	5217

Code	Value	Code	Value	Code	Value	Code	Value
LM	5224	P61	4343	S5	4299	VS	2420*
LS	4189	P70	3015	S7	2943*	W1	4795
LS3	2656	PE	5116	S8	4223	W2	5251
LS4	2908	PF	4666, 5024*	S9	S S Turner	W3	4862
LS6	4119	PG	P Goulding	S10	G-BXGZ*	W4	3874
LS7	4597	PH	1467*	S13	2425*	W5	4859
LS8	4237	PH1	4577	S19	4580	W7	4861*
LT	4538	PK	4990	S20	4041	W8	4574
LW	5118	PM3	4723	S22	4191	W9	5225
LX	4376	PN	P C Naegeli	S27	4834	W10	4641
LY	2650	PS	3571	S30	2380	W17	2595
LZ	4338*	PT	4721	S33	4710*	W19	4410
M	3205	PW5	4311	S60	4848	W20	D C Heath
M2	5048	PZ	4058	S75	5046*	W22	4852
M4	4368	Q5	3278	S81	3722*	W27	4407
M5	2494	R1	4475	S83	4268*	W54	4231
M6	G-MSIX	R2	5041	SA1	2986*	W81	5215
M7	2939	R3	4688	SC	4654	WA1	4487
M8	4278	R4	4600	SH	G-BXSH*	WA2	4452
M9	4904	R6	5288	SH1	Surrey & Hants GC	WE	4431
M11	5183	R7	4581*	SH2	4800	WE4	4993*
M19	4793*	R8	4471	SH3	3322	WK	4216*
M25	4480	R9	3216	SH4	3538	X	S Godleman
M80	4804	R10	4590	SH6	Surrey & Hants GC	X1	4783
MB	5025	R11	4896	SH7	4924	X4	5080
MF	2801	R12	5130*	SH8	3192	X5	4750
ML	2893	R17	RAFGSA	SH9	4740	X7	N G Hackett
MM	4969, 5160*	R18	5213	SI	5002	X8	4330
MS	4966	R20	4578*	SK	4727	X9	5252
MY	4975	R21	4572	SK1	5032	X11	5064
N	5023	R22	4614	SM	R Acreman, 4908*	X15	4785
N1	4443	R23	4629*	SO1	4863	X17	5098
N2	3420	R25	4587	SP	P G Scott	X19	3846
N3	5078	R28	5079*	SR	4430	X50	4341
N4	1914	R30	(ASK 13, Odiham)*	SW	4562	X56	2955
N5	4207	R32	4675*	T1	G-OPHT	X70	4211*
N6	3736	R33	4582*	T2	4406	X96	2414
N8	4352*	R35	2888*	T3	5071	X97	3955
N11	2142	R36	4612*	T4	5097	XD2	5099
N12	4960	R37	4636*	T5	4301	XE	5255
N15	3548	R38	4837*	T6	4881	XS	5285
N16	3657	R39	4601	T8	I Mountain	Y4	4280
N19	4132	R41	4730*	T9	5291	Y7	5205
N21	673	R43	4530*	T10	1612	Y11	5056*
N25	4598	R46	4620*	T11	5067	Y44	4853
N28	3482	R48	4570*	T12	4840	YG	1908*
N29	3254	R49	4621*	T19	4123	Z	P M Wells, 1873*, 3368*
N36	3864*	R53	4503	T21	K J Scott, 3290*	Z1	4789
N51	2987	R55	4470	T22	Surrey & Hants GC	Z2	4788
N52	1551*	R56	4684*	T27	4716	Z3	4762
N53	Seahawk GC	R57	4603	T34	2397	Z4	3340
N55	1118*, 4883	R59	4683*	T40	5275	Z5	4267
N56	3505	R61	4633*	T42	D E Williams	Z6	3654*
NC	5219	R63	4622	T45	873*	Z7	G-DCDC
NG	N F Goudie	R67	4697	T49	1203	Z8	4190
NG1	4987	R69	RAFGSA	T51	1164	Z9	4696
NH	4962	R71	3064*	T54	3756	Z10	4575
NJ1	N J Irving, 4844*	R73	4555	T65	2800	Z12	4704
NT	2318	R75	4604*	T99	4980	Z19	4784*
NU	4953	R77	4736	TB2	3733	Z25	2427*
NU2	Notts Univ GC	R80	4752*	TC	A J McNamara	Z27	5173
NW	2934	R83	960*	TL2	4679	Z33	4275
NX	2898*	R88	4680*	U1	4335	Z35	4865
OD	5245	R92	4707	U2	4131	Z45	4040
OL	5253	R93	2207*	U9	4378	Z55	5185
OV	D V Wilson	RA	5158	UP2	5063	Z99	4068
OZ	4458	RB	R Brown, 4989*	UWE	4734*		
P	3274	RB1	4890*	UY	4841*		
P1	4567	RC	5009	V1	4546		
P2	4442	RH	2785	V2	R Jones		
P3	4363*	RJ	3463	V5	4034	Note:	
P4	4648	RM	5204*	V6	5006	Codes "SY" to "ZZ" are allocated to	
P5	4152	RNT	2831*	V7	2695	the Air Cadets Central Gliding School	
P6	P J Pengilly	RP1	4233	V8	4982		
P7	E R Smith	RS	4713	V9	5073		
P8	4373*	RT	R Tietema, 3969*	V10	3622		
P9	2443	RW	4671	V11	4292		
P10	4923	RY	4084	V12	5195		
P19	1707	RZ	2282	V17	4758		
P20	2136	S	3642	V26	4976		
P23	4615*	S1	4821	V66	4776		
P30	4571	S2	4118	V2C	4921		
P31	4017*	S3	3580	V2T	4664		
P50	4691	S4	4293	VE	3006*		

PART 2 (iii) – CIVIL REGISTRATION and MILITARY SERIAL DECODE INDEX

Several former British military gliders carry their former service serials for authenticty A few imported vintage specimens also carry their previous UK and overseas civil registrations. Whilst details of marks carried are included in Part 1, Column 3 this specific decode Index is including for ease of reference. Examples known are shown below.

Country	Regn or Serial	BGA No.
UK		
	G-ALRH	629
	G-ALRK	490
RAF		
	RA905	1143
	TS291	852
	VM684	791
	VM687	794
	WB920	3221
	WB922	4366
	WB924	3901
	WB935	4110
	WB943	2941
	WB944	3160
	WB961	4856
	WB962	3836
	WB971	3324
	WB975	3288
	WB981	3238
	WB988	4877
	WE990	2583
	WE992	2692
	WG498	3245
	WJ306	2720*, 3240
	WT871	3149
	WT898	4412
	WT900	3272
	WT908	3487
	WT910	3953
	WT913	3239
	WT914	3194
	WT918	3241
	WZ819	3498
	WZ828	4421
	XA240	4556
	XA295	3336
	XA302	3786
	XA310	4963
	XE786	4033
	XE790	4926
	XE807	3545
	XN185	4077
	XN186	3905
	XN187	3903
	XN243	3145
	XN419	3255
	XP463	4372
	XS652	1107
	XT653	3469
GERMANY		
	D-12-354	1711
	D-1265	2276
	D-4667	3142
	D-5084	2688
	D-5627	1872
	D-5826	3186
	D-6173	4336
SWITZERLAND		
	HB-474	2474
CZECH REPUBLIC		
	OK-0833	4884
	OK-0927	4286
	OK-0975	5015
	OK-8592	655
SLOVAKIA		
	OM-0973	4970

PART 3 – IRISH GLIDING AND SOARING ASSOCIATION REGISTER

The system is similar to the British Gliding Association and until 2007 the register was maintained by the Irish Gliding & Soaring Association. Originally this was kept by the Irish Aviation Club using the prefix "IAC". From 1960 until 1967 gliders were allocated with a number prefixed "IGA". The IGSA listing is updated from Air-Britain sources. In March 2007 responsibility for glider registration was taken over by the Irish Aviation Authority and all active gliders were re-registered in the sequence from EI-GLA. The remaining aircraft are shown below.

No. Code	Type	Construction No	Previous Identity	Date	Registered Owner (Operator) (Unconfirmed) Base	Status
IGA 6	Slingsby T.8 Tutor	Not known	IAC 6	.56	Meath Aero Museum Ashbourne, County.Meath	N 3.01
			VM657			
EI-100	SZD-12A Mucha 100A	494	OY-XAN	.95	P Bedford Dromod	N 6.07
					(Preserved at Cavan & Leitrim Railway)	
EI-102	Slingsby T.26 Kite 2	Not known	IGA 102	.54	Dublin Gliding Club Gowran Grange	N 5.03
			IAC 102, BGA		*(Reserved as EI-GMG)*	
EI-105	Schleicher K7	775	IGA 7	.60	Dublin Gliding Club (Roscommon)	N 6.03
					(Sold to private syndicate)	
EI-118	EoN AP.8 Baby	EoN/B/001	BGA 608	.73	B Douglas Gowran Grange	
			RAFGSA 217, BGA 608, G-ALLU, BGA 608 *(Reserved as EI-GMK)*			
EI-120	LET L-13 Blanik	175205	RAFGSA	.75	Private Syndicate Gowran Grange	N 4.06
			BGA 1730			
EI-124 124	Grob G102 Astir CS 77 (Astir Standard)	1761		.80	Nutgrove Shopping Centre Churchtown, Dublin	N 6.07
					(On display)	
EI-127	Schleicher Ka 6CR	662	PH-259	??	N van Kuyk *(Reserved as EI-GLG)* Not known	
EI-130	Scheibe L-Spatz	200	BGA 2199	??	J J Sullivan Gowran Grange	
			D-4707		*"White Cloud" (Reserved as EI-GMI)*	
EI-133 33	Schleicher K 8B	8557	D-8517	.91	Dublin Gliding Club Gowran Grange	A10.01
			D-9367		*(Reserved as EI-GLE)*	
EI-134 34	Schleicher ASW 15B	15249	D-1087	.91	Not known *(Reserved as EI-GLX)* Gowran Grange	
EI-135	Slingsby T.38 Grasshopper	758	WZ762	.91	(Syndicate) Gowran Grange	N 4.06
	(Wings from WZ756 or WZ768)				*(Stored as "WZ762")*	
EI-139	Slingsby T.31B	902	BGA 3485	.93	P Bedford Dromod	N 6.07
			G-BOKG, XE789		*(Preserved at Cavan & Leitrim Railway; reserved as EI-GMG)*	
EI-140	SZD-12A Mucha 100A	491	HB-647	.93	D Mongey *(Reserved as EI-GMJ)* Gowran Grange	
EI-143	Schleicher ASK 13	13112	BGA 1501	.94	Dublin Gliding Club *(To BGA 1501 @ 4.07)*	
EI-144	Scheibe SF 27A Zugvogel V	6049	(EI-142)	.94	M L Kelly Gowran Grange	
			D-1444		*(Reserved as EI-GLY)*	
EI-154	LET L-13 Blanik	173214	BGA 1500	6.02	J Selman Ardagh	
			G-ATCG			
EI-157	Slingsby T.21B	1158	BGA 1465	.02	Dublin Gliding Club Gowran Grange	
			RAFGSA 333, XN154		*(Reserved as EI-GLZ)*	
EI-160	Grob G103 Twin Astir	Not known		.04	Not known *(Stored)* Kilkenny	N 6.07
EI-162	Centrair 101A Pégase	101A0311	BGA 3458	.04	Not known Gowran Grange	
					(Hit tree on field landing Clonegal, County Wexford 7. 8.06)	

Re-registrations in 2007:

From:	To:		From:	To:
EI-108	EI-GLF		EI-150	EI-GLA
EI-111	EI-GLM		EI-151	EI-GMA; G-CKRM
EI-112	EI-GLD		EI-153	EI-GLV
EI-113	EI-GMF		EI-153	EI-GLV
EI-115	EI-GLP		EI-158	EI-GMD
EI-128	EI-GLW		EI-159	EI-GLI
EI-132	EI-GMB		EI-161	EI-GLU
EI-136	EI-GMC		EI-163	EI-GLC
EI-145	EI-GLJ		EI-164	EI-GLB
EI-146	EI-GLO		EI-165	EI-GLN
EI-147	EI-GLL		EI-167	EI-GLR
EI-148	EI-GLK		EI-169	EI-GLH
EI-149	EI-GLT		EI-177	EI-GLS

SECTION 7

PART 1 – OVERSEAS REGISTRATION PREFIX INDEX

The previous identity origins of many of the current UK and Irish registered aircraft are many and varied. Therefore, we include both current and historical lists of ICAO national country allocations so the reader can deduce, in brief, the aircraft's provenance. Thanks to Mike Cain for an update this year

Current Prefixes:

Prefix	Country	Commenced	Historical Prefix(es)	Prefix	Country	Commenced	Historical Prefix(es)
AP-	Pakistan	1947		LY-	Lithuania	1936	LY-, RY-, CCCP-
A2-	Botswana	1972	VQ-ZE -VQ-Z	LZ-	Bulgaria	1929	
A3-	Tonga	1971	VQ-F	M-	Isle of Man	2007	G-
A4O-	Oman	1974		N	United States	1921	
A5-	Bhutan	1983		OB-	Peru	1940	OA-
A6-	United Arab Emirates-	1977	A6-	OD-	Lebanon	1951	F-, LR-
A7-	Qatar	1975		OE-	Austria	1936	A-
A8-	Liberia	2003	LI-, EL-	OH-	Finland	1931	K-S
A9C-	Bahrain	1977		OK-	Czech Republic	1929	L-B
B-	China (Peoples' Republic of)	1975	XT	OM-	Slovakia	19xx	OK-
B-	China (Republic of)	1949	XT	OO-	Belgium	1929	O-B
B-H, -K, -L-	Hong Kong	1997	VR-H	OY-	Denmark	1929	T-D
B-M-	Macau	1999	CR-M	P-	Korea (North)	1953	
C-	Canada	1974	G-C, CF-	PH-	Netherlands	1929	H-N
CC-	Chile	1929		PJ-	Netherlands Antilles	1929	
CN-	Morocco	1952	F-D	PK-	Indonesia	1929	
CP-	Bolivia	1954	CB	PP-	Brazil	1932	P-B
CS-	Portugal	1929	C-P	PR-	Brazil	1950	
CU-	Cuba	1947	NM-	PT-	Brazil	1950	
CX-	Uruguay	1929		PU-	Brazil (ultralights)	1950	
C2-	Nauru	1971	VH-	PZ-	Suriname	1929	
C3-	Andorra	1993		P2-	Papua New Guinea	1974	VH-
C5-	Gambia	1978	VP-X	P4-	Aruba	1986	PJ-
C6-	Bahamas	1975	VP-B	RA-	Russia	1991	RR-, CCCP-
C9-	Mozambique	1975	CR-A, CR-B	RDPL-	Laos	1975	F-L, XW-
D-	Germany	1929		RP-	Philippines	1975	PI-
DQ-	Fiji	1971	VQ-F	SE-	Sweden	1929	S-A
D2-	Angola	1975	CR-L	SP-	Poland	1929	P-P
D4-	Cape Verde Islands	1975	CR-C	ST-	Sudan	1959	SN-
D6-	Comoros	1975	F-O	SU-	Egypt	1931	
EC-	Spain	1929	M-	SU-Y	Palestine	1995	VQ-P (1930-48)
EI-, EJ-	Ireland	1928		SX-	Greece	1929	
EK-	Armenia	1991	CCCP-	S2-	Bangladesh	1972	AP-
EP-	Iran	1944	RV-		(Formerly East Pakistan)		
ER-	Moldova	1991	CCCP-	S5-	Slovenia	1993	YU-, SL-
ES-	Estonia	1929	ES-, CCCP-	S7-	Seychelles	1976	VQ-S
ET-	Ethiopia	1945		S9-	Sao Tome	1977	CR-S
EW-	Belarus	1991	CCCP-	TC-	Turkey	1929	
EX-	Kyrgyzstan	1991	CCCP-	TF-	Iceland	1937	
EY-	Tajiikstan	1991	CCCP-	TG-	Guatemala	1948	LG-
EZ-	Turkmenistan	1993	CCCP-	TI-	Costa Rica	1927	
E3-	Eritrea	1994	ET-	TJ-	Cameroon	1960	F-O, VR-N
F-	France	1919		TL-	Central African Republic	1961	F-O
F-O	French Overseas Territories	1929		TN-	Congo (Peoples' Republic of)	1960	F-O
G-	United Kingdom	1919		TR-	Gabon	1960	F-O
HA-	Hungary	1935	H-M	TS-	Tunisia	1956	F-O
HB-	Switzerland	1935	CH-	TT-	Chad	1960	F-O
HC-	Ecuador	1929		TU-	Ivory Coast	1960	F-O
HH-	Haiti	1929		TY-	Benin	1960	F-O
HI-	Dominican Republic	1929		TZ-	Mali	1960	F-O
HK-	Colombia	1946	C-	T3-	Kiribati	1983	VP-P
HL-	Korea (South)	1948		T7-	San Marino	1997	
HP-	Panama	1952	R-, RX-	T8A-	Palau	2004	V6-
HR-	Honduras	1961	XH-		(Formerly part of Micronesia)		
HS-	Thailand	1929	H-S	T9-	Bosnia Herzegovina	1992	YU-
HV-	Vatican state	1929			(Reportedly allocated E7- in 2008)		
HZ-	Saudi Arabia	1945	UH-	UK-	Uzbekistan	1991	CCCP-
H4-	Solomon Islands	1978	VP-P	UN-	Kazakhstan	1991	CCCP-
I-	Italy	1929		UR-	Ukraine	1991	CCCP-
JA-	Japan	1948	J-	VH-	Australia	1929	G-AU
JU-	Mongolia	1998	MT-, HMAY-	VN-	Vietnam	1975	F-VN, XV-
JY-	Jordan	1954	TJ- ,VQ-P	VP-A	Anguilla	1997	
J2-	Djibouti	1977	F-O	VP-B	Bermuda	1997	VR-B
J3-	Grenada	1974	VQ-G	VP-C	Cayman Islands	1997	VR-C
J5-	Guinea Bissau	1979	CR-G	VP-F	Falkland Islands	1929	
J6-	St. Lucia	1981	VQ-L	VP-G	Gibraltar	1997	VR-G
J7-	Dominica	1978	VP-L	VP-LVA	British Virgin Islands	1971	
J8-	St. Vincent	1979	VP-V	to VP-LZZ			
LN-	Norway	1931	N-	VQ-H	St. Helena	1929	
LQ-	Argentina (Government)	1932		VQ-T	Turks and Caicos Islands	1980	VP-J
LV-	Argentina	1932	R-	VT-	India	1930	G-IA, CR-I
LX-	Luxembourg	1935	UL-	V2-	Antigua	1981	VP-L, VP-A

Prefix	Country	Commenced	Historical Prefix(es)
V3-	Belize	1983	VP-H--
V4--	St.Kitts and Nevis	1983	VP-LKA-LLZ
V5-	Namibia	1990	ZS-
V6--	Micronesia	1990	
V7--	Marshall Islands	1991	MI-
V8-	Brunei	1984	VR-U-
XA-	Mexico *(Commercial)*	1929	X-
XB-	Mexico *(Private)*	1929	X-
XC-	Mexico *(Government)*	1929	X-
XT-	Burkina Faso	1984	F-O
	(Formerly Upper Volta)		
XU-	Cambodia	1954	F-KH, KW-
XY-	Myanmar	1938	VT- *(Formerly Burma)*
YA-	Afghanistan	1929	
YI-	Iraq	1931	
YJ-	Vanuatu	1933	F-O or VP-P marks
	(Formerly New Hebrides)		until 1980
YK-	Syria	1949	F-, SR-
YL-	Latvia	1929	YL-, CCCP
YN-	Nicaragua	1981	YN-, AN-
YR-	Romania	1936	CV-
YS-	El Salvador	1939	
YU-	Serbia and Montenegro	1933	X-S, UN
	(Formerly part of Yugoslavia until 1992. Montenegro having		
	declared independence in 2008 may take up new marks in due		
	course, 4O being suggested.)		
YV-	Venezuela	1929	
Z-	Zimbabwe	1980	VP-W, VP-Y
ZA-	Albania	1946	
ZK-, ZM-	New Zealand	1929	G-NZ
ZP-	Paraguay	1929	
ZS-, ZU-	South Africa	1929	G-U
Z3-	Macedonia	1992	YU
3A-	Monaco	1959	CZ, MC
3B-	Mauritius	1959	VQ-M
3C-	Equatorial Guinea	1970	EC-
3D-	Swaziland	1971	VQ-ZIA - ZLZ
3X-	Guinea	1958	F-O
4K-	Azerbaijan	1991	CCCP-

Prefix	Country	Commenced	Historical Prefix(es)
4L-	Georgia	1991	CCCP-
4R-	Sri Lanka	1954	VP-C, CY-
4X-	Israel	1948	
5A-	Libya	1959	I-
5B-	Cyprus	1960	VQ-C
5H-	Tanzania	1964	
	(Formerly Zanzibar (VP-Z) and Tanganyika VR-T)		
5N-	Nigeria	1960	VR-N
5R-	Madagasgar	1960	F-O
5T-	Mauritania	1960	F-O
5U-	Niger	1960	F-O
5V-	Togo	1976	F-O
5W-	Western Samoa	1962	ZK-
5X-	Uganda	1962	VP-U
5Y-	Kenya	1963	VP-K
6O-	Somalia	1969	I-, 6OS-
6V-	Senegal	1960	F-O
6Y-	Jamaica	1964	VP-J
7O-	Yemen	1974	YE-, 4W-
7P-	Lesotho	1967	VQ-ZAA -ZDZ
7Q-	Malawi	1964	VP-Y
7T-	Algeria	1962	F-O
8P-	Barbados	1968	VQ-B
8Q-	Maldive Republic	1976	(VP-)
8R-	Guyana	1967	VP-G
9A-	Croatia	1991	YU-, RC-
9G-	Ghana	1957	VP-A
9H -	Malta	1968	VP-M
9J-	Zambia	1964	VP-Y
9K-	Kuwait	1960	K-
9L-	Sierra Leone	1961	VR-L
9M-	Malaysia	1963	VR-J, -O, -R, -S, -W
9N-	Nepal	1960	
9Q-	Congo (Democratic Republic)	1962	OO-C, 9O-
	(Formerly Belgian Congo and Zaïre)		
9U-	Burundi	1966	OO-C, BR-
9V-	Singapore	1966	VR-S, 9M-
9XR-	Rwanda	1966	OO-C
9Y-	Trinidad and Tobago	1965	VP-T

Historical Prefixes:

Prefix	Country	Period	Current Prefix
A-	Austria	1929-1939	OE-
AN-	Nicaragua	1936-1981	YN-
BR-	Burundi	1962-1965	9U-
C-	Colombia	1929-1946	HK-
CB-	Bolivia	1929-1954	CP-
CCCP-	Soviet Union	1929-1991	RA- (Russia)
CF-	Canada	1929-1974	C
CH--	Switzerland	1929-1936	HB-
CR-A, -M	Mozambique	1929-1975	C9-
CR-B, -H	Mozambique	1971-1975	C9-
CR-C	Cape Verde Islands	1929-1975	D4-
CR-G	Portuguese Guinea (Guinea Bissau) 1929-1975		J5-
CR-I	Portuguese India	1929-1961	VT-
CR-L	Angola	1929-1975	D2-
CR-S	Sao Tome and Principe	1929-1977	S9-
CR-T	Timor	1929-1976	PK-
CV-	Romania	1929-1936	YR-
CY-	Ceylon	1948-1954	4R-
CZ-	Monaco	1929-1949	MC
DDR-	East Germany	1981-1990	D
DM-	East Germany	1955-1981	DDR-
EL-	Liberia	1952-2003	A8-.
ES-	Estonia	1929-1939	Merged into Soviet Union CCCP
EZ-	Saarland	1929-1933	SL-
F-D	French Morocco	1929-1952	CN-
F-KH	Cambodia	1953-1960	XU-
F-LA	Laos	1955-1959	XW-
F-O	Algeria	1929-1962	7T-

Prefix	Country	Period	Current Prefix
F-O	Benin	1929-1960	TY-
F-O	Cameroon	1929-1960	TJ-
F-O	Chad	1929-1960	TT-
F-O	Congo	1929-1960	TN-
F-O	Djibouti	1929-1977	J2-.
F-O	Gabon	1929-1960	TR-
F-O	Guinea	1929-1958	3X-
F-O	Indo-China	1948-1950s	see Cambodia, Laos, Vietnam
F-O	Ivory Coast	1929-1960	TU-
F-O	Madagascar	1929-1960	5R-
F-O	Mali	1929-1960	TZ-
F-O	Mauritania	1929-1960	5T-
F-O	Niger	1929-1960	5U-
F-O	Senegal	1929-1960	6V-
F-O	Togo	1929-1976	5V-.
F-O	Tunisia	1929-1956	TS-
F-O	Ubangi-Shari	1929-1960	TL-
F-O	Upper Volta	1929-1960	XT-
F-VN	French Indo-China	1949-1959	XV- Vietnam
FC-	Free French	1940-1944	F-
G-AU	Australia	1921-1928	VH-
G-C	Canada	1920-1928	CF-
G-IA	India	1919-1928	VT-
G-K	Kenya	1928-1928	VP-K
G-NZ	New Zealand	1921-1928	ZK-
G-U	Union of South Africa	1927-1928	ZS-
H-M	Hungary	19xx-1935	HA-.
HMAY	Mongolia	19xx-1998	MT- (or JU-?)

Prefix	Country	Period	Current Prefix
H-S	Siam	1919-1929	HS-.
J-	Japan	1929-1945	JA
JZ-	Dutch East Indies	1954-1963	PK-
K-	Kuwait	1967-1968	Interim - 9K
K-S	Finland	19xx-1931	OH-
KA-	Katanga	1961-1963	Unofficial - 9O
KW-	Cambodia	1954-1954	XU-
L-B	Czechoslovakia	1919-1929	OK-.
LG	Guatemala	1936-1948	TG
LI-	Liberia	1929-1952	EL-, now A8-
LR-	Lebanon	1944-1954	OD-
LY-	Lithuania	1929-1939	Merged into Soviet Union CCCP-
M-	Spain	1929-1933	EC-
MC-	Monaco	1949-1959	3A-
MT-	Mongolia	1948-1998	JU
N-	Norway	1919-1931	LN-.
O-B	Belgium,	1919-1929	OO-.
OA-	Peru	1929-1938	OB-
OO-C	Belgian Congo	1929-1960	9O-
OK-	Czechoslovakia	1929-1993	OK- (Czech Rep) OM- (Slovakia)
P-B	Brazil	1927-1932	PP-
P-P	Poland	1919-1929	SP-
PI-	Philippines	1945-1973	RP-
R-	Argentina *(three digits)*	1928-1937	LV-
R-	Argentina *(four letters)*	1927-1931	
R-	Panama *(two digits)*	1929-1943	RX-
RR	Russia	1922-1929	CCCP-
RV-	Persia *(Iran)*	1929-1944	EP-
RX-	Panama	1943-1952	HP-
RY-	Lithuania	1929-1939	Merged into Soviet Union CCCP-
S-A	Sweden	1929-1929	SE-.
SA-	Saudi Arabia	1946 1952	HZ-
SL-	Saarland	1953-1957	D-
SL-	Slovenia	1991-1991	Unofficial, to S5-.
SN-	Sudan	1929-1955	ST-
SR-	Syria	1946-1951	YK-.
T-D	Denmark	1919-1929	OY-.
TJ-	Transjordan	1946-1954	JY-
TS-	Saar Territory	1930-1931	Unofficial, to EZ-.
UL-	Luxembourg	1929-1935	LX-
UN-	Yugoslavia	1928-1933	YU-
VO-	Newfoundland	1934-1949	Merged into Canada CF-
VP-A	Gold Coast	1929-1957	9G- (Ghana)
VP-B	Bahamas	1929-1973	C6-
VP-C	Ceylon	1929-1948	CY-
VP-G	British Guiana	1929-1967	8R-
VP-H	British Honduras *(Belize)*	1947-1983	V3-
VP-J	Jamaica	1930-1962	6Y-(Jamaica) & VQ-T (Turks & Caicos Islands)
VP-K	Kenya	1929-1963	5Y-
VP-LAA to -LIZ	Leeward Is (Antigua)	1929-1981	V2-
VP-LKA to -LLZ	Leeward Is (St. Kitts, Nevis)	1929-1983	V4-
VP-LLA to -LLZ	Leeward Is (Anguilla)	1929-1997	VP-A
VP-LMA to -LMZ	Leeward Is (Dominica)	1929-1978	J7-
	(Montserrat)	1929-1997	VP-M
VP-LVA to -LZZ	Leeward Is (BVI)	1929-1997	VP-L

Prefix	Country	Period	Current Prefix
VP-M	Malta	1929-1968	9H-
VP-N	Nyasaland	1929-1953	VP-Y
VP-P	Western Pacific Islands	1929- 1978	H4- (Solomon Islands) &
		1929-1981	T3- (Kiribati) VP-
VP-R	Northern Rhodesia	1929-1953	VP-Y (Central African Federation)
VP-S	Somaliland	1929-1960	6OS-
VP-T	Trinidad and Tobago	1931-1965	9Y-
VP-U	Uganda	1929-1962	5X-
VP-V	St. Vincent & Grenadines	1959-1979	J8-
VP-W	Wei-Hai-Wei (Shantung, China)	1929-1930	XT-
VP-W, VP-Y	(Southern) Rhodesia	1965-1980	Z- (Zimbabwe)
VP-X	The Gambia	1929-1945	C5-.
VP-Y	Central African Federation	1953-1965	became VP-W (Rhodesia), 7Q- (Malawi) & 9J- (Zambia)
VP-Z	Zanzibar	1929-1963	5H- (Tanzania)
VQ-B	Barbados	1952-1968	8P-
VQ-C	Cyprus	1952-1960	5B-
VQ-F	Fiji, Tonga and Friendly Isles	1929-1971	DQ- (Fiji), A3- (Tonga)
VQ-G	Grenada	1962-1974	J3-
VQ-L	St. Lucia	1965-1981	J6-
VQ-M	Mauritius	1929-1968	3B-
VQ-P	Palestine	1930-1948	either TJ- or 4X-
VQ-S	Seychelles	1929-1977	S7-
VQ-ZAA to -ZDZ	Basutoland	1929-1967	7P- (Lesotho)
VQ-ZEA to -ZHZ	Bechuanaland	1929-1968	A2- (Botswana)
VQ-ZIA to -ZLZ	Swaziland	1929-1975	3D-
VR-A	Aden	1939-1969	4W- (Yemen)
VR-B	Bermuda	1931-1997	VP-B
VR-C	Cayman Islands	1968-1997	VP-C
VR-G	Gibraltar	1929-1997	VP-G
VR-H	Hong Kong	1929-1997	B-H
VR-J	Johore	1929-1957	9M-
VR-L	Sierra Leone	1929-1961	9L-
VR-N	British Cameroons	1929-1960	either TJ- or 5N
VR-O	Sabah *(North Borneo)*	1929-1963	9M-
VR-R	Malaya	1929-1959	9M-
VR-S	Singapore	1929-1963	9M- , then 9V- 1965
VR-T	Tanganyika	1930-1963	5H- (Tanzania)
VR-U	Brunei	1929-1984	V8-
VR-W	Sarawak	1929-1963	9M-
X-	Mexico	1929-1934	XA-, XB- & XC-.
X-S	Yugoslavia	1927-1928	UN-.
XH-	Honduras	1929-1960	HR-
XT	China	1929-1949	B-
XV-	South Vietnam	1959-1975	VN-
XW-	Laos	1959-1975	RDPL-
YE-	Yemen	1955-1969	4W-
YL-	Latvia	1929-1939	Merged into Soviet Union CCCP-
YN-	Nicaragua	1929-1936	AN-
4W-	Yemen	1969-1990	Merged into 7O-
6OS	Somalia	1960-1969	6O-
9O-	Zaïre	1960-1966	9Q-

PART 2 – MILITARY SERIALS DECODE

In certain circumstances the Civil Aviation Authority may permit the operation of aircraft without the need to carry regulation size national registration letters. These conditions are referred to as "exemptions". The CAA issues to operators Exemption Certificates which are usually valid for two years. The basic requirements are that the owner undertakes to notify the CAA of the markings carried and may not fly overseas, without specific permission of the overseas country. In the case of aircraft wearing military marks the authority of the relevant department at the Ministry of Defence is required for UK markings whilst an equivalent establishment must sanction any overseas markings to be carried.

Below are current details of aircraft which are known to be wearing military and, in a very few cases, other markings. The information is compiled from members' observations and includes any BAPC and "B" Conditions identitites known to be located in the UK and Ireland. Full details of BAPC markings are carried in SECTION 3 and c/ns for the others can be found in their respective Sections. We should point out that some of the serials used are spurious. The Glider de-code is at SECTION 5, Part 2 (iii)

Country	Serial	Code	Regn	Type
UNITED KINGDOM (RAF unless otherwise shown)				
	01		G-BPVE	Bleriot Type XI 1909 replica
	4		BAPC.11	English Electric Wren composite
	12A		BAPC.2	Bristol Boxkite reconstruction
	14		BAPC.6	Roe Triplane Type I
	168		G-BFDE	Sopwith Tabloid Scout replica *(Royal Navy Air Service)*
	304		BAPC.62	Cody Type V Biplane *(Royal Flying Corps)*
	687		BAPC.181	Royal Aircraft Factory BE.2b replica *(Royal Flying Corps)*
	1881		BAPC.122	Avro 504 fsm
	2345		G-ATVP	Vickers FB.5 Gunbus replica *(Royal Flying Corps)*
	2882		BAPC.234	Vickers FB.5 Gunbus replica *(Royal Flying Corps)*
	3066		G-AETA	Caudron G.III *(RNAS)*
	5964		BAPC.112	AirCo DH.2 fsm *(Royal Flying Corps)*
	5964		G-BFVH	AirCo DH.2
	6232		BAPC.41	Royal Aircraft Factory BE.2c replica *(Royal Flying Corps)*
	9917		G-EBKY	Sopwith Pup *(Royal Flying Corps)*
	A485		BAPC.176	Royal Aircraft Factory SE.5a replica *(Royal Flying Corps)*
	A1742		BAPC.38	Bristol Scout D fsm *(Royal Flying Corps) Corps)*
	A7317		BAPC.179	Sopwith Pup fsm *(Royal Flying Corps)*
	A8226		G-BIDW	Sopwith "1½" Strutter replica *(Royal Flying Corps)*
	B-415		BAPC.163	AFEE 10/42 Rotachute Rotabuggy reconstruction
	B595	W	G-BUOD	SE.5A replica *(Royal Flying Corps)*
	B1807	A7	G-EAVX	Sopwith Pup *(Royal Flying Corps)- intended marks*
	B2458	R	G-BPOB	Sopwith F1 Camel replica *(Royal Flying Corps)*
	B4863		BAPC.113	Royal Aircraft Factory SE.5a fsm
	B5577	W	BAPC.59	Sopwith Camel fsm *(Royal Flying Corps)*
	B6401		G-AWYY	Sopwith F1 Camel replica *(Royal Flying Corps)*
	B7270		G-BFCZ	Sopwith F1 Camel replica *(Royal Flying Corps)*
	C1904	Z	G-PFAP	Royal Aircraft Factory SE.5a (Currie Wot) *(RFC)*
	C3009	B	G-BFWD	Royal Aircraft Factory SE.5a (Currie Wot) *(RFC)*
	C3011	S	G-SWOT	Royal Aircraft Factory SE.5a (Currie Wot) *(RFC)*
	C4451		BAPC.210	Avro 504J *(Royal Flying Corps)*
	C4912		BAPC.135	Bristol 20 M.1C Monoplane fsm
	C4918		G-BWJM	Bristol 20 M.1C Monoplane replica
	C4988		G-BPLT	Bristol 20 M.1C Monoplane replica
	C4994		G-BLWM	Bristol 20 M.1C Monoplane replica
	C5430	V	G-CCXG	Royal Aircraft Factory SE.5a replica *(Royal Flying Corps)*
	C6468	A	G-CEKL	Royal Aircraft Factory SE.5a replica *(Royal Flying Corps))*
	C9533	M	G-BUWE	Royal Aircraft Factory SE.5a replica *(Royal Flying Corps)*
	D276	A	BAPC.208	Royal Aircraft Factory SE.5a replica *(Royal Flying Corps)*
	D7889		G-AANM	Bristol F.2b Fighter
	D8096	D	G-AEPH	Bristol F.2b Fighter
	E449		G-EBJE	Avro 504K
	E2466		BAPC.165	Bristol F.2b Fighter
	E2939		G-ATXL	Avro 504K replica
	E3747		G-BYKV	Avro 504K replica
	E8894		G-CDLI	Airco DH.9
	F-141	G	G-SEVA	Royal Aircraft Factory SE.5a replica *(Royal Flying Corps)*
	F235	B	G-BMDB	Royal Aircraft Factory SE.5a replica *(Royal Flying Corps)*
	F904		G-EBIA	Royal Aircraft Factory SE.5a replica *(Royal Flying Corps)*
	F938		G-EBIC	Royal Aircraft Factory SE.5a replica *(Royal Flying Corps)*
	F-943		G-BIHF	Royal Aircraft Factory SE.5a replica *(Royal Flying Corps)*
	F943		G-BKDT	Royal Aircraft Factory SE.5a replica *(Royal Flying Corps)*
	F5447	N	G-BKER	Royal Aircraft Factory SE.5a replica *(Royal Flying Corps)*
	F5459	Y	G-INNY	Royal Aircraft Factory SE.5a replica *(Royal Flying Corps)*
	F5459	Y	BAPC.142	Royal Aircraft Factory SE.5a replica *(Royal Flying Corps)*
	F5475	A	BAPC.250	Royal Aircraft Factory SE.5a replica *(Royal Flying Corps)*
	F8010	Z	G-BDWJ	Royal Aircraft Factory SE.5a replica *(Royal Flying Corps)*
	F8614		G-AWAU	Vickers FB.27A Vimy replica
	H1968		BAPC.42	Avro 504K replica
	H3426		BAPC.68	Hawker Hurricane replica
	H5199		G-ADEV	Avro 504K
	J7326		G-EBQP	de Havilland DH.53 Humming Bird *(Intended marks)*
	J9941		G-ABMR	Hawker Hart II
	K-123		G-EACN	BAT FK.23 Bantam
	K1786		G-AFTA	Hawker Tomtit
	K1930		G-BKBB	Hawker Fury II
	K2048		G-BZNW	Hawker (Isaacs) Fury
	K2050		G-ASCM	Hawker (Isaacs) Fury
	K2059		G-PFAR	Hawker (Isaacs) Fury
	K2075		G-BEER	Hawker (Isaacs) Fury
	K2227		G-ABBB	Bristol Bulldog IIA
	K-2567		G-MOTH	de Havilland DH.82A Tiger Moth
	K2572		G-AOZH	de Havilland DH.82A Tiger Moth
	K-2585		G-ANKT	de Havilland DH.82A Tiger Moth
	K2587		G-BJAP	de Havilland DH.82A Tiger Moth

Serial	Code	Registration	Type
K3241		G-AHSA	Avro Tutor
K3661	562	G-BURZ	Hawker Nimrod I
K3731		G-RODI	Hawker (Isaacs) Fury
K4232		SE-AZB	Cierva C.30A
K4235		G-AHMJ	Cierva C.30A
K-4259	71	G-ANMO	de Havilland DH.82A Tiger Moth
K5054		G-BRDV	Supermarine Spitfire Prototype replica
K5054		BAPC.190	Supermarine Spitfire Prototype fsm
K5054		BAPC.214	Supermarine Spitfire Prototype fsm
K5414	XV	G-AENP	Hawker Afghan Hind
K5673		BAPC.249	Hawker Fury I fsm
K5673		G-BZAS	Hawker Fury I replica
K7271		BAPC.148	Hawker Fury II fsm
K7271		G-CCKV	Hawker (Isaacs) Fury II
K7985		G-AMRK	Gloster Gladiator I
K8203		G-BTVE	Hawker Demon I
K8303	D	G-BWWN	Hawker (Isaacs) Fury
K9926	JH-C	BAPC.217	Supermarine Spitfire fsm
L1070	XT-A	BAPC.227	Supermarine Spitfire fsm
L1679	JX-G	BAPC.241	Hawker Hurricane 1 fsm
L1710	AL-D	BAPC.219	Hawker Hurricane fsm
L2301		G-AIZG	Supermarine Walrus 1 (Royal Navy)
L6906		G-AKKY	Miles Magister
L7005	PS-B	BAPC.281	Boulton Paul Defiant fsm
L8353		G-AMMC	Miles M.14A Hawk Trainer 3
N248		BAPC.164	Wight Quadraplane Type 1 fsm
N500		G-BWRA	Sopwith Triplane replica
N1854		G-AIBE	Fairey Fulmar 2 (RN)
N1977	8	G-BWMJ	Nieuport Scout 17/23 replica (French AF)
N2532	GZ-H	BAPC.272	Hawker Hurricane fsm
N3194	GR-Z	BAPC.220	Supermarine Spitfire fsm
N3289	DW-K	BAPC.65	Supermarine Spitfire fsm
N3313	KL-B	BAPC.69	Supermarine Spitfire fsm
N3317	AI-A	BAPC.268	Supermarine Spitfire fsm
N3788		G-AKPF	Miles M.14A Hawk Trainer
N4877	MK-V	G-AMDA	Avro 652A Anson 1
N5182		G-APUP	Sopwith Pup replica (Royal Navy Air Service)
N5195		G-ABOX	Sopwith Pup (Royal Navy Air Service)
N5199		G-BZND	Sopwith Pup replica
N5492	B	BAPC.111	Sopwith Triplane fsm (Royal Navy Air Service)
N5903		G-GLAD	Gloster Gladiator II
N6290		G-BOCK	Sopwith Triplane replica (Royal Navy Air Service)
N6452		G-BIAU	Sopwith Pup replica (Royal Navy Air Service)
N-6466		G-ANKZ	de Havilland DH.82A Tiger Moth
N-6473		G-AOBO	de Havilland DH.82A Tiger Moth
N6720	VX	G-BYTN	de Havilland DH.82A Tiger Moth
N-6797		G-ANEH	de Havilland DH.82A Tiger Moth
N6847		G-APAL	de Havilland DH.82A Tiger Moth
N6965	FL-J	G-AJTW	de Havilland DH.82A Tiger Moth
N-9192	RCO-N	G-DHZF	de Havilland DH.82A Tiger Moth
N9389		G-ANJA	de Havilland DH.82A Tiger Moth
P641		BAPC.123	Vickers FB.5 Gunbus fsm
P2790		G-ORGI	Hawker Hurricane IIB
P2793	SD-M	BAPC.236	Hawker Hurricane fsm
P2902	DX-X	G-ROBT	Hawker Hurricane I
P2921	GZ-L	BAPC.273	Hawker Hurricane fsm
P2954	WX-E	BAPC.267	Hawker Hurricane fsm
P2970	US-X	BAPC.291	Hawker Hurricane fsm
P3059	SD-N	BAPC.64	Hawker Hurricane fsm
P3208	SD-T	BAPC.63	Hawker Hurricane fsm
P3679	GZ-K	BAPC.278	Hawker Hurricane fsm
P3873	YO-H	BAPC.265	Hawker Hurricane fsm
P6382	C	G-AJRS	Miles Magister
P6775	YT-J	BAPC.299	Vickers-Supermarine Spitfire fsm
P7350	XT-D	G-AWIJ	Vickers-Supermarine Spitfire F.IIA
P8140	ZP-K	BAPC.71	Vickers-Supermarine Spitfire fsm
P8448	UM-D	BAPC.225	Vickers-Supermarine Spitfire replica
R1914		G-AHUJ	Miles Magister
R3821	UX-N	G-BPIV	Bristol Blenheim IV
R4118	UP-W	G-HUPW	Hawker Hurricane I
R-5136		G-APAP	de Havilland DH.82A Tiger Moth
R5172	FIJE	G-AOIS	de Havilland DH.82A Tiger Moth
R6690	PR-A	BAPC.254	Vickers-Supermarine Spitfire 1 fsm
S1287	5	G-BEYB	Fairey Flycatcher replica (FAA)
S1595		BAPC.156	Supermarine S.6B fsm
S1579	571	G-BBVO	Hawker Nimrod (Isaacs Fury) (Royal Navy)
S1581	573	G-BWWK	Hawker Nimrod 1 (FAA)
T5672		G-ALRI	de Havilland DH.82A Tiger Moth
T-5854		G-ANKK	de Havilland DH.82A Tiger Moth
T-5879	RUC-W	G-AXBW	de Havilland DH.82A Tiger Moth
T6313		G-AHVU	de Havilland DH.82A Tiger Moth
T-6953		G-ANNI	de Havilland DH.82A Tiger Moth
T-7230		G-AFVE	de Havilland DH.82A Tiger Moth
T7245		G-ANEJ	de Havilland DH.82A Tiger Moth
T7281		G-ARTL	de Havilland DH.82A Tiger Moth
T7328		G-APPN	de Havilland DH.82A Tiger Moth
T7793		G-ANKV	de Havilland DH.82A Tiger Moth
T-7842		G-AMTF	de Havilland DH.82A Tiger Moth
T9707		G-AKKR	Miles M.14A Hawk Trainer
T9738		G-AKAT	Miles M.14A Hawk Trainer

T7909		G-ANON	de Havilland DH.82A Tiger Moth
T-7997		G-AHUF	de Havilland DH.82A Tiger Moth
V3388		G-AHTW	Airspeed Oxford 1V
V6799	SD-X	BAPC.72	Hawker Hurricane fsm
V7467	LE-D	BAPC.223	Hawker Hurricane fsm {1}
V7467	LE-D	BAPC.288	Hawker Hurricane fsm {2}
V9367	MA-B	G-AZWT	Westland Lysander IIIA
V9673	MA-J	G-LIZY	Westland Lysander III
W2068	68	VH-ASM	Avro 652A Anson I
W2718	AA5Y	G-RNLI	Vickers-Supermarine Walrus (Royal Navy)
W5856	A2A	G-BMGC	Fairey Swordfish II
W9385	YG-L	G-ADND	de Havilland DH.87B Hornet Moth
X4683	EB-N	G-CDPM	Jurca MJ.100 Spitfire (80% scale replica Spitfire)
Z2033	N/275	G-ASTL	Fairey Firefly TT.1
Z5140	HA-C	G-HURI	Hawker Hurricane IIB
Z5252	GO-B	G-BWHA	Hawker Hurricane IIB
Z7015	7-L	G-BKTH	Hawker Sea Hurricane IB (Royal Navy)
Z7197		G-AKZN	Percival Proctor III
AB196		G-CCGH	Super Marine Spitfire Mk.26
AB550	GE-P	BAPC.230	Vickers-Supermarine Spitfire fsm
AB910	IR-G	G-AISU	Vickers-Supermarine Spitfire LF.Vb
AP507	KX-P	G-ACWP	Cierva C.30A
AR501	NN-A	G-AWII	Vickers-Supermarine Spitfire Vc
AR614	DU-Z	G-BUWA	Vickers-Supermarine Spitfire Vc
BB807		G-ADWO	de Havilland DH.82A Tiger Moth
BD707	AE-C	G-HURR	Hawker Hurricane XII (IIB)
BE421	XP-G	BAPC.205	Hawker Hurricane IIc fsm
BL924	AZ-G	BAPC.242	Vickers-Supermarine Spitfire Vb fsm
BM597	U-2	G-MKVB	Vickers-Supermarine Spitfire Vb
BM631	XR-C	BAPC.269	Vickers-Supermarine Spitfire V fsm
BN230	FT-A	BAPC.218	Hawker Hurricane fsm
BR600	SH-V	BAPC.222	Vickers-Supermarine Spitfire fsm
BR600		BAPC.224	Vickers-Supermarine Spitfire fsm
DE-208		G-AGYU	de Havilland DH.82A Tiger Moth
DE470	16	G-ANMY	de Havilland DH.82A Tiger Moth
DE623		G-ANFI	de Havilland DH.82A Tiger Moth
DE673		G-ADNZ	de Havilland DH.82A Tiger Moth
DE730		G-ANFW	de Havilland DH.82A Tiger Moth
DE992		G-AXXV	de Havilland DH.82A Tiger Moth
DF112		G-ANRM	de Havilland DH.82A Tiger Moth
DF128	RCO-U	G-AOJJ	de Havilland DH.82A Tiger Moth
DF155		G-ANFV	de Havilland DH.82A Tiger Moth
DR828	PB-1	N18V	Beech Traveler
EM720		G-AXAN	de Havilland DH.82A Tiger Moth
EN343		BAPC.226	Vickers-Supermarine Spitfire fsm
EN398		BAPC.184	Vickers-Supermarine Spitfire IX fsm
EN526	SZ-G	BAPC.221	Vickers-Supermarine Spitfire replica
EP120	AE-A	G-LFVB	Supermarine Spitfire Vb
FB226	MT-A	G-BDWM	North American Mustang (Bonsall Mustang)
FE695	94	G-BTXI	North American Harvard IIB
FE788		G-CTKL	Noorduyn AT-16 Harvard IIB
FE905		LN-BNM	North American Harvard IIB
FH153	58	G-BBHK	Noorduyn AT-16-ND Harvard IIB (RCAF c/s)
FR886		G-BDMS	Piper Cub
FS628		G-AIZE	Fairchild Argus
FT375		G-BWUL	North American Harvard IIB
FT391		G-AZBN	North American Harvard IIB
FX301	FD-NQ	G-JUDI	North American Harvard III
FZ625		G-AMPO	Douglas Dakota 3
HB275		G-BKGM	Beech Expeditor
HG691		G-AIYR	de Havilland DH.89A Dragon Rapide
HH268		BAPC.261	General Aircraft Hotspur replica
HM580	KX-K	G-ACUU	Cierva C.30A
HS503		BAPC.108	Fairey Swordfish IV
JF343*	JW-P	G-CCZP	Super Marine Spitfire Mk.26
JG891	T-B	G-LFVC	Vickers Supermarine 349 Spitfire L.Vc
JV828		N423RS	Consolidated-Vultee PBY-5A Catalina
KB889	NA-I	G-LANC	Avro Lancaster X
KD345	130	G-FGID	Vought FG-1D Corsair (RN)
KF584	RAI-X	G-RAIX	North American Harvard IV
KF729		G-BJST	CCF Harvard 4
KJ351		BAPC.80	Airspeed AS.58 Horsa II
KK116		G-AMPY	Douglas C-47B-15-DK Dakota 3
KZ321	JV-N	G-HURY	Hawker Hurricane IV
LB264		G-AIXA	Taylorcraft Plus D (Auster I)
LB312		G-AHXE	Taylorcraft Plus D (Auster I)
LB367		G-AHGZ	Taylorcraft Plus D (Auster I)
LB375		G-AHGW	Taylorcraft Plus D (Auster I)
LB381		G-AHKO	Taylorcraft Plus D (Auster I)
LF789	R2-K	BAPC.186	de Havilland DH.82B Queen Bee composite
LF858		G-BLUZ	de Havilland DH.82B Queen Bee
LH291		BAPC 279	Airspeed AS51 Horsa I
LS326	L 2	G-AJVH	Fairey Swordfish II
LZ766		G-ALCK	Percival Proctor III
MAV467	R-O	BAPC.202	Vickers-Supermarine Spitfire V fsm
MH415	FU-N	BAPC.209	Vickers-SupermarineSpitfire LF.IXC fsm
MH434	ZD-B	G-ASJV	Vickers-Supermarine Spitfire IXB
MH486	FF-A	BAPC.206	Vickers-Supermarine Spitfire IX fsm
MJ627	9G-P	G-BMSB	Vickers-Supermarine Spitfire IX
MJ832	DN-Y	BAPC.229	Vickers-Supermarine Spitfire fsm

MK732	3W-17	G-HVDM	Vickers-Supermarine Spitfire IXc
MK805	SH-B	-----------	Vickers-Supermarine Spitfire IX replica
(Built TDL Reproduction Aircraft)			"Peter John III" in RAF 64 Sqn c/s
ML407	OU-V	G-LFIX	Vickers-Supermarine Spitfire IX
MP425		G-AITB	Airspeed Oxford I
MT197		G-ANHS	Auster 4
MT438		G-AREI	Auster III
MT928	ZX-M	G-BKMI	Vickers-Supermarine Spitfire VIIIc
MV268	JE-J	G-SPIT	Vickers-Supermarine Spitfire XIVe
MV370		G-FXIV	Vickers-Supermarine Spitfire XIVc
MW763	HF-A	G-TEMT	Hawker Tempest II
NJ203		G-AKNP	Short S.45 Solent 3
NJ633		G-AKXP	Auster 5
NJ673		G-AOCR	Auster 5
NJ695		G-AJXV	Auster 4
NJ719		G-ANFU	Auster 5 - intended marks
NL750		G-AOBH	de Havilland DH.82A Tiger Moth
NL913		G-AOFR	de Havilland DH.82A Tiger Moth
NL985		G-BWIK	de Havilland DH.82A Tiger Moth
NM181		G-AZGZ	de Havilland DH.82A Tiger Moth
NP336		G-AGTB	Percival Proctor V
NS519		G-MOSI	de Havilland DH.98 Mosquito TT.35
NX611	LE-C:DX-C	G-ASXX	Avro Lancaster B.VII
PL965	R	G-MKXI	Vickers-Supermarine Spitfire PR.XI
PL983	JV-F	G-PRXI	Vickers-Supermarine Spitfire XI
PS853	C	G-RRGN	Vickers-Supermarine Spitfire PR.XIX
PT462	SW-A	G-CTIX	Vickers-Supermarine Spitfire IX
PV303	ON-B	G-CCJL	Super Marine Spitfire Mk.26
PZ865	JX-E	G-AMAU	Hawker Hurricane IIc
RB412	DW-B	G-CEFC	Super Marine Spitfire Mk.26
RG333		G-AIEK	Miles Messenger
RM221		G-ANXR	Percival Proctor IV
RR232		G-BRSF	Vickers-Supermarine Spitfire IXc
RT486	PF-A	G-AJGJ	Auster 5
RT610		G-AKWS	Auster 5A
SM845	GZ-J	G-BUOS	Vickers-Supermarine Spitfire XVIIIe
SX336	VL-105	G-KASX	Vickers Supermarine Seafire F.XVII (Royal Navy)
TA634	8K-K	G-AWJV	de Havilland DH.98 Mosquito TT.35
TA719	6 T	G-ASKC	de Havilland DH.98 Mosquito TT.35
TA805	FX-M	G-PMNF	Vickers-Supermarine Spitfire IX
TB252	GW-H	G-XVIE	Vickers-Supermarine Spitfire XVIe
TD248	CR-S	G-OXVI	Vickers-Supermarine Spitfire XVIe
TJ398		BAPC.70	Auster AOP.5
TJ534		G-AKSY	Auster 5
TJ565		G-AMVD	Auster 5
TJ569		G-AKOW	Auster 5
TJ672	DT-S	G-ANIJ	Auster 5
TJ704	JA	G-ASCD	Beagle A.61 Terrier 2 (Auster AOP.6)
TS423		N147DC	Douglas C-47A-75-DL Dakota (Army Air Force)
TS798		G-AGNV	Avro 685 York C.1
TW439		G-ANRP	Auster 5
TW467		G-ANIE	Auster 5
TW511		G-APAF	Auster 5 (AAC)
TW536	T-SV	G-BNGE	Auster AOP.6
TW591		G-ARIH	Auster AOP.6 (AAC)
TW641		G-ATDN	Auster AOP.6
TX310		G-AIDL	de Havilland DH.89A Dragon Rapide 6
VF512	PF-M	G-ARRX	Auster AOP.6
VF516		G-ASMZ	Auster AOP.6
VF526	T	G-ARXU	Auster AOP.6 (AAC)
VF581		G-ARSL	Auster AOP.6
VL348		G-AVVO	Avro Anson C.19 Series 2
VL349	V7-Q	G-AWSA	Avro Anson C.19 Series 2
VM286		G-BPUR	Piper J-3L-65 Cub
VM360		G-APHV	Avro Anson C.19 Series 2
VN799		G-CDSX	English Electric Canberra T.Mk.4 (Prototype)
VP519		G-AVVR	Avro 652A Anson 19 Series.2 (Cockpit only)
VP955		G-DVON	de Havilland DH.104 Devon C.2/2
VP981		G-DHDV	de Havilland DH.104 Devon C.2/2
VR192		G-APIT	Percival Prentice T.1
VR249	FA-EL	G-APIY	Percival Prentice T.1
VR259	M	G-APJB	Percival Prentice T.1
VS356		G-AOLU	Percival Prentice T.1
VS623		G-AOKZ	Percival Prentice T.1
VT871		G-DHXX	de Havilland DH.100 Vampire FB.6
VV612		G-VENI	de Havilland DH.112 Venom FB.1
VX113	36	G-ARNO	Auster AOP.6 (AAC)
VX147		G-AVIL	Ercoupe 415
VX927		G-ASYG	Beagle A 61 Terrier 2 (AAC)
VZ345		D-CATA	Hawker Sea Fury T.20 (RN)
VZ638		G-JETM	Gloster Meteor T.7 (RN and FRU)
VZ728		G-AGOS	Reid and Sigrist Bobsleigh
WB188		G-HUNT	Hawker Hunter F.51
WB188		G-BZPB	Hawker Hunter GA.Mk.11
WB188		G-BZPC	Hawker Hunter GA.Mk.11
WB533		G-DEVN	de Havilland DH.104 Devon C.2/2
WB565	X	G-PVET	de Havilland DHC-1 Chipmunk T.10 (AAC)
WB569	R	G-BYSJ	de Havilland DHC-1 Chipmunk T.10
WB571	34	G-AOSF	de Havilland DHC-1 Chipmunk T.10
WB585	M	G-AOSY	de Havilland DHC-1 Chipmunk T.10

WB588	D	G-AOTD	de Havilland DHC-1 Chipmunk T.10
WB615	E	G-BXIA	de Havilland DHC-1 Chipmunk T.10
WB654	U	G-BXGO	de Havilland DHC-1 Chipmunk T.10
WB671	910	G-BWTG	de Havilland DHC-1 Chipmunk T.10 (Royal Navy)
WB697	95	G-BXCT	de Havilland DHC-1 Chipmunk T.10
WB702		G-AOFE	de Havilland DHC-1 Chipmunk T.10
WB703		G-ARMC	de Havilland DHC-1 Chipmunk T.10
WB711		G-APPM	de Havilland DHC-1 Chipmunk T.10
WB726	E	G-AOSK	de Havilland DHC-1 Chipmunk T.10
WD286		G-BBND	de Havilland DHC-1 Chipmunk T.10
WD292		G-BCRX	de Havilland DHC-1 Chipmunk T.10
WD310	B	G-BWUN	de Havilland DHC-1 Chipmunk T.10
WD331		G-BXDH	de Havilland DHC-1 Chipmunk T.10
WD347		G-BBRV	de Havilland DHC-1 Chipmunk T.10
WD363		G-BCIH	de Havilland DHC-1 Chipmunk T.10
WD373	12	G-BXDI	de Havilland DHC-1 Chipmunk T.10
WD379	K	G-APLO	de Havilland DHC-1 Chipmunk T.10
WD390	68	G-BWNK	de Havilland DHC-1 Chipmunk T.10
WD413		G-VROE	Avro 652A Anson T.21
WE569		G-ASAJ	Beagle Terrier (Auster T.7)
WE591	Y	G-ASAK	Beagle Terrier (Auster T.7)
WF118		G-DACA	Percival P.57 Sea Prince T.1
WG288	153:P	G-SALY	Hawker Sea Fury FB.XI (RN)
WG308	8	G-BYHL	de Havilland DHC-1 Chipmunk T.10
WG316		G-BCAH	de Havilland DHC-1 Chipmunk T.10
WG321	G	G-DHCC	de Havilland DHC-1 Chipmunk T.10 (AAC)
WG348		G-BBMV	de Havilland DHC-1 Chipmunk T.10
WG350		G-BPAL	de Havilland DHC-1 Chipmunk T.10
WG407	67	G-BWMX	de Havilland DHC-1 Chipmunk T.10
WG422	16	G-BFAX	de Havilland DHC-1 Chipmunk T.10
WG458	G	N458BG	de Havilland DHC.1 Chipmunk T.10
WG465		G-BCEY	de Havilland DHC-1 Chipmunk T.10
WG469	72	G-BWJY	de Havilland DHC-1 Chipmunk T.10
WG472		G-AOTY	de Havilland DHC-1 Chipmunk T.10
WG719		G-BRMA	Westland Dragonfly HR.5
WJ358		G-ARYD	Auster AOP.6
WJ945	21	G-BEDV	Vickers Varsity T.1
WK126	843	N2138J	English Electric Canberra TT.18
WK163		G-BVWC	English Electric Canberra B.2
WK436		G-VENM	de Havilland DH.112 Venom FB.50 (FB.1)
WK512	A	G-BXIM	de Havilland DHC-1 Chipmunk T.10 (AAC)
WK514		G-BBMO	de Havilland DHC-1 Chipmunk T.10
WK517		G-ULAS	de Havilland DHC-1 Chipmunk T.10
WK522		G-BCOU	de Havilland DHC-1 Chipmunk T.10
WK549		G-BTWF	de Havilland DHC-1 Chipmunk T.10
WK577		G-BCYM	de Havilland DHC-1 Chipmunk T.10
WK585		G-BZGA	de Havilland DHC-1 Chipmunk T.10
WK586	V	G-BXGX	de Havilland DHC-1 Chipmunk T.10 (AAC)
WK590	69	G-BWVZ	de Havilland DHC-1 Chipmunk T.10
WK609	93	G-BXDN	de Havilland DHC-1 Chipmunk T.10
WK611		G-ARWB	de Havilland DHC-1 Chipmunk T.10
WK622		G-BCZH	de Havilland DHC-1 Chipmunk T.10
WK624	M	G-BWHI	de Havilland DHC-1 Chipmunk T.10
WK628		G-BBMW	de Havilland DHC-1 Chipmunk T.10
WK630		G-BXDG	de Havilland DHC-1 Chipmunk T.10
WK633	B	G-BXEC	de Havilland DHC-1 Chipmunk T.10
WK640	C	G-BWUV	de Havilland DHC-1 Chipmunk T.10
WK642		G-BXDP	de Havilland DHC-1 Chipmunk T.10
WL626	P	G-BHDD	Vickers Varsity T.1
WM167		G-LOSM	Armstrong-Whitworth Meteor NF.11
WP308	572	G-GACA	Hunting Percival P.57 Sea Prince T.1
WP788		G-BCHL	de Havilland DHC-1 Chipmunk T.10
WP790	T	G-BBNC	de Havilland DHC-1 Chipmunk T.10
WP795	901	G-BVZZ	de Havilland DHC-1 Chipmunk T.10 (Royal Navy)
WP800	2	G-BCXN	de Havilland DHC-1 Chipmunk T.10
WP803		G-HAPY	de Havilland DHC-1 Chipmunk T.10
WP805		G-MAJR	de Havilland DHC-1 Chipmunk T.10
WP808		G-BDEU	de Havilland DHC-1 Chipmunk T.10
WP809	78	G-BVTX	de Havilland DHC-1 Chipmunk T.10 (Royal Navy)
WP833		G-BZDU	de Havilland DHC-1 Chipmunk T.10
WP840	9	G-BXDM	de Havilland DHC-1 Chipmunk T.10
WP844		G-BWOX	de Havilland DHC-1 Chipmunk T.10
WP857	24	G-BDRJ	de Havilland DHC-1 Chipmunk T.10
WP859	E	G-BXCP	de Havilland DHC-1 Chipmunk T.10
WP860	6	G-BXDA	de Havilland DHC-1 Chipmunk T.10
WP870	12	G-BCOI	de Havilland DHC-1 Chipmunk T.10
WP896		G-BWVY	de Havilland DHC-1 Chipmunk T.10
WP901		G-BWNT	de Havilland DHC-1 Chipmunk T.10
WP903		G-BCGC	de Havilland DHC-1 Chipmunk T.10 (Queens Flight)
WP925	C	G-BXHA	de Havilland DHC-1 Chipmunk T.10 (AAC)
WP928	D	G-BXGM	de Havilland DHC-1 Chipmunk T.10 (AAC)
WP929		G-BXCV	de Havilland DHC-1 Chipmunk T.10
WP930	J	G-BXHF	de Havilland DHC-1 Chipmunk T.10 (AAC)
WP971		G-ATHD	de Havilland DHC-1 Chipmunk T.10
WP983	B	G-BXNN	de Havilland DHC-1 Chipmunk T.10
WP984	H	G-BWTO	de Havilland DHC-1 Chipmunk T.10
WR360		G-DHSS	de Havilland DH.112 Venom FB.1
WR410		G-DHUU	de Havilland DH.112 Venom FB.1
WR421		G-DHTT	de Havilland DH.112 Venom FB.1
WR470		G-DHVM	de Havilland DH.112 Venom FB.1

WS774	4	G-ANSO	Gloster Meteor T.7
WT333		G-BVXC	English Electric Canberra B(I).8
WT722	878:VL	G-BWGN	Hawker Hunter T.8C *(Royal Navy)*
WT723	866:VL	G-PRII	Hawker Hunter PR.11 *(Royal Navy)*
WV198	K	G-BJWY	Sikorsky Whirlwind HAR.21
WV318	D	G-FFOX	Hawker Hunter T.7B
WV322	Y	G-BZSE	Hawker Hunter T.11
WV372	R	G-BXFI	Hawker Hunter T.7
WV499	G	G-BZRF	Hunting Percival P.56 Provost T.1
WV493	29:A-P	G-BDYG	Percival Provost T.1
WV740		G-BNPH	Hunting Percival Pembroke C.1
WV783		(G-ALSP)	Bristol 171 Sycamore 3
WW421	P	G-BZRE	Hunting Percival Provost T.1
WZ507	74	G-VTII	de Havilland DH.115 Vampire T.11
WZ584	K	G-BZRC	de Havilland DH.115 Vampire T.11
WZ662		G-BKVK	Auster AOP.9 *(Army)*
WZ706		G-BURR	Auster AOP.9 *(Army)*
WZ847	F	G-CPMK	de Havilland DHC-1 Chipmunk T.10
WZ868	H	G-ARMF	de Havilland DHC-1 Chipmunk T.10
WZ872	E	G-BZGB	de Havilland DHC-1 Chipmunk T.10
WZ879	X	G-BWUT	de Havilland DHC-1 Chipmunk T.10
WZ882	K	G-BXGP	de Havilland DHC-1 Chipmunk T.10 *(AAC)*
XA880		G-BVXR	de Havilland DH.104 Devon C.2 *(RAE)*
XB259		G-AOAI	Blackburn Beverley C.1
XD693	Z-Q	G-AOBU	Percival Jet Provost T.1
XE489		G-JETH	Armstrong-Whitworth Sea Hawk FGA.6
XE601		G-ETPS	Hawker Hunter FGA.Mk.9 *(ETPS)*
XE665	876:VL	G-BWGM	Hawker Hunter T.8C *(RN)*
XE685	871:VL	G-GAII	Hawker Hunter T.8C *(RN)*
XE689	864:VL	G-BWGK	Hawker Hunter GA.11 *(RN)*
XE897		G-DHVV	de Havilland DH.115 Vampire T.55
XE920	A	G-VMPR	de Havilland DH.115 Vampire T.11
XE956		G-OBLN	de Havilland DH.115 Vampire T.11
XF515	R	G-KAXF	Hawker Hunter F.6A
XF597	AH	G-BKFW	Percival Provost T.1
XF603		G-KAPW	Percival Provost T.1
XF690		G-MOOS	Percival Provost T.1
XF785		G-ALBN	Bristol 173 Mk.1
XF836		G-AWRY	Percival Provost T.1
XF868		G-BGSB	Hunting-Percival P.56 Provost T.1
XF877	JX	G-AWVF	Percival Provost T.1
XG160	U	G-BWAF	Hawker Hunter F.6A
XG452		G-BRMB	Bristol Belvedere HC.1
XG547	T-S	G-HAPR	Bristol Sycamore HC.14
XG588		G-BAMH	Westland S-55 Whirlwind Series.3
XG775		G-DHWW	de Havilland DH.115 Vampire T.11 *(Royal Navy)*
XH313	E	G-BZRD	de Havilland DH.115 Vampire T.11
XH558		G-VLCN	Avro Vulcan B.2
XJ348		G-AMXX	de Havilland DH.104 Dove 2A
XJ389		G-AJJP	Fairey Jet Gyrodyne
XJ398		G-BDBZ	Westland WS-55 Whirlwind 2
XJ729		G-BVGE	Westland Whirlwind HAR.10
XJ771		G-HELV	de Havilland DH.115 Vampire T.55
XK895	CU-19	G-SDEV	de Havilland DH.104 Sea Devon C.20 *(Royal Navy)*
XK940		G-AYXT	Westland Whirlwind HAS.7
XL426		G-VJET	Avro Vulcan B.2
XL502		G-BMYP	Fairey Gannet AEW.3 *(RN)*
XL571	V	G-HNTR	Hawker Hunter T.7 *(Blue Diamonds c/s)*
XL573		G-BVGH	Hawker Hunter T.7
XL577	V	G-BXKF	Hawker Hunter T.7 *(Blue Diamonds c/s)*
XL587	Z	G-HPUX	Hawker Hunter T.7
XL602		G-BWFT	Hawker Hunter T.8M
XL621		G-BNCX	Hawker Hunter T.7
XL714		G-AOGR	de Havilland DH.82A Tiger Moth
XL-716		G-AOIL	de Havilland DH.82A Tiger Moth
XL809		G-BLIX	Saro Skeeter AOP.12 *(AAC)*
XL812		G-SARO	Saro Skeeter AOP.12
XL954		G-BXES	Percival Pembroke C.1
XM223		G-BWWC	de Havilland DH.104 Devon C.2
XM365		G-BXBH	Hunting Jet Provost T.3A
XM424		G-BWDS	Hunting Jet Provost T.3A
XM478		G-BXDL	Hunting Jet Provost T.3A
XM479	54	G-BVEZ	Hunting Jet Provost T.3A
XM496		G-BDUP	Bristol 175 Britannia Series 253
XM556		G-HELI	Saro Skeeter AOP.12
XM575		G-BLMC	Avro Vulcan B.2A
XM655		G-VULC	Avro Vulcan B.2A
XM685	PO:513	G-AYZJ	Westland Whirlwind HAS.7
XM819		G-APXW	Lancashire Aircraft EP.9 *(AAC)*
XN332	759	G-APNV	Saunders-Roe P.531-1
XN441		G-BGKT	Auster AOP.9 *(AAC)*
XN459		G-BWOT	Hunting Jet Provost T.3A
XN629	49	G-KNOT	Hunting Jet Provost T.3A
XP254		G-ASCC	Auster AOP.11 *(AAC)*
XP279		G-BWKK	Auster AOP.9 *(AAC)*
XP355	A	G-BEBC	Westland Whirlwind HAR.10
XP524	134	G-CVIX	de Havilland DH.110 Sea Vixen D.3
XP672	03	G-RAFI	Hunting Jet Provost T.4
XP693		G-FSIX	English Electric Lightning F.6
XP772		G-DHCZ	de Havilland DHC.2 Beaver AL.1 *(AAC)*

XP907		G-SROE	Westland Scout AH.1
XR240		G-BDFH	Auster AOP.9 *(AAC)*
XR241		G-AXRR	Auster AOP.9 *(AAC)*
XR246		G-AZBU	Auster AOP.9
XR486		G-RWWW	Westland Whirlwind HCC.12 *(Queens Flight)*
XR537		G-NATY	Folland Gnat T.1
XR538	01	G-RORI	Folland Gnat T.1 *(Training c/s)*
XR592		G-AMWI	Bristol 171 Sycamore 4
XR595	M	G-BWHU	Westland Scout AH.1 *(AAC)*
XR673		G-BXLO	Hunting Jet Provost T.4
XR724		G-BTSY	English Electric Lightning F.6
XR773		G-OPIB	English Electric Lightning F.6
XR944		G-ATTB	Wallis WA.116
XR991		G-MOUR	Folland Gnat T.1 *(Yellowjacks c/s)*
XR993		G-BVPP	Folland Gnat T.1 *(Red Arrows c/s)*
XS111		G-TIMM	Folland Gnat T.1
XS165	37	G-ASAZ	Hiller UH-12E-4
XS235		G-CPDA	de Havilland DH.106 Comet 4C
XS451		G-LTNG	English Electric Lightning T.5
XS587		G-VIXN	de Havilland DH.110 Sea Vixen FAW.2 *(Royal Navy)*
XS765		G-BSET	Beagle Basset CC.1
XS770		G-HRHI	Beagle Basset CC.1 *(Queens Flight)*
XT223		G-XTUN	Westland Sioux AH.1 *(AAC)*
XT420	606	G-CBUI	Westland Wasp HAS.1 *(RN)*
XT435	430	G-RIMM	Westland Wasp HAS.1 *(RN)*
XT634		G-BYRX	Westland Scout AH.1 *(AAC)*
XT787		G-KAXT	Westland Wasp HAS.1 *(Royal Navy)*
XT788	474	G-BMIR	Westland Wasp HAS.1 *(Royal Navy)*
XT793	456	G-BZPP	Westland Wasp HAS.1 *(Royal Navy)*
XV130	R	G-BWJW	Westland Scout AH.1 *(AAC)*
XV134	P	G-BWLX	Westland Scout AH.1 *(AAC)*
XV137		G-CRUM	Westland Scout AH.1 *(AAC)*
XV140	K	G-KAXL	Westland Scout AH.1 *(AAC)*
XV268		G-BVER	de Havilland DHC.2 Beaver *(AAC)*
XW289	73	G-JPVA	BAC Jet Provost T.5A
XW293	Z	G-BWCS	BAC Jet Provost T.5
XW324	K	G-BWSG	BAC Jet Provost T.5
XW325	E	G-BWGF	BAC Jet Provost T.5A
XW333		G-BVTC	BAC Jet Provost T.5A
XW354		G-JPTV	BAC Jet Provost T.5A
XW422		G-BWEB	BAC Jet Provost T.5A
XW423	14	G-BWUW	BAC Jet Provost T.5A
XW433		G-JPRO	BAC Jet Provost T.5A *(CFS)*
XW635		G-AWSW	Beagle Husky
XW784	VL	G-BBRN	Mitchell-Procter Kittiwake *(Royal Navy)*
XW799		G-BXSL	Westland Scout AH.Mk.1
XW854		G-CBSD	Westland Gazelle HT.2 *(Royal Navy)*
XW857		G-LEDR	Westland Gazelle HT.2 *(Royal Navy)*
XW858	C	G-DMSS	Westland Gazelle HT.3
XW861	CU-52	G-BZFJ	Westland Gazelle HT.2
XW898	G	G-CBXT	Westland Gazelle HT.3 *(Royal Navy)*
XX110		BAPC.169	Sepecat Jaguar GR.1 fsm
XX226	74	BAPC.152	BAe Hawk T.1A fsm
XX253		BAPC.171	BAe Hawk T.1 *(Red Arrows c/s)*
XX406	P	G-CBSH	Westland SA.341D Gazelle HT.3
XX436	CU-39	G-ZZLE	Westland SA.341C Gazelle HT.2 *(Royal Navy)*
XX467	86	G-TVII	Hawker Hunter T.7 *(TWU)*
XX513	10	G-CCMI	Scottish Aviation Bulldog
XX514		G-BWIB	Scottish Aviation Bulldog
XX515	4	G-CBBC	Scottish Aviation Bulldog
XX518	S	G-UDOG	Scottish Aviation Bulldog
XX521	H	G-CBEH	Scottish Aviation Bulldog
XX522	06	G-DAWG	Scottish Aviation Bulldog
XX524	04	G-DDOG	Scottish Aviation Bulldog
XX525	8	G-CBJJ	Scottish Aviation Bulldog
XX528	D	G-BZON	Scottish Aviation Bulldog
XX534	B	G-EDAV	Scottish Aviation Bulldog
XX537	C	G-CBCB	Scottish Aviation Bulldog
XX538	O	G-TDOG	Scottish Aviation Bulldog
XX543	F	G-CBAB	Scottish Aviation Bulldog
XX546	03	G-WINI	Scottish Aviation Bulldog
XX549	6	G-CBID	Scottish Aviation Bulldog
XX551	E	G-BZDP	Scottish Aviation Bulldog
XX554	09	G-BZMD	Scottish Aviation Bulldog
XX561	7	G-BZEP	Scottish Aviation Bulldog
XX611	7	G-CBDK	Scottish Aviation Bulldog
XX612	A03	G-BZXC	Scottish Aviation Bulldog
XX614	V	G-GGRR	Scottish Aviation Bulldog
XX619	T	G-CBBW	Scottish Aviation Bulldog
XX621	H	G-CBEF	Scottish Aviation Bulldog
XX622	B	G-CBGX	Scottish Aviation Bulldog
XX624	E	G-KDOG	Scottish Aviation Bulldog
XX625	01	G-CBBR	Scottish Aviation Bulldog
XX626	W:02	G-CDVV	Scottish Aviation Bulldog
XX628	9	G-CBFU	Scottish Aviation Bulldog
XX629	V	G-BZXZ	Scottish Aviation Bulldog
XX630	25	G-SIJW	Scottish Aviation Bulldog
XX631	W	G-BZXS	Scottish Aviation Bulldog
XX636	Y	G-CBFP	Scottish Aviation Bulldog
XX638		G-DOGG	Scottish Aviation Bulldog

XX658	03	G-BZPS	Scottish Aviation Bulldog
XX667	16	G-BZFN	Scottish Aviation Bulldog
XX668	I	G-CBAN	Scottish Aviation Bulldog
XX692	A	G-BZMH	Scottish Aviation Bulldog
XX693	07	G-BZML	Scottish Aviation Bulldog
XX694	E	G-CBBS	Scottish Aviation Bulldog
XX695	3	G-CBBT	Scottish Aviation Bulldog
XX698	9	G-BZME	Scottish Aviation Bulldog
XX699	F	G-CBCV	Scottish Aviation Bulldog
XX700	17	G-CBEK	Scottish Aviation Bulldog
XX702		G-CBCR	Scottish Aviation Bulldog
XX704		G-BCUV	Scottish Aviation Bulldog
XX707	4	G-CBDS	Scottish Aviation Bulldog
XX711	X	G-CBBU	Scottish Aviation Bulldog
XX713	2	G-CBJK	Scottish Aviation Bulldog
XX725	GU	BAPC.150	Sepecat Jaguar GR.1
XX885		G-HHAA	Hawker Siddeley Buccaneer S.2B
XZ329		G-BZYD	Westland Gazelle AH.1 *(Army)*
XZ363	A	BAPC.151	Sepecat Jaguar GR.1A
XZ934	U	G-CBSI	Westland SA.341C Gazelle HT.2 *(RN)*
ZA556		BAPC.155	Panavia Tornado GR.1 fsm
ZA634	C	G-BUHA	Slingsby T.61F Venture T.2
ZA652		G-BUDC	Slingsby T.61F Venture T.2
ZB500		G-LYNX	Westland Lynx 800 *(AAC)*
ZB627	A	G-CBSK	Westland SA.314G Gazelle HT.3
ZB629		G-CBZL	Westland SA.314G Gazelle HT.3
ZB647	40	G-CBSF	Westland SA.314G Gazelle HT.2
ZF592		G-AWON	English Electric Lightning F.53
ZH139	01	BAPC.191	BAe Harrier GR.7
ZJ116		G-OIOI	EH Industries EH-101 Heliliner
8449M		G-ASWJ	Beagle B.206
	F	G-RUMW	Grumman FM-2 Wildcat *(FAA)*
	12	G-ARSG	Roe Triplane IV replica

"B" Conditions markings

G-17-3		G-AVNE	Westland Wessex 60
G-29-1		G-APRJ	Avro Lincoln B.2 *(Fuselage only)*
U-0247		G-AGOY	Miles M.38 Messenger - *intended marks*
W-2		BAPC.85	Weir W-2
X-25		BAPC.274	Boulton and Paul P.6 fsm

Other markings

SR-XP020		G-BZUG	TLAC RL7A XP Sherwood Ranger

OTHER ARMED FORCES
AUSTRALIA

A2-4		VH-ALB	Supermarine Seagull
A16-199	SF-R	G-BEOX	Lockheed Hudson IIIA
A17-48		G-BPHR	DH.82A Tiger Moth
A21-14		G-AFOR	de Havilland DH.94 Moth Minor
A77-851		G-METE	Gloster Meteor F.8
A81-17		G-AIMI	Bristol 170 Freighter 21E
A84-234		G-BURM	English Electric Canberra TT.18
N6-766		G-SPDR	DH.115 Sea Vampire T.55 *(Navy)*

BELGIUM

66		BAPC.19	Bristol F2b Fighter fuselage frame
B-06		G-BDPU	Britten-Norman BN-2A-21 Islander
B-11		G-BEED	Britten-Norman BN-2A-21 Islander
HD-75		G-AFDX	Hanriot HD.1
T-24	UR-1	G-AMJD	de Havilland DH.82A Tiger Moth

BOLIVIA

FAB-184		G-SIAI	SIAI-Marchetti SF.260W

BURKINA FASO

BF8431	31	G-NRRA	SIAI-Marchetti SF.260W

CANADA

622		N6699D	Piasecki HUP-3 Retreiver *(RCN)*
RCAF 671		G-BNZC	de Havilland DHC-1 Chipmunk
920	QN-	CF-BXO	Supermarine Stranraer
3349	-	G-BYNF	North American NA-64 Yale I
4188	-	G-ANOS	de Havilland DH.82A Tiger Moth
5403		G-HHII	Hawker Hurricane X
5429	Z	G-KAMM	Hawker Hurricane XIIA
16693	693	G-BLPG	Auster J/1N *(AOP.6 c/s)*
18013	013	G-TRIC	de Havilland DHC-1 Chipmunk
18393		G-BCYK	Avro Canada CF.100 Canuck IV
20310	310	G-BSBG	North American Harvard IV

PEOPLES' REPUBLIC OF CHINA (including HONG KONG*)

	68	G-BVVG	Nanchang CJ-6A *(Chinese AF)*
50051		G-BAJJ	Hawker Siddeley HS.121 Trident 2E Series 108
50055		G-BBWG	Hawker Siddeley HS.121 Trident 2E Series 109
50258		G-ASDS	Vickers 843 Viscount
HKG-6*		G-BPCL	Scottish Aviation Bulldog
HKG-11*		G-BYRY	Slingsby T.67M-200 Firefly
HKG-13*		G-BXKW	Slingsby T.67M-200 Firefly

FINLAND

AV-57		G-EBNU	Avro 504K

FRANCE

1 4513	S	G-BFYO	SPAD XIIi replica
19		BAPC.136	Deperdussin 1913 Monoplane fsm
20	315-SQ	G-BWGG	Max Holste Broussard *(ALAT)*
78		G-BIZK	Nord 3202 *(Air Force)*
124		G-BOSJ	Nord 3400

Country	Serial	Code	Registration	Aircraft type
	143		G-MSAL	Morane-Saulnier MS.733 (Aéronavale)
	156		G-NIFE	Stampe SV-4A (Air Force)
	157	01	G-AVEB	Morane Saulnier MS.230 (Air Force)
	185	44-CA	G-BWLR	Max Holste Broussard
	208	IR	G-YYYY	Max Holste Broussard
	394		G-BIMO	Stampe SV-4C (Air Force)
	MS.824		G-AWBU	Morane-Saulnier N replica (Air Force)
	18-5395	CDG	G-CUBJ	Piper L-18C Super Cub (ALAT)
	51-7545	119	N14113	North American T-28B Trojan (Air Force)
	517692	142	G-TROY	North American T-28A Trojan
GERMANY	1		G-BWUE	Hispano HA.1112-MIL Buchon
	1+4		G-BSLX	WAR FW190 scale replica
	2+1	7334	G-SYFW	WAR FW190 scale replica
	4+--		G-AWHS	Hispano HA.1112-MIL Buchon
	8+--		G-WULF	WAR FW190 scale replica
	- + 9		G-CCFW	WAR FW190 scale replica
	14		BAPC.67	Messerschmitt Bf.109 fsm
	+14		G-BSMD	Nord 1101 (Messerschmitt guise)
	17+TF		G-BZTJ	Bücker Bü.133C Jungmeister
	50 483	CW+BG	G-BXBD	CASA 1131 Jungmann
	97+04		G-APVF	Putzer Elster B
	99+32		G-BZGK	North American OV-10B Bronco
	102/17		BAPC.88	Fokker Dr.1 5/8th scale model
	152/17		G-ATJM	Fokker Dr.1 replica
	210/16		BAPC.56	Fokker E.III replica
	403/17		G-CDXR	Fokker Dr.1 Triplane replica (German Army Air Service)
	422/15		G-AVJO	Fokker E-III replica
	425/17		BAPC.133	Fokker Dr.1 Triplane replica
	450/17		G-BVGZ	Fokker Dr.1 Triplane replica (German Army Air Service)
	477/17		G-FOKK	Fokker Dr.1 Triplane replica
	694		BAPC.239	Fokker D.VIII 5/8th scale model
	1480	6	BAPC.66	Messerschmitt Bf.109 replica
	C.L.1.1801/18		G-BNPV	Bowers Fly Baby (German Army Air Service)
	C.L.1.1803/18		G-BUYU	Bowers Fly Baby (German Army Air Service)
	2292		BAPC.138	Hansa Brandenberg W.29 fsm
	4477	GD+EG	G-RETA	CASA 1131E Jungmann Series 2000
	5125/18		BAPC.110	Fokker D.VIIF fsm
	6357	6	BAPC.74	Messerschmitt Bf.109 replica
	7198/18		G-AANJ	LVG C.VI
	10639	6 (Black)	G-USTV	Messerschmitt Bf.109G-2
	191454		BAPC.271	Messerschmitt Me 163B Komet fsm
	C19/15		BAPC.118	Albatros D.Va fsm
	D692		G-BVAW	Staaken Flitzer
	D-2692		G-STIG	Focke-Wulf FW.44J Stieglit
	D5397/17		G-BFXL	Albatros D.VA replica
	DR1/17		BAPC.139	Fokker Dr.1 Triplane fsm
		6G+ED	G-BZOB	Slepcev Storch
		BU+CC	G-BUCC	CASA 1131E Jungmann
		BU+CK	G-BUCK	CASA 1131E Jungmann
		CC+43	G-CJCI	Pilatus P.2 (Arado Ar.96B guise)
		CF+HF	EI-AUY	Morane-Saulnier MS.502 Criquet
		DM+BK	G-BPHZ	Morane-Saulnier MS.505 Criquet
		FI+S	G-BIRW	Morane-Saulnier MS.505 Criquet
		GL+SU	G-GLSU	Bucker Bu.181B-1 Bestmann
		KG+EM	G-ETME	Nord 1002 Pingouin
		N8+AA	G-BFHD	CASA 352L
		N9+AA	G-BECL	CASA.352L
		NJ+C11	G-ATBG	Messerschmitt Bf.108 (Nord 1002)
		S4+A07	G-BWHP	CASA 1131E Jungmann
		S5+B06	G-BSFB	CASA 1131E Jungmann
		VK-NZ	G-BFHG	CASA 352L
HUNGARY	503		G-BRAM	MiG 21PF (Russian c/s)
IRELAND	176		G-AMDD	de Havilland DH.104 Dove 6
	177		G-BLIW	Percival Provost T.51
ISRAEL	13		G-AHAY	Auster V J/1 Autocrat
	171		G-AJMC	Bristol 156 Beaufighter TF.X
ITALY		W7	G-AGFT	Avia FL.3
	MM12822	20	G-FIST	Fiesler Fi.156C-3 Storch
	MM53211	ZI-4	BAPC.79	Fiat G.46-4B
	44mm52801		97-4	G-BBII	Fiat G.46-3B
JAPAN	15-1585		BAPC.58	Yokosuka MXY-7 Ohka II
	24		BAPC.83	Kawasaki Ki 100-1b
	997		BAPC.98	Yokosuka MXY-7 Ohka II
JORDAN	A-410		G-AIPW	Taylorcraft Auster 5A Series 160 (Arab Legion AF c/s)
	109		G-BVPO	de Havilland DH.100 Vampire FB.6
	209		G-BVLM	de Havilland DH.115 Vampire T.55
	712	E	G-BWKC	Hawker Hunter F.58
	800		G-BOOM	Hawker Hunter T.7 (T.53)
	843		G-BWKC	Hawker Hunter F.58
KUWAIT	53-418		G-AXEE	English Electric Lightning F.53
MEXICO	52		N4238C	Mudry CAP.10B (Air Force)

NETHERLANDS	174	K		G-BEPV	Fokker S.11 Instructor (Navy)
	BI-005			G-BUVN	CASA 1131E Jungmann
	E-15			G-BIYU	Fokker S.11 Instructor
	H-98			G-CCCA	Vickers Supermarine 509 Spitfire Tr.IX (Air Force)
	H-99			G-ILDA	Vickers Supermarine 509 Spitfire Tr.IX (Air Force)
	N-321			G-BWGL	Hawker Hunter T.8C
	R-55	(Also carries 52-2466)		G-BLMI	Piper L-18C Super Cub (Air Force)
	R-151			G-BIYR	Piper L-21B Super Cub
	R-156			G-ROVE	Piper L-21B Super Cub (Air Force)
	R-163	(Also carries 54-2453)		G-BIRH	Piper L-21B Super Cub (Air Force)
	R-167			G-LION	Piper L-21B Super Cub (Air Force)
NEW ZEALAND	NZ4115			G-AHJR (2)	Short S.25 Sunderland MR.5
	NZ6001			G-ARTR	de Havilland DHC-2 Beaver 1
NORTH KOREA	No marks			G-BMZF	MiG-15
NORWAY	56321			G-BKPY	Saab Safir
OMAN	417			G-RSAF	BAC 167 Strikemaster Mk.82A
	425			G-SOAF	BAC 167 Strikemaster Mk.82A
POLAND	1018			G-ISKA	WSK-PZL Mielec TS-11 Iskra
	PLW-6247			G-OMIG	WSK SBLim-2A
PORTUGAL	1365			G-DHPM	de Havilland DHC-1 Chipmunk
	1373			G-CBJG	de Havilland DHC-1 Chipmunk
	1377			G-BARS	de Havilland DHC-1 Chipmunk
	1747			G-BGPB	CCF Harvard 4
RUSSIA	1 (White)			G-BZMY	Yakovlev Yak C-11 (Soviet AF)
	01 (Yellow)			G-YKSZ	Yakovlev Yak-52 (Soviet AF)
	07 (Yellow)			G-BMJY	Yakovlev Yak-18 (Soviet AF)
	9 (White)			G-OYAK	Yakovlev Yak-11(Soviet AF)
	09 (Yellow)			G-BVMU	Yakovlev Yak-52 (DOSAAF)
	10 (Yellow)			G-BTZB	Yakovlev Yak-50 (DOSAAF)
	11 (Yellow)			G-YCII	Yakovlev Yak C-11 (Soviet AF)
	21 (White)			G-CDBJ	Yakovlev Yak-3 (Russian AF c/s)
	26 (Grey)			G-BVXK	Yakovlev Yak-52 (DOSAAF)
	27 (Red)			G-YAKX	Yakovlev Yak-52 (DOSAAF)
	31 (Black)			G-YAKV	Yakovlev Yak-52 (DOSAAF)
	33 (White)			G-YAKH	Yakovlev Yak-52 (Soviet AF)
	33 (Red)			G-YAKZ	Yakovlev Yak-50 (Soviet AF)
	36 (White)			G-IYAK	Yakovlev Yak C-11 (DOSAAF)
	36 (White)			G-KYAK	Yakovlev Yak C-11 (DOSAAF)
	39			G-XXVI	Sukhoi Su-26M
	42 (White)			G-CBRU	Yakovlev Yak-52 (DOSAAF)
	48 (Grey)			G-CBSN	Yakovlev Yak-52 (DOSAAF)
	49 (Red)			G-YAKU	Yakovlev Yak-50 (Soviet AF)
	50 (Grey)			G-CBRW	Yakovlev Yak-52 (DOSAAF)
	55 (Grey)			G-BVOK	Yakovlev Yak-52 (DOSAAF)
	61(Red)			G-YAKM	Yakovlev Yak-50 (Soviet AF)
	66 (Red)			G-YAKN	Yakovlev Yak-52 (Soviet AF)
	139 (Yellow)			G-BWOD	Yakovlev Yak-52 (DOSAAF)
	503			G-BRAM	See HUNGARY above
SAUDI ARABIA	1104			G-SMAS	BAC 167 Strikemaster Mk.80A
	1133			G-AMZW	Douglas C-47B-20-DK Dakota
SOUTH AFRICA	92			G-BYCX	Westland Wasp HAS.Mk.1 (Navy)
	6850			G-BYCX	Westland Wasp HAS.Mk.1 (Navy)
SOUTH ARABIA (South Yemen))	104			G-PROV	Hunting Percival P.84 Jet Provost T.52A (T.4)
SPAIN	E3B-153	781-75		G-BPTS	CASA 1131 Jungmann
	E3B-350	05-97		G-BHPL	CASA 1131 Jungmann
	E3B-369	781-32		G-BPDM	CASA 1131 Jungmann
	E3B-494	81-47		G-CDLC	CASA 1131 Jungmann
SRI LANKA	CR-822			G-AMJY	Douglas C-47B-40-DK Dakota
	CX-123			G-AKEE	de Havilland DH.82A Tiger Moth
SWEDEN	Fv5555			G-EBNO	de Havilland DH.60 Moth
SWITZERLAND	A-10			G-BECW	CASA 1131E Jungmann
	A-12			G-CCHY	Bücker Bü.131 Jungmann
	A-50			G-CBCE	CASA 1131E Jungmann replica
	A-57			G-BECT	CASA 1131E Jungmann
	A-125			G-BLKZ	Pilatus P.2-05
	A-806			G-BTLL	Pilatus P.3
	C-552			G-DORN	EKW C-3605
	J-1167			G-MKVI	de Havilland DH.100 Vampire FB.6
	J-1573			G-VICI	de Havilland DH.112 Venom FB.50
	J-1605			G-BLID	de Havilland DH.112 Venom FB.50
	J-1758			G-BLSD	de Havilland DH.112 Venom FB.50
	J-4021			G-HHAC	Hawker Hunter F.58
	J-4031			G-BWFR	Hawker Hunter F.58
	J-4058			G-HHAD	Hawker Hunter F.58
	J-4072			G-HHAB	Hawker Hunter F.58

J-4081		G-HHAF	Hawker Hunter F.58
J-4090		G-SIAL	Hawker Hunter F.58
U-80		G-BUKK	Bücker Bü.133 Jungmeister
U-95		G-BVGP	Bücker Bü.133 Jungmeister
U-99		G-AXMT	Bücker Bü.133 Jungmeister
U-110		G-PTWO	Pilatus P.2
V-54		G-BVSD	SE.3130 Alouette II

UNITED STATES

001		G-BYPY	Ryan ST3-KR *(Army)*
00195700		G-OIDW	Cessna F150G *(Pseudo Air Force)*
02538		N33870	Fairchild PT-19 Cornell *(Army Air Corps)*
07539	143	N63590	Boeing Stearman Kaydet *(Navy)*
14		G-ISDN	Boeing Stearman Kaydet *(Army)*
17-6532	15	G-BSKS	Nieuport 28C-1
18-0012		G-BLXT	Royal Aircraft Factory SE.5A
18-2001		G-BIZV	Piper L-18C Super Cub *(Army)*
112		G-BSWC	Boeing Stearman Kaydet *(Army Air Corps)*
118		G-BSDS	Boeing Stearman Kaydet *(Army Air Corps)*
169		N52485	Boeing Stearman Kaydet *(Navy)*)
1102	102	G-AZLE	Boeing Stearman Kaydet *(Navy)*
1164		G-BKGL	Beech C-45 *(Army)*
14863		G-BGOR	North American AT-6D Texan *(Army Air Force)*
16037		G-BSFD	Piper J-3C-65 Cub *(Army)*
16136	205	G-BRUJ	Boeing Stearman Kaydet *(Navy)*
18263	822	N38940	Boeing Stearman Kaydet *(Army Air Corps)*
111836	JZ-6	G-TSIX	North American AT-6C Texan *(Navy)*
111989		N33600	Cessna L-19A Bird Dog *(Army)*
115042	TA-042	G-BGHU	North American T-6G Texan *(Air Force)*
115227		G-BKRA	North American T-6G Texan *(Navy)*
115302	TP	G-BJTP	Piper L-18C Super Cub *(Marin*
115373	A-373	G-AYPM	Piper L-21A Super Cub *(Army)*
115684	VM	G-BKVM	Piper L-21A Super Cub *(Army)*
124485	DF-A	G-BEDF	Boeing B-17G Flying Fortress *(Army Air Corps)*
126603		G-BHWH	Weedhopper JC-24C *(Navy)*
146289	2W	N99153	North American T-28C Trojan
151632		G-BWGR	North American TB-25N Mitchell *(Air Force)*
23		N49272	Fairchild PT-23 Cornell *(Army Air Corps)*
26		G-BAVO	Boeing Stearman Kaydet *(Army)*
27		G-AGYY	Ryan PT-21 *(Army Air Corps)*
21714	201B	G-RUMM	Grumman F8F-2P Bearcat *(Navy)*
24550	GP	G-PDOG	Cessna O-1E Bird Dog *(Air Force)*
24582		G-VDOG	Cessna L-1E Bird Dog *(Army)*
26922	AK 402	G-RADR	Douglas AD-4NA Skyraider *(Navy)*
28521	TA-521	G-TVIJ	North American T-6J Harvard *(Air Force)*
29261		G-CDET	Culver Cadet *(Army Air Force)*
212540	RD 40	G-BBHK	Noorduyn AT-16-ND Harvard IIB *(Navy)*
217786	25	CF-EQS	Boeing Stearman Kaydet *(Army Air Force)*
219993		G-CEJU	Bell P-39Q Airacobra
226413	ZU-N	N47DD	Republic P-47D Thunderbolt *(Army Air Force)*
228473		G-BLZW	Republic P-47D-30-RA Thunderbolt
231983	IY-G	F-BDRS	Boeing B-17G Flying Fortress *(Army Air Force)*
236657	D-72	G-BGSJ	Piper L-4A-PI *(Army Air Corps)*
237123		BAPC.157	Waco CG-4A Hadrian
238410	A-44	G-BHPK	Piper L-4A *(Army Air Corps)*
243809		BAPC.185	WACO CG-4A Hadrian Glider
252983		N66630	Schweizer TG-3A *(Army Air Corps)*
298177	R-8	N6438C	Stinson L-5C Sentinel
3		BAPC.140	Curtiss 42A R3C2 fsm *(Army)*
3-1923		G-BRHP	Aeronca O-58B Grasshopper *(Army)*
379		G-ILLE	Boeing Stearman Kaydet *(Army Air Corps)*
3072	72	G-TEXN	North American T-6G-NT Texan *(Navy)*
3397	174	G-OBEE	Boeing Stearman A75N-1 *(Navy)*
30274		N203SA	Piper AE-1 Cub Cruiser *(Navy)*
31145	G-26	G-BBLH	Piper L-4B *(Army)*
31171		N7614C	North American B-25J Mitchell *(Marines)*
31430		G-BHVV	Piper J-3C-65 Cub *(Army Air Force)*
31952		G-BRPR	Aeronca L-3C Grasshopper *(Army)*
314887		G-AJPI	Fairchild UC-61 Forwarder *(Army Air Force)*
315211	JB-Z	N1944A	Douglas C-47A
315509	W7-S	G-BHUB	Douglas C-47A Dakota *(Army Air Force)*
329405	A-23	G-BCOB	Piper L-4H *(Army Air Corps)*
329417		G-BDHK	Piper L-4A *(Army Air Corps)*
329471	F-44	G-BGXA	Piper L-4H *(Army Air Corps)*
329601	D-44	G-AXHR	Piper L-4H *(Army Air Corps)*
329854	R-44	G-BMKC	Piper L-4H *(Army Air Corps)*
329934	B-72	G-BCPH	Piper L-4H *(Army Air Corps)*
330238	A-24	G-LIVH	Piper L-4H *(Army Air Corps)*
330485	C-44	G-AJES	Piper L-4H *(Army Air Corps)*
343251	27	G-NZSS	Boeing Stearman Kaydet *(Army Air Corps)*
41-33275	CE	G-BICE	North American AT-6C Texan *(Army Air Corps)*
42-17553	716	N1731B	Boeing A75N-1 Stearman
42-35870	129	G-BWLJ	Taylorcraft DCO-65 O *(Navy)*
42-58678	IY	G-BRIY	Taylorcraft L-2A *(Army Air Corps)*
42-78044		G-BRXL	Aeronca L-3F *(Army)*
42-84555	EP-H	G-ELMH	North American AT-6D Harvard *(Army Air Corps)*
42-100766		6W-SAF	Douglas C-47A-65-DL *(Nose section only)*
43	SC	G-AZSC	North American AT-16 Texan *(Army Air Force)*
44		G-RJAH	Boeing Stearman Kaydet *(Army Air Corps)*
44-9063		EI-ARS (2)	Douglas C-54E-5-DO Skymaster
44-30861		N9089Z	North American B-25J Mitchell *(Army Air Corps)*

44-42914		N31356	Douglas DC-4-1009
44-79609	S-44	G-BHXY	Piper L-4H *(Army Air Force)*
44-83184	7	G-RGUS	Fairchild UC-61K Forwarder *(Army)*
44-83868	N	N5237V	Boeing B-17G Flying Fortress *(Army Air Force)*
45-0951		G-BLFL	Douglas C-47B-45-DK Dakota
46-16130		G-BGCF	Douglas C-47A-90-DL Dakota
49		G-KITT	Curtiss TP-40M Kittyhawk *(Air Force)*
441		G-BTFG	Boeing Stearman Kaydet *(Navy)*
4406	12	G-ONAF	Naval Aircraft Factory N3N-3 *(Navy)*
40467	19	G-BTCC	Grumman F6F Hellcat *(Navy)*
46214	X-3	CF-KCG	Grumman TBM-3E Avenger *(Navy)*
413317	VF-B	N51RT	North American P-51D Mustang *(Army Air Corps)*
413573	B6-K	N6526D	North American P-51D Mustang *(Army Air Corps)*
413704	B7-H	G-BTCD	North American P-51D Mustang *(Army Air Force)*
414419	LH-F	G-MSTG	North American P-51D Mustang *(Army Air Force)*
433915		G-PBYA	Consolidated PBY-5A Catalina *(USAAF)*
436021		G-BWEZ	Piper L-4 *(Army Air Corps)*
454467	J-44	G-BILI	Piper L-4J *(Army Air Corps)*
454537	J-04	G-BFDL	Piper L-4J *(Army Air Corps)*
461748	Y	G-BHDK	Boeing B-29A Superfortress *(Air Force)*
463209	WZ-S	BAPC.255	North American P-51D Mustang *(Army Air Corps)*
463864	HL-W	G-CBNM	North American P-51D Mustang *(Army Air Corps)*
472035		G-SIJJ	North American P-51D Mustang *(Army Air Force)*
472216	HO-M	G-BIXL	North American P-51D Mustang *(Army Air Corps)*
472218	WZ-I	G-HAEC	North American P-51D Mustang *(Army Air Force)*
479651		EI-CFO	Piper L-4H *(Army Air Corps)*
479744	49-M	G-BGPD	Piper L-4H *(Army Air Corps)*
479766	63-D	G-BKHG	Piper L-4H *(Army Air Corps)*
479897	JD	G-BOXJ	Piper L-4H *(Army Air Corps)*
480015	M-44	G-AKIB	Piper L-4H *(Army Air Corps)*
480133	B-44	G-BDCD	Piper L-4J *(Army Air Corps)*
480173	H-57	G-RRSR	Piper L-4J *(Army Air Corps)*
480321	H-44	G-FRAN	Piper L-4J *(Army Air Corps)*
480480	E-44	G-BECN	Piper L-4J *(Army Air Corps)*
480636	A-58	G-AXHP	Piper L-4J *(Army Air Corps)*
480723	E5-J	G-BFZB	Piper L-4J *(Army Air Corps)*
480752	E-39	G-BCXJ	Piper L-4J *(Army Air Corps)*
480762		EI-BBV	Piper L-4J *(Army Air Corps)*
493209	ANG	G-DDMV	North American T-6G Texan *(California Air Nat.Guard)*
5	146-11083	G-BNAI	SPAD replica *(Wolf W.II) (Army Air Corps)*
51-11701A	AF258	G-BSZC	Beech C-45H *(Air Force)*
51-15319	A-319	G-FUZZ	Piper L-18C Super Cub *(Army)*
54-2445	A-445	G-OTAN	Piper L-21B Super Cub *(Army)*
54-2447		G-SCUB	Piper L-21B Super Cub *(Army)*
54884	D-57-	N61787	Piper J-3C-65 Cub
56498		N44914	Douglas C-54D Skymaster
6-1042	7	G-BMZX	SPAD replica *(Wolf W.II) (Army Air Corp*
624	D-39	G-BVMH	Piper L-4 *(Wag-Aero Cuby) (Army Air Corps)*
669		G-CCXA	Boeing Stearman A75N1 *(Army Air Corps)*
699		G-CCXB	Boeing Stearman A75N1 *(Army Air Corps)*
72-21509	129	G-UHIH	Bell UH-1H Iroquois *(Army)*
7797		G-BFAF	Aeronca L-16A *(Army)*
85		G-BTBI	Republic P-47 Thunderbolt scale replica *(Air Force)*
854		G-BTBH	Ryan PT-22 *(Army Air Corps)*
855		N56421	Ryan PT-22 *(Army Air Corps)*
897	E	G-BJEV	Aeronca Chief *(Navy)*
8178	FU-178	G-SABR	North American F-86A Sabre *(Air Force)*
8242	FU-242	N196B	North American F-86A Sabre *(Air Force)*
80105	19	G-CCBN	Replica SE5A *(US Air Service)*
90678	27	G-BRVG	North American SNJ-7 Texan *(Navy)*
92844	8	G-BXUL	Vought FG-1D Corsair *(Navy)*
93542	LTA-542	G-BRLV	North American T-6 Texan *(Air Force)*
C1661-TA		G-BTUV	Aeronca 65TAC Defender *(Air Force)*
	G-57	G-AKAZ (2)	Piper L-4A *(Army Air Corps)*

VENUEZULA	2531	G-AMXS	de Havilland DH.104 Dove 2A
YUGOSLAVIA	146	G-BSXD	Soko P-2 Kraguj
	30149	149	G-SOKO	Soko P-2 Kraguj
UNATTRIBUTED	164	BAPC.106	Bleriot Type XI
	5439	BAPC.84	Mitsubishi Ki 46 III (Dinah)
	442795	BAPC.199	Fieseler Fi 103 (V-1)
	GBH-7	BAPC.234	Vickers FB.5 Gunbus fsm
	LHS-1	BAPC.147	Bensen B.7 Gyroglider
	QP-30	G-BFDV	Westland WG.13 Lynx HC.28 *(SEAE)*

PART 3 – "B CONDITIONS" MARKINGS

Air Navigation Order (ANO2000) promulgates the specific circumstances under which aerospace manufacturers can pursue the conduct of aircraft trials without the need for valid Certificates of Airworthiness. ANO2000 establishes both "A" and "B" conditions but we are only concerned here with the latter requirements which stipulate the use of identity marks as approved by the CAA for the purposes of "B Conditions" flight.

In brief, under "B Conditions" an aircraft must fly only for the purpose of:
    (a) experimenting with or testing the aircraft (including any engines installed thereon) or any equipment installed or carried in the aircraft;
    (b) enabling it to qualify for the issue of a certificate of airworthiness or the validation thereof or the approval of a modification of the aircraft or the issue of a permit to fly;
    (c) demonstrating and displaying the aircraft, any engines installed thereon or any equipment installed or carried in the aircraft with a view to the sale thereof or of other similar aircraft, engines or equipment;
    (d) demonstrating and displaying the aircraft to employees of the operator;
    (e) the giving of flying training to or the testing of flight crew employed by the operator or the training or testing of other persons employed by the operator; or
    (f) proceeding to or from a place at which any experiment, inspection, repair, modification, maintenance, approval, test or weighing of the aircraft, the installation of equipment in the aircraft, demonstration, display or training is to take place or at which installation of furnishings in, or the painting of, the aircraf is to be undertaken.

The flight must be operated by a person approved by the CAA for the purposes of these Conditions and subject to any additional conditions which may be specified in such an approval. If not registered in the United Kingdom the aircraft must be marked in a manner approved by the CAA for the purposes of these Conditions. The aircraft must carry such flight crew as may be necessary to ensure the safety of the aircraft. No person can act as pilot in command of the aircraft except a person approved for the purpose by the CAA.

Prompted by the SBAC a radically new system was introduced in 1948. In essence, this remains in existence today. Whilst deemed "current" many Companies included have long since merged or ceased to trade and so, by coincidence, the table below enscapsulates in miniature the absorbing changes within the UK aircraft industry which have occurred during the period 1948 to date. The same can also be said for the original series covering the period from 1929 to 1948. Thanks to Barry V Taylor for new information this year.

CURRENT SERIES

Prefix	Company	Period	Issued	Remarks
G-1-	Sir W G Armstrong-Whitworth Aircraft Ltd	1948-1967	1.1.48	Cancelled
G-1-	Rolls-Royce Ltd (Bristol Engines Division)	1949-19xx	9.4.69	Cancelled
G-2-	Blackburn Aircraft Ltd	1949-1967	1.1.48	Cancelled
G-3-	Boulton Paul Aircraft Ltd	1948-1973	1.1.48	Cancelled 31.12.73
G-03	BAE Systems (Operating) Ltd	19xx-		Current
G-4-	Portsmouth Aviation Ltd	1948-1949	1.1.48	Cancelled 23.5.49
G-4-	Miles Aviation and Transport (R & D) Ltd	1969-19xx	1.5.69	Cancelled
G-04	BAe Systems (Operating) Ltd	19xx-		Current
G-5-	The de Havilland Aircraft Co Ltd	1948-	1.1.48	Current
	(became Raytheon Services Ltd)			
G-6-	Fairey Aviation Ltd	1948-1969	1.1.48	Cancelled 17.1.69
G-7-	Gloster Aircraft Ltd	1948-1961	1.1.48	Cancelled
G-7-	Slingsby Sailplanes Ltd	1971-	21.10.71	Current
	(became Slingsby Aviation Ltd)			
G-8-	Handley Page Ltd	1948-1970	1.1.48	Cancelled 28.2.70
G-08	BAE Systems (Operating) Ltd	19xx-		Current
G-9-	Hawker Aircraft Ltd (became British Aerospace Defence Ltd)	1948-1996	1.1.48	Cancelled
G-10-	Reid and Sigrist Ltd	1948-1953	1.1.48	Cancelled 1.4.53
G-11-	A.V.Roe and Co. Ltd	1948-	1.1.48	Current
	(became BAe Systems (Operations) Ltd)			
G-12-	Saunders-Roe Ltd	1948-1967	1.1.48	Cancelled 9.6.67
G-13-	Not allocated			
G-14-	Short Brothers and Harland Ltd	1948-	1.1.48	Current
	(became Short Brothers plc)			
G-15-	Vickers Armstrong Ltd, Supermarine Division	1948-1968	1.1.48	Cancelled 17.10.68
G-16-	Vickers Armstrong Ltd, Weybridge Division	1948-1999	1.1.48	Cancelled
	(became British Aerospace Airbus Ltd)			
G-17-	Westland Aircraft Ltd	1948-	1.1.48	Current
	(became GKN Westland Helicopters Ltd)			
G-18-	The Bristol Aeroplane Co.Ltd	1948-1975	1.1.48	Cancelled 31.7.75
G-19-	Heston Aircraft Ltd	1948-1960	1.1.48	Cancelled 4.2.60
G-20-	General Aircraft Ltd	1948-1949	1.1.48	Cancelled 23.5.49
G-21-	Miles Aircraft Ltd (H P Reading Ltd)	1948-1963	1.1.48	Cancelled 11.2.63
G-22-	de Havilland Aircraft Co Ltd, Airspeed Division	1948-1952	1.1.48	Cancelled 23.5.52
G-23-	Percival Aircraft Ltd	1948-1966	1.1.48	Cancelled 31.5.66
G-24-	Cunliffe-Owen Aircraft Ltd	1948-1949	1.1.48	Cancelled 23.5.49
G-25-	Auster Aircraft Ltd	1948-1962	1.1.48	Cancelled
G-26-	Slingsby Sailplanes Ltd	1948-1949	1.1.48	Cancelled 19.12.49
G-27-	English Electric Co Ltd Aircraft Division	1948-1991	1.1.48	Cancelled
	(became British Aerospace Military Aircraft Division Ltd)			
G-28-	British European Airways Corporation (Helicopters)	1948-	1.1.48	Current
	(became Brintel Helicopters Ltd)			
G-29-	D Napier and Son Ltd	1948-1962	1.1.48	Cancelled 9.11.62
G-30-	Pest Control Ltd	1952-1957	1.1.48	Cancelled 4.3.57
G-31-	Scottish Aviation Ltd	1948-	1.1.48	Current
	(became BAe Systems (Operations) Ltd)			
G-32-	Cierva Autogiro Co. Ltd	1948-1951	1.1.48	Cancelled 9.3.51
G-33-	Flight Refuelling Ltd	Not known		
G-34-	Chrislea Aircraft Ltd	1948-1952	1.1.48	Cancelled
G-35-	F.G.Miles Ltd (became Beagle Aircraft Ltd)	1951-1970	9.8.54	Cancelled 29.6.70
G-36-	College of Aeronautics	1954-	9.8.54	Current
	(became Cranfield Aerospace Ltd)			
G-37-	Rolls-Royce Ltd	1954-1971	9.8.54	Cancelled 17.9.71
G-38-	de Havilland Propellers Ltd (became Hawker Siddeley Dynamics)	1954-1975	9.8.54	Cancelled 22.10.75
G-39-	Folland Aircraft Ltd	1954-1965	9.8.54	Cancelled 2.4.65
G-40-	Wiltshire School of Flying Ltd	Not known		Not taken up
G-41-	Aviation Traders (Engineering) Ltd	1956-1976	3.10.56	Cancelled 27.2.76
G-42-	Armstrong Siddeley Motors Ltd	1956-1959	13.11.56	Cancelled 28.8.59
G-43-	Edgar Percival Aircraft Ltd	1956-1959	21.11.56	Cancelled 26.6.59

G-44-	Agricultural Aviation Ltd	1959-1959	17.4.59	Cancelled 14.12.59
G-45-	Bristol Siddeley Engines Ltd	1959-1969	27.5.59	Cancelled 8.4.69
G-46-	Saunders-Roe Ltd, Helicopter Division	1959-1962	15.6.59	Cancelled 3.5.62
G-47-	Lancashire Aircraft Co. Ltd	1960-19xx	8.2.60	Cancelled
G-48-	Westland Aircraft Ltd, Bristol Division	1960-1969	7.7.60	Cancelled 28.2.69
G-49-	F.G.Miles Engineering Ltd	1965-1969	23.7.65	Cancelled c.1969
G-50-	Alvis Ltd	1967-1975	16.2.67	Cancelled
G-51-	Britten-Norman Ltd (became BN Group Ltd)	1967-	20.9.67	Current
G-52-	Marshalls of Cambridge (Engineering) Ltd (became Marshalls of Cambridge Aerospace Ltd)	1968-	18.1.68	Current
G-53-	Norman Aeroplane Co. Ltd	1977-19xx	23.5.77	Cancelled
G-54-	Cameron Balloons Ltd	197x-	Not known	Current
G-55-	W.Vinten Ltd	19xx-19xx	Not known	Cancelled
G-56-	Edgley Aircraft Ltd	19xx-19xx	Not known	Cancelled
G-57-	Airship Industries (UK) Ltd	19xx-19xx	Not known	Cancelled
G-58-	ARV Aviation (became Island Aircraft)	19xx-19xx	Not known	Cancelled
G-59-	Mainair Sports Ltd	19xx	7.05	Cancelle
G-60-	FR Aviation Ltd	19xx-	Not known	(Current together with G-71)
G-61-	Aviation Enterprises Ltd	19xx-	Not known	Current
G-62-	Curtiss and Green Ltd	19xx-19xx	Not known	Cancelled
G-63-	Thunder and Colt Balloons Ltd	1994-19xx	c.1994	Cancelled
G-64-	Brooklands Aerospace Group plc	19xx-19xx	Not known	Cancelled
G-65-	Solar Wings Aviation Ltd	19xx-1995	Not known	Cancelled
G-66-	Aerial Arts Ltd	19xx-19xx	Not known	Cancelled
G-67-	Atlantic Aerengineering Ltd	19xx	Not known	Current
G-68-	Medway Microlights Ltd	19xx	Not known	Current
G-69-	Cyclone Airsports Ltd (formerly Aerial Arts)	19xx	7.05	Cancelled
G-70-	FLS Aerospace (Lovaux) Ltd	19xx	1997	Cancelled
G-71-	FR Aviation Ltd	19xx	Not known	Current
G-72-	Lindstrand Balloons Ltd	19xx	Not known	Current
G-73-	Aviation (Scotland) Ltd	19xx	1995	Cancelled
G-74-	Fleaplanes UK Ltd	19xx	2001	Cancelled
G-75-	Chichester Miles Consultants Ltd	19xx	Not known	Current
G-76-	Police Aviation Services Ltd	19xx	Not known	Current
G-77-	Thruster Air Services Ltd	19xx	Not known	Current
G-78-	Bristow Helicopters Ltd	19xx	Not known	Current
G-79-	McAlpine Helicopters Ltd	19xx	Not known	Current
G-80-	British Microlight Aircraft Association	19xx	Not known	Current
G-81-	Cooper Aerial Services	19xx	Not known	Cancelled
G-82-	European Helicopters Ltd	19xx	1999	Cancelled
G-83-	Mann Aviation Group (Engineering) Ltd	19xx	Not known	Current
G-84-	Intora-Firebird plc	19xx	Not known	Cancelled
G-85-	CFM Aircraft Ltd	19xx	2004	
G-86-	Advanced Technologies Group Ltd	19xx	Not known	Current
G-87-	CHC Scotia Ltd	19xx	Not known	Current
G-88-	Air Hanson Engineering	19xx	Not known	Current
G-89	Not known			
G-90	Not known			
G-91	Bella Aviation	2004-2005		
G-92	Not known			
G-93	P&M Aviation Ltd	7.2005		
G-94	Rotorsport UK Ltd	2006		

ORIGINAL SERIES

Prefix	Company	Period	Issued	Remarks
A	The Sir W G Armstrong Whitworth Aircraft Ltd	1929-1948	23.12.29	
B	Blackburn Aeroplane and Motor Co.Ltd	1929-1948	23.12.29	
C	Boulton and Paul Ltd	1929-1948	23.12.29	
D	Bristol Aeroplane Co.	Not taken up		
D	Cunliffe Owen Aircraft Ltd	Not taken up		
D	Portsmouth Aviation Ltd	1947-1948	1947	
E	de Havilland Aircraft Co Ltd	1929-1948	23.12.29	
F	The Fairey Aviation Co Ltd	1929-1948	23.12.29	
G	Gloster Aircraft Ltd	1929-1948	23.12.29	
H	Handley Page Ltd	1929-1948	23.12.29	
I	H G Hawker Engineering Co Ltd	1929-1948	23.12.29	
J	George Parnall and Co (became Parnall Aircraft Ltd)	1929-1946	23.12.29	Cancelled 1946
J	Reid and Sigrist Ltd	1947-1948	1947	
K	A V Roe and Co Ltd	1929-1948	23.12.29	
L	Saunders-Roe Ltd	1929-1948	23.12.29	
M	Short Bros (Rochester & Bedford) Ltd	1929-1948	23.12.29	
N	Supermarine Aviation Works (Vickers) Ltd	1929-1948	23.12.29	
O	Vickers (Aviation) Ltd	1929-1948	23.12.29	
P	Westland Aircraft Works	1929-1948	23.12.29	
R	The Bristol Aeroplane Co.Ltd	1929-1948	23.12.29	
S	Spartan Aircraft Ltd	1930-1936	30.8.30	Cancelled 29. 2.36
S	Heston Aircraft Ltd	1936-1948	15.5.36	
S	Comper Aircraft Co. Ltd	Not taken up		
T	General Aircraft Ltd	1933-1948	8.5.33	
U	Phillips & Powis Aircraft Ltd	1934-1948	5.2.34	
V	Airspeed (1934) Ltd	1934-1948	27.6.34	
W	G & J Weir Ltd	1933-1948	8.5.33	Cancelled 1946
X	Percival Aircraft Ltd	1936-1948	21.1.36	
Y	The British Aircraft Manufacturing Co.Ltd	1936-1938	1936	Cancelled 1938
Y	Cunliffe Owen Aircraft Ltd	1940-1948	28.10.40	
Z	Taylorcraft Aeroplanes (England) Ltd	1946-1948	12.1.46	
AA	Believed not allocated			
AB	Slingsby Sailplanes Ltd	1947-1948	1947	

PART 4 – FICTITIOUS MARKINGS

Registration	Type	Rematks	Location
"K.158"	Austin Whippet replica	See BAPC.207 - (a)	Doncaster
"EI-ABH"	Mignet HM.14 Pou-Du-Ciel replica	(b)	Meath, Ireland
"F-OCMF"	Sud SA.321F Super Frelon	See F-BTRP - (a)	Weston-super-Mare
"G-EASQ"	Bristol 30/46 Babe III replica	See BAPC.87 - (a)	Kemble
"G-EBED"	Vickers 60 Viking IV replica	See BAPC.114 - (a)	Brooklands
"G-EBVO"	Blackburn Lincock fsm	See BAPC.287 - (a)	Brooklands
"G-AAAH"	de Havilland DH.60 Moth replica	See BAPC.270 - (a)	Elvington
"G-AAAH"	de Havilland DH.60G Moth replica	See BAPC.168 - (a)	Croydon
"G-AACA"	Avro 504K replica	See BAPC.177 - (a)	Brooklands
"G-ABUL"	de Havilland DH.82A Tiger Moth	See G-AOXG - (b)	RNAS Yeovilton
"G-ACSS"	de Havilland DH.88 Comet	See BAPC.216 - (a)	London Colney
"G-ACSS"	de Havilland DH.88 Comet model	See BAPC.257 - (a)	Hatfield
"G-ADNV"	de Havilland DH.82A Tiger Moth	See G-AMLF - (b)	Santa Paula, California, US
"G-ADRG"	Mignet HM.14 Pou-Du-Ciel replica	See BAPC.77 - (b)	Stondon
"G-ADRX"	Mignet HM.14 Pou-Du-Ciel replica	See BAPC.231 - (a)	Haverigg
"G-ADRY"	Mignet HM.14 Pou-Du-Ciel replica	See BAPC.29 - (a)	Dover
"G-ADVU"	Mignet HM.14 Pou-Du-Ciel replica	See BAPC.211 - (a)	Sunderland
"G-ADYV"	Mignet HM.14 Pou-Du-Ciel replica	See BAPC.243 - (a)	Malvern Wells
"G-ADZW"	Mignet HM.14 Pou-Du-Ciel replica	See BAPC.253 - (a)	Southampton
"G-AEAJ"	de Havilland DH.89 Dragon Rapide replica	See BAPC.280 - (a)	Liverpool
"G-AEOF"	Mignet HM.14 Pou-Du-Ciel replica	See BAPC.22 - (a)	Schipol, Netherlands
"G-AFAP"	CASA 352L	(c)	Cosford
"G-AFFI"	Mignet HM.14 Pou-Du-Ciel	See BAPC.76 - (a)	Elvington
"G-AFUG"	Luton LA.4 Minor	See BAPC 97 - (a)	Sunderland
"G-AGIH"	Lockheed 18-56 Lodestar	See G-BMEW - (b)	Gardermoen, Norway
"G-AJOV"	Westland WS-51 Dragonfly HR.3	(c)	Cosford
"G-AJOZ"	Fairchild F.24W-41A Argus 1	(c)	Woodhall Spa
"G-AJPR"	de Havilland DH.104 Dove 6	See G-ARDE - (b)	Al Mahata Museum, The Sharjah Aviation Museum,, Sharjah,UAE
"G-ALVD"	de Havilland DH.104 Dove 2B	See G-ALCU (c)	Coventry
"G-AMZZ" (2)	Douglas C-47A-DK Dakota [12254,]	Al Mahata Museum, The Sharjah Aviation Museum	
	(ex 42-92452 - to RCAF FZ669, CAF12943, C-GCXE, HI-502, N688EA),		Sharjah,UAE
"G-AOXL"	de Havilland DH.114 Heron 2D	See G-ANUO - (b)	Croydon
"G-BMAF"	Cessna 150J	See G-BOWC - (b)	Croft Farm, Defford
"G-CARS"	Pitts S-2A Special	See BAPC.134 - (a)	(Northampton)
"G-CDBS"	MBB Bö.105DD	See G-BCXO - (b)	Land's End Cornwall
"G-ESKY"	Piper PA-23-250 Aztec D	See G-BADI - (c)	North Weald
"G-FIRE"	British Aircraft Corporation One-Eleven 401AK	See 5N-HHH - (b) *(Note authentic G-FIRE (e)*	Southend
"G-FIRE"	Embraer EMB.110P2 Bandeirante	See SX-BNL - (b) *(Note authentic G-FIRE (e)*	Southend
"G-MAZY"	de Havilland DH.82A Tiger Moth	H.Hodgson *"Maisie"*	Newark
	(On loan from Cotswold Aircraft Restoration Group: rebuilt for static display as composite ex Newark components and G-AMBB/T6801; also reported as ex DE561 [lost at sea 1942])		
"G-OOAT"	Piper PA-28-151 Cherokee Warrior	See G-BCTA - (c)	Fairoaks
"G-OOAT"	Piper PA-28R-200 Cherokee Arrow II	See G-BDKV - (c)	Fairoaks
"G-OPAS"	Agusta A109A-II	See D-HCKV - (b)	Gloucestershire
"G-PRAT"	Gulfstream AA-5A Cheetah	*See* G-BIVV - (c)	North Weald
"G-RAFM"	Robinson R22 Beta	See G-OTHL - (b)	Hendon
"G-SHOG"	Colomban MC-15 Cri-Cri	V.S.E.Norman *(Static model 1999)*	Rendcomb
"G-SMOKE"	Hawker Siddeley HS.121 Trident 2E	*See* G-AVFG - (c)	Manchester
"VH-FDT"	de Havilland DHA.3 Drover 2	See G-APXX - (b)	Lasham
"ZK-POZ"	CSS-13 Aeroklubowy	See G-BSSY - (b)	Old Warden

PART 5 – NO EXTERNAL MARKINGS

These are listed by Type to ease identification.

Registration	Type	Comments
G-AANI	Blackburn Monoplane	(c)
G-AANG	Bleriot XI	(c)
G-AANH	Deperdussin Monoplane	(c)
G-EBNV	English Electric Wren	(d)
G-BAAF	Manning-Flanders MF.1	(c)
G-BFIP	Wallbro Monoplane	(b)
G-TURP	Aérospatiale SA341G Gazelle 1	(b)

PART 4 and PART 5 Notes:

(a) Details at SECTION 5, Part 2
(b) Details at SECTION 5, Part 1
(c) Details at SECTION 1, Part 2
(d) Details at SECTION 1, Part 1
(e) Details at SECTION 1, Part 3

PART 6 – GLIDER TYPE INDEX (UK AND IRELAND)

Below is a summary of BGA and IGSA numbers. All BGA certified gliders are referenced below under their BGA numbers rather than Tri-graph reference. Those allocated G- registrations are shown in the relevant Index at SECTION 7, Part 9.

FLUGWISSENSCHAFTLICHEN VERENIGUNG **A**ACHEN
FVA-10B RHEINLAND
    BGA 1711

ABBOTT-BAYNES SAILPLANES LTD
SCUD I replica
    BGA 3922
SCUD II
    BGA 231
SCUD III
    BGA 283 684

AEROMERE see CARMAM

AKAFLIEG BRAUNSCHWEIG
SB.5
    BGA 2690 2719

ALLGAIER
GEIER
    BGA 2557

AMS-FLIGHT see GLASER-DIRKS

AVIA
40P
    BGA 680

AVIASTROITEL see FEDOROV
AC-4
    BGA 4802

AVIALSA see SCHEIBE

AVIONAUTICA RIO see CARMAM

BAC
VII replica
    BGA 2878

BIRMINGHAM GUILD LTD including SWALES and YORKSHIRE SAILPLANES
BG.135, SD.3 and YS-55 CONSORT
    BGA 1741 1891 1921 2212

BÖLKOW
PHOEBUS
    BGA 1542 1547 1570 1577 1595 4537 5190

BREGUET
905 FAUVETTE
    BGA 2112 2679 2915

CAPRONI VIZZOLA COSTRUZIONI AERONAUTICHE SpA
CALIF A-21
    BGA 5219

SOCIÉTÉ **CARMAM** see AEROMERE and AVIONAUTICA RIO
M.100S MESANGE
    BGA 1416 2082 2383 2867 4114
M.200 FOEHN
    BGA 2877 2978 3839
JP-15/34 KIT-CLUB and JP-15/36A AIGLON
    BGA 2485 2593 3169 4017 4055

SOCIÉTÉ **NOUVELLE CENTRAIR** see SCHLEICHER
101 PÉGASE
    BGA 2865 2901 2911 2924 2936 2939 2980 2987 2990 3107 3144 3146
    3198 3217 3231 3259 3271 3296 3304 3368 3394 3470 3474 3476 3559
    3560 3561 3567 3593 3594 3599 3613 3710 3737 3854 3871 3891 4083
    4084 4140 4329 4698 4930 4950 5067 5081 5105 5151 5197 EI-162
201 MARIANNE
    BGA 4854 4865
SNC-34 ALLIANCE
    BGA 4531

CHARD see KING-ELLIOTT-STREET

COLDITZ
COCK replica - designs unrelated
    BGA 4732 4757

DFS see GRUNAU, EoN, NORD, FOCKE-WULF, WEIHE and SCHLEICHER production
KRANICH
    BGA 1147
OLYMPIA-MEISE
    BGA 449
WEIHE
    BGA 448 1021 1093 1230 2602

DG FLUGZEUGBAU see GLASER-DIRKS and ROLLADEN-SCHNEIDER
DG-1000
    BGA 5058 5167 5179 5191 5211 5220 5222 5239 5249 5292

DITTMAR
CONDOR IV
    BGA 4905

EICHELSDORFER
SB.5
    BGA 2690 2719

EIRI including MOLINO
PIK-20
    BGA 2073 2078 2124 2129 2136 2153 2164 2182 2197 2211 2231 2232
    2271 2303 2326 2412 2416 2444 2513 2535 2537 2550 4379 4501 4809
    4859 5050

ELLIOTTS OF NEWBURY see DFS and NORD
EoN AP.5 OLYMPIA
    BGA 503 505 509 538 544 562 678 726 795 834 909 962 973 997 1029
    1035 1037 1040 1055 1056 1057 1059 1153 1303 1382 1386 1539 1554
    1718 1800 1974 2279
EoN AP.6 OLYMPIA 401, 403 and 419 variants
    BGA 1051 1052 1278 1960 2372
EoN AP.7 PRIMARY and ETON TX.1
    BGA 580 588 589 1461 1625 3214
EoN AP.8 BABY
    BGA 628 629 1252 EI-118
EoN AP.10 460, 463 and 465 variants
    BGA 1156 1171 1172 1177 1201 1217 1223 1225 1253 1270 1283 1286
    1288 1300 1307 1328 1334 1355 1373 1389 1394 2776

FAUVEL
AV.22S
    BGA 2344
AV.36
    BGA 2932

FEDOROV see AVIA STROITEL
Me-7 MECHTA
    BGA 4060 4102 4217 4490 4492

FFA FLUGZEUGWERKE AG
DIAMANT
    BGA 1455 1469 1532 1537 3940 5309

FOCKE-WULF see DFS WEIHE
KRANICH III
    BGA 2814

GLASER-DIRKS
DG-100 and DG-101
    BGA 2081 2125 2126 2127 2216 2310 2402 2604 2605 2749 2826 2850
    3126 3139 3233 3638 4053 4264 4467 4660 4666 4719 4759 4866 4892
    5020 5112 5198
DG-200 and DG-202
    BGA 2357 2368 2394 2436 2464 2482 2559 2603 2736 2788 2802 2869
    3433 3794 3804 3858 4352 4368 4423 4433 4536 4569 4575 4681 4721
    4818 4846 4878 4928 4994 5016 5019
DG-300 and DG-303 ELAN
    BGA 2918 3103 3124 3154 3187 3256 3302 3303 3308 3337 3356 3399
    3494 3500 3519 3534 3542 3543 3583 3664 3676 3708 3805 3845 3849
    3866 4043 4156 4238 4349 4439 4651 4711 4766 4769 4815 4944 4955
    5124 5152 5259 5297
DG-500 and DG-505 ELAN
    BGA 3715 3814 3880 3942 3955 4061 4134 4304 4432 4690 4754 4903

4911 4946 4947 5096 5125 5227 5263 5264 5269
DG-600
   BGA 3312 3400 3427 4949 4966
DG-800 and DG-808
   BGA 4547 5272
DG-1000 see DG FLUGZEUGBAU

GLASFLÜGEL ING EUGEN HANLE
H.201 STANDARD LIBELLE
   BGA 1513 1517 1518 1519 1598 1615 1628 1629 1630 1632 1636 1637
   1648 1655 1656 1657 1660 1661 1662 1669 1670 1671 1673 1678 1686
   1688 1699 1737 1750 1752 1755 1756 1768 1775 1802 1816 1840 1844
   1858 1860 1871 1875 1876 1877 1887 1908 2000 2229 2247 3352 3645
   3686 3750 3767 3777 3780 3796 3841 3969 3986 4253 4257 4364 4377
   4462 4515 4524 4643 4848 4985
H.205 CLUB LIBELLE
   BGA 1987 2059 2415 3110 3626 3732 3781 4937 5004 5225
H.206 HORNET
   BGA 2168 2176 5174
H.301 LIBELLE
   BGA 3680 4027
H.303 MOSQUITO
   BGA 2225 2270 2321 2366 2376 2378 2379 2382 2427 2429 2438 2441
   2443 2452 2472 2529 2575 2584 2599 2600 3131 3587 4054 4451 4652
   4771 4777
304
   BGA 2706 2825 4048 5232
604
   BGA 2585

GROB (BURKHART GROB LUFT und RAUMFAHRT GmbH) see SCHEMPP-HIRTH
G102 ASTIR VARIANTS
   BGA 2084 2144 2155 2162 2180 2181 2183 2185 2186 2196 2200 2220
   2226 2228 2239 2241 2246 2269 2275 2283 2286 2289 2291 2300 2318
   2327 2329 2340 2351 2391 2401 2442 2446 2460 2480 2504 2514 2522
   2525 2540 2555 2582 2630 2741 2772 2859 2985 2986 3134 3151 3172
   3192 3196 3212 3216 3248 3280 3283 3294 3465 3479 3486 3502 3512
   3518 3685 3700 3701 3726 3753 3764 3811 3812 3819 3924 3990 3995
   4005 4096 4125 4132 4159 4182 4183 4185 4194 4215 4236 4276 4287
   4298 4326 4371 4395 4401 4411 4416 4471 4520 4522 4528 4584 4603
   4622 4637 4672 4697 4702 4712 4720 4722 4736 4740 4742 4790 4797
   4844 4880 4891 4924 4948 4953 4960 4987 5026 5040 5077 5194 5296
   5305 EI-124
G103 TWIN ASTIR VARIANTS
   BGA 2323 2341 2343 2676 2873 3006 3013 3015 3024 3064 3076 3191
   3440 3574 3808 3810 3826 3835 4124 4271 4583 4611 4691 4729 4840
   4990 5052 5069 5210 5275 5299 EI-160
G104 SPEED ASTIR
   BGA 2545 3596 4669

GRUNAU including DFS,FOKKER and HAWKRIDGE production
BABY
   BGA 277 370 578 615 1410 1463 1663 1747 1910 2238 2384 2433 2709
   2804 5066

HALFORD
JSH SCORPION
   BGA 2146

HAWKRIDGE
DAGLING
   BGA 491 493

HOLS-DER-TEUFEL
REPLICA
   BGA 3277

HÜTTER
H.17
   BGA 490 2847
H.28 replica
   BGA 3982

ICA
IS-28B2
   BGA 2050 2051 2206 2207 2511 2704 2708 2712 4044
IS-29D
   BGA 1980 2065
IS-30
   BGA 3180
IS-32A
   BGA 3114

ISF including VALENTIN production
MISTRAL C
   BGA 4376 4529 4725 4796 4803

SOCIÉTÉ ISSOIRE AVIATION
E78 SILENE
   BGA 2548 4085 4787 5262

JASTREB see SCHEMPP-HIRTH

KING-ELLIOTT-STREET
OSPREY
   BGA 2021

LAK
LAK-12 LIETUVA
   BGA 3611 3669 3717 3724 3881 3937 3938 3944 3958 3967 4115 4133
   4170 4184 4388 4394 3724 3881 3937 3938 3944 3958 3967 4115 4133
   4170 4184 4388 4394 4488 4692 4888
LAK-17
   BGA 4703 4813 4989 5098 5159 5171 5207 5250
LAK-19
   BGA 5193 5214 5241 5261 5267 5284

LANAVERRE see SCHEMPP-HIRTH

LET
L-13 BLANIK
   BGA 1280 1321 1326 1830 1831 2066 2067 2106 2172 2407 2991 3186
   3677 4201 4438 4658 EI-120 EI-154
L-23 SUPER BLANIK
   BGA 3609 3635
L-33 SOLO
   BGA 3667

LETOV (VOJENSKÁ továrna na letadla LETOV)
LF-107 LUNAK
   BGA 4286 4884 4970 5015 5208 5258

MANUEL
CONDOR
   BGA 2161
WILLOW WREN
   BGA 162

MARCO
J-5
   BGA 4014

MARGANSKI
MDM-1 FOX
   BGA 4566
SWIFT S-1
   BGA 4915 5240

MAUPIN
WOODSTOCK
   BGA 3833 4091

MOLINO see EIRI

MONNETT
MONERAI
   BGA 2988

MÜLLER
MOSWEY III
   BGA 2474

MÜNCHEN
MÜ-13D
   BGA 1937 2267

NEUKOM
STANDARD ELFE S-2
   BGA 3374
ELFE S4
   BGA 4497 4875 5276

NORD see EoN
2000
   BGA 2840

OBERLERCHNER see SCHEMPP-HIRTH
Mg19a STEINADLER
   BGA 2903

PENROSE
PEGASUS
BGA 4002

PFENNINGER-MARKWALDER
ELFE PM3
BGA 4723

PIK see EIRI
PIK-16C VASAMAss
BGA 1540

PILATUS FLUGZEUGWERKE
B4 PC-11
BGA 1772 1773 1780 1809 1810 1821 1823 1836 1839 1841 1849 1902 1904 1911 1929 1976 2189 2240 2296 2322 2352 2874 3851 3855 4020 4234 4874

POTTIER see CARMAM

PZL-BIELSKO see SZD

PZL-SWIDNIK
PW-5 SMYK
BGA 4311 4325 4402 4440 4565 4568 4988

ROLLADEN-SCHNEIDER FLUGZEUGBAU GmbH
LS1
BGA 3454 4738 4750 5104
LS3
BGA 2251 2581 2621 2632 2637 2639 2656 2663 2668 2979 3671 3739 3751 4307 4428 4899 5095 5144 5212
LS4
BGA 2697 2698 2755 2777 2785 2789 2790 2801 2806 2808 2812 2856 2899 2906 2908 2926 2934 2947 2950 2959 3109 3273 3298 3317 3340 3401 3552 3627 3709 3747 3885 4015 4019 4058 4080 4082 4095 4246 4293 4299 4335 4346 4393 4457 4541 4577 4595 4596 4734 4753 4841 4945 4975 4984 5007 5024 5034 5056 5169 5178 5183 5186 5234
LS6
BGA 3123 3156 3361 3455 3683 3698 3706 3707 3727 3791 3803 3809 3892 3895 3898 3910 3913 3936 3954 3964 3965 3973 3976 3991 4046 4088 4119 4131 4153 4155 4214 4300 4385 4390 4426 4650 4814 4952 4957 5035
LS7
BGA 3381 3410 3437 3438 3522 3525 3544 3555 3562 3577 3580 3590 3600 3621 3629 3640 3663 3702 3714 3799 3801 3872 3882 4452 4597 4741 4772 4925 5042 5110 5206
LS8
BGA 4178 4189 4190 4192 4195 4222 4223 4232 4237 4245 4261 4262 4267 4278 4288 4296 4305 4330 4337 4373 4386 4406 4409 4418 4424 4429 4437 4442 4444 4450 4478 4489 4508 4534 4538 4549 4558 4567 4574 4576 4600 4625 4628 4630 4631 4638 4645 4646 4648 4657 4668 4671 4676 4688 4709 4718 4747 4751 4767 4768 4779 4783 4784 4785 4871 4904 4973 4974 5032 5039 5045 5057 5065 5107 5121 5192 5196

SCHEIBE-FLUGZEUBAU GmbH including AVIALSA/ROCHETAU production
BERGFALKE
BGA 1464 2547 2855 4111 5092
L-SPATZ and A60 FAUCONNET
BGA 2276 2278 2388 2498 2652 3840 4265 4517 EI-130
ZUGVOGEL III
BGA 2560 2779 3471 3497 3558 3624 4013 4064 4162 4275
SF-26 STANDARD
BGA 2319 2735
SF-27A ZUGVOGEL V
BGA 2515 2752 2956 3285 3358 3436 3442 3531 3539 3579 3655 3687 3703 3759 4036 4161 4176 4219 4235 EI-144
SF-34
BGA 2843

SCHEMPP-HIRTH FLUGZEUGBAU GmbH including GROB, JASTREB and OBERLERCHNER production
Gö 3 MINIMOA
BGA 1639
GÖ 4 GOEVIER
BGA 1992
STANDARD AUSTRIA
BGA 1127 2166
SHK
BGA 1391 1392 1426 1467 1538 1544 1578 1579 1581 1837 2157 2222 2363 2574 3310 3646
CIRRUS and CIRRUS VTC
BGA 1456 1473 1475 1506 1543 1584 1631 1822 1834 1869 1870 2033 2426 3730 3894 4197 4213 4218 4705 4773 5022 5038 5123
HS.4 STANDARD CIRRUS
BGA 1616 1617 1667 1677 1706 1724 1727 1734 1743 1748 1785 1801

1913 1916 1919 1966 2022 2037 2071 2091 2097 2114 2138 2195 2420 2462 2501 2628 2673 3120 3155 3257 3355 3376 3377 3463 3478 3564 3628 3653 3675 3719 3775 3789 3798 3904 3929 3983 3992 3996 3997 4009 4010 4012 4059 4072 4141 4174 4250 4254 4256 4273 4297 4332 4342 4343 4380 4404 4408 4414 4436 4459 4463 4468 4504 4514 4516 4523 4548 4551 4609 4619 4689 4701 4715 4726 4761 4799 4823 4836 4967 5021 5023 5046 5055 5087 5102 5111 5120 5122 5195 5218 5221 5278
HS.5 NIMBUS 2
BGA 1722 1725 1726 1958 2025 2115 2137 2175 2224 2243 2375 2491 2495 2528 2531 2625 2641 2645 2657 2680 2701 2705 2751 2756 3159 3420 3457 3553 3806 3821 4065 4068 4121 4499 4624 4632
HS.6 JANUS
BGA 2359 2723 2875 2876 4062 4168 4180 4186 4210 4348 4472 4647 4824 5126 5133 5177
HS.7 MINI NIMBUS
BGA 2268 2337 2346 2466 2469 2539 2549 2553 2597 2631 2684 3269 4130 4145 4510 4765 4894 4912 4951 5053 5287
NIMBUS 3
BGA 2820 2821 2868 2898 3106 3130 3224 3244 4263 4324 4344 4420 4822 4932 5119 5187 5298
NIMBUS 3D
BGA 3581 3610 3827 4008 4322 4458 4735 4835 4853 5116
NIMBUS 4
BGA 3920 4413 4443 4546 5205
NIMBUS 4D
BGA 4079 4482
DISCUS A, B and CS variants
BGA 3141 3199 3206 3207 3232 3236 3278 3322 3339 3365 3373 3393 3397 3398 3453 3523 3535 3538 3607 3631 3632 3641 3733 3754 3760 3837 3856 3874 3879 3886 3887 3932 3933 3939 3946 3960 3961 3978 3981 3994 4004 4016 4030 4032 4034 4040 4047 4050 4051 4092 4100 4106 4117 4120 4123 4128 4147 4152 4158 4163 4169 4226 4242 4283 4301 4318 4328 4355 4360 4362 4363 4387 4392 4405 4417 4430 4470 4502 4503 4507 4527 4543 4544 4563 4579 4585 4590 4601 4608 4615 4674 4679 4685 4687 4694 4724 4737 4782 4800 4806 4810 4811 4826 4827 4838 4863 4868 4883 4908 4933 4939 5149 5219 5245 5257 5268
DISCUS 2
BGA 4533 4641 4642 4659 4794 4820 4843 4890 5047 5093 5156 5175 5188 5202 5217 5243 5244 5252 5273 5288
DUO DISCUS
BGA 4066 4073 4081 4113 4151 4175 4252 4350 4455 4473 4475 4511 4553 4661 4699 4775 4792 4873 4893 4931 4941 4993 5002 5033 5041 5063 5075 5103 5115 5150 5154 5162 5170 5180 5182 5203 5209 5226 5242 5247 5248 5251 5253 5271 5274 5281 5290 5306
VENTUS A, B and C variants
BGA 2695 2743 2744 2766 2775 2816 2853 2960 2968 2981 3115 3136 3152 3171 3197 3279 3301 3371 3395 3411 3417 3456 3533 3540 3549 3568 3575 3622 3651 3681 3684 3785 3878 3899 3918 3921 3935 3959 4225 4258 4291 4378 4400 4449 4461 4483 4562 4571 4586 4743 4839 4847 4862 5017 5118 5128 5146 5224
VENTUS 2
BGA 4165 4216 4231 4244 4249 4251 4292 4310 4340 4465 4505 4588 4606 4664 4700 4776 4786 4795 4805 4850 4886 4895 4896 4913 4921 4934 4942 4943 4956 4959 4976 4977 4978 4981 4998 5006 5012 5048 5059 5060 5064 5070 5071 5072 5073 5080 5084 5108 5147 5148 5155 5158 5165 5166 5199 5231 5233 5277 5302

ALEXANDER **SCHLEICHER SEGELFLUGZEUGBAU** including CENTRAIR production
RHÖNBUSSARD
BGA 337
Ka 2 RHÖNSCHWALBE
BGA 1026 2274 2324 2913 3425 4336
Ka 3
BGA 2689
RHÖNLERCHE II
BGA 1789 1872 1873
Ka 6, BR, CR RHÖNSEGLER
BGA 1027 1039 1094 1098 1219 1222 1257 1273 1279 1281 1284 1323 1340 1341 1348 1375 1412 1423 1433 1591 1970 2044 2058 2064 2102 2123 2145 2156 2171 2177 2202 2257 2258 2287 2290 2301 2309 2312 2313 2331 2339 2355 2395 2410 2478 2483 2486 2516 2570 2573 2598 2636 2782 2852 2870 3142 3182 3247 3286 3311 3318 3329 3332 3351 3370 3396 3441 3483 3504 3508 3528 3572 3659 3670 3688 3696 3722 3743 3744 3763 3773 3778 3815 3876 3900 3985 4099 4167 4212 4331 4419 4464 4999 5076 5201 EI-127
Ka 6E
BGA 1351 1380 1381 1383 1393 1425 1428 1431 1435 1440 1443 1444 1449 1450 1452 1454 1472 1483 1484 1487 1493 1495 1507 1522 1524 1525 1533 1546 1568 1603 1640 1696 2099 2128 2134 2193 2227 2294 2334 2396 2411 2430 2459 2527 2651 2699 2738 2757 2929 3158 3386 3426 3459 3495 3571 3598 3612 3614 3758 3790 3974 4357 4358 4519 4526 4607 4739
Ka 7 RHÖNADLER
BGA 936 1031 1157 1174 1259 1499 1626 1634 1647 1664 1694 1862 1959 2139 2158 2187 2218 2223 2306 2320 2432 2440 2463 2477 2489 2538 2594 2601 2721 2803 2851 2943 2946 2966 2977 2982 3201 3258 3262 3281 3307 3344 3382 3421 3449 3521 3603 3682 3783 3838 3980 4069 4616 EI-105

K 8
BGA 1458 1502 1528 1529 1563 1574 1580 1653 1807 1925 2032 2093
2117 2142 2154 2167 2192 2205 2214 2219 2221 2260 2298 2307 2328
2332 2338 2369 2386 2390 2434 2619 2627 2646 2688 2717 2747 2849
2879 2912 2925 2931 2935 3127 3170 3275 3328 3342 3349 3383 3434
3435 3446 3514 3515 3548 3582 3597 3616 3722 3740 3748 3769 3792
3850 3863 3873 3919 3975 4003 4025 4045 4067 4139 4148 4255 4268
4312 4320 4321 4345 4365 4485 4493 4495 4513 4525 4604 4649 4686
4693 4708 4745 4869 4897 4898 5005 5200 EI-133

Ka 10
BGA 2983

ASK 13
BGA 1396 1421 1427 1429 1430 1436 1438 1442 1445 1446 1447 1448
1494 1497 1503 1508 1535 1565 1608 1611 1612 1650 1746 1753 1861
2023 2169 2191 2234 2256 2285 2317 2385 2405 2406 2425 2554 2567
2610 2739 2830 2845 2860 2861 2944 2954 2989 3112 3163 3205
3215 3254 3274 3366 3428 3482 3550 3566 3573 3642 3656 3692 3787
3853 4056 4089 4166 4187 4206 4208 4221 4241 4247 4284 4289 4295
4479 4512 4581 4592 4593 4598 4602 4620 4626 4633 4634 4636 4663
4680 4683 4730 4752 4830 4837 4864 4882 4906 5054 5061 5101 5127
5164 5172 5293 EI-143

ASW 15
BGA 1562 1582 1606 1938 3121 3122 3165 3167 3306 3315 3363 3369
3375 3408 3432 3464 3506 3618 3731 3736 3755 3761 3770 3883 3928
3993 4078 4129 4181 4327 4359 4396 4431 4435 4447 4498 4561 4682
4713 4825 4845 5308 EI-134

ASW 17
BGA 1691 1788 2595 2667

ASK 18
BGA 2150 2190 2245 2261 2973 4143 4173 4530 4570 4582 4612 4621
4675 4684 4756 5229

ASW 19
BGA 2282 2354 2361 2414 2417 2473 2502 2518 2552 2623 2727 2760
2831 2836 2862 2893 2894 2895 2896 3228 3252 3390 3585 3595 3716
3831 3846 3870 3890 3930 3956 4011 4029 4038 4063 4203 4280 4294
4381 4389 4410 4486 4532 4550 4580 4654 4710 4728 4793 4801 4804
5037 5043 5088

ASW 20
BGA 2350 2370 2397 2423 2453 2461 2479 2494 2524 2556 2565 2596
2618 2620 2624 2635 2640 2644 2648 2649 2650 2659 2677 2691 2707
2711 2726 2740 2754 2778 2783 2827 2828 2837 2848 2864 2880 2951
2955 2961 2974 3101 3119 3133 3162 3222 3266 3291 3321 3414 3419
3424 3462 3475 3513 3516 3537 3588 3654 3820 3834 3859 3861 3889
3943 3963 3988 4041 4087 4112 4118 4164 4196 4211 4220 4240 4248
4309 4341 4347 4448 4476 4477 4539 4770 4860 4909 4996 5000 5044
5099 5129 5215 5291

ASK 21
BGA 2588 2591 2612 2687 2702 2742 2764 2817 2835 2871 2887 2888
2905 2922 2928 3138 3625 3639 3673 3674 3679 3693 3697 3704 3711
3848 4031 4104 4105 4146 4198 4233 4308 4316 4317 4339 4351 4367
4369 4383 4487 4496 4500 4555 4564 4572 4573 4578 4587 4614 4629
4706 4828 4832 4991 4997 5003 5011 5030 5031 5068 5078 5079 5091
5130 5163 5189 5213 5228 5260 5282 5300

ASW 22
BGA 3261 3388 3713 4191 4852

ASK 23
BGA 2995 2996 2997 2998 3721 4007

ASW 24
BGA 3372 3389 3604 3756 3757 3762 3802 3807 4303 4399 4445 4454
4727 4758 4764 4870

ASH 25
BGA 3496 3532 3592 3606 3623 3643 3720 3909 4039 4290 4415 4425
4480 5009

ASW 27
BGA 4207 4279 4315 4338 4407 4422 4545 4557 4610 4677 4678 4696
4704 4716 4749 4762 4788 4789 4791 4816 4819 4831 4834 4876 4881
4923 4971 4980 4986 5010 5014 5018 5025 5049 5097 5100 5157 5160
5173 5304

ASW 28
BGA 4821 4829 4861 4914 4935 4936 4961 4968 4969 4982 5082 5089
5114 5117 5131 5132 5145 5153 5161 5184 5204 5216 5223 5237 5238
5294

ASG 29
BGA 5235 5236 5246 5254 5255 5256 5265 5266 5270 5285 5286 5295
5301 5303 5307

SCHWEYER
RHÖNSPERBER
BGA 260

SCOTT
VIKING
BGA 416

SHENSTONE
HARBINGER
BGA 1091

SHORT
NIMBUS
BGA 470

SIEBERT
SIE 3
BGA 2642 3461

SLINGSBY SAILPLANES LTD including YORKSHIRE SAILPLANES production
T.1 FALCON 1
BGA 266 3166
T.6 KITE 1
BGA 236 251 285 310 400
T.7 CADET
BGA 731 1143
T.8 TUTOR
BGA 442 466 485 791 794 804 833 852 858 895 904 1424 1599 1698 1745
1759 1770 2288 IGA 6
T.12 GULL I
BGA 378 902
T.13 PETREL
BGA 651
T.15 GULL III
BGA 643 3825
T.21
BGA 570 601 614 646 665 666 673 711 765 782 856 869 875 945 948 960
1000 1014 1081 1085 1144 1215 1218 1254 1315 1354 1482 1588 1965
2010 2024 2036 2720 2767 2900 2941 2964 2975 3148 3160 3189 3195
3221 3225 3235 3238 3240 3243 3245 3250 3255 3264 3287 3288 3290
3292 3324 3385 3423 3774 3836 3901 3903 3905 4077 4110 4135 4366
4707 4833 4856 4877 5230 EI-157
T.25 GULL 4
BGA 565
T.26 KITE 2
BGA 521 663 689 751 EI-102
T.30 PREFECT
BGA 599 625 701 815 1152 1601 2333 2380 2517 2546 2583 2692
T.31B
BGA 1346 1376 1559 3145 3149 3181 3185 3194 3229 3239 3241 3272
3299 3336 3487 3545 3786 3953 4033 4228 4412 4746 4926 4963 5283
EI-139
T.34 SKY
BGA 685 686 694 698 1053 2284 4670
T.37 SKYLARK 1
BGA 725
T.38 GRASSHOPPER
BGA 3359 3480 3481 3488 3498 3979 4098 4229 4361 4372 4421 4552
4556 5074 EI-135
T.41 SKYLARK 2
BGA 724 729 733 745 759 778 793 801 802 814 822 826 845 896 899 1441
1549 1757 2002
T.42 EAGLE
BGA 740 780 825 828 830 841 880
T.43 SKYLARK 3
BGA 735 736 742 761 763 806 813 823 844 864 867 870 871 916 920 922
925 927 929 950 957 985 988 996 1004 1013 1023 1251
T.45 SWALLOW
BGA 873 890 910 921 1003 1008 1017 1018 1061 1107 1109 1136 1165
1167 1169 1211 1263 1291 1319 1364 1365 1398 2762 2793 3469 3823
T.49 CAPSTAN
BGA 1009 1106 1118 1131 1132 1133 1134 1135 1163 1183 1191 1196
1203 1204 1237 1249 1360
T.50 SKYLARK 4
BGA 1019 1043 1047 1050 1063 1066 1087 1088 1089 1095 1100 1102
1103 1104 1115 1117 1115 1117 1119 1121 1124 1138 1189 1193 1194
1202 1210 1220 1239 2881 3601
T.51 DART
BGA 1164 1180 1181 1185 1187 1197 1198 1207 1240 1262 1265 1266
1268 1269 1290 1293 1295 1296 1298 1299 1310 1312 1313 1316 1317
1330 1332 1336 1356 1359 1361 1400 1401 1975
T.53 and YS 53
BGA 1811 1897 2132
T.59 KESTREL
BGA 1514 1681 1683 1684 1685 1689 1720 1723 1744 1761 1763 1765
1769 1792 1794 1795 1797 1798 1799 1850 1852 1854 1855 1857 1859
1889 1914 1940 1941 1944 1945 1940 1941 1944 1945 1946 1982 1983
1986 1988 1989 1990 2047 2470 2481 2902 3176
T.65 VEGA
BGA 2445 2448 2455 2456 2457 2458 2496 2497 2507 2508 2509 2523
2526 2544 2576 2577 2578 2579 2592 2611 2613 2614 2615 2616 2622
2660 2669 2670 2671 2672 2681 2682 2685 2694 2700 2710 2713 2714
2715 2716 2728 2729 2763 2774 2792 2794 2796 2797 2799 2800 2807
3392

STANDARD AUSTRIA see SCHEMPP-HIRTH

START+FLUG
H101 SALTO
BGA 4778

SWALES see BIRMINGHAM GUILD

SZD

SZD-8 JASKOLKA
  BGA 2512
SZD-9bis BOCIAN
  BGA 998 1078 1474 1605 1668 1676 1843 1994 1995 2034 2242 2734 2904
  3345
SZD-12A MUCHA
  BGA 3776 3862 EI-100 EI-140
SZD-22 MUCHA STANDARD
  BGA 4857 5176
SZD-24 and SZD-32 FOKA
  BGA 1367 1377 1646 3945
SZD-30 PIRAT
  BGA 1470 1485 1551 1555 1596 1674 1707 1709 1714 1779 1803 1805
  1819 1832 1845 1888 1905 1930 1932 1934 1962 1963 1968 1977 1993
  2031 2042 2089 2100 2140 2141 2209 2254 2377 2857
SZD-36A COBRA 15
  BGA 1732 1846 1847 1885 1952 1998
SZD-38A JANTAR-1
  BGA 1969 2026 2079 3387
SZD-41A and SZD-48 JANTAR-STANDARD
  BGA 2090 2119 2151 2152 BGA 2413 2745 2829 2917 2937 3188 3282
  3448 3511 3817 4204 5013
SZD-42 JANTAR-2
  BGA 2255
SZD-50-3 PUCHACZ
  BGA 2957 2992 3203 3510 3546 3576 3589 3620 3630 3658 3695 3725
  3734 3772 3779 3782 3793 3829 3832 3864 3888 3906 4157 4313 4446
  4714 4717 4748 4938 5113
SZD-51-1 JUNIOR
  BGA 3234 3237 3268 3418 3505 3541 3644 3649 3657 3718 3842 3847
  3852 3869 3884 3950 3884 3950 3951 4042 4070 4127 4138 4594 4618
  4635 4807 5094 5106 5109 5168 5280
SZD-55-1
  BGA 3689 3877 3962 4230 4763 4962 5185
SZD-59 ACRO
  BGA 4272

TORVA

SPRITE
  BGA 1702

VFW-FOKKER GmbH

FK-3
  BGA 3971

VALENTIN see ISF

VOGT

LO-100 ZWERGREIHER
  BGA 2770

VTC (VAZDUHOPLOVNO TEHNICKI CENTAR) see SCHEMPP-HIRTH

SOCIÉTÉ DES ETABLISSMENTS BENJAMIN **W**ASSMER

WA21 JAVELOT II
  BGA 1575
WA22 SUPER JAVELOT
  BGA 1480
WA26P SQUALE
  BGA 2629 3923 3968
WA28F ESPADON
  BGA 4441 4855
WA30 BIJAVE
  BGA 2753 3404

YORKSHIRE SAILPLANES see BIRMINGHAM GUILD

ZAKLAD SZYBOWCOWY JEZOW

PW-6U
  BGA 5289

ZLIN (ZLINSKA LETECKNA AKCIOVA)
24 KRAJANEK
  BGA 655

PART 7 – AIRCRAFT TYPE INDEX (OVERSEAS)

This Index covers entries in SECTION 5, Part 1 and 2.

AERO VODOCHODY NÁRODNÍ PODNIK see LET
L-29 DELFIN
  YL-PAF YL-PAG

AERONCA AIRCRAFT CORPORATION
A65A CHIEF
  NC33884

AEROPO
EUROFOX
  I-6929

AEROSPACELINES
377SGT SUPER GUPPY
  F-BTGV

AÉROSPATIALE including EUROCOPTER production and see SUD-AVIATION
AS.350B ECUREUIL
  N9FJ N214AE N350AY N350UK
AS.355 TWIN SQUIRREL
  N766AM
EC.155
  N604FD N672LE P4-HEC
SA.365 DAUPHIN 2
  F-WQAP VP-BUL 5N-BDA 5N-BET

AEROSTYLE GmbH
BREEZER
  D-MBRG

COSTRUZIONI AERONAUTICHE GIOVANNI **AGUSTA SpA**
A109 variants
  D-HCKV N2NR N8UF N35AG N61FM N74PM N91TH N109AB N109AG
  N109AN N109MJ N109NL N109TD N109TF N109TK N109WF N188S
  N195NJ N449J N517TS N591JM N745HA N800WK N877SW N7242N
  RP-C2900 SX-HCF S5-HPC
A119
  N65TG N119BM VH-PSR

AIRBUS INDUSTRIE
A319
  A6-ESH
A320
  SX-BLX

AMERICAN AVIATION CORPORATION see GRUMMAN-AMERICAN

ANTONOV
AN-2
  HA-MKE HA-MKF LY-BIG LY-MHC RA-01641 YL-LEU YL-LEV YL-LEW
  YL-LEX YL-LEY YL-LEZ YL-LFA YL-LFB YL-LFC YL-LFD

AUSTER AIRCRAFT LTD
Model H AUSTER 5
  F-BBSO
B.8 AGRICOLA
  ZK-BMI ZK-CCU

AVIATIKA JOINT STOCK COMPANY
MAI-890
  YL-MIG

AVIATION TRADERS ENGINEERING LIMITED
ATL98 CARVAIR
  CF-EPV

A V ROE and CO LTD including BAe and HAWKER SIDDELEY AVIATION design
and production
652A ANSON
  VH-ASM
671 - see CIERVA
748
  N748D VH-AHL VH-AMQ VH-AYS ZS-ODJ

BAE SYSTEMS (OPERATIONS) LTD including BRITISH AEROSPACE plc
BRITISH AEROSPACE (REGIONAL AIRCRAFT) Ltd, HANDLEY-PAGE and SCOTTISH AVIATION
production
JETSTREAM variants to Series 32
  N14234
146 including Avro variants
  I-TERB I-TERV LZ-TIM N9070L N9086L SE-DRB
ATP
  PK-MTV

BEAGLE AIRCRAFT LTD
B.121 PUP
  HB-NAV N556MA
B.206
  N181WW

BEECH AIRCRAFT CORPORATION Including HAWKER BEECHCRAFT
CORPORATION
17 TRAVELER
  N18V NC18028
18/3NM, 3TM and C-45
  N2500 N96240
C23 MUSKETEER
  N6632L
B24R SIERRA 200
  D-EDEQ N39TA
33 DEBONAIR and BONANZA
  N35SN N42FW
F33A BONANZA
  N78GG N121JF N999F N2299L
A35, C35, K35, and V35B BONANZA models
  N59VT N150JC N675BW N3023W N60256
36 BONANZA
  D-EKDN N4VQ N36NB N36SU N250TP N364AB N671B N715BC
  N767CM N836TP N7205T N7251Y N8258F N24136 N36665
56, and 58 BARON models
  D-IBPN N27MW N28TE N55BN N55EN N58GT N58YD N64VB N65MJ
  N79AP N125AV N142TW N258RP N418WS N468DB N554RB N581AF
  N717HL N951SF N1835W N2061K N7148R N7219L N7223Y N23659
  N60526
60 DUKE
  N60NZ N322RJ N1024L N3669D
65, 70 and 80 QUEEN AIR models
  N70AA
76 DUCHESS
  D-GEWU N800VM
90 KING AIR
  N30FL N34RF N41AK N46BM N59GG N146FL N200RE N402BL
  N456PP N521LB N683GW N712DB N816RL N1092H N9838Z
200, 300 and 350 SUPER KING AIR models
  N27HK N64GG N73MW N250TM N288GS N500CS N983AJ N2341S
  N3103L N37172
400 BEECHJET
  N79EL N497XP N709EL N719EL

BELL HELICOPTER TEXTRON CANADA INC including AGUSTA BELL
HELICOPTER and WESTLAND HELICOPTERS LTD production
47 variants
  N201W N7801R OO-SHW
206A and 206B JETRANGER variants
  N56GH N64JG N206HE N206MF N208ER N784F OE-XBA
206L LONG RANGER
  N96HC N340AJ N707BM N720B
212
  5N-AJT 5N-AJU 5N-AJV 5N-AJW 5N-BHN
222
  N40EA N153H N222WX N510W N800HL N2105J
407
  N37LP N120HH N222LB N407AG N407CG N407CL N407WD N477KA
  N686RH N775SB N8010M N9133D N30562 N42527
430
  N901RL N5120 VP-BKQ
UH-1 IROQUOIS
  N116HS N454CC N911DN

BELLANCA-AIRCRAFT CORPORATION
8KCAB-180 SUPER DECATHLON
  N669MM

BOEING AIRCRAFT CO including BOEING COMPANY

B-17G FORTRESS
F-BDRS N5237V
247
N18E
707
N707QJ VP-BDF
727-100 series
OO-DHN OO-DHR P4-MMG VP-BAA VP-BAB VP-CKA
727-200 series
EC-CFA EC-DDX HZ-AB3 TC-ALM
737-200 series
C-GWJO OO-SDK TF-ELL
737-700 series
A6-HRS VP-BBW VP-BNZ VP-BWR
737-800 series
A6-HEH A6-MRM N737M
747-100 series
N852FT
747-200 series
N218BA SX-OAD
747SP
VP-BAT

BOEING AIRPLANE CO

STEARMAN 75 KAYDET, N2S, PT-13, PT-17; variants
CF-EQS N43SV N126SE N707TJ N731 N1325M N1731B N3922B
N4596N N4712V N5057V N10053 N38940 N52485 N54922 N59269
N62842 N63590 N65200 N65565 N68427 N74189 SE-BOG XB-RIY

BÖLKOW APPARATEBAU GmbH including MALMO and MBB production

BÖ.102 HELITRAINER
D-HMQV
BÖ.105
LQ-BLT
BÖ.207
D-EBLI D-EBLO D-EFQE D-EFTI D-EHKY D-EHLA D-EHOP D-EHUQ
D-EHYX D-EJBI
BÖ.208 JUNIOR
D-EAMB D-ECGI D-EDNA D-EEAH D-EMUH F-BRHN
BÖ.209 MONSUN
D-EAAH D-EAAW D-EFJG D-EGHW

BOMBARDIER INC

CANADAIR CL-600 CHALLENGER variants
HB-IVR HZ-SJP3 N800BN OE-IFB VP-BGO VP-CAP VP-CEO VP-CFT
VP-CHU VP-CIC VP-CJA VP-COP
CANADAIR CRJ 200 REGIONAL JET
OE-LRE VP-BCC VP-BCI
BD-100 CHALLENGER 300
VP-CLV
BD-700 GLOBAL variants
N456MS N171JJ OY-ILG VP-BAM VP-BOW VP-CEB VP-CRC

BRANTLY HELICOPTER CORPORATION

B.2
N19GL N276SA

BRIGHTON MA AND COMPANY LTD

Balloon (Hot Air)
MAB-65
HB-BOU

BRISTOL AEROPLANE CO LTD

SCOUT D replica
N5419
175 BRITANNIA
EL-WXA

BRITISH AIRCRAFT CORPORATION (BAC)

ONE-ELEVEN
VR-BEB 5N-HHH
BAC167 STRIKEMASTER
N21419

BRITTEN-NORMAN LTD

BN 2 ISLANDER
N54EW N121MT N2536Y

BROCK MANUFACTURING

KB2 GYROCOPTER
PH-TWR

BÜCKER

Bü.133 JUNGMEISTER
OO-EII

CAMERON BALLOONS LTD see CAMERON-COLT and CAMERON-THUNDER

Airship (Hot Air)
Zero 25
OO-JAT
Balloon (Hot Air)
77 variants
C-GYZI
84 series
N413JB
140 variants
5Y-SIL

CESSNA AIRCRAFT COMPANY including REIMS AVIATION SA production
(F.prefix)

C.34 AIRMASTER
NC16403
120
N77342
140
N76402
150
N105SK N3084F N3109X N4337K N6819F N7263S N11824
A150 AEROBAT
N7374A OO-WIO
152
N4770B N4779B N47351
170
D-EEVY N170AZ N2366D N5428C
172 SKYHAWK
D-EAGC D-EFZO F-GLTR N75TC N172AM N259SA N355GW N525DB
N937DR N1554E N5043X N6182G N9680Q N13253 N19753 N20981
N21927 N50029 N75822 N80533 N95409 OY-DRS OY-EGZ SE-IFB
172RG CUTLASS
N1937Z
R172K HAWK XP
D-EBXR N78XP
REIMS FR172 ROCKET variants
D-EKJD D-EMZCt
175A SKYLARK
N6907E
177(RG) CARDINAL
N177SA N278SA N442BJ N707XJ N8225Y N53103
180 and SKYWAGON
N180BB N180FN N36362 N71763 PH-KRC
182 SKYLANE variants
D-EIIP D-EJLY N14MT N22NN N25XZ N182GC N277DS N369AN
N382AS N409SA N656JM N681EW N735BZ N735CX N883DP
N888MY N1320S N1329T N1424C N1745M N2231F N2379C N2445V
N2454Y N4102D N5020A N6078T
190 and 195 models
N999MH N1551D
206 SUPER SKYLANE, SUPER SKYWAGON and STATIONAIR models
N191ME N206CF N566N
208 and 208B (GRAND) CARAVAN
D-FBPS D-FLOH N208B N208NJ
210 CENTURION
D-EBWS D-EEHW N23KY N210AD N210CP N210EU N210NM N249SP
N277CD N761JU N1778X N6593W N9533Y N30593
T303 CRUSADER
N11FV N57MT N154DJ N289CW N889VF N6498V N9870C
305 BIRD DOG (L-19)
N134TT N33600
310
N31GN N218Y N310QQ N310WT N438DD N747YK N1757H
320 SKYKNIGHT
N4173T
337 SUPER SKYMASTER
N19F N80N N337UK N2216X N456TL SE-LTE
340
N3HK N27BG N66SW N85LB N340DW N340GJ N340SC N340YP
N1711G N8702K
401
N401JN N9146N

414
N414AK N414FZ
421 GOLDEN EAGLE variants
N1FY N9AY N26HE N37VB N60GM N64LA N75FW N132CK N202AA
N421CA N421DD N421EA N900CB N37379 N41098 N80056
425 CORSAIR and 425 CONQUEST II
N90YA N425DR N425SL N1262K
441 CONQUEST II
N22CG
500 and 501 CITATION 1
N324JC N527EW N909PS N80364 VP-BGE VP-CAT VP-COM
510 CITATION MUSTANG
N80HQ N814WS
525 CITATIONJET
N50VC N198JH N224CJ N242ML N380CR N498YY N511TC N524SF
N665CH   VP-CJI
525A CITATIONJET 2
N122SM N309CJ N525PM N569DM
525B CITATIONJET 3
N80HB N96MR N100JS
550, S550 CITATION BRAVO and 551 CITATION II models
N46PJ N48NS N60LW N127BU N145DF N365WA N550LD N550PD
N7070A VP-CED
560 CITATION ULTRA and ENCORE
N535CE N652NR N846MA VP-CSN
560XL CITATION EXCEL
N188WS N560TH N575NR
650 CITATION III and CITATION VI
N373DJ N606AT
680 SOVEREIGN
N680GG
750 CITATION X
N750GF N750NS N5113S P4-LJG

CFM METAL-FAX
SHADOW
OO-A95

CGS
HAWK
N216HK

CHAMPION AIRCRAFT CORPORATION see BELLANCA
CITABRIA,SKYTRAC
N51ER N94SA

CHAYAIR MANUFACTURING AND AVIATION (PTY) LTD
SYCAMORE
ZU-DCX

CHRISTEN INDUSTRIES INC including AVIAT and see PITTS
A-1 and A-1B HUSKY vriants
N49BH N78HB N8754J SE-KBU

CIERVA
C.30A (AVRO 671)
SE-AZB

CIRRUS DESIGN CORPORATION
SR20
N131CD N147CD N164SR N184CD N203CD N262BM N470RD
N520DR N781CD N840CD N994SR N5336Z N8159Q
SR22
N9SZ N10MC N12SJ N17UK N40GD N80NS N108SR N112SR
N121HT N122MG N123DV N141HT N147GT N147KA N147LD N147LK
N147VC N150ZZ N151CG N160SR N192SR N199ZZ N220RJ N221CH
N222ED N222SW N297SR N327BM N352CD N376SR N434A N482CD
N521CD N542CD N573VE N588CD N590CD N593CD N663CD
N702SR N719CD N730WF N741CD N753TW N771SR N799CD N800C
N820CD N834CD N843SR N852CD N866C N900UK N902SR N916CD
N922CE N956CD N982CD N986SR N1569C N5084V N54105

COLT BALLOONS LTD including CAMERON BALLOONS LTD, THUNDER and
COLT LTD BALLOONS production and see COLTING BALLOONS
Balloon (Hot Air)
77 variants
OY-BOW
90 series
D-Pamgas

COMMANDER AIRCRAFT COMPANY see ROCKWELL

CONSOLIDATED VULTEE AIRCRAFT see STINSON AIRCRAFT
CORPORATION
BT-15 VALIANT
N58566
PBY CATALINA
N423RS VP-BPS

CURTISS-WRIGHT CORPORATION
P-40N WARHAWK
N9950

Dallach
FASCINATION D4 BK
PH-3P3

AVIONS MARCEL **DASSAULT**
FALCON 7X
N999BE
FALCON 20 and 200 models
N357PS 9M-BCR
FALCON 50
N200UP N950H VP-BMP
FALCON 900 and 900EX models
HZ-OFC5 LX-FTA N900NS
FALCON 2000 and 2000EX models
VP-BDL VP-CMD

DE HAVILLAND AIRCRAFT LTD
DH.80A PUSS MOTH
VH-UQB
DH.82A TIGER MOTH
F-BGCJ F-BGEQ
DH.83 FOX MOTH
ZK-AGM
DH.84 DRAGON
VH-SNB
DH.104 DOVE
D-IFSB VP-YKF
DH.106 COMET
F-BGNX
DH.125 see **HAWKER SIDDELEY**

DE HAVILLAND (AUSTRALIA)
DHA-3 DROVER
VH-FDT

DE HAVILLAND (CANADA) including BOMBARDIER INC and OGMA production
DHC-1 CHIPMUNK
N458BG
DHC-2 BEAVER
OY-JRR
DHC-3 OTTER
VP-FAK

DIAMOND AIRCRAFT INDUSTRIES GmbH
DA.40(D) STAR
N39SE OE-KKC
DA.42 TWIN STAR
N35AL

DORNIER
DO.28 SKYSERVANT
HA-ACL HA-ACO HA-VOC
228
D-CALM

DOUGLAS AIRCRAFT COMPANY INC
A-26 INVADER
N4806E
DC-3, C-47 DAKOTA and SKYTRAIN variants
N147DC N473DC N1944A N4565L N9050T ZS-MRU 6W-SAF
DC-4
N31356 N44914
DC-8
9G-MKA

DYN'AÉRO SA
MCR-01
21YV

Eclipse Aviation Corporation
ECLIPSE 500
N500UK

ELA Aviación S.L
ELA 07
EC-EP6

EMBRAER
110 BANDEIRANTE
N97121 SX-BNL

ENGLISH ELECTRIC CO LTD (AVRO production)
CANBERRA
N2138J

ENSTROM HELICOPTER CORPORATION
280 SHARK
D-HGBX
480
N480BB N480DD N480JB N480KP

ERCO including ALON and FORNEY production
ERCOUPE 415
N3188H N6620W N93938

EXTRA FLUGZEUGBAU GmbH
EA.200
D-EXGC
EA.300
D-ETTO
EA.400
N400YY

Fairchild Engine and AIRPLANE
24 ARGUS
NC1328 N16676
CORNELL
N33870 N49272
C-119
N2700

FAIREY AVIATION CO LTD
FIREFLY
SE-BRG

FARMAN
F.40
F-HMFI

FARNBOROUGH AIRCRAFT CORPORATION LTD
F1C3 KESTREL
N352F

FARRINGTON AIRCRAFT CORP
TWINSTARR GYROCOPTER
31-WI N96XW

FIRE BALLOONS
Balloon (Hot Air)
3000
D-Opha

FOKKER BV
F.27 FRIENDSHIP
TC-MBE
F.27-050 (FOKKER 50)
LN-KKA
F.28-010 (FOKKER 100)
N897US N898US

AVIONS FOURNIER
RF-3
D-KMDP

General Aircraft LTD
MONOSPAR ST.12
VH-UTH

GLASFLÜGEL ING EUGEN HANLE
H303 MOSQUITO
SX-122

GOVERNMENT AIRCRAFT FACTORY
N22 NOMAD
N6302W OY-NMH

GROB-WERKE GMB&Co KG
G.109
D-KGLM

GRUMMAN AIRCRAFT ENGINEERING
G.21 GOOSE
N4575C
TBM-3 AVENGER
CF-KCG

GRUMMAN AMERICAN AVIATION CORPORATION (1),
AMERICAN GENERAL AVIATION (2) and GULFSTREAM AMERICAN CORPORATION (3) production
GRUMMAN AA-5 TRAVELLER (1)
D-EFDL
GRUMMAN AA-5A CHEETAH (1)
N674BW OO-GCO
GRUMMAN AA-5B TIGER (1)
D-EGDC D-ENTO F-GKGN
GULFSTREAM AA-5B TIGER (3)
N31RB N666GA N2121T
AMERICAN GENERAL AG-5B TIGER (2)
N136SA

GULFSTREAM AEROSPACE CORPORATION
G1159 GULFSTREAM II
5N-AGV
GULFSTREAM IV and V variants
HB-ITF HZ-ARK N841WS VP-BBX VP-BEP VP-BGN VP-BKI VP-BKZ
VP-BLA VP-BLR VP-BLW VP-BNL VP-BNO VP-BUS VP-CBX VP-CFF
VP-CGN VP-CLA VP-CMR VP-CSF

Hawker Aircraft LTD
TEMPEST
N7027E
SEA FURY
D-CATA

HAWKER SIDDELEY AVIATION including BAe, CORPORATE JETS LTD,
DE HAVILLAND and RAYTHEON-HAWKER production
HS.125
N228TM N249SR N485LT N800UK N5736 VP-BKK VP-BNK VP-CFS
VP-COD VP-CPT VP-CSP VP-CXP VT-UBG 5N-AAN

HILLER HELICOPTERS INC
UH-12 (360)
N21UH N57CR N212W N780ND N831M N5025J N5315V N5317V
N33514 N38763 N62171 N90724

HOWARD
500
N500LN

HUGHES TOOL CO and HUGHES HELICOPTERS INC including
SCHWEIZER AIRCRAFT CORPORATION (269 wef 1986) and McDONNELL- DOUGLAS
(369 wef 1983) production
269
N994K N8990F N17596
369
N59SD N239MY N252JP N259BK N322MC N369HL N500RK N500SY
N500TY N500XV N696XX N2742Y N5264Q N7172Z N9057F OY-HGB

Impulse Aircraft
IMPULSE
D-MDMM

Jabiru Aircraft (PTY) LTD
JABIRU J160
VH-JRQ

JODEL including CEA, SAN and WASSMER production and see ROBIN
DR.250/160
D-EIAR

DR.300/120
  F-BSPQ
DR.360
  F-BROC

JORA spol sro
JORA
  OK-DUA 14

Kamov COMPANY

Ka.26
  D-HOAY DDR-SPY

KAVANAGH BALLOONS PTY LIMITED

Balloon (Hot Air)
D-77
  VH-AYY

LEIGHTFLUGZEUGBAU **KLEMM** GMBH - see BA
KL.35
  D-EQXD

Lake AIRCRAFT CORPORATION INC

LA-4 BUCCANEER
  C-FQIP N84142

LEARJET INC including BOMBARDIER AEROSPACE production

LEARJET Model 25
  N121EL N309LJ
LEARJET Model 31
  N2FU
LEARJET Model 40
  N40XR
LEARJET Model 45
  N66DN N66SG N708SP OY-OCV
LEARJET Model 60
  N69LJ VP-CRB

LET NARODNI PODNIK KUNOVICE

L-410 TURBOLET
  HA-LAQ HA-YFC OY-PBH UR-VTV

LIBERTY AEROSPACE INC

XL-2
  N518XL

LOCKHEED AIRCRAFT CORPORATION including LOCKHEED-CALIFORNIA

CO and CANADAIR production
10 ELECTRA
  NC5171N
L.188 ELECTRA
  N2RK N4HG
L.749 CONSTELLATION
  N7777G
L.1011 TRISTAR
  TF-ABP
JETSTAR
  N6NE
T-33A
  N36TH

LUSCOMBE AIRPLANE CORPORATION

8 SILVAIRE
  N1604K

McDONNELL DOUGLAS CORPORATION

MD-80
  LV-WTY

McDONNELL DOUGLAS HELICOPTER CO see HUGHES and
MD HELICOPTERS

AVIONS **MAX HOLSTE**
MH.1521 BROUSSARD
  F-BXCP

MAULE AIRCRAFT CORPORATION

M-4
  N9861M

M-5 LUNAR ROCKET
  N346X N775RG N5632R N5647S N56643
M-6 SUPER ROCKET
  N6130X N56462
M(XT)-7 SUPER, STAR ROCKET and STARCRAFT models
  N14HF N280SA N535TK N882JH N1027G

MD HELICOPTERS INC

MD.520N
  N18GH
MD.600N
  N70457
MD.900
  N555WA N902JW N90011 N92001

MIL

Mil-2
  SP-SAY YL-LHN YL-LHO

MILES AIRCRAFT LTD

M.25 MARTINET
  TF-SHC

MITSUBISHI

MU-2
  N33EW N80JN N973BB

MOONEY AIRCRAFT CORPORATION

M.20 and M.252 variants
  D-EANS HB-DFT N12ZX N20UK N61MF N90BE N101UK N123UK
  N192JM N201YK N212MZ N278DB N305RD N305SE N321KL N900RK
  N937BP N4305H N7423V N97821 OY-DFD

MORANE-SAULNIER including GEMS, MORANE, SEEMS and SOCATA production
MS.880, MS.885, MS.887, MS.892 and MS.894 variants
  D-EGKE F-GFGH OO-NAT PH-ZZY

AVIONS **MUDRY AND CIE** including AKROTECH EUROPE and CONSTRUCTIONS
AÉRONAUTIQUES DE BOURGOGNE
CAP.10
  N73AE N80MC N501DW N503DW N4238C
CAP.222, CAP.231 and CAP.232 variants
  F-GKMZ F-GOTC F-GOZO F-GXDB F-GYRO

Nardi

FN.305
  I-TOMI

NEICO

LANCAIR 360
  N250JF PH-PAB
LANCAIR COLUMBIA variants
  N79HR N209DW N350DG N400HF N400UK N1376C N1417W

NOORDUYN AVIATION LTD see NORTH AMERICAN

NORD

1002 PINGOUIN
  LV-RIE
1203 NORECRIN
  OO-AJK

NORTH AMERICAN AVIATION INC and including CAC, CCF, NOORDUYN

AVIATION LTD and NORTH AMERICAN ROCKWELL production
B-25 MITCHELL
  N7614C N9089Z N9115Z N25644
F-86 SABRE
  N196B
P-51 MUSTANG
  N51RT NX251RJ N6526D N7098V
AT-16 HARVARD
  LN-AMY LN-BNM
T-28 TROJAN
  N14113 N99153

JOSEF **Oberlerchner HOLZINDUSTRIE**
JOB 15
  D-ECFE

OMEGA BALLOONS
Balloon (Hot Air)
80
  OY-BOB

PACIFIC AEROSPACE CORPORATION
PAC 750
  ZK-JQK ZK-KAY

PARTENAVIA COSTRUZIONI AERONAUTICHE SpA
P.68
  N75CY N98AG

PEGASUS AVIATION
QUANTUM
  I-6943

PERCIVAL AIRCRAFT CO LTD
P.66 PEMBROKE
  N46EA

PIAGGIO AERO INDUSTRIES including FOCKE WULF production
P.149
  D-EHJL D-EOAJ OO-MEL

PIASECKI HELICOPTER CORPORATION
HUP-3 RETRIEVER
  N6699D

PICCARD BALLOONS
Balloon (Hot Air)
  OO-BFH

PILATUS AIRCRAFT LTD
PC.6 PORTER
  F-GODZ ZK-PCI
PC.12
  N12AG N234RG N660WB VP-BLS

PIPER AIRCRAFT CORPORATION including TAYLOR AIRCRAFT CO LTD *
and THE NEW PIPER AIRCRAFT INC production
J-2 CUB *
  OY-FAA
J-3C CUB (L-4 and O-59 versions)
  F-BMHM HB-OBP N61787
J-5A CUB CRUISER
  N203SA
PA-15 VAGABOND
  NC4531H
PA-16 CLIPPER
  N5240H N5730H N5900H
PA-18 SUPER CUB variants
  I-EIXM N123SA N652P N662KK N4085E N7238X N45458 N45462
  N45477 N45507 N45526 N45531 N45543 N45552 OO-DFS VH-JVL
PA-22-108 COLT
  D-EGEU N209SA N243SA
PA-22 TRI-PACER
  N2652P N6830B
PA-23 APACHE variants,
  N2086P PH-NLK
PA-23-250 AZTEC variants
  N37LW N171WM N250BW N250TB N370SA N485ED N747WW
  N818MJ N989Y N2401Z N4422P N6601Y N54211 N70844
PA-24 COMANCHE variants
  N25KB N84VK N218SA N250CC N500AV N673SA N5052P N5839P
  N7348P N7456P N7832P N8829P N9381P N26634 N61970 SE-IIV
PA-28-140 CHEROKEE (CRUISER)
  HB-OLP N277SA N519MC N6602Y 9J-RBC
PA-28-161 (CHEROKEE) WARRIOR
  N123DU N161FF N2929W N5915V N8241Z SE-GPU
PA-28-180 CHEROKEE
  N180LK SE-EOS
PA-28-181 (CHEROKEE) ARCHER
  D-EAOB N65JF N73GR N411BC N499MS N661KK N2273Q N2405Y
  N4514X N75048
PA-28-235 CHEROKEE
  D-EBWE N235PF
PA-28-236 DAKOTA
  N6339U N81188 OO-MHB

PA-28R (CHEROKEE) ARROW variants
  D-EAWW D-EGVA N171JB N187SA N200GK N216GC N747MM
  N808VT N9325N N38273 N47494 SX-AJM
PA-28RT ARROW variants
  D-EKHW N2CL N691J N799JH N2136E N2943D N8105Z N8153E
  N8412B N29566 N84718
PA-30 TWIN COMANCHE - also see PA-39
  D-GPEZ N7EY N8MZ N25PR N30NW N35AD N41FT N230MJ N359DW
  N499AG N502TC N818Y N918Y N7976Y N8523Y
PA-31 NAVAJO (CHIEFTAIN) variants
  N5LL N31NB N95TA N189SA N250AC N250MD N350PB N449TA N642P
  N666AW N2480X N3586D OY-BTZ ST-AHZ SX-BFM
PA-31T CHEYENNE
  F-GPBF
PA-32 CHEROKEE SIX variants
  D-EDEL N61DE N112WM N129SC N132LE N257SA N562RR N2923N
  N2967N N2989M N3400W N5277T
PA-32R-300 (CHEROKEE) LANCE
  N101DW N6954J N7640F N38945
PA-32R-301 SARATOGA variants
  N8YG N32LE N48CA N51AH N67SP N77YY N88NA N123AX N380CA
  N515SC N551TT N808CA N957T N4178W N9123X N30614 N31008
PA-32RT LANCE
  N646JR
PA-34 SENECA variants
  N37US N43GG N61HB N95D N123NN N145DR N199PS N245CB
  N375SA N559C N3044B N4168D N6920B N21381 N32625 N39605
PA-38 TOMAHAWK
  D-EGLW F-GCTU N24730 PH-TMH SE-GVH
PA-39 TWIN COMANCHE C/R - also see PA-30
  N320MR N613F N971RJ N4297A N8911Y
PA-44-180 SEMINOLE
  N440GC N629RS
PA-46 MALIBU variants
  N45PJ N46PL N46WK N71WZ N177MA N186CB N295S N338DB
  N343RR N352CM N638DB N866LP N955SH N5320N N9122N N9275Y
  N92562
PA-60-601P AEROSTAR 601 (TED SMITH production)
  N69LP N70VB N711TL

PITTS
S-1
  N80BA N85WS N666BM N697RB
S-2
  N61PS N74DC N414MB N531RM N80035

POLIKARPOV
PO-2 (CSS-13)
  N588NB
I-15
  FLARF02089

AVIONS **POTEZ**
840
  F-BMCY

POWER ASSIST
SWIFT
  95MR

PZL WARSZAWA-OKECIE SA
PZL-101 GAWRON
  SP-CHD
PZL-110 KOLIBER
  D-EIVF

RAVEN INDUSTRIES
Balloon (Hot Air)
S.40
  N1196R
S.50
  N12006

RAYTHEON HAWKER see HAWKER SIDDELEY AVIATION
RB390 PREMIER
  N72GD N800FR

REPUBLIC AVIATION CORPORATION
P-47 THUNDERBOLT
  N47DD

AVIONS PIERRE **ROBIN** including CONSTRUCTIONS AÉRONAUTIQUES DE BOURGOGNE
DR.400 and DR..500 variants
D-EAPF D-EIKR D-ELSR F-GOXD
HR.100
CS-ARI F-BTKO F-GMHH
ATL
F-GFOR F-GJQI

ROBINSON HELICOPTER CO INC
R.44 RAVEN I, II
N13DT N393N N999RL

ROCKWELL INTERNATIONAL CORPORATION including GULFSTREAM
and COMMANDER AIRCRAFT COMPANY (**114**) production
500, 680, 685 and 690 COMMANDER variants
N51WF N71VE N125MM N690CL N808NC N840PN N840TC N980HB
N3596T N91384 VP-BCT VP-BMZ
COMMANDER 112 and 114
D-EWAT N14AF N50AY N112JA N114ED N115MD N115TB N395TC
N411DP N1350J N1407J N4599W N4698W N5834N N6010Y N6024V
N6039X N6081F N6088F N6088Z N6095A ZS-MBI

ROTORWAY HELICOPTERS INTERNATIONAL
SCORPION
SE-HXF

RUSCHMEYER LUFTFAHRTTECHNIK GmbH
RUSHMEYER R90
D-EFFA N12AB

RYAN AERONAUTICAL CORPORATION
ST3KR, PT-22
N1344 N56421
NAVION
D-ECDL NC285RS N2548T N3864

SCHEIBE-FLUGZEUGBAU GmbH
SFS-31 MILAN
D-KIFF
SF-25 FALKE (inc SLINGSBY T.61)
SE-UCF

SCHEMPP-HIRTH FLUGZEUGBAU GmbH
CIRRUS
D-2782
DISCUS
ZK-GIL

ALEXANDER **SCHLEICHER** GmbH and CO
K.8B
D-1155
ASW 22
D-KKAM
ASW 28
D-9004
ASG 29
D-KAAD D-KBJG D-KEEJ D-KLCC D-KNZG D-KPRA D-KPRB D-KPRC
D-7429 D-9729

SCHROEDER FIRE BALLOONS
Balloon (Hot Air)
3000
D-Opha

SCHWEIZER AIRCRAFT CORPORATION
TG-3
N66630

SCOTTISH AVIATION
BULLDOG
HA-TVA

SHORT BROTHERS LTD
S.16 SCION
VH-UUP
S.24 SANDRINGHAM
VH-BRC
SD.3-30
OY-MUB

SIAI-MARCHETTI SpA
S.205/208
D-EFZC
SF.260
I-LELF N61FD N260AP

SIKORSKY AIRCRAFT see WESTLAND
S-76
N70QJ N399BH VP-BNI VP-BNM
S-92
N908W

SOCATA see MORANE-SAULNIER
TB-9 TAMPICO and TB-10 TOBAGO
F-GJPB F-GLAO I-IAFS N99ET N770RM
TB-20, TB-21 TRINIDAD and TB-200 TOBAGO GT/XL
N1FD N20AG N33NW N34FA N37EL N91ME N97GP N113AC N297GT
N345TB N575GM N709AM
TBM-700 and TBM-850
N181PC N223JG N228CX N257JM N262J N324JS N582C N700EL
N700GY N700KV N700S N700VA N700VB N702MB N850LH N851WA
N997JM

SOKO
G-2 GALEB
YU-YAB

STEARMAN see BOEING-STEARMAN

STINSON AIRCRAFT CORPORATION
JUNIOR R
NC2612
L-5 SENTINEL
N6438C N57783

STODDARD-HAMILTON
GLASAIR
PH-DUC

SUD-AVIATION and including AéROSPATIALE, SOKO and WESTLAND HELICOPTERS
production
SE.313 and SE318 ALOUETTE II
F-GXFP HA-IDL HA-LFZ HA-PPC N297CJ
SA.315 LAMA
F-BPFP
SA.321 SUPER FRELON
F-BTRP
SA.330 PUMA
9L-LSA 9L-LSG
SA.341 and SA.342 GAZELLE
F-GIBU HA-LFB HA-LFH HA-LFM HA-LFQ HA-PPY N505HA N565F
N58283 YU-HEH YU-HEI YU-HES YU-HET YU-HEVYU-HEY YU-MAN
YU-PJB

SUKHOI
Su-29
HA-HUD HA-YAO HA-YAR HA-YAW

COSTRUZIONI AERONAUTICHE **T**ECNAM Srl
P.2002 SIERRA
LX-TRE

SCF **TECHNOAVIA**
SMG-92 FINIST
HA-NAH HA-YDF

THUNDER BALLOONS LTD including THUNDER and COLT LTD
Balloon (Hot Air)
Ax7 series
N4990T OO-BRM
Ax10 series
DQ-PBF

TL ULTRALIGHT Sro
TL-2000 STING
OK-IUA 69

URBAN AIR
UFM-10 SAMBA
OK-GUA 16 OK-GUA 28 OK-JUA 03 OK-KUA 16 OK-KUA 26
OK-LUA 36

UFM-11/13 LAMBADA
  OK-DUU 15 OK-FUA 05

UTVA AIRCRAFT FACTORY
UTVA 56
YU-DLG

Van's AIRCRAFT INC
RV-8
  PH-PWA

VELOCITY INC
VELOCITY
  N173RG

VFW-FOKKER GmbH
VFW-614
  D-ASDB

VICKERS
VIMY FB-27
  NX71MY
700 series VISCOUNT
  F-BGNR
(SUPER) VC-10
  A40-AB

VICKERS SUPERMARINE LTD
228 SEAGULL
  VH-ALB
304 STRANRAER
  CF-BXO
361 SPITFIRE
  N382RW

Waco AIRCRAFT CORPN
YMF
  N999PD

société WASSMER
WA.52 EUROPA
  D-EFVS
WA.54 ATLANTIC
  D-EEPI
WA.81 PIRANA
  F-GAIF

WESTLAND HELICOPTERS LTD see SIKORSKY
WESTLAND-SIKORSKY S-55 WHIRLWIND
  VR-BEP VR-BEU
WG.30
  N112WG N114WG N116WG N118WG N5820T N5840T N5880T

Yakovlev including ACROSTAR, IAV-BACHAU, LET, NANCHANG, SPP and
WSK production
Yak-12
  LY-AHD HA-HUB
Yak-18T
  HA-HUA HA-HUE HA-JAB HA-JAC HA-SMD HA-YAB HA-YAD HA-YAE
  HA-YAF HA-YAG HA-YAH HA-YAJ HA-YAK HA-YAM HA-YAN HA-YAP
  HA-YAU HA-YAV HA-YAZ RA01370
Yak-52
  LY-ALT FLARF01035 RA-01378 YL-CBJ
Yak-55
  RA-01274

Zenair
ZENITH 100
  F-PYOY
CH-600 ZODIAC variants
  PH-3W6

PART 8 – AIRCRAFT TYPE INDEX (IRELAND)

This Index covers entries in SECTION 2, Part 1 and SECTION 4.

737-400 series
EI-COH COI COJ COK CUA CUD CUN CWE CWF CWW CWX CXI CXJ CXK CXM CZG CZK DDK DDY DFD DFE DFF DGL DGM DNM DOR DOS DOV DXC DXG DXO
737-500 series
EI-CDD CDE CDF CDG CDH DTU DTV DTW DTX DUD DUE
737-700 series
EI-DMX DMY DNB DNC DRD DRE DZC
737-800 series
EI-CSF CSG CSH CSI-CSJ CSM CSN CSO CSP CSQ CSR CSS CST CSV CSW CSX CSY CSZ CTA CTB CXV DAC DAD DAE DAF DAG DAH DAI DAJ DAK DAL DAM DAN DAO DAP DAR DAS DAT DAV DAW DAX DAY DAZ DCB DCC DCD DCE DCF DCG DCH DCI DCJ DCK DCL DCM DCN DCO DCP DCR DCS DCT DCV DCW DCX DCY DCZ DGZ DHA DHB DHC DHD DHE DHF DHG DHI DHJ DHK DHM DHN DHS DHT DHV DHW DHX DHY DHZ DJR DJU DKD DLB DLC DLD DLE DLF DLG DLH DLI DLJ DLK DLL DLM DLN DLO DLR DLS DLT DLV DLW DLX DLY DLZ DMZ DND DPA DPB DPC DPD DPE DPF DPG DPH DPI DPJ DPK DPL DPM DPN DPO DPP DPR DPS DPT DPV DPW DPX DPY DPZ DRA DRB DRC DRE DWA DWB DWC DWD DWE DWF DWG DWH DWI DWJ DWK DWL DWM DWO DWP DWR DWS DWT DWV DWW DWX DWY DWZ DYA DYB DYC DYD DYE DYF DYG
757-200 series
EI-CEY CEZ DKL DNA DUA DUC IGA IGB IGC LTO LTY
767-200 series
EI-CXZ CZD DBW DMH DMP GAA GBA
767-300 series
EI-CRD CRF CRL CRM CRO CXO CZH DBF DBG DBP DBU DDW DFS DMJ DOF UNB
777-200 series
EI-DBK DBL DBM DDH

BÖLKOW
PHOEBUS
EI-GMD

BOMBARDIER INC
CANADAIR CL-600 REGIONAL JET
EI-DOT DOU DRI DRJ DRK DUK DUM DUU DUX DUY DVP DVR DVS DVT
CANADAIR CL604 CHALLENGER
EI-IRE

BOX
DUET
EI-BOX

BRITISH AIRCRAFT MANUFACTURING COMPANY LTD (BA)
L 25C SWALLOW 2
EI-AFF

BRITTEN-NORMAN LTD
BN.2A ISLANDER
EI-AYN BCE CUW

BROCK MANUFACTURING
KB2 GYROCOPTER
EI-CVY

CAMERON BALLOONS LTD
Balloon (Hot Air)
65 variants
EI-BSN
77 variant
EI-CKJ
84 variant
(EI-BAY)
90 variant
EI-DGW POP
105 variant
EI-CUE

CARLSON
SPARROW
EI-COO

SOCIÉTÉ NOUVELLE CENTRAIR
101A PÉGASE
EI-GLC

CESSNA AIRCRAFT COMPANY including REIMS AVIATION SA production (F.prefix)
150
EI-APF AST AVM BAT BFE BHW BYF CDV CHM CIN CML CMV
A150 AEROBAT
EI-AUC AYF CTI
152
EI-BGJ BIB BMM BMN CCJ CCK CCL CCM CGT CRU DGX

A152 AEROBAT
EI-BJM
172 SKYHAWK
EI-AOK AYK BAG BAS BCK BIC BIR BKF BPL BRS BSC BUA CAA CFP CFY CGD CHS CLQ COT CUJ DDC DDX EAZ GSE GWY ING MCF NFW OFM SAC SKP STT
R172 HAWK XP
EI-BJO CCV
REIMS FR172 ROCKET
EI-BJI
177(RG) CARDINAL
EI-BHC POD
(R)182 SKYLANE (RG)
EI-BCL CAP CDP FBG GSM
206 SUPER SKYLANE, STATIONAIR
EI-BNK SBP SPB
210 CENTURION
EI-AWH BUF CAX CDX CGH
310
EI-AOS
335
EI-CUP
337 SUPER SKYMASTER
EI-AVC BHM
340
EI-CIJ
441 CONQUEST
EI-DMG
551 CITATION II
EI-CIR

CFM METAL-FAX
(STREAK) SHADOW
EI-CHR CZC DBH DXL DXS

CHAMPION AIRCRAFT CORPORATION see AERONCA and BELLANCA
7EC TRAVELLER
EI-BHV
7ECA CITABRIA
EI-ANT
7FC TRI-TRAVELLER
EI-BBE
7GCAA CITABRIA
EI-BYX

COLT BALLOONS LTD
Balloon (Hot Air)
14A CLOUDHOPPER
EI-DZB
21A
EI-DZA
77A
EI-BGT

COMCO IKARUS GmbH
IKARUS C42
EI-DXA

CVJETKOVIC
CA-65
EI-BNT

CYCLONE AIRSPORTS LTD
AX3
EI-DXP

DE HAVILLAND AIRCRAFT CO LTD
DH.82A TIGER MOTH
EI-AHI AUB AWP
DH.84 DRAGON
EI-ABI

DOUGLAS
DC-3A and C-47 variants
EI-ALR ALT AYO
C-54E-5-DO SKYMASTER
EI-ARS

DRUINE
D.62 CONDOR
EI-BCP BXT

EIPPER
QUICKSILVER
EI-BLE BLN BOH BPP

EIRI-AVION O/Y
PIK-20D
  EI-GME

ELA AVIACIÓN S.L
ELA 07
  EI-DKN DTT DXU

ELLIOTTS OF NEWBURY see DFS and NORD
EoN AP.5 OLYMPIA 2B
  EI-GLP

EMBRAER
EMB-170
  EI-DFG DFH DFI DFJ DFK DFL

ERCO
ERCOUPE 415
  EI-CGG CIH CVL

EUROCOPTER
EC120 COLIBRI
  EI-DDB EUR FAB FGL MIK NZO PJW
EC130B
  EI-HOK LKS LNX

EUROPA AVIATION
EUROPA
  EI-COE

EUROWING
GOLDWING
  EI-BNF CMK

EVANS
VP-1
  EI-AYY BBD BRU
VP-2
  EI-BDL BNJ BVT

EVEKTOR
EV-97 EUROSTAR
  EI-CXY DFM DKW DOI DRW DUJ

EXTRA FLUGZEUGBAU GmbH
EA.300/200
  EI-SAM

FLEXIFORM
STRIKERr
  EI-BPN
TRIKE
  EI-BRK

FOKKER BV including FAIRCHILD-HILLER (1) and FOKKER-VFW NV (2) production
D.VII/65 replica
  EI-APT APU APV
F.27
  EI-AKA
FH.227 (1)
  EI-CAZ
F.28-100 (2)
  EI-DGE

FORNEY
F-1A AIRCOUPE
  EI-AUT

FOUGA
CM-170 MAGISTER
  EI-BXO

GARDAN
GY-80 HORIZON
  EI-AYB

GLASER-DIRKS FLUGZEUGBAU GmbH
DG-200 series
  EI-GLJ GLL

GLASFLÜGEL ING EUGEN HANLE
H.201 STANDARD LIBELLE
  EI-GLN

GROB-WERKE GmbH and Co KG
G.109
  EI-HCS
G.115
  EI-CAC CAD CAE CCD DJY

GRUMMAN AMERICAN AVIATION CORPORATION (1) including
AMERICAN AVIATION CORPORATION (2) and GULFSTREAM AMERICAN CORPORATION (4) production production
AMERICAN AA-5 TRAVELER (2)
  EI-BMV BNR
GRUMMAN AA-5 TRAVELLER (1)
  EI-AYD
GULFSTREAM GA-7 COUGAR (3)
  EI-DUI

GULFSTREAM AEROSPACE CORPORATION
GULFSTREAM V SP
  EI-GDL

GYROSCOPIC ROTORCRAFT
GYROPLANE
  EI-COG

HAWKER SIDDELEY AVIATION including BRITISH AEROSPACE PLC,
CORPORATE JETS LTD and RAYTHEON-HAWKER production
HS.125 Series 700
  EI-WJN
800XP
  EI-WXP
850XP
  EI-KJC

HIWAY HANG GLIDERS LTD
SKYTRIKE with Demon & Vulcan wings
  EI-BMW BNH BPU BRV

HOAC FLUGZEUGWERKE (HOFFMANN FLUGZEUGBAU FRIESACH)
DV-20 KATANA
  EI-CLA
H-36 DIMONA
  EI-CRV

HOVEY
DELTA BIRD
  EI-BRW

HOWELL SIDNEY
TWINSTARR
  EI-DJX

HUGHES TOOL CO and HUGHES HELICOPTERS INC including
SCHWEIZER AIRCRAFT CORPORATION (269 wef 1986)
269 (Srs 300)
  EI-CVM CZL CZP DDI DMC DNU

HUNT
AVON trike
  EI-CKF CKG
PEGASUS XL
  EI-DBJ

ICP SRL
MXP-740 SAVANNAH
  EI-DGI DKB

III (INIZIATIVE INDUSTRIALI ITALIANE) SpA
SKY ARROW
  EI-CPX

JODEL including CEA, SAN and WASSMER production
D.9 BÉBÉ
  EI-BUC
D.112
  EI-BSB
D.120 PARIS-NICE
  EI-CJS
D.18
  EI-CKZ
DR.1050
  EI-ARW

JORA SPOL SRO
JORA
  EI-NVL

LAK including AB SPORTINE AVIAICIJA production
LAK-17A
  EI-GLH

LAKE AIRCRAFT CORPORATION
LA-4 BUCCANEER
  EI-BUH

LEARJET INC including BOMBARDIER AEROSPACE production
LEARJET Model 31
  EI-MAX
LEARJET Model 60
  EI-DXW IAW REX VIV

LETOV AIR
LK-2M SLUKA
  EI-CNA

LINDSTRAND BALLOONS LTD
Balloon (Hot Air)
LBL 31
  EI-DJZ
LBL 90A
  EI-CRB

LOCKHEED-CALIFORNIA CO
L.382 HERCULES
  EI-JIV

McCANDLESS
M.4 GYROPLANE
  EI-ASR

McDONNELL DOUGLAS CORPORATION
DC-9-82, and DC-9-83
  EI-CBR CBS CBY CBZ CCC CCE CDY CEP CEQ CER CFZ CIW CKM
  CNR CRE CRH CRW
MD-11
  EI-UPA UPE UPI UPO UPU

MAGNI GYRO of ITALY
SPARTAN
  EI-DBX

MAINAIR SPORTS LTD
BLADE
  EI-DOW DRH
GEMINI FLASH
  EI-CKT
MERCURY
  EI-CMU

MALMÖ
MFI-9 JUNIOR
  EI-AWR

MAULE AIRCRAFT CORPORATION
MX-7
  EI-CUT GER

MEDWAY MICROLIGHTS LTD
ECLIPSE R
  EI-CRY CTC ELL

MESSERSCHMITT-BÖLKOW-BLOHM GmbH including EUROCOPTER
DEUTSCHLAND GmbH production
BÖ.105 varriants
  EI-BLD LIT

MIGNET
HM.14 POU-DU-CIEL replica
  ("EI-ABH"")

MONNETT
MONI
  EI-BMU

MOONEY AIRCRAFT CORPORATION
M.20
  EI-CAY

MORANE-SAULNIER
MS.502 CRIQUET
  EI-AUY

MOSKITO
MOSKITO 2
  EI-CJV

PARTENAVIA COSTRUZIONI AERONAUTICHE SpA
P.68
  EI-BWH

PEGASUS AVIATION
QUANTUM
  EI-CNU
QUASAR
  EI-DKC

PFALZ
D.III replica
  EI-ARC

PHOENIX
LUTON LA-4 MINOR
  EI-ATP
LUTON LA-5A MAJOR
  EI-CGF

PIEL
CP.301 EMERAUDE
  EI-CFG

PIEL AVIATION including SCINTEX production
CP.301 EMERAUDE
  EI-CFG
CP.1310-C3 SUPER EMERAUDE
  EI-DUK

PILATUS AIRCRAFT LTD
PC.12
  EI-IAN

PIPER AIRCRAFT CORPORATION
J-3C CUB
  EI-AFE AKM BBV BCM BCN BCO BEN BFO BIO BSX BYY CFO CHK COY
  CPP
J-5A CUB CRUISER
  EI-CGV
PA-12 SUPER CRUISER
  EI-ADV CFF CFH CMN
PA-18 SUPER CUB
  EI-ANY AVE BID BIK CIG CKH DTS
PA-22-108 COLT
  EI-BAV
PA-22-150 TRI-PACER
  EI-UFO
PA-22-160 TRI-PACER
  EI-AWD
PA-23-250 AZTEC
  EI-BDM WAC WMN
PA-28-140 CHEROKEE (CRUISER)
  EI-AOB ATK BSO CGP CIV CMB COZ
PA-28-151 CHEROKEE WARRIOR
  EI-WRN
PA-28-161 (CHEROKEE) WARRIOR
  EI-CTT DJM SKW
PA-28-180 CHEROKEE
  EI-BBC BDR CIF
PA-28-181 (CHEROKEE) ARCHER
  EI-DDZ KDH
PA-28R-200 CHEROKEE ARROW II
  EI-EDR
PA-28RT-201 ARROW IV
  EI-SKU
PA-31-350 NAVAJO CHIEFTAIN
  EI-DIF
PA-34-200T SENECA II
  EI-CMT
PA-34-220T SENECA III
  EI-BSL
PA-38-112 TOMAHAWK
  EI-BJT BVK
PA-44-180 SEMINOLE
  EI-SKB SKR SKT

PROGRESSIVE AERODYNE INC
SEAREY AMPHIBIAN
  EI-SEA

PTERODACTYL LTD
MICROLIGHT
  EI-BOA

PZL WARSZAWA-OKECIE SA
PZL-110 KOLIBER
  EI-DOY

Raj HAMSA
X'AIR
  EI-CXC DBI DBV DCA DDJ DFY DGG DGH DGJ DGK DKT DKY DNR DRL
  DRX DXM DXX KEV TON

RAND-ROBINSON
KR-2
  EI-BNL BOV

REALITY AIRCRAFT
ESCAPADE
  EI-DKZ

AVIONS PIERRE ROBIN
HR.200/120B
  EI-YLG
DR.400 vraiants
  EI-CRG SKE SKG SKL
R.1180T AIGLON
  EI-BIS ROB
R.2160D
  EI-SKS SKV

ROBINSON HELICOPTER CO INC
R22 variants
  EI-CFE CFX CPO CWL CWR DIZ DKI DXI DXJ EHB EHE EHG EMG EXG
  GAV GKL GPT GTY JWM KHR MAG TGF TKI
R44 variants
  EI-CZM DDA DFW DJW DRN DTR DVX DVZ DXH DXK DZI EBJ EGG EGR
  EJR ESK EXC EXH EXM FAR FOX GPZ HAZ JAL JAR JFD JWP KEY LAJ
  LOC MCC MJR MMO MOR MPW MUL MVK NBD NBP NJA OLI PEC RAV
  RON SGF SGN SUB SWD TMH TOY UNI VIC WWI

ROLLADEN-SCHNEIDER FLUGZEUGBAU GmBH
LS7-WL
  EI-GLS

ROTORWAY
EXECUTIVE
  EI-BNP CMW

RUTAN
LONG-EZE
  EI-CMR CPI

Scheibe-FLUGZEUBAU GmbH including AVIALSA/ROCHETAU production
ZUGVOGEL III
  EI-GLO

ALEXANDER SCHLEICHER GmbH and Co
Ka 6CR
  EI-GLG GLM GLU GLW
K 8B
  EI-GLF
ASK 13
  EI-GLD GMF
ASK 14
  EI-APS
ASK 16
  EI-AYR
ASW 17
  EI-GMB
ASK 16
  EI-AYR
ASW 18
  EI-GMC
ASW 20L
  EI-GLR
ASK 21
  EI-GLA GLB]

SCHEMPP-HIRTH FLUGZEUBAU GmbH
CIRRUS
  EI-GLk
DISCUS B
  EI-GLT
DUO DISCUS T
  EI-GLI

SIKORSKY AIRCRAFT
S-61N
  EI-CNL CXS CZN GCE MES RCG SAR

SKYHOOK
SABRE
  EI-BPT

SLINGSBY SAILPLANES LTD
T.21 CADET
  EI-CJT
T.31 MOTOR TUTOR
  EI-CKJ
T.56 SE.5 replica
  EI-ARH ARM

SNCAN STAMPE including AIA production
STAMPE SV.4A/C
  EI-BAJ BLB CJR

SOCATA including MORANE-SAULNIER, SEEMS (wef 1962) and GEMS (wef 1965) production
MS.880B RALLYE CLUB
  EI-ATS AWU AYA AYI BCW BDH BGB BGC BGD BGU BHK BIM BIW BMA
  BMH BNU CFV CHN CIA
(MS.880B) RALLYE 100, 110 and 150 series
  EI-BBG BBI BBJ BCS BCU BDK BEA BFI BFP BFR BGA BHY BJK BKN
  BMB BMJ
MS.885 SUPER RALLYE
  EI-BKE
MS.892A RALLYE COMMODORE 150
  EI-BEP BHF BKU BUJ
MS.892E RALLYE 150GT and 180GT
  EI-BGG BBO BGS CEG
MS.893A RALLYE COMMODORE 180
  EI-BHN BHP BUT
MS.894A RALLYE MINERVA 220
  EI-AUG AYT
MS.887 RALLYE 125
  EI-BIT
ST.10 DIPLOMATE
  EI-BUG
TB-9 TAMPICO
  EI-BMI BSK BYG CRX GFC
TB-10 TOBAGO
  EI-BOE
TBM-700
  EI-TBM

SOLAR WINGS LTD
PEGASUS XL-Q and XL-R
  EI-BSW CGJ CGM CGN CHT CKU DIA DNW DOX

SOUTHDOWN SAILWINGS LTD
PUMA and SPRINT
  EI-BPO DDP

SPARTAN AIRCRAFT LTD
3-SEATER II
  (EI-ABU)

STEEN AERO LAB.INC
SKYBOLT
  EI-CIZ SAT

STINSON AIRCRAFT CORPORATION
108 STATION WAGON
  EI-CGC

STODDARD-HAMILTON
GLASAIR
  EI-CTG

Taylor
JT.1 MONOPLANE
  EI-BKK

TAYLORCRAFT AIRCRAFT CORPORATION
PLUS D
  EI-AGD ALH AMF
BC-65
  EI-CES

TEAM
MINI-MAX
  EI-CNC CGB

CONSTRUZIONI AERONAUTICHE **TECNAM SRL**
P92/EM ECHO
  EI-DRU
P2002
  EI-DRO LFC

THRUSTER AIR SERVICES LTD
TST
  EI-BYA CKI
T.300/T600
  EI-CEN DKJ

THUNDER BALLOONS LTD
Balloon (Hot Air)
AX8
  EI-BAR

URBAN AIR SRO
UFM-10 SAMBA variants
  EI-DRM DXT DXZ DZE JIM XLA
UFM-11 LAMBADA
  EI-DGA DGP DGR DGT DGY DNV

VAN'S AIRCRAFT INC
RV-7
  EI-HUM

VIKING
DRAGONFLY
  EI-BPE

WHITTAKER
MW5
  EI-BUL CAN CTL
MW6
  EI-BVB CJZ CKN CLL COM DMU

ZENAIR see HEINTZ and COLOMBAN
CH.200 and 250 ZENITH variants
  EI-BKM BVY BYL
CH.601
  EI-DXN
CH.701
  EI-DOB SMK

ZLIN
526 TRENER MASTER
  EI-BIG

PART 9 – AIRCRAFT TYPE INDEX (ISLE OF MAN)

This Index covers entries in SECTION 3.

COSTRUZIONI AERONAUTICHE GIOVANNI **AGUSTA SpA**
A109E POWERr
  M-IDAS
AW139
  M-ERIT

AMERCAN-GENERAL AVIATION
AG-5B TIGER
  M-PHML

BEECH AIRCRAFT CORPORATION includng RAYTHEON AIRCRAFT
COMPANY production
A36 BONANZA
  M-FOUR
G58 BARON
  M-NINE

BOMBARDIER INC
BD-100 CHALLENGER 300
  M-NEWT TAGB
BD-700 GLOBAL 5000
  M-LLGC
CL-600 CHALLENGER
  M-BIGG

BRITISH AEROSPACE PLC
BAe 125 Series 800B
  M-HDAM

CESSNA AIRCRAFT COMPANY
172N SKYHAWK
  M-BONO
208B GRAND CARAVAN
  M-YAKW
425 CONQUEST
  M-MANX
525 CITATIONJET variants
  M-AJDM ELON ICRO XONE
560 (XL) CITATION variants
  M-ANSL BWFC
680 CiTATION SOVEREIGN
  M-AGIC

DASSAULT AVIATION
FALCON 50
  M-DASO
FALCON 900
  M-FALC RURU SAIR
FALCON 2000 variants
  M-CHEM YJET

EMBRAER
EMB-135BJ LEGACY
  M-YNJC

GULFSTREAM AEROSPACE CORPORATION
GULFSTREAM IV
  M-GULF

LET KUNOVICE
L-200A MORAVA
  M-RAVA

PILATUS AIRCRAFT LTD
PC.12
  M-ICKY

PIPER AIRCRAFT CORPORATION
PA-28
  M-AZDA
PA-30 TWIN COMANCHE
  M-ALAN
PA-32-301XTC SARATOGA
  M-SUEC
PA-34-200T SENECA
  M-EDIA

RAYTHEON AIRCRAFT COMPANY
HAWKER BEECH 350 KING AIRi
  M-OORE
RB390 PREMIER
  M-YSKY

SIKORSKY AIRCRAFT
S-76B
  M-ONTY

SOCATA
TB-20 TRINIDAD
  M-ANIN GINZ

PART 10 – AIRCRAFT TYPE INDEX (UK)

This Index covers all entries in SECTION 1, Parts 1 to 3, and entries in SECTION 4, Part 1 plus selected default Engine details for which see also note under 'Type' page viii.

ABBOTT-BAYNES SAILPLANES LTD
SCUD III
  G-ALJR

ABINGDON
Balloon (Hot Air)
SPHERICAL FREE
  G-ATXR

ACE AVIATION
MAGIC LASER
  G=CENP

ACRO
ADVANCED
  G-BPAA

ETABLISSEMENTS AERONAUTIQUES **R ADAM**
RA.14 LOISIR
  G-BHIK

ADVANCED AIRSHIP CORPORATION
Airship (Gas-Filled)
ANR-1
  G-MAAC

ADVANCED TECHNOLOGIES INC
FIREBIRD CH1 ATI
  G-BXZN

AERIAL ARTS (LTD)
ALPHA (Rotax 277)
  G-MNIT MNZS
CHASER (Rotax 377) with 110SX and 130SX wings
  G-MNTD MNYD MNYE MNYF MTCP MTDD MTDE MVOD MWGO
CHASER S (Rotax 377)
  G-MVDK MVDL MVDP MVDR MVGA MVGF MVGG MVGH (MVGI) MVHA
  MVIE MVJF MVJG MVJH MVJI MVJJ MVJK MVKZ MVLA MVLB MVLC
  MVLD MVLE MVLF MVLG MVLS MVLT MVLW MVML MVMM MVOP
  MVRG MVRL MVSG MVTF MVTL MVTM MVUS MVVU MVYY MVZM
  MWWZ MWXW MWXX MWXY MWXZ MWYM MYBU MYCB MYEI MYEJ
  MYFO MYGK MYIL MYIT MYJO MYJW MYKD MYMY MYRE MYSA MYSV
  MYWN MYWS MYYD MZCB MZTS

AÉRIANE SA
SWIFT'LIGHT PAS
  G-CEVX

AERO SP ZOO
AT-3 variants
  G-DPEP SACX SACY SPAT SWLL SYEL SYWL UKAT

AERO COMMANDER INC
-680 COMMANDER
  G-AWOE

AERO DESIGNS
PULSAR X (Rotax 582)
  G-BSFA BTDR BTRF BTWY BUDI BUJL BUSR BUYB BVLN BVSF BVTW
  BXDU CCBZ CCIG IIAN LUED LWNG MCMS RMAN
PULSAR XP (Rotax 912 and 912-UL)
  G-BUOW BUZB CBLA CEDJ EPOX LEEN OOXP PLSA XPXP
PULSAR 3 (Rotax 912-ULS)
  G-BYJL CDNF

AERO DYNAMICS LTD
SPARROW HAWK
  G-BOZU

AERO VODOCHODY NÁRODNÍ PODNIK see CZL and LET
C-104
  G-CCOB
L-29 DELFIN
  G-BYCT BZNT DELF ODAT
L-39 ALBATROS
  G-BZDI BZVL CCWB

SB Lim-2A
  G-BMZF OMIG
Lim-5
  G-MIGG

AEROCAR
TAYLOR COOT A
  G-COOT
TAYLOR MINI IMP
  G-BLWW

AEROCHUTE INDUSTRIES PTY LTD
DUAL
  G-CDPO CEZH

AERODYNE SYSTEMS INC
VECTOR
  G-MBTW MJAZ

AEROFAB INC see LAKE

AEROLA LTD
ALATUS-M
  G-CEWG

AEROMERE SpA see AVIAMILANO

AEROMOT INDUSTRIA MECANICO METALURGICA LTDA
AMT-200 SUPER XIMANGO
  G-BWNY CECJ JTPC KHOM LLEW MOAN RFIO XMGO

AERONAUTICAL CORPORATION OF AMERICA
AERONCA C.3
  G-ADRR ADYS AEFT AESB CDUW

AERONAUTICAL CORPORATION OF GB LTD
AERONCA 100
  G-AETG AEVS AEWU AEXD

AERONCA AIRCRAFT CORPORATION
AERONCA K
  G-ONKA
7AC CHAMPION
  G-AJON AKTR AOEH ATHK AVDT AWVN BGWV BPFM BPGK BRAR
  BRCV BRER BRWA BRXG BTGM BTNO BVCS LEVI OTOE TECC
7ACA CHAMP
  G-HAMP
7BCM CHAMPION (L-16)
  G-AKTO BFAF TIMP
7BM CHAMPION
  G-DHAH
7DC CHAMPION
  G-BRFI
11AC CHIEF,
  G-AKTK AKUO AKVN BJEV BPRA BPRX BPXY BRCW BRFJ BRWR BRXF
  BRXL BSTC BTFL BTSR BUAB BUTF IIAC IVOR
11CC SUPER CHIEF
  G-BBJNY BTRI
15AC SEDAN
  G-AREX
65C(TAC) SUPER CHIEF
  G-BTRG BTUV
O-58B (L-3) GRASSHOPPER
  G-BRHP BRPR

AEROPHILE SA
Balloon (Gas-Filled)
AEROPHILE 5500
  G-CCYF

AEROPRAKT
A22 FOXBAT (Rotax 912-ULS)
  G-CBGJ CBJH CBYH CCCE CCJV CDDW CDTZ CEOP CESI CEWR
  CHAD COXS CWTD FBAT FBTT FJTH FOXB FXBT GFOX MOWG MRAF
  NJTC PHOX SDOI TADC VROD

AEROS COMPANY
*DISCUS c/w **D**elta **T**rikes **A**viation ALIZE trike*
G-CENZ

AÉROSPATIALE including EUROCOPTER production also see AÉROSPATIALE, ALENIA, ATR and SOCATA
AS.332L SUPER PUMA including EC.225LP variant
G-BKZE BKZG BLPM BLXR BMCW BMCX BUZD BWWI BWZX CDSV
CEYJ CHCF CHCG CHCH CHCI CHCL CHCM JSAR PUMA PUMB PUMD
PUME PUMN PUMO PUMS REDJ REDK REDL REDM REDN REDO
REDP TIGC TIGE TIGF TIGG TIGH TIGJ TIGO TIGS TIGV TIGZ ZZSA
ZZSB ZZSC ZZSD ZZSE ZZSF
AS.350B ECUREUIL
G-BRVO BVJE BVXM BXGA BZVG CBHL CDTD DEMM DOIT ECOU
EFTF EJOC FIBS HELM HRAK IANW IFBP JBBZ JCOP JESI KELY LARR
MAAV MURP NUTY OAWD ODMC OLFA OMCC OOIO OOTT ORKY
PDGF PDGR PLMB PLMH PROB PROM REAL SCHI SMDJ SPVK TATS
VKVK WHAM WHST
AS.355 ECUREUIL 2
G-BOSN BPRI BPRJ BPRL BSTE BSYI BUFW BVLG BYPA BYZA CAMB
CCWK CDLP CPOL DANZ DBOK DEUX DFOX DOOZ EMHH FFRI ICSG
HBRO HEAN JEMH JETU JPAL LECA LENI LHEL LINE LNTY LUVY NETR
NTWK OASP OHCP OHMS OLCP ORDH ORMA OTSP PASH PDGT
REEM RIDA SEPA SEPB SEPC SEWP SKYN SKYW STON STRL SYPA
TAKE TBHH TOPC TOPS TVHD ULES VGMC VONE VONF VONG VONH
VONK WENA WIRE XLLL XOIL ZITZ
AS.365 (and SA.365) DAUPHIN variants
G-BKXD BLEZ BLUM BLUN BTEU BTNC CEUK DAUF DORF DPHN
HEMS LCPL MLTY MRMJ OLNT PDGN PLMI

AÉROSPATIALE-ALENIA
ATR.-42
G-CDFF DRFC IONA RHUM SSEA
ATR -72
G-BWDA BWDB BXTN

AEROSPOOL SPOL S.R.O.
WT9 UK DYNAMIC
G-CENO DYMC DYNA DYNM EECC GRMN JFDI JFLO RMHE OTIV TDYN

AEROSPORT
SCAMP
G-BKFL BKPB BOOW
WOODY PUSHER including Woods production
G-AWWP AYVP BSFV SHUV

AEROSTAR SA and YAKOVELEV

AEROTECH INTERNATIONAL LTD see WHITTAKER

AEROTEK INC see PITTS

AESL see VICTA

AQUILA TECHNISCHE ENTWICKLUNGEN GmbH
AT01
G-DCHO OKTI ROWA UILA WTWO

COSTRUZIONI AERONAUTICHE GIOVANNI **AGUSTA SpA**
A109 variants
G-BWNZ CCUK CDWY CERO CGRI DBOY DNHI DPPF ELTE EMHB
EMHC ETOU FUFU GDSG GRND HBEK HDTV IFRH IMAR IWRB JJJL
JMON JMXA JODI JONW MDPI MEDS MENY MOMO NWAR OCMM ONEL
"OPAS" ORLE PBEK PLPL SAMP SCII SCOI SDCT STGR STNS TBGL
TELY TGRA TMUR TYCN UKAW USTC USTH USTS VIPH WELY WNAA
WOFM WRBI ZIZZ
AW139
G-CGIJ CGWB CHCP CHCT CHCV SARD

AHERNE
BARRACUDA
G-BZSV

AIR AND SPACE MANUFACTURING INC
AIR AND SPACE 18A GYROPLANE
G-BVWK BVWL

AIR COMMAND MANUFACTURING INC
503 (COMMANDER)
G-BOAS BOIK BPAO BRSP KENB
532 ELITE
G-BOGV BOKF BOOJ BPPU BPUE BPUG BRGO BRKX BRLB BSND

BSXP OGTS TFRB YROI
582 SPORT
G-BTCB URRR

AIR CRÉATION
503 FUN 18 GT
G-MYMM MYOL MYTZ MYUA MYVI MYXF
582, KISS
G-BZXP CBEB CBJL CBKE CBKS CBLX CBMX CBNY CBRZ CCEK CCFA
CCGM CCHJ CCHM CCPA CHKN COXY KIZZ PGHM SNOG TEDW TFLY
TRYK
IXESS (TANARG) 912
G-CDRJ CEBH CEBY CEDT CEIV DJST ELSI FWKS IMUP IXES NARG
OOLL SYUT TANA TARG TEAS TNRG WYKD

AIR ET ADVENTURE
SATURNE S11OK
G-NORB

AIR NAVIGATION AND ENGINEERING CO
ANEC II
G-EBJO
ANEC IV MISSEL THRUSH
G-FBPI

AIRBORNE WINDSPORTS PTY LTD
XT912
G-CDGE CDRD CEHH CEHZ EDLY LVPL XTEE XTHT XTNI XTNR

AIRBUS SAS including AIRBUS INDUSTRIE
A300
G-MAJS MONR MONS OJMR
A319
G-DBCA DBCB DBCC DBCD DBCE DBCF DBCG DBCH DBCI DBCJ
DBCK EJAR EJJB EUOA EUOB EUOC EUOD EUOE EUOF EUOG EUOH
EUOI EUPA EUPB EUPC EUPB EUPD EUPE EUPF EUPG EUPH
EUPJ EUPK EUPL EUPM EUPN EUPO EUPP EUPR EUPS EUPT EUPU
EUPV EUPW EUPX EUPY EUPZ EZAA EZAB EZAC EZAD EZAE EZAF
EZAG EZAH EZAI EZAJ EZAK EZAL EZAM EZAN EZAO EZAP EZAS
EZAT EZAU EZAV EZAW EZAX EZAY EZAZ EZBA EZBB EZBC EZBD
EZBE EZBF ZEZG EZBH EZBI EZBJ EZBK EZBL EZBM EZBN EZBO
EZBP EZBR EZBT EZBU EZBV EZBW EZBX EZBY EZBZ EZDA EZDB
EZDC EZDD EZDE EZDF EZDH EZDI EZDJ EZEA EZEB EZEC EZED
EZEF EZEG EZEJ EZEK EZEO EZEP EZET EZEU EZEV EZEW EZEZ
EZIA EZIC EZID EZIE EZIG EZIH EZII EZIJ EZIK EZIL EZIM EZIN EZIO
EZIP EZIR EZIS EZIT EZIU EZIV EZIW EZIX EZIY EZIZ EZMH EZMS
EZNC EZNM EZPG EZSM NMAK
A320
G-BUSD BUSG BUSH BUSI BUSJ BUSK BYTH CRPH EUKA EUKB EUKC
EUKD EUKE EUKF EUKG EUKH EUKI EUKJ EUKK EUKL EUUA EUUB
EUUC EUUD EUUE EUUF EUUG EUUH EUUI EUUJ EUUK EUUL EUUM
EUUN EUUO EUUP EUUR EUUS EUUT EUUU EUUV EUUW EUUX EUUY
EUUZ EUYA EUYB EUYC EUYD EUYE EUYF EUYG EUYH EUYI EUYJ
EUYK EUYL FTDF DHJZ MEDE MEDH MEDK MEDL MIDO MIDP MIDR
MIDS MIDT MIDU MIDV MIDX MIDY MIDZ MONX MPCD MRCK OOAR
OOAU OOAW OOPU OOPW OOPX OZBB OZBK TTOB TTOC TTOD
TTOE TTOF TTOG TTOH TTOI TTOJ TTOK VCED
A321
G-DHJH EUXC EUXD EUXE EUXF EUXG EUXH EUXI EUXJ EUXK EUXL
EUXM MEDF MEDG MEDJ MEDL MEDM MIDC MIDJ MIDL MIDO MARA
NIKO OJEG OMYJ OOAE OOAV OOPE OOPH OOPH OZBE OZBF OZBG
OZBH OZBI OZBL OZBN OZBO OZBP OZBR OZBS SMTJ TTIA TTIC TTID
TTIE TTIF TTIG TTIH TTII
A330
G-EOMA MDBD MLJL OJMB OJMC OMYT SMAN TCXA WWBB WWBC
WWBD WWBM
A340
G-VAIR VATL VBLU VBUG VBUS VEIL VELD VFAR VFIT VFIZ VFOX
VFUN VGAS VGOA VHOL VMEG VNAP VOGE VRED VSEA VSHY VSSH
VSUN VWEB VWIN VWKD VYOU

AIRCRAFT DESIGNS LTD
SHERIFF SA-1
G-FRJB

AIRCRAFT MANUFACTURING CO (AIRCO)
DH.2 replica
G-BFVH
DH.6
G-EAML
DH.9
G-EAQM CDLI

AIRSHIP INDUSTRIES (UK) LTD including AEROSPACE DEVELOPMENTS
Airship (Hot Air)
AD 500
　G-BECE
Airship (Gas Filled)
SKYSHIP 500
　G-BIHN

AIRSPEED LTD
AS.40 OXFORD
　G-AHTW AITB AITF
AS.57 AMBASSADOR
　G-ALZO
AS.65 CONSUL
　G-AIKR AJLR

AIRTOUR BALLOON CO LTD
Balloon (Hot Air)
31 series
　G-BKVY BLVA
56 series
　"G-OAFC" G-BKVW BKVX BLVB BSGH BWPL
77 series
　G-BLYT BOBH IVAC

ALLPORT
Balloon (Minimum Lift)
HOT AIR FREE
　G-BJIA BJSS

ALON INC see ERCOUPE

SOCIÉTÉ **ALPAVIA** see FOURNIER

ALPI AVIATION SRL
PIONEER 200
　G-CDSB CEVJ CEWL
PIONEER 300 (HAWK)
　G-CDPA CDSD CDYY CDZA CEAR CEEG CEIX CEMY CEPW CETX
　DEBT EKIM EWES FAJC GBOB HORK IPKA ITBT KITH LEAH LLOY LXUS
　OLAA OPFA PCCC PION RABS SRAW TREX XCIT VIXX VOLO YVES
　ZZZG

AMERICAN AEROLIGHTS INC
EAGLE
　G-MBCU MBEP MBFS MBHE MBIO MBJD MBJK MBKY MBRD MBRS
　MBWE MBZV MJAE MJBL MJBV MJEO MJNM MJNO MMTV

AMERICAN AIRCRAFT
FALCON
　G-BUYF

AMERICAN AVIATION CORPORATION see GRUMMAN-AMERICAN

AMERICAN BLIMP CORPORATION
Airship (Gas-Filled)
A-60+
　G-TLEL

AMERICAN CHAMPION AIRCRAFT CORPORATION
7ECA CITABRIA AURORA
　G-CDGJ EGWN WEBS
7GCBC EXPLORER
　G-EXPL GCBC
8KCAB SUPER DECATHLON
　G-CEOE CEUY DDGJ EEEZ IGLZ IZZZ ZZAP

AMERICAN MOTH CORPORATION see DE HAVILLAND

AMF MICROFLIGHT LTD including AMF AVIATION ENTERPRISES LTD
CHEVVRON (Konig SD570)
　G-MNFL MTFG MVGC MVGD MVGE MVIP MVOO MVUO MVVV MVXX
　MVZZ MWHS MWNO MWPW MWRZ MWUI MWZB MYGN MYYP MZCK
　MZDP MZFH MZMK

ANDERSON
EA-1 KINGFISHER AMPHIBIAN
　G-BUTE BXBC

ANDREASSON including CROSBY
BA.4B
　G-AWPZ AYFV BEBS BFXF JEDS YPSY

ANONIMA POIAZIONARA VERCELLESE IND. AERONAUTICHE
AVIA FL.3
　G-AGFT

ARBITER SERVICES
Trike with Aerial Arts 130SX wing
　G-MNWL

ARKLE see MITCHELL

ARMSTRONG-WHITWORTH AIRCRAFT see GLOSTER and HAWKER
AW.650 ARGOSY
　G-AOZZ APRL ASXM ASXN BEOZ

ARROW AIRCRAFT (LEEDS) LTD
ACTIVE
　G-ABVE

ARROW AIRCRAFT AND MOTORS CORPORATION
ARROW SPORT A2-60
　G-AARO

ARROWFLIGHT LTD see CGS

ARV AVIATION LTD
ARV-1 variants (Hewland AE75)
　G-BMOK BMWF BMWM BNGV BNGW BNGY BNHB BOGK BPMX BSRK
　BWBZ DEXP ERMO OARV ORIX OTAL POOL STWO XARV YARV ZARV

AUSTER AIRCRAFT LTD including BEAGLE-AUSTER AIRCRAFT LTD and
BEAGLE AIRCRAFT LTD production
PLUS C.2
　G-AFTN
PLUS D
　G-AHCR AHGW AHGZ AHKO AHSD AHUG AHWJ AHXE AIXA
Model E AUSTER III
　G-AHLK AREI BUDL
Model G AUSTER, 4
　G-A JXV AJXY ANHS ANHU
Model H AUSTER 5 and AUSTER 5D ALPHA 5 vairants
　G-AGLK AIKE AIPE AJGJ AJXC AKOW AKSY AKSZ AKWS AKWT AKXP
　ALBJ ALBK ALFA ALNV ALXZ ALYB ALYG AMVD ANFU ANHM ANHR
　ANHW ANHX ANIE ANIJ ANIU ANRP AOCP AOCR AOCU AOFJ AOVW
　APAF APAH APBE APBW APRF APTU BDFX BICD BXKX
V J/1 AUTOCRAT and variants
　G-AFWN AGOH AGTO AGTT AGVG AGVN AGXS AGXV AGYK AHAM
　AHAP AHAT AHAU AHAY AHHE AHHK AHSP AIBM AIBX AIBY AIGD AIJI
　AIPW AIPW AIRC AIZU AIZW AIZY AJEB AJEC AJEE AJEM AJIH AJIT
　AJIU AJRB AJRE AJRHN AJUD AJUE AJYB AMTM APKM AXUJ BRKC
　BVGT CDPG JAYI
J/1N ALPHA
　G-AGXN AGXU AGYD AGYH AGYT AHAL AHAV AHCL AHCN AHHH
　AHHT AHSO AHSS AIBH AIBR AIBW AIFZ AIGF AIGT AJAE AJAJ AJAS
　AJEH AJEI AJIS AJIW AJUL AJYB APIK APJZ APKN APTR ARRL ARUY
　BLPG TENT
V J/1B AIGLET
　G-AMKU ANGV ARBM
J/1U WORKMASTER
　G-APMH APSR OJAS
V J/2 ARROW
　G-AJAM AWLX BEAH
V J/4 ARCHER
　G-AIJK AIJM AIJS AIJT AIPR
J/5B, J/5G, J/5P, and J/5V AUTOCAR vairants
　G-AOHZ AOIY APUW ARKG ARLY ARNB ARUG ASFK AXMN
J/5F, J/5K and J/5/L AIGLET TRAINER variants
　G-AMMS AMRF AMTA AMTD AMUI AMYD AMZI AMZT AMZU ANNW
　ANWX AOFS APLG APVG BGKZ
J/5Q and J/5R ALPINE vriants
　G-ANXC AOGV AOZL APCB
6A, AOP.6 and TUGMASTER variants
　G-ARGB ARGI ARHM ARIH ARRX ARXU ARYD ASEF ASIP ASOC ASTI
　BKXP BNGE
AOP.9, AOP.11 and BEAGLE E.3 variants
　G-ASCC AVHT AVXY AXRR AXWA AYUA AZBU BDFH BGKT BGTC BJXR
　BKVK BURR BWKK BXON CEHR
B.4
　G-AMKL
B.8 AGRICOLA
　G-CBOA

AUSTIN
WHIPPET replica
 "K.158"

AUTOMOBILOVE ZAVODY MRAZ
M.1 SOKOL
 G-AIXN

AVENGER
Balloon (Minimum Lift)
T.200-2112
 G-BHMJ BHMK BHMM BIGM BIGR BIPW BIRL

AVIAMILANO SRL including AEROMERE, LAVERDA and SEQUOIA production
F.8L FALCO
 G-BVDP BWYO BYLL CCOR CWAG CYLL FALC FALO GANE LMAX
 OCAD OGKB ORJW PDGG REEC RJAM
F.14 NIBBIO
 G-OWYN

AVIASUD ENGINEERING SA
MISTRAL
 G-MGAG MVSJ MVUP MVWW MVWZ MVXN MVXV MVZR MWIB MYSL
 MZJB

AVIAT AIRCRAFT INC see CHRISTEN

AVIATION COMPOSITES CO LTD see EUROPA AVIATION

AVIATION ENTERPRISES LTD
MAGNUM
 G-CDBC

AVID AIRCRAFT INC
*AVID FLYER (Rotax 582) including AEROBAT, HAULER and SPEEDWING
variants*
 G-BSPW BTGL BTHU BTKG BTMS BTRC BUFV BUIR BUJJ BUJV BULC
 BULY BUON BUZE BUZM-BVBR BVBV BVFO BVHT BVIV BVLW BVSN
 BVYX BWRC BXNA CURV EFRY ELKS IJAC IMPY LAPN LORT NANO
 OVID OZEE PILL RAFV SPAM

AVRO AIRCRAFT LTD see ENGLISH ELECTRIC and HAWKER
CF-100 CANUCK
 G-BCYK

A V ROE and CO LTD including BAe and HAWKER SIDDELEY AVIATION design
and production
AVRO ROE 1 replica
 G-ROEI
TRIPLANE replica
 G-ARSG
504K, 504L and replicas
 G-EASD EBJE EBNU
 "G-AACA" G-ABAA ADEV ATXL BYKV

534 BABY
 G-EACQ
581, 594 and 616 AVIAN
 G-EBOV EBZM
 G-AAHD ABLF ABLK ACGT EUJG
620 - see CIERVA
621 TUTOR
 G-AHSA
652A ANSON and AVRO NINETEEN
 G-AGPG AHKX AMDA APHV AVVO AVVR AWRS AWSA AYWA VROE
671 - see CIERVA
683 LANCASTER
 G-ASXX BCOH BVBP LANC
685 YORK
 G-AGNV ANTK
694 LINCOLN
 G-APRJ
698 VULCAN
 G-BLMC VJET VLCN VULC
748
 G-ATMI ATMJ AVXI AYIM BEJD BGMO BIUV BORM BPNJ BURJ BVOU
 BVOV OPFW ORAL OSOE OTBA SOEI

AVTECH PTY LTD including JABIRU AIRCRAFT COMPANY PTY LTD
JABIRU SK, SPL and UL variants (Jabiru 2200A)
 G-BXAO BXSI BYBM BYBZ BYCZ BYFC BYIA BYIM BYJD BYNR BYNS
 BYSF BYTK BYTV BYYL BYYT BYZS BZAP BZDZ BZEN BZFI BZGT

 BZHR BZIV BZLV BZMC BZST BZSZ BZTY BZUL BZWK BZXN BZYK
 CBFZ CBGR CBIF CBJM CBJY CBKY CBOP CBPP CBPR CBSU CBZM
 CCAE CCBY CCEL CCMC CCRX CCVN CDFK CDNY CDZX CECE CECG
 CEKM CNAB CEOM COVE CSDJ DANY DJAY DMAC DRCI DWMS ENRE
 EPIC EPOC EUAN EWBC GPAS HINZ IKEV IPAT IZOD JAAB JABB JABE
 JABS JABY JABZ JACO JAJP JAXS JBSP JPMA JSPL JUDD KKER LEEE
 LOIS LUMA LYPG MGCA MIRA NIGC OCDW ODGS OGSA OJAB OMHP
 OPUS OZZI PBUS PHYS PRLY RODG ROYC RUFS RYAL SIMP SUTD
 SVDG THOT TJAL TUBB TYKE UJAB UJGK UKOZ UNNA VILA VJAB
JABIRU J400 and J430 variants (Jabiru 3300A)
 G-CCGG CCID CCPV CCYA CDCP CDBD CDJL CDLS CDSI CDTL CDUT
 CDXJ CEFP CEKW CEPM ESGJ GPSF JABI JABJ JABU JJAB KEVI KIDD
 LUBY MLAL MUTZ NJSP NMBG OZIE PUKA RCST RDCO SAZY SIZZ

BAC (1935) **LTD** including KRONFELD LTD
DRONE
 G-ADPJ AEDB AEKV

BAE SYSTEMS (OPERATIONS) LTD including BRITISH AEROSPACE plc,
BRITISH AEROSPACE (REGIONAL AIRCRAFT) Ltd, HANDLEY-PAGE and SCOTTISH AVIATION
production
HARRIER
 G-CBCU CBGK
JETSTREAM variants to Series 32
 G-BBBV BBYM BLKP BTXG BUVC BUVD BWWW CBEP CCPW EIGG
 ISLB ISLC ISLD IJYS JSSD JURA JXTA JXTC LOVB NFLA OJSA PLAJ
 RAVL UIST
JETSTREAM Series 41 variants
 G-CDYI GCJL JMAC MAJA MAJB MAJC MAJD MAJE MAJF MAJG MAJH
 MAJI MAJJ MAJK MAJL MAJM MAJN MAJP MAJT MAJU MAJV MAJW
 MAJX MAJY MAJZ
ATP and JETSTREAM Series 61
 G-BTPA BTPC BTPE BTPF BTPG BTPH BTPJ BTPL BTPN BTTO BTZG
 BTZH BTZK BUKJ BUUP BUUR BUWM JEMA JEMC JEMD JEME MANH
 MANL MANP OAAF PLXI
146 including Avro variants
 G-BLRA BPNT BXAR BXAS BZAT BZAU BZAV BZAW BZAX BZAY BZAZ
 CBAE CCJC CCJP CDCN CDRK CDXH CDZP CEBN CEBU CEFW CEIC
 CEIH CEVF CFAA CLHD DEFM FLTA FLTB FLTC GNTZ IRJX JEAJ JEAM
 JEAO JEAS JEAT JEAX JEAY JEBA JEBB JEBD JEBE JEBF JEBG LCYB
 LUXE MANS MIMA OFMC OFOA OFOM OINV ORJX OZRH TBAE TBIC
 ZAPK ZAPN ZAPO ZAPR

BAILEY AVIATION
QUATTRO 175 (DUDEK reACTION SPORT Wing)
 G-CEOT CEVT

BALONY-KUBICEK Spol SrO
Balloon (Hot Air)
BB20
 G-CCWT CEBL DNGA
BB22 variants
 G-CDRZ CERM
BB26
 G-CEBG CRBV DBSR
BB30
 G-NIMA
BB37
 G-CDWA

THE **BALLOON WORKS**
Balloon (Hot Air)
FIREFLY 7
 G-CBPG

BARKER
CHARADE
 G-CBUN

BARNETT ROTORCRAFT
BARNETT J4B-2
 G-BRVR BRVS BWCW

BARON
Balloon (Minimum Lift)
TIGER T.200
 G-BIMK

BEAGLE AIRCRAFT LTD
A.109 AIREDALE
 G-ARNP AROJ ARRO ARXB ARXC ARXD ARYZ ARZS ASAI ASBH ASBY
 ASCB ASRK ASWF ATCC AVKP AWGA

B.121 PUP
G-AVDF AVLM AVLN AVZN AVZP AWKM AWKO AWVC AWWE AWYJ AWYO AXCX AXDU AXDV AXDW AXEV AXHO AXIA AXIE AXIF AXJH AXJI AXJJ AXJO AXMW AXMX AXNN AXNP AXNR AXNS AXOJ AXOZ AXPA AXPB AXPC AXPM AXPN AXSC AXSD AXUA AZCK AZCL AZCM AZCN AZCP AZCT AZCU AZCV AZCZ AZDA AZDG AZEV AZEW AZEY AZFA AZGF AZSW BAKW BASP BDCO IPUP JIMB OPUP PUPP TSKY

B.206
G-ARRM ASOF ASWJ ATDD AVLK BSET FLYP HRHI

BEAGLE-AUSTER AIRCRAFT LTD

A.61 TERRIER
G-ARLP ARLR ARNO ARSL ARTM ARUI ASAJ ASAK ASAX ASCD ASCF ASDK ASMZ ASOI ASOM ASRL ASUI ASYG ASZE ASZX ATBU ATDN ATHU AVYK AYDW AYDX TIMG

D.4
G-ARLG

D.5 HUSKY
G-ASNC ATCD ATMH AVSR AWSW AXBF

D.6
G-ARCS ARDJ

BEDE see BROOKMOOR BEDE AIRCRAFT

BEECH AIRCRAFT CORPORATION includng RAYTHEON AIRCRAFT
COMPANY production

17 TRAVELER
G-BRVE LAJT

18/3NM, 3TM and C-45
G-ASUG BKGL BKGM BKRG BKRN BSZC

19A MUSKETEER SPORT III,
G-AWFZ AWTS AWTV

A23 MUSKETEER II
G-ATBI

A23-24 MUSKETEER SUPER III
G-TAMS

B24R SIERRA 200
G-BBSC

C23 SUNDOWNER 180
G-AYYU BAHO BARH BASN BBSB BBTY BUXN GUCK

C24R MUSKETEER SUPER R
G-BYDG BZPG CBCY

F33, F33A and F33C BONANZA
G-BGSW BTHW BTZA COLA GRYZ HOPE HOSS JUST MOAC OAHC VICM

35, G35, H35, N35, P35 S35 and V35B BONANZA
G-APTY ARKJ ARZN ASJL ATSR BBTS BONZ EHMJ NEWT REST VTAL

A36 BONANZA
G-BMYD BSEY CDJV EISG FOZZ JLHS LOLA MAPR POPA ZLOJ

95-A55A and 95-B55A BARON
G-ASOH BFLZ BLJM BNBY BXDF BZIT FABM MDJN RICK SWEE UROP WOOD

55 BARON variants
G-AWAJ FLAK MOSS

58 BARON variants
G-BLKY BMLM BNUN BTFT BXPM BYDY CIZZ CCVP DAFY FLTZ IOCO OSDI VCML WWIZ

60 DUKE
G-IASL

65 QUEENAIR variants
G-AVDS AWKX

76 DUCHESS
G-BGHP BGRG BGVH BIMZ BNTT BNUO BNYO BODX BOFC BRPU BXHD BXWA BXXT BYNY BZNN BZOY BZPJ BZRT CBBF GBSL GCCL GDMW JLRW MULT OADY OBLC OPAT TRAN WACI WACJ

90 KING AIR variants
G-BMKD OJRO ORTH RACI

95 TRAVELAIR variants
G-ASMF ASYJ

200 and 300 SUPER KING AIR variants
G-BGRE BPPM BVMA BYCP BZNE CDFY CDZT CEGP CEGR CGAW CLOW FPLB FPLD FPLE FRYI FSEU GBMR IMEA JENC JIMG JOAL KLYN KVIP MAMD MEGN MOUN NICY OCEG OMGI ONAL ORJA OTCS PCOP PFFN POWB RAFO RAFP SASC SASD SAXN SERC SGEC SPOR SYGA TAGH WATJ WCCP WVIP

BELL
Balloon (Minimum Lift)

FD 31T
G-BITY

BELL AIRCRAFT CORPORATION
P-39Q AIRACOBRA
G-CEJU

BELL HELICOPTER TEXTRON INC including AGUSTA BELL HELICOPTER CO,
BELL HELICOPTER TEXTRON CANADA, IPTN (412) and WESTLAND HELICOPTERS LTD
production

*47D and 47G **(WESTLAND)***
G-ARXH ASOL AXKO AXKS AXKX AXKY BAXS BBRI BBZL BFEF BFYI BHAR BHBE BHNV BPAI CHOP CIGY GGTT LHCI MASH XTUN

*47H and 47J **(AGUSTA-BELL)***
G-ASLR AZYB BFPP

206A and 206B JETRANGER variants
G-AVII AVSZ BARP BBCA BBNG BBOR BEWY BKEW BKZI BLGV BLZN BNYD BOLO BPWI BSBW BTFX BTHY BUZZ BVGA BXAY BXKL BXNS BXNT BXRY BXUF BYBA BYBC BYBI BYSE BZEE BZNI CBYX CCBL CCVO CDGV CDYS CHGL CLAY COIN CORN CPTS CRDY CRLH CVIP DNCN DOFY ELLI ENES EWAW FEZZ FOXM GAND GEZZ GSJH GUST HANY HEBE HELE HMPH HMPT HMSS HOLZ HPAD HSDW IBIG ISPH IVAS JAES JBDB JBHH JETX JLEE JWBI KETH LBDC LILY LSPA MFMF MILI MOTA NEWZ OAMG OAMI OBAM OBYT OCFD OCST OETI OFCH OFST OJPS OMDR ONOW ONTV ONYX OPEN OSMD OYST PEAK PERZ PORT PSHR RAMI RAMY RKEL RNBW SDCI SELY SHMS SKII SPEY STER SUEZ TAMF TBAH TCMM TEGS TGRZ TILI TOYZ TREE TTMB WBHH WIIZ WIZZ WLLY XBCI XBOX XXIV ZAPH

206L LONG RANGER
G-CBXD CDYR CSWL CYRS ELIT EYRE FANY GANG JGBI LEEZ LILA LIMO LONE MAAX ODCC OGCE OHHI OLDN PWIT RCOM SUEY

212
G-BALZ BFER BIXV

222
G-NOIR VOND

407
G-CEOA MAYE OZAC

412
G-CCYX CDAF OIBU

UH-1H IROQUOIS
G-HUEY UHIH

BELLANCA AIRCRAFT CORPORATION including AERONCA, CHAMPION
and AMERICAN CHAMPION production

7ECA CITABRIA
G-BLHS BOID BOTO BPMM BSLW IDD

7GCAA CITABRIA
G-BFHP BUGE JOIE ZOSA

7GCBC CITABRIA
G-BBEN BBXY BDBH BGGA BGGB BGGC BIZW BKBP BRJW BVLT CONR HUNI

7KCAB CITABRIA
G-AYXU BOLG

8GCBC SCOUT
G-BCSM BGGD

8KCAB DECATHLON
G-BTXX

17-30A SUPER VIKING
G-VIKE

BENSEN AIRCRAFT CORPORATION including CAMPBELL-BENSEN and
MONTGOMERIE-BENSEN production

B.7 GYROPLANE variants
G-APSY APUD ARBF ASCT ASLP ASNY

B.8 GYROPLANE variants
G-ARTJ ASME ASWN ATLP ATOZ ATWT AWDW AWPY AXBG AZAZ BCGB BGIO BHEM BHFE BIFN BIGP BIGU BIHX BIPY BIVK BIVL BJAO BKBS BLLA BLLB BMBW BMOT BMYF BMZW BNJL BOUV BOWZ BOZW BPCV BPNN BPOO BPSK BPTV BRBS BRCF BREA BREU BRHL BRXN BSBX BSJB BSMG BSMX BSNL BSNY BSZM BTBL BTFW BTIG BTJN BTJS BTTD BUJK BUPF BVAZ BVIF BVJF BVMG BVPX BWAH BWEY BWJN BWSZ BXCL BYTS BZID BZIP BZOF CBFW CBNX CBSV CCXS CDBE CDMK CDVJ FGSI IPFM OOJC OTIM SCUD YJET YROS YROY

BENSEN-PARSONS see PARSONS

BEST OFF
SKY RANGER (SWIFT) variants
G-CBIV CBVR CBVS CBWW CBXS CCAF CCBA CCBG CCBJ CCCK CCCM CCCR CCCY CCDG CCDH CCDW CCDY CCEH CCIK CCIO CCIY CCJA CCJT CCJW CCKF CCKG CCLF CCLU CCMX CCMZ CCNJ CCNR CCNS CCNU CCPF CCPL CCRR CCRV CCSX CCTR CCUD CCUF CCVR CCWC CCWU CCXH CCXL CCXM CCXN CCYM CDAY CDBA CDBO CDBV CDCH CDDR CDDU CDFJ CDFP CDHA CDHE CDIJ CDIP CDIU CDJC CDJP CDKH CDKI CDKX CDLG CDLK CDMP CDMV CDNE CDOV CDPE CDPV CDTP CDUL CDUS CDVA CDWB CDWM CDYJ CECP CEDI CEDZ CEHD CEKK CENG CENS CERB CESD CETO CETU CETV CEUJ CEXM CEZE CFBL CFBS CFBY CFCD CFCK CFWR CRAB CUBE CZMI DOIN ERTE EVAJ FLDG FONZ FRNK GLHI HABI HIYA HULK INCE

ISEL JAYS JEZZ JPWM KULA LASN LDAH LUMB MARO MLZZ MOPS
NOTS NUFC OBAZ OKIM OMSS OSKR OTCV OVOL PAWS POLL PSKY
PTAR RAFR REVO RHAM RSKY SKPG SKRA SKRG SKSW SOPH SPMM
TEDI TFOG TMCB TYGR UACA UMMY UPHI UPTA VVVV WAZP WEEK
WLSN XLAM XYJY ZADA ZSKY

BETTS
TB.1
  G-BVUG

BIERINX and DUGOURD
POU du CIEL BI-FLY
  G-POUX

BILSAM ENTERPRISES POLSKA SP ZOO
SKY CRUISER
  G-CECR

BINDER AVIATIK GmbH see PIEL

BIRDMAN ENTERPRISES LTD
WT-11 CHINOOK
  G-MMKE

BLACKBURN AEROPLANE AND MOTOR CO LTD
LINCOCK fsm
  "G-EBVO"
MONOPLANE
  G-AANI
B.2
  G-AEBJ

BLACKBURN AND GENERAL AIRCRAFT LTD
BEVERLEY
  G-AOAI
BLAKE
BLUETIT
  G-BXIY

BLERIOT CIE
XI
  G-AANG AVXV BLXI BPVE LOTI

BOEING AIRCRAFT CO including BOEING COMPANY
B-17G FORTRESS
  G-BEDF FORT
B-29 SUPERFORTRESS
  G-BHDK
707-300 series
  G-AYAG
707-400 series
  G-APFG APFJ
737-200 series
  G-BYYK CEAE CEAF CEAG CEAH FIGP GPFI
737-300 series
  G-BYZJ CELA CELB CELC CELD CELE CELF CELG CELH CELI CELJ
  CELK CELO CELP CELR CELS CELU CELV CELW CELX CELY CELZ
  EZYR GSPN LGTE LGTF LGTG LGTH LGTI OBMP ODSK OFRA OGBD
  OGBE OTDA POWC STRA STRI STRJ THOE THOF THOG THOH THOI
  THOJ THOK THOL THON THOO THOP TOYA TOYB TOYC TOYD TOYE
  TOYF TOYG TOYH TOYI TOYJ TOYK ZAPV ZAPW ZAPZ
737-400 series
  G-DOCA DOCB DOCE DOCF DOCG DOCH DOCL DOCN DOCO DOCS
  DOCT DOCU DOCV DOCW DOCX DOCY DOCZ GBTA GBTB
737-500 series
  G-BVKB BVKD BVZE BVZG BVZI GFFA GFFB GFFD GFFE GFFF GFFG
  GFFH GFFI GFFJ THOC THOD
737-600 series
  G-CDKD CDKT CDRA CDRB
737-700 series
  G-EZJA EZJB EZJC EZJF EZJG EZJH EZJI EZJJ EZJK EZJL EZJM EZJN EZJO
  EZJP EZJS EZJT EZJU EZJV EZJW EZJX EZJY EZJZ EZKA EZKB EZKC EZKD
  EZKE EZKF EZKG MSJF SEFC STRF STRH
737-800 series
  G-CDEG CDZH CDZI CDZL CDZM CEJO CEJP DLCH FDZA FDZB FDZD
  FDZE FDZF FDZG FDZJ FDZO FZDP OXLC SAAW THOK XLAA XLAB
  XLAD XLAH XLAI XLAJ XLAK XLAM XLAN XLAO
747-200 series
  G-BDXG BDXH BDXJ MKAA MKBA MKCA MKDA MKEA MKFA MKGA
  MKHA VBEE

747-400 series
  G-BNLA BNLB BNLC BNLD BNLE BNLF BNLG BNLH BNLI BNLJ BNLK
  BNLL BNLM BNLN BNLO BNLP BNLR BNLS BNLT BNLU BNLV BNLW
  BNLX BNLY BNLZ BYGA BYGB BYGC BYGD BYGE BYGF BYGG CIVA
  CIVB CIVC CIVD CIVE CIVF CIVG CIVH CIVI CIVJ CIVK CIVL CIVM CIVN
  CIVO CIVP CIVS CIVT CIVU CIVV CIVW CIVX CIVY CIVZ GSSA
  GSSB GSSC VAST VBIG VFAB VGAL VHOT VLIP VROC VROM VROS
  VROY VTOP VWOW VXLG
757-200 series
  G-BIKC BIKF BIKG BIKI BIKJ BIKK BIKM BIKN BIKO BIKP BIKS BIKU BIKV
  BIKZ BMRA BMRB BMRC BMRD BMRE BMRF BMRH BMRJ BPEC BPED
  BPEE BPEI BPEJ BPEK BYAD BYAE BYAF BYAH BYAI BYAJ BYAK BYAL
  BYAO BYAP BYAR BYAS BYAT BYAU BYAW BYAX BYAY CEJM CPEL
  CPEM CPEN CPEO CPEP CPER CPES CPET DAJB FCLA FCLB FCLC
  FCLD FCLE FCLF FCLG FCLH FCLI FCLJ FCLK FJEB JMCE JMCF JMCG
  LSAA LSAB LSAC LSAD LSAE LSAF LSAG LSAH LSAI MONB MONC
  MOND MONE MONJ MONK OJIB OOBA OOBC OOBD OOBE OOBF OOBI
  OOBJ OOOK OOOX OOPK OPJB STRX STRY STRZ TCBA ZAPU ZAPX
757-300 series
  G-JMAA JMAB
767-200 series
  G-BOPB BYAA BYAB CECU CEMK SJET SILC SLVR
767-300 series
  G-BNWA BNWB BNWC BNWD BNWH BNWI BNWM BNWN BNWO BNWR
  BNWS BNWT BNWU BNWV BNWW BNWX BNWY BNWZ BZHA BZHB
  BZHC CDPT CEFG CEOD CZNA DAJC DBLA DIMB OOBM OBYB OBYD
  OBYE OBYF OBYG OBYH OBYI OBYJ OOAN OOBK OOBL OOPN PJLO
  TCCA UKZM VKNG VKNI
777-200 series
  G-RAES VIIA VIIB VIIC VIID VIIE VIIF VIIG VIIH VIIJ VIIK VIIL VIIM VIIN
  VIIO VIIP VIIR VIIS VIIT VIIU VIIV VIIW VIIX VIIY YMMA YMMB YMMC
  YMMD YMME YMMF YMMG YMMH YMMI YMMJ YMMK YMML YMMM
  YMMN YMMO YMMP YMMR YMMS YMMT YMMU ZZZA ZZZB ZZZC

BOEING AIRPLANE CO
STEARMAN 75 KAYDET, N2S, PT-13, PT-17
  G-AROY AWLO AZLE BAVN BAVO BHUW BIXN BNIW BRHB BRSK BRTK
  BRUJ BSDS BSGR BSWC BTFG CCXA CCXB IIIG ILLE ISDN NZSS RJAH
  THEA

BOLAND
Balloon (Hot Air)
52-12
  G-BYMW

BÖLKOW
PHOEBUS B1- see WAGGON-U MASCHINENBAU AG

BÖLKOW APPARATEBAU GmbH including MALMO, MBB and WAGGON-U
MASCHINENBAU AG production
PHOEBUS variants
  G-CKLX DCJB
BÖ.207
  G-EFTE
BÖ 208 JUNIOR
  G-ASFR ASZD ATDO ATRI ATSI ATSX ATTR ATUI ATVX ATXZ AVKR
  AVLO AVZI BIJD BJEX BOKW BSME CLEM ECGO
BÖ 209 MONSUN
  G-AYPE AZBB AZDD AZOA AZOB AZRA AZTA AZVA AZVB EMHK

BOMBARDIER INC
CANADAIR CL-600 series CHALLENGER
  G-CHAI CJMB CMBL DGET EMLI FTSL HARK IMAC JMCW JMMD JMMP
  LGKO LVLV LWDC OCSC OCSD PRKR REYS STCC TAGA VVPA
CANADAIR REGIONAL JET series
  G-DUOD ELNX
BD-100 CHALLENGER 300
  G-KALS UYGB
BD-700 GLOBAL EXPRESS
  G-LXRS XXRS

BONSALL
DB-1 MUSTANG
  G-BDWM

BOULTON PAUL AIRCRAFT LTD
P.108 BALLIOL
  G-APCN

BOWERS
FLY BABY
  G-BFRD BNPV BUYU

BRADSHAW
Balloon (Hot Air)
HAB-76
  G-AXXP

BRANDLI
BX-2 CHERRY
  G-BXUX

BRANTLY HELICOPTER CORPORATION
B.2
  G-ASHD ASXD ATFG AVIP AWDU BPIJ OAPR OMAX ROTR
305
  G-ASXF

BREMNER see MITCHELL wing

BRIGHTON MA AND COMPANY LTD
Balloon (Hot Air)
Ax7-65
  G-AVTL AWJB

BRISTOL AEROPLANE CO LTD
BOXKITE
  G-ASPP
F.2B FIGHTER
  G-AANM AEPH
20 M.1C replica
  G-BLWM BPLT BWJM
30/46 BABE III replica
  "G-EASQ"
105 BULLDOG
  G-ABBB
149 BOLINGBROKE (BLENHEIM)
  G-BPIV
156 BEAUFIGHTER
  G-AJMC DINT
170 FREIGHTER
  G-AICH AIMI AINT
171 SYCAMORE
  G-ALSP ALSX AMWI HAPR
173
  G-ALBN
175 BRITANNIA
  G-ALRX ANCF AOVF AOVT BDUP
192 BELVEDERE
  G-BRMB

BRITISH AERIAL TRANSPORT COMPANY LTD
FK-23 BANTAM
  G-EACN

BRITISH AIRCRAFT CORPORATION (BAC) see HUNTING
ONE-ELEVEN
  "G-FIRE" G-ASJD ASYD AVMJ AVMO AVMT AVMU AWYV AZMF
CONCORDE
  G-AXDN BBDG BOAA BOAB BOAC BOAD BOAE BOAF BOAG SSST

BRITISH AIRCRAFT MANUFACTURING COMPANY LTD see
BRITISH KLEMM and KLEMM
EAGLE 2
  G-AFAX
SWALLOW 2
  G-ADPS AEVZ AFCL AFGC AFGD AFGE

BRITISH KLEMM AEROPLANE CO sse KLEMM
L.25 SWALLOW
  G-ACXE

BRITTEN-NORMAN LTD including BRITTEN-NORMAN (BEMBRIDGE) LTD,
FAIREY BRITTEN-NORMAN LTD,IRMA and PILATUS (BN-2) production
BN.1F
  G-ALZE
BN.2A, BN2B, BN2T ISLANDER, and DEFENDER
  G-AVCN AWID AWNT AXUB AXZK AYAZ AYRU AZBV BCEN BCWR
  BCZS BDJV BDPN BDPU BDZI BEDW BEED BEEG BEFI BELF BFNU
  BJEE BJEF BJEJ BJOP BJWO BLDV BLNH BLNJ BPCA BSPT BSWR
  BUBN BVHY CEIO CEIP CEIR CEUA CEUB CEUC CEUD CEUE CHES
  CHEZ CIAS CZNE GMPB HEBS IOWA JSAT LEAP MAFF OBNC OBNL
  ORED OSEA PASV SBUS SEIL SELX SICA SICB SJCH SSKY XAXA
BN.2A III TRISLANDER
  G-BBYO BDOT BDTN BDTO BEDP BEVR BEVT BEVV FTSE JOEY LCOC
  OJAV PCAM RBCI RHOP RLON XTOR

CONSTRUCTIONS AERONAUTIQUE MAURICE **BROCHET**
MB.50 PIPISTRELLE
  G-AVKB BADV

BROOKLANDS AERO LTD
MOSQUITO
  G-AWIF

BROOKLANDS AIRCRAFT CO see OPTICA

BROOKMOOR BEDE AIRCRAFT
BD-4
  G-BEKL BKZV BOPD BYLS
BD-5
  G-BGLB BJPI

BRÜGGER
MB.2 COLIBRI
  G-BKCI BKRH BNDP BNDT BPBP BRWV BUDW BUTY BVIS BVVN BXVS
  HRLM KARA PRAG

BÜCKER including CASA and DORNIER-WERKE AG production
Bü.131 JUNGMANN (CASA 1-131)
  G-BECT BECW BHPL BHSL BIRI BJAL BPDM BPTS BPVW BSAJ BSFB
  BSLH BTDT BTDZ BUCC BUCK BUOR BUVN BVPO BWHP BYIJ BZJV
  CCHY CDJU CDLC CDRU DUDS EHBJ EMJA JGMN JUNG JWJW RETA
  TAFF WIBS
Bü.133 JUNGMEISTER
  G-AEZX AXMT AYFO BUKK BUTX BVJP BVXJ BZTJ PTDP TAFI
Bü 181 BESTMANN
  G-AMYA CBKB GLSU

BUSBY
Balloon (Minimum Lift)
BUZ B20N
  G-FYGH

BUSHBY-LONG see LOEHLE
MIDGET MUSTANG
  G-AWIR BXHT CEKU IIMT MIDG

BYRNE
Balloon (Minimum Lift)
ODYSSEY 4000
  G-BCFE

CAB see MINICAB

CALL AIRCRAFT CO see IMCO

CAMBRIDGE HOT-AIR BALLOONING ASSOCIATION
Balloon (Hot Air)
CHABA 42
  G-BBGZ

CAMERON BALLOONS LTD see CAMERON-COLT and CAMERON-THUNDER
Airship (Gas-Filled)
DG-19
  G-BKIK
Zero 25
  G-BMUR
Airship (Hot Air)
D-38
  G-SMHK
DP-70
  G-BMEZ BNXG-BPFF BRDT
DP-80
  G-UPPY VIBA
D-96
  G-BAMK BEPZ
Balloon (Gas/Hot Air)
R-15
  G-CICI
R-36
  G-ROZY
R-42
  G-BLIO
R-77
  G-BUFA BUFC BUFE

Balloon (Hot Air)

20 variants
G-BIBS BJUV BOYO BRCJ BRCO

21 series
G-BTXM

24 series
G-BSCK BVCY

31 variants
G-BEJK BEUY BGHS BKIX BMST BPUB BRMT BVFB BZYR CBIH CBLN CCHP CDFI CEJT CESX CESY CEYD IHOP LEAU NOMO PRTT RBMV TOHS WETI

34 series
G-BRKL BUCB BVZX BYNW BZBT EROS EZER FZZI IAMP OBLU RAPP

42 variants
G-AZER BCDL BCEU BMWU BPHD BPXG BUPP BWEE BWGX BXJH BXTG BYRK CCAY CCJY CCSI HOPI SKOT

56 variants
G-AZKK BBYU BCOJ BCXZ BDPK BDSF BDUI BDUZ BDYH BECK BEEH BEND BENN BERT BEXX BEXZ BFAB BFFT BFKL BGOI BHGF BHSN BICU BKRS BKZF BMYA BNZN BOWM BRIR BRSA BTHZ BZKK CDJZ HOFM HOOV LENN ODAY OVET SWPR WAAC WYNT

60 series
G-BTZU BVDM BVDY BWRT BXJZ CBJS CBVD CENN CEOI IFIF ROGY

65 variants
G-AZIP AZUP AZUV AZXB BAOW BAYC BBGR BBYR BCAP BCFN BCRI BDRK BDSK BEIF BGJU BHKH BHNC BHND BHOT BIBO BIGL BISH BIWK BIWU BIYI BJAW BJWJ BJZA BKGR BKWR BLEP BLJF BLPK BLZB BMCD BMJN BMKY BMPD BMVW BMYJ BNAN BNAU BNAW BOAL BOOB BOWV BPGD BPPA BPXF BREH BRMI BROE BROG BSAS BSGP BTUH BWBA BWHG BXGY BXUU BZPD BYZL CEVH GLUE HENS KAFE MUIR NATX OERX PMAM PYRO RUDD SMIG WELS

70 variants
G-BXOT BYJX BZEK CCPP PIRO RAMA WJAC

77 variants
G-BAXF BBCK BBOC BBYL BCNP BCRE BCZO BDBI BDNZ BDSE BEPO BFUZ BFYK BGAY BGAZ BGHV BHDV BHHB BHHK BHHN BHII BHYO BIEF BIET BIRY BJGK BKNP BKPN BKTR BKWW BKZB BLFY BLIP BLJH BLLD BLPP BLSH BLYJ BLZS BMAD BMKJ BMKP BMKW BMLJ BMLW BMOH BMPP BMTN BMTX BMZB BNCB BNCH BNCJ BNDN BNDV BNEO BNFG BNFO BNGJ BNGN BNHI BNIN BNIU BNJG BNKT BNMA BNMG BNNC BNNE BNPE BNTW BNTZ BNUC BOAU BOBR BOEK BOFF BOGP BOGY BOJB BOJD BOJU BOOZ BORB BORN BOTW BOVV BOWB BOWL BOXG BOYS BOZN BPBV BPBY BPDF BPDG BPHH BPHJ BPLF BPLV BPPP BPSH BPSR BPTD BPVC BPVM BPWC BPYI BPYS BPYT BPYV BRBO BRFE BRFO BRIE BRKW BRLX BRMU BRMV BRNW BRRF BRRR BRSD BRTV BRUE BRUV BRZA BRZT BSBI BSBM BSBR BSDX BSEV BSHO BSHT BSIC BSIJ BSLI BSKD BSMS BSUV BSWV BSWY BSXM BTAG BTJH BTKZ BTOP BTPT BTRX BTWJ BTWM BTXW BTZV BUAF BUAM BUDU BUEV BUGD BUGP BUGS BUHM BUNG BUOX BUPI BUTJ BUWU BUZK BVBS BVBU BVDR BVFF BVHK BVMF BVUK BVXB BWAJ BWAN BWHC BWPC BWTJ BWYN BXAX BXSX BXTJ BXVT BYBN BYHY BYLY BYNJ BZBI BZPW CBHX CBKV CCAR CCHW CCPO CCSP CEJA CEJC CEPU CEPV CGOD CHUK CTGR CXHK DRYI EIIR ENNY EPDI ERIK FABB FELT FUZY GEES GEEZ GEUP GPPN GUNS HARE HENY IDDI JINI JLMW KEYY KODA KTEE LAZR LEGO LEXI LIBB LIOT LOAG LOAN LOLL LUBE MAMO MITTS MOFF MOKE MRTY NBSI NWPR OATV OCND OEDP OHSA OJEN OKYA OMRB ONZO ORPR PADI POLY PUSS RAPH RCMF RONI SAFE SAIX SCAH SCFO SLAC SNAP SNOW SUCH SUSI TECK TUDR ULIA UPUP VODA VOLT WAIT WBEV WELI XSKY ZINT ZUMP

80 series
G-BUYC BVEK BVEN BVGJ BVUU BVZN BWAO BWGP BXJP BXLG BXSC BXSJ BYER BYJJ BYTJ BZMV BZPK CBEY CCYN CDJY CEEB CELM CEMF CEMU EVET LIMP MCAP NMOS OARG OBTS OGJM ONIX RECE RMAX SLCE UPHL WIEZ

84 series
G-AYAJ AYJZ AYVA AZBH AZDF AZNT AZRN AZSP BAAX BAGY BAKO BALD BAND BAST BBLL BCEZ BNFP BNXR BOWU BOYM BREX BRGD BSKE BSKU BSMK BVXD BWLN MOSY STAV

90 variants
G-BMFU BMJZ BNII BOOP BOWK BPSO BPUJ BROY BRPJ BRZC BSCA BSNJ BSWX BTBP BTCM BTHF BTJU BTTB BTTL BTWV BTXF BUAJ BUFJ BUFX BUGY BUIE BUIU BUIZ BUOE BUUO BUVW BVBX BVDX BVFP BVHO BVHR BVKV BVMR BVOC BVOP BVPK BVTN BWAU BWBC BWDU BWIP BWJI BWNO BWNS BWPT BWUU BWVU BXAM BXJO BXVV BYDT BYHC BYIU BYJC BYKX BYMY BYNN BYOK BYOX BYTW BYZX BZEY BZFD BZIX BZJH BZKX BZOX BZRU BZTK BZUU BZXR BZYY CBAT CBED CBKI CBKJ CBLU CBRV CBUO CCBB CCBT CCJF CCMN CCNN CCPT CCUJ CCXF CDHS CDHY CDIO CDOB CDOI CDPC CDRF CECD CEES CEJZ CEOS CEPR CERH CESH CEUV COMP CONC CPSF CTEL CXCX DEKA DHLB DIAL DRYS EEFA ELLE FBMW FOGG FVEL GLAW GOCX GOGW HBUG IBEV IBLU IGEL IGLE INSR ITOI IWON JMJR JULU KAYI LAAC LAGR LTSB LULA MFLI MILE MOFZ MSON OJBM OJMS OKCC OMEN OXBY PATG PERC PINC

PRNT RISE RIXY RIZE RIZI SALE SBIZ SIAM SLII SORT SRVO STRM TANK TEDF TETI TINS TMCC TRIG VKUP VRVI WIFI YUMM YUPI YVET ZSKD

100 series
G-CEFS NPWR

105 variants
G-BAVU BMEE BMOV BNFN BOTD BOTK BPBW BPJE BRFR BRLL BSNZ BSRD BTEA BTFM BTIZ BTKW BTPB BTRL BUAV BUHU BULD BURX BUWF BVCA BVEU BVHV BVNR BVUA BVXA BWDH BWEW BWKF BWOW BWPZ BWRY BWSU BXBM BXBY BXEN BXGC BXOW BXXG BXXL BYFJ BYHU BYIL BYKI BYMX BYNX BYPD BZDJ BZDN BZKU BZVU BZXO CAMP CBEC CBHW CBMC CBNW CCFN CCGY CCIU CCOT CCVD CCYI CDIT CDMC CDWD CDYG CDZW CEDA CEDF CEEK CEGC CEHU CEIN CEJR CEKS CESC CITR CLIC DOOM DRGN ELEE ENRY FFAB FOWS FUSE GFAB HONK JOSH JSON KSKS LOSI METH MHBD NLYB NZGL OAFR OAML OFAA OJBS OSAT OUCH OUVI POPP SAXC SDLW SEDO SEPT SERV SFSL SSTI SUCK TORK TUTU ULTR VSGE WNGS XHOT YLYB

120 variants
G-BNEX BOHL BOZY BPSS BPTX BPZK BRXA BSYB BTEE BTKN BTOU BTUU BTXS BUFT BURN BVSO BVXF BWAG BWKD BWLD BWYS BXBR BXVJ BXWI BYSV CBFF CBMK CBOW CBVV CCEN CCTS CCVZ CCXE CDIK CDLB CDRI CEXN ENZO FLOA GHIA HOTT LOBO MEUP MOFB NERO OLUG OMFG TING VALZ VIKY XPDA

133 series
G-BWAA BZVE CBUW

140 series
G-AZUW BVYU BWTE DSPK FLTG OXBC

145 series
G-CETK DENT HIBM

160 series
G-CBHD

165 series
G-BIAZ

180 variants
G-BRZI BSWZ BSYD BTYE BUJR BUKC BVKL BXMM OBRY RWHC SKYR

200 series
G-BXOS BZJU CCJG

210 series
G-BUOC BVBN BWZK BXBA BXJC BXRM BYMG BYSM BZBE BZXF CCNV CVBF GURL JHNY JOJO ORGY RPBM SKYU SKYX

225 series
G-CCBV CCPZ CDRN

250 series
G-BUBR BUXR BVIG BWKU BWKX BWZJ BXPK BYHX BYYD BZIK CBFY CCGZ CDDV HIUP MOLI OBUN OVBF OVIC SKYY STPI XRLD

275 series
G-BWML BXBG BXIC BXMW BXTE BYSK BYZG BZTT CBYC CBZZ CCNC CCSG CCSJ CCZI CDDC CDIH CDRZ CFCC OOTW SKYK TCAS

300 series
G-BZNU CBAW SNIF

315 series
G-BZSU CCRH KNIX OBRA SIMI SKYJ

340 series
G-BZUO KVBF RVBF

350 series
G-CCOS CCSA CDDL CDIB CERC EVBF VBFG VBFH VBFI VBFJ VBFK

375 series
G-BBGN

400 series
G-ZVBF

425 series
G-CCGT

1600 series
G-VPSI

Special Shapes

SHAPE	REGISTRATION(S)
ACTION MAN PARACHUTIST	G-RIPS
APPLE	G-BWSO
BALL	G-RNIE
BEER BARREL	G-PINT
BEER CAN	G-IBET
BEER CRATE	G-FGSK
BEETHOVEN BUST	G-BNJU
BELLOWS	G-BIUL
BELLS WHISKY BOTTLE	G-BUUU
BENIHANA	G-BMVS
BERENTZEN BOTTLE	G-KORN
BERTIE BASSETT	G-BXAL BZTS
BIBENDUM	G-GRIP
BIERKRUG	G-BXFY
BOWLER	G-OPKF

BRADFORD AND BINGLEY	G-BWMY
BUDDY	G-WLVE
BUDWEISER CAN	G-BPFJ
BULB	G-BVWI
BULL	G-CBON
BUS	G-BUSS
CABIN	G-SHAK
CAN	G-BXPR CDMO OFIZ PURE
CARROTS	G-BWSP HUCH
CHAMPION SPARK PLUG	G-BETF
CHATEAU DE BALLEROY	G-BKBR BTCZ
CHESTIE	G-USMC
CHICK	G-BYEI
CLOWN	G-CLWN
CLUB	G-BWNP
COCA COLA BOTTLE	G-BXSB BYIV BYIW BYIX
COOLING TOWER	G-WATT
COTTAGE	G-COTT
DRAGON	G-GBGF
DUDE	G-OIFM
EAGLE	G-BVMJ
FABERGE EGG	G-BNFK
ELEPHANT	G-BLRW BMKX BPRC
EGG	G-OEGG
FIRE EXTINGUISHER	G-BZJA
FLAME	G-CBIU
FORKLIFT	G-BZVE
FORBES' MAGAZINE	G-BPOV
FURNESS BUILDING	G-BSIO
GOLFBALL	G-PUTT
GOLLY	G-OLLI
GRAND ILLUSION	G-MAGC
HARLEY	G-BMUN
HELIX OILCAN	G-HLIX
HOFMEISTER LAGER BEAR	G-HEYY
HOME SPECIAL	G-BWZP
ICE CREAM CONE	G-BZTL
IKEA	G-IKEA
JAGUAR XK8 SPORTS CAR	G-OXKB
KATALOG	G-OTTO
KP CHOC DIPS TUB	G-DIPI
LIGHTBULB	G-BVWI LAMP
LIPS	G-LIPS
LOCOMOTION	G-LOKO
MACAW	G-BRWZ
MINAR E PAKISTAN	G-BKNN
MONSTER	G-MSTR
MONSTER TRUCK	G-BWMU
MR PEANUT	G-NUTS
MUG	G-RMUG
N ELE	G-WBMG
OIL CAN	G-UNIP
ORANGE	G-CDXW
OTTI	G-OTTI
PERRIER BOTTLE	G-PERR
PIG	G-HOGS
POT	G-CHAM
PRINTER	G-BYFK
PYLON	G-PYLN
ROBINSON'S BARLEY WATER	G-BKES
RUPERT BEAR	G-BTML
RUSSIAN DOLL	G-USSR
SAMSUNG COMPUTER	G-SEUK
SANTA MARIA SHIP	G-BPSP
SATURN	G-DREX
SAUCER	G-GUFO
SCOTTISH PIPER	G-PIPY
SIGN	G-UCCC
SONIC THE HEDGEHOG	G-SEGA
SPARKASSE BOX	G-BXKH
SPHERE	G-BVFU BYJW IBBC SATL
SPHINX	G-BLFE
STRAWBERRY	G-BXTF
SUGAR BOX	G-BZDX BZDY BZKR
SULTAN	G-TURK
TEMPLE	G-BMWN
TENNENT'S LAGER GLASS	G-BTSL
TRAIN	G-BTMY
TRAINER'S SHOE	G-BUDN
TRUCK	G-BLDL DERV
TV	G-TVTV
UNCLE SAM	G-USAM
VAN	G-ORAC
WITCH	G-WYCH
WINE BOX	G-STOW

CAMPBELL AIRCRAFT LTD including BENSEN and EVERETT GYROPLANES LTD production
COUGAR
G-BAPS
CRICKET
G-AXPZ AXRC AXVK AXVM AYBX AYCC AYHI AYPZ BHBA BKVS BORG BRLF BSPJ BSRL BTEI BTMP BUIG BVDJ BVIT BVLD BVOH BWSD BWUA BWUZ BXCJ BXHU BXUA BYMO BYMP BZKN CBWN CCPD CDXV CFCH GYRO KGED RUGS

CANADIAN HOME ROTORS
SAFARI
G-CCKJ

CAPRONI VIZZOLA COSTRUZIONI AERONAUTICHE SpA
CALIF A-21
G-CKNC

CARLSON
SPARROW
G-BSUX BVVB

SOCIÉTÉ CARMAM
JP-15/36A AIGLON
G-CHMU DEDB

CASA see BUCKER (1131), HEINKEL (2111) and JUNKERS (352L)

CASSUTT including MUSSO SPECIAL, SPEED TWO and WILSON variants
RACER
G-BFMF BNJZ BOMB BOXW BPVO BXMF CXDZ FRAY NARO RAGE RUNT

AVIONS CAUDRON
G.III
G-AETA

CCF see HAWKER and NORTH AMERICAN

CEA see JODEL and ROBIN

SOCIÉTÉ NOUVELLE CENTRAIR
MOTO-DELTA
G-MBPJ
101 PÉGASE variants
G-CEVE CFCB CFEH CFFC CFFS CFGW CFJK CFMK CFNM CFRR CFRV CFRX CFVM CFVN CFVP CFVV CFWY CFWD CGBU CHDD CHNZ CKBA CKHM CKKB CKMF DESH DESW DETJ DETM DEVM DHES PEGZ REER SVEN
201 MARIANNE
G-CJXB CJXN
SNC-34 ALLIANCE
G-CJHR

CESSNA AIRCRAFT COMPANY including REIMS AVIATION SA production (F.prefix)
C.165 AIRMASTER
G-BTDE
120
G-AJJS AJJT AKTS AKVM BHLW BJML BPWD BPZB BRJC BRPE BRPF BRPG BRPH BRUN BRXH BSUH BTBW BTEW BTVG BTYW BTYX BUHZ BUJM BUKO BVUZ JOLY OVFM
140 variants
G-AKUR ALOD ALTO ANGK BOCI BPHW BPHX BPKO BPUU BTOS BUHO BYCD HALJ
150
"G-BMAF" G-APXY ARFI ARFO ASMS ASMW ASST ASUE ASYP ASZB ASZU ATEF ATHV ATHZ ATKF ATMC ATML ATMM ATMN ATMY ATNE ATNL ATOD ATRK ATRM ATUF ATYM ATZY AVAA AVAR AVEM AVEN AVER AVGU AVHM AVIA AVIB AVIT AVMD AVMF AVNC AVPH AVUG AVUH AVVL AVZU AWAW AWAX AWBX AWCP AWES AWFF AWGK AWLA AWMT AWOT AWPJ AWPU AWRK AWTJ AWTX AWUG AWUH AWUJ AWUK AWUL AWUN AWUO AWUT AWUU AXGG AXPF AYBD AYGC AYRF AZLH AZLY AZZR AZXC BABC BAEU BAHI BAIK BAIP BAMC BAXU BAXV BAYO BAYP BAZS BBBC BBCI BBDT BBJX BBKA BBKB BBKE BBKY BBNJ BCBX BCCC BCRT BCUH BCUJ BDBU BDFJ BDFZ BDOD BDSL BDTX BDUM BDUO BDZC BEIG BELT BEOK BEWP BFIY BFOG BFSR BFVU BFWL BGBI BGEA BGOJ BHIY BIFY BIOC BJOV BLVS BMBB BMLX BMXJ BNFI BOBV BOIV BOMN BORY BOTP BOUJ BOUZ BOVT BOWC BPAB BPAW BPAX BPCJ BPEM BPGZ BPNA BPOS BPRP BPWG BPWM BPWN BRBH BRJT BRLR BRNC BRTC BRTJ BSBZ BSEJ BSJU BSJZ BSKA BSOB BSYV BSYW BSZU BSZV BTES BTGP BTHE BTIN BTSN BTTE BTYC BUCS BUCT BUGG BURH BUTT BWII BWVL BZJW CDIS CEOK CFBD SBM CSFC DENA DENB DENC DEND ECBH EJMG FAYE FFEN FINA GBLR GCNZ GFLY GLED GOLY HFCB

HFCI HIVE HULL IANJ JWDS LUCK KMCL MABE NSTG OIDW OJVH
OKED OSTY PHAA PLAN SADE SALL SAMZ SMCL TAIL TEDB UFLY YIII

A150 AEROBAT
G-AXRT AXSW AXUF AYCF AYOZ AYRO AZID AZJY AZOZ AZUZ AZZX
BABD BACN BACO BACP BAEP BAEV BAEZ BAII BAOP BAPI BAPJ
BBTB BBXB BCDY BCFR BCKU BCKV BCTU BCUY BCVG BCVH BDAI
BDEX BDOW BDRD BEIA BEKN BEMY BEOE BEOY BFGG BFGX BFGZ
BFIE BFRR BHRH BIBN BJTB BLPH BMEX BOFW BOFX BOYU BPJW
BTFS BUCA BUTT CLUB FMSG HFCA JAGS JHAC OISO OPIC OSND
PHLY PHOR PHUN PNIX

152
G-BFEK BFFC BFFE BFFW BFHU BFHV BFKG BFKH BFLU BFOE BFOF
BGAA BGAB BGAE BGFX BGGO BGGP BGHI BGIB BGLG BGNT BHAA
BHAI BHAV BHCP BHDM BHDR BHDS BHDW BHEC BHFC BHFI BHHG
BHIN BHPY BHRB BHRN BHSA BHUI BHUP BHWA BHWB BHYX BHZH
BICG BIDH BIJV BIJW BIJX BILR BILS BIOK BITF BITH BIUM BIXH BIZG
BJKY BJNF BJVJ BJVT BJWH BJYD BKAZ BKFC BKGW BKTV BKWY
BLJO BLWV BLZE BLZH BLZP BMCV BMFZ BMGG BMJB BMJC BMJD
BMMM BMSU BMTA BMTB BMTJ BMVB BMXA BMXB BMXC BMXX BNAJ
BNDO BNFR BNFS BNHJ BNHK BNID BNIV BNJB BNJC BNJD BNJH
BNKC BNKI BNKP BNKR BNKS BNKV BNMC BNMD BNME BNMF BNNR
BNOZ BNPY BNRK BNRL BNSI BNSM BNSN BNSU BNSV BNUL BNUS
BNUT BNYL BNYN BOAI BODO BOFL BOFM BOGC BOHI BOHJ BOIO
BOIR BOKY BOLV BOLW BONW BOOI BORJ BOTG BOYL BOZR BPBJ
BPBK BPEO BPFZ BPGM BPHT BPIY BPME BPTU BRBF BRBP BRND
BRNE BRNK BRNN BRPV BRTD BRTP BRUA BSCP BSCZ BSDO BSDP
BSFP BSFR BSTO BSTP BSWH BSZI BSZO BSZW BTAL BTCE BTDW
BTFC BTGH BTGR BTGW BTGX BTIK BTVW BTVX BTYT BUEF BUEG
BVTM BWEU BWEV BWNB BWNC BWND BXJM BXTB BXVB BXVY
BXWC BXYU BYFA BYMH BYMJ BZAD BZAE BZEB BZEC BZHE BZHF
BZWH CCHT CCTW CDTX CEFM CEPX CEUS CEZM CHIK CPFC DACF
DRAG ENTT ENTW FIGA FIGB FLOP GFIA GFIB GFIC HART HFCL HFCT
IBRO JIMH KATT LAMS LSMI MASS OAFT OBEN ODAC OFRY OIMC
OLEE OPAM OPJC OVMC OWAC OWAK OWOW PFSL POCO SACB
TALA TALB TALC TALD TAYS WACB WACE WACF WACG WACT

A152 AEROBAT
G-BFGL BFKF BFMK BFRV BFZN BFZT BFZU BGAF BGLN BHAD BHED
BHEN BHJA BHMG BHMH BILJ BILK BIMT BLAC BLAX BMUO BMYG
BOPX BOSO BOYB BRUM BZEA FIFE FLAP FLIP JEET JONI LEIC MPBH
OCPC OWFS RLFI TFCI WACH WACU ZOOL

170
G-AORB APVS AWOU BCLS MDAY

172 SKYHAWK and CUTLASS variants
G-APSZ ARID ARLU ARMO ARMR AROA ARWO ARWR ARYI ARYK
ARYS ASFA ASIB ASMJ ASNW ASOK ASSS ASUP ASVM ASWL ATAF
ATFY ATKT ATLM ATSL ATWJ AVEC AVHH AVIC AVIS AVJF AVKG AVPI
AVTP AVVC AVZV AWGD AWLF AWMP AWMZ AWUX AWUZ AWVA
AXBH AXBJ AXDI AXSI AXVB AYCT AYRG AYRT AYUV AZDZ AZJV
AZKW AZKZ AZLM AZLV AZTK AZTS AZUM AZXD AZZV BAEO BAEY
BAIW BAIX BANX BAOB BAOS BAVB BAXY BAZT BBDH BBJY BBJZ
BBKI BBKZ BBNZ BBOA BBTG BBTH BCCD BCHK BCOL BCPK BCRB
BCUF BCVJ BCYR BCZM BDCE BDNU BDZD BEHV BEMB BENK BEUX
BEWR BEZK BEZO BEZR BEZV BFGD BFKB BFMX BFOV BFPH BFPM
BFRS BFTH BFZV BGAG BGBR BGHJ BGIU BGIY BGLO BGMP BGND
BGRO BGSV BHAW BHCC BHCM BHDX BHDZ BHMI BHPZ BHSB
BHUG BHUJ BHVR BHYP BHYR BIBW BIDF BIGJ BIHI BIIB BIIE BIOB
BITM BIZF BJDE BJDW BJGY BJVM BJWI BJWW BJXZ BKCE BKEP
BKEV BKII BKIJ BKLO BLHJ BLVW BMCI BMHS BMIG BNKE BNRR
BNST BNTP BNXD BNYM BOEN BOHH BOIL BOIX BOIY BOJR BOJS
BOLI BOLY BOMS BONR BONS BOOL BORW BOUE BOUF BOVG
BOYP BPML BPRM BPTL BPVA BPVY BPWS BRAK BRBI BRBJ BRCM
BRWX BRZS BSEP BSHR BSNG BSOG BSOO BSPE BSTM BTMA BTMR
BTRE BUJN BULH BURD BUZN BXGV BXOI BXSD BXSE BXSR BXXK
BYBD BYEA BYES BYET BYNA BZBF BZGH BZPM BZZD CBFO CBME
CBOR CBXJ CCTT CDDK CDMM CEKI CEMH CESS CFLY CLUX COCO
CSCS CXSM DCKK DEMH DODD DRBG DUNK DUVL ECGC ECON
EETG EGEG EICK ENII ENNK ENOA EOLX ETAT ETDC FACE FLOW
FNLD FNLY GBFF GBLP GBTL GEHL GFEA GFMT GFSA GRAY GWYN
GYAV GZDO HERC HILS ICOM ILPY IZZS IZZY JFWI JHPA JMKE JONZ
LACI LANE LAVE LENX LICK LSCM MALK MCLY MELT MFAC MICK MILA
NOUS NWFC NWFG OAKR OBMS OERS OFCM OJAG OOLE OPIT
OPYE ORMG OSII OSPK OSKY OTAM OVFR OWST OZOO PDSI PFCL
PLBI RATI RARB RGAP RJCC ROLY ROOK ROUP RSWO RUIA RVRI
SACD SBAE SEVE SEXI SHSP SHWK SKAN SKKY SMRS TAMR TASH
TDRA TIML TOBI TOBY TRAX TRIO TYMS TYRE UFCB UFCC UFCD
UFCE UFCF UFCG UFCH UFCI UFCJ WACL WACW WACY YFZT YNYS
YORK YSPY ZACE

172RG CUTLASS
G-BHVC BHYC BILU PARI

R172K HAWK XP
G-BHYD BPCI BPWR BTMK EPIM FANL XPII

REIMS FR172 ROCKET variants
G-AWCN AWDR AWWU AWYB AYGX AYJW BAIL BARC BBKG BBXH
BCTK BDOE BFSS BLPF BZVB DRAM DRID EDTO JANS LOYA MFEF
RABA YBAA ROKT THIN

REIMS FR172K HAWK XP
G-BFIG BFIU DAVD EFBP PJTM STAY YIPI

175 SKYLARK
G-ARCV ARML ARMN AROC ARRI ARUZ ARWS

177(RG) CARDINAL
G-AYPG AYPH AYSX AYSY AZTF AZTW AZVP BAGN BAIS BAJA BAJB
BAJE BBHI BBJV BCUW BEBN BFIV BFMH BFPZ BPSL BRDO BRPS
BTSZ BUJE FIJJ FNEY GBFR LNYS OAMP OSFS TOTO

180 including 180K SKYWAGON
G-ARAT ASIT AXZO BEOD BETG BNCS BOIA BTSM BUPG CIBO DAPH

(T) 182 SKYLANE variants
G-ARAW ASLH ASSF ASXZ ATCX ATLA ATPT AVCV AVDA AVGY AVID
AWJA AXNX AXZU AYOW AYWD AZNO BAAT BAFL BAHD BAHX BAMJ
BBGX BBYH BBYS BCWB BDBJ BDIG BEKO BFSA BFZD BGAJ BGPA
BHDP BHIB BHIC BHVP BHYA BJVH BKHJ BKKN BKKO BMMK BMUD
BNMO BNRY BOPH BOTH BOWO BPUM BRKR BRRK BSDW BSRR BTHA
BUVO BWMC BWRR BXEZ BXZM BYEM BZVO CBIL CBMP CBVX CCAN
CCYS CDRC CDSL CDXI CEFV DATG DAVZ DOVE DRGS DTFF EEZS
EFAM EIRE EIWT EKOS ENRM EOHL ESME ESSL FAUX GBUN GCYC
GHOW GUMS HEDI HRND HRNT HUFF IATU IBZS IFAB IJAG IOPT IRPC
ISEH IZZI JBRN JENI JOBS JOON KEMY KTWO KWAX LANS LEGG LVES
MICI MILN MISH MOUT NLEE NOCK NYZS OBBO OHAC OJHC OJRM
OLDG OMAG OPCG OPST ORAY OWCS OWRT OZOI PDHJ PLEE POPW
POWL PUGS RACY RCWK ROWE SAAM SHAR SKYL THRE TPSL VALI
VIPA WARP WHDP WIFE WMLT XLTG ZBLT ZGZG

185 SKYWAGON variants
G-AYNN BBEX BDKC BKPC BLOS BWWF BXRH BYBP RNRM

195A
G-BSPK

205(A)
G-ASNK ASOX

(T)P206D SUPER SKYLANE
G-AWUA AYCJ

(U)206 SUPER SKYWAGON variants
G-ASVN ATCE ATLT BGWR BMHC BPGE DROP LEMO

(U)206 STATIONAIR variants
G-AZRZ BAGV BMOF BOFD BSUE BXDB BXRO CCSN LEMO PEPA
SBKS SEAI STAT

(U)206 TURBO STATIONAIR variants
G-BFCT BYIC CCRC CTFF OLLS OSSA SEMR SKYE

207 SKYWAGON
G-NJAG

208 CARAVAN and 208B GRAND CARAVAN
G-BZAH EELS ETHY GOTF MDJE OAFF WIKY

210 CENTURION variants
G-ASXR BENF BEYV BNZM BSGT CDMH DECK EMLS MANT MPRL
OFLY OWAN PIIX SEEK TOTN VMDE

T303 CRUSADER
G-BSPF CMOS CRUZ CYLS DOLY GAME IKAP INDC JUIN OAPE PUSI
ROCH UILT

305 BIRD DOG (L-19)
G-PDOG VDOG

310 variants
G-APNJ ARCI ASSZ AXLG AYGB AYND AZUY BALN BARG BARV BBXL
BGTT BHEH BIFA BJMR BODY BPIL BRIA BTFF BWYE BWYG BXUY
BXYG EGEE EGLT FFWD FISH IMLI LLMC MIWS MPBI ODLY REDB
REDD RIST RODD SOUL TKPZ TROP VDIR XLKF YHPV

335
G-FITZ

(T)337 SUPER SKYMASTER variants
G-AXHA BCBZ BMJR HIVA RGEN

REIMS F337 SUPER SKYMASTER variants
G-AZKO BFGH BFJR BOYR BTVV

340
G-BVES CCXJ FEBE HAFG LIZA LUND PUFN REEN SAMM

401 variants
G-AVKN AZFR AZRD DACC OVNE

402 variants
BXJA EYES MAPP NOSE

404 TITAN
G-BWLF EXEX FIFA MIND OOSI TASK

REIMS F406 CARAVAN II
G-BVJT FIND LEAF MAFA MAFB SFPA SFPB TURF

414A CHANCELLOR
G-SMJJ

421 GOLDEN EAGLE variants
G-BAGO BFTT BHKJ BLST CSNA FTAX GILT HIJK JACK KWLI PVIP SVIP
TAMY TREC UVIP VVIP

425 CORSAIR
G-KRMA

500 CITATION
G-DJAE JTNC LOFT ORHE

501 CITATION 1
  G-VUEM
510 MUSTANNG
  G-LEAI
525(A) CITATIONJET variants
  G-BVCM CITJ CJAD CJDB EDCJ EDCK EDCL EEBJ GEBJ HCSA HGRC
  HMMV IUAN OEBJ OCJT OODM OSOH PWNS SEAJ SFCJ TBEA ZIZI
550 CITATION II
  G-CEUO DWJM EJEL ESTA FCDB FIRM FJET GHPG IDAB IKOS IPAL
  JBIS JBIZ JETC JETJ JETO JMDW ORDB RDBS SOVA SPUR VUEA
  VUEZ
550 CITATION BRAVO
  G-OJMW OMRH WAIN
551 CITATION variants
  G-FLVU LUXY
560 CITATION V
  G-JOPT PPLC
560 CITATION ULTRA variants
  G-KDMA OBCC
560 XL CITATION EXCEL
  G-CBRG CIEL ELOA IPAX LDFM REDS SIRS WINA XLMB
560 XL CITATION XLS
  G-NSJS OMEA OROO OXLS PKRG RSXL XBEL
680 CITATION SOVEREIGN
  G-SVSB XBLU
750 CITATION X
  G-CDCX CEDK

CFM METAL-FAX including CFM AIRCRAFT LTD
IMAGE
  G-BTUD
SHADOW Series B and BD (Rotax 447)
  G-MNZP MNZR MTFU MTGN MTHV MTTH MTWL MVBB MVCW MVIG
  MVRS MVRT MVYZ MYKE
SHADOW Series C and CD (Rotax 503)
  G-BZLF CAIN MGUY MJVF MNCM MNER MNIS MNTK MNTP MNVI MNVJ
  MNVK MNWY MNXX MNZJ MNZZ MTBE MTCA MTCT MTDU MTFU MTFZ
  MTGV MTGW MTHT MTKR MTMX MTMY MTWH MTWK MTXR MVAC
  MVAM MVCC MVEI MVEN MVFH MVHD MVLJ MVLP MVOH MVPK
  MVRO MVRP MVRR MVVT MWAE MWDB MWDN MWEN MWEZ MWFB
  MWIZ MWJF MWLD MWMU MWON MWPN MWRL MWRY MWSZ MWTJ
  MWTN MWTP MWUA MWVG MWVH MWYD MYBC MYBL MYCM MYDD
  MYDE MYEP MYIF MYIP MYLV MYOH MYON MYOS MYPL MYPT MYSM
  MYTH MYUS MYWF MYWM MYXY MZBN MZCT MZRS PSUE
SHADOW Series DD (Rotax 582)
  G-BXZY BYCJ CCMW DARK DMWW LYNK MGTW MYZP MZBS MZGS
  MZKH MZNH MZOM ODVB PBEL
SHADOW D Series SS (Rotax 912)
  G-MZLP
STREAK SHADOW and STARSTREAK SHADOW
  G-BONP BROI BRSO BRWP BRZZ BSMN BSOR BSPL BSRX BSSV
  BTDD BTEL BTGT BTKP BTZZ BUGM BUIL BULJ BUOB BUTB BUVX
  BUWR BUXC BVDT BVFR BVLF BVOR BVPY BVTD BWAI BWCA BWOZ
  BWPS BXFK BXVD BXWR BYAZ BYFI BYOO BZEZ BZMZ BZWJ BZWY
  CBCZ CBGI CBNO CEZU CZBE DOTT ENEE FAME GORE HLCF MEOW
  MGGT MGPH MWPP MYNX MYTY OLGA OPIT ORAF OTCH RINT ROTS
  SHIM SNEV STRK TEHL TTOY WESX WHOG WYAT

CGS including ARROWFLIGHT AVIATION LTD
HAWK
  G-MWYS MYTP MZGU

CHAMPION AIRCRAFT CORPORATION see AERONCA and BELLANCA
7FC TRI-TRAVELER
  G-APYT ARAP ARAS

CHANCE-VOUGHT see VOUGHT

CHARGUS GLIDING CO LTD see HIWAY
T.250
  G-MBEU MBJG
VORTEX 120
  G-MJWH

CHICHESTER-MILES CONSULTANTS LTD including DESIGNABILITY LTD
LEOPARD
  G-BKRL BRNM

CHILTON AIRCRAFT
DW.1 and 2 variants
  G-AESZ AFGH AFGI AFSV BWGJ CDXU DWIA DWIB

CHOWN
Balloon (Minimum Lift)
OSPREY variants
  G-BBJHI BJHJ BJHN BJHO BJHP BJHR BJHW BJHY BJHZ BJIC BJID
  BJIK BJKV BJKZ BJLE BJMH BJMT BJND BJNH BJHI BJPL BJPT BJRA
  BJRG BJRL BJRO BJSC BJSD BJSF BJSI BJSK BJTZ FYBO
PORTSWOOD variants
  G-FYBB FYBX

CHRISLEA AIRCRAFT CO LTD
LC.1 AIRGUARD
  G-AFIN
CH.3 SUPER ACE
  G-AKUW AKVD AKVF
CH.3 Series 4 SKYJEEP
  G-AKVR

CHRISTEN INDUSTRIES INC including AVIAT AIRCRAFT INC and see PITTS
EAGLE
  G-CCYO CENC EEGL EGAL EGEL EGIL EGLE EGUL ELKA IXII NEST
  NUTA OEGL
A-1 HUSKY variants
  G-BUVR CDOD DBLX DOGY HAIB HSKI HUSK JJDC LTMM OCLC OGGY
  USKY WATR

CHRIS TENA
MINI COUPE
  G-BPDJ

CIERVA AUTOGYRO COMPANY including DE HAVILLAND AIRCRAFT CO LTD
and A V ROE and CO LTD variants
C.8
  G-EBYY
C.19 (AVRO 620)
  G-ABXH
C.24
  G-ABLM
C.30A (AVRO 671)
  G-ACUU ACWM ACWP ACXA AHMJ

CIRRUS DESIGN CORPORATION
SR20
  G-CDLY CIRI EDHO GEMM ONEC OPSS OSPY SMKM SRVA SRZO
  TAAA TAAC TABI VGAG ZZDG
SR22
  G-CGRD DUAL ETFL HEJB MACL NETB OONK RBMS TAAB VBCA
  WTEC ZRZZ

CIVILIAN AIRCRAFT CO
CAC.1 COUPE
  G-ABNT

CLIFF SIMS
AZTEC trike
  G-MMFY

CLUTTON
FRED (Volkswagen 1834)
  G-BBBW BDBF BGFF BGHZ BISG BITK BJAD BKAF BKDP BKEY BKVF
  BKZT BLNO BMAX BMMF BMOO BMSL BNZR BOLS BPAV BVCO BWAP
  MANX ORAS PFAF PFAL RONW USTY

COATES
SWALESONG
  G-AYDV

COLT BALLOONS LTD including THUNDER and COLT LTD and
CAMERON BALLOONS LTD (2) production
Airship (Gas-Filled)
GA-42
  G-BKXM MATS ZEPI
Airship (Hot Air)
AS-56
  G-BNKF BTXH NOVO
AS-80 (Rotax 462)
  G-BPCG BPGT BPKN
AS-105 (Rotax 462)
  G-BTSW BWKE BWMV BXEY BXNV BXYF OVAX RBOS
AS-120 (Rotax 582)
  G-BXKU
AS-261
  G-BPLD

Balloon (Hot Air)

12A Cloudhopper
G-BHOJ

14A Cloudhopper
G-BHKN BHKR BHPN

17A Cloudhopper
G-BIDV BIYT BJWV BKBO BKDS BKIU BKXM BLHI BONV BPXH BUDY HELP HEXE

21 series
G-BLVY BLXG BMKI BNFM BOLN BOLP BOLR BPFX BSAK BSIG BTXM BUEU BWBJ LLAI SOOS

H-24
G-BZUV

25 series
G-BSOF BUPH BVAO OKBT

31 series
G-BHIG BROJ BSDV BSMM BVTL BXXU DNGR DHLZ DOWN HOUS IMAN MUTE PIXE PONY

42 series
G-BJZR SEAT

56 series
G-BHEX BHRY BICM BISX BIXW BJXP BJYF BKSD BLLW BLOT BTZY BUGO BVCN BVOZ BVUC CCYP CFBI EZXO FZZZ ILEE MERC POSH TTWO WIMP

65D
G-BLCH

69 series
G-BLEB BOVW BPAH BSHC BSHD BTMO BVDD COLR FZZY JBJB OABC OBUD TCAN TWEY

77 series
G-BGOD BIGT BKOW BLTA BLUE BMYN BOCF BOGT BOHD BORA BORE BORT BPEZ BPFB BPJK BRLT BRVF BRVU BSCI BSUB BSUK BTDS BTTS BTZS BUJH BUKS BULF BURG BUVE BUVS BUVT BUYO BVAX BXFN BXIE BYFX CDUY CHEL CURE DING DRAW DURX EZVS FLAG GGOW GOBT HOME HOTI HOTZ IMAG JONO LSHI MAUK MKAK OAWS OBJH OCAR ODAD OLPG ONCL OSST READ SGAS SIXX STOK TTFG TRUX UPPP UZLE WHAT WHIM WOOL WRIT

90 series
G-BPUW BRHG BRRU BSIU BTCS BTPVI BXUW FOWL IRLY JNNB OBBC OLDV OMMM PEGG PHSI SAUF SEND TOFT

105 series
G-BLHK BLMZ BMBS BNAG BPZS BRUH BSCC BSHS BSNU BTHX BURL BUSV BWMA BWRM BYIO DYNG FVRY OWEL PLUG POPP RAIL

120 series
G-BXCO BYDJ BZIL BZNF CBEJ OBIB VYGR

180 series
G-BMXM BOGR BONK CUCU MUMM

210 series
G-BTYZ BULN BUXA BVFY BZYO

240 series
G-IGLA LCIO

260 series
G-HUGO

315 series
G-CCIE VVBF

2500 series
G-USUK

Special Shapes

SHAPE	REGISTRATION(S)
AGFA FILM CASSETTE	G-OHDC
APPLE	G-BRZV
ARIEL BOTTLE	G-BNHN
BEER GLASS	G-BNHL PUBS
BIBENDUM	G-PNEU
BLACK KNIGHT	G-BNMI
BOTTLE	G-BOTL
BUDWEISER CAN	G-BUET BVIO
CLOWN	G-GWIZ
CYLINDER	G-CHUB
DRACHENFISCH	G-BMUJ
EGG	G-BWWL
FILM CAN	G-OXRG
FINANCIAL TIMES	G-ETFT FTFT
FLAME	G-BLKU
FLYING JEANS	G-JCJC
FLYING MITT	G-WCAT
FLYING YACHT	G-BXXJ
GAS FLAME	G-BGOO
HEAD	G-HEAD
HOP	G-MALT
ICE CREAM CONE	G-BWBE BWBF OJHB
J and B WHISKY BOTTLE	G-JANB
JUMBO	G-OVAA
KINDERMOND	G-BMUL

MAXWELL HOUSE COFFEE JARS	G-BVBJ BVBK
MICKEY MOUSE	G-BTRB
OLD PARR WHISKY BOTTLE	G-PARR
PANASONIC BATTERY	G-PSON
PIG	G-BUZS
PIGGY BANK	G-BXVW
SANTA CLAUS	G-HOHO
SATZENBRAU BOTTLE	G-BIRE
STORK	G-BRGP
TANK	G-BXND
UFO	G-BMUK
WORLD	G-DHLI

COLOMBAN

MC-12 and MC-15 CRI-CRI variants
"G-SHOG" G-BOUT BWFO CDNJ CRIC CRIK MCXV OCRI SHOG

COLTING BALLOONS LTD

Balloon (Hot Air)

AX8-105A
G-BGAS

COMCO IKARUS GmbH including AEROSPORT LTD (formerly FLYBUY ULTRALIGHTS LTD) production

IKARUS C42 variants
G-CBFV CBGP CBIJ CBJW CBKU CBPD CBRF CBTG CBVY CBXC CCCT CCFZ CCLS CCNT CCPS CCYR CCZL CDBU CDCG CDCM CDCO CDIX CDJK CDMS CDNR CDOK CDOT CDPP CDRO CDRP CDRY CDSW CDUK CDVI CDWI CDYD CDYO CDYT CDZG CEAK CEAN CECC CECL CEDC CEDR CEEW CEFA CEGL CEGZ CEHG CEHV CEJW CEPY CETR CETZ CEVA CEWY CEZA CFOG CLIF CVAL CWAY DASS DJBC DMCI DNKS DOZI DTOY DUGE EDEE EGGI FBII FIFT FLYB FLYC FLYM FROM GNJW GRPA GSCV HBBH HIJN HNGE IBAZ IAJS ICRS IKRS IKUS ILRS INJA JWDB MGPA MROY MSKY NCCI NDPA NORA NPPL NSBB OAJL OFBU OJDS ORMW OROS OSTL OVAL OVLA RBSN RODJ ROZZ RTMY SARM SFLA SFLB SGEN SIMM SJEN ULSY WILT WOLV WSSX YADA ZAVI

COMMANDER AIRCRAFT COMPANY see ROCKWELL

COMMONWEALTH AIRCRAFT CORPORATION PTY LTD see NORTH AMERICAN

COMPER AIRCRAFT CO

CLA.7 SWIFT
G-ABTC ABUS ABUU ACTF ECTF LCGL OBUU

CONSOLIDATED VULTEE AIRCRAFT CORPORATION see STINSON AIRCRAFT CORPORATION

CV.32-3 LIBERATOR
G-AGZI

PBY-5A CATALINA
G-PBYA

CONVAIR see GENERAL DYNAMICS CORPORATION

COOK

ARIES P
G-MYXI

COPE

BUG
G-BXTV

CORBEN

BABY ACE
G-BTSB BUAA

JUNIOR ACE
G-BSDI

CORBETT FARMS LTD see MICROFLIGHT AIRCRAFT LTD

CORBY

CJ-1 STARLET
G-BVVZ CBHP CCHN CCXO ILSE

COSMIK AVIATION LTD

SUPERCHASER
G-DREG

COSMOS

TRIKE with La Mouette wing
G-MVCK

ETABLISSEMENT **COUESNON** - see JODEL

CRANFIELD INSTITUTE OF TECHNOLOGY
A.1-400 EAGLE
  G-COAI

CREMER
Balloon (Minimum Lift)
HOT AIR FREE
  G-BJLX BJLY BJRP BJRR BJRV

CROSBY see ANDREASSON

CROSSLEY
*RACER*r
  G-BKRU

CSS see POLIKARPOV

CUB PROSPECTOR see PIPER

CULVER
LCA CADET
  G-CDET

CURRIE
WOT variants
  G-APNT ARZW ASBA AVEY AYMP AYNA BANV BDFB BFAH BFWD
  BKCN BLPB BXMX CWBM CWOT PFAP SWOT

CURTISS-WRIGHT AIRCRAFT CORPORATION
TRAVEL AIR 12Q TRAVELAIR
  G-AAOK

CURTISS-WRIGHT CORPORATION
P-40B TOMAHAWK
  G-CDWH
P-40N KITTYHAWK
  G-KITT

CURTISS ROBERTSON
ROBIN C.2
  G-BTYY HFBM

CUSTOMCRAFT BALLOON SERVICES
Balloon (Hot Air)
A25
  G-CCKZ DUMP

CYCLONE AIRSPORTS LTD see PEGASUS AVIATION and SOLAR WINGS
(AVIATION)
70 trike (Rotax 377/277) with Aerial Arts 110SX &130SX wings
  G-MMYL MNMY
AX3
  G-BVJG MYFI MYFV MYFW MYFZ MYGD MYHG MYHH MYHJ MYHM
  MYHR MYIJ MYIU MYKA MYKT MYME MYMW MYMZ MYOY MYPM
  MYPR MYRO MYRU MYRV MYSO MYTM MYUI MYVN MYXH MYYL
  MYZC MYZF MYZG MZDS MZEL
AX2000
  G-BYJM CBGS CBMB CBUX JONY MGUN MYER MZER MZFA MZFX
  MZGA MZGB MZGC MZGM MZGP MZHR MZIV MZJF MZJL MZJR MZKC
  MZLM MZLS MZLU MZMX MZOE OAJB ROMW STRG WAKY

CZECH AIRCRAFT WORKS (CZAW)
*SPORTCRUISER*r
  G-CESZ CFEZ CZAW EDDS ENST FELX MUTT SASI SCRZ VIIZ ZAAP
  ZECH

Dan Rihn
DR.107 ONE DESIGN
  G-CEPZ CVII IDII IIID LOAD ONED RIHN TAZZ

DART AIRCRAFT LTD
KITTEN
  G-AEXT

DASSAULT AVIATION including AVIONS MARCEL DASSAULT and
AVIONS MARCEL DASSAULT-BREGUET AVIATION production
FALCON 10
  G-ECJI

FALCON 20
  G-FFRA FRAD FRAF FRAH FRAI FRAJ FRAK FRAL FRAO FRAP FRAR
  FRAS FRAT FRAU FRAW FRBA
(MYSTERE) FALCON 900 variants
  G-CBHT FNES GALX HAAM HMEI HMEV JMMX JPSX SIRO
FALCON 2000 variants
  G-GEDY JETF KWIN OJAJ

DAVIS
DA-2A
  G-BPFL

DE HAVILLAND AIRCRAFT LTD including AMERICAN MOTH CORPORATION,
DE HAVILLAND AIRCRAFT PTY LTD, F + W, MORANE-SAULNIER, MORRIS MOTORS and
OGMA production - also see AIRCO and HAWKER SIDDELEY AVIATION
DH.51
  G-EBIR
DH.53 HUMMING BIRD
  G-EBHX EBQP
DH.60G and DH.60M MOTH variants including reps
  G-EBLV EBWD
  "G-AAAH" x 2* G-AAAH AADR AAEG AAHI AAHY AAJT AALY AAMX
  AAMY AAMZ AANL AANO AANV AAOR AAWO AAYT AAZG ABAG ABDA
  ABDX ABEV ABSD ABYA ABZB ACGZ ACNS ACXB ACXK ADHD ATBL
  EBNO EBZN BVNG
DH.71 TIGER MOTH
  G-ECDX
DH.80A PUSS MOTH
  G-AAZP ABDW ABIH ABLS AEOA AHLO FAVC
*DH.82 TIGER MOTH variants and replicas**
  "G-ABUL"* "G-ACDR"* "G-MAZY" G-ACDA ACDC ACDI ACMD ADGT
  ADGV ADGZ ADIA ADJJ ADNZ ADPC ADWJ ADWO ADXT AFGZ AFVE
  AFWI AGEG AGHY AGNJ AGPK AGYU AGZZ AHAN AHIZ AHLT AHOO
  AHPZ AHUF AHUV AHVU AHVV AIDS AIRI AIRK AIXJ AJHS AJOA AJTW
  AJVE AKEE AKUE AKXS ALBD ALIW ALJL ALNA ALND ALRI ALUC ALVP
  ALWS ALWW AMBB AMCK AMCM AMHF AMIU AMIV AMJD AMLF AMJR
  AMNN AMOU AMPM AMRM AMTF AMTK AMTP AMTV AMVS ANCN
  ANCS ANCX ANCY ANDE ANDM ANDP ANEH ANEJ ANEL ANEM ANEN
  ANEW ANEZ ANFC ANFI ANFL ANFM ANFP ANFV ANFW ANHK ANJA
  ANJD ANJG ANKK ANKT ANKV ANKZ ANLD ANLS ANMO ANMY ANNB
  ANNC ANNE ANNG ANNI ANNK ANOH ANOM ANON ANOO ANOS
  ANPE ANPK ANRF ANRM ANRN ANRX ANSG ANSM ANTE ANZS ANZU
  ANZZ AOAA AOBH AOBX AODR AODT AOEI AOEL AOES AOET
  AOFR AOGI AOGJ AOGR AOHY AOIL AOIM AOIS AOJJ AOJK AOJX
  AOUR AOYU AOXG AOXN AOZH APAL APAM APAO APAP APBI APCC
  APFU APGL APIH APJO APJP APLU APMX APPN APPT ARAZ AREH
  ARTL ASKP ASPV AVPJ AXAN AXBW AXBZ AXXV AYDI AYIT AZDY
  AZGZ AZZZ BACK BAFG BBRB BYLB BEWN BFHH BHLT BHUM BJAP
  BJZF BMPY BOGW BPAJ BPHR BRHW BTOG BWIK BWMK BWMS
  BWVT BYTN CDJO DHTM DHZF ECDS EMSY ERDS MOTH OOSY
  PWBE TIGA
DH.82B QUEEN BEE
  G-BLUZ
DH.83 FOX MOTH variants
  G-ACCB ACEJ AOJH
DH.84 DRAGON
  G-ACET ACIT AJKF ECAN
DH.85 LEOPARD MOTH
  G-ACLL ACMA ACMN ACOJ ACUS AIYS
DH.87B HORNET MOTH
  G-ADKC ADKK ADKL ADKM ADLY ADMT ADND ADNE ADOT ADRH
  ADUR AELO AESE AHBL AHBM AMZO
*DH.88 COMET including reps**
  "G-ACSS" x 2* G-ACSP ACSS
*DH.89 DRAGON RAPIDE variants including replica**
  "G-AEAJ"* G-ACPP ACYR ACZE ADAH AEML AERN AGJG AGSH AGTM
  AHAG AHED AHGD AIDL AIWY AIYR AJBJ AJCL AKDW AKGV AKIF
  AKNV AKOE AKRP AKRS ALGB ALXT ALZF
DH.90 DRAGONFLY
  G-AEDU
DH.94 MOTH MINOR
  G-AFNG AFNI AFNJ AFOB AFOJ AFOR AFOW AFPN
DH.98 MOSQUITO
  G-ASKB ASKC AWJV MOSI
DH.100 VAMPIRE
  G-BVPD DHXX FBIX MKVI
DH.104 DOVE and (SEA) DEVON including Riley conversions
  "G-ALVD" G-AHRI ALCU ALFT ALFU AMDD AMFU AMXR AMXS AMXX
  ANOV ANUW ANVU AOUF APSO ARBE ARDE AREA ARHW ARHX ARJB
  ARUE ATGJ ATGK AWFM BAHB BVXR BWWC DEVN DHDV DVON HBBC
  KOOL OEWA OPLC SDEV
DH.106 COMET
  G-ANAV AOJT AOVU APAS APDB APDF APYD BDIW BDIX BEEX CPDA

DH.110 SEA VIXEN
G-CVIX VIXN
DH.112 VENOM
G-BLID BLKA BLSD DHSS DHTT DHUU DHVM VENI VENM VICI VNOM
DH.114 HERON and SEA HERON
"G-AOXL" G-ALZL ANPV ANUO ANXB AOGW AORG AOTI AOXL APXG ASCX ASFI ASVC
DH.115 VAMPIRE and SEA VAMPIRE
G-BVLM BZRC BZRD DHVV DHWW DUSK HELV OBLN SPDR VTII
DH.121 TRIDENT see **HAWKER SIDDELEY**
DH.125 see **HAWKER SIDDELEY**

DE HAVILLAND AIRCRAFT PTY LTD
DHA.3 DROVER
G-APXX

DE HAVILLAND CANADA including DE HAVILLAND INC, BOMBARDIER INC *
and OGMA production
DHC-1 CHIPMUNK
G-AKDN ALWB AMMA AMUF ANWB AOFE AOJR AORW AOSF AOSK AOSP AOSY AOTD AOTF AOTR AOTY AOUO AOUP AOZP APLO APPA APPM APTS APYG ARGG ARMC ARMD ARMF ARMG ARWB ATHD ATVF BAPB BARS BAVH BBMN BBMO BBMR BBMT BBMV BBMW BBMX BBMZ BBNA BBNC BBND BBRV BBSS BCAH BCCX BCEY BCGC BCHL BCHV BCIH BCKN BCOI BCOO BCOU BCOY BCPU BCRX BCSA BCSL BCXN BCYM BCZH BDCC BDDD BDEU BDRJ BFAW BFAX BFDC BNZC BPAL BTWF BVTX BVZZ BWHI BWJY BWJZ BWMX BWNK BWNT BWOX BWTG BWTO BWUN BWUT BWUV BWVY BWVZ BXCP BXCT BXCV BXDA BXDG BXDH BXDI BXDM BXDN BXDP BXEC BXGL BXGM BXGO BXGP BXGX BXHA BXHF BXIA BXIM BXNN BYHL BYSJ BZDU BZGA BZGB BZXE CBJG CERD CHPY CPMK DHCC DHPM HAPY HDAE ITWB MAJR OACP PVET TRIC UANO ULAS
DHC-2 BEAVER
G-BVER DHCZ
DHC-6 TWIN OTTER
G-BIHO BVVK BZFP CBML
DHC-8 DASH EIGHT variants*
G-ECOA ECOB ECOC ECOD ECOE ECOF ECOG ECOH ECOI ECOJ ECOK JECE JECF JECG JECH JECI JECJ JECK JECL JECM JECN JECO JECP JECR JECS JECT JECU JECV JECW JECX JECY JEDI JEDJ JEDK JEDL JEDM JEDN JEDO JEDP JEDR JEDT JEDU JEDV JEDW WOWA WOWB WOWC WOWD WOWE

DEMON see HIWAY

DENNEY AEROCRAFT COMPANY including SKYSTAR
KITFOX (Rotax 582)
G-BNYX BONY BPII BPKK BRCT BSAZ BSCG BSCH BSFX BSFY BSGG BSHK BSIF BSIK BSRT BSSF BSUZ BSVK BTAT BTBG BTBN BTDC BTDN BTIF BTIR BTKD BTMT BTNR BTOL BTSV BTTY BTVC BTWB BUDR BUIP BUKF BUKP BULZ BUNM BUOL BUPW BUWS BUYK BUZA BVAH BVCT BVEY BVGO BWAR BWHV BWSJ BWSN BWWZ BWYI BXBP BXCW BXWH BZAR CBDI CBTX CDXY CJUD CRES CTOY DJNH ELIZ EYAS FBOY FOXC FOXD FOXF FOXG FOXI FOXS FOXX FOXZ FSHA HOBO HUTT KAWA KFOX KITF KITY KTTY LACR LEED LESJ LESZ LOST MSCM OFOX OPDS PHYL PPPP RAYA RFOX RSSF RWSS TFOX TOMZ TWTW

DEPERDUSSIN CIE
MONOPLANE
G-AANH

DESIGNABILITY LTD see CHICHESTER-MILES

DESOUTTER AIRCRAFT COMPANY
DESOUTTER 1
G-AAPZ

CONSTRUCTIONS AÉRONAUTIQUES EMILE **DEWOITINE**
D.26
G-BBMI

DG FLUGZEUGBAU GmbH incluidng AMS-FLIGHT DOO, ELAN OVARNA
SPORTNEGA ORODJA N.SOL.O and GLASER-DIRKS FLUGZEUGBAU GmbH production
DG-100 ELAN series
G-CFBH CFBW CFFU CFYU CJNZ CJRL CJXP CKDY CKHV CKMG DDHJ DDHK DDHL DDMD DEPU DGIO
DG-300 (CLUB) ELAN and ELAN ACRO series
G-CFAJ CFJR CFJS CFJX CFLC CFLX CFNS CFSR CFTS CFUJ CFUU CFWM CFZW CHBE CHDR CHMB CJDV CJNO CJRC CJTK CJTN CJVL CKBF CKRF CKJH CKOR DESO DHCU DJAB PAFR

DG-400
G-BLJD BLRM BNXL BPIN BPXB BRTW BYTG CKCC DIRK HAJJ INCA KESS LEES OAPW
DG-500 ELAN series
G-BRRG BZYG CGBZ CHEF CHGV CHNA CHYE CHRC CJZB CJZK CKAW CKAX CKHC CKKJ CKNK CKOW CKOX SOOM SORA XBGA
DG-600
G-CFNT CKBS KOFM
DG-800 variants
G-BVJK BXSH BXUI BYEC CCRA CJJH DGCL DGIV IANB MSIX OBUP ORIG TRTM
DG-1000 variants
G-CKFN CKLY CKKV CKND CKNF CKOH DGIK RIEF WYVN

DIAMOND AIRCRAFT INDUSTRIES GmbH
DA.20 KATANA
G-BXGH BXJV BXJW BXMZ BXOF BXPC BXPD BXTS BYMB IKAT NIKK OBDA
DA.40(D) STAR
G-CBFA CCFP CCFR CCFS CCFU CCHA CCHB CCHC CCHD CCHE CCHF CCHG CCHK CCKH CCKI CCLB CCLC CCLV CCLW CCMF CCPX CCUS CCXU CCZU CDEJ CDEK CDEL CDSF CDSZ DAKM DIAM DSPL EMDM EMMM HASO JKMF JKMG KAFT LAFT MAFT MOPB OCCD OCCE OCCF OCCG OCCH OCCK OCCL OCCM OCCN OCCO OCCP OCCR OCCS OCCT OCCU OCCV OTDI SFLY SOHO WBVS ZANY
DA.42 TWIN STAR
G-CDKR CDSZ CDTG CEWN CTCD CTCE CDTF CDXK CEFX CTCH DJET DMND DMVV ELSE ENGA FCAB GSYJ HAFT HANG IANV ITFL JKMH JKMJ KELV LLMW LULV MHJK OCCW OCCX OCCY OCCZ OPFR ORZA PETS RASA SELC SERE SLCT SUEA VVTV

DOLGOPRUDNENSKOGO DESIGN BUREAU OF AUTOMATION
Balloon (Hot Air)
DKBA AT 0301-0
G-DKBA

DORNIER including AG fur DORNIER-FLUGZEUGE, DORNIER GmbH, DORNIER
WERKE AG, DORNIER LUFTAHRT GmbH and see BUCKER
DO.27
G-BMFG
DO.28 SKYSERVANT
G-ASUR BWCO
228
G-MAFE MAFI OMAF
328
G-BWIR BWWT BYHG BYMK BYML BZOG CCGS CJAB

DOUGLAS AIRCRAFT COMPANY INC including DOUGLAS AIRCRAFT
CORPORATION and see McDONNELL DOUGLAS
AD-4 SKYRAIDER
G-BMFB RADR
C-47 DAKOTA, and C-53 STORMTROOPER
"G-AMSU" "G-AMZZ" G-AGYX AHLX AIYT AJAV AKLL ALFO ALWC AMCA AMHJ AMJY AMNL AMPO AMPY AMRA AMSM AMYJ AMZH AMZW ANAF BGCF BHUB BLFL DAKK
DC-6
G-APSA SIXC
DC-7C
G-AOIE

DRAGON BALLOONS
Balloon (Hot Air)
G77
G-BKRZ

DRAGON LIGHT AIRCRAFT CO LTD
DRAGON 150 and 200
G-MJSL MJVY MMAC MMAE MMAI MMML MMNH MMPR MNJF

DRAYTON BALLOONS
Balloon (Hot Air)
B-56
G-BITS

DRUINE including ROLLASON AIRCRAFT and ENGINES LTD (D.31/D.62) production
D.31 TURBULENT
G-AJCP APIZ APNZ APOL APTZ APUY APVN APVZ APWP ARBZ ARGZ ARIM ARLZ ARMZ ARNZ ARRU ARRZ ASFX ASHT ASMM ASSY ASTA ATBS AVPC AWBM AWDO AWMR AWWT BFXG BGBF BKXR BLTC BUKH BVLU BWID OJJF
D.53 TURBI, D.54 TURBI
G-AOTK APBO APFA
D.62 CONDOR (Continental O-200-A)
G-ARHZ ARVZ ASEU ASRB ASRC ATAU ATAV ATOH ATUG ATVW

AVAW AVEX AVJH AVMB AVOH AVXW AWAT AWEI AWFN AWFO AWFP
AWSN AWSP AWSS AWST AXGS AXGU AXGV AXGZ AYFC AYFD AYFF
AYFG AYZS BADM BUOF RELL YNOT

DUDEK PARAGLIDING - see BAILEY AVIATION

DYKE
DELTA
  G-DYKE
SOCIÉTÉ **DYN'AÉRO**
CR100
  G-BZGY
MCR-01 variants (Rotax 912)
  G-BYEZ BYTM BZXG CBNL CBZX CCFG CCMM CCPN CCTE CCUI
  CCWH CDBY CDGG CDLL CDWG CENA CUTE CWMT DECO DGHI
  HARD KARK LMLV NONE OHIO PGAC POOP RESG TDVB TOOT

E_{AA}
ACROSPORT
  G-BJHK BKCV BLCI BPGH BSHY BTAK BTWI BVVL CCFX NEGG OJDA
  OMLC TANY TSOL VCIO
BIPLANE
  G-ATEP AVZW BBMH BPUA PFAA PFAY

EAGLE see AMERICAN AEROLIGHTS

EAVES
Balloon (Minimum Lift)
DODO variants
  G-BJGF BJGG BJIC BJJD BJJE BJJF BJJG
EUROPEAN variants
  G-BJMG BJRB BJRC BJRD FYBP FYDB FYDC FYDN FYFA FYFG FYFH
  FYFI

ECLIPSE GLIDERS
SUPER EAGLE
  G-BGWZ

EDGAR PERCIVAL including LANCASHIRE AIRCRAFT COMPANY production
EP.9 PROSPECTOR
  G-APAD APXW ARDG

EDGE
360
  G-ZVKO

EDWARDS
GYROCOPTER
  G-ASDF

FLUGZEUGBAU **EICHELSDORFER**
SB.5
  G-DEJH

EH INDUSTRIES LTD
EH-101
  G-EHIL OIOI

EIPPER AIRCRAFT INC
QUICKSILVER MX
  G-MBBM MBCK MBFO MBYM MJAM MJBT MJDW MJIR MJJK MJPV
  MJVP MJVU MMBU MMMG MMNA MMNB MMNC MMWC MNCO MTDO
  MWDZ

EIRI-AVION O/Y ncluding MOLINO
PIK-20 series
  G-BHNP CJBH CJDK CJVE CJXG CKFE DDFK DDJN DDKT DDLY DDPL
  DDRT DDVN DDZT DEAR EDMV OPIK PIKD POPE SOAR

EKW see DORNIER-WERKE AG
C-3605
  G-CCYZ DORN

ELA AVIACIÓN S.L
ELA 07
  G-CECB CEDP CEEA CEEF CEER CEFH CEGY CEHO CENFCENR
  CETW

ELECTRA FLYING CORPORATION
EAGLE
MBRB

ELLIOTTS OF NEWBURY
EoN AP.5 OLYMPIA 2B
  G-ALJZ
EoN AP.7 PRIMARY
  G-ALMN
EoN AP.10 460
  G-APWL

ELMWOOD
CA-05 CHRISTAVIA
  G-MRED

EMBRAER
EMB-110 BANDEIRANTE
  "G-FIRE" G-FLTY TABS
EMB-135BJ LEGACY
  G-CJMD CMAF FECR MGYB RBRO RRAZ SIRA SYLJ WCCI
EMB-135ER
  G-CDFS RJXJ RJXK RJXL
EMB-145 variants
  G-CCYH EMBC EMBD EMBE EMBH EMBI EMBJ EMBK EMBL EMBM
  EMBN EMBO EMBP EMBU EMBV EMBW EMBX EMBY ERJA ERJB ERJC
  ERJD ERJE ERJF ERJG RJXA RJXB RJXC RJXD RJXE RJXF RJXG
  RJXH RJXI RJXM RJXN RJXO SYLJ
EMB-312 TUCANO
  G-BTUC CEHJj
ERJ190-200LR (Embraer 195)
  G-FBEA FBEB FBEC FBED FBEE FBEF FBEG FBEH FBEI FBEJ FBEK
  FBEL FBEM FBEN

ENGLISH ELECTRIC CO LTD including AVRO (CANBERRA) production
WREN
  G-EBNV
CANBERRA
  G-BURM BVWC BVXC CDSX OMHD
LIGHTNING
  G-AWON AXEE BTSY FSIX LTNG OPIB

ENSTROM HELICOPTER CORPORATION
F-28
  G-BBHE BBIH BBPN BBPO BDKD BHAX BONG BRZG BURI BWOV BXLW
  BXXW BYKF BZHI EGAN MHCE MHCJ OABO ONUP PASN WSEC
280 SHARK
  G-BEYA BIBJ BPXE BSDZ BSLV BXFD BXRD BYSW CKCK COLL GKAT
  HDIX HYST IDUP MHCB MHCD MHCF MHCG MHCI MHCK MHCL MHCM
  MOTR OGES OITV OJBB OJMF OPDM OTHE PBYY SHAA SHRK SHUU
  SOPP VETS VRTX VVWW WIZI WRFM WRSY WSKY
480
  G-ENHP IGHH IJBB JPTT LADD LADZ MEEK OSKP OZAR REAN RIBZ
  TOIL TRUD TRYX UZZY WOOF

ENGINEERING AND RESEARCH CORPORATION including
AIR PRODUCTS LTD (FORNEY) and ALON INC (A-2) production
ALON A-2
  G-AVIL HARY
ERCOUPE 415 variants
  G-AVTT BZNO COUP EGHB ERCO
FORNEY F-1A
  G-ARHB ARHC AROO ONHH

EUROCOPTER see AÉROSPATIALE, SUD-AVIATION and MBB
EC.120 COLIBRI
  G-BXYD CBNB DEVL DRLH EIZO ETIM FCKD FEDA GTJM HEHE HVRZ
  IGPW ISSY JJFB LHCC LHMS MKII MODE OLDO OTFL PDGE RCNB
  TBLY TGGR VIPR WUSH WZRD ZADY ZWAR ZZOE ZZZS
EC.130
  G-ECBO
EC.155
  G-CEOJ CEXZ EURT EWAT ISST ISSV ISSW NIVA WJCJ
EC.225LP SUPER PUMA - see AÉROSPATIALE

EUROCOPTER DEUTSCHLAND GmbH
EC.135
  G-BZRS CCAU CHSU CPSH DAAT DORS EMAA EMID ESEX EWRT
  FEES IWRC KRNW LASU MSPT NEAU NESV NMID NWAA NWPS PLAL
  PSNI RWLA SASA SASB SPAO SPHU SSXX SUFF SURY TAGG VGMB
  WCAO WHIN WMAO WMAS WONN XMII

EUROPA AVIATION including AVIATION COMPOSITES CO LTD
EUROPA variants (Rotax 912 variants)
  G-BVGF BVIZ BVJN BVKF BVLV BVOS BVOW BVRA BVUV BVVH BVVP
  BVWM BWCV BWDP BWDX BWEG BWFH BWFX BWIJ BWIV BWJH

BWKG BWNL BWON BWRO BWUP BWVS BWWB BWYD BWZA BXCH
BXDY BXFG BXGG BXHY BXII BXIJ BXLK BXNC BXTD BXUM BYFG BYIK
BYJI BYPM BYSA BZAM BZHS BZNY BZTH BZTI BZTN CBES CBHI CBOF
CBWP CBXW CBYN CCEF CCFK CCGW CCJX CCOV CCRJ CCUL CCUY
CDBX CDEX CDPY CDVS CEBV CEMI CEOW CERI CEYK CHAH CHEB
CHET CHOX CHUG CEIW CLAV CORA CROB CROY CUTY DAMY DAYS
DDBD DEBR DLCB DRMM DURO EENI EESA EIKY EMIN EMSI EOFS
EORJ EUAB EURX EXES EZZA FELL FIZY FLOR FLOX FLYT FOGI GBXS
GCAC GIDY GIWT HOLM HUEW IANI IBBS IGII IKRK ILUM IMAB IOWE
IRON IVER IVET JAMY JERO JHKP JHYS JIMM JOST JULZ KDCC KIMM
KIRB KITS LABS LACE LAMM LEBE LILP LINN MAAN MAUS MEGG MFHI
MIME NDOL NEAT NESA NHRJ NIGL OBDM OBEV OBJT ODJG ODTW
OEZY OGAN OIZI OJHL OKEV OMIK OPJK OPRC ORPC OSJN OSLD
OUHI OURO OWWW OZEF PATF PATS PATZ PEGY PHXS PLPM PTAG
PTYE PUDS PUPY RATZ RBBB RBJW RDHS REJP RICS RIKS RIXS
RJWX RMAC RMMT ROBD RONA ROOV ROWI RPAF RPCC RWLY SAMY
SELF SHSH SMDH SNOP SNOZ SRYY STUE SUSE SYCO TAGR TERN
TKAY TOPK TSUE VKIT VPSJ WUFF WWWG XSDJ YURO ZORO ZTED

EUROWING LTD
GOLDWING
G-MBDG MBFZ MBPM MBPX MBZH MJAJ MJAY MJDP MJOE MJRL
MJRO MJRS MJSY MJUU MJWB MJWS MMBN MMLE MMTZ MMWL
MNNS MNZU

EVANS
VP-1
G-AYUJ AYXW BAAD BAJC BAPP BBXZ BCTT BDAR BDTB BDTL BDUL
BEIS BEKM BFAS BFHX BFJJ BGFK BGLF BHMT BHYV BIDD BIFO BKFI
BLCW BLWT BMJM BVAM BVEL BVJU BVUT BWFJ EVPI GVPI PFAG
PFAH PFAO PFAW TEDY VPAT VPCB
VP-2
G-BCVE BEYN BFYL BGFC BGPM BJVC BJZB BMSC BPBB BTAZ BTHJ
BTSC BUGI BUKZ BVPM BXOC CCEI RASC

EVEKTOR including COSMIK AVIATION LTD production
EV-97(A) (TEAM)EUROSTAR (Rotax 912-UL)
G-CBIY CBJR CBMZ CBNK CBRR CBVM CBWE CBWG CCAC CCBK
CCBM CCCO CCDX CCEJ CCEM CCKL CCMO CCMP CCPH CCPJ
CCSR CCTH CCTI CCTO CCTP CCUT CCVA CCVK CCWP CCZZ CDAC
CDAP CDAZ CDCC CDCT CDEP CDIY CDJR CDNG CDNI CDNM CDNP
CDOA CDOZ CDPL CDTA CDTU CDVD CDVP CDVU CDXM CDYP CEAM
CEBF CEBP CECY CEDV CEDX CEFK CEFZ CEHL CEGO CEKJ CEME
CENB CEND CERE CESF CESV CETT CEVS CEYY CEZD CEZF CFEE
CFTJ CSMK CTAV DATH DODG DOMS DSKI EMLE EVRO EZZY GHEE
ICMT IDOL IFLE IHOT JEEP JLAT JUGE JVBP KEJY LBUZ LOSY LYNI
NICC NIDG OCMT ODRY OSPD OTUN OTYE PROW RCHY RJRJ RMPY
SDFM SHMI SJES TINT TIVV UURO UZUP VORN XIXI ZZAC

EVERETT GYROPLANES LTD including R J EVERETT ENGINEERING and
see CAMPBELL
GYROPLANE variants
G-BIPI BMZN BMZP BMZS BTMV BTVB BUAI BULT BUZC BWCK LAXY
MICY OFRB OGOS ULPS

EXPERIMENTAL AVIATION
BERKUT
G-REDX

EXTRA FLUGZEUGBAU GmbH
EA.230/260
G-CBUA EXTR ROMP XTRA
EA.300
G-BZFR BZII CDYN DUKK EEEK EXEA FIII IIDI IIEI IIEX IIMI IIUI IIXI IIZI
IXTI JJIL JOKR KAYH KIII MIII MRKI OFFO SIII TENG XCCC XOXO XXTR
ZEXL ZXCL ZXEL

EXTREME SARL
SILEX
G-BZKG

F + W see DE HAVILLAND

FAIRCHILD ENGINE and AIRPLANE CORPORATION
24R ARGUS including repllica
"G-AJOZ"* G-AIZE AJOZ AJPC AJPI AKIZ BCBH BCBL FANC RGUS
M-62 CORNELL
G-CEVL

FAIREY AVIATION CO LTD
FLYCATCHER
G-BEYB

FIREFLY
G-ASTL
FULMAR
G-AIBE
GANNET
G-BMYP KAEW
FB.2 JET GYRODYNE
G-AJJP
SWORDFISH
G-AJVH BMGC
ULTRA-LIGHT HELICOPTER
G-APJJ

FAIRTRAVEL LTD
LINNET 2
G-ASMT ASZR

FALCONAR
F-9
G-AYEG
F-11
G-AWHY WBTS
F-12
G-BGHT CBWV TIMS

FEDOROV
Me-7 MECHTA
G-CHPT CHUO

FEWSDALE TIGERCRAFT LTD
GYROPLANE
G-ATLH

FFA FLUGZEUGWERKE AG
DIAMANT
G-CHGT DCDW DCGS

FIAT AERONAUTICA D'ITALIA
FIAT CR.42
G-CBLS

FIAT-SEZIONE AERITALIA
FIAT G.46
G-BBII

FIESELER WERKE GmbH
Fi/156c-3 STORCH
G-FIST STCH STOR

FISHER FLYING PRODUCTS INC
SUPER KOALA variants
G-BTBF BUVL MMTY

FLAGLOR
SKY SCOOTER
G-BDWE

FLEET AIRCRAFT OF CANADA LTD
80 CANUCK
G-FLCA

FLEXIFORM SKY SAILS see GARLAND, HIWAY and MAINAIR
TRIKE
G MMNT

FLIGHT DESIGN GmbH
CT2K (Rotax 912-ULS)
G-CBAI CBDH CBDJ CBEW CBEX CBIB CBIE CBLV CBNA CBUF CBVZ
CBWA CCNG CCNP CDJF CDPZ COMU CTDH DMCT GGCT IDSL KKCW
MCOY NULA POGO PRAH TOMJ
CTSW
G-CDWJ CDWS CDXL CEDE CEDM CEEO CEIE CEKT CENE CERA
CESW CETF CETH CEWT CEZZ CFAZ CJHP CLEG CTDW CTSW DEFT
FICS IROE KFLY KUPP LCKY OCDP RILA SAAA SDAT SWCT TODG
TORN VINH

FLYLIGHT AIRPORTS LTD
DOODLE BUG-TARGET
G-BZKH BZKI BZKJ CBZY
LIGHTLY-DISCUS
G-CEOL

FLS AEROSPACE (LOVAUX) LTD
SPRINT
  G-BVNU BXWU BXWV OAGI SAHI SCLX

FOCKE-WULF FLUGZEUGBAU GmbH see PIAGGIO
FW 44J Stieglitz
  G-STIG
FW 190 variants
  G-DORA FOKW FWAB

FOKKER BV including FOKKER VFW NV, ROYAL NETHERLANDS AIRCRAFT
FACTORY production and replicas.
Dr.1
  G-ATJM BVGZ CDXR FOKK
E.III
  G-AVJO
S.11 INSTRUCTOR
  G-BEPV BIYU
F.27 FRIENDSHIP
  G-BAUR BDVS BHMY BMXD BNIZ BVOB ECAT JEAI
F.27-050 (Fokker 50)
  G-UKTA

FOLLAND AIRCRAFT LTD
GNAT
  G-BVPP FRCE MOUR NAAT NATY RORI TIMM

FORNEY see ERCOUPE

FOSTER WIKNER AIRCRAFT CO LTD
GM.1 WICKO
  G-AFJB

AVIONS **FOURNIER** including ALPAVIA and SPORTAVIA-PÜTZER
RF3
  G-ATBP AYJD BCWK BFZA BHLU BIIA BIPN BLXH BNHT
RF4D
  G-AVHY AVKD AVNZ AVWY AWBJ AWEK AWEL AWEM AWGN AWLZ
  BHJN BIIF BUPJ BXLN IVEL
RF5 and RF5B SPERBER
  G-AYME AZJC AZPF AZRK AZRM BACE BEVO BJXK BPWK CBPC KCIG
  RFSB SSWV
RF6B-100
  G-BKIF BLWH BOLC
RF7
  G-LTRF

FRED see CLUTTON

FRESH BREEZE MÜLLER & WERNER GBR
FLYKE trike and Silex L sailwing & Monster paramotor
  G-CESL

FUJI HEAVY INDUSTRIES LTD
FA.200
  G-BAPM BBGI BBRC BBZN BCFF BCKS BCKT BCNZ BDFR BEUK BFGO
  CEYT FEWG FUJI HAMI HECB KARI MCOX

GADFLY AIRCRAFT CO LTD
HDW-1
  G-AVKE

GAERTNER
Balloon (Hot Air)
AX4 SKYRANGER
  G-BSGB

GARDAN see MINICAB

GARLAND-BIANCHI AIRCRAFT CO LTD
LINNET 1
  G-APNS

GAZEBO BALLOONS
Balloon (Hot Air)
AX6-65
  G-BCGP

GAZELLE see SOUTHERN MICROLIGHT

GEFA-FLUG GmbH
Airship (Hot Air)
AS 105 GD
  G-PEYO

GENERAL AIRCRAFT LTD
MONOSPAR ST.25 AMBULANCE
  G-AEYF
GAL.42 CYGNET
  G-AGBN

GENERAL AVIA
F22
  G-FZZA

GENERAL DYNAMICS CORPORATION
CONVAIR CV-440-54
  G-CONV

GIPPSLAND AERONAUTICS PTY LTD
GA-8 AIRVAN
  G-CDYA SCOL TVCO VANA VAND

GLASER-DIRKS FLUGZEUGBAU GmbH
DG-200 series
  G-CHBD CJAE CJAW CJDP CJKM CJVP CJWT CKDU CKDX DADJ DDTA
  DDTM DDXN DEDM DEME DHDH DEMU EEBR EEKA ONEZ

GLASFLÜGEL ING EUGEN HANLE
H201 STANDARD LIBELLE
  G-AXZH CFZB CHJR CHWC CJAS CJEU CJHJ CJNG CJWV DCFX DCLP
  DCLV DCMH DCMO DCMS DCMV DCNG DCNJ DCNY DCPM DCRB
  DCRO DCRV DCRW DCSR DCTU DCUJ DCWE DCWG DCWX DCYG
  DDBP DDCC DDMS DENO DFAR DHAA DHAD DHCO ECLW ECPA EHAV
  LIBL LIBY YOHO
H205 CLUB LIBELLE
  G-CKAM CKNI DDEO
H206 HORNET
  G-CKLC DDKD
H303 MOSQUITO
  G-CFBN CHMT CJEH CJNR CJTO DDTK DDTV DDTX DDTY DDWL
  DDWR DDXW DEAK DEDJ MOZI
304
  G-CHMM DAWZ DEHU

GLOBE AIRCRAFT CORPORATION
GC-1B SWIFT
  G-AHUN ARNN BFNM

GLOSTER AIRCRAFT CO LTD including ARMSTRONG-WHITWORTH
production
GAMECOCK replica
  G-CBTS
GLADIATOR
  G-AMRK CBHO GLAD
METEOR variants
  G-ANSO ARCX BPOA BWMF JETM LOSM METE

GOULD-TAYLORCRAFT see TAYLORCRAFT

GOWLAND
GWG.2 JENNY WREN
  G-ASRF

GRANGER
ARCHAEOPTERYX
  G-ABXL

GREAT LAKES AIRCRAFT INC see OLDFIELD
2T-1A SPORT TRAINER
  G-BIIZ BUPV GLII GLST

GREEN
Balloon (Hot Air)
S-25
  G-BSON

GREENSLADE
TRIKE with Flexiform wing
  G-MMWG

GRIFFITHS
GH.4
  G-ATGZ

GROB-WERKE GMB & CO KG including GROB FLUGZEUGBAU GmbH &CO KG and BURKHART GROB LUFT-UND RAUMFAHRT GMBH & CO KG

G102 ASTIRr
G-CEWP CEWW CFCJ CFEF CFFB CFGK CFHT CFHW CFRL CFSH CFSZ CFTK CFTR CGBJ CGBK CGCL CGDO CHBT CHGB CHKB CHRA CHSE CHTD CHTE CHTR CHUN CHVK CHXY CJCF CJLR CJMV CJSD CJSK CJUS CJWR CJYC CJYP CKAY CKBD CKBL CKEE CKGH CKMC CKRN DDJD DDJX DDKU DDKW DDKX DDLH DDMR DDNC DDNE DDNK DDOB DDOR DDPO DDPY DDRU DDRW DDSH DDSU DDUL DDUX DDWU DDXJ DDYF DEAF DEAW DELN DHTG EEBM FECO GCMW GSST ONAT

G103 TWIN ASTIR
G-CFHO CFOC CJLZ CJWM CKRH

G103 TWIN ACRO variants
G-CFWC CHBH CHWW CJKV CJOG CKFG CKMT DEWP DEWR DEXA NUGC

G104 SPEED ASTIR
G-CFXA FEBB

G109
G-BIXZ BJVK BJZX BLMG BLUV BMCG BMFY BMGR BMLK BMLL BMMP BXSP BXXI BYJH BZLY CBLY CDNA CEYN CHAR DKDP IPSI KEMC KNEK LLAN LREE LULU NDGC RASH ROBZ SAGA SAMG TACK UILD WAVE WAVY

G115 variants
G-BOPT BOPU BPKF BVHC BVHD BVHE BVHF BVHG BYDB BYFD BYUA BYUB BYUC BYUD BYUE BYUF BYUG BYUH BYUI BYUJ BYUK BYUL BYUM BYUN BYUO BYUP BYUR BYUS BYUT BYUU BYUV BYUW BYUX BYUY BYUZ BYVA BYVB BYVC BYVD BYVE BYVF BYVG BYVH BYVI BYVJ BYVK BYVL BYVM BYVN BYVO BYVP BYVR BYVS BYVT BYVU BYVV BYVW BYVX BYVY BYVZ BYWA BYWB BYWC BYWD BYWE BYWF BYWG BYWH BYWI BYWJ BYWK BYWL BYWM BYWN BYWO BYWP BYWR BYWS BYWT BYWU BYWV BYWW BYWX BYWY BYWZ BYXA BYXB BYXC BYXD BYXE BYXF BYXG BYXH BYXI BYXJ BYXK BYXL BYXM BYXN BYXO BYXP BYXR BYXS BYXT BYXX BYXY BYXZ BYYA BYYB GROE MERF RAFA RAFB TAYI

GRUMMAN AIRCRAFT ENGINEERING

G.44 WIDGEON
G-DUCK

F-6F HELLCAT
G-BTCC

F-8F BEARCAT
G-BUCF RUMM

FM-2 WILDCAT
G-RUMW

GRUMMAN AMERICAN AVIATION CORPORATION (3) including
AMERICAN AVIATION CORPORATION (1), AMERICAN GENERAL AVIATION (2) and
GULFSTREAM AMERICAN CORPORATION (4) production

AMERICAN AA-1 YANKEE (1)
G-AYLP BFOJ SEXY

AMERICAN AA-1A TRAINER (1)
G-AYHA AZKS RUMN

GRUMMAN AA-1B TRAINER (3)
G-BBFC BBWZ BCLW BDNW BDNX BERY

GRUMMAN AA-1C LYNX (3)
G-BEXN BTLP

AMERICAN AA-5 TRAVELLER (1)
G-AZMJ AZVG BAFA BAJN BAJO BIWW

GRUMMAN AA-5 TRAVELLER (3)
G-BAOU BASH BAVR BAVS BBBI BBCZ BBDL BBDM BBLS BBRZ BBSA BBUE BBUFCCCJ BCCK BCEE BCEF BCEO BCEP BCIJ BCLI BCPN BDCL BDFY BEZC BEZF BEZG BEZH BEZI BIAY BLFW BMYI BSTR MALC NONI OBMW

GRUMMAN AA-5A CHEETAH (3)
G-BDLO BEBE BFIJ BFIN BFLX BFZO BNVB BXHH BXOX CHTA JAJB JNAS JUDY MILY MOGI OPWK PURR REEK

GULFSTREAM AA-5A CHEETAH (4)
G-BGCM BGFG BGFI BGVV BHZO BIVV BJDO CCAT DOEA IFLI KINE LSFI MSTC OCAM OMOG OPPL OSSF OSTC OSTU PADD PAWS PING RATE

GRUMMAN AA-5B TIGER (3)
G-BCRR BDRB BFTF BFTG BFVS BFXW BFZP BHLX BIPA BKPS BOXU BXTT ERRY PORK REET ROWL RUBB WINK ZARI ZERO

GULFSTREAM AA-5B TIGER (4)
G-BFXX BGPH BGVY BHZK BIBT BIPV BJAJ BOZO BOZZ BPIZ BTII DAVO DINA DONI GAJB IRIS JENN NODE OTIG TGER TYGA WMTM

AMERICAN GENERAL AG-5B TIGER (2)
G-BTUZ BYDX CCXX CDGS GIRY NODY OABR RICO

GA-7 COUGAR (3)
G-BOXR OOGO

GA-7 COUGAR (4)
G-BGNV BGON BGSY BLHR BOOE CDND CYMA EENY GOTC HIRE OOGA OOGI OOGS TANI

GULFSTREAM AEROSPACE CORPORATION

G159 GULFSTREAM I
G-BNCE

GULFSTREAM G-IV
G-EVLN MATF TAYC

GULFSTREAM GV-SP (Gulfstream 550)
G-EGNS GSSO HRDS JCBC

GULFSTREAM-AMERICAN CORPORATION see GRUMMAN AMERICAN

GYROFLIGHT

BROOKLAND HORNET
G-BRPP MIKE PHIL

Hadland

WILLOW
G-MMMH

HALLAM

FLECHE
G-FLCT

HANDLEY PAGE LTD

O/400 replica
G-BKMG

HP.39 GUGNUNC
G-AACN

HP.81 HERMES
G-ALDG

HANDLEY PAGE (READING) LTD

HPR.7 DART HERALD
G-APWA APWJ ASKK ASVO ATIG AVEZ AVPN BAZJ BEYF CEXP

HANRIOT ET CIE

HD.1
G-AFDX

HAPI

CYGNET SF-2A
G-BRZD BWFN BXCA BXHJ BYYC CCKT

HARKER

DH WASP
G-MJSZ

HARMON

ROCKET
G-RCKT

HASELDINE

HUMMELBIRD
G-CETN

HATZ

CB-1
G-BRSY BXXH CBYW HATZ TIKO

AÉRONAUTIQUE **HAVRAISE** see MINICAB

HAWKER AIRCRAFT LTD including AVRO and CCF production and see
ARMSTRONG WHITWORTH and W.A.R

AUDAX
G-BVVI

CYGNET
G-CAMM EBJI EBMB

DEMON
G-BTVE

FURY (Biplane)
G-BKBB

FURY
 G-BWOL CBEL CBZP

HART
G-ABMR

HIND
G-AENP CBLK

HUNTER
G-BNCX BOOM BUEZ BVGH BVWG BVWV BWAF BWFR BWFT BWGK BWGL BWGM BWGN BWKA BWKC BWOU BXFI BXKF BZPB BZPC BZSE BZSR EGHH ETPS FFOX GAII HHAB HHAC HHAF HNTR HPUX HUNT HVIP KAXF PRII PSST SIAL TVII VETA

HURRICANE
G-AMAU BYDL CBOE HHII HRLI HUPW HURI HURR ROBT

NIMROD
  G-BURZ BWWK
SEA FURY
  G-BUCM RNHF SALY
SEA HAWK see ARMSTRONG WHITWORTH
SEA HURRICANE
  G-BKTH
TEMPEST
  G-PEST TEMT
TOMTIT
  G-AFTA

HAWKER SIDDELEY AVIATION including BRITISH AEROSPACE PLC,
CORPORATE JETS LTD and RAYTHEON-HAWKER production
DH.121 TRIDENT, HS.121 TRIDENT
  G-ARPH ARPO AVFB AVFE AVFG AVFH AVFJ AWZI AWZJ AWZM AWZP
  AWZR AWZS AWZU AZFW BAJJ BBVU BBVV BBVW BBVZ BBWG
DH 125, HS.125 and HAWKER 800 variants
  G-ARYB ARYC ASSM ATPD BOCB BYHM BZNR CDLT DCTA FINK GMAB
  IFTE IFTF IWDB JETI JJSI JMAX LAOR OHEA OJWB OLDD RDMV VIPI
  WYNE YUGO
BUCCANEER
  G-HHAA
HARRIER
  G-VTOL

HEAD BALLOONS INC
Balloon (Hot Air)
Ax8-105
  G-UKUK

HEINKEL
CASA 2111 (He.111H-16)
  G-AWHA AWHB

HEINTZ see ZENAIR

HELIO
SUPER COURIER
  G-BAGT BGIX

HELTON AIRCRAFT CORPORATION
LARK 95
  G-LARK

R J HEMMING
TRIKE with Solar Wings Typhoon wing
  G-MMPU

HILL see MAXAIR

HILLER HELICOPTERS INC
UH-12 (360)
  G-ASAZ ASTP ATKG

HINDUSTAN AERONAUTICS LTD
PUSHPAK
  G-AVPO BXTO

HISPANO see MESSERSCHMITT

HIWAY HANG GLIDERS LTD
SKYTRIKE with Demon, Excalibur, Flexiform, Gold Marque, Hiway,
Solar Wings, Super Scorpion & Vulcan wings
  G-MBAA MBBJ MBCL MBEU MBFK MBIA MBIT MBJF MBJX MBKZ MBPU
  MJAN MJAV MJDJ MJDR MJFZ MJHV MJKF MJKO MJKP MJMD MJMS
  MJPE MJSO MJXY MMCN MMCV MMHG MMHK MMHL MMLH MMRH
  MMUR MNGO MNME MVDS MYBN

HOAC FLUGZEUGWERKE (HOFFMANN FLUGZEUGBAU FRIESACH) including
DIAMOND AIRCRAFT INDUSTRIES GmbH production
DV.20 KATANA
  G-BWFI BWFV BWGY BWLP BWLS BWYM TENS
H 36 DIMONA/
  G-BKPA BLCV BNUX CEUT KOKL LYDA OMDG RIET
HK 36 SUPER DIMONA variants
  G- BYFL FMKA GEOS IMOK LIDA OSFA SLMG XKKA

HOLMAN
BRISTOL TYPE 2000
  G-CCGP

HORNET MICROLIGHTS LTD
HORNET 250 with Airwave Nimrod wing (Fuji-Robin EC-25-PS)
  G-MBCX MBJL
HORNET DUAL TRAINER with Southdown Raven wing (Rotax462)
  G-MNRI MNRK MNRM MTGX MTJX MTMP MTMR MTRL MTXE MVHZ
HORNET R variants (Combi) (Rotax 462)
  G-MVUR MVUU MVYK MVYL MVYN MVZW MWBP MWBR MWBS MWBU
  MWBW MWBY MWDE MWDI MWEU MWEY MWKE

HOVEY
BETA BIRD
  G-BKRV
WD-II/III WHING DING
  G-MBAB MNVO

HOWARD
SPECIAL T-MINUS
  G-BRXS

HOWES
Balloon (Hot Air)
AX6
  G-BDWO

HUGHES TOOL CO and HUGHES HELICOPTERS INC including
SCHWEIZER AIRCRAFT CORPORATION (**269** wef 1986) and McDONNELL- DOUGLAS
(**369** wef 1983) production
269 (Series 300)
  G-BAXE BMWA BOVX BOXT BPJB BPPY BRTT BSML BSVR BUEX
  BWAV BWDV BWNJ BWWJ BWZY BXMY BXRP BZXJ CBCN CCVG CDOJ
  CDTK CDTW CDYW CEAW CEBE CECO CEOY DASY DCBI ECBI FCBI
  HCBI IBHH IRYC JAMA JMDI LINX MARE OCBI OCJK ODNH OJAE OOGL
  OSLO PKPK PLOW PLPC RHCB RIFB ROCR SBHH SHPP STEP TAMA
  TAMB TAMC TAMD TAME TASS TSLC VNUS WARK WHRL XCBI
369 (Series 500)
  G-AYIA BIOA BPLZ BRTL BTRP CCKS CCPY CCUO DADS DIZZ ERIS
  GSOO GSPG HAUS HKHM HSOO HUES HUKA IDWR JETZ JIVE KSWI
  LIBS LINC LOGO MACE MLSN MRAJ MRRR OGJP OMDH OPCS ORRR
  RISK SOOC SSCL SWEL TCEE TRUE TVEE VICE

HUNT
AVON Trike variants with HIWAY & HUNT wings
  G-BZRG BZTW BZUZ MNCA MGTR MMGT MNCA MYTV MYUR MYWC
  MYWH MYYE MYYJ MZCX MZDZ MZFE MZGH

HUNTAIR LTD
PATHFINDER
  G-MBWG MBYK MBYL MJBZ MJDE MJDH MJFM MJJA MJOC MJUV
  MJWK MMBV MMCB MMDR MMOG

HUNTING PERCIVAL AIRCRAFT LTD including BRITISH AIRCRAFT
CORPORATION (BAC) and see PERCIVAL
P.66 PEMBROKE
  G-BNPG BNPH BXES
P.66 PRESIDENT
  G-AOJG
P.84 JET PROVOST variants
  G-AOBU AOHD BKOU BVEZ BVSP BWDR BWDS BWGT BWOT BWSG
  BWSH BXBH BXDL BXLO KNOT PROV RAFI TORE VIVM
BAC.145 JET PROVOST variants
  G-BVTC BWCS BWEB BWGF BWGS BWOF BYED BWUU JPRO JPTV
  JPVA
BAC.167 STRIKEMASTER variants
  G-AXEF AYHS BESY BFOO CDHB CFBK FLYY MXPH RSAF SMAS
  UVNR

HYBRED see MEDWAY

IAV-BACHAU see YAKOVLEV

ICA (INTREPRINDEREA DE CONSTRUCTII AERONAUTICE-BRASOV)
IS-28A
  G-DDEG DDLT DDZR DEHW DEJA
IS-28M
  G-BKXN BMMV BMOM
IS-29D
  G-DDEW

ICP SRL
MXP-740 SAVANNAH variants
  G-CBBM CCII CCJO CCJU CCLP CCSV CCXP CDAT CDCR CDEH CDJD
  CDKN CDKO CDLR CDSH CDTT CDTY CDUV CDVK CDZU CEBC CECK
  CEED CEEX CEFY CEGK CENU CEVU CEZB CSUE VGVG

III (INIZIATIVE INDUSTRIALI ITALIANE) **SpA**
SKY ARROW (Rotax 912)
  G-BXGT BYCY BYZR BZVT CBTB CIAO FINZ GULP IOIA ROME SKYT
  SUTN

ILYUSHIN
Il-2
  G-BZVW BZVX

INTERAVIA
Balloon (Hot Air)
70TA
  G-BUUT
80TA
  G-BZYT

INTERPLANE AIRCRAFT INC
ZJ-VIERA
  G-CFAP

ISAACS
FURY
  G-ASCM AYJY BBVO BCMT BEER BIYK BKFK BKZM BMEU BWWN
  BZAS BZNW CCKV EHMF FURI PFAR RODI
SPITFIRE
  G-BBJI BXOM

JACKAROO AIRCRAFT see THRUXTON

JACOBS
Balloon (Hot Air)
V35 AIRCHAIRr
  G-CEWF

JASTREB see SCHEMPP-HIRTH

JODEL including CEA, SAN and WASSMER production and see FALCONAR and ROBIN
D.9 and D.92 variants
  G-AVPD AWFT AXKJ AXYU AZBL BAGF BDEI BDNT BGFJ BURE BZBZ
  KDIX
D.11, D.112, D.117 and, D.119 variants
  G-ARDO ARNY ASIS ASJZ ASXY ATIN ATIZ ATJN ATWB AVPM AWFW
  AWMD AWVB AWVZ AWWI AXAT AXCG AXCY AXFN AXHV AXWT
  AXXW AXZT AYBP AYBR AYCP AYEB AYGA AYHX AYKJ AYKK AYKT
  AYMU AYWH AYXP AZFF AZHC AZII AZKP AZVL BAAW BAKR BAPR
  BARF BATJ BAUH BAZM BBPS BCGW BCLU BDBV BDDG BDIH BDJD
  BDMM BEDD BEZZ BFEH BFGK BFNG BFXR BGTX BGWO BHCE BHEL
  BHFF BHHX BHKT BHNL BHNX BIAH BIDX BIEO BIOU BIPT BITO BIVB
  BIVC BIWN BIYW BIZY BJOT BKAO BKIR BMIP BOOH BPFD BRCA BRVZ
  BUFF BVEH BVPS BVVE BWMB DAVE INNI
D.18
  G-BODT BSYA BTRZ BUAG BUPR BWVC BWVV BXFC CBRC CBRD
  JRKD OJOD OLEM TREK WIBB
D.120 PARIS-NICE
  G-ASPF ASXU ATLV AVLY AVYV AXNJ AYGG AYLV AYRS AZEF AZGA
  AZLF BACJ BANU BCGM BDDF BDEH BDWX BFOP BHGJ BHNK BHPS
  BHXD BHXS BHZV BICR BIEN BJFM BJOE BJYK BKAE BKCW BKCZ
  BKGB BKJS BKPX BMDS BMID BMLB BMYU BOWP BYBE CCBR DIZO
D.140 MOUSQUETAIRE
  G-ARDZ ARLX AROW ARRY ATKX AYFP BJOB BSPC BWAB CVST DCXL
  EGUR EHIC JRME OBAN REES TOAD YRUS
D.150 MASCARET variants
  G-ASKL ASRT AVEF AZBI BACL BFEB BHEG BHEZ BHVF BIDG BLAT
  BLXO BMEH BVSS BVST CECH CEZW DISO EDGE FARR IEJH JDEL
  LDWS MASC OABB TIDS
DR.1050, and DR.1051 variants
  G-ARFT ARRD ARRE ARUH ARXT ASXS ATAG ATEV ATFD ATGE ATIC
  ATJA ATLB ATWA AVGJ AVGZ AVHL AVJK AVOA AWUE AWVE AWWN
  AWWO AXLS AXSM AXUK AYEH AYEJ AYEV AYEW AYGD AYJA AYKD
  AYLC AYLF AYLL AYUT AYYO AYYT AYZK AZOU AZWF BAEE BDMW
  BEAB BEYZ BFBA BGBE BGRI BHHE BHOL BHSY BHTC BHUE BIOI
  BKDX BLKM BLRJ BPLH BTHH BXIO BXYJ BYCS BYFM CCNA CEIS
  CESA DANA IOSI IOSO JODL JWIV LAKI RIVE SPOG
DR.200, DR.220 and DR.221 variants
  G-AVOC AVOM AYDZ BANA BFHR BHRW BLCT BLLH BMKF BUTH
  CPCD GREG MLLE RRCU STEV
DR.250 and DR.253 variants
  G-ATTM AWKP AWYL AXWV AYUB BJBO BKPE BOSM BSZF BUVM
  BXCG BYEH BYHP
DR.300, DR.315, DR.340 and DR.360 variants
  G-AXDK AYCO AZIJ AZJN BGVB BICP BLAM BLGH BLHH BOEH BOZV
  BVYG BVYM BXOU DRSV DRZF KIMB

JORDAN AVIATION
DUET
  G-MBWH MMKY

JUNKERS FLUGZEUG UND MOTORENWERKE AG including CASA
production
Ju 87/R4
  G-STUK
CASA 352L
  "G-AFAP" G- BECL BFHD BFHE BFHG

JURCA
MJ.2 TEMPETE
  G-ASUS AYTV
MJ.5 SIROCCO
  G-CEAO CLAX RECO
MJ.100 SPITFIRE
  G-CDPM

K & S
JUNGSTER
  G-BLDC DAJW OWEN
SA.102.5 CAVALIER
  G-AZHH BCKF BCMJ BCRK BDKJ BDLY BUNJ BWSI

KAY
GYROPLANE
  G-ACVA

KEIRS
HEATED AIR TUBE)
  G-BGZS

KEN BROCK
KB-2 (Rotax 582)
  G-BSEG BUZV BVMN BVUJ

KENSINGER
KF
  G-ASSV

KING
Balloon (Minimum Lift)
KINGRAM 01
  G-BJDV

KIRK
Balloon (Minimum Lift)
SKYRIDER
  G-BJTF

LEIGHTFLUGZEUGBAU **KLEMM** GMBH - see BA
L.25-1A
  G-AAUP
KL.35
  G-KLEM

KNIGHT see PAYNE

KOLB
TWINSTAR (Rotax 582)
  G-BUZT BYTA CCFJ CCRB CDFA CDZS CODY CEBI CYRA IANN KOLB
  MGPX MWWM MYDP MYIK MYKB MYLN MYLP MYMI MYNY MYOG
  MYOO MYOR MYPC MYVA MYWP MYXS MZGJ MZZT PLAD

KRONFELD LTD see BAC (1935) LTD

L**A** MOUETTE
PROFIL (Wing)
  G-MVCK

LAFAYETTE
HI-NUSKI Mk.1
  G-MBWI

LAK including AB SPORTINE AVIAICIJA production
LAK-12 LIETUVA
  G-CHGR CHHM CHHW CHRB CHTF CJBS CJBY DHSR GLAK

LAK-17 series
G-CJOU CJVJ CKCR CKHE CKKK CKMP CKOI DAVS
LAK-19T
G-CKOU CKPA EWEW

LAKE AIRCRAFT CORPORATION including AEROFAB INC and
CONSOLIDATED AERONAUTIC INC)
LA-4
G-BASO BOLL
LA-250 RENEGADE
G-LAKE SIVW

LAMBERT AIRCRAFT ENGINEERING BVBA
MISSION M212-100
G-XFLY

LANCAIR see NEICO

LANCASHIRE
MICRO-TRIKE with Flexiiform & Wasp wings
G-MJYW MMFG MMPL

LANCASHIRE AIRCRAFT see EDGAR PERCIVAL

LANGE FLUGZEUGBAU GmbH
E1 ANTARES
G-DCDC

LASER
LAZER Z200, Z230
G-BWKT CBHR CDDP LAZA VILL

LAVERDA see AVIAMILANO

LAZAIR see ULTRAFLIGHT

TONY LE VIER ASSOCIATES INC
COSMIC WIND
G-ARUL BAER

LEARJET INC including BOMBARDIER AEROSPACE production
LEARJET Model 40
G-MEET MOOO STUF
LEARJET Model 45
G-CDNK CDSR GMAA GOMO IOOX JANV LLOD OLDK OLDT OLDW
RWGW SOVB SOVC ZXZX
LEARJET Model 60
G-HOIL LGAR SXTY

LEDERLIN
38OL LADYBUG
G-AYMR

SOCIÉTÉ DES AVIONS LEOPOLDORFF
L-6
G-BYKS
L-7
G-AYKS

LET NARODNI PODNIK KUNOVICE
L-13 BLANIK
G-CHTY CJDU CJNX DCVB DDEX DDVD
ZLIN Z.37 CMELAK (Bumble Bee)
G-AVZB

LETOV LTD
LF-107 LUNAK
G-CKMR
LK-2M SLUKA
G-BYLJ MYRP MYRR MYUP MYVG MYVT MYXO MZBF MZBK MZDX
MZES MZFC MZGF MZLY MZNZ MZOI MZOX XPBI

LEVI
LEVI GO-PLANE RL6 Srs 1
G-BCMF

LIBERTY AEROSPACE INC
XL-2
G-OIVN

LIGHTNING see SOUTHDOWN

LILLIPUT BALLOONS UK
Balloon (Minimum Lift)
TYPE 1
G-HONY
TYPE 4
G-GRWL

LINDSTRAND (HOT AIR) BALLOONS LTD
Airship (Hot Air)
HS 110
G-BZFU HSTH LRBW TRIB
Balloon (Gas)
LBL 14A
G-BWBB BXAJ
Balloon (Hot Air)
LBL 9A
G-CEHX
LBL 21 series
G-BVRL BYEY CBYS OJNB
LBL 25 CLOUDHOPPER
G-BVUI BXHM BYYJ CBZJ CDAD CEGG EECO HOPR OLAW OOER
RIME
LBL 31A
G-BWHD BXIZ BXUH BZIH BZNV BZUK CDUJ CDXF CEOU FFFT LELE
ONCB
LBL 35A CLOUDHOPPER
G-CDIW HOPA
LBL 42A
G-BWCG CBLO
LBL 56 series
G-COSY DBAT
LBL 60 series
G-CCBP IRLZ OERR CDZO
LBL 69 series
G-BVDS BVGG BVIR BWLA BYKA CBBX HSBC LBLI REAR
LBL 77 series
G-BUBS BUWI BUZR BVPV BVRR BWAW BWBO BWFK BWKZ BWMH
BWTU BXDR BYJG BYJR BYKW BYLW BYRZ BYYE BZBJ BZGV BZKE
CCFV CDWX CDYL CDYX ERRI HERD ICKY LBUK MCOW MERE MUCK
NUNI PATP PSAX TAJF
LBL 90 series
G-VWW BVZT BWBT BWTN BWWE BWZU BXLF BXXO BXZF BXZI BZLU
BZPV CBIM CBNI CCJH CCOI CCSS CDDM CDDN CDEU CDHJ CDIV
CHLL DUGI EDRE FLEW FWAY GOGB JEMI MINN MRKT OBJB ODJF
OSUP PATX PROF RAYO SJKR TSWI UNER UNGE
LBL 105 series
G-BUYJ BUZJ BVDO BVON BVRU BWGA BWRZ BWSB BWTB BWWY
BXDZ BXHE BXJG BXUO BYFU BYIY BYJN BYJZ BYLX BZAG BZUD
CBPH CBPW CCIA CCSM CCVF CCXD CDLV CDMW CECS CEJI CEMV
ENRI FLGT FRIL GOAL GULF HAPI ICOI IOFR ITVM JENO LPAD OAER
ODAF ODDY OPMT OUMC OVIA PIZZ RAPI RIMB ROMS RROW RXUK
SNAK VITL ZETA
LBL 120 series
G-BVLZ BWDM BWEA BZBL CBTR CBVH DUBI ENBD OGSS UPUZ
LBL 150A
G-BVEW BXCM CDHP CEOV IRTH
LBL 180A
G-BVIX CBZU KNOB OTUP WIZD
LBL 210A
G-BVLL BVML BXNX BZDE CCKX CCRS DVBF FBVF HVBF JVBF NVBF
OCBS SSLF WVBF
LBL 240A
G-BXBL CCKY OWYE
LBL 260 series
G-PVBF SMRT VIZA
LBL 310A
G-BZPE CBIW TVBF
LBL 317 series
G-CDHN YVBF
LBL 330A
G-BXVE CCWE CDHK CDHL LRGE LVBF XVBF
LBL 360A
G-CENX VBFF
LBL 400A
G-UVBF

Special Shapes

SHAPE	REGISTRATION(S)
ARMCHAIR	G-LAZY
BABY BEL	G-BXUG
BATTERY	G-OKCP
BANANAS	G-CEMW
BEAR	G-BWTF
BIRTHDAY CAKE	G-WISH
BULB	G-DINK

CAKE	G-BZNZ
DOG	G-CDOG
FLOWERS	G-ODBN
FOUR	G-BVVU
HOUSE	G-CDWV
HUMPTY DUMPTY	G-EGGG
J & B BOTTLE	G-OJBW
NEWSPAPER	G-BVGK FFTT
PIG	G-PIGG
PINK PANTHER	G-PINX
POP CAN	G-BXHN
RACING CAR	G-TKGR
SUN	G-BZIC
TELEWEST SPHERE	G-BXHO
TULIPS	G-TULP

LINDSTRAND TECHNOLOGIES LTD
Balloon (Gas)
LTL 203T
   G-CFBF LAPS

LOCKHEED AIRCRAFT CORPORATION including LOCKHEED-CALIFORNIA
CO and CANADAIR production
10 ELECTRA
   G-LIOA
18 LODESTAR
   G-AGCN AGIJ BMEW
414 HUDSON
   G-BEOX
L.188 ELECTRA
   G-FIJR FIJV FIZU LOFA LOFB LOFC LOFD LOFE LOFF LOFG OFRT
L.749 CONSTELLATION
   G-CONI
L.1011 TRISTAR
   G-IOIT
T-33A
   G-BYOY WGHB

LORIMER
IOLAIRE
   G-MZFI

LOVEGROVE see BENSEN
AV-8 GYROPLANE
   G-BXXR
SHEFFY GYROPLANE
   G-CDFW

LUSCOMBE AIRCRAFT COMPANY
RATTLER
   G-BKPG

LUSCOMBE AIRPLANE CORPORATION
8 variants
   G-AFUP AFYD AFZK AFZN AGMI AHEC AICX AJAP AJJU AJKB AKTI
AKTN AKTT AKUF AKUG AKUH AKUI AKUJ AKUK AKUL AKUM AKUP
AKVP BNIO BNIP BPOU BPPO BPVZ BPZA BPZC BPZE BRDJ BRGF
BRGG BRHX BRHY BRJA BRJK BROO BRPZ BRRB BRSW BRUG BSHH
BSHI BSNE BSNT BSOE BSOX BSSA BSTX BSUD BSYF BSYH BTCH
BTCJ BTDF BTIJ BTJA BTJB BTJC BUAO BUKT BUKU BULO BVEP
BVGW BVGY BWOB CCRK DAIR EITE KENM LUSC LUSI LUST NIGE
ROTI SAGE YRIL

LVG
C.VI
   G-AANJ

LYNDEN
AURORA
   G-CBZS

R and W McCANDLESS
M.2 GYROPLANE
   G-ARTZ (1)
M.4 GYROPLANE
   G-ARTZ (2) ATXX AXVN BVLE

McCULLOCH AIRCRAFT CORPORATION
J.2 GYROPLANE
   G-HEKY

McDONNELL DOUGLAS CORPORATION
MD-82
   G-CEPA CEPB CEPC CEPD CEPE CEPF CEFG CEFH CEPI CEPJ
   CEPK
MD-83
   G-FLTK FLTL FLTM
DC-10-30
   G-DCMA

McDONNELL DOUGLAS HELICOPTER CO see HUGHES and
MD HELICOPTERS

MACAIR
MERLIN
   G-BWEN

MAGNI GYRO of ITALY - see VPM

MAINAIR SPORTS LTD see PEGASUS/FLASH and SOUTHDOWN INTERNATIONAL
BLADE (Rotax 912)
   G-BYCW BYHN BYHO BYHS BYJB BYKC BYKD BYNM BYON BYOS
BYOW BYRO BYRP BYRR BYTL BYTU BYZB BZAA BZAL BZDC BZDD
BZEG BZEL BZFO BZFS BZGM BZGS BZGW BZJL BZJN BZMS BZNS
BZPA BZPN BZPZ BZRB BZRW BZTM BZTR BZTV BZTX BZUB BZUN
BZWB BZXM BZXT CBAD CBBG CBDD CBDL CBDN CBDP CBEM CBET
CBGT CBHG CBHJ CBHM CBJT CBKM CBKN CBKO CBLD CBLM CBLT
CBMM CBNC CBOG CBOM CBOO CBOV CBRE CBRJ CBRM CBSM
CBSZ CBTE CBTM CBTW CBVG CBWM CBXM CBXV CBYF CBYM CBZA
CBZB CBZD CCAB CCAG CCAM CCAW CCDM CCFM CCGK CCIF CCPM
CCTM CCWL CCXR CCZW CDAG CDCU CDOR CEGM CEMR CLFC
EEYE ENVY FERN FLYF JAIR JBEN JMAN JOOL LENF MAIN MYLT
MYRC MYRD MYTD MYTG MYTL MYTU MYUC MYUN MYVB MYVE
MYVH MYVO MYVY MYVZ MYXJ MYXM MYXN MYYA MYYG MYYH
MYYW MYYY MZAA MZAB MZAE MZAF MZAG MZAJ MZAM MZAP MZAR
MZAS MZAT MZAU MZAV MZAY MZAZ MZBA MZBL MZCC MZCD MZCE
MZCG MZCN MZCU MZDF MZDK MZDT MZEB MZED MZEG MZEJ
MZEW MZFB MZFS MZFZ MZGI MZGW MZHB MZIH MZIR MZIS MZIT
MZIW MZJA MZJD MZJK MZJV MZJX MZJZ MZKG MZKJ MZKK MZKM
MZKV MZKZ MZLC MZLZ MZMD MZMJ MZML MZMM MZMP MZMV
MZMY MZMZ MZNC MZNI MZNJ MZNL MZNO MZOC MZOF MZOP MZOR
MZPH MZSD MZSM MZZY NNON NOOK NOWW OBMI OHVA ORBS
OSEP OYES REED REEF RIKI RINN RUFF RYPH SHUF WAKE WLMS
YZYZ
GEMINI wih Flexiform and Southdown wings
   G-JESA MBST MBTF MBTG MJYP MJZU MMAR MMDP MMHE MMJT
MMKM MMOB MMPJ MMRP MMRW MMSO MMTG MMTL MMTX MMUX
MMXW MNJG MNMC
GEMINI FLASH variants (Rotax 503)
   G-MMDP MMKL MMPO MMSP MMTG MMUO MMUT MMUW MMVP
MMWA MMXD MMXJ MMXL MMXU MMXV MMZA MMZB MMZF MMZJ
MMZK MMZM MMZN MMZV MNAC MNAE MNBD MNBF MNBG MNBN
MNBP MNBR MNBS MNBT MNBV MNBW MNCF MNCG MNCJ MNDC
MNDF MNDM MNEF MNEG MNEH MNET MNEV MNEY MNFF MNFM
MNFN MNFP MNGK MNGM MNGT MNGU MNGW MNIA MNID MNIE MNIF
MNIG MNIH MNII MNIZ MNJU MNLI MNLY MNMG MNMI MNMO MNMV
MNNF MNNJ MNNL MNNR MNPC MNPG MNRW MNRX MNSA MNSI
MNSJ MNTI MNTS MNTU MNTV MNTZ MNUA MNUF MNUG MNUO MNUR
MNVT MNVV MNVW MNWD MNWI MNWZ MNXS MNXU MNYJ MNYK
MNZB MNZC MNZD MNZF MTAB MTAC MTAE MTAF MTAG MTAH MTAR
MTBD MTBH MTBJ MTBW MTBX MTBY MTCE MTCU MTCW MTDF MTDR
MTDW MTDY MTEI MTEJ MTEK MTEY MTFI MTGA MTGH MTGO MTHW
MTHZ MTIA MTIB MTIL MTIM MTIN MTJA MTJB MTJC MTJD MTJE MTJL
MTJT MTJV MTJW MTJZ MTKN MTKW MTKX MTKZ MTLB MTLC MTLL
MTMA MTMC MTML MTMT MTMV MTMW MTNC MTNG MTNH MTNI
MTNJ MTNL MTNM MTNY MTPA MTPB MTRA MTRZ MTSC MTTI MTTM
MTTP MTTR MTTW MTUU MTUV MTVH MTVI MTVJ MTWF MTWG MTWR
MTWS MTWX MTXM MTXP MTXS MTXZ MTZG MTZH MTZL MTZM MTZO
MTZV MTZW MTZX MTZY MTZZ MVAA MVAB MVAD MVAO MVAP MVBD
MVBF MVBG MVBI MVBK MVBL MVBM MVBN MVBO MVCE MVCF MVCY
MVCZ MVDA MVDT MVEH MVEJ MVEK MVEL MVEO MVER MVES MVET
MVEV MVGM MVHE MVHF MVHG MVHH MVIB MVIH MVIX MVIY MVIZ
MVJA MVJC MVJE MVJL MVKC MVLL MVLR MVMO MVMR MVMT MVMU
MVMV MVMW MVMX MVMY MVMZ MVNM MVNW MVNX MVNY MVNZ
MVOB MVOF MVON MVOR MVPA MVPB MVPC MVPD MVPE MVPI MVRA
MVRB MVRC MVRD MVRM MVSN MVSO MVSP MVST MVSV MVTC
MVUA MVXB MVXC MVXR MVXS MVYS MVZS MWAB MWCE MWCW
MWDJ MWEL MWGG MWHI MWHO MWHR MWIA MWIG MWIH MWIV
MWJY MWLP MWLT MWLX MWMM MWMS MWMT MWMX MWMY MWNE
MWNS MWNT MWNU MWOJ MWPB MWPC MWPD MWPF MWPO MWRB
MWRC MWRD MWRE MWRF MWRG MWRH MWRI MWRJ MWRR MWSB
MWSL MWSM MWTG MWTH MWTO MWTR MWTY MWTZ MWVN MWVO
MWVR MWVS MWVT MWVY MWVZ MWWB MWWC MWWI MWWJ
MWWK MWWN MWXA MWXB MWXC MWXL MWXN MWXU MWXV

MWYA MWYG MWYH MWYL MWYT MWYV MWZC MWZG MWZL MWZN
MYAO MYAS MYAU MYBJ MYCK MYCR MYCS MYDV MYEU MYFP MYFR
MYFU MYGZ MYHF MYHL MYHN MYIH MYIV MYIY MYJC MYJM MYKC
MYKG MYKH MYKV MYLG MYLR MYMK MYMO MYMV MYND MYOM
MYOW MYPE MYPW MYSJ MZCF OLJT

MERCURY (Rotax 503)
  G-MTVG MWVK MWXF MWXJ MWXK MWZA MYAI MYCJ MYCL MYCN
MYCV MYDC MYGJ MYJR MYKX MYKY MYLS MYML   MYNC MYNF
MYNJ MYOB MYOF MYOV MYOX MYPV MYRW MYSG MYSZ MYTB
MYTK MYTX MYUB MYUD MYUE MYUK MYUW MYVL MYVS MYWA
MYYU MZAK MZCO MZEK RAVE

RAPIER (Rotax 503)
  G-BYBV BYOZ BZAB BZUF BZWR CCHV MFLY MJYV MZEP MZEV MZFD
MZGL MZHJ MZHL MZIL MZIM MZJE MZKN MZND MZNU MZON YARR

SCORCHER SOLO (Rotax 447)
  G-MNDD MNNM MNPV MNPY MNPZ MNRE MNRZ MVBE MYFT MZKI
MZKN

(DUAL) TRI-FLYER trike with Flexiform, Solar Wings & Southdown wings
  G-CCVX MBCJ MBHK MBIZ MBMT MBPG MBZO MJEE MJHR MJIF
MJMN MJMR MJPE MJRA MJTP MJXE MJYX MMCZ MMDK MMDN MMEJ
MMFD MMFE MMFV MMJG MMKR MMLI MMTD MMUH MMYV MNFA
MNJD MNUI MVBC

MALMO see BÖLKOW

MANNING-FLANDERS
MF.1 replica
  G-BAAF

MANUEL
LADYBIRD
  G-MJPB

MARGAN'SKI & MYSLOWSKI ZAKLADY LOTNICZE Sp.z.o.o.
MDM-1 FOX
  G-CFOX
SWIFT S-1
  G-EIER IZII

MARQUART
MA.5 CHARGER
  G-BHBT BVJX

MAULE AIRCRAFT CORPORATION
M-5-180C LUNAR ROCKET
  G-BVFZ
M-5-235C LUNAR ROCKET
  G-BHJK BICX BIES BPMB BVFT CCBF FMGG OJGT RAIN RJWW
M-6-235 SUPER ROCKET
  G-BKGC MOUL
M-7-235 SUPER ROCKET
  G-TAFC
MT-7-235 SUPER ROCKET
  G-HIND
MX-7-180 SUPER ROCKET variants
  G-BSKG JREE LOFM MLHI OMOL RAZZ URUS WALY
MX-7-235 SUPER ROCKET
  G-ITON
MXT-7-160 SUPER, ROCKET
  G-BUXD
MXT-7-180 SUPER, ROCKET
  G-BTXT BUEP BVIK BVIL CROL GROL

AVIONS MAX HOLSTE
MH.1521 BROUSSARD variants
  G-BWGG BWLR CBGL YYYY

MAXAIR
DRIFTER
  G-MYBB
HUMMER
  G-MBYH MJCF MMZZ MNIM

MD HELICOPTERS INC
MD.500N NOTAR
  G-NEEN SIVN SMAC
MD.600N
  G-NELY PEPL THUG
MD.900 EXPLORER
  G-BXZK CMBS EHMS GMPS GMPX GNAA HPOL KAAT KSSH LNAA
SASH SIVR SUSX SYPS WPAS YPOL

MEDWAY MICROLIGHTS LTD see RAVEN and SOUTHDOWN
AV8R
  G-CCGO
ECLIPSER (Rotax 912-UL)
  G-BYBO BYSS BYXV BYXW BZWI CBMR CBMS CCCI CCZR ZZOW
HALF PINT trike (JPX PUL 425) with Aerial Arts 130SX wing
  G-MMZI MNDE MNEK MNTT MNVL
HYBRED 44XL (Fuji-Robin EC-44)
  G-MJVE MMEK MMKG MMKH MNCU MNCV MNEI MNJX
HYBRED 44XLR (Rotax 447)
  G-BYBJ BYRH MNMN MNXO MTFC MTJG MTLX MTNE MTNF MTUX
MVCD MVDJ MVEE MVGB MVGY MVKB MVMK MVPF MVPL MVRY
MVRZ MVSI MVUD MVVH MVVI MVVR MVWV MVXD MVXE MVXI MVXJ
MVXM MVYP MVYR MVZO MWCY MWCZ MWGC MWIL MWJP MWJR
MWLB MWLS MWRM MWSS MWST MWSU MWVU MYVV MYVX
SLA 80 EXECUTIVE
  G-CCJJ CDZY CEII
SLA 95I
  G-CENJ
SLA 100 EXECUTIVE
  G-CDXD CEHE RSMC

SOCIÉTÉ **MENAVIA** see PIEL

MESSERSCHMITT AG including HISPANO HA.1112 * versions
Bf.108D-1 TAIFUN
  G-AKZY
Bf.109
  G-AWHE* AWHJ* AWHL* AWHN* AWHO* AWHS* BWUE* AYDS CDTI
EMIL HUNN* USTV

MESSERSCHMITT-BÖLKOW-BLOHM GmbH including EUROCOPTER DEUTSCHLAND GmbH production
BÖ.105 variants
  "G-CDBS" G-BATC BCXO BFYA BTHV BTKL BUXS CDBS EYNL NAAA
NAAB NDAA ENVO PASB PASG PASX TVAM WAAN WAAS WYPA
BK-117C-1
  G-DCPA OEMT RESC
BK-117C-2 (EC145)
  G-MPSA MPSB MPSC

MICKLEBURGH
L107 SPARROW
  G-BZVC

MICRO AVIATION
B-22 BANTAM (Rotax 582)
  G-BXZU BZYS MZEY MZLX

MICRO BIPLANE AVIATION
TIGER CUB 440 (Fuji-Robin EC-44)
  G-MJRU MJSP MJSU MJUC MJUW MJWF MJWJ MJWW MJXD MJXF
MJYD MJZE MMAG MMBE MMBH MMBT MMCX MMFS MMGF MMGL
MMHN MMIE MMIH MMIX MMJV MMKP MMLB MMUM MNJC MNKM
MWFT

MICRO ENIGINEERING (AVIATON) LTD (MEA)
MISTRAL
  G-MBET MBOH

MICROFLIGHT AIRCRAFT LTD including CORBETT FARMS production
SPECTRUM (Rotax 503)
  G-MVJM MVSU MWCG MWKX MWOF MWPG MWPH MWTD MWTE
MWWR MYAY

MIDLAND ULTRALIGHTS LTD
SIROCCO
  G-MNDU MNRT MTRC MVSM

MIGNET
HM.14 POU-DU-CIEL reps
  "G-ADRG" "G-ADRX" "G-ADRY" "G-ADVU" "G-ADYV" "G-ADZW" "G-AEOF"
"G-AFFI"
HM.14 POU-DU-CIEL
  G-ADXS AEBB AEEH AEFG AEGV AEHM AEJZ AEKR MYSI
HM.293
  G-AXPG

SOCIÉTÉ D'EXPLOITATION DES AERONEFS HENRI **MIGNET**
HM-1000 BALERIT (Rotax 582)
  G-MRAM MYDZ MYXL MZIX MZLI MZMW MZPB MZTA

MOSKOVSKII MASHINOSTROITELNYY ZAVOD IMIENI AI **MIKOYANA**
MiG-21
  G-BRAM

MILES AIRCRAFT LTD including PHILLIPS AND POWIS AIRCRAFT LTD
M.2L HAWK SPEED SIX
  G-ADGP
M.2W HAWK TRAINER
  G-ADWT
M.3 FALCON
  G-ADLS AEEG
M.5 SPARROWHAWK
  G-ADNL
M.11A WHITNEY STRAIGHT
  G-AERV AEUJ AFGK
M.12 MOHAWK
  G-AEKW
M.14A HAWK TRAINER 3
  G-AFBS AHUJ AIUA AJRS AKAT AKKR AKKY AKPF AMMC ANWO
M.17 MONARCH
  G-AFJU AFLW AFRZ
M.18
  G-AHKY
M.38 MESSENGER variants
  G-AGOY AIEK AJKG AJOC AJOE AJVL AJWB AKAO AKBO AKIN AKIS
  AKVZ ALBP
M.65 GEMINI variants
  G-AISD AJTI AKDK AKEL AKEN AKGE AKHP AKHU AKKA AKKB AKKH
  ALCS
M.75 ARIES
  G-AOGA
M.100 STUDENT
  G-MIOO

MILLER
NEXUS MUSTANG
  G-NXUS

MILLS
MH-1
  G-OMHI

MINICAB including AÉRONAUTIQUE HAVRAISE, CONSTRUCTIONS AERONAUTIQUE
  DE BEARN, GARDAN, NOUVELLE SOC COMETAL and SRCM production
GY-20 and GY-201 MINICAB
  G-ATPV AVRW AWEP AWUB AWWM AZJE BANC BBFL BCER BCNC
  BCPD BDGB BEBR BGKO BGMJ BGMR

MIRAGE see ULTRAFLIGHT

MITCHELL
U-2 SUPER WING
  G-MMNS

MITCHELL-PROCTER see PROCTER
KITTIWAKE
  G-ATXN BBRN

MONNETT see SONEX
MONI
  G-BMVU CBTL INOW MONI TRIM
SONERAI
  G-BGEH BGLK BICJ BJBM BJLC BKDC BKFA BKNO BLAI BMIS BOBY
  BSGJ BVCC CCOZ LOWE PFAT

MONOCOUPE CORPORATION
90A
  G-AFEL

MONTGOMERIE-BENSEN see BENSEN

MOONEY AIRCRAFT CORPORATION
M.20 variants
  G-APVV ASUB ATOU AWLP BCJH BDTV BHBI BHJI BIBB BIWR BJHB
  BKMA BKMB BPCR BPFC BSXI BWJG BWTW BXML BYEE CEJN CERT
  DBYE DESS DEST FLYA GCKI GJKK JAKI JAST JDIX JENA MALS MUNI
  NRYL OBAL ODJH OEAC OJAC OJJB OONE OPWS OSUS RAFW

MORANE-SAULNIER including GEMS, SOCIÉTÉ LEVASSEUR, MORANE,
SEEMS,and SOCATA production and see DE HAVILLAND and FIESELER
TYPE N
  G-AWBU

MS.230 PARASOL
  G-AVEB BJCL
MS.315
  G-BZNK
MS.502 CRIQUET
  G-BIRW BPHZ
MS.733 ALCYON
  G-MSAL
MS.800 series RALLYE variants
  G-ARXW ASAT ASAU ATWE AVIN AVTV AVVJ AVZX AWKT AWOA
  AWYX AXCM AXGE AXHS AXHT AXOH AXOS AXOT AYRH AYTA AYYX
  AZEE AZGL AZKC AZKE AZMZ AZUT AZVF AZVH AZVI AZYD BAAI
  BAOH BAOJ BAOM BBED BBGC BBLM BCLT BCOR BCST BCVC BCXB
  BDEC BDWA BDWH BECA BECB BEIL BERA BERC BETO BEVB BEVC
  BEVW BFAK BFDF BFGS BFTZ BGKC BGMT BGSA BHWK BIAC BIIK
  BIRB BJDF BKBF BKGA BKGT BKJF BKOA BKVA BKVB BLGS BLIY BPJD
  BRDN BTIU BTOW BTUG BUKR BWWG BXZT BYPN BZNX CCZA EISO
  EXIT FARM FOSY GIGI HENT HHAV KHRE MELV OACI OMIA PIGS
  WCEI

MORAVA see LET NARODNI PODNIK KUNOVICE

MORAVAN NARODNI PODNIK
ZLIN Z-226T TRENER SPEZIAL
  G-EJGO
ZLIN Z-242L
  G-BWTC BWTD EKMN
ZLIN Z-326 TRENER MASTER
  G-BEWO BKOB
ZLIN Z-50LX
  G-MATE
ZLIN Z-526 TRENER MASTER variants (Walter Minor 6-3)
  G-AWJX AWJY AWSH BLMA BPNO PCDP TINY ZLIN

MORETON
Balloon (Minimum Lift)
ORIENTAL
  G-BINY

MORRIS
Balloon (Minimum Lift)
SCRUGGS BL2 series
  G-BILE BILG BINL BINM BINX BIOS BIPH BISL BISM BISS BIST
SCRUGGS RS5000
  G-BIWB BIWC BIWD BJEN BJES BJGN

MORRIS MOTORS LTD see DE HAVILLAND

MOSS BROS AIRCRAFT LTD
MOSS MA.1
  G-AFHA
MOSS MA.2
  G-AFJV

MOTO-DELTA see CENTRAIR

MOULT
TRIKE with Flexiform wing
  G-MTFK

AVIONS **MUDRY** ET CIE including AKROTECH EUROPE and CONSTRUCTIONS
AÉRONAUTIQUES DE BOURGOGNE
CAP.10
  G-BECZ BKCX BLVK BRDD BXBK BXBU BXFE BXRA BXRB BXRC BYFY
  CAPI CAPX CCNX CCXC CDCE CDIF CPDW CPXC CZCZ GDTU IVAL
  LORN MOZZ ODIN OIOB RIFN SLEA WIXI
CAP.20 and CAP.21
  G-BIPO BPPS
CAP.231 and CAP.232
  G-GKKI IIAI IIVI OGBR SKEW

MURPHY
QUICKSILVER GT500
  G-CEWY

MURPHY AIRCRAFT MANUFACTURING LTD
ELITE
  G-CBRT ONIG
MAVERICK
  G-BYCV CBGO CBVF CDYM MZJJ MZJS MZLE ONFL

REBEL (Lycoming O-235)
  G-BUTK BVHS BWCY BWFZ BWLL BYBK BYPP BZFT CBFK CCPK DIKY
  LJCC YELL
RENEGADE SPIRIT UK (Rotax 582)
  G-BYBU MGOO MVZP MVZX MWAJ MWDM MWKA MWMW MWNF
  MWNR MWOO MWPS MWPZ MWUH MWVP MWWD MYAM MYAZ MYCO
  MYFM MYRK MYUF MYXR MZIZ REBB TBMW
RENEGADE 912
  G-BTHN BTKB BWPE FIRZ NINE RCMC TBAG

NANCHANG see YAKOVLEV

NASH see PROCTER

NAVAL AIRCRAFT FACTORY
N3N-3
  G-ONAF

NDN AIRCRAFT LTD
NDN-6 FIELDMASTER
  G-NRDC

NEICO
LANCAIR 200, 235, 320
  G-BSRI BUNO CBAF FOPP JBAS PJMT UILE

THE **NEW KOLB AIRCRAFT COMPANY**
FIREFLY
  G-CEPN

NICOLLIER
HN.700 MENESTREL
  G-BVHL CCCJ CCDS CCKN CCVW CDHZ CDZR MINS VIVO

NIEUPORT
SCOUT 17/23
  G-BWMJ
28C-1
  G-BSKS

NOBLE HARDMAN AVIATION LTD including THE SNOWBIRD AEROPLANE CO LTD
SNOWBIRD (Rotax 532)
  G-BZYV MTXL MTXU MVCI MVCJ MVIL MVIM MVIN MVIO MVOJ MVOL
  MVYT MVYU MVYV MVYW MVYX RUMI

NOORDUYN AVIATION LTD see NORTH AMERICAN

SOCIÉTÉ NATIONALE DE CONSTRUCTIONS AÉRONAUTIQUES DU **NORD** (SNCAN)
1002 PINGOUIN
  G-ASTG ATBG ETME
1101 NORALPHA
  G-ATDB ATHN BSMD MESS
1203 NORECRIN
  G-BAYL BEDB
3202
  G-BIZK BIZM BPMU
3400
  G-BOSJ

THE **NORMAN AEROPLANE CO LTD**
NAC-2 FREELANCE
  G-NACA NACI

NORTH AMERICAN AVIATION INC see LOEHLE and including CAC, CCF,
NOORDUYN AVIATION LTD and NORTH AMERICAN ROCKWELL production
B-25 MITCHELL
  G-BWGR BYDS
F-86 SABRE
  G-BZNL SABR
P-51 MUSTANG
  G-BIXL BTCD CBNM CEBW HAEC MRLL MSTG SIJJ UAKE
NA-64 YALE
  G-BYNF
OV-10B BRONCO
  G-BZGK BZGL
(A) T-6 TEXAN, AT-16 HARVARD variants
  G-AZBN AZSC BBHK BGGR BGHU BGOR BGPB BICE BJST BKRA BRBC
  BRLV BRVG BSBG BTXI BUKY BWUL BZHL CCOY CTKL DDMV ELMH
  HRVD JUDI RAIX TEXN TOMC TSIX TVIJ
T-28/A TROJAN
  G-TROY

NORTH WING DESIGN
STRATUS-ATF
  G-CEYP

NOSTALGAIR
N.3 PUP
  G-BVEA

NOTT
Balloon (Hot Air)
Various
  G-CCSW NOTT

NOTT-CAMERON
Balloon (Hot Air)
NCA ULD- 2
  G-BNXK

NOVA VERTRIEBSGESELLSCHAFT GmbH
Paragliders
VERTEX
  G-BYLI BYZT BZVI CCET
PHOCUS
  G-BZYI
PHILOU
  G-BZXI
X LARGE 37
  G-BZJI

OLDFIELD
BABY LAKES
  G-BBGL BGEI BGLS BKHD BMIY BTZL BWMO POND SWAK

OMEGA BALLOONS
Balloon (Hot Air)
O-20
  G-AXMD
56
  G-AYAL
84
  G-AWMO AXJB AXVU

OPTICA INDUSTRIES LTD including FLS production
OA.7 OPTICA
  G-BMPL BOPO BOPR

ORLICAN
L-40 META-SOKOL
  G-APUE APVU

OZONE/ADVENTURE SA
ROADSTER-ADVENTURE FUNFLYER QUATTRO
  G-TMAN

PACIFIC AIRWAVE
PULSE 2 - SKYCYLE Trike)
  G-CEZN

PAKES
JACKDAW
  G-MBOF

PARAMANIA -see PASSION'ALLES

G **PARNALL and COMPANY**
PARNALL ELF
  G-AAIN
PARNALL PIXIE
  G-EBJG

PARSONS including BENSEN-PARSONS and MONTGOMERIE-PARSONS
TWO PLACE GYROPLANE
  G-BPIF BTFE BUWH BVOD CBOU CDGT IIXX IVYS UNIV

PARTENAVIA COSTRUZIONI AERONAUTICHE SpA
P.64B OSCAR
  G-BMDP
P.68B and C
  G-BCDK BFBU BHBZ BHJS BMOI ENCE FJMS HUBB KIMK OLMA ORVR
  PART RVRE SAMJ

PASSION'ALLES
CHARIOT Z trike- PARAMANIA ACTION GT26 sailwing
G-CEOZ

PAYNE
Balloon (Hot Air)
FREE
G-AZRI
AX7-62
G-BFMZ

PAYNE
KNIGHT TWISTER
G-BRAX

PAZMANY
PL-1
G-BDHJ
PL-2
G-OPAZ
PL-4A
G-BMMI BRFX FISK PAZY PLIV

PEARSON
Balloon (Minimum Lift)
Series 2
G-BIXX

PEGASUS AVIATION including CYCLONEAIRSPORTS LTD, MAINAIR SPORTS LTD and
P&M Ltd production.
QUANTUM series (Rotax 912)
G-BYDZ BYEW BYFF BYFE BYFF BYHR BYIS BYIZ BYJK BYKT BYLC
BYMF BYMI BYMT BYND BYOG BYOV BYPB BYPJ BYPL BYRJ BYRU
BYSR BYSX BYTC BYYN BYYP BYYY BZAI BZBR BZDL BZDS BZED BZFC
BZFH BZGZ BZHN BZHO BZIM BZIW BZJF BZJO BZJZ BZLL BZLX BZLZ
BZMI BZMW BZNB BZNC BZNM BZOD BZOE BZOO BZOU BZOV BZRJ
BZRP BZRR BZSA BZSG BZSI BZSM BZSS BZSX BZUC BZUE BZUI BZUJ
BZVJ BZVV BZWS BZWU BZXV BZXX BZYN CBAY CBBB CBBN CBBP
CBCD CBCF CBCX CBDX CBDZ CBEN CBEU CBEV CBGG CBHK CBHN
CBHY CBIZ CBJO CBKW CBLL CBMV CBNT CBOY CBSP CBTD CBTZ
CBUD CBUS CBUU CBUZ CBYI CBYV CCCD CCDK CCDZ CCFT CCIH
CCJD CCNE CCNW CCOC CCRF CCRT CCUR CCWN CCWO CCWW
CCYL CCZB CDAA CDAO CDCY CDCZ CDDF CDEN CDFR CDGX CDHM
CDIL CDIR CDLZ CDOD CDPW CDRR CDTB CDTC CDVH CDXG CFBM
DINO DSLL EDMC EMLY EOFW FESS FFUN GBJP ICWT ISEW JAWC
JGSI KAZI KICK MCEL MCJL MDBC MGDL MGEF MGFK MGFO MGGG
MGGV MGMC MGTG MHMR MROC MSPY MYLC MYLE MYLH MYLI MYLK
MYLL MYLM MYLZ MYMB MYMC MYMX MYNB MYNK MYNL MYNN MYNO
MYNP MYNR MYNS MYNT MYNV MYNZ MYOU MYPH MYPI MYPN MYPX
MYPY MYRF MYRM MYRN MYRS MYRT MYRY MYRZ MYSB MYSC MYSR
MYSW MYSX MYSY MYTI MYTJ MYTN MYUO MYUU MYUV MYVC MYVJ
MYVK MYVM MYVR MYWG MYWI MYWJ MYWK MYWL MYWO MYWR
MYWT MYWU MYWW MYWY MYXE MYXT MYXW MYXX MYXZ MYYB
MYYC MYYI MYYK MYYN MYYX MYZB MYZJ MYZK MYZL MYZM MYZY
MZAN MZAW MZAX MZBB MZBC MZBI MZBM MZBO MZBT MZBY MZCI
MZCJ MZCM MZCR MZCV MZCY MZDB MZDC MZDD MZDE MZDH MZDN
MZDU MZDV MZDY MZEC MZEE MZEH MZEM MZEX MZEZ MZFG MZFM
MZFT MZFV MZGG MZGK MZGN MZGO MZGV MZHI MZHK MZHN MZHP
MZIB MZIC MZIE MZIF MZIJ MZIU MZJG MZJH MZJA MZJO MZJT
MZJW MZJY MZKA MZKD MZKF MZKL MZKY MZLA MZLD MZLF MZLJ
MZLN MZLT MZLV MZLW MZMC MZMF MZMG MZMH MZMN MZMT MZNB
MZNG MZNP MZNR MZNS MZNT MZOD MZOG MZOJ MZOS MZOV
MZOW MZPD MZRC MZRH MZRM MZSC NAPO OAMF OATE OBJP OELD
OLDM OLFB OHKS OTJH PEGA PIXI PRSI REDC REPH RUSA SILY SITA
SMBM TBBC TFIX TRAM TUSA WHEE ZZXX
QUIK variants (Rotax 912-UL(S))
G-CBRY CBVN CBYE CBYO CBZH CBZT CCAD CCAS CCAZ CCCG
CCDB CCDD CCDF CCDO CCEA CCEW CCFB CCFL CCGC CCGI CCHH
CCHI CCHO CCIV CCJM CCKM CCKO CCLM CCLX CCMD CCME CCML
CCMS CCNM CCOG CCOK CCOU CCOW CCPC CCPG CCRW CCSD
CCSF CCSH CCSL CCSY CCTC CCTD CCTU CCTZ CCUA CCVR CCWR
CCWV CCXT CCXZ CCYE CCYJ CCZO CDAR CDAX CDBB CDCF CDCI
CDCK CDEC CDEW CDFG CDFO CDGC CDGD CDGO CDKK CDKM
CDLA CDLD CDLJ CDMJ CDML CDMU CDMZ CDNH CDOC CDOM CDOP
CDOW CDPD CDRG CDRT CDRW CDSA CDSM CDSS CDTO CDTR
CDUH CDUU CDVG CDVN CDVO CDVR CDVZ CDWO CDWP CDWR
CDWS CDWW CDWZ CDXM CDXN CEBD CEBM CEBT CECA CECM
CEDN CEEI CEEM CEGJ CEGT CEGV CEGW CEHC CEHI CEHW CEJJ
CEJX CEKG CEMB CEML CEMM CEMO CEMT CEMZ CENL CENV
CEPP CERN CERV CERW CESG CESR CETL CETM CEUF CEUH
CEUZ CEVB CEVG CEVP CEVW CEWD CEWH CEZT CEZX CFAT CJAI
CJAY CJGG CWEB CWIC CWIK CWMC CWVY DCMI DECX DDDY EEWZ
EJMM EZAR FEET FLEX FFIT FRGT GAZN GBEE GCEA GEMX GTFC

GTEE GTGT GTJD GTSO GTTP HAMS HALT JOBA JULE KEVS KUIK
KWIC LSKY LUNE LYTB MASI MAXS MFLJ MLAW MRJJ NJPW NUTT
OFDT OJJV OKEM OLDP OLFZ OMIW OMPW ORLA OUIK PEAR PIPI
PVSS RAYB RCRC RIBA RIKY RITT SEEE SHEE SHEZ SISU SOCK
SUEL TARR TBJP TBLB TCNY TERR TJAV TONN TPWL WBLY WFLY
WIZS XDWE XJJM YSMO

PENN-SMITH
GYROPLANE
G-AXOM

PERCIVAL AIRCRAFT CO LTD including HUNTING PERCIVAL AIRCRAFT
LTD production
Type D GULL FOUR
G-ACGR
Type D GULL SIX
G-ACUP ADPR AERD
Type E MEW GULL
G-AEXF
Type K VEGA GULL
G-AEZJ
Type Q SIX
G-AFFD
PROCTOR variants
G-AGTB AHDI AHTE AHVG AHZY AKEX AKIU AKZN ALCK ALIS ALJF
ANXR AOGE
P.40 PRENTICE
G-AOKL AOKO AOKZ AOLK AOLU AOMF AOPL AOPO APIT APIY APJB
APPL
P.50 PRINCE
G-AMLZ
P.56 PROVOST
G-AWPH AWRY AWTD AWVF BDYG BGSB BKFW BLIW BZRE BZRF
KAPW MOOS TMKI
P.57 SEA PRINCE
G-BIDN BRFC DACA GACA RACA

PEREIRA
OSPREY
G-BVGI CCCW GEOF PREY

PHANTOM see SKYRIDER

PHILLIPS
ST.1 SPEEDTWIN
G-GPST
ST.2 SPEEDTWIN
G-STDL

PHILLIPS AND POWIS AIRCRAFT LTD - see MILES AIRCRAFT LTD

PHOENIX
*LUTON LA-4, LA-4A MINOR including Ord-Hume O-H7, Parker CA-4 and
Phoenix Duet versions and including replica*
G-AFIR AFIU "AFUG"* AMAW ARIF ARXP ASAA ASCY ASEA ASEB ASML
ASXJ ATCJ ATFW ATKH ATWS AVDY AVUO AWIP AWMN AXGR AXKH
AYDY AYSK AYTT AZHU AZPV BANF BBCY BBEA BCFY BDJG BIJS
BKHR BRWU
LA-5A MAJOR
G-ARAD

INDUSTRIE AERONAUTICHE E MECCANICHE RINALDO **PIAGGIO SpA** incluidng
PIAGGIO AERO INDUSTRIES SpA and FOCKE-WULF FLUGZEUGBAU GMBH production
P.149
G-RORY
P.166
G-APWY

DON **PICCARD BALLOONS INC**
Balloon (Hot Air)
Piccard Balloon
G-ATTN
AX6
G-AWCR AZHR

PIEL AVIATION including COOPAVIA, ROUSSEAU, SOCIÉTÉ MENAVIA and SOCIÉTÉ
SCINTEX production
CP.301 EMERAUDE
G-ARDD ARRS ARUV ASCZ ASLX ASVG AXXC AYCE AYEC AYTR AZGY
AZYS BBKL BCCR BDCI BDDZ BDKH BHRR BIDO BIJU BIVF BKFR BKNZ
BKUR BLRL BPRT BSVE BXAH BXYE DENS PIEL

CP.328 SUPER EMERAUDE
G-SAZZ
CP.1310-C3 SUPER EMERAUDE
G-ASMV ASNI BCHP BGVE BJCF BJVS BLXI BXRF
CP.1315-C3 SUPER EMERAUDE
G-BHEK
CP.1320
G-SAFI
CP.1330 SUPER EMERAUDE
G-BANW

PIETENPOL
AIRCAMPER
G-ADRA BBSW BKVO BMDE BMLT BNMH BRXY BUCO BUXK BUZO
BVYY BWAT BWVB BXZO BYFT BYKG BYLD BYZY CCKR DAYZ ECOX
ECVB EDFS IMBY KIRC LEOD OFFA OHAL OPJS PCAF PIET RAGS SILS
TARN UNGO VALS

PIK see EIRI and SIREN

PILATUS AIRCRAFT LTD
P.2
G-BLKZ CJCI PTWO
P.3
G-BTLL
PC.6 TURBO PORTER
G-BYNE CECI WGSC
PC.12 variants
G-CCWY ILMD INTO MATX OCLE OLTT PVPC TRAT WINT ZUMO

PILATUS FLUGZEUGWERKE AG
B4-PC11 variants
G-CHDA CHDE CHLC CJXX DCSN DCUB DCUT DCVG DCVK DCVM DCVV
DCYA DCZD DDLA DDND DDSV DEOU ECSW PILY

PIPER AIRCRAFT CORPORATION including TAYLOR AIRCRAFT CO LTD,
and THE NEW PIPER AIRCRAFT INC production
J-2 CUB
G-AEXZ AFFH JTWO
J-3 CUB variants
G-AFDO AGAT AGIV AGVV AHIP AIIH AISS AISX AJAD AJES AKAA AKAZ
AKIB AKRA AKTH AKUN ASPS ATKI ATZM AXGP AXHP AXHR AYCN
AYEN BAET BBHJ BBLH BBUU BBXS BCNX BCOB BCOM BCPH BCPJ
BCUB BCXJ BDCD BDEY BDEZ BDHK BDJP BDMS BDOL BECN BEDJ
BEUI BFBY BFDL BFHI BFZB BGPD BGSJ BGTI BGXA BHPK BHVV
BHXY BHZU BIJE BILI BJAF BJAY BJSZ BJTO BKHG BLPA BMKC ANXP
BOTU BOXJ BPCF BPUR BPVH BPYN BREB BROR BSBT BSFD BSNF
BSTI BSVH BSYO BTBX BTET BTSP BTUM BTZX BVAF BVPN BWEZ
CCOX CCUB COPS CUBS CUBY FRAN HEWI KIRK KUUI LFOR LIVH
LOCH NCUB OCUB OINK OLEZ POOH RAMP RIXA RRSR SEED TCUB
J-4 CUB COUPÉ variants
G-AFGM AFWH AFZA BRBV BSDJ BUWL
J-5A CUB CRUISER
G-BRIL BRLI BSDK BSXT BTKA
PA-12 SUPER CRUISER
G-AMPG ARTH AWPW AXUC BCAZ BOWN BSYG CDCS PAIZ
PA-15 VAGABOND
G-ALGA ASHU AWOF BDVB BOVB BRJL BRPY BRSX BSFW BTFJ BTOT
BUKN CCEE FKNH
PA-16 CLIPPER
G-BAMR BBUG BIAP BSVI BSWF
PA-17 VAGABOND
G-AKTP ALEH ALIJ AMYL AWKD AWOH BCVB BDVA BDVC BIHT BLMP
BSMV BSWG BTBY BTCI BUXX
PA-18 SUPER CUB
G-AMEN APZJ ARAM ARAN ARAO AREO ARGV ARVO ATRG AVOO
AWMF AXLZ AYPM AYPO AYPS AYPT AZRL BAFT BAFV BAKV BBOL
BBYB BCFO BCMD BEOI BEUA BEUU BFFP BGPN BGPW BGYN BHGC
BHOM BIDJ BIDK BIID BIJB BIMM BIRH BITA BIYJ BIYR BIYY BIZV BJBK
BJCI BJEI BJFE BJIV BJTP BJWX BJWZ BKET BKJB BKRF BKTA BKVM
BLHM BLIH BLLN BLLO BLMI BLMR BLMT BLPE BLRC BMAY BMEA
BMKB BNXM BOOC BPJG BPJH BPUL BROZ BRRL BSHV BTBU BTUR
BVIE BVIW BVMI BVRZ BWOR BWUB BZGD BZHT CCKW CDPR CUBB
CUBI CUBJ CUBN CUBP CVMI DADG ECUB EGPG FUZZ HACK HELN
JCUB KAMP LCUB LION MGMM NESY NETY NNAC OFER OOMF OROD
OSPS OTAN OTUG OVON PIPR PUDL ROVE SCUB SUPA TUGG WCUB
WGCS WLAC XCUB YCUB ZAZA
PA-20 PACER (Conversions ex PA-22 standard*)
G-APXT* APYI* APZX* ARBS* ARGY* ATBX ATXA* AVDV* BFMR BIYP
ARBS BSED* BTLM* BUDE* BUOI BUXV* BWWU* BXBB PAXX
PA-22-108 COLT
G-ARGO ARJE ARJF ARJH ARKK ARKM ARKN ARKP ARKS ARND ARNE
ARNG ARNJ ARNK ARNL ARON ARSU CBEI GGLE

PA-22-135 TRI-PACER
G-BMCS BUVA TJAY
PA-22-150 TRI-PACER
G-APXU
PA-22-150 CARIBBEAN,
G-APYW ARAX ARCC ARCF ARDS AREL ARFB ARHN ARHR ARIK ARIL
AWLI AZRS BRNX TLDK
PA-22-160 TRI-PACER
G-APUR APXR APYN APZL ARAI ARBV ARDT ARET AREV ARFD ARHP
ARYH BTKV EMSB HALL
PA-23-160 APACHE,
G-APFV APMY ARCW ARJS ARJT ARJU ARJV ARMA ASMY ATOA BICY
BEXO
PA-(E)23-250 AZTEC
"G-ESKY" G-ASEP ASER ASHH ATFF AXDC AYBO AYMO AZXG AZYU
BADI BADJ BAPL BATN BAUA BAUI BAUJ BAVL BBCC BBDO BBHF BBIF
BBMJ BBNO BBRA BBTJ BCBG BCCE BCEX BCRP BFBB BFWE BGTG
BGWW BHNG BJNZ BJXX BKJW BKVT BLLM BMFD BNUV BSVP CALL
ESKY KEYS LIZZ MLFF NRSC OART OPME OSJF OXTC RVRC RVRD
RVRJ RVRW TAPE TAXI TOPO UNDD XSFT
PA-24 COMANCHE (-180)
G-ARHI ARUO AXMA AZKR BRDW BWNI MOTO
PA24-250 COMANCHE
G-APXJ ARBO ARDB ARLB ARLK ARXG ARYV ASCJ ASEO BAHJ BYTI
DISK TALF
PA-24-260 COMANCHE
G-ATJL ATNV ATOY AVCM AVGA AXTO AZWY BRXW KSVB PETH
PA-25 PAWNEE
G-ATFR
PA-25-235 PAWNEE
G-ASIY ASVP AVPY AVXA AXED AZPA BAUC BCBJ BDDS BDPJ BEII
BETL BETM BFBP BFEV BFEY BFPR BFPS BFSC BFSD BILL BNZV
BPWL BSTH BUXY BVYP BXST CMGC CTUG LYND NYMF TUGS
PA25-260 PAWNEE
G-BFRY BHUU BLDG CCUV DSGC PAWN PSGC SATN TOWS
PA-28-140 CHEROKEE, CRUISER and FLITELINER
G-ASSW ASVZ ATEZ ATJG ATMW ATOI ATOJ ATOK ATOL ATOM ATON
ATOO ATOP ATOR ATPN ATRO ATRP ATRR ATTI ATTK ATTV ATUB
ATUD ATVK ATVO AVFR AVFX AVFZ AVGC AVGD AVGE AVGI AVLB
AVLC AVLE AVLF AVLG AVLH AVLI AVLJ AVLT AVRP AVSI AVUS AVUT
AVUU AVWA AVWD AVWE AVWG AVWI AVWJ AVWL AVWM AVYP
AVYR AWBE AWBG AWBH AWBS AWEV AWEX AWPS AXAB AXIO AXIR
AXJV AXJX AXSZ AXTA AXTC AXTH AXTJ AXTL AYIG AYJP AYJR AYKW
AYMK AYNF AYNJ AYPV AYRM AYWE AZEG AZFC AZMX AZRH AZWB
AZWD AZZO BAFU BAFW BAGX BAHE BAHF BAKH BASL BATW BAWK
BAXZ BBBY BBDC BBEF BBEV BBIL BBIX BBYP BBZF BCDJ BCGI BCGJ
BCGN BCJM BCJN BCJP BDGY BDSH BDWY BEAC BEEU BEFF BEYT
BFXK BGAX BGPU BGRC BHXK BIYX BOFY BOSR BRBW BRPK BRPL
BRWO BSLU BSSE BSTZ BTEX BTGO BTON BULR BXPL BYCA BZWG
CCLJ CGHM COLH DENE DIAT EEKY ENGL FIAT GCAT JDJM KATS
LFSC LFSI LTFB LTFC MATZ MIDD MKAS NHRH OFTI OKYM OMAT
PAWL PETR PIKK RECK RVRA RVRT SCPL SMTH TEFC TEWS UANT
WOLF ZANG ZEBY
PA-28-150 CHEROKEE
G-BIFB
PA-28-160 CHEROKEE
G-ARVT ARVU ARVV ATDA ATIS BSER BSLM BWYB JAKS LIZI
PA-28-180 CHEROKEE, CHALLENGER and ARCHER
G-ARYR ASFL ASHX ASII ASIJ ASIL ASKT ASRW ASUD ASWX ATAS
ATEM ATHR ATNB ATOT ATTX ATUL ATVS ATXM ATYS ATZK AVAX
AVBG AVBH AVBS AVBT AVGK AVNN AVNO AVNP AVNS AVNU AVNW
AVOZ AVPV AVRK AVRU AVRY AVRZ AVSA AVSB AVSC AVSD AVSE
AVSF AVSP AVYL AVYM AVZR AWDP AWIT AWSL AWTL AWXR AWXS
AXSG AXTP AXZD AXZF AYAB AYAR AYAT AYAW AYEE AYEF AYPJ
AYUH AZDX AZLN AZYF BABG BAJR BASJ BATV BBBN BBEC BBHY
BBKX BBPP BBPY BCCF BCLL BEYL BGTJ BKCC BODM BOHM BRBG
BRGI BSEF BSGD BUTZ BUUX BUYY BXJD CBMO CDEO CJBC DEVS
DLTR EFCM GALA GBRB HOCK HRYZ ITUG KEES LFSG NINB NINC
NIND NITA OIBO ONET OTYP SOOT TEMP WACP YULL
PA-28-151 CHEROKEE WARRIOR
G-BBXW BCIE BCIR BCRL BCTF BCTA BDGM BDPA BEBZ BEFA BHFK
BIEY BNMB BNNT BOHR BOTF BPEL BPKR BPMF BPPK BRBD BRTX
BTNT BTUW BVBF BXLY CCZV CDMA CEGU CPTM FMAM FPIG GUSS
JAMP LUSH PSRT ROWS TALG VIVS
PA-28-161 (CHEROKEE) WARRIOR II
G-BFBR BFDK BFMG BFNIBFNK BFWB BFWK BFYM BGKS BGOG BGPJ
BGPL BGVK BGYH BHJO BHOR BHRC BHVB BICW BIIT BIUW BJBW
BJBX BJCA BJSV BLVL BMFP BMKR BMTR BMUZ BNCR BNEL BNJT
BNNO BNNS BNNY BNNZ BNOE BNOF BNOH BNOJ BNOM BNON BNOP
BNRG BNSY BNSZ BNTD BNXE BNXT BNXU BNZB BNZZ BOAH BODB
BODC BODD BODE BODR BOER BOFZ BOHA BOHO BOIG BOJW BOJZ
BOKB BOKK BOKX BOMY BOPC BORK BORL BOTI BOTN BOUP BOVK
BOXA BOXB BOXC BOYH BOYI BOZI BPAF BPBM BPCK BPDT BPFH
BPHL BPIU BPKM BPMR BPOM BPRN BPRY BPWE BRBA BRBB BRBE
BRDF BRDG BRDM BRFM BRSE BRUB BSAW BSBA BSCV BSCY BSGL

BSHP BSJX BSLK BSLT BSOK BSOZ BSPI BSPM BSSC BSSW BSSX
BSVG BSVM BSXA BSXB BSXC BSYY BSYZ BSZT BTAW BTBC BTDV
BTFO BTGY BTID BTIV BTKT BTNE BTNH BTNV BTRK BTRS BTRY BTSJ
BUFH BUFY BUIF BUIJ BUIK BUJO BUJP BUKX BURT BVJZ BXAB BXVU
BYHI BYKP BZLH CBAL CCYY CDDG CDER CDMX CDMY CDON CEGS
CEIZ CEJF CEMD CETD CETE CEXO CEXR CGDJ CKEY CLAC CLEA
CSGT DKEY EDGA EDGI EEGU EGLL EGTB EKKL ELZN ELZY EMSL
EOLD ERFS ESFT EVIE EVTO EXXO FIZZ FLAV FPSA GALB GBAB
GHKX GRRC GURU HAMR HMES IKBP ISDB JASE JAVO KART KBPI
KNAP KYTE LACA LACB LAZL LBMM LFSJ LFSK LSFT MAYO MSFT
NINA OAAA OANI OJWS OPTI OPUK OWAP OWAR PJCC RIZZ
RSKR RVRN SACI SACO SARH SEJW SEXX SLYN SNUZ SRWN SUZN
SVEA VICC WARE WARR WFFW WNTR XAVI XENA XINE

PA-28-161 WARRIOR III
G-BXOJ BYHH BZBS BZDA BZIO BZMT CBKR CBWD CBYU CEEV CEEY
CEEZ CEJD COVA COVB DOME FNPT GFTA GFTB GOTH GYTO HMED
ISHA JACA OBDN OBFC OBFS OMST OOFT WARA WARB WARH WARO
WARS WARU WARV WARW WARX WARY WARZ WAVS

PA-28-161 CADET
G-BPJO BPJP BPJR BPJS BPJU BRJV BTIM BWOH BWOI BWOJ BXJJ
BXTY BXTZ CDEF CEEN CEEU CEJV CEZI CEZL CEZO EGTR EJRS
EKIR EXON EXXO FOXA GFCA GFCB JLIN KCIN KDET LORC OCTU
ODEN OLSF OXOM SACR SACS SACT TLET

PA-28-181 (CHEROKEE) ARCHER II
G-BDSB BEIP BEMW BEXW BFDI BFSY BFVG BGBG BGVZ BGWM BHNO
BHWZ BHZE BIIV BIUY BJAG BLFI BMIW BMPC BMSD BNGT BNPO
BNRP BNVE BNYP BOBZ BOEE BOJM BOMP BOMU BOOF BOPA BORS
BOSE BPAY BPFI BPGU BPOT BPTE BPXA BPYO BRBX BRME BRNV
BRUD BRXD BSCS BSEU BSIM BSIZ BSKW BSNX BSVB BSXS BSZJ
BTAM BTGZ BTKX BTYI BUMP BVNS BWPH BXEX BXIF BXOZ BXRG
BXWO BYKL BYSP CBSO CBTT CCAV CDGW CHAS CHIP CIFR DJJA
EFIR EHGF EHLX ERNI FBRN GASP HARN ILLY JANA JANT JCAS JJAN
JJEN JOYT KAIR KITE MALA MASF MDAC MELS NIKE NUKA ODUD
OGEM OJEH OMJA OODW OPET PALY RADI RAZY RNCH SARA SGSE
SHED SOBI TALE TERY TIMK TSGJ TWEL USSY WISE WWAY YANK
ZMAM

PA-28-181 ARCHER III
G-BWUH BXTW BYHK BZHK BZHV CCHL CCWA DIXY EGLS FEAB
FORR GFPA GFPB IDPH ISAX JACB JACC JACS JADJ JONM JOYZ
KEMI KEVB LACD LKTB LORR MPAA NOTE ORAR PACT PEJM PUKB
SUEB VAAC VOAR WLGC

PA-28-201T TURBO DAKOTA
G-BNYB BOKA BXCC

PA-28-235 CHEROKEE and PATHFINDER)
G-ASLV AWSM BAMM BXYM BZEH CCBH EWME

PA-28-236 DAKOTA
G-BGXS BHTA BPCX BRKH CSBD DAKO FRGN FWPW KOTA LEAM
ODAK TART

PA-28R-180 CHEROKEE ARROW
G-AVWN AVWO AVWR AVWT AVWU AVWV AVXF AVYS AVYT AWAZ
AWBA AWBB AWBC AWEZ AWFB AWFC AWFD AWFJ AZWS BAPW
BWNM CCIJ CSWH FBWH NELI NIJM OKAG SBMM WWAL

PA-28R-200 CHEROKEE ARROW
G-AXCA AXWZ AYAC AYII AYPU AYRI AZAJ AZDE AZFI AZFM AZRV
BCPG BFZH BMJG BTLG CBVU GYMM

PA-28R-200 CHEROKEE ARROW II
G-AZNL AZOG AZSF BAHS BAIH BAMY BAWG BBDE BBEB BBFD BBZH
BBZV BCGS BCJO BDKV BHEV BHGY BHWY BIKE BIZO BKFZ BKXF
BLXP BMGB BMKK BMNL BMOE BTRT BZDH CBEE DMCS DSFT EDVL
ELUT EPTR FULL GDOG HALC MACK ODOG OMNI RACO RONG STEA
TORC VFAS

PA-28R-201 (CHEROKEE) ARROW III
G-BEWX BGKU BGKV BIDI BMLS BMPR BNEE BNSG BOBA BYHJ BYYO
BZKL BZMB CBPI CBZR CEOF CEOG FROS HERB IBFW IRKB MEME
OARA OARI OARO OARU OTGA RJMS TEBZ THSL TOLL TSGA UTSY
WAMS

PA-28R-201T TURBO (CHEROKEE) ARROW III
G-BEOH BFDO BFLI BFTC BGOL BMIV BNNX BNVT BOIC BOYV BSNP
BSPN DDAY DIZY DNCS ECJM JESS MEGA OBAK OJIM OKEN OOTC
SABA SHAY SHUG

PA-28RT-201 ARROW IV
G-BGVN BHAY BOET BOJI BONC BPZM BREP BUUM BVDH BXYO BXYP
BXYR BXYT CDYC CEDD GEHP GHRW ISCA JANO LAOL LBRC MERL
MRST OARC OMHC VOID WEND

PA-28RT-201T TURBO ARROW IV
G-BHFJ BMHT BNJR BNTC BNTS BOGM BOOG BOWY BPBO BPXJ
BRLG BRRJ BUND BUNH BWMI BYKP DAAH DAAZ DONS EXAM GPMW
IJOE LZZY OPEP OPJD RATV RUBY SKYV TAPS TCTC YAWW

PA-30 TWIN COMANCHE - also see PA-39
G-ASRO ASSB ASSP ASWW ASYK ATEW ATFK ATMT ATSZ ATWR
ATXD AVCY AVJJ AVKL AVPS AVVI AWBN AWBT AXAU AYSB AZAB
BAKJ BAWN BLOR BZRO CDHF COMB ELAM RROD SURG TCOM UAVA

PA-31 TURBO NAVAJO
G-BBDS BEZL BFIB BLFZ BPYR CBTN EEJE EGLG FILL GURN IMEC
ISFC LYDD ONAV OWLC RHYM UMMI VICT

PA-31-325 NAVAJO C/R
G-BWHF

PA-31-350 (NAVAJO) CHIEFTAIN
G-BASU BBNT BVYF CEBK CITY EMAX GLTT HVRD IFIT JAJK LIDE
LYDB LYDC LYDF NERC NEWR OBNW OETV OJIL ONPA OSGB PLAC
PZAZ PZIZ STHA VIPP VIPU VIPV VIPY VIPX YEOM

PA-31T2 CHEYENNE IIXL
G-CHEY FCED

PA-32-260 CHEROKEE SIX
G-ATJV ATRW ATRX BBFV BHGO BRGT CCFI ELDR ETBY NEAL OCTI
OEVA OSIX RAYE

PA-32-300 CHEROKEE SIX
G-AVFU AVUZ AZDJ BAGG BBSM BEZP BGUB BKEK BRNZ BSTV BXWP
CDUX CSIX DENI DIGI DIWY FRAG IFFR ILTS KFRA KNOW NEON OSCC
OTBY PECK SALA SIMY SIXD WINS

PA-32-301FT 6x
G-RAGT RYNS

PA-32-301 SARATOGA
G-BMDC BVWZ WAIR

PA-32-301T TURBO SARATOGA
G-MOLL

PA-32R-300 (CHEROKEE) LANCE
G-BDWP BEHH BHBG BSYC BTCA CEYE VERN

PA-32R-301 SARATOGA variants
G-BJCW BKMT BMJA BPVI BYFR BYPU CCST EENA ELLA GOBD HDEW
HYLT JPOT MOVI NIOS OIHC OPSL PURL RAMS RIGH ROLF TSDS
YSTT

PA-32R-301T TURBO SARATOGA variants
G-BOGO BPVN CLOP GOTO MAIE NJIM SVPN SYDE VONS

PA-32RT-300 LANCE II
G-BFUB BFYC BOTV BRHA BSUF JUPP NROY OJCW RHHT TFYN

PA-32RT-300T TURBO LANCE II
G-LUNA SAWI TFIN

PA-34-200 SENECA
G-AZIK AZOL AZVJ BABK BACB BADL BAIG BAKD BASM BATR BBLU
BBNH BBNI BBPX BBXK BCGA BCID BPAD BRHO BVEV EMER EXEC
EZYU FLYI OCFM OPAG TEST

PA-34-200T SENECA II
G-BCVY BDUN BEAG BEHU BEJV BEVG BFLH BGFT BHFH BHYG BLWD
BMUT BNEN BNRX BOCG BOFE BOIZ BORH BOSD BOUK BOUL BOUM
BOWE BPON BPXX BSDN BSGK BSHA BSII BSPG BSUW BTGV BYBH
CAHA CBWB CDPV CHEM CLOS CLUE CTWW CVLH DAZY DCEA ELIS
FILE GAFA GFEY GOAC GOGS GUYS IEIO IFLP JDBC JLCA LORD MAIR
MAXI OACG PEGI ROUS RSHI RVRB SENE SENX VVBK XKEN

PA-34-220T SENECA III
G-BLYK BMDK BMJO BOJK BUBU BWDT DARA GFCD HCSL HMJB
HTRL JANN LENY MPWT NESW OOON OWAL POPS

PA-34-220T SENECA IV
G-DISD MAIK PFCI

PA-34-220T SENECA V
G-BZTG GSYS NSUK OBNA OTVR

PA-38-112 TOMAHAWK
G-BGBK BGBN BGBW BGGE BGGG BGGI BGGL BGGM BGGN BGIG
BGKY BGLA BGRM BGRN BGRR BGRX BGSH BGWN BGXB BGXO
BGZF BHCZ BJNN BJUR BJUS BJYN BKAS BLWP BMKG BMSF BMTO
BMVL BMVM BNCO BNDE BNEK BNGR BNHG BNIM BNKH BNNU BNPL
BNPM BNSL BNUY BNVD BNXV BNYK BODP BODS BOHS BOHT BOHU
BOLD BOLE BOLF BOMO BOMZ BPES BPHI BPIK BPPE BPPF BRFL
BRFN BRHR BRJR BRLO BRLP BRML BRSJ BSFE BSKL BSOT BSOU
BSOV BSYK BSYL BSYM BTAP BTAR BTAS BTFP BTIL BTJK BTJL BTND
BVHM BVLP BWNU BWSC BXET BXZA BYMC BYMD CHER CWFA
CWFB DFLY DTOO EDNA EGNR EMMS EORG GALL GTHM LFSA LFSB
LFSD LFSH LFSM LFSN MSFC NCFC NCFE OEDB OLFC OPSF OTFT
PRIM RECS RVRF RVRG RVRK RVRL RVRM RVRO RVRR SION SUKI
TOMS VMCG XALT

PA-39 TWIN COMANCHE C/R - also see PA-30
G-ASMA AYZE LARE OAJS OGET SIGN

PA-42-720 CHEYENNE 111A
G-GZRP

PA-44-180 SEMINOLE
G-BGCO BGTF BHFE BHRP BRUI BRUX CFSA DENZ GAFT OACA PDOC
SEMI TWIN

PA-44-180T TURBO SEMINOLE
G-GHSI

PA-46-350P MALIBU MIRAGE
G-DIPM DNOP EODE GREY JCAR VRST WADI

PA-46-500TP MALIBU MERIDIAN
G-CEJB DERI DERK

PA-60-601P AEROSTAR 601 (**TED SMITH** production)
G-MOVE RIGS

PIPER
CP.1 METISSE
  G-BVCP

PITTS AVIATION ENTERPRISES INC including AEROTEK INC, AVIAT INC and CHRISTEN INDUSTRIES INC
S-1 variants
  G-AXNZ AZCE AZPH BADZ BBOH BETI BHSS BIRD BKDR BKKZ BKPZ
  BKVP BLAG BMTU BOXH BOXV BOZS BPDV BPRD BPZY BRAA BRBN
  BRCE BRCI BRJN BRVL BRZL BRZX BSRH BTEF BTOO BUWJ BVSZ
  BXAF BXAU BXFB BXTI BYIR BYJP BZSB CCFO CCXK CEOB FARL
  FCUK FLIK FORZ IIIL IIIR IIIX IIIV JAWZ LITZ LOOP LUNY MAGG MAXG
  MINT OKAY ONSO OODI OSIC OSIS OSIT OWAZ PARG REAP SIIS
  SKNT STYL SWON VOOM WAZZ WIGY WILD XRED YOYO
S-2 variants
  G-BADW BOEM BPLY BRVT BTTR BTUK BTUL BYIP CCTF EWIZ FDPS
  FOLY HISS ICAS IICI IIDY IIIE IIII IIIT ITII KITI ODDS OSZA OSZB PIIT
  PITS PITZ PTTS ROLL SIIB SIIE SKNT SPIN STUA STUB TIII WREN
  XATS ZIII

PLUMB
BGP.1 BIPLANE
  G-BGPI FUNN

POBER
P-9 PIXIE
  G-BUXO

POLIKARPOV
Po-2 (CSS-13)
  G-BXYA

PORTERFIELD AIRPLANE CO
CP-50
  G-AFZL
CP-65
  G-BVWY

PORTSLADE SCHOOL
Balloon (Hot Air)
FREE BALLOON
  G-AZYL

AVIONS POTTIER
P.80S
  G-BTYH

POWERCHUTE SYSTEMS INTERNATIONAL LTD
KESTREL (Rotax 503
  G-MVRV MWCI MWCK MWCM MWCN MWCO MWCP MWCS MWFG
  MWFI MWFL MWGU MWGV MWGW MWGZ MWMB MWMC MWMD
  MWMG MWMH MWNV MWNX MWOC MWOD MWOE MYCX MYCY MYCZ
  MYDA MYEX MYHS
RAIDER (Rotax 447)
  G-MVHB MVHC MVNA MVNB MVNC MVNJ MVNK MVNL MVVZ MVWJ

PRACTAVIA
PILOT SPRITE
  G-AZZH BALY BCVF BCWH ROSS

PRESTWICK MPA GROUP
DRAGONFLY MPA Mk 1
  G-BDFU

PRICE
Balloon (Hot Air)
AX7-77
  G-BMDJ

PRIVATEER see SLINGSBY

PROCTER see MITCHELL
PETREL
  G-AXSF

PROGRESSIVE AERODYNE INC
SEAREY AMPHIBIAN
  G-CREY

PROTECH
PT-2C
  G-EWAN

PTERODACTYL LTD see SOLEAIR
PFLEDGLING, PTRAVELER
  G-MBAW MBHZ MBPB MJST MMPI

ALFONS PUTZER KG
ELSTER B
  G-APVF BMWV

PZL-BIELSKO includiing SZYBOWCOWY ZAKLAD DOSWIADCZALNY (SZD)
SZD-9bis BOCIAN
  G-DBJD DCEB DDBX
SZD-24-4 FOKA
  G-DBZZ
SZD-30 PIRAT
  G-DCKD DCZE DCZJ DDAN DDAP DDBV DDFW DDNT
SZD-32A FOKA
  G-DCMF
SZD-36A COBRA
  G-DDAC DDCA DCVS DCVT DDAC
SZD-38A JANTAR-1
  G-DDDE DDFL
SZD-41A JANTAR STANDARD 1
  G-DDHC DDJL
SZD-45A OGAR
  G-BEBG BKTM BMFI OGAR
SZD-48 JANTAR STANDARD 2 & 3
  G-CFHV CFOT DESP DFTJ
SZD-50-3 PUCHACZ
  G-CFEN CFTH CFUY CFWE CFWT CFXO CFYA CFYL CGBD CGCU
  CGEL CHAF CHDP CHEP CHFH CHSC CJEC CJRF CJRJ CKAN CKHW
  DEUF DHCF
SZD-51-1 JUNIOR
  G-CFFV CFFY CFHF CFPM CFTC CFUS CFZA CFZF CFZP CGCC CHDB
  CHDU CHEK CHHE CHMA CHNK CHOV CHRG CJLG CJMY CJVC CKHA
  CKHN CKHR CKPN DHCR DHCW
SZD-55-1 PROMYK
  G-CHEC CHHR CKBN CKLR
SZD-59 ACRO
  G-CHWX

PZL-SWIDNIK
PW-5 SMYK
  G-CEUP CJCG CKPX

PZL WARSZAWA-OKECIE SA
PZL-104 WILGA variants
  G-BUNC BWDF BXBZ EPZL RIIN RTRT WILG
PZL-110 KOLIBER variants
  G-BUDO BVAI BXLR BXLS BYSI BZAJ BZLC CBGA CDDE CCIZ KOLI
  LOKM

QAC
QUICKIE
  G-BKFM BKSE BMFN BMVG BNJO BPMW BSPA BSSK BWIZ BXOY CUIK
  IMBI KUTU KWKI OSAW WAHL
TRI-Q
  G-BWIZ FARY

QUAD CITY including BFC kits
CHALLENGER (Rotax 503)
  G-BYKU BZHP CAMR CBDU CCFD IBFC MGAA MGRH MVZK MWFU
  MWFV MWFX MWFY MWFZ MYAG MYDN MYDS MYFH MYGM MYIA
  MYIX MYOZ MYPZ MYRH MYRJ MYSD MYTO MYTT MYUL MYXC MYXK
  MYXV MYYF MZAC MZBW MZBZ MZEA MZHO MZKW MZNA

RAJ HAMSA
X'AIR (FALCON and HAWK) variants
  G-BYCL BYHV BYJU BYLT BYMR BYNT BYOH BYOJ BYOR BYPO BYPW
  BYRV BYSY BYTR BYTZ BYYM BYYR BYZF BYZW BZAF BZAK BZBP
  BZDK BZEJ BZER BZEU BZEX BZFF BZGN BZGU BZGX BZHJ BZIA BZIS
  BZIY BZKC BZLT BZMR BZNG BZUP BZVH BZVK BZVR BZWC BZYM BZYX
  BZXA CBAH CBAV CBBH CBCI CBCM CBDO CBDV CBDW CBDY CBFE
  CBHB CBHV CBIC CBII CBIS CBJX CBKL CBLF CBLH CBLP CBLW CBMA
  CBNJ CBOC CBPU CBTK CBUC CBUJ CBVC CBVE CBVO CBWY CBXA
  CBXR CCBI CCBU CCBX CCCV CCCZ CCDJ CCDL CCDP CCDR CCEF
  CCES CCEY CCGJ CCGR CCHS CCIW CCKJ CCMK CCNF CCNL CCNZ
  CCOH CCOO CCRI CCSO CCVJ CCWF CCWZ CCZJ CCZS CDDH CDDO
  CDEM CDFM CDHO CDKC CDPS CDSN CDWL CEDO CEEC CEOH CEON
  CESJ CFCE CWAL HARI HITM IWIN MITE NEMO ODJD OHWV RAJA SPDY
  TANJ THAT TSKD UFAW XAYR XIOO ZRAF XRXR

RAND-ROBINSON

KR-2
G-BETW BLDN BNML BOLZ BOUN BPRR BRJX BRJY BRSN BSTL BTGD BUDF BUDS BURF BUWT BVIA BVZJ BYLP CBAU CEHT DGWW JCMW KISS KRII OFMB UTSI XRAY

RANGO BALLOON AND KITE COMPANY

Balloon (Minimum Lift)
NA variants
G-BINZ BJAS BJRH FYFW FYFY FYGI

RANS

S-4 COYOTE (Rotax 447)
G-MWBO MWEP MWES MWFW MWGN MWIO MWLA MWLZ MWWP MYWV
S-5 COYOTE (Rotax 447)
G-MVPJ MWFF MWGA MYDO MYFN MZGD
S-6 COYOTE variants (Rotax 503)
G-BSMU BSSI BSTT BSUA BSUT BTNW BTXD BUEW BUOK BUTM BUWK BVCL BVFM BVIN BVOI BVPW BVRK BVUM BVZO BVZV BWHK BWWP BWYR BXCU BXRZ BXWK BYBR BYCM BYCN BYIB BYID BYJO BYMN BYMU BYMV BYNP BYOT BYOU BYPT BYPZ BYRG BYRS BYSN BYZO BZBC BZBX BZEW BZGF BZGR BZKF BZKO BZLE BZMJ BZNH BZNJ BZRA BZRY BZUH BZVM BZYA BZYL CBAS CBAZ CBFX CBNV CBOK CBOS CBTO CBUY CBXZ CBYD CBZG CBZN CCDC CCEG CCJN CCLH CCNB CCNH CCOF CCTV CCTX CCZN CDFU CDGB CDGH CDKE CDVF CDYB CETY CLEE HTWE IZIT KEPP MGEC MGND MIKI MWCH MWHP MWIF MWSC MWTT MWUK MWUL MWUN MWVL MWWL MWYE MYAJ MYBA MYBI MYDK MYDX MYES MYGH MYGP MYGR MYHI MYHK MYHP MYIR MYIS MYJD MYJY MYKN MYLD MYLF MYLO MYLW MYMH MYMP MYMR MYMS MYNE MYNH MYOA MYOI MYOT MYPA MYPJ MYSP MYSU MYTE MYUZ MYVP MYXB MYXG MYXP MYYV MYZR MYZV MZAH MZBD MZBH MZBU MZBV MZCA MZDA MZDG MZDM MZDR MZEN MZEO MZEU MZFL MZFN MZFY MZIY MZJI MZJM MZKE MZLG MZLL MZMS MZMU MZNV MZOZ MZUB OYTE RDNS RINS RTHS RTMS SAUK SOOZ SSIX TIVS TSOB WYLE WZOY
S-7 COURIER
G-BVNY BWKJ BWMN CBNF CEEJ KATI OJKM
S-9 CHAOS
G-BSEE
S-10 SAKOTA (Rotax 532)
G-BRPT BRZW BSBV BSGS BSMT BSWB BTCR BTGG BTJX BTWZ BUAX BUKB BVFA BVHI BWIA BWIL JSCL RANS RANZ
S-12 AIRAILE
G-BZAO

RAYTHEON AIRCRAFT COMPANY

RB390 PREMIER
G-CJAG CJAH FRYL OEWD OMJC PHTO PREI VONJ
400A
G-EDCS STOB
850A
G-CERX

REALITY AIRCRAFT LTD

EASY RAIDER
G-CBKF CBXE CBXF CCEZ CCHR CCJS CCMJ OESY OEZI SLIP SRII
ESCAPADE
G-CCYB CDCW CDEV CDIZ CDKL CDLE CDSK CDTJ CECF CEDB CEIL CFAS CFBO DIZI ECKB ESCA ESCC ESCP ESGA ESKA IMNY LSJE MCUB PADE POZA SCPD VNON ZHKF

REARWIN AIRCRAFT and ENGINES INC

175 SKYRANGER
G-BTGI RWIN
8125 CLOUDSTER
G-EVLE
8500 SPORTSTER
G-AEOF

REECE

SKY RANGER
G-MJRR

REID and SIGRIST

RS.4 DESFORD
G-AGOS

REIMS AVIATION SA see CESSNA

RENEGADE see MURPHY

REPLICA PLANS

SE.5a
G-BDWJ BIHF BKER BMDB BUOD BUWE CCBN CCXG CEKL INNY SEVA

REPUBLIC AVIATION CORPORATION

P-47 THUNDERBOLT
G-BLZW CDVX THUN

REVOLUTION HELICOPTERS

MINI-500
G-BWCZ OREV PDWI

RIDOUT

Balloon (Minimum Lift)
ARENA
G-BIRP BJNA
EUROPEAN
G-BJDK BJFC BJMZ
JARRE
G-BJMX
STEVENDON SKYREACHER
G-BIWA
WARREN
G-BIWF
ZELENSKI
G-BIWG

RIGG

Balloon (Minimum Lift)
SKYLINER II
G-BIAR

AVIONS PIERRE **ROBIN** including ALPHA AVIATION MANUFACTURING LTD (*R2160*), CONSTRUCTIONS AÉRONAUTIQUES DE BOURGOGNE and ROBIN AVIATION production
DR.400 variants
G-BAEB BAEM BAEN BAFP BAFX BAGC BAGR BAGS BAHL BAJY BAJZ BAKM BALF BALG BALH BALI BALJ BAMS BAMT BAMU BAMV BANB BAPV BAPX BAZC BBAX BBAY BBCH BBCS BBDP BBJU BBMB BCXE BDUY BEUP BFJZ BGRH BGWC BHAJ BHJU BHLE BHLH BHOA BIHD BIZI BJUD BKDH BKDI BKDJ BKVL BNFV BOGI BPHG BPZP BRBK BRBL BRBM BRNT BRNU BSDH BSFF BSLA BSSP BSVS BSYU BSZD BTRU BUGJ BUYS BXRT BYHT BZMM CBBA CBEZ CBMT CBZK CCKP CCWM CCZX CDAI CDBM CDIM CDOY CEKE CETB CONB DUDZ EGGS EHMM ELEN ELUN EOMK ETIV EUSO EYCO FCSP FTIL FTIM FTIN FUEL GAOH GAOM GBUE GBVX GCUF GDEF GDKR GGJK GLKE GOSL HAIR HANS HXTD IEYE IOOI JBDH JBUZ JEDH JMTS JUDE KIMY LARA LEKT LEOS LGCA LGCB LGCC MAGZ MIFF NBDD NFNF OACF ONGC ORRG OTIB OYIO PAYD PVCV PVML RONS RTUG SELL TUGY UAPA XLXL YOGI ZACH ZIGI ZIPI
DR.500-200i PRÉSIDENT
G-BYIT BZIJ CDMD CHIX DPYE GSRV IYCO KENW MOTI PREZ RNDD TYER
HR.100-200B ROYAL
G-AZHB AZHK BBCN BXWB CBFN
HR.100-210 SAFARI II
G-BAPY BAWR BAYR BBAW BBCN BBIO BLWF HRIO MPWI RUES
HR.100-285 TIARA
G-BEUD BLHN
HR.200 variants
G-BBOE BCCY BETD BFBE BGXR BLTM BNIK BVMM BWFG BXDT BXGW BXOR BXVK BYLH BYNK BYSG BZET BZLG BZXK GBJS GBXF GMKD GMKE HHUK HRCC JPAT NSOF WAVA WAVI WAVN WAVV
R.1180T(D) AIGLON
G-BGHM BIRT BJVV GBAO GDER GEEP PACE ROBN VECD VITE
R.2100 SUPER CLUB,
G-BKXA
R.2100A,
G-BGBA BICS
R.2112 ALPHA
G-BIVA BZFB CBNG EWHT PLAY RAFC TOUR
R.2120
G-CBLECBVB ECAC
R.2160 (ALPHA SPORT)
G-BLWY BVYO BWZG BYBF CETG ILUA MATT OCFC PGSI PSFG SACK SBMO VECG WAVT
R.3000 variants
G-BLYP BOLU BZOL CCCN ENNI PAVL
ATL variants
G-GFNO GFRD GFRO GGHZ

ROBINSON AIRCRAFT CO

REDWING
G-ABNX

ROBINSON HELICOPTER CO INC

R22 variants

"G-RAFM" G-BJUC BLDK BLME BLTF BOAM BOCN BODZ BOEW BOVR BOYC BOYX BPGV BPIT BPNI BPTZ BRBY BROX BRRY BRVI BRWD BRXV BSCE BSEK BSGF BTBA BTDI BTHI BTNA BTOC BUBW BVGS BVPR BWHY BWTH BXOA BXSG BXSY BXUC BXXN BXYK BYCF BYIE BYTE BYZP BYZZ BZBU BZJJ BZMO BZYE CBBK CBVL CBWZ CBXK CBXN CBZF CCAP CCDE CCGE CCGF CCMR CCVU CCVY CDAW CDED CDBF CDBG CDDD CDMG CDSU CESN CESU CHAN CHIS CHPA CHPR CHYL CHZN CMSN CRAY CTRL DAAM DABS DEER DEFY DELB DERB DGOD DLDL DMCD DODB DODR EFGH EFOF EGGY EIBM EPAR ERBL EROM ETIN FIRS FLYH FOGY FOLI GEGE GJCD GOUP HARR HBMW HIEL HIPO HIZZ HONI HRBS HRHE HSLA HUGS HURN IAGD IBED ICCL IIFR IIPT INKY IORG ISMO JARA JATD JBII JCAP JERS JHEW JONB JONH JOYD JSAK JWFT KNIB KNOX KUKI LAIN LHCA LHCB LIPE LSWL LYNC MACA MATY MAVI MDGE MDKD MICH MOGY MRSN NJSH NORT NWDC OASH OAVA OBIL OBIO OCOV ODCS ODJB OEAT OFAS OGOH OHSL OICV OIIO OJAN OKEY OLAU OLRT OMMG ONMT ORMB OSEE OSHL OTED OTHL OTOY OVNR OZZY PACL PBRL PERE RALD RATA REDY RENT RIAT RIDD RIDL RNGO ROTF ROUT ROVY RSVP RSWW RWIA SBUT SCHO SIMS SLNW SPEE SUCT SUMX TAGT TATO TGRD TGRE TGRS THLA TILE TIMH TINK TOLY TOMM TORS TOSH TTHC TUNE VCJH VEYE VMSL VOCE WADS WAGG WFOX WIRL WIZA WIZR WIZY WRWR YACB YMBO ZAPY ZFLY

R44 variants

G-BVMC BWVH BYCE BYKK BZGO BZLP BZMG BZOP BZPL BZTA BZXY CBAK CBEG CBFJ CBOT CBRO CBVI CBYY CBZE CCFC CCNY CCRD CCTL CCWD CCWI CCWJ CCYC CCYG CCYT CCZG CCZH CDCB CDCV CDHH CDKU CDKY CDSE CDXX CDJZ CDMI CDSY CDUE CDWK CDXA CDXB CEAU CECW CECX CEDG CEEE CEHK CEHY CEIM CEKF CEKX CEMC CENY CERS CESB CESO CEST CEUU CEUX CEVI CEWV CEYA CEYB CFAN CGGG CHAP CHUM CIDA CJLL CKEM CMCC CMXX CRIB CROW CULF DAVG DAVV DBUG DCON DCSE DCSG DGHD DIGG DKMK DMRA DMRS DOVS DRIV DSPI DSPZ DWCE DYCE EDES EECH EEZA EGTC EJRC EJTC EKKO EKYD ELMO EMEL EMMI ESSY ETFF ETNT EZZR FABI FAKE FARE FCUM FEAR FLBI FLYS FLYX FOFO FUNY GACB GATE GATT GBEN GDAV GDJF GDOV GENI GEST GGNG GGRH GHDC GIBB GILI GLIB GOES GRWW GSPY HFLY HGRB HHOG HMPF HRHS HRPN HTEL HVER IAJJ ICAB IFDM IFTS IGNL IJNK ILET ILLG IMBS INDX ITPH IVEN IVIV JAJA JAKF JANI JBKA JCWM JEFA JILY JKAY JORD JPJR JRED JTSA JWEB KEIF KELI KIDG KLAS KNYT KPAO KSPB KYDD LAID LARY LEVO LLIZ LMBO LMCG LOCO LOTA LOYN LRSN LUKI LUKY LWAY MAKI MAPL MAYB MCAI MCCG MDDT MDPY MGAN MGWI MIKS MITC MRDC MRKS MRRY MURY MUSH NANI NESH NICI NIOG NOSY NSEW NYLE OAJC OBBY OBSM OCHM OCON ODHB ODOC OEJC OFIL OHLI OHJV OHVR OJAZ OJRH OLFO OLOW OMCD OMEL OMGH OMKA ONEP ONGA OOFR OONA OPDG OPHA OPTF ORBK OSJL OSSI OTJB OTNA OTTZ OTVI OWND PBEE PEPS PFML PGGY PIDG PIMP PIXL PIXX PPTS PRET PROJ RALA RAVN RDEL REDI REGE RFUN RGNT RMBM ROAD ROCT ROGE ROTG ROWR ROZI RROB RTWO RTWW RULE RUZZ RWEW RWGS RYZZ SAIG SBRA SEFI SHAF SHAN SHRT SIRD SLOK SPJE SPYS SSJP STAA STOP STPH STUY SUMZ SUNN SWAT TAND TBTB TEXT TGDL TGDT TIMC TOLI TRAC TRCW TRCY TRNT UTTS UTZI VALV VEIT VVBL WAFU WAGS WALI WEGO WLDN WMBT WMWM WTAV WWOW WYSP XELA XLIV XTEK XTRM YEAH YIIK ZBED ZOOT

ROCKWELL INTERNATIONAL CORPORATION including COMMANDER

AIRCRAFT COMPANY (COMMANDER 114B) production

COMMANDER 112 variants

G-BDAK BDFW BDIE BDKW BDLT BEBU BEDG BENJ BEPY BFPO BFZM BHRO BIOJ BLTK BMWR BPTG CNCN CRIL DASH EHXP ERIC FLPI HROI IMPX JILL LITE OVIN PLAZ SAAB

COMMANDER 114 and 114A variants

G-BDYD BERI BERW BFAI BFXS BGBZ BHSE BKAY BMJL BOLT BUSW BYKB DANT DDIG DIME HILO JURG LADS NATT OIBM OLFT OMUM RCED TECH TWIZ ZIPA

COMMANDER 114B

G-EMCA FATB HMBJ HPSB HPSE HPSF HPSL KEEF NOOR OECM OOJP PJNZ VICS

COMMANDER 685

G-OMAP

COMMANDER 690

G-CECN

ROGER HARDY

RH7B TIGER LIGHT

G-MZGT

ROGERSON

HORIZON 1

G-DOGZ

ROLLADEN-SCHNEIDER FLUGZEUGBAU GmbH includng

DG FLUGZEUGBAU GmbH production

LS1 variants

G-CFOZ CJST LSIF

LS3 variants

G-CEVD CEVV CGDA CJDJ CKHB CKMV DECP DEEF DEES DEEX DEGE LSGM ILBO

LS4 variantst

G-CFAO CFHL CFJM CFKG CFNU CHKX CHMX CHNV CHPL CHVV CHXT CHXZ CHZM CHZY CJEP CJKP CJLC CJLH CJSW CJUB CKAV CKCB CKDK CKEC CKFL CKKX CKLG CKLN CKLS CKNS DEHK DEHL DEKV DEMB DEMF DEMG DEMT DEOA DETG DETY DEUH DHNX DKEN EELT EENE EESY FERV GBPP LSED LSFR LSLS SVNC XCIV

LS6 variants

G-CFCP CGBG CGBO CGBR CGCM CHAO CHBC CHHH CHHT CHHU CHJC CHJF CHMK CHOZ CHPD CHSA CHYA CJDG CJNP CKBH DFRA DHET DHEZ DHUM LSCP LSED LSGB LSVI STEU

LS7 variants

G-CEVN CFMY CFTV CFTY CFUV CFVH CFWU CFYB CFYK CFYW CFZV CGBL CHAY CHBA CHDX CHEH CJLK CJSJ CJTR CJZZ CKHS CKMO DFOG EUFO LSFB

LS8 variants

G-CHUW CHVF CHTM CHTS CHUV CHVL CHVU CHWL CHWS CHXC CHXW CHYF CHZG CJCP CJDE CJDK CJDT CJEA CJFL CJFX CJGS CJHY CJJK CJKD CJKL CJKN CJLN CJMO CJMT CJMU CJNJ CJOD CJPH CJPL CJPR CJRA CJSU CJTM CJTM CJTY CJUE CKEL CKEZ CKFM CKFV CKHP CKJE CKMA CKME CKPM CTAG DSVN GZIP LLLL LSKV RIEV WDGC WLLS XWON

ROLLASON AIRCRAFT and ENGINES LTD see DRUINE

BETA

G-AWHX BADC BETE BUPC

ROMAIN

COBRA BIPLANE

G-MNLH

ROOKE & HOUNSELL

Balloon (Minimum Lift)

BITTERNE MK.1

G-BJJM

ROOSTER see LIGHTWING

ROTARY AIR FORCE INC

RAF 2000 variants (Subaru EJ22)

G-BUYL BVSM BWAD BWAE BWHS BWTK BXAC BXDD BXDE BXEA BXEB BXGS BXKM BXMG BYIN BYJA CBCJ CBHC CBHZ CBIT CBJE CBJN CCEU CCUH CDJN HEKK HOWL IRAF JEJE ONON PHLB RAFZ SAYS TXSE YRAF YROJ YROO

ROTEC ENGINEERING INC

RALLY 2B

G-MBGS MBMG MJPA MVRF

ROTORSPORT (UK) LTD

UK MT-03

G-CDYF CDZZ CEHM CEHN CEIA CEOX CERF CEUI CEVY CEXX CEYR CFAI CFAK CFAR CFCL JBRE JYRO KENG KEVG LUNG MAZA MEPU NAGG PILZ PPLG RIFS RSMT TELC UMAS YROM YROX

ROTORWAY

(SCORPION) EXECUTIVE

G-BNZL BNZO BPCM BRGX BSRP BUJJ BURP BUSN BVOY BVTV BWLY BWUJ BYNH BYNI BZBW BZES BZOM BZXD CBIK CBJV CBWO CBWU CBYB CBZI CCFY CCMU CDBK CDRS CHTG EFFI ESUS FLIT JONG KENI MAMC NEEL NJBA OHOV PILE PURS RATH RAWS REID RHYS RISH RWAY SFOX SSEX VART WHOO YEWS ZHWH

ATELIERS AERONAUTIQUE **ROUSSEAU** see PIEL

ROYAL AIRCRAFT FACTORY see REPLICA PLANS and SLINGSBY

BE.2C

G-AWYI

SE.5, SE.5A

G-EBIA

G--EBIB EBIC BKDT

RUSCHMEYER LUFTFAHRTTECHNIK GmbH

RUSHMEYER R90

G-EERH TTHL UAPO

RUTAN
COZY
G-BXDO BXVX BYLZ CESP COZI OGJS SCUL SPFX
DEFIANT
G-OTWO
LONG-EZ
G-BKXO BLLZ BLMN BLTS BMHA BMIM BMUG BOOX BPWP BRFB BSIH
BUPA BZMF CBLZ HAIG ICON LEZE LGEZ LUKE MUSO OMJT PUSH
RAEM RAFT RPEZ SENA
VARIEZE
G-BEZE BEZY BIMX BKST BVAY BVKM EZDG EMMY IPSY KENZ LASS
OOSE SKCI TIMB VEZE

RYAN AERONAUTICAL CORPORATION
ST3KR, PT-22
G-AGYY BTBH BYPY

SAAB-SCANIA AB including SVENSKA AEROPLAN AB (SAAB)
32 LANSEN
G-BMSG
91 SAFIR
G-BCFW HRLK SAFR
SF.340 variants
G-GNTB GNTF LGNA LGNB LGNC LGND LGNE LGNF LGNG LGNH LGNI
LGNJ LGNK LGNL
2000
G-CDEA CDEB CDKA CDKB CERY CERZ

SAFFERY MODEL BALLOONS including CUPRO SAPHIRE LTD
Balloon (Minimum Lift)
S.200
G-BIHU
S.200 RIGG SKYLINER
G-BHLJ
S.330
G-BERN BFBM
SMITH PRINCESS
G-FYGM

SAN see JODEL

SAUNDERS-ROE LTD
A.19 CLOUD
G-ACGO
P.531-2
G-APNV APVL
SKEETER
G-APOI BLIX HELI SARO

SCALLAN
Balloon (Minimum Lift)
EAGLE
G-FYEO
FIREFLY
G-FYEZ

SCHEIBE-FLUGZEUGBAU GmbH
BERGFALKE
G-CKGY EEBD
ZUGVOGEL
G-CFRS CHKV
SF24 MOTORSPATZ
G-BZPF
SF25 FALKE variants including SLINGSBY T.61 derivatives*
G-AVIZ AXEO AXIW AXJR AYBG AYSD* AYUM* AYUN* AYUP* AYUR*
AYYL* AYZU* AYZW* AZHD* AZIL* AZMC* AZMD* AZPC* AZYY* BADH*
BAIZ* BAKY* BAMB* BDZA BECF BEGG BFPA BFUD BGMV BHSD BIGZ
BKVG BLCU BLTR BLZA BMBZ BMVA BODU BPIR BPZU BRRD BRWT
BSEL* BSUO BSWL* BSWM* BTDA* BTRW* BTTZ* BTUA* BTWC*
BTWD* BTWE* BUDA* BUDB* BUDC* BUDT* BUED* BUEK* BUFG*
BUFN* BUFR* BUGL* BUGT* BUGV* BUGW* BUGZ* BUHA* BUHR*
BUIH* BUJA* BUJB* BUJI* BUJX* BUNB* BUXJ* BVKK* BVKU* BVLX*
BWTR* BXAN BXMV CCHX CDFD CDSC CKNN* FEFE FHAS FLKE FLKS
GBGA HBOS KAOM KDEY KFAN KGAO KWAK MFMM MILD OHGC OSUT
OWGC* SEXE
SF27A
G-CFOF CGAV CHSX DEKS
SF28A TANDEM FALKE
G-BARZ BYEJ CCIS

SCHEMPP-HIRTH FLUGZEUBAU GmbH including SCHEMPP-HIRTH KG
and SCHEMPP-HIRTH GMBH & CO KG
SHK-1
G-CFJZ DCCB DCGT
(STANDARD) CIRRUS variants including BURKHART GROB FLUGZEUGBAU,
JASTREB FABRIKA AVIONAI JEDRILICA.,LANAVERRE INDUSTRIE, and
VAZDUHOPLOVNO TEHNICKI CENTAR production
G-CDDB CFBB CFCN CFLW CFMT CFMU CFVS CFYJ CGAH CGEP
CHAX CHFF CHGG CHJY CHKC CHKD CHKR CHKS CHMY CHNM CHSV
CHTU CHUR CHVZ CHZJ CHZU CJCJ CJCN CJCU CJDS CJER CJEV
CJFA CJGN CJJJ CJMH CJOS CJOW CJRG CJRT CJUU CJVU CKEA
CKEB CKES CKFA CKJF CKHT CKJG CKJT CKFK CKMD CKMD CKNB
CKNE CTWO DCDH DCFK DCGY DCJR DCKZ DCLA DCNC DCOR DCOY
DCRH DCTB DCVE DCWR DCYM DCYT DDAS DDDA DDDM DDDR
DDGE DDVS DDVY DDXL DEEN DEHK KCHG SCNN
DISCUS variants including ORLICAN AKCIOVA, SPOLECNOST production
G-CEUN CEWZ CFCA CFDM CFEJ CFES CFFT CFFX CFHR CFLE CFMO
CFNL CFNR CFOY CFTW CFUL CFYM CFYN CGCT CGDX CHDZ CHEN
CHGK CHGS CHHO CHJH CHJL CHKA CHKY CHLN CHLS CHLY CHMO
CHOM CHOR CHOW CHPI CHPX CHRS CHRX CHSD CHSO CHUZ
CHXH CHZE CJAO CJBR CJBW CJCK CJFC CJGL CJGM CJGR CJHM
CJJZ CJKR CJKX CJLC CJLP CJLW CJNE CJOA CJOC CJPP CJRR CJSE
CJUP CJUV CJVB CJVX CJWK CJXL CJXR CJYF CJYN CJZG CKAH
CKAP CKFB CKFT CKJZ CKLD CKLV CKOD CKOK CKPB CKPG DHCL
DHEM DHGL DHKL DHMP DHPR DHSJ DJAN DJMD DTWO HOJO IDER
KOBH RGTS SAJA SAOC TWOA TWOT
DUO DISCUS T
G-CHNF CHNW CHRW CHSW CJCX CJEM CJFF CJFH CJJP CJOO
CJPA CJTU CJUM CJXW CKCV CKEV CKGF CKHK CKKE CKKN CKKY
CKML CKNJ CKOJ CKOL CKPE CKPO CKPY DDJF DUOT DUOX HKAA
JIFI ODUO OKLL PHNX RDDT SAXT SISI TLTL XDUO
JANUS variants
G-BMBJ BXJS CHTB CHUH CJFE CKJK CKLF CTAA DEOV DEOW DJAA
JNSC JNUS
(MINI) NIMBUS variants
G-CDTH CENK CEWE CFAM CFCS CFGF CFHG CFWK CFZO CHBV
CHFX CHNH CHNU CHOY CHYY CHZA CJCT CJED CJMN CJMV CJTJ
CJWG CJXA CJYS CJZL CKBG CKFH CKJC CKLP CKPL CKPV DDAJ
DDGY DDKL DDMM DDNG DDTU DDXT DDYU DEAJ DEAM DEEK DEFF
DEGS DEHP DEON DEVF ECOL EEBF EEBK EEER EENN EHCB HAUT
HJSM IVDM KEPE KOYY NIMB NYMB NIVT OJNE OZOZ
VENTUS variants
G-CEUR CFBT CFDE CFEG CFFK CFMN CFNN CFPE CFPL CFRB CFUH
CFVW CFYC CFZH CGAS CHFV CHFY CHUY CHVE CHVT CHWH CHXR
CJEX CJFR CJKY CJOR CJSL CJVA CJWX CJYU CJZM CKAJ CKAS
CKBK CKCH CKDA CKDO CKDV CKFC CKFP CKFU CKGA CKGB CKGB
CKGC CKGD CKGL CKJB CKJM CKKF CKNO CKNR CKPK CVZT DEKJ
DELG DELR DEPX DEUJ DEUS DFAW DHSL DHYL DKFU EVII FORA
IFWD HAAH IICT IICX IIIO IRLE KHCC KPLG KTCC NJET ORCW OTCZ
RBCT SWSW TWOC UNIN VCXT VENC VENT VNTS VSIX VTCT VTUS
VTWO WONE XJON XXVB YODA ZENN

ALEXANDER SCHLEICHER SEGELFLUGZEUGBAU GmbH and Co
including SA CENTRAIR and JUBI GMBH SPORTFLUGZEUGBAU production *
Ka 6 variants
G-CEVK CEWO CFBZ CFCR CFDR CFKY CFND CFTB CFVZ CFWA
CFXU CGCP CGDE CHAB CHFB CHJP CHPO CHSN CJEW CJHD CJHL
CJSG CKDB CKMJ DBUZ DBVR DBVZ DBYL DBYM DBYU DBYX DCAE
DCAG DCAS DCCL DCCR DCCU DCDF DCEM DCEY DCGB
DCGE DCLZ DCPJ DDAW DDEV DDGK DDHM DDSY DDHT DDJE DDKN
DDLP DDMO DDNW DDNX DDOF DDOK DDRD DDSB DDSY DDUR
DDVG DDWC DDXH DDYC DDYJ DEAH DECF DEEW DEKC DGAW
DHAL ECDB EELY FGAZ HCAC
K 7 variants
G-CFJW CFOU CFXH DBVB DCLT DCMG DDAK DDML DDOX DDRM
DDWN DEDK DELX
K 8 variants
G-CFLH CFNA CFWL CFXW CGDB CGDK CHDN CHDY CHKK CHYW
CHYX CJAT CJFT CJGD CJHK CJLS CJNN CJOJ CKDH CKMI DCGH
DDGA DDJB DDMB DDMG DDOY DDRZ DDSF DDUF DDUK DDWG
DEEM DEPT DESJ EHCZ
*ASK 13 **
G-CFGR CFHM CFMH CFPX CFSD CFVC CFVU CFWB CFZN CHPE
CHSM CHUD CHUF CHUU CHVW CHXJ CHXV CJGW CJLO CJMP CJMW
CJMZ CJPV CJPY CJWB CJWJ CJXM CJYE CJZE CKFJ CKHH CHXP
CKJL CKKR CKLA CKRB DCBW DCCE DCCF DCCP DCCT DCCW DCCX
DCCY DCEX DCFA DCFG DCGO DCKV DCMK DCRT DCWH DDKE
DDMX DDOA DDVB DEDU DEKD DEPP DETS DFAT DHAL DJLL EEBZ
ASK 14
G-BKSP BSIY KOHF
ASW 15 variants
G-CFBC CFDA CFML CFMS CFOB CFRK CFTD CGCR CGDS CGDY
CHEJ CHZD CJDM CJDR CJJX CJPX CJRE CJVW CKRR DCHT DHOX
DJGG GTWO

ASK 16
  G-BCHT BCTI
ASW 17
  G-DCPD DCTE
ASK 18
  G-CHRN CJHO CJKG CJMK CJPO CJPZ CJSZ CKNM DDLB DDNJ DDPA
  EEUX
ASW 19
  G-CEWI CEXY CFGP CFNH CFWP CFWZ CGCA CHHK CHLM CHLV
  CHNC CHUA CHXE CHXU CJBK CJBT CJFU CJKS CJNT CJRB CJUZ
  CKEX CKGU DDHX DDSX DDTE DDVL DDVP DDXX DDZG DEJR DELA
  DEPE DERP DERS DHCE DHER DHCV FEBJ
ASW 20
  G-BUCG CEVZ CFBA CFHD CFJE CFKL CFPH CFPN CFRW CFTL CFTP
  CFUN CFWS CFZL CHBU CHDJ CHDL CHEO CHGW CHHS CHPC CHUJ
  CHUT CHVP CHVX CHZZ CJEE CJFJ CJFK CJHZ CJTP CJZH CKCY
  CKDC CKER CKHF CKJN CKMY CKPZ DDST DDTP DDXB DDYE DEBX
  DECC DEEC DEFE DEFV DEHV DEHZ DEKU DELZ DENV DEOJ DEPF
  DEPS DERA DERH DETZ DEUD DEUK DEUY DFAF DHCH DHOK EEDE
  EEFK EENW EFLY EKEY MAGK MEEE
ASK 21
  G-CEWC CFBV CFYV CGAF CGAG CGAM CGBB CGBF CGBN CGBV
  CHLP CHPV CHPW CHTV CHYT CHZR CJAV CJAX CJBM CJGJ CJJR
  CJKA CJKJ CJKO CJKU CJKZ CJOX CJTR CJVZ CJWD CKCT CKCZ
  CKDF CKEK CKGX CKFY CKJP CKKP CKGK CKLW CKMW CKNL CKOT
  CKPP DECZ DEGZ DEHO DEKG DERH DESB DESU DHCX DHRR DJAD
  EENK PNGC
ASW 22
  G-CGBX CHTN CJWZ LDER
ASK 23
  G-CGCF DEVW DEVX DEVY DEYV
ASW 24
  G-CFNG CGDT CGDU CGDZ CHBB CHBG CHYD CJCD CJEB CJEL
  CJRU CJTB CJTH CJXT OTRY
ASH 25 variants
  G-CFST CFWW CHLX CHXO CWLC GBBB RAIR SINK
ASH 26E
  G-BWBY CCLR CDPX KEAM OPHT ZZAJ
ASW 27
  G-CEUG CHXD CHYR CHZO CJCM CJDC CJJF CJLY CJPS CJPT
  CJRH CJSS CJVM CJXZ CJYD CJZX CKCN CKDN CKDS CKDW CKED
  CKFD CKHD CKHG CKKH CKLB CKOM CKRM LIDY OASG OASW SASG
  THRM
ASW 28
  G-CJVS CJWA CJZN CKAL CKBM CKBU CKBV CKCJ CKGN CKGV CKHX
  CKJA CKKD CKJN CKJS CKJV CKKD CKKM CKLP CKMM CKMZ CKNG
  CKNV CKRC GLID TRBO
ASG 29
  G-CKOE CKON CKOO CKOY CKOZ VLCC XOAR XXIX

SCHROEDER FIRE BALLOONS GmbH
Balloon (Hot Air)
G
  G-CBVK

SCHWEIZER AIRCRAFT CORPORATION see HUGHES

SOCIÉTÉ **SCINTEX** see PIEL

SCOTTISH AVIATION
TWIN PIONEER
  G-APHY APJT APRS AYFA BBVF
BULLDOG variants
  G-ASAL AXEH AXIG AYZM AZAK AZET AZJO AZWO BCUO BCUP BCUS
  BCUV BDIN BDOG BHXA BHZR BHZS BHZT BPCL BULL BWIB BZDP
  BZEP BZFN BZMD BZME BZMH BZML BZON BZPS BZXS BZXZ CBAB
  CBAN CBBC CBBL CBBR CBBS CBBT CBBU CBBW CBCB CBCR CBCV
  CBDK CBDS CBEF CBEH CBEK CBFP CBFU CBGX CBID CBJJ CBJK
  CCMI CCOA CDVV DAWG DDOG DISA DOGE DOGG EDAV GGRR
  GRRR JWCM KDOG RAIG RNRS SIJW TDOG UDOG ULHI WINI

SE see ROYAL AIRCRAFT.FACTORY, SLINGSBY and REPLICA PLANS

SEEMS see MORANE-SAULNIER

SERVOTECH LTD
GRASSHOPPER
  G-ARVN AWRP AXFM AZAU

SHAW
TWIN-EZE
  G-IVAN

SHERRY
BUZZARD
  G-MMNN

SHERWOOD RANGER see TLAC

SHIELD
XYLA
  G-AWPN

SHORT BROTHERS LTD see EMBRAER
S.16 SCION
  G-ACUX
S.25 SANDRINGHAM/SUNDERLAND
  G-AHJR AKCO BJHS
S.45 SOLENT
  G-AKNP
SA.6 SEALAND
  G-AKLS AKLW
SC.5 BELFAST
  G-BEPS
SC.7 SKYVAN
  G-BDVO BEOL PIGY
SD.3-30
  G-BDBS BEWT BKIE BKMW OGIL SSWA
SD.3-60
  G-BKMX BMLC BOEG BPFN CEAL CLAS EXPS JEMX OBHD ROND
  SSWE SSWM SSWO SSWR TMRA TMRB TMRO XPSS

SIAI-MARCHETTI SpA
S.205
  G-AVEH AYXS BBRX BFAP VELA
SF.260
  G-BAGB IGIE MACH NRRA SIAI
SM.1019
  G-LISO

SIKORSKY AIRCRAFT see VERTICAL AVIATION TECHNOLOGIES (**S-52**)
and WESTLAND
S-51
  "G-AJOV" G-AJHW
S-61 variants
  G-ATBJ ATFM AYOY BBHL BBVA BCEA BCEB BCLD BDIJ BDOC BFFJ
  BFRI BGWJ BGWK BHOG BHOH BIMU BPWB
S-76 variants
  G-BHBF BIBG BIEJ BISZ BJFL BJGX BMAL BOYF BURS BVCX BYDF
  BYOM CEYZ CFDV CHCD DRNT EEBB FULM JCBA JCBJ KAZA KAZB
  KAZD LJRM SSSC SSSD SSSE VIPZ VONA VONB VONC XJCB XXEA
S-92
  G-CGMU CGOD CHCK IACA IACB IACC IACD IACE IACF SARB SARC

SILENCE
TWISTER
  G-CDKJ RIOT TWSR TWST XSEL

SIPA
903, S91
  G-AMSG ATXO AWLG BBBO BBDV BDAO BDKM BGME BHMA DWEL
  SIPA

SKANDINAVISK AERO INDUSTRI
KRAMME KZ.VIII
  G-AYKZ

SKY BALLOONS LTD including CAMERON BALLOONS
Balloon (Hot Air)
16 series
  G-BWVP
21 series
  G-BYCB
25 series
  G-BXWX BZSL
31 series
  G-BWOY BXVP OSVY
56 series
  G-BWYP
65 series
  G-BWUS BXKO BXUS DUNG
70 series
  G-PGUY
77 series
  G-BWSL BXHL BXVG BXXP BZLS CDAM CLRK KSKY LOWS MAGL
  OBET RCML

80 series
  G-BYBS BYOI SETI
90 series
  G-BWKR BXGD BXJT BXLP BXPP BXVR BXWL BYZV BZKV CLOE CZAG
  GPEG LEAS VINO ZABC
105 series
  G-BWDZ BWOA BWPP BXCN BXDV BXIW BXXS BYNV BZFG
120 series
  G-BWIX BWJR BWPF BWYU BXLC BXWG BYEX CFAY OBFE
140 series
  G-BYKZ
160 series
  G-BWUK
180 series
  G-BWIW BXVL
200 series
  G-BWST BXIH
220 series
  G-SPEL
240 series
  G-BXUE MRLN
260
  G-KTKT
Special Shape

SHAPE	REGISTRATION
FLYING MAP	G-MAPS

SKYCRAFT (UK) LTD
SCOUT
  G-MBBB MBUZ

SKYFOX
CA-25N GAZELLE
  G-IDAY

SKYHOOK SAILWINGS LTD
TR1 Trike with Cutlass, Pixie and Zeus wings
  G-MJFX MJNU MJNY MMVS

SKYRIDER AVIATION
AIRSPORTS PHANTOM
  G-MJSE MJSF MJTE MJTX MJTZ MJUR MJUX MJVX MMKX MNCS MTTN

SKYSTAR see DENNEY

SLEPCEV
STORCH
  G-BZOB

SLINGSBY AIRCRAFT CO LTD see TIPSY

SLINGSBY SAILPLANES LTD including SLINGSBY ENGINEERING LTD and
see FOURNIER, SCHEIBE and SOPWITH
T.6 KITE 1
  G-ALNH
T.30 KIRKBY PREFECT
  G-ALLF
T.31 MOTOR CADET derivatives
  G-AYAN BCYH BDSM BEMM BNPF BODH BOOD BPIP BRVJ BUAC
  BVFS BZLK
T.51 DART
  G-DBRY DBSA DBUF DBVH DBWJ DBWM DBWO DBWP DBWS DBXH
  DCAZ DCBA
T.53
  G-DDHE
T.59 KESTREL
  G-BDWZ BDXG BDZG CETJ DCAZ DCNW DCOJ DCSD DCSF DCSK
  DCTJ DCTM DCTO DCVY DCWA DCWB DCWF DCXM DCZR DDBN
  KESY
T.61 see SCHEIBE
T.65 (SPORT) VEGA variants
  G-BGBV DDWT DDXD DDXE DDZA DDZP DECL DEDY DEEG DEFW
  DEGH DEGJ DEGX DEHG DEJC DEJE DELD DEMJ DEMN DEMP DEMZ
  EEAD EECK VEGA
T.67A and T.67M FIREFLY
  G-BIOW BJIG BJNG BJXA BJXB BJZN BKAM BKTZ BLLP BLLR BLLS
  BLPI BLRF BLRG BLTU BLTW BLUX BLVI BNSO BNSP BNSR BOCL
  BOCM BONT BONU BUUA BUUB BUUC BUUD BUUE BUUF BUUI BUUJ
  BUUK BUUL BWGO BWXA BWXB BWXC BWXD BWXE BWXF BWXG
  BWXH BWXI BWXJ BWXK BWXL BWXM BWXN BWXO BWXP BWXR
  BWXS BWXT BWXU BWXW BWXW BWXY BWXZ BXKW BYBX
  BYOB BYOD BYRY BYYG CBWX CDHC EFSM FLYG HONG KONG ONES
  OPUB RAFG SFTZ SKYC SKYO TONS ZEIN

SMD
GAZELLE with FlexiformSealander sailwing
  G-MMGU MMHS

SMITH
DSA-1 MINIPLANE
  G-BTGJ

SMYTH
MODEL S SIDEWINDER
  G-BRVH

SNCAN including AIA DE MAISON-BLANCHE(1), SAN(3) and SOCIÉTÉ STAMPE ET
RENAULT(2) **(SV-4)** production
NC854
  G-BCGH BGEW BIUP BJEL BJLB NORD
NC856 NORVEGIE
  G-CDWE
NC858
  G-BDJR BDXX BPZD
SV-4A (DH Gipsy Major 10)
  G-AZNK BLOL
SV-4A (Renault 4P)
  G-BHYI BZSY(3) NIFE STMP(3)
SV-4B (DH Gipsy Major 10)
  G-AIYG AWIW AYIJ AZSA(2) BRMC2)
SV-4C (DH Gipsy Major 10)
  G-AXRP BEPC BIMO BPLM(1) BRXP OODE
SV-4C (LycomIng IO-360)
  G-BMNV
SV-4C (Renault 4P)
  G-AMPI ATIR(1) AWXZ AXCZ AXHC AXNW AYCG AYDR AYGE AYZI
  AZGC AZGE BAKN BEPF BHFG BKRK BKSX BTIO BWRS BXSV BYDK
  EEUP FORC GMAX HJSS(1)
SV-4C(G) (DH Gipsy Major 1C)
  G-ASHS
SV-4C(G) (DH Gipsy Major 10)
  G-AWEF AYCK(1) AYJB AYWT(1) AZCB BWEF FORD SVIV
SV-4E (LycomIng O-360)
  G-BNYZ

SNIAS see SUD and AéROSPATIALE

SOCATA see MORANE-SAULNIER
ST.10 DIPLOMATE
  G-AYKG AZIB HOLY
TB-9 TAMPICO
  G-BHIT BHOZ BIBA BIXA BIXB BIZE BIZR BJKF BKCR BKIB BKIT BKUE
  BKVC BLCM BRIV BTWX BTZP CMED DLEE GHZJ GMSI INIT RUSI
TB-10 TOBAGO
  G-BGXC BGXD BGXT BHDE BHGP BHJF BITE BKBN BKBV BKBW BKIS
  BLCG BLYE BMYC BNDR BNRA BOIT BSDL BTIE CBGC CBHA CBPE
  CFME CONL CTCL DAND EDEN FAIR FLEA GBHI GKUE GOLF HALP
  HELA HILT IANC IANH IGGL JBMC JURE MOOR MRTN OFIT PATN PCAT
  PHTG POPI RENO RIAM SBKR SERL SKYF SONA TBIO TBOK TBTN
  TEDS TINA TOBA TZEE VMJM
TB-200 TOBAGO GT
  G-BXLT BXVA EGAG HEVN MLLA OBEI
TB-20 TRINIDAD
  G-BLXA BLYD BMIX BNXX BPAS BPTI BSCN BTZO BYJS BYTB BZPI
  CCGL CADDA CDDT CEPT CORB CPMS CTIO CTZO DLOM DMAH EGJA
  FFTI FIFI GOOD HGPI HOOD JDEE KKES KPTT OALD OBGC OOTB
  OTUI PEKT PTRE RRFC SAPM SCBI SCIP SLTN TANS TBGT TBSV
  TBXX TBZO THZL TMOL TOAK TRIN TYNE WERY
TB-21 TRINIDAD GT TURBO
  G-BZLI CBFM TBZI VALY
TBM-700
  G-MCMC PMHT

FABRIKA VAZDUHOPLOVA SOKA
SOKO P-2 KRAGUJ
  G-BSXD RADA SOKO

SOLAR WINGS LTD and SOLAR WINGS AVIATION LTD including
HOLD CONTROL PLC and seeCYCLONE AIRSPORTS LTD and PEGASUS AVIATION
PANTHER XL (Fuji-Robin EC-44-PM)
  G-MMBY MMKA MMTS
PANTHER XL-R (Rotax 447)
  G-MNBI
PANTHER XL-S (Fuji-Robin EC-44-PM)
  G-MJWZ MMGS MMJF MMMN MMOK MMSA MMSG MMSH MMZG MNAH
  MNAI MNAK MNHH

PEGASUS XL-Q (Rotax 462)
G-BZWM DEAN MGCB MNKO MTJS MTNO MTNP MTPN MTPS MTRV
MTTD MTTE MTTX MTTY MTTZ MTUN MTUP MTUR MTUS MTUT MTUY
MTVX MTXI MTXJ MTXH MTXK MTYA MTYC MTYD MTYE MTYF MTYH
MTYI MTYL MTYP MTYR MTYS MTYT MTYU MTZP MTZR MTZS MVAW
MVAX MVAY MVCL MVCM MVCN MVCP MVCR MVCS MVCT MVCV MVEX
MVEZ MVFA MVFB MVFC MVFD MVFE MVFF MVGU MVGW MVHP MVHR
MVHS MVHW MVHY MVJN MVJO MVJP MVJR MVJS MVJT MVJU MVJW
MVKN MVKO MVKP MVKS MVKT MVKU MVKV MVKW MVLK MVLV MVMA
MVMC MVPR MVPS MVPX MVPY MVRH MVRI MVRJ MVRU MVRW MVRX
MVSB MVSD MVSE MVSW MVSX MVSY MVSZ MVTA MVTI MVTJ MVTK
MVUF MVUG MVUI MVUJ MVUK MVUL MVUM MVVN MVVO MVVP MVYC
MVYD MVZJ MVZL MVZT MVZU MVZV MWAC MWAD MWAL MWAT MWBK
MWCB MWCF MWDD MWDK MWDL MWEE MWEF MWEG MWEH MWER
MWFS MWGL MWGM MWGR MWHC MWHF MWHG MWHL MWHX MWIE
MWIR MWIS MWJN MWKO MWKP MWKY MWKZ MWLL MWLM MWMN
MWMO MWMP MWMZ MWNA MWNB MWNC MWNG MWOR MWOY MWPE
MWPJ MWPK MWRW MWRX MWSD MWSJ MWSK MWTB MWTC MWTI
MWTK MWTL MWUO MWUX MWUY MWUZ MWVA MWWG MWWH MWWV
MWXP MWXR MWYB MWYC MWYU MWYY MWYZ MYAC MYAE MYAF
MYBF MYBS MYBV MYBW MYBY MYBZ MYEA MYEC MYFX MYPG MYTC
MYUH MZLR

PEGASUS XL-R variants (Rotax 447)
G-MGPD MMOH MMRL MMTA MMTC MMTR MMYA MMYN MNAR MNAW
MNAX MNAY MNAZ MNBA MNBB MNBC MNGG MNHC MNHD MNHE
MNHF MNHI MNHJ MNHK MNHL MNHM MNHN MNHR MNHS MNHT
MNMK MNUX MNVB MNVC MNVE MNWW MNYC MNYU MNYV MNYW
MNYX MNZK MTAA MTAI MTAJ MTAO MTAV MTAW MTAX MTAY MTAZ
MTBA MTBL MTBR MTBU MTBV MTCH MTCN MTCO MTDG MTDH MTDI
MTDV MTEC MTED MTEE MTES MTET MTEU MTEW MTEX MTFA MTFB
MTFM MTFO MTFP MTFR MTFT MTGJ MTGK MTGL MTGM MTHG MTHH
MTHI MTHJ MTHN MTIE MTIH MTIJ MTIO MTIP MTIR MTIS MTIU MTIW
MTIX MTIY MTIZ MTKG MTKH MTKI MTLG MTLI MTLJ MTLT MTLV MTLY
MTME MTMF MTMG MTMH MTOA MTOB MTOD MTOE MTOF MTOG
MTOH MTOJ MTOK MTON MTOO MTOP MTOR MTOS MTOT MTOU
MTOY MTOZ MTPE MTPF MTPG MTPH MTPI MTPJ MTPK MTPL MTPM
MTPP MTPR MTRM MTRO MTRS MTSN MTSO MTSP MTSR MTSS
MTSY MTSZ MTTA MTTB MTTU MTUA MTUI MTUK MTUL MTVB MTVK
MTVL MTVN MTVO MTWB MTWD MTYY MTZJ MTZK MVAR MVAT
MVAV MBVJ MVBY MVBZ MVCA MVCB MVDV MVDW MVDX MVDY
MVDZ MVEC MVED MVEF MVEG MVFP MVFS MVFT MVFV MVFY MVFZ
MVGN MVGO MVGP MVJD MVKF MVKH MVKJ MVKK MVKL MVKM
MVVK MVVM MWAF MWAG MWAV MWBL MWCC MWCU MWDC MWLE
MWLF MWLG MWLU MWMR MWMV MWOH MWOI MWPX MWRN MWRP
MWRT MWRU MWRV MWSE MWSF MWSO MWSP MWSR MWTU MWUB
MWUC MWUD MWUF MWUP MWUR MWUS MWUU MWUV MWVE
MWVF MWZI MWZJ MWZT MWZU MWZV MWZW MWZY MWZZ MYAB
MYBG MYBO MYBP MYDJ MYED MYEG MYEH MYFS MYGT MYGU
MYGV

PEGASUS FLASH (Rotax 447)
G-MNDO MNJH MNJJ MNJL MNJN MNJR MNKP MNKV MNKW MNKX
MNNY MNNZ MNPA MNSH MNSN MNUD MNUE MNVG MNVH MNWU
MNXP MNYA MNYZ MTCK MTJH

PEGASUS QUASAR (Rotax 503)
G-MWHT MWHU MWIM MWIU MWIW MWIX MWIY MWJH MWJI MWJJ
MWJK MWJS MWJT MWJV MWLH MWLJ MWLK MWMI MWMJ MWMK
MWML MWNK MWNL MWOM MWOP MWPU MWSI MWVM MWXG
MWXH MWYI MWYJ MWZD MWZE MWZF MWZO MWZP MWZR MWZS
MYAK MYBD MYBE MYBT MYCE MYEK MYEM MYEN MYEO MYFK
MYFL MYIM MYIN MYIO MYJJ MYJK MYJS MYJT MYJU MYKP MYKR
MYKS MYTR MYXD MZMA MZPW REKO

PEGASUS PHOTON (Solo 210)
G-MNIK MNIU MNKB MNKC MNKD MNKE MNKG MNKK MNVZ MNXB
MTAL

TRIKE with Typhoon wing
G-MMBZ

SOLENT BALLOON GROUP
Balloon (Minimum Lift)
OSPREY variants
G-BJTN BJTY BJUE BJUU FYAV FYBD FYBE FYBF FYBG FYBH FYBI
FYCL FYCT FYCV FYCZ FYDF FYDG FYDO FYDS FYDU FYEV FYFN

SOMERS-KENDAL
SK.1
G-AOBG

SONEX AIRCRAFT   see MONNETT
SONEX
G-CEFJ ZONX

SOPWITH AVIATION CO LTD
CAMEL including reps
G-AWYY BFCZ BPOB BZSC

DOVE including reps
G-EAGA
PUP including reps
G-EBKY
G-ABOX APUP BIAT BIAU BZND EAVX
1½ STRUTTER replica
G-BIDW
TABLOID SCOUT
G-BFDE
TRIPLANE including reps
G-BOCK BWRA

SORRELL AVIATION
SNS-7 HYPERBIPE (Lycoming IO-360)
G-BPDK HIPE

SOUTHDOWN AEROSTRUCTURE LTD
PIPISTRELLE
G-MJTM

SOUTHDOWN INTERNATIONAL LTD/SOUTHDOWN SAILWINGS LTD
including MEDWAY MICROLIGHTS LTD and RAVEN AIRCRAFT INTERNATIONAL production
PUMA SPRINT
G-MJEB MJTR MJZK MMAO MMAZ MMIW MMJD MMLW MMPH MMRN
MMTJ MMUA MMUV MMVA MMVI MMVX MMVZ MMWX MMXO MMYF
MMYO MMYT MMYU MMYY MMYZ MMZW MNAV MNBE MNBM MNCI
MNCP MNDY MNFB MNFG MNFX MNGX MNIL MNJS MNKU MNML
MVAF MWBJ MWCR MWJX
PUMA RAVEN (Fuji-Robin EC-44-PM)
G-MNMU MNVN MNXF MNYG
RAVEN variants (Rotax 447)
G-MGOD MMVH MNJB MNJT MNKZ MNLM MNLN MNLT MNLZ MNMD
MNNA MNNB MNNC MNNO MNRP MNRS MNSL MNSX MNSY MNTC
MNTE MNTM MNTN MNTY MNUU MNUW MNVP MNWG MNXE MNXG
MNXI MNYL MNYM MNYP MNZW MNZX MTAP MTBB MTBK MTBN
MTBO MTBZ MTCM MTIK MTMO MTPC MTRT MTRW MTYV MTYW
MTYX MVIF MYKL MYLX MYLY MYMJ MYYZ MYZO MZBR MZDJ
WILD CAT Mk.II
G-MMDF
TRIKE with SIGMA wing
G-MBDM
TRIKE with LIGHTNING wing
G-MMIZ MYJE

SOUTHERN AIRCRAFT LTD
MARTLET
G-AAYX

SPAD
XIII
G-BFYO

SPARTAN AIRCRAFT LTD
ARROW
G-ABWP
CRUISER
G-ACYK

SPEICH
AIR COMMAND GYROPLANE
G-BPGC

SPEZIO
DAL-1 TUHOLER
G-NGRM NOBI

SPORTAVIA-PÜTZER GmbH see FOURNIER
RS.180 SPORTSMAN
G-VIZZ

SPP see YAKOVLEV
AERO 45
G-APRR AYLZ
SUPER AERO 145
G-ATBH
MORAVA L-200A
G-ASFD

SQUIRES
DRAGONFLY 250-II
G-MJLK
LIGHTFLY Trike with Solar Wings wing
G-MNNG

SRCM see MINICAB

STAAKEN
Z-1 FLITZER, Z-21(A) FLITZER
  G-BVAW BYYZ ERDA ERIW ERTI FLIZ FLZR FZIS WIDZ

STANSTED BALLOON GROUP
Balloon (Minimum Lift)
All variants
  G-BIVS BJLN BJLP

STARCK
AS.80
  G-BJAE

STAR-LITE
SL-1
  G-BUZH FARO SOLA

STEARMAN see BOEING-STEARMAN

STEEN AERO LAB INC
SKYBOLT (Lycoming O-360)
  G-BGRT BIMN BRIS BUXI BVXE BZWV ENGO BWPJ CBYJ CCPE KEST
  RODC SBLT SBOL SKIE

STEMME GmbH and Co KG
S 10 variants (Limbach L2400)
  G-BVYZ BXGZ BXHR BZSP EXPD JCKT JULL STEM STEN STME

STEPHENS
AKRO
  G-RIDE

STERN
ST.80 BALADE
  G-BWVI

STINSON AIRCRAFT CORPORATION
HW-75
  G-AFYO BMSA
V-77 RELIANT
  G-BUCH
108 VOYAGER (Consolidated Vultee Aircraft production)
  G-BHMR BPTA BRZK WAGN

STITS
SA.3A PLAYBOY
  G-BDRL BGLZ BVVR

STODDARD-HAMILTON
GLASAIR
  G-BKHW BMIO BODI BOVU BSAI BUBT BUHS BZBO CDAB ICBM IIRG
  KRES KSIR LAIR LASR OPNH TRUK USSI
GLASTAR (Lycoming 320)
  G-BYEK BZDM CBAR CBCL CBJD CTEC ETCW GERY IARC IKES LAZZ
  LSTR MHGS SACH SKUA

STOLP AIRCRAFT CORPORATION
SA.100 STARDUSTER
  G-BSZG IIIM
SA.200 STARDUSTER TOO
  G-WINN
SA.300 STARDUSTER TOO
  G-BNNA BOBT BRVB BSZB BTGS BUPB BZKD CDBR CEZK DUST JIII
  KEEN NARR OTOO STOO UINN
SA.500 STARLET
  G-AZTV
SA.750 ACRODUSTER TOO
  G-BLES BUGB
SA.900 V-STAR
  G-BLAF

STOREY
TSR.3
  G-AWIV

STRIPLIN
LONE RANGER
  G-MBDL MBJM
SKY RANGER
  G-MJKB MMFZ

STROJIRNY PRVNI PETILESKY (SPP) (sopsee MORAVA

STROJNIK
S-2A
  G-BMPS

SUD-AVIATION including AÉROSPATIALE, ICA-BRASOV and WESTLAND HELICOPTERS
LTD *(GAZELLE)* production
SE.313 ALOUETTE II variants
  G-BVSD BZGG UGLY
SE.316 ALOUETTE IIi
  G-CDSG CDSJ
SA.315B LAMA
  G-LAMA
SA.341 and SA.342 GAZELLE
  G-BCHM BXTH BZDV BZYD CBGZ CBJZ CBKA CBKC CBKD CBSD CBSF
  CBSH CBSI CBSK CBXT CBZL CDJT CDNO CDNS CDXE DFKI DMSS
  EHUP EROL EZEL FUKM GAZA GAZZ GZLE KANE LEDR LOYD MANN
  OGAZ OGEO OLDH SFTA SIVJ SWWM TOPZ TURP UZEL VOIP WCRD
  WDEV ZELE ZLLE ZZEL ZZLE

SUKHOI
Su-26M
  G-IIIS IIIZ SIID XXVI

SUPER SCORPION see HIWAY

SUPER MARINE AIRCRAFT (PTY)
SPITFIRE Mk.26
  G-CCGH CCJL CCZP CEFC CENI CEPL HABT PIXY

UNIVERSITY OF **SUSSEX BALLOONING SOCIETY**
Balloon (Gas -Filled)
GAS BALLOON
  G-AWOK

SWALLOW AEROPLANE CO
SWALLOW B
  G-MJBK

SWEARINGEN AIRCRAFT CORPN
SA.226TC METRO II
  G-CEGE

SZD see PZL

Tarjani
Trike wih Solar Wings Typhoon wing
  G-MJCU

TAYLOR
JT.1 MONOPLANE (Volkswagen 1600)
  G-APRT AWGZ AXYK AYSH AYUS BBBB BDAD BDAG BDNC BDNG
  BDNO BEUM BEVS BEYW BFBC BFDZ BFOU BGCY BGHY BILZ BJMO
  BKEU BKHY BLDB BMAO BMET BRUO BUXL BYAV CDGA CRIS DRAY
  SUZY WARD
JT.2 TITCH
  G-AYZH BABE BARN BDRG BFID BGCX BGMS BIAX BKWD BVNI EOFF
  MISS MOLE OJON RKET TICH VIVI

TAYLOR see AEROCAR

TAYLOR-WATKINSON
DINGBAT
  G-AFJA

TAYLOR AIRCRAFT CO INC see PIPER

TAYLORCRAFT see AUSTER

TAYLORCRAFT AIRCRAFT CORPORATION
BC-12D
  G-AHNR AKVO BIGK BOLB BPHO BPHP BPPZ BREY BRIH BRPX BRXE
  BSDA BTFK BVDZ BVXS
BC-65
  G-BSCW
BL-65
  G-BVRH
DCO-65
  G-BWLJ

_DF-65_
G-BRIY
_F-19_
G-BRIJ
_F-21_
G-BPJV
F-22 varants
G-BVOX BWBI

TEAM
HI-MAX (Rotax 447)
G-CBNZ MZHM MZIA
MINI-MAX (Rotax 447)
G-BVSB BVSX BVYK BXCD BXSU BYBW BYFV BYII BYJE BYYX BZFK
BZOR BZTC CBIN CBPL CBXU CCGB CEDL CEDW MWFC MWFD
MWHH MWLW MWSA MWWE MWZM MYAT MYBM MYCT MYDF MYGF
MYII MYIZ MYKJ MYKZ MYLB MYNI MYRG MYRL MYSK MYXA MYYR
MYYS MYZE MZCS MZII MZMO MZNM MZNN MZOY MZPJ NADS OJLH
OPEJ OSCO THEO

CONSTRUZIONI AERONAUTICHE **TECNAM SRL**
P92 ECHO variants (Jabiru 2200)
G-BZHG BZWT CBAX CBDM CBGE CBLB CBUG CBYZ CCAL CCDU
CDSJ CDZK DWPF OALH PGFG PLOD SDOZ TCNM TECM WHEN
P2002 SIERRA variants
G-CDTE CDTV CENH CEOC CEVM NESE RAYZ RLMW SDOB TECS
TESI TESR TEMB TSAC

TEMAN
MONO-FLY
G-MMJX MMPZ

TEVERSON
BISPORT
G-CBGH

THE LIGHT AIRCRAFT COMPANY (TLAC)
SHERWOOD RANGER variants
G-BZUG CBHU CCBW CDPH GKFC HVAN MWND PUSY WZOL

THORN
Balloon (Gas-Filled)
COAL GAS BALLOON
G-ATGN

THORP AERO INC including AD AEROSPACE LTD and VENTURE LIGHT
AIRCRAFT RESOURCES production
_T.18_
G-BLIT BSVN BYBY HATF
_T.211_
G-BTHP BYJF CCXI TZII

THRUSTER AIR SERVICES LTD including THRUSTER AIRCRAFT (UK) LTD
TST Mk.1 (Rotax 503)
G-MTGB MTGC MTGD MTGE MTGF MTGR MTGS MTGT MTGU MTKA
MTKB MTKD MTKE MTLM MTLN MTNR MTNT MTNU MTNV MTPT MTPU
MTPW MTPX MTPY MTSH MTSJ MTSK MTSM MTUB MTUC MTUD
MTUE MTUF MTVP MTVR MTVS MTVT MTVV MTWY MTWZ MTXA MTXB
MTXC MTXD MTZA MTZB MTZC MTZD MTZF MVAG MVAH MVAI MVAJ
MVAK MVAL MVBP MVBT MVDD MVDE MVDF MVDG MVDH MVFJ MVFK
MVFL MVFM MVFO MVHI MVHJ MVHK MVHL MVIR MVIT MVIU MVIV
MVIW MVME MVMG MVMI MVOT MVOV MVOW MVOX MVOY MVXL
MVYE MWIU MYWZ
T.300 variants
G-MGWH MVUB MVWN MVWR MVWS MVZA MVZC MVZD MVZG MVZI
MWAN MWAP MWAR MWDS MWWS MYAR MYDR MYDT MYDU MYJF
MYXU
T.600 (Jabiru 2200A)
G-BYPF BYPG BYPH BZDB BZGP BZIG BZJC BZJD BZNP BZTD CBDC
CBGU CBGV CBGW CBIO CBIP CBIR CBKG CBPN CBVA CBWI CBWJ
CBXG CBXH CBYT CCBC CCCB CCCF CCCU CCDV CCEB CCIC CCMT
CCRN CCRP CCUZ CCXV CCXW CDBZ CDDI CDDX CDGI CDIA CDJE
CDRH CDSO CSAV CXIP DIDY EVEY FJCE INGE IRAL KDCD KIPP KYLE
MARZ _MCCF_ MGTV MOMA MYWD MYWE MZFO MZFR MZFU MZGX
MZGY MZGZ MZHA MZHD MZHE MZHF MZHS MZHU MZHV MZHW
MZHY MZKR MZKS MZKT MZKU MZNX MZNY NDOT OASJ OBAX OHYE
OJSH OMAL OOFE ORDS ORUG OWMC PGSA PSUK PVST PYNE RAFH
RAFS REDZ RIVR UDGE ULLY WORM

THRUXTON see JACKAROO AIRCRAFT
JACKAROO
G-ANZT AOEX AOIR APAJ

THUNDER BALLOONS LTD including CAMERON BALLOONS LTD and THUNDER
and COLT LTD
Airship (Hot Air)
_AS-33_
G-ERMS
Balloon (Hot Air)
_O.5_
G-BBOD
Ax3 SKY CHARIOT
G-BHUR BKBD BKIY BKMR NEIL
Ax4 series
G-LORY
Ax5 series
G-BDAY BEMU BLOV
Ax6 series
G-BBDJ BBOO BCCH BDVG BECS BEEE BEJB BERD BETH BFIT BFOS
BFOZ BGPF BHTG BIIL BIZU BJVU BLWB BPSJ BPUF DICK LDYS LIFE
RTBI THOM TNTN
Ax7 series
G-BAXK BBOX BCAR BCAS BCCG BCIN BCNR BCSX BDGH BDGO
BDMO BDON BEVI BFIX BGRS BGST BHAT BHEU BHHH BHIS BHSP
BHZX BJSW BJZC BKDK BKUU BLAH BLCC BLCY BLET BLGX BLKJ
BLTN BLUI BLZF BMCC BMHJ BMMW BMMY BMOG BMUU BMVT BMYS
BNBL BNBV BNBW BNCC BNCU BNGO BNMX BNXZ BNZK BOAO BOIJ
BORD BOSB BPGF BPHU BPNU BPVU BPYZ BRDE BRLS BRVN BRXB
BRZE BSAV BSCF BSCO BSOJ BSZH BTAN BTAU BTHK BTRR BTSX
BTTW BTVA BTXK BUDK BUIN BUKI BULB BUNV BUPU BVDB BVUH
BYNU BZBH CDFN FUND GASS GGGG GHIN HOWE LENS LYTE MLWI
NEGS NIGS NWPB OFBJ OJDC OONI PIAF PIES PUFF RAFE RBOW
REGS RIGB RINO ROCK ROSI SFRY SOFT THOS USIL VIVA WDEB
WINE
Ax8 series
G-BGHW BJMW BOHF BORR BOTE BPZZ BRVY BSCX BSKI BSPB BSTK
BSTY BTBB BTHM BTJD BTRO BUBL BUBY BUEI BUJW BUXW BUYD
BVDW BVGB BVKH BVPA BVWB BWKW BYLV CBFH GEMS HAZE INGA
KBKB OMDD OTEL PUNK SUED TOOL ZEBO
Ax9 series
G-BTJO BTOZ BTRN BTUJ BUAT BULK BVKZ BZBN FABS OIOZ
Ax10 series
G-BTJF BTYF BUNZ BUOZ BUVZ BWNX BZGJ CCEO CDKZ OLEO
WORK
Ax11 series
G-BXAD BZHX BZRZ

Special Shapes

SHAPE	REGISTRATION(S)
ICE CREAM	G-ICES
JUMBO JET	G-VJIM
WHISKY BOTTLE	G-RARE

THURSTON
TEAL
G-OWET

TIPSY AIRCRAFT CO LTD including AVIONS FAIREY SA, COBELAVIA SA
and SLINGSBY _(for NIPPER AIRCRAFT LTD*)_ production
_S2_
G-AFVH
BELFAIR
G-APIE APOD
JUNIOR
G-AMVP
NIPPER variants
G-APYB ARBG ARDY ARFV ARXN ASXI ASZV ATBW ATUH AVKI* AVKK*
AVKT* AVTC* AVXD* AWDA* BWHR AWJE* AWJF* AWLR* AWLS* AXLI*
AXZM* BLMW BRIK BRPM BWCT BYLO CBCK CCFE CORD* ENIE NIPA*
NIPP* NIPR* ONCS OVAG TIPS
TRAINER I
G-AFJR AFRV AFSC AFVN AFWT AISA AISC

TLAC see The Light Aircraft Company formerly The LIttle Aircraft Company

TL ULTRALIGHT COMPANY
TL-2000 STING
G-CEPS

TRAGO MILLS see FLS

TRI-R TECHNOLOGIES
KIS
G-BVTA BVZD BZDR MANW OKIS OKMA OKPW TKIS
KIS CRUISER
G-BYZD

TROTTER
Balloon (Hot Air)
AX3-20
　G-BRBT

TURNER
SUPER T-40A
　G-BRIO

TWAMLEY
TRIKE
　G-MBGF MJWI

ULTRAFLIGHT LTD including AMF Microflight Ltd production
LAZAIR
　G-MBYI MNRD MTFL MVGZ

ULTRALIGHT AVIATION SYSTEMS
STORM BUGGY trike with Lightning & Solar Wings wings
　G-MBGX MJBS

ULTRAMAGIC SA
Balloon (Hot Air)
H-31
　G-BZIZ BZPY CEFB CEJL
H-42
　G-CEAY OOCH
M-56
　G-CEJG
M-65C
　G-CEBO RACR
77 variants
　G-BXPT BZKW BZSH BZSO CBRK CBWK CCLO CCRG CERR CERL DAIV
　DWPH DXCC HOLI KNEE LOKI PIMM RWRW
90 variants
　G-CCYU CEEL CEIK CSFD KEWT LEEH MAXR PENH
105 variants
　G-BZPX BZRX CBRB CCOP CDGF CDPN CEAV CEKH CELN CEMG
　CEUL EPSN GBGB
M-120
　G-CDJI CDNZ CEUM
S-130
　G-CBKK CBZV CEAX CEMN
M-145
　G-BZGI
T-150
　G-OMOO
S-160
　G-CDFC
T-180
　G-CCTN CCUE
210 variants
　G-BZPR BZPT CDWN
N-250
　G-BZJX CBUE CDST VBFA VBFC VBFD
N-300
　G-CBPZ
N-355
　G-VBFB VBFE

ULTRASPORTS
PANTHER trike with Flexiform wing
　G-MJVR
PUMA trike with Southdown wing
　G-MJCE MMBL MMCI
TRI-PACER trike with Excalibur, Flexiform, Hiway, Solar Wings, Southdown &
Wasp wings
　G-MBIY MBLK MBLU MBPY MBTJ MJER MJFB MJHC MJIA MJIC MJOI
　MJTC MJVN MMPG MMRK MMWS MNGD MNSD MTTL MZLK

ULTRAVIA
PELICAN variants
　G-BWWA MPAC MWRS

UNICORN GROUP
Balloon (Minimum Lift)
UE variants
　G-BINR BINS BINT BIWJ BJAA BJDY BJGM BJLF BJLG BJSX BJUO FYEK

VAHDAT-HAGH
SEMICOPTER
　G-BZEV
SHIRAZ
　G-CCUU

VALENTIN FLUGZEUGBAU GMBH
MISTRAL C
　G-DJHP DKBW
TAIFUN 17E
　G-BMSE OACE TFUN

VAN'S AIRCRAFT INC
RV-3 variants
　G-BVDC CCTG RODZ RVRH
RV-4
　G-BOHW BULG BVDI BVLR BVRV BVUN BVVS BXPI BXRV BZPH CDJB
　CEID CEVC FTUO IIGI IKON INTS MARX MAXV MUMY NADZ ORCA PIPS
　RATC RIIV RMIT RVDP RVIV RVJW RVMJ RVNS RVPM RVRV SARV
　VANS
RV-6 variants
　G-BUEC BUTD BVCG BXJY BXVM BXVO BXWT BXYX BYDV BYEL BZOZ
　BZRV BZUY BZVN BZWZ BZXB CBCP CBUK CCJI CCVS CDAE CDVT
　CEYM CSPR DFUN EDRV EERV ESTR EYOR GDRV GLUC GPAG GRIN
　GRVE HACE HAMY HOPY JAEE JIMZ JSRV KELL MURG NPKJ OJVA
　OJVL OMDB ONUN OORV ORVE ORVG OTRV PJSY PWUL REAS REVE
　RIVT RRVX RUSL RVAN RVAW RVBC RVCE RVCG RVCL RVDJ RVDR
　RVEE RVET RVGA RVIA RVIB RVIC RVIN RVIT RVJM RVMT RVPW
　RVSA RVSH RVSX RVTE RVVI SIXY TEXS TJDM TOGO USRV VANZ
　XVOM
RV-7 variants
　G-CBJU CCVM CCZD CDJW CDME CDRM CDYZ CECV CEIG CEIT CETS
　COLS COPZ CTED DIDG FIXX GERT HUTY IMCD ISMA IVII JFRV JMRV
　JTEM KAOS KELS MROD MRVL NAPP OKER ORAE OVII PBEC PPLL
　PROS PYPE RIDG RISY RMRV RVAB RVAC RVII RVMC RVTT RVUK
　RVRP SEVN STAF UZZL VANN XIII
RV-8 variants
　G-BZWN CCIR CDDY CDPJ CEGI CETI DAZZ DUDE EGBS HILZ JBTR
　JILS KELZ LEXX LEXY LSPH LUDM MHRV PHMG PHVM RVAL RVBA
　RVCH RVIS RVLC RVMZ RVPH RVPL RVSR TUCK XSEA ZAAZ ZUMI
RV-9 variants
　G-CCGU CCND CCZT CCZY CDCD CDMF CDMN CDRV CDXT CDZD
　CEEP CEGH CERK CETP ENTS GNRV HOXN HUMH IINI KMRV NIEN
　ONER OPVM ORVS RPRV RUVY RVDG RVIX RVJO RVJP RVMB RVNH
　RVSD RVSG THMB TTRL XSAM
RV-10
　G-OHIY RVIO RVTN XRVX

VAN DEN BEMDEN
Balloon (Gas-Filled)
FREE
　G-BBFS BIHP BWCC
OMEGA III
　G-BDTU

VARGA
2150A KACHINA
　G-BLHW BPVK CHTT DJCR VARG

VENTURE LIGHT AIRCRAFT RESOURCES see THORP

VFW-FOKKER GmbH
FK-3
　G-CHJA

VICKERS-ARMSTRONGS (AIRCRAFT) LTD
FB.5 GUNBUS replica
　G-ATVP
FB.27 VIMY (including replica)*
　G-EAOU
　G-AWAU*
60 VIKING IV replica
　"G-EBED"
600 series VIKING
　G-AGRU AGRW AHOT
668 VARSITY
　G-BEDV BHDD
700 series VISCOUNT
　G-ALWF AMOG AMOI ANHD AOFX
800 series VISCOUNT
　G-APIM ASDS AVHE AVJB AZLC AZLP AZLS BAPF OPAS
953 VANGUARD MERCHANTMAN
　G-APEJ APEP APES

VC-10
G-ARVF ARVM ASIX
SUPER VC-10
G-ASGC

VICKERS SUPERMARINE LTD including WESTLAND AIRCRAFT LTD production
236 WALRUS
G-AIZG RNLI
SPITFIRE variants including replica*
G-AIDN AIST AISU ALGT ASJV AVAV AWII AWIJ BJSG BKMI BMSB BRAF
BRDV* BRSF BUOS BUWA BYDE CBNU CCCA CCVV CDGU CDGY CTIX
CZAF FIRE FXII FXIV ILDA IXCC LFIX LFVB LFVC MCDB MKIA MKVB
MXVI MKXI OXVI PMNF PRXI RRGN SPIT SXVI VIII WWII XVIB
SEAFIRE variants
G-BWEM CDTM KASX
552 SWIFT
G-SWIF

VICTA including AESL production
AIRTOURER
G-ATCL ATEX ATHT ATJC AWMI AWVG AXIX AYLA AYWM AZBE AZHI
AZHT AZMN AZOE AZOF AZRP

VIKING
DRAGONFLY
G-BKPD BNEV BRKY DKGF

VOISIN
Replica
G-BJHV

VOLMER
VJ.22 SPORTSMAN
G-BAHP
VJ.24W
G-MBBZ

VOUGHT
F4U CORSAIR
G-CCMV FGID

VPM SNC and SRL including Magni Gyro
M-14 SCOUT
G-BUEN
M-16 TANDEM TRAINER
G-BUPM BUZL BXEJ BXIX BZJM BZXW CBUP CCAH CERG CVPM DBDB
IBFP IJMC ODPJ UNIX YFLY

WACO
UPF-7
G-UPFS WACO
YKS-7
G-BWAC
YMF
G-WOCO YMFC

WAG-AERO INC
CUBY SPORT TRAINER
G-BTWL BVMH BZHU
SUPER SPORT
G-DTUG
WAG-A-BOND
G-BNJA

WALLBRO
MONOPLANE
G-BFIP

WALLINGFORD MODEL BALLOONS
Balloon (Minimum Lift)
WMB.2 WINDTRACKER
G-BIAI BIBX BILB

WALLIS AUTOGYROS LTD including BEAGLE-MILES AIRCRAFT LTD,
BEAGLE- WALLIS LTD and VINTEN-WALLIS LTD production
WA.116
G-ARRT ARZB ASDY ATHM ATTB AVDG AXAS BGGU BLIK BMJX SCAN
VIEW
WA.117
G-AVJV VTEN

WA.118
G-AVJW
WA.120
G-AYVO BGGV
WA.121
G-BAHH
WA.122
G-BGGW
WA.201
G-BNDG

W.A.R.
FOCKE-WULF FW190 reps
G-BSLX CCFW JABO SYFW WULF
VOUGHT F-4U CORSAIR replica
G-BJNB

WARD
ELF
G-MMUL
GNOME
G-AXEI

SOCIÉTÉ DES ETABLISSMENTS BENJAMIN **WASSMER** see JODEL
WA26P SQUALE
G-DEEP
WA28F ESPADON
G-CJDX CJXC
WA.41 SUPER BALADOU
G-ATSY ATZS AVEU
WA.51 PACIFIC
G-AZYZ
WA.52 EUROPA
G-BTLB OELZ
WA.81 PIRANHA
G-BKOT

WATKINSON see TAYLOR-WATKINSON

JOHN **WEBB**
TRIKE with Flexiform wing
G-MMYV

WEEDHOPPER OF UTAH INC
JC-24
G-BHWH MJMB MMNV MTNK

WELLS
Balloon (Minimum Lift)
AIRSPEED 300
G-FYGJ

WEST
Balloon (Hot Air)
AX3-15
G-BCFD

WESTERN
Balloon (Hot Air)
20
G-AYMV
O-31
G-AZPX
65 series
G-AYUK AZJI AZOO BBCB BBUT

WESTLAND AIRCRAFT LTD see FAIREY and SUPERMARINE
WIDGEON
G-EBUB
LYSANDER
G-AZWT BCWL CCOM LIZY

WESTLAND HELICOPTERS LTD see SIKORSKY and SUD AVIATION
WESTLAND-SIKORSKY S-51 DRAGONFLY
G-ALMB AMHB AMJW BRMA
WESTLAND-SIKORSKY S-51/2 WIDGEON
G-ANLW AOZE APTW
WESTLAND-SIKORSKY S-55 WHIRLWIND
G-AMJT ANFH ANJV AODA APWN APXA APXB ATKV AYXT AYZJ BAMH
BDBZ BEBC BJWY BVGE RWWW
WESTLAND-SIKORSKY S-58 WESSEX
G-ATBZ AVNE AWOX BYRC CCUP
WG.13 LYNX
G- BFDV LYNX

WG.30
G-BGHF BKFD BKFF BKGD BLTY EFIS ELEC HAUL
SCOUT
G-BWHU BWJW BWLX BXRR BXRS BXSL BYKJ BYRX BZBD CBUH CRUM NOTY SCTA SROE
WASP
G-BMIR BYCX BZPP CBUI KANZ KAXT RIMM

WESTLAND-AGUSTA see EH INDUSTRIES

WESTLAND-BELL see BELL

W H EKIN (ENGINEERING) CO LTD
WHE AIRBUGGY
G-AXYZ AXZB

WHEELER
SCOUT
G-MJAL MNKN

RON WHEELER AIRCRAFT SALES PTY
SLYMPH
G-ABOI

WHITTAKER including AEROTECH INTERNATIONAL LTD
MW2B EXCALIBUR
G-BDDX
MW4
G-MBTH
MW5 SORCERER series (Rotax 447)
G-BZWX BZXL CBBO CDTF CEFT MMGV MNMM MNXZ MTAS MTBP MTBR MTBS MTBT MTDK MTFN MTHB MTLZ MTRX MVNN MVNO MVNP MVNR MVNS MVNT MVNU MWEK MWEO MWGI MWGJ MWGK MWIC MWJW MWSX MWSY MYAH MYAN MYJZ MYRB MZOH
MW6 MERLIN, MW6-S FATBOY FLYER and MW6-T
G-BUOA BYTX BZYU CBMU CBWS CBYP CCWG MGCK MNMW MTTF MTXO MURR MVPH MVPM MVPN MVTD MVXA MWAW MWHM MWIP MWLN MWLO MWOV MWPR MWSW MYCA MYCP MYCU MYDM MYDW MYEF MYET MYEV MYGE MYIE MYKO MYMN MYPP MYPS MYZA MYZN MZBG MZBX MZCH MZDL MZFK MZHG MZHT MZID MZJP MZNE MZOK SIXS
MW7 (Rotax 532)
G-BOKH BPHK BPUP BREE BRMW BSXX BTFV BTUS BWVN BZOW

WILD
Balloon (Minimum Lift)
BVS SPECIAL
G-BJUB

WILLIAMS
KFZ-1 TIGERFALCK
G-KFZI

WILLIAMS
Balloon (Minimum Lift)
All variants
G-FYAN FYAO FYAP FYAU FYDI FYDP FYFJ

WILLIAMS FLUGZEUGBAU
ALBATROSS D.Va replica
G-BFXL

WILLS
AERA 2
G-BJKW

WINDSOR BALLOON GROUP
Balloon (Minimum Lift)
WINDSOR MK.4 MLB
G-BJFW

WINTER
LF-1 ZAUNKÖNIG
G-ALUA

WITTMAN
W.8 and W.10 TAILWIND (Continental O-200-A)
G-BCBR BDAP BDBD BJWT BMHL BNOB BOHV BOIB BPYJ CEJE CFON WYND ZIPY

WOLF
W-II BOREDOM FIGHTER
G-BMZX BNAI

WOMBAT
GYROCOPTER
G-BWLZ WBAT

WOODS see AEROSPORT

WSK see YAKOVLEV

WSK PZL MIELEC
TS-11 ISKRA
G-BXVZ ISKA

YAKOVLEV including ACROSTAR, IAV-BACHAU, LET, NANCHANG AIRCRAFT
MANUFACTURING COMPANY (NAMC CJ-6A*) and SPP + production
Yak-1
G-BTZD
Yak-3
G-BTHD CDBJ
Yak-9
G-YAKP
Yak-11 (C-11)
G-BTUB BTZE BZMY KYAK OYAK YCII
Yak-18 variants
G-BMJY+ BVVG* BXZB* CEIB
Yak-50
G-BTZB BWFM BWWX BWYK CBPM EYAK FUNK GYAK HAMM IIYK IVAR JYAK SKPH SOCT SVET VLAD YAAK YAKA YAKK YAKM YAKU YAKZ YKSO
Yak-52
G-BVMU BVOK BVVA BVVW BVXK BWFP BWOD BWSV BWVR BXAK BXAV BXID BXJB BZJB BZTF CBLJ CBMD CBMI CBOZ CBPY CBRH CBRL CBRP CBRU CBRW CBSL CBSR CBSS CBVT CCCP CCJK CCSU CDFE CDJJ CUPS ETHI FLSH HYAK IMIC IUII LAOK LENA LYAK LYFA MCCY OCBT RNAC TYAK XYAK YAKB YAKC YAKD YAKF YAKH YAKI YAKN YAKO YAKR YAKT YAKV YAKX YAKY YFUT YKCT YKSZ YKYK YOTS YYAK ZYAK
Yak-55
G-OHNO NOIZ YKSS

YORKSHIRE
Balloon (Hot Air)
A66
G-BHOO

ZEBEDEE BALLOON SERVICE
Balloon (Hot Air)
V-31 HAB
G-BXIT

ZENAIR see HEINTZ AND /COLOMBAN
CH.250 ZENITH variants
G-BIRZ BTXZ GFKY RAYS
CH.601 ZODIAC variants (Rotax 912)
G-BRII BRJB BUTG BUZG BVAB BVAC BVPL BVVM BVZR BYEO BYJT BYLF BYPR BZFV CBAP CBDG CBDT CBGB CBIX CBJP CBPV CBRX CBUR CCAK CCED CCLL CCTA CCVL CCVT CCZK CDAK CDAL CDDS CDFL CDGP CDJG CDJM CDLW CDMT CDNT CDPI CDWU CDXO CDZB CEAT CEBA CEBZ CECZ CEUW CEZS CEZV CFRY CLEO CSZM CZAC DAGJ DONT DROO EEZZ EXLL EZUB FOXL JAME KHOP KIMA OANN OMEZ OMWE OOSH PATO RUVI RWMW XLNT YOXI ZAIR ZENI ZODY
CH.701 variants (Rotax 912)
G-BRDB BTMW BXIG BZJP BZVA CBCH CBGD CBMW CBZW CCIT CCJB CCSK CCVI CDGR CDYU CEWS EOIN FAMH IMME JFMK OMEX RAYH TTDD ZENA

ZIVKO AERONAUTICS INC
EDGE 540
G-EDGY

ZLIN see LET NARODNI PODNIK KUNOVICE and MORAVAN NARODNI PODNIK

NOTES

AIR-BRITAIN SALES

Companion volumes to this publication are also available by post-free mail order from
Air-Britain Sales Department (Dept UKI08)
41 Penshurst Road, Leigh, Tonbridge, Kent TN11 8HL

Orders may also be placed by Answerphone/Fax 01732 835637 or by e-mail to
sales@air-britain.co.uk

For a full list of current titles and details of how to order, visit our e-commerce site at www.air-britain.co.uk
Visa Credit / Visa Debit / Mastercard / Solo / Maestro accepted - please give full details of card number, security
number, start date or issue number where appropriate and expiry date. We cannot accept Amex cards.

ANNUAL PUBLICATIONS - 2008

UK and IRELAND QUICK REFERENCE 2008 £6.95 (Members) £7.95 (Non-members)
Basic easy-to-carry current registration and type listing of UK, Eire and Isle of Man, foreign aircraft based in UK and
Ireland, current military serials of both countries, aircraft museums and base index. A5 size, 168 pages.

BUSINESS JETS & TURBOPROPS QUICK REFERENCE 2008 £6.95 (Members) £7.95 (Non-members)
Now expanded to include all purpose-built business jets and business turboprops, in both civil and military use, in
registration or serial order by country. Easy-to-carry A5 size, 144 pages.

AIRLINE FLEETS QUICK REFERENCE 2008 £6.95 (Members) £7.95 (Non-members)
Pocket guide now includes airliners of over 19 seats of 1,700 major operators likely to be seen worldwide; regn, type,
c/n, fleet numbers. Contains 27,500 entries, listed by country and airline. A5 size, 232 pages.

BUSINESS JETS INTERNATIONAL 2008 *Available June* Prices to be announced
Complete production listings of all business jet types in c/n order, giving full identities, fates and a comprehensive
cross-reference index containing over 50,000 registrations. Available in hardback at approx 500 pages.

AIRLINE FLEETS 2008 £19.95 (Members) £26.00 (Non-members)
Almost 3000 fleets listed by country with registrations, c/ns, line numbers, fleet numbers and names, plus numerous
appendices including airliners in non-airline service, IATA and ICAO airline and base codes, operator index, etc. Now
800 pages A5 size hardback.

EUROPEAN REGISTERS HANDBOOK 2008 *Available lateMay* Prices to be announced
Current civil registers of 44 European countries, all powered aircraft, balloons, gliders, microlights. Full previous
identities and many extra permit and reservation details. Now in A4 softback format with new layout this year.

EUROPEAN REGISTERS QUICK REFERENCE 2008 *From April. Each* £5.95 (Members) £6.95 (Non-members)
Two issues this year: **Southern Europe** covering from Portugal to Turkey; and **Northern & Eastern Europe** from
Scandinavia to the Black Sea. Both including balloons, ulms, gliders and military listings in registration/type Quick-
Reference A5 size softback format. Ideal for touring! ERQR 2006 covering Germany and the Benelux countries and
ERQR 2007 covering France, Austria and Switzerland are still available at £5.95/£6.95.

MANY OTHER CIVIL and MILITARY AIRCRAFT PUBLICATIONS ARE AVAILABLE NOW, INCLUDING:

AVIATION MUSEUMS AND COLLECTIONS OF MAINLAND EUROPE £22.50 (Members) £28.00 (Non-members)
Revised and expanded with full details of location, detailed listings of exhibits, many photographs including colour
sections and maps. 608 pages A5 hardback.

JET AIRLINERS OF THE WORLD 1949-2007 £26.50 (Members) £37.50 (Non-members)
This 2-volume edition contains the production listings of all jet airliners - over 33,000 aircraft - including military transport versions and all Soviet types, together with a cross-reference index listing nearly 75,000 registrations and serials,
a total of 944 pages!

Air-Britain also publishes a comprehensive range of military titles, please check for latest details of RAF Serial
Registers, detailed RAF aircraft type histories, Squadron histories and Royal Navy aircraft histories.

IMPORTANT NOTE – Members receive substantial discounts on prices of all the above Air-Britain publications,
as shown. For details of membership see the following page or visit our website at www.air-britain.co.uk

AIR-BRITAIN MEMBERSHIP

Check out our website at www.air-britain.co.uk

If you are not currently a member of Air-Britain, the publishers of this book, you may be interested in what we have on offer to provide for your interest in aviation.

About Air-Britain

Formed 60 years ago, we are the world's most progressive aviation society, and exist to bring together aviation enthusiasts with every type of interest. Our members include aircraft historians, aviation writers, spotters and pilots – and those who just have a fascination with aircraft and aviation. Air-Britain is a non-profit organisation, which is independently audited, and any financial surpluses are used to provide services to the ever-growing membership. Our current membership now stands at around 4,000 worldwide.

Membership of Air-Britain

Membership is open to all. A basic membership fee is charged and every member receives a copy of the quarterly house magazine, Air-Britain Aviation World, and is entitled to use all the Air-Britain specialist services and to buy **Air-Britain publications at discounted prices**. A membership subscription includes the choice to add any or all of our other 3 magazines, News and/or Archive and/or Aeromilitaria. Air-Britain publishes 10-20 books per annum (around 70 titles in stock at any one time). Membership runs January - December each year, but new members have a choice of options periods to get their initial subscription started.

Air-Britain Aviation World is the quarterly 48-page house magazine containing not only news of Air-Britain activities, but also a wealth of features, often illustrated in colour, on many different aviation subjects, contemporary and historical, contributed by our members.

Air-Britain News is the world aviation news monthly, containing data on Aircraft Registrations worldwide, and news of Airlines and Airliners, Business Jets, Local Airfield News, Civil and Military Air Show Reports and International Military Aviation. An average 160 pages of lavishly–illustrated information for the dedicated enthusiast.

Air-Britain Archive is the quarterly 48-page specialist journal of civil aviation history. Packed with the results of historical research by Air-Britain specialists into aircraft types, overseas registers and previously unpublished photographs and facts about the rich heritage of civil aviation. Around 100 photographs per issue, some in colour.

Air-Britain Aeromilitaria is the quarterly 48-page unique source for meticulously researched details of military aviation history edited by the acclaimed authors of Air-Britain's military monographs, featuring British, Commonwealth, European and U.S. Military aviation articles. Illustrated in colour and black and white.

Other Benefits

Additional to the above, members have exclusive access to the Air-Britain e-mail Information Exchange Service (ab-ix) where they can exchange information and solve each other's queries, and to an on-line UK airfield residents database. Other benefits include numerous Branches, use of the Specialists' Information Service; Air-Britain trips and access to black and white and colour photograph libraries. During the summer we also host our own popular FLY-IN. Each autumn we host an Aircraft Recognition Contest.

Membership Subscription Rates – from £18 per annum.

Membership subscription rates start from as little as £18 per annum (2008), and this amount provides a copy of 'Air-Britain Aviation World' quarterly as well as all the other benefits covered above. Subscriptions to include any or all of our other three magazines vary between £25 and £62 per annum (slightly higher to overseas).

 Join in 2008 for two years (2008-2009) and save £5.00 off the total subscription

Join on-line at membership@air-britain.co.uk or, write to 'Air-Britain' at 1 Rose Cottages, 179 Penn Road, Hazlemere, High Wycombe, Bucks HP15 7NE, UK, or telephone/fax on 01394 450767 (+44 1394 450767) and ask for a membership pack containing the full details of subscription rates, samples of our magazines and a book list.